Published by Aut

CW00508843

THE
ROYAL AIR FORCE
RETIRED LIST

2006

LONDON: TSO

ISBN 0 11 773039 4

ISSN 0266 8610

CONTENTS

NOTES

The Royal Air Force Retired List is published biennially, showing officers who have retired from permanent commissions and received immediate pension (retired pay).

Officers are placed on the Retired List in their substantive ranks. Where the Defence Council has permitted officers to retain as courtesy titles in civil life ranks higher than their substantive ranks, this is shown by "rtg ...."

The branches shown against Retired officers' names are those in which they were serving on leaving the Active List and reflect the computer record upon exit.

The ranks shown in respect of former Royal Air Force Chaplains are the relative ranks which the Defence Council has permitted them to retain on retirement.

Retired officers who succeed to peerages, baronetcies or courtesy titles, are required to notify the Editor requesting their inclusion in the Retired List and records of the Ministry of Defence.

Readers who notice errors or omissions are invited to notify the Editor quoting the relevant page number. To enable correction of entries for the next edition, all notifications should reach the Editor by 1 March 2006. Such communications should not be sent to the printers or publishers.

The Editor controls the master Distribution List for the free issue of the Air Force List. Defence Storage and Distribution Centre (DSDC) at Llangennech is responsible for the issue of the publication strictly in accordance with the Distribution List. Units are asked to ensure the Editor and DSDC are informed of any reduction in requirements. Unit requests for additional copies and amendment to the master Distribution List should be addressed to DSDC at Llangennech (normally using form MOD 999—Demand for Forms and Publications) and include a clear supporting case for the increase.

Correspondence to the Editor should be addressed to:

> Editor of The Air Force Lists
> PMA IM 1a1 (RAF)
> RAF Personnel Management Agency
> Room 5, Building 248A
> RAF Innsworth
> Gloucester
> GL3 1EZ

The following abbreviations are used throughout the book:

Ranks

Air Chief Marshal	ACM
Air Marshal	AM
Air Vice-Marshal	AVM
Air Commodore	A Cdre
*Air Commandant PMRAFNS	A Cdt
Group Captain	Gp Capt
*Group Officer PMRAFNS	Gp Offr
Wing Commander	Wg Cdr
*Wing Officer PMRAFNS	Wg Offr
Squadron Leader	Sqn Ldr
*Squadron Officer PMRAFNS	Sqn Offr
Flight Lieutenant	Flt Lt
*Flight Officer PMRAFNS	Flt Offr
Flying Officer	Fg Offr
Pilot Officer	Plt Offr

*These ranks are also held by WRAF officers who retired before 1 August 1968.

Branches

ACB	Airfield Construction	
ADMIN	Administrative	
ASD	Administrative and Special duties	
CAT	Catering	Note 1
DEL	Dental	
DM	Director of Music	
EDN	Education	Note 1
ENG	Engineer and former Technical	
FLY	Flying	Note 5
GD	General Duties	Note 6
(GD(G))	General Duties (Ground and former Aircraft Control, Balloon and Fighter Control)	Note 3
LGL	Legal	
MAF	Marine	
MED	Medical	
MED(SEC)	Medical Secretarial	Note 4
MED SPT	Medical Support	
MED TECH	Medical Technican	Note 7
OPS SPT	Operations Support	
PE	Physical Education and former Physical Fitness	Note 1
PI	Photographic Interpretation	
PRT	Provost	Note 2
RGT	Royal Air Force Regiment	Note 3
SEC	Secretarial and former Accountant	
SUP	Supply and former Equipment	
SY	Security	

Notes:
1 These branches are shown as ADMIN after 1975.
2 This branch is shown as ADMIN from 1 April 1975.
3 These branches are shown as OPS SPT from 1 April 1997.
4 This branch is shown as MED SPT from 1 April 2000.
5 From 1 April 2003 this branch replaces the former GD branch for those officers of Sqn Ldr rank or below.
6 From 1 April 2003 the new GD branch includes all Wg Cdrs and GP Capts not in specialist branches.
7 This branch is shown as MED SPT from 1 July 2003.

LIST OF RETIRED OFFICERS OF THE ROYAL AIR FORCE

A

ABAYAKOON J.V.F. Born 16/8/34. Commd 29/12/69. Flt Lt 29/12/69. Retd SUP 29/12/77.
ABBOTT H.M. Born 13/2/40. Commd 28/11/69. Fg Offr 28/11/69. Retd SEC 4/12/71.
ABBOTT J.A. Born 13/6/20. Commd 3/6/44. Flt Lt 26/3/60. Retd GD(G) 22/6/70.
ABBOTT J.A. Born 11/2/20. Commd 6/6/46. Sqn Ldr 1/1/60. Retd SEC 30/5/70.
ABBOTT J.D.F. BSc CEng MIMechE. Born 12/9/56. Commd 7/1/76. Wg Cdr 1/7/97. Retd GD 16/9/04.
ABBOTT J.H. Born 23/9/45. Commd 17/10/71. Sqn Ldr 1/7/85. Retd ENG 1/7/88.
ABBOTT L.E. Born 11/7/35. Commd 30/5/69. Sqn Ldr 1/7/91. Retd ENG 1/7/94.
ABBOTT L.S. MBE. Born 17/6/20. Commd 21/7/55. Sqn Ldr 1/7/66. Retd ENG 18/9/74.
ABBOTT M.J. Born 25/6/44. Commd 5/3/65. A Cdre 1/7/92. Retd GD 25/6/94.
ABBOTT M.J. BSc. Born 4/10/47. Commd 28/2/69. Flt Lt 28/5/74. Retd ENG 4/10/85.
ABBOTT N.J. Born 9/8/63. Commd 2/9/84. Flt Lt 2/9/89. Retd SUP 6/1/97.
ABBOTT R.E. Born 22/9/27. Commd 2/3/49. Sqn Ldr 1/7/59. Retd GD 22/9/65.
ABBOTT R.J. MBE. Born 24/1/41. Commd 20/7/78. Sqn Ldr 1/1/90. Retd ADMIN 2/4/95.
ABBOTT W.T. Born 18/11/11. Commd 25/3/43. Fg Offr 29/1/44. Retd ENG 13/3/46. rtg Flt Lt
ABBOTT-WRIGHT J.C. Born 11/10/49. Commd 13/1/72. Flt Lt 22/6/78. Retd ADMIN 14/3/97.
ABBS M.R. Born 28/7/65. Commd 26/9/91. Sqn Ldr 1/1/01. Retd ENGINEER 1/1/04.
ABEL G.W. Born 15/4/26. Commd 29/6/50. Flt Lt 15/4/64.
ABEL W.G. Born 29/1/24. Commd 3/9/43. Gp Capt 1/1/69. Retd GD 5/2/77.
ABELA P.P. MCMI. Born 26/6/46. Commd 21/10/66. Sqn Ldr 1/1/81. Retd ENG 26/6/84.
ABELL P.J. The Rev. Born 8/1/45. Commd 1/9/74. Retd Wg Cdr 2/12/98.
ABER C.P. Born 3/4/44. Commd 22/2/63. Wg Cdr 1/7/88. Retd GD 3/4/99.
ABEY-KOCH L.K. MA BA LLB. Born 17/6/50. Commd 16/12/79. Sqn Ldr 1/1/88. Retd ADMIN 16/12/95.
ABLITT B.P. BA. Born 30/10/57. Commd 16/6/92. Flt Lt 16/6/94. Retd ADMIN 14/3/97.
ABRA J.E. MBE. Born 10/5/46. Commd 8/9/77. Wg Cdr 1/7/99. Retd GD 12/12/03.
ABRAHAM W.B. BSc. Born 27/3/44. Commd 22/7/68. Sqn Ldr 22/1/76. Retd ADMIN 22/7/84.
ABRAM C.J. Born 10/5/46. Commd 18/8/67. Flt Lt 18/8/70. Retd GD 31/5/75.
ABRAM E.A. BA. Born 13/11/66. Commd 11/11/90. Flt Lt 11/5/93. Retd ADMIN 14/3/97.
ABREY J.W. OBE FCMI. Born 13/2/24. Commd 26/1/45. Gp Capt 1/1/73. Retd GD 13/2/75.
ABRUTAT D.J. BSc. Born 13/6/73. Commd 6/2/00. Plt Offr 6/2/00. Retd OPS SPT 27/9/02.
ACHILLES J.C.P. Born 11/10/41. Commd 23/11/78. Sqn Ldr 1/1/88. Retd ENG 2/6/94.
ACKLAM G. Born 13/7/30. Commd 30/1/52. Wg Cdr 1/1/81. Retd GD 13/7/85.
ACKROYD A.C.C. MA. Born 10/6/37. Commd 5/1/60. Sqn Ldr 13/3/71. Retd ADMIN 25/6/76.
ACKROYD D.F.W. MMedSci MB BS MRCGP MFOM DRCOG DAvMed. Born 4/1/54. Commd 17/2/80. Wg Cdr 18/8/91. Retd MED 4/12/97.
ACKROYD D.G.S. Born 2/4/42. Commd 5/9/69. Wg Cdr 1/7/83. Retd GD(G) 2/3/96.
ACKROYD E. Born 25/11/22. Commd 26/4/43. Flt Lt 20/10/46. Retd GD 15/2/58.
ACKROYD S.J. Born 30/3/44. Commd 1/4/65. Flt Lt 1/10/70. Retd GD 31/7/75.
ACONS E.G.N. Born 1/5/45. Commd 9/12/65. Wg Cdr 1/7/89. Retd OPS SPT 1/5/00.
ACRES A.J. Born 30/6/21. Commd 4/5/46. Flt Lt 14/9/46. Retd SUP 27/10/55.
ADAIR P.J. Born 9/10/31. Commd 6/12/51. Flt Lt 17/4/57. Retd GD 29/4/78.
ADAM A.E. MA MB BS MRCPath. Born 7/6/39. Commd 23/1/67. Sqn Ldr 14/8/75. Retd MED 12/5/83.
ADAM G.W. Born 7/9/14. Commd 9/3/43. Flt Lt 9/9/46. Retd ENG 31/3/62.
ADAM I.W. BSc. Born 24/5/44. Commd 28/9/64. Sqn Ldr 1/7/78. Retd ENG 24/5/99.
ADAM J. BSc. Born 2/12/62. Commd 3/5/83. Flt Lt 15/1/87. Retd GD 2/3/01.
ADAM J.H.M. Born 26/2/35. Commd 14/1/54. Flt Lt 7/3/62. Retd GD 26/8/93.
ADAMS A.C.T. Born 20/5/49. Commd 1/4/71. Flt Lt 3/11/73. Retd GD 28/11/86.
ADAMS A.H.D. Born 2/3/30. Commd 19/12/63. Flt Lt 19/12/68. Retd ENG 2/3/92.
ADAMS A.W. Born 14/8/19. Commd 7/11/46. Sqn Ldr 1/7/63. Retd ENG 14/8/74.
ADAMS B.S. BA. Born 13/5/56. Commd 18/11/79. Flt Lt 18/2/81. Retd GD 19/11/88.
ADAMS C.J. Born 30/5/39. Commd 1/8/61. Sqn Ldr 1/1/74. Retd GD 1/1/98.
ADAMS C.M. Born 29/7/21. Commd 19/3/42. Sqn Ldr 1/7/60. Retd SEC 16/7/61.
ADAMS C.R. Born 18/1/36. Commd 6/2/54. Wg Cdr 1/1/86. Retd GD 18/1/91.
ADAMS C.R. CBE AFC FCIPD. Born 1/4/40. Commd 1/8/61. A Cdre 1/1/90. Retd GD 1/4/95.

ADAMS D. Born 11/1/24. Commd 2/1/50. Wg Cdr 1/7/66. Retd GD 11/1/79.
ADAMS D.A. MCMI. Born 27/8/49. Commd 6/10/69. Wg Cdr 1/7/89. Retd ENG 17/1/97.
ADAMS D.B. MA PhD BSc. Born 26/4/27. Commd 19/10/49. Wg Cdr 1/4/69. Retd EDN 31/3/74.
ADAMS D.N. BSc FRAeS. Born 28/4/46. Commd 22/9/65. A Cdre 1/1/97. Retd GD 11/12/01.
ADAMS E.R. Born 26/3/34. Commd 12/8/59. Sqn Ldr 1/9/68. Retd EDN 12/8/75.
ADAMS J.H. Born 25/8/32. Commd 17/1/52. Flt Lt 29/4/59. Retd GD 20/10/70.
ADAMS J.H.A. Born 30/8/35. Commd 30/7/57. Sqn Ldr 1/7/68. Retd GD 31/8/74.
ADAMS K.M. Born 18/5/46. Commd 31/8/78. Sqn Ldr 1/1/88. Retd ENG 6/12/96.
ADAMS K.S. Born 24/4/58. Commd 1/12/77. Flt Lt 1/6/83. Retd GD 30/9/88.
ADAMS M.K. CB AFC FRAeS. Born 23/1/34. Commd 18/3/53. AVM 1/7/83. Retd GD 2/10/88.
ADAMS M.P. MRAeS MCMI. Born 22/10/40. Commd 13/2/60. Wg Cdr 1/1/93. Retd GD 1/1/96.
ADAMS M.T.H. DFC. Born 20/1/20. Commd 30/5/39. Sqn Ldr 1/7/55. Retd GD 20/1/69.
ADAMS N.J. Born 11/5/30. Commd 26/7/51. Flt Lt 14/11/56. Retd GD 5/11/68.
ADAMS N.M. Born 22/4/59. Commd 20/9/79. Sqn Ldr 1/1/95. Retd GD 1/10/98.
ADAMS N.R. Born 30/6/48. Commd 23/3/68. Sqn Ldr 1/7/82. Retd GD 28/2/93.
ADAMS P.B. Born 16/6/33. Commd 30/1/52. Flt Lt 13/11/57. Retd GD 16/6/88.
ADAMS P.G. DFC. Born 29/4/18. Commd 22/5/48. Sqn Ldr 1/7/55. Retd GD 29/4/61.
ADAMS P.S.G. MBE. Born 10/4/47. Commd 10/6/66. Sqn Ldr 1/1/80. Retd GD 14/3/96.
ADAMS R.C. MBE. Born 20/3/49. Commd 20/9/68. Sqn Ldr 1/1/90. Retd GD(G) 20/3/93.
ADAMS R.H.D. Born 19/11/33. Commd 10/9/52. Sqn Ldr 1/7/69. Retd GD 19/9/84.
ADAMS R.J. Born 29/12/28. Commd 5/12/51. Flt Lt 6/6/60. Retd GD 29/12/86.
ADAMS R.M. MB ChB. Born 6/7/62. Commd 13/11/84. Sqn Ldr 1/8/93. Retd MED 8/1/97.
ADAMS R.W.G. Born 28/5/37. Commd 16/12/58. Sqn Ldr 1/1/69. Retd SUP 5/6/82.
ADAMS S.J. Born 28/3/27. Commd 6/6/57. Flt Lt 6/12/60. Retd GD 28/3/82.
ADAMS S.M. MCIPS. Born 5/10/30. Commd 30/3/61. Wg Cdr 1/1/79. Retd SUP 1/4/85.
ADAMS T.F. Born 27/4/30. Commd 4/2/71. Flt Lt 4/2/74. Retd ENG 1/10/84.
ADAMS W.H. Born 29/11/17. Commd 20/11/42. Flt Lt 20/5/46. Retd GD 23/10/55.
ADAMSON A.N.G. BSc CEng MIERE MIEE MCMI. Born 20/11/33. Commd 6/10/60. Flt Lt 25/11/62.
    Retd ENG 1/11/80.
ADAMSON D.T. Born 29/5/25. Commd 1/4/45. Sqn Ldr 1/10/55. Retd GD 1/9/62.
ADAMSON E. DFM. Born 9/4/22. Commd 3/3/44. Flt Lt 29/6/50. Retd ADMIN 9/4/77.
ADAMSON G.N. BTech. Born 16/5/55. Commd 2/9/73. Sqn Ldr 1/1/87. Retd ENG 16/5/93.
ADAMSON N.C. Born 5/9/38. Commd 28/7/59. Flt Lt 7/3/62. Retd GD 31/7/69.
ADAMSON W.M. Born 19/3/34. Commd 18/3/52. Flt Lt 15/2/65. Retd GD 1/1/69.
ADCOCK B.R. Born 7/2/39. Commd 11/7/64. Flt Lt 26/7/67. Retd GD 7/2/77.
ADCOCK C.B. BA FCMI. Born 5/4/41. Commd 31/7/62. Gp Capt 1/1/91. Retd GD 1/1/97.
ADCOCK D.F. Born 6/5/21. Commd 9/10/42. Sqn Ldr 1/7/54. Retd GD 8/5/64.
ADCOCK K.C. Born 20/3/27. Commd 4/6/52. Flt Lt 9/7/59. Retd GD 20/3/65.
ADCOCK T.L. Born 19/4/38. Commd 24/4/56. Wg Cdr 1/7/76. Retd GD 30/9/84.
ADCOCK T.R. OBE MRAeS. Born 1/10/43. Commd 22/5/64. Sqn Ldr 1/1/78. Retd GD 1/10/81. Re-entered 28/4/82.
    Sqn Ldr 29/7/78. Retd GD 18/4/99
ADDIS M.H. MSc BSc. Born 6/5/55. Commd 31/8/75. Sqn Ldr 1/7/87. Retd ENG 6/5/94.
ADDIS P.J. Born 28/8/24. Commd 14/11/51. Flt Lt 20/6/55. Retd GD(G) 28/8/82.
ADDISON D. BA. Born 11/8/74. Commd 21/8/00. Flt Lt 9/8/99. Retd ADMIN (TRG) 1/6/03.
ADDISON J.M. Born 15/12/63. Commd 8/5/86. Flt Lt 9/6/90. Retd GD 15/12/01.
ADDISON T. Born 23/10/46. Commd 1/10/65. Sqn Ldr 1/7/85. Retd SY 1/11/87.
ADES A.V. MBE MBA FCMI. Born 29/11/43. Commd 10/11/61. Gp Capt 1/7/96. Retd GD 1/7/99.
ADEY D.D. Born 6/5/63. Commd 6/10/94. Flt Lt 6/10/96. Retd ADMIN 6/10/02.
ADHEMAR P.N. Born 7/2/47. Commd 25/2/66. Flt Lt 25/8/71. Retd GD 1/4/76.
ADKINSON C.R. Born 7/3/64. Commd 27/3/88. Fg Offr 27/3/88. Retd ENG 6/7/89.
ADLINGTON L.E. AFM. Born 6/6/26. Commd 28/1/60. Flt Lt 28/7/63. Retd GD 31/3/74.
ADOLPH M.P.N. MSc MB BCh BAO DAvMed. Born 8/3/31. Commd 16/7/62. Wg Cdr 25/10/74. Retd MED 16/7/78.
ADRIAN G.K. Born 27/3/56. Commd 1/7/90. Flt Lt 9/12/85. Retd ADMIN 1/7/96.
AGER S.M. DPhysEd. Born 14/5/42. Commd 14/9/65. Sqn Ldr 1/7/80. Retd GD 14/9/87.
AGER W.G.A. Born 26/4/22. Commd 24/2/43. Flt Lt 24/8/46. Retd GD 26/4/65.
AGNEW B.M. Born 23/7/34. Commd 5/5/55. Sqn Ldr 1/7/69. Retd SUP 25/9/88.
AGNEW G.R. BA MCMI. Born 7/1/46. Commd 6/11/64. Wg Cdr 1/7/88. Retd GD 14/9/96.
AGNEW R. Born 28/7/12. Commd 19/11/42. Flt Lt 19/5/46. Retd ENG 3/7/58.
AHERNE R.B. MBE. Born 8/2/35. Commd 5/11/70. Sqn Ldr 1/1/84. Retd ENG 8/1/86.
AHMED R.R.A. BA. Born 7/7/63. Commd 30/8/81. Flt Lt 15/10/85. Retd GD 14/3/96.
AIKEN R. Born 14/5/32. Commd 28/1/53. Flt Lt 17/6/58. Retd GD 14/5/92.
AINGE D.B. Born 7/7/43. Commd 17/12/64. Sqn Ldr 1/1/78. Retd GD 7/7/81.
AINLEY P. DFC. Born 4/11/23. Commd 26/5/43. Sqn Ldr 1/1/54. Retd GD 5/7/66. rtg Wg Cdr
AINSLIE E.J. BEM. Born 14/2/35. Commd 12/7/79. Flt Lt 12/7/84. Retd ENG 14/2/85.
AINSLIE I.M.C.P. Born 11/5/47. Commd 8/7/65. Sqn Ldr 1/7/89. Retd OPS SPT(ATC) 11/5/03.
AINSWORTH A.M. MCMI DipMgmt. Born 16/12/64. Commd 22/11/84. Sqn Ldr 1/7/96. Retd SUP 16/12/02.

AINSWORTH D.P. BSc. Born 4/12/63. Commd 8/5/88. Flt Lt 8/11/90. Retd GD 8/5/00.
AINSWORTH H. Born 2/10/17. Commd 27/2/47. Flt Lt 27/8/51. Retd SUP 1/12/61.
AINSWORTH J. Born 8/3/19. Commd 10/12/42. Sqn Ldr 1/1/57. Retd ENG 8/3/74.
AINSWORTH J.C. CEng MRAeS MCMI. Born 4/9/26. Commd 4/3/54. Gp Capt 1/7/73. Retd ENG 3/9/77.
AINSWORTH S.J. MDA BSc MCIPS MCIT MILT MCMI. Born 19/11/61. Commd 31/8/80. Sqn Ldr 1/7/91.
    Retd SUP 13/12/99.
AIREY F.C. MBE. Born 26/6/16. Commd 26/4/43. Wg Cdr 1/1/61. Retd ENG 26/6/72.
AIREY I.S. BSc. Born 23/2/43. Commd 14/12/62. Flt Lt 14/12/65. Retd GD 31/12/71.
AIREY N.D. Born 11/7/58. Commd 11/1/79. Sqn Ldr 1/1/95. Retd GD 5/7/98.
AIRS K.A. Born 28/10/41. Commd 28/9/62. Flt Lt 28/3/68. Retd GD 23/10/79.
AITKEN A.I. Born 7/11/38. Commd 23/6/61. Flt Lt 1/4/66. Retd GD 7/11/76.
AITKEN W.M. BEd. Born 25/2/54. Commd 9/10/77. Sqn Ldr 1/7/87. Retd ADMIN 29/8/96.
AKDENIZ S.O. BSc. Born 12/2/63. Commd 2/9/84. Flt Lt 2/3/88. Retd SY 1/10/91.
AKED G.A. Born 20/6/25. Commd 17/8/50. Flt Lt 17/2/55. Retd GD 20/6/71.
AKEHURST C.S.L. MCMI. Born 1/12/21. Commd 17/3/55. Sqn Ldr 1/7/69. Retd ENG 1/1/72.
AKEHURST P.B. LVO OBE BTech CEng MRAeS. Born 31/1/51. Commd 22/9/74. Gp Capt 1/1/99. Retd GD 30/6/04.
AKEHURST R. Born 14/12/61. Commd 11/6/81. Flt Lt 1/1/97. Retd GD 1/8/01.
AKEHURST DE VISME P.M. Born 7/6/48. Commd 1/8/69. Fg Offr 1/2/70. Retd GD 30/11/72.
AKEROYD W.S. DFM FCMI. Born 23/10/20. Commd 29/10/42. Gp Capt 1/1/70. Retd GD(G) 23/10/76.
AKERS S.J. MBA GradInstPS. Born 4/12/58. Commd 13/12/79. Sqn Ldr 1/7/92. Retd SUP 14/3/97.
AKERS-DOUGLAS A.A. Born 17/9/43. Commd 24/6/65. Flt Lt 9/2/68. Retd GD 11/4/73.
AKHURST D.H. Born 9/12/39. Commd 17/5/63. Flt Lt 17/11/68. Retd GD 6/10/79.
AKISTER W.H. Born 5/8/32. Commd 27/8/52. Flt Lt 12/2/58. Retd GD 5/8/87.
AKRED R.L. Born 17/4/64. Commd 6/10/94. Flt Lt 6/10/96. Retd ADMIN 6/10/02.
ALABASTER J.C. Born 4/3/36. Commd 10/3/60. Fg Offr 10/9/61. Retd ENG 24/1/65.
ALBONE D.P.J.F. Born 10/2/23. Commd 22/8/63. Flt Lt 22/8/66. Retd GD 16/2/73.
ALCOCK A.J.H. MBE. Born 3/5/44. Commd 22/5/64. Gp Capt 1/7/90. Retd GD 3/5/99.
ALCOCK G.R. AFC*. Born 2/3/43. Commd 10/12/65. Flt Lt 1/7/69. Retd GD 2/3/81.
ALCOCK J.M. MRAeS. Born 3/10/32. Commd 14/7/54. Wg Cdr 1/7/72. Retd GD 3/10/90.
ALCOCK Sir Michael GCB KBE DSc FEng FIMechE FRAeS. Born 11/7/36. Commd 30/12/58. ACM 30/6/93.
    Retd ENG 25/6/96.
ALCOCK M.R. Born 2/1/41. Commd 19/6/64. Flt Lt 19/12/69. Retd GD 2/3/80. Re-instated 4/6/84. Flt Lt 15/4/74.
    Retd GD 3/1/91.
ALCOCK R.C.K. Born 3/3/34. Commd 31/12/52. Flt Lt 6/6/61. Retd GD 5/9/76.
ALDEN D.R. Born 14/1/45. Commd 28/4/65. Flt Lt 28/10/70. Retd GD 11/11/75.
ALDEN L.S. Born 1/5/22. Commd 10/3/44. Flt Lt 10/9/47. Retd GD 3/2/68.
ALDER I.T. Born 29/7/46. Commd 23/9/82. Sqn Ldr 1/7/98. Retd SUP 29/7/01.
ALDERSMITH M.F. Born 13/9/26. Commd 14/6/46. Wg Cdr 1/7/69. Retd GD 13/9/81.
ALDERSON B. Born 29/1/41. Commd 24/2/61. Flt Lt 24/8/71. Retd GD 29/1/96.
ALDERSON G.L.D. MEd BA BSc(Econ). Born 31/7/31. Commd 3/1/61. Wg Cdr 1/7/78. Retd ADMIN 3/5/84.
ALDERSON M.J.D. Born 16/10/29. Commd 1/8/51. Flt Lt 1/8/56. Retd SEC 30/1/60.
ALDERSON N.C. Born 15/4/44. Commd 28/4/67. Flt Lt 28/10/72. Retd GD 16/1/83.
ALDERSON O.W. AFC. Born 16/5/31. Commd 28/12/51. Sqn Ldr 1/7/72. Retd GD 16/11/93.
ALDINGTON J.D. Born 23/12/42. Commd 28/10/81. Sqn Ldr 1/7/87. Retd GD 14/10/90.
ALDOUS D.I. Born 14/3/44. Commd 19/4/63. Sqn Ldr 1/7/75. Retd GD 14/3/88.
ALDRED J.D. Born 14/4/33. Commd 24/1/52. Sqn Ldr 1/7/64. Retd GD 14/4/91.
ALDRED J.R. Born 15/5/42. Commd 6/4/72. Flt Lt 19/12/69. Retd GD 15/5/80.
ALDRED R.H. Born 22/8/40. Commd 6/4/72. Flt Lt 6/4/74. Retd ADMIN 23/10/90.
ALDRICH J.R.A. MSc BSc CEng MIEE. Born 30/7/57. Commd 30/8/78. Sqn Ldr 1/7/89. Retd ENG 30/7/95.
ALDRIDGE A. Born 25/7/18. Commd 11/8/40. Sqn Ldr 1/8/47. Retd GD 27/6/58.
ALDRIDGE B.J. MSc MRAeS. Born 6/8/35. Commd 2/10/61. Sqn Ldr 1/7/70. Retd GD 11/6/76.
ALDRIDGE F.S.J. Born 26/6/24. Commd 17/6/54. Sqn Ldr 1/7/71. Retd GD 30/9/75.
ALDRIDGE K. Born 14/5/46. Commd 21/1/66. Flt Lt 21/7/71. Retd GD 27/7/91.
ALDRIDGE M.R. MBA MCMI. Born 3/12/57. Commd 1/7/82. Sqn Ldr 1/7/90. Retd ENG 1/7/01.
ALDWINCKLE J.P. MA. Born 13/9/22. Commd 13/3/50. Wg Cdr 1/1/68. Retd ADMIN 13/9/77.
ALEXANDER C.D. FHCIMA. Born 1/5/39. Commd 28/7/60. Gp Capt 1/1/88. Retd SUP 3/4/92.
ALEXANDER C.R. Born 15/12/49. Commd 14/3/72. Flt Lt 15/10/74. Retd ENG 1/6/79.
ALEXANDER D.A.M. Born 27/2/26. Commd 22/8/43. Sqn Ldr 1/7/64. Retd GD(G) 27/2/76.
ALEXANDER G. BSc. Born 6/6/42. Commd 14/9/64. Sqn Ldr 1/1/75. Retd GD 14/9/80.
ALEXANDER G.B. Born 25/2/25. Commd 29/5/52. Sqn Ldr 1/7/72. Retd GD 30/11/75.
ALEXANDER J.G. Born 2/5/47. Commd 27/3/80. Flt Lt 27/3/82. Retd GD(G) 17/7/95.
ALEXANDER J.R. DFC DFM. Born 6/6/22. Commd 2/6/44. Flt Lt 1/7/54. Retd GD 6/6/73.
ALEXANDER R.D. OBE AFC. Born 7/4/23. Commd 27/6/51. Wg Cdr 1/1/72. Retd GD 7/4/78.
ALEXANDER R.S. Born 28/2/37. Commd 14/5/60. Flt Lt 14/11/65. Retd GD 26/4/75.
ALEXANDER-BOWEN M. Born 7/10/54. Commd 18/12/80. Flt Lt 18/6/87. Retd ADMIN 14/4/96.
ALFANDARY C.M. BA. Born 20/4/49. Commd 16/2/86. Flt Lt 16/2/84. Retd ADMIN 16/2/02.

ALFORD B.J. Born 1/11/48. Commd 28/4/67. Flt Lt 28/10/72. Retd GD 5/4/86.
ALFORD J. BA. Born 23/8/32. Commd 2/8/68. Sqn Ldr 2/8/76. Retd ADMIN 31/12/83.
ALFORD R. Born 27/3/44. Commd 9/8/63. Flt Lt 9/2/69. Retd GD(G) 27/3/82.
ALFORD T.A. BA. Born 4/11/32. Commd 23/11/56. Sqn Ldr 23/8/65. Retd EDN 23/11/74.
ALGAR H.K.M. Born 18/2/24. Commd 27/1/55. Flt Lt 27/1/61. Retd GD 30/4/68.
ALISON R.H. MBE. Born 28/8/24. Commd 12/6/45. Wg Cdr 1/7/73. Retd SEC 28/8/79.
ALISTER-JONES N.A. Born 29/9/42. Commd 14/1/65. Flt Lt 8/3/72. Retd SY 1/10/77.
ALLAIN A.M. Born 9/3/36. Commd 30/3/61. Flt Lt 1/4/71. Retd GD(G) 9/3/93.
ALLAM C.M. Born 29/1/56. Commd 21/4/77. Sqn Ldr 1/7/87. Retd GD 29/1/94.
ALLAM J.W. Born 3/10/24. Commd 6/2/44. Flt Lt 6/8/47. Retd GD 29/8/54.
ALLAN A.S.M. Born 16/3/32. Commd 14/12/50. Flt Lt 14/12/56. Retd SEC 16/9/70.
ALLAN C.F. Born 4/4/56. Commd 21/4/77. Flt Lt 21/10/82. Retd GD 21/9/87.
ALLAN D. Born 26/9/46. Commd 16/12/66. Sqn Ldr 1/1/91. Retd GD 1/10/87.
ALLAN D.D. Born 9/7/46. Commd 2/8/73. Gp Capt 1/7/94. Retd ENG 31/8/98.
ALLAN D.R. MBE BSc. Born 25/9/47. Commd 22/9/65. Gp Capt 1/1/91. Retd ENG 9/7/94.
ALLAN G.L.A. Born 16/8/40. Commd 14/1/65. Flt Lt 14/7/70. Retd GD 7/7/80.
ALLAN J.McM. MSc BA CEng MIEE. Born 12/11/53. Commd 23/5/85. Sqn Ldr 1/1/92. Retd ENG 23/5/99.
ALLAN K.T. BDS. Born 28/1/61. Commd 1/9/85. Wg Cdr 4/3/98. Retd DEL 1/9/01.
ALLAN N. Born 5/2/52. Commd 4/4/96. Flt Lt 4/4/00. Retd ADMIN 9/12/00.
ALLAN P.H.W. ACIS. Born 6/8/30. Commd 28/7/49. Sqn Ldr 1/7/64. Retd SEC 25/7/75.
ALLARD D. Born 26/3/31. Commd 12/3/64. Flt Lt 12/3/70. Retd PE 1/9/73.
ALLARD S. Born 15/6/11. Commd 6/10/41. Flt Lt 30/4/44. Retd ENG 7/2/46. rtg Sqn Ldr
ALLARDYCE D.C. Born 12/11/43. Commd 17/7/64. Flt Lt 22/5/69. Retd GD 27/8/76.
ALLAWAY W.J. Born 12/1/45. Commd 30/4/81. Sqn Ldr 1/1/89. Retd GD 7/10/97.
ALLBON J.D. Born 11/3/42. Commd 5/6/67. Fg Offr 5/6/69. Retd SEC 5/6/71.
ALLCHIN B.C. Born 21/4/38. Commd 14/2/56. Sqn Ldr 1/7/66. Retd GD 1/10/87.
ALLCORN B.E. Born 12/8/41. Commd 2/9/63. Wg Cdr 1/7/82. Retd SY 9/9/96.
ALLDIS C.A. CBE DFC AFC MA. Born 28/9/18. Commd 3/10/39. Gp Capt 1/7/59. Retd GD 26/1/66. rtg A Cdre
ALLDRITT D.P.G. Born 9/4/60. Commd 11/9/86. Flt Lt 11/9/88. Retd SY 12/12/95.
ALLEN A.F. Born 17/9/37. Commd 31/1/66. Sqn Ldr 1/1/74. Retd ADMIN 21/3/78.
ALLEN A.G. Born 19/8/32. Commd 22/7/71. Flt Lt 22/7/73. Retd SUP 19/8/87.
ALLEN B.R. Born 12/4/32. Commd 3/2/65. Flt Lt 3/2/65. Retd GD(G) 3/2/73.
ALLEN C. Born 8/8/55. Commd 27/2/75. Wg Cdr 1/1/93. Retd ADMIN 8/8/99.
ALLEN C.R. Born 15/6/47. Commd 8/9/77. Sqn Ldr 1/1/85. Retd ENG 16/6/97.
ALLEN D.F. Born 29/5/63. Commd 12/3/87. Flt Lt 12/9/92. Retd GD 27/5/96.
ALLEN D.G. Born 18/1/24. Commd 28/1/45. Flt Lt 22/7/51. Retd GD 12/4/68.
ALLEN D.G. Born 18/10/40. Commd 26/10/61. Flt Lt 23/8/68. Retd RGT 18/10/78.
ALLEN D.M. CEng MIEE MRAeS CDip AF. Born 23/2/43. Commd 15/7/64. Wg Cdr 1/7/79. Retd ENG 23/2/87.
ALLEN D.R. MSc BDS MGDSRCS(Edin). Born 23/12/42. Commd 16/9/62. Wg Cdr 15/6/80. Retd DEL 1/4/91.
    Re-entered 1/9/92. Gp Capt 1/1/94. Retd DEL 23/12/00.
ALLEN D.W. Born 30/10/33. Commd 23/7/52. Sqn Ldr 1/1/71. Retd GD 30/10/93.
ALLEN F. Born 22/11/32. Commd 20/3/52. Gp Capt 1/1/82. Retd GD 2/9/83.
ALLEN F.D. MSc BSc CEng MIMechE. Born 14/6/35. Commd 4/9/59. Sqn Ldr 4/3/70. Retd EDN 4/9/75.
ALLEN F.G. BA MInstAM MCMI. Born 7/5/29. Commd 11/2/65. Sqn Ldr 1/7/77. Retd GD 31/3/85.
ALLEN F.G. Born 8/12/38. Commd 25/7/60. Wg Cdr 1/7/78. Retd SUP 8/12/93.
ALLEN G.E. Born 24/3/38. Commd 4/10/63. Flt Lt 4/4/69. Retd GD 18/6/79.
ALLEN G.H. Born 5/11/14. Commd 9/10/42. Sqn Ldr 1/1/60. Retd GD(G) 5/11/64.
ALLEN G.H. Born 8/9/36. Commd 9/3/62. Flt Lt 1/4/66. Retd GD 8/9/74.
ALLEN G.P. Born 9/8/35. Commd 9/4/57. Sqn Ldr 1/7/75. Retd ADMIN 9/4/90.
ALLEN H. MCMI. Born 4/4/14. Commd 26/4/45. Wg Cdr 1/7/65. Retd SEC 4/4/69.
ALLEN H.A. Born 18/5/57. Commd 6/7/80. Flt Lt 6/1/85. Retd ADMIN 31/3/97.
ALLEN J. Born 9/12/34. Commd 10/10/63. Sqn Ldr 1/1/85. Retd GD 1/10/87.
ALLEN J.D. Born 18/3/61. Commd 28/2/80. Wg Cdr 1/1/98. Retd SUP 1/1/01.
ALLEN J.G. Born 26/10/58. Commd 3/11/77. Flt Lt 3/5/83. Retd GD 1/10/89.
ALLEN J.H. DFC. Born 30/7/23. Commd 28/7/44. Flt Lt 10/8/54. Retd SEC 1/1/75.
ALLEN J.H. Born 10/12/45. Commd 1/4/66. Flt Lt 6/10/71. Retd GD 1/5/87.
ALLEN J.M. Born 28/12/47. Commd 22/9/88. Flt Lt 22/9/90. Retd SUP 1/8/01.
ALLEN J.W. Born 10/6/31. Commd 7/11/51. Sqn Ldr 1/1/66. Retd GD 6/9/85.
ALLEN K.E. Born 26/7/24. Commd 22/6/45. Wg Cdr 1/1/67. Retd GD 24/7/76.
ALLEN L.J. Born 30/3/18. Commd 18/10/51. Flt Offr 18/4/56. Retd GD(G) 30/3/68.
ALLEN M.D.P. Born 29/5/50. Commd 1/4/71. Sqn Ldr 1/1/84. Retd GD(G) 1/10/92.
ALLEN M.J.W. BSc. Born 15/10/49. Commd 26/2/71. Flt Lt 26/11/75. Retd ENG 15/10/87.
ALLEN M.K.C. Born 25/7/52. Commd 22/5/75. Flt Lt 22/11/80. Retd GD 3/2/91.
ALLEN M.S. Born 26/10/56. Commd 16/9/76. Flt Lt 16/3/82. Retd GD 11/10/88.
ALLEN N.E. MSc BSc(Econ) MCMI. Born 8/7/34. Commd 4/1/56. Sqn Ldr 5/3/69. Retd EDN 1/10/79.
ALLEN N.J. Born 11/10/60. Commd 20/6/91. Flt Lt 20/6/93. Retd ADMIN 14/9/96.

ALLEN P. Born 2/10/23. Commd 27/8/64. Flt Lt 27/8/67. Retd GD 30/6/73.
ALLEN P.J. Born 19/2/34. Commd 30/1/58. Flt Lt 30/7/62. Retd GD 21/7/72.
ALLEN R. MBE BA. Born 28/2/59. Commd 17/8/80. Sqn Ldr 1/1/93. Retd ADMIN 5/11/00.
ALLEN R.A.E. AFC* MCMI. Born 28/11/22. Commd 9/11/44. Wg Cdr 1/7/62. Retd GD 28/11/77.
ALLEN R.C. CBE BSc. Born 21/8/31. Commd 18/3/53. A Cdre 1/1/82. Retd GD 21/8/86.
ALLEN R.J. FRAeS. Born 20/6/49. Commd 7/6/68. Gp Capt 1/1/99. Retd GD 1/5/04.
ALLEN R.N.G. CBE DFC. Born 8/11/20. Commd 17/4/41. Gp Capt 1/7/61. Retd GD 8/2/73.
ALLEN R.R. Born 16/11/42. Commd 6/4/62. Flt Lt 6/10/67. Retd GD 31/12/85. Re-entered 2/12/90. Flt Lt 7/9/72.
    Retd GD 31/3/99.
ALLEN S. Born 24/3/18. Commd 10/9/43. Flt Lt 10/3/47. Retd GD 10/7/58.
ALLEN S.B. BA. Born 5/2/57. Commd 14/1/79. Flt Lt 14/10/80. Retd GD 14/1/87.
ALLEN T.J. ACIS MCMI. Born 1/5/37. Commd 25/7/60. Sqn Ldr 1/7/72. Retd ADMIN 1/9/82.
ALLEN T.N. BSc. Born 23/9/44. Commd 28/9/64. Sqn Ldr 1/1/80. Retd GD 14/1/87.
ALLEN W.G. Born 30/9/25. Commd 6/2/50. Flt Lt 11/11/68. Retd GD 30/9/77.
ALLENBY W. BSc. Born 14/8/25. Commd 29/8/51. Flt Lt 30/4/53. Retd GD 13/11/57.
ALLERTON R.C. CB. Born 7/12/35. Commd 9/12/54. Flt Lt 1/7/87. Retd SUP 15/4/90.
ALLFREE D.N. Born 29/12/15. Commd 8/3/45. Fg Offr 3/5/46. Retd SEC 21/9/53. rtg Flt Lt
ALLGOOD R.S. MBE FAAI MInstAM(Dip) MCIPD. Born 28/12/34. Commd 17/6/54. Wg Cdr 1/7/78.
    Retd ADMIN 1/10/87.
ALLIES E.M. MBE DFC BA. Born 11/4/20. Commd 6/8/40. Gp Capt 1/1/72. Retd EDN 11/4/75.
ALLIN G.R. Born 5/8/33. Commd 30/4/52. Flt Lt 6/11/57. Retd GD 5/8/71.
ALLINSON J.E. Born 10/10/31. Commd 16/5/51. Flt Lt 16/2/57. Retd GD 10/10/69.
ALLINSON P.A. Born 18/1/26. Commd 4/9/49. Flt Lt 11/12/56. Retd GD 26/7/65.
ALLISON A. Born 15/9/64. Commd 29/7/87. Flt Lt 29/7/93. Retd OPS SPT 15/9/02.
ALLISON C. BA. Born 13/11/39. Commd 19/9/71. Sqn Ldr 1/7/88. Retd ADMIN 13/11/94.
ALLISON D. CBE. Born 5/8/31. Commd 15/12/53. A Cdre 1/7/83. Retd GD 4/8/85.
ALLISON D. CB. Born 15/10/32. Commd 6/4/54. AVM 1/7/85. Retd GD 12/1/87.
ALLISON J. Born 27/7/21. Commd 27/5/54. Flt Lt 27/5/60. Retd GD 28/9/68.
ALLISON Sir John KCB CBE FRAeS. Born 24/3/43. Commd 28/7/64. ACM 8/3/96. Retd GD 6/9/99.
ALLISON J.S. BSc. Born 12/3/49. Commd 28/2/72. Flt Lt 28/5/75. Retd PI 24/10/82.
ALLISON P.B. MBE BEng CEng MRAeS. Born 30/6/66. Commd 3/8/88. Sqn Ldr 1/1/99. Retd ENGINEER 1/7/03.
ALLISON R.M. BEd. Born 30/3/57. Commd 9/10/79. Sqn Ldr 1/1/90. Retd ADMIN 9/10/95.
ALLISON R.W.I. Born 17/12/42. Commd 24/6/65. Flt Lt 24/12/67. Retd GD 23/12/72.
ALLISON T.S. Born 15/10/52. Commd 22/9/88. Flt Lt 22/9/92. Retd SUP 31/3/94.
ALLISSTONE M.J. CBE FInstPet FCMI MCIPS. Born 13/2/33. Commd 27/7/54. A Cdre 1/1/84. Retd SUP 2/4/88.
ALLKINS C.R. Born 4/10/44. Commd 9/10/64. Sqn Ldr 1/7/80. Retd GD 1/5/92.
ALLKINS R.D. Born 28/6/47. Commd 11/1/81. Sqn Ldr 1/1/91. Retd ADMIN 1/1/94.
ALLOTT M.G. CB FCMI. Born 28/12/18. Commd 12/1/44. A Cdre 1/7/73. Retd SUP 28/12/76.
ALLOWAY H.V. Born 25/6/14. Commd 1/9/33. Wg Cdr 1/7/47. Retd GD 22/9/57.
ALLPORT D.K. DSO DFC*. Born 13/4/17. Commd 26/3/42. Wg Cdr 1/7/65. Retd GD 13/4/72.
ALLPORT M.K. MBE. Born 6/3/44. Commd 24/1/65. Wg Cdr 1/1/91. Retd GD 6/9/99.
ALLSO C.E. MBE. Born 30/7/21. Commd 13/12/43. Sqn Ldr 1/7/60. Retd GD 25/4/75.
ALLSOP D.A. Born 11/3/63. Commd 26/9/85. Flt Lt 26/3/91. Retd GD 10/1/03.
ALLSOP K. Born 8/1/26. Commd 7/10/48. Flt Lt 7/4/52. Retd GD 8/1/69.
ALLSOP N.G. Born 20/4/23. Commd 26/8/45. Flt Lt 27/5/54. Retd GD 3/10/67.
ALLSOPP R.F. Born 8/9/35. Commd 27/1/67. Flt Lt 27/1/69. Retd PRT 27/1/75.
ALLSOPP W. Born 20/3/16. Commd 10/6/38. Sqn Ldr 1/1/54. Retd GD 25/4/59.
ALLTON M.C. BSc. Born 23/8/62. Commd 11/12/83. Sqn Ldr 1/7/97. Retd GD 1/2/02.
ALM G.A. Born 11/7/48. Commd 20/9/79. Flt Lt 20/9/81. Retd SUP 20/9/87.
ALMOND J.S. BEM. Born 1/6/21. Commd 12/12/46. Sqn Ldr 1/1/69. Retd SUP 14/12/74.
ALSFORD J.E. BSc. Born 24/3/54. Commd 26/10/75. Sqn Ldr 1/7/85. Retd GD 1/4/88.
ALSOP D. Born 9/7/46. Commd 24/6/71. Flt Lt 24/6/73. Retd ENG 9/7/93.
ALSOP E.G. The Rev. ALCD. Born 19/4/12. Commd 13/9/39. Retd Gp Capt 19/4/67.
ALTERSKYE J.A. Born 20/11/44. Commd 5/12/63. Flt Lt 4/5/72. Retd GD(G) 30/12/72.
ALTON J.S. Born 16/7/50. Commd 6/4/72. Wg Cdr 1/7/91. Retd ENG 29/4/02.
ALVEY M.J. Born 6/11/60. Commd 27/7/89. Sqn Ldr 1/1/01. Retd ADMIN (SEC) 2/4/04.
AMBLER J. BEng MRAeS. Born 1/3/39. Commd 2/10/61. Wg Cdr 1/7/82. Retd GD 4/10/91.
AMBLER K.T.W. MBE. Born 22/3/32. Commd 12/12/51. Sqn Ldr 1/7/69. Retd GD 27/2/76.
AMBLER M.J. Born 2/9/42. Commd 16/9/71. Sqn Ldr 1/7/81. Retd ADMIN 1/10/87.
AMBRIDGE E.G. Born 28/9/07. Commd 8/1/32. Wg Cdr 1/7/48. Retd SUP 28/9/60.
AMBRIDGE F. Born 15/7/29. Commd 1/6/72. Flt Lt 1/6/76. Retd ENG 10/12/84.
AMBROSE D.W. Born 22/3/34. Commd 4/7/69. Flt Lt 4/7/73. Retd ENG 22/3/94.
AMBROSE E.A. AFC. Born 25/2/26. Commd 31/8/50. Flt Lt 27/5/54. Retd GD 31/1/76.
AMBROSE M.D. Born 17/12/36. Commd 20/5/82. Flt Lt 20/5/85. Retd ADMIN 18/12/88.
AMBROSE M.P.W. Born 25/3/35. Commd 8/5/56. Flt Lt 8/11/61. Retd GD 10/2/89.
AMDOR J.A.R. BSocSc MCIPD MCMI. Born 13/12/40. Commd 5/1/65. Sqn Ldr 1/7/76. Retd ADMIN 26/4/91.

AMES J.G. Born 5/5/21. Commd 30/9/54. Flt Lt 10/3/59. Retd ENG 21/1/69.
AMEY P.N. BSc. Born 30/7/54. Commd 17/9/72. Sqn Ldr 1/1/87. Retd ENG 30/7/92.
AMIES D.R. MB BS FRCS(Edin) MRCS LRCP. Born 18/10/34. Commd 30/9/62. Wg Cdr 14/8/71. Retd MED 1/10/74.
AMIES J.N. Born 14/8/38. Commd 7/6/68. Flt Lt 7/6/70. Retd ENG 30/10/76.
AMIES N.F. CEng MIMechE. Born 22/11/40. Commd 4/2/64. Sqn Ldr 1/7/77. Retd ENG 22/11/95.
AMIN J.S. Born 24/10/44. Commd 4/10/63. Flt Lt 4/4/69. Retd GD 1/9/76.
AMOR G. MBE. Born 7/10/22. Commd 30/5/45. Wg Cdr 1/7/65. Retd GD 7/10/77.
AMOR S.R.W. Born 19/10/15. Commd 23/1/39. Sqn Ldr 1/7/48. Retd SUP 23/10/64. rtg Wg Cdr
AMOR T.J. MB ChB. Born 6/8/57. Commd 5/9/78. Wg Cdr 1/8/94. Retd MED 6/8/95.
AMOS A.K. Born 3/7/30. Commd 26/3/52. Gp Capt 1/7/73. Retd GD 3/7/85.
AMOS D.G. MBE. Born 8/4/32. Commd 29/10/64. Flt Lt 29/10/69. Retd ENG 1/9/86.
AMOS S.A. Born 9/10/62. Commd 22/11/84. Flt Lt 3/11/87. Retd ADMIN 9/10/00.
AMOS V.E. Born 24/9/33. Commd 31/3/59. Sqn Ldr 31/10/67. Retd EDN 31/3/75.
AMROLIWALLA F.K. BSc MB BS FRCP DPH DIH DAvMed. Born 21/2/33. Commd 2/5/66. A Cdre 19/11/91.
    Retd MED 21/2/98.
ANCELL G. Born 12/11/53. Commd 18/1/73. Sqn Ldr 1/7/92. Retd GD 23/12/95.
ANDERS J.N. BSc. Born 3/7/40. Commd 9/9/63. Flt Lt 9/12/64. Retd GD 9/9/79.
ANDERS R.G. Born 9/7/39. Commd 25/10/73. Flt Lt 25/10/75. Retd SEC 25/10/81.
ANDERSON A. Born 9/2/34. Commd 15/7/53. Flt Lt 5/10/60. Retd GD 10/12/87.
ANDERSON A.J. CEng MIEE MRAeS. Born 19/1/42. Commd 15/7/63. Sqn Ldr 1/1/73. Retd ENG 19/1/80.
ANDERSON A.W. Born 25/6/43. Commd 10/12/65. Flt Lt 6/10/71. Retd GD 31/1/76.
ANDERSON B.E. Born 4/8/32. Commd 27/1/67. Flt Lt 27/1/69. Retd SUP 27/1/75.
ANDERSON B.M. MCMI. Born 2/12/36. Commd 8/5/56. Flt Lt 7/3/62. Retd GD 2/12/94.
ANDERSON B.R. Born 4/2/34. Commd 12/3/60. Flt Lt 12/9/65. Retd GD 5/2/77.
ANDERSON B.S. Born 21/2/32. Commd 14/5/57. Sqn Ldr 1/1/68. Retd GD 1/1/71.
ANDERSON C.G. BEd. Born 8/1/56. Commd 30/3/86. Flt Lt 30/9/89. Retd SUP 14/3/96.
ANDERSON C.McK. BA. Born 28/5/62. Commd 30/10/83. Flt Lt 30/4/87. Retd ADMIN 22/10/89.
ANDERSON C.S.M. MBE. Born 30/4/39. Commd 13/12/60. Sqn Ldr 1/1/73. Retd GD 13/12/85.
ANDERSON D.D. MBE. Born 22/2/33. Commd 27/3/52. A Cdre 1/1/84. Retd SY 22/8/87.
ANDERSON D.J. Born 2/1/32. Commd 17/12/52. Sqn Ldr 1/7/65. Retd SUP 2/1/75.
ANDERSON D.M. BSc CEng MRAeS. Born 24/6/46. Commd 28/9/64. A Cdre 1/1/93. Retd ENG 1/12/95.
ANDERSON D.S. BSc. Born 9/5/61. Commd 11/12/83. Flt Lt 11/6/86. Retd GD 11/12/99.
ANDERSON G.G. MHCIMA. Born 28/1/54. Commd 11/10/84. Flt Lt 11/10/86. Retd ADMIN 14/3/96.
ANDERSON I.V. MB ChB DPH. Born 14/3/29. Commd 2/2/58. Wg Cdr 23/3/70. Retd MED 2/2/74.
ANDERSON J.A. Born 2/5/29. Commd 4/7/51. Flt Lt 17/10/56. Retd GD 3/5/71.
ANDERSON J.D. Born 22/4/22. Commd 18/11/53. Flt Lt 18/11/58. Retd GD(G) 31/1/73.
ANDERSON J.D. BSc. Born 20/10/40. Commd 5/12/66. Flt Lt 5/9/68. Retd GD 7/11/82.
ANDERSON J.D. MBE. Born 18/3/57. Commd 20/5/82. Sqn Ldr 1/1/91. Retd ADMIN 18/3/98.
ANDERSON J.D. BSc. Born 20/10/40. Commd 5/12/66. Flt Lt 5/9/68. Retd GD 1/4/94.
ANDERSON J.G. BSc. Born 23/4/39. Commd 3/12/61. Sqn Ldr 1/7/74. Retd GD 23/4/94.
ANDERSON J.P. OBE. Born 23/11/43. Commd 14/8/64. Wg Cdr 1/7/85. Retd GD 23/11/98.
ANDERSON K.L. MCMI. Born 4/11/47. Commd 1/8/69. Sqn Ldr 1/1/81. Retd ADMIN 4/11/88.
ANDERSON L.E. Born 19/11/46. Commd 11/6/81. Sqn Ldr 1/1/89. Retd ADMIN 19/5/01.
ANDERSON L.J. MBE CEng MIEE MCMI. Born 30/11/29. Commd 5/12/51. Wg Cdr 1/1/75. Retd ENG 1/10/82.
ANDERSON M. DPhysEd. Born 1/1/39. Commd 15/8/65. Flt Lt 19/3/68. Retd ADMIN 1/9/76.
ANDERSON M.F. Born 6/3/43. Commd 8/11/68. Fg Offr 22/3/71. Retd SUP 28/7/73.
ANDERSON M.I.S. MVO. Born 22/9/31. Commd 28/8/52. Sqn Ldr 1/7/83. Retd GD 22/4/92.
ANDERSON M.J. MSc BSc. Born 1/7/53. Commd 25/9/74. Sqn Ldr 1/7/87. Retd ENG 1/12/92.
ANDERSON M.N. BSc. Born 22/1/64. Commd 20/8/93. Flt Lt 20/3/92. Retd ENG 4/5/92.
ANDERSON N.J.C. Born 9/9/54. Commd 28/11/74. Sqn Ldr 1/7/89. Retd GD 15/7/93.
ANDERSON R. Born 27/11/29. Commd 12/3/52. Flt Lt 12/9/56. Retd GD 27/11/67.
ANDERSON R. BSc. Born 31/12/49. Commd 14/7/74. Sqn Ldr 1/1/90. Retd FLY(N) 31/12/04.
ANDERSON R.C. BSc. Born 12/3/42. Commd 30/9/61. Sqn Ldr 1/7/73. Retd ENG 12/3/80.
ANDERSON R.W. Born 8/9/46. Commd 21/4/67. Flt Lt 4/5/72. Retd GD 1/10/76.
ANDERSON S.E. Born 5/6/47. Commd 6/9/68. Flt Lt 9/11/74. Retd SEC 22/1/79.
ANDERSON T.L. BSc MRAeS. Born 20/2/31. Commd 9/7/54. Sqn Ldr 1/7/70. Retd GD 1/7/73.
ANDERSZ S.T.R. Born 16/3/18. Commd 1/9/39. Flt Lt 1/7/46. Retd SEC 1/4/73.
ANDERSZ T. DFC. Born 27/9/18. Commd 1/3/41. Flt Lt 15/3/53. Retd GD(G) 27/9/73.
ANDERTON D.J. Born 13/2/44. Commd 28/10/66. Flt Lt 28/4/72. Retd GD 7/10/78.
ANDERTON M.B. Born 12/4/42. Commd 29/11/63. Flt Lt 29/5/69. Retd GD 14/1/76. Re-instated 6/10/72 to 21/12/82.
ANDREW A.G. Born 29/10/60. Commd 15/10/81. Flt Lt 15/4/87. Retd GD 27/12/98.
ANDREW D. MBE AFC. Born 26/1/23. Commd 14/7/58. Flt Lt 1/7/58. Retd GD 26/1/72.
ANDREW D. Born 5/11/40. Commd 8/11/68. Sqn Ldr 1/1/77. Retd GD 1/1/91.
ANDREW D.R. MB ChB. Born 20/6/55. Commd 24/10/78. Sqn Ldr 1/2/87. Retd MED 24/10/94.
ANDREW J.M.T. Born 25/8/54. Commd 6/7/80. Flt Lt 6/7/85. Retd ADMIN 1/10/88.
ANDREW R. MBE. Born 12/6/24. Commd 26/2/44. Sqn Ldr 1/7/71. Retd SEC 12/6/79.

ANDREWS A. MSc BSc(Eng) CEng ACGI MRAeS. Born 9/7/34. Commd 22/12/55. A Cdre 1/1/83.
  Retd ENG 3/11/85.
ANDREWS A.E. Born 6/12/30. Commd 8/11/62. Sqn Ldr 1/1/80. Retd ENG 15/3/83.
ANDREWS A.W. MA PhD MSc BSc CPhys CChem MRSC MInstP MCIPD. Born 30/10/46. Commd 18/8/85.
  Sqn Ldr 1/7/90. Retd ADMIN 3/10/01.
ANDREWS C.W. BSc DCAe CEng MRAeS MIEE. Born 3/3/34. Commd 2/2/56. Sqn Ldr 2/8/66. Retd EDN 3/3/72.
ANDREWS D.C. MBE FRIN. Born 1/4/44. Commd 12/7/63. A Cdre 1/1/96. Retd GD 1/4/99.
ANDREWS E.R. The Rev. Born 17/8/33. Commd 29/12/69. Retd Wg Cdr 1/5/88.
ANDREWS F.L. BA. Born 6/1/55. Commd 16/9/73. Flt Lt 15/10/79. Retd SUP 15/7/88.
ANDREWS F.S. Born 8/9/37. Commd 11/6/60. Flt Lt 26/7/67. Retd GD(G) 19/1/76.
ANDREWS G.D. Born 28/5/37. Commd 29/7/58. Sqn Ldr 1/1/69. Retd GD 24/10/69.
ANDREWS G.N. Born 14/1/43. Commd 10/11/80. Sqn Ldr 1/7/91. Retd ADMIN 14/1/98.
ANDREWS G.P. Born 22/3/49. Commd 14/2/99. Flt Lt 14/2/99. Retd OPS SPT(FLTOPS) 22/3/04.
ANDREWS G.R. Born 1/12/38. Commd 30/10/57. Flt Lt 18/2/64. Retd PRT 31/7/65.
ANDREWS J. Born 20/9/35. Commd 15/2/62. Flt Lt 1/4/66. Retd GD 20/9/73.
ANDREWS J.B. CEng MIEE FRAeS. Born 25/4/36. Commd 23/7/58. Gp Capt 1/7/79. Retd ENG 28/5/83.
ANDREWS J.W.T. TD CEng MIMechE. Born 25/4/33. Commd 20/2/72. Wg Cdr 1/7/82. Retd ENG 25/6/91.
ANDREWS M.A. Born 27/12/32. Commd 4/9/58. Flt Lt 4/12/64. Retd ADMIN 30/9/67. Re-employed 1/3/71.
  Sqn Ldr 1/7/74. Retd ADMIN 1/6/83.
ANDREWS M.L. Born 19/5/60. Commd 11/1/79. Flt Lt 11/7/84. Retd GD 19/5/98.
ANDREWS N.K. MB ChB BSc DRCOG. Born 13/7/69. Commd 5/8/99. Sqn Ldr 23/8/99. Retd MEDICAL 19/5/03.
ANDREWS P.D. BEM. Born 26/7/57. Commd 26/9/91. Flt Lt 26/9/93. Retd ADMIN 14/3/96.
ANDREWS R. BA. Born 15/10/33. Commd 18/10/55. Sqn Ldr 1/7/64. Retd GD 18/10/71.
ANDREWS R.M. Born 6/9/50. Commd 10/9/70. Flt Lt 10/3/77. Retd GD(G) 6/9/88.
ANDREWS S.A. Born 12/10/47. Commd 28/11/69. Flt Lt 28/5/75. Retd GD 12/10/85.
ANDREWS S.C. Born 26/9/42. Commd 13/1/72. Flt Lt 13/1/74. Retd GD 14/4/96.
ANDREWS W.D.B. Born 8/3/32. Commd 30/9/53. Sqn Ldr 1/7/82. Retd GD 23/8/88.
ANFIELD J.E. Born 16/2/52. Commd 8/9/83. Flt Lt 8/9/85. Retd ADMIN 8/9/92.
ANGEL B.L. Born 27/4/33. Commd 29/5/56. Flt Lt 13/4/60. Retd GD 1/12/83.
ANGEL R. Born 10/12/53. Commd 3/1/78. Flt Lt 3/1/80. Retd GD 31/7/93.
ANGELA D.W.F. Born 19/7/38. Commd 19/9/60. Gp Capt 1/1/86. Retd GD 17/5/95.
ANGELL A.P. Born 27/5/44. Commd 28/6/79. Flt Lt 28/6/82. Retd GD 31/12/93.
ANGELL E.E.M. AFC. Born 18/9/14. Commd 10/2/36. Wg Cdr 1/7/47. Retd GD 10/11/61.
ANGELL H.E. DFC. Born 1/11/16. Commd 29/6/36. Wg Cdr 1/7/52. Retd GD 1/11/71.
ANGELL K.G. Born 18/4/20. Commd 17/7/43. Flt Lt 14/11/56. Retd GD 20/2/68.
ANGELL T.J. BSc CEng MIEE. Born 6/6/12. Commd 28/1/43. Fg Offr 29/1/44. Retd ENG 28/3/46. rtg Flt Lt
ANGUS D.A. Born 12/6/48. Commd 28/2/69. Wg Cdr 1/1/92. Retd GD 12/6/03.
ANGUS G. Born 27/10/25. Commd 6/7/45. Flt Lt 1/3/61. Retd GD 7/5/73.
ANGUS I.J.Mcl. Born 2/7/39. Commd 23/9/66. Sqn Ldr 1/7/91. Retd GD 2/7/94.
ANGUS J.A. Born 29/3/47. Commd 1/3/68. Plt Offr 1/3/68. Retd GD 20/11/68.
ANGUS P.J.M. MBE BA. Born 15/2/55. Commd 9/12/76. Wg Cdr 1/7/93. Retd OPS SPT 6/4/01.
ANGUS S.G. Born 28/3/58. Commd 9/12/76. Flt Lt 9/6/83. Retd ADMIN 30/12/86.
ANNABLE K. Born 6/8/22. Commd 19/6/44. Sqn Ldr 1/7/62. Retd GD 5/9/69.
ANNAL E. CEng MIEE MRAeS. Born 23/10/33. Commd 5/5/60. Sqn Ldr 1/7/72. Retd ENG 2/4/85.
ANNAN R.H. DSO. Born 8/8/17. Commd 3/11/40. Wg Cdr 1/7/52. Retd GD 12/3/55.
ANNAND K.P. MA MSc. Born 9/7/37. Commd 30/9/55. Sqn Ldr 1/1/67. Retd ENG 9/7/75.
ANNING J.A. BA. Born 9/10/36. Commd 6/4/62. Fg Offr 6/10/62. Retd GD 30/8/65.
ANNING T.V. Born 24/12/42. Commd 17/5/79. Flt Lt 17/5/84. Retd GD 17/4/93.
ANSCOMBE M.R.J. Born 7/9/38. Commd 30/5/59. Sqn Ldr 1/1/74. Retd GD 1/4/79.
ANSDELL D.J. Born 19/5/27. Commd 3/11/51. Flt Lt 14/5/58. Retd GD 19/5/65.
ANSELL A.N. Born 8/8/24. Commd 23/1/50. Flt Lt 21/12/59. Retd GD 12/7/65.
ANSELL V.B. DFC. Born 29/4/15. Commd 2/6/44. Flt Lt 2/6/50. Retd GD(G) 23/8/61.
ANSELL W.T.K. Born 15/2/30. Commd 6/4/50. Flt Lt 19/11/53. Retd GD 20/8/71.
ANSLEY J.H. Born 3/11/32. Commd 2/7/52. Flt Lt 27/11/57. Retd GD 3/11/70.
ANSTEAD E.W. Born 4/3/34. Commd 11/6/52. Flt Lt 28/9/60. Retd GD 9/9/79.
ANSTEAD J.S. Born 15/10/46. Commd 3/4/67. Flt Lt 28/4/75. Retd GD 3/1/75.
ANSTEE S.D. Born 9/11/66. Commd 28/7/95. Flt Lt 28/7/97. Retd ADMIN (SEC) 9/11/04.
ANSTEY B.G. MInstAM. Born 10/12/37. Commd 26/3/59. Gp Capt 1/7/83. Retd SY(PRT) 10/12/87.
ANSTISS R. MPhil CPhys CEng DipTech DipSoton MInstP MIEE. Born 30/1/40. Commd 13/2/72. Sqn Ldr 1/1/78.
  Retd ENG 13/2/88.
ANTHONY E. MD ChB FRCPsych DCH DPM. Born 26/10/30. Commd 3/2/57. Gp Capt 3/2/80. Retd MED 30/8/89.
ANTHONY J.D.E. Born 7/2/57. Commd 28/10/76. Flt Lt 28/4/82. Retd GD 1/8/94.
ANTHONY K. MCMI. Born 5/12/26. Commd 14/11/51. Sqn Ldr 1/1/62. Retd GD 12/11/73.
ANTHONY K.F. Born 1/3/43. Commd 2/6/77. Flt Lt 2/6/79. Retd GD 2/6/85.
ANTHONY S.T. Born 30/8/58. Commd 17/7/87. Flt Lt 17/8/90. Retd OPS SPT 30/8/99.
ANTLIFF D.M. Born 28/3/48. Commd 24/11/67. Flt Lt 24/5/73. Retd GD 28/3/86.

ANTON D.J. MSc MB BS MFOM MRCS LRCP DAvMed. Born 25/1/46. Commd 27/1/69. Wg Cdr 25/5/85. Retd MED 1/4/93.
ANTONIAK T.P. Born 26/6/20. Commd 17/5/56. Sqn Ldr 1/1/72. Retd GD 26/6/75.
APIAFI H. Born 8/9/41. Commd 23/9/66. Flt Lt 1/7/69. Retd GD 8/9/79.
APPLEBOOM K.J. MCMI. Born 18/5/26. Commd 3/5/46. Wg Cdr 1/7/69. Retd GD 18/5/81.
APPLEBY B.K. Born 12/5/46. Commd 6/5/66. Sqn Ldr 1/7/96. Retd GD 12/5/01.
APPLEBY M.W. Born 29/9/47. Commd 31/7/86. Flt Lt 31/7/90. Retd ENG 1/10/93.
APPLEBY N.E. Born 31/12/44. Commd 26/9/62. Flt Lt 4/11/70. Retd GD 31/12/82.
APPLEFORD K.E. AFC. Born 11/2/25. Commd 6/1/55. Sqn Ldr 1/1/70. Retd GD 11/2/83.
APPLEGARTH P.N.J. BSc. Born 29/10/57. Commd 5/9/76. Flt Lt 15/4/81. Retd GD 6/1/89.
APPLEGATE D.S. Born 2/10/31. Commd 23/9/53. Sqn Ldr 1/7/65. Retd ENG 2/10/69.
APPLETON J.G. Born 8/6/17. Commd 7/5/53. Sqn Ldr 1/7/62. Retd ENG 5/8/67.
APPLETON J.H. Born 18/4/19. Commd 23/10/43. Flt Lt 23/4/47. Retd GD 18/4/62.
APPLETON S.G. Born 1/5/48. Commd 1/8/69. Gp Capt 1/7/94. Retd ADMIN 14/3/96.
APPLEYARD B. Born 11/8/22. Commd 29/10/43. Flt Lt 7/1/52. Retd GD 11/8/77.
APPLEYARD D.R. Born 22/4/32. Commd 22/5/75. Flt Lt 22/5/78. Retd GD 7/9/83.
APPLEYARD F. FCMI. Born 4/7/37. Commd 18/4/51. Gp Capt 1/1/78. Retd GD 4/7/86.
APPLEYARD G.K. BA. Born 7/4/35. Commd 12/7/57. Sqn Ldr 15/3/65. Retd EDN 18/4/78.
APPLEYARD K.D. Born 24/3/48. Commd 11/5/78. Sqn Ldr 1/1/85. Retd SUP 11/5/92.
APPLEYARD R.J. MSc BEng CEng MRAeS. Born 12/6/55. Commd 5/9/76. Sqn Ldr 1/1/90. Retd ENG 12/6/93.
APPS R.M. Born 25/2/45. Commd 11/4/85. Sqn Ldr 1/7/96. Retd ENG 25/8/00.
ARAM G.D. MBE. Born 10/6/43. Commd 12/1/62. Sqn Ldr 1/7/81. Retd GD 10/6/98.
ARATHOON W.J. Born 30/12/61. Commd 9/4/81. Sqn Ldr 1/1/98. Retd GD 1/7/01.
ARBER J.C. Born 23/4/28. Commd 25/5/50. Sqn Ldr 1/1/62. Retd GD 22/6/74.
ARCHBELL T.H. DFC. Born 23/10/14. Commd 16/5/38. Sqn Ldr 1/9/45. Retd GD 11/7/47. rtg Wg Cdr
ARCHBOLD D.A. BA MCMI. Born 20/2/45. Commd 15/7/66. Sqn Ldr 1/1/76. Retd ADMIN 20/2/89. rtg Wg Cdr
ARCHBOLD F. Born 29/6/21. Commd 16/6/44. Flt Lt 16/12/47. Retd GD 28/6/70.
ARCHBOLD J.F.P. Born 28/8/21. Commd 1/4/45. Sqn Ldr 1/7/66. Retd GD(G) 28/8/76.
ARCHER D.F. Born 10/8/27. Commd 22/8/63. Flt Lt 22/8/68. Retd ENG 29/8/75.
ARCHER D.F. MBE MSc MCIPS. Born 14/6/48. Commd 27/2/70. Gp Capt 1/7/02. Retd GD 31/7/04.
ARCHER G.M. BSc. Born 24/5/64. Commd 23/9/83. Sqn Ldr 1/1/95. Retd GD 24/5/02.
ARCHER H.D. DFC. Born 10/7/22. Commd 5/9/42. Wg Cdr 1/1/61. Retd GD 10/7/77.
ARCHER H.M. AFC MRAeS. Born 25/3/27. Commd 21/3/52. Gp Capt 1/1/73. Retd GD 2/9/80.
ARCHER J.A. Born 28/11/47. Commd 11/10/84. Flt Lt 11/10/88. Retd ENG 31/12/96.
ARCHER J.P. Born 18/8/37. Commd 19/2/76. Sqn Ldr 1/1/86. Retd GD 2/8/95.
ARCHER L.G. CEng FCMI MIEE. Born 6/11/44. Commd 17/12/64. Gp Capt 1/1/91. Retd ENG 1/5/94.
ARCHER M.G. BSc. Born 3/12/62. Commd 30/1/81. Flt Lt 15/10/87. Retd ENG 1/6/92.
ARCHER P.J. Born 19/2/10. Commd 18/9/41. Flt Lt 1/9/45. Retd ENG 4/10/59. rtg Sqn Ldr
ARCHER-JONES K.E. BSc. Born 6/6/54. Commd 16/9/73. Gp Capt 1/7/97. Retd ENG 1/5/99.
ARCHIBALD D. Born 23/2/50. Commd 3/1/69. Flt Lt 1/6/76. Retd SUP 23/4/77.
ARDEN J.P. Born 18/10/64. Commd 19/7/84. Sqn Ldr 1/7/97. Retd FLY(N) 23/6/03.
ARDEN R.W. ACA. Born 2/9/47. Commd 7/3/71. Fg Offr 7/9/71. Retd SEC 30/11/74.
ARDLEY B. Born 10/12/34. Commd 19/12/59. Gp Capt 1/1/84. Retd SY 20/1/87.
ARDLEY J.C. MBE. Born 11/5/47. Commd 3/12/70. Sqn Ldr 1/7/93. Retd GD 11/5/02.
ARGALL I.H.A. MCIPS MCMI. Born 5/4/38. Commd 5/3/57. Sqn Ldr 1/7/70. Retd SUP 5/4/96.
ARGUE D.W. BEM. Born 3/4/31. Commd 8/11/68. Sqn Ldr 1/7/82. Retd ENG 29/9/86.
ARKELL-HARDWICK G.H. Born 20/5/40. Commd 23/12/58. Sqn Ldr 1/1/70. Retd GD 1/2/79.
ARKIESON D.S. Born 13/8/56. Commd 22/5/75. Flt Lt 22/11/81. Retd GD(G) 13/8/85.
ARKLE N. BSc. Born 9/7/57. Commd 20/1/80. Sqn Ldr 1/7/94. Retd SUP 1/10/02.
ARKLEY J.D. BA. Born 11/9/36. Commd 31/8/62. Flt Lt 15/2/64. Retd GD 23/11/82.
ARM D.A. Born 19/5/25. Commd 21/4/44. Sqn Ldr 1/10/55. Retd GD 30/1/76.
ARMIGER N.S. Born 21/4/39. Commd 23/12/58. Sqn Ldr 1/1/84. Retd GD(G) 21/4/94.
ARMITAGE A. Born 3/12/33. Commd 13/8/52. Flt Lt 20/2/58. Retd GD 3/12/88.
ARMITAGE A. BA. Born 2/4/47. Commd 13/10/85. Sqn Ldr 1/7/89. Retd ADMIN 22/10/94.
ARMITAGE F.S. Born 3/6/29. Commd 6/5/65. Flt Lt 6/5/68. Retd GD 3/6/87.
ARMITAGE G.D. Born 6/2/31. Commd 10/8/59. Flt Lt 27/6/61. Retd GD(G) 6/2/86.
ARMITAGE J. Born 9/4/16. Commd 12/6/58. Sqn Ldr 6/7/67. Retd MED(T) 1/5/70.
ARMITAGE Sir Michael KCB CBE. Born 25/8/30. Commd 14/4/53. ACM 1/7/86. Retd GD 5/4/90.
ARMOUR P.MacD. Born 12/5/28. Commd 4/4/50. Flt Lt 5/10/52. Retd GD 15/10/54.
ARMSON B.R. The Rev. AIB. Born 21/6/46. Commd 17/8/86. Retd Flt Lt 31/7/87.
ARMSTRONG B. BA. Born 19/11/56. Commd 16/12/79. Sqn Ldr 1/7/89. Retd GD 7/12/97.
ARMSTRONG B.R. Born 9/9/56. Commd 23/11/78. Wg Cdr 1/1/95. Retd GD 31/7/98.
ARMSTRONG C. MCMI. Born 22/5/23. Commd 20/4/50. Wg Cdr 1/1/73. Retd SUP 31/3/77.
ARMSTRONG C. CEng MIMechE MRAeS. Born 18/3/35. Commd 2/11/62. Sqn Ldr 1/7/69. Retd ENG 7/11/78.
ARMSTRONG C. Born 24/4/52. Commd 16/3/73. Sqn Ldr 1/1/81. Retd GD 24/4/90.
ARMSTRONG D. Born 3/11/37. Commd 24/9/59. Flt Lt 1/4/66. Retd ENG 3/11/75.

ARMSTRONG D.B. BDS MGDSRCSEng LDSRCS DGDP(UK). Born 21/9/46. Commd 11/4/89. Gp Capt 1/7/96.
Retd DENTAL 31/10/03.
ARMSTRONG E.P. Born 19/3/36. Commd 19/9/59. Flt Lt 19/3/65. Retd GD 15/10/88.
ARMSTRONG G.P. Born 3/2/39. Commd 19/2/76. Flt Lt 19/2/81. Retd ENG 12/12/83.
ARMSTRONG G.R. BSc. Born 28/2/55. Commd 25/2/79. Flt Lt 25/5/80. Retd GD 1/6/99.
ARMSTRONG J. Born 4/2/35. Commd 13/12/55. Sqn Ldr 1/1/68. Retd GD 4/2/73.
ARMSTRONG J.C. MCIPS. Born 10/11/46. Commd 25/8/67. Gp Capt 1/1/95. Retd SUP 10/11/02.
ARMSTRONG J.D. MBE. Born 9/3/37. Commd 19/9/57. Wg Cdr 1/7/81. Retd GD 9/3/92.
ARMSTRONG J.G. Born 12/11/23. Commd 13/4/44. Sqn Ldr 1/1/55. Retd GD 12/11/61.
ARMSTRONG J.M. Born 29/5/60. Commd 28/6/79. Flt Lt 28/12/84. Retd GD 31/7/98.
ARMSTRONG J.S. Born 30/9/29. Commd 8/11/51. Flt Lt 24/4/68. Retd GD 16/5/81.
ARMSTRONG L.I. MCIPS. Born 4/5/43. Commd 24/4/70. Sqn Ldr 1/7/84. Retd SUP 2/5/89.
ARMSTRONG M.H. BA. Born 17/7/46. Commd 11/1/79. Wg Cdr 1/7/00. Retd ENG 17/7/01.
ARMSTRONG M.J. FHCIMA. Born 23/6/45. Commd 9/11/65. Gp Capt 1/7/90. Retd ADMIN 14/3/96.
ARMSTRONG N.I. BA. Born 7/2/34. Commd 21/6/56. Sqn Ldr 21/12/66. Retd EDN 30/6/72.
ARMSTRONG N.J. MCIPS. Born 9/11/44. Commd 3/10/69. Sqn Ldr 1/1/83. Retd SUP 14/3/96.
ARMSTRONG P.J. Born 15/4/30. Commd 11/4/51. Sqn Ldr 1/1/62. Retd GD 5/12/75.
ARMSTRONG P.W. Born 4/5/41. Commd 3/1/64. Sqn Ldr 1/1/74. Retd GD 13/8/79.
ARMSTRONG P.W. Born 20/9/60. Commd 7/8/87. Flt Lt 27/9/90. Retd ENG 23/4/94.
ARMSTRONG R. MBE. Born 13/12/23. Commd 12/6/44. Flt Lt 3/7/48. Retd GD 21/12/61.
ARMSTRONG R.L. CEng MIEE. Born 26/1/20. Commd 18/11/43. Sqn Ldr 1/1/56. Retd ENG 17/12/73.
ARMSTRONG S.W. Born 3/1/31. Commd 20/6/51. Flt Lt 20/12/55. Retd GD 3/1/69.
ARMSTRONG T. CEng MIEE. Born 9/5/30. Commd 27/4/65. Flt Lt 27/1/67. Retd ENG 1/10/76.
ARMSTRONG W. MBE. Born 29/1/44. Commd 17/5/79. Sqn Ldr 1/1/88. Retd ADMIN 28/5/94.
ARMSTRONG W.J.A. Born 26/5/23. Commd 11/9/42. Flt Lt 29/3/51. Retd GD 28/1/68.
ARNAUD J.R. DFC. Born 23/8/20. Commd 11/1/43. Sqn Ldr 1/1/68. Retd GD 23/8/75.
ARNEY J.W. Born 22/6/14. Commd 27/7/35. Wg Cdr 1/7/47. Retd GD 31/10/57.
ARNOLD A.V. Born 22/7/34. Commd 28/4/61. Flt Lt 9/2/68. Retd GD 21/12/76.
ARNOLD C. Born 12/3/35. Commd 7/1/71. Flt Lt 7/1/73. Retd SUP 7/1/79.
ARNOLD D.J.B. Born 25/11/36. Commd 27/3/56. Flt Lt 1/8/62. Retd GD(G) 3/4/80.
ARNOLD L.E. BA MCIPD. Born 1/3/63. Commd 1/4/85. Sqn Ldr 1/7/96. Retd ADMIN 29/8/01.
ARNOLD M. OBE BSc(Eng) CEng MRAeS MCMI. Born 24/12/38. Commd 12/9/61. Gp Capt 1/1/85.
Retd GD 24/12/93.
ARNOLD M.D. Born 24/2/28. Commd 15/8/51. Flt Lt 15/5/57. Retd GD 25/1/67.
ARNOLD M.E. Born 9/10/62. Commd 25/2/82. Flt Lt 25/8/87. Retd GD 9/8/91.
ARNOLD P. Born 7/6/49. Commd 2/5/69. Sqn Ldr 1/7/84. Retd SUP 7/6/93.
ARNOLD S. Born 24/5/64. Commd 15/3/84. Flt Lt 16/12/89. Retd SUP 25/5/02.
ARNOLD S. MBE MCMI. Born 14/12/18. Commd 26/4/45. Sqn Ldr 1/7/55. Retd RGT 14/12/73.
ARNOLD S.P. Born 18/10/63. Commd 28/7/88. Flt Lt 24/5/92. Retd GD(G) 14/3/96.
ARNOLD W.J. Born 7/3/21. Commd 21/10/54. Sqn Ldr 1/7/69. Retd ENG 7/6/73.
ARNOT T.M.K. OBE. Born 7/1/47. Commd 19/8/71. Gp Capt 1/7/96. Retd ADMIN 7/1/02.
ARNOTT R.D. CBE FCMI MCIPD. Born 4/3/39. Commd 7/1/58. A Cdre 1/7/87. Retd GD 28/6/96.
ARNOTT R.M.H. Born 28/9/40. Commd 22/5/64. Flt Lt 22/11/69. Retd GD 1/6/86.
ARNOTT W. AFC. Born 13/3/16. Commd 31/8/40. Flt Lt 1/9/45. Retd GD(G) 13/3/71. rtg Sqn Ldr
ARROWSMITH F.B. BSc. Born 25/3/30. Commd 15/11/51. Sqn Ldr 25/3/63. Retd EDN 25/3/68.
ARROWSMITH R.H. BEM. Born 8/11/41. Commd 7/3/85. Flt Lt 1/9/91. Retd ENG 2/7/93.
ARSCOTT J.R.D. Born 19/4/47. Commd 23/3/66. AVM 1/7/99. Retd OPS SPT 18/4/01.
ARSCOTT K.M. Born 15/1/43. Commd 21/10/64. Flt Lt 21/10/70. Retd SEC 1/3/73.
ARSCOTT P.M. Born 13/7/34. Commd 27/2/70. Flt Lt 28/8/75. Retd GD 23/5/81.
ARSCOTT R.H. CBE. Born 18/9/24. Commd 11/8/44. Gp Capt 1/1/70. Retd GD 3/4/79.
ARTHUR J.R.G. BSc. Born 9/6/54. Commd 6/5/76. Sqn Ldr 1/1/90. Retd GD 14/9/96.
ARTHUR L. DFC. Born 15/10/19. Commd 28/7/43. Flt Lt 28/1/47. Retd GD 2/7/47.
ARTHUR L.T. Born 9/5/35. Commd 2/1/54. Sqn Ldr 1/1/68. Retd GD 9/5/73.
ARTHUR P.J. MBE. Born 17/4/36. Commd 23/7/58. Gp Capt 1/1/81. Retd ENG 17/4/90.
ARTUS E.D. Born 22/4/20. Commd 7/3/47. Flt Lt 7/9/51. Retd SUP 27/5/56.
ARTUS E.G. BSc CEng MIOSH MRAeS MCMI. Born 22/12/46. Commd 22/9/65. Wg Cdr 1/1/91. Retd ENG 14/3/97.
ARULANANDAM E.A.A. Born 12/7/44. Commd 25/8/67. Flt Lt 25/2/74. Retd SUP 7/2/83. Re-entered 6/7/90.
Flt Lt 6/7/90. Retd SUP 6/7/96.
ARUNDEL I. BEM. Born 2/1/54. Commd 16/2/89. Flt Lt 16/2/89. Retd ENG 1/1/93.
ARUNDELL W.H. Born 10/1/21. Commd 10/5/44. Flt Lt 1/9/45. Retd PE 10/1/76.
ASBURY M.J.A. Born 30/4/39. Commd 24/9/59. Flt Lt 1/7/68. Retd GD 30/4/77.
ASH C.S. BSc. Born 8/8/52. Commd 3/9/72. Flt Lt 15/4/76. Retd GD 14/9/96.
ASH J.R.L. The Rev. Born 13/6/17. Commd 10/2/50. Retd Wg Cdr 13/9/72.
ASH J.S. BA. Born 15/7/53. Commd 17/6/79. Flt Lt 17/9/82. Retd SUP 2/1/85.
ASH P.D. Born 8/7/31. Commd 5/12/51. Flt Lt 5/6/56. Retd GD 31/10/75.
ASHBY M.F. Born 14/11/33. Commd 7/5/52. Flt Lt 2/10/57. Retd GD 14/11/71.

ASHBY P.M.c.E. Born 15/3/60. Commd 5/4/79. Flt Lt 5/10/84. Retd GD 1/5/91.
ASHCROFT G.A. Born 28/5/46. Commd 2/3/78. Wg Cdr 1/1/94. Retd SUP 26/9/00.
ASHCROFT J.B. MB BCh FRCR DMR(D). Born 29/1/47. Commd 27/1/69. Wg Cdr 26/7/84. Retd MED 29/1/85.
ASHDOWN B. Born 23/8/19. Commd 15/4/43. Sqn Ldr 1/1/57. Retd ENG 23/8/68.
ASHE M.J. Born 23/12/23. Commd 13/3/46. Sqn Ldr 1/1/60. Retd RGT 23/12/68.
ASHFORD A.M. BSc. Born 7/4/65. Commd 15/9/86. Flt Lt 15/1/90. Retd GD 15/7/99.
ASHFORD F. FTCL ARCM. Born 30/10/36. Commd 15/6/83. Flt Lt 15/3/81. Retd DM 31/10/89.
ASHFORD R.G. CBE LLB. Born 2/5/31. Commd 27/2/52. AVM 1/7/83. Retd GD 12/9/85.
ASHFORD-SMITH R.P. Born 10/5/25. Commd 29/4/53. Flt Lt 29/4/59. Retd GD 10/5/63.
ASHFORTH-SMITH A.J. BA. Born 8/2/54. Commd 11/9/83. Sqn Ldr 1/7/94. Retd SUP 14/3/97.
ASHLEIGH-THOMAS P.D. BSc BSc CEng MIEE MRAeS MCMI. Born 29/1/40. Commd 6/8/63. Sqn Ldr 1/7/75.
    Retd ENG 7/8/88. rtg Wg Cdr
ASHLEY B.A. AFC. Born 10/1/28. Commd 21/3/51. Wg Cdr 1/1/69. Retd GD 6/5/77.
ASHLEY G.M. MInstAM(Dip). Born 20/12/34. Commd 20/6/63. Flt Lt 17/3/71. Retd ADMIN 20/12/89.
ASHLEY K.F. OBE BDS FDSRCS FRCS LRCP. Born 3/4/34. Commd 29/2/60. Gp Capt 19/4/82. Retd DEL 1/9/88.
ASHLEY M.S. Born 1/7/42. Commd 26/8/81. Flt Lt 25/9/69. Retd GD 12/1/93.
ASHLEY N.J. Born 6/9/42. Commd 25/1/63. Flt Lt 6/3/68. Retd GD 6/9/80.
ASHMAN J.K. Born 6/6/30. Commd 20/12/51. Flt Lt 22/5/57. Retd GD 6/6/68.
ASHMAN R.J.L. BA. Born 21/7/56. Commd 4/6/87. Flt Lt 4/6/89. Retd ENG 4/6/01.
ASHMORE P.A. MRIN. Born 2/6/38. Commd 3/7/56. Sqn Ldr 1/1/73. Retd GD 2/6/88.
ASHMORE P.E. BSc. Born 14/7/51. Commd 25/2/72. Sqn Ldr 1/1/84. Retd ENG 1/6/91.
ASHOVER D.R. AFC. Born 8/6/31. Commd 17/5/51. Flt Lt 6/9/56. Retd GD 5/4/72.
ASHTON D. Born 20/6/49. Commd 3/10/69. Sqn Ldr 1/1/90. Retd GD(G) 1/10/95.
ASHTON E.R. Born 28/4/21. Commd 29/4/45. Flt Lt 10/11/55. Retd GD 14/12/69.
ASHTON J.M. Born 25/11/39. Commd 26/10/66. Sqn Ldr 1/7/76. Retd GD 18/7/88. Re-instated 15/8/90.
    Sqn Ldr 29/7/78. Retd GD 25/11/94.
ASHTON J.T. Born 15/8/46. Commd 21/1/66. Flt Lt 21/7/71. Retd GD 26/8/77.
ASHTON L.J. The Venerable CB. Born 27/6/15. Commd 15/5/45. Retd AVM 1/7/73.
ASHTON M.A. MB BS MRCPath. Born 6/3/57. Commd 20/9/81. Wg Cdr 20/9/94. Retd MED 14/3/96.
ASHTON M.D. Born 3/3/43. Commd 22/2/63. Flt Lt 22/8/68. Retd GD 3/3/81.
ASHTON R. Born 16/2/36. Commd 14/8/56. Flt Lt 14/2/62. Retd GD 16/2/91.
ASHTON T. Born 2/9/28. Commd 11/1/50. Flt Lt 30/11/55. Retd GD 2/9/66.
ASHTON-JONES K. Born 13/5/42. Commd 12/6/62. Gp Capt 1/7/87. Retd ADMIN 2/4/94.
ASHURST D. Born 25/11/46. Commd 27/6/71. Flt Lt 27/3/74. Retd ENG 18/10/75.
ASHWORTH A.D. Born 23/10/26. Commd 25/7/52. Flt Lt 5/12/55. Retd GD 19/6/73.
ASHWORTH D.C. BSc. Born 2/6/63. Commd 8/8/97. Flt Lt 19/8/91. Retd FLY(N) 19/2/05.
ASHWORTH D.R. MDefStud. Born 10/3/62. Commd 29/1/87. Sqn Ldr 1/1/98. Retd ADMIN (SEC) 9/2/03.
ASHWORTH J. Born 9/8/42. Commd 11/8/77. Sqn Ldr 1/1/91. Retd GD(G) 22/4/94.
ASHWORTH J.N.L. BA. Born 11/9/48. Commd 5/10/75. Wg Cdr 5/10/85. Retd LGL 5/10/91.
ASHWORTH K. Born 15/9/63. Commd 10/5/90. Flt Lt 10/5/92. Retd SUP 14/3/96.
ASHWORTH R.C.B. Born 3/8/28. Commd 11/4/51. Sqn Ldr 1/7/72. Retd GD 17/6/77.
ASHWORTH S.P. Born 24/4/66. Commd 4/7/85. Flt Lt 4/1/90. Retd GD 12/5/97.
ASKER H.A. DFC DFM. Born 24/2/20. Commd 8/11/41. Sqn Ldr 1/7/51. Retd GD 22/4/63.
ASKHAM W.D. OBE CEng FCMI MRAeS. Born 19/3/31. Commd 12/2/53. Gp Capt 1/1/74. Retd ENG 20/6/88.
ASPIN P.D. Born 15/11/31. Commd 7/6/68. Sqn Ldr 1/7/78. Retd ENG 15/4/82.
ASPINALL K.P. Born 5/6/45. Commd 19/12/79. Sqn Ldr 1/1/87. Retd SUP 1/5/90.
ASPINALL M. BA. Born 30/5/59. Commd 4/7/82. Sqn Ldr 1/7/91. Retd ADMIN 4/1/97.
ASPINALL R.M. MA. Born 7/1/47. Commd 12/1/69. Sqn Ldr 1/1/88. Retd GD 1/9/02.
ASPLIN D.J. Born 30/7/56. Commd 27/3/75. Flt Lt 1/1/93. Retd GD(G) 1/1/96.
ASSHETON W.R. DFC. Born 12/12/17. Commd 6/3/39. Sqn Ldr 1/8/47. Retd GD 22/11/57.
ASTILL M.C. BSc. Born 1/5/63. Commd 13/9/81. Sqn Ldr 1/1/99. Retd GD 1/1/02.
ASTLE M.H. MBE. Born 29/4/43. Commd 12/1/62. Sqn Ldr 1/7/91. Retd GD 3/5/94.
ASTLEY P.M. Born 27/11/15. Commd 1/8/36. Wg Cdr 12/9/45. Retd GD 15/12/47. rtg Gp Capt
ASTLEY-COOPER N.F. BEng. Born 11/7/49. Commd 16/1/72. Sqn Ldr 1/1/83. Retd ENG 16/1/91.
ASTON A.A. Born 1/9/37. Commd 17/5/56. Sqn Ldr 1/7/69. Retd SUP 1/4/77.
ASTON A.B. Born 2/3/44. Commd 4/3/71. Flt Lt 13/6/76. Retd GD 13/6/84.
ASTON B.J. Born 7/9/29. Commd 19/8/71. Sqn Ldr 1/7/84. Retd ENG 7/5/88.
ASTON C.J. Born 29/8/48. Commd 13/9/70. Sqn Ldr 1/1/81. Retd ADMIN 13/9/86.
ATCHISON I.W. BDS. Born 20/12/26. Commd 29/9/50. Wg Cdr 17/7/63. Retd DEL 29/9/66.
ATCHISON J.D. BA. Born 7/1/64. Commd 3/1/88. Flt Lt 3/7/91. Retd OPS SPT(FC) 3/1/04.
ATHERLEY D.M.K. Born 11/4/31. Commd 30/7/52. Wg Cdr 1/7/80. Retd GD 11/4/86.
ATHERTON D.A. FCMI. Born 2/4/31. Commd 9/4/52. A Cdre 1/7/82. Retd ADMIN 1/8/84.
ATHERTON D.W. Born 26/8/36. Commd 11/1/79. Sqn Ldr 1/1/89. Retd MED(SEC) 1/6/93.
ATHERTON S.E. Born 17/2/66. Commd 23/8/95. Flt Lt 30/9/95. Retd OPS SPT(ATC) 20/6/04.
ATHERTON S.P. Born 16/5/57. Commd 9/8/79. Wg Cdr 1/1/96. Retd SUP 21/11/98.
ATKIN C.H. Born 26/4/21. Commd 7/9/44. Flt Lt 12/12/52. Retd GD 29/1/63.

ATKINS A.R. CEng MIEE. Born 30/4/26. Commd 25/5/50. Wg Cdr 1/1/67. Retd ENG 1/5/74.
ATKINS C.V. Born 14/2/29. Commd 7/12/49. Flt Lt 27/12/55. Retd GD 14/2/67.
ATKINS C.W.F. Born 6/11/45. Commd 11/3/65. Flt Lt 11/9/71. Retd ENG 12/3/75.
ATKINS D.MacD. Born 2/9/40. Commd 5/11/59. Flt Lt 9/2/68. Retd SEC 21/8/68.
ATKINS P.B. OBE MCMI. Born 31/5/43. Commd 9/3/62. Wg Cdr 1/7/85. Retd GD 17/3/93.
ATKINS P.C. Born 30/7/37. Commd 29/7/58. Gp Capt 1/7/86. Retd SUP 30/7/92.
ATKINS P.J. Born 8/11/40. Commd 18/12/62. Sqn Ldr 1/1/77. Retd GD 8/11/95.
ATKINS S. Born 18/3/50. Commd 19/12/85. Sqn Ldr 1/7/96. Retd ADMIN 17/9/02.
ATKINS W.A. Born 10/2/21. Commd 11/6/45. Flt Lt 19/6/52. Retd GD 25/2/65.
ATKINSON A.B. Born 26/3/43. Commd 17/5/63. Flt Lt 17/11/68. Retd GD 2/10/73.
ATKINSON A.J. Born 16/11/36. Commd 12/11/80. Flt Lt 25/2/67. Retd GD 16/11/93.
ATKINSON A.R. Born 2/4/14. Commd 3/2/44. Flt Lt 3/8/47. Retd ENG 24/10/53.
ATKINSON A.T. OBE MCMI. Born 20/4/35. Commd 25/10/61. Wg Cdr 1/7/72. Retd GD 20/4/93.
ATKINSON A.W.W. OBE AFC. Born 4/9/24. Commd 9/6/45. Gp Capt 1/1/74. Retd GD 31/3/78.
ATKINSON B.C. OBE. Born 20/6/36. Commd 7/12/61. Wg Cdr 1/7/76. Retd ADMIN 20/6/94.
ATKINSON Sir David KBE MB ChB FRCP(Edin) FFCM FFOM. Born 29/9/24. Commd 3/3/49. AM 1/7/81.
    Retd MED 29/9/84.
ATKINSON D.M. BEng CEng FIIE MIEE CDipAF. Born 30/3/58. Commd 13/9/81. Flt Lt 15/7/86. Retd ENG 30/3/97.
ATKINSON D.R. Born 17/3/29. Commd 9/4/52. Sqn Ldr 1/7/62. Retd GD 14/5/76. Re-instated 9/7/80.
    Sqn Ldr 26/8/66. Retd GD 17/3/89.
ATKINSON E.J. CEng FIEE DipEl. Born 21/10/23. Commd 1/9/45. Wg Cdr 1/1/67. Retd ENG 17/3/78.
ATKINSON E.L. MBE. Born 7/9/25. Commd 14/11/51. Wg Cdr 1/1/71. Retd ADMIN 7/9/80.
ATKINSON G.B. BSc CEng MIMechE MRAeS. Born 20/2/45. Commd 15/7/65. Flt Lt 15/4/70. Retd ENG 31/7/76.
ATKINSON G.E. Born 27/9/18. Commd 22/2/44. Flt Lt 24/2/50. Retd SEC 6/2/65.
ATKINSON H.E. IEng. Born 11/11/30. Commd 31/10/69. Flt Lt 31/10/74. Retd ENG 9/1/91.
ATKINSON I.C. BSc DLUT CEng FIMechE FRAeS. Born 27/11/49. Commd 26/2/71. Gp Capt 1/7/00.
    Retd GD 31/8/04.
ATKINSON J. Born 26/6/26. Commd 25/6/53. Flt Lt 25/12/56. Retd GD 26/6/64.
ATKINSON J. Born 11/5/33. Commd 30/1/52. Flt Lt 13/11/57. Retd GD 11/5/71.
ATKINSON J.A. Born 10/6/20. Commd 11/10/41. Sqn Ldr 1/1/53. Retd GD 10/6/63.
ATKINSON J.C. CBE FCMI. Born 15/10/28. Commd 27/7/49. A Cdre 1/1/77. Retd GD 12/11/83.
ATKINSON K.R. Born 5/9/52. Commd 2/1/75. Sqn Ldr 1/1/91. Retd GD 1/1/94.
ATKINSON M.R. Born 13/7/42. Commd 17/12/64. Sqn Ldr 1/1/80. Retd GD 1/4/96.
ATKINSON P. Born 19/2/31. Commd 2/7/64. Sqn Ldr 1/7/76. Retd GD(AEO) 30/4/89.
ATKINSON P.R. Born 31/7/59. Commd 25/9/80. Flt Lt 25/3/86. Retd GD 31/7/97.
ATKINSON R.C. BSc. Born 4/4/54. Commd 17/9/72. Flt Lt 15/10/76. Retd GD 15/7/87.
ATKINSON R.C. AFC. Born 4/12/41. Commd 9/10/64. Sqn Ldr 1/1/82. Retd GD 11/10/97.
ATKINSON R.E. Born 9/5/34. Commd 17/12/52. Sqn Ldr 1/7/65. Retd GD 10/5/74.
ATKINSON R.F. Born 5/9/24. Commd 21/4/44. Sqn Ldr 1/4/55. Retd GD 3/7/76.
ATKINSON S.D. Born 17/2/36. Commd 30/8/62. Sqn Ldr 1/7/75. Retd ADMIN 1/10/82.
ATKINSON T.E. Born 15/11/48. Commd 22/9/69. Flt Lt 22/3/76. Retd ENG 15/11/86.
ATLAY P.A. Born 15/9/43. Commd 20/6/63. Wg Cdr 1/1/90. Retd GD(G) 14/9/96.
ATTARD A.M. DFM. Born 28/2/20. Commd 18/4/45. Flt Lt 4/12/52. Retd SUP 28/2/69.
ATTENBOROUGH R.G. MRCS LRCP. Born 25/2/28. Commd 18/7/54. Flt Lt 18/7/55. Retd MED 8/10/60. rtg Sqn Ldr
ATTEWELL D.J. Born 22/12/66. Commd 19/6/86. Flt Lt 13/12/92. Retd OPS SPT(ATC) 22/12/04.
ATTLEE D.L. CB MVO DL. Born 2/9/22. Commd 28/1/44. AVM 1/7/75. Retd GD 2/9/77.
ATTON D.H. Born 30/1/45. Commd 30/5/71. Sqn Ldr 1/7/82. Retd ENG 30/5/90.
ATTON T.W. Born 23/3/30. Commd 25/6/66. Flt Lt 25/6/71. Retd SUP 1/5/75.
ATTRIDGE A.R. MBE. Born 21/3/29. Commd 28/7/60. Wg Cdr 1/1/77. Retd ADMIN 21/3/84.
ATTRILL A.J. Born 27/6/34. Commd 30/7/59. Sqn Ldr 1/7/76. Retd SUP 30/6/84.
ATTRYDE R.A.J. Born 30/8/43. Commd 18/12/80. Flt Lt 18/12/84. Retd GD 30/3/94.
ATTWOOD A.I. MB BS FRCS(Edin) MRCS LRCP. Born 6/5/48. Commd 29/7/68. Wg Cdr 30/8/85. Retd MED 1/1/94.
ATTWOOD D.J. Born 11/4/50. Commd 15/9/69. Flt Lt 26/8/75. Retd GD 22/10/94.
AUBREY K. Born 21/3/52. Commd 28/7/88. Flt Lt 28/7/92. Retd MED(SEC) 10/10/95.
AUBREY N. BSc CEng MIMechE MINucE. Born 30/9/36. Commd 15/1/63. Sqn Ldr 1/7/70. Retd ENG 6/11/76.
AUDET D.W. BSc. Born 29/1/63. Commd 8/5/88. Flt Lt 8/11/90. Retd GD 5/12/01.
AUDHLAM-GARDINER B.G.P. MMar MCMI. Born 22/1/34. Commd 22/10/63. Sqn Ldr 22/10/63.
    Retd GD(G) 22/1/92.
AUDLEY H.M. Born 19/3/30. Commd 3/2/52. Flt Lt 9/9/62. Retd SEC 22/6/75.
AUDSLEY D.MacR. Born 20/5/38. Commd 26/5/61. Flt Lt 26/11/66. Retd GD 16/7/68.
AUGUST G.I. BA. Born 1/7/50. Commd 2/2/75. Wg Cdr 1/1/90. Retd GD 1/3/03.
AUKETT J. Born 14/1/35. Commd 29/4/54. Sqn Ldr 1/7/75. Retd ADMIN 14/1/90.
AULT J. DFC. Born 3/9/33. Commd 8/6/59. Wg Cdr 1/1/76. Retd GD 29/1/87.
AUNGER D.J. MSc BSc. Born 24/12/61. Commd 5/1/86. Sqn Ldr 1/7/94. Retd ENGINEER 10/6/03.
AUST W.F. Born 23/11/24. Commd 9/12/48. Flt Lt 3/12/52. Retd GD 23/11/62.
AUSTEN-SMITH Sir Roy KBE CB DFC. Born 28/6/24. Commd 7/4/44. AM 1/7/79. Retd GD 1/11/81.

AUSTIN D.A. Born 11/5/23. Commd 12/4/45. Sqn Ldr 1/1/56. Retd GD 14/5/66.
AUSTIN F.H.P. OBE. Born 11/8/16. Commd 7/9/40. Wg Cdr 1/1/54. Retd GD 3/4/65.
AUSTIN G.P. BA. Born 22/11/46. Commd 4/6/72. Flt Lt 4/9/73. Retd GD 4/6/88.
AUSTIN J.A.G. Born 21/7/12. Commd 24/8/40. Flt Offr 1/9/45. Retd SEC 21/7/61.
AUSTIN J.R. Born 26/12/44. Commd 28/2/64. Flt Lt 12/11/69. Retd GD 26/6/82.
AUSTIN J.W. Born 26/7/21. Commd 23/8/56. Flt Lt 23/8/59. Retd GD 27/9/68.
AUSTIN K.P. Born 3/1/34. Commd 14/12/54. Sqn Ldr 1/1/66. Retd SEC 29/7/75.
AUSTIN P.D.A. AFC. Born 20/7/31. Commd 4/4/51. Wg Cdr 1/7/69. Retd GD 23/7/74.
AUSTIN P.G. Born 20/1/43. Commd 8/12/61. Sqn Ldr 1/1/80. Retd GD 26/4/84.
AUSTIN Sir Roger KCB AFC FRAeS. Born 9/3/40. Commd 18/2/58. AM 6/4/92. Retd GD 22/5/97.
AUSTIN R.A. Born 30/1/30. Commd 25/5/50. Wg Cdr 1/7/75. Retd GD(G) 30/1/85.
AUSTIN R.P. Born 10/3/66. Commd 28/2/85. Flt Lt 28/8/90. Retd FLY(P) 10/3/04.
AUSTIN T.S. Born 14/9/38. Commd 8/1/57. Sqn Ldr 1/7/73. Retd GD 14/9/93.
AUSTIN W.R. BSc. Born 24/4/46. Commd 28/2/72. Flt Lt 28/5/73. Retd GD 14/9/96.
AUSTIN-VAUTIER S.W. BSc. Born 16/2/53. Commd 14/9/75. Wg Cdr 1/7/90. Retd ADMIN 2/12/93.
AUTIE P.G. Born 25/9/39. Commd 6/4/62. Sqn Ldr 1/7/73. Retd SUP 26/9/94.
AUTON K.N. Born 2/11/32. Commd 12/7/51. Flt Lt 20/2/62. Retd GD 1/10/75.
AVENS R.B. MCIPD MCMI. Born 27/4/38. Commd 28/2/57. Sqn Ldr 1/1/72. Retd SY 1/10/86.
AVERY D.G. Born 7/5/47. Commd 31/10/69. Sqn Ldr 1/1/92. Retd GD 14/12/98.
AVERY J.D. PhD BSc. Born 18/2/45. Commd 14/11/71. Sqn Ldr 6/8/76. Retd ADMIN 14/11/90.
AVERY V.G. Born 12/9/29. Commd 19/6/52. Flt Lt 19/12/55. Retd GD 21/6/80.
AVISS H.G. MBE. Born 1/6/11. Commd 2/4/53. Sqn Ldr 1/1/62. Retd ENG 1/6/68.
AVORY I.H. Born 8/5/47. Commd 3/5/60. Flt Lt 3/11/73. Retd GD 8/5/85.
AWAD H.H.F. MB ChB MRCOG. Born 20/6/52. Commd 19/11/89. Sqn Ldr 19/11/87. Retd MED 13/9/96.
AXFORD R. MBE. Born 3/8/36. Commd 12/4/73. Sqn Ldr 1/1/82. Retd ENG 6/5/87.
AXFORD-HAWKES I.A. Born 11/4/65. Commd 29/3/90. Flt Lt 7/2/93. Retd OPS SPT(ATC) 11/4/03.
AYEE P.C. CBE CEng FIEE FRAeS. Born 14/1/42. Commd 5/12/63. A Cdre 1/1/94. Retd ENG 14/1/97.
AYERS C.R. Born 1/3/42. Commd 28/3/63. Sqn Ldr 1/7/84. Retd SUP 1/3/97.
AYERS J.H. Born 9/3/44. Commd 16/8/68. Sqn Ldr 1/7/93. Retd GD 9/6/01.
AYERS J.R. Born 28/10/32. Commd 28/7/53. Flt Lt 28/1/56. Retd GD 28/10/70.
AYERS P.S. Born 25/1/56. Commd 9/5/91. Flt Lt 9/5/95. Retd ADMIN 14/12/96.
AYERS-BERRY R.L.W. Born 4/3/50. Commd 2/8/68. Flt Lt 18/1/75. Retd GD(G) 1/5/75.
AYERST P.V. DFC MCMI. Born 4/11/20. Commd 14/12/38. Wg Cdr 1/7/68. Retd GD 5/5/73.
AYKROYD G.M. Born 5/4/43. Commd 21/12/62. Sqn Ldr 1/7/74. Retd GD 14/12/82.
AYLIFFE A.C. MBE MA FRIN. Born 25/2/54. Commd 19/10/75. Flt Lt 19/1/77. Retd FLY(N) 30/4/04.
AYLING C.J. MHCIMA. Born 26/5/39. Commd 23/10/59. Sqn Ldr 1/1/72. Retd ADMIN 26/5/77.
AYLING L.J. MBE. Born 13/1/25. Commd 6/5/46. Sqn Ldr 1/1/60. Retd SEC 1/7/67.
AYLING R.J. Born 30/8/18. Commd 26/12/46. Flt Lt 26/12/52. Retd SEC 30/8/73.
AYLOTT L.H. Born 29/10/37. Commd 28/5/57. Flt Lt 21/8/63. Retd GD 29/10/94.
AYLWARD A.J. Born 19/4/35. Commd 9/12/53. Wg Cdr 1/1/73. Retd SUP 2/4/80.
AYLWARD D. Born 31/7/41. Commd 8/1/62. Wg Cdr 1/7/78. Retd GD 31/7/85.
AYLWARD G.A.S. Born 4/2/11. Commd 24/10/45. Flt Lt 4/1/51. Retd SEC 29/7/59.
AYO J.E. Born 21/5/36. Commd 19/8/71. Flt Lt 19/8/72. Retd ADMIN 21/5/86.
AYRE G.A. BA. Born 1/12/41. Commd 23/6/63. Flt Lt 1/7/67. Retd GD 30/3/69.
AYRE K.W.A. Born 8/9/24. Commd 9/1/45. Sqn Ldr 1/7/69. Retd GD 2/7/73.
AYRES G.A. Born 22/2/14. Commd 2/6/49. Sqn Ldr 1/1/63. Retd SEC 3/7/64.
AYRES M.L. MB BS FRCS. Born 1/2/39. Commd 13/4/70. Wg Cdr 13/9/78. Retd MED 13/4/86.
AYRES N. Born 23/10/27. Commd 2/12/53. Flt Lt 2/12/57. Retd PE 30/11/68.
AYRES S.A. MSc BSc CPhys MInstP. Born 5/12/54. Commd 19/6/83. Flt Lt 19/12/82. Retd ADMIN 5/1/91.
AYRES V.E. BA. Born 25/3/45. Commd 24/6/65. Sqn Ldr 1/1/78. Retd GD 25/3/83.
AYRIS F.R.S. AFM. Born 25/1/38. Commd 4/7/69. Flt Lt 4/5/72. Retd GD 4/7/77.
AYSHFORD J.M. Born 12/11/21. Commd 8/4/41. Gp Capt 1/1/66. Retd GD 12/11/76.
AYTON C.H. Born 30/3/58. Commd 18/10/79. Flt Lt 18/4/85. Retd GD 7/4/02.
AZIZ S.I. BSc DMS FCMI. Born 3/10/37. Commd 24/6/68. Fg Offr 5/9/67. Retd SEC 31/10/70.
AZZARO P.G. Born 19/12/41. Commd 30/7/63. Flt Lt 13/10/69. Retd GD 30/5/94.

B

BAATZ A.P. Born 21/3/60. Commd 10/2/83. Flt Lt 10/8/88. Retd GD 14/3/96.
BABBINGTON J.D. BTech. Born 21/6/51. Commd 15/9/71. Sqn Ldr 1/1/87. Retd GD 1/1/90.
BABINGTON J.P. BA. Born 3/4/50. Commd 17/1/72. Gp Capt 1/1/99. Retd GD 16/4/04.
BABLER P.E.O. CEng MRAeS. Born 29/7/38. Commd 30/7/59. Sqn Ldr 1/1/71. Retd ENG 4/8/76.
BACH G.I. BSc CEng MRAeS MIEE MCMI. Born 5/5/33. Commd 7/9/56. Gp Capt 1/1/77. Retd ENG 22/8/78.
BACK A.H.C. MBE AFC MA BSc. Born 30/5/30. Commd 21/10/51. Sqn Ldr 1/7/60. Retd GD 21/7/69.
BACK R.C. BA. Born 23/8/48. Commd 24/9/67. Flt Lt 15/10/71. Retd GD 23/8/86.
BACKHOUSE D.H.W. BTech. Born 19/3/45. Commd 27/10/70. Wg Cdr 1/1/88. Retd ENG 31/10/00.
BACON A. Born 28/6/42. Commd 19/8/71. Wg Cdr 1/1/86. Retd ADMIN 1/2/89.
BACON C.E. Born 13/3/41. Commd 25/8/67. Sqn Ldr 1/1/78. Retd GD(G) 13/3/96.
BACON D.R. Born 2/12/48. Commd 20/5/82. Sqn Ldr 1/1/91. Retd SUPPLY 2/12/03.
BACON D.T. Born 27/6/51. Commd 8/12/83. Sqn Ldr 1/7/92. Retd ADMIN (SEC) 1/11/04.
BACON F.C.G. Born 27/3/31. Commd 21/10/66. Sqn Ldr 1/1/86. Retd ENG 27/12/91.
BACON G.A. Born 19/8/51. Commd 3/8/75. Fg Offr 3/2/76. Retd GD 6/9/77.
BACON J.C. Born 9/3/60. Commd 15/8/85. Flt Lt 12/5/88. Retd ADMIN 29/3/91.
BACON L.D. MA MSc BSc CEng MRAeS DIC. Born 11/7/62. Commd 31/8/80. Wg Cdr 1/1/99. Retd ENG 1/1/02.
BACON S.H. Born 7/4/19. Commd 19/8/42. Sqn Ldr 1/7/53. Retd ENG 7/4/68.
BACON S.W.G. ACMA MCMI. Born 25/10/38. Commd 1/3/68. Wg Cdr 1/7/86. Retd ADMIN 25/10/88.
BACON T.J. OBE. Born 30/5/42. Commd 12/7/79. Wg Cdr 1/1/92. Retd ADMIN 3/6/96.
BADCOCK H.F. Born 16/1/22. Commd 22/10/59. Sqn Ldr 1/7/71. Retd ENG 16/7/75.
BADCOCK P.C. MBE . Born 15/12/46. Commd 26/1/70. Gp Capt 1/7/94. Retd GD 15/12/04.
BADDELEY E.S. CEng FRAeS FCMI. Born 6/12/23. Commd 16/9/43. A Cdre 1/1/74. Retd ENG 25/3/78.
BADDOCK R.J. Born 30/9/33. Commd 30/12/55. Flt Lt 30/6/61. Retd GD 30/9/71.
BADLEY P.I. Born 18/6/22. Commd 20/11/43. Flt Lt 5/7/49. Retd GD(G) 30/3/77.
BAERSELMAN J.C.K. Born 7/8/36. Commd 9/4/57. Sqn Ldr 1/7/67. Retd GD 8/1/77.
BAFF R.N. Born 27/2/27. Commd 9/1/50. Flt Lt 11/11/54. Retd GD 7/10/65.
BAGG W.L. OBE DFC. Born 17/9/20. Commd 12/9/42. Wg Cdr 1/1/64. Retd SUP 17/4/75.
BAGGALEY W.N. Born 4/7/24. Commd 3/1/46. Sqn Ldr 1/7/74. Retd GD(G) 7/5/76.
BAGGLEY K.J. Born 31/1/60. Commd 11/1/79. Sqn Ldr 1/7/90. Retd GD 31/1/98.
BAGGOTT J.P. MBE MA MSc CEng MIEE. Born 18/1/57. Commd 5/9/76. Sqn Ldr 1/1/88. Retd ENG 18/1/95.
BAGGULEY W. Born 9/7/36. Commd 29/4/58. Flt Lt 7/8/64. Retd GD 10/4/88.
BAGLEY C. Born 27/2/39. Commd 2/2/78. Sqn Ldr 1/1/88. Retd ENG 2/9/93.
BAGLEY D.C. Born 6/10/60. Commd 16/2/89. Flt Lt 16/2/91. Retd ENG 6/10/98.
BAGLEY L. BA. Born 1/7/39. Commd 6/9/61. Fg Offr 6/9/63. Retd SEC 23/4/65.
BAGLEY W.K. BA. Born 13/2/32. Commd 9/9/54. Sqn Ldr 17/2/63. Retd EDN 9/9/70.
BAGNALL A.C. BA. Born 11/12/62. Commd 7/12/86. Flt Lt 7/6/90. Retd ADMIN 14/3/97.
BAGNALL J.C. BSc. Born 11/11/45. Commd 27/10/70. Sqn Ldr 1/1/84. Retd GD 1/5/96.
BAGNALL R.A. Born 17/7/44. Commd 14/8/64. Sqn Ldr 1/1/95. Retd GD 17/7/99.
BAGSHAW D.R. AFC. Born 28/2/37. Commd 4/6/62. Sqn Ldr 1/7/82. Retd GD 28/2/92.
BAGSHAW F. Born 15/10/06. Commd 23/4/53. Flt Lt 23/4/56. Retd ENG 23/4/63.
BAGSHAW G. Born 13/1/32. Commd 14/1/53. Sqn Ldr 1/1/68. Retd GD 13/1/87.
BAGSHAW M. MB BCh MRCS LRCP DAvMed AFOM MRAeS. Born 9/7/46. Commd 29/11/70. Sqn Ldr 26/7/79. Retd MED 29/11/86.
BAGSHAW T.W. MRAeS MCMI. Born 26/7/20. Commd 15/4/43. Sqn Ldr 1/1/63. Retd ENG 25/5/73.
BAIGENT P. Born 22/2/33. Commd 19/8/53. Flt Lt 15/8/62. Retd GD 22/2/71.
BAILEY A.A. Born 6/4/36. Commd 26/3/64. Flt Lt 16/6/69. Retd GD(G) 14/12/77.
BAILEY A.A. Born 2/7/47. Commd 8/4/82. Sqn Ldr 1/1/90. Retd ENG 31/3/94.
BAILEY A.C. Born 11/2/33. Commd 11/11/71. Sqn Ldr 1/1/81. Retd ENG 6/4/83.
BAILEY A.P. BEng MRAeS. Born 17/7/63. Commd 2/8/89. Sqn Ldr 1/7/01. Retd ENGINEER 1/7/04.
BAILEY B.J. MSc BSc CEng MRAeS. Born 22/8/51. Commd 15/9/69. Sqn Ldr 1/1/84. Retd ENG 12/12/89.
BAILEY C. Born 27/11/46. Commd 1/4/66. Flt Lt 1/10/71. Retd GD 6/12/75.
BAILEY C.A. BEM MCMI. Born 24/4/28. Commd 11/3/65. Flt Lt 11/3/70. Retd ENG 16/1/79. Re-instated 17/9/80 to 12/12/86.
BAILEY C.T. Born 8/1/55. Commd 15/12/88. Flt Lt 15/12/30. Retd GD 1/8/96.
BAILEY D.A. DFC. Born 28/4/20. Commd 2/11/42. Sqn Ldr 1/1/56. Retd GD 12/6/69.
BAILEY D.A.F. MCMI ACIS. Born 3/10/41. Commd 24/9/64. Wg Cdr 1/7/80. Retd ADMIN 5/4/93.
BAILEY D.G. CB CBE FCMI. Born 12/9/24. Commd 26/1/48. AVM 1/7/76. Retd GD 28/7/80.
BAILEY D.J. Born 27/10/49. Commd 3/12/70. Flt Lt 27/4/75. Retd GD 27/10/87.
BAILEY D.M. MB BS. Born 5/2/66. Commd 26/2/92. Flt Lt 1/8/95. Retd MED 7/2/96.
BAILEY E.A. MBE. Born 25/5/13. Commd 20/5/43. Fg Offr 23/7/46. Retd SUP 17/12/47. rtg Flt Lt
BAILEY G. MSc CBiol MIBiol FIMLS MCMI. Born 31/10/32. Commd 2/1/70. Wg Cdr 1/7/75. Retd MED(T) 1/7/88.

BAILEY G.H. Born 30/3/25. Commd 6/2/50. Flt Lt 6/2/54. Retd MAR 1/3/59.
BAILEY G.P.B. Born 28/3/22. Commd 16/6/44. Wg Cdr 1/7/64. Retd GD 19/10/67.
BAILEY I.C. Born 20/5/43. Commd 26/5/67. Flt Lt 15/9/70. Retd ENG 20/5/82.
BAILEY J.D. Born 18/4/47. Commd 28/2/66. Flt Lt 25/8/71. Retd GD 18/4/85.
BAILEY J.F. BSc. Born 15/3/36. Commd 28/11/58. Sqn Ldr 18/8/68. Retd EDN 30/8/75.
BAILEY J.H. Born 8/2/53. Commd 16/9/76. Sqn Ldr 1/7/88. Retd ENG 1/7/91.
BAILEY J.W. Born 16/1/47. Commd 20/10/83. Sqn Ldr 1/1/92. Retd MED(SEC) 14/3/96.
BAILEY K.J. Born 25/7/30. Commd 1/10/55. Sqn Ldr 1/1/64. Retd GD 2/10/83.
BAILEY L.M. MBE. Born 16/10/23. Commd 14/12/45. Sqn Ldr 1/7/59. Retd GD 16/10/66.
BAILEY M.J. Born 3/3/24. Commd 10/3/44. Flt Lt 10/9/47. Retd GD 15/3/67.
BAILEY N.P. Born 24/9/56. Commd 8/10/87. Flt Lt 8/10/89. Retd GD(G) 8/10/95.
BAILEY R. MRAeS. Born 1/7/51. Commd 4/7/69. Sqn Ldr 1/1/87. Retd GD 1/1/90.
BAILEY R. FHCIMA MCIPD. Born 28/4/35. Commd 9/6/54. Sqn Ldr 1/1/68. Retd ADMIN 28/4/93.
BAILEY R. AFC. Born 1/10/14. Commd 13/6/40. Sqn Ldr 1/8/47. Retd SEC 14/12/68.
BAILEY R.C. Born 28/9/35. Commd 15/9/60. Flt Lt 15/3/65. Retd GD 28/9/73.
BAILEY R.C. Born 21/4/52. Commd 16/3/73. Flt Lt 16/3/76. Retd GD 21/4/90.
BAILEY R.W. The Rev. Born 30/1/49. Commd 29/6/75. Retd Wg Cdr 29/6/99.
BAILEY T.G. BA BEd. Born 27/6/43. Commd 21/7/65. Flt Lt 15/4/70. Retd GD 30/4/76. Re-instated 3/7/79.
    Flt Lt 3/7/79. Retd ADMIN 30/4/90.
BAILEY W.B. Born 13/8/46. Commd 30/1/70. Fg Offr 30/1/72. Retd GD 3/8/76.
BAILLIE M.B. Born 7/8/39. Commd 24/8/72. Flt Lt 24/8/74. Retd GD 15/4/82.
BAILLIE S. OBE. Born 17/9/22. Commd 15/9/44. A Cdre 1/1/74. Retd SUP 31/3/77.
BAIN C.J. Born 5/4/44. Commd 28/9/62. Sqn Ldr 1/7/81. Retd GD 1/10/94.
BAIN G.D.P. LLB. Born 27/7/45. Commd 31/10/66. Flt Lt 31/7/68. Retd GD 1/3/75.
BAIN R. MSc. Born 30/1/51. Commd 7/5/92. Sqn Ldr 4/6/00. Retd MED(T) 29/11/02.
BAINBRIDGE A.C. Born 23/8/61. Commd 13/3/80. Sqn Ldr 1/7/94. Retd OPS SPT 26/12/99.
BAINBRIDGE A.R. BA. Born 1/7/29. Commd 6/2/52. Flt Offr 6/8/57. Retd SEC 1/1/58.
BAINBRIDGE A.S. Born 15/9/55. Commd 3/8/83. Sqn Ldr 1/1/97. Retd OPS SPT(ATC) 7/4/04.
BAINBRIDGE B. MBE DFC. Born 20/12/22. Commd 7/7/44. Wg Cdr 1/7/62. Retd GD(G) 20/12/71.
BAINBRIDGE R.G. Born 12/4/24. Commd 12/2/46. Flt Lt 26/5/55. Retd GD 12/4/67.
BAINBRIDGE R.T. AFC. Born 21/6/16. Commd 22/6/41. Wg Cdr 1/1/55. Retd GD 23/7/66.
BAINBRIDGE S.C. BA. Born 21/6/53. Commd 16/11/72. Flt Lt 4/3/78. Retd GD(G) 16/11/78. Re-entered 4/1/88.
    Flt Lt 22/4/87. Retd OPS SPT (ATC) 22/1/04.
BAINBRIDGE S.W. OBE MRAeS. Born 25/7/26. Commd 27/3/52. Gp Capt 1/1/78. Retd GD 25/7/81.
BAINES A.P. Born 2/12/33. Commd 1/12/59. Flt Lt 11/10/63. Retd GD 23/1/78.
BAINES W.S. Born 18/11/44. Commd 15/7/66. Sqn Ldr 1/7/86. Retd GD 29/2/96.
BAIRD B.S.Mcl. Born 2/11/58. Commd 28/2/82. Flt Lt 28/2/87. Retd ENG 1/3/90.
BAIRD G.M. Born 28/10/13. Commd 13/3/39. Flt Lt 1/9/45. Retd GD(G) 2/12/63.
BAIRD Sir John KBE MB ChB FRCP(Edin) FRCS(Edin) FFOM FRAeS DAvMed. Born 25/7/37. Commd 3/11/63.
    AM 24/2/97. Retd MED 16/6/00.
BAIRD P.D.A. Born 19/1/20. Commd 12/11/43. Flt Lt 30/6/57. Retd GD(G) 6/9/64.
BAIRSTO Sir Peter KBE CB AFC CCMI. Born 3/8/26. Commd 10/5/46. AM 1/7/81. Retd GD 17/4/84.
BAIRSTOW G. Born 27/5/47. Commd 1/8/69. Flt Lt 1/2/72. Retd GD 27/5/91.
BAKER A.C. BSc MRAeS MCMI. Born 25/4/36. Commd 30/11/58. Sqn Ldr 1/1/72. Retd GD 23/9/75.
BAKER A.J.R. Born 24/5/23. Commd 2/3/61. Flt Lt 2/3/64. Retd GD 13/4/73.
BAKER A.K. MCMI. Born 17/1/24. Commd 31/7/58. Sqn Ldr 1/7/74. Retd ENG 6/5/78.
BAKER A.R. Born 20/11/36. Commd 11/5/62. Flt Lt 1/7/68. Retd GD(G) 8/1/79. Re-instated 5/3/80. Flt Lt 6/1/70.
    Retd ADMIN 20/11/91.
BAKER B.A.F. Born 13/4/47. Commd 26/8/66. Flt Lt 17/12/72. Retd OPS SPT 7/4/98.
BAKER C. Born 24/10/42. Commd 29/4/63. Flt Lt 24/10/68. Retd PRT 2/9/72.
BAKER C. Born 15/4/47. Commd 20/8/65. Flt Lt 20/2/71. Retd GD 1/6/77.
BAKER C.C.M. OBE FCMI MCIPD. Born 7/10/19. Commd 29/11/37. A Cdre 1/7/68. Retd GD 31/7/71.
BAKER C.P. CB FCMI FCIPS. Born 14/6/38. Commd 2/10/58. AVM 1/1/90. Retd SUP 14/6/93.
BAKER D.H.G. MBE BA. Born 12/4/39. Commd 30/9/58. Gp Capt 1/1/81. Retd ENG 1/5/88.
BAKER D.M. OBE FCMI. Born 4/1/48. Commd 8/9/69. Gp Capt 1/1/92. Retd ADMIN 8/9/00.
BAKER D.V. Born 29/8/33. Commd 22/7/55. Wg Cdr 1/7/76. Retd ENG 31/8/83.
BAKER E.J. OBE MCMI MCIPS. Born 29/4/23. Commd 24/6/43. Wg Cdr 1/7/64. Retd SUP 30/9/77.
BAKER E.J. Born 2/9/28. Commd 8/7/54. Flt Lt 1/10/67. Retd GD 2/9/83.
BAKER E.M. Born 11/9/10. Commd 24/2/43. Sqn Offr 1/7/59. Retd SEC 1/7/62.
BAKER F. Born 11/4/32. Commd 13/8/52. Flt Lt 9/1/58. Retd GD 11/4/70.
BAKER F.J. Born 24/7/24. Commd 26/11/53. Flt Lt 26/5/57. Retd GD 3/11/63.
BAKER F.M.A. Born 1/2/25. Commd 26/8/45. Sqn Ldr 1/7/64. Retd SUP 1/3/68.
BAKER G.G. Born 1/8/09. Commd 27/7/53. Flt Lt 27/1/47. Retd ENG 20/5/62.
BAKER G.H. Born 24/10/32. Commd 28/7/53. Sqn Ldr 1/7/61. Retd GD 1/9/62.
BAKER H. MBE DFC. Born 15/9/14. Commd 16/12/40. Flt Lt 16/6/44. Retd GD(G) 15/9/69.
BAKER H.M. Born 24/4/46. Commd 2/11/88. Flt Lt 2/11/92. Retd OPS SPT 28/4/97.

BAKER I.I. Born 25/5/14. Commd 1/9/45. Flt Offr 1/9/45. Retd SEC 31/7/52.
BAKER J.E. Born 1/4/64. Commd 24/3/83. Flt Lt 24/9/89. Retd SY 7/3/93.
BAKER J.F. Born 21/2/11. Commd 10/8/44. Sqn Ldr 1/1/53. Retd SUP 3/4/60.
BAKER J.M. Born 1/7/13. Commd 18/8/41. Flt Offr 1/9/45. Retd SEC 30/4/54.
BAKER J.T. Born 27/12/45. Commd 26/5/57. Flt Lt 18/2/70. Retd GD 7/10/75.
BAKER J.W. Born 12/12/45. Commd 5/2/65. Flt Lt 5/8/70. Retd GD 26/4/75.
BAKER L.A.B. AFC. Born 25/4/33. Commd 3/9/52. Wg Cdr 1/7/71. Retd GD 25/4/88.
BAKER L.M. Born 2/4/45. Commd 19/10/80. Flt Lt 26/2/87. Retd ADMIN 5/12/91.
BAKER M.E. Born 25/1/36. Commd 23/11/78. Flt Lt 23/11/83. Retd ENG 1/9/89.
BAKER M.G. MVO. Born 15/4/23. Commd 10/3/44. Sqn Ldr 1/9/65. Retd GD 30/9/69.
BAKER M.J. Born 18/9/32. Commd 30/1/58. Flt Lt 30/7/62. Retd GD 30/11/72.
BAKER M.J. BA. Born 4/3/39. Commd 25/3/60. Sqn Ldr 1/7/77. Retd GD 4/3/94.
BAKER M.P.C. Born 20/9/44. Commd 6/11/64. Flt Lt 4/5/72. Retd GD 22/10/94.
BAKER N.G. Born 21/7/24. Commd 29/9/45. Flt Lt 29/3/49. Retd GD 4/2/70.
BAKER P. Born 1/7/53. Commd 8/8/74. Flt Lt 8/2/81. Retd GD 1/7/91.
BAKER P. BA. Born 13/10/59. Commd 5/10/79. Flt Lt 15/4/83. Retd GD 31/1/99.
BAKER P.F. Born 29/7/37. Commd 22/7/62. Sqn Ldr 1/7/73. Retd ENG 22/1/80.
BAKER P.J. Born 13/7/41. Commd 22/5/75. Flt Lt 22/5/77. Retd GD 22/5/85.
BAKER P.P. AFC. Born 2/9/25. Commd 19/10/45. Sqn Ldr 1/7/56. Retd GD 17/7/59.
BAKER P.T. MBE. Born 13/12/43. Commd 17/12/65. Wg Cdr 1/1/86. Retd GD 1/2/93.
BAKER R. OBE BSc(Eng) CEng MRAeS MCMI. Born 25/8/38. Commd 28/11/66. Wg Cdr 1/7/80.
    Retd ENG 29/11/90.
BAKER R.A.H. Born 29/6/33. Commd 1/8/69. Flt Lt 1/8/73. Retd ENG 1/8/75.
BAKER R.D.F. BA. Born 29/3/73. Commd 6/4/97. Flt Lt 6/10/99. Retd FLY(N) 20/3/04.
BAKER R.D.F. BA. Born 29/3/73. Commd 6/4/97. Flt Lt 6/10/99. Retd FLY(N) 14/6/04.
BAKER R.F. BSc. Born 31/5/37. Commd 15/3/60. Sqn Ldr 15/9/70. Retd EDN 15/3/76.
BAKER R.F. Born 30/7/33. Commd 27/3/70. Flt Lt 27/3/75. Retd SEC 3/4/78.
BAKER R.J. BSc. Born 6/7/33. Commd 11/4/57. Wg Cdr 1/1/75. Retd ENG 29/10/85.
BAKER R.P. Born 14/6/34. Commd 7/6/68. Flt Lt 7/6/70. Retd ENG 1/11/80.
BAKER S. DSO* DFC*. Born 19/11/18. Commd 24/11/41. Wg Cdr 1/7/55. Retd GD 20/6/66.
BAKER S.A. BEng. Born 4/9/63. Commd 31/7/91. Flt Lt 15/7/94. Retd ENG 4/9/01.
BAKER S.E. Born 10/6/39. Commd 15/7/58. Wg Cdr 1/7/78. Retd SUP 6/4/90.
BAKER S.E. MSc BSc CEng MIEE MCMI. Born 2/3/59. Commd 11/9/77. Sqn Ldr 1/1/90. Retd ENG 19/7/98.
BAKER T.H. DFC DFM. Born 16/8/13. Commd 9/4/41. Wg Cdr 1/1/55. Retd GD 28/1/58.
BAKER V.W. Born 25/3/40. Commd 14/10/71. Flt Lt 14/10/73. Retd GD 14/10/81.
BAKER W.E. DFC. Born 24/3/24. Commd 17/5/47. Flt Lt 29/6/50. Retd GD 24/10/55.
BAKER W.J. MSc CEng MIEE MRAeS. Born 7/4/34. Commd 30/8/62. Sqn Ldr 23/5/70. Retd ADMIN 12/1/86.
BAKER W.J. BA. Born 1/7/26. Commd 19/10/49. Flt Offr 19/4/53. Retd EDN 8/4/60.
BAKEWELL G. BSc(Eng) CEng MIMechE MRAeS. Born 4/11/48. Commd 27/2/70. Sqn Ldr 1/7/83.
    Retd ENGINEER 4/11/03.
BALAAM A.W.L. BSc. Born 30/4/66. Commd 15/9/85. Sqn Ldr 1/1/98. Retd FLY(P) 1/6/04.
BALCHIN D.P.G. Born 9/8/20. Commd 21/2/46. Flt Lt 21/8/50. Retd SUP 9/8/69.
BALD G. Born 10/6/38. Commd 16/9/76. Flt Lt 16/9/77. Retd ADMIN 16/9/84.
BALDCHIN L.A. Born 9/3/23. Commd 21/8/42. Sqn Ldr 1/10/55. Retd GD 9/3/66.
BALDIE I.S. Born 25/6/44. Commd 31/1/64. Flt Lt 31/7/69. Retd GD 1/3/75.
BALDING P.D.M. Born 29/4/42. Commd 11/5/62. Sqn Ldr 1/7/80. Retd GD(G) 29/4/86.
BALDING R. Born 4/8/46. Commd 24/2/67. Wg Cdr 1/1/90. Retd SUP 14/3/97.
BALDOCK E.J. MBE. Born 27/9/13. Commd 10/5/45. Sqn Ldr 1/1/58. Retd SEC 27/9/62.
BALDOCK K.W. OBE. Born 23/9/40. Commd 28/7/67. Wg Cdr 1/7/90. Retd ADMIN 30/4/96.
BALDOCK S.D. MBE DFM MCMI. Born 19/2/21. Commd 14/6/43. Wg Cdr 1/7/62. Retd GD 19/2/76.
BALDWIN C.C. Born 9/5/48. Commd 1/8/69. Flt Lt 4/5/72. Retd GD 9/5/86.
BALDWIN C.J. AFC. Born 19/11/37. Commd 3/7/56. Sqn Ldr 1/1/73. Retd GD 19/11/92.
BALDWIN D.A.M. Born 3/9/32. Commd 31/5/51. Flt Lt 28/11/56. Retd GD 1/5/61.
BALDWIN D.J. BA. Born 18/6/48. Commd 3/1/69. Sqn Ldr 1/1/82. Retd GD 18/6/86.
BALDWIN G.F. Born 5/10/32. Commd 2/7/52. Flt Lt 27/11/57. Retd GD 4/1/71.
BALDWIN N.B. CB CBE. Born 20/9/41. Commd 31/7/62. AVM 1/7/93. Retd GD 20/6/96.
BALDWIN P.A. Born 10/1/64. Commd 28/7/88. Flt Lt 18/4/91. Retd SUP 3/1/96.
BALDWIN S.A. MBE. Born 17/9/42. Commd 11/5/62. A Cdre 1/7/90. Retd GD 14/9/96.
BALDWYN M. MILT. Born 17/9/42. Commd 15/8/85. Flt Lt 15/8/87. Retd ADMIN 13/9/96.
BALE N.T. MLitt BSc MCMI. Born 13/12/52. Commd 17/9/72. Gp Capt 1/1/02. Retd GD 14/4/04.
BALEAN P.B. Born 25/8/20. Commd 23/12/39. Sqn Ldr 1/8/47. Retd GD 12/6/50.
BALES S.J. Born 24/2/50. Commd 21/6/90. Sqn Ldr 1/1/01. Retd ENGINEER 28/11/03.
BALES S.S. DPhysEd. Born 11/7/48. Commd 2/4/72. Sqn Ldr 1/7/82. Retd ADMIN 13/9/86.
BALFOUR A.J.C. CBE MA MB BChir FRCPath LMSSA DCP DTM&H MRAeS. Born 19/11/26. Commd 15/3/54.
    A Cdre 22/9/89. Retd MED 19/11/91.
BALFOUR T. Born 10/11/29. Commd 6/12/51. Flt Lt 30/6/57. Retd GD 10/11/67.

BALFRE A.L.J. Born 26/6/49. Commd 16/9/71. Flt Lt 16/3/77. Retd GD 25/6/87.
BALGARNIE N. MBE. Born 29/1/44. Commd 12/4/73. Sqn Ldr 1/1/82. Retd ADMIN 31/1/96.
BALL Sir Alfred KCB DSO DFC. Born 18/1/21. Commd 23/12/39. AM 1/7/75. Retd GD 7/4/79.
BALL A.J.W. Born 11/1/43. Commd 19/8/66. Flt Lt 16/6/69. Retd GD 11/1/81.
BALL B.J. DFC. Born 20/5/27. Commd 5/4/50. Wg Cdr 1/7/63. Retd GD 31/10/78.
BALL B.W. OBE MCIT MILT MCMI. Born 16/4/39. Commd 4/6/59. Wg Cdr 1/1/77. Retd SUP 16/9/91.
BALL C.A. Born 15/1/32. Commd 2/7/52. Flt Lt 27/11/57. Retd GD 17/1/52.
BALL D. Born 23/3/20. Commd 21/2/49. Wg Cdr 1/1/66. Retd ENG 30/12/72.
BALL D. Born 13/10/29. Commd 23/8/51. Wg Cdr 1/1/72. Retd GD 9/8/83.
BALL D.B. Born 5/4/51. Commd 28/10/76. Sqn Ldr 1/7/85. Retd ENG 5/4/89.
BALL D.C. Born 27/3/31. Commd 26/3/53. Sqn Ldr 1/1/77. Retd PI 2/4/81.
BALL D.E. BSc. Born 1/11/61. Commd 29/4/84. Sqn Ldr 1/1/97. Retd OPS SPT 29/4/00.
BALL E.H. BSc. Born 14/8/52. Commd 13/9/70. Sqn Ldr 1/7/83. Retd GD 1/7/86.
BALL F.C. DFC. Born 9/2/20. Commd 1/12/42. Flt Lt 1/6/46. Retd GD 3/3/54.
BALL H.J. Born 26/4/57. Commd 26/9/90. Sqn Ldr 1/7/00. Retd ADMIN (CAT) 26/9/04.
BALL J.A. AFC . Born 14/5/48. Commd 28/2/69. Gp Capt 1/7/93. Retd GD 14/7/03.
BALL J.A. Born 22/4/40. Commd 10/2/72. Flt Lt 10/2/74. Retd GD(G) 22/4/95.
BALL J.A.C. Born 11/7/40. Commd 20/9/59. Sqn Ldr 3/8/70. Retd DEL 11/7/78.
BALL J.C. Born 20/10/41. Commd 19/12/63. Sqn Ldr 1/7/73. Retd SUP 20/10/79.
BALL J.F. Born 28/12/10. Commd 2/9/43. Sqn Ldr 1/1/56. Retd ENG 28/12/65.
BALL K.A. Born 11/5/32. Commd 9/9/54. Flt Lt 9/6/56. Retd GD 9/9/70.
BALL L.A. Born 6/12/17. Commd 2/6/49. Flt Lt 2/12/52. Retd SEC 1/4/55.
BALL M.G. DFC. Born 7/4/63. Commd 24/3/83. Sqn Ldr 1/1/95. Retd GD 7/4/01.
BALL M.J. Born 4/10/37. Commd 9/11/55. Sqn Ldr 1/7/78. Retd GD(G) 4/10/92.
BALL M.W. AFC. Born 22/4/47. Commd 2/8/68. Gp Capt 1/7/91. Retd GD 23/4/97.
BALL P.G. CEng MIMechE MRAeS. Born 5/1/26. Commd 5/4/71. Sqn Ldr 5/4/71. Retd ENG 11/9/87.
BALL S.M. MInstAM ACIS. Born 29/10/50. Commd 12/12/71. Sqn Ldr 1/1/83. Retd ADMIN 2/2/92.
BALL S.W. BSc. Born 9/7/64. Commd 7/12/86. Sqn Ldr 1/7/99. Retd FLY(P) 7/12/04.
BALL T.A. Born 9/6/28. Commd 20/4/55. Sqn Ldr 1/1/65. Retd CAT 10/5/71.
BALL T.F. BSc MRAeS. Born 4/6/46. Commd 26/5/67. Sqn Ldr 1/1/80. Retd ENG 4/6/90.
BALLANCE D.J. BSc. Born 21/4/67. Commd 10/10/85. Flt Lt 15/1/91. Retd FLY(P) 21/4/05.
BALLANTINE A.G. Born 18/4/24. Commd 28/9/61. Flt Lt 28/9/66. Retd GD 18/4/82.
BALLANTYNE A. MB ChB. Born 23/1/34. Commd 6/1/63. Sqn Ldr 13/8/64. Retd MED 1/6/68.
BALLANTYNE A.C. Born 13/8/62. Commd 4/10/85. Flt Lt 4/4/91. Retd GD 5/8/01.
BALLANTYNE J.A. Born 3/8/40. Commd 3/10/74. Sqn Ldr 1/7/83. Retd ENG 3/8/85.
BALLINGER F.G. Born 26/3/34. Commd 14/12/72. Fg Offr 14/12/72. Retd GD(G) 8/7/75.
BALLINGER J. Born 11/2/44. Commd 22/3/63. Sqn Ldr 1/7/76. Retd GD 11/2/82.
BALMER M.T. Born 24/5/65. Commd 26/9/90. Flt Lt 24/1/93. Retd ADMIN (SEC) 30/5/03.
BALMFORD D.E. Born 6/7/34. Commd 5/6/56. Flt Lt 6/3/63. Retd GD(G) 2/8/72.
BALMFORTH-SLATER D.L. Born 2/12/62. Commd 24/3/83. Flt Lt 24/9/89. Retd OPS SPT 2/12/00.
BALSHAW J.K. BSc. Born 9/3/30. Commd 20/8/52. Sqn Ldr 9/3/63. Retd ADMIN 20/8/80.
BAMBERGER C.S. DFC*. Born 4/5/19. Commd 9/2/42. Sqn Ldr 1/1/57. Retd GD 29/1/59.
BAMBERGER J. Born 8/11/55. Commd 1/9/74. APO 1/9/74. Retd GD 3/11/77.
BAMFIELD R.H. MBE MCMI. Born 3/7/43. Commd 8/10/70. Wg Cdr 1/1/90. Retd ADMIN 1/7/93.
BAMFORD M.N. Born 2/8/55. Commd 20/1/80. Sqn Ldr 1/7/88. Retd ADMIN 20/1/96.
BAMPTON A.F. Born 5/5/36. Commd 10/11/61. Flt Lt 28/4/66. Retd GD 25/6/77.
BANCE A.E. AFC. Born 12/11/23. Commd 19/11/53. Flt Lt 19/11/59. Retd GD 8/3/68.
BANCE D.E. Born 2/11/31. Commd 18/4/74. Flt Lt 1/1/91. Retd ENG 1/1/94.
BANCROFT J.J. Born 12/9/36. Commd 24/2/61. Sqn Ldr 1/1/85. Retd GD 12/9/91.
BANCROFT J.K. Born 13/12/29. Commd 11/6/52. Flt Lt 18/12/57. Retd GD 13/12/72. Re-instated 21/5/81 to 13/12/84.
BANCROFT-PITMAN G. Born 7/11/35. Commd 20/10/65. Wg Cdr 1/1/78. Retd GD(G) 2/4/94. rtg Gp Capt
BANCROFT-PITMAN S.C. Born 29/10/44. Commd 6/11/80. Sqn Ldr 1/1/92. Retd GD 29/10/99.
BANCROFT-WILSON A. BSc. Born 3/2/58. Commd 26/7/81. Flt Lt 26/10/84. Retd ADMIN 28/4/88.
BANCROFT-WILSON H.A. BEng. Born 6/2/55. Commd 26/7/81. Flt Lt 26/1/82. Retd ENG 1/12/96.
BANEY T.H. Born 29/10/35. Commd 2/10/58. Flt Lt 2/4/69. Retd GD 2/10/74.
BANFIELD A.F. Born 8/2/38. Commd 23/10/56. Sqn Ldr 1/7/88. Retd GD 1/7/88.
BANFIELD E.L. AFC. Born 21/8/32. Commd 11/4/60. Sqn Ldr 1/7/87. Retd GD 21/8/92.
BANFIELD M.W.F. Born 18/4/32. Commd 6/12/51. Sqn Ldr 1/1/64. Retd GD 1/8/79.
BANGAY J.M. MCMI. Born 21/10/21. Commd 24/10/45. Sqn Ldr 1/7/64. Retd SY 21/10/76.
BANGAY W.G.E. Born 7/5/30. Commd 6/7/50. Flt Lt 6/7/56. Retd SEC 7/5/68.
BANKS A.J.R. OBE FCIS FCIPD. Born 29/6/47. Commd 4/5/72. Gp Capt 1/7/92. Retd ADMIN 10/12/96.
BANKS C.O. Born 13/6/54. Commd 22/2/79. Sqn Ldr 1/1/90. Retd GD 8/2/93.
BANKS C.P. Born 4/11/61. Commd 28/7/93. Flt Lt 28/7/95. Retd OPS SPT 28/7/01.
BANKS D.R. Born 29/9/47. Commd 27/2/70. Flt Lt 14/5/74. Retd ENG 4/4/85.
BANKS E. OBE FLCM LRAM LGSM ARCM. Born 2/4/32. Commd 20/12/62. Wg Cdr 1/7/83. Retd DM 2/4/89.
BANKS E.F. FCMI. Born 29/4/29. Commd 11/4/51. Gp Capt 1/1/75. Retd SUP 29/4/84.

BANKS F.W.J. Born 8/8/31. Commd 6/12/51. Flt Lt 27/6/57. Retd GD 8/8/74.
BANKS G.E. MA. Born 17/2/41. Commd 6/11/64. Flt Lt 6/2/66. Retd GD 17/7/93.
BANKS G.F. Born 9/10/24. Commd 11/3/65. Flt Lt 11/3/68. Retd GD 31/7/73.
BANKS I.N. Born 24/7/53. Commd 2/10/72. Sqn Ldr 1/7/91. Retd ADMIN 12/4/94.
BANKS K.J. Born 9/2/45. Commd 20/9/79. Flt Lt 20/9/81. Retd ENG 20/9/87.
BANKS L.F. DFC AFC. Born 9/2/20. Commd 6/6/42. Wg Cdr 1/1/57. Retd GD 10/11/63.
BANKS M.C.F. Born 11/10/30. Commd 19/1/50. Wg Cdr 1/7/75. Retd SUP 11/10/85.
BANKS M.L. Born 18/9/33. Commd 24/3/61. Fg Offr 21/3/58. Retd GD 16/8/66.
BANKS M.R. MB ChB DO. Born 10/9/44. Commd 11/1/65. Sqn Ldr 12/8/73. Retd MED 1/8/80.
BANKS P.A. BSc. Born 19/5/54. Commd 5/5/83. Sqn Ldr 1/7/91. Retd ADMIN (SEC) 1/9/04.
BANKS P.C. MBE BSc CertEd. Born 10/11/45. Commd 20/5/79. Sqn Ldr 1/1/90. Retd ADMIN 30/4/99.
BANKS R.L. Born 3/9/39. Commd 20/11/60. Flt Lt 20/5/65. Retd GD 3/9/77.
BANKS R.W. Born 5/3/24. Commd 25/8/60. Flt Lt 25/8/63. Retd ENG 6/12/74.
BANNARD R.J. FCMI. Born 8/6/30. Commd 9/4/52. Gp Capt 1/7/71. Retd GD 15/10/81.
BANNATYNE J.A. CBE BA. Born 12/2/11. Commd 27/1/40. Gp Offr 1/7/60. Retd SEC 6/12/64.
BANNERMAN A. Born 1/1/29. Commd 25/8/52. Flt Lt 25/3/56. Retd GD 1/1/72.
BANNERMAN H. MB BS DOMS. Born 9/10/08. Commd 8/1/33. Wg Cdr 1/10/46. Retd MED 1/6/55.
BANNING D.C. Born 12/11/37. Commd 22/5/70. Sqn Ldr 1/7/82. Retd GD(G) 13/11/88.
BANNISTER A.J. MCMI. Born 25/10/18. Commd 17/4/39. Wg Cdr 1/7/67. Retd SUP 25/10/73.
BANNISTER D.R. Born 2/8/48. Commd 20/12/73. Wg Cdr 1/7/89. Retd GD 3/12/99.
BANNISTER M. BA. Born 26/2/39. Commd 31/12/79. Sqn Ldr 11/7/77. Retd ADMIN 1/9/85.
BANNISTER P. Born 15/5/37. Commd 16/12/58. Sqn Ldr 1/1/69. Retd SUP 15/5/75.
BANNISTER R.A. Born 19/1/54. Commd 1/7/76. Sqn Ldr 1/7/90. Retd GD 1/2/98.
BANNON R.P. BSc MB BS FRCR MRCS LRCP DCH. Born 6/1/47. Commd 27/4/70. Sqn Ldr 22/8/79.
    Retd MED 28/10/86.
BANYARD A.E. CEng MIMechE. Born 8/5/42. Commd 10/10/63. Sqn Ldr 1/7/78. Retd ENG 8/5/86.
BANYARD G.F. OBE. Born 23/7/21. Commd 23/10/43. Wg Cdr 1/7/61. Retd GD 23/7/76.
BAPTISTE P.J. Born 9/3/62. Commd 28/2/85. Flt Lt 16/2/89. Retd GD(G) 19/12/95.
BAPTY P.C. BEng. Born 12/5/59. Commd 4/7/82. Flt Lt 4/10/83. Retd GD 14/3/97.
BARBER A.F.H. Born 31/10/20. Commd 9/6/43. Flt Lt 9/3/47. Retd ENG 1/11/61.
BARBER A.W. BSc. Born 14/11/33. Commd 25/6/55. Flt Lt 25/6/58. Retd GD 25/9/72.
BARBER D.J. Born 22/8/12. Commd 1/1/37. Wg Cdr 1/1/50. Retd SUP 1/11/60.
BARBER D.J. Born 11/12/44. Commd 25/3/64. Sqn Ldr 1/1/82. Retd GD 1/1/85.
BARBER D.W. OBE. Born 11/3/22. Commd 2/1/42. Gp Capt 1/7/72. Retd GD 11/3/77.
BARBER F.W.A. Born 14/9/19. Commd 19/7/56. Sqn Ldr 1/1/66. Retd ENG 14/9/77.
BARBER G.M. BA. Born 23/1/25. Commd 5/9/48. Sqn Ldr 1/1/62. Retd GD 1/1/65.
BARBER J. Born 18/5/56. Commd 9/10/75. Flt Lt 9/4/81. Retd GD 18/5/94.
BARBER J.C. DFM. Born 10/6/21. Commd 28/9/45. Sqn Ldr 1/1/70. Retd GD(G) 1/5/75.
BARBER J.R. BA. Born 22/1/60. Commd 8/5/83. Sqn Ldr 1/7/91. Retd SUP 8/5/99.
BARBER K. Born 31/3/24. Commd 24/1/52. Sqn Ldr 1/7/62. Retd ENG 1/7/65.
BARBER L.A. Born 1/12/28. Commd 11/10/49. Sqn Ldr 1/7/62. Retd GD 1/12/66.
BARBER L.T.G. OBE AFC. Born 18/1/10. Commd 21/2/30. Wg Cdr 1/10/46. Retd GD 18/1/57. rtg Gp Capt
BARBER M.I. BEng. Born 19/2/60. Commd 1/8/86. Flt Lt 25/7/90. Retd ENG 31/3/99.
BARBER N.J.H. Born 13/9/62. Commd 5/2/81. Flt Lt 5/8/86. Retd GD 14/3/96.
BARBER P. Born 6/2/52. Commd 27/9/73. Flt Lt 1/4/93. Retd GD 27/3/79.
BARBER P. OBE DFC. Born 2/5/23. Commd 19/9/42. Wg Cdr 1/1/60. Retd GD 2/5/70.
BARBER R. Born 23/9/59. Commd 5/4/79. Sqn Ldr 1/1/91. Retd GD 23/9/97.
BARBER R.E. BSc CEng MIEE. Born 5/8/40. Commd 2/9/73. Sqn Ldr 1/1/83. Retd ENG 2/9/89.
BARBER R.H. Born 17/9/47. Commd 27/1/67. Flt Lt 25/5/07. Retd GD(G) 17/9/85.
BARBER R.S. Born 21/4/45. Commd 3/1/64. Flt Lt 3/7/69. Retd GD 21/4/83.
BARBER R.V.W. Born 10/4/47. Commd 21/10/66. Flt Lt 25/2/73. Retd GD(G) 10/4/85.
BARBER S.B.J. MA. Born 5/8/55. Commd 21/3/74. Wg Cdr 1/1/98. Retd GD 3/4/03.
BARBER W.D. Born 20/3/21. Commd 14/3/46. Flt Lt 10/8/55. Retd GD 18/7/64.
BARBER W.J. Born 31/8/42. Commd 16/9/71. Flt Lt 16/9/73. Retd ENG 31/8/80.
BARBOUR T.M. BA. Born 31/5/55. Commd 30/4/78. Flt Lt 30/1/80. Retd GD 14/3/97.
BARCILON R.L. AFC. Born 17/3/34. Commd 5/4/55. A Cdre 1/7/86. Retd GD 13/7/87.
BARCLAY A.B.G. Born 11/2/17. Commd 8/5/41. Flt Lt 10/11/55. Retd CAT 7/4/64.
BARCLAY B.N. Born 14/9/24. Commd 14/4/49. Flt Lt 14/10/52. Retd GD 30/3/68.
BARCLAY E.J.A. MSc BSc. Born 13/3/65. Commd 17/5/94. Sqn Ldr 1/1/98. Retd SUPPLY 1/10/03.
BARCLAY R.T. Born 21/12/21. Commd 28/2/57. Flt Lt 27/8/60. Retd GD 6/4/68.
BARCLAY S.J. OBE MCIPD. Born 11/5/42. Commd 6/5/65. Gp Capt 1/7/90. Retd ADMIN 14/3/96.
BARCROFT A.M.L. Born 15/10/49. Commd 31/7/70. Wg Cdr 1/1/89. Retd SUP 14/3/97.
BARDELL T. Born 22/9/46. Commd 9/12/65. Sqn Ldr 1/7/91. Retd GD(G) 14/3/96.
BARDELL-COX T.A. MBA BSc(Econ) MCMI. Born 27/12/61. Commd 7/6/87. Sqn Ldr 1/7/01.
    Retd OPS SPT(INT) 1/7/04.
BARDEN D.W. Born 15/5/39. Commd 23/12/58. Wg Cdr 1/7/77. Retd GD 7/4/82.

BARDEN J.A. Born 11/5/54. Commd 2/6/77. Flt Lt 2/12/82. Retd GD 14/4/93.
BARDON P.J. DFC AFC. Born 15/4/29. Commd 14/12/49. Wg Cdr 1/1/65. Retd GD 31/7/68.
BARDON R.T. Born 20/4/54. Commd 3/11/77. Flt Lt 3/5/80. Retd GD 20/10/92.
BARDSLEY A. BSc. Born 13/5/31. Commd 3/8/55. Sqn Ldr 1/1/65. Retd ENG 25/6/85.
BAREHAM D.M. MSc BEng CEng GradCIPD MRAeS LCIPD. Born 13/1/66. Commd 3/8/88. Sqn Ldr 1/1/00.
     Retd ENGINEER 13/1/05.
BARFIELD D.B. Born 11/5/34. Commd 11/11/71. Flt Lt 11/11/75. Retd SY 11/5/82.
BARFOOT D.B. Born 5/12/23. Commd 6/7/44. Sqn Ldr 1/7/55. Retd GD 25/2/72.
BARFOOT W.E. Born 31/10/19. Commd 27/3/43. Sqn Ldr 1/1/53. Retd GD 5/6/59.
BARGEWELL T.A. IEng MIIE. Born 19/3/46. Commd 8/9/83. Sqn Ldr 1/1/93. Retd ENG 3/3/99.
BARGH R.A. BSc. Born 31/7/31. Commd 8/12/59. Flt Lt 18/3/64. Retd ENG 22/9/89.
BARHAM C.L. Born 7/7/47. Commd 26/4/84. Flt Lt 26/4/88. Retd GD 1/4/90.
BARHAM D.G.A. MA. Born 22/5/37. Commd 7/10/48. Wg Cdr 25/5/68. Retd EDN 24/11/75.
BARHAM E.M. Born 29/7/29. Commd 17/5/62. Sqn Ldr 1/7/73. Retd PRT 2/4/81.
BARHAM M.W. Born 13/7/34. Commd 21/9/62. Wg Cdr 1/1/83. Retd SUP 26/2/89.
BARKEL J. Born 31/10/22. Commd 11/4/57. Flt Lt 14/2/66. Retd GD(G) 31/10/77.
BARKER A. Born 11/3/44. Commd 4/12/64. Flt Lt 4/6/70. Retd GD 18/8/76.
BARKER A.C. MBE MSc. Born 9/7/53. Commd 18/4/76. Wg Cdr 1/7/93. Retd ENG 31/5/01.
BARKER A.M. Born 22/6/55. Commd 3/7/80. Sqn Ldr 1/1/89. Retd ADMIN 15/11/92.
BARKER B.G. EDN 22/12/35. Commd 11/11/65. Sqn Ldr 11/8/73. Retd EDN 22/12/73.
BARKER C.M.I. MA. Born 7/4/54. Commd 22/5/75. Wg Cdr 1/1/96. Retd GD 29/9/01.
BARKER D. BSc. Born 6/4/57. Commd 26/11/78. Flt Lt 26/8/80. Retd GD 6/4/95.
BARKER D.H. MSc BSc BSc MRAeS AFIMA. Born 16/7/45. Commd 22/9/65. Sqn Ldr 15/1/78. Retd ADMIN 16/7/89.
BARKER D.J. Born 28/3/41. Commd 19/7/74. Flt Lt 16/9/73. Retd ENG 16/9/79.
BARKER D.S. MA BSc MCMI. Born 27/7/34. Commd 23/9/55. Sqn Ldr 1/7/66. Retd SEC 16/11/68.
BARKER H. Born 31/5/34. Commd 13/8/52. Flt Lt 29/4/59. Retd GD 31/5/72.
BARKER J. Born 14/6/45. Commd 31/1/64. Wg Cdr 1/1/93. Retd GD 31/3/99.
BARKER J. Born 9/8/35. Commd 24/1/63. Sqn Ldr 1/7/72. Retd GD(G) 1/4/86.
BARKER J.A. MB ChB DLO MRAeS. Born 13/12/39. Commd 21/1/63. Wg Cdr 2/8/76. Retd MED 3/4/82.
BARKER J.E. CEng FCMI MIEE. Born 10/1/30. Commd 30/9/54. Gp Capt 1/1/82. Retd ENG 10/1/88.
BARKER J.L. CB CBE DFC BA. Born 12/11/10. Commd 6/7/31. Gp Capt 1/1/53. Retd GD 26/2/63. rtg AVM
BARKER J.R.L. Born 1/11/70. Commd 29/5/97. Flt Lt 9/6/03. Retd OPS SPT(FLTOPS) 1/9/03.
BARKER J.S. Born 2/12/21. Commd 23/8/56. Sqn Ldr 1/1/69. Retd ENG 4/12/71.
BARKER M.A. BSc. Born 9/8/55. Commd 15/9/74. Sqn Ldr 1/1/87. Retd ENG 1/4/95.
BARKER N.C.W. Born 17/5/43. Commd 17/12/65. Sqn Ldr 1/7/73. Retd GD 27/4/93.
BARKER P. Born 3/12/49. Commd 5/8/73. Wg Cdr 1/7/00. Retd GD 3/12/04.
BARKER R. Born 19/9/08. Commd 1/3/41. Flt Lt 1/9/45. Retd ENG 30/5/48.
BARKER R.A. Born 29/7/32. Commd 25/1/66. Flt Lt 9/12/66. Retd EDN 9/12/73.
BARKER R.A. BSc. Born 23/2/52. Commd 13/9/70. Sqn Ldr 1/1/84. Retd ENG 10/8/90.
BARKER R.A. BSc. Born 24/4/66. Commd 22/2/93. Sqn Ldr 1/1/02. Retd FLY(P) 1/1/05.
BARKER R.H.C. Born 21/10/17. Commd 3/8/42. Flt Lt 31/12/50. Retd SEC 29/4/61.
BARKER R.J. Born 29/12/57. Commd 17/7/87. Flt Lt 17/7/89. Retd OPS SPT 19/2/01.
BARKER R.P. Born 6/11/47. Commd 2/12/66. Flt Lt 2/6/72. Retd GD 22/10/94.
BARKER S.J. CEng DipSoton MIEE. Born 1/2/34. Commd 22/7/55. Wg Cdr 1/7/77. Retd ENG 1/2/87.
BARKER W.W. BSc. Born 24/9/30. Commd 15/10/52. Sqn Ldr 1/1/65. Retd GD 12/5/85.
BARKWAY A.F. Born 2/8/44. Commd 18/4/74. Sqn Ldr 1/7/84. Retd SUP 14/3/96.
BARKWAY R.J. Born 26/7/37. Commd 1/4/65. Flt Lt 26/7/92. Retd SUP 26/7/92.
BARLEE L.W. Born 24/5/19. Commd 21/9/50. Sqn Ldr 1/7/59. Retd ENG 24/5/68.
BARLEX A.N. Born 29/12/31. Commd 12/9/51. Wg Cdr 1/7/79. Retd GD 29/12/86.
BARLEY M.J. Born 11/1/61. Commd 20/1/85. Sqn Ldr 1/1/00. Retd SUP 11/1/03.
BARLOW D.E. Born 23/7/59. Commd 15/8/85. Flt Lt 5/9/88. Retd OPS SPT 23/7/97.
BARLOW I.G. MCMI. Born 5/10/38. Commd 14/4/49. Sqn Ldr 1/7/70. Retd GD 1/4/78.
BARLOW J.F. BA. Born 9/3/27. Commd 24/1/56. Fg Offr 24/7/56. Retd ENG 7/6/60.
BARLOW M.A. BEng. Born 7/11/65. Commd 6/11/88. Flt Lt 6/5/90. Retd GD 14/3/97.
BARLOW P.E.C. Born 4/5/51. Commd 15/2/73. Wg Cdr 1/1/91. Retd ADMIN 13/1/97.
BARLOW R.A.G. Born 22/11/23. Commd 7/11/46. Flt Lt 30/7/48. Retd ENG 12/4/62. rtg Sqn Ldr
BARLOW R.C. Born 26/12/17. Commd 14/10/41. Flt Lt 1/9/45. Retd GD 26/2/55.
BARLOW T.F. Born 7/2/10. Commd 22/7/43. Flt Lt 22/1/48. Retd SEC 30/5/64.
BARLTROP D.F. MBE. Born 1/1/34. Commd 16/9/71. Sqn Ldr 1/1/82. Retd ENG 1/1/94.
BARLTROP W.S. Born 1/3/40. Commd 20/10/64. Sqn Ldr 1/7/81. Retd GD(G) 1/3/95.
BARMBY A.S. Born 15/3/35. Commd 24/6/53. Flt Lt 25/11/58. Retd GD 15/3/73.
BARMBY J. Born 16/2/63. Commd 25/2/82. Flt Lt 26/8/88. Retd GD(G) 7/8/89.
BARNARD E.F.E. Born 21/1/09. Commd 30/4/35. Wg Cdr 1/10/46. Retd GD 13/4/56.
BARNARD J. Born 7/6/20. Commd 6/1/55. Flt Lt 6/1/58. Retd GD(G) 7/6/75.
BARNARD J.B. BA. Born 22/8/33. Commd 6/4/54. Flt Lt 11/3/60. Retd GD 22/8/93.
BARNARD J.B. Born 3/5/44. Commd 6/7/62. Sqn Ldr 1/7/88. Retd GD 1/6/98.

BARNARD M.H. Born 21/7/38. Commd 9/4/60. Sqn Ldr 1/7/71. Retd GD 21/7/76.
BARNARD P.J. Born 5/4/31. Commd 1/9/52. Flt Lt 1/3/57. Retd GD 5/4/69.
BARNARD P.Q. MBE IEng. Born 4/5/43. Commd 23/11/78. Sqn Ldr 1/1/87. Retd ENG 4/5/00.
BARNARD R.G. Born 18/6/30. Commd 24/1/52. Flt Lt 15/5/57. Retd GD 3/8/76.
BARNARD T.A. Born 29/12/40. Commd 4/4/59. Flt Lt 4/10/64. Retd GD 29/12/78.
BARNARD W.G. Born 4/3/29. Commd 4/6/52. Flt Lt 20/3/58. Retd MAR 15/1/68.
BARNES C.H. Born 16/5/37. Commd 24/9/64. Sqn Ldr 1/7/72. Retd GD 10/3/85.
BARNES C.R. Born 5/9/68. Commd 26/9/91. Flt Lt 19/3/95. Retd OPS SPT(PROVSY) 3/11/03.
BARNES D.A.W. BA. Born 30/5/36. Commd 3/1/58. Sqn Ldr 23/3/68. Retd EDN 30/5/74.
BARNES D.H. OBE. Born 28/3/37. Commd 30/3/61. Gp Capt 1/1/82. Retd GD 5/4/85.
BARNES D.J. MBE CEng MRAeS MCMI. Born 1/10/20. Commd 13/4/44. Wg Cdr 1/7/68. Retd ENG 3/6/78.
BARNES D.J. Born 6/8/44. Commd 29/7/83. Sqn Ldr 1/7/92. Retd ADMIN 2/12/97.
BARNES D.N. Born 2/8/46. Commd 23/3/66. Sqn Ldr 1/7/78. Retd ADMIN 15/10/01.
BARNES F. AFC MRAeS MCMI. Born 29/9/22. Commd 25/3/44. Wg Cdr 1/7/69. Retd GD 1/5/72.
BARNES F.G. BSc. Born 12/3/35. Commd 10/10/56. Flt Lt 18/3/64. Retd SUP 29/11/74.
BARNES F.O. Born 1/12/42. Commd 6/7/62. Flt Lt 6/1/68. Retd GD 15/4/02.
BARNES H. Born 19/4/23. Commd 23/12/45. Flt Lt 19/6/52. Retd ENG 16/9/76.
BARNES H.J.C. Born 31/3/26. Commd 21/12/45. Sqn Ldr 1/1/57. Retd GD 1/4/68.
BARNES I.A. Born 8/4/22. Commd 11/5/48. Flt Lt 11/5/52. Retd SUP 9/5/62.
BARNES J. Born 9/2/20. Commd 27/6/53. Flt Lt 25/6/56. Retd SEC 30/5/64.
BARNES J.A. Born 27/5/42. Commd 17/5/63. Flt Lt 17/11/68. Retd GD 31/5/72.
BARNES J.H. Born 1/5/44. Commd 11/9/64. Sqn Ldr 1/7/77. Retd GD 1/5/82.
BARNES K.M. Born 20/10/38. Commd 10/2/72. Flt Lt 10/2/74. Retd GD(G) 11/8/81.
BARNES L.J.F. MSc. Born 4/7/51. Commd 25/2/72. Gp Capt 1/7/00. Retd GD 11/4/04.
BARNES M. Born 10/8/39. Commd 22/3/63. A Cdre 1/7/89. Retd GD 22/4/92.
BARNES N.I. Born 15/9/55. Commd 25/2/82. Flt Lt 20/12/84. Retd ENG 15/9/99.
BARNES P.E. Born 23/6/44. Commd 6/11/64. Plt Offr 6/11/65. Retd GD 13/5/67.
BARNES S.G. DFC BSc. Born 22/3/62. Commd 14/9/80. Wg Cdr 1/7/97. Retd GD 24/4/01.
BARNES W.H. MSc. Born 9/10/36. Commd 31/10/71. Sqn Ldr 31/10/71. Retd ENG 3/10/75.
BARNETT A. DFM. Born 8/1/22. Commd 21/11/43. Flt Lt 21/5/47. Retd ENG 10/9/59.
BARNETT C.A. Born 11/10/42. Commd 23/11/62. A Cdre 1/7/94. Retd GD(G) 1/12/95.
BARNETT G.W. Born 16/3/18. Commd 29/10/43. Sqn Ldr 1/1/63. Retd ENG 30/3/68.
BARNETT J.C. Born 12/4/38. Commd 22/5/64. Flt Lt 22/5/68. Retd GD 3/2/80. Re-entered 6/3/85. Flt Lt 21/6/73.
   Retd GD 12/4/98.
BARNETT J.J. Born 6/6/49. Commd 31/7/70. Wg Cdr 1/7/86. Retd GD 14/11/89.
BARNETT J.N. BSc. Born 6/1/62. Commd 2/9/84. Flt Lt 2/3/86. Retd GD 3/1/93.
BARNETT J.R. Born 21/7/63. Commd 10/6/94. Sqn Ldr 1/1/99. Retd FLY(P) 6/1/04.
BARNETT M.J.R. Born 30/1/44. Commd 12/7/63. Sqn Ldr 1/7/83. Retd GD 2/4/93.
BARNETT R.E.J. Born 12/5/23. Commd 26/8/43. Wg Cdr 1/7/65. Retd ENG 31/12/77.
BARNETT W. Born 24/2/45. Commd 23/9/65. Gp Capt 1/1/97. Retd ADMIN 24/2/00.
BARNEY J. MBE. Born 8/1/34. Commd 2/12/55. A Cdre 1/1/85. Retd ADMIN 29/8/87.
BARNEY J.S. MB ChB. Born 12/9/59. Commd 29/3/83. Wg Cdr 1/8/97. Retd MED 29/3/00.
BARNFATHER B.J. Born 19/12/63. Commd 24/3/83. Flt Lt 24/9/88. Retd GD 31/12/92.
BARNFATHER C.L. BA CEng MIEE MRAeS MCMI. Born 21/6/37. Commd 23/7/58. Wg Cdr 1/7/84.
   Retd ENG 21/6/92.
BARNICOAT D.R. MCMI. Born 21/7/25. Commd 19/10/45. Wg Cdr 1/1/67. Retd GD 1/11/75.
BARNINGHAM R.A. Born 17/11/54. Commd 8/9/83. Sqn Ldr 1/7/91. Retd SUP 14/3/96.
BARNOWSKI B. Born 15/9/22. Commd 25/1/51. Flt Lt 10/11/55. Retd GD 17/8/73.
BARNWELL L.M.L. BA. Born 12/8/43. Commd 3/2/73. Flt Lt 3/2/78. Retd SEC 22/9/81.
BARON D.A. OBE. Born 3/2/41. Commd 24/2/61. Gp Capt 1/7/85. Retd GD 3/2/96.
BARON G. Born 14/9/46. Commd 10/6/66. Flt Lt 10/6/71. Retd GD 29/6/83.
BARON R.A. Born 13/8/53. Commd 6/4/72. Flt Lt 6/10/77. Retd GD 23/10/80.
BARON R.J.M. MBE. Born 5/6/26. Commd 15/11/45. Flt Lt 10/10/51. Retd GD 1/7/57.
BARR A. Born 25/8/47. Commd 1/4/66. Flt Lt 30/9/72. Retd GD 25/8/02.
BARR D.M. FRAeS FCMI. Born 17/9/47. Commd 1/4/66. Gp Capt 1/1/94. Retd GD 3/1/97.
BARR J.J. Born 25/7/21. Commd 19/8/39. Gp Capt 1/1/67. Retd GD 30/4/72.
BARR J.W. Born 20/7/42. Commd 28/8/75. Flt Lt 28/8/77. Retd ENG 28/8/83.
BARR-SIM I.E. Born 11/8/29. Commd 13/12/50. Flt Lt 19/11/53. Retd GD 18/7/56.
BARRACLOUGH Sir John KCB CBE DFC AFC FRAeS FRSA. Born 2/5/18. Commd 7/5/38. ACM 3/9/73.
   Retd GD 3/4/76.
BARRACLOUGH R.H. Born 27/10/30. Commd 8/2/51. Sqn Ldr 1/1/63. Retd GD 6/5/77. Re-instated 15/10/80.
   Sqn Ldr 12/6/66. Retd GD 16/6/91.
BARRACLOUGH S.M. Born 2/4/17. Commd 28/6/41. Sqn Ldr 1/8/47. Retd GD 28/5/58.
BARRADELL D.J. Born 27/2/44. Commd 12/1/62. Flt Lt 12/7/67. Retd GD 28/9/98.
BARRAS-SMITH D.I. Born 6/11/20. Commd 25/2/43. Flt Lt 25/8/46. Retd GD 6/11/63. rtg Sqn Ldr
BARRASS J.A. BSc. Born 31/3/59. Commd 18/10/81. Wg Cdr 1/7/98. Retd GD 10/4/01.

BARRASS K. Born 10/7/58. Commd 15/2/90. Flt Lt 15/2/92. Retd ENG 15/2/98.
BARRATT D. Born 5/3/60. Commd 28/5/98. Flt Lt 28/5/02. Retd ADMIN (SEC) 5/11/04.
BARRATT J.F. Born 25/12/31. Commd 21/4/67. Flt Lt 21/4/70. Retd GD 1/8/74.
BARRATT M.A. Born 4/9/31. Commd 12/8/54. Sqn Ldr 1/1/83. Retd GD 4/9/89.
BARRATT P. The Rev. Born 25/3/56. Commd 5/4/79. Retd Flt Lt 2/9/87. Re-entered 2/7/90. Retd 31/12/97. Sqn Ldr
BARRATT P.C.S. MBE BSc. Born 10/3/50. Commd 19/11/72. Sqn Ldr 1/1/83. Retd GD 1/4/90.
BARRATT P.L. MA MSc BEng. Born 25/12/63. Commd 15/10/85. Sqn Ldr 1/7/99. Retd ENGINEER 1/7/03.
BARRATT S.G. Born 18/7/25. Commd 30/8/55. Flt Lt 16/11/64. Retd ADMIN 18/7/84.
BARRETT A. Born 31/3/47. Commd 1/7/82. Sqn Ldr 1/1/91. Retd ENG 14/3/96.
BARRETT A.H. BSc. Born 24/1/60. Commd 19/6/83. Sqn Ldr 1/1/92. Retd ENG 19/6/99.
BARRETT B.C. Born 26/3/46. Commd 26/5/67. Sqn Ldr 1/1/80. Retd ENG 26/3/84.
BARRETT B.D. Born 1/11/17. Commd 17/7/42. Sqn Ldr 1/7/60. Retd PRT 30/9/70. rtg Wg Cdr
BARRETT C.J. Born 19/8/44. Commd 27/1/74. Flt Lt 27/1/74. Retd GD(G) 19/8/82.
BARRETT D.C. Born 1/6/53. Commd 9/9/81. Flt Lt 21/1/80. Retd ADMIN 11/11/87.
BARRETT D.G. Born 4/8/37. Commd 7/6/73. Flt Lt 7/6/75. Retd GD(G) 7/6/81.
BARRETT D.W.R. Born 12/1/31. Commd 19/1/50. Wg Cdr 1/7/75. Retd ADMIN 26/9/83.
BARRETT F.J. Born 18/5/27. Commd 7/10/48. Sqn Ldr 1/7/59. Retd GD 7/9/68.
BARRETT F.O. CBE DFC. Born 2/12/18. Commd 25/10/38. A Cdre 1/1/70. Retd GD 8/2/73.
BARRETT H. CEng MIMechE MRAeS MCMI. Born 27/7/26. Commd 30/4/51. Sqn Ldr 1/1/61. Retd ENG 7/9/74.
BARRETT I. BSc. Born 29/5/48. Commd 13/5/73. Sqn Ldr 1/1/90. Retd FLY(N) 29/5/04.
BARRETT J.H. Born 21/7/13. Commd 4/3/35. Sqn Ldr 1/9/40. Retd GD 15/8/47.
BARRETT P. BSc ARSM. Born 20/11/53. Commd 23/9/73. Sqn Ldr 1/1/88. Retd GD 20/11/91.
BARRETT P.A. OBE BSc FRAeS. Born 5/7/47. Commd 17/9/73. Gp Capt 1/1/96. Retd GD 3/9/04.
BARRETT R.J. BA. Born 28/2/31. Commd 16/12/54. Flt Lt 1/3/71. Retd PI 6/7/74.
BARRETT R.J. Born 6/8/37. Commd 28/7/59. Wg Cdr 1/7/83. Retd GD 6/8/92.
BARRETT R.T. CEng MIEE MRAes. Born 1/9/40. Commd 18/7/61. Sqn Ldr 1/7/70. Retd ENG 1/9/78.
BARRETT R.W. Born 27/3/43. Commd 31/10/70. Flt Lt 31/10/76. Retd ADMIN 31/10/82.
BARRETT S.A. Born 7/9/21. Commd 23/10/43. Sqn Ldr 1/4/55. Retd GD 5/3/65.
BARRETT S.T. BSc. Born 10/8/61. Commd 2/9/84. Flt Lt 12/4/89. Retd ENG 2/5/94.
BARRETT T. Born 20/2/34. Commd 29/10/52. Wg Cdr 1/7/74. Retd GD 31/5/83.
BARREY C.J. DFC AFC DFM. Born 13/12/19. Commd 10/7/43. Sqn Ldr 1/7/61. Retd GD 13/12/74.
BARRIBALL E.R. Born 4/9/33. Commd 9/6/69. Wg Cdr 1/7/79. Retd GD(G) 31/12/86.
BARRINGER M.J. Born 25/10/38. Commd 25/7/60. Sqn Ldr 1/7/70. Retd GD 1/11/80.
BARRINGTON A. Born 13/8/23. Commd 9/3/44. Sqn Ldr 1/7/57. Retd SEC 1/9/67.
BARRINGTON D.E. Born 27/9/54. Commd 3/1/88. Flt Lt 3/1/88. Retd ADMIN 16/2/97.
BARRITT J.B. MCMI. Born 10/4/30. Commd 22/7/66. Sqn Ldr 1/7/82. Retd ENG 10/4/85.
BARRON J. Born 1/2/33. Commd 6/2/52. Flt Lt 22/1/58. Retd GD 11/1/75.
BARRON J.D. Born 12/12/56. Commd 14/10/84. Flt Lt 14/4/90. Retd ADMIN 14/3/97.
BARROW B.A.J. MB BS MRCS LRCP DPM. Born 26/12/29. Commd 18/7/54. Wg Cdr 5/7/67. Retd MED 18/7/70.
BARROW J.F.V. Born 7/8/20. Commd 4/6/59. Sqn Ldr 1/7/70. Retd GD 7/8/75.
BARROW J.I. Born 2/10/34. Commd 13/12/55. Gp Capt 1/1/85. Retd SUP 21/7/89.
BARROW J.L. Born 24/11/44. Commd 26/11/64. Sqn Ldr 1/1/82. Retd GD 1/1/85.
BARROW P.A. Born 9/7/34. Commd 14/12/54. Flt Lt 14/6/57. Retd GD 9/7/72.
BARROW S. Born 30/11/62. Commd 11/10/84. Sqn Ldr 1/7/95. Retd OPS SPT 30/6/01.
BARRY G.P. FCMI. Born 18/4/20. Commd 18/1/45. Gp Capt 1/7/70. Retd SUP 18/4/75.
BARRY J.S. MBE. Born 4/8/44. Commd 31/8/78. Wg Cdr 1/1/92. Retd GD(G) 30/11/94.
BARTER C. Born 11/9/39. Commd 17/9/57. Sqn Ldr 1/1/91. Retd GD 11/9/94.
BARTER G.B. Born 6/11/33. Commd 5/10/58. Sqn Ldr 1/1/71. Retd CAT 15/10/74.
BARTER J.F. Born 21/4/61. Commd 5/2/81. Sqn Ldr 1/1/94. Retd OPS SPT 22/4/98.
BARTHOLOMEW E. DFC. Born 29/11/22. Commd 24/11/44. Flt Lt 24/5/48. Retd GD 1/9/62.
BARTHOLOMEW J. Born 21/8/48. Commd 28/11/69. Flt Lt 28/5/75. Retd GD 31/5/75.
BARTHROPP P.P.C. DFC AFC. Born 9/11/20. Commd 31/10/38. Sqn Ldr 1/8/47. Retd GD 28/12/57. rtg Wg Cdr
BARTLE C.J. Born 19/9/41. Commd 20/8/65. Sqn Ldr 1/7/87. Retd GD 19/9/96.
BARTLE D.G. Born 29/7/33. Commd 29/3/56. Wg Cdr 1/1/78. Retd GD(G) 2/5/88.
BARTLE G.L. Born 18/8/44. Commd 14/2/63. Fg Offr 14/2/66. Retd ENG 23/10/66.
BARTLE M. BSc. Born 27/11/41. Commd 22/5/64. Sqn Ldr 1/7/72. Retd GD 4/2/80.
BARTLE S.J. BEng. Born 3/11/73. Commd 7/2/92. Fg Offr 15/1/95. Retd ENG 16/4/97.
BARTLETT C. AFC. Born 27/10/20. Commd 8/9/44. Wg Cdr 1/1/64. Retd GD 27/10/75.
BARTLETT C.S.M.c.D. Born 31/8/23. Commd 24/5/46. Sqn Ldr 1/1/58. Retd GD 2/9/66.
BARTLETT G.C.C. AFC. Born 19/8/12. Commd 29/6/36. Wg Cdr 1/10/46. Retd GD 29/9/59.
BARTLETT J. Born 1/3/32. Commd 23/8/51. Sqn Ldr 1/7/78. Retd PI 8/11/84.
BARTLETT J.E. Born 26/1/47. Commd 13/1/67. Flt Lt 13/1/72. Retd GD 27/1/90.
BARTLETT J.W. Born 24/11/37. Commd 6/9/63. Flt Lt 26/7/67. Retd GD 24/11/75.
BARTLETT K.W. BA MBCS. Born 9/3/57. Commd 25/2/82. Flt Lt 25/8/85. Retd ADMIN 16/11/96.
BARTLETT L.H. DSO. Born 20/6/16. Commd 31/7/41. Gp Capt 1/1/60. Retd GD 20/6/66.
BARTLETT M.A. Born 6/3/45. Commd 20/10/67. Flt Lt 4/5/72. Retd GD 1/4/76.

BARTLETT M.S. MVO CEng MIMechE. Born 15/1/45. Commd 11/2/65. Wg Cdr 1/1/82. Retd ENG 18/9/84.
BARTLETT M.T. Born 24/2/23. Commd 30/3/45. Sqn Ldr 1/7/59. Retd GD 26/2/66.
BARTLETT R.J. Born 23/11/12. Commd 30/10/41. Wg Cdr 1/7/58. Retd ENG 23/11/66.
BARTLETT S.E.J. Born 27/1/14. Commd 15/1/43. Flt Lt 15/7/47. Retd PE 27/1/62.
BARTLETT S.M. Born 30/7/64. Commd 7/11/85. Flt Lt 12/9/90. Retd OPS SPT 30/7/02.
BARTLETT T.R. CEng MIEE. Born 13/1/24. Commd 7/12/61. Sqn Ldr 13/9/68. Retd EDN 13/9/78.
BARTLETT W.R.J. Born 10/1/55. Commd 28/7/88. Flt Lt 27/7/90. Retd ENG 28/7/96.
BARTLEY D.C. Born 31/10/42. Commd 16/8/68. Fg Offr 16/8/70. Retd GD 20/12/72.
BARTMAN C.D. Born 21/5/22. Commd 10/3/43. Sqn Ldr 1/1/53. Retd GD 21/5/65.
BARTON A.D. Born 17/5/36. Commd 19/12/59. Flt Lt 19/6/64. Retd GD 17/5/74.
BARTON A.E.Mack. CEng MRAeS. Born 31/1/24. Commd 14/10/44. Sqn Ldr 1/1/58. Retd GD 31/8/67.
BARTON D.H. MCMI. Born 16/8/25. Commd 21/4/45. Sqn Ldr 1/7/58. Retd SEC 25/4/78.
BARTON D.I. Born 14/10/22. Commd 15/6/44. Flt Lt 19/6/52. Retd GD(G) 18/4/56.
BARTON E.J. Born 9/2/38. Commd 3/8/62. Flt Lt 1/4/66. Retd GD 1/9/78.
BARTON L. Born 3/2/32. Commd 2/1/56. Sqn Ldr 1/1/70. Retd GD(G) 4/2/82.
BARTON M.A. Born 22/9/59. Commd 13/12/79. Flt Lt 13/6/85. Retd GD 14/9/96.
BARTON N. Born 14/12/48. Commd 31/7/70. Flt Lt 31/7/73. Retd GD 14/12/86.
BARTON P.C. BSc. Born 17/6/51. Commd 15/8/69. Flt Lt 15/4/74. Retd GD 1/4/86.
BARTON P.R. BSc. Born 2/7/59. Commd 2/9/86. Wg Cdr 1/7/98. Retd GD 1/5/04.
BARTON R.A. OBE DFC*. Born 7/6/16. Commd 27/1/36. Wg Cdr 1/7/47. Retd GD 27/2/59.
BARTON R.H. Born 28/6/39. Commd 24/2/61. Flt Lt 24/8/66. Retd GD 1/3/77.
BARTRAM J.A. MSc FCMI FREC MRAeS. Born 10/6/52. Commd 29/4/71. Wg Cdr 1/1/96. Retd GD 31/7/03.
BARTRUM J. AFC. Born 12/4/24. Commd 27/2/47. Flt Lt 11/11/54. Retd GD 12/4/62.
BARWELL C.H. Born 16/5/23. Commd 19/2/44. Sqn Ldr 1/4/56. Retd GD 16/5/68.
BARWELL J.D. AFC. Born 31/3/31. Commd 17/10/51. Sqn Ldr 1/1/60. Retd SEC 19/5/68.
BARWELL R.D. BA. Born 6/11/35. Commd 10/10/58. Sqn Ldr 10/4/69. Retd ADMIN 30/6/87.
BARWOOD A.J. OBE MRCS LRCP DPH DIH FRAeS. Born 1/4/15. Commd 7/2/41. Gp Capt 1/7/59.
    Retd MED 1/4/80.
BARWOOD A.T. MRCS LRCP DPH. Born 7/7/24. Commd 3/8/50. Wg Cdr 3/8/62. Retd MED 24/11/66.
BASCOMBE A.R.H. BSc. Born 25/12/54. Commd 2/9/73. Flt Lt 15/10/77. Retd GD 5/11/86.
BASEY P.A.B. Born 3/9/59. Commd 8/9/83. Sqn Ldr 1/1/95. Retd GD 29/7/99.
BASHALL I. Born 31/5/34. Commd 18/3/53. Flt Lt 3/9/58. Retd GD 15/8/64.
BASHFORD G.J. Born 20/5/22. Commd 5/2/44. Flt Lt 15/9/65. Retd GD 20/5/77.
BASKERVILLE G.J. BSc. Born 16/3/35. Commd 2/11/56. Sqn Ldr 10/3/65. Retd EDN 16/3/73.
BASKETT C.A. DFC. Born 19/9/11. Commd 16/11/36. Wg Cdr 1/1/51. Retd GD 13/1/58.
BASNETT M.A. CBE. Born 1/4/46. Commd 1/4/65. Gp Capt 1/1/90. Retd SY 3/7/93.
BASS G.C. Born 7/2/21. Commd 22/9/55. Flt Lt 22/9/61. Retd ENG 30/6/73.
BASS J. Born 22/1/42. Commd 19/12/85. Flt Lt 19/12/89. Retd SY 22/1/92.
BASS J.M. Born 28/7/30. Commd 11/6/52. Flt Lt 18/12/57. Retd GD 28/7/68.
BASS R.H. Born 14/10/66. Commd 23/1/64. Sqn Ldr 1/1/86. Retd MED 14/3/96.
BASSETT J.W. Born 17/11/31. Commd 17/5/62. Flt Lt 17/5/68. Retd GD 8/1/77.
BASSETT R.G. Born 21/3/38. Commd 2/4/56. Sqn Ldr 1/7/69. Retd GD 21/3/76.
BASSFORD P.G. Born 2/5/30. Commd 19/1/50. Flt Lt 17/1/57. Retd GD 2/5/68.
BASSINGTHWAIGHTE K. Born 19/1/43. Commd 11/3/68. Wg Cdr 11/3/81. Retd LGL 11/3/84. rtg Gp Capt
BASTABLE A.W.R. Born 26/1/38. Commd 10/3/77. Sqn Ldr 1/7/87. Retd ENG 1/4/94.
BASTEN P.F. Born 25/9/36. Commd 9/4/60. Flt Lt 9/10/65. Retd GD 25/9/74.
BASTIAN M.A. Born 2/10/35. Commd 5/12/63. Fg Offr 1/4/64. Retd GD(G) 26/10/67.
BASTIN J.E. LLB. Born 8/3/29. Commd 12/12/51. Sqn Ldr 1/1/62. Retd SUP 8/3/67.
BASTON I.J. Born 5/5/61. Commd 16/9/79. Flt Lt 10/5/86. Retd GD 5/5/99.
BATCHELAR E. Born 7/9/21. Commd 10/6/41. Gp Capt 1/7/66. Retd GD 7/7/72.
BATCHELOR A.B. Born 17/9/50. Commd 24/10/73. Wg Cdr 1/1/97. Retd GD 2/4/03.
BATCHELOR L.E. Born 23/10/35. Commd 21/12/62. Flt Lt 1/4/66. Retd GD 31/3/69.
BATCHELOR P.D. Born 4/10/44. Commd 9/4/65. Sqn Ldr 1/7/78. Retd GD(G) 4/10/82.
BATCHELOR P.J. MB BS FRCS DLO. Born 24/8/26. Commd 29/6/53. Wg Cdr 29/6/64. Retd MED 29/6/69.
BATCHELOR W.A. BEd DPhysEd. Born 6/5/26. Commd 5/9/51. Wg Cdr 1/7/71. Retd PE 16/11/79.
BATCHELOR W.B. Born 19/6/08. Commd 19/9/40. Flt Lt 1/4/33. Retd ENG 19/7/48. rtg Sqn Ldr
BATE B.G. Born 12/2/49. Commd 14/12/72. Gp Capt 1/1/95. Retd ENG 6/5/02.
BATE L.C. Born 3/8/46. Commd 2/8/68. Sqn Ldr 1/7/84. Retd ENG 14/3/96.
BATEMAN A.J. BSc. Born 20/9/55. Commd 1/9/74. Sqn Ldr 1/7/88. Retd GD 30/6/94.
BATEMAN J.M. MB BS MRCP(UK). Born 31/1/58. Commd 17/3/80. Sqn Ldr 1/8/88. Retd MED 14/3/96.
BATEMAN R.E. MBE MCMI. Born 11/10/29. Commd 11/2/65. Sqn Ldr 1/7/75. Retd ENG 11/10/87.
BATEMAN R.H. BA. Born 18/5/24. Commd 11/2/44. Flt Lt 10/11/55. Retd GD 6/4/65.
BATEMAN R.I. MSc BA MCIT MILT MRAeS. Born 8/8/54. Commd 2/9/73. Gp Capt 1/7/98. Retd SUP 1/1/02.
BATES C. BSc. Born 24/12/33. Commd 7/12/56. Sqn Ldr 7/6/67. Retd EDN 1/1/75.
BATES C.R. BSc CEng FIEE. Born 2/8/39. Commd 12/9/61. Gp Capt 1/1/87. Retd ENG 2/8/94.
BATES D.F. CB FCMI. Born 10/4/28. Commd 5/4/50. AVM 1/1/80. Retd ADMIN 11/12/82.

BATES D.L. Born 23/3/33. Commd 8/11/51. Wg Cdr 1/1/80. Retd GD 23/3/88.
BATES E. Born 7/6/28. Commd 15/7/52. Flt Lt 15/4/58. Retd GD 7/6/66.
BATES G.A. MBE. Born 19/4/24. Commd 25/8/60. Sqn Ldr 1/7/74. Retd ENG 30/4/76.
BATES J. Born 13/7/38. Commd 19/8/58. Flt Lt 15/2/65. Retd GD 18/10/75.
BATES J. BA. Born 16/12/44. Commd 1/3/68. Sqn Ldr 1/1/80. Retd ENG 1/1/83.
BATES J.L. Born 30/10/30. Commd 5/12/51. Flt Lt 14/11/56. Retd GD 30/10/68.
BATES J.O. BSc CEng MIEE MRAeS. Born 8/9/45. Commd 9/10/67. Wg Cdr 1/1/85. Retd ENG 8/9/00.
BATES J.S. Born 29/12/28. Commd 10/4/52. Sqn Ldr 1/1/65. Retd GD 29/12/83.
BATES P.F. Born 27/11/36. Commd 14/11/59. Flt Lt 14/5/65. Retd GD 27/11/74.
BATES R. Born 7/10/30. Commd 28/5/66. Sqn Ldr 1/7/84. Retd ENG 7/10/88.
BATES R.C. BSc. Born 28/2/55. Commd 16/9/73. Sqn Ldr 1/7/87. Retd ENG 28/8/94.
BATES R.D. AFC FCMI. Born 13/3/34. Commd 27/7/54. Gp Capt 1/1/76. Retd GD 5/5/86.
BATES R.G. Born 28/8/47. Commd 15/6/83. Sqn Ldr 1/1/92. Retd ENG 14/3/97.
BATES R.J.S. BA CEng MRAeS. Born 21/2/39. Commd 30/9/57. Wg Cdr 1/7/75. Retd ENG 9/5/79.
BATES W.N. Born 17/4/62. Commd 29/7/83. Flt Lt 29/1/89. Retd GD 17/4/00.
BATESON A.M. Born 21/1/53. Commd 3/1/88. Flt Lt 3/1/94. Retd ADMIN 14/3/97.
BATESON D. Born 12/6/60. Commd 15/3/79. Flt Lt 8/7/85. Retd ADMIN 14/3/96.
BATEY R. Born 3/7/11. Commd 19/8/43. Flt Lt 19/2/47. Retd ENG 3/7/48.
BATH D.S.G. MB ChB DLO. Born 8/3/35. Commd 6/11/60. Sqn Ldr 16/10/65. Retd MED 7/3/69.
BATHER R.A. Born 16/8/58. Commd 18/10/79. Flt Lt 28/6/83. Retd GD 16/8/96.
BATHGATE A. Born 27/7/64. Commd 15/12/88. Flt Lt 31/3/93. Retd SUP 27/7/02.
BATHGATE P. BEng. Born 13/4/64. Commd 1/8/86. Sqn Ldr 1/1/99. Retd ENG 13/4/02.
BATSON P.K. MBE. Born 17/8/51. Commd 8/1/76. Sqn Ldr 1/7/89. Retd FLY(P) 27/4/03.
BATSTONE A.E. PhD BSc. Born 9/11/30. Commd 2/9/53. Sqn Ldr 1/1/63. Retd GD 2/9/69.
BATT B.B. FCMI. Born 26/7/35. Commd 21/4/54. A Cdre 1/7/88. Retd GD 2/4/91.
BATT M.K. MBE. Born 23/4/33. Commd 20/7/59. Gp Capt 1/1/85. Retd SY(RGT) 23/4/88.
BATT W.L. Born 16/2/22. Commd 18/3/46. Flt Lt 30/4/53. Retd GD 1/4/65.
BATTEN R.L. Born 30/5/21. Commd 8/12/48. Flt Lt 8/12/48. Retd GD 17/5/66.
BATTEN R.M. Born 7/12/21. Commd 29/10/41. Flt Lt 19/6/51. Retd GD(G) 20/9/66.
BATTERSBY R.S.H. BA. Born 15/5/59. Commd 5/2/84. Sqn Ldr 1/7/95. Retd ADMIN 5/2/00.
BATTEY F.J. BA. Born 11/1/62. Commd 11/9/83. Flt Lt 15/1/88. Retd ADMIN 11/8/00.
BATTLE J.B.R. Born 24/10/21. Commd 14/11/42. Sqn Ldr 1/7/54. Retd GD 24/10/64.
BATTLEY S.P. Born 27/12/49. Commd 22/7/71. Wg Cdr 1/7/96. Retd ADMIN 8/12/01.
BATTY P. Born 8/11/35. Commd 28/11/69. Flt Lt 4/5/72. Retd GD(G) 28/11/77. Re-instated 1/2/80 to 16/11/85.
BATTY P.H. Born 7/3/25. Commd 26/5/60. Sqn Ldr 1/1/69. Retd GD(G) 7/3/83.
BATTY S.T. MILT. Born 16/6/68. Commd 8/10/87. Fg Offr 8/4/90. Retd SUP 1/5/93.
BAUGH D.L. OBE. Born 18/8/43. Commd 28/7/64. Gp Capt 1/7/89. Retd GD 2/6/97.
BAUGH S.P. BA. Born 5/5/64. Commd 2/9/84. Flt Lt 15/1/88. Retd GD 14/9/96.
BAUGHAN D.S. IEng MIEIE. Born 10/4/54. Commd 8/10/87. Flt Lt 8/10/89. Retd ENG 15/12/00.
BAUGHAN M.J. Born 27/7/34. Commd 26/8/66. Flt Lt 26/8/67. Retd EDN 26/8/74.
BAUMGARTNER H.N. Born 7/4/50. Commd 29/3/68. Flt Lt 29/9/73. Retd GD 21/8/76.
BAVERSTOCK M.J. BEd. Born 29/9/60. Commd 13/2/83. Flt Lt 13/11/84. Retd GD 13/2/99.
BAVERSTOCK T. Born 15/7/46. Commd 2/3/70. Flt Lt 2/9/75. Retd GD 22/9/89.
BAXANDALL J.D.C. MB BS FRCOG. Born 21/3/32. Commd 17/6/57. A Cdre 17/10/88. Retd MED 14/9/96.
BAXTER A. Born 1/5/46. Commd 28/11/74. Sqn Ldr 1/7/84. Retd OPS SPT 1/12/99.
BAXTER A. MSc BEng. Born 15/3/70. Commd 28/8/88. Flt Lt 15/1/94. Retd FLY(P) 15/7/03.
BAXTER G.G. BSc. Born 23/12/34. Commd 20/12/57. Sqn Ldr 20/6/67. Retd EDN 12/9/73.
BAXTER G.R. MA BA FCMI. Born 16/12/25. Commd 7/10/48. Gp Capt 1/7/66. Retd GD 7/5/80.
BAXTER H. MBE. Born 18/2/28. Commd 20/10/49. Gp Capt 1/7/81. Retd GD 18/2/83.
BAXTER J.T. Born 3/4/20. Commd 21/6/56. Flt Lt 21/6/62. Retd GD(G) 11/8/67.
BAXTER K. Born 7/7/63. Commd 19/12/91. Flt Lt 19/12/93. Retd OPS SPT 7/7/01.
BAXTER M.E. BSc. Born 8/4/66. Commd 14/2/88. Flt Lt 14/8/90. Retd FLY(P) 8/4/04.
BAXTER P.R. Born 21/9/36. Commd 9/6/55. Sqn Ldr 1/1/72. Retd GD 4/6/83.
BAXTER P.S. CEng MIEE. Born 23/3/35. Commd 24/6/58. Sqn Ldr 1/1/69. Retd ENG 17/4/74.
BAXTER S.G.L. Born 26/2/61. Commd 3/7/80. Flt Lt 17/12/86. Retd SUP 1/10/89.
BAXTER W.J. Born 2/9/18. Commd 26/5/60. Flt Lt 26/5/63. Retd ENG 2/9/73.
BAXTER W.L. Born 10/9/22. Commd 12/2/44. Sqn Ldr 1/1/55. Retd GD 10/9/71.
BAYER P. Born 17/10/50. Commd 20/9/68. Wg Cdr 1/1/00. Retd GD 17/10/03.
BAYES C.R. Born 16/2/46. Commd 15/10/81. Sqn Ldr 1/7/94. Retd ENG 14/3/96.
BAYLEY J.L. Born 13/11/17. Commd 23/9/44. Wg Cdr 1/7/68. Retd GD 2/12/72.
BAYLEY W.J. FAAI MCMI. Born 2/8/31. Commd 27/9/51. Sqn Ldr 1/7/68. Retd ADMIN 1/9/85.
BAYLISS D. Born 17/8/62. Commd 5/5/88. Flt Lt 5/5/90. Retd GD 2/4/02.
BAYLISS D.G. Born 26/10/53. Commd 2/8/90. Flt Lt 2/8/94. Retd ADMIN(SEC) 2/4/03.
BAYLISS G.G. DFC AFC. Born 28/4/29. Commd 19/4/60. Flt Lt 19/4/60. Retd GD 19/9/71.
BAYLISS J.A. MBE. Born 3/4/41. Commd 18/12/62. Wg Cdr 1/1/89. Retd GD 3/4/96.
BAYLISS R.O. The Rev. RMN. Born 21/7/44. Commd 2/8/81. Retd Gp Capt 31/8/01.

BAYLISS V. MCMI. Born 28/5/24. Commd 23/12/44. Wg Cdr 1/1/70. Retd GD(G) 28/5/79.
BAYLY A.E. BSc CEng MIEE. Born 27/6/43. Commd 30/9/62. Sqn Ldr 1/1/74. Retd ENG 15/5/76.
BAYLY R.C. MBE. Born 9/1/24. Commd 18/9/44. Sqn Ldr 1/1/70. Retd PE 9/1/79.
BAYNE D.P. Born 3/6/37. Commd 28/7/67. Flt Lt 4/5/72. Retd GD 4/6/74.
BAYNE R.M. Born 28/2/39. Commd 13/12/60. Sqn Ldr 1/7/74. Retd GD 1/9/79.
BAYNES K.G. Born 16/3/32. Commd 24/9/52. Gp Capt 1/7/80. Retd GD 31/3/85.
BAYNTON J.G. BSc. Born 6/3/53. Commd 14/1/73. Sqn Ldr 1/7/84. Retd GD 6/3/90.
BAYNTON W.G. Born 18/10/24. Commd 27/5/44. Sqn Ldr 1/4/55. Retd GD 30/3/68.
BEACH M.D. Born 6/10/32. Commd 6/2/57. Flt Lt 21/8/63. Retd ADMIN 30/9/83.
BEACHAM W.J. Born 4/1/30. Commd 31/8/50. Sqn Ldr 1/7/68. Retd GD 4/1/88.
BEADLE P.J.C. Born 30/7/57. Commd 24/7/81. Sqn Ldr 1/1/92. Retd GD 14/3/96.
BEADLE T. Born 18/4/48. Commd 23/2/68. Flt Lt 23/8/73. Retd GD 18/4/86.
BEADLE T.C. LLB. Born 28/3/61. Commd 17/7/81. Flt Lt 15/10/83. Retd GD 19/10/87.
BEADLE W.W. Born 4/10/18. Commd 26/2/54. Flt Lt 26/2/59. Retd ENG 5/1/62.
BEADMAN J.F. Born 4/10/44. Commd 29/10/64. Sqn Ldr 1/1/84. Retd SUP 4/10/92.
BEAK P. BEd. Born 9/3/49. Commd 18/11/79. Flt Lt 18/11/83. Retd ADMIN 18/1/95.
BEAL D.G. OBE CEng MRAeS MinstP FINucE. Born 6/4/18. Commd 7/1/43. Wg Cdr 1/1/62. Retd ENG 6/7/73.
BEAL M.A. BSc. Born 13/5/67. Commd 6/11/89. Flt Lt 25/3/91. Retd FLY(P) 14/6/05.
BEAL M.J. Born 9/11/41. Commd 24/3/61. Flt Lt 10/2/67. Retd GD 9/11/79.
BEAL R.V. FACCA. Born 17/8/06. Commd 15/9/39. Sqn Ldr 1/8/47. Retd SEC 15/9/58.
BEALER R.A. Born 17/6/45. Commd 3/3/67. Wg Cdr 1/1/91. Retd GD 17/6/00.
BEAMENT H.T. Born 22/7/43. Commd 31/1/64. Flt Lt 4/11/70. Retd GD 1/8/75.
BEAMISH D.T. CBE MMAR MCMI. Born 25/9/20. Commd 19/10/49. Gp Capt 1/1/71. Retd MAR 25/9/75.
BEAMISH O.T. Born 30/12/38. Commd 19/2/76. Sqn Ldr 1/7/85. Retd GD 30/12/93.
BEAN E. MBE. Born 1/4/18. Commd 3/8/44. Sqn Ldr 1/10/55. Retd ENG 1/4/69.
BEAN J.D. Born 25/7/44. Commd 27/2/75. Flt Lt 27/2/77. Retd GD 27/2/83.
BEANE D. Born 5/9/38. Commd 7/12/61. Flt Lt 1/4/66. Retd GD 5/9/76.
BEANE M.J. Born 7/5/39. Commd 9/9/58. Sqn Ldr 1/7/92. Retd GD 7/5/94.
BEANEY G.P.E. FRCS MB BS MRCS LRCP DLO. Born 8/4/33. Commd 4/1/59. Sqn Ldr 4/7/63. Retd MED 1/5/68.
BEAR E.A. BSc(Eng) CEng FCMI MRAeS MIMechE. Born 7/3/29. Commd 24/9/52. A Cdre 1/1/78. Retd ENG 7/3/84.
BEARBLOCK C.D.A.F. BSc. Born 3/1/66. Commd 16/9/84. Flt Lt 15/1/90. Retd GD 15/7/99.
BEARD A.F.P. MBE. Born 12/11/18. Commd 20/7/43. Wg Cdr 1/1/64. Retd SUP 1/2/69.
BEARD A.J. Born 16/11/39. Commd 12/7/79. Sqn Ldr 1/1/89. Retd GD 1/8/91.
BEARD D.H. Born 17/8/26. Commd 5/12/63. Sqn Ldr 1/7/73. Retd PE 30/6/81.
BEARD D.J.R. Born 6/3/30. Commd 11/10/51. Sqn Ldr 1/7/64. Retd GD 6/3/68.
BEARD D.M. Born 5/11/43. Commd 13/12/79. Flt Lt 13/12/84. Retd SUP 5/11/99.
BEARD J.N. Born 8/8/23. Commd 10/4/52. Flt Lt 10/11/55. Retd GD 8/8/78.
BEARD J.S. Born 8/11/45. Commd 6/5/66. Flt Lt 6/11/71. Retd GD 2/4/90.
BEARD M.E. Born 13/10/34. Commd 19/11/52. Flt Lt 15/4/58. Retd GD 30/9/77.
BEARD S.W.B. Born 24/3/35. Commd 16/6/69. Flt Lt 16/6/71. Retd PRT 5/1/73.
BEARDMORE J. CEng MIEE. Born 4/3/23. Commd 27/5/43. Sqn Ldr 1/10/55. Retd ENG 6/7/63.
BEARDS J.B. Born 9/9/43. Commd 24/6/65. Flt Lt 24/12/67. Retd GD 13/4/73.
BEARDSALL D.H. Born 20/3/34. Commd 17/12/64. Flt Lt 17/12/70. Retd GD 1/11/75.
BEARDSLEY R.A. DFC. Born 9/1/20. Commd 28/6/41. Sqn Ldr 1/7/65. Retd GD(G) 1/8/70.
BEARDSMORE J. BA DPhysEd. Born 30/6/46. Commd 7/8/67. Sqn Ldr 1/7/79. Retd ADMIN 30/6/90.
BEARNE G. CB. Born 5/11/08. Commd 28/6/29. AVM 1/7/56. Retd GD 5/11/61.
BEARRYMAN F.G. Born 13/5/25. Commd 19/7/57. Sqn Ldr 1/1/71. Retd ENG 10/6/75.
BEASANT N.C.A. BSc. Born 9/7/50. Commd 18/4/71. Sqn Ldr 1/1/83. Retd GD 16/7/88.
BEASLEY D.A. MBE FHCIMA. Born 13/2/21. Commd 11/5/53. Wg Cdr 1/1/67. Retd CAT 31/8/73.
BEASLEY G.J. Born 24/3/43. Commd 8/12/61. Flt Lt 9/2/68. Retd GD 1/6/94.
BEAT P.A. Born 20/7/64. Commd 27/7/89. Sqn Ldr 1/7/00. Retd OPS SPT(ATC) 1/7/03.
BEATON A.J. Born 12/12/47. Commd 17/2/67. Sqn Ldr 1/7/81. Retd GD 3/8/85.
BEATON H.B. Born 6/1/63. Commd 20/10/83. Plt Offr 19/8/84. Retd ADMIN 15/12/85.
BEATON H.W. Born 25/8/31. Commd 6/12/51. Sqn Ldr 1/7/67. Retd GD 20/8/76.
BEATON J. Born 28/6/19. Commd 9/9/39. Flt Lt 30/1/47. Retd SUP 19/11/60. rtg Sqn Ldr
BEATON J.L. BA MMar. Born 5/12/32. Commd 11/4/61. Sqn Ldr 11/7/72. Retd ADMIN 11/4/77.
BEATON K.A. Born 20/3/48. Commd 1/7/82. Flt Lt 1/7/84. Retd ADMIN 1/6/94.
BEATON M.J. Born 13/8/52. Commd 25/2/79. Sqn Ldr 1/1/93. Retd ADMIN 14/3/96.
BEATON P.K. Born 20/6/35. Commd 27/10/67. Flt Lt 27/10/69. Retd GD 27/10/75.
BEATSON R.MacL. Born 15/11/33. Commd 11/6/52. Flt Lt 14/5/58. Retd GD 15/11/71.
BEATSON T.R. MB BS FRCS LRCP. Born 4/3/28. Commd 5/8/52. Wg Cdr 5/7/64. Retd MED 5/8/68.
BEATTIE D.L. Born 5/1/32. Commd 22/9/55. Flt Lt 5/10/60. Retd GD 29/1/70.
BEATTIE J.G. Born 31/1/41. Commd 16/1/60. Flt Lt 28/7/65. Retd GD 31/1/79.
BEATTIE J.G. Born 31/1/41. Commd 16/1/60. Flt Lt 28/7/65. Retd GD 30/1/79.
BEATTIE N.G. Born 10/4/44. Commd 13/12/79. Sqn Ldr 1/1/91. Retd ENG 3/1/97.
BEATTIE T.W. Born 4/2/23. Commd 6/3/53. Sqn Ldr 1/1/66. Retd GD 31/8/68.

BEAUMONT D. Born 20/11/18. Commd 17/7/45. Sqn Ldr 1/1/57. Retd SEC 22/5/65.
BEAUMONT D.L. Born 26/4/41. Commd 17/5/63. Flt Lt 8/1/69. Retd GD 26/4/79.
BEAUMONT K.M. MA. Born 4/11/19. Commd 1/9/41. Sqn Ldr 1/3/56. Retd EDN 1/2/58.
BEAUTEMENT P. MSc BSc PGCE. Born 14/6/51. Commd 2/9/84. Sqn Ldr 1/7/91. Retd ADMIN 14/3/97.
BEAVAN A.J.P. Born 18/6/43. Commd 11/8/67. Flt Lt 4/5/72. Retd GD 10/2/77.
BEAVERS F.P.P. MSc BChD LDSRCS MGDSRCS(Ed). Born 2/6/53. Commd 9/4/78. Wg Cdr 15/5/89. Retd DEL 9/4/94.
BEAVES B.R. BA DPhysEd. Born 1/6/43. Commd 13/9/70. Sqn Ldr 13/3/74. Retd ADMIN 13/9/86.
BEAVIS Sir Michael KCB CBE AFC CCMI. Born 8/3/29. Commd 25/8/49. ACM 1/7/84. Retd GD 3/1/87.
BEAZLEY F. IEng. Born 18/4/31. Commd 26/5/67. Sqn Ldr 1/1/80. Retd ENG 1/5/89.
BEAZLEY R.H. CBE AFC FRAeS. Born 15/9/41. Commd 5/3/65. Gp Capt 1/1/90. Retd GD 15/12/96.
BEBBINGTON F.S. Born 22/10/43. Commd 9/3/62. Sqn Ldr 1/1/77. Retd GD 31/1/82.
BEBBINGTON H.A. Born 29/4/37. Commd 31/10/69. Flt Lt 4/5/72. Retd GD 31/10/77.
BEBBINGTON J.K. Born 9/1/35. Commd 23/9/66. Flt Lt 23/9/71. Retd ENG 6/9/74.
BECK B. Born 6/8/12. Commd 1/9/41. Flt Lt 10/1/45. Retd ENG 13/1/46. rtg Sqn Ldr
BECK C.O. Born 6/8/14. Commd 12/8/42. Sqn Ldr 1/1/55. Retd GD(G) 9/11/61.
BECK G. BSc. Born 7/3/66. Commd 12/2/95. Flt Lt 12/8/98. Retd ADMIN 18/4/00.
BECK H.W.B. Born 10/6/33. Commd 15/5/58. Sqn Ldr 1/1/72. Retd GD 5/5/78.
BECK M.P. BA MRAeS. Born 22/7/36. Commd 21/4/67. Wg Cdr 1/7/79. Retd ENG 8/5/86.
BECK P.R. Born 26/6/44. Commd 28/10/66. Flt Lt 28/4/72. Retd GD 7/12/72.
BECKER A.F. Born 19/1/29. Commd 31/1/52. Flt Lt 31/1/57. Retd ENG 6/8/60.
BECKER B.H. CEng MRAeS. Born 12/6/12. Commd 15/7/33. Gp Capt 1/7/53. Retd ENG 1/5/55.
BECKER K.H. Born 18/10/43. Commd 29/11/63. Sqn Ldr 1/7/80. Retd GD 18/10/99.
BECKETT G.A.J. CEng MIEE. Born 2/12/23. Commd 5/12/51. Wg Cdr 1/7/69. Retd ENG 21/12/73.
BECKETT J.D. Born 28/8/35. Commd 23/2/60. Sqn Ldr 11/7/71. Retd EDN 23/2/76.
BECKETT J.H. MCMI. Born 7/12/23. Commd 15/9/60. Sqn Ldr 1/7/74. Retd ADMIN 6/8/77.
BECKETT J.R. MCIPS. Born 18/9/42. Commd 23/9/66. Sqn Ldr 1/7/74. Retd SUP 18/9/97.
BECKINGHAM A.T.H. Born 27/6/39. Commd 6/8/60. Flt Lt 16/10/67. Retd ADMIN 18/7/77.
BECKLEY D.H. Born 4/5/30. Commd 30/5/69. Flt Lt 30/5/73. Retd GD(G) 4/5/80.
BECKLEY P.A. FCMI. Born 17/7/29. Commd 9/8/51. Gp Capt 1/7/81. Retd ADMIN 1/12/83.
BECKLEY R.B. Born 9/10/20. Commd 2/2/45. Flt Lt 7/6/56. Retd GD 9/6/64.
BECKNELLE P.V. Born 15/1/39. Commd 27/1/61. Flt Lt 27/7/66. Retd GD 28/4/72.
BEDDOES A.B. Born 28/6/45. Commd 17/1/85. Sqn Ldr 1/1/94. Retd ENG 14/3/97.
BEDDOWS A.J. Born 28/1/46. Commd 26/5/67. Flt Lt 26/11/73. Retd ADMIN 28/1/84.
BEDFORD A.W. AFC. Born 18/11/20. Commd 14/11/42. Flt Lt 14/5/46. Retd GD 15/9/51.
BEDFORD B. Born 11/3/29. Commd 2/7/52. Flt Lt 8/1/58. Retd GD 21/1/68.
BEDFORD B.K. Born 2/2/32. Commd 28/11/51. Flt Lt 28/5/56. Retd GD 2/2/70.
BEDFORD D.J. Born 5/2/63. Commd 2/2/84. Flt Lt 2/8/89. Retd GD 28/4/00.
BEDFORD E. Born 28/10/46. Commd 28/2/69. Flt Lt 6/10/71. Retd GD 10/6/91.
BEDFORD G.R. MB ChB. Born 30/7/12. Commd 2/5/41. Gp Capt 1/7/62. Retd MED 2/8/70.
BEDFORD P.A. AFC MRAeS. Born 28/5/46. Commd 26/5/67. Gp Capt 1/1/92. Retd GD 17/1/99.
BEDFORD R. MBE BSc DCAe MRAeS. Born 10/8/34. Commd 22/11/56. Sqn Ldr 1/1/66. Retd ENG 16/8/72.
BEDFORD S.H. Born 22/2/51. Commd 17/7/70. Sqn Ldr 1/1/87. Retd GD 1/5/89.
BEDNALL M.P. BSc MRAeS. Born 24/2/43. Commd 30/9/62. Flt Lt 1/1/79. Retd ENG 1/1/82.
BEDWELL R.S.W. Born 26/9/23. Commd 17/10/57. Sqn Ldr 1/1/71. Retd ENG 7/4/78.
BEDWIN P.G.W. MBE. Born 4/11/43. Commd 4/11/64. Sqn Ldr 1/1/79. Retd GD 1/1/82.
BEDWORTH M.A. BSc. Born 23/1/40. Commd 4/7/66. Flt Lt 4/7/67. Retd EDN 1/10/71.
BEE M.E. AFC. Born 31/12/37. Commd 29/7/58. Wg Cdr 1/1/73. Retd GD 11/7/78.
BEEBE P.S.J. Born 17/1/33. Commd 14/11/57. Gp Capt 1/7/79. Retd ADMIN 11/9/82.
BEEBY C.W. BA. Born 20/7/48. Commd 28/12/80. Sqn Ldr 1/1/89. Retd SUP 14/3/96.
BEEBY J.M. MRAeS MCMI. Born 6/6/20. Commd 17/11/49. Sqn Ldr 1/1/58. Retd ENG 2/1/71.
BEECH M.D. AFC BSc. Born 21/10/51. Commd 13/9/70. Sqn Ldr 1/7/82. Retd GD 20/11/88.
BEECH P.D. BSc. Born 19/5/53. Commd 11/7/76. Flt Lt 11/10/77. Retd GD 11/7/88.
BEECH-ALLAN M.D. Born 13/8/47. Commd 28/4/67. Flt Lt 28/10/72. Retd GD 1/4/76.
BEECHAM R.S. OBE. Born 28/1/33. Commd 21/8/52. Gp Capt 1/7/79. Retd ADMIN 3/4/82.
BEECROFT J. DFM. Born 25/9/20. Commd 8/6/43. Flt Lt 8/12/46. Retd GD 25/9/63.
BEEDIE A.I.B. Born 28/4/49. Commd 23/2/68. Gp Capt 1/1/95. Retd GD 2/4/05.
BEEDIE W. FInstAM MCMI. Born 17/9/48. Commd 8/11/68. Wg Cdr 1/7/87. Retd ADMIN 14/3/97.
BEEDIE W.A. CEng MRAeS. Born 29/7/23. Commd 2/9/43. Wg Cdr 1/7/73. Retd ENG 24/12/76.
BEER D.V. The Rev. PhL STL. Born 21/5/31. Commd 11/1/66. Retd Wg Cdr 21/5/86.
BEER G.C. Born 12/6/43. Commd 4/12/64. Flt Lt 8/1/69. Retd GD 30/10/76.
BEER M.E. MBE. Born 10/2/44. Commd 19/4/63. Sqn Ldr 1/7/82. Retd GD 9/9/95.
BEER P.G. CB CBE LVO. Born 16/7/41. Commd 11/5/62. AVM 1/7/91. Retd GD 16/11/95.
BEER R.B.E. Born 2/11/24. Commd 12/9/63. Sqn Ldr 1/1/74. Retd ENG 28/8/79.
BEES R.G. BSc. Born 6/11/56. Commd 14/10/76. Sqn Ldr 1/7/88. Retd GD 6/11/94.
BEESLEY J.H. Born 19/7/28. Commd 17/7/58. Sqn Ldr 1/7/77. Retd GD 2/4/85.
BEESTON M.D. MA. Born 6/10/65. Commd 2/9/84. Flt Lt 15/1/90. Retd FLY(P) 7/6/05.

BEET G.T.W. BSc. Born 20/5/60. Commd 6/9/81. Sqn Ldr 1/1/95. Retd GD 20/5/99.
BEETLESTONE T.J. Born 30/11/35. Commd 6/4/72. Flt Lt 6/4/75. Retd GD 30/11/93.
BEGG A. MBE. Born 27/9/25. Commd 21/11/51. Flt Lt 21/5/56. Retd GD 28/3/69.
BEGG A.L. Born 24/5/39. Commd 13/2/60. Sqn Ldr 1/7/72. Retd GD 25/5/76.
BEGG G.I. BSc. Born 15/3/56. Commd 14/9/75. Flt Lt 15/10/79. Retd GD 1/5/88.
BEGG W. ACCS. Born 18/10/23. Commd 23/12/61. Flt Lt 23/12/64. Retd SEC 17/1/68.
BEGGS B.D. Born 20/1/36. Commd 9/4/57. Flt Lt 9/10/59. Retd GD 27/10/67.
BEGLAN P.M. Born 11/4/43. Commd 28/2/64. Flt Lt 13/6/72. Retd GD 11/4/81.
BEHRENS R.W. CEng MIEE. Born 14/2/42. Commd 26/5/64. Sqn Ldr 1/7/75. Retd ENG 8/7/83.
BEILBY I.D.C. Born 14/12/29. Commd 11/2/65. Flt Lt 11/2/70. Retd ENG 14/12/89.
BEITH-JONES H. OBE FCMI. Born 21/3/44. Commd 28/3/63. Wg Cdr 1/1/85. Retd ADMIN 27/3/96.
BELBEN M.J. BA CEng MIEE MRAeS MCMI. Born 21/11/37. Commd 27/1/67. Flt Lt 27/1/69. Retd ENG 21/11/75.
BELBIN A.T. CEng MRAeS. Born 7/10/41. Commd 11/3/68. Flt Lt 11/11/70. Retd ENG 30/9/86.
BELCHAMBER N.W. Born 4/11/30. Commd 30/3/61. Flt Lt 30/3/66. Retd GD 4/11/85.
BELCHER D. Born 28/10/29. Commd 12/3/52. Sqn Ldr 1/7/64. Retd GD 5/12/75.
BELCHER F.D. Born 3/4/33. Commd 30/5/69. Flt Lt 30/5/75. Retd GD(G) 4/4/79.
BELCHER H.G. Born 13/7/15. Commd 17/8/39. Wg Cdr 1/7/54. Retd SUP 28/6/58.
BELFITT F. DFM. Born 10/8/17. Commd 18/2/43. Flt Lt 18/8/46. Retd GD(G) 10/8/69.
BELK P. Born 16/12/38. Commd 15/6/83. Sqn Ldr 1/1/90. Retd ENG 20/1/95.
BELL A.A. Born 8/2/36. Commd 5/5/60. Flt Lt 5/11/64. Retd GD 8/2/74.
BELL A.E. Born 2/12/23. Commd 3/1/44. Flt Lt 29/6/50. Retd SEC 12/11/50.
BELL A.G. Born 6/8/57. Commd 23/11/78. Sqn Ldr 1/7/92. Retd SY 1/4/97.
BELL A.J. Born 2/7/25. Commd 18/10/51. Flt Lt 18/4/55. Retd GD(G) 2/7/80.
BELL A.P. MRAeS. Born 1/4/43. Commd 9/2/62. Wg Cdr 1/1/83. Retd GD 2/4/93.
BELL A.R. Born 27/10/39. Commd 25/7/60. Flt Lt 25/1/63. Retd GD 27/10/94.
BELL C.E. BA. Born 12/6/36. Commd 26/10/79. Sqn Ldr 26/10/76. Retd ENG 7/7/87.
BELL C.G. BA MRAeS MRIN MCMI. Born 25/8/33. Commd 5/11/52. Wg Cdr 1/7/79. Retd GD 25/8/88.
BELL C.R. Born 10/9/23. Commd 20/10/46. Flt Lt 20/4/50. Retd GD 15/1/62.
BELL C.R.L. BSc CEng MIMechE. Born 6/8/44. Commd 15/7/65. Wg Cdr 1/1/86. Retd ENG 6/8/99.
BELL D.A. Born 24/1/33. Commd 29/12/54. Flt Lt 29/6/60. Retd GD 28/11/71.
BELL D.A. Born 5/4/39. Commd 11/11/64. Sqn Ldr 1/1/86. Retd GD(G) 1/5/89.
BELL D.A.J. MBE. Born 13/10/24. Commd 28/7/67. Flt Lt 28/7/70. Retd ENG 13/10/79.
BELL E. AFC. Born 21/2/16. Commd 31/1/42. Sqn Ldr 1/7/54. Retd GD 21/2/59.
BELL G. MMar MNI. Born 26/6/33. Commd 11/3/68. Wg Cdr 1/7/84. Retd ADMIN 4/6/90.
BELL G. Born 2/1/35. Commd 28/6/79. Sqn Ldr 1/1/88. Retd ENG 30/4/90.
BELL G.B. AFC. Born 6/12/24. Commd 25/8/49. Sqn Ldr 1/7/58. Retd GD 8/4/74.
BELL G.E. Born 13/12/36. Commd 23/3/55. Flt Lt 1/1/67. Retd GD 13/12/74.
BELL G.F. Born 23/7/41. Commd 30/8/64. Sqn Ldr 1/7/87. Retd GD 23/7/96.
BELL G.F.A. Born 16/2/52. Commd 29/7/83. Flt Lt 29/7/85. Retd GD(G) 29/7/91.
BELL H. ACIS. Born 13/1/30. Commd 11/3/65. Sqn Ldr 1/7/74. Retd SEC 5/5/79.
BELL H.W. BA. Born 23/12/48. Commd 1/11/71. Flt Lt 1/2/73. Retd GD 1/11/83.
BELL J. MBE. Born 14/2/41. Commd 11/5/78. Sqn Ldr 1/7/88. Retd SUP 14/6/96.
BELL J.A. OBE FCMI. Born 16/9/34. Commd 26/7/55. A Cdre 1/1/83. Retd GD 1/10/89.
BELL J.D. OBE. Born 21/5/45. Commd 11/8/77. Wg Cdr 1/7/90. Retd ADMIN 30/6/00.
BELL J.D. BA. Born 1/4/48. Commd 16/8/70. Sqn Ldr 1/7/79. Retd ENG 16/8/86.
BELL J.J. Born 19/8/40. Commd 21/3/64. Flt Lt 20/6/70. Retd GD(G) 19/8/80.
BELL J.J. Born 19/8/40. Commd 24/11/80. Sqn Ldr 1/7/87. Retd SUP 10/12/92.
BELL J.L. Born 30/7/43. Commd 8/6/62. Flt Lt 8/12/67. Retd GD 15/5/72.
BELL J.R. DFC MBE. Born 25/3/23. Commd 22/2/44. Wg Cdr 1/7/72. Retd PI 31/3/77.
BELL J.R. BEng BA. Born 17/4/61. Commd 1/9/86. Flt Lt 15/1/93. Retd ENG 1/9/02.
BELL J.S. BSc. Born 27/10/42. Commd 7/10/63. Sqn Ldr 1/1/74. Retd GD 27/10/80.
BELL J.S.W. OBE AFC. Born 23/9/24. Commd 24/3/44. Gp Capt 1/7/71. Retd GD 29/6/78.
BELL J.T. Born 7/2/40. Commd 15/9/61. Flt Lt 15/3/72. Retd GD 7/8/90.
BELL J.V. CBE. Born 29/10/40. Commd 5/3/65. Gp Capt 1/7/87. Retd GD 29/7/96.
BELL K. Born 8/1/29. Commd 13/2/64. Sqn Ldr 1/7/75. Retd ADMIN 8/7/82.
BELL K. Born 26/2/41. Commd 6/5/83. Sqn Ldr 1/7/92. Retd SY 26/2/96.
BELL M.A. BA. Born 16/3/59. Commd 18/10/81. Sqn Ldr 1/1/93. Retd SUP 14/9/96.
BELL M.C. BSc. Born 16/5/54. Commd 3/9/72. Flt Lt 15/4/79. Retd ENG 16/5/92.
BELL M.F. Born 20/7/41. Commd 26/5/61. Wg Cdr 1/1/94. Retd GD 20/7/96.
BELL M.J. BSc. Born 12/7/48. Commd 3/1/69. Flt Lt 15/10/70. Retd GD 1/1/82.
BELL M.J. Born 4/1/43. Commd 1/7/82. Flt Lt 1/3/87. Retd ENG 16/5/93.
BELL N.G. Born 16/4/44. Commd 12/7/63. Wg Cdr 16/4/02. Retd GD 16/4/02.
BELL P. MBE. Born 28/9/22. Commd 1/5/47. Flt Lt 4/6/53. Retd PE 30/4/70.
BELL P.A. BSc. Born 22/6/62. Commd 27/10/82. Sqn Ldr 1/1/98. Retd GD 1/1/01.
BELL P.G. CEng MRAeS. Born 11/9/39. Commd 18/7/61. Wg Cdr 1/1/77. Retd ENG 21/6/85.
BELL P.J. Born 20/7/58. Commd 20/7/78. Flt Lt 20/1/84. Retd GD 20/7/96.

BELL R.L.B. Born 17/9/36. Commd 12/1/55. Sqn Ldr 1/7/69. Retd GD 17/9/74.
BELL S. Born 26/5/64. Commd 28/2/85. Flt Lt 28/8/90. Retd GD 30/6/02.
BELL S.H. Born 5/5/26. Commd 14/11/51. Flt Lt 14/5/56. Retd GD 5/5/81.
BELL W.A. BA. Born 6/4/40. Commd 1/10/62. Wg Cdr 1/1/80. Retd GD 1/10/89.
BELL W.E.B. Born 1/9/33. Commd 26/8/52. Flt Lt 31/7/57. Retd GD 1/1/65.
BELL W.G. Born 21/10/23. Commd 27/1/55. Flt Lt 27/1/61. Retd GD 31/8/68.
BELLAMY D.W. Born 17/8/63. Commd 13/8/82. Flt Lt 13/2/88. Retd GD 1/4/92.
BELLAMY R.M. BTech. Born 1/2/44. Commd 30/12/69. Flt Lt 30/3/73. Retd ENG 11/5/79.
BELLAMY S.R.J. MB BS DCP. Born 22/10/34. Commd 1/1/64. Gp Capt 4/2/86. Retd MED 14/9/96.
BELLAMY-KNIGHTS P.G. Born 21/4/32. Commd 19/3/52. Wg Cdr 1/7/75. Retd GD 13/10/86.
BELLARS B.P. Born 11/12/59. Commd 11/8/86. Sqn Ldr 1/7/92. Retd ADMIN (SEC) 11/12/03.
BELLERGY P.A. Born 27/12/20. Commd 4/6/45. Gp Capt 1/7/71. Retd SEC 30/4/74.
BELLERS W.R. Born 1/2/36. Commd 13/7/61. Flt Lt 1/4/66. Retd RGT 14/10/75.
BELLINGALL J.E. Born 7/12/43. Commd 25/4/69. Flt Lt 25/10/74. Retd GD 7/12/00.
BELLWOOD B. BA DPhysEd. Born 22/8/31. Commd 25/3/54. Flt Lt 7/3/62. Retd SUP 30/8/75.
BELSHAM P.M. Born 30/8/33. Commd 18/6/52. Flt Lt 1/3/61. Retd GD 30/4/76.
BELSON D.J. Born 13/7/31. Commd 9/4/52. Sqn Ldr 1/7/61. Retd GD 13/7/69.
BELTON A.C. MA. Born 6/10/70. Commd 28/8/88. Flt Lt 15/1/94. Retd FLY(P) 1/8/03.
BEMAN K. Born 22/2/37. Commd 31/12/62. Flt Lt 22/4/68. Retd GD 23/2/75.
BENBOW G.T. Born 1/4/32. Commd 5/3/57. Flt Lt 21/8/63. Retd GD 1/4/94.
BENCKE R.G. Born 2/9/40. Commd 19/12/61. Sqn Ldr 1/1/76. Retd GD 1/7/80.
BENDALL D.H. Born 24/2/48. Commd 1/4/71. Sqn Ldr 1/7/00. Retd FLY(P) 31/8/03.
BENDELL A.J. OBE AFC. Born 30/3/36. Commd 3/3/54. Wg Cdr 1/7/74. Retd GD 19/6/87.
BENDELL T.W. Born 4/4/44. Commd 8/9/77. Flt Lt 8/9/79. Retd ENG 8/9/85.
BENDY R.A. Born 26/3/50. Commd 28/11/74. Flt Lt 28/5/80. Retd GD 12/8/90.
BENDYSHE-BROWN W.J. BA. Born 7/11/47. Commd 29/3/68. Wg Cdr 1/1/89. Retd SUP 25/6/94.
BENEY T.J. FCMI. Born 20/1/48. Commd 28/2/69. Gp Capt 1/7/93. Retd GD 20/1/03.
BENFIELD D. Born 25/1/32. Commd 23/6/67. Flt Lt 23/6/72. Retd GD(G) 8/4/78.
BENFIELD J.M. Born 25/10/43. Commd 1/8/62. Flt Lt 26/4/68. Retd GD 20/8/76.
BENFORD T.J. BA MCIPS. Born 22/4/47. Commd 1/3/68. Sqn Ldr 1/7/79. Retd SUP 22/4/85.
BENHAM D.I. OBE DFC* AFC. Born 30/12/17. Commd 21/3/41. Sqn Ldr 1/8/47. Retd GD 30/12/57. rtg Wg Cdr
BENHAM T.M. Born 14/10/59. Commd 1/2/87. Sqn Ldr 1/1/02. Retd OPS SPT(ATC) 1/7/05.
BENN L.V. BA. Born 31/3/48. Commd 28/2/69. Flt Lt 28/2/72. Retd GD 14/10/86.
BENNEDIK P.R. MBE. Born 16/3/21. Commd 4/9/58. Sqn Ldr 1/7/70. Retd ENG 1/3/78.
BENNETT A.R. MVO. Born 24/12/41. Commd 29/11/63. Flt Lt 29/5/69. Retd GD 22/5/93.
BENNETT A.W. BEM MCMI. Born 2/9/20. Commd 9/9/54. Sqn Ldr 1/7/66. Retd ENG 2/2/76.
BENNETT B.C. AFC. Born 9/10/17. Commd 14/12/38. A Cdre 1/1/66. Retd GD 25/10/71.
BENNETT C.R. MIIE. Born 21/3/61. Commd 1/5/80. Sqn Ldr 1/7/96. Retd ENG 1/11/99.
BENNETT D. Born 25/3/47. Commd 10/1/69. Sqn Ldr 1/1/86. Retd GD 26/5/01.
BENNETT D.A. MBE. Born 10/10/27. Commd 26/5/60. Wg Cdr 1/1/75. Retd ENG 26/4/78.
BENNETT D.G. Born 25/6/43. Commd 22/2/63. Flt Lt 22/8/68. Retd GD 13/12/75.
BENNETT D.H. Born 4/4/27. Commd 22/7/47. Wg Cdr 1/7/66. Retd GD 4/4/82.
BENNETT D.J.C. Born 30/1/46. Commd 10/6/66. Sqn Ldr 1/1/84. Retd GD 2/10/94.
BENNETT D.P. Born 18/7/26. Commd 6/3/52. Wg Cdr 1/1/76. Retd GD 18/7/81.
BENNETT Sir Erik KBE CB. Born 3/9/26. Commd 22/1/48. AVM 1/1/82. Retd GD 10/6/91.
BENNETT F.R. Born 26/6/30. Commd 13/2/52. Flt Lt 1/10/67. Retd GD 9/7/68.
BENNETT F.W. Born 3/9/20. Commd 6/5/43. Sqn Ldr 1/7/69. Retd SEC 31/8/73.
BENNETT G. CEng MRAeS. Born 16/2/29. Commd 30/1/52. Wg Cdr 1/1/76. Retd ENG 12/4/79.
BENNETT G. Born 20/7/32. Commd 27/7/71. Sqn Ldr 22/7/79. Retd EDN 1/11/83.
BENNETT G.A. Born 6/1/19. Commd 13/6/46. Flt Lt 13/12/50. Retd RGT 1/7/58.
BENNETT G.W. Born 23/12/17. Commd 5/3/53. Flt Lt 5/3/56. Retd ENG 25/6/60.
BENNETT H.E. Born 23/10/22. Commd 9/8/47. Flt Lt 9/2/51. Retd GD 8/11/77.
BENNETT H.F.G. Born 1/11/15. Commd 29/1/46. Flt Lt 11/11/54. Retd RGT 30/12/57.
BENNETT H.T. Born 26/10/10. Commd 26/12/30. Gp Capt 1/7/50. Retd GD 23/6/61.
BENNETT I. BSc FCIPD. Born 4/3/43. Commd 19/9/71. Wg Cdr 1/1/93. Retd ADMIN 13/4/96.
BENNETT I.M.H. BSc. Born 2/2/49. Commd 12/12/71. Flt Lt 12/3/72. Retd GD 28/10/88.
BENNETT I.T. Born 18/6/30. Commd 7/5/52. Flt Lt 13/4/60. Retd SEC 18/3/66.
BENNETT J. Born 19/9/22. Commd 10/12/43. Flt Lt 7/6/51. Retd GD 31/1/62.
BENNETT J.A. Born 17/9/41. Commd 17/4/68. Flt Lt 16/11/74. Retd SUP 16/11/80.
BENNETT J.B. Born 15/7/47. Commd 25/6/66. Wg Cdr 1/7/93. Retd SUP 15/7/02.
BENNETT J.C. LDSRCS. Born 27/5/41. Commd 20/9/59. Flt Lt 10/6/65. Retd DEL 27/7/68.
BENNETT J.F. MRAeS AIIP. Born 19/4/33. Commd 26/3/52. Sqn Ldr 1/7/71. Retd ENG 27/8/86.
BENNETT J.N. BSc CEng MIEE. Born 21/5/52. Commd 23/1/74. Flt Lt 23/4/77. Retd ENG 30/4/83.
BENNETT J.S. AFC. Born 20/3/22. Commd 22/3/50. Sqn Ldr 1/7/68. Retd GD 20/3/77.
BENNETT J.S. Born 2/3/49. Commd 21/4/77. Fg Offr 4/8/79. Retd ADMIN 2/6/82.
BENNETT J.W. Born 27/1/49. Commd 30/10/79. Flt Lt 30/10/79. Retd GD 30/10/87.

BENNETT K. Born 17/11/30. Commd 11/9/56. Flt Lt 11/3/62. Retd GD 5/6/72. rtg Sqn Ldr
BENNETT K. Born 3/4/61. Commd 16/2/86. Fg Offr 16/2/88. Retd SY 1/11/91.
BENNETT K.G. BSc CEng MIEE. Born 10/1/41. Commd 30/9/60. Gp Capt 1/1/87. Retd ENG 27/8/90.
BENNETT K.J. Born 28/8/36. Commd 3/4/58. Sqn Ldr 1/1/75. Retd SUP 28/8/91.
BENNETT K.M. Born 15/12/70. Commd 9/5/91. Flt Lt 9/11/97. Retd ADMIN 17/2/00.
BENNETT K.N. Born 24/9/55. Commd 1/7/82. Flt Lt 1/7/84. Retd GD 1/2/00.
BENNETT L. DFC*. Born 4/6/11. Commd 1/4/40. Sqn Ldr 1/8/47. Retd GD(G) 4/6/61.
BENNETT M.G. DFC. Born 7/1/25. Commd 7/7/49. Wg Cdr 1/1/65. Retd GD 10/5/69.
BENNETT N.H. BSc CEng MRAeS. Born 5/3/50. Commd 10/1/72. Flt Lt 15/4/77. Retd ENG 5/3/88.
BENNETT P.B. Born 27/7/57. Commd 26/11/81. Flt Lt 29/9/84. Retd ADMIN 27/7/95.
BENNETT P.D.S. DFC*. Born 18/3/18. Commd 20/10/37. Sqn Ldr 1/9/45. Retd GD 31/12/57. rtg Wg Cdr
BENNETT P.G.N. Born 20/6/40. Commd 10/12/65. Flt Lt 14/7/71. Retd GD 26/7/84.
BENNETT P.J. Born 14/5/47. Commd 2/8/68. Sqn Ldr 1/1/84. Retd GD 1/1/87.
BENNETT R.J. Born 20/7/35. Commd 9/4/57. Gp Capt 1/1/82. Retd ADMIN 1/3/86.
BENNETT R.J. BSc. Born 4/1/54. Commd 30/9/73. Wg Cdr 1/1/95. Retd GD 1/11/98.
BENNETT R.L. AFC. Born 14/8/27. Commd 7/7/49. Wg Cdr 1/7/66. Retd GD 14/5/82.
BENNETT R.W. BEM. Born 7/9/40. Commd 11/10/84. Flt Lt 11/10/88. Retd SY 7/9/94.
BENNETT S.C.S. Born 28/4/23. Commd 24/4/50. Sqn Ldr 1/7/66. Retd GD 9/4/73.
BENNETT T. Born 25/2/12. Commd 15/10/43. Flt Lt 15/4/47. Retd ENG 15/7/48.
BENNETT T.A. CBE. Born 21/12/28. Commd 27/7/49. A Cdre 1/1/82. Retd GD 1/1/84.
BENNETT T.R. MMar. Born 12/8/52. Commd 2/3/80. Flt Lt 2/3/80. Retd GD 14/3/97.
BENNETT W.G. Born 4/9/20. Commd 1/1/43. Sqn Ldr 1/7/58. Retd GD 15/5/61.
BENNETT W.R. Born 31/12/45. Commd 28/2/64. Flt Lt 28/8/69. Retd GD 1/5/92.
BENNINGTON G.W. DFM MCMI. Born 4/5/23. Commd 24/7/44. A Cdre 1/1/73. Retd SUP 31/1/76.
BENNISON S. Born 18/11/49. Commd 18/8/69. Sqn Ldr 1/1/91. Retd ADMIN 19/10/92.
BENNISON S.W. BSc CEng MIEE. Born 10/11/59. Commd 6/9/81. Sqn Ldr 1/1/91. Retd ENG 10/11/97.
BENOIST J.D. Born 2/10/46. Commd 27/2/75. Sqn Ldr 1/1/88. Retd OPS SPT 2/4/98.
BENSAID K.A. Born 23/8/20. Commd 24/1/63. Flt Lt 24/1/68. Retd ENG 23/8/75.
BENSLEY D. BA. Born 26/11/34. Commd 25/4/63. Sqn Ldr 10/2/68. Retd ADMIN 12/6/82.
BENSON A.N.W. Born 28/10/49. Commd 22/5/70. Flt Lt 22/11/75. Retd GD 28/10/87.
BENSON D.R. OBE. Born 17/11/46. Commd 3/7/65. Gp Capt 1/7/97. Retd SUP 11/11/01.
BENSON G. MCMI. Born 12/9/40. Commd 12/1/61. Sqn Ldr 1/1/74. Retd ADMIN 12/9/86.
BENSON G.E. CEng MRAeS. Born 30/3/37. Commd 23/2/60. Sqn Ldr 1/1/71. Retd ENG 23/2/76.
BENSON J.W. BA. Born 21/3/32. Commd 25/11/53. Sqn Ldr 6/6/65. Retd EDN 6/11/72.
BENSON N.R. BSc. Born 27/11/61. Commd 5/2/84. Sqn Ldr 1/1/96. Retd GD 5/2/00.
BENSON R. Born 26/5/23. Commd 26/4/44. Flt Lt 15/8/48. Retd GD 30/4/57.
BENSON T.E. Born 1/9/31. Commd 12/6/31. A Cdre 1/1/85. Retd GD 15/4/87.
BENSON T.J. BSc. Born 14/6/55. Commd 7/11/76. Sqn Ldr 1/1/90. Retd GD 14/6/93.
BENSTEAD A.H. Born 2/6/44. Commd 2/6/77. Flt Lt 2/6/79. Retd GD 14/3/96.
BENT B. DFC. Born 22/8/19. Commd 24/4/43. Flt Lt 27/5/54. Retd GD(G) 5/12/70.
BENT R.C.T. MVO BSc ACGI. Born 17/5/47. Commd 22/9/65. Wg Cdr 1/7/87. Retd ENG 31/3/94.
BENTHAM P. BEng. Born 5/1/40. Commd 2/10/61. Wg Cdr 1/1/91. Retd GD 5/11/95.
BENTLEY A.J. BSc CEng FIEE. Born 26/3/42. Commd 15/7/63. A Cdre 1/7/92. Retd ENG 25/7/94.
BENTLEY A.M. OBE AFC. Born 28/1/16. Commd 1/8/36. Wg Cdr 1/7/47. Retd GD 9/5/49. rtg Gp Capt
BENTLEY D.E. Born 25/5/47. Commd 17/1/69. Wg Cdr 1/1/90. Retd ADMIN 7/5/01.
BENTLEY I. Born 24/3/37. Commd 29/7/58. Plt Offr 29/7/58. Retd GD 5/12/59.
BENTLEY J.P. Born 14/6/22. Commd 1/5/42. Sqn Ldr 1/1/73. Retd SUP 14/2/76.
BENTLEY M.J. Born 3/7/50. Commd 7/1/80. Sqn Ldr 1/1/87. Retd ADMIN 7/1/96.
BENTLEY T.H.J. Born 24/3/24. Commd 12/2/45. Sqn Ldr 1/1/59. Retd GD 24/4/64.
BERESFORD I.M. MBE. Born 6/5/64. Commd 30/3/89. Sqn Ldr 1/1/99. Retd ENGINEER 16/11/03.
BERESFORD J.D. OBE. Born 20/6/15. Commd 29/10/41. Wg Cdr 1/1/55. Retd GD 27/6/70.
BERESFORD N.E.L. LVO. Born 10/10/48. Commd 7/6/68. Gp Capt 1/7/00. Retd GD 10/6/03.
BERESFORD S.E. Born 24/2/53. Commd 12/3/87. Flt Lt 12/3/89. Retd ENG 31/10/97.
BERGH I.L.e.C. Born 9/8/26. Commd 19/6/47. Flt Lt 4/7/56. Retd GD 12/2/65.
BERGIN J.P. Born 26/5/56. Commd 18/12/80. Sqn Ldr 1/7/92. Retd SUP 14/3/97.
BERGIN T.A. Born 30/9/21. Commd 3/8/50. Sqn Ldr 1/7/68. Retd GD(G) 30/9/76.
BERKELEY P.R.A. Born 31/12/30. Commd 5/3/57. Flt Lt 5/9/62. Retd GD 31/12/68.
BERNARD D.C. MBE FRAeS MILT MCMI. Born 19/7/47. Commd 28/7/67. Gp Capt 1/7/97. Retd SUP 19/7/02.
BERNARD D.H. MBE CEng MIEE MCMI. Born 23/5/20. Commd 12/6/47. Wg Cdr 1/1/67. Retd ENG 23/5/75.
BERNAU K.H. Born 8/9/22. Commd 26/5/67. Flt Lt 15/12/70. Retd GD(G) 30/5/81.
BERNERS-PRICE C. Born 13/1/57. Commd 27/1/77. Flt Lt 27/7/82. Retd GD 1/3/89.
BERRESFORD C.S. Born 28/11/43. Commd 23/2/68. Flt Lt 23/8/73. Retd GD 14/3/96.
BERRIDGE A.D. Born 12/10/46. Commd 31/10/69. Flt Lt 30/4/75. Retd GD 7/8/76.
BERRIMAN S.C. BTech CEng MIMechE. Born 20/9/52. Commd 26/7/81. Sqn Ldr 1/1/88. Retd ENG 14/10/98.
BERRY A.J. CEng MIEE CDipAF. Born 10/9/47. Commd 12/12/71. Wg Cdr 1/1/86. Retd ENG 1/1/89.

BERRY D.E.de. BEd. Born 26/9/33. Commd 7/5/52. Flt Lt 2/10/57. Retd GD 14/10/75. Re-instated 31/8/78. Sqn Ldr 1/7/86. Retd 26/9/91.
BERRY E.R. Born 8/8/38. Commd 24/6/71. Flt Lt 24/6/73. Retd SUP 24/6/79.
BERRY I.F. Born 20/12/62. Commd 5/1/86. Sqn Ldr 1/7/98. Retd ENG 1/3/02.
BERRY K.H. Born 15/4/41. Commd 1/10/52. Flt Lt 1/4/67. Retd GD 12/9/70.
BERRY M.A. Born 20/3/37. Commd 28/6/60. Sqn Ldr 1/1/69. Retd ENG 20/3/92.
BERRY N.A. Born 25/5/30. Commd 9/3/66. Sqn Ldr 1/1/78. Retd SUP 31/5/80.
BERRY R.D. Born 18/3/48. Commd 21/3/69. Sqn Ldr 1/1/89. Retd SUP 14/3/97.
BERRY-DAVIES C.W.K. The Rev. Born 21/4/48. Commd 15/12/92. Retd Wg Cdr 21/4/03.
BERRYMAN J.A. Born 8/3/44. Commd 28/2/64. Flt Lt 12/11/69. Retd GD 7/11/75.
BERRYMAN K.F. BSc. Born 5/3/44. Commd 11/10/70. Sqn Ldr 11/4/78. Retd EDN 11/10/79.
BERRYMAN N.W. Born 13/12/45. Commd 26/5/67. Sqn Ldr 1/7/79. Retd GD 7/3/91.
BERTRAM S. Born 21/7/11. Commd 21/11/44. Flt Lt 29/11/51. Retd GD(G) 1/10/64.
BERTRAND F.R. BDS. Born 8/1/24. Commd 16/12/60. Sqn Ldr 2/1/62. Retd DEL 7/8/66.
BESANT J.H. Born 26/2/23. Commd 11/1/44. Flt Lt 7/6/51. Retd GD 1/8/73.
BESLEY J. FCA AMCIPD. Born 19/3/33. Commd 16/5/57. Sqn Ldr 1/1/67. Retd SEC 22/9/71.
BESSANT D.E.L. Born 27/2/38. Commd 4/7/69. Flt Lt 4/7/71. Retd ENG 4/7/79.
BESSANT P. Born 9/1/41. Commd 13/7/61. Sqn Ldr 1/1/78. Retd SY 10/1/91.
BEST B.V. BA. Born 3/4/38. Commd 9/8/60. Sqn Ldr 9/2/69. Retd ADMIN 9/8/76.
BEST E.F. Born 17/10/38. Commd 2/5/69. Flt Lt 2/5/71. Retd SUP 2/5/77.
BEST I.G. Born 26/11/16. Commd 22/8/41. Wg Cdr 1/7/64. Retd SEC 26/11/71.
BEST M.A. Born 10/5/53. Commd 29/6/72. Sqn Ldr 1/1/87. Retd GD(G) 5/7/91.
BEST P.A. Born 1/10/22. Commd 21/1/55. Flt Lt 21/10/59. Retd GD 1/10/77.
BEST R.E. AFC. Born 18/7/45. Commd 21/3/69. Wg Cdr 1/7/89. Retd GD 18/7/01.
BEST R.M. CEng MIMechE MIProdE. Born 22/10/42. Commd 16/8/70. A Cdre 1/1/91. Retd ENG 14/9/96.
BESWETHERICK A.T. Born 14/11/25. Commd 11/3/53. Flt Lt 11/12/58. Retd GD 29/1/66.
BESZANT G.W. BSc. Born 9/3/49. Commd 2/7/72. Flt Lt 2/4/76. Retd PI 2/7/84.
BETHELL R.A. Born 9/4/22. Commd 7/2/42. Flt Lt 19/11/48. Retd GD 28/6/55.
BETSON C. Born 12/6/43. Commd 30/5/69. Flt Lt 30/11/74. Retd GD 1/7/75.
BETTEL D.C. Born 24/8/21. Commd 19/7/44. Sqn Ldr 1/7/70. Retd SUP 24/8/76.
BETTEL M.R. OBE BSc FCMI MInstAM. Born 16/10/49. Commd 5/7/68. Gp Capt 1/1/97. Retd OPS SPT 7/11/02.
BETTELL M.J. OBE. Born 12/3/44. Commd 28/9/62. A Cdre 1/7/89. Retd GD 16/4/99.
BETTERIDGE A.J. Born 20/7/39. Commd 18/69. Flt Lt 4/5/72. Retd ADMIN 1/8/77.
BETTERIDGE H. Born 31/5/28. Commd 11/2/65. Flt Lt 11/2/70. Retd ENG 12/12/74.
BETTERIDGE J. Born 14/1/24. Commd 6/5/47. Flt Lt 20/1/54. Retd GD 14/1/62.
BETTERIDGE M.P. BDS. Born 4/9/54. Commd 16/11/75. Wg Cdr 8/4/91. Retd DEL 4/9/92.
BETTERIDGE P.A. MA MBA DipMgmt. Born 28/11/59. Commd 13/8/82. Wg Cdr 1/7/99. Retd ADMIN 1/8/01.
BETTERIDGE R.S.J. Born 22/11/23. Commd 11/8/54. Sqn Ldr 1/1/68. Retd GD 1/4/73.
BETTERIDGE T.J. MB ChB MRCPath DCP. Born 8/10/31. Commd 10/7/60. Wg Cdr 18/8/71. Retd MED 10/7/76.
BETTERTON B.D. Born 19/12/38. Commd 30/4/57. Gp Capt 1/7/88. Retd GD 19/12/93.
BETTERTON T.J. Born 5/4/36. Commd 18/8/54. Flt Lt 18/2/60. Retd GD 5/4/96.
BETTINSON L.G. DFC. Born 2/10/19. Commd 25/8/40. Flt Lt 15/11/46. Retd GD 1/5/50.
BETTS C.J. BSc. Born 26/3/60. Commd 11/12/83. Flt Lt 11/6/85. Retd GD 11/12/95.
BETTS C.S. CBE MA. Born 8/4/19. Commd 11/7/41. AVM 1/1/72. Retd ENG 8/4/74.
BETTS D.E. Born 3/8/31. Commd 23/10/80. Sqn Ldr 12/6/75. Retd GD 3/8/91.
BETTS D.J. MSc CEng MBCS MCMI AIDPM. Born 20/11/45. Commd 26/5/67. Sqn Ldr 1/1/77. Retd SUP 20/2/92.
BETTS J.W. MBE. Born 30/9/23. Commd 24/5/51. Sqn Ldr 1/1/69. Retd GD 30/9/78.
BETTS L.J. BSc. Born 8/7/54. Commd 7/11/76. Flt Lt 7/2/78. Retd GD 7/11/88.
BETTS M. Born 22/7/42. Commd 28/2/64. Sqn Ldr 1/7/76. Retd GD 1/7/80.
BETTS N.G. Born 31/5/48. Commd 28/2/69. Flt Lt 28/8/74. Retd ENG 5/1/82.
BETTS P.J. BSc(Econ). Born 22/7/48. Commd 2/2/70. Fg Offr 2/2/72. Retd SEC 2/2/76. Re-entered 31/10/77. Wg Cdr 1/1/92. Retd SY 14/9/96.
BETTS R.C. BA. Born 7/1/42. Commd 30/7/63. Wg Cdr 1/7/77. Retd GD 18/1/83.
BEVAN A.W. BEM. Born 12/3/29. Commd 15/6/61. Sqn Ldr 1/7/75. Retd ENG 12/3/84.
BEVAN B. Born 28/10/28. Commd 2/3/61. Flt Lt 2/3/66. Retd GD 1/3/68.
BEVAN D.C. Born 9/12/44. Commd 12/7/63. Sqn Ldr 1/7/93. Retd GD 30/4/94.
BEVAN D.L. BSc. Born 14/2/49. Commd 1/11/71. Sqn Ldr 1/7/79. Retd ENG 1/11/87.
BEVAN D.L. Born 21/11/46. Commd 14/8/70. Sqn Ldr 1/1/85. Retd SUPPLY 21/11/04.
BEVAN E.W.J. Born 21/2/13. Commd 5/12/47. Sqn Ldr 1/7/51. Retd RGT 19/10/57.
BEVAN G.G. Born 15/2/14. Commd 15/4/43. Sqn Ldr 1/1/57. Retd ENG 15/2/63.
BEVAN J.H. Born 26/1/44. Commd 31/8/78. Sqn Ldr 1/7/86. Retd GD(G) 2/3/94.
BEVAN M. Born 4/2/20. Commd 4/4/44. Flt Lt 20/10/47. Retd ENG 4/2/69.
BEVAN S.J. BEM. Born 7/11/20. Commd 23/12/60. Flt Lt 23/12/66. Retd ENG 15/7/67.
BEVAN T.E. Born 11/4/49. Commd 10/3/77. Flt Lt 22/3/79. Retd GD 11/4/87.
BEVAN W.J. BA. Born 30/11/38. Commd 1/9/64. Wg Cdr 1/1/87. Retd ADMIN 21/10/91.
BEVAN-JOHN D.R.S. OBE. Born 25/2/17. Commd 30/7/38. Gp Capt 1/1/57. Retd GD 30/1/59.

BEVERIDGE A.W. BSc. Born 18/8/45. Commd 13/2/72. Sqn Ldr 19/12/76. Retd ADMIN 13/2/88.
BEVERIDGE D.A. Born 1/3/53. Commd 29/4/71. Flt Lt 29/10/76. Retd GD 1/3/91.
BEVERIDGE G.J. Born 4/11/29. Commd 8/7/54. Wg Cdr 1/1/80. Retd ADMIN 4/11/84.
BEVERLEY I.M. MDA BA MCIPS. Born 23/4/57. Commd 3/5/81. Sqn Ldr 1/1/89. Retd SUPPLY 3/5/03.
BEVERLEY O.E. Born 3/1/25. Commd 1/3/62. Flt Lt 1/3/57. Retd GD 15/1/76.
BEVIS C.G.S. Born 10/2/15. Commd 7/5/56. Flt Lt 7/5/56. Retd MAR 30/9/67.
BEWLEY D.I.W. MHCIMA MCMI. Born 29/12/30. Commd 25/9/52. Wg Cdr 1/1/74. Retd ADMIN 16/6/82.
BEWSHER J.E.S. MSc BSc DMS MILT. Born 22/2/66. Commd 26/8/94. Sqn Ldr 1/7/00. Retd SUPPLY 9/1/05.
BEYNON G.G. Born 9/3/48. Commd 17/7/87. Flt Lt 17/7/89. Retd GD 30/9/94.
BHATIA R.J. Born 14/5/62. Commd 28/5/85. Flt Lt 23/11/90. Retd GD 30/9/94.
BIANCO D. Born 23/5/43. Commd 21/2/74. Sqn Ldr 1/1/83. Retd SUP 23/5/93.
BIBBEY A. Born 16/5/22. Commd 4/9/58. Sqn Ldr 1/7/73. Retd ENG 16/5/77.
BIBBY G. Born 29/3/39. Commd 25/9/80. Fg Offr 25/9/79. Retd PI 1/10/85.
BIBBY G.T. BA. Born 21/3/27. Commd 7/10/48. Flt Lt 4/12/52. Retd GD 23/1/60.
BIBBY G.W. Born 25/1/22. Commd 23/8/50. Sqn Ldr 1/7/66. Retd GD(G) 25/1/72.
BIBBY M.J. OBE. Born 3/12/44. Commd 2/6/67. Wg Cdr 1/1/87. Retd GD 14/3/96.
BIBBY W.W. Born 12/8/22. Commd 1/10/43. Sqn Ldr 1/7/54. Retd GD 20/5/68.
BIBEY M.A. Born 13/7/50. Commd 9/5/91. Flt Lt 9/5/95. Retd ENG 1/6/96.
BICHARD K. OBE. Born 23/7/33. Commd 27/7/54. Wg Cdr 1/1/74. Retd GD 23/7/89.
BICKERS R.A. Born 9/1/43. Commd 27/2/75. Sqn Ldr 1/1/90. Retd GD 12/1/96.
BICKERS R.L.T. Born 5/7/17. Commd 22/7/43. Flt Lt 22/7/50. Retd GD(G) 16/8/57.
BICKERS S.M. Born 27/9/61. Commd 24/3/83. Sqn Ldr 1/7/96. Retd SUP 1/1/01.
BICKFORD-SMITH D.G. Born 5/11/22. Commd 16/2/43. Sqn Ldr 1/1/57. Retd GD(G) 1/6/67.
BICKNELL D.W. AFC. Born 31/1/17. Commd 13/5/43. Flt Lt 13/11/46. Retd GD 15/9/53.
BIDDINGTON D.V.W. Born 13/4/47. Commd 23/4/87. Sqn Ldr 1/1/97. Retd ENG 24/2/01.
BIDDISCOMBE P.G. Born 10/7/32. Commd 26/7/55. Sqn Ldr 1/1/65. Retd GD 7/9/85.
BIDIE C.H. AFC* MCMI. Born 27/3/26. Commd 9/3/50. Wg Cdr 1/1/66. Retd GD 30/3/77.
BIDSTON P.M. Born 30/8/49. Commd 17/7/70. Flt Lt 17/1/76. Retd GD 30/8/87.
BIEBER S.M. FRCS LRCP DIH DPH DTM&H. Born 27/7/12. Commd 9/7/38. Wg Cdr 1/1/58. Retd MED 1/9/60.
BIGGAR G. Born 5/12/27. Commd 29/6/48. Gp Capt 1/7/76. Retd SY 5/12/82.
BIGGIE C.J.R. Born 21/8/39. Commd 24/9/63. Flt Lt 24/11/67. Retd ENG 24/9/79.
BIGGIN S.J.C. BA. Born 6/6/72. Commd 25/5/00. Flt Lt 25/5/02. Retd OPS SPT(INT) 6/7/03.
BIGGS D. Born 20/2/64. Commd 29/7/91. Flt Lt 27/11/93. Retd GD(G) 14/3/96.
BIGGS J.P.C. IEng AMRAeS. Born 12/12/61. Commd 16/2/89. Flt Lt 7/11/91. Retd ENG 14/3/96.
BIGGS M.J. Born 12/8/24. Commd 27/2/58. Sqn Ldr 1/1/72. Retd GD 12/8/83.
BIGGS R.V.A. Born 3/8/30. Commd 22/12/49. Flt Lt 22/6/53. Retd GD 29/3/69.
BIGGS T.W.G. Born 20/4/57. Commd 29/1/79. Flt Lt 21/4/85. Retd GD 7/9/88.
BIGLANDS S. BSc. Born 24/6/48. Commd 17/1/72. Flt Lt 17/4/73. Retd GD 17/1/88.
BIGMORE H.J. Born 2/7/11. Commd 18/3/43. Fg Offr 1/1/44. Retd ENG 9/8/46. rtg Flt Lt
BILLETT R.T. Born 11/1/16. Commd 24/4/41. Wg Cdr 1/7/52. Retd GD 21/2/71.
BILLING M. Born 2/4/27. Commd 30/7/59. Flt Lt 18/8/64. Retd ENG 15/1/72.
BILLINGE P.A. Born 14/7/38. Commd 15/12/59. Flt Lt 15/6/62. Retd GD 1/12/78.
BILLINGS E.H. Born 14/1/43. Commd 25/5/80. Flt Lt 22/5/83. Retd GD 14/1/98.
BILLINGS G.J. Born 24/6/50. Commd 24/4/70. Sqn Ldr 1/7/83. Retd SUP 24/6/88.
BILLINGS N.G. Born 17/1/36. Commd 4/7/69. Sqn Ldr 1/7/75. Retd ENG 1/7/78.
BILLINGS S.J. BSc DipEd. Born 26/9/54. Commd 6/9/81. Flt Lt 6/3/84. Retd ENG 6/9/97.
BILLINGTON D.P. Born 25/6/60. Commd 30/8/84. Sqn Ldr 1/1/97. Retd GD 30/4/00.
BILLS D.T. FCIPD ACIS. Born 30/6/47. Commd 1/8/69. Wg Cdr 1/1/86. Retd SY 14/3/96.
BILLS M.A. Born 6/7/54. Commd 31/8/78. Flt Lt 18/11/80. Retd GD 18/7/85.
BILLSON R.A. Born 17/6/37. Commd 11/5/78. Flt Lt 11/5/81. Retd GD 17/6/92.
BILTCLIFFE A.J. Born 20/4/27. Commd 13/2/52. Flt Lt 12/6/57. Retd GD 20/4/65.
BINDLOSS K.M. Born 17/7/15. Commd 3/6/42. Flt Offr 3/12/46. Retd SEC 16/11/53.
BINDON T.R. Born 17/6/25. Commd 10/10/63. Flt Lt 10/10/68. Retd GD 28/2/78.
BINEDELL A.C.G. DFC. Born 9/3/17. Commd 1/9/45. Flt Lt 1/9/45. Retd GD(G) 27/3/63.
BINFIELD G.H. Born 16/4/48. Commd 25/2/82. Wg Cdr 1/7/96. Retd GD 16/4/03.
BING N.J. Born 6/12/41. Commd 18/12/62. Flt Lt 28/7/65. Retd GD 6/12/79.
BINGHAM D.C. Born 7/5/32. Commd 11/12/51. Flt Lt 17/10/56. Retd GD 1/10/83.
BINGHAM J.D. Born 8/2/46. Commd 4/7/85. Flt Lt 4/7/89. Retd OPS SPT(ATC) 29/8/04.
BINGHAM P.C. Born 8/3/47. Commd 21/1/66. Gp Capt 1/7/96. Retd GD 14/9/96.
BINGHAM S.A. BA. Born 22/11/55. Commd 3/5/81. Sqn Ldr 1/1/93. Retd GD(G) 14/3/96.
BINGHAM W.G. Born 15/12/23. Commd 24/9/64. Sqn Ldr 1/7/73. Retd SUP 15/12/78.
BINHAM P.P. Born 6/2/53. Commd 30/9/73. Sqn Ldr 1/1/86. Retd GD 21/11/91.
BINKS E. DFM. Born 21/2/18. Commd 5/3/51. Sqn Ldr 1/7/52. Retd GD 26/9/59.
BINKS H. Born 11/8/26. Commd 11/11/50. Wg Cdr 1/1/70. Retd GD 16/8/75.
BINNIE D. AFC. Born 4/3/46. Commd 14/8/64. Sqn Ldr 1/1/78. Retd GD 10/12/86.
BINNINGTON A.W. Born 19/6/39. Commd 23/6/61. Flt Lt 1/4/66. Retd GD 14/2/94.

BINNS C.C. Born 7/4/12. Commd 18/6/52. Sqn Offr 1/4/58. Retd SEC 1/10/63.
BINNS C.G. Born 29/1/38. Commd 2/2/60. Sqn Ldr 1/7/71. Retd CAT 2/2/76.
BINNS H. OBE MInstPkg MCIPS MILT. Born 17/8/40. Commd 15/2/62. Wg Cdr 1/1/85. Retd SUP 20/11/92.
BINNS J.H. MB ChB FRCS. Born 27/4/31. Commd 30/1/57. Wg Cdr 30/1/70. Retd MED 3/3/73.
BIRBECK S. Born 20/12/42. Commd 29/6/72. Flt Lt 29/6/74. Retd ENG 21/7/83.
BIRCH C.N. AFC. Born 27/11/18. Commd 14/11/38. Sqn Ldr 1/8/47. Retd GD 28/3/58.
BIRCH D.N. Born 15/12/35. Commd 14/7/63. Flt Lt 1/7/68. Retd GD 1/9/86.
BIRCH J.L. BSc. Born 27/11/24. Commd 24/11/48. Wg Cdr 1/7/74. Retd SY 31/7/76.
BIRCH J.Y. Born 7/9/11. Commd 5/5/52. Flt Lt 30/11/45. Retd ENG 14/11/62.
BIRCH P.H.B. BEng. Born 30/5/63. Commd 3/8/88. Flt Lt 15/7/91. Retd ENG 30/5/01.
BIRCH R.F. MBE. Born 6/12/38. Commd 25/7/60. Sqn Ldr 1/1/69. Retd GD 27/8/76.
BIRCH R.J. BA. Born 24/1/41. Commd 1/10/62. Sqn Ldr 1/7/75. Retd GD 24/1/79.
BIRCHALL P. Born 14/4/46. Commd 11/10/84. Flt Lt 11/10/88. Retd ENG 30/8/96.
BIRCHALL R.A. Born 28/9/30. Commd 1/8/51. Plt Offr 1/8/51. Retd SEC 24/12/52.
BIRD C. Born 8/3/48. Commd 23/4/87. Flt Lt 23/4/91. Retd ADMIN 14/3/97.
BIRD D.L. Born 10/11/30. Commd 19/1/50. Sqn Ldr 1/1/66. Retd SEC 31/8/68.
BIRD G.D. Born 12/5/25. Commd 19/1/45. Wg Cdr 1/1/68. Retd GD 8/5/76.
BIRD H. Born 15/3/19. Commd 5/10/50. Sqn Ldr 1/7/61. Retd ENG 27/3/71.
BIRD H.S. Born 3/11/38. Commd 3/5/68. Sqn Ldr 1/7/78. Retd SUP 14/11/81. Re-instated 1/7/87. Sqn Ldr 15/2/84.
  Retd SUP 3/11/91.
BIRD J.B. BSc. Born 5/12/34. Commd 20/12/57. Sqn Ldr 20/6/67. Retd EDN 19/9/73.
BIRD J.C. Born 26/1/60. Commd 28/6/79. Flt Lt 28/12/84. Retd GD 26/8/98.
BIRD J.K. Born 21/5/33. Commd 7/5/52. Sqn Ldr 1/7/74. Retd ADMIN 21/5/91.
BIRD J.O. Born 4/1/66. Commd 11/5/89. Fg Offr 11/5/91. Retd GD 1/7/93.
BIRD J.R. Born 15/4/28. Commd 11/5/51. Flt Lt 6/9/56. Retd GD 31/3/70.
BIRD J.S. Born 3/7/39. Commd 5/2/65. Flt Lt 14/5/68. Retd GD 3/7/94.
BIRD L.A. Born 11/9/30. Commd 4/2/53. Sqn Ldr 1/1/62. Retd CAT 18/10/69.
BIRD M.J. MHCIMA. Born 5/9/31. Commd 24/9/63. Sqn Ldr 1/7/77. Retd ADMIN 5/9/86.
BIRD P.D. Born 9/10/20. Commd 22/5/42. Gp Capt 1/7/67. Retd GD 9/4/71.
BIRD P.R. Born 20/11/47. Commd 11/8/67. Sqn Ldr 1/7/88. Retd SY 14/3/96.
BIRD R.C. Born 7/7/44. Commd 22/5/70. Sqn Ldr 1/1/92. Retd GD 7/1/01.
BIRD R.V. Born 1/4/44. Commd 11/9/64. Flt Lt 4/5/72. Retd GD 1/4/82.
BIRD W.F. Born 2/10/34. Commd 25/5/61. Flt Lt 1/10/67. Retd GD 25/5/77.
BIRD W.J. MBE MA. Born 13/4/52. Commd 2/2/75. Sqn Ldr 1/1/87. Retd GD 2/2/91.
BIRDLING W.R. DFC. Born 10/9/22. Commd 30/6/45. Flt Lt 30/12/47. Retd GD 21/3/61.
BIRKBECK P.C.L. BSc. Born 12/1/49. Commd 24/9/67. Sqn Ldr 1/1/89. Retd OPS SPT 30/9/01.
BIRKENHEAD G.B. MSc BSc CEng MIEE. Born 4/7/62. Commd 22/7/93. Sqn Ldr 1/7/98. Retd ENGINEER 26/4/05.
BIRKETT A.C. BDS. Born 9/3/62. Commd 19/1/86. Wg Cdr 2/1/98. Retd DEL 1/10/02.
BIRKETT C.R. BSc. Born 6/2/57. Commd 14/9/75. Plt Offr 15/7/78. Retd GD 5/5/79.
BIRKETT G.M.R. Born 25/9/15. Commd 1/5/52. Wg Cdr 19/6/68. Retd MED(T) 25/9/70.
BIRKS B.G. Born 6/12/42. Commd 6/7/62. Flt Lt 6/1/68. Retd GD 30/4/85.
BIRLISON R.K. Born 7/8/22. Commd 6/9/56. Sqn Ldr 1/1/70. Retd ENG 13/1/73.
BIRNIE R.E.R. BA. Born 26/6/66. Commd 2/9/84. Sqn Ldr 1/1/01. Retd OPS SPT(FC) 26/6/04.
BIRRELL D. Born 26/6/21. Commd 25/1/43. Flt Lt 25/7/46. Retd GD 2/6/48.
BIRRELL W.D. MSc BSc MCIPD MCMI. Born 9/10/36. Commd 8/8/60. Sqn Ldr 11/8/69. Retd EDN 1/10/78.
BIRSE D.L. Born 18/8/20. Commd 21/9/50. Sqn Ldr 1/1/64. Retd SUP 17/8/70.
BIRT A.E. BSc. Born 11/3/37. Commd 25/9/62. Sqn Ldr 14/12/74. Retd ADMIN 11/4/93.
BIRTLES R. MA MCIPD MInstAM MCMI. Born 4/5/49. Commd 12/12/71. Wg Cdr 1/1/89. Retd ADMIN 12/12/93.
BIRTLES T.D. MBE MB ChB DAvMed AFOM. Born 24/12/35. Commd 28/4/64. Wg Cdr 3/4/74. Retd MED 28/4/80.
BISBEY J. Born 4/9/21. Commd 9/12/48. Flt Lt 9/6/52. Retd GD 4/9/64.
BISH D. Born 25/6/26. Commd 25/10/46. Sqn Ldr 1/1/60. Retd GD 1/3/68.
BISHOP A.M. Born 14/7/47. Commd 23/10/86. Flt Lt 23/10/88. Retd GD 15/7/97.
BISHOP A.P. The Venerable CB MPhil LTh FRSA. Born 24/5/46. Commd 5/10/75. Retd AVM 1/1/02.
BISHOP B.M. BDS LDSRCS. Born 28/3/37. Commd 19/7/57. Wg Cdr 28/2/76. Retd DEL 1/10/77.
BISHOP D.A. BSc. Born 5/9/58. Commd 29/8/77. Sqn Ldr 1/1/92. Retd ENG 5/9/96.
BISHOP D.E. Born 23/2/46. Commd 5/2/65. Flt Lt 4/11/70. Retd FLY(P) 23/2/04.
BISHOP D.G. Born 4/4/50. Commd 25/2/72. Flt Lt 25/8/77. Retd SUP 1/4/79.
BISHOP G.M. Born 12/1/26. Commd 19/1/56. Flt Offr 5/10/60. Retd SEC 5/12/67.
BISHOP J.H. Born 30/4/28. Commd 12/12/51. Gp Capt 1/1/73. Retd SEC 11/1/75.
BISHOP J.L. AFC BA MRAeS. Born 6/3/45. Commd 3/3/67. Wg Cdr 1/1/83. Retd GD 22/7/91.
BISHOP J.M. MA FIL. Born 9/7/48. Commd 3/1/69. Wg Cdr 1/7/86. Retd ADMIN 16/3/93.
BISHOP J.M. MCMI. Born 11/10/43. Commd 10/5/73. Sqn Ldr 1/1/86. Retd GD(G) 14/3/96.
BISHOP J.N. MBE. Born 5/7/21. Commd 15/9/60. Sqn Ldr 1/7/71. Retd ENG 31/3/74.
BISHOP J.S.V.C. Born 21/11/24. Commd 21/6/56. Flt Lt 21/6/62. Retd GD 21/11/74.
BISHOP M.J. BSc. Born 17/5/38. Commd 1/10/62. Sqn Ldr 1/1/71. Retd GD 1/10/78.
BISHOP M.R.M. Born 22/9/23. Commd 29/7/44. Sqn Ldr 1/1/69. Retd GD 22/9/81.

BISHOP N.A. BEng. Born 27/2/65. Commd 10/5/86. Flt Lt 15/1/89. Retd GD 21/2/96.
BISHOP R.G. BChD LDSRCS. Born 6/9/40. Commd 20/9/59. Sqn Ldr 21/9/70. Retd DEL 2/4/78.
BISHOP R.J. BA. Born 2/4/43. Commd 9/10/75. Flt Lt 9/10/77. Retd ENG 3/4/93.
BISHOP R.J. Born 23/10/38. Commd 22/8/61. Flt Lt 22/8/65. Retd ADMIN 22/8/77.
BISHOP R.S. Born 19/11/44. Commd 11/10/84. Sqn Ldr 1/7/95. Retd ADMIN 19/11/99.
BISHOP T.R. Born 28/9/20. Commd 1/5/42. Flt Lt 1/11/46. Retd GD(G) 1/4/65.
BISHOPP J.B. Born 23/4/48. Commd 27/2/70. Wg Cdr 1/7/91. Retd GD 23/4/03.
BISSELL N. Born 1/1/31. Commd 27/8/52. Flt Lt 5/2/58. Retd GD 1/1/69.
BISSELL R.J. BA. Born 7/5/61. Commd 8/1/89. Flt Lt 8/1/91. Retd OPS SPT(PROVSY) 8/1/05.
BISSHOPP G.W. Born 19/4/41. Commd 21/1/73. Flt Lt 21/1/75. Retd ENG 20/4/84.
BITTEL E. BSc(Eng) ACGI. Born 29/6/48. Commd 2/8/71. Sqn Ldr 1/7/83. Retd ENG 22/6/96.
BLACK A.W. MB ChB FRCPsych DPM. Born 6/5/25. Commd 24/11/52. Gp Capt 22/10/74. Retd MED 6/5/85.
BLACK E.J. FRAeS FCMI. Born 12/7/46. Commd 25/2/66. A Cdre 1/7/97. Retd GD 5/5/99.
BLACK F.S. MB BCh BAO MFCM DPH. Born 15/4/24. Commd 2/12/62. Wg Cdr 1/5/67. Retd MED 1/12/76.
BLACK G.P. CB OBE AFC*. Born 10/7/32. Commd 19/1/53. AVM 1/1/85. Retd GD 10/7/87.
BLACK I.C. Born 11/5/59. Commd 22/2/79. Flt Lt 20/6/84. Retd GD 11/5/97.
BLACK J.B. OBE DFC. Born 20/4/14. Commd 16/3/34. Wg Cdr 1/7/47. Retd GD 17/2/49. rtg Gp Capt
BLACK J.B. Born 26/6/33. Commd 29/6/59. Flt Lt 29/6/59. Retd GD 31/8/87.
BLACK J.H.W. MBE. Born 14/8/35. Commd 2/10/58. Wg Cdr 1/1/80. Retd GD 14/9/90.
BLACK J.McL. The Rev. MA BD. Born 11/7/36. Commd 20/10/69. Retd Wg Cdr 11/7/91.
BLACK M. BA. Born 7/9/54. Commd 7/11/76. Sqn Ldr 1/1/92. Retd GD 23/9/93.
BLACK P.D. BSc MB BS FRCS LRCP DO. Born 14/11/43. Commd 11/1/65. Sqn Ldr 3/2/74. Retd MED 14/11/81.
BLACK W. Born 13/6/29. Commd 25/6/53. Flt Lt 25/12/56. Retd GD 13/6/67.
BLACK W.A. Born 23/7/33. Commd 13/8/52. Sqn Ldr 1/7/84. Retd GD 23/7/93.
BLACK MA D.V. MCMI. Born 14/11/20. Commd 1/4/43. Sqn Ldr 3/11/59. Retd ENG 18/6/82.
BLACK-ROBERTS J.D. Born 25/9/32. Commd 26/6/57. Fg Offr 26/6/57. Retd SUP 10/1/65.
BLACKBURN D.A. Born 3/2/30. Commd 28/11/51. Flt Lt 28/5/56. Retd GD 3/2/68.
BLACKBURN G.J. BA. Born 3/10/60. Commd 20/1/85. Flt Lt 20/1/01. Retd ADMIN 20/1/01.
BLACKBURN L.E. MBE. Born 4/4/28. Commd 20/12/51. Sqn Ldr 1/7/68. Retd GD 4/4/83.
BLACKBURN N.J.S. Born 21/10/57. Commd 14/8/80. Flt Lt 14/2/86. Retd GD 14/4/96.
BLACKBURN R. MBE. Born 29/4/32. Commd 19/4/51. Sqn Ldr 1/1/68. Retd GD 25/9/78.
BLACKBURN R.H. BSc. Born 3/5/47. Commd 13/9/71. Sqn Ldr 1/7/88. Retd GD 14/9/96.
BLACKBURN R.M. BSc. Born 17/11/57. Commd 8/2/81. Sqn Ldr 1/1/90. Retd SUP 1/6/96.
BLACKBURN S.A. Born 19/7/50. Commd 27/3/70. Sqn Ldr 1/1/86. Retd ADMIN 6/4/88.
BLACKFORD B.M. Born 10/1/45. Commd 22/5/64. Wg Cdr 1/1/90. Retd GD 16/8/93.
BLACKFORD D.W. Born 9/6/33. Commd 10/9/52. Flt Lt 13/4/60. Retd GD(G) 9/6/88.
BLACKFORD J.L. Born 26/10/35. Commd 31/7/56. Sqn Ldr 1/1/67. Retd GD 1/3/77.
BLACKFORD P. MB ChB MRCGP DRCOG DAvMed. Born 22/5/54. Commd 22/7/75. Wg Cdr 30/8/91.
    Retd MED 22/5/92.
BLACKFORD P.A. Born 9/7/48. Commd 17/2/67. Gp Capt 1/1/97. Retd GD 31/5/02.
BLACKFORD P.F. Born 22/11/20. Commd 23/12/39. Sqn Ldr 1/8/47. Retd GD 1/5/58.
BLACKHAM W. DPhysEd. Born 8/9/24. Commd 13/8/52. Flt Lt 13/8/56. Retd PE 7/3/66.
BLACKLEY A.B. CBE AFC BSc. Born 28/9/37. Commd 16/11/59. AVM 1/1/89. Retd GD 30/11/93.
BLACKLOCK D.W. Born 5/9/34. Commd 10/3/60. Flt Lt 10/9/64. Retd GD 30/9/87.
BLACKLOCK G.B. OBE DFC DFM. Born 23/6/14. Commd 28/8/40. Gp Capt 1/7/56. Retd GD 28/8/61.
BLACKMAN A.L. BA. Born 6/4/28. Commd 9/12/48. Flt Lt 7/6/51. Retd GD 6/8/56.
BLACKMAN J.P. OBE MSc BSc MCMI. Born 24/5/46. Commd 22/2/71. Wg Cdr 1/7/85. Retd ENG 7/1/96.
BLACKMORE D.J. MBE MPhil MIBiol. Born 24/9/32. Commd 18/10/62. Flt Lt 11/10/68. Retd MED(T) 1/6/73.
BLACKMORE F.C. AFC. Born 16/2/16. Commd 9/4/41. Sqn Ldr 1/8/47. Retd GD 27/6/59. rtg Wg Cdr
BLACKMORE N.J. BEng. Born 20/10/67. Commd 3/8/88. Flt Lt 25/9/93. Retd ENGINEER 6/11/03.
BLACKMORE-HEAL D.C. IEng MIIE. Born 4/5/53. Commd 29/3/90. Flt Lt 29/3/94. Retd ENG 2/10/00.
BLACKNEY A.B. MBA CEng FIMechE FCMI. Born 29/11/34. Commd 3/1/61. Gp Capt 1/1/80. Retd ENG 9/12/85.
BLACKSHAW S.G. Born 26/9/48. Commd 8/10/70. Flt Lt 8/4/76. Retd GD 22/10/94.
BLACKWELL J. AFC. Born 13/1/50. Commd 21/3/69. Wg Cdr 1/1/85. Retd GD 11/12/88.
BLACKWOOD T.V. Born 20/12/46. Commd 23/3/67. Sqn Ldr 1/1/84. Retd GD 20/12/90.
BLACKWOOD W.D. BDS. Born 24/1/34. Commd 11/1/59. Wg Cdr 19/11/71. Retd DEL 11/1/75.
BLAGBROUGH R.B. Born 6/5/43. Commd 17/12/64. Sqn Ldr 1/7/75. Retd GD 6/5/81.
BLAGDEN A.G. Born 13/2/12. Commd 9/5/40. Flt Lt 9/5/42. Retd GD 14/12/45.
BLAGROVE C.N. MBE BSc. Born 13/1/56. Commd 30/10/77. Sqn Ldr 1/7/87. Retd GD 13/1/00.
BLAIK M.A. Born 19/9/42. Commd 27/1/67. Wg Cdr 1/1/83. Retd SUP 19/9/86.
BLAIN A.A. BSc. Born 15/1/41. Commd 6/8/63. Sqn Ldr 1/1/73. Retd ENG 6/8/79.
BLAIN D.F. ACA. Born 2/12/10. Commd 4/9/36. Sqn Ldr 1/6/45. Retd SEC 1/8/47. rtg Wg Cdr
BLAIR D.A. Born 16/10/22. Commd 12/4/45. Flt Lt 4/1/51. Retd GD 16/10/65.
BLAIR G.J. Born 20/5/75. Commd 28/9/00. Fg Off 2/6/02. Retd SUPPLY 28/2/04.
BLAIR H. Born 22/2/23. Commd 3/8/50. Sqn Ldr 1/1/69. Retd ADMIN 22/2/78.
BLAIR J. DFM. Born 19/7/18. Commd 4/10/43. Sqn Ldr 1/7/67. Retd SUP 19/7/73.

BLAIR J.C. DFC AFC. Born 8/4/20. Commd 15/11/42. Wg Cdr 1/7/58. Retd GD 13/5/64.
BLAIR J.J. DFC. Born 16/2/19. Commd 28/1/44. Flt Lt 28/7/47. Retd GD 30/7/63.
BLAIR M.J. BSc. Born 18/3/43. Commd 17/5/62. Sqn Ldr 1/7/77. Retd ENG 1/5/93.
BLAIR R.C. Born 27/4/65. Commd 26/4/84. Sqn Ldr 1/7/97. Retd FLY(P) 23/6/03.
BLAIR-HICKMAN W.N. Born 11/9/42. Commd 30/7/63. Flt Lt 30/1/66. Retd GD 23/8/75.
BLAKE A.H. Born 17/12/14. Commd 29/7/41. Wg Cdr 1/1/53. Retd RGT 30/6/55.
BLAKE A.H. Born 1/10/40. Commd 18/12/62. Sqn Ldr 1/7/73. Retd GD 1/5/79.
BLAKE C. Born 21/7/38. Commd 11/5/62. Sqn Ldr 1/7/71. Retd GD 8/8/78.
BLAKE D.J. Born 6/8/40. Commd 9/2/62. Flt Lt 20/7/70. Retd PRT 6/8/78.
BLAKE H.R. Born 25/12/11. Commd 1/11/45. Sqn Ldr 9/7/57. Retd MED(T) 26/12/66.
BLAKE J.D. Born 5/8/39. Commd 14/5/57. Sqn Ldr 1/7/75. Retd GD 13/6/84.
BLAKE P. OBE. Born 13/12/28. Commd 1/5/52. Wg Cdr 1/1/77. Retd GD 3/1/84.
BLAKE P.G. FCMI. Born 20/8/38. Commd 28/7/59. Gp Capt 1/7/85. Retd GD 20/8/93.
BLAKE R.G. Born 18/11/46. Commd 23/3/67. Wg Cdr 1/1/90. Retd GD 18/11/01.
BLAKE V.R.H. Born 7/11/33. Commd 26/5/54. Flt Lt 7/3/62. Retd GD 7/11/71.
BLAKELEY J. OBE BSc CEng FRAeS. Born 26/10/42. Commd 15/7/63. A Cdre 1/1/90. Retd ENG 1/5/91.
BLAKEMAN G. OBE MCMI. Born 26/7/21. Commd 23/10/42. Wg Cdr 1/1/60. Retd GD 26/7/68.
BLAKEMORE R.C. Born 30/7/39. Commd 28/1/60. Sqn Ldr 1/7/71. Retd ADMIN 1/10/84.
BLAKEY J.H.N.M. BSc. Born 16/10/46. Commd 27/10/68. Flt Lt 27/7/70. Retd GD 12/8/77.
BLAKEY R.W. Born 18/8/32. Commd 13/8/52. Flt Lt 9/1/58. Retd GD 18/8/69.
BLAKLEY R.J. Born 28/11/22. Commd 1/1/62. Flt Lt 24/11/65. Retd ENG 27/8/77.
BLANCHARD-SMITH R.M. BSc CertEd. Born 28/6/51. Commd 13/12/79. Sqn Ldr 1/7/94. Retd ADMIN (SEC) 27/4/03.
BLANCHFIELD G. BSc. Born 23/10/48. Commd 13/1/45. Wg Cdr 1/1/90. Retd GD 13/12/96.
BLAND P.C. Born 25/5/45. Commd 17/5/79. Sqn Ldr 1/7/95. Retd GD 4/8/02.
BLANE D.C. PhD BA FIMA MCMI. Born 20/7/35. Commd 31/12/58. Sqn Ldr 31/8/69. Retd EDN 28/11/79.
BLANK K.R. Born 3/5/32. Commd 5/7/68. Flt Lt 5/7/73. Retd ADMIN 3/5/92.
BLANN A.D. BSc. Born 28/10/30. Commd 17/12/52. Flt Lt 17/3/54. Retd GD 28/10/68.
BLASZAK R.M. Born 1/2/15. Commd 1/3/41. Flt Lt 1/7/46. Retd PE 4/4/69.
BLATCH J.R. AFC. Born 23/2/31. Commd 6/12/51. Sqn Ldr 1/1/64. Retd GD 27/8/76.
BLATCHFORD K.G. Born 10/3/42. Commd 27/1/61. Flt Lt 27/7/66. Retd GD 10/3/80.
BLAYMIRES M.E.F. Born 11/2/19. Commd 10/6/43. Flt Lt 10/12/46. Retd ENG 30/7/60. rtg Sqn Ldr
BLEACH D.G. MCMI. Born 12/2/23. Commd 10/9/43. Wg Cdr 1/1/70. Retd GD 1/8/74.
BLEADEN J.A. Born 2/7/40. Commd 28/7/60. Flt Lt 10/2/67. Retd GD 2/7/78.
BLEASDALE P.D. Born 11/9/41. Commd 16/7/62. Flt Lt 16/1/68. Retd GD 2/4/76.
BLEASE S.C.P. MB ChB. Born 14/11/58. Commd 12/1/82. Sqn Ldr 1/8/88. Retd MED 30/1/96.
BLEE W.H.P. MCMI. Born 5/12/23. Commd 28/3/45. Wg Cdr 1/7/68. Retd ADMIN 30/10/76.
BLENCOWE M.R. Born 25/10/45. Commd 19/8/65. Flt Lt 2/12/71. Retd SEC 25/10/83.
BLENKINSOP C.M. Born 14/9/47. Commd 10/5/73. Flt Lt 10/11/79. Retd ADMIN 25/9/88.
BLENKINSOP G.E. MIFireE. Born 22/5/47. Commd 8/11/68. Flt Lt 20/9/74. Retd SY 22/5/85.
BLENKINSOP J.W. Born 25/9/46. Commd 21/1/66. Sqn Ldr 1/7/80. Retd FLY(N) 25/9/04.
BLENKIRON T.J. Born 13/3/49. Commd 29/6/72. Flt Lt 29/12/78. Retd ADMIN 13/3/88.
BLEVINS D. Born 16/5/38. Commd 7/9/80. Sqn Ldr 1/1/88. Retd SUP 16/5/93.
BLEVINS P.R. Born 20/5/64. Commd 6/10/94. Flt Lt 6/10/96. Retd ENG 6/10/02.
BLEVINS S.J. Born 19/3/58. Commd 20/1/80. Flt Lt 20/1/85. Retd ADMIN 21/12/87.
BLEZARD D.N. Born 8/4/49. Commd 2/8/68. Flt Lt 18/1/75. Retd GD(G) 1/4/78.
BLICQ R.S. Born 2/5/25. Commd 20/10/52. Flt Lt 26/5/55. Retd GD 16/5/57.
BLINMAN M.G. Born 29/12/34. Commd 10/4/56. Sqn Ldr 1/7/69. Retd SUP 30/4/92.
BLINMAN T.V. Born 15/7/17. Commd 30/1/44. Flt Lt 30/7/47. Retd SEC 15/7/61.
BLISS D.A. Born 31/5/16. Commd 15/11/46. Sqn Ldr 1/1/52. Retd RGT 23/3/58.
BLISS N.A. Born 24/12/56. Commd 30/4/81. Sqn Ldr 1/7/91. Retd GD(G) 24/12/94.
BLISS R.J. Born 9/5/44. Commd 3/8/62. Sqn Ldr 1/7/78. Retd GD 26/8/92.
BLISS W.E. CBE. Born 4/10/28. Commd 7/7/49. Gp Capt 1/1/76. Retd GD 4/10/85.
BLISSETT H. Born 17/12/22. Commd 19/7/51. Sqn Ldr 1/7/61. Retd ENG 21/12/78. Re-instated 13/6/62 to 17/12/82.
BLOCK K.J. Born 8/5/50. Commd 2/11/88. Flt Lt 2/11/92. Retd ENG 1/8/01.
BLOCKEY J.W. Born 3/4/37. Commd 17/12/57. Flt Lt 17/6/63. Retd GD 2/4/92.
BLOCKEY P.D. Born 16/7/33. Commd 9/10/56. Sqn Ldr 1/7/68. Retd GD 16/7/71.
BLOCKI J. Born 24/12/21. Commd 15/4/47. Flt Lt 1/7/47. Retd GD(G) 24/12/76.
BLOME-JONES L.M. DFC. Born 17/1/12. Commd 17/2/36. Sqn Ldr 9/6/47. Retd SEC 8/3/58. rtg Wg Cdr
BLOMFIELD O.H.D. Born 28/9/12. Commd 14/8/34. Wg Cdr 1/10/46. Retd GD 10/3/49.
BLOMLEY D.L. MBE. Born 22/10/43. Commd 17/12/65. Sqn Ldr 1/1/75. Retd SUP 22/10/81. Re-entered 18/7/84.
    Wg Cdr 1/7/92. Retd SUP 31/8/00.
BLOOD D.M.W. BSc. Born 23/11/61. Commd 31/8/80. Flt Lt 15/10/84. Retd GD 1/9/00.
BLOOD D.M.W. LLO MB BCh MRCP. Born 17/3/52. Commd 26/6/73. Sqn Ldr 17/8/81. Retd MED 13/3/86.
BLOOMFIELD J.N. Born 2/8/33. Commd 3/4/58. Sqn Ldr 1/7/69. Retd GD 11/11/81.
BLOOMFIELD P.B. Born 24/5/30. Commd 18/6/52. Flt Lt 13/11/57. Retd GD 24/5/68.
BLOOR R.N. MRCPsych MRCS LRCP. Born 20/12/49. Commd 14/2/71. Sqn Ldr 24/9/80. Retd MED 20/12/87.

BLORE C.E. Born 23/10/50. Commd 12/10/78. Sqn Ldr 1/1/88. Retd ENG 1/1/91.
BLOUNT C.C. MVO. Born 2/2/25. Commd 19/10/45. Sqn Ldr 1/1/56. Retd GD 18/10/60.
BLOW G.J. Born 18/5/51. Commd 25/2/72. Wg Cdr 1/1/90. Retd SUP 29/2/92.
BLOWER A.P. MB MChir FRCS DMRD. Born 31/1/27. Commd 30/3/53. Wg Cdr 5/3/65. Retd MED 19/3/70.
BLOWERS A.L. Born 1/5/29. Commd 14/12/70. Flt Lt 14/12/70. Retd ADMIN 16/5/84.
BLOWFIELD G.E. Born 17/8/16. Commd 28/3/46. Sqn Ldr 1/7/68. Retd SUP 17/8/71.
BLUNDELL M.D. MB ChB FFARCS DA. Born 13/2/41. Commd 28/9/64. Wg Cdr 8/8/81. Retd MED 15/3/83.
BLUNDEN D. Born 10/4/30. Commd 5/3/52. Flt Lt 5/9/56. Retd GD 31/3/70.
BLUNDEN R.F. BA MRAeS MCMI MBCS. Born 10/9/48. Commd 12/7/68. Wg Cdr 1/1/92. Retd GD 2/4/03.
BLUNKELL M.E. MBE CEng MIEE. Born 17/6/42. Commd 14/2/63. Wg Cdr 1/7/83. Retd ENG 17/4/93.
BLUNT A.S. Born 17/8/41. Commd 18/7/61. Wg Cdr 1/7/85. Retd ENG 17/4/89.
BLUNT C.A. MCMI MCIPD. Born 9/1/31. Commd 9/11/50. Wg Cdr 1/7/72. Retd SEC 4/4/81.
BLUNT I.R. Born 26/8/40. Commd 30/7/64. Gp Capt 1/7/86. Retd ENG 1/5/91.
BLYTH A.G. Born 22/1/21. Commd 14/3/49. Flt Lt 4/6/56. Retd GD 2/2/70.
BLYTH A.J.G. MCMI. Born 29/5/42. Commd 21/7/61. Sqn Ldr 1/7/78. Retd GD 1/7/81.
BLYTH C.I. DFC* AFC*. Born 1/4/25. Commd 24/5/45. Sqn Ldr 1/1/56. Retd GD 1/4/63.
BLYTH G.F. Born 27/5/11. Commd 24/3/43. Flt Lt 24/9/46. Retd ENG 8/3/47.
BLYTH G.G. BA. Born 2/11/48. Commd 24/9/67. Flt Lt 15/10/73. Retd SUP 2/11/86.
BLYTH I. Born 7/5/54. Commd 7/11/91. Flt Lt 7/11/95. Retd ENG 1/7/02.
BLYTH I.D. Born 22/3/37. Commd 15/9/60. Wg Cdr 1/7/82. Retd GD(AEO) 1/1/90.
BLYTHE A.C. DFC. Born 26/7/21. Commd 11/5/41. Gp Capt 1/1/60. Retd GD 18/5/70.
BLYTHE W.D. Born 10/7/17. Commd 11/7/46. Sqn Ldr 1/1/58. Retd SEC 31/1/63.
BLYTHE-BROOK D. Born 10/3/40. Commd 21/4/67. Sqn Ldr 1/7/82. Retd SUP 10/3/95.
BOAGEY J.G. MBE. Born 1/10/19. Commd 28/2/46. Wg Cdr 1/1/63. Retd ENG 1/6/70.
BOAK D.C. MCMI. Born 14/8/39. Commd 19/1/66. Wg Cdr 1/1/85. Retd ADMIN 4/1/87.
BOARDMAN C.L. Born 2/10/36. Commd 12/6/58. Sqn Ldr 1/7/70. Retd CAT 12/8/75.
BOARDMAN H.J. MBE BSc CEng MIMechE MCMI. Born 12/12/50. Commd 26/2/71. Sqn Ldr 1/1/82. Retd ENG 12/12/88.
BOARDS D.A. DFM. Born 1/2/17. Commd 13/8/43. Flt Lt 1/4/56. Retd GD 5/2/60.
BOAST R.S. CBE DFC AE. Born 21/12/20. Commd 16/6/40. Gp Capt 1/7/61. Retd GD 24/7/65.
BOATWRIGHT P.H. CBE FCMI FRAeS. Born 3/4/37. Commd 26/3/64. Gp Capt 1/1/87. Retd GD(G) 3/4/92.
BOBART R. Born 29/6/22. Commd 11/8/44. Flt Lt 26/5/55. Retd GD 23/6/67.
BOBISHKO-BIGGS P.V. BDS. Born 20/12/57. Commd 1/4/84. Flt Lt 7/8/82. Retd DEL 28/7/86.
BOCKING I. Born 6/10/47. Commd 29/1/87. Flt Lt 29/1/91. Retd OPS SPT 29/7/98.
BODDINGTON J.A. BA DPhysED MCMI. Born 12/5/43. Commd 10/8/65. Sqn Ldr 1/1/77. Retd PE 10/8/81.
BODDY G.M. OBE. Born 16/9/37. Commd 5/2/56. A Cdre 1/1/90. Retd GD(G) 1/7/92.
BODEN A.N. BA FRSA LHSM. Born 21/4/38. Commd 19/1/66. Gp Capt 1/7/87. Retd MED(SEC) 1/7/89.
BODEN D.E.G. Born 13/7/29. Commd 20/11/51. Flt Lt 28/5/56. Retd GD 13/7/84.
BODEN G.R. Born 5/8/28. Commd 7/7/52. Sqn Ldr 1/1/63. Retd GD 5/8/66.
BODEN J. Born 9/4/40. Commd 24/11/67. Flt Lt 15/4/70. Retd SEC 9/4/78.
BODEN J.M. MCMI. Born 28/6/30. Commd 30/7/52. Wg Cdr 1/1/76. Retd ADMIN 28/2/78.
BODEN R.A. Born 28/9/46. Commd 21/2/74. Flt Lt 3/2/77. Retd GD(G) 14/3/96.
BODENHAM B. Born 8/11/50. Commd 15/8/85. Flt Lt 15/8/87. Retd ENG 15/8/93.
BODIAM A.R. BSc. Born 8/6/51. Commd 26/9/69. Sqn Ldr 1/1/88. Retd GD 1/3/91.
BODIE J.W. Born 14/11/52. Commd 15/3/73. Sqn Ldr 1/7/86. Retd ADMIN 14/12/90.
BODY W.R.S. CEng MRAeS. Born 13/9/22. Commd 4/11/58. Sqn Ldr 1/7/70. Retd ENG 13/9/73.
BOE I.C.C. Born 3/5/48. Commd 11/8/67. Flt Lt 11/2/74. Retd SY(RGT) 3/5/88.
BOETIUS J.M. CEng MRAeS MIMechE. Born 4/6/33. Commd 28/10/57. Flt Lt 28/10/62. Retd ENG 28/10/73.
BOETIUS P.A. Born 1/7/34. Commd 11/8/55. Flt Offr 11/8/61. Retd SEC 16/12/61.
BOFFEY B.G.A. Born 28/10/31. Commd 20/11/58. Flt Lt 14/4/65. Retd SUP 17/3/71.
BOGG R. Born 14/6/42. Commd 11/5/62. A Cdre 11/5/62. Retd GD 14/6/97.
BOGGIA R. BDS MGDSRCS(Ed) MGDSRCS(Eng) LDSRCS. Born 7/3/39. Commd 30/6/63. Sqn Ldr 22/12/67. Retd DEL 30/6/66. Re-entered 22/6/75. Gp Capt 1/1/91. Retd DEL 7/2/97.
BOGGIS M.F. Born 8/3/35. Commd 6/2/54. Flt Lt 6/8/59. Retd GD(G) 14/9/87.
BOGGIS P.J.S. DFC. Born 29/9/18. Commd 8/8/39. Flt Lt 1/9/45. Retd GD(G) 7/10/67. rtg Sqn Ldr
BOGUE P.J. Born 24/11/30. Commd 30/7/52. Flt Lt 30/1/55. Retd GD 25/11/68.
BOHL M.J. BA. Born 23/9/61. Commd 11/9/83. Flt Lt 11/3/86. Retd ADMIN 14/3/97.
BOHM E.B. ACIS. Born 23/7/48. Commd 17/5/79. Wg Cdr 1/7/95. Retd ADMIN 1/12/98.
BOLAM G.D. MA BSc CEng MIEE DUS. Born 1/8/19. Commd 24/8/49. Wg Cdr 24/9/66. Retd EDN 17/11/71.
BOLAM S.F. MHCIMA AInstAM(Dip) CMC. Born 11/1/50. Commd 29/8/72. Wg Cdr 1/1/92. Retd GD 11/1/05.
BOLD G. Born 15/1/25. Commd 29/6/50. Sqn Ldr 1/1/62. Retd GD 31/1/75.
BOLE L.T. Born 10/4/50. Commd 26/4/84. Sqn Ldr 1/7/92. Retd ENGINEER 10/4/05.
BOLER F.F. Born 5/6/25. Commd 9/6/44. Flt Lt 9/6/50. Retd GD(G) 1/10/69.
BOLEY P.G. IEng MIIE MILT. Born 17/1/43. Commd 26/9/82. Sqn Ldr 1/7/92. Retd ENG 26/9/98.
BOLINGBROKE P.V. Born 26/9/22. Commd 22/6/50. Flt Lt 22/6/56. Retd SEC 1/5/74.
BOLLANS G.D. Born 26/9/57. Commd 17/5/79. Flt Lt 17/11/84. Retd GD 13/12/95.

BOLSOVER D.R. Born 9/10/53. Commd 22/5/75. Wg Cdr 1/1/96. Retd GD 17/8/01.
BOLT C.R. MBE MCIPS. Born 29/3/47. Commd 2/8/68. Wg Cdr 1/1/91. Retd SUP 14/9/96.
BOLT J.L. Born 8/7/35. Commd 7/5/60. Sqn Ldr 1/1/70. Retd ENG 17/5/76.
BOLTON B.N. Born 7/2/49. Commd 27/2/70. Wg Cdr 1/7/89. Retd GD 7/2/04.
BOLTON C.A. Born 5/11/20. Commd 3/7/57. Sqn Ldr 1/1/64. Retd SEC 29/12/73.
BOLTON C.A. BSc CEng MIEE AMBCS MIDPM. Born 23/4/50. Commd 17/10/71. Sqn Ldr 1/7/84. Retd ENG 23/4/88.
BOLTON C.A. Born 15/6/45. Commd 5/12/63. Gp Capt 1/1/92. Retd ADMIN 2/12/96.
BOLTON C.C.I. Born 12/1/46. Commd 6/11/64. Flt Lt 4/5/72. Retd GD 16/10/76.
BOLTON D. MCMI. Born 15/4/32. Commd 22/10/53. Gp Capt 1/7/78. Retd SY 23/9/80.
BOLTON G.E. Born 20/10/48. Commd 26/2/71. Sqn Ldr 1/7/84. Retd SUP 20/10/02.
BOLTON J.A. Born 6/5/37. Commd 2/5/59. Sqn Ldr 1/7/71. Retd GD 1/10/78.
BOLTON J.F. Born 3/8/28. Commd 22/7/50. Flt Lt 22/7/55. Retd RGT 12/1/68.
BOLTON J.W.A. BSc MRAeS. Born 17/12/44. Commd 30/8/66. Gp Capt 1/1/89. Retd GD 1/10/93.
BOLTON M.W. MCMI. Born 28/3/43. Commd 12/4/66. Sqn Ldr 1/1/88. Retd GD 1/9/02.
BOLTON P.J. Born 30/4/57. Commd 6/4/95. Flt Lt 6/4/99. Retd ENGINEER 10/4/05.
BOLTON P.M. Born 30/1/44. Commd 22/3/63. Flt Lt 22/9/68. Retd GD 29/3/74.
BOLTON R.A. Born 7/9/48. Commd 29/11/68. Flt Lt 29/5/74. Retd GD 14/10/78.
BOLTON R.J. Born 26/3/36. Commd 24/9/64. Flt Lt 24/9/66. Retd GD 24/8/74.
BOLTON W. Born 22/12/20. Commd 9/10/42. Flt Lt 26/5/55. Retd GD 31/1/68.
BOLTON-KING J. Born 9/7/36. Commd 23/12/58. Flt Lt 7/8/64. Retd GD 9/9/72.
BOLTON-KING R. BA. Born 23/2/40. Commd 17/8/64. Sqn Ldr 1/1/75. Retd GD 17/8/80.
BOMBER K.J. Born 6/10/45. Commd 22/5/64. Sqn Ldr 1/7/77. Retd GD 6/10/83.
BONAS R.H. Born 6/6/34. Commd 29/10/73. Sqn Ldr 1/1/80. Retd GD 13/2/87.
BOND A.D. Born 21/9/48. Commd 19/6/70. Flt Lt 1/12/74. Retd GD 21/9/86.
BOND C. BEng. Born 29/1/42. Commd 9/9/63. Sqn Ldr 1/7/78. Retd GD 29/1/97.
BOND C.C. Born 22/2/33. Commd 9/4/52. Flt Lt 17/4/61. Retd GD 17/10/75.
BOND C.F. DFC. Born 7/10/18. Commd 22/1/43. Flt Lt 15/7/52. Retd SEC 7/10/73.
BOND C.P. Born 21/4/60. Commd 21/6/90. Flt Lt 21/6/92. Retd GD 21/6/98.
BOND E.D.B. Born 23/6/31. Commd 22/12/53. Flt Lt 7/3/62. Retd GD 1/9/69.
BOND G. Born 15/11/46. Commd 25/2/82. Flt Lt 25/2/85. Retd GD 1/10/91.
BOND G.H. BSc. Born 17/4/56. Commd 21/10/79. Flt Lt 21/1/81. Retd GD 6/6/89.
BOND M.N. Born 16/10/38. Commd 16/5/60. Sqn Ldr 1/1/71. Retd GD 16/10/76.
BOND N.P. Born 14/12/47. Commd 23/9/66. Flt Lt 18/3/73. Retd SUP 1/1/76.
BOND P.R. Born 29/5/33. Commd 3/9/52. Gp Capt 1/7/81. Retd GD 9/7/91.
BOND R.A.V. MILT. Born 13/8/47. Commd 1/3/68. Wg Cdr 1/1/91. Retd SUP 17/7/96.
BOND R.N. Born 24/12/23. Commd 6/12/56. Flt Lt 6/12/62. Retd GD 2/4/68.
BOND T.A.M. Born 14/12/32. Commd 14/12/54. Sqn Ldr 1/7/69. Retd SUP 1/7/72.
BOND T.M. Born 17/11/36. Commd 30/12/54. Flt Lt 1/3/61. Retd GD 17/11/74.
BONE A.L. Born 27/6/26. Commd 21/11/51. Flt Lt 21/5/56. Retd GD 31/12/69.
BONE C.E. MB ChB. Born 18/4/56. Commd 1/11/81. Sqn Ldr 1/11/85. Retd MED 6/6/86. Re-entered 26/4/91.
    Wg Cdr 25/11/97. Retd MED 21/9/02.
BONE D.J. Born 15/7/61. Commd 15/8/85. Flt Lt 15/2/91. Retd GD 6/8/94.
BONE J.H. FINucE. Born 23/6/27. Commd 4/2/48. Flt Lt 4/2/54. Retd SEC 1/2/78.
BONE R.D. MBE. Born 29/1/24. Commd 19/11/53. Flt Lt 19/11/59. Retd GD 29/1/79.
BONELLA T.R. MSc BSc. Born 24/5/52. Commd 25/9/71. Wg Cdr 1/7/91. Retd ENG 2/12/98.
BONFIELD F.W.L. Born 17/9/41. Commd 26/5/61. Sqn Ldr 1/7/73. Retd GD 17/9/79.
BONFIELD K.M. Born 3/2/64. Commd 23/5/85. Fg Offr 23/5/87. Retd GD 17/9/90.
BONHAM-SMITH I.H. Born 1/3/40. Commd 23/6/60. Flt Lt 23/9/66. Retd ADMIN 1/3/78.
BONNER W.H.McC. OBE MCIPD MCMI. Born 12/12/33. Commd 13/9/51. Wg Cdr 1/7/73. Retd GD 9/2/86.
BONNEY G.W. Born 25/10/25. Commd 5/11/46. Flt Lt 4/11/53. Retd GD 30/6/65.
BONNEY K.G.B. CEng FRAeS FInstMC FCMI. Born 27/6/22. Commd 9/3/50. Wg Cdr 1/1/70. Retd ENG 27/6/77.
BONNEY-JAMES R.M. Born 2/6/46. Commd 26/5/67. Wg Cdr 1/1/90. Retd GD 2/6/02.
BONNOR N. FRIN FRAeS. Born 29/7/39. Commd 25/7/60. A Cdre 1/1/89. Retd GD 2/4/91.
BONNY G.L. MCMI. Born 18/2/24. Commd 26/8/48. Wg Cdr 1/7/64. Retd GD 1/3/73.
BONSALL P.J. BSc CEng MRAeS MCMI. Born 11/11/49. Commd 4/10/68. Sqn Ldr 1/1/87. Retd ENG 1/1/90.
BONSEY J.D. Born 8/4/33. Commd 26/9/52. Flt Lt 5/11/58. Retd GD(G) 8/4/93.
BOOKER E.J. OBE MM MCMI. Born 6/11/20. Commd 5/4/43. Wg Cdr 1/7/59. Retd ENG 6/11/75.
BOOKER G.S.F. BSc CEng MIMechE MRAeS. Born 16/11/47. Commd 27/2/70. Wg Cdr 1/7/88. Retd ENG 14/3/97.
BOOKER H.J. Born 21/5/23. Commd 2/7/64. Flt Lt 2/7/67. Retd GD 21/5/78.
BOOKER L.A.J. BEM. Born 29/10/17. Commd 26/9/57. Flt Lt 26/9/60. Retd ENG 23/11/63.
BOOKER S.A. MBE. Born 25/4/22. Commd 18/5/43. Sqn Ldr 1/1/72. Retd GD 30/6/73.
BOOKER T.T. Born 3/3/44. Commd 21/4/77. Sqn Ldr 1/7/86. Retd MED(SEC) 3/3/99.
BOOKHAM R.P. BA. Born 24/4/48. Commd 20/7/78. Sqn Ldr 1/7/86. Retd ENG 23/4/02.
BOOLY M.I.E. Born 30/8/54. Commd 7/11/91. Flt Lt 7/11/95. Retd SUP 1/10/98.
BOON J.F. CBE FCIPD FCMI. Born 27/4/35. Commd 18/2/54. A Cdre 1/7/85. Retd ADMIN 28/4/93.
BOON T.R. Born 26/8/46. Commd 23/3/67. Sqn Ldr 1/1/85. Retd GD 15/9/00.

BOONHAM A. OBE CEng MIEE. Born 24/9/16. Commd 29/3/41. Gp Capt 1/1/64. Retd ENG 24/9/71.
BOORMAN P. Born 11/3/35. Commd 13/9/50. Flt Lt 15/3/65. Retd GD 1/3/73.
BOORMAN P.S. Born 19/7/49. Commd 6/11/80. Sqn Ldr 1/1/91. Retd OPS SPT 1/10/97.
BOOTH A.E. Born 17/6/35. Commd 24/4/70. Flt Lt 12/7/74. Retd MED(T) 1/9/76.
BOOTH C.J. Born 26/6/40. Commd 1/8/61. Wg Cdr 1/7/91. Retd GD 26/6/95.
BOOTH D.M.C. Born 22/3/50. Commd 31/7/86. Flt Lt 31/7/90. Retd ENGINEER 22/3/05.
BOOTH D.P. Born 15/7/45. Commd 18/8/67. Sqn Ldr 1/7/79. Retd SUP 7/12/98.
BOOTH E.D. Born 14/5/23. Commd 10/3/44. Flt Lt 24/6/54. Retd SEC 28/8/64.
BOOTH E.M. MSc MB ChB MFCM MFOM DIH. Born 29/1/32. Commd 6/1/63. Wg Cdr 23/12/71. Retd MED 31/10/81.
BOOTH F. Born 27/8/31. Commd 23/8/51. Sqn Ldr 1/7/65. Retd GD 27/8/86.
BOOTH G.A. Born 19/7/62. Commd 19/7/87. Sqn Ldr 1/7/97. Retd ENG 19/7/02.
BOOTH L.W.N. DFC. Born 2/9/18. Commd 20/3/43. Sqn Ldr 1/7/62. Retd SUP 31/8/72.
BOOTH M.R. Born 18/2/56. Commd 24/6/76. Flt Lt 24/12/81. Retd GD 29/5/88.
BOOTH P. MB ChB MRCP DCH. Born 14/10/54. Commd 22/7/75. Wg Cdr 1/8/92. Retd MED 14/10/92.
BOOTH P.M. BSc. Born 8/10/23. Commd 3/1/61. Sqn Ldr 14/2/66. Retd ADMIN 3/1/77.
BOOTH R. Born 27/9/37. Commd 16/9/55. Sqn Ldr 1/1/72. Retd GD 27/9/75.
BOOTH R.E. Born 19/11/38. Commd 9/7/60. Sqn Ldr 1/7/78. Retd GD 19/11/93.
BOOTH R.I. Born 31/8/42. Commd 9/2/62. Flt Lt 9/8/67. Retd GD 1/4/76.
BOOTH R.S. Born 27/5/51. Commd 25/2/72. Sqn Ldr 1/1/88. Retd SY 2/6/93.
BOOTH T.A. Born 18/9/44. Commd 31/8/62. Flt Lt 1/7/69. Retd GD 3/7/82.
BOOTH T.I. Born 19/11/43. Commd 12/1/62. Flt Lt 1/7/68. Retd GD 19/11/81.
BOOTHBY A. MCMI. Born 18/12/22. Commd 25/8/43. Sqn Ldr 1/1/68. Retd RGT 18/6/79.
BOOTHBY H.E. OBE BA. Born 1/11/22. Commd 2/6/43. Gp Capt 1/7/72. Retd ADMIN 1/11/77.
BOOTHBY P.E. Born 16/10/56. Commd 20/9/79. Flt Lt 20/3/85. Retd GD 2/3/98.
BOOTHROYD P.V. Born 27/12/46. Commd 5/2/65. Flt Lt 4/11/70. Retd GD 14/3/96.
BORE J.E. OBE. Born 14/10/32. Commd 13/9/51. A Cdre 1/7/81. Retd GD 1/7/83.
BOREHAM P.J. Born 30/7/37. Commd 4/4/59. Wg Cdr 1/1/80. Retd ENG 30/7/87.
BOREHAM P.M. Born 8/9/43. Commd 8/9/63. Sqn Ldr 1/1/79. Retd GD 1/1/82.
BOREHAM R.J. Born 2/7/31. Commd 19/8/71. Flt Lt 19/8/74. Retd GD(G) 1/3/83.
BORLAND D.A. AFM. Born 5/11/22. Commd 26/11/53. Flt Lt 26/11/59. Retd GD 5/11/72.
BORLEY W.D. Born 7/8/66. Commd 26/9/91. Flt Lt 26/7/95. Retd OPS SPT(ATC) 7/8/04.
BORRILL C.P. BSc. Born 20/7/61. Commd 14/10/84. Sqn Ldr 1/7/92. Retd SUP 14/10/00.
BORROWS K. BSc CEng MRAeS MCMI. Born 3/11/37. Commd 4/9/59. Sqn Ldr 1/1/67. Retd ENG 4/9/89.
BOSANCO-MITCHELL D.W. Born 7/6/44. Commd 4/7/85. Sqn Ldr 1/1/94. Retd ENG 13/4/99.
BOSANQUET C.C. Born 19/12/46. Commd 4/5/70. Flt Lt 15/4/72. Retd GD 13/9/75.
BOSELEY K. Born 9/1/58. Commd 19/12/91. Flt Lt 19/12/93. Retd SUP 14/3/96.
BOSHER J.H. Born 18/10/32. Commd 23/8/51. Flt Lt 22/5/57. Retd GD 29/5/72.
BOSSY M.J. Born 31/10/45. Commd 1/6/72. Wg Cdr 1/7/96. Retd GD 31/10/00.
BOSTOCK S.N. MSc FCMI. Born 9/8/43. Commd 17/12/65. A Cdre 1/7/94. Retd GD 23/12/96.
BOSTON G.A. Born 12/7/26. Commd 22/2/47. Flt Lt 7/6/51. Retd GD 12/7/69.
BOSTON J. Born 27/4/45. Commd 30/8/84. Sqn Ldr 1/1/96. Retd ADMIN 27/4/00.
BOSWORTH G.W. Born 24/3/58. Commd 15/12/88. Flt Lt 15/12/90. Retd ADMIN 23/4/92.
BOSWORTH J. Born 28/8/31. Commd 18/2/53. Flt Lt 20/7/58. Retd GD(G) 28/8/89.
BOSWORTH J.M. Born 20/4/63. Commd 8/12/83. Flt Lt 8/6/90. Retd SUP 1/10/90.
BOTELER W.E. DFC. Born 13/6/20. Commd 4/6/43. Sqn Ldr 1/10/55. Retd GD 13/6/63.
BOTHAM J.A. Born 26/3/48. Commd 2/12/66. Sqn Ldr 1/1/85. Retd GD 26/3/92.
BOTHAMS J. Born 4/10/21. Commd 17/3/49. Wg Cdr 1/1/66. Retd SEC 1/5/74.
BOTSFORD F.A. AFM. Born 19/8/23. Commd 30/11/50. Flt Lt 30/5/54. Retd GD 31/8/68.
BOTT A.K. Born 17/2/20. Commd 16/1/47. Flt Lt 16/7/51. Retd SEC 28/10/67.
BOTTELEY R.J. BSc. Born 9/12/43. Commd 3/10/66. Sqn Ldr 3/4/77. Retd ADMIN 3/10/82.
BOTTERILL P.G. CBE AFC FCMI. Born 14/1/32. Commd 14/11/51. Gp Capt 1/1/77. Retd GD 14/1/87.
BOTTERY P.A. Born 8/8/49. Commd 18/69. Sqn Ldr 1/7/81. Retd ENG 1/1/88.
BOTTING L.E. CBE DFC. Born 29/7/13. Commd 16/8/41. Gp Capt 1/1/57. Retd GD 31/8/60.
BOTTOME N.L. Born 21/6/20. Commd 7/1/42. Sqn Ldr 1/7/54. Retd GD 21/6/63.
BOTTOMLEY J.C. BSc. Born 22/1/64. Commd 18/8/85. Sqn Ldr 1/1/98. Retd GD 22/4/02.
BOTTOMLEY M.V. Born 5/5/39. Commd 27/8/64. Wg Cdr 1/7/81. Retd SUP 5/5/94.
BOTWRIGHT P. Born 28/2/30. Commd 14/11/51. Flt Lt 22/5/57. Retd GD 28/2/68.
BOUCAUT R.P. Born 29/9/45. Commd 29/3/68. Fg Offr 29/3/70. Retd GD 30/11/72.
BOUCH P.A. Born 23/10/35. Commd 1/2/56. Sqn Ldr 1/7/88. Retd GD 1/7/91.
BOUCH R. Born 10/7/58. Commd 10/3/77. Sqn Ldr 1/1/90. Retd GD 10/7/96.
BOUCHARD A.M. MBE. Born 15/1/51. Commd 5/7/73. Sqn Ldr 1/7/88. Retd GD(G) 19/3/95.
BOUCHER J.F. Born 3/10/29. Commd 24/10/51. Flt Lt 24/4/56. Retd GD 26/9/75.
BOUGHTON A.H. Born 18/6/08. Commd 3/1/41. Sqn Ldr 1/7/48. Retd SEC 4/12/58.
BOUGHTON T.V.J. MBE. Born 19/7/20. Commd 15/4/43. Flt Lt 15/10/46. Retd ENG 18/7/73.
BOULD G.R. CEng MIMechE MRAeS. Born 7/4/41. Commd 10/1/70. Flt Lt 10/4/73. Retd ENG 14/1/82.
BOULDING N.J. BA. Born 28/11/53. Commd 3/9/72. Sqn Ldr 1/7/84. Retd ENG 28/11/91.

BOULIND P.R. MB ChB MRCOG. Born 11/3/43. Commd 27/1/69. Wg Cdr 11/8/83. Retd MED 27/1/85.
BOULNOIS D.P. Born 25/10/21. Commd 11/5/41. Sqn Ldr 1/7/52. Retd GD 20/7/58.
BOULT R.d.e.V. Born 27/8/31. Commd 17/12/52. Sqn Ldr 1/7/61. Retd GD 16/10/76.
BOULTER P.A. Born 9/11/38. Commd 30/5/69. Flt Lt 4/5/72. Retd GD 30/5/77.
BOULTON D.H. Born 4/3/46. Commd 30/1/75. Flt Lt 7/6/81. Retd GD 15/7/90.
BOULTON M.S. BA. Born 6/11/63. Commd 11/10/87. Flt Lt 11/4/90. Retd FLY(N) 11/10/03.
BOULTON R.D.B. Born 11/12/29. Commd 20/12/51. Flt Lt 4/4/57. Retd GD 11/12/67.
BOUNDY B.M. Born 21/4/30. Commd 19/4/50. Flt Lt 19/10/54. Retd GD 21/4/68.
BOUNDY P.J. BSc. Born 7/8/61. Commd 13/2/83. Flt Lt 13/5/84. Retd GD 23/3/01.
BOUNTIFF A. Born 30/1/24. Commd 14/4/49. Sqn Ldr 1/7/61. Retd GD 15/5/75.
BOURKE D. MBE. Born 19/6/15. Commd 11/6/53. Sqn Ldr 1/1/64. Retd ENG 19/6/70.
BOURKE D.L. Born 17/12/16. Commd 18/11/53. Flt Lt 18/11/58. Retd ENG 24/12/66.
BOURN J.J. Born 18/10/28. Commd 14/12/49. Sqn Ldr 1/1/62. Retd GD 5/2/71.
BOURNE A. MBE. Born 4/4/24. Commd 4/10/60. Sqn Ldr 1/1/72. Retd GD(G) 4/4/79.
BOURNE A.G. AFM. Born 9/1/25. Commd 6/9/56. Flt Lt 13/4/60. Retd GD 21/4/70.
BOURNE B.A. Born 19/10/21. Commd 30/1/44. Sqn Ldr 1/4/55. Retd GD 19/10/70.
BOURNE D.R. Born 23/1/33. Commd 6/4/54. Sqn Ldr 1/1/73. Retd GD 19/4/83.
BOURNE E. Born 5/8/29. Commd 9/4/52. Fg Offr 9/4/52. Retd GD 27/7/54.
BOURNE G.F. BA BSc. Born 31/12/44. Commd 1/4/76. Sqn Ldr 1/7/82. Retd GD 1/9/98.
BOURNE H. The Rev. Born 1/2/34. Commd 7/8/67. Retd Wg Cdr 7/1/88.
BOURNE L. Born 16/10/54. Commd 31/1/80. Sqn Ldr 1/1/94. Retd OPS SPT 31/10/97.
BOUSFIELD F.P. Born 13/6/18. Commd 25/8/60. Flt Lt 25/8/65. Retd ENG 7/10/67.
BOUTIN J.L.B. MCMI. Born 17/1/34. Commd 7/11/60. Sqn Ldr 1/7/66. Retd GD 7/11/76.
BOWART P. Born 10/5/44. Commd 20/5/82. Flt Lt 1/3/87. Retd ADMIN 14/3/97.
BOWATER M.V. MCMI. Born 7/10/28. Commd 7/6/51. Sqn Ldr 1/7/81. Retd ADMIN 12/1/82.
BOWDEN A.J. Born 2/2/48. Commd 9/3/72. Flt Lt 9/9/78. Retd GD(G) 1/10/92.
BOWDEN D.B. Born 23/6/47. Commd 27/2/70. Sqn Ldr 1/7/80. Retd SUP 23/6/85.
BOWDEN G.S. BSc CEng M DipEl MIEE. Born 13/9/31. Commd 19/8/54. Wg Cdr 17/2/73. Retd ADMIN 19/6/76.
BOWDEN M.W. Born 20/9/47. Commd 1/3/68. Flt Lt 6/7/74. Retd GD(G) 20/9/85.
BOWDITCH K.H. Born 21/11/32. Commd 21/11/51. Flt Lt 21/5/56. Retd GD 31/8/74.
BOWELL S.J.P. MBA BSc. Born 1/4/61. Commd 2/9/79. Flt Lt 15/10/83. Retd GD 1/4/99.
BOWEN A. Born 22/6/34. Commd 10/12/52. Sqn Ldr 1/7/82. Retd GD 22/6/92.
BOWEN A.J. Born 1/11/44. Commd 5/2/65. Sqn Ldr 1/7/90. Retd GD 31/3/94.
BOWEN D.E. Born 13/12/23. Commd 19/11/44. Wg Cdr 1/7/68. Retd GD(G) 3/4/73.
BOWEN D.E. Born 31/5/37. Commd 27/9/73. Flt Lt 27/9/78. Retd SEC 2/10/81.
BOWEN G.A. Born 9/6/20. Commd 27/6/46. Sqn Ldr 1/7/57. Retd SEC 1/5/68.
BOWEN J.B. BSc. Born 16/1/59. Commd 11/9/77. Sqn Ldr 1/1/98. Retd GD 18/12/00.
BOWEN J.L. Born 4/6/44. Commd 4/6/64. Flt Lt 24/12/70. Retd SUP 1/2/77.
BOWEN R.D.F. Born 22/4/25. Commd 19/10/45. Flt Lt 15/12/49. Retd GD 1/10/52.
BOWEN R.N. MSc BSc CEng MInstNDT DIC. Born 27/12/58. Commd 23/10/80. Sqn Ldr 1/1/92. Retd ENG 27/12/96.
BOWEN T.R. The Rev. BA. Born 30/6/20. Commd 30/12/53. Retd Gp Capt 26/7/75.
BOWEN W.V. Born 7/8/17. Commd 7/6/44. Flt Lt 7/12/48. Retd GD(G) 7/8/67.
BOWER A.H. AFC. Born 6/7/34. Commd 24/9/52. Flt Lt 21/5/58. Retd GD 6/7/72.
BOWER K.A. Born 3/5/24. Commd 28/7/67. Flt Lt 28/7/72. Retd ENG 3/5/79.
BOWER R. MA CEng MIEE. Born 26/4/48. Commd 1/12/69. Sqn Ldr 1/7/83. Retd ENG 1/7/86.
BOWERMAN G.T. BSc. Born 25/11/49. Commd 23/9/68. Flt Lt 15/10/72. Retd GD 6/9/80.
BOWERS D.V. Born 16/10/35. Commd 23/8/65. Flt Lt 23/9/67. Retd SEC 16/1/74.
BOWERS R.C. MBE. Born 18/5/22. Commd 5/10/50. Wg Cdr 1/7/70. Retd ENG 18/5/77.
BOWES F.T. Born 11/2/20. Commd 9/2/42. Flt Lt 7/6/51. Retd GD 7/2/66.
BOWES J.M.B. Born 11/7/32. Commd 15/12/53. Fg Offr 15/12/53. Retd GD 1/3/56.
BOWES J.W. BEM. Born 13/2/33. Commd 19/6/70. Flt Lt 19/6/72. Retd SEC 19/6/78.
BOWES R.E.M. BSc. Born 31/5/51. Commd 15/9/69. Sqn Ldr 1/7/84. Retd ENG 9/9/96.
BOWHILL K.R. OBE BA. Born 31/1/22. Commd 16/9/42. Wg Cdr 1/7/58. Retd GD 31/1/69.
BOWIE A.G. The Rev. CBE BA BSc. Born 10/5/28. Commd 7/1/55. Retd Gp Capt 22/10/84.
BOWIE J.J. Born 10/2/29. Commd 4/8/49. Flt Lt 23/11/55. Retd GD 10/2/67.
BOWIE R. MBE. Born 21/5/26. Commd 3/5/46. Sqn Ldr 1/7/56. Retd GD 21/5/84.
BOWKER M.P. Born 7/9/33. Commd 16/7/52. Sqn Ldr 1/1/67. Retd GD 17/7/87.
BOWLES D.J. Born 21/2/58. Commd 12/8/79. Sqn Ldr 1/1/96. Retd ADMIN 1/1/99.
BOWLES E.B. Born 20/8/24. Commd 1/8/69. Flt Lt 1/8/72. Retd GD(G) 20/8/76.
BOWLEY J.L.A. Born 31/5/30. Commd 5/4/36. Flt Lt 25/1/57. Retd GD 31/5/68.
BOWMAN A.M. MBE. Born 5/4/36. Commd 18/2/58. Gp Capt 1/7/84. Retd GD 3/4/89.
BOWMAN D.H.J. BSc MRAeS. Born 12/7/40. Commd 14/9/64. Flt Lt 14/6/66. Retd GD 14/9/80.
BOWMAN J.C. Born 7/8/43. Commd 15/7/64. Flt Lt 15/7/69. Retd ENG 30/8/73.
BOWMAN J.H. Born 16/12/13. Commd 2/12/43. Flt Lt 2/6/48. Retd GD(G) 16/12/63.
BOWMAN J.R. Born 18/9/35. Commd 23/2/54. Flt Lt 1/10/67. Retd GD 18/9/90.
BOWMAN M.A. Born 9/7/48. Commd 27/3/86. Flt Lt 27/3/90. Retd ADMIN 13/10/00.

BOWMAN M.N. BSc(Eng). Born 1/9/60. Commd 4/9/78. Sqn Ldr 1/1/94. Retd GD 1/9/98.
BOWMER J.L. DFC DFM. Born 10/5/23. Commd 14/6/44. Flt Lt 14/12/47. Retd GD 1/9/73. rtg Sqn Ldr
BOWN A.R. Born 2/11/49. Commd 14/8/70. Wg Cdr 1/1/94. Retd GD 2/11/04.
BOWN J.A. Born 10/9/25. Commd 4/10/56. Flt Lt 4/10/62. Retd GD(G) 10/9/75.
BOWNS A. ARRC RNT. Born 6/3/37. Commd 20/10/68. Sqn Ldr 20/10/80. Retd MED(SEC) 30/1/81.
BOWRING C.M. DFM. Born 12/5/19. Commd 10/3/43. Flt Lt 10/9/47. Retd SEC 12/5/68.
BOWRING D.J. BSc. Born 22/4/53. Commd 22/8/76. Flt Lt 22/11/77. Retd GD 22/8/92.
BOWRING J.I.R. CB CBE CEng FCMI FRAeS. Born 28/3/23. Commd 27/4/44. AVM 1/7/74. Retd ENG 4/1/78.
BOWRON C.F. Born 25/9/48. Commd 29/3/68. Flt Lt 29/9/73. Retd GD 27/4/02.
BOWS R.W. BDS BA MGDSRCS(Ed). Born 23/9/59. Commd 17/8/86. Wg Cdr 22/8/96. Retd DEL 17/8/02.
BOWSHER D.S. Born 24/7/59. Commd 17/5/79. Flt Lt 17/11/84. Retd GD 24/7/97.
BOWYER E.C. Born 2/3/32. Commd 13/8/52. Flt Lt 9/1/58. Retd GD 2/3/70.
BOWYER R.G. FCMI. Born 29/8/32. Commd 14/4/53. Gp Capt 1/7/79. Retd GD 18/7/80.
BOX A.G. BSc. Born 24/10/33. Commd 25/6/57. Sqn Ldr 1/7/66. Retd GD 30/9/75.
BOXALL A.C.W. Born 26/10/44. Commd 24/6/65. Sqn Ldr 1/7/88. Retd FLY(P) 26/10/04.
BOXALL C.J. Born 22/3/41. Commd 31/8/62. Flt Lt 29/2/68. Retd GD 22/3/79.
BOXALL K.Y. BSc. Born 14/8/45. Commd 27/2/75. Flt Lt 27/2/77. Retd GD 13/8/84.
BOXALL-HUNT A.E. Born 23/1/48. Commd 24/11/67. Sqn Ldr 1/1/64. Retd GD 1/1/87.
BOXELL R. MBE BEM. Born 27/3/29. Commd 14/8/70. Flt Lt 14/8/75. Retd ADMIN 1/9/84.
BOXER H.E.C. CB OBE. Born 28/7/14. Commd 27/7/35. A Cdre 1/1/59. Retd GD 29/11/67.
BOXER J.A. Born 21/3/52. Commd 9/3/72. Flt Lt 9/9/77. Retd GD 21/3/90.
BOXER W.D. Born 20/4/30. Commd 11/4/63. Flt Lt 11/4/69. Retd ADMIN 31/10/84.
BOXSEY C.R. MCMI. Born 13/8/19. Commd 26/9/57. Sqn Ldr 1/1/67. Retd ENG 16/8/69.
BOXX P.J. MB ChB FRCOG. Born 5/5/39. Commd 28/4/65. Gp Capt 22/7/88. Retd MED 1/1/91.
BOYACK C. AFC MCMI. Born 24/6/33. Commd 9/4/52. Wg Cdr 1/7/85. Retd GD 24/6/88.
BOYCE J. Born 23/5/56. Commd 28/6/79. Flt Lt 10/3/82. Retd GD 23/5/94.
BOYCE J.S. Born 14/11/12. Commd 22/8/45. Flt Offr 17/5/56. Retd SEC 23/1/62.
BOYCE M.D. BA. Born 21/11/35. Commd 13/10/64. Sqn Ldr 5/11/72. Retd EDN 5/5/81.
BOYCE P.A. Born 11/1/77. Commd 3/10/96. Fg Off 3/10/98. Retd FLY(P) 12/6/03.
BOYCE S.G.J. Born 7/1/57. Commd 22/2/79. Flt Lt 22/2/84. Retd GD 10/10/89.
BOYCE T.S.B. MCMI. Born 8/4/31. Commd 15/12/53. Wg Cdr 1/1/76. Retd GD 2/12/85.
BOYD A.F. OBE DFC. Born 11/4/21. Commd 30/3/42. Wg Cdr 1/1/62. Retd GD 20/2/71.
BOYD A.J.W. Born 2/3/49. Commd 27/2/70. Wg Cdr 1/1/92. Retd GD 2/3/04.
BOYD K.L. Born 9/8/28. Commd 22/10/53. Sqn Ldr 1/1/74. Retd GD 9/8/83.
BOYD M.N.R. Born 19/1/58. Commd 28/6/79. Flt Lt 28/12/84. Retd GD 1/9/96.
BOYD P.C. BDS. Born 6/9/42. Commd 26/1/66. Wg Cdr 26/1/79. Retd DEL 26/1/82.
BOYD P.M. Born 5/12/44. Commd 5/7/73. Wg Cdr 1/1/90. Retd ENG 9/12/94.
BOYD S. Born 11/1/62. Commd 23/4/87. Flt Lt 23/10/92. Retd FLY(N) 8/5/03.
BOYDE G.W. Born 31/7/23. Commd 14/1/44. Flt Lt 17/5/65. Retd GD 30/8/68.
BOYDELL F. IEng. Born 12/2/52. Commd 1/7/82. Flt Lt 1/7/84. Retd ENG 1/3/90.
BOYENS A.R. Born 10/9/50. Commd 13/10/72. Flt Lt 13/4/78. Retd GD 1/12/85.
BOYER K. Born 23/11/60. Commd 24/4/80. Flt Lt 24/10/85. Retd GD 13/9/99.
BOYES D.R. MA. Born 24/4/41. Commd 1/4/66. Sqn Ldr 1/7/72. Retd GD 26/1/84.
BOYES R. Born 9/12/25. Commd 16/9/71. Flt Lt 16/9/74. Retd GD 9/12/83.
BOYLAND P.S. AFC BSc. Born 12/5/61. Commd 26/9/82. Sqn Ldr 1/1/96. Retd GD 17/1/02.
BOYLE A.A. Born 20/4/35. Commd 10/4/56. Flt Lt 10/10/58. Retd GD 29/1/64.
BOYLE E.J. Born 8/12/45. Commd 18/8/67. Flt Lt 18/8/70. Retd GD 1/5/94.
BOYLE J.S. Born 12/6/30. Commd 14/4/53. Flt Lt 22/5/57. Retd GD 12/6/68.
BOYLE M.P. BSc. Born 31/5/61. Commd 24/6/93. Sqn Ldr 1/7/00. Retd OPS SPT(ATC) 11/10/03.
BOYLE M.S. Born 17/12/32. Commd 9/1/57. Flt Lt 15/8/62. Retd GD 9/1/73.
BOYLE P. BSc MB ChB MRCGP. Born 3/6/49. Commd 28/9/86. Wg Cdr 28/9/92. Retd MED 14/9/96.
BOYLE P.R. BSc CEng MIEE MRAeS. Born 19/2/49. Commd 1/9/70. Flt Lt 1/12/71. Retd GD 17/12/87.
BOYLE T.L. OBE. Born 21/9/50. Commd 21/1/74. Gp Capt 1/7/00. Retd GD 30/9/01.
BOYLES M.L. BTech. Born 24/5/54. Commd 3/9/72. Sqn Ldr 1/7/88. Retd ENG 24/5/92.
BOYMAN R.S. Born 16/10/27. Commd 29/3/62. Flt Lt 29/3/67. Retd ENG 16/10/85.
BOYNE H.G. Born 12/9/29. Commd 12/11/51. Sqn Ldr 1/1/67. Retd GD 28/11/75.
BOYNE R. Born 1/2/39. Commd 27/7/72. Sqn Ldr 1/7/81. Retd ADMIN 29/7/91.
BOYNS J.H.A. Born 25/6/18. Commd 18/3/42. Flt Lt 18/9/42. Retd SUP 31/1/65.
BOYS D.R. Born 13/6/34. Commd 7/5/64. Sqn Ldr 1/1/77. Retd ENG 13/6/89.
BOYS-STONES P.A. Born 27/10/28. Commd 15/10/52. Sqn Ldr 1/7/61. Retd GD 20/5/68.
BOZIER V. Born 3/9/47. Commd 1/3/68. Flt Lt 3/9/74. Retd GD(G) 3/9/88.
BRABAN R.L. Born 28/5/38. Commd 1/3/68. Wg Cdr 1/1/88. Retd ADMIN 2/6/90.
BRABBINS R.W. BTech. Born 17/11/50. Commd 15/9/69. Sqn Ldr 1/1/86. Retd GD 1/1/89.
BRACE E.A. MBE. Born 30/9/20. Commd 23/1/45. Flt Lt 21/10/55. Retd SEC 17/10/70.
BRACE F.E. Born 17/2/50. Commd 20/12/73. Flt Lt 27/9/77. Retd GD(G) 17/2/88.
BRACEBRIDGE M.C. MB BS. Born 30/9/44. Commd 24/4/67. Sqn Ldr 24/7/75. Retd MED 24/4/83.

BRACKEN E.W. Born 3/3/39. Commd 9/12/65. Sqn Ldr 1/1/75. Retd ENG 25/8/84.
BRACKENBOROUGH F.A. Born 29/5/23. Commd 29/7/65. Flt Lt 29/7/70. Retd GD 1/6/73.
BRACKENBURY I. CB OBE BSc CEng FIMechE. Born 28/8/45. Commd 26/5/67. AVM 1/1/98. Retd ENG 28/8/00.
BRACKENBURY S. Born 27/5/54. Commd 10/5/32. Sqn Ldr 1/1/86. Retd GD(G) 27/5/92.
BRACKETT J.E. MCMI. Born 3/3/38. Commd 14/3/57. Wg Cdr 1/1/75. Retd SUP 7/4/91. rtg Gp Capt
BRACKLEY M.J. Born 7/6/35. Commd 30/4/62. Sqn Ldr 1/7/74. Retd ADMIN 7/6/85.
BRACKPOOL M.J. BA. Born 31/7/46. Commd 15/10/81. Sqn Ldr 1/1/91. Retd ENG 26/5/98.
BRACKSTONE K.G. LLB. Born 17/10/53. Commd 3/9/72. Sqn Ldr 1/7/94. Retd ADMIN 18/10/98.
BRADBEER P.A. Born 25/4/61. Commd 23/4/87. Sqn Ldr 1/1/97. Retd ENGINEER 25/4/05.
BRADBEER R. Born 15/3/19. Commd 20/4/44. Sqn Ldr 1/1/67. Retd GD(G) 30/3/74.
BRADBURN N.P. Born 7/2/60. Commd 5/2/84. Flt Lt 5/2/89. Retd ADMIN 14/3/96.
BRADBURY T.J. Born 22/10/26. Commd 14/2/27. Flt Lt 14/8/50. Retd GD 8/7/68.
BRADEN E.G.A. BEM. Born 13/12/28. Commd 7/9/61. Sqn Ldr 1/1/76. Retd ENG 13/12/83.
BRADFORD D.A. BA. Born 16/7/42. Commd 30/7/63. Flt Lt 30/10/65. Retd GD 16/7/00.
BRADFORD M.R. Born 20/11/18. Commd 18/11/54. Sqn Ldr 1/1/67. Retd ENG 21/11/70.
BRADFORD M.W.B. MBE. Born 31/1/41. Commd 19/4/64. Sqn Ldr 1/7/78. Retd GD 29/9/95.
BRADFORD T. Born 16/8/17. Commd 14/2/46. Flt Lt 15/12/49. Retd ENG 24/4/54.
BRADGATE J.K. MSc BEng CEng MIEE. Born 7/10/64. Commd 3/8/88. Flt Lt 27/2/92. Retd ENGINEER 27/7/04.
BRADING R. Born 10/1/33. Commd 3/11/53. Flt Lt 21/1/59. Retd GD 27/2/71.
BRADLEY B.R. AFM. Born 3/12/24. Commd 21/7/55. Flt Lt 21/7/61. Retd GD 3/12/74.
BRADLEY C.E. Born 11/5/15. Commd 1/5/39. Sqn Ldr 1/8/47. Retd SUP 11/5/64. rtg Wg Cdr
BRADLEY D.J. BSc. Born 9/12/39. Commd 23/10/62. Sqn Ldr 23/4/71. Retd EDN 23/10/78.
BRADLEY D.L. Born 26/7/35. Commd 19/8/71. Sqn Ldr 26/10/82. Retd MED(T) 21/6/86.
BRADLEY G.M. BSc. Born 1/12/64. Commd 1/2/87. Flt Lt 1/8/89. Retd GD 1/2/99.
BRADLEY H. Born 1/7/23. Commd 14/10/42. Flt Offr 14/10/47. Retd SEC 3/4/54.
BRADLEY J.D. AFC. Born 12/2/22. Commd 26/5/47. Flt Lt 26/5/55. Retd GD 1/12/61.
BRADLEY K. OBE MA MCIPD. Born 16/7/35. Commd 30/1/58. Gp Capt 1/1/85. Retd ADMIN 16/7/91.
BRADLEY M.G. AFC BA. Born 22/9/28. Commd 12/10/50. Wg Cdr 1/7/66. Retd GD 22/9/83.
BRADLEY M.J. MB BCh BAO. Born 30/4/34. Commd 20/8/61. Flt Lt 20/8/61. Retd MED 17/2/66.
BRADLEY M.M. Born 22/10/19. Commd 10/11/41. Sqn Ldr 1/1/63. Retd SEC 1/11/69.
BRADLEY P.J. Born 7/9/23. Commd 1/4/65. Sqn Ldr 1/7/75. Retd ADMIN 29/3/78.
BRADLEY P.L.F. Born 4/3/33. Commd 26/1/55. Flt Lt 15/8/62. Retd GD 1/10/71.
BRADLEY R.W. MBE. Born 5/4/24. Commd 21/2/52. Sqn Ldr 1/1/65. Retd GD 5/4/72.
BRADLEY T. MBE BA MRAeS. Born 19/9/41. Commd 13/1/67. Wg Cdr 1/7/86. Retd GD 10/11/91.
BRADLEY T.J. BEng. Born 25/3/36. Commd 1/1/57. Flt Lt 12/11/63. Retd GD 12/2/78.
BRADLEY W.G. MBE MSc(Eng) MSc CEng MRAeS. Born 17/10/38. Commd 27/4/65. Wg Cdr 1/7/83.
   Retd ENG 17/10/93.
BRADLEY W.H.M. MCMI. Born 26/2/33. Commd 18/2/63. Sqn Ldr 1/7/72. Retd ADMIN 26/2/83.
BRADLY P. MRIN. Born 10/7/43. Commd 26/10/62. Gp Capt 1/1/91. Retd GD 10/5/93.
BRADSHAW A. DFC. Born 22/8/22. Commd 13/1/43. Flt Lt 13/7/46. Retd GD 28/8/65.
BRADSHAW A. BSc MCGI. Born 23/12/66. Commd 12/3/87. Flt Lt 12/9/92. Retd FLY(N) 23/12/04.
BRADSHAW E. Born 1/3/38. Commd 5/11/70. Flt Lt 5/11/72. Retd GD(G) 6/11/75. Re-instated 12/11/80. Flt Lt 12/11/77.
   Retd GD(G) 1/10/94.
BRADSHAW G.W. Born 20/10/28. Commd 23/9/81. Flt Lt 4/7/65. Retd GD 20/10/88.
BRADSHAW J.C. MSc BSc. Born 13/5/49. Commd 1/8/69. Sqn Ldr 1/1/85. Retd ENG 13/11/00.
BRADSHAW J.R. MCIPS MIDPM MCMI. Born 26/3/30. Commd 17/12/52. Gp Capt 1/7/78. Retd SUP 26/3/85.
BRADSHAW J.T. Born 10/6/44. Commd 23/9/66. Sqn Ldr 1/7/80. Retd SY 1/7/85.
BRADSHAW K.M.J. BEng. Born 26/11/57. Commd 6/7/80. Sqn Ldr 1/7/89. Retd ENG 9/6/97.
BRADSHAW P.N. MSc. Born 21/1/52. Commd 25/5/80. Sqn Ldr 1/1/89. Retd GD(G) 25/5/96.
BRADSHAW P.R. BSc. Born 11/4/54. Commd 3/10/76. Flt Lt 30/1/80. Retd GD(G) 3/10/92.
BRADSHAW W.H.A. DFC. Born 21/2/21. Commd 19/1/42. Gp Capt 1/1/68. Retd GD(G) 1/5/71.
BRADY D. Born 12/4/60. Commd 29/7/83. Flt Lt 29/1/90. Retd GD(G) 21/1/92.
BRADY G.A. Born 10/6/46. Commd 2/4/65. Flt Lt 8/3/72. Retd GD 10/6/84.
BRADY J.P. BA. Born 16/5/47. Commd 19/8/66. Wg Cdr 1/1/86. Retd GD 16/5/97.
BRADY J.W. Born 19/3/33. Commd 15/7/53. Sqn Ldr 1/1/71. Retd GD 19/3/91.
BRADY N.H. Born 21/9/60. Commd 31/1/80. Sqn Ldr 1/1/93. Retd GD 1/1/99.
BRADY R.P. BSc. Born 15/10/54. Commd 2/9/73. Flt Lt 15/4/78. Retd GD 15/7/88.
BRADY T.A. Born 24/10/45. Commd 7/1/71. Sqn Ldr 1/7/85. Retd ADMIN 24/10/00.
BRAGG E.J. Born 2/1/31. Commd 2/4/57. Fg Offr 9/4/59. Retd GD 2/4/62.
BRAGG G.W. Born 11/11/64. Commd 19/12/91. Flt Lt 12/3/95. Retd ADMIN 1/11/96.
BRAGG R.H. Born 8/5/30. Commd 12/12/51. Wg Cdr 1/1/70. Retd GD 29/9/72.
BRAILSFORD E.E. BEM. Born 12/7/20. Commd 10/1/57. Flt Lt 10/1/63. Retd SUP 18/7/70.
BRAIN J. AFC. Born 11/1/16. Commd 4/3/39. Sqn Ldr 1/1/53. Retd GD 9/2/63.
BRAIN P.M. Born 2/8/34. Commd 26/11/60. Sqn Ldr 1/1/80. Retd GD 2/8/89.
BRAIN R.J. AFC. Born 31/5/21. Commd 30/5/44. Sqn Ldr 1/1/55. Retd GD 31/5/61.
BRAITHWAITE R.G. AFC. Born 11/7/39. Commd 29/4/58. Sqn Ldr 1/7/87. Retd GD 1/8/92.

BRAITHWAITE S.H. Born 13/2/15. Commd 25/8/44. Sqn Ldr 1/1/56. Retd SEC 17/2/65.
BRAITHWAITE S.M. Born 13/10/63. Commd 24/3/83. Flt Lt 24/9/88. Retd GD 1/10/97.
BRAKE C.R. BSc. Born 18/11/63. Commd 13/11/89. Sqn Ldr 1/7/01. Retd OPS SPT(PROVSY) 1/7/04.
BRAKES D.M.P. Born 10/12/53. Commd 17/9/72. Fg Offr 6/4/77. Retd GD(G) 31/3/79.
BRAMALL D.C. MSc BEng CEng MIMechE MCMI. Born 28/1/42. Commd 13/10/64. Wg Cdr 1/1/78.
    Retd ENG 13/10/83.
BRAMBLES J.P. Born 18/9/63. Commd 2/11/88. Sqn Ldr 1/7/00. Retd SUPPLY 9/5/04.
BRAMBLEY F.R. AFC. Born 21/4/33. Commd 6/12/51. Wg Cdr 1/1/79. Retd GD 5/11/84.
BRAMELD I.N. Born 25/1/39. Commd 28/7/60. Wg Cdr 1/7/79. Retd SUP 2/4/82.
BRAMHAM P.M. Born 21/10/52. Commd 3/7/83. Sqn Ldr 1/1/89. Retd GD 1/1/92.
BRAMLEY D.W. DPhysEd. Born 5/8/41. Commd 16/4/63. Wg Cdr 1/7/79. Retd GD 5/8/85.
BRAMLEY P.A.McC. Born 21/3/29. Commd 31/7/50. Flt Lt 26/3/56. Retd GD 21/3/67.
BRAMWELL R.W. MRCS LRCP. Born 7/4/32. Commd 4/11/62. Sqn Ldr 27/9/64. Retd MED 23/9/68.
BRAMWELLS W.H. LDS. Born 16/12/27. Commd 27/3/60. Gp Capt 1/1/79. Retd DEL 1/3/85.
BRANAGH N. OBE BEd. Born 8/11/46. Commd 12/12/71. Sqn Ldr 1/1/85. Retd ADMIN 1/1/88. Re-entered 2/5/89.
    Wg Cdr 1/1/93. Retd ADMIN 8/11/01.
BRANCH K.G. MB ChB FFARCS Dip Soton DA. Born 23/10/32. Commd 2/2/58. Wg Cdr 2/2/71. Retd MED 2/2/74.
BRAND M.S. Born 16/11/45. Commd 4/7/85. Flt Lt 4/7/87. Retd GD 31/10/95.
BRAND R.S. DFC. Born 28/7/26. Commd 16/4/47. Sqn Ldr 1/1/59. Retd GD 3/5/68.
BRANDIE W.J. Born 25/7/49. Commd 30/5/69. Flt Lt 30/11/74. Retd GD 2/4/01.
BRANDON J.H. Born 16/10/35. Commd 18/2/58. Wg Cdr 1/1/85. Retd GD 16/10/93.
BRANDON V.G. Born 8/8/61. Commd 8/11/90. Flt Lt 8/11/92. Retd ENG 26/1/02.
BRANKIN W.R. BEM. Born 28/10/29. Commd 20/6/63. Sqn Ldr 1/1/80. Retd PE 1/8/80.
BRANNAN E.S. Born 24/2/60. Commd 6/5/83. Sqn Ldr 1/1/96. Retd GD 5/1/99.
BRANSBURY J.M. Born 8/12/47. Commd 1/10/65. Flt Lt 1/4/71. Retd GD 14/3/96.
BRANSON R.A. AFC. Born 18/6/16. Commd 14/5/44. Flt Lt 14/11/47. Retd GD(G) 5/10/63.
BRANT J.M. CEng MRAeS. Born 15/9/31. Commd 6/7/50. Gp Capt 1/1/79. Retd ENG 15/9/86.
BRANTHWAITE P.A. Born 8/4/47. Commd 6/5/66. Flt Lt 6/11/71. Retd GD 22/4/01.
BRANTON G.J. Born 14/12/46. Commd 2/8/73. Flt Lt 19/6/76. Retd GD(G) 14/12/84.
BRANTON J.F. BSc. Born 16/1/32. Commd 1/3/56. Gp Capt 1/7/78. Retd ENG 24/1/84.
BRASSINGTON C.S. Born 25/5/35. Commd 21/10/66. Flt Lt 21/10/72. Retd ENG 27/7/74.
BRATBY M.J. MSc BA. Born 25/2/45. Commd 27/10/70. Wg Cdr 1/1/89. Retd SUP 25/2/00.
BRATLEY D.B. Born 4/10/47. Commd 8/12/83. Flt Lt 27/7/88. Retd ADMIN 1/10/99.
BRAUEN P.D. MBE MCMI. Born 6/11/30. Commd 31/8/50. Sqn Ldr 1/7/67. Retd SEC 6/11/80.
BRAUN E.R. BEM CEng MRAeS MCMI. Born 30/7/22. Commd 22/9/49. Wg Cdr 1/1/73. Retd ENG 5/1/74.
BRAUN P.D. Born 15/7/48. Commd 2/5/69. Sqn Ldr 1/1/83. Retd ENG 16/7/89.
BRAUND R.E. Born 5/3/27. Commd 11/4/51. Flt Lt 11/1/57. Retd GD 22/11/65.
BRAWN F.R. MBE. Born 24/3/21. Commd 3/6/65. Flt Lt 3/6/70. Retd ENG 30/6/77.
BRAWN R.H. Born 14/12/41. Commd 30/5/69. Fg Offr 30/7/63. Retd GD 25/2/66.
BRAY A.M.J. Born 28/2/59. Commd 3/11/77. Sqn Ldr 1/7/89. Retd GD 10/10/99.
BRAY A.N. Born 24/3/13. Commd 17/12/32. Plt Offr 17/12/32. Retd GD 6/12/33.
BRAY D.B. Born 27/12/44. Commd 22/5/64. Sqn Ldr 1/1/81. Retd GD 2/12/97.
BRAY D.R.M. Born 16/3/21. Commd 14/2/47. Fg Offr 14/2/47. Retd RGT 24/6/50.
BRAY J.H. Born 2/12/42. Commd 14/2/63. Flt Lt 2/12/69. Retd ENG 2/12/80.
BRAY J.J. DFC. Born 20/7/18. Commd 15/1/42. Flt Lt 1/9/45. Retd GD 30/8/53. rtg Sqn Ldr
BRAY M.S. Born 2/4/47. Commd 10/12/65. Flt Lt 10/6/71. Retd GD 30/9/77.
BRAY R.W. LHA. Born 12/7/32. Commd 7/2/70. Flt Lt 7/2/74. Retd MED(SEC) 17/1/76.
BRAY R.W. Born 1/7/28. Commd 6/4/50. Wg Cdr 1/1/66. Retd GD 1/7/83.
BRAY-SMITH A.J. Born 5/6/58. Commd 8/9/77. Flt Lt 8/3/83. Retd GD 14/1/96.
BRAYSHAW S. BSc CEng MIEE. Born 29/12/41. Commd 15/7/63. Wg Cdr 1/1/88. Retd ENG 19/12/98.
BRAYSHER S.P. Born 25/6/52. Commd 14/10/71. Fg Offr 14/4/74. Retd SUP 22/4/75.
BRAZENDALE S.R.L. BSc. Born 8/9/49. Commd 2/7/72. Sqn Ldr 1/1/85. Retd ENG 2/7/88.
BRAZIEL C.J. Born 13/1/50. Commd 15/8/85. Flt Lt 15/8/89. Retd SY 28/2/94.
BRAZIER J.A. Born 29/8/34. Commd 10/10/79. Sqn Ldr 17/1/76. Retd SUP 1/11/87.
BRAZIER J.F. OBE. Born 23/10/32. Commd 9/2/55. Wg Cdr 1/7/74. Retd GD 1/8/85.
BRAZIER P.D. Born 26/5/53. Commd 9/3/72. Flt Lt 5/8/78. Retd GD(G) 2/12/90.
BREADMORE K.G.W. Born 5/12/49. Commd 21/3/69. Flt Lt 21/9/74. Retd GD 1/6/78.
BREADNER D.G.J. BSc CEng FIEE FIMechE FIIM FRAeS FCMI. Born 26/7/36. Commd 7/8/58. A Cdre 1/7/83.
    Retd ENG 30/11/89.
BREADNER J.H. Born 28/3/23. Commd 12/12/45. Wg Cdr 1/1/69. Retd ENG 28/3/78.
BREALEY D.J. MSc BSc. Born 3/7/52. Commd 2/10/72. Sqn Ldr 15/1/84. Retd ADMIN 3/7/90.
BREARLEY R.H. MA MSc AFIMA MCMI. Born 17/9/40. Commd 8/12/64. Sqn Ldr 8/6/75. Retd ADMIN 8/12/80.
BRECKEN S. Born 24/6/25. Commd 4/7/57. Sqn Ldr 1/7/68. Retd GD 4/11/75.
BRECKENRIDGE M.J. Born 16/1/42. Commd 14/1/82. Sqn Ldr 1/1/93. Retd ENG 16/1/97.
BREDDY P.B. BSc. Born 22/6/66. Commd 1/9/85. Flt Lt 15/1/91. Retd GD 15/7/00.
BREDENKAMP J. Born 24/3/34. Commd 5/4/55. Wg Cdr 1/1/75. Retd GD 24/3/89.

BREEDS P.W. Born 29/9/49. Commd 11/4/85. Sqn Ldr 1/7/01. Retd OPS SPT(INT) 29/9/04.
BREEZE A. Born 13/2/32. Commd 7/5/52. Flt Lt 2/10/57. Retd GD 13/2/92.
BREEZE R.S. DFM. Born 17/9/15. Commd 20/9/45. Sqn Ldr 1/7/64. Retd SEC 8/2/69.
BREGEON G.E. Born 31/5/32. Commd 27/5/53. Wg Cdr 1/7/78. Retd GD 4/6/86.
BREMNER C.M. Born 22/11/50. Commd 4/5/72. Flt Lt 4/11/77. Retd GD 13/8/82.
BREMNER D.A.G. Born 11/9/45. Commd 18/8/67. Gp Capt 1/1/91. Retd OPS SPT 11/9/00.
BREMNER J.A. Born 6/4/42. Commd 14/2/63. Sqn Ldr 1/7/79. Retd SY 1/7/87.
BREMNER-YOUNG J.E. Born 22/2/25. Commd 6/8/52. Flt Lt 7/2/57. Retd GD 5/9/66.
BRENNAN B. CertEd. Born 17/6/53. Commd 14/12/81. Sqn Ldr 1/1/99. Retd FLY(N) 6/4/03.
BRENNAN C. Born 6/3/57. Commd 16/6/88. Flt Lt 21/4/94. Retd MED(T) 15/8/97.
BRENNAN D.E. Born 6/4/30. Commd 4/7/51. Flt Lt 14/11/56. Retd GD 6/4/68.
BRENNAN D.H. MA MB LMSSA DO. Born 30/7/30. Commd 5/5/57. Wg Cdr 5/5/70. Retd MED 1/1/75.
BRENNAN D.J. Born 15/3/29. Commd 24/9/59. Flt Lt 24/9/64. Retd GD 1/1/77.
BRENNAN J.P. Born 8/9/52. Commd 8/6/84. Flt Lt 8/6/86. Retd ADMIN 31/3/94.
BRENNAN P.S. MA BA PGCE MCIPD MCMI. Born 14/3/50. Commd 2/8/90. Sqn Ldr 1/7/99. Retd ADMIN 7/7/01.
BRENNAN V.T. Born 4/5/33. Commd 17/1/52. Flt Lt 8/5/57. Retd GD 4/5/71.
BRENT E.A. Born 16/2/20. Commd 24/5/48. Flt Lt 28/11/60. Retd GD 29/8/67.
BRENT M.J. Born 16/7/33. Commd 10/4/56. Flt Lt 10/10/61. Retd GD 21/3/75.
BRERETON MARTIN W.S. CBE. Born 6/5/43. Commd 24/6/65. Gp Capt 1/1/89. Retd SY 5/5/94.
BRESLIN C.J. BSc. Born 1/6/53. Commd 10/11/85. Sqn Ldr 1/1/91. Retd ADMIN 1/11/96.
BRETON P.M. Born 14/12/23. Commd 25/6/43. Flt Lt 20/6/48. Retd GD 15/8/55.
BRETT D.E. Born 15/9/32. Commd 13/9/51. Wg Cdr 1/1/75. Retd GD 15/2/84.
BRETT G.A. Born 23/4/64. Commd 22/11/84. Flt Lt 22/5/90. Retd GD 14/9/96.
BRETT J.D. MA. Born 11/7/35. Commd 23/2/60. Wg Cdr 1/7/79. Retd ADMIN 31/7/85.
BRETT W.H. Born 3/4/03. Commd 7/3/40. Sqn Ldr 1/8/47. Retd SEC 6/12/53.
BRETTELL I.C.B. Born 6/10/31. Commd 17/12/52. Sqn Ldr 1/1/63. Retd GD 6/10/69.
BREW R.A. Born 1/4/34. Commd 10/9/52. Flt Lt 7/2/58. Retd GD 1/4/72.
BREWER A. Born 11/11/31. Commd 17/5/51. Flt Lt 6/9/56. Retd GD 11/11/69.
BREWER A.F. AFC. Born 3/1/33. Commd 13/5/53. Sqn Ldr 1/7/79. Retd GD 3/1/93.
BREWER A.R. BEng. Born 13/11/44. Commd 9/10/67. Flt Lt 9/1/71. Retd ENG 17/7/88.
BREWER C.W. Born 6/8/45. Commd 29/12/69. Wg Cdr 1/7/90. Retd SUP 30/10/92.
BREWER F.R. Born 27/10/20. Commd 14/10/57. Sqn Ldr 1/1/68. Retd CAT 28/1/75.
BREWER H.E. DFC. Born 31/1/16. Commd 9/10/42. Sqn Ldr 1/1/66. Retd SEC 28/11/69.
BREWER N.C. Born 19/4/49. Commd 23/6/67. Gp Capt 1/7/99. Retd OPS SPT 1/7/01.
BREWER R.B. MCMI. Born 9/4/49. Commd 27/10/67. Wg Cdr 1/7/86. Retd GD(G) 1/10/89.
BREWERTON N. BA MRAeS MCMI. Born 7/11/54. Commd 30/9/73. Gp Capt 1/7/97. Retd GD 23/5/01.
BREWIN E. Born 29/1/20. Commd 5/5/44. Sqn Ldr 1/7/55. Retd GD 8/7/66.
BREWINGTON A.H. Born 1/5/34. Commd 26/10/61. Flt Lt 1/4/66. Retd GD(G) 31/7/87. Re-instated 9/4/90.
   Flt Lt 9/12/68. Retd GD(G) 9/4/93.
BREWSTER D. Born 22/12/22. Commd 3/12/44. Flt Lt 2/2/51. Retd SEC 1/11/68.
BREWSTER E.M. Born 1/7/14. Commd 9/12/42. Flt Offr 9/12/47. Retd SEC 13/12/51.
BREWSTER M.G. Born 14/12/54. Commd 20/9/79. Sqn Ldr 1/1/91. Retd SUP 14/3/96.
BREX J.T. Born 14/11/37. Commd 5/2/57. Flt Lt 15/8/62. Retd GD 9/8/76.
BRICE D.V. AFC. Born 9/6/30. Commd 31/7/58. Sqn Ldr 1/1/70. Retd GD 9/6/85.
BRICE E.J. CBE MRAeS DPhysEd. Born 12/2/17. Commd 28/6/40. A Cdre 1/1/69. Retd PE 17/4/71.
BRICE W.R. FCIS. Born 7/11/41. Commd 11/11/65. Gp Capt 1/7/87. Retd ADMIN 1/6/94.
BRICKWOOD Sir Basil Born 21/5/23. Commd 10/5/45. Flt Lt 14/5/58. Retd RGT 26/2/60.
BRIDGE A.J. MCMI. Born 27/3/32. Commd 21/1/53. Sqn Ldr 1/7/68. Retd SEC 1/7/71.
BRIDGE B.J. Born 25/9/47. Commd 8/12/83. Sqn Ldr 1/7/93. Retd ENG 2/4/98.
BRIDGE D. Born 8/1/38. Commd 30/9/63. Sqn Ldr 1/7/83. Retd GD 1/1/87.
BRIDGE R.W. AFC. Born 3/3/34. Commd 16/7/52. Sqn Ldr 1/7/66. Retd GD 3/3/72.
BRIDGEMAN D.A. MCMI ACIS. Born 6/2/35. Commd 24/2/67. Flt Lt 24/2/69. Retd SEC 1/9/73.
BRIDGER C. MBBS FRCP. Born 3/9/39. Commd 10/6/63. Gp Capt 27/11/87. Retd MED 1/7/96.
BRIDGER D.G. Born 17/12/28. Commd 26/3/52. Sqn Ldr 1/7/76. Retd GD 25/5/83.
BRIDGER P.S. Born 21/10/25. Commd 18/1/46. Wg Cdr 1/1/69. Retd GD 26/3/76.
BRIDGES A.G. CBE. Born 4/4/35. Commd 26/7/55. Gp Capt 1/7/78. Retd GD 4/4/92.
BRIDGES F.W. AIIP. Born 31/1/23. Commd 19/5/49. Flt Lt 19/11/53. Retd ENG 12/5/73.
BRIDGES G.E. Born 15/9/40. Commd 1/8/61. Sqn Ldr 1/1/72. Retd GD 16/12/79.
BRIDGES J.D. Born 26/5/62. Commd 5/10/81. APO 5/10/81. Retd GD 10/1/85.
BRIDGES M.D. MBE. Born 11/5/50. Commd 15/8/85. Sqn Ldr 1/1/94. Retd SUP 14/3/97.
BRIDGES R.C. Born 5/10/62. Commd 19/12/85. Flt Lt 19/6/91. Retd GD 14/3/96.
BRIDGES S.J. Born 31/10/60. Commd 30/8/84. Flt Lt 1/3/91. Retd OPS SPT 30/4/00.
BRIDGEWATER K. MA CEng MIEE. Born 31/10/27. Commd 29/12/53. Sqn Ldr 1/1/63. Retd ENG 29/12/69.
BRIDGHAM T.H. Born 23/1/45. Commd 19/8/66. Sqn Ldr 1/7/84. Retd GD 29/2/96.
BRIDLE A.L.M. BEd. Born 8/9/56. Commd 21/10/79. Flt Lt 21/10/83. Retd ADMIN 21/10/95.
BRIDLE D.W. Born 14/3/40. Commd 6/10/69. Sqn Ldr 1/7/84. Retd PRT 1/2/91.

BRIDLE N.H. Born 25/12/21. Commd 7/9/44. Flt Lt 27/6/55. Retd SUP 27/2/65.
BRIDSON D.S. AFC. Born 20/7/31. Commd 14/11/51. Sqn Ldr 1/1/67. Retd GD 31/8/73.
BRIDSON D.W. MSc. Born 31/3/37. Commd 30/9/58. Sqn Ldr 1/7/71. Retd ENG 21/10/78.
BRIDSON G.T. Born 3/8/33. Commd 13/9/51. Flt Lt 4/1/57. Retd GD 3/8/76.
BRIERLEY G. MCMI. Born 14/2/28. Commd 8/11/51. Wg Cdr 1/1/77. Retd SUP 14/2/83.
BRIERLEY G.N. OBE AFC BA DPhysEd. Born 4/11/25. Commd 25/8/52. Gp Capt 1/1/71. Retd PE 3/4/79.
BRIERS D.J. Born 21/3/40. Commd 31/10/63. Flt Lt 15/2/70. Retd GD(G) 21/3/95.
BRIGDEN K. Born 9/11/39. Commd 26/3/64. Flt Lt 25/7/70. Retd GD(G) 1/1/80. Re-instated 1/4/81. Flt Lt 23/10/71. Retd GD(G) 1/4/91.
BRIGGS D.A. Born 9/4/32. Commd 26/7/51. Flt Lt 6/10/56. Retd GD 9/4/70.
BRIGGS D.W. DFC. Born 7/5/24. Commd 30/9/44. Flt Lt 30/3/48. Retd GD 8/12/73.
BRIGGS E.H. CEng MIEE. Born 26/9/21. Commd 23/12/43. Wg Cdr 1/7/67. Retd ENG 2/4/75.
BRIGGS J.F. BSc. Born 23/10/48. Commd 8/9/74. Sqn Ldr 1/1/91. Retd GD 2/9/97.
BRIGGS K.R. Born 17/7/33. Commd 27/7/54. Gp Capt 1/1/81. Retd GD 12/12/85.
BRIGGS P.N. Born 28/2/53. Commd 22/7/71. Fg Offr 11/12/73. Retd GD(G) 1/10/75.
BRIGGS R. Born 21/1/23. Commd 25/8/60. Flt Lt 25/8/65. Retd ENG 13/4/74.
BRIGGS R. Born 28/10/51. Commd 4/2/71. Sqn Ldr 1/1/86. Retd GD 28/10/89.
BRIGGS T. CEng MIEE MCMI. Born 2/2/34. Commd 22/10/59. Sqn Ldr 1/7/69. Retd ENG 31/1/76.
BRIGHT A. Born 12/1/33. Commd 15/12/53. Sqn Ldr 1/1/67. Retd SUP 12/1/71.
BRIGHT D.M.F. MSc BA CEng MRAeS. Born 26/10/34. Commd 26/9/53. Wg Cdr 1/7/71. Retd ENG 9/12/86.
BRIGHT P.T. Born 24/1/48. Commd 28/2/69. Fg Offr 28/2/71. Retd SUP 3/8/75.
BRIGHT R.M. Born 22/4/47. Commd 26/5/67. Sqn Ldr 1/7/84. Retd ENG 1/11/01.
BRIGHT S. Born 18/11/18. Commd 9/8/45. Sqn Ldr 1/7/57. Retd SEC 18/11/68.
BRIGHT T.A.G. Born 16/6/43. Commd 24/3/83. Flt Lt 24/3/87. Retd ENG 29/4/92.
BRIGHTMAN P.S. Born 24/6/49. Commd 8/9/83. Flt Lt 8/9/85. Retd OPS SPT(REGT) 24/6/04.
BRIGHTON P. BSc CEng MRAeS MCMI. Born 26/3/33. Commd 3/8/55. Wg Cdr 1/7/68. Retd ENG 3/8/71.
BRIGHTON R.H. Born 10/6/25. Commd 26/3/52. Sqn Ldr 1/7/68. Retd GD 1/5/76.
BRIGHTWELL P.M. Born 16/9/42. Commd 6/4/62. Flt Lt 6/4/69. Retd SUP 1/5/76.
BRIGNALL T.A. MBE. Born 14/7/56. Commd 26/4/84. Wg Cdr 1/1/97. Retd OPS SPT 1/2/01.
BRIMELOW B. BA DCAe. Born 31/1/35. Commd 25/9/54. Sqn Ldr 1/7/65. Retd ENG 31/1/73. rtg Wg Cdr
BRIMMELL B.D. Born 23/4/58. Commd 10/12/88. Flt Lt 15/12/90. Retd ENG 15/12/96.
BRIMSON C.D. Born 5/12/36. Commd 4/7/57. Sqn Ldr 1/1/71. Retd GD 21/11/78.
BRIMSON I.D. MCMI. Born 10/2/34. Commd 27/7/54. Gp Capt 1/7/74. Retd GD 3/4/81.
BRINDLE A. AFC. Born 21/12/25. Commd 24/7/52. Flt Lt 17/5/56. Retd GD 31/1/74.
BRINDLE C.F. BA. Born 28/12/41. Commd 4/8/64. Sqn Ldr 4/2/73. Retd ADMIN 4/8/80.
BRINDLE G. Born 22/6/44. Commd 1/10/68. Gp Capt 1/1/89. Retd GD 22/6/04.
BRINDLE P.J. MPhil FCMI MInstD. Born 5/6/48. Commd 20/12/73. Gp Capt 1/7/94. Retd ADMIN 21/8/96.
BRINDLEY J. BSc CEng MRAeS. Born 9/4/49. Commd 11/3/73. Sqn Ldr 1/1/81. Retd ENG 11/3/89.
BRINDLEY P.R.H. CEng MIMechE. Born 31/1/39. Commd 13/6/71. Wg Cdr 1/7/84. Retd ENG 31/1/89.
BRINE K.C. CEng MIEE MRAes MCMI. Born 20/2/33. Commd 22/7/55. Wg Cdr 1/7/74. Retd ENG 22/2/83.
BRINICOMBE P.M. MEd BA. Born 27/3/45. Commd 11/5/71. Sqn Ldr 1/1/90. Retd ADMIN 1/1/93.
BRIODY P.J. Born 8/4/41. Commd 17/7/62. Sqn Ldr 1/7/76. Retd ENG 1/7/79.
BRISBANE G.M. DSO DFC DFM. Born 11/1/11. Commd 21/8/40. Wg Cdr 1/7/53. Retd GD 3/3/58.
BRISCOE L.B. Born 18/6/22. Commd 14/11/57. Sqn Ldr 1/7/70. Retd ENG 13/8/73.
BRISDION G.A. MSc BSc. Born 10/11/54. Commd 20/1/85. Flt Lt 20/7/88. Retd OPS SPT 20/1/01.
BRISTOW C.F. Born 8/3/35. Commd 19/4/93. Flt Lt 27/9/61. Retd GD 8/3/93.
BRISTOW J. BTech CEng MIMechE. Born 12/8/50. Commd 8/1/73. Wg Cdr 1/7/87. Retd ENG 8/1/95.
BRISTOW P.A. Born 9/8/34. Commd 16/7/52. Flt Lt 6/2/58. Retd GD 9/8/72.
BRITTAIN A.A. Born 18/4/43. Commd 12/2/64. Flt Lt 6/4/69. Retd SEC 19/8/78.
BRITTAIN D.R. Born 9/2/33. Commd 4/10/51. Sqn Ldr 1/1/81. Retd GD 9/2/93.
BRITTAIN E.A. AFC. Born 11/8/21. Commd 11/6/43. Sqn Ldr 1/7/53. Retd GD 11/8/64.
BRITTAIN J.N. Born 13/8/38. Commd 23/10/56. Flt Lt 21/8/63. Retd GD 13/8/76.
BRITTAIN R.D. CBE FCMI MCIPS. Born 27/6/30. Commd 11/4/51. A Cdre 1/1/80. Retd SUP 27/6/85.
BRITTEN-AUSTIN H.G. MSc BSc CEng FIEE. Born 3/2/48. Commd 26/2/71. Gp Capt 1/1/99. Retd GD 3/2/03.
BRITTON C.A. MCIPD. Born 29/11/48. Commd 13/12/68. Wg Cdr 1/7/94. Retd ADMIN 20/1/03.
BRITTON D. MCMI. Born 8/3/35. Commd 18/10/62. Flt Lt 10/2/67. Retd SEC 18/7/78.
BRITTON G.E. Born 5/4/37. Commd 6/4/62. Sqn Ldr 1/1/88. Retd GD 30/4/91.
BRITTON G.S. Born 30/12/46. Commd 27/1/67. Wg Cdr 1/1/88. Retd SUP 30/12/01.
BRITTON P.D. Born 13/6/46. Commd 12/7/79. Sqn Ldr 1/1/87. Retd GD 22/10/00.
BRITTON R.D. Born 23/6/32. Commd 25/11/55. Sqn Ldr 1/1/71. Retd GD 22/12/80.
BRITTON R.E. Born 13/5/25. Commd 27/3/57. Sqn Ldr 1/7/72. Retd SUP 17/6/77.
BROAD B.A. Born 24/11/33. Commd 20/11/75. Sqn Ldr 1/1/89. Retd ENG 1/1/92.
BROAD L.C. MSc CEng MRAeS. Born 21/5/35. Commd 26/4/60. Sqn Ldr 5/3/73. Retd ADMIN 26/4/76. Re-instated 3/9/79 to 21/6/85.
BROAD M.H.D. Born 1/2/30. Commd 12/12/51. Flt Lt 12/12/56. Retd SUP 30/9/75.
BROAD R.N. MA. Born 7/7/29. Commd 7/7/49. Sqn Ldr 1/7/59. Retd GD 7/7/67.

BROADBENT A.C. Born 4/7/62. Commd 19/11/87. Flt Lt 19/11/89. Retd GD 2/2/97.
BROADBENT J.A. DSO. Born 14/9/47. Commd 24/4/70. Gp Capt 1/1/93. Retd GD 12/12/96.
BROADBENT J.W. Born 27/1/36. Commd 22/7/65. Flt Lt 22/7/71. Retd GD(G) 2/4/80.
BROADBENT M.E. CEng MIMechE MRAeS. Born 31/3/39. Commd 24/9/63. Sqn Ldr 1/7/71. Retd ENG 24/9/79.
BROADBENT R. DFC. Born 23/8/19. Commd 1/9/45. Wg Cdr 1/1/56. Retd GD 30/11/63.
BROADHEAD R. Born 2/9/28. Commd 19/7/50. Flt Lt 19/1/61. Retd GD 2/9/66.
BROADHURST I. BA. Born 23/4/55. Commd 29/9/85. Flt Lt 29/3/89. Retd SUP 3/4/93.
BROADHURST P.W.T. Born 27/12/34. Commd 10/12/52. Sqn Ldr 1/7/76. Retd SUP 9/2/89.
BROADLEY D.F. Born 15/3/27. Commd 9/6/48. Sqn Ldr 1/1/66. Retd SY 7/5/77.
BROADLEY S.M. Born 21/7/63. Commd 16/2/89. Flt Lt 10/2/93. Retd ADMIN 21/7/01.
BROADMEADOW H. MCMI. Born 18/6/24. Commd 22/9/44. Wg Cdr 1/1/69. Retd GD 18/6/79.
BROADWAY S.J.H. Born 13/10/55. Commd 17/7/75. Flt Lt 17/1/81. Retd OPS SPT(FC) 2/4/03.
BROADWITH D.T. Born 17/11/35. Commd 24/6/55. Sqn Ldr 1/7/68. Retd GD 14/12/74.
BROATCH K.A. BEd. Born 20/4/64. Commd 5/1/92. Flt Lt 5/7/94. Retd ADMIN 14/9/96.
BROCK I.R. Born 15/2/34. Commd 26/7/56. Flt Lt 1/3/61. Retd GD 15/2/77.
BROCKLEBANK A. Born 2/6/41. Commd 4/5/72. Flt Lt 28/10/78. Retd SUP 17/1/88.
BROCKLEBANK B.A. Born 3/7/27. Commd 24/2/64. Sqn Ldr 1/7/75. Retd SUP 8/10/81.
BROCKLEBANK R.A. BA AFRIN DipEurHum. Born 25/4/43. Commd 11/5/62. Flt Lt 11/11/66. Retd GD 25/10/00.
BROCKLESBY P.M. BA. Born 10/2/50. Commd 25/7/71. Flt Lt 25/10/74. Retd SUP 16/4/77.
BROCKLEY R.S. PhD MSc BSc. Born 2/12/52. Commd 6/11/80. Sqn Ldr 1/7/90. Retd GD 6/7/96.
BROCKMAN R.F. BSc. Born 18/3/41. Commd 11/9/86. Flt Lt 11/9/88. Retd GD 18/3/96.
BRODERICK H.J. Born 14/9/23. Commd 12/9/63. Flt Lt 12/9/66. Retd GD 14/9/78.
BRODERICK J.A. OBE MCIT MILT MCMI. Born 23/3/42. Commd 23/9/65. Wg Cdr 1/7/89. Retd SUP 23/6/98.
BRODIE G.E. BSc CEng MIMechE. Born 8/7/64. Commd 3/8/86. Sqn Ldr 1/7/95. Retd ENG 12/10/02.
BRODIE I.M. Born 2/6/17. Commd 9/3/36. Sqn Ldr 1/7/62. Retd GD(G) 12/1/74.
BRODIE J.G. MBE AFC. Born 6/12/22. Commd 29/11/44. Wg Cdr 1/1/66. Retd GD 6/12/77.
BRODIE R.C.G. BSc MRAeS. Born 25/12/39. Commd 1/2/61. Sqn Ldr 1/7/73. Retd GD 1/10/84.
BROEKHUIZEN P. Born 3/5/44. Commd 4/9/81. Sqn Ldr 1/1/87. Retd ADMIN 3/1/89.
BROGAN G.E. Born 23/12/65. Commd 8/1/89. Flt Lt 8/7/90. Retd GD 7/3/91.
BROGAN M.J. Born 13/5/15. Commd 20/8/42. Flt Lt 17/5/56. Retd GD(G) 21/1/69.
BROMIDGE H.D. BA. Born 1/6/44. Commd 5/7/73. Sqn Ldr 1/7/81. Retd ENG 1/7/84.
BROMLEY C.J. Born 22/6/20. Commd 9/8/47. Flt Lt 9/2/52. Retd SUP 22/6/69.
BROMLEY D. Born 19/7/31. Commd 17/12/52. Sqn Ldr 1/1/66. Retd GD 1/9/73.
BROMLEY H.J. Born 10/4/26. Commd 15/11/48. Flt Lt 9/6/52. Retd GD 31/3/74.
BROMLEY P.E. Born 15/8/45. Commd 5/3/65. Flt Lt 5/9/70. Retd GD 25/9/75. Re-instated 27/8/80 to 16/3/82. GD(G)
BROOK C.J. Born 6/8/50. Commd 25/2/72. Flt Lt 25/2/75. Retd GD 25/8/82.
BROOK D.C.G. CB CBE. Born 23/12/35. Commd 31/7/56. AVM 1/7/86. Retd GD 22/12/89.
BROOK E.D.C. Born 28/1/29. Commd 23/9/65. Flt Lt 23/9/70. Retd ENG 13/10/73.
BROOK J.M. CB MB ChB FRCGP MFOM DAvMed. Born 26/5/34. Commd 15/2/59. AVM 1/1/92. Retd MED 26/5/94.
BROOK P.A. Born 15/11/30. Commd 12/3/52. Flt Lt 10/7/57. Retd GD 15/11/68.
BROOKE C.L. Born 5/6/44. Commd 22/8/71. Sqn Ldr 1/1/85. Retd ADMIN 31/3/94.
BROOKE G.U. Born 2/8/26. Commd 4/5/50. Flt Lt 26/5/55. Retd GD 2/8/64.
BROOKE K. Born 7/12/24. Commd 24/9/64. Flt Lt 24/9/67. Retd GD 14/10/75.
BROOKE M.C. AFC. Born 22/4/44. Commd 11/5/62. Wg Cdr 1/7/86. Retd GD 31/3/94.
BROOKE R. MCIPS MCMI. Born 24/8/48. Commd 30/5/69. Wg Cdr 1/7/91. Retd SUP 31/3/94.
BROOKE-SMITH B.A. Born 6/8/46. Commd 29/4/71. Flt Lt 29/10/75. Retd GD 9/8/87.
BROOKER J.A. Born 4/8/10. Commd 19/6/41. Flt Lt 25/7/47. Retd SEC 1/3/51.
BROOKES A.J. MBA BA FRSA. Born 16/2/45. Commd 5/1/66. Wg Cdr 1/1/88. Retd GD 25/6/99.
BROOKES M. Born 11/9/42. Commd 4/10/63. Flt Lt 11/3/68. Retd GD 3/1/80.
BROOKES M.W. BA. Born 25/2/38. Commd 7/8/59. Wg Cdr 1/1/78. Retd ADMIN 4/4/85.
BROOKFIELD C. Born 24/12/42. Commd 30/8/84. Flt Lt 30/8/88. Retd ENG 2/5/93.
BROOKING D. Born 5/5/47. Commd 28/2/69. Sqn Ldr 1/7/84. Retd GD 7/3/87.
BROOKS A. Born 26/10/27. Commd 28/7/67. Flt Lt 28/7/70. Retd GD 26/10/82.
BROOKS A.J. Born 11/3/33. Commd 21/11/51. Sqn Ldr 1/1/84. Retd GD 11/3/91.
BROOKS C.A. BDS MGDSRCS(Eng). Born 17/12/41. Commd 17/9/61. Wg Cdr 22/12/79. Retd DEL 14/3/97.
BROOKS C.L. Born 22/10/20. Commd 7/1/42. Sqn Ldr 1/7/50. Retd GD 1/10/61. rtg Wg Cdr
BROOKS D. BSc. Born 12/1/43. Commd 14/9/64. Sqn Ldr 1/7/76. Retd GD 10/5/99.
BROOKS D. Born 13/11/15. Commd 24/1/45. Sqn Offr 1/7/60. Retd SUP 30/11/62.
BROOKS D.A. BSc CEng MIMechE MRAeS MCMI. Born 20/3/34. Commd 20/12/57. Sqn Ldr 4/5/67.
    Retd ADMIN 9/11/85.
BROOKS D.G. Born 13/3/31. Commd 28/6/51. Flt Lt 10/10/56. Retd GD 13/3/69.
BROOKS D.J. Born 3/5/64. Commd 19/11/87. Sqn Ldr 1/1/02. Retd OPS SPT(FC) 1/1/04.
BROOKS D.R. BSc. Born 9/4/53. Commd 22/5/85. Sqn Ldr 1/1/91. Retd ADMIN (TRG) 24/10/03.
BROOKS E.A.S. BDS. Born 29/5/63. Commd 6/7/86. Wg Cdr 6/7/99. Retd DEL 6/7/02.
BROOKS G.S. MSc BA FRGS ACMA. Born 22/7/65. Commd 21/6/93. Sqn Ldr 1/7/99. Retd ADMIN (SEC) 14/2/04.
BROOKS J.H. Born 18/10/50. Commd 11/9/86. Sqn Ldr 1/1/97. Retd FLY(AEO) 20/10/03.

BROOKS J.L. Born 8/5/39. Commd 23/7/65. Flt Lt 6/4/74. Retd GD 6/4/80.
BROOKS K.A. Born 25/10/53. Commd 10/5/90. Sqn Ldr 1/1/99. Retd GD 31/5/01.
BROOKS L.M. Born 26/8/31. Commd 3/5/51. Flt Lt 23/11/57. Retd GD 12/11/71.
BROOKS N.J. BSc. Born 21/10/45. Commd 8/9/69. Flt Lt 8/12/70. Retd GD 18/11/88.
BROOKS N.N. BA. Born 12/2/52. Commd 13/2/92. Flt Lt 13/2/94. Retd ADMIN 7/8/00.
BROOKS P. Born 9/10/58. Commd 27/3/80. Flt Lt 27/9/86. Retd GD(G) 15/5/89.
BROOKS P.E. BA. Born 15/11/48. Commd 28/8/72. Flt Lt 29/11/75. Retd ADMIN 29/8/88.
BROOKS R. Born 3/9/31. Commd 7/11/51. Flt Lt 7/5/56. Retd PI 2/7/82.
BROOKS R.F. DFM. Born 1/2/25. Commd 27/10/67. Flt Lt 27/10/70. Retd GD(G) 1/2/83.
BROOKS W.J. Born 26/11/28. Commd 3/5/51. Sqn Ldr 1/1/64. Retd GD(G) 28/2/79.
BROOKWICK T.R.W. BSc. Born 26/3/61. Commd 13/2/83. Flt Lt 13/5/84. Retd GD 17/8/95.
BROOM B.A. Born 31/7/45. Commd 15/10/81. Sqn Ldr 1/7/91. Retd ADMIN 1/1/97.
BROOM C.J. Born 12/9/56. Commd 6/10/77. Sqn Ldr 1/7/90. Retd GD 12/9/94.
BROOM C.J. MBE. Born 4/12/22. Commd 24/1/52. Sqn Ldr 1/1/68. Retd GD 4/12/77.
BROOM T.A. Born 16/4/31. Commd 5/5/51. Flt Lt 5/11/55. Retd GD 16/4/69.
BROOME M.J. BA. Born 28/9/60. Commd 4/1/83. Sqn Ldr 1/1/96. Retd GD 4/1/99.
BROOMFIELD J.D. Born 26/8/47. Commd 22/9/67. Flt Lt 23/12/73. Retd ADMIN 30/9/77.
BROOMFIELD W.T.H. Born 21/8/28. Commd 22/7/66. Flt Lt 22/7/69. Retd ENG 1/1/85.
BROTHERHOOD W.R. CBE. Born 22/1/12. Commd 17/2/32. A Cdre 1/7/56. Retd GD 13/2/61.
BROTHERS P.M. CBE DSO DFC*. Born 30/9/17. Commd 23/3/36. A Cdre 1/7/66. Retd GD 4/4/73.
BROTHERTON I.P. Born 6/11/30. Commd 29/11/50. Sqn Ldr 1/1/66. Retd GD 18/3/77.
BROTHERTON J. Born 17/4/25. Commd 13/7/45. Sqn Ldr 20/6/63. Retd EDN 28/8/70.
BROTHERTON J. BEng. Born 6/6/64. Commd 14/2/88. Flt Lt 14/8/89. Retd FLY(N) 14/2/04.
BROTHERTON S.C.D. BSc. Born 14/11/59. Commd 27/3/83. Flt Lt 27/6/86. Retd ADMIN 31/3/92.
BROUGH I.S. BSc. Born 14/11/59. Commd 27/3/83. Flt Lt 27/6/86. Retd ADMIN 31/3/92.
BROUGH J.H. Born 20/1/62. Commd 26/4/84. Sqn Ldr 1/1/97. Retd GD 20/4/00.
BROUGH S.G. BEng CEng MRAeS. Born 27/7/54. Commd 8/10/75. Sqn Ldr 1/1/88. Retd ENG 31/1/01.
BROUGHTON A. MSc MB ChB MRCPath DCP DTM&H. Born 19/6/35. Commd 4/9/60. Wg Cdr 4/9/72.
    Retd MED 4/9/73.
BROUGHTON D.W. MBE BA FRIN. Born 27/12/39. Commd 28/9/60. Gp Capt 1/1/90. Retd GD 5/4/91.
BROUGHTON J. FCMI. Born 18/2/34. Commd 24/9/52. A Cdre 1/7/86. Retd GD 1/1/89.
BROUGHTON J.C.W. Born 18/11/41. Commd 3/5/68. Sqn Ldr 1/7/87. Retd GD(G) 1/5/93.
BROUGHTON K. Born 26/8/30. Commd 11/4/51. Flt Lt 11/1/57. Retd GD 14/9/70.
BROUGHTON P.J. Born 1/7/18. Commd 11/8/41. Sqn Offr 1/1/52. Retd SEC 5/10/52.
BROUGHTON R.P. Born 30/6/32. Commd 19/7/51. Flt Lt 13/4/60. Retd GD 30/6/70.
BROUGHTON T.W. Born 24/7/36. Commd 5/11/70. Flt Lt 5/11/72. Retd GD 31/7/76.
BROWN A. Born 26/4/47. Commd 3/7/80. Sqn Ldr 1/1/91. Retd ENGINEER 12/2/05.
BROWN A. MIIM MCMI. Born 15/12/31. Commd 29/7/63. Sqn Ldr 29/4/73. Retd ADMIN 15/12/91.
BROWN A.C. Born 2/5/25. Commd 28/12/43. Flt Lt 18/9/54. Retd GD 11/12/65.
BROWN A.C. Born 15/3/38. Commd 11/5/78. Sqn Ldr 1/1/89. Retd SUP 29/3/90.
BROWN A.D. MBE AFC. Born 12/9/48. Commd 10/9/70. Flt Lt 10/3/76. Retd GD 29/4/89.
BROWN A.D. Born 19/5/63. Commd 23/5/85. Sqn Ldr 1/1/98. Retd GD 19/5/01.
BROWN A.J. BA. Born 22/9/73. Commd 30/11/97. Flt Lt 30/5/01. Retd ADMIN (SEC) 26/1/04.
BROWN A.P. Born 13/3/20. Commd 22/9/44. Flt Lt 22/3/48. Retd GD 13/3/63.
BROWN A.S. Born 7/9/37. Commd 20/8/55. Sqn Ldr 1/1/69. Retd GD 7/9/74.
BROWN A.S. Born 18/2/56. Commd 31/1/80. Flt Lt 8/3/84. Retd ADMIN 25/10/94.
BROWN A.S.E. Born 8/8/47. Commd 11/8/86. Sqn Ldr 1/7/96. Retd ENG 8/8/02.
BROWN A.W.J. Born 14/12/30. Commd 9/9/54. Sqn Ldr 1/1/76. Retd GD 3/4/84.
BROWN B. OBE. Born 28/11/11. Commd 28/8/41. Wg Cdr 1/1/61. Retd ENG 27/10/62.
BROWN C. Born 26/2/27. Commd 8/11/68. Flt Lt 8/11/73. Retd ENG 17/12/77.
BROWN C.G. BA. Born 25/12/43. Commd 23/9/68. Flt Lt 23/3/73. Retd ENG 20/9/87.
BROWN C.J. MILT MCIPD. Born 23/8/50. Commd 8/5/86. Flt Lt 8/5/90. Retd SUP 2/4/93.
BROWN C.McD. Born 11/5/35. Commd 28/2/57. Sqn Ldr 1/1/67. Retd GD 11/5/73.
BROWN C.N.A. BSc CEng MIMechE. Born 27/8/52. Commd 22/6/75. Sqn Ldr 1/1/84. Retd ENG 2/6/97.
BROWN C.R. Born 14/10/41. Commd 15/10/71. Sqn Ldr 14/10/77. Retd ADMIN 19/4/83.
BROWN C.R. Born 16/5/46. Commd 10/6/66. Flt Lt 10/12/71. Retd GD 16/5/84.
BROWN D.A. Born 15/9/27. Commd 15/6/50. Sqn Ldr 1/7/62. Retd SUP 15/9/65.
BROWN D.A. Born 3/5/56. Commd 2/2/78. Wg Cdr 1/1/97. Retd GD 10/7/00.
BROWN D.A. Born 8/12/36. Commd 7/12/54. Sqn Ldr 1/1/90. Retd GD 8/12/94.
BROWN D.C. OBE. Born 20/4/45. Commd 31/10/63. Gp Capt 1/1/90. Retd SUP 22/4/94.
BROWN D.G.P. MB ChB. Born 3/10/24. Commd 12/1/52. Wg Cdr 12/1/64. Retd MED 28/1/78.
BROWN D.J. Born 20/5/44. Commd 22/2/63. Sqn Ldr 1/7/75. Retd GD 30/5/88.
BROWN D.J. Born 8/11/45. Commd 31/1/64. Flt Lt 28/3/70. Retd GD 31/3/94.
BROWN D.M.H. Born 14/9/33. Commd 27/3/75. Sqn Ldr 1/1/84. Retd ENG 14/12/92.
BROWN D.N. MBE. Born 27/12/28. Commd 28/9/61. Wg Cdr 1/1/80. Retd ENG 1/7/83.
BROWN D.O. Born 9/8/18. Commd 16/8/41. Sqn Ldr 1/7/49. Retd GD 14/4/58.

BROWN D.P. Born 25/2/31. Commd 14/9/54. Flt Lt 14/3/59. Retd GD 14/9/70.
BROWN D.P. Born 8/1/57. Commd 11/6/81. Flt Lt 11/12/86. Retd GD 10/11/96.
BROWN D.P. Born 21/1/54. Commd 6/11/80. Sqn Ldr 1/1/90. Retd ADMIN 31/8/94.
BROWN D.S. BA MCIPD MCMI DipEd. Born 6/8/36. Commd 7/8/63. Gp Capt 1/7/90. Retd ADMIN 1/7/93.
BROWN D.T. MRAeS. Born 2/4/19. Commd 19/8/42. Wg Cdr 1/1/63. Retd ENG 13/1/71.
BROWN D.W. Born 2/3/46. Commd 26/5/67. Flt Lt 4/11/70. Retd GD 5/5/79.
BROWN D.W. BEM MInstAM. Born 15/1/41. Commd 6/5/83. Sqn Ldr 1/7/92. Retd ADMIN 15/1/96.
BROWN E. MRAeS. Born 21/4/17. Commd 15/4/43. Wg Cdr 1/7/64. Retd ENG 1/11/68.
BROWN E.A. Born 6/11/36. Commd 23/11/78. Sqn Ldr 1/1/87. Retd ENG 6/11/94.
BROWN E.F. DFC AFC. Born 23/12/23. Commd 14/5/43. Wg Cdr 1/7/59. Retd GD 23/9/68.
BROWN E.G. Born 15/8/35. Commd 4/8/53. Sqn Ldr 1/1/68. Retd GD 15/4/77.
BROWN E.J.B. Born 16/12/18. Commd 4/4/49. Wg Cdr 1/7/56. Retd RGT 24/12/68.
BROWN E.M. MA MCIPD. Born 3/4/44. Commd 16/1/72. Sqn Ldr 16/3/77. Retd ADMIN 16/1/88.
BROWN E.McN. Born 2/11/39. Commd 19/6/61. Flt Lt 19/12/66. Retd GD 28/6/73.
BROWN E.N.L. Born 30/12/23. Commd 10/7/52. Flt Offr 10/7/58. Retd SEC 2/5/68.
BROWN E.S. Born 21/4/57. Commd 28/10/76. Wg Cdr 1/7/95. Retd GD 2/8/02.
BROWN E.W. Born 26/2/32. Commd 4/6/52. Sqn Ldr 1/1/84. Retd GD 26/2/87.
BROWN F. BSc CEng DipSoton FCMI MIEE. Born 10/3/34. Commd 22/11/56. Gp Capt 1/1/83. Retd ADMIN 30/11/84.
BROWN F.J. Born 7/8/31. Commd 10/10/63. Flt Lt 10/10/68. Retd CAT 29/9/73.
BROWN F.L. Born 30/6/17. Commd 6/6/57. Sqn Ldr 1/7/69. Retd ENG 30/6/72.
BROWN G.A. Born 1/3/34. Commd 15/10/52. Flt Lt 17/9/58. Retd GD 30/9/75.
BROWN G.B. Born 20/11/45. Commd 5/11/65. Sqn Ldr 1/1/96. Retd FLY(P) 20/11/03.
BROWN G.G. Born 16/11/21. Commd 6/1/44. Sqn Ldr 1/7/55. Retd ENG 9/8/69.
BROWN G.G. Born 3/9/30. Commd 7/12/61. Flt Lt 7/12/66. Retd GD 21/4/77.
BROWN G.H. Born 8/2/14. Commd 16/3/45. Flt Lt 19/12/51. Retd SUP 6/9/58.
BROWN G.J. Born 1/4/39. Commd 21/10/66. Sqn Ldr 1/7/80. Retd ENG 4/5/90.
BROWN G.J. MIOSH. Born 19/6/53. Commd 22/6/89. Flt Lt 22/6/91. Retd FLY(AEO) 12/12/03.
BROWN G.P. Born 3/11/47. Commd 2/12/66. Sqn Ldr 1/7/84. Retd GD 1/7/87.
BROWN G.R. CEng MRAeS MIEE. Born 8/8/32. Commd 14/1/54. Wg Cdr 1/7/74. Retd ENG 15/1/76.
BROWN H.J. Born 4/12/35. Commd 9/8/60. Sqn Ldr 1/1/71. Retd ADMIN 9/8/76.
BROWN H.J.R. Born 25/9/10. Commd 11/2/43. Flt Lt 14/7/54. Retd SUP 26/10/65.
BROWN H.M. MSc BA. Born 17/7/51. Commd 17/11/81. Sqn Ldr 1/7/86. Retd ADMIN 14/3/96.
BROWN H.M.K. MCMI. Born 5/4/28. Commd 27/7/49. Sqn Ldr 1/1/61. Retd GD 25/6/76.
BROWN H.T. DFC MCMI. Born 17/2/22. Commd 7/8/47. Wg Cdr 1/1/61. Retd GD 28/7/76.
BROWN I. Born 23/9/54. Commd 8/4/82. Fg Offr 8/10/84. Retd GD 26/6/87.
BROWN I.P. Born 30/5/59. Commd 31/1/80. Sqn Ldr 1/7/91. Retd ADMIN 30/6/98.
BROWN J. Born 4/4/33. Commd 27/2/52. Wg Cdr 1/1/80. Retd GD(G) 4/4/88.
BROWN J. BA. Born 12/5/47. Commd 17/7/70. Sqn Ldr 1/1/80. Retd ENG 12/5/91.
BROWN J. Born 21/2/44. Commd 15/6/83. Flt Lt 15/6/87. Retd ENG 10/7/98.
BROWN J. BA. Born 3/6/47. Commd 16/9/76. Wg Cdr 1/1/91. Retd ENG 3/7/02.
BROWN J. Born 18/8/28. Commd 4/9/58. Sqn Ldr 1/1/78. Retd GD 18/8/86.
BROWN J. Born 16/10/13. Commd 24/2/55. Flt Lt 24/2/58. Retd SEC 16/10/68.
BROWN J. Born 3/8/21. Commd 26/9/57. Sqn Ldr 1/7/72. Retd ENG 29/3/74.
BROWN J.A. Born 15/4/47. Commd 2/12/66. Sqn Ldr 1/7/78. Retd GD 15/4/85.
BROWN J.C. Born 2/3/32. Commd 15/12/53. Sqn Ldr 1/7/64. Retd GD 11/3/70.
BROWN J.D. Born 5/9/31. Commd 29/12/51. Flt Lt 25/4/57. Retd GD(G) 25/6/77.
BROWN J.E. Born 20/10/21. Commd 30/10/44. Sqn Ldr 1/1/68. Retd GD 19/4/73.
BROWN J.E. Born 7/1/38. Commd 16/12/58. Wg Cdr 1/1/80. Retd GD 1/6/84.
BROWN J.E. Born 4/10/61. Commd 6/5/83. Sqn Ldr 1/7/95. Retd GD 4/10/99.
BROWN J.G.V. Born 14/2/40. Commd 1/7/82. Flt Lt 1/7/85. Retd GD(G) 31/3/95.
BROWN J.H. Born 31/1/41. Commd 2/3/61. Sqn Ldr 1/1/74. Retd SUP 2/4/93.
BROWN J.H.F. Born 11/1/29. Commd 19/6/52. Wg Cdr 1/1/80. Retd GD 11/1/84.
BROWN J.J.D. MA CEng MRAeS DCAe. Born 8/8/35. Commd 25/9/54. Wg Cdr 1/1/75. Retd ENG 8/8/90.
BROWN J.L.L. Born 16/10/41. Commd 28/4/67. Flt Lt 6/12/69. Retd GD 16/10/79.
BROWN J.M. OBE CEng FIEE MCMI. Born 17/9/33. Commd 26/9/71. Wg Cdr 1/7/76. Retd ENG 17/9/88.
BROWN J.M. Born 31/5/34. Commd 10/9/70. Flt Lt 10/9/73. Retd GD 5/8/77.
BROWN J.McC. BSc. Born 22/2/46. Commd 20/1/80. Fg Offr 20/1/78. Retd ADMIN 20/2/82.
BROWN J.R. Born 12/1/45. Commd 25/3/64. Wg Cdr 1/1/88. Retd GD 8/12/97.
BROWN J.S. Born 18/11/47. Commd 3/10/74. Flt Lt 3/10/76. Retd ENG 18/11/85.
BROWN J.W.J. MCSP MCMI. Born 30/7/30. Commd 1/6/72. Sqn Ldr 1/7/85. Retd MED(SEC) 23/11/88.
BROWN K. DFC. Born 28/11/23. Commd 17/9/43. Sqn Ldr 1/7/72. Retd GD 28/11/73.
BROWN K.C. Born 11/4/14. Commd 24/3/43. Sqn Ldr 1/1/66. Retd SEC 15/5/69.
BROWN K.M.A. Born 1/5/46. Commd 9/3/72. Sqn Ldr 1/7/90. Retd ADMIN 1/1/98.
BROWN K.R. The Rev. BA. Born 17/3/48. Commd 22/4/79. Retd Wg Cdr 22/4/95.
BROWN L. MBE. Born 29/8/36. Commd 7/5/64. Wg Cdr 1/7/85. Retd ENG 29/8/88.
BROWN L.B. Born 20/8/37. Commd 2/8/68. Sqn Ldr 1/1/76. Retd ADMIN 20/8/87.

BROWN L.B. AFM. Born 13/2/17. Commd 3/8/50. Flt Lt 1/8/55. Retd GD 26/5/62.
BROWN L.I. Born 14/1/23. Commd 20/10/43. Sqn Ldr 1/7/71. Retd GD(G) 14/1/78.
BROWN L.W. Born 1/3/45. Commd 1/2/65. Flt Lt 28/8/70. Retd GD(G) 1/3/83.
BROWN M. Born 2/7/33. Commd 12/11/57. Sqn Ldr 1/1/70. Retd GD 15/2/76.
BROWN M.A. MSc CEng MRAeS. Born 10/8/63. Commd 29/4/84. Sqn Ldr 1/7/98. Retd ENGINEER 29/7/03.
BROWN M.H. Born 4/11/46. Commd 15/12/88. Flt Lt 15/12/92. Retd ENGINEER 4/11/03.
BROWN M.J. BA MCMI. Born 3/1/37. Commd 11/10/65. Sqn Ldr 1/7/77. Retd SUP 3/1/93.
BROWN M.J.D. MA CEng MRAeS MRIN. Born 9/5/36. Commd 25/9/54. AVM 1/7/86. Retd ENG 9/5/91.
BROWN M.R. Born 31/5/35. Commd 17/9/57. Sqn Ldr 1/7/71. Retd GD 28/9/88.
BROWN M.R. MIIM MCMI. Born 2/6/43. Commd 4/11/82. Sqn Ldr 1/1/91. Retd ENG 2/6/98.
BROWN M.S. Born 16/3/50. Commd 22/5/70. Flt Lt 22/11/75. Retd GD 16/6/80.
BROWN M.S. BA. Born 11/2/32. Commd 17/12/52. Sqn Ldr 1/7/65. Retd ADMIN 2/6/84.
BROWN M.T. Born 16/10/35. Commd 17/7/59. Flt Lt 7/7/64. Retd EDN 19/9/65.
BROWN M.W. Born 10/5/45. Commd 3/3/67. Flt Lt 3/9/69. Retd GD 11/5/76.
BROWN M.W. Born 30/9/47. Commd 18/9/66. Wg Cdr 1/1/98. Retd GD 8/7/01.
BROWN N. Born 19/12/50. Commd 3/7/80. Flt Lt 3/7/82. Retd GD 1/9/86.
BROWN N.A. Born 28/4/65. Commd 2/11/88. Flt Lt 2/5/94. Retd GD 14/3/97.
BROWN N.F. Born 14/12/19. Commd 19/2/45. Flt Lt 23/9/47. Retd GD 27/7/63.
BROWN N.J.B. Born 18/9/52. Commd 8/10/87. Fg Offr 8/10/87. Retd ENG 25/4/93. rtg Flt Lt
BROWN O.C. Born 18/7/13. Commd 23/2/43. Flt Lt 27/5/54. Retd GD(G) 14/2/62.
BROWN P.A. Born 24/4/47. Commd 24/4/80. Flt Lt 24/4/82. Retd ENG 24/4/88.
BROWN P.A. Born 8/1/57. Commd 2/2/84. Flt Lt 8/5/86. Retd SUP 23/6/95.
BROWN P.C. Born 24/2/37. Commd 10/2/59. Sqn Ldr 1/1/90. Retd GD 1/1/93.
BROWN P.J. BSc. Born 18/10/40. Commd 9/9/63. Sqn Ldr 1/7/78. Retd GD 9/3/93.
BROWN P.M.D. BSc CEng MRAeS MCMI. Born 17/7/52. Commd 25/9/71. Wg Cdr 1/1/96. Retd ENG 1/10/02.
BROWN P.S. DFC. Born 1/12/23. Commd 22/2/45. Flt Lt 29/12/55. Retd GD(G) 30/6/69.
BROWN R. Born 1/7/35. Commd 28/7/67. Flt Lt 28/7/69. Retd GD 7/1/75.
BROWN R. McN. Born 3/12/32. Commd 15/12/53. Wg Cdr 1/1/71. Retd GD 1/5/85.
BROWN R. Born 18/1/33. Commd 12/3/52. Sqn Ldr 1/7/68. Retd GD 13/11/84.
BROWN R. Born 2/12/47. Commd 16/8/68. Flt Lt 2/12/74. Retd SUP 1/1/76.
BROWN R. Born 29/12/31. Commd 11/10/69. Sqn Ldr 1/12/79. Retd MED(T) 30/5/85.
BROWN R. Born 21/7/34. Commd 4/3/71. Flt Lt 4/3/73. Retd SUP 4/3/79.
BROWN R.A. Born 4/5/28. Commd 21/12/48. Flt Lt 22/1/55. Retd PI 31/8/78.
BROWN R.A. Born 19/4/47. Commd 26/8/66. Flt Lt 17/12/72. Retd GD(G) 27/1/79.
BROWN R.B. Born 9/11/46. Commd 11/5/86. Flt Lt 11/5/92. Retd ADMIN 11/5/02.
BROWN R.D. Born 11/12/41. Commd 29/1/63. Flt Lt 3/6/69. Retd GD 3/2/79. Re-instated 19/1/83. Sqn Ldr 1/1/93.
   Retd GD 1/5/96.
BROWN R.E. Born 2/6/24. Commd 8/8/51. Sqn Ldr 1/1/67. Retd GD 2/6/84.
BROWN R.F. MA BM BCh FRCS (Eng). Born 11/9/25. Commd 3/3/52. A Cdre 1/7/83. Retd MED 9/4/89.
BROWN R.G.H. Born 4/1/41. Commd 17/7/64. Flt Lt 6/10/71. Retd GD 2/9/80.
BROWN R.J. Born 27/12/60. Commd 20/5/82. Flt Lt 20/11/87. Retd GD 14/9/96.
BROWN R.R. The Rev. BA BD. Born 24/3/36. Commd 7/8/67. Retd Gp Capt 31/10/94.
BROWN R.S. MBE MCIPD MCMI. Born 26/1/23. Commd 4/6/44. Wg Cdr 1/7/63. Retd ADMIN 4/9/76.
BROWN R.W. Born 10/6/31. Commd 3/6/65. Sqn Ldr 9/5/76. Retd MED(SEC) 10/2/79.
BROWN R.W. Born 10/4/30. Commd 30/8/62. Sqn Ldr 1/1/77. Retd ENG 1/5/80.
BROWN S.D. Born 17/12/48. Commd 23/3/67. Flt Lt 23/9/72. Retd GD 17/12/86.
BROWN S.K. Born 11/4/46. Commd 22/5/64. Flt Lt 15/4/70. Retd GD 11/4/01.
BROWN S.P. BSc CEng MRAeS. Born 28/5/51. Commd 15/9/69. Sqn Ldr 1/7/87. Retd ENG 29/5/01.
BROWN T.C.L. GM MB BS MRCS LRCP DPH DIH. Born 1/9/24. Commd 31/10/47. Wg Cdr 1/4/62. Retd MED 1/5/64.
BROWN T.H. Born 8/11/48. Commd 27/2/70. Flt Lt 27/2/73. Retd GD 22/9/87.
BROWN T.L. BEM. Born 9/1/21. Commd 15/9/60. Sqn Ldr 1/1/72. Retd ENG 7/4/73.
BROWN W. Born 1/7/31. Commd 11/11/65. Sqn Ldr 15/7/73. Retd EDN 15/10/74.
BROWN W.A. CEng MRAeS. Born 9/12/47. Commd 3/5/68. Sqn Ldr 1/7/82. Retd ENG 9/12/85.
BROWN W.G. Born 24/10/11. Commd 26/7/45. Flt Lt 4/1/51. Retd SEC 1/7/54.
BROWN W.H.P. FIIP MCMI. Born 10/3/31. Commd 29/10/52. Sqn Ldr 1/7/69. Retd PI 11/4/81.
BROWN W.J. CEng MRAeS MIEE. Born 8/8/32. Commd 14/1/54. Wg Cdr 1/7/74. Retd ENG 15/1/76.
BROWN W.P.W. BSc. Born 5/12/53. Commd 7/3/76. Sqn Ldr 1/1/88. Retd GD 7/3/92.
BROWNBRIDGE S.M. BA. Born 29/7/52. Commd 25/9/71. Flt Lt 15/4/79. Retd SY 11/6/80.
BROWNE B.R. Born 3/3/23. Commd 25/5/43. Sqn Ldr 1/1/60. Retd GD 13/6/72.
BROWNE C.D.A. CB DFC FCMI. Born 8/7/22. Commd 1/6/41. A Cdre 1/1/68. Retd GD 8/1/73.
BROWNE D.F.M. CBE AFC* FCMI. Born 3/7/24. Commd 14/1/44. A Cdre 1/1/74. Retd GD 30/9/77.
BROWNE D.K. Born 7/3/42. Commd 7/6/73. Flt Lt 7/6/75. Retd GD 7/3/97.
BROWNE G.B. OBE. Born 30/3/35. Commd 26/7/55. Wg Cdr 1/1/78. Retd GD 30/3/93.
BROWNE J.F.P. MBE MCMI AIDPM. Born 10/5/37. Commd 25/7/60. Wg Cdr 1/7/78. Retd SUP 28/2/89.
BROWNE J.P.R. CBE BSc(Eng) CEng FRAeS FICE FCMI. Born 27/4/37. Commd 17/9/58. AVM 1/7/89.
   Retd ENG 27/4/92.

BROWNE P.H. Born 6/3/58. Commd 1/12/77. Flt Lt 6/3/96. Retd GD 6/3/96.
BROWNE P.J. Born 10/10/30. Commd 17/5/62. Sqn Ldr 1/1/74. Retd ENG 19/1/82.
BROWNE R.D. Born 4/4/31. Commd 23/7/52. Flt Lt 25/7/66. Retd GD 4/4/74.
BROWNE R.M.c.V. BSc CEng MRAeS MCMI. Born 16/8/40. Commd 14/9/65. Gp Capt 1/1/86. Retd ENG 16/8/95.
BROWNE W.E. LHA. Born 16/6/27. Commd 7/12/61. Wg Cdr 1/7/75. Retd MED(SEC) 16/6/82.
BROWNE W.N. DFC. Born 20/8/47. Commd 15/9/67. Sqn Ldr 1/1/91. Retd GD 1/10/01.
BROWNING B.E.L. OBE BA. Born 2/6/27. Commd 31/7/56. Sqn Ldr 1/1/73. Retd SEC 4/6/77.
BROWNING D.A.V. Born 14/2/33. Commd 27/3/70. Flt Lt 27/3/76. Retd SEC 30/9/83.
BROWNING G.R.C. Born 2/5/46. Commd 28/10/66. Flt Lt 4/5/72. Retd GD 4/5/75.
BROWNING H.H.J. Born 11/7/30. Commd 11/4/51. Sqn Ldr 1/7/61. Retd GD 15/10/71.
BROWNING I.M.R. DFC. Born 17/9/20. Commd 6/2/39. Sqn Ldr 1/8/47. Retd GD 18/9/58.
BROWNING N.J. Born 1/12/46. Commd 18/11/66. Flt Lt 6/5/73. Retd SY 1/12/84.
BROWNLEE A.A. Born 12/12/13. Commd 11/11/42. Flt Offr 11/11/47. Retd SUP 11/3/63.
BROWNLOW B. CB OBE AFC FRAeS. Born 13/1/29. Commd 7/7/49. AVM 1/1/80. Retd GD 13/1/84.
BROWNLOW R.P. Born 9/9/39. Commd 19/9/59. Gp Capt 1/1/91. Retd GD 9/9/94.
BROWNLOW S.M. Born 12/12/62. Commd 26/4/84. Sqn Ldr 1/7/97. Retd GD 16/3/01.
BROWSE C.R. Born 6/2/38. Commd 26/5/61. Flt Lt 26/11/71. Retd GD 29/11/76.
BROWSE J.S.A.McM. Born 12/8/38. Commd 8/12/61. Flt Lt 8/6/67. Retd GD 22/8/77.
BRUCE A. MA AHSM. Born 27/10/49. Commd 26/11/81. Sqn Ldr 1/1/90. Retd MED(SEC) 2/4/93.
BRUCE A.I. DPhysEd. Born 11/12/22. Commd 25/9/45. Wg Cdr 1/7/69. Retd PE 1/7/73.
BRUCE A.J. Born 2/10/43. Commd 27/2/70. Wg Cdr 1/7/88. Retd ADMIN 26/11/94.
BRUCE C.W. OBE. Born 28/11/35. Commd 10/4/56. A Cdre 1/1/88. Retd GD 2/4/91.
BRUCE D. Born 14/10/45. Commd 25/2/66. Wg Cdr 1/7/90. Retd GD 25/11/00.
BRUCE D.A. Born 2/6/48. Commd 5/8/76. Sqn Ldr 1/1/88. Retd ENG 31/10/00.
BRUCE D.V. Born 25/8/58. Commd 22/6/89. Flt Lt 22/6/91. Retd ENG 22/6/97.
BRUCE L. Born 21/4/32. Commd 3/11/60. Sqn Ldr 1/7/76. Retd GD 2/12/86.
BRUCE M.J. Born 20/8/46. Commd 8/1/65. Gp Capt 1/7/91. Retd GD 14/3/96.
BRUCE P.R. Born 4/2/47. Commd 2/8/68. Sqn Ldr 1/1/80. Retd GD 4/8/02.
BRUCE R.P. BEng. Born 23/6/64. Commd 26/10/86. Sqn Ldr 1/1/98. Retd GD 26/10/02.
BRUFF K.J. Born 14/6/62. Commd 27/8/87. Sqn Ldr 1/1/98. Retd ADMIN (SEC) 2/7/04.
BRUFF S.A.F. BSc. Born 27/6/55. Commd 13/4/80. Flt Lt 13/4/83. Retd ENG 7/5/96.
BRUMAGE M.W. MA CertEd. Born 15/2/46. Commd 18/11/79. Wg Cdr 1/7/94. Retd ADMIN 2/11/00.
BRUMBY F. Born 24/10/36. Commd 8/4/82. Flt Lt 8/4/85. Retd ENG 31/7/91.
BRUMPTON R. BA FRAeS. Born 4/1/47. Commd 21/4/67. A Cdre 1/7/97. Retd ENG 4/1/02.
BRUNGER W.D. Born 3/4/27. Commd 21/11/51. Sqn Ldr 1/7/63. Retd GD 2/6/76.
BRUNING M.P.W.C.E. Born 1/11/42. Commd 6/11/67. Sqn Ldr 1/7/85. Retd OPS SPT 1/11/97.
BRUNNING R. Born 25/4/43. Commd 10/9/70. Sqn Ldr 1/1/84. Retd GD(G) 1/1/87.
BRUNSDEN J.P. Born 14/3/43. Commd 28/4/65. Sqn Ldr 1/7/79. Retd GD 14/3/98.
BRUNSDEN-BROWN R.A.T. Born 25/8/32. Commd 28/6/51. Flt Lt 14/5/58. Retd GD 25/8/70.
BRUNSKILL J. Born 7/9/32. Commd 4/6/52. Flt Lt 14/10/53. Retd GD 1/1/76.
BRUNT R. Born 7/4/43. Commd 21/5/65. Flt Lt 8/3/72. Retd GD 7/11/75.
BRUNTON I.A.J. Born 2/6/45. Commd 18/8/67. Flt Lt 1/7/69. Retd GD 30/12/75.
BRUSHNEEN R.P. Born 11/1/45. Commd 27/1/77. Flt Lt 10/9/79. Retd ADMIN 30/4/83.
BRUTON I.F. BA. Born 8/11/50. Commd 3/1/71. Gp Capt 1/7/97. Retd GD 31/5/03.
BRUYN A.A. Born 28/4/36. Commd 9/2/55. Sqn Ldr 1/7/89. Retd GD 1/7/92.
BRYAN A.S. Born 24/11/58. Commd 3/7/80. Flt Lt 17/12/86. Retd SUP 13/3/92.
BRYAN C.J. BEM. Born 17/3/29. Commd 23/9/66. Flt Lt 23/9/68. Retd ENG 23/9/74.
BRYAN D.R. Born 9/12/24. Commd 26/4/50. Sqn Ldr 1/1/61. Retd GD 31/5/67.
BRYAN G. OBE MCMI. Born 5/9/25. Commd 25/8/49. Wg Cdr 1/7/67. Retd GD 8/4/78.
BRYAN J.H. CEng FIEE FCMI MRAeS MIIM. Born 14/11/33. Commd 30/4/59. Wg Cdr 1/7/76. Retd ENG 1/11/87.
BRYAN N.A. The Rev. BA. Born 7/9/39. Commd 11/8/69. Retd Wg Cdr 7/9/94.
BRYAN P.S. Born 21/4/34. Commd 31/10/69. Sqn Ldr 1/7/80. Retd ENG 21/4/84.
BRYAN W.A.M. Born 17/6/40. Commd 20/9/79. Flt Lt 20/9/81. Retd ADMIN 20/9/87.
BRYAN W.J. Born 19/6/22. Commd 3/12/59. Flt Lt 3/12/65. Retd ENG 19/6/73.
BRYANS J.C.W. MSc BA BSc CEng MIEE. Born 9/3/45. Commd 1/11/79. Wg Cdr 1/7/94. Retd ADMIN 21/12/99.
BRYANT D.T. CB OBE. Born 1/11/33. Commd 23/7/52. AVM 1/1/85. Retd GD 7/4/89.
BRYANT F.P. MSc. Born 29/12/43. Commd 9/8/63. Sqn Ldr 1/1/74. Retd GD 6/12/82.
BRYANT J.M. Born 14/7/66. Commd 14/7/84. Wg Cdr 1/7/84. Retd GD 28/4/90.
BRYANT M.K. DLUT. Born 18/12/42. Commd 5/11/70. Sqn Ldr 1/7/80. Retd ENG 1/7/83.
BRYANT P.N.R. Born 1/11/53. Commd 30/8/84. Sqn Ldr 1/7/94. Retd ADMIN 30/8/98.
BRYANT R.F. Born 17/5/29. Commd 5/5/51. Wg Cdr 1/1/75. Retd GD 14/10/83.
BRYANT S.H. Born 17/12/10. Commd 27/12/43. Fg Offr 27/12/43. Retd ASD 20/1/46.
BRYDEN R.W. Born 12/7/41. Commd 5/3/65. Gp Capt 1/7/89. Retd ADMIN 17/9/94.
BRYDON R.J. AFC AFM. Born 10/3/22. Commd 15/3/44. Flt Lt 7/3/62. Retd GD 10/3/77.
BRYETT D.B. BSc. Born 1/8/33. Commd 2/11/56. Sqn Ldr 2/5/66. Retd ADMIN 12/1/87.
BRYSON L.C. Born 12/7/48. Commd 29/11/68. Flt Lt 29/5/74. Retd GD 1/9/85.

BUCHAN A. Born 21/12/46. Commd 7/1/71. Gp Capt 1/7/93. Retd SUP 14/3/97.
BUCHAN D.J. Born 20/9/42. Commd 3/8/62. Sqn Ldr 1/7/80. Retd OPS SPT 20/9/97.
BUCHAN F.N. Born 17/5/25. Commd 27/5/54. Flt Lt 27/11/57. Retd GD 17/5/63.
BUCHAN J.T. Born 2/11/19. Commd 18/12/43. Flt Lt 29/6/50. Retd GD(G) 2/11/74.
BUCHAN J.W. Born 30/3/65. Commd 26/2/89. Flt Lt 15/5/91. Retd OPS SPT(ATC) 30/3/03.
BUCHAN T.G. Born 2/11/20. Commd 23/3/66. Flt Lt 23/3/72. Retd SUP 20/11/73.
BUCHANAN D.R. MCMI. Born 10/8/22. Commd 4/5/53. Wg Cdr 1/7/71. Retd SEC 12/10/75.
BUCHANAN I.K. Born 15/5/57. Commd 13/12/79. Wg Cdr 1/1/98. Retd ADMIN 13/8/01.
BUCHANAN J.L. Born 21/8/57. Commd 9/8/79. Flt Lt 20/12/85. Retd SUP 25/7/93.
BUCHANAN N.J. Born 14/3/65. Commd 2/7/91. Flt Lt 7/3/89. Retd ADMIN (P ED) 14/9/03.
BUCHANAN N.W. Born 14/11/44. Commd 21/10/63. Gp Capt 1/1/87. Retd SUP 10/4/90.
BUCHANAN W.D. Born 20/2/47. Commd 25/2/66. Sqn Ldr 1/7/94. Retd GD 20/2/02.
BUCHER T.J.P. MB BS FRCS(Edin). Born 19/4/33. Commd 17/8/58. Flt Lt 17/8/59. Retd MED 16/8/61.
    Re-instated 1/9/63. A Cdre 3/12/91. Retd MED 2/5/94.
BUCK B.W. Born 15/1/23. Commd 13/9/44. Flt Lt 13/3/48. Retd GD 31/3/62.
BUCK C.W.D. MA. Born 13/7/46. Commd 16/1/72. Sqn Ldr 1/1/83. Retd ENG 13/7/01.
BUCK D.G. BSc. Born 15/1/42. Commd 14/9/64. Flt Lt 14/12/65. Retd GD 14/9/80.
BUCKBY D.M. Born 7/3/58. Commd 18/10/81. Flt Lt 18/10/85. Retd ADMIN 18/10/97.
BUCKE P.J. Born 27/2/44. Commd 21/12/62. Flt Lt 21/6/68. Retd GD 13/7/76.
BUCKEL A.K. Born 28/2/47. Commd 18/10/81. Flt Lt 15/10/86. Retd ENG 1/5/93.
BUCKELL E.A.C. MB BS MRCS LRCP DObstRCOG. Born 23/3/30. Commd 27/6/54. Sqn Ldr 1/4/62. Retd MED 27/6/64.
BUCKHAM H. Born 18/12/34. Commd 9/4/57. Sqn Ldr 1/1/69. Retd GD 18/12/72.
BUCKINGHAM A.E. Born 12/12/34. Commd 21/3/69. Sqn Ldr 1/7/79. Retd GD(G) 12/12/89.
BUCKINGHAM C.F. Born 15/4/49. Commd 11/4/85. Flt Lt 11/4/89. Retd GD 15/4/00.
BUCKLAND E.S. DFC. Born 10/1/23. Commd 26/11/42. Flt Lt 26/11/48. Retd GD(G) 10/1/68.
BUCKLAND J.R. Born 6/7/31. Commd 12/8/54. Flt Lt 12/2/59. Retd GD 6/7/69.
BUCKLAND N.A. Born 26/11/48. Commd 28/2/69. Gp Capt 1/7/89. Retd GD 14/3/96.
BUCKLAND P.G. Born 13/4/45. Commd 15/7/66. Sqn Ldr 1/7/83. Retd GD 13/4/89.
BUCKLAND P.J.L. Born 3/12/43. Commd 11/8/77. Flt Lt 11/8/79. Retd ADMIN 11/8/91.
BUCKLE D.M. Born 27/2/49. Commd 7/6/68. Sqn Ldr 1/7/83. Retd SY(RGT) 1/10/89.
BUCKLE E. Born 16/7/29. Commd 12/9/57. Flt Lt 12/12/63. Retd SEC 4/4/73.
BUCKLE F.G. CEng MRAeS MIEE. Born 10/2/29. Commd 9/7/59. Wg Cdr 1/1/75. Retd ENG 18/11/78.
BUCKLER J.L. Born 22/7/46. Commd 18/8/67. Gp Capt 1/1/95. Retd GD 22/7/01.
BUCKLEY E. DFM. Born 4/9/14. Commd 29/3/43. Flt Lt 29/9/47. Retd SEC 9/5/54.
BUCKLEY G.C.A. DFC. Born 15/3/54. Commd 2/6/77. Wg Cdr 1/1/98. Retd GD 14/2/00.
BUCKLEY J. Born 19/1/22. Commd 26/7/45. Gp Capt 1/7/73. Retd SEC 26/9/75.
BUCKLEY J.E.D. Born 23/3/25. Commd 14/3/46. Flt Lt 27/5/54. Retd SUP 23/3/63.
BUCKLEY J.N.G. Born 25/11/32. Commd 9/4/52. Flt Lt 29/4/59. Retd SEC 19/5/71.
BUCKLEY J.W. Born 3/11/19. Commd 27/2/46. Flt Lt 30/8/48. Retd GD 22/11/62.
BUCKLEY M. Born 22/4/36. Commd 23/6/67. Flt Lt 4/5/72. Retd GD 23/6/75.
BUCKLEY N.J. Born 1/10/47. Commd 13/1/67. Gp Capt 1/7/88. Retd OPS SPT 7/4/01.
BUCKLEY R.W.W. CEng MIEE MRAeS. Born 18/12/14. Commd 10/12/42. Flt Lt 4/9/46. Retd ENG 29/11/54.
BUCKLEY T.P. MCMI. Born 18/5/43. Commd 3/1/64. Wg Cdr 1/7/92. Retd ADMIN 18/5/98.
BUDD G.E. Born 11/3/42. Commd 14/9/63. Flt Lt 19/10/68. Retd GD 11/3/80.
BUDD P.H. Born 13/12/53. Commd 30/1/75. Wg Cdr 1/1/00. Retd GD 30/9/03.
BUDDEN W.C.G. MBE BEM. Born 18/6/19. Commd 28/7/49. Flt Lt 5/11/58. Retd ENG 18/6/68.
BUDDIN T. Born 2/7/43. Commd 8/1/65. Flt Lt 4/11/70. Retd GD 29/11/75. Re-instated 22/9/78. Flt Lt 28/8/73.
    Retd GD 2/2/92.
BUDKIEWICZ K.S. Born 12/8/46. Commd 8/6/84. Flt Lt 8/6/88. Retd ENG 4/10/00.
BUFTON K.D. Born 2/8/56. Commd 27/1/77. Sqn Ldr 1/1/92. Retd GD 29/9/96.
BUFTON T. MSc BSc CEng FCMI MIEE DIC. Born 26/11/46. Commd 26/5/67. Gp Capt 1/1/97. Retd ENG 26/11/01.
BUGG S.L. MSc CEng MIMechE MRAeS MIIM MCMI. Born 7/5/29. Commd 25/9/52. Wg Cdr 1/1/77.
    Retd ENG 7/5/84.
BUICK A.E.F. Born 21/6/24. Commd 29/5/46. Flt Lt 1/1/58. Retd GD 31/12/73.
BUICK F.D. BSc. Born 6/3/31. Commd 23/9/53. Wg Cdr 1/7/71. Retd ENG 10/12/85.
BUICK J.M. Born 7/11/30. Commd 31/7/51. Flt Lt 5/10/60. Retd GD 31/1/69.
BUIST S.L. Born 9/6/59. Commd 1/12/77. Wg Cdr 1/7/97. Retd GD 9/6/03.
BULFORD P.J. DFC. Born 6/8/30. Commd 26/9/51. Sqn Ldr 1/7/64. Retd GD 6/8/88.
BULFORD S.E. AFC. Born 2/9/19. Commd 23/12/40. Sqn Ldr 1/7/49. Retd GD 19/9/58.
BULL A.E. Born 16/12/16. Commd 4/4/38. Sqn Ldr 1/1/53. Retd GD 1/1/58.
BULL E.F. BEM. Born 6/6/29. Commd 24/11/60. Sqn Ldr 1/1/78. Retd ENG 6/6/79.
BULL K.A. Born 24/5/47. Commd 25/11/68. Wg Cdr 1/1/90. Retd GD 11/4/02.
BULL K.M. Born 20/7/46. Commd 2/2/84. Sqn Ldr 1/1/94. Retd ADMIN 20/7/01.
BULL M. Born 11/2/45. Commd 15/2/90. Flt Lt 15/2/94. Retd ENG 1/2/00.
BULL N.J. Born 1/12/16. Commd 15/4/44. Flt Lt 1/1/58. Retd GD(G) 30/12/71.
BULL R.M. Born 21/12/48. Commd 27/5/78. Sqn Ldr 1/7/90. Retd OPS SPT 1/9/00.

BULL R.P. BSc CEng MRAeS. Born 17/2/48. Commd 28/2/69. Wg Cdr 1/1/89. Retd ENG 10/2/97.
BULLEN A.G. MBE. Born 26/7/15. Commd 16/10/44. Wg Cdr 1/7/65. Retd PRT 30/6/69.
BULLEN P. MILT. Born 14/12/58. Commd 30/3/89. Flt Lt 30/3/91. Retd SUP 25/8/96.
BULLEN R. CB GM MA FCMI. Born 19/10/20. Commd 28/6/42. AVM 1/7/72. Retd SEC 19/10/75.
BULLEN R.J. Born 13/3/43. Commd 13/2/64. Sqn Ldr 1/1/75. Retd ADMIN 13/3/81.
BULLEN R.K. Born 31/1/43. Commd 19/3/81. Sqn Ldr 1/1/90. Retd ENG 31/7/98.
BULLERS R.F. Born 18/11/29. Commd 27/3/57. Sqn Ldr 1/7/75. Retd GD(G) 18/11/89.
BULLEY B. BSc. Born 25/4/45. Commd 28/9/64. Sqn Ldr 1/1/78. Retd GD 25/4/89.
BULLEY R.A. MBE. Born 3/12/41. Commd 30/5/69. Flt Lt 30/5/71. Retd GD 1/7/94.
BULLEY W.B. Born 5/1/32. Commd 18/4/51. Sqn Ldr 1/7/72. Retd GD 1/12/75.
BULLICK G.B. Born 12/7/66. Commd 31/7/86. Flt Lt 31/1/92. Retd FLY(P) 12/7/04.
BULLIFENT A.D. BSc. Born 9/7/65. Commd 14/5/89. Flt Lt 14/11/91. Retd GD 14/3/97.
BULLOCK A.B. MBE. Born 3/12/32. Commd 29/10/52. Sqn Ldr 1/1/71. Retd GD(G) 3/12/87.
BULLOCK C. Born 17/9/41. Commd 25/3/64. Flt Lt 25/9/69. Retd GD 12/8/75.
BULLOCK C.T. Born 15/4/36. Commd 11/6/81. Flt Lt 11/6/84. Retd GD 11/6/91.
BULLOCK E. BSc. Born 12/5/32. Commd 18/11/54. Wg Cdr 1/1/75. Retd ENG 11/7/84.
BULLOCK G. BA MCMI. Born 12/12/46. Commd 6/1/69. Sqn Ldr 1/1/77. Retd ADMIN 6/1/85.
BULLOCK J.M. BSc. Born 18/9/20. Commd 6/9/50. Wg Cdr 1/7/64. Retd EDN 16/4/71.
BULLOCK J.P. CEng MRAeS MCMI. Born 22/1/20. Commd 19/8/42. Wg Cdr 1/7/61. Retd ENG 22/1/75.
BULLOCK J.P.L. Born 31/3/38. Commd 8/10/70. Sqn Ldr 1/7/79. Retd SUP 31/3/96.
BULLOCK J.S. Born 4/11/33. Commd 18/2/53. Wg Cdr 1/1/77. Retd GD 4/11/88.
BULLOCK K.W. Born 25/9/23. Commd 14/1/44. Flt Lt 27/5/54. Retd GD 15/12/64.
BULLOCK M.C. BSc. Born 14/11/49. Commd 12/12/71. Wg Cdr 1/7/87. Retd ADMIN 12/12/99.
BULLOCK M.J. BSc. Born 26/6/43. Commd 6/10/69. Sqn Ldr 1/7/76. Retd ENG 8/4/78.
BULLOCK R.W. Born 5/8/28. Commd 10/10/63. Sqn Ldr 1/7/77. Retd ADMIN 5/8/80.
BULLOCK S.L. Born 11/5/53. Commd 27/8/87. Flt Lt 27/8/89. Retd ENG 27/8/95.
BULLOCKE M.B. Born 24/7/38. Commd 25/7/60. Wg Cdr 1/7/77. Retd GD 24/7/93.
BULMAN J.C. BA. Born 12/3/43. Commd 17/7/75. Sqn Ldr 1/1/88. Retd ENG 19/8/94.
BULMER M.G. BA. Born 10/6/73. Commd 8/2/98. Flt Lt 8/8/01. Retd OPS SPT(FC) 27/6/03.
BULPETT E.H. Born 3/7/39. Commd 28/8/75. Sqn Ldr 1/1/88. Retd GD(G) 3/1/90.
BUMSTEAD G.E.S. FCMI. Born 24/9/21. Commd 9/8/48. A Cdre 1/1/73. Retd SY 24/9/76.
BUNCE D.F. BSc. Born 24/9/36. Commd 3/1/58. Sqn Ldr 3/7/66. Retd EDN 24/9/74.
BUNCE S.C. Born 2/5/61. Commd 15/10/81. APO 15/10/81. Retd GD 13/6/82.
BUNCE S.M. BEd. Born 31/8/61. Commd 29/9/85. Flt Lt 29/3/88. Retd ADMIN 3/3/89.
BUNCE T.N. Born 13/10/41. Commd 17/7/87. Flt Lt 17/7/89. Retd ENG 2/9/93.
BUNCH B.R. Born 14/10/39. Commd 3/8/62. Flt Lt 1/7/68. Retd GD 10/4/78.
BUNCHER C.P. Born 9/6/49. Commd 19/6/70. Sqn Ldr 1/1/85. Retd GD 1/1/88.
BUNCHER R.H. Born 16/4/41. Commd 1/10/65. Flt Lt 1/10/68. Retd GD 28/9/74.
BUNDOCK P. Born 18/4/50. Commd 28/3/91. Sqn Ldr 1/7/99. Retd FLY(ALM) 9/3/05.
BUNN O.G. CBE. Born 16/4/41. Commd 15/9/61. Gp Capt 1/1/88. Retd GD 2/4/93.
BUNNER A.J. Born 29/11/20. Commd 14/2/46. Flt Lt 16/12/51. Retd ENG 5/9/56.
BUNNEY C.J. Born 29/6/38. Commd 10/9/70. Sqn Ldr 1/7/81. Retd ADMIN 29/6/88.
BUNNEY K.M. Born 18/6/52. Commd 16/72. Flt Lt 1/12/78. Retd ADMIN 26/7/86.
BUNNING F.W. Born 2/2/26. Commd 27/6/51. Flt Lt 27/3/57. Retd GD 26/5/66.
BUNTING H.V. OBE. Born 6/6/13. Commd 1/4/40. Wg Cdr 1/7/52. Retd GD 6/6/68.
BUNTING P.J. Born 15/8/45. Commd 1/10/65. Flt Lt 4/5/72. Retd GD 7/11/75.
BUNTING V.G. Born 31/3/40. Commd 28/4/65. Flt Lt 9/2/68. Retd GD 31/3/78.
BURBOROUGH W.R. Born 14/7/43. Commd 28/11/69. Flt Lt 12/8/73. Retd GD 14/7/81.
BURCH J.C. MCMI. Born 16/10/20. Commd 17/4/44. Sqn Ldr 1/4/55. Retd GD 16/10/69.
BURCH M.W. Born 6/3/57. Commd 5/8/76. Sqn Ldr 1/1/95. Retd GD(G) 14/3/96.
BURCH P.F.R. Born 6/2/44. Commd 6/4/72. Flt Lt 6/10/78. Retd SUP 6/2/99.
BURCH R.M. Born 27/8/35. Commd 18/5/61. Sqn Ldr 1/1/73. Retd GD 28/8/90.
BURCHALL R.F. Born 21/3/46. Commd 9/8/79. Flt Lt 9/8/80. Retd ADMIN 9/8/87.
BURCHELL C.R. Born 13/9/34. Commd 22/12/53. Flt Lt 23/6/59. Retd GD(G) 13/9/91.
BURCHELL D.J. Born 11/12/45. Commd 8/7/65. Sqn Ldr 1/1/87. Retd GD(G) 14/3/96.
BURD T.F. OBE. Born 11/11/21. Commd 10/10/46. Gp Capt 1/1/68. Retd SUP 11/11/76.
BURDEKIN P.A. Born 20/11/45. Commd 10/10/66. Flt Lt 28/4/72. Retd GD 31/3/95.
BURDEN A.R. MISM MCMI. Born 26/2/27. Commd 16/5/57. Sqn Ldr 1/1/70. Retd GD(G) 26/2/82.
BURDEN D.S. MBE AFC MRIN. Born 18/11/30. Commd 23/4/53. Sqn Ldr 1/1/76. Retd GD 18/11/88.
BURDEN F.W. BSc CEng MIEE. Born 15/3/48. Commd 24/2/74. Sqn Ldr 1/1/84. Retd ENG 24/2/90.
BURDEN G.H.StJ. Born 28/3/27. Commd 27/6/51. Flt Lt 29/7/63. Retd GD 29/7/71.
BURDEN R.A. Born 29/2/56. Commd 23/10/86. Flt Lt 23/10/88. Retd GD(G) 23/10/94.
BURDEN R.C. Born 7/6/53. Commd 7/6/73. Sqn Ldr 1/1/91. Retd GD 7/6/94.
BURDESS A.R.E. MSc BSc CEng MIEE. Born 15/10/61. Commd 11/9/83. Sqn Ldr 1/7/92. Retd ENG 15/10/99.
BURDESS C.R. Born 25/12/51. Commd 22/5/75. Flt Lt 22/11/80. Retd GD 1/6/92.
BURDESS S.B. BEng CEng FRAeS. Born 17/9/46. Commd 28/9/64. A Cdre 1/7/95. Retd ENG 2/1/97.

BURDETT B.B. Born 11/9/36. Commd 18/8/54. Flt Lt 5/10/60. Retd GD 11/9/73. rtg Sqn Ldr
BURDETT P.N. Born 24/8/57. Commd 4/11/82. Flt Lt 4/5/85. Retd GD 24/8/95.
BURDETT R.E. Born 3/6/41. Commd 6/5/66. Flt Lt 17/3/71. Retd SUP 2/2/74.
BURDETT R.F. BA. Born 21/11/47. Commd 13/12/74. Wg Cdr 1/1/91. Retd GD 11/4/05.
BURDETT T.F. MBE CEng MIMechE. Born 10/10/40. Commd 10/1/71. Sqn Ldr 1/1/86. Retd ENG 10/10/95.
BUREAU P. Born 19/4/30. Commd 30/7/52. Flt Lt 10/11/55. Retd GD 19/4/68.
BURFORD K.A. Born 7/5/44. Commd 9/7/72. Wg Cdr 1/1/89. Retd GD(G) 30/12/93.
BURGE F.G. MCMI. Born 13/6/44. Commd 16/6/69. Wg Cdr 1/1/89. Retd SY 1/8/96.
BURGE W.J. MBE. Born 15/10/34. Commd 24/1/74. Flt Lt 24/1/77. Retd GD(G) 1/2/85.
BURGES J.R. BSc CEng FIEE FRAeS. Born 18/10/19. Commd 13/9/40. A Cdre 1/7/70. Retd ENG 18/10/74.
BURGESS A.E. Born 12/1/20. Commd 2/12/43. Sqn Ldr 1/4/56. Retd ENG 19/10/68.
BURGESS A.S. MB BS. Born 4/2/60. Commd 6/10/81. Sqn Ldr 1/8/90. Retd MED 1/3/91.
BURGESS A.V. MCMI. Born 10/4/33. Commd 18/7/63. Wg Cdr 1/7/82. Retd SY 10/4/91.
BURGESS G.H. CBE FCMI. Born 16/5/22. Commd 26/6/42. Gp Capt 1/7/68. Retd GD 30/3/77.
BURGESS I.A. Born 26/4/16. Commd 1/1/43. Flt Lt 1/1/43. Retd GD(G) 10/8/63.
BURGESS J.G. Born 28/11/51. Commd 16/3/73. Flt Lt 16/3/76. Retd GD 28/11/89.
BURGESS J.H. Born 17/9/46. Commd 31/10/74. Wg Cdr 14/3/96. Retd ENG 14/3/96.
BURGESS K.J. Born 10/12/27. Commd 28/10/51. Sqn Ldr 1/7/62. Retd GD 28/11/75. Re-instated 3/9/80 to 14/4/85.
BURGESS M.J. Born 18/8/23. Commd 16/4/43. Sqn Ldr 1/1/53. Retd RGT 7/4/64.
BURGESS P. Born 25/9/30. Commd 1/2/62. Flt Lt 1/2/68. Retd PE 30/9/80.
BURGESS S.D. Born 17/7/29. Commd 6/12/56. Flt Lt 16/8/61. Retd PI 28/2/73.
BURGESS S.F. BSc. Born 22/11/62. Commd 2/9/84. Flt Lt 2/3/88. Retd ADMIN 31/1/97.
BURGHAM A.P. BA. Born 3/12/55. Commd 27/3/80. Sqn Ldr 1/1/91. Retd SUP 21/1/97.
BURGIS W.S. Born 21/4/52. Commd 4/3/71. Flt Lt 4/9/76. Retd GD 21/4/90.
BURKBY J.A. Born 9/4/41. Commd 1/10/65. Sqn Ldr 1/7/87. Retd GD 9/4/96.
BURKE B. Born 25/8/46. Commd 20/11/75. Sqn Ldr 1/1/86. Retd GD 31/3/94.
BURKE E.S.R. Born 9/11/42. Commd 25/1/63. Flt Lt 4/11/68. Retd GD 22/10/94.
BURKE H.R. Born 24/5/59. Commd 19/6/86. Flt Lt 6/12/92. Retd GD(G) 14/3/96.
BURKE J.G. MBA DipMgmt. Born 18/7/51. Commd 23/10/86. Sqn Ldr 1/7/99. Retd ENG 19/7/02.
BURKE J.J. BSc CEng FIEE DipEL MRAeS. Born 12/4/30. Commd 12/11/53. A Cdre 1/1/78. Retd ENG 12/4/85.
BURKE K.S. MSc BSc. Born 28/11/58. Commd 1/1/82. Sqn Ldr 1/1/91. Retd ENG 17/1/98.
BURKE O.G. Born 16/4/14. Commd 23/8/44. Sqn Offr 1/1/58. Retd PRT 28/4/61.
BURKE R.H. Born 28/6/39. Commd 4/8/44. Sqn Ldr 1/1/74. Retd GD 28/6/97.
BURKE T.E. BA CEng MIMechE MRAeS. Born 11/3/34. Commd 14/5/63. Sqn Ldr 1/7/75. Retd ENG 14/5/79.
BURKE T.F. Born 16/4/40. Commd 10/6/63. Gp Capt 1/7/94. Retd GD(G) 16/4/95.
BURKE T.J.d'E. BA. Born 30/3/27. Commd 13/1/49. Sqn Ldr 1/7/59. Retd ENG 30/3/85.
BURKEY J.W. Born 19/2/40. Commd 28/6/79. Flt Lt 28/6/82. Retd GD 19/2/95.
BURLEIGH G.H. AFC. Born 31/12/31. Commd 30/7/52. Gp Capt 1/1/76. Retd GD 31/12/86.
BURLES D.R. Born 17/10/31. Commd 28/7/53. Flt Lt 28/1/56. Retd GD 18/4/70.
BURLEY B.M. Born 27/6/30. Commd 11/4/51. Gp Capt 1/1/81. Retd GD 26/5/83.
BURLEY G. Born 29/11/46. Commd 19/10/72. Sqn Ldr 1/1/00. Retd FLY(N) 29/11/03.
BURLINGTON-GREEN E.A. Born 3/8/18. Commd 18/7/46. Sqn Ldr 1/7/63. Retd ENG 3/8/73.
BURLOW N.E. DFC. Born 12/8/22. Commd 25/8/55. Flt Lt 25/8/58. Retd GD 12/8/72.
BURMAN B.G. Born 16/11/41. Commd 12/9/63. Wg Cdr 1/7/83. Retd SY 3/7/93.
BURMAN M.H. BSc. Born 21/5/61. Commd 30/10/83. Flt Lt 30/4/86. Retd GD 30/10/99.
BURN N. Born 1/6/57. Commd 1/1/95. Retd GD 1/6/01.
BURNELL C.M. Born 11/6/55. Commd 11/7/74. Flt Lt 11/1/81. Retd SUP 28/2/81.
BURNESS S.A. Born 10/12/16. Commd 17/3/49. Sqn Ldr 1/4/58. Retd SEC 10/4/70.
BURNET-SMITH W.J. Born 29/12/22. Commd 28/3/44. Flt Lt 30/10/58. Retd GD 1/1/73.
BURNETT Sir Brian GCB DFC AFC BA. Born 10/3/13. Commd 27/6/32. ACM 7/10/67. Retd GD 11/3/72.
BURNETT B.StL. Born 27/12/45. Commd 5/3/65. Flt Lt 5/9/70. Retd GD 30/12/82.
BURNETT D.J. Born 3/4/45. Commd 17/12/65. Flt Lt 1/7/68. Retd GD 17/9/97.
BURNETT D.J. Born 11/2/44. Commd 22/5/64. Flt Lt 22/11/69. Retd FLY(AEO) 11/2/04.
BURNETT P.G. Born 2/1/42. Commd 7/7/62. Flt Lt 15/4/72. Retd ENG 2/1/80.
BURNETT R.J. Born 31/8/35. Commd 30/1/58. Sqn Ldr 1/7/69. Retd GD 31/8/73.
BURNETT W.J. DSO OBE DFC AFC. Born 8/11/15. Commd 5/9/37. A Cdre 1/7/63. Retd GD 21/5/68.
BURNETT W.M. Born 19/7/44. Commd 24/6/66. Gp Capt 1/1/91. Retd GD 8/7/93.
BURNHAM A.F.R. Born 3/11/29. Commd 16/12/49. Flt Lt 16/12/54. Retd RGT 3/11/67.
BURNINGHAM J. Born 1/4/31. Commd 26/5/60. Flt Lt 26/5/66. Retd GD 15/4/84.
BURNINGHAM J.K. MBE Dip Soton. Born 22/11/31. Commd 29/12/53. Gp Capt 1/7/74. Retd ENG 24/2/80.
BURNS A.H.F. Born 20/5/44. Commd 8/5/86. Sqn Ldr 1/7/93. Retd ADMIN 14/3/96.
BURNS B. Born 3/3/50. Commd 16/1/00. Flt Lt 16/1/00. Retd OPS SPT(FLTOPS) 3/3/05.
BURNS C.S. Born 22/7/46. Commd 18/8/67. Wg Cdr 1/1/91. Retd GD 17/4/04.
BURNS F.W. DPhysEd. Born 14/3/36. Commd 17/7/62. Flt Lt 17/7/66. Retd PE 5/9/78.
BURNS G.F. Born 5/5/47. Commd 1/4/71. Flt Lt 1/10/76. Retd GD 30/9/77.
BURNS I.D. MCMI. Born 4/8/34. Commd 15/3/60. Sqn Ldr 1/7/76. Retd ADMIN 1/10/84.

BURNS I.D. Born 13/11/48. Commd 30/5/69. Flt Lt 30/11/74. Retd GD 8/10/81.
BURNS J. CBE. Born 27/7/33. Commd 9/4/52. Gp Capt 1/7/79. Retd GD 27/7/93.
BURNS J.C. Born 27/9/43. Commd 26/3/64. Flt Lt 25/7/70. Retd GD(G) 27/9/82.
BURNS J.G. Born 27/11/27. Commd 8/4/49. Flt Lt 8/10/51. Retd GD 12/2/58.
BURNS J.R. Born 24/2/23. Commd 12/11/43. Sqn Ldr 1/1/67. Retd GD 24/2/78.
BURNS K.D. Born 21/8/46. Commd 1/3/68. Wg Cdr 1/1/90. Retd GD 31/12/93.
BURNS M.H.C. Born 7/4/19. Commd 1/7/46. Flt Lt 1/7/46. Retd RGT 1/5/58.
BURNS N.J. Born 9/5/38. Commd 9/11/64. Sqn Ldr 1/7/84. Retd SUP 23/7/92.
BURNS P. BSc. Born 11/3/54. Commd 20/8/89. Flt Lt 20/2/90. Retd ADMIN 1/11/02.
BURNS P.J. Born 13/5/59. Commd 22/2/79. Flt Lt 22/8/84. Retd GD 24/2/91.
BURNS P.R.S. MB ChB. Born 11/3/42. Commd 14/5/74. Sqn Ldr 1/8/82. Retd MED 27/4/89.
BURNS S. Born 4/4/47. Commd 6/5/66. Flt Lt 6/11/71. Retd GD 4/6/76.
BURNS T.J. Born 25/5/35. Commd 13/12/55. Sqn Ldr 1/1/71. Retd GD 1/1/74.
BURNS T.P. Born 17/5/33. Commd 21/5/52. Wg Cdr 1/1/85. Retd GD(G) 17/11/91.
BURNS W.L. Born 14/5/25. Commd 6/5/65. Flt Lt 6/5/71. Retd SUP 1/8/84.
BURNSIDE D.H. OBE DSO DFC*. Born 26/1/12. Commd 28/10/35. Gp Capt 1/7/54. Retd GD 23/3/62.
BURNSIDE P.A.L. BSc. Born 18/1/54. Commd 15/1/74. Sqn Ldr 1/1/88. Retd GD 18/1/92.
BURR R.A.M. Born 2/10/38. Commd 30/5/59. Flt Lt 19/1/65. Retd GD 2/10/76.
BURR R.H. DFM. Born 3/9/16. Commd 28/11/43. Flt Lt 28/5/47. Retd GD 24/10/57.
BURRAGE P.A. Born 14/11/26. Commd 21/1/53. Flt Lt 21/7/56. Retd GD 13/7/79.
BURRAGE W.C. Born 12/6/21. Commd 21/10/59. Flt Lt 22/10/62. Retd ENG 12/6/71.
BURRELL A.G. Born 4/8/42. Commd 6/11/80. Sqn Ldr 1/1/91. Retd ENG 30/4/97.
BURRELL J.D. Born 6/3/37. Commd 24/4/70. Wg Cdr 1/7/84. Retd ADMIN 15/6/87.
BURRELLS J.S.S. Born 1/10/37. Commd 19/12/63. Sqn Ldr 1/7/73. Retd SUP 2/5/79.
BURRETT I.C. Born 21/3/60. Commd 11/10/78. Wg Cdr 1/1/96. Retd GD 2/5/00.
BURREY J.D. Born 6/12/50. Commd 22/5/75. Flt Lt 22/11/80. Retd GD 3/2/91.
BURRIDGE J. MCMI. Born 6/11/24. Commd 1/12/44. Gp Capt 1/1/72. Retd SUP 31/3/78.
BURRILL B.C. Born 12/9/45. Commd 20/10/83. Sqn Ldr 1/1/91. Retd ADMIN 23/4/94.
BURROUGH R.F. BSc(Eng) BA. Born 12/8/48. Commd 9/8/71. Gp Capt 1/1/96. Retd GD 12/8/03.
BURROWS A.R. Born 21/4/68. Commd 21/12/89. Fg Offr 21/12/91. Retd GD 25/4/93.
BURROWS D.S. Born 22/9/31. Commd 30/7/52. Wg Cdr 1/7/76. Retd GD 22/9/86.
BURROWS H.C. MCMI. Born 5/6/31. Commd 7/3/51. Sqn Ldr 1/7/64. Retd GD 17/7/74.
BURROWS J.A. Born 21/4/46. Commd 25/4/69. Sqn Ldr 1/1/86. Retd FLY(N) 21/4/05.
BURROWS J.S. BSc. Born 22/8/50. Commd 13/9/71. Sqn Ldr 1/1/81. Retd ENG 22/12/88.
BURROWS N. Born 23/6/44. Commd 24/6/65. Flt Lt 24/12/67. Retd GD 6/4/74.
BURROWS P.G. Born 21/8/53. Commd 17/7/75. Flt Lt 17/1/81. Retd GD 15/4/01.
BURROWS R.S. AFC FRAeS FCMI. Born 18/10/43. Commd 3/8/62. Gp Capt 1/7/86. Retd GD 1/7/88.
BURROWS S.E. Born 17/12/68. Commd 28/7/88. Flt Lt 20/12/94. Retd ADMIN 28/1/97.
BURROWS T.G. Born 19/8/39. Commd 3/7/80. Flt Lt 3/7/85. Retd SUP 19/8/94.
BURROWS W.D. Born 9/11/32. Commd 4/7/51. Sqn Ldr 1/7/67. Retd SEC 9/11/70.
BURRY S.J. BSc(Eng) CEng MRAeS ACGI. Born 7/1/53. Commd 25/9/71. Wg Cdr 1/1/94. Retd ENG 7/1/97.
BURSCOUGH B. Born 22/11/48. Commd 16/6/88. Flt Lt 16/6/92. Retd SUP 14/3/97.
BURT A.T. Born 26/7/32. Commd 13/9/51. Sqn Ldr 1/7/69. Retd GD 17/9/76.
BURT S.J. Born 27/7/25. Commd 25/8/55. Flt Lt 25/8/61. Retd GD 27/7/80.
BURT V.A. Born 21/6/43. Commd 5/3/65. Flt Lt 5/9/70. Retd GD 21/6/81.
BURTENSHAW A.J. Born 19/4/57. Commd 21/4/77. Sqn Ldr 1/1/88. Retd GD 9/12/95.
BURTON A.A. Born 15/4/40. Commd 11/6/60. Flt Lt 10/2/67. Retd GD 15/4/78.
BURTON A.J. MEd BA. Born 15/1/54. Commd 14/9/86. Sqn Ldr 1/1/93. Retd ADMIN 14/12/02.
BURTON A.J. OBE BSc(Econ) FCIS FCIPD. Born 11/11/50. Commd 30/7/72. AVM 1/1/99. Retd GD 10/10/03.
BURTON A.R.K. BSc CEng MRAeS MIEE. Born 17/8/23. Commd 14/10/42. Wg Cdr 1/1/62. Retd ENG 8/6/68.
BURTON B.E. Born 3/3/28. Commd 5/11/53. Wg Cdr 1/1/75. Retd GD 3/3/83.
BURTON B.H. Born 30/6/53. Commd 15/2/90. Flt Lt 15/2/94. Retd ENG 14/3/97.
BURTON B.M. Born 6/6/35. Commd 11/11/71. Flt Lt 11/11/74. Retd GD 12/11/76.
BURTON D.E. Born 16/2/24. Commd 1/4/45. Flt Lt 17/3/49. Retd GD 31/8/63.
BURTON D.O. Born 22/9/47. Commd 22/11/84. Flt Lt 22/11/88. Retd SUP 1/10/93.
BURTON D.P. Born 4/12/60. Commd 23/10/86. Flt Lt 23/10/88. Retd GD 4/12/98.
BURTON G.E.W. BSc MRCS LRCP. Born 16/1/48. Commd 9/7/81. Sqn Ldr 3/7/90. Retd MED 6/5/96.
BURTON G.O. Born 23/7/45. Commd 19/6/70. Gp Capt 1/7/90. Retd ENG 23/7/00.
BURTON H.M. Born 22/9/59. Commd 5/4/79. Flt Lt 5/10/84. Retd GD 25/9/89.
BURTON J.C. Born 14/6/44. Commd 24/6/65. Sqn Ldr 1/1/74. Retd SUP 14/6/82.
BURTON J.E. Born 24/2/24. Commd 27/6/45. Wg Cdr 1/1/67. Retd GD 26/4/74.
BURTON J.K. Born 14/2/35. Commd 22/7/66. Flt Lt 22/7/68. Retd ENG 22/7/74.
BURTON J.M. MBE. Born 4/2/50. Commd 31/8/78. Sqn Ldr 1/7/86. Retd ENG 1/10/96.
BURTON J.M. Born 15/4/57. Commd 15/10/78. Sqn Ldr 1/7/91. Retd ADMIN 14/3/97.
BURTON K.C. RNT. Born 4/9/22. Commd 12/6/58. Flt Lt 27/5/64. Retd MED(T) 10/11/68.
BURTON K.W. Born 7/6/29. Commd 30/7/64. Sqn Ldr 1/1/77. Retd GD(G) 23/5/83.

BURTON M. JC OBE FRIN FCMI. Born 12/8/32. Commd 30/1/52. A Cdre 1/1/85. Retd GD 12/8/87.
BURTON P.F.J. AFC MCMI. Born 22/10/40. Commd 1/8/61. Wg Cdr 1/7/76. Retd GD 30/7/80.
BURTWELL K.W. Born 10/12/44. Commd 24/1/77. Flt Lt 24/6/77. Retd ADMIN 16/2/87.
BURTWELL P.A. BSc. Born 19/7/50. Commd 22/10/72. Sqn Ldr 1/1/86. Retd ADMIN 1/1/89.
BURWELL C.C.N. MBE. Born 12/9/51. Commd 25/2/72. Gp Capt 1/7/93. Retd GD 27/7/99.
BURWOOD M.K. Born 23/8/42. Commd 19/8/65. Fg Offr 29/12/67. Retd GD 23/4/70.
BURY J.E. CEng MIEE MCMI. Born 6/12/17. Commd 12/9/42. Flt Lt 12/3/46. Retd ENG 6/12/69.
BURY R.F. BSc MB BS FRCS. Born 10/8/48. Commd 8/8/71. Wg Cdr 22/11/87. Retd MED 6/2/88.
BUSBY C.A. BSc. Born 18/4/60. Commd 20/1/85. Flt Lt 20/7/88. Retd OPS SPT 20/1/01.
BUSBY J.M. BSc. Born 16/1/48. Commd 10/4/68. Sqn Ldr 1/7/82. Retd GD 16/1/03.
BUSCH W. Born 13/11/43. Commd 11/11/71. Flt Lt 11/11/73. Retd GD(G) 13/11/81.
BUSFIELD D.B. Born 22/2/42. Commd 11/6/60. Flt Lt 11/12/65. Retd GD 22/2/80.
BUSH G.R. Born 21/10/48. Commd 21/12/89. Gp Capt 1/7/94. Retd OPS SPT 7/4/98.
BUSH J.D. Born 28/5/68. Commd 21/12/89. Fg Offr 23/5/92. Retd ADMIN 30/7/96.
BUSH M.J. Born 31/8/40. Commd 5/6/62. Sqn Ldr 1/7/74. Retd GD 31/8/78.
BUSH P.J. Born 12/5/48. Commd 12/7/68. Wg Cdr 1/1/90. Retd MED(SEC) 23/8/98.
BUSH R.F.J. Born 20/6/44. Commd 12/2/68. Flt Lt 1/9/71. Retd EDN 4/4/78.
BUSH T.H. BSc CEng FIMechE MRAeS MCMI. Born 29/12/40. Commd 15/7/63. Wg Cdr 1/1/79. Retd ENG 17/4/88.
BUSH V.R. MSc IEng MIIE. Born 3/12/52. Commd 19/12/85. Wg Cdr 1/7/03. Retd GD 18/4/04.
BUSHBY R.D. MDA BA MInstPet MCIT MILT. Born 17/4/48. Commd 22/8/71. Wg Cdr 1/7/93. Retd ADMIN 17/4/03.
BUSHELL G.K. OBE. Born 18/4/22. Commd 5/3/43. Wg Cdr 1/7/62. Retd GD 3/4/73.
BUSK D.G. Born 18/1/45. Commd 13/3/80. Flt Lt 13/3/83. Retd GD 1/8/01.
BUSSEREAU V.R.D. Born 7/7/42. Commd 21/5/65. Wg Cdr 1/7/94. Retd GD 7/7/97.
BUSSEY J.E. MBE. Born 7/8/34. Commd 7/9/61. Wg Cdr 1/7/80. Retd GD 18/9/82.
BUSSEY W.T. MVO OBE BEM. Born 13/12/13. Commd 23/12/43. Wg Cdr 1/1/62. Retd ENG 1/9/67.
BUSUTTIL W. MB ChB. Born 5/11/59. Commd 9/7/81. Wg Cdr 1/8/97. Retd MED 5/11/97.
BUSWELL B.D. Born 26/12/27. Commd 19/5/49. Flt Lt 19/11/53. Retd GD 26/12/65.
BUTCHARD J.E. Born 2/6/41. Commd 15/9/61. Flt Lt 2/12/66. Retd GD 1/10/86.
BUTCHER A.J. BSc. Born 3/8/55. Commd 2/1/77. Wg Cdr 1/1/91. Retd ADMIN 1/1/94.
BUTCHER A.J. The Rev. MA. Born 20/10/43. Commd 26/3/72. Retd GD 26/3/88.
BUTCHER C.A. Born 1/7/39. Commd 26/3/59. Flt Offr 29/5/65. Retd GD(G) 3/12/66.
BUTCHER D.J. Born 18/10/45. Commd 26/5/67. Sqn Ldr 1/1/87. Retd GD(G) 1/10/96.
BUTCHER E. Born 12/1/20. Commd 21/10/54. Flt Lt 21/10/57. Retd GD 12/1/70.
BUTCHER E.T. Born 11/2/20. Commd 27/3/41. Flt Lt 27/3/43. Retd GD(G) 11/2/75.
BUTCHER F.A. Born 23/3/33. Commd 17/1/52. Flt Lt 8/5/57. Retd GD 11/5/76.
BUTCHER H.R. MCIPS. Born 18/4/39. Commd 31/10/69. Sqn Ldr 1/7/80. Retd SUP 18/4/94.
BUTCHER P.C. OBE BA MRAeS MCMI. Born 9/12/47. Commd 1/3/68. Gp Capt 1/1/93. Retd GD 4/10/94.
BUTCHER T.A. Born 12/12/42. Commd 6/7/62. Flt Lt 6/1/68. Retd GD 12/12/80.
BUTLER A.A. Born 12/10/32. Commd 6/9/68. Flt Lt 1/1/73. Retd GD 12/10/92.
BUTLER B.J.McG. Born 19/12/37. Commd 5/11/70. Sqn Ldr 1/1/83. Retd SY(RGT) 18/6/88.
BUTLER B.R.M. Born 30/11/23. Commd 23/9/43. Flt Lt 30/10/52. Retd MAR 29/10/58.
BUTLER C.W.J. Born 17/1/36. Commd 30/12/54. Sqn Ldr 1/1/71. Retd GD 17/1/91.
BUTLER D.J. Born 9/2/41. Commd 30/5/59. Flt Lt 15/2/65. Retd GD 13/10/94.
BUTLER D.P. MSc BSc. Born 30/1/61. Commd 4/1/83. Sqn Ldr 1/1/92. Retd ENG 30/1/99.
BUTLER D.W. AFC. Born 26/6/22. Commd 27/3/43. Sqn Ldr 1/7/54. Retd GD 25/8/60.
BUTLER D.W.J. DFC MHCIMA. Born 27/4/20. Commd 25/8/43. Sqn Ldr 1/1/69. Retd CAT 30/9/72.
BUTLER H.W.T. Born 18/9/31. Commd 3/11/51. Flt Lt 3/5/56. Retd GD 18/9/86.
BUTLER I. Born 9/3/65. Commd 29/7/91. Sqn Ldr 1/7/02. Retd ADMIN (SEC) 1/10/03.
BUTLER J.C. Born 3/5/29. Commd 27/9/51. Sqn Ldr 1/7/64. Retd GD 1/3/74.
BUTLER J.G. Born 10/5/32. Commd 7/5/53. Flt Lt 7/11/57. Retd GD 10/5/70.
BUTLER M.A. BA. Born 31/1/42. Commd 10/3/77. Wg Cdr 1/7/91. Retd GD 31/1/97.
BUTLER M.B. Born 2/9/32. Commd 28/6/51. Sqn Ldr 1/7/67. Retd GD 3/6/77.
BUTLER M.J. Born 26/2/42. Commd 23/12/60. A Cdre 1/7/90. Retd GD 26/2/97.
BUTLER M.P.J. BSc. Born 17/3/51. Commd 19/2/73. Sqn Ldr 1/7/84. Retd GD 17/3/89.
BUTLER P. Born 15/11/26. Commd 24/1/52. Flt Lt 15/5/57. Retd GD 15/11/69.
BUTLER P.P. MBE. Born 28/9/14. Commd 2/1/39. Sqn Ldr 1/1/49. Retd SUP 24/2/62.
BUTLER P.W.P. Born 23/12/55. Commd 30/1/75. Sqn Ldr 1/7/94. Retd GD 14/3/97.
BUTLER R.A. BSc. Born 9/5/55. Commd 1/6/77. Flt Lt 6/8/79. Retd GD 6/11/89.
BUTLER R.L.S. Born 16/4/46. Commd 1/8/61. Flt Lt 1/2/64. Retd GD 16/5/78.
BUTLER R.M. MSc BDS FFGDP(UK) MGDSRCS(Ed). Born 20/5/44. Commd 21/7/68. A Cdre 1/7/97. Retd DEL 20/5/01.
BUTLER T.G.W. BSc. Born 28/1/56. Commd 27/4/74. Flt Lt 15/10/79. Retd GD 20/11/94.
BUTLER W.C. Born 20/4/23. Commd 1/8/44. Flt Lt 4/4/51. Retd SUP 20/5/55.
BUTLER W.F. Born 28/1/18. Commd 31/7/58. Flt Lt 1/1/67. Retd ENG 28/4/70.
BUTT L.C. Born 24/11/45. Commd 24/4/64. Sqn Ldr 1/7/79. Retd GD 24/11/00.
BUTT M.R.D. Born 13/3/34. Commd 14/1/54. Sqn Ldr 1/1/81. Retd GD 13/3/89.
BUTT P.C. Born 24/4/47. Commd 1/3/68. Gp Capt 1/1/88. Retd ADMIN 24/4/91.

BUTT R.H.S. Born 1/11/20. Commd 9/10/47. Sqn Ldr 1/7/70. Retd ENG 6/1/74.
BUTT W.E. FIMLT. Born 5/9/35. Commd 5/9/69. Flt Lt 20/5/74. Retd MED(T) 1/4/77.
BUTTAR M.S. MCMI. Born 30/1/32. Commd 12/7/62. Sqn Ldr 1/7/73. Retd SUP 30/1/87.
BUTTER H.A.J. MCMI. Born 19/12/32. Commd 24/8/56. Sqn Ldr 24/2/64. Retd EDN 6/4/78.
BUTTERFIELD C.T. BSc. Born 17/10/56. Commd 14/1/79. Flt Lt 14/4/80. Retd GD 14/1/87.
BUTTERFIELD D.I. Born 22/7/22. Commd 15/9/60. Flt Lt 15/9/63. Retd GD 22/7/77.
BUTTERFIELD L.J. CEng MIMechE. Born 3/12/30. Commd 6/8/52. Sqn Ldr 1/7/66. Retd ENG 21/8/74.
BUTTERISS J. MBE. Born 6/3/21. Commd 21/11/43. Sqn Ldr 1/1/64. Retd GD(G) 1/6/74.
BUTTERISS M. BA MB BChir MRCGP MRCS LRCP DRCOG DAVMED. Born 10/8/45. Commd 24/7/67.
    Sqn Ldr 2/8/76. Retd MED 24/1/84.
BUTTERS D.J. DFC* MCMI. Born 19/7/22. Commd 21/8/44. Sqn Ldr 1/1/63. Retd SUP 19/9/73.
BUTTERS G.K. Born 2/5/42. Commd 18/10/62. Sqn Ldr 1/7/79. Retd ENG 2/5/86.
BUTTERWORTH B. BA. Born 18/3/31. Commd 18/11/53. Sqn Ldr 1/1/69. Retd GD 30/9/74.
BUTTERWORTH J.D.T. MBE. Born 14/5/36. Commd 12/4/73. Sqn Ldr 1/7/82. Retd ENG 14/5/92.
BUTTERWORTH R. BSc. Born 16/12/48. Commd 23/9/68. Flt Lt 15/4/72. Retd GD 22/10/94.
BUTTERWORTH R.J. Born 16/12/44. Commd 7/7/67. Flt Lt 7/7/72. Retd GD 28/3/83.
BUTTERWORTH W.D. Born 9/5/42. Commd 21/7/61. Wg Cdr 1/7/93. Retd GD 5/12/98.
BUTTERWORTH W.H. Born 7/11/23. Commd 26/10/48. Flt Lt 19/6/52. Retd GD(G) 15/7/63.
BUTTON D.H. DFM. Born 21/1/18. Commd 19/1/43. Sqn Ldr 1/7/54. Retd ENG 22/6/68.
BUXEY M.R. Born 10/10/41. Commd 27/1/61. Sqn Ldr 1/1/82. Retd GD 20/8/94.
BUXTON C.T. Born 14/4/56. Commd 27/2/75. Sqn Ldr 1/1/91. Retd GD 14/4/94.
BUXTON D.G. Born 25/4/56. Commd 28/10/76. Flt Lt 28/2/82. Retd GD 25/4/94.
BUXTON D.O. MRAeS. Born 31/10/19. Commd 27/4/44. Sqn Ldr 1/1/55. Retd ENG 20/1/61.
BYCROFT P.C. Born 22/1/39. Commd 9/2/62. Flt Lt 1/4/66. Retd GD 17/10/77.
BYERS C.W. Born 4/4/26. Commd 23/4/52. Flt Lt 5/9/62. Retd GD 12/11/75.
BYRAM P.A. MBE. Born 14/12/45. Commd 21/1/66. Sqn Ldr 1/1/86. Retd GD 1/12/95.
BYRNE B.N. Born 13/7/23. Commd 26/2/43. Sqn Ldr 1/4/55. Retd GD 11/11/61.
BYRNE E.G. Born 9/4/45. Commd 4/12/86. Flt Lt 4/12/90. Retd ENG 14/9/96.
BYRNE G.C.H. Born 22/9/36. Commd 2/8/66. Sqn Ldr 1/7/78. Retd GD 12/6/81.
BYRNE H.D. AFC. Born 24/11/17. Commd 1/9/45. Wg Cdr 1/1/57. Retd GD 26/11/64.
BYRNE J.J. Born 11/2/33. Commd 19/8/53. Fg Offr 20/8/55. Retd GD 31/1/64.
BYRNE K.C. Born 16/10/48. Commd 28/2/69. Sqn Ldr 1/7/80. Retd ENG 16/10/86.
BYRNE M.J. Born 27/12/17. Commd 19/9/46. Fg Offr 19/9/46. Retd RGT 27/12/48.
BYRNE R.F. MBE. Born 11/7/33. Commd 4/6/52. Sqn Ldr 1/7/79. Retd GD 5/11/84.
BYRNE-BURNS P.J. Born 20/6/45. Commd 28/4/65. Flt Lt 4/11/70. Retd GD 21/6/94.
BYRNE-BURNS R.M. Born 22/8/43. Commd 23/1/64. Sqn Ldr 1/7/79. Retd ADMIN 1/7/82.
BYRON A.N. MSc CEng MRAeS. Born 12/6/22. Commd 3/3/43. Sqn Ldr 1/1/55. Retd ENG 12/6/82.
BYWATER D.L. FRAeS FCMI. Born 16/7/37. Commd 1/4/58. A Cdre 1/1/89. Retd GD 1/8/92.
BYWATER E.B. Born 28/9/34. Commd 19/11/52. Wg Cdr 1/1/83. Retd GD 28/9/92.
BYWATER R.D. Born 20/3/64. Commd 30/8/84. Flt Lt 20/2/90. Retd GD 30/3/98.

C

CABLE B.F. MBE. Born 30/1/43. Commd 26/5/61. Wg Cdr 1/1/91. Retd GD 22/4/94.
CABLE J.A. Born 8/7/22. Commd 5/12/43. Sqn Ldr 1/7/62. Retd SUP 8/7/77.
CABORN J.R. Born 25/10/43. Commd 17/12/64. Sqn Ldr 1/1/77. Retd GD 25/10/81.
CABOURNE P.J. BA FCMI. Born 4/8/27. Commd 12/10/52. A Cdre 1/1/81. Retd GD 5/2/83.
CADDICK D.J. MBE MA MLitt BA FCIPD FCMI MInstD. Born 29/5/61. Commd 16/9/79. Sqn Ldr 1/1/91. Retd OPS SPT 23/7/01.
CADE A.S. OBE. Born 16/9/17. Commd 24/10/41. Wg Cdr 1/7/58. Retd GD 16/9/72.
CADIOT C.J. BSc. Born 25/1/51. Commd 28/10/73. Flt Lt 1/6/81. Retd SUP 28/10/92.
CADLE C.P. Born 7/11/46. Commd 15/9/67. Fg Offr 15/9/69. Retd GD 14/2/71.
CADOGAN C.I.G. Born 26/6/41. Commd 28/2/80. Sqn Ldr 1/7/88. Retd ENG 1/2/96.
CADOGAN S.W. Born 23/7/47. Commd 5/1/70. Gp Capt 1/7/94. Retd ADMIN 14/9/96.
CADWALLADER D.G. Born 2/12/44. Commd 3/3/67. Sqn Ldr 1/1/79. Retd GD 19/10/97.
CAESAR I.R. Born 21/10/58. Commd 8/10/87. Sqn Ldr 1/1/03. Retd OPS SPT(REGT) 31/5/05.
CAFFERKY P.W.P. Born 25/1/62. Commd 8/9/83. Sqn Ldr 1/7/95. Retd GD 25/1/00.
CAHILL I.G. Born 28/8/61. Commd 4/11/82. Sqn Ldr 1/1/87. Retd GD 1/1/00.
CAIGER A.B.E. Born 9/12/34. Commd 9/4/57. Sqn Ldr 1/7/67. Retd SUP 9/12/72.
CAILES C.P. Born 6/12/63. Commd 19/11/87. Flt Lt 26/10/93. Retd ADMIN 14/3/97.
CAILLARD D.P. Born 10/8/61. Commd 8/4/82. Fg Offr 10/8/84. Retd SY 1/4/86.
CAILLARD H.A. CB. Born 16/4/27. Commd 8/4/49. AVM 1/1/80. Retd GD 8/5/82.
CAIN B.W. BA. Born 9/6/47. Commd 1/11/70. Flt Lt 1/5/73. Retd ADMIN 1/7/77.
CAIN P.T. Born 14/1/45. Commd 24/6/76. Flt Lt 24/6/78. Retd ENG 24/6/84.
CAINES C.J. Born 24/1/49. Commd 25/9/80. Flt Lt 25/9/82. Retd ENG 24/1/99.
CAINES J. Born 12/7/49. Commd 13/1/72. Flt Lt 13/7/77. Retd GD 20/9/87.
CAINEY D.J. BA MCMI ACIS. Born 25/7/33. Commd 1/9/64. Sqn Ldr 11/12/73. Retd ADMIN 3/2/83.
CAIRD A.R. Born 18/11/47. Commd 27/10/67. Flt Lt 27/4/74. Retd SUP 18/11/85.
CAIRD M.S. Born 10/5/50. Commd 2/1/70. Wg Cdr 1/7/94. Retd SUP 14/3/97.
CAIRD R. CEng MRAeS MCMI. Born 21/9/22. Commd 26/8/43. Wg Cdr 1/7/62. Retd ENG 28/4/73.
CAIRNES A.E. Born 6/7/13. Commd 16/12/33. Sqn Ldr 1/6/42. Retd GD 6/6/46. rtg Wg Cdr
CAIRNS A. Born 8/10/33. Commd 9/10/67. Sqn Ldr 1/1/79. Retd MAR 11/10/83.
CAIRNS D.R. MA. Born 21/5/63. Commd 2/4/84. Flt Lt 15/1/87. Retd GD 23/10/89.
CAIRNS G.C. CBE AFC MRAeS. Born 21/5/26. Commd 22/2/46. AVM 1/1/75. Retd GD 21/5/80.
CAIRNS H.W.D. Born 15/9/42. Commd 15/12/60. Gp Capt 1/7/88. Retd ADMIN 2/7/94.
CAIRNS J.D. Born 18/5/36. Commd 9/2/66. Sqn Ldr 1/1/74. Retd ENG 1/1/77.
CAIRNS J.G. Born 29/10/44. Commd 23/9/66. Sqn Ldr 1/1/90. Retd GD 30/9/94.
CAIRNS J.L. Born 5/1/46. Commd 10/2/72. Sqn Ldr 1/1/91. Retd FLY(N) 1/6/04.
CAIRNS J.P.W. DFC*. Born 19/2/16. Commd 3/6/42. Flt Lt 2/11/51. Retd GD(G) 1/5/68.
CAIRNS J.W.McL. Born 9/5/42. Commd 17/2/64. Flt Lt 9/11/67. Retd GD 1/10/75.
CAIRNS W.D. MCMI. Born 29/1/21. Commd 25/8/55. Flt Lt 25/8/61. Retd ENG 30/6/73.
CAIRNS W.J. FInstPet. Born 9/11/31. Commd 28/5/66. Flt Lt 1/2/72. Retd SUP 31/1/83.
CAKEBREAD J.R.G. DFC. Born 18/4/22. Commd 27/10/43. Flt Lt 27/4/47. Retd ENG 1/9/61.
CALAME M.R. Born 25/3/42. Commd 19/8/66. Sqn Ldr 1/7/82. Retd GD 1/10/94.
CALDER G.R.D. MSc CEng FIMechE FRAeS FCMI. Born 16/9/23. Commd 27/4/44. A Cdre 1/7/73. Retd ENG 2/4/74.
CALDER I.M. MBE. Born 15/1/33. Commd 17/1/52. Sqn Ldr 1/1/71. Retd GD 15/1/83.
CALDER J. ACMA. Born 26/10/55. Commd 8/6/84. Wg Cdr 1/1/01. Retd ADMIN 27/1/02.
CALDER R.J.G. Born 13/9/48. Commd 1/8/69. Fg Offr 1/2/70. Retd GD 1/9/72.
CALDER-JONES H.L. OBE FCMI. Born 20/8/24. Commd 15/10/43. Gp Capt 1/7/65. Retd GD 21/11/69.
CALDERWOOD L.D. Born 24/12/64. Commd 19/7/84. Sqn Ldr 1/1/98. Retd GD 24/12/02.
CALDON M. MA BA. Born 19/9/48. Commd 25/2/79. Flt Lt 25/2/81. Retd ADMIN 1/10/85.
CALDOW W.F. DSO AFC DFM. Born 12/3/21. Commd 20/10/42. Flt Lt 20/4/46. Retd GD 21/7/55. rtg Sqn Ldr
CALDWELL D.E. Born 28/7/32. Commd 13/9/51. A Cdre 1/7/84. Retd GD 10/6/85.
CALDWELL T.S. MCMI. Born 28/3/39. Commd 11/9/64. Sqn Ldr 1/1/72. Retd GD 29/10/91.
CALEY J.R. MBE. Born 17/1/22. Commd 13/6/46. Flt Lt 4/6/53. Retd SY 17/1/77.
CALEY M.C. BTech CEng MIMechE. Born 28/7/38. Commd 9/7/61. Sqn Ldr 1/1/72. Retd ENG 9/7/79.
CALEY P.R. BEM. Born 22/5/28. Commd 19/9/60. Sqn Ldr 1/7/71. Retd GD(G) 31/8/82.
CALFORD A.J. DPhysEd. Born 19/2/29. Commd 18/4/56. Flt Lt 18/4/60. Retd SUP 25/12/71.
CALLADINE W.J. CEng MIEE. Born 17/2/32. Commd 9/9/54. Gp Capt 1/7/73. Retd ENG 17/1/76.
CALLAGHAN G.G. FCMI. Born 28/12/30. Commd 6/9/56. Wg Cdr 1/1/72. Retd SEC 1/10/74.
CALLAGHAN J. BA MIL. Born 19/3/49. Commd 11/8/74. Sqn Ldr 1/7/08. Retd ADMIN 30/6/92.
CALLAGHAN J.F. Born 24/3/38. Commd 10/9/62. Sqn Ldr 1/1/78. Retd GD 16/5/80.
CALLAGHAN P.R. Born 21/1/37. Commd 30/9/55. Sqn Ldr 1/7/67. Retd GD 21/1/95.
CALLAN P. BA. Born 11/9/34. Commd 18/7/63. Gp Capt 1/7/84. Retd ADMIN 1/11/85.

CALLAWAY A. Born 16/9/32. Commd 19/10/67. Wg Cdr 1/8/85. Retd GD 17/4/87.
CALLAWAY A.B. CEng FIMechE FCMI. Born 8/7/34. Commd 24/4/59. Gp Capt 1/7/81. Retd ENG 20/2/87.
CALLEJA A.A. Born 16/9/43. Commd 28/4/67. Flt Lt 28/6/73. Retd ADMIN 31/12/83.
CALLEY Sir Henry DSO DFC. Born 9/12/14. Commd 1/11/41. Wg Cdr 1/7/47. Retd GD 10/8/48.
CALLIS A. BEM MCMI. Born 30/11/20. Commd 25/8/60. Sqn Ldr 1/7/72. Retd SEC 30/11/75.
CALLISTER C.W. BA DipEd. Born 14/6/40. Commd 24/9/63. Sqn Ldr 24/3/71. Retd ADMIN 14/6/95.
CALLISTER J.W. Born 11/8/58. Commd 9/11/89. Flt Lt 9/11/91. Retd ENG 1/10/94.
CALLOW A.R. Born 10/12/63. Commd 29/7/83. Sqn Ldr 1/1/98. Retd OPS SPT 10/12/01.
CALNAN J.M.P. CB CEng FIMechE. Born 22/4/36. Commd 25/10/57. AVM 1/7/90. Retd ENG 10/7/92.
CALTON S. AFC. Born 21/5/51. Commd 27/3/70. Sqn Ldr 1/1/85. Retd GD 21/5/89. Re-entered 13/5/91.
    Sqn Ldr 24/12/86. Retd GD 4/12/98.
CALVERT D.J. Born 23/2/41. Commd 9/3/62. Flt Lt 1/7/68. Retd GD 23/2/79.
CALVERT D.P. MBE BSc. Born 24/3/51. Commd 15/9/69. Wg Cdr 1/1/91. Retd GD 30/7/03.
CALVERT D.T. Born 4/1/44. Commd 15/9/67. Wg Cdr 1/1/87. Retd GD 11/10/97.
CALVERT J.A. MCMI. Born 15/4/33. Commd 15/11/51. Wg Cdr 1/7/76. Retd ADMIN 3/4/79.
CALVERT L.G. MC. Born 25/6/23. Commd 4/2/48. Flt Lt 4/8/52. Retd RGT 29/3/59.
CALVERT R.A. Born 26/7/31. Commd 14/4/53. Sqn Ldr 1/7/61. Retd GD 26/7/69.
CALVERT R.D. BA. Born 12/2/47. Commd 21/1/66. Sqn Ldr 1/7/83. Retd GD 1/7/86.
CALVERT S.A. Born 3/2/70. Commd 28/3/91. Fg Offr 28/9/93. Retd ADMIN 15/12/96.
CALVERT S.E. Born 29/5/62. Commd 7/11/85. Flt Lt 4/12/90. Retd OPS SPT 29/5/00.
CAMBRIDGE F.W.J. Born 17/1/16. Commd 27/2/47. Flt Lt 27/8/51. Retd SEC 10/1/56.
CAMBROOK I.D. MBE MDA BA. Born 17/8/55. Commd 17/7/77. Sqn Ldr 1/7/92. Retd ADMIN 31/7/02.
CAMERON A.D.C. Born 25/8/56. Commd 27/1/77. Wg Cdr 1/7/95. Retd ADMIN 15/4/00.
CAMERON A.F. BSc. Born 10/3/50. Commd 29/8/72. Sqn Ldr 1/7/85. Retd GD 29/8/89.
CAMERON C.H. Born 13/2/24. Commd 16/5/57. Flt Lt 1/4/63. Retd GD 1/10/68.
CAMERON D.F. BSc MB ChB MFOM DAvMed. Born 25/3/29. Commd 1/9/63. Wg Cdr 16/2/71. Retd MED 15/10/82.
CAMERON D.G. MCMI. Born 16/3/26. Commd 20/1/45. Wg Cdr 1/1/71. Retd GD(G) 16/3/86.
CAMERON D.N. Born 29/7/34. Commd 9/4/53. Wg Cdr 1/7/79. Retd GD 1/8/85.
CAMERON I.A. Born 20/6/47. Commd 6/5/66. Wg Cdr 1/1/96. Retd GD 20/7/02.
CAMERON K.A. MB ChB MFCM DipSocMed. Born 4/4/29. Commd 1/1/62. Wg Cdr 9/11/66. Retd MED 7/12/75.
CAMERON M.J. Born 11/6/43. Commd 2/5/71. Sqn Ldr 1/7/85. Retd SY 18/12/93.
CAMERON S. AFC DPhysEd. Born 26/10/30. Commd 7/1/57. Sqn Ldr 1/7/67. Retd PE 31/7/75.
CAMMELL G.W. Born 11/5/23. Commd 3/9/51. Flt Lt 3/9/51. Retd GD 4/9/67.
CAMP A.J. AFC. Born 12/9/21. Commd 9/12/46. Flt Lt 26/5/55. Retd GD 1/4/62.
CAMP P.J. DFM. Born 13/11/16. Commd 25/8/40. Sqn Ldr 1/8/47. Retd GD 1/8/58.
CAMPBELL A. Born 28/6/48. Commd 11/4/85. Sqn Ldr 1/1/94. Retd ADMIN 31/8/02.
CAMPBELL A. BSc. Born 18/9/49. Commd 24/9/72. Gp Capt 1/1/96. Retd GD 31/5/02.
CAMPBELL A.D.K. Born 8/6/41. Commd 18/12/62. Wg Cdr 1/7/84. Retd GD 8/6/96.
CAMPBELL C. Born 17/3/34. Commd 28/7/60. Sqn Ldr 1/1/70. Retd GD 1/1/73.
CAMPBELL C. FCMI. Born 16/9/32. Commd 30/7/52. Wg Cdr 1/1/79. Retd GD 4/4/88.
CAMPBELL C.A. MB BS FRCS(Edin) MRCS LRCP. Born 15/1/42. Commd 15/10/62. Wg Cdr 3/1/80.
    Retd MED 31/12/83.
CAMPBELL C.C.W. Born 14/2/58. Commd 8/9/77. Flt Lt 8/3/83. Retd GD 16/2/95.
CAMPBELL C.D. Born 6/10/46. Commd 25/6/65. Sqn Ldr 1/1/76. Retd GD 6/10/84.
CAMPBELL C.H. Born 21/10/41. Commd 17/1/85. Sqn Ldr 1/1/93. Retd ENG 21/10/96.
CAMPBELL C.J.A. Born 17/12/60. Commd 28/9/89. Sqn Ldr 1/1/98. Retd ADMIN 1/1/01.
CAMPBELL C.T. Born 18/7/34. Commd 19/12/63. Wg Cdr 1/7/77. Retd ADMIN 15/9/84.
CAMPBELL D. Born 20/3/22. Commd 10/4/45. Fg Offr 10/4/46. Retd GD 20/3/55.
CAMPBELL D. Born 8/8/32. Commd 16/7/52. Flt Lt 12/12/57. Retd GD 8/10/70.
CAMPBELL D.A. Born 23/11/58. Commd 2/3/78. Sqn Ldr 1/1/94. Retd GD 1/9/97.
CAMPBELL D.C. Born 25/4/62. Commd 4/7/85. Sqn Ldr 1/1/97. Retd GD 17/6/01.
CAMPBELL D.H. Born 1/11/28. Commd 1/10/54. Flt Lt 4/1/56. Retd GD 12/8/80.
CAMPBELL D.M. Born 12/6/32. Commd 22/10/59. Flt Lt 28/7/65. Retd GD 12/6/70.
CAMPBELL E.C. Born 26/3/46. Commd 13/9/70. Flt Lt 13/3/75. Retd ENG 31/3/94.
CAMPBELL G. Born 2/12/19. Commd 31/12/42. Sqn Ldr 6/3/63. Retd EDN 28/6/66.
CAMPBELL G.F. Born 2/12/41. Commd 3/11/60. Sqn Ldr 1/1/75. Retd GD 2/12/78.
CAMPBELL H.D. DFM. Born 3/4/23. Commd 17/3/45. Flt Lt 12/7/54. Retd GD(G) 20/11/61.
CAMPBELL I.M. Born 18/5/52. Commd 29/6/72. Sqn Ldr 1/1/90. Retd OPS SPT(ATC) 5/12/03.
CAMPBELL J. Born 23/2/36. Commd 20/12/73. Sqn Ldr 1/1/86. Retd GD(G) 28/12/89.
CAMPBELL J.A. Born 30/8/35. Commd 22/1/54. Flt Lt 22/7/59. Retd GD 30/9/84.
CAMPBELL J.R. Born 19/2/22. Commd 6/4/44. Flt Lt 26/5/55. Retd GD 1/1/66.
CAMPBELL J.T. BSc. Born 15/12/62. Commd 30/8/81. Flt Lt 15/10/85. Retd GD 7/2/96.
CAMPBELL K.A. CB MSc BSc CEng MRAeS. Born 3/5/36. Commd 25/9/54. AVM 1/7/85. Retd ENG 2/2/90.
CAMPBELL M. BSc CEng. Born 6/4/48. Commd 18/4/69. Sqn Ldr 1/7/83. Retd ENG 1/7/87.
CAMPBELL M.C. Born 24/10/54. Commd 22/5/75. Sqn Ldr 1/1/89. Retd GD(G) 24/10/92.
CAMPBELL N. MCIPS MCIT MILT MCMI. Born 16/2/45. Commd 3/3/67. Sqn Ldr 1/7/76. Retd SUP 1/5/86.

CAMPBELL P.A. BSc. Born 17/8/62. Commd 6/4/93. Wg Cdr 1/1/00. Retd GD 30/4/03.
CAMPBELL P.E. IEng. Born 27/9/50. Commd 19/6/88. Flt Lt 19/6/88. Retd ENG 2/10/01.
CAMPBELL P.P. The Rev. BD. Born 26/2/55. Commd 27/2/83. Retd Sqn Ldr 31/3/90.
CAMPBELL R.D. Born 25/4/60. Commd 3/7/80. Flt Lt 3/1/87. Retd OPS SPT 25/4/98.
CAMPBELL R.I. Born 29/11/32. Commd 6/5/52. Wg Cdr 1/1/80. Retd GD 1/7/86.
CAMPBELL R.M.C.L. Born 24/12/41. Commd 24/3/61. Wg Cdr 1/1/90. Retd GD 24/12/96.
CAMPBELL R.S. Born 7/6/45. Commd 3/7/80. Sqn Ldr 1/7/91. Retd ENG 6/2/98.
CAMPBELL W.M. Born 20/8/47. Commd 2/8/68. Flt Lt 6/10/71. Retd GD 1/5/76.
CAMPBELL W.M. Born 5/7/44. Commd 25/6/65. Flt Lt 25/12/70. Retd GD 1/6/89.
CAMPBELL W.Mc. AFC. Born 12/6/40. Commd 10/11/61. Sqn Ldr 1/1/88. Retd GD 15/12/92.
CAMPBELL-PERRETT B.J. BA BSc CEng MRAeS. Born 25/11/49. Commd 4/7/85. Sqn Ldr 1/7/99.
    Retd ENGINEER 25/11/04.
CAMPBELL-VOULLAIRE E.G. DFC. Born 10/6/12. Commd 14/9/34. Wg Cdr 1/10/46. Retd GD 15/4/52.
CAMPEY A. AFC. Born 22/10/23. Commd 20/5/44. Sqn Ldr 1/7/55. Retd GD 27/4/68.
CAMPIN C.G. Born 15/9/25. Commd 13/3/52. Flt Lt 13/3/56. Retd RGT 26/2/67.
CAMPING R.A. BSc. Born 21/9/44. Commd 14/9/65. Gp Capt 1/1/94. Retd ENG 18/9/98.
CAMPION A.J. Born 14/12/38. Commd 18/8/61. Flt Lt 18/8/66. Retd GD 28/7/72.
CAMPION G.E. Born 1/7/22. Commd 13/10/41. Sqn Offr 1/1/53. Retd SEC 3/7/56.
CAMPION N.J. BSc. Born 27/11/55. Commd 19/9/76. Flt Lt 15/10/78. Retd GD 15/7/89.
CAMPION P. Born 6/2/39. Commd 22/5/75. Sqn Ldr 1/7/90. Retd ADMIN 6/2/94.
CAMPION W.D. MBE. Born 12/3/22. Commd 2/10/58. Sqn Ldr 1/1/70. Retd ENG 12/3/78.
CAMPLING K.R. Born 6/2/45. Commd 16/8/68. Flt Lt 16/2/74. Retd GD 6/5/84.
CAMPODONIC B.P. Born 1/7/22. Commd 18/10/44. Flt Offr 1/3/52. Retd SEC 22/12/53.
CANAVAN M.B.M. MA. Born 20/10/41. Commd 17/12/63. Wg Cdr 1/1/86. Retd GD 20/10/96.
CANAWAY J.F. Born 21/1/21. Commd 13/3/45. Flt Lt 12/3/51. Retd SEC 21/8/67.
CANDY G.R. Born 17/8/22. Commd 13/2/59. Sqn Ldr 1/1/74. Retd ENG 17/8/77.
CANDY S.N. Born 5/4/21. Commd 21/7/55. Flt Lt 21/7/58. Retd GD 15/4/76.
CANE P.J. Born 13/6/51. Commd 11/5/89. Fg Offr 11/5/89. Retd SY 2/1/93.
CANE R. Born 26/10/41. Commd 31/7/62. Flt Lt 31/1/65. Retd GD 3/4/73.
CANFER B.J. Born 1/12/46. Commd 21/1/66. Sqn Ldr 1/1/83. Retd GD 11/2/95.
CANN B.S. Born 12/5/20. Commd 8/7/43. Sqn Ldr 1/7/68. Retd ENG 24/4/73.
CANN M.L. MCMI. Born 8/5/29. Commd 13/12/50. Wg Cdr 1/1/76. Retd SUP 8/5/84.
CANN M.R. Born 15/10/43. Commd 28/10/66. Flt Lt 28/4/72. Retd GD 31/1/76.
CANNELL F.G. BSc. Born 19/7/57. Commd 14/12/75. Flt Lt 15/10/79. Retd GD 15/7/90.
CANNELL J.M.B. Born 6/5/21. Commd 13/2/47. Wg Cdr 1/1/70. Retd SUP 6/5/76.
CANNIFORD B.J. Born 20/7/37. Commd 3/5/56. Flt Lt 28/3/63. Retd SEC 22/7/72.
CANNING E.J. MCMI. Born 5/1/26. Commd 1/5/47. Flt Lt 28/2/66. Retd SUP 6/3/74.
CANNING J.A. Born 26/7/47. Commd 2/8/68. Flt Lt 2/8/71. Retd GD 26/7/02.
CANNING J.J. DFC. Born 28/1/20. Commd 31/7/42. Sqn Ldr 1/1/54. Retd GD 1/5/71.
CANNING J.W. Born 8/8/35. Commd 31/7/56. Wg Cdr 1/7/77. Retd GD 16/4/89.
CANNING P.F.A. Born 24/3/39. Commd 13/12/60. Gp Capt 1/1/88. Retd ADMIN 31/8/93.
CANNOCK N.J.M. BSc. Born 3/1/55. Commd 6/7/80. Flt Lt 6/4/82. Retd ENG 22/12/84.
CANNOCK P.J. BSc. Born 25/8/59. Commd 17/8/80. Wg Cdr 1/1/98. Retd SUP 1/7/02.
CANNON B.O. Born 21/1/11. Commd 6/1/36. Sqn Ldr 1/6/43. Retd SUP 24/3/50. rtg Wg Cdr
CANNON G.J. BSc. Born 18/11/61. Commd 21/1/82. Flt Lt 15/10/85. Retd GD 20/12/98.
CANNON G.T. AFC. Born 6/9/30. Commd 17/8/50. Wg Cdr 1/1/70. Retd GD 10/1/72.
CANNON M.R. Born 27/3/36. Commd 13/10/61. Wg Cdr 1/1/86. Retd ADMIN 4/4/90.
CANNON M.R. BEng. Born 9/11/54. Commd 16/9/73. Sqn Ldr 1/1/91. Retd SY 14/3/96.
CANNON P. Born 8/10/35. Commd 10/3/77. Flt Lt 10/3/81. Retd ENG 10/10/86.
CANNON S.J. Born 4/11/40. Commd 12/3/64. Flt Lt 12/9/70. Retd ENG 15/5/71.
CANT A.F. Born 24/11/47. Commd 1/8/69. Sqn Ldr 1/1/88. Retd SUP 24/11/91.
CANT C.I.H. Born 1/2/43. Commd 28/7/64. Flt Lt 28/1/67. Retd GD 3/10/78.
CANTON B.V. CEng MRAeS MIEE. Born 24/2/41. Commd 26/5/65. Sqn Ldr 1/7/77. Retd ENG 1/7/80.
CANTON E.J. DFC. Born 30/11/20. Commd 20/4/43. Flt Lt 4/12/52. Retd GD 1/8/68.
CANTWELL E.W. Born 12/5/21. Commd 11/11/65. Flt Lt 11/11/70. Retd ENG 12/5/76.
CANTWELL P.J. BSc. Born 26/2/63. Commd 30/8/81. Flt Lt 15/10/85. Retd GD 14/3/97.
CAPE G.A. Born 15/10/32. Commd 31/1/62. Sqn Ldr 1/1/81. Retd GD 30/9/88.
CAPE N.J. OBE. Born 22/8/21. Commd 22/5/44. Wg Cdr 1/7/62. Retd GD 18/6/72.
CAPEWELL H.J. Born 3/4/27. Commd 22/5/52. Flt Lt 12/6/57. Retd GD 1/4/74.
CAPP C.H. Born 28/9/24. Commd 28/2/57. Flt Lt 28/2/63. Retd GD 28/9/74.
CAPP T.R. BSc. Born 23/2/34. Commd 8/8/65. Sqn Ldr 1/1/67. Retd GD 8/8/72.
CAPPER A.C. AFC. Born 25/11/23. Commd 8/10/45. Flt Lt 29/6/50. Retd GD 8/3/52.
CAPPS J.J. BSc. Born 4/3/49. Commd 27/2/74. Gp Capt 1/1/97. Retd GD 2/5/03.
CAPSTICK R.A. BEM MCIPS MCMI. Born 20/11/35. Commd 2/8/68. Wg Cdr 1/1/85. Retd SUP 1/8/90.
CARD D.E. CEng MRAeS MIEE MCMI. Born 8/6/23. Commd 12/4/51. Wg Cdr 1/7/69. Retd ENG 29/9/77.
CARD D.R. Born 23/1/48. Commd 11/8/67. Flt Lt 11/2/73. Retd GD 16/8/77.

CARD J. Born 15/5/21. Commd 10/3/44. Flt Lt 10/9/47. Retd GD 15/5/54.
CARD R.W.F. Born 8/1/38. Commd 19/8/65. Flt Lt 19/8/67. Retd ADMIN 1/10/77. Re-instated 23/11/79. Sqn Ldr 1/7/84. Retd ADMIN 1/11/90.
CARD S.J.G. Born 21/10/34. Commd 13/12/55. Flt Lt 5/11/58. Retd GD 21/10/72.
CARDALE B.B. Born 3/6/16. Commd 17/11/41. Flt Offr 1/9/45. Retd SEC 25/8/65.
CARDEN D.R. AFC. Born 17/2/39. Commd 14/8/64. Wg Cdr 1/1/88. Retd GD 17/2/94.
CARDEN H.C. Born 4/9/59. Commd 26/11/81. Flt Lt 8/5/86. Retd SY 14/3/96.
CARDER A.M. BA. Born 28/5/31. Commd 21/1/54. Sqn Ldr 17/2/63. Retd ADMIN 2/1/77.
CARDER A.S. Born 5/4/33. Commd 17/1/52. Sqn Ldr 1/7/67. Retd GD 2/12/85.
CARDUS D.M. Born 22/1/47. Commd 1/4/66. Flt Lt 1/10/71. Retd GD 22/1/88.
CARDWELL J.B. MB ChB MRCGP DTM&H. Born 30/8/30. Commd 14/10/56. Wg Cdr 17/11/06. Retd MED 19/1/73.
CARDWELL J.S. MRCS LRCP. Born 24/1/25. Commd 1/5/52. Sqn Ldr 19/7/58. Retd MED 4/8/62.
CARDWELL M.A. BSc. Born 28/5/46. Commd 25/6/66. Sqn Ldr 1/1/83. Retd ADMIN 28/5/02.
CARDY D.K.J. Born 6/8/29. Commd 2/3/61. Flt Lt 2/3/67. Retd SY 6/8/87.
CARDY J.B. FInstPet MCIPS MCMI. Born 25/3/35. Commd 7/7/55. Sqn Ldr 1/1/68. Retd SUP 11/6/85.
CARDY K.T. Born 24/3/33. Commd 3/5/68. Sqn Ldr 1/7/80. Retd ENG 3/4/85.
CARELESS R.J. Born 27/1/27. Commd 12/3/52. Flt Lt 12/12/57. Retd GD 21/11/66.
CAREY D.J. Born 24/6/45. Commd 18/3/73. Sqn Ldr 1/1/86. Retd GD 2/3/93.
CAREY D.K. Born 30/12/43. Commd 4/7/69. Sqn Ldr 1/7/78. Retd SUP 14/9/96.
CAREY I. Born 25/9/43. Commd 1/11/79. Sqn Ldr 1/9/90. Retd ADMIN 25/9/98.
CAREY R. Born 14/4/48. Commd 20/12/73. Flt Lt 20/6/76. Retd GD 14/4/86.
CARFOOT B.G. OBE. Born 5/5/14. Commd 12/9/38. Wg Cdr 13/2/45. Retd SUP 22/3/46. rtg Gp Capt
CARGILL J. Born 27/11/21. Commd 7/7/55. Sqn Ldr 1/7/66. Retd ENG 11/8/73.
CARGILL N.S. MCMI. Born 30/8/38. Commd 14/5/57. Sqn Ldr 1/7/72. Retd GD(G) 30/8/76.
CARLE F.G. OBE. Born 14/9/10. Commd 28/8/36. Wg Cdr 1/7/48. Retd SUP 10/6/58.
CARLE G.S. Born 15/2/44. Commd 24/2/67. Sqn Ldr 1/1/83. Retd GD(G) 1/12/88.
CARLESS D. Born 16/8/46. Commd 24/11/67. Flt Lt 24/5/73. Retd GD 27/4/77.
CARLETON G.W. CB. Born 22/9/35. Commd 18/6/59. Plt Offr 24/12/59. Retd LGL 12/7/61. Re-entered 31/5/65. AVM 1/1/93. Retd LGL 22/9/97.
CARLETON R.K. MSc BEng CEng MIEE. Born 18/4/67. Commd 23/6/94. Sqn Ldr 1/1/99. Retd ENGINEER 18/4/05.
CARLEY K.J. Born 8/1/34. Commd 3/7/67. Wg Cdr 1/1/80. Retd SUP 1/10/87.
CARLEY T.E. Born 29/9/21. Commd 17/4/50. Flt Lt 23/10/56. Retd GD 24/11/66.
CARLING G. Born 5/8/54. Commd 10/5/90. Flt Lt 10/5/90. Retd ENG 1/8/93.
CARLISLE P.H. Born 17/5/44. Commd 14/6/63. Sqn Ldr 1/1/76. Retd GD 12/12/84.
CARLSON J.E. Born 18/3/36. Commd 28/1/58. Flt Lt 30/7/63. Retd GD 18/3/74.
CARLTON D. Born 16/7/58. Commd 8/11/90. Sqn Ldr 1/7/01. Retd ENGINEER 6/9/04.
CARLTON P. Born 3/3/65. Commd 19/6/86. Flt Lt 19/12/91. Retd FLY(P) 4/4/04.
CARLTON T.W.G. FCMI FRAeS. Born 7/5/37. Commd 29/7/58. A Cdre 1/7/86. Retd GD 8/5/88.
CARMAN R.D. Born 24/10/44. Commd 24/8/71. Flt Lt 24/8/73. Retd GD(G) 24/8/83.
CARMEN T.R.E. Born 17/1/44. Commd 17/12/65. Sqn Ldr 1/7/79. Retd SUP 17/1/00.
CARMICHAEL A.G. Born 2/4/25. Commd 5/5/55. Sqn Ldr 1/1/64. Retd GD 1/4/74.
CARMICHAEL B.K. BSc. Born 13/9/45. Commd 27/4/69. Wg Cdr 1/7/90. Retd GD 14/9/96.
CARMICHAEL W.J. MCIPD. Born 19/2/50. Commd 7/3/76. Sqn Ldr 1/7/86. Retd ADMIN 7/3/93.
CARN P.E. Born 29/8/20. Commd 27/4/61. Flt Lt 27/4/66. Retd ENG 2/10/71.
CARNAZZA C.J. Born 26/5/59. Commd 28/6/79. Flt Lt 28/12/84. Retd GD 21/10/96.
CARNEGIE D.N. Born 4/7/44. Commd 17/5/63. Flt Lt 17/11/68. Retd GD 28/1/76.
CAROLAN A.J. Born 9/12/46. Commd 5/11/65. Flt Lt 20/7/71. Retd GD 9/12/84.
CARPENTER C.J. MSc BSc MCIPD MRAeS. Born 3/11/44. Commd 13/9/70. Sqn Ldr 13/3/79. Retd ADMIN 13/9/86.
CARPENTER D.R. Born 28/5/38. Commd 25/6/66. Sqn Ldr 1/1/83. Retd GD(G) 1/7/92.
CARPENTER D.W. BSc. Born 22/9/46. Commd 22/2/71. Flt Lt 22/11/72. Retd GD 7/2/88.
CARPENTER H.J. Born 27/6/34. Commd 19/11/52. Flt Lt 15/4/58. Retd GD 27/6/72.
CARPENTER R.R.T. Born 4/4/29. Commd 26/2/53. Sqn Ldr 1/7/67. Retd SUP 4/4/84.
CARPENTER R.S.T.G. AFC. Born 8/11/35. Commd 23/9/81. Sqn Ldr 1/1/89. Retd GD 8/11/93. Re-instated 27/4/84. Sqn Ldr 24/7/67. Retd SUP 4/9/88.
CARPENTER T.H. Born 3/2/33. Commd 15/6/53. Flt Lt 17/9/58. Retd GD 3/1/85.
CARPENTER W.C.A. Born 13/2/26. Commd 30/7/59. Flt Lt 30/7/64. Retd ENG 1/6/76.
CARPMAEL R.M. Born 28/9/30. Commd 1/11/56. Sqn Ldr 1/1/72. Retd GD(G) 20/9/85.
CARR B.M. BSc. Born 12/9/32. Commd 2/2/55. Flt Lt 2/11/59. Retd SUP 2/9/71.
CARR C.L.J. BSc. Born 6/11/41. Commd 27/2/63. Flt Lt 17/5/66. Retd PI 19/8/77.
CARR C.P. Born 4/4/37. Commd 28/11/69. Flt Lt 4/5/72. Retd GD 1/1/75.
CARR D.R. MCMI. Born 12/1/26. Commd 24/5/53. Sqn Ldr 1/1/63. Retd GD 12/1/84.
CARR E. MILT MCIPD. Born 15/4/46. Commd 8/12/83. Sqn Ldr 1/7/94. Retd SUP 14/3/96.
CARR E.W. DCAe. Born 12/11/25. Commd 3/8/45. Sqn Ldr 1/7/57. Retd ENG 12/11/63.
CARR I.R. Born 22/6/40. Commd 22/2/63. Flt Lt 22/8/68. Retd GD 30/10/78.
CARR J.H. MSc BSc (Eur Ing) CEng MIMechE. Born 3/9/62. Commd 14/10/84. Flt Lt 14/4/87. Retd ENG 14/10/00.
CARR J.V. BTech. Born 23/6/57. Commd 6/9/81. Sqn Ldr 1/7/96. Retd GD 1/7/99.

CARR M.C. Born 21/11/45. Commd 1/4/65. Sqn Ldr 1/7/84. Retd SUP 21/11/00.
CARR M.J.I. Born 28/4/36. Commd 21/4/54. Flt Lt 13/4/60. Retd GD 1/1/76.
CARR N.J. MB BS MRCPath. Born 11/1/60. Commd 8/10/84. Wg Cdr 22/9/97. Retd MED 8/10/00.
CARR P.G. BSc. Born 6/4/59. Commd 15/1/79. Flt Lt 15/4/82. Retd GD 24/11/98.
CARR P.H. Born 7/11/59. Commd 11/6/81. Sqn Ldr 1/7/91. Retd GD 4/1/98.
CARR P.S. Born 17/5/33. Commd 27/3/70. Sqn Ldr 1/1/80. Retd ENG 12/3/86.
CARR P.W. AFC. Born 30/3/25. Commd 4/9/46. Sqn Ldr 1/7/58. Retd GD 27/2/60.
CARR P.W. BA. Born 14/5/48. Commd 1/2/87. Flt Lt 1/2/92. Retd ADMIN 5/2/96.
CARR R.F.R. MBE . Born 18/5/47. Commd 10/6/66. Gp Capt 1/1/91. Retd GD 18/5/04.
CARR R.H. DFM. Born 15/9/16. Commd 23/12/42. Flt Lt 4/6/53. Retd GD(G) 19/9/71.
CARR S.E. Born 11/9/29. Commd 24/9/64. Flt Lt 24/9/69. Retd ENG 29/4/78.
CARR S.J. Born 9/6/42. Commd 4/7/69. Flt Lt 21/2/73. Retd GD 1/1/89.
CARR S.R. DFC . Born 4/5/63. Commd 24/3/83. Sqn Ldr 1/1/00. Retd FLY(P) 31/1/05.
CARR T.J. Born 4/2/41. Commd 17/7/62. Sqn Ldr 1/7/73. Retd ENG 2/3/79.
CARR W.R. OBE FInstPet MCMI. Born 25/5/29. Commd 24/9/59. Wg Cdr 1/7/76. Retd SUP 2/7/82.
CARR-GLYNN K.A. Born 4/3/42. Commd 5/3/65. Flt Lt 9/2/68. Retd GD 6/3/79.
CARR-WHITE C.I. Born 23/6/37. Commd 6/12/58. Sqn Ldr 1/1/70. Retd GD 11/12/77.
CARRAN R.J. Born 9/6/38. Commd 18/7/63. Flt Lt 1/4/66. Retd GD 10/6/75.
CARRELL P.C. CEng MCMI MRAeS. Born 12/5/41. Commd 19/1/66. Sqn Ldr 1/7/75. Retd ENG 12/11/95.
CARREY R.A.J. Born 8/11/31. Commd 31/10/51. Flt Lt 31/7/57. Retd GD 8/11/69.
CARRINGTON C.J.M. BA. Born 16/9/41. Commd 30/7/63. Wg Cdr 1/7/83. Retd GD 31/12/91.
CARRINGTON D.J. BSc(Eng) CEng MRAeS ACGI. Born 21/4/48. Commd 20/9/66. Wg Cdr 1/1/88. Retd ENG 21/4/92.
CARRINGTON P.C.R. Born 7/7/18. Commd 19/7/46. Wg Cdr 1/7/62. Retd RGT 31/10/64.
CARRINGTON P.J. BSc. Born 16/1/34. Commd 16/12/56. Sqn Ldr 6/6/67. Retd EDN 30/8/72.
CARROLL B. BSc MRAeS MCMI. Born 22/2/31. Commd 6/2/52. Wg Cdr 1/7/68. Retd GD 22/9/84.
CARROLL D. Born 26/1/41. Commd 25/8/60. Flt Lt 25/11/66. Retd ADMIN 1/9/91.
CARROLL F.A. BEM. Born 29/3/43. Commd 11/10/84. Sqn Ldr 1/1/90. Retd SUP 21/8/93.
CARROLL M.J. MB ChB DAvMed. Born 16/1/53. Commd 23/1/74. Wg Cdr 15/8/90. Retd MED 31/7/91.
CARROLL M.J. BChD FDSRCS. Born 14/5/41. Commd 24/3/63. Sqn Ldr 20/3/70. Retd DEL 7/3/78.
CARROLL P. Born 9/7/59. Commd 7/8/87. Flt Lt 15/7/91. Retd ENG 9/7/97.
CARROLL P.J. Born 21/4/51. Commd 27/3/70. Flt Lt 27/9/75. Retd GD 21/4/89.
CARROLL P.T.J. Born 14/3/42. Commd 15/9/67. Wg Cdr 1/7/89. Retd GD 15/11/92.
CARROLL R.M. MSc BSc. Born 9/10/52. Commd 3/7/83. Flt Lt 1/5/78. Retd ADMIN 25/3/92.
CARROLL S.D. Born 7/9/68. Commd 28/7/88. Fg Offr 28/1/91. Retd SY 20/8/93.
CARROLL T.F. Born 5/8/23. Commd 3/9/44. Flt Lt 11/12/54. Retd GD(G) 12/11/64.
CARROLL W.H. Born 9/4/30. Commd 26/3/52. Flt Lt 31/7/57. Retd GD 1/4/76.
CARROTT I.C. Born 31/10/27. Commd 14/4/49. Sqn Ldr 1/7/61. Retd GD 24/2/79.
CARRUTHERS J.A. MA CEng MIEE. Born 6/7/37. Commd 30/9/56. Wg Cdr 1/7/79. Retd ENG 6/7/92.
CARRUTHERS J.B. BSc. Born 15/9/26. Commd 20/11/47. Wg Cdr 1/1/66. Retd GD 15/12/82.
CARRUTHERS R. Born 20/7/40. Commd 15/6/83. Flt Lt 15/6/87. Retd ADMIN 31/10/93.
CARSON A.V. Born 24/12/61. Commd 12/3/87. Sqn Ldr 1/7/97. Retd ENG 1/7/00.
CARSON G.P. BEd FCMI DPhysEd. Born 13/2/46. Commd 11/8/69. Gp Capt 1/1/92. Retd ADMIN 8/9/95.
CARSON T.A. DFC. Born 14/7/23. Commd 3/8/44. Flt Lt 13/12/48. Retd GD 5/10/61.
CARSTAIRS T. BEM. Born 31/3/37. Commd 1/6/72. Sqn Ldr 1/7/83. Retd ENG 1/7/92.
CARTER A.J.R. Born 9/2/45. Commd 24/4/64. Flt Lt 24/10/69. Retd GD 1/2/71.
CARTER A.M. Born 3/12/37. Commd 31/1/64. Wg Cdr 1/1/87. Retd GD 30/6/93.
CARTER A.R. Born 20/5/38. Commd 17/7/56. Sqn Ldr 1/7/68. Retd GD 20/5/76.
CARTER B.R. Born 11/11/32. Commd 27/1/55. Sqn Ldr 1/7/67. Retd GD 31/1/70.
CARTER C.A. BSc. Born 22/8/63. Commd 14/10/84. Flt Lt 14/4/87. Retd GD 22/9/01.
CARTER C.G. Born 29/2/44. Commd 19/4/63. Flt Lt 19/10/68. Retd GD 14/9/96.
CARTER C.N. BSc. Born 6/3/52. Commd 22/3/81. Flt Lt 22/9/84. Retd OPS SPT 6/3/99.
CARTER C.S. Born 25/9/44. Commd 11/1/79. Flt Lt 11/1/81. Retd GD 11/1/87.
CARTER D.E. Born 21/6/42. Commd 18/12/62. Flt Lt 18/6/65. Retd GD 29/12/73.
CARTER D.E. Born 14/2/41. Commd 11/6/60. Flt Lt 14/2/66. Retd GD 14/2/79.
CARTER D.E. MBE . Born 19/5/44. Commd 7/1/71. Sqn Ldr 1/7/98. Retd FLY(P) 19/5/04.
CARTER D.J. Born 9/2/42. Commd 3/8/62. Flt Lt 3/2/68. Retd GD 9/2/80.
CARTER D.McG. Born 8/12/23. Commd 30/7/61. Sqn Ldr 1/1/73. Retd ADMIN 9/12/77.
CARTER E.M.A. MBA BA. Born 9/10/59. Commd 4/1/83. Sqn Ldr 1/7/97. Retd OPS SPT 1/10/99.
CARTER E.R. Born 29/8/27. Commd 11/4/57. Sqn Ldr 1/7/69. Retd GD 2/6/76.
CARTER G.H. AFC. Born 1/6/17. Commd 14/3/45. Flt Lt 29/6/50. Retd GD(G) 13/8/64.
CARTER G.R. Born 13/9/24. Commd 27/5/54. Flt Lt 27/5/60. Retd GD 29/1/72.
CARTER G.W. Born 28/6/22. Commd 9/6/52. Flt Lt 7/3/62. Retd SEC 15/5/69.
CARTER I.C. Born 17/2/32. Commd 25/2/63. Flt Lt 24/11/67. Retd GD(G) 17/2/89.
CARTER J.A. Born 16/11/36. Commd 12/9/63. Wg Cdr 1/1/78. Retd ADMIN 1/9/87.
CARTER J.A. Born 28/11/24. Commd 16/4/44. Flt Lt 23/1/49. Retd GD 31/12/55.
CARTER J.A. Born 7/2/30. Commd 30/6/54. Flt Lt 5/10/60. Retd GD 2/12/68.

CARTER J.C. Born 10/7/59. Commd 29/8/77. APO 29/8/77. Retd ENG 28/9/78.
CARTER J.D. Born 13/9/61. Commd 1/7/82. Sqn Ldr 1/1/93. Retd GD 13/9/99.
CARTER J.F. Born 10/9/35. Commd 31/7/59. Fg Offr 31/7/59. Retd GD 15/5/66.
CARTER J.G. Born 28/9/28. Commd 4/6/52. Wg Cdr 1/1/75. Retd GD 1/1/82.
CARTER J.G. MA CEng MIEE MRAeS. Born 30/9/35. Commd 25/9/54. Sqn Ldr 1/1/67. Retd ENG 30/9/73.
CARTER J.H. AFC. Born 29/4/34. Commd 8/4/53. Wg Cdr 1/7/78. Retd GD 1/10/84.
CARTER J.S.R.B. Born 25/1/29. Commd 20/6/63. Flt Lt 20/6/66. Retd GD 14/11/79.
CARTER J.V.E.P. Born 17/3/26. Commd 22/2/46. Wg Cdr 1/7/63. Retd GD 17/3/81.
CARTER J.W. DFM. Born 16/8/18. Commd 14/12/46. Flt Lt 7/6/51. Retd GD 1/1/54.
CARTER M.A. Born 11/8/58. Commd 21/4/77. Flt Lt 21/10/82. Retd GD 22/3/91.
CARTER N.D.R. MB ChB. Born 24/11/63. Commd 27/1/94. Wg Cdr 21/8/02. Retd MEDICAL 1/8/03.
CARTER N.T. OBE. Born 6/4/42. Commd 24/1/63. A Cdre 1/1/90. Retd SUP 1/10/94.
CARTER P.R. Born 24/4/35. Commd 2/4/65. Flt Lt 4/11/70. Retd GD 30/1/73.
CARTER P.R. Born 16/9/46. Commd 18/11/66. Wg Cdr 1/7/88. Retd GD(G) 14/3/96.
CARTER R. Born 2/8/35. Commd 23/6/67. Sqn Ldr 1/7/80. Retd ENG 10/7/86.
CARTER R.A.C. CB DSO DFC MRAeS. Born 15/9/10. Commd 23/7/32. A Cdre 1/7/56. Retd GD 25/4/64.
CARTER S.J. MB BS DA FFARCS. Born 5/4/32. Commd 16/6/57. Gp Capt 17/11/79. Retd MED 16/10/85.
CARTER S.J. Born 23/9/62. Commd 8/11/90. Sqn Ldr 1/1/00. Retd ENGINEER 31/1/04.
CARTER T.F. MBE AFC. Born 5/9/31. Commd 2/7/52. Sqn Ldr 1/7/77. Retd GD 3/10/91.
CARTER V.W. IEng. Born 24/2/45. Commd 8/6/84. Flt Lt 8/6/88. Retd ENG 1/9/94.
CARTLICH S.A. Born 11/6/23. Commd 24/5/59. Flt Lt 24/9/64. Retd ENG 1/9/77.
CARTLIDGE A.W.F. Born 9/10/29. Commd 13/12/50. Flt Lt 13/12/55. Retd SUP 9/10/67.
CARTLIDGE J.K. Born 1/4/48. Commd 1/8/69. Flt Lt 1/2/75. Retd ENG 15/7/77.
CARTLIDGE P.F. Born 30/11/36. Commd 23/6/61. Fg Offr 23/6/63. Retd GD 30/4/69.
CARTMELL A.E. BA MA. Born 15/8/32. Commd 14/7/55. Wg Cdr 1/1/75. Retd EDN 5/1/82.
CARTNER E. DPhysEd. Born 3/12/39. Commd 26/5/64. Wg Cdr 1/7/90. Retd ADMIN 11/8/93.
CARTWRIGHT A.A. MA. Born 9/1/28. Commd 23/2/50. Gp Capt 1/1/74. Retd ADMIN 20/9/80.
CARTWRIGHT B.A. Born 30/1/32. Commd 28/7/67. Flt Lt 15/4/70. Retd GD 17/11/75. Re-instated 18/12/97 to 15/5/90.
CARTWRIGHT J. Born 8/2/37. Commd 1/4/58. Flt Lt 8/10/63. Retd GD 26/6/69.
CARTWRIGHT J.B. BSc. Born 5/4/32. Commd 8/8/56. Sqn Ldr 22/7/64. Retd ADMIN 17/8/84.
CARTWRIGHT J.E. Born 16/2/38. Commd 5/11/70. Sqn Ldr 1/7/77. Retd GD(G) 16/2/93.
CARTWRIGHT R.J. MRIN MCMI. Born 17/11/44. Commd 14/6/63. Wg Cdr 1/1/88. Retd GD 31/3/94.
CARTWRIGHT S.A. BA. Born 29/4/52. Commd 22/10/72. Flt Lt 22/7/76. Retd SUP 22/10/84.
CARTWRIGHT-TERRY I.S. Born 27/4/49. Commd 26/2/71. Flt Lt 26/2/74. Retd GD 14/3/97.
CARTWRIGHT-TERRY L.G.G. MBE BA. Born 10/9/47. Commd 28/2/69. Wg Cdr 1/7/99. Retd ENG 10/9/02.
CARTY P.J. Born 26/11/25. Commd 3/5/46. Sqn Ldr 1/7/60. Retd GD 1/9/72.
CARUANA P.A. Born 5/10/53. Commd 2/11/88. Flt Lt 2/11/92. Retd SUP 8/6/93.
CARUS D.A. BSc. Born 14/10/51. Commd 13/9/70. Flt Lt 15/10/76. Retd ENG 22/1/80.
CARVELL C.J. Born 9/4/45. Commd 5/11/70. Sqn Ldr 1/1/88. Retd GD(G) 14/3/96.
CARVELL D.R. AFC. Born 28/10/46. Commd 1/3/68. Flt Lt 1/3/71. Retd GD 28/10/84.
CARVELL R.M. BA. Born 22/4/56. Commd 6/11/77. Flt Lt 6/2/80. Retd ADMIN 2/2/86.
CARVELLO P.E. Born 24/2/37. Commd 25/9/59. Flt Lt 28/7/65. Retd ENG 25/9/75.
CARVER H.D. FCMI. Born 14/1/24. Commd 3/3/45. Gp Capt 1/1/74. Retd GD 29/4/78.
CARVER H.S. CBE LVO FCMI. Born 30/9/28. Commd 5/4/50. A Cdre 1/7/77. Retd GD 1/3/84.
CARVER M.J. Born 24/8/38. Commd 28/4/65. Flt Lt 8/1/69. Retd GD 29/8/75.
CARVER N.J. AFC. Born 5/8/22. Commd 3/7/42. Sqn Ldr 1/7/62. Retd GD 31/8/63.
CARVOSSO A.F. Born 18/1/23. Commd 3/7/42. Wg Cdr 1/1/62. Retd GD 29/11/72.
CARVOSSO K.G. Born 1/11/46. Commd 29/4/71. Sqn Ldr 1/1/86. Retd GD 1/1/89.
CASANO M.P. MC. Born 7/6/13. Commd 12/6/35. Flt Lt 1/6/45. Retd SEC 24/3/58.
CASE G.A. Born 7/8/52. Commd 13/9/70. Sqn Ldr 1/7/85. Retd GD 7/8/90.
CASE R.A. Born 6/3/51. Commd 15/9/69. Flt Lt 13/3/76. Retd GD 5/10/88.
CASE V.L. Born 11/12/57. Commd 27/1/77. Flt Lt 4/6/83. Retd GD(G) 11/12/95.
CASE W.C. BA. Born 9/3/38. Commd 2/10/61. Sqn Ldr 14/8/68. Retd ADMIN 2/10/77.
CASEMENT P.R. DSO DFC* AFC. Born 22/5/21. Commd 21/7/40. Gp Capt 1/1/60. Retd GD 29/6/68.
CASEY B.J. Born 18/6/50. Commd 14/1/79. Fg Offr 14/1/79. Retd ADMIN 23/11/82.
CASEY D.M. Born 18/10/42. Commd 18/4/74. Wg Cdr 1/1/89. Retd GD 31/10/92.
CASEY G.A. Born 28/1/66. Commd 5/10/95. Flt Lt 5/10/97. Retd SUPPLY 28/1/04.
CASEY H. BSc. Born 9/6/57. Commd 2/3/80. Flt Lt 2/6/83. Retd GD(G) 7/9/83.
CASEY J.P. Born 5/2/60. Commd 3/7/80. Sqn Ldr 1/7/93. Retd OPS SPT 1/5/02.
CASEY L. MBE. Born 31/5/15. Commd 25/5/44. Sqn Ldr 1/1/64. Retd GD(G) 31/7/70.
CASEY T.M. Born 8/5/39. Commd 25/6/66. Flt Lt 12/11/69. Retd GD 31/7/73.
CASEY W.M. Born 23/7/23. Commd 15/9/47. Flt Lt 25/11/53. Retd GD 23/7/66.
CASEY W.P. Born 3/4/48. Commd 23/3/67. Sqn Ldr 1/1/85. Retd GD(G) 3/4/92.
CASH P.B. Born 8/3/31. Commd 28/7/53. Wg Cdr 1/7/80. Retd GD 8/3/86.
CASKIE J. Born 13/9/39. Commd 9/2/62. Flt Lt 9/8/67. Retd GD 17/10/77.
CASLEY V.G.S. Born 16/6/16. Commd 6/9/42. Sqn Ldr 1/1/55. Retd GD 1/7/58.

CASS A.C. MBE. Born 15/2/39. Commd 5/2/57. Sqn Ldr 1/1/91. Retd GD 15/2/94.
CASS J.M. BA. Born 25/3/61. Commd 27/3/83. Sqn Ldr 1/1/96. Retd GD 18/3/00.
CASS R.P. BSc CEng MIEE MIMechE MRAeS. Born 29/5/28. Commd 15/7/52. Wg Cdr 1/1/66. Retd ENG 29/5/83.
CASSADY R.J. Born 7/2/43. Commd 25/1/63. Wg Cdr 1/1/88. Retd GD 5/5/03.
CASSADY R.J. Born 7/2/43. Commd 25/1/63. Wg Cdr 1/1/88. Retd GD 1/2/04.
CASSELL D.B. Born 17/4/24. Commd 15/8/51. Flt Lt 28/3/57. Retd GD(G) 31/8/68. Re-instated 10/6/71 to 17/4/82.
CASSELS C.McI. Born 11/8/23. Commd 10/7/44. Sqn Ldr 1/7/53. Retd GD 11/8/66.
CASSELS J.R. DFC*. Born 2/4/22. Commd 21/7/43. Sqn Ldr 1/1/53. Retd GD 2/4/65.
CASSELS J.R.G. Born 10/9/41. Commd 28/4/61. Sqn Ldr 1/1/75. Retd GD 8/3/76.
CASSELY A.A. Born 2/3/23. Commd 21/4/67. Flt Lt 21/4/70. Retd GD(G) 2/7/48.
CASSELY I.H. BSc. Born 10/8/53. Commd 6/3/77. Flt Lt 6/3/93. Retd GD 6/3/93.
CASSIA S.H. MA. Born 1/5/57. Commd 5/9/76. Flt Lt 15/10/82. Retd ENG 25/4/86.
CASSIDY A.C. MA CEng MRAeS. Born 7/4/49. Commd 15/9/69. Sqn Ldr 1/7/80. Retd ENG 7/2/90. rtg Wg Cdr
CASSIDY A.J. Born 6/3/48. Commd 21/1/66. Flt Lt 21/7/71. Retd GD 30/10/74.
CASSIDY E.M. Born 26/3/47. Commd 13/5/73. Flt Lt 13/11/74. Retd SEC 24/5/75.
CASSIDY M.J.V. The Rt Rev Mgr. Born 15/2/37. Commd 3/9/68. Retd Gp Capt 11/4/92.
CASSIDY P.J. MA BSc. Born 29/3/48. Commd 5/2/84. Sqn Ldr 1/7/91. Retd ADMIN 14/2/97.
CASSON D.S. Born 3/2/23. Commd 21/1/45. Flt Lt 7/12/49. Retd GD 10/6/59.
CASSON E.A. DMS. Born 9/3/32. Commd 22/1/55. Sqn Ldr 1/1/66. Retd GD 1/11/76.
CASTAGNOLA J. DSO DFC*. Born 20/4/22. Commd 13/12/43. Sqn Ldr 1/7/55. Retd GD 15/11/61.
CASTLE D.A. BSc. Born 14/7/55. Commd 2/9/73. Wg Cdr 1/1/97. Retd GD 19/10/01.
CASTLE D.E. Born 8/7/36. Commd 25/1/63. Flt Lt 26/7/67. Retd GD 3/9/78.
CASTLE D.J.D. Born 11/12/32. Commd 21/5/52. Sqn Ldr 1/7/70. Retd GD 13/11/75.
CASTLE G. BA. Born 9/2/48. Commd 13/9/70. Gp Capt 1/1/93. Retd SY 2/6/95.
CASTLE K.A. Born 24/9/41. Commd 9/3/62. Flt Lt 9/9/67. Retd GD 26/11/76.
CASTLE L.L.G. Born 14/6/13. Commd 7/7/55. Flt Lt 7/7/58. Retd ENG 1/7/67.
CASTLE R.C. MILT MCIPD MCMI. Born 3/6/49. Commd 22/5/70. Sqn Ldr 1/7/83. Retd SUP 3/6/87.
CASTLE R.G. Born 10/7/30. Commd 5/3/53. Flt Lt 5/9/57. Retd GD 31/3/70.
CASTLE T.B. Born 6/10/36. Commd 26/10/61. Flt Lt 4/8/66. Retd GD 6/10/74.
CASTLING D.P. MB ChB. Born 3/12/56. Commd 17/7/80. Sqn Ldr 1/8/88. Retd MED 14/3/96.
CASTLING H.C. Born 19/3/22. Commd 25/9/46. Flt Lt 4/12/52. Retd SY 26/3/77.
CASTLING S.H.P. LLB. Born 20/11/53. Commd 17/9/72. Flt Lt 30/3/80. Retd LGL 1/9/83.
CASWELL A.G. Born 2/7/37. Commd 28/2/57. Flt Lt 21/8/63. Retd SY 2/7/92.
CATER G. CEng MIMechE. Born 27/12/34. Commd 12/9/61. Sqn Ldr 1/1/73. Retd ENG 9/8/86.
CATER J.H. AFC. Born 10/11/16. Commd 16/10/40. Sqn Ldr 1/7/58. Retd ENG 28/11/65.
CATER M.J.G. Born 21/9/43. Commd 22/3/63. Flt Lt 17/3/71. Retd GD 27/11/76.
CATER R.L. MBE CEng MRAeS. Born 6/10/17. Commd 29/9/41. Sqn Ldr 1/1/54. Retd ENG 6/10/72.
CATER R.S.C. MA MRAeS. Born 10/11/11. Commd 4/4/39. Gp Capt 1/7/64. Retd EDN 8/8/70.
CATLIN B. MCMI. Born 10/2/19. Commd 5/10/50. Sqn Ldr 1/7/61. Retd ENG 10/12/77.
CATLOW M.W. Born 2/7/41. Commd 14/8/64. Flt Lt 14/2/70. Retd GD 11/7/80.
CATON G. Born 2/1/49. Commd 29/11/68. Sqn Ldr 1/7/84. Retd GD 14/9/96.
CATON J.E. Born 22/1/17. Commd 9/9/43. Sqn Ldr 1/7/58. Retd SEC 22/1/64.
CATON T.G.C. Born 31/10/28. Commd 5/4/50. Flt Lt 27/2/55. Retd GD 31/10/83.
CATT D.G. Born 14/11/36. Commd 4/2/63. Flt Lt 4/2/63. Retd GD 14/11/86.
CATT R.D. Born 3/5/30. Commd 22/3/51. Flt Lt 22/3/57. Retd SEC 30/12/61.
CATT W.R. Born 28/12/39. Commd 9/11/84. Sqn Ldr 1/1/93. Retd GD 31/3/95.
CATTERALL R.P. Born 1/3/67. Commd 11/9/86. Sqn Ldr 1/7/01. Retd FLY(P) 1/3/05.
CATTERSON D.G. BSc. Born 12/1/51. Commd 8/7/73. Sqn Ldr 1/1/86. Retd GD 14/9/96.
CATTLE A.P. Born 26/9/37. Commd 9/2/62. Sqn Ldr 1/7/89. Retd GD 26/9/97.
CATTLE F.H.P. AFC. Born 29/6/26. Commd 14/6/46. Wg Cdr 1/1/66. Retd GD 23/2/79.
CAULFIELD W. BA. Born 13/3/33. Commd 31/10/61. Sqn Ldr 9/3/66. Retd ADMIN 31/10/77.
CAUSER D.R. BSc ACGI. Born 7/12/50. Commd 24/3/74. Flt Lt 2/7/76. Retd GD 2/4/92.
CAUSTON M.J. Born 19/4/40. Commd 2/6/77. Flt Lt 2/6/81. Retd GD(G) 1/5/90. Re-instated 9/9/91. Flt Lt 11/10/82.
  Retd GD(G) 1/8/94.
CAVANAGH J.C. BSc MCMI. Born 5/12/52. Commd 28/12/71. Sqn Ldr 1/7/84. Retd GD 5/12/90.
CAVANAGH J.P. Born 17/2/42. Commd 11/3/65. Sqn Ldr 15/2/83. Retd GD 31/3/94.
CAVE A.P.D. MB ChB FRCR DRCOG. Born 19/3/50. Commd 28/9/70. Wg Cdr 16/4/87. Retd MED 14/3/96.
CAVE G.S. BSc. Born 19/4/58. Commd 12/8/79. Sqn Ldr 1/7/95. Retd ADMIN 14/3/97.
CAVE L.W. MBE. Born 8/5/30. Commd 13/7/61. Sqn Ldr 1/1/71. Retd SUP 8/2/73.
CAVE R.A. Born 7/3/48. Commd 23/3/67. Flt Lt 23/9/72. Retd GD 7/3/86.
CAVE T.S. BA. Born 2/8/58. Commd 22/3/81. Flt Lt 22/6/82. Retd GD 22/11/93.
CAVEY V.W. Born 25/3/28. Commd 22/9/55. Wg Cdr 1/7/74. Retd ADMIN 1/12/82.
CAWDERY P.H. MSc BSc. Born 18/10/43. Commd 30/9/63. Sqn Ldr 1/1/76. Retd ENG 18/10/81.
CAWSEY A.W. Born 26/7/35. Commd 10/2/54. Flt Lt 10/8/59. Retd GD 2/1/73.
CAWSEY M.J. Born 21/5/32. Commd 9/12/71. Sqn Ldr 1/1/82. Retd GD 1/8/87.
CAWTHORNE C.A. DFM CEng MRAeS MCMI. Born 22/2/24. Commd 11/5/44. Wg Cdr 1/1/67. Retd ENG 4/7/74.

CAYGILL M.N. Born 1/12/44. Commd 3/3/67. Gp Capt 1/7/86. Retd GD 23/4/90.
CEMM N.A. BSc. Born 20/8/60. Commd 12/2/80. Sqn Ldr 1/7/93. Retd GD 20/8/98.
CHABROWSKI H.B. Born 4/8/47. Commd 16/12/66. Flt Lt 16/6/73. Retd SUP 3/10/78.
CHACKSFIELD A.W. Born 4/8/47. Commd 1/8/69. Fg Offr 1/8/70. Retd RGT 18/10/74.
CHADDERTON A.P. Born 29/3/59. Commd 3/7/80. Flt Lt 3/1/86. Retd GD 29/3/97.
CHADWICK D. Born 5/10/39. Commd 10/11/61. Flt Lt 10/11/66. Retd GD 5/10/77.
CHADWICK D.B. CEng MIMechE. Born 12/4/43. Commd 22/8/71. Flt Lt 22/7/74. Retd ENG 5/4/90.
CHADWICK D.P.C. Born 12/9/46. Commd 19/1/66. Sqn Ldr 1/7/78. Retd SUP 9/7/90.
CHADWICK L.A. Born 2/9/64. Commd 28/7/94. Flt Lt 28/7/96. Retd GD 30/9/02.
CHADWICK P. Born 8/8/25. Commd 6/7/45. Flt Lt 12/10/51. Retd GD 28/9/68.
CHADWICK P.J. AFC FCMI MRAeS. Born 22/11/44. Commd 14/7/63. Wg Cdr 1/1/86. Retd GD 31/3/94.
CHADWICK-HIGGINS S.G. Born 6/7/57. Commd 21/6/90. Sqn Ldr 1/7/01. Retd ADMIN (SEC) 1/10/03.
CHAFER S.N. BA. Born 23/4/59. Commd 4/11/82. Flt Lt 4/5/88. Retd GD 5/7/98.
CHAFFE R. Born 29/12/31. Commd 2/1/64. Sqn Ldr 2/1/69. Retd EDN 24/10/74.
CHAFFEY W.K.T. CEng MRAeS. Born 13/2/39. Commd 30/1/70. Sqn Ldr 1/1/77. Retd ENG 13/2/94.
CHAIKIN D. Born 26/11/22. Commd 22/5/45. Flt Lt 27/5/54. Retd GD 26/11/77.
CHAKRAVERTY A.C. MB BS MChOrth FRCSEd. Born 5/9/36. Commd 17/91. Gp Capt 31/5/89. Retd MED 7/3/99.
CHALKLEY K.B. MBE. Born 19/1/45. Commd 15/7/66. Sqn Ldr 1/7/80. Retd GD 9/12/96.
CHALKLEY W.G. Born 18/10/22. Commd 19/8/65. Flt Lt 19/8/70. Retd ENG 18/10/77.
CHALLANS P.G. BSc CEng MIEE. Born 17/4/46. Commd 31/3/70. Wg Cdr 1/1/91. Retd ENG 1/11/96.
CHALLEN J.M. Born 24/8/32. Commd 6/12/51. Flt Lt 27/3/57. Retd GD(G) 24/8/93.
CHALLINOR J.A. MVO DFM. Born 12/6/23. Commd 5/8/44. Sqn Ldr 1/1/68. Retd GD 12/6/78.
CHALLIS P. BSc. Born 5/12/47. Commd 6/10/69. Wg Cdr 1/1/88. Retd GD 27/6/94.
CHALLONDER A.S. Born 10/11/64. Commd 26/9/91. Sqn Ldr 1/7/00. Retd ENGINEER 1/7/03.
CHALMERS B.L. Born 23/3/21. Commd 15/5/52. Sqn Ldr 1/7/70. Retd SEC 1/1/75.
CHALMERS G.S. Born 27/11/21. Commd 24/4/42. Sqn Ldr 1/10/54. Retd GD 27/11/70.
CHALMERS I.G.C. MCMI. Born 15/8/33. Commd 16/7/52. Wg Cdr 1/7/75. Retd GD 17/1/86.
CHALMERS I.MacD. Born 31/3/29. Commd 2/7/52. Flt Lt 22/8/59. Retd GD 1/9/86.
CHALMERS R.D. Born 3/4/36. Commd 3/11/77. Flt Lt 3/11/81. Retd ENG 1/1/90.
CHALONER C.R. AFC. Born 10/9/47. Commd 11/11/71. Flt Lt 16/8/74. Retd GD 10/9/85.
CHALONER J. DFM. Born 3/6/21. Commd 19/1/44. Flt Lt 19/7/47. Retd GD(G) 30/12/67.
CHAMBERLAIN D.B. BSc. Born 20/1/50. Commd 15/9/69. Sqn Ldr 1/1/84. Retd GD 20/1/88.
CHAMBERLAIN E.J. Born 29/3/27. Commd 28/6/51. Flt Lt 10/10/56. Retd GD 21/11/75.
CHAMBERLAIN K.G. DFC MCIPD. Born 24/3/21. Commd 3/9/42. Wg Cdr 1/7/64. Retd SEC 24/3/76.
CHAMBERLAIN S.J. MSc BEng CEng MIMechE. Born 4/2/56. Commd 1/9/74. Sqn Ldr 1/1/88. Retd ENG 11/9/01.
CHAMBERS B.R.G. BSc CEng MIMechE MRAeS. Born 23/1/43. Commd 25/11/68. Wg Cdr 1/1/88. Retd ENG 23/1/98.
CHAMBERS C.M. Born 12/2/47. Commd 1/3/68. A Cdre 1/1/95. Retd GD 6/4/02.
CHAMBERS D.C. Born 7/5/21. Commd 26/9/57. Flt Lt 1/4/63. Retd ENG 9/12/71.
CHAMBERS H. Born 9/1/19. Commd 30/4/59. Sqn Ldr 15/3/68. Retd MED(SEC) 9/1/74.
CHAMBERS H.J. Born 1/9/30. Commd 5/12/51. Flt Lt 22/5/57. Retd GD 22/8/75.
CHAMBERS J.A.R. Born 10/1/23. Commd 28/5/43. Sqn Ldr 1/7/58. Retd SEC 10/1/73.
CHAMBERS M.A. Born 18/12/45. Commd 23/9/65. Wg Cdr 1/7/98. Retd GD 18/12/03.
CHAMBERS M.A. Born 5/12/80. Commd 28/9/00. Plt Off 28/3/01. Retd OPS SPT(ATC) 19/3/03.
CHAMBERS M.G. MBE. Born 27/5/47. Commd 26/4/84. Sqn Ldr 1/1/99. Retd OPS SPT 1/9/01.
CHAMBERS P.J. Born 17/3/44. Commd 6/4/92. Sqn Ldr 1/1/86. Retd GD(G) 1/6/93.
CHAMBERS R.C. AFC. Born 17/1/36. Commd 19/1/61. Sqn Ldr 1/7/67. Retd GD 17/1/69.
CHAMBERS R.P. BSc. Born 31/8/58. Commd 5/9/76. Sqn Ldr 1/1/88. Retd GD 31/8/96.
CHAMBERS S.P. Born 20/10/58. Commd 20/7/78. Flt Lt 20/1/84. Retd GD 2/4/92.
CHAMBRE A.C.F. BSc DipEl. Born 7/8/20. Commd 4/9/62. Wg Cdr 4/9/62. Retd EDN 1/6/65.
CHAMP R.A. Born 8/2/41. Commd 24/2/67. Flt Lt 12/11/69. Retd GD(G) 8/2/96.
CHAMPION J.H. Born 4/11/32. Commd 27/11/54. Sqn Ldr 1/1/68. Retd SUP 2/6/84.
CHAMPION J.L. Born 24/10/30. Commd 18/3/63. Flt Lt 18/3/63. Retd GD 18/3/71.
CHAMPION M. Born 23/9/48. Commd 3/5/68. Sqn Ldr 1/7/78. Retd GD 10/2/86.
CHAMPION M.C. Born 2/10/43. Commd 15/7/64. Sqn Ldr 1/1/74. Retd ENG 2/10/81.
CHAMPION R.S. Born 16/10/22. Commd 9/3/53. Flt Lt 9/3/57. Retd SEC 12/11/65.
CHAMPNISS P.H. AFC. Born 1/2/33. Commd 6/4/54. Gp Capt 1/1/74. Retd GD 30/9/78.
CHANCE J.P. BSc CEng DipSoton MRAeS. Born 3/9/34. Commd 23/9/55. Wg Cdr 1/7/76. Retd ENG 10/5/86.
CHANDLER C.C. Born 18/3/47. Commd 2/8/68. Sqn Ldr 1/7/80. Retd GD 18/3/91.
CHANDLER D.N. Born 17/9/38. Commd 4/6/64. Flt Lt 26/4/88. Retd ENG 26/4/94.
CHANDLER H.A. MSc MB BS FRCPath MRCS(Eng) LRCP. Born 18/9/38. Commd 5/11/90. Gp Capt 30/6/91.
    Retd MED 14/9/96.
CHANDLER H.C.H. Born 1/9/14. Commd 3/2/45. Flt Lt 17/9/55. Retd SEC 14/5/62.
CHANDLER H.F. Born 14/10/24. Commd 17/11/44. Flt Lt 17/5/48. Retd GD 14/10/82.
CHANDLER H.T. Born 21/11/46. Commd 1/3/68. Flt Lt 1/3/71. Retd GD 1/5/90.
CHANDLER J.A.W. Born 19/10/32. Commd 28/6/51. Flt Lt 10/10/56. Retd GD(G) 19/10/82.
CHANDLER J.E. CBE CEng FRAeS. Born 26/10/47. Commd 28/2/69. Air Cdre 1/1/99. Retd GD 11/1/05.

CHANDLER J.H. BEM BSc. Born 6/10/47. Commd 27/3/86. Flt Lt 27/3/90. Retd ENG 1/12/02.
CHANDLER M.F. Born 31/10/34. Commd 21/10/66. Flt Lt 21/10/71. Retd GD 31/3/87.
CHANDLER N.R. MBE LLB. Born 25/10/58. Commd 17/8/80. Gp Capt 1/1/98. Retd SUP 1/5/01.
CHANDLER P.L. BSc. Born 10/11/53. Commd 27/7/75. Sqn Ldr 1/1/86. Retd GD 10/11/94.
CHANDLER P.M. Born 27/12/56. Commd 18/10/79. Flt Lt 8/10/83. Retd GD 1/1/91.
CHANDLER R.F. Born 19/10/19. Commd 1/5/42. Flt Lt 13/7/49. Retd GD 1/2/58.
CHANDLER R.J. Born 18/3/61. Commd 15/10/81. Flt Lt 18/4/87. Retd GD 17/10/92.
CHANDLER R.M. Born 26/9/45. Commd 2/4/65. Flt Lt 2/10/70. Retd GD 26/9/83.
CHANDLER R.W. Born 12/7/36. Commd 9/4/57. Flt Lt 1/7/69. Retd GD 1/12/75.
CHANEY P.D. MCMI. Born 14/6/49. Commd 29/11/68. Sqn Ldr 1/7/84. Retd GD 14/3/96.
CHANNON J.H. MBE. Born 11/11/43. Commd 6/4/72. Wg Cdr 1/1/90. Retd GD 11/11/98.
CHANT T.J. Born 12/8/59. Commd 11/9/86. Sqn Ldr 1/7/96. Retd ADMIN 1/7/02.
CHANTLER A.H. Born 4/9/23. Commd 17/10/51. Flt Lt 24/7/55. Retd GD 3/3/62.
CHAPLIN A.J. Born 22/11/36. Commd 17/12/57. Gp Capt 1/7/84. Retd GD 22/11/91.
CHAPMAN A. Born 15/3/34. Commd 24/9/52. Flt Lt 1/4/58. Retd GD 4/7/85.
CHAPMAN A.D. Born 13/4/46. Commd 6/5/66. Flt Lt 8/3/72. Retd GD 13/4/01.
CHAPMAN A.R. BA. Born 24/10/67. Commd 12/11/89. Flt Lt 12/5/92. Retd GD 14/9/96.
CHAPMAN B. AE. Born 16/8/19. Commd 9/2/43. Sqn Ldr 1/1/63. Retd SUP 16/10/70.
CHAPMAN C.H. Born 6/4/21. Commd 1/2/62. Sqn Ldr 1/1/72. Retd GD 31/5/75.
CHAPMAN C.R. BEng. Born 16/4/64. Commd 2/8/89. Flt Lt 15/7/92. Retd ENG 16/4/02.
CHAPMAN D. Born 29/3/26. Commd 21/12/45. Sqn Ldr 1/4/56. Retd GD 30/3/68.
CHAPMAN D.J.W. ERD. Born 13/6/32. Commd 5/12/71. Sqn Ldr 5/12/71. Retd SUP 5/12/87.
CHAPMAN D.P. Born 30/7/59. Commd 8/11/90. Flt Lt 8/11/96. Retd ENG 25/6/96.
CHAPMAN D.R. Born 19/9/44. Commd 7/6/68. Flt Lt 7/12/73. Retd GD 26/2/84.
CHAPMAN D.S.J. CEng MIEE. Born 19/10/16. Commd 11/6/53. Sqn Ldr 1/7/61. Retd ENG 6/5/67.
CHAPMAN D.StJ. Born 6/1/37. Commd 20/12/73. Sqn Ldr 1/1/83. Retd GD 6/1/94.
CHAPMAN E.G. CEng MIEE. Born 21/3/38. Commd 30/7/64. Sqn Ldr 1/7/73. Retd ENG 21/3/93.
CHAPMAN F.N. Born 19/3/29. Commd 26/5/60. Sqn Ldr 1/7/72. Retd ENG 9/8/79.
CHAPMAN F.W. BA. Born 18/11/58. Commd 11/9/77. Flt Lt 15/4/82. Retd GD 18/11/96.
CHAPMAN G.C. Born 3/11/32. Commd 31/5/51. Sqn Ldr 1/1/71. Retd GD 3/11/92.
CHAPMAN G.K. Born 19/7/15. Commd 19/8/44. Sqn Ldr 1/1/54. Retd RGT 29/9/57.
CHAPMAN I.J. Born 20/5/56. Commd 14/1/88. Flt Lt 29/6/90. Retd ENG 30/3/93.
CHAPMAN J.H. BSc. Born 19/3/16. Commd 3/12/42. Wg Cdr 1/7/62. Retd EDN 30/11/70.
CHAPMAN J.S. Born 27/10/42. Commd 6/11/64. Flt Lt 6/5/70. Retd GD 27/10/80.
CHAPMAN K. MPhil BA. Born 21/3/39. Commd 24/2/61. Gp Capt 7/7/84. Retd GD 21/3/94.
CHAPMAN M.A. Born 11/3/60. Commd 22/11/84. Sqn Ldr 1/1/99. Retd ENG 4/7/02.
CHAPMAN N.S. OBE. Born 23/6/12. Commd 25/4/40. Wg Cdr 1/1/60. Retd SEC 23/6/67.
CHAPMAN P.E. Born 11/5/20. Commd 17/6/54. Flt Lt 1/6/57. Retd ENG 11/8/62.
CHAPMAN P.G. Born 12/1/35. Commd 15/7/53. Flt Lt 8/1/59. Retd GD 12/1/73.
CHAPMAN P.J. Born 13/9/53. Commd 18/1/73. Wg Cdr 1/1/01. Retd GD 4/1/05.
CHAPMAN P.R.C. Born 31/7/44. Commd 19/4/63. Sqn Ldr 1/7/75. Retd GD 30/6/84.
CHAPMAN R. BSc. Born 5/10/22. Commd 10/7/42. Sqn Ldr 4/3/59. Retd EDN 18/3/64.
CHAPMAN R.H. Born 21/12/33. Commd 25/2/53. Flt Lt 17/8/58. Retd GD 21/12/71.
CHAPMAN R.W. RMN RNT. Born 9/5/29. Commd 24/2/67. Fg Offr 24/2/69. Retd MED(T) 27/2/71.
CHAPMAN S.D. Born 12/3/35. Commd 9/7/57. Sqn Ldr 1/1/73. Retd GD 12/3/93.
CHAPMAN S.M. BA. Born 22/5/29. Commd 26/3/52. Sqn Ldr 1/7/63. Retd SEC 26/6/69.
CHAPMAN-ANDREWS D.F.J. BDS FDS RCS. Born 21/10/33. Commd 3/3/63. Gp Capt 15/12/80. Retd DEL 31/12/91.
CHAPPELL D. IEng MIIE MCMI. Born 6/8/46. Commd 28/10/76. Sqn Ldr 1/1/85. Retd ENGINEER 6/8/04.
CHAPPELL J.D. Born 4/6/38. Commd 10/10/61. Flt Lt 10/5/67. Retd GD 25/7/77.
CHAPPELL M.J. Born 9/6/37. Commd 4/7/57. Sqn Ldr 1/7/74. Retd ADMIN 9/6/89.
CHAPPELL M.R. Born 13/5/62. Commd 22/6/92. Sqn Ldr 1/7/01. Retd OPS SPT(FC) 1/7/04.
CHAPPELL P.D.W. Born 25/3/21. Commd 24/11/40. Sqn Ldr 1/1/53. Retd GD 30/8/61.
CHAPPELL R. Born 2/1/20. Commd 25/5/50. Sqn Ldr 1/1/68. Retd SUP 30/1/70.
CHAPPLE B.A.C. AFC. Born 30/10/41. Commd 18/6/63. Sqn Ldr 1/7/80. Retd GD 30/10/96.
CHAPPLE M.W.P. OBE AFC. Born 11/10/43. Commd 22/9/63. Wg Cdr 1/1/89. Retd GD 5/8/96.
CHAPPLE R. CB MB BS MFPHM MFOM MRCS MCMI LRCP DPH. Born 2/5/34. Commd 6/11/60. AVM 1/1/92.
   Retd MED 1/7/94.
CHAPPLE R.C. Born 5/6/36. Commd 3/8/68. Sqn Ldr 1/1/90. Retd GD 1/1/92.
CHAPPLE S.C. Born 5/6/21. Commd 2/1/43. Flt Lt 25/8/46. Retd GD 29/7/54.
CHARLES G. Born 11/12/42. Commd 9/12/65. Flt Lt 9/6/72. Retd ENG 28/2/76.
CHARLES G.A. MBE. Born 16/10/19. Commd 17/9/43. Flt Lt 28/5/50. Retd GD 25/10/68. rtg Sqn Ldr
CHARLES G.W.F. MRAeS. Born 14/4/29. Commd 26/7/50. Gp Capt 1/1/78. Retd GD 22/3/83.
CHARLES M.M. AFC. Born 27/10/41. Commd 28/4/61. Sqn Ldr 1/7/73. Retd GD 27/10/79.
CHARLES N.W. BSc. Born 11/6/56. Commd 15/9/74. Flt Lt 15/4/79. Retd GD 15/7/89.
CHARLESWORTH A.M. DFC. Born 9/8/22. Commd 6/7/41. Sqn Ldr 1/7/57. Retd GD 30/9/67.
CHARLESWORTH J.M. FCMI. Born 29/4/31. Commd 24/1/52. Gp Capt 1/1/81. Retd GD 29/4/86.

CHARLESWORTH P.B. BSc. Born 24/9/56. Commd 28/9/80. Sqn Ldr 1/1/90. Retd ENG 28/9/96.
CHARLETT-GREEN J.A. MBE. Born 15/8/39. Commd 22/7/66. Wg Cdr 1/1/79. Retd ENG 15/8/94.
CHARLICK S.F. Born 10/2/29. Commd 24/1/52. Flt Lt 15/5/57. Retd GD 15/2/75.
CHARLTON A.R. BSc. Born 19/11/50. Commd 13/9/70. Sqn Ldr 1/7/83. Retd ENG 25/7/90.
CHARLTON B.J. CEng MIEE. Born 13/3/38. Commd 28/7/67. Wg Cdr 1/7/85. Retd ENG 13/3/93.
CHARLTON D. Born 8/5/49. Commd 8/5/86. Wg Cdr 1/7/96. Retd ADMIN 1/7/97.
CHARLTON E.M. BSc. Born 9/4/58. Commd 17/1/82. Flt Lt 17/4/82. Retd GD 28/10/95.
CHARLTON G.K. BSc. Born 24/3/47. Commd 1/9/70. Sqn Ldr 1/7/86. Retd GD 25/9/97.
CHARLTON J.P. Born 21/7/41. Commd 16/1/60. Sqn Ldr 1/1/77. Retd ENG 1/1/80.
CHARLTON M.C. Born 30/3/45. Commd 26/5/67. Wg Cdr 1/1/90. Retd ENG 14/9/96.
CHARLTON P.E. MC MCMI. Born 13/4/25. Commd 20/9/48. Sqn Ldr 1/1/55. Retd SY 30/9/78.
CHARLTON R.A. Born 31/10/39. Commd 9/2/62. Flt Lt 9/8/67. Retd GD 31/10/77.
CHARMAN C.A. Born 4/3/23. Commd 3/9/53. Flt Lt 22/5/57. Retd GD(G) 4/3/78.
CHARMAN J.W. Born 9/8/24. Commd 8/9/44. Flt Lt 8/3/48. Retd GD 9/8/62.
CHARMAN K.P. Born 9/9/24. Commd 6/2/44. Flt Lt 7/6/51. Retd GD 20/11/63.
CHARNLEY N.S. BSc. Born 24/5/62. Commd 14/9/80. Flt Lt 15/4/85. Retd GD 24/5/01.
CHARNOCK P.M. Born 27/7/59. Commd 26/9/90. Flt Lt 26/9/92. Retd ADMIN 26/9/98.
CHARTERS S.J.D. Born 2/6/12. Commd 18/2/42. Flt Lt 1/9/45. Retd ENG 2/6/61. rtg Sqn Ldr
CHARTRES R.W. AFC. Born 12/5/23. Commd 30/9/42. Wg Cdr 1/7/66. Retd GD 2/8/68.
CHASE M.H. Born 14/8/16. Commd 1/8/46. Flt Lt 14/11/56. Retd SUP 14/8/73.
CHASE R.J. Born 2/6/34. Commd 2/7/52. Flt Lt 16/8/61. Retd GD 2/6/72.
CHASE S.W. BA FCIPD FBIFM FCMI MInstAM. Born 22/5/55. Commd 16/9/73. Gp Capt 1/1/95. Retd ADMIN 10/7/97.
CHATER H.A. AFC. Born 6/4/17. Commd 3/5/37. Wg Cdr 1/7/55. Retd GD 6/4/72. rtg Gp Capt
CHATFIELD F.H. Born 28/6/25. Commd 16/9/53. Flt Lt 16/9/60. Retd SEC 28/6/63.
CHATTAWAY A.M. BA. Born 24/7/61. Commd 30/10/83. Flt Lt 30/4/87. Retd SY 14/3/96.
CHATTAWAY C. Born 12/5/57. Commd 20/1/76. Flt Lt 16/4/84. Retd GD 1/4/92.
CHATTERTON M. LLB. Born 19/6/54. Commd 5/1/76. Sqn Ldr 1/1/88. Retd GD 13/2/97.
CHEADLE B.B. Born 11/10/32. Commd 12/9/63. Flt Lt 12/9/69. Retd SEC 1/11/72.
CHEAL T. Born 31/7/59. Commd 20/7/78. Sqn Ldr 1/1/91. Retd GD 31/7/97.
CHEATER B.J. Born 16/5/38. Commd 28/7/59. Sqn Ldr 1/7/68. Retd GD 16/5/76.
CHECKETTS Sir David CVO. Born 23/8/30. Commd 31/8/48. Sqn Ldr 1/7/61. Retd GD 23/8/67.
CHEESBROUGH J. Born 6/12/26. Commd 30/1/52. Wg Cdr 1/1/67. Retd GD 4/4/81.
CHEESEBROUGH D. Born 24/10/37. Commd 1/10/60. Sqn Ldr 1/1/84. Retd GD 24/10/95.
CHEESEMAN N.D. Born 3/6/60. Commd 24/9/92. Sqn Ldr 1/7/02. Retd OPS SPT(PROVSY) 19/7/04.
CHEESEMAN S.B. BSc. Born 30/3/51. Commd 15/9/69. Sqn Ldr 1/1/84. Retd GD 30/3/89.
CHEESMAN C.J. BSc CEng MIEE. Born 8/1/37. Commd 11/9/62. Gp Capt 1/7/89. Retd ENG 1/7/92.
CHEESMAN G.J. Born 4/1/45. Commd 22/5/64. Wg Cdr 1/7/85. Retd ADMIN 4/1/89.
CHEESMAN M. MCMI. Born 17/1/37. Commd 23/7/58. Wg Cdr 1/1/77. Retd ENG 13/5/91.
CHEESMAN P.F. Born 8/2/36. Commd 6/8/60. Flt Lt 6/2/66. Retd GD 12/4/76.
CHEETHAM G.E. Born 23/7/53. Commd 2/2/84. Flt Lt 2/2/86. Retd ADMIN 2/2/92.
CHEETHAM J.D. Born 21/3/38. Commd 21/3/74. Flt Lt 21/3/77. Retd GD 22/9/90.
CHEETHAM J.L. Born 10/2/45. Commd 12/7/63. Flt Lt 12/1/69. Retd GD 26/8/76.
CHEETHAM P.D. BSc. Born 13/5/58. Commd 9/11/80. Flt Lt 9/2/82. Retd GD 9/11/96.
CHELMICK E. MBE. Born 20/6/20. Commd 24/4/45. Wg Cdr 1/7/64. Retd SUP 6/4/68.
CHELU R. Born 13/7/54. Commd 12/7/79. Flt Lt 12/7/81. Retd GD 15/2/01.
CHERRY A.V. Born 5/12/32. Commd 9/4/52. Flt Lt 5/9/57. Retd GD 5/12/70.
CHERRY D.F. Born 9/9/48. Commd 7/6/68. Sqn Ldr 1/1/00. Retd FLY(N) 9/9/03.
CHERRY P. Born 14/9/21. Commd 17/12/43. Sqn Ldr 1/1/56. Retd GD 14/9/64.
CHERRY P.D. OBE DFC DFM. Born 21/4/19. Commd 31/12/41. Wg Cdr 1/1/60. Retd ENG 27/4/68. rtg Gp Capt
CHERRY R.A. MBE BEng CEng MIEE MCMI. Born 28/5/42. Commd 30/5/69. Sqn Ldr 1/1/77. Retd ENG 28/5/97.
CHESHER B.C. Born 17/11/24. Commd 26/1/45. Wg Cdr 1/7/76. Retd GD(G) 30/3/78.
CHESHIRE C. Born 27/7/25. Commd 19/1/45. Wg Cdr 1/7/64. Retd GD 23/3/69.
CHESHIRE Sir John KBE CB FRAeS. Born 4/9/42. Commd 17/12/63. ACM 11/3/97. Retd GD 4/9/00.
CHESHIRE R.C. Born 7/8/40. Commd 13/2/72. Flt Lt 13/11/73. Retd ENG 7/8/95.
CHESNEY A. BSc. Born 15/11/56. Commd 2/9/73. Sqn Ldr 1/1/90. Retd SY 15/11/94.
CHESSALL M.P. Born 9/10/44. Commd 22/5/64. Flt Lt 22/11/69. Retd GD 21/12/76.
CHESSHIRE A. MB BS DA. Born 22/5/21. Commd 9/6/63. Wg Cdr 15/12/67. Retd MED 9/6/82.
CHESTERMAN W.G. Born 16/10/18. Commd 21/9/43. Wg Cdr 1/7/62. Retd SEC 1/5/73.
CHESWORTH G.A. CB OBE DFC. Born 4/6/30. Commd 1/10/53. AVM 1/1/81. Retd GD 3/6/84.
CHETWYND K.J. BSc CEng MIEE. Born 26/8/63. Commd 13/9/81. Flt Lt 15/10/87. Retd ENG 11/3/94.
CHEVERTON B.J. Born 20/12/36. Commd 28/4/61. Flt Lt 1/4/66. Retd GD 1/1/75.
CHEVIN R.W. Born 10/7/47. Commd 19/7/84. Sqn Ldr 1/1/92. Retd MED(SEC) 14/3/96.
CHEW C.P. BA BArch. Born 19/8/56. Commd 6/9/81. Flt Lt 6/12/82. Retd GD 6/9/97.
CHEW J.W.T. Born 10/3/37. Commd 11/6/60. Fg Offr 11/6/63. Retd SEC 10/12/65.
CHEW S.R. Born 12/4/42. Commd 17/12/63. Flt Lt 17/6/66. Retd GD 13/4/79.
CHEYNE J.J. Born 27/5/44. Commd 8/6/62. Sqn Ldr 1/7/75. Retd GD 27/5/82.

CHICHESTER-CONSTABLE G.R. BSc. Born 25/11/55. Commd 28/9/80. Flt Lt 28/12/83. Retd ENG 15/7/88.
CHICK J.F.H. Born 9/1/29. Commd 13/12/50. Wg Cdr 1/7/70. Retd GD 9/1/84. rtg Gp Capt
CHICK R. Born 19/3/32. Commd 15/8/51. Sqn Ldr 1/1/70. Retd GD 8/5/90.
CHICK S.D. BSc. Born 11/3/64. Commd 17/11/83. Flt Lt 15/1/88. Retd GD 15/7/97.
CHICKEN R. Born 26/8/10. Commd 6/9/40. Sqn Ldr 1/8/47. Retd SEC 7/9/59.
CHICKEN S.H. BSc. Born 17/8/60. Commd 4/8/78. Sqn Ldr 1/7/94. Retd ENG 23/1/98.
CHIDDENTION S. MBE. Born 10/10/64. Commd 6/3/92. Wg Cdr 1/1/02. Retd GD 19/11/04.
CHILD J.A. MMAR BSc. Born 9/3/50. Commd 4/10/82. Sqn Ldr 1/7/90. Retd OPS SPT(FC) 9/3/05.
CHILD J.G. Born 14/12/49. Commd 26/10/62. Sqn Ldr 1/1/78. Retd GD 14/12/88.
CHILDS A.P. Born 21/10/45. Commd 26/5/67. Wg Cdr 1/7/91. Retd GD 21/10/00.
CHILDS C. BEng CEng MIEE. Born 29/12/66. Commd 2/8/89. Sqn Ldr 1/7/00. Retd ENGINEER 29/12/04.
CHILDS I.J. Born 24/6/42. Commd 17/12/64. Wg Cdr 1/7/89. Retd GD 24/6/97.
CHILDS L.A. Born 12/8/13. Commd 25/12/41. Sqn Ldr 1/7/51. Retd RGT 23/9/58.
CHILDS M. BSc. Born 22/1/31. Commd 21/10/54. Wg Cdr 1/7/75. Retd ENG 2/4/85.
CHILLAS I.S. Born 6/4/34. Commd 10/9/70. Sqn Ldr 1/7/83. Retd GD 6/4/94.
CHILLERY B.J. Born 13/6/40. Commd 19/8/66. Flt Lt 19/8/68. Retd GD(G) 30/6/90.
CHILTON T.B. Born 7/3/31. Commd 5/11/52. Flt Lt 24/3/58. Retd GD(G) 7/3/86.
CHILVERS A. BSc CEng MRAeS. Born 28/1/47. Commd 26/5/57. Sqn Ldr 1/7/81. Retd ENG 17/2/99.
CHILVERS H.S. Born 10/10/37. Commd 6/7/62. Flt Lt 1/4/66. Retd GD 11/10/91.
CHIMES B.V. BSc. Born 12/7/56. Commd 15/10/78. Sqn Ldr 1/7/91. Retd GD 14/3/96.
CHINERY M.A. Born 15/12/61. Commd 8/9/83. Flt Lt 8/3/90. Retd OPS SPT 15/12/99.
CHINN C.W. BTech. Born 9/7/49. Commd 23/9/68. Sqn Ldr 1/7/85. Retd ENG 1/7/88.
CHINN D. Born 10/9/49. Commd 4/7/69. Flt Lt 4/7/74. Retd GD 1/4/77.
CHINNECK M.R.S. MSc BSc. Born 21/2/51. Commd 26/2/71. Wg Cdr 1/7/99. Retd ENG 2/4/02.
CHIPP M.J. Born 28/6/48. Commd 16/8/68. Sqn Ldr 1/1/85. Retd GD 1/1/88.
CHIPPINGTON C.J. BSc. Born 16/12/43. Commd 15/7/65. Sqn Ldr 1/7/77. Retd ENG 16/12/81.
CHIPPINGTON D.W.B. MBE. Born 7/2/32. Commd 13/6/60. Gp Capt 1/7/78. Retd GD(G) 7/2/87.
CHIPPS B.G. Born 21/11/48. Commd 24/7/81. Flt Lt 24/7/83. Retd GD(ENG) 18/8/88.
CHISHOLM C.G. Born 5/12/32. Commd 28/3/63. Sqn Ldr 1/7/80. Retd GD(AEO) 5/12/87.
CHISHOLM I.M. MCIPD. Born 27/5/40. Commd 26/5/61. Sqn Ldr 1/7/83. Retd GD 25/4/94.
CHISHOLM J. DFC. Born 25/4/23. Commd 17/6/44. Flt Lt 17/6/50. Retd SEC 5/10/58.
CHISLETT C. Born 14/7/60. Commd 5/4/79. Fg Offr 5/10/81. Retd GD(G) 3/7/85.
CHISLETT P.J.A. CBE. Born 31/10/32. Commd 6/12/54. A Cdre 1/1/85. Retd GD(G) 31/10/87.
CHISWICK D.H. Born 20/7/33. Commd 29/12/51. Flt Lt 22/5/57. Retd GD 20/7/76.
CHIVERS R.A. Born 17/4/48. Commd 28/2/69. Flt Lt 4/5/72. Retd GD 28/1/96.
CHIVERS T.A. MA. Born 7/9/33. Commd 12/8/63. Sqn Ldr 14/2/66. Retd ADMIN 4/4/85.
CHO-YOUNG C. MSc CEng FCMI FRAeS DipSoton MIEE AFIMA. Born 9/5/45. Commd 19/8/71. Gp Capt 1/7/91.
    Retd ADMIN 14/3/96.
CHOLERTON P.W. BSc. Born 13/10/49. Commd 26/2/71. Flt Lt 26/5/76. Retd ENG 13/10/87.
CHORLEY A.A. AIIP. Born 1/7/18. Commd 2/10/58. Sqn Ldr 1/1/69. Retd ENG 1/7/73.
CHORLTON I. MB BS MRCPath DCP. Born 31/7/37. Commd 27/8/62. Wg Cdr 22/8/75. Retd MED 27/8/78.
CHOTHIA G.M. Born 31/1/44. Commd 28/7/67. Wg Cdr 1/7/96. Retd OPS SPT 10/4/98.
CHOWN B.A. Born 27/11/47. Commd 1/12/77. Sqn Ldr 1/1/87. Retd ADMIN 27/11/02.
CHOWN B.A.J. Born 1/5/43. Commd 7/7/67. Sqn Ldr 1/1/80. Retd GD 3/1/83.
CHOWN J.F. BEM. Born 14/11/32. Commd 14/3/52. Flt Lt 14/11/75. Retd PI 1/10/81.
CHOY E. Born 22/8/23. Commd 15/10/43. Flt Lt 15/10/45. Retd GD 17/9/73.
CHRISP C.R. CEng MRAeS. Born 9/3/24. Commd 21/10/63. Sqn Ldr 10/2/67. Retd EDN 21/10/79.
CHRISPIN D.S. Born 30/10/34. Commd 31/12/52. Sqn Ldr 1/7/66. Retd GD 30/10/72.
CHRISTENSEN C.K. MBE MSc CEng MIEE DipElEng. Born 25/7/48. Commd 2/1/74. Wg Cdr 1/7/99.
    Retd ENG 3/2/03.
CHRISTIAN D.A. Born 7/6/35. Commd 10/4/56. Flt Lt 29/4/59. Retd GD 7/6/73.
CHRISTIAN D.A. Born 31/8/26. Commd 27/2/52. Flt Lt 15/2/65. Retd SEC 9/12/71.
CHRISTIE A. BSc. Born 14/6/30. Commd 11/10/52. Flt Lt 1/6/57. Retd ENG 4/9/63.
CHRISTIE A.M. AFC MRAeS. Born 20/10/28. Commd 12/12/51. Gp Capt 1/1/77. Retd GD 20/10/83.
CHRISTIE C.M. FCMI. Born 3/5/32. Commd 2/7/52. Gp Capt 1/1/82. Retd GD 3/9/87.
CHRISTIE G. BSc. Born 26/1/43. Commd 27/3/80. Flt Lt 27/3/82. Retd ENG 27/3/88.
CHRISTIE J.L. BSc MB ChB MRCPath DCP DMJ. Born 13/12/39. Commd 3/10/66. Wg Cdr 15/10/78.
    Retd MED 3/10/82.
CHRISTIE J.McL. MSc BSc. Born 17/5/42. Commd 30/8/66. Sqn Ldr 28/2/74. Retd ADMIN 10/2/90.
CHRISTIE N.G. Born 25/9/47. Commd 14/7/66. Flt Lt 4/5/72. Retd GD 25/9/85.
CHRISTIE S.G. MSc BSc. Born 10/12/49. Commd 15/9/69. Sqn Ldr 1/7/81. Retd ENG 10/3/88.
CHRISTIE S.J. Born 7/5/47. Commd 6/5/83. Sqn Ldr 1/7/93. Retd ADMIN 1/12/00.
CHRISTIE-MILLER I.R. Born 4/5/42. Commd 18/12/62. Flt Lt 18/6/65. Retd GD 24/11/77.
CHRISTISON J.D. MBE. Born 21/8/33. Commd 2/7/52. Sqn Ldr 1/7/80. Retd GD 21/8/93.
CHRISTMAS D.F. Born 5/4/31. Commd 28/6/51. Flt Lt 22/5/77. Retd GD 31/7/77.
CHRISTY M.G. Born 24/7/43. Commd 28/7/64. Flt Lt 26/7/67. Retd GD 24/7/88.

CHRISTY M.P. BSc. Born 2/5/60. Commd 28/1/82. Sqn Ldr 1/1/95. Retd GD 2/5/98.
CHUBB A.B. BSc. Born 3/2/81. Commd 19/2/73. Sqn Ldr 1/7/85. Retd GD 19/2/89.
CHUBB M.A. MA BSc MCMI. Born 26/8/58. Commd 29/11/81. Wg Cdr 1/1/01. Retd GD 29/2/04.
CHURCH J.E.A. Born 24/2/64. Commd 14/1/88. Flt Lt 14/7/94. Retd OPS SPT 22/9/02.
CHURCH J.E.H. Born 2/11/24. Commd 15/9/60. Sqn Ldr 1/1/72. Retd ENG 2/11/79.
CHURCH J.M. BA. Born 12/9/33. Commd 21/11/56. Sqn Ldr 1/7/67. Retd SEC 21/11/72.
CHURCHER C.F.S. MBE CEng MRAeS. Born 12/8/18. Commd 19/8/42. Sqn Ldr 1/1/54. Retd ENG 12/8/76.
CHURCHER D.A. Born 24/4/25. Commd 24/5/44. Flt Lt 4/12/52. Retd GD 28/7/66.
CHURCHER L.C. Born 14/10/20. Commd 2/11/44. Flt Lt 2/7/53. Retd GD 20/5/75.
CHURCHER R.G. DSO MVO DFC*. Born 9/5/22. Commd 29/5/41. Gp Capt 1/1/70. Retd GD 31/3/77.
CHURCHER T.F.C. Born 12/2/20. Commd 4/4/38. Sqn Ldr 1/8/47. Retd GD 12/2/63.
CHURCHER W.J. Born 25/2/27. Commd 19/1/49. Wg Cdr 1/7/76. Retd RGT 7/4/79.
CHURCHILL A.W. Born 23/12/38. Commd 2/5/68. Flt Lt 10/2/74. Retd GD(G) 10/2/80.
CHURCHILL E.J. AFC. Born 20/4/21. Commd 27/9/43. Sqn Ldr 1/4/55. Retd GD 20/4/64.
CHURCHILL I.M. BSc. Born 1/9/63. Commd 2/9/84. Flt Lt 2/3/87. Retd GD 1/9/01.
CHURCHILL J.H. BA MRAeS. Born 25/12/40. Commd 10/11/61. Gp Capt 1/7/88. Retd GD(G) 2/4/93.
CHURCHILL P.S. Born 11/11/59. Commd 5/4/79. Flt Lt 5/10/84. Retd GD 27/6/88.
CHURCHMAN N.J. Born 2/4/67. Commd 7/11/90. Sqn Ldr 1/1/01. Retd ADMIN (SEC) 2/4/05.
CHURCHMAN S.C. Born 25/12/30. Commd 19/6/70. Sqn Ldr 1/1/80. Retd ADMIN 2/6/84.
CLACK A.S.A. Born 9/1/39. Commd 2/1/70. Flt Lt 2/1/72. Retd GD 2/10/80.
CLACK S.B. Born 13/3/20. Commd 16/11/61. Flt Lt 16/11/67. Retd ENG 3/8/68.
CLACKETT M.R. Born 23/11/47. Commd 8/9/77. Sqn Ldr 1/1/86. Retd ENG 14/6/88.
CLAMP W.E. Born 22/3/36. Commd 3/12/54. Flt Lt 3/6/60. Retd GD 22/3/91.
CLANCY L.J. BSc MRAeS DCAe. Born 15/3/29. Commd 22/8/51. Sqn Ldr 1/4/61. Retd EDN 22/8/67.
CLAPP B.D. BA. Born 3/6/45. Commd 18/3/66. Flt Lt 3/12/67. Retd GD 5/3/75.
CLARE A.J. MCMI. Born 18/11/45. Commd 11/11/65. Wg Cdr 1/1/96. Retd OPS SPT 18/11/00.
CLARE B.G. Born 2/1/21. Commd 2/1/56. Flt Lt 22/5/57. Retd SEC 2/10/74.
CLARE D. DFC. Born 6/4/20. Commd 16/8/41. Gp Capt 1/1/63. Retd GD 25/6/74.
CLARE H.R. Born 23/5/21. Commd 29/10/43. Flt Lt 19/11/53. Retd GD 11/5/68.
CLARIDGE G.J.B. CBE. Born 23/2/30. Commd 1/11/50. A Cdre 1/1/79. Retd GD 27/2/84.
CLARIDGE J.G. DFC AFC. Born 13/5/20. Commd 28/8/43. Wg Cdr 1/1/59. Retd GD 26/3/59.
CLARIDGE P.G. BSc CEng MIEE. Born 23/6/35. Commd 10/10/58. Sqn Ldr 10/7/68. Retd ADMIN 23/6/93.
CLARIDGE R.V. Born 26/11/30. Commd 27/2/52. Flt Lt 7/3/62. Retd GD 29/3/69.
CLARK A. Born 5/12/43. Commd 8/1/76. Sqn Ldr 1/1/87. Retd ADMIN 5/12/98.
CLARK A.A. BSc CEng MRAeS ACGI. Born 7/9/37. Commd 2/10/58. Sqn Ldr 1/7/70. Retd GD 7/9/75.
CLARK A.B. MCMI ACIS. Born 30/9/36. Commd 12/7/62. Wg Cdr 1/1/80. Retd ADMIN 8/12/87.
CLARK A.J.C. Born 17/3/29. Commd 10/12/52. Flt Lt 5/5/58. Retd GD 15/7/68.
CLARK A.M. BA. Born 19/12/49. Commd 4/7/69. Flt Lt 18/10/75. Retd ADMIN 17/12/87.
CLARK A.R. Born 18/9/42. Commd 28/7/64. Flt Lt 28/1/76. Retd GD 18/9/80.
CLARK B.E. MBE. Born 19/3/39. Commd 27/8/64. Sqn Ldr 1/1/76. Retd PRT 1/1/79.
CLARK B.J. BSc. Born 27/8/62. Commd 1/7/93. Sqn Ldr 1/7/93. Retd SUP 27/8/00.
CLARK B.M. Born 20/1/46. Commd 13/8/80. Sqn Ldr 1/7/86. Retd FLY(N) 13/6/03.
CLARK B.S. Born 2/10/19. Commd 9/7/53. Sqn Ldr 1/1/62. Retd ENG 30/11/73.
CLARK B.S. Born 6/9/38. Commd 14/8/56. Flt Lt 25/1/71. Retd GD 25/1/79.
CLARK C.D. Born 5/7/17. Commd 29/5/47. Flt Lt 29/11/51. Retd SUP 19/8/60.
CLARK C.E. Born 27/2/25. Commd 29/12/51. Flt Lt 26/2/58. Retd GD 11/1/60.
CLARK C.F. MSc MILT. Born 10/11/46. Commd 9/2/66. Sqn Ldr 1/7/83. Retd SUP 14/3/97.
CLARK C.J.J. BEM. Born 1/9/39. Commd 7/1/71. Flt Lt 7/1/73. Retd ADMIN 1/10/77.
CLARK C.P. Born 1/5/43. Commd 6/4/62. Flt Lt 6/10/67. Retd GD 21/2/72.
CLARK C.W. Born 2/1/21. Commd 15/9/44. Wg Cdr 1/1/61. Retd GD 2/1/76.
CLARK D. MSc BA. Born 13/12/43. Commd 12/8/79. Sqn Ldr 1/1/88. Retd ADMIN 1/11/97.
CLARK D.H. Born 25/9/40. Commd 26/5/61. Sqn Ldr 1/7/79. Retd GD 25/9/95.
CLARK D.H.G. The Rev. Born 17/1/26. Commd 13/2/61. Retd Wg Cdr 15/9/82. rtg Gp Capt
CLARK D.J. Born 27/12/56. Commd 14/9/75. Sqn Ldr 1/7/97. Retd OPS SPT 20/2/02.
CLARK D.J. Born 27/12/56. Commd 14/9/75. Sqn Ldr 1/1/90. Retd SUP 14/3/97.
CLARK D.M. Born 10/2/48. Commd 3/5/68. Sqn Ldr 1/7/79. Retd GD 26/4/86.
CLARK D.P.C.V. BA. Born 7/2/62. Commd 2/9/84. Wg Cdr 1/1/97. Retd ADMIN 2/9/00.
CLARK D.R. Born 15/7/28. Commd 30/7/59. Sqn Ldr 1/7/73. Retd SY 30/7/77.
CLARK D.S.J. Born 31/7/22. Commd 2/4/43. Flt Lt 2/10/46. Retd GD 16/11/61.
CLARK E. BA. Born 9/2/50. Commd 15/9/69. Flt Lt 15/4/77. Retd SY(RGT) 9/8/88.
CLARK E.S.C. Born 9/2/23. Commd 12/3/53. Fg Offr 12/3/55. Retd SEC 9/11/57.
CLARK F.D.G. CBE BA. Born 2/11/29. Commd 1/7/53. AVM 1/1/80. Retd GD 10/11/84.
CLARK G. Born 15/9/39. Commd 10/6/66. Flt Lt 10/12/71. Retd GD 14/5/82.
CLARK G. BSc. Born 16/2/62. Commd 29/9/85. Sqn Ldr 1/7/95. Retd GD 5/6/01.
CLARK G. Born 28/11/45. Commd 19/6/64. Flt Lt 19/12/69. Retd GD 3/12/98.
CLARK G.J. AFC. Born 26/4/23. Commd 26/5/45. Sqn Ldr 1/7/65. Retd GD 26/4/78.

CLARK G.S. IEng MCIT MILT MRAeS MHSM. Born 25/2/45. Commd 26/3/72. Wg Cdr 1/1/90. Retd SUP 25/2/00.
CLARK H.G. MBE. Born 5/6/25. Commd 6/7/45. Wg Cdr 1/7/67. Retd GD 4/10/75.
CLARK H.J. BA. Born 24/11/42. Commd 27/2/75. Flt Lt 27/2/77. Retd GD 28/11/87.
CLARK I.F. LLB. Born 11/11/44. Commd 15/7/66. Flt Lt 15/1/69. Retd GD 11/11/82.
CLARK I.G. Born 5/10/21. Commd 22/7/66. Flt Lt 22/7/69. Retd SEC 6/2/76.
CLARK J.B. Born 29/5/53. Commd 22/5/75. Flt Lt 22/11/80. Retd GD 1/8/93.
CLARK J.C. Born 28/8/38. Commd 4/2/64. Sqn Ldr 1/7/83. Retd ENG 1/5/91.
CLARK J.D. Born 4/2/41. Commd 26/5/61. Flt Lt 26/11/66. Retd GD 4/8/79.
CLARK J.F. Born 19/8/30. Commd 24/9/52. Sqn Ldr 1/7/62. Retd ENG 24/9/68.
CLARK J.J. Born 13/11/48. Commd 22/11/84. Wg Cdr 1/1/99. Retd ADMIN 29/1/03.
CLARK J.M. BSc MRAeS. Born 8/10/56. Commd 31/8/75. Sqn Ldr 1/7/89. Retd GD 8/10/94.
CLARK J.R.T. Born 16/5/47. Commd 2/8/68. Flt Lt 8/3/72. Retd GD 1/10/75.
CLARK K. Born 4/8/30. Commd 17/9/52. Plt Offr 16/12/53. Retd GD 1/1/55.
CLARK K.A. BSc MRAeS. Born 13/2/37. Commd 16/11/59. Sqn Ldr 1/7/69. Retd GD 13/2/95.
CLARK L.D. BA BSc MRAeS. Born 3/3/45. Commd 28/9/64. Sqn Ldr 1/7/75. Retd GD 12/12/83.
CLARK L.E.D. The Rev. MBE . Born 31/1/52. Commd 22/8/89. Retd Wg Cdr 15/2/03.
CLARK L.J. BEd. Born 17/11/52. Commd 12/8/79. Sqn Ldr 1/1/90. Retd ADMIN 12/8/01.
CLARK M.B. BSc DipEl ARCS. Born 27/6/33. Commd 26/1/56. Wg Cdr 26/7/74. Retd ADMIN 30/9/76.
CLARK M.J. Born 25/11/31. Commd 1/1/63. Flt Lt 1/10/71. Retd CAT 1/9/79.
CLARK M.V. Born 21/6/45. Commd 25/3/64. Flt Lt 6/10/69. Retd GD 21/6/83.
CLARK P. AFM. Born 21/1/25. Commd 21/10/54. Flt Lt 21/10/60. Retd GD 30/4/68.
CLARK P.C. FCMI. Born 18/5/33. Commd 22/1/53. Gp Capt 1/7/76. Retd SY 26/7/83.
CLARK P.D. CB BA CEng FRAeS. Born 19/3/39. Commd 28/7/60. AVM 1/7/91. Retd ENG 25/4/94.
CLARK P.J.W. Born 12/12/42. Commd 22/2/63. Flt Lt 22/8/68. Retd GD 1/12/80.
CLARK R. MBE. Born 21/10/22. Commd 2/10/47. Flt Lt 27/5/54. Retd PE 22/10/65.
CLARK R. BEM. Born 28/10/47. Commd 14/8/80. Sqn Ldr 1/7/91. Retd ADMIN 14/8/91.
CLARK R.E.V. MSc BA BSc. Born 23/2/52. Commd 23/1/74. Wg Cdr 1/1/96. Retd ADMIN 15/9/00.
CLARK R.I. Born 5/12/25. Commd 29/1/62. Flt Lt 29/1/62. Retd GD 21/1/72.
CLARK R.J. Born 10/3/29. Commd 26/8/66. Sqn Ldr 1/7/79. Retd ENG 10/3/84.
CLARK R.W. OBE CEng FIEE. Born 6/4/44. Commd 7/6/68. A Cdre 1/7/96. Retd ENG 22/7/00.
CLARK S.E. BSc CEng MRAeS. Born 8/12/44. Commd 28/9/04. A Cdre 1/7/91. Retd ENG 2/8/93.
CLARK S.J. Born 13/7/32. Commd 22/3/51. Flt Lt 1/9/59. Retd GD 1/12/65.
CLARK T.J. Born 18/6/61. Commd 25/9/83. Flt Lt 29/6/89. Retd OPS SPT 25/9/99.
CLARK T.J. MSc BSc CEng MIEE ACGI. Born 16/5/58. Commd 18/10/81. Sqn Ldr 1/7/95. Retd ENGINEER 1/10/04.
CLARK T.R. Born 2/8/47. Commd 23/6/67. Wg Cdr 1/1/90. Retd ENG 2/8/02.
CLARK W.A. Born 12/7/62. Commd 23/10/86. Flt Lt 23/4/93. Retd OPS SPT 23/6/02.
CLARKE A.J. AFC MRAeS. Born 30/7/23. Commd 18/11/46. Sqn Ldr 1/7/57. Retd GD 30/7/66.
CLARKE A.K. Born 23/8/49. Commd 31/7/70. Sqn Ldr 1/7/83. Retd GD 7/3/87.
CLARKE B.R. Born 17/6/25. Commd 29/3/45. Wg Cdr 1/1/66. Retd ADMIN 25/10/77.
CLARKE C.C. Born 9/2/53. Commd 1/6/72. Flt Lt 1/12/78. Retd ENG 1/4/83.
CLARKE C.H. FCMI. Born 25/11/23. Commd 1/3/43. A Cdre 1/1/74. Retd SUP 25/11/78.
CLARKE C.J.G. Born 26/4/42. Commd 16/6/88. Flt Lt 16/6/92. Retd SUP 2/4/93.
CLARKE D.B. BA DipEd MIPM MCMI. Born 9/5/33. Commd 25/8/55. Sqn Ldr 25/2/65. Retd EDN 25/8/71.
CLARKE D.C. Born 13/8/46. Commd 20/8/78. Sqn Ldr 1/1/92. Retd OPS SPT(PROVSY) 13/8/03.
CLARKE D.E. Born 6/2/38. Commd 22/5/70. Flt Lt 22/5/74. Retd GD 30/4/76.
CLARKE D.J. BA. Born 17/11/52. Commd 3/10/76. Sqn Ldr 1/1/00. Retd GD 17/11/02.
CLARKE D.J. Born 23/7/63. Commd 4/5/84. Flt Lt 15/9/93. Retd OPS SPT 23/7/01.
CLARKE D.J. MB ChB FRCS. Born 11/12/34. Commd 21/7/65. Wg Cdr 21/10/75. Retd MED 1/6/83.
CLARKE D.J. LDSRCS. Born 8/11/21. Commd 6/1/63. Wg Cdr 6/1/69. Retd DEL 6/1/79.
CLARKE E.J. Born 24/3/20. Commd 25/5/45. Flt Lt 22/11/48. Retd GD 22/6/54.
CLARKE F. Born 13/5/30. Commd 12/9/63. Sqn Ldr 1/7/78. Retd ENG 1/5/81.
CLARKE F.A. Born 28/6/11. Commd 18/1/45. Fg Offr 18/1/45. Retd ASD 15/3/46.
CLARKE F.J. BSc. Born 10/11/51. Commd 13/9/70. Wg Cdr 1/7/95. Retd ENG 30/12/96.
CLARKE G. MA. Born 18/9/27. Commd 19/9/51. Wg Cdr 1/7/64. Retd GD 31/12/69.
CLARKE G. MA MSc. Born 17/2/49. Commd 28/1/79. Flt Lt 28/1/79. Retd ADMIN 28/1/95.
CLARKE G.H. Born 11/5/47. Commd 21/7/65. Gp Capt 1/1/97. Retd GD 15/7/01.
CLARKE G.J. Born 8/4/35. Commd 21/3/74. Sqn Ldr 21/3/86. Retd MED(T) 8/4/90.
CLARKE H.O. Born 13/3/33. Commd 18/8/61. Fg Offr 18/8/63. Retd GD 13/3/71.
CLARKE H.S. Born 29/8/26. Commd 2/7/52. Sqn Ldr 1/1/72. Retd GD(G) 29/8/81.
CLARKE J. Born 30/5/64. Commd 11/3/92. Flt Lt 27/1/91. Retd OPS SPT(ATC) 30/5/04.
CLARKE J.L. Born 12/9/24. Commd 1/6/45. Flt Lt 7/6/51. Retd SEC 1/6/57.
CLARKE J.P. Born 20/5/30. Commd 16/6/52. Flt Lt 11/12/56. Retd GD 20/5/68.
CLARKE K. Born 4/2/49. Commd 17/7/87. Flt Lt 17/7/91. Retd ENGINEER 5/4/03.
CLARKE K.A. BA. Born 12/9/36. Commd 8/8/74. Sqn Ldr 1/1/84. Retd ENG 11/10/86.
CLARKE K.P. BEng MSc MRAeS. Born 14/9/37. Commd 23/9/59. Sqn Ldr 20/5/74. Retd EDN 1/10/79.
CLARKE L.G. BA MCIPS. Born 23/5/47. Commd 10/5/73. Wg Cdr 1/1/92. Retd SUP 20/7/96.

CLARKE M.C.A. Born 12/12/42. Commd 6/7/62. Sqn Ldr 1/1/85. Retd OPS SPT 12/12/97.
CLARKE M.G.A. Born 7/12/25. Commd 25/5/50. Sqn Ldr 1/7/62. Retd ENG 1/7/65.
CLARKE N. MBE IEng MIIE. Born 6/9/62. Commd 10/5/90. Sqn Ldr 1/7/99. Retd ENGINEER 1/5/03.
CLARKE N.K. Born 17/11/40. Commd 9/3/72. Flt Lt 9/3/74. Retd GD(G) 9/3/80.
CLARKE P.C. Born 13/4/25. Commd 5/7/53. Flt Lt 13/4/60. Retd GD 13/4/83.
CLARKE P.J. Born 10/11/45. Commd 26/5/64. Flt Lt 22/11/69. Retd GD 10/11/83.
CLARKE P.M. MSc. Born 17/2/49. Commd 6/4/72. Flt Lt 6/10/78. Retd ADMIN 7/4/99.
CLARKE P.S. Born 14/4/45. Commd 26/5/67. Flt Lt 26/11/71. Retd GD 19/4/88.
CLARKE R.D. Born 29/8/43. Commd 11/4/63. Wg Cdr 1/7/80. Retd SY 29/8/87.
CLARKE R.D. BA. Born 23/10/58. Commd 27/3/83. Flt Lt 27/6/86. Retd GD(G) 11/8/89.
CLARKE R.E. Born 29/1/46. Commd 30/5/69. Flt Lt 30/11/74. Retd GD 31/1/76.
CLARKE R.E. Born 26/12/24. Commd 24/10/49. Flt Lt 10/10/55. Retd GD 5/10/57.
CLARKE R.G. Born 14/7/44. Commd 5/7/73. Sqn Ldr 1/7/86. Retd ENG 14/9/96.
CLARKE R.J. Born 31/8/28. Commd 12/7/50. Flt Lt 14/5/56. Retd GD 31/8/66.
CLARKE R.J. MSc MInstPS MIDPM MCMI. Born 20/6/48. Commd 25/8/67. Sqn Ldr 1/7/83. Retd ADMIN 15/12/87.
CLARKE R.P. Born 25/8/44. Commd 10/2/72. Flt Lt 10/2/74. Retd ADMIN 26/8/94.
CLARKE S. Born 14/6/44. Commd 4/7/69. Flt Lt 24/1/73. Retd GD 1/7/75.
CLARKE S.M. CEng MRAeS. Born 6/4/24. Commd 22/9/49. Gp Capt 1/1/72. Retd ENG 5/9/78.
CLARKE T.J.R. BSc. Born 20/9/33. Commd 22/11/57. Sqn Ldr 22/5/68. Retd EDN 22/11/73.
CLARKE T.M. Born 12/3/33. Commd 24/1/52. Flt Lt 29/5/57. Retd GD 12/3/71.
CLARKE V.G. Born 16/5/22. Commd 12/5/44. Wg Cdr 1/7/62. Retd GD 18/5/65.
CLARKIN B.T. Born 13/10/42. Commd 3/11/77. Sqn Ldr 1/1/88. Retd ADMIN 3/1/97.
CLARKSON D. BSc. Born 12/6/49. Commd 23/4/87. Sqn Ldr 1/7/99. Retd ENGINEER 12/6/04.
CLARKSON J. AFC. Born 30/11/45. Commd 5/2/65. Wg Cdr 1/1/91. Retd GD 22/4/94.
CLARKSON T.W. DFC. Born 1/7/21. Commd 16/4/43. Flt Lt 5/5/63. Retd GD 1/7/76.
CLAUSE D.M. AFC FCMI MRAeS. Born 1/8/23. Commd 20/2/43. Gp Capt 1/1/65. Retd GD 31/10/76.
CLAXTON J.F. MA. Born 23/1/32. Commd 26/9/53. Sqn Ldr 1/7/65. Retd ENG 23/1/70.
CLAXTON K. Born 1/4/53. Commd 7/7/73. Wg Cdr 1/7/89. Retd GD 14/7/92.
CLAY A.R.F. BA. Born 9/6/57. Commd 14/9/75. Flt Lt 15/10/79. Retd GD 15/7/90.
CLAY E.F. Born 24/11/13. Commd 9/8/47. Flt Lt 9/2/52. Retd SEC 1/3/68.
CLAY J.M. Born 30/7/36. Commd 14/10/71. Flt Lt 14/10/75. Retd ENG 14/8/84.
CLAY L.S. Born 11/6/52. Commd 18/12/80. Flt Lt 18/2/82. Retd ADMIN 18/12/96.
CLAY P. BSc CEng MRAeS. Born 12/6/23. Commd 8/6/44. Sqn Ldr 1/10/56. Retd ENG 12/6/78.
CLAYDON K.W. Born 12/6/29. Commd 14/11/51. Sqn Ldr 1/7/67. Retd GD 2/4/73.
CLAYFIELD W.E. DFC. Born 11/10/19. Commd 28/1/43. Wg Cdr 1/7/70. Retd SEC 11/10/74.
CLAYPHAN A.A.A. Born 11/2/32. Commd 21/5/52. Sqn Ldr 1/7/67. Retd GD 12/1/74.
CLAYSON J.L. MBE FCMI. Born 21/11/31. Commd 21/8/52. Gp Capt 1/7/76. Retd ADMIN 30/7/84. rtg A Cdre
CLAYTON B.A. AFC. Born 6/3/29. Commd 8/9/47. Flt Lt 23/12/58. Retd SUP 6/3/67.
CLAYTON C.P. Born 24/10/45. Commd 29/7/65. Sqn Ldr 1/1/89. Retd ENG 24/12/95.
CLAYTON D.A. CEng MIMechE MRAeS. Born 9/6/33. Commd 25/7/56. Gp Capt 1/1/79. Retd ENG 9/12/87.
CLAYTON J.D. BSc. Born 10/7/30. Commd 19/9/51. Sqn Ldr 1/7/61. Retd GD 10/7/68.
CLAYTON J.McK. Born 24/3/25. Commd 15/6/61. Flt Lt 15/6/64. Retd GD 11/0/75.
CLAYTON K.R. BSc. Born 26/7/61. Commd 30/3/86. Flt Lt 30/9/89. Retd OPS SPT 30/9/02.
CLAYTON L.C.F. Born 22/3/43. Commd 27/1/61. Flt Lt 27/7/66. Retd GD 3/12/68.
CLAYTON N. Born 13/3/22. Commd 30/10/44. Flt Lt 30/4/48. Retd GD 1/6/62.
CLAYTON R.H. Born 9/3/37. Commd 14/10/71. Flt Lt 14/10/73. Retd ENG 17/7/81.
CLAYTON R.J. Born 25/7/44. Commd 4/2/71. Fg Offr 4/8/73. Retd SUP 3/1/76.
CLAYTON R.M. Born 3/4/38. Commd 18/12/56. Gp Capt 1/7/87. Retd GD 3/7/93.
CLAYTON S. Born 3/6/63. Commd 26/11/81. Sqn Ldr 1/7/96. Retd GD 10/1/00.
CLAYTON-JONES G.S. MRAeS. Born 22/3/42. Commd 14/5/60. Wg Cdr 1/1/85. Retd GD 22/3/97.
CLEARY G.A.L. Born 23/1/45. Commd 14/1/82. Flt Lt 1/3/87. Retd GD(G) 1/10/89.
CLEAVE N.H.L.W. Born 13/9/39. Commd 31/7/62. Flt Lt 15/2/65. Retd GD 13/9/94.
CLEAVER A.G. Born 4/7/39. Commd 21/7/61. Gp Capt 1/7/89. Retd GD 4/7/94.
CLEAVER L.D. Born 27/9/23. Commd 26/2/46. Sqn Ldr 1/1/67. Retd GD(G) 16/3/74.
CLEE P.A. Born 28/5/36. Commd 30/12/54. Sqn Ldr 1/1/71. Retd GD 1/8/88.
CLEE R.B. Born 2/12/22. Commd 6/2/44. Flt Lt 4/12/52. Retd GD 28/11/67.
CLEGG D. Born 1/7/20. Commd 22/9/41. Flt Offr 1/9/45. Retd SEC 21/5/55.
CLEGG J.R. Born 26/9/43. Commd 25/6/66. Flt Lt 25/12/72. Retd ENG 1/9/83.
CLEGG M.A. Born 10/8/42. Commd 17/12/64. Sqn Ldr 1/1/72. Wg Cdr 1/1/96. Retd GD 2/4/98.
CLEIFE V.E. Born 22/12/10. Commd 23/3/42. Flt Lt 23/3/44. Retd GD 29/9/46.
CLELAND S.E.J. BA. Born 24/8/74. Commd 12/8/01. Fg Off 12/2/01. Retd SUPPLY 10/2/04.
CLELAND-SMITH D.J. Born 13/11/48. Commd 13/1/72. Wg Cdr 1/1/96. Retd GD 13/6/03.
CLELLAND D.H. Born 23/3/26. Commd 9/4/52. Flt Lt 21/8/57. Retd GD 23/3/76.
CLEMAS L.H. Born 17/2/17. Commd 23/1/39. Flt Lt 18/2/52. Retd SUP 17/2/66. rtg Sqn Ldr
CLEMENTS A.J.B. CEng FCMI MIEE DipEl. Born 2/12/21. Commd 9/8/45. A Cdre 1/7/74. Retd ENG 2/12/76.
CLEMENTS D.M. BA. Born 17/12/33. Commd 12/7/57. Sqn Ldr 12/1/65. Retd ADMIN 29/3/87.

CLEMENTS G.D. Born 2/11/52. Commd 1/4/76. Flt Lt 1/10/81. Retd GD 8/12/91.
CLEMENTS H.E. OBE MCMI. Born 3/1/28. Commd 14/12/49. Wg Cdr 1/1/69. Retd GD 1/11/75.
CLEMENTS H.H. Born 22/1/15. Commd 5/8/43. Sqn Ldr 1/7/54. Retd ENG 10/1/62.
CLEMENTS J.B. Born 20/1/41. Commd 15/3/84. Sqn Ldr 1/1/92. Retd SY 20/6/96.
CLEMENTS J.M.a.c.S. Born 14/9/45. Commd 25/6/65. Flt Lt 8/3/72. Retd GD 14/9/86.
CLEMENTS M.F. DUS. Born 31/5/36. Commd 23/7/58. Sqn Ldr 1/7/68. Retd ENG 31/5/74.
CLEMENTS M.P.M. BSc CEng MRAeS ACGI. Born 20/2/52. Commd 24/9/76. Sqn Ldr 1/1/89. Retd ENG 24/9/92.
CLEMENTS P.H.R. Born 10/6/38. Commd 14/8/64. Flt Lt 1/7/68. Retd GD 10/6/76.
CLEMENTS R.D. MBA BSc. Born 1/3/46. Commd 12/7/70. Wg Cdr 1/1/88. Retd GD 14/9/96.
CLEMENTS R.E. Born 18/6/43. Commd 3/5/68. Sqn Ldr 1/7/79. Retd GD 21/9/97.
CLEMENTS S.H. MBA MCMI. Born 29/12/48. Commd 8/1/78. Sqn Ldr 1/7/88. Retd ADMIN 8/1/94.
CLEMENTSON J. MA. Born 29/5/36. Commd 30/7/80. Sqn Ldr 28/8/77. Retd ADMIN 1/4/92.
CLEMETT A.L. BSc. Born 13/8/43. Commd 25/2/68. Sqn Ldr 1/7/80. Retd GD 13/8/02.
CLEMINSON A. Born 19/9/55. Commd 13/1/02. Flt Lt 13/1/02. Retd FLY(AEO) 14/6/03.
CLEMITSON J.M. OBE. Born 29/10/35. Commd 27/2/70. Wg Cdr 1/7/82. Retd GD(G) 13/2/87.
CLEMPSON P. Born 30/7/65. Commd 13/1/97. Sqn Ldr 1/1/97. Retd SUPPLY 30/7/03.
CLERICI A.E. Born 19/4/16. Commd 24/11/41. Flt Offr 1/9/45. Retd SEC 4/9/60.
CLERK R.D. Born 13/2/20. Commd 1/7/43. Flt Lt 1/1/47. Retd ENG 23/12/56.
CLEVERLEY D.H.H. DFM. Born 15/6/20. Commd 1/5/42. Flt Lt 1/11/46. Retd GD(G) 19/5/54. rtg Sqn Ldr
CLEVERLEY J.W. BA. Born 2/10/27. Commd 24/4/59. Sqn Ldr 28/6/64. Retd EDN 31/12/75.
CLEVERLEY N.A. Born 2/12/51. Commd 16/9/71. Flt Lt 16/3/77. Retd GD 4/9/81.
CLEVERLEY R.A.R. Born 4/5/19. Commd 1/3/62. Flt Lt 1/3/65. Retd ENG 4/5/74.
CLEVERLY R.K. Born 2/5/36. Commd 30/11/55. Flt Lt 28/8/61. Retd GD 25/5/66.
CLEVERLY R.M. Born 20/7/49. Commd 25/8/67. Flt Lt 3/2/74. Retd GD(G) 3/4/76.
CLEVES K.G. BA. Born 10/11/31. Commd 15/7/54. Sqn Ldr 15/1/65. Retd EDN 15/7/70.
CLEWS J.D. Born 2/3/17. Commd 16/2/44. Sqn Ldr 1/1/69. Retd SEC 2/3/72.
CLIFF F.H. Born 26/1/37. Commd 19/6/70. Flt Lt 1/7/75. Retd ENG 19/6/78. Re-instated 1/7/81. Sqn Ldr 1/1/89.
    Retd ENG 26/1/95.
CLIFF M.E. Born 13/3/38. Commd 8/1/76. Flt Lt 8/1/81. Retd ADMIN 31/8/89.
CLIFF M.J.H. Born 24/9/60. Commd 13/12/79. Sqn Ldr 1/7/93. Retd GD 24/9/98.
CLIFF P.D. OBE. Born 19/3/35. Commd 17/6/53. Wg Cdr 1/7/79. Retd GD 17/7/82.
CLIFFE R.B. Born 30/10/52. Commd 24/6/76. Wg Cdr 1/1/93. Retd ENG 1/11/98.
CLIFFE S.M. BEd. Born 29/7/59. Commd 29/11/81. Sqn Ldr 1/1/91. Retd ADMIN 14/3/96.
CLIFFORD A.W. Born 20/10/22. Commd 10/5/46. Flt Lt 19/11/53. Retd GD 31/3/70.
CLIFFORD B.B. Born 27/8/34. Commd 24/9/52. Flt Lt 17/9/58. Retd GD 27/8/92.
CLIFFORD B.J. Born 1/6/43. Commd 17/12/65. Sqn Ldr 1/1/73. Retd GD 1/6/81.
CLIFFORD D.P. Born 30/9/54. Commd 16/5/74. Flt Lt 5/10/80. Retd OPS SPT 30/9/99.
CLIFFORD G.F. Born 16/10/49. Commd 25/2/72. Sqn Ldr 1/1/88. Retd GD 16/10/93.
CLIFFORD G.M. BSc. Born 16/6/58. Commd 28/2/82. Flt Lt 28/8/85. Retd ADMIN 31/10/87.
CLIFFORD J.M. MSc MB BChir. Born 17/4/29. Commd 21/11/54. Wg Cdr 21/11/67. Retd MED 28/10/73.
CLIFFORD J.N. Born 25/12/46. Commd 25/7/71. Flt Lt 7/1/75. Retd PI 25/12/85.
CLIFFORD K.C. MBE. Born 28/3/33. Commd 4/6/64. Sqn Ldr 1/1/76. Retd ENG 28/10/93.
CLIFFORD M.W.A. Born 4/6/34. Commd 26/4/60. Sqn Ldr 18/9/69. Retd EDN 23/1/76.
CLIFFORD P.H.R. MCMI. Born 1/6/33. Commd 26/3/52. Sqn Ldr 1/1/63. Retd GD 1/6/71.
CLIFFORD R.I. MCMI. Born 25/4/44. Commd 25/6/65. Flt Lt 25/12/70. Retd GD 26/1/73. Re-entered 6/6/74.
    Sqn Ldr 1/7/87. Retd ADMIN 5/1/98.
CLIFFORD-JONES W.E. MB BS MRCS LRCP DO. Born 13/9/29. Commd 1/5/55. Gp Capt 26/3/78. Retd MED 3/5/78.
CLIFT D.G. Born 15/3/19. Commd 1/4/39. Sqn Ldr 1/1/71. Retd GD(G) 2/7/74.
CLIFTON A.G. Born 21/9/32. Commd 29/9/54. Fg Offr 30/12/53. Retd GD 9/7/57.
CLIFTON D.J. Born 17/9/51. Commd 27/3/75. Flt Lt 27/9/80. Retd GD 2/12/90.
CLIFTON P.J. Born 16/10/22. Commd 8/6/43. Sqn Ldr 1/10/55. Retd GD 16/10/65.
CLINCH B.A. Born 12/12/51. Commd 18/12/80. Flt Lt 18/12/82. Retd SUP 12/12/89.
CLINCH B.F.A. Born 13/2/36. Commd 5/5/54. Flt Lt 5/10/60. Retd GD 30/3/74.
CLINGAN B.R. Born 30/5/42. Commd 19/6/70. Flt Lt 19/6/72. Retd ENG 20/5/88.
CLINGING D. MBE. Born 15/11/49. Commd 20/12/73. Sqn Ldr 1/7/89. Retd GD(G) 31/8/92.
CLINKER S.P. Born 21/12/53. Commd 30/8/84. Flt Lt 30/8/86. Retd SUP 14/9/96.
CLINKSKEL J.W.C. Born 23/8/57. Commd 23/3/81. Fg Offr 23/3/83. Retd SUP 1/10/86.
CLINTON E.M. MBE. Born 17/7/31. Commd 11/2/65. Flt Lt 11/2/71. Retd SUP 17/7/89.
CLINTON I.J. Born 5/2/38. Commd 15/6/61. Flt Lt 1/4/66. Retd SEC 5/2/76.
CLIPSHAM J.R. AMCIPD. Born 8/8/58. Commd 18/4/74. Sqn Ldr 1/7/88. Retd GD(G) 14/9/96.
CLISBY B.E. CEng MIEE. Born 16/3/37. Commd 23/10/59. Sqn Ldr 1/7/71. Retd ENG 23/10/75.
CLISH R.E. Born 11/12/11. Commd 27/3/44. Flt Lt 7/6/51. Retd SUP 28/9/53.
CLITHEROW A.F. BSc. Born 1/12/57. Commd 19/9/76. Flt Lt 15/10/80. Retd GD 11/11/96.
CLIVE-GRIFFIN J.B. Born 1/7/14. Commd 30/6/51. Flt Offr 30/6/55. Retd CAT 18/4/64.
CLODE R.F. Born 12/4/41. Commd 7/6/68. Flt Lt 28/2/72. Retd GD 31/7/94.
CLOGGER P.A. CEng MRAeS. Born 17/6/45. Commd 13/2/64. Wg Cdr 1/7/83. Retd ENG 17/6/89.

CLOHERTY J.K. MB BCh FRCS(Edin) FCOphth DO. Born 8/12/28. Commd 11/8/57. A Cdre 3/4/89. Retd MED 8/12/93.
CLOKE B.E. Born 13/4/43. Commd 16/6/69. Wg Cdr 1/7/89. Retd SY 14/4/93.
CLOKE J.A. BSc. Born 8/3/47. Commd 28/7/67. Sqn Ldr 1/1/80. Retd ENG 8/3/85.
CLOKE R. AFC FCMI. Born 8/7/38. Commd 28/7/59. Gp Capt 1/1/88. Retd GD 21/6/89.
CLOKE S.R. MSc BA FCIT FILT FCIPD. Born 3/6/58. Commd 4/9/81. Sqn Ldr 1/1/90. Retd SUP 23/10/98.
CLOSE A.P. Born 27/10/34. Commd 23/9/65. Sqn Ldr 1/7/73. Retd SY(PRT) 1/6/88.
CLOSE J.A. Born 12/4/39. Commd 2/5/59. Flt Lt 28/7/65. Retd ENG 12/11/70. Re-instated 14/9/71. Sqn Ldr 1/1/87. Retd ENG 12/4/94.
CLOSE T.D. Born 15/11/51. Commd 19/6/70. Flt Lt 19/12/75. Retd GD 29/1/82.
CLOSE W.E. Born 21/7/32. Commd 15/12/53. Wg Cdr 1/1/72. Retd GD 1/12/84.
CLOTHIER P.R. MB ChB FRCS. Born 14/4/49. Commd 10/1/71. Wg Cdr 9/9/87. Retd MED 25/2/95.
CLOUDER B.E.W. Born 25/9/45. Commd 14/10/71. Flt Lt 14/4/74. Retd GD 25/9/83.
CLOUGH G. Born 5/3/50. Commd 28/11/74. Sqn Ldr 1/1/87. Retd OPS SPT(FC) 5/3/05.
CLOUGH J.H. DFC. Born 27/10/19. Commd 8/3/41. Flt Lt 1/9/45. Retd GD 30/10/48. rtg Wg Cdr
CLOUGH P.J. BSc CEng MIEE. Born 1/3/46. Commd 15/7/66. Wg Cdr 1/7/83. Retd ENG 1/7/86.
CLOUTMAN D.H. Born 26/6/40. Commd 1/4/65. Sqn Ldr 1/7/77. Retd SUP 14/8/95.
CLOVER B.J. Born 9/7/64. Commd 29/7/83. Sqn Ldr 1/1/00. Retd GD 1/1/03.
CLOVIS M. Born 6/4/48. Commd 28/2/69. Sqn Ldr 1/7/83. Retd ENG 1/7/86.
CLOWES R.G. Born 1/11/59. Commd 19/3/81. Flt Lt 10/10/84. Retd GD 14/3/97.
CLUBB J.A.W. Born 14/5/29. Commd 15/12/49. Sqn Ldr 1/1/61. Retd GD 6/5/76.
CLUBBE H.M. Born 7/5/12. Commd 2/8/45. Sqn Ldr 1/7/62. Retd SUP 7/5/68.
CLUBBE P. OBE FCMI MCIPS. Born 30/1/28. Commd 7/10/48. Gp Capt 1/1/77. Retd SUP 30/1/83.
CLUBLEY G. DFC. Born 24/10/22. Commd 2/4/44. Sqn Ldr 1/10/54. Retd GD 1/6/70.
CLUCAS B.P. MInstPet. Born 17/6/46. Commd 18/8/67. Sqn Ldr 1/7/80. Retd SUP 6/12/99.
CLUCAS R.D. Born 27/8/40. Commd 13/12/79. Sqn Ldr 1/7/89. Retd ENG 1/5/93.
CLUER C.B. Born 17/9/37. Commd 28/10/63. Sqn Ldr 1/1/71. Retd GD 1/4/75.
CLUER R.J. Born 22/6/57. Commd 16/9/76. Sqn Ldr 1/7/94. Retd GD 22/6/99.
CLULOW M.A. Born 20/8/39. Commd 28/8/75. Wg Cdr 1/1/91. Retd GD(G) 20/8/94.
CLUTTERBUCK A.N. Born 30/12/53. Commd 30/4/81. Flt Lt 1/11/84. Retd SY 7/12/92.
CLUTTON N.A. BSc. Born 27/5/49. Commd 1/9/70. Flt Lt 1/12/71. Retd GD 1/4/91.
CLYDE G.A. BSc. Born 18/11/48. Commd 6/3/77. Wg Cdr 1/7/92. Retd ADMIN 9/10/99.
COAK A.F.H. DipPE. Born 11/12/43. Commd 16/8/70. Sqn Ldr 1/7/81. Retd ADMIN 16/8/86.
COALES M.R. Born 16/3/43. Commd 19/6/64. Flt Lt 19/12/69. Retd GD 16/3/81.
COATES A.N. Born 15/10/34. Commd 24/2/67. Flt Lt 24/2/69. Retd PRT 24/2/75.
COATES D.J. MBE. Born 6/10/29. Commd 19/8/53. Sqn Ldr 1/7/67. Retd GD 5/11/73.
COATES F.B. Born 24/11/20. Commd 2/10/58. Sqn Ldr 1/7/69. Retd ENG 23/5/73.
COATES H. DFC. Born 10/10/18. Commd 5/4/43. Sqn Ldr 1/7/54. Retd GD 3/5/59.
COATES J. Born 30/12/50. Commd 5/8/76. Flt Lt 6/6/79. Retd ADMIN 18/5/83.
COATES J.B. BSc CEng MIEE. Born 10/4/46. Commd 15/7/66. Flt Lt 15/10/70. Retd ENG 10/4/84.
COATES J.G. BSc CEng MRAeS. Born 19/4/49. Commd 27/2/70. Wg Cdr 1/7/90. Retd ENG 14/9/96.
COATES R.A. Born 31/1/55. Commd 8/8/74. Flt Lt 8/2/79. Retd GD 9/11/87.
COATES S.G. BEng. Born 11/12/62. Commd 16/9/84. Flt Lt 7/4/89. Retd ENG 1/1/96.
COATESWORTH G.A. MCMI. Born 8/11/31. Commd 17/12/52. Sqn Ldr 1/1/66. Retd GD 8/11/69.
COBB D.C. MSc DPhysEd CDipAF. Born 20/11/43. Commd 10/8/65. Sqn Ldr 1/7/77. Retd ADMIN 18/6/82.
COBB H.J. DSO DFC AFC. Born 31/5/22. Commd 7/1/43. Wg Cdr 1/1/62. Retd GD 3/12/67.
COBB J.A. MCMI. Born 11/8/48. Commd 19/2/76. Sqn Ldr 1/1/84. Retd GD(G) 2/2/96.
COBB J.W. MBE. Born 20/9/41. Commd 11/8/69. Sqn Ldr 1/7/90. Retd SY 9/12/96.
COBB N.A. Born 26/1/60. Commd 30/4/81. Sqn Ldr 1/1/96. Retd GD 1/1/99.
COBB R.D. BSc. Born 2/5/64. Commd 5/9/82. APO 5/9/82. Retd GD 11/12/85.
COBB S.D. Born 12/5/61. Commd 1/7/82. Flt Lt 1/1/89. Retd ADMIN 11/12/96.
COBBOLD J.W. Born 21/1/21. Commd 15/5/47. Flt Lt 15/11/51. Retd SEC 21/1/70.
COBLEY R.A. Born 25/9/34. Commd 1/4/71. Sqn Ldr 1/1/80. Retd SUP 25/9/89.
COBURN E.W. CBE CEng FIMechE MRAeS. Born 29/12/25. Commd 22/4/53. A Cdre 1/7/76. Retd ENG 25/4/80.
COBURN K. BA CEng MIEE MRAeS. Born 11/12/42. Commd 22/7/71. Wg Cdr 1/7/86. Retd ENG 31/3/94.
COCHRAN D. Born 17/12/45. Commd 6/5/66. Flt Lt 17/6/71. Retd GD 30/9/77.
COCHRANE C.G. BSc CEng MIEE. Born 2/7/44. Commd 15/7/65. Sqn Ldr 1/1/74. Retd ENG 2/7/82.
COCHRANE J. Born 26/7/30. Commd 9/4/52. Sqn Ldr 1/7/60. Retd GD 29/9/62.
COCHRANE J. Born 24/8/47. Commd 28/7/88. Flt Lt 28/7/90. Retd OPS SPT 1/9/00.
COCHRANE J.E. Born 13/12/25. Commd 7/1/71. Flt Lt 7/1/74. Retd GD 7/1/84.
COCHRANE R.A. Born 14/2/30. Commd 24/9/59. Flt Lt 24/9/64. Retd GD 12/8/77.
COCHRANE R.B.S. Born 2/8/16. Commd 30/1/47. Sqn Ldr 1/7/63. Retd GD 28/9/70.
COCKARILL T.J. Born 31/5/47. Commd 28/4/65. Flt Lt 17/3/71. Retd GD 8/11/75.
COCKAYNE W.N. Born 16/4/18. Commd 28/1/43. Flt Lt 28/7/46. Retd ENG 7/8/54.
COCKBURN D. Born 29/4/48. Commd 2/8/68. Flt Lt 2/8/71. Retd GD 22/10/94.
COCKCROFT W. Born 28/1/29. Commd 28/7/60. Sqn Ldr 1/1/82. Retd ENG 28/1/89.

COCKER F.S. DFC CEng MIEE. Born 3/2/20. Commd 1/5/42. Wg Cdr 1/7/68. Retd ENG 30/11/77.
COCKERAM J.L. Born 27/11/10. Commd 6/3/52. Flt Lt 23/8/54. Retd MED(T) 29/11/60.
COCKERELL T.F. AFC. Born 13/5/39. Commd 26/5/61. Gp Capt 1/1/89. Retd GD 1/2/90.
COCKERILL D. Born 6/2/63. Commd 4/7/85. Flt Lt 4/1/91. Retd GD 10/6/02.
COCKERILL G.W. MRIN MCMI. Born 29/6/24. Commd 23/10/47. Sqn Ldr 1/7/73. Retd GD 15/5/76. Re-instated 22/10/80 to 29/6/84.
COCKERILL L.G. Born 26/1/30. Commd 9/4/52. Flt Lt 9/10/54. Retd GD 26/1/68.
COCKFIELD G. Born 5/5/29. Commd 28/2/57. Sqn Ldr 1/1/76. Retd GD 5/5/84.
COCKFIELD J.E. OBE. Born 20/11/21. Commd 21/6/44. Gp Capt 1/7/69. Retd GD 13/12/76.
COCKING J.S. Born 20/12/38. Commd 23/6/67. Wg Cdr 1/7/86. Retd ENG 2/4/93.
COCKING R.K. BSc. Born 11/10/46. Commd 22/9/68. Sqn Ldr 1/1/83. Retd FLY(N) 11/10/04.
COCKLE A.V. Born 12/1/28. Commd 26/8/66. Flt Lt 26/8/72. Retd SUP 12/1/89.
COCKLE J.A. Born 29/4/37. Commd 28/6/67. Flt Lt 2/8/67. Retd GD 2/10/85.
COCKMAN A. FCA. Born 3/1/15. Commd 25/7/41. Sqn Ldr 1/1/50. Retd SEC 3/4/64. rtg Wg Cdr
COCKMAN P.R. Born 7/10/55. Commd 13/6/74. Sqn Ldr 1/1/87. Retd GD 1/8/01.
COCKMAN P.S. Born 28/9/23. Commd 9/11/50. Sqn Ldr 1/1/61. Retd GD 29/6/68.
COCKRAM H. Born 25/12/11. Commd 21/11/44. Fg Offr 21/5/45. Retd GD(G) 18/12/45. Re-called 18/8/47. Flt Lt 7/6/51. Retd 25/12/61.
COCKRELL D.J. BSc ACGI DIC. Born 28/3/26. Commd 20/11/47. Flt Lt 28/3/51. Retd EDN 31/7/55.
COCKRILL M.J. MBE. Born 1/10/46. Commd 25/6/65. Wg Cdr 1/1/89. Retd GD 14/9/96.
COCKS A.J. Born 17/6/14. Commd 27/8/41. Flt Lt 1/9/45. Retd ENG 28/9/53. rtg Sqn Ldr
COCKS G. Born 5/5/25. Commd 9/6/55. Flt Lt 9/12/58. Retd GD 24/9/70.
COCKS J.H. Born 3/3/51. Commd 31/10/74. Flt Lt 1/5/81. Retd GD(G) 15/7/90.
COCKS J.H. Born 16/6/14. Commd 2/1/39. Wg Cdr 1/7/52. Retd SUP 8/2/60.
COCKSEDGE M.P. Born 17/9/48. Commd 27/2/70. Wg Cdr 1/7/89. Retd GD 20/1/00.
COCKSEDGE R.D. Born 7/11/42. Commd 6/11/64. Flt Lt 6/5/70. Retd GD 23/8/74.
COCKSHOTT C.R.G. Born 8/4/37. Commd 30/3/61. Sqn Ldr 1/7/71. Retd SUP 1/9/83.
CODD M.H. OBE. Born 26/3/39. Commd 14/12/72. Wg Cdr 1/1/87. Retd ADMIN 26/8/94.
CODY A. DFC AFC DFM. Born 15/5/18. Commd 15/6/41. Flt Lt 1/9/45. Retd GD 30/9/64.
CODY C.F.K. Born 22/3/54. Commd 29/6/72. Fg Offr 9/12/74. Retd GD(G) 1/8/75.
CODY C.T.K. Born 4/8/22. Commd 13/6/42. Wg Cdr 1/7/69. Retd GD 31/3/73.
COE M.J. Born 18/10/42. Commd 11/5/78. Sqn Ldr 1/1/92. Retd ENG 18/10/97.
COE M.R. AFC. Born 22/11/44. Commd 17/7/66. Wg Cdr 1/1/86. Retd GD 31/3/94.
COGGINS M.G. Born 15/10/38. Commd 28/7/60. Gp Capt 1/7/81. Retd ENG 22/11/88.
COGGON B. CEng MIEE MRAeS. Born 15/11/29. Commd 3/12/54. Wg Cdr 1/1/75. Retd ENG 15/11/84.
COGGON M.G. Born 24/1/48. Commd 16/3/74. Sqn Ldr 1/1/91. Retd OPS SPT(FC) 24/1/05.
COHEN A.G. MBE BSc. Born 12/8/55. Commd 30/8/78. Flt Lt 28/2/79. Retd GD 30/8/94.
COHU T.R. Born 15/3/34. Commd 26/7/55. Wg Cdr 1/1/84. Retd GD 14/2/87.
COIA E.G. Born 6/11/35. Commd 7/5/64. Sqn Ldr 1/1/74. Retd ENG 2/9/81.
COKER J.D. Born 5/10/43. Commd 20/12/64. Flt Lt 20/6/70. Retd GD 22/10/94.
COKER P.A. OBE FRAeS FCMI. Born 1/4/56. Commd 24/6/76. Air Cdre 1/7/02. Retd GD 2/7/04.
COKER R.T. Born 21/1/35. Commd 6/2/54. Flt Lt 6/8/59. Retd GD 21/1/73.
COLAM G. Born 1/7/34. Commd 1/7/53. Flt Lt 7/3/62. Retd GD 1/7/72.
COLBECK R. Born 22/4/26. Commd 22/2/46. A Cdre 1/7/78. Retd GD 22/4/81.
COLBECK W.J. MA MB BCh FFARCS DipSoton. Born 26/1/28. Commd 31/8/53. Wg Cdr 29/8/65. Retd MED 31/8/69.
COLBOURNE G.A. Born 25/11/26. Commd 24/9/51. Flt Lt 22/8/55. Retd GD 21/12/69.
COLBOURNE S.J. IEng. Born 23/12/40. Commd 19/2/76. Sqn Ldr 1/1/87. Retd ENG 23/12/95.
COLCHESTER A.C.F. BA BM BCh MRCP. Born 4/10/47. Commd 18/6/72. Sqn Ldr 24/7/80. Retd MED 11/9/81.
COLCLOUGH D.H. BA BSc MCIPD CertEd. Born 28/9/47. Commd 2/11/88. Flt Lt 2/11/90. Retd ADMIN 31/1/97.
COLDICOTT T.S.t.G. Born 10/9/45. Commd 26/5/67. Flt Lt 18/2/70. Retd GD 10/9/82.
COLDREY M.J.M. Born 28/2/45. Commd 5/2/65. Flt Lt 5/8/70. Retd GD 28/2/83.
COLE A.J. CEng MIEE MRAeS MBCS. Born 12/4/33. Commd 23/9/55. Wg Cdr 1/1/76. Retd ENG 24/9/83.
COLE B.C. OBE. Born 12/3/48. Commd 22/11/73. Wg Cdr 1/1/89. Retd ADMIN 1/1/97.
COLE C.L.P. BSc DUS. Born 18/3/25. Commd 3/1/46. Wg Cdr 18/3/66. Retd EDN 19/4/69.
COLE D.J. Born 16/10/42. Commd 10/9/70. Sqn Ldr 1/7/79. Retd GD 1/7/82.
COLE D.J.R. BA DPhysEd. Born 21/12/44. Commd 7/8/67. Wg Cdr 1/7/89. Retd ADMIN 21/6/97.
COLE G.E. Born 5/12/59. Commd 27/3/80. Flt Lt 27/9/86. Retd OPS SPT 5/12/97.
COLE G.H. Born 2/10/30. Commd 2/2/56. Flt Lt 2/8/60. Retd GD 2/10/85.
COLE I. Born 3/4/19. Commd 20/10/40. Sqn Offr 1/1/54. Retd SEC 17/12/62.
COLE J.B. Born 19/9/32. Commd 25/9/56. Sqn Ldr 1/1/71. Retd GD 10/8/84.
COLE J.G. DFC. Born 11/2/20. Commd 28/12/38. Sqn Ldr 1/8/47. Retd GD 29/5/58. rtg Wg Cdr
COLE J.M. Born 1/10/58. Commd 12/10/78. Flt Lt 3/3/85. Retd GD(G) 14/3/96.
COLE J.M. Born 16/12/32. Commd 27/9/51. Flt Lt 11/1/57. Retd GD 16/12/70.
COLE J.T. Born 20/4/15. Commd 20/10/44. Flt Lt 20/4/49. Retd CAT 20/4/64.
COLE K.N. Born 25/12/25. Commd 7/1/49. Flt Lt 11/11/54. Retd GD 25/12/68.

COLE M.E. OBE DPhysEd. Born 10/4/35. Commd 25/9/62. Sqn Ldr 1/7/73. Retd ADMIN 30/9/87.
COLE M.E. IEng. Born 30/10/49. Commd 7/11/91. Flt Lt 7/11/95. Retd ENGINEER 30/10/04.
COLE M.J. Born 10/10/61. Commd 24/10/81. Flt Lt 24/4/86. Retd GD 1/12/91.
COLE P.E. Born 11/1/51. Commd 31/8/78. Sqn Ldr 1/7/85. Retd ADMIN 18/8/89.
COLE P.L. Born 12/5/46. Commd 26/4/84. Sqn Ldr 1/7/92. Retd ENG 12/5/98.
COLE P.S. Born 28/3/32. Commd 27/9/51. Wg Cdr 1/7/75. Retd GD 15/1/87.
COLE R.A. Born 24/10/48. Commd 1/8/69. Sqn Ldr 1/7/90. Retd FLY(P) 24/10/03.
COLE R.D. Born 26/7/41. Commd 31/7/62. Flt Lt 31/1/65. Retd GD 26/7/79.
COLE T.M. Born 3/11/57. Commd 24/7/97. Flt Lt 24/7/01. Retd ENGINEER 1/5/04.
COLEBROOK R. Born 18/11/21. Commd 4/12/42. Flt Lt 23/4/51. Retd GD 1/10/68.
COLEBY B.F. MBE. Born 11/8/45. Commd 2/6/77. Sqn Ldr 1/7/91. Retd GD 6/7/96.
COLEMAN A.H. Born 10/10/31. Commd 9/4/52. Flt Lt 5/9/57. Retd GD 10/10/69.
COLEMAN C.J.F. MA. Born 10/8/46. Commd 18/9/66. Flt Lt 15/4/70. Retd GD 31/3/86.
COLEMAN D.A. BSc. Born 10/10/50. Commd 21/1/73. Sqn Ldr 1/1/85. Retd ENG 21/1/89.
COLEMAN D.E. Born 19/12/23. Commd 1/11/43. Sqn Ldr 1/1/57. Retd GD 31/12/61.
COLEMAN D.R. Born 18/8/48. Commd 16/8/70. Sqn Ldr 1/1/80. Retd ADMIN 30/9/87.
COLEMAN E.R.T. Born 26/4/53. Commd 3/9/72. Flt Lt 4/5/80. Retd GD 26/4/91.
COLEMAN F.A. MA MRAeS. Born 18/7/14. Commd 4/4/39. Gp Capt 1/1/67. Retd EDN 18/7/74.
COLEMAN I.M. Born 1/11/48. Commd 27/2/70. Sqn Ldr 1/7/87. Retd FLY(N) 1/11/03.
COLEMAN J.F. The Rev. BD. Born 25/10/53. Commd 1/9/78. Retd Wg Cdr 1/9/94.
COLEMAN J.R. Born 21/8/30. Commd 1/8/51. Flt Lt 1/2/54. Retd GD 21/8/68.
COLEMAN P.T. Born 14/6/42. Commd 29/6/72. Wg Cdr 1/1/96. Retd ENG 14/6/97.
COLEMAN R.H. Born 3/3/40. Commd 10/11/61. Flt Lt 10/5/67. Retd GD 19/10/67.
COLEMAN R.J. MMS MCMI. Born 26/1/34. Commd 25/2/53. Gp Capt 1/1/80. Retd GD 26/1/90.
COLES A. BA. Born 9/10/37. Commd 23/6/61. Sqn Ldr 1/1/72. Retd GD 31/1/87. rtg Wg Cdr
COLES A.J. Born 15/3/32. Commd 21/11/51. Sqn Ldr 1/1/64. Retd GD 15/3/70.
COLES G.B. Born 9/11/36. Commd 4/10/63. Flt Lt 9/2/68. Retd GD 9/11/74.
COLES G.T. Born 25/1/25. Commd 2/7/52. Flt Lt 27/11/57. Retd GD 25/9/75.
COLES J.G. Born 11/6/23. Commd 1/5/52. Sqn Ldr 1/1/69. Retd GD 11/6/71.
COLES P.K.L. MB ChB MRCGP DRCOG DAvMed AFOM. Born 31/1/48. Commd 20/2/72. Gp Capt 1/7/94.
    Retd MED 31/7/99.
COLES R.E. BSc. Born 20/10/57. Commd 19/9/76. Sqn Ldr 1/1/91. Retd ENG 1/10/97.
COLES R.G. Born 30/11/41. Commd 22/2/63. Flt Lt 12/11/69. Retd GD(G) 1/10/75. Re-entered 8/7/81. Sqn Ldr 1/7/87.
    Retd OPS SPT 8/7/97.
COLES S.E. BSc. Born 7/9/47. Commd 22/9/65. Flt Lt 1/3/71. Retd GD 23/9/75.
COLESKY A.D. Born 19/3/38. Commd 9/3/62. Flt Lt 1/7/69. Retd GD 13/6/70.
COLEY D.G.L. Born 19/2/20. Commd 29/8/45. Sqn Ldr 1/7/55. Retd RGT 19/11/60.
COLEY N. Born 3/4/56. Commd 17/7/75. Sqn Ldr 1/7/91. Retd GD 14/3/97.
COLGAN A.J. BEd. Born 15/12/62. Commd 10/11/85. Flt Lt 10/11/88. Retd ADMIN (P ED) 31/12/03.
COLGAN F.J. Born 27/2/20. Commd 23/9/46. Sqn Ldr 1/7/53. Retd RGT 31/7/61.
COLHOUN D.N.T. Born 23/12/48. Commd 29/3/68. Flt Lt 29/9/73. Retd GD 23/12/86.
COLHOUN M.S. Born 12/8/42. Commd 8/12/61. Flt Lt 8/6/67. Retd GD 12/8/83.
COLLARD R. Born 20/7/35. Commd 1/12/54. Flt Lt 1/6/60. Retd GD 20/7/73.
COLLEN B.A. DFM. Born 20/11/23. Commd 27/4/61. Flt Lt 27/4/64. Retd GD 30/9/73.
COLLENETTE M.C.J. Born 11/11/44. Commd 19/12/63. Wg Cdr 1/7/87. Retd ADMIN 18/11/89.
COLLER A.J. MPhil BA MILT MCIPS MCMI. Born 5/7/61. Commd 11/9/83. Sqn Ldr 1/1/94. Retd SUP 31/7/02.
COLLETT D.M. Born 25/8/38. Commd 8/12/61. Flt Lt 28/5/66. Retd GD 2/5/77.
COLLEY D.T. Born 30/9/55. Commd 31/8/78. Flt Lt 14/9/83. Retd PI 1/9/89.
COLLEY P.J. Born 3/9/48. Commd 25/10/68. Sqn Ldr 1/7/81. Retd SY(RGT) 31/12/87.
COLLIER A.S. MSc BSc BSc FRGS. Born 10/8/63. Commd 19/6/88. Flt Lt 19/12/91. Retd OPS SPT(INT) 19/6/04.
COLLIER C.P. Born 24/7/41. Commd 11/2/65. Flt Lt 11/2/69. Retd SUP 25/7/91.
COLLIER D.S. AFC. Born 19/3/23. Commd 11/2/44. Sqn Ldr 1/10/55. Retd GD 19/3/66.
COLLIER J.C. Born 23/9/37. Commd 9/12/65. Gp Capt 1/7/85. Retd ENG 3/1/90.
COLLIER J.D.D. DSO DFC*. Born 10/11/16. Commd 29/6/36. Wg Cdr 1/7/47. Retd GD 9/3/59. rtg Gp Capt
COLLIER J.M. Born 5/5/43. Commd 28/7/64. Gp Capt 1/7/87. Retd GD 5/11/98.
COLLIER N.D. Born 11/8/37. Commd 12/9/56. Fg Offr 15/10/59. Retd SUP 19/3/63.
COLLIER P.G. Born 25/10/34. Commd 26/11/64. Sqn Ldr 3/9/72. Retd EDN 26/11/72.
COLLIER P.R.S. BA. Born 1/12/56. Commd 18/3/85. Sqn Ldr 1/1/95. Retd FLY(N) 1/6/03.
COLLIER S.J. Born 4/7/66. Commd 26/9/85. Sqn Ldr 1/7/99. Retd FLY(P) 4/7/04.
COLLIER V. Born 1/11/33. Commd 3/6/65. Flt Lt 3/6/71. Retd ENG 17/11/72. Re-instated 7/5/80. Sqn Ldr 1/7/85.
    Retd ENG 1/11/88.
COLLIER-BAKER A.D. Born 6/2/57. Commd 15/2/90. Flt Lt 15/2/92. Retd ENG 15/2/98.
COLLIN M.A.B. Born 22/6/38. Commd 25/7/60. Sqn Ldr 1/7/69. Retd GD 7/4/77.
COLLINGE M.J. Born 2/4/62. Commd 26/4/84. Sqn Ldr 1/7/93. Retd ENG 2/4/00.
COLLINGE R.A. MBE MCMI. Born 23/4/35. Commd 29/4/54. Wg Cdr 1/7/79. Retd SY 29/7/85.

COLLINGS J.C. MB BS(Lond) MRCS(Eng) LRCP(Lond). Born 20/2/34. Commd 2/7/62. Wg Cdr 20/2/74.
Retd MED 2/7/78.
COLLINGS S.J. Born 5/5/38. Commd 28/11/69. Flt Lt 28/11/71. Retd PI 28/11/77.
COLLINGSWOOD P.D. Born 10/12/67. Commd 9/2/95. Flt Lt 19/3/97. Retd SUPPLY 10/12/04.
COLLINGWOOD D.C. Born 1/2/38. Commd 25/6/62. Flt Lt 25/6/62. Retd GD 20/12/68.
COLLINGWOOD D.J. Born 8/7/30. Commd 4/7/51. Flt Lt 13/11/57. Retd GD 8/7/73.
COLLINGWOOD W. Born 30/3/13. Commd 7/10/43. Sqn Ldr 1/4/56. Retd ENG 30/3/62.
COLLINS A. AFC DFM. Born 26/10/19. Commd 10/8/43. Sqn Ldr 1/10/54. Retd GD 15/8/68. rtg Wg Cdr
COLLINS A.C. Born 4/9/36. Commd 4/9/61. Wg Cdr 1/1/83. Retd GD 4/4/90.
COLLINS A.D. DPhysEd. Born 1/3/25. Commd 11/8/52. Sqn Ldr 1/1/64. Retd PE 14/1/68.
COLLINS A.F. MLitt BA. Born 19/9/45. Commd 20/8/67. Sqn Ldr 1/1/92. Retd GD 16/3/98.
COLLINS A.J. Born 29/1/44. Commd 4/10/63. Sqn Ldr 1/1/94. Retd GD 24/1/01.
COLLINS A.J.F. Born 8/11/44. Commd 31/10/74. Flt Lt 31/10/76. Retd ADMIN 8/11/82.
COLLINS B.E. Born 11/4/32. Commd 3/11/51. Flt Lt 3/5/56. Retd GD(G) 1/9/77. Re-instated 7/1/80. Flt Lt 27/8/62.
Retd GD(G) 1/8/89.
COLLINS D. Born 26/8/33. Commd 9/4/52. Flt Lt 21/8/57. Retd GD 11/4/78. Re-instated 19/11/80. Flt Lt 31/3/60.
Retd GD 26/8/88.
COLLINS D.A.I. Born 21/2/46. Commd 3/10/69. Flt Lt 3/4/75. Retd GD 19/5/85.
COLLINS D.C. MCIPS MCMI. Born 22/6/38. Commd 2/9/57. A Cdre 1/1/90. Retd SUP 4/4/92.
COLLINS D.G. Born 8/7/30. Commd 29/10/64. Sqn Ldr 1/7/84. Retd ENG 8/7/88.
COLLINS D.S. MCIPD. Born 13/3/48. Commd 15/6/83. Flt Lt 15/6/87. Retd SY 5/1/97.
COLLINS E.T. CEng MRAeS MIEE. Born 20/10/34. Commd 28/11/69. Flt Lt 28/11/71. Retd ENG 28/11/77.
COLLINS G. Born 5/2/21. Commd 14/4/44. Flt Lt 9/5/58. Retd GD(G) 2/3/71.
COLLINS G.E. Born 19/1/51. Commd 5/2/81. Flt Lt 5/2/83. Retd GD(G) 5/2/95.
COLLINS G.P. Born 18/4/49. Commd 10/9/70. Wg Cdr 1/7/88. Retd GD 2/6/90.
COLLINS I.S. Born 20/1/57. Commd 19/11/87. Flt Lt 19/11/89. Retd ENG 19/11/95.
COLLINS J.B.V. Born 6/4/35. Commd 31/7/56. Sqn Ldr 1/7/70. Retd GD 1/7/73.
COLLINS J.H. Born 15/8/36. Commd 13/12/68. Sqn Ldr 1/1/78. Retd GD(G) 1/10/80.
COLLINS J.P. Born 7/5/36. Commd 10/11/61. Flt Lt 10/2/67. Retd GD 7/5/74.
COLLINS J.R. Born 5/12/35. Commd 21/10/66. Flt Lt 21/10/68. Retd SUP 21/10/74.
COLLINS K. BSc. Born 25/1/50. Commd 25/11/73. Flt Lt 25/5/74. Retd GD 22/10/94.
COLLINS L.J. Born 2/6/24. Commd 26/11/43. Flt Lt 4/6/53. Retd GD(G) 13/4/66.
COLLINS M.A. Born 8/11/33. Commd 28/4/61. Flt Lt 1/4/66. Retd GD 8/5/91.
COLLINS M.D. Born 12/5/65. Commd 23/10/86. Flt Lt 2/5/90. Retd FLY(N) 13/9/04.
COLLINS M.W.F. MBE. Born 24/4/47. Commd 1/12/69. Sqn Ldr 1/1/83. Retd SUP 10/12/99.
COLLINS M.W.G. Born 14/4/24. Commd 19/4/44. Gp Capt 1/7/73. Retd SEC 14/4/79.
COLLINS P.I. Born 26/4/52. Commd 3/10/74. Flt Lt 25/8/78. Retd GD 26/4/90.
COLLINS P.J. BSc. Born 22/4/54. Commd 3/9/72. Sqn Ldr 1/1/87. Retd GD 1/1/93.
COLLINS P.J. Born 21/4/48. Commd 16/9/76. Flt Lt 14/12/78. Retd ENG 21/4/86.
COLLINS P.S. CB AFC BA FCMI. Born 19/3/30. Commd 17/10/51. AVM 1/7/83. Retd GD 1/7/85.
COLLINS R. Born 26/4/56. Commd 28/7/93. Flt Lt 28/7/97. Retd ENG 9/8/98.
COLLINS R.D. Born 18/7/43. Commd 19/6/64. Sqn Ldr 1/7/90. Retd GD 18/7/00.
COLLINS R.M. MCMI. Born 28/12/39. Commd 28/11/69. Sqn Ldr 1/1/85. Retd GD 4/5/92.
COLLINS S.M.StC. MBE. Born 7/5/41. Commd 24/3/61. Sqn Ldr 1/7/74. Retd GD 7/5/79.
COLLINS S.P. Born 26/11/63. Commd 10/5/90. Flt Lt 10/5/92. Retd ADMIN 14/3/96.
COLLINS T.J. Born 24/12/55. Commd 14/7/77. Flt Lt 12/6/83. Retd GD 1/10/98.
COLLIS D.J. Born 25/11/39. Commd 12/12/59. Flt Lt 12/6/65. Retd GD 14/3/78.
COLLIS J.J. Born 27/4/49. Commd 7/6/68. Sqn Ldr 1/1/86. Retd GD 14/6/90. Re-entered 13/9/91. Sqn Ldr 13/9/91.
Retd FLY(P) 27/4/04.
COLLIS L. BA. Born 10/11/40. Commd 26/11/62. Sqn Ldr 1/7/72. Retd GD 1/10/87.
COLMAN A.E. Born 8/1/31. Commd 10/7/52. Sqn Ldr 1/1/67. Retd GD 21/5/76.
COLMAN M.H.J. Born 13/2/24. Commd 28/1/44. Wg Cdr 1/1/66. Retd GD 13/10/70.
COLMAN N.A. MSc MCIT MILT MCIPS MCMI. Born 22/8/45. Commd 4/6/64. Gp Capt 1/7/91. Retd SUP 30/3/94.
COLQUHOUN C.I. MBE DFC AFC. Born 25/8/23. Commd 18/12/43. Wg Cdr 1/1/69. Retd ENG 30/6/78.
COLQUHOUN I.F. Born 6/10/31. Commd 17/3/55. Sqn Ldr 1/7/64. Retd PE 22/9/70.
COLQUHOUN W.M. BA. Born 14/6/61. Commd 15/10/80. Sqn Ldr 1/7/99. Retd GD 1/7/02.
COLSON E.B. DSO. Born 26/5/10. Commd 30/5/50. Sqn Ldr 30/5/50. Retd RGT 11/8/55.
COLSTON J.F.A. BSc. Born 13/12/26. Commd 28/6/51. Sqn Ldr 1/7/69. Retd GD 2/9/75.
COLSTON R.J. Born 4/7/22. Commd 1/9/45. Sqn Ldr 1/7/54. Retd GD 6/7/61.
COLSTON W.B. Born 7/10/30. Commd 17/5/51. Flt Lt 6/9/56. Retd GD 7/10/68.
COLTART G. Born 6/3/21. Commd 19/5/44. Sqn Ldr 1/1/69. Retd ENG 15/9/73.
COLTERJOHN E.D. MB ChB DObstRCOG. Born 6/8/30. Commd 10/10/56. Sqn Ldr 1/4/62. Retd MED 3/10/67.
COLTMAN J.D. Born 22/6/34. Commd 18/3/53. Wg Cdr 1/1/76. Retd GD 1/5/82.
COLTON R.A. BSc. Born 27/12/40. Commd 10/9/63. Flt Lt 26/7/67. Retd ENG 10/9/79.
COLVER R.J. OBE. Born 12/4/45. Commd 13/8/65. Gp Capt 1/1/94. Retd GD 14/3/96.
COLVIN N.G. Born 22/1/31. Commd 25/5/50. Gp Capt 1/7/76. Retd GD(G) 13/11/82.

COLWELL G.P. BA. Born 6/8/38. Commd 14/8/59. Wg Cdr 1/7/86. Retd GD 6/8/93.
COLWELL V.W.E. Born 6/4/23. Commd 1/8/50. Flt Lt 5/9/56. Retd GD 17/12/66.
COLWILL D.P. Born 20/5/19. Commd 15/7/45. Flt Lt 15/1/50. Retd SEC 25/4/70.
COLWILL S.J. FRAeS. Born 20/8/51. Commd 27/3/70. Gp Capt 1/7/94. Retd GD(G) 19/10/96.
COLYER D.R. Born 29/7/37. Commd 11/9/56. Flt Lt 11/3/62. Retd GD 29/7/75.
COLYER R.B. MCMI. Born 27/12/39. Commd 23/3/66. Sqn Ldr 1/1/75. Retd ENG 10/4/90.
COMBER N. Born 25/12/23. Commd 4/11/45. Sqn Ldr 1/1/56. Retd GD 31/7/69.
COMINA B.J. Born 19/6/52. Commd 27/5/71. Flt Lt 14/10/77. Retd ADMIN 20/7/79. Re-entered 20/8/80.
    Gp Capt 1/7/98. Retd ADMIN 30/4/01.
COMINA P.S.C. Born 1/12/48. Commd 31/10/69. Sqn Ldr 1/12/02. Retd OPS SPT 1/12/02.
COMMANDER R.J. Born 16/5/48. Commd 23/3/67. Flt Lt 23/9/72. Retd GD 1/6/85.
COMMON M.F.F. MBE. Born 20/1/44. Commd 14/9/64. Wg Cdr 1/1/89. Retd GD 20/7/02.
COMMON W.W. Born 17/11/27. Commd 9/1/51. Flt Lt 26/9/56. Retd GD 20/2/66.
COMPTON D. Born 23/4/29. Commd 26/5/60. Sqn Ldr 1/1/76. Retd ENG 1/5/79.
COMPTON J.F. Born 1/10/14. Commd 5/5/44. Flt Lt 29/6/50. Retd CAT 1/10/66. rtg Sqn Ldr
COMPTON P.A.G. Born 20/6/47. Commd 4/2/71. Flt Lt 21/7/74. Retd ENG 20/7/86.
COMPTON P.J. Born 21/2/48. Commd 1/4/66. Sqn Ldr 1/1/87. Retd GD 19/9/94.
COMRIE A.C. Born 20/3/39. Commd 4/3/71. Flt Lt 4/3/73. Retd SUP 3/9/77.
CONANT G.T.G. Born 7/10/24. Commd 8/7/46. Flt Lt 8/7/52. Retd GD(G) 6/3/53.
CONBA T.W.T. ACIS. Born 20/8/33. Commd 25/8/67. Flt Lt 25/8/69. Retd SEC 2/2/74.
CONCHIE B.J. AFC. Born 11/9/30. Commd 2/7/52. Sqn Ldr 1/1/77. Retd GD 1/1/80.
CONDIE J.P. Born 26/4/36. Commd 8/1/76. Flt Lt 8/1/79. Retd GD 27/4/86.
CONDIE R.H. Born 1/9/32. Commd 11/4/58. Flt Lt 11/10/67. Retd EDN 11/4/74.
CONDLIFF T.D. Born 28/8/44. Commd 5/11/70. Flt Lt 1/4/74. Retd GD 28/8/82.
CONDON R. FRGS MInstAM MCMI. Born 19/2/46. Commd 18/8/67. Wg Cdr 1/1/89. Retd ADMIN 2/4/95.
CONDREN M.A. Born 27/10/58. Commd 29/5/97. Flt Lt 29/5/01. Retd ADMIN (P ED) 2/4/04.
CONGDON P.S.M. Born 1/3/46. Commd 18/11/66. Sqn Ldr 1/7/84. Retd SY 11/7/87.
CONLON T.P. Born 11/9/44. Commd 12/7/68. Sqn Ldr 1/7/88. Retd GD 6/8/96.
CONN A. BSc. Born 6/8/73. Commd 5/10/97. Flt Lt 5/4/00. Retd OPS SPT(FLTOPS) 18/1/04.
CONNARTY A.O. Born 21/11/48. Commd 8/8/74. Wg Cdr 1/1/94. Retd GD(G) 14/3/96.
CONNELL E. Born 13/11/22. Commd 11/1/45. Flt Lt 6/4/53. Retd GD 8/8/64.
CONNELL J.L. BSc. Born 17/5/57. Commd 15/3/87. Sqn Ldr 1/1/95. Retd ADMIN 14/3/97.
CONNELL M.B. Born 30/5/50. Commd 30/5/69. Sqn Ldr 1/7/84. Retd GD 19/5/90.
CONNELLY J.S. BA MCMI. Born 19/10/34. Commd 10/4/56. Sqn Ldr 1/1/76. Retd GD(G) 1/10/85.
CONNER A.C. BSc. Born 30/9/70. Commd 20/3/91. Flt Lt 15/1/94. Retd FLY(N) 15/7/04.
CONNING W.J.J. Born 16/5/32. Commd 23/4/52. Flt Lt 19/9/57. Retd GD 16/5/87.
CONNOLLY B.T. BSc. Born 18/12/59. Commd 31/7/83. Sqn Ldr 1/1/96. Retd GD 31/12/01.
CONNOLLY D.M. MB BS MRCGP MRAeS DAvMed. Born 7/2/59. Commd 21/7/85. Wg Cdr 2/3/97.
    Retd MED 21/7/01.
CONNOLLY E. MSc BTech CEng MIEE. Born 14/3/50. Commd 11/8/74. Sqn Ldr 1/1/87. Retd ENG 18/11/01.
CONNOLLY G.A.W. LLB. Born 26/11/50. Commd 20/10/74. Flt Lt 20/7/76. Retd GD 20/10/90.
CONNOLLY J. AFC FRAeS. Born 5/2/52. Commd 4/2/71. A Cdre 1/1/98. Retd GD 28/8/01.
CONNOLLY T.V. Born 25/6/22. Commd 19/12/54. Sqn Ldr 1/7/71. Retd GD(G) 25/6/77.
CONNOR E.L. MCMI. Born 29/12/22. Commd 1/10/43. Wg Cdr 1/7/63. Retd GD 2/10/73.
CONNOR J.P. AFC BSc(Eng). Born 11/10/46. Commd 20/8/67. Sqn Ldr 1/7/81. Retd GD 11/10/90.
CONNOR M.R.H. OBE MSc. Born 22/3/45. Commd 8/7/65. Gp Capt 1/7/92. Retd SUP 18/4/00.
CONNORS D.P. MPhil BA. Born 26/11/74. Commd 1/6/03. Plt Off 1/6/03. Retd ADMIN (TRG) 26/4/04.
CONNORS J.J. Born 20/10/23. Commd 29/3/45. Flt Lt 29/11/51. Retd GD 16/12/64.
CONNORTON J. Born 2/12/43. Commd 27/7/72. Sqn Ldr 1/1/89. Retd ENG 2/12/98.
CONOLLY R.G. Born 3/11/47. Commd 15/9/67. Sqn Ldr 1/1/84. Retd GD 21/1/94.
CONQUER N.P.W. Born 16/2/21. Commd 24/8/41. Wg Cdr 1/7/58. Retd GD 16/2/68.
CONRAD J.A. Born 7/11/48. Commd 29/8/72. Sqn Ldr 1/1/81. Retd ADMIN 14/3/96.
CONRADI I.G. BSc. Born 19/4/37. Commd 27/10/57. Flt Lt 2/4/63. Retd GD 19/4/75.
CONRADI K.R. BSc. Born 14/2/62. Commd 14/9/80. Flt Lt 15/10/84. Retd GD 17/12/96.
CONRAN-SMITH D.R. Born 5/11/39. Commd 19/12/61. Sqn Ldr 1/1/72. Retd GD 5/11/83.
CONRY J.D. Born 29/8/23. Commd 7/11/44. Sqn Ldr 1/4/55. Retd GD 9/12/67.
CONSTABLE D.C.J. Born 7/3/45. Commd 30/5/69. Sqn Ldr 1/1/97. Retd GD 1/12/99.
CONSTABLE E.C. MCMI. Born 8/9/49. Commd 21/3/69. Sqn Ldr 1/1/82. Retd FLY(P) 5/4/04.
CONSTABLE F.G. DFM. Born 19/12/19. Commd 16/4/41. Sqn Ldr 1/7/53. Retd GD 17/1/59.
CONSTABLE J.E. BA. Born 20/5/57. Commd 19/9/76. Flt Lt 15/10/82. Retd SY 1/10/87.
CONSTABLE P.F. AFC. Born 19/6/37. Commd 24/6/55. Wg Cdr 1/7/80. Retd GD 1/2/90.
CONSTABLE R.E. Born 19/4/35. Commd 30/8/62. Sqn Ldr 1/1/71. Retd SUP 3/5/78.
CONSTANTI D. Born 11/1/31. Commd 18/6/52. Flt Lt 13/11/57. Retd GD 30/1/69.
CONSTANTINE K.W. Born 13/6/22. Commd 19/7/51. Sqn Ldr 1/7/67. Retd ADMIN 13/6/77.
CONWAY D.B. Born 18/11/37. Commd 9/2/62. Flt Lt 25/7/66. Retd GD 4/3/88.
CONWAY H.D. MB ChB DPH DIH. Born 11/11/10. Commd 30/3/35. Wg Cdr 1/7/47. Retd MED 9/11/63.

CONWAY L.B.J. Born 25/11/24. Commd 12/3/52. Sqn Ldr 1/7/72. Retd GD 25/5/76.
CONWAY S.D. Born 12/5/45. Commd 21/7/65. Flt Lt 21/1/71. Retd GD 16/2/77.
CONYERS G.G. Born 29/7/17. Commd 4/3/43. Sqn Ldr 1/4/56. Retd ENG 29/7/66.
COODE I.C.S.M. Born 25/2/32. Commd 6/5/65. Flt Lt 26/7/67. Retd SUP 6/5/73.
COOK A.K. DFC. Born 7/10/11. Commd 1/4/40. Flt Lt 1/4/42. Retd GD 15/12/45. rtg Sqn Ldr
COOK B.H. Born 14/5/32. Commd 21/5/52. Flt Lt 15/10/57. Retd GD(G) 4/11/75.
COOK B.W. Born 14/2/23. Commd 19/3/52. Sqn Ldr 1/7/65. Retd GD 5/3/76.
COOK C. BDS. Born 17/10/56. Commd 8/8/89. Wg Cdr 4/1/00. Retd DEL 4/1/03.
COOK C.E. BSc. Born 20/2/46. Commd 28/9/64. Sqn Ldr 1/1/83. Retd GD 14/3/97.
COOK C.J. Born 22/11/42. Commd 14/2/69. Sqn Ldr 1/1/88. Retd GD 22/11/00.
COOK C.M. Born 14/6/54. Commd 16/9/76. Sqn Ldr 1/7/92. Retd ADMIN 14/6/00.
COOK C.M. IEng MIIE. Born 4/6/68. Commd 31/3/91. Sqn Ldr 1/7/01. Retd ENGINEER 31/12/03.
COOK D. OBE MCMI. Born 27/9/30. Commd 19/4/50. Gp Capt 1/7/76. Retd 27/9/85.
COOK D.A. MILT. Born 7/1/46. Commd 11/5/78. Sqn Ldr 1/1/88. Retd SUP 20/4/96.
COOK D.E. MMedSci MB ChB DIH DAvMed AFOM MRAeS. Born 31/5/56. Commd 18/1/77. Wg Cdr 1/8/93.
    Retd MED 18/6/97.
COOK D.F. Born 1/4/49. Commd 27/2/70. Sqn Ldr 1/1/81. Retd GD 1/1/01.
COOK D.G. Born 28/4/29. Commd 18/7/63. Sqn Ldr 1/7/77. Retd GD(G) 1/8/79.
COOK E.J. MBE. Born 1/7/18. Commd 30/9/42. Sqn Offr 1/7/50. Retd SEC 5/5/54.
COOK F.J. Born 13/1/32. Commd 2/2/63. Flt Lt 25/7/66. Retd GD 24/8/76.
COOK G.H. Born 18/1/26. Commd 20/10/59. Flt Lt 22/10/65. Retd ENG 26/11/76.
COOK H.T. BSc. Born 31/12/51. Commd 13/9/70. Sqn Ldr 1/7/85. Retd GD 20/4/90.
COOK I.V. BSc. Born 8/6/66. Commd 19/7/87. Flt Lt 19/1/90. Retd FLY(P) 8/6/04.
COOK J. Born 20/2/21. Commd 26/9/45. Sqn Ldr 1/7/68. Retd GD(G) 2/2/71.
COOK J.B. MILDM. Born 26/6/34. Commd 21/10/65. Sqn Ldr 1/7/78. Retd SUP 30/4/90.
COOK J.D. BA. Born 16/6/23. Commd 14/8/43. Sqn Ldr 1/10/55. Retd GD 11/11/61.
COOK J.H. CEng MIEE MRAeS MCMI. Born 31/5/24. Commd 21/6/56. Wg Cdr 1/1/70. Retd ENG 1/1/72.
COOK J.K. Born 4/5/18. Commd 6/10/44. Flt Lt 6/4/48. Retd GD 17/7/54.
COOK K.H.H. DFC. Born 9/4/23. Commd 22/1/43. Wg Cdr 1/1/60. Retd GD 13/1/68.
COOK M.E. Born 26/11/32. Commd 26/3/52. Flt Lt 8/8/57. Retd GD 26/11/70.
COOK M.J. BSc(Eng). Born 19/12/63. Commd 11/9/83. Flt Lt 15/1/89. Retd GD 15/7/98.
COOK N.C. MILAM. Born 20/1/47. Commd 19/1/66. Wg Cdr 1/1/86. Retd RGT 20/1/91.
COOK P. Born 17/2/35. Commd 18/2/54. Flt Lt 1/3/61. Retd CAT 17/2/73.
COOK P.J. Born 28/7/40. Commd 18/12/80. Flt Lt 18/12/83. Retd GD(ENG) 23/5/89.
COOK R. CBE BTech DMS. Born 19/2/53. Commd 24/4/77. Air Cdre 1/7/01. Retd GD 17/6/05.
COOK R.M. Born 3/8/38. Commd 8/12/61. Flt Lt 28/11/67. Retd SUP 1/5/77.
COOK R.M.S. MBE. Born 23/1/41. Commd 28/4/61. Sqn Ldr 1/1/88. Retd GD 24/7/95.
COOK R.T. Born 20/2/26. Commd 20/11/50. Flt Lt 26/5/55. Retd GD 30/6/69.
COOK W. Born 3/3/54. Commd 13/1/72. Plt Offr 6/5/72. Retd GD(G) 2/10/72.
COOKE A.J. Born 3/7/31. Commd 3/6/65. Flt Lt 3/6/71. Retd GD(G) 3/7/89.
COOKE A.K. BTech BEng. Born 19/1/60. Commd 11/9/83. Flt Lt 11/3/86. Retd ADMIN 11/9/95.
COOKE B.H. MCMI. Born 4/3/30. Commd 5/11/53. Sqn Ldr 1/1/74. Retd SEC 24/10/81.
COOKE C.K. Born 15/4/24. Commd 1/10/43. Gp Capt 1/7/71. Retd GD 29/5/75.
COOKE D. Born 4/7/21. Commd 10/5/43. Flt Lt 10/11/46. Retd GD 4/7/64.
COOKE F.I. CEng MIEE. Born 22/4/35. Commd 25/8/60. Flt Lt 14/2/66. Retd ENG 22/4/73.
COOKE G. The Rev. Born 11/1/38. Commd 2/10/67. Retd Sqn Ldr 20/10/71.
COOKE G.G. MBE. Born 3/1/46. Commd 20/9/79. Sqn Ldr 1/1/90. Retd ENG 3/7/01.
COOKE H. Born 23/7/44. Commd 16/12/66. Flt Lt 16/3/73. Retd PI 24/1/76.
COOKE I.E. PhD BSc. Born 1/5/48. Commd 22/10/72. Flt Lt 22/10/73. Retd EDN 28/11/75.
COOKE J. Born 20/4/28. Commd 23/1/64. Flt Lt 23/1/69. Retd GD 20/4/88.
COOKE J.D. BA. Born 1/8/23. Commd 2/7/51. Sqn Ldr 1/1/64. Retd PE 31/5/73.
COOKE J.J. BA. Born 21/10/45. Commd 9/6/68. Gp Capt 1/7/90. Retd SUP 24/10/92.
COOKE J.M. Born 17/1/38. Commd 24/6/71. Flt Lt 24/6/73. Retd ENG 21/9/89.
COOKE J.M. Born 7/8/21. Commd 19/7/44. Flt Lt 19/1/48. Retd GD 12/6/51.
COOKE J.N.C. CB OBE MD BS FRCP FRCP(Edin) MFOM MRCS. Born 16/1/22. Commd 1/11/45. AVM 1/9/79.
    Retd MED 15/6/85.
COOKE M.S. Born 20/6/37. Commd 18/1/56. Flt Lt 18/7/61. Retd GD 26/4/64.
COOKE P.K. Born 12/5/27. Commd 19/7/51. Flt Lt 19/1/55. Retd GD 12/5/65.
COOLEDGE R.C. Born 10/9/18. Commd 26/1/45. Flt Lt 26/7/48. Retd GD 23/11/57.
COOMBER A.M. BA. Born 28/12/73. Commd 7/4/96. Flt Lt 7/10/99. Retd OPS SPT(INT) 1/9/03.
COOMBES C. Born 19/7/34. Commd 10/4/56. Flt Lt 1/3/61. Retd GD 18/6/81.
COOMBES D.L. Born 8/10/67. Commd 31/7/86. Flt Lt 21/1/93. Retd ADMIN 27/6/96.
COOMBES D.W. Born 9/11/25. Commd 20/4/50. Sqn Ldr 1/1/68. Retd GD 9/7/76.
COOMBES P.K. Born 5/11/27. Commd 9/8/51. Flt Lt 28/11/56. Retd GD 5/11/82.
COOMBES R.E. Born 5/10/58. Commd 5/1/86. Wg Cdr 1/7/02. Retd GD 20/4/05.
COOMBES S.R.A. BSc. Born 4/8/60. Commd 26/9/82. Sqn Ldr 1/1/94. Retd GD 26/9/98.

COOMBS B. BA. Born 21/7/47. Commd 30/1/70. Wg Cdr 1/7/98. Retd OPS SPT 1/12/00.
COOMBS M.J. Born 2/8/36. Commd 27/1/67. Flt Lt 27/1/69. Retd PRT 27/1/75.
COON W.J.B. BSc CEng MRAeS. Born 14/9/32. Commd 22/1/55. Wg Cdr 1/7/75. Retd ENG 1/10/82.
COONEY E.F. Born 1/7/15. Commd 22/6/50. Fg Offr 22/6/52. Retd SEC 16/7/55.
COONEY P.J. Born 17/3/61. Commd 1/11/79. Sqn Ldr 1/1/94. Retd GD 17/3/99.
COOP G.A. MRAeS. Born 13/10/46. Commd 11/8/67. Wg Cdr 1/7/88. Retd GD 13/10/01.
COOPER A.C. MBE. Born 4/6/14. Commd 29/11/43. Sqn Ldr 1/1/56. Retd ENG 4/6/69.
COOPER A.D. Born 30/3/43. Commd 22/5/75. Sqn Ldr 1/7/87. Retd GD 14/3/96.
COOPER A.F. Born 9/3/54. Commd 17/7/75. Flt Lt 9/9/79. Retd GD 14/3/96.
COOPER A.H. Born 23/2/29. Commd 24/9/64. Sqn Ldr 1/1/77. Retd ENG 3/4/79.
COOPER A.J. Born 2/1/63. Commd 15/2/90. Sqn Ldr 1/7/99. Retd ENG 1/7/02.
COOPER A.R.C. Born 23/6/83. Commd 1/4/18. Sqn Ldr 1/4/18. Retd GD 22/8/28. Re-called 26/10/39 to 28/10/43.
COOPER B.C. Born 30/3/10. Commd 14/2/46. Flt Lt 14/8/48. Retd ENG 30/3/65.
COOPER B.F. MSc BSc CEng MRAeS. Born 8/10/37. Commd 10/8/65. Sqn Ldr 1/1/75. Retd ENG 8/2/96.
COOPER B.V. Born 24/5/27. Commd 20/12/62. Flt Lt 20/12/68. Retd ADMIN 24/5/85.
COOPER C.A. MA. Born 3/7/33. Commd 26/9/53. Wg Cdr 1/7/74. Retd ENG 3/7/88.
COOPER C.C. Born 1/10/65. Commd 9/5/91. Flt Lt 19/4/94. Retd FLY(P) 1/10/03.
COOPER C.E.F. Born 16/8/28. Commd 12/12/51. Sqn Ldr 1/7/71. Retd SUP 6/9/78.
COOPER C.F. CBE BA MCMI MCIPS. Born 5/10/44. Commd 11/11/71. A Cdre 1/7/93. Retd SUP 2/5/01.
COOPER C.G. BTech. Born 6/4/51. Commd 15/9/69. Sqn Ldr 1/7/84. Retd ENG 6/4/89.
COOPER C.R. OBE FCMI CertEd. Born 5/3/45. Commd 30/1/70. Gp Capt 1/7/93. Retd ADMIN 8/9/99.
COOPER D.A. AFC. Born 27/9/30. Commd 12/12/51. Wg Cdr 1/7/67. Retd GD 1/7/70.
COOPER D.F. BSc. Born 26/3/36. Commd 9/8/57. Sqn Ldr 12/8/70. Retd ADMIN 11/11/76.
COOPER D.R. MSc BSc. Born 18/7/43. Commd 5/1/70. Sqn Ldr 5/3/75. Retd ADMIN 18/7/98.
COOPER E.E. Born 22/12/12. Commd 12/9/46. Sqn Ldr 1/1/63. Retd SUP 22/12/67.
COOPER F.A. Born 27/4/23. Commd 4/7/44. Sqn Ldr 1/7/61. Retd GD 26/2/65.
COOPER F.B. CEng MIMechE MIQA MRAeS. Born 30/9/37. Commd 1/1/62. Wg Cdr 1/1/84. Retd ENG 30/9/91.
COOPER F.T. Born 13/2/23. Commd 3/2/45. Sqn Ldr 1/7/56. Retd GD 13/2/66.
COOPER G. Born 14/8/46. Commd 18/1/73. Sqn Ldr 1/1/90. Retd GD 14/8/98.
COOPER G.B. DPhysEd. Born 12/3/28. Commd 6/8/52. Flt Lt 6/8/56. Retd PE 6/8/68.
COOPER G.D. MBE. Born 7/11/19. Commd 31/12/41. Wg Cdr 1/1/58. Retd ENG 7/11/74.
COOPER G.E. Born 15/5/39. Commd 16/9/71. Flt Lt 16/9/73. Retd GD 15/5/94.
COOPER G.M.G. BSc CEng FRAeS FCMI. Born 12/9/31. Commd 24/9/52. A Cdre 1/7/81. Retd ENG 30/11/82.
COOPER G.P. Born 25/6/52. Commd 16/3/73. Sqn Ldr 1/7/86. Retd SUP 25/6/90.
COOPER G.S. OBE. Born 25/10/25. Commd 21/12/45. A Cdre 1/7/75. Retd GD 1/9/78.
COOPER H. BDS LDS RCS MGDSRCS(Eng). Born 31/1/42. Commd 18/9/60. Wg Cdr 5/1/78. Retd DEL 31/3/88.
COOPER I.D. Born 9/9/55. Commd 13/12/79. Flt Lt 19/1/84. Retd GD 1/4/89.
COOPER J. DPhysEd. Born 30/9/39. Commd 5/1/65. Flt Lt 5/7/70. Retd GD 15/9/77.
COOPER J.A. Born 5/12/22. Commd 10/9/44. Flt Lt 10/3/48. Retd GD 12/5/73.
COOPER J.E. Born 22/5/33. Commd 6/4/54. Gp Capt 1/7/85. Retd SUP 18/5/88.
COOPER J.H. Born 12/2/51. Commd 14/10/71. Sqn Ldr 1/7/85. Retd GD 12/2/89.
COOPER J.J. OBE MCMI. Born 12/1/23. Commd 6/8/44. Wg Cdr 1/1/64. Retd GD 12/1/78.
COOPER J.W. BA. Born 16/8/30. Commd 18/6/52. Flt Lt 13/11/57. Retd GD 16/9/90.
COOPER K.C. Born 27/12/23. Commd 19/7/51. Flt Lt 19/1/55. Retd GD(G) 1/10/77.
COOPER K.G. Born 1/1/31. Commd 4/1/56. Flt Lt 4/7/61. Retd GD 1/12/70.
COOPER K.J. MHCIMA. Born 12/10/21. Commd 17/10/57. Flt Lt 1/4/63. Retd CAT 18/10/75.
COOPER L.A. BSc. Born 16/12/38. Commd 31/10/60. Flt Lt 31/7/62. Retd GD 12/11/77.
COOPER M.A. Born 12/7/46. Commd 21/5/80. Flt Lt 21/3/74. Retd GD 25/2/87.
COOPER M.B. Born 30/11/14. Commd 2/1/39. Sqn Ldr 1/6/45. Retd GD 28/4/49.
COOPER P.A. BSc CEng DipEl MIEE. Born 30/1/28. Commd 23/2/50. Sqn Ldr 1/4/61. Retd EDN 9/10/73.
COOPER P.A.L. Born 29/8/18. Commd 9/9/39. Wg Cdr 1/1/55. Retd SEC 31/12/60.
COOPER P.R. BEng. Born 12/7/50. Commd 17/1/72. Sqn Ldr 1/7/85. Retd GD 12/7/88.
COOPER R.A. BA. Born 6/3/50. Commd 13/9/70. Flt Lt 15/4/73. Retd GD 6/3/88.
COOPER R.A. Born 24/2/38. Commd 7/6/68. Sqn Ldr 1/1/78. Retd ENG 21/4/83.
COOPER R.A. Born 24/8/56. Commd 29/3/90. Flt Lt 29/3/92. Retd OPS SPT(INT) 29/3/04.
COOPER R.B.A. Born 16/12/28. Commd 8/2/51. Sqn Ldr 1/1/66. Retd SUP 1/1/69.
COOPER R.E. BEM. Born 21/1/32. Commd 4/7/64. Sqn Ldr 4/7/71. Retd EDN 4/7/74.
COOPER R.H. Born 27/6/29. Commd 18/9/50. Flt Lt 5/10/60. Retd GD 27/6/67.
COOPER R.H. Born 29/9/19. Commd 21/10/54. Sqn Ldr 1/1/63. Retd ENG 1/9/70.
COOPER R.M. Born 8/12/41. Commd 29/10/60. Sqn Ldr 1/1/72. Retd GD 8/12/79.
COOPER R.W.L. Born 4/2/45. Commd 4/7/69. Flt Lt 14/11/75. Retd GD(G) 11/3/85.
COOPER S.H. Born 26/7/20. Commd 27/8/59. Flt Lt 27/9/64. Retd SUP 26/1/71.
COOPER S.R. Born 17/9/35. Commd 1/8/69. Flt Lt 1/8/71. Retd ADMIN 10/9/76.
COOPER T.K.N. Born 20/10/43. Commd 11/5/86. Sqn Ldr 29/12/86. Retd MED(T) 1/7/88.
COOPER T.W. AFM. Born 21/5/24. Commd 29/6/50. Sqn Ldr 1/1/61. Retd GD 23/4/76.
COOTE C.H. Born 23/5/58. Commd 5/4/79. Flt Lt 5/10/84. Retd GD 5/4/87.

COOTE S.M. BSc. Born 25/7/65. Commd 11/10/87. Flt Lt 11/4/90. Retd FLY(P) 17/8/04.
COOTER C.E. BA. Born 15/8/34. Commd 9/8/60. Sqn Ldr 24/5/69. Retd EDN 16/7/74.
COPE A.W. MBE AFC FRAeS. Born 13/2/47. Commd 1/3/68. Gp Capt 1/1/97. Retd GD 13/2/02.
COPE S.E. Born 13/4/20. Commd 1/5/47. Flt Lt 1/11/51. Retd SUP 3/10/59.
COPE LEWIS R. Born 25/6/35. Commd 9/6/54. Flt Lt 9/12/59. Retd GD 5/10/73.
COPE-LEWIS M.M. Born 24/7/39. Commd 20/12/62. Sqn Ldr 1/7/73. Retd SEC 26/9/78.
COPELAND P.J. Born 22/7/34. Commd 19/1/66. Sqn Ldr 1/1/74. Retd ENG 7/9/88.
COPELAND S.J. Born 23/9/60. Commd 26/4/84. Flt Lt 27/9/90. Retd ADMIN 11/12/96.
COPLAND J.H. MCMI. Born 17/3/33. Commd 4/5/53. Sqn Ldr 1/1/67. Retd GD 19/3/76.
COPLESTON D.J. Born 6/4/23. Commd 22/8/46. Flt Lt 22/2/50. Retd ENG 6/4/56.
COPNALL P.I. BSc. Born 20/4/63. Commd 29/9/85. Flt Lt 29/3/93. Retd GD 15/12/92.
COPPARD E.G. Born 11/11/26. Commd 18/3/52. Flt Lt 22/5/57. Retd GD 6/1/82.
COPPING G.C.A. Born 26/8/55. Commd 22/5/75. Sqn Ldr 1/7/91. Retd ADMIN 12/6/98.
COPPINS D.V.H. Born 2/2/26. Commd 22/8/63. Flt Lt 22/8/66. Retd GD 2/2/84.
COPSEY G.J. MBA BSc CEng MRAeS MCMI. Born 11/2/51. Commd 25/2/72. Sqn Ldr 1/1/85. Retd ENG 26/2/90.
COPSEY J.E. Born 6/1/44. Commd 2/8/66. Flt Lt 17/3/71. Retd GD 6/1/82.
CORBELL B. Born 23/11/32. Commd 10/9/79. Sqn Ldr 20/5/76. Retd ADMIN 10/9/80.
CORBET D.J. Born 13/12/22. Commd 14/6/44. Wg Cdr 1/7/62. Retd GD 30/7/66.
CORBETT A.F. Born 31/1/31. Commd 6/9/56. Flt Lt 6/3/61. Retd GD 31/1/91.
CORBETT A.J. BA. Born 12/7/60. Commd 7/11/82. Flt Lt 7/5/86. Retd ADMIN 5/11/95.
CORBIN C.J. MRCS LRCP. Born 24/3/53. Commd 22/1/74. Sqn Ldr 1/8/82. Retd MED 1/4/90.
CORBIN L.G. Born 10/7/20. Commd 26/9/43. Flt Lt 26/3/47. Retd GD 10/7/75.
CORBITT A.G. Born 13/6/48. Commd 27/2/70. Wg Cdr 1/7/90. Retd SUP 1/6/95.
CORBITT A.L. Born 30/5/49. Commd 1/3/68. Flt Lt 1/6/74. Retd SEC 1/3/78.
CORBITT I.S. MSc CDipAF. Born 30/7/47. Commd 1/3/68. AVM 1/1/00. Retd GD 30/7/02.
CORBRIDGE W. Born 16/5/25. Commd 24/4/70. Flt Lt 24/4/76. Retd MED(T) 16/5/80.
CORBY J. Born 9/2/38. Commd 25/3/70. Sqn Ldr 1/1/81. Retd GD 9/2/93.
CORDEN A.M. Born 22/2/46. Commd 5/2/65. Flt Lt 5/2/71. Retd GD 1/10/75.
CORDEN J.S. BSc ACGI. Born 3/6/57. Commd 23/9/79. Sqn Ldr 1/1/92. Retd GD 31/12/96.
CORDEROY G.T. The Rev. BA. Born 15/4/31. Commd 1/1/62. Retd Gp Capt 23/10/87.
CORDERY C. BEd FCIPD. Born 20/9/52. Commd 3/5/81. Wg Cdr 1/1/93. Retd ADMIN 6/8/01.
CORDING R.F. Born 20/4/28. Commd 20/4/48. Flt Lt 28/6/60. Retd GD 29/1/68.
CORDUROY F.G. MSc BSc. Born 23/10/30. Commd 10/10/51. Flt Lt 10/4/56. Retd GD 23/10/68.
CORFE A.G. Born 24/7/25. Commd 29/12/44. Sqn Ldr 1/1/58. Retd GD 3/12/76.
CORFIELD B.T. Born 6/12/20. Commd 3/11/44. Flt Lt 3/5/48. Retd GD 6/12/63.
CORFIELD J. Born 28/2/23. Commd 17/10/57. Sqn Ldr 1/1/78. Retd ENG 28/2/83.
CORFIELD P.W. Born 21/11/40. Commd 10/9/70. Flt Lt 10/9/72. Retd SEC 21/11/78.
CORIAT H. BA. Born 9/10/37. Commd 15/12/59. Gp Capt 1/1/86. Retd GD 31/10/88.
CORKE B.C. MB ChB. Born 16/2/38. Commd 16/7/62. Sqn Ldr 16/7/67. Retd MED 3/4/74.
CORKE D. Born 1/7/18. Commd 19/12/41. Sqn Offr 1/7/51. Retd SEC 1/2/54.
CORKER R.C. DFC. Born 10/11/20. Commd 5/7/44. Sqn Ldr 1/7/69. Retd GD(G) 10/11/75.
CORKERTON W.C. Born 27/8/30. Commd 5/12/51. Flt Lt 5/6/56. Retd GD 27/8/68.
CORLEY B.R. Born 4/4/34. Commd 8/10/52. Flt Lt 6/3/58. Retd GD 4/4/72.
CORMACK B.A. BTech CEng MRAeS MCMI. Born 5/8/53. Commd 25/9/71. Sqn Ldr 1/1/86. Retd ENG 5/8/91.
CORMACK B.G. MA. Born 5/7/40. Commd 1/8/66. Sqn Ldr 1/3/73. Retd ADMIN 1/8/88.
CORMACK P.G. MCMI. Born 23/1/36. Commd 5/5/55. Wg Cdr 1/7/74. Retd RGT 9/5/81.
CORNABY P.J. DPhysEd MCMI. Born 9/7/30. Commd 16/1/57. Wg Cdr 1/1/74. Retd SUP 3/9/83.
CORNALL C.J. Born 23/9/51. Commd 11/4/85. Flt Lt 11/4/87. Retd GD 22/1/95.
CORNELIUS J. Born 2/8/17. Commd 4/11/43. Flt Lt 4/5/47. Retd ENG 31/10/53.
CORNELIUS S.J. Born 24/2/39. Commd 6/12/59. Sqn Ldr 1/1/86. Retd GD 24/2/94.
CORNES B.R. Born 19/10/58. Commd 25/2/82. Flt Lt 25/8/87. Retd FLY(P) 28/2/05.
CORNFIELD K.L. OBE MA. Born 27/11/55. Commd 1/9/74. Gp Capt 1/1/00. Retd GD 2/4/03.
CORNFORD A.L. Born 29/8/14. Commd 8/1/39. Wg Cdr 1/7/53. Retd SUP 17/11/64.
CORNFORD D.A. Born 21/2/45. Commd 23/5/85. Flt Lt 23/5/89. Retd ENG 1/9/99.
CORNISH A.H.P. Born 1/1/30. Commd 1/8/51. Sqn Ldr 1/1/64. Retd GD 5/3/76.
CORNISH C.W. Born 20/5/23. Commd 28/5/43. Wg Cdr 1/7/59. Retd GD 10/9/68.
CORNISH C.W. CEng MINucE MRAeS. Born 11/3/21. Commd 17/5/56. Sqn Ldr 1/1/68. Retd ENG 10/8/74.
CORNISH J.H. Born 7/3/27. Commd 13/2/64. Sqn Ldr 1/7/69. Retd ENG 7/3/85.
CORNTHWAITE J.D. Born 14/4/34. Commd 17/7/70. Sqn Ldr 1/7/80. Retd ENG 31/10/86.
CORNWELL B.A. BSc ARCS. Born 24/12/48. Commd 29/8/72. Wg Cdr 1/1/94. Retd GD 1/11/03.
CORNWELL M.R. Born 16/10/45. Commd 21/7/65. Flt Lt 21/1/71. Retd GD 16/10/83.
CORNWELL N.H. Born 12/9/24. Commd 12/9/63. Flt Lt 12/9/68. Retd ENG 12/9/79.
CORP G.G. Born 30/5/14. Commd 27/5/54. Flt Lt 27/5/57. Retd GD 28/2/59.
CORPS S.G. Born 2/11/29. Commd 1/4/53. Flt Lt 3/9/58. Retd GD 20/12/62.
CORRANS K.D. MCMI. Born 28/10/38. Commd 18/2/81. Wg Cdr 1/7/91. Retd ADMIN 18/2/97.
CORRIE H.C.D. Born 31/10/16. Commd 3/10/46. Sqn Ldr 1/1/65. Retd SUP 1/11/71.

CORRIETTE R.H. Born 16/3/61. Commd 8/2/96. Flt Lt 8/2/98. Retd SUPPLY 8/2/04.
CORRIN J.E. Born 17/9/42. Commd 2/1/75. Sqn Ldr 1/7/82. Retd SUP 24/7/93.
CORSER V.J. MCMI. Born 23/1/18. Commd 13/2/47. Wg Cdr 1/1/64. Retd SUP 23/1/73.
CORSER W.J.L. BA. Born 5/1/44. Commd 22/5/64. Sqn Ldr 1/7/90. Retd GD 30/4/96.
CORSER W.P. Born 10/10/15. Commd 27/1/55. Sqn Ldr 1/1/64. Retd ENG 4/8/67.
CORSON J.P. Born 4/4/31. Commd 19/4/51. Flt Lt 17/10/56. Retd GD 4/4/69.
CORTON S. Born 3/3/38. Commd 12/1/62. Flt Lt 1/7/66. Retd GD 3/3/88.
COSBY D.R. AFC. Born 7/12/43. Commd 9/2/62. Flt Lt 12/11/69. Retd GD 7/12/81.
COSGROVE J.A. CBE. Born 13/10/43. Commd 21/7/65. Gp Capt 1/1/92. Retd GD 22/5/98.
COSHAM A.R. Born 6/1/47. Commd 28/11/69. Flt Lt 17/8/73. Retd GD 2/9/75.
COSSAR A.K. MSc BSc(Eng) CEng MIEE. Born 2/12/48. Commd 27/2/70. Gp Capt 1/1/02. Retd GD 1/1/04.
COSTAIN H.D. MBE MCMI. Born 27/3/22. Commd 6/3/43. Wg Cdr 1/1/70. Retd GD 27/3/77.
COSTELLO J.M. Born 12/4/19. Commd 31/10/43. Flt Lt 3/4/47. Retd GD(G) 12/4/63.
COSTICK E.H. QGM. Born 5/10/28. Commd 6/4/64. Sqn Ldr 1/7/76. Retd ENG 5/10/83.
COSTIN W.J. Born 13/12/47. Commd 14/8/70. Flt Lt 14/2/76. Retd GD 13/12/85.
COSTLEY J.A. Born 2/3/32. Commd 23/1/64. Flt Lt 23/1/69. Retd GD 16/8/75.
COSTLEY J.M. BSc. Born 8/3/31. Commd 11/2/54. Sqn Ldr 11/8/64. Retd EDN 28/10/69.
COSWAY D.P. Born 17/2/66. Commd 15/3/87. Flt Lt 15/9/93. Retd OPS SPT(FLTOPS) 31/5/05.
COTTAM B.M. Born 19/3/45. Commd 26/5/67. Gp Capt 1/1/92. Retd GD 5/12/96.
COTTAM J. MB BS LMSSA FRCS(Edin). Born 25/3/30. Commd 26/9/54. Wg Cdr 3/9/67. Retd MED 26/9/70.
COTTER J.D. DFC. Born 21/9/23. Commd 4/11/43. Sqn Ldr 1/10/55. Retd GD 21/3/62.
COTTERELL S.C. Born 6/6/20. Commd 21/5/49. Flt Lt 6/3/63. Retd GD(G) 11/1/69.
COTTERILL P.A.S. Born 23/7/30. Commd 2/6/49. Flt Lt 6/3/56. Retd GD 23/7/68.
COTTINGHAM A.S. Born 25/10/34. Commd 17/12/57. Sqn Ldr 1/1/70. Retd GD 25/11/75.
COTTON A.E. MCMI. Born 24/9/32. Commd 15/5/58. Flt Lt 15/5/64. Retd SUP 24/6/73.
COTTON G.J. Born 31/1/50. Commd 4/7/69. Sqn Ldr 1/7/85. Retd GD 1/7/88.
COTTON M.J. IEng AMRAeS. Born 28/4/58. Commd 11/9/86. Flt Lt 11/9/88. Retd ENG 28/4/96.
COTTON R.J. Born 4/10/33. Commd 11/10/51. Sqn Ldr 1/7/63. Retd GD 3/1/89.
COTTON S.J. Born 26/10/41. Commd 8/4/70. Flt Lt 8/3/72. Retd GD 19/5/80.
COTTON W.F. Born 3/6/41. Commd 14/8/70. Sqn Ldr 1/7/80. Retd SUP 2/4/92.
COTTRELL A. Born 7/9/15. Commd 25/8/44. Sqn Ldr 1/7/58. Retd PRT 24/5/69.
COTTRELL F.R. Born 11/9/23. Commd 2/4/45. Flt Lt 28/6/56. Retd GD(G) 15/12/60.
COUBAN S.J. ACA. Born 26/12/05. Commd 30/5/41. Sqn Ldr 1/8/47. Retd SEC 30/11/58.
COUCH A.P. BTech. Born 19/5/50. Commd 23/9/68. Wg Cdr 1/7/86. Retd GD 14/11/89.
COUCH S.J. BSc. Born 20/10/60. Commd 13/2/83. Flt Lt 15/5/86. Retd ENG 13/2/93.
COUCH T.J. Born 15/6/36. Commd 24/2/55. Sqn Ldr 1/1/72. Retd SUP 30/4/77.
COUCHER J.J. AFM. Born 24/11/21. Commd 7/2/57. Flt Lt 7/2/60. Retd GD 29/10/68.
COUCHMAN A.J. AFC. Born 5/10/19. Commd 5/3/43. Sqn Ldr 1/1/70. Retd GD 5/10/74.
COUCHMAN C.M. MBE. Born 23/5/54. Commd 8/9/83. Flt Lt 8/9/85. Retd GD(G) 23/5/92.
COUCHMAN H.M.C. Born 3/7/45. Commd 6/5/65. Sqn Ldr 1/1/85. Retd GD 14/3/97.
COUCHMAN M.J. Born 26/12/47. Commd 23/1/87. Flt Lt 23/1/93. Retd GD(G) 14/3/96.
COUCILL G.C. BSc. Born 18/10/29. Commd 10/4/52. Sqn Ldr 1/7/63. Retd GD 21/1/77.
COUGHLAN D.A. Born 16/11/43. Commd 26/10/62. Flt Lt 26/4/68. Retd GD 14/6/77.
COUGHLIN C.C. BA. Born 20/12/55. Commd 15/9/74. Flt Lt 15/10/80. Retd ADMIN 1/10/83.
COUKHAM A.T. FIMLS. Born 18/8/32. Commd 13/1/72. Flt Lt 26/9/74. Retd MED(T) 31/12/76.
COULCHER C.P.J. MCMI. Born 17/3/37. Commd 17/12/57. Wg Cdr 1/7/77. Retd GD 17/3/92.
COULES E.W. Born 26/10/26. Commd 6/6/51. Flt Lt 22/5/57. Retd GD 1/12/66.
COULSON L.R. IEng MIIE AMRAeS. Born 14/2/44. Commd 26/4/84. Sqn Ldr 1/1/94. Retd ENG 14/3/96.
COULSON P. Born 6/9/41. Commd 18/12/62. Flt Lt 28/7/65. Retd GD 15/2/74.
COULSON P.A. Born 13/5/54. Commd 4/7/85. Sqn Ldr 1/7/92. Retd GD 1/7/95.
COULSON R.L.S. CBE. Born 18/2/20. Commd 5/11/41. Gp Capt 1/1/65. Retd GD 18/2/70.
COULSON S.P. DSO DFC. Born 6/7/16. Commd 19/12/36. Gp Capt 1/1/57. Retd GD 30/9/65.
COULTER D.N. Born 26/12/37. Commd 13/2/58. Flt Lt 21/8/63. Retd GD 26/12/75.
COULTER E.G. MSc CEng MIEE. Born 23/5/47. Commd 12/2/76. Wg Cdr 1/7/94. Retd ENG 23/5/02.
COULTON R.G. Born 7/6/21. Commd 27/4/49. Flt Lt 27/4/55. Retd SEC 28/10/65. Re-instated 28/4/71 to 28/4/74.
COUMBE D.J. Born 16/1/35. Commd 9/2/66. Sqn Ldr 1/1/80. Retd GD(G) 13/9/86.
COUNTER R.T. MB BS FRCS(Edin) MRCS LRCP DLO. Born 10/4/45. Commd 19/7/65. Sqn Ldr 18/7/74.
    Retd MED 27/4/77.
COURCHEE J.W. Born 3/9/37. Commd 22/7/71. Sqn Ldr 1/7/78. Retd ENG 1/1/88.
COURCOUX J. Born 24/6/46. Commd 1/4/66. Sqn Ldr 1/7/78. Retd GD 21/10/78.
COURSE P.K. Born 16/3/45. Commd 9/3/72. Flt Lt 9/3/74. Retd GD 31/3/78.
COURT A.R. Born 15/6/32. Commd 9/4/52. Flt Lt 12/2/58. Retd GD 15/6/70.
COURT C.J. BSc MBA MCIPD. Born 18/3/50. Commd 11/5/75. Sqn Ldr 1/7/84. Retd ADMIN 11/5/91.
COURT D.M. BSc. Born 2/8/60. Commd 4/1/83. Flt Lt 4/4/84. Retd GD 12/12/95.
COURT D.T. Born 23/3/31. Commd 21/3/49. Flt Lt 7/11/57. Retd GD 2/8/68.
COURT F.J. Born 28/5/11. Commd 30/7/53. Flt Lt 1/12/56. Retd ENG 28/5/66.

COURT J.M.A. BSc. Born 25/7/17. Commd 1/9/48. Sqn Ldr 1/6/56. Retd EDN 1/9/56.
COURT L.R. Born 20/3/23. Commd 9/11/43. Sqn Ldr 1/10/55. Retd GD 26/7/57.
COURT P.G. BSc. Born 10/1/59. Commd 5/2/98. Sqn Ldr 1/7/02. Retd MEDICAL SUPPORT 14/7/04.
COURT-SMITH D.StJ. Born 5/2/32. Commd 21/5/52. Sqn Ldr 1/7/78. Retd GD 6/2/90.
COURTENAY L.M. CEng MIEE. Born 2/5/22. Commd 12/3/42. Wg Cdr 1/7/58. Retd ENG 24/10/64.
COURTENAY R.T. MB BS DAvMed. Born 29/9/59. Commd 18/6/81. Wg Cdr 1/8/97. Retd MED 29/9/97.
COURTMAN B. Born 10/9/35. Commd 3/3/54. Sqn Ldr 1/1/73. Retd GD 1/5/88.
COURTNAGE K. OBE AFC. Born 7/2/23. Commd 1/5/45. Gp Capt 1/7/68. Retd GD 30/4/75.
COURTNEY G.H.H. Born 30/11/41. Commd 2/2/68. Flt Lt 27/4/74. Retd GD(G) 10/10/83.
COUSENS R.J. Born 17/4/59. Commd 5/2/81. Flt Lt 5/8/86. Retd GD 5/2/96.
COUSINS Sir David KCB AFC BA. Born 20/1/42. Commd 17/12/63. ACM 1/8/97. Retd GD 11/11/98.
COUSINS E.S.J. Born 2/3/24. Commd 19/7/57. Flt Lt 1/4/63. Retd GD 7/4/79.
COUSINS L.D. Born 6/9/09. Commd 2/4/53. Flt Lt 2/4/56. Retd ENG 6/9/64.
COUSINS L.W.J. CEng MIEE. Born 7/10/20. Commd 5/11/42. Wg Cdr 1/1/67. Retd ENG 7/10/75.
COUSINS P. Born 22/7/33. Commd 29/3/56. Flt Lt 1/10/67. Retd SEC 22/7/71.
COUSTON T. Born 22/8/64. Commd 26/4/84. Sqn Ldr 1/1/99. Retd FLY(P) 22/2/03.
COUTHARD C.W. CB AFC* FRAeS. Born 27/2/21. Commd 2/8/41. AVM 1/7/72. Retd GD 27/2/76.
COUTTS J. Born 16/10/33. Commd 23/7/52. Flt Lt 29/4/59. Retd GD(G) 16/10/93.
COUTTS J.A. MA. Born 11/1/41. Commd 9/6/62. Flt Lt 9/6/65. Retd GD 11/9/79.
COUTTS-SMITH A. Born 25/2/26. Commd 7/7/49. Sqn Ldr 1/7/58. Retd GD 30/3/68.
COUZENS D.C. MA MBA CEng FIMechE FRAeS FCMI DLUT. Born 15/10/49. Commd 23/9/68. AVM 1/1/99.
    Retd GD 18/12/04.
COUZENS E.L. Born 13/11/19. Commd 21/4/45. Flt Lt 15/12/49. Retd GD(G) 28/5/66.
COUZENS M.C.A. Born 1/9/62. Commd 31/7/86. Sqn Ldr 1/7/99. Retd ADMIN 1/7/02.
COVELL R.G. BA MB BChir MFCM MRCS LRCP DPH. Born 17/11/26. Commd 1/4/52. Gp Capt 1/1/73.
    Retd MED 29/1/76.
COVENEY A.J. Born 21/2/43. Commd 6/11/67. Sqn Ldr 1/1/78. Retd SUP 5/12/97.
COVENEY D.L. MBE MSc. Born 9/4/30. Commd 29/12/53. Wg Cdr 1/7/70. Retd ENG 3/6/80.
COVENTRY J.F. MSc BDS LDSRCS. Born 1/6/41. Commd 18/9/60. Wg Cdr 23/12/77. Retd DEL 1/6/79.
COVENTRY P.P. Born 11/8/22. Commd 20/9/41. Sqn Ldr 1/7/57. Retd GD 29/7/63.
COVENTRY W.C. Born 21/6/33. Commd 1/9/54. Flt Lt 30/11/61. Retd GD 6/1/66.
COVERDALE A.T.L. Born 3/3/43. Commd 17/12/65. Flt Lt 17/6/68. Retd GD 18/7/71.
COVILLE Sir Christopher KCB BA FCIPD FRAeS. Born 2/6/45. Commd 26/5/67. Air Mshl 6/8/98. Retd GD 1/6/03.
COWAN A. Born 19/10/22. Commd 10/3/44. Sqn Ldr 1/1/66. Retd GD 19/10/77.
COWAN C.W. DFC DFM. Born 24/9/19. Commd 19/6/41. Sqn Ldr 1/7/54. Retd GD 2/4/59.
COWAN D.M. Born 12/5/28. Commd 3/11/51. Sqn Ldr 1/7/64. Retd GD 31/7/71.
COWAN J.A. MBE BA. Born 8/10/45. Commd 27/2/70. Sqn Ldr 1/1/86. Retd GD 23/4/98.
COWAN J.L. MRCS LRCP DTM&H. Born 10/5/24. Commd 29/6/50. Wg Cdr 28/12/62. Retd MED 7/10/69.
COWAP M. MBE. Born 10/11/32. Commd 28/5/66. Flt Lt 28/5/72. Retd PRT 30/6/73.
COWAP M.J. Born 24/4/39. Commd 3/6/58. Flt Lt 7/8/64. Retd GD 26/9/77.
COWARD D.J. OBE FInstAM. Born 20/5/37. Commd 4/6/64. Wg Cdr 1/1/89. Retd ADMIN 26/11/92.
COWARD J.B. AFC. Born 18/5/15. Commd 28/1/37. A Cdre 1/7/62. Retd GD 8/9/69.
COWARD M.R. BA MCMI. Born 17/4/53. Commd 25/9/71. Sqn Ldr 1/1/89. Retd ADMIN 28/7/91.
COWDEN E.M.L. Born 28/6/28. Commd 26/3/59. Flt Lt 26/6/65. Retd ADMIN 18/11/80.
COWE R.I. Born 12/6/51. Commd 9/11/89. Flt Lt 9/11/91. Retd GD 30/6/01.
COWELL D.H. Born 12/2/26. Commd 4/7/51. Flt Lt 17/5/56. Retd GD 14/12/69. Re-instated 13/4/58 to 12/2/83.
COWELL J.R. Born 28/7/41. Commd 8/11/68. Sqn Ldr 1/1/80. Retd GD 1/12/84.
COWELL J.R.D. Born 21/4/22. Commd 26/3/43. Flt Lt 26/3/47. Retd GD 31/5/52.
COWELL R.W. Born 8/2/47. Commd 14/7/66. Sqn Ldr 1/7/85. Retd GD(G) 2/7/94.
COWEN H.E. Born 6/5/17. Commd 22/12/44. Flt Lt 22/6/48. Retd SEC 6/5/61.
COWEN P.G. Born 23/8/40. Commd 1/8/61. Sqn Ldr 1/7/73. Retd GD 6/12/75.
COWEN R.I. BA. Born 30/12/48. Commd 2/7/72. Flt Lt 2/10/75. Retd SEC 1/4/78.
COWEY P.A. Born 1/7/29. Commd 2/9/54. Flt Offr 2/9/60. Retd SEC 19/11/60.
COWEY W.H. Born 24/6/24. Commd 20/10/44. Flt Lt 1/4/63. Retd GD 31/7/73.
COWHAM A.T. Born 11/9/33. Commd 1/11/56. Flt Lt 9/2/63. Retd GD(G) 6/8/72.
COWIE A.J. BSc. Born 8/3/67. Commd 18/8/91. Flt Lt 18/2/94. Retd GD 14/3/01.
COWIE C. Born 9/9/41. Commd 9/8/63. Flt Lt 9/2/69. Retd GD 9/9/79.
COWIE I.W. Born 13/5/46. Commd 2/8/68. Flt Lt 4/5/72. Retd GD(G) 13/5/90.
COWIE T.F. MA. Born 24/3/24. Commd 30/4/62. Sqn Ldr 6/2/68. Retd EDN 30/4/78.
COWLAND R.A. CEng MIMechE. Born 2/8/29. Commd 28/11/51. Sqn Ldr 12/3/67. Retd EDN 12/9/79.
COWLES G.W. Born 10/9/31. Commd 23/4/52. Flt Lt 19/9/57. Retd GD 10/9/92.
COWLEY A. BSc. Born 10/3/60. Commd 13/2/83. Sqn Ldr 1/1/91. Retd ENG 5/1/93.
COWLEY A.T. Born 1/4/47. Commd 23/3/67. Flt Lt 23/9/72. Retd GD 3/9/77.
COWLEY D.A. AFC BA. Born 15/4/36. Commd 30/7/57. A Cdre 1/7/86. Retd GD 15/4/91.
COWLEY G.R. Born 30/1/51. Commd 5/8/76. Fg Offr 5/8/78. Retd ADMIN 27/2/82.
COWLING R.A. Born 19/7/29. Commd 12/3/52. Sqn Ldr 1/1/70. Retd GD 12/7/84.

COWMEADOW G.V. MSc BSc(Eng). Born 8/2/21. Commd 17/10/41. Wg Cdr 1/1/58. Retd ENG 8/2/77.
COWNIE A.G.H. BSc. Born 20/10/56. Commd 1/2/79. Sqn Ldr 1/7/91. Retd GD 4/4/98.
COWPE R.A. BSc. Born 9/11/47. Commd 18/8/68. Flt Lt 9/5/70. Retd GD 22/8/80.
COWPER P.M. Born 16/8/39. Commd 9/12/76. Sqn Ldr 1/1/88. Retd ADMIN 16/8/94.
COWPER R. Born 30/9/48. Commd 3/7/80. Sqn Ldr 1/1/88. Retd SUP 14/3/97.
COWTON J.B. Born 31/3/25. Commd 1/4/45. Wg Cdr 1/1/69. Retd GD 27/3/76.
COX A.F. MA BSc CEng MIEE MCMI. Born 3/5/62. Commd 31/8/80. Wg Cdr 1/1/98. Retd ENG 1/1/01.
COX A.H. MB BS. Born 21/11/27. Commd 4/2/52. Wg Cdr 2/2/64. Retd MED 11/11/80.
COX B.G. Born 2/3/33. Commd 6/4/54. Sqn Ldr 1/7/64. Retd GD 2/3/71.
COX B.R.A. OBE AFC MCMI. Born 4/9/26. Commd 20/9/48. Gp Capt 1/1/73. Retd GD 4/9/81.
COX C.S. Born 21/8/55. Commd 28/2/82. Flt Lt 28/8/86. Retd GD 1/12/95.
COX C.W. MA. Born 5/11/20. Commd 2/5/49. Wg Cdr 1/1/66. Retd EDN 21/7/71.
COX D.J. Born 28/7/30. Commd 27/8/52. Sqn Ldr 1/7/79. Retd GD 28/7/85.
COX D.N. Born 13/4/62. Commd 29/7/83. Flt Lt 29/1/89. Retd GD 1/5/99.
COX D.S. Born 19/4/36. Commd 7/5/64. Flt Lt 1/4/67. Retd ENG 19/4/74.
COX E.M.P.S. Born 20/2/44. Commd 17/5/63. Plt Offr 17/5/64. Retd GD 30/9/65.
COX E.R. Born 9/11/39. Commd 13/12/60. Gp Capt 1/7/87. Retd GD 9/11/94.
COX F.W.P. Born 20/4/22. Commd 27/6/45. Sqn Ldr 1/1/71. Retd GD 20/4/77. Re-instated 14/9/79 to 20/4/82.
COX G. Born 3/3/42. Commd 21/12/66. Flt Lt 21/6/70. Retd GD 3/3/80.
COX G.L. Born 21/5/43. Commd 28/4/67. Fg Offr 28/4/69. Retd GD 26/9/69.
COX H.R. Born 8/1/45. Commd 17/2/67. Sqn Ldr 1/7/81. Retd GD 8/1/89.
COX J.E. Born 25/4/37. Commd 13/6/74. Sqn Ldr 1/1/89. Retd ADMIN 25/4/94.
COX J.L. Born 13/2/60. Commd 8/10/87. Flt Lt 8/4/94. Retd OPS SPT(FC) 8/6/03.
COX J.R. Born 11/4/25. Commd 7/4/44. Sqn Ldr 1/1/62. Retd ENG 28/9/68.
COX M.G.T. BEng. Born 20/5/61. Commd 1/8/86. Flt Lt 15/7/89. Retd ENG 20/5/99.
COX P. Born 9/7/25. Commd 18/5/61. Flt Lt 18/5/66. Retd GD 16/12/67.
COX P.A. Born 25/7/42. Commd 30/7/63. Flt Lt 30/1/66. Retd GD 22/10/94.
COX R.A.P. Born 3/11/42. Commd 24/9/64. Wg Cdr 1/1/83. Retd SUP 18/2/86.
COX R.E.N. Born 13/10/44. Commd 2/12/66. Sqn Ldr 1/7/83. Retd OPS SPT 1/12/00.
COX R.M. CEng FINucE MIEE MCMI. Born 1/12/22. Commd 11/12/43. Sqn Ldr 1/7/62. Retd ENG 28/2/78.
COX R.S. Born 13/6/26. Commd 24/1/52. Flt Lt 15/5/57. Retd GD 31/7/68.
COX R.S.S. Born 26/1/38. Commd 14/8/56. Flt Lt 14/2/62. Retd GD 10/10/64.
COX S.B. BSc. Born 25/11/42. Commd 24/1/66. Sqn Ldr 1/1/88. Retd GD 25/11/97.
COX S.C. DFC DFM. Born 16/12/17. Commd 17/4/42. Flt Lt 26/5/48. Retd GD(G) 13/3/55.
COX S.H. Born 28/10/24. Commd 1/7/44. Sqn Ldr 1/4/56. Retd GD 10/10/67.
COX T.J. Born 19/5/36. Commd 17/3/67. Flt Lt 17/3/71. Retd SUP 17/3/75.
COXELL D.J. Born 12/8/21. Commd 25/5/43. Flt Lt 26/5/55. Retd GD 8/8/68.
COXELL W.J. Born 29/4/15. Commd 24/6/43. Flt Lt 8/10/52. Retd GD(G) 28/8/65.
COXHEAD D.J.M. AFC. Born 1/11/16. Commd 14/8/43. Flt Lt 15/11/48. Retd GD 2/9/58.
COY A. BA. Born 20/10/48. Commd 1/9/70. Sqn Ldr 1/1/96. Retd GD 1/5/99.
COY S.J. OBE. Born 29/11/44. Commd 15/7/66. Gp Capt 1/7/92. Retd GD 29/11/99.
COY-BURT R.H.E. Born 14/3/54. Commd 19/2/76. Flt Lt 3/7/82. Retd GD(G) 14/3/92.
COYLE P.J. Born 15/3/57. Commd 22/3/81. Sqn Ldr 1/1/91. Retd ENG 22/9/97.
COYLE W.L.J. BSc CEng MRAeS. Born 14/12/48. Commd 27/2/70. Sqn Ldr 1/7/80. Retd ENG 14/12/86.
COYNE N.A. Born 27/10/58. Commd 6/10/94. Fg Offr 1/1/89. Retd ADMIN 14/9/96.
COYNE T. AIIP. Born 17/12/32. Commd 13/2/52. Sqn Ldr 1/7/82. Retd ENG 3/3/85.
COZENS G.A. Born 26/9/22. Commd 10/12/45. Flt Lt 7/6/51. Retd GD 29/11/66.
COZENS G.T.J. Born 19/1/37. Commd 4/1/60. Sqn Ldr 4/7/70. Retd EDN 4/1/76.
COZENS R.S.G. Born 23/12/20. Commd 8/7/54. Sqn Ldr 1/1/69. Retd GD 30/11/73.
COZENS R.W. DFC. Born 27/7/21. Commd 24/11/43. Flt Lt 4/1/51. Retd GD(G) 10/8/76.
CRABB A.S.G. Born 23/11/60. Commd 14/9/80. Sqn Ldr 1/7/94. Retd GD 1/7/99.
CRABB C.M. Born 23/2/24. Commd 9/9/44. Sqn Ldr 1/7/68. Retd GD 20/6/73.
CRABB G.A. OBE CEng FCMI MRAeS MIProdE. Born 16/3/18. Commd 29/4/42. Gp Capt 1/1/69. Retd ENG 21/4/73.
CRABTREE R.A.K. OBE. Born 26/7/38. Commd 13/12/60. Wg Cdr 1/7/79. Retd GD 5/6/85.
CRABTREE S. SRN. Born 3/4/50. Commd 26/5/74. Flt Lt 26/3/81. Retd GD(G) 22/3/84.
CRACROFT H.G. Born 23/12/36. Commd 1/4/58. Wg Cdr 1/1/76. Retd GD 1/3/85.
CRADDEN B.P. Born 26/9/42. Commd 31/1/90. Flt Lt 31/1/84. Retd ENG 1/6/93.
CRADDEN C.M. BSc. Born 14/8/48. Commd 27/10/70. Flt Lt 27/7/74. Retd SUP 27/10/86.
CRADDOCK G.A. Born 3/12/66. Commd 8/10/87. Flt Lt 8/4/94. Retd OPS SPT(FC) 3/12/04.
CRADDOCK N.J.B. Born 5/12/45. Commd 21/10/66. Sqn Ldr 1/1/87. Retd ENG 1/10/89.
CRAGG J. Born 18/10/26. Commd 2/4/54. Flt Lt 22/9/72. Retd GD 18/10/84.
CRAGGS F.T. Born 22/9/24. Commd 23/6/60. Flt Lt 23/6/66. Retd SUP 22/9/79.
CRAGGS M.B. Born 6/1/47. Commd 12/12/78. Sqn Ldr 1/1/84. Retd ADMIN 12/12/94.
CRAGHILL W.M. Born 29/3/40. Commd 18/2/58. A Cdre 1/7/90. Retd GD 29/7/93.
CRAIG A.J. Born 1/7/51. Commd 13/9/70. Flt Lt 22/4/78. Retd GD 1/7/90.
CRAIG A.J. CEng MRAeS MIMechE. Born 11/5/40. Commd 18/7/61. Sqn Ldr 1/7/70. Retd ENG 4/9/79.

CRAIG A.R. MCMI. Born 17/8/32. Commd 14/12/54. Wg Cdr 1/7/79. Retd ADMIN 16/7/88.
CRAIG C.N. Born 25/12/35. Commd 2/1/67. Sqn Ldr 14/10/72. Retd ADMIN 24/12/86.
CRAIG G.J. Born 27/12/36. Commd 6/4/32. Sqn Ldr 1/1/72. Retd ADMIN 7/4/87.
CRAIG G.P. Born 7/7/26. Commd 7/5/52. Flt Lt 2/10/57. Retd GD 6/7/76.
CRAIG I.J. MBE. Born 1/7/49. Commd 24/8/72. Wg Cdr 1/7/01. Retd GD 2/2/04.
CRAIG J. Born 20/9/37. Commd 10/11/61. Flt Lt 10/5/67. Retd GD 22/8/77.
CRAIG J.S.D. Born 1/4/33. Commd 25/10/51. Flt Lt 22/5/57. Retd GD 1/4/71.
CRAIG K.D. MB BCh MRCPsych. Born 9/7/49. Commd 21/11/71. Wg Cdr 28/7/88. Retd MED 31/1/96.
CRAIG R. DFC. Born 14/11/20. Commd 7/8/44. Sqn Ldr 1/1/70. Retd SUP 31/5/73.
CRAIG R. Born 4/11/41. Commd 20/10/83. Flt Lt 20/10/87. Retd ENG 2/3/93.
CRAIG R.F. Born 28/1/35. Commd 25/7/67. Sqn Ldr 1/1/77. Retd ADMIN 28/1/85.
CRAIGEN R.K. Born 1/9/44. Commd 9/8/63. Flt Lt 9/2/69. Retd GD 1/9/93.
CRAIGMYLE A.A. Born 12/3/22. Commd 9/7/59. Sqn Ldr 1/1/70. Retd ENG 12/3/77.
CRAMB B.L. Born 5/8/44. Commd 24/7/81. Flt Lt 1/3/87. Retd MED(SEC) 31/8/89.
CRAMER V.N. OBE FCMI. Born 22/9/23. Commd 28/6/45. Gp Capt 1/1/68. Retd GD 23/9/73.
CRAMP C. Born 8/6/14. Commd 15/6/42. Sqn Ldr 1/7/54. Retd ENG 8/6/69.
CRAMP D.C. BSc. Born 27/2/52. Commd 27/1/70. Flt Lt 15/4/76. Retd ADMIN 27/2/93.
CRAMPTON J. DFC AFC*. Born 21/8/21. Commd 1/9/41. Sqn Ldr 1/7/50. Retd GD 1/6/57.
CRAMPTON P.P. Born 21/12/21. Commd 20/4/50. Sqn Ldr 1/1/68. Retd GD 21/12/76.
CRANE C.D. Born 3/7/57. Commd 5/4/79. Sqn Ldr 1/7/90. Retd GD(G) 3/7/95.
CRANE D. MDA BSc CEng MIEE. Born 13/4/63. Commd 2/9/84. Sqn Ldr 1/7/94. Retd ENG 1/8/01.
CRANE D.L. Born 24/2/35. Commd 6/5/53. Sqn Ldr 1/1/71. Retd GD 8/8/88.
CRANE J. OBE CEng MRAeS. Born 4/7/19. Commd 19/8/42. Wg Cdr 1/7/59. Retd ENG 4/7/74.
CRANE J.S. Born 21/5/33. Commd 17/1/52. Sqn Ldr 1/1/66. Retd GD 29/6/74.
CRANE R. Born 25/7/23. Commd 21/4/45. Flt Lt 4/12/52. Retd GD 12/8/66.
CRANE T. Born 19/4/49. Commd 17/5/79. Flt Lt 17/5/81. Retd GD 17/5/87.
CRANFIELD J.T.O'B. MB BS FFARCS MRCS LRCP. Born 9/10/44. Commd 23/1/67. Wg Cdr 3/7/83.
    Retd MED 27/10/85.
CRANSWICK C.E. BSc. Born 4/2/48. Commd 10/4/68. Sqn Ldr 1/7/83. Retd FLY(P) 9/4/05.
CRAVEN I.W. Born 19/3/62. Commd 15/3/84. Flt Lt 15/9/89. Retd GD 19/1/01.
CRAVEN J.S. Born 19/9/64. Commd 2/9/93. Flt Lt 6/11/89. Retd OPS SPT(FC) 1/6/03.
CRAVEN J.T. Born 29/6/42. Commd 17/12/63. Sqn Ldr 1/1/76. Retd GD 1/10/86.
CRAVEN-GRIFFITHS J.K. OBE BA MInstPS. Born 29/4/31. Commd 9/4/52. Gp Capt 1/1/82. Retd SUP 9/11/83.
CRAWFORD A.I. MA. Born 18/11/56. Commd 5/2/76. Flt Lt 15/4/82. Retd ADMIN 28/12/87.
CRAWFORD A.J. Born 10/11/55. Commd 4/7/85. Flt Lt 4/7/87. Retd GD 29/10/93.
CRAWFORD B. Born 15/10/14. Commd 10/6/38. Flt Lt 10/6/42. Retd SEC 19/3/50. rtg Sqn Ldr
CRAWFORD B.J. MVO. Born 29/3/34. Commd 26/11/52. Sqn Ldr 1/7/81. Retd GD 29/3/92.
CRAWFORD D. BSc. Born 3/10/49. Commd 2/9/73. Flt Lt 2/9/76. Retd ENG 2/9/89.
CRAWFORD D.E.G. Born 30/10/33. Commd 16/12/66. Sqn Ldr 1/1/80. Retd ADMIN 30/10/91.
CRAWFORD G.J. MCMI MRAeS. Born 25/10/55. Commd 11/8/77. Wg Cdr 1/1/95. Retd GD 25/10/99.
CRAWFORD J.A. BSc. Born 14/6/60. Commd 4/9/78. Sqn Ldr 1/7/94. Retd GD 14/6/98.
CRAWFORD J.S. Born 31/5/21. Commd 20/2/43. Sqn Ldr 1/7/62. Retd GD 26/7/71.
CRAWFORD J.S. Born 29/4/21. Commd 4/4/45. Flt Lt 30/6/49. Retd GD 29/4/76.
CRAWFORD P.A. AFC BSc. Born 11/1/50. Commd 3/10/68. A Cdre 1/7/96. Retd GD 10/11/00.
CRAWFORD P.D. Born 17/2/57. Commd 11/1/81. Flt Lt 18/10/84. Retd ADMIN 17/2/95.
CRAWFORD R.S. Born 4/5/18. Commd 15/3/37. Flt Lt 1/12/42. Retd GD 28/8/51. rtg Sqn Ldr
CRAWLEY H.L. DFC. Born 7/9/29. Commd 26/3/52. Flt Lt 7/8/57. Retd GD 2/8/71.
CRAWLEY I.C. Born 15/2/43. Commd 7/3/68. Flt Lt 4/11/70. Retd SY 21/5/84.
CRAWLEY L.F. MBE. Born 5/8/17. Commd 17/6/43. Wg Cdr 1/1/65. Retd SEC 5/8/72.
CRAWLEY M.A. MB ChB MRCP DPhysMed. Born 15/1/34. Commd 17/8/58. Wg Cdr 2/8/71. Retd MED 1/7/77.
CRAWLEY N.R. Born 30/11/65. Commd 8/10/87. Flt Lt 8/4/93. Retd FLY(N) 30/11/04.
CRAWLEY T.W. Born 6/6/58. Commd 29/7/83. Sqn Ldr 1/7/94. Retd MED(SEC) 14/3/96.
CRAWLEY M. BSc CEng MRAeS. Born 5/1/53. Commd 25/9/71. Sqn Ldr 1/7/83. Retd ENG 5/1/91.
CRAWSHAW J.A.L. MBE MCMI. Born 13/7/29. Commd 12/12/51. Sqn Ldr 1/7/63. Retd SEC 14/7/74.
CRAWSHAW P.H. MBE. Born 21/2/30. Commd 21/3/51. Sqn Ldr 1/1/67. Retd GD 31/7/80.
CRAWSHAW R.D. Born 22/9/45. Commd 31/1/64. Flt Lt 31/7/69. Retd GD 23/6/73.
CRAWSHAY-WILLIAMS P.G. Born 20/11/23. Commd 3/9/43. Flt Lt 3/3/47. Retd GD 20/11/61.
CRAXTON L.V. Born 4/3/21. Commd 27/3/41. Wg Cdr 1/1/60. Retd GD 4/3/68.
CRAY R.D. BSc. Born 12/11/60. Commd 11/12/83. Fg Offr 11/12/82. Retd GD 7/8/86.
CREAGH P.W.M. Born 13/10/43. Commd 15/4/61. Sqn Ldr 1/1/88. Retd ADMIN 1/1/91.
CREASEY A.G. Born 29/1/18. Commd 12/6/47. Flt Lt 12/12/51. Retd SUP 29/1/67.
CREASEY B.R. MCMI. Born 16/8/29. Commd 20/6/63. Flt Lt 20/6/68. Retd ENG 21/8/76.
CREASEY W.A. OBE CEng MIMechE. Born 6/1/37. Commd 26/2/71. A Cdre 1/7/89. Retd ENG 6/1/92.
CREE T.S. Born 2/9/44. Commd 19/3/81. Flt Lt 19/3/84. Retd GD 30/6/89.
CREED T. Born 27/1/45. Commd 1/4/66. Sqn Ldr 1/7/79. Retd GD 27/1/83.
CREIGH P.J.W. Born 20/5/37. Commd 4/5/58. Sqn Ldr 1/7/70. Retd GD 25/9/73.

CREIGHTON W.H. Born 30/7/43. Commd 11/5/78. Flt Lt 11/5/80. Retd GD 31/7/99.
CRESSWELL A.P. BSc. Born 16/6/56. Commd 15/9/74. Flt Lt 15/4/79. Retd GD 15/7/89.
CRESSWELL G.J. MB ChB. Born 6/5/49. Commd 26/6/73. Sqn Ldr 8/7/81. Retd MED 26/6/89.
CRESSWELL J.S. Born 17/10/33. Commd 5/4/53. Wg Cdr 1/1/69. Retd GD 17/10/88.
CRESSWELL J.V. Born 29/5/42. Commd 22/2/63. Flt Lt 9/2/68. Retd GD 29/5/80.
CRESSWELL K.N.A.B. Born 25/12/27. Commd 10/3/60. Flt Lt 10/3/65. Retd GD 3/5/77.
CRESSWELL R.F. BA MCIPS MILT MCMI. Born 23/4/44. Commd 15/7/66. Sqn Ldr 1/7/77. Retd SUP 27/10/97.
CRESSWELL T.J. Born 1/8/30. Commd 1/8/51. Flt Lt 1/2/54. Retd GD 1/8/68.
CRETNEY F.D. Born 24/4/33. Commd 30/4/53. Sqn Ldr 1/7/64. Retd GD 1/10/70.
CREWE G.P. Born 18/5/44. Commd 14/2/69. Flt Lt 14/8/74. Retd GD 20/8/76.
CREWS P. Born 30/5/23. Commd 6/10/60. Flt Lt 6/10/63. Retd GD 24/3/78.
CRIBB P.H. CBE DSO* DFC. Born 28/9/18. Commd 30/7/38. A Cdre 1/1/62. Retd GD 28/9/66.
CRICK S.E. Born 11/10/47. Commd 17/12/69. Flt Lt 10/3/74. Retd FLY(N) 1/8/03.
CRIGHTON M. BSc. Born 12/2/64. Commd 2/9/91. Sqn Ldr 1/7/98. Retd SUPPLY 3/2/03.
CRIGHTON S.M. Born 7/5/63. Commd 12/11/89. Fg Offr 12/11/90. Retd SUP 15/5/95.
CRILLEY D.J.F. Born 26/1/40. Commd 21/2/69. Flt Lt 21/2/71. Retd GD(G) 30/9/82.
CRIPPS A.G. CEng MIMechE MRAeS. Born 4/3/42. Commd 8/11/62. Sqn Ldr 1/1/97. Retd ENG 4/3/97.
CRIPPS B.D. Born 14/5/37. Commd 21/10/65. Flt Lt 9/2/68. Retd GD(G) 14/5/87.
CRIPPS J.S. CEng MIEE MIMechE. Born 3/7/37. Commd 1/8/63. Sqn Ldr 1/7/70. Retd ENG 3/7/75.
CRIPPS R.H. Born 4/7/27. Commd 29/7/65. Sqn Ldr 21/10/70. Retd EDN 29/7/73.
CRIPPS R.W. Born 29/7/37. Commd 4/7/69. Wg Cdr 1/7/86. Retd ENG 29/7/92.
CRIPPS T.M. BA. Born 21/1/38. Commd 25/9/62. Sqn Ldr 14/9/72. Retd ADMIN 1/5/87.
CRIPPS T.P. Born 15/6/37. Commd 30/9/55. Sqn Ldr 1/1/68. Retd GD 15/6/75.
CRISPIN J.A. Born 9/6/24. Commd 10/3/44. Sqn Ldr 1/10/54. Retd GD 9/6/67.
CRISPIN P. BA MRIN MCMI. Born 22/4/45. Commd 15/7/66. Sqn Ldr 1/1/80. Retd GD 22/4/89.
CRISTINACCE G. Born 30/7/23. Commd 23/7/51. Flt Lt 8/1/58. Retd GD 23/7/67.
CRITCHLEY F.J.E. Born 15/2/51. Commd 28/11/69. Flt Lt 28/5/75. Retd GD 8/2/79.
CRITCHLEY P.G. Born 19/4/53. Commd 9/3/72. Sqn Ldr 1/1/85. Retd GD 19/4/91.
CROASDALE G.P.H. Born 4/10/52. Commd 4/5/72. Sqn Ldr 1/7/86. Retd GD 4/10/90.
CROCKATT A.B. AFC. Born 12/9/50. Commd 26/2/71. Wg Cdr 1/1/91. Retd GD 5/4/01.
CROCKATT D.R. MRCS LRCP DAvMed FCMI. Born 12/7/27. Commd 8/4/56. Gp Capt 1/1/79. Retd MED 2/4/85.
CROCKER A.E. Born 15/1/21. Commd 30/5/46. Flt Lt 7/6/51. Retd GD(G) 5/10/68.
CROCKER A.P. Born 14/4/66. Commd 22/11/84. Plt Offr 22/5/85. Retd GD(G) 24/6/86.
CROCKER C.E. Born 23/9/23. Commd 6/5/44. Sqn Ldr 1/7/60. Retd SUP 1/4/73.
CROCKER L.R. BA. Born 15/6/32. Commd 28/10/54. Sqn Ldr 1/7/67. Retd SUP 1/7/82.
CROCKER R.G. DFC. Born 2/3/21. Commd 28/8/42. Flt Lt 6/5/46. Retd GD 12/3/47.
CROCKETT T. Born 23/3/39. Commd 9/2/62. Sqn Ldr 1/7/79. Retd GD 23/3/94.
CROCKFORD B.W. Born 17/4/39. Commd 30/3/65. Flt Lt 15/4/70. Retd ENG 30/3/81.
CROCOMBE M. MIIE. Born 28/4/50. Commd 9/8/79. Wg Cdr 1/7/99. Retd ENG 12/12/02.
CROFT G.J. Born 30/11/43. Commd 31/10/74. Flt Lt 31/10/76. Retd GD(G) 31/10/82.
CROFT I. BSc CEng MICE MRAeS. Born 11/12/39. Commd 25/2/64. Sqn Ldr 1/1/71. Retd ENG 25/2/80.
CROFT K.F. BSc MB ChB DRCOG. Born 22/1/48. Commd 17/9/74. Wg Cdr 3/8/91. Retd MED 14/3/96.
CROFT M.H. Born 8/12/56. Commd 4/9/81. Flt Lt 4/3/88. Retd OPS SPT 4/5/97.
CROFT P.A. Born 2/8/42. Commd 6/2/67. Sqn Ldr 1/7/74. Retd SY 6/2/83.
CROFT R. MCMI. Born 7/9/23. Commd 6/11/58. Sqn Ldr 1/7/71. Retd ENG 26/3/77.
CROFTON D.N. Born 5/3/50. Commd 1/4/71. Wg Cdr 1/7/94. Retd OPS SPT 1/10/02.
CROFTS P.G. Born 24/9/34. Commd 23/10/56. Flt Lt 23/4/62. Retd ENG 24/9/72.
CROFTS R. Born 11/8/50. Commd 8/11/90. Flt Lt 6/11/92. Retd ENG 2/7/93.
CROIZAT J.P. MBE. Born 15/8/32. Commd 7/5/53. Sqn Ldr 1/1/63. Retd CAT 15/8/70.
CROMACK B.J. MSc BSc. Born 1/7/29. Commd 28/9/80. Sqn Ldr 1/7/87. Retd ADMIN 7/2/88.
CROMACK R. BSc. Born 18/2/40. Commd 8/9/69. Sqn Ldr 8/3/73. Retd ADMIN 8/9/87.
CROMAR A.D. Born 5/1/12. Commd 13/1/42. Fg Offr 1/12/42. Retd ENG 8/1/46. rtg Flt Lt
CROMAR R. Born 2/5/14. Commd 8/9/42. Flt Lt 14/3/51. Retd GD(G) 29/8/64.
CROMARTY I.J. MSc MB ChB MRCGP DRCOG DAvMed. Born 20/2/56. Commd 2/9/75. Wg Cdr 1/8/92. Retd MED 20/2/00.
CROMARTY J.I. MB ChB MFCM DPH. Born 28/12/28. Commd 29/9/52. Gp Capt 1/7/74. Retd MED 6/8/76.
CROMARTY N.W. Born 28/4/58. Commd 14/7/77. Gp Capt 1/1/99. Retd GD 18/4/03.
CROMBIE D.J.C. MBE. Born 15/11/42. Commd 28/4/65. Sqn Ldr 1/7/84. Retd GD 15/11/01.
CROMBIE G.J. MBE. Born 11/12/45. Commd 26/5/67. Sqn Ldr 1/1/97. Retd GD 1/5/99.
CROMBIE K.S. Born 16/8/53. Commd 25/4/82. Sqn Ldr 1/1/94. Retd GD 25/4/98.
CROMPTON D.J. BA MBCS. Born 28/11/32. Commd 24/8/56. A Cdre 1/7/83. Retd ADMIN 31/1/86.
CROMPTON D.M. Born 24/10/28. Commd 13/8/58. Sqn Ldr 1/7/70. Retd SUP 24/10/83.
CROMPTON J.W. Born 15/8/27. Commd 9/12/48. Flt Lt 28/2/55. Retd GD 7/10/61.
CROMPTON R.M. Born 1/7/29. Commd 16/10/52. Flt Offr 16/10/58. Retd SEC 7/7/61.
CRONE H.J. AFC MCMI. Born 16/2/41. Commd 9/12/61. Sqn Ldr 1/1/71. Retd GD 16/2/79.
CRONING D.I.R. Born 21/11/41. Commd 3/10/74. Flt Lt 3/10/76. Retd SUP 3/10/82.

CROOK B.A. MPhil. Born 30/5/44. Commd 17/5/63. Wg Cdr 1/7/83. Retd GD 30/5/88.
CROOK C. MBE. Born 17/10/31. Commd 30/7/52. Sqn Ldr 1/7/64. Retd GD 17/10/69.
CROOK G.C. Born 13/9/25. Commd 23/9/52. Flt Lt 26/2/64. Retd GD 23/9/68.
CROOK G.D.W. MB ChB MRCP(UK). Born 1/2/56. Commd 10/3/77. Wg Cdr 1/8/93. Retd MED 1/2/94.
CROOK G.T. LDSRCS. Born 7/6/23. Commd 22/8/46. A Cdre 1/7/80. Retd DEL 1/7/82.
CROOK M.R.W. Born 24/5/45. Commd 3/3/67. Sqn Ldr 1/7/79. Retd GD 30/11/85.
CROOK P.W. Born 22/2/41. Commd 18/12/62. Sqn Ldr 1/1/73. Retd GD 22/2/79.
CROOKS F.R. Born 9/8/35. Commd 5/7/68. Sqn Ldr 1/7/76. Retd ENG 9/8/90.
CROPPER E.W. Born 15/12/23. Commd 30/1/44. Gp Capt 1/7/70. Retd GD 23/3/74.
CROSBIE J.L. OBE. Born 31/7/14. Commd 15/12/34. Gp Capt 1/1/53. Retd GD 31/7/64.
CROSBIE J.P. Born 8/5/56. Commd 8/10/87. Flt Lt 8/10/89. Retd ENG 8/10/95.
CROSBY B.W. CEng MIEE MRAeS. Born 26/8/37. Commd 13/10/64. Flt Lt 13/10/69. Retd ENG 13/10/80.
CROSBY C.R.C. Born 18/7/41. Commd 31/8/62. Flt Lt 18/1/67. Retd GD 23/9/68.
CROSBY D.M.M. Born 23/4/50. Commd 9/12/71. Sqn Ldr 1/7/97. Retd FLY(P) 23/4/05.
CROSBY K.B. FCMI MCIT MILT MRAeS. Born 21/7/19. Commd 23/9/43. Gp Capt 1/7/70. Retd GD(G) 21/7/74.
CROSBY M.A. Born 20/12/63. Commd 24/3/83. Sqn Ldr 1/7/94. Retd GD 31/12/97.
CROSLAND M.R. Born 2/12/31. Commd 22/7/53. Flt Lt 7/1/59. Retd GD 4/12/69.
CROSS A.R.D. BA. Born 23/12/59. Commd 19/6/83. Sqn Ldr 1/7/94. Retd ENG 19/6/99.
CROSS E.J. Born 27/12/32. Commd 11/4/51. Flt Lt 11/1/57. Retd GD 11/10/61.
CROSS J.A. Born 18/5/49. Commd 29/4/71. Flt Lt 14/8/77. Retd ADMIN 18/5/87.
CROSS K.J. MCMI. Born 13/10/34. Commd 6/10/60. Sqn Ldr 1/1/72. Retd GD(G) 9/4/80.
CROSS M.J. BA. Born 7/1/59. Commd 11/4/82. Sqn Ldr 1/1/92. Retd ADMIN 11/4/98.
CROSS P.A. Born 31/12/44. Commd 8/12/83. Sqn Ldr 1/7/92. Retd ENG 1/1/93.
CROSS P.B. Born 28/3/26. Commd 5/9/56. Flt Lt 13/4/60. Retd GD 5/5/81.
CROSS P.D. Born 28/8/39. Commd 22/5/75. Sqn Ldr 1/1/83. Retd GD(G) 1/1/85.
CROSS P.R. Born 22/4/47. Commd 16/8/68. Flt Lt 16/2/73. Retd GD 22/10/94.
CROSS T. CEng MIEE. Born 25/6/20. Commd 3/6/43. Wg Cdr 1/1/62. Retd ENG 27/3/71.
CROSS W.E.J. Born 30/11/12. Commd 6/5/43. Fg Offr 26/2/44. Retd ENG 8/2/46.
CROSS W.M.N. OBE. Born 26/2/42. Commd 31/7/62. Gp Capt 1/1/93. Retd GD 26/5/97.
CROSSE J.P. MA. Born 25/1/56. Commd 10/10/77. Flt Lt 15/10/81. Retd SY 1/3/86.
CROSSFIELD R.J. Born 8/3/66. Commd 13/2/92. Flt Lt 14/4/92. Retd ADMIN 14/9/96.
CROSSLEY C. BSc. Born 16/9/57. Commd 26/7/81. Flt Lt 26/1/85. Retd GD(G) 4/3/93.
CROTTY M.P. CBE MSc BA FCIT FILT FILDM MCIPS. Born 14/4/41. Commd 17/7/62. A Cdre 1/1/89.
   Retd SUP 18/10/95.
CROUCH A.M. Born 1/7/21. Commd 3/5/44. Flt Offr 8/8/54. Retd SEC 31/7/60.
CROUCH C.A. Born 8/1/50. Commd 8/8/69. Sqn Ldr 1/7/85. Retd GD 27/9/87.
CROUCH I.A. Born 18/4/50. Commd 25/2/72. Fg Offr 25/2/73. Retd SUP 31/7/76.
CROUCH J.R. MSc BSc. Born 8/4/48. Commd 11/8/74. Sqn Ldr 1/7/84. Retd ADMIN 11/8/90.
CROUCH P.C. AFM. Born 29/6/23. Commd 5/9/57. Sqn Ldr 1/7/71. Retd GD 29/6/78.
CROUCH P.T. Born 27/6/56. Commd 2/1/75. Wg Cdr 1/7/92. Retd GD(G) 1/7/95.
CROUCHEN D.H. DFC. Born 3/8/21. Commd 9/3/41. Flt Lt 13/11/57. Retd GD(G) 14/10/67. rtg Sqn Ldr
CROUCHER D.G. Born 6/6/24. Commd 11/2/44. Gp Capt 1/1/70. Retd GD 28/5/76.
CROW A.T. Born 23/2/39. Commd 15/9/60. Flt Lt 1/4/66. Retd SUP 10/1/90.
CROW J.T.M.D.O. Born 25/10/37. Commd 10/8/60. Flt Lt 4/5/72. Retd CAT 7/12/73.
CROW T. Born 24/11/11. Commd 22/4/43. Sqn Ldr 1/1/54. Retd SUP 24/11/66.
CROWDEN-LONGSTREATH P.D. Born 11/1/16. Commd 18/7/44. Flt Lt 13/11/57. Retd SUP 25/2/71.
CROWDER R.B. MCMI. Born 22/1/39. Commd 28/7/59. Wg Cdr 1/1/76. Retd GD 2/4/89.
CROWDER S.J. Born 8/7/65. Commd 9/6/92. Sqn Ldr 1/1/96. Retd ADMIN (SEC) 8/7/03.
CROWE G.V. Born 21/9/44. Commd 13/6/74. Flt Lt 13/6/76. Retd ENG 21/9/82.
CROWE J.A. Born 14/5/64. Commd 29/1/87. Flt Lt 29/7/92. Retd FLY(P) 18/3/04.
CROWE M. Born 14/2/25. Commd 20/3/52. Flt Lt 1/1/56. Retd SEC 14/2/63. Re-appointed 1/11/67 to 1/11/72.
CROWE P. Born 4/8/29. Commd 31/12/52. Flt Lt 26/5/58. Retd GD(G) 9/4/76.
CROWE P.A. BSc(Eng) MMS MCMI. Born 3/11/42. Commd 30/9/62. Sqn Ldr 1/1/78. Retd GD 3/11/97.
CROWHURST G. MIDPM. Born 9/3/39. Commd 2/2/70. Wg Cdr 1/1/80. Retd GD(G) 1/4/86.
CROWHURST J.H. Born 14/1/32. Commd 5/9/57. Wg Cdr 1/7/80. Retd ADMIN 9/5/86.
CROWLE A.J.W. Born 26/8/61. Commd 8/11/92. Flt Lt 8/11/92. Retd ENG 26/8/99.
CROWLE J.D. Born 15/8/41. Commd 6/10/60. Wg Cdr 1/7/78. Retd SUP 15/8/96.
CROWLE P.W. Born 4/2/49. Commd 2/7/78. Flt Lt 20/7/80. Retd ENG 4/2/87.
CROWLEY A.C. Born 4/10/55. Commd 2/11/88. Flt Lt 2/11/90. Retd SUP 2/4/93.
CROWLEY J.M. AFC CEng MRAeS. Born 30/8/27. Commd 8/4/49. Wg Cdr 1/1/63. Retd GD 31/8/68.
CROWLEY J.W. Born 7/6/48. Commd 20/9/68. Sqn Ldr 1/1/82. Retd GD 7/6/86. Re-entered 21/3/89. Gp Capt 1/1/99.
   Retd GD 1/10/02.
CROWLEY K.A. BA. Born 3/2/44. Commd 24/6/65. Flt Lt 24/3/67. Retd GD 19/6/71.
CROWLEY L.J. Born 24/1/36. Commd 22/1/57. Sqn Ldr 1/7/70. Retd GD 24/1/74.
CROWLEY M.B. Born 2/10/15. Commd 25/7/45. Sqn Offr 1/7/58. Retd SUP 2/10/64.
CROWLEY R.J. BSc. Born 31/12/55. Commd 1/9/74. Flt Lt 15/10/78. Retd GD 10/6/88.

CROWSON D. MBE. Born 25/3/36. Commd 26/9/57. Sqn Ldr 1/7/72. Retd GD 25/3/86.
CROWSON F.J. Born 14/8/38. Commd 1/4/65. Sqn Ldr 1/7/79. Retd GD(G) 1/10/85.
CROWTHER A.J. Born 23/3/45. Commd 29/11/63. Flt Lt 4/11/70. Retd GD 23/3/83.
CROY A.O. Born 6/4/20. Commd 8/6/54. Flt Lt 8/6/59. Retd ENG 6/4/62.
CROYDON W.H. CBE. Born 8/9/33. Commd 9/4/52. A Cdre 1/1/84. Retd GD 8/8/88.
CROZIER I.D. AFC MRAeS. Born 18/1/22. Commd 7/7/42. Wg Cdr 1/7/59. Retd GD 1/11/67.
CROZIER P.C. Born 10/3/42. Commd 23/12/60. Fg Offr 19/6/63. Retd GD 24/12/65.
CROZIER W.J. AFC. Born 23/3/17. Commd 9/10/42. Flt Lt 24/3/47. Retd GD(G) 24/5/66.
CRUICKSHANK A. Born 22/8/16. Commd 22/2/44. Sqn Ldr 1/1/52. Retd RGT 1/4/58.
CRUICKSHANK J.H. MBE. Born 12/4/20. Commd 27/8/59. Sqn Ldr 1/1/70. Retd ENG 12/4/75.
CRUICKSHANKS C.J. AFC* FRAeS. Born 7/1/45. Commd 17/12/65. A Cdre 1/7/94. Retd GD 7/1/00.
CRUICKSHANKS R.E. BSc. Born 27/7/32. Commd 22/12/55. Sqn Ldr 14/2/66. Retd EDN 15/9/71.
CRUMBIE G.C. Born 30/5/40. Commd 13/12/60. Sqn Ldr 1/1/69. Retd GD 30/5/80.
CRUMPTON R.H. MBE. Born 2/4/29. Commd 7/5/52. Sqn Ldr 1/1/64. Retd GD 19/12/75.
CRUSE C. Born 12/3/47. Commd 1/6/69. Wg Cdr 1/1/87. Retd SUP 12/3/97.
CRUSE J.G. AFC. Born 2/6/27. Commd 23/3/51. Sqn Ldr 1/1/61. Retd GD 9/8/61.
CRUSH M.W.A. Born 28/8/49. Commd 25/4/69. Flt Lt 25/10/74. Retd GD 9/10/76.
CRUTCHLOW R.L. Born 9/12/33. Commd 3/12/59. Wg Cdr 1/1/85. Retd GD 8/4/88.
CRUWYS G.E. Born 27/2/20. Commd 12/5/40. Sqn Ldr 1/7/53. Retd GD 27/2/63.
CRWYS-WILLIAMS D.O. CB FCIPD. Born 24/12/40. Commd 1/8/61. AVM 1/7/88. Retd GD 1/4/93.
CRYER N.C. Born 8/4/68. Commd 28/7/88. Flt Lt 28/1/95. Retd OPS SPT 1/10/01.
CRYMBLE M.J. Born 24/3/54. Commd 24/8/72. Flt Lt 24/2/78. Retd GD 5/4/00.
CUBBERLEY F.J. Born 11/6/33. Commd 10/3/60. Sqn Ldr 1/7/81. Retd GD 8/8/88.
CUBBY G. MBE. Born 20/12/20. Commd 12/12/42. Gp Capt 1/1/67. Retd SEC 16/1/71.
CUBIN A. MBE. Born 9/10/62. Commd 26/11/81. Sqn Ldr 1/1/98. Retd GD 1/1/01.
CUBITT R.J. Born 4/12/51. Commd 8/9/83. Flt Lt 8/9/85. Retd SUP 8/9/91.
CUDLIPP R.M. Born 27/1/48. Commd 28/7/88. Sqn Ldr 1/1/01. Retd ENGINEER 31/8/04.
CUDMORE A.F.J. Born 19/7/58. Commd 7/11/91. Flt Lt 7/11/93. Retd SUP 31/3/94.
CUDMORE M.C. Born 8/2/62. Commd 20/5/90. Flt Lt 10/1/88. Retd GD 1/8/00.
CUDWORTH J.E. Born 30/4/27. Commd 28/2/57. Flt Lt 28/5/63. Retd SEC 5/11/69.
CUGLEY J. OBE MB BS. Born 13/10/46. Commd 9/4/85. Wg Cdr 8/2/95. Retd MED 17/9/99.
CUGNONI K.F. BA. Born 11/9/34. Commd 23/10/59. Flt Lt 23/2/64. Retd SEC 6/9/78.
CULL M.S. Born 3/12/35. Commd 2/3/61. Sqn Ldr 1/7/72. Retd GD 11/9/81.
CULLEN A.M. Born 25/11/45. Commd 26/11/81. Sqn Ldr 1/1/89. Retd ADMIN 25/11/00.
CULLEN G.M. AFC. Born 11/9/24. Commd 11/6/53. Sqn Ldr 1/7/81. Retd GD 11/9/84.
CULLEN H.G. DFC. Born 1/9/21. Commd 15/8/46. Sqn Ldr 1/1/51. Retd GD 1/9/64.
CULLEN P.G. Born 27/9/31. Commd 8/5/53. Flt Lt 18/8/58. Retd GD(G) 27/9/88.
CULLEN R.J. BTh CertEd DipPasTh. Born 27/4/55. Commd 30/4/78. Flt Lt 30/6/82. Retd ADMIN 30/4/83.
    Re-entrant 9/5/84. Sqn Ldr 1/11/91. Retd ADMIN 14/9/96.
CULLEN S.A. MD MB ChB FRCPath FRAeS. Born 18/7/39. Commd 18/12/68. Air Cdre 6/4/92.
    Retd MEDICAL 12/7/04.
CULLIFORD F.J. Born 2/5/23. Commd 17/8/43. Wg Cdr 1/7/63. Retd ENG 2/8/77.
CULLIFORD J. Born 27/1/16. Commd 16/9/35. Sqn Ldr 1/1/50. Retd SEC 7/3/71.
CULLIGAN S.A. Born 12/8/50. Commd 9/10/75. Sqn Ldr 1/1/92. Retd SUP 31/3/94.
CULLING S.R. BSc CEng MIMechE MRAeS MCMI. Born 12/2/40. Commd 30/9/59. Sqn Ldr 1/1/74. Retd ENG 1/4/87.
CULLINGTON G.G. CBE AFC BSc. Born 8/5/44. Commd 28/9/64. Gp Capt 1/1/91. Retd GD 8/2/00.
CULLINGWORTH R. Born 29/8/51. Commd 16/3/73. Sqn Ldr 1/1/88. Retd GD 1/1/91.
CULLIS C. Born 9/10/37. Commd 21/10/66. Sqn Ldr 1/7/80. Retd GD 9/10/95.
CULLUM P.J.G. MCMI. Born 16/4/47. Commd 1/3/68. Wg Cdr 1/7/90. Retd GD 16/4/05.
CULLUM W.B.J. Born 18/10/27. Commd 26/8/66. Flt Lt 26/8/71. Retd ENG 31/3/78.
CULMER A.W. MBE MSc BSc CEng FIMechE FRAeS ACGI. Born 19/2/23. Commd 21/1/45. Gp Capt 1/7/69.
    Retd ENG 19/3/77.
CULMER B.E. Born 4/11/43. Commd 22/5/75. Flt Lt 22/5/77. Retd OPS SPT 3/4/98.
CULMER D.R. CEng MIEE qs. Born 4/4/39. Commd 23/3/66. Gp Capt 22/12/92. Retd ENG 21/12/92.
CULPAN J. Born 18/5/16. Commd 12/4/45. Flt Lt 12/10/49. Retd SEC 13/8/55.
CULPIN B.W. DSO DFC. Born 27/12/21. Commd 11/7/43. Sqn Ldr 1/7/55. Retd GD 27/12/76.
CULPIN R.W. Born 8/5/63. Commd 19/12/85. Sqn Ldr 1/6/00. Retd GD 1/1/03.
CULPITT G.E. OBE. Born 1/6/36. Commd 9/2/55. Gp Capt 1/7/84. Retd GD 1/5/90.
CULVERHOUSE P.C. MBE. Born 18/9/43. Commd 9/10/64. Sqn Ldr 1/7/79. Retd GD 18/9/98.
CUMBERLAND M.J. MBA BSc MILT. Born 26/4/64. Commd 15/8/85. Flt Lt 15/2/92. Retd SUPPLY 26/4/04.
CUMBERLAND T. MCMI. Born 18/10/38. Commd 13/12/60. Wg Cdr 1/1/77. Retd SUP 1/1/81.
CUMMING D. Born 18/6/45. Commd 4/3/71. Flt Lt 4/3/73. Retd GD 16/8/95.
CUMMING F.G. MBE MB ChB. Born 5/3/25. Commd 15/7/48. Wg Cdr 1/4/62. Retd MED 1/6/67.
CUMMING J. CEng MIEE MRAeS. Born 4/4/36. Commd 10/8/55. Sqn Ldr 1/7/77. Retd ENG 16/7/82.
CUMMING J.A. MB BS. Born 18/2/40. Commd 24/9/62. Sqn Ldr 17/6/69. Retd MED 3/1/73.
CUMMING L.L. BSc. Born 18/10/29. Commd 26/11/49. Sqn Ldr 1/7/60. Retd GD 17/9/68.

CUMMING P.L. BDS. Born 18/12/30. Commd 3/1/60. Gp Capt 1/1/80. Retd DEL 18/12/88.
CUMMING R.G. Born 11/2/45. Commd 1/4/71. Wg Cdr 1/7/91. Retd GD 3/5/99.
CUMMING R.G.F. Born 10/9/34. Commd 27/2/70. Sqn Ldr 1/7/87. Retd ENG 10/9/92.
CUMMINGS A.E. BA. Born 4/8/40. Commd 21/2/63. Sqn Ldr 26/10/71. Retd EDN 19/2/79.
CUMMINGS C.J. MBCS MIDPM. Born 3/2/44. Commd 12/3/64. Wg Cdr 1/1/88. Retd SUP 10/5/94.
CUMMINGS D. CEng MIEE MRAeS. Born 26/1/30. Commd 20/12/51. Gp Capt 1/1/78. Retd ENG 30/8/80.
CUMMINGS L.M. Born 12/10/46. Commd 9/2/66. Sqn Ldr 1/1/78. Retd ADMIN 12/10/84.
CUMMINGS W.J. Born 15/3/51. Commd 4/5/72. Sqn Ldr 1/1/89. Retd GD 15/3/95.
CUMMINS J.B. Born 1/5/28. Commd 11/3/53. Flt Lt 24/11/58. Retd GD 20/1/69.
CUMMINS R.P. Born 14/5/13. Commd 31/12/42. Sqn Ldr 1/1/54. Retd SEC 14/5/62.
CUMMINS T.M. Born 12/4/31. Commd 6/8/63. Flt Lt 12/11/69. Retd GD(G) 12/4/92.
CUNDALL H.J. CBE DSO DFC AFC. Born 7/4/19. Commd 17/12/38. Gp Capt 1/1/57. Retd GD 27/11/61.
CUNDY P.J. DSO DFC AFC TD. Born 3/10/16. Commd 11/4/40. Wg Cdr 1/1/52. Retd GD 3/10/63.
CUNLIFFE D.A. BA MRIN. Born 15/12/38. Commd 6/7/59. Sqn Ldr 1/1/70. Retd GD 25/11/89.
CUNLIFFE T.F.G. The Rev. Born 13/6/23. Commd 8/9/53. Retd Wg Cdr 13/6/78.
CUNLIFFE V. Born 25/8/55. Commd 13/12/79. Flt Lt 13/6/85. Retd GD 31/5/91.
CUNNANE A. Born 17/9/35. Commd 5/5/60. Sqn Ldr 1/7/73. Retd GD 2/10/84.
CUNNIFFE T.J. LLB. Born 2/5/38. Commd 13/11/62. Wg Cdr 1/7/79. Retd ADMIN 17/9/90.
CUNNINGHAM D.J. MBE. Born 15/5/53. Commd 12/12/83. Sqn Ldr 1/7/98. Retd OPS SPT 1/7/01.
CUNNINGHAM F.McK. Born 7/9/30. Commd 6/5/53. Flt Lt 6/2/59. Retd GD 7/9/68.
CUNNINGHAM G.W. MSc BSc CEng MRAeS. Born 3/2/50. Commd 23/9/68. Wg Cdr 1/7/88. Retd ENG 18/5/96.
CUNNINGHAM J.A.D.J. FRCS FRCS(I) LRCP&S. Born 21/1/24. Commd 1/1/51. Wg Cdr 1/4/62. Retd MED 1/3/67.
CUNNINGHAM M.J. OBE. Born 22/5/43. Commd 5/11/65. Gp Capt 1/7/88. Retd GD 2/5/89.
CUNNINGHAM M.R.C. MA. Born 11/12/26. Commd 10/5/54. Sqn Ldr 2/3/63. Retd EDN 11/12/81.
CUNNINGHAM M.R.S. MBE MCMI. Born 1/1/24. Commd 19/9/43. Sqn Ldr 1/7/55. Retd GD 1/7/72.
CUNNINGHAM P.D. MBE. Born 5/9/35. Commd 22/7/71. Sqn Ldr 1/7/80. Retd SUP 5/9/92.
CUNNINGHAM P.J. DFM. Born 7/1/35. Commd 5/5/60. Flt Lt 5/11/64. Retd GD 7/1/73.
CUNNINGHAM P.M.D. BSc. Born 30/9/62. Commd 14/9/86. Sqn Ldr 1/1/00. Retd FLY(P) 21/10/03.
CUNNINGHAM P.W.J. Born 1/9/37. Commd 30/7/59. Sqn Ldr 1/7/71. Retd GD 1/6/78.
CUNNINGHAM R.A. MRAeS MIEE. Born 30/3/23. Commd 27/2/44. Sqn Ldr 1/1/61. Retd ENG 1/1/64.
CUNNINGHAM R.H. Born 22/4/33. Commd 27/9/51. Flt Lt 26/1/57. Retd GD 1/4/75. rtg Sqn Ldr
CUNNINGHAM S. BSc. Born 15/11/60. Commd 27/8/87. Flt Lt 18/7/91. Retd ENG 15/11/01.
CUNNINGHAM S.P. GM. Born 29/8/08. Commd 27/5/43. Flt Lt 27/11/45. Retd ENG 30/9/58.
CUNNINGHAM T. The Rev. Born 28/11/31. Commd 24/9/62. Retd Wg Cdr 24/9/78.
CUNNINGHAM V.A.L.M. Born 18/3/52. Commd 15/2/84. Flt Lt 18/8/78. Retd GD(G) 23/9/89.
CUNNINGHAM-SMITH H.C. Born 4/3/44. Commd 12/3/72. Flt Lt 29/5/74. Retd ADMIN 12/3/88.
CUNNINGTON G.H. OBE. Born 5/5/26. Commd 20/7/50. Wg Cdr 1/7/70. Retd GD 4/2/81.
CUNNINGTON P.C. MA. Born 5/5/40. Commd 30/9/59. Sqn Ldr 1/7/74. Retd ENG 5/5/95.
CUPPLES J.M. Born 1/7/19. Commd 7/4/41. Sqn Offr 1/7/51. Retd SEC 4/11/53.
CUPPLES S.E. MB BCh DPH. Born 10/6/18. Commd 20/3/42. Wg Cdr 1/7/56. Retd MED 18/9/71.
CURD B.R. Born 18/6/37. Commd 28/7/67. Flt Lt 28/7/69. Retd GD 28/7/75.
CURE A.G. MA. Born 9/9/46. Commd 22/9/74. Wg Cdr 1/1/94. Retd ADMIN 14/3/96.
CURETON C. Born 7/10/38. Commd 5/3/57. Sqn Ldr 1/1/73. Retd GD 27/10/78.
CURLEY M.T. AFC. Born 26/2/46. Commd 3/1/64. Sqn Ldr 1/7/86. Retd GD 31/12/96.
CURNOW J. Born 25/8/42. Commd 31/8/62. Flt Lt 15/4/70. Retd GD 25/8/80.
CURRAN E.T. MBE BSc CEng DCAe MIMechE MRAeS. Born 13/1/30. Commd 10/2/49. Wg Cdr 1/1/66.
    Retd ENG 14/1/69.
CURRANT C.F. DSO DFC*. Born 14/12/11. Commd 1/4/40. Wg Cdr 1/7/47. Retd GD 14/12/58.
CURREY K.F. BA CEng MIEE MRAeS MCMI. Born 14/2/20. Commd 29/3/45. Sqn Ldr 1/7/64. Retd ENG 14/3/80.
CURRIE I. Born 30/6/46. Commd 15/9/67. Flt Lt 15/3/73. Retd GD 30/6/84.
CURRIE I.A. MCMI. Born 14/12/50. Commd 1/4/71. Flt Lt 1/7/77. Retd ADMIN 14/12/88.
CURRIE I.G. MB ChB. Born 20/1/29. Commd 24/10/54. Gp Capt 1/1/77. Retd MED 5/1/83.
CURRIE J. CEng MIMechE MRAeS. Born 20/6/26. Commd 3/10/61. Sqn Ldr 1/1/68. Retd ENG 30/9/81.
CURRIE J.H. Born 2/7/41. Commd 31/7/62. Flt Lt 31/1/65. Retd GD 22/10/94.
CURRIE R.I. MSc BSc CEng MRAeS. Born 26/11/63. Commd 14/10/82. Sqn Ldr 1/1/95. Retd ENG 26/11/01.
CURRUMS G.D. Born 2/9/53. Commd 9/10/75. Sqn Ldr 1/1/88. Retd GD 17/10/94.
CURRY A.C. OBE FCMI. Born 13/1/34. Commd 7/5/52. A Cdre 1/1/87. Retd GD 13/1/89.
CURRY B.G. Born 25/9/43. Commd 8/9/83. Sqn Ldr 1/7/90. Retd ADMIN 31/3/94.
CURRY D.J. Born 22/11/39. Commd 1/8/61. Sqn Ldr 1/1/72. Retd GD 22/11/77.
CURRY P.M. Born 22/6/47. Commd 19/8/66. Sqn Ldr 1/1/91. Retd GD 10/2/98.
CURRY R.G. Born 7/5/41. Commd 27/6/59. A Cdre 1/7/89. Retd GD 5/8/96.
CURTIES D.M. BSc. Born 4/2/52. Commd 26/6/75. Sqn Ldr 1/1/86. Retd GD 22/12/91.
CURTIN P.B. AFC. Born 7/6/37. Commd 1/4/58. Sqn Ldr 1/7/70. Retd GD 1/10/77.
CURTIS A.C. Born 11/4/66. Commd 8/11/90. Flt Lt 8/11/92. Retd FLY(P) 11/4/04.
CURTIS A.L. Born 1/10/35. Commd 1/11/53. Wg Cdr 1/7/74. Retd GD 1/6/87.
CURTIS C.F.A. Born 13/12/26. Commd 16/1/48. Sqn Ldr 1/7/57. Retd GD 11/10/62.

CURTIS D.G. MBE. Born 21/6/44. Commd 1/7/82. Sqn Ldr 1/1/92. Retd GD(G) 14/3/96.
CURTIS F.A. Born 25/8/62. Commd 26/9/85. Flt Lt 22/9/90. Retd ADMIN 14/9/96.
CURTIS J.A.B. DFC. Born 23/6/12. Commd 1/3/43. Flt Lt 1/3/48. Retd GD(G) 29/3/59.
CURTIS K.J. BSc. Born 20/12/52. Commd 13/8/70. Sqn Ldr 1/1/85. Retd ENG 20/12/90.
CURTIS K.R. Born 21/11/22. Commd 18/11/53. Sqn Ldr 1/1/72. Retd GD 2/5/75.
CURTIS M.I.M. BA CEng MIEE DipEE. Born 1/1/41. Commd 31/3/64. Sqn Ldr 1/7/83. Retd ENG 31/7/95.
CURTIS M.R. MBE. Born 21/6/37. Commd 19/7/56. Wg Cdr 1/1/74. Retd SEC 16/1/79.
CURTIS P.H. Born 26/9/15. Commd 2/1/39. Sqn Ldr 8/6/45. Retd SUP 14/5/50. rtg Wg Cdr
CURTIS R.A. BSc. Born 27/3/43. Commd 2/5/71. Flt Lt 2/5/73. Retd ENG 2/5/87.
CURTIS R.R. Born 24/7/34. Commd 26/5/60. Sqn Ldr 1/7/70. Retd GD 2/10/79.
CURTIS R.S. Born 17/4/42. Commd 4/6/64. Wg Cdr 1/7/88. Retd GD(G) 16/4/94.
CURTIS R.W.J. BA. Born 5/2/57. Commd 27/8/87. Flt Lt 27/8/89. Retd ADMIN 7/3/97.
CURTIS T.B. Born 15/9/64. Commd 27/8/87. Flt Lt 12/12/91. Retd OPS SPT 15/9/02.
CURTIS W.A. Born 11/7/46. Commd 22/5/64. Flt Lt 22/11/69. Retd GD 1/11/72.
CURTISS Sir John KCB KBE CCMI. Born 6/12/24. Commd 27/10/44. AM 1/1/81. Retd GD 13/6/83.
CURZON F. Born 21/4/31. Commd 22/8/63. Flt Lt 22/8/66. Retd SEC 29/9/73.
CURZON H.N. MA. Born 22/1/62. Commd 11/9/83. Flt Lt 11/3/87. Retd ADMIN 11/9/89.
CUSHION B.C. Born 10/3/47. Commd 1/3/68. Flt Lt 1/3/71. Retd GD 9/7/90.
CUSSEN O.A. DFC*. Born 20/3/16. Commd 8/5/43. Flt Lt 8/11/45. Retd GD(G) 1/4/63.
CUTBUSH D.H.D. Born 20/3/45. Commd 28/7/88. Flt Lt 28/7/92. Retd ENG 31/1/97.
CUTCHEY P.H. DFC. Born 8/6/22. Commd 28/3/42. Flt Lt 28/9/45. Retd GD(G) 11/8/66.
CUTHBERT-JOHNSTONE E. Born 12/1/08. Commd 19/3/41. Fg Offr 8/4/42. Retd ASD 25/6/46. rtg Flt Lt
CUTHBERTSON D. Born 6/5/59. Commd 13/12/79. Sqn Ldr 1/7/91. Retd GD 6/5/97.
CUTHEW J. Born 23/5/33. Commd 27/2/52. Flt Lt 26/6/57. Retd GD 23/5/71.
CUTHILL C.R. DFC AFC. Born 12/5/23. Commd 30/9/44. Flt Lt 30/3/48. Retd GD 12/5/61.
CUTHILL J. DFC. Born 28/6/23. Commd 16/10/44. Flt Lt 26/5/55. Retd GD 29/8/69.
CUTHILL R.T. Born 19/1/46. Commd 1/3/68. Wg Cdr 1/7/86. Retd GD 15/6/97.
CUTHILL S.M. BA BA BSc(Eng) CEng MRAeS. Born 19/4/47. Commd 10/4/68. Sqn Ldr 1/1/80. Retd ENG 15/7/88.
CUTLER A. BSc. Born 12/5/50. Commd 3/9/72. Flt Lt 15/4/80. Retd ENG 3/9/88.
CUTLER A.M. MHCIMA. Born 20/6/51. Commd 8/7/73. Sqn Ldr 1/1/85. Retd ADMIN 8/7/89.
CUTLER D.P. Born 28/7/47. Commd 21/10/65. Flt Lt 4/5/72. Retd GD(G) 14/2/88.
CUTLER D.R. Born 1/7/44. Commd 20/11/64. Sqn Ldr 1/7/79. Retd GD(G) 1/7/82.
CUTLER P.E.C. Born 2/6/33. Commd 4/7/51. Flt Lt 19/7/58. Retd RGT 2/6/64.
CUTLER P.S. BA. Born 4/4/44. Commd 16/1/72. Flt Lt 16/10/75. Retd GD(G) 1/4/77.
CUTTER N.F. Born 22/6/30. Commd 23/8/56. Flt Lt 23/2/61. Retd GD 22/6/68.
CUTTILL D.A. ACIS. Born 24/7/31. Commd 19/6/52. Sqn Ldr 1/7/64. Retd SEC 24/7/69.
CUTTING D.J. BA. Born 20/6/36. Commd 20/1/64. Sqn Ldr 1/1/72. Retd GD 20/1/80.
CUTTLE D.A. CEng MIMechE MRAeS. Born 23/10/41. Commd 24/1/63. Sqn Ldr 1/1/75. Retd ENG 23/10/96.
CUTTS P.D. Born 29/4/47. Commd 29/3/68. Wg Cdr 1/1/87. Retd ENG 1/9/91.
CYSTER C.D. Born 23/3/44. Commd 20/10/67. Sqn Ldr 1/7/80. Retd GD 10/7/89.
CZARNECKI Z.H. Born 12/1/21. Commd 26/9/57. Flt Lt 26/9/60. Retd GD 12/1/71.

D

D'ARCY R.S.G. Born 19/10/40. Commd 13/10/61. Flt Lt 13/4/72. Retd GD 19/10/95.
D'ARCY S.H.R.L. Born 19/11/29. Commd 11/4/51. Sqn Ldr 1/7/61. Retd GD 1/5/76. Re-instated 5/11/80 to 30/7/87.
D'AUTHREAU A. Born 1/7/26. Commd 28/8/52. Flt Offr 28/8/58. Retd SEC 1/11/67.
D'OLIVEIRA B. OBE. Born 5/2/28. Commd 4/5/50. Wg Cdr 1/7/69. Retd GD 1/11/75.
DA COSTA F.A. MBE. Born 5/10/39. Commd 28/1/58. Sqn Ldr 1/1/85. Retd GD 5/10/01.
DABIN V.R. Born 28/12/31. Commd 6/2/61. Sqn Ldr 1/1/75. Retd GD 1/11/86.
DACHTLER A.H. BSc. Born 15/6/43. Commd 12/7/63. Flt Lt 15/6/66. Retd GD 15/6/81.
DACRE J.P. Born 22/7/41. Commd 22/2/63. Gp Capt 1/1/90. Retd GD 12/1/95.
DADD R.S.M. BSc. Born 6/3/27. Commd 15/3/49. Sqn Ldr 1/1/62. Retd ENG 26/10/65.
DADSWELL L.D. BSc DIC. Born 16/3/13. Commd 1/1/34. Gp Capt 1/1/56. Retd ENG 1/10/63.
DAFFARN G.C. BSc FCMI. Born 14/4/49. Commd 9/9/69. Gp Capt 1/7/99. Retd GD 15/1/05.
DAGG M. Born 13/12/25. Commd 19/12/63. Flt Lt 19/12/68. Retd ENG 18/8/78.
DAIMOND J.E. The Rev. BA. Born 19/11/39. Commd 6/1/66. Retd Wg Cdr 4/10/91.
DAINTY G.P. Born 6/3/45. Commd 5/3/65. Flt Lt 5/9/70. Retd GD 6/3/82.
DAINTY J.D.G. Born 30/8/39. Commd 12/9/63. Wg Cdr 1/1/81. Retd SUP 21/7/91.
DAINTY P.C. OBE. Born 12/10/14. Commd 10/10/40. Gp Capt 1/1/62. Retd SEC 9/10/67.
DAISH J.R. Born 18/3/39. Commd 11/12/61. Wg Cdr 1/1/87. Retd GD 16/5/94.
DAKIN A.G. BSc. Born 9/8/58. Commd 18/7/78. Wg Cdr 1/1/99. Retd GD 25/5/05.
DALBY A.P. MBA MSc MHSM MCMI DipHSM. Born 18/8/58. Commd 25/4/82. Sqn Ldr 1/7/95. Retd MED SPT 3/4/02.
DALBY D. MRAeS. Born 28/5/20. Commd 23/9/43. Sqn Ldr 1/7/54. Retd ENG 28/5/69.
DALE A.A. Born 29/4/45. Commd 20/8/65. Flt Lt 29/10/70. Retd GD(G) 29/4/89.
DALE A.J. Born 18/1/58. Commd 24/7/81. Flt Lt 21/1/84. Retd GD 18/1/96.
DALE B.H. Born 3/2/36. Commd 22/1/55. Wg Cdr 1/7/79. Retd GD 18/8/87.
DALE D.C. Born 31/3/56. Commd 10/5/90. Flt Lt 10/5/92. Retd SUP 1/7/00.
DALE D.M. BSc. Born 6/2/38. Commd 24/5/59. Sqn Ldr 1/7/72. Retd GD 28/3/77.
DALE H.L. Born 21/9/12. Commd 1/6/42. Fg Offr 14/12/42. Retd ENG 31/5/46. rtg Flt Lt
DALE I.P. MSc BA. Born 3/3/59. Commd 29/8/77. Sqn Ldr 1/7/92. Retd ENG 29/9/98.
DALE J. Born 12/5/57. Commd 6/10/77. Wg Cdr 1/7/99. Retd ADMIN 2/4/01.
DALE J.D. Born 14/3/44. Commd 17/12/65. Sqn Ldr 1/1/75. Retd SY 8/5/82. Re-instated 14/5/84. Wg Cdr 1/1/85. Retd SY 1/8/87.
DALE J.R.F. Born 13/3/51. Commd 24/4/70. Flt Lt 8/8/76. Retd GD(G) 28/5/82.
DALE P.G. Born 13/3/23. Commd 20/9/44. Flt Offr 1/7/51. Retd PRT 23/7/56.
DALE P.P. Born 6/11/30. Commd 31/12/52. Flt Lt 15/2/65. Retd GD 22/11/70.
DALE R.W. ACIS. Born 19/5/35. Commd 20/6/63. Flt Lt 1/4/66. Retd SEC 19/5/73.
DALE T.B. BA MInstAM MCMI. Born 6/10/38. Commd 17/11/59. Wg Cdr 1/7/87. Retd ADMIN 6/10/93.
DALE T.E. Born 28/3/31. Commd 26/8/66. Sqn Ldr 1/1/79. Retd ENG 20/1/84.
DALES M. Born 7/9/40. Commd 30/7/63. Sqn Ldr 1/1/72. Retd GD 7/9/78. Re-instated 1/4/82. Sqn Ldr 26/7/75. Retd GD 7/9/95.
DALEY F.W. Born 19/6/33. Commd 10/4/56. Sqn Ldr 1/7/67. Retd GD 30/9/73.
DALGLEISH R.F. Born 22/11/46. Commd 17/7/70. Flt Lt 22/4/74. Retd GD 1/12/89.
DALGLEISH W.H. Born 18/1/26. Commd 22/2/46. Sqn Ldr 1/7/56. Retd GD 18/1/64.
DALGLIESH D.C. Born 27/5/47. Commd 23/3/67. Flt Lt 23/9/72. Retd GD 27/5/85.
DALKIN J.L. Born 26/5/33. Commd 17/12/64. Sqn Ldr 2/10/74. Retd ADMIN 1/2/84.
DALLAS G.C. Born 10/9/52. Commd 2/2/84. Flt Lt 2/2/86. Retd ENG 14/3/97.
DALLEY J.O. OBE DFM. Born 7/4/20. Commd 28/8/42. Gp Capt 1/7/62. Retd GD 26/4/75.
DALLEY K.P. Born 25/3/42. Commd 2/3/61. Flt Lt 9/2/68. Retd GD 24/3/80. Re-entered 11/3/81. Sqn Ldr 1/1/87. Retd GD 15/4/00.
DALLIMORE G. Born 26/1/37. Commd 24/9/63. Sqn Ldr 1/7/71. Retd ENG 5/4/91.
DALLIMORE J.M. Born 26/11/38. Commd 7/5/64. Sqn Ldr 1/7/73. Retd ENG 26/11/76.
DALLISON D.M. Born 14/1/26. Commd 4/5/50. Flt Lt 11/6/53. Retd GD 15/12/57.
DALLISON P.M. MCIPD MCMI. Born 21/7/45. Commd 3/3/65. Sqn Ldr 1/1/83. Retd GD 14/3/96.
DALTON A.G. Born 5/12/64. Commd 15/3/84. Flt Lt 15/9/89. Retd FLY(P) 31/5/04.
DALTON C. Born 15/12/57. Commd 27/9/89. Flt Lt 27/7/91. Retd ADMIN 14/3/96.
DALTON G. Born 13/11/46. Commd 7/7/67. Sqn Ldr 1/1/93. Retd GD(G) 1/4/94.
DALTON I.R. MBE. Born 21/4/45. Commd 19/3/81. Sqn Ldr 1/1/90. Retd ADMIN 22/4/97.
DALTON J.A.H. Born 16/11/21. Commd 30/12/43. Flt Lt 7/9/47. Retd GD(G) 16/11/76.
DALTON J.G. Born 23/11/15. Commd 30/3/53. Flt Lt 11/11/54. Retd SEC 23/11/73.
DALTON R.A. BSc. Born 28/5/63. Commd 29/4/83. Sqn Ldr 1/1/98. Retd GD 28/2/02.
DALTON-MORRIS S.E.J. Born 24/6/34. Commd 24/9/52. Sqn Ldr 1/7/76. Retd GD 18/12/86.
DALY J.H.D. Born 3/4/29. Commd 30/7/52. Sqn Ldr 1/7/62. Retd GD 3/4/67.

DALY M.J. MBE. Born 27/12/52. Commd 12/7/79. Sqn Ldr 1/1/90. Retd SY 1/1/93.
DALY M.J. Born 16/6/33. Commd 13/2/52. Sqn Ldr 1/7/66. Retd GD(G) 19/7/81.
DALY P.K. Born 28/6/60. Commd 28/2/80. Plt Offr 28/2/81. Retd GD 9/5/82.
DALY W.O. Born 27/3/20. Commd 3/8/50. Wg Cdr 1/7/61. Retd SUP 27/3/75.
DALZELL S.R. Born 29/10/55. Commd 26/9/85. Sqn Ldr 1/7/92. Retd ENG 1/7/95.
DALZIEL L.M.c.A. BA. Born 14/7/56. Commd 11/4/82. Flt Lt 11/10/85. Retd GD(G) 15/9/89.
DALZIEL S.M. BSc. Born 11/6/48. Commd 18/7/66. Flt Lt 25/11/73. Retd ENG 11/6/86.
DAMMENT J.F.D. Born 12/3/32. Commd 17/12/53. Sqn Ldr 1/7/69. Retd SUP 18/12/84.
DAMPIER E.P. Born 23/3/87. Commd 1/4/18. Fg Offr 1/10/19. Retd GD 23/12/22. rtg Flt Lt
DANBY C.I. Born 10/12/42. Commd 20/12/62. Flt Lt 15/2/70. Retd GD 10/99.
DANBY J.E. Born 28/10/20. Commd 26/7/45. Sqn Ldr 1/1/68. Retd SEC 1/12/70.
DANBY T. Born 31/3/33. Commd 2/4/57. Sqn Ldr 1/7/79. Retd GD 14/4/85.
DANCE N.R. Born 1/2/48. Commd 17/2/67. Flt Lt 17/8/72. Retd GD 30/9/85.
DANCKWARDT F.P.J.L. Born 20/6/24. Commd 21/8/44. Sqn Ldr 1/4/56. Retd GD 20/6/74.
DANDEKER K. DFC. Born 14/12/17. Commd 6/1/43. Wg Cdr 1/7/67. Retd ENG 1/6/72.
DANDEKER P. Born 15/2/46. Commd 1/10/65. Sqn Ldr 1/1/86. Retd GD 1/10/89.
DANDO D.F. Born 31/1/34. Commd 18/6/52. Flt Lt 29/4/59. Retd GD(G) 15/8/85.
DANDY R. Born 6/7/46. Commd 3/5/68. Flt Lt 3/11/73. Retd GD 4/5/77.
DANE M.B. MBE. Born 15/2/35. Commd 15/2/73. Sqn Ldr 1/7/81. Retd GD 15/2/93.
DANIEL C.R.D. MCIT. Born 12/9/45. Commd 14/1/65. Sqn Ldr 1/1/77. Retd SUP 12/9/83.
DANIEL J.A. Born 8/12/37. Commd 2/1/75. Flt Lt 8/12/92. Retd GD(G) 8/12/92.
DANIEL M.P. Born 26/12/40. Commd 22/9/67. Sqn Ldr 1/7/78. Retd ADMIN 7/1/86.
DANIEL N.S. Born 28/2/41. Commd 17/5/79. Flt Lt 17/5/84. Retd GD(G) 28/2/96.
DANIEL T.P. Born 8/4/32. Commd 4/10/51. Flt Lt 4/4/57. Retd GD 8/4/70.
DANIELI G.A. Born 19/9/39. Commd 27/1/61. Flt Lt 10/2/67. Retd GD 19/9/77.
DANIELL D.H. BA. Born 18/12/25. Commd 28/7/60. Sqn Ldr 1/1/73. Retd SEC 18/12/75.
DANIELL P.A. BSc BA CEng MIEE MCMI. Born 8/3/28. Commd 5/12/51. Wg Cdr 1/1/76. Retd ENG 18/3/78.
DANIELS B.A. CEng MIEE MRAeS. Born 20/7/34. Commd 24/7/57. Sqn Ldr 1/7/66. Retd ENG 20/7/72.
DANIELS B.V. BSc. Born 5/7/29. Commd 27/4/54. Wg Cdr 1/1/69. Retd ENG 5/9/81.
DANIELS G.A. Born 2/10/44. Commd 5/11/70. Sqn Ldr 1/1/84. Retd GD 2/10/99.
DANIELS J.G. Born 19/11/28. Commd 22/1/54. Sqn Ldr 1/1/79. Retd GD 16/8/87.
DANIELS K.R. MA MSc MB BChir MRCGP DCH DRCOG DAvMed. Born 23/11/47. Commd 27/7/70. Wg Cdr 9/9/87.
  Retd MED 14/3/96.
DANIELS L.F. Born 20/11/22. Commd 24/1/63. Flt Lt 24/1/68. Retd ENG 20/11/77.
DANIELS M.E.J. Born 22/1/30. Commd 24/2/67. Sqn Ldr 1/7/80. Retd ENG 22/6/92.
DANIELS P.J. Born 20/5/43. Commd 23/9/66. Flt Lt 8/3/72. Retd GD 30/9/77.
DANIELS R.E. Born 8/11/29. Commd 13/8/52. Wg Cdr 1/1/77. Retd GD 8/11/84.
DANKS E.T.M. Born 24/1/45. Commd 3/3/67. Sqn Ldr 1/1/76. Retd GD 24/1/89.
DANKS P.I. BSc CEng MRAeS MCMI. Born 17/12/48. Commd 4/11/73. Wg Cdr 1/7/97. Retd ENG 6/11/99.
DANN G.H. Born 6/10/23. Commd 10/3/45. Flt Lt 14/7/58. Retd GD(G) 9/2/68.
DANNING J.M. Born 9/10/44. Commd 10/1/69. Sqn Ldr 1/1/81. Retd GD 16/11/91.
DANTON B.E. Born 20/12/34. Commd 14/1/53. Flt Lt 3/6/58. Retd GD 20/12/89.
DANVERS K.V. BTech. Born 27/12/55. Commd 20/11/78. Flt Lt 20/2/79. Retd GD 20/11/86.
DARBY B.T. Born 3/10/37. Commd 22/3/63. Flt Lt 1/7/69. Retd GD(G) 8/4/91.
DARBY J.E. Born 11/9/44. Commd 19/6/64. Sqn Ldr 1/7/80. Retd GD 11/9/88.
DARBY K. Born 7/10/28. Commd 3/8/49. Flt Lt 15/7/55. Retd GD 7/10/66.
DARBY M.C. MVO BSc. Born 1/8/37. Commd 30/9/56. A Cdre 1/1/86. Retd ENG 7/4/90.
DARBYSHIRE P. MA BSc. Born 19/8/50. Commd 17/7/77. Wg Cdr 1/7/91. Retd ADMIN 14/9/96.
DARGAN J.C. Born 8/7/26. Commd 25/10/46. Sqn Ldr 1/7/60. Retd GD 8/7/64.
DARK C.J. Born 9/1/40. Commd 21/8/58. Sqn Ldr 1/1/88. Retd GD 9/1/95.
DARK M.E. Born 9/10/30. Commd 9/4/52. Sqn Ldr 1/1/63. Retd GD 24/7/70.
DARLING D. OBE CEng FRAeS. Born 2/5/31. Commd 11/2/53. Gp Capt 1/1/76. Retd ENG 4/4/80.
DARLING J.G.A. MCMI. Born 20/12/18. Commd 12/6/53. Sqn Ldr 1/7/66. Retd ENG 2/1/71.
DARLING M.H.O. Born 5/12/41. Commd 22/2/63. Sqn Ldr 1/1/91. Retd GD 5/12/96.
DARLING S.J. BEd. Born 25/1/63. Commd 10/11/85. Flt Lt 10/5/88. Retd ADMIN 31/3/95.
DARLING T. BEM. Born 24/8/39. Commd 22/11/84. Flt Lt 29/3/93. Retd ENG 22/4/93.
DARLINGTON G.C. BTech. Born 21/8/50. Commd 13/9/70. Sqn Ldr 1/7/86. Retd ENG 1/7/89.
DARLOW T. MBE. Born 26/10/23. Commd 29/10/64. Sqn Ldr 1/1/80. Retd ENG 26/10/83.
DARNELL A.R. BEM. Born 12/5/19. Commd 30/7/59. Flt Lt 30/7/64. Retd ENG 31/12/69.
DARNELL R. Born 28/10/44. Commd 31/1/64. Flt Lt 12/11/69. Retd GD(G) 14/3/96.
DARNEY D.H. Born 22/6/21. Commd 14/8/42. Flt Lt 21/9/46. Retd GD 9/5/66.
DARRANT D.E. Born 1/7/20. Commd 29/7/42. Flt Offr 29/1/47. Retd SEC 30/6/54.
DARROCH D.G. Born 3/1/44. Commd 31/1/64. Flt Lt 31/7/69. Retd GD 1/4/77.
DARROCH T.J. BSc. Born 15/4/33. Commd 17/7/55. Sqn Ldr 17/2/65. Retd EDN 14/9/72.
DART A.C. Born 21/2/57. Commd 30/4/88. Flt Lt 11/10/81. Retd GD 30/4/96.
DART A.P. CBE DSO DFC. Born 4/4/16. Commd 7/10/41. Gp Capt 1/1/61. Retd GD 4/4/71.

DART C.J. Born 9/7/43. Commd 20/8/65. Flt Lt 4/5/72. Retd GD 27/10/89.
DART J.N. FIIP. Born 7/4/49. Commd 25/10/73. Sqn Ldr 1/7/88. Retd GD 1/11/02.
DART R.E. BSc. Born 7/10/27. Commd 24/7/52. Sqn Ldr 1/4/61. Retd EDN 15/4/68.
DART W.A.C. Born 1/3/55. Commd 11/7/74. Flt Lt 11/1/80. Retd GD 24/8/82.
DARWIN R.B. BSc. Born 20/12/39. Commd 14/5/63. Sqn Ldr 1/1/74. Retd GD 19/11/90.
DASH D.M. BSc. Born 9/10/47. Commd 17/1/72. Flt Lt 17/10/73. Retd GD 2/6/79.
DASTON H.N.M. Born 11/8/14. Commd 18/5/40. Flt Lt 18/5/56. Retd SEC 11/8/69.
DATTNER D. OBE AFC. Born 20/1/22. Commd 6/6/44. Sqn Ldr 1/1/60. Retd GD 30/1/65.
DAULBY D.J. BSc. Born 13/2/46. Commd 11/5/71. Sqn Ldr 1/1/85. Retd GD 1/7/94.
DAULBY K.J. BSc. Born 23/10/63. Commd 29/9/85. Flt Lt 29/3/88. Retd GD 23/10/01.
DAUM R.E.O. MB BS FFARCS. Born 13/6/54. Commd 19/11/74. Wg Cdr 1/2/92. Retd MED 13/6/92.
DAUNCEY R.H.H. MCMI. Born 21/2/31. Commd 9/4/52. Wg Cdr 1/1/76. Retd ADMIN 29/2/84.
DAVENPORT A. Born 27/7/43. Commd 5/11/65. Flt Lt 5/5/71. Retd GD 6/7/77.
DAVENPORT R.J. CBE AFC MCMI. Born 15/2/25. Commd 27/7/45. A Cdre 1/1/78. Retd GD 2/4/81.
DAVENPORT-GOOD A.M. Born 2/12/61. Commd 11/6/81. Sqn Ldr 1/7/93. Retd OPS SPT 1/8/97.
DAVEY C. MCMI. Born 20/4/41. Commd 25/2/63. Sqn Ldr 1/1/77. Retd ENG 1/1/80.
DAVEY D.N. Born 18/11/31. Commd 18/7/63. Sqn Ldr 1/7/74. Retd ENG 31/1/88.
DAVEY G.G. Born 17/9/23. Commd 9/9/54. Flt Lt 9/3/58. Retd GD 19/1/63.
DAVEY H.A. Born 13/2/31. Commd 28/1/60. Sqn Ldr 1/1/79. Retd GD(G) 19/9/85.
DAVEY J.M. Born 15/12/43. Commd 21/4/77. Sqn Ldr 1/1/88. Retd SUP 26/7/93.
DAVEY K.E. Born 7/7/22. Commd 19/5/45. Flt Lt 29/11/51. Retd GD(G) 1/6/62.
DAVEY K.M. DFC. Born 27/4/20. Commd 26/1/43. Flt Lt 26/7/46. Retd GD 3/5/63.
DAVEY L.B. OBE FCMI. Born 26/11/19. Commd 30/4/43. A Cdre 1/1/71. Retd SUP 3/1/73.
DAVEY P.J.O. Born 9/9/35. Commd 22/1/55. Sqn Ldr 1/7/83. Retd GD(G) 9/9/90.
DAVEY R.C. Born 3/3/47. Commd 17/3/67. Sqn Ldr 1/1/78. Retd ADMIN 3/10/88.
DAVEY R.G. Born 10/4/31. Commd 9/4/52. Wg Cdr 1/1/81. Retd SUP 10/4/86.
DAVEY R.J. Born 25/3/34. Commd 24/9/90. Sqn Ldr 3/7/81. Retd GD 25/3/93.
DAVEY S.B. Born 30/7/44. Commd 31/8/62. Wg Cdr 1/7/83. Retd SY(RGT) 30/7/88.
DAVID E.W. DPhysEd. Born 17/9/36. Commd 6/7/62. Sqn Ldr 1/1/73. Retd GD 31/5/79.
DAVID J.M. Born 6/12/34. Commd 19/10/60. Flt Lt 19/10/60. Retd GD 19/10/76.
DAVID K.F. MBE. Born 22/9/33. Commd 26/8/66. Flt Lt 26/8/71. Retd GD 3/5/72.
DAVID R.J.M. Born 14/4/34. Commd 19/8/53. Gp Capt 1/1/83. Retd GD 14/4/89.
DAVID W.D. CBE DFC* AFC. Born 25/7/18. Commd 4/4/38. Gp Capt 1/7/60. Retd GD 26/5/67.
DAVID W.I. Born 12/12/31. Commd 23/1/52. Flt Lt 14/11/56. Retd GD 13/1/71.
DAVIDGE E.H. MCIPD. Born 12/3/50. Commd 14/1/88. Flt Lt 14/1/92. Retd ADMIN 13/11/97.
DAVIDGE M.C.F. MA MIISec. Born 1/10/47. Commd 13/4/80. Sqn Ldr 1/1/89. Retd SY 31/10/96.
DAVIDSON A. Born 27/9/34. Commd 26/3/53. Sqn Ldr 1/7/69. Retd GD 29/9/87.
DAVIDSON A.C. Born 2/12/49. Commd 19/6/70. Sqn Ldr 1/7/87. Retd SY(RGT) 1/10/89.
DAVIDSON D.K. Born 21/2/60. Commd 5/5/88. Flt Lt 28/7/90. Retd ADMIN 13/10/96.
DAVIDSON G.McG. Born 20/1/18. Commd 23/12/43. Flt Lt 23/5/56. Retd GD(G) 27/9/67.
DAVIDSON H. OBE. Born 10/10/30. Commd 12/6/51. A Cdre 1/7/79. Retd GD 8/8/81.
DAVIDSON I. Born 7/2/55. Commd 28/10/76. Flt Lt 28/4/82. Retd GD 9/6/99.
DAVIDSON I.F. BA. Born 3/4/46. Commd 8/1/65. Wg Cdr 1/1/94. Retd GD 3/4/01.
DAVIDSON I.W.B. MCMI. Born 12/5/49. Commd 24/9/67. Flt Lt 25/5/74. Retd GD 1/10/89.
DAVIDSON J.C. Born 6/3/51. Commd 29/1/87. Flt Lt 29/1/91. Retd ENG 3/4/93.
DAVIDSON J.E. DFC AFC. Born 30/9/22. Commd 19/9/44. Flt Lt 19/3/49. Retd GD(G) 30/6/61.
DAVIDSON J.J. Born 15/7/52. Commd 28/8/75. Sqn Ldr 1/7/86. Retd GD(G) 12/5/91.
DAVIDSON J.N. BTech MCIT MILT. Born 30/5/53. Commd 26/11/78. Flt Lt 26/11/79. Retd SUP 16/12/84.
DAVIDSON M.C.F. MDA MSc BSc CEng MRAeS MCMI. Born 24/2/57. Commd 19/9/76. Sqn Ldr 1/1/91.
Retd ENGINEER 1/6/04.
DAVIDSON M.F. Born 10/6/38. Commd 4/7/57. Sqn Ldr 1/1/75. Retd SY(RGT) 10/6/88.
DAVIDSON M.W. Born 8/6/37. Commd 18/2/58. Flt Lt 7/8/64. Retd GD 20/12/68.
DAVIDSON N. Born 28/3/33. Commd 7/1/71. Flt Lt 7/1/76. Retd SEC 1/10/83.
DAVIDSON P.M. Born 17/10/51. Commd 19/8/71. Flt Lt 18/12/77. Retd SUP 19/8/81. Re-entered 14/9/83.
Sqn Ldr 1/1/91. Retd SUP 9/1/00.
DAVIDSON R. Born 21/2/51. Commd 16/3/73. Sqn Ldr 1/7/88. Retd ADMIN 15/4/92.
DAVIDSON R. BSc PGCE FInstLM MCMI LCIPD LCGI. Born 2/7/55. Commd 14/2/99. Flt Lt 14/2/99. Retd ADMIN
(TRG) 4/4/04.
DAVIDSON R.B. DFC MCMI. Born 9/5/20. Commd 24/11/41. Wg Cdr 1/1/64. Retd GD 9/5/75.
DAVIDSON R.H.C. MA. Born 27/1/47. Commd 18/9/66. Sqn Ldr 1/1/79. Retd GD 11/7/89.
DAVIDSON R.N. Born 6/1/34. Commd 11/6/52. Sqn Ldr 1/7/70. Retd GD(G) 2/7/87.
DAVIDSON S. Born 9/4/33. Commd 14/5/53. Flt Lt 13/4/60. Retd SEC 9/4/71. rtg Sqn Ldr
DAVIDSON S.M. Born 1/9/56. Commd 20/7/78. Flt Lt 20/1/84. Retd GD 1/9/94.
DAVIDSON T.J. Born 25/7/56. Commd 5/8/76. Sqn Ldr 1/7/88. Retd GD 25/7/94.
DAVIDSON W. Born 7/7/19. Commd 2/10/41. Flt Lt 1/9/45. Retd ENG 14/11/53.
DAVIDSON W.A. IEng FIIE. Born 6/2/47. Commd 5/1/78. Sqn Ldr 1/1/86. Retd ENG 6/2/02.

DAVIE A. OBE MA MBA. Born 21/11/48. Commd 27/2/70. Gp Capt 1/7/02. Retd GD 1/8/04.
DAVIE D. Born 25/9/28. Commd 18/9/47. Flt Lt 19/12/55. Retd GD 25/9/66.
DAVIE P.E. BA MBCS. Born 10/8/30. Commd 28/11/51. A Cdre 1/1/80. Retd SEC 28/11/81.
DAVIE R.C. MB BS DA DAvMed. Born 9/6/32. Commd 10/7/60. Gp Capt 1/7/81. Retd MED 31/12/87.
DAVIES A. Born 24/8/48. Commd 31/7/70. Flt Lt 31/7/73. Retd GD 31/3/94.
DAVIES A. MA BA. Born 25/1/66. Commd 2/9/84. Flt Lt 15/1/90. Retd GD 2/12/96.
DAVIES A.B. BEng. Born 15/8/61. Commd 16/9/84. Flt Lt 11/8/88. Retd ENG 2/5/94.
DAVIES A.C. MBE CEng MIProdE MCMI. Born 11/2/41. Commd 7/12/65. Wg Cdr 1/7/81. Retd ENG 11/2/91.
DAVIES A.C. Born 17/1/39. Commd 2/2/68. Flt Lt 4/11/70. Retd SUP 17/1/77.
DAVIES A.J. Born 20/9/43. Commd 5/11/70. Flt Lt 5/11/72. Retd GD(G) 20/9/81.
DAVIES A.J. BA. Born 8/6/36. Commd 23/9/59. Wg Cdr 1/1/81. Retd GD 2/3/87.
DAVIES A.J.I. BA MCMI. Born 6/11/30. Commd 15/7/54. Sqn Ldr 17/2/63. Retd EDN 22/10/73.
DAVIES A.T. Born 11/5/52. Commd 29/3/90. Flt Lt 29/3/94. Retd GD 26/10/01.
DAVIES B. Born 27/5/25. Commd 17/11/44. Flt Lt 17/11/50. Retd GD 15/10/64.
DAVIES B.D. AFC. Born 11/7/20. Commd 5/9/42. Sqn Ldr 1/7/54. Retd GD 11/7/63.
DAVIES B.J. BSc. Born 23/11/44. Commd 16/2/69. Flt Lt 16/11/70. Retd GD 17/8/74.
DAVIES C. Born 8/7/16. Commd 21/2/46. Wg Cdr 1/7/62. Retd SUP 28/11/64.
DAVIES C.D. Born 13/2/49. Commd 19/6/70. Sqn Ldr 1/1/90. Retd FLY(N) 13/2/05.
DAVIES C.G. Born 17/6/23. Commd 23/3/50. Fg Offr 23/3/51. Retd ENG 27/3/54.
DAVIES C.W. Born 8/3/40. Commd 2/8/73. Flt Lt 2/8/75. Retd ENG 2/8/82.
DAVIES D.A. BA. Born 19/8/34. Commd 9/8/57. Wg Cdr 1/7/81. Retd ADMIN 19/8/84.
DAVIES D.B.A.L. BSc MB BS FRCGP MFCM MFOM MRCS LRCP DRCOG DAvMed. Born 4/2/32. Commd 29/1/58.
    AVM 1/1/89. Retd MED 4/2/92.
DAVIES D.C. OBE BSc MInstP. Born 24/7/21. Commd 2/9/42. Wg Cdr 24/7/63. Retd ADMIN 24/7/76.
DAVIES D.E. DFC AFC*. Born 6/2/17. Commd 29/3/39. Sqn Ldr 1/9/45. Retd GD 4/3/58. rtg Wg Cdr
DAVIES D.E. Born 23/11/35. Commd 19/8/71. Flt Lt 18/9/76. Retd ENG 10/10/93.
DAVIES D.G. Born 10/11/47. Commd 11/11/71. Flt Lt 8/8/76. Retd GD(G) 1/11/85.
DAVIES D.I. MRCS LRCP. Born 1/6/21. Commd 27/7/50. Gp Capt 1/7/71. Retd MED 7/4/79.
DAVIES D.S. Born 14/1/36. Commd 28/9/61. Sqn Ldr 1/7/76. Retd SUP 1/5/89.
DAVIES D.T. FCMI. Born 6/3/39. Commd 8/6/62. A Cdre 1/1/91. Retd ADMIN 6/3/94.
DAVIES E. Born 17/1/11. Commd 23/2/43. Fg Offr 20/10/43. Retd ENG 15/3/46. rtg Flt Lt
DAVIES E.A. Born 5/2/33. Commd 15/11/51. Flt Lt 22/5/57. Retd GD 5/2/71.
DAVIES E.H. Born 20/7/23. Commd 21/5/46. Flt Lt 4/12/53. Retd GD 20/7/68.
DAVIES E.J.L. Born 16/7/16. Commd 16/3/44. Flt Lt 16/9/47. Retd ENG 24/7/65.
DAVIES E.O. Born 23/12/31. Commd 13/12/51. Sqn Ldr 1/1/63. Retd SUP 1/1/66.
DAVIES F.H. Born 10/12/36. Commd 3/12/54. Flt Lt 3/6/60. Retd GD 10/12/91.
DAVIES F.R. DFC BA. Born 11/9/15. Commd 17/10/42. Flt Lt 7/5/47. Retd GD(G) 11/9/70.
DAVIES F.W.J. BA MCMI. Born 18/3/24. Commd 3/5/46. Sqn Ldr 1/7/56. Retd GD 27/5/78.
DAVIES G. Born 22/3/24. Commd 19/5/45. Flt Lt 19/5/51. Retd GD 9/3/63.
DAVIES G. MBE BA. Born 12/9/33. Commd 9/4/53. Flt Lt 14/5/62. Retd GD 12/9/93.
DAVIES G.E. DFC. Born 24/9/23. Commd 5/5/44. Sqn Ldr 1/7/55. Retd GD 31/3/62.
DAVIES G.G. AFC. Born 23/1/29. Commd 2/7/52. Wg Cdr 1/7/70. Retd GD 2/10/73.
DAVIES G.J. Born 3/12/70. Commd 14/2/93. Plt Offr 14/2/93. Retd ENG 10/5/94.
DAVIES G.M.D. Born 12/6/20. Commd 22/2/44. Fg Offr 5/2/47. Retd PE 7/2/56. rtg Flt Lt
DAVIES G.R. Born 14/1/24. Commd 2/2/44. Sqn Ldr 1/7/69. Retd GD(G) 29/1/77.
DAVIES G.W. BM BS BMedSci MRCGP DRCOG DAvMed. Born 25/6/52. Commd 16/7/74. Wg Cdr 27/7/89.
    Retd MED 16/1/97.
DAVIES H.A. BSc. Born 10/1/56. Commd 30/8/78. Sqn Ldr 1/1/88. Retd GD 30/8/94.
DAVIES H.B. BEng. Born 26/2/67. Commd 3/8/93. Flt Lt 15/7/96. Retd ENGINEER 26/2/05.
DAVIES H.D. Born 2/3/25. Commd 22/10/44. Sqn Ldr 1/1/67. Retd GD 4/6/73.
DAVIES H.D. Born 21/2/41. Commd 20/5/82. Sqn Ldr 1/1/90. Retd SUP 21/2/96.
DAVIES H.E.J. BSc. Born 13/7/51. Commd 15/9/69. Sqn Ldr 1/7/85. Retd ENG 1/1/02.
DAVIES H.J. Born 29/6/27. Commd 16/1/47. Sqn Ldr 1/1/57. Retd GD 30/9/68.
DAVIES H.L. MB BCh FRCS(Edin) FRCS LRCP. Born 30/8/35. Commd 6/11/60. Wg Cdr 8/8/73. Retd MED 6/11/76.
DAVIES H.M. BA. Born 5/7/39. Commd 12/6/62. Flt Lt 1/7/74. Retd GD 5/7/94.
DAVIES H.M.F. BA DipEd. Born 7/6/31. Commd 15/8/65. Sqn Ldr 15/2/67. Retd ADMIN 21/10/88.
DAVIES H.N.R. Born 26/7/51. Commd 25/10/73. Flt Lt 30/6/80. Retd GD(G) 26/7/89.
DAVIES I.J. MBE FCMI. Born 3/11/17. Commd 5/10/44. Gp Capt 1/7/66. Retd SUP 27/12/72.
DAVIES I.K. MA PhD MSc. Born 19/12/30. Commd 25/8/55. Wg Cdr 17/2/71. Retd EDN 23/2/72.
DAVIES I.T. Born 10/2/51. Commd 12/3/87. Flt Lt 12/3/91. Retd SUP 1/10/93.
DAVIES J. BSc. Born 26/6/42. Commd 22/10/72. Sqn Ldr 1/1/81. Retd ENG 22/10/91.
DAVIES J. MIDPM MCMI. Born 20/8/51. Commd 15/9/69. Sqn Ldr 1/1/86. Retd SUP 14/3/97.
DAVIES J. BA. Born 21/8/20. Commd 15/7/43. Sqn Ldr 5/11/58. Retd EDN 7/4/72.
DAVIES J. CEng MIMechE. Born 1/7/34. Commd 20/7/65. Sqn Ldr 1/1/72. Retd ENG 20/7/79.
DAVIES J. Born 11/4/58. Commd 14/7/77. Sqn Ldr 1/1/94. Retd GD 28/7/98.
DAVIES J.A. DFC BA. Born 24/10/22. Commd 26/1/45. Sqn Ldr 23/4/57. Retd EDN 14/8/63.

DAVIES J.A.M. MBE. Born 5/8/21. Commd 13/4/45. Sqn Ldr 1/1/61. Retd PE 31/5/73.
DAVIES J.B. Born 10/3/38. Commd 16/4/57. Flt Lt 7/8/64. Retd GD 10/3/76.
DAVIES J.C. Born 31/1/41. Commd 17/5/63. Sqn Ldr 1/7/82. Retd GD 31/1/96.
DAVIES J.C.W. Born 18/2/14. Commd 11/1/43. Sqn Ldr 1/7/52. Retd GD 18/2/57.
DAVIES J.E. Born 29/8/37. Commd 16/2/61. Flt Lt 1/4/66. Retd SEC 29/8/75.
DAVIES J.F. Born 5/2/34. Commd 8/10/52. Flt Lt 6/3/58. Retd GD 5/2/89.
DAVIES J.F. Born 20/3/35. Commd 9/5/54. Wg Cdr 1/7/83. Retd GD 28/4/89.
DAVIES J.G. Born 18/2/46. Commd 26/5/67. Flt Lt 18/2/70. Retd GD 18/2/90.
DAVIES J.G. AFC. Born 28/9/27. Commd 28/11/51. Flt Lt 28/5/56. Retd GD 3/8/76.
DAVIES J.H. Born 25/1/26. Commd 18/5/61. Sqn Ldr 1/7/73. Retd ADMIN 1/6/77.
DAVIES J.H. Born 14/4/57. Commd 23/1/88. Wg Cdr 1/1/02. Retd GD 8/4/05.
DAVIES J.I. CBE MCMI. Born 8/6/30. Commd 15/6/50. Wg Cdr 1/7/67. Retd GD 29/6/74.
DAVIES J.L. OBE MA MRIN. Born 9/5/46. Commd 28/9/64. Gp Capt 1/7/92. Retd GD 30/7/94.
DAVIES J.M. Born 6/3/35. Commd 14/10/71. Flt Lt 14/10/73. Retd SUP 14/10/78.
DAVIES J.M.B. BA MCIPS. Born 13/6/47. Commd 2/8/68. Gp Capt 1/7/92. Retd SUP 16/4/94.
DAVIES J.P. Born 21/6/54. Commd 19/12/85. Sqn Ldr 1/1/92. Retd SY 2/1/95.
DAVIES J.R. MInstAM. Born 13/2/30. Commd 30/7/52. Wg Cdr 1/7/72. Retd SUP 13/2/85.
DAVIES J.S. Born 30/3/50. Commd 5/11/70. Wg Cdr 1/1/95. Retd GD 30/3/05.
DAVIES J.T. Born 3/2/31. Commd 2/7/52. Flt Lt 14/5/58. Retd GD 3/2/69.
DAVIES J.W. Born 27/12/38. Commd 21/10/65. Wg Cdr 1/1/85. Retd ADMIN 27/12/93.
DAVIES J.W.A. Born 24/3/35. Commd 4/7/69. Flt Lt 4/4/71. Retd ENG 4/7/77.
DAVIES K.F. Born 16/7/28. Commd 23/3/66. Sqn Ldr 1/7/78. Retd ENG 16/7/83.
DAVIES L. AFC. Born 15/2/20. Commd 26/6/43. Wg Cdr 1/7/65. Retd GD 3/7/73.
DAVIES L.H. BA. Born 28/12/39. Commd 31/3/64. Flt Lt 30/12/65. Retd GD 1/5/90.
DAVIES L.K. BEd. Born 9/8/53. Commd 13/4/80. Flt Lt 13/2/82. Retd ADMIN 31/8/89.
DAVIES L.V. DFM. Born 7/7/19. Commd 7/8/41. Flt Lt 1/9/45. Retd SEC 29/2/64. rtg Sqn Ldr
DAVIES M. MSc BSc CEng MIMechE. Born 11/1/49. Commd 1/8/69. Gp Capt 1/7/93. Retd ENG 13/9/96.
DAVIES M.J. BSc. Born 10/7/60. Commd 19/6/83. Flt Lt 19/12/85. Retd ENG 19/6/99.
DAVIES M.J. Born 4/11/50. Commd 22/5/70. Flt Lt 22/11/75. Retd GD 8/8/81.
DAVIES M.J. MSc. Born 20/2/47. Commd 4/1/83. Sqn Ldr 1/7/94. Retd ENG 2/7/01.
DAVIES M.J. Born 17/5/59. Commd 20/7/78. Fg Offr 12/1/81. Retd SUP 31/7/82.
DAVIES M.J.A. DPhysEd. Born 3/2/33. Commd 17/1/52. Sqn Ldr 1/7/72. Retd PE 15/9/75.
DAVIES M.J.P. Born 7/4/21. Commd 18/4/45. Sqn Ldr 1/1/56. Retd GD 27/4/64.
DAVIES M.P. Born 2/3/25. Commd 26/2/46. Sqn Ldr 1/7/56. Retd GD 12/3/63.
DAVIES M.R. BSc. Born 21/1/64. Commd 5/9/82. Sqn Ldr 1/1/98. Retd ENGINEER 21/1/05.
DAVIES N.A. Born 20/12/27. Commd 7/12/48. Flt Lt 20/12/54. Retd GD 20/12/65.
DAVIES N.C. Born 18/12/22. Commd 26/10/44. Sqn Ldr 1/7/70. Retd PI 28/3/78.
DAVIES N.E. BSc CEng MRAeS. Born 8/7/36. Commd 30/9/58. Sqn Ldr 1/1/76. Retd ENG 8/7/94.
DAVIES P. Born 24/12/41. Commd 26/3/69. Sqn Ldr 1/7/79. Retd SUP 22/5/93.
DAVIES P.A. BA CertEd. Born 13/9/39. Commd 17/7/62. Sqn Ldr 8/10/75. Retd ADMIN 17/7/78.
DAVIES P.A. BSc. Born 5/3/58. Commd 18/10/81. Flt Lt 18/1/81. Retd GD 1/8/93.
DAVIES P.A.G. BSc. Born 9/1/46. Commd 5/12/71. Sqn Ldr 1/7/80. Retd ADMIN 18/4/01.
DAVIES P.F. Born 24/5/57. Commd 11/6/81. Flt Lt 11/12/87. Retd GD(G) 1/10/88.
DAVIES P.J. BTech. Born 6/2/55. Commd 15/9/74. Flt Lt 27/3/80. Retd ENG 1/10/83.
DAVIES P.V. Born 4/4/48. Commd 17/7/70. Flt Lt 17/1/76. Retd GD 4/4/86.
DAVIES R. FCMI. Born 25/6/22. Commd 16/2/45. Gp Capt 1/7/72. Retd SUP 13/7/74.
DAVIES R. Born 8/11/42. Commd 17/12/64. Flt Lt 9/2/68. Retd GD 29/4/94.
DAVIES R.E. Born 4/9/30. Commd 31/5/50. Sqn Ldr 1/7/61. Retd GD 16/9/76.
DAVIES R.J. Born 26/11/47. Commd 28/4/67. Flt Lt 28/10/72. Retd GD 26/11/02.
DAVIES R.J. MB BCh MRCPsych DPM. Born 13/2/33. Commd 20/8/65. Wg Cdr 28/8/72. Retd MED 8/11/80.
DAVIES R.M. Born 23/5/43. Commd 26/11/60. Flt Lt 26/5/66. Retd GD 4/7/75.
DAVIES R.McQ. Born 4/10/23. Commd 14/7/44. Sqn Ldr 1/7/71. Retd ADMIN 30/10/76.
DAVIES R.W. Born 30/8/49. Commd 3/12/70. Flt Lt 3/6/76. Retd GD 22/10/94.
DAVIES R.W. BSc. Born 12/9/52. Commd 25/9/71. Wg Cdr 1/7/00. Retd GD 9/4/05.
DAVIES S. Born 5/1/68. Commd 4/6/87. Flt Lt 4/12/92. Retd FLY(P) 16/1/05.
DAVIES S. Born 26/4/13. Commd 28/6/45. Flt Lt 4/1/51. Retd SEC 26/4/62.
DAVIES S.H. Born 18/3/37. Commd 22/1/55. Sqn Ldr 1/7/73. Retd GD 18/3/94.
DAVIES S.J. Born 12/2/15. Commd 30/1/47. Sqn Ldr 1/7/63. Retd SEC 4/12/65.
DAVIES S.P. Born 21/5/48. Commd 23/3/67. Flt Lt 23/9/72. Retd GD 14/10/77.
DAVIES S.W. The Rev. AKC. Born 12/8/26. Commd 24/10/61. Retd Sqn Ldr 24/10/77.
DAVIES T.C. MSc BSc CEng MIEE. Born 4/1/40. Commd 24/9/63. Flt Lt 24/3/66. Retd ADMIN 24/9/82.
DAVIES T.C. BSc CEng FIEE FRAeS MInstP. Born 21/10/42. Commd 13/4/64. A Cdre 1/1/91. Retd ENG 21/10/97.
DAVIES T.K. Born 5/5/48. Commd 4/3/71. Flt Lt 4/9/76. Retd GD 22/10/94.
DAVIES T.N. CEng MIMechE MRAeS. Born 2/8/37. Commd 5/1/60. Sqn Ldr 5/1/70. Retd EDN 5/1/76.
DAVIES T.V. CEng FIMechE FRAeS. Born 20/10/38. Commd 3/2/69. Gp Capt 1/7/87. Retd ENG 20/10/93.
DAVIES W.C.S. CEng MRAeS. Born 26/11/20. Commd 19/10/49. Flt Lt 11/11/54. Retd ENG 3/4/69.

DAVIES W.G. Born 10/6/42. Commd 2/6/77. Sqn Ldr 1/7/87. Retd ADMIN 28/11/92.
DAVIES W.I. Born 4/5/19. Commd 17/3/49. Flt Lt 17/9/53. Retd GD(G) 4/5/62.
DAVIES W.J. Born 27/11/26. Commd 17/10/51. Flt Lt 7/8/55. Retd GD 18/3/65.
DAVIES-THOMAS J.B. Born 30/9/34. Commd 30/5/59. Sqn Ldr 1/7/71. Retd ADMIN 1/10/84.
DAVIS A.H. Born 23/8/43. Commd 9/9/63. Sqn Ldr 1/7/92. Retd GD 23/8/98.
DAVIS A.M.c.B. OBE. Born 24/11/44. Commd 22/5/64. Wg Cdr 1/1/90. Retd GD 24/11/99.
DAVIS A.R. Born 13/6/33. Commd 13/2/52. Sqn Ldr 1/1/64. Retd GD 13/6/71.
DAVIS B. Born 12/11/14. Commd 6/9/56. Flt Lt 6/9/59. Retd SEC 19/6/72.
DAVIS C.A. Born 9/2/55. Commd 8/8/74. Sqn Ldr 1/1/89. Retd GD(G) 9/2/93.
DAVIS C.D. Born 22/9/49. Commd 22/3/81. Fg Offr 22/1/84. Retd GD(G) 5/1/85. Re-entered 8/12/89. Fg Offr 22/1/84.
    Retd GD(G) 5/1/85.
DAVIS C.H. FCMI. Born 11/3/29. Commd 27/2/52. Wg Cdr 1/7/73. Retd SEC 18/10/83.
DAVIS C.H. Born 11/11/31. Commd 29/4/53. Flt Lt 30/9/58. Retd GD 11/11/69.
DAVIS C.J. Born 16/1/33. Commd 8/5/53. Sqn Ldr 1/7/78. Retd GD 27/3/89.
DAVIS C.K. Born 22/10/16. Commd 9/12/45. Sqn Ldr 1/1/66. Retd ENG 22/10/73.
DAVIS C.L. Born 31/8/39. Commd 10/12/57. Sqn Ldr 1/1/88. Retd GD 31/8/95.
DAVIS D. Born 27/12/23. Commd 26/5/60. Flt Lt 26/5/65. Retd GD 4/6/73.
DAVIS D.A. MBE. Born 6/7/28. Commd 30/7/59. Sqn Ldr 1/1/72. Retd ENG 6/7/78.
DAVIS F.W.T. Born 20/6/22. Commd 22/9/43. Flt Lt 15/12/49. Retd GD 20/6/77.
DAVIS G. Born 21/4/45. Commd 2/5/71. Flt Lt 2/6/75. Retd GD 2/5/87.
DAVIS J. Born 6/5/24. Commd 20/5/44. Flt Lt 20/11/47. Retd GD 30/11/68.
DAVIS J.A.S. Born 4/11/22. Commd 27/5/54. Flt Lt 27/11/57. Retd GD 30/5/64.
DAVIS J.D. Born 23/3/34. Commd 18/3/53. Wg Cdr 1/7/73. Retd GD 30/9/88.
DAVIS J.D. Born 22/6/37. Commd 16/12/66. Flt Lt 16/12/68. Retd GD 23/8/74.
DAVIS J.D. BSc. Born 13/10/35. Commd 8/4/57. Flt Lt 18/6/61. Retd ENG 6/4/66.
DAVIS J.F. OBE DFC AFC. Born 28/2/17. Commd 10/4/40. A Cdre 1/1/64. Retd GD 1/1/65.
DAVIS J.H.W. OBE. Born 1/12/39. Commd 7/1/58. A Cdre 1/1/90. Retd GD 30/6/91.
DAVIS J.L. AFC. Born 3/9/26. Commd 15/10/50. Sqn Ldr 1/1/69. Retd GD 26/8/76.
DAVIS J.S.C. Born 16/3/31. Commd 2/7/52. Flt Lt 27/11/57. Retd GD 16/3/69.
DAVIS K.G. Born 28/7/71. Commd 10/5/90. Plt Offr 10/11/90. Retd ENG 26/3/93.
DAVIS K.J.M. MCMI. Born 23/2/29. Commd 1/8/51. Sqn Ldr 1/1/62. Retd GD 1/2/75.
DAVIS L.A.E. Born 28/4/34. Commd 24/9/52. Flt Lt 21/2/58. Retd GD 1/5/76.
DAVIS M.C.A. Born 6/12/34. Commd 17/12/52. Gp Capt 1/1/80. Retd GD 10/9/89.
DAVIS M.L. Born 24/9/61. Commd 11/4/85. Flt Lt 4/2/88. Retd GD 14/3/97.
DAVIS M.R. Born 6/12/51. Commd 16/2/89. Sqn Ldr 1/1/98. Retd GD 4/2/00.
DAVIS N.W. Born 7/8/46. Commd 5/2/65. Flt Lt 5/8/71. Retd GD(G) 16/10/96.
DAVIS P.H. Born 19/4/46. Commd 23/3/67. Flt Lt 23/9/72. Retd GD 19/4/84.
DAVIS P.P. Born 11/5/43. Commd 2/12/66. Flt Lt 15/4/70. Retd GD 30/12/75.
DAVIS P.R. ACIS. Born 2/4/34. Commd 26/7/55. Wg Cdr 1/7/78. Retd ADMIN 22/8/83.
DAVIS R. MSc BSc CEng MIMechE. Born 24/10/54. Commd 14/6/81. Sqn Ldr 1/1/90. Retd ENG 7/2/00.
DAVIS R.C. Born 26/11/22. Commd 25/3/54. Sqn Ldr 1/1/71. Retd GD 10/11/73.
DAVIS R.F. DFM. Born 19/9/16. Commd 1/1/42. Sqn Ldr 1/7/54. Retd SUP 19/9/76.
DAVIS R.G. BSc. Born 11/5/35. Commd 2/10/58. Flt Lt 14/2/66. Retd GD 2/10/74.
DAVIS R.G. BSc. Born 5/7/44. Commd 30/9/64. Sqn Ldr 1/1/76. Retd GD 23/2/84.
DAVIS R.K. Born 8/8/56. Commd 20/9/79. Sqn Ldr 1/1/93. Retd ADMIN 1/1/96.
DAVIS R.L. CB. Born 22/3/30. Commd 17/12/52. AVM 1/1/81. Retd GD 13/7/83.
DAVIS R.N. DPhysEd. Born 25/5/46. Commd 22/8/71. Sqn Ldr 1/7/85. Retd ADMIN 23/4/94.
DAVIS R.S. Born 10/8/26. Commd 26/11/64. Flt Lt 26/11/67. Retd GD 2/4/76.
DAVIS S. Born 8/6/43. Commd 8/1/76. Sqn Ldr 1/1/94. Retd FLY(AEO) 8/6/04.
DAVIS S.L. Born 6/2/61. Commd 24/7/81. Flt Lt 8/12/86. Retd GD 27/3/92.
DAVIS W. MBE. Born 27/3/43. Commd 17/7/87. Flt Lt 17/7/91. Retd ADMIN 1/8/96.
DAVISON C. MBE FCMI DPhysEd. Born 26/9/47. Commd 11/8/69. AVM 1/7/00. Retd ADMIN 28/6/01.
DAVISON C.M. BSc CEng FIEE MCMI. Born 24/9/48. Commd 27/2/70. A Cdre 1/7/97. Retd ENG 4/4/01.
DAVISON D. Born 3/3/44. Commd 30/3/89. Flt Lt 14/1/87. Retd DM 1/4/95.
DAVISON D.P. Born 8/10/30. Commd 30/7/52. Flt Lt 26/5/55. Retd GD 8/10/68.
DAVISON F.W. Born 2/8/21. Commd 1/9/45. Wg Cdr 1/1/58. Retd GD 29/9/68.
DAVISON G. DFC AFC. Born 1/5/14. Commd 24/10/40. Sqn Ldr 1/8/47. Retd GD 24/2/57.
DAVISON J.L. MBE MSc MCIPS. Born 14/2/48. Commd 27/2/70. Sqn Ldr 1/1/81. Retd SUP 16/9/86.
DAVISON T.A. MCMI. Born 1/11/47. Commd 20/8/65. Wg Cdr 1/7/88. Retd GD(G) 1/11/91.
DAVY A.M.J. BA. Born 31/12/45. Commd 24/11/67. Sqn Ldr 1/7/88. Retd GD 31/12/00.
DAVY J.W. MCIPD MCMI. Born 12/8/44. Commd 21/12/62. Sqn Ldr 1/7/75. Retd GD 12/8/82.
DAVY P.J. BDS LDSRCS. Born 27/2/42. Commd 18/9/60. Wg Cdr 23/12/77. Retd DEL 14/3/97.
DAVY T.H. Born 6/6/22. Commd 28/3/45. Flt Lt 8/2/53. Retd GD 1/8/68.
DAW N. Born 3/4/42. Commd 5/11/65. Flt Lt 5/5/71. Retd GD 26/7/81.
DAW S. Born 3/12/09. Commd 25/3/43. Flt Lt 4/2/52. Retd SUP 21/3/62.
DAWE A.G. BA. Born 13/12/64. Commd 11/9/83. Flt Lt 15/1/89. Retd FLY(P) 2/4/04.

DAWE D.T. LDS DPD. Born 4/6/30. Commd 4/1/54. Wg Cdr 21/8/66. Retd DEL 29/3/72.
DAWES A.D.R. MCMI. Born 4/11/30. Commd 12/12/51. Sqn Ldr 1/1/62. Retd GD 5/11/80.
DAWES E.L. Born 1/2/37. Commd 23/11/78. Sqn Ldr 1/7/88. Retd ENG 1/2/95.
DAWES J.P.H. BSc. Born 25/5/37. Commd 2/10/58. Sqn Ldr 1/7/73. Retd GD 1/7/76.
DAWES L.H. Born 16/9/10. Commd 6/8/40. Flt Lt 1/9/45. Retd SUP 12/3/55. rtg Sqn Ldr
DAWES L.H. DFC. Born 11/2/21. Commd 21/11/41. Sqn Ldr 1/10/55. Retd GD 1/5/58.
DAWES M.R. BSc. Born 12/4/48. Commd 13/9/71. Sqn Ldr 1/7/81. Retd ENG 14/12/96.
DAWES P. MBE. Born 3/6/23. Commd 22/9/44. Sqn Ldr 1/10/55. Retd GD 3/6/72.
DAWES P.A. BSc. Born 29/5/44. Commd 6/9/65. Sqn Ldr 1/7/78. Retd ENG 29/5/82.
DAWKES A. Born 9/4/66. Commd 11/4/85. Fg Offr 11/4/87. Retd GD 31/1/90.
DAWKINS B.D. MSc BSc BSc CEng FIIP MRAeS MCMI. Born 16/7/44. Commd 4/6/64. Sqn Ldr 1/1/75. Retd ENG
  22/7/82.
DAWKINS T.G.D. Born 10/10/25. Commd 25/9/50. Flt Lt 4/12/52. Retd GD 8/8/57.
DAWLING R.I. RVM. Born 31/1/52. Commd 28/7/93. Sqn Ldr 1/1/04. Retd ADMIN (CAT) 1/3/05.
DAWS A.StJ. Born 2/6/65. Commd 19/6/86. Flt Lt 19/12/91. Retd GD 14/3/96.
DAWSON A. MCMI. Born 9/9/36. Commd 6/5/55. Wg Cdr 1/1/75. Retd GD 12/7/77.
DAWSON A.F. Born 12/5/44. Commd 31/1/64. Wg Cdr 1/1/86. Retd GD 8/10/98.
DAWSON A.N. MBE BEM. Born 1/4/22. Commd 17/5/56. Sqn Ldr 1/7/70. Retd ENG 1/4/77.
DAWSON C.L. Born 13/5/52. Commd 29/4/71. Wg Cdr 1/7/90. Retd ADMIN 10/10/00.
DAWSON D.A. Born 15/8/28. Commd 10/10/63. Sqn Ldr 1/1/74. Retd SEC 15/11/78.
DAWSON D.J. Born 17/1/41. Commd 10/11/61. Flt Lt 10/5/67. Retd GD 31/10/73.
DAWSON D.M. Born 29/10/42. Commd 20/6/63. Sqn Ldr 1/7/75. Retd ADMIN 29/10/80.
DAWSON E. CBE BSc DipSoton CEng FIEE MRAeS FCMI. Born 17/12/28. Commd 20/12/51. A Cdre 1/1/74.
  Retd ENG 1/1/81.
DAWSON F.P. Born 2/10/13. Commd 1/1/37. Wg Cdr 1/7/50. Retd SUP 28/11/57.
DAWSON G.P.M. IEng MIIE. Born 10/5/50. Commd 4/7/85. Sqn Ldr 1/7/93. Retd ENG 9/4/01.
DAWSON G.S. Born 1/4/48. Commd 16/9/76. Flt Lt 22/10/79. Retd ENG 1/3/91.
DAWSON G.W. DFM. Born 14/10/17. Commd 24/7/42. Sqn Ldr 1/1/53. Retd SEC 14/10/66.
DAWSON H.H. MCMI. Born 1/11/14. Commd 17/7/58. Flt Lt 17/7/63. Retd ENG 1/11/69.
DAWSON H.M. Born 14/5/42. Commd 26/11/60. Flt Lt 4/5/72. Retd OPS SPT 14/5/97.
DAWSON J.B. MSc CEng MIEE. Born 20/7/34. Commd 3/6/65. Sqn Ldr 3/3/73. Retd EDN 1/10/75.
DAWSON M.J. Born 9/8/50. Commd 8/1/76. Sqn Ldr 1/1/88. Retd GD(G) 1/1/91.
DAWSON M.J. Born 21/11/27. Commd 7/3/51. Wg Cdr 1/7/78. Retd GD 3/7/78.
DAWSON N.S. BSc(Eng) ACGI. Born 11/11/57. Commd 12/8/79. Wg Cdr 1/1/00. Retd GD 10/6/03.
DAWSON P. Born 27/8/79. Commd 1/4/99. Plt Offr 1/10/99. Retd OPS SPT 31/1/02.
DAWSON R. BSc MS DCAe CEng MRAeS. Born 13/4/27. Commd 28/8/48. Wg Cdr 1/1/70. Retd ENG 1/6/78.
DAWSON R.D. BEng. Born 27/11/62. Commd 30/6/84. Flt Lt 30/12/86. Retd GD 1/6/93.
DAWSON R.J.C. OBE. Born 25/9/47. Commd 28/2/69. Wg Cdr 1/7/87. Retd ENG 7/12/91.
DAWSON S. Born 28/7/47. Commd 17/2/67. Flt Lt 17/8/72. Retd GD 1/4/87.
DAWSON S.D. BSc. Born 10/3/57. Commd 1/10/75. Flt Lt 15/10/81. Retd ENG 1/4/87.
DAWSON T.L.I. Born 21/2/38. Commd 7/2/57. Sqn Ldr 1/1/69. Retd SUP 3/5/75.
DAWSON W.E. BEng. Born 13/2/57. Commd 20/11/78. Flt Lt 20/8/80. Retd GD 1/12/97.
DAWSON W.H. Born 9/9/44. Commd 14/11/82. Flt Lt 1/3/87. Retd ENG 29/11/91.
DAY A.C. ACII. Born 28/6/55. Commd 25/5/80. Plt Offr 25/5/80. Retd ADMIN 7/10/81.
DAY B.G. Born 22/4/32. Commd 19/4/51. Flt Lt 17/10/56. Retd GD 22/10/70.
DAY C.G. Born 18/2/17. Commd 26/8/43. Sqn Ldr 1/7/54. Retd ENG 7/9/68.
DAY C.J. BSc. Born 11/8/65. Commd 11/9/86. Flt Lt 7/2/91. Retd FLY(N) 11/8/03.
DAY D.A.G. Born 30/10/34. Commd 9/8/60. Wg Cdr 1/1/81. Retd GD 1/11/84.
DAY F.B.W.E. Born 22/12/54. Commd 5/8/76. Fg Offr 4/12/78. Retd GD(G) 10/8/82. Re-entered 20/9/85. Sqn Ldr 1/7/91.
  Retd OPS SPT 1/12/02.
DAY G.C. Born 19/5/24. Commd 13/9/45. Flt Lt 29/11/51. Retd GD 19/5/62.
DAY G.R. BA. Born 31/5/46. Commd 28/9/70. Sqn Ldr 1/7/85. Retd GD 1/7/88.
DAY J.G. Born 17/11/50. Commd 27/5/71. Flt Lt 27/11/76. Retd GD 30/5/81.
DAY J.R. Sir John KCB OBE BSc. Born 15/7/47. Commd 22/9/65. Air Chf Mshl 5/4/01. Retd GD 1/9/03.
DAY L.J. DFC. Born 17/7/23. Commd 20/5/46. Sqn Ldr 1/7/59. Retd GD 31/1/62.
DAY M. BSc. Born 11/4/63. Commd 7/7/85. Sqn Ldr 1/1/00. Retd ADMIN 1/1/03.
DAY M. Born 12/9/42. Commd 14/8/80. Flt Lt 14/8/83. Retd GD 12/9/00.
DAY N.J. CBE BSc(Eng) ACGI. Born 13/2/49. Commd 24/9/67. AVM 1/1/02. Retd GD 15/5/04.
DAY P. OBE AFC. Born 4/4/42. Commd 6/4/62. Sqn Ldr 1/7/76. Retd GD 2/4/01.
DAY P. Born 30/5/50. Commd 8/8/74. Flt Lt 8/2/81. Retd OPS SPT 29/1/99.
DAY P.A. Born 1/7/36. Commd 12/9/63. Wg Cdr 1/7/82. Retd SUP 1/7/91.
DAY P.J. Born 23/8/45. Commd 28/2/64. Wg Cdr 1/7/84. Retd GD 8/6/90.
DAY P.W. AFC. Born 25/1/44. Commd 19/4/63. Gp Capt 1/1/90. Retd GD 25/1/99.
DAY R.F. Born 3/2/36. Commd 22/5/55. Wg Cdr 1/7/73. Retd GD(G) 1/7/76.
DAY R.H. Born 10/1/39. Commd 19/1/66. Wg Cdr 1/7/91. Retd ENG 1/7/94.
DAY S.H. Born 18/8/51. Commd 27/3/70. Flt Lt 27/9/75. Retd GD 1/6/77.

DAY T.H. Born 3/5/43. Commd 18/5/61. Flt Lt 1/7/68. Retd GD(G) 3/5/81.
DAYBELL D.J. MA. Born 9/10/18. Commd 5/8/47. Sqn Ldr 5/8/52. Retd EDN 5/8/65.
DAYBELL P.J. MBE MA BA. Born 14/10/50. Commd 15/9/69. Wg Cdr 1/7/91. Retd ADMIN 28/1/00.
DAYKIN K.F. MBE MSc BSc CEng MRAeS. Born 8/10/46. Commd 2/5/71. Wg Cdr 1/7/85. Retd ENG 31/3/89.
DAYMON C.P.F. Born 3/6/52. Commd 6/4/72. Flt Lt 6/10/77. Retd GD 11/6/84.
DAYSH R.E. Born 7/7/27. Commd 3/2/49. Sqn Ldr 1/1/59. Retd GD 7/7/65.
DE BELDER K.R.J. OBE MB BS FRCS LRCP. Born 3/6/27. Commd 1/9/52. Gp Capt 3/11/70. Retd MED 30/11/73.
DE BELDER M.J.K. MA MB BChir MRCGP DAvMed. Born 3/7/52. Commd 26/6/73. Wg Cdr 1/8/90. Retd MED 1/8/91.
DE BLAC I.J.M.A. Born 16/6/24. Commd 24/7/50. Flt Lt 22/8/60. Retd GD 25/5/68.
DE BURCA P.J. Born 3/2/41. Commd 22/2/63. Flt Lt 17/3/71. Retd GD(G) 3/2/79. Re-entered 6/8/80. Flt Lt 17/9/72. Retd GD(G) 3/2/96.
DE BURGH M. MCMI. Born 11/3/29. Commd 17/5/51. Wg Cdr 1/7/67. Retd GD 9/4/79.
DE BURIATTE A.H. Born 8/2/24. Commd 12/9/50. Flt Lt 26/5/55. Retd GD(G) 8/2/62. Re-appointed 25/4/66 to 8/2/79.
DE BURLET R.P.A.J. Born 12/4/21. Commd 23/10/39. Sqn Ldr 1/7/52. Retd ENG 31/3/62.
DE CAMPS P.S. Born 7/10/50. Commd 8/8/74. Flt Lt 8/2/81. Retd ADMIN 14/3/96.
DE COURCIER M.H. Born 1/5/53. Commd 13/1/72. Flt Lt 13/7/77. Retd GD 1/5/91.
DE FLEURY C.G. Born 7/2/41. Commd 22/7/71. Sqn Ldr 1/7/80. Retd ENG 7/6/99.
DE GARIS D.R.W. Born 16/10/37. Commd 16/10/58. Wg Cdr 1/7/80. Retd GD 16/10/92.
DE GARIS L. AFC. Born 16/11/26. Commd 14/6/46. Wg Cdr 1/1/63. Retd GD 1/4/68.
DE GARIS M.G. Born 23/10/33. Commd 10/9/52. Flt Lt 7/2/58. Retd GD 23/10/71. rtg Sqn Ldr
DE IONGH B.E. Born 15/5/24. Commd 10/6/44. Gp Capt 1/1/70. Retd GD 31/3/76.
DE LA COUR G. OBE BSc. Born 12/6/62. Commd 7/10/82. Sqn Ldr 1/1/97. Retd GD 12/9/00.
DE LA HOYDE D.E. Born 29/10/16. Commd 29/11/37. Flt Lt 3/8/46. Retd GD(G) 30/3/60.
DE LABAT A.C.P. Born 1/1/52. Commd 6/10/74. Sqn Ldr 1/7/87. Retd ADMIN 1/1/91.
DE LEACY J.R. Born 3/4/28. Commd 15/5/61. Flt Lt 30/8/88. Retd SEC 1/10/74.
DE MARCO M.L. Born 19/12/44. Commd 9/10/64. Flt Lt 9/10/67. Retd GD 1/5/76.
DE NAEYER P.J. Born 10/4/17. Commd 23/12/61. Flt Lt 23/12/66. Retd SUP 30/4/71.
DE NAEYER R.E.S. Born 8/8/19. Commd 17/8/50. Sqn Ldr 1/7/61. Retd SUP 10/4/70.
DE PROCHNOW N.S.H. Born 12/7/48. Commd 8/12/70. Flt Lt 8/12/76. Retd ADMIN 8/12/86.
DE ROSBOURG A.E.G. AFC. Born 17/8/20. Commd 1/8/44. Flt Lt 19/11/53. Retd GD 21/1/68.
DE SALIS T.W.F. OBE AFC. Born 13/7/26. Commd 14/6/46. Wg Cdr 1/1/66. Retd GD 13/7/81.
DE SOUZA R.G. Born 5/5/26. Commd 26/3/59. Flt Lt 26/3/65. Retd GD 25/11/67.
DE SOUZA T.P. Born 1/7/40. Commd 11/7/74. Flt Lt 11/7/76. Retd ENG 11/7/82.
DE SOYZA A.A. MSc DUS CEng MRAeS. Born 6/7/36. Commd 30/7/59. Sqn Ldr 1/7/69. Retd ENG 29/5/76.
DE SOYZA K.W. MSc BSc. Born 19/1/62. Commd 30/8/81. Sqn Ldr 1/7/95. Retd ENG 15/1/02.
DE THIER L.R. CEng MRAeS. Born 3/6/20. Commd 18/8/42. Sqn Ldr 1/7/53. Retd ENG 22/2/78.
DE VECCHIS B. Born 25/1/42. Commd 23/6/67. Flt Lt 8/10/69. Retd SEC 23/6/72.
DE VERTEUIL R.A.P. Born 4/12/40. Commd 2/10/61. Flt Lt 2/4/67. Retd GD 4/12/78.
DE VILLE F. Born 1/11/43. Commd 6/1/69. Plt Offr 6/1/69. Retd SEC 1/7/72.
DE'ATH J.G. MBE MA FIIM FCMI. Born 29/4/32. Commd 6/4/54. A Cdre 1/1/83. Retd SUP 4/2/86.
DE'ATH J.J.D. CEng MIEE. Born 17/12/31. Commd 29/12/53. Sqn Ldr 1/7/66. Retd ENG 29/12/69.
DE'NAHLIK A.J.J.A. MCMI. Born 27/2/20. Commd 13/9/43. Wg Cdr 1/1/65. Retd SEC 14/9/68.
DE-ROHAN-WILLNER G.P. BSc. Born 16/2/64. Commd 15/10/84. Plt Offr 15/7/86. Retd ENG 20/2/87.
DE-SALIS M.S.F. Born 12/5/65. Commd 22/11/84. Fg Offr 22/5/91. Retd SY 1/4/93.
DEACON C.E. MBE CEng MRAeS MCMI. Born 16/2/21. Commd 10/1/57. Sqn Ldr 1/7/66. Retd ENG 1/3/74.
DEACON D.F. BSc. Born 24/6/60. Commd 12/10/78. Flt Lt 15/10/82. Retd GD 15/7/93.
DEACON R.J.S. MCIPS. Born 5/11/34. Commd 23/3/66. Wg Cdr 1/9/81. Retd SUP 1/5/85.
DEACON R.L. Born 9/4/22. Commd 25/5/46. Flt Lt 19/1/55. Retd GD 1/12/61.
DEACON V.H.W. MHCIMA. Born 10/10/26. Commd 28/9/51. Sqn Ldr 1/1/72. Retd ADMIN 31/1/78.
DEACON ELLIOTT R.C. Born 30/5/49. Commd 1/8/69. Flt Lt 1/8/72. Retd GD 30/5/87.
DEACON-ELLIOTT A.S. BSc. Born 4/11/50. Commd 13/9/70. Sqn Ldr 1/1/88. Retd GD 1/1/91.
DEADMAN C.D. Born 5/8/27. Commd 3/8/52. Flt Lt 20/2/58. Retd GD 14/4/82.
DEADMAN D.E. AFC. Born 1/11/32. Commd 29/5/52. Flt Lt 27/8/57. Retd GD 1/11/70.
DEAKIN P.J. MCMI MCIPD. Born 6/10/30. Commd 30/7/52. Sqn Ldr 1/1/63. Retd GD 26/8/77.
DEAKIN P.V. Born 5/4/40. Commd 19/12/61. Sqn Ldr 1/1/74. Retd GD 5/4/95.
DEAKIN P.V. Born 5/10/39. Commd 1/8/61. Gp Capt 1/1/90. Retd GD 5/10/94.
DEAKIN S.J. Born 8/3/43. Commd 4/7/69. Sqn Ldr 1/1/95. Retd GD 16/4/96.
DEAL J.P. Born 28/2/21. Commd 6/12/44. Flt Lt 11/11/54. Retd GD 28/2/76.
DEALTRY R.A. Born 2/10/45. Commd 19/6/76. Flt Lt 19/6/77. Retd ADMIN 16/9/84.
DEAN B. MBE. Born 1/6/46. Commd 1/4/71. Sqn Ldr 1/7/84. Retd SUP 1/8/96.
DEAN B.T. Born 2/5/32. Commd 12/3/52. Flt Lt 10/7/57. Retd GD 31/10/68.
DEAN G.M. LLB. Born 3/12/53. Commd 18/4/76. Flt Lt 18/4/82. Retd ADMIN 14/9/96.
DEAN G.W. BA. Born 30/7/36. Commd 23/5/63. Flt Lt 23/5/64. Retd EDN 21/8/71.
DEAN H.M. BSc CEng MRAeS MinstP. Born 30/1/22. Commd 9/1/43. Gp Capt 1/7/71. Retd EDN 1/7/73.
DEAN H.P.E. Born 19/2/06. Commd 8/11/40. Flt Lt 1/9/45. Retd ENG 14/12/47. rtg Sqn Ldr
DEAN J.D.E. BSc. Born 19/3/52. Commd 2/10/72. Flt Lt 15/4/76. Retd GD 19/3/90.

DEAN J.H. Born 23/2/32. Commd 1/3/62. Sqn Ldr 1/7/72. Retd GD(G) 23/2/90.
DEAN M.H. Born 6/4/38. Commd 3/2/63. Wg Cdr 21/9/76. Retd MED 17/7/82.
DEAN M.J. Born 3/8/38. Commd 29/4/58. Sqn Ldr 1/7/78. Retd GD 24/11/90.
DEAN M.J. MCIPS. Born 7/3/48. Commd 26/9/85. Sqn Ldr 1/1/03. Retd SUPPLY 1/1/05.
DEAN M.S. Born 15/2/72. Commd 13/2/92. Flt Lt 13/8/97. Retd FLY(P) 23/10/03.
DEAN M.S. MBE. Born 20/7/43. Commd 15/7/66. Sqn Ldr 1/7/76. Retd ENG 31/3/93.
DEAN O.V.C. Born 8/7/22. Commd 26/12/42. Flt Lt 26/6/46. Retd GD 31/3/62.
DEAN R.C. Born 26/6/44. Commd 21/12/62. Sqn Ldr 1/7/79. Retd GD 17/2/84.
DEAN R.H. DFC. Born 10/7/10. Commd 26/3/43. Flt Lt 18/7/49. Retd SEC 4/8/58. rtg Sqn Ldr
DEAN R.J.H. Born 1/2/34. Commd 4/6/59. Sqn Ldr 1/7/79. Retd SY 23/6/84.
DEAN T.R.L. BSc. Born 26/1/48. Commd 6/10/69. Sqn Ldr 1/1/02. Retd FLY(P) 1/1/05.
DEAN W.G. Born 15/12/43. Commd 21/4/77. Sqn Ldr 1/1/84. Retd SUP 21/4/91.
DEANS D.A. Born 19/2/46. Commd 20/11/75. Flt Lt 20/11/77. Retd GD 14/3/96.
DEAR A.J. Born 7/12/46. Commd 2/12/66. Wg Cdr 1/1/95. Retd GD 5/4/04.
DEARDEN A. Born 27/10/30. Commd 24/2/55. Sqn Ldr 1/7/66. Retd ENG 20/11/91.
DEARDS S.J. Born 26/8/23. Commd 10/3/44. Wg Cdr 1/1/67. Retd GD 26/8/78.
DEARMAN K.J. Born 29/12/39. Commd 25/7/60. Gp Capt 1/1/88. Retd GD 29/12/94.
DEARN I.E.M. Born 4/7/35. Commd 18/5/55. Sqn Ldr 1/7/69. Retd GD 4/7/73.
DEARSLEY E. BEM. Born 8/6/39. Commd 29/7/83. Sqn Ldr 1/7/90. Retd ENG 8/6/94.
DEAS R.P. Born 1/12/33. Commd 7/5/52. Flt Lt 5/5/61. Retd GD 6/7/74.
DEBELLE F.A. Born 7/12/28. Commd 1/9/54. Flt Lt 13/4/60. Retd GD 8/1/73.
DEBENHAM B.C. BA. Born 26/9/52. Commd 25/9/71. Wg Cdr 1/7/91. Retd ADMIN 26/9/96.
DEBNAM C. Born 31/7/41. Commd 3/5/68. Sqn Ldr 1/7/80. Retd ENG 30/6/82.
DEBNEY P.J. Born 6/10/42. Commd 17/10/65. Flt Lt 30/11/67. Retd GD 30/8/82.
DEBUSE A.W. MSc BSc CEng MIMechE MCIPD MRAeS CertEd. Born 23/10/45. Commd 19/9/71. Sqn Ldr 22/4/75. Retd ADMIN 31/3/94.
DECKER D.W.M. Born 19/10/36. Commd 20/10/65. Sqn Ldr 1/1/77. Retd CAT 1/1/80.
DEDMAN N.J.P. Born 10/3/57. Commd 14/9/84. Sqn Ldr 1/7/91. Retd GD 10/3/95.
DEE A.G.O. Born 2/1/49. Commd 31/7/70. Gp Capt 1/7/97. Retd GD 2/1/04.
DEEBANK A.E. BSc. Born 28/2/54. Commd 23/9/79. Wg Cdr 1/7/94. Retd ADMIN 14/9/96.
DEEKS F.J. DFC. Born 10/4/22. Commd 17/5/42. Flt Lt 25/11/49. Retd GD 19/10/61.
DEEKS N.B. Born 27/2/33. Commd 28/11/69. Sqn Ldr 29/6/80. Retd MED(SEC) 30/7/83.
DEELEY C.R. FRIN FIAP MCMI. Born 20/3/36. Commd 30/5/59. Wg Cdr 1/1/86. Retd GD 20/3/94.
DEEMAN S.H. Born 28/12/29. Commd 17/3/67. Sqn Ldr 12/10/76. Retd MED(SEC) 28/12/84.
DEEN R.J.E. Born 16/1/52. Commd 17/5/79. Flt Lt 15/5/81. Retd SY(PRT) 16/1/90.
DEEPAN K.V. Born 16/3/40. Commd 29/10/64. Sqn Ldr 1/1/76. Retd GD 16/3/95.
DEERE W. Born 27/3/30. Commd 24/1/52. Flt Lt 15/5/57. Retd GD 27/3/68.
DEFFEE H.McL.D. Born 8/1/15. Commd 4/2/44. Flt Lt 5/4/54. Retd GD(G) 8/1/65.
DEIGHTON G.B. Born 30/7/25. Commd 6/7/45. Flt Lt 6/7/45. Retd GD 30/7/68.
DELAFIELD J. MRAeS. Born 31/1/38. Commd 16/12/58. A Cdre 1/1/89. Retd GD 11/5/91.
DELAHAYE P.F. Born 2/10/23. Commd 27/5/44. Flt Lt 22/4/48. Retd GD 2/10/66.
DELAHUNT-RIMMER P.R. Born 27/11/55. Commd 20/7/78. Sqn Ldr 20/7/83. Retd GD 20/3/94.
DELANEY D.D. Born 10/12/23. Commd 18/1/50. Sqn Ldr 1/1/61. Retd GD 1/1/64. rtg Sqn Ldr
DELANY D.B. AFC. Born 10/12/21. Commd 3/4/41. Wg Cdr 1/7/59. Retd GD 10/12/68.
DELANY J.F.B. AFC. Born 8/5/22. Commd 4/5/50. Sqn Ldr 1/7/72. Retd GD 29/3/77.
DELANY O.D.L. OBE BA FBIFM FCMI. Born 12/10/49. Commd 13/9/70. A Cdre 1/7/97. Retd ADMIN 14/12/98.
DELAP D.V.M.A. Born 8/10/37. Commd 30/9/56. Wg Cdr 1/1/76. Retd ENG 30/9/82.
DELAP T.H.F. Born 6/11/35. Commd 17/12/57. Sqn Ldr 1/7/65. Retd GD 6/11/73.
DELBRIDGE K.S. DFC. Born 8/9/22. Commd 22/11/43. Sqn Ldr 1/10/55. Retd SUP 8/9/60.
DELDERFIELD V.A.J. Born 3/6/58. Commd 13/8/82. Sqn Ldr 1/1/91. Retd ENG 3/6/96.
DELL C.J. BSc. Born 31/10/58. Commd 17/8/80. Sqn Ldr 1/7/94. Retd SUP 8/12/98.
DELL J.L. OBE. Born 23/8/24. Commd 15/11/44. Sqn Ldr 1/7/55. Retd GD 12/12/59.
DELL P.E. Born 29/3/34. Commd 26/11/52. Flt Lt 2/6/58. Retd GD 29/3/93.
DELLBRIDGE J.H. Born 27/2/09. Commd 4/12/40. Sqn Ldr 1/1/51. Retd ENG 27/2/58.
DELLOW J.E. Born 29/4/25. Commd 5/2/51. Flt Lt 16/11/60. Retd GD 8/8/66.
DELMEGE G.H. Born 19/2/45. Commd 28/2/64. Flt Lt 28/8/69. Retd GD 14/3/96.
DELVE H. Born 22/12/43. Commd 25/1/63. Gp Capt 1/7/95. Retd GD 22/7/00.
DELVE K. BA. Born 7/7/54. Commd 17/9/72. Flt Lt 15/10/76. Retd GD 1/11/94.
DEMERY N.J. Born 30/1/54. Commd 3/9/72. Flt Lt 9/3/80. Retd GD 8/4/88.
DEMMER P.S. BA FCMI. Born 23/7/32. Commd 31/5/51. Gp Capt 1/7/84. Retd GD 3/11/85.
DEMPSEY J. Born 15/10/56. Commd 15/12/88. Flt Lt 20/9/91. Retd SY 24/5/93.
DEMPSTER H.M.c.I. Born 20/4/28. Commd 5/7/68. Flt Lt 5/7/71. Retd SEC 1/11/75.
DENCER S.D. BSc. Born 1/3/56. Commd 5/9/77. Flt Lt 5/6/81. Retd ENG 12/1/88.
DENCH K.V. Born 6/6/27. Commd 22/8/63. Sqn Ldr 1/7/74. Retd SUP 6/5/78.
DENCH R.L.H. Born 22/10/22. Commd 20/7/43. Flt Lt 1/1/52. Retd GD 22/10/77.
DENHAM D.C. BA CEng MIMechE. Born 21/1/44. Commd 15/7/66. Wg Cdr 1/1/82. Retd ENG 1/5/96.

DENHAM E. Born 2/5/22. Commd 24/2/55. Flt Lt 23/2/60. Retd GD 3/12/73.
DENHAM J.D. Born 14/8/35. Commd 20/11/56. Sqn Ldr 1/7/69. Retd GD 31/12/73.
DENHOLM I.T. MBE BSc. Born 13/7/54. Commd 3/9/72. Gp Capt 1/7/00. Retd GD 9/7/03.
DENISON D.F. Born 7/1/27. Commd 20/6/50. Sqn Ldr 1/7/75. Retd GD 7/1/87.
DENISON D.M. PhD MB BS BSc. Born 7/3/33. Commd 1/9/63. Wg Cdr 15/10/75. Retd MED 1/3/76.
DENMAN K.R. Born 4/2/37. Commd 26/3/64. Sqn Ldr 1/1/83. Retd GD 1/9/92.
DENMAN W.J. MBE. Born 12/7/41. Commd 7/1/71. Sqn Ldr 1/7/77. Retd GD 26/1/84.
DENNAY V.R. BEng. Born 3/8/55. Commd 5/9/76. Sqn Ldr 1/7/90. Retd ENG 3/8/99.
DENNETT J.A. BSc CEng MRAeS. Born 9/10/38. Commd 30/9/58. Wg Cdr 1/1/81. Retd ENG 10/10/88.
DENNETT T.A. Born 14/5/50. Commd 19/8/71. Sqn Ldr 1/7/86. Retd ADMIN 28/1/93.
DENNEY J.A. BEd. Born 18/9/55. Commd 15/10/78. Flt Lt 15/7/80. Retd GD 21/8/82.
DENNEY R.A. Born 22/5/22. Commd 26/7/43. Sqn Ldr 1/7/66. Retd GD 1/10/68.
DENNING J.R. Born 4/8/48. Commd 21/4/67. Flt Lt 21/10/73. Retd SUP 1/3/78.
DENNING L.A. BDS LDSRCS. Born 14/10/52. Commd 9/12/84. Wg Cdr 20/12/91. Retd DEL 14/3/97.
DENNING R.J. BSc. Born 31/1/63. Commd 30/8/81. Flt Lt 15/10/87. Retd ENG 1/5/92.
DENNING T.W.E. Born 13/7/44. Commd 24/11/67. Sqn Ldr 1/1/94. Retd GD 13/7/00.
DENNIS B.W. MBE MA PhD CEng MIEE MIMechE MRAeS MCMI. Born 9/9/37. Commd 30/9/57. Wg Cdr 1/1/76.
   Retd ENG 3/1/86.
DENNIS D.E.P. Born 30/6/46. Commd 15/10/81. Flt Lt 1/3/87. Retd ADMIN 1/10/87.
DENNIS G.J. Born 8/12/46. Commd 11/4/85. Sqn Ldr 1/1/98. Retd ENG 4/3/02.
DENNIS N.C.H. Born 23/7/42. Commd 9/2/62. Flt Lt 9/2/67. Retd GD 23/7/80.
DENNIS R.V. Born 2/6/18. Commd 28/5/43. Sqn Ldr 1/7/68. Retd GD(G) 1/8/71.
DENNIS S. Born 7/7/36. Commd 22/7/71. Sqn Ldr 1/1/86. Retd GD 7/7/94.
DENNIS T.E. Born 29/11/32. Commd 28/2/52. Flt Lt 5/9/57. Retd GD 29/11/70.
DENNISON J.P. Born 29/5/29. Commd 1/3/56. Flt Lt 1/4/60. Retd GD 30/12/68.
DENNY A.C.H. OBE BA FCIS FCIPD FCMI. Born 13/2/30. Commd 28/7/53. Wg Cdr 1/7/78. Retd ADMIN 26/2/82.
DENNY G.R. Born 27/4/40. Commd 19/9/59. Flt Lt 19/3/65. Retd GD 27/6/69.
DENNY I.J. Born 20/1/47. Commd 29/7/83. Flt Lt 29/7/87. Retd ADMIN 31/1/97.
DENNY T.O. BSc MRAeS. Born 22/1/29. Commd 2/1/52. Wg Cdr 1/7/78. Retd ADMIN 22/1/84.
DENOVEN A. MBE DFM. Born 3/3/22. Commd 27/3/43. Flt Lt 25/6/49. Retd ADMIN 5/11/77.
DENT B. Born 4/12/32. Commd 10/9/52. Flt Lt 9/3/70. Retd GD 7/5/64. Re-instated 9/3/70. Sqn Ldr 2/3/92.
DENT B.J. Born 9/11/33. Commd 20/3/57. Flt Lt 3/2/61. Retd GD 9/11/91.
DENT C.R. Born 24/7/38. Commd 25/7/60. Flt Lt 17/4/65. Retd GD 24/7/93.
DENT L. BA MCMI. Born 10/6/31. Commd 6/4/54. Flt Lt 6/4/59. Retd SEC 10/2/70.
DENT R.A. Born 5/3/11. Commd 12/11/42. Flt Lt 12/5/46. Retd ENG 1/9/50.
DENTON C.A.F. CEng MIEE MCMI. Born 5/2/22. Commd 25/4/46. Sqn Ldr 1/10/56. Retd ENG 5/2/77.
DENTON P.K. Born 4/1/51. Commd 27/3/70. Flt Lt 27/9/75. Retd GD 4/1/89.
DENTON-POWELL F.M. MBE FCIPD MCMI. Born 31/7/42. Commd 24/1/74. Wg Cdr 2/4/93. Retd ENG 2/4/93.
DENWOOD V.R. MBE . Born 13/5/46. Commd 28/2/69. Sqn Ldr 1/7/87. Retd ENGINEER 13/5/03.
DENYER L.S. Born 25/1/23. Commd 16/9/43. Sqn Ldr 1/1/55. Retd ENG 25/1/83.
DEPOLO M.J. Born 7/7/49. Commd 4/12/86. Sqn Ldr 1/1/98. Retd OPS SPT 8/7/99.
DERBYSHIRE E.G. BSc. Born 9/5/28. Commd 6/1/53. Flt Lt 6/7/57. Retd GD 6/1/69.
DERBYSHIRE I. MBE MSc BA CEng MIEE MInstP. Born 26/10/48. Commd 6/10/71. Wg Cdr 1/7/02. Retd GD 1/7/04.
DERBYSHIRE P.N. Born 26/4/48. Commd 1/8/69. Flt Lt 1/8/72. Retd GD 26/4/92.
DERRICK J.W. Born 9/7/45. Commd 10/1/69. Flt Lt 10/7/74. Retd GD 23/9/84.
DERRICK T. Born 29/12/19. Commd 12/7/44. Flt Lt 12/1/48. Retd GD 1/12/67.
DERRINGTON T.F. Born 21/7/52. Commd 10/2/72. Flt Lt 10/8/77. Retd GD 14/9/79.
DESAI A.K. MCMI. Born 13/7/47. Commd 20/9/68. Sqn Ldr 1/1/84. Retd FLY(N) 21/11/03.
DESMOND G.J. Born 16/9/18. Commd 9/7/42. Sqn Ldr 1/1/57. Retd GD 18/1/58.
DESMOND P. MBE. Born 25/3/33. Commd 13/8/52. Wg Cdr 1/7/80. Retd GD 25/3/88.
DETAIN L.W.G. Born 20/2/21. Commd 13/2/47. A Cdre 1/7/73. Retd SUP 20/2/76.
DEUBERT R.A. Born 3/3/46. Commd 2/4/65. Flt Lt 2/10/70. Retd GD 3/5/84.
DEVANY T.J. The Rev Mgr. Born 5/7/43. Commd 7/1/88. Retd Gp Capt 1/7/04.
DEVEREUX J.G. BA CertEd MIL. Born 21/2/49. Commd 2/2/75. Sqn Ldr 1/1/91. Retd ADMIN 2/7/94.
DEVEREUX P. Born 1/9/36. Commd 15/10/78. Flt Lt 15/10/84. Retd ENG 6/4/89.
DEVEREUX R.O. Born 16/7/39. Commd 4/10/63. Sqn Ldr 1/7/74. Retd GD 16/7/89.
DEVERILL J.J. Born 24/2/22. Commd 26/4/41. Sqn Ldr 1/7/54. Retd GD 24/2/65. rtg Wg Cdr
DEVERSON M. Born 22/6/25. Commd 8/7/54. Flt Lt 8/1/58. Retd GD 22/6/76.
DEVERSON P.O. Born 15/1/23. Commd 9/4/43. Flt Lt 28/5/51. Retd GD 11/3/67.
DEVESON K.H. BA BSc MRAeS. Born 24/9/47. Commd 18/9/66. Sqn Ldr 1/7/85. Retd GD 8/2/99.
DEVEY SMITH T.W.A. MCMI. Born 2/9/29. Commd 11/4/51. Sqn Ldr 1/1/61. Retd GD 14/5/76.
DEVILLEZ E.A. Born 26/3/22. Commd 19/9/47. Sqn Ldr 1/1/58. Retd GD 14/8/71.
DEVINE D. Born 10/4/46. Commd 28/5/66. Wg Cdr 1/7/87. Retd GD(G) 14/3/96.
DEVINE S.P. Born 13/11/48. Commd 31/10/69. Fg Offr 31/10/71. Retd GD 30/1/75.
DEVLIN D. BSc(Eng) CEng MBCS ARSM. Born 8/6/49. Commd 30/7/72. Sqn Ldr 1/1/87. Retd ADMIN (SEC) 8/6/04.
DEVLIN H.T. Born 2/5/47. Commd 26/7/70. Sqn Ldr 1/7/93. Retd GD 2/9/98.

DEVONSHIRE C.H. BSc. Born 7/8/51. Commd 15/9/69. Flt Lt 15/4/77. Retd SUP 1/10/84. rtg Sqn Ldr
DEW R.S. Born 21/3/47. Commd 29/4/71. Flt Lt 29/10/75. Retd GD 11/1/87.
DEWAR R. Born 9/5/12. Commd 23/3/50. Flt Lt 23/9/54. Retd SUP 9/5/67.
DEWELL F.W. AFC. Born 9/1/12. Commd 1/4/40. Wg Cdr 1/7/58. Retd GD 9/1/65.
DEWEY G.F. DFM. Born 17/4/16. Commd 17/9/42. Sqn Ldr 1/7/54. Retd GD 10/5/59.
DEWHURST D.P. Born 1/8/31. Commd 27/10/54. Flt Lt 27/4/60. Retd GD 7/12/54.
DEXTER G. BA. Born 8/1/61. Commd 29/4/84. Flt Lt 29/10/86. Retd ADMIN 14/2/92.
DEXTER R.A. MCIPD MCMI. Born 21/12/29. Commd 14/7/55. Wg Cdr 1/1/76. Retd ADMIN 21/12/84.
DEXTER R.W. Born 21/7/32. Commd 5/11/70. Flt Lt 5/11/73. Retd GD 19/7/75.
DEYTRIKH A. AFC. Born 24/10/21. Commd 5/11/41. Sqn Ldr 1/1/57. Retd GD 24/10/67. rtg Wg Cdr
DEZONIE L.J. Born 6/10/60. Commd 3/7/80. Sqn Ldr 1/1/91. Retd ADMIN 6/10/98.
DEZONIE V.C. Born 25/3/27. Commd 21/10/65. Flt Lt 21/10/71. Retd ADMIN 25/3/82.
DHENIN Sir Geoffrey KBE AFC* GM MA MD MChir MRCS LRCP FFCM DPH FRAeS. Born 2/4/18. Commd 11/2/43. AM 1/1/74. Retd MED 31/3/78.
DHESE I.R. Born 17/4/43. Commd 24/7/81. Sqn Ldr 1/1/89. Retd ADMIN 17/4/98.
DIACK H.W. Born 6/12/43. Commd 23/9/68. Flt Lt 23/6/72. Retd CAT 1/4/78.
DIAMANDOPOULOS D. BSc CEng MRAeS. Born 14/1/43. Commd 15/7/60. Wg Cdr 1/7/88. Retd ENG 1/10/91.
DIAMOND P.A. BEng CEng MIEE. Born 15/9/63. Commd 7/8/87. Sqn Ldr 1/7/87. Retd ENG 15/12/01.
DIAPER E.D.J. MB ChB DAvMed AFOM. Born 18/11/30. Commd 2/2/58. Gp Capt 1/1/85. Retd MED 16/10/92.
DIAPER G.H.H. MBE. Born 2/2/23. Commd 15/6/61. Sqn Ldr 1/1/75. Retd ENG 4/12/82.
DIBB P.G.R. Born 9/7/60. Commd 12/9/86. Sqn Ldr 1/1/94. Retd GD 2/12/97.
DIBBENS D.T. Born 19/9/52. Commd 28/10/76. Flt Lt 28/4/82. Retd GD 12/7/92.
DIBBERN R.V. Born 5/7/22. Commd 24/8/44. Flt Lt 7/6/51. Retd GD 29/5/58.
DICK A.H. Born 4/3/24. Commd 23/8/44. Wg Cdr 1/7/64. Retd GD 31/3/75.
DICK A.R. MSc BSc. Born 16/6/47. Commd 3/8/80. Sqn Ldr 1/1/92. Retd ADMIN 14/9/96.
DICK E.A. Born 15/10/20. Commd 27/6/43. Sqn Ldr 1/1/59. Retd GD 9/4/71.
DICK I.C.H. MBE AFC. Born 23/7/42. Commd 18/12/62. Gp Capt 1/7/86. Retd GD 23/11/97.
DICK I.R. Born 2/2/26. Commd 29/7/48. Sqn Ldr 1/1/75. Retd GD 26/2/81.
DICK N.M.c.L. Born 16/4/32. Commd 9/4/52. Flt Lt 9/1/58. Retd GD 2/6/66.
DICK R. CB. Born 18/10/31. Commd 30/7/52. AVM 1/1/85. Retd GD 15/8/88.
DICK R. Born 21/3/45. Commd 29/7/65. Flt Lt 28/10/71. Retd ADMIN 21/3/83.
DICK-CLELAND A.S. Born 28/1/35. Commd 27/6/59. Flt Lt 27/12/64. Retd GD 6/3/75.
DICKEN A.B. MCMI. Born 13/4/30. Commd 8/7/54. Wg Cdr 1/1/80. Retd GD 13/10/85.
DICKEN M.J.C.W. CB FCMI. Born 13/7/35. Commd 29/7/58. AVM 1/7/89. Retd ADMIN 3/4/92.
DICKENS B.C. BSc CEng MRAeS MCMI. Born 8/2/45. Commd 31/1/64. Gp Capt 1/7/92. Retd ENG 15/5/01.
DICKENS J.S. AFC. Born 10/7/45. Commd 3/5/65. Flt Lt 28/10/70. Retd GD 10/7/83.
DICKENS M.D. Born 18/11/55. Commd 22/5/80. Flt Lt 22/2/86. Retd GD 25/5/90.
DICKENS R.E. Born 20/10/15. Commd 20/5/46. Flt Lt 4/1/51. Retd SEC 20/9/70.
DICKENSON P.M. Born 11/4/36. Commd 23/2/55. Sqn Ldr 1/7/73. Retd GD 28/11/75.
DICKER A.H.G. Born 21/5/24. Commd 26/1/45. Flt Lt 26/1/48. Retd GD 17/7/62.
DICKER R.W. Born 30/6/31. Commd 3/8/51. Gp Capt 1/7/76. Retd SY 20/9/80.
DICKIE D.G. AFM. Born 18/3/24. Commd 11/1/47. Flt Lt 7/6/56. Retd GD 31/8/67.
DICKINS T.P. CEng MIEE MRAeS. Born 19/8/31. Commd 4/3/58. Wg Cdr 1/1/76. Retd ENG 1/4/83.
DICKINSON B. Born 15/9/50. Commd 27/2/70. Flt Lt 18/7/76. Retd SUP 15/9/88.
DICKINSON B. MBE MA DCAe CEng FIMA FInstP MRAeS. Born 15/8/27. Commd 13/1/49. Wg Cdr 15/8/68. Retd EDN 5/2/72.
DICKINSON D.P. Born 15/9/42. Commd 24/3/83. Flt Lt 24/3/87. Retd ENG 15/9/97.
DICKINSON D.W.K. Born 8/6/53. Commd 22/5/75. Sqn Ldr 1/1/89. Retd GD(G) 17/10/89.
DICKINSON J.H. Born 15/6/55. Commd 22/5/75. Wg Cdr 1/7/91. Retd GD 15/6/96.
DICKINSON K. Born 25/12/52. Commd 2/11/88. Flt Lt 2/11/92. Retd ADMIN (P ED) 17/9/04.
DICKINSON M.J. Born 6/4/46. Commd 30/8/84. Sqn Ldr 1/1/94. Retd ENG 5/1/96.
DICKINSON N.M. BSc. Born 4/5/56. Commd 15/9/74. Flt Lt 15/10/78. Retd GD 15/7/90.
DICKINSON R.H. BA. Born 21/4/59. Commd 22/10/76. Sqn Ldr 1/1/94. Retd GD 21/4/97.
DICKINSON R.J.F. AFC. Born 19/8/26. Commd 20/12/46. Gp Capt 1/1/73. Retd GD 19/8/81.
DICKINSON W.D. Born 3/4/26. Commd 25/5/50. Sqn Ldr 1/7/58. Retd GD 3/4/71.
DICKISON L.V.W. Born 19/2/17. Commd 14/8/50. Flt Lt 26/5/55. Retd GD(G) 19/2/67.
DICKS E.C.R. MRAeS. Born 19/4/44. Commd 17/12/64. Wg Cdr 1/1/91. Retd GD 19/4/99.
DICKSON E.I.D. MCMI. Born 30/1/24. Commd 11/1/51. Sqn Ldr 1/1/62. Retd ENG 24/3/78.
DICKSON H.M. Born 16/9/37. Commd 1/6/61. Wg Cdr 1/1/86. Retd ADMIN 16/9/88.
DICKSON J.A. BA. Born 9/8/36. Commd 30/9/58. Flt Lt 9/4/64. Retd GD 9/8/94.
DICKSON J.E. BA. Born 4/6/67. Commd 5/4/95. Sqn Ldr 1/1/97. Retd ADMIN (TRG) 4/6/05.
DICKSON J.J.H. LVO MBE AE. Born 11/4/34. Commd 5/11/52. Wg Cdr 1/7/76. Retd GD 10/8/85.
DICKSON L.G. Born 23/1/28. Commd 8/4/49. Sqn Ldr 1/7/61. Retd GD 24/1/73.
DICKSON M.W. Born 27/10/62. Commd 4/7/85. Flt Lt 4/1/92. Retd OPS SPT 4/3/01.
DICKSON W.H.E. DPhysEd. Born 7/12/49. Commd 29/8/72. Flt Lt 29/8/76. Retd ADMIN (P ED) 7/12/04.
DIFFEY G.E. MBE. Born 29/5/52. Commd 20/7/78. Wg Cdr 1/1/99. Retd OPS SPT 28/2/01.

DIFFEY K.S. BA. Born 22/3/34. Commd 8/8/56. Wg Cdr 1/1/77. Retd ADMIN 22/3/89.
DIGBY A.P. Born 16/4/47. Commd 15/2/73. Flt Lt 15/2/75. Retd GD 1/4/92.
DIGBY B.N. ACIS. Born 8/1/35. Commd 6/10/60. Sqn Ldr 1/1/72. Retd ADMIN 31/12/77.
DIGBY J.R. Born 19/8/36. Commd 16/12/58. Wg Cdr 1/7/86. Retd ADMIN 8/4/89.
DIGGANCE P.J. Born 4/10/39. Commd 20/12/57. Flt Lt 30/6/63. Retd GD 4/10/77.
DIGGLE G. Born 28/10/43. Commd 2/6/77. Sqn Ldr 1/7/90. Retd ADMIN 2/7/93.
DIGINGS N.L. BSc. Born 5/8/51. Commd 13/9/70. Flt Lt 15/4/75. Retd GD 5/8/89.
DIGMAN J.I.S. OBE DFC. Born 4/9/23. Commd 25/6/43. Gp Capt 1/1/69. Retd GD 4/9/71.
DIGNAN J.C. Born 14/7/46. Commd 28/4/67. Sqn Ldr 1/7/82. Retd GD 19/12/86.
DIGNAN P.B. Born 14/7/19. Commd 4/1/48. Sqn Ldr 1/10/55. Retd GD 8/7/64. rtg Wg Cdr
DIGNEN B. Born 16/9/30. Commd 28/6/51. Flt Lt 1/6/57. Retd GD 16/9/68.
DILLON J.L. MCMI. Born 29/3/29. Commd 12/9/50. Gp Capt 1/7/76. Retd GD 28/8/83.
DILLON J.Y. BEd. Born 30/5/57. Commd 23/7/78. Flt Lt 23/1/82. Retd GD(G) 14/3/96.
DILLON J.A. Born 2/10/45. Commd 2/8/68. Flt Lt 6/10/71. Retd GD 1/7/76.
DILLON K. Born 6/12/46. Commd 2/8/68. Wg Cdr 1/1/92. Retd GD 14/3/96.
DILLON R.B.R. Born 28/11/31. Commd 8/10/52. Flt Lt 27/6/59. Retd SEC 28/11/69.
DILWORTH R.L. BSc. Born 26/4/44. Commd 28/9/64. Flt Lt 15/4/68. Retd GD 27/5/81.
DIMENT A.J. Born 16/9/47. Commd 27/10/67. Wg Cdr 1/7/91. Retd SY 30/9/94.
DIMMER A.H. Born 22/8/46. Commd 1/4/65. Sqn Ldr 1/1/78. Retd SUP 22/8/84.
DIMMER F.J.L. Born 18/3/33. Commd 26/3/52. Flt Lt 31/7/57. Retd GD 18/3/71.
DIMMER G.E. Born 12/2/17. Commd 3/9/39. Wg Cdr 1/7/60. Retd SUP 22/4/72.
DIMMER J.F.E. BSc. Born 25/8/51. Commd 17/11/74. Flt Lt 17/2/75. Retd GD 17/11/90.
DIMMER T.W. Born 13/11/30. Commd 17/11/59. Sqn Ldr 8/3/72. Retd EDN 17/11/75.
DIMOCK D.H.T. Born 2/7/25. Commd 22/6/45. Wg Cdr 1/1/66. Retd GD 14/2/76.
DINEEN M.G. Born 7/9/43. Commd 9/9/63. Wg Cdr 1/1/91. Retd GD 1/9/93.
DINGLE B.T. Born 24/11/48. Commd 2/8/76. Gp Capt 1/1/96. Retd OPS SPT 4/1/03.
DINGWALL P.C. BA ACIS. Born 10/1/48. Commd 13/9/70. Wg Cdr 1/1/88. Retd ADMIN 14/3/97.
DINGWALL R.H. Born 2/5/30. Commd 17/6/54. Flt Lt 17/12/58. Retd GD 2/5/90.
DINGWALL R.L. Born 20/2/39. Commd 16/12/66. Sqn Ldr 1/1/88. Retd GD(G) 20/2/94.
DINMORE D. MBE. Born 11/8/44. Commd 17/12/65. Flt Lt 17/6/68. Retd GD 31/3/80.
DINMORE G.W. Born 4/3/38. Commd 30/1/75. Wg Cdr 1/1/91. Retd GD(G) 31/8/92.
DINNING G.A. BSc. Born 19/2/66. Commd 15/9/86. Flt Lt 15/1/90. Retd GD 14/3/96.
DINNIS J.J.J. Born 13/4/32. Commd 27/7/54. Sqn Ldr 1/7/69. Retd SUP 1/7/72.
DIPPER O.D. Born 16/6/34. Commd 11/11/53. Sqn Ldr 1/1/72. Retd GD 1/1/85.
DIPROSE D.A. BA. Born 23/6/46. Commd 18/8/67. Flt Lt 18/8/70. Retd GD 23/6/90.
DIQUE M.J.A. BEng. Born 25/9/61. Commd 7/8/87. Flt Lt 7/1/93. Retd ENG 23/7/01.
DISCOMBE F.H. Born 30/3/23. Commd 25/5/43. Flt Lt 26/5/57. Retd GD 30/3/66.
DISNEY H.A.S. OBE MA. Born 9/7/17. Commd 8/3/38. Gp Capt 1/1/58. Retd GD 23/8/63.
DITCHBURN A. Born 15/4/44. Commd 31/10/69. Flt Lt 20/7/73. Retd GD 1/1/76.
DITCHBURN A.W. BA IEng AMRAeS. Born 20/5/54. Commd 30/3/89. Flt Lt 30/3/91. Retd ENG 30/3/97.
DIVE L.S. BEng. Born 27/4/29. Commd 17/12/52. Sqn Ldr 28/1/66. Retd EDN 2/4/81.
DIVERS A.R. MB BS. Born 30/11/52. Commd 20/2/73. Wg Cdr 29/6/89. Retd MED 30/11/90.
DIVERS D.M. MVO. Born 11/2/24. Commd 20/4/50. Wg Cdr 1/1/68. Retd GD 30/1/73.
DIVERS J.M. Born 10/5/56. Commd 22/9/88. Flt Lt 22/9/90. Retd ENG 22/9/96.
DIX K.J. OBE AFC MIEE MRAeS MCMI . Born 12/9/30. Commd 25/9/52. Wg Cdr 1/7/71. Retd GD 1/1/83.
DIX M. BSc. Born 15/3/52. Commd 25/9/71. Sqn Ldr 1/7/87. Retd RGT 1/7/90.
DIX R.E. Born 13/1/61. Commd 19/12/91. Flt Lt 19/12/93. Retd OPS SPT 19/12/99.
DIX R.J. Born 29/7/42. Commd 29/11/63. Sqn Ldr 1/7/76. Retd GD 29/7/80.
DIXON A. Born 2/12/32. Commd 25/10/51. Flt Lt 25/4/57. Retd GD 30/3/73.
DIXON A. BSc. Born 8/8/55. Commd 23/9/73. Flt Lt 15/4/78. Retd GD 4/1/00.
DIXON A.H. Born 5/12/21. Commd 29/9/57. Flt Lt 1/4/63. Retd ADMIN 5/12/76.
DIXON A.J. Born 20/8/57. Commd 22/5/80. Flt Lt 22/11/85. Retd GD 1/4/00.
DIXON C.F. MSc MCMI. Born 7/10/39. Commd 19/12/61. Wg Cdr 1/1/77. Retd SUP 1/12/89.
DIXON D.J. Born 21/3/31. Commd 22/7/66. Flt Lt 22/7/67. Retd EDN 22/7/74.
DIXON D.P. Born 23/4/65. Commd 16/6/88. Flt Lt 24/6/91. Retd GD 3/1/88.
DIXON E.R. Born 1/7/15. Commd 15/7/42. Flt Offr 15/1/47. Retd SEC 6/10/56.
DIXON G.K. Born 11/1/58. Commd 11/10/84. Flt Lt 6/11/88. Retd ADMIN 3/6/96.
DIXON H.P. Born 3/1/33. Commd 18/1/52. Wg Cdr 1/1/77. Retd GD(G) 3/1/88.
DIXON J. MA. Born 19/2/37. Commd 22/8/58. Wg Cdr 1/7/76. Retd ADMIN 24/10/89.
DIXON J.E. Born 1/12/45. Commd 5/2/65. Flt Lt 5/8/70. Retd GD 1/12/84.
DIXON J.E. Born 18/10/22. Commd 1/5/44. Sqn Ldr 1/7/70. Retd ADMIN 17/10/77.
DIXON J.M. Born 16/7/45. Commd 3/3/67. Flt Lt 3/9/69. Retd OPS SPT 7/10/00.
DIXON J.P.S. Born 29/6/32. Commd 6/4/54. Flt Lt 14/11/56. Retd GD 29/6/70.
DIXON K.R. BA BEd. Born 13/3/45. Commd 20/1/80. Flt Lt 20/1/81. Retd ADMIN 20/1/96.
DIXON M. Born 21/12/45. Commd 2/8/68. Flt Lt 2/2/71. Retd GD 1/7/89.
DIXON M. BA. Born 23/11/36. Commd 15/10/58. Wg Cdr 1/1/77. Retd ADMIN 26/2/83.

DIXON M.E. Born 1/7/18. Commd 27/10/43. Flt Offr 19/6/52. Retd SEC 15/2/55.
DIXON N.D. Born 22/7/48. Commd 2/3/78. Sqn Ldr 1/7/85. Retd ENG 1/7/88.
DIXON N.G. BA. Born 1/2/41. Commd 30/9/61. Wg Cdr 1/7/81. Retd ENG 31/3/96.
DIXON P.M. Born 29/8/46. Commd 22/12/67. Sqn Ldr 1/1/83. Retd GD 29/8/01.
DIXON P.R. MBA BSc(Eng) MRAeS. Born 10/10/49. Commd 24/9/67. Wg Cdr 1/7/94. Retd GD 23/4/03.
DIXON P.S. AFC. Born 18/5/46. Commd 28/9/64. Sqn Ldr 1/1/85. Retd GD 28/1/02.
DIXON R. OBE MCIPS MCMI. Born 8/3/44. Commd 17/12/65. Gp Capt 1/7/88. Retd SUP 7/3/94.
DIXON R.H.B. Born 15/5/25. Commd 8/12/45. Wg Cdr 1/7/61. Retd GD 24/3/77. rtg Gp Capt
DIXON R.L. BSc. Born 7/5/48. Commd 2/2/70. Air Cdre 1/1/98. Retd GD 7/5/03.
DIXON R.S. Born 11/3/47. Commd 2/12/66. Sqn Ldr 1/1/87. Retd GD 30/12/91.
DIXON R.T. OBE. Born 29/5/32. Commd 12/9/51. Gp Capt 1/7/78. Retd GD 19/9/87.
DIXON R.T. Born 15/4/46. Commd 27/7/72. Sqn Ldr 1/7/88. Retd ENG 13/9/96.
DIXON S.J. Born 25/6/76. Commd 2/4/98. Flt Lt 1/10/02. Retd OPS SPT(FLTOPS) 5/1/04.
DIXON S.R. DFC AFC. Born 31/7/20. Commd 24/11/41. Sqn Ldr 1/1/53. Retd GD 31/7/75.
DIXON T.S.J. Born 14/12/32. Commd 2/7/52. Flt Lt 27/11/57. Retd GD 14/12/70.
DJUMIC M. MSc BSc. Born 3/6/59. Commd 18/10/81. Wg Cdr 1/1/97. Retd SUP 1/1/00.
DOBB A.L. BSc. Born 25/11/41. Commd 26/5/70. Sqn Ldr 1/1/83. Retd ENG 2/7/93.
DOBBIE D.A. AFC. Born 18/6/21. Commd 28/3/43. Sqn Ldr 1/7/53. Retd GD 18/6/70.
DOBBIE J.A.A. BSc. Born 30/11/38. Commd 28/9/60. Flt Lt 28/3/65. Retd GD 31/5/90.
DOBBS A.C. Born 29/5/43. Commd 24/6/65. Sqn Ldr 1/7/83. Retd GD 26/6/98.
DOBBS P.F. Born 26/12/46. Commd 1/3/68. Sqn Ldr 1/7/80. Retd ENG 12/11/90.
DOBBS S.S. OBE. Born 10/3/12. Commd 22/4/43. Wg Cdr 1/7/59. Retd ENG 10/3/67.
DOBBY V. Born 20/3/43. Commd 11/6/81. Flt Lt 11/6/84. Retd GD 12/10/97.
DOBEL M.J. Born 29/4/42. Commd 1/3/68. Sqn Ldr 1/1/74. Retd SEC 29/4/81.
DOBIE I.M. Born 3/4/46. Commd 15/6/83. Sqn Ldr 1/7/91. Retd ENG 14/12/96.
DOBIE T.G. OBE MD ChB. Born 23/6/23. Commd 23/7/43. Gp Capt 1/7/69. Retd MED 30/9/72.
DOBLE L.A. OBE FRAeS. Born 6/1/47. Commd 28/4/67. A Cdre 1/1/96. Retd GD 29/12/00.
DOBSON C.W. Born 27/4/21. Commd 13/2/47. Flt Lt 13/2/53. Retd SEC 1/8/64.
DOBSON G.C. Born 7/3/31. Commd 20/1/51. Flt Lt 10/11/55. Retd GD 8/5/85.
DOBSON G.J. DFC BSc. Born 22/5/63. Commd 13/9/81. Flt Lt 15/1/87. Retd GD 21/7/98.
DOBSON G.M. Born 4/5/50. Commd 29/4/71. Flt Lt 29/10/76. Retd GD 1/6/91.
DOBSON J.B. Born 22/8/40. Commd 15/9/67. Sqn Ldr 1/7/82. Retd GD 22/8/95.
DOBSON J.B.M. Born 3/7/33. Commd 27/7/54. Sqn Ldr 1/1/65. Retd GD 3/7/71.
DOBSON M. Born 2/8/22. Commd 3/1/46. Flt Lt 22/5/57. Retd GD 1/10/68.
DOBSON M.F.H. AFC. Born 10/9/24. Commd 7/7/49. Sqn Ldr 1/7/59. Retd GD 9/10/73.
DOBSON M.H. Born 31/5/47. Commd 1/3/68. Sqn Ldr 1/1/81. Retd GD 31/5/91.
DOBSON R.G.R. Born 17/5/26. Commd 22/12/49. Flt Lt 22/6/53. Retd GD 18/5/64.
DOBSON W.J. Born 13/8/25. Commd 26/9/51. Flt Lt 26/3/56. Retd GD 1/10/68.
DOBSON W.J. Born 27/12/33. Commd 27/2/52. Flt Lt 26/6/57. Retd GD 20/12/75.
DOCHERTY J. Born 26/7/36. Commd 1/4/65. Flt Lt 1/4/67. Retd GD 17/12/74.
DOCHERTY J. BDS. Born 27/8/32. Commd 21/7/55. Sqn Ldr 21/8/62. Retd DEL 30/8/66.
DOCKER C.E. Born 25/7/59. Commd 13/3/80. Flt Lt 24/7/86. Retd SUP 31/8/91.
DOCKERTY R. Born 11/9/28. Commd 25/6/66. Flt Lt 25/6/69. Retd GD 1/1/77.
DODD B.J.H. LHA AMCMI. Born 3/6/36. Commd 21/2/69. Sqn Ldr 1/5/80. Retd MED(SEC) 5/1/84.
DODD C.G. MA. Born 16/3/35. Commd 25/10/57. Sqn Ldr 25/4/65. Retd EDN 25/10/73.
DODD D. Born 19/7/33. Commd 17/10/59. Sqn Ldr 1/1/77. Retd GD 3/11/84.
DODD J.B. Born 31/8/46. Commd 18/8/67. Sqn Ldr 1/1/87. Retd GD 14/9/96.
DODD L. Born 27/4/35. Commd 27/4/61. Sqn Ldr 1/7/73. Retd ADMIN 4/11/85.
DODD M.T.B. Born 28/4/39. Commd 28/1/60. Sqn Ldr 1/1/72. Retd ADMIN 28/4/77.
DODD R.L. Born 21/10/36. Commd 3/11/60. Sqn Ldr 1/1/74. Retd GD 1/6/89.
DODDS A. BEM AIIP. Born 18/3/30. Commd 30/7/64. Sqn Ldr 1/7/78. Retd ENG 23/8/80.
DODDS C.N. Born 23/11/40. Commd 12/1/62. Sqn Ldr 1/7/76. Retd GD 1/6/82.
DODDS F.K. Born 1/7/47. Commd 15/2/90. Flt Lt 15/2/94. Retd ENGINEER 1/7/04.
DODDS G. BSc. Born 1/4/40. Commd 2/10/61. Sqn Ldr 1/7/70. Retd GD 26/3/79.
DODDS K.M. Born 29/10/36. Commd 6/4/72. Flt Lt 6/4/78. Retd ADMIN 29/10/86.
DODDS L.W.M. Born 11/2/26. Commd 16/2/49. Flt Lt 19/11/53. Retd GD 8/10/67.
DODDS T.E.D. Born 11/1/38. Commd 9/1/57. Flt Lt 14/1/64. Retd SUP 28/9/67.
DODHY B.M.A. MB ChB. Born 15/6/39. Commd 24/2/75. Wg Cdr 1/8/81. Retd MED 7/4/94.
DODIMEAD D.J. OBE. Born 13/12/24. Commd 24/10/46. Gp Capt 1/7/71. Retd GD 13/12/79.
DODKINS W.J. Born 17/4/23. Commd 19/9/44. Sqn Ldr 1/1/68. Retd SUP 17/4/78.
DODSON G.A.F. Born 2/2/60. Commd 16/12/82. Flt Lt 16/6/88. Retd GD 13/12/99.
DODWORTH P. CB OBE AFC BSc. Born 12/9/40. Commd 2/10/61. AVM 1/1/91. Retd GD 1/10/96.
DOE R.F.T. DSO DFC*. Born 10/3/20. Commd 20/3/39. Wg Cdr 1/1/56. Retd GD 1/4/66.
DOE R.J. Born 17/8/34. Commd 9/4/53. Flt Lt 18/8/58. Retd GD 17/8/72.
DOEL J.E. Born 11/10/39. Commd 14/8/80. Sqn Ldr 1/1/88. Retd ENG 11/10/94.
DOGGART J.M. Born 8/6/47. Commd 28/2/69. Sqn Ldr 1/7/79. Retd GD 3/12/90.

DOGGETT A.C. Born 1/6/31. Commd 17/12/52. Sqn Ldr 1/7/65. Retd GD 1/9/73.
DOGGETT B.P. Born 15/5/49. Commd 12/7/68. A Cdre 1/7/99. Retd GD 30/9/01.
DOGGETT P.G. Born 19/10/35. Commd 11/11/71. Sqn Ldr 1/1/83. Retd SUP 1/8/86.
DOHERTY B.D. BEng AMIEE. Born 23/7/65. Commd 31/7/91. Flt Lt 13/3/96. Retd ENGINEER 24/11/03.
DOHERTY F.W. Born 10/12/22. Commd 23/7/43. Wg Cdr 1/7/61. Retd GD 21/8/70.
DOHERTY G.P. BSc. Born 8/12/61. Commd 11/5/86. Flt Lt 11/11/88. Retd GD 7/8/02.
DOHERTY I.E. Born 21/8/44. Commd 14/2/63. Sqn Ldr 1/7/74. Retd ENG 21/8/88.
DOHERTY J. MSc. Born 7/6/38. Commd 12/9/61. Sqn Ldr 1/1/71. Retd ENG 12/9/77.
DOHERTY L.A. MBE. Born 26/2/64. Commd 20/10/83. Wg Cdr 1/1/00. Retd GD 19/3/05.
DOHERTY M.R. Born 20/4/30. Commd 14/11/51. Flt Lt 14/5/56. Retd GD 20/4/85.
DOHERTY M.V. LLB. Born 16/12/35. Commd 18/8/57. Sqn Ldr 1/1/68. Retd GD 29/6/85.
DOIG C.G. Born 10/6/50. Commd 27/2/70. Sqn Ldr 1/7/86. Retd FLY(N) 10/6/05.
DOIG U.M. Born 9/5/46. Commd 11/8/77. Flt Lt 11/2/84. Retd GD(G) 9/5/84.
DOLAN D.M. Born 6/12/50. Commd 14/8/70. Flt Lt 14/2/76. Retd GD 31/1/98.
DOLBY J.R. MBE. Born 24/1/16. Commd 25/4/43. Sqn Ldr 1/1/63. Retd ENG 17/2/72.
DOLE T.F. MCMI. Born 27/1/37. Commd 1/11/56. Gp Capt 1/7/85. Retd ADMIN 27/1/92.
DOLEMAN R.A. Born 21/3/46. Commd 23/9/66. Flt Lt 14/1/73. Retd GD 21/3/84.
DOLING G.J. Born 31/5/51. Commd 29/6/72. Flt Lt 29/12/77. Retd GD 31/5/89.
DOLING G.J. Born 31/5/51. Commd 29/6/72. Flt Lt 29/12/77. Retd GD 31/5/89.
DOLING P.E. Born 28/4/34. Commd 30/5/58. Sqn Ldr 3/10/68. Retd EDN 6/10/79.
DOLLIMORE R.P. MA. Born 7/7/27. Commd 4/11/48. Wg Cdr 1/7/69. Retd ENG 16/5/78.
DOLMAN A.T. MBE BSc. Born 27/5/47. Commd 16/1/72. Wg Cdr 1/7/89. Retd ENG 21/5/91.
DOLMAN G.H. Born 30/6/34. Commd 26/3/53. Sqn Ldr 1/1/80. Retd GD 30/6/89.
DOLPHIN L. Born 17/6/23. Commd 24/4/47. Sqn Ldr 1/1/73. Retd GD 1/7/78.
DOLTON D.J. BSc. Born 14/2/60. Commd 6/9/81. Flt Lt 6/12/84. Retd GD(G) 15/2/91.
DOMMETT J.B. Born 5/2/33. Commd 14/8/70. Sqn Ldr 1/7/80. Retd ENG 3/4/84.
DON J. BSc. Born 11/10/48. Commd 10/1/71. Flt Lt 10/10/74. Retd OPS SPT(ATC) 11/10/03.
DONACHY J. OBE FCCA. Born 12/6/37. Commd 5/6/67. Wg Cdr 1/7/84. Retd ADMIN 7/8/92.
DONALD A.W.M. Born 16/4/60. Commd 20/10/77. Flt Lt 14/2/85. Retd GD 1/2/93.
DONALD B. Born 6/3/40. Commd 2/5/69. Flt Lt 18/10/75. Retd GD(G) 6/9/90.
DONALD Sir John KBE MB ChB FRCGP FFOM MFCM DTM&H FCMI. Born 7/11/27. Commd 31/8/53. AM 1/7/84.
    Retd MED 31/7/86.
DONALD M. Born 5/6/35. Commd 29/7/54. Flt Lt 5/10/60. Retd GD 1/11/68.
DONALD M.H. Born 8/6/51. Commd 23/10/86. Sqn Ldr 1/1/97. Retd ENGINEER 21/4/03.
DONALDSON M.P. MBE. Born 22/7/43. Commd 22/2/63. AVM 1/7/93. Retd GD 14/9/96.
DONALDSON W.F. Born 7/9/29. Commd 11/10/51. Flt Lt 25/1/57. Retd GD 30/11/68.
DONALDSON-DAVIDSON D. Born 28/2/23. Commd 26/11/53. Sqn Ldr 1/1/70. Retd GD 7/1/72.
DONDERS B. Born 22/12/32. Commd 8/11/51. Sqn Ldr 1/7/77. Retd GD 20/1/84.
DONEY G.E. Born 15/7/45. Commd 11/6/81. Sqn Ldr 1/1/91. Retd ENG 22/4/94.
DONEY T.M. BA. Born 13/10/76. Commd 7/2/99. Fg Off 7/8/98. Retd OPS SPT(FC) 3/6/03.
DONKIN P.E. Born 15/5/48. Commd 28/4/67. Flt Lt 28/10/72. Retd GD 17/5/93.
DONLAN P. Born 8/2/38. Commd 26/8/66. Wg Cdr 1/7/80. Retd GD(G) 8/2/93.
DONMALL N.E.G. Born 12/12/22. Commd 8/11/41. Flt Lt 17/5/56. Retd GD(G) 12/12/77.
DONNELLY B. Born 14/12/41. Commd 13/10/61. Flt Lt 13/4/67. Retd GD 14/12/79.
DONNELLY D.A. MRIN. Born 6/2/45. Commd 15/7/66. Wg Cdr 1/1/90. Retd GD 6/6/00.
DONNELLY J. AFM*. Born 19/3/44. Commd 19/3/81. Flt Lt 19/3/84. Retd GD 19/9/01.
DONNELLY J.M. Born 29/7/43. Commd 6/11/64. Wg Cdr 1/1/86. Retd GD 1/2/94.
DONNELLY P.P. MA. Born 12/2/49. Commd 19/9/71. Sqn Ldr 1/1/86. Retd ADMIN (SEC) 12/2/04.
DONNISON E. BSc BDS BA LDSRCS. Born 12/5/38. Commd 7/8/59. Gp Capt 1/1/92. Retd DEL 12/5/96.
DONOHOE W.J. Born 26/10/30. Commd 30/7/52. Sqn Ldr 1/1/68. Retd ENG 31/8/69.
DONOHUE A. Born 5/4/36. Commd 5/9/69. Flt Lt 5/9/71. Retd PRT 28/2/75.
DONOHUE P.F. MCMI. Born 1/4/28. Commd 24/12/53. Sqn Ldr 1/7/68. Retd ADMIN 1/4/80.
DONOVAN C.P. Born 18/12/24. Commd 27/1/45. Gp Capt 1/7/72. Retd GD 18/12/82.
DONOVAN F.T. Born 28/2/13. Commd 9/12/54. Flt Lt 9/12/57. Retd SEC 22/6/64.
DOOLE W.J. Born 28/7/48. Commd 25/8/67. Fg Offr 21/12/70. Retd RGT 12/5/74.
DOONAN D.K. BSc. Born 22/3/61. Commd 30/10/83. Flt Lt 30/4/87. Retd ADMIN 30/10/99.
DOONAN J.S. MCMI. Born 24/10/34. Commd 28/4/61. Sqn Ldr 1/7/76. Retd GD 24/10/89.
DOORNE R.L. BA. Born 2/3/34. Commd 26/9/53. Sqn Ldr 1/7/67. Retd ENG 2/3/72.
DORA M.J. MSc BSc MCMI. Born 11/5/54. Commd 3/9/72. Sqn Ldr 1/7/87. Retd SUP 14/3/97.
DORAN A.P. Born 20/10/33. Commd 19/1/56. Sqn Ldr 1/7/71. Retd SEC 20/11/81.
DORAN F.E. OBE. Born 8/9/22. Commd 28/4/45. Gp Capt 1/1/75. Retd GD(G) 30/3/78.
DOREY A.J. Born 20/2/48. Commd 27/2/70. Flt Lt 27/8/72. Retd GD 28/8/93.
DORLING R.F. BMedSci MB ChB MRCGP DRCOG DAvMed AFOM. Born 3/4/49. Commd 21/11/71. Sqn Ldr 4/9/80.
    Retd MED 18/7/88.
DORMAN T.R. BA. Born 27/4/55. Commd 15/9/74. Sqn Ldr 1/1/88. Retd SUP 31/10/00.
DORMAN-JACKSON C.I. Born 20/3/38. Commd 10/12/57. Sqn Ldr 1/7/77. Retd GD 21/11/88.

DORN A. Born 13/2/49. Commd 2/2/68. Flt Lt 23/5/74. Retd GD(G) 13/2/87.
DORNAN C.R. Born 7/2/35. Commd 1/2/60. Flt Lt 1/2/60. Retd GD 1/2/76.
DORRETT I. Born 27/4/39. Commd 25/7/60. Gp Capt 1/7/87. Retd SUP 28/2/95.
DORRICOTT G.H. Born 3/3/30. Commd 7/5/52. Sqn Ldr 1/1/70. Retd GD 27/7/73.
DORSETT R.C.T. Born 4/1/24. Commd 21/7/55. Flt Lt 21/7/61. Retd GD 13/7/74.
DORWARD P.J.G. Born 11/8/57. Commd 9/5/91. Fg Offr 26/3/84. Retd ENG 2/4/93.
DORWARD S.G. FCMI. Born 6/2/49. Commd 26/5/67. Wg Cdr 1/1/86. Retd GD(G) 14/3/96.
DOSWELL B.E. Born 25/4/42. Commd 20/9/68. Flt Lt 12/5/72. Retd GD 1/11/75.
DOUBLE J. DFC. Born 23/11/21. Commd 27/2/44. Flt Lt 27/8/47. Retd GD 23/11/64.
DOUBLE L. Born 11/6/20. Commd 10/8/44. Flt Lt 30/6/49. Retd SUP 14/2/50.
DOUBLEDAY M. CEng MIEE. Born 1/2/22. Commd 20/4/54. Flt Lt 20/4/59. Retd ENG 5/2/72.
DOUBLEDAY M. BA. Born 20/6/34. Commd 27/9/57. Sqn Ldr 27/3/65. Retd EDN 29/6/68.
DOUCE R.J. Born 26/6/55. Commd 29/4/81. Flt Lt 30/4/83. Retd GD 1/2/91.
DOUCH A.J. MA MRAeS FCMI. Born 26/10/17. Commd 25/6/38. Wg Cdr 1/1/53. Retd GD 8/6/72.
DOUGAN W.W. Born 22/10/17. Commd 6/1/55. Flt Lt 6/1/58. Retd GD 18/7/68.
DOUGHTY R. Born 28/7/48. Commd 20/6/91. Flt Lt 20/6/95. Retd ENGINEER 28/7/03.
DOUGLAS A.G. CBE MC. Born 6/2/17. Commd 14/12/38. A Cdre 1/1/67. Retd RGT 7/8/70.
DOUGLAS A.G. BA. Born 13/9/38. Commd 28/9/60. Flt Lt 28/6/62. Retd GD 27/12/67.
DOUGLAS G.A. MB ChB FFARCS. Born 13/2/48. Commd 30/9/68. Wg Cdr 8/8/85. Retd MED 12/7/87.
DOUGLAS G.J. IEng AMRAeS. Born 26/7/58. Commd 29/1/87. Flt Lt 29/1/89. Retd ENG 26/7/96.
DOUGLAS I. Born 7/10/35. Commd 2/8/68. Sqn Ldr 1/7/80. Retd ENG 7/10/93.
DOUGLAS I.A.McC. Born 7/1/39. Commd 1/4/58. Wg Cdr 1/7/85. Retd GD 7/1/94.
DOUGLAS J.P. Born 17/6/27. Commd 9/12/48. Sqn Ldr 1/1/61. Retd GD 17/6/61.
DOUGLAS J.R.H. BSc CEng MRAeS. Born 9/6/49. Commd 23/9/68. Sqn Ldr 1/1/81. Retd ENG 9/6/88.
DOUGLAS J.S. OBE. Born 24/4/45. Commd 25/3/64. Wg Cdr 1/1/89. Retd GD 24/4/00.
DOUGLAS K.M. Born 3/2/46. Commd 8/1/65. Wg Cdr 1/1/86. Retd GD 4/6/03.
DOUGLAS R.M. Born 24/1/45. Commd 20/9/68. Flt Lt 10/7/71. Retd GD 1/5/76.
DOUGLAS S. Born 1/2/64. Commd 23/5/85. Fg Offr 31/7/86. Retd GD(G) 25/9/89.
DOUGLAS S.S. Born 3/3/23. Commd 7/4/44. Sqn Ldr 1/7/55. Retd GD 4/4/66.
DOUGLAS-BEVERIDGE A.J. CEng MRAeS MIEE. Born 10/3/40. Commd 18/7/61. Sqn Ldr 1/7/70.
    Retd ENG 10/3/78.
DOUGLASS M.P. AFC. Born 11/9/49. Commd 8/8/69. Sqn Ldr 1/7/87. Retd GD 1/7/90.
DOURISH G.A. Born 11/10/46. Commd 14/2/91. Flt Lt 14/2/95. Retd ENGINEER 11/10/03.
DOUTY P.A. OBE CEng MIMechE MRAeS. Born 8/5/34. Commd 25/7/56. Wg Cdr 1/1/73. Retd ENG 7/11/85.
DOUXCHAMPS F. Born 11/11/15. Commd 15/3/50. Flt Offr 15/3/56. Retd GD(G) 11/11/65.
DOVE A.N.E. BSc. Born 18/12/62. Commd 30/8/87. Flt Lt 28/2/89. Retd GD 14/9/96.
DOVE B. AFC. Born 25/11/43. Commd 8/12/61. Wg Cdr 1/7/81. Retd GD 18/10/97.
DOVE-DIXON B.W. Born 19/2/33. Commd 4/10/51. Sqn Ldr 1/1/71. Retd GD(G) 13/4/79.
DOVER I.P. Born 22/5/62. Commd 22/11/84. Flt Lt 22/5/90. Retd GD 22/5/00.
DOVESTON A.E.J. MIDPM. Born 28/3/47. Commd 17/7/70. Sqn Ldr 1/7/84. Retd SUP 27/6/88.
DOVEY A.R. Born 17/2/31. Commd 12/11/54. Flt Lt 16/8/61. Retd GD 1/8/82.
DOW A.M. Born 7/7/32. Commd 11/10/51. Flt Lt 25/1/57. Retd GD 12/11/86.
DOW E.M. OBE. Born 1/7/15. Commd 17/6/40. Wg Offr 1/1/50. Retd SEC 17/10/54. rtg Gp Offr
DOW I.H. Born 24/11/46. Commd 2/8/68. Sqn Ldr 1/1/76. Retd GD 24/11/96.
DOWD R.K. BSc. Born 23/9/45. Commd 22/9/65. Flt Lt 15/4/69. Retd GD 1/4/85.
DOWDALL N.P. MB ChB MRCGP DRCOG DAvMed. Born 1/8/57. Commd 1/1/79. Wg Cdr 1/8/95.
    Retd MED 31/12/96.
DOWDESWELL D. MCMI. Born 17/1/27. Commd 2/6/61. Gp Capt 1/1/80. Retd MED(SEC) 1/1/83.
DOWDESWELL J.L. BSc. Born 3/2/65. Commd 18/12/92. Sqn Ldr 1/7/99. Retd FLY(P) 3/9/03.
DOWDS T. MSc BA. Born 20/6/48. Commd 2/3/78. Sqn Ldr 1/1/86. Retd ENG 14/5/01.
DOWELL A.McL. BA MCSP DipTP. Born 14/11/31. Commd 6/9/68. Sqn Ldr 23/10/79. Retd MED(T) 2/6/81.
DOWER N.S. FCMI. Born 11/4/21. Commd 8/3/43. Gp Capt 1/1/67. Retd GD(G) 16/6/72.
DOWER W.D.K. Born 10/11/21. Commd 4/10/60. Flt Lt 4/10/63. Retd GD(G) 30/5/70.
DOWLER R.R.J. Born 9/10/46. Commd 1/3/68. Flt Lt 1/3/71. Retd GD 3/10/78.
DOWLING B.R.C. CEng MRAes MIMechE. Born 17/6/39. Commd 28/7/60. Sqn Ldr 1/1/70. Retd ENG 7/8/84.
DOWLING D.E. Born 13/4/23. Commd 13/2/64. Flt Lt 13/2/69. Retd ENG 1/10/74.
DOWLING D.E.B. AFC. Born 18/6/30. Commd 11/4/51. Gp Capt 1/7/74. Retd GD 12/6/81.
DOWLING F.J. MCMI. Born 10/10/30. Commd 30/1/70. Sqn Ldr 1/7/80. Retd ADMIN 31/8/85.
DOWLING F.N. Born 3/9/41. Commd 28/3/66. Flt Lt 13/4/70. Retd RGT 31/3/73.
DOWLING F.W. OBE. Born 30/5/15. Commd 25/4/40. Wg Cdr 1/7/57. Retd SEC 30/5/70.
DOWLING J.E. Born 20/4/51. Commd 8/8/69. Sqn Ldr 1/7/87. Retd GD 1/7/90.
DOWN A.M. Born 7/8/46. Commd 14/8/64. Sqn Ldr 1/1/84. Retd GD 1/1/91.
DOWN B.J. Born 24/5/36. Commd 23/6/67. Flt Lt 4/11/70. Retd ENG 23/6/75.
DOWN L.M. MSc BEng CEng MIMechE. Born 15/10/50. Commd 22/4/71. Wg Cdr 1/1/87. Retd ENG 30/9/90.
DOWNER R.R. Born 31/5/44. Commd 4/11/82. Sqn Ldr 1/7/89. Retd ADMIN 1/6/97.
DOWNER S.V.B. Born 29/1/33. Commd 12/11/54. Flt Lt 26/2/64. Retd GD 29/1/71.

DOWNES B.R. Born 8/8/31. Commd 13/9/51. Sqn Ldr 1/7/66. Retd ADMIN 1/12/83.
DOWNES C.B.W. Born 14/1/23. Commd 30/5/44. Sqn Ldr 1/1/55. Retd GD 27/10/61.
DOWNES D.T. Born 13/5/45. Commd 16/5/74. Sqn Ldr 1/7/81. Retd ENG 10/8/98.
DOWNES M. Born 16/12/16. Commd 7/4/44. Sqn Ldr 1/10/54. Retd GD 6/3/58.
DOWNES N.J. Born 22/1/42. Commd 20/8/65. Flt Lt 20/2/71. Retd GD 3/5/81.
DOWNES R.N. BSc MB BS. Born 29/4/52. Commd 22/1/74. Wg Cdr 23/1/91. Retd MED 10/8/92.
DOWNEY D.B.G. MBE. Born 10/10/35. Commd 5/5/54. Sqn Ldr 1/7/85. Retd GD 12/10/88.
DOWNEY J.C.T. CB DFC AFC. Born 26/11/20. Commd 24/6/39. AVM 1/1/70. Retd GD 13/12/75.
DOWNEY T.R. Born 20/1/30. Commd 13/2/52. Sqn Ldr 1/7/67. Retd GD 12/4/76.
DOWNEY W.R.H. MB BCh FRCP DCH. Born 8/2/30. Commd 6/1/57. Gp Capt 8/1/79. Retd MED 3/4/85.
DOWNING J.W. CEng MIEE MRAeS. Born 19/6/40. Commd 15/12/60. Sqn Ldr 1/1/72. Retd ENG 30/7/77.
DOWNING M.R. Born 25/5/43. Commd 9/3/62. Flt Lt 9/9/67. Retd GD 27/5/76.
DOWNING P.W. Born 22/12/24. Commd 19/5/49. Flt Lt 19/11/52. Retd GD 13/3/64.
DOWNING R.E. Born 10/7/32. Commd 22/1/54. Flt Lt 22/7/59. Retd GD 10/7/70.
DOWNING W.G. Born 6/3/20. Commd 22/2/51. Sqn Ldr 1/1/66. Retd GD 31/7/68.
DOWNS D.E. Born 22/1/35. Commd 19/11/63. Flt Lt 1/4/66. Retd GD 22/1/73.
DOWNS D.H. OBE. Born 13/6/22. Commd 4/12/42. Wg Cdr 1/7/67. Retd GD 31/7/73.
DOWNS E.J. MBE. Born 24/9/21. Commd 23/11/43. Sqn Ldr 1/4/55. Retd GD 24/9/70.
DOWNS E.J.R. Born 19/6/25. Commd 27/11/46. Sqn Ldr 1/1/61. Retd GD 30/8/68.
DOWNS E.L. BSc. Born 11/1/62. Commd 31/8/80. Flt Lt 15/4/85. Retd GD 1/4/96.
DOWNS J.W. Born 11/4/31. Commd 3/1/54. Flt Lt 21/7/61. Retd GD(G) 11/4/69.
DOWNS R.D. Born 10/8/31. Commd 30/12/54. Sqn Ldr 1/1/71. Retd GD 11/1/84.
DOYE C.C. Born 2/2/45. Commd 8/4/82. Wg Cdr 1/7/95. Retd ENG 10/4/98.
DOYLE A.J.R. AFC. Born 17/1/34. Commd 19/12/58. Sqn Ldr 1/7/68. Retd GD 19/1/73.
DOYLE B.J. Born 27/4/44. Commd 17/12/64. Flt Lt 17/6/67. Retd GD 1/1/76.
DOYLE B.M. OBE. Born 10/10/40. Commd 29/11/63. Wg Cdr 1/7/84. Retd GD 26/12/95.
DOYLE J.F. Born 21/4/35. Commd 3/2/63. Sqn Ldr 26/8/64. Retd MED 1/2/72.
DOYLE K. Born 2/5/51. Commd 7/11/91. Fg Offr 7/11/91. Retd ENG 2/4/93.
DOYLE L. Born 23/11/65. Commd 28/9/89. Flt Lt 1/9/94. Retd SUP 14/3/96.
DOYLE P.E. Born 3/6/24. Commd 17/6/54. Sqn Ldr 1/7/73. Retd GD 2/4/80.
DOYLE P.J. BSc. Born 8/1/70. Commd 14/8/94. Flt Lt 14/2/97. Retd SUPPLY 14/8/03.
DOYLE-DAVIDSON M.J.S. MCMI. Born 16/1/38. Commd 1/4/58. Gp Capt 1/1/92. Retd GD 16/1/93.
DRABBLE K.W. Born 11/3/18. Commd 20/12/45. Sqn Ldr 1/1/58. Retd ENG 11/3/73.
DRAGE F.L.G. Born 17/1/24. Commd 8/9/44. Sqn Ldr 1/7/58. Retd GD 17/1/84.
DRAKE B. DSO DFC*. Born 20/12/17. Commd 7/9/36. Wg Cdr 1/1/53. Retd GD 1/7/63. rtg Gp Capt
DRAKE B.R. Born 5/9/40. Commd 9/10/64. Sqn Ldr 1/7/73. Retd GD 30/9/82.
DRAKE D.A. Born 1/9/47. Commd 7/7/67. Flt Lt 7/1/73. Retd GD 30/9/75.
DRAKE D.R. Born 8/5/44. Commd 22/2/63. Flt Lt 12/11/69. Retd GD 8/5/82.
DRAKE E.L.D. DFC* AFC. Born 10/10/20. Commd 27/3/42. Wg Cdr 1/7/58. Retd GD 16/7/66.
DRAKE P.H. MB BS MRCS MRCOG LRCP. Born 21/6/25. Commd 1/6/58. Gp Capt 1/7/74. Retd MED 4/8/77.
DRAKE R.J. Born 9/2/22. Commd 22/2/67. Flt Lt 22/9/70. Retd ENG 9/2/82.
DRAKE W.M. Born 25/10/25. Commd 29/3/45. Sqn Ldr 1/1/60. Retd GD 28/1/77.
DRANE S.A. Born 2/4/24. Commd 1/4/52. Wg Cdr 1/1/72. Retd ADMIN 1/4/77.
DRAPER A.B. Born 14/3/39. Commd 23/12/60. Flt Lt 23/6/66. Retd GD 5/4/84.
DRAPER A.R. Born 3/12/28. Commd 2/3/49. Flt Lt 9/9/60. Retd SUP 3/12/66.
DRAPER E.E.J. Born 18/4/42. Commd 5/1/70. Sqn Ldr 1/1/81. Retd ENG 17/4/93.
DRAPER W.J.B.P. Born 21/2/38. Commd 28/2/56. Flt Lt 15/2/65. Retd GD 11/12/72.
DRAYTON D.L.J.A. Born 8/7/30. Commd 22/7/66. Fg Offr 22/7/66. Retd SUP 8/9/68.
DREA T.A.F. Born 31/7/19. Commd 6/6/57. Flt Lt 1/4/63. Retd ENG 17/12/67.
DREW C.D. Born 1/6/36. Commd 30/7/57. Flt Lt 30/7/62. Retd SEC 1/6/74.
DREW C.D. Born 6/11/49. Commd 1/12/77. Sqn Ldr 1/7/87. Retd ENG 1/7/90.
DREW D.J. Born 31/7/47. Commd 1/5/68. Flt Lt 1/5/71. Retd GD 31/7/02.
DREW F.R. CBE. Born 2/5/09. Commd 27/7/29. Gp Capt 1/7/47. Retd GD 1/6/57.
DREW G. BA MCMI. Born 25/10/31. Commd 14/7/55. Sqn Ldr 17/2/65. Retd EDN 14/7/71.
DREW H.A.W. AFC FCMI. Born 17/11/38. Commd 2/5/59. Gp Capt 1/1/87. Retd GD 20/4/90.
DREW J.K. Born 15/3/36. Commd 4/5/59. Flt Lt 28/6/64. Retd GD 4/5/75.
DREW J.M. Born 6/11/22. Commd 23/6/60. Flt Lt 23/6/63. Retd GD 6/11/73.
DREWERY C.C. Born 28/2/63. Commd 13/8/82. Sqn Ldr 1/1/94. Retd GD 28/5/01.
DREWITT B. MA CEng MRAeS. Born 9/12/40. Commd 30/9/59. Sqn Ldr 1/1/73. Retd ENG 9/5/81.
DRING B.N. Born 31/7/37. Commd 8/10/79. Sqn Ldr 5/10/78. Retd SUP 6/10/87.
DRING C.A. Born 29/7/50. Commd 19/3/81. Flt Lt 19/3/83. Retd OPS SPT 16/9/00.
DRINKELL W.G. DFC AFC. Born 23/11/21. Commd 26/4/43. Sqn Ldr 1/10/54. Retd GD 20/4/68.
DRINKWATER E. Born 18/7/32. Commd 6/12/51. Flt Lt 13/11/57. Retd GD 18/7/90.
DRINKWATER G.M. Born 8/4/65. Commd 26/9/91. Flt Lt 26/9/93. Retd FLY(P) 24/8/03.
DRINKWATER R. Born 8/2/36. Commd 6/4/72. Flt Lt 6/4/77. Retd ADMIN 1/10/77.
DRISCOLL G.P. BSc. Born 15/7/54. Commd 17/9/72. Sqn Ldr 1/7/84. Retd ENG 18/9/92.

DRISSELL P. BA. Born 2/5/57. Commd 28/9/80. Sqn Ldr 1/1/87. Retd ADMIN 14/3/96.
DRIVER A.C. Born 2/7/16. Commd 17/10/42. Fg Offr 28/12/49. Retd GD 1/3/51. rtg Flt Lt
DRIVER D.F. Born 22/7/30. Commd 2/7/52. Flt Lt 8/1/58. Retd GD 29/8/64.
DRIVER J.W. DFC. Born 21/1/12. Commd 6/7/44. Flt Lt 6/7/50. Retd GD(G) 29/1/62.
DRIVER K.C. Born 14/5/30. Commd 11/11/65. Wg Cdr 1/7/84. Retd ENG 14/5/88.
DRIVER R.E.A. Born 26/1/24. Commd 22/3/51. Flt Lt 14/11/56. Retd GD 26/1/82.
DRIVER V.R. BA. Born 15/10/41. Commd 3/10/74. Sqn Ldr 1/7/81. Retd ENG 8/1/96.
DROWN R.W. Born 6/11/21. Commd 6/5/44. Sqn Ldr 1/7/73. Retd GD 6/11/76. Re-instated 29/12/76 to 4/12/82.
DRU DRURY S.G. MBE CEng MIEE. Born 29/4/39. Commd 2/3/65. Sqn Ldr 1/7/73. Retd ENG 29/4/94.
DRUITT R.K. BSc. Born 6/3/50. Commd 23/9/68. Sqn Ldr 1/1/89. Retd FLY(P) 6/3/05.
DRUMMOND G.K. Born 11/8/34. Commd 10/10/63. Flt Lt 10/10/69. Retd GD 26/10/74.
DRUMMOND J.A. BSc AMBCS. Born 2/6/42. Commd 19/8/68. Wg Cdr 1/1/88. Retd ADMIN 2/10/90.
DRUMMOND J.M. Born 16/5/33. Commd 15/12/53. Flt Lt 15/12/58. Retd SEC 27/1/68.
DRUMMOND-HAY P.D.F. Born 28/8/21. Commd 19/8/44. Sqn Ldr 1/1/61. Retd GD(G) 28/9/70.
DRUREY S.J. Born 25/12/58. Commd 28/6/79. Sqn Ldr 1/1/95. Retd GD 1/1/98.
DRURY K.A. DFM. Born 9/6/23. Commd 12/5/44. Sqn Ldr 1/7/73. Retd GD 9/6/83.
DRURY R.G. BSc. Born 26/2/54. Commd 17/9/72. Flt Lt 15/10/78. Retd ENG 15/7/87.
DRYBURGH G.D. Born 6/5/46. Commd 11/10/84. Flt Lt 11/10/88. Retd ENG 2/4/99.
DRYBURGH J. Born 15/12/25. Commd 5/1/55. Flt Lt 22/1/62. Retd GD 20/7/66.
DRYBURGH J.J. Born 27/1/32. Commd 1/2/62. Sqn Ldr 1/7/73. Retd ENG 7/10/83.
DRYDEN D.W. MCMI. Born 2/12/48. Commd 2/6/67. Sqn Ldr 1/1/89. Retd GD(G) 2/6/94.
DRYDEN W.E. Born 4/12/41. Commd 31/8/78. Sqn Ldr 1/1/90. Retd SY 11/7/94.
DRYLAND G.N. Born 12/12/44. Commd 15/7/66. Flt Lt 15/1/69. Retd GD 30/4/76.
DRYSDALE J.D. CBE FCMI. Born 1/8/33. Commd 1/9/54. Gp Capt 1/7/80. Retd GD 1/11/87.
DRYSDALE P.A. Born 20/4/27. Commd 14/11/51. Flt Lt 14/5/56. Retd GD 20/4/70.
DRYSDALE S.C.Y. Born 1/12/28. Commd 2/1/52. Flt Lt 2/1/58. Retd GD 1/6/67.
DU BOULAY J.F.H. CBE DFC. Born 1/1/13. Commd 17/12/32. Wg Cdr 1/6/41. Retd GD 3/6/46. rtg Gp Capt
DU FEU D.F. Born 7/5/30. Commd 8/11/51. Flt Lt 23/2/57. Retd GD 7/6/68.
DU PLESSIS R.P. Born 22/3/30. Commd 2/7/52. Sqn Ldr 1/7/66. Retd GD 1/7/69.
DUBIENIEC A.P. Born 2/6/56. Commd 22/8/80. Flt Lt 15/4/84. Retd ADMIN 2/6/94.
DUBOCK R.M. OBE AFC. Born 20/10/22. Commd 29/1/43. Wg Cdr 1/1/69. Retd GD 30/4/77.
DUCKENFIELD B.L. AFC. Born 15/4/17. Commd 1/4/40. Gp Capt 1/1/66. Retd GD 28/6/69.
DUCKER M.G. Born 22/6/53. Commd 27/7/72. Flt Lt 27/1/78. Retd GD 1/9/79.
DUCKETT E.T. Born 1/6/24. Commd 29/6/44. Wg Cdr 1/7/71. Retd SEC 1/6/74.
DUCKETT R.B. CVO AFC. Born 5/6/42. Commd 30/7/63. A Cdre 1/7/88. Retd GD 4/5/96.
DUCKHAM J.L. BSc. Born 3/7/51. Commd 26/9/69. Sqn Ldr 1/7/87. Retd GD 1/7/90.
DUCKMANTON G.R. Born 24/5/46. Commd 24/4/70. Sqn Ldr 1/7/84. Retd SUP 16/7/94.
DUCKWORTH D.J. MCMI. Born 28/1/44. Commd 5/5/69. Sqn Ldr 1/1/81. Retd ADMIN 11/1/96.
DUCKWORTH P. MBE. Born 26/6/38. Commd 22/2/63. Sqn Ldr 1/7/73. Retd GD 3/7/84.
DUDDY J. Born 4/11/42. Commd 4/7/85. Sqn Ldr 27/6/93. Retd MED(T) 24/4/96.
DUDGEON M.G. OBE. Born 6/11/43. Commd 17/12/65. Wg Cdr 1/1/92. Retd GD 6/11/00.
DUDLEY E.E. Born 3/8/33. Commd 28/1/53. Flt Lt 17/6/58. Retd GD 3/8/71.
DUDLEY M.J. Born 29/9/58. Commd 13/12/79. Flt Lt 13/6/85. Retd GD 18/3/91.
DUDLEY P.T.McD. Born 25/3/27. Commd 14/11/51. Flt Lt 14/5/56. Retd GD 25/3/65.
DUDLEY T.H. Born 25/9/16. Commd 12/9/46. Flt Lt 27/5/54. Retd SUP 13/5/55.
DUFF I.R. Born 6/8/40. Commd 25/6/65. Sqn Ldr 1/1/81. Retd ADMIN 25/11/84.
DUFF L. Born 31/12/46. Commd 11/2/65. Wg Cdr 1/1/92. Retd ADMIN 31/8/96.
DUFF M.C. Born 14/2/34. Commd 8/1/57. Flt Lt 1/7/62. Retd GD 1/11/75.
DUFFIELD A.F. Born 29/2/20. Commd 27/12/43. Sqn Ldr 1/7/56. Retd GD 1/6/62.
DUFFILL G.E. Born 30/11/22. Commd 2/10/58. Flt Lt 2/10/64. Retd ENG 10/11/77.
DUFFIN P.A.R. BA BA MRIN MRAeS. Born 14/3/44. Commd 24/7/63. Wg Cdr 1/1/91. Retd GD 14/3/99.
DUFFIN S.V. BSc(Eng) CEng MRAeS ACGI. Born 29/9/46. Commd 23/9/65. Wg Cdr 1/7/85. Retd ENG 29/9/90.
DUFFUS J.C. Born 9/9/57. Commd 20/1/80. Sqn Ldr 1/7/90. Retd ADMIN 19/8/96.
DUFFY G.J.M. Born 11/2/62. Commd 17/7/87. Flt Lt 21/1/91. Retd SUP 11/2/03.
DUFFY J. DFM. Born 25/9/21. Commd 4/6/44. Sqn Ldr 1/7/58. Retd GD(G) 25/9/76.
DUFFY M.G. MMar. Born 27/6/39. Commd 28/2/66. Sqn Ldr 1/7/75. Retd MAR 28/2/82.
DUFTON A. MCIPD MCMI. Born 23/11/32. Commd 27/7/54. Wg Cdr 1/7/73. Retd ADMIN 29/1/77.
DUFTON H. FCMI MCIPS. Born 16/11/21. Commd 16/1/50. Gp Capt 1/7/70. Retd SUP 16/11/76.
DUGDALE A. Born 27/11/17. Commd 5/3/53. Flt Lt 12/8/58. Retd ENG 31/8/68.
DUGDALE A.T. DFC. Born 27/6/22. Commd 22/6/44. Flt Lt 22/12/47. Retd GD 31/12/61.
DUGDALE K.R. MSc BSc ARCS. Born 15/9/46. Commd 13/9/70. Sqn Ldr 13/3/77. Retd ADMIN 13/9/86.
DUGDALE M.R. MB ChB MRCS LRCP DRCOG. Born 28/7/49. Commd 16/4/72. Wg Cdr 14/9/86. Retd MED 14/10/88.
DUGGAN C.E. Born 30/5/64. Commd 7/11/91. Flt Lt 7/11/93. Retd SUP 2/12/96.
DUGGAN G.H. Born 9/1/30. Commd 7/12/56. Sqn Ldr 1/7/67. Retd CAT 3/8/69.
DUGGAN T.E. Born 1/5/47. Commd 28/2/69. Sqn Ldr 1/7/81. Retd GD 1/6/98.
DUGUID A.G. MA. Born 14/1/25. Commd 12/7/50. Gp Capt 1/1/76. Retd ADMIN 14/1/80.

DUGUID M. Born 10/4/48. Commd 22/9/69. Wg Cdr 1/7/93. Retd ENG 27/10/01.
DUGUID M.D. MA MCMI. Born 18/4/47. Commd 24/9/67. Wg Cdr 1/1/88. Retd SUP 19/2/97.
DUKE P.M. Born 29/5/43. Commd 6/7/62. Flt Lt 6/1/68. Retd GD 1/1/73.
DUKE R.C.E. Born 23/9/32. Commd 4/7/51. Flt Lt 22/5/57. Retd GD 23/9/77. Re-instated 8/4/81. Retd 8/5/87.
DULAKE E.A. Born 1/10/57. Commd 3/5/81. Sqn Ldr 1/1/91. Retd ADMIN 5/7/91.
DULAKE I.G.L. Born 9/7/47. Commd 2/1/77. Sqn Ldr 1/1/88. Retd ADMIN 2/1/93.
DULSON P.P. Born 8/2/48. Commd 14/8/70. Flt Lt 14/8/75. Retd GD 31/3/86.
DULY S.V. MBE. Born 23/8/38. Commd 5/12/63. Sqn Ldr 1/7/74. Retd SUP 23/8/93.
DUMMER F.G. CEng MRAeS MCMI. Born 17/7/19. Commd 15/4/43. Wg Cdr 1/7/59. Retd ENG 17/7/74.
DUMMER P.J. BA. Born 30/10/38. Commd 28/9/60. Sqn Ldr 1/7/73. Retd GD 10/10/97.
DUNBAR R.C. DFM MCMI MCIPD. Born 7/10/21. Commd 20/11/42. Wg Cdr 1/7/68. Retd SEC 15/4/72.
DUNCALF R.J. Born 3/1/56. Commd 27/1/77. Flt Lt 27/7/82. Retd GD 1/10/97.
DUNCAN A. BSc DCAe CEng MIEE. Born 31/1/34. Commd 2/4/59. Sqn Ldr 11/10/65. Retd ENG 24/4/75.
DUNCAN B.C. Born 4/7/60. Commd 20/12/90. Flt Lt 20/12/92. Retd ENG 20/12/98.
DUNCAN D. Born 23/7/22. Commd 27/2/58. Flt Lt 27/2/61. Retd ENG 23/7/77.
DUNCAN D. MSc CEng MRAeS. Born 27/10/22. Commd 26/8/43. Wg Cdr 1/7/63. Retd ENG 27/10/77.
DUNCAN G. Born 20/6/60. Commd 8/5/86. Flt Lt 16/2/89. Retd GD 31/8/98.
DUNCAN G.D. Born 18/8/32. Commd 26/12/51. Sqn Ldr 1/1/80. Retd GD 18/8/93.
DUNCAN H.K.A. BSc. Born 29/6/65. Commd 3/1/88. Sqn Ldr 1/7/94. Retd ADMIN 2/3/97.
DUNCAN I.B. Born 28/1/32. Commd 30/1/52. Flt Lt 30/10/57. Retd GD 25/8/70.
DUNCAN J.C. Born 26/8/28. Commd 21/3/51. Wg Cdr 1/7/75. Retd GD 8/5/81.
DUNCAN J.C. Born 23/7/49. Commd 18/4/74. Wg Cdr 1/1/01. Retd GD 30/4/04.
DUNCAN M.J. Born 21/1/60. Commd 26/11/81. Flt Lt 26/5/88. Retd ADMIN 19/1/96.
DUNCAN P.J. Born 30/9/51. Commd 9/3/72. Sqn Ldr 1/7/87. Retd GD 30/9/90.
DUNCAN R. Born 1/1/31. Commd 17/5/51. Flt Lt 6/9/56. Retd GD 1/1/69.
DUNCAN R.F. Born 2/8/30. Commd 31/3/60. Flt Lt 31/3/66. Retd GD 28/9/76.
DUNCAN R.J. Born 3/12/45. Commd 6/5/66. Flt Lt 6/11/71. Retd GD 13/1/76.
DUNCAN R.P. BSc. Born 28/1/42. Commd 24/1/66. Flt Lt 24/10/67. Retd GD 24/1/82.
DUNCAN T.F. Born 27/6/21. Commd 2/3/45. Flt Lt 2/9/48. Retd GD 28/11/55.
DUNCAN W. Born 19/12/35. Commd 6/9/68. Flt Lt 6/3/71. Retd GD 18/9/76.
DUNCOMBE D.J. BA. Born 23/6/35. Commd 10/9/63. Sqn Ldr 27/2/66. Retd EDN 31/8/72.
DUNCOMBE J.J. AFC. Born 13/6/23. Commd 29/10/45. Wg Cdr 1/1/63. Retd GD 28/2/78.
DUNCOMBE R.A. Born 23/4/21. Commd 27/10/43. Flt Lt 25/1/46. Retd GD 31/8/54.
DUNCOMBE R.F. Born 30/6/20. Commd 15/11/48. Sqn Ldr 1/1/52. Retd RGT 1/11/61.
DUNDAS H.S.L. DSO* DFC. Born 22/7/20. Commd 1/12/42. Wg Cdr 1/5/45. Retd GD 25/1/47. rtg Gp Capt
DUNFORD B.E. MBE. Born 6/11/40. Commd 26/5/67. Wg Cdr 1/7/91. Retd ENG 30/11/95.
DUNGATE J. MBE AFM. Born 17/7/40. Commd 14/8/70. Sqn Ldr 1/1/87. Retd GD 17/7/95.
DUNKLEY P.A. Born 21/2/61. Commd 23/10/86. Flt Lt 23/10/88. Retd GD 25/4/00.
DUNKLEY P.R. IEng MIIE. Born 30/11/45. Commd 27/7/71. Sqn Ldr 1/7/85. Retd ENG 30/6/01.
DUNKLEY R.L. MBE. Born 25/8/22. Commd 26/7/44. Sqn Ldr 1/4/56. Retd GD 25/8/65.
DUNLEAVY B.T. MBE. Born 22/6/51. Commd 23/4/87. Sqn Ldr 1/1/95. Retd ADMIN 1/1/99.
DUNLOP J.G. MA. Born 11/8/27. Commd 5/11/52. Sqn Ldr 5/5/63. Retd EDN 5/11/68.
DUNLOP J.S. BSc. Born 22/1/56. Commd 8/1/89. Flt Lt 8/7/92. Retd ADMIN 14/9/96.
DUNLOP K.E. MBE. Born 20/7/46. Commd 19/8/71. Sqn Ldr 1/1/82. Retd GD(G) 5/4/88.
DUNLOP P. AFC*. Born 14/12/48. Commd 4/2/71. Wg Cdr 1/7/86. Retd GD 14/10/90.
DUNN A. MBE BSc. Born 15/6/23. Commd 19/12/42. Wg Cdr 1/1/65. Retd GD 31/3/78.
DUNN A.P. Born 15/12/23. Commd 16/6/44. Sqn Ldr 1/1/56. Retd GD 31/3/62.
DUNN D.J. BA. Born 1/3/47. Commd 31/8/78. Sqn Ldr 1/7/85. Retd ADMIN 1/7/88.
DUNN Sir Eric KBE CB BEM CEng MRAeS. Born 27/11/27. Commd 12/2/53. AM 1/7/83. Retd ENG 1/7/86.
DUNN E.H. Born 1/11/45. Commd 23/9/66. Wg Cdr 1/1/91. Retd GD 14/3/96.
DUNN I. BDS LDSRCS. Born 18/3/41. Commd 26/2/78. Wg Cdr 29/9/80. Retd DEL 1/4/89.
DUNN J.H. BSc. Born 1/10/52. Commd 25/9/71. Flt Lt 15/4/77. Retd GD 1/10/90.
DUNN J.R. Born 10/5/61. Commd 15/6/83. Sqn Ldr 1/1/95. Retd OPS SPT 10/5/99.
DUNN J.S. Born 13/7/42. Commd 28/9/62. Flt Lt 28/3/68. Retd GD 13/11/80.
DUNN M. Born 2/3/43. Commd 21/12/62. Sqn Ldr 1/7/79. Retd GD(G) 2/3/84. Re-entered 17/4/89. Sqn Ldr 1/7/93. Retd OPS SPT 17/4/99.
DUNN M. Born 7/12/37. Commd 27/5/71. Sqn Ldr 1/1/90. Retd GD 1/6/92.
DUNN M.J. Born 7/12/41. Commd 8/11/70. Flt Lt 30/11/78. Retd SUP 7/1/84.
DUNN M.K. Born 29/8/64. Commd 15/3/84. Sqn Ldr 1/1/98. Retd SUP 29/8/02.
DUNN R.A.E. Born 12/10/32. Commd 27/9/51. Sqn Ldr 1/7/78. Retd GD 3/4/85.
DUNN R.E.L. Born 3/5/36. Commd 28/5/66. Flt Lt 1/7/68. Retd PI 28/5/74.
DUNN S.F. Born 14/8/17. Commd 18/11/53. Flt Lt 18/11/58. Retd GD(G) 9/3/66.
DUNN W.A. Born 13/1/43. Commd 6/4/62. Flt Lt 29/6/69. Retd GD(G) 1/1/74.
DUNN W.H. Born 21/10/30. Commd 6/6/57. Sqn Ldr 1/1/69. Retd GD 1/11/80.
DUNNACHIE D.J. Born 1/3/33. Commd 7/7/66. Sqn Ldr 1/1/85. Retd GD 1/6/91.
DUNNE J. Born 23/1/23. Commd 7/9/61. Flt Lt 7/9/66. Retd GD(G) 1/7/76.

DUNNE J.M. Born 21/10/33. Commd 31/10/63. Sqn Ldr 1/7/79. Retd ENG 18/2/85.
DUNNE P.F. Born 12/2/36. Commd 9/10/75. Sqn Ldr 1/7/87. Retd SUP 12/4/90.
DUNNE T.E.M. MCMI. Born 21/6/25. Commd 14/10/44. Wg Cdr 1/7/66. Retd GD 21/6/80.
DUNNET J.B. Born 25/12/19. Commd 28/5/42. Flt Lt 15/10/51. Retd GD(G) 30/4/66.
DUNNETT E.W. Born 18/1/26. Commd 10/10/63. Flt Lt 10/10/68. Retd SEC 1/2/69.
DUNNETT N.A.W. CEng MIMechE MRAeS. Born 15/10/39. Commd 28/4/64. Sqn Ldr 1/7/72. Retd ENG 28/4/82.
DUNNING A. DFC. Born 2/2/13. Commd 9/8/41. Sqn Ldr 1/7/53. Retd PRT 26/3/55.
DUNNINGHAM N.J.J. Born 4/1/23. Commd 14/8/43. Sqn Ldr 1/7/64. Retd GD 28/8/74.
DUNNINGTON N. FCMI. Born 12/2/38. Commd 5/7/68. Wg Cdr 1/1/81. Retd ADMIN 2/10/85.
DUNPHY D.G. CEng MIMechE MRAeS MCMI. Born 11/7/18. Commd 22/10/41. Wg Cdr 1/7/58. Retd ENG 15/4/67.
DUNSCOMBE F.L. Born 26/10/23. Commd 10/3/44. Sqn Ldr 1/1/62. Retd GD(G) 30/4/66.
DUNSFORD E.C. BEM MCMI. Born 20/10/31. Commd 19/12/63. Sqn Ldr 1/1/75. Retd GD(AEO) 20/10/89.
DUNSFORD R.J. BSc. Born 28/1/49. Commd 28/9/67. Gp Capt 1/7/02. Retd GD 1/7/04.
DUNSMORE M. Born 23/5/37. Commd 22/10/59. Sqn Ldr 1/7/69. Retd GD 14/5/71.
DUNSMORE S.M. BSc. Born 9/11/65. Commd 27/8/87. Sqn Ldr 1/1/00. Retd FLY(N) 9/11/03.
DUNSMUIR D.B. DPhysEd. Born 5/3/49. Commd 13/9/70. Sqn Ldr 1/1/87. Retd ADMIN 1/1/93.
DUNSTALL M.R. Born 24/11/60. Commd 17/1/85. Sqn Ldr 1/1/99. Retd OPS SPT 1/7/02.
DUNSTAN P.N. Born 16/4/37. Commd 31/10/63. Sqn Ldr 1/1/73. Retd GD 17/4/87.
DUNSTONE D.J. Born 12/4/33. Commd 8/5/53. Flt Lt 1/3/61. Retd GD 29/9/70.
DUNTON D.B. Born 13/11/45. Commd 25/6/66. Sqn Ldr 1/7/77. Retd GD 13/11/83.
DUNWOODIE A. Born 24/2/42. Commd 16/9/76. Flt Lt 16/9/77. Retd ADMIN 16/9/84.
DUNWOODIE J.S. Born 28/6/34. Commd 8/5/53. Flt Lt 18/4/67. Retd GD 10/3/71.
DUPENOIS N.G. Sol. Born 29/4/47. Commd 1/3/71. Flt Lt 1/3/71. Retd LGL 1/3/73.
DUPERE J.G. MB BS. Born 28/8/42. Commd 6/4/64. Flt Lt 10/7/68. Retd MED 10/7/73.
DUPRE R.A.C. Born 26/5/19. Commd 17/9/43. Sqn Ldr 1/10/57. Retd SEC 29/5/67.
DURACK C.B. Born 11/7/41. Commd 6/11/80. Sqn Ldr 1/7/96. Retd ENG 11/7/96.
DURAND B.E. Born 2/9/37. Commd 6/8/60. Wg Cdr 1/1/84. Retd GD 2/9/92.
DURANT-LEWIS J.A. MSc BSc CEng MRAeS MCMI. Born 8/7/45. Commd 28/9/64. Sqn Ldr 1/7/75. Retd ENG 8/7/83.
DURBIDGE K. DFC DFM. Born 1/6/21. Commd 28/2/43. Sqn Ldr 1/4/55. Retd GD 1/6/64.
DURBIN W. Born 10/2/44. Commd 15/10/81. Flt Lt 15/10/86. Retd ENG 6/5/93.
DURBRIDGE C.J. Born 19/1/50. Commd 29/8/72. Flt Lt 1/3/78. Retd GD 19/1/91.
DURHAM A.StJ.L. Born 2/2/52. Commd 15/2/73. Sqn Ldr 1/7/89. Retd ADMIN 1/7/92.
DURHAM E. Born 29/12/35. Commd 21/4/54. Gp Capt 1/1/87. Retd GD 17/7/89.
DURHAM M.W. MSc BSc DIC. Born 19/10/54. Commd 30/8/78. Flt Lt 30/11/79. Retd GD 1/1/95.
DURHAM W. BTech. Born 21/6/49. Commd 1/11/71. Flt Lt 1/8/72. Retd GD 3/12/92.
DURKIN G.E. Born 26/2/38. Commd 17/1/69. Flt Lt 17/1/71. Retd ENG 17/1/77.
DURKIN P. Born 7/9/42. Commd 19/8/71. Flt Lt 20/7/75. Retd GD(G) 19/12/82. Re-entered 30/11/87. Flt Lt 1/7/80.
    Retd OPS SPT 7/9/98.
DURLING A.M. Born 9/9/16. Commd 26/4/45. Sqn Ldr 1/10/56. Retd SEC 3/4/69.
DURLING D.F. Born 16/4/34. Commd 24/9/52. Flt Lt 14/5/58. Retd GD(G) 16/4/72. Re-instated 26/10/79. Flt Lt 23/11/65.
    Retd GD(G) 17/5/88.
DURLING D.H. Born 11/12/21. Commd 5/3/43. Flt Lt 5/9/46. Retd GD 11/12/64.
DURLING R.A.R. MSc BSc. Born 17/6/56. Commd 14/7/79. Sqn Ldr 1/1/89. Retd ENG 13/1/03.
DURMAN P.M. Born 22/10/19. Commd 20/4/44. Wg Cdr 1/7/67. Retd ENG 3/5/74.
DURN I.P. MSc BSc CEng MIEE. Born 20/10/48. Commd 26/2/71. Sqn Ldr 1/1/80. Retd ENG 1/1/91.
DURNAN C.J. Born 9/6/44. Commd 12/9/63. Flt Lt 12/12/69. Retd SEC 29/9/73.
DURNFORD A.C. Born 21/6/51. Commd 27/3/70. Flt Lt 27/9/75. Retd GD 22/1/85.
DURNFORD H.T.M. MCMI. Born 2/9/33. Commd 10/4/56. Sqn Ldr 1/1/70. Retd SUP 30/9/84.
DUROSE C.G. MSc BSc MCMI. Born 16/3/44. Commd 8/9/69. Sqn Ldr 8/3/75. Retd ADMIN 8/9/85.
DURRANT C. Born 17/3/28. Commd 16/10/51. Sqn Ldr 1/1/65. Retd GD 28/5/76.
DURRANT D.B. Born 25/5/28. Commd 1/8/51. Flt Lt 1/2/54. Retd GD 25/5/66.
DURRANT F.J. MBE. Born 1/1/21. Commd 26/9/57. Sqn Ldr 1/7/66. Retd ENG 1/1/75.
DURRANT J.H. Born 30/7/24. Commd 19/12/63. Flt Lt 19/12/66. Retd SEC 31/10/72.
DURRANT P.J. BSc(Eng) CEng MIMechE MRAeS. Born 26/10/43. Commd 22/9/63. Wg Cdr 1/7/78.
    Retd ENG 12/12/83.
DURSTON I. Born 27/9/46. Commd 21/7/65. Flt Lt 4/5/72. Retd GD 1/3/85.
DURSTON L.S.W. MBE. Born 5/10/19. Commd 20/6/46. Sqn Ldr 1/7/60. Retd ENG 30/5/70.
DUTHIE A.B. MA. Born 17/7/45. Commd 22/9/63. Flt Lt 15/10/68. Retd GD 17/7/83.
DUTTON A.D. BSc. Born 29/7/41. Commd 8/1/68. Sqn Ldr 1/7/75. Retd ENG 29/7/93.
DUTTON A.G.B. MB ChB FRCOG. Born 6/11/38. Commd 26/9/71. Gp Capt 1/10/88. Retd MED 6/11/92.
DUTTON F.R. Born 18/5/35. Commd 21/10/61. Sqn Ldr 1/1/74. Retd CAT 2/9/80.
DUTTON J.J. OBE. Born 13/4/18. Commd 23/1/40. Wg Cdr 1/1/55. Retd SUP 30/9/56.
DUTTON L.M. MSc BA MRIN MRAeS. Born 1/10/46. Commd 7/7/67. Wg Cdr 1/1/90. Retd GD 15/1/96.
DUTTON M.J.R. Born 13/8/35. Commd 1/7/53. Flt Lt 7/3/62. Retd GD 20/12/91.
DUTTON M.R.G. Born 15/7/49. Commd 14/8/70. Flt Lt 14/8/75. Retd GD 12/3/88.
DUVAL D.V. Born 27/9/36. Commd 30/7/57. Wg Cdr 1/7/74. Retd GD 27/10/89.

DWYER M.W. Born 7/3/36. Commd 14/8/70. Sqn Ldr 1/7/80. Retd ENG 7/3/94.
DYCHE R. BSc CEng MRAeS MIEE MCMI. Born 14/1/32. Commd 27/9/57. Wg Cdr 1/1/76. Retd ENG 2/5/78.
DYDE S.A.J. Born 19/2/60. Commd 28/2/80. Sqn Ldr 1/1/91. Retd GD 30/6/97.
DYE P.D. AFC BSc. Born 18/9/49. Commd 15/9/69. Sqn Ldr 1/1/85. Retd GD 1/1/88.
DYE R.M. Born 4/11/24. Commd 11/8/44. Sqn Ldr 1/1/56. Retd GD 4/11/67.
DYE R.P. Born 5/12/26. Commd 16/9/50. Sqn Ldr 1/7/72. Retd GD 5/12/82.
DYER B. BSc. Born 2/9/46. Commd 25/11/68. Sqn Ldr 25/5/78. Retd ADMIN 25/11/84.
DYER B.H. Born 18/11/44. Commd 29/11/63. Flt Lt 29/5/69. Retd GD 21/12/74.
DYER G.C. MBE BA FRIN MCMI. Born 5/4/34. Commd 5/7/53. Wg Cdr 1/1/73. Retd ENG 19/6/78.
DYER G.L.S. MA. Born 2/9/37. Commd 30/9/56. Flt Lt 15/10/62. Retd GD 2/9/75.
DYER H.W. Born 31/3/17. Commd 11/1/51. Sqn Ldr 1/7/62. Retd GD(G) 31/3/72.
DYER J. Born 21/5/45. Commd 24/6/71. Wg Cdr 1/7/89. Retd ADMIN 21/5/00.
DYER J.T.F. BSc. Born 22/12/52. Commd 27/7/75. Flt Lt 27/10/76. Retd GD 29/9/84.
DYER N.R. Born 31/3/44. Commd 24/6/65. Flt Lt 24/12/67. Retd GD 5/7/74.
DYER P.C. MCMI. Born 22/3/38. Commd 3/12/62. Flt Lt 14/2/66. Retd GD(G) 22/3/93.
DYER R.A. BSc CEng. Born 14/6/49. Commd 16/9/73. Flt Lt 30/11/76. Retd ENG 14/6/87.
DYER-PERRY A.H.C. BSc MRAeS. Born 15/2/45. Commd 23/2/68. Wg Cdr 1/1/88. Retd GD 15/2/02.
DYKES P.H. Born 5/11/26. Commd 30/7/59. Flt Lt 16/9/64. Retd ENG 5/11/81.
DYMOND F.E. Born 6/3/20. Commd 16/1/42. Sqn Ldr 1/10/54. Retd GD 6/3/69.
DYMOND J.N. Born 20/12/32. Commd 6/4/54. Flt Lt 22/5/57. Retd GD 20/12/70.
DYNES D.R. Born 7/5/39. Commd 29/4/71. Flt Lt 29/4/73. Retd SEC 29/4/79.
DYSON C.J.F. Born 18/6/38. Commd 19/9/59. Flt Lt 19/3/70. Retd GD 18/6/76.
DYSON J.B. Born 19/11/45. Commd 28/10/66. Flt Lt 28/4/72. Retd GD 19/11/83.
DYSON K.F. Born 8/12/31. Commd 1/6/72. Flt Lt 1/6/74. Retd MED(SEC) 30/9/87.
DYSON M.L. MRCS LRCP DMRT. Born 13/5/22. Commd 27/10/50. Sqn Ldr 27/1/55. Retd MED 26/2/60.
DYSON R.E. DFC. Born 3/9/21. Commd 8/8/42. Sqn Ldr 1/7/51. Retd GD 3/9/76. rtg Wg Cdr
DYSON R.K. Born 11/5/60. Commd 1/7/82. Sqn Ldr 1/7/97. Retd FLY(P) 19/4/05.
DYSON T.M. Born 20/1/35. Commd 13/1/56. Sqn Ldr 1/7/67. Retd GD 12/4/74.

E

EACOPO M.J. Born 4/1/48. Commd 23/2/68. Sqn Ldr 1/1/91. Retd GD 14/3/96.
EADES J.A. Born 15/3/30. Commd 22/6/50. Flt Offr 22/5/57. Retd SEC 23/6/58.
EADIE C.J. BL LLB FCIS. Born 18/9/34. Commd 25/4/58. Gp Capt 1/1/79. Retd LGL 26/12/89.
EADY C.J. MSc BSc. Born 5/2/63. Commd 2/9/84. Sqn Ldr 1/1/97. Retd ENG 5/2/01.
EAGERS C.J. Born 7/10/46. Commd 31/10/74. Wg Cdr 1/7/89. Retd SUP 14/9/96.
EAGLES T.W. Born 23/3/44. Commd 9/3/72. Flt Lt 7/2/75. Retd GD(G) 23/3/94.
EAMES P.F. Born 23/4/16. Commd 31/5/38. Sqn Ldr 1/8/47. Retd GD 1/11/57.
EARL A.C. Born 29/12/63. Commd 20/10/83. Flt Lt 20/4/90. Retd GD(G) 1/10/90.
EARL D.L.T. Born 18/3/43. Commd 17/12/63. Wg Cdr 1/1/84. Retd GD 1/10/88.
EARLAND J.M. Born 23/9/22. Commd 27/3/43. Flt Lt 10/9/47. Retd GD 31/3/62.
EARLE B.P. Born 16/5/31. Commd 5/5/51. Gp Capt 1/1/76. Retd GD 17/4/86.
EARLE D.J. Born 30/8/45. Commd 15/7/66. Sqn Ldr 1/7/75. Retd ENG 31/12/77.
EARLE P.J. BSc. Born 9/6/52. Commd 16/2/86. Flt Lt 16/2/88. Retd ADMIN 16/2/02.
EARLE-WELBY G.R. MA. Born 14/8/21. Commd 10/10/49. Sqn Ldr 14/8/55. Retd EDN 14/9/68.
EARNDEN K.C. BA CEng MRAeS. Born 18/2/56. Commd 5/4/79. Wg Cdr 1/7/97. Retd ENG 7/2/02.
EARNSHAW C.W. DFC. Born 7/3/23. Commd 13/3/44. Flt Lt 13/9/47. Retd ENG 11/3/53.
EARNSHAW P.T. Born 17/11/49. Commd 13/6/74. Flt Lt 13/12/79. Retd GD 25/2/90.
EARP D.A. Born 21/5/51. Commd 14/8/70. Sqn Ldr 1/1/88. Retd GD 1/1/91.
EARP J.R. Born 16/8/47. Commd 7/1/71. Flt Lt 1/4/74. Retd GD 6/1/76.
EASBY M. BSc. Born 2/5/40. Commd 27/10/62. Wg Cdr 1/7/85. Retd ADMIN 2/5/95.
EASEY J.A. Born 8/4/39. Commd 5/2/57. Sqn Ldr 1/7/84. Retd GD 9/4/88.
EASLEY M.J. Born 26/1/49. Commd 4/7/69. Flt Lt 4/1/75. Retd GD 26/1/87.
EASON A.S. BA. Born 12/5/65. Commd 15/8/97. Sqn Ldr 1/7/01. Retd OPS SPT(ATC) 25/9/04.
EASON R.F. Born 10/8/35. Commd 1/6/72. Flt Lt 1/6/74. Retd MED(SEC) 2/10/76.
EAST A. BSc. Born 22/10/59. Commd 15/11/81. Flt Lt 15/10/82. Retd GD 15/7/93.
EAST A.C. AFC. Born 21/4/34. Commd 7/5/52. Flt Lt 2/10/57. Retd GD 31/12/72.
EAST D.R. Born 4/2/56. Commd 27/8/87. Flt Lt 27/8/89. Retd ADMIN 27/8/95.
EAST F.C. CEng MIEE. Born 26/1/42. Commd 9/3/66. Sqn Ldr 1/1/78. Retd ENG 1/1/81.
EAST M.J. Born 10/1/47. Commd 5/3/65. Wg Cdr 1/1/90. Retd GD 14/3/96.
EAST R.T. Born 23/10/17. Commd 15/11/50. Sqn Ldr 31/7/61. Retd EDN 1/9/65.
EASTER G.K. Born 26/3/18. Commd 18/8/45. Flt Lt 18/2/48. Retd GD 21/6/61.
EASTERBROOK R.L. Born 17/7/24. Commd 6/6/46. Gp Capt 1/1/71. Retd GD 17/10/79.
EASTERBROOK T. Born 17/6/44. Commd 4/5/72. Flt Lt 4/11/76. Retd GD 27/10/81.
EASTERBROOK W.J. Born 14/8/20. Commd 15/11/51. Flt Lt 26/5/55. Retd GD 28/6/67.
EASTERLING G.G. Born 28/1/25. Commd 25/8/44. Flt Lt 13/3/51. Retd GD(G) 28/1/63.
EASTMEAD B.P. Born 5/7/29. Commd 13/12/50. Sqn Ldr 1/7/64. Retd SUP 13/9/67.
EASTMENT R.M. OBE MRAeS. Born 16/3/49. Commd 12/7/68. Wg Cdr 1/7/89. Retd GD 4/12/98.
EASTMOND D.H. Born 20/11/40. Commd 24/4/64. Sqn Ldr 1/1/75. Retd GD 3/2/80.
EASTON B.R.L. MA CEng FIMechE MRAeS. Born 14/6/34. Commd 25/9/54. A Cdre 1/7/80. Retd ENG 11/6/88.
EASTON I.F. CEng FRAeS FCMI. Born 11/2/21. Commd 19/8/42. Gp Capt 1/7/70. Retd ENG 11/2/76.
EASTON J.H. Born 26/10/43. Commd 19/8/66. Wg Cdr 1/1/87. Retd GD 26/10/98.
EASTON M.S. Born 18/4/64. Commd 19/11/87. Flt Lt 17/1/91. Retd FLY(P) 18/4/03.
EASTON S.J. BSc. Born 14/7/64. Commd 29/9/83. Flt Lt 15/1/88. Retd GD 15/7/97.
EASTWOOD D. Born 12/10/37. Commd 10/10/58. Sqn Ldr 6/10/71. Retd ADMIN 12/4/76.
EASTWOOD J.C.E. Born 16/4/41. Commd 25/1/63. Flt Lt 25/7/68. Retd GD 1/10/74.
EASTWOOD S.P. Born 10/1/60. Commd 29/1/87. Flt Lt 29/1/89. Retd GD(G) 14/3/96.
EASY C.A. Born 19/3/45. Commd 3/6/56. Flt Lt 25/7/72. Retd ADMIN 13/2/84.
EASY W.R. MB ChB DCH. Born 23/1/44. Commd 24/7/67. Wg Cdr 27/10/86. Retd MED 31/1/89.
EATON C.W. DFC*. Born 18/11/22. Commd 17/4/44. Flt Lt 17/10/47. Retd GD 18/11/65.
EATON K.A. MSc BDS MGDSRCS LDSRCS. Born 20/4/45. Commd 11/12/78. Wg Cdr 25/7/81. Retd DEL 29/4/90.
EATON K.C. Born 25/3/54. Commd 18/1/73. Sqn Ldr 1/7/87. Retd GD 25/3/92.
EATON N.G. MCMI. Born 9/1/36. Commd 9/3/55. Sqn Ldr 1/7/66. Retd GD 9/1/74.
EATON S.J. DFC. Born 4/12/21. Commd 25/9/42. Wg Cdr 1/1/61. Retd GD 30/10/72.
EATON-SHORE J.H. CEng MRAeS MCMI. Born 19/5/21. Commd 9/12/43. Wg Cdr 1/1/67. Retd ENG 19/5/76.
EATWELL E.E. FRIN. Born 11/8/31. Commd 26/11/69. Wg Cdr 1/1/80. Retd GD 11/8/86.
EAVES J.G. Born 21/10/29. Commd 16/7/52. Flt Lt 16/11/64. Retd GD(G) 16/11/72.
EBBAGE D.A. Born 1/9/42. Commd 25/9/69. Retd GD 9/1/76.
ECCLES G. Born 16/4/16. Commd 28/10/43. Flt Lt 4/6/53. Retd SEC 1/3/69.
ECCLES H.H. MA MRAeS. Born 5/6/19. Commd 26/9/39. Gp Capt 1/1/60. Retd GD 10/7/64.
ECCLES J.V.R. Born 22/1/30. Commd 6/12/51. Wg Cdr 1/7/76. Retd ADMIN 1/10/80.
ECCLES R. AFC. Born 2/2/45. Commd 21/5/65. Sqn Ldr 1/1/82. Retd GD 1/1/85.

ECKEL A.M. Born 28/9/32. Commd 24/9/52. Flt Lt 21/2/58. Retd GD 28/9/70.
ECKERSLEY A.M. Born 1/5/63. Commd 4/11/82. Sqn Ldr 1/1/95. Retd GD 1/2/02.
ECKERT P.M. BSc CEng MIEE MRAeS. Born 23/10/49. Commd 24/9/67. Sqn Ldr 1/7/83. Retd ENG 23/10/87.
EDDELL J.P. BSc. Born 6/10/49. Commd 7/12/75. Sqn Ldr 1/1/86. Retd ADMIN 7/12/91.
EDDY G.P. Born 24/5/23. Commd 12/7/62. Flt Lt 12/7/67. Retd GD 24/5/78.
EDE H. Born 28/4/47. Commd 9/3/72. Sqn Ldr 1/1/95. Retd FLY(N) 28/4/05.
EDELSTEN P. MCMI MCIPD. Born 23/5/23. Commd 5/9/42. Sqn Ldr 1/1/55. Retd GD 23/5/72.
EDEN D.F.E. MBE. Born 10/1/34. Commd 26/7/55. Wg Cdr 1/7/84. Retd SUP 10/1/93.
EDEN F.R. Born 6/10/21. Commd 30/1/45. Sqn Ldr 1/1/67. Retd GD(G) 6/10/72.
EDEN J.J. BSc. Born 11/1/67. Commd 19/2/89. Sqn Ldr 1/1/02. Retd OPS SPT(REGT) 19/2/05.
EDEN N.C. Born 1/10/50. Commd 25/2/72. Flt Lt 25/2/74. Retd GD 1/10/88.
EDEN P.C. Born 11/7/28. Commd 15/12/47. Sqn Ldr 1/1/63. Retd GD 12/8/78.
EDEN R.E. MBE. Born 24/10/66. Commd 4/3/94. Sqn Ldr 1/7/02. Retd OPS SPT(ATC) 19/11/04.
EDENBROW G.R. MBE. Born 8/9/23. Commd 8/9/44. Wg Cdr 1/1/70. Retd PE 31/3/74.
EDENBROW R.A.O. BSc. Born 30/4/50. Commd 15/9/69. Flt Lt 15/12/73. Retd GD 14/3/97.
EDGAR C.H. MBE AE. Born 15/3/21. Commd 17/7/46. Sqn Ldr 1/7/72. Retd RGT 29/11/75.
EDGAR J.D. BSc CEng MRAeS. Born 25/10/60. Commd 2/9/79. Wg Cdr 1/7/99. Retd GD 25/10/04.
EDGAR S. MHCIMA. Born 30/6/48. Commd 24/11/76. Wg Cdr 1/7/87. Retd GD 4/4/03.
EDGCUMBE G.D.T. Born 3/5/55. Commd 11/9/86. Sqn Ldr 1/7/96. Retd SY 14/4/00.
EDGE F.D. MBE. Born 16/3/19. Commd 4/5/50. Flt Lt 1/7/54. Retd PRT 30/6/62.
EDGE G. Born 28/9/57. Commd 9/12/76. Flt Lt 9/6/82. Retd GD 9/1/95.
EDGE P.M. Born 10/9/23. Commd 26/3/53. Sqn Ldr 1/1/73. Retd GD 10/4/78.
EDGELEY C.V. Born 2/7/40. Commd 11/11/65. Flt Lt 7/6/68. Retd ENG 2/7/78.
EDGELL J.A. Born 10/4/54. Commd 30/4/81. Sqn Ldr 1/1/89. Retd SUP 10/9/92.
EDGERLEY A.G. Born 26/3/23. Commd 9/11/43. Sqn Ldr 1/7/60. Retd GD 26/3/78.
EDGINGTON J.F. FCMI. Born 27/9/36. Commd 6/5/55. Gp Capt 1/1/78. Retd ADMIN 30/9/80.
EDINGTON D.J. Born 3/11/48. Commd 31/7/70. Flt Lt 31/1/76. Retd SUP 21/3/78.
EDINGTON J.A. Born 28/4/20. Commd 17/11/44. Flt Lt 17/5/48. Retd GD(G) 5/11/73.
EDKINS A.C. Born 31/12/46. Commd 21/3/74. Flt Lt 29/6/80. Retd OPS SPT 6/7/97.
EDKINS A.J.A. CEng MRAeS MCMI. Born 4/12/38. Commd 17/7/62. Sqn Ldr 1/7/71. Retd ENG 17/7/78.
EDMONDS A.C. Born 21/8/42. Commd 9/8/79. Sqn Ldr 1/1/85. Retd ADMIN 21/8/94.
EDMONDS A.J. Born 13/4/44. Commd 24/11/67. Flt Lt 24/5/73. Retd GD 13/6/01.
EDMONDS C.C. BSc. Born 23/3/48. Commd 15/4/73. Wg Cdr 1/7/93. Retd GD 30/9/03.
EDMONDS K.R. FCMI. Born 14/4/34. Commd 17/12/52. Gp Capt 1/7/84. Retd GD 14/4/89.
EDMONDS M.A. Born 6/3/36. Commd 7/12/54. Sqn Ldr 1/1/71. Retd GD 16/6/74.
EDMONDS P.J. Born 27/12/35. Commd 21/10/66. Flt Lt 21/10/68. Retd SEC 21/10/74.
EDMONDS R.J. DFM. Born 29/9/17. Commd 8/9/42. Wg Cdr 1/1/60. Retd ENG 30/6/65.
EDMONDS R.J. Born 18/2/11. Commd 24/4/41. Flt Lt 1/9/45. Retd ENG 8/12/49.
EDMONDSON C.S. Born 3/7/45. Commd 17/5/79. Sqn Ldr 1/1/86. Retd ENG 3/4/89.
EDMONDSON F.R. DFC. Born 12/9/21. Commd 6/4/47. Flt Lt 4/1/51. Retd GD 12/9/64.
EDMONDSON S. DFC. Born 6/4/21. Commd 1/11/43. Flt Lt 19/11/53. Retd GD 14/9/68.
EDMONDSON-JONES J.R. Born 23/1/28. Commd 14/12/49. Plt Offr 14/12/49. Retd GD 31/7/52.
EDMONSTON A.C. Born 31/3/62. Commd 30/4/81. Flt Lt 30/10/86. Retd GD 31/3/93.
EDMUND R.C.P. BSc CEng MIEE. Born 9/12/41. Commd 30/9/61. Sqn Ldr 1/7/73. Retd ENG 9/12/96.
EDMUNDS A.C. Born 23/9/35. Commd 30/7/57. Wg Cdr 1/1/85. Retd GD 23/9/93.
EDMUNDS A.R. Born 22/12/35. Commd 16/9/55. Flt Lt 6/3/63. Retd GD 22/12/78.
EDMUNDS D.J. BA. Born 28/12/41. Commd 31/8/78. Sqn Ldr 1/1/89. Retd GD(G) 19/2/94.
EDMUNDS K.W. Born 30/10/56. Commd 25/2/88. Sqn Ldr 1/1/01. Retd FLY(AEO) 14/5/03.
EDMUNDSON M. Born 29/6/49. Commd 11/3/79. Flt Lt 11/3/88. Retd SY 31/5/95.
EDNEY P.A. BSc. Born 28/6/38. Commd 23/9/59. Sqn Ldr 8/4/73. Retd ADMIN 28/6/76.
EDSALL K.C. MB BS MRCS LRCP. Born 30/5/40. Commd 18/6/72. Wg Cdr 26/5/89. Retd MED 9/1/95.
EDWARD A.F. BA MCIPS MCMI. Born 12/1/48. Commd 27/10/67. Sqn Ldr 1/1/80. Retd SUP 12/1/86.
EDWARDE J.D. Born 1/7/44. Commd 21/7/65. Flt Lt 21/1/71. Retd GD 21/3/77.
EDWARDS A. BSc. Born 22/10/60. Commd 16/9/79. Sqn Ldr 1/1/94. Retd GD 1/6/99.
EDWARDS A.K. MBE. Born 1/4/21. Commd 13/8/44. Flt Lt 13/2/48. Retd GD 1/4/64.
EDWARDS A.W. Born 25/5/44. Commd 29/3/68. Flt Lt 4/5/72. Retd GD(G) 25/5/82. Re-instated 20/3/90. Flt Lt 20/3/84. Retd GD(G) 14/3/96.
EDWARDS B. Born 2/8/37. Commd 3/8/62. Flt Lt 1/4/71. Retd GD 2/8/75.
EDWARDS B.M. Born 26/12/47. Commd 13/5/73. Sqn Ldr 1/1/86. Retd ENG 1/5/91.
EDWARDS C.B.F. Born 12/12/19. Commd 28/7/60. Flt Lt 28/7/63. Retd SEC 22/3/69.
EDWARDS C.R. Born 19/11/38. Commd 26/8/66. Wg Cdr 1/1/80. Retd PI 4/5/84.
EDWARDS D. Born 8/8/51. Commd 16/3/73. Flt Lt 16/3/74. Retd GD 18/9/01.
EDWARDS D.A. Born 31/12/65. Commd 30/3/89. Fg Offr 30/3/91. Retd SUP 14/3/96.
EDWARDS D.A.H. CEng MIEE MRAeS. Born 23/3/38. Commd 24/9/59. Gp Capt 1/7/85. Retd ENG 31/10/90.
EDWARDS D.G. Born 29/8/36. Commd 9/6/55. Sqn Ldr 1/1/71. Retd ADMIN 23/9/87.
EDWARDS D.L. Born 13/1/34. Commd 12/3/52. Gp Capt 1/7/79. Retd GD 13/1/84.

EDWARDS D.P. Born 4/4/33. Commd 24/2/67. Flt Lt 24/2/72. Retd ENG 24/10/75.
EDWARDS D.W.J. Born 19/11/46. Commd 24/4/70. Sqn Ldr 1/7/80. Retd ENG 19/11/84.
EDWARDS E.J. BA. Born 6/1/28. Commd 30/6/54. Sqn Ldr 7/9/61. Retd EDN 30/9/73.
EDWARDS E.T.D. Born 12/7/32. Commd 21/5/52. Flt Lt 16/10/57. Retd GD 12/7/70.
EDWARDS F.G. Born 19/12/37. Commd 19/6/70. Flt Lt 19/6/72. Retd ENG 19/12/87.
EDWARDS G.C. Born 12/3/45. Commd 25/2/66. Flt Lt 1/11/72. Retd GD 12/3/83.
EDWARDS G.D. BSc. Born 22/9/63. Commd 7/6/87. Sqn Ldr 1/1/01. Retd ENGINEER 1/1/04.
EDWARDS G.G. Born 7/9/31. Commd 5/9/49. Flt Lt 14/11/56. Retd GD(G) 7/9/69. Re-instated 31/12/70 to 30/6/82.
EDWARDS H. DFC MCMI. Born 7/6/22. Commd 4/10/41. Wg Cdr 1/1/60. Retd SEC 1/1/74.
EDWARDS H.J. Born 31/8/49. Commd 31/10/69. Flt Lt 27/3/76. Retd SUP 1/11/78.
EDWARDS I.P. BSc. Born 4/6/64. Commd 18/8/85. Flt Lt 18/2/88. Retd GD 18/8/97.
EDWARDS J.A. Born 26/6/31. Commd 30/8/50. Flt Lt 26/5/55. Retd GD 31/12/68.
EDWARDS J.A.F. Born 5/3/39. Commd 11/8/69. Flt Lt 11/8/71. Retd ENG 9/12/81.
EDWARDS J.A.K. MBE MCIPD. Born 9/5/31. Commd 14/1/54. Sqn Ldr 1/7/74. Retd SY(RGT) 9/5/89.
EDWARDS J.D. Born 21/1/35. Commd 3/3/54. Flt Lt 3/9/59. Retd GD 14/2/76.
EDWARDS J.D. Born 19/7/22. Commd 16/7/43. Wg Cdr 1/1/70. Retd ENG 5/9/75.
EDWARDS J.M. MInstAM MCMI. Born 21/8/41. Commd 24/2/67. Wg Cdr 1/7/90. Retd ADMIN 2/4/93.
EDWARDS J.M. Born 5/5/29. Commd 26/3/59. Fg Offr 26/6/61. Retd SEC 5/5/67.
EDWARDS J.R.W. Born 20/4/33. Commd 17/9/57. Wg Cdr 1/7/80. Retd SUP 11/2/85.
EDWARDS J.W. Born 17/9/51. Commd 13/9/70. Sqn Ldr 1/1/88. Retd ADMIN 1/1/91.
EDWARDS K. MBE FCIPD. Born 8/11/40. Commd 25/8/67. Gp Capt 1/1/88. Retd ADMIN 5/4/91.
EDWARDS K. BA(Econ). Born 10/7/44. Commd 8/5/67. Gp Capt 1/1/90. Retd ADMIN 11/4/95.
EDWARDS K.A. BSc. Born 12/3/51. Commd 13/9/70. Fg Offr 15/10/72. Retd GD 5/7/75. Re-entered 22/5/83.
    Sqn Ldr 1/7/90. Retd SUP 15/10/99.
EDWARDS M. Born 22/5/32. Commd 14/4/53. Sqn Ldr 1/1/63. Retd GD 14/4/65.
EDWARDS M.C. BTech. Born 10/6/53. Commd 13/2/77. Sqn Ldr 1/1/88. Retd ENG 13/2/93.
EDWARDS M.J. BA. Born 26/3/32. Commd 29/3/56. Sqn Ldr 23/6/71. Retd ADMIN 30/9/73. Re-instated 7/5/80 to
    26/3/87.
EDWARDS M.S. The Rev. BD. Born 13/2/44. Commd 25/4/82. Retd Sqn Ldr 19/1/96.
EDWARDS P. Born 22/1/43. Commd 12/7/63. Gp Capt 1/7/90. Retd GD 12/2/01.
EDWARDS P.A. Born 1/4/45. Commd 1/4/65. Flt Lt 1/7/71. Retd ADMIN 1/4/83.
EDWARDS P.G.C. Born 29/12/32. Commd 27/9/51. Flt Lt 13/11/57. Retd GD 29/12/70.
EDWARDS P.J. Born 10/11/26. Commd 3/5/46. Flt Lt 3/11/49. Retd GD 19/3/53.
EDWARDS P.W. Born 17/4/53. Commd 31/10/74. Sqn Ldr 1/1/91. Retd GD 14/3/97.
EDWARDS R.A. OBE. Born 30/1/32. Commd 15/12/53. Gp Capt 1/1/81. Retd GD 30/1/87.
EDWARDS R.M. BSc. Born 7/5/34. Commd 20/9/57. Sqn Ldr 20/3/67. Retd EDN 20/9/73.
EDWARDS S.A. OBE. Born 24/11/34. Commd 9/4/57. Gp Capt 1/1/83. Retd GD 2/1/85.
EDWARDS T.A. BSc. Born 23/6/63. Commd 10/11/85. Flt Lt 10/5/88. Retd GD 28/11/97.
EDWARDS T.A. Born 11/1/25. Commd 15/9/60. Flt Lt 15/9/65. Retd GD 1/11/73.
EDWARDS T.P. Born 16/3/21. Commd 11/2/44. Flt Lt 11/8/47. Retd GD 25/11/61.
EDWARDS W. AFC. Born 14/8/26. Commd 20/12/46. Gp Capt 1/7/74. Retd GD 29/10/80.
EDWARDS W.A. Born 17/11/35. Commd 31/7/56. Sqn Ldr 1/7/69. Retd SUP 17/11/73.
EDWORTHY P.J. Born 16/2/38. Commd 27/7/59. Sqn Ldr 1/7/71. Retd GD 3/1/85.
EEDLE D.S. BSc. Born 25/5/28. Commd 25/5/50. Gp Capt 1/7/79. Retd GD 25/5/83.
EELES J.S. Born 5/5/25. Commd 26/3/53. Flt Lt 26/9/56. Retd GD 16/12/70.
EELES T. BA. Born 14/9/42. Commd 30/7/63. Gp Capt 1/7/90. Retd GD 14/9/97.
EGAN I. BSc. Born 24/6/58. Commd 5/9/76. Sqn Ldr 1/7/91. Retd GD 24/6/96.
EGAN J.J. DFC. Born 30/10/23. Commd 14/6/50. Flt Lt 10/11/55. Retd GD 19/8/64.
EGAN-WYER D.G. ACCS. Born 6/12/26. Commd 9/11/59. Sqn Ldr 1/7/68. Retd SUP 8/1/71.
EGERTON A.J. MA MBA. Born 27/9/64. Commd 30/8/84. Wg Cdr 1/7/98. Retd ADMIN 27/9/02.
EGGINTON J.T. AFC. Born 14/3/33. Commd 7/5/52. Sqn Ldr 1/1/73. Retd GD 1/11/73.
EGGLESTONE B.J. Born 21/12/43. Commd 15/8/82. Flt Lt 4/11/70. Retd GD(G) 25/12/80.
EGGLESTONE M. Born 30/4/48. Commd 21/6/90. Sqn Ldr 1/1/01. Retd ADMIN (PROVSY) 30/4/03.
EGGLETON M.B. Born 10/4/34. Commd 4/2/53. Flt Lt 24/6/58. Retd GD 1/7/68.
EGLINGTON W.D.S. Born 6/6/25. Commd 24/1/52. Flt Lt 13/11/57. Retd GD 16/3/68.
EGRE C.H. Born 30/5/49. Commd 27/2/70. Sqn Ldr 1/1/91. Retd GD(G) 1/4/94.
EIDSFORTH A.R.J. Born 18/5/39. Commd 19/12/61. Flt Lt 19/12/66. Retd SUP 18/5/77.
EIGHTEEN D.E. OBE. Born 14/6/46. Commd 16/9/76. Wg Cdr 1/7/96. Retd ENG 16/6/01.
EISLER J.J. Born 27/12/39. Commd 21/10/64. Flt Lt 21/10/64. Retd GD 21/10/80.
EKE D.V. BA MSRG. Born 21/3/38. Commd 9/7/60. Flt Lt 9/1/60. Retd GD 21/3/93.
EKE P. Born 27/3/34. Commd 5/7/53. Flt Lt 15/8/62. Retd GD 6/10/84.
EKINS D.J. BSc. Born 14/1/61. Commd 15/8/82. Sqn Ldr 1/7/93. Retd GD 14/1/99.
ELBURN A.J. BA. Born 25/4/33. Commd 26/9/53. Sqn Ldr 1/7/69. Retd ENG 1/7/72.
ELDER P.R. Born 28/8/41. Commd 2/10/61. Flt Lt 2/4/67. Retd GD 28/8/79.
ELDER R.D. CBE FRAeS. Born 27/5/46. Commd 1/3/68. AVM 1/7/96. Retd GD 8/2/99.
ELDER W.J. MB BS DCH MRCP. Born 8/9/29. Commd 3/4/55. Wg Cdr 5/3/68. Retd MED 3/4/71.

ELEY D.L. Born 27/1/26. Commd 21/12/45. Wg Cdr 1/1/65. Retd GD 7/2/77.
ELEY M.M. Born 9/10/48. Commd 8/8/74. Sqn Ldr 1/1/88. Retd GD 22/4/94.
ELEY T.E.A. Born 15/3/36. Commd 28/9/61. Wg Cdr 1/1/79. Retd GD 16/3/86.
ELFORD C.B. FCIPD MCMI. Born 11/10/19. Commd 26/3/42. Wg Cdr 1/7/62. Retd ADMIN 22/10/74.
ELIAS J.W.A. Born 2/2/31. Commd 9/9/55. Sqn Ldr 1/7/72. Retd GD 27/5/84.
ELING C.I. Born 28/5/50. Commd 20/9/79. Flt Lt 20/9/81. Retd GD 28/10/87.
ELIOT R.C. Born 7/5/60. Commd 13/12/79. Flt Lt 13/6/85. Retd GD 7/5/98.
ELISTON J.A. AFM. Born 7/5/24. Commd 29/7/65. Sqn Ldr 1/1/75. Retd GD 9/1/80.
ELKINGTON J.F.D. Born 23/12/20. Commd 14/7/40. Wg Cdr 1/7/61. Retd GD 23/12/75.
ELKINGTON K.A. Born 16/7/43. Commd 21/7/61. Sqn Ldr 1/1/79. Retd GD 1/1/82.
ELKINS C.A. MSc BSc. Born 5/10/50. Commd 15/9/69. Wg Cdr 1/7/90. Retd ENG 14/3/96.
ELLACOMBE J.L.W. CB DFC* FCMI. Born 28/2/20. Commd 23/3/40. A Cdre 1/7/68. Retd GD 16/4/73.
ELLAM C. CEng MIMechE MRAeS. Born 28/6/32. Commd 26/9/71. Sqn Ldr 26/9/71. Retd ENG 28/6/92.
ELLAM D.J. MB BS MRCS LRCP DA. Born 15/5/34. Commd 7/2/60. Wg Cdr 7/2/73. Retd MED 1/11/84.
ELLAWAY M.J. Born 16/2/51. Commd 5/11/70. Wg Cdr 1/7/90. Retd GD 19/11/04.
ELLENDER A.R. Born 3/8/42. Commd 28/7/64. Sqn Ldr 1/7/74. Retd GD 3/8/86.
ELLERD-STYLES L. BSc CEng MIMechE MRAeS DCAe. Born 31/10/14. Commd 3/10/41. Gp Capt 1/1/64.
    Retd ENG 31/10/69.
ELLERTON D.R.D. Born 9/7/22. Commd 11/5/43. Sqn Ldr 1/7/53. Retd GD 1/1/56.
ELLES-HILL W.J. Born 16/2/33. Commd 20/3/52. Fg Offr 6/8/61. Retd GD 10/4/66.
ELLICOTT R.A.C. Born 25/8/30. Commd 4/4/51. Sqn Ldr 1/1/75. Retd GD 21/8/84.
ELLIMAN J.N. Born 6/2/25. Commd 7/9/46. Sqn Ldr 1/1/61. Retd GD 30/4/73.
ELLINGWORTH R.A. Born 17/12/35. Commd 17/5/56. Sqn Ldr 1/1/75. Retd GD(G) 25/7/89.
ELLIOT A.H. Born 14/9/24. Commd 15/11/44. Flt Lt 18/5/64. Retd GD 31/8/73.
ELLIOT J.R. Born 29/9/33. Commd 22/1/53. Flt Lt 16/12/59. Retd SEC 29/9/71. rtg Sqn Ldr
ELLIOT-WILLIAMS B.H. Born 5/4/36. Commd 22/7/66. Flt Lt 1/7/69. Retd GD(G) 23/7/74.
ELLIOTT C.B. Born 15/6/32. Commd 8/5/56. Flt Lt 8/11/61. Retd GD 15/6/70.
ELLIOTT D.G. Born 5/10/48. Commd 27/2/75. Flt Lt 16/3/77. Retd GD 5/10/86.
ELLIOTT F.C.P. Born 17/3/21. Commd 5/2/44. Wg Cdr 1/7/65. Retd GD 17/3/76.
ELLIOTT G.C. Born 2/9/41. Commd 4/3/71. Flt Lt 4/9/77. Retd SUP 9/11/86.
ELLIOTT H.J. Born 18/10/61. Commd 19/3/81. Sqn Ldr 1/1/98. Retd GD 1/1/01.
ELLIOTT J.E. Born 24/5/42. Commd 13/12/79. Sqn Ldr 1/7/90. Retd ENG 20/7/93.
ELLIOTT J.G. MBE. Born 24/11/46. Commd 1/3/68. Wg Cdr 1/7/96. Retd GD 24/11/01.
ELLIOTT J.H. Born 16/6/24. Commd 29/3/45. Wg Cdr 1/1/67. Retd GD 18/4/70.
ELLIOTT K.T. Born 18/6/51. Commd 2/1/70. Flt Lt 7/3/76. Retd ADMIN 18/6/89.
ELLIOTT L.C. MBE. Born 1/4/14. Commd 22/8/41. Sqn Ldr 1/7/60. Retd ENG 1/4/69.
ELLIOTT M.R. Born 27/3/47. Commd 1/4/71. Flt Lt 1/10/76. Retd GD 30/4/88.
ELLIOTT N.P.G. MSc BSc. Born 21/8/47. Commd 8/1/73. Sqn Ldr 1/7/84. Retd ENG 8/1/89.
ELLIOTT P. Born 22/1/47. Commd 31/7/86. Flt Lt 31/7/90. Retd ENG 2/4/93.
ELLIOTT P.J.B. MBE. Born 16/9/41. Commd 2/1/70. Sqn Ldr 1/7/76. Retd GD 16/9/96.
ELLIOTT P.W. FIISec. Born 17/6/47. Commd 14/10/71. Flt Lt 17/11/74. Retd SY 17/6/85.
ELLIOTT R.L. Born 3/5/29. Commd 26/9/51. Flt Lt 23/9/70. Retd GD 1/5/76.
ELLIOTT R.P. Born 15/3/53. Commd 2/9/73. Wg Cdr 1/1/94. Retd SUP 1/10/01.
ELLIOTT R.P. DSO DFC*. Born 13/4/17. Commd 1/3/37. Sqn Ldr 1/7/52. Retd GD 20/12/57. rtg Wg Cdr
ELLIOTT R.T. Born 27/7/41. Commd 10/4/67. Flt Lt 10/4/71. Retd ADMIN 1/10/87.
ELLIOTT S.W. Born 27/7/46. Commd 8/1/76. Sqn Ldr 1/1/01. Retd GD 1/1/03.
ELLIOTT T.E. MINucE. Born 4/12/20. Commd 26/9/57. Sqn Ldr 1/7/68. Retd ENG 2/1/71.
ELLIOTT T.J. Born 3/10/44. Commd 29/11/63. Flt Lt 1/7/69. Retd GD 22/10/94.
ELLIS A.C. BSc. Born 15/10/46. Commd 23/9/68. Flt Lt 23/3/70. Retd EDN 9/10/71.
ELLIS D. Born 25/11/28. Commd 5/12/51. Flt Lt 5/6/56. Retd GD(G) 25/11/88.
ELLIS D. Born 5/8/43. Commd 12/1/62. Flt Lt 12/7/67. Retd GD 5/8/76.
ELLIS D.C. MSc BSc CEng MIMechE. Born 18/9/57. Commd 23/9/79. Sqn Ldr 1/1/89. Retd ENG 30/4/00.
ELLIS D.J.A. Born 23/6/25. Commd 15/6/61. Sqn Ldr 1/7/74. Retd ENG 3/6/78.
ELLIS G.L. Born 25/9/30. Commd 6/9/68. Flt Lt 6/9/74. Retd SEC 17/10/81.
ELLIS H.R.W. Born 15/8/38. Commd 2/1/70. Flt Lt 15/2/65. Retd GD 11/9/76.
ELLIS H.W. BSc. Born 16/10/54. Commd 2/9/73. Flt Lt 15/10/77. Retd GD 15/7/88.
ELLIS J.C. Born 13/10/62. Commd 26/9/90. Flt Lt 26/9/92. Retd ADMIN 3/3/96.
ELLIS J.C. OBE CEng MIMechE MRAeS. Born 15/6/15. Commd 23/9/43. Wg Cdr 1/7/61. Retd ENG 25/11/67.
ELLIS J.D. Born 2/12/40. Commd 23/12/58. Flt Lt 1/7/64. Retd GD 15/5/76.
ELLIS J.R. Born 3/8/56. Commd 22/4/87. Flt Lt 23/4/89. Retd ADMIN 23/4/95.
ELLIS L.E. DFC. Born 19/6/12. Commd 12/7/37. Sqn Ldr 1/1/45. Retd GD 19/6/55. rtg Wg Cdr
ELLIS P.W. DFC. Born 23/1/43. Commd 31/1/43. Flt Lt 1/1/54. Retd GD 13/3/58.
ELLIS R. Born 5/9/40. Commd 22/5/70. Sqn Ldr 1/1/77. Retd GD(G) 1/1/80.
ELLIS R.A. Born 10/7/24. Commd 22/2/60. Sqn Ldr 1/7/65. Retd SUP 2/12/71.
ELLIS R.A. BA CertEd. Born 29/8/47. Commd 15/3/87. Sqn Ldr 1/7/98. Retd ADMIN (SEC) 15/3/03.
ELLIS R.A. Born 12/11/58. Commd 2/6/77. Flt Lt 2/12/82. Retd GD 7/12/00.

ELLIS R.H. MB BChir MRCOG. Born 8/7/32. Commd 16/2/59. Wg Cdr 16/2/72. Retd MED 16/2/75.
ELLIS R.M. Born 10/3/46. Commd 26/11/81. Flt Lt 16/10/86. Retd SUP 6/5/95.
ELLIS S. Born 30/5/52. Commd 30/1/75. Flt Lt 30/5/79. Retd GD(G) 29/5/81.
ELLIS T.D. Born 4/10/36. Commd 28/7/67. Flt Lt 28/7/69. Retd GD 5/8/75.
ELLIS T.J. MA. Born 18/8/52. Commd 2/1/74. Flt Lt 15/1/75. Retd GD 23/11/75.
ELLIS-MARTIN P. Born 1/8/55. Commd 2/11/88. Sqn Ldr 1/1/02. Retd MEDICAL SUPPORT 20/7/04.
ELLISON C.O. DFC. Born 28/9/19. Commd 19/3/43. Sqn Ldr 1/1/54. Retd GD 16/3/59.
ELLISON I. MCMI. Born 12/7/45. Commd 8/7/65. Wg Cdr 1/7/90. Retd ADMIN 12/7/00.
ELLISON J.T. ACIS. Born 30/7/19. Commd 22/3/43. Sqn Ldr 1/7/55. Retd SEC 1/7/71.
ELLISON T.B. Born 8/2/59. Commd 8/4/82. Flt Lt 8/4/87. Retd GD 8/3/96.
ELMES T.J.W. Born 30/6/26. Commd 23/4/47. Sqn Ldr 1/1/69. Retd SY 31/7/76.
ELMITT J.W. Born 5/12/32. Commd 13/9/51. Flt Lt 11/6/57. Retd GD 5/12/75.
ELPHICK A.P. Born 5/7/25. Commd 4/7/50. Sqn Ldr 1/7/72. Retd GD 31/8/73.
ELRICK A.D. Born 7/1/48. Commd 23/4/87. Flt Lt 23/4/91. Retd ADMIN 7/5/94.
ELSAM M.B. FCMI. Born 28/10/40. Commd 2/5/59. Gp Capt 1/7/84. Retd GD 11/6/90.
ELSDEN L.P. Born 22/11/23. Commd 6/6/45. Flt Lt 6/6/51. Retd RGT 31/12/59.
ELSDON I.J. Born 1/7/20. Commd 25/8/41. Flt Offr 1/9/45. Retd SEC 14/5/50. rtg Sqn Offr
ELSEGOOD A.W. Born 25/3/33. Commd 17/12/52. Flt Lt 12/5/58. Retd GD 25/3/71.
ELSEGOOD W.W. Born 30/9/33. Commd 8/5/53. Sqn Ldr 1/7/70. Retd GD 1/1/73.
ELSOM B. Born 13/10/36. Commd 18/11/64. Flt Lt 18/11/64. Retd GD 20/5/67.
ELTON D.H. Born 20/3/31. Commd 28/8/57. Fg Offr 28/8/57. Retd GD 26/2/64.
ELTON E.A. BA. Born 7/11/44. Commd 28/9/64. Sqn Ldr 1/7/75. Retd GD 3/5/02.
ELTON P. Born 24/9/32. Commd 5/9/69. Sqn Ldr 1/7/79. Retd GD(G) 5/4/85.
ELTON P.H. MCMI. Born 1/3/31. Commd 14/4/53. Gp Capt 1/1/81. Retd SUP 1/3/86.
ELTON P.J.G. BA MCIPD MCMI. Born 17/8/29. Commd 26/7/50. Sqn Ldr 1/7/61. Retd GD 31/12/80.
ELVIN E.A. MCMI. Born 15/6/20. Commd 27/2/58. Flt Lt 1/4/63. Retd ENG 25/6/75.
ELWAY D.R. Born 1/11/33. Commd 21/1/53. Sqn Ldr 1/1/67. Retd ADMIN 30/9/80.
ELWELL R.F. Born 21/5/36. Commd 1/2/56. Flt Lt 1/8/61. Retd GD(G) 21/5/91.
ELWORTHY The Hon Sir Timothy KCVO CBE. Born 27/1/38. Commd 28/7/59. A Cdre 1/7/87. Retd GD 27/1/93.
ELWY W.N. MRAeS. Born 6/8/12. Commd 10/4/31. Wg Cdr 1/7/48. Retd ENG 1/11/57. rtg Gp Capt
ELY P. MInstAM MCMI. Born 22/12/35. Commd 5/9/69. Sqn Ldr 1/7/76. Retd ADMIN 16/7/86.
EMBERSON K.J. Born 4/9/58. Commd 30/8/84. Flt Lt 30/8/86. Retd GD 4/9/96.
EMBLETON G.A. Born 11/10/31. Commd 26/9/51. Flt Lt 17/5/56. Retd GD 11/10/89.
EMERSON C. MBE. Born 19/12/48. Commd 19/6/86. Sqn Ldr 1/7/93. Retd ENG 1/1/97.
EMERSON J.E. Born 24/9/43. Commd 8/6/84. Sqn Ldr 1/7/93. Retd ENG 12/10/97.
EMERSON J.R. Born 4/2/25. Commd 4/9/58. Flt Lt 4/9/63. Retd ENG 5/2/75.
EMERSON K.J. MPhil BSc. Born 3/7/60. Commd 13/2/83. Sqn Ldr 1/1/94. Retd GD 13/2/99.
EMERY D.A. Born 27/10/32. Commd 3/12/56. Wg Cdr 1/1/76. Retd GD(G) 27/10/87.
EMERY J.V. OBE CEng MRAeS MCMI. Born 5/12/39. Commd 30/9/59. Wg Cdr 1/7/77. Retd ENG 5/12/89.
EMERY M.J.R. Born 12/4/38. Commd 14/6/63. Flt Lt 8/1/69. Retd GD 20/11/88.
EMERY S.J. Born 4/7/49. Commd 16/5/74. Flt Lt 16/11/79. Retd FLY(N) 21/4/03.
EMMERSON D. CBE AFC. Born 6/9/39. Commd 30/7/57. AVM 1/1/90. Retd GD 1/5/91.
EMMERSON D.E. Born 3/6/17. Commd 26/5/43. Flt Lt 4/6/53. Retd GD(G) 3/6/71.
EMMERSON J.G. Born 21/5/43. Commd 6/9/65. Flt Lt 6/9/69. Retd GD 6/9/81. Re-entered 3/11/86. Sqn Ldr 1/7/94.
    Retd GD 21/5/98.
EMMERSON R.J. Born 7/5/37. Commd 24/2/61. Flt Lt 25/7/66. Retd GD 5/5/74.
EMMETT P.C. PhD MSc BSc CEng MIEE. Born 2/6/51. Commd 29/9/85. Sqn Ldr 1/7/95. Retd ENG 29/9/01.
EMMETT W.A.C. Born 3/7/16. Commd 15/3/37. Sqn Ldr 1/7/51. Retd GD 30/4/58.
EMPSON D.K. MBE. Born 14/6/31. Commd 12/9/51. Gp Capt 1/1/81. Retd GD 16/6/83.
EMPSON H.G. CEng MRAeS MCMI. Born 10/2/28. Commd 25/8/60. Wg Cdr 1/1/76. Retd ENG 8/9/82.
EMPSON J.G. MSc MSc BEng CEng MIEE. Born 31/7/65. Commd 3/8/88. Sqn Ldr 1/1/00. Retd ENGINEER 31/7/03.
EMPTAGE J.A. BSc. Born 4/7/52. Commd 19/10/75. Flt Lt 19/1/76. Retd GD 1/3/99.
EMRYS-EVANS S. DFC MCMI. Born 3/6/20. Commd 3/7/44. Sqn Ldr 1/7/68. Retd GD(G) 9/6/75.
EMTAGE J.A. BSc. Born 5/4/64. Commd 5/9/82. Sqn Ldr 1/1/02. Retd FLY(P) 3/3/04.
ENDACOTT R. Born 14/1/31. Commd 21/11/51. Flt Lt 21/5/56. Retd GD 14/7/68.
ENDERBY G. Born 11/2/42. Commd 12/7/62. Gp Capt 1/7/87. Retd RGT 30/5/90.
ENGLAND D.C.E. MA. Born 5/7/33. Commd 6/4/54. Sqn Ldr 1/7/69. Retd GD 1/7/72.
ENGLAND H.A. DFC. Born 14/1/19. Commd 9/7/38. Wg Cdr 1/1/54. Retd GD 14/1/74.
ENGLAND H.G.C. Born 4/1/38. Commd 30/7/64. Sqn Ldr 1/7/81. Retd ADMIN 4/1/93.
ENGLAND J.D.L. MBE LLB MCIPD. Born 22/7/49. Commd 9/11/80. Wg Cdr 1/1/00. Retd GD 22/1/05.
ENGLAND K. Born 11/8/22. Commd 25/2/44. Flt Lt 17/5/56. Retd GD(G) 11/8/77.
ENGLAND R.J. Born 24/4/62. Commd 4/9/81. Flt Lt 4/3/87. Retd GD 1/3/89.
ENGLISH D.F. Born 15/9/40. Commd 15/10/81. Sqn Ldr 1/1/91. Retd ENG 1/10/93.
ENGLISH D.P. Born 11/8/29. Commd 1/8/51. Sqn Ldr 1/7/66. Retd GD 30/9/77.
ENGLISH H.A. MCMI. Born 10/1/21. Commd 9/9/54. Sqn Ldr 1/7/69. Retd ENG 9/4/73.
ENGLISH J.P. Born 16/2/54. Commd 13/9/80. Sqn Ldr 1/7/90. Retd GD 31/12/94.

ENGLISH K.A. Born 11/9/16. Commd 27/10/55. Flt Lt 27/10/58. Retd ENG 12/9/63.
ENGLISH R.G. DFC. Born 10/7/14. Commd 31/10/38. Sqn Ldr 1/8/47. Retd GD 3/8/57.
ENGWELL M.J. OBE. Born 9/9/44. Commd 31/8/62. Wg Cdr 1/1/83. Retd GD 9/9/01.
ENKEL P.A. AIIP. Born 27/4/35. Commd 21/10/66. Flt Lt 21/10/68. Retd ENG 21/10/84. Re-instated 2/6/77 to 2/6/85.
ENSTON J.N. Born 7/8/45. Commd 2/4/65. Flt Lt 2/10/70. Retd GD 7/8/00.
ENTICKNAP R.G. Born 6/10/15. Commd 1/12/40. Sqn Ldr 1/7/50. Retd ENG 8/12/51.
ENTWISLE B. Born 24/4/33. Commd 13/2/52. Gp Capt 1/1/85. Retd GD 20/6/87.
ENTWISLE P.A. Born 1/8/23. Commd 27/2/58. Sqn Ldr 1/7/75. Retd ADMIN 1/8/83.
ENVIS I.F.C. Born 10/3/49. Commd 27/3/70. Sqn Ldr 1/7/86. Retd SUP 1/7/89.
EPISCOPO S. MBE. Born 16/1/38. Commd 11/6/60. Sqn Ldr 1/7/87. Retd GD 14/4/93.
EPPS E.J.G. Born 29/2/20. Commd 26/2/45. Flt Lt 26/8/48. Retd GD 28/11/53.
EPPS W.R. Born 22/2/35. Commd 15/5/61. Flt Lt 15/5/62. Retd RGT 1/7/70.
EPTON O.W. Born 24/8/41. Commd 24/6/65. Sqn Ldr 1/7/74. Retd GD 30/9/78.
ERNSTING J. CB OBE PhD MB BS BSc FRAeS FRCP MFOM MRCS. Born 21/4/28. Commd 27/6/54. AVM 18/7/90.
    Retd MED 21/4/93.
ERRINGTON J.H. Born 26/10/21. Commd 14/7/44. Sqn Ldr 1/1/68. Retd GD(G) 26/10/76.
ERRINGTON M.E. Born 10/11/43. Commd 28/6/79. Sqn Ldr 1/1/93. Retd FLY(AEO) 10/11/03.
ERRY D.S. BEng. Born 14/12/65. Commd 14/8/88. Flt Lt 14/2/91. Retd GD 14/8/00.
ERSKINE C.E. Born 18/12/32. Commd 24/2/67. Sqn Ldr 1/7/76. Retd ENG 1/8/84.
ERSKINE H.G. Born 22/3/45. Commd 14/7/66. Flt Lt 14/1/72. Retd GD 11/12/76.
ERSKINE CRUM W.S. OBE. Born 26/3/42. Commd 30/7/63. Wg Cdr 1/1/86. Retd GD 26/6/97.
ERVINE T.E. Born 12/9/20. Commd 5/4/43. Flt Lt 24/2/50. Retd GD 17/6/54.
ERWICH J.A. Born 12/3/25. Commd 19/11/52. Flt Lt 20/10/60. Retd SEC 9/7/68.
ERWIN P.G. Born 8/8/42. Commd 23/11/78. Sqn Ldr 1/1/89. Retd ENG 20/4/96.
ERWOOD T.K. Born 26/5/21. Commd 7/7/49. Sqn Ldr 1/1/73. Retd GD 26/5/76.
ESCOTT B.E. BA MCMI. Born 23/12/29. Commd 15/2/61. Sqn Ldr 12/10/70. Retd ADMIN 23/12/85.
ESPLEY R.H. BEM. Born 27/12/06. Commd 5/11/42. Flt Lt 5/5/46. Retd ENG 28/12/61.
ESPLIN I.G. CB OBE DFC MA BEc. Born 26/2/14. Commd 19/10/40. AVM 1/1/63. Retd GD 8/9/65.
ESSERY J.C. AFC BEM. Born 2/7/45. Commd 1/4/85. Sqn Ldr 1/7/88. Retd GD 1/10/91.
ESSEX B.J.N. AFC. Born 28/9/44. Commd 28/2/64. Wg Cdr 1/7/81. Retd GD 2/11/85.
ESSON D.G. Born 5/6/47. Commd 23/9/66. Sqn Ldr 1/7/82. Retd GD 1/7/85.
ETCHELLS K. Born 3/12/22. Commd 17/2/45. Flt Lt 17/8/48. Retd GD 1/3/61.
ETCHES R.A.W. Born 25/2/58. Commd 31/8/78. Flt Lt 29/2/84. Retd GD 1/10/98.
ETHEREDGE G.H. Born 29/4/08. Commd 5/8/41. Flt Lt 12/5/44. Retd ENG 14/1/46. rtg Sqn Ldr
ETHERIDGE E.K. Born 22/7/13. Commd 9/3/44. Flt Lt 19/6/52. Retd SUP 22/7/60.
ETHERIDGE J. Born 28/5/58. Commd 8/5/86. Wg Cdr 1/1/99. Retd ENG 28/5/02.
ETHERINGTON R.F. Born 2/2/24. Commd 25/3/45. Flt Lt 25/9/48. Retd GD 26/11/55.
ETKINS J. Born 11/10/25. Commd 11/5/45. Sqn Ldr 1/7/61. Retd GD 1/7/64.
ETTRIDGE A.G. Born 8/8/35. Commd 30/7/57. Sqn Ldr 1/7/68. Retd GD 8/8/73.
EUSTACE P.H. Born 5/8/42. Commd 12/1/62. A Cdre 1/1/91. Retd GD 3/4/98.
EVA H.J. Born 24/2/36. Commd 30/4/59. Wg Cdr 1/1/78. Retd ADMIN 24/2/91.
EVA V.J. Born 23/4/11. Commd 19/1/50. Flt Lt 19/7/52. Retd ENG 1/5/59.
EVANS A. Born 6/11/35. Commd 1/4/58. Flt Lt 26/2/64. Retd GD 5/2/77.
EVANS A. BSc. Born 6/11/45. Commd 1/3/68. Sqn Ldr 1/1/83. Retd ENG 20/7/96.
EVANS A.A. Born 23/5/22. Commd 15/5/45. Sqn Ldr 1/7/58. Retd GD 23/5/65.
EVANS A.J. Born 18/2/46. Commd 1/3/68. Flt Lt 8/3/72. Retd GD 18/2/84.
EVANS A.M. Born 12/7/48. Commd 27/2/70. Flt Lt 27/8/75. Retd GD 12/7/89.
EVANS B. MBE MRAeS. Born 4/2/34. Commd 11/2/64. Sqn Ldr 1/7/75. Retd ENG 4/2/94.
EVANS B.A. BSc. Born 13/4/65. Commd 11/10/84. Flt Lt 15/1/89. Retd GD 15/7/98.
EVANS B.D. Born 18/6/43. Commd 27/2/70. Flt Lt 25/9/72. Retd GD(G) 18/6/81.
EVANS B.K.J. BSc. Born 18/6/40. Commd 22/10/63. Sqn Ldr 22/4/73. Retd EDN 22/10/79.
EVANS C. MBE. Born 7/11/38. Commd 27/6/59. Flt Lt 14/2/60. Retd GD 7/11/93.
EVANS C.D. MB BS MRCP DObstRCOG DPhysMed. Born 15/11/32. Commd 21/6/59. Wg Cdr 24/9/71.
    Retd MED 21/6/75.
EVANS C.D. OBE. Born 4/4/48. Commd 1/8/69. Gp Capt 1/7/97. Retd ADMIN 18/8/02.
EVANS C.E. CBE. Born 21/4/37. Commd 4/5/53. AVM 1/1/89. Retd GD 21/4/92.
EVANS C.H. Born 24/3/36. Commd 9/7/57. Flt Lt 26/5/69. Retd SUP 9/2/77.
EVANS C.J. BSc. Born 12/12/51. Commd 18/3/84. Flt Lt 18/9/80. Retd ADMIN 18/3/00.
EVANS C.R. OBE. Born 21/6/25. Commd 29/3/45. Wg Cdr 1/1/64. Retd GD 12/2/77.
EVANS C.W. Born 10/2/23. Commd 28/7/45. Wg Cdr 1/1/74. Retd ADMIN 13/1/78.
EVANS D. AFC. Born 16/6/24. Commd 5/5/45. Flt Lt 5/11/47. Retd GD 16/6/67.
EVANS Sir David GCB CBE CCMI. Born 14/7/24. Commd 7/4/44. ACM 31/3/78. Retd GD 9/8/83.
EVANS D. Born 2/12/47. Commd 11/4/85. Sqn Ldr 1/1/96. Retd ENGINEER 3/4/05.
EVANS D.A.T. Born 21/9/39. Commd 29/11/63. Flt Lt 15/10/66. Retd GD 21/9/80.
EVANS D.B.L. BSc. Born 18/6/71. Commd 11/2/96. Flt Lt 11/8/99. Retd SUPPLY 31/8/03.
EVANS D.C. MB ChB MRCOG. Born 15/3/47. Commd 21/11/71. Wg Cdr 6/8/88. Retd MED 21/11/88.

EVANS D.C. Born 19/4/58. Commd 26/9/90. Flt Lt 26/9/92. Retd ADMIN 26/9/98.
EVANS D.C. Born 12/10/26. Commd 18/7/63. Sqn Ldr 1/1/78. Retd PRT 1/9/79.
EVANS D.G. Born 8/2/38. Commd 4/12/64. Flt Lt 8/1/69. Retd GD 30/6/72.
EVANS D.J. Born 17/4/29. Commd 11/6/53. Flt Lt 11/12/56. Retd GD 17/4/67.
EVANS D.J. Born 18/7/50. Commd 19/12/85. Sqn Ldr 1/7/96. Retd SUP 13/8/01.
EVANS D.J. Born 18/1/65. Commd 8/11/90. Flt Lt 25/6/93. Retd ENG 18/1/03.
EVANS D.K. Born 16/4/35. Commd 25/7/56. Sqn Ldr 1/1/80. Retd ENG 16/4/93.
EVANS D.M. Born 8/3/36. Commd 29/3/56. Sqn Ldr 1/7/70. Retd SEC 1/5/79.
EVANS D.N. MCIPD MRIN. Born 28/8/34. Commd 30/7/52. Sqn Ldr 1/1/80. Retd GD 1/10/85.
EVANS D.O. Born 10/12/23. Commd 1/10/43. Sqn Ldr 1/1/61. Retd GD 25/2/65.
EVANS D.R. Born 20/2/31. Commd 29/3/50. Flt Lt 29/9/54. Retd GD 15/3/69.
EVANS D.R.E. Born 19/10/52. Commd 16/3/73. Gp Capt 1/1/98. Retd GD 4/4/05.
EVANS D.R.J. MA CEng MIEE DipEL. Born 27/4/31. Commd 26/9/53. Wg Cdr 1/7/69. Retd ENG 27/4/83.
EVANS D.S. Born 7/2/50. Commd 2/5/69. Fg Offr 2/11/71. Retd PI 1/2/73.
EVANS D.T. OBE. Born 17/10/24. Commd 16/2/45. Wg Cdr 1/1/68. Retd GD 17/10/82.
EVANS E. Born 11/2/57. Commd 24/4/80. Flt Lt 24/10/85. Retd GD 30/6/89.
EVANS E. OBE. Born 5/9/21. Commd 3/7/42. Wg Cdr 1/7/59. Retd GD 6/8/66.
EVANS E.E. Born 25/10/29. Commd 7/1/61. Flt Lt 27/2/72. Retd ADMIN 27/2/78.
EVANS E.G. Born 24/1/16. Commd 27/1/45. Flt Lt 27/3/51. Retd GD(G) 30/1/65.
EVANS E.J. Born 26/12/20. Commd 27/10/55. Sqn Ldr 1/7/67. Retd ENG 9/6/73.
EVANS F.E. Born 16/4/13. Commd 12/8/40. Wg Cdr 1/1/57. Retd SEC 16/4/65.
EVANS G.A. Born 20/5/38. Commd 28/1/60. Flt Lt 28/7/66. Retd ENG 20/5/76.
EVANS G.E.W. MCMI. Born 2/10/31. Commd 5/11/52. Wg Cdr 1/1/77. Retd GD 4/10/85.
EVANS G.H. MSc BSc CEng MIEE MRAeS. Born 4/2/55. Commd 28/7/88. Flt Lt 28/7/90. Retd ENG 29/9/98.
EVANS G.H. BSc. Born 25/11/59. Commd 6/9/81. Flt Lt 6/12/82. Retd GD 25/11/97.
EVANS G.H.D. DSO DFC. Born 29/6/17. Commd 18/12/37. Wg Cdr 1/1/49. Retd GD 29/5/68.
EVANS G.M. Born 6/10/21. Commd 12/8/47. Flt Lt 12/2/52. Retd SEC 27/10/55.
EVANS G.P. Born 28/8/49. Commd 31/7/70. Flt Lt 31/7/73. Retd GD 2/9/81.
EVANS G.R. MRAeS. Born 12/6/56. Commd 20/7/78. Gp Capt 1/1/98. Retd GD 7/4/00.
EVANS H.J. Born 12/2/61. Commd 15/8/85. Flt Lt 30/1/89. Retd GD 14/3/96.
EVANS H.N. Born 22/2/32. Commd 3/11/51. Flt Lt 17/5/56. Retd GD 30/12/63.
EVANS I. Born 22/3/48. Commd 17/2/67. Gp Capt 1/1/95. Retd GD 1/3/00.
EVANS I.M. Born 5/7/40. Commd 15/6/83. Sqn Ldr 1/7/92. Retd ENG 5/7/95.
EVANS J. Born 5/10/39. Commd 1/8/61. Gp Capt 1/1/90. Retd GD 5/10/94.
EVANS J.A. BA. Born 3/1/44. Commd 31/10/63. Wg Cdr 1/1/88. Retd ADMIN 22/6/94.
EVANS J.E.C. MB BCh DAvMed. Born 5/9/49. Commd 23/1/72. Wg Cdr 14/7/88. Retd MED 26/7/90.
EVANS J.G. MBE MBA BA. Born 1/5/55. Commd 16/9/73. Wg Cdr 1/1/94. Retd OPS SPT 7/5/00.
EVANS J.J. BA. Born 19/8/32. Commd 30/9/54. Sqn Ldr 15/2/65. Retd EDN 30/9/71.
EVANS J.L.D. Born 2/8/23. Commd 29/6/50. Fg Offr 29/6/51. Retd RGT 15/7/55.
EVANS J.M. DFC. Born 5/12/33. Commd 24/1/52. Flt Lt 29/5/57. Retd GD 15/10/73.
EVANS J.M. Born 28/12/14. Commd 15/3/35. Sqn Ldr 1/3/45. Retd GD(G) 30/4/61. rtg Wg Cdr
EVANS J.P. Born 20/12/39. Commd 6/4/62. Wg Cdr 1/7/91. Retd GD 3/7/93.
EVANS J.R. MDA BSc CEng MRAeS. Born 30/9/60. Commd 2/9/79. Sqn Ldr 1/1/93. Retd ENG 15/12/98.
EVANS J.R. Born 13/8/19. Commd 6/11/45. Flt Lt 6/11/50. Retd SEC 5/11/55.
EVANS J.V. Born 30/3/43. Commd 6/9/63. Flt Lt 6/3/69. Retd GD 30/3/84.
EVANS J.V. MCIPS MCMI. Born 12/7/26. Commd 6/8/63. Sqn Ldr 1/1/69. Retd SUP 6/11/85.
EVANS J.W. Born 24/9/35. Commd 25/6/67. Flt Lt 26/5/69. Retd SUP 19/7/74.
EVANS K. Born 18/12/41. Commd 30/7/63. Sqn Ldr 1/1/74. Retd GD 17/5/79.
EVANS K.A.D. Born 30/8/41. Commd 14/8/62. Flt Lt 14/2/68. Retd GD 31/8/79.
EVANS K.B.G. Born 24/1/20. Commd 18/9/47. Flt Lt 29/11/51. Retd PI 24/1/75.
EVANS K.R. Born 10/2/40. Commd 27/3/63. Flt Lt 27/9/66. Retd GD 31/10/70.
EVANS K.W.S. DFC. Born 24/12/19. Commd 10/6/42. Flt Lt 23/4/51. Retd GD 6/10/64.
EVANS L. DPhysEd. Born 29/11/38. Commd 25/9/62. Flt Lt 25/9/66. Retd PE 25/9/78.
EVANS L.H. Born 11/2/11. Commd 12/3/42. Sqn Ldr 1/1/53. Retd ENG 19/6/65.
EVANS L.N. Born 8/6/59. Commd 24/3/83. Flt Lt 24/9/88. Retd ENG 2/1/99.
EVANS M. Born 16/12/49. Commd 4/2/71. Flt Lt 1/4/75. Retd GD 1/10/90.
EVANS M.C. Born 18/1/41. Commd 26/8/66. Flt Lt 28/1/73. Retd ADMIN 18/1/96.
EVANS M.D. Born 26/2/39. Commd 25/7/60. Sqn Ldr 1/7/70. Retd GD 30/9/85.
EVANS M.E.S. Born 24/11/26. Commd 14/6/46. Flt Lt 15/12/49. Retd GD 24/11/64.
EVANS M.H. IEng FIEE. Born 4/10/44. Commd 25/10/73. Sqn Ldr 1/1/85. Retd ENG 4/10/99.
EVANS M.J. CEng MIMechE MRAeS. Born 12/6/35. Commd 23/7/58. A Cdre 1/7/84. Retd ENG 1/7/86.
EVANS M.N. Born 5/4/40. Commd 4/4/59. Gp Capt 1/1/90. Retd GD 5/4/95.
EVANS M.P. MSc. Born 7/8/55. Commd 30/8/84. Sqn Ldr 1/1/00. Retd ENGINEER 2/8/04.
EVANS M.R. BSc. Born 3/3/58. Commd 3/5/77. Flt Lt 15/10/80. Retd GD 26/11/96.
EVANS M.W. BA. Born 22/10/59. Commd 28/2/82. Flt Lt 28/8/85. Retd ADMIN 17/6/89.
EVANS N. Born 27/11/44. Commd 19/6/64. Flt Lt 15/4/70. Retd GD 1/7/76.

EVANS N.M. Born 26/2/50. Commd 30/5/69. Gp Capt 1/7/93. Retd GD(G) 5/4/96.
EVANS N.V. Born 31/1/37. Commd 21/4/64. Fg Offr 21/10/64. Retd ENG 1/3/68.
EVANS P. MEd BA. Born 6/3/62. Commd 20/1/85. Sqn Ldr 1/7/94. Retd ADMIN 20/1/02.
EVANS P.A. Born 5/5/53. Commd 29/6/72. Sqn Ldr 1/7/89. Retd GD 1/5/01.
EVANS P.G. CEng MRAeS MIEE. Born 29/12/30. Commd 22/12/55. Sqn Ldr 1/7/66. Retd ENG 7/9/71.
EVANS P.I. MSc MBA BSc. Born 15/2/60. Commd 23/11/80. Sqn Ldr 1/1/92. Retd ENG 15/2/98.
EVANS P.L. Born 19/9/39. Commd 27/2/75. Flt Lt 12/6/70. Retd ADMIN 27/2/83.
EVANS P.R. AFC. Born 13/9/34. Commd 26/7/55. Flt Lt 26/1/58. Retd GD 13/9/72.
EVANS P.R. Born 16/6/29. Commd 15/6/61. Fg Offr 15/6/61. Retd ENG 17/12/66.
EVANS P.W. BSc. Born 14/11/65. Commd 6/4/94. Sqn Ldr 1/7/00. Retd OPS SPT(FC) 14/11/03.
EVANS R. Born 4/8/30. Commd 4/9/58. Wg Cdr 1/1/80. Retd GD 1/9/85.
EVANS R. Born 30/10/57. Commd 10/3/77. Flt Lt 10/9/82. Retd GD 29/3/95.
EVANS R.A. Born 21/8/43. Commd 29/6/72. Flt Lt 29/6/74. Retd GD 12/01.
EVANS R.C. Born 11/8/23. Commd 24/11/44. Flt Lt 18/2/49. Retd GD 16/1/60.
EVANS R.J. CEng MRAeS. Born 29/7/35. Commd 4/1/60. Sqn Ldr 1/1/76. Retd ENG 29/7/89.
EVANS R.W.D. Born 15/9/24. Commd 19/4/56. Sqn Ldr 1/4/56. Retd GD 5/10/63.
EVANS S.J.R. Born 22/4/18. Commd 29/10/42. Sqn Ldr 1/7/53. Retd ENG 22/4/73.
EVANS S.M. BSc. Born 24/9/51. Commd 13/9/70. Sqn Ldr 1/1/89. Retd GD 1/1/92.
EVANS S.R. BA. Born 3/7/46. Commd 2/4/71. Flt Lt 15/10/69. Retd GD 31/10/72.
EVANS T.E.W. BA. Born 4/7/15. Commd 20/5/41. Sqn Ldr 29/9/51. Retd EDN 1/9/66.
EVANS T.L. BSc. Born 24/7/51. Commd 28/9/70. Sqn Ldr 1/1/85. Retd GD 24/7/89.
EVANS T.N. Born 14/11/44. Commd 13/2/86. Flt Lt 13/2/90. Retd GD(G) 7/12/96.
EVANS T.W. BSc. Born 1/10/24. Commd 12/9/61. Sqn Ldr 12/3/65. Retd ADMIN 12/9/77.
EVANS W.D. Born 13/12/12. Commd 8/8/40. Flt Lt 8/8/42. Retd 23/5/47.
EVANS W.E. DFC. Born 4/9/21. Commd 26/7/43. Sqn Ldr 1/4/56. Retd GD 4/9/64.
EVANS W.E. Born 1/10/13. Commd 14/3/46. Sqn Ldr 1/7/58. Retd SUP 16/10/62.
EVANS W.G. OBE. Born 5/1/53. Commd 16/9/73. Gp Capt 1/7/02. Retd GD 9/5/03.
EVANS W.H. DFC AFC. Born 15/12/16. Commd 24/10/44. Flt Lt 29/11/51. Retd GD(G) 16/12/71.
EVANS W.J. Born 17/7/40. Commd 20/5/82. Flt Lt 1/3/87. Retd ENG 17/7/95.
EVE J. Born 19/8/12. Commd 24/6/40. Flt Lt 1/9/45. Retd GD(G) 31/8/64. rtg Sqn Ldr
EVE J.S. Born 24/2/52. Commd 12/10/78. Flt Lt 25/4/81. Retd GD 24/2/90.
EVELEIGH G.C. CB OBE. Born 25/10/12. Commd 16/12/33. AVM 1/1/61. Retd GD 27/3/65.
EVELEIGH M. OBE MCMI. Born 9/12/48. Commd 7/6/68. Wg Cdr 1/7/92. Retd SY 14/3/97.
EVERALL N.D. Born 8/4/59. Commd 23/11/78. Wg Cdr 1/7/00. Retd GD 1/10/04.
EVEREST K. Born 1/11/39. Commd 19/4/63. Sqn Ldr 1/1/86. Retd GD 1/11/94.
EVEREST L.H. Born 11/4/23. Commd 3/4/43. Flt Lt 8/1/49. Retd GD 30/3/77.
EVERETT B.D. MBE BA FCMI MCIPS MInstAM(Dip) MRAeS. Born 17/6/35. Commd 26/9/57. Wg Cdr 1/1/75.
    Retd SUP 1/9/85.
EVERETT E.W. Born 25/6/18. Commd 30/12/42. Sqn Ldr 1/7/54. Retd SEC 25/6/73.
EVERITT A.J. MSc BEd DIC. Born 11/7/45. Commd 20/1/80. Sqn Ldr 1/7/88. Retd ADMIN 10/8/91.
EVERITT G.H. CBE DSO DFC*. Born 29/12/17. Commd 9/6/40. Gp Capt 1/7/58. Retd GD 29/12/67.
EVERITT J.W. MBE MCMI. Born 12/3/24. Commd 9/11/44. Sqn Ldr 1/7/67. Retd GD 12/3/79.
EVERITT W.M. CEng MRAeS. Born 31/10/39. Commd 17/7/62. Wg Cdr 1/1/78. Retd ENG 1/2/94.
EVERS E.D. Born 6/11/36. Commd 5/3/55. Sqn Ldr 1/7/67. Retd GD 1/1/74.
EVERSHED T.A. BA MB BCh MRCS MFCM LRCP DPH DIH. Born 17/10/21. Commd 18/4/46. A Cdre 19/10/74.
    Retd MED 18/1/75.
EVERSON D.G. DFM. Born 13/12/21. Commd 8/2/43. Flt Lt 8/8/46. Retd GD(G) 13/12/76.
EVERSON R.C. OBE AFC. Born 16/2/20. Commd 29/5/43. Wg Cdr 1/1/59. Retd GD 16/2/67.
EVERSON R.M. Born 13/11/57. Commd 5/4/79. Flt Lt 5/10/84. Retd GD 13/5/96.
EVERY T. Born 18/2/22. Commd 19/9/43. Flt Lt 27/5/54. Retd GD 24/10/63.
EVES D.G.E.D. Born 28/7/49. Commd 24/11/67. Flt Lt 24/5/74. Retd ADMIN 1/8/94.
EVES D.V. Born 2/1/29. Commd 10/3/59. Flt Lt 10/3/65. Retd GD(G) 2/1/67.
EVESHAM D.A. MSc BSc MBCS. Born 11/7/53. Commd 2/3/80. Sqn Ldr 1/1/89. Retd ADMIN 2/3/96.
EVETTS P.C. Born 8/11/33. Commd 29/12/51. Flt Lt 25/10/57. Retd GD 2/7/65.
EVETTS R. Born 19/11/20. Commd 11/4/57. Sqn Ldr 1/7/68. Retd ENG 19/11/73.
EWAN J. MA. Born 25/1/30. Commd 28/6/55. Wg Cdr 1/1/72. Retd GD 25/6/85.
EWEN G.P. MA. Born 13/2/66. Commd 14/2/88. Flt Lt 14/8/91. Retd OPS SPT(ATC) 14/2/04.
EWENS A.V. Born 25/11/31. Commd 2/6/52. Flt Lt 27/11/57. Retd GD 11/4/91.
EWENS W.W.H. MCMI. Born 23/11/35. Commd 19/8/54. Sqn Ldr 1/7/69. Retd GD 21/8/76.
EWER A.C. Born 16/1/37. Commd 25/7/59. Sqn Ldr 1/7/72. Retd GD 1/4/94.
EWER R.M. Born 8/6/63. Commd 25/2/82. Flt Lt 25/8/87. Retd GD 1/2/96.
EWER R.P. Born 14/2/65. Commd 15/2/90. Flt Lt 15/8/96. Retd OPS SPT(FLTOPS) 25/6/05.
EWING M.I.H. Born 3/2/27. Commd 17/1/49. Sqn Ldr 1/7/70. Retd SY 1/6/77.
EWING P.M.M. CEng MRAeS. Born 20/3/30. Commd 15/7/54. Sqn Ldr 26/2/64. Retd ADMIN 1/10/77.
EXELL P.F. Born 10/7/33. Commd 23/12/53. Sqn Ldr 1/7/68. Retd ENG 10/7/71.
EXLER R.W. Born 21/2/51. Commd 4/7/69. Flt Lt 4/1/75. Retd GD 2/8/89.

EXLEY B.J.A. Born 13/5/36. Commd 7/3/65. Flt Lt 8/3/72. Retd ADMIN 30/1/78. Re-instated 19/10/83. Sqn Ldr 1/1/89.
    Retd ADMIN 31/10/91.
EXLEY D. Born 4/12/33. Commd 11/6/52. Flt Lt 18/12/57. Retd GD 4/12/71.
EXLEY D.A. MBE. Born 3/1/26. Commd 22/8/63. Sqn Ldr 1/1/74. Retd GD(G) 31/1/86.
EXTON M.H. DFC. Born 8/12/16. Commd 6/11/42. Sqn Ldr 1/1/52. Retd GD 3/5/59.
EXTON S.W. Born 24/10/49. Commd 18/4/74. Wg Cdr 1/1/94. Retd GD 24/10/99.
EXWOOD I.W.R. CEng MRAeS. Born 10/1/38. Commd 28/7/60. Sqn Ldr 1/7/60. Retd ENG 10/1/76.
EYLES E.J. MSc CEng MIEE. Born 21/2/31. Commd 25/9/62. Sqn Ldr 4/1/68. Retd EDN 27/9/83.
EYNON A.V. Born 6/7/12. Commd 31/12/41. Flt Lt 22/10/45. Retd ENG 30/12/57. rtg Sqn Ldr
EYNON J.F. Born 21/2/28. Commd 5/11/52. Sqn Ldr 1/1/72. Retd ADMIN 29/11/80.
EYRE J.W. AFC. Born 8/10/32. Commd 6/12/51. Flt Lt 13/11/57. Retd GD 9/10/79.
EZRA W.A. Born 25/6/17. Commd 6/8/44. Sqn Ldr 1/7/65. Retd SUP 12/7/72.

F

FABIAN G.C. MSc BSc CEng MRAeS. Born 28/11/56. Commd 17/8/80. Sqn Ldr 1/1/91. Retd ENG 1/1/97.
FACE P.P. CEng MRAeS MCMI. Born 26/12/23. Commd 28/3/46. Wg Cdr 1/1/72. Retd ENG 31/3/78.
FACER P. Born 1/3/56. Commd 1/7/82. Flt Lt 1/7/84. Retd GD 1/3/94.
FACEY D.E. FCA. Born 11/5/32. Commd 4/7/57. Sqn Ldr 1/7/70. Retd ADMIN 11/5/82.
FAGG A.J. Born 11/8/52. Commd 10/2/72. Sqn Ldr 1/1/86. Retd GD(G) 11/8/90.
FAGG G.A. BSc. Born 31/1/59. Commd 13/10/77. Flt Lt 15/10/81. Retd GD 31/1/97.
FAGG P.S. MB BS. Born 2/3/51. Commd 19/2/74. Wg Cdr 7/9/89. Retd MED 22/8/90.
FAHY P.E. DFC AFC. Born 14/6/21. Commd 18/5/44. Flt Lt 6/2/48. Retd GD 9/8/58.
FAIERS J.H. Born 19/4/43. Commd 14/8/80. Sqn Ldr 1/1/90. Retd ENG 19/4/98.
FAINT P.E. Born 16/2/38. Commd 30/11/56. Flt Lt 24/5/63. Retd GD 13/7/78.
FAIR G.P. Born 24/8/48. Commd 11/8/77. Sqn Ldr 1/7/92. Retd GD 1/8/94.
FAIR P.C. Born 18/5/06. Commd 15/11/26. Flt Lt 1/8/33. Retd GD 8/4/37.
FAIRBAIRN A.D. Born 16/2/45. Commd 24/2/67. Sqn Ldr 1/7/80. Retd SUP 14/3/97.
FAIRBAIRN D. BSc. Born 26/8/21. Commd 14/2/49. Sqn Ldr 1/7/67. Retd GD 26/8/76.
FAIRBAIRN J.M. Born 7/1/59. Commd 25/9/80. Sqn Ldr 1/7/95. Retd GD 6/10/97.
FAIRBRASS P. MInstAM. Born 23/6/60. Commd 16/2/86. Sqn Ldr 1/7/00. Retd ADMIN (SEC) 1/7/03.
FAIRBURN M.R. Born 8/6/57. Commd 11/2/93. Sqn Ldr 1/7/03. Retd OPS SPT(FLTOPS) 1/7/05.
FAIREY M.J. Born 25/7/31. Commd 22/1/54. Flt Lt 22/7/59. Retd GD(G) 6/10/69.
FAIRFOOT C.F. Born 20/1/17. Commd 20/10/41. Sqn Ldr 1/7/52. Retd SUP 1/8/64.
FAIRGRIEVE J.C. DFC. Born 17/2/18. Commd 1/5/42. Flt Lt 1/11/45. Retd GD 4/1/54.
FAIRGRIEVE P.J. Born 14/5/38. Commd 2/6/77. Flt Lt 2/6/82. Retd GD(G) 30/7/90.
FAIRHEAD I.F. BSc(Eng). Born 29/8/39. Commd 1/1/63. Sqn Ldr 1/1/71. Retd ENG 29/8/94.
FAIRHURST E.A. DFC TD. Born 14/4/18. Commd 13/5/40. Wg Cdr 1/1/55. Retd GD 22/5/65.
FAIRHURST G.L. Born 21/6/52. Commd 27/3/86. Flt Lt 27/3/88. Retd GD(ENG) 10/10/89.
FAIRHURST P. MBE. Born 7/4/27. Commd 27/9/50. Sqn Ldr 1/1/62. Retd ENG 7/4/82. rtg Wg Cdr
FAIRWEATHER A.J. BSc(Eng) ACGI. Born 31/12/38. Commd 2/10/61. Gp Capt 1/1/93. Retd GD 1/1/96.
FAIRWEATHER J.M. Born 23/4/30. Commd 1/2/56. Sqn Ldr 1/1/70. Retd PRT 1/4/76.
FAITH M.M. Born 1/7/12. Commd 17/1/41. Sqn Offr 1/1/50. Retd SEC 10/12/61.
FALCONER D.G. Born 28/5/11. Commd 2/11/44. Flt Lt 2/2/52. Retd GD(G) 28/5/61.
FALCONER G. BEM. Born 14/4/23. Commd 22/7/63. Flt Lt 22/7/69. Retd SEC 14/4/73.
FALCONER N. BSc MRAeS FIS. Born 9/7/33. Commd 18/10/55. Flt Lt 18/7/57. Retd GD 18/1/72.
FALCONER N.A. Born 13/12/14. Commd 13/6/46. Flt Lt 29/11/51. Retd RGT 28/11/57.
FALCONER R.J. Born 29/12/33. Commd 10/3/77. Flt Lt 10/3/82. Retd ENG 16/11/87.
FALK V.S. Born 1/7/16. Commd 5/4/44. Flt Offr 4/1/51. Retd SUP 1/7/54.
FALKINER R.J.T. Born 28/8/41. Commd 28/7/64. Sqn Ldr 1/7/75. Retd SUP 28/8/79.
FALL L.A. Born 21/10/46. Commd 6/5/65. Flt Lt 5/8/71. Retd SEC 31/1/73.
FALL R.M. FHCIMA MCMI. Born 5/12/46. Commd 11/8/69. Sqn Ldr 1/1/79. Retd ADMIN 11/8/85.
FALLON F. MRAeS. Born 12/1/20. Commd 19/8/42. Sqn Ldr 1/1/61. Retd ENG 13/1/68.
FALLON P. BA. Born 25/7/37. Commd 7/8/59. Sqn Ldr 7/2/67. Retd EDN 7/8/75.
FALLON R.D. MBE. Born 29/11/44. Commd 22/12/67. Sqn Ldr 1/7/88. Retd GD 29/11/02.
FALLOW D. Born 25/12/55. Commd 22/9/88. Sqn Ldr 1/7/97. Retd ENG 2/4/01.
FANNON J.V. Born 29/2/16. Commd 30/1/47. Flt Lt 30/7/51. Retd SUP 1/3/65.
FARAGHER G.E. CEng MIEE MRAeS. Born 5/9/37. Commd 28/7/60. Sqn Ldr 1/7/69. Retd ENG 5/9/75.
FARCI V.I.A. Born 14/6/57. Commd 9/5/91. Sqn Ldr 1/7/97. Retd GD 1/7/00.
FARDELL J.B. Born 12/9/35. Commd 3/5/60. Flt Lt 3/3/66. Retd GD 12/9/73.
FARES D.B. MInstAM MHSM MCMI. Born 20/3/48. Commd 8/9/77. Wg Cdr 1/7/89. Retd MED(SEC) 14/3/96.
FAREY M.J. Born 26/11/41. Commd 17/5/62. Sqn Ldr 1/7/77. Retd SY 1/7/83.
FARISH T.J. BSc. Born 26/12/55. Commd 15/9/74. Sqn Ldr 1/7/87. Retd GD 26/12/93.
FARLAM G.A. BSc. Born 14/3/34. Commd 26/7/55. Flt Lt 26/1/58. Retd GD 14/3/72.
FARLEY G.G. Born 29/7/26. Commd 7/10/48. Gp Capt 1/1/78. Retd GD 16/2/79.
FARLEY G.H. AFC. Born 10/4/22. Commd 24/5/44. Flt Lt 11/11/54. Retd GD 17/10/61.
FARLEY J.F. AFC. Born 17/4/33. Commd 21/9/55. Flt Lt 14/6/61. Retd GD 6/9/67.
FARLEY R.F. Born 5/6/57. Commd 19/3/81. Sqn Ldr 1/7/93. Retd FLY(P) 1/3/03.
FARLEY R.H. MCMI. Born 14/2/30. Commd 12/12/51. Sqn Ldr 1/7/69. Retd SEC 30/8/80.
FARLEY R.M. Born 31/3/34. Commd 18/2/53. Wg Cdr 1/7/76. Retd GD(G) 10/11/88.
FARMAN R.J. BSc. (Eur Ing) CEng CDipAF MiMechE MCIBSE MBIFM. Born 18/6/52. Commd 13/9/70.
    Sqn Ldr 1/1/90. Retd ENG 18/6/93.
FARMER A.T. Born 22/1/39. Commd 19/1/66. Sqn Ldr 1/1/81. Retd GD 15/1/93.
FARMER B.L. BSc CEng MIMechE MRAeS MCMI. Born 3/10/45. Commd 23/8/83. Sqn Ldr 1/7/89. Retd ENG 1/7/93.
FARMER D.J. MSc BSc MB ChB FRSH MRCGP DRCOG DAvMed DPDerm. Born 7/3/61. Commd 6/11/83.
    Wg Cdr 6/8/99. Retd MED 30/9/02.

FARMER H.A. Born 11/1/60. Commd 8/6/84. Flt Lt 8/12/90. Retd SUP 31/3/94.
FARMER H.T.C. Born 1/10/28. Commd 6/9/51. Gp Capt 1/1/74. Retd GD 2/4/77.
FARMER L.R. MBE. Born 16/4/22. Commd 2/10/58. Sqn Ldr 1/1/70. Retd ENG 21/7/73.
FARMER M.E. Born 26/12/39. Commd 27/3/75. Sqn Ldr 1/7/87. Retd ENG 26/12/94.
FARMER M.J. Born 22/4/45. Commd 16/9/76. Sqn Ldr 1/7/84. Retd ENG 22/4/00.
FARMER M.K. Born 20/1/48. Commd 24/11/67. Sqn Ldr 1/7/88. Retd GD 1/5/02.
FARMER R.A. Born 4/2/42. Commd 9/12/71. Flt Lt 9/6/78. Retd GD(G) 28/6/88.
FARMER R.G. BSc. Born 23/9/31. Commd 23/9/55. Sqn Ldr 23/3/65. Retd EDN 23/9/71.
FARMER R.M.L. MILT MCIT. Born 12/12/65. Commd 29/7/91. Flt Lt 16/6/94. Retd SUPPLY 12/12/03.
FARMER T.J. CEng MIEE. Born 1/6/38. Commd 11/4/63. Flt Lt 10/6/68. Retd ENG 10/8/76.
FARMER-WRIGHT I.P. Born 15/11/29. Commd 17/12/52. Sqn Ldr 1/1/72. Retd ADMIN 15/11/87.
FARNES P.C.P. DFM. Born 16/7/18. Commd 27/11/40. Sqn Ldr 1/9/45. Retd GD 27/6/58. rtg Wg Cdr
FARNES R.H. Born 7/3/41. Commd 20/8/65. Flt Lt 1/7/68. Retd GD 13/7/74.
FARNFIELD K.D. Born 6/9/50. Commd 14/8/70. Sqn Ldr 1/1/85. Retd GD 6/9/88.
FARNLEY L.A. Born 4/9/08. Commd 20/2/43. Flt Lt 20/8/46. Retd ENG 29/8/57.
FARQUHAR D.B. AFC MA. Born 20/2/49. Commd 10/4/68. Wg Cdr 1/7/86. Retd GD 31/3/95.
FARQUHAR J.G. Born 20/9/34. Commd 11/3/57. Sqn Ldr 1/1/67. Retd GD 1/10/87.
FARQUHAR K.G. Born 17/3/18. Commd 4/10/56. Flt Lt 4/10/59. Retd SEC 29/9/62.
FARQUHAR W.E. Born 28/5/41. Commd 3/5/68. Flt Lt 21/9/74. Retd GD 7/11/83.
FARQUHAR-SMITH H.W. BA FIL MRAeS MCMI. Born 7/11/39. Commd 30/1/61. Gp Capt 1/1/91. Retd GD 7/11/94.
FARQUHARSON A.J.M. Born 5/2/23. Commd 12/6/47. Sqn Ldr 1/7/60. Retd SEC 1/7/63.
FARQUHARSON D. BSC. Born 6/7/46. Commd 27/4/69. Flt Lt 27/10/73. Retd GD 31/12/76.
FARQUHARSON F.H.K. Born 23/1/51. Commd 16/9/76. Wg Cdr 1/7/95. Retd ENG 14/3/97.
FARQUHARSON G.M. Born 2/7/36. Commd 14/8/70. Flt Lt 14/8/72. Retd SUP 14/8/78. Re-instated 14/1/80.
   Sqn Ldr 1/1/88. Retd SUP 5/8/91.
FARQUHARSON W.L. DFC* FCMI. Born 28/9/20. Commd 14/2/42. Gp Capt 1/7/66. Retd GD 28/1/76.
FARR J.L. OBE. Born 8/6/24. Commd 10/12/43. Sqn Ldr 1/1/59. Retd GD 8/7/67.
FARR P.G.D. CB OBE DFC FCMI. Born 26/8/17. Commd 12/7/37. AVM 1/7/70. Retd GD 6/11/72.
FARR-VOLLER G.E.A. BA. Born 5/7/47. Commd 30/3/89. Flt Lt 30/3/91. Retd GD 14/7/96.
FARRAND B.M. Born 1/7/26. Commd 9/6/55. Fg Offr 9/6/57. Retd SUP 1/3/61.
FARRANDS R.A. FCIS MCMI. Born 19/4/23. Commd 5/3/45. Gp Capt 1/1/74. Retd ADMIN 19/3/77.
FARRANT E.H. Born 5/12/32. Commd 17/5/70. Flt Lt 17/7/74. Retd GD 5/12/87.
FARRAR A.MCK. Born 12/5/46. Commd 29/6/72. Flt Lt 29/12/77. Retd GD 22/10/94.
FARRAR-HOCKLEY H.A. Born 14/10/54. Commd 20/9/79. Flt Lt 26/11/84. Retd ADMIN 14/10/93.
FARRELL B.G. Born 26/4/44. Commd 13/12/79. Sqn Ldr 1/1/89. Retd ENG 26/4/99.
FARRELL C.L. MA. Born 14/4/38. Commd 30/9/57. Wg Cdr 1/7/80. Retd ENG 14/4/93.
FARRELL J.A.J. Born 4/6/24. Commd 4/5/50. Sqn Ldr 1/1/69. Retd GD 16/7/73.
FARRELL W. Born 10/7/23. Commd 6/9/56. Flt Lt 6/9/62. Retd GD 20/8/63.
FARRER B.C. MBE. Born 25/7/34. Commd 9/4/53. A Cdre 1/1/86. Retd GD 25/7/89.
FARRER G.B.J. BSc. Born 31/8/61. Commd 11/12/83. Sqn Ldr 1/7/98. Retd SUP 1/7/01.
FARRER W.R. AFM. Born 20/2/24. Commd 17/5/56. Flt Lt 17/5/62. Retd GD 20/2/74. rtg Sqn Ldr
FARRIER C.D. MB BS FRCS FRCS(Edin) LRCP. Born 30/11/30. Commd 21/8/55. Wg Cdr 26/12/68. Retd MED 10/9/76.
FARRINGTON J.A. Born 18/1/34. Commd 23/2/55. Flt Lt 23/8/60. Retd GD 18/1/72.
FARROW A.G. Born 29/3/44. Commd 11/9/78. Flt Lt 11/5/80. Retd GD 1/4/85.
FARROW H. BEM. Born 16/4/15. Commd 4/7/57. Flt Lt 1/4/63. Retd SEC 10/7/69.
FARROW P.J. Born 21/9/40. Commd 22/2/63. Sqn Ldr 1/7/74. Retd GD 21/9/95.
FARTHING D.E. Born 27/12/26. Commd 6/1/71. Flt Lt 7/1/75. Retd GD 27/12/81.
FARTHING P.J. MA. Born 26/5/38. Commd 23/10/59. Sqn Ldr 1/1/69. Retd SEC 23/10/75.
FAUCHON F.T. Born 20/9/35. Commd 21/6/56. Wg Cdr 1/1/77. Retd GD(G) 20/9/90.
FAULKNER B.E.F. OBE FCMI. Born 17/6/29. Commd 11/4/51. Gp Capt 1/1/77. Retd SEC 17/5/80.
FAULKNER E.C.H. MBE. Born 2/1/09. Commd 19/9/41. Sqn Ldr 1/8/47. Retd ENG 2/1/58.
FAULKNER H.M. BSc. Born 18/12/57. Commd 11/12/83. Sqn Ldr 1/1/04. Retd OPS SPT(FC) 12/7/04.
FAULKNER J.H. Born 24/1/27. Commd 8/6/53. Flt Lt 17/5/56. Retd GD 26/3/67.
FAULKNER K.O. Born 1/10/49. Commd 19/3/81. Flt Lt 19/3/83. Retd GD 19/6/89.
FAULKNER M. BA. Born 28/6/49. Commd 24/9/72. Sqn Ldr 1/7/89. Retd GD 10/8/94.
FAULKNER V. BSc. Born 29/9/35. Commd 19/10/58. Flt Lt 23/3/64. Retd GD 23/9/75.
FAUSCH A.V. Born 15/6/28. Commd 30/5/51. Flt Lt 30/11/55. Retd GD 30/1/67.
FAWCETT J.H. AFC BSc MRAeS. Born 8/4/40. Commd 27/7/62. Flt Lt 9/12/64. Retd GD 1/1/76.
FAWCETT K.A. Born 17/1/31. Commd 8/8/57. Sqn Ldr 1/7/74. Retd ADMIN 19/5/76.
FAWCETT M. MBE MCMI. Born 31/3/22. Commd 24/3/55. Sqn Ldr 1/1/69. Retd SUP 31/3/77.
FAWCETT P. Born 9/9/39. Commd 1/8/39. Wg Cdr 1/7/90. Retd GD(G) 29/4/93.
FAWCETT W.J. Born 13/2/39. Commd 13/12/79. Sqn Ldr 1/7/90. Retd ENG 29/10/93.
FAWCUS K.A. Born 16/11/46. Commd 29/7/68. Flt Lt 4/5/72. Retd SY 16/11/84.
FAWCUS P.C.A. Born 17/12/43. Commd 25/2/66. Flt Lt 25/8/71. Retd GD 17/12/81.
FAWCUS T.F. Born 11/9/21. Commd 30/5/45. Flt Lt 1/12/51. Retd SUP 30/4/73.

FAWSON S.E. CEng FCMI MRAeS. Born 25/7/22. Commd 13/9/43. Gp Capt 1/7/71. Retd ENG 25/7/82.
FAZACKERLEY M.D. Born 17/7/53. Commd 10/2/72. Fg Offr 10/2/74. Retd GD 11/11/77.
FAZAKERLEY I. Born 25/5/41. Commd 31/7/62. Wg Cdr 1/1/85. Retd SUP 25/5/96.
FAZEY F. Born 18/8/18. Commd 26/11/42. Sqn Ldr 1/1/54. Retd ENG 1/8/64.
FEAKES G.W. Born 30/9/34. Commd 20/8/53. Flt Lt 22/5/61. Retd GD 30/9/72.
FEAKES R. Born 25/8/35. Commd 9/4/57. Sqn Ldr 1/7/65. Retd GD 27/8/85.
FEALEY P.E. MCMI. Born 28/2/28. Commd 26/4/60. Sqn Ldr 1/1/73. Retd SUP 28/2/88.
FEAR F.L. Born 28/2/23. Commd 12/10/44. Sqn Ldr 1/1/68. Retd GD(G) 28/2/78.
FEAR T.J. CEng MIMechE. Born 11/4/50. Commd 26/2/71. Sqn Ldr 1/7/87. Retd ENG 30/6/90.
FEAR T.J. Born 26/3/45. Commd 9/8/63. Flt Lt 9/2/69. Retd GD 29/6/74.
FEARN M.H. Born 4/2/58. Commd 25/9/80. Flt Lt 18/11/84. Retd GD(G) 4/2/96.
FEAST D.T.H. MCMI. Born 15/1/31. Commd 18/10/62. Sqn Ldr 1/1/69. Retd ADMIN 18/1/84.
FEAST R.C. Born 26/6/50. Commd 21/3/69. Wg Cdr 1/7/90. Retd GD 1/3/97.
FEATHER D.R. Born 30/9/25. Commd 6/7/45. Sqn Ldr 1/7/58. Retd GD 30/9/63.
FEATHERSTONE A.J. OBE MMS MCMI. Born 23/12/37. Commd 5/6/56. Wg Cdr 1/7/82. Retd GD 23/12/92.
FEATHERSTONE D.F.W. Born 20/2/38. Commd 19/6/64. Flt Lt 9/2/68. Retd GD 20/2/76.
FEATHERSTONE J.C. Born 15/4/43. Commd 17/12/64. Gp Capt 1/7/91. Retd ADMIN 15/4/98.
FEATHERSTONE J.R. MSc BA. Born 18/8/46. Commd 17/10/71. Sqn Ldr 1/7/86. Retd SUP 1/9/96.
FEATONBY W.G. Born 28/9/34. Commd 24/5/53. Sqn Ldr 1/1/68. Retd GD 18/5/86.
FEEK C.D. Born 9/10/45. Commd 3/3/67. Wg Cdr 1/1/86. Retd SY 2/9/93.
FEELEY H.J. MBE MRAeS. Born 8/5/30. Commd 30/3/61. Sqn Ldr 1/7/74. Retd ENG 8/5/80.
FEENAN M.L. CBE MA FCMI. Born 18/9/47. Commd 1/9/70. A Cdre 1/7/96. Retd GD 18/9/02.
FEENEY C.M. Born 7/3/54. Commd 24/7/81. Flt Lt 24/7/83. Retd GD 7/3/92.
FEENEY J. Born 23/3/42. Commd 14/7/66. Sqn Ldr 1/1/92. Retd GD 14/8/96.
FEESEY J.D.L. AFC MRAeS. Born 11/10/42. Commd 12/1/62. AVM 1/1/94. Retd GD 30/1/99.
FEETHAM G.C. Born 27/4/34. Commd 18/7/54. Sqn Ldr 1/7/67. Retd GD(G) 31/8/69.
FEIRN R. MCMI. Born 12/4/21. Commd 18/5/61. Sqn Ldr 1/1/73. Retd ENG 12/4/82.
FEIST M. Born 12/12/44. Commd 14/6/63. Flt Lt 15/4/70. Retd GD 16/5/92.
FEIST N.R. Born 30/10/37. Commd 29/11/63. Flt Lt 25/7/66. Retd GD 30/3/86.
FELGER C.F.W. Born 5/12/43. Commd 12/7/63. Wg Cdr 1/7/85. Retd GD 5/12/02.
FELIX R. LVO MCMI. Born 30/9/39. Commd 9/7/57. Wg Cdr 1/7/78. Retd GD 15/3/83.
FELL C.M. CBE AFC. Born 12/10/18. Commd 26/1/41. A Cdre 1/7/68. Retd GD 12/8/71.
FELL E.E. AFC* MCMI. Born 20/4/22. Commd 5/3/53. Sqn Ldr 1/1/67. Retd GD 23/4/74.
FELL J.C. BSc CEng MRAeS. Born 15/8/21. Commd 1/8/43. Sqn Ldr 1/10/56. Retd ENG 25/1/69.
FELL M.C. Born 27/9/49. Commd 19/6/70. Flt Lt 14/11/76. Retd GD(G) 27/9/87.
FELL P.A. Born 18/3/26. Commd 19/7/56. Flt Lt 19/7/62. Retd GD 1/11/75.
FELL W.B. MCMI. Born 7/9/22. Commd 24/7/52. Sqn Ldr 1/7/74. Retd SUP 7/9/77.
FELLOWES D. MSc BSc. Born 28/10/41. Commd 13/9/70. Wg Cdr 1/7/87. Retd ADMIN 7/12/91.
FELLOWES T.P. Born 25/6/17. Commd 17/1/49. Sqn Ldr 1/7/50. Retd RGT 1/2/54.
FELLOWS L. BEd MIL. Born 22/4/46. Commd 22/3/81. Sqn Ldr 1/1/89. Retd ADMIN 14/3/97.
FELLOWS T.A. Born 3/1/57. Commd 13/12/79. Sqn Ldr 1/7/94. Retd SUP 13/7/97.
FELMING P.C.H. Born 24/12/23. Commd 8/8/51. Sqn Ldr 1/1/63. Retd CAT 30/9/67.
FELTON F. Born 25/9/36. Commd 29/7/65. Flt Lt 29/7/67. Retd PRT 25/9/74.
FELTON M.C.D. Born 28/3/33. Commd 23/8/51. Wg Cdr 1/7/75. Retd ADMIN 25/2/84.
FELTS P.A. BA. Born 22/8/47. Commd 2/3/80. Flt Lt 2/12/83. Retd SUP 2/3/96.
FELTS W. Born 4/6/46. Commd 20/9/79. Flt Lt 20/9/80. Retd ADMIN 20/9/87.
FELWICK D.L. Born 9/11/44. Commd 24/6/65. Wg Cdr 1/1/80. Retd SY 1/1/83.
FENBOW C.G. Born 12/9/38. Commd 25/7/59. Flt Lt 22/2/65. Retd GD 15/8/68.
FENECH F. Born 12/12/22. Commd 12/6/47. Flt Lt 7/8/56. Retd SUP 9/8/64.
FENLON K.S. Born 29/1/36. Commd 27/3/75. Flt Lt 27/3/80. Retd ENG 29/1/94.
FENLON-SMITH P.A. Born 4/5/60. Commd 12/7/79. Sqn Ldr 1/1/93. Retd GD 4/5/98.
FENN A.K. BDS. Born 20/3/58. Commd 1/9/86. Sqn Ldr 28/6/93. Retd DEL 20/3/98.
FENN M.G. Born 15/8/33. Commd 11/10/51. Flt Lt 27/7/59. Retd GD 15/8/71. rtg Sqn Ldr
FENN R.J. Born 31/10/45. Commd 11/9/64. Flt Lt 4/11/70. Retd GD 31/10/85.
FENNELL G.R. Born 27/1/30. Commd 13/9/51. Flt Lt 30/4/57. Retd GD 3/2/76.
FENNELL J. MBE AFC. Born 7/1/25. Commd 24/7/47. Gp Capt 1/7/69. Retd GD 7/1/80.
FENNELL J.R. Born 9/6/42. Commd 31/8/62. Sqn Ldr 1/7/94. Retd GD 9/6/97.
FENNELL P.R. Born 2/4/39. Commd 22/2/64. Wg Cdr 1/7/86. Retd GD 2/4/94.
FENNELL S.M. Born 9/6/44. Commd 24/9/64. Flt Lt 10/12/70. Retd SEC 5/5/73.
FENNER M.D. MCMI. Born 16/2/29. Commd 5/4/50. Gp Capt 1/1/74. Retd GD 31/3/77.
FENNESSY D.C. LLB. Born 24/11/37. Commd 14/5/63. Sqn Ldr 31/3/73. Retd EDN 14/5/79.
FENNING R.C. Born 4/3/31. Commd 5/11/58. Flt Lt 5/11/58. Retd GD 16/6/71.
FENNY D.R. Born 5/2/61. Commd 29/7/83. Flt Lt 29/1/89. Retd GD 28/3/99.
FENTON G.N. Born 2/5/48. Commd 2/8/68. Flt Lt 8/3/72. Retd GD 20/5/85.
FENTON M.J. CEng MIMechE. Born 28/9/42. Commd 23/12/61. Flt Lt 23/6/68. Retd ENG 28/9/82.
FENTON S.C. Born 22/2/43. Commd 8/9/83. Flt Lt 8/9/87. Retd ENG 30/11/88.

FENTON T.J. MBE. Born 20/4/62. Commd 8/10/87. Sqn Ldr 1/1/98. Retd ADMIN 1/8/01.
FENTON W.J.F. Born 15/1/17. Commd 9/9/39. Wg Cdr 1/7/56. Retd SUP 10/8/61.
FENTUM M.D. Born 12/7/48. Commd 20/10/67. Sqn Ldr 1/1/86. Retd GD 1/11/96.
FENWICK-WILSON R.M. AFC. Born 29/7/14. Commd 24/8/34. Sqn Ldr 1/9/40. Retd GD 11/3/46. rtg Wg Cdr
FEREDAY W.L. Born 1/7/14. Commd 3/6/42. Sqn Offr 1/1/53. Retd SEC 30/6/59.
FERENCZY G.I. CEng FIEE FCMI. Born 15/6/34. Commd 12/6/58. A Cdre 1/7/80. Retd ENG 11/6/85.
FERGUSON A. FCMI. Born 24/7/44. Commd 20/6/66. Gp Capt 1/1/89. Retd GD 16/10/93.
FERGUSON A.D. Born 3/11/12. Commd 15/7/33. Plt Offr 15/7/33. Retd GD 4/4/34.
FERGUSON A.M. CEng FIEE. Born 21/3/44. Commd 15/7/65. A Cdre 1/1/95. Retd ENG 14/7/99.
FERGUSON A.P. BSc CEng MRAeS MCMI. Born 2/7/53. Commd 3/9/72. Sqn Ldr 1/7/85. Retd ENG 2/7/91.
FERGUSON C.G. Born 11/4/41. Commd 14/5/60. Sqn Ldr 1/7/76. Retd GD 1/12/79.
FERGUSON D.A. Born 4/3/35. Commd 19/8/54. Flt Lt 7/3/62. Retd GD 1/10/86. rtg Sqn Ldr
FERGUSON D.C. AFC. Born 9/6/33. Commd 27/2/52. Wg Cdr 1/1/76. Retd GD 9/6/88.
FERGUSON D.W.B. BSc. Born 29/9/55. Commd 26/5/85. Flt Lt 26/11/86. Retd ENG 31/3/94.
FERGUSON G.M. CB CBE. Born 15/4/38. Commd 28/7/60. AVM 1/7/91. Retd SUP 1/7/94.
FERGUSON I.C. BA. Born 19/2/60. Commd 11/9/83. Flt Lt 11/3/85. Retd GD 29/2/96.
FERGUSON I.J. Born 9/2/54. Commd 5/2/81. Sqn Ldr 1/7/90. Retd GD(G) 2/7/96.
FERGUSON I.K. Born 16/4/51. Commd 7/6/73. Flt Lt 7/12/78. Retd GD 30/9/91.
FERGUSON J. Born 8/6/26. Commd 8/7/65. Sqn Ldr 31/8/74. Retd MED(SEC) 30/4/77.
FERGUSON L.H. DFM. Born 1/5/21. Commd 23/10/42. Flt Lt 13/12/48. Retd GD 1/5/64. rtg Sqn Ldr
FERGUSON M.C. MBE. Born 26/3/22. Commd 19/1/50. Gp Capt 1/1/71. Retd ENG 8/6/74.
FERGUSON P.D. Born 11/6/24. Commd 15/12/44. Sqn Ldr 1/1/69. Retd GD 28/4/79.
FERGUSON R.A.W. MBE. Born 17/8/18. Commd 17/5/56. Flt Lt 17/5/59. Retd ENG 30/5/64.
FERN R.A. Born 22/11/62. Commd 26/11/81. Flt Lt 26/5/88. Retd GD(G) 22/4/89.
FERNEE M.F. Born 14/3/44. Commd 3/8/62. Flt Lt 3/2/68. Retd GD 4/8/81.
FERNIE J.E. Born 21/8/57. Commd 31/8/75. Sqn Ldr 1/1/89. Retd GD 21/8/95.
FERNIE W.A. MSc BSc(Eng) CEng MRAeS. Born 2/11/49. Commd 4/10/71. Sqn Ldr 1/1/85. Retd ENG 1/1/90.
FERRAR D. CertEd. Born 21/4/44. Commd 29/4/71. Wg Cdr 1/7/96. Retd ADMIN 21/8/01.
FERREN T.B. Born 23/11/29. Commd 21/10/66. Sqn Ldr 1/7/82. Retd ENG 23/11/89.
FERRIDAY D.W. MSc MMedSci MB BCh FFOM MRCGP DRCOG. Born 13/10/52. Commd 4/9/73. Sqn Ldr 4/8/82.
    Retd MED 1/2/83. Re-entered 13/2/87. Wg Cdr 13/2/93. Retd MED
FERRIER J.A. Born 16/9/65. Commd 28/2/88. Sqn Ldr 1/7/98. Retd GD 19/9/02.
FERRIES A.I. BSc. Born 8/4/48. Commd 3/11/71. Wg Cdr 1/7/94. Retd GD 25/12/04.
FERRILL B. BEM. Born 13/3/32. Commd 26/6/65. Flt Lt 3/6/71. Retd ADMIN 29/6/84.
FERRILL M.B.A. BSc. Born 8/3/62. Commd 31/8/80. Flt Lt 15/10/86. Retd SUP 8/12/96.
FERRIS R.B. DPhysEd. Born 21/1/29. Commd 28/9/55. Sqn Ldr 1/7/68. Retd SUP 28/9/71.
FEWELL D.J. Born 23/11/32. Commd 21/5/52. Flt Lt 16/10/57. Retd GD 31/7/76.
FEWING W.R.J. CBE MA MSc CEng MRAeS MCMI. Born 30/5/34. Commd 26/9/53. A Cdre 1/7/85.
    Retd ENG 30/5/89.
FEWTRELL C.G. Born 14/4/31. Commd 15/6/53. Flt Lt 14/10/58. Retd GD 14/4/69.
FEWTRELL E.C.S. DFC. Born 3/7/16. Commd 23/3/36. Wg Cdr 1/1/52. Retd GD 3/7/71. rtg Gp Capt 21/9/00.
FEWTRELL G.H.S. Born 26/12/24. Commd 21/4/45. Flt Lt 11/6/53. Retd GD 15/5/68.
FFRENCH-CONSTANT M.C. BA BM BCh. Born 27/9/29. Commd 4/4/55. Wg Cdr 4/4/68. Retd MED 4/4/71.
FIDLER P.P. Born 13/1/42. Commd 8/9/83. Flt Lt 8/9/87. Retd ENG 10/3/93.
FIELD B.C. FInstPet MCIPS. Born 7/8/34. Commd 26/5/64. Sqn Ldr 1/1/73. Retd SUP 12/10/79.
FIELD C.P. Born 5/3/33. Commd 15/12/53. Fg Offr 15/12/53. Retd GD 25/11/59.
FIELD C.R. Born 6/7/45. Commd 1/4/65. Sqn Ldr 1/1/81. Retd SY 1/10/85.
FIELD H.O. Born 14/4/29. Commd 1/6/51. Sqn Ldr 1/7/62. Retd GD 14/4/67.
FIELD J. DPhysEd. Born 13/6/45. Commd 10/6/66. Wg Cdr 1/7/88. Retd ADMIN 14/9/96.
FIELD J. MBE. Born 5/10/30. Commd 13/7/61. Sqn Ldr 1/7/74. Retd ENG 6/8/83.
FIELD M.J.G. Born 10/3/39. Commd 6/9/68. Flt Lt 6/9/70. Retd GD 10/3/77.
FIELD M.K. BA. Born 24/12/34. Commd 14/5/60. Flt Lt 14/2/62. Retd GD 17/3/87.
FIELD P.A. MBE MCMI. Born 4/9/34. Commd 23/3/64. Wg Cdr 1/7/79. Retd ADMIN 8/4/88.
FIELD P.V. BSc CEng MRAeS. Born 3/3/28. Commd 25/5/50. Wg Cdr 1/1/67. Retd ENG 1/11/73.
FIELD S.E.B. Born 10/6/43. Commd 15/7/64. Flt Lt 15/7/69. Retd ENG 1/10/74.
FIELD-RICHARDS N.J. CEng MRAeS. Born 7/7/39. Commd 28/7/60. Wg Cdr 1/7/75. Retd ENG 26/3/79.
FIELDING D. Born 24/8/52. Commd 28/9/89. Flt Lt 28/9/91. Retd ENG 5/4/99.
FIELDING F.W. MBE AFC. Born 1/9/25. Commd 23/4/53. Sqn Ldr 1/1/68. Retd GD 1/9/79.
FIELDING J.G. OBE MCMI. Born 7/11/28. Commd 22/9/49. Wg Cdr 1/1/73. Retd ADMIN 7/11/84.
FIELDING P. Born 11/8/44. Commd 11/2/65. Sqn Ldr 1/7/78. Retd ADMIN 11/8/82.
FIELDING S. Born 23/7/32. Commd 12/10/54. Flt Lt 16/8/61. Retd GD 23/10/70.
FIELDING S. BSc. Born 18/1/60. Commd 14/9/80. Flt Lt 15/10/83. Retd FLY(P) 29/8/04.
FIGGINS P.D. Born 21/3/40. Commd 1/11/79. Sqn Ldr 1/7/91. Retd SY 21/2/95.
FIGGURES J.M.F. BSc CEng MIEE. Born 26/11/44. Commd 28/9/64. Sqn Ldr 1/1/85. Retd ENG 26/5/00.
FILBEY C.H. Born 2/9/21. Commd 27/2/47. Sqn Ldr 1/7/66. Retd SUP 13/9/68.
FILBEY K.D. CBE FRAeS. Born 16/12/47. Commd 28/2/69. AVM 1/1/98. Retd GD 17/1/03.

FILDES R.A. Born 30/8/22. Commd 28/7/60. Flt Lt 28/7/65. Retd SEC 1/1/76.
FILING T.J. AFC. Born 3/11/33. Commd 11/6/52. Flt Lt 18/12/57. Retd GD 3/11/71.
FILLINGHAM A.P. Born 5/3/61. Commd 8/12/83. Flt Lt 8/6/89. Retd GD 14/3/96.
FILLINGHAM K. DFC. Born 16/5/23. Commd 3/4/44. Flt Lt 19/11/53. Retd GD 13/12/67.
FINCH A.J. MA MEd BA PGCE MCIPD DipEd. Born 4/10/57. Commd 11/9/83. Sqn Ldr 1/1/91. Retd ADMIN 14/3/97.
FINCH C.R. MIExpE. Born 28/9/47. Commd 13/9/70. Sqn Ldr 1/1/91. Retd ENG 12/10/96.
FINCH E.D. Born 15/6/27. Commd 8/4/49. Sqn Ldr 1/7/57. Retd GD 15/6/65.
FINCH F.W. Born 11/7/12. Commd 7/5/53. Sqn Ldr 1/7/61. Retd ENG 1/8/64.
FINCH G.P. Born 19/2/47. Commd 11/8/67. Flt Lt 11/2/73. Retd GD 19/4/92.
FINCH J. CBE DFC AFC. Born 18/8/20. Commd 13/4/41. Gp Capt 1/7/61. Retd GD 6/1/68.
FINCH J.E. BSc. Born 17/5/28. Commd 4/10/50. Flt Lt 19/6/52. Retd GD 23/4/55.
FINCH J.S.G. Born 15/7/32. Commd 25/3/52. Flt Lt 7/8/57. Retd GD 15/7/87.
FINCH P.F. Born 10/5/28. Commd 9/12/65. Flt Lt 9/12/71. Retd SUP 24/5/75.
FINCH P.S. Born 2/3/59. Commd 23/10/86. Flt Lt 17/11/88. Retd SY 2/3/97.
FINCH R.B. Born 3/11/49. Commd 27/2/75. Flt Lt 27/8/80. Retd GD 3/11/90.
FINCH R.I. FCIPD FSCA. Born 24/11/35. Commd 9/4/57. Wg Cdr 1/7/77. Retd ADMIN 24/11/90.
FINCH R.T.A. BSc MCIPS. Born 20/9/49. Commd 15/9/69. Flt Lt 15/10/75. Retd SUP 1/7/78.
FINCHAM P.J. Born 26/7/44. Commd 15/3/73. Sqn Ldr 1/1/80. Retd ENG 26/7/88.
FINCHER J.F. CEng MIMechE. Born 7/7/32. Commd 15/7/54. Sqn Ldr 1/1/65. Retd ENG 7/7/92.
FINDING A.R. Born 19/8/51. Commd 4/2/71. Sqn Ldr 1/1/86. Retd ADMIN 6/3/89.
FINDING P. CEng MRAeS MCMI. Born 12/5/22. Commd 10/12/43. Sqn Ldr 1/1/62. Retd ENG 9/11/74.
FINDLATER J. Born 22/10/33. Commd 27/2/56. Wg Cdr 1/7/80. Retd GD 11/6/86.
FINDLAY D.W. MA. Born 12/3/55. Commd 9/6/54. Flt Lt 15/4/77. Retd GD 15/7/87.
FINDLAY G.S. OBE BSc FCMI. Born 21/11/35. Commd 22/8/61. Gp Capt 1/7/89. Retd ADMIN 2/7/91.
FINDLAY J. Born 2/3/13. Commd 14/11/46. Plt Offr 14/11/46. Retd SUP 13/6/48.
FINDLAY M.D.deR. Born 22/7/42. Commd 28/7/64. Flt Lt 26/7/67. Retd GD 17/9/71.
FINE B.H.P. Born 24/11/35. Commd 14/6/63. Flt Lt 25/7/66. Retd GD 24/11/73.
FINEGAN C.M. BSc MCMI. Born 25/1/33. Commd 7/12/65. Sqn Ldr 1/1/74. Retd SUP 25/1/91.
FINELY N.H.M. Born 16/10/44. Commd 30/8/73. Wg Cdr 1/1/96. Retd OPS SPT 28/4/01.
FINKLE R. Born 2/1/34. Commd 12/7/57. Sqn Ldr 1/7/66. Retd ENG 12/7/73.
FINLAY D.L.A. MCMI. Born 25/1/24. Commd 8/8/44. Sqn Ldr 1/4/57. Retd SEC 22/11/75.
FINLAY G. BSc. Born 8/7/57. Commd 26/7/81. Flt Lt 26/10/81. Retd GD 14/3/96.
FINLAY J.I. MCMI. Born 26/11/24. Commd 17/8/50. Sqn Ldr 1/7/62. Retd GD 1/10/73.
FINLAYSON J.S. MA. Born 20/1/44. Commd 16/1/67. Sqn Ldr 1/7/77. Retd GD 25/11/93.
FINLAYSON P.J.S. AFC. Born 9/12/20. Commd 14/1/39. Wg Cdr 1/1/54. Retd GD 9/12/75. rtg Gp Capt
FINN B.B. Born 23/2/19. Commd 1/4/46. Flt Lt 9/2/51. Retd ENG 18/9/54.
FINN-KELCEY C.J. MBE. Born 28/6/51. Commd 17/7/70. Flt Lt 17/1/76. Retd GD 29/6/82.
FINNERON T.J. MCMI. Born 14/9/50. Commd 25/2/72. Sqn Ldr 1/1/82. Retd GD 9/12/90.
FINNEY P. BSc(Eng) MSc CEng MRAeS. Born 5/10/39. Commd 9/7/63. Wg Cdr 1/1/78. Retd ENG 9/7/85.
FINNEY S.F. MBE. Born 5/8/50. Commd 29/6/72. Sqn Ldr 1/7/85. Retd ADMIN 5/8/00.
FINNIE A.J. BA MCIPD. Born 23/6/30. Commd 8/2/52. Wg Cdr 1/1/75. Retd SEC 4/2/78.
FINNIE J.B. Born 13/12/41. Commd 20/8/65. Flt Lt 20/8/71. Retd GD 24/8/74.
FINNIS J.F.S. Born 21/1/22. Commd 28/7/44. Flt Lt 27/5/54. Retd GD 21/1/77.
FIRMIN P.A. BSc. Born 18/3/61. Commd 5/2/84. Flt Lt 5/8/85. Retd GD 1/12/00.
FIRMSTON-WILLIAMS R.A. Born 28/12/57. Commd 5/2/81. Flt Lt 5/8/86. Retd GD 29/4/97.
FIRTH C.J. Born 11/7/29. Commd 24/1/52. Flt Lt 29/10/57. Retd GD 29/3/69.
FIRTH H.V. Born 2/5/48. Commd 16/6/88. Sqn Ldr 1/1/96. Retd SUPPLY 2/9/03.
FIRTH J.F. MBE MCMI. Born 26/10/20. Commd 14/3/46. Sqn Ldr 1/7/65. Retd ENG 31/8/78.
FIRTH J.R. Born 2/8/41. Commd 18/8/61. Flt Lt 22/9/68. Retd GD 2/4/81.
FIRTH J.V. MA BA. Born 1/1/30. Commd 11/12/52. Gp Capt 1/7/83. Retd ADMIN 1/1/85.
FIRTH P.A. Born 28/2/33. Commd 24/5/53. Sqn Ldr 1/7/78. Retd GD 28/2/88.
FISH D. Born 22/1/24. Commd 6/7/50. Sqn Ldr 1/1/62. Retd GD 22/3/68.
FISH I.D. BSc. Born 3/10/46. Commd 13/9/70. Sqn Ldr 1/7/85. Retd GD(G) 31/10/90.
FISH L. DFC DFM. Born 5/2/20. Commd 25/6/42. Flt Lt 20/1/47. Retd GD(G) 3/3/70.
FISH M. MA BA. Born 5/11/60. Commd 14/4/85. Sqn Ldr 1/7/95. Retd ADMIN 30/9/01.
FISH M.A. MBE. Born 4/2/31. Commd 23/5/51. Sqn Ldr 1/1/69. Retd GD 26/10/76.
FISH P.A. Born 20/10/41. Commd 27/1/61. Flt Lt 15/4/70. Retd GD 20/10/79.
FISHER A. AFC MRAeS. Born 19/8/33. Commd 9/4/52. Sqn Ldr 1/1/70. Retd GD 31/12/73.
FISHER A. Born 22/9/50. Commd 4/3/71. Sqn Ldr 1/1/86. Retd SY(PRT) 1/1/89.
FISHER B.N.M.S. Born 17/6/41. Commd 10/6/66. Flt Lt 10/12/71. Retd GD 22/2/96.
FISHER C. Born 28/5/32. Commd 22/7/66. Flt Lt 22/7/68. Retd SEC 30/9/78.
FISHER C.J. Born 5/3/43. Commd 24/11/67. Sqn Ldr 1/7/81. Retd SUP 1/7/84. Re-entered 17/2/89. Sqn Ldr 17/2/86. Retd SUP 5/3/98.
FISHER C.R. BSc. Born 20/7/49. Commd 17/1/72. Flt Lt 17/4/73. Retd GD 17/1/88.
FISHER D. Born 30/12/20. Commd 17/6/54. Flt Lt 27/8/57. Retd GD 30/3/68.
FISHER D.J. AFC. Born 9/8/46. Commd 26/5/67. Sqn Ldr 1/7/80. Retd GD 31/10/89.

FISHER D.W. IEng MIIE MCMI. Born 31/5/47. Commd 16/12/66. Sqn Ldr 1/7/83. Retd ENG 31/5/91.
FISHER E.H. Born 27/5/20. Commd 26/9/57. Sqn Ldr 18/4/67. Retd DEL 30/8/69.
FISHER E.T. Born 4/5/19. Commd 2/3/45. Flt Lt 4/1/51. Retd GD 31/8/68.
FISHER F.E. MBE BSc CEng MRAeS. Born 21/3/49. Commd 11/8/74. Wg Cdr 1/7/94. Retd GD 21/4/04.
FISHER G.W.O. OBE DFC*. Born 10/7/21. Commd 19/8/39. Wg Cdr 1/1/55. Retd GD 5/5/61.
FISHER H.M. AFC. Born 18/7/28. Commd 28/6/51. Flt Lt 10/10/56. Retd GD 16/10/66.
FISHER H.W.H. DFC. Born 19/3/17. Commd 6/2/39. Wg Cdr 1/7/52. Retd GD 27/2/56.
FISHER J.A. CEng MIEE. Born 5/2/30. Commd 18/5/65. Wg Cdr 1/1/75. Retd ENG 4/4/81.
FISHER J.F. AFC MRAeS. Born 5/6/43. Commd 17/12/63. Sqn Ldr 1/1/78. Retd GD 5/6/81.
FISHER J.R. Born 21/10/16. Commd 3/4/39. Sqn Ldr 1/8/47. Retd SUP 21/10/66.
FISHER J.S. BSc CEng MIEE. Born 27/3/47. Commd 6/9/71. Flt Lt 6/3/74. Retd ADMIN 6/9/87.
FISHER J.W. Born 8/4/52. Commd 3/12/70. Sqn Ldr 1/1/88. Retd SUP 1/1/91.
FISHER M. BA. Born 18/8/36. Commd 10/10/58. Sqn Ldr 10/4/67. Retd EDN 11/10/75.
FISHER M.G.P. BA MB BChir MFOM DRCOG DCH DAvMed. Born 21/11/30. Commd 14/10/56. Gp Capt 1/7/79.
    Retd MED 29/8/85.
FISHER M.G.W. Born 31/3/43. Commd 29/10/64. Sqn Ldr 1/7/77. Retd ADMIN 31/3/84. Re-entered 16/1/87.
    Wg Cdr 1/7/90. Retd ADMIN 1/10/00.
FISHER P.A. Born 22/5/44. Commd 22/3/63. Flt Lt 22/9/68. Retd GD 1/6/77.
FISHER P.T. Born 15/1/59. Commd 6/5/83. Flt Lt 23/10/86. Retd GD(G) 26/9/89.
FISHER R.A. Born 19/9/44. Commd 28/2/64. Flt Lt 28/8/69. Retd GD 3/1/76.
FISHER R.I. Born 9/5/43. Commd 28/4/67. Wg Cdr 1/1/94. Retd GD 9/5/98.
FISHER R.J. Born 6/8/33. Commd 21/5/52. Flt Lt 26/11/57. Retd GD 6/8/71.
FISHER W. Born 28/9/27. Commd 21/4/67. Flt Lt 21/4/70. Retd GD 28/9/82.
FISHER W.I.J. Born 17/12/38. Commd 14/8/70. Flt Lt 14/8/76. Retd MED(SEC) 28/8/76.
FISHWICK H. MBE FCMI. Born 4/3/20. Commd 28/6/43. Gp Capt 1/1/72. Retd ENG 4/3/75.
FISHWICK R.J. Born 18/6/45. Commd 18/8/67. Gp Capt 1/7/90. Retd OPS SPT 15/10/02.
FITCH S.A. Born 22/8/71. Commd 20/12/90. Flt Lt 20/6/96. Retd FLY(P) 15/5/03.
FITCHARD R.H. MRIN MMS MCMI. Born 25/12/36. Commd 29/9/55. Sqn Ldr 1/1/72. Retd GD 25/12/94.
FITCHEN E.E. DFC. Born 24/2/12. Commd 16/10/40. Flt Lt 1/9/45. Retd SEC 1/1/54. rtg Sqn Ldr
FITCHEW K.E. Born 28/6/27. Commd 16/7/52. Flt Lt 12/12/57. Retd GD 18/11/75.
FITHEN G. BSc FCMI. Born 7/1/28. Commd 21/1/55. A Cdre 1/7/77. Retd EDN 3/11/81.
FITNESS J.H. Born 26/10/63. Commd 12/3/87. Sqn Ldr 1/7/97. Retd OPS SPT 27/2/02.
FITT G.R. Born 26/8/45. Commd 15/7/66. Fg Offr 15/7/71. Retd SUP 14/2/76. Re-entered 11/12/77. Sqn Ldr 1/7/86.
    Retd SUP 11/12/99.
FITTON J. Born 1/10/13. Commd 9/9/54. Sqn Ldr 1/1/64. Retd ENG 9/11/68.
FITTON K. Born 27/6/17. Commd 29/8/44. Sqn Ldr 1/1/66. Retd SUP 29/6/68.
FITTON M.M. AFM. Born 6/8/34. Commd 4/2/71. Flt Lt 4/2/74. Retd GD(G) 6/8/89.
FITTUS J.C. Born 25/3/41. Commd 31/7/62. Flt Lt 14/2/66. Retd GD 10/10/70.
FITZ-GERALD S.F. Born 14/3/57. Commd 1/11/81. Flt Lt 1/4/85. Retd GD(G) 31/3/96.
FITZCHARLES M. Born 18/2/35. Commd 19/8/65. Flt Lt 19/8/70. Retd GD 1/5/73.
FITZGERALD D. MBE DFC MRAeS. Born 1/9/22. Commd 2/9/42. Wg Cdr 1/1/64. Retd GD 1/9/68.
FITZGERALD J.F. BEng. Born 2/9/66. Commd 1/9/85. Sqn Ldr 1/7/01. Retd FLY(P) 3/2/05.
FITZGERALD M.A. Born 1/4/43. Commd 31/10/69. Flt Lt 8/9/74. Retd SY 16/1/83.
FITZGERALD P.E. BSc. Born 8/8/46. Commd 1/10/70. Sqn Ldr 1/1/83. Retd GD 22/4/94.
FITZGERALD-LOMBARD D.A.I. MBE. Born 29/10/47. Commd 30/1/70. Sqn Ldr 1/1/86. Retd SUP 29/10/91.
FITZGERALD-LOMBARD D.M.B. Born 5/8/06. Commd 18/10/37. Sqn Ldr 1/7/48. Retd MAR 21/6/58. rtg Wg Cdr
FITZGERALD-LOMBARD R.M.S. CEng FIEE MRAeS. Born 9/10/39. Commd 18/7/61. A Cdre 1/7/90.
    Retd ENG 9/10/94.
FITZMAURICE A.F.N. Born 12/11/63. Commd 11/10/91. Sqn Ldr 1/1/97. Retd OPS SPT(FC) 31/7/04.
FITZPATRICK A.G. Born 15/8/41. Commd 31/8/62. Flt Lt 8/1/69. Retd GD 15/8/79.
FITZPATRICK C. Born 12/2/49. Commd 27/2/70. Sqn Ldr 1/7/95. Retd GD 1/10/98.
FITZPATRICK D. Born 2/10/27. Commd 21/11/51. Flt Lt 29/4/59. Retd GD 16/5/67.
FITZPATRICK Sir John KBE CB. Born 15/12/29. Commd 28/7/53. AM 1/1/84. Retd GD 31/3/86.
FITZPATRICK J.D. BEng CEng MRAeS. Born 7/7/64. Commd 3/8/88. Sqn Ldr 1/1/02. Retd ENGINEER 1/1/05.
FITZPATRICK K.L. Born 18/12/42. Commd 30/7/63. Wg Cdr 1/7/78. Retd GD 1/7/81.
FITZPATRICK P. Born 14/2/27. Commd 24/2/66. Flt Lt 24/2/72. Retd SUP 2/4/77. Re-instated 13/8/80. Retd 14/2/87.
FITZPATRICK P. MBE. Born 21/7/33. Commd 9/2/55. Flt Lt 10/8/60. Retd GD 29/11/76.
FITZPATRICK P.J. Born 30/3/41. Commd 17/3/67. Sqn Ldr 1/1/80. Retd SUP 1/6/87.
FITZROY K.C. Born 20/9/28. Commd 30/1/52. Flt Lt 18/4/57. Retd GD 30/1/68.
FITZSIMMONS A.P. BA. Born 30/1/50. Commd 10/6/73. Flt Lt 10/9/76. Retd GD(G) 10/6/89.
FITZSIMMONS D.J. AFC. Born 12/4/42. Commd 13/2/60. Flt Lt 13/8/65. Retd GD 12/4/79.
FIXTER M.R. Born 25/9/63. Commd 8/9/83. Sqn Ldr 1/1/97. Retd OPS SPT 25/9/01.
FIXTER S.R. Born 23/11/58. Commd 7/8/87. Flt Lt 15/7/90. Retd ENG 23/11/96.
FLACK G.G. MBE. Born 27/12/37. Commd 4/10/56. Sqn Ldr 1/1/70. Retd SY 20/2/77.
FLACK G.N. BSc. Born 12/1/54. Commd 3/9/72. Flt Lt 15/10/76. Retd GD 15/7/87. Re-instated 3/12/90. Sqn Ldr 1/7/92.
    GD 1/7/95.

FLACK R.P.B. Born 3/12/40. Commd 9/9/63. Flt Lt 9/3/69. Retd GD 23/12/80.
FLAHERTY S.D. Born 7/8/51. Commd 13/1/72. Sqn Ldr 1/7/84. Retd GD 18/9/85.
FLAKE A.J. CEng MIEE. Born 1/5/15. Commd 25/11/41. Sqn Ldr 1/1/52. Retd ENG 1/11/64.
FLANAGAN N.G. MB ChB MRCP MRCPath DCP DMJ. Born 3/4/36. Commd 28/4/63. Wg Cdr 31/10/75.
    Retd MED 28/4/79.
FLANAGAN R.C. Born 10/3/18. Commd 30/10/41. Flt Lt 19/2/46. Retd ENG 10/3/67.
FLANAGAN T.C. MSc BA MCMI. Born 11/4/33. Commd 10/7/52. Gp Capt 1/1/81. Retd GD 4/5/83.
FLANDERS J.R. CEng MIEE. Born 10/10/40. Commd 2/8/68. Flt Lt 2/8/70. Retd ENG 10/10/78.
FLANNERY T.J. Born 24/5/20. Commd 12/7/46. Flt Lt 10/6/54. Retd ENG 22/10/61.
FLATT H. BSc MCIPD. Born 18/2/60. Commd 2/12/88. Sqn Ldr 1/1/96. Retd ADMIN (SEC) 31/5/03.
FLAVELL D.M. Born 21/4/43. Commd 11/4/85. Sqn Ldr 1/7/95. Retd ENG 24/4/98.
FLAVELL E.J.G. AFC. Born 25/4/22. Commd 24/10/44. Sqn Ldr 1/1/56. Retd GD 1/6/68.
FLAVIN J. Born 9/4/63. Commd 1/7/82. Flt Lt 13/11/88. Retd ADMIN 1/3/91.
FLAXMAN D.J. Born 24/2/37. Commd 30/11/56. Sqn Ldr 1/7/75. Retd GD(G) 1/7/78.
FLECKNEY C.F. MSc BSc BSc DIC. Born 28/6/46. Commd 24/11/77. Sqn Ldr 1/3/78. Retd ENGINEER 24/11/03.
FLECKNEY W.T.H. DFC LLB MCMI. Born 27/6/22. Commd 15/9/44. Sqn Ldr 1/7/70. Retd GD 26/6/73.
FLEET S.J. Born 31/8/39. Commd 20/8/65. Flt Lt 20/2/70. Retd GD 3/5/81.
FLEGG H.G. MA DCAe MRAeS. Born 10/6/24. Commd 11/1/45. Sqn Ldr 6/9/60. Retd EDN 12/5/65.
FLEMING A.W.P. Born 14/5/31. Commd 27/2/70. Flt Lt 27/2/76. Retd ADMIN 1/7/77.
FLEMING C.J. BSc. Born 27/12/61. Commd 11/9/83. Flt Lt 11/3/86. Retd GD 14/3/96.
FLEMING E.M. Born 18/12/25. Commd 23/5/63. Flt Lt 23/5/69. Retd GD(G) 17/8/79.
FLEMING H.C. FCA. Born 16/12/11. Commd 12/6/36. Wg Cdr 1/7/53. Retd SEC 15/6/59.
FLEMING J.B.A. OBE. Born 23/2/16. Commd 13/5/40. Wg Cdr 1/7/53. Retd GD 5/3/63.
FLEMING J.H. Born 14/3/17. Commd 17/10/57. Sqn Ldr 1/1/69. Retd SUP 9/7/73.
FLEMING J.McL. Born 18/8/26. Commd 27/5/53. Fg Offr 19/2/58. Retd SUP 4/2/64.
FLEMING P. OBE. Born 14/9/15. Commd 16/3/34. Gp Capt 1/1/55. Retd GD 14/10/65.
FLEMING P.J. MCSP DPhysEd. Born 13/5/47. Commd 11/8/69. Sqn Ldr 1/7/86. Retd ADMIN 14/3/96.
FLEMMINGS M.S. Born 28/12/52. Commd 16/3/73. Sqn Ldr 1/1/85. Retd GD 28/12/90.
FLETCHER A. Born 11/12/44. Commd 8/11/70. Sqn Ldr 1/1/88. Retd ENG 2/4/93.
FLETCHER A.K. Born 14/7/46. Commd 28/4/65. Sqn Ldr 1/1/84. Retd GD 14/7/01.
FLETCHER A.P.R. The Rev. BTh DipPasTh. Born 7/9/46. Commd 14/5/78. Retd Wg Cdr 14/5/00.
FLETCHER A.W.G. The Rev. BA. Born 23/4/24. Commd 6/6/61. Retd Wg Cdr 31/7/72.
FLETCHER B. MCMI. Born 22/10/35. Commd 27/10/67. Sqn Ldr 1/1/75. Retd SEC 1/1/78.
FLETCHER B.M.G. Born 22/3/38. Commd 1/3/62. Sqn Ldr 1/7/74. Retd SUP 1/7/77.
FLETCHER C.F. Born 23/10/20. Commd 30/4/44. Flt Lt 26/6/51. Retd GD(G) 23/10/70.
FLETCHER C.W. Born 17/11/15. Commd 29/5/41. Sqn Ldr 1/1/54. Retd ENG 1/4/60.
FLETCHER D.B. Born 17/8/35. Commd 19/8/53. Flt Lt 21/10/59. Retd GD 17/8/73.
FLETCHER D.K. Born 8/7/52. Commd 5/8/76. Sqn Ldr 1/1/91. Retd GD 10/5/97.
FLETCHER E.B. Born 23/2/25. Commd 30/1/52. Flt Lt 29/4/59. Retd GD 6/11/70.
FLETCHER E.M.D. Born 18/5/09. Commd 18/8/41. Sqn Offr 1/7/50. Retd SEC 31/5/58.
FLETCHER G.R.K. AFC. Born 11/12/26. Commd 8/4/49. Wg Cdr 1/1/64. Retd GD 1/8/68.
FLETCHER J.T. Born 15/7/21. Commd 3/8/50. Sqn Ldr 1/1/61. Retd ENG 15/8/73.
FLETCHER K.D. BSc MB ChB. Born 6/11/55. Commd 5/9/78. Sqn Ldr 1/8/87. Retd MED 5/9/94.
FLETCHER L.A. CEng MIEE MRAeS. Born 13/8/32. Commd 13/8/52. Flt Lt 20/5/58. Retd ENG 30/5/71.
FLETCHER L.G. Born 9/12/23. Commd 6/3/52. Flt Lt 6/9/56. Retd SUP 23/1/68.
FLETCHER L.W. Born 26/2/18. Commd 28/4/45. Wg Cdr 1/7/65. Retd SEC 2/3/74.
FLETCHER M.D. Born 22/12/43. Commd 14/1/82. Flt Lt 14/1/84. Retd ENG 14/9/90.
FLETCHER M.J. Born 7/5/34. Commd 18/5/53. Sqn Ldr 1/7/85. Retd GD 3/7/86.
FLETCHER N. MA. Born 25/3/22. Commd 19/6/42. Wg Cdr 1/1/64. Retd GD 26/9/68.
FLETCHER N.K. Born 5/6/46. Commd 20/11/75. Flt Lt 20/11/77. Retd GD 1/10/84.
FLETCHER P. DPhysEd. Born 19/4/30. Commd 24/4/57. Sqn Ldr 1/1/68. Retd SUP 1/9/74.
FLETCHER P.G.C. BA. Born 20/7/30. Commd 14/5/54. Flt Lt 15/4/60. Retd RGT 29/7/60.
FLETCHER P.J. ACIS. Born 4/3/50. Commd 19/6/70. Sqn Ldr 1/7/81. Retd ADMIN 4/3/88.
FLETCHER R.B. Born 5/11/43. Commd 2/5/69. Flt Lt 3/8/71. Retd SUP 5/11/81.
FLETCHER R.H. Born 27/4/46. Commd 19/7/84. Flt Lt 19/7/86. Retd ADMIN 19/7/92.
FLETCHER R.H. BSc CEng MIMechE MRAeS. Born 17/2/47. Commd 26/5/67. A Cdre 1/7/95. Retd ENG 7/8/99.
FLETCHER R.N. Born 14/10/47. Commd 14/10/71. Sqn Ldr 1/1/89. Retd ADMIN 1/9/96.
FLETCHER R.S. MSc BSc(Eng) CEng MIEE. Born 1/4/47. Commd 16/1/72. Sqn Ldr 1/1/80. Retd ENG 16/1/88.
FLETCHER T. DFC DFM*. Born 7/9/14. Commd 12/9/43. Flt Lt 12/3/47. Retd GD(G) 7/9/64.
FLETCHER W.D.M. CEng MRAeS. Born 12/7/42. Commd 7/12/65. Wg Cdr 1/7/82. Retd ENG 12/7/97.
FLETT K.McD. Born 22/8/26. Commd 1/10/50. Sqn Ldr 1/1/59. Retd GD 22/8/81.
FLETTON R.J. Born 20/12/45. Commd 28/11/69. Flt Lt 28/5/75. Retd GD 22/10/94.
FLEWITT A.J. BSc CEng MIEE MRAeS. Born 25/2/51. Commd 13/11/72. Sqn Ldr 1/7/81. Retd ENG 25/2/89.
FLIGHT J.P. MMS MCMI. Born 4/7/31. Commd 15/9/71. Sqn Ldr 1/7/80. Retd ADMIN 2/4/86.
FLINN P.W. Born 4/5/27. Commd 8/4/49. Flt Lt 8/10/51. Retd GD 4/5/65.
FLINN T.J. Born 12/1/49. Commd 27/2/70. Wg Cdr 1/7/86. Retd GD 1/7/89.

FLINT C.J. MILT MCMI. Born 22/2/43. Commd 26/5/67. Wg Cdr 1/7/84. Retd SUP 22/2/98.
FLINT C.J. Born 20/9/33. Commd 5/5/54. Fg Offr 18/5/65. Retd GD(G) 20/11/66.
FLINT H.P. Born 29/8/30. Commd 26/3/52. Flt Lt 31/7/57. Retd GD 11/9/68.
FLINT P.A. Born 27/2/48. Commd 28/11/69. Sqn Ldr 1/1/90. Retd GD 22/12/00.
FLIPPANT F.W.J. DFC. Born 25/2/25. Commd 14/11/57. Flt Lt 1/4/63. Retd GD(G) 1/8/79.
FLITCROFT K.W. Born 21/3/40. Commd 23/11/78. Sqn Ldr 1/7/88. Retd ENG 21/3/95.
FLOATE N.J. BSc. Born 20/12/33. Commd 11/4/58. Sqn Ldr 11/10/67. Retd EDN 11/4/74.
FLOCKHART D. Born 11/4/38. Commd 7/1/71. Flt Lt 7/1/73. Retd SUP 11/4/93.
FLOOD D.M. Born 12/1/21. Commd 25/1/51. Sqn Ldr 1/7/71. Retd SEC 12/1/76.
FLOOD F.J. Born 21/5/25. Commd 23/8/56. Flt Lt 23/8/62. Retd GD 1/8/68.
FLOOD J. Born 10/7/46. Commd 26/5/67. Sqn Ldr 1/7/83. Retd GD 1/7/86.
FLOOD P.J. Born 21/2/57. Commd 28/2/80. Flt Lt 26/8/83. Retd SY 21/2/95.
FLOOD R.G. Born 6/5/28. Commd 10/10/63. Flt Lt 10/10/68. Retd ENG 19/10/68.
FLOOD R.P. AFC. Born 6/10/25. Commd 5/6/45. Wg Cdr 1/7/68. Retd GD 2/10/75.
FLOOD T. Born 13/10/35. Commd 20/6/63. Flt Lt 1/4/66. Retd GD 13/10/90.
FLORCZAK F. MBE BA MCMI. Born 12/8/19. Commd 16/7/41. Sqn Ldr 1/1/63. Retd ENG 12/8/77.
FLORENCE W.H. Born 16/8/28. Commd 29/3/62. Sqn Ldr 1/7/74. Retd ENG 16/8/83.
FLOWER R.G. Born 21/3/23. Commd 3/8/61. Flt Lt 3/8/64. Retd GD 30/6/73.
FLOWERDEW B.N. Born 11/10/46. Commd 8/1/65. Wg Cdr 1/7/90. Retd GD 11/10/04.
FLOYD J.M. BSc CEng MRAeS. Born 24/11/43. Commd 3/10/66. Sqn Ldr 1/7/81. Retd ENG 1/7/84.
FLOYDD W.F. MBE BEM. Born 29/1/32. Commd 28/5/66. Wg Cdr 1/1/84. Retd SY 2/11/85.
FLUCKER C.J.R. BSc. Born 11/10/63. Commd 7/6/01. Sqn Ldr 1/8/98. Retd MEDICAL 1/3/03.
FLYNN C.T. MBE MB ChB MRCP. Born 13/11/30. Commd 22/5/64. Wg Cdr 1/3/72. Retd MED 16/1/76.
FLYNN J.B. Born 7/7/34. Commd 11/4/63. Sqn Ldr 1/1/77. Retd GD 7/7/84.
FLYNN J.R. Born 17/2/27. Commd 27/3/70. Flt Lt 11/7/73. Retd DEL 17/8/82.
FLYNN M.R. Born 12/2/44. Commd 1/2/62. Sqn Ldr 1/1/82. Retd GD 12/2/88.
FOALE C.H. Born 10/6/30. Commd 12/12/51. A Cdre 1/1/77. Retd GD 14/7/79.
FOARD D.J.S. Born 27/8/25. Commd 25/8/49. Sqn Ldr 1/1/60. Retd GD 30/3/68.
FODEN D. MBE. Born 17/10/42. Commd 17/5/79. Sqn Ldr 1/1/88. Retd ENG 1/11/95.
FODEN J.B. BA FHCIMA MCMI AMRSH. Born 7/5/26. Commd 17/1/49. Wg Cdr 1/1/70. Retd ADMIN 7/5/84.
FOERS R. MBE MHCIMA. Born 30/12/35. Commd 6/6/57. Sqn Ldr 1/1/76. Retd ADMIN 30/12/92.
FOGARTY M. BEM. Born 11/11/26. Commd 2/2/68. Flt Lt 2/2/73. Retd ADMIN 11/11/84.
FOGARTY R.J. BCom. Born 11/10/62. Commd 16/2/85. Flt Lt 18/10/87. Retd GD 25/9/98.
FOGG W.G. Born 4/2/39. Commd 4/10/63. Flt Lt 1/2/70. Retd GD 18/6/79.
FOGGIE P.R. BSc CEng MIEE. Born 4/9/44. Commd 15/7/65. Sqn Ldr 1/7/77. Retd ENG 4/9/82.
FOGGIN R.W. Born 6/12/29. Commd 18/7/68. Flt Lt 18/7/68. Retd ENG 7/12/79.
FOGGO C.H. Born 17/8/50. Commd 2/11/88. Flt Lt 2/11/90. Retd FLY(ENG) 4/8/04.
FOGGO R.C. Born 8/7/40. Commd 6/11/80. Sqn Ldr 1/7/90. Retd ENG 30/11/95.
FOGGO W.N. Born 22/5/43. Commd 19/2/76. Sqn Ldr 1/1/91. Retd GD 2/4/93.
FOLEY A.J. Born 11/5/44. Commd 21/12/62. Flt Lt 15/4/70. Retd GD 5/4/77.
FOLEY H.A.W. Born 27/9/28. Commd 17/6/54. Flt Lt 17/12/59. Retd GD 9/2/70.
FOLEY J.F. MBE BSc. Born 6/6/50. Commd 13/9/71. Sqn Ldr 1/7/86. Retd GD 14/9/96.
FOLEY J.W.A. Born 9/5/45. Commd 31/1/64. Flt Lt 4/5/72. Retd GD 30/7/76.
FOLEY T. Born 4/7/40. Commd 27/9/73. Sqn Ldr 1/7/80. Retd ADMIN 1/1/91.
FOLLETT P. Born 15/2/36. Commd 27/2/75. Sqn Ldr 1/1/84. Retd SUP 16/8/89.
FOLLEY R.F. Born 15/11/11. Commd 6/1/36. Gp Capt 1/7/54. Retd SUP 6/4/67.
FOLLIS R.G.C. DFC. Born 13/9/23. Commd 12/9/42. Sqn Ldr 1/7/59. Retd GD(G) 15/9/63.
FOLLIS R.J.C. Born 7/1/44. Commd 17/5/62. Flt Lt 2/9/69. Retd GD 7/1/81.
FONFE F.D.C. Born 16/8/49. Commd 27/10/67. Fg Offr 14/3/70. Retd RGT 26/3/72.
FONFE M.D.C. MBE. Born 21/2/45. Commd 26/5/67. Wg Cdr 1/7/87. Retd OPS SPT 21/2/00.
FOORD I.J. BSc. Born 24/6/51. Commd 15/9/69. Flt Lt 15/10/73. Retd GD 4/7/80.
FOOT C.W.J. Born 28/12/34. Commd 18/3/53. Flt Lt 6/2/59. Retd GD 28/12/72.
FOOT F.G. OBE. Born 29/3/13. Commd 4/4/38. Wg Cdr 1/1/52. Retd GD 14/1/58. rtg Gp Capt
FOOT G.E.P. MBE. Born 21/11/23. Commd 29/11/44. Sqn Ldr 1/10/55. Retd GD 21/11/66.
FOOT W.J. Born 13/11/31. Commd 5/11/53. Flt Lt 5/5/58. Retd GD 13/11/76. Re-instated 22/6/79. Flt Lt 12/12/60.
  Retd GD 13/11/88.
FOOTE D.A. Born 2/12/63. Commd 20/10/83. Sqn Ldr 1/1/98. Retd GD 1/6/02.
FOOTER S.G. MBE . Born 13/5/57. Commd 15/7/79. Wg Cdr 1/1/98. Retd GD 1/5/03.
FOPP D. AFC AE* MCMI. Born 13/3/20. Commd 3/11/41. Sqn Ldr 1/9/65. Retd GD 13/3/75.
FORBEAR J.S. Born 30/4/46. Commd 23/3/66. Fg Offr 23/9/68. Retd ENG 19/12/70.
FORBES D.J. FCMI. Born 26/3/45. Commd 24/9/64. Gp Capt 1/7/90. Retd SUP 7/7/96.
FORBES D.L. Born 23/9/22. Commd 25/9/46. Flt Lt 29/11/51. Retd GD 30/9/58.
FORBES D.M. Born 8/4/44. Commd 6/5/65. Flt Lt 4/5/72. Retd GD(G) 8/1/82.
FORBES F.A. Born 7/12/21. Commd 15/9/60. Sqn Ldr 1/1/73. Retd ENG 31/7/74.
FORBES G.A. BSc. Born 11/10/50. Commd 15/9/69. Sqn Ldr 1/1/85. Retd GD 30/1/88.
FORBES G.S. Born 12/10/49. Commd 4/2/71. Sqn Ldr 1/1/83. Retd GD 12/10/87.

FORBES J.C. DFM MCMI. Born 20/8/21. Commd 18/12/41. Gp Capt 1/1/65. Retd GD 20/8/76.
FORBES J.M. Born 10/8/16. Commd 16/3/45. Sqn Ldr 1/7/53. Retd SUP 7/4/62.
FORBES K.J. MBE. Born 12/8/22. Commd 6/6/57. Sqn Ldr 1/7/66. Retd ENG 10/9/77.
FORBES L.J.C. FInstLM MCIPD. Born 23/6/51. Commd 29/6/72. Sqn Ldr 1/7/88. Retd GD 1/7/91.
FORBES P.B. MB ChB MRCOG. Born 29/1/51. Commd 16/5/72. Wg Cdr 6/8/88. Retd MED 31/7/91.
FORBES S.J. Born 27/3/44. Commd 17/12/64. Flt Lt 17/6/71. Retd ENG 10/3/73.
FORBES S.M. Born 21/10/19. Commd 7/4/44. Flt Lt 11/3/48. Retd GD(G) 1/8/62.
FORD A.T. Born 18/12/45. Commd 26/5/67. A Cdre 1/7/97. Retd ADMIN 23/5/99.
FORD C.G. Born 7/12/41. Commd 24/3/61. Sqn Ldr 1/1/75. Retd GD 7/12/96.
FORD C.P. Born 31/12/22. Commd 30/4/59. Flt Lt 30/4/62. Retd GD 1/3/68.
FORD E.A. BSc. Born 30/6/51. Commd 25/2/72. Sqn Ldr 1/1/89. Retd ENG 6/8/01.
FORD F.R. Born 22/11/23. Commd 30/1/45. Flt Lt 10/8/48. Retd GD 3/12/66.
FORD Sir Geoffrey KBE CB BSc FEng FIEE DipEl. Born 6/8/23. Commd 21/10/42. AM 1/7/78. Retd ENG 6/4/81.
FORD G.C. BA. Born 7/7/50. Commd 15/9/69. Flt Lt 15/10/73. Retd GD 28/4/74.
FORD G.W. AFM. Born 12/9/24. Commd 26/5/54. Fg Offr 26/5/56. Retd GD 31/7/57.
FORD H.A. Born 28/7/30. Commd 31/12/52. Wg Cdr 1/7/77. Retd GD 28/7/85.
FORD J. OBE CEng MRAeS. Born 24/1/20. Commd 15/4/43. Wg Cdr 1/7/61. Retd ENG 24/1/75.
FORD J.A. BSc. Born 7/6/57. Commd 8/2/81. Flt Lt 8/5/81. Retd GD 8/2/97.
FORD J.A.F. FCMI. Born 19/6/44. Commd 24/6/65. A Cdre 1/7/94. Retd GD 24/5/98.
FORD J.M. Born 27/10/30. Commd 18/6/52. Flt Lt 17/8/58. Retd GD 14/6/71.
FORD J.P. AFC. Born 16/6/21. Commd 16/3/47. Wg Cdr 1/1/62. Retd GD 16/6/76. rtg Gp Capt
FORD M.A. MBE BDS FDRCS. Born 19/4/36. Commd 19/2/61. Wg Cdr 21/6/73. Retd DEL 30/9/77.
FORD M.A. Born 24/11/56. Commd 20/7/78. Flt Lt 20/1/84. Retd GD 14/3/97.
FORD M.S. MSc MPhil. Born 11/10/57. Commd 13/9/81. Sqn Ldr 1/1/92. Retd SUPPLY 13/9/03.
FORD N.A. BSc. Born 1/7/60. Commd 4/9/78. Flt Lt 15/10/84. Retd ENG 28/5/89.
FORD N.L. Born 19/11/41. Commd 21/12/62. Sqn Ldr 1/7/74. Retd GD 19/11/79.
FORD P.C.C. BSc. Born 15/6/47. Commd 1/1/67. Flt Lt 15/6/70. Retd GD 15/6/85.
FORD P.J. Born 14/7/44. Commd 22/3/63. Flt Lt 20/11/68. Retd GD 14/10/82.
FORD P.M. Born 6/10/38. Commd 23/6/67. Wg Cdr 1/1/87. Retd ENG 6/10/93.
FORD W.A. MBE BA ACIS. Born 14/1/34. Commd 19/10/59. Wg Cdr 1/1/75. Retd ADMIN 14/1/89.
FORDE W.L.T. Born 2/8/41. Commd 18/12/62. Sqn Ldr 1/7/74. Retd ADMIN 19/12/94.
FORDER R.A. Born 10/11/44. Commd 15/7/66. Flt Lt 1/7/69. Retd GD 10/8/72.
FORDER R.M. CEng MIMechE MRAeS. Born 28/9/39. Commd 28/5/66. Sqn Ldr 1/1/77. Retd ENG 28/9/94.
FORDHAM A. MA. Born 24/3/25. Commd 29/3/45. Sqn Ldr 1/7/57. Retd GD 5/6/65.
FORDHAM G.C. BSc. Born 18/9/45. Commd 26/5/67. Sqn Ldr 1/7/76. Retd ENG 1/10/87.
FORDHAM K. Born 4/8/44. Commd 5/1/70. Sqn Ldr 1/1/81. Retd ENG 5/1/86.
FOREMAN M.C. Born 3/8/59. Commd 29/8/77. Sqn Ldr 1/7/97. Retd GD 3/8/97.
FOREMAN R. Born 17/3/36. Commd 6/1/64. Sqn Ldr 1/1/85. Retd GD 17/3/94.
FORESHEW W.P. Born 30/12/12. Commd 23/3/50. Flt Lt 23/9/53. Retd SEC 17/11/58.
FORMAN G.N. CB. Born 30/11/30. Commd 27/11/57. AVM 1/7/82. Retd LGL 3/11/89.
FORMBY M.L. MRAeS. Born 19/6/13. Commd 12/3/34. Wg Cdr 1/7/53. Retd ENG 20/5/67.
FORREST J.E.N. Born 21/1/20. Commd 9/8/47. Flt Lt 7/6/51. Retd GD(G) 21/1/75.
FORREST M.J. Born 9/12/31. Commd 7/12/51. Flt Lt 16/2/57. Retd GD 2/10/65.
FORREST P.F. MSc BSc CEng MIEE. Born 22/1/59. Commd 14/10/84. Sqn Ldr 1/7/92. Retd ENG 14/10/00.
FORREST P.G. Born 28/4/63. Commd 22/6/89. Flt Lt 22/6/91. Retd ADMIN 28/8/96.
FORREST S.A.E. MBE CEng MIEE. Born 4/8/24. Commd 15/1/63. Sqn Ldr 1/12/65. Retd EDN 4/8/79.
FORRESTER A.J. BSc. Born 8/1/68. Commd 3/8/88. Flt Lt 30/6/92. Retd GD 7/2/96.
FORRESTER A.J. BSc. Born 18/2/56. Commd 29/4/84. Flt Lt 29/10/83. Retd ADMIN 14/3/97.
FORRESTER C. Born 25/8/30. Commd 19/7/51. Flt Lt 30/10/56. Retd GD 25/8/92.
FORRESTER I.C. Born 29/6/29. Commd 7/5/52. Flt Lt 2/10/57. Retd GD 16/10/67.
FORRESTER J.M. Born 16/8/65. Commd 23/10/86. Flt Lt 23/4/93. Retd OPS SPT(FC) 16/8/03.
FORRESTER P.A.W. Born 2/8/24. Commd 3/5/56. Sqn Ldr 1/7/71. Retd GD 5/3/73.
FORRESTER R.A. OBE BA. Born 2/6/44. Commd 22/3/63. Wg Cdr 1/7/87. Retd GD 17/10/98.
FORROW T.H. AMCIPD. Born 24/6/52. Commd 28/11/74. Sqn Ldr 1/1/89. Retd GD(G) 1/1/92.
FORSHAW D.J. Born 1/7/41. Commd 13/12/79. Flt Lt 13/12/85. Retd ENG 31/3/94.
FORSHAW J.F. ACIS MCIPD MCMI. Born 5/3/37. Commd 27/4/55. Wg Cdr 1/1/76. Retd SEC 5/1/82.
FORSHAW T.K.G. Born 19/6/23. Commd 20/4/50. Flt Lt 19/11/53. Retd GD 19/12/63.
FORSSANDER D.R. Born 19/12/14. Commd 20/6/41. Sqn Ldr 1/1/49. Retd SUP 1/1/50.
FORSTER B.J. Born 29/3/65. Commd 15/3/84. Flt Lt 15/9/89. Retd GD 7/10/92.
FORSTER B.R.W. MBE DFC AFC. Born 7/7/17. Commd 19/5/42. Wg Cdr 1/7/56. Retd GD 30/7/60.
FORSTER C.P. Born 1/7/25. Commd 6/12/50. Flt Offr 6/6/56. Retd SEC 28/8/56.
FORSTER F.O. Born 24/5/22. Commd 1/8/42. Flt Lt 2/3/50. Retd GD 22/6/65.
FORSTER I. DPhysEd. Born 31/1/49. Commd 16/8/70. Fg Offr 31/1/71. Retd PE 1/9/73.
FORSTER I.H. OBE BA FCIPD FCMI. Born 2/8/33. Commd 12/9/56. A Cdre 1/1/56. Retd ADMIN 1/12/87.
FORSTER J.A. Born 1/7/34. Commd 1/6/72. Flt Lt 1/6/78. Retd SY 1/6/85.
FORSTER J.A.F. Born 20/5/24. Commd 6/9/56. Flt Lt 6/9/62. Retd GD 16/11/67.

FORSTER J.B. Born 25/8/41. Commd 25/2/66. Flt Lt 25/8/72. Retd GD(G) 25/8/87.
FORSTER P.J. Born 7/1/41. Commd 1/4/65. Sqn Ldr 1/1/73. Retd SEC 7/1/79.
FORSTER P.R. Born 21/9/35. Commd 13/11/62. Sqn Ldr 1/1/75. Retd SEC 13/11/78.
FORSTER R.A.A. BA MILT MCMI. Born 7/5/48. Commd 17/1/72. Sqn Ldr 1/1/88. Retd SUP 14/3/97.
FORSTER R.D. Born 5/6/42. Commd 5/1/78. Flt Lt 5/1/80. Retd ENG 5/1/86.
FORSYTH B. BA. Born 24/11/45. Commd 17/12/64. Wg Cdr 1/7/83. Retd ENG 24/11/89.
FORSYTH D.R.G. MBE MSc FCIPS MIL. Born 25/11/47. Commd 2/8/68. Gp Capt 1/1/90. Retd SUP 13/7/95.
FORSYTH J.G. Born 12/5/42. Commd 27/4/70. Sqn Ldr 1/7/89. Retd ENG 1/9/93.
FORSYTHE J.R. CBE DFC. Born 10/7/20. Commd 10/11/42. A Cdre 1/1/71. Retd GD 10/11/75.
FORSYTHE R.A. OBE. Born 18/6/48. Commd 22/9/67. Wg Cdr 1/7/89. Retd GD 15/6/02.
FORTE C.B. Born 19/2/49. Commd 7/7/85. Wg Cdr 1/7/98. Retd GD 19/2/04.
FORTEATH J.H. Born 18/1/31. Commd 1/10/55. Gp Capt 1/7/79. Retd GD 14/4/84.
FORTESCUE D.C. Born 11/9/17. Commd 21/6/45. Wg Cdr 1/1/64. Retd SEC 18/2/66.
FORTEY R.G. Born 13/6/29. Commd 15/3/57. Flt Lt 15/9/61. Retd GD 11/10/71.
FORTUNE D.B. CEng MIMechE. Born 7/12/28. Commd 13/6/60. Wg Cdr 1/1/77. Retd ENG 24/7/82.
FORTUNE M.B. Born 22/7/37. Commd 6/7/62. Flt Lt 6/1/67. Retd GD 23/6/68.
FORTUNE T.F. Born 6/7/47. Commd 26/9/85. Sqn Ldr 1/7/93. Retd FLY(ENG) 6/7/03.
FORWARD B.M.E. OBE MRAeS. Born 20/10/35. Commd 10/2/59. Wg Cdr 1/7/80. Retd GD 18/5/86.
FORWARD C.W. Born 17/9/08. Commd 3/1/41. Flt Lt 1/9/45. Retd SUP 23/10/54. rtg Sqn Ldr
FOSH J.S. CBE MMAR MNI. Born 28/5/35. Commd 14/6/63. Gp Capt 1/7/84. Retd MAR 25/5/85.
FOSKETT G.W. Born 25/5/25. Commd 2/1/48. Sqn Ldr 1/7/54. Retd RGT 25/5/63. rtg Wg Cdr
FOSKETT L.B. OBE AFC. Born 17/8/21. Commd 1/1/43. Gp Capt 1/1/65. Retd GD 17/8/76.
FOSTER A. Born 11/11/37. Commd 2/9/55. Flt Lt 2/3/61. Retd GD 24/3/65.
FOSTER A. BSc CEng MIEE. Born 18/7/48. Commd 7/9/70. Sqn Ldr 1/1/79. Retd ENG 1/9/92.
FOSTER A.F. Born 21/11/36. Commd 6/5/65. Flt Lt 6/5/71. Retd GD 21/11/94.
FOSTER A.R. BSc. Born 24/6/47. Commd 6/10/69. Flt Lt 6/1/71. Retd GD 6/10/85.
FOSTER B.G.A. Born 21/11/46. Commd 16/9/76. Sqn Ldr 1/1/87. Retd ENG 14/3/97.
FOSTER D.F. MB ChB MFOM DRCOG DAvMed. Born 17/4/31. Commd 14/11/66. Gp Capt 1/1/82. Retd MED 11/1/85.
FOSTER D.J.G. AFC BSc CEng MRAeS. Born 24/7/36. Commd 23/3/55. Wg Cdr 1/1/76. Retd GD 1/1/79.
FOSTER E.C. Born 6/6/50. Commd 19/6/70. Gp Capt 1/1/99. Retd ADMIN 7/6/01.
FOSTER F.W. Born 21/1/48. Commd 1/8/69. Sqn Ldr 1/7/80. Retd GD 30/12/89.
FOSTER G. Born 2/11/31. Commd 2/7/52. Flt Lt 2/3/58. Retd GD 29/4/71.
FOSTER G.R. Born 15/3/21. Commd 12/1/45. Sqn Ldr 1/1/72. Retd GD 15/3/76.
FOSTER G.R. Born 17/8/47. Commd 17/2/67. Flt Lt 17/8/72. Retd GD 31/1/85.
FOSTER G.R. Born 6/6/36. Commd 20/1/64. Flt Lt 20/1/64. Retd SUP 4/6/67.
FOSTER G.S. Born 29/1/37. Commd 17/10/59. Sqn Ldr 1/7/77. Retd GD 9/10/89.
FOSTER J.A. Born 16/10/44. Commd 1/4/66. Flt Lt 1/10/71. Retd GD 16/10/82.
FOSTER J.A. Born 23/11/40. Commd 28/4/61. Flt Lt 28/10/66. Retd GD 23/11/95.
FOSTER J.A. MSc BSc CEng MIEE CDipAF. Born 3/10/51. Commd 15/9/69. Wg Cdr 1/1/94. Retd GD 4/4/04.
FOSTER J.E. MRIN MCMI. Born 17/7/40. Commd 8/12/61. Sqn Ldr 1/7/74. Retd GD 17/7/95.
FOSTER J.E. Born 24/1/29. Commd 11/4/63. Flt Lt 11/4/66. Retd GD 4/6/68.
FOSTER J.M. BA. Born 22/6/55. Commd 29/3/73. Flt Lt 1/10/77. Retd GD 1/10/87.
FOSTER J.P. Born 22/12/54. Commd 1/11/79. Sqn Ldr 1/1/90. Retd SY 1/1/93.
FOSTER J.W. DFC AFC. Born 1/8/22. Commd 18/9/42. Gp Capt 1/1/67. Retd GD 14/9/75.
FOSTER K.C. OBE. Born 14/10/42. Commd 27/1/61. Wg Cdr 1/1/82. Retd GD 3/1/93.
FOSTER M.A. Born 3/5/48. Commd 27/9/73. Sqn Ldr 1/1/86. Retd GD(G) 19/3/89.
FOSTER M.G.L. AFC. Born 15/4/13. Commd 24/2/37. Wg Cdr 1/10/46. Retd GD 15/4/60.
FOSTER M.M. OBE. Born 20/11/29. Commd 1/8/51. Wg Cdr 1/7/71. Retd GD 20/11/84.
FOSTER P.J. BSc. Born 13/4/48. Commd 17/10/71. Flt Lt 17/7/75. Retd ADMIN 17/10/87.
FOSTER R. Born 11/12/49. Commd 8/8/69. Wg Cdr 1/7/90. Retd GD 11/12/04.
FOSTER R.G. Born 1/10/22. Commd 11/8/44. Flt Lt 11/2/48. Retd GD 1/10/65.
FOSTER R.K. BSc. Born 14/2/36. Commd 23/6/61. Flt Lt 23/12/66. Retd GD 28/3/77.
FOSTER R.W.J. Born 5/2/65. Commd 16/2/89. Flt Lt 16/8/94. Retd GD 14/3/96.
FOSTER S.F. BEng. Born 27/3/62. Commd 2/8/89. Flt Lt 15/7/92. Retd ENG 7/5/01.
FOSTER S.R. Born 15/9/49. Commd 24/6/71. Flt Lt 24/12/76. Retd GD 1/5/87.
FOSTER V.A. Born 27/8/29. Commd 18/10/62. Flt Lt 18/10/68. Retd ENG 31/7/71.
FOSTER W.E. Born 30/5/19. Commd 30/7/59. Sqn Ldr 1/1/70. Retd ENG 1/9/76.
FOSTER W.H. Born 3/5/32. Commd 15/5/58. Flt Lt 15/5/64. Retd SEC 3/5/70.
FOSTER-PEGG R.I. Born 16/2/66. Commd 23/5/88. Flt Lt 23/11/90. Retd GD 14/3/96.
FOTHERGILL W.T. MB BS DipSoton DA FFARCS. Born 11/3/29. Commd 1/10/53. Wg Cdr 10/9/65. Retd MED 1/10/69.
FOULGER D.A. MBE. Born 28/11/44. Commd 15/7/66. Sqn Ldr 1/7/79. Retd GD 6/3/93.
FOULKES B.V. MCMI. Born 30/7/37. Commd 26/5/67. Flt Lt 26/5/73. Retd MED(SEC) 3/10/75.
FOULKES D.D. Born 3/10/41. Commd 26/3/64. Flt Lt 3/10/68. Retd SEC 14/9/73.
FOULKES R.L. BSc. Born 12/3/54. Commd 13/5/76. Flt Lt 15/10/77. Retd GD 13/5/92.
FOUND D.G. Born 15/1/41. Commd 3/8/62. Fg Offr 3/8/64. Retd GD 25/11/66.
FOUNTAIN C. FCMI. Born 9/10/25. Commd 14/11/49. A Cdre 1/1/76. Retd GD 1/5/79.

FOUNTAIN J.S. Born 19/5/43. Commd 24/6/65. Flt Lt 29/11/70. Retd GD 26/8/76.
FOURIE V.H. Born 1/10/24. Commd 29/8/45. Sqn Ldr 1/1/57. Retd GD 18/12/62.
FOVARQUE A.J. BSc. Born 4/9/46. Commd 17/1/72. Wg Cdr 1/7/94. Retd GD 16/1/99.
FOWLE A.P.D. Born 10/4/76. Commd 5/10/95. Plt Offr 5/10/96. Retd GD 16/2/98.
FOWLE C.J.D. BSc CEng MInstP MRAeS MCMI. Born 15/5/22. Commd 5/8/42. Wg Cdr 1/7/68. Retd ENG 20/8/77.
FOWLE M.D. Born 13/7/48. Commd 7/10/69. Wg Cdr 1/1/92. Retd ADMIN 14/9/96.
FOWLER A.K. Born 13/8/57. Commd 27/3/80. Flt Lt 15/5/84. Retd GD(G) 7/1/97.
FOWLER C.R. Born 19/11/45. Commd 28/11/69. A Cdre 1/1/96. Retd ADMIN 19/12/00.
FOWLER D. BSc CEng MRAeS. Born 7/8/45. Commd 15/7/66. Sqn Ldr 1/1/76. Retd ENG 7/8/83.
FOWLER D. Born 9/7/47. Commd 19/6/70. Sqn Ldr 1/7/84. Retd GD 1/7/87.
FOWLER D.F. Born 27/2/21. Commd 18/12/44. Flt Lt 18/6/47. Retd GD 2/3/54.
FOWLER D.J. AFC. Born 19/3/20. Commd 22/4/44. Sqn Ldr 1/10/54. Retd GD 19/3/69.
FOWLER F.A. Born 11/2/20. Commd 5/3/53. Sqn Ldr 1/7/67. Retd ENG 11/2/78.
FOWLER F.B.L. MRAeS. Born 2/7/15. Commd 10/6/43. Sqn Ldr 1/7/54. Retd ENG 2/8/64.
FOWLER G.A. Born 12/12/35. Commd 2/2/60. Wg Cdr 1/1/79. Retd EDN 1/4/81.
FOWLER J.C. MSc BA MCIPS. Born 23/4/48. Commd 26/5/70. Sqn Ldr 1/7/82. Retd SUP 14/3/96.
FOWLER J.G. MA MB BChir MRCGP DAvMed. Born 22/12/37. Commd 15/10/62. Wg Cdr 2/9/76. Retd MED 15/10/78.
FOWLER K.E. BSc. Born 8/10/61. Commd 16/9/79. Sqn Ldr 1/1/98. Retd GD 8/5/01.
FOWLER L.W. MBE MCMI. Born 31/3/25. Commd 10/8/45. Sqn Ldr 1/1/63. Retd GD 31/3/78.
FOWLER M.L. Born 9/5/65. Commd 12/3/87. Flt Lt 12/9/92. Retd FLY(P) 23/8/03.
FOWLER M.S. Born 9/2/46. Commd 21/7/65. Flt Lt 21/1/71. Retd GD 21/9/84.
FOWLER R. AFC. Born 2/2/38. Commd 25/1/63. Gp Capt 1/1/84. Retd GD 29/12/89.
FOWLER S.G. Born 5/8/38. Commd 31/7/58. Wg Cdr 1/1/83. Retd ADMIN 23/9/88.
FOWLER S.M. Born 4/7/45. Commd 28/11/69. Flt Lt 28/5/75. Retd GD 14/5/00.
FOWLER T.A.M. Born 5/4/41. Commd 22/12/61. Flt Lt 18/4/67. Retd RGT 9/8/72.
FOWLIE D.G. MB ChB MRCPsych. Born 16/1/46. Commd 25/9/67. Sqn Ldr 6/8/76. Retd MED 12/11/83.
FOWNES P.W. Born 28/2/31. Commd 18/10/62. Sqn Ldr 1/7/80. Retd GD 3/10/81.
FOX A.M. Born 17/8/50. Commd 1/11/81. Flt Lt 9/2/79. Retd GD 15/1/93.
FOX A.R. OBE DCAe CEng MRAeS DipEl. Born 2/6/24. Commd 24/10/51. Gp Capt 1/1/73. Retd ENG 12/9/78.
FOX B.C.A. OBE LLB FCMI. Born 7/9/16. Commd 14/7/39. Gp Capt 1/7/67. Retd SUP 1/9/70.
FOX B.L. Born 16/4/33. Commd 8/7/65. Flt Lt 8/7/71. Retd MED(T) 1/10/75.
FOX C.J.H. MBE. Born 28/1/23. Commd 3/8/50. Sqn Ldr 1/1/64. Retd GD 1/6/79.
FOX C.W. BEM. Born 10/9/35. Commd 21/9/72. Sqn Ldr 1/7/85. Retd ENG 21/5/90.
FOX D.A. Born 23/5/40. Commd 12/3/60. Flt Lt 12/9/65. Retd GD 2/4/93.
FOX E.A. Born 31/8/33. Commd 30/7/64. Flt Lt 30/7/70. Retd SEC 5/9/73.
FOX E.D. MCMI. Born 15/12/16. Commd 21/2/46. Sqn Ldr 1/7/70. Retd SUP 1/7/73.
FOX G.H. Born 17/10/49. Commd 26/2/71. Sqn Ldr 1/1/85. Retd SY 14/3/96.
FOX J. MIIM. Born 11/6/48. Commd 17/5/79. Flt Lt 17/5/81. Retd ENG 17/5/87.
FOX J.A. Born 31/12/41. Commd 10/5/73. Flt Lt 1/5/75. Retd ENG 10/5/81.
FOX J.B. CEng MIEE MCMI. Born 3/5/33. Commd 11/1/57. Sqn Ldr 1/7/66. Retd ENG 15/5/84.
FOX J.E. Born 24/10/42. Commd 19/4/63. Flt Lt 19/10/68. Retd GD 31/7/76.
FOX L. MA. Born 12/9/55. Commd 29/5/85. Wg Cdr 1/1/94. Retd GD 1/4/03.
FOX M.A. Born 22/11/41. Commd 2/4/65. Flt Lt 4/11/70. Retd GD 7/12/80.
FOX M.J. Born 22/4/55. Commd 27/2/75. Sqn Ldr 1/7/87. Retd GD 22/4/93.
FOX N.A. MCMI. Born 18/9/35. Commd 31/7/56. Wg Cdr 1/1/75. Retd SUP 23/5/89.
FOX N.G. BA. Born 28/5/50. Commd 8/11/68. Wg Cdr 1/1/90. Retd GD 1/10/03.
FOX N.H. BSc. Born 8/2/49. Commd 7/5/72. Flt Lt 7/2/74. Retd GD 7/5/88.
FOX O.A. DFM. Born 27/7/17. Commd 21/6/43. Flt Lt 21/12/46. Retd ENG 27/7/66.
FOX P.N. Born 25/7/49. Commd 16/8/68. Sqn Ldr 1/1/96. Retd GD 9/4/02.
FOX R. MBE BEM. Born 28/8/17. Commd 7/12/61. Flt Lt 7/12/64. Retd PE 10/10/72.
FOX R.G. Born 17/4/35. Commd 31/7/56. Sqn Ldr 1/7/65. Retd GD 17/4/73. Re-instated 23/9/81. Sqn Ldr 7/12/73.
 Retd GD 17/4/95.
FOX R.O. BSc. Born 27/8/46. Commd 20/4/71. Flt Lt 20/7/71. Retd GD 20/4/87.
FOX R.W. Born 7/6/44. Commd 22/2/63. Flt Lt 8/1/69. Retd GD 14/3/96.
FOX R.W. Born 18/8/29. Commd 12/12/51. Flt Lt 12/6/54. Retd GD 18/8/67.
FOX-EDWARDS A. BSocSc. Born 13/7/62. Commd 14/9/80. Sqn Ldr 1/7/94. Retd GD 13/7/00.
FOY M.A. BM FRCS(Edin). Born 8/12/52. Commd 18/11/85. Wg Cdr 4/8/91. Retd MED 30/11/93.
FOYLE D.A. Born 16/8/19. Commd 21/2/55. Flt Lt 21/2/55. Retd SEC 1/12/64.
FOYLE D.J. Born 30/7/44. Commd 11/7/74. Sqn Ldr 1/1/81. Retd ENG 30/7/88.
FOZARD M.J. CEng MRAeS. Born 12/12/46. Commd 2/8/68. Wg Cdr 1/7/87. Retd ENG 12/12/01.
FRADLEY D. Born 7/12/40. Commd 31/7/62. Sqn Ldr 1/1/72. Retd GD 5/2/80.
FRAGEL N.J. Born 17/9/64. Commd 15/3/84. Fg Offr 15/9/86. Retd ADMIN 1/10/89.
FRAME L.S. BSc. Born 24/8/38. Commd 1/1/61. Wg Cdr 1/1/77. Retd GD 1/1/80.
FRAME O.S. Born 27/3/19. Commd 5/8/42. Flt Lt 19/3/51. Retd GD(G) 28/6/69.
FRAME P.J. Born 13/1/33. Commd 13/9/51. Sqn Ldr 1/7/64. Retd GD 28/1/77. Re-instated 30/3/83. Sqn Ldr 30/8/70.
 Retd GD 13/1/91.

FRAMPTON J.H. Born 25/2/19. Commd 4/3/38. Sqn Ldr 1/1/51. Retd GD 24/2/59.
FRANCE B.N. Born 30/6/42. Commd 4/7/69. Flt Lt 4/5/72. Retd RGT 12/11/73.
FRANCE J.D. Born 21/11/37. Commd 22/1/57. Sqn Ldr 1/1/78. Retd GD(G) 2/4/92.
FRANCEY A.I. Born 28/3/47. Commd 1/4/66. Fg Offr 1/4/68. Retd GD 26/10/71.
FRANCEY M.D. BSc. Born 4/6/60. Commd 8/5/92. Flt Lt 7/11/85. Retd GD 9/5/00.
FRANCIS A.D. Born 28/7/38. Commd 28/2/80. Flt Lt 28/2/84. Retd ENG 19/9/88.
FRANCIS A.G. Born 16/4/43. Commd 2/6/82. Sqn Ldr 1/1/89. Retd FLY(N) 16/10/03.
FRANCIS C. Born 11/7/63. Commd 28/3/91. Flt Lt 28/3/93. Retd ADMIN 11/11/96.
FRANCIS C.F. Born 9/5/13. Commd 12/12/46. Flt Lt 12/6/50. Retd SUP 27/8/58.
FRANCIS C.P. Born 12/5/28. Commd 27/7/49. Sqn Ldr 1/7/58. Retd GD 1/4/67.
FRANCIS C.V. Born 24/4/35. Commd 6/9/55. Flt Lt 6/3/61. Retd GD 1/3/69.
FRANCIS G. DFC AFC*. Born 4/9/16. Commd 16/3/47. Flt Lt 5/2/48. Retd GD(G) 4/9/74.
FRANCIS G.A. Born 16/10/26. Commd 3/5/46. Sqn Ldr 1/1/57. Retd GD 30/12/67.
FRANCIS G.R. Born 5/1/37. Commd 30/7/57. Sqn Ldr 1/7/70. Retd GD 1/4/87.
FRANCIS H.T. DFC. Born 3/3/15. Commd 1/1/43. Sqn Ldr 1/8/47. Retd GD 7/5/58.
FRANCIS I.C. DPhysEd MCMI. Born 8/5/31. Commd 24/2/55. Sqn Ldr 1/7/68. Retd SUP 26/2/74.
FRANCIS I.E. Born 31/3/38. Commd 26/5/60. Wg Cdr 1/1/78. Retd GD 23/6/90.
FRANCIS I.P. BA. Born 16/2/37. Commd 7/8/59. Sqn Ldr 7/2/67. Retd EDN 7/8/75.
FRANCIS I.R. BSc. Born 12/5/63. Commd 20/1/85. Sqn Ldr 1/7/98. Retd FLY(N) 7/7/03.
FRANCIS L.E. CEng MRAeS FCMI. Born 9/8/18. Commd 1/12/41. Gp Capt 1/7/69. Retd ENG 9/8/72.
FRANCIS N.J. Born 30/11/48. Commd 21/3/69. Fg Offr 20/9/71. Retd GD(G) 23/12/74.
FRANCIS N.P. BSc. Born 7/8/61. Commd 29/4/84. Flt Lt 29/10/86. Retd GD 14/9/96.
FRANCIS P.H. Born 25/10/18. Commd 28/7/49. Sqn Ldr 1/7/58. Retd ENG 26/10/67.
FRANCIS R.H. BA. Born 23/7/30. Commd 22/9/49. Sqn Ldr 1/7/75. Retd SEC 23/7/80.
FRANCIS R.J. Born 12/3/43. Commd 20/7/78. Sqn Ldr 1/7/86. Retd ENG 15/1/95.
FRANCIS R.W. DFC. Born 18/1/25. Commd 11/11/44. Sqn Ldr 1/7/69. Retd GD 30/8/75.
FRANCIS W.G. Born 25/5/39. Commd 22/10/59. Wg Cdr 1/7/89. Retd ADMIN 21/8/90.
FRANCIS W.K. Born 10/12/29. Commd 13/7/61. Flt Lt 13/7/67. Retd SEC 19/8/67.
FRANK C.G.H. BSc CEng MRAeS MIEE. Born 26/5/27. Commd 6/11/47. Wg Cdr 1/7/71. Retd ENG 1/3/79.
FRANK E.A. Born 1/7/20. Commd 4/10/44. Flt Offr 9/11/52. Retd SEC 13/1/55.
FRANK M.J.C. Born 6/4/45. Commd 15/9/67. Sqn Ldr 1/7/80. Retd GD 1/11/89.
FRANKCOM G.P. BA. Born 15/4/42. Commd 17/9/67. Sqn Ldr 1/7/77. Retd GD 17/9/83.
FRANKLAND M.J. Born 26/9/51. Commd 29/4/71. Sqn Ldr 1/7/85. Retd GD 14/3/97.
FRANKLAND R. Born 11/8/53. Commd 5/8/76. Flt Lt 5/2/82. Retd GD 20/4/92.
FRANKLIN C.E. Born 6/9/34. Commd 14/10/71. Flt Lt 14/10/75. Retd ENG 19/9/84.
FRANKLIN D.B. Born 12/8/32. Commd 27/9/51. Flt Lt 29/4/57. Retd GD 12/8/87.
FRANKLIN D.G.T. AFC. Born 25/5/26. Commd 20/4/50. Sqn Ldr 1/7/58. Retd GD 31/5/76.
FRANKLIN D.J.P. Born 26/1/48. Commd 26/5/67. Flt Lt 26/11/72. Retd GD 29/11/75.
FRANKLIN G.S. AFC. Born 25/11/35. Commd 10/11/63. Flt Lt 25/7/66. Retd GD 7/12/74.
FRANKLIN K.T. Born 1/7/20. Commd 20/10/04. Sqn Offr 1/1/55. Retd SEC 11/12/55.
FRANKLIN N.E. Born 7/10/28. Commd 25/6/66. Sqn Ldr 1/7/79. Retd ENG 2/4/82.
FRANKLIN P.R. Born 17/9/40. Commd 22/5/70. Flt Lt 22/5/72. Retd GD(G) 17/9/78.
FRANKLIN T.J. Born 21/10/32. Commd 24/9/64. Flt Lt 24/9/69. Retd ENG 1/2/73.
FRANKLIN-JONES A. BSc MRAeS. Born 3/11/13. Commd 22/8/39. Wg Cdr 1/1/58. Retd EDN 17/9/66.
FRANKLING M.B. MSc CEng MRAeS. Born 22/12/43. Commd 16/9/76. Sqn Ldr 1/1/87. Retd ADMIN 16/9/90.
FRANKS C. Born 27/12/41. Commd 10/3/77. Sqn Ldr 1/7/91. Retd ENG 27/6/93.
FRANKS D.M. Born 15/9/45. Commd 6/9/68. Flt Lt 6/3/75. Retd GD 12/3/84.
FRANKS J.N. Born 3/6/34. Commd 18/5/55. Flt Lt 23/11/60. Retd GD 3/6/89.
FRASER A.L. CEng MIMechE. Born 28/12/33. Commd 28/10/55. Wg Cdr 1/7/73. Retd ENG 29/11/85.
FRASER A.L. Born 30/9/40. Commd 5/12/63. Sqn Ldr 1/1/80. Retd ENG 30/9/95.
FRASER A.W. Born 15/3/34. Commd 18/3/53. A Cdre 1/7/77. Retd GD 24/7/79.
FRASER B. BA DPhysEd. Born 30/1/46. Commd 15/12/70. Sqn Ldr 1/1/87. Retd ADMIN 30/1/01.
FRASER B.F.J. Born 4/5/35. Commd 4/7/69. Flt Lt 4/7/71. Retd ADMIN 4/7/77.
FRASER E.M. Born 1/7/19. Commd 17/5/41. Flt Offr 1/9/45. Retd SEC 15/8/50.
FRASER G.W. MA MA. Born 13/5/44. Commd 4/9/67. Wg Cdr 1/1/83. Retd ADMIN 1/1/86.
FRASER I. Born 13/6/35. Commd 23/1/64. Flt Lt 1/4/66. Retd SEC 13/6/73.
FRASER J. Born 6/8/41. Commd 6/9/63. Sqn Ldr 1/7/91. Retd GD 6/8/98.
FRASER J.C.A. BSc. Born 23/10/56. Commd 15/9/74. Sqn Ldr 1/7/90. Retd GD 23/10/00.
FRASER J.W. MBE. Born 11/10/24. Commd 3/6/53. Sqn Ldr 1/7/62. Retd CAT 9/8/69.
FRASER K. Born 26/9/05. Commd 3/6/29. Sqn Ldr 1/12/43. Retd SEC 7/5/46. rtg Wg Cdr
FRASER N.A.S. Born 10/9/62. Commd 24/7/81. Sqn Ldr 1/7/94. Retd OPS SPT 10/9/00.
FRASER N.M.J. Born 14/3/35. Commd 13/12/55. Wg Cdr 1/7/80. Retd GD 22/2/89.
FRASER N.N. Born 24/12/37. Commd 25/1/63. Flt Lt 25/7/68. Retd GD 2/10/78.
FRASER R.G. BSc. Born 8/6/53. Commd 14/11/76. Wg Cdr 1/1/99. Retd GD 31/7/00.
FRASER W.A. MBE MCMI. Born 31/10/19. Commd 5/5/60. Sqn Ldr 1/7/68. Retd ENG 31/10/74.
FRATER S. MCIPD MCMI. Born 12/3/45. Commd 4/5/72. Wg Cdr 1/7/88. Retd ADMIN 1/4/92.

FRAZER C.F. Born 20/9/45. Commd 3/3/64. Flt Lt 17/3/71. Retd GD 30/4/76.
FRAZER K.D. Born 18/7/42. Commd 16/9/71. Sqn Ldr 1/7/79. Retd ENG 18/7/97.
FRAZER W.M. BSc. Born 28/12/46. Commd 6/10/69. Flt Lt 6/7/71. Retd GD 23/5/91.
FREARSON W.C. MCMI. Born 13/1/21. Commd 5/12/42. Sqn Ldr 1/1/70. Retd SEC 13/1/76.
FREARY W.T.W. BEM. Born 31/3/36. Commd 27/10/67. Sqn Ldr 1/1/75. Retd ADMIN 29/4/77.
FRECKNALL I.T. BA. Born 17/7/67. Commd 31/3/91. Flt Lt 30/9/93. Retd FLY(N) 31/3/03.
FREEBORN A.J. Born 16/10/28. Commd 2/3/49. Wg Cdr 1/1/70. Retd GD 4/9/76.
FREEGUARD T.S. Born 24/4/40. Commd 14/10/71. Sqn Ldr 1/1/78. Retd ADMIN 1/7/82.
FREEMAN A.R. Born 4/3/41. Commd 30/7/63. Sqn Ldr 1/1/72. Retd GD 20/12/80.
FREEMAN B.G. OBE. Born 20/3/45. Commd 27/5/71. Gp Capt 1/1/94. Retd GD 1/1/98.
FREEMAN G. Born 18/9/32. Commd 12/7/51. Flt Lt 20/5/64. Retd GD 1/2/72.
FREEMAN K.S. DFM. Born 22/1/18. Commd 25/4/43. Flt Lt 25/10/46. Retd GD 2/8/53.
FREEMAN N.B. AFC. Born 15/4/19. Commd 27/7/40. Wg Cdr 1/7/56. Retd GD 23/4/66.
FREEMAN R.E.M. Born 30/7/37. Commd 16/12/58. Wg Cdr 1/1/79. Retd GD 20/6/83.
FREEMAN S.J. BSc. Born 2/2/30. Commd 6/8/63. Sqn Ldr 15/4/70. Retd ADMIN 6/8/79.
FREEMAN T.J. CEng MIEE. Born 26/4/40. Commd 19/1/66. Flt Lt 23/1/70. Retd ENG 26/4/78.
FREER Sir Robert GBE KCB CCMI. Born 1/9/23. Commd 25/9/43. ACM 1/1/80. Retd GD 3/4/82.
FREESTON D.J. Born 23/9/29. Commd 24/9/52. Flt Lt 1/4/58. Retd GD 29/9/84.
FREESTONE-WALKER A. Born 28/5/41. Commd 8/11/68. Sqn Ldr 1/1/77. Retd SUP 1/1/80.
FREKE C.J. Born 26/11/55. Commd 13/8/82. Fg Offr 13/2/85. Retd GD(G) 1/2/87.
FRENCH A. OBE FRIN MRAeS. Born 11/6/32. Commd 17/6/54. Gp Capt 1/7/77. Retd GD 8/4/87.
FRENCH A.P.W. Born 22/2/58. Commd 19/9/76. Flt Lt 12/3/83. Retd GD 22/2/96.
FRENCH B.T.A. Born 24/2/31. Commd 22/8/71. Sqn Ldr 22/8/71. Retd SUP 26/11/88.
FRENCH D.R. CB MBE CEng MRAeS. Born 11/12/37. Commd 6/10/60. AVM 1/7/91. Retd ENG 1/1/94.
FRENCH E.G. BSc. Born 19/12/25. Commd 24/4/49. Sqn Ldr 19/11/63. Retd ADMIN 24/4/75.
FRENCH H.F. Born 8/6/36. Commd 24/6/71. Sqn Ldr 1/1/84. Retd ENG 30/4/88.
FRENCH J.F. Born 13/11/42. Commd 28/2/64. Sqn Ldr 1/7/88. Retd GD 22/5/93.
FRENCH K.G.H. Born 29/3/44. Commd 24/6/65. Flt Lt 24/12/67. Retd GD 29/1/82.
FRENCH K.H. Born 15/6/38. Commd 9/4/60. Flt Lt 9/10/65. Retd GD 1/10/76.
FRENCH M.R. Born 19/6/39. Commd 1/4/58. Gp Capt 1/1/85. Retd GD 16/9/88.
FRENCH P.F.G. MSc BSc CEng MIEE. Born 17/12/52. Commd 19/3/78. Sqn Ldr 1/1/85. Retd ADMIN 19/3/94.
FRENCH R. Born 17/11/26. Commd 3/5/46. Flt Lt 28/2/50. Retd GD(G) 17/1/73.
FRENCH R.A. Born 3/12/41. Commd 26/5/61. Flt Lt 26/11/66. Retd GD 22/10/94.
FRENCH R.E. Born 27/1/40. Commd 23/6/61. Fg Offr 23/6/63. Retd GD 5/8/66.
FRENCH T.H. MBE. Born 28/2/15. Commd 29/11/43. Flt Lt 24/4/50. Retd SUP 28/2/64. Re-commissioned 7/3/66 to 7/3/69.
FRENCH T.J. CEng MRAeS MIEE. Born 24/3/33. Commd 25/7/56. Wg Cdr 1/1/76. Retd ENG 24/3/87.
FREWER P.J. Born 3/9/34. Commd 9/12/53. Flt Lt 3/9/61. Retd GD 3/9/72.
FREYNE T. The Rev. Born 25/11/17. Commd 28/7/42. Retd Wg Cdr 15/3/62.
FRIAR P.D. MSc BSc (Eur Ing) CEng MRAeS. Born 25/2/56. Commd 4/1/81. Sqn Ldr 1/1/90. Retd ENG 4/1/97.
FRICK T. BDS. Born 10/1/64. Commd 23/4/93. Wg Cdr 2/8/00. Retd DENTAL 2/8/03.
FRICKER C.J. Born 2/1/42. Commd 2/8/68. Sqn Ldr 1/1/78. Retd ENG 1/1/87. Re-entered 21/12/87. Sqn Ldr 21/12/87. Retd ENG 2/1/97.
FRICKER G.A. OBE. Born 26/10/08. Commd 9/9/41. Wg Cdr 1/7/54. Retd ENG 26/10/60.
FRIDAY S.J. Born 25/8/63. Commd 25/2/82. Flt Lt 25/8/87. Retd GD 4/4/92.
FRIDGE A.R. Born 6/12/32. Commd 21/10/66. Sqn Ldr 1/1/78. Retd GD(G) 1/8/83.
FRIPP A.G. Born 13/6/14. Commd 12/6/47. Sqn Ldr 1/1/64. Retd ENG 13/6/69.
FRIPP M.D. BA. Born 28/5/37. Commd 30/9/56. Sqn Ldr 1/1/69. Retd ENG 28/5/75.
FRIPP W.A. DFC. Born 20/10/21. Commd 25/8/44. Flt Lt 21/1/53. Retd SUP 10/6/61.
FRISCH M.A.F. Born 1/9/43. Commd 15/12/88. Flt Lt 15/12/90. Retd ENG 1/9/98.
FRITCHLEY E. BSc. Born 16/10/53. Commd 26/10/75. Flt Lt 26/7/79. Retd ENG 26/10/91.
FRITH E.D. CBE AFC*. Born 12/9/33. Commd 27/7/54. Gp Capt 1/7/78. Retd GD 12/9/88.
FRITH E.L. CB ACIS. Born 18/3/19. Commd 20/8/38. AVM 1/7/71. Retd SEC 18/3/74.
FRITH J.E. BSc CEng MIEE DipEl. Born 1/2/21. Commd 22/8/41. Gp Capt 1/7/61. Retd ENG 9/8/69.
FRITH M.C. IEng. Born 24/4/44. Commd 5/7/73. Wg Cdr 1/7/88. Retd ENG 1/1/98.
FRIZZELL J.S. Born 12/7/46. Commd 23/9/66. Sqn Ldr 1/1/83. Retd GD 18/1/90.
FRIZZELLE D.St.C.A. The Rev. Born 1/8/17. Commd 10/12/45. Retd Wg Cdr 10/9/72.
FROELICH B. Born 21/5/14. Commd 7/1/45. Fg Offr 7/7/45. Retd GD(G) 18/12/45. Re-commissioned 14/5/50. Flt Lt 19/11/53. Retd 24/4/66.
FROGGATT D.G. Born 9/4/56. Commd 3/11/77. Sqn Ldr 1/7/88. Retd GD 9/4/94.
FROGLEY R.T. CBE DFC MRAeS. Born 30/5/16. Commd 31/7/37. Gp Capt 1/7/55. Retd GD 30/5/66.
FROST A.F. Born 15/1/23. Commd 3/7/42. Flt Lt 5/10/60. Retd GD(G) 15/1/78. rtg Sqn Ldr
FROST A.K. BSc. Born 6/5/56. Commd 20/10/86. Sqn Ldr 1/7/90. Retd ENG 1/10/91.
FROST D.F. BA CEng MIMechE. Born 22/2/35. Commd 1/3/71. Sqn Ldr 1/3/71. Retd ENG 22/4/93.
FROST D.J.C. Born 13/2/10. Commd 20/2/41. Sqn Ldr 1/8/47. Retd ENG 13/2/60.
FROST D.W. Born 6/9/48. Commd 27/2/70. Sqn Ldr 1/1/88. Retd FLY(P) 6/9/03.

FROST G.B. Born 24/1/36. Commd 21/12/62. Flt Lt 25/7/66. Retd SEC 24/1/74.
FROST G.L. Born 13/5/30. Commd 16/11/51. Sqn Ldr 1/7/77. Retd GD 13/5/88.
FROST I.E. Born 24/3/46. Commd 6/11/64. Sqn Ldr 1/7/83. Retd GD 1/7/86.
FROST I.M. Born 10/8/51. Commd 25/2/72. Sqn Ldr 1/7/84. Retd GD 10/8/89.
FROST J. Born 12/10/34. Commd 10/3/60. Sqn Ldr 1/1/69. Retd ENG 13/10/77. Re-instated 28/7/82. Sqn Ldr 15/10/73. Retd ENG 12/10/92.
FROST J.R. MCMI. Born 15/11/13. Commd 21/1/43. Sqn Ldr 1/7/54. Retd ENG 20/11/68.
FROST J.W. CBE DFC DL. Born 30/7/21. Commd 2/5/42. A Cdre 1/7/68. Retd GD 11/10/76.
FROST M. Born 28/9/63. Commd 19/6/86. Flt Lt 19/12/91. Retd GD 17/2/02.
FROST P.A. BSc. Born 10/2/66. Commd 7/3/94. Flt Lt 28/2/90. Retd FLY(P) 10/2/04.
FROST P.C. Born 17/2/46. Commd 19/8/66. Flt Lt 17/2/73. Retd ENG 17/2/84.
FROST R.G. Born 6/6/51. Commd 4/5/72. Flt Lt 4/11/77. Retd GD 22/10/94.
FROST T.P. Born 23/2/23. Commd 16/7/48. Flt Lt 4/11/53. Retd GD 29/7/55.
FROST W.S. CEng MRAeS MCMI. Born 30/5/18. Commd 9/3/44. Wg Cdr 1/7/62. Retd ENG 30/9/72.
FROUD J.R.J. Born 14/10/31. Commd 4/6/52. Sqn Ldr 1/7/82. Retd GD 14/10/91.
FROUDE H. RM. Born 23/1/51. Commd 10/11/74. Sqn Offr 1/6/85. Retd MED 10/11/93.
FRUIN-BALL V.C. Born 22/2/28. Commd 18/6/52. Sqn Ldr 1/1/67. Retd SEC 1/1/70.
FRY B.J. DFC. Born 16/6/24. Commd 24/3/45. Sqn Ldr 1/4/56. Retd GD 16/6/67.
FRY D.J. Born 16/6/61. Commd 22/5/80. Sqn Ldr 1/7/95. Retd GD 16/6/99.
FRY F.J. Born 2/1/25. Commd 2/11/49. Flt Lt 23/10/56. Retd GD 2/1/63.
FRY G.P. MBE BSc MCMI. Born 24/5/30. Commd 20/8/52. Wg Cdr 1/1/71. Retd ADMIN 1/10/77.
FRY P. OBE. Born 5/8/33. Commd 18/7/63. Wg Cdr 1/1/81. Retd GD 6/8/83.
FRY P.J. DFC. Born 19/12/22. Commd 26/11/44. Sqn Ldr 1/7/55. Retd GD 1/2/61.
FRY R.D. MHCIMA. Born 22/2/55. Commd 30/3/75. Wg Cdr 1/7/92. Retd ADMIN 14/9/96.
FRY W.E.C. Born 23/11/30. Commd 30/7/59. Sqn Ldr 1/7/72. Retd GD(G) 30/8/75.
FRYER A.H. Born 29/9/24. Commd 19/5/44. Sqn Ldr 1/10/55. Retd GD 29/9/67.
FRYER D. MSc BEng CEng MIEE. Born 14/7/62. Commd 7/8/87. Sqn Ldr 1/7/99. Retd ENGINEER 1/7/03.
FRYER D.F. Born 19/4/44. Commd 25/3/64. Flt Lt 25/9/69. Retd GD 2/6/76.
FRYER J.A. Born 4/1/30. Commd 11/4/51. Sqn Ldr 1/1/62. Retd GD 4/1/70.
FRYER J.M. DFM. Born 2/1/22. Commd 5/6/43. Wg Cdr 1/1/71. Retd GD(G) 3/1/73.
FRYER T.P. Born 10/10/52. Commd 18/4/74. Sqn Ldr 1/1/89. Retd GD(G) 1/1/92.
FRYER W.C. Born 13/2/25. Commd 20/4/50. Flt Lt 20/10/53. Retd GD 1/10/68.
FRYETT B.W. Born 1/4/54. Commd 11/9/86. Flt Lt 11/9/88. Retd ADMIN 11/9/96.
FRYETT D.B. Born 22/6/39. Commd 26/10/62. Flt Lt 26/4/68. Retd GD 10/7/78. Re-instated 28/7/81. Sqn Ldr 1/1/90. Retd ADMIN 30/9/91.
FUDGE R.A. BEM. Born 14/5/30. Commd 11/2/65. Sqn Ldr 1/7/75. Retd SEC 1/8/80.
FULENA P.N. Born 28/2/45. Commd 17/7/64. Flt Lt 17/1/70. Retd GD 1/5/76.
FULFORD J.W. BA MCMI. Born 1/9/35. Commd 23/10/56. Wg Cdr 1/7/80. Retd GD 1/9/90.
FULFORD K.T. BEM. Born 25/12/28. Commd 13/2/64. Sqn Ldr 1/7/74. Retd ENG 30/12/78.
FULLARTON B.M. Born 27/4/39. Commd 26/6/61. Flt Lt 1/4/71. Retd GD 28/11/73.
FULLBROOK D.J. MPhil CEng MIMechE MRAeS. Born 2/12/39. Commd 6/10/74. Sqn Ldr 1/1/80. Retd ENG 5/5/99.
FULLER A.B. Born 18/2/46. Commd 5/3/65. Sqn Ldr 1/1/77. Retd GD 27/4/98.
FULLER B.A. MSc CEng MRAeS. Born 8/6/37. Commd 25/4/60. Sqn Ldr 18/8/70. Retd EDN 1/7/78.
FULLER B.G. Born 18/9/32. Commd 1/4/53. Wg Cdr 1/7/76. Retd SUP 18/9/87.
FULLER D.P. BA. Born 26/6/40. Commd 30/9/59. Sqn Ldr 1/1/71. Retd ENG 26/6/78.
FULLER G.D. FCMI. Born 23/6/24. Commd 20/10/44. Gp Capt 1/1/76. Retd GD 23/6/79.
FULLER J.D. Born 13/3/39. Commd 6/4/62. Fg Offr 6/4/64. Retd GD 19/3/66.
FULLER J.H. Born 13/5/16. Commd 5/7/45. Fg Offr 30/8/47. Retd CAT 18/8/50. rtg Flt Lt
FULLER K. Born 8/11/34. Commd 3/3/65. Flt Lt 30/4/68. Retd SUP 9/12/86.
FULLER K.D.J. Born 13/8/31. Commd 21/5/52. Flt Lt 16/10/57. Retd GD 13/8/69.
FULLER M.J. Born 22/10/50. Commd 21/3/69. A Cdre 1/1/00. Retd OPS SPT 1/6/02.
FULLER M.J.D. Born 2/5/38. Commd 28/7/59. Sqn Ldr 1/1/71. Retd GD 2/4/76.
FULLER N.D. DFC. Born 6/7/22. Commd 8/10/43. Flt Lt 8/4/47. Retd GD 31/3/62.
FULLER R.F. Born 9/10/46. Commd 2/8/68. Sqn Ldr 1/1/80. Retd ENG 9/10/84.
FULLER S.C. OBE BEM. Born 21/10/44. Commd 16/8/70. Gp Capt 1/7/94. Retd SY 21/8/96.
FULLER W. Born 16/1/45. Commd 3/3/67. Flt Lt 3/9/69. Retd GD 26/10/73.
FULLERTON J.A. The Rev. MA. Born 9/8/25. Commd 8/1/53. Retd Wg Cdr 20/2/69.
FULLERTON R.G. BSc. Born 30/3/60. Commd 18/3/84. Flt Lt 18/9/86. Retd GD 19/8/02.
FULLFORD A.C. Born 10/12/58. Commd 23/11/78. Flt Lt 23/5/84. Retd GD 10/12/94.
FULLILOVE W.G. Born 26/9/28. Commd 21/5/52. Flt Lt 2/3/58. Retd GD 10/6/71.
FULLUCK D.J. Born 7/8/35. Commd 10/2/54. Flt Lt 10/2/61. Retd GD 5/4/74.
FULTON M.J. Born 14/7/43. Commd 25/6/65. Flt Lt 1/7/69. Retd GD 24/3/94.
FULTON T.J.N. BSc. Born 10/2/42. Commd 30/8/66. Wg Cdr 1/1/89. Retd GD 10/2/98.
FUNNELL I.S. Born 30/3/32. Commd 24/9/52. Flt Lt 29/4/59. Retd GD 24/4/72.
FUNNELL S.N.G. Born 24/5/44. Commd 31/7/86. Flt Lt 31/7/90. Retd ENG 24/5/94.
FURLONG C.D. Born 10/11/37. Commd 4/12/56. Sqn Ldr 1/7/72. Retd GD 10/11/75.

FURLONG J.A. MA BSc. Born 28/4/37. Commd 22/10/59. Sqn Ldr 1/4/70. Retd EDN 1/10/78.
FURLONG R. Born 5/7/49. Commd 31/7/70. Flt Lt 31/7/73. Retd GD 17/9/81.
FURNEAUX S.J. Born 9/4/13. Commd 9/8/41. Sqn Ldr 1/8/47. Retd RGT 19/5/58. rtg Wg Cdr
FURNELL P.C. Born 26/5/43. Commd 15/8/85. Flt Lt 15/8/89. Retd ADMIN 26/5/93.
FURNER D.J. CBE DFC AFC. Born 14/11/21. Commd 31/7/42. AVM 1/1/74. Retd GD 31/1/76.
FURNESS M.J. Born 3/6/36. Commd 12/3/64. Sqn Ldr 1/7/71. Retd GD 3/6/78.
FURNESS T.H.-.B. MCMI. Born 6/1/23. Commd 30/5/45. Sqn Ldr 1/7/61. Retd ADMIN 6/1/78.
FURNEY J.G.L. Born 13/6/43. Commd 18/7/63. Sqn Ldr 1/1/79. Retd SUP 1/1/85.
FURNISS P. DFC. Born 16/7/19. Commd 31/1/42. AVM 1/1/79. Retd LGL 1/4/82.
FURR R.D. Born 29/4/44. Commd 1/11/63. Flt Lt 1/7/69. Retd GD 22/5/02.
FURSE D.C. DFC. Born 21/6/21. Commd 9/3/41. Wg Cdr 1/7/61. Retd GD 1/5/72.
FURZE R.MacA. AFC. Born 9/11/28. Commd 27/7/49. Wg Cdr 1/7/66. Retd GD 9/11/83.
FYFE I. BA. Born 16/9/35. Commd 30/9/55. Flt Lt 1/10/67. Retd ENG 6/11/76.
FYFE J.N.MCD. MA. Born 16/5/57. Commd 27/9/78. Flt Lt 15/4/81. Retd GD 15/1/92.
FYNES C.J.S. AFC. Born 21/9/44. Commd 11/8/77. Sqn Ldr 1/7/91. Retd GD 24/3/01.
FYNES P.N.S. Born 16/2/43. Commd 19/12/63. Flt Lt 9/5/70. Retd GD(G) 1/6/82.

G

GADD N. Born 5/5/40. Commd 8/9/68. Wg Cdr 1/1/89. Retd GD(G) 5/5/95.
GADD R.P. BL LLB. Born 5/7/33. Commd 17/5/62. Flt Lt 17/5/68. Retd GD 31/8/74.
GAGE P.S. Born 5/12/15. Commd 18/10/41. Wg Cdr 1/7/58. Retd ENG 5/3/71.
GAGE V. ACIS MCMI. Born 3/10/43. Commd 27/1/67. Wg Cdr 1/1/83. Retd ADMIN 6/11/87.
GAIR G.A. Born 28/9/35. Commd 28/9/62. Flt Lt 8/1/69. Retd GD 9/10/73.
GAIT B. Born 17/9/24. Commd 26/8/45. Flt Lt 4/6/53. Retd GD 20/12/66.
GAIT-SMITH F.E. Born 20/8/37. Commd 1/1/64. Flt Lt 1/1/64. Retd GD 26/8/66.
GAJOWSKYJ J.B. Born 27/1/54. Commd 31/7/86. Fg Offr 6/9/88. Retd RGT 18/6/91.
GALBRAITH E.A. Born 4/7/20. Commd 12/6/57. Flt Lt 12/6/57. Retd CAT 1/6/63.
GALBRAITH M.A. BSc. Born 10/12/72. Commd 6/10/96. Flt Lt 6/4/00. Retd OPS SPT(FLTOPS) 2/10/03.
GALBRAITH T.F. Born 10/11/16. Commd 22/10/41. Flt Lt 8/5/51. Retd SEC 1/8/53.
GALBRAITH-GUNNER R.V. Born 7/6/20. Commd 3/12/44. Flt Lt 3/12/50. Retd SEC 19/8/67.
GALE B.D. Born 2/5/22. Commd 14/10/43. Flt Lt 27/5/54. Retd GD 2/9/67.
GALE D.W. MVO. Born 27/12/46. Commd 14/7/66. Sqn Ldr 1/7/83. Retd GD 27/12/90.
GALE I.T. Born 4/2/60. Commd 12/7/79. Sqn Ldr 1/7/91. Retd GD 4/2/98.
GALE J. OBE. Born 22/6/23. Commd 11/8/44. Wg Cdr 1/7/66. Retd GD 29/9/72.
GALE J.F. Born 19/5/30. Commd 13/12/50. Sqn Ldr 1/7/62. Retd GD 5/3/85.
GALE R.A.A. Born 14/12/32. Commd 14/11/57. Sqn Ldr 1/7/69. Retd SUP 30/9/78.
GALEA A.P. MCMI. Born 23/7/42. Commd 28/7/64. Sqn Ldr 1/1/75. Retd GD 28/7/79.
GALES A.J. BA. Born 23/4/64. Commd 28/8/83. Flt Lt 15/1/89. Retd GD 11/8/02.
GALKOWSKI R.A. MSc BEng MRAeS. Born 6/3/63. Commd 2/8/85. Sqn Ldr 1/7/96. Retd ENG 6/3/01.
GALLACHER A.S. BSc. Born 26/2/56. Commd 16/12/73. Sqn Ldr 1/7/88. Retd GD 26/2/94.
GALLAFENT M.D. Born 22/10/32. Commd 29/12/51. Flt Lt 22/5/57. Retd GD 26/6/78.
GALLAGHER H. Born 14/7/31. Commd 14/7/72. Flt Lt 14/7/72. Retd PRT 7/1/75.
GALLAGHER R. Born 11/1/43. Commd 6/9/63. Sqn Ldr 1/7/84. Retd GD 11/1/98.
GALLAGHER S.F. BSc. Born 12/5/39. Commd 14/9/65. Wg Cdr 1/1/86. Retd GD 12/5/94.
GALLAGHER T.A. Born 14/4/16. Commd 1/1/43. Sqn Ldr 1/1/54. Retd GD 21/8/57.
GALLAGHER W. LVO AFC. Born 20/7/15. Commd 16/5/42. Wg Cdr 1/7/62. Retd SUP 10/2/72.
GALLAGHER W.F. Born 8/10/39. Commd 1/4/66. Flt Lt 1/10/71. Retd GD 13/12/81.
GALLANDERS P.A. Born 27/7/46. Commd 23/9/65. Wg Cdr 1/7/89. Retd GD(G) 30/3/95.
GALLAUGHER R.A. MBE. Born 30/7/46. Commd 1/3/68. Sqn Ldr 1/1/88. Retd SUP 30/7/01.
GALLETLY G.E.G. MCMI. Born 27/5/24. Commd 20/3/45. Sqn Ldr 1/7/57. Retd GD 27/5/73.
GALLETTI I. Born 26/4/33. Commd 24/4/56. Flt Lt 24/10/61. Retd GD(G) 26/4/71. Re-instated 24/5/73 to 27/2/84.
GALLEY B.W. Born 6/11/43. Commd 10/1/71. Sqn Ldr 1/7/86. Retd ADMIN 10/1/01.
GALLEY J. Born 21/8/29. Commd 28/11/51. Flt Lt 28/5/56. Retd GD 21/8/84.
GALLIENNE W.C. Born 24/5/22. Commd 24/2/67. Flt Lt 24/2/72. Retd ENG 30/3/77.
GALLIVER D.R. MCMI. Born 29/1/17. Commd 21/2/46. Wg Cdr 1/1/68. Retd SUP 29/1/72.
GALLON J.D. Born 20/5/43. Commd 4/6/64. Sqn Ldr 1/7/82. Retd GD(G) 30/6/85. Re-instated 17/7/89. Flt Lt 17/7/89.
  Retd GD(G) 1/9/95.
GALLOP H.J. Born 13/3/41. Commd 24/4/70. Flt Lt 4/5/72. Retd GD 1/10/80.
GALLOW A.F.A. Born 8/9/33. Commd 24/7/61. Wg Cdr 1/7/79. Retd GD 4/11/88.
GALLOW N.R.A. Born 11/4/62. Commd 18/12/80. Flt Lt 18/6/86. Retd GD 21/3/89.
GALLOWAY E.W. BA. Born 27/1/49. Commd 6/5/83. Flt Lt 6/5/84. Retd ADMIN 6/5/91.
GALLOWAY T.A. Born 29/6/50. Commd 2/2/71. Flt Lt 26/2/74. Retd GD 25/9/89.
GALLWEY I.D. Born 2/5/36. Commd 30/7/57. Sqn Ldr 1/1/68. Retd GD 2/5/74.
GALPIN D.N. MRIN. Born 13/4/29. Commd 15/12/49. Gp Capt 1/1/77. Retd GD 13/4/84. Re-instated 28/11/84.
  Sqn Ldr 30/7/78. Retd 19/5/89.
GALYER J.T. Born 8/1/43. Commd 10/11/61. Sqn Ldr 1/7/74. Retd GD 8/1/81.
GALYER R.P. Born 6/1/36. Commd 1/10/54. Sqn Ldr 1/1/68. Retd GD 6/12/75.
GAMBLE A.T. Born 9/10/20. Commd 28/7/44. Flt Lt 28/1/48. Retd GD(G) 9/10/70.
GAMBLE D.H. Born 23/6/29. Commd 30/7/52. Wg Cdr 1/7/76. Retd SUP 4/8/79.
GAMBLE J.L. Born 4/6/45. Commd 14/6/63. Sqn Ldr 1/1/82. Retd GD 26/4/85.
GAMBLE R. Born 23/9/16. Commd 28/10/43. Flt Lt 22/2/48. Retd ENG 14/10/54.
GAMBLE R.E. Born 17/6/30. Commd 13/12/50. Flt Lt 19/11/53. Retd GD 17/6/69.
GAMBLE W.M. BSc. Born 13/5/49. Commd 30/9/79. Sqn Ldr 1/1/84. Retd ENG 30/4/90.
GAMBLIN R.W. AFC. Born 8/9/44. Commd 31/8/62. Wg Cdr 1/7/81. Retd GD 1/7/84.
GAMBOLD W.G. Born 23/11/38. Commd 9/4/60. A Cdre 1/7/91. Retd GD(G) 23/11/93.
GAME D.I. Born 27/6/25. Commd 21/5/46. Flt Lt 1/4/63. Retd GD 29/3/69.
GAMMAGE P.A. Born 17/9/46. Commd 6/4/70. Flt Lt 17/4/78. Retd GD(G) 6/4/92.
GAMMON N.W. Born 4/12/21. Commd 8/9/44. Sqn Ldr 1/1/71. Retd GD(G) 30/4/76.
GAMMON R.M. Born 5/3/32. Commd 22/8/51. Sqn Ldr 1/1/63. Retd GD 5/3/70.

GAMSON J.A. Born 5/12/32. Commd 12/7/51. Wg Cdr 1/7/84. Retd SUP 5/12/87.
GANN M.D. LDSRCS. Born 18/11/36. Commd 6/1/63. Wg Cdr 17/3/75. Retd DEL 6/1/79.
GANNON D.H. DFC AFC. Born 5/8/23. Commd 10/12/43. Flt Lt 7/6/51. Retd GD 5/8/66.
GANNON D.M. Born 30/8/47. Commd 20/9/79. Sqn Ldr 1/7/90. Retd SUPPLY 30/8/03.
GANT J. MBE DFM DPhysEd. Born 10/2/23. Commd 5/9/51. Sqn Ldr 1/1/63. Retd PE 24/5/70.
GAPPER L.F. AFM. Born 8/9/24. Commd 28/1/60. Sqn Ldr 1/7/75. Retd GD 8/9/82.
GARBUTT M.J.B. Born 18/1/31. Commd 14/11/59. Fg Offr 14/11/61. Retd GD 20/2/65.
GARDEN E.R. BSc(Eng) CEng MIMechE MRAeS. Born 1/7/45. Commd 22/9/63. Sqn Ldr 1/1/75. Retd ENG 1/7/83. Re-entered 2/6/86. Sqn Ldr 2/12/77. Retd ENG 1/7/01.
GARDEN S.R. AFC. Born 27/3/18. Commd 10/3/45. Flt Lt 30/6/49. Retd GD 30/3/68.
GARDEN Sir Timothy KCB MA MPhil FRAeS. Born 23/4/44. Commd 22/9/63. AM 21/3/94. Retd GD 23/4/96.
GARDENER A.M. Born 31/8/29. Commd 21/5/52. Flt Lt 16/10/57. Retd GD 31/8/84.
GARDENER J.I. Born 28/1/32. Commd 18/10/62. Sqn Ldr 1/7/88. Retd GD 28/1/93.
GARDHAM R.H. Born 1/7/23. Commd 6/9/44. Flt Offr 19/6/52. Retd SUP 13/10/54.
GARDINER A. Born 5/2/24. Commd 30/7/59. Sqn Ldr 1/1/73. Retd ENG 29/6/78.
GARDINER C.A. BA MCIPS. Born 14/5/45. Commd 15/7/66. Gp Capt 1/1/96. Retd SUP 14/5/00.
GARDINER D.R. Born 1/7/12. Commd 5/5/41. Sqn Offr 1/1/50. Retd SEC 16/3/53.
GARDINER G.J. BA. Born 10/7/53. Commd 7/11/82. Wg Cdr 1/7/96. Retd ADMIN 8/11/99.
GARDINER I.F. BEd. Born 16/2/61. Commd 19/6/88. Flt Lt 19/12/88. Retd ADMIN 1/10/94.
GARDINER J.C. MBE. Born 1/9/50. Commd 19/12/85. Sqn Ldr 1/1/94. Retd SUP 24/5/01.
GARDINER J.C. BA DPhysEd. Born 7/1/46. Commd 22/8/71. Wg Cdr 1/1/92. Retd ADMIN 7/1/01.
GARDINER M.J. OBE BSc FRAeS. Born 13/6/46. Commd 28/9/84. AVM 1/1/99. Retd GD 12/6/02.
GARDINER P.M. MCMI. Born 31/10/44. Commd 1/4/65. Wg Cdr 1/7/87. Retd GD(G) 20/1/94.
GARDINER P.M.R. Born 3/7/42. Commd 21/12/64. Flt Lt 1/7/68. Retd GD 31/1/76.
GARDINER P.O. Born 26/10/50. Commd 21/2/74. Sqn Ldr 1/1/88. Retd GD 1/1/91.
GARDINER S.V. Born 5/4/49. Commd 29/6/72. Wg Cdr 1/7/94. Retd ADMIN 14/9/96.
GARDNER A.J. LLB. Born 18/9/32. Commd 27/6/58. Sqn Ldr 27/4/68. Retd ADMIN 18/9/92.
GARDNER B.R. Born 19/7/47. Commd 5/11/70. Flt Lt 12/7/74. Retd GD 1/4/92.
GARDNER C.M.S. OBE DFC. Born 7/10/13. Commd 1/9/45. Wg Cdr 1/7/47. Retd GD 22/4/52.
GARDNER D.F. Born 21/3/26. Commd 17/10/57. Sqn Ldr 1/7/75. Retd GD 21/9/84.
GARDNER G. Born 26/6/46. Commd 10/6/66. Sqn Ldr 1/7/76. Retd GD 1/7/85.
GARDNER J. Born 18/6/32. Commd 10/9/52. Sqn Ldr 1/7/64. Retd GD 1/7/69.
GARDNER J.A. Born 13/6/42. Commd 15/7/63. Sqn Ldr 1/1/75. Retd ENG 30/10/82.
GARDNER J.E. Born 28/11/20. Commd 2/10/42. Sqn Ldr 1/1/72. Retd GD 28/11/75.
GARDNER J.R. Born 14/6/18. Commd 1/4/39. Wg Cdr 1/1/54. Retd GD 14/6/65. rtg Gp Capt
GARDNER M.J. Born 26/11/41. Commd 15/9/67. Sqn Ldr 1/1/93. Retd GD 26/11/96.
GARDNER N. CEng MRAeS MIMechE DCAe. Born 19/1/29. Commd 28/11/51. Sqn Ldr 1/7/61. Retd ENG 28/11/67.
GARDNER N.T. Born 29/12/32. Commd 30/7/52. Flt Lt 2/12/58. Retd GD 29/12/75.
GARDNER P.B. Born 16/9/39. Commd 24/3/61. Wg Cdr 1/1/84. Retd GD 1/3/92.
GARDNER P.M. DFC. Born 1/7/18. Commd 29/11/37. Sqn Ldr 1/8/47. Retd GD 31/7/48.
GARDNER R. BEM. Born 26/8/24. Commd 5/5/60. Sqn Ldr 1/7/70. Retd ENG 2/12/75.
GARDNER R.C. Born 25/3/35. Commd 5/11/70. Flt Lt 5/11/72. Retd SUP 5/11/78.
GARDNER R.M. Born 23/11/60. Commd 11/4/85. Flt Lt 31/1/88. Retd SY 23/2/93.
GARDNER R.S. Born 3/3/51. Commd 22/5/70. Flt Lt 22/11/76. Retd OPS SPT 6/8/99.
GARDNER T.R. Born 13/4/34. Commd 28/1/53. Sqn Ldr 1/1/76. Retd GD(G) 19/12/85.
GARFIELD R.F. Born 1/5/43. Commd 17/5/63. Flt Lt 1/11/68. Retd GD 1/5/76.
GARGETT J.P. Born 31/5/44. Commd 26/11/81. Sqn Ldr 1/7/90. Retd ENG 3/12/97.
GARLAND A.H. Born 13/11/11. Commd 1/2/30. Gp Capt 1/1/50. Retd GD 30/4/58.
GARLAND A.R. MBE BSc FRGS MCMI. Born 1/5/43. Commd 24/2/67. Wg Cdr 1/7/88. Retd GD(G) 1/9/94.
GARLAND R. Born 18/9/27. Commd 27/6/51. Flt Lt 10/7/55. Retd GD 7/1/73.
GARLICK J. Born 12/7/34. Commd 17/6/53. Flt Lt 7/3/62. Retd GD 12/7/72.
GARLICK R.J. BA CEng MRAeS. Born 26/3/36. Commd 25/7/56. Gp Capt 1/1/87. Retd ENG 26/5/91.
GARNER A.S. BSc CEng MRAeS. Born 24/3/61. Commd 2/9/79. Wg Cdr 1/1/00. Retd GD 2/4/04.
GARNER B.R. BSc. Born 14/10/35. Commd 5/1/60. Sqn Ldr 27/3/68. Retd ADMIN 14/10/92.
GARNER J.T. Born 10/4/34. Commd 14/1/65. Sqn Ldr 1/1/87. Retd GD 10/4/92.
GARNER P.J. Born 16/5/62. Commd 29/7/91. Fg Offr 29/7/93. Retd MED(T) 8/12/95.
GARNER R.W.C. Born 11/5/64. Commd 11/4/85. Sqn Ldr 1/1/03. Retd FLY(N) 4/7/04.
GARNETT C.H. BSc CEng MRAeS MIEE. Born 21/2/35. Commd 24/11/55. Sqn Ldr 1/7/64. Retd ENG 29/5/71.
GARNETT P.E. Born 1/7/21. Commd 8/8/45. Flt Offr 30/6/52. Retd SUP 16/9/52.
GARNON-COX D.G. MILT MInstPet. Born 31/12/66. Commd 28/7/95. Flt Lt 28/7/97. Retd SUPPLY 31/12/04.
GARNONS-WILLIAMS J.S. BSc. Born 3/8/46. Commd 18/8/68. Sqn Ldr 1/1/81. Retd GD 18/8/84.
GARRATT D.R. Born 13/5/47. Commd 31/8/75. Gp Capt 1/7/99. Retd LGL 1/7/93.
GARRATT W.H. Born 19/6/63. Commd 8/5/86. Flt Lt 25/2/89. Retd GD 19/6/01.
GARRETT G.E. BA MCIPD MCMI CertEd. Born 15/5/47. Commd 1/7/79. Sqn Ldr 1/1/85. Retd ADMIN 1/7/89.
GARRETT K.A.S. Born 12/8/30. Commd 15/6/50. Flt Lt 26/4/56. Retd GD 12/8/68.
GARRETT S.J. BSc. Born 3/11/58. Commd 29/11/81. Sqn Ldr 1/1/95. Retd GD 11/9/98.

GARRETTS A. MBE. Born 3/4/22. Commd 13/10/45. Sqn Ldr 1/7/57. Retd GD 3/4/71.
GARRETY M.J. Born 26/6/68. Commd 16/6/88. Fg Offr 16/6/90. Retd GD 19/2/93.
GARRIGAN M. CEng MIMechE. Born 4/12/39. Commd 4/7/66. Gp Capt 1/1/89. Retd ENG 26/8/91.
GARRITT P.C. CEng MIEE. Born 2/7/34. Commd 28/7/67. Flt Lt 28/7/69. Retd ENG 28/7/75. Re-instated 29/4/81.
    Sqn Ldr 1/1/87. Retd ENG 2/7/94.
GARRITY M.J. Born 6/3/32. Commd 2/1/52. Sqn Ldr 1/1/79. Retd GD 6/3/92.
GARRITY R.D. Born 21/3/62. Commd 24/7/81. Flt Lt 24/1/88. Retd OPS SPT 21/3/00.
GARROCH A.W. OBE MPhil BSc(Eng) MRAeS. Born 25/8/47. Commd 18/9/66. Wg Cdr 1/7/86. Retd GD 1/1/94.
GARROD A.E. Born 8/4/12. Commd 14/6/40. Flt Lt 1/9/45. Retd GD(G) 8/4/67.
GARROD M.D. Born 23/8/64. Commd 22/11/84. Flt Lt 22/5/90. Retd GD 4/12/01.
GARROD S.J. Born 6/8/51. Commd 16/5/74. Flt Lt 16/11/79. Retd GD 28/1/90.
GARSIDE M. Born 12/4/64. Commd 27/8/87. Flt Lt 27/2/94. Retd ADMIN 14/3/97.
GARSIDE P. Born 13/7/40. Commd 2/12/66. Flt Lt 2/6/72. Retd GD 22/8/82.
GARSTIN A. Born 1/7/29. Commd 18/10/50. Flt Offr 21/1/55. Retd CAT 19/10/60.
GARSTIN J.C. BSc. Born 7/11/49. Commd 15/9/69. Sqn Ldr 1/1/84. Retd SUPPLY 7/11/04.
GARSTIN L.K. MB BS MRCS LRCP. Born 7/5/23. Commd 2/4/51. Gp Capt 1/1/74. Retd MED 3/1/81.
GARTH P.A. BA. Born 20/6/34. Commd 7/9/56. Gp Capt 1/7/85. Retd ADMIN 20/6/89.
GARTHWAITE B. Born 28/8/57. Commd 27/1/77. Sqn Ldr 1/1/90. Retd GD 28/8/95.
GARTON A.C. Born 8/9/45. Commd 10/6/66. Sqn Ldr 1/1/78. Retd GD 28/10/97.
GARTON I.H.A. BA. Born 30/11/42. Commd 30/9/62. Flt Lt 15/4/69. Retd ENG 1/5/74.
GARWOOD H.G. Born 16/8/18. Commd 22/10/44. Sqn Ldr 1/7/55. Retd GD 15/8/58.
GARWOOD M. Born 19/3/60. Commd 2/2/84. Wg Cdr 1/1/03. Retd GD 1/2/05.
GARWOOD R.H. DFC. Born 26/8/22. Commd 10/5/43. Sqn Ldr 1/9/55. Retd GD 1/11/73.
GASCOYNE A.W. Born 2/8/22. Commd 6/3/52. Flt Lt 6/9/56. Retd SEC 28/10/60.
GASCOYNE B.A. BA. Born 4/5/42. Commd 3/5/68. Sqn Ldr 1/7/84. Retd SUP 4/5/97.
GASH C.A. Born 13/6/50. Commd 25/2/72. Flt Lt 25/2/74. Retd GD 22/10/94.
GASH R.F. MRAeS. Born 11/12/20. Commd 21/9/44. Sqn Ldr 1/1/56. Retd ENG 26/9/64.
GASH W.J. Born 18/9/18. Commd 14/11/46. Wg Cdr 1/7/65. Retd ENG 1/10/70.
GASKELL D. Born 15/7/41. Commd 9/3/63. Sqn Ldr 1/7/91. Retd SUP 15/7/96.
GASKIN L.A. Born 23/4/58. Commd 28/7/95. Flt Lt 28/7/99. Retd OPS SPT(REGT) 4/1/04.
GASKIN P.P.V. OBE . Born 23/10/47. Commd 22/9/67. Gp Capt 1/7/95. Retd GD 23/4/03.
GASSON D.R. MBE. Born 21/11/44. Commd 31/3/68. Sqn Ldr 1/1/81. Retd GD 31/3/84. Re-entered 2/6/86.
    Wg Cdr 1/7/90. Retd GD 15/8/97.
GASSON T.P. Born 16/4/31. Commd 15/10/52. Flt Lt 22/4/58. Retd GD 16/4/69.
GASTRELL D. Born 31/3/28. Commd 23/6/60. Flt Lt 23/6/65. Retd GD 23/5/68.
GATELEY P. BSc. Born 5/1/50. Commd 17/1/72. Flt Lt 17/10/73. Retd GD 17/1/88.
GATENBY M.H. BSc. Born 3/8/58. Commd 28/9/80. Sqn Ldr 1/1/94. Retd ADMIN 28/9/99.
GATES A.C. Born 24/11/38. Commd 4/10/71. Flt Lt 6/10/76. Retd ENG 14/10/79. Re-instated 6/10/82. Sqn Ldr 1/7/88.
    Retd ENG 24/8/94.
GATES E.S. DFC MA. Born 25/3/22. Commd 19/6/43. Wg Cdr 1/4/69. Retd EDN 1/7/73.
GATES F.G. MBE. Born 20/4/30. Commd 27/8/64. Sqn Ldr 1/7/76. Retd SUP 1/10/84.
GATES J.A. MBE. Born 9/1/33. Commd 3/7/55. Gp Capt 1/1/83. Retd GD(G) 15/1/89.
GATES M. BEng. Born 16/1/65. Commd 7/8/87. Flt Lt 21/2/92. Retd ENG 17/8/00.
GATES P. CEng MRAeS. Born 31/10/42. Commd 10/4/67. Sqn Ldr 1/1/78. Retd ENG 10/4/89.
GATES P.N. Born 11/6/26. Commd 15/9/60. Sqn Ldr 1/7/74. Retd ENG 7/4/81.
GATES W. Born 27/5/27. Commd 9/2/50. Flt Lt 24/3/56. Retd GD 10/9/72.
GATHERCOLE D.C. Born 14/8/30. Commd 12/9/51. Sqn Ldr 1/1/67. Retd GD 1/1/70.
GATHERER G. Born 28/4/42. Commd 11/7/74. Sqn Ldr 1/1/89. Retd ENG 1/7/93.
GATHERER J.A. Born 9/11/43. Commd 10/11/61. Flt Lt 4/5/72. Retd GD 9/11/81.
GATISS J.W. Born 26/5/45. Commd 8/7/65. Flt Lt 7/10/71. Retd SY 11/6/82.
GATLAND A.J. Born 13/6/50. Commd 31/7/70. Flt Lt 31/7/73. Retd GD 31/3/79.
GATTER P.G.E. BSc. Born 10/6/34. Commd 6/9/55. Sqn Ldr 1/1/71. Retd GD 9/10/79.
GATTRELL R.L.B. Born 4/5/38. Commd 19/6/64. Wg Cdr 1/7/82. Retd SUP 4/5/93.
GATWARD V.J. Born 14/5/33. Commd 30/1/52. Flt Lt 29/5/57. Retd GD 14/5/91.
GAUDEN-ING R. Born 23/11/41. Commd 4/10/63. Flt Lt 17/3/71. Retd GD 30/12/72.
GAUGHAN P.J. Born 14/3/63. Commd 22/11/84. Flt Lt 22/5/90. Retd GD 14/3/01.
GAULT A.J. Born 2/12/40. Commd 21/12/62. Flt Lt 4/11/70. Retd GD 2/12/78.
GAULT I. Born 6/6/48. Commd 26/6/77. Sqn Ldr 1/1/87. Retd GD(G) 14/3/96.
GAULT J. Born 6/6/25. Commd 28/9/06. Flt Lt 28/9/68. Retd MAR 6/6/83.
GAULT R.K. OBE. Born 5/11/52. Commd 29/6/72. Wg Cdr 1/7/90. Retd GD 27/4/02.
GAULT R.W. Born 25/9/44. Commd 5/2/65. Gp Capt 1/7/90. Retd GD 25/9/99.
GAULT W. MBE. Born 18/2/46. Commd 1/4/66. Sqn Ldr 1/1/84. Retd GD 8/6/99.
GAUNT D. Born 23/1/47. Commd 19/3/81. Flt Lt 19/3/83. Retd GD 14/3/96.
GAUNTLETT D.W. Born 26/3/63. Commd 21/12/89. Flt Lt 21/12/91. Retd GD 26/3/01.
GAUSDEN P.H. AFC. Born 2/4/37. Commd 3/3/57. Sqn Ldr 1/1/86. Retd GD 2/4/95.
GAUTREY D.H. Born 8/3/16. Commd 3/1/51. Sqn Ldr 14/11/56. Retd EDN 1/6/66.

GAUTREY M.S. Born 5/5/33. Commd 23/7/52. Wg Cdr 1/1/73. Retd GD 30/3/77.
GAVIN G.A. Born 20/7/26. Commd 13/2/64. Flt Lt 13/2/69. Retd ENG 2/11/76.
GAWN I.L. MCMI. Born 17/2/44. Commd 30/4/80. Wg Cdr 1/7/91. Retd ADMIN 1/9/93.
GAY A. CEng MIMechE. Born 8/11/41. Commd 19/10/65. Flt Lt 12/11/69. Retd ENG 19/10/81.
GAY L.W.J. Born 12/1/20. Commd 16/11/42. Flt Lt 16/5/46. Retd SUP 11/11/55.
GAYER W.A. Born 23/3/33. Commd 29/12/51. Sqn Ldr 1/7/67. Retd GD 23/3/71.
GAYFER H.W. Born 30/12/19. Commd 14/2/46. Fg Offr 14/8/47. Retd ENG 23/3/49.
GAYFORD W.M. Born 25/6/29. Commd 14/10/51. Flt Lt 14/4/56. Retd GD 30/6/79.
GAYLER L.W. CEng MIEE. Born 7/11/18. Commd 30/5/42. Sqn Ldr 1/1/54. Retd ENG 15/12/73.
GAZZARD T.A. Born 14/6/44. Commd 6/9/63. Flt Lt 17/3/71. Retd GD 14/6/82.
GEACH C.R. Born 25/11/37. Commd 25/7/60. Sqn Ldr 1/1/72. Retd GD 25/11/93.
GEACH S.R. Born 22/2/54. Commd 28/2/85. Flt Lt 25/1/87. Retd ADMIN 28/2/93.
GEAR K.C. Born 7/10/25. Commd 5/5/55. Flt Lt 5/11/58. Retd ADMIN 30/7/77.
GEAREY D.T. MSc. Born 28/12/47. Commd 16/5/74. Wg Cdr 1/1/89. Retd ENG 1/11/95.
GEARING J.N. BA DCAe. Born 12/7/34. Commd 25/10/57. Wg Cdr 1/7/83. Retd ADMIN 12/7/92.
GEARS H. Born 29/8/17. Commd 17/4/47. Flt Lt 17/10/51. Retd SUP 10/1/57.
GEARY N.F. Born 10/7/25. Commd 7/4/55. Sqn Ldr 1/1/74. Retd GD 10/7/76.
GEDDES E.I.G. Born 29/7/34. Commd 3/12/59. Sqn Ldr 1/1/71. Retd ADMIN 26/1/86.
GEDDES M.S. Born 7/8/32. Commd 7/6/51. Sqn Ldr 1/7/70. Retd SUP 7/8/73.
GEDDES R.G. BSc. Born 4/5/47. Commd 14/11/71. Sqn Ldr 1/1/95. Retd GD 1/3/01.
GEDGE P.W. Born 19/12/42. Commd 28/4/67. Sqn Ldr 1/7/90. Retd SUP 19/12/97.
GEE B.J. BSc. Born 11/9/30. Commd 25/2/53. Wg Cdr 1/7/70. Retd GD 1/7/73.
GEE E.J. MCMI. Born 26/9/26. Commd 17/1/49. Sqn Ldr 1/7/66. Retd RGT 14/4/78.
GEE F.W. Born 24/2/22. Commd 21/6/56. Flt Lt 21/6/62. Retd ENG 31/7/68.
GEE G.S. MRAeS. Born 5/1/20. Commd 15/4/43. Sqn Ldr 1/1/54. Retd SUP 5/1/75.
GEE P.W. MBE AFC. Born 4/1/25. Commd 20/10/49. Sqn Ldr 1/1/65. Retd GD 25/6/76.
GEENTY W.J. MCMI. Born 1/4/24. Commd 16/3/47. Wg Cdr 1/7/67. Retd GD 1/4/79.
GEESON J.A. BEng. Born 19/6/75. Commd 6/10/96. Fg Offr 6/4/97. Retd ENG 6/12/99.
GEFFRYES S.D. Born 12/2/27. Commd 27/6/51. Flt Lt 27/3/57. Retd GD 6/3/67.
GEGG J.D.J. Born 1/7/48. Commd 14/6/71. Sqn Ldr 1/7/95. Retd FLY(N) 1/7/05.
GELDARD A.P. Born 26/8/64. Commd 8/9/83. Flt Lt 8/3/89. Retd GD 1/9/98.
GELDART M.B. Born 2/7/30. Commd 26/7/51. Flt Lt 13/11/57. Retd GD 30/7/83.
GELL A.P. BSc. Born 14/5/66. Commd 2/9/84. Flt Lt 15/1/90. Retd FLY(P) 14/5/04.
GENESE H.N.H. MRCS LRCP. Born 17/12/18. Commd 19/7/43. Sqn Ldr 19/7/51. Retd MED 1/9/55.
GENT A.J. Born 8/6/65. Commd 15/3/84. Sqn Ldr 1/1/98. Retd FLY(P) 8/6/03.
GENT B. Born 10/1/34. Commd 19/6/70. Sqn Ldr 1/7/84. Retd SUP 10/1/94.
GENT E.W. Born 22/2/42. Commd 10/11/61. Flt Lt 10/5/67. Retd GD 26/1/74.
GENT J.B. Born 4/11/35. Commd 26/8/66. Sqn Ldr 1/1/78. Retd ADMIN 17/9/92.
GENTLE D.H. Born 3/7/32. Commd 26/12/51. Sqn Ldr 1/1/63. Retd GD 3/7/88.
GENTLEMAN J. Born 8/1/44. Commd 15/9/67. Sqn Ldr 1/7/77. Retd GD 1/10/91.
GEOGHEGAN M. Born 3/7/52. Commd 22/10/72. Sqn Ldr 1/7/89. Retd ADMIN 1/5/99.
GEOGHEGAN M.F.C. Born 20/11/50. Commd 14/10/71. Flt Lt 14/4/77. Retd GD 14/3/97.
GEORGE A.M. MBE. Born 11/6/47. Commd 29/3/68. Sqn Ldr 1/1/88. Retd OPS SPT 11/6/02.
GEORGE B. Born 12/3/29. Commd 13/2/64. Sqn Ldr 1/7/74. Retd ENG 12/7/79.
GEORGE D.R. MCMI. Born 17/4/23. Commd 21/8/43. Wg Cdr 1/1/67. Retd GD 26/10/77.
GEORGE E.R. MBE MILT. Born 18/1/64. Commd 2/8/90. Sqn Ldr 1/1/00. Retd SUP 1/1/03.
GEORGE E.V. DFM. Born 2/2/24. Commd 7/6/68. Flt Lt 7/6/71. Retd GD 2/2/84.
GEORGE G.H.E. Born 9/7/46. Commd 22/7/71. Flt Lt 11/12/77. Retd OPS SPT 7/4/98.
GEORGE N. OBE. Born 5/5/22. Commd 28/7/49. Wg Cdr 1/1/67. Retd ADMIN 30/3/77.
GEORGE R.B.W.A. Born 9/6/28. Commd 27/7/49. Sqn Ldr 1/7/59. Retd GD 17/3/77.
GEORGE R.C.E. Born 29/3/23. Commd 23/4/45. Flt Lt 23/10/48. Retd GD 25/3/77.
GEORGE R.J. Born 26/8/47. Commd 9/3/72. Flt Lt 9/9/77. Retd GD 14/9/96.
GEORGE W.G. AFC. Born 17/9/22. Commd 9/8/47. Flt Lt 7/6/51. Retd GD 1/9/73.
GERIG C.M. MVO MSc BSc CEng MRAeS ACGI. Born 6/1/46. Commd 28/9/64. Sqn Ldr 1/1/78. Retd ENG 6/1/84.
GERMAIN D.J. MCMI. Born 11/8/32. Commd 28/6/51. Sqn Ldr 1/7/64. Retd GD 11/8/87.
GERMAN A. Born 21/6/33. Commd 30/9/55. Sqn Ldr 1/7/73. Retd GD 21/6/91.
GERMAN R.D. Born 19/12/50. Commd 12/8/76. Flt Lt 21/5/80. Retd GD 5/8/90.
GERMANEY R.C. Born 31/3/52. Commd 20/7/78. Sqn Ldr 1/7/96. Retd OPS SPT 20/3/00.
GERRARD D.W. Born 15/9/40. Commd 30/5/59. Gp Capt 1/1/90. Retd GD 15/9/95.
GERRARD T.J. BA MCMI ACIS. Born 29/7/50. Commd 20/9/75. Wg Cdr 1/1/88. Retd ADMIN 1/1/91.
GERRARD W.G. Born 26/5/23. Commd 6/11/42. Flt Lt 13/1/55. Retd SUP 17/6/68.
GERRY B.T. Born 16/8/39. Commd 6/4/62. Flt Lt 6/10/67. Retd GD 12/12/77.
GETGOOD L.V. Born 7/1/21. Commd 7/10/43. Flt Lt 19/10/50. Retd SEC 3/1/59.
GETHING R.T. CB OBE AFC. Born 11/8/11. Commd 15/3/32. Gp Capt 1/7/50. Retd GD 29/1/60. rtg A Cdre
GEVAUX W.G. BSc. Born 12/1/38. Commd 5/8/59. Flt Lt 28/6/62. Retd GD 28/9/76.
GHAIL R.S. Born 22/11/39. Commd 20/11/67. Flt Lt 20/11/67. Retd ENG 22/11/77.

GHENT P.W.B. Born 2/9/49. Commd 4/7/85. Flt Lt 4/7/89. Retd ENG 1/5/93.
GIBB A.H. FCMI. Born 27/2/20. Commd 29/12/40. Gp Capt 1/1/69. Retd GD 23/4/71.
GIBB G.P. MRAeS. Born 7/8/33. Commd 4/2/53. Wg Cdr 1/7/82. Retd GD 2/4/85.
GIBB I.B. MBE DipTechEd MILT MInstPet. Born 2/6/44. Commd 30/5/69. Wg Cdr 1/7/91. Retd SUP 2/6/00.
GIBB R.W. Born 7/4/40. Commd 1/8/61. Wg Cdr 1/1/88. Retd GD 7/4/95.
GIBBARD B.D. Born 14/1/42. Commd 17/2/66. Wg Cdr 1/1/85. Retd SY(PRT) 17/2/88.
GIBBARD C.P. Born 24/12/49. Commd 11/11/71. Fg Offr 22/4/74. Retd SUP 1/11/75.
GIBBARD R.W. MBE. Born 8/3/29. Commd 19/11/52. Sqn Ldr 1/7/66. Retd GD 15/4/76.
GIBBINS P. Born 27/1/38. Commd 14/12/70. Wg Cdr 1/1/84. Retd SUP 1/5/92.
GIBBON A.J. Born 4/9/47. Commd 29/6/72. Flt Lt 29/12/77. Retd GD 14/3/96.
GIBBON J. MBE. Born 8/4/34. Commd 22/12/53. Wg Cdr 1/1/75. Retd GD 9/1/81.
GIBBON P.C. Born 21/5/43. Commd 5/2/65. Flt Lt 5/8/70. Retd GD 16/9/76.
GIBBON R.M. Born 3/6/43. Commd 4/9/64. Wg Cdr 1/1/91. Retd ENG 3/6/98.
GIBBONS B.K.W. BCom MCMI ACIS ACCA. Born 6/11/26. Commd 7/5/56. Sqn Ldr 1/1/67. Retd SUP 1/10/73.
GIBBONS C. Born 4/3/48. Commd 17/3/67. Sqn Ldr 1/1/88. Retd GD 1/10/90.
GIBBONS D.G. Born 25/10/24. Commd 9/8/51. Flt Lt 13/11/57. Retd GD 2/4/68.
GIBBONS D.R. Born 4/6/49. Commd 27/3/70. Flt Lt 27/9/75. Retd GD 4/6/87.
GIBBONS G. Born 5/7/24. Commd 23/8/56. Flt Lt 23/8/59. Retd GD 1/10/68.
GIBBONS G.R. Born 5/8/47. Commd 2/12/67. Flt Lt 17/8/72. Retd GD 1/5/01.
GIBBONS J.R. AFC. Born 24/10/23. Commd 9/4/43. Gp Capt 1/7/63. Retd GD 9/3/67.
GIBBONS M.J. Born 5/9/37. Commd 16/12/58. Sqn Ldr 1/7/70. Retd GD 5/9/93.
GIBBONS P.C. Born 18/11/39. Commd 31/10/63. Flt Lt 31/1/70. Retd SEC 16/4/79.
GIBBONS T.E. Born 13/6/45. Commd 19/3/81. Sqn Ldr 1/1/90. Retd ENG 13/6/00.
GIBBS A.G. Born 21/1/18. Commd 30/1/47. Flt Lt 30/3/52. Retd SEC 16/2/57.
GIBBS A.J. BSc. Born 14/6/43. Commd 30/9/61. Flt Lt 14/12/67. Retd ENG 14/6/74.
GIBBS B. FCIS MCMI. Born 5/12/32. Commd 15/7/53. Wg Cdr 1/1/72. Retd SEC 1/5/75.
GIBBS C.M. CB CBE DFC. Born 11/6/21. Commd 16/1/47. AVM 1/7/74. Retd GD 1/7/76.
GIBBS D.J. Born 28/7/29. Commd 1/2/62. Flt Lt 1/2/68. Retd PE 27/9/75.
GIBBS F. Born 11/11/11. Commd 9/12/41. Sqn Ldr 1/7/54. Retd ENG 11/11/60.
GIBBS I.C. Born 18/7/36. Commd 30/5/59. Sqn Ldr 1/7/71. Retd GD 30/9/78.
GIBBS I.W.B. Born 4/12/42. Commd 11/5/62. Flt Lt 11/11/67. Retd GD 4/12/80.
GIBBS J.S. MBE CEng MRAeS MCMI. Born 17/1/21. Commd 4/6/43. Sqn Ldr 1/1/63. Retd ENG 17/1/76.
GIBBS R.P.M. DSO DFC*. Born 2/4/15. Commd 1/8/36. Sqn Ldr 1/9/42. Retd GD 24/2/44. rtg Wg Cdr
GIBLEN J.T. Born 10/6/33. Commd 6/6/57. Sqn Ldr 1/7/86. Retd GD 10/6/91.
GIBLIN B.J. Born 30/7/41. Commd 6/11/64. Flt Lt 4/5/72. Retd GD 15/9/80.
GIBSON A.D. AFC DFM. Born 7/1/23. Commd 15/9/47. Sqn Ldr 1/1/57. Retd GD 7/1/72.
GIBSON A.J. Born 15/9/35. Commd 17/12/57. Sqn Ldr 1/7/71. Retd GD 29/12/88.
GIBSON A.J. Born 11/3/45. Commd 6/4/72. Sqn Ldr 1/1/82. Retd GD 11/3/89.
GIBSON A.W.M. The Rev. Born 6/7/34. Commd 6/6/66. Retd Wg Cdr 6/7/89.
GIBSON B. DFC DPhysEd. Born 3/1/23. Commd 30/10/43. Flt Lt 26/8/53. Retd PE 1/5/65.
GIBSON B.M. Born 17/5/25. Commd 29/1/46. Flt Lt 19/6/52. Retd RGT 12/10/59.
GIBSON B.S. Born 28/5/13. Commd 14/9/41. Sqn Ldr 1/7/43. Retd GD 28/5/56. rtg Wg Cdr
GIBSON C.R. Born 21/9/58. Commd 29/9/80. Sqn Ldr 1/7/97. Retd OPS SPT(FC) 31/5/03.
GIBSON D.A. MBE MA MA MIL MCMI. Born 18/11/62. Commd 14/9/80. Wg Cdr 1/1/00. Retd GD 22/7/03.
GIBSON D.A. MRAeS. Born 24/8/08. Commd 16/8/32. Gp Capt 1/7/49. Retd ENG 1/11/52.
GIBSON D.W. Born 19/8/34. Commd 16/5/74. Sqn Ldr 1/7/83. Retd ADMIN 1/6/87.
GIBSON E.E. Born 17/7/10. Commd 8/1/44. Flt Lt 10/8/48. Retd SUP 3/2/58.
GIBSON G.G. BSc. Born 16/1/32. Commd 30/9/54. Gp Capt 1/7/83. Retd ADMIN 16/1/89.
GIBSON G.J. Born 4/3/46. Commd 28/2/85. Flt Lt 28/2/89. Retd OPS SPT(FC) 4/3/04.
GIBSON G.M. Born 28/5/35. Commd 9/12/65. Flt Lt 1/7/68. Retd ENG 9/12/73.
GIBSON G.W. CBE. Born 19/1/41. Commd 17/1/69. Gp Capt 1/7/89. Retd ENG 14/12/96.
GIBSON J.A. BSc. Born 31/3/62. Commd 16/2/84. Flt Lt 15/1/87. Retd GD 1/5/01.
GIBSON J.A.A. DSO DFC. Born 24/8/16. Commd 16/5/38. Sqn Ldr 1/1/53. Retd GD 31/12/54.
GIBSON J.D. AFC. Born 20/2/26. Commd 22/3/51. Flt Lt 22/9/54. Retd GD 20/2/64.
GIBSON J.H. Born 6/11/55. Commd 28/4/85. Sqn Ldr 1/7/91. Retd GD(G) 1/7/94.
GIBSON J.M.M. BA. Born 10/3/61. Commd 27/8/87. Sqn Ldr 1/1/95. Retd ENG 10/10/00.
GIBSON J.N. Born 9/12/23. Commd 9/9/59. Sqn Ldr 21/2/70. Retd ADMIN 11/5/76.
GIBSON K.S. Born 6/3/31. Commd 4/2/53. Flt Lt 24/6/58. Retd PI 6/3/86.
GIBSON L. Born 4/3/36. Commd 25/9/59. Sqn Ldr 1/1/72. Retd SUP 5/11/76.
GIBSON L. BSc. Born 24/9/41. Commd 1/8/66. Sqn Ldr 1/1/77. Retd GD 24/9/96.
GIBSON M. BEng CEng MIMechE. Born 19/6/63. Commd 2/9/84. Sqn Ldr 1/1/96. Retd ENG 19/6/01.
GIBSON M.J. CB OBE BSc FRAeS ACGI. Born 2/1/39. Commd 13/7/59. AVM 1/7/91. Retd GD 2/1/94.
GIBSON M.T. Born 3/6/22. Commd 18/12/50. Flt Lt 1/9/54. Retd GD 29/10/62.
GIBSON P.G. OBE. Born 17/2/28. Commd 22/7/50. Gp Capt 1/1/83. Retd SY 1/9/84.
GIBSON P.J. Born 4/11/44. Commd 12/7/63. Flt Lt 15/4/70. Retd GD 4/11/82.
GIBSON R.H. Born 19/7/38. Commd 1/8/61. Flt Lt 26/2/64. Retd GD 31/12/68.

GIBSON S.J. MBE. Born 21/3/47. Commd 17/7/75. Sqn Ldr 1/7/84. Retd ENG 21/3/91.
GIBSON T. Born 29/5/27. Commd 8/11/62. Sqn Ldr 1/7/79. Retd ENG 29/5/88.
GIBSON T.C. Born 8/10/62. Commd 29/1/87. Flt Lt 29/7/92. Retd GD 14/3/96.
GIBSON T.J. MBA BSc. Born 17/2/50. Commd 11/8/74. Sqn Ldr 1/1/88. Retd ENG 1/12/97.
GIBSON T.M. PhD MPhil MB ChB FFOM FRAeS DAvMed DDAM. Born 6/3/47. Commd 22/1/68. A Cdre 1/7/97. Retd MED 1/9/02.
GIBSON V.S. Born 20/12/20. Commd 4/11/44. Flt Lt 4/5/48. Retd GD 30/8/68.
GIBSON W.R. Born 9/7/30. Commd 9/8/51. Sqn Ldr 1/1/66. Retd GD 1/4/83.
GIDDA G.S. MBA. Born 22/9/65. Commd 2/8/90. Flt Lt 16/6/94. Retd ENGINEER 22/10/03.
GIDDINGS H.W. The Rev. AKC. Born 7/10/30. Commd 2/1/67. Retd Wg Cdr 1/5/83.
GIDDINGS Sir Michael KCB OBE DFC AFC* MRAeS. Born 27/8/20. Commd 1/11/41. AM 1/1/74. Retd GD 19/6/76.
GIDNEY A.J. BEng. Born 19/7/44. Commd 22/6/64. Flt Lt 30/5/68. Retd GD 8/9/73.
GIFFIN N.C.W. Born 18/11/50. Commd 19/6/70. Flt Lt 19/12/76. Retd ADMIN 1/7/84.
GIFFIN N.H. Born 13/5/31. Commd 30/7/52. Flt Lt 30/1/55. Retd GD 13/5/69.
GIFFORD F.C.M. Born 16/8/49. Commd 3/12/70. Sqn Ldr 1/1/88. Retd OPS SPT 16/8/99.
GIFFORD R. Born 18/3/35. Commd 23/9/53. Flt Lt 6/6/61. Retd GD 13/1/65.
GIGGINS R.P. Born 28/11/46. Commd 16/8/68. Flt Lt 28/5/72. Retd GD 1/7/85.
GIGGS A.F. Born 31/5/39. Commd 24/6/76. Sqn Ldr 1/7/88. Retd ADMIN 2/10/92.
GILBERT A.C. DFC. Born 5/10/21. Commd 26/10/44. Sqn Ldr 1/1/64. Retd ADMIN 5/10/76.
GILBERT A.I. Born 10/5/51. Commd 24/7/81. Sqn Ldr 1/1/93. Retd ADMIN 15/11/01.
GILBERT B.H.T. BA. Born 22/6/38. Commd 19/1/66. Sqn Ldr 1/7/75. Retd ENG 7/5/89.
GILBERT C.D. Born 26/9/32. Commd 6/12/51. Sqn Ldr 1/1/63. Retd GD 1/10/76.
GILBERT D.J. MSc BSc(Eng) DIC MBCS. Born 26/2/45. Commd 28/9/64. Sqn Ldr 1/7/80. Retd ENG 26/2/89.
GILBERT D.M. Born 1/7/15. Commd 9/12/42. Flt Offr 9/12/47. Retd GD(G) 16/1/57.
GILBERT E.L. LMSSA. Born 22/8/20. Commd 2/3/53. Wg Cdr 1/4/62. Retd MED 7/2/78.
GILBERT E.S. Born 8/6/34. Commd 8/10/52. Wg Cdr 1/7/75. Retd GD(G) 4/4/80.
GILBERT G.H. AFC FCMI. Born 8/11/30. Commd 30/11/50. Gp Capt 1/7/74. Retd GD 8/11/85.
GILBERT J. Born 16/1/49. Commd 21/3/69. Sqn Ldr 1/1/85. Retd GD 7/2/01.
GILBERT Sir Joseph KCB CBE BA CCMI. Born 15/6/31. Commd 17/9/52. ACM 1/1/87. Retd GD 9/8/89.
GILBERT J.C. MBE BSc. Born 22/1/45. Commd 29/9/64. Gp Capt 1/7/91. Retd ENG 22/1/00.
GILBERT J.L. CVO DFC. Born 19/12/21. Commd 28/10/43. Gp Capt 1/1/66. Retd GD 31/1/68.
GILBERT J.S. MA. Born 8/7/32. Commd 3/8/55. Sqn Ldr 10/2/67. Retd EDN 19/11/71.
GILBERT J.W. BDS LDSRCS. Born 2/7/33. Commd 5/5/57. Wg Cdr 22/1/70. Retd DEL 31/10/88.
GILBERT J.W. Born 30/10/41. Commd 14/10/71. Sqn Ldr 1/1/81. Retd SY 2/4/93.
GILBERT K.V.E. Born 2/12/29. Commd 5/4/50. Sqn Ldr 1/7/60. Retd GD 2/12/67.
GILBERT M.P. BSc CEng MIEE. Born 30/10/59. Commd 30/3/86. Sqn Ldr 1/7/93. Retd ENG 30/4/02.
GILBERT M.StJ.J. BSc. Born 8/1/61. Commd 11/12/83. Flt Lt 11/6/86. Retd GD 9/10/00.
GILBERT N.P. Born 26/8/65. Commd 5/10/90. Flt Lt 24/7/90. Retd FLY(P) 26/8/03.
GILBERT P.G. BSc. Born 7/1/32. Commd 18/11/54. Sqn Ldr 1/1/65. Retd ENG 18/11/70.
GILBERT P.N. Born 4/3/59. Commd 28/2/85. Flt Lt 2/11/87. Retd OPS SPT 4/8/97.
GILBERT R. BA MCMI. Born 14/4/42. Commd 22/10/63. Sqn Ldr 22/4/72. Retd ADMIN 14/4/83.
GILBERT R.L. MBE BSc CEng MBCS. Born 9/11/46. Commd 2/4/65. Sqn Ldr 1/7/85. Retd ADMIN 9/11/01.
GILBERT R.W. Born 26/2/49. Commd 3/10/74. Flt Lt 3/4/79. Retd GD 17/6/90.
GILBERT T.J. MB BS. Born 26/6/62. Commd 11/12/84. Wg Cdr 10/9/99. Retd MED 11/12/00.
GILBODY P.G.A. Born 19/9/50. Commd 8/3/73. Flt Lt 10/11/79. Retd GD(G) 14/5/89.
GILBY D.A. Born 23/5/20. Commd 30/1/47. Sqn Ldr 1/7/58. Retd SUP 17/4/65.
GILCHRIST A.B. Born 19/4/46. Commd 19/3/80. Flt Lt 9/5/77. Retd SY 26/6/86.
GILCHRIST A.J. MSc BSc MRAeS. Born 5/3/46. Commd 24/9/67. Sqn Ldr 15/1/78. Retd ADMIN 6/1/97.
GILCHRIST C.C.R. Born 16/7/48. Commd 28/2/69. Flt Lt 28/2/72. Retd GD 16/7/86.
GILCHRIST J.I. Born 28/6/46. Commd 2/8/68. Sqn Ldr 1/1/91. Retd GD(G) 31/3/95.
GILCHRIST J.K. Born 24/2/23. Commd 23/4/51. Sqn Ldr 1/7/73. Retd GD(G) 24/2/83.
GILCHRIST N.S.F. AFC. Born 8/5/36. Commd 5/8/76. Sqn Ldr 1/7/90. Retd GD 14/9/96.
GILDERSLEEVES J.P.V. Born 25/8/58. Commd 22/5/80. Sqn Ldr 1/1/97. Retd OPS SPT 25/8/02.
GILDING C.R. CEng MRAeS CDipAF. Born 14/1/40. Commd 28/7/60. Sqn Ldr 1/7/76. Retd ENG 14/1/95.
GILDING J.L. Born 2/10/44. Commd 20/6/63. Flt Lt 20/12/69. Retd ENG 3/4/71.
GILDING M.J. MSc BSc BA CEng FIEE. Born 8/8/47. Commd 22/9/65. A Cdre 1/7/96. Retd ENG 5/5/01.
GILES A.F. BSc CEng MIMechE MIEE MRAeS ACGI. Born 17/11/37. Commd 14/5/63. Sqn Ldr 1/7/71. Retd ENG 14/5/79.
GILES J.A. BSc. Born 9/7/48. Commd 5/1/70. Sqn Ldr 1/7/84. Retd GD 1/7/87.
GILES J.A. BSc. Born 20/8/52. Commd 25/7/76. Flt Lt 25/4/78. Retd GD 20/8/92.
GILES P.W. OBE MA PhD. Born 14/12/45. Commd 15/9/69. A Cdre 1/1/97. Retd ENG 11/3/02.
GILES R.W. Born 3/10/41. Commd 18/12/62. Flt Lt 18/12/67. Retd SEC 27/5/74.
GILES W.J. BA. Born 15/6/44. Commd 16/9/76. Sqn Ldr 1/7/85. Retd ENG 1/12/98.
GILL A.A. Born 17/8/48. Commd 7/10/73. Wg Cdr 1/1/88. Retd GD(G) 17/3/92.
GILL A.C. Born 14/3/66. Commd 11/4/85. Sqn Ldr 1/1/97. Retd OPS SPT(ATC) 14/3/04.
GILL A.M. OBE DFC AE MRAeS MCIPD MCMI. Born 24/2/16. Commd 6/9/40. Wg Cdr 1/7/55. Retd GD 3/3/71.

GILL C. Born 29/8/23. Commd 27/1/55. Flt Lt 27/1/61. Retd GD 29/8/73.
GILL D.A. Born 27/4/45. Commd 22/5/64. Flt Lt 22/11/69. Retd GD 29/3/73.
GILL D.N. BA BSc CEng MRAeS. Born 25/4/62. Commd 11/9/83. Sqn Ldr 1/7/93. Retd ENG 25/4/00.
GILL E.A. MSc BSc MILT MCMI CDipAF. Born 7/1/63. Commd 18/8/85. Sqn Ldr 1/1/95. Retd SUPPLY 1/10/03.
GILL F. Born 11/5/30. Commd 3/11/51. Flt Lt 3/5/56. Retd GD 1/5/68.
GILL H. CB OBE. Born 30/10/22. Commd 1/1/43. AVM 1/1/77. Retd SUP 25/8/79.
GILL J. Born 1/2/42. Commd 20/7/78. Flt Lt 20/7/83. Retd GD 1/2/97.
GILL J.R. MSc BEng MRAeS. Born 15/4/64. Commd 2/8/85. Sqn Ldr 1/7/97. Retd ENG 15/9/02.
GILL L.W.G. DSO MCIPD. Born 31/3/18. Commd 28/11/37. AVM 1/1/68. Retd GD 31/3/73.
GILL M. MCMI. Born 18/11/29. Commd 11/4/51. Sqn Ldr 1/7/64. Retd GD 31/3/75.
GILL N.J. BSc. Born 14/4/36. Commd 23/9/59. Flt Lt 23/3/64. Retd GD 23/9/75.
GILL P.H.R. MSc MFOM MRCS LRCP DAvMed. Born 30/1/42. Commd 11/1/65. Gp Capt 5/9/92. Retd MED 14/1/98.
GILL P.J. BSc. Born 19/6/51. Commd 13/6/74. Sqn Ldr 1/7/88. Retd GD 1/8/91.
GILL P.W.R. Born 18/6/32. Commd 2/1/52. Flt Lt 2/7/56. Retd GD 4/4/77.
GILL R.A. CBE MS BSc. Born 22/5/40. Commd 30/9/60. A Cdre 1/7/90. Retd ENG 1/1/94.
GILL R.L. BSc. Born 10/4/60. Commd 2/9/79. Wg Cdr 1/1/99. Retd ENG 1/1/99.
GILL T.E. MBE BSc MRAeS. Born 26/5/31. Commd 7/10/53. Sqn Ldr 1/7/64. Retd GD 24/6/73.
GILL V.A. Born 7/5/38. Commd 24/8/72. Flt Lt 24/2/79. Retd ADMIN 8/5/88.
GILL W. DFC. Born 27/3/21. Commd 15/2/45. Fg Offr 15/11/46. Retd GD 11/5/54.
GILL W.A. Born 29/4/26. Commd 9/1/50. Flt Lt 9/11/54. Retd GD 9/1/66.
GILL W.A. Born 17/4/42. Commd 4/7/85. Flt Lt 4/7/89. Retd GD(G) 17/4/92.
GILLAN A.M.F. Born 9/9/44. Commd 5/7/68. Flt Lt 21/11/74. Retd RGT 4/12/74.
GILLANDERS D.C. Born 29/2/40. Commd 4/4/59. Sqn Ldr 1/7/71. Retd GD 26/3/79.
GILLARD E.P. Born 28/6/32. Commd 23/1/52. Flt Lt 23/7/56. Retd GD 28/9/70.
GILLARD L.F. CEng MRAeS. Born 18/5/29. Commd 19/2/53. Sqn Ldr 1/7/64. Retd ENG 4/7/70.
GILLARD N.J. BA. Born 14/11/49. Commd 24/9/72. Sqn Ldr 1/1/83. Retd ADMIN 1/12/89.
GILLEN D. Born 27/11/31. Commd 3/12/61. Fg Offr 16/8/92. Retd PRT 3/12/69.
GILLEN J.M. Born 22/7/07. Commd 2/6/43. Wg Cdr 1/7/53. Retd PRT 11/5/61.
GILLESPIE A.V.I. MB ChB MRCOG. Born 13/7/50. Commd 9/5/71. Wg Cdr 31/7/87. Retd MED 31/8/89.
GILLESPIE I.R. MBE BA. Born 26/8/41. Commd 9/9/63. Sqn Ldr 1/7/88. Retd GD 26/8/96.
GILLESPIE J.P. AE BL. Born 22/8/39. Commd 6/9/65. Sqn Ldr 1/7/76. Retd GD 22/8/94.
GILLESPIE J.R. Born 10/1/45. Commd 20/5/82. Sqn Ldr 1/7/90. Retd ADMIN 10/1/00.
GILLESPIE M. BSc DipSoton. Born 13/6/37. Commd 19/2/63. Sqn Ldr 3/3/68. Retd ADMIN 19/2/83.
GILLETT A.F. Born 1/6/53. Commd 1/6/72. Flt Lt 1/12/77. Retd GD 14/1/85.
GILLETT B.T. Born 20/11/61. Commd 12/1/92. Flt Lt 30/5/86. Retd SUP 1/12/95.
GILLETT M.J. Born 26/12/40. Commd 24/4/64. Flt Lt 8/3/72. Retd GD 3/2/80.
GILLIATT Z.E. Born 9/2/39. Commd 28/4/60. Sqn Ldr 1/1/74. Retd ADMIN 30/6/77.
GILLIES J.R.C. BSc CertEd. Born 23/11/64. Commd 25/9/88. Sqn Ldr 1/7/01. Retd ADMIN (TRG) 25/9/04.
GILLIES R.L. MA. Born 10/3/64. Commd 7/7/97. Flt Lt 25/3/91. Retd ADMIN (TRG) 26/11/04.
GILLIES S.C. Born 14/3/63. Commd 11/4/85. Sqn Ldr 1/1/97. Retd FLY(P) 11/11/04.
GILLING T. BA. Born 12/12/31. Commd 17/12/64. Sqn Ldr 1/1/75. Retd ADMIN 9/11/85.
GILLMORE J.N. Born 29/12/36. Commd 17/7/56. Sqn Ldr 1/1/72. Retd GD 25/4/90.
GILLOTT S.M. BSc. Born 1/1/60. Commd 26/5/85. Flt Lt 26/11/88. Retd OPS SPT 26/11/02.
GILLOW C.H.P. BA. Born 11/8/57. Commd 3/10/77. Sqn Ldr 1/1/89. Retd GD 12/12/95.
GILMER W.N. OBE AFC. Born 7/5/23. Commd 17/7/44. Wg Cdr 1/1/61. Retd GD 12/8/75.
GILMORE T.K. Born 11/8/37. Commd 3/6/58. Flt Lt 5/12/63. Retd GD 13/10/73.
GILMOUR A. Born 19/9/49. Commd 30/8/73. Flt Lt 29/2/76. Retd GD 31/1/96.
GILMOUR K.C. Born 14/1/18. Commd 19/9/47. Flt Lt 16/9/50. Retd GD(G) 14/1/73.
GILMOUR P.S. Born 12/10/53. Commd 8/1/85. Sqn Ldr 1/1/92. Retd GD 1/1/92.
GILPIN H.V. DPhysEd. Born 2/4/28. Commd 27/10/54. Flt Lt 1/3/61. Retd SUP 28/11/70.
GILPIN J. MBE. Born 16/11/31. Commd 12/3/64. Flt Lt 12/3/69. Retd GD 2/6/84.
GILPIN P.W. CBE DFC. Born 30/9/22. Commd 19/6/42. Gp Capt 1/7/65. Retd GD 30/9/77.
GILPIN R.C. Born 28/11/32. Commd 28/7/53. Flt Lt 28/1/56. Retd GD 30/11/62.
GILRAY G. MB ChB MFCM DPH. Born 6/11/29. Commd 1/5/55. Wg Cdr 5/4/66. Retd MED 8/1/76.
GILROY C.N. BSc. Born 18/8/45. Commd 20/2/67. Sqn Ldr 1/1/80. Retd GD 18/8/85.
GILROY J.W. Born 31/1/49. Commd 5/7/68. Flt Lt 14/12/74. Retd GD(G) 31/1/87.
GILROY N.S. Born 27/5/59. Commd 23/7/98. Flt Lt 23/7/02. Retd OPS SPT(ATC) 1/8/03.
GILROY P.P. Born 29/6/41. Commd 30/7/63. Sqn Ldr 1/7/72. Retd GD 6/10/73.
GILSON J.I. Born 26/2/42. Commd 1/1/62. Wg Cdr 1/1/87. Retd ADMIN 30/9/92.
GILSON M.Q. Born 17/7/44. Commd 5/3/65. Sqn Ldr 1/1/82. Retd GD 17/7/88.
GILVARY R.B. Born 19/5/37. Commd 1/4/58. Wg Cdr 1/1/76. Retd GD 1/4/90.
GIMBLETT G.R.G. MBE. Born 6/3/20. Commd 25/11/42. Sqn Ldr 1/7/72. Retd GD 6/3/75.
GINGELL A.S. BSc. Born 15/11/55. Commd 15/9/74. Sqn Ldr 1/1/87. Retd SUP 15/11/93.
GINGELL Sir John GBE KCB. Born 3/2/25. Commd 16/4/51. ACM 1/1/82. Retd GD 22/6/84.
GINGELL R.R. Born 20/2/50. Commd 6/1/71. Sqn Ldr 1/1/86. Retd GD 1/1/89.
GINN A.W. Born 22/7/32. Commd 14/4/53. Sqn Ldr 1/7/64. Retd GD 1/9/84.

GINN M.C. AFC. Born 15/10/35. Commd 31/7/56. Sqn Ldr 1/7/64. Retd GD 1/2/68.
GIRDLER E.E.G. Born 8/7/37. Commd 14/8/64. Flt Lt 26/7/67. Retd GD 8/7/75.
GIRDWOOD K.R.H. BSc. Born 29/4/65. Commd 11/9/83. Sqn Ldr 1/7/98. Retd FLY(P) 29/4/03.
GIRDWOOD W.S. FCIPS. Born 22/1/36. Commd 7/7/55. Gp Capt 1/1/84. Retd SUP 6/4/90.
GIRVEN C.F. BSc. Born 8/8/61. Commd 2/9/84. Flt Lt 2/3/87. Retd GD 2/3/01.
GISSING H.C. Born 26/9/24. Commd 16/2/45. Flt Lt 21/11/48. Retd GD 30/9/67.
GITSHAM G.T. Born 1/5/24. Commd 23/12/43. Flt Lt 21/7/61. Retd GD 29/3/69.
GJERTSEN A.B. BSc. Born 2/12/48. Commd 28/2/72. Flt Lt 28/5/73. Retd GD 6/10/77.
GLADDING R.E. CBE. Born 17/6/29. Commd 9/4/52. A Cdre 1/1/76. Retd SUP 17/6/84.
GLADSTONE J. AFC*. Born 6/9/22. Commd 12/6/51. Sqn Ldr 1/9/65. Retd GD 6/9/73.
GLADSTONE P.G. Born 13/10/20. Commd 6/2/45. Sqn Ldr 1/7/56. Retd GD 21/11/63.
GLADWELL B.N. Born 2/9/28. Commd 22/7/66. Flt Lt 22/7/69. Retd GD 2/9/83.
GLADWELL I.M. DFM. Born 28/2/23. Commd 7/6/43. Flt Lt 7/12/46. Retd GD 28/2/66.
GLADWIN D.W. Born 4/10/44. Commd 3/8/62. Flt Lt 3/2/68. Retd GD 29/12/73.
GLAISTER D.H. PhD BSc MB BS. Born 13/3/34. Commd 21/6/59. Gp Capt 21/6/82. Retd MED 23/12/94.
GLAISTER J.L.G. DFC. Born 28/12/15. Commd 26/6/39. Flt Lt 1/9/45. Retd SEC 5/8/52. rtg Sqn Ldr
GLANCY W.C. Born 2/5/52. Commd 11/4/83. Flt Lt 11/4/87. Retd ENG 9/2/93.
GLANFIELD P. ACT(Batt) MHCIMA. Born 21/7/34. Commd 8/12/59. Sqn Ldr 1/7/70. Retd CAT 8/12/75.
GLAS J.A. BA. Born 25/9/50. Commd 3/1/71. Sqn Ldr 1/7/85. Retd GD 25/9/88.
GLASER E.D. DFC. Born 20/4/21. Commd 11/7/40. Flt Lt 1/9/45. Retd GD 26/6/53. rtg Sqn Ldr
GLASGOW G.H. Born 14/3/39. Commd 10/12/57. Sqn Ldr 1/1/75. Retd GD 1/1/78.
GLASIER J. Born 26/4/60. Commd 26/9/91. Fg Offr 5/3/94. Retd ADMIN 14/3/97.
GLASS E.S.A. Born 2/6/41. Commd 1/12/77. Flt Lt 1/12/82. Retd ADMIN 1/4/87.
GLASS J.R. CEng MIMechE MRAeS MCMI. Born 10/2/36. Commd 2/2/60. Sqn Ldr 1/1/68. Retd ENG 2/2/76.
GLASS M.R. BEng CEng MIMechE. Born 1/9/60. Commd 8/8/85. Sqn Ldr 1/7/95. Retd ENG 1/9/98.
GLASS N.J. Born 15/1/31. Commd 12/12/51. Sqn Ldr 1/7/66. Retd GD 1/7/69.
GLASSPOOL I.D. Born 13/8/41. Commd 17/1/69. Sqn Ldr 1/7/76. Retd GD(G) 13/8/96.
GLAZIER D.W. Born 28/10/35. Commd 30/5/69. Flt Lt 30/5/71. Retd ENG 30/9/78.
GLAZIER M.J. Born 27/4/31. Commd 4/6/64. Sqn Ldr 1/7/74. Retd GD 4/6/83.
GLEADEN A.W. BSc. Born 21/11/28. Commd 10/11/54. Sqn Ldr 1/7/62. Retd GD 8/11/75.
GLEAVE M. OBE. Born 5/7/47. Commd 5/11/65. Gp Capt 1/7/91. Retd GD 6/9/02.
GLEBOCKI J. Born 4/1/13. Commd 1/1/37. Flt Lt 1/7/46. Retd SEC 8/10/61.
GLEDHILL J.P. Born 8/8/24. Commd 9/12/48. Sqn Ldr 1/1/58. Retd GD 11/5/68.
GLEDHILL J.S. Born 29/5/30. Commd 19/8/06. Sqn Ldr 1/7/75. Retd ENG 9/10/81.
GLEDHILL T.C. AFC. Born 20/12/24. Commd 28/10/44. Gp Capt 1/7/66. Retd GD 27/9/75.
GLEED D.R. MCMI. Born 27/4/45. Commd 10/10/63. Wg Cdr 1/1/86. Retd GD(G) 28/2/94.
GLEN M.C. CEng MIIM MRAeS MCMI. Born 29/12/36. Commd 24/7/57. Wg Cdr 1/7/77. Retd ENG 1/2/87.
GLENDINNING B.W. Born 9/8/40. Commd 19/8/65. Sqn Ldr 1/1/79. Retd SY 1/10/82.
GLENDINNING H.D. Born 29/6/21. Commd 8/7/54. Sqn Ldr 1/1/68. Retd GD 30/8/76.
GLENN G.H.W. DFC*. Born 19/10/20. Commd 17/12/41. Sqn Ldr 1/1/55. Retd GD 10/10/63.
GLENN H. Born 19/4/20. Commd 17/6/43. Flt Lt 19/8/51. Retd SUP 25/8/53.
GLENN J.A. BSc DPhysEd. Born 1/12/32. Commd 4/7/57. Sqn Ldr 20/9/66. Retd ADMIN 1/12/92.
GLENN W.J. AFC DFM. Born 28/9/19. Commd 17/11/42. Flt Lt 17/5/46. Retd GD 20/4/63.
GLENNIE D.J. Born 21/10/43. Commd 3/5/68. Sqn Ldr 1/7/87. Retd GD 21/1/92.
GLENNIE J. BSc. Born 9/6/40. Commd 9/11/65. Sqn Ldr 1/1/79. Retd ENG 1/1/82.
GLENTON J.A. Born 25/1/43. Commd 28/9/62. Flt Lt 1/7/68. Retd GD 25/1/98.
GLEW W. Born 26/4/54. Commd 16/5/74. Sqn Ldr 1/1/89. Retd SUP 8/8/96.
GLIDLE C.S. Born 18/8/29. Commd 26/3/52. Sqn Ldr 1/7/67. Retd GD 28/11/75.
GLINN J.W. Born 16/3/15. Commd 18/9/41. Flt Lt 1/9/45. Retd ENG 1/9/50.
GLOAG A.D. Born 12/7/40. Commd 9/2/64. Flt Lt 14/3/69. Retd GD 21/4/81.
GLOVER A.G. Born 20/9/43. Commd 28/9/62. Flt Lt 8/1/69. Retd GD 3/8/76.
GLOVER A.S. BSc. Born 22/5/63. Commd 17/7/02. Flt Lt 15/1/02. Retd LEGAL 17/12/04.
GLOVER G.H. CEng FIMechE MRAeS. Born 7/12/36. Commd 17/7/59. Gp Capt 1/7/84. Retd ENG 16/4/90.
GLOVER H.F. CEng MRAeS. Born 27/3/23. Commd 7/10/43. A Cdre 1/7/75. Retd ENG 27/3/78.
GLOVER J. Born 29/10/42. Commd 4/7/85. Flt Lt 4/7/89. Retd ADMIN 29/10/94.
GLOVER J.W. BA. Born 2/4/54. Commd 3/9/72. Sqn Ldr 1/1/86. Retd GD 15/12/96.
GLOVER N.D. Born 5/8/22. Commd 24/11/44. Flt Lt 11/11/54. Retd PI 5/8/77.
GLOVER P.B. Born 25/9/45. Commd 26/5/67. Flt Lt 4/5/72. Retd GD 13/12/75.
GLOVER R.A.H. Born 8/1/21. Commd 27/8/64. Flt Lt 27/8/69. Retd ENG 8/1/76.
GLOVER R.B. Born 18/2/31. Commd 1/9/70. Sqn Ldr 1/7/76. Retd SUP 25/8/84.
GLOVER R.E. DFC. Born 29/3/18. Commd 17/8/40. Wg Cdr 1/7/54. Retd GD 29/3/73.
GLOVER R.G. Born 27/6/65. Commd 26/4/84. Flt Lt 26/10/89. Retd GD 28/2/93.
GLOVER R.G. Born 6/7/42. Commd 21/12/62. Flt Lt 21/6/68. Retd GD 6/7/80. rtg Sqn Ldr
GLOVER R.W. BSc. Born 27/5/33. Commd 12/1/53. Sqn Ldr 1/1/62. Retd GD 27/5/71.
GLUNING S.L. Born 26/8/34. Commd 22/5/75. Sqn Ldr 1/7/85. Retd ENG 26/8/92.
GLYDE P.L. Born 8/5/47. Commd 23/3/67. Flt Lt 23/9/72. Retd GD 8/5/02.

GOADBY A. Born 18/8/31. Commd 9/5/51. Flt Lt 9/11/55. Retd GD 18/2/71.
GOADBY J.W. MRCS LRCP MFOM DRCOG DAvMed. Born 14/3/38. Commd 22/4/63. Wg Cdr 23/8/80.
    Retd MED 19/5/83.
GOATER J.N. BA. Born 12/1/53. Commd 14/4/86. Flt Lt 22/10/80. Retd SUP 19/1/92.
GOATHAM J. MSc BSc PGCE. Born 10/9/62. Commd 16/1/84. Flt Lt 15/1/87. Retd OPS SPT(FLTOPS) 1/7/05.
GOATHAM J.R. Born 24/7/34. Commd 19/1/66. Flt Lt 19/1/71. Retd GD 1/6/73.
GOATLEY B.J. MBCS. Born 23/4/28. Commd 11/4/51. Wg Cdr 1/7/73. Retd SUP 1/12/77.
GOBLE T.J.L. BA. Born 26/4/57. Commd 11/5/77. Plt Offr 15/7/79. Retd GD 26/2/79.
GODBY P.R. Born 27/8/14. Commd 6/3/39. Wg Cdr 1/7/55. Retd GD 6/9/61.
GODDARD A.F. BSc CEng MRAeS. Born 24/1/37. Commd 23/7/58. Wg Cdr 1/7/74. Retd ENG 18/9/82. rtg Gp Capt
GODDARD B. Born 5/10/48. Commd 9/12/71. Flt Lt 9/6/77. Retd GD 29/1/96.
GODDARD D.E. Born 12/9/31. Commd 26/3/53. Flt Lt 5/8/58. Retd GD(G) 12/9/91.
GODDARD G.M. MSc BSc CEng MIMechE ACGI. Born 13/12/45. Commd 28/9/64. Wg Cdr 1/1/86. Retd ENG 13/12/00.
GODDARD J.A. BSc. Born 17/8/48. Commd 6/4/70. Sqn Ldr 1/7/83. Retd GD 7/2/87.
GODDARD J.F. BSc CEng MIEE DipEl. Born 27/1/25. Commd 9/6/45. Wg Cdr 11/12/68. Retd ADMIN 3/4/76.
GODDARD J.J. BSc. Born 9/5/29. Commd 4/10/51. Sqn Ldr 9/5/61. Retd ADMIN 9/5/86.
GODDARD J.S. Born 30/1/44. Commd 31/12/62. Fg Offr 21/12/64. Retd GD 10/7/65.
GODDARD M.J.S. BSc. Born 17/6/49. Commd 14/1/79. Wg Cdr 1/1/91. Retd ADMIN 14/3/96.
GODDARD P.J. CB AFC. Born 17/10/43. Commd 22/3/63. AVM 1/1/94. Retd GD 17/4/98.
GODDARD P.R. Born 9/2/52. Commd 25/80. Flt Lt 22/5/82. Retd GD 14/3/96.
GODDARD R. BA. Born 10/9/57. Commd 19/9/76. Fg Offr 15/4/78. Retd GD 5/6/80.
GODDEN D.R.P. BDS MB ChB FDSRCS(Eng) FRCS(Eng). Born 28/12/58. Commd 13/1/80. Plt Offr 13/1/80.
    Retd DEL 8/12/86. Re-entered 28/8/88. Sqn Ldr 1/8/92. Retd DEL 28/9/97.
GODFREY A. MCMI. Born 1/4/51. Commd 24/6/76. Sqn Ldr 1/1/87. Retd ADMIN 1/1/90.
GODFREY A.G. Born 16/4/13. Commd 16/3/44. Sqn Ldr 1/7/55. Retd ENG 16/6/62.
GODFREY A.R. Born 20/11/40. Commd 1/8/69. Sqn Ldr 1/7/80. Retd ADMIN 20/11/95.
GODFREY A.V. Born 17/1/23. Commd 22/6/45. Flt Lt 30/6/49. Retd GD 21/11/64.
GODFREY I.P. Born 1/8/48. Commd 10/6/66. Flt Lt 4/5/72. Retd GD 1/7/90.
GODFREY M.F. BSc. Born 28/5/49. Commd 19/9/71. Sqn Ldr 1/1/89. Retd ADMIN 23/12/00.
GODFREY M.V. AFC . Born 1/9/49. Commd 2/2/70. Wg Cdr 1/7/89. Retd GD 1/9/04.
GODFREY R.W. Born 9/8/36. Commd 1/2/65. Flt Lt 26/7/67. Retd GD 9/8/74.
GODFREY S.J.G. Born 22/4/40. Commd 25/3/64. Flt Lt 25/9/69. Retd GD 3/12/79.
GODFREY T.W. MBE. Born 1/7/34. Commd 28/5/66. Gp Capt 1/1/87. Retd SY(PRT) 17/6/89.
GODLEY P.R. Born 16/5/46. Commd 4/7/69. Flt Lt 4/1/76. Retd ADMIN 24/3/85.
GODMAN M.E. Born 25/2/39. Commd 10/2/59. Flt Lt 12/8/64. Retd GD 21/8/78.
GODSALL-STANTON J.R. Born 16/4/31. Commd 5/5/51. Flt Lt 10/11/55. Retd GD 16/4/92.
GODSELL S.J. LLB. Born 25/8/53. Commd 16/2/86. Flt Lt 16/8/87. Retd ADMIN 1/1/93.
GODSMARK F.R. Born 23/5/18. Commd 4/3/39. Sqn Ldr 1/1/60. Retd SEC 23/5/73.
GODWIN A.F. Born 13/6/22. Commd 25/6/43. Flt Lt 25/12/46. Retd GD 1/2/59.
GODWIN C.L. AFC. Born 3/5/24. Commd 20/8/43. A Cdre 1/1/70. Retd GD 2/5/79.
GOFF J.H. Born 24/9/29. Commd 31/3/60. Sqn Ldr 1/7/68. Retd GD 26/8/74.
GOFF R. Born 23/2/44. Commd 3/1/64. Flt Lt 7/7/69. Retd GD 1/5/76.
GOGGIN T.E. MCMI. Born 6/9/28. Commd 11/4/63. Sqn Ldr 1/7/77. Retd SUP 30/11/78.
GOLBY D.H. MA MCMI. Born 3/4/37. Commd 14/8/61. Sqn Ldr 1/1/70. Retd ADMIN 2/2/91.
GOLD E.J. BSc DCAe CEng MRAeS. Born 16/3/34. Commd 5/9/57. Wg Cdr 14/1/73. Retd ADMIN 30/9/76.
GOLDBY J.L. DFC. Born 28/6/22. Commd 6/11/42. Sqn Ldr 1/1/56. Retd GD 30/6/62.
GOLDBY M.B. Born 9/12/49. Commd 4/9/81. Sqn Ldr 1/7/90. Retd ENG 14/9/96.
GOLDEN E. Born 26/4/49. Commd 30/5/69. Sqn Ldr 1/7/85. Retd GD 1/7/88. Re-entered 21/4/89. Sqn Ldr 21/4/86.
    Retd GD 29/5/00.
GOLDEN M.J. Born 7/2/46. Commd 26/1/66. Sqn Ldr 1/7/90. Retd GD 7/2/01.
GOLDFIELD R.H. Born 7/1/48. Commd 13/6/74. Sqn Ldr 1/7/83. Retd GD(G) 29/4/88.
GOLDIE J. Born 25/12/61. Commd 23/10/86. Flt Lt 19/2/90. Retd SY 20/3/93.
GOLDIE J.M. Born 27/5/21. Commd 22/9/48. Flt Lt 22/9/54. Retd SEC 25/5/70.
GOLDING C.G.L. Born 14/2/24. Commd 20/8/43. Flt Lt 7/11/47. Retd GD 4/1/49.
GOLDS A.F. Born 8/11/34. Commd 14/11/59. Flt Lt 14/5/65. Retd GD 8/11/89.
GOLDS C.C. AFC. Born 16/9/36. Commd 29/12/54. Sqn Ldr 1/7/66. Retd GD 13/2/71.
GOLDSMITH T.W. Born 16/10/19. Commd 27/12/44. Flt Lt 7/6/51. Retd SEC 16/10/52.
GOLDSTEIN M. MBE BA. Born 17/6/34. Commd 12/7/57. Wg Cdr 1/1/77. Retd ADMIN 7/4/86.
GOLDSWORTHY G.R. Born 18/4/23. Commd 18/6/62. Sqn Ldr 1/1/80. Retd CAT 18/4/83.
GOLLINS J.H. Born 1/10/34. Commd 3/10/60. Sqn Ldr 1/7/73. Retd SY 17/1/87.
GOMES R.S. Born 11/9/41. Commd 22/5/80. Flt Lt 22/5/86. Retd ENG 9/5/87.
GOMMO R.D. MA CEng. Born 14/6/34. Commd 25/9/54. Gp Capt 1/1/78. Retd ENG 16/6/81.
GOOCH J.E. Born 5/4/30. Commd 25/8/60. Sqn Ldr 1/7/74. Retd ENG 5/4/88.
GOOCH N.W. Born 17/10/18. Commd 31/7/58. Flt Lt 31/7/63. Retd ENG 30/11/68.
GOOD M.J. MCMI. Born 11/1/49. Commd 11/10/71. Air Cdre 1/7/98. Retd OPS SPT 9/1/03.
GOODACRE F.H. AFC. Born 23/12/15. Commd 10/11/42. Flt Lt 10/5/46. Retd GD(G) 30/12/65.

GOODALL J. MBE. Born 18/10/21. Commd 26/9/57. Sqn Ldr 1/7/69. Retd ENG 18/10/81.
GOODALL J.F. Born 1/7/32. Commd 2/1/52. Sqn Ldr 1/7/69. Retd GD 1/7/72.
GOODALL M.P. Born 16/5/51. Commd 17/1/85. Sqn Ldr 1/7/92. Retd ENG 13/12/99.
GOODALL P.J. MCMI. Born 27/6/30. Commd 14/4/53. Wg Cdr 1/7/67. Retd GD 15/8/75.
GOODALL Sir Roderick KBE CB AFC* FRAeS. Born 19/1/47. Commd 1/3/68. Air Mshl 1/9/99. Retd GD 4/2/04.
GOODE A.G. MCMI. Born 31/10/20. Commd 13/6/43. Sqn Ldr 1/1/69. Retd SUP 1/11/74.
GOODE A.T.R. The Rev. MA. Born 10/12/42. Commd 18/7/71. Retd Wg Cdr 10/12/97.
GOODE G.E.F. OBE DFC. Born 8/4/17. Commd 17/11/40. Wg Cdr 1/7/56. Retd GD 15/6/68.
GOODENOUGH P.J. Born 19/2/28. Commd 8/8/51. Flt Lt 8/5/57. Retd GD 10/7/67.
GOODEY L.G. DFC. Born 26/4/16. Commd 23/8/42. Wg Cdr 1/7/60. Retd ENG 16/5/71.
GOODFELLOW B.H. Born 6/4/41. Commd 23/1/64. Sqn Ldr 1/1/75. Retd SEC 6/4/79.
GOODFELLOW J.H. MA CEng MIEE MCMI. Born 19/7/37. Commd 2/2/60. Sqn Ldr 1/1/71. Retd ENG 2/2/76.
GOODFELLOW J.V. MSc BSc CEng MRAeS AFIMA. Born 10/6/38. Commd 25/9/59. Sqn Ldr 25/3/68.
    Retd ADMIN 10/6/76.
GOODFELLOW M.S. Born 15/3/30. Commd 16/1/52. Sqn Ldr 1/7/60. Retd GD 15/3/68.
GOODFELLOW W. Born 4/2/38. Commd 5/12/63. Sqn Ldr 1/1/73. Retd SEC 4/2/76.
GOODHEAD D.G.C. CEng MRAeS MIProdE MCMI. Born 16/6/30. Commd 11/6/53. Sqn Ldr 1/7/64. Retd ENG 1/7/78.
GOODHEW A.N. Born 31/10/29. Commd 5/12/51. Flt Lt 5/6/56. Retd GD 31/10/67.
GOODING D.J. Born 14/6/50. Commd 25/2/72. Flt Lt 25/8/77. Retd ADMIN 14/6/88.
GOODING J. Born 11/6/33. Commd 13/12/68. Flt Lt 13/12/73. Retd ENG 11/6/92.
GOODING P.J. AFC. Born 23/11/43. Commd 24/6/65. Gp Capt 1/1/90. Retd GD 28/2/99.
GOODINSON H.J. Born 20/5/34. Commd 18/11/58. Sqn Ldr 1/7/68. Retd ADMIN 3/4/85.
GOODLIFFE I.R. Born 6/8/38. Commd 16/12/66. Sqn Ldr 1/7/73. Retd ADMIN 1/5/82.
GOODMAN A.G. Born 5/11/51. Commd 5/7/68. Flt Lt 4/11/70. Retd GD 5/11/96.
GOODMAN A.M. Born 14/4/37. Commd 16/12/58. Sqn Ldr 1/1/71. Retd GD 14/10/97.
GOODMAN E.J. Born 25/4/33. Commd 8/7/65. Gp Capt 1/1/83. Retd MED 30/6/87.
GOODMAN G.J. OBE MRIN. Born 30/12/46. Commd 2/8/68. Wg Cdr 1/7/88. Retd GD 30/12/01.
GOODMAN J.R. DFC* AFC AE*. Born 10/1/21. Commd 6/5/42. Gp Capt 1/1/66. Retd SEC 10/1/76.
GOODMAN K.M. Born 21/4/10. Commd 11/7/45. Flt Offr 19/11/53. Retd SEC 3/7/59.
GOODMAN L.S. Born 24/9/20. Commd 24/4/42. Sqn Ldr 1/1/61. Retd GD 1/1/64.
GOODMAN P. Born 15/8/37. Commd 18/2/64. Wg Cdr 1/1/81. Retd GD 15/8/92.
GOODMAN P.J. Born 3/10/38. Commd 13/12/60. Sqn Ldr 1/1/72. Retd GD 3/10/96.
GOODMAN P.S.T. Born 23/3/65. Commd 30/8/84. Flt Lt 28/2/90. Retd FLY(P) 23/3/03.
GOODMAN R.N. BSc. Born 14/5/53. Commd 17/9/72. Flt Lt 15/4/78. Retd GD 5/4/00.
GOODRIDGE V.D. Born 21/3/42. Commd 19/2/76. Sqn Ldr 13/2/87. Retd MED(T) 6/4/92.
GOODRIDGE W.M. Born 25/6/38. Commd 29/1/72. Sqn Ldr 1/1/84. Retd ENG 1/10/84.
GOODRUM J.R. Born 14/4/40. Commd 24/4/80. Sqn Ldr 1/7/89. Retd GD 14/4/95.
GOODRUM R.M. Born 21/1/64. Commd 16/12/82. Flt Lt 16/6/88. Retd FLY(P) 21/7/04.
GOODRUM S. Born 23/1/31. Commd 5/11/05. Wg Cdr 1/1/76. Retd GD 1/10/85.
GOODSELL B.D. Born 16/2/29. Commd 13/12/50. Flt Lt 13/12/55. Retd SEC 16/2/67. rtg Sqn Ldr
GOODSELL B.H. Born 23/9/20. Commd 15/4/43. Flt Lt 20/3/48. Retd ENG 23/9/69.
GOODSELL G.V. Born 20/12/49. Commd 8/8/69. Wg Cdr 1/1/91. Retd GD 20/12/04.
GOODSIR D.H. AFC. Born 20/2/32. Commd 28/2/52. Flt Lt 14/5/58. Retd GD 7/7/73.
GOODSON J.C. DFM. Born 9/4/20. Commd 5/4/43. Flt Lt 5/4/45. Retd GD(G) 9/4/75.
GOODWILL J.P. BSc. Born 18/2/32. Commd 25/8/55. Sqn Ldr 25/2/63. Retd EDN 19/1/74.
GOODWILL W.M.G. BSc. Born 12/10/62. Commd 26/8/86. Flt Lt 22/12/88. Retd GD 22/6/98.
GOODWIN B.M.P. Born 20/8/55. Commd 14/7/77. Sqn Ldr 1/1/91. Retd SY 1/1/94.
GOODWIN C.W.D. Born 3/8/57. Commd 29/7/76. Sqn Ldr 1/1/91. Retd GD 1/6/98.
GOODWIN D.M. Born 17/5/31. Commd 14/11/51. Wg Cdr 1/1/70. Retd GD 21/5/86.
GOODWIN D.M. Born 4/2/35. Commd 12/1/55. Flt Lt 1/3/61. Retd GD 14/7/73.
GOODWIN F.W. AFC. Born 8/2/24. Commd 23/5/63. Flt Lt 23/5/66. Retd PI 31/5/78.
GOODWIN G.J. Born 8/1/14. Commd 21/7/55. Flt Lt 27/1/59. Retd ENG 8/1/69.
GOODWIN J. Born 7/7/30. Commd 5/11/52. Flt Lt 1/3/61. Retd GD 7/7/85.
GOODWIN K.J. CBE AFC. Born 2/5/28. Commd 7/7/49. A Cdre 1/7/80. Retd GD 1/7/82.
GOODWIN M.F. Born 14/7/27. Commd 3/2/49. Flt Lt 3/8/52. Retd GD 29/8/65.
GOODWIN M.J. Born 2/5/38. Commd 3/3/57. Flt Lt 12/1/66. Retd GD 19/8/75.
GOODWIN M.J. Born 7/5/59. Commd 11/8/74. Flt Lt 11/8/78. Retd ADMIN 11/8/90.
GOODWIN N.P. Born 11/9/46. Commd 27/10/67. Fg Offr 11/9/69. Retd RGT 6/12/72.
GOODWIN P.M. Born 13/8/32. Commd 10/12/52. Flt Lt 15/11/61. Retd GD 1/3/65.
GOODWIN W.A. Born 20/1/18. Commd 20/4/54. Flt Lt 20/4/59. Retd ENG 1/5/64.
GOODWYN C.R. BA. Born 28/11/58. Commd 27/3/83. Flt Lt 27/6/86. Retd OPS SPT 27/3/99.
GOODYER G.C.D. MVO. Born 25/11/27. Commd 15/12/49. A Cdre 1/1/75. Retd GD 26/6/79.
GOOLD I.G. BA. Born 11/3/66. Commd 14/2/88. Flt Lt 14/8/90. Retd GD 14/7/01.
GOORNEY A.B. BSc MB ChB DIH DPM. Born 16/1/27. Commd 1/5/51. Wg Cdr 18/8/63. Retd MED 1/9/67.
GOOSE E.J.T. MA. Born 23/7/23. Commd 9/9/43. A Cdre 1/1/73. Retd ENG 23/3/78.
GOPSILL W.G. Born 2/6/32. Commd 17/7/58. Flt Lt 17/1/63. Retd GD 31/10/75.

GORDDARD R.C. Born 23/12/09. Commd 3/1/41. Flt Lt 8/1/45. Retd SUP 24/7/46. rtg Sqn Ldr
GORDINE G.A.P. Born 23/4/27. Commd 16/12/50. Sqn Ldr 1/1/66. Retd GD 16/10/76. Re-instated 12/11/79 to 17/9/84.
GORDON A.L. BSc MCMI. Born 22/7/43. Commd 6/9/65. Wg Cdr 1/1/91. Retd GD 2/4/93.
GORDON A.McP. MA. Born 18/10/52. Commd 11/11/71. Wg Cdr 1/7/94. Retd ADMIN 7/2/99.
GORDON A.T. BSc. Born 15/8/43. Commd 14/12/65. Flt Lt 28/1/67. Retd GD 15/8/81.
GORDON B. Born 30/6/49. Commd 5/5/88. Flt Lt 5/5/92. Retd ENGINEER 4/8/03.
GORDON C.R. MVO MCMI. Born 9/7/23. Commd 6/10/44. Gp Capt 1/1/68. Retd GD 29/1/76.
GORDON D.C. Born 4/4/23. Commd 5/12/42. Sqn Ldr 1/7/56. Retd GD 23/4/64.
GORDON D.F.M. Born 12/8/43. Commd 12/1/62. Sqn Ldr 1/7/78. Retd GD 1/4/90.
GORDON D.J. Born 21/3/25. Commd 25/9/45. Wg Cdr 1/1/64. Retd GD 2/7/68.
GORDON E.D. MA. Born 24/4/26. Commd 13/11/62. Sqn Ldr 13/5/64. Retd EDN 28/11/64.
GORDON E.N. Born 9/9/56. Commd 4/7/85. Fg Offr 4/1/88. Retd GD(G) 7/8/88.
GORDON E.R. AFC. Born 23/12/22. Commd 6/11/47. Flt Lt 27/5/54. Retd GD 14/10/61.
GORDON G.D. Born 10/8/48. Commd 1/6/72. Flt Lt 1/12/77. Retd GD 22/10/94.
GORDON J.A. CEng MIMechE MRAeS. Born 7/11/40. Commd 18/7/61. Flt Lt 15/4/66. Retd ENG 1/8/70.
GORDON K.D.M. CEng MIMechE MRAeS. Born 24/9/37. Commd 30/7/59. Wg Cdr 1/1/77. Retd ENG 20/2/88.
GORDON M.A. MBE DFC BA. Born 27/4/57. Commd 26/11/78. Wg Cdr 1/7/92. Retd GD 1/7/95.
GORDON M.H. Born 6/9/37. Commd 10/5/73. Flt Lt 10/5/78. Retd ENG 1/10/81.
GORDON P. Born 12/12/40. Commd 26/4/84. Flt Lt 26/4/88. Retd ENG 12/12/95.
GORDON R.W. Born 20/3/25. Commd 1/4/52. Sqn Ldr 1/1/62. Retd GD 20/7/80.
GORDON R.W.A. Born 29/3/42. Commd 4/10/63. Sqn Ldr 1/7/75. Retd GD 1/4/93.
GORDON W. MBE. Born 17/11/30. Commd 8/4/53. Sqn Ldr 1/7/62. Retd SUP 5/11/84.
GORDON W. Born 13/6/32. Commd 28/3/66. Flt Lt 4/5/72. Retd ADMIN 13/6/92.
GORDON W.H. MBE DFC. Born 16/4/22. Commd 5/9/42. Flt Lt 5/3/46. Retd ENG 31/3/77. rtg Sqn Ldr
GORDON-CUMMING A.R. Born 10/9/24. Commd 23/9/44. Gp Capt 1/7/63. Retd GD 16/11/69.
GORDON-HALL P.J. DFC. Born 16/12/20. Commd 12/6/39. Sqn Ldr 1/7/51. Retd GD 24/12/53.
GORDON-JOHNSON P. Born 11/11/44. Commd 12/7/63. Sqn Ldr 1/7/74. Retd GD 1/12/79.
GORDON-JONES Sir Edward KCB CBE DSO DFC. Born 31/8/14. Commd 7/10/35. AM 1/7/67. Retd GD 22/8/69.
GORDON-SMITH G.E. Born 9/7/35. Commd 10/4/62. Flt Lt 10/4/62. Retd RGT 6/7/68.
GORE P.C. Born 26/4/20. Commd 26/8/43. Flt Lt 15/12/49. Retd GD(G) 26/1/71.
GORMAN A. BSc. Born 23/10/56. Commd 17/1/82. Flt Lt 17/4/85. Retd OPS SPT 17/1/98.
GORMAN E.B.T. Born 6/5/37. Commd 30/9/58. Sqn Ldr 1/7/72. Retd GD 1/7/75.
GORMAN K. MBCS MIDPM. Born 31/12/47. Commd 2/8/68. Sqn Ldr 1/7/81. Retd GD(G) 31/12/85.
GORMAN M.J. Born 20/8/49. Commd 27/7/89. Flt Lt 27/7/93. Retd ADMIN 14/3/97.
GORNALL J.H. MCMI. Born 14/2/39. Commd 7/6/68. Sqn Ldr 1/7/79. Retd ENG 14/2/89.
GORRINGE-SMITH P.L. Born 16/5/24. Commd 10/8/45. Flt Lt 10/8/51. Retd SUP 16/5/62.
GORTON S.H. Born 11/10/57. Commd 14/9/75. Sqn Ldr 1/7/89. Retd GD 2/1/97.
GOSLING J.R. Born 24/6/61. Commd 24/4/80. Sqn Ldr 1/1/94. Retd GD 24/6/99.
GOSLING S.J. Born 24/11/47. Commd 10/3/65. Wg Cdr 1/1/87. Retd GD 25/11/90.
GOSLYN H.I. Born 30/3/42. Commd 26/11/64. Fg Offr 26/11/64. Retd GD 30/6/69.
GOSNEY G.A. Born 5/11/19. Commd 5/11/43. Flt Lt 5/5/47. Retd GD 21/12/53.
GOSS A.R. MBE. Born 16/5/26. Commd 26/12/51. Sqn Ldr 1/7/75. Retd GD 16/5/84.
GOSS C.R.J. Born 22/12/49. Commd 3/10/69. Wg Cdr 1/1/87. Retd SUP 1/1/90.
GOSS E.J. Born 17/5/25. Commd 3/2/49. Wg Cdr 1/7/71. Retd SUP 17/5/80.
GOSS J.P. BA. Born 7/2/49. Commd 6/7/80. Flt Lt 6/10/83. Retd GD 31/3/94.
GOSS M.E. Born 8/10/25. Commd 25/5/50. Wg Cdr 1/1/75. Retd ENG 2/9/77.
GOSS T.A. BEng CEng MIEE. Born 26/6/47. Commd 13/2/72. Sqn Ldr 1/1/84. Retd ENG 13/2/91.
GOSSLAND D.M. Born 20/5/21. Commd 23/1/41. Flt Lt 28/3/47. Retd GD 31/10/56.
GOSTELOW T.F. Born 19/2/23. Commd 4/6/64. Flt Lt 4/6/67. Retd GD 6/4/68.
GOSTLING A.E. BSc. Born 2/10/29. Commd 24/9/52. Sqn Ldr 24/3/63. Retd EDN 24/9/68.
GOSWELL G.A. Born 25/7/32. Commd 7/5/52. Flt Lt 1/10/67. Retd GD 25/7/70.
GOTHARD A. Born 2/9/31. Commd 7/6/68. Flt Lt 7/6/73. Retd ENG 19/6/93.
GOTHARD E.L. MBE. Born 11/2/39. Commd 13/12/60. Flt Lt 15/2/65. Retd GD 6/2/94.
GOTTS S. Born 4/1/13. Commd 1/11/56. Flt Lt 1/11/59. Retd SEC 4/1/68.
GOUCHER D. Born 7/10/36. Commd 29/7/58. Gp Capt 1/7/79. Retd ADMIN 22/9/87.
GOUCK R.F. MMS. Born 10/5/41. Commd 27/3/70. Sqn Ldr 1/7/79. Retd SUP 1/2/83.
GOUGH D.C. Born 23/9/45. Commd 13/8/82. Sqn Ldr 1/1/90. Retd ENG 1/1/93.
GOUGH E.C. Born 29/7/23. Commd 7/5/43. Sqn Ldr 1/1/54. Retd GD 29/7/66.
GOUGH H.G. Born 17/4/22. Commd 8/11/46. Flt Lt 9/6/52. Retd GD 30/11/60.
GOUGH J.W. BSc. Born 2/4/48. Commd 4/1/68. Flt Lt 22/6/71. Retd GD 17/2/81.
GOUGH P.D. Born 1/3/24. Commd 10/12/43. Flt Lt 29/6/55. Retd GD(G) 9/12/65.
GOUGH V.A. AFC MCIPD MCMI. Born 14/12/21. Commd 4/4/44. Wg Cdr 1/7/67. Retd GD 14/12/76.
GOUGH V.R. MCMI. Born 29/12/33. Commd 24/6/71. Flt Lt 24/6/76. Retd ENG 1/10/79.
GOULBORN M.C. Born 12/2/59. Commd 2/2/78. Flt Lt 17/6/84. Retd SUP 31/8/86.
GOULBORN P.A.G. Born 7/8/24. Commd 30/5/69. Sqn Ldr 1/7/76. Retd GD(G) 7/8/79.
GOULD C.E. Born 23/5/38. Commd 3/7/56. Gp Capt 1/7/81. Retd GD 1/2/87.

GOULD D.J. Born 1/4/09. Commd 18/12/40. Fg Offr 1/10/41. Retd SEC 20/8/46. rtg Flt Lt
GOULD E.A. Born 24/7/47. Commd 1/4/66. Sqn Ldr 1/1/84. Retd GD 1/1/87.
GOULD J.C. MBE. Born 19/5/61. Commd 17/1/85. Sqn Ldr 1/1/99. Retd SUP 1/1/02.
GOULD M.B. LLB. Born 1/8/51. Commd 13/9/71. Sqn Ldr 1/7/86. Retd ADMIN 6/9/89.
GOULD R.H. CBE MA FRAeS. Born 22/1/45. Commd 5/1/66. A Cdre 1/1/92. Retd GD 22/1/00.
GOULD R.J. Born 7/2/15. Commd 2/8/45. Flt Lt 18/5/56. Retd CAT 10/3/66.
GOULD T.D. Born 24/4/41. Commd 10/9/70. Sqn Ldr 1/1/87. Retd SUP 24/4/96.
GOULDEN A.A. Born 30/8/37. Commd 4/3/71. Sqn Ldr 1/1/79. Retd SUP 8/10/88.
GOULDING B.S. Born 16/2/57. Commd 26/9/90. Flt Lt 13/5/95. Retd MED(T) 12/10/97.
GOULDING G. BSc. Born 4/2/35. Commd 9/8/57. Wg Cdr 1/1/81. Retd ADMIN 20/6/88.
GOULDING N.B. Born 27/11/43. Commd 17/5/63. Sqn Ldr 1/7/00. Retd FLY(P) 31/3/03.
GOULT J.P. BSc. Born 14/3/52. Commd 27/7/75. Flt Lt 27/10/76. Retd GD 27/7/87.
GOULTHORPE P.J. CBE MA CEng MRAeS. Born 20/4/30. Commd 6/10/53. A Cdre 1/7/78. Retd ENG 13/2/84.
GOURD D.A. MBE. Born 21/6/22. Commd 27/10/67. Flt Lt 27/10/70. Retd SY 23/6/82.
GOVAN M.G. Born 1/7/21. Commd 30/5/45. Flt Offr 16/12/51. Retd SUP 1/10/59.
GOVER P.D.L. AFC BSc FRAeS FCMI. Born 17/7/38. Commd 28/11/60. A Cdre 1/1/87. Retd GD 17/7/93.
GOW D.G. BSc. Born 21/6/63. Commd 14/4/85. Sqn Ldr 1/1/99. Retd FLY(P) 31/5/05.
GOW F.J. Born 17/10/21. Commd 26/5/60. Sqn Ldr 1/7/72. Retd ENG 17/12/76.
GOW J.A. LDSRCS. Born 13/8/22. Commd 22/8/46. Sqn Ldr 22/4/54. Retd DEL 2/3/57.
GOWER S.D. Born 27/5/57. Commd 26/4/84. Flt Lt 11/8/89. Retd ENG 31/3/94.
GOWER-JONES J.E. BA MCMI. Born 16/6/20. Commd 17/4/47. Wg Cdr 1/1/68. Retd SUP 17/4/75.
GOWERS A.E. BSc CEng MIEE. Born 2/1/50. Commd 4/3/74. Sqn Ldr 1/7/84. Retd ENG 4/3/90.
GOWERS C.J. Born 28/11/53. Commd 5/7/73. Wg Cdr 1/7/91. Retd GD 9/5/95.
GOWERS C.S. Born 20/12/52. Commd 11/8/77. Sqn Ldr 1/7/93. Retd GD 31/12/93.
GOWERS K.G. Born 12/6/31. Commd 1/4/53. Sqn Ldr 1/7/69. Retd GD 12/6/91.
GOWING A.J. Born 28/11/40. Commd 14/1/63. Flt Lt 20/5/67. Retd GD 1/3/73.
GOWING A.R. IEng MIIE. Born 18/4/46. Commd 30/8/84. Sqn Ldr 1/1/98. Retd ENG 18/10/02.
GOWING D. Born 5/11/20. Commd 26/11/43. Flt Lt 19/11/53. Retd GD 7/7/67.
GOWING K. MA CEng MIMechE MRAeS. Born 14/5/45. Commd 28/9/64. Gp Capt 1/7/91. Retd ENG 14/5/00.
GOWING W.H. BSc. Born 12/2/50. Commd 15/9/69. Flt Lt 15/10/72. Retd GD 2/4/87.
GOWLING B.J. MBE. Born 23/11/31. Commd 21/5/52. Wg Cdr 1/1/81. Retd GD 23/11/89.
GOWRING R.J. CBE. Born 29/6/40. Commd 16/1/60. Gp Capt 1/1/88. Retd GD 29/6/95.
GOY G.S.W. MSc BSc (Eur Ing) CEng FRAeS. Born 14/2/32. Commd 19/8/54. Wg Cdr 17/2/71. Retd ADMIN 4/12/76.
GRACE E.T. BA. Born 27/4/48. Commd 25/2/88. Flt Lt 25/2/90. Retd ENG 25/2/96.
GRACE I.B. BSc. Born 18/2/57. Commd 26/11/78. Flt Lt 26/2/80. Retd ENG 26/11/87.
GRACE J.W. Born 10/6/35. Commd 14/10/71. Sqn Ldr 1/7/89. Retd GD 1/7/92.
GRACE R. Born 17/1/46. Commd 4/7/85. Flt Lt 4/8/89. Retd ENG 31/10/98.
GRACEY D.G.T. BSocSc. Born 24/4/64. Commd 22/6/86. Sqn Ldr 1/1/98. Retd ADMIN 22/6/02.
GRACIE K.M.R. BSc. Born 3/8/42. Commd 15/7/63. Sqn Ldr 1/1/73. Retd ENG 13/9/75.
GRADLEY J.A. Born 25/3/36. Commd 8/1/76. Sqn Ldr 1/1/86. Retd ENG 11/11/88.
GRAEME-COOK B.G. Born 1/3/60. Commd 4/9/81. Sqn Ldr 1/1/95. Retd GD 1/5/98.
GRAFHAM A.C. Born 9/3/35. Commd 27/10/54. Flt Lt 1/3/61. Retd GD 9/3/93.
GRAFTON G. MBE. Born 1/3/46. Commd 17/1/69. Sqn Ldr 1/7/79. Retd GD 24/9/84.
GRAFTON J.E. Born 6/7/66. Commd 25/2/88. Flt Lt 25/8/93. Retd FLY(N) 22/7/04.
GRAHAM A. Born 21/2/44. Commd 31/10/63. Flt Lt 17/12/72. Retd ADMIN 8/1/84.
GRAHAM A.R. Born 11/4/41. Commd 6/9/63. Sqn Ldr 1/1/88. Retd GD 11/4/96.
GRAHAM B.S. CEng MRAeS. Born 31/1/39. Commd 23/3/66. Wg Cdr 1/1/78. Retd ENG 1/7/83.
GRAHAM D. Born 11/8/30. Commd 24/10/51. Wg Cdr 1/1/79. Retd GD(G) 1/1/81.
GRAHAM D. Born 16/10/46. Commd 23/10/86. Sqn Ldr 1/7/95. Retd ENG 17/10/96.
GRAHAM D.F. Born 29/5/31. Commd 17/3/55. Flt Lt 17/9/59. Retd GD 30/7/74.
GRAHAM D.H.M. OBE. Born 27/9/12. Commd 6/1/36. Gp Capt 1/1/57. Retd SUP 6/10/61.
GRAHAM D.J. Born 27/5/31. Commd 26/3/52. Flt Lt 1/10/57. Retd GD 27/5/69.
GRAHAM D.M. Born 20/1/46. Commd 12/7/68. Sqn Ldr 1/7/81. Retd GD 14/9/96.
GRAHAM E.C. CEng MIEE. Born 5/3/39. Commd 28/7/60. Sqn Ldr 1/1/71. Retd ENG 5/3/77.
GRAHAM G.G. DFM MCMI. Born 26/4/17. Commd 20/5/43. Flt Lt 20/11/46. Retd SEC 3/4/71.
GRAHAM G.W. Born 12/12/32. Commd 7/5/52. Flt Lt 13/4/60. Retd GD 9/10/86.
GRAHAM H. MSc BSc. Born 8/8/64. Commd 1/6/94. Sqn Ldr 1/7/98. Retd ENGINEER 14/8/04.
GRAHAM I.J.A. BSc. Born 16/9/48. Commd 28/2/72. Flt Lt 28/11/72. Retd GD 30/9/84.
GRAHAM I.S. Born 19/5/47. Commd 23/3/67. Flt Lt 23/9/72. Retd GD 7/12/76.
GRAHAM J. Born 3/6/38. Commd 28/7/59. Wg Cdr 1/1/75. Retd GD 9/12/85.
GRAHAM K.H. Born 24/10/37. Commd 8/12/61. Flt Lt 10/2/67. Retd GD 24/10/75.
GRAHAM K.M. Born 6/2/50. Commd 31/7/70. Flt Lt 31/7/73. Retd GD 6/2/88.
GRAHAM K.P. BSc. Born 3/11/59. Commd 20/3/79. Flt Lt 15/10/82. Retd GD 3/11/97.
GRAHAM M.B. Born 3/7/46. Commd 21/3/74. Sqn Ldr 1/7/81. Retd GD 3/7/94.
GRAHAM M.G.C. Born 25/8/63. Commd 8/9/83. Sqn Ldr 1/7/95. Retd GD 15/12/00.
GRAHAM N.P. Born 21/4/33. Commd 9/12/53. Flt Lt 16/8/61. Retd GD 26/5/72.

GRAHAM P.J. Born 30/11/46. Commd 29/1/87. Flt Lt 29/1/91. Retd SY 1/10/93.
GRAHAM R. Born 28/4/47. Commd 21/1/66. Sqn Ldr 1/1/81. Retd GD 4/9/97.
GRAHAM R.H. Born 21/2/35. Commd 11/11/53. Flt Lt 15/4/59. Retd GD 29/4/72.
GRAHAM-CUMMING A.N. MB BS MRCGP MRCS MFOM LRCP DAvMed MRAeS. Born 17/12/48. Commd 23/1/72.
Gp Capt 1/1/98. Retd MED 6/8/00.
GRAINGE R.J. CEng MRAeS MIMechE. Born 20/11/30. Commd 16/6/55. Sqn Ldr 1/1/65. Retd ENG 1/1/72.
GRAINGER B.J. Born 2/6/37. Commd 18/5/55. Sqn Ldr 1/7/68. Retd GD 1/8/87.
GRAINGER D. Born 24/7/43. Commd 23/11/78. Flt Lt 23/11/82. Retd ENG 24/3/89.
GRAINGER P.D. Born 12/11/49. Commd 6/11/80. Sqn Ldr 1/1/88. Retd ENG 1/1/91.
GRAND-SCRUTTON J. Born 29/7/37. Commd 10/9/63. Sqn Ldr 1/7/84. Retd ENG 29/7/95.
GRANDY N. BA. Born 5/10/54. Commd 22/1/77. Flt Lt 2/4/78. Retd GD 2/1/89.
GRANGE M. Born 24/7/71. Commd 26/9/90. Fg Offr 26/9/92. Retd GD 30/3/94.
GRANGE M.J. Born 2/6/38. Commd 18/2/60. Wg Cdr 1/1/89. Retd GD 5/2/93.
GRANGE R.J. Born 10/3/46. Commd 28/4/67. Flt Lt 28/10/72. Retd GD 27/4/76.
GRANGER D.W. MBE BSc MCMI. Born 5/9/33. Commd 20/9/57. Sqn Ldr 20/3/67. Retd EDN 1/1/74.
GRANGER H.J. CEng MIEE. Born 10/6/22. Commd 16/1/47. Wg Cdr 1/1/67. Retd ENG 30/3/77.
GRANT B.C.E. Born 6/8/44. Commd 18/11/66. Wg Cdr 1/1/95. Retd OPS SPT 6/8/99.
GRANT B.P. MCIPS MCMI. Born 19/5/35. Commd 7/3/56. Gp Capt 1/1/81. Retd SUP 3/4/82.
GRANT D. MCIPS MCIT MILT. Born 7/7/44. Commd 9/2/66. Gp Capt 1/7/93. Retd SUP 7/7/94.
GRANT D.I.G. ACMA. Born 24/8/36. Commd 27/8/64. Sqn Ldr 1/7/71. Retd SEC 2/10/79. rtg Wg Cdr
GRANT H.J. Born 9/5/14. Commd 1/1/45. Sqn Ldr 1/1/63. Retd SEC 9/5/69.
GRANT H.S. MB ChB MFOM DRCOG DAvMed MRAeS. Born 23/8/47. Commd 29/7/68. Gp Capt 1/7/95.
Retd MED 30/4/96.
GRANT I. Born 11/4/41. Commd 3/8/62. Flt Lt 11/10/66. Retd GD 11/4/79.
GRANT I.H. Born 26/10/22. Commd 26/10/43. Sqn Ldr 1/1/71. Retd GD 12/4/74.
GRANT J.A. MBE MCMI. Born 27/1/18. Commd 2/4/53. Wg Cdr 28/8/70. Retd MED(T) 27/1/73.
GRANT J.C. IEng FIEE. Born 7/12/38. Commd 31/1/80. Sqn Ldr 1/7/89. Retd ENG 7/12/93.
GRANT K.R. Born 26/11/38. Commd 3/10/69. Wg Cdr 1/7/87. Retd MED(SEC) 3/7/89.
GRANT L.J. Born 10/6/22. Commd 24/3/44. Flt Lt 24/9/47. Retd GD 31/3/74.
GRANT N.G. Born 16/10/31. Commd 20/11/52. Wg Cdr 1/1/79. Retd ADMIN 16/10/86.
GRANT P. Born 27/7/30. Commd 26/3/57. Sqn Ldr 1/1/74. Retd GD(G) 27/7/85.
GRANT P.A. Born 24/5/25. Commd 6/10/60. Flt Lt 6/10/65. Retd GD(G) 5/10/74.
GRANT P.R.M. Born 12/5/52. Commd 4/2/71. Flt Lt 4/8/76. Retd GD 4/8/90.
GRANT P.W. Born 20/7/25. Commd 21/6/56. Flt Lt 16/8/61. Retd GD 5/6/70.
GRANT R.G.H. Born 29/10/20. Commd 4/6/64. Flt Lt 4/6/69. Retd ENG 29/5/71.
GRANT T. DFC. Born 12/7/20. Commd 25/6/48. Flt Lt 16/10/57. Retd GD(G) 21/10/66.
GRANT T.A. MSc BA. Born 3/10/49. Commd 24/8/72. Sqn Ldr 1/1/85. Retd SUP 1/4/99.
GRANT T.J. BSc CEng MRAeS. Born 18/6/47. Commd 18/9/66. Sqn Ldr 1/7/78. Retd ENG 1/10/87.
GRANTHAM A.R.A. Born 27/6/46. Commd 10/12/65. Flt Lt 10/6/71. Retd GD 1/2/73.
GRANVILLE B. MCMI. Born 15/7/43. Commd 21/1/77. Wg Cdr 1/7/91. Retd ADMIN 31/3/94.
GRANVILLE-MARTIN H. Born 1/7/12. Commd 7/11/49. Flt Lt 7/11/49. Retd SUP 16/6/58.
GRANVILLE-WHITE C. CBE. Born 3/7/41. Commd 31/7/62. Gp Capt 1/7/87. Retd GD 3/7/96.
GRATER C.L. MHCIMA. Born 3/6/39. Commd 23/6/60. Sqn Ldr 1/7/71. Retd ADMIN 3/6/77.
GRATTAN R.C. Born 19/1/42. Commd 17/7/61. Flt Lt 26/7/67. Retd GD 28/8/76.
GRATTAN R.F. BA. Born 21/8/31. Commd 1/11/50. Gp Capt 1/7/78. Retd GD 30/6/79.
GRATTAN W.J. Born 24/12/39. Commd 1/11/79. Sqn Ldr 1/1/89. Retd SUP 1/1/94.
GRATTON J.B. Born 5/2/33. Commd 15/12/53. Sqn Ldr 1/7/67. Retd GD 5/2/71.
GRAVELEY A.F. Born 22/4/45. Commd 14/2/63. Wg Cdr 1/7/88. Retd SY 1/7/93.
GRAVELL S.W. Born 7/2/32. Commd 4/1/53. Flt Lt 3/6/58. Retd GD 7/2/70.
GRAVES A.W. Born 2/6/52. Commd 16/6/88. Flt Lt 16/6/90. Retd GD 14/3/97.
GRAVES J.R.C.H. OBE. Born 15/4/22. Commd 27/4/41. Wg Cdr 1/7/60. Retd GD 6/7/68.
GRAVES O.W. FCA. Born 27/6/35. Commd 5/5/60. Flt Lt 5/5/66. Retd SEC 26/10/75.
GRAVES S.C. Born 19/4/53. Commd 7/6/73. Flt Lt 7/12/78. Retd GD 1/7/87.
GRAY A.J. Born 24/4/27. Commd 28/7/49. Wg Cdr 1/1/68. Retd ADMIN 20/5/82.
GRAY A.R. Born 15/3/47. Commd 30/4/81. Sqn Ldr 1/7/88. Retd ADMIN 1/7/91.
GRAY A.R.N. Born 26/10/46. Commd 28/11/74. Flt Lt 28/11/79. Retd ADMIN 26/10/86.
GRAY A.S. Born 2/7/17. Commd 29/5/46. Sqn Ldr 1/7/57. Retd SEC 31/8/63.
GRAY C.R. BSc. Born 1/1/39. Commd 10/11/64. Sqn Ldr 30/4/73. Retd ADMIN 15/10/90.
GRAY C.W. Born 26/4/23. Commd 1/3/62. Flt Lt 1/3/65. Retd GD 26/4/78.
GRAY D. BA. Born 27/9/43. Commd 6/5/83. Wg Cdr 1/7/94. Retd ADMIN 14/3/96.
GRAY D.M. Born 12/10/64. Commd 8/6/84. Sqn Ldr 1/1/99. Retd FLY(P) 1/8/03.
GRAY D.S. Born 13/6/39. Commd 16/12/65. Flt Lt 16/6/72. Retd SEC 19/6/78.
GRAY D.V.M. Born 14/2/10. Commd 30/4/41. Sqn Offr 1/1/50. Retd SEC 17/2/59. rtg Wg Offr
GRAY E.G. Born 3/10/30. Commd 10/12/52. Flt Lt 5/5/58. Retd GD 3/10/68.
GRAY G. Born 13/9/54. Commd 16/12/82. Flt Lt 16/12/84. Retd GD 13/9/94.
GRAY G. MBE. Born 2/9/24. Commd 8/6/44. Sqn Ldr 1/4/56. Retd GD 2/9/73.

GRAY G. BSc. Born 16/5/40. Commd 22/10/63. Sqn Ldr 23/2/73. Retd ADMIN 16/5/95.
GRAY G. DFC AFC. Born 23/8/16. Commd 8/5/42. Sqn Ldr 1/7/50. Retd GD 19/12/51.
GRAY G.B. Born 2/11/49. Commd 25/2/72. Sqn Ldr 1/7/83. Retd GD 2/11/87.
GRAY H. BA. Born 3/12/18. Commd 3/8/48. Sqn Ldr 3/5/54. Retd EDN 15/9/70.
GRAY H.B. Born 26/9/26. Commd 7/6/48. Flt Lt 1/6/52. Retd SY 26/10/77.
GRAY J. Born 27/7/23. Commd 4/10/56. Flt Lt 4/4/60. Retd GD 5/9/71.
GRAY J. Born 13/10/11. Commd 10/6/42. Sqn Offr 1/1/60. Retd SEC 16/11/66.
GRAY J. Born 6/6/41. Commd 4/5/72. Sqn Ldr 1/7/88. Retd ENG 7/10/91.
GRAY J.C. MSc BSc BDS. Born 10/7/33. Commd 27/1/56. Wg Cdr 8/10/73. Retd DEL 7/5/85.
GRAY J.T.W. DFC. Born 4/1/19. Commd 21/12/43. Flt Lt 26/5/55. Retd GD(G) 25/1/63.
GRAY M. Born 1/7/19. Commd 2/9/42. Flt Offr 20/5/48. Retd SEC 11/8/50.
GRAY M.C. Born 12/12/27. Commd 8/7/54. Flt Lt 8/1/58. Retd GD 12/12/86.
GRAY M.J. AFC. Born 16/8/44. Commd 12/7/63. Wg Cdr 1/1/85. Retd GD 16/8/88.
GRAY P. DFC. Born 3/10/24. Commd 5/12/51. Flt Lt 5/6/56. Retd GD 12/8/68.
GRAY P.B. MHCIMA. Born 20/2/31. Commd 25/2/64. Sqn Ldr 1/1/77. Retd ADMIN 20/2/89.
GRAY P.J. Born 25/9/40. Commd 19/9/59. Gp Capt 1/1/85. Retd GD(G) 1/9/89.
GRAY P.L. Born 9/1/32. Commd 14/4/53. Gp Capt 1/1/76. Retd GD 28/5/87.
GRAY R. Born 13/3/38. Commd 2/10/58. Sqn Ldr 1/1/73. Retd GD 11/5/88.
GRAY R.J. BSc. Born 2/3/72. Commd 9/10/94. Fg Offr 9/10/93. Retd GD 17/4/98.
GRAY R.K. MIEH. Born 4/8/29. Commd 5/11/52. Wg Cdr 5/5/70. Retd ADMIN 1/8/78.
GRAY R.W. Born 1/9/21. Commd 16/7/45. Flt Lt 27/5/54. Retd GD 1/9/76.
GRAY T.L. Born 21/8/21. Commd 3/5/56. Flt Lt 3/5/62. Retd SEC 30/11/67.
GRAY W.A. Born 26/9/26. Commd 16/7/52. Flt Lt 12/5/62. Retd GD 26/9/69.
GRAY-WALLIS H.F. Born 1/8/50. Commd 1/8/69. Wg Cdr 1/7/92. Retd OPS SPT 3/8/01.
GRAYDON G.O. OBE. Born 10/1/30. Commd 26/4/50. Gp Capt 1/1/80. Retd GD 30/4/84.
GRAYSON R.J. Born 23/8/40. Commd 21/12/62. Flt Lt 21/6/68. Retd GD 10/12/91.
GREALY P.G.R. Born 9/11/23. Commd 18/6/43. Sqn Ldr 1/1/54. Retd GD 9/11/72.
GREATOREX M. Born 16/7/55. Commd 27/1/77. Wg Cdr 1/7/96. Retd GD 10/4/04.
GREAVES A.J. BA. Born 23/11/51. Commd 1/6/83. Flt Lt 15/10/76. Retd ADMIN 1/4/81. Re-instated 1/6/83.
    Sqn Ldr 1/7/87. Retd ADMIN 23/1/91.
GREAVES C.G.R. CEng MRAeS. Born 28/11/40. Commd 28/1/60. Wg Cdr 1/7/79. Retd ENG 28/11/95.
GREAVES J.R. Born 27/5/19. Commd 14/1/43. Flt Lt 14/7/47. Retd SEC 27/5/69.
GREAVES R.B. MCMI. Born 15/8/35. Commd 4/2/71. Flt Lt 4/2/73. Retd SUP 4/2/79.
GREEN A. Born 4/2/41. Commd 19/12/61. Wg Cdr 1/1/79. Retd GD 1/1/82.
GREEN A.J. Born 4/7/31. Commd 27/2/52. Flt Lt 27/2/56. Retd GD 4/7/69.
GREEN A.J. LLM MB BS MRCPath MRCS LRCP. Born 5/4/50. Commd 14/5/78. Wg Cdr 27/2/89. Retd MED 14/9/96.
GREEN A.J. Born 28/12/57. Commd 18/10/81. Sqn Ldr 1/1/91. Retd ENG 10/5/99.
GREEN A.N. BA. Born 29/9/54. Commd 11/5/76. Wg Cdr 1/1/92. Retd MED(SEC) 14/3/96.
GREEN A.P. Born 18/3/59. Commd 19/10/80. Sqn Ldr 1/7/90. Retd GD(G) 18/3/97.
GREEN A.R. Born 9/7/36. Commd 24/2/67. Flt Lt 24/2/73. Retd ADMIN 3/4/76.
GREEN B.B. BSc CEng MIMechE MRAeS MCMI. Born 16/4/34. Commd 23/9/55. Wg Cdr 1/7/76. Retd ENG 4/10/78.
GREEN B.N. Born 27/4/28. Commd 11/4/63. Sqn Ldr 1/7/84. Retd ENG 1/9/86.
GREEN B.W. Born 7/9/15. Commd 1/4/45. Sqn Ldr 1/1/54. Retd PRT 5/1/64.
GREEN C.L.D. Born 4/10/34. Commd 19/12/54. Flt Lt 9/2/68. Retd GD 15/5/85.
GREEN D.A. Born 29/10/46. Commd 18/8/67. Sqn Ldr 1/7/83. Retd SUP 3/7/00.
GREEN D.D.G. Born 6/6/23. Commd 20/10/43. Flt Lt 14/11/56. Retd GD 28/5/67.
GREEN D.E. CEng FIEE MRAeS. Born 5/2/21. Commd 25/8/60. Flt Lt 25/8/65. Retd ENG 26/6/71.
GREEN D.G.P. Born 27/7/51. Commd 30/1/75. Sqn Ldr 1/1/93. Retd GD(G) 14/3/96.
GREEN D.J. CEng MRAeS. Born 23/12/39. Commd 17/7/62. Sqn Ldr 1/1/72. Retd ENG 23/12/77.
GREEN D.J. FCMI. Born 29/10/22. Commd 10/7/43. Gp Capt 1/1/72. Retd GD 29/10/77.
GREEN D.L. Born 21/2/29. Commd 15/2/51. Flt Lt 15/8/54. Retd GD 21/2/84.
GREEN D.R. OBE. Born 17/9/42. Commd 30/7/63. Wg Cdr 1/1/78. Retd GD 31/12/85.
GREEN D.W. Born 22/12/38. Commd 17/5/63. Flt Lt 7/6/67. Retd GD 22/12/76.
GREEN D.W. BA. Born 2/6/33. Commd 9/8/57. Sqn Ldr 9/2/65. Retd ADMIN 23/8/89.
GREEN D.W.J. BSc. Born 18/7/58. Commd 29/11/81. Sqn Ldr 1/1/95. Retd SY 13/1/96.
GREEN E. Born 7/2/35. Commd 9/6/54. Flt Lt 9/12/59. Retd GD 7/2/72.
GREEN G.N. Born 17/5/47. Commd 2/8/68. Sqn Ldr 1/7/89. Retd ENG 17/3/02.
GREEN G.P. BSc. Born 15/9/58. Commd 28/12/80. Flt Lt 1/11/84. Retd RGT 11/5/91.
GREEN J. MCMI. Born 8/7/32. Commd 8/10/70. Sqn Ldr 27/2/81. Retd MED(SEC) 11/7/84.
GREEN J. BSc. Born 6/9/44. Commd 15/7/66. Sqn Ldr 1/7/79. Retd ENG 6/9/82.
GREEN J.B. BA. Born 3/10/68. Commd 8/2/90. Plt Offr 19/11/87. Retd GD(G) 15/1/93.
GREEN J.D. Born 17/3/44. Commd 25/6/66. Flt Lt 15/10/72. Retd GD(G) 17/3/82.
GREEN J.E. Born 9/4/34. Commd 22/1/57. Sqn Ldr 1/7/76. Retd GD 19/4/94.
GREEN J.H. BSc(Econ). Born 14/4/54. Commd 16/9/73. Wg Cdr 1/1/91. Retd ADMIN 10/1/97.
GREEN K.W.J. Born 22/6/44. Commd 28/10/76. Wg Cdr 1/7/94. Retd ADMIN 22/6/99.
GREEN M.D. Born 27/10/60. Commd 18/6/84. Wg Cdr 1/7/01. Retd GD 27/10/04.

GREEN M.J. DPhysEd. Born 4/9/39. Commd 1/9/64. Wg Cdr 1/1/80. Retd ADMIN 1/7/88.
GREEN M.K. MBE. Born 10/10/47. Commd 7/6/68. Flt Lt 10/10/74. Retd GD(G) 1/10/90.
GREEN M.R. OBE. Born 8/7/14. Commd 8/7/42. Wg Cdr 1/7/61. Retd SEC 14/7/69.
GREEN N.B. MBA BA. Born 15/4/63. Commd 21/4/93. Sqn Ldr 1/7/98. Retd ENG 11/1/03.
GREEN N.E. Born 12/5/27. Commd 10/10/63. Sqn Ldr 1/7/77. Retd GD 12/5/82.
GREEN P.F. Born 7/8/30. Commd 25/5/50. Wg Cdr 1/1/81. Retd ADMIN 1/2/85.
GREEN P.F. DPhysEd. Born 28/9/39. Commd 7/6/39. Sqn Ldr 1/1/79. Retd ADMIN 13/2/84.
GREEN P.G. Born 24/9/41. Commd 2/6/77. Flt Lt 2/6/81. Retd GD 11/8/92.
GREEN P.L. Born 11/11/31. Commd 1/3/62. Sqn Ldr 1/7/74. Retd ENG 15/12/84.
GREEN P.O.V. AFC FCMI. Born 16/6/20. Commd 20/8/38. A Cdre 1/1/67. Retd GD 1/12/73.
GREEN P.S. Born 31/7/42. Commd 13/3/80. Flt Lt 13/3/83. Retd GD 1/11/89.
GREEN R. BA. Born 23/6/32. Commd 16/9/71. Sqn Ldr 16/9/78. Retd ADMIN 16/9/80.
GREEN R.A. Born 16/5/47. Commd 9/8/79. Sqn Ldr 1/7/87. Retd ADMIN 1/7/90.
GREEN R.A. Born 2/12/19. Commd 2/8/42. Flt Lt 10/11/55. Retd SEC 20/12/68.
GREEN R.A.S. Born 3/8/51. Commd 2/3/80. Flt Lt 2/3/84. Retd ENG 2/3/96.
GREEN R.C.E. Born 3/4/44. Commd 25/3/64. Flt Lt 29/10/69. Retd GD 2/6/76.
GREEN R.D. Born 28/12/60. Commd 30/4/81. Sqn Ldr 1/1/94. Retd SUP 28/12/98.
GREEN R.E. CEng MIEE MRAeS. Born 15/7/40. Commd 18/7/61. Sqn Ldr 1/1/71. Retd ENG 15/7/78.
GREEN R.J. Born 28/5/23. Commd 17/2/44. Flt Lt 17/8/47. Retd ENG 28/5/56.
GREEN R.J.C. MRIN MCMI. Born 27/1/40. Commd 10/2/59. Wg Cdr 1/1/81. Retd GD 27/1/95.
GREEN R.M. Born 16/12/43. Commd 30/7/64. Flt Lt 28/11/70. Retd GD(G) 14/3/96.
GREEN R.T. Born 26/6/32. Commd 25/11/53. Flt Lt 25/5/59. Retd GD 26/6/70.
GREEN R.W. Born 11/12/38. Commd 25/2/82. Flt Lt 25/2/87. Retd ADMIN 11/12/93.
GREEN S.C. MSc MCGI MRAeS. Born 4/6/63. Commd 28/2/85. Flt Lt 28/8/90. Retd GD 4/6/01.
GREEN S.D.J. BA. Born 10/11/53. Commd 2/9/73. Flt Lt 15/10/77. Retd GD 15/7/88.
GREEN S.J. Born 2/7/47. Commd 28/2/70. Flt Lt 28/2/72. Retd GD 25/5/76.
GREEN S.J. BSc (Eur Ing) CEng CPhys MInstP MRAeS. Born 13/6/54. Commd 30/9/73. Sqn Ldr 1/1/89.
  Retd ENG 9/8/92.
GREEN W. Born 16/10/21. Commd 29/4/45. Flt Lt 25/2/54. Retd GD(G) 16/2/62.
GREEN W.L. OBE DFC. Born 24/5/23. Commd 15/1/44. Gp Capt 1/1/71. Retd GD 2/11/75.
GREEN W.S. AFC. Born 12/4/21. Commd 12/7/45. Flt Lt 4/1/51. Retd GD 12/4/64.
GREENAWAY P.C. Born 21/2/40. Commd 22/3/63. Flt Lt 22/9/68. Retd GD 2/10/78.
GREENE B.A. BSc. Born 26/9/47. Commd 18/9/66. Flt Lt 15/4/72. Retd GD 26/8/74.
GREENFIELD M.D. BSc. Born 25/1/61. Commd 26/9/82. Flt Lt 26/12/83. Retd GD 14/2/86.
GREENFIELD N. MSc BA FCMA ACIS. Born 12/10/53. Commd 17/9/72. Wg Cdr 1/7/84. Retd ADMIN 31/12/91.
GREENHALGH B.S. Born 5/7/29. Commd 12/12/51. Flt Lt 4/7/59. Retd GD 7/3/62.
GREENHALGH I.F. The Rev. Born 11/1/49. Commd 10/7/97. Retd Wg Cdr 1/7/04.
GREENHALGH J. Born 31/3/16. Commd 16/4/35. Wg Cdr 1/7/47. Retd GD 18/9/53. rtg Gp Capt
GREENHALGH J.L. MBE. Born 23/12/44. Commd 27/1/67. Wg Cdr 1/7/90. Retd ADMIN 2/12/98.
GREENHALGH N. Born 7/10/24. Commd 22/6/45. Wg Cdr 1/7/67. Retd GD 7/10/84.
GREENHALGH S.A. MRCS LRCP DPH DTM&H. Born 10/9/27. Commd 4/3/56. Wg Cdr 4/3/69. Retd MED 1/9/73.
GREENHALGH S.B. Born 20/11/46. Commd 22/5/80. Flt Lt 22/5/82. Retd GD 14/9/96.
GREENHALGH W.R. Born 13/5/43. Commd 23/1/64. Sqn Ldr 1/7/79. Retd SY 1/7/83.
GREENHALL R.L. CEng MRAeS MIProdE MIMechE MCMI. Born 13/7/34. Commd 23/6/58. Wg Cdr 1/1/76.
  Retd ENG 10/9/85.
GREENHAM P.M. Born 22/11/62. Commd 2/10/97. Flt Lt 2/10/99. Retd OPS SPT(ATC) 10/1/05.
GREENHILL J.G. FCMI. Born 10/10/26. Commd 14/6/46. A Cdre 1/1/80. Retd GD 1/1/82.
GREENHILL-HOOPER T.J. Born 15/11/32. Commd 15/12/53. Sqn Ldr 1/7/66. Retd GD 15/11/70.
GREENHOUGH G.H. BA BD. Born 3/4/36. Commd 7/11/58. Sqn Ldr 16/1/69. Retd EDN 2/2/75.
GREENHOW M. DPhysEd. Born 5/7/33. Commd 19/9/59. Sqn Ldr 1/1/71. Retd GD 14/10/83.
GREENHOW N. Born 16/1/25. Commd 25/5/50. Sqn Ldr 1/7/72. Retd GD 15/9/77.
GREENLAND B.J.L. AFC. Born 20/12/22. Commd 19/4/43. Sqn Ldr 1/7/55. Retd GD 29/1/62.
GREENLAND J.M. Born 3/9/28. Commd 11/11/50. Flt Lt 26/5/55. Retd GD 3/9/83.
GREENLEAF E.J. DSO DFC. Born 7/2/15. Commd 19/1/42. Sqn Ldr 1/8/47. Retd GD 21/2/58.
GREENSLADE F.W. Born 27/1/31. Commd 30/1/70. Sqn Ldr 1/1/82. Retd ENG 27/1/89.
GREENSLADE R.E. Born 11/7/30. Commd 29/3/62. Flt Lt 29/3/67. Retd GD 6/9/75.
GREENSTREET G.G. MBE. Born 21/9/34. Commd 29/10/52. Sqn Ldr 1/1/67. Retd GD 21/9/89.
GREENWAY A.M. MSc BEng CEng MIEE. Born 2/10/65. Commd 16/9/84. Sqn Ldr 1/7/98. Retd ENGINEER 2/10/04.
GREENWAY D.F. MCMI. Born 31/8/34. Commd 24/9/52. Sqn Ldr 1/7/77. Retd Pl 7/4/87.
GREENWAY D.H.A. OBE FCMI. Born 15/2/39. Commd 26/6/57. Gp Capt 1/1/86. Retd GD 15/2/94.
GREENWAY J. Born 6/2/44. Commd 28/2/85. Sqn Ldr 1/7/94. Retd ADMIN 16/2/97.
GREENWAY T.C. Born 20/11/38. Commd 11/5/78. Sqn Ldr 26/5/88. Retd MED(T) 19/11/93.
GREENWOOD A. BA. Born 23/7/65. Commd 28/8/83. Sqn Ldr 1/1/02. Retd OPS SPT(FC) 1/1/05.
GREENWOOD A.S. Born 16/6/32. Commd 14/5/53. Wg Cdr 1/7/80. Retd ADMIN 2/7/83.
GREENWOOD A.W. Born 1/10/32. Commd 27/2/52. Wg Cdr 1/7/84. Retd GD(G) 1/9/88.
GREENWOOD B. BSc CEng MRAeS. Born 3/11/49. Commd 5/1/75. Sqn Ldr 1/1/84. Retd ENG 30/4/00.

GREENWOOD B.J. MHCIMA MCMI. Born 24/9/31. Commd 5/7/54. Wg Cdr 1/7/83. Retd ADMIN 24/9/86.
GREENWOOD D. BSc. Born 28/4/42. Commd 1/9/64. Sqn Ldr 1/7/86. Retd ADMIN 28/4/97.
GREENWOOD D.E. Born 23/9/31. Commd 25/6/66. Flt Lt 25/6/71. Retd ADMIN 7/5/77.
GREENWOOD D.F. CEng MRAeS MIEE. Born 27/3/24. Commd 19/7/51. Wg Cdr 1/1/67. Retd ENG 7/9/74.
GREENWOOD D.J. AFM. Born 21/1/34. Commd 28/9/61. Flt Lt 28/3/66. Retd GD 6/7/79.
GREENWOOD E.W. BSc. Born 9/4/32. Commd 11/8/52. Sqn Ldr 1/7/67. Retd GD 31/1/74.
GREENWOOD J. Born 22/8/25. Commd 7/7/44. Flt Lt 19/11/53. Retd GD 1/8/73.
GREENWOOD P. Born 27/12/63. Commd 4/4/96. Flt Lt 4/4/98. Retd ENGINEER 4/4/05.
GREENWOOD R.K. Born 26/11/44. Commd 22/3/63. Sqn Ldr 1/1/81. Retd GD 1/7/93.
GREEP D.F. Born 26/8/46. Commd 14/7/69. Wg Cdr 1/7/91. Retd ENG 15/7/93.
GREETHURST A.P.L. Born 30/3/25. Commd 8/7/54. Flt Lt 21/10/59. Retd GD 30/3/63.
GREEVES B.J. BSc. Born 28/4/50. Commd 15/9/69. Flt Lt 15/6/73. Retd GD 8/12/81.
GREGG J.L. Born 11/10/30. Commd 2/5/51. Wg Cdr 1/1/67. Retd GD 11/3/78.
GREGORY A. BA. Born 22/3/37. Commd 14/3/57. Sqn Ldr 1/7/69. Retd GD 17/2/77.
GREGORY B. Born 4/1/30. Commd 6/6/57. Flt Lt 6/12/61. Retd GD 8/6/62.
GREGORY C.M. MSc BSc CEng MIEE. Born 3/4/58. Commd 6/9/81. Sqn Ldr 1/1/89. Retd ENG 6/9/97.
GREGORY D.G. FCIPD FCMI. Born 24/7/30. Commd 11/4/51. A Cdre 1/7/79. Retd SEC 27/4/81.
GREGORY E.J. Born 4/4/49. Commd 21/2/69. Flt Lt 12/7/75. Retd GD(G) 4/6/80.
GREGORY E.J.W. MCIPD ACGI. Born 4/11/34. Commd 26/10/61. Sqn Ldr 1/7/80. Retd GD 4/11/92.
GREGORY H.E. Born 15/3/24. Commd 14/7/44. Flt Lt 29/9/48. Retd GD 1/10/68.
GREGORY J.J. Born 1/8/21. Commd 13/7/45. Flt Lt 26/5/55. Retd GD 14/8/65.
GREGORY J.L. Born 7/6/27. Commd 27/9/51. Flt Lt 21/10/59. Retd PI 19/12/81. rtg Sqn Ldr
GREGORY J.M. MHCIMA. Born 16/7/24. Commd 19/4/48. Flt Lt 1/10/51. Retd CAT 25/10/78.
GREGORY M.J. MA MSc CEng MRAeS MIEE. Born 30/10/40. Commd 30/9/59. Wg Cdr 1/1/84. Retd ENG 1/5/96.
GREGORY N.A. BA ACII. Born 31/8/47. Commd 29/3/68. Gp Capt 1/7/99. Retd OPS SPT 31/8/02.
GREGORY P.S. Born 17/3/47. Commd 21/9/72. Flt Lt 21/3/78. Retd GD 8/2/89.
GREGORY R.D. Born 10/5/49. Commd 31/7/70. Sqn Ldr 1/1/91. Retd GD 9/5/01.
GREGORY R.G. Born 1/2/23. Commd 10/3/60. Flt Lt 10/3/65. Retd GD 17/1/68.
GREGORY R.J. Born 23/4/63. Commd 20/10/83. Flt Lt 20/4/89. Retd GD 1/9/01.
GREGORY R.P. BM. Born 17/4/59. Commd 19/12/79. Sqn Ldr 1/8/88. Retd MED 23/2/96.
GREGORY W.G. Born 31/10/23. Commd 26/11/53. Sqn Ldr 1/1/68. Retd GD 1/5/73.
GREGSON B.P. Born 6/5/48. Commd 19/2/76. Sqn Ldr 1/1/87. Retd GD(G) 27/10/91.
GREIG J.R. OBE MSc MB ChB MFOM DIH. Born 14/5/36. Commd 30/9/62. A Cdre 1/7/91. Retd MED 30/9/96.
GREIG J.R. BM BS. Born 26/2/69. Commd 6/9/89. Flt Lt 1/8/93. Retd MED 31/5/96.
GREIG K.D. BA CEng MIEE. Born 31/8/38. Commd 11/4/63. Wg Cdr 1/1/86. Retd ENG 31/8/93.
GREIG R.C.C. Born 24/5/36. Commd 24/4/70. Sqn Ldr 1/7/81. Retd GD 24/5/91.
GREIG S.A. Born 28/5/51. Commd 9/12/71. Flt Lt 9/6/77. Retd GD 28/11/89.
GREIG S.M.c.N. Born 14/1/14. Commd 12/9/38. Wg Cdr 1/1/60. Retd SUP 10/10/64.
GRENFELL J. Born 16/12/38. Commd 1/10/60. Sqn Ldr 1/7/76. Retd GD 1/7/81.
GRESHAM J.W. Born 6/6/47. Commd 22/7/66. Fg Offr 26/11/68. Retd GD(G) 1/12/72. Re-entered 11/3/81.
    Sqn Ldr 1/11/89. Retd OPS SPT 6/6/02.
GRESWELL J.H. CB CBE DSO DFC. Born 28/7/16. Commd 30/9/35. A Cdre 1/1/62. Retd GD 28/7/68.
GREVES E.W. Born 24/3/41. Commd 14/5/60. Flt Lt 14/11/65. Retd GD 24/3/96.
GREVILLE N. Born 17/8/22. Commd 4/7/42. Flt Lt 4/1/46. Retd GD 22/11/55.
GREY D.M. Born 15/2/46. Commd 22/5/64. Wg Cdr 1/1/84. Retd GD 10/8/85.
GREY P.R. FCA. Born 8/10/15. Commd 10/6/39. Sqn Ldr 1/8/47. Retd SEC 8/10/70.
GREY S.H. BA. Born 2/5/29. Commd 5/9/51. Sqn Ldr 1/4/61. Retd EDN 30/3/74.
GRIBBLE W.L. Born 18/8/21. Commd 10/2/45. Fg Offr 4/6/47. Retd GD 3/12/48.
GRICE P.W. BA. Born 12/6/52. Commd 2/10/72. Sqn Ldr 1/1/87. Retd GD 13/8/89.
GRIERSON M.J. Born 7/12/45. Commd 7/7/67. Flt Lt 5/2/75. Retd GD 22/4/94.
GRIERSON-JACKSON M.W. Born 19/12/20. Commd 18/5/41. Flt Lt 1/9/45. Retd GD 1/1/53. rtg Sqn Ldr
GRIESHABER D.C. Born 12/4/33. Commd 19/8/71. Flt Lt 19/8/76. Retd ENG 4/2/88.
GRIEVE A.J.M. Born 13/2/41. Commd 8/12/61. Flt Lt 26/7/67. Retd GD 13/2/96.
GRIEVE B.S. Born 17/10/36. Commd 29/12/54. Flt Lt 15/8/62. Retd GD 15/12/67.
GRIEVE D.J.W. BA. Born 23/12/54. Commd 18/3/84. Flt Lt 18/9/86. Retd ADMIN 18/3/00.
GRIEVE I.P. Born 9/6/42. Commd 3/8/62. Sqn Ldr 1/1/75. Retd GD 28/12/93.
GRIFFIN A.J. AFC. Born 3/8/45. Commd 15/7/66. A Cdre 1/7/92. Retd GD 14/3/96.
GRIFFIN C.A. BEng. Born 14/4/59. Commd 29/11/81. Flt Lt 29/2/84. Retd ENG 29/11/97.
GRIFFIN E.K. Born 4/5/48. Commd 26/5/70. Flt Lt 26/11/75. Retd GD 20/6/93.
GRIFFIN F.J. Born 23/5/19. Commd 11/4/46. Sqn Ldr 1/7/59. Retd ENG 23/5/68.
GRIFFIN J. Born 13/3/51. Commd 3/7/80. Flt Lt 3/7/82. Retd MED(SEC) 13/3/89.
GRIFFIN J.T. Born 22/5/43. Commd 25/6/65. Sqn Ldr 1/1/89. Retd FLY(N) 22/5/03.
GRIFFIN K.G. Born 13/8/48. Commd 2/6/67. Sqn Ldr 1/1/84. Retd GD 1/1/87.
GRIFFIN M.E.L. BSc. Born 15/12/62. Commd 7/12/86. Flt Lt 7/6/90. Retd GD(G) 1/10/91.
GRIFFIN N.P. The Rev. BA. Born 23/1/37. Commd 24/2/69. Retd Wg Cdr 24/2/85.
GRIFFIN S.A. BSc CEng MRAeS. Born 10/7/59. Commd 10/10/79. Wg Cdr 1/1/96. Retd ENG 1/1/99.

GRIFFIN S.E. Born 28/8/46. Commd 2/8/68. Flt Lt 2/8/71. Retd GD 28/8/84.
GRIFFIN S.J. Born 12/10/59. Commd 8/11/90. Sqn Ldr 1/1/01. Retd FLY(AEO) 11/10/04.
GRIFFIN T.E. Born 29/4/15. Commd 24/12/42. Flt Lt 16/8/47. Retd ENG 2/3/68.
GRIFFITH D.V. BSc. Born 27/6/63. Commd 13/9/81. Flt Lt 15/10/85. Retd GD 15/7/96.
GRIFFITH H.D. BSc. Born 2/5/29. Commd 17/9/52. Sqn Ldr 1/1/63. Retd ENG 8/7/84.
GRIFFITH M.D. Born 7/12/46. Commd 11/10/84. Flt Lt 11/10/88. Retd MED(SEC) 14/3/96.
GRIFFITH R.J. BA. Born 30/10/49. Commd 29/1/87. Flt Lt 29/1/89. Retd ADMIN 29/1/95.
GRIFFITH-JONES G.L.S. CBE MA. Born 3/5/11. Commd 7/4/32. Gp Capt 1/7/52. Retd ENG 3/5/66.
GRIFFITHS A. Born 19/10/41. Commd 27/1/67. Wg Cdr 1/7/81. Retd SY 20/4/93.
GRIFFITHS A. BSc DUS CEng MIEE MInstP. Born 19/11/35. Commd 4/9/59. Wg Cdr 4/3/75. Retd ADMIN 17/5/76.
GRIFFITHS A.W. OBE. Born 26/5/23. Commd 29/10/43. Wg Cdr 1/7/60. Retd GD 30/9/69.
GRIFFITHS B.T. MBE BA MCMI. Born 29/9/30. Commd 3/9/52. Wg Cdr 17/2/71. Retd EDN 18/11/73.
GRIFFITHS C.E. Born 13/6/46. Commd 5/3/65. Flt Lt 4/11/70. Retd GD 19/9/75.
GRIFFITHS D.A. Born 12/3/39. Commd 27/8/64. Flt Lt 4/12/66. Retd SUP 12/3/77.
GRIFFITHS D.A. OBE AFC. Born 20/7/42. Commd 30/7/63. Gp Capt 1/1/85. Retd GD 22/7/86.
GRIFFITHS D.A. BSc CEng MIEE MCMI. Born 8/5/33. Commd 30/4/72. Sqn Ldr 30/4/72. Retd ENG 8/5/93.
GRIFFITHS D.B. Born 25/4/16. Commd 25/11/43. Wg Offr 1/7/55. Retd SEC 29/6/63.
GRIFFITHS D.F. Born 8/6/21. Commd 3/10/46. Flt Lt 3/4/51. Retd SUP 19/6/54.
GRIFFITHS D.I. DFC. Born 29/12/21. Commd 23/5/42. Sqn Ldr 1/7/57. Retd GD 29/12/64.
GRIFFITHS D.J. Born 4/4/32. Commd 16/12/66. Sqn Ldr 1/1/79. Retd ENG 12/12/85.
GRIFFITHS D.J. AFC BSc. Born 21/8/41. Commd 8/1/65. Sqn Ldr 1/1/75. Retd GD 21/8/96.
GRIFFITHS D.J. Born 12/7/65. Commd 8/6/84. Sqn Ldr 1/1/99. Retd OPS SPT(REGT) 12/7/03.
GRIFFITHS D.P.L. DPhysEd. Born 15/10/46. Commd 18/10/79. Sqn Ldr 1/7/90. Retd ADMIN 1/11/96.
GRIFFITHS D.W. DFC*. Born 7/8/21. Commd 27/7/42. Sqn Ldr 1/1/57. Retd GD 7/8/64.
GRIFFITHS E.J. MCMI. Born 26/8/20. Commd 1/5/42. Sqn Ldr 1/4/57. Retd SEC 26/8/69.
GRIFFITHS E.P. Born 30/11/11. Commd 18/1/45. Sqn Ldr 1/7/57. Retd SEC 2/3/59.
GRIFFITHS E.R. OBE MB BS FRCSEng. Born 10/7/24. Commd 5/2/51. Wg Cdr 1/4/62. Retd MED 6/8/67.
GRIFFITHS F.P. Born 11/6/44. Commd 10/3/77. Flt Lt 10/3/79. Retd GD(G) 30/9/86.
GRIFFITHS G. OBE. Born 7/1/23. Commd 9/3/44. Wg Cdr 1/1/71. Retd GD(G) 7/1/78.
GRIFFITHS G. Born 24/4/46. Commd 9/3/66. Wg Cdr 1/7/88. Retd ADMIN 14/3/96.
GRIFFITHS G.B. Born 9/2/41. Commd 28/11/74. Sqn Ldr 1/7/83. Retd ENG 30/9/94.
GRIFFITHS G.D. MSc BSc. Born 24/6/62. Commd 23/4/87. Sqn Ldr 1/1/97. Retd ENG 9/9/00.
GRIFFITHS H.A. Born 16/6/34. Commd 3/3/54. Gp Capt 1/7/87. Retd GD 16/6/92.
GRIFFITHS H.M. Born 1/5/18. Commd 23/3/50. Sqn Ldr 1/7/59. Retd PRT 31/7/64.
GRIFFITHS H.M. MB ChB DPhysMed. Born 15/9/43. Commd 25/7/66. Wg Cdr 27/8/83. Retd MED 19/5/84.
GRIFFITHS H.W. BSc. Born 13/4/53. Commd 3/9/78. Wg Cdr 1/7/92. Retd ADMIN 14/9/96.
GRIFFITHS J. Born 25/11/17. Commd 28/3/46. Sqn Ldr 1/1/57. Retd SUP 15/9/62.
GRIFFITHS J.D. MBE. Born 4/11/21. Commd 15/5/58. Sqn Ldr 1/7/69. Retd ENG 30/6/76.
GRIFFITHS J.D. Born 11/8/48. Commd 21/4/67. Sqn Ldr 1/1/85. Retd GD 1/1/88.
GRIFFITHS J.D. BSc. Born 8/6/46. Commd 7/2/71. Flt Lt 7/11/74. Retd GD 1/1/86.
GRIFFITHS M.A. BEd. Born 3/5/56. Commd 4/1/83. Flt Lt 4/1/87. Retd ADMIN 4/1/87.
GRIFFITHS M.J. Born 15/12/34. Commd 13/12/55. Flt Lt 13/6/58. Retd GD 10/2/62.
GRIFFITHS M.J. BSc MB BS. Born 30/5/63. Commd 13/11/85. Sqn Ldr 1/8/94. Retd MED 14/3/96.
GRIFFITHS M.L. Born 4/4/38. Commd 2/2/60. Sqn Ldr 24/7/71. Retd ADMIN 4/4/76.
GRIFFITHS N.A. BA FCIPS FCMI. Born 27/4/44. Commd 15/7/66. A Cdre 1/1/93. Retd SUP 2/12/98.
GRIFFITHS P. Born 30/10/61. Commd 7/8/87. Flt Lt 15/7/90. Retd ENG 16/1/94.
GRIFFITHS P.A. Born 10/3/43. Commd 28/7/64. Wg Cdr 1/1/91. Retd GD 31/3/94.
GRIFFITHS P.D. Born 16/4/50. Commd 12/4/73. Sqn Ldr 1/7/85. Retd SUP 1/7/88.
GRIFFITHS P.R. BSc. Born 2/12/51. Commd 13/8/70. Sqn Ldr 1/7/83. Retd ENG 2/12/90.
GRIFFITHS P.S. Born 15/4/47. Commd 2/4/65. Flt Lt 2/10/70. Retd GD 28/9/84.
GRIFFITHS R.D. Born 17/1/25. Commd 5/11/59. Flt Lt 5/11/65. Retd SUP 1/5/69.
GRIFFITHS R.E. MSc BSc(Eng) ACGI. Born 22/10/39. Commd 30/9/58. Wg Cdr 1/7/87. Retd ENG 22/10/94.
GRIFFITHS R.G.E. CEng MRAeS. Born 23/10/16. Commd 4/11/43. Sqn Ldr 1/7/54. Retd ENG 23/3/68.
GRIFFITHS R.H. Born 19/7/41. Commd 30/3/61. Wg Cdr 1/1/87. Retd ENG 19/7/96.
GRIFFITHS R.P.A. BSc. Born 22/4/54. Commd 2/1/77. Fg Offr 2/7/74. Retd ADMIN 1/5/79.
GRIFFITHS S. MInstLM. Born 6/2/65. Commd 6/4/93. Sqn Ldr 1/7/98. Retd OPS SPT(REGT) 6/2/03.
GRIFFITHS S.C. BA. Born 1/5/65. Commd 15/4/93. Wg Cdr 1/7/02. Retd GD 1/7/05.
GRIFFITHS S.C. BEng. Born 12/1/63. Commd 31/7/90. Flt Lt 15/7/93. Retd ENG 12/1/01.
GRIFFITHS S.G. MBE MBA. Born 2/6/48. Commd 28/2/69. Wg Cdr 1/1/87. Retd GD 29/2/00.
GRIFFITHS S.M. Born 29/2/64. Commd 23/5/85. Flt Lt 23/11/90. Retd FLY(P) 2/8/04.
GRIFFITHS W. Born 15/9/23. Commd 18/5/44. Sqn Ldr 1/7/62. Retd SUP 3/3/78.
GRIFFITHS W. Born 28/3/44. Commd 14/1/65. Sqn Ldr 1/7/78. Retd GD 28/3/82.
GRIFFITHS W.L. Born 10/10/21. Commd 5/6/42. Sqn Ldr 1/1/54. Retd GD 14/11/64.
GRIGG G.A.F. BA. Born 16/11/32. Commd 15/7/54. Flt Lt 26/2/64. Retd EDN 30/6/65.
GRIGG R.F. Born 11/10/28. Commd 12/9/63. Sqn Ldr 1/1/74. Retd ENG 10/11/78.

GRIGGS D.S. AFC BA. Born 1/9/50. Commd 6/4/70. Gp Capt 1/1/96. Retd GD 1/9/00.
GRIGGS R.W.R. Born 5/2/24. Commd 6/12/56. Flt Lt 6/6/66. Retd GD 5/2/67.
GRIGGS T.C. Born 15/5/48. Commd 25/10/73. Flt Lt 25/4/79. Retd GD 22/10/94.
GRIGOR H.S. Born 19/1/50. Commd 15/9/69. Flt Lt 15/3/77. Retd GD 19/1/88.
GRIGSON M.W.S. OBE MA CEng DipEl MIEE. Born 13/12/33. Commd 26/9/53. Wg Cdr 1/1/73. Retd ENG 1/8/79.
Re-instated 22/10/80. Wg Cdr 24/3/74. Retd ENG 18/4/88.
GRILLI P.J.P. Born 15/3/38. Commd 20/12/62. Wg Cdr 1/7/81. Retd ADMIN 3/5/90.
GRIMA F.X. MD MSc MRCGP MFOM MCMI DPH. Born 28/8/31. Commd 9/7/61. Gp Capt 1/7/85. Retd MED 28/8/92.
GRIME G.H. BDS. Born 19/5/38. Commd 26/1/66. Wg Cdr 13/1/79. Retd DEL 21/4/92.
GRIME J.R.A. Born 16/12/66. Commd 19/12/85. Sqn Ldr 1/1/98. Retd FLY(P) 16/12/04.
GRIMER J.O. Born 25/9/43. Commd 28/2/66. Wg Cdr 1/7/87. Retd SUP 14/3/96.
GRIMES M.K. Born 28/8/48. Commd 7/6/68. Flt Lt 7/12/74. Retd GD(G) 28/8/86.
GRIMSDALE G.E. Born 14/3/26. Commd 17/10/57. Flt Lt 1/4/63. Retd GD 21/9/68.
GRIMSEY J.M. Born 1/7/31. Commd 12/3/53. Flt Offr 12/3/59. Retd SEC 12/3/61.
GRIMSHAW E.B. Born 9/12/30. Commd 2/1/70. Flt Lt 2/1/76. Retd SUP 14/2/76.
GRIMSHAW F. Born 3/7/31. Commd 20/12/51. Flt Lt 4/4/57. Retd GD 15/1/70.
GRIMSHAW G. Born 24/11/31. Commd 11/8/53. Flt Lt 6/2/59. Retd GD 24/11/69.
GRIMSHAW J.D. Born 16/4/22. Commd 14/5/43. Sqn Ldr 1/7/57. Retd GD 30/3/62.
GRIMSTON D.F. CEng MIEE. Born 17/4/37. Commd 30/7/59. Wg Cdr 1/1/90. Retd ENG 21/4/92.
GRINDLEY G.L. OBE. Born 20/12/33. Commd 13/8/52. Gp Capt 1/1/87. Retd SY 2/7/87.
GRINTER R.K. CEng MIMechE MRAeS. Born 26/3/35. Commd 24/4/59. Wg Cdr 1/1/83. Retd ENG 1/4/85.
GRIPTON M.J. Born 24/6/56. Commd 15/12/88. Flt Lt 15/12/90. Retd ENG 2/4/93.
GRISBROOK D. MBE BSc. Born 25/8/29. Commd 5/11/52. Sqn Ldr 5/5/63. Retd EDN 5/11/68.
GRISDALE J.N.J. MBE. Born 4/1/47. Commd 13/4/66. Gp Capt 1/7/94. Retd GD 4/1/02.
GRIST M.J. CEng MIMechE MCMI. Born 2/9/36. Commd 5/7/60. Sqn Ldr 1/1/70. Retd ENG 5/7/76.
GRITTEN A.J. MBE. Born 28/3/47. Commd 2/8/68. Wg Cdr 1/7/86. Retd OPS SPT 28/3/02.
GROBELNY W. AFC. Born 21/5/19. Commd 24/1/52. Sqn Ldr 1/7/67. Retd GD 1/8/73.
GROCOTT D.F.H. CBE AFC. Born 8/2/23. Commd 15/10/43. A Cdre 25/9/76. Retd GD 29/9/77.
GROCOTT J.C. Born 24/4/48. Commd 12/2/67. Sqn Ldr 1/1/86. Retd GD 1/1/89.
GROCOTT R.G. Born 7/6/24. Commd 25/3/44. Wg Cdr 1/7/69. Retd GD(G) 3/12/77.
GROGAN C.D. AFC. Born 10/5/23. Commd 5/3/53. Flt Lt 5/9/56. Retd GD 23/2/63.
GROGAN J.B. Born 15/7/46. Commd 4/12/64. Wg Cdr 1/7/81. Retd GD 15/7/87.
GROOCOCK D.W. AFC. Born 28/6/22. Commd 1/1/44. Gp Capt 1/1/70. Retd GD 1/6/74.
GROOM G.R. Born 8/5/15. Commd 3/3/44. Sqn Ldr 1/7/55. Retd SEC 3/6/65.
GROOM J.A. MHCIMA. Born 4/8/50. Commd 19/11/72. Flt Lt 19/12/76. Retd CAT 3/10/79.
GROOMBRIDGE P.L. MBE. Born 2/12/31. Commd 30/7/64. Wg Cdr 1/7/82. Retd SUP 1/8/84.
GROOMBRIDGE R.C. Born 17/11/39. Commd 6/10/60. Sqn Ldr 1/7/74. Retd GD 17/11/77. Re-entrant 3/12/79.
Sqn Ldr 17/7/76. Retd GD 14/12/97.
GROSE G.M. BSc MCIPS. Born 11/10/53. Commd 3/9/72. Sqn Ldr 1/1/85. Retd SUP 11/10/91.
GROSE L.A. Born 24/1/42. Commd 1/10/65. Flt Lt 1/4/71. Retd GD 21/9/82. Re-entered 23/4/86. Sqn Ldr 1/7/99.
Retd GD 24/1/02.
GROSE N.J. AFC. Born 17/4/53. Commd 22/7/71. Flt Lt 22/1/77. Retd GD 1/6/83.
GROSE R.J. BEM. Born 15/1/23. Commd 26/9/57. Sqn Ldr 1/1/68. Retd ADMIN 1/5/76.
GROSS A.J. BEng. Born 25/8/40. Commd 16/10/61. Gp Capt 1/1/92. Retd GD 25/8/95.
GROSSE H.M. AFC. Born 23/2/44. Commd 6/7/62. Wg Cdr 1/7/82. Retd GD 23/2/88.
GROSSET M.J. Born 9/12/47. Commd 23/6/67. Sqn Ldr 1/1/78. Retd ADMIN 15/2/85.
GROSSET P.M. MCMI. Born 7/5/43. Commd 17/12/65. Gp Capt 1/1/90. Retd ADMIN 22/4/94.
GROSVENOR D.E. Born 20/11/32. Commd 20/12/51. Wg Cdr 1/7/72. Retd ADMIN 2/4/85.
GROSVENOR L. Born 9/1/44. Commd 23/9/66. Flt Lt 23/3/72. Retd GD 5/2/84. Re-entered 3/4/85. Flt Lt 18/5/73.
Retd GD 9/7/00.
GROUT M.D. Born 1/7/16. Commd 20/10/41. Sqn Offr 1/7/50. Retd SEC 16/10/51.
GROVE A.D.W. Born 17/1/47. Commd 3/6/65. Sqn Ldr 1/1/84. Retd OPS SPT 17/1/02.
GROVE N. DFM. Born 13/1/24. Commd 28/2/57. Flt Lt 28/2/63. Retd GD 11/2/73.
GROVER P.E. Born 26/2/32. Commd 6/6/57. Flt Lt 6/12/61. Retd GD 26/2/70.
GROVES B.A. Born 24/3/36. Commd 10/2/72. Flt Lt 10/2/74. Retd ADMIN 10/2/82.
GROVES B.A. BSc. Born 16/5/48. Commd 7/12/75. Flt Lt 7/3/77. Retd GD 7/12/91.
GROVES E.R. Born 8/6/29. Commd 30/3/61. Sqn Ldr 1/7/79. Retd MED 8/6/87.
GROVES F.J. MBE MB BCh MRCGP DRCOG DAvMed MRAeS. Born 30/9/56. Commd 9/7/81. Wg Cdr 10/8/94.
Retd MED 9/7/98.
GROVES J.A. Born 28/4/54. Commd 22/6/89. Sqn Ldr 1/7/97. Retd ADMIN 1/7/00.
GROVES R.L. Born 15/6/22. Commd 19/7/51. Wg Cdr 1/7/66. Retd ENG 17/2/73.
GROVES W.R. MBE. Born 17/11/15. Commd 24/3/45. Wg Cdr 1/7/66. Retd SUP 12/6/70.
GROZIER J. Born 10/11/22. Commd 4/5/50. Flt Lt 4/11/53. Retd GD 11/7/72.
GRUBB D.W. Born 12/4/24. Commd 9/8/47. Sqn Ldr 1/1/62. Retd GD 9/7/76.
GRUMBLEY K.G. Born 4/12/45. Commd 18/8/67. Wg Cdr 1/1/86. Retd GD 4/12/00.
GRUNDON B.I. MCIPD. Born 11/9/36. Commd 19/9/71. Flt Lt 19/9/73. Retd ENG 19/9/87.

GRUNDY B.G. OBE. Born 28/9/20. Commd 1/9/45. A Cdre 1/7/71. Retd SEC 30/11/72.
GRUNDY F.H. Born 25/9/56. Commd 27/2/75. Sqn Ldr 1/7/90. Retd GD 1/10/96.
GRUNDY L.V. MIPD. Born 25/5/44. Commd 4/6/64. Sqn Ldr 1/7/75. Retd ADMIN 1/8/91.
GRUNDY R. Born 11/2/32. Commd 22/12/53. Flt Lt 21/10/59. Retd GD 11/2/70.
GRUNDY R.C. MMS. Born 19/12/40. Commd 21/7/70. Sqn Ldr 1/1/82. Retd ADMIN 2/1/93.
GRUNDY R.W. MBE BTech. Born 8/2/51. Commd 13/9/71. Sqn Ldr 1/7/87. Retd GD 14/3/97.
GRUNER S.C. Born 18/2/45. Commd 3/3/67. Sqn Ldr 1/7/80. Retd GD 21/9/84.
GUARD F.R. Born 10/10/32. Commd 25/10/53. Wg Cdr 1/1/85. Retd GD 1/1/88.
GUBBINS R.B. FCMI. Born 4/6/32. Commd 27/7/54. Gp Capt 1/1/76. Retd GD 9/3/87.
GUEST C.A. MCMI. Born 4/9/18. Commd 11/11/43. Sqn Ldr 1/7/54. Retd ENG 7/8/71.
GUEST C.B. Born 15/1/42. Commd 3/9/62. Sqn Ldr 1/1/75. Retd GD 15/1/80.
GUEST D.M. Born 2/10/47. Commd 28/2/69. Wg Cdr 1/1/86. Retd GD 2/10/02.
GUEST G.R. Born 21/11/14. Commd 16/5/42. Flt Lt 16/11/46. Retd SEC 9/12/63. rtg Sqn Ldr
GUEST M.J. MA MSc CEng MRAeS. Born 20/5/34. Commd 26/9/53. Gp Capt 1/1/76. Retd ENG 17/6/92.
GUEST R. MSc MB ChB MRCGP DIH MFOM. Born 14/12/54. Commd 30/3/76. Wg Cdr 6/8/84. Retd MED 14/12/92.
GUILFOYLE A.A. Born 5/8/37. Commd 20/7/78. Flt Lt 20/7/81. Retd GD 30/9/85.
GUILFOYLE D. BA. Born 6/6/41. Commd 7/6/68. Sqn Ldr 1/1/76. Retd ENG 1/10/87.
GULLICK R. BSc. Born 31/7/53. Commd 1/9/75. Sqn Ldr 1/1/88. Retd ENG 1/10/93.
GULLIVER J. Born 30/3/48. Commd 12/7/68. Flt Lt 12/1/74. Retd FLY(N) 30/9/03.
GULLIVER M.B. Born 23/4/29. Commd 24/8/48. Fg Offr 20/7/51. Retd GD 10/12/55.
GULLIVER M.C.H. BSc CEng MIMechE MCMI ACGI. Born 24/1/41. Commd 20/7/65. Sqn Ldr 1/7/73.
  Retd ENG 20/7/81.
GUNDRY A.F. Born 8/12/23. Commd 28/7/60. Flt Lt 28/7/63. Retd GD 8/12/81.
GUNN A.C. MA LLB(EDIN) LLB(LOND) BL. Born 6/2/30. Commd 5/9/57. Wg Cdr 1/7/58. Retd LGL 1/7/71.
GUNN A.J. Born 19/10/29. Commd 30/7/52. Flt Lt 27/12/57. Retd GD 1/8/73.
GUNN A.R. Born 9/8/24. Commd 29/1/46. Flt Lt 29/1/52. Retd RGT 29/1/64.
GUNN D.C.E. MCMI. Born 19/4/48. Commd 10/1/69. Sqn Ldr 1/7/85. Retd ADMIN (PROVSY) 19/4/03.
GUNN D.J. Born 27/5/60. Commd 20/5/82. Sqn Ldr 1/1/96. Retd GD 18/8/00.
GUNN G.A. Born 4/5/26. Commd 15/6/48. Sqn Ldr 1/7/58. Retd GD 30/12/59.
GUNN J. Born 26/4/42. Commd 24/3/83. Sqn Ldr 1/1/92. Retd ENG 1/7/95.
GUNN R.H. Born 15/9/34. Commd 24/2/55. Flt Lt 24/2/61. Retd SEC 10/7/64.
GUNNELL P. Born 4/7/44. Commd 29/4/71. Flt Lt 29/4/73. Retd SUP 1/9/77.
GUNNELL S.D. DFM. Born 2/12/22. Commd 23/3/43. Flt Lt 9/3/47. Retd GD 1/10/66.
GUNNING R.D. Born 23/4/38. Commd 28/7/59. Flt Lt 28/1/62. Retd GD 22/5/66.
GUNNS P.E. CEng MIMechE MRAeS MCMI. Born 18/5/36. Commd 23/7/58. Wg Cdr 1/1/74. Retd ENG 18/5/91.
GUNTRIP J.J. Born 23/5/28. Commd 14/12/49. Flt Lt 14/6/52. Retd GD 23/5/66.
GUNYON H.W. Born 16/2/28. Commd 4/8/53. Flt Lt 23/10/57. Retd GD 24/2/68.
GURDEN M. BEng. Born 27/1/64. Commd 2/8/85. Flt Lt 21/8/91. Retd ENG 27/1/02.
GURNEY D.J. Born 20/1/43. Commd 29/5/64. Sqn Ldr 1/1/75. Retd GD 20/1/81.
GURNEY J.A. Born 14/1/44. Commd 17/2/67. Flt Lt 17/8/72. Retd GD 16/12/76.
GUTHRIE D. Born 26/5/28. Commd 27/7/49. Sqn Ldr 1/1/60. Retd GD 26/5/66.
GUTHRIE I. BA. Born 7/9/57. Commd 8/5/83. Sqn Ldr 1/7/93. Retd SUP 8/5/99.
GUTHRIE J.M. BSc FInstAM FInstLM. Born 26/5/45. Commd 22/5/80. Sqn Ldr 1/7/91. Retd ADMIN (SEC) 26/5/03.
GUTHRIE P.F. Born 11/11/59. Commd 4/7/82. Sqn Ldr 1/1/92. Retd ENG 4/7/98.
GUTTERIDGE A.C. Born 1/5/45. Commd 28/4/65. Sqn Ldr 1/7/77. Retd GD 1/5/89.
GUTTERIDGE J.L. BEM CEng MRAeS. Born 16/8/22. Commd 26/2/53. Sqn Ldr 1/1/63. Retd ENG 1/11/75.
GUTTRIDGE A.H. MVO MBE. Born 27/10/43. Commd 2/12/66. Sqn Ldr 1/1/91. Retd GD 27/10/98.
GUTTRIDGE D.A.E. Born 10/10/34. Commd 17/11/59. Wg Cdr 1/7/78. Retd ENG 1/8/87.
GUY B.T. MRAeS. Born 17/7/26. Commd 29/3/56. Flt Lt 29/9/59. Retd GD 8/9/76.
GUY E.L. Born 8/5/29. Commd 17/12/64. Sqn Ldr 1/1/78. Retd GD 8/5/84.
GUY L. Born 11/8/58. Commd 24/4/80. Sqn Ldr 1/1/91. Retd ADMIN 11/8/96.
GUY P.N. BA. Born 4/2/39. Commd 23/10/62. Sqn Ldr 23/4/72. Retd EDN 13/12/79.
GUY R.F.B. FCIS. Born 3/11/12. Commd 1/1/37. Wg Cdr 1/1/53. Retd SUP 1/7/60.
GUY R.J. Born 11/4/24. Commd 17/7/58. Sqn Ldr 1/7/69. Retd GD 9/4/77.
GUY R.W. CEng MIEE MRAeS. Born 26/10/34. Commd 25/7/56. Wg Cdr 1/1/73. Retd ENG 26/8/89.
GUYATT D.J. Born 26/12/48. Commd 10/1/69. Flt Lt 26/6/74. Retd GD 14/9/96.
GUYER M.L. Born 10/8/32. Commd 19/4/51. Flt Lt 17/10/55. Retd GD 4/6/65.
GUZ N. BSc. Born 3/2/60. Commd 26/7/81. Wg Cdr 1/7/99. Retd GD 3/2/04.
GWINNELL E.B.C. Born 17/4/30. Commd 18/8/54. Flt Lt 18/1/60. Retd GD 23/5/70.
GWYNNE G.B. Born 5/9/31. Commd 1/10/55. Gp Capt 1/1/82. Retd GD 15/9/84.
GWYNNE R.C. Born 19/5/30. Commd 28/11/69. Sqn Ldr 1/1/80. Retd GD 2/1/84.
GWYTHER V.R. Born 9/5/22. Commd 28/2/57. Sqn Ldr 1/7/73. Retd GD 31/3/77.
GYLES S.W. Born 27/9/46. Commd 11/1/66. Sqn Ldr 1/1/87. Retd GD 10/10/90.

H

HAARHOFF H.A. DFC. Born 25/9/12. Commd 17/1/40. Sqn Ldr 1/1/50. Retd ENG 29/11/59.
HACK D.R. Born 19/7/58. Commd 2/2/78. Sqn Ldr 1/1/93. Retd GD(G) 16/12/96.
HACK K.S. Born 15/5/43. Commd 17/5/79. Sqn Ldr 1/1/88. Retd SY 31/3/94.
HACKE L.E.A. Born 29/1/22. Commd 3/6/44. Sqn Ldr 1/7/57. Retd GD 29/1/65.
HACKE N.S. BSc. Born 7/11/61. Commd 29/4/84. Flt Lt 29/10/86. Retd GD 31/7/89.
HACKETT A.D.B.P. Born 13/8/42. Commd 29/3/68. Flt Lt 11/11/73. Retd SUP 13/8/80.
HACKETT G.R. Born 22/12/43. Commd 28/9/62. Flt Lt 28/1/70. Retd GD 22/4/94.
HACKFORD D.M.McC. Born 18/7/44. Commd 22/8/63. Sqn Ldr 1/7/75. Retd SUP 18/8/82. Re-entered 5/8/83.
    Sqn Ldr 20/7/76. Retd SUP 14/9/96.
HACKMAN G.E.H. AFC. Born 9/8/19. Commd 20/6/42. Sqn Ldr 1/1/53. Retd GD 6/2/59. rtg Wg Cdr
HACKNEY A.C. Born 18/5/36. Commd 6/4/55. Flt Lt 6/10/60. Retd GD 18/5/94.
HACKNEY P.S. BSc. Born 9/7/53. Commd 4/10/71. Flt Lt 15/10/75. Retd GD 9/7/92.
HACKNEY R.G. MB ChB. Born 2/9/57. Commd 30/1/79. Wg Cdr 1/5/96. Retd MED 1/12/99.
HADDOCK P. Born 2/7/22. Commd 5/2/45. Flt Lt 19/6/52. Retd GD(G) 6/3/64.
HADDOW R.W. OBE AFM MSc CEng MIEE MRAeS. Born 20/5/36. Commd 4/9/67. Sqn Ldr 13/10/72.
    Retd ADMIN 4/9/83.
HADLAND J.V. DFC. Born 23/5/14. Commd 17/8/41. Sqn Ldr 1/1/49. Retd SUP 20/12/58.
HADLEY D. BSc. Born 13/3/47. Commd 27/10/70. Flt Lt 27/7/74. Retd GD(G) 6/12/74.
HADLEY T.G. Born 7/8/33. Commd 5/8/54. Sqn Ldr 1/1/67. Retd RGT 8/9/73.
HADLINGTON P.B. Born 5/10/31. Commd 19/11/52. Flt Lt 15/4/58. Retd GD(G) 5/10/88.
HADLOW R.K.J. Born 20/4/35. Commd 21/4/54. Sqn Ldr 1/7/66. Retd GD 20/4/73.
HADNETT D.T.J. Born 26/7/47. Commd 30/5/69. Wg Cdr 1/7/99. Retd SUP 31/12/02.
HAFFENDEN N.C. Born 23/12/36. Commd 23/11/78. Flt Lt 23/11/83. Retd ENG 24/12/90.
HAGAN G.E. Born 26/9/23. Commd 27/5/54. Flt Lt 27/5/60. Retd GD 31/1/69.
HAGAN J.G. BSc. Born 10/5/56. Commd 21/11/82. Sqn Ldr 1/1/90. Retd OPS SPT 1/8/01.
HAGAN P.V. Born 12/3/65. Commd 28/9/89. Flt Lt 21/1/94. Retd SUP 14/9/96.
HAGE A.E. Born 20/4/29. Commd 13/2/64. Flt Lt 13/2/69. Retd ENG 11/3/75. Re-employed 21/5/80. Retd 25/10/83.
HAGEL G. Born 16/11/32. Commd 11/10/51. Sqn Ldr 1/7/63. Retd GD 25/2/77.
HAGGAR H.T. MBE DFM FCMI. Born 7/5/17. Commd 6/4/43. Gp Capt 1/1/69. Retd SEC 7/5/72.
HAGGAR N.A.T. Born 4/11/47. Commd 23/3/67. Flt Lt 23/9/72. Retd GD 27/7/00.
HAGGARTY E. MSc BSc CertEd. Born 5/3/61. Commd 11/10/87. Flt Lt 11/4/88. Retd ENGINEER 11/10/03.
HAGGERTY F.M. MBE. Born 17/11/43. Commd 12/7/63. Flt Lt 12/11/69. Retd GD 22/10/94.
HAGGERTY M.E.O. Born 5/5/33. Commd 29/12/51. Sqn Ldr 1/7/64. Retd GD 5/5/71.
HAGGETT N.L. MBE MRAeS DPhysEd. Born 8/7/26. Commd 8/8/56. Sqn Ldr 1/1/68. Retd ADMIN 8/3/85.
HAGUE L. OBE MCMI. Born 4/3/21. Commd 23/10/43. Wg Cdr 1/1/65. Retd GD 14/12/74.
HAGUE S.J. Born 20/8/59. Commd 14/1/81. Flt Lt 6/3/86. Retd SUP 31/3/94.
HAIG J.C.H. BA. Born 6/1/38. Commd 5/6/56. Flt Lt 5/12/61. Retd GD 6/1/81.
HAIG T.L. Born 1/9/40. Commd 16/9/71. Sqn Ldr 1/1/84. Retd GD(G) 1/9/95.
HAIGH A.J. MIEE MCMI. Born 22/6/49. Commd 15/9/69. Sqn Ldr 1/1/83. Retd ENG 22/6/87.
HAIGH C.F. MBE. Born 7/2/43. Commd 2/9/63. Sqn Ldr 1/7/85. Retd GD 7/2/98.
HAIGH D. Born 16/10/17. Commd 23/6/44. Sqn Ldr 1/7/58. Retd SEC 16/10/66.
HAIGH I.G. Born 3/12/33. Commd 23/7/52. Flt Lt 29/1/58. Retd GD 3/12/71.
HAIGH J.P.C. Born 29/3/49. Commd 20/9/68. Flt Lt 20/3/74. Retd GD 16/11/74.
HAIGH P. BTech. Born 21/2/43. Commd 22/2/71. Flt Lt 22/5/72. Retd GD 22/2/87.
HAIGH-JONES R.C. Born 2/7/46. Commd 4/2/71. Sqn Ldr 1/1/82. Retd GD(G) 1/1/85.
HAIL I.S. Born 3/2/47. Commd 25/2/66. Flt Lt 8/3/72. Retd GD 3/2/85. Re-instated 23/9/87. Flt Lt 26/10/74.
    Retd GD 23/12/95.
HAILE J.E.T. Born 8/3/18. Commd 30/7/38. Wg Cdr 1/7/49. Retd GD 31/7/54.
HAIMES R.C. Born 4/5/23. Commd 13/7/61. Flt Lt 13/7/64. Retd GD(G) 31/3/77.
HAINE R.C. OBE DFC FCMI. Born 1/10/16. Commd 1/4/40. Gp Capt 1/7/62. Retd GD 1/10/70.
HAINES C.V. AFC*. Born 11/3/12. Commd 1/4/40. Sqn Ldr 1/7/55. Retd SEC 29/3/59.
HAINES F.C. Born 11/11/21. Commd 25/12/43. Sqn Ldr 1/4/55. Retd GD 11/11/64.
HAINES G.C. LDSRCS. Born 10/3/33. Commd 19/8/62. Wg Cdr 13/9/72. Retd DEL 10/9/91.
HAINES G.S. Born 22/1/16. Commd 3/12/42. Sqn Ldr 1/7/53. Retd SEC 28/12/62.
HAINES H.G. AFC. Born 2/4/24. Commd 18/11/55. Sqn Ldr 1/7/63. Retd GD 2/4/79.
HAINES J.H. OBE. Born 17/10/45. Commd 8/1/65. A Cdre 1/1/96. Retd GD 1/2/02.
HAINES P.J.J. BSc. Born 16/7/61. Commd 19/11/72. Gp Capt 1/1/04. Retd GD 30/4/05.
HAINES P.W.R. Born 17/8/47. Commd 1/3/68. Flt Lt 6/7/74. Retd GD(G) 17/8/85.
HAINES R.A. Born 4/10/28. Commd 17/5/51. Flt Lt 22/5/57. Retd GD 4/10/66.
HAIR W.J. Born 29/1/51. Commd 16/3/73. Flt Lt 16/3/76. Retd GD 29/1/89.
HAISELDEN J.C. Born 7/11/38. Commd 28/10/76. Flt Lt 28/10/78. Retd ENG 28/10/84.

HAISLEY J.R. LLB. Born 13/5/37. Commd 2/10/67. Flt Lt 2/10/67. Retd GD(G) 2/10/75.
HAKIN L. OBE. Born 9/7/42. Commd 6/9/63. Gp Capt 1/7/90. Retd GD 9/7/97.
HALDANE G.E. BA. Born 5/11/47. Commd 4/6/72. Flt Lt 4/3/74. Retd GD 4/6/88.
HALDANE I. Born 14/5/42. Commd 1/4/66. Flt Lt 4/5/72. Retd GD 8/11/77.
HALE A. OBE BEM. Born 5/7/20. Commd 14/11/46. A Cdre 1/1/73. Retd SUP 5/7/75.
HALE E.J. DFC AFC. Born 6/12/13. Commd 26/10/42. Flt Lt 26/4/47. Retd GD(G) 31/3/60. rtg Sqn Ldr
HALE M.W. Born 14/12/24. Commd 21/4/44. Sqn Ldr 1/4/56. Retd GD 14/12/62.
HALE R.A. Born 28/3/25. Commd 30/4/46. Wg Cdr 1/1/67. Retd GD 27/3/76.
HALE R.M. Born 23/12/46. Commd 14/7/66. Sqn Ldr 1/7/80. Retd GD 23/12/84.
HALEEM S.A.B.A. Born 19/7/43. Commd 10/7/64. Flt Lt 19/1/69. Retd GD 18/3/69.
HALEEM S.M. Born 22/6/67. Commd 16/6/88. Flt Lt 16/12/93. Retd GD 14/3/97.
HALES A.E.G. MCMI. Born 10/11/33. Commd 31/10/62. A Cdre 1/1/85. Retd SY 1/1/87.
HALES D.W. BEng. Born 13/10/66. Commd 21/7/87. Sqn Ldr 1/1/02. Retd FLY(P) 1/1/05.
HALEY J.W.J. MCMI. Born 31/1/25. Commd 26/8/45. Wg Cdr 1/1/67. Retd SUP 4/9/79.
HALEY M.J.B. Born 1/4/37. Commd 7/1/58. Flt Lt 21/8/63. Retd SY 25/9/76.
HALEY R.C. BSc. Born 23/4/62. Commd 11/9/83. Flt Lt 11/3/86. Retd GD 11/9/95.
HALFACREE K.D. Born 27/9/23. Commd 20/5/44. Flt Lt 26/5/55. Retd ENG 30/6/78.
HALFORD W.T.H. Born 9/6/40. Commd 6/8/63. Flt Lt 26/7/67. Retd SUP 6/8/79.
HALFPENNY B.N. The Venerable CB MA. Born 7/6/36. Commd 20/10/65. Retd AVM 7/10/91.
HALFTER P.N. BA. Born 14/2/50. Commd 10/7/72. Wg Cdr 1/7/90. Retd ADMIN 6/4/02.
HALKES J.S. Born 17/7/39. Commd 17/7/60. Sqn Ldr 1/7/68. Retd GD 1/1/71.
HALL A.N.C.M.-. Born 4/7/47. Commd 21/7/65. Sqn Ldr 1/7/94. Retd GD 4/7/00.
HALL A.T. Born 3/10/50. Commd 5/4/91. Sqn Ldr 5/4/89. Retd ENG 14/7/97.
HALL A.V. Born 29/10/45. Commd 1/3/68. Gp Capt 1/7/91. Retd ENG 14/9/96.
HALL B.E. Born 23/12/37. Commd 14/8/64. Flt Lt 3/2/70. Retd ADMIN 6/4/89.
HALL B.J. Born 21/8/38. Commd 8/1/57. Wg Cdr 1/7/75. Retd GD 10/4/92.
HALL C.A. Born 15/1/47. Commd 1/4/71. Flt Lt 1/10/76. Retd GD 24/4/82.
HALL C.R. Born 26/10/37. Commd 28/2/64. Flt Lt 10/2/67. Retd GD 1/8/73.
HALL C.R. Born 14/11/43. Commd 8/9/69. Wg Cdr 1/7/89. Retd SY 23/4/94.
HALL C.S. Born 15/7/41. Commd 28/2/66. Sqn Ldr 1/1/78. Retd ENG 28/2/82.
HALL D. Born 28/3/31. Commd 30/7/52. Flt Lt 21/1/58. Retd GD(G) 28/3/89.
HALL D. Born 23/1/46. Commd 26/5/67. Flt Lt 4/11/70. Retd GD 23/1/90.
HALL D.B. Born 25/7/34. Commd 14/1/53. Flt Lt 3/6/58. Retd PI 5/12/85.
HALL D.C. Born 5/5/28. Commd 28/4/51. Flt Lt 13/10/60. Retd GD 6/5/69.
HALL D.I. Born 5/8/31. Commd 19/8/54. Sqn Ldr 1/7/67. Retd ENG 19/8/81.
HALL E. Born 9/11/34. Commd 11/9/56. Flt Lt 15/8/62. Retd GD 25/6/65.
HALL F.P. CEng MRAeS. Born 13/5/39. Commd 11/10/70. Sqn Ldr 1/7/81. Retd ENG 12/11/91.
HALL G.A. AFM. Born 23/11/23. Commd 27/1/55. Sqn Ldr 1/1/72. Retd GD 1/10/73.
HALL G.G. Born 1/7/16. Commd 16/9/42. Sqn Offr 1/4/57. Retd SEC 1/9/58.
HALL G.H.E. Born 5/7/33. Commd 18/11/66. Flt Lt 18/11/68. Retd GD(G) 18/11/74.
HALL G.R. BEng. Born 27/4/65. Commd 15/9/86. Fg Offr 15/7/86. Retd GD 17/5/88.
HALL G.T. Born 30/11/33. Commd 16/7/52. Flt Lt 21/10/59. Retd GD 30/11/76.
HALL G.W.B. BEng. Born 8/7/37. Commd 4/4/61. Sqn Ldr 1/7/72. Retd GD 16/12/79.
HALL H.B. Born 15/2/37. Commd 5/3/57. Flt Lt 5/9/62. Retd GD 4/5/74.
HALL H.D. CB CBE AFC FCMI. Born 3/6/25. Commd 20/9/48. AVM 1/7/79. Retd GD 6/12/82.
HALL H.W. CBE. Born 28/2/39. Commd 28/4/65. A Cdre 1/7/89. Retd GD 1/6/94.
HALL I. MBE. Born 15/5/40. Commd 1/4/58. Sqn Ldr 1/7/70. Retd GD 15/5/78.
HALL I.S. BA. Born 9/9/48. Commd 13/1/67. Gp Capt 1/1/96. Retd GD 1/10/98.
HALL J. Born 28/12/34. Commd 17/9/52. Flt Lt 17/6/58. Retd GD 20/8/66.
HALL J.A. BA. Born 2/7/49. Commd 27/2/70. Wg Cdr 1/7/86. Retd GD 14/4/97.
HALL J.D. Born 15/2/45. Commd 15/8/85. Flt Lt 15/8/89. Retd ENG 2/4/93.
HALL J.D. Born 9/8/51. Commd 9/5/91. Flt Lt 9/5/93. Retd ADMIN 2/12/96.
HALL J.D.M. Born 21/4/34. Commd 23/1/59. Flt Lt 27/8/62. Retd GD 23/1/71.
HALL J.F. OBE FIIP CEng MRAeS MCMI. Born 28/6/20. Commd 28/7/43. Wg Cdr 1/7/66. Retd ENG 28/6/75.
HALL J.H. Born 20/10/45. Commd 15/9/67. Flt Lt 15/3/73. Retd GD 14/2/77.
HALL J.R. Born 26/3/35. Commd 10/4/56. Flt Lt 10/10/58. Retd GD 26/3/73.
HALL J.S. CBE MSc MB BS FFOM DIH DAvMed. Born 25/10/31. Commd 3/3/57. A Cdre 1/7/87. Retd MED 4/4/92.
HALL K. BSc. Born 23/7/46. Commd 13/9/67. Sqn Ldr 15/1/76. Retd ADMIN 23/7/84.
HALL M.E. Born 8/11/34. Commd 26/5/54. Flt Lt 26/11/59. Retd GD 8/11/72.
HALL M.G. Born 12/10/31. Commd 29/12/51. Flt Lt 25/4/57. Retd GD 18/7/73. Re-employed 11/3/81 to 20/2/82.
HALL M.R. BA. Born 6/1/43. Commd 13/4/66. Wg Cdr 1/1/86. Retd GD 17/10/97.
HALL N.A. Born 2/1/63. Commd 20/1/85. Flt Lt 20/7/88. Retd OPS SPT 20/1/01.
HALL P.M. BA. Born 28/12/40. Commd 17/3/67. Gp Capt 1/7/88. Retd ADMIN 1/7/94.
HALL P.T. MBE. Born 7/8/24. Commd 1/5/45. Wg Cdr 1/7/66. Retd GD 31/7/76.
HALL R.D. Born 15/10/28. Commd 6/7/49. Sqn Ldr 1/7/66. Retd GD 16/7/73.
HALL R.J. MRIN. Born 17/9/46. Commd 4/7/68. Sqn Ldr 1/1/81. Retd FLY(N) 31/3/05.

HALL R.J.J. Born 5/6/19. Commd 20/6/46. Sqn Ldr 1/1/65. Retd ENG 5/6/74.
HALL R.P.W. Born 4/4/50. Commd 19/6/70. Sqn Ldr 1/1/90. Retd FLY(N) 16/2/05.
HALL S.C. Born 11/11/36. Commd 9/2/55. Sqn Ldr 1/7/66. Retd GD 11/11/74.
HALL S.R. MA BA MCIPD MRIN. Born 27/12/43. Commd 9/4/72. Sqn Ldr 12/3/74. Retd ADMIN 27/12/98.
HALL T.D. Born 22/4/20. Commd 19/7/44. Wg Cdr 1/7/74. Retd ENG 18/1/50.
HALL V.C.J. LLB. Born 28/4/77. Commd 4/10/98. Flt Lt 4/4/02. Retd SUPPLY 8/4/03.
HALL W.P. BSc. Born 22/9/63. Commd 14/2/94. Flt Lt 8/11/91. Retd OPS SPT(ATC) 8/5/04.
HALLAM G.P. Born 5/5/36. Commd 9/2/66. Flt Lt 1/7/68. Retd ENG 1/10/75.
HALLAM J.R. Born 21/2/18. Commd 30/3/61. Flt Lt 30/3/66. Retd GD(G) 31/1/69.
HALLAM M.E. MEng BSc CEng MIMechE. Born 18/7/37. Commd 7/5/72. Sqn Ldr 1/6/74. Retd ADMIN 26/10/90.
HALLAM W.B.L. MA. Born 9/2/35. Commd 25/9/54. Flt Lt 15/8/62. Retd ENG 9/2/73.
HALLATT W.H. Born 12/3/22. Commd 5/11/45. Sqn Ldr 1/4/56. Retd GD 12/11/60.
HALLER D. Born 5/10/37. Commd 28/7/59. Sqn Ldr 1/1/69. Retd GD 1/8/80.
HALLETT A.C. Born 24/11/48. Commd 21/12/67. Sqn Ldr 1/1/86. Retd SY(RGT) 1/1/89.
HALLETT A.W. MBE DFC AFC. Born 12/11/21. Commd 24/4/44. Flt Lt 24/4/50. Retd CAT 12/11/70.
HALLETT C.A. Born 26/2/33. Commd 16/9/71. Flt Lt 16/9/74. Retd GD 26/2/88.
HALLIDAY B.W. BSc. Born 27/6/32. Commd 6/1/55. Sqn Ldr 17/2/65. Retd EDN 23/9/70.
HALLIDAY D.G. MBE. Born 16/5/47. Commd 30/1/75. Flt Lt 15/2/82. Retd SUPPLY 16/5/85. Re-entered 1/6/90.
    Sqn Ldr 1/7/95. Retd SUPPLY 16/5/04.
HALLIDAY N.G. MSc MBCS. Born 30/12/34. Commd 27/5/53. Wg Cdr 1/7/83. Retd GD 2/11/85.
HALLING G.R. MBE. Born 31/7/17. Commd 8/7/43. Flt Lt 8/1/47. Retd ENG 14/8/65.
HALLION G. Born 17/7/31. Commd 29/12/51. Flt Lt 13/11/57. Retd GD 17/7/69.
HALLIWELL N.J. Born 23/9/54. Commd 16/5/74. Sqn Ldr 1/7/89. Retd GD 23/9/92.
HALLIWELL S. DFC* MCMI. Born 25/7/21. Commd 19/4/43. Wg Cdr 1/7/68. Retd GD 10/8/76.
HALLORAN G.M. Born 28/7/44. Commd 6/9/68. Sqn Ldr 1/7/86. Retd ADMIN 17/1/91.
HALLOWAY I. BEng. Born 26/2/64. Commd 1/8/86. Flt Lt 27/2/91. Retd ENG 14/9/96.
HALLOWS B.R.W. OBE DFC. Born 3/6/16. Commd 7/3/40. Wg Cdr 1/1/52. Retd GD 16/6/60.
HALLS B.J. Born 21/2/31. Commd 13/8/52. Flt Lt 9/1/58. Retd GD 21/2/69.
HALLS B.R. Born 10/2/41. Commd 19/1/68. Flt Lt 29/6/74. Retd ENG 29/6/80.
HALLS B.R. Born 10/2/41. Commd 10/7/87. Sqn Ldr 1/1/91. Retd ENG 31/3/93.
HALLS M.D. Born 22/1/38. Commd 25/7/59. Flt Lt 25/1/65. Retd GD(G) 6/4/79.
HALLS R.A. Born 31/1/19. Commd 29/8/46. Flt Lt 7/6/51. Retd SUP 8/5/56.
HALLUMS P.L. Born 8/6/18. Commd 6/12/56. Flt Lt 6/12/59. Retd ENG 8/6/73.
HALLWORTH B. MSc BSc. Born 30/12/35. Commd 3/1/61. Sqn Ldr 17/6/70. Retd ADMIN 3/1/77.
HALSALL M.C. MBCS MIEE. Born 13/3/53. Commd 1/7/82. Flt Lt 1/7/84. Retd ENG 13/3/91.
HALSEY J.C. MSc BSc(Eng) ACGI. Born 14/11/54. Commd 2/9/73. Sqn Ldr 1/7/89. Retd ENG 15/11/91.
HALSTEAD J.S. Born 22/8/46. Commd 20/10/67. Flt Lt 22/2/72. Retd GD 12/10/93.
HALSTEAD R.G. DFC. Born 10/6/22. Commd 7/1/44. Flt Lt 4/12/52. Retd GD 28/10/64.
HAM G. Born 26/3/47. Commd 28/2/85. Sqn Ldr 1/1/97. Retd ENGINEER 13/3/03.
HAMBIDGE C.D. BEM. Born 19/4/22. Commd 26/8/66. Flt Lt 26/8/68. Retd SEC 26/8/74.
HAMBIDGE J.E. MB BS. Born 14/9/58. Commd 29/8/80. Sqn Ldr 1/8/89. Retd MED 1/3/96.
HAMBLETON J.R. Born 24/2/39. Commd 31/7/62. Flt Lt 15/2/65. Retd GD 20/12/82.
HAMBLIN B.E. Born 22/4/46. Commd 28/4/65. Flt Lt 4/11/70. Retd GD 12/11/76. Re-instated 4/8/78. Flt Lt 28/7/72.
    Retd GD 1/4/90.
HAMBLING B.F. Born 29/11/46. Commd 3/12/70. Sqn Ldr 1/7/78. Retd ENG 29/11/84.
HAMBLY F.E.W. Born 11/6/31. Commd 21/5/52. Sqn Ldr 1/7/85. Retd GD 1/5/90.
HAMBLY P.F. Born 1/7/59. Commd 5/2/81. Sqn Ldr 1/7/92. Retd SUP 14/3/97.
HAMBRY E.V. Born 23/12/11. Commd 6/6/40. Sqn Ldr 1/8/47. Retd SEC 23/12/60.
HAMER J.L. Born 16/8/47. Commd 1/8/69. Flt Lt 1/2/75. Retd ENG 22/6/79.
HAMER N.J.T. Born 29/3/43. Commd 13/12/79. Sqn Ldr 1/1/90. Retd GD 14/9/96.
HAMER T.L. BSc. Born 19/1/51. Commd 21/1/73. Sqn Ldr 1/7/82. Retd GD(G) 21/1/89.
HAMER T.M. AFC AFM. Born 10/11/23. Commd 24/2/55. Sqn Ldr 1/1/69. Retd GD 24/1/82.
HAMES C.S. Born 29/9/22. Commd 1/1/43. Flt Lt 1/7/46. Retd GD 28/9/55.
HAMILL J.W. Born 31/10/40. Commd 26/5/61. Sqn Ldr 1/1/88. Retd GD 2/12/92.
HAMILL P.A. Born 31/12/29. Commd 16/9/50. Wg Cdr 1/1/74. Retd GD 1/8/84.
HAMILL R. BSc. Born 7/4/51. Commd 5/5/71. Flt Lt 15/4/74. Retd GD 7/4/89.
HAMILL-KEAYS W.J.P. Born 11/3/40. Commd 16/9/76. Sqn Ldr 1/7/84. Retd ADMIN 1/7/87.
HAMILTON A.F. DSO DFC. Born 15/12/12. Commd 12/8/32. Wg Cdr 1/10/46. Retd GD 23/12/59.
HAMILTON A.G. MCMI. Born 3/2/29. Commd 30/7/52. Sqn Ldr 1/7/63. Retd SEC 8/9/72.
HAMILTON A.G. Born 23/12/47. Commd 2/12/66. Flt Lt 2/6/72. Retd GD 15/6/76.
HAMILTON B. CBE DFC AFC FRIN MRAeS FCMI. Born 18/10/23. Commd 1/7/46. A Cdre 1/7/69. Retd GD 9/6/78.
HAMILTON B.I.L. MRAeS. Born 7/10/34. Commd 10/2/54. Sqn Ldr 1/1/72. Retd GD 4/5/88.
HAMILTON C.I. Born 23/10/43. Commd 13/1/67. Sqn Ldr 1/7/01. Retd FLY(N) 15/1/04.
HAMILTON D.A. BTech. Born 23/12/50. Commd 13/11/72. Wg Cdr 1/1/00. Retd GD 1/1/02.
HAMILTON D.B. Born 10/2/49. Commd 8/11/73. Wg Cdr 1/7/94. Retd GD 10/2/04.
HAMILTON D.R. Born 24/7/48. Commd 28/4/67. Gp Capt 1/1/95. Retd GD 12/9/97.

HAMILTON F.B. Born 28/4/21. Commd 28/7/43. Sqn Ldr 1/1/55. Retd GD 11/5/64.
HAMILTON F.J. MCMI. Born 21/6/36. Commd 2/4/57. Gp Capt 1/1/86. Retd GD 21/6/91.
HAMILTON G. Born 18/4/47. Commd 1/9/86. Flt Lt 15/10/73. Retd GD 2/4/93.
HAMILTON G.A. Born 27/6/66. Commd 19/5/93. Flt Lt 15/6/95. Retd OPS SPT(ATC) 15/8/04.
HAMILTON I.B. Born 23/6/33. Commd 24/5/53. Sqn Ldr 1/1/66. Retd GD 23/6/71.
HAMILTON I.B. Born 30/3/37. Commd 23/1/64. Flt Lt 1/4/66. Retd PRT 30/3/75.
HAMILTON I.G. BSc. Born 21/4/67. Commd 1/7/97. Sqn Ldr 1/7/00. Retd ADMIN (TRG) 21/4/05.
HAMILTON I.P. Born 17/6/47. Commd 2/7/72. Wg Cdr 1/7/95. Retd ENG 1/11/01.
HAMILTON J.M. BSc. Born 19/6/53. Commd 17/9/72. Sqn Ldr 1/7/88. Retd ENG 30/11/92.
HAMILTON M.B. Born 3/4/11. Commd 19/12/31. Wg Cdr 1/10/46. Retd GD 2/6/48. rtg Gp Capt
HAMILTON M.L. DFC. Born 31/1/18. Commd 25/9/42. Sqn Ldr 1/10/55. Retd GD 22/10/57.
HAMILTON N.I. Born 13/8/43. Commd 10/5/64. A Cdre 1/1/96. Retd GD 1/2/98.
HAMILTON P.D. BMet. Born 23/3/61. Commd 29/1/82. Flt Lt 15/4/84. Retd GD 23/3/99.
HAMILTON R.C.F. Born 31/8/27. Commd 12/6/51. Flt Lt 17/5/56. Retd GD(G) 14/12/74.
HAMILTON R.J. BSc. Born 2/1/50. Commd 22/10/72. Sqn Ldr 1/1/84. Retd GD 22/10/88.
HAMILTON R.McC. Born 16/8/23. Commd 11/8/44. Flt Lt 15/5/48. Retd GD 16/8/68. rtg Sqn Ldr
HAMILTON T.E. Born 29/11/44. Commd 21/10/65. Gp Capt 1/1/95. Retd GD(G) 14/9/96.
HAMILTON T.S. Born 6/11/60. Commd 30/3/89. Flt Lt 30/3/91. Retd ENG 6/5/94.
HAMILTON-IRVINE W.D. Born 27/7/41. Commd 8/12/61. Flt Lt 10/2/67. Retd GD 18/7/72.
HAMILTON-RUMP D.J. Born 23/4/43. Commd 17/12/64. A Cdre 1/1/93. Retd GD 8/1/94.
HAMLETT D.M. BA. Born 23/9/12. Commd 30/8/51. Sqn Offr 1/1/65. Retd SEC 4/2/68.
HAMLEY D.B.D. Born 9/4/27. Commd 7/4/48. Wg Cdr 1/1/65. Retd GD 1/6/78.
HAMLEY P.O.V. Born 24/3/22. Commd 22/2/45. Flt Lt 19/6/52. Retd GD 30/5/56.
HAMLIN D.E. MA. Born 21/4/32. Commd 28/9/54. Flt Lt 28/12/55. Retd GD 28/9/70.
HAMLIN D.P.A. BA. Born 18/9/59. Commd 11/9/77. Flt Lt 15/10/81. Retd GD 8/8/00.
HAMLYN G.M. Born 9/12/46. Commd 15/12/67. Flt Lt 15/3/73. Retd GD 9/12/01.
HAMLYN K. Born 12/4/46. Commd 13/12/79. Sqn Ldr 1/1/91. Retd SUP 14/3/97.
HAMM D.J. Born 16/4/36. Commd 22/4/68. Flt Lt 15/8/73. Retd ADMIN 22/4/84.
HAMMANS G.D. Born 4/7/28. Commd 11/4/51. Fg Offr 11/4/53. Retd SUP 12/4/56.
HAMMANS M.P. Born 3/8/59. Commd 20/1/81. Sqn Ldr 1/1/95. Retd GD 1/1/98.
HAMMATT D.A. AFC DFM*. Born 17/11/19. Commd 30/3/42. Sqn Ldr 1/7/50. Retd GD 12/12/58.
HAMMETT G.G. Born 14/9/54. Commd 27/2/75. Sqn Ldr 1/7/89. Retd OPS SPT 6/8/02.
HAMMETT R.J. BSc. Born 27/6/50. Commd 24/9/72. Wg Cdr 1/7/91. Retd SY 14/3/96.
HAMMOND B.G. FCA. Born 23/4/34. Commd 11/4/57. Gp Capt 1/1/81. Retd ADMIN 15/9/84.
HAMMOND D.J. FHCIMA MCMI. Born 9/10/36. Commd 5/10/56. Wg Cdr 1/7/76. Retd ADMIN 11/2/85.
HAMMOND D.R. Born 2/10/51. Commd 21/9/72. Sqn Ldr 1/1/87. Retd GD 1/1/90.
HAMMOND E.J. CEng MRAeS MIEE. Born 24/7/33. Commd 30/4/59. Wg Cdr 1/1/74. Retd ENG 26/7/83.
HAMMOND J. BSc. Born 13/1/65. Commd 20/3/95. Sqn Ldr 1/1/99. Retd ENGINEER 8/5/04.
HAMMOND L.C. Born 16/6/42. Commd 9/11/70. Sqn Ldr 1/1/80. Retd SUP 16/6/97.
HAMMOND L.J.C. Born 26/7/35. Commd 22/1/54. Sqn Ldr 1/1/71. Retd GD 1/1/74.
HAMMOND M.K. BSc CEng MIEE. Born 1/3/58. Commd 17/8/80. Sqn Ldr 1/1/90. Retd ENG 17/8/96.
HAMMOND O.M. Born 30/10/45. Commd 8/1/65. Flt Lt 8/7/70. Retd GD 31/12/75.
HAMMOND P.R.A. Born 30/11/41. Commd 1/4/71. Fg Offr 1/10/73. Retd SUP 22/11/74.
HAMMOND R.J. Born 21/4/34. Commd 14/1/53. Flt Lt 21/10/59. Retd GD 21/4/72.
HAMMOND S.H.J. BEM. Born 7/7/14. Commd 27/10/55. Flt Lt 27/10/61. Retd ENG 23/7/69.
HAMMOND S.M. BSc. Born 3/5/63. Commd 20/6/94. Sqn Ldr 1/1/02. Retd FLY(P) 1/1/05.
HAMMOND S.P. Born 17/6/47. Commd 28/10/66. Flt Lt 28/4/72. Retd GD 17/6/02.
HAMMOND T.L. Born 7/6/53. Commd 5/7/73. Flt Lt 5/1/79. Retd GD 12/8/90.
HAMMOND T.M. MB ChB MRCGP DRCOG DAvMed. Born 12/9/58. Commd 19/12/80. Sqn Ldr 1/2/90.
    Retd MED 19/12/96.
HAMMOND-DOUTRE G.I. Born 15/2/36. Commd 22/8/59. Sqn Ldr 1/1/81. Retd GD 15/2/91.
HAMON S. Born 13/5/47. Commd 2/11/88. Flt Lt 2/11/92. Retd GD(G) 14/3/96.
HAMPER K.L. BSc. Born 7/7/56. Commd 23/9/79. Flt Lt 23/12/82. Retd GD(G) 23/9/95.
HAMPSON L. MCMI. Born 23/7/24. Commd 13/5/44. Gp Capt 1/7/76. Retd GD 24/4/79.
HAMPSON S.T.J. Born 20/4/21. Commd 11/8/43. Sqn Ldr 1/7/56. Retd GD 20/4/71.
HAMPSON-JONES C. BEng. Born 5/6/63. Commd 3/8/88. Sqn Ldr 1/1/99. Retd ENG 5/6/01.
HAMPTON A.G.N. Born 13/3/30. Commd 30/7/52. Flt Lt 30/1/55. Retd GD 1/10/58.
HAMPTON G. OBE DFC. Born 26/8/19. Commd 26/8/42. Wg Cdr 1/1/58. Retd GD 28/8/66.
HAMPTON I.J. Born 28/11/46. Commd 21/1/66. Sqn Ldr 1/1/82. Retd FLY(N) 28/11/03.
HAMPTON R. AFC. Born 1/5/24. Commd 3/8/45. Gp Capt 1/7/71. Retd GD 1/5/79.
HANAGAN R.M. MBE. Born 26/6/12. Commd 23/4/53. Flt Lt 1/6/56. Retd CAT 16/7/68. rtg Sqn Ldr
HANBURY T.J. BDS LDSRCS. Born 26/9/37. Commd 18/9/60. Wg Cdr 6/8/65. Retd DEL 31/12/82.
HANCOCK C.S. Born 10/8/38. Commd 13/10/61. Sqn Ldr 1/1/80. Retd ADMIN 10/4/86.
HANCOCK D.J. Born 23/10/24. Commd 14/2/45. Flt Lt 14/8/48. Retd GD 23/10/67.
HANCOCK J.E.G. DFC AE. Born 18/6/11. Commd 5/5/40. Sqn Ldr 1/7/50. Retd GD(G) 2/9/61.
HANCOCK J.L. MDA BSc CEng MRAeS. Born 24/11/55. Commd 14/3/77. Wg Cdr 1/7/93. Retd ENG 31/1/02.

HANCOCK L.T.F. Born 1/9/13. Commd 12/11/42. Sqn Ldr 1/7/53. Retd ENG 1/9/68.
HANCOCK R.A. OBE CEng MRAeS MIEE. Born 26/12/30. Commd 16/11/51. Wg Cdr 1/1/72. Retd ENG 12/8/85.
HANCOX I.R. BSc CEng MRAeS. Born 18/2/49. Commd 24/1/73. Flt Lt 24/4/75. Retd ENG 24/4/82.
HAND G.J. AFC DPhysEd. Born 4/6/47. Commd 11/8/69. Sqn Ldr 1/7/81. Retd ADMIN 14/3/96.
HANDFIELD R. Born 19/4/49. Commd 31/7/70. Flt Lt 31/7/73. Retd GD 2/2/82.
HANDLEY C. MA BM BCh FRCS(Edin). Born 15/10/49. Commd 20/2/73. Wg Cdr 16/7/88. Retd MED 20/2/95.
HANDLEY D.J. Born 17/7/46. Commd 4/7/85. Flt Lt 4/7/89. Retd ADMIN 14/3/97.
HANDLEY F.M. Born 22/8/12. Commd 26/9/41. Flt Lt 17/10/47. Retd SUP 22/8/67.
HANDLEY R. Born 12/4/30. Commd 9/12/65. Sqn Ldr 27/12/72. Retd EDN 9/12/73.
HANDS E.C. Born 30/12/47. Commd 17/7/75. Flt Lt 17/7/77. Retd ENG 30/12/85.
HANDS G.T. Born 19/11/13. Commd 18/2/43. Sqn Ldr 1/1/54. Retd ENG 19/5/72.
HANDS M.W. Born 30/5/42. Commd 27/1/61. Flt Lt 27/7/66. Retd GD 15/2/80.
HANDS P.J.F. IEng MCMI. Born 20/10/40. Commd 23/11/78. Sqn Ldr 1/1/88. Retd ENG 1/5/95.
HANDSCOMB K.L. Born 26/12/29. Commd 11/1/55. Sqn Ldr 1/7/83. Retd GD 26/12/87.
HANDY R.B. MCIPD. Born 4/10/43. Commd 30/7/64. Sqn Ldr 1/1/87. Retd OPS SPT 19/4/99.
HANFORD F.J. BA. Born 26/8/41. Commd 14/11/71. Flt Lt 14/5/74. Retd SUP 23/6/96.
HANKIN E.C.H. Born 23/6/07. Commd 16/1/47. Flt Lt 4/1/51. Retd SUP 8/11/55.
HANKINSON K. Born 18/9/24. Commd 23/4/53. Flt Lt 23/10/56. Retd GD 13/12/78.
HANKINSON K.W. BA. Born 19/4/52. Commd 12/1/75. Flt Lt 12/4/76. Retd GD 1/10/91.
HANKINSON R.C.D. MSc BA MBCS. Born 12/7/52. Commd 24/6/71. Sqn Ldr 1/1/84. Retd SUP 12/7/90.
HANLEY-LANDERS J.E. Born 5/1/50. Commd 14/10/71. Flt Lt 11/3/78. Retd GD(G) 5/1/88.
HANLON D.J. BSc. Born 15/8/49. Commd 22/10/72. Flt Lt 22/7/73. Retd GD 22/10/88.
HANLON R.E. Born 7/8/41. Commd 12/7/68. Sqn Ldr 1/7/80. Retd GD 5/4/93.
HANLON T.G. FRAeS FCMI. Born 10/7/47. Commd 5/11/65. Gp Capt 1/1/95. Retd GD 26/4/00.
HANMORE D. Born 22/2/25. Commd 9/6/45. Flt Lt 27/5/54. Retd GD 24/4/66.
HANN C.D. Born 1/8/66. Commd 27/7/89. Flt Lt 24/12/94. Retd OPS SPT(FC) 3/4/05.
HANN D.W. Born 22/8/35. Commd 9/7/54. AVM 1/1/85. Retd GD 17/8/89.
HANN M.P. BA. Born 24/8/37. Commd 7/10/63. Sqn Ldr 1/7/76. Retd GD 7/10/79.
HANN P.G. BEM CEng MRAeS MCMI. Born 13/8/16. Commd 12/4/51. Wg Cdr 1/1/68. Retd ENG 5/9/71.
HANNA M.A. Born 6/8/59. Commd 20/7/78. Flt Lt 20/1/84. Retd GD 8/10/88.
HANNA R.G. AFC*. Born 28/8/28. Commd 2/5/51. Sqn Ldr 1/1/68. Retd GD 14/5/71.
HANNABY A.R. BSc CEng MRAeS. Born 16/4/58. Commd 5/9/76. Wg Cdr 1/7/97. Retd ENG 16/4/02.
HANNAFORD A.G. Born 19/2/38. Commd 23/10/59. Sqn Ldr 1/7/72. Retd SEC 19/2/76.
HANNAFORD E.R. Born 27/8/43. Commd 9/2/62. Wg Cdr 1/1/90. Retd GD 4/12/98.
HANNAH K.J.E. MVO AFC. Born 16/8/26. Commd 3/5/46. Wg Cdr 1/1/70. Retd GD 14/2/76.
HANNAH M. Born 16/8/22. Commd 10/9/43. Wg Cdr 1/7/72. Retd GD 16/8/77.
HANNAM G.I. Born 1/8/48. Commd 29/4/71. Sqn Ldr 1/1/85. Retd GD 1/1/88.
HANNANT J.W. DFC. Born 19/2/15. Commd 5/1/42. Flt Lt 1/9/45. Retd PE 26/4/69.
HANNAWAY P. MA. Born 10/12/58. Commd 6/6/86. Sqn Ldr 1/7/92. Retd SUPPLY 14/12/03.
HANNAY T.J. Born 2/9/29. Commd 14/8/53. Flt Lt 12/4/59. Retd GD 30/9/75.
HANNEY J.P. Born 12/12/33. Commd 12/3/52. Flt Lt 12/12/57. Retd GD 26/10/62.
HANNIGAN C.R. Born 28/1/23. Commd 13/1/52. Flt Lt 13/7/55. Retd GD 14/3/68.
HANNIGAN J.B. The Rev. Born 20/4/30. Commd 18/10/61. Retd Wg Cdr 18/10/81.
HANNINGTON R.H. CEng MRAeS. Born 8/7/40. Commd 17/7/62. Sqn Ldr 1/7/72. Retd ENG 8/7/78.
HANNINGTON R.P.H. MBA BEng CEng MIEE MCMI. Born 27/11/52. Commd 12/1/75. Wg Cdr 1/7/89. Retd ENG 12/1/97.
HANNS D.W.G. Born 3/12/37. Commd 17/5/79. Sqn Ldr 1/7/89. Retd GD 3/12/93.
HANSEN E.J. Born 3/5/32. Commd 8/10/52. Flt Lt 6/3/58. Retd GD 14/11/71.
HANSLIP N.C. MSc MRAeS DCAe. Born 14/5/23. Commd 9/8/50. Sqn Ldr 9/7/57. Retd EDN 3/2/65.
HANSLOW M.G. Born 18/9/46. Commd 24/3/83. Sqn Ldr 1/7/94. Retd ENG 18/9/01.
HANSON B. Born 22/8/39. Commd 10/12/65. Sqn Ldr 1/7/75. Retd GD 18/7/83.
HANSON B.T. Born 28/10/29. Commd 22/3/51. Flt Lt 13/2/57. Retd GD 30/7/70.
HANSON J.H. Born 16/6/35. Commd 24/6/63. Flt Lt 29/4/59. Retd GD 8/3/73.
HANSON P.C. Born 26/1/54. Commd 11/2/93. Flt Lt 11/2/97. Retd ADMIN 15/9/97.
HARBISON W. CB CBE AFC. Born 11/4/22. Commd 6/11/42. AVM 1/1/75. Retd GD 31/3/77.
HARBORD H.R. CEng MRAeS MCMI. Born 12/5/22. Commd 19/6/52. Wg Cdr 1/1/71. Retd ENG 31/3/77.
HARBORNE M.P. BSc. Born 29/5/56. Commd 15/9/74. Flt Lt 15/4/79. Retd GD 29/5/94.
HARBORNE P.N. Born 10/8/47. Commd 26/2/71. Wg Cdr 1/1/98. Retd GD 11/8/02.
HARCOMBE R.T. Born 18/12/31. Commd 24/1/63. Sqn Ldr 1/1/77. Retd ENG 18/1/84.
HARCOURT-SMITH B. Born 18/7/34. Commd 18/6/52. Wg Cdr 1/7/73. Retd GD 25/2/85.
HARCOURT-SMITH Sir David GBE KCB DFC FRAeS. Born 14/10/31. Commd 30/7/52. ACM 1/1/87. Retd GD 20/5/89.
HARDAKER S. Born 5/5/21. Commd 28/9/61. Sqn Ldr 1/1/72. Retd ENG 30/3/76.
HARDCASTLE J.E.F. Born 15/9/30. Commd 19/4/50. Sqn Ldr 1/1/62. Retd SEC 15/9/68.
HARDCASTLE W.D. Born 20/2/32. Commd 27/1/77. Flt Lt 27/1/80. Retd ADMIN 28/5/82.
HARDEN K.J. Born 16/4/44. Commd 12/7/79. Wg Cdr 1/7/91. Retd ADMIN 16/4/99.
HARDEN R.H. Born 16/2/43. Commd 14/2/69. Flt Lt 6/10/71. Retd GD 18/2/81.
HARDHAM J.A. Born 18/10/28. Commd 8/9/53. Flt Lt 22/5/57. Retd GD 25/10/66.

HARDIE C.B.H. Born 30/4/40. Commd 19/12/61. Flt Lt 19/6/64. Retd GD 29/9/83.
HARDIE C.H.C. Born 27/10/33. Commd 16/7/52. Flt Lt 12/12/57. Retd GD 27/10/71.
HARDIE J.D.V. Born 8/9/48. Commd 1/8/69. Flt Lt 1/8/72. Retd GD 3/2/81.
HARDIE J.W. Born 5/9/37. Commd 4/3/71. Flt Lt 4/3/73. Retd GD 4/3/79.
HARDIE P.D. Born 23/1/49. Commd 2/12/66. Sqn Ldr 1/1/85. Retd GD 14/3/96.
HARDIE T.J. AFC. Born 22/8/29. Commd 12/6/51. Flt Lt 12/12/55. Retd GD 22/8/67.
HARDING A.G. MSc BSc. Born 10/6/48. Commd 27/2/70. Sqn Ldr 1/7/84. Retd ENG 1/10/89.
HARDING C.D.E. Born 14/9/64. Commd 15/3/84. Flt Lt 15/9/90. Retd OPS SPT 14/3/00.
HARDING D.A.W. Born 14/4/37. Commd 23/9/66. Flt Lt 23/9/68. Retd GD 14/12/85.
HARDING J.V. CBE. Born 9/5/40. Commd 31/7/62. Gp Capt 1/1/90. Retd GD 9/8/95.
HARDING J.W. Born 15/1/34. Commd 27/5/53. Flt Lt 29/4/59. Retd GD 15/1/72.
HARDING J.W.W. Born 14/10/45. Commd 7/7/67. Sqn Ldr 1/1/82. Retd GD(G) 8/11/93.
HARDING K.A. Born 10/4/65. Commd 19/7/84. Flt Lt 19/1/90. Retd GD 29/7/96.
HARDING K.O. OBE. Born 10/12/37. Commd 19/2/57. Gp Capt 1/1/86. Retd GD 2/4/91.
HARDING M.S. Born 6/7/60. Commd 27/3/80. Flt Lt 27/9/85. Retd GD 12/7/99.
HARDING P.E. DPhysEd. Born 27/3/42. Commd 11/8/69. Sqn Ldr 1/7/84. Retd ADMIN 15/8/94.
HARDING P.G. MBE. Born 3/6/20. Commd 18/7/49. Flt Lt 4/1/51. Retd RGT 19/12/51.
HARDING P.J. MCMI. Born 13/7/39. Commd 4/9/58. Sqn Ldr 1/1/70. Retd SUP 13/7/77.
HARDING P.J. Born 5/7/48. Commd 1/8/69. Sqn Ldr 1/1/81. Retd SY 5/7/87.
HARDING P.J. CB CBE AFC. Born 1/6/40. Commd 12/3/60. AVM 1/1/89. Retd GD 1/6/98.
HARDING P.M. Born 1/7/25. Commd 6/10/51. Flt Offr 12/3/59. Retd SEC 6/5/61.
HARDING R.M. PhD BSc MB BS DAvMed AFOM MRAeS. Born 17/7/50. Commd 5/3/72. Wg Cdr 12/7/89.
   Retd MED 21/4/95.
HARDING R.R. Born 16/3/26. Commd 1/10/54. Wg Cdr 1/7/67. Retd GD 16/3/84.
HARDING S.J. Born 19/11/41. Commd 24/4/80. Sqn Ldr 1/7/90. Retd ENG 29/7/95.
HARDING S.J. Born 4/11/57. Commd 28/2/80. Sqn Ldr 1/1/93. Retd ADMIN 1/1/96.
HARDING-MORRIS S. Born 31/3/56. Commd 10/5/90. Flt Lt 2/9/95. Retd MED(T) 14/3/96.
HARDINGE N.G. Born 26/3/36. Commd 6/7/62. Flt Lt 1/4/66. Retd GD 23/6/74.
HARDISTY R.W. Born 29/4/44. Commd 22/2/63. Flt Lt 22/8/68. Retd GD 28/4/76.
HARDLESS J.W. Born 16/8/30. Commd 17/1/51. Flt Lt 17/7/55. Retd GD 16/8/68.
HARDMAN C. Born 29/3/21. Commd 21/9/43. Sqn Ldr 1/7/63. Retd GD 31/7/68.
HARDMAN K.P. BSc CEng MRAeS. Born 17/3/28. Commd 30/11/50. Sqn Ldr 17/2/65. Retd EDN 14/7/73.
HARDS P.H. Born 9/4/17. Commd 24/4/43. Sqn Ldr 1/7/56. Retd GD 28/10/72.
HARDSTAFF J. MBE. Born 28/2/35. Commd 27/5/53. A Cdre 1/1/84. Retd GD 1/4/88.
HARDWICK B.J. Born 7/10/30. Commd 24/2/67. Flt Lt 24/2/72. Retd GD 12/3/77.
HARDWICK E.A. Born 17/8/47. Commd 26/5/67. Sqn Ldr 1/7/81. Retd ENG 17/8/86.
HARDWICK J.R. Born 13/10/33. Commd 17/12/52. Gp Capt 1/7/80. Retd GD 6/5/88.
HARDWICK M. Born 12/7/48. Commd 30/7/72. Sqn Ldr 1/1/89. Retd ENGINEER 6/4/04.
HARDY A.J. BPhil MCIPD DPhysEd DipTM CertEd. Born 6/6/35. Commd 14/9/79. Sqn Ldr 1/7/86. Retd ADMIN 6/6/93.
HARDY F.O.C. Born 26/3/29. Commd 27/2/50. Flt Lt 22/4/66. Retd GD 26/3/67.
HARDY M.J. Born 15/3/34. Commd 12/1/52. Gp Capt 1/7/74. Retd GD 26/11/76.
HARDY N.J. Born 14/6/63. Commd 1/7/82. Flt Lt 1/1/88. Retd GD 14/6/01.
HARDY O.L. DFC* AFC. Born 31/7/22. Commd 1/9/45. Wg Cdr 1/1/59. Retd GD 20/8/69.
HARDY R. MBE. Born 14/6/27. Commd 4/2/48. Wg Cdr 1/1/70. Retd SY 31/7/76.
HARDY R.A. Born 25/5/49. Commd 8/9/77. Flt Lt 8/3/84. Retd SUP 23/5/93.
HARDY R.J. Born 24/7/51. Commd 13/9/70. Fg Offr 13/9/73. Retd GD 24/12/74.
HARDY W.W.G. Born 21/6/37. Commd 26/9/57. Sqn Ldr 1/1/71. Retd SY 21/6/77.
HARDY-GILLINGS B. Born 31/5/48. Commd 7/7/67. Sqn Ldr 1/7/97. Retd FLY(N) 31/5/03.
HARDY-SMITH B.A. Born 10/12/41. Commd 11/7/64. Flt Lt 4/5/72. Retd GD 10/12/79.
HARE E.W.F. OBE FCMI MRAeS. Born 12/9/23. Commd 12/11/43. Gp Capt 1/7/69. Retd GD 12/9/73.
HARE J.M. Born 22/7/33. Commd 30/9/53. Sqn Ldr 1/1/64. Retd GD 14/9/73.
HARE M.W.J. AFC LLB. Born 9/1/55. Commd 16/9/73. Sqn Ldr 1/1/86. Retd GD 12/4/88.
HARGRAVE G.W. Born 11/1/24. Commd 1/1/63. Flt Lt 1/1/63. Retd EDN 31/8/67.
HARGREAVES A.S. Born 24/9/43. Commd 17/7/64. Wg Cdr 1/1/88. Retd ADMIN 6/1/97.
HARGREAVES D.A. Born 28/9/57. Commd 19/12/76. Flt Lt 19/6/79. Retd GD 1/1/97.
HARGREAVES D.J. Born 1/4/44. Commd 17/12/65. Sqn Ldr 1/1/78. Retd GD 1/4/94.
HARGREAVES G. CEng MRAeS CChem MRSC. Born 1/12/35. Commd 2/1/62. Wg Cdr 1/7/78. Retd ENG 1/6/86.
HARGREAVES J.G. CBE. Born 17/3/37. Commd 6/8/58. A Cdre 1/1/93. Retd SUP 1/1/93.
HARGREAVES K. Born 10/7/43. Commd 14/6/63. Flt Lt 14/12/68. Retd GD 10/7/81. Re-entered 19/5/82. Sqn Ldr 19/5/82.
   Sqn Ldr 1/7/90. Retd GD 10/7/99.
HARGREAVES L.J. Born 18/3/34. Commd 30/7/52. Sqn Ldr 1/1/65. Retd GD 22/3/72.
HARGREAVES L.N.M. PhD BSc MB ChB DAvMed. Born 25/9/50. Commd 19/7/78. Wg Cdr 4/8/95. Retd MED 14/9/96.
HARGREAVES M. Born 3/7/44. Commd 14/6/63. Flt Lt 14/12/69. Retd SUP 3/7/82.
HARGREAVES R.S. BSc(Eng) MRAeS. Born 26/1/33. Commd 4/4/59. Wg Cdr 1/7/80. Retd GD 3/5/85.
HARKER F.G. Born 8/8/19. Commd 27/10/55. Flt Lt 27/10/61. Retd SUP 3/10/64.
HARKER G.S. MDA FRAeS. Born 4/5/50. Commd 15/9/69. Gp Capt 1/7/97. Retd ENG 31/5/02.

HARKER W.D. Born 12/9/18. Commd 29/6/54. Flt Lt 29/6/59. Retd ENG 22/10/61.
HARKIN A.G. BSocSc. Born 20/8/63. Commd 26/4/87. Flt Lt 26/10/89. Retd ADMIN 14/9/96.
HARKIN D.J. BA. Born 25/1/52. Commd 20/9/71. Sqn Ldr 1/1/85. Retd GD 25/1/90.
HARLAND A.J. CEng MIMechE MRAeS. Born 12/6/33. Commd 20/2/55. Wg Cdr 1/7/79. Retd ENG 12/7/88.
HARLAND L.L. DFC*. Born 12/2/20. Commd 19/7/42. Wg Cdr 1/1/58. Retd GD 24/2/67.
HARLAND M.C. Born 17/4/63. Commd 8/4/82. Sqn Ldr 1/1/97. Retd FLY(N) 7/1/04.
HARLAND Sir Reginald KBE CB AE* MA CEng FIMechE FIEE FRAeS CCMI. Born 30/5/20. Commd 3/10/39.
    AM 1/1/74. Retd ENG 8/8/77.
HARLAND W.G.F. BA. Born 27/5/48. Commd 1/10/70. Flt Lt 1/7/71. Retd GD 14/5/96.
HARLE D.D. Born 28/3/51. Commd 25/2/72. Flt Lt 25/2/75. Retd GD 28/3/89.
HARLEY G.P. Born 28/10/64. Commd 4/12/86. Flt Lt 4/6/92. Retd GD 14/3/97.
HARLING R. DFC. Born 25/10/20. Commd 14/1/45. Flt Lt 14/7/48. Retd GD 31/3/62.
HARLOW D.M. Born 8/1/41. Commd 14/5/62. Flt Lt 9/2/68. Retd GD 31/7/76.
HARLOW E.J.A. Born 10/3/43. Commd 17/7/64. Flt Lt 17/1/70. Retd GD 10/3/98.
HARLOW J. Born 16/9/21. Commd 21/4/44. Flt Lt 16/2/48. Retd GD 1/9/60.
HARLOW R.A. MB BS LMSSA MRCOG. Born 3/3/32. Commd 13/4/58. Wg Cdr 4/7/70. Retd MED 13/4/74.
HARMAN G.T. Born 19/12/16. Commd 9/8/41. Sqn Ldr 1/8/47. Retd GD 30/5/58.
HARMAN J.D. Born 17/12/45. Commd 14/8/64. Flt Lt 14/2/70. Retd GD 23/11/83.
HARMAN P.J. Born 5/4/45. Commd 28/2/64. Flt Lt 28/8/69. Retd GD 21/1/76.
HARMSTON R.W. Born 15/4/37. Commd 24/2/67. Flt Lt 24/2/69. Retd SEC 15/4/75.
HARNETT E.E. Born 25/6/40. Commd 30/1/70. Sqn Ldr 1/1/79. Retd ADMIN 31/7/90.
HARPER A. AFC CEng MRAeS MCMI. Born 20/2/24. Commd 22/9/45. Wg Cdr 1/1/62. Retd GD 20/2/79.
HARPER B.A.H. CEng MRAeS. Born 5/2/41. Commd 30/8/66. Flt Lt 30/1/71. Retd ENG 30/8/82.
HARPER B.J. Born 22/4/37. Commd 24/6/55. Sqn Ldr 1/1/67. Retd GD 17/8/87.
HARPER B.L.S. Born 9/3/43. Commd 10/11/61. Sqn Ldr 1/7/73. Retd GD 9/3/98.
HARPER D.J. OBE AFC MCMI. Born 28/3/24. Commd 8/11/44. Wg Cdr 1/7/62. Retd GD 1/9/76.
HARPER D.J. Born 9/5/27. Commd 2/3/49. Flt Lt 2/2/55. Retd GD 1/10/68.
HARPER D.P. Born 10/9/48. Commd 30/1/70. Fg Offr 18/7/72. Retd SUP 20/5/76.
HARPER H.R. Born 25/1/46. Commd 8/1/65. Sqn Ldr 1/1/89. Retd GD 14/3/96.
HARPER I.F. MBE. Born 3/6/49. Commd 29/3/68. Wg Cdr 1/7/93. Retd GD 10/8/01.
HARPER J.R. Born 18/5/31. Commd 17/12/52. Sqn Ldr 1/7/67. Retd GD 1/7/70.
HARPER J.W. DFC. Born 25/5/20. Commd 13/1/43. Sqn Ldr 1/1/64. Retd GD(G) 25/5/75.
HARPER K.A. MSc BDS FDSRCSEng MGDSRCSEng MRD. Born 29/8/61. Commd 17/11/88. Wg Cdr 1/8/96.
    Retd DENTAL 21/7/04.
HARPER K.I. Born 7/4/57. Commd 25/2/82. Flt Lt 13/2/86. Retd GD(G) 7/4/95.
HARPER R.A. Born 22/1/37. Commd 25/6/57. Flt Lt 28/7/65. Retd GD 1/5/75.
HARPER R.B.B. DPhysEd. Born 20/9/19. Commd 27/8/52. Flt Lt 27/8/56. Retd PE 28/4/69.
HARPER R.D. Born 12/1/47. Commd 3/10/69. Sqn Ldr 1/1/87. Retd GD 22/4/94.
HARPER S.E.R. Born 29/6/24. Commd 22/6/46. Flt Lt 4/1/51. Retd GD 29/6/67.
HARPER S.R.J. DFC BA. Born 15/10/21. Commd 16/7/44. Flt Lt 5/8/53. Retd SEC 4/11/61.
HARPER T.A. Born 19/8/51. Commd 16/3/73. Wg Cdr 1/7/91. Retd GD 4/4/05.
HARPHAM S.T. DFM. Born 6/6/16. Commd 29/10/42. Flt Lt 29/4/47. Retd SEC 28/9/63.
HARPUR W. Born 30/7/36. Commd 9/3/62. Flt Lt 22/5/68. Retd SUP 4/8/76. Re-instated 7/1/81. Flt Lt 25/10/72.
    Retd SUP 1/10/89.
HARRALL M.R.M. Born 13/1/40. Commd 25/7/59. Flt Lt 25/1/65. Retd GD 14/11/74.
HARRELD J.J. Born 14/7/33. Commd 17/1/52. Flt Lt 8/5/57. Retd GD 14/7/72.
HARRIDENCE R.P.S. DFC MCMI. Born 12/7/22. Commd 20/11/42. Sqn Ldr 1/1/67. Retd GD(G) 1/10/74.
HARRIES G.O. Born 19/8/46. Commd 3/5/68. Sqn Ldr 1/1/81. Retd GD 19/8/90.
HARRIES H.R.M. The Rev. MBE. Born 6/6/30. Commd 30/10/58. Retd Wg Cdr 30/10/72.
HARRIES J.M. BA. Born 11/11/39. Commd 3/10/61. Sqn Ldr 11/5/71. Retd ADMIN 30/1/78.
HARRIES K.J. MA ACIS. Born 10/2/27. Commd 7/10/48. Sqn Ldr 1/1/62. Retd SEC 10/2/65.
HARRIES W.D. Born 15/5/34. Commd 25/2/53. Flt Lt 14/7/58. Retd GD 15/5/77.
HARRIES W.J.L. OBE MB BS FRCS LRCP. Born 17/10/21. Commd 2/1/47. Gp Capt 3/1/69. Retd MED 1/9/82.
HARRIES-JENKINS G. MA MPhil LLB. Born 13/7/31. Commd 18/11/53. Sqn Ldr 13/4/63. Retd EDN 11/3/70.
HARRILD D.J. DFC. Born 9/5/20. Commd 21/4/44. Sqn Ldr 1/1/69. Retd GD(G) 9/5/75.
HARRINGTON B.R. Born 17/11/20. Commd 24/6/44. Flt Lt 20/5/55. Retd SEC 17/11/75.
HARRINGTON D.G. BA CEng FIEE MCMI. Born 14/1/38. Commd 23/7/58. A Cdre 1/1/87. Retd ENG 2/4/89.
HARRINGTON D.H. BSc DipSoton CEng MIEE. Born 31/10/33. Commd 23/9/55. Sqn Ldr 29/4/65. Retd EDN 17/1/76.
HARRINGTON J. Born 9/12/48. Commd 31/7/70. Flt Lt 31/7/73. Retd GD 18/6/76.
HARRINGTON L. Born 16/7/26. Commd 23/8/46. Sqn Ldr 1/7/56. Retd GD 16/7/64.
HARRINGTON M.V.P.H. CVO BA FCMI. Born 19/9/36. Commd 17/12/57. Gp Capt 1/7/81. Retd GD 19/9/91.
HARRINGTON W.T. OBE. Born 31/5/07. Commd 30/6/41. Wg Cdr 1/1/54. Retd ENG 31/5/58.
HARRIS A. BSc CertEd. Born 12/8/50. Commd 11/8/74. Gp Capt 1/7/95. Retd ADMIN 4/6/02.
HARRIS A. MCIPS. Born 10/7/23. Commd 22/9/44. Wg Cdr 1/7/68. Retd SUP 30/3/78.
HARRIS A.D. Born 30/7/55. Commd 8/6/84. Sqn Ldr 1/1/94. Retd GD 14/3/96.
HARRIS A.E. BSc. Born 6/11/43. Commd 10/7/67. Wg Cdr 1/7/83. Retd ADMIN 1/10/93.

HARRIS A.J. AFC. Born 11/10/22. Commd 4/5/50. Flt Lt 4/11/53. Retd GD 11/1/63.
HARRIS A.J. Born 2/3/47. Commd 2/8/68. Sqn Ldr 1/1/80. Retd GD(G) 2/3/85.
HARRIS A.J. MSc BSc. Born 11/11/62. Commd 8/9/81. Sqn Ldr 1/1/94. Retd ENG 11/11/00.
HARRIS A.J. Born 28/12/16. Commd 22/9/55. Flt Lt 22/9/58. Retd SEC 12/2/72.
HARRIS A.J. The Rt Rev Mgr. Born 6/5/40. Commd 24/10/77. Retd Gp Capt 5/4/94.
HARRIS B. Born 21/6/31. Commd 22/7/55. Wg Cdr 1/1/70. Retd ENG 2/4/82.
HARRIS B. Born 13/10/37. Commd 22/8/59. Flt Lt 22/2/65. Retd GD 13/10/75.
HARRIS B.H. Born 26/12/27. Commd 27/2/52. Flt Lt 11/5/58. Retd GD 26/12/65.
HARRIS C.P.A. BSc. Born 31/7/44. Commd 22/12/71. Flt Lt 22/5/72. Retd GD 22/10/94.
HARRIS D.B.R. Born 8/3/29. Commd 1/10/53. Wg Cdr 1/1/71. Retd GD 8/3/84.
HARRIS D.J. MBE MSc. Born 1/11/38. Commd 29/3/62. Sqn Ldr 1/7/73. Retd ENG 3/1/78.
HARRIS D.J. Born 30/5/46. Commd 17/7/70. Flt Lt 17/1/76. Retd FLY(P) 30/5/04.
HARRIS D.P. CEng MIMarE. Born 29/8/35. Commd 27/7/70. Sqn Ldr 1/1/75. Retd ENG 30/4/82.
HARRIS E.A. Born 7/8/47. Commd 3/10/69. Wg Cdr 1/1/91. Retd GD(G) 14/9/96.
HARRIS E.A. MBE. Born 5/3/37. Commd 30/12/55. Gp Capt 1/7/89. Retd GD 5/8/92.
HARRIS E.C. DFC. Born 18/9/21. Commd 13/12/48. Flt Lt 11/11/54. Retd GD 22/3/68.
HARRIS E.H. BA MITD MCMI. Born 30/9/32. Commd 24/12/64. Sqn Ldr 24/8/70. Retd ADMIN 22/11/84.
HARRIS G. OBE. Born 29/1/47. Commd 2/2/68. Wg Cdr 1/7/86. Retd ADMIN 11/6/96.
HARRIS H.S.T. DFC. Born 16/7/23. Commd 17/10/44. Flt Lt 17/4/48. Retd GD 1/5/68.
HARRIS I.W. DFC. Born 16/10/20. Commd 18/10/41. Sqn Ldr 1/1/55. Retd GD 16/10/63.
HARRIS J. OBE DFC. Born 21/9/20. Commd 2/8/41. Wg Cdr 1/1/58. Retd GD 21/9/67.
HARRIS Sir John KCB CBE. Born 3/6/38. Commd 25/6/58. AM 1/5/92. Retd GD 29/6/96.
HARRIS J. Born 25/7/41. Commd 22/2/63. Sqn Ldr 1/1/74. Retd GD 25/7/79.
HARRIS J.C. BSc. Born 5/1/64. Commd 29/11/94. Flt Lt 2/10/92. Retd OPS SPT(REGT) 2/4/05.
HARRIS J.F. Born 26/11/27. Commd 7/8/59. Sqn Ldr 29/5/67. Retd ADMIN 1/4/77.
HARRIS J.G. Born 16/12/25. Commd 13/6/46. Flt Lt 15/8/62. Retd RGT 19/9/71.
HARRIS J.H. Born 21/10/22. Commd 25/8/60. Sqn Ldr 1/7/72. Retd ENG 23/7/73.
HARRIS J.P. Born 25/1/34. Commd 4/2/71. Sqn Ldr 1/7/84. Retd ENG 25/1/93.
HARRIS J.S. Born 31/3/57. Commd 20/5/82. Flt Lt 2/2/85. Retd ENG 31/3/95.
HARRIS J.V. Born 21/12/31. Commd 26/5/60. Flt Lt 26/5/66. Retd GD 17/2/67.
HARRIS K. Born 30/11/38. Commd 19/2/76. Sqn Ldr 1/1/85. Retd GD(G) 16/9/90.
HARRIS K.A. Born 6/10/30. Commd 7/1/71. Sqn Ldr 1/1/84. Retd ENG 4/10/86.
HARRIS K.B. MBE. Born 9/8/25. Commd 22/8/63. Sqn Ldr 1/1/76. Retd ENG 9/8/83.
HARRIS K.J. BSc CEng MIEE. Born 20/3/46. Commd 26/5/67. Wg Cdr 1/1/89. Retd ENG 20/3/01.
HARRIS L. MCMI. Born 25/3/32. Commd 16/7/52. Wg Cdr 1/1/77. Retd GD(G) 25/3/87.
HARRIS L.A. Born 11/2/60. Commd 28/7/94. Flt Lt 28/7/96. Retd GD 28/7/02.
HARRIS M.C. Born 18/6/40. Commd 12/8/63. Fg Offr 26/10/65. Retd GD(G) 11/2/67.
HARRIS M.C.S. Born 11/12/40. Commd 18/12/62. Flt Lt 10/2/67. Retd GD 10/1/79.
HARRIS M.J. MA. Born 16/6/56. Commd 1/9/74. Flt Lt 15/10/78. Retd GD 16/6/94.
HARRIS N.G. DFC. Born 27/11/20. Commd 31/8/44. Flt Lt 28/2/49. Retd GD(G) 27/11/70.
HARRIS N.J. Born 13/3/44. Commd 27/3/70. Flt Lt 27/9/75. Retd GD 1/2/88.
HARRIS P.C. BEM. Born 21/9/38. Commd 11/6/81. Flt Lt 11/6/85. Retd ENG 7/4/89.
HARRIS P.F. MBE. Born 11/7/29. Commd 10/2/55. Wg Cdr 1/7/75. Retd GD 11/7/84.
HARRIS P.G. MHCIMA. Born 16/5/48. Commd 19/6/83. Wg Cdr 1/7/97. Retd GD 16/5/03.
HARRIS P.I. Born 13/5/40. Commd 21/5/65. Flt Lt 26/7/67. Retd GD 21/9/74.
HARRIS P.T. Born 5/7/47. Commd 10/12/65. Sqn Ldr 1/1/84. Retd GD(G) 1/9/94.
HARRIS P.V. AFC FRAeS. Born 4/3/49. Commd 27/2/70. AVM 1/7/99. Retd GD 30/4/02.
HARRIS R. ACIS MCMI. Born 27/11/35. Commd 18/11/66. Sqn Ldr 1/1/75. Retd SEC 3/7/79.
HARRIS R.C. Born 14/5/49. Commd 18/12/80. Wg Cdr 1/7/96. Retd SUP 1/6/01.
HARRIS R.C. BSc. Born 28/10/50. Commd 23/9/68. Flt Lt 15/10/72. Retd GD 28/10/88.
HARRIS R.D. Born 27/5/37. Commd 23/7/58. Sqn Ldr 1/1/70. Retd ENG 27/5/92.
HARRIS R.F. OBE MB ChB FRCP DCH. Born 22/6/42. Commd 16/9/63. Wg Cdr 7/8/80. Retd MED 19/3/89.
HARRIS R.G. MBE. Born 23/1/38. Commd 5/9/57. Sqn Ldr 1/1/76. Retd PI 3/8/78.
HARRIS R.J.L. FRSH MIDSH. Born 10/8/30. Commd 16/12/66. Wg Cdr 1/1/80. Retd MED(T) 10/8/85.
HARRIS R.M. BSc CEng MIEE. Born 10/2/49. Commd 4/1/68. Wg Cdr 1/7/91. Retd GD 20/10/03.
HARRIS R.W. MCMI. Born 15/11/52. Commd 24/4/80. Flt Lt 24/7/83. Retd ADMIN 23/4/93.
HARRIS S.A. DFC. Born 8/6/21. Commd 2/10/44. Sqn Ldr 1/7/55. Retd GD 8/6/70.
HARRIS S.G. Born 7/10/19. Commd 22/9/55. Sqn Ldr 1/1/66. Retd ENG 31/3/77.
HARRIS S.W. Born 19/1/58. Commd 4/11/82. Flt Lt 22/10/85. Retd ENG 2/9/93.
HARRIS T.C. Born 28/1/49. Commd 14/2/99. Flt Lt 14/2/99. Retd MED TECH 98 28/1/04.
HARRIS T.S. DFC. Born 2/12/22. Commd 9/5/42. Sqn Ldr 1/7/51. Retd GD 30/11/54.
HARRIS T.W.P. Born 31/7/45. Commd 3/6/65. Flt Lt 4/5/72. Retd SEC 3/5/78.
HARRIS W.C. BA. Born 23/12/41. Commd 5/11/65. Flt Lt 5/8/67. Retd GD 21/6/81.
HARRIS W.H. Born 25/1/20. Commd 21/4/45. Flt Lt 21/10/48. Retd GD 15/5/54.
HARRISON A. BA. Born 23/7/43. Commd 15/9/67. Sqn Ldr 1/7/79. Retd GD 1/7/85.
HARRISON A.J. CB CBE. Born 9/11/43. Commd 22/2/63. AVM 1/1/95. Retd GD 4/5/98.

HARRISON A.J. Born 9/10/42. Commd 17/5/63. Flt Lt 1/7/69. Retd GD 9/10/80.
HARRISON A.L. The Rev. ALCD. Born 6/2/22. Commd 24/8/54. Retd Sqn Ldr 3/8/67.
HARRISON A.R. Born 13/7/49. Commd 9/3/72. Flt Lt 9/9/77. Retd GD 15/11/87.
HARRISON B.P. BA. Born 29/8/56. Commd 28/9/80. Flt Lt 28/3/84. Retd ADMIN 28/9/96.
HARRISON D.E. Born 8/12/63. Commd 25/6/89. Flt Lt 25/6/93. Retd ADMIN 4/5/01.
HARRISON D.J. Born 13/7/42. Commd 2/4/65. Flt Lt 4/5/72. Retd PI 9/11/80.
HARRISON D.J. CBE FCMI. Born 2/7/37. Commd 5/10/56. A Cdre 1/7/86. Retd ADMIN 2/7/92.
HARRISON E.C. MBE . Born 31/8/49. Commd 18/8/69. Wg Cdr 1/1/01. Retd GD 31/8/04.
HARRISON E.G.G. Born 8/4/21. Commd 29/7/44. Sqn Ldr 1/4/55. Retd GD 1/8/68.
HARRISON E.M. Born 7/3/20. Commd 5/6/43. Sqn Ldr 1/1/55. Retd SEC 7/3/69.
HARRISON G.J. Born 26/9/50. Commd 28/7/88. Flt Lt 28/7/90. Retd SUP 8/5/93.
HARRISON G.S. BA. Born 9/5/63. Commd 13/9/81. Sqn Ldr 1/7/95. Retd GD 9/5/01.
HARRISON G.S. BA. Born 8/6/44. Commd 30/5/71. Wg Cdr 1/1/87. Retd SUP 8/9/94.
HARRISON H. AFC. Born 20/4/26. Commd 1/10/50. Gp Capt 1/1/74. Retd GD 27/4/81.
HARRISON I. Born 20/12/41. Commd 2/5/69. Flt Lt 8/3/72. Retd SEC 20/12/79.
HARRISON I.R. Born 12/10/33. Commd 18/11/65. Flt Lt 1/5/72. Retd GD(G) 1/5/80.
HARRISON J.A. Born 26/12/25. Commd 6/10/50. Sqn Ldr 1/1/61. Retd GD 15/1/67. rtg Wg Cdr
HARRISON J.D. MIL. Born 18/7/46. Commd 28/11/69. Flt Lt 27/4/74. Retd ADMIN 12/6/84.
HARRISON J.G. AFC. Born 22/12/18. Commd 4/12/42. Sqn Ldr 1/1/52. Retd GD 20/1/54.
HARRISON J.G.M. MRCS LRCP. Born 3/2/25. Commd 26/11/51. Wg Cdr 26/11/63. Retd MED 26/11/67.
HARRISON J.L. Born 22/6/31. Commd 17/12/52. Flt Lt 17/6/55. Retd GD 22/6/69.
HARRISON J.R. BSc. Born 5/7/52. Commd 2/1/77. Flt Lt 2/11/78. Retd ENG 1/8/83.
HARRISON K.A. BSc. Born 7/12/38. Commd 31/7/59. Flt Lt 28/3/65. Retd GD 7/12/76.
HARRISON L.H. Born 8/9/29. Commd 10/8/50. Flt Lt 16/5/56. Retd GD 1/3/69.
HARRISON M.E.J. BSc. Born 30/10/33. Commd 5/9/57. Sqn Ldr 1/1/69. Retd ENG 29/4/77.
HARRISON N.A. MMedSci MB BS MRCP(UK) DTM&H DAvMed. Born 27/9/54. Commd 12/2/79. Wg Cdr 1/8/93.
    Retd MED 9/7/96.
HARRISON N.F. DSO AFC*. Born 5/5/20. Commd 17/12/51. Wg Cdr 1/7/62. Retd GD 1/12/66.
HARRISON P.J. CEng MIMechE MRAeS MCMI. Born 23/12/44. Commd 15/7/66. Sqn Ldr 1/1/79. Retd ENG 23/12/82.
HARRISON P.M. BEng. Born 19/10/66. Commd 16/9/84. Fg Offr 15/1/87. Retd ENG 6/2/90.
HARRISON R.A. CEng MIMechE MRAeS. Born 4/8/29. Commd 16/6/55. Wg Cdr 1/1/69. Retd ENG 5/7/75.
HARRISON R.A.W. DFC. Born 25/6/24. Commd 18/7/44. Sqn Ldr 1/7/58. Retd GD 10/5/66.
HARRISON R.B. Born 25/4/16. Commd 21/11/39. Wg Cdr 1/1/60. Retd SUP 21/4/64.
HARRISON R.F.J. Born 18/1/44. Commd 12/7/63. Sqn Ldr 1/1/79. Retd GD 18/1/82.
HARRISON R.J. Born 29/8/11. Commd 26/11/41. Sqn Ldr 1/8/47. Retd GD 29/8/56.
HARRISON R.J. BA MCMI CertEd DPhysEd. Born 13/6/48. Commd 9/7/81. Flt Lt 16/8/74. Retd ADMIN 16/8/75.
    Re-entered 30/7/79. Wg Cdr 1/1/92. Retd GD 18/4/04.
HARRISON R.L. DPhysEd. Born 1/5/47. Commd 16/8/70. Sqn Ldr 1/1/86. Retd ADMIN 1/5/02.
HARRISON R.M. Born 13/3/44. Commd 5/7/67. Wg Cdr 1/7/94. Retd ENG 13/3/99.
HARRISON R.S. Born 19/9/37. Commd 6/8/63. Flt Lt 6/8/66. Retd EDN 31/12/69.
HARRISON R.S. MMS MCMI. Born 27/11/46. Commd 21/4/67. Flt Lt 21/10/73. Retd ENG 27/11/84.
HARRISON S.E. DFC DFM. Born 13/9/19. Commd 2/7/42. Sqn Ldr 1/7/50. Retd GD 28/8/59.
HARRISON T.E. BA. Born 9/6/28. Commd 6/9/50. Sqn Ldr 1/1/61. Retd SEC 23/9/67.
HARRISON W.E. Born 26/10/21. Commd 27/10/44. Flt Lt 19/11/53. Retd GD 26/10/64.
HARRISON W.P. Born 10/6/44. Commd 1/10/65. Flt Lt 1/4/71. Retd GD 4/10/85.
HARROD J.B. Born 8/3/27. Commd 27/9/51. Flt Lt 13/2/57. Retd GD 8/3/65.
HARROP D. CEng MRAeS. Born 27/11/40. Commd 13/10/64. Sqn Ldr 1/7/92. Retd ENG 13/4/95.
HARROP D.R. MRAeS MIDPM. Born 17/11/38. Commd 22/6/60. Wg Cdr 1/7/90. Retd GD(G) 17/11/93.
HARROP G.G. Born 9/12/32. Commd 20/12/51. Flt Lt 4/4/57. Retd GD 9/12/90.
HARROP J.M. MSc BSc CEng MRAeS. Born 11/6/58. Commd 31/7/83. Sqn Ldr 1/7/99. Retd ENG 1/7/02.
HARROP P.A. MA BA MIPD MCMI. Born 12/10/51. Commd 20/6/72. Sqn Ldr 1/1/85. Retd ADMIN 12/10/88.
HARROP W.S. CEng MRAeS MCMI. Born 10/4/22. Commd 23/8/56. Sqn Ldr 1/1/69. Retd ENG 31/12/75.
HARROW C.T. BSc CEng MRAeS. Born 26/3/42. Commd 15/7/63. Gp Capt 1/1/91. Retd ENG 26/3/94.
HARROW J.F. Born 2/3/27. Commd 23/4/47. Wg Cdr 1/1/79. Retd SY 2/3/84.
HARRYMAN M.J. Born 29/6/40. Commd 5/8/76. Sqn Ldr 1/1/88. Retd ADMIN 29/6/95.
HART C.M. BA MCMI. Born 19/8/36. Commd 10/5/73. Sqn Ldr 1/1/84. Retd ENG 19/8/93.
HART D. Born 17/2/45. Commd 31/8/78. Sqn Ldr 1/7/85. Retd ADMIN 31/3/94.
HART D.C. BSc. Born 14/3/59. Commd 29/8/77. Sqn Ldr 1/1/92. Retd GD 14/3/97.
HART E.M. Born 24/5/45. Commd 26/4/84. Flt Lt 26/4/88. Retd ENG 23/4/94.
HART F.K. CEng MIMechE MRAeS. Born 22/3/27. Commd 23/1/52. Sqn Ldr 1/7/67. Retd ENG 22/3/87.
HART G. Born 27/9/32. Commd 20/8/52. Flt Lt 26/5/58. Retd GD 27/9/70.
HART I.B. Born 7/8/14. Commd 22/12/43. Flt Offr 22/12/49. Retd SEC 9/9/63.
HART J.S. FCMI. Born 21/9/22. Commd 20/9/41. Gp Capt 1/7/67. Retd GD 31/5/71.
HART K.L. Born 2/9/37. Commd 2/9/55. Sqn Ldr 1/1/71. Retd GD 3/9/74.
HART L.R. Born 25/1/39. Commd 4/2/71. Sqn Ldr 1/7/89. Retd ADMIN 25/1/94.
HART M.C. BSc. Born 1/10/62. Commd 14/4/85. Flt Lt 14/10/87. Retd GD 14/10/01.

HART P.J. Born 1/8/31. Commd 31/12/52. Flt Lt 26/5/58. Retd GD 1/8/69.
HART P.T. Born 8/9/61. Commd 8/9/83. Sqn Ldr 1/1/94. Retd ADMIN 8/9/99.
HART R.E.E. OBE. Born 19/3/46. Commd 4/6/64. A Cdre 1/7/91. Retd ADMIN 30/6/94.
HART R.J.A. Born 30/3/43. Commd 23/3/67. Flt Lt 23/9/72. Retd GD(G) 5/12/85.
HARTE J.K. OBE. Born 14/10/43. Commd 24/4/70. Wg Cdr 1/7/92. Retd GD 14/10/98.
HARTILL D.R. Born 24/3/51. Commd 27/3/75. Sqn Ldr 1/1/90. Retd GD 1/10/98.
HARTLAND D.V. MBE. Born 19/2/33. Commd 21/11/51. Sqn Ldr 1/1/70. Retd SUP 19/2/93.
HARTLEY I.G. Born 21/5/46. Commd 18/8/67. Sqn Ldr 1/7/86. Retd GD 12/6/99.
HARTLEY J. MBE CEng MRAeS MCMI. Born 24/11/17. Commd 15/11/45. Wg Cdr 1/7/69. Retd ENG 24/11/72.
HARTLEY J. Born 24/9/43. Commd 19/5/69. Wg Cdr 1/7/88. Retd ADMIN 31/1/92.
HARTLEY J.C. Born 28/9/42. Commd 15/7/63. Fg Offr 15/1/64. Retd ENG 18/5/68.
HARTLEY J.W. Born 10/2/37. Commd 29/7/58. Flt Lt 13/5/64. Retd GD 1/1/76.
HARTLEY K.A. Born 26/8/48. Commd 27/2/70. Flt Lt 27/2/73. Retd GD 22/12/79.
HARTLEY M. CEng FRAeS MCMI. Born 15/8/35. Commd 24/7/57. Sqn Ldr 1/1/67. Retd ENG 28/4/89.
HARTLEY R.M. MBE. Born 14/12/21. Commd 10/10/44. Sqn Ldr 15/2/65. Retd ADMIN 10/8/76.
HARTLEY R.P.H. Born 27/7/45. Commd 11/8/67. Flt Lt 11/2/73. Retd GD 1/10/87.
HARTLEY S.McK. Born 25/11/47. Commd 17/7/70. Flt Lt 17/1/77. Retd GD(G) 5/1/89.
HARTLEY V. MA BA. Born 18/12/47. Commd 13/9/70. Sqn Ldr 15/1/81. Retd ADMIN 13/9/86.
HARTLEY-WOOLLEY A.H. Born 30/6/45. Commd 17/5/79. Sqn Ldr 1/1/89. Retd GD(G) 17/5/93.
HARTMAN G. DFC. Born 24/10/17. Commd 13/7/40. Sqn Ldr 1/1/57. Retd GD 27/2/59.
HARTNELL-PARKER B.K. Born 17/7/18. Commd 29/5/47. Sqn Ldr 1/1/62. Retd SUP 21/9/68.
HARTNETT F.E.L. OBE BSc. Born 3/9/40. Commd 10/8/65. Wg Cdr 1/1/80. Retd ADMIN 1/7/87.
HARTRIDGE B.W.A. Born 9/10/31. Commd 14/8/70. Flt Lt 14/8/73. Retd GD 15/7/75.
HARTWELL N.R.G. Born 6/7/23. Commd 26/8/43. Sqn Ldr 1/7/57. Retd ENG 30/6/78.
HARTY C.J. Born 8/9/62. Commd 23/10/86. Fg Offr 23/10/88. Retd GD 23/10/89.
HARTY T.A. Born 21/9/20. Commd 2/4/53. Flt Lt 1/6/56. Retd RGT 2/9/72.
HARVARD I.C. Born 14/8/56. Commd 22/11/84. Flt Lt 22/11/86. Retd OPS SPT 14/8/00.
HARVEY A.D. MBE. Born 27/6/21. Commd 28/11/46. Wg Cdr 1/7/63. Retd SUP 27/6/66.
HARVEY B. Born 26/3/23. Commd 13/5/44. Flt Lt 1/5/52. Retd GD 1/4/64.
HARVEY D.L. Born 22/9/20. Commd 4/3/39. Wg Cdr 1/1/57. Retd GD 3/8/66.
HARVEY D.V.R. The Rev. MTh BA. Born 2/4/37. Commd 9/12/65. Retd Wg Cdr 2/4/92.
HARVEY G.C. MSc BSc AFIMA. Born 22/7/29. Commd 10/11/64. Wg Cdr 10/5/74. Retd ADMIN 30/9/77.
HARVEY G.F. Born 13/4/22. Commd 26/5/60. Flt Lt 26/5/63. Retd GD(G) 13/4/77.
HARVEY H. Born 20/3/13. Commd 28/12/40. Wg Cdr 1/7/56. Retd ENG 16/4/68.
HARVEY H. GM. Born 14/6/22. Commd 13/7/48. Flt Lt 19/6/52. Retd GD 9/5/66.
HARVEY H.A. MCMI. Born 26/1/28. Commd 2/3/49. Wg Cdr 1/7/65. Retd GD 2/11/76.
HARVEY H.G. MA MCMI. Born 15/7/36. Commd 3/9/59. Wg Cdr 1/7/86. Retd GD 1/5/90.
HARVEY I.R. MBE BSc. Born 15/8/51. Commd 15/9/69. Wg Cdr 1/1/88. Retd GD 18/6/91.
HARVEY J.C. CEng MRAeS. Born 23/1/41. Commd 17/7/62. Sqn Ldr 1/7/74. Retd ENG 23/1/79.
HARVEY J.D. Born 26/5/32. Commd 26/7/55. Wg Cdr 1/1/74. Retd GD 10/3/84.
HARVEY J.F. Born 1/7/20. Commd 24/1/44. Flt Lt 24/1/50. Retd GD(G) 16/9/67.
HARVEY J.J. Born 30/10/26. Commd 8/10/52. Flt Lt 6/3/58. Retd GD 27/5/68.
HARVEY J.T. Born 18/5/32. Commd 29/12/51. Sqn Ldr 1/1/63. Retd GD 18/6/70.
HARVEY K.L. Born 12/10/60. Commd 30/4/81. Flt Lt 30/10/87. Retd GD(G) 1/6/93.
HARVEY M.A. Born 16/9/36. Commd 30/12/65. A Cdre 1/7/86. Retd GD(G) 2/4/91.
HARVEY M.J.A. Born 28/1/42. Commd 24/6/65. Flt Lt 8/3/72. Retd GD(G) 21/1/80.
HARVEY M.McD. Born 26/10/28. Commd 14/12/49. Sqn Ldr 1/7/61. Retd GD 30/9/74.
HARVEY P.J.R. MSc BSc. Born 3/2/46. Commd 1/11/81. Sqn Ldr 1/1/91. Retd ENG 3/2/01.
HARVEY P.M. FCMI. Born 16/2/23. Commd 17/9/43. Gp Capt 1/1/70. Retd GD 29/7/74.
HARVEY S. BSc. Born 8/1/61. Commd 14/4/85. Sqn Ldr 1/7/96. Retd ADMIN 14/4/01.
HARVEY S.R. Born 10/5/47. Commd 25/6/65. Flt Lt 4/5/72. Retd GD 18/11/99.
HARVEY T. Born 24/10/52. Commd 9/5/91. Flt Lt 9/5/95. Retd MED(SEC) 4/9/96.
HARVEY T.J. Born 26/6/36. Commd 31/8/62. Flt Lt 25/7/66. Retd GD 5/3/90.
HARVEY V.N.W. Born 4/7/14. Commd 29/10/43. Flt Lt 17/5/56. Retd GD(G) 7/10/67.
HARVEY-BENNETT P.G. BSc(Eng) DipSoton. Born 30/3/40. Commd 30/9/58. Sqn Ldr 1/7/69. Retd ENG 1/9/83.
HARWELL G.G.M. BSc. Born 29/8/63. Commd 30/8/81. Flt Lt 15/10/85. Retd GD 29/8/01.
HARWOOD A.R. Born 28/4/40. Commd 26/3/64. Sqn Ldr 1/1/81. Retd GD 29/4/90.
HARWOOD C.A. Born 15/1/38. Commd 28/8/56. Wg Cdr 1/7/79. Retd GD(G) 18/1/90.
HARWOOD-GRAYSON M. MA. Born 4/12/52. Commd 14/11/76. Wg Cdr 1/1/90. Retd ADMIN 1/1/93.
HASKELL G.P. MCIPS. Born 29/6/39. Commd 9/3/66. Sqn Ldr 1/1/74. Retd SUP 6/5/85.
HASKINS S.W. Born 5/1/61. Commd 31/1/80. Flt Lt 31/7/85. Retd GD 7/6/98.
HASLAM A.S. MSc BSc CEng MRAeS. Born 13/2/47. Commd 17/1/82. Sqn Ldr 1/1/89. Retd ADMIN 13/2/02.
HASLAM R.J. Born 11/2/23. Commd 5/9/57. Flt Lt 5/9/60. Retd GD 31/5/68.
HASLER P.R. Born 8/4/38. Commd 20/11/75. Sqn Ldr 1/7/89. Retd ENG 8/4/96.
HASSALL M.G. Born 8/11/33. Commd 27/3/75. Flt Lt 27/3/80. Retd ENG 28/3/85.
HASSELL R.S. Born 24/2/29. Commd 5/6/50. Flt Lt 5/9/56. Retd GD 24/9/67.

HASSELSTROM W.H. Born 29/8/20. Commd 17/4/42. Sqn Ldr 1/1/54. Retd SEC 30/12/67.
HASTINGS A. Born 6/10/48. Commd 24/4/80. Sqn Ldr 1/1/87. Retd ADMIN 1/8/95.
HASTINGS C.N. BSc. Born 31/1/63. Commd 30/8/81. Sqn Ldr 1/1/98. Retd GD 31/1/01.
HASTINGS J.B. Born 11/6/46. Commd 17/7/75. Wg Cdr 1/7/88. Retd ENG 11/6/01.
HASTINGS M.C. Born 23/4/30. Commd 21/11/51. Flt Lt 21/5/56. Retd GD 23/4/68.
HASTINGS T.A. OBE. Born 14/8/29. Commd 18/6/52. Gp Capt 1/1/78. Retd GD 13/2/82.
HASTINGS W.J.G. BEM. Born 15/4/13. Commd 25/8/55. Flt Lt 25/8/58. Retd ENG 15/4/68.
HASZELDINE D.R. MSc BSc. Born 5/4/53. Commd 3/9/72. Sqn Ldr 1/7/84. Retd ENG 5/4/91.
HATCHER A.I. Born 2/5/54. Commd 20/6/91. Flt Lt 20/6/93. Retd ENG 2/9/00.
HATCHER F.J. Born 27/1/42. Commd 12/2/68. Sqn Ldr 1/7/80. Retd ENG 12/2/84.
HATCHER L. Born 5/12/43. Commd 28/4/65. Flt Lt 28/10/70. Retd GD 5/6/82.
HATCHER P.J. Born 29/11/24. Commd 23/9/66. Flt Lt 23/9/69. Retd GD 30/6/72.
HATCHER R.G. CEng MIEE MRAeS. Born 20/12/44. Commd 15/7/65. Sqn Ldr 1/7/74. Retd ENG 20/12/82.
HATCHER T.M. Born 28/2/66. Commd 30/8/84. Flt Lt 28/2/90. Retd GD 29/2/96.
HATHAWAY J.H.T. Born 10/7/39. Commd 29/3/68. Sqn Ldr 1/1/81. Retd GD 10/7/94.
HATHAWAY R.L.S. AFC MCMI. Born 30/4/21. Commd 25/10/47. Sqn Ldr 1/7/62. Retd GD 30/4/76.
HATLEY E.M. MHCIMA. Born 5/9/42. Commd 7/12/65. Gp Capt 1/7/91. Retd ADMIN 30/7/95.
HATT G.D. Born 18/4/24. Commd 24/8/44. Flt Lt 6/10/63. Retd GD 16/10/75.
HATTEN A.F. BEM. Born 15/4/43. Commd 13/12/79. Sqn Ldr 1/1/88. Retd ENG 20/10/95.
HATTER A.J. Born 14/9/45. Commd 29/7/65. Flt Lt 4/5/72. Retd SUP 16/3/74.
HATTON D. Born 19/10/38. Commd 14/5/60. Flt Lt 8/1/69. Retd GD(G) 30/9/82.
HATTON G.A. Born 26/8/18. Commd 10/3/44. Sqn Ldr 1/7/67. Retd GD(G) 26/8/73.
HATTON J.F. Born 7/7/20. Commd 23/12/39. Wg Cdr 1/1/54. Retd GD 7/7/67.
HATTON P.A. Born 11/5/48. Commd 8/11/68. Sqn Ldr 1/1/89. Retd SY 25/7/96.
HATTON S. OBE. Born 5/10/22. Commd 11/8/44. Wg Cdr 1/7/65. Retd GD 19/7/75.
HAUGHTON D.J. Born 12/6/46. Commd 10/12/65. Sqn Ldr 1/1/82. Retd GD 12/6/90.
HAVEN R.C. Born 7/7/32. Commd 21/5/52. Sqn Ldr 1/7/70. Retd GD 12/8/77.
HAW C. DFC DFM. Born 8/5/20. Commd 6/3/42. Flt Lt 10/2/46. Retd GD 19/9/51. rtg Sqn Ldr
HAW D.G. Born 28/1/27. Commd 3/8/61. Sqn Ldr 1/7/73. Retd PE 4/8/81.
HAWARD C.W.A. Born 8/11/45. Commd 2/4/65. Flt Lt 2/10/70. Retd GD 9/12/95.
HAWARD F.W.W. DFC. Born 31/1/20. Commd 5/12/42. Flt Lt 26/5/59. Retd GD(G) 31/1/70.
HAWARD P.J. MBE. Born 17/11/46. Commd 10/12/65. Sqn Ldr 1/7/93. Retd GD 1/10/94.
HAWES A.S. Born 20/3/21. Commd 25/9/46. Fg Offr 25/9/48. Retd PE 23/10/55.
HAWES C.D. BDS. Born 22/5/41. Commd 30/12/62. Wg Cdr 23/12/77. Retd DEL 22/5/79.
HAWES C.M.H. BA. Born 29/6/48. Commd 7/6/68. Wg Cdr 1/1/91. Retd GD 17/1/03.
HAWES K.N.J. Born 28/11/38. Commd 30/7/57. Sqn Ldr 1/7/72. Retd GD 11/12/77.
HAWES M.J. LVO. Born 18/10/32. Commd 4/7/51. Sqn Ldr 1/7/73. Retd GD 18/10/92.
HAWES M.R. The Rev. AKC. Born 28/10/31. Commd 15/6/65. Retd Wg Cdr 28/10/86.
HAWES R.G.O. Born 22/3/24. Commd 4/9/58. Flt Lt 22/9/61. Retd ENG 12/4/75.
HAWES W.G. Born 21/12/33. Commd 15/10/52. Flt Lt 21/10/58. Retd GD 21/12/92.
HAWKE J.M. BA MCMI. Born 30/8/32. Commd 23/9/55. Wg Cdr 1/1/74. Retd SUP 3/10/78.
HAWKEN P.H.G. BA. Born 26/4/40. Commd 29/4/58. Sqn Ldr 1/1/72. Retd PRT 26/4/78.
HAWKER H.C.V. DFC. Born 25/9/22. Commd 28/2/42. Flt Lt 5/12/47. Retd GD 13/1/58.
HAWKER P.B. AFM. Born 16/3/25. Commd 29/7/52. Flt Lt 3/11/59. Retd GD 15/3/69.
HAWKER S.R. BEd. Born 12/12/55. Commd 9/11/86. Flt Lt 9/5/82. Retd ADMIN 1/7/86.
HAWKES A.J. Born 28/2/37. Commd 21/9/55. Flt Lt 30/6/61. Retd GD 1/10/68.
HAWKEY J.A. Born 24/4/23. Commd 18/6/44. Sqn Ldr 1/7/59. Retd 31/3/62.
HAWKHEAD H. Born 13/5/11. Commd 24/12/44. Sqn Ldr 1/1/56. Retd PRT 13/5/60.
HAWKINS B.J.R. Born 6/3/56. Commd 17/5/79. Sqn Ldr 1/7/88. Retd OPS SPT 6/3/00.
HAWKINS C.H. DFC AFC. Born 7/12/16. Commd 1/11/41. Flt Lt 16/7/51. Retd GD(G) 28/2/62.
HAWKINS D.E. CB CBE DFC*. Born 27/12/19. Commd 7/5/38. AVM 1/7/69. Retd GD 31/7/74.
HAWKINS D.G. Born 16/5/19. Commd 12/9/63. Flt Lt 12/9/68. Retd SEC 31/12/68.
HAWKINS D.G. PhD BSc. Born 1/6/41. Commd 21/1/68. Gp Capt 1/1/87. Retd GD 3/12/97.
HAWKINS D.J. Born 24/2/46. Commd 13/3/80. Flt Lt 13/3/82. Retd GD 1/2/96.
HAWKINS D.R. CB MBE FCIPD FCMI. Born 5/4/37. Commd 17/12/59. AVM 1/7/91. Retd SY 1/7/93.
HAWKINS I.P.W. MCMI. Born 21/10/24. Commd 29/3/45. Wg Cdr 1/7/65. Retd GD 1/11/75.
HAWKINS J.W.J. CEng MIEE MRAeS. Born 24/7/30. Commd 17/12/52. Wg Cdr 1/1/75. Retd ENG 14/4/84.
HAWKINS M.J. Born 1/9/31. Commd 27/3/50. Sqn Ldr 1/1/64. Retd GD 1/9/69.
HAWKINS M.L. BSc CEng FRAeS MIMechE. Born 28/9/40. Commd 30/9/60. Gp Capt 1/7/87. Retd ENG 28/9/95.
HAWKINS N.M. BA. Born 7/9/32. Commd 5/12/60. Sqn Ldr 29/1/72. Retd ADMIN 31/5/84.
HAWKINS P.J. Born 11/12/48. Commd 23/9/66. Flt Lt 23/3/72. Retd FLY(N) 20/11/03.
HAWKINS P.R. Born 30/3/19. Commd 12/6/47. Sqn Ldr 1/4/58. Retd SEC 14/8/65.
HAWKSLEY P. Born 20/7/42. Commd 14/8/64. Flt Lt 14/2/70. Retd GD 20/7/80.
HAWKSWORTH P.R. Born 18/12/40. Commd 19/4/63. Gp Capt 1/1/91. Retd GD 6/6/93.
HAWLEY G.A. Born 27/2/50. Commd 24/3/83. Sqn Ldr 1/7/98. Retd ENGINEER 27/2/05.
HAWLEY N.H. Born 19/12/35. Commd 4/4/71. Flt Lt 4/4/73. Retd ENG 19/12/85.

HAWORTH D.A. Born 2/9/32. Commd 19/4/51. Sqn Ldr 1/1/73. Retd GD(G) 1/3/89.
HAWORTH G. DFC DFM. Born 4/9/15. Commd 17/7/41. Sqn Ldr 1/8/47. Retd GD 28/12/57.
HAWTHORN I.E. MB BS FRCS(Edin) MRCS LRCP. Born 22/3/57. Commd 18/10/77. Wg Cdr 1/8/94. Retd MED 22/3/95.
HAWTHORNE J.F. CEng MIEE MRAeS. Born 27/2/20. Commd 10/12/42. Sqn Ldr 1/10/55. Retd ENG 31/10/63.
HAWTIN J.D.C. Born 9/12/33. Commd 26/7/55. Wg Cdr 1/7/73. Retd GD 9/12/88.
HAY A.W. Born 16/3/12. Commd 21/2/46. Sqn Ldr 1/1/57. Retd SUP 30/5/61.
HAY B.D.T. MCIT MILT MRAeS. Born 7/12/46. Commd 23/9/65. Wg Cdr 1/7/90. Retd SUP 6/6/02.
HAY I.J. Born 20/11/36. Commd 10/9/70. Flt Lt 10/9/72. Retd SEC 10/9/78.
HAY J.C. BA. Born 17/9/46. Commd 29/6/72. Wg Cdr 1/7/99. Retd ENG 17/9/01.
HAY J.S.S. AFC. Born 2/12/23. Commd 29/3/45. Sqn Ldr 1/9/65. Retd GD 1/10/68.
HAY M. Born 19/10/53. Commd 15/2/73. Sqn Ldr 1/7/90. Retd GD(G) 1/7/93.
HAY P. Born 17/9/42. Commd 10/12/65. Flt Lt 10/6/71. Retd GD 1/9/81.
HAY P.G. Born 1/5/38. Commd 10/2/59. Fg Offr 12/2/61. Retd GD 11/2/66.
HAY P.McN. Born 24/5/33. Commd 20/3/52. Sqn Ldr 1/1/69. Retd GD 24/5/93.
HAY W.P. Born 22/10/33. Commd 19/11/57. Flt Lt 7/8/64. Retd GD(G) 22/10/88.
HAY W.T.H. Born 6/4/22. Commd 23/4/45. Flt Lt 23/4/51. Retd PE 30/4/58.
HAYCOCK M. Born 15/3/40. Commd 24/11/67. Flt Lt 24/11/69. Retd PE 15/9/78.
HAYDAY J.C. Born 15/11/32. Commd 4/6/52. Flt Lt 30/10/57. Retd GD 15/11/70.
HAYDEN B. BSc. Born 12/7/57. Commd 11/9/83. Flt Lt 11/3/85. Retd ADMIN 31/10/86.
HAYDEN M.J. Born 16/5/33. Commd 16/7/52. Wg Cdr 1/7/76. Retd GD 23/11/87.
HAYDON D.A. Born 12/2/47. Commd 1/1/67. Flt Lt 1/7/72. Retd GD 28/2/76.
HAYES A.P. Born 11/5/50. Commd 25/2/72. Wg Cdr 1/1/89. Retd ENG 11/5/94.
HAYES C.G. Born 19/7/62. Commd 19/12/91. Flt Lt 21/11/94. Retd ENG 23/10/00.
HAYES C.W. OBE. Born 11/5/17. Commd 6/5/42. Gp Capt 1/1/68. Retd GD 15/3/70.
HAYES D.T.C. Born 31/3/26. Commd 21/9/50. Sqn Ldr 1/7/62. Retd GD 28/11/75.
HAYES E. MBE. Born 22/3/34. Commd 17/3/67. Flt Lt 17/3/72. Retd GD 22/6/92.
HAYES E. Born 1/7/13. Commd 13/1/43. Flt Offr 13/1/48. Retd SUP 21/8/55.
HAYES E.C. Born 25/3/13. Commd 3/12/41. Flt Lt 9/9/45. Retd ENG 3/10/53. rtg Sqn Ldr
HAYES K. BSc. Born 26/11/30. Commd 17/10/51. Sqn Ldr 1/1/61. Retd GD 26/11/68.
HAYES L.J. Born 6/4/47. Commd 19/3/81. Flt Lt 19/3/83. Retd GD 1/6/95.
HAYES N.R. Born 14/3/24. Commd 6/9/68. Flt Lt 6/9/71. Retd GD 14/9/78.
HAYES S.G. Born 6/6/51. Commd 24/4/70. Sqn Ldr 1/7/85. Retd SUP 6/6/89.
HAYHOW K.J. Born 12/4/23. Commd 23/12/43. Flt Lt 10/11/55. Retd SEC 11/8/65.
HAYLER P. Born 29/11/33. Commd 25/6/66. Flt Lt 25/6/68. Retd SUP 25/6/74.
HAYLETT M. Born 16/11/18. Commd 27/11/52. Flt Offr 17/7/47. Retd SUP 21/1/60.
HAYLETT M.G. Born 7/5/50. Commd 6/11/80. Flt Lt 6/11/82. Retd GD(ENG) 6/11/88.
HAYLEY C.A. DFC. Born 15/4/21. Commd 16/4/43. Flt Lt 16/10/46. Retd GD 15/4/67.
HAYLEY J.T. Born 21/12/23. Commd 22/7/63. Sqn Ldr 1/7/75. Retd GD 21/12/81.
HAYLOCK E.K.A. MCMI. Born 18/12/22. Commd 15/10/43. Sqn Ldr 1/7/67. Retd ADMIN 18/12/77.
HAYMAN D.J. BA. Born 26/9/42. Commd 28/7/64. Wg Cdr 1/7/87. Retd SUP 26/9/93.
HAYMAN J. Born 12/8/31. Commd 1/3/62. Flt Lt 1/3/68. Retd ENG 1/6/77.
HAYMAN M.J. Born 24/9/47. Commd 24/6/71. Flt Lt 14/10/77. Retd SEC 1/8/78.
HAYMAN W.F. MBE MRAeS. Born 23/12/31. Commd 10/10/63. Sqn Ldr 1/7/76. Retd ENG 23/12/92.
HAYNE R.D. Born 26/4/58. Commd 15/6/83. Flt Lt 15/6/85. Retd ENG 26/4/96.
HAYNES A.R. BSc. Born 7/2/47. Commd 26/5/67. Sqn Ldr 1/7/79. Retd ENG 7/2/02.
HAYNES C.J.P. BSc MCMI. Born 24/12/46. Commd 22/9/65. Sqn Ldr 1/1/78. Retd ENG 24/12/84.
HAYNES D.M. MCMI ACIS. Born 8/11/40. Commd 27/8/59. Sqn Ldr 1/7/78. Retd SEC 1/7/81.
HAYNES H.M. BA BEd. Born 17/7/56. Commd 7/11/85. Flt Lt 7/5/87. Retd ADMIN 14/3/97.
HAYNES J.H. Born 25/3/38. Commd 14/3/57. Flt Lt 5/8/64. Retd SUP 8/8/67.
HAYNES J.M. BA. Born 29/4/64. Commd 20/10/83. Sqn Ldr 1/7/99. Retd FLY(P) 1/5/03.
HAYNES P.C. Born 26/5/66. Commd 21/6/90. Flt Lt 21/12/95. Retd GD 14/3/97.
HAYNES P.W. Born 26/9/47. Commd 23/6/67. Sqn Ldr 1/1/79. Retd SY 26/9/85.
HAYNES R. Born 6/6/19. Commd 6/11/43. Flt Lt 6/5/47. Retd GD(G) 6/6/76.
HAYNES R.G. Born 23/9/44. Commd 28/9/62. Flt Lt 28/3/68. Retd GD 23/9/82.
HAYS L. Born 5/7/23. Commd 4/9/44. Flt Lt 4/9/50. Retd ADMIN 6/7/76.
HAYSOM C.C. Born 1/10/41. Commd 30/7/63. Flt Lt 30/1/66. Retd GD 6/1/79.
HAYSOM K.J. Born 13/8/46. Commd 1/11/79. Flt Lt 1/11/81. Retd GD 31/3/94.
HAYTER A.J. MCMI. Born 11/3/22. Commd 10/7/44. Sqn Ldr 1/1/58. Retd GD 11/3/71.
HAYTER D.E.F. Born 4/2/23. Commd 29/6/50. Sqn Ldr 1/7/60. Retd ENG 15/8/64.
HAYTER L.A. Born 6/4/20. Commd 3/2/44. Flt Lt 27/7/55. Retd GD(G) 8/12/71.
HAYTER M.D. Born 1/3/50. Commd 10/9/70. Flt Lt 10/3/76. Retd GD 22/10/94.
HAYTER R.J. CEng MIMechE MRAeS. Born 3/8/29. Commd 18/7/51. Wg Cdr 1/7/79. Retd ENG 3/8/84.
HAYTER S.J. Born 12/12/47. Commd 10/6/66. Sqn Ldr 1/7/78. Retd SUP 11/12/85.
HAYTER-PRESTON P. Born 19/12/21. Commd 7/1/42. Flt Lt 8/5/51. Retd GD(G) 17/7/57.
HAYTON P. MA. Born 11/4/50. Commd 5/5/71. Flt Lt 15/1/73. Retd GD 12/5/78.
HAYWARD B.A. MBE. Born 9/11/32. Commd 7/12/61. Flt Lt 7/12/66. Retd GD 2/9/72.

HAYWARD D. Born 3/7/31. Commd 1/6/72. Sqn Ldr 19/8/81. Retd MED(T) 3/7/89.
HAYWARD D. OBE. Born 22/2/45. Commd 15/7/66. Gp Capt 1/1/89. Retd GD 14/3/96.
HAYWARD E.J.N. Born 15/6/40. Commd 25/9/80. Flt Lt 15/12/82. Retd GD 19/7/85.
HAYWARD F. Born 22/5/26. Commd 21/6/56. Sqn Ldr 1/7/74. Retd GD 22/5/84.
HAYWARD H.R. Born 26/6/29. Commd 10/10/63. Flt Lt 10/10/68. Retd GD 29/3/69.
HAYWARD K.R. AFC. Born 15/5/21. Commd 30/9/54. Sqn Ldr 1/1/66. Retd GD 28/8/68.
HAYWARD L.C. Born 13/10/24. Commd 25/8/49. Flt Lt 25/2/53. Retd GD 13/10/67.
HAYWARD N.R. AFC. Born 4/5/40. Commd 1/8/61. Wg Cdr 1/7/75. Retd GD 1/7/78.
HAYWARD R. Born 11/11/44. Commd 12/7/68. Sqn Ldr 1/1/81. Retd GD 30/5/97.
HAYWARD R.A. AFC. Born 12/7/23. Commd 15/1/45. Flt Lt 15/7/48. Retd GD 12/7/66.
HAYWARD S.A. Born 19/10/64. Commd 15/3/84. Sqn Ldr 1/1/99. Retd GD 19/10/02.
HAYWARD T.F. OBE MRIN MCMI. Born 23/9/36. Commd 20/8/55. Wg Cdr 1/7/76. Retd GD 20/7/84.
HAYWARD V.F. BA. Born 12/5/33. Commd 25/8/55. Wg Cdr 1/7/77. Retd ADMIN 9/5/87.
HAYWOOD J.W. MSc BEng CEng. Born 29/4/44. Commd 28/11/76. Sqn Ldr 1/1/84. Retd ADMIN 4/1/99.
HAYWOOD K.M. MCMI. Born 27/9/39. Commd 17/5/79. Sqn Ldr 1/1/90. Retd ADMIN 7/7/93.
HAYWOOD V.M. MA MCIPD MBIFM CertEd AdvDipEd(Open) DPhysEd. Born 17/9/52. Commd 2/1/77.
    Sqn Ldr 1/1/90. Retd ADMIN 13/12/99.
HAZAN T.S.W. Born 15/11/50. Commd 15/9/69. Flt Lt 30/1/78. Retd GD 14/3/97.
HAZELL A.R.E. BSc. Born 14/1/34. Commd 5/10/56. Sqn Ldr 5/4/66. Retd ADMIN 2/1/87.
HAZLEHURST N.R. BSc(Eng) ACGI. Born 23/8/54. Commd 6/11/77. Flt Lt 6/8/79. Retd GD 6/11/89.
HAZLEWOOD F.S. CB CBE AFC* FRAeS FCMI. Born 13/5/21. Commd 16/4/43. AVM 1/1/73. Retd GD 15/1/77.
HEAD D. Born 9/7/42. Commd 24/4/70. Flt Lt 4/5/72. Retd GD 9/7/80.
HEAD D.A. Born 17/6/52. Commd 19/8/71. Flt Lt 19/2/77. Retd GD 17/6/90.
HEAD D.G. Born 23/10/37. Commd 11/11/65. Sqn Ldr 1/1/78. Retd GD 23/10/92.
HEAD G.J.A. Born 4/11/22. Commd 14/7/44. Sqn Ldr 1/1/75. Retd ADMIN 4/11/77.
HEAD I.C. Born 16/1/33. Commd 5/3/59. Flt Lt 18/3/64. Retd ENG 15/9/74.
HEAD J.W.M. Born 13/1/43. Commd 28/7/64. Flt Lt 9/2/68. Retd GD 6/4/80.
HEAD M.G. Born 6/7/40. Commd 19/12/61. Wg Cdr 1/1/81. Retd GD 1/5/93.
HEAD M.J. MMar. Born 19/11/36. Commd 2/1/67. Sqn Ldr 2/1/75. Retd MAR 2/1/83.
HEAD R.A. Born 27/10/43. Commd 22/5/64. Flt Lt 22/11/69. Retd GD 1/6/82.
HEADLAND M.J. BSc. Born 7/7/50. Commd 26/4/72. Flt Lt 15/4/77. Retd ENG 1/9/77.
HEADLAND R.J. Born 17/3/26. Commd 21/6/56. Sqn Ldr 1/1/73. Retd GD 31/12/75.
HEADLEY I.S. OBE. Born 24/12/33. Commd 26/3/52. Wg Cdr 1/1/81. Retd GD 24/12/91.
HEADLEY P.J. Born 26/2/40. Commd 1/8/61. Flt Lt 7/8/64. Retd GD 27/5/73.
HEAL C.W.C. OBE FInstPet FCMI. Born 24/11/32. Commd 8/8/58. Gp Capt 1/7/80. Retd SUP 23/11/86.
HEAL J.C.F. Born 2/7/64. Commd 27/8/87. Flt Lt 27/2/93. Retd GD 14/3/97.
HEALD M.A.R. MBE. Born 14/7/25. Commd 5/10/50. Flt Lt 5/4/54. Retd GD 14/7/80.
HEALEY D.E. Born 3/1/19. Commd 30/9/41. Sqn Ldr 1/1/53. Retd RGT 29/8/59.
HEALEY J.A. Born 6/8/43. Commd 25/1/63. Flt Lt 1/7/69. Retd GD 31/3/94.
HEALEY P.M. Born 9/2/42. Commd 6/4/62. Sqn Ldr 1/1/77. Retd GD 22/4/94.
HEALY D. BSc ACGI. Born 24/5/23. Commd 16/9/43. Sqn Ldr 1/7/54. Retd ENG 31/8/61.
HEALY D.J. BSc. Born 6/6/61. Commd 2/9/84. Flt Lt 2/3/87. Retd SUP 14/3/96.
HEALY P.C.F. CEng MIEE MCMI. Born 15/3/34. Commd 31/12/64. Sqn Ldr 1/1/69. Retd ENG 1/10/80.
HEANEY R.C. Born 21/1/52. Commd 27/2/75. Flt Lt 27/8/81. Retd GD(G) 4/11/90.
HEANEY S.R. Born 30/9/64. Commd 7/12/86. Flt Lt 7/6/89. Retd GD 7/12/02.
HEAP E. Born 14/5/56. Commd 11/5/78. Sqn Ldr 1/7/88. Retd GD 14/5/94.
HEAP F.W. Born 1/5/26. Commd 17/5/62. Sqn Ldr 1/1/76. Retd GD 1/5/84.
HEAP P.J. Born 31/3/42. Commd 11/5/78. Flt Lt 11/5/83. Retd SUP 2/10/85.
HEARD A.W. Born 7/1/59. Commd 25/2/62. Flt Lt 25/8/87. Retd GD 19/10/97.
HEARD L.J. Born 18/5/12. Commd 21/2/46. Fg Offr 1/11/47. Retd SUP 17/3/48.
HEARD N.J. BSc. Born 21/12/59. Commd 4/9/78. Sqn Ldr 1/7/93. Retd GD 21/12/97.
HEARLE D.C. The Rev. MA BD. Born 20/4/20. Commd 23/8/44. Retd Gp Capt 20/4/75.
HEARMON P.C. Born 8/5/31. Commd 13/9/51. Flt Lt 4/1/57. Retd GD 8/5/71.
HEARN M.P. Born 9/1/48. Commd 4/7/69. Flt Lt 4/1/75. Retd GD 9/1/89.
HEARN P.G. AFC BA. Born 31/8/32. Commd 25/8/53. Gp Capt 1/1/80. Retd ADMIN 31/8/87.
HEARN P.J. Born 9/1/21. Commd 19/2/43. Sqn Ldr 1/7/51. Retd SUP 9/8/70.
HEARN P.J. MBE MCMI. Born 22/8/42. Commd 2/4/65. Sqn Ldr 1/1/82. Retd GD 31/12/97.
HEARN P.J. Born 1/12/44. Commd 6/9/68. Flt Lt 8/2/75. Retd SUP 20/5/84.
HEARNDEN D.M. Born 4/6/06. Commd 8/7/42. Flt Offr 8/1/47. Retd SEC 23/1/57.
HEARNE P.J. Born 6/2/19. Commd 28/7/42. Sqn Ldr 1/7/54. Retd GD 24/2/62.
HEARNSHAW T. BA. Born 8/8/34. Commd 7/2/57. Sqn Ldr 7/8/65. Retd EDN 25/10/72.
HEASELGRAVE D.R. Born 20/5/67. Commd 11/9/86. Sqn Ldr 1/1/98. Retd OPS SPT(ATC) 20/5/05.
HEASMAN D.A. Born 28/7/22. Commd 11/12/45. Flt Lt 19/11/53. Retd RGT 30/9/61.
HEATH A.D. Born 9/4/47. Commd 28/2/69. Flt Lt 8/3/72. Retd GD 1/4/88.
HEATH B.D. Born 8/2/38. Commd 20/11/75. Sqn Ldr 1/7/90. Retd ENG 1/7/93.
HEATH B.P. Born 2/8/27. Commd 6/6/51. Flt Lt 5/9/56. Retd GD 4/5/76.

HEATH E.L. Born 30/4/22. Commd 3/7/43. Sqn Ldr 1/7/54. Retd GD 30/4/69.
HEATH F.G. Born 28/5/14. Commd 15/10/53. Sqn Ldr 22/2/63. Retd MED(T) 31/12/66.
HEATH G. Born 11/3/45. Commd 28/10/66. Sqn Ldr 1/7/89. Retd GD 9/1/96.
HEATH G.F. BA. Born 27/10/38. Commd 23/6/61. Flt Lt 23/12/66. Retd GD 27/10/93.
HEATH J.G. Born 11/10/44. Commd 11/9/64. Flt Lt 15/4/70. Retd GD 31/3/93.
HEATH J.R. MBE. Born 27/6/37. Commd 4/11/82. Sqn Ldr 1/1/89. Retd ENG 4/11/92.
HEATH J.W.H. Born 27/7/31. Commd 31/12/52. Flt Lt 13/4/60. Retd GD 31/8/68.
HEATH P.G. BSc. Born 16/6/49. Commd 19/5/74. Flt Lt 19/8/75. Retd GD 19/5/90.
HEATH P.J. Born 14/4/40. Commd 22/5/75. Sqn Ldr 1/1/90. Retd ENG 2/4/93.
HEATH R.A.J. Born 29/3/55. Commd 11/1/79. Sqn Ldr 1/1/89. Retd GD 30/9/98.
HEATH R.O. Born 3/4/11. Commd 12/6/35. Fg Offr 12/6/36. Retd SEC 9/12/39. Re-called 7/10/40. Flt Lt 13/11/42.
    Retd 9/6/47. rtg Sqn Ldr
HEATH-WHYTE R.W. BSc CEng MIEE MRAeS. Born 24/5/40. Commd 30/9/59. Sqn Ldr 1/7/73. Retd ENG 24/5/78.
HEATHCOTE D.F. MCIPD MRIN MCMI. Born 10/1/37. Commd 6/10/60. Wg Cdr 1/7/87. Retd GD 31/7/93.
HEATHCOTE E. Born 9/2/15. Commd 8/9/41. Sqn Ldr 1/7/52. Retd ENG 9/2/62.
HEATHCOTE G. BSc. Born 20/6/63. Commd 15/3/87. Flt Lt 15/9/89. Retd FLY(P) 15/3/03.
HEATHER G.A. Born 13/11/21. Commd 10/3/44. Flt Lt 10/9/47. Retd ADMIN 13/11/76.
HEATHER G.W. Born 21/12/09. Commd 9/10/31. Wg Cdr 1/10/46. Retd GD 1/8/56.
HEATHERILL J.A. OBE MCMI. Born 27/11/22. Commd 26/11/43. Wg Cdr 1/7/61. Retd GD 27/11/77.
HEATHFIELD A.J. BEd. Born 19/6/63. Commd 14/9/86. Sqn Ldr 1/1/01. Retd ADMIN (TRG) 31/7/04.
HEATON A. Born 7/4/34. Commd 10/8/60. Flt Offr 14/2/66. Retd CAT 22/9/67.
HEATON E.A. Born 22/7/41. Commd 20/9/68. Sqn Ldr 1/1/91. Retd GD 23/4/96.
HEATON M.G. BA. Born 23/2/57. Commd 8/12/77. Sqn Ldr 1/1/90. Retd GD 23/2/95.
HEATON M.R. BSc. Born 22/2/64. Commd 18/8/85. Flt Lt 18/2/88. Retd GD 11/9/01.
HEAVER P.L. Born 25/7/33. Commd 28/1/53. Flt Lt 14/12/61. Retd GD 25/7/71.
HEAVERS I.D. Born 25/9/26. Commd 2/10/50. Flt Lt 3/3/56. Retd GD 24/3/66.
HEBBEN S.J. Born 17/3/65. Commd 15/8/85. Plt Offr 15/2/86. Retd ADMIN 24/2/89.
HEBBES D.G. BEd. Born 16/11/57. Commd 18/8/85. Flt Lt 18/8/86. Retd ADMIN 2/11/96.
HEBBLETHWAITE J.E. Born 8/1/43. Commd 28/9/62. Flt Lt 28/3/68. Retd GD 8/1/81.
HEBBORN K. MBE BSc CEng DipEL MIEE. Born 1/2/31. Commd 5/8/53. Gp Capt 1/7/76. Retd ADMIN 31/12/84.
HEDGCOCK T.J. Born 30/11/36. Commd 8/12/61. Flt Lt 1/4/66. Retd GD 30/11/91.
HEDGECOCK B. Born 23/9/32. Commd 26/9/72. Sqn Ldr 1/1/84. Retd ENG 14/9/89.
HEDGECOCK R.B.G. MSc. Born 11/7/35. Commd 20/2/59. Wg Cdr 1/7/74. Retd ENG 3/3/87.
HEDGELAND P.M.S. CB OBE BSc CEng FIEE FCGI. Born 24/11/22. Commd 10/6/42. AVM 1/1/75. Retd ENG 31/3/78.
HEDGER J.H. Born 15/4/23. Commd 13/12/42. Gp Capt 1/7/73. Retd GD(G) 31/3/78.
HEDGER S.C. Born 21/1/19. Commd 1/9/64. Flt Lt 30/10/65. Retd GD(G) 21/1/74.
HEDGES A.G.F. Born 19/4/32. Commd 14/1/53. Flt Lt 3/6/58. Retd GD 1/10/75.
HEDGES D.P. Born 2/3/48. Commd 22/9/67. Air Cdre 1/7/01. Retd GD 5/9/03.
HEDGES J.W. Born 23/2/10. Commd 1/5/42. Flt Lt 20/11/45. Retd ENG 17/1/50.
HEDGES R.W.H. CBE. Born 2/5/44. Commd 17/12/65. Gp Capt 1/7/87. Retd GD 1/11/91.
HEDLEY B. Born 12/8/28. Commd 26/3/64. Flt Lt 26/3/69. Retd PE 12/8/83.
HEELEY J.M. Born 24/9/57. Commd 18/10/79. Flt Lt 5/10/83. Retd OPS SPT 24/9/01.
HEELEY W.J. Born 25/2/21. Commd 21/11/42. Wg Cdr 1/7/65. Retd GD 26/8/68.
HEGARTY J.F. Born 24/7/31. Commd 28/10/81. Flt Lt 22/5/75. Retd GD 23/7/87. Re-instated 23/11/82 to 24/7/87.
HEGLAND G. DSC. Born 15/5/17. Commd 17/10/49. Sqn Ldr 17/10/57. Retd MAR 17/10/65.
HEGLEY I.S. Born 8/6/47. Commd 23/2/68. Sqn Ldr 1/1/83. Retd SUP 8/6/91.
HEITHUS C. MCIPS MILT MCMI. Born 13/1/44. Commd 3/3/67. Wg Cdr 1/7/94. Retd SUP 13/1/99.
HELD F.P. Born 20/1/26. Commd 30/10/61. Flt Lt 30/10/61. Retd ADMIN 20/1/86.
HELLARD G.P. Born 16/7/62. Commd 15/8/85. Sqn Ldr 1/1/02. Retd OPS SPT(REGT) 3/9/03.
HELLARD S.M. BEng. Born 12/1/67. Commd 3/8/88. Sqn Ldr 1/7/99. Retd ENGINEER 12/1/05.
HELLAWELL K. FCMI. Born 14/10/20. Commd 1/5/42. A Cdre 1/1/73. Retd ENG 14/10/75.
HELLINGS K.E. Born 28/8/24. Commd 4/3/45. Flt Lt 4/9/48. Retd GD 29/6/69.
HELLYER C. MRIN. Born 5/12/43. Commd 3/1/64. Wg Cdr 1/7/92. Retd GD 31/3/94.
HELLYER R.J. Born 21/5/44. Commd 27/3/75. Sqn Ldr 1/7/89. Retd GD 26/1/93.
HELSBY C.M. CEng. Born 25/8/34. Commd 27/11/58. Sqn Ldr 17/1/69. Retd ADMIN 22/10/76.
HELSBY E.W. BA MinstAM DPhysEd. Born 16/10/29. Commd 4/9/59. Wg Cdr 1/1/78. Retd ADMIN 16/11/84.
HELY M.H.M. MA DUS CEng MIEE. Born 12/12/36. Commd 30/9/55. Sqn Ldr 1/7/67. Retd SUP 12/12/74.
HEMBROW S.P. Born 24/2/61. Commd 11/10/84. Flt Lt 11/10/90. Retd GD 14/3/96.
HEMINGWAY J.A. DFC. Born 17/7/19. Commd 7/5/38. Gp Capt 1/7/69. Retd GD 12/9/69.
HEMMING B.H. Born 12/7/36. Commd 21/1/74. Flt Lt 21/2/77. Retd GD 1/1/85.
HEMMING W.J. DFC. Born 23/11/20. Commd 21/10/43. Flt Lt 21/4/47. Retd GD(G) 23/11/66.
HEMMINGS D.J. AFC. Born 2/10/45. Commd 6/5/64. Sqn Ldr 1/1/77. Retd GD 4/11/83.
HEMMINGS W.J. Born 18/9/20. Commd 21/6/56. Flt Lt 21/6/62. Retd GD(G) 18/9/75.
HEMPSEED J.C. Born 21/8/17. Commd 17/10/46. Fg Offr 17/10/46. Retd ENG 26/10/54.
HEMPSTEAD M.C. AFC. Born 15/5/28. Commd 28/6/51. Sqn Ldr 1/7/68. Retd GD 15/3/77.
HEMSLEY H.C. Born 5/3/27. Commd 11/3/65. Flt Lt 11/3/70. Retd SUP 30/9/72.

HEMSLEY S.E. Born 15/8/36. Commd 31/7/56. Flt Lt 16/8/61. Retd PRT 15/8/74.
HEMSLEY T. AFC. Born 19/8/20. Commd 17/12/44. Flt Lt 4/12/52. Retd GD 7/8/64.
HEMSLEY-HALL H.S. Born 9/8/13. Commd 14/8/40. Sqn Ldr 1/7/50. Retd GD(G) 31/3/60.
HEMSON E.A. Born 11/7/42. Commd 9/9/63. Flt Lt 9/9/67. Retd GD 11/10/80.
HEMSWORTH J.R. Born 13/8/18. Commd 3/6/44. Sqn Ldr 1/4/55. Retd GD 31/1/58.
HENCHIE S.D. Born 13/5/38. Commd 28/4/61. Sqn Ldr 1/1/84. Retd GD(G) 3/7/90.
HENCHOZ A.T. Born 18/1/46. Commd 9/3/66. Flt Lt 30/7/72. Retd SUP 18/1/84.
HENCKEN D.C. BSocSc. Born 10/3/43. Commd 22/9/63. Gp Capt 1/7/91. Retd GD 20/9/98.
HENDERSON A.E. AFC. Born 24/11/19. Commd 1/9/45. Sqn Ldr 1/10/54. Retd GD 24/11/62.
HENDERSON C. BSc DipEl CEng MIEE. Born 28/4/28. Commd 11/10/50. Wg Cdr 1/4/69. Retd ADMIN 29/9/76.
HENDERSON C.J. Born 21/9/44. Commd 23/3/67. Wg Cdr 1/1/92. Retd GD 27/8/94.
HENDERSON D. Born 9/8/33. Commd 21/4/54. Flt Lt 7/3/62. Retd GD 9/8/71.
HENDERSON D.F.A. CBE. Born 24/4/48. Commd 28/2/69. AVM 1/7/94. Retd GD 2/1/96.
HENDERSON D.I. Born 21/12/57. Commd 9/8/79. Flt Lt 2/2/84. Retd GD 21/12/95.
HENDERSON E.C. MBE. Born 15/4/17. Commd 12/9/46. Sqn Ldr 1/7/57. Retd SEC 15/4/66.
HENDERSON G.S. BEd. Born 12/11/64. Commd 1/2/93. Sqn Ldr 1/1/99. Retd OPS SPT(ATC) 30/8/03.
HENDERSON H.R. Born 28/6/56. Commd 23/9/79. Sqn Ldr 1/1/90. Retd ADMIN 23/9/98.
HENDERSON I. AFC. Born 2/9/36. Commd 1/4/58. Sqn Ldr 1/7/68. Retd GD 12/2/75. rtg Wg Cdr
HENDERSON J.A. Born 3/5/50. Commd 13/1/72. Sqn Ldr 1/7/85. Retd ADMIN 1/7/88.
HENDERSON J.H. CEng MIEE. Born 19/4/20. Commd 6/5/43. Sqn Ldr 1/1/63. Retd ENG 19/4/75.
HENDERSON J.M. AMBCS. Born 8/11/46. Commd 9/3/66. Wg Cdr 1/1/91. Retd SUP 11/9/01.
HENDERSON J.S. Born 18/9/42. Commd 1/11/63. Flt Lt 4/5/72. Retd OPS SPT 18/9/97.
HENDERSON K. MCMI. Born 28/12/33. Commd 24/9/80. Sqn Ldr 22/10/70. Retd GD 28/12/89.
HENDERSON K. MA MSc DIC CEng MIEE. Born 9/9/50. Commd 6/3/77. Sqn Ldr 1/7/85. Retd ADMIN 31/12/94.
HENDERSON P.G.R. Born 3/10/22. Commd 5/5/60. Flt Lt 5/5/63. Retd GD(G) 15/1/70.
HENDERSON P.W. CB MBE BSc CEng FRAeS. Born 5/11/45. Commd 26/5/67. AVM 1/1/98. Retd ENG 5/11/00.
HENDERSON R.C. Born 12/12/36. Commd 30/10/61. Sqn Ldr 1/7/86. Retd GD 12/12/94.
HENDERSON S.K. Born 13/3/63. Commd 10/5/87. Flt Lt 5/9/91. Retd OPS SPT 24/1/02.
HENDERSON W.J.T. Born 26/5/22. Commd 6/12/41. Sqn Ldr 1/7/53. Retd GD 31/3/62.
HENDLEY I.F. FIDPM MILT MBCS. Born 22/4/44. Commd 27/2/70. Gp Capt 22/4/99. Retd ADMIN 22/4/99.
HENDRA T.H. Born 15/1/17. Commd 28/10/43. Flt Lt 14/2/57. Retd GD(G) 20/4/69.
HENDRICK R.J. Born 8/4/32. Commd 8/10/70. Flt Lt 8/10/73. Retd GD(ENG) 2/8/77. Re-instated 14/1/81. Flt Lt 22/3/77.
    Retd GD(ENG) 21/11/89.
HENDRICK R.O. Born 30/1/46. Commd 30/1/70. Flt Lt 30/7/75. Retd GD 14/9/96.
HENDRIE A. PhD BSc MB ChB MRCGP DRCOG DAvMed. Born 2/12/46. Commd 5/9/72. Wg Cdr 3/8/89.
    Retd MED 3/12/96.
HENDRY L.J.T. MBE. Born 26/6/53. Commd 18/1/73. Sqn Ldr 1/1/87. Retd ENG 16/8/91.
HENDRY R. Born 11/7/32. Commd 21/5/52. Flt Lt 11/5/58. Retd GD 19/4/71.
HENDRY R.W. Born 18/11/54. Commd 12/1/92. Flt Lt 15/5/86. Retd GD 12/2/00.
HENDY J.V. Born 3/3/44. Commd 10/9/70. Flt Lt 10/9/72. Retd GD(G) 3/3/83.
HENLEY B.S. Born 28/11/52. Commd 10/2/72. Sqn Ldr 1/1/85. Retd GD 28/11/90.
HENLEY I.M. Born 8/6/43. Commd 8/6/62. Wg Cdr 1/1/87. Retd GD 8/6/98.
HENLEY J.F. Born 25/5/19. Commd 8/3/45. Fg Offr 8/3/46. Retd GD 15/5/54.
HENLEY P. Born 30/6/30. Commd 16/4/57. Wg Cdr 1/1/75. Retd GD 1/1/78.
HENLEY P.G. Born 28/2/61. Commd 8/4/82. Flt Lt 8/10/88. Retd OPS SPT 28/2/99.
HENLY J.D.E. Born 3/12/29. Commd 2/7/52. Flt Lt 27/11/57. Retd GD 3/12/67.
HENNESSEY M.A. Born 18/11/46. Commd 26/8/66. Flt Lt 26/2/73. Retd SUP 1/1/76.
HENNESSEY P.deP. Born 1/9/23. Commd 31/8/45. Sqn Ldr 1/1/57. Retd GD 1/6/68.
HENNESSEY W.A. Born 24/4/27. Commd 3/11/60. Flt Lt 3/11/65. Retd GD 24/4/82.
HENNESSY B.M. Born 16/5/46. Commd 13/1/72. Flt Lt 22/6/78. Retd ADMIN 23/8/89.
HENNESSY D.F. DPhysEd. Born 31/8/45. Commd 13/9/70. Sqn Ldr 1/7/85. Retd ADMIN 1/3/91.
HENNINGTON J.T. MBE BSc CEng MRAeS. Born 12/11/46. Commd 22/9/65. Wg Cdr 1/7/85. Retd ENG 1/3/90.
HENRY A.W. Born 27/9/26. Commd 3/5/46. Flt Lt 4/1/51. Retd GD 27/9/64.
HENRY B.L. MBE. Born 23/10/44. Commd 4/12/64. Sqn Ldr 1/7/86. Retd GD 23/10/01.
HENRY E.J. MCMI. Born 16/4/48. Commd 9/12/76. Sqn Ldr 1/1/86. Retd ADMIN 1/1/89.
HENRY K. Born 17/4/31. Commd 2/1/52. Sqn Ldr 1/7/64. Retd GD 10/5/80.
HENRY L.C. BSc. Born 4/12/70. Commd 9/12/97. Fg Offr 9/8/96. Retd ADMIN 23/4/00.
HENRY L.H. Born 31/8/47. Commd 12/7/68. Sqn Ldr 1/1/89. Retd SUP 31/8/02.
HENRY P.G. BEng. Born 13/11/59. Commd 2/9/84. Flt Lt 23/6/87. Retd ENG 13/11/97.
HENRY R.G. Born 15/12/21. Commd 17/11/49. Flt Lt 17/11/49. Retd GD 30/9/58.
HENRY R.W. Born 20/11/52. Commd 14/12/72. Gp Capt 1/1/98. Retd GD 13/1/99.
HENRY W.M. BSc. Born 18/11/46. Commd 1/11/71. Sqn Ldr 1/1/79. Retd ENG 1/11/87.
HENSHAW A.E. Born 29/4/47. Commd 24/6/76. Sqn Ldr 1/7/86. Retd ADMIN 2/6/93.
HENSHAW J.A. OBE MCIPD. Born 10/7/20. Commd 11/7/43. Gp Capt 1/1/72. Retd SEC 10/7/75.
HENSHAW M.J. Born 7/2/49. Commd 29/8/72. Wg Cdr 1/7/89. Retd ADMIN 1/10/96.
HENSHAW W.R. Born 30/8/44. Commd 14/7/66. Sqn Ldr 1/1/82. Retd GD 1/10/86.

HENSON J.M. OBE. Born 20/9/40. Commd 3/8/62. Wg Cdr 1/7/91. Retd GD 2/4/93.
HENWOOD B.N. Born 17/3/35. Commd 8/7/53. Sqn Ldr 1/1/81. Retd GD 10/5/85.
HEPBURN R.M. BSocSc. Born 6/10/54. Commd 2/9/73. Fg Offr 15/4/75. Retd ADMIN 4/2/78.
HEPPENSTALL S. BSc. Born 7/8/50. Commd 27/1/70. Flt Lt 15/4/73. Retd GD 7/8/88.
HEPPENSTALL S.G. Born 14/6/47. Commd 25/1/71. Wg Cdr 1/7/90. Retd GD 14/9/96.
HEPWORTH M.E. Born 31/7/44. Commd 15/3/84. Sqn Ldr 1/1/91. Retd ENG 31/12/98.
HERBERT C.A. Born 30/8/34. Commd 5/4/55. Gp Capt 1/7/77. Retd GD 30/6/86.
HERBERT G.J. BSc. Born 7/3/62. Commd 31/7/83. Sqn Ldr 1/7/97. Retd GD 17/5/01.
HERBERT G.S.R. BSc. Born 2/3/65. Commd 26/4/87. Sqn Ldr 1/7/00. Retd ENGINEER 1/7/04.
HERBERT J.R. Born 12/12/43. Commd 11/8/67. Flt Lt 11/2/73. Retd GD 15/12/85.
HERBERT P.C.J. OBE MCMI. Born 12/2/42. Commd 12/3/60. Wg Cdr 1/7/82. Retd GD 12/2/97.
HERBERT S.J. Born 3/9/41. Commd 3/9/60. Flt Lt 9/2/68. Retd GD 1/5/73.
HERBERT W.R. Born 15/8/20. Commd 7/1/42. Wg Cdr 1/7/65. Retd GD 15/8/75.
HERBERTSON J.M. Born 28/11/51. Commd 16/3/73. Flt Lt 16/3/76. Retd GD 15/8/81.
HERBERTSON J.N. Born 28/12/38. Commd 15/12/59. Wg Cdr 1/1/78. Retd GD 5/1/91.
HERCLIFFE F. Born 8/5/22. Commd 2/4/51. Sqn Ldr 1/1/71. Retd GD 1/8/73.
HERCUS W.G. Born 8/9/41. Commd 5/2/65. Flt Lt 21/8/67. Retd GD 8/9/79.
HERD H.D. OBE. Born 25/6/36. Commd 15/12/59. Wg Cdr 1/1/80. Retd ADMIN 21/12/88.
HERDMAN A. Born 18/7/42. Commd 30/8/73. Sqn Ldr 1/7/85. Retd ADMIN 20/4/93.
HERDMAN I.A. MRAeS MCMI. Born 15/12/45. Commd 3/6/65. Sqn Ldr 1/7/79. Retd GD(G) 4/7/89.
HERDMAN T.J. Born 29/5/35. Commd 18/11/53. Flt Lt 23/8/59. Retd GD 29/11/60.
HEREFORD J.N. MA. Born 25/7/32. Commd 31/1/66. Sqn Ldr 31/7/69. Retd ADMIN 25/7/87.
HEREFORD P.J. OBE . Born 17/8/48. Commd 21/2/74. Wg Cdr 1/7/91. Retd GD 17/8/04.
HERITAGE M.J.H. BEM MCIPS. Born 13/7/33. Commd 22/5/70. Flt Lt 22/5/74. Retd SUP 14/7/83.
HERMER G.P. AFC MRAeS. Born 28/8/45. Commd 26/5/67. Sqn Ldr 1/7/81. Retd GD 1/7/84.
HERMISTON M. MBE CEng FRAeS MIMechE. Born 29/12/15. Commd 5/7/40. Gp Capt 1/7/61. Retd ENG 4/1/71.
HERMITAGE G.M. Born 17/7/26. Commd 7/4/48. Gp Capt 1/7/69. Retd GD 29/9/76.
HERMOLLE M.A. Born 7/8/43. Commd 11/6/81. Flt Lt 11/6/84. Retd GD 2/4/93.
HERN J.M. Born 21/12/32. Commd 13/2/57. Flt Lt 13/2/63. Retd SEC 1/7/75.
HERN P. Born 20/9/45. Commd 10/12/65. Flt Lt 20/3/71. Retd GD 20/9/83.
HERN R.W. Born 2/2/20. Commd 11/4/57. Flt Lt 1/4/63. Retd ENG 2/8/64.
HEROD J.R. MBE. Born 21/3/63. Commd 8/12/83. Sqn Ldr 1/7/97. Retd GD 21/9/01.
HEROLD C.J.W. MBE FIIP. Born 5/11/20. Commd 13/11/43. Gp Capt 1/1/71. Retd ENG 31/8/74.
HERON A.F. The Rev. BA LTh. Born 11/2/28. Commd 1/2/62. Retd Wg Cdr 1/2/78.
HERON A.V. MBE. Born 27/7/28. Commd 10/10/63. Sqn Ldr 1/1/77. Retd ENG 27/7/86.
HERON J.D. OBE. Born 14/6/36. Commd 17/12/57. Gp Capt 1/7/83. Retd GD 14/5/87.
HERON S.W. Born 5/1/60. Commd 1/7/82. Sqn Ldr 1/7/91. Retd ENG 5/1/98.
HERON-WEEBER D.R. Born 1/11/20. Commd 6/12/54. Flt Lt 6/12/54. Retd PRT 31/3/62.
HERRETT D.E. Born 28/6/31. Commd 28/6/51. Sqn Ldr 1/7/72. Retd GD 28/6/89.
HERRICK N. BEng. Born 27/12/60. Commd 19/6/84. Flt Lt 1/8/87. Retd ENG 1/5/88.
HERRIDGE W.E. Born 27/4/34. Commd 6/10/77. Flt Lt 6/10/80. Retd PI 1/8/86.
HERRIGTON W.J. CB FCMI. Born 18/5/28. Commd 27/7/49. AVM 1/7/78. Retd GD 3/4/82.
HERRING G.R. Born 8/7/43. Commd 17/12/63. Sqn Ldr 1/1/74. Retd GD 8/7/87.
HERRING K. Born 2/2/10. Commd 13/9/41. Sqn Ldr 1/8/47. Retd ENG 2/2/59.
HERRING K.A. Born 4/9/46. Commd 25/2/88. Flt Lt 25/2/92. Retd ENG 3/4/93.
HERRING P. Born 26/11/22. Commd 23/3/66. Flt Lt 23/3/71. Retd ENG 26/11/82.
HESELWOOD R. Born 24/8/46. Commd 27/3/70. Flt Lt 4/12/73. Retd GD 12/3/92.
HESKETH P.M. BA. Born 6/2/31. Commd 4/11/53. Sqn Ldr 26/2/64. Retd EDN 1/2/75.
HESKETT D. Born 27/12/46. Commd 11/10/84. Flt Lt 11/10/88. Retd SUP 11/7/93.
HESLAM-ELEY D. Born 4/9/42. Commd 19/6/64. Flt Lt 8/3/72. Retd GD 4/9/80.
HESLIN T. MBE MBA. Born 19/6/50. Commd 20/9/79. Sqn Ldr 1/7/91. Retd SUPPLY 19/6/05.
HESLOP J. Born 27/2/25. Commd 2/1/62. Sqn Ldr 1/1/71. Retd GD(G) 4/4/75.
HESMONDHALGH E.J. Born 10/7/21. Commd 17/4/47. Flt Lt 17/10/51. Retd SUP 1/6/61.
HESSEY B. Born 7/1/24. Commd 19/7/57. Flt Lt 1/10/67. Retd GD 28/6/72.
HESTER E.R. Born 5/2/22. Commd 19/8/41. Sqn Ldr 1/7/52. Retd ENG 10/9/52.
HESTER V.A. DFC. Born 16/11/19. Commd 25/11/41. Sqn Ldr 11/7/53. Retd GD 16/11/58.
HETHERINGTON A.J. MA. Born 12/11/38. Commd 9/5/66. Flt Lt 9/2/68. Retd GD 10/4/86.
HETHERINGTON D.T. Born 4/1/46. Commd 28/4/67. Sqn Ldr 1/1/91. Retd GD 14/3/96.
HETHERINGTON H. BA. Born 4/8/20. Commd 30/9/52. Sqn Ldr 30/12/58. Retd EDN 9/3/73.
HETHERINGTON J.M. BSc. Born 23/4/56. Commd 14/8/77. Wg Cdr 1/7/94. Retd GD 1/1/98.
HEWARD M. Born 15/11/09. Commd 1/12/41. Flt Offr 1/12/47. Retd CAT 29/5/62.
HEWAT C.J.S. MBE . Born 3/4/50. Commd 12/7/79. Wg Cdr 1/7/97. Retd GD 3/4/05.
HEWETT B.P.G. MBE. Born 3/1/37. Commd 28/2/56. Flt Lt 1/1/73. Retd SY 3/1/92.
HEWETT G.M. MBE. Born 20/5/61. Commd 25/9/80. Wg Cdr 1/1/98. Retd GD 1/1/01.
HEWETT-HICKS P.E. Born 9/7/20. Commd 23/2/48. Flt Lt 22/7/48. Retd SEC 9/7/75.
HEWITT A.R. Born 23/10/22. Commd 3/10/43. Plt Offr 3/10/48. Retd SEC 7/5/51.

HEWITT D.N. Born 10/11/39. Commd 2/3/65. Sqn Ldr 1/7/74. Retd ENG 2/3/81. Re-entered 4/10/90. Sqn Ldr 4/10/90. Retd ENG 10/7/96.
HEWITT I.S. Born 10/1/43. Commd 25/3/64. Flt Lt 12/11/69. Retd GD 31/5/80. Re-instated 8/12/82. Flt Lt 21/5/72. Retd GD 25/6/93.
HEWITT J.A. Born 21/7/36. Commd 26/5/67. Sqn Ldr 1/1/75. Retd ENG 31/8/90.
HEWITT J.G.F. DSM. Born 4/1/30. Commd 9/4/52. Gp Capt 1/7/77. Retd GD 5/4/83.
HEWITT J.P. Born 18/6/64. Commd 8/9/83. Sqn Ldr 1/1/99. Retd GD 20/9/02.
HEWITT M. Born 30/12/45. Commd 11/8/67. Flt Lt 30/6/71. Retd GD 14/3/96.
HEWITT P.A. Born 24/10/45. Commd 22/7/71. Flt Lt 21/7/74. Retd GD 14/3/96.
HEWITT R.C. Born 14/12/46. Commd 21/1/66. Sqn Ldr 1/1/83. Retd GD 12/1/92.
HEWITT S.G. AFC*. Born 18/12/22. Commd 28/5/43. Sqn Ldr 1/7/53. Retd GD 25/12/61.
HEWLETT T.C. OBE. Born 9/2/49. Commd 27/2/70. Gp Capt 1/1/95. Retd GD 29/4/01.
HEXT J.H.G. Born 12/4/30. Commd 9/6/54. Sqn Ldr 1/7/76. Retd GD 3/10/79.
HEXTALL R. Born 3/11/34. Commd 23/5/63. Wg Cdr 1/1/79. Retd SUP 3/4/82.
HEYES M.R.H. MA MSc CEng FIEE FCMI MRAeS. Born 22/7/34. Commd 25/9/54. Gp Capt 1/1/79. Retd ENG 10/4/87.
HEYES T.A. Born 27/12/47. Commd 17/2/67. Sqn Ldr 1/1/80. Retd GD 27/12/85.
HEYLAND C.R.K. Born 12/10/45. Commd 9/12/65. Sqn Ldr 1/1/85. Retd SUP 1/1/92.
HEYS P.J. IEng FIIE. Born 6/1/47. Commd 1/3/68. Sqn Ldr 1/1/83. Retd ENG 14/3/96.
HEYWARD P.J. Born 25/6/23. Commd 22/9/49. Flt Lt 22/3/54. Retd SEC 24/10/61.
HEYWOOD D.G.L. MCMI. Born 20/11/26. Commd 25/10/46. Gp Capt 1/1/70. Retd GD 1/10/76.
HEYWOOD J.N. Born 25/12/45. Commd 23/3/67. Sqn Ldr 1/7/84. Retd SY 16/8/93.
HEYWOOD T.D.L. Born 2/2/48. Commd 9/3/72. Flt Lt 24/6/78. Retd GD(G) 15/11/89.
HIBBERD N.R.W. AFC. Born 8/10/44. Commd 28/2/64. Sqn Ldr 1/1/80. Retd GD 1/6/97.
HIBBERT C.J. BA. Born 18/8/44. Commd 15/7/66. Flt Lt 15/7/69. Retd GD 18/8/77.
HIBBERT W.J. DFC. Born 12/7/20. Commd 13/4/42. Sqn Ldr 1/1/54. Retd GD 15/11/61.
HIBBIN D.J. Born 13/6/37. Commd 3/11/77. Flt Lt 3/11/81. Retd ENG 4/8/93.
HICK A.R. Born 20/11/23. Commd 18/9/44. Flt Lt 13/11/57. Retd GD 1/5/68.
HICK M.R. FCMI MCIPD. Born 4/4/37. Commd 13/9/60. Gp Capt 1/7/75. Retd ADMIN 2/10/87.
HICKEY C.D. Born 4/9/20. Commd 14/11/46. Flt Lt 14/5/51. Retd SUP 30/5/64.
HICKEY G.A. MCMI. Born 23/1/33. Commd 1/10/57. Gp Capt 1/7/79. Retd SY 1/5/81.
HICKEY J.J. Born 6/6/16. Commd 16/5/47. Sqn Ldr 1/7/65. Retd SUP 6/6/71.
HICKEY L.D. AFC. Born 19/7/21. Commd 6/7/50. Flt Lt 11/11/55. Retd GD 10/4/68.
HICKEY P.L. CBE MSc MB BS DObstRCOG DAvMed. Born 21/6/45. Commd 19/7/65. Gp Capt 1/7/92. Retd MED 10/10/94.
HICKEY S.A. OBE FRAeS FCMI. Born 23/5/46. Commd 16/12/66. Gp Capt 1/7/95. Retd GD 6/4/01.
HICKEY S.D. MCMI. Born 7/5/48. Commd 5/11/70. Wg Cdr 1/7/01. Retd GD 1/7/04.
HICKIE J.A. Born 9/5/29. Commd 22/7/66. Sqn Ldr 1/1/79. Retd ENG 9/5/87.
HICKLEY P.A.M. BA. Born 29/1/44. Commd 31/1/64. Flt Lt 31/7/69. Retd GD 1/10/92.
HICKLING A.I. Born 29/8/27. Commd 30/11/59. Flt Lt 30/11/59. Retd GD 3/1/69.
HICKMAN C.StJ. Born 8/8/39. Commd 19/4/63. Flt Lt 19/10/68. Retd GD 8/8/94.
HICKMAN K.P. Born 6/10/43. Commd 11/7/74. Sqn Ldr 1/1/86. Retd ENG 6/4/96.
HICKMORE G.G.A. MBE. Born 25/11/35. Commd 4/5/55. Sqn Ldr 1/7/82. Retd GD 25/11/93.
HICKMOTT J.A. Born 7/10/34. Commd 8/7/53. Sqn Ldr 1/1/70. Retd GD 1/1/73.
HICKMOTT M.E.J. DFC MRAeS. Born 11/7/24. Commd 26/8/45. Sqn Ldr 1/1/59. Retd GD 11/6/73.
HICKOX A.J.L. DFC*. Born 3/6/22. Commd 1/5/42. Flt Lt 29/3/49. Retd GD 30/10/62.
HICKS A.G. MA CEng MIEE MRAeS. Born 18/2/36. Commd 9/8/57. A Cdre 1/7/87. Retd GD 18/10/91.
HICKS B. MBE. Born 3/10/44. Commd 14/7/69. Wg Cdr 1/1/88. Retd PRT 14/7/91.
HICKS C.P. Born 26/12/48. Commd 31/7/70. Wg Cdr 1/7/96. Retd GD 26/4/04.
HICKS D. Born 2/10/33. Commd 2/7/52. Flt Lt 14/5/58. Retd GD(G) 2/10/83.
HICKS D.S. Born 4/5/33. Commd 27/5/69. Sqn Ldr 1/1/82. Retd GD 4/5/91.
HICKS F.H. Born 15/5/21. Commd 24/10/45. Flt Lt 15/12/49. Retd GD 1/10/57.
HICKS G.A. Born 15/9/28. Commd 20/5/63. Flt Lt 23/5/68. Retd GD(G) 15/9/83.
HICKS G.F. Born 23/9/23. Commd 21/7/55. Sqn Ldr 1/7/75. Retd GD 31/7/82.
HICKS H. MBE BA. Born 13/7/23. Commd 31/1/45. Gp Capt 1/7/72. Retd ADMIN 31/3/76.
HICKS J.S.R. MA. Born 6/11/35. Commd 5/3/60. Sqn Ldr 1/7/71. Retd GD 1/4/80. Re-instated 4/2/81. Sqn Ldr 6/5/72. Retd GD 30/9/89.
HICKS P. Born 21/7/30. Commd 31/7/58. Flt Lt 31/1/62. Retd GD 1/4/77.
HICKS P.G. MBE BSc. Born 5/8/57. Commd 4/9/78. Wg Cdr 1/7/99. Retd GD 19/2/04.
HICKS P.K.V. Born 9/7/22. Commd 11/11/44. Wg Cdr 1/7/64. Retd GD 1/9/67.
HICKS T.P. MBE. Born 9/9/48. Commd 8/6/84. Sqn Ldr 1/1/91. Retd ENG 5/4/96.
HICKSON C. Born 3/3/44. Commd 6/4/62. Flt Lt 6/10/67. Retd GD 31/10/94.
HICKSON P.R. BSc. Born 22/7/65. Commd 13/4/93. Sqn Ldr 1/1/00. Retd OPS SPT(REGT) 8/5/04.
HIDE D.C. Born 14/12/42. Commd 28/4/65. Flt Lt 28/10/70. Retd GD 12/1/81.
HIDE W.R. DFC. Born 10/7/17. Commd 14/10/42. Flt Lt 14/4/47. Retd GD(G) 10/7/72.
HIFLE R. Born 24/4/39. Commd 13/1/72. Sqn Ldr 1/7/85. Retd GD 8/11/89.
HIGGINBOTTOM D.H. Born 20/8/48. Commd 27/5/48. Sqn Ldr 1/1/87. Retd GD(G) 7/12/92.

HIGGINS B.H. Born 21/6/37. Commd 9/2/62. Wg Cdr 1/7/89. Retd ADMIN 21/6/92.
HIGGINS C.R.M. BA. Born 9/12/34. Commd 27/2/61. Flt Lt 1/5/61. Retd GD(G) 9/12/92.
HIGGINS E.B. Born 8/8/19. Commd 6/9/56. Flt Lt 6/9/62. Retd GD(G) 31/10/72.
HIGGINS J. Born 3/4/64. Commd 23/7/98. Flt Lt 23/7/00. Retd ENGINEER 25/6/05.
HIGGINS J.W. CEng MRAeS MCMI. Born 12/5/21. Commd 28/7/49. Wg Cdr 1/1/73. Retd ENG 12/5/76.
HIGGINS M.P. Born 22/9/34. Commd 4/6/64. Flt Lt 10/2/67. Retd SEC 22/9/72.
HIGGINSON A.G. MB ChB MRCPath. Born 19/4/43. Commd 11/1/65. Wg Cdr 7/9/80. Retd MED 9/11/81.
HIGGOTT G.D. CEng MRAeS. Born 20/10/40. Commd 4/12/67. Flt Lt 4/12/72. Retd ENG 4/12/83.
HIGGS A.R.N. OBE MA. Born 6/2/34. Commd 3/1/58. Wg Cdr 1/7/80. Retd ADMIN 10/4/93.
HIGGS B. CBE. Born 22/8/34. Commd 19/11/52. AVM 1/1/86. Retd GD 29/10/87.
HIGGS D.M. Born 30/11/36. Commd 6/4/55. Wg Cdr 1/1/81. Retd ADMIN 27/4/84.
HIGGS E.L.C. MCMI. Born 11/1/25. Commd 6/7/45. Wg Cdr 1/1/70. Retd SUP 3/4/79.
HIGGS J.F. MCMI. Born 8/9/33. Commd 3/6/65. Sqn Ldr 1/7/78. Retd ADMIN 6/4/83.
HIGGS P.R. BSc. Born 22/6/54. Commd 3/1/88. Flt Lt 3/7/88. Retd ENG 23/9/95.
HIGGS S.K. Born 29/1/66. Commd 7/11/85. Flt Lt 7/5/91. Retd FLY(P) 29/1/04.
HIGGS S.M. Born 9/1/61. Commd 28/2/80. Flt Lt 28/8/86. Retd OPS SPT 1/1/01.
HIGH M.N.S. Born 11/10/56. Commd 9/12/76. Flt Lt 9/6/82. Retd GD 11/10/94.
HIGH R. Born 3/12/20. Commd 7/10/44. Flt Lt 19/11/53. Retd GD(G) 1/3/68.
HIGH W.D. Born 1/7/10. Commd 10/6/42. Flt Offr 10/12/46. Retd SEC 29/10/50.
HIGHAM D. MBE. Born 13/9/31. Commd 22/9/55. Sqn Ldr 1/7/66. Retd ENG 1/3/85.
HIGHAM F.J. OBE DFC. Born 2/5/15. Commd 14/7/04. Wg Cdr 1/7/55. Retd GD 2/5/62.
HIGHAM P. Born 2/12/48. Commd 19/6/86. Flt Lt 19/6/90. Retd ADMIN 14/3/96.
HIGHMAN P. Born 26/7/22. Commd 7/6/51. Flt Lt 7/12/55. Retd MAR 18/9/63.
HIGHMORE H.G. Born 14/8/30. Commd 3/6/65. Sqn Ldr 1/1/77. Retd ENG 2/6/82.
HIGHTON P.T. Born 13/1/34. Commd 28/9/54. Sqn Ldr 1/1/69. Retd GD 31/7/73.
HIGLEY G.R. Born 7/7/34. Commd 28/1/53. Flt Lt 29/4/59. Retd GD 7/7/72.
HIGNELL A.F. OBE MA MB BChir MFCM MRCGP DPH. Born 6/7/28. Commd 26/9/54. Gp Capt 1/7/77.
    Retd MED 1/4/80.
HIGNELL R.A. BSc. Born 23/8/54. Commd 2/9/73. Flt Lt 15/10/79. Retd ENG 1/5/83.
HIGNETT D.R. Born 2/3/46. Commd 22/9/65. Flt Lt 28/8/72. Retd ENG 2/3/84.
HIGSON D.J. BA. Born 14/2/49. Commd 30/7/72. Sqn Ldr 1/7/79. Retd ADMIN 30/7/88.
HILDAGE A.R. MCMI. Born 31/12/52. Commd 8/9/83. Wg Cdr 1/7/96. Retd ADMIN 1/5/98.
HILDITCH C.H. BSc. Born 24/9/34. Commd 20/11/56. Flt Lt 20/8/58. Retd GD 24/9/89.
HILDITCH L.E. Born 22/9/47. Commd 27/10/67. Fg Offr 24/2/70. Retd GD(G) 15/9/73. Re-entered 31/10/84.
    Flt Lt 31/10/87. Retd OPS SPT 31/10/00.
HILDITCH S.L. BSc FRAeS. Born 2/9/54. Commd 30/9/73. Gp Capt 1/1/02. Retd GD 28/3/05.
HILDRETH P. Born 15/4/22. Commd 23/1/43. Flt Lt 23/1/48. Retd RGT 25/6/58. rtg Sqn Ldr
HILES A.N. BA. Born 11/3/41. Commd 10/11/64. Flt Lt 10/8/68. Retd SEC 1/7/75.
HILL A.G. Born 23/4/44. Commd 2/2/68. Wg Cdr 1/1/94. Retd ADMIN 14/3/96.
HILL A.J. Born 17/6/17. Commd 6/3/39. Sqn Ldr 1/8/47. Retd GD 25/10/57.
HILL A.K. Born 11/2/47. Commd 21/1/86. Sqn Ldr 1/7/97. Retd GD 11/2/02.
HILL A.M. Born 20/3/47. Commd 1/1/82. Sqn Ldr 1/7/91. Retd SY 2/12/96.
HILL A.R. Born 6/9/31. Commd 14/4/53. Flt Lt 14/10/55. Retd GD 6/9/69.
HILL A.R. BSc. Born 10/7/45. Commd 2/8/71. Wg Cdr 1/1/92. Retd ENG 13/1/95.
HILL A.R. Born 22/6/38. Commd 6/5/66. Flt Lt 4/11/70. Retd GD(G) 18/11/77.
HILL B.H. Born 30/6/42. Commd 12/4/73. Wg Cdr 1/1/92. Retd GD 30/6/97.
HILL C. Born 29/1/39. Commd 28/10/63. Flt Lt 20/12/67. Retd GD 31/1/84.
HILL C.J. FIMIS MCMI. Born 28/5/46. Commd 3/10/66. Wg Cdr 1/7/92. Retd GD 10/6/03.
HILL D. Born 15/7/45. Commd 2/6/67. Sqn Ldr 1/1/80. Retd GD 1/6/98.
HILL D. CEng MRAeS. Born 15/3/21. Commd 19/8/42. Gp Capt 1/7/71. Retd ENG 15/9/73.
HILL D.B.R. Born 8/3/26. Commd 3/5/46. Fg Offr 3/5/47. Retd GD 15/6/49.
HILL D.F.E. BA. Born 28/12/33. Commd 22/5/62. Sqn Ldr 26/7/65. Retd EDN 22/5/78.
HILL D.P. Born 4/11/39. Commd 16/12/66. Sqn Ldr 1/1/91. Retd GD 4/11/94.
HILL D.S. BEM. Born 7/8/31. Commd 7/9/61. Flt Lt 7/9/67. Retd ENG 1/12/81.
HILL D.W. BEM. Born 26/12/24. Commd 18/5/61. Flt Lt 18/5/66. Retd ENG 1/1/77.
HILL E.G.F. CBE. Born 1/10/17. Commd 4/3/39. A Cdre 1/1/70. Retd SUP 3/1/73.
HILL E.J. Born 23/1/30. Commd 30/8/62. Sqn Ldr 1/7/84. Retd ENG 23/1/88.
HILL E.J.R. Born 19/4/51. Commd 4/2/71. Wg Cdr 1/1/97. Retd GD 1/7/04.
HILL E.P. The Rev Mgr. Born 8/8/43. Commd 14/9/82. Retd Gp Capt 5/5/00.
HILL F. Born 3/9/11. Commd 20/4/44. Flt Lt 20/10/47. Retd ENG 2/6/48.
HILL Dame Felicity DBE. Born 12/12/15. Commd 25/4/41. A Cdre 1/4/66. Retd SEC 9/8/69.
HILL H.F. Born 21/2/24. Commd 20/11/58. Flt Lt 1/2/63. Retd GD(G) 21/2/82.
HILL I.J.C. Born 20/10/38. Commd 20/9/59. Sqn Ldr 1/1/72. Retd GD 1/2/73. Re-employed 13/11/78. Retd 1/11/83.
HILL I.R. OBE MA PhD MD MB BChir MRCPath LDS AMRAeS. Born 26/11/39. Commd 25/11/68. Wg Cdr 29/3/84.
    Retd MED 28/5/91.
HILL J.B. AFC. Born 14/5/43. Commd 24/6/65. Gp Capt 1/7/86. Retd GD 13/5/93.

HILL J.E. BA. Born 16/5/59. Commd 18/10/81. Flt Lt 14/5/83. Retd ADMIN 14/3/97.
HILL J.G. MA. Born 7/1/33. Commd 25/8/55. Sqn Ldr 25/2/63. Retd EDN 31/10/73.
HILL J.R.E. Born 21/5/40. Commd 8/12/64. Sqn Ldr 1/1/76. Retd ENG 8/12/87.
HILL L.C.V. Born 21/7/23. Commd 19/12/63. Flt Lt 19/12/68. Retd ENG 21/7/77.
HILL L.R. Born 3/3/23. Commd 19/11/45. Flt Lt 30/6/49. Retd GD 3/3/62.
HILL M. Born 13/5/50. Commd 4/2/71. Flt Lt 4/8/77. Retd OPS SPT(ATC) 13/5/05.
HILL M.A. BEng. Born 13/11/46. Commd 24/7/68. Flt Lt 1/6/72. Retd GD 5/4/75.
HILL M.D. Born 18/8/34. Commd 17/3/54. Flt Lt 15/8/62. Retd GD 28/3/77.
HILL M.J. Born 23/10/51. Commd 16/3/73. Sqn Ldr 1/7/85. Retd GD 23/10/89.
HILL N. BSc. Born 17/5/55. Commd 7/11/85. Wg Cdr 1/1/00. Retd GD 4/1/05.
HILL P.A. MCMI. Born 18/11/32. Commd 25/9/52. Sqn Ldr 1/1/69. Retd ADMIN 18/11/87.
HILL P.F. Born 25/3/38. Commd 24/2/61. Flt Lt 1/4/66. Retd GD 2/9/75.
HILL P.G. Born 14/3/22. Commd 30/4/41. Gp Capt 1/1/67. Retd GD 14/3/77.
HILL P.J.R. Born 1/2/43. Commd 26/5/61. Sqn Ldr 1/1/81. Retd GD 1/1/84.
HILL P.M. Born 16/11/23. Commd 21/7/55. Flt Lt 21/7/61. Retd GD 16/11/73.
HILL P.R. MBE. Born 26/6/22. Commd 29/9/44. Wg Cdr 1/1/74. Retd GD(G) 30/6/76.
HILL R. MRAeS. Born 1/10/17. Commd 19/11/42. Sqn Ldr 1/7/53. Retd ENG 1/10/67.
HILL R. DPhysEd. Born 17/8/42. Commd 22/9/64. Fg Offr 22/9/64. Retd ADMIN 22/9/82.
HILL R. Born 11/2/23. Commd 25/8/49. Sqn Ldr 1/1/73. Retd GD 10/9/77.
HILL R.A. Born 2/6/44. Commd 14/7/66. Wg Cdr 1/7/83. Retd GD 10/6/88.
HILL R.B. MHCIMA. Born 27/5/25. Commd 7/5/56. Flt Lt 5/11/58. Retd CAT 7/6/75.
HILL R.G. MCMI LHA. Born 2/3/34. Commd 22/7/66. Sqn Ldr 21/9/77. Retd MED(SEC) 2/5/84.
HILL R.L. Born 28/8/50. Commd 27/1/77. Flt Lt 27/7/81. Retd GD 30/3/94.
HILL S.C.A. Born 19/4/34. Commd 2/7/52. Sqn Ldr 1/7/67. Retd SEC 19/4/72.
HILL S.J. MSc BSc. Born 1/8/47. Commd 30/5/71. Sqn Ldr 1/1/80. Retd ENG 30/5/87.
HILL S.R. OBE BA CEng FIMechE FCMI FRAeS CertDipAF. Born 27/3/42. Commd 28/11/66. A Cdre 1/7/89. Retd ENG 28/2/91.
HILL W. Born 4/2/33. Commd 1/12/54. Wg Cdr 1/7/78. Retd GD 11/5/87.
HILL W.W. Born 16/8/32. Commd 26/3/52. Flt Lt 26/12/63. Retd GD 2/1/76.
HILL W.W. MBE. Born 8/3/30. Commd 17/5/51. Sqn Ldr 1/1/67. Retd GD 18/3/88.
HILL-TREVOR N.E. Born 25/4/31. Commd 25/5/50. Fg Offr 30/1/54. Retd RGT 16/7/60.
HILLER D.W. CEng MRAeS MCMI. Born 24/3/35. Commd 16/5/57. Gp Capt 1/1/85. Retd ENG 1/12/89.
HILLIARD A.J. Born 22/9/35. Commd 3/3/54. Flt Lt 3/9/59. Retd GD 22/9/90.
HILLIARD F.H. Born 3/1/26. Commd 6/3/52. Flt Lt 6/9/55. Retd GD 3/1/76.
HILLIARD G.H. Born 28/10/56. Commd 28/10/76. Flt Lt 28/4/82. Retd GD(G) 28/10/96.
HILLIARD T. Born 6/6/32. Commd 23/4/52. Sqn Ldr 1/1/64. Retd GD 2/8/69.
HILLIER B.E. Born 18/11/44. Commd 8/10/70. Flt Lt 28/1/73. Retd ENG 18/11/82.
HILLIER C. Born 8/3/18. Commd 5/10/50. Sqn Ldr 1/1/62. Retd ENG 8/3/69.
HILLIER D.J. CEng MRAeS. Born 12/3/43. Commd 15/7/65. Sqn Ldr 1/7/74. Retd ENG 30/6/81.
HILLIER P.F.J. Born 23/11/22. Commd 2/3/45. Flt Lt 29/11/51. Retd GD 25/5/61.
HILLIER P.S. BSc CEng MRAeS. Born 17/7/46. Commd 3/2/69. Wg Cdr 1/7/90. Retd ENG 17/7/01.
HILLIKER C. Born 6/6/46. Commd 6/5/66. Wg Cdr 1/1/91. Retd GD 31/7/00.
HILLMAN C.G. MILAM DPhysEd. Born 19/3/48. Commd 13/9/70. Wg Cdr 1/1/89. Retd ADMIN 13/9/92.
HILLMAN R. Born 20/4/35. Commd 16/9/53. Sqn Ldr 1/7/67. Retd GD 31/12/91.
HILLS B.F. MBE. Born 18/7/25. Commd 3/9/46. Wg Cdr 1/1/73. Retd GD 18/7/80.
HILLS C.C. Born 2/3/34. Commd 15/10/52. Flt Lt 22/4/58. Retd GD 11/4/72.
HILLS D.G.M. CB OBE MB BS MFCM DPH. Born 28/2/25. Commd 29/6/50. AVM 1/4/83. Retd MED 1/4/85.
HILLS D.W. CEng MIEE. Born 25/8/21. Commd 6/6/46. Wg Cdr 1/1/66. Retd ENG 1/2/78.
HILLS E.D. CB CBE. Born 26/1/17. Commd 23/1/39. AVM 1/7/71. Retd SUP 1/9/73.
HILLS J. Born 5/12/46. Commd 7/1/71. Sqn Ldr 1/7/81. Retd GD 31/5/85.
HILLS N.G.R. Born 29/10/63. Commd 23/4/87. Flt Lt 21/8/93. Retd ADMIN 14/3/96.
HILLS P.L. MCMI. Born 13/10/20. Commd 26/9/57. Sqn Ldr 1/1/68. Retd ENG 17/10/70.
HILLS P.L. MSc BSc CEng MIEE. Born 29/7/43. Commd 15/7/65. Sqn Ldr 1/7/77. Retd ENG 26/7/01.
HILLS R.J. Born 31/10/62. Commd 11/10/87. Flt Lt 11/10/93. Retd ADMIN 29/1/97.
HILLS T.A. Born 7/8/56. Commd 17/7/75. Flt Lt 17/1/81. Retd GD 7/8/94.
HILLSMITH K.R. Born 30/12/62. Commd 20/10/83. Flt Lt 20/4/89. Retd GD 30/1/01.
HILTON A.A. Born 9/8/26. Commd 4/7/51. Flt Lt 24/4/57. Retd GD 25/8/71.
HILTON A.P. Born 16/9/33. Commd 5/4/55. Sqn Ldr 1/1/70. Retd GD 1/1/73.
HILTON B.S. Born 18/12/33. Commd 15/3/55. Flt Lt 24/3/58. Retd ADMIN 1/4/84.
HILTON J.B.S. Born 11/4/48. Commd 27/2/70. Flt Lt 27/8/75. Retd ADMIN 1/10/90.
HILTON P.W. Born 3/9/37. Commd 21/10/65. Gp Capt 1/7/89. Retd SUP 3/9/92.
HILTON R.B. BSc. Born 9/7/51. Commd 25/9/71. Fg Offr 15/4/74. Retd ENG 10/4/79.
HILTON T.F. Born 19/7/45. Commd 26/5/67. Flt Lt 4/5/72. Retd GD 26/9/72.
HINCHCLIFFE P.M. Born 22/11/28. Commd 6/12/50. Flt Lt 6/9/56. Retd GD 27/11/66.
HINCHLIFFE D.A.R. Born 6/5/40. Commd 10/2/59. Sqn Ldr 1/1/79. Retd GD 6/5/95.
HINCHLIFFE N.B. Born 24/9/53. Commd 20/1/80. Flt Lt 20/1/81. Retd ADMIN 20/1/99.

HINCHLIFFE P.C. Born 20/8/24. Commd 26/3/45. Flt Lt 16/3/57. Retd GD(G) 10/8/67.
HIND J.M. MCMI. Born 15/6/32. Commd 6/1/51. Sqn Ldr 1/7/67. Retd SUP 1/7/77.
HIND K. Born 2/12/33. Commd 22/7/55. Fg Offr 15/10/56. Retd ENG 16/10/59.
HIND L. Born 10/11/42. Commd 27/9/73. Flt Lt 27/9/75. Retd GD 1/5/93.
HIND P.J. Born 8/12/35. Commd 14/1/65. Flt Lt 26/7/67. Retd GD 30/6/77.
HINDE C.J. MBA MCMI. Born 25/4/46. Commd 11/5/75. Flt Lt 11/2/79. Retd ADMIN 11/5/91.
HINDLE I. MSc BDS FDSRCS FFDRCSIrel. Born 28/7/45. Commd 31/7/66. Flt Lt 18/12/68. Retd DEL 18/12/73.
   Re-entered 2/4/79. Gp Capt 20/12/91. Retd DEL 3/4/97.
HINDLE M.P. ACIS. Born 19/12/45. Commd 25/8/67. Wg Cdr 1/7/85. Retd ADMIN 19/12/89.
HINDLEY A. OBE AFC. Born 19/3/15. Commd 23/10/39. Wg Cdr 1/7/54. Retd GD 1/1/58.
HINDLEY F. MBE. Born 24/6/37. Commd 21/10/66. Flt Lt 1/7/69. Retd GD 24/6/95.
HINDLEY M.A. Born 25/3/43. Commd 22/2/63. Sqn Ldr 1/7/74. Retd GD 25/3/94.
HINDMARSH A.D. AFC. Born 22/7/15. Commd 9/4/43. Sqn Ldr 1/7/52. Retd GD 21/11/58.
HINDMARSH J. Born 2/2/29. Commd 20/6/63. Sqn Ldr 1/7/74. Retd ENG 2/2/84.
HINDMARSH T.J. OBE BA. Born 19/9/37. Commd 24/4/64. Gp Capt 1/1/89. Retd GD 24/10/92.
HINDS C.D. BSc. Born 4/2/45. Commd 15/7/66. Sqn Ldr 1/7/75. Retd ENG 6/11/76.
HINE A.T. Born 27/2/47. Commd 19/8/66. Flt Lt 8/3/72. Retd GD 27/2/85.
HINE D.J. Born 22/4/35. Commd 26/5/54. A Cdre 1/1/87. Retd GD 18/11/88.
HINE Sir Patrick GCB GBE FRAeS CCMI. Born 14/7/32. Commd 22/3/51. ACM 1/7/85. Retd GD 1/9/91.
HINES F.M.A. Born 14/3/33. Commd 5/4/55. Wg Cdr 1/7/70. Retd GD 27/10/84.
HING T.J. Born 18/8/50. Commd 30/1/70. Fg Offr 18/7/72. Retd SUP 31/3/76.
HINGE C.J. Born 2/2/39. Commd 21/10/65. Flt Lt 29/7/68. Retd GD 2/2/77.
HINGLEY H.B. OBE BMus LRAM ARCM. Born 4/3/38. Commd 24/3/67. Wg Cdr 1/7/89. Retd DM 4/3/95.
HINGSTON-JONES G.F. OBE CCMI MInstPS. Born 20/4/31. Commd 18/6/71. Wg Cdr 1/1/79. Retd SUP 18/7/87.
HINKLEY R.W. BEM. Born 7/12/55. Commd 14/2/99. Flt Lt 14/2/99. Retd OPS SPT(REGT) 2/7/04.
HINKLEY SMITH K.L. MA. Born 12/10/39. Commd 27/4/65. Sqn Ldr 1/7/79. Retd ADMIN 1/4/97.
HINNELL K.G. Born 10/10/19. Commd 15/11/45. Sqn Ldr 1/1/66. Retd ENG 10/10/74.
HINSHELWOOD W.E.D. MSc BTech. Born 22/12/48. Commd 18/4/69. Sqn Ldr 1/7/83. Retd ENG 1/10/88.
HINTON D.H.E. Born 29/6/32. Commd 17/12/52. Flt Lt 17/5/56. Retd GD 29/1/70. Re-instated 14/9/79 to 29/1/84.
HINTON N.G. CEng MRAeS. Born 3/10/37. Commd 10/8/65. Sqn Ldr 1/7/74. Retd ENG 10/8/81.
HINTON P.N. MCMI. Born 5/5/47. Commd 1/4/66. Sqn Ldr 1/7/83. Retd GD 1/9/00.
HINTON R.H. Born 12/4/22. Commd 15/3/45. Sqn Ldr 1/1/59. Retd GD 14/4/65.
HINWOOD J.A. Born 5/6/22. Commd 12/3/43. Flt Lt 19/11/53. Retd GD(G) 5/6/77.
HIPKINS B.G. Born 17/10/25. Commd 9/8/47. Sqn Ldr 1/7/76. Retd ADMIN 7/10/78.
HIPKINS J.R.D. Born 29/11/68. Commd 15/12/88. Fg Offr 15/6/91. Retd SUP 1/5/93.
HIPPERSON D.G. Born 22/4/35. Commd 18/8/54. Flt Lt 26/2/60. Retd GD 22/4/73.
HIPPERSON G. Born 17/6/41. Commd 22/3/63. Flt Lt 22/9/68. Retd GD 17/6/82.
HIRD D.W. Born 14/1/25. Commd 10/4/52. Flt Lt 10/4/52. Retd GD 14/1/83.
HIRD R. Born 8/12/57. Commd 22/9/88. Flt Lt 22/9/90. Retd ENG 22/9/96.
HIRONS P.J. Born 22/3/37. Commd 26/5/67. Sqn Ldr 1/7/75. Retd ENG 31/5/77.
HIRPARA R.H. MB BS MCMI DAvMed. Born 2/4/43. Commd 1/2/80. Wg Cdr 22/5/92. Retd MED 14/9/96.
HIRST C.A.R. BSc. Born 9/4/50. Commd 28/2/72. Flt Lt 28/5/73. Retd GD 9/4/88.
HIRST C.W. Born 24/6/52. Commd 27/1/77. Flt Lt 7/12/80. Retd OPS SPT 1/10/97.
HIRST F. Born 16/8/20. Commd 28/2/46. Sqn Ldr 1/1/63. Retd ENG 28/4/68.
HIRST J.K. Born 6/1/37. Commd 24/11/60. Sqn Ldr 6/11/69. Retd ADMIN 30/5/76.
HIRST K.L. Born 5/6/26. Commd 14/6/46. Sqn Ldr 1/7/59. Retd GD 1/10/73.
HIRST P.B. Born 2/2/40. Commd 28/7/60. Sqn Ldr 1/7/74. Retd ENG 2/2/78.
HIRST P.J. Born 12/4/32. Commd 24/1/52. Wg Cdr 1/7/74. Retd GD 10/2/86.
HISCOCK P.G. Born 7/12/33. Commd 22/5/59. Sqn Ldr 20/8/68. Retd ADMIN 24/5/77. Re-instated 2/1/80 to 13/7/84.
HISLOP I.G. Born 20/6/33. Commd 8/7/54. Sqn Ldr 1/1/70. Retd SUP 3/3/76.
HITCHCOCK C.W. Born 13/5/48. Commd 17/3/67. Flt Lt 17/9/73. Retd SUP 12/7/80.
HITCHCOCK J.E. Born 11/11/28. Commd 24/10/51. Flt Lt 24/4/56. Retd GD 11/11/66.
HITCHCOCK K.J. CBE. Born 23/8/25. Commd 22/9/49. A Cdre 1/7/76. Retd SEC 17/11/79.
HITCHCOCK P.G. Born 23/9/47. Commd 6/5/66. Wg Cdr 1/7/87. Retd GD 13/5/99.
HITCHEN G.P. BA. Born 2/10/31. Commd 23/9/53. Sqn Ldr 17/2/63. Retd ADMIN 1/5/76.
HITCHEN N. Born 25/12/32. Commd 11/10/51. Sqn Ldr 1/7/76. Retd PI 27/4/84.
HITCHEN S. MVO AFC. Born 8/5/35. Commd 11/2/55. Wg Cdr 1/1/75. Retd GD 4/4/80.
HITCHEN S.T. Born 18/8/19. Commd 17/7/57. Sqn Ldr 17/2/64. Retd EDN 18/8/74.
HITCHINGS G.M. CEng FIEE FCMI MRAeS. Born 25/7/38. Commd 23/7/58. Gp Capt 1/7/89. Retd ENG 25/7/93.
HITCHINS D.K. MSc CEng MIEE MRAeS. Born 28/6/35. Commd 30/7/59. Sqn Ldr 1/7/68. Retd ENG 1/1/74.
HIVES D.B. Born 9/6/31. Commd 14/4/53. Gp Capt 1/1/79. Retd GD 9/6/86.
HOAD N.E. CVO CBE AFC* FCMI. Born 27/3/23. Commd 1/5/43. AVM 1/7/74. Retd GD 31/3/78.
HOAR B.A. Born 5/2/34. Commd 23/3/70. Sqn Ldr 1/7/81. Retd SY 4/7/84.
HOAR L.J. Born 26/5/25. Commd 1/12/44. Flt Lt 1/6/48. Retd GD 26/5/68.
HOAR R.J. Born 2/7/42. Commd 2/6/67. Sqn Ldr 1/1/88. Retd GD 2/7/97.
HOARE D.S. Born 22/10/17. Commd 16/11/36. Gp Capt 1/7/60. Retd GD 22/7/67.

HOARE M.G.N. BA. Born 17/12/34. Commd 1/10/63. Sqn Ldr 1/7/69. Retd GD 1/2/84.
HOARE P. DMS FRIN. Born 30/6/23. Commd 28/1/44. Sqn Ldr 1/7/59. Retd GD 30/6/72.
HOARE P.F. BA. Born 9/7/48. Commd 27/10/70. Sqn Ldr 1/7/83. Retd GD 27/10/86.
HOARE P.H. Born 31/7/43. Commd 23/11/78. Flt Lt 23/11/83. Retd ENG 1/5/85.
HOARE R. Born 13/8/32. Commd 15/12/53. Flt Lt 15/6/56. Retd GD 13/8/70.
HOARE W.A. Born 5/4/37. Commd 12/1/61. Wg Cdr 1/1/79. Retd GD 30/6/81.
HOARE W.H.C. Born 29/8/45. Commd 15/7/66. Sqn Ldr 1/7/75. Retd ENG 29/8/00.
HOBART D.A. CB MPhil LLB FRAeS MCMI. Born 24/12/51. Commd 25/2/72. AVM 1/7/01. Retd GD 10/1/05.
HOBBS D.J. Born 10/9/49. Commd 2/5/69. Flt Lt 19/7/75. Retd SEC 21/6/81.
HOBBS E.J. MCMI MCIPD. Born 20/5/32. Commd 22/3/51. Sqn Ldr 1/7/68. Retd SEC 1/10/74.
HOBBS E.W. BSc MCGI. Born 23/5/53. Commd 4/7/82. Flt Lt 4/4/86. Retd OPS SPT 4/7/98.
HOBBS J. Born 2/7/28. Commd 19/7/50. Flt Lt 14/5/56. Retd GD 2/7/66.
HOBBS J.B. Born 26/2/50. Commd 11/11/71. Flt Lt 11/5/77. Retd GD 13/6/89.
HOBBS J.R. Born 21/3/47. Commd 12/7/68. Flt Lt 12/1/74. Retd GD 1/10/75.
HOBBS L.G. Born 24/12/21. Commd 21/12/43. Flt Lt 21/6/47. Retd GD 17/2/56. rtg Sqn Ldr
HOBBS M.A.A. Born 6/9/30. Commd 24/5/53. Sqn Ldr 1/1/66. Retd GD 10/4/75.
HOBBS P.C. OBE CEng FRAeS MCIPD MCMI. Born 21/3/41. Commd 2/3/65. Gp Capt 1/1/91. Retd ENG 4/4/93.
HOBBS P.F. Born 10/4/33. Commd 25/1/54. Sqn Ldr 1/1/80. Retd GD 10/4/93.
HOBBS R.K. Born 4/5/21. Commd 17/3/44. Flt Lt 17/9/47. Retd GD(G) 30/3/76.
HOBBS S. BEd. Born 27/8/61. Commd 30/8/83. Sqn Ldr 1/7/94. Retd ADMIN 14/3/97.
HOBBY W.E. AFC. Born 23/2/32. Commd 17/3/55. Wg Cdr 1/1/78. Retd GD 27/8/86.
HOBDAY D.E. Born 9/11/30. Commd 1/8/51. Flt Lt 27/8/54. Retd GD 9/11/68.
HOBDAY P. MSc BA. Born 5/12/48. Commd 10/6/84. Sqn Ldr 1/1/91. Retd ADMIN 5/7/98.
HOBDEN M.F. OBE. Born 12/3/22. Commd 20/3/42. Gp Capt 1/7/70. Retd RGT 5/7/72.
HOBGEN C.W. Born 31/10/22. Commd 23/1/44. Gp Capt 1/1/73. Retd PRT 18/1/75.
HOBKINSON J.T. LDSRCS. Born 1/7/40. Commd 27/12/61. Wg Cdr 13/7/77. Retd DEL 1/7/98.
HOBLYN F.J. Born 22/2/17. Commd 7/7/42. Sqn Ldr 1/7/62. Retd ENG 29/3/73.
HOBSON J.F. MB ChB MFCM MFOM DPH DIH. Born 5/3/25. Commd 27/10/50. A Cdre 1/7/76. Retd MED 20/12/83.
HOBSON M.E. CBE AFC FCMI. Born 1/12/26. Commd 23/8/46. Gp Capt 1/7/66. Retd GD 1/8/73.
HOBSON R.M. MCMI. Born 23/11/40. Commd 2/6/77. Flt Lt 2/6/81. Retd ADMIN 23/11/86.
HOBSON W.R.T. Born 6/4/34. Commd 24/8/54. Flt Lt 29/6/59. Retd GD 7/4/72.
HOCHMAL A. Born 18/12/14. Commd 2/8/40. Flt Lt 12/11/49. Retd GD(G) 29/1/70. rtg Sqn Ldr
HOCKIN J.W. Born 29/5/44. Commd 14/8/64. Flt Lt 4/11/70. Retd GD 29/5/82. Re-entered 1/4/85. Flt Lt 28/10/73.
    Retd GD 29/5/99.
HOCKING E.J. Born 12/4/34. Commd 5/11/52. Flt Lt 1/4/66. Retd SEC 12/4/74.
HOCKING J.M. Born 5/5/23. Commd 13/11/45. Sqn Ldr 1/7/56. Retd GD 5/5/72.
HOCKING M.C. Born 1/10/57. Commd 28/2/80. Flt Lt 28/8/85. Retd GD 22/10/95.
HOCKLEY C.J. OBE CEng MRAeS. Born 2/3/48. Commd 28/2/69. Wg Cdr 1/1/87. Retd GD 2/3/03.
HOCKLEY S.P. Born 23/5/59. Commd 5/5/88. Flt Lt 5/5/90. Retd ENGINEER 23/5/04.
HOCKNELL J.S. OBE MSc BSc CertEd. Born 13/9/42. Commd 10/7/67. Wg Cdr 1/1/85. Retd ADMIN 13/9/00.
HOCTOR B.P. CEng MIEE. Born 3/9/43. Commd 15/7/65. Sqn Ldr 1/1/75. Retd ENG 3/9/98.
HODDER C.A. Born 25/4/10. Commd 3/2/41. Flt Lt 1/7/43. Retd ENG 5/1/46. rtg Sqn Ldr
HODDER R.W. Born 1/2/15. Commd 7/11/43. Sqn Ldr 1/4/56. Retd ENG 1/2/64.
HODDINOTT G. BEM. Born 15/7/23. Commd 2/7/47. Sqn Ldr 1/7/58. Retd RGT 15/7/68.
HODGE A.J. BEM. Born 23/9/19. Commd 21/7/55. Sqn Ldr 1/7/65. Retd ENG 23/9/74.
HODGE B.J. BEng. Born 26/4/63. Commd 13/9/81. Flt Lt 15/1/87. Retd GD 15/7/96.
HODGE D.J. Born 2/6/45. Commd 1/4/65. Gp Capt 1/1/97. Retd OPS SPT 3/5/99.
HODGE K.B. IEng MIIE. Born 19/9/44. Commd 19/6/86. Flt Lt 19/6/90. Retd ENG 1/4/93.
HODGE M.V. Born 14/2/22. Commd 22/7/42. Wg Cdr 1/1/65. Retd GD 20/9/67.
HODGE T.D.A. BSc. Born 28/2/63. Commd 13/2/81. Flt Lt 15/4/86. Retd GD 15/7/96.
HODGES F.A. Born 21/7/12. Commd 14/10/43. Sqn Ldr 1/7/56. Retd GD(G) 27/5/61.
HODGES F.G. BA. Born 22/4/27. Commd 25/8/54. Flt Lt 25/8/60. Retd SEC 3/12/68.
HODGES J.T. Born 10/10/22. Commd 28/2/42. Flt Lt 1/9/45. Retd GD 4/6/54.
HODGES Sir Lewis KCB CBE DSO* DFC*. Born 1/3/18. Commd 17/12/38. ACM 1/5/71. Retd GD 2/5/76.
HODGES M.G.M. Born 11/2/41. Commd 9/2/62. Wg Cdr 1/7/91. Retd GD(G) 28/2/95.
HODGES M.T. CEng MIEE. Born 5/5/41. Commd 17/7/62. Gp Capt 1/1/89. Retd ENG 2/4/96.
HODGES R. BA MCIPD ACIS. Born 29/1/38. Commd 18/7/61. Sqn Ldr 1/10/69. Retd ADMIN 18/7/77.
HODGKIN C.W. Born 13/5/21. Commd 17/3/55. Sqn Ldr 1/1/69. Retd ENG 1/8/73.
HODGKINS W.M. Born 22/6/39. Commd 6/11/66. Flt Lt 29/9/67. Retd GD 4/11/80.
HODGKINSON Sir Derek KCB CBE DFC AFC. Born 27/12/17. Commd 25/1/37. ACM 22/4/74. Retd GD 8/5/76.
HODGKINSON V.A. Born 14/2/30. Commd 9/4/52. Wg Cdr 1/7/69. Retd ADMIN 4/3/78.
HODGKINSON W.J. Born 14/2/30. Commd 4/4/53. Sqn Ldr 1/7/67. Retd GD 1/7/70.
HODGSON C.P. Born 29/5/63. Commd 8/12/83. Flt Lt 8/6/89. Retd FLY(P) 8/4/03.
HODGSON D.C. Born 10/3/63. Commd 1/7/82. Sqn Ldr 1/7/98. Retd GD 1/7/01.
HODGSON G.F. BA. Born 19/10/47. Commd 1/8/69. Sqn Ldr 1/1/85. Retd GD 21/9/99.
HODGSON I. Born 21/8/49. Commd 23/2/68. Sqn Ldr 1/1/89. Retd FLY(N) 27/11/03.

HODGSON J. MBE. Born 17/12/18. Commd 14/11/57. Sqn Ldr 1/7/70. Retd ENG 17/12/73.
HODGSON J.W. Born 2/5/41. Commd 17/5/63. Sqn Ldr 1/7/80. Retd GD 2/3/92.
HODGSON K.C. Born 17/2/27. Commd 13/8/52. Sqn Ldr 1/1/70. Retd GD 3/8/76.
HODGSON M. Born 19/12/45. Commd 10/6/66. Sqn Ldr 1/1/93. Retd GD 14/3/96.
HODGSON P.E. Born 28/9/35. Commd 12/1/61. Flt Lt 12/7/65. Retd GD 28/9/73.
HODGSON R.B. MBA BA FCMI. Born 2/7/49. Commd 25/4/68. Air Cdre 1/1/02. Retd GD 2/7/04.
HODGSON R.E. Born 25/2/36. Commd 12/9/63. Flt Lt 29/1/70. Retd SUP 12/6/79.
HODGSON R.P. Born 30/3/53. Commd 3/1/82. Flt Lt 30/4/78. Retd GD 30/3/91.
HODGSON S.W.S. MSc BSc CEng MRAeS. Born 23/1/52. Commd 25/9/71. Sqn Ldr 1/1/86. Retd ENG 1/10/92.
HODGSON T.H. Born 18/11/21. Commd 28/6/46. Flt Lt 4/1/51. Retd SEC 18/11/61.
HODKINSON C.G. Born 9/8/23. Commd 25/8/55. Flt Lt 25/8/61. Retd GD 9/8/78.
HODKINSON R.G.W. Born 8/7/20. Commd 27/1/55. Flt Lt 27/1/58. Retd GD 10/2/68.
HODNETT N.J.G. CBE. Born 3/6/37. Commd 15/2/56. A Cdre 1/1/88. Retd GD 3/6/92.
HODSON B.T. Born 31/5/26. Commd 27/3/47. Sqn Ldr 1/7/64. Retd SUP 1/7/67.
HODSON I. Born 15/2/43. Commd 7/6/68. Sqn Ldr 1/7/82. Retd GD 30/11/99.
HODSON K.G. OBE. Born 28/5/19. Commd 25/11/42. Sqn Ldr 1/1/57. Retd GD 28/5/74.
HODSON N. Born 1/7/15. Commd 27/10/43. Flt Offr 18/5/56. Retd SEC 8/11/64.
HOFFLER I.H. BSc. Born 21/12/49. Commd 13/9/71. Flt Lt 13/12/72. Retd GD 1/6/94.
HOFFMAN DE VISME G.F.A. BSc DipEl. Born 3/5/23. Commd 30/1/50. Sqn Ldr 3/5/57. Retd EDN 20/11/62.
HOFFORD D.H. Born 25/4/25. Commd 27/5/44. Flt Lt 4/6/54. Retd GD 26/1/66.
HOGAN B.E. Born 18/5/20. Commd 31/12/41. Wg Cdr 1/7/71. Retd GD 17/8/73.
HOGAN F.J. Born 16/10/25. Commd 6/12/50. Flt Lt 6/9/56. Retd GD 20/1/66.
HOGAN G.J.C. DFC AFC FCMI. Born 19/6/20. Commd 9/7/38. Gp Capt 1/7/65. Retd GD 17/5/72.
HOGAN J.S. Born 25/3/48. Commd 4/4/71. Wg Cdr 1/1/89. Retd ADMIN 4/4/93.
HOGAN P.J. Born 15/1/21. Commd 15/1/44. Sqn Ldr 1/7/66. Retd GD(G) 15/1/76.
HOGARTH P.W.F. Born 15/7/33. Commd 2/4/57. Flt Lt 6/3/63. Retd GD 15/7/71.
HOGG A.W. BSc. Born 11/9/59. Commd 12/2/83. Flt Lt 13/8/84. Retd GD 14/11/95.
HOGG J.E. Born 26/11/28. Commd 27/5/53. Flt Lt 11/11/58. Retd GD 20/1/69.
HOGG J.K. Born 23/4/63. Commd 13/8/82. Sqn Ldr 1/7/96. Retd GD 1/1/02.
HOGG J.S. Born 12/1/30. Commd 26/3/59. Flt Lt 26/3/65. Retd GD 12/1/85.
HOGG M.C. Born 12/2/42. Commd 28/2/64. Flt Lt 28/8/69. Retd GD 12/2/80.
HOGG P.F. MB BS MRCS MRCP DMRD. Born 20/5/39. Commd 29/12/65. Wg Cdr 25/9/76. Retd MED 22/7/80.
HOGG R.I. Born 14/3/46. Commd 26/5/67. Gp Capt 1/1/95. Retd ENG 14/3/01.
HOGG R.P. Born 6/9/20. Commd 13/6/44. Sqn Ldr 1/1/52. Retd RGT 27/11/61.
HOILE J.F. CEng MIMechE. Born 5/7/33. Commd 7/2/57. Sqn Ldr 1/7/65. Retd ENG 20/1/86.
HOLBEN F.B. Born 7/1/45. Commd 17/12/65. Flt Lt 17/6/69. Retd GD 7/1/83.
HOLBOURN A.C.E. OBE BA MRAeS. Born 7/3/36. Commd 1/4/58. Wg Cdr 1/7/82. Retd GD 3/4/86.
HOLBOURN A.S. Born 26/4/16. Commd 12/6/47. Flt Lt 26/5/55. Retd PE 19/5/64.
HOLBOURN P.E. Born 5/5/31. Commd 7/11/51. Sqn Ldr 1/7/65. Retd GD(G) 5/5/69.
HOLBROOK G.F. DFC. Born 17/9/21. Commd 12/7/44. Sqn Ldr 1/7/69. Retd GD 1/9/73.
HOLBROOK T.H. Born 3/6/27. Commd 1/8/69. Sqn Ldr 1/1/81. Retd ENG 3/6/87.
HOLBURN R.T. OBE. Born 26/7/27. Commd 26/9/49. Wg Cdr 1/7/73. Retd RGT 1/10/79.
HOLCROFT D. OBE. Born 17/9/36. Commd 19/1/66. Wg Cdr 1/7/85. Retd ENG 26/5/91.
HOLDEN A.E. Born 4/6/24. Commd 1/7/53. Flt Lt 11/7/57. Retd GD(G) 6/7/66.
HOLDEN B.D. Born 20/5/34. Commd 27/4/61. Flt Lt 27/10/65. Retd GD 20/5/72.
HOLDEN D.J. CEng MIMechE. Born 3/4/38. Commd 19/5/69. Flt Lt 19/5/71. Retd ENG 1/8/74.
HOLDEN E.A. BSc. Born 17/5/76. Commd 8/12/99. Flt Lt 30/5/01. Retd OPS SPT(INT) 31/7/03.
HOLDEN G. BA. Born 29/1/56. Commd 5/2/84. Flt Lt 5/8/87. Retd ADMIN 13/5/96.
HOLDEN G.A. MMar. Born 27/11/41. Commd 16/6/69. Sqn Ldr 1/7/80. Retd ADMIN 1/5/96.
HOLDEN J.F. Born 24/8/21. Commd 14/4/49. Flt Lt 14/10/52. Retd GD(G) 27/2/65. Re-appointed 10/10/66 to 24/8/76.
HOLDEN P.J. MA MSc. Born 12/11/60. Commd 2/9/79. Sqn Ldr 1/7/96. Retd ENG 1/7/99.
HOLDEN P.J. AIB. Born 14/8/54. Commd 23/9/79. Wg Cdr 1/7/93. Retd ADMIN 4/4/97.
HOLDEN R.E. BSc. Born 5/6/50. Commd 15/9/69. Sqn Ldr 1/1/85. Retd GD 5/12/88.
HOLDEN T.C.W. DipEurHum. Born 13/12/50. Commd 14/8/88. Flt Lt 14/8/90. Retd ADMIN 14/8/96.
HOLDEN W.V. MBE BSc MRAeS. Born 7/11/26. Commd 24/8/50. Wg Cdr 1/1/66. Retd ENG 7/11/81.
HOLDEN-RUSHWORTH P. Born 11/12/29. Commd 27/2/58. Sqn Ldr 1/7/75. Retd GD 1/8/80.
HOLDER E.H.M. Born 25/4/29. Commd 18/5/55. Sqn Ldr 5/3/70. Retd EDN 5/9/74.
HOLDER M.T. Born 31/12/45. Commd 5/3/65. Flt Lt 5/9/70. Retd GD 31/1/96.
HOLDER N.R. Born 24/12/45. Commd 26/5/67. Sqn Ldr 1/7/78. Retd GD 24/12/83.
HOLDER R.R. BSc(Eng). Born 13/9/12. Commd 15/3/35. A Cdre 1/1/64. Retd ENG 15/9/67.
HOLDER S. BSc. Born 12/3/63. Commd 11/10/83. Wg Cdr 1/1/99. Retd ENG 1/1/02.
HOLDING B.C. AFC. Born 6/12/52. Commd 2/8/72. Flt Lt 2/2/78. Retd GD 6/12/88.
HOLDING J. Born 4/4/22. Commd 12/2/53. Flt Lt 12/2/56. Retd ENG 4/4/77. rtg Sqn Ldr
HOLDSTOCK A.C. MA CEng MIMechE. Born 11/12/51. Commd 25/9/71. Sqn Ldr 1/1/88. Retd ENG 1/1/91.
HOLDSTOCK A.J. Born 25/5/16. Commd 20/10/48. Flt Lt 29/3/56. Retd GD(G) 31/8/60.
HOLDSWORTH A.D. Born 31/7/58. Commd 18/9/89. Flt Lt 6/2/88. Retd GD 26/6/96.

HOLDSWORTH M.T. BA. Born 17/1/47. Commd 2/8/68. Sqn Ldr 1/1/79. Retd ADMIN 17/1/85.
HOLDSWORTH P. Born 20/5/58. Commd 8/4/82. Flt Lt 8/7/87. Retd GD 1/12/99.
HOLDSWORTH T.M.J. MCMI. Born 7/10/43. Commd 23/6/67. Wg Cdr 1/1/86. Retd GD(G) 6/7/94. rtg Gp Capt
HOLDWAY J.C. Born 1/11/33. Commd 5/4/55. Sqn Ldr 1/1/68. Retd GD 2/11/83.
HOLE E.M. OBE. Born 10/2/20. Commd 23/9/42. Wg Offr 1/7/61. Retd SEC 16/5/63.
HOLE J.D. Born 25/4/42. Commd 30/9/60. Flt Lt 17/7/67. Retd ENG 24/5/70.
HOLE P.K. Born 20/11/40. Commd 19/9/59. Flt Lt 10/2/67. Retd GD 10/4/71. Re-instated 13/2/80. Flt Lt 16/12/75.
  Retd GD 30/9/88.
HOLES D.G. Born 9/8/33. Commd 27/10/54. Flt Lt 5/10/60. Retd GD 25/4/74.
HOLF J.V. Born 20/6/20. Commd 17/8/43. Sqn Ldr 1/1/72. Retd GD 20/6/75.
HOLLAND B.C. MA. Born 9/2/36. Commd 23/11/59. Sqn Ldr 1/1/71. Retd GD 9/8/91.
HOLLAND D.A. Born 14/2/51. Commd 14/8/70. Wg Cdr 1/1/02. Retd GD 21/2/04.
HOLLAND D.T. BA. Born 12/2/34. Commd 6/12/56. Sqn Ldr 6/6/64. Retd ADMIN 29/5/76.
HOLLAND G.M. Born 12/6/53. Commd 19/3/81. Flt Lt 15/3/84. Retd ADMIN 12/6/91.
HOLLAND J.E. DFC. Born 18/4/20. Commd 11/7/40. Wg Cdr 1/7/56. Retd GD 18/4/67.
HOLLAND J.P. Born 14/11/46. Commd 2/6/67. Flt Lt 2/12/72. Retd GD(G) 12/11/94.
HOLLAND J.P. BA. Born 11/7/30. Commd 11/12/58. Flt Lt 11/12/63. Retd GD 1/12/82.
HOLLAND P. MBE. Born 7/3/35. Commd 17/6/54. Gp Capt 1/7/86. Retd SUP 7/3/90.
HOLLAND P. BSc. Born 7/12/31. Commd 29/10/59. Sqn Ldr 29/4/64. Retd EDN 29/10/72.
HOLLAND P. Born 16/4/42. Commd 4/2/71. Flt Lt 4/2/73. Retd ADMIN 16/4/83.
HOLLAND P.L. BSc. Born 26/7/62. Commd 11/9/83. Sqn Ldr 1/7/95. Retd OPS SPT 26/7/00.
HOLLAND R.M.J. Born 13/5/46. Commd 20/8/65. Wg Cdr 1/1/92. Retd GD 13/5/96.
HOLLAND T.R. AFC. Born 9/4/26. Commd 20/12/46. Wg Cdr 1/1/67. Retd GD 3/4/76.
HOLLAND V.G. AFM. Born 1/3/33. Commd 7/9/61. Fg Offr 7/9/61. Retd GD 22/3/69.
HOLLAND W.H. AInstAM. Born 10/11/34. Commd 24/1/74. Flt Lt 24/1/76. Retd GD(G) 10/11/89.
HOLLAND-SMITH T.R.M. Born 28/2/42. Commd 18/8/61. Flt Lt 8/1/69. Retd GD 28/2/80.
HOLLANDS K.E.H. MCMI. Born 1/9/40. Commd 11/11/71. Wg Cdr 1/7/87. Retd ADMIN 3/1/91.
HOLLANDS S.A. MCMI. Born 19/2/48. Commd 22/9/67. Wg Cdr 1/7/90. Retd GD 19/2/03.
HOLLETT G.K.A. OBE MCMI. Born 14/4/20. Commd 7/10/43. Wg Cdr 1/1/68. Retd SEC 20/4/72.
HOLLETT R.A.F. Born 31/12/42. Commd 4/11/82. Sqn Ldr 1/1/92. Retd ENG 31/12/97.
HOLLETT R.L. Born 21/6/40. Commd 6/7/62. Wg Cdr 1/1/85. Retd GD 21/6/95.
HOLLEY B.J. PhD MSc BSc CEng CPhys MInstP CertEd. Born 6/2/53. Commd 16/2/86. Sqn Ldr 1/7/94.
  Retd ADMIN 16/5/02.
HOLLEY J.C. Born 26/8/11. Commd 29/4/42. Flt Lt 3/12/45. Retd ENG 2/6/48.
HOLLIDAY A.M.R. Born 10/3/52. Commd 24/4/70. Sqn Ldr 1/7/85. Retd SUP 10/3/90.
HOLLIDAY D.J. Born 13/11/41. Commd 14/12/63. Wg Cdr 1/1/91. Retd GD 31/3/94.
HOLLIDAY D.M. AFC CDipAF MCMI. Born 9/1/36. Commd 6/4/55. Wg Cdr 1/1/80. Retd GD 9/1/86.
HOLLIDAY G.S.C. Born 14/2/17. Commd 2/5/38. Sqn Ldr 1/8/47. Retd GD 13/2/58.
HOLLIDAY R.A. Born 1/2/27. Commd 22/7/66. Flt Lt 22/7/71. Retd SEC 8/11/75.
HOLLIDAY R.C. DCAe CEng MRAeS MIMechE. Born 15/11/35. Commd 18/7/71. Sqn Ldr 18/7/71. Retd ENG 20/3/89.
HOLLIDAY R.E. OBE. Born 5/9/38. Commd 11/9/56. Gp Capt 1/7/83. Retd GD 5/9/93.
HOLLIN D. MCMI. Born 6/4/44. Commd 8/11/68. Gp Capt 1/7/94. Retd OPS SPT 1/11/99.
HOLLINGDALE M.D. BSc(Eng) ACGI. Born 10/7/57. Commd 21/10/79. Flt Lt 21/1/81. Retd GD 21/10/87.
HOLLINGSWORTH A. Born 8/11/21. Commd 24/4/43. Sqn Ldr 1/7/66. Retd GD 8/11/76.
HOLLINGSWORTH A.C. Born 18/2/22. Commd 21/8/42. Gp Capt 1/1/65. Retd GD 2/4/73.
HOLLINGSWORTH D. Born 22/6/27. Commd 23/8/56. Flt Lt 23/8/62. Retd GD 16/4/73.
HOLLINGSWORTH M.J. Born 4/12/60. Commd 15/3/87. Sqn Ldr 1/1/98. Retd ADMIN (SEC) 16/3/03.
HOLLINGTON H.B. CEng MIEE MRAeS. Born 23/9/31. Commd 25/8/55. Sqn Ldr 1/1/68. Retd GD 11/2/77.
HOLLINGWORTH I. BSc. Born 11/12/55. Commd 19/9/76. Flt Lt 15/10/79. Retd GD 14/10/88.
HOLLINGWORTH M. Born 11/12/35. Commd 6/9/68. Flt Lt 6/9/70. Retd GD 6/9/76.
HOLLIS D.J. BSc LLB MCMI. Born 4/12/32. Commd 14/12/54. Gp Capt 1/7/74. Retd SUP 21/9/77.
HOLLIS I.A. CEng MIERE. Born 15/11/35. Commd 9/10/67. Flt Lt 4/11/70. Retd ENG 15/11/90.
HOLLOWAY A.F. Born 1/7/15. Commd 29/9/41. Flt Offr 16/4/52. Retd SEC 31/10/59.
HOLLOWAY E.J. DFC. Born 3/4/18. Commd 6/12/41. Wg Cdr 1/7/56. Retd GD 1/9/61.
HOLLOWAY G.M.N. MB ChB FRCS. Born 19/11/45. Commd 17/9/72. Wg Cdr 28/10/83. Retd MED 16/10/92.
HOLLOWAY R.A. Born 6/5/53. Commd 16/6/81. Flt Lt 11/6/83. Retd GD 29/12/96.
HOLLOWAY R.E. MBE. Born 16/11/32. Commd 12/7/51. Wg Cdr 1/7/81. Retd GD 16/11/90.
HOLLOWAY R.J.B. Born 1/2/50. Commd 3/12/70. Flt Lt 3/6/76. Retd GD 10/1/80.
HOLLOWAY T.M. FRAeS. Born 5/1/45. Commd 18/11/66. Gp Capt 1/7/91. Retd SUP 14/3/96.
HOLLOWAY W.F.J. MBE MCMI. Born 5/9/30. Commd 18/5/61. Sqn Ldr 1/7/72. Retd ENG 7/9/76. Re-instated 2/1/80.
  Retd ENG 5/9/85.
HOLLOWOOD J.W. Born 1/10/45. Commd 1/3/68. Gp Capt 1/7/94. Retd SUP 14/9/96.
HOLMAN A.C. Born 26/12/47. Commd 2/8/68. Sqn Ldr 1/1/82. Retd GD 1/10/96.
HOLMAN C.V. Born 15/2/27. Commd 30/11/50. Sqn Ldr 1/7/67. Retd GD 1/2/75.
HOLMAN M.J. Born 23/6/59. Commd 6/10/94. Flt Lt 6/10/96. Retd FLY(ALM) 6/10/03.
HOLMAN P.J. Born 17/8/34. Commd 23/6/67. Sqn Ldr 1/1/76. Retd ENG 20/4/83.

HOLMAN R.A. OBE. Born 9/10/35. Commd 12/9/63. Gp Capt 1/7/85. Retd ADMIN 9/10/90.
HOLME B.P. Born 30/9/32. Commd 22/8/59. Flt Lt 22/2/65. Retd GD 28/7/78. Re-instated 30/1/80. Flt Lt 27/8/66.
   Retd GD 30/9/92.
HOLME D. Born 31/3/39. Commd 23/9/59. Sqn Ldr 1/1/79. Retd GD 27/5/89.
HOLME H. MBE. Born 8/3/10. Commd 26/8/41. Sqn Ldr 1/1/56. Retd ENG 8/3/59.
HOLMES E. DFC. Born 29/1/21. Commd 4/9/43. Flt Lt 4/3/47. Retd GD 1/2/62.
HOLMES E.F.O. MBE. Born 22/11/22. Commd 2/5/50. Sqn Ldr 1/7/66. Retd GD 22/11/73.
HOLMES F.M. Born 19/8/44. Commd 8/11/68. Sqn Ldr 1/1/84. Retd SUP 23/7/90.
HOLMES G. ACCA ACIS. Born 3/11/32. Commd 19/7/56. Sqn Ldr 1/7/65. Retd SEC 21/11/71.
HOLMES J.A. DFC*. Born 30/6/17. Commd 17/12/38. Gp Capt 1/1/57. Retd GD 30/6/67. rtg A Cdre
HOLMES J.W. Born 12/2/07. Commd 6/6/40. Sqn Ldr 1/8/47. Retd SEC 12/12/53.
HOLMES K. Born 22/6/48. Commd 6/9/68. Flt Lt 21/12/74. Retd GD(G) 15/3/77.
HOLMES K.W. MBE. Born 15/9/23. Commd 22/9/44. Wg Cdr 1/1/68. Retd GD(G) 1/5/75.
HOLMES L.G. OBE DFC AFC FCMI. Born 15/4/21. Commd 10/10/42. Gp Capt 1/7/63. Retd GD 18/2/75.
HOLMES M.E. Born 12/1/22. Commd 19/7/57. Flt Lt 19/7/60. Retd ENG 2/12/67.
HOLMES M.K. Born 29/9/58. Commd 11/6/81. Sqn Ldr 1/7/91. Retd GD 9/2/97.
HOLMES M.R. Born 17/11/28. Commd 21/2/49. Flt Lt 16/3/55. Retd GD 17/11/66.
HOLMES M.S. Born 11/10/45. Commd 5/3/65. Gp Capt 1/1/94. Retd GD 11/4/01.
HOLMES P.B. Born 10/3/32. Commd 28/6/51. Wg Cdr 1/1/77. Retd ADMIN 10/2/87.
HOLMES R. BEng. Born 29/3/60. Commd 2/8/89. Flt Lt 15/7/92. Retd ENG 29/3/01.
HOLMES R.G. Born 15/1/45. Commd 6/9/63. Flt Lt 6/3/69. Retd GD 15/1/00.
HOLMES R.H. Born 7/5/39. Commd 15/12/59. Sqn Ldr 1/1/70. Retd GD 7/5/77.
HOLMES R.J. BSc. Born 12/1/64. Commd 18/8/85. Flt Lt 18/2/88. Retd FLY(P) 19/8/03.
HOLMES R.L. MBE. Born 5/7/33. Commd 6/4/54. Wg Cdr 1/7/75. Retd GD 5/7/88.
HOLMES R.M. Born 27/4/24. Commd 17/2/45. Fg Offr 14/1/50. Retd GD 4/2/56.
HOLMES S.L. BSc. Born 28/3/73. Commd 30/11/94. Flt Lt 14/2/98. Retd SUPPLY 1/11/03.
HOLMES S.W. MCMI. Born 21/4/31. Commd 24/7/52. Wg Cdr 1/1/72. Retd GD 26/7/84.
HOLMES V.R. Born 15/7/30. Commd 30/7/52. Flt Lt 30/3/58. Retd GD 30/4/76.
HOLMES W.G. Born 3/12/27. Commd 7/10/48. Wg Cdr 1/1/68. Retd GD 3/11/79.
HOLMYARD D.P. Born 13/5/47. Commd 16/8/68. Sqn Ldr 1/1/95. Retd GD 2/1/97.
HOLROYD Sir Frank KBE CB MSc CEng FIEE FRAeS. Born 30/8/35. Commd 1/10/59. Air Mshl 4/7/88. Retd GD 5/12/91.
HOLROYD J. Born 24/7/40. Commd 20/11/75. Sqn Ldr 1/1/86. Retd ENG 24/7/95.
HOLT G.F. Born 26/3/41. Commd 13/2/60. Flt Lt 14/2/66. Retd GD 26/6/91.
HOLT I.W. Born 14/1/44. Commd 27/1/67. Sqn Ldr 1/1/87. Retd GD(G) 31/7/96.
HOLT R.J. MSc BSc CEng MIEE. Born 14/8/45. Commd 22/9/63. A Cdre 1/1/94. Retd ENG 14/3/97.
HOLT S.D.H. MA MB BChir FRCS. Born 16/7/51. Commd 22/1/74. Sqn Ldr 14/9/82. Retd MED 7/8/90.
HOLTBY H. Born 28/10/41. Commd 21/2/69. Sqn Ldr 1/7/87. Retd GD 28/10/96.
HOLTBY P.R. MBE CEng FIEE FRAeS. Born 19/7/39. Commd 18/7/61. Gp Capt 1/7/87. Retd ENG 19/7/90.
HOLTON J.P.L. MCMI. Born 17/3/36. Commd 12/7/62. Sqn Ldr 1/1/71. Retd SUP 2/4/76.
HOLYOAKE A.A. AFC. Born 28/9/26. Commd 13/2/60. Sqn Ldr 1/1/75. Retd GD 28/9/86.
HOLYOAKE A.P. MBE. Born 1/7/78. Commd 9/3/66. Sqn Ldr 1/7/78. Retd ENG 27/11/86.
HOME S.M. BSc. Born 27/10/46. Commd 27/6/70. Flt Lt 27/3/75. Retd ADMIN 27/6/87.
HOMER C.R.C. Born 9/9/37. Commd 28/7/60. Sqn Ldr 1/1/88. Retd GD(G) 9/9/92.
HOMER D.St John. Born 8/3/36. Commd 30/7/57. Gp Capt 1/7/78. Retd GD 31/5/87.
HOMES C.J. AFC. Born 20/2/19. Commd 19/2/44. Sqn Ldr 1/10/54. Retd GD 19/2/59.
HONE A.J. Born 10/8/25. Commd 21/6/45. Sqn Ldr 1/1/59. Retd SUP 10/8/63.
HONE B.S. Born 10/2/49. Commd 12/10/78. Flt Lt 12/10/80. Retd GD(G) 10/2/87.
HONE S.J. Born 19/7/20. Commd 12/8/54. Sqn Ldr 1/7/72. Retd ENG 19/7/75.
HONEY A. MRCS LRCP. Born 16/10/27. Commd 31/8/53. Wg Cdr 6/6/65. Retd MED 31/8/72.
HONEY G.W. OBE. Born 22/5/35. Commd 29/7/55. Wg Cdr 1/7/77. Retd GD 1/11/87.
HONEY N.J. MSc BSc CEng. Born 4/5/55. Commd 28/2/82. Sqn Ldr 1/7/89. Retd ENG 31/3/02.
HONEY R.J. Born 9/5/63. Commd 14/2/88. Flt Lt 14/12/93. Retd FLY(N) 14/2/04.
HONEY R.J. CB CBE FCIPD. Born 3/12/36. Commd 26/1/55. AVM 1/7/87. Retd GD 12/6/94.
HONEY R.O.H. Born 28/7/40. Commd 3/8/62. Flt Lt 3/5/66. Retd GD 28/7/78.
HONEYBALL D.C. Born 23/4/46. Commd 13/4/78. Flt Lt 5/1/80. Retd GD(G) 5/1/89.
HONEYMAN D.B. Born 1/6/29. Commd 7/6/68. Sqn Ldr 1/1/83. Retd ENG 1/12/89.
HONEYMAN D.J.M. BSc. Born 19/5/61. Commd 19/6/83. Wg Cdr 1/1/02. Retd GD 19/6/05.
HONEYMAN G. Born 17/2/24. Commd 10/5/45. Sqn Ldr 1/10/55. Retd GD 17/2/73.
HONLEY A.D.A. CBE AFC FCMI. Born 5/12/25. Commd 19/12/45. A Cdre 1/7/79. Retd GD 3/4/82.
HONOUR G.W. Born 4/6/30. Commd 26/10/61. Flt Lt 26/10/67. Retd GD 25/8/69.
HOOD B. Born 19/2/41. Commd 19/6/64. Flt Lt 26/11/67. Retd GD 19/9/81. Re-instated 14/3/88. Flt Lt 21/5/74.
   Retd GD 19/2/96.
HOOD E.J. AFC. Born 12/6/29. Commd 13/9/51. Flt Lt 4/1/57. Retd GD 3/4/70.
HOOD E.J.R.F. Born 7/7/41. Commd 18/12/62. Flt Lt 28/7/65. Retd GD 20/6/68.
HOOD I.A. Born 1/8/45. Commd 2/5/71. Sqn Ldr 1/7/86. Retd ENG 9/8/98.
HOOD J. Born 25/11/47. Commd 30/1/75. Flt Lt 28/6/81. Retd GD(G) 15/7/90.

HOOD J.H.G. Born 27/4/20. Commd 24/1/42. Flt Lt 21/11/48. Retd PI 5/8/72.
HOOD M.G.H. Born 28/8/60. Commd 17/4/96. Flt Lt 2/7/92. Retd ENGINEER 2/4/05.
HOOD P.R. Born 15/8/28. Commd 6/12/56. Flt Lt 6/12/62. Retd GD 27/9/68.
HOOK L. Born 26/7/23. Commd 12/8/54. Sqn Ldr 1/7/73. Retd GD 26/7/83.
HOOK N.B. Born 21/4/28. Commd 26/3/64. Flt Lt 26/6/70. Retd SEC 8/1/80.
HOOKER M.R. MCMI. Born 5/3/50. Commd 31/10/69. Wg Cdr 1/7/90. Retd GD 5/3/05.
HOOKS R.K. CBE BSc(Eng) CEng FRAeS. Born 7/8/29. Commd 5/9/51. AVM 1/1/81. Retd ENG 5/5/84.
HOOLEY D.P. Born 29/11/43. Commd 2/8/68. Sqn Ldr 1/7/77. Retd GD(G) 29/3/83.
HOOLEY D.R.A. MCIPS MCMI. Born 28/9/24. Commd 9/3/45. Sqn Ldr 1/1/60. Retd SUP 31/12/76.
HOOPER A.L. Born 17/11/38. Commd 15/12/59. Sqn Ldr 1/7/71. Retd GD 28/6/98.
HOOPER C.A. Born 1/3/46. Commd 26/5/67. Sqn Ldr 1/7/82. Retd GD 1/6/01.
HOOPER G.M. The Rev. Born 11/5/39. Commd 15/9/69. Retd Sqn Ldr 4/4/74.
HOOPER H. Born 10/11/46. Commd 23/4/87. Flt Lt 23/4/91. Retd ENG 2/4/93.
HOOPER J.A. Born 26/4/66. Commd 28/7/95. Flt Lt 28/7/97. Retd OPS SPT(INT) 26/4/04.
HOOPER J.E. Born 18/9/37. Commd 27/10/67. Flt Lt 15/4/70. Retd GD 28/9/74.
HOOPER R.T. Born 7/8/62. Commd 27/8/87. Sqn Ldr 1/1/00. Retd GD 1/1/03.
HOOPER-SMITH C.J. BSc. Born 30/6/45. Commd 13/4/67. Flt Lt 15/4/71. Retd GD 1/2/89.
HOPE A.H. MCMI. Born 15/4/17. Commd 15/8/41. Wg Cdr 1/7/60. Retd ENG 16/4/72.
HOPE N. Born 17/9/64. Commd 20/12/90. Sqn Ldr 1/7/02. Retd OPS SPT(ATC) 1/7/05.
HOPE V.G. DFC. Born 27/11/18. Commd 19/1/43. Flt Lt 19/7/46. Retd GD 27/10/47. rtg Sqn Ldr
HOPER B.P. Born 8/2/51. Commd 31/7/86. Sqn Ldr 1/1/95. Retd ADMIN 3/4/01.
HOPGOOD M.S. Born 7/12/42. Commd 10/11/61. Flt Lt 1/7/69. Retd GD 7/12/80.
HOPKIN P.M.A. BSc. Born 8/6/44. Commd 19/8/68. Sqn Ldr 19/2/76. Retd ADMIN 19/8/84.
HOPKINS A.J. AFC. Born 11/5/35. Commd 26/5/55. Wg Cdr 1/1/71. Retd GD 1/1/74.
HOPKINS B. Born 17/9/34. Commd 28/1/53. Sqn Ldr 1/7/66. Retd GD 17/9/72.
HOPKINS C.C. Born 29/10/31. Commd 19/8/54. Wg Cdr 1/1/76. Retd ENG 1/3/80.
HOPKINS D.B. Born 8/12/30. Commd 29/4/53. Flt Lt 10/9/58. Retd GD 8/12/68.
HOPKINS E.E. AFC. Born 13/8/17. Commd 3/5/43. Flt Lt 29/11/51. Retd GD(G) 1/1/62.
HOPKINS E.W. Born 16/1/33. Commd 25/10/51. Flt Lt 25/4/57. Retd GD 16/1/71.
HOPKINS H.E. CBE DFC AFC. Born 29/8/12. Commd 12/10/36. Gp Capt 1/7/63. Retd GD 29/8/62.
HOPKINS H.E. Born 23/2/20. Commd 6/9/47. Flt Lt 6/3/52. Retd SEC 30/11/68.
HOPKINS H.L. MSc BSc CEng MRAeS MInstP. Born 25/11/30. Commd 28/10/55. Wg Cdr 20/2/74. Retd ADMIN 30/9/77.
HOPKINS J.D.N. Born 20/11/37. Commd 10/2/56. Flt Lt 1/1/76. Retd GD 30/4/91. rtg Gp Capt
HOPKINS J.P. MB ChB DRCOG. Born 8/3/52. Commd 15/1/89. Wg Cdr 15/1/95. Retd MED 14/3/97.
HOPKINS L. MBE. Born 20/4/19. Commd 19/5/49. Sqn Ldr 1/7/58. Retd ENG 23/7/66.
HOPKINS N.K. MBE. Born 21/7/30. Commd 11/4/51. Sqn Ldr 1/7/62. Retd SEC 21/7/68.
HOPKINS P.A. Born 22/3/51. Commd 25/2/72. Sqn Ldr 1/7/81. Retd GD 28/9/85.
HOPKINS P.J.A. BA. Born 16/8/50. Commd 19/2/73. Sqn Ldr 1/1/83. Retd GD 19/2/89.
HOPKINS R.J. DSO MCMI. Born 17/12/21. Commd 19/9/42. Wg Cdr 1/7/61. Retd GD 9/12/75.
HOPKINS R.S.A.E. Born 28/7/37. Commd 11/1/79. Flt Lt 11/1/82. Retd GD 28/7/94.
HOPKINS W.B.G. AFC. Born 29/5/34. Commd 2/7/52. Gp Capt 1/1/79. Retd GD 1/2/86.
HOPKINSON F.E. Born 15/9/21. Commd 29/6/43. Flt Lt 30/8/47. Retd GD 25/11/67.
HOPKINSON M.I.T. Born 16/5/49. Commd 5/3/68. Flt Lt 3/11/73. Retd GD 24/1/76. Re-entered 6/8/80. Flt Lt 16/5/78. Retd GD 14/3/97.
HOPKINSON M.J. BSc. Born 13/6/61. Commd 31/8/80. Sqn Ldr 1/7/93. Retd GD 30/8/98.
HOPKINSON P.E. BSc. Born 19/9/60. Commd 15/3/87. Flt Lt 15/9/89. Retd FLY(P) 15/3/03.
HOPKIRK J.A.C. BA MB BChir MRCP. Born 3/3/43. Commd 11/1/65. Wg Cdr 4/9/81. Retd MED 3/3/87.
HOPPER A.G. Born 30/12/44. Commd 15/11/65. Gp Capt 1/7/91. Retd GD 14/3/96.
HOPPER B. Born 13/6/42. Commd 7/1/63. Fg Offr 7/1/65. Retd GD 15/5/66.
HOPPER H.E. Born 25/8/18. Commd 4/11/44. Flt Lt 4/5/48. Retd GD(G) 25/8/68.
HOPPER I.G. CEng MRAeS. Born 6/2/41. Commd 17/7/62. Sqn Ldr 1/7/73. Retd ENG 6/2/79.
HOPPER K. MA CEng MIEE MRAeS. Born 11/7/35. Commd 9/5/54. Sqn Ldr 1/1/66. Retd ENG 15/6/75.
HOPPS D. Born 22/11/27. Commd 1/8/69. Flt Lt 1/8/72. Retd GD 1/5/75.
HOPTON D. MBE. Born 9/12/18. Commd 25/8/60. Sqn Ldr 1/1/69. Retd ENG 31/5/74.
HOPTON D.St.J. Born 10/3/29. Commd 6/12/56. Sqn Ldr 1/7/66. Retd PRT 1/10/74.
HOPWOOD P.G. BSc. Born 22/9/39. Commd 3/1/64. Sqn Ldr 1/1/78. Retd GD 1/1/81.
HORAH D.E. Born 6/12/22. Commd 25/5/45. Flt Lt 16/10/61. Retd GD(G) 1/7/75.
HORAN J.F. Born 4/7/39. Commd 18/12/80. Sqn Ldr 18/12/80. Retd ENG 17/8/93.
HORDER G.E. Born 2/6/45. Commd 5/1/66. Fg Offr 15/10/66. Retd GD 31/8/68.
HORDLEY M.J. BSc. Born 5/6/55. Commd 2/9/73. Flt Lt 15/4/80. Retd ENG 30/9/83.
HORE N.E. Born 21/5/14. Commd 9/5/40. Flt Lt 1/1/43. Retd GD 23/7/53. rtg Sqn Ldr
HORLOCK G.L. Born 10/10/48. Commd 21/3/69. Sqn Ldr 1/7/83. Retd ENG 10/10/86.
HORLOCK K.J. Born 29/5/51. Commd 16/5/72. Flt Lt 15/4/77. Retd ADMIN 30/5/88.
HORLOCK N.J. Born 7/10/63. Commd 19/12/85. Flt Lt 19/6/91. Retd GD 7/10/01.
HORLOCK R.E. BA. Born 24/10/57. Commd 18/10/81. Sqn Ldr 1/1/90. Retd ENG 18/10/97.
HORN C. MBE. Born 6/4/21. Commd 21/12/43. Sqn Ldr 1/9/65. Retd GD 11/5/68.

HORN G.W. Born 24/2/32. Commd 22/7/66. Sqn Ldr 1/7/83. Retd ENG 24/2/87.
HORNBY I.L.I. Born 29/9/09. Commd 28/7/41. Sqn Offr 1/5/50. Retd SEC 14/5/59.
HORNE A.W. DFC AFC. Born 25/10/19. Commd 7/3/38. Wg Cdr 1/7/55. Retd GD 10/9/68.
HORNE B.P. BA IEng FIIE AMRAeS. Born 14/8/53. Commd 15/8/85. Sqn Ldr 1/7/97. Retd ENG 30/9/01.
HORNE C.J.L. Born 9/12/37. Commd 15/2/60. Flt Lt 15/8/65. Retd GD 15/2/76.
HORNE D.A. Born 13/10/48. Commd 21/3/69. Sqn Ldr 1/1/86. Retd SY(RGT) 1/1/89.
HORNE M.J. MSc CEng MIEE. Born 3/3/44. Commd 15/7/65. Sqn Ldr 1/7/74. Retd ENG 3/3/82.
HORNE R. BA PGCE MCIPD. Born 27/6/42. Commd 14/11/71. Sqn Ldr 14/5/79. Retd ADMIN 28/5/93.
HORNE R.J. BEd MILAM. Born 18/9/47. Commd 29/8/72. Sqn Ldr 1/7/88. Retd ADMIN 16/11/92.
HORNE S.L. Born 4/11/45. Commd 5/3/65. Flt Lt 6/10/71. Retd GD 4/11/84.
HORNE W.J. MBE. Born 12/4/34. Commd 8/5/53. Sqn Ldr 1/1/78. Retd GD 28/11/88.
HORNING G.B. Born 17/4/30. Commd 21/11/51. Sqn Ldr 1/7/83. Retd GD 17/4/88.
HORNSBY E. The Rev. AKC. Born 25/12/23. Commd 16/9/55. Retd Sqn Ldr 14/5/69.
HORNSBY N.A. Born 27/8/62. Commd 18/3/84. Flt Lt 18/9/87. Retd OPS SPT 27/8/00.
HORNSEY R. Born 26/9/34. Commd 8/5/56. Flt Lt 8/11/61. Retd GD 26/9/72.
HOROBIN C. Born 16/12/41. Commd 1/10/65. Flt Lt 14/3/69. Retd GD 16/12/79.
HORRELL J.A. OBE BSc. Born 1/10/28. Commd 10/1/51. Gp Capt 1/7/80. Retd GD 18/5/84.
HORROCKS C.A. Born 16/6/56. Commd 17/1/85. Flt Lt 17/1/87. Retd GD(G) 16/6/94.
HORROCKS I. Born 10/3/34. Commd 26/11/52. A Cdre 1/7/85. Retd GD 22/12/89.
HORROCKS J. DFC. Born 25/6/22. Commd 21/12/43. Flt Lt 4/6/53. Retd GD 25/6/73.
HORROCKS J.S. Born 8/7/23. Commd 17/3/55. Flt Lt 17/3/61. Retd GD 8/7/78. rtg Sqn Ldr
HORROCKS P.A. BSc CEng MIEE. Born 3/9/44. Commd 4/6/72. Sqn Ldr 1/1/86. Retd ENG 3/9/01.
HORSCROFT H.M. Born 17/8/31. Commd 30/5/69. Sqn Ldr 1/7/77. Retd GD 30/9/81.
HORSCROFT J.R. Born 28/7/45. Commd 12/7/63. Flt Lt 12/1/69. Retd GD 31/7/76.
HORSFALL G.J. Born 24/12/11. Commd 25/3/44. Flt Lt 25/3/50. Retd GD(G) 1/9/64.
HORSFALL J.A. AFC. Born 21/3/38. Commd 15/12/59. Sqn Ldr 1/7/70. Retd GD 2/4/88.
HORSFIELD R. Born 19/10/34. Commd 5/4/55. Wg Cdr 1/7/70. Retd GD 1/11/77.
HORSHAM-BATLEY D.J.W. BTech. Born 18/4/58. Commd 29/3/90. Flt Lt 29/3/92. Retd MED(SEC) 29/3/98.
HORSLEY C.J. Born 8/7/37. Commd 15/12/59. Wg Cdr 1/1/85. Retd GD 8/7/92.
HORSLEY R.G. Born 29/9/49. Commd 4/5/72. Flt Lt 4/11/78. Retd GD(G) 17/10/90.
HORSLEY R.M. DFC AFC. Born 4/5/21. Commd 20/4/42. Wg Cdr 1/7/60. Retd GD 1/7/68.
HORSLEY-HEATHER J.S.B. Born 21/2/35. Commd 25/7/56. Sqn Ldr 1/7/69. Retd ENG 21/2/73.
HORSTED K.T. Born 26/5/59. Commd 22/6/89. Flt Lt 22/6/91. Retd ENG 22/6/97.
HORTH H.S. MBE AFC. Born 26/1/21. Commd 25/2/44. Sqn Ldr 1/10/54. Retd GD 26/1/76.
HORTON D. Born 31/7/45. Commd 6/5/66. Sqn Ldr 1/1/85. Retd FLY(P) 31/7/04.
HORTON G.R. BA BSc. Born 2/3/51. Commd 5/8/73. Flt Lt 5/11/74. Retd GD 15/12/95.
HORTON M.P. MCMI. Born 16/3/45. Commd 26/5/67. Sqn Ldr 1/7/75. Retd GD 16/3/83.
HORTON P. Born 27/3/48. Commd 29/7/83. Sqn Ldr 1/7/94. Retd ADMIN (SEC) 27/3/05.
HORTON T.W. DSO DFC*. Born 29/12/19. Commd 6/5/43. Wg Cdr 1/1/56. Retd GD 29/12/66.
HORWOOD G.M. Born 24/4/49. Commd 16/8/68. Wg Cdr 1/1/92. Retd GD 24/4/04.
HORWOOD J.V. MCMI. Born 11/8/26. Commd 24/9/47. Wg Cdr 1/1/63. Retd GD 1/11/75.
HORWOOD R.J. CBE FRAeS. Born 28/9/49. Commd 7/6/68. Air Cdre 1/1/99. Retd GD 19/5/04.
HOSE P.S. Born 13/8/18. Commd 15/8/46. Wg Cdr 1/7/65. Retd SUP 13/8/73.
HOSIER J.D. Born 26/4/38. Commd 17/1/69. Flt Lt 17/1/71. Retd GD 17/1/77.
HOSKIN D.P. Born 23/7/44. Commd 29/7/83. Flt Lt 29/7/87. Retd GD 23/7/99.
HOSKINS B.R. AFC MRAeS MCMI. Born 14/9/43. Commd 22/5/64. Gp Capt 1/1/89. Retd GD 14/9/94.
HOSKINS F.D. Born 25/12/29. Commd 12/12/51. Wg Cdr 1/1/70. Retd GD 25/11/75.
HOSKINS J.H. DSO DFC. Born 20/1/16. Commd 17/5/41. Wg Cdr 1/1/52. Retd GD 24/2/63.
HOSKINS J.W. Born 19/2/36. Commd 1/4/58. Sqn Ldr 1/7/71. Retd GD 1/10/75.
HOSKINS P.A. ACIS. Born 24/5/30. Commd 12/12/51. Sqn Ldr 1/1/65. Retd SEC 20/10/73.
HOSKINS P.J. BA MIL. Born 6/2/48. Commd 28/2/69. Gp Capt 1/7/91. Retd GD 1/5/98.
HOTCHKISS A.E. Born 12/3/32. Commd 19/4/51. Gp Capt 1/7/79. Retd GD 12/3/87.
HOTCHKISS E.L. Born 18/10/21. Commd 11/3/46. Flt Lt 7/6/51. Retd GD 18/10/76.
HOTSON C.C.J. Born 4/6/31. Commd 22/10/53. Flt Lt 22/4/58. Retd GD 21/2/76.
HOUCHIN C.R. Born 30/7/44. Commd 31/7/64. Flt Lt 31/7/69. Retd GD 31/5/75.
HOUGH A.E. Born 21/3/21. Commd 9/8/47. Sqn Ldr 1/7/62. Retd ENG 28/3/68.
HOUGH A.L. BA. Born 7/6/41. Commd 30/8/84. Flt Lt 30/8/88. Retd ENG 19/1/93.
HOUGH J.D. MMAR. Born 27/12/46. Commd 8/9/74. Sqn Ldr 1/7/81. Retd MAR 1/4/86.
HOUGH J.M.P. Born 13/3/40. Commd 19/10/60. Sqn Ldr 1/7/72. Retd GD 8/9/78.
HOUGH R.J. Born 3/3/25. Commd 21/12/45. Flt Lt 1/1/56. Retd GD 2/3/60.
HOUGHAM R.W. Born 7/6/18. Commd 9/8/48. Sqn Ldr 1/7/69. Retd RGT 7/6/73.
HOUGHTON A.J. Born 15/11/43. Commd 11/8/67. Flt Lt 4/12/71. Retd GD 24/10/84.
HOUGHTON A.P. Born 25/10/64. Commd 10/5/90. Sqn Ldr 1/7/00. Retd ENGINEER 14/7/03.
HOUGHTON A.W. Born 8/9/36. Commd 30/12/55. Wg Cdr 1/7/73. Retd GD 5/5/88.
HOUGHTON F.A. MBE MRAeS. Born 7/4/18. Commd 26/7/41. Sqn Ldr 1/7/52. Retd ENG 7/1/63. rtg Wg Cdr
HOUGHTON J.A. MB BS. Born 17/11/61. Commd 26/11/93. Wg Cdr 1/8/01. Retd MEDICAL 16/8/03.

HOUGHTON J.E. AFC FCMI. Born 25/5/40. Commd 27/6/59. A Cdre 1/7/87. Retd GD 25/5/95.
HOUGHTON N.B. Born 26/2/47. Commd 10/2/72. Flt Lt 10/8/77. Retd GD 2/3/93.
HOUGHTON P.G. BA. Born 19/7/51. Commd 15/9/69. Sqn Ldr 1/1/83. Retd GD 19/7/89.
HOUGHTON R. MBE. Born 8/2/23. Commd 11/7/44. Wg Cdr 1/1/73. Retd GD 8/2/78.
HOUGHTON R. Born 7/5/34. Commd 17/12/52. Wg Cdr 1/1/83. Retd GD 7/5/92.
HOUGHTON R.W.J. Born 16/7/25. Commd 1/7/53. Flt Lt 11/12/58. Retd GD 23/2/65.
HOULBROOK L. Born 3/3/60. Commd 19/11/87. Flt Lt 19/11/89. Retd OPS SPT 3/3/98.
HOULGATE F.V. Born 26/1/23. Commd 10/2/44. Flt Lt 25/4/48. Retd GD 9/8/57.
HOULSTON P. Born 17/3/48. Commd 13/1/67. Fg Offr 16/2/69. Retd GD 3/4/71.
HOUNSELL G.E. Born 4/9/30. Commd 11/5/55. Sqn Ldr 1/7/66. Retd GD 1/7/69.
HOUNSELL L.J. Born 27/11/32. Commd 28/2/80. Sqn Ldr 1/7/89. Retd ENG 27/11/98.
HOUNSLOW R.J. FCMI FRAeS. Born 19/11/50. Commd 9/3/72. Gp Capt 1/1/96. Retd GD 2/12/04.
HOURSTON D.I. Born 14/12/59. Commd 5/4/79. Sqn Ldr 1/1/92. Retd SUP 14/12/97.
HOURSTON I.M. MB ChB. Born 29/10/31. Commd 31/3/57. A Cdre 1/7/85. Retd MED 1/7/87.
HOURY R. Born 17/5/40. Commd 26/5/61. Flt Lt 1/11/67. Retd GD 2/4/76.
HOUSBY G. BSc. Born 14/8/61. Commd 26/3/92. Flt Lt 26/3/94. Retd ENG 26/3/00.
HOUSBY S.J. Born 20/5/52. Commd 4/5/72. Flt Lt 4/11/77. Retd GD 4/8/89.
HOUSE C.W. Born 7/10/19. Commd 28/12/42. Flt Lt 1/11/51. Retd GD(G) 22/11/66.
HOUSE D. Born 30/9/65. Commd 28/9/89. Flt Lt 28/3/96. Retd OPS SPT(ATC) 19/2/05.
HOUSE E.D. Born 1/4/16. Commd 27/6/43. Sqn Ldr 1/1/57. Retd SUP 4/5/65.
HOUSE G.W. Born 12/8/45. Commd 5/12/63. Wg Cdr 1/7/88. Retd GD(G) 14/3/96.
HOUSE J.R. Born 25/4/29. Commd 27/8/59. Sqn Ldr 1/1/76. Retd ENG 23/11/82.
HOUSE L.G. Born 23/5/22. Commd 9/7/59. Flt Lt 9/7/64. Retd ENG 23/9/73.
HOUSEMAN W.A. BSc. Born 12/7/47. Commd 1/8/69. Sqn Ldr 1/1/83. Retd GD 19/7/89.
HOUSLEY T.J. BA. Born 2/6/59. Commd 29/8/77. Flt Lt 15/10/83. Retd SUP 1/10/88.
HOUSTON E. BA LLB. Born 14/7/46. Commd 18/9/66. Flt Lt 15/10/69. Retd GD 1/10/85.
HOUTHEUSEN H.J. DFC. Born 16/5/15. Commd 4/8/42. Sqn Ldr 1/1/63. Retd GD(G) 8/4/66.
HOVER R.A. Born 6/7/40. Commd 24/9/63. Sqn Ldr 1/1/75. Retd ENG 6/7/95.
HOW D. Born 30/8/53. Commd 3/7/80. Sqn Ldr 1/1/91. Retd SUP 14/3/96.
HOW M.S.F. Born 31/7/37. Commd 12/12/59. Sqn Ldr 1/7/71. Retd GD 31/7/75.
HOWARD A.C. LLB. Born 1/11/60. Commd 25/10/87. Sqn Ldr 25/10/91. Retd LGL 15/7/99.
HOWARD A.E. Born 17/5/32. Commd 25/11/53. Flt Lt 25/5/59. Retd GD 17/5/72. rtg Sqn Ldr
HOWARD A.H. Born 12/1/35. Commd 5/11/70. Sqn Ldr 1/7/79. Retd ADMIN 7/3/90.
HOWARD B.H. DFC. Born 8/4/24. Commd 10/7/43. Wg Cdr 1/7/61. Retd GD 16/8/68.
HOWARD E. BSc. Born 11/11/55. Commd 14/8/77. Flt Lt 14/11/77. Retd GD 14/8/89.
HOWARD E.E. Born 5/3/29. Commd 11/1/50. Flt Lt 3/5/56. Retd GD 5/3/67.
HOWARD G. Born 31/3/45. Commd 15/7/66. Flt Lt 12/11/69. Retd GD 10/9/76.
HOWARD H.J. Born 27/3/44. Commd 22/5/70. Flt Lt 7/1/74. Retd GD 27/3/00.
HOWARD J.C.E. Born 31/12/51. Commd 5/5/88. Sqn Ldr 1/7/01. Retd ENGINEER 22/8/03.
HOWARD M.R. BSc. Born 4/3/49. Commd 28/12/71. Flt Lt 15/10/76. Retd ENG 28/12/87.
HOWARD N.R.S. Born 27/3/30. Commd 24/10/51. Wg Cdr 1/1/72. Retd GD 14/5/83.
HOWARD P. Born 2/4/46. Commd 24/3/83. Sqn Ldr 1/7/91. Retd ENG 2/4/01.
HOWARD P. CB OBE PhD MB BS FRCP FFOM FRAeS. Born 15/12/25. Commd 20/8/51. AVM 1/8/85. Retd MED 17/10/88.
HOWARD P.D. Born 19/10/23. Commd 27/8/59. Sqn Ldr 1/7/73. Retd SEC 30/8/75.
HOWARD P.I. BDS MGDSRCS(Eng) MCIPD. Born 7/12/58. Commd 13/1/80. Wg Cdr 5/12/94. Retd DEL 7/12/96.
HOWARD P.J. ACIS. Born 24/11/38. Commd 28/12/66. Wg Cdr 1/1/87. Retd ADMIN 14/5/89.
HOWARD P.V. Born 17/2/15. Commd 17/9/43. Flt Lt 29/6/50. Retd GD(G) 26/3/70.
HOWARD R.F.G. BEM FCIPS FCMI. Born 23/3/23. Commd 17/8/50. Gp Capt 1/7/72. Retd ADMIN 23/3/78.
HOWARD R.J. AFC. Born 9/11/38. Commd 25/7/60. Gp Capt 1/7/87. Retd GD 9/11/93.
HOWARD R.M. Born 21/2/48. Commd 9/8/79. Sqn Ldr 1/7/92. Retd SUP 6/1/03.
HOWARD R.T. AFC. Born 28/9/20. Commd 18/2/44. Sqn Ldr 1/1/58. Retd GD 28/9/69.
HOWARD S.M. BSc. Born 18/2/66. Commd 12/6/86. Sqn Ldr 1/7/00. Retd FLY(P) 18/2/04.
HOWARD W.J. Born 14/7/39. Commd 25/7/60. Flt Lt 1/7/72. Retd GD 3/11/81.
HOWARD W.T. BEM. Born 1/1/23. Commd 13/7/61. Sqn Ldr 1/7/73. Retd ENG 15/1/77.
HOWARD-JONES G.M. DFC FCMI MCIPD. Born 11/9/19. Commd 24/6/39. Gp Capt 1/7/69. Retd SEC 27/4/74.
HOWARTH G.W.L. BTech PGCE. Born 30/11/53. Commd 6/9/81. Sqn Ldr 1/1/89. Retd ADMIN 14/3/97.
HOWARTH P. BSc CEng MRAeS. Born 8/7/41. Commd 1/8/66. Sqn Ldr 1/1/75. Retd ENG 1/8/82.
HOWARTH P.D. Born 17/2/44. Commd 1/4/66. Flt Lt 18/1/76. Retd GD 13/12/77. Re-entered 1/4/81. Wg Cdr 1/7/95.
  Retd ADMIN 14/12/96.
HOWAT A.H. Born 21/5/48. Commd 24/2/67. Flt Lt 24/8/72. Retd GD 18/6/74.
HOWAT M.C.M. BSc. Born 17/6/42. Commd 26/3/63. Flt Lt 17/6/65. Retd GD 9/10/77.
HOWAT T.McC. Born 15/4/41. Commd 27/6/59. Sqn Ldr 1/7/87. Retd GD 15/4/96.
HOWDEN M.J. BSc. Born 1/7/19. Commd 16/6/43. Flt Offr 6/8/50. Retd SEC 4/5/63.
HOWDEN R.I.C. Born 31/7/35. Commd 11/2/55. Wg Cdr 1/1/73. Retd GD 1/2/75.
HOWE E.J. Born 31/3/41. Commd 18/8/61. Flt Lt 30/9/66. Retd GD 31/3/79.
HOWE I.McG.G. Born 11/5/57. Commd 5/8/76. Wg Cdr 1/7/94. Retd GD 1/12/97.

HOWE J.F.G. CB CBE AFC. Born 26/3/30. Commd 4/10/54. AVM 1/7/80. Retd GD 30/11/85.
HOWE J.L. BSc. Born 28/2/43. Commd 13/4/64. Sqn Ldr 1/7/74. Retd GD 28/2/81. Re-instated 14/11/84. Retd GD 7/3/86.
HOWE R. Born 11/2/46. Commd 27/1/67. Flt Lt 15/7/73. Retd SUP 11/2/84.
HOWE R.S. Born 9/9/45. Commd 26/5/67. Sqn Ldr 1/7/92. Retd GD 9/9/00.
HOWE R.S.L. MSc CEng MIEE. Born 23/3/30. Commd 18/2/54. Sqn Ldr 18/6/64. Retd EDN 18/2/70.
HOWELL E.A. BEd. Born 21/3/56. Commd 3/9/78. Sqn Ldr 1/1/89. Retd ADMIN 3/9/00.
HOWELL E.M.T. CBE CEng FRAeS. Born 11/9/13. Commd 15/12/34. AVM 1/1/66. Retd ENG 17/3/67.
HOWELL F.C. Born 19/1/19. Commd 19/7/45. Flt Lt 19/1/50. Retd SEC 11/10/53.
HOWELL G.P. MB BS FRCS(Edin) LMSSA. Born 12/12/53. Commd 18/2/75. Wg Cdr 16/2/92. Retd MED 30/10/96.
HOWELL J.K. MB ChB DCH DObstRCOG. Born 12/9/30. Commd 17/2/56. Wg Cdr 17/2/69. Retd MED 4/3/73.
HOWELL M.D. Born 18/6/51. Commd 25/2/72. Flt Lt 25/2/75. Retd GD 1/9/83.
HOWELL R.A. Born 30/12/59. Commd 3/7/80. Flt Lt 31/12/83. Retd GD 14/1/91.
HOWELL R.T. Born 7/3/38. Commd 22/12/61. Sqn Ldr 1/1/74. Retd GD 1/10/80.
HOWELLS J.R. BSc CEng MRAeS. Born 24/4/39. Commd 30/9/59. Wg Cdr 1/7/76. Retd ENG 1/7/79.
HOWELLS L. Born 1/5/48. Commd 25/10/73. Sqn Ldr 1/7/89. Retd OPS SPT(ATC) 1/5/03.
HOWELLS M.A. BA FInstPet MCMI. Born 9/10/32. Commd 27/7/54. Wg Cdr 1/7/72. Retd SUP 30/7/83.
HOWELLS P.M. BA. Born 20/12/40. Commd 2/2/65. Sqn Ldr 1/7/77. Retd SEC 2/2/81.
HOWELLS R.L. Born 27/10/50. Commd 19/6/70. Flt Lt 13/2/77. Retd GD(G) 18/7/81.
HOWELLS V.B. CBE. Born 14/2/38. Commd 15/12/59. A Cdre 1/7/88. Retd SUP 14/8/95.
HOWES A.M.McC. Born 19/7/30. Commd 12/12/51. Wg Cdr 1/7/69. Retd SUP 1/9/82.
HOWES C.E. OBE. Born 25/5/15. Commd 8/12/41. Wg Offr 1/7/56. Retd SEC 28/3/61.
HOWES G.P. Born 3/1/59. Commd 30/4/81. Sqn Ldr 1/1/92. Retd GD 3/1/97.
HOWES M. Born 19/8/45. Commd 2/6/67. Sqn Ldr 1/1/80. Retd GD 19/8/89.
HOWES M.E. Born 18/11/43. Commd 21/12/62. Flt Lt 1/7/69. Retd GD 18/11/81.
HOWES M.J.N. The Rev. BA. Born 17/4/43. Commd 22/10/72. Retd Wg Cdr 22/10/88.
HOWEY J.H. Born 6/12/34. Commd 30/5/59. Flt Lt 10/2/67. Retd GD(G) 5/12/74.
HOWIE A. Born 11/9/30. Commd 12/9/50. Wg Cdr 1/1/72. Retd GD 11/9/85.
HOWIE D.G. Born 21/7/33. Commd 15/3/60. Sqn Ldr 1/1/73. Retd GD 21/7/88.
HOWIE T.D. Born 17/11/61. Commd 19/3/81. Flt Lt 19/9/87. Retd OPS SPT 17/11/99.
HOWITT J.S. AFC MRCS LRCP. Born 24/12/16. Commd 10/9/40. Gp Capt 1/1/59. Retd MED 11/9/64.
HOWITT M.G. Born 15/10/51. Commd 17/7/87. Sqn Ldr 1/1/96. Retd ENG 9/11/02.
HOWLAND R.J.L. BSc. Born 3/10/66. Commd 16/9/84. Fg Offr 15/1/87. Retd ENG 15/6/88.
HOWLES P.A.H. Born 6/1/33. Commd 28/1/53. Sqn Ldr 1/1/71. Retd GD 1/1/74.
HOWLETT D.J. Born 31/10/49. Commd 4/2/71. Sqn Ldr 1/7/94. Retd SUPPLY 30/4/03.
HOWLETT N.S. CB. Born 17/4/27. Commd 2/10/47. AVM 1/1/79. Retd GD 17/4/82.
HOWLETT P.C. Born 7/2/31. Commd 21/12/67. Sqn Ldr 1/7/83. Retd ENG 7/2/93.
HOWLETT P.W. AFC. Born 19/2/46. Commd 21/5/65. Sqn Ldr 1/7/93. Retd GD 19/2/01.
HOWORTH D.M. OBE. Born 28/7/19. Commd 27/7/40. Wg Cdr 1/7/66. Retd GD(G) 28/7/74.
HOWSEGO G.M. Born 6/5/62. Commd 11/6/81. Flt Lt 11/12/87. Retd SY 14/3/96.
HOWSON G. BSc. Born 1/5/49. Commd 14/11/73. Sqn Ldr 1/1/82. Retd ENG 14/11/89.
HOXEY K.H. Born 28/5/23. Commd 15/12/44. Sqn Ldr 1/7/74. Retd GD 28/5/78.
HOY S.L. Born 2/10/43. Commd 14/8/70. Flt Lt 14/8/72. Retd ENG 2/10/81.
HOY W. DFC AFC. Born 23/12/18. Commd 30/10/39. Wg Cdr 1/1/51. Retd GD 5/4/66.
HOYER W. Born 9/10/33. Commd 8/11/51. Flt Lt 23/2/57. Retd GD 14/6/74.
HOYES M.P. BSc. Born 5/1/48. Commd 13/9/70. Sqn Ldr 1/1/89. Retd ENG 13/9/92.
HOYLE A. Born 16/10/39. Commd 26/5/61. Sqn Ldr 1/1/83. Retd GD 11/10/85.
HRUSKA A.L. Born 23/6/15. Commd 2/8/40. Sqn Ldr 1/7/60. Retd GD(G) 23/6/70.
HUBBARD F.W. MBE MCMI. Born 14/9/21. Commd 8/6/44. Wg Cdr 1/1/62. Retd GD 26/4/74.
HUBBARD G.E.F. RD. Born 9/7/21. Commd 8/5/57. Flt Lt 8/5/57. Retd MAR 3/5/71.
HUBBARD J.W. Born 14/9/66. Commd 2/11/89. Flt Lt 2/5/95. Retd OPS SPT(FC) 14/9/04.
HUBBARD K.G. OBE DFC AFC. Born 26/2/20. Commd 6/5/41. Gp Capt 1/7/61. Retd GD 1/1/66.
HUBBARD L.H. Born 16/6/42. Commd 22/5/68. Flt Lt 22/5/74. Retd GD(G) 11/6/75.
HUBBARD M.R. MSc BSc CEng MIEE. Born 18/12/47. Commd 21/4/67. Sqn Ldr 1/7/80. Retd ENG 18/12/88.
HUBBARD P.U. Born 14/12/24. Commd 7/7/49. Sqn Ldr 1/7/58. Retd GD 14/12/62.
HUBBARD R.G.M. MCMI. Born 10/4/22. Commd 10/5/46. Wg Cdr 1/7/65. Retd SY 26/3/77.
HUBBARD S.J. DFC AFC* MRAeS. Born 25/3/21. Commd 15/7/44. Wg Cdr 1/1/60. Retd GD 30/6/65.
HUBBLE C.M. BSc. Born 7/12/50. Commd 13/9/71. Flt Lt 15/10/76. Retd ENG 1/10/81.
HUBBLE P.N. MSc BSc MCMI. Born 25/7/58. Commd 6/9/81. Wg Cdr 1/7/98. Retd GD 6/9/03.
HUBBLE R.C. The Rev. Born 11/10/30. Commd 1/6/64. Retd Wg Cdr 11/10/85.
HUCKER M.F. The Rev. MBE MA BD. Born 1/5/33. Commd 1/9/62. Retd Gp Capt 10/11/90.
HUDDLESTON C.J. Born 6/7/60. Commd 22/7/84. Flt Lt 22/7/90. Retd SUP 22/7/00.
HUDDLESTON F.A. Born 13/12/46. Commd 21/5/65. Wg Cdr 1/7/93. Retd GD 13/12/03.
HUDDLESTON G.R. The Rev. MA. Born 22/1/36. Commd 7/7/69. Retd Wg Cdr 7/7/85.
HUDDLESTONE J.A. BEd. Born 11/11/62. Commd 13/10/83. Sqn Ldr 1/7/00. Retd ADMIN (TRG) 1/7/03.
HUDGELL E.E.L. Born 22/6/13. Commd 1/3/41. Sqn Offr 1/7/54. Retd SEC 10/4/56.
HUDSON A. Born 8/6/23. Commd 1/5/47. Flt Lt 4/1/51. Retd ENG 8/6/56.

HUDSON A.M. Born 1/7/56. Commd 3/11/97. Sqn Ldr 1/7/03. Retd FLY(P) 1/11/04.
HUDSON D.B. BSc. Born 26/8/48. Commd 27/2/70. Sqn Ldr 1/7/83. Retd ENG 26/8/92.
HUDSON D.J. Born 12/4/58. Commd 9/8/79. Sqn Ldr 1/7/91. Retd GD 30/6/01.
HUDSON E.G. Born 15/11/35. Commd 1/4/58. Sqn Ldr 1/7/90. Retd GD 15/11/95.
HUDSON J.A. Born 18/8/42. Commd 21/12/62. Flt Lt 8/1/69. Retd GD 18/8/80.
HUDSON J.D. BA. Born 3/10/74. Commd 15/11/96. Flt Lt 15/1/00. Retd FLY(P) 17/5/03.
HUDSON K.B. Born 23/1/45. Commd 24/6/76. Flt Lt 24/6/78. Retd GD 24/6/84.
HUDSON M. MA BA. Born 10/11/49. Commd 30/10/83. Flt Lt 30/4/87. Retd ADMIN 10/1/01.
HUDSON M.E. MCMI. Born 13/2/49. Commd 11/5/78. Sqn Ldr 1/7/86. Retd ADMIN 13/2/93.
HUDSON M.J. Born 3/9/63. Commd 19/7/84. Sqn Ldr 1/7/97. Retd GD 3/9/01.
HUDSON N.R. BSc. Born 25/12/47. Commd 7/6/71. Sqn Ldr 1/1/79. Retd ENG 7/6/87.
HUDSON R. MB BS DAvMed. Born 10/12/55. Commd 28/3/84. Wg Cdr 1/6/95. Retd MED 14/3/97.
HUDSON R.A. Born 9/11/19. Commd 24/3/44. Sqn Ldr 1/4/57. Retd SEC 10/2/68.
HUDSON R.A. BA CertEd. Born 13/5/48. Commd 7/5/91. Sqn Ldr 1/1/83. Retd FLY(N) 13/5/03.
HUDSON R.A.H.R. DFM. Born 20/5/24. Commd 2/5/45. Flt Lt 2/11/48. Retd GD 2/1/68.
HUDSON R.I. Born 5/10/24. Commd 10/12/44. Flt Lt 4/12/52. Retd SEC 22/11/68.
HUDSON R.J.S. Born 14/8/28. Commd 27/9/50. Flt Lt 27/9/53. Retd GD 5/9/56.
HUDSON R.S. Born 29/6/37. Commd 16/9/71. Sqn Ldr 1/7/91. Retd SUP 1/7/94.
HUDSON S. Born 25/12/21. Commd 7/4/44. Sqn Ldr 1/1/56. Retd GD 31/8/68.
HUDSON S.G. Born 15/4/60. Commd 1/11/79. Flt Lt 1/5/86. Retd SY 16/4/87.
HUDSON T.F.H. Born 26/8/15. Commd 3/4/39. Wg Cdr 1/1/52. Retd SUP 31/8/59.
HUDSPETH J.D. Born 9/12/45. Commd 17/7/70. Flt Lt 25/2/74. Retd GD 11/12/75.
HUES C.F. Born 18/10/38. Commd 20/2/72. Flt Lt 21/8/73. Retd ADMIN 20/2/83.
HUETT P.S. Born 20/1/46. Commd 6/5/66. Sqn Ldr 1/7/79. Retd GD 7/12/86.
HUGGARD W.M. Born 6/1/16. Commd 8/6/43. Flt Lt 17/9/51. Retd GD(G) 5/12/62.
HUGGETT D.F. AFC. Born 12/12/33. Commd 20/5/52. Flt Lt 20/2/58. Retd GD 4/12/65.
HUGGINS D.G. DPhysEd. Born 23/6/49. Commd 22/8/71. Sqn Ldr 1/7/88. Retd ADMIN 1/3/94.
HUGGINS J.C. Born 3/7/48. Commd 2/2/68. Flt Lt 22/6/74. Retd SUP 11/11/77.
HUGGINS W. MBE. Born 11/12/31. Commd 17/1/69. Flt Lt 17/1/73. Retd ADMIN 31/1/88.
HUGH J.A.C. MPhil BSc CEng MIEE. Born 15/10/41. Commd 6/10/69. Sqn Ldr 1/1/76. Retd ENG 6/10/85.
HUGHES A.G. Born 12/6/46. Commd 4/7/85. Flt Lt 4/7/89. Retd GD(G) 6/1/97.
HUGHES B. Born 2/3/30. Commd 11/4/51. A Cdre 1/1/76. Retd SUP 2/3/85.
HUGHES B. BSc(Eng) CEng MIEE MRAeS. Born 30/11/40. Commd 30/9/60. Wg Cdr 1/1/79. Retd ENG 1/4/86.
HUGHES B.J. MSc MRAeS MCMI. Born 27/4/37. Commd 21/8/61. Wg Cdr 1/7/78. Retd GD 1/9/82.
HUGHES B.J. Born 10/1/47. Commd 8/7/65. Gp Capt 1/1/91. Retd SY 22/6/94.
HUGHES B.M. Born 7/3/64. Commd 18/11/90. Flt Lt 25/1/93. Retd GD 21/4/98.
HUGHES C.E. Born 4/1/47. Commd 27/2/70. Flt Lt 18/4/74. Retd ADMIN 4/1/85.
HUGHES C.J. AFC. Born 14/12/37. Commd 19/4/63. Flt Lt 1/4/66. Retd GD 14/12/75.
HUGHES C.O. Born 1/12/32. Commd 18/6/52. Flt Lt 13/11/57. Retd GD(G) 1/12/87.
HUGHES C.W.G. Born 2/4/34. Commd 30/7/52. Sqn Ldr 1/7/73. Retd GD 2/4/92.
HUGHES D.G.M. BSc. Born 12/6/43. Commd 4/4/66. Flt Lt 4/1/68. Retd GD 4/4/82.
HUGHES D.H. CEng MRAeS MCMI MIIM. Born 20/7/26. Commd 21/2/51. Wg Cdr 1/7/73. Retd ENG 20/7/84.
HUGHES D.J.S. FIFA. Born 6/6/40. Commd 18/7/63. Sqn Ldr 1/7/76. Retd ADMIN 8/7/90.
HUGHES D.L. Born 14/7/63. Commd 23/10/86. Sqn Ldr 1/1/02. Retd OPS SPT(ATC) 1/2/04.
HUGHES D.N. Born 4/8/59. Commd 11/6/81. Flt Lt 11/12/87. Retd OPS SPT 4/8/97.
HUGHES E.J.A. MBE. Born 14/10/33. Commd 11/10/51. Sqn Ldr 1/7/84. Retd GD 14/10/89.
HUGHES F. MA MSc. Born 30/9/41. Commd 1/9/64. Sqn Ldr 30/3/71. Retd EDN 1/11/75.
HUGHES G.F. BA. Born 12/2/55. Commd 1/9/74. Wg Cdr 1/7/94. Retd ADMIN 21/12/96.
HUGHES G.J. MSc. Born 30/7/54. Commd 7/7/83. Sqn Ldr 1/1/91. Retd ENGINEER 14/7/04.
HUGHES G.K. BSc. Born 17/10/63. Commd 14/9/86. Sqn Ldr 1/7/98. Retd ENG 14/9/02.
HUGHES G.T. Born 5/8/25. Commd 11/11/50. Flt Lt 11/2/55. Retd GD 4/7/65.
HUGHES H.W. BSc. Born 24/12/38. Commd 28/9/60. Wg Cdr 1/1/80. Retd GD 24/12/93.
HUGHES I.C.J. Born 19/9/41. Commd 30/7/63. Wg Cdr 1/7/83. Retd GD 1/1/93.
HUGHES J. Born 5/2/43. Commd 28/7/64. Flt Lt 28/1/67. Retd GD 5/3/80.
HUGHES J.A. Born 6/4/46. Commd 30/5/69. Sqn Ldr 1/1/94. Retd GD 14/3/96.
HUGHES J.C. BDS. Born 8/4/41. Commd 20/9/59. Wg Cdr 23/6/77. Retd DEL 8/4/01.
HUGHES J.G. Born 21/7/41. Commd 6/7/62. Flt Lt 9/2/68. Retd GD 21/7/79.
HUGHES J.G. Born 11/6/38. Commd 26/11/81. Flt Lt 10/3/87. Retd SY(PRT) 10/11/89.
HUGHES J.H. BA MCIPD. Born 25/12/38. Commd 12/9/61. Sqn Ldr 1/7/73. Retd ADMIN 12/9/85.
HUGHES J.M. Born 27/9/26. Commd 23/4/52. Flt Lt 29/4/59. Retd GD 31/10/67.
HUGHES J.P. Born 22/12/15. Commd 16/5/57. Flt Lt 16/5/60. Retd ENG 22/12/70.
HUGHES J.T. BA. Born 3/8/55. Commd 20/11/78. Wg Cdr 1/7/97. Retd OPS SPT 6/4/02.
HUGHES K.A. Born 5/7/28. Commd 26/11/64. Flt Lt 26/11/67. Retd GD 5/7/78.
HUGHES K.L. DFC. Born 27/8/21. Commd 11/4/43. Sqn Ldr 1/7/52. Retd GD 11/2/56.
HUGHES K.L. AFC. Born 2/11/23. Commd 17/9/43. Sqn Ldr 1/10/54. Retd GD 31/12/61.
HUGHES K.R. Born 30/3/15. Commd 16/10/39. Flt Lt 1/1/43. Retd GD 1/7/50.

HUGHES L.J. Born 19/6/29. Commd 20/5/53. Flt Lt 6/3/63. Retd SUP 19/6/90.
HUGHES M. Born 5/3/30. Commd 1/8/51. Wg Cdr 1/1/69. Retd GD 25/10/80.
HUGHES M.J. Born 18/1/43. Commd 17/12/63. Flt Lt 17/6/66. Retd GD 31/3/73.
HUGHES M.K. Born 4/3/60. Commd 16/6/88. Flt Lt 16/6/90. Retd GD(G) 4/12/95.
HUGHES M.S. MSc MB BS FRIPHH MRCS LRCP DAvMed DIH MFOM. Born 21/12/32. Commd 2/9/64. Wg Cdr 25/4/75. Retd MED 5/1/83.
HUGHES N.D. OBE. Born 13/1/45. Commd 22/2/63. Wg Cdr 1/1/86. Retd GD 31/3/94.
HUGHES N.J. Born 24/3/41. Commd 18/12/62. Wg Cdr 1/1/87. Retd GD 24/3/96.
HUGHES N.J. BA. Born 19/2/67. Commd 29/9/91. Flt Lt 29/3/95. Retd ADMIN 30/9/96.
HUGHES P. Born 30/8/47. Commd 5/11/65. Flt Lt 3/9/71. Retd GD 30/9/77.
HUGHES P.A. CBE DFC. Born 18/11/18. Commd 29/7/39. Gp Capt 1/1/61. Retd GD 11/6/68. rtg A Cdre
HUGHES P.B. Born 1/8/46. Commd 28/4/65. Sqn Ldr 1/7/87. Retd ADMIN 1/8/01.
HUGHES R. Born 18/2/32. Commd 17/7/58. Flt Lt 17/1/63. Retd GD 18/11/71.
HUGHES R.M.H. Born 17/5/47. Commd 17/7/70. Wg Cdr 1/1/95. Retd GD 17/5/02.
HUGHES R.P. BSc. Born 22/8/59. Commd 19/6/83. Flt Lt 19/12/84. Retd GD 19/6/99.
HUGHES S.D. Born 4/10/59. Commd 15/10/81. Sqn Ldr 1/7/93. Retd GD 4/10/97.
HUGHES S.G. BL. Born 16/2/31. Commd 27/8/59. Flt Lt 27/11/65. Retd SEC 28/4/73.
HUGHES S.J. BDS. Born 13/10/45. Commd 30/8/66. Wg Cdr 13/9/81. Retd DEL 14/3/97.
HUGHES S.J. Born 25/2/57. Commd 20/9/79. APO 20/9/79. Retd GD 29/11/80.
HUGHES S.P. Born 1/8/42. Commd 17/12/63. Flt Lt 17/6/66. Retd GD 18/4/68.
HUGHES T. Born 1/10/29. Commd 28/2/52. Sqn Ldr 1/7/67. Retd SUP 14/1/85.
HUGHES T.F. Born 15/5/38. Commd 8/12/61. Sqn Ldr 1/1/76. Retd GD(G) 28/12/88.
HUGHES W. Born 29/10/22. Commd 20/11/44. Sqn Ldr 1/7/73. Retd GD 10/6/77.
HUGHES W.F. Born 19/7/35. Commd 21/7/55. Gp Capt 1/7/83. Retd ADMIN 19/7/90.
HUGHES W.H. Born 27/10/30. Commd 28/7/67. Sqn Ldr 1/1/81. Retd ADMIN 27/10/85.
HUGHES W.O. BSc. Born 30/11/31. Commd 9/9/54. Sqn Ldr 1/7/65. Retd GD 9/9/70.
HUGHES W.P.G. Born 11/12/46. Commd 8/10/70. Sqn Ldr 1/7/83. Retd ADMIN 1/7/86.
HUGHES-LEWIS A.B. Born 20/3/44. Commd 17/12/64. Wg Cdr 1/1/86. Retd GD 3/4/89.
HUGHESDON A.D. Born 6/8/33. Commd 16/7/52. Flt Lt 1/11/61. Retd GD 1/11/77.
HUGILL J. DFC. Born 30/5/19. Commd 13/7/43. Flt Lt 13/7/45. Retd GD(G) 30/5/74.
HUGILL J. Born 24/6/31. Commd 15/2/51. Flt Lt 13/4/50. Retd GD 7/9/70.
HUGO V. MRIN. Born 15/7/38. Commd 22/8/59. Sqn Ldr 1/1/72. Retd GD 2/12/77.
HUIE R.G. FCIPD MCMI. Born 13/10/23. Commd 6/6/45. Wg Cdr 1/1/67. Retd SEC 13/10/78.
HUKE C.W.N. BA. Born 26/5/64. Commd 30/5/86. Flt Lt 30/9/88. Retd GD 26/5/02.
HULBERT J. DFM. Born 23/1/21. Commd 21/6/45. Flt Lt 7/6/51. Retd GD 13/2/64.
HULIN W.H. Born 7/2/20. Commd 9/4/43. Flt Lt 15/12/49. Retd SEC 4/11/53.
HULL A.F.R. Born 13/8/23. Commd 26/9/51. Flt Lt 30/4/62. Retd GD 13/8/66.
HULL D. Born 1/5/38. Commd 19/4/63. Sqn Ldr 1/7/84. Retd GD 1/5/93.
HULL D.H. MA MB BChir FRCP. Born 21/8/31. Commd 11/8/57. AVM 28/4/94. Retd MED 21/8/96.
HULL P. BEM. Born 16/8/52. Commd 14/2/99. Flt Lt 14/2/99. Retd ENGINEER 10/4/04.
HULL W.B. BSc. Born 22/7/37. Commd 12/9/61. Sqn Ldr 12/3/69. Retd ADMIN 22/6/88.
HULLAH D. Born 20/10/25. Commd 28/5/66. Flt Lt 28/5/71. Retd SY 1/11/77.
HULLAND G.R. Born 25/6/48. Commd 22/9/69. Sqn Ldr 1/1/84. Retd ENGINEER 18/10/03.
HULLEY S.F. Born 26/1/67. Commd 8/5/86. Sqn Ldr 1/1/01. Retd FLY(N) 26/1/05.
HULM F.R. BDS. Born 10/5/31. Commd 16/6/63. A Cdre 1/7/83. Retd DEL 11/7/86.
HULME A.N. MBE. Born 16/4/33. Commd 6/9/54. Wg Cdr 1/1/77. Retd GD 28/1/82.
HULME L.M. Born 29/6/45. Commd 30/1/70. Sqn Ldr 1/7/95. Retd GD 29/6/00.
HULME S. Born 18/9/38. Commd 25/8/60. Sqn Ldr 1/1/72. Retd ENG 18/9/76.
HULSE D.S. Born 9/1/37. Commd 30/11/55. Flt Lt 30/5/61. Retd GD 9/1/95.
HULSE K.G. Born 3/10/45. Commd 18/8/68. Flt Lt 15/4/72. Retd GD 3/10/83.
HULYER M.C. MCMI. Born 2/6/45. Commd 5/3/65. Sqn Ldr 1/1/83. Retd GD 1/10/88.
HUMAN P.R. Born 11/2/44. Commd 23/4/87. Flt Lt 23/4/91. Retd ENG 5/5/93.
HUMBERSTONE G.F. Born 18/11/35. Commd 23/6/61. Flt Lt 1/4/66. Retd GD 1/9/76.
HUMBLE B. OBE BSc(Eng). Born 11/9/37. Commd 3/10/61. Wg Cdr 1/1/81. Retd ENG 9/8/88.
HUMBLE T.L. Born 10/3/19. Commd 28/3/46. Sqn Ldr 1/7/63. Retd ENG 28/6/69.
HUME D. Born 20/7/45. Commd 6/5/83. Flt Lt 6/5/87. Retd ADMIN 15/11/93.
HUME D.C. BSc CEng MIEE. Born 1/10/54. Commd 2/9/73. Sqn Ldr 1/7/88. Retd ENG 1/10/92.
HUMPHERSON R. Born 27/3/32. Commd 17/12/52. Flt Lt 17/6/55. Retd GD 27/3/70.
HUMPHREY A.S. Born 1/7/22. Commd 2/9/42. Flt Offr 2/9/47. Retd SEC 14/6/52.
HUMPHREY C.A. Born 24/1/45. Commd 3/3/67. Wg Cdr 1/1/88. Retd GD 14/3/96.
HUMPHREY J.A. Born 23/4/62. Commd 7/11/85. Flt Lt 22/10/89. Retd MED 31/8/90.
HUMPHREY M. BA MCMI. Born 16/7/49. Commd 5/9/69. Flt Lt 17/1/76. Retd GD(G) 1/9/90.
HUMPHREY M.H. Born 29/12/46. Commd 28/6/79. Sqn Ldr 1/7/95. Retd GD 29/12/01.
HUMPHREY P.G. IEng MIIE. Born 10/8/48. Commd 16/9/76. Sqn Ldr 1/1/87. Retd ENGINEER 10/8/03.
HUMPHREY R. Born 8/12/37. Commd 4/12/56. Flt Lt 12/6/62. Retd GD 1/7/88.
HUMPHREY R. Born 11/5/37. Commd 29/7/58. Sqn Ldr 1/1/71. Retd GD 1/10/96.

HUMPHREY R.C. BSc MSc CEng MRAeS. Born 4/12/35. Commd 7/11/58. Sqn Ldr 12/3/68. Retd ADMIN 4/12/80.
HUMPHREY R.J. Born 29/11/36. Commd 21/12/67. Wg Cdr 1/7/85. Retd GD 16/5/87.
HUMPHREY S.F. Born 28/5/24. Commd 11/11/47. Flt Lt 10/11/55. Retd GD 13/7/67.
HUMPHREYS G.A. BSc. Born 17/7/58. Commd 11/9/77. Sqn Ldr 1/7/89. Retd GD 1/12/97.
HUMPHREYS M.W. Born 14/5/40. Commd 2/7/64. Wg Cdr 1/7/88. Retd ADMIN 1/7/90.
HUMPHREYS P.J. Born 28/4/60. Commd 2/8/87. Flt Lt 26/9/85. Retd FLY(P) 10/4/05.
HUMPHREYS-EVANS D.H. AFC. Born 8/1/40. Commd 9/2/62. Sqn Ldr 1/1/87. Retd GD 12/8/90.
HUMPHREYSON R.C. MBE AFC. Born 9/6/38. Commd 30/10/58. Gp Capt 1/7/80. Retd GD 1/2/90.
HUMPHRIES A.G. BA. Born 1/1/46. Commd 28/2/80. Flt Lt 28/2/82. Retd GD 14/3/96.
HUMPHRIES A.S. PhD MBA FCMI MIMIS. Born 2/6/49. Commd 26/2/71. Gp Capt 1/7/00. Retd GD 2/6/04.
HUMPHRIES B.M. CBE BSc CEng MIMechE. Born 13/3/43. Commd 15/7/63. A Cdre 1/1/89. Retd ENG 10/1/90.
HUMPHRIES H.V.J. Born 23/12/47. Commd 8/9/83. Flt Lt 8/9/87. Retd ENG 14/9/96.
HUMPHRIES J.R. Born 28/5/35. Commd 27/5/73. Flt Lt 24/3/62. Retd GD(G) 2/4/90.
HUMPHRIES J.S. Born 13/10/21. Commd 15/2/51. Flt Lt 15/8/54. Retd ENG 13/10/70.
HUMPHRIES P.J. FIMLT. Born 12/1/29. Commd 7/12/61. Sqn Ldr 13/2/73. Retd MED(T) 6/12/73.
HUMPHRIES R.L. MSc BDS. Born 12/6/39. Commd 27/12/61. Wg Cdr 29/11/76. Retd DEL 2/10/80.
HUMPHRYS P.J.C. Born 24/4/48. Commd 17/7/70. Flt Lt 17/1/76. Retd GD 3/11/88.
HUMPSTON E.A.R. CEng MRAeS. Born 17/9/29. Commd 3/3/54. Wg Cdr 1/1/72. Retd ENG 17/9/84.
HUNKIN E. Born 25/11/49. Commd 31/7/70. Sqn Ldr 1/1/85. Retd GD 1/1/88.
HUNNISETT S.P. Born 17/8/51. Commd 5/4/79. Sqn Ldr 17/8/51. Retd SUP 31/3/94.
HUNT A. Born 27/10/47. Commd 11/10/70. Sqn Ldr 1/7/85. Retd ENG 1/7/88.
HUNT A. Born 21/4/21. Commd 13/8/44. Flt Lt 13/8/48. Retd RGT 2/9/60.
HUNT A.A. Born 23/2/47. Commd 20/10/83. Flt Lt 20/10/87. Retd GD(G) 21/10/90.
HUNT A.J.F. Born 1/8/41. Commd 31/7/62. Flt Lt 31/1/65. Retd GD 20/9/75.
HUNT B. Born 1/10/40. Commd 30/5/69. Wg Cdr 1/1/88. Retd GD 31/10/93.
HUNT B. Born 3/7/43. Commd 21/1/73. Sqn Ldr 1/7/83. Retd ENG 28/1/95.
HUNT B.C. BSc. Born 23/4/39. Commd 1/10/62. Wg Cdr 1/7/87. Retd GD 23/4/94.
HUNT B.D. Born 25/4/47. Commd 10/6/66. Flt Lt 10/12/71. Retd GD 25/12/85. Re-entered 7/9/87. Sqn Ldr 1/7/96.
  Retd FLY(P) 20/4/04.
HUNT C. MB ChB BAO MRCGP DAvMed. Born 15/12/52. Commd 24/6/84. Wg Cdr 20/11/90. Retd MED 14/3/96.
HUNT C.C. BDS. Born 24/7/53. Commd 14/5/74. Wg Cdr 25/11/89. Retd DEL 24/7/91.
HUNT C.D. Born 12/12/44. Commd 3/1/64. Flt Lt 3/7/69. Retd GD 12/12/82.
HUNT D. Born 5/5/34. Commd 10/12/52. Flt Lt 20/7/58. Retd GD 5/6/72.
HUNT D. Born 13/3/33. Commd 22/7/66. Sqn Ldr 1/7/76. Retd ADMIN 10/6/85.
HUNT E.S.J. Born 3/2/65. Commd 4/10/96. Sqn Ldr 1/1/99. Retd FLY(P) 10/6/03.
HUNT G.K. Born 31/3/20. Commd 15/6/61. Sqn Ldr 1/7/69. Retd SUP 15/9/72.
HUNT H.A. MB ChB FRCGP DRCOG DCH. Born 16/3/33. Commd 5/4/59. Gp Capt 1/1/82. Retd MED 5/4/85.
HUNT K.D. BEM. Born 5/3/22. Commd 6/11/58. Flt Lt 6/11/63. Retd ENG 31/12/66.
HUNT M.J. Born 10/1/45. Commd 25/6/65. Sqn Ldr 1/1/87. Retd FLY(P) 10/1/05.
HUNT M.L. MInstPet. Born 18/3/46. Commd 26/8/66. Sqn Ldr 16/6/83. Retd SUP 31/3/94.
HUNT N.B. MSc. Born 19/8/50. Commd 26/2/71. Sqn Ldr 1/1/85. Retd SUP 30/9/90.
HUNT N.B. BSc. Born 1/8/59. Commd 11/9/77. Sqn Ldr 1/1/95. Retd GD 1/1/98.
HUNT N.J. Born 15/7/59. Commd 24/7/81. Flt Lt 24/1/87. Retd GD 20/12/96.
HUNT P.E. Born 3/11/47. Commd 19/7/84. Flt Lt 19/7/84. Retd ENG 25/8/93.
HUNT P.M. Born 26/9/31. Commd 14/1/65. Flt Lt 14/1/68. Retd SEC 30/1/75.
HUNT R.G. Born 13/1/41. Commd 11/6/60. Flt Lt 11/12/65. Retd GD 13/1/79.
HUNT R.G.T. MBE MCMI. Born 5/10/45. Commd 8/10/70. Wg Cdr 1/1/91. Retd ADMIN 14/3/96.
HUNT S.D. Born 2/5/60. Commd 23/11/78. Flt Lt 23/5/84. Retd GD 2/5/97.
HUNT S.W. CBE. Born 21/10/47. Commd 1/8/69. Gp Capt 1/7/90. Retd GD 14/9/96.
HUNTER A.F.C. CBE AFC MA LLB DL. Born 8/3/39. Commd 1/10/62. AVM 1/7/89. Retd GD 1/7/93.
HUNTER B.J. OBE CEng FIEE MRAeS. Born 22/2/41. Commd 18/7/61. Gp Capt 1/7/81. Retd ENG 1/6/89.
HUNTER B.V. Born 19/12/21. Commd 6/9/41. Sqn Ldr 1/10/55. Retd GD 1/10/58.
HUNTER C.E. Born 12/9/16. Commd 16/10/43. Flt Lt 16/4/47. Retd GD 17/7/53.
HUNTER D.A. BA. Born 7/2/58. Commd 14/4/85. Sqn Ldr 1/1/95. Retd ADMIN 14/4/01.
HUNTER D.A. Born 25/12/54. Commd 16/9/73. Sqn Ldr 1/1/91. Retd GD 1/1/94.
HUNTER D.I. Born 18/10/50. Commd 27/3/70. Flt Lt 18/7/76. Retd SUP 1/12/79.
HUNTER D.M. Born 4/3/47. Commd 19/6/70. Flt Lt 19/12/75. Retd GD 22/3/87.
HUNTER F.J.W. Born 14/5/35. Commd 28/2/56. Sqn Ldr 1/1/70. Retd GD 16/1/76.
HUNTER G. Born 14/5/48. Commd 28/5/69. Sqn Ldr 1/1/81. Retd OPS SPT(INT) 14/5/03.
HUNTER I. Born 13/1/48. Commd 21/4/67. Sqn Ldr 1/7/81. Retd SUP 13/1/92.
HUNTER I.M. MA. Born 2/3/51. Commd 4/6/70. Sqn Ldr 1/1/86. Retd GD 2/3/89.
HUNTER I.P.N.M. Born 11/7/43. Commd 20/2/64. Flt Lt 11/5/69. Retd RGT 11/7/81.
HUNTER J. Born 28/10/46. Commd 15/3/73. Wg Cdr 1/1/91. Retd ADMIN 31/3/94.
HUNTER J. Born 23/8/34. Commd 14/1/54. Flt Lt 14/7/59. Retd GD 31/8/72.
HUNTER J.A.L. Born 12/7/20. Commd 9/3/44. Sqn Ldr 1/7/63. Retd ENG 12/7/75.
HUNTER K. BSc. Born 27/10/27. Commd 16/6/53. Wg Cdr 1/1/69. Retd GD 20/9/78.

HUNTER K. Born 30/4/44. Commd 2/11/88. Flt Lt 2/11/92. Retd ENG 5/10/00.
HUNTER K.E. Born 14/9/37. Commd 25/7/71. Sqn Ldr 1/1/86. Retd ENG 30/4/89.
HUNTER K.G. CBE FCMI. Born 18/4/26. Commd 25/8/49. Gp Capt 1/1/77. Retd GD 18/7/83.
HUNTER M.R. Born 2/2/41. Commd 14/6/63. Flt Lt 4/5/72. Retd GD 2/2/96.
HUNTER N. Born 1/7/17. Commd 22/9/39. Gp Offr 1/7/50. Retd SEC 17/11/51.
HUNTER N.B. Born 21/10/48. Commd 1/8/69. Sqn Ldr 1/7/85. Retd GD 1/7/88.
HUNTER P. Born 9/6/68. Commd 26/9/90. Plt Offr 26/3/91. Retd SY 24/3/93.
HUNTER S.C. Born 7/6/48. Commd 7/9/80. Flt Lt 7/9/80. Retd GD(G) 1/2/91.
HUNTER S.J. BSc MB BS. Born 12/9/33. Commd 16/1/83. Sqn Ldr 17/3/85. Retd MED 22/11/91.
HUNTER W.D. OBE CEng FRAeS. Born 20/4/20. Commd 19/8/42. A Cdre 1/7/72. Retd ENG 5/10/74.
HUNTER-TOD G.R.A. Born 21/2/20. Commd 8/8/45. Sqn Offr 1/10/57. Retd SEC 25/5/60.
HUNTER-TOD J.F. Born 3/12/60. Commd 8/6/84. Flt Lt 6/12/90. Retd SUP 1/8/99.
HUNTLEY A.S. Born 18/11/43. Commd 22/5/64. Wg Cdr 1/1/83. Retd OPS SPT 18/11/98.
HUNTLEY L.S. MB BCh. Born 31/8/58. Commd 9/1/79. Sqn Ldr 1/8/87. Retd MED 14/3/96.
HUNWICK P.F. Born 11/1/34. Commd 26/7/55. Flt Lt 14/5/58. Retd GD(G) 30/7/72.
HUPPLER A.B. Born 21/2/33. Commd 24/6/53. Flt Lt 21/10/59. Retd GD 21/2/71.
HURCOMBE M.J.L. Born 9/1/46. Commd 26/5/67. Wg Cdr 1/7/85. Retd ENG 18/10/96.
HURLEY D. LVO AFC. Born 5/8/32. Commd 12/7/51. Sqn Ldr 1/7/78. Retd GD 30/11/88.
HURLEY D.J. MBE. Born 13/3/50. Commd 25/3/69. Wg Cdr 1/1/91. Retd GD 3/12/01.
HURLEY J.B. Born 2/2/28. Commd 6/8/49. Flt Lt 25/9/58. Retd GD 2/2/66.
HURLEY K. Born 30/10/48. Commd 20/9/68. Sqn Ldr 1/7/79. Retd GD 17/1/87.
HURLEY P.R.J. Born 24/4/50. Commd 9/12/76. Sqn Ldr 1/7/90. Retd ADMIN 24/4/94.
HURLOCK W.J. FCMI MCIPD. Born 15/10/21. Commd 30/8/44. Gp Capt 1/1/73. Retd SEC 27/3/76.
HURLOW-JONES W.P.F. MSc CEng MIMechE MRAeS. Born 1/6/36. Commd 23/7/58. Flt Lt 15/4/63. Retd ENG 26/9/80.
HURRELL A.J. BSc. Born 7/5/54. Commd 30/9/73. Sqn Ldr 1/7/90. Retd GD 14/9/96.
HURRELL A.J. BA. Born 28/6/60. Commd 15/9/69. Sqn Ldr 1/1/83. Retd GD 14/3/97.
HURRELL D.A. CB AFC FRAeS. Born 29/4/43. Commd 2/12/63. AVM 1/7/95. Retd GD 29/4/98.
HURRELL F.C. CB OBE FFOM MB BS MRCS LRCP DAvMed. Born 24/4/28. Commd 27/4/53. AVM 1/7/84.
Retd MED 24/4/88.
HURRELL I.E. CEng MIEE. Born 7/12/45. Commd 18/11/66. Sqn Ldr 1/1/79. Retd ENG 7/12/89.
HURRELL L.G. Born 27/4/22. Commd 30/10/43. Sqn Ldr 1/1/55. Retd GD 27/4/65.
HURRELL M.C. Born 26/9/45. Commd 29/4/71. Flt Lt 29/10/76. Retd GD 11/1/87.
HURRELL M.D. Born 21/1/35. Commd 4/12/56. Flt Lt 12/6/62. Retd GD 10/12/68.
HURRELL T. Born 20/9/33. Commd 1/4/53. Sqn Ldr 1/7/66. Retd GD 20/9/88.
HURREN D.G. MBA BA. Born 14/12/52. Commd 8/5/83. Sqn Ldr 1/1/94. Retd SUP 8/5/99.
HURRY A.J. Born 23/2/50. Commd 21/3/69. Sqn Ldr 1/7/89. Retd OPS SPT(REGT) 23/2/05.
HURRY D.P. Born 3/9/33. Commd 10/10/57. Flt Lt 1/1/62. Retd PRT 25/10/73.
HURRY J. DSO DFC FCMI. Born 2/1/20. Commd 23/10/39. Gp Capt 1/7/64. Retd GD 2/1/74.
HURST A.J. MCIPS. Born 19/8/45. Commd 1/3/68. Sqn Ldr 1/7/78. Retd SUP 19/8/83.
HURST J.P. Born 16/1/24. Commd 7/8/46. Flt Lt 4/1/51. Retd GD 2/7/55.
HURST L. Born 12/8/41. Commd 27/1/61. Flt Lt 27/6/66. Retd GD 12/8/79.
HURST M.W.M. BA CEng MIMechE. Born 2/9/42. Commd 30/9/62. Wg Cdr 1/1/79. Retd ENG 1/1/85.
HURST R.H. BSc. Born 5/4/49. Commd 30/1/75. Sqn Ldr 1/7/87. Retd ENG 29/7/90.
HURST R.W. Born 13/7/13. Commd 19/9/40. Gp Capt 1/1/63. Retd SEC 15/7/65.
HURST W. MBE. Born 28/6/21. Commd 2/9/44. Flt Lt 2/3/49. Retd SEC 29/6/71.
HURST W.E.B. CEng MRAeS MCMI. Born 1/6/18. Commd 7/1/43. Wg Cdr 1/7/66. Retd ENG 1/6/76.
HURST W.J. AFC. Born 26/3/21. Commd 12/7/41. Sqn Ldr 1/7/51. Retd GD 31/8/61.
HURWORTH P.W.J. Born 26/5/31. Commd 28/7/67. Flt Lt 28/7/69. Retd SY 1/4/77.
HUSBAND A.J. CEng MIEE. Born 26/4/38. Commd 12/9/61. Sqn Ldr 1/1/80. Retd ENG 30/4/92.
HUSBAND G.S. BA. Born 16/2/44. Commd 30/5/69. Flt Lt 7/1/72. Retd ENG 16/9/82.
HUSBAND R.E. MBE. Born 14/4/41. Commd 11/5/78. Sqn Ldr 1/1/88. Retd SUP 14/4/96.
HUSH W. BSc. Born 19/4/50. Commd 5/1/70. Wg Cdr 1/7/93. Retd GD 25/7/03.
HUSHER R.P. Born 24/5/44. Commd 24/4/70. Flt Lt 24/4/72. Retd GD 24/5/82.
HUSKISSON N.D. BSc. Born 12/4/65. Commd 28/8/83. Flt Lt 15/1/89. Retd GD 15/7/98.
HUSSEY G.T. Born 11/8/34. Commd 16/9/53. Flt Lt 16/3/59. Retd GD 1/11/61.
HUSSEY K. Born 24/10/52. Commd 2/11/88. Flt Lt 2/11/92. Retd ADMIN 1/12/95.
HUSSEY R.J.C. BSc. Born 6/2/58. Commd 21/10/79. Sqn Ldr 1/1/90. Retd ENG 6/2/96.
HUSTON J.T. BSc CEng MIEE MCMI. Born 6/8/38. Commd 18/7/61. Sqn Ldr 1/7/70. Retd ENG 18/7/77.
HUSTWAYTE W.R. Born 21/3/33. Commd 25/10/51. Flt Lt 22/5/57. Retd GD 21/3/91.
HUSTWITH R.H.C. OBE BA. Born 8/10/22. Commd 2/4/43. Wg Cdr 1/1/66. Retd GD 2/7/68.
HUTCHESON R.J. BSc. Born 16/7/34. Commd 16/4/59. Sqn Ldr 1/7/73. Retd GD 16/7/91.
HUTCHINGS J. Born 11/2/48. Commd 17/3/67. Wg Cdr 1/1/88. Retd SUP 11/2/92.
HUTCHINGS P.J.P. Born 1/5/38. Commd 8/7/65. Gp Capt 1/1/87. Retd GD(G) 1/5/93.
HUTCHINGS R.G. BSc. Born 13/4/51. Commd 13/9/70. Sqn Ldr 1/1/83. Retd ADMIN 13/4/89.
HUTCHINGS R.J. Born 18/4/30. Commd 27/8/52. Gp Capt 1/7/76. Retd GD 18/4/85.
HUTCHINS B.R.J. Born 18/8/50. Commd 19/2/76. Sqn Ldr 1/1/93. Retd GD 14/3/96.

HUTCHINS G.I. Born 20/12/62. Commd 12/1/92. Flt Lt 3/5/91. Retd GD 30/3/01.
HUTCHINS P. OBE. Born 5/11/25. Commd 13/6/46. Gp Capt 1/1/74. Retd RGT 16/1/79.
HUTCHINS P.F.W. CEng MIEE. Born 14/6/42. Commd 15/6/65. Wg Cdr 1/7/88. Retd ENG 14/6/97.
HUTCHINSON A.A. MA. Born 21/1/27. Commd 9/12/48. Wg Cdr 1/7/72. Retd GD 21/1/82.
HUTCHINSON A.C. BSc AIIP CEng MRAeS. Born 11/2/40. Commd 21/10/66. Sqn Ldr 1/7/76. Retd ENG 1/10/86.
HUTCHINSON B. MSc CEng MIMechE MRAeS. Born 18/1/36. Commd 5/1/60. Sqn Ldr 21/7/68. Retd EDN 5/1/76.
HUTCHINSON C.R. Born 6/11/32. Commd 30/7/57. Flt Lt 15/2/63. Retd GD 3/5/73.
HUTCHINSON D.E.K. Born 20/9/60. Commd 7/5/92. Flt Lt 7/5/94. Retd GD 19/11/02.
HUTCHINSON D.W. Born 14/6/21. Commd 19/8/42. Sqn Ldr 1/4/56. Retd ENG 14/6/76.
HUTCHINSON G.C. Born 23/3/25. Commd 8/9/45. Flt Lt 4/12/52. Retd GD 13/11/57.
HUTCHINSON H.W.F. CEng MIMechE MRAeS. Born 2/8/38. Commd 18/7/61. Sqn Ldr 1/7/71. Retd ENG 25/9/76.
HUTCHINSON I. Born 13/11/18. Commd 5/8/41. Sqn Ldr 1/1/55. Retd GD 1/12/57.
HUTCHINSON I.F.C. Born 17/11/38. Commd 15/12/59. Sqn Ldr 1/1/70. Retd GD 30/10/70.
HUTCHINSON J.C. Born 24/12/58. Commd 11/4/82. Flt Lt 11/4/87. Retd ENG 11/4/98.
HUTCHINSON J.D. Born 14/8/34. Commd 14/12/54. Gp Capt 1/1/80. Retd GD 26/11/85.
HUTCHINSON L.H. Born 29/6/23. Commd 9/11/43. Flt Lt 31/7/50. Retd GD(G) 31/3/62.
HUTCHINSON P.T. MSc. Born 7/1/66. Commd 4/6/87. Sqn Ldr 1/7/99. Retd FLY(N) 1/10/04.
HUTCHINSON R.S. MCMI. Born 19/12/29. Commd 17/12/52. Wg Cdr 1/1/72. Retd SUP 3/1/81.
HUTCHINSON T.H. Born 8/5/21. Commd 20/2/43. Sqn Ldr 1/7/54. Retd GD 8/5/70. rtg Wg Cdr
HUTCHINSON W.R. Born 18/6/18. Commd 13/2/45. Flt Lt 13/8/48. Retd GD 12/6/58.
HUTCHISON A.G.L. Born 26/3/31. Commd 29/10/52. Gp Capt 1/1/75. Retd GD 2/12/80.
HUTCHISON A.S. Born 8/11/33. Commd 16/7/52. Flt Lt 29/4/59. Retd GD 8/11/71.
HUTCHISON B. BA. Born 2/7/57. Commd 3/8/86. Sqn Ldr 1/1/94. Retd ADMIN 3/8/02.
HUTCHISON C. BSc. Born 24/1/54. Commd 30/4/78. Plt Offr 30/4/07. Retd GD(G) 20/9/78.
HUTCHISON G.W. MSc BSc CEng DipSoton FCMI MIEE MCIPD. Born 12/8/35. Commd 11/4/58. Wg Cdr 11/10/76.
   Retd ADMIN 1/9/84.
HUTCHISON J.C. Born 24/12/58. Commd 11/4/82. Flt Lt 11/4/87. Retd ENG 11/4/98.
HUTCHISON P.B. MSc BEng. Born 19/3/67. Commd 20/9/87. Sqn Ldr 1/7/03. Retd ENGINEER 1/11/04.
HUTCHISON P.D.J. BSc. Born 8/3/63. Commd 13/9/81. Flt Lt 15/10/85. Retd GD 15/7/97.
HUTCHISON P.J.I. BSc. Born 20/8/51. Commd 24/1/74. Sqn Ldr 1/7/88. Retd PRT 1/7/91.
HUTCHISON R.C. Born 9/9/24. Commd 25/2/44. Flt Lt 7/3/48. Retd GD 29/3/69.
HUTT H.G. Born 1/4/31. Commd 21/10/66. Flt Lt 4/5/72. Retd SUP 21/10/74.
HUTTON A. Born 19/1/21. Commd 5/9/57. Sqn Ldr 1/1/71. Retd GD(G) 19/1/76.
HUTTON J.C. DFC. Born 27/1/21. Commd 16/3/41. Wg Cdr 1/1/56. Retd GD 31/1/64.
HUTTON J.H. CEng MIMechE. Born 21/1/36. Commd 17/10/57. Wg Cdr 1/1/76. Retd ENG 3/7/87.
HUTTON L. Born 13/11/20. Commd 25/8/45. Sqn Ldr 1/10/56. Retd ENG 13/3/64.
HUTTON L.H. Born 27/9/37. Commd 20/6/61. Sqn Ldr 1/7/73. Retd ENG 20/6/77.
HUTTON P.A.J. Born 4/1/46. Commd 3/3/67. Flt Lt 3/9/69. Retd GD 1/8/72.
HUTTON P.C. Born 7/6/24. Commd 30/8/51. Flt Offr 30/8/57. Retd SEC 31/5/62.
HUTTON T.W.A. OBE DFC FCMI. Born 27/4/23. Commd 1/9/45. Gp Capt 1/1/66. Retd GD 11/2/78.
HUXLEY B. CB CBE. Born 14/9/31. Commd 17/12/52. AVM 1/1/85. Retd GD 21/3/87.
HUXLEY-JONES R.J. Born 11/6/59. Commd 30/4/81. Flt Lt 1/8/85. Retd SUP 13/8/85.
HUYTON H.G. Born 6/10/22. Commd 17/3/45. Sqn Ldr 1/1/59. Retd GD 16/10/65.
HUZZARD I.J. Born 17/1/49. Commd 17/7/70. Sqn Ldr 1/7/83. Retd GD 17/1/87.
HYAM C. Born 6/11/34. Commd 23/2/54. Sqn Ldr 1/1/74. Retd GD 1/10/77.
HYATT C.J. MA CEng MRAeS MCMI. Born 25/12/34. Commd 25/9/54. Wg Cdr 1/7/76. Retd ENG 26/9/78.
HYDE C.B. OBE. Born 6/7/41. Commd 23/6/61. Wg Cdr 1/1/85. Retd SY 1/10/95.
HYDE D.C. MSc MSc BSc. Born 30/3/43. Commd 22/8/71. Wg Cdr 1/1/87. Retd ENG 30/9/01.
HYDE J.A. Born 23/4/33. Commd 7/1/57. Sqn Ldr 1/7/79. Retd GD 28/4/91.
HYDE J.H. MCIPD MCMI. Born 27/9/30. Commd 14/7/52. Wg Cdr 1/7/75. Retd GD(G) 2/4/82.
HYDE K. Born 26/7/43. Commd 28/6/79. Flt Lt 28/6/82. Retd GD 26/7/98.
HYDE O.L. CEng MRAeS. Born 22/2/20. Commd 30/8/40. Gp Capt 1/1/72. Retd ENG 22/2/75.
HYDE T.J.G. Born 2/7/35. Commd 9/12/53. Flt Lt 7/3/62. Retd GD(G) 3/11/81.
HYDER C.W. Born 20/4/35. Commd 6/6/57. Sqn Ldr 1/1/73. Retd GD 20/4/93.
HYGATE J.P. Born 3/1/43. Commd 3/11/77. Flt Lt 3/11/79. Retd ENG 3/1/98.
HYLAND A.D. Born 24/11/15. Commd 24/11/41. Sqn Offr 1/1/54. Retd SEC 15/12/64.
HYLAND D.M. Born 29/9/42. Commd 23/5/63. Sqn Ldr 1/1/75. Retd SUP 25/7/81.
HYLAND N.E. Born 27/7/31. Commd 9/4/52. Flt Lt 5/9/57. Retd GD 27/4/71.
HYLTON B.R.V. MBE BSc CEng MIEE. Born 25/2/40. Commd 30/9/59. Wg Cdr 1/7/75. Retd ENG 1/7/78.
HYMAN D.M. Born 25/1/25. Commd 14/1/44. Sqn Ldr 1/1/71. Retd GD(G) 25/1/83.
HYMANS J.A. BSc. Born 4/9/63. Commd 29/9/85. Flt Lt 29/3/87. Retd GD 14/3/96.
HYMANS R.E. Born 9/10/36. Commd 9/2/55. Sqn Ldr 1/1/70. Retd GD 9/10/74. Re-instated 21/11/79. Retd GD 7/9/87.
HYMERS A.W. Born 3/3/33. Commd 6/4/54. Flt Lt 6/10/56. Retd GD 22/7/57.
HYNES G.P. MBE MCIPS. Born 18/1/36. Commd 22/7/66. Sqn Ldr 1/7/74. Retd SUP 18/1/86.
HYNES V.S. Born 6/8/13. Commd 22/9/41. Flt Offr 1/9/45. Retd SEC 27/6/60.
HYSON P.G. FCMI. Born 5/12/23. Commd 6/1/46. Gp Capt 1/7/75. Retd GD 15/3/78.

I

IBBETSON B. Born 13/7/34. Commd 17/12/64. Flt Lt 10/2/67. Retd SUP 17/12/72.
IBBETSON H.E. Born 18/1/36. Commd 3/10/69. Sqn Ldr 3/10/77. Retd ADMIN 1/12/87.
IBBOTT R.I. Born 7/2/47. Commd 4/12/64. Flt Lt 4/6/70. Retd GD 7/2/85.
IBISON G.B. Born 15/1/29. Commd 19/6/52. Flt Lt 19/3/56. Retd GD 28/6/68.
IDDENDEN P. Born 29/4/47. Commd 24/3/83. Sqn Ldr 1/1/95. Retd ENG 29/4/02.
IDDON B.R. Born 19/3/56. Commd 20/7/78. Flt Lt 11/1/82. Retd GD 19/3/93.
IDE J.M. Born 5/7/31. Commd 4/1/60. Flt Lt 4/1/60. Retd GD 5/7/86.
IFOULD K.W. CBE AFC FRAeS MIL. Born 14/1/46. Commd 5/2/65. Gp Capt 1/7/94. Retd GD 14/1/01.
IGNATOWSKI K. AFC DFM. Born 28/11/19. Commd 24/5/49. Sqn Ldr 1/7/71. Retd GD 28/11/74.
IGOE C.P. Born 15/10/52. Commd 13/1/72. Air Cdre 1/7/01. Retd GD 15/7/03.
IKIN D.R. MCMI. Born 5/4/32. Commd 23/7/52. Sqn Ldr 1/1/70. Retd GD 19/5/90.
ILBERT J.C. Born 24/11/43. Commd 17/7/64. Flt Lt 6/10/71. Retd GD 22/11/75.
ILCHESTER The Earl of, CEng FINucE FCMI MRAeS. Born 1/4/20. Commd 28/3/46. Wg Cdr 1/7/66. Retd ENG 27/3/76.
    rtg Gp Capt
ILES M.G. Born 11/8/41. Commd 22/5/64. Flt Lt 22/11/69. Retd GD 12/3/80.
ILETT R.P. Born 20/2/60. Commd 28/6/79. Sqn Ldr 1/1/91. Retd GD 31/7/98.
ILEY C. Born 11/11/28. Commd 11/3/65. Flt Lt 11/3/68. Retd GD 31/5/75.
ILEY L.A. Born 6/10/44. Commd 4/6/64. Flt Lt 29/8/70. Retd GD(G) 12/4/75.
ILIFFE C.R. Born 11/5/15. Commd 2/1/39. Wg Cdr 1/7/51. Retd SUP 27/2/59.
ILLINGWORTH P.F. Born 29/4/17. Commd 21/12/36. Sqn Ldr 1/8/47. Retd GD 16/4/58.
ILLSLEY C.W. Born 30/5/43. Commd 30/8/66. Wg Cdr 1/7/90. Retd GD 10/12/98.
ILSLEY D.J. Born 23/10/31. Commd 28/7/53. Sqn Ldr 1/1/67. Retd GD 1/1/70.
ILSLEY J.M. BSc. Born 27/11/25. Commd 12/3/49. Flt Lt 19/11/53. Retd GD 20/8/60.
IMBER H.Mack. BEng. Born 1/3/66. Commd 25/9/88. Flt Lt 25/3/90. Retd GD 14/9/96.
IMPEY A.C. FCIPS. Born 6/9/36. Commd 3/5/56. A Cdre 1/1/85. Retd SUP 23/3/93.
IMS M.K. Born 28/3/61. Commd 1/7/82. Flt Lt 1/1/88. Retd GD 28/6/99.
INCE E.K.P. DFC. Born 3/1/16. Commd 3/1/41. Sqn Ldr 1/7/51. Retd RGT 1/7/54.
INCE J.B. Born 1/7/41. Commd 15/9/67. Flt Lt 12/11/69. Retd GD 1/7/79.
INCE J.G. Born 1/2/29. Commd 14/4/49. Sqn Ldr 1/7/64. Retd GD 3/2/72.
INCE-JONES H. Born 5/11/32. Commd 7/7/69. Flt Lt 7/7/69. Retd GD(G) 7/7/85.
INCH J.D.R. Born 4/8/49. Commd 2/2/68. Flt Lt 18/7/74. Retd SEC 4/2/78.
INCLEDON-WEBBER G. Born 19/2/30. Commd 4/7/51. Flt Lt 3/11/56. Retd GD 19/8/68.
INGALLS R.D. Born 8/8/24. Commd 1/11/56. Sqn Ldr 1/7/71. Retd GD 8/8/79.
INGAMELLS J.R. Born 13/11/38. Commd 22/2/63. Wg Cdr 1/1/81. Retd GD 17/5/89.
INGELBRECHT A.C. Born 13/11/59. Commd 20/9/79. Flt Lt 20/3/85. Retd GD 14/9/96.
INGHAM B.H. Born 30/3/37. Commd 26/5/67. Sqn Ldr 1/1/81. Retd ENG 30/3/92.
INGHAM G.R. Born 13/3/40. Commd 1/4/65. Sqn Ldr 1/1/85. Retd ADMIN 13/3/95.
INGHAM J.E. Born 7/1/40. Commd 14/8/70. Flt Lt 14/8/72. Retd GD(G) 30/3/77. Re-instated 24/8/80. Flt Lt 4/11/75.
    Retd GD(G) 1/11/92.
INGHAM R.A. AFC BEng. Born 14/2/51. Commd 19/11/72. Sqn Ldr 1/7/84. Retd GD 14/1/96.
INGLE C.M. Born 28/8/46. Commd 2/12/66. Flt Lt 2/6/72. Retd GD 26/8/77.
INGLE M.W. CEng MRAeS. Born 27/9/36. Commd 27/3/58. Sqn Ldr 1/7/68. Retd ENG 27/9/74.
INGLE N.J.W. MBE . Born 10/6/66. Commd 11/9/86. Sqn Ldr 1/1/02. Retd FLY(P) 1/1/05.
INGLIS M.J. Born 27/1/65. Commd 19/7/87. Flt Lt 19/7/93. Retd ADMIN 14/9/96.
INGOE P. Born 13/6/46. Commd 2/8/68. Sqn Ldr 1/1/84. Retd GD 13/6/90.
INGOLD S.L. Born 21/12/32. Commd 24/4/70. Flt Lt 4/5/72. Retd SEC 24/4/78.
INGRAM J. BSc CEng MIMechE. Born 25/2/35. Commd 31/10/71. Sqn Ldr 31/10/71. Retd ENG 25/8/93.
INGRAM J.A. DFC. Born 19/7/13. Commd 24/8/36. Sqn Ldr 1/8/47. Retd GD 19/10/56.
INGRAM J.R. The Rev. Born 20/3/24. Commd 14/12/48. Retd Wg Cdr 26/4/77.
INGRAM J.W. Born 3/9/40. Commd 6/7/62. Sqn Ldr 1/7/87. Retd GD 3/9/95.
INGRAM M. The Rev. Born 27/5/28. Commd 6/1/60. Retd Wg Cdr 6/1/76.
INGWELL S.M. BSc CEng MIEE. Born 14/6/45. Commd 20/10/71. Sqn Ldr 1/1/79. Retd ENG 20/10/87.
INIONS E.T. Born 17/5/22. Commd 14/8/45. Flt Lt 1/7/52. Retd PRT 26/3/62.
INNES B.M.C. Born 10/8/48. Commd 8/3/69. Flt Lt 14/3/76. Retd GD(G) 10/8/86.
INNES C.R. Born 31/8/12. Commd 7/8/49. Flt Lt 7/8/49. Retd SUP 30/12/57.
INNES D.S. Born 10/3/34. Commd 28/7/55. Flt Lt 6/3/62. Retd GD 30/11/68.
INNES G. CBE FCMI. Born 26/11/23. Commd 31/3/45. A Cdre 1/7/76. Retd SY 1/7/78.
INNES G.A.R. Born 18/10/47. Commd 26/5/67. Sqn Ldr 1/1/81. Retd GD(G) 18/6/91.
INNES P.E. MA BSc. Born 18/1/28. Commd 24/9/52. Sqn Ldr 24/3/63. Retd EDN 24/9/68.
INNES R.R. OBE FCMI CDipAF. Born 6/12/52. Commd 2/2/84. Gp Capt 1/1/01. Retd GD 3/5/05.
INNES R.T.A. Born 29/9/28. Commd 30/1/52. Flt Lt 29/5/57. Retd GD 28/11/69.

INNES W.J.A. MA. Born 11/10/34. Commd 28/7/54. Sqn Ldr 1/7/65. Retd GD 11/10/72.
INNES-SMITH N.A. OBE. Born 7/6/30. Commd 12/12/51. Wg Cdr 1/1/68. Retd GD 7/6/88.
INVERARITY A.D. BA. Born 24/11/44. Commd 6/10/69. Flt Lt 6/1/71. Retd GD 22/4/94.
INVERARITY G.A. DFC. Born 23/9/19. Commd 28/8/43. Sqn Ldr 1/7/69. Retd GD(G) 16/7/72.
IONS G. Born 27/5/37. Commd 30/7/64. Sqn Ldr 1/7/71. Retd SUP 30/9/82.
IREDALE R.D. Born 27/5/47. Commd 2/4/65. Gp Capt 1/1/94. Retd GD 27/5/01.
IREDALE T.P. Born 7/3/43. Commd 9/2/66. Flt Lt 29/4/70. Retd SUP 7/7/75.
IRELAND B.J. Born 24/4/49. Commd 4/5/72. Flt Lt 4/11/77. Retd GD 31/5/01.
IRELAND D.S.J. Born 3/7/21. Commd 23/9/44. Flt Lt 27/5/54. Retd GD 31/7/76.
IRELAND N.C.V. Born 22/8/39. Commd 13/12/60. Flt Lt 7/8/64. Retd GD 22/8/77. Re-instated 2/8/91. Flt Lt 2/8/81.
     Retd ENG 22/8/94.
IRELAND W.S. OBE. Born 16/7/27. Commd 13/2/52. Wg Cdr 1/7/72. Retd GD 20/9/80.
IRISH R.G.V. FCMI MCIPS. Born 24/5/33. Commd 27/2/52. Wg Cdr 1/1/77. Retd SUP 1/12/87.
IRONS A.J. Born 1/3/61. Commd 15/10/81. APO 15/10/81. Retd GD 10/4/83.
IRONSIDE H.H.A. Born 31/8/15. Commd 16/4/35. Flt Lt 1/3/45. Retd GD(G) 23/12/45. Re-employed 24/12/49.
     Sqn Ldr 1/1/52. Retd 31/8/65. rtg Wg Cdr
IRONSIDE J.J.N.A. Born 26/3/42. Commd 6/4/62. Flt Lt 6/10/67. Retd GD 26/3/80.
IRVIN J.H. OBE. Born 30/5/15. Commd 21/10/35. Wg Cdr 1/7/47. Retd GD 20/6/60. rtg Gp Capt
IRVINE H.R. Born 17/3/25. Commd 11/2/57. Flt Lt 11/2/57. Retd ADMIN 7/4/83.
IRVINE K.F. MCMI. Born 20/4/29. Commd 7/9/61. Flt Lt 7/9/66. Retd ENG 31/5/74.
IRVINE M.C.G. MB BS. Born 28/6/60. Commd 25/6/89. Sqn Ldr 8/6/91. Retd MED 14/3/96.
IRVINE T.G. BSc. Born 3/7/59. Commd 29/8/77. Flt Lt 15/9/83. Retd GD 14/9/00.
IRVINE W.G. Born 8/7/31. Commd 28/9/51. Flt Lt 28/3/56. Retd GD 8/7/69.
IRVINE-BROWN M. Born 4/5/49. Commd 9/12/71. Fg Offr 9/6/74. Retd GD(G) 1/11/75.
IRVING H.J. Born 16/7/25. Commd 9/6/44. Wg Cdr 1/1/72. Retd GD 23/8/75.
IRVING J. Born 24/3/33. Commd 23/8/51. Flt Lt 3/12/57. Retd GD 10/10/75.
IRVING J.N.B. MBE PhD BSc CEng FRAeS. Born 31/5/30. Commd 11/11/56. Gp Capt 1/7/73. Retd ENG 3/5/79.
IRVING N.R. AFC. Born 19/2/47. Commd 23/3/67. A Cdre 1/1/95. Retd GD 14/3/96.
IRWIN A.F. BSc. Born 5/12/50. Commd 15/9/69. Sqn Ldr 1/1/83. Retd GD 5/12/88.
IRWIN G.S. Born 10/2/41. Commd 1/4/84. Wg Cdr 1/1/94. Retd MED(SEC) 4/4/96.
IRWIN R.H. Born 29/5/25. Commd 24/9/64. Fg Offr 24/9/64. Retd SUP 20/4/70.
IRWIN S.R.C. BA IEng MISM AMRAeS. Born 16/2/48. Commd 2/8/90. Flt Lt 2/8/92. Retd ADMIN 14/3/97.
ISAACSON A. Born 5/6/23. Commd 14/7/51. Sqn Ldr 1/5/65. Retd EDN 21/9/73.
ISABEL J.R. Born 12/12/45. Commd 23/9/66. Plt Offr 23/9/67. Retd GD 12/12/68.
ISHAM D.C. CEng MCMI MIEE. Born 26/6/26. Commd 26/9/57. Wg Cdr 1/1/71. Retd ENG 15/7/77.
ISHAM L.J. Born 4/3/20. Commd 22/9/55. Sqn Ldr 1/7/67. Retd ENG 4/3/75.
ISHERWOOD P.B. Born 14/7/37. Commd 4/1/56. Sqn Ldr 1/1/70. Retd GD 31/5/75.
ISHERWOOD R. Born 1/11/22. Commd 14/3/42. Sqn Ldr 1/9/65. Retd GD 29/11/77.
IVELAW P.I. BSc CEng MIMechE MIEE MRAeS. Born 21/8/20. Commd 1/4/42. Sqn Ldr 1/4/56. Retd ENG 31/10/64.
IVES P.F. BSc. Born 15/6/31. Commd 7/9/56. Sqn Ldr 7/3/66. Retd EDN 15/6/73.
IVES R.C. Born 10/2/40. Commd 15/6/61. Flt Lt 6/8/68. Retd GD(G) 24/2/87.
IVES W.J. CBE MCMI. Born 8/11/21. Commd 11/11/42. Gp Capt 1/1/71. Retd GD 8/11/76.
IVESON R.D. AFC. Born 18/8/47. Commd 2/6/67. Gp Capt 1/1/94. Retd GD 19/8/99.
IVESON T.C. DFC. Born 11/9/19. Commd 1/5/42. Flt Lt 11/4/48. Retd GD 12/7/49.
IWACHOW K.J.W. Born 15/6/21. Commd 25/5/50. Flt Lt 11/11/54. Retd GD 15/6/64.
IZATT G.N. AIB. Born 26/1/47. Commd 16/8/68. Flt Lt 16/2/74. Retd GD 26/1/02.
IZZARD J. OBE CEng FIMechE. Born 18/4/45. Commd 14/4/69. Wg Cdr 1/1/85. Retd ENG 18/4/00.
IZZARD J. Born 21/8/13. Commd 24/5/45. Fg Offr 24/11/45. Retd SEC 17/5/47. rtg Flt Lt
IZZARD P.W. MBE. Born 10/11/42. Commd 4/10/63. Wg Cdr 1/1/94. Retd GD 10/11/97.

J

JACEWICZ J. DFM. Born 24/4/20. Commd 1/9/48. Sqn Ldr 1/1/57. Retd GD 24/4/69.
JACK D.A. Born 13/7/42. Commd 5/9/69. Wg Cdr 1/7/87. Retd SUP 2/4/97.
JACK J. MBE. Born 15/10/33. Commd 24/2/67. Sqn Ldr 1/7/74. Retd SY 1/7/77.
JACK J.M.A. ACIS. Born 28/1/46. Commd 1/4/65. Sqn Ldr 1/7/80. Retd ADMIN 28/1/90.
JACKLIN D. Born 7/5/42. Commd 29/4/71. Sqn Ldr 29/10/77. Retd ADMIN 1/10/80.
JACKMAN L.C. Born 11/3/47. Commd 29/4/71. Sqn Ldr 1/1/92. Retd GD 31/3/94.
JACKMAN S.M. Born 20/9/59. Commd 27/8/87. Sqn Ldr 1/1/97. Retd ADMIN 1/8/01.
JACKSON A. DPhysEd. Born 11/9/41. Commd 7/8/67. Sqn Ldr 1/7/78. Retd ADMIN 7/8/83.
JACKSON A.D. CBE BSc CEng FIEE AInstP. Born 16/10/15. Commd 25/4/39. A Cdre 1/1/63. Retd ENG 17/10/70.
JACKSON A.E. Born 30/9/61. Commd 31/1/80. Sqn Ldr 1/1/94. Retd GD 1/5/95.
JACKSON A.F. OBE. Born 22/7/34. Commd 25/9/59. Gp Capt 1/7/86. Retd ADMIN 22/7/94.
JACKSON A.I. Born 2/7/45. Commd 28/2/64. Flt Lt 31/8/69. Retd GD 31/8/94.
JACKSON C. Born 15/11/39. Commd 2/3/61. Flt Lt 19/3/67. Retd GD 3/10/70.
JACKSON C. Born 5/2/43. Commd 21/5/65. Flt Lt 4/5/72. Retd GD 5/2/84.
JACKSON C.S. MBE FCMI MInstPS. Born 11/3/26. Commd 16/1/47. Gp Capt 1/7/75. Retd SUP 11/3/81.
JACKSON D. Born 24/10/49. Commd 15/8/85. Flt Lt 15/8/89. Retd ENG 1/8/01.
JACKSON D.E. Born 23/11/31. Commd 23/4/52. Flt Lt 25/9/57. Retd GD 23/11/69.
JACKSON D.H. BSc. Born 3/11/42. Commd 6/8/63. Wg Cdr 1/1/94. Retd GD 3/11/97.
JACKSON D.L. Born 30/4/29. Commd 18/6/52. Flt Lt 13/11/57. Retd GD 18/5/84.
JACKSON D.L. Born 15/3/49. Commd 11/4/85. Sqn Ldr 1/7/94. Retd ENG 4/12/96.
JACKSON D.S. Born 15/12/35. Commd 30/7/62. Flt Lt 30/7/62. Retd GD 15/12/93.
JACKSON D.V. MCMI. Born 21/5/30. Commd 17/12/52. Sqn Ldr 1/1/63. Retd SUP 21/5/68.
JACKSON E.D. MCMI. Born 18/12/22. Commd 22/9/49. Wg Cdr 1/1/66. Retd ENG 7/8/76.
JACKSON G.W. DFC. Born 9/10/20. Commd 16/4/43. Flt Lt 16/4/45. Retd GD(G) 9/10/75.
JACKSON H.M. Born 1/7/13. Commd 7/9/42. Sqn Ldr 1/7/55. Retd GD(G) 1/7/63.
JACKSON I.A. DFC. Born 21/1/14. Commd 4/4/43. Flt Lt 4/1/51. Retd SEC 16/2/63.
JACKSON I.R. Born 14/11/44. Commd 23/1/64. Gp Capt 1/7/87. Retd PRT 24/8/90.
JACKSON J. Born 24/8/46. Commd 28/8/75. Sqn Ldr 1/1/84. Retd ENG 1/1/87.
JACKSON J.A. Born 7/12/65. Commd 11/4/85. Flt Lt 11/10/90. Retd GD 7/12/02.
JACKSON J.D. BA. Born 5/7/40. Commd 17/7/64. Sqn Ldr 3/7/74. Retd ADMIN 5/7/95.
JACKSON J.D. BSc DUS. Born 15/12/34. Commd 25/9/54. Flt Lt 15/4/61. Retd ENG 27/7/68.
JACKSON J.G. BA. Born 8/5/39. Commd 15/6/61. Sqn Ldr 1/1/73. Retd SUP 1/7/79.
JACKSON J.J. Born 6/7/30. Commd 13/9/51. Flt Lt 13/4/60. Retd GD 2/9/83.
JACKSON J.K. MBE MHCIMA. Born 13/2/28. Commd 22/9/49. Gp Capt 1/7/73. Retd CAT 11/3/75.
JACKSON J.M. Born 4/5/41. Commd 28/4/67. Flt Lt 28/10/72. Retd GD 17/1/83.
JACKSON J.R. AFC. Born 19/10/29. Commd 11/9/52. Wg Cdr 1/1/78. Retd GD 19/10/84.
JACKSON J.W. Born 20/2/40. Commd 27/6/59. Flt Lt 27/12/64. Retd GD 29/10/90.
JACKSON K. Born 12/8/35. Commd 15/10/81. Flt Lt 15/10/86. Retd ENG 12/8/93.
JACKSON K.F. Born 4/10/30. Commd 1/7/53. Sqn Ldr 1/7/61. Retd GD 30/12/68.
JACKSON K.R. MBE AFC. Born 5/9/23. Commd 12/4/51. Sqn Ldr 1/1/74. Retd GD 5/9/83.
JACKSON L.J. Born 3/4/31. Commd 2/6/67. Flt Lt 4/5/72. Retd PE 24/2/75.
JACKSON M.A. Born 24/12/26. Commd 27/2/70. Sqn Ldr 1/7/81. Retd ENG 25/5/88.
JACKSON M.L. Born 29/6/71. Commd 29/3/90. Fg Offr 29/3/92. Retd GD 25/5/93.
JACKSON M.L. OBE MA FCIPD. Born 29/3/46. Commd 29/7/65. A Cdre 1/1/92. Retd ADMIN 14/3/97.
JACKSON M.R. Born 14/4/48. Commd 16/12/66. Sqn Ldr 1/7/84. Retd OPS SPT 2/7/01.
JACKSON M.R. CB. Born 28/12/41. Commd 17/12/63. AVM 1/7/96. Retd GD 1/7/98.
JACKSON N. CBE CEng FRAeS FIMechE. Born 16/11/35. Commd 27/9/57. A Cdre 1/1/79. Retd ENG 2/1/81.
JACKSON R. Born 4/7/15. Commd 17/4/47. Flt Lt 17/10/51. Retd SEC 12/5/56.
JACKSON Sir Ralph KBE CB FRCP(Edin) FRCP(Lond) MRCS. Born 22/6/14. Commd 16/5/36. AVM 1/9/69. Retd MED 30/9/75.
JACKSON R.A. Born 12/2/33. Commd 5/4/55. Sqn Ldr 1/7/65. Retd GD 12/2/91.
JACKSON R.A. Born 1/5/52. Commd 29/6/72. Sqn Ldr 1/1/88. Retd GD 1/1/90.
JACKSON R.K. Born 4/4/44. Commd 15/7/66. Sqn Ldr 1/1/82. Retd GD 1/6/89.
JACKSON R.M. Born 16/11/31. Commd 11/4/63. Flt Lt 11/4/69. Retd SEC 1/1/72.
JACKSON S. MBE MCMI. Born 14/7/21. Commd 2/7/44. Wg Cdr 1/1/70. Retd SUP 30/12/75.
JACKSON T.A. MVO AFC. Born 30/10/22. Commd 23/7/43. Sqn Ldr 1/9/65. Retd GD 30/10/77.
JACKSON T.H. Born 24/1/23. Commd 23/9/43. Wg Cdr 1/1/70. Retd ENG 24/1/78.
JACKSON T.W. Born 28/10/42. Commd 25/6/65. Flt Lt 4/10/68. Retd GD 28/10/80.
JACKSON V.L. DFC. Born 11/4/22. Commd 2/4/43. Flt Lt 2/10/46. Retd GD(G) 14/10/64.
JACKSON W.S. Born 6/8/22. Commd 30/4/43. Wg Cdr 1/1/65. Retd ADMIN 25/3/77.
JACOBS G.H. Born 1/1/39. Commd 2/2/68. Sqn Ldr 1/7/78. Retd SY(RGT) 1/10/88.

JACOBS R. Born 23/7/43. Commd 6/9/63. Sqn Ldr 1/7/85. Retd GD 23/7/98.
JACOBS V.K. Born 18/9/18. Commd 1/9/45. Sqn Ldr 1/1/49. Retd GD 15/12/57.
JACOBS W. Born 3/7/20. Commd 28/2/47. Sqn Ldr 1/7/66. Retd SUP 15/6/73.
JACOBS W.F. Born 26/4/30. Commd 13/12/50. Sqn Ldr 1/7/60. Retd GD 26/4/68.
JACOTINE A.E.D. Born 19/12/32. Commd 2/1/70. Flt Lt 2/1/73. Retd GD 3/4/85.
JACQUES B. Born 15/12/46. Commd 6/5/65. Sqn Ldr 1/1/84. Retd GD(G) 15/12/90.
JAGO P. Born 15/8/55. Commd 5/1/78. Sqn Ldr 1/7/89. Retd OPS SPT 12/9/99.
JAGO W.P. Born 4/8/37. Commd 29/7/58. Sqn Ldr 1/1/68. Retd GD 6/8/74.
JAKEMAN C.M. BM MB BS BMedSci FRCS(Edin). Born 18/10/56. Commd 12/2/80. Wg Cdr 1/8/94.
   Retd MED 12/2/96.
JAMES A.G.T. OBE. Born 8/8/15. Commd 16/3/35. Wg Cdr 1/7/47. Retd GD 28/3/58.
JAMES A.J.S. Born 17/10/37. Commd 13/1/56. Flt Lt 26/2/64. Retd GD 17/10/74.
JAMES A.S.L. BA. Born 20/2/19. Commd 26/10/49. Flt Lt 26/10/49. Retd SEC 7/4/68.
JAMES B. Born 29/11/41. Commd 25/9/80. Sqn Ldr 1/1/89. Retd ENG 1/10/91.
JAMES B.A. MC. Born 17/4/15. Commd 1/5/39. Flt Lt 1/1/43. Retd RGT 11/6/58. rtg Sqn Ldr
JAMES B.E. Born 12/4/31. Commd 2/7/52. Sqn Ldr 1/7/69. Retd GD 11/12/76.
JAMES B.P. BMet CEng MIEE DipEl. Born 8/8/29. Commd 22/11/50. Sqn Ldr 1/1/62. Retd ENG 22/8/67.
JAMES C.P. FCIPS. Born 10/7/31. Commd 27/7/54. A Cdre 1/7/78. Retd SUP 1/10/83.
JAMES D.A.Z. AFC. Born 13/4/44. Commd 17/12/64. Flt Lt 17/6/67. Retd GD 13/5/89.
JAMES D.J. MVO. Born 27/2/33. Commd 4/7/51. Sqn Ldr 1/1/80. Retd GD 27/2/93.
JAMES E.R. Born 11/8/22. Commd 12/5/44. Sqn Ldr 1/1/73. Retd GD 11/8/77.
JAMES E.W. Born 27/4/23. Commd 14/3/57. Flt Lt 14/3/63. Retd GD 29/3/78.
JAMES E.W. Born 20/6/32. Commd 27/8/52. Flt Lt 23/1/58. Retd GD 24/4/92.
JAMES F. Born 27/6/25. Commd 20/12/51. Wg Cdr 1/7/76. Retd PI 27/6/80.
JAMES F.D. Born 7/2/34. Commd 24/9/64. Flt Lt 9/2/68. Retd GD(G) 12/12/73.
JAMES F.R. Born 11/1/25. Commd 17/3/45. Sqn Ldr 1/1/67. Retd GD 15/9/73.
JAMES G.H.J. Born 18/6/29. Commd 22/10/59. Sqn Ldr 1/1/72. Retd SEC 28/9/74.
JAMES G.R. MCMI. Born 4/6/43. Commd 21/12/62. Gp Capt 1/1/88. Retd SUP 30/4/91.
JAMES G.T. BSc. Born 26/11/52. Commd 18/7/72. Sqn Ldr 1/1/86. Retd ENG 26/11/90.
JAMES H.G. AFC* DFM. Born 3/10/21. Commd 12/2/44. Sqn Ldr 1/10/54. Retd GD 31/7/65.
JAMES H.M. Born 17/10/25. Commd 4/5/50. Sqn Ldr 1/7/69. Retd GD 17/10/80.
JAMES I. MHCIMA MRSH. Born 16/7/59. Commd 27/3/83. Flt Lt 27/9/87. Retd ADMIN 27/3/99.
JAMES J.M. Born 22/12/31. Commd 11/3/65. Flt Lt 11/3/71. Retd SEC 13/11/74.
JAMES J.N. Born 6/10/45. Commd 8/7/65. Flt Lt 7/10/07. Retd SY 2/10/85.
JAMES J.R. BA. Born 6/9/41. Commd 22/5/80. Sqn Ldr 1/1/90. Retd ADMIN 1/9/95.
JAMES J.W.G. DFC. Born 3/11/20. Commd 11/2/42. Sqn Ldr 1/7/56. Retd GD 31/3/62.
JAMES M.F.C. OBE MSc BSc CEng MRAeS. Born 20/4/46. Commd 7/1/71. Wg Cdr 1/7/89. Retd ENG 25/8/97.
JAMES M.J. Born 20/8/37. Commd 5/7/73. Flt Lt 5/7/78. Retd ENG 19/8/78. Re-instated 27/8/80. Flt Lt 13/7/80.
   Retd ENG 4/3/88.
JAMES M.K.B. Born 7/6/19. Commd 1/9/45. Sqn Ldr 1/1/59. Retd SEC 3/10/64.
JAMES M.N. FIMLS. Born 14/11/31. Commd 3/10/74. Sqn Ldr 28/12/82. Retd MED(T) 14/11/86.
JAMES N.B.W. The Rev. Born 23/9/39. Commd 13/8/72. Retd Wg Cdr 12/11/93.
JAMES N.G.R. BA. Born 17/6/48. Commd 24/9/72. Gp Capt 1/7/92. Retd ADMIN 4/4/96.
JAMES N.H. MSc BDS BPharm. Born 25/12/36. Commd 23/10/59. A Cdre 1/1/91. Retd DEL 24/10/93.
JAMES N.K. Born 25/3/44. Commd 7/3/71. Flt Lt 7/9/74. Retd ENG 7/3/87.
JAMES P.H.D. Born 29/10/21. Commd 23/7/43. Flt Lt 29/6/50. Retd GD(G) 29/10/65.
JAMES P.W.S. Born 21/3/23. Commd 26/11/43. Flt Lt 26/5/47. Retd GD 27/6/55. rtg Sqn Ldr.
JAMES R. Born 19/4/25. Commd 14/7/45. Sqn Ldr 1/1/60. Retd GD 25/6/76.
JAMES R. BA. Born 21/1/48. Commd 6/10/69. Sqn Ldr 1/7/80. Retd GD 21/1/86.
JAMES R.A.B. CEng MRAeS. Born 28/8/19. Commd 19/8/42. Wg Cdr 1/7/60. Retd ENG 7/2/74.
JAMES R.P. MBE. Born 30/9/22. Commd 14/8/42. Sqn Ldr 1/1/52. Retd GD 30/9/65.
JAMES S.L. BSc. Born 26/11/51. Commd 25/2/73. Flt Lt 15/10/74. Retd GD 17/7/90.
JAMES S.P. Born 28/7/56. Commd 8/11/89. Flt Lt 9/11/91. Retd ENG 30/3/94.
JAMES T.A. Born 12/6/40. Commd 11/5/78. Sqn Ldr 1/1/88. Retd SUP 12/6/95.
JAMES T.A.L. Born 24/2/29. Commd 7/3/52. Flt Lt 17/2/65. Retd EDN 29/8/67.
JAMES T.M. Born 14/1/48. Commd 5/1/78. Flt Lt 5/1/80. Retd GD 1/12/99.
JAMES W.A. Born 19/10/19. Commd 27/5/43. Sqn Ldr 1/7/55. Retd ENG 30/4/74.
JAMES W.B. Born 11/11/37. Commd 2/1/70. Flt Lt 2/1/72. Retd GD 11/11/92.
JAMES W.C. MBE MA. Born 15/2/26. Commd 6/11/47. Wg Cdr 1/1/62. Retd ENG 1/1/65.
JAMES W.D. Born 2/9/33. Commd 4/7/69. Flt Lt 4/7/75. Retd ENG 12/6/84.
JAMES W.D. Born 19/9/46. Commd 16/8/70. Sqn Ldr 16/2/77. Retd ADMIN 11/2/97.
JAMES W.J.M. AFC. Born 2/4/38. Commd 23/12/60. Sqn Ldr 1/7/84. Retd GD 2/10/99.
JAMESON S.V. Born 8/9/44. Commd 4/7/85. Sqn Ldr 1/1/94. Retd ENG 8/9/99.
JAMIESON A.D. MLitt BSc. Born 8/11/40. Commd 7/10/63. Flt Lt 7/1/65. Retd GD 7/10/79.
JAMIESON B.W. BSc. Born 28/7/64. Commd 3/8/86. Flt Lt 3/8/91. Retd ADMIN 3/8/02.
JAMIESON D.W. Born 27/10/13. Commd 2/9/45. Sqn Ldr 1/10/57. Retd SEC 11/1/63.

JAMIESON E.C. MB ChB DAvMed. Born 19/4/43. Commd 25/7/66. Sqn Ldr 2/8/73. Retd MED 31/8/74.
JAMIESON H.C. OBE MRAeS. Born 31/3/30. Commd 28/1/53. Wg Cdr 1/1/69. Retd ENG 1/1/72.
JAMIESON J. Born 6/2/23. Commd 5/5/60. Sqn Ldr 1/7/71. Retd ENG 6/2/76.
JAMIESON J. IEng MIIE. Born 9/4/57. Commd 14/1/88. Sqn Ldr 1/7/99. Retd ENGINEER 14/5/04.
JAMIESON J.G. BSc CEng MRAeS. Born 4/9/45. Commd 26/5/67. Sqn Ldr 1/7/77. Retd ENG 1/10/86.
JAMIESON L.K. Born 21/9/25. Commd 22/10/59. Flt Lt 22/10/65. Retd ADMIN 12/4/76.
JAMIESON M.J. Born 13/9/46. Commd 1/4/66. Flt Lt 8/3/72. Retd GD 13/9/84.
JAMISON D. BA. Born 18/5/36. Commd 25/9/62. Sqn Ldr 18/11/67. Retd EDN 17/9/83.
JANAWAY C.D. Born 22/8/66. Commd 23/4/87. Flt Lt 22/3/91. Retd FLY(P) 23/12/04.
JANE R.D. DPhysEd. Born 11/10/24. Commd 23/8/50. Sqn Ldr 1/7/61. Retd PE 30/5/70.
JANERING B.D. Born 6/2/42. Commd 24/12/67. Flt Lt 11/11/73. Retd GD(G) 6/2/80.
JANES J.E. Born 30/4/21. Commd 3/6/44. Sqn Ldr 1/7/55. Retd ADMIN 30/4/76.
JANES M.F. Born 14/9/30. Commd 25/5/05. Flt Lt 21/10/56. Retd RGT 14/9/68.
JANES P.J. Born 8/4/33. Commd 15/9/60. Flt Lt 1/4/66. Retd SEC 12/11/72.
JANIUREK J.D. Born 16/11/55. Commd 1/11/79. Sqn Ldr 1/1/92. Retd GD 2/7/95.
JANKIEWICZ M. Born 18/1/23. Commd 24/5/48. Flt Lt 7/2/61. Retd GD 21/8/67.
JANNATY Y. BSc. Born 17/7/63. Commd 14/5/97. Flt Lt 26/10/89. Retd FLY(N) 26/4/03.
JAQUARELLO A.R. Born 6/1/39. Commd 24/2/67. Flt Lt 24/2/69. Retd GD 6/1/77.
JAQUES A.F. Born 3/8/28. Commd 30/9/54. Flt Lt 21/10/59. Retd GD 11/2/71.
JAQUES P. BA. Born 7/4/45. Commd 9/8/79. Sqn Ldr 1/7/85. Retd ADMIN 9/8/93.
JAQUES P.S. BA. Born 9/3/47. Commd 11/10/70. Sqn Ldr 1/7/84. Retd GD(G) 11/10/92.
JAQUES S.A. Born 7/3/23. Commd 30/10/45. Flt Lt 23/10/55. Retd SEC 28/3/70.
JARDINE D. Born 4/7/22. Commd 22/3/51. Flt Lt 22/9/54. Retd ENG 13/10/61.
JARDINE J.A. BA. Born 20/9/44. Commd 27/2/75. Flt Lt 27/2/77. Retd GD(G) 27/2/83. Re-entered 30/4/90.
    Flt Lt 30/4/86. Retd OPS SPT 22/5/98.
JARMAIN S.P. Born 27/4/48. Commd 28/11/69. Wg Cdr 1/1/02. Retd GD 1/5/04.
JARMAN B.C. MHCIMA MCMI. Born 14/2/53. Commd 27/3/77. Sqn Ldr 1/1/90. Retd ADMIN 1/10/94.
JARMY J.F.D. DFC. Born 26/4/22. Commd 20/11/42. Sqn Ldr 1/1/53. Retd SUP 26/4/77.
JARRETT F. Born 22/8/22. Commd 12/8/54. Sqn Ldr 1/1/71. Retd GD 1/1/74.
JARRETT R.W.E. Born 26/11/11. Commd 6/4/45. Fg Offr 6/4/45. Retd GD 17/4/46.
JARRON J.C. Born 18/1/48. Commd 2/8/68. Air Cdre 1/1/00. Retd GD 18/1/03.
JARRON T.E.L. Born 21/12/42. Commd 17/12/63. A Cdre 1/1/92. Retd GD 21/4/94.
JARVIS A.J. Born 20/10/32. Commd 27/2/58. Sqn Ldr 1/1/69. Retd SEC 25/12/74.
JARVIS A.S. MBE. Born 3/8/27. Commd 14/8/51. Flt Lt 14/8/57. Retd SEC 18/7/64.
JARVIS D.B. DFC. Born 11/8/21. Commd 25/9/42. Flt Lt 25/9/44. Retd GD 8/5/47.
JARVIS E.A. Born 29/7/17. Commd 1/9/45. Flt Lt 1/9/45. Retd GD(G) 29/7/67.
JARVIS G.H. Born 13/7/26. Commd 10/5/50. Wg Cdr 1/1/70. Retd GD 10/7/76.
JARVIS G.J. Born 12/7/32. Commd 11/2/65. Flt Lt 11/2/71. Retd SUP 16/1/74.
JARVIS J.A. MBE MHSM RMN. Born 13/7/46. Commd 12/10/78. Sqn Ldr 1/1/86. Retd MED(SEC) 1/8/89.
    Re-entered 13/11/89. Wg Cdr 1/7/93. Retd MED SPT 31/8/01.
JARVIS K.W. Born 3/7/42. Commd 30/7/63. Wg Cdr 1/1/81. Retd GD 3/7/86.
JARVIS R.A. CertEd. Born 4/4/48. Commd 1/2/87. Flt Lt 1/2/87. Retd ADMIN (TRG) 4/4/03.
JARVIS R.C. Born 17/2/39. Commd 17/1/69. Flt Lt 17/1/71. Retd GD(G) 30/9/82. Re-instated 8/6/86. Flt Lt 25/12/74.
    Retd GD(G) 4/8/91.
JARVIS R.H. Born 6/6/28. Commd 18/10/62. Flt Lt 18/10/68. Retd SUP 30/7/82.
JARVIS R.H. Born 8/8/37. Commd 14/12/55. Sqn Ldr 1/7/71. Retd GD 24/11/81. Re-entered 13/3/87. Sqn Ldr 18/10/76.
    Retd GD 8/8/98.
JARVIS R.J. OBE. Born 5/1/23. Commd 28/5/43. Gp Capt 1/7/71. Retd GD 23/1/78.
JARVIS R.M. Born 3/1/34. Commd 19/1/66. Sqn Ldr 1/7/83. Retd GD 18/1/95.
JARVIS S.G. Born 19/8/36. Commd 27/6/60. Flt Lt 1/10/67. Retd GD 27/6/76.
JARVIS T. Born 9/7/59. Commd 1/7/82. Flt Lt 1/1/88. Retd GD 1/3/01.
JASINSKI N.Z.R. Born 7/2/50. Commd 25/2/72. Sqn Ldr 1/7/84. Retd OPS SPT(REGT) 3/4/03.
JASPER N.J. Born 28/2/33. Commd 8/11/51. Flt Lt 22/5/57. Retd GD 28/2/71.
JAY J.B. MCMI. Born 23/4/24. Commd 11/4/44. Wg Cdr 1/7/62. Retd GD 15/1/72.
JAY J.M. Born 3/8/33. Commd 8/7/54. Sqn Ldr 1/7/68. Retd GD 3/8/76.
JAY P.A. MSc BSc. Born 16/8/50. Commd 24/3/74. Sqn Ldr 1/7/01. Retd OPS SPT(INT) 8/1/05.
JAY R.H. Born 5/10/29. Commd 16/7/52. Flt Lt 15/4/59. Retd SUP 14/9/68.
JAY W.J. Born 19/7/15. Commd 12/11/42. Flt Lt 12/5/46. Retd ENG 19/10/60.
JAYAKODY-ARACHCHIGE D. MSc BSc(Eng) CEng MIMechE MRAeS. Born 10/12/45. Commd 2/8/68. Sqn Ldr 1/1/81.
    Retd ENG 1/10/87. Re-entered 15/2/88. Sqn Ldr 18/5/81. Retd ENG 14/9/96.
JEAPES J.M. Born 14/6/33. Commd 4/2/71. Flt Lt 4/2/74. Retd GD 27/12/83.
JEE E.A. Born 28/8/22. Commd 21/9/42. Sqn Ldr 1/7/68. Retd GD 1/5/74.
JEFFERIES D.J. Born 24/12/31. Commd 23/12/61. Sqn Ldr 1/7/74. Retd SUP 24/12/82.
JEFFERIES I.S. Born 15/11/43. Commd 24/6/76. Sqn Ldr 1/1/93. Retd GD 15/5/02.
JEFFERIES R.E. OBE AFC. Born 6/7/23. Commd 25/8/49. Wg Cdr 1/1/67. Retd GD 20/12/75.
JEFFERS J. Born 14/9/22. Commd 6/6/57. Sqn Ldr 1/7/73. Retd ENG 24/3/78.

JEFFERS P. Born 23/1/46. Commd 18/8/67. A Cdre 1/1/96. Retd GD 11/5/02.
JEFFERSON B. Born 1/9/46. Commd 24/4/70. Flt Lt 24/10/75. Retd GD 1/12/85.
JEFFERY E. Born 10/12/47. Commd 28/7/88. Flt Lt 28/7/92. Retd ENG 26/3/96.
JEFFERY E.G.P. Born 13/8/26. Commd 14/6/46. A Cdre 1/1/77. Retd GD 13/8/81.
JEFFERY J.M. Born 2/9/52. Commd 9/3/72. Sqn Ldr 1/7/86. Retd ADMIN 6/1/01.
JEFFERYS A.D. Born 24/8/33. Commd 30/7/52. Flt Lt 27/12/57. Retd GD 24/8/71.
JEFFORD C.G. MBE BA. Born 13/9/40. Commd 16/1/60. Wg Cdr 1/7/87. Retd GD 11/9/91.
JEFFORD C.W. Born 28/4/13. Commd 12/11/42. Sqn Ldr 1/1/54. Retd ENG 28/4/68.
JEFFORD J.E. MBE. Born 16/7/43. Commd 7/6/73. Sqn Ldr 1/1/82. Retd ENG 1/1/85.
JEFFREY E. Born 10/12/47. Commd 28/7/88. Flt Lt 28/7/92. Retd ENG 26/3/96.
JEFFREY J.E. BA MRAeS. Born 31/1/44. Commd 17/12/64. Gp Capt 1/7/97. Retd GD 31/1/99.
JEFFREY T.M. Born 14/8/34. Commd 6/2/54. Sqn Ldr 1/1/69. Retd GD 1/12/86.
JEFFRIES A.H. Born 2/9/17. Commd 7/5/53. Sqn Ldr 1/1/67. Retd ENG 15/4/72.
JEFFS F.R. AFC. Born 7/12/13. Commd 11/5/36. Wg Cdr 1/7/47. Retd GD 31/10/56.
JEFFS G.J. BA. Born 22/1/63. Commd 10/11/85. Sqn Ldr 1/7/99. Retd OPS SPT 1/7/02.
JEFFS W.J. Born 28/9/47. Commd 13/1/82. Flt Lt 13/1/87. Retd GD(G) 18/4/96.
JELL R.A. DFC AFC. Born 28/7/19. Commd 23/4/41. Wg Cdr 1/7/55. Retd GD 28/7/74.
JELLIE J.M.E. Born 1/5/24. Commd 27/8/52. Sqn Ldr 1/1/67. Retd SEC 25/9/73.
JENKING D. MCMI. Born 13/7/43. Commd 5/11/70. Wg Cdr 1/7/84. Retd ADMIN 13/7/87.
JENKINS B. OBE MCMI. Born 9/4/26. Commd 21/5/47. Wg Cdr 1/1/67. Retd GD 9/4/81.
JENKINS B. BEng CEng MRAeS MIEE. Born 15/10/40. Commd 30/9/59. Wg Cdr 1/1/84. Retd ENG 1/1/87.
JENKINS D.T. Born 24/5/20. Commd 25/9/45. Flt Lt 10/11/55. Retd RGT 24/5/65.
JENKINS D.V. Born 28/1/17. Commd 5/6/43. Flt Lt 19/11/53. Retd PI 28/1/72.
JENKINS E.H. CBE CEng FRAeS FCMI. Born 13/2/20. Commd 19/8/42. A Cdre 1/7/71. Retd ENG 15/8/73.
JENKINS G.R. BA. Born 7/10/32. Commd 27/10/55. Sqn Ldr 1/2/64. Retd EDN 27/10/71.
JENKINS H.A. DFC. Born 15/11/20. Commd 21/7/40. Wg Cdr 1/1/52. Retd GD 1/1/66.
JENKINS H.H. Born 19/11/17. Commd 8/2/43. Flt Lt 1/7/52. Retd GD 1/3/60.
JENKINS H.J.F. Born 13/1/50. Commd 11/10/70. Sqn Ldr 1/1/81. Retd ADMIN 13/1/88.
JENKINS I.P. Born 8/2/58. Commd 1/12/77. Wg Cdr 1/7/96. Retd OPS SPT 7/2/02.
JENKINS J. Born 21/12/43. Commd 22/11/84. Flt Lt 1/3/87. Retd GD 31/3/94.
JENKINS J.C. MB ChB DPM MRCPsych. Born 17/9/34. Commd 30/9/62. Sqn Ldr 2/10/64. Retd MED 29/4/72.
JENKINS J.C. Born 15/8/35. Commd 28/1/60. Flt Lt 25/7/66. Retd GD(G) 2/4/75.
JENKINS J.K. DPhysEd. Born 15/6/28. Commd 6/8/52. Sqn Ldr 1/1/69. Retd ADMIN 1/5/80.
JENKINS J.R. Born 20/2/38. Commd 2/10/58. Wg Cdr 1/7/82. Retd GD(G) 4/4/89.
JENKINS L.H. MBE DPhysEd. Born 1/7/31. Commd 4/9/59. Wg Cdr 1/7/79. Retd ADMIN 1/7/86.
JENKINS M. MCMI. Born 4/3/31. Commd 4/7/51. Wg Cdr 1/7/69. Retd GD 2/4/81.
JENKINS M.D. Born 12/1/41. Commd 12/7/63. Flt Lt 12/1/69. Retd GD 26/3/79.
JENKINS M.R. MBE BA IEng MCMI AMRAeS. Born 25/11/46. Commd 22/5/80. Wg Cdr 1/7/01. Retd GD 1/7/04.
JENKINS N. BSc. Born 27/3/51. Commd 15/9/69. Sqn Ldr 1/7/85. Retd ADMIN 9/11/00.
JENKINS P. MSc BSc MIMechE MCMI. Born 20/12/46. Commd 1/9/71. Wg Cdr 1/7/90. Retd ENG 1/9/93.
JENKINS P.G. MA MS. Born 14/8/45. Commd 28/9/64. Sqn Ldr 1/7/76. Retd ENG 12/5/84.
JENKINS P.J. BSc ACGI. Born 24/11/50. Commd 15/9/69. Sqn Ldr 1/1/85. Retd ENG 24/11/88.
JENKINS P.R. CEng MRAeS. Born 24/10/36. Commd 16/4/63. Sqn Ldr 1/1/72. Retd ENG 9/6/78. Re-instated 19/3/80. Sqn Ldr 11/10/73. Retd ENG 24/10/93.
JENKINS R.M. AFC* FCMI. Born 20/12/23. Commd 2/10/47. Gp Capt 1/1/70. Retd GD 20/12/78.
JENKINS S.R. BSc. Born 11/12/57. Commd 28/9/80. Sqn Ldr 1/1/92. Retd GD 14/3/96.
JENKINS T.J. CEng MIEE. Born 2/10/26. Commd 9/5/66. Wg Cdr 1/7/78. Retd ENG 9/5/82.
JENKINS V. BSc. Born 14/1/36. Commd 19/2/63. Sqn Ldr 26/2/70. Retd EDN 19/2/79.
JENKINSON C.R.D. BA. Born 6/6/59. Commd 28/9/80. Flt Lt 14/10/81. Retd GD 31/8/96.
JENKINSON D. BSc MCIPD. Born 6/8/34. Commd 7/9/56. Sqn Ldr 7/3/64. Retd EDN 7/9/72.
JENKINSON J.D. Born 13/8/31. Commd 12/2/53. Wg Cdr 1/1/78. Retd GD(G) 12/8/83.
JENKINSON T.R. MB ChB. Born 11/11/58. Commd 14/8/83. Sqn Ldr 14/8/88. Retd MED 19/2/96.
JENKS M.W. BSc. Born 6/8/64. Commd 7/6/87. Flt Lt 7/12/89. Retd SY(PRT) 19/4/92.
JENKYNS T.J.B. The Rev. BA. Born 18/10/31. Commd 1/6/64. Retd Wg Cdr 31/12/85.
JENNER P.W.I. AFC. Born 1/3/23. Commd 25/5/50. Flt Lt 25/11/53. Retd GD 28/3/61.
JENNER R.M. Born 22/8/53. Commd 6/4/72. Gp Capt 1/1/97. Retd GD 29/4/04.
JENNER Sir Timothy KCB FRAeS. Born 31/12/45. Commd 26/5/67. AM 17/9/98. Retd GD 24/5/01.
JENNER T.R. Born 30/3/38. Commd 12/2/62. Sqn Ldr 1/1/91. Retd GD 12/2/96.
JENNINGS B.A.T. MA CEng MIEE MCMI. Born 19/1/34. Commd 26/9/53. Sqn Ldr 1/1/67. Retd ENG 19/1/72.
JENNINGS B.L. Born 25/2/27. Commd 21/9/46. Flt Lt 19/6/52. Retd RGT 25/2/65.
JENNINGS D.R. Born 13/5/36. Commd 2/5/69. Flt Lt 8/3/72. Retd GD 21/2/76.
JENNINGS E.N. Born 18/6/12. Commd 21/8/41. Sqn Ldr 1/7/54. Retd ENG 18/6/61.
JENNINGS J.K. Born 27/3/33. Commd 27/7/54. Flt Lt 27/1/57. Retd GD 27/3/71.
JENNINGS J.T. DFC FInstAM FCMI. Born 22/2/24. Commd 4/7/46. Gp Capt 1/7/67. Retd GD 22/2/79.
JENNINGS L.M. BA. Born 6/3/52. Commd 14/6/81. Sqn Ldr 1/1/92. Retd SUP 27/11/96.
JENNINGS P.T. Born 22/3/42. Commd 28/10/66. Flt Lt 28/4/72. Retd GD 22/3/02.

JENNINGS R. MBE . Born 15/5/50. Commd 22/9/88. Sqn Ldr 1/1/98. Retd ADMIN (SEC) 15/5/05.
JENNINGS R.T. Born 21/4/33. Commd 9/4/52. Flt Lt 5/9/57. Retd PI 6/4/82.
JENNINGS S.A. DFC. Born 27/7/17. Commd 6/11/42. Flt Lt 6/11/48. Retd GD(G) 27/7/74.
JENNINGS S.G. Born 20/11/44. Commd 5/3/65. Wg Cdr 1/7/84. Retd GD 1/10/89.
JENNISON G.M. Born 27/6/59. Commd 23/9/79. Flt Lt 23/6/83. Retd ADMIN 9/8/89.
JENNISON R.W. BSc. Born 29/7/53. Commd 30/9/73. Flt Lt 15/4/76. Retd GD 3/1/94.
JENSEN F.D. MSc BSc CEng MIEE. Born 21/10/49. Commd 24/9/72. Wg Cdr 1/7/91. Retd ENG 1/10/97.
JENSEN T.A. BSc. Born 31/12/47. Commd 12/5/70. Flt Lt 12/2/72. Retd GD 14/6/74.
JENVEY M.D. Born 20/9/57. Commd 17/5/79. Flt Lt 22/3/83. Retd GD 20/9/95.
JEPSON C.D. MBE . Born 24/8/65. Commd 15/3/84. Sqn Ldr 1/7/01. Retd FLY(P) 31/3/05.
JEPSON H. Born 29/5/25. Commd 8/7/45. Sqn Ldr 1/7/57. Retd GD 28/9/68.
JERMYN P. Born 6/9/20. Commd 8/7/43. Sqn Ldr 1/7/57. Retd GD(G) 4/9/65.
JERRUM E.W. Born 14/3/24. Commd 31/10/66. Flt Lt 31/10/66. Retd GD 1/1/74.
JERVIS D.A. Born 19/10/49. Commd 27/2/70. Flt Lt 27/8/75. Retd GD 31/3/77.
JERVIS N. Born 12/4/23. Commd 2/12/46. Flt Lt 3/8/52. Retd GD 31/8/66.
JERVIS W.L.A. Born 5/10/29. Commd 18/6/52. Flt Lt 7/3/62. Retd GD 27/6/74. rtg Sqn Ldr.
JESSON F. Born 26/9/18. Commd 17/7/43. Wg Cdr 1/1/61. Retd GD(G) 31/7/62.
JESSOP I.J. Born 31/5/12. Commd 27/5/42. Flt Offr 27/11/46. Retd SEC 7/7/67.
JESSUP A.B. Born 10/4/39. Commd 24/11/67. Flt Lt 4/11/70. Retd ENG 17/3/84.
JEVONS P.J. Born 22/5/42. Commd 9/7/60. Wg Cdr 1/1/85. Retd GD 22/5/97.
JEVONS R.C. MBE BSc. Born 22/1/46. Commd 7/5/72. Flt Lt 7/5/74. Retd SUP 1/4/81.
JEW I.T. Born 19/11/41. Commd 21/2/74. Sqn Ldr 1/7/84. Retd PRT 21/11/91.
JEWELL B.D. Born 25/12/41. Commd 8/1/65. Flt Lt 6/10/71. Retd GD 14/9/80.
JEWELL B.R. MSc BSc CEng MRAeS. Born 20/9/29. Commd 1/5/52. Gp Capt 1/1/78. Retd ENG 20/9/79.
JEWELL C.G. Born 23/7/55. Commd 8/10/87. Flt Lt 8/10/89. Retd ENG 8/10/95.
JEWELL P.M. Born 22/9/33. Commd 3/12/54. Sqn Ldr 1/7/85. Retd GD 22/9/91.
JEWISS J.O. Born 18/8/37. Commd 2/4/57. Wg Cdr 1/7/75. Retd GD 24/5/80.
JEWITT R.E.R. Born 12/7/13. Commd 6/11/58. Flt Lt 6/11/64. Retd ENG 13/11/68.
JEWKES P. Born 21/3/44. Commd 18/4/74. Sqn Ldr 1/1/87. Retd ENG 4/8/96.
JEWSBURY S.J. MCMI. Born 20/12/29. Commd 7/4/55. Sqn Ldr 1/1/69. Retd SUP 14/11/81.
JEWSBURY T.A. MCMI. Born 6/5/37. Commd 1/6/72. Sqn Ldr 1/7/79. Retd ADMIN 29/7/88.
JEWSON J.A. Born 10/10/17. Commd 19/3/58. Sqn Ldr 19/3/58. Retd SUP 10/10/72.
JINMAN J.A.V. Born 11/8/32. Commd 28/8/52. Sqn Ldr 1/1/79. Retd GD 11/8/87.
JOBLING K.A. Born 19/10/42. Commd 17/5/63. Flt Lt 17/11/68. Retd GD 2/4/93.
JOBLING P.L. Born 29/10/36. Commd 9/7/55. Flt Lt 1/3/61. Retd GD 29/10/74.
JOCELYN M.A. BSc. Born 12/9/53. Commd 3/9/72. Wg Cdr 1/7/91. Retd GD 12/9/97.
JOHN G.A. BA CEng MIEE MRAeS MCMI. Born 4/2/38. Commd 30/9/58. Wg Cdr 1/7/77. Retd ENG 9/7/89.
JOHN H. The Rev. Born 11/5/28. Commd 12/6/62. Retd Wg Cdr 12/6/78.
JOHN J.L. MBE. Born 27/8/29. Commd 28/11/69. Sqn Ldr 1/7/89. Retd ENG 8/10/92.
JOHN L.O. Born 19/5/31. Commd 14/5/53. Flt Lt 14/5/59. Retd SEC 19/5/69.
JOHN P.D.M. MBE MCIPS MCMI. Born 17/2/45. Commd 8/7/65. Wg Cdr 1/1/85. Retd SUP 17/2/89.
JOHN P.S. BSc. Born 7/7/52. Commd 13/9/70. Flt Lt 15/4/75. Retd GD 7/7/90.
JOHN R.S. BSc CEng MIMechE MRAeS. Born 11/2/63. Commd 2/9/84. Flt Lt 2/3/88. Retd ENG 11/2/01.
JOHNCOCK D.A. Born 18/6/48. Commd 22/9/67. Wg Cdr 1/7/89. Retd ENG 19/6/02.
JOHNCOCK E.D. MBE. Born 15/3/25. Commd 2/7/59. Sqn Ldr 1/7/72. Retd ADMIN 15/3/85.
JOHNS L.T. Born 22/4/36. Commd 17/11/65. Sqn Ldr 1/7/87. Retd ADMIN 22/4/94.
JOHNS R.A. Born 13/7/21. Commd 17/10/41. Flt Lt 17/4/46. Retd SEC 13/7/70.
JOHNSON A. AFC. Born 13/12/18. Commd 14/2/45. Sqn Ldr 1/1/56. Retd GD 13/1/58.
JOHNSON A.A.B. DPhysEd. Born 13/11/36. Commd 11/4/61. Sqn Ldr 1/1/73. Retd PE 26/3/79.
JOHNSON A.F. MSc MB BS MRCGP MRCS LRCP DObstRCOG DAvMed AFOM. Born 15/5/41. Commd 22/4/68.
    A Cdre 1/1/92. Retd MED 15/12/95.
JOHNSON A.K. BSc DPhysEd. Born 14/3/33. Commd 20/9/57. Sqn Ldr 20/3/67. Retd ADMIN 14/3/88.
JOHNSON A.R. Born 4/3/48. Commd 21/1/66. Flt Lt 21/7/71. Retd GD 4/3/86.
JOHNSON A.R.A. BSc. Born 18/12/59. Commd 19/6/83. Flt Lt 19/12/85. Retd GD 25/8/00.
JOHNSON A.T. MB ChB FRAeS MFCM MFOM DAvMed. Born 3/3/31. Commd 11/8/57. AVM 1/1/89.
    Retd MED 11/8/91.
JOHNSON B. BSc. Born 7/1/31. Commd 2/2/56. Sqn Ldr 2/8/65. Retd EDN 21/9/72.
JOHNSON B. PhD MSc BSc MinstP. Born 20/2/41. Commd 23/9/68. Gp Capt 1/7/88. Retd ADMIN 4/4/92.
JOHNSON B.A. Born 4/2/49. Commd 4/7/69. Flt Lt 4/1/75. Retd GD 22/10/94.
JOHNSON B.B. MCMI. Born 23/9/16. Commd 23/1/39. Wg Cdr 1/1/55. Retd SUP 23/10/72.
JOHNSON B.C. OBE. Born 21/3/39. Commd 25/7/60. Gp Capt 1/7/84. Retd GD 21/6/96.
JOHNSON B.D. MCIPS MCMI. Born 9/3/38. Commd 1/4/58. Gp Capt 1/7/87. Retd SUP 1/7/91.
JOHNSON B.H. Born 24/8/37. Commd 23/1/64. Flt Lt 13/4/69. Retd GD(G) 3/12/82.
JOHNSON B.L. Born 10/12/40. Commd 12/12/59. Sqn Ldr 1/1/71. Retd ENG 10/12/78.
JOHNSON B.L. Born 24/8/49. Commd 4/5/72. Flt Lt 4/11/77. Retd GD 17/1/88.
JOHNSON B.M. Born 26/9/16. Commd 5/9/51. Fg Offr 5/3/53. Retd SEC 25/8/54.

JOHNSON B.W. Born 21/6/43. Commd 19/1/64. Wg Cdr 1/1/88. Retd GD 21/6/00.
JOHNSON C. BSc. Born 4/12/49. Commd 14/7/74. Flt Lt 14/4/76. Retd GD 14/7/90.
JOHNSON C.I. OBE CEng MIEE MRAeS. Born 25/2/40. Commd 28/7/60. Gp Capt 1/7/83. Retd ENG 4/6/86.
JOHNSON C.R. OBE AFC MCMI. Born 20/2/21. Commd 3/9/43. Wg Cdr 1/1/61. Retd GD 30/6/73.
JOHNSON D. Born 6/12/34. Commd 22/5/59. Sqn Ldr 3/9/68. Retd ADMIN 31/8/86.
JOHNSON D.A.V. BSc. Born 6/10/31. Commd 29/9/55. Sqn Ldr 1/1/63. Retd GD 7/6/71.
JOHNSON D.B.W. Born 30/12/23. Commd 14/3/45. Flt Lt 29/11/51. Retd GD 25/5/68.
JOHNSON D.L. MCIPD MCMI. Born 6/12/38. Commd 12/9/61. Sqn Ldr 4/3/93. Retd ADMIN 1/4/93.
JOHNSON D.M. Born 13/3/39. Commd 12/4/66. Sqn Ldr 1/7/86. Retd GD 5/4/89.
JOHNSON D.R. BA. Born 16/8/60. Commd 13/2/83. Flt Lt 13/5/83. Retd GD 13/2/91.
JOHNSON D.T. Born 25/11/46. Commd 27/9/73. Sqn Ldr 1/7/84. Retd ENG 1/7/87.
JOHNSON F. Born 7/12/11. Commd 1/7/43. Fg Offr 26/2/44. Retd ASD 4/2/46.
JOHNSON F.A. DFC. Born 6/10/19. Commd 3/2/45. Sqn Ldr 1/7/54. Retd GD 7/11/58.
JOHNSON F.S.R. CB OBE CCMI. Born 4/8/17. Commd 9/4/43. AVM 1/1/71. Retd SUP 1/1/74.
JOHNSON G.L. DFM. Born 25/11/21. Commd 29/11/43. Sqn Ldr 1/4/55. Retd GD 15/9/62.
JOHNSON H.D. DFC. Born 10/6/18. Commd 16/3/42. Sqn Ldr 1/1/52. Retd GD 14/3/58.
JOHNSON H.R. BSc. Born 30/4/58. Commd 2/3/80. Flt Lt 2/12/81. Retd GD 14/3/97.
JOHNSON I.A. Born 21/8/29. Commd 16/8/61. Flt Lt 16/8/61. Retd GD 16/8/69.
JOHNSON J.D. Born 8/1/15. Commd 11/4/45. Flt Lt 4/1/51. Retd SEC 8/1/64.
JOHNSON J.E. CB CBE DSO** DFC*. Born 9/3/15. Commd 10/8/40. AVM 1/1/63. Retd GD 15/3/66.
JOHNSON J.F. Born 10/9/15. Commd 1/12/42. Flt Lt 19/2/45. Retd GD 12/8/47.
JOHNSON J.H. DFC. Born 26/11/20. Commd 9/5/41. Wg Cdr 1/1/56. Retd GD 10/12/57.
JOHNSON J.R. Born 28/7/31. Commd 14/4/53. Wg Cdr 1/1/74. Retd GD 28/7/86.
JOHNSON K. Born 26/3/23. Commd 26/6/44. Wg Cdr 1/7/61. Retd GD 27/9/68.
JOHNSON K.W. DFC. Born 18/9/24. Commd 1/4/45. Sqn Ldr 1/1/59. Retd GD 15/10/67.
JOHNSON L.C. MVO. Born 2/2/61. Commd 15/5/91. Sqn Ldr 1/1/99. Retd OPS SPT(ATC) 28/2/03.
JOHNSON L.F. OBE. Born 9/10/09. Commd 20/6/41. Sqn Ldr 1/1/61. Retd SUP 9/10/64.
JOHNSON M. Born 8/5/55. Commd 2/3/80. Sqn Ldr 1/1/88. Retd ADMIN 14/3/96.
JOHNSON M. Born 13/6/48. Commd 1/7/82. Sqn Ldr 1/1/91. Retd ADMIN 1/7/96.
JOHNSON M. Born 17/10/61. Commd 20/5/82. Sqn Ldr 1/7/94. Retd SUP 17/10/99.
JOHNSON M. MSc BSc(Eng) CEng MRAeS ACGI. Born 16/11/55. Commd 15/9/74. Sqn Ldr 1/1/88.
   Retd ENG 5/4/96.
JOHNSON M.A. Born 14/5/47. Commd 22/11/84. Flt Lt 22/11/88. Retd ADMIN 14/3/96.
JOHNSON M.A. Born 17/5/39. Commd 15/12/59. Flt Lt 15/6/62. Retd GD 11/6/91.
JOHNSON M.C. Born 28/10/47. Commd 13/1/67. Sqn Ldr 1/1/80. Retd GD 28/10/85. Re-entered 23/8/88.
   Sqn Ldr 26/10/82. Retd GD 14/3/97.
JOHNSON M.H. CEng MRAeS. Born 12/4/36. Commd 16/11/61. Sqn Ldr 1/7/71. Retd ENG 26/8/75.
JOHNSON M.K. AFC. Born 16/7/50. Commd 19/8/71. Sqn Ldr 1/7/82. Retd GD 16/7/88.
JOHNSON M.W. Born 12/4/32. Commd 26/3/52. Flt Lt 7/8/57. Retd GD 5/1/68.
JOHNSON M.W. BD MCMI. Born 9/5/48. Commd 2/8/68. Sqn Ldr 1/7/84. Retd ADMIN 1/7/87.
JOHNSON N. BSc. Born 20/5/49. Commd 18/4/71. Flt Lt 15/4/72. Retd GD 2/12/91.
JOHNSON P. Born 26/3/49. Commd 17/12/72. Wg Cdr 1/7/91. Retd ENG 31/10/98.
JOHNSON P.G. OBE BA FRAeS FCMI. Born 8/6/44. Commd 14/6/63. A Cdre 1/7/94. Retd GD 24/8/99.
JOHNSON P.J. Born 6/10/30. Commd 24/9/64. Flt Lt 24/9/69. Retd ENG 7/10/80.
JOHNSON R. Born 10/6/34. Commd 31/12/52. Flt Lt 5/11/58. Retd GD 10/6/72.
JOHNSON R. Born 6/7/37. Commd 6/8/60. Flt Lt 6/2/66. Retd GD 6/7/92.
JOHNSON R.A. BSc CEng MRAeS. Born 19/10/51. Commd 25/9/71. Sqn Ldr 1/7/85. Retd ENG 14/3/97.
JOHNSON R.D. BSc. Born 31/3/49. Commd 3/1/69. Wg Cdr 1/7/86. Retd SUP 1/7/89.
JOHNSON R.H. DL. Born 17/1/24. Commd 29/7/43. Wg Cdr 1/1/61. Retd ENG 1/1/64.
JOHNSON R.H. CEng MRAeS. Born 24/6/45. Commd 19/8/65. Sqn Ldr 1/1/80. Retd ENG 24/6/83.
JOHNSON R.H.O. Born 3/2/44. Commd 24/6/65. A Cdre 1/1/96. Retd SUP 3/2/99.
JOHNSON R.O. Born 2/5/66. Commd 28/9/89. Flt Lt 28/6/96. Retd OPS SPT(REGT) 14/5/05.
JOHNSON R.S. Born 22/2/39. Commd 10/11/06. Flt Lt 1/7/68. Retd GD 3/11/72.
JOHNSON S. BEd. Born 2/9/55. Commd 14/4/85. Sqn Ldr 1/1/96. Retd OPS SPT 14/4/01.
JOHNSON S. Born 19/7/49. Commd 25/2/72. Sqn Ldr 1/7/84. Retd ADMIN 19/7/87.
JOHNSON S.A. Born 14/7/66. Commd 11/4/85. Flt Lt 11/10/90. Retd GD 14/3/96.
JOHNSON S.D. BEM. Born 18/12/19. Commd 20/10/55. Sqn Ldr 1/7/67. Retd ENG 18/7/70.
JOHNSON S.P. DFC BEM. Born 28/2/22. Commd 10/11/43. Sqn Ldr 1/10/54. Retd GD 28/2/71.
JOHNSON S.R. BSc(Econ). Born 12/2/48. Commd 27/4/70. Sqn Ldr 1/1/80. Retd GD 27/4/86.
JOHNSON T.E. DFC. Born 23/6/22. Commd 13/11/43. Sqn Ldr 1/10/54. Retd GD 23/6/71.
JOHNSON W.A. BSc. Born 16/6/43. Commd 17/8/64. Wg Cdr 1/7/87. Retd GD 16/6/98.
JOHNSON W.H. Born 17/2/22. Commd 29/7/45. Sqn Ldr 1/7/70. Retd GD 23/2/72.
JOHNSON W.R. Born 29/3/38. Commd 24/4/64. Flt Lt 24/10/69. Retd GD 7/1/80.
JOHNSTON B. Born 10/2/38. Commd 16/12/58. Flt Lt 6/3/63. Retd GD 1/8/89.
JOHNSTON B.E. BSc. Born 18/12/41. Commd 30/7/63. Gp Capt 1/7/86. Retd GD 1/4/97.
JOHNSTON C.K. Born 10/8/20. Commd 22/12/44. Flt Lt 22/6/49. Retd GD(G) 10/8/70.

JOHNSTON C.W.H. Born 21/5/48. Commd 7/6/68. Sqn Ldr 1/7/87. Retd ADMIN (SEC) 21/5/03.
JOHNSTON D.C. Born 30/8/61. Commd 30/4/81. Sqn Ldr 1/7/96. Retd OPS SPT 8/1/02.
JOHNSTON G. Born 24/4/24. Commd 20/4/50. Sqn Ldr 1/7/69. Retd GD 24/4/84.
JOHNSTON G.A. Born 19/7/47. Commd 1/3/68. Sqn Ldr 1/1/79. Retd ENG 1/8/91.
JOHNSTON G.MacA. Born 6/10/51. Commd 15/2/73. Flt Lt 15/8/79. Retd GD(G) 12/12/81.
JOHNSTON H. Born 18/10/47. Commd 2/6/67. Wg Cdr 1/1/95. Retd GD 31/7/99.
JOHNSTON I.A.B. Born 17/12/50. Commd 30/8/73. Sqn Ldr 1/1/90. Retd ADMIN (SEC) 16/5/05.
JOHNSTON J.A. DPhysEd. Born 13/1/43. Commd 23/2/68. Wg Cdr 1/7/89. Retd ADMIN 14/3/96.
JOHNSTON M.J. Born 7/3/55. Commd 26/9/90. Flt Lt 26/9/94. Retd OPS SPT 1/7/02.
JOHNSTON N.A. BSc. Born 10/1/64. Commd 3/8/86. Flt Lt 3/2/88. Retd GD 3/8/02.
JOHNSTON N.M. Born 10/6/50. Commd 8/8/69. Fg Offr 8/8/71. Retd GD(G) 25/10/72. Re-instated 8/11/74.
  Flt Lt 22/8/77. Retd GD(G) 24/6/89.
JOHNSTON P.J.C. Born 11/2/38. Commd 3/11/77. Wg Cdr 1/7/90. Retd ADMIN 2/4/92.
JOHNSTON R. Born 5/6/31. Commd 19/11/52. Flt Lt 15/4/58. Retd GD 5/6/69.
JOHNSTON R.A. Born 29/9/37. Commd 16/12/58. Sqn Ldr 1/1/72. Retd GD 29/9/95.
JOHNSTON R.C.R. MBE BA CEng MIEE. Born 3/4/42. Commd 15/7/64. Gp Capt 1/1/88. Retd ENG 4/4/93.
JOHNSTON R.C.R. MBE MCMI. Born 6/9/19. Commd 4/6/59. Sqn Ldr 1/7/67. Retd ENG 27/11/71.
JOHNSTON S.B. MCMI. Born 12/8/38. Commd 15/12/59. Sqn Ldr 1/1/68. Retd GD 31/8/79.
JOHNSTON S.J. MBE MA MREC. Born 26/12/56. Commd 11/10/90. Wg Cdr 1/1/01. Retd GD 20/5/05.
JOHNSTON T.A. Born 18/3/38. Commd 25/3/64. Fg Offr 25/3/66. Retd GD 22/6/69.
JOHNSTONE A. Born 31/10/42. Commd 9/8/63. Flt Lt 9/2/69. Retd GD 1/11/79.
JOHNSTONE D.B. Born 11/9/22. Commd 4/8/54. Flt Lt 4/8/59. Retd ENG 11/9/64.
JOHNSTONE D.N. BA MB BCh BAO MRCP MRCPsych DPM. Born 27/11/29. Commd 3/6/50. Gp Capt 3/6/79.
  Retd MED 1/1/89.
JOHNSTONE F.E. MBE. Born 13/12/22. Commd 18/11/66. Flt Lt 18/11/69. Retd ENG 26/2/78.
JOHNSTONE J.C. Born 28/1/32. Commd 3/11/60. Sqn Ldr 1/1/79. Retd GD(G) 2/4/83.
JOINT J.M. BSc CEng MIMechE. Born 1/3/47. Commd 22/9/65. Wg Cdr 1/7/84. Retd ENG 1/7/87.
JOLLEY M.S. Born 1/7/25. Commd 12/3/53. Fg Offr 12/3/55. Retd SEC 1/12/63.
JOLLIE P.McF.O. MRCS LRCP DObstRCOG. Born 28/4/30. Commd 11/11/56. Wg Cdr 30/8/69. Retd MED 11/1/72.
JOLLIFFE F.S.W. Born 27/7/23. Commd 20/3/45. Wg Cdr 1/7/66. Retd GD 1/10/77.
JOLLY D. Born 2/9/28. Commd 1/8/51. Fg Offr 1/8/51. Retd GD 25/3/54.
JOLLY P.D.R. BA FCMI. Born 19/9/45. Commd 3/1/64. Wg Cdr 1/7/85. Retd GD 1/10/94.
JOLLY R.M. CBE CCMI. Born 4/8/20. Commd 7/1/43. A Cdre 1/1/71. Retd SEC 4/8/75.
JONAS C.A.C. BA. Born 27/5/27. Commd 27/7/47. Flt Lt 27/7/50. Retd GD 15/12/53.
JONATHAN P.W. Born 14/12/46. Commd 7/7/67. Flt Lt 7/1/73. Retd GD 22/4/94.
JONES A. Born 19/4/65. Commd 23/5/85. Sqn Ldr 1/7/98. Retd ADMIN 22/6/02.
JONES A. MBE. Born 31/5/50. Commd 3/10/74. Wg Cdr 1/7/92. Retd ADMIN 15/9/00.
JONES A.C. MA. Born 10/11/23. Commd 27/9/50. Sqn Ldr 1/1/65. Retd SUP 31/3/74.
JONES A.C. Born 5/2/30. Commd 23/4/52. Sqn Ldr 1/7/69. Retd ENG 5/2/88.
JONES A.D.G. AFC DipPE. Born 12/4/39. Commd 30/8/66. Wg Cdr 1/7/90. Retd ADMIN 14/7/91.
JONES A.E. MBE. Born 10/6/33. Commd 3/8/53. Sqn Ldr 1/1/74. Retd RGT 10/6/91.
JONES A.E. Born 16/10/48. Commd 27/2/70. Flt Lt 27/2/73. Retd GD 1/3/78.
JONES A.F. Born 18/1/45. Commd 18/8/67. Sqn Ldr 1/1/80. Retd GD 18/1/83.
JONES A.G. Born 24/4/49. Commd 27/1/77. Flt Lt 27/1/79. Retd GD 24/4/99.
JONES A.H. Born 19/8/41. Commd 31/7/62. Flt Lt 31/1/87. Retd GD 10/5/92.
JONES A.J. Born 20/4/58. Commd 8/5/91. Flt Lt 9/5/93. Retd ADMIN 18/9/96.
JONES A.M. BSc. Born 23/6/55. Commd 2/9/73. Flt Lt 15/4/78. Retd GD 13/2/80.
JONES A.P.S. Born 9/7/39. Commd 15/12/59. Flt Lt 21/8/63. Retd GD 28/9/70.
JONES A.S. Born 11/9/61. Commd 15/3/84. Flt Lt 15/9/90. Retd OPS SPT 11/9/99.
JONES A.S. MSc BSc. Born 18/7/62. Commd 16/2/86. Sqn Ldr 1/1/00. Retd ENGINEER 16/2/04.
JONES A.T. Born 21/11/41. Commd 17/7/70. Sqn Ldr 1/7/85. Retd GD 21/4/93.
JONES A.W. BSc. Born 22/5/36. Commd 25/10/57. A Cdre 1/7/85. Retd ENG 25/6/90.
JONES A.W. Born 2/5/44. Commd 10/6/66. Flt Lt 4/5/72. Retd GD 1/11/75.
JONES A.W. BSc MCIPD. Born 28/5/44. Commd 6/1/69. Sqn Ldr 6/3/76. Retd ADMIN 6/1/85.
JONES B.A. BSc. Born 27/3/47. Commd 22/2/71. Wg Cdr 1/1/87. Retd ENG 30/9/99.
JONES B.B. Born 9/2/36. Commd 12/11/57. Wg Cdr 1/1/84. Retd GD(G) 9/2/91.
JONES B.C. Born 4/3/35. Commd 21/11/61. Sqn Ldr 1/7/75. Retd GD(G) 1/7/78.
JONES B.C.E. BSc CEng MRAeS. Born 6/7/28. Commd 11/10/50. Wg Cdr 1/1/67. Retd ENG 13/8/77.
JONES B.C.S. Born 22/7/34. Commd 28/7/55. Wg Cdr 1/7/78. Retd SY(RGT) 10/5/89.
JONES B.D. OBE FHCIMA. Born 7/9/37. Commd 17/11/59. A Cdre 1/1/90. Retd ADMIN 7/9/92.
JONES B.E. Born 15/5/52. Commd 30/4/81. Sqn Ldr 1/7/89. Retd ADMIN 4/1/93.
JONES B.E. Born 14/10/41. Commd 18/8/61. Flt Lt 9/2/68. Retd GD 14/10/79.
JONES B.H. Born 6/2/33. Commd 14/12/54. Sqn Ldr 1/1/67. Retd GD 6/2/93.
JONES B.J. Born 27/8/32. Commd 4/8/53. Flt Lt 5/10/60. Retd GD 27/8/70.
JONES B.L. BA. Born 15/4/33. Commd 26/3/52. Sqn Ldr 1/1/74. Retd SUP 15/4/93.
JONES B.L. BSc. Born 12/9/30. Commd 21/10/66. Flt Lt 21/10/71. Retd GD 15/11/75.

JONES B.R. Born 9/4/40. Commd 1/4/58. Fg Offr 13/8/61. Retd SUP 28/4/65.
JONES B.R.R. Born 6/4/48. Commd 2/8/68. Sqn Ldr 1/1/80. Retd GD 24/11/86.
JONES C.A. BSc. Born 12/10/54. Commd 19/3/78. Flt Lt 19/9/79. Retd ADMIN 14/3/96.
JONES C.B.S. Born 12/2/47. Commd 31/7/83. Flt Lt 31/7/83. Retd ENG 16/1/89.
JONES C.C. Born 14/9/48. Commd 29/11/68. Sqn Ldr 1/7/84. Retd GD 1/7/87.
JONES C.F.J. CEng MIMechE. Born 26/6/38. Commd 17/7/62. Sqn Ldr 1/7/69. Retd ENG 18/10/74.
JONES C.G. IEng MIIE. Born 17/10/47. Commd 11/10/84. Sqn Ldr 1/7/95. Retd ENGINEER 16/4/04.
JONES C.L. BA MCMI. Born 21/10/61. Commd 19/11/87. Wg Cdr 1/7/01. Retd GD 1/5/05.
JONES C.M. Born 9/1/24. Commd 16/10/52. Flt Offr 2/11/61. Retd SEC 19/10/65.
JONES C.V. MHCIMA. Born 19/11/52. Commd 11/9/77. Flt Lt 11/3/81. Retd ADMIN 11/9/93.
JONES D. Born 30/5/31. Commd 8/11/68. Sqn Ldr 1/7/83. Retd ENG 6/4/87.
JONES D.A. BA DPhysEd. Born 4/5/30. Commd 20/8/52. Flt Lt 20/11/56. Retd SUP 20/8/68. rtg Sqn Ldr.
JONES D.B. MSc BSc. Born 9/11/49. Commd 24/4/77. Sqn Ldr 1/7/84. Retd ADMIN 24/4/93.
JONES D.C. DFC. Born 26/4/22. Commd 12/6/44. Sqn Ldr 1/4/56. Retd GD 26/4/65.
JONES D.C. Born 17/3/30. Commd 20/1/51. Flt Lt 14/11/56. Retd GD 24/9/80.
JONES D.C. Born 28/5/60. Commd 24/7/81. Sqn Ldr 1/1/94. Retd GD 28/5/98.
JONES D.G. MCMI FINucE. Born 31/5/32. Commd 20/5/53. Sqn Ldr 1/7/67. Retd RGT 2/7/71.
JONES D.G. Born 29/6/46. Commd 8/9/69. Flt Lt 8/12/70. Retd GD 8/9/85.
JONES D.G. MRCS LRCP DLO. Born 16/2/17. Commd 18/4/46. Gp Capt 18/4/68. Retd MED 19/4/80.
JONES D.H.S. BSc. Born 1/5/44. Commd 30/8/66. Flt Lt 30/5/68. Retd GD 30/8/82.
JONES D.I.P. Born 10/12/36. Commd 30/12/55. Flt Lt 30/6/61. Retd GD 21/4/77.
JONES D.J. MB BS FRCS LRCP DRCOG. Born 11/1/51. Commd 17/10/71. Wg Cdr 2/12/87. Retd MED 12/8/90.
JONES D.J. MBE. Born 1/1/15. Commd 8/7/54. Sqn Ldr 1/7/66. Retd PE 2/7/68.
JONES D.J. Born 5/8/44. Commd 14/1/65. Gp Capt 1/1/90. Retd GD 14/3/96.
JONES D.J.C. Born 25/12/19. Commd 25/8/60. Sqn Ldr 1/1/71. Retd ENG 25/12/74.
JONES D.J.R. Born 2/1/45. Commd 30/1/75. Flt Lt 9/3/94. Retd GD(G) 6/4/94.
JONES D.L. Born 2/5/39. Commd 7/1/58. Flt Lt 9/7/63. Retd GD 2/5/77.
JONES D.L. BEng. Born 27/5/62. Commd 15/9/85. Flt Lt 15/3/90. Retd ENG 3/12/96.
JONES D.M. BSc. Born 21/8/56. Commd 11/9/83. Sqn Ldr 1/1/92. Retd ADMIN 11/9/99.
JONES D.M. Born 15/2/50. Commd 17/1/69. Flt Lt 19/4/75. Retd SEC 30/11/75.
JONES D.M. Born 31/7/34. Commd 18/5/56. Sqn Ldr 1/1/69. Retd GD 20/8/76.
JONES D.M. Born 28/6/48. Commd 2/8/68. Gp Capt 1/1/94. Retd GD 28/6/03.
JONES D.McK. Born 21/6/48. Commd 22/8/71. Sqn Ldr 1/7/85. Retd ADMIN 1/7/88.
JONES D.R. Born 22/7/38. Commd 2/1/61. Wg Cdr 1/7/80. Retd GD 5/9/90.
JONES D.R.C. BA. Born 26/9/42. Commd 1/4/66. Flt Lt 1/7/67. Retd GD 14/3/96.
JONES D.R.H. Born 12/1/15. Commd 8/8/41. Sqn Ldr 1/1/55. Retd PRT 18/1/64.
JONES E. LDS. Born 9/5/16. Commd 30/12/43. Flt Lt 30/12/44. Retd DEL 14/6/50.
JONES E. Born 18/5/18. Commd 13/6/45. Sqn Offr 1/7/59. Retd SUP 18/5/62.
JONES E. Born 17/6/20. Commd 28/3/46. Sqn Ldr 1/1/65. Retd SUP 16/2/68.
JONES E.A. AMCIPD. Born 16/10/43. Commd 24/6/65. Wg Cdr 1/7/85. Retd GD 2/8/93.
JONES E.A. DFM. Born 18/3/24. Commd 16/10/44. Sqn Ldr 1/7/73. Retd ADMIN 30/6/78.
JONES E.E. AFC. Born 6/10/32. Commd 17/3/54. Wg Cdr 1/1/78. Retd GD 8/5/87.
JONES E.G. OBE BSc MB ChB. Born 2/2/53. Commd 30/8/78. Wg Cdr 1/7/93. Retd GD 30/8/97.
JONES F.H. Born 15/5/26. Commd 13/9/51. Flt Lt 4/1/57. Retd GD 1/10/83.
JONES F.J. BSc. Born 6/3/39. Commd 1/9/64. Flt Lt 26/11/68. Retd GD(G) 5/1/83.
JONES G. Born 23/7/39. Commd 27/8/59. Sqn Ldr 1/1/71. Retd ADMIN 1/9/76.
JONES G. Born 27/2/62. Commd 19/3/81. Sqn Ldr 1/1/99. Retd OPS SPT 1/1/02.
JONES G. Born 3/6/29. Commd 31/5/51. Wg Cdr 1/1/69. Retd GD 3/4/81.
JONES G. The Rev. Born 19/5/35. Commd 22/4/68. Retd Wg Cdr 1/1/86.
JONES G.A. Born 6/5/32. Commd 15/9/60. Flt Lt 15/9/66. Retd GD 6/5/87.
JONES G.B. BSc CEng FIMechE. Born 1/4/50. Commd 25/2/72. Sqn Ldr 1/1/87. Retd ENGINEER 22/4/05.
JONES G.C. Born 14/12/46. Commd 28/4/65. Wg Cdr 1/1/85. Retd GD 26/10/90.
JONES G.G. BSc. Born 29/9/35. Commd 31/7/56. Sqn Ldr 1/7/69. Retd GD 15/10/80.
JONES G.M. BEd. Born 25/1/59. Commd 6/9/81. Sqn Ldr 1/1/92. Retd SY 14/3/96.
JONES G.M. Born 23/7/17. Commd 3/6/42. Flt Offr 3/12/46. Retd SEC 1/5/53.
JONES G.P. Born 5/5/48. Commd 1/6/72. Flt Lt 1/12/78. Retd GD(G) 14/2/88.
JONES G.V. BSc. Born 2/7/63. Commd 2/9/84. Flt Lt 2/3/87. Retd FLY(N) 24/9/03.
JONES G.W. Born 21/5/31. Commd 8/7/54. Flt Lt 8/1/59. Retd GD 23/5/69.
JONES G.W.H. The Rev. Born 30/5/24. Commd 12/5/52. Retd Sqn Ldr 25/4/67. rtg Wg Cdr.
JONES H. Born 21/9/30. Commd 6/8/52. Flt Lt 6/2/57. Retd GD 21/9/68.
JONES H. MBE. Born 28/3/39. Commd 5/8/76. Sqn Ldr 1/7/87. Retd ADMIN 1/5/92.
JONES H.D. MB BS FFARCS DA DipSoton. Born 3/6/27. Commd 29/8/54. Wg Cdr 30/1/66. Retd MED 29/8/70.
JONES H.G. Born 1/8/28. Commd 9/5/55. Wg Cdr 1/1/72. Retd SEC 1/9/73.
JONES H.V. Born 7/6/39. Commd 31/1/64. Sqn Ldr 1/1/85. Retd GD 1/1/91.
JONES H.W. Born 9/3/60. Commd 15/3/84. Flt Lt 15/9/90. Retd OPS SPT 31/10/99.
JONES I. AFC. Born 28/12/23. Commd 4/9/46. Flt Lt 7/3/62. Retd SUP 13/6/74.

JONES I. Born 20/4/56. Commd 24/4/80. Fg Offr 24/10/82. Retd SUP 30/6/84.
JONES I. CEng MIMechE MRAeS FIEE MCMI. Born 31/12/24. Commd 27/6/51. Sqn Ldr 1/1/63. Retd ENG 27/6/67.
JONES I.M. Born 28/6/44. Commd 11/10/70. Sqn Ldr 1/1/79. Retd ENG 11/10/89.
JONES I.M. Born 5/9/61. Commd 8/11/90. Flt Lt 8/11/92. Retd ENG 31/3/94.
JONES I.R. Born 11/9/48. Commd 11/8/77. Flt Lt 11/8/79. Retd ADMIN 11/10/86.
JONES J. Born 8/11/40. Commd 26/68. Flt Lt 7/6/70. Retd ENG 30/6/78.
JONES J.B.L. BSc. Born 10/5/63. Commd 30/8/81. Flt Lt 15/4/86. Retd GD 15/7/96.
JONES J.B.M. Born 7/4/35. Commd 29/4/54. Gp Capt 1/1/84. Retd ADMIN 7/4/90.
JONES J.D. MBE MA DUS. Born 27/2/27. Commd 24/11/48. A Cdre 1/7/74. Retd ENG 15/3/78.
JONES J.D.M. The Rev. MA. Born 17/8/24. Commd 17/11/59. Retd Sqn Ldr 29/4/66.
JONES J.E. DCM. Born 7/4/20. Commd 26/5/51. Flt Lt 31/3/59. Retd SEC 1/12/64.
JONES J.H. DFM. Born 9/4/17. Commd 4/3/44. Flt Lt 4/3/49. Retd SEC 18/9/65.
JONES J.H. Born 1/10/33. Commd 17/7/58. Sqn Ldr 4/1/69. Retd ADMIN 1/10/93.
JONES J.H. Born 21/10/39. Commd 23/5/63. Flt Lt 1/12/69. Retd SUP 20/2/79.
JONES J.I. BSc. Born 21/1/20. Commd 24/4/42. Flt Lt 19/11/53. Retd GD 13/3/64.
JONES J.L. BSc MInstP MBCS. Born 14/11/44. Commd 13/8/72. Sqn Ldr 29/3/78. Retd ADMIN 13/8/88.
JONES J.M. BEng. Born 21/6/66. Commd 30/8/87. Flt Lt 28/2/90. Retd GD 30/8/99.
JONES J.M. CB BDS FDSRCS(Eng). Born 27/1/31. Commd 16/10/55. AVM 1/7/83. Retd DEL 26/2/88.
JONES J.M. MB BCh DAvMed AFOM. Born 14/10/46. Commd 30/9/68. Gp Capt 1/7/96. Retd MED 2/4/01.
JONES J.McK. Born 20/6/24. Commd 2/7/47. Flt Lt 23/11/60. Retd GD 1/1/69.
JONES J.R. MB BCh MRCGP DRCOG DAvMed. Born 6/9/56. Commd 5/11/79. Wg Cdr 1/8/94. Retd MED 5/11/95.
JONES J.S. CBE BSc CEng MRAeS. Born 10/12/40. Commd 13/10/64. A Cdre 1/1/92. Retd ENG 10/12/95.
JONES J.T. Born 4/5/40. Commd 13/12/68. Flt Lt 13/12/70. Retd GD 7/10/77.
JONES J.V. Born 2/7/29. Commd 15/6/48. Flt Lt 6/9/55. Retd GD(G) 2/7/67.
JONES J.W.H. Born 12/6/17. Commd 22/9/49. Sqn Ldr 1/7/59. Retd ENG 2/3/68.
JONES K.A. MBE. Born 27/3/47. Commd 14/8/69. Sqn Ldr 1/7/93. Retd GD 7/4/01.
JONES K.A. BSc. Born 18/3/62. Commd 30/10/83. Flt Lt 30/4/86. Retd GD 18/3/00.
JONES K.C. Born 24/7/46. Commd 7/6/68. Flt Lt 24/1/72. Retd GD 6/7/84.
JONES K.E. Born 18/1/38. Commd 30/11/55. Sqn Ldr 1/1/76. Retd GD 18/1/76.
JONES K.G. Born 16/1/24. Commd 19/10/44. Sqn Ldr 1/1/72. Retd GD 16/1/79.
JONES K.H.R. DFC. Born 5/1/23. Commd 11/12/45. Sqn Ldr 1/1/74. Retd GD(G) 5/1/78.
JONES K.R. Born 19/8/63. Commd 4/7/85. Flt Lt 4/1/91. Retd FLY(N) 30/4/03.
JONES K.W.P. Born 22/9/30. Commd 21/10/65. Sqn Ldr 1/7/79. Retd ENG 14/9/84.
JONES L. Born 19/12/27. Commd 25/7/47. Flt Lt 14/4/53. Retd GD 19/12/65.
JONES M. OBE. Born 16/8/47. Commd 21/4/67. Wg Cdr 1/7/87. Retd PRT 1/9/90.
JONES M. Born 22/8/21. Commd 24/1/42. Sqn Ldr 1/1/52. Retd GD 22/8/64. rtg Wg Cdr.
JONES M.A. Born 19/9/38. Commd 7/5/64. Wg Cdr 1/7/82. Retd ENG 20/9/88.
JONES M.D. Born 5/11/43. Commd 17/5/63. Plt Offr 17/5/64. Retd GD 11/3/65.
JONES M.F. The Rev. Born 20/7/44. Commd 2/9/73. Retd Sqn Ldr 1/5/81.
JONES M.H. Born 2/12/41. Commd 28/9/62. Sqn Ldr 1/7/74. Retd GD 2/12/79.
JONES M.H. BSc CEng MIEE. Born 10/2/48. Commd 28/2/69. Sqn Ldr 1/7/79. Retd ENG 10/2/86.
JONES M.H. OBE. Born 20/8/47. Commd 5/8/76. Wg Cdr 1/1/91. Retd ADMIN 20/8/02.
JONES M.J. OBE MCMI. Born 2/8/41. Commd 20/12/62. Wg Cdr 1/1/81. Retd SUP 31/3/97.
JONES M.J. Born 9/10/27. Commd 13/3/47. Sqn Ldr 1/1/75. Retd SUP 6/5/76.
JONES M.J. Born 29/5/39. Commd 14/8/64. Flt Lt 15/4/70. Retd GD 20/8/81.
JONES M.P. BSc. Born 17/7/63. Commd 22/7/84. Flt Lt 22/1/87. Retd GD 12/2/01.
JONES M.P. Born 22/3/55. Commd 10/2/83. Flt Lt 15/12/85. Retd OPS SPT(ATC) 22/5/04.
JONES M.S. BSc. Born 22/4/63. Commd 22/7/84. Flt Lt 22/1/87. Retd GD 23/7/00.
JONES M.S. Born 18/2/48. Commd 2/8/68. Flt Lt 2/8/71. Retd GD 4/9/73.
JONES M.S. Born 5/2/41. Commd 3/8/62. Fg Offr 3/8/64. Retd GD 8/9/65.
JONES N. BSc. Born 10/2/29. Commd 19/4/51. Wg Cdr 1/1/66. Retd GD 1/1/69.
JONES N.E. Born 9/5/47. Commd 28/2/69. Flt Lt 28/2/72. Retd GD 1/1/75.
JONES N.G. DFC BSc. Born 13/5/20. Commd 6/12/41. Sqn Ldr 1/4/56. Retd GD 17/5/68.
JONES N.H. Born 1/6/50. Commd 24/4/70. Flt Lt 24/10/75. Retd GD 1/6/88.
JONES N.M. Born 23/1/18. Commd 10/12/42. Sqn Ldr 1/7/53. Retd ENG 27/4/68.
JONES O. Born 16/12/24. Commd 6/9/56. Flt Lt 6/9/62. Retd GD 16/12/83.
JONES O.N. CGM MCMI. Born 25/12/23. Commd 18/3/44. Sqn Ldr 1/7/62. Retd GD(G) 19/1/74.
JONES P. Born 20/1/48. Commd 2/11/88. Sqn Ldr 1/1/97. Retd ENG 19/9/01.
JONES P. Born 24/11/29. Commd 4/8/54. Flt Lt 22/8/59. Retd GD 16/3/69.
JONES P.A. BTech. Born 14/3/62. Commd 2/9/84. Sqn Ldr 1/7/96. Retd GD 2/9/00.
JONES P.A.R. BSc. Born 22/4/41. Commd 9/9/63. Sqn Ldr 1/1/74. Retd GD 9/9/79.
JONES P.D. BA. Born 5/10/32. Commd 29/12/53. Sqn Ldr 17/2/63. Retd EDN 5/10/70.
JONES P.D. Born 17/6/55. Commd 2/3/78. Flt Lt 2/9/83. Retd GD 25/1/88.
JONES P.F.P. BSc. Born 17/3/48. Commd 11/8/74. Sqn Ldr 1/7/86. Retd GD 13/4/98.
JONES P.J. Born 21/2/34. Commd 12/7/66. Flt Lt 12/7/66. Retd GD(G) 1/10/82.
JONES P.K. BEng. Born 9/10/61. Commd 20/1/85. Flt Lt 20/7/87. Retd GD 30/9/97.

JONES P.M. BA. Born 10/7/30. Commd 13/2/64. Sqn Ldr 1/7/84. Retd ENG 4/7/86.
JONES P.N. Born 29/9/32. Commd 24/2/67. Flt Lt 24/2/73. Retd ENG 1/4/82.
JONES P.N. Born 13/2/41. Commd 11/9/64. Sqn Ldr 1/1/83. Retd GD 13/2/96.
JONES P.R. BSc. Born 25/8/67. Commd 18/9/85. Flt Lt 15/1/91. Retd GD 15/7/00.
JONES P.R. DFC MCMI. Born 21/10/20. Commd 28/2/44. Sqn Ldr 1/7/66. Retd GD(G) 23/9/75.
JONES P.R. Born 26/10/65. Commd 28/2/85. Flt Lt 28/2/91. Retd GD 14/3/96.
JONES P.R.C. Born 9/7/40. Commd 18/12/62. Sqn Ldr 1/7/72. Retd GD 9/7/78.
JONES P.W. MCMI. Born 20/12/53. Commd 5/4/79. Sqn Ldr 1/7/88. Retd SY 14/9/96.
JONES R. Born 20/6/28. Commd 28/11/51. Sqn Ldr 1/1/64. Retd GD 25/10/75.
JONES R. Born 10/8/40. Commd 11/11/71. Flt Lt 11/11/73. Retd GD 30/9/89.
JONES R. Born 19/3/30. Commd 6/12/51. Flt Lt 28/1/58. Retd GD 29/3/69.
JONES R. BA. Born 30/12/33. Commd 1/11/56. Sqn Ldr 1/5/64. Retd EDN 30/8/72.
JONES R.A. BA. Born 30/7/60. Commd 20/10/83. Flt Lt 18/4/90. Retd ENG 20/6/99.
JONES R.A. Born 24/4/37. Commd 22/2/71. Wg Cdr 1/1/90. Retd MED(SEC) 1/1/92.
JONES R.A.J. MBE CEng MRAeS. Born 27/3/33. Commd 26/3/59. Wg Cdr 1/1/76. Retd ENG 28/9/85.
JONES R.B. Born 15/6/34. Commd 17/3/67. Flt Lt 4/4/69. Retd GD(G) 15/11/78.
JONES R.C. BA. Born 13/11/32. Commd 12/7/57. Sqn Ldr 1/7/63. Retd EDN 13/10/74.
JONES R.G. Born 7/8/29. Commd 28/11/51. Sqn Ldr 1/1/82. Retd GD 7/8/84.
JONES R.G.A. CEng MRAeS. Born 12/12/21. Commd 20/12/57. Sqn Ldr 1/7/70. Retd ENG 12/12/76.
JONES R.I. Born 30/4/30. Commd 13/12/50. Wg Cdr 1/7/68. Retd SUP 2/5/75.
JONES R.L. MCIPD CertEd. Born 8/12/45. Commd 15/10/81. Sqn Ldr 1/1/87. Retd ADMIN 15/10/92.
JONES R.L. MBE. Born 13/8/49. Commd 25/2/88. Flt Lt 25/2/90. Retd GD 29/1/02.
JONES R.M. CEng MIMechE MRAeS. Born 25/1/44. Commd 15/7/65. Sqn Ldr 1/1/75. Retd ENG 25/1/82.
JONES R.M. MSc MB BS MRCP MRCPath DRCOG. Born 9/5/48. Commd 4/6/80. Wg Cdr 28/8/85.
    Retd MED 27/9/89.
JONES R.M. Born 7/10/28. Commd 23/6/67. Flt Lt 23/6/70. Retd GD 7/10/88.
JONES R.M.G. Born 19/5/61. Commd 16/9/79. Flt Lt 2/9/85. Retd GD 11/4/91.
JONES R.N. Born 17/12/47. Commd 13/1/72. Flt Lt 13/7/77. Retd GD 20/9/87.
JONES R.N. IEng MIIE. Born 21/4/45. Commd 9/8/79. Sqn Ldr 1/1/87. Retd ENG 20/8/98.
JONES R.P. Born 5/3/63. Commd 13/4/86. Sqn Ldr 1/7/96. Retd GD 13/4/02.
JONES R.R. MSc BA. Born 2/12/44. Commd 9/10/67. Sqn Ldr 1/7/75. Retd SUP 12/12/84.
JONES R.R. Born 7/8/62. Commd 15/3/84. Flt Lt 15/9/89. Retd GD 1/7/01.
JONES R.T. AFC. Born 11/12/22. Commd 11/2/44. Flt Lt 11/8/47. Retd GD 31/3/62.
JONES R.T.B. CB FRCS LRCP. Born 16/11/25. Commd 1/9/52. AVM 17/9/87. Retd MED 18/7/90.
JONES R.W. Born 19/4/29. Commd 27/8/59. Flt Lt 27/8/65. Retd ENG 19/4/74.
JONES R.W. Born 31/5/54. Commd 15/3/73. Sqn Ldr 1/7/91. Retd GD(G) 14/3/96.
JONES R.W. BChD LDS. Born 18/9/42. Commd 20/10/74. Wg Cdr 17/3/80. Retd DEL 14/3/87.
JONES S. Born 10/12/42. Commd 21/7/61. Flt Lt 9/2/68. Retd GD 22/10/94.
JONES S.A. Born 8/3/52. Commd 21/12/89. Flt Lt 21/12/93. Retd ENG 19/4/02.
JONES S.A. Born 2/6/54. Commd 13/6/74. Wg Cdr 1/7/90. Retd GD(G) 1/7/93.
JONES S.A. CBE BA. Born 30/9/34. Commd 18/10/62. A Cdre 1/1/87. Retd ADMIN 20/1/90.
JONES S.B. Born 29/3/48. Commd 28/2/69. Sqn Ldr 1/1/84. Retd SUP 14/3/97.
JONES S.J. Born 11/1/62. Commd 7/5/92. Flt Lt 7/5/94. Retd ENG 7/5/00.
JONES S.O. Born 3/2/52. Commd 13/1/72. Flt Lt 13/7/77. Retd GD 3/2/90.
JONES S.W. Born 11/12/26. Commd 12/1/61. Sqn Ldr 1/1/76. Retd ENG 11/12/82.
JONES T. Born 15/2/13. Commd 26/6/42. Sqn Ldr 1/1/52. Retd SUP 15/2/68.
JONES T. BA. Born 2/12/34. Commd 17/5/76. Sqn Ldr 5/4/66. Retd ADMIN 17/5/76.
JONES T.C. MBE. Born 20/2/23. Commd 26/5/60. Sqn Ldr 1/1/72. Retd ENG 31/3/78.
JONES T.E. BSc. Born 22/5/34. Commd 8/8/56. Wg Cdr 1/7/79. Retd ADMIN 22/5/89.
JONES T.L. MA. Born 18/5/33. Commd 28/2/56. Sqn Ldr 1/7/84. Retd GD 1/1/88.
JONES T.P.F. Born 3/10/45. Commd 31/10/63. Wg Cdr 1/1/81. Retd SY 1/1/84.
JONES T.R. Born 16/5/39. Commd 20/1/69. Gp Capt 1/1/87. Retd LGL 3/11/97.
JONES T.S.C. AFC. Born 31/5/33. Commd 27/2/52. Wg Cdr 1/7/72. Retd GD 12/6/81.
JONES T.W. Born 11/2/30. Commd 10/10/63. Flt Lt 10/10/68. Retd ENG 1/10/77.
JONES T.W. Born 20/8/46. Commd 17/7/64. Sqn Ldr 1/1/84. Retd GD 1/1/87.
JONES V.G. Born 18/2/50. Commd 22/11/73. Flt Lt 22/5/80. Retd SUP 6/8/89.
JONES W.C. MBE. Born 3/7/48. Commd 16/6/92. Flt Lt 16/6/94. Retd ADMIN 1/9/97.
JONES W.D. Born 8/10/29. Commd 28/4/64. Gp Capt 1/1/80. Retd GD 8/10/84.
JONES W.J.C. MCMI. Born 23/12/19. Commd 15/1/43. Sqn Ldr 1/1/58. Retd GD 23/12/74.
JONES W.O. Born 27/11/11. Commd 7/11/33. Wg Cdr 1/7/47. Retd RGT 1/2/58.
JONES W.R.D. Born 14/7/43. Commd 12/7/63. Sqn Ldr 1/1/82. Retd GD 14/7/00.
JONSON J.R. Born 30/7/36. Commd 11/12/58. Wg Cdr 1/1/77. Retd MED 10/9/88.
JOOSSE C.A. Born 2/1/44. Commd 11/1/79. Sqn Ldr 1/7/89. Retd ENG 2/12/97.
JORDAN A.D.G. FCA. Born 9/5/16. Commd 23/8/40. Sqn Ldr 1/8/47. Retd SEC 9/5/65.
JORDAN A.G. BSc. Born 21/5/48. Commd 27/2/70. Sqn Ldr 1/7/80. Retd ENG 21/5/86.
JORDAN A.R. Born 26/6/23. Commd 11/9/43. Sqn Ldr 1/7/58. Retd GD 26/9/66.

JORDAN E.I.R. MBE BEM. Born 26/11/22. Commd 25/8/60. Sqn Ldr 1/1/72. Retd ENG 26/11/77.
JORDAN H.E. Born 13/12/31. Commd 2/7/52. Flt Lt 27/11/57. Retd GD 31/12/69.
JORDAN J. Born 21/4/16. Commd 12/5/43. Sqn Ldr 1/7/54. Retd ENG 27/6/70.
JORDAN J.B. Born 23/6/33. Commd 28/5/57. Flt Lt 6/12/62. Retd GD 23/6/71.
JORDAN K. MB BS FRCS(Edin) DO. Born 28/10/47. Commd 23/2/70. Wg Cdr 6/2/86. Retd MED 9/6/89.
JORDAN M.F. Born 1/10/43. Commd 14/6/63. Wg Cdr 1/1/88. Retd ADMIN 3/4/00.
JORDAN M.W. Born 24/6/38. Commd 24/2/61. Flt Lt 24/2/68. Retd RGT 30/11/68.
JORDAN P.A. Born 17/5/25. Commd 31/3/44. Sqn Ldr 1/7/67. Retd GD 15/5/76.
JORDAN R.J.B. BSc. Born 3/2/60. Commd 11/12/83. Flt Lt 11/6/86. Retd GD 11/12/95.
JORDAN R.K. Born 1/1/41. Commd 6/8/60. Flt Lt 4/2/67. Retd GD(G) 1/1/79.
JORDAN R.W. DFC AFC. Born 2/9/23. Commd 5/3/43. Gp Capt 1/7/65. Retd GD 13/4/70.
JORDAN T.A. BA. Born 18/3/35. Commd 7/9/56. Sqn Ldr 7/3/65. Retd EDN 7/9/74.
JORDAN T.E. MB BS MRCS LRCP. Born 15/12/44. Commd 28/9/64. Sqn Ldr 6/9/73. Retd MED 23/6/77.
JOSEPH M.M. CEng MIEE. Born 26/4/30. Commd 3/10/66. Sqn Ldr 6/10/71. Retd EDN 3/10/83.
JOSEPH R.W. CBE BSc. Born 6/10/49. Commd 2/9/73. Air Cdre 1/1/03. Retd GD 30/4/04.
JOSEPHY T.W. Born 2/7/48. Commd 23/3/67. Sqn Ldr 1/7/96. Retd GD 1/6/99.
JOSEY D.A. DFC. Born 1/6/20. Commd 22/5/42. Flt Lt 19/12/48. Retd GD(G) 7/7/68.
JOSLIN J.M. CEng MIMechE MRAeS MCMI. Born 7/7/38. Commd 28/7/60. Sqn Ldr 1/1/73. Retd ENG 18/10/75.
JOSS D.A. MBE JP MCIPD MCMI. Born 15/5/21. Commd 24/9/44. Sqn Ldr 1/7/56. Retd SEC 27/6/69.
JOY A. Born 11/2/30. Commd 25/10/51. Flt Lt 27/4/57. Retd GD 11/2/68.
JOY A.I.P. MCMI. Born 12/12/44. Commd 1/9/70. Flt Lt 8/12/72. Retd GD 30/1/84.
JOY H.F. Born 21/7/25. Commd 27/5/54. Sqn Ldr 1/7/68. Retd GD 31/3/74.
JOY R.M. MBE. Born 15/8/44. Commd 3/3/67. Sqn Ldr 1/1/78. Retd GD 22/11/96.
JOYCE C.J. Born 27/8/28. Commd 17/12/52. Flt Lt 5/11/58. Retd GD 15/10/72.
JOYCE M.H. BA. Born 2/6/38. Commd 30/9/57. Wg Cdr 1/7/80. Retd ENG 2/6/93.
JOYCE M.P.R. Born 28/5/37. Commd 20/9/61. Flt Lt 1/10/67. Retd GD 20/9/71.
JOYCE R.L. PhD BSc CEng MIM MRAeS. Born 28/3/37. Commd 11/12/61. Gp Capt 1/7/83. Retd GD 13/12/87.
JOYCE W.T. MBE MCMI. Born 15/9/20. Commd 16/8/46. Wg Cdr 1/1/69. Retd SEC 30/7/73.
JOYNER C.D. MBE. Born 7/5/47. Commd 1/8/69. Wg Cdr 1/1/91. Retd GD 1/1/97.
JUDD D.G.M. MSc MSc BSc. Born 12/1/62. Commd 30/10/83. Sqn Ldr 1/7/95. Retd ENG 15/1/02.
JUDD J.A. Born 15/1/23. Commd 14/4/49. Sqn Ldr 1/7/59. Retd GD 22/1/71.
JUDD L.J. Born 4/10/41. Commd 28/9/62. Sqn Ldr 1/7/78. Retd GD 4/10/96.
JUDGE A.M. Born 19/3/59. Commd 9/8/79. Flt Lt 9/2/85. Retd GD 30/11/96.
JUDSON G.W. Born 16/2/29. Commd 11/4/51. Flt Lt 11/4/56. Retd SEC 28/3/58.
JUDSON M.T. Born 8/3/11. Commd 5/1/43. Sqn Ldr 1/7/54. Retd ENG 8/3/60.
JUKES A.R. BDS MCMI. Born 19/7/39. Commd 12/12/76. Sqn Ldr 6/2/76. Retd DEL 12/12/84.
JUKES B.A. Born 10/12/46. Commd 10/12/65. Sqn Ldr 1/7/89. Retd GD 14/3/96.
JUKES M.H. BSc. Born 23/3/48. Commd 24/9/67. Sqn Ldr 1/7/88. Retd FLY(P) 23/3/03.
JUNGMAYR E.W. MBE RSCN. Born 9/4/58. Commd 14/8/83. Sqn Ldr 1/1/93. Retd MED(SEC) 14/3/96.
JUNOR I.O. Born 7/9/40. Commd 18/12/62. Gp Capt 1/1/86. Retd GD 2/4/93.
JUPE D.B. Born 12/4/56. Commd 22/2/79. Flt Lt 20/7/82. Retd GD 10/1/99.
JUPP M.F. Born 24/6/42. Commd 6/11/67. Wg Cdr 1/7/86. Retd ENG 6/11/89.
JURY A.R. IEng AMRAeS. Born 13/3/41. Commd 21/9/72. Sqn Ldr 1/1/91. Retd ENG 13/3/96.
JURY J.G. Born 22/7/65. Commd 2/8/90. Flt Lt 4/10/92. Retd FLY(P) 22/7/03.
JURY N.M.A. Born 28/10/63. Commd 21/6/90. Flt Lt 31/7/92. Retd FLY(P) 27/6/03.
JUST E.J. BSc ARCS CEng MRAeS MIEE. Born 10/4/32. Commd 24/11/54. Sqn Ldr 1/1/67. Retd ENG 24/11/70.

K

KAIN K.V. Born 1/7/20. Commd 7/10/42. Flt Offr 7/10/47. Retd SEC 7/7/54.
KANAGASABAY S. MSc MB BS MFCM. Born 9/7/28. Commd 15/11/59. Wg Cdr 6/6/69. Retd MED 27/8/76.
KANE E.J. Born 27/5/23. Commd 1/5/45. Sqn Ldr 1/1/72. Retd GD 31/8/73.
KANE J.H. Born 12/5/45. Commd 26/3/64. Sqn Ldr 1/7/76. Retd ADMIN 12/5/87.
KANE J.I. BSc CEng MIEE MCMI. Born 30/10/53. Commd 30/9/73. Air Cdre 1/1/01. Retd GD 25/11/03.
KANE T.M. MCMI. Born 9/10/20. Commd 17/9/38. Wg Cdr 1/7/69. Retd GD(G) 29/5/74.
KANE W.B. Born 24/10/46. Commd 28/7/67. Wg Cdr 1/7/87. Retd ADMIN 24/10/90.
KANHAI R.I. Born 4/10/64. Commd 16/8/89. Sqn Ldr 1/1/00. Retd OPS SPT(ATC) 4/10/04.
KARL H.L. Born 12/2/51. Commd 20/9/69. Sqn Ldr 1/7/84. Retd GD 12/2/89.
KARLE D. Born 7/3/51. Commd 20/12/90. Flt Lt 20/12/94. Retd OPS SPT 22/5/99.
KARRAN J.A.C. AFC. Born 24/3/13. Commd 16/4/35. Sqn Ldr 1/9/41. Retd GD 12/1/48. rtg Wg Cdr.
KATON R.C. CEng MIMechE MRAeS. Born 2/7/41. Commd 17/7/62. Sqn Ldr 1/1/72. Retd ENG 31/8/78.
KAY A.F.G. Born 5/11/23. Commd 6/3/52. Flt Lt 6/9/56. Retd SEC 31/3/62.
KAY D. Born 29/7/39. Commd 5/11/70. Flt Lt 5/11/72. Retd SEC 5/11/78.
KAY D.J. Born 18/3/29. Commd 6/7/49. Flt Lt 23/10/57. Retd GD 18/9/67.
KAY E. Born 6/5/15. Commd 20/6/41. Flt Lt 26/5/55. Retd SEC 30/9/61.
KAY G.C. Born 25/10/46. Commd 21/1/66. Flt Lt 21/7/71. Retd GD 25/10/84.
KAY M.I. LLB. Born 17/8/48. Commd 1/9/70. Flt Lt 1/6/72. Retd GD 15/11/87.
KAY R. Born 14/1/21. Commd 7/10/43. Flt Lt 7/4/48. Retd SUP 17/10/58.
KAY R.P. Born 2/2/19. Commd 12/4/45. Sqn Ldr 1/7/59. Retd ENG 2/2/74.
KAYE G. Born 11/6/33. Commd 26/3/52. Sqn Ldr 1/7/77. Retd SUP 14/5/86.
KAYE J.F.M. BSc. Born 13/11/47. Commd 27/10/70. Flt Lt 27/1/71. Retd GD 27/10/86.
KAYE M. Born 4/4/21. Commd 7/4/43. Wg Cdr 1/1/71. Retd GD 31/5/75.
KAYE M.P. BA. Born 2/4/44. Commd 17/12/64. Sqn Ldr 1/7/76. Retd GD 2/4/82.
KAYE P.M. Born 29/4/59. Commd 11/1/79. Wg Cdr 1/1/97. Retd OPS SPT 8/4/02.
KEAM P.C. Born 15/4/38. Commd 29/7/72. Sqn Ldr 29/8/78. Retd ADMIN 27/7/86.
KEAN T.F. MBE CEng MIMechE MRAeS. Born 25/4/39. Commd 28/7/60. Sqn Ldr 1/7/69. Retd ENG 10/7/89.
KEANE A.M. Born 10/12/41. Commd 28/10/63. Sqn Ldr 1/7/80. Retd GD 1/7/80.
KEANE C. BSc CertEd. Born 23/8/63. Commd 1/2/87. Flt Lt 1/8/89. Retd ADMIN (TRG) 1/2/03.
KEANE L. Born 20/3/61. Commd 20/10/83. Flt Lt 20/4/89. Retd GD 1/10/90.
KEAREY J.R. BSc CEng MRAeS. Born 7/1/48. Commd 2/8/68. Sqn Ldr 1/7/80. Retd ENG 1/10/87.
KEARL I.A.R. Born 23/11/33. Commd 27/7/54. Sqn Ldr 1/1/69. Retd SUP 29/5/76.
KEARNEY A.J. CBE BSc(Econ). Born 26/5/45. Commd 3/3/67. Gp Capt 1/1/93. Retd GD 26/5/00.
KEARNEY C.J. Born 6/1/59. Commd 6/10/94. Fg Offr 19/10/89. Retd ADMIN 29/11/96.
KEARNEY J.J. MBE. Born 19/4/28. Commd 24/1/52. Sqn Ldr 1/1/64. Retd GD 30/6/77.
KEARNS D.C.L. AFC DSC. Born 24/12/16. Commd 23/4/43. Sqn Ldr 1/7/54. Retd GD 17/3/60.
KEARNS M.E. BA. Born 4/2/36. Commd 28/11/58. Sqn Ldr 28/5/69. Retd EDN 1/7/75.
KEARSEY M.H. Born 8/10/58. Commd 1/12/77. Plt Offr 1/6/78. Retd SUP 6/3/79.
KEARY D.H. DFC. Born 1/4/16. Commd 1/5/41. Wg Cdr 1/7/56. Retd SEC 30/5/64.
KEAST R.J. BSc CEng MRAeS. Born 20/8/37. Commd 30/9/57. Sqn Ldr 1/7/69. Retd ENG 20/8/75.
KEATING P.J. BA MRIN. Born 6/11/41. Commd 21/7/61. Sqn Ldr 1/1/89. Retd GD 6/9/94.
KEATING S.F. Born 12/3/24. Commd 17/5/62. Flt Lt 17/5/65. Retd ENG 12/3/79.
KEATLEY R.F. Born 6/11/22. Commd 23/12/43. Sqn Ldr 1/4/55. Retd GD 6/11/65.
KEATS D.J.B. Born 10/1/31. Commd 2/12/51. Sqn Ldr 1/1/73. Retd GD 10/1/69.
KEATS T.S. Born 5/12/40. Commd 31/7/62. Sqn Ldr 1/7/73. Retd GD 5/12/78.
KEAY V.C. Born 21/5/23. Commd 20/11/42. Sqn Ldr 1/1/60. Retd GD 21/9/73.
KEDAR A. BSc CEng MRAeS MCMI. Born 16/9/30. Commd 23/9/53. Gp Capt 1/1/74. Retd ENG 16/9/85.
KEDDIE D.G. Born 23/5/09. Commd 5/9/31. Gp Capt 1/7/50. Retd GD 25/1/57.
KEDDIE J.B.F. Born 29/1/20. Commd 8/2/44. Flt Lt 8/8/47. Retd GD 26/12/58.
KEE W. Born 18/3/18. Commd 6/5/43. Flt Lt 6/11/47. Retd SEC 1/1/55.
KEEBLE P.N. Born 9/11/45. Commd 18/8/67. Flt Lt 4/5/72. Retd GD 1/1/76. Re-entered 22/4/81. Flt Lt 24/11/75. Retd GD 2/3/97.
KEEBLE P.W. Born 16/5/47. Commd 6/5/66. Flt Lt 6/11/71. Retd GD 1/6/94.
KEECH A.J. BEM MCMI. Born 27/7/28. Commd 7/6/68. Sqn Ldr 1/7/83. Retd ENG 27/7/86.
KEECH R.A. BSc. Born 9/3/52. Commd 30/10/72. Sqn Ldr 1/1/87. Retd GD 9/3/90.
KEEDLE B.D. Born 15/11/33. Commd 23/7/52. Flt Lt 29/1/58. Retd GD 15/4/71.
KEELEY A.F.W. Born 27/10/31. Commd 17/12/52. Flt Lt 17/6/55. Retd GD 21/1/73.
KEELEY T.J. Born 31/1/29. Commd 4/6/64. Flt Lt 4/6/67. Retd GD 31/1/84.
KEELING A.G. BSc CEng MRAeS. Born 7/2/43. Commd 22/10/70. Flt Lt 22/10/70. Retd ENG 26/6/83.
KEELING R.F.N. Born 6/4/25. Commd 24/9/56. Sqn Ldr 1/1/64. Retd PRT 1/1/67.
KEELING T.W. Born 16/1/45. Commd 13/9/70. Sqn Ldr 1/7/84. Retd ENG 9/6/97.

KEEN R.D. MBCS. Born 30/8/46. Commd 9/12/65. Sqn Ldr 1/7/78. Retd GD 15/7/87.
KEEN S.S. Born 5/2/46. Commd 22/7/71. Sqn Ldr 1/1/80. Retd ENG 31/3/85. Re-entered 8/3/91. Wg Cdr 1/1/96.
 Retd ENG 11/12/98.
KEEN W.H. Born 14/11/19. Commd 20/1/44. Sqn Ldr 1/7/63. Retd GD(G) 14/11/69.
KEENAN D.J. OBE . Born 10/2/48. Commd 15/9/67. Wg Cdr 1/1/90. Retd GD 10/2/05.
KEENAN E.J. DFC. Born 21/11/19. Commd 29/5/41. Flt Lt 27/4/54. Retd SEC 1/8/63.
KEENAN J.F. Born 19/9/44. Commd 5/11/70. Flt Lt 21/7/74. Retd GD 21/11/75.
KEENE D.A. BDS DOrthRCS. Born 26/3/40. Commd 20/9/59. Wg Cdr 29/7/77. Retd DEL 26/3/78.
KEEP D.J. MA MSc BSc CEng MIEE. Born 22/11/61. Commd 31/8/80. Wg Cdr 1/1/99. Retd ENG 1/1/02.
KEEP M.G. Born 1/11/25. Commd 25/8/55. Flt Lt 25/8/61. Retd GD 30/3/68.
KEEP R.P. Born 22/11/61. Commd 25/2/83. Sqn Ldr 1/7/95. Retd SUP 22/11/99.
KEER D.C. Born 15/4/33. Commd 27/2/70. Sqn Ldr 1/1/79. Retd ENG 16/4/83.
KEER M. BA. Born 7/1/71. Commd 24/4/97. Flt Lt 10/10/97. Retd SEC 22/6/73.
KEETON P. MBA BSc CEng MRAeS. Born 4/9/62. Commd 30/8/81. Sqn Ldr 1/1/95. Retd ENGINEER 8/1/05.
KEEVES J.E. Born 6/12/21. Commd 28/9/61. Flt Lt 28/9/66. Retd ENG 6/12/76.
KEFALAS D. LLB BA. Born 26/6/35. Commd 4/6/58. Flt Lt 9/11/70. Retd SEC 22/6/73.
KEHOE P. BSc. Born 21/4/59. Commd 15/3/79. Flt Lt 15/10/84. Retd GD(G) 20/9/87.
KEHOE S. Born 25/6/29. Commd 22/8/51. Flt Lt 22/2/56. Retd GD(G) 25/6/87.
KEILLER D.E.S. Born 19/3/31. Commd 3/7/56. Flt Lt 3/1/62. Retd GD 17/1/64.
KEILLER F.E.S. MBE MB ChB FRCS(Edin) FRCS. Born 20/7/27. Commd 1/7/56. Wg Cdr 21/8/68. Retd MED 1/7/72.
KEILY J.A. Born 15/10/28. Commd 11/4/51. Sqn Ldr 1/7/62. Retd SUP 15/10/66.
KEITCH M.P. BA IEng CDipAF. Born 10/5/42. Commd 9/5/66. Sqn Ldr 1/1/80. Retd ENG 1/1/83. Re-entered 12/5/86.
 Sqn Ldr 12/5/83. Retd ENG 10/5/97.
KEITH G.T. Born 10/4/47. Commd 25/5/66. Gp Capt 1/7/89. Retd OPS SPT 15/6/98.
KEKEWICH H.C. BA. Born 27/8/56. Commd 10/6/84. Flt Lt 10/12/86. Retd SUP 14/9/96.
KEKWICK A.R. Born 17/7/33. Commd 7/11/52. Sqn Ldr 1/7/66. Retd RGT 13/6/70.
KELL G.W. Born 10/3/53. Commd 11/5/78. Sqn Ldr 1/1/97. Retd OPS SPT 1/8/98.
KELLACHAN P.A. BSc CertEd. Born 22/9/62. Commd 10/4/95. Sqn Ldr 1/7/96. Retd ADMIN (TRG) 12/2/05.
KELLARD C.A. MCSP. Born 15/12/51. Commd 30/3/89. Flt Lt 30/3/93. Retd OPS SPT 1/5/02.
KELLAWAY H. Born 24/7/10. Commd 11/2/43. Flt Lt 11/8/46. Retd SEC 3/3/58.
KELLEHER K.P. Born 22/10/23. Commd 9/8/45. Sqn Ldr 1/1/71. Retd GD 22/10/78.
KELLETT B.M. MSc BSc. Born 29/9/55. Commd 15/9/74. Wg Cdr 1/7/93. Retd SUP 29/9/99.
KELLETT M. DFC. Born 25/9/17. Commd 7/9/40. Sqn Ldr 1/9/45. Retd GD 19/6/56. rtg Wg Cdr.
KELLEY J.W.D. BA. Born 27/11/30. Commd 10/1/61. Sqn Ldr 1/9/68. Retd ADMIN 17/12/74.
KELLEY W.E.J. Born 22/3/30. Commd 21/2/69. Flt Lt 21/2/72. Retd GD 17/1/76.
KELLY A.F. Born 10/11/37. Commd 28/4/61. Flt Lt 1/4/66. Retd GD 16/1/75.
KELLY A.G. Born 6/3/20. Commd 9/7/47. Flt Lt 9/1/52. Retd SUP 4/4/64.
KELLY A.W. BSc. Born 31/8/54. Commd 27/3/83. Flt Lt 27/3/84. Retd ADMIN 14/3/96.
KELLY B.J. Born 11/3/37. Commd 29/6/72. Sqn Ldr 1/1/80. Retd ENG 19/5/90.
KELLY B.R. BEng. Born 24/5/66. Commd 24/11/83. Sqn Ldr 1/7/01. Retd FLY(P) 1/7/04.
KELLY C.J. Born 9/4/47. Commd 21/1/66. Flt Lt 4/5/72. Retd GD 1/12/73.
KELLY D.J. Born 3/9/21. Commd 19/9/44. Fg Offr 1/7/46. Retd RGT 25/9/50. rtg Flt Lt.
KELLY G. Born 13/11/42. Commd 10/6/66. Flt Lt 4/5/72. Retd GD 30/4/76.
KELLY G.C. Born 14/4/43. Commd 28/10/66. Flt Lt 28/4/72. Retd GD 18/1/83.
KELLY H.B. CB MVO MD BS FRCP MRCS DCH. Born 12/8/21. Commd 23/11/53. AVM 1/9/78. Retd MED 26/3/83.
KELLY J.D.C. BM BCh FRCS LRCP. Born 15/3/30. Commd 16/10/55. Wg Cdr 16/10/68. Retd MED 16/10/71.
KELLY L.E. CEng MRAeS. Born 12/4/32. Commd 28/10/55. Wg Cdr 1/7/75. Retd ENG 12/4/90.
KELLY M. Born 18/5/39. Commd 25/7/59. Flt Lt 25/1/65. Retd GD 18/5/77.
KELLY P. Born 14/10/46. Commd 21/7/65. Sqn Ldr 1/7/77. Retd GD 12/8/80.
KELLY P.A. OBE. Born 30/1/38. Commd 30/7/59. A Cdre 1/7/89. Retd ENG 2/7/91.
KELLY P.M. Born 1/7/60. Commd 20/9/79. Gp Capt 1/7/03. Retd GD 20/9/04.
KELLY P.N. Born 22/8/38. Commd 9/10/75. Sqn Ldr 31/3/86. Retd MED(T) 25/4/91.
KELLY R.H. DPhysEd. Born 27/8/28. Commd 5/9/51. Flt Lt 5/9/55. Retd PE 26/3/67.
KELLY R.V. Born 4/6/26. Commd 1/3/62. Sqn Ldr 1/7/72. Retd SUP 4/6/84.
KELLY R.W. MCMI. Born 20/3/22. Commd 24/12/44. Wg Cdr 1/7/71. Retd GD(G) 30/3/78.
KELLY W.E. The Rev. MA. Born 25/5/31. Commd 6/6/66. Retd Wg Cdr 6/6/82.
KELLY W.E. Born 9/4/28. Commd 27/9/50. Gp Capt 1/1/71. Retd GD 30/6/78.
KELLY W.J.R. BSc CEng MIMechE. Born 2/12/49. Commd 26/2/71. Sqn Ldr 1/7/90. Retd ENGINEER 2/12/04.
KELSEY H.C. DSO DFC*. Born 19/10/20. Commd 25/6/41. Wg Cdr 1/7/56. Retd GD 19/10/67.
KELSEY R.J. Born 17/7/17. Commd 29/6/36. Wg Cdr 1/7/50. Retd GD 15/6/59.
KELSON G.M. Born 3/5/35. Commd 3/1/64. Flt Lt 4/5/72. Retd GD 10/9/79.
KELSON M. Born 7/3/31. Commd 7/3/69. Flt Lt 7/3/72. Retd GD 7/4/88.
KEMBALL Sir John KCB CBE DL BA. Born 31/1/39. Commd 12/11/57. AM 10/11/89. Retd GD 30/4/93.
KEMBLE R. Born 13/1/41. Commd 9/10/64. Flt Lt 6/10/71. Retd GD 26/9/75. Re-instated 18.5.79. Flt Lt 28/5/75.
 Retd GD 13/1/96.
KEMLEY M.J. BA. Born 5/3/55. Commd 16/9/73. Wg Cdr 1/7/96. Retd ADMIN 18/8/00.

KEMMETT R.J. Born 19/1/35. Commd 23/3/66. Sqn Ldr 1/7/84. Retd GD 19/1/93.
KEMP B.V. BEng. Born 11/10/65. Commd 3/10/84. Sqn Ldr 1/1/99. Retd FLY(P) 11/10/03.
KEMP C.A. Born 27/5/44. Commd 8/10/70. Flt Lt 8/4/76. Retd GD 1/4/92.
KEMP E.A. Born 20/8/43. Commd 18/10/62. Fg Offr 18/1/65. Retd SEC 17/10/68.
KEMP G.G.J.N. BSc MRAeS. Born 17/8/31. Commd 6/3/52. Sqn Ldr 4/3/65. Retd EDN 17/5/74.
KEMP G.J. CB. Born 14/7/21. Commd 3/12/41. AVM 1/7/73. Retd SEC 8/11/75.
KEMP H.A. Born 30/8/51. Commd 16/9/71. Plt Offr 23/12/71. Retd RGT 24/7/73.
KEMP I.H. CEng MRAeS. Born 7/4/26. Commd 21/6/56. Sqn Ldr 1/1/64. Retd ENG 7/4/84.
KEMP J.A. Born 28/9/15. Commd 18/11/41. Sqn Ldr 1/8/47. Retd RGT 28/5/58.
KEMP M.J. Born 30/4/34. Commd 20/1/64. Sqn Ldr 1/1/82. Retd GD 30/4/92.
KEMP N.L.D. DFC. Born 24/7/19. Commd 7/9/40. Flt Lt 25/9/48. Retd GD 31/8/66.
KEMP P. BSc. Born 12/2/47. Commd 1/11/71. Flt Lt 1/5/76. Retd GD 1/11/87.
KEMP P.J. Born 16/1/39. Commd 25/7/60. Gp Capt 1/7/83. Retd GD 1/10/89.
KEMP P.J. Born 26/7/36. Commd 31/7/61. Flt Lt 10/2/67. Retd RGT 31/7/77.
KEMP R.G. QVRM AE FRIN. Born 24/3/47. Commd 21/1/66. Sqn Ldr 1/1/78. Retd GD 24/3/85.
KEMP R.J.M. MBE BSc. Born 14/11/52. Commd 3/10/76. Sqn Ldr 1/7/87. Retd SY 2/4/93.
KEMP W.J. Born 21/12/40. Commd 18/12/62. Sqn Ldr 1/1/75. Retd GD 21/12/90.
KEMPEN E.McM. Born 7/1/15. Commd 13/3/46. Flt Lt 7/6/51. Retd RGT 17/4/54.
KEMPSELL A.J. BSc. Born 30/9/53. Commd 29/7/72. Flt Lt 15/10/79. Retd ENG 30/9/91.
KEMPSTER M.J. BSc. Born 22/7/41. Commd 13/6/66. Sqn Ldr 1/1/82. Retd GD 22/7/96.
KEMSLEY R.W. Born 15/3/20. Commd 9/2/43. Wg Cdr 1/1/71. Retd ENG 26/2/77.
KENDAL S.R. Born 14/9/18. Commd 26/3/38. Flt Lt 27/11/45. Retd GD 1/11/61. rtg Sqn Ldr.
KENDALL E.P. MBE MCMI. Born 19/10/37. Commd 17/7/56. Wg Cdr 1/1/87. Retd GD 19/10/92.
KENDALL F.M. Born 31/3/12. Commd 9/5/41. Flt Lt 1/9/45. Retd SUP 20/7/57. rtg Sqn Ldr.
KENDALL J.F. Born 14/2/49. Commd 24/11/67. Wg Cdr 1/1/01. Retd GD 14/2/04.
KENDALL P.J. Born 21/10/38. Commd 12/10/63. Flt Lt 10/2/67. Retd GD 25/7/85.
KENDALL R.A. Born 8/10/49. Commd 17/7/87. Flt Lt 17/7/91. Retd OPS SPT(ATC) 7/5/03.
KENDELL M.R.J. Born 10/5/48. Commd 19/12/85. Flt Lt 19/12/89. Retd ADMIN (SEC) 10/5/05.
KENDRA P.G. Born 2/7/18. Commd 9/7/53. Sqn Ldr 1/1/65. Retd ENG 5/10/68.
KENDRICK C.E. Born 19/8/39. Commd 6/9/63. Flt Lt 15/4/70. Retd GD 21/5/79. Re-instated 1/8/90. Flt Lt 1/8/84. Retd GD 19/8/94.
KENDRICK D.A. BA. Born 5/3/45. Commd 15/7/66. Wg Cdr 1/1/85. Retd ENG 16/9/89.
KENDRICK D.I. MIDPM. Born 4/2/47. Commd 4/3/71. Gp Capt 1/1/97. Retd SUP 18/5/01.
KENDRICK E.C. Born 8/9/31. Commd 7/10/57. Sqn Ldr 1/7/68. Retd GD 1/7/71.
KENDRICK F.W. Born 11/10/21. Commd 9/7/44. Sqn Ldr 1/1/59. Retd PRT 11/10/68. rtg Wg Cdr.
KENDRICK I. LRAM ARCM. Born 17/2/40. Commd 21/4/77. Sqn Ldr 5/10/86. Retd DM 8/5/90.
KENDRICK J.D. Born 5/10/42. Commd 30/7/63. Sqn Ldr 1/7/73. Retd GD 5/10/80.
KENDRICK J.M. Born 20/5/45. Commd 26/9/72. Flt Lt 10/5/79. Retd GD(G) 27/6/92.
KENDRICK K.R. IEng. Born 4/12/42. Commd 9/2/66. Sqn Ldr 1/7/79. Retd ENG 4/7/97.
KENDRICK L. CBE MRAeS. Born 16/4/19. Commd 5/11/41. Gp Capt 1/1/64. Retd ENG 1/8/67.
KENDRICK O.M.J. Born 17/10/32. Commd 19/9/59. Flt Lt 19/3/70. Retd GD 17/10/70.
KENDRICK V.B. BA FCMI. Born 27/6/32. Commd 24/8/56. Gp Capt 1/7/77. Retd ADMIN 1/9/83.
KENNEDY A.G. Born 13/1/63. Commd 7/12/86. Flt Lt 7/6/89. Retd OPS SPT 7/12/02.
KENNEDY A.J. Born 3/3/11. Commd 5/2/32. Wg Cdr 1/10/46. Retd GD 29/8/47.
KENNEDY A.K.M. Born 16/12/13. Commd 6/10/41. Flt Offr 1/9/45. Retd SEC 14/8/52.
KENNEDY B.J.O. Born 13/11/49. Commd 9/10/75. Wg Cdr 1/7/92. Retd ADMIN 13/5/00.
KENNEDY C.G. MSc MB BS MRCGP DRCOG DAvMed. Born 8/6/54. Commd 20/8/78. Wg Cdr 20/8/91. Retd MED 31/7/97.
KENNEDY C.J. Born 28/12/48. Commd 31/7/70. Sqn Ldr 1/1/97. Retd GD 31/5/00.
KENNEDY C.W.N. MBE. Born 28/8/27. Commd 31/5/50. Wg Cdr 1/7/71. Retd GD 1/5/79.
KENNEDY D.A. Born 19/6/49. Commd 10/5/73. Flt Lt 10/11/78. Retd GD 22/1/89.
KENNEDY E.O. Born 1/6/20. Commd 4/4/45. Wg Cdr 1/7/69. Retd PRT 31/1/73.
KENNEDY G. AFC DFM. Born 11/4/12. Commd 1/4/40. Wg Cdr 1/1/54. Retd GD 11/4/59.
KENNEDY G.A.A. Born 23/4/33. Commd 2/3/61. Flt Lt 2/9/65. Retd GD 30/5/86.
KENNEDY G.F. Born 30/7/12. Commd 5/9/55. Wg Cdr 5/9/68. Retd GD(G) 5/9/72.
KENNEDY G.S. Born 9/2/44. Commd 21/12/62. Sqn Ldr 1/7/75. Retd GD 9/3/97.
KENNEDY I.D. BSc. Born 21/3/52. Commd 14/9/75. Flt Lt 14/12/76. Retd GD 14/9/87.
KENNEDY J. Born 9/10/29. Commd 16/9/71. Sqn Ldr 1/7/79. Retd ADMIN 16/6/83.
KENNEDY J.D. BA. Born 23/8/46. Commd 27/4/69. A Cdre 1/1/97. Retd GD 23/8/02.
KENNEDY J.M. BSc CertEd. Born 1/11/47. Commd 11/3/73. Wg Cdr 1/1/98. Retd GD 6/4/05.
KENNEDY K.T. Born 9/4/39. Commd 9/3/66. Wg Cdr 1/1/80. Retd GD(G) 22/10/86.
KENNEDY M. Born 17/5/36. Commd 31/10/69. Flt Lt 4/5/72. Retd ENG 31/10/77.
KENNEDY M.H. Born 20/11/44. Commd 4/7/69. Flt Lt 4/1/75. Retd GD 6/10/98.
KENNEDY P.A. DSO DFC AFC. Born 15/5/17. Commd 7/3/42. A Cdre 1/7/67. Retd GD 15/12/67.
KENNEDY P.A.M. MCMI ACII. Born 9/11/46. Commd 28/11/69. Wg Cdr 1/1/96. Retd GD 9/11/04.
KENNEDY P.J. Born 4/2/56. Commd 27/2/75. Flt Lt 27/8/80. Retd GD 1/10/89.

KENNEDY P.R. Born 30/10/37. Commd 8/11/68. Flt Lt 29/11/71. Retd SUP 20/6/78.
KENNEDY R.N. Born 16/1/43. Commd 6/4/62. Flt Lt 6/10/67. Retd GD 1/2/75.
KENNEDY S. Born 25/12/56. Commd 30/4/81. Sqn Ldr 1/7/94. Retd GD 14/3/96.
KENNEDY T. Born 7/5/44. Commd 22/11/84. Sqn Ldr 1/6/94. Retd ENG 7/5/99.
KENNEDY Sir Thomas GCB AFC*. Born 19/5/28. Commd 8/4/49. ACM 1/7/83. Retd GD 10/5/86.
KENNELL J.M. MSc. Born 11/11/42. Commd 26/11/60. Gp Capt 1/7/93. Retd GD 11/5/98.
KENNELLY B.C. Born 28/2/33. Commd 4/10/51. Sqn Ldr 1/7/65. Retd GD 19/11/73.
KENNETT P. Born 16/1/30. Commd 30/7/52. Flt Lt 17/5/56. Retd GD 16/1/68.
KENNETT R.J. Born 12/1/31. Commd 20/5/57. Flt Lt 13/12/59. Retd SEC 2/3/69.
KENNETT R.J. MSc BA FInstPet MCIPS MIMIS. Born 11/7/44. Commd 15/7/66. Wg Cdr 1/1/96. Retd SUP 11/7/99.
KENNEY E.StB. BA BAI. Born 14/7/20. Commd 4/1/45. Wg Cdr 1/1/65. Retd ACB 19/7/75.
KENNEY K.L. Born 20/5/36. Commd 12/11/54. Flt Lt 12/5/60. Retd GD 20/5/74.
KENNISH B.E. Born 12/9/65. Commd 27/3/86. Sqn Ldr 1/1/01. Retd FLY(N) 1/1/04.
KENNY T.J. Born 9/6/37. Commd 29/7/55. Flt Lt 7/3/62. Retd GD 9/6/75.
KENRICK M.E. Born 4/2/32. Commd 27/2/52. Sqn Ldr 1/1/89. Retd GD 9/2/90.
KENT A.J. BSc CEng MIEE. Born 1/1/45. Commd 15/7/66. Wg Cdr 1/1/82. Retd ENG 1/1/89.
KENT H.M. MSc CEng MRAeS. Born 7/2/29. Commd 17/1/51. Gp Capt 1/1/83. Retd ENG 7/2/84.
KENT J.W.L. CEng MIMechE. Born 23/3/37. Commd 17/11/59. Wg Cdr 1/7/77. Retd ENG 2/10/84.
KENT K.J. Born 26/9/42. Commd 31/7/86. Flt Lt 31/7/90. Retd OPS SPT 26/9/97.
KENT L.D. Born 11/11/12. Commd 10/12/42. Fg Offr 10/6/43. Retd ENG 15/6/47. rtg Flt Lt.
KENT P.E.M. Born 15/7/37. Commd 16/12/58. Wg Cdr 1/7/74. Retd SUP 19/1/79.
KENT P.L. MB ChB MRCGP DRCOG DAvMed. Born 5/8/49. Commd 6/7/86. Wg Cdr 6/7/92. Retd MED 14/3/97.
KENT R.J. Born 11/10/44. Commd 22/5/64. Sqn Ldr 1/1/81. Retd SUP 31/3/94.
KENT W. AFC. Born 14/1/21. Commd 9/7/43. Gp Capt 1/1/66. Retd GD 14/1/71.
KENT W.W. Born 1/9/24. Commd 12/9/51. Flt Lt 12/6/56. Retd GD 21/9/65.
KENTISH L. Born 6/10/28. Commd 3/4/59. Sqn Ldr 1/1/71. Retd ENG 7/4/79.
KENVYN I.P. BSc. Born 17/8/50. Commd 15/9/69. Sqn Ldr 1/1/84. Retd GD 17/8/88.
KENWARD R.N. The Rev. MA. Born 12/6/34. Commd 1/1/64. Retd Wg Cdr 12/6/89.
KENWORTHY D.I. BSc. Born 12/12/66. Commd 13/9/88. Flt Lt 15/1/92. Retd FLY(P) 6/3/05.
KENWORTHY F.C. BA. Born 13/8/16. Commd 3/1/51. Sqn Ldr 3/11/54. Retd EDN 1/11/64.
KENWORTHY J.M. Born 10/3/20. Commd 11/4/44. Flt Lt 11/4/46. Retd SEC 12/3/74.
KENYON A. Born 2/4/21. Commd 17/9/43. Flt Lt 18/10/65. Retd GD 30/3/68.
KENYON B. Born 7/8/31. Commd 4/3/71. Flt Lt 4/3/75. Retd ADMIN 19/2/88.
KENYON G.B. CEng MIMechE. Born 25/10/35. Commd 27/11/58. Wg Cdr 1/1/74. Retd ENG 11/7/88.
KEOGH J.McK. Born 19/12/17. Commd 6/10/44. Sqn Ldr 1/1/60. Retd SEC 12/1/73.
KEOGH R.P. Born 3/8/25. Commd 8/10/57. Flt Lt 7/6/51. Retd GD 17/12/57.
KEOGH T.C. Born 6/5/29. Commd 15/9/60. Flt Lt 15/9/66. Retd PE 14/9/68.
KEPPEL-COMPTON R.W. Born 24/1/38. Commd 6/6/57. Gp Capt 1/1/85. Retd ADMIN 1/12/88.
KEPPIE I.H. AFC. Born 22/7/33. Commd 27/7/54. Gp Capt 1/1/73. Retd GD 29/3/75.
KER N.R. Born 14/11/12. Commd 16/2/49. Flt Lt 3/7/49. Retd GD 14/11/64.
KER R.F. Born 17/12/37. Commd 21/7/61. Flt Lt 25/7/66. Retd GD 31/1/70.
KERBY R.S. Born 8/9/22. Commd 24/1/42. Wg Cdr 1/1/62. Retd GD 16/9/68.
KERMEEN R.W. MSc BSc PGCE FBCS. Born 1/4/41. Commd 30/8/66. Sqn Ldr 1/3/73. Retd ADMIN 30/8/82.
 Re-instated 4/5/83. Wg Cdr 1/1/87. Retd ADMIN 1/10/95.
KERMODE R.E.T. Born 9/7/23. Commd 3/2/44. Sqn Ldr 1/10/55. Retd ENG 4/4/69.
KERNS R.K. MSc BTech. Born 5/9/48. Commd 1/9/71. Sqn Ldr 1/7/79. Retd ENG 1/9/87.
KERR C. MCMI. Born 7/3/17. Commd 21/10/54. Sqn Ldr 1/1/66. Retd ENG 7/6/74.
KERR D.B. Born 12/5/33. Commd 6/5/53. Flt Lt 7/3/62. Retd GD 9/4/72.
KERR D.C. Born 6/12/33. Commd 8/9/54. Flt Lt 6/3/63. Retd GD 6/6/77.
KERR G.J.A. AFC. Born 21/2/24. Commd 25/9/52. Sqn Ldr 1/1/70. Retd GD 21/2/79.
KERR K.J. Born 26/9/28. Commd 28/2/51. Flt Lt 28/11/56. Retd GD 26/9/66.
KERR R.G. Born 16/5/35. Commd 17/12/57. Sqn Ldr 1/7/66. Retd GD 16/5/73.
KERR T. Born 26/10/48. Commd 11/5/78. Sqn Ldr 1/1/87. Retd SUP 31/10/96.
KERRIDGE G.E. Born 12/2/18. Commd 10/8/40. Sqn Ldr 1/7/51. Retd GD 11/12/57.
KERRIDGE M.H. Born 12/1/41. Commd 11/8/77. Flt Lt 11/8/78. Retd ADMIN 11/8/85.
KERRIDGE R.S. BEng. Born 23/5/38. Commd 23/10/59. Flt Lt 2/7/63. Retd GD 2/10/77.
KERRIGAN C.P. Born 13/6/53. Commd 15/8/85. Sqn Ldr 1/1/93. Retd ENG 15/1/96.
KERRIGAN J.G. Born 8/4/33. Commd 27/7/54. Gp Capt 1/7/84. Retd SEC 8/12/86.
KERRISON P.I. BSc CEng MIMechE MRAeS. Born 24/10/42. Commd 15/7/64. Sqn Ldr 1/7/77. Retd ENG 24/10/99.
KERSHAW J. Born 22/6/46. Commd 20/8/69. Wg Cdr 1/1/92. Retd GD 22/6/01.
KERSHAW J.B. MB ChB MRCPath. Born 17/4/47. Commd 27/4/70. Sqn Ldr 13/8/78. Retd MED 14/7/86.
KERSHAW M.E. DPhysEd MCMI. Born 6/3/47. Commd 19/8/68. Sqn Ldr 1/1/82. Retd ADMIN 21/5/01.
KERSHAW R.M. Born 24/2/20. Commd 29/6/50. Sqn Ldr 1/7/61. Retd SUP 15/10/70.
KERSS T.J. MBE BSc. Born 29/6/57. Commd 31/8/75. Wg Cdr 1/7/93. Retd GD 1/7/96.
KERSWELL R.H. Born 9/2/22. Commd 21/7/44. Flt Lt 29/6/50. Retd GD 15/10/62.
KERTLAND R.J. MCMI. Born 13/1/19. Commd 22/3/51. Sqn Ldr 1/7/62. Retd ENG 14/4/72.

KESSELER P.J. Born 11/5/37. Commd 5/11/59. Gp Capt 1/1/86. Retd SUP 11/5/92.
KESTERTON P. BA. Born 17/1/54. Commd 7/6/73. Flt Lt 7/12/79. Retd GD(G) 23/4/82.
KETCHER L.S. AFM. Born 14/11/23. Commd 4/3/44. Sqn Ldr 1/1/75. Retd GD 30/9/77.
KETTELL L.P. Born 3/12/60. Commd 31/1/80. Sqn Ldr 1/1/91. Retd SUP 3/12/98.
KETTLE A. MBE. Born 22/11/19. Commd 25/8/55. Sqn Ldr 1/7/74. Retd GD(G) 8/9/77.
KETTLE J.D.N. MA CEng FIEE. Born 5/4/36. Commd 30/9/56. Gp Capt 1/1/79. Retd ENG 7/5/90.
KETTLEWELL G.V.W. Born 30/1/16. Commd 31/7/37. Wg Cdr 1/1/49. Retd GD 1/4/59.
KEVAN G.J. Born 25/10/48. Commd 30/1/75. Wg Cdr 1/1/02. Retd GD 1/1/04.
KEVAN R.G. BA. Born 14/12/38. Commd 15/1/63. Sqn Ldr 29/4/70. Retd EDN 15/1/79.
KEWIN J.A. Born 22/1/43. Commd 9/3/62. Flt Lt 9/9/67. Retd GD 27/5/96.
KEY G.C. OBE DFC MA. Born 1/1/14. Commd 4/5/36. Gp Capt 1/7/55. Retd GD 1/1/64.
KEY S.W.R.A. Born 12/9/34. Commd 26/7/55. Sqn Ldr 1/1/66. Retd GD 12/9/94.
KEYS A.R. DFC BSc. Born 21/2/29. Commd 29/12/51. Wg Cdr 1/1/66. Retd GD 2/7/70.
KEYS D. Born 22/4/28. Commd 12/1/55. Flt Lt 29/4/59. Retd GD 18/6/66.
KEYS P.E. Born 2/12/34. Commd 19/8/65. Flt Lt 19/8/70. Retd GD 3/4/79.
KEYTE H.W. Born 1/11/16. Commd 4/1/47. Sqn Ldr 1/7/62. Retd SUP 1/11/74. rg Gp Capt.
KEYTE S.W. OBE BA. Born 27/12/41. Commd 6/7/62. Wg Cdr 1/7/86. Retd GD 3/4/93.
KEYWORTH G. Born 2/1/47. Commd 25/2/66. Flt Lt 25/8/72. Retd SUP 2/1/85.
KHAN F.A. MSc BSc CEng MIExpE MIMechE. Born 24/6/48. Commd 15/6/71. Sqn Ldr 1/1/83. Retd ENG 14/3/97.
KHAN R. BEng. Born 4/7/60. Commd 1/8/86. Flt Lt 3/7/91. Retd ENG 5/7/99.
KHAN R. MB BS. Born 4/10/65. Commd 6/2/00. Sqn Ldr 1/8/97. Retd MEDICAL 14/9/04.
KHAREGAT R.P. Born 16/2/36. Commd 31/7/56. Sqn Ldr 1/7/66. Retd GD 16/2/74.
KIDD A.M. BSc. Born 25/7/56. Commd 30/10/77. Sqn Ldr 1/7/89. Retd ENG 25/7/00.
KIDD B.J.G. MCMI. Born 20/3/32. Commd 2/2/56. Gp Capt 1/1/77. Retd ENG 1/4/85.
KIDD C. Born 8/6/20. Commd 10/8/43. Flt Lt 10/11/55. Retd GD 1/11/61.
KIDD D.A. MBE CEng MIERE. Born 17/8/33. Commd 6/6/57. Gp Capt 1/1/85. Retd ENG 17/8/88.
KIDD E.A. Born 7/5/45. Commd 22/5/83. Flt Lt 27/7/76. Retd GD 1/8/94.
KIDD M.A.M. Born 13/7/44. Commd 25/10/63. Gp Capt 1/7/94. Retd ADMIN 14/7/96.
KIDD W.R. Born 21/3/37. Commd 25/6/57. Flt Lt 3/1/63. Retd GD 5/4/75.
KIDDLE P.G. Born 5/3/45. Commd 31/1/64. Sqn Ldr 1/1/82. Retd GD 5/3/89.
KIDNEY R. AFC. Born 9/11/35. Commd 30/7/57. Gp Capt 1/1/87. Retd GD 16/7/88.
KIELY C.T. Born 5/8/50. Commd 28/2/80. Sqn Ldr 1/7/90. Retd OPS(ATC) 3/7/04.
KIERNAN A.H. Born 1/4/13. Commd 7/1/43. Flt Lt 7/7/47. Retd PE 21/4/68.
KIGGELL L.J. Born 18/4/41. Commd 22/7/66. Wg Cdr 1/7/85. Retd GD(G) 5/2/96.
KIGGELL P.S. OBE. Born 27/4/43. Commd 3/1/64. Gp Capt 1/1/92. Retd GD 2/1/94.
KILBURN P. BSc. Born 29/1/30. Commd 2/1/52. Sqn Ldr 21/6/63. Retd ADMIN 1/11/86.
KILBY K.R. Born 5/3/54. Commd 8/12/83. Flt Lt 8/12/85. Retd ENG 2/4/93.
KILCOYNE J.G. Born 20/5/39. Commd 18/10/79. Sqn Ldr 1/1/88. Retd SY 20/5/94.
KILFORD P.C. Born 8/11/54. Commd 24/4/80. Sqn Ldr 1/1/88. Retd ENG 31/3/94.
KILFORD R.I. BSc. Born 6/1/59. Commd 29/8/77. Sqn Ldr 1/1/90. Retd ENG 6/1/97.
KILGORE D.I. Born 14/4/44. Commd 2/4/65. Flt Lt 4/5/72. Retd GD(G) 2/12/77.
KILLICK M.R. Born 4/10/38. Commd 30/4/57. Gp Capt 1/7/87. Retd GD 4/10/93.
KILLINGRAY A.J. Born 24/5/44. Commd 3/7/80. Sqn Ldr 1/1/90. Retd ENG 19/11/97.
KILMINSTER M.R. Born 25/6/47. Commd 27/11/68. Fg Offr 12/10/69. Retd GD 31/5/73.
KILNER A. Born 23/9/34. Commd 30/8/66. Flt Lt 30/8/66. Retd PI 4/3/78.
KILPATRICK N.D. BA MB BChir MRCS LRCP FRCOG. Born 8/12/31. Commd 4/1/59. Wg Cdr 2/2/71. Retd MED 2/11/78.
KIMBER A.B. Born 6/11/40. Commd 17/5/63. Fg Offr 17/5/65. Retd GD 6/4/66.
KIMBER C.J. BEd. Born 19/10/61. Commd 30/3/86. Flt Lt 30/9/89. Retd OPS SPT 30/3/02.
KIMBER P.L. Born 24/9/20. Commd 18/3/45. Flt Lt 22/10/48. Retd GD 20/7/65.
KIMBERLEY R.G. Born 10/8/48. Commd 29/10/68. Flt Lt 29/5/74. Retd GD 19/10/80.
KIME A.B. Born 24/6/34. Commd 27/2/70. Sqn Ldr 1/1/78. Retd ENG 24/6/92.
KIME K.C. Born 17/9/33. Commd 16/2/59. Sqn Ldr 1/1/83. Retd GD(G) 31/12/85.
KIME K.G. Born 25/4/37. Commd 19/2/76. Sqn Ldr 1/1/89. Retd ENG 25/4/95.
KIMMINGS R.W. MBE. Born 29/4/22. Commd 24/2/55. Sqn Ldr 1/1/71. Retd GD 29/4/77.
KINCH D.G. DFM. Born 6/6/29. Commd 9/9/54. Sqn Ldr 1/1/65. Retd GD 8/6/79.
KINDELL H.D. BA. Born 5/11/62. Commd 10/6/91. Sqn Ldr 1/1/97. Retd ADMIN (TRG) 8/3/03.
KINDER E. FCIS MCMI. Born 3/5/31. Commd 15/6/50. Gp Capt 1/7/76. Retd SEC 7/10/81.
KINDER J.R. Born 31/10/62. Commd 8/4/82. Flt Lt 8/10/87. Retd GD 30/11/00.
KINDER R. Born 9/10/23. Commd 7/7/49. Sqn Ldr 1/7/59. Retd GD 9/10/72.
KING A.D. Born 16/9/23. Commd 22/11/56. Flt Lt 22/5/60. Retd GD 27/2/82.
KING A.F. CEng MIMechE. Born 23/3/33. Commd 30/5/61. Sqn Ldr 1/7/69. Retd ENG 27/5/83.
KING A.J. MInstPet MCIPS. Born 25/6/43. Commd 12/7/63. Sqn Ldr 1/1/76. Retd SUP 17/7/93.
KING A.J. Born 3/2/58. Commd 30/4/81. Wg Cdr 1/7/01. Retd GD 1/8/04.
KING A.R. MCMI. Born 19/8/31. Commd 21/11/56. Wg Cdr 1/7/76. Retd GD 19/4/85.
KING A.S. CEng MRACS MIEE. Born 15/3/35. Commd 2/10/57. Wg Cdr 1/7/75. Retd ENG 1/4/87.

KING A.V. Born 26/5/16. Commd 1/11/45. Flt Lt 4/1/51. Retd ENG 17/7/54.
KING B. Born 15/3/33. Commd 21/10/65. Sqn Ldr 1/1/78. Retd SUP 15/5/80.
KING B.A.R. Born 1/4/19. Commd 1/5/47. Flt Lt 1/11/51. Retd SUP 31/7/64.
KING B.H. Born 25/3/38. Commd 21/7/61. Flt Lt 9/5/66. Retd GD 25/3/76.
KING B.J. Born 8/8/33. Commd 4/6/52. Flt Lt 30/10/57. Retd GD 8/8/70.
KING B.M. Born 1/7/10. Commd 27/1/43. Flt Offr 27/1/48. Retd SEC 5/1/50.
KING B.W. Born 12/2/48. Commd 28/2/69. Flt Lt 28/2/72. Retd GD 12/8/92.
KING C. OBE CEng MRAeS MCMI. Born 2/9/21. Commd 24/5/51. Gp Capt 1/1/71. Retd ENG 2/10/75.
KING C. Born 13/12/49. Commd 28/11/69. Sqn Ldr 1/7/90. Retd GD 22/4/94.
KING C.H. Born 16/3/19. Commd 29/8/45. Flt Lt 4/12/52. Retd SEC 24/9/69.
KING D. Born 20/9/34. Commd 24/2/61. Flt Lt 1/4/66. Retd GD 20/9/72.
KING D. Born 13/9/30. Commd 28/2/51. Flt Lt 20/12/56. Retd GD 31/7/62.
KING E. DFC. Born 8/3/19. Commd 3/4/48. Flt Lt 3/4/48. Retd GD 31/3/62.
KING E. Born 20/1/36. Commd 16/9/71. Flt Lt 17/8/76. Retd MED(T) 21/1/78.
KING E.H. OBE. Born 6/3/18. Commd 15/4/39. Wg Cdr 1/7/56. Retd GD 6/3/65.
KING E.T. MB BS DPH LMSSA. Born 21/3/22. Commd 29/6/50. Wg Cdr 15/12/62. Retd MED 30/10/73.
KING E.T.I. MRAeS MCMI. Born 26/5/44. Commd 3/1/64. Gp Capt 1/1/86. Retd GD 20/4/87.
KING F.W. The Rev. Born 4/2/24. Commd 20/5/55. Retd Wg Cdr 18/6/70.
KING G.A. MCMI. Born 28/6/32. Commd 5/2/53. Wg Cdr 1/1/74. Retd GD 12/9/83.
KING G.A. Born 13/8/47. Commd 28/6/79. Sqn Ldr 1/1/86. Retd ADMIN 27/11/95.
KING H. OBE. Born 11/5/18. Commd 19/12/42. Gp Capt 1/1/64. Retd GD 11/5/73.
KING I.D. Born 28/11/63. Commd 26/4/93. Flt Lt 21/8/93. Retd ADMIN (SEC) 23/4/04.
KING J. Born 6/11/20. Commd 12/6/43. Sqn Ldr 1/4/55. Retd GD 1/3/62.
KING J. Born 14/6/30. Commd 13/8/52. Sqn Ldr 1/7/66. Retd GD 1/1/69.
KING J. BSc. Born 29/12/50. Commd 14/11/69. Flt Lt 15/10/73. Retd GD 1/2/88.
KING J.A. AFC. Born 31/12/43. Commd 22/2/63. Gp Capt 1/1/91. Retd GD 31/12/98.
KING J.A. Born 13/9/31. Commd 6/9/56. Sqn Ldr 1/1/83. Retd GD 13/9/88.
KING J.F. BEM. Born 27/4/16. Commd 31/7/58. Flt Lt 31/7/61. Retd SEC 7/11/65.
KING J.G. MRCS. Born 26/7/30. Commd 18/8/56. Gp Capt 28/8/79. Retd MED 10/4/87.
KING J.G. Born 30/8/42. Commd 22/7/71. Sqn Ldr 1/7/80. Retd ENG 7/6/97.
KING J.H. BA. Born 4/11/13. Commd 6/9/40. Wg Cdr 1/7/58. Retd SUP 13/4/67.
KING J.M. Born 15/1/35. Commd 1/2/62. Sqn Ldr 1/1/77. Retd SEC 4/4/87.
KING J.P. Born 12/6/37. Commd 1/5/61. Flt Lt 9/3/68. Retd GD 9/4/76.
KING J.S. Born 3/2/44. Commd 4/11/82. Sqn Ldr 1/7/91. Retd ENG 14/3/96.
KING J.W. DFC DFM FCIS. Born 26/5/22. Commd 8/12/42. Gp Capt 1/7/67. Retd GD 26/10/73.
KING M.D.J. BSc MIL. Born 20/5/51. Commd 2/1/70. Wg Cdr 1/1/92. Retd GD 20/5/95.
KING M.G. Born 28/11/30. Commd 1/8/51. Wg Cdr 1/7/72. Retd GD 29/11/80.
KING M.J. Born 13/2/65. Commd 19/7/87. Flt Lt 19/1/92. Retd FLY(N) 13/8/04.
KING N.A. Born 1/1/62. Commd 11/5/78. Flt Lt 26/5/87. Retd GD 9/8/91.
KING N.M. Born 6/1/54. Commd 11/5/78. Flt Lt 11/11/83. Retd GD 10/10/93.
KING P. CBE FCMI. Born 3/4/35. Commd 27/10/54. A Cdre 1/7/85. Retd GD 27/5/88.
KING P.F. CB OBE FRCS(Edin) MFOM MRCS LRCP DLO MRAeS. Born 17/9/22. Commd 14/8/45. AVM 1/7/83. Retd MED 17/9/87.
KING P.M. BSc. Born 26/2/56. Commd 1/8/76. Wg Cdr 1/7/93. Retd SUP 26/2/02.
KING P.T. MB BS FRCR DMRD. Born 24/7/36. Commd 21/1/63. Wg Cdr 4/12/77. Retd MED 19/11/78.
KING R. Born 31/8/23. Commd 6/6/57. Flt Lt 1/4/63. Retd GD 28/2/70.
KING R.A. Born 19/9/44. Commd 24/4/64. Sqn Ldr 1/1/89. Retd GD 19/9/02.
KING R.A.D. Born 15/11/45. Commd 20/9/68. Flt Lt 20/3/74. Retd GD 17/10/86.
KING R.F. MVO . Born 2/12/46. Commd 18/8/67. Sqn Ldr 1/7/82. Retd FLY(P) 2/12/03.
KING R.J. Born 4/9/12. Commd 22/4/43. Sqn Ldr 1/7/54. Retd ENG 30/4/66.
KING R.P.J. Born 27/8/29. Commd 12/12/51. Sqn Ldr 1/1/61. Retd GD 26/12/67.
KING R.S. BA. Born 12/3/32. Commd 1/2/69. Sqn Ldr 1/2/69. Retd EDN 1/5/80.
KING R.W. Born 9/6/47. Commd 1/3/68. Wg Cdr 1/1/91. Retd GD 9/6/02.
KING S.E. Born 29/4/22. Commd 3/8/61. Flt Lt 3/8/64. Retd ENG 29/4/72.
KING T.A. Born 31/1/48. Commd 4/10/78. Flt Lt 19/7/74. Retd GD(G) 21/2/93.
KING T.N. Born 2/10/34. Commd 10/4/56. Wg Cdr 1/7/82. Retd GD 2/10/89.
KING V.D. OBE. Born 25/2/33. Commd 8/10/56. Wg Cdr 1/1/74. Retd SUP 25/2/88.
KING W.C. AFC. Born 23/2/26. Commd 7/5/53. Flt Lt 7/11/56. Retd GD 3/8/64.
KING W.F. Born 18/1/43. Commd 21/2/74. Sqn Ldr 1/1/74. Retd ADMIN 18/1/98.
KING W.J. MBE. Born 26/12/19. Commd 30/7/59. Flt Lt 30/7/64. Retd ENG 31/5/73.
KINGAN J.G. MB ChB MFCM AFOM DPH. Born 27/11/23. Commd 2/6/49. Gp Capt 1/7/76. Retd MED 27/11/81.
KINGDOM A.A. Born 2/11/30. Commd 8/1/62. Sqn Ldr 1/1/74. Retd SEC 1/9/81.
KINGDOM R.J. MBE. Born 12/5/22. Commd 11/6/45. Flt Lt 4/1/51. Retd GD 13/6/67.
KINGDON A.A. Born 8/5/48. Commd 17/7/87. Sqn Ldr 1/7/94. Retd FLY(ALM) 8/5/03.
KINGDON R.C.N. Born 21/10/32. Commd 26/3/52. Flt Lt 18/9/57. Retd GD(G) 21/10/88.
KINGHORN R.A. MCMI. Born 4/6/32. Commd 19/4/51. Wg Cdr 1/1/77. Retd SUP 1/10/84.

KINGS A.F. BSc. Born 2/7/59. Commd 3/9/79. Sqn Ldr 1/1/91. Retd ENG 2/7/97.
KINGS R.A. Born 22/10/14. Commd 3/8/40. Flt Lt 1/9/45. Retd GD(G) 27/10/64. rtg Sqn Ldr.
KINGSFORD P.G. BSc. Born 30/6/50. Commd 1/11/71. Sqn Ldr 1/1/84. Retd GD 30/6/88.
KINGSHOTT K. CBE DFC. Born 8/7/24. Commd 21/1/46. AVM 1/1/78. Retd GD 29/1/80.
KINGSLEY J.T. Born 21/11/36. Commd 10/8/55. Flt Lt 15/2/65. Retd GD 23/11/73.
KINGSTON D.W. Born 8/8/23. Commd 25/10/44. Flt Lt 25/4/48. Retd GD 8/8/66.
KINGSTON J.M. MB BS MRCS LRCP DAvMed. Born 20/5/43. Commd 11/5/80. Wg Cdr 11/5/86.
    Retd MED 14/3/96.
KINGSTON R. Born 10/11/44. Commd 17/12/65. Sqn Ldr 1/1/76. Retd GD 10/11/82.
KINGSTON R.A. Born 7/9/34. Commd 21/12/67. Sqn Ldr 1/1/77. Retd GD(G) 4/9/79.
KINGSTON-BROWN D. Born 29/7/51. Commd 16/9/76. Sqn Ldr 1/7/92. Retd ADMIN 31/8/95.
KINGSWOOD C.J. Born 12/12/58. Commd 11/1/79. Flt Lt 11/7/84. Retd GD 12/12/96.
KINGTON-BLAIR-OLIPHANT D.N. CB OBE BA. Born 22/12/11. Commd 17/3/33. A Cdre 1/7/58. Retd ENG 14/4/66.
    rtg AVM.
KINGWILL P.M. Born 14/8/46. Commd 23/3/66. Sqn Ldr 1/7/79. Retd SUP 14/8/84. Re-entered 1/3/88.
    Sqn Ldr 17/1/83. Retd SUP 14/8/01.
KINGWILL P.N. Born 24/11/14. Commd 9/5/54. Wg Cdr 1/7/59. Retd SUP 14/8/65.
KINNAIRD S. BA. Born 30/1/61. Commd 16/9/79. Sqn Ldr 1/7/92. Retd GD 1/9/99.
KINNARD R.M. Born 28/9/17. Commd 29/6/50. Sqn Ldr 1/7/65. Retd SUP 28/9/72.
KINNEAR J.T. Born 16/8/26. Commd 4/6/64. Flt Lt 4/6/67. Retd ENG 1/6/74.
KINNELL R. Born 25/5/58. Commd 22/11/84. Sqn Ldr 1/1/01. Retd OPS SPT(REGT) 11/12/03.
KINNIN V. Born 18/5/42. Commd 22/5/80. Sqn Ldr 1/1/90. Retd ENG 18/5/97.
KINVER J.A. Born 15/10/19. Commd 20/8/43. Flt Lt 31/12/47. Retd GD 20/6/64.
KINVIG G.A. Born 8/1/64. Commd 24/3/83. Sqn Ldr 1/7/95. Retd ADMIN (SEC) 8/7/04.
KINZETT R.H. BA FCIPD MInstAM. Born 23/9/49. Commd 17/1/72. Gp Capt 1/7/97. Retd ADMIN 1/10/00.
KIRALFY R.J.C. MSc BSc CEng FCMI FIEE. Born 13/9/50. Commd 15/9/69. Gp Capt 1/1/99. Retd GD 1/7/04.
KIRBY B.C. BA. Born 24/12/37. Commd 23/7/58. Wg Cdr 1/7/80. Retd ENG 29/5/89.
KIRBY E.F. MCMI. Born 23/6/25. Commd 6/10/44. Wg Cdr 1/7/62. Retd GD 19/6/76.
KIRBY M.A. Born 25/12/45. Commd 2/2/68. Flt Lt 2/8/74. Retd SUP 5/5/79.
KIRBY N.R. Born 29/5/46. Commd 5/2/65. Sqn Ldr 1/7/79. Retd GD 29/5/90.
KIRBY R.A. Born 5/9/44. Commd 17/7/64. Sqn Ldr 1/1/79. Retd GD 5/9/84.
KIRBY R.S. BA. Born 11/9/52. Commd 29/9/71. Flt Lt 15/4/78. Retd ADMIN 1/2/83.
KIRBY T. MBE. Born 5/2/51. Commd 20/9/79. Gp Capt 1/7/99. Retd GD 16/4/05.
KIRBY W.J. MBE. Born 8/10/36. Commd 15/2/56. Wg Cdr 1/7/79. Retd GD 8/4/87.
KIRK A.N. Born 20/12/31. Commd 7/12/54. Sqn Ldr 1/1/63. Retd ENG 9/12/70.
KIRK A.P. Born 9/5/47. Commd 20/9/68. Wg Cdr 1/1/93. Retd GD 5/1/01.
KIRK A.W. MB ChB DAvMed DRCOG ALCM. Born 13/12/52. Commd 22/1/74. Wg Cdr 7/2/91. Retd MED 22/7/93.
KIRK G.H. Born 17/11/43. Commd 9/3/62. Flt Lt 9/9/67. Retd GD 17/11/81. re-entrant 14/9/83. Sqn Ldr 1/7/90.
    Retd GD 17/11/98.
KIRK J.E. OBE. Born 18/9/03. Commd 28/7/34. Gp Capt 1/1/53. Retd GD 18/9/58.
KIRK J.M. MB ChB MRCGP. Born 16/5/43. Commd 18/4/66. Sqn Ldr 1/8/74. Retd MED 18/4/82.
KIRK J.N. Born 11/2/62. Commd 31/1/80. Wg Cdr 1/1/99. Retd OPS SPT 23/7/02.
KIRK J.S. MBE. Born 16/5/34. Commd 13/8/52. Sqn Ldr 1/7/79. Retd GD 30/12/84.
KIRK J.S. Born 28/6/50. Commd 31/10/69. Flt Lt 30/4/75. Retd GD 28/6/88.
KIRK M.A. Born 2/2/44. Commd 24/6/65. Flt Lt 1/7/68. Retd GD 10/9/76.
KIRK R. MCMI. Born 13/6/33. Commd 23/3/55. Sqn Ldr 1/1/66. Retd GD 13/6/71.
KIRK W.E. Born 8/2/31. Commd 9/4/52. Wg Cdr 1/1/73. Retd GD 20/5/83.
KIRKBRIDE R. Born 10/5/24. Commd 2/6/44. Flt Lt 10/11/55. Retd GD 30/11/78.
KIRKHAM A.J.A. BSc. Born 20/1/57. Commd 2/3/80. Flt Lt 2/6/83. Retd GD(G) 2/3/96.
KIRKHAM R.N. Born 19/1/43. Commd 21/7/65. Flt Lt 12/11/69. Retd GD 19/8/81.
KIRKHAM R.R. Born 15/7/33. Commd 1/7/83. Sqn Ldr 1/7/83. Retd ENG 28/11/86.
KIRKHOPE T. BSc. Born 9/10/49. Commd 17/10/71. Wg Cdr 1/7/94. Retd GD 4/8/01.
KIRKLAND B.S. Born 18/2/41. Commd 3/10/61. Sqn Ldr 1/1/72. Retd SEC 18/2/79.
KIRKLAND D.W. Born 29/10/33. Commd 27/3/56. Flt Lt 7/7/63. Retd GD 24/7/73.
KIRKLAND G. BSc. Born 23/10/43. Commd 26/9/66. Flt Lt 26/6/68. Retd GD 26/9/82.
KIRKMAN W.G. Born 20/6/29. Commd 26/11/53. Flt Lt 26/5/58. Retd GD 16/1/64.
KIRKPATRICK P.S. Born 29/1/47. Commd 27/1/77. Flt Lt 27/1/79. Retd MED 29/1/85.
KIRKPATRICK R.B.J. MB BS DAvMed. Born 29/4/61. Commd 9/11/92. Wg Cdr 26/4/99. Retd MEDICAL 31/1/04.
KIRKPATRICK W.J. BA. Born 10/8/53. Commd 19/10/75. Wg Cdr 1/7/91. Retd GD 1/2/98.
KIRKPATRICK W.J. BSc. Born 26/2/53. Commd 30/10/72. Flt Lt 15/10/75. Retd GD 30/10/84.
KIRKUP A.P.J. Born 21/6/51. Commd 16/3/73. Flt Lt 16/3/76. Retd GD 1/7/01.
KIRMAN C.K. Born 7/11/47. Commd 26/4/84. Flt Lt 26/4/88. Retd ADMIN 7/11/02.
KIRTLEY S. Born 6/11/21. Commd 25/4/42. Wg Cdr 1/1/61. Retd GD 1/9/68.
KIRTON P.A.M. Born 8/3/61. Commd 14/1/88. Flt Lt 14/1/90. Retd GD 2/1/96.
KIRTON P.J. BEng. Born 22/9/49. Commd 18/4/71. Flt Lt 15/10/73. Retd GD 22/9/87.
KISSANE R.C. Born 2/1/33. Commd 12/10/54. Flt Lt 12/4/60. Retd GD(G) 26/4/87.

KITCHEN S. Born 27/2/16. Commd 19/3/44. Flt Lt 19/9/47. Retd GD 9/5/58.
KITCHENER B. Born 8/9/35. Commd 21/7/61. Fg Offr 21/7/63. Retd GD 23/7/66.
KITCHIN J.S.F. Born 15/8/46. Commd 25/6/65. Flt Lt 25/12/70. Retd GD 1/3/77.
KITCHING D.J. Born 7/10/42. Commd 1/8/69. Wg Cdr 1/1/91. Retd GD 2/4/93.
KITCHING R. Born 23/5/33. Commd 5/9/57. Flt Lt 5/3/62. Retd GD 23/5/71.
KITCHINGMAN B.F. Born 27/11/23. Commd 2/3/61. Flt Lt 2/3/66. Retd SEC 10/9/68.
KITLEY A.J.H. MCMI. Born 15/7/22. Commd 18/11/41. Wg Cdr 1/1/59. Retd GD 15/7/69.
KITSON D.A. Born 27/2/31. Commd 17/12/52. Fg Offr 17/12/54. Retd SEC 17/12/55.
KITT A.P. BA. Born 20/11/59. Commd 13/2/83. Sqn Ldr 1/1/97. Retd OPS SPT(REGT) 13/2/05.
KIVER P.A. BSc. Born 9/4/57. Commd 26/11/78. Sqn Ldr 1/1/90. Retd GD(G) 9/4/95.
KLEBOE D.E. Born 19/10/21. Commd 24/12/41. Flt Lt 1/9/45. Retd ENG 19/10/76. rtg Sqn Ldr.
KLEIN C.J. Born 23/12/58. Commd 24/7/81. Fg Offr 24/1/82. Retd GD(G) 29/5/85.
KLEYNHANS J.W. Born 7/8/28. Commd 7/5/57. Flt Lt 7/11/61. Retd GD 7/5/73.
KNAPP J.D. AFC. Born 15/12/30. Commd 8/10/52. Sqn Ldr 1/1/81. Retd GD 15/12/91.
KNAPP P.D. Born 21/1/50. Commd 16/11/72. Sqn Ldr 1/1/91. Retd GD 14/3/96.
KNAPPER W.F. OBE. Born 6/7/28. Commd 5/4/50. Gp Capt 1/1/72. Retd GD 14/1/83.
KNAPTON P.A. OBE DFC. Born 4/5/21. Commd 19/2/42. Wg Cdr 1/7/60. Retd GD 8/4/75.
KNELL J.C. Born 4/9/30. Commd 4/7/51. Flt Lt 17/10/56. Retd GD 4/9/68.
KNEVITT H.J. BSc DCAe MIMechE MRAeS ACGI. Born 20/1/17. Commd 20/11/39. Wg Cdr 1/1/56.
    Retd ENG 10/3/62.
KNIGHT A.C.E. The Rev. BSc. Born 22/3/42. Commd 2/9/73. Retd Wg Cdr 2/9/95.
KNIGHT A.E. Born 17/9/61. Commd 8/9/83. Flt Lt 1/8/89. Retd GD 17/9/99.
KNIGHT A.F.H. Born 7/10/23. Commd 20/9/60. Sqn Ldr 20/9/68. Retd ADMIN 20/9/76.
KNIGHT B.J.S. Born 24/12/25. Commd 5/2/48. Flt Lt 1/1/59. Retd GD 4/8/76.
KNIGHT B.R.R. CEng MRAeS. Born 12/9/35. Commd 7/2/58. Sqn Ldr 1/7/66. Retd ENG 7/2/74.
KNIGHT C.A. Born 30/12/50. Commd 22/5/70. Sqn Ldr 1/1/90. Retd FLY(N) 12/6/05.
KNIGHT D. MSc BSc. Born 27/2/43. Commd 31/10/66. Sqn Ldr 10/8/73. Retd ADMIN 31/10/82.
KNIGHT D.A. MBE MA BA. Born 23/5/55. Commd 2/9/73. Wg Cdr 1/1/94. Retd ENG 15/11/00.
KNIGHT D.A. Born 18/8/54. Commd 17/9/72. Flt Lt 12/2/80. Retd GD 18/8/92.
KNIGHT F.K. Born 10/10/20. Commd 6/12/41. Wg Cdr 1/7/71. Retd SUP 10/10/75.
KNIGHT H.I. MSc BDS MGDSRCSEng LDSRCS DDPHRCS. Born 29/10/57. Commd 15/2/96. Wg Cdr 30/1/96.
    Retd DENTAL 16/9/03.
KNIGHT J. Born 5/1/39. Commd 3/8/62. Flt Lt 3/2/68. Retd GD 10/4/78.
KNIGHT J. BSc. Born 9/7/49. Commd 2/1/74. Flt Lt 2/1/76. Retd ADMIN 1/4/82.
KNIGHT J.C. Born 29/1/32. Commd 27/3/52. Sqn Ldr 1/7/63. Retd CAT 29/1/70.
KNIGHT J.M. Born 29/11/35. Commd 25/8/67. Flt Lt 4/5/72. Retd GD 31/8/73.
KNIGHT J.S. Born 25/5/26. Commd 7/7/49. Flt Lt 4/6/53. Retd GD 3/10/73.
KNIGHT K.A.R. Born 15/4/43. Commd 9/8/63. Sqn Ldr 1/7/79. Retd GD 25/4/87.
KNIGHT Sir Michael KCB AFC DLitt BA FRAeS. Born 23/11/32. Commd 28/9/54. ACM 1/7/86. Retd GD 18/11/89.
KNIGHT M.F.J. Born 26/1/15. Commd 25/7/45. Sqn Ldr 1/7/60. Retd SEC 26/1/68.
KNIGHT M.H. MA BA. Born 15/5/39. Commd 12/9/61. Sqn Ldr 12/3/72. Retd EDN 1/10/79.
KNIGHT M.J. Born 16/1/49. Commd 27/2/70. Flt Lt 27/2/73. Retd GD 16/1/87.
KNIGHT O.J.A. Born 21/6/38. Commd 6/10/59. Wg Cdr 1/7/83. Retd GD 25/9/93.
KNIGHT P. Born 30/11/62. Commd 20/10/83. Flt Lt 20/4/89. Retd GD 3/11/01.
KNIGHT P.C. MSc. Born 29/9/45. Commd 11/11/65. Wg Cdr 1/7/88. Retd SUP 1/12/99.
KNIGHT P.G. Born 18/5/37. Commd 25/7/71. Flt Lt 25/11/74. Retd ENG 31/12/87.
KNIGHT P.N. MB BS DObstRCOG DPhysMed. Born 5/2/31. Commd 26/6/55. Wg Cdr 26/6/68. Retd MED 26/3/73.
KNIGHT R. Born 26/7/26. Commd 23/8/46. Sqn Ldr 1/4/56. Retd GD 26/7/64.
KNIGHT R. Born 3/4/27. Commd 20/12/46. Sqn Ldr 1/7/57. Retd GD 4/4/64.
KNIGHT R. Born 23/5/36. Commd 22/10/59. Sqn Ldr 1/1/72. Retd GD 23/5/92.
KNIGHT R.I. Born 14/9/43. Commd 21/4/77. Flt Lt 21/4/79. Retd MED(SEC) 21/4/85.
KNIGHT R.M. Born 9/8/47. Commd 6/5/66. Sqn Ldr 1/7/00. Retd FLY(P) 9/8/04.
KNIGHT S.M. Born 28/1/61. Commd 27/3/80. Flt Lt 27/9/85. Retd GD 14/9/96.
KNIGHT T.B. CEng MIMechE MRAeS. Born 2/12/43. Commd 15/7/65. Sqn Ldr 1/1/75. Retd ENG 2/12/81.
KNIGHTON E.A. AFC MCMI. Born 11/10/23. Commd 20/11/45. Wg Cdr 1/1/61. Retd GD 15/3/78.
KNIGHTS E.C.R. Born 25/10/20. Commd 15/7/43. Fg Offr 24/12/45. Retd ENG 24/11/47. rtg Flt Lt.
KNIGHTS P.R. Born 20/12/50. Commd 10/5/73. Flt Lt 10/11/78. Retd GD 22/10/94.
KNIGHTS P.W. Born 2/6/38. Commd 4/3/71. Flt Lt 4/3/73. Retd GD 4/3/79.
KNILL A.P. Born 3/8/55. Commd 2/9/73. Sqn Ldr 1/1/87. Retd GD(G) 3/8/93.
KNILL T.S. MSc BSc(Eng). Born 30/1/60. Commd 4/9/78. Sqn Ldr 1/7/91. Retd ENG 30/1/98.
KNOPP G.E. Born 16/9/33. Commd 18/6/52. Flt Lt 15/4/70. Retd GD 13/10/74.
KNOTT K.S. Born 25/12/21. Commd 20/11/54. Sqn Ldr 1/7/70. Retd GD 25/12/76.
KNOTT L.J. Born 24/4/23. Commd 5/11/53. Flt Lt 4/11/58. Retd GD(G) 24/4/78.
KNOTTS R.M.H. MBA BA. Born 14/1/36. Commd 1/4/71. Sqn Ldr 1/7/78. Retd ENG 1/10/89.
KNOWLES D.W. Born 18/8/48. Commd 2/6/77. Wg Cdr 1/1/94. Retd GD 18/8/03.
KNOWLES J.R. BSc. Born 21/2/51. Commd 28/2/72. Flt Lt 28/5/73. Retd GD 5/10/76.

KNOWLES M.C. Born 10/3/38. Commd 19/2/63. Sqn Ldr 1/7/73. Retd ENG 1/12/90.
KNOWLES P.A. Born 26/1/42. Commd 3/11/77. Sqn Ldr 1/7/87. Retd ENG 31/5/96.
KNOWLES S.J.R. BSc. Born 18/8/47. Commd 25/7/71. Sqn Ldr 1/1/85. Retd ENG 1/1/88.
KNOWLES W.J. CEng FRAeS FCMI FINucE. Born 27/2/18. Commd 3/6/43. Gp Capt 1/7/66. Retd ENG 30/5/70.
KNOX A.E. MBE MCMI. Born 3/4/39. Commd 28/5/66. A Cdre 1/1/88. Retd GD(G) 12/10/92.
KNOX A.G. MSc BA. Born 3/9/45. Commd 23/3/66. Wg Cdr 1/7/87. Retd SUP 13/9/94.
KNOX G.J. Born 4/10/47. Commd 12/7/68. Flt Lt 12/1/74. Retd GD 1/4/78.
KOCH M.E.J. Born 15/12/33. Commd 17/7/56. Flt Lt 7/3/62. Retd GD 1/10/84.
KOCHER C.J. AIIP. Born 18/11/32. Commd 24/10/51. Flt Lt 22/5/57. Retd GD 18/11/70.
KOPP A.K. Born 12/5/50. Commd 18/10/79. Sqn Ldr 1/1/88. Retd SUP 11/9/91.
KORNER J.R. Born 15/9/37. Commd 17/7/56. Flt Lt 21/8/63. Retd GD(G) 6/8/89.
KORNICKI F. Born 18/12/16. Commd 25/6/51. Sqn Ldr 1/1/61. Retd CAT 8/1/72.
KOTLARCHUK S.J. Born 31/5/61. Commd 4/2/99. Flt Lt 23/12/97. Retd OPS SPT(FC) 17/3/04.
KRAUZE I.A. MSc BEng CEng MIEE. Born 9/11/65. Commd 3/8/88. Sqn Ldr 1/7/02. Retd ENGINEER 1/7/05.
KRECKELER M.K. BSc. Born 18/12/60. Commd 2/9/79. Flt Lt 15/9/86. Retd ENG 18/12/00.
KRISTER S.J. MRCS LRCP DPH DIH. Born 12/2/23. Commd 17/10/46. Wg Cdr 3/3/61. Retd MED 17/10/62.
KUIPERS R.D. Born 4/7/39. Commd 27/1/61. Flt Lt 10/2/67. Retd GD 4/7/79.
KUUN D.R. Born 14/12/37. Commd 29/7/58. Wg Cdr 1/1/74. Retd GD 14/12/92.
KYFFIN R.G.M. BA. Born 9/2/61. Commd 19/6/83. Flt Lt 19/12/86. Retd OPS SPT 19/6/99.
KYLE J. DFM. Born 20/9/22. Commd 1/5/44. Flt Lt 19/11/53. Retd GD(G) 20/9/74.
KYLE J.W.P. MBE MCMI. Born 14/4/32. Commd 15/5/58. Wg Cdr 1/1/78. Retd SY 1/6/85.
KYLE R.H. CB MBE BSc(Eng) CEng FRAeS. Born 4/1/43. Commd 30/9/61. AVM 1/1/92. Retd ENG 8/9/97.
KYLE V.T. Born 20/3/32. Commd 26/8/66. Flt Lt 26/8/71. Retd ENG 2/10/79. Re-instated 11/2/81. Flt Lt 5/1/73. Retd ENG 20/3/89.
KYLES J.G. MCMI. Born 7/3/22. Commd 5/5/44. Wg Cdr 1/1/68. Retd SUP 4/3/77.

L

L'ESTRANGE J.P. AFC AFM. Born 26/4/26. Commd 26/9/51. Sqn Ldr 1/7/67. Retd GD 24/8/84.
LA TOUCHE T.P.D. Born 28/3/25. Commd 1/11/48. Wg Cdr 1/1/68. Retd GD 28/3/82.
LABERCOMBE A.J. MCMI. Born 14/12/44. Commd 3/3/67. Wg Cdr 1/7/91. Retd GD 14/9/96.
LABOUCHERE C.M. MA. Born 2/12/38. Commd 30/9/57. Sqn Ldr 1/1/69. Retd ENG 1/1/77.
LACE F.J. Born 18/2/33. Commd 21/11/51. Flt Lt 6/3/57. Retd GD 6/4/76. Re-instated 4/8/31 to 3/6/85.
LACEY K.M. Born 28/8/56. Commd 11/5/78. Flt Lt 30/9/84. Retd GD(G) 9/1/97.
LACEY M. BSc(Eng) CEng MIMechE ACGI. Born 28/10/36. Commd 30/9/56. Wg Cdr 1/7/75. Retd ENG 15/5/90.
LACEY N.V. BTech. Born 17/5/52. Commd 13/9/70. Sqn Ldr 1/1/89. Retd GD 25/7/96.
LACEY T.A. BSc. Born 20/9/48. Commd 25/2/88. Flt Lt 25/2/92. Retd ENG 31/1/02.
LACEY W. Born 17/7/51. Commd 13/1/72. Wg Cdr 1/7/92. Retd SY 14/3/97.
LACY F.S. MBE AE* BA MCMI. Born 27/5/18. Commd 17/9/42. Sqn Ldr 1/1/60. Retd SEC 27/5/75.
LACY P.A. Born 8/8/41. Commd 14/10/71. Sqn Ldr 1/10/76. Retd EDN 14/10/79.
LADBROOK P.R. IEng MRAeS. Born 9/5/47. Commd 4/6/87. Sqn Ldr 1/7/00. Retd ENGINEER 1/7/03.
LADBROOKE D.R. Born 5/3/42. Commd 4/10/63. Flt Lt 5/9/67. Retd GD 16/6/85.
LADDS R.G. BSc CEng MBCS. Born 19/10/50. Commd 26/9/69. Sqn Ldr 1/1/86. Retd ENGINEER 31/1/04.
LADMORE W. Born 28/6/35. Commd 26/5/67. Sqn Ldr 1/7/73. Retd ENG 1/7/76.
LADRO E.A. DFC*. Born 17/7/13. Commd 1/9/44. Flt Lt 1/9/44. Retd GD 29/8/58.
LAGNADO E.J. Born 4/9/28. Commd 17/12/53. Flt Lt 17/12/59. Retd SEC 5/1/69.
LAIDLAY A.M. DFC. Born 14/8/24. Commd 24/3/44. Sqn Ldr 1/1/61. Retd GD 26/3/76.
LAIDLER A.J. Born 23/2/43. Commd 4/10/63. Sqn Ldr 1/1/83. Retd GD 23/2/00.
LAIDLER W.J. FCMI MRAeS. Born 22/4/24. Commd 3/6/44. Gp Capt 1/7/68. Retd GD 25/3/77.
LAINCHBURY I.M. BEng CEng MIEE. Born 3/11/63. Commd 3/8/88. Sqn Ldr 1/7/01. Retd ENGINEER 1/7/04.
LAINES C.J. Born 24/1/49. Commd 25/9/80. Flt Lt 25/9/82. Retd ENG 24/1/99.
LAING C.W. Born 5/5/14. Commd 17/8/39. Sqn Ldr 1/8/47. Retd SUP 17/5/63.
LAING D. Born 31/12/57. Commd 22/9/88. Flt Lt 22/9/90. Retd ADMIN 14/9/96.
LAING G.H.B. MA. Born 29/10/49. Commd 13/9/70. Sqn Ldr 1/1/82. Retd FLY(P) 29/10/04.
LAING J.S. Born 2/3/33. Commd 28/11/60. Flt Lt 28/11/60. Retd GD 2/3/71.
LAING S.J. Born 6/1/65. Commd 8/9/83. Flt Lt 8/7/90. Retd GD(G) 1/6/91.
LAIRD B.C. Born 7/2/41. Commd 16/1/60. Flt Lt 14/2/66. Retd GD 7/2/79.
LAIRD D. MMAR MNI MCMI. Born 10/4/33. Commd 14/8/62. Sqn Ldr 4/8/70. Retd MAR 14/8/78.
LAIRD P.E. DFC AFC. Born 24/2/18. Commd 13/7/43. Flt Lt 13/1/47. Retd GD 1/6/61. rtg Sqn Ldr.
LAITE B.C. Born 8/6/44. Commd 19/4/63. A Cdre 1/1/94. Retd GD 4/6/98.
LAITHWAITE L.J. Born 18/8/35. Commd 17/3/67. Flt Lt 17/3/73. Retd SY 18/12/76.
LAKE A.R. Born 19/7/63. Commd 17/1/85. Flt Lt 17/7/90. Retd GD 19/7/01.
LAKE C.T. Born 28/6/30. Commd 27/6/51. Flt Lt 27/12/55. Retd GD 28/6/68.
LAKE E.E. MVO CEng MRAeS MCMI. Born 3/2/23. Commd 1/10/44. Gp Capt 1/1/75. Retd ENG 3/2/78.
LAKE H.B. MBE. Born 30/7/35. Commd 12/12/59. Wg Cdr 1/7/79. Retd GD 1/3/84.
LAKE P. Born 1/10/29. Commd 24/6/52. Flt Lt 5/11/58. Retd GD 1/10/67.
LAKEN D.E. Born 17/7/28. Commd 7/1/71. Flt Lt 7/1/74. Retd GD(G) 10/8/82.
LAKER J.G.S. MCMI. Born 25/5/48. Commd 8/11/68. Sqn Ldr 1/1/87. Retd OPS SPT 25/5/98.
LAKEY M.J. GM. Born 23/9/47. Commd 25/2/66. Sqn Ldr 1/1/84. Retd GD 1/1/87. Re-entrant 16/8/91.
　　Sqn Ldr 16/8/88. Retd GD 1/10/00.
LAMB A.L. BA. Born 27/6/73. Commd 5/4/98. Flt Lt 5/10/01. Retd SUPPLY 15/9/03.
LAMB C.A. Born 9/10/34. Commd 16/12/66. Flt Lt 16/12/68. Retd ENG 31/12/74.
LAMB D. MIEE. Born 5/2/35. Commd 24/9/64. Flt Lt 28/3/67. Retd ENG 5/2/73.
LAMB E. Born 2/6/38. Commd 10/4/67. Flt Lt 4/5/72. Retd ENG 10/4/83.
LAMB E.W. MVO MCMI. Born 18/1/23. Commd 27/4/44. Flt Lt 27/4/63. Retd ENG 28/4/76.
LAMB F.N. MBE. Born 22/6/16. Commd 6/12/56. Sqn Ldr 1/1/65. Retd GD(G) 28/2/70.
LAMB G.C. CB CBE AFC FCMI. Born 23/7/23. Commd 4/12/42. AVM 1/7/75. Retd GD 31/3/78.
LAMB G.J. Born 10/7/46. Commd 18/11/66. Flt Lt 18/5/72. Retd GD 1/1/89.
LAMB I.C. BA. Born 12/11/54. Commd 15/3/87. Flt Lt 15/3/92. Retd ADMIN 13/9/96.
LAMB J. Born 11/10/33. Commd 3/9/52. Sqn Ldr 1/7/72. Retd GD(G) 30/1/77.
LAMB J.A. Born 6/4/30. Commd 7/5/53. Sqn Ldr 1/1/64. Retd GD 19/3/76.
LAMB J.D. BEM. Born 24/10/50. Commd 14/2/99. Flt Lt 14/2/99. Retd ENGINEER 12/4/04.
LAMB J.R. MSc BSc. Born 22/6/33. Commd 8/8/56. Sqn Ldr 8/2/66. Retd ADMIN 2/4/85.
LAMB K. Born 17/8/40. Commd 9/3/62. Flt Lt 1/7/68. Retd GD 17/8/78.
LAMB M.P. MB BS MRCOG MRCS(Eng) LRCP. Born 26/3/45. Commd 25/7/66. Sqn Ldr 2/6/75. Retd MED 26/3/83.
LAMB N. Born 14/10/25. Commd 6/9/56. Sqn Ldr 1/1/66. Retd GD 14/10/83.
LAMB R. Born 27/5/30. Commd 3/8/61. Flt Lt 3/8/67. Retd GD 28/3/69.
LAMB R.B. BA MCMI. Born 27/7/31. Commd 18/10/55. Sqn Ldr 1/7/63. Retd GD 24/9/84.
LAMB T.D. AFC. Born 4/11/18. Commd 19/4/45. Sqn Ldr 1/7/59. Retd GD 2/7/62.

LAMBDIN G.S. Born 19/4/17. Commd 22/9/55. Flt Lt 22/9/58. Retd ENG 21/2/61.
LAMBDON S.G. Born 17/1/31. Commd 27/5/53. Flt Lt 1/3/61. Retd GD 30/9/83.
LAMBE G.F. Born 8/12/44. Commd 17/7/64. Sqn Ldr 1/7/82. Retd GD 8/4/89.
LAMBE M.T. BA MCMI. Born 8/4/32. Commd 21/10/54. Sqn Ldr 16/10/66. Retd ADMIN 9/4/82.
LAMBERT A.D. DFC. Born 6/8/19. Commd 15/6/40. Sqn Ldr 1/8/47. Retd GD 19/5/56.
LAMBERT A.J. Born 29/9/52. Commd 25/9/71. Flt Lt 19/5/78. Retd GD 29/9/90.
LAMBERT A.P.N. MPhil. Born 12/10/48. Commd 27/2/70. Air Cdre 1/1/01. Retd GD 12/10/03.
LAMBERT A.R. Born 31/3/54. Commd 5/8/76. Sqn Ldr 1/1/89. Retd SY 14/9/96.
LAMBERT C.R. BSc. Born 19/12/55. Commd 15/9/74. Flt Lt 15/10/78. Retd GD 15/7/89.
LAMBERT C.R. Born 24/6/54. Commd 20/8/80. Wg Cdr 1/7/94. Retd SY 14/9/96.
LAMBERT E.V. Born 13/5/32. Commd 23/9/66. Sqn Ldr 1/7/80. Retd ADMIN 3/5/85.
LAMBERT G.D. AFC. Born 16/5/31. Commd 19/8/53. Sqn Ldr 1/1/82. Retd GD 16/5/93.
LAMBERT I.A. The Rev. MTh BA. Born 9/2/43. Commd 5/11/75. Retd Wg Cdr 10/2/98.
LAMBERT J.D. MCMI. Born 1/1/32. Commd 6/12/51. Wg Cdr 1/7/74. Retd SUP 15/9/86.
LAMBERT J.R. OBE MA MRAeS. Born 3/2/30. Commd 17/12/52. A Cdre 1/1/77. Retd SUP 4/2/87.
LAMBERT K.M. Born 1/7/24. Commd 23/5/51. Flt Offr 23/5/55. Retd CAT 10/12/57.
LAMBERT L.H. DFC AFC. Born 21/10/19. Commd 13/2/42. Wg Cdr 1/7/56. Retd GD 13/2/61.
LAMBERT P.C. Born 29/4/38. Commd 6/5/65. Sqn Ldr 1/7/86. Retd GD 29/7/94.
LAMBERT R.W. Born 2/2/25. Commd 15/6/50. Flt Lt 27/5/54. Retd GD 2/2/63.
LAMBERT T.M. MA. Born 6/9/17. Commd 19/5/48. Sqn Ldr 1/1/65. Retd SUP 6/9/72.
LAMBIE P.S. BTech MCMI. Born 26/6/46. Commd 24/4/77. Sqn Ldr 1/7/88. Retd ENG 26/6/01.
LAMBLE D.A. Born 29/10/28. Commd 3/11/60. Flt Lt 3/11/66. Retd ENG 1/10/75.
LAMBOURNE A.J. Born 19/10/43. Commd 6/4/62. Sqn Ldr 1/1/77. Retd GD 24/10/80.
LAMBTON D. MB ChB MRCGP MFOM DRCOG DAvMed. Born 30/8/31. Commd 3/3/57. Gp Capt 1/7/80. Retd MED 25/6/83.
LAMBTON K.P. Born 28/5/52. Commd 2/1/75. Flt Lt 7/10/79. Retd GD 6/6/80.
LAMING H.J. Born 17/7/18. Commd 10/8/43. Flt Lt 10/2/47. Retd ENG 14/11/53.
LAMMING B. Born 18/1/32. Commd 27/2/70. Sqn Ldr 1/7/79. Retd ENG 31/7/84.
LAMOND A.J. BA. Born 2/12/58. Commd 7/11/82. Flt Lt 7/8/84. Retd GD 4/11/95.
LAMOND H.W. Born 26/8/15. Commd 4/1/39. Wg Cdr 1/7/53. Retd GD 15/9/62.
LAMONT C.R. Born 27/9/36. Commd 4/5/55. Sqn Ldr 30/11/78. Retd GD 27/9/94.
LAMONT J.P. Born 25/7/40. Commd 11/5/62. Flt Lt 9/2/68. Retd GD 25/7/78.
LAMONT-TURNER A.R. Born 12/6/20. Commd 12/8/44. Flt Lt 12/8/48. Retd RGT 1/3/58.
LAMPARD C.J. BSc(Eng) CEng MRAeS ACGI. Born 22/3/46. Commd 28/9/64. Gp Capt 1/7/91. Retd ENG 31/1/03.
LAMPARD I.B. Born 23/8/35. Commd 9/9/54. Sqn Ldr 1/7/70. Retd SUP 23/8/90.
LAMPER C.G. BEM. Born 30/11/44. Commd 22/5/80. Sqn Ldr 1/7/94. Retd ADMIN 10/7/96.
LAMPITT M.L. Born 22/1/47. Commd 27/7/72. Sqn Ldr 1/7/86. Retd GD 9/6/92.
LANCASTER D.E. BSc. Born 13/9/62. Commd 30/8/81. Flt Lt 15/10/85. Retd GD 1/4/00.
LANCASTER D.W. Born 1/10/30. Commd 10/12/52. Flt Lt 5/5/58. Retd GD 1/10/68.
LANCASTER J.E. Born 15/4/33. Commd 27/5/53. Flt Lt 28/10/58. Retd GD 15/10/71.
LANCASTER J.S.R. Born 31/1/35. Commd 1/10/63. Flt Lt 7/3/66. Retd GD 31/1/73.
LANCASTLE G.J. BSc. Born 19/2/43. Commd 23/9/68. Sqn Ldr 23/3/76. Retd ADMIN 18/9/94.
LANCE R.M. MCMI. Born 24/2/39. Commd 22/10/59. Sqn Ldr 1/7/74. Retd ADMIN 1/7/77.
LANCE V.R. Born 2/9/60. Commd 14/10/84. Flt Lt 14/10/89. Retd SUP 14/10/96.
LANCHBURY G.J. Born 25/8/42. Commd 25/1/63. Wg Cdr 1/1/90. Retd GD 1/8/93.
LANCHBURY R.W. Born 25/2/35. Commd 21/4/67. Flt Lt 21/4/69. Retd GD 1/6/74.
LAND W.A. MBE AFC. Born 15/1/20. Commd 28/6/42. Flt Lt 10/5/51. Retd SEC 1/6/63.
LANDELLS A.B. MBE DFC. Born 23/3/24. Commd 19/9/44. Wg Cdr 1/7/65. Retd GD 30/1/73.
LANDELLS S.H. Born 13/10/66. Commd 23/10/86. Flt Lt 23/4/92. Retd GD 14/3/96.
LANDER P.J. BTech. Born 6/1/51. Commd 2/10/72. Sqn Ldr 1/1/88. Retd GD 1/1/91.
LANDERYOU J.N. BA FCMI MIL. Born 30/12/38. Commd 5/3/57. Wg Cdr 1/1/79. Retd GD 14/4/94.
LANDESS L. Born 20/12/32. Commd 16/11/64. Flt Lt 16/11/64. Retd GD 20/12/89.
LANDON E.P. DFC FCMI. Born 4/9/20. Commd 24/4/42. Gp Capt 1/1/64. Retd GD 15/7/71.
LANDSBURGH A. Born 2/8/48. Commd 10/3/77. Sqn Ldr 1/7/87. Retd FLY(AEO) 30/4/05.
LANDY J.N. MSc MBCS MCMI. Born 18/3/44. Commd 26/8/66. Sqn Ldr 1/7/78. Retd SUP 1/10/85.
LANE A. Born 1/7/49. Commd 14/2/99. Flt Lt 14/2/99. Retd ADMIN (P ED) 1/7/05.
LANE A.H.J. The Rev. MBE BA. Born 13/9/49. Commd 20/8/78. Retd Wg Cdr 20/8/92.
LANE C.B. Born 24/4/38. Commd 6/12/61. Sqn Ldr 1/1/73. Retd SY 15/4/77.
LANE C.D. Born 1/7/39. Commd 22/5/80. Flt Lt 22/5/83. Retd ADMIN 2/5/93.
LANE H.R. Born 24/12/23. Commd 3/11/44. Flt Lt 27/5/54. Retd GD 23/11/65.
LANE I.E.P. BA. Born 1/7/30. Commd 20/1/60. Flt Offr 18/3/64. Retd EDN 29/8/64.
LANE J.F. Born 23/8/46. Commd 6/5/66. Flt Lt 6/11/71. Retd GD 6/12/76.
LANE J.G.A. MBE. Born 13/3/17. Commd 12/12/46. Sqn Ldr 1/7/60. Retd PE 14/3/72.
LANE K. Born 1/6/47. Commd 13/12/68. Sqn Ldr 1/1/81. Retd SUP 1/6/85.
LANE L.S. BSc. Born 19/6/30. Commd 10/4/58. Sqn Ldr 19/6/63. Retd EDN 13/10/83.
LANE M.J. MCMI. Born 17/11/34. Commd 14/1/54. Gp Capt 1/7/82. Retd ADMIN 17/11/90.
LANE M.T. Born 28/3/46. Commd 2/6/67. Flt Lt 2/12/72. Retd GD 28/3/84.

LANE P.D. Born 27/11/43. Commd 22/3/63. Flt Lt 22/9/68. Retd GD 27/11/98.
LANE R. BSc. Born 24/7/47. Commd 8/1/84. Flt Lt 8/1/83. Retd LGL 1/4/85.
LANE R.G. Born 12/5/42. Commd 23/6/67. Sqn Ldr 1/1/77. Retd ENG 12/5/80.
LANE R.J. MSc BDS DGDPRCS. Born 25/11/39. Commd 23/2/66. Gp Capt 1/1/87. Retd DEL 30/4/94.
LANE R.W. Born 28/1/44. Commd 11/8/77. Sqn Ldr 1/1/85. Retd ENG 15/8/97.
LANE S.E.J. Born 9/1/44. Commd 9/3/62. Wg Cdr 1/7/90. Retd GD(G) 1/2/95.
LANE W.A.N. Born 22/2/36. Commd 21/7/55. Sqn Ldr 1/7/69. Retd GD 31/12/71.
LANE W.F. BEM MCMI. Born 3/8/20. Commd 9/9/54. Sqn Ldr 1/7/67. Retd ENG 26/6/71.
LANFORD J.B. Born 26/5/33. Commd 21/10/66. Sqn Ldr 1/1/79. Retd ENG 31/1/86.
LANG A.C. MBE BA CEng FIMechE FRAeS. Born 19/10/47. Commd 23/3/67. A Cdre 1/1/98. Retd ENG 19/10/02.
LANG A.G. DFC. Born 26/10/19. Commd 17/12/41. Sqn Ldr 1/1/50. Retd GD 18/2/58.
LANG A.J. Born 11/5/63. Commd 11/10/84. Flt Lt 11/10/89. Retd GD 18/7/92.
LANG B. Born 30/6/47. Commd 17/7/70. Wg Cdr 1/1/90. Retd SY 1/9/94.
LANG D.E.R. AFC. Born 6/4/25. Commd 5/12/43. Flt Lt 1/8/53. Retd GD 26/3/64.
LANG J.A. BA. Born 2/4/37. Commd 1/9/70. Sqn Ldr 1/7/78. Retd ADMIN 2/4/96.
LANG K.R. Born 23/4/25. Commd 28/4/44. Sqn Ldr 1/1/57. Retd GD 8/9/72.
LANG R.A.M. Born 22/12/23. Commd 27/11/43. Flt Lt 4/6/53. Retd SUP 21/12/59.
LANGAN P.J. Born 18/4/40. Commd 27/2/70. Flt Lt 27/2/72. Retd GD(G) 20/4/90.
LANGAN-FOX C.P. Born 18/11/44. Commd 9/3/72. Flt Lt 9/3/74. Retd GD(G) 18/11/82.
LANGDON A.C. OBE. Born 26/12/20. Commd 25/5/42. Wg Cdr 1/1/57. Retd GD 26/12/67.
LANGDON L.M. Born 20/12/36. Commd 27/1/77. Flt Lt 27/1/83. Retd ADMIN 20/12/86.
LANGDON N.R. BEM MCMI. Born 14/6/38. Commd 19/8/66. Sqn Ldr 1/7/74. Retd GD 10/9/88.
LANGDON P.G. DFM. Born 10/2/22. Commd 4/12/43. Sqn Ldr 1/7/69. Retd GD 30/3/77.
LANGDOWN P. Born 17/12/37. Commd 30/9/58. Flt Lt 9/4/64. Retd GD 12/8/76.
LANGER J.F. CBE AFC FCMI MRAeS. Born 24/6/25. Commd 6/2/44. A Cdre 1/7/73. Retd GD 29/9/79.
LANGFORD T.W.R. Born 17/7/36. Commd 30/7/57. Flt Lt 30/1/60. Retd GD 17/7/94.
LANGHAM M.B. Born 11/9/42. Commd 17/12/64. Wg Cdr 1/1/80. Retd GD 31/3/94.
LANGHAM R.T. Born 20/9/18. Commd 18/11/53. Flt Lt 18/11/58. Retd GD(G) 20/9/68.
LANGLEY A. Born 22/4/33. Commd 5/11/70. Sqn Ldr 1/1/80. Retd ADMIN 22/4/83.
LANGLEY J.D. BA. Born 12/3/32. Commd 6/4/54. Flt Lt 6/10/56. Retd GD 2/4/91.
LANGLEY M.J. Born 15/2/44. Commd 9/3/62. Wg Cdr 1/1/85. Retd GD 2/3/98.
LANGLEY P.J. DFC. Born 24/10/24. Commd 14/1/44. Flt Lt 19/11/53. Retd GD 26/2/66.
LANGLEY W.F. BEM. Born 13/8/20. Commd 12/9/46. Sqn Ldr 1/1/59. Retd SUP 11/5/63.
LANGRIDGE H.A. OBE MCMI. Born 12/5/23. Commd 10/7/51. Wg Cdr 1/1/69. Retd SEC 13/5/75.
LANGRILL P. OBE. Born 22/7/38. Commd 11/6/60. Gp Capt 1/1/90. Retd GD 22/7/93.
LANGSTAFF R. OBE AFC. Born 17/1/28. Commd 27/6/51. Gp Capt 1/1/80. Retd GD 20/11/82.
LANGSTAFF R.J. MA BA MB BCh FRCS(Edin). Born 29/2/56. Commd 25/8/77. Wg Cdr 11/8/95. Retd MED 30/11/95.
LANGSTAFF-ELLIS J.W. BEd. Born 6/1/50. Commd 17/8/80. Flt Lt 17/2/84. Retd ADMIN 7/1/00.
LANGSTON J. CBE. Born 30/6/24. Commd 4/2/44. A Cdre 1/7/75. Retd GD 26/7/79.
LANGTON R.P. BA. Born 3/6/31. Commd 19/10/59. Wg Cdr 1/7/77. Retd ADMIN 9/9/88.
LANGWORTHY W.A. AFC. Born 16/4/35. Commd 21/10/53. Sqn Ldr 1/7/78. Retd GD 29/11/85.
LANIGAN D.S. Born 29/6/41. Commd 31/7/62. Flt Lt 31/1/65. Retd GD 29/6/79.
LANNEN C.A. BSc. Born 21/4/50. Commd 15/9/69. Sqn Ldr 1/1/81. Retd ENG 26/10/90.
LANNING H. DFC. Born 7/12/19. Commd 24/9/42. Sqn Ldr 1/7/56. Retd ENG 7/12/74.
LANNON P.M.H. Born 6/1/29. Commd 25/8/60. Sqn Ldr 1/7/72. Retd ENG 11/4/80.
LANSDELL C.H. Born 23/12/33. Commd 30/6/54. Flt Lt 16/8/61. Retd GD 25/12/71.
LANSDOWN M.L.E. Born 11/8/55. Commd 8/11/90. Sqn Ldr 1/1/02. Retd SUPPLY 1/3/04.
LAPHAM E.F. MBE MCMI. Born 7/9/21. Commd 11/9/42. Sqn Ldr 1/1/58. Retd SEC 12/9/70.
LAPPIN K.E. BA. Born 31/7/37. Commd 11/10/60. Sqn Ldr 31/3/71. Retd ADMIN 11/10/76.
LAPRAIK R.D. BSc(Eng). Born 1/10/49. Commd 24/9/67. Sqn Ldr 1/7/79. Retd GD 18/11/86.
LAPSLEY J.C.W. Born 25/6/48. Commd 28/2/69. Sqn Ldr 1/7/80. Retd ENG 25/6/86.
LAPWOOD G.E. Born 1/8/19. Commd 7/7/55. Sqn Ldr 1/1/66. Retd GD(G) 1/5/71.
LARARD F.N. DFM. Born 19/1/24. Commd 5/9/44. Flt Lt 5/9/50. Retd SEC 19/1/62.
LARBEY J.P.S. Born 10/10/42. Commd 7/5/64. Flt Lt 4/11/70. Retd OPS SPT 10/10/97.
LARKIN D.E. CBE MRAeS. Born 11/7/33. Commd 25/7/59. Gp Capt 1/1/86. Retd GD 11/7/94.
LARKIN P.J. BA. Born 9/3/66. Commd 16/9/84. Sqn Ldr 1/1/02. Retd SUPPLY 1/1/05.
LARKIN W.J. Born 13/2/21. Commd 2/3/45. Flt Lt 4/1/51. Retd GD 30/3/68.
LARKING R.G. Born 12/8/53. Commd 15/3/73. Sqn Ldr 1/1/88. Retd GD 12/8/91.
LARKINS G.S. Born 17/5/33. Commd 6/4/54. Flt Lt 6/4/59. Retd SUP 16/9/64.
LARKWORTHY L.T. Born 17/10/25. Commd 19/6/52. Sqn Ldr 1/7/67. Retd ENG 17/6/77.
LARKWORTHY W. MB BS FRCP DCH. Born 29/3/33. Commd 20/9/59. Wg Cdr 3/9/71. Retd MED 20/9/78.
LARNER J. Born 28/4/24. Commd 8/9/69. Flt Lt 1/8/72. Retd RGT 1/11/74.
LARNEY G.K. DFC MRAeS. Born 18/10/12. Commd 29/6/39. Sqn Ldr 1/7/56. Retd ENG 19/11/61.
LARTER M.H. Born 18/2/67. Commd 11/2/93. Sqn Ldr 1/1/01. Retd ADMIN (SEC) 18/2/05.
LARTER P.J. Born 7/9/44. Commd 4/2/71. Sqn Ldr 1/1/85. Retd SUP 30/8/96.
LASHBROOK W.I. DFC AFC DFM. Born 3/1/13. Commd 27/5/41. Flt Lt 10/10/42. Retd GD 23/11/48. rtg Sqn Ldr.

LASSETER W. Born 4/9/52. Commd 6/4/72. Sqn Ldr 1/6/84. Retd GD 14/3/97.
LAST R.W. BA. Born 21/1/59. Commd 16/9/79. Sqn Ldr 1/1/95. Retd GD 24/6/98.
LAST V.E. DPhysEd. Born 8/1/44. Commd 7/8/67. Flt Lt 8/3/72. Retd ADMIN 1/1/87.
LATCHAM J. BSc MInstP DipEl. Born 22/12/17. Commd 24/8/49. Wg Cdr 24/8/66. Retd EDN 22/12/72.
LATCHEM R.E. Born 21/4/33. Commd 17/1/52. Flt Lt 24/7/57. Retd GD 21/4/88.
LATHAM F. OBE DSc MD ChB. Born 7/3/20. Commd 23/5/46. Wg Cdr 23/1/58. Retd MED 23/5/60.
LATHAM P.A. CB AFC. Born 18/6/25. Commd 22/2/46. AVM 1/1/78. Retd GD 2/4/81.
LATHAM P.E.S. Born 14/10/61. Commd 8/10/87. Flt Lt 8/10/89. Retd GD 14/10/99.
LATHAM T. BSc. Born 9/8/59. Commd 29/8/77. Sqn Ldr 1/7/88. Retd ENG 1/10/90.
LATIMER M.B. Born 10/11/37. Commd 24/9/59. Flt Lt 1/4/66. Retd ENG 10/11/75.
LATIN R.V. MS BSc CEng MIEE. Born 15/5/39. Commd 30/9/58. Sqn Ldr 1/1/69. Retd ENG 15/5/77. rtg Wg Cdr.
LATTIMER B.C. BCom. Born 20/3/44. Commd 3/11/69. Flt Lt 3/8/71. Retd GD 1/3/75.
LAU G.S. OBE MCIPD MCMI. Born 7/5/19. Commd 7/5/45. Sqn Ldr 1/4/56. Retd GD 6/10/69.
LAUCHLAN J.P. Born 6/3/64. Commd 19/7/84. Flt Lt 13/12/90. Retd ADMIN 14/3/96.
LAUGHLIN M. BSc. Born 5/4/41. Commd 3/7/62. Sqn Ldr 1/7/72. Retd GD 29/3/77.
LAUGHTON L.S. OBE. Born 30/8/22. Commd 28/3/42. Wg Cdr 1/1/59. Retd GD 7/7/73.
LAUNDY M.J. Born 11/1/45. Commd 15/7/66. Flt Lt 15/1/69. Retd GD 11/1/89.
LAURANCE M.A. MCMI. Born 27/5/35. Commd 17/3/55. Sqn Ldr 1/7/66. Retd ADMIN 28/6/85.
LAURENSON J.A.W.S. Born 13/5/40. Commd 19/12/61. Sqn Ldr 1/1/74. Retd GD 13/5/95.
LAURIE G.H. MVO. Born 15/12/45. Commd 8/1/65. Sqn Ldr 1/7/77. Retd GD 15/12/00.
LAURIE I.H. AFC. Born 16/11/27. Commd 7/7/55. Sqn Ldr 1/1/83. Retd GD 16/11/85.
LAURIE R.I. Born 9/11/34. Commd 4/3/71. Flt Lt 4/3/74. Retd GD 2/10/79.
LAVELLE P.J. Born 25/3/30. Commd 29/3/68. Sqn Ldr 1/7/83. Retd ENG 31/5/89.
LAVENDER B.W. OBE AFC FCMI. Born 25/4/35. Commd 16/9/53. Gp Capt 1/7/78. Retd GD 18/12/89.
LAVER R.A. CEng MIEE. Born 18/3/42. Commd 15/7/64. Sqn Ldr 1/1/91. Retd ENG 18/3/97.
LAVERACK W.P. Born 29/9/27. Commd 12/3/64. Sqn Ldr 1/4/74. Retd MED(T) 19/7/79.
LAW A.B. Born 8/12/37. Commd 20/7/64. Sqn Ldr 1/1/83. Retd GD 2/8/89.
LAW A.L. DFC AFC*. Born 28/11/15. Commd 2/5/40. Sqn Ldr 1/7/49. Retd GD 27/5/57.
LAW A.W. Born 18/5/31. Commd 9/4/52. Gp Capt 1/7/76. Retd SEC 29/1/81.
LAW B.A. Born 9/3/08. Commd 20/4/41. Flt Lt 1/9/45. Retd SEC 20/1/58. rtg Sqn Ldr.
LAW G.A. Born 29/1/21. Commd 10/12/43. Sqn Ldr 1/7/57. Retd GD 29/1/64.
LAW J. AFM. Born 8/7/11. Commd 1/11/56. Sqn Ldr 1/7/71. Retd GD 8/7/74.
LAW J. Born 4/1/31. Commd 16/12/51. Flt Lt 14/5/58. Retd GD 4/1/86.
LAW J.S. MA. Born 23/6/50. Commd 8/9/74. Sqn Ldr 1/1/87. Retd GD(G) 8/9/90.
LAW M.D. Born 25/1/30. Commd 13/12/51. Sqn Ldr 1/1/77. Retd SY 8/4/81.
LAW P.A. CEng MIEE. Born 24/11/27. Commd 14/12/49. Gp Capt 1/7/74. Retd ENG 25/11/76.
LAW R.C.E. DSO DFC MA. Born 2/11/17. Commd 21/2/39. Wg Cdr 1/1/52. Retd GD 28/4/60. rtg Gp Capt.
LAW S.A.T. BA MB ChB MRCGP DA DAvMed. Born 21/12/53. Commd 14/8/83. Wg Cdr 14/8/92. Retd MED 15/12/97.
LAW S.H. Born 6/2/59. Commd 12/7/79. Flt Lt 12/1/86. Retd SY 6/2/97.
LAWER A. BSc MRAeS. Born 31/3/56. Commd 14/1/79. Sqn Ldr 1/1/89. Retd GD 14/1/97.
LAWES J.W. FCMI MInstAM. Born 23/6/37. Commd 8/7/65. Gp Capt 1/1/84. Retd GD(G) 16/1/90.
LAWLEY B.J. MB ChB. Born 18/5/28. Commd 3/7/52. Sqn Ldr 3/7/59. Retd MED 26/2/61.
LAWLOR A.E.M. MBE MHCIMA. Born 22/5/49. Commd 4/12/86. Sqn Ldr 1/7/96. Retd ADMIN (CAT) 22/5/04.
LAWLOR W.J. BA. Born 21/9/36. Commd 22/10/63. Sqn Ldr 9/3/72. Retd EDN 22/10/79.
LAWN B.E.T. CEng MIEE. Born 9/1/38. Commd 12/9/61. Sqn Ldr 1/1/74. Retd ENG 3/4/82.
LAWRANCE M.J.B. MBE. Born 11/4/35. Commd 10/4/56. Sqn Ldr 1/7/72. Retd GD 11/4/93.
LAWRENCE A.G.E. Born 16/4/27. Commd 17/10/57. Flt Lt 1/4/63. Retd GD 16/4/76.
LAWRENCE A.J. Born 19/6/41. Commd 22/7/71. Flt Lt 22/7/73. Retd SUP 22/7/79.
LAWRENCE B. Born 17/5/43. Commd 17/12/65. Flt Lt 17/6/06. Retd GD 17/5/81.
LAWRENCE C.G. Born 8/8/20. Commd 1/5/42. Flt Lt 20/8/46. Retd GD(G) 1/4/69.
LAWRENCE C.H. BSc CEng MRAeS. Born 22/1/50. Commd 26/2/71. Wg Cdr 1/7/93. Retd GD 22/1/05.
LAWRENCE C.M. Born 12/4/57. Commd 21/11/84. Flt Lt 15/3/87. Retd SY 12/4/95.
LAWRENCE C.T. MBE BSc. Born 11/9/56. Commd 30/10/77. Sqn Ldr 1/7/87. Retd GD 11/9/94.
LAWRENCE D. MCMI ACIS. Born 30/8/38. Commd 15/12/59. Sqn Ldr 1/7/70. Retd ADMIN 1/9/95.
LAWRENCE D.B. Born 10/3/30. Commd 23/3/51. Flt Lt 13/11/57. Retd GD 10/3/68.
LAWRENCE D.F. CBE CEng MIMechE. Born 29/4/35. Commd 19/7/57. A Cdre 1/7/84. Retd ENG 29/6/90.
LAWRENCE G.F. OBE BA CEng MIEE MRAeS. Born 22/4/39. Commd 18/7/61. Gp Capt 1/1/81. Retd ENG 3/10/89.
LAWRENCE H.H. DFC. Born 30/7/19. Commd 19/10/43. Flt Lt 17/5/47. Retd GD 30/7/62.
LAWRENCE I.C. Born 26/5/35. Commd 28/7/53. Sqn Ldr 1/1/81. Retd GD 27/11/89.
LAWRENCE I.M. Born 22/5/49. Commd 28/7/94. Flt Lt 28/7/96. Retd FLY(ALM) 22/11/04.
LAWRENCE J. Born 23/1/59. Commd 17/9/84. Sqn Ldr 1/7/94. Retd SUP 4/7/96.
LAWRENCE J. Born 26/2/19. Commd 12/6/47. Sqn Ldr 1/1/61. Retd SUP 5/3/69.
LAWRENCE J.T. CB CBE AFC. Born 16/4/20. Commd 5/8/41. AVM 1/7/71. Retd GD 16/4/75.
LAWRENCE N.J. BSc. Born 27/6/59. Commd 30/3/86. Flt Lt 30/9/89. Retd OPS SPT 30/3/02.
LAWRENCE P. BSc. Born 30/8/63. Commd 14/4/85. Flt Lt 14/10/88. Retd PI 28/4/91.
LAWRENCE P.J. LLB. Born 20/5/52. Commd 13/9/70. Sqn Ldr 1/7/82. Retd GD 20/5/89.

LAWRENCE P.W.F. Born 10/2/43. Commd 17/7/64. Flt Lt 17/1/70. Retd GD 13/1/79.
LAWRENCE R.F. Born 3/2/33. Commd 11/4/51. Flt Lt 15/1/57. Retd GD 9/7/65.
LAWRENCE R.H. Born 12/12/47. Commd 28/2/69. Flt Lt 28/2/72. Retd GD 12/12/85. Re-entered 18/12/87.
   Sqn Ldr 1/7/97. Retd FLY(P) 12/12/03.
LAWRENCE R.J. MBE. Born 31/1/33. Commd 13/2/52. Flt Lt 30/6/57. Retd GD 31/1/88.
LAWRENCE R.N. Born 11/11/47. Commd 1/8/69. Fg Offr 1/2/71. Retd RGT 27/11/73.
LAWRENCE V.J.W. Born 1/9/28. Commd 11/4/51. Wg Cdr 1/7/72. Retd SEC 13/7/75.
LAWRENCE W.T.J. Born 11/8/45. Commd 18/8/67. Flt Lt 18/2/73. Retd SUP 11/8/83.
LAWRENSON A.J. BA. Born 6/4/67. Commd 19/2/89. Flt Lt 19/8/91. Retd GD 14/3/97.
LAWRENSON R.F. DFM. Born 28/10/21. Commd 21/7/44. Flt Lt 19/6/52. Retd GD 2/3/63.
LAWRENSON R.I. FHCIMA FCMI. Born 14/9/32. Commd 29/5/52. Gp Capt 1/1/76. Retd ADMIN 16/9/82.
LAWRIE J.R.G. MCMI. Born 8/10/24. Commd 1/10/52. Wg Cdr 1/7/79. Retd SY 8/10/82.
LAWRY K.J. Born 21/4/47. Commd 2/6/67. Sqn Ldr 1/1/82. Retd GD 21/6/00.
LAWS A.P. MBE. Born 24/5/63. Commd 20/10/83. Sqn Ldr 1/1/97. Retd OPS SPT 24/5/01.
LAWS D.F. Born 14/6/32. Commd 28/9/51. Flt Lt 28/3/56. Retd GD 15/11/75.
LAWS L.R. Born 11/3/40. Commd 24/6/71. Flt Lt 13/11/77. Retd GD(G) 8/3/87.
LAWSON A.A. Born 17/2/32. Commd 28/2/52. Flt Lt 5/9/57. Retd GD 29/5/65.
LAWSON D. Born 1/1/50. Commd 27/3/70. Flt Lt 1/7/75. Retd GD 1/11/88.
LAWSON D.E. Born 11/4/43. Commd 2/8/68. Flt Lt 10/6/74. Retd ENG 11/4/81.
LAWSON E.A. MA. Born 17/2/54. Commd 2/1/77. Sqn Ldr 1/1/86. Retd ADMIN 2/1/93.
LAWSON E.W. MBE CEng MRAeS MCMI. Born 16/7/21. Commd 6/3/52. Sqn Ldr 1/1/62. Retd ENG 16/7/71.
LAWSON G.C. AInstAM. Born 18/3/54. Commd 19/3/81. Flt Lt 19/9/87. Retd ADMIN 10/11/96.
LAWSON G.G. BA. Born 25/7/37. Commd 24/4/56. Wg Cdr 1/1/79. Retd GD 25/7/92.
LAWSON J.D. Born 9/10/66. Commd 4/12/86. Sqn Ldr 1/7/02. Retd FLY(P) 1/7/05.
LAWSON K.W. Born 31/10/24. Commd 30/6/45. Flt Lt 30/12/48. Retd GD(G) 31/10/79.
LAWSON M.C. Born 1/7/10. Commd 23/8/44. Flt Offr 1/5/50. Retd PRT 11/3/60.
LAWSON P.G. Born 17/9/27. Commd 23/4/52. Flt Lt 27/8/58. Retd GD 17/9/70.
LAWSON P.W. AFM. Born 4/2/25. Commd 30/7/64. Flt Lt 30/7/67. Retd GD 21/3/78.
LAWSON R.J. Born 5/10/65. Commd 24/9/84. Sqn Ldr 1/1/99. Retd GD 14/11/02.
LAWSON S.P. BSc. Born 24/10/61. Commd 11/5/89. Sqn Ldr 11/5/01. Retd MEDICAL SUPPORT 7/11/04.
LAWTON D.G. MBE. Born 24/7/25. Commd 26/8/66. Flt Lt 26/8/69. Retd GD 15/1/80.
LAWTON G.C.S. Born 21/7/15. Commd 7/2/42. Flt Lt 9/9/46. Retd MAR 21/7/64.
LAWTON H.J. Born 18/6/37. Commd 25/6/66. Flt Lt 1/7/68. Retd GD 18/6/75.
LAWTON J.M. Born 12/5/44. Commd 3/11/77. Flt Lt 3/11/78. Retd ADMIN 3/11/85.
LAWTON J.V. Born 30/12/43. Commd 17/5/63. Sqn Ldr 1/7/78. Retd GD 30/6/84.
LAWTON J.W.H. Born 13/9/28. Commd 9/2/66. Sqn Ldr 1/7/78. Retd ENG 13/9/84.
LAWTON M.C. Born 10/3/52. Commd 9/3/72. Sqn Ldr 1/7/88. Retd GD 1/7/91.
LAWTON R.E. Born 11/2/42. Commd 21/7/61. Flt Lt 21/1/67. Retd GD 11/7/85.
LAWTON R.E. Born 31/7/51. Commd 13/2/86. Flt Lt 13/2/88. Retd ENG 22/8/91.
LAX B. CEng MIEE MRAeS MCMI. Born 15/9/24. Commd 14/2/45. Wg Cdr 1/7/70. Retd ENG 30/10/76.
LAX F.C. Born 3/3/11. Commd 14/12/44. Flt Lt 15/12/49. Retd SEC 25/5/56.
LAX I.A.W. Born 24/3/60. Commd 18/10/79. Flt Lt 18/4/85. Retd GD 16/2/94.
LAXON P.B. Born 10/12/19. Commd 13/10/41. Flt Lt 1/9/45. Retd SEC 10/12/68.
LAY C.J. Born 13/4/68. Commd 22/6/89. Sqn Ldr 1/1/01. Retd FLY(P) 1/5/03.
LAY P.C. Born 25/1/50. Commd 14/2/99. Flt Lt 14/2/99. Retd OPS SPT(ATC) 25/1/05.
LAYBOURN R.A. OBE BEM BA. Born 20/11/43. Commd 25/2/82. Wg Cdr 1/1/96. Retd ENG 13/6/98.
LAYBOURNE K.R. Born 5/11/57. Commd 24/7/81. Flt Lt 3/12/84. Retd SY 14/3/96.
LAYCOCK A.D. Born 21/11/30. Commd 28/6/51. Sqn Ldr 1/7/65. Retd GD 21/5/76.
LAYCOCK J. Born 25/4/38. Commd 27/7/59. Gp Capt 1/7/80. Retd GD 1/11/89.
LAZZARI J.N. Born 8/9/49. Commd 28/6/79. Sqn Ldr 1/1/95. Retd GD 2/4/01.
LE BAIGUE E.A. Born 20/11/31. Commd 6/6/57. Sqn Ldr 1/7/67. Retd GD 1/12/71.
LE BROCQ R.H.B. AFC. Born 15/1/36. Commd 17/12/57. Wg Cdr 1/7/71. Retd GD 29/5/76.
LE BRUN J.L.J.C. AFC. Born 2/3/38. Commd 1/11/61. Flt Lt 26/7/67. Retd GD 24/12/82.
LE CHEMINANT Sir Peter GBE KCB DFC*. Born 17/6/20. Commd 23/12/39. ACM 2/2/76. Retd GD 27/8/79.
LE CLERCQ L.R.W. MCMI. Born 31/7/48. Commd 2/8/73. Sqn Ldr 1/7/86. Retd GD(G) 31/7/92.
LE CORNU C.C. Born 16/9/39. Commd 25/7/60. Wg Cdr 1/1/84. Retd GD 16/9/94.
LE COUNT E.W. Born 23/9/37. Commd 10/9/70. Sqn Ldr 1/7/90. Retd GD 1/7/93.
LE CRERAR J.L. Born 6/1/18. Commd 27/1/44. Flt Lt 27/7/47. Retd ENG 30/6/54. rtg Sqn Ldr.
LE CUDENEC R. DFC. Born 13/12/22. Commd 13/12/42. Flt Lt 13/12/42. Retd GD 13/8/77.
LE DIEU N. CEng MRAeS. Born 26/9/39. Commd 4/9/61. Gp Capt 1/1/91. Retd ENG 26/9/94.
LE DREW L.R. Born 20/11/36. Commd 18/6/62. Flt Lt 18/6/62. Retd GD 18/6/78.
LE GALLOUDEC S.J. Born 25/9/58. Commd 26/9/70. Flt Lt 26/9/92. Retd ENG 10/10/01.
LE GRAS J.M. Born 26/8/32. Commd 24/10/51. Flt Lt 16/2/57. Retd GD 26/8/70.
LE GRESLEY A.I. Born 11/3/28. Commd 1/3/49. Sqn Ldr 1/1/63. Retd GD 11/3/66.
LE HEUZE D.P.J. Born 11/10/55. Commd 9/5/91. Flt Lt 9/5/93. Retd ADMIN 14/3/97.
LE JEUNE P.V. Born 31/10/46. Commd 28/2/69. Flt Lt 4/5/72. Retd GD 2/11/76.

LE LORRAIN R.C. Born 31/1/28. Commd 28/6/51. Flt Lt 28/6/57. Retd SUP 31/1/83.
LE MARIE M.J. Born 5/9/49. Commd 7/6/68. Sqn Ldr 1/7/84. Retd ADMIN 1/7/87.
LE MARQUAND P.E. Born 18/12/35. Commd 15/2/56. Gp Capt 1/1/86. Retd GD 5/7/88.
LE MOINE J. Born 16/6/35. Commd 11/11/71. Sqn Ldr 1/1/80. Retd ADMIN 16/1/87.
LE-MONNIER P.R. Born 26/3/69. Commd 28/7/88. Fg Offr 28/1/91. Retd SY 31/3/93.
LEA R.F. Born 2/4/44. Commd 3/8/62. Flt Lt 3/2/68. Retd GD 2/4/81.
LEA R.G. Born 14/10/12. Commd 14/7/44. Fg Offr 14/1/45. Retd GD 2/1/46.
LEA R.J. BSc. Born 17/5/63. Commd 2/9/84. Sqn Ldr 1/7/95. Retd GD 17/5/01.
LEA S.M. BSc. Born 5/4/63. Commd 2/9/84. Sqn Ldr 1/1/94. Retd SUP 5/4/01.
LEA T.C. Born 28/2/24. Commd 14/4/49. Flt Lt 14/10/52. Retd GD 15/4/59.
LEACH A.J. CEng MIEE MRAeS. Born 21/12/43. Commd 15/7/65. Flt Lt 15/10/70. Retd ENG 21/12/81.
LEACH C.W. CEng MIEE. Born 19/2/21. Commd 15/7/43. Wg Cdr 1/1/63. Retd ENG 19/2/76.
LEACH D.Q.R. Born 11/12/43. Commd 10/1/69. Flt Lt 10/7/74. Retd GD 2/12/91.
LEACH P.A.G. MBE CEng MIEE MRAeS. Born 20/5/39. Commd 2/3/65. Wg Cdr 1/1/85. Retd ENG 20/5/94.
LEACH P.W. BSc. Born 10/12/62. Commd 16/11/83. Flt Lt 15/1/87. Retd GD 15/7/01.
LEACH R.E. MBE BA MCMI. Born 10/2/36. Commd 27/6/59. Sqn Ldr 1/7/74. Retd GD 28/8/88.
LEACH R.M. BSc. Born 23/9/35. Commd 30/4/58. Sqn Ldr 1/1/69. Retd GD 22/12/69.
LEACH W.T. BSc. Born 23/4/62. Commd 31/8/80. Flt Lt 15/10/84. Retd GD 23/4/00.
LEADBEATER R.A.L. Born 17/1/40. Commd 13/12/79. Sqn Ldr 1/7/92. Retd ENG 17/1/95.
LEADBETTER P.M. MVO MCMI. Born 20/3/49. Commd 27/2/70. Wg Cdr 1/7/92. Retd GD 20/3/04.
LEADON F.R. Born 9/1/23. Commd 11/10/44. Flt Lt 17/5/56. Retd GD 1/10/68.
LEAH L.E. ACIS. Born 30/7/20. Commd 1/6/43. Flt Lt 6/12/49. Retd SEC 1/10/60.
LEAH M.H. Born 2/4/29. Commd 27/8/59. Sqn Ldr 1/1/73. Retd ENG 22/11/85.
LEAHY A.McL. Born 31/5/57. Commd 25/2/82. Sqn Ldr 1/1/90. Retd ENG 31/5/95.
LEAHY J.J. BA FCMI. Born 26/8/38. Commd 28/5/66. Gp Capt 1/1/88. Retd SUP 26/8/93.
LEAN P.A. BSc IEng MIIE. Born 24/10/50. Commd 3/7/80. Sqn Ldr 1/7/92. Retd ENGINEER 31/7/04.
LEANEY G. Born 18/6/45. Commd 3/3/67. Sqn Ldr 1/7/80. Retd ADMIN 18/6/89.
LEANING P.T.W. FILT MCIPS. Born 6/2/48. Commd 19/6/70. A Cdre 1/7/98. Retd SUP 2/8/00.
LEAR G.G. Born 9/6/35. Commd 27/2/70. Sqn Ldr 1/7/77. Retd GD(G) 27/2/86.
LEARMONTH C. MBE MCMI. Born 13/6/33. Commd 23/6/67. Wg Cdr 1/7/80. Retd SY 18/9/86.
LEARMOUNT D.W. Born 3/5/47. Commd 8/10/70. Flt Lt 8/4/75. Retd GD 1/6/79.
LEARNER P.F.G. BSc MCMI. Born 19/3/53. Commd 25/9/71. Sqn Ldr 1/1/88. Retd ADMIN (SEC) 6/4/05.
LEARNER R.H. CEng MIProdE MRAeS. Born 23/8/48. Commd 14/9/75. Wg Cdr 1/7/90. Retd ENG 19/7/93.
LEARY J.D. Born 1/6/32. Commd 14/4/53. Gp Capt 1/1/85. Retd GD 1/6/88.
LEARY J.M. AFC BSc. Born 29/5/28. Commd 25/11/54. Sqn Ldr 1/1/63. Retd GD 30/1/76.
LEARY M.V. MBE. Born 9/3/40. Commd 12/7/65. Flt Lt 8/3/72. Retd PE 12/7/81.
LEARY N.O. DFC. Born 19/10/34. Commd 27/5/53. Sqn Ldr 1/1/69. Retd GD 1/11/85.
LEATHAM G.H. Born 9/5/36. Commd 3/11/77. Sqn Ldr 1/1/91. Retd ENG 1/4/95.
LEATHERDALE F.R. DFC. Born 3/11/22. Commd 5/2/42. Sqn Ldr 1/4/56. Retd GD 3/11/65.
LEAVER G. CBE MCMI MHSM. Born 27/10/34. Commd 9/3/66. Gp Capt 1/7/89. Retd MED(SEC) 1/7/93.
LEAVEY D. Born 11/2/34. Commd 20/1/56. Sqn Ldr 1/1/72. Retd GD 23/1/82.
LECKENBY I.P. Born 28/8/46. Commd 18/8/67. Flt Lt 18/8/70. Retd GD 1/7/78.
LECKENBY P.J. MBE. Born 23/4/44. Commd 21/12/62. Sqn Ldr 1/7/77. Retd GD 23/4/82. Re-entered 15/1/90.
   Sqn Ldr 15/1/90. Retd FLY(N) 23/4/04.
LECKEY J. Born 1/11/54. Commd 10/3/77. Wg Cdr 1/7/94. Retd GD 6/12/04.
LECKEY R.G. MSc ARIC. Born 13/5/33. Commd 28/9/60. Flt Lt 28/12/61. Retd ADMIN 29/5/84.
LECKIE R. AFC. Born 12/3/35. Commd 5/7/53. Sqn Ldr 1/1/69. Retd GD 20/9/75. Re-instated 3/9/81.
   Sqn Ldr 15/12/75. Retd GD 30/9/90.
LEDDY A. Born 12/4/25. Commd 26/11/69. Flt Lt 28/11/72. Retd PI 2/11/77.
LEDGARD J.C. The Rev. BA. Born 3/6/41. Commd 1/9/70. Retd Wg Cdr 1/9/86.
LEDGER C.L.K. Born 21/12/39. Commd 22/8/59. Sqn Ldr 1/7/77. Retd ADMIN 21/12/94.
LEDGER R. Born 24/9/49. Commd 3/8/68. Fg Offr 10/8/70. Retd SEC 14/7/71.
LEDLIE E.P. MBE. Born 26/9/23. Commd 4/2/48. Wg Cdr 1/1/73. Retd RGT 18/1/74.
LEDWARD J. Born 4/9/33. Commd 4/6/52. Sqn Ldr 1/1/84. Retd GD 4/9/93.
LEE A. Born 4/7/57. Commd 24/6/76. Flt Lt 24/12/81. Retd GD 11/2/90.
LEE A.L. Born 10/2/45. Commd 27/5/71. Flt Lt 27/5/73. Retd GD(G) 10/2/83.
LEE A.N. BSc. Born 16/4/65. Commd 10/11/85. Flt Lt 22/6/89. Retd ENG 14/9/96.
LEE B.A. BSc CEng MIEE. Born 5/10/49. Commd 26/2/71. Wg Cdr 1/1/81. Retd ENG 6/6/94.
LEE B.J. Born 24/2/32. Commd 9/2/66. Flt Lt 9/2/71. Retd GD 26/8/75.
LEE B.R. Born 13/12/54. Commd 4/11/82. Flt Lt 4/11/84. Retd GD(G) 1/4/93.
LEE B.R. Born 15/1/42. Commd 6/7/62. Gp Capt 1/1/90. Retd GD 27/7/96.
LEE C.H. BSc. Born 22/11/62. Commd 2/9/84. Flt Lt 2/3/87. Retd GD 14/9/96.
LEE C.L. Born 22/5/52. Commd 16/4/78. Sqn Ldr 1/1/89. Retd ADMIN 5/10/92.
LEE Sir David GBE CB. Born 4/9/12. Commd 23/7/32. ACM 7/10/67. Retd GD 19/3/71.
LEE D.A. BSc. Born 14/9/51. Commd 15/9/69. Sqn Ldr 1/7/84. Retd ENG 14/9/89.
LEE D.E. Born 10/9/22. Commd 18/7/45. Flt Lt 10/4/57. Retd SEC 3/6/65.

LEE D.G. MBE. Born 7/11/45. Commd 20/10/67. Sqn Ldr 1/1/78. Retd GD 7/11/83.
LEE D.W. Born 16/1/38. Commd 28/7/59. Sqn Ldr 1/1/84. Retd GD 16/7/98.
LEE D.W.H. Born 28/10/30. Commd 30/9/53. Sqn Ldr 1/7/76. Retd GD 28/10/88.
LEE F.H. Born 21/2/38. Commd 3/8/62. Sqn Ldr 1/1/90. Retd GD 21/11/94.
LEE G. Born 5/5/39. Commd 10/2/64. Wg Cdr 1/7/80. Retd GD 3/10/89.
LEE G. BSc. Born 2/3/25. Commd 3/1/46. Wg Cdr 1/7/63. Retd ENG 31/3/78.
LEE G.A. CEng MIEE MRAeS MCMI. Born 20/9/43. Commd 15/7/64. Sqn Ldr 1/7/77. Retd ENG 2/12/97.
LEE G.G. Born 11/5/28. Commd 27/7/49. Sqn Ldr 1/7/59. Retd GD 26/8/77.
LEE G.R. Born 1/6/27. Commd 27/8/59. Sqn Ldr 1/7/72. Retd SY 2/6/77.
LEE J.E. Born 29/6/23. Commd 26/7/44. Flt Lt 26/1/48. Retd GD 29/6/66.
LEE J.F.W. Born 20/3/20. Commd 17/5/56. Flt Lt 17/5/62. Retd ENG 20/6/73.
LEE J.G.J. CEng MRAeS MIMechE. Born 29/7/38. Commd 28/7/60. Sqn Ldr 1/1/74. Retd ENG 7/8/81.
LEE J.J. AFC BSc. Born 18/8/39. Commd 23/10/59. Sqn Ldr 1/7/72. Retd GD 1/9/73.
LEE J.W. Born 16/4/36. Commd 9/3/72. Sqn Ldr 1/7/87. Retd ADMIN 30/6/91.
LEE M.E. Born 7/11/42. Commd 4/11/82. Flt Lt 4/11/86. Retd ENG 10/6/93.
LEE M.E. Born 9/4/55. Commd 23/5/85. Sqn Ldr 1/7/94. Retd ENG 7/9/98.
LEE M.J.W. CBE BSc. Born 23/2/30. Commd 10/3/54. Gp Capt 1/1/78. Retd GD 7/4/84.
LEE M.K. MBE . Born 23/1/48. Commd 26/4/84. Sqn Ldr 1/7/92. Retd ADMIN (P ED) 23/7/03.
LEE N.C. MB BS MRCS LRCP DAvMed. Born 11/7/33. Commd 21/2/52. Sqn Ldr 19/7/71. Retd MED 30/8/74.
LEE N.P. Born 17/4/57. Commd 27/1/77. Flt Lt 27/7/82. Retd GD 24/11/88.
LEE O.R. Born 6/9/23. Commd 19/2/43. Flt Lt 19/8/46. Retd GD 20/12/47. rtg Sqn Ldr.
LEE P.A. MB ChB BAO DPH DIH. Born 11/6/11. Commd 7/9/35. Gp Capt 1/1/57. Retd MED 7/6/67.
LEE P.A. Born 4/4/37. Commd 26/11/60. Flt Lt 26/5/66. Retd GD 9/8/76.
LEE P.D. MBE. Born 24/9/20. Commd 10/5/48. Wg Cdr 1/1/63. Retd RGT 1/4/71.
LEE P.H. AIIP. Born 27/12/23. Commd 1/2/45. Sqn Ldr 1/1/70. Retd ENG 30/6/78.
LEE P.N. Born 1/1/20. Commd 7/7/44. Sqn Ldr 1/7/58. Retd GD 1/1/63.
LEE R.E. Born 20/10/29. Commd 28/7/60. Flt Lt 28/1/66. Retd GD 1/5/85.
LEE R.E. Born 4/10/48. Commd 24/4/70. Sqn Ldr 1/1/82. Retd GD 4/10/86.
LEE R.K. CEng MIMechE. Born 25/10/45. Commd 7/3/71. Flt Lt 7/8/74. Retd ENG 29/5/98.
LEE R.R.G. Born 31/3/47. Commd 20/9/79. Flt Lt 20/9/81. Retd OPS SPT 31/3/02.
LEE S.W. MILT. Born 31/10/65. Commd 12/6/92. Flt Lt 12/9/93. Retd SUPPLY 31/10/03.
LEE W.B. MBE BEM. Born 11/11/36. Commd 22/2/79. Sqn Ldr 1/7/88. Retd ENG 11/11/91.
LEE W.G. Born 30/12/43. Commd 21/5/65. Fg Offr 21/5/67. Retd GD 9/1/70.
LEE-POTTER J.P. MB BS MRCS LRCP DTM&H DCP MCPath. Born 30/8/34. Commd 3/1/60. Sqn Ldr 25/11/64. Retd MED 24/2/68.
LEE-PRESTON P.C. Born 23/4/47. Commd 25/2/66. Flt Lt 25/8/71. Retd GD 23/4/85.
LEECH B.J. Born 22/7/36. Commd 21/4/67. Flt Lt 21/4/73. Retd GD(G) 31/8/89.
LEECH D.W. MSc BEng BA CEng MIEE. Born 24/3/64. Commd 5/9/82. Wg Cdr 1/7/01. Retd GD 1/7/04.
LEECH J.W. Born 11/1/36. Commd 27/7/66. Flt Lt 22/7/72. Retd MAR 12/1/78.
LEEDHAM M.L. MCMI. Born 18/11/39. Commd 19/12/61. Sqn Ldr 1/1/72. Retd SUP 18/11/77.
LEEDS P.F. Born 25/3/42. Commd 31/10/74. Wg Cdr 1/1/91. Retd PRT 31/10/92.
LEEFARR B. MCMI. Born 6/9/35. Commd 22/4/55. Wg Cdr 1/1/76. Retd GD 6/9/90.
LEEMING G.H. Born 14/9/42. Commd 28/4/61. Sqn Ldr 1/7/78. Retd GD 1/10/90.
LEEMING J. The Rev. Born 10/11/34. Commd 1/6/64. Retd Wg Cdr 11/11/84.
LEEMING R.D. FRCS LRCP&S(I) DLO. Born 15/6/31. Commd 7/2/60. Wg Cdr 2/9/71. Retd MED 1/10/76.
LEEMING T. Born 26/4/32. Commd 9/8/51. Flt Lt 28/11/56. Retd GD 27/7/70.
LEEMING-LATHAM L. MMedSc MB ChB DAvMed MFOM. Born 13/4/51. Commd 23/1/72. Wg Cdr 4/6/88. Retd MED 24/4/96.
LEES B.D. BSc CEng MIEE. Born 30/9/61. Commd 14/9/80. Flt Lt 15/10/86. Retd ENG 10/6/94.
LEES B.E. Born 15/11/29. Commd 1/3/62. Sqn Ldr 1/7/80. Retd ENG 15/11/89.
LEES C.Q. FIFA. Born 15/7/39. Commd 27/8/59. Sqn Ldr 1/1/72. Retd ADMIN 15/7/94.
LEES J.R. MBE. Born 14/10/35. Commd 9/4/57. Sqn Ldr 1/1/74. Retd GD 14/10/93.
LEES M.N. Born 3/12/50. Commd 5/11/70. Gp Capt 1/1/95. Retd GD 14/12/01.
LEES M.R. Born 25/12/47. Commd 23/2/68. Flt Lt 23/8/73. Retd GD 25/12/85.
LEES N. BA. Born 12/11/37. Commd 30/9/57. Sqn Ldr 1/7/69. Retd ENG 12/11/75.
LEES P.D. Born 12/4/61. Commd 29/7/83. Sqn Ldr 1/7/95. Retd GD 14/12/99.
LEES P.D. Born 6/11/55. Commd 27/2/75. Flt Lt 27/8/80. Retd GD 27/6/87.
LEES P.J. Born 16/11/46. Commd 10/12/65. Flt Lt 10/6/72. Retd GD 16/11/84.
LEES R.A. Born 29/10/32. Commd 27/8/53. Sqn Ldr 1/7/66. Retd GD 23/12/65.
LEES R.L. CB MBE FCIPD FCMI. Born 27/2/31. Commd 9/4/52. AVM 1/1/83. Retd ADMIN 3/3/86.
LEESE A.D.W. IEng FIEIE. Born 16/1/34. Commd 30/5/69. Flt Lt 30/5/74. Retd ENG 16/1/94.
LEESE I.D. Born 22/10/57. Commd 23/10/86. Flt Lt 23/10/88. Retd SY 22/10/95.
LEFFLER T. Born 25/9/63. Commd 2/5/84. Flt Lt 2/8/90. Retd OPS SPT 25/9/01.
LEFLEY R. MSc BEng. Born 27/10/64. Commd 30/9/90. Flt Lt 15/7/93. Retd ENG 27/10/02.
LEGG A.E. Born 18/5/41. Commd 24/2/61. Sqn Ldr 1/1/74. Retd GD 18/5/79.
LEGG B.R. MBE. Born 7/1/24. Commd 3/11/60. Flt Lt 3/11/65. Retd RGT 9/12/69.

LEGG P.D. MA FCMI MRAeS. Born 24/5/55. Commd 15/9/74. Wg Cdr 1/7/93. Retd GD 24/5/99.
LEGG S.J.E. BSc. Born 18/1/51. Commd 22/4/71. Sqn Ldr 1/1/86. Retd GD 6/5/88.
LEGGE A.F. Born 4/6/44. Commd 3/3/67. Fg Offr 3/9/67. Retd GD 19/12/68.
LEGGE G.P.E. BEng. Born 28/10/62. Commd 3/9/89. Flt Lt 15/7/92. Retd ENGINEER 28/10/03.
LEGGE P.N. Born 24/3/31. Commd 30/7/52. Sqn Ldr 1/7/62. Retd GD 24/3/69.
LEGGET E.H. MRAeS MCMI. Born 28/6/30. Commd 1/8/51. Wg Cdr 1/1/69. Retd GD 1/5/76.
LEGGETT A.J. OBE FBCS MCMI. Born 9/11/30. Commd 18/2/54. Gp Capt 1/7/77. Retd ADMIN 5/4/83. rtg A Cdre.
LEGGETT C.J. Born 17/11/42. Commd 8/12/61. Wg Cdr 1/1/95. Retd GD 17/11/98.
LEGGETT D.N.J.P. Born 17/4/14. Commd 3/3/33. Wg Cdr 1/7/47. Retd ENG 19/6/51. rtg Gp Capt
LEGGETT P.G. Born 14/2/21. Commd 31/8/40. Sqn Ldr 1/7/49. Retd GD 23/5/58.
LEGGETT R.W. Born 3/4/22. Commd 10/1/42. Wg Cdr 1/7/56. Retd GD 1/4/68.
LEGGOTT R.H. Born 6/9/30. Commd 24/9/64. Sqn Ldr 1/7/74. Retd ENG 6/9/92.
LEGGOTT S.P. BSc. Born 15/3/63. Commd 13/4/83. Flt Lt 15/1/87. Retd GD 15/7/96.
LEGH-SMITH J.R. Born 10/9/39. Commd 19/12/61. Gp Capt 1/1/89. Retd GD 10/9/94.
LEHEUP M.D. BA. Born 12/1/29. Commd 5/5/60. Flt Lt 5/5/66. Retd ENG 30/7/80.
LEIGH A.M. Born 23/1/46. Commd 21/3/69. Flt Lt 1/11/72. Retd GD 3/2/76.
LEIGH B.N.B. Born 31/3/48. Commd 1/8/69. Sqn Ldr 1/1/80. Retd ADMIN 31/3/86.
LEIGH J.M. Born 20/1/46. Commd 20/8/65. Wg Cdr 1/7/89. Retd GD 13/9/96.
LEIGH M.E. Born 18/8/43. Commd 14/6/63. Sqn Ldr 1/1/77. Retd EDN 18/8/81.
LEIGH R.G. Born 27/1/44. Commd 14/6/63. Flt Lt 14/12/68. Retd GD 27/1/02.
LEIGH U.D.B. Born 1/7/15. Commd 29/11/44. Fg Offr 29/11/46. Retd SUP 6/10/50. rtg Flt Offr.
LEIGHTON G.S. Born 8/11/47. Commd 29/6/72. Flt Lt 29/12/78. Retd SUP 21/2/84.
LEIGHTON R. Born 16/11/33. Commd 30/7/52. Sqn Ldr 1/7/71. Retd GD 16/11/88.
LEIGHTON-PORTER S.E. BSc. Born 26/3/57. Commd 5/9/76. Sqn Ldr 1/1/92. Retd GD 26/3/95.
LEINSTER I.A. BSc. Born 18/8/29. Commd 8/5/52. Sqn Ldr 1/7/62. Retd GD 2/6/71.
LEIPNIK W.A.M. Born 4/6/61. Commd 4/11/82. Flt Lt 30/4/89. Retd GD(G) 7/12/92.
LEITCH A.H. Born 9/4/51. Commd 16/3/73. Flt Lt 16/3/76. Retd GD 4/8/87.
LEITCH D.G. MB ChB MRCP DCH. Born 17/5/39. Commd 15/10/62. Wg Cdr 28/9/78. Retd MED 1/2/79.
LEITH D.I. BA. Born 12/1/38. Commd 1/1/63. Sqn Ldr 1/7/70. Retd EDN 19/4/74.
LEITH D.J. OBE. Born 6/11/25. Commd 22/6/45. Gp Capt 1/7/77. Retd GD 6/11/80.
LELLIOT R.G. Born 31/1/32. Commd 22/8/63. Flt Lt 16/6/68. Retd SEC 15/5/79.
LEMARE D.A.C. Born 11/8/46. Commd 28/4/67. Sqn Ldr 1/1/87. Retd GD 27/4/00.
LEMON B.J. MBE AFC FCMI. Born 18/2/34. Commd 9/11/54. A Cdre 1/1/81. Retd GD 14/6/89.
LEMON G.T. Born 27/12/22. Commd 29/1/44. Flt Lt 1/12/55. Retd GD 30/12/68.
LEMON J.H. MB BS DAvMed. Born 4/6/32. Commd 10/9/52. Wg Cdr 17/8/71. Retd MED 17/8/74.
LEMON P.C. DSO DFC. Born 16/6/18. Commd 12/10/36. Sqn Ldr 1/8/47. Retd GD 1/12/57.
LENAGHAN P. Born 28/2/38. Commd 18/2/58. Flt Lt 15/2/65. Retd GD 28/2/93.
LENNON P. Born 17/3/34. Commd 5/11/52. Flt Lt 24/3/58. Retd GD 1/6/76.
LENNON P.C.C. Born 8/5/42. Commd 15/9/61. Fg Offr 15/9/63. Retd GD 5/5/67.
LENNON R.B. Born 30/11/51. Commd 27/9/73. Sqn Ldr 1/1/88. Retd GD 1/1/91.
LENNOX D. Born 27/2/19. Commd 22/5/42. Flt Lt 16/7/51. Retd ENG 1/5/61. rtg Sqn Ldr.
LENNOX D.S. OBE CEng MRAeS. Born 12/2/37. Commd 23/7/58. Gp Capt 1/7/80. Retd ENG 1/8/87.
LENOIR R.J. MA MB BChir FFARCS DRCOG. Born 2/5/46. Commd 10/5/87. Wg Cdr 10/5/93. Retd MED 23/10/02.
LENTON W.S. Born 18/2/40. Commd 27/7/60. Flt Lt 2/7/63. Retd GD 18/2/78.
LEONARD A. OBE BEM. Born 15/3/42. Commd 14/8/80. Wg Cdr 1/7/93. Retd ENG 3/1/98.
LEONARD B.J. MCIPS MCMI. Born 19/3/26. Commd 3/5/46. Wg Cdr 1/7/67. Retd SUP 31/3/77. rtg Gp Capt
LEONARD G. BA. Born 24/4/64. Commd 2/9/84. Flt Lt 2/3/88. Retd ADMIN 14/3/97.
LEONARD G.H.J. DFC. Born 14/2/23. Commd 10/3/44. Sqn Ldr 1/7/61. Retd SEC 31/8/68.
LEONARD H.A. Born 23/4/33. Commd 28/3/53. Flt Lt 5/8/58. Retd GD 23/4/71.
LEONARD R.G. OBE. Born 23/7/52. Commd 16/3/73. Gp Capt 1/1/01. Retd GD 1/3/05.
LEONARD W. Born 11/6/22. Commd 19/7/57. Sqn Ldr 1/1/70. Retd ENG 11/10/77.
LEONCZEK M.R. BSc. Born 5/5/61. Commd 30/10/83. Sqn Ldr 1/7/97. Retd GD 1/7/00.
LEPPARD D.E. Born 13/5/38. Commd 13/12/60. A Cdre 1/7/86. Retd GD 9/9/89.
LEPPARD R.W. OBE CEng MIERE MCMI. Born 23/9/21. Commd 13/12/45. Gp Capt 1/7/76. Retd ENG 29/11/78.
LERWILL G.F. DFC. Born 12/3/15. Commd 15/3/35. Gp Capt 1/1/59. Retd GD 12/4/65.
LESLIE A.B. Born 26/11/35. Commd 23/11/78. Flt Lt 23/11/83. Retd ADMIN 6/4/90.
LESLIE D.M. Born 16/1/34. Commd 3/9/52. Wg Cdr 1/7/72. Retd GD 24/2/85.
LESLIE G.E. BSc. Born 30/3/29. Commd 19/12/52. Flt Lt 17/5/56. Retd GD 14/1/69.
LESLIE J. Born 1/1/55. Commd 27/3/75. Flt Lt 27/3/80. Retd GD 13/1/93.
LESLIE W.A. Born 26/5/12. Commd 26/5/41. Fg Offr 26/5/42. Retd ENG 18/10/47. rtg Flt Lt.
LETCHFORD C.W.G. Born 2/5/38. Commd 6/4/72. Flt Lt 6/4/74. Retd GD 13/6/78.
LETHER H.V. CBE. Born 5/6/45. Commd 4/10/63. Gp Capt 1/7/91. Retd GD 3/12/96.
LETTON M.H. Born 21/7/35. Commd 3/3/54. Flt Lt 3/9/59. Retd GD 21/7/73.
LEUCHARS C.G. BSc. Born 5/6/46. Commd 26/5/67. Flt Lt 26/5/70. Retd GD 14/3/96.
LEVENE I. Born 2/5/22. Commd 6/11/43. Flt Lt 26/12/57. Retd GD(G) 17/10/63.
LEVER R.A. Born 10/2/52. Commd 24/1/71. Flt Lt 24/12/76. Retd GD 10/2/90.

LEVERSON J.J. Born 1/11/37. Commd 1/6/72. Flt Lt 1/6/74. Retd GD(G) 1/6/80.
LEVETT G. Born 25/2/32. Commd 2/7/52. Sqn Ldr 1/7/66. Retd ENG 25/2/70.
LEVICK P. Born 9/4/58. Commd 15/9/81. Sqn Ldr 1/7/94. Retd FLY(N) 9/4/04.
LEVIN R. Born 10/10/20. Commd 25/8/60. Flt Lt 25/8/65. Retd ENG 6/4/68.
LEVISEUR R.H. Born 9/10/23. Commd 19/6/47. Sqn Ldr 1/1/60. Retd GD 9/9/72.
LEVISTON A.M. BSc. Born 5/12/57. Commd 26/9/82. Sqn Ldr 1/1/95. Retd GD 26/9/98.
LEVISTON A.R. Born 19/12/43. Commd 30/5/69. Sqn Ldr 1/7/89. Retd ENG 2/6/93.
LEVITT A.W. Born 19/6/44. Commd 29/6/72. Gp Capt 1/7/93. Retd ENG 4/4/94.
LEVY M.H. MBE. Born 18/1/27. Commd 1/1/47. Sqn Ldr 1/1/57. Retd GD 26/10/68.
LEWARNE J.O.H. BA. Born 30/8/30. Commd 5/5/54. Flt Lt 3/12/56. Retd GD 5/5/70.
LEWENDON A.J. LLB. Born 16/3/53. Commd 31/7/83. Flt Lt 31/1/87. Retd ADMIN 24/4/92.
LEWENDON J.M. Born 14/4/30. Commd 12/12/51. Gp Capt 1/1/76. Retd ADMIN 31/12/83.
LEWENDON M.J. Born 16/8/49. Commd 10/2/72. Flt Lt 17/2/77. Retd GD 18/10/87.
LEWER J.H. Born 19/2/41. Commd 3/8/62. Flt Lt 3/2/68. Retd GD 19/2/79.
LEWER J.S. Born 5/6/37. Commd 21/3/69. Sqn Ldr 30/11/80. Retd MED(SEC) 7/4/88.
LEWIN E.R. Born 6/4/13. Commd 29/8/42. Flt Lt 10/11/55. Retd SUP 10/6/62.
LEWIN P. Born 31/8/32. Commd 28/2/52. Sqn Ldr 1/7/86. Retd GD 31/8/92.
LEWINGTON D.I. Born 1/7/55. Commd 22/11/73. Sqn Ldr 1/1/86. Retd GD(G) 10/9/93.
LEWINGTON E.J. Born 21/10/22. Commd 3/1/46. Flt Lt 4/1/51. Retd GD 21/10/65.
LEWINGTON G.E. Born 20/2/45. Commd 5/3/65. Flt Lt 5/9/70. Retd GD 26/12/72.
LEWINGTON L. Born 17/8/17. Commd 21/2/40. Sqn Ldr 1/7/50. Retd ENG 1/1/55. rtg Wg Cdr.
LEWINS D.M. Born 10/8/59. Commd 12/7/79. Sqn Ldr 1/7/91. Retd GD 10/8/97.
LEWIS A.E. Born 30/1/19. Commd 27/8/59. Sqn Ldr 1/1/70. Retd ENG 28/2/76.
LEWIS A.G. MBE. Born 23/6/20. Commd 1/3/45. Sqn Ldr 1/10/55. Retd ENG 26/10/62.
LEWIS A.O. Born 24/12/16. Commd 5/3/53. Sqn Ldr 1/7/61. Retd ENG 24/12/71.
LEWIS A.R. Born 11/10/30. Commd 28/7/53. Flt Lt 28/1/56. Retd GD 11/10/68.
LEWIS B. MCMI. Born 5/10/24. Commd 13/9/45. Wg Cdr 1/1/71. Retd GD 5/11/75.
LEWIS B.A. Born 14/4/31. Commd 27/3/52. Flt Lt 27/12/57. Retd GD 14/11/68.
LEWIS B.H.J. BSc. Born 6/9/37. Commd 3/12/58. Flt Lt 4/1/66. Retd GD 6/9/75.
LEWIS C.B. Born 29/7/28. Commd 28/6/51. Flt Lt 10/10/56. Retd GD 14/2/63.
LEWIS C.G. Born 1/12/20. Commd 1/10/43. Wg Cdr 1/7/59. Retd GD 1/12/67.
LEWIS D. Born 29/9/50. Commd 23/4/87. Sqn Ldr 1/7/97. Retd ENG 1/10/99.
LEWIS D. MB ChB DObstRCOG. Born 18/10/39. Commd 13/8/72. Sqn Ldr 20/4/70. Retd MED 16/12/77.
LEWIS D.G. Born 26/9/29. Commd 6/12/51. Flt Lt 27/3/57. Retd GD 25/8/70.
LEWIS D.H. Born 6/5/51. Commd 24/1/74. Sqn Ldr 1/1/89. Retd GD 1/10/97.
LEWIS D.I. AFC. Born 4/3/43. Commd 28/4/61. Wg Cdr 1/7/81. Retd GD 17/6/93.
LEWIS D.J. MSc BA PGCE. Born 1/3/59. Commd 11/9/83. Sqn Ldr 1/1/94. Retd ADMIN 11/9/99.
LEWIS D.M. MB ChB MRCGP DAvMed. Born 22/8/59. Commd 13/8/79. Sqn Ldr 1/8/88. Retd MED 31/1/89.
    Re-entered 3/7/89. Wg Cdr 1/8/96. Retd MED 22/8/99.
LEWIS D.R. Born 11/8/31. Commd 27/3/52. Flt Lt 22/2/56. Retd GD 6/7/87.
LEWIS E.W. Born 15/2/30. Commd 26/3/52. Flt Lt 7/8/57. Retd GD 14/11/70.
LEWIS G. MCMI. Born 13/11/25. Commd 9/6/55. Sqn Ldr 1/7/69. Retd PRT 1/2/74.
LEWIS G.G. Born 17/1/31. Commd 6/12/51. Flt Lt 5/6/57. Retd GD 24/4/68.
LEWIS G.J. MA MEd BA PGCE MCIPD. Born 20/7/53. Commd 28/9/80. Sqn Ldr 1/7/89. Retd ADMIN 14/9/96.
LEWIS G.L.C. Born 13/10/48. Commd 10/9/70. Flt Lt 10/3/76. Retd GD 13/10/86.
LEWIS G.N. AFC. Born 7/6/31. Commd 16/7/52. Sqn Ldr 1/1/63. Retd GD 1/3/75.
LEWIS H.E. Born 8/9/35. Commd 6/5/64. Flt Lt 6/5/70. Retd GD 1/10/83.
LEWIS H.E. Born 5/5/24. Commd 15/9/60. Sqn Ldr 1/7/75. Retd ENG 30/9/77.
LEWIS H.P. Born 9/7/47. Commd 24/4/70. Flt Lt 7/1/74. Retd GD 30/9/77.
LEWIS I.V. Born 25/1/46. Commd 8/8/74. Sqn Ldr 1/1/85. Retd ENG 15/8/01.
LEWIS J. Born 26/9/18. Commd 24/4/42. Sqn Ldr 1/7/69. Retd GD(G) 26/9/73.
LEWIS J.A. Born 5/6/25. Commd 19/7/51. Flt Lt 10/11/55. Retd GD(G) 10/10/72.
LEWIS J.A.H. Born 6/8/34. Commd 19/12/59. Flt Lt 19/6/64. Retd GD 30/6/68.
LEWIS J.C.W. BA. Born 20/9/14. Commd 16/2/48. Sqn Ldr 16/1/52. Retd EDN 1/9/65.
LEWIS J.E. Born 3/6/19. Commd 30/7/42. Flt Offr 30/1/47. Retd SEC 10/7/54.
LEWIS J.G. MBE. Born 29/10/28. Commd 16/7/52. Flt Lt 12/12/57. Retd GD 18/3/69.
LEWIS J.G. Born 11/9/40. Commd 19/7/84. Flt Lt 19/7/88. Retd ENG 1/3/96.
LEWIS J.H. MA LMSSA DPH. Born 17/4/10. Commd 4/1/37. Gp Capt 1/10/57. Retd MED 1/12/65.
LEWIS J.H. BSc. Born 16/4/63. Commd 14/5/89. Flt Lt 14/11/91. Retd OPS SPT(ATC) 14/5/05.
LEWIS J.J.W. DFM. Born 20/1/16. Commd 21/11/41. Sqn Ldr 1/8/47. Retd GD 20/1/58.
LEWIS J.R. Born 3/7/23. Commd 19/7/51. Flt Lt 19/1/56. Retd RGT 3/7/68.
LEWIS J.T.S. AFC. Born 19/9/37. Commd 29/7/58. Sqn Ldr 1/7/68. Retd GD 1/2/72.
LEWIS K.G. CEng FRAeS FIEE FCMI. Born 19/3/30. Commd 21/2/52. Gp Capt 1/1/76. Retd ENG 19/3/85.
LEWIS K.J. Born 31/3/31. Commd 7/5/52. Flt Lt 2/10/57. Retd GD 1/4/68.
LEWIS K.L. Born 25/4/23. Commd 17/6/44. Wg Cdr 1/1/72. Retd GD 23/4/77.
LEWIS L.W.C. MCMI. Born 1/12/16. Commd 3/3/44. Wg Cdr 1/1/59. Retd PRT 1/12/68.

LEWIS M. MSc BSc CEng MIEE. Born 10/12/49. Commd 8/9/74. Wg Cdr 1/7/90. Retd ENG 7/5/94.
LEWIS N.R. MA MB BCh MRCS LRCP DPhysMed. Born 21/7/25. Commd 29/9/52. Wg Cdr 2/4/65. Retd MED 29/9/68.
LEWIS P. MCMI. Born 9/10/33. Commd 11/6/63. Sqn Ldr 1/1/71. Retd SEC 1/1/76.
LEWIS P.E. DFC. Born 20/5/17. Commd 25/10/37. Sqn Ldr 1/9/45. Retd GD 25/5/58. rtg Wg Cdr.
LEWIS P.G. Born 7/1/48. Commd 27/5/71. Sqn Ldr 1/7/83. Retd GD(G) 8/2/87.
LEWIS P.H. OBE. Born 25/8/31. Commd 17/12/52. Wg Cdr 1/7/69. Retd GD 26/8/81. Re-instated on Retired List 28/8/86.
LEWIS P.H.T. OBE BEng CEng FIMechE MRAeS MCMI. Born 24/10/25. Commd 6/6/46. Gp Capt 1/1/74. Retd ENG 24/10/80.
LEWIS P.J. LLB FCIPD FBIFM. Born 21/1/56. Commd 17/7/77. Gp Capt 1/1/96. Retd ADMIN 21/2/00.
LEWIS P.J.H. AFC. Born 10/1/33. Commd 6/4/54. Sqn Ldr 1/7/64. Retd GD 2/2/74.
LEWIS P.R. MA CEng MRAeS MCMI. Born 16/6/35. Commd 30/9/55. Sqn Ldr 1/1/72. Retd ENG 6/2/88.
LEWIS R. BSc. Born 16/11/40. Commd 1/10/62. Sqn Ldr 1/7/72. Retd ENG 18/1/80.
LEWIS R.A. Born 27/9/26. Commd 19/11/52. Flt Lt 15/4/58. Retd GD 28/5/68.
LEWIS R.A. Born 11/8/42. Commd 5/8/64. Flt Lt 28/1/70. Retd ENG 11/8/80.
LEWIS R.A. BA. Born 31/8/30. Commd 20/8/58. Sqn Ldr 17/2/63. Retd ADMIN 31/8/85.
LEWIS R.A. Born 25/3/44. Commd 16/9/71. Wg Cdr 1/1/90. Retd ENG 30/11/00.
LEWIS R.C.J. Born 24/5/61. Commd 24/7/81. Flt Lt 24/1/87. Retd GD 25/5/00.
LEWIS R.J. BSc. Born 14/3/15. Commd 21/6/40. Gp Capt 1/1/63. Retd ENG 2/11/68.
LEWIS R.O. MBE MCMI. Born 9/6/45. Commd 26/8/66. Sqn Ldr 1/1/80. Retd SY(RGT) 9/6/89.
LEWIS R.P. Born 30/10/47. Commd 11/11/71. Flt Lt 11/5/77. Retd GD 26/7/87.
LEWIS R.P.R. Born 2/5/24. Commd 4/10/44. Flt Lt 4/4/48. Retd GD 2/11/48.
LEWIS R.R. Born 1/7/42. Commd 27/1/61. Flt Lt 27/7/71. Retd GD 15/9/72.
LEWIS R.R. Born 22/10/58. Commd 19/9/76. Fg Offr 20/9/80. Retd SUP 3/9/82.
LEWIS S.A. BSc. Born 2/7/45. Commd 28/9/64. Flt Lt 15/10/70. Retd ENG 27/10/72.
LEWIS S.C. Born 12/2/51. Commd 4/9/81. Flt Lt 4/9/83. Retd GD(G) 2/5/91.
LEWIS S.K. Born 11/9/44. Commd 10/12/65. Flt Lt 11/3/70. Retd GD 12/9/92.
LEWIS T.C. Born 4/10/30. Commd 11/2/65. Flt Lt 11/2/70. Retd ENG 1/9/76.
LEWIS T.G. Born 4/4/16. Commd 9/6/55. Flt Lt 18/11/58. Retd GD(G) 4/4/71.
LEWIS T.J. Born 20/1/63. Commd 25/5/89. Flt Lt 6/9/88. Retd GD 14/10/95.
LEWIS W.D. Born 10/9/13. Commd 29/6/44. Sqn Ldr 1/7/65. Retd SEC 10/9/68.
LEWIS W.E. Born 31/12/14. Commd 27/10/55. Flt Lt 27/10/58. Retd ENG 31/12/70.
LEWIS W.R. Born 20/7/44. Commd 24/6/65. Sqn Ldr 1/1/82. Retd GD 8/4/88.
LEWIS-LLOYD J. Born 24/6/31. Commd 30/7/52. Sqn Ldr 1/7/61. Retd GD 14/8/64.
LEWIS-MORRIS M.J. MSc BSc. Born 1/2/46. Commd 29/4/84. Sqn Ldr 1/1/92. Retd ADMIN 1/5/02.
LEWRY A.M. Born 26/11/52. Commd 28/10/76. Flt Lt 28/10/81. Retd GD 9/8/92.
LEY K.A.M.M. Born 11/5/43. Commd 3/8/61. Sqn Ldr 1/7/79. Retd RGT 11/5/87.
LEYLAND M. BSc. Born 20/11/35. Commd 6/1/69. Sqn Ldr 30/11/71. Retd ADMIN 20/11/85.
LEYLAND R.G. Born 5/11/45. Commd 30/8/84. Flt Lt 1/3/87. Retd GD 2/4/93.
LEYLAND R.H. Born 22/1/30. Commd 30/12/54. Sqn Ldr 1/1/82. Retd GD 1/4/84.
LEZEMORE R.B. Born 24/5/14. Commd 9/7/53. Flt Lt 9/7/56. Retd ENG 24/5/69.
LIDBETTER G.H. Born 10/8/39. Commd 6/4/72. Sqn Ldr 1/1/87. Retd GD 10/8/94.
LIDDELL D. Born 12/1/39. Commd 7/6/68. Sqn Ldr 1/7/86. Retd GD 12/1/94.
LIDDELL G.K.H. Born 18/8/22. Commd 11/9/52. Flt Lt 11/3/57. Retd SEC 31/10/64.
LIDDELL H.M. AFC BA. Born 27/9/24. Commd 14/4/49. Sqn Ldr 1/7/71. Retd GD 27/9/82.
LIDDELL P. CB BSc CEng FIEE FRAeS. Born 9/10/48. Commd 18/9/66. AVM 1/7/99. Retd GD 21/10/03.
LIDDIARD B. MCMI. Born 23/7/30. Commd 19/7/51. Wg Cdr 1/1/80. Retd GD 31/10/83.
LIDDIARD M.T.N. OBE MCMI. Born 25/12/34. Commd 26/7/55. Wg Cdr 1/1/75. Retd SUP 1/11/79.
LIDDLE A.G. BSc. Born 6/8/36. Commd 28/11/56. Flt Lt 2/7/60. Retd GD 30/10/68.
LIDDLE W. Born 7/9/27. Commd 17/5/56. Flt Lt 17/11/60. Retd GD 11/1/71.
LIDSTONE H.R.G. Born 9/3/13. Commd 28/3/46. Sqn Ldr 1/1/57. Retd SUP 9/3/62.
LIDSTONE J.H. Born 20/11/39. Commd 21/2/69. Flt Lt 21/2/71. Retd SEC 5/5/78.
LIGGAT A.M.S. Born 9/5/58. Commd 6/6/78. Sqn Ldr 1/7/92. Retd GD 9/5/96.
LIGGINS R.O. Born 11/6/53. Commd 8/2/81. Flt Lt 8/8/85. Retd ENG 2/6/93.
LIGGITT D.J. Born 10/3/40. Commd 25/7/60. Wg Cdr 1/7/77. Retd GD 1/11/88.
LIGHT G.A. BA. Born 19/10/58. Commd 15/5/79. Fg Offr 15/4/79. Retd SY 24/1/82.
LIGHT O.C.S. Born 24/4/31. Commd 14/9/64. Flt Lt 29/11/68. Retd SEC 7/3/73.
LIGHTBODY P.D. Born 14/7/64. Commd 6/5/83. Flt Lt 6/11/88. Retd GD 9/2/93.
LIGHTFOOT R.D. AFC. Born 30/3/40. Commd 1/8/61. A Cdre 1/7/87. Retd GD 28/6/93.
LIGHTOWLERS A. Born 5/3/23. Commd 10/3/44. Sqn Ldr 1/7/57. Retd GD 5/6/72.
LILES A.J. MBE. Born 19/11/31. Commd 14/1/53. Sqn Ldr 1/7/63. Retd ENG 26/10/76.
LILES T.N.F. Born 10/12/42. Commd 30/7/63. Flt Lt 30/1/66. Retd GD 10/12/80.
LILLEY C.G. MBE FCMI MinstPS. Born 7/7/24. Commd 7/4/44. Gp Capt 1/7/74. Retd SUP 7/7/79.
LILLEY D.S. Born 12/6/30. Commd 30/7/52. Sqn Ldr 1/1/65. Retd SUP 2/8/80.
LILLEY E.C.J. MHCIMA. Born 19/1/55. Commd 8/4/82. Sqn Ldr 1/7/93. Retd ADMIN 1/6/98.
LILLEY G. Born 1/7/43. Commd 5/7/73. Flt Lt 5/7/75. Retd ADMIN 5/7/82.
LILLEY K.G. Born 25/4/41. Commd 18/12/62. Sqn Ldr 1/7/72. Retd GD 10/8/85.
LILLEY R.L. Born 6/1/43. Commd 17/12/63. Sqn Ldr 1/1/74. Retd ADMIN 6/1/81.

LILLEY S.R. Born 11/6/23. Commd 21/6/56. Flt Lt 21/6/62. Retd GD 1/10/68.
LILLEYSTONE J.T. MCMI. Born 25/12/21. Commd 12/9/42. Wg Cdr 1/7/68. Retd GD 25/12/76.
LILLIS J. Born 28/7/45. Commd 26/5/67. Sqn Ldr 1/1/90. Retd FLY(N) 28/7/04.
LIM C.S. MCIT MIDPM MCMI. Born 22/2/31. Commd 28/7/53. Wg Cdr 1/1/73. Retd SUP 22/2/86.
LIMB B.J.M. QGM. Born 7/6/36. Commd 8/1/59. Sqn Ldr 1/7/84. Retd GD 7/6/92.
LIMB M.A. BA. Born 27/12/40. Commd 15/11/89. Flt Lt 23/11/69. Retd GD 2/4/93.
LIMBERT J.J. Born 5/4/53. Commd 2/8/90. Flt Lt 2/8/94. Retd ADMIN 15/4/02.
LIMBREY B.M. MSc. Born 26/8/44. Commd 17/9/72. Wg Cdr 1/7/86. Retd ADMIN 2/4/91.
LINALE J.R. Born 27/7/35. Commd 10/3/60. Flt Lt 10/9/64. Retd GD 5/8/80.
LINCOLN T.G. DFC MCMI. Born 5/11/22. Commd 24/3/44. Flt Lt 24/3/50. Retd SUP 3/4/73. rtg Sqn Ldr.
LINCOLN W.D. Born 24/6/24. Commd 1/7/52. Sqn Ldr 1/7/72. Retd GD 1/7/76.
LIND R.E. DFC. Born 13/1/18. Commd 7/6/44. Flt Lt 7/6/50. Retd GD(G) 13/1/73.
LINDER G.R. Born 15/3/38. Commd 16/12/66. Sqn Ldr 1/7/78. Retd SUP 20/11/88.
LINDLEY A.J. Born 30/1/46. Commd 23/1/64. Flt Lt 20/6/70. Retd GD 30/1/84.
LINDLEY R.A. The Venerable CBE BA. Born 21/11/20. Commd 12/9/46. Retd Wg Cdr 29/11/70.
LINDLEY R.F. Born 21/7/47. Commd 2/12/66. Flt Lt 2/6/72. Retd GD 25/8/76.
LINDO R.W. BSc. Born 14/4/49. Commd 22/4/71. Sqn Ldr 1/1/85. Retd GD 1/2/88.
LINDSAY A.H. Born 8/7/26. Commd 29/4/53. Flt Lt 16/8/61. Retd GD 21/10/68.
LINDSAY A.J. BA. Born 24/8/64. Commd 18/8/85. Wg Cdr 1/7/00. Retd ADMIN 24/8/02.
LINDSAY G.H. Born 13/7/62. Commd 23/10/86. Flt Lt 23/4/93. Retd OPS SPT 23/6/02.
LINDSAY G.J. BA PGCE. Born 28/11/63. Commd 18/8/91. Flt Lt 18/2/94. Retd ADMIN 10/11/96.
LINDSAY I.D. MA MSc MB BChir MRCGP DRCOG DAvMed AFOM. Born 1/3/48. Commd 26/10/70.
   Gp Capt 1/1/97. Retd MED 12/12/99.
LINDSAY I.R. CBE MSc MB ChB DPH MFOM. Born 17/8/25. Commd 12/8/48. A Cdre 1/1/83. Retd MED 9/1/88.
LINDSAY P.F. MBE FInstNDT. Born 5/11/50. Commd 23/4/87. Wg Cdr 1/7/01. Retd GD 3/5/04.
LINDSAY W.R.S. Born 20/10/38. Commd 25/6/65. Flt Lt 17/3/71. Retd GD 20/10/93.
LINDSEY A.M. Born 26/1/39. Commd 22/3/63. Sqn Ldr 1/1/77. Retd GD(G) 7/9/93.
LINDSEY-HALLS D.J. BA MCMI. Born 12/8/40. Commd 18/8/61. Wg Cdr 1/7/81. Retd GD 1/10/87.
LINE C.R. Born 5/4/55. Commd 13/12/79. Fg Offr 13/6/82. Retd GD(G) 1/8/85.
LINE K.M. Born 24/2/33. Commd 26/3/52. Flt Lt 7/3/62. Retd GD 11/9/71.
LINE R.C. Born 20/2/59. Commd 25/9/80. Flt Lt 25/3/86. Retd GD 20/2/97.
LINES A. Born 12/7/23. Commd 21/12/67. Flt Lt 21/12/72. Retd ENG 16/10/76.
LINES A.N. Born 14/2/46. Commd 19/10/72. Flt Lt 2/6/77. Retd GD(G) 15/7/85.
LINES C. Born 13/12/43. Commd 27/5/71. Flt Lt 27/11/76. Retd GD 31/12/93.
LINES J.A. Born 28/9/50. Commd 9/12/71. Flt Lt 9/6/77. Retd GD 28/9/88.
LINES P.J. Born 17/5/35. Commd 15/9/61. Flt Lt 1/4/66. Retd GD 12/5/89.
LINES P.J. Born 1/3/64. Commd 24/3/83. Sqn Ldr 1/1/98. Retd GD 24/6/01.
LINES R.P. Born 9/7/38. Commd 21/11/67. Flt Lt 14/12/74. Retd ADMIN 14/12/80.
LINFOOT J.A. Born 1/6/24. Commd 10/9/60. Flt Lt 10/9/65. Retd GD(G) 24/12/71.
LINFORD G.P. Born 16/3/50. Commd 28/10/68. Flt Lt 1/2/76. Retd ADMIN 20/8/77.
LINFORD R.J. OBE. Born 3/6/24. Commd 5/5/45. Wg Cdr 1/7/66. Retd GD 5/5/80.
LING C.W.M. DFC. Born 27/6/11. Commd 25/7/31. Wg Cdr 12/4/45. Retd GD 5/6/46. rtg Gp Capt.
LING H.T.N. Born 19/11/25. Commd 26/12/51. Flt Lt 26/6/56. Retd GD 19/11/85.
LINGARD D.I. Born 16/4/44. Commd 7/1/71. Flt Lt 7/7/76. Retd GD 16/4/99.
LINGARD R. DFC. Born 16/10/22. Commd 25/4/43. Sqn Ldr 1/7/54. Retd GD 16/10/61.
LINGWOOD K.E. Born 1/12/24. Commd 6/1/56. Flt Lt 6/1/56. Retd GD(G) 11/5/73.
LINK D. Born 18/6/23. Commd 2/9/44. Fg Offr 2/3/45. Retd GD 14/7/47. rtg Flt Lt.
LINNELL R.J. Born 19/10/63. Commd 10/2/83. Flt Lt 10/8/88. Retd GD 17/12/96.
LINNEY D.W. AFC. Born 8/8/47. Commd 15/9/67. Sqn Ldr 1/7/82. Retd GD 8/8/85.
LINNIT R.W. Born 1/6/08. Commd 19/8/40. Flt Lt 1/1/43. Retd GD 4/6/48. rtg Sqn Ldr.
LINTHUNE V.H. DFC. Born 18/4/18. Commd 18/2/42. Sqn Ldr 1/1/51. Retd GD 18/11/57.
LINTON M.G. Born 30/1/36. Commd 9/12/53. Sqn Ldr 1/1/91. Retd GD 1/1/94.
LINTOTT A.G. MCIPS. Born 17/11/31. Commd 12/2/53. Wg Cdr 1/1/76. Retd SUP 17/11/86.
LINTOTT D.P. BA. Born 13/9/40. Commd 29/4/71. Flt Lt 29/4/73. Retd GD 30/9/78.
LIQUORISH A.W. Born 10/7/10. Commd 2/10/41. Fg Offr 1/10/42. Retd SUP 9/8/46. rtg Flt Lt.
LISETT T.S. Born 4/2/55. Commd 15/3/84. Flt Lt 15/3/86. Retd ENG 4/2/93.
LISHER B.J. MB BS DAvMed. Born 25/11/43. Commd 24/1/66. Sqn Ldr 5/6/74. Retd MED 24/1/82.
LISHMAN C.W.P. Born 14/5/13. Commd 25/2/44. Sqn Ldr 1/4/58. Retd SEC 7/6/68.
LISHMAN P.J.S. Born 16/12/43. Commd 4/10/63. Flt Lt 4/4/69. Retd GD 21/5/85.
LISKUTIN M. DFC AFC. Born 23/8/19. Commd 3/7/43. Sqn Ldr 1/1/57. Retd GD 23/8/62.
LISLE E.J. DFC*. Born 9/5/20. Commd 9/8/41. Sqn Ldr 1/1/54. Retd GD 9/5/63.
LISTER C.W.M. MCMI. Born 8/9/31. Commd 2/7/52. Sqn Ldr 1/1/67. Retd GD 17/1/77.
LISTER H.J. Born 8/3/16. Commd 6/2/43. Flt Lt 6/8/46. Retd GD 8/3/71.
LISTER J.A. MB ChB MRCPsych DPM. Born 4/10/33. Commd 26/3/53. Wg Cdr 21/11/72. Retd MED 15/8/76.
LISTER K. DFC. Born 7/8/21. Commd 21/7/42. Wg Cdr 1/1/60. Retd GD 7/2/68.
LISTER T.H.W. Born 23/11/18. Commd 24/6/43. Flt Lt 19/6/52. Retd GD(G) 10/3/61.

LISTON E.G. BSc. Born 20/9/51. Commd 11/8/74. Sqn Ldr 1/7/86. Retd GD 1/7/86.
LISTON M.J. Born 31/8/49. Commd 11/5/89. Flt Lt 11/5/91. Retd OPS SPT(FLTOPS) 11/10/03.
LITHGOW P. Born 17/11/24. Commd 13/3/46. Sqn Ldr 1/7/59. Retd RGT 1/10/69.
LITTLE A.J. Born 17/12/45. Commd 27/2/70. Wg Cdr 1/7/90. Retd ADMIN 17/12/00.
LITTLE A.S. BSc. Born 8/5/39. Commd 30/9/58. Sqn Ldr 1/1/72. Retd ENG 8/5/77.
LITTLE A.S. Born 16/6/29. Commd 1/10/57. Sqn Ldr 1/1/78. Retd GD 3/1/80.
LITTLE B.V. MBE. Born 7/5/28. Commd 2/7/52. Flt Lt 27/11/57. Retd GD 2/5/79.
LITTLE C. BEd. Born 5/9/55. Commd 12/2/86. Sqn Ldr 1/1/95. Retd ADMIN (SEC) 3/6/04.
LITTLE G.D. Born 10/9/40. Commd 2/3/78. Sqn Ldr 1/1/88. Retd ADMIN 1/1/90.
LITTLE M.J. MBE FCMI. Born 2/4/30. Commd 1/10/58. Gp Capt 1/7/79. Retd GD(G) 2/6/82.
LITTLE P.C. Born 26/12/33. Commd 21/10/53. Sqn Ldr 1/1/65. Retd GD 9/5/74.
LITTLE R. Born 17/2/58. Commd 12/10/78. Flt Lt 10/3/85. Retd OPS SPT 29/1/99.
LITTLE R.G. MBE. Born 30/5/19. Commd 5/4/43. Wg Cdr 1/7/59. Retd ENG 30/5/77.
LITTLE S.H. Born 9/2/43. Commd 20/9/69. Flt Lt 20/9/73. Retd GD 9/2/81.
LITTLE W. Born 10/2/52. Commd 29/6/72. Flt Lt 29/12/77. Retd GD 1/5/85.
LITTLEBOY W.E. MBE CEng MRAeS MCMI. Born 4/9/32. Commd 2/11/55. Sqn Ldr 1/1/68. Retd ENG 4/9/87.
LITTLEFIELD D.B. Born 19/6/34. Commd 26/5/61. Flt Lt 1/4/66. Retd GD 19/6/72.
LITTLEJOHN R.J. Born 7/5/29. Commd 11/4/51. Sqn Ldr 1/1/62. Retd GD 2/4/82.
LITTLEJOHN R.K. MA MCIPD. Born 17/3/46. Commd 10/4/68. Wg Cdr 1/1/87. Retd ADMIN 14/3/97.
LITTLER L.R. Born 10/2/35. Commd 2/10/58. Sqn Ldr 1/1/70. Retd SUP 10/10/70.
LITTLER M.R. Born 9/1/49. Commd 3/7/80. Sqn Ldr 1/1/91. Retd GD 14/3/96.
LITTLER R.T. Born 11/6/43. Commd 22/6/70. Flt Lt 22/9/71. Retd GD 30/11/74.
LITTLER W.T. Born 15/5/31. Commd 11/2/65. Flt Lt 11/2/71. Retd ENG 15/5/76.
LITTLEWOOD M. Born 29/1/64. Commd 20/12/90. Flt Lt 20/12/92. Retd ENG 14/9/96.
LIVERMORE N.K. BA. Born 7/1/57. Commd 20/3/80. Flt Lt 2/6/81. Retd GD 1/10/97.
LIVERMORE R. AFM. Born 13/12/23. Commd 10/2/56. Flt Lt 10/2/61. Retd GD 2/7/68.
LIVERSIDGE B.M.W. Born 7/5/44. Commd 25/8/67. Wg Cdr 1/1/85. Retd SY(RGT) 9/5/89.
LIVESEY N.J. BSc. Born 2/12/58. Commd 18/10/81. Flt Lt 18/7/82. Retd GD 18/10/97.
LIVESEY P.J. Born 4/6/61. Commd 31/1/80. Flt Lt 31/7/85. Retd GD 27/10/91.
LIVETT E. Born 6/4/20. Commd 5/12/43. Flt Lt 18/8/48. Retd GD 17/4/63.
LIVINGSTON G. MB ChB MFCM MFOM DPH DIH. Born 2/8/28. Commd 5/5/58. AVM 1/1/85. Retd MED 16/4/89.
LIVINGSTON N. Born 8/7/63. Commd 11/10/84. Flt Lt 11/4/90. Retd GD 31/5/01.
LIVINGSTON R.J. Born 14/7/41. Commd 23/9/66. Sqn Ldr 1/7/78. Retd GD(G) 10/11/92.
LIVINGSTONE S. BSc MCMI. Born 14/2/59. Commd 6/9/81. Sqn Ldr 1/1/89. Retd ADMIN 14/3/96.
LLEWELLYN D.G. BSc. Born 14/12/60. Commd 16/9/79. Fg Offr 15/4/81. Retd GD 14/11/83.
LLEWELLYN-SMITH M. Born 17/12/56. Commd 10/10/87. Flt Lt 8/10/89. Retd ADMIN 8/10/95.
LLOYD A. AFC. Born 16/10/16. Commd 20/8/43. Sqn Ldr 1/7/54. Retd GD 13/1/60.
LLOYD A. CEng MRAeS. Born 27/6/20. Commd 27/2/43. Wg Cdr 1/7/67. Retd ENG 2/7/70.
LLOYD A.G. MMar. Born 28/11/30. Commd 3/1/66. Flt Lt 31/1/72. Retd SUP 31/1/82.
LLOYD B.E. Born 16/12/44. Commd 31/10/63. Flt Lt 31/1/70. Retd SEC 12/2/77.
LLOYD D. CEng MIEE MRAeS. Born 29/12/39. Commd 18/7/61. Sqn Ldr 1/7/70. Retd ENG 30/9/79. rtg Wg Cdr.
LLOYD D.A.O. Born 27/3/23. Commd 18/7/46. Flt Lt 13/11/57. Retd GD 27/3/66.
LLOYD D.C.A. CB FCMI. Born 5/11/28. Commd 5/4/50. AVM 1/1/76. Retd GD 28/5/83.
LLOYD D.G. Born 29/4/47. Commd 25/2/66. Sqn Ldr 1/1/83. Retd GD 7/12/91.
LLOYD D.M. Born 21/6/36. Commd 6/9/56. Sqn Ldr 1/1/74. Retd SEC 1/3/79.
LLOYD E.N. BSc. Born 22/10/30. Commd 10/9/52. Sqn Ldr 22/10/62. Retd EDN 22/10/68.
LLOYD G.K.N. AFC MRAeS MCMI. Born 24/4/23. Commd 20/5/42. Wg Cdr 1/7/59. Retd GD 30/11/68.
LLOYD J. Born 27/4/31. Commd 21/5/52. Flt Lt 29/4/59. Retd GD 27/5/92.
LLOYD J.D. Born 12/7/47. Commd 2/8/68. Flt Lt 2/8/71. Retd GD 22/6/99.
LLOYD J.D. Born 12/2/33. Commd 4/10/51. Sqn Ldr 1/7/65. Retd GD 12/2/93.
LLOYD J.R. Born 5/12/40. Commd 24/3/61. Sqn Ldr 1/7/73. Retd GD 5/12/78.
LLOYD K.F. Born 22/6/28. Commd 3/11/51. Flt Lt 3/5/56. Retd GD 22/6/83.
LLOYD K.T. Born 18/12/45. Commd 29/4/71. Sqn Ldr 1/7/85. Retd ADMIN 20/4/96.
LLOYD M.G. Born 4/10/47. Commd 15/9/67. Wg Cdr 1/1/88. Retd GD 7/8/98.
LLOYD M.H. Born 21/1/02. Commd 19/11/87. Flt Lt 27/8/90. Retd GD 14/3/96.
LLOYD M.J. BSc. Born 12/8/55. Commd 7/11/76. Flt Lt 7/2/80. Retd ADMIN 12/8/93.
LLOYD M.J. Born 21/2/21. Commd 1/1/43. Flt Lt 1/7/46. Retd GD 21/2/64.
LLOYD P.R.J. BSc. Born 21/8/54. Commd 22/8/76. Sqn Ldr 1/1/88. Retd GD 22/8/92.
LLOYD P.U. Born 14/7/24. Commd 26/7/51. Flt Lt 13/11/57. Retd SEC 27/2/65.
LLOYD R.B. Born 4/2/40. Commd 25/7/60. Sqn Ldr 1/7/70. Retd GD 31/7/79.
LLOYD R.H. Born 11/9/39. Commd 13/12/60. Sqn Ldr 1/1/74. Retd GD 11/9/94.
LLOYD R.I. Born 30/5/37. Commd 26/11/60. Sqn Ldr 1/7/85. Retd GD 30/9/87.
LLOYD R.J.C. Born 25/12/47. Commd 21/3/67. Flt Lt 21/3/76. Retd GD(G) 25/12/85.
LLOYD R.S. Born 21/10/26. Commd 23/8/46. Wg Cdr 1/7/64. Retd GD 1/11/75.
LLOYD R.S.R. BSc FCIPD FCMI DipEd. Born 24/4/36. Commd 4/9/59. Gp Capt 1/1/88. Retd ADMIN 24/4/94.
LLOYD S.J. BSc FRAeS FCMI. Born 8/5/51. Commd 13/9/70. Gp Capt 1/1/97. Retd GD 15/12/03.

LLOYD T.E.L. AFC. Born 16/2/37. Commd 29/12/54. Sqn Ldr 25/12/71. Retd GD 16/2/94.
LLOYD T.J. Born 2/7/54. Commd 20/9/79. Sqn Ldr 1/1/90. Retd ENG 1/1/93.
LLOYD W.A.C. Born 19/7/28. Commd 29/3/56. Flt Lt 29/9/60. Retd SEC 19/7/83.
LLOYD W.F. MBE. Born 20/6/47. Commd 13/9/70. Sqn Ldr 1/1/80. Retd ENG 13/9/88.
LLOYD W.S. OBE FCMI. Born 4/8/18. Commd 27/12/42. Gp Capt 1/1/68. Retd SEC 4/8/73.
LLOYD-MORRISON S.G. AFC BSc. Born 2/8/45. Commd 20/8/67. Sqn Ldr 1/1/83. Retd GD 20/8/89.
LLOYD-ROACH D.J. BSc. Born 30/6/60. Commd 9/11/78. Sqn Ldr 1/1/90. Retd ENG 30/6/98.
LOADER J.P. MBE. Born 3/5/55. Commd 18/4/74. Wg Cdr 1/7/99. Retd GD 20/3/04.
LOADER R.B. MBE. Born 16/3/23. Commd 5/3/59. Flt Lt 27/2/63. Retd ENG 16/3/78.
LOASBY B.L. Born 1/6/32. Commd 14/11/59. Flt Lt 14/5/65. Retd GD 1/6/70.
LOAT J. AFC. Born 25/8/20. Commd 17/9/38. Sqn Ldr 1/7/70. Retd GD 25/8/75.
LOBBAN I.C. Born 2/10/48. Commd 6/5/81. Flt Lt 15/2/74. Retd GD 6/5/89.
LOBLE S.J. Born 3/5/48. Commd 6/4/72. Flt Lt 6/10/78. Retd GD(G) 13/12/87.
LOBLEY B. Born 28/8/46. Commd 28/3/91. Flt Lt 28/3/95. Retd ENG 30/6/00.
LOBLEY G.V. CEng FIEE FRAeS. Born 26/4/35. Commd 22/7/55. A Cdre 1/7/78. Retd ENG 1/5/86.
LOBLEY J.V. MBE MCMI. Born 30/5/39. Commd 10/12/57. Wg Cdr 1/7/74. Retd GD 31/12/77.
LOBO R.B.M. DPhysEd. Born 28/10/47. Commd 9/3/72. Sqn Ldr 1/7/87. Retd ADMIN 1/7/90.
LOCK A.A. Born 5/5/31. Commd 15/2/51. Flt Lt 17/5/56. Retd GD 5/5/69.
LOCK A.W. Born 13/2/31. Commd 20/12/51. Flt Lt 4/4/57. Retd GD 13/2/69.
LOCK D.A. Born 12/5/31. Commd 26/10/50. Sqn Ldr 1/1/65. Retd GD 12/5/69.
LOCK D.M. Born 26/4/47. Commd 8/6/84. Sqn Ldr 1/7/96. Retd ADMIN (SEC) 1/5/03.
LOCK F.J.H.C. CEng MIMechE MRAeS MCMI. Born 27/1/33. Commd 24/5/53. Wg Cdr 1/7/74. Retd ENG 27/1/88.
LOCK P.C.R. MBE. Born 26/7/23. Commd 19/8/65. Sqn Ldr 18/12/76. Retd MED(T) 26/7/78.
LOCK P.J. Born 9/2/45. Commd 11/11/65. Wg Cdr 1/1/94. Retd ENG 9/2/00.
LOCK R.K. Born 14/1/66. Commd 22/6/89. Sqn Ldr 1/1/04. Retd OPS SPT(ATC) 1/2/05.
LOCK T.N. BSc. Born 10/11/55. Commd 31/8/75. Flt Lt 14/5/79. Retd GD 15/7/90.
LOCKE D.R. OBE. Born 7/12/23. Commd 9/7/43. Gp Capt 1/7/70. Retd GD 7/12/78.
LOCKE G.H. Born 11/10/40. Commd 24/9/64. Sqn Ldr 1/1/75. Retd GD(G) 11/10/95.
LOCKE J.E. BA. Born 16/3/74. Commd 5/10/97. Fg Offr 5/4/98. Retd OPS SPT 29/6/99.
LOCKE M.A. MCMI. Born 26/3/43. Commd 12/1/62. Sqn Ldr 1/1/75. Retd GD 13/11/96.
LOCKE P.D. Born 8/1/42. Commd 14/8/64. Flt Lt 9/2/68. Retd GD 8/1/80. Re-entrant 22/10/82. Sqn Ldr 1/7/88.
    Retd GD 8/1/97.
LOCKE T.F. Born 13/7/45. Commd 1/3/68. Flt Lt 4/5/72. Retd GD 13/7/89.
LOCKETT E.B. BSc CEng MRAeS. Born 3/10/45. Commd 3/10/68. Wg Cdr 1/1/88. Retd ENG 3/3/91.
LOCKETT P. Born 16/1/42. Commd 19/8/71. Flt Lt 13/1/78. Retd ADMIN 3/5/87.
LOCKETT R.J. CEng MRAeS. Born 29/8/39. Commd 18/7/61. Wg Cdr 1/1/80. Retd ENG 1/12/87.
LOCKHART D.S. DFC. Born 26/2/33. Commd 4/10/51. Sqn Ldr 1/7/65. Retd GD 27/8/76.
LOCKHART P. MBA. Born 2/1/62. Commd 11/11/87. Sqn Ldr 1/1/99. Retd ENGINEER 22/5/03.
LOCKHART R.E. Born 12/3/25. Commd 31/3/45. Sqn Ldr 1/7/67. Retd GD 30/6/76.
LOCKHURST T.E. MBE. Born 17/7/42. Commd 3/11/77. Sqn Ldr 1/1/85. Retd ENG 16/7/97.
LOCKIE D.I. Born 25/6/51. Commd 19/6/70. Flt Lt 19/12/75. Retd GD 22/10/94.
LOCKWOOD G. Born 24/8/33. Commd 16/7/52. Flt Lt 12/12/57. Retd GD(G) 24/8/93.
LOCKWOOD G.A. Born 21/1/35. Commd 17/3/67. Flt Lt 3/7/72. Retd MED(SEC) 31/1/75.
LOCKWOOD G.J. MBE MCMI. Born 19/4/23. Commd 20/2/43. Flt Lt 20/2/48. Retd SEC 19/4/75.
LOCKWOOD R.J. Born 22/2/18. Commd 28/10/43. Flt Lt 28/4/48. Retd SEC 14/3/67. rtg Sqn Ldr.
LOCKWOOD T. Born 12/3/25. Commd 25/2/44. Sqn Ldr 1/1/61. Retd SEC 12/9/81.
LOCKWOOD V.C. MCMI MRAeS. Born 6/6/49. Commd 25/6/65. Wg Cdr 1/1/90. Retd GD 30/9/91.
LOCKYEAR K.O. MRAeS. Born 7/4/20. Commd 15/4/43. Wg Cdr 1/7/60. Retd ENG 13/7/68.
LOCKYER D.E.C. BEM CEng MIERE. Born 1/10/19. Commd 28/2/46. Sqn Ldr 1/10/56. Retd ENG 13/3/71.
LOCKYER F.R. OBE. Born 28/6/29. Commd 26/7/50. Gp Capt 1/7/69. Retd GD 5/3/76.
LODGE A.M. BSc CertEd. Born 26/6/56. Commd 20/5/79. Flt Lt 20/9/82. Retd ADMIN 20/5/01.
LODGE T.F. Born 2/11/41. Commd 1/7/63. Sqn Ldr 1/1/74. Retd GD 2/11/79.
LOEB R.M. Born 28/2/47. Commd 22/3/81. Flt Lt 22/3/85. Retd ADMIN 30/9/87.
LOFFHAGEN D.A. MBE. Born 7/11/32. Commd 14/7/53. Wg Cdr 1/7/71. Retd SEC 16/6/74.
LOFTHOUSE A.J. Born 19/11/48. Commd 23/2/68. Flt Lt 23/8/73. Retd GD 9/4/86.
LOFTHOUSE B.W. ACIS. Born 27/4/25. Commd 25/8/44. Wg Cdr 1/1/64. Retd GD 27/2/76.
LOFTHOUSE C.J. OBE DFC. Born 26/9/21. Commd 6/5/41. Sqn Ldr 1/1/54. Retd GD 1/7/66.
LOFTING P.J.D. Born 16/8/21. Commd 12/1/44. Fg Offr 20/5/48. Retd GD 1/11/55.
LOFTING R.G. AFC. Born 28/10/21. Commd 22/9/43. Wg Cdr 1/1/62. Retd GD 28/3/75.
LOFTS D. Born 21/6/32. Commd 10/10/58. Sqn Ldr 1/1/72. Retd ADMIN 21/6/87.
LOFTS P.D. Born 5/11/62. Commd 20/5/82. Sqn Ldr 1/1/97. Retd GD 5/11/00.
LOGAN A.M. BA. Born 6/3/54. Commd 7/6/74. Flt Lt 1/12/79. Retd RGT 17/1/81.
LOGAN D.J.C. Born 23/8/11. Commd 3/6/41. Flt Lt 1/9/45. Retd ENG 22/10/53.
LOGAN H. MBE. Born 20/11/18. Commd 25/3/54. Flt Lt 25/3/57. Retd GD(G) 20/11/68.
LOGAN I.E.D.B. MCMI. Born 21/1/34. Commd 24/9/52. Sqn Ldr 1/1/76. Retd ADMIN 20/5/92.
LOGAN K.A. MSc FISM FCIPD. Born 6/5/58. Commd 20/8/90. Sqn Ldr 1/7/98. Retd ADMIN 3/4/02.

LOGAN K.G. Born 30/8/40. Commd 21/12/62. Flt Lt 1/7/68. Retd GD 30/8/95.
LOGAN L.J. Born 13/8/18. Commd 29/5/48. Sqn Ldr 1/7/59. Retd SUP 13/8/64.
LOGAN P.S. Born 27/11/43. Commd 22/5/64. Sqn Ldr 1/1/93. Retd GD 29/5/00.
LOGAN R.H. Born 6/8/31. Commd 13/6/74. Sqn Ldr 1/7/83. Retd ADMIN 6/8/85.
LOGAN R.N. Born 25/5/55. Commd 30/1/80. Sqn Ldr 1/1/85. Retd ADMIN 25/5/96.
LOGAN S.E.K. BSc. Born 9/12/43. Commd 1/8/66. Sqn Ldr 8/6/73. Retd ADMIN 1/8/82.
LOGAN S.T. BSc. Born 17/3/44. Commd 30/8/66. Flt Lt 30/5/68. Retd GD 2/12/97.
LOGSDON C.L. MHCIMA. Born 12/4/65. Commd 16/4/93. Flt Lt 7/12/91. Retd ADMIN (CAT) 12/4/03.
LOHAN K.H. Born 13/10/22. Commd 25/4/42. Sqn Ldr 1/4/56. Retd GD 13/10/65.
LOHSE K.R. Born 25/6/48. Commd 30/5/69. Flt Lt 30/11/75. Retd SY(RGT) 30/4/88.
LOLE R.W. Born 16/11/52. Commd 1/6/72. Flt Lt 1/12/77. Retd GD 16/2/91.
LOMAS D.J. Born 1/2/27. Commd 6/11/47. Sqn Ldr 1/1/60. Retd GD 3/12/76.
LOMAS J.G. Born 16/4/30. Commd 20/12/51. Flt Lt 4/4/57. Retd GD 16/4/68.
LOMAS R.L. OBE. Born 27/2/46. Commd 14/2/69. Wg Cdr 1/7/87. Retd GD 28/10/90.
LOMAS R.W. BSc CEng FCMI MRAeS. Born 5/9/32. Commd 9/12/54. Gp Capt 1/7/78. Retd ENG 17/10/81.
LONDESBOROUGH A. Born 11/3/43. Commd 19/6/64. Flt Lt 19/12/69. Retd GD 3/4/88.
LONERGAN W.J. Born 3/9/37. Commd 15/2/60. Flt Lt 15/8/65. Retd GD 15/2/76.
LONG B.C. LLB MCMI ACIS. Born 24/6/32. Commd 28/6/51. Flt Lt 10/10/56. Retd SEC 23/10/70.
LONG C. MBE MCMI. Born 7/2/31. Commd 2/1/67. Sqn Ldr 1/7/77. Retd ADMIN 7/2/86.
LONG C.J. Born 5/1/47. Commd 2/8/68. Flt Lt 2/8/71. Retd GD 5/1/85.
LONG C.W. The Rev. MBE BTh BA. Born 12/12/47. Commd 13/9/85. Retd Wg Cdr 4/4/05.
LONG D. BSc. Born 3/10/40. Commd 4/12/64. Flt Lt 4/9/66. Retd GD 14/9/80.
LONG G.A. Born 5/11/11. Commd 6/9/45. Sqn Ldr 1/1/60. Retd SUP 3/12/66.
LONG I.J. BSc. Born 28/4/65. Commd 11/9/83. Flt Lt 15/1/89. Retd GD 15/7/98.
LONG J.A.W. AFC FCMI. Born 14/4/22. Commd 19/10/42. Gp Capt 1/1/67. Retd GD 31/3/77.
LONG J.J.F. Born 21/3/20. Commd 12/2/44. Wg Cdr 1/7/66. Retd ENG 1/1/76.
LONG J.R. BA. Born 11/11/48. Commd 25/7/71. Flt Lt 25/7/72. Retd ADMIN 25/7/75. Re-entered 1/4/76.
    Wg Cdr 1/7/95. Retd ADMIN 30/9/96.
LONG J.T.C. Born 14/1/33. Commd 29/10/52. Flt Lt 24/3/58. Retd GD 14/1/71.
LONG M.A. Born 9/12/38. Commd 15/7/58. Flt Lt 16/4/64. Retd GD 9/12/93.
LONG P.R. RMN. Born 17/11/50. Commd 30/4/81. Flt Lt 30/10/87. Retd GD(G) 29/12/96.
LONG R.A.D. Born 26/6/41. Commd 14/6/63. Flt Lt 4/5/72. Retd GD 22/4/94.
LONG R.C. Born 26/8/31. Commd 8/10/70. Sqn Ldr 1/7/81. Retd ENG 30/3/84.
LONG R.G. Born 15/4/49. Commd 16/9/76. Flt Lt 23/7/79. Retd ENG 30/5/88.
LONG R.J. Born 5/4/45. Commd 30/4/81. Flt Lt 30/4/85. Retd GD(G) 31/7/87.
LONG S. OBE MA BSc. Born 20/8/59. Commd 8/5/83. Wg Cdr 1/7/98. Retd ENG 1/1/01.
LONG S.L. Born 19/7/51. Commd 17/5/79. Flt Lt 27/9/84. Retd GD(G) 9/8/96.
LONG T.J. CEng MRAeS. Born 18/11/23. Commd 25/8/60. Sqn Ldr 1/7/72. Retd ENG 1/10/77.
LONG V.E. AFC. Born 26/6/21. Commd 21/12/42. Sqn Ldr 1/7/52. Retd GD 26/6/64.
LONG W.R.H. Born 6/3/35. Commd 16/4/57. Sqn Ldr 1/7/87. Retd GD(G) 1/7/90.
LONGBONE N.J. MA. Born 1/12/29. Commd 5/8/59. Wg Cdr 1/1/78. Retd SUP 1/12/84.
LONGDEN A.G. CEng MIMechE MRAeS. Born 29/3/31. Commd 23/1/52. Gp Capt 1/7/76. Retd ENG 20/3/86.
LONGDEN D.A. MBE CEng MIEE MRAeS. Born 11/9/41. Commd 8/10/80. Wg Cdr 1/7/91. Retd ENG 11/4/93.
LONGDEN J.P. Born 30/3/47. Commd 22/11/73. Flt Lt 22/5/76. Retd GD 9/8/88.
LONGDON S.J. Born 7/8/59. Commd 21/6/90. Flt Lt 21/6/92. Retd ENG 21/6/98.
LONGHURST B.M. Born 11/8/49. Commd 31/7/70. Flt Lt 31/7/73. Retd GD 3/10/78.
LONGHURST D.N. BSc. Born 31/10/61. Commd 14/9/80. Flt Lt 15/10/84. Retd GD 31/10/99.
LONGHURST E. Born 25/10/21. Commd 26/5/60. Flt Lt 26/5/66. Retd ENG 24/10/73.
LONGHURST J. Born 16/6/33. Commd 27/2/52. Sqn Ldr 1/7/82. Retd GD 16/6/88.
LONGHURST R. Born 28/11/44. Commd 22/11/84. Flt Lt 22/11/88. Retd GD(G) 30/9/96.
LONGLEY R.D. Born 4/9/45. Commd 19/12/63. Wg Cdr 1/1/89. Retd GD(G) 3/4/92.
LONGLEY R.G. Born 31/3/24. Commd 29/5/45. Wg Cdr 1/7/66. Retd SUP 16/6/74.
LONGMAN B.D. OBE CEng MRAeS MIEE MCMI. Born 25/2/45. Commd 15/7/66. Wg Cdr 1/7/86. Retd ENG 25/2/00.
LONGMIRE K. BA. Born 27/11/57. Commd 11/4/85. Sqn Ldr 1/7/94. Retd ADMIN 25/1/96.
LONGMUIR J.J. Born 16/1/42. Commd 11/1/79. Sqn Ldr 1/1/94. Retd GD 29/2/96.
LONGSTAFF B.N. Born 5/1/43. Commd 18/11/66. Flt Lt 15/10/70. Retd GD(G) 5/1/93.
LONGSTAFF D.J. Born 6/5/32. Commd 28/7/60. Flt Lt 1/4/66. Retd GD(G) 1/10/73.
LONGSTAFF R.B. Born 7/8/42. Commd 24/2/67. Sqn Ldr 1/1/77. Retd SUP 1/11/84.
LONGSTAFF R.J. OBE. Born 19/10/17. Commd 13/3/47. Wg Cdr 1/7/68. Retd SEC 19/10/72.
LOOKER I. MSc BSc. Born 14/8/60. Commd 29/4/84. Sqn Ldr 1/7/96. Retd ENG 10/1/02.
LOOSELEY K.D. Born 18/12/46. Commd 14/7/66. Flt Lt 8/3/72. Retd GD 10/1/98.
LOOSELEY M. Born 7/8/53. Commd 4/7/72. Flt Lt 4/11/77. Retd GD 29/7/00.
LOPES C.A. Born 17/9/27. Commd 24/2/67. Flt Lt 24/2/72. Retd ENG 17/9/85.
LORAM W.H. Born 12/6/35. Commd 3/11/77. Sqn Ldr 1/7/86. Retd ENG 12/6/95.
LORD D.P. BSc. Born 30/4/53. Commd 22/8/76. Sqn Ldr 1/7/94. Retd FLY(P) 2/4/04.
LORD D.V. Born 10/8/36. Commd 3/12/54. Flt Lt 3/6/60. Retd GD 10/8/91.

LORD G. Born 15/8/25. Commd 20/1/51. Flt Lt 20/10/55. Retd GD 11/5/70.
LORD H. Born 28/12/20. Commd 9/9/54. Flt Lt 3/10/59. Retd ENG 2/6/73.
LORD J. Born 6/8/26. Commd 29/3/50. Flt Lt 29/9/53. Retd GD 7/2/73.
LORD R.K. Born 29/12/29. Commd 9/8/51. Flt Lt 28/11/56. Retd GD 29/12/67.
LORIGAN M.P. Born 20/4/39. Commd 26/8/66. Flt Lt 14/11/71. Retd GD(G) 8/4/80.
LORIMER H. OBE MCMI. Born 2/7/22. Commd 15/8/44. Wg Cdr 1/7/63. Retd SUP 2/7/77.
LORIMER J.M. Born 18/6/20. Commd 29/3/45. Flt Lt 30/6/49. Retd GD 19/6/63.
LORRAINE C.J. Born 10/7/54. Commd 13/6/74. Sqn Ldr 1/7/86. Retd GD 10/7/92.
LORRIMAN B. BSc. Born 30/10/40. Commd 19/6/64. Sqn Ldr 1/7/71. Retd GD 2/3/80.
LORRIMAN G.A. Born 29/1/17. Commd 16/9/43. Sqn Ldr 1/7/54. Retd ENG 1/6/68.
LORTON J.A. Born 10/11/29. Commd 2/2/68. Flt Lt 1/1/73. Retd GD 16/11/73.
LORY G.I. BSc. Born 31/12/65. Commd 29/10/84. Sqn Ldr 1/7/97. Retd SUPPLY 31/12/03.
LOS R. MBE MRAeS MCMI. Born 28/6/17. Commd 11/2/42. Wg Cdr 1/7/59. Retd ENG 4/4/70.
LOSH S. Born 6/11/62. Commd 16/6/88. Sqn Ldr 1/7/00. Retd ENGINEER 1/7/03.
LOTEN A.D. Born 21/9/18. Commd 29/6/50. Sqn Ldr 1/1/62. Retd SEC 21/9/73.
LOTINGA R.E. Born 16/5/53. Commd 4/5/72. Sqn Ldr 1/7/87. Retd GD 1/3/92.
LOTT D.C. Born 8/5/40. Commd 1/8/61. Sqn Ldr 1/7/73. Retd GD 8/5/78.
LOTT E.J. Born 14/12/17. Commd 8/12/52. Flt Lt 8/12/52. Retd SEC 14/12/72.
LOTT M.A. Born 15/5/42. Commd 8/6/62. Flt Lt 8/12/67. Retd GD 31/1/76.
LOTT W.R. Born 6/12/16. Commd 14/5/43. Sqn Ldr 1/1/62. Retd SUP 7/12/71.
LOUBERT J.A.R.R. Born 21/5/32. Commd 15/10/62. Flt Lt 15/10/62. Retd GD 15/7/64.
LOUDON K. CEng MRAeS. Born 28/1/28. Commd 14/8/62. Sqn Ldr 14/8/67. Retd ADMIN 31/3/79.
Re-instated 9/4/80. Sqn Ldr 23/8/68. Retd ADMIN 21/8/88.
LOUDON S.M. Born 23/3/62. Commd 8/4/82. Flt Lt 15/9/88. Retd SUP 14/3/97.
LOUGH A.E. Born 14/8/20. Commd 19/12/55. Sqn Ldr 1/1/72. Retd ADMIN 14/8/75.
LOUGHBOROUGH I.P.G. MBE MCMI. Born 30/6/43. Commd 19/12/63. Wg Cdr 1/7/87. Retd RGT 1/7/90.
LOUIS P.G. DFC DFM. Born 31/5/18. Commd 21/11/41. Wg Cdr 1/7/52. Retd GD 17/2/55.
LOUTH J.P.W. BSc. Born 17/3/66. Commd 30/8/87. Sqn Ldr 1/7/97. Retd ADMIN (SEC) 17/3/04.
LOVATT P. PhD BA FCMI. Born 16/11/24. Commd 1/5/47. Sqn Ldr 1/1/60. Retd RGT 16/11/79.
LOVE D.B. BJur MCIPD. Born 9/9/47. Commd 17/1/72. Gp Capt 1/1/97. Retd ADMIN 3/6/00.
LOVE J.M. Born 23/4/33. Commd 27/2/52. Sqn Ldr 1/1/66. Retd GD 23/10/91.
LOVE J.R. Born 27/2/24. Commd 6/1/50. Flt Lt 6/7/52. Retd GD 27/2/67.
LOVE P.V. Born 13/10/31. Commd 16/7/52. Flt Lt 2/10/58. Retd ENG 13/10/69.
LOVEDAY B.W. Born 3/11/42. Commd 9/3/62. Flt Lt 9/2/68. Retd GD 3/11/80.
LOVEDAY D.V. Born 30/5/43. Commd 24/6/65. Sqn Ldr 1/1/77. Retd GD 23/8/80.
LOVEDAY E.C. Born 23/11/30. Commd 28/7/53. Sqn Ldr 1/7/65. Retd GD 23/11/68.
LOVEDAY R. MA CEng MRAeS. Born 19/7/36. Commd 30/9/55. Sqn Ldr 1/7/67. Retd ENG 30/6/89.
LOVEGROVE C.F. Born 14/1/45. Commd 15/7/66. Sqn Ldr 1/1/79. Retd ADMIN 14/1/83.
LOVEGROVE G.B. Born 6/4/43. Commd 24/2/61. Sqn Ldr 1/1/76. Retd GD 6/4/84. Re-entered 27/3/87. Sqn Ldr 22/12/78.
Retd GD 6/4/00.
LOVEGROVE G.B. Born 6/12/41. Commd 16/2/61. Flt Lt 16/5/67. Retd GD(G) 16/6/73.
LOVEGROVE J.M. Born 1/7/19. Commd 6/10/41. Flt Offr 1/9/45. Retd SEC 7/6/52.
LOVEGROVE M.C. Born 12/8/43. Commd 14/11/76. Flt Lt 14/11/80. Retd ENG 14/11/92.
LOVEGROVE P.L. Born 19/11/24. Commd 9/12/48. Sqn Ldr 1/7/64. Retd GD 30/3/68.
LOVEJOY E.W. DFC. Born 14/2/20. Commd 3/3/43. Flt Lt 4/12/50. Retd GD 10/9/65.
LOVEJOY F. MBE. Born 24/3/44. Commd 5/4/79. Sqn Ldr 1/1/88. Retd ENG 24/3/99.
LOVELACE R.E. Born 26/6/19. Commd 19/1/50. Sqn Ldr 1/1/61. Retd ENG 26/6/74.
LOVELAND A.S. MCMI. Born 9/11/29. Commd 13/12/50. Sqn Ldr 1/7/63. Retd SUP 9/11/67.
LOVELAND R.S. CEng MRAeS. Born 29/11/20. Commd 19/8/42. Wg Cdr 1/7/58. Retd ENG 29/11/75.
LOVELESS G.E.W. MBE. Born 3/3/18. Commd 1/7/57. Sqn Ldr 1/7/66. Retd CAT 3/1/75.
LOVELESS M.F. The Rev. Born 8/2/46. Commd 28/9/86. Retd Wg Cdr 28/9/02.
LOVELL A.G. Born 7/10/27. Commd 6/12/51. Flt Lt 13/4/60. Retd SEC 31/1/68.
LOVELL F.W. Born 18/6/29. Commd 17/9/52. Flt Lt 17/9/56. Retd SUP 17/9/68.
LOVELL J.W. Born 26/2/16. Commd 18/9/39. Wg Cdr 1/1/56. Retd SUP 28/1/61.
LOVELL K.A. Born 11/6/24. Commd 22/8/49. Flt Lt 18/5/58. Retd GD 31/8/68.
LOVENBURY L.M. Born 25/11/18. Commd 3/5/51. Sqn Ldr 1/7/63. Retd SUP 28/4/73.
LOVERIDGE D.C.E. CDipAF. Born 24/10/36. Commd 14/8/70. Sqn Ldr 1/7/82. Retd ENG 24/10/94.
LOVERIDGE D.J. OBE FCMI. Born 21/10/37. Commd 28/7/59. A Cdre 1/1/88. Retd GD 14/4/91.
LOVERIDGE P.A. Born 20/7/45. Commd 15/7/66. Sqn Ldr 1/1/83. Retd ENG 14/3/96.
LOVERING P.R. Born 17/6/53. Commd 26/11/81. Sqn Ldr 1/7/90. Retd ENG 6/1/96.
LOVERING T.E. Born 20/12/36. Commd 21/10/66. Flt Lt 21/10/68. Retd PE 12/1/74.
LOVETT A.J. Born 5/12/44. Commd 11/8/67. Sqn Ldr 1/1/82. Retd GD 1/5/89.
LOVETT A.M. Born 1/1/35. Commd 12/11/57. Sqn Ldr 1/1/80. Retd GD 1/1/94.
LOVETT C.B. BA CEng MRAeS. Born 10/4/40. Commd 17/7/62. Sqn Ldr 1/7/77. Retd ENG 27/9/88.
LOVETT D.M. MVO. Born 30/10/31. Commd 17/3/58. Sqn Ldr 1/1/79. Retd GD 31/10/81.
LOVETT K.J. CBE. Born 4/8/35. Commd 17/3/54. A Cdre 1/7/86. Retd GD 5/4/91.

LOVETT M.S. Born 28/1/38. Commd 17/10/59. Wg Cdr 1/7/81. Retd GD 30/9/88.
LOW I.N. Born 18/1/57. Commd 18/12/80. Flt Lt 18/6/87. Retd SY 14/8/96.
LOW J.H. Born 3/11/22. Commd 1/10/43. Wg Cdr 1/7/70. Retd ADMIN 3/11/77.
LOW R.A.C. Born 21/4/57. Commd 22/2/79. Wg Cdr 1/7/96. Retd GD 21/4/01.
LOWDEN R.W. Born 1/6/15. Commd 3/2/44. Sqn Ldr 1/1/55. Retd ENG 2/6/64. rtg Wg Cdr.
LOWDON J.G. Born 12/4/41. Commd 26/10/62. Flt Lt 8/1/69. Retd GD 12/4/79.
LOWE Sir Douglas GCB DFC AFC. Born 14/3/22. Commd 4/1/43. ACM 3/11/75. Retd GD 22/8/83.
LOWE D.R. Born 21/5/33. Commd 16/4/57. Wg Cdr 1/1/78. Retd GD 9/4/88.
LOWE D.W. FCMI. Born 2/2/29. Commd 9/4/52. Gp Capt 1/1/80. Retd GD 2/2/83.
LOWE E.W. Born 10/11/19. Commd 18/12/43. Flt Lt 18/6/47. Retd GD 6/6/53.
LOWE G. Born 6/11/38. Commd 24/6/71. Sqn Ldr 1/7/77. Retd ENG 18/7/80.
LOWE G.M. Born 5/3/49. Commd 11/11/71. Flt Lt 22/4/78. Retd SY 3/5/87.
LOWE M.R. Born 14/10/31. Commd 21/10/66. Sqn Ldr 1/1/82. Retd ENG 10/1/84.
LOWE P.D. Born 4/7/23. Commd 19/3/43. Flt Lt 15/4/49. Retd GD 29/1/63.
LOWE P.P.W. Born 16/11/40. Commd 23/12/60. Sqn Ldr 1/1/77. Retd GD 1/1/80.
LOWE R.F. MRCS LRCP DCP. Born 27/5/18. Commd 25/5/42. Wg Cdr 23/10/63. Retd MED 17/2/66.
LOWE T. The Rev. MA. Born 1/3/39. Commd 6/10/77. Retd Wg Cdr 1/3/94.
LOWERY A.J. CEng MIEE MRAeS MCMI. Born 26/3/36. Commd 23/7/58. A Cdre 1/7/88. Retd ENG 31/8/92.
LOWERY D.J. AFC. Born 13/12/25. Commd 17/3/55. Sqn Ldr 1/9/65. Retd GD 21/12/74.
LOWERY H.J.L. Born 5/5/25. Commd 2/7/64. Flt Lt 2/7/67. Retd GD 12/11/73.
LOWES D.W. Born 17/4/28. Commd 26/7/50. Flt Lt 26/7/55. Retd SEC 17/4/66.
LOWES M.S. Born 16/2/52. Commd 6/4/72. Flt Lt 6/10/77. Retd GD 12/12/81.
LOWLES I.E. MB ChB MRCOG. Born 3/4/49. Commd 8/8/71. Sqn Ldr 7/8/79. Retd MED 8/2/88.
LOWMAN S. Born 16/10/54. Commd 7/11/91. Flt Lt 7/11/95. Retd OPS SPT(ATC) 30/10/04.
LOWNDES R.L. BSc. Born 16/7/57. Commd 8/2/81. Flt Lt 8/11/82. Retd GD 5/4/01.
LOWRIE B. Born 12/2/54. Commd 8/9/77. Sqn Ldr 1/1/89. Retd ADMIN 1/2/89.
LOWRY D.H. BSc. Born 10/9/42. Commd 11/11/73. Sqn Ldr 1/7/83. Retd GD(G) 30/9/90.
LOWRY K.G. Born 8/4/20. Commd 23/3/50. Sqn Ldr 1/1/63. Retd ENG 29/9/73.
LOWRY M.R.J. Born 3/8/65. Commd 7/11/85. Flt Lt 7/5/91. Retd FLY(P) 3/8/03.
LOWRY P. CEng FIEE MRAeS. Born 2/9/28. Commd 18/7/71. Sqn Ldr 18/7/71. Retd ENG 2/9/92.
LOWRY W.A. FINucE. Born 14/9/22. Commd 21/9/50. Wg Cdr 1/7/72. Retd ENG 14/9/77.
LOWTHER J.R. Born 26/11/14. Commd 28/2/57. Flt Lt 28/2/60. Retd ACB 11/10/63.
LOWTHER W.B. BA. Born 13/2/32. Commd 6/3/61. Wg Cdr 1/7/79. Retd GD 13/10/86.
LOWTON A.L. Born 5/8/38. Commd 24/9/64. Flt Lt 24/9/66. Retd GD 1/7/77.
LOXTON J.A. BA. Born 5/7/31. Commd 28/10/55. Sqn Ldr 17/2/63. Retd EDN 28/10/71.
LOYNES R.A. Born 12/11/52. Commd 17/9/84. Sqn Ldr 1/1/92. Retd GD 19/7/98.
LUBY J.S. Born 31/5/21. Commd 26/10/44. Flt Lt 26/4/48. Retd GD 3/5/76.
LUCAS A.M. Born 19/3/56. Commd 22/5/75. Flt Lt 22/11/80. Retd GD 26/2/88.
LUCAS B.H. The Venerable. CB BA. Born 20/1/40. Commd 22/6/70. Retd AVM 31/10/95.
LUCAS D. MCMI. Born 3/12/23. Commd 75/5/53. Wg Cdr 1/1/71. Retd ADMIN 1/3/78.
LUCAS D.G. AFC MBA BA. Born 5/7/37. Commd 16/12/58. Wg Cdr 1/1/75. Retd GD 1/1/78. Re-instated 28/1/81.
  Wg Cdr 21/8/78. Retd GD 1/12/87.
LUCAS E.D. Born 28/3/33. Commd 21/5/52. Sqn Ldr 1/1/71. Retd GD 28/3/91.
LUCAS G.H. Born 24/2/32. Commd 6/2/52. Flt Lt 14/8/57. Retd GD 1/5/69.
LUCAS I.T. Born 13/9/48. Commd 28/2/85. Flt Lt 28/2/89. Retd ENG 31/3/94.
LUCAS K.P. MNI. Born 23/4/24. Commd 9/7/56. Wg Cdr 1/1/71. Retd MAR 23/4/79.
LUCAS M. Born 23/10/48. Commd 20/9/79. Flt Lt 20/9/81. Retd ENG 20/9/87.
LUCAS R.G. MSc BSc. Born 30/7/55. Commd 2/9/73. Sqn Ldr 1/1/86. Retd ENG 30/7/93.
LUCIE F.J.F. Born 28/3/15. Commd 31/12/41. Flt Lt 1/9/45. Retd GD(G) 31/3/60. rtg Sqn Ldr.
LUCK D.C. Born 21/3/30. Commd 13/12/50. Gp Capt 1/7/73. Retd GD 21/3/85.
LUCKHAM R.J. BSc. Born 26/1/54. Commd 12/8/79. Sqn Ldr 1/7/90. Retd ENG 31/3/94.
LUCKHURST T.E. MBE. Born 17/7/42. Commd 3/11/77. Sqn Ldr 1/1/85. Retd ENG 16/7/97.
LUCKING J.W. AFC. Born 16/3/34. Commd 27/5/53. Sqn Ldr 1/1/69. Retd GD 16/3/89.
LUCKING R.R. Born 15/9/38. Commd 25/7/60. Sqn Ldr 1/1/85. Retd GD 15/9/93.
LUCKINS G. Born 7/10/25. Commd 24/1/52. Flt Lt 15/5/57. Retd GD 7/1/74.
LUCY K.P.F. Born 20/8/19. Commd 29/7/44. Flt Lt 29/1/48. Retd SEC 2/2/55.
LUDFORD J.S. Born 18/12/51. Commd 16/11/72. Sqn Ldr 1/7/87. Retd GD 18/3/91.
LUDGATE F.E. CEng FIEE. Born 7/2/15. Commd 20/6/40. Gp Capt 1/7/58. Retd ENG 7/2/70.
LUDGATE L.G. Born 22/7/27. Commd 8/4/49. Wg Cdr 1/1/72. Retd SUP 24/3/78.
LUDLOW B.P. MMedSci MB BS MRAeS MRCS DAvMed LRCP AFOM. Born 4/3/55. Commd 18/11/75. Wg Cdr 1/8/92.
  Retd MED 4/3/99.
LUDLOW S. Born 11/2/62. Commd 23/5/85. Flt Lt 23/11/90. Retd GD 24/11/01.
LUDLOW V.J. MSc CEng MIEE. Born 13/4/34. Commd 24/12/64. Sqn Ldr 24/12/71. Retd ADMIN 1/10/76.
LUERY D.J. Born 27/3/30. Commd 5/5/60. Wg Cdr 1/7/80. Retd SUP 27/3/85.
LUFFMAN F.T. Born 28/11/26. Commd 5/5/60. Sqn Ldr 1/7/77. Retd SUP 28/11/78.
LUFFMAN G. Born 11/6/35. Commd 5/5/54. Sqn Ldr 1/7/70. Retd ADMIN 11/6/93.

LUGG A. MBE. Born 20/9/19. Commd 8/7/42. Sqn Offr 1/7/53. Retd SEC 21/6/57.
LUKE D.O. MCMI. Born 31/3/23. Commd 19/6/42. Wg Cdr 1/1/61. Retd GD 31/3/78.
LUKE J.C.O. CBE BSc. Born 7/8/49. Commd 23/9/68. A Cdre 1/1/98. Retd ADMIN 1/9/00.
LUMB B.E. Born 15/5/16. Commd 14/7/43. Gp Capt 1/1/67. Retd SEC 1/6/71.
LUMB C.P. CBE. Born 30/10/43. Commd 6/9/63. A Cdre 1/1/90. Retd GD 30/10/95.
LUMB R.J. BSc. Born 12/12/43. Commd 28/9/64. Wg Cdr 1/1/90. Retd GD 10/6/93.
LUMSDEN I.A. Born 22/9/56. Commd 17/5/79. Wg Cdr 1/7/94. Retd SY 28/8/96.
LUMSDEN J.G. OBE AFC FCMI. Born 21/12/40. Commd 31/7/62. A Cdre 1/7/90. Retd GD 10/6/96.
LUNAN T.D.A. Born 28/4/23. Commd 11/8/44. Sqn Ldr 1/4/56. Retd GD 3/2/67.
LUND B. BA. Born 16/6/31. Commd 21/10/53. Wg Cdr 1/7/71. Retd EDN 1/11/75.
LUND F.R. Born 15/10/30. Commd 12/12/51. Flt Lt 11/11/54. Retd GD 15/10/69.
LUND R.A. Born 3/11/47. Commd 3/5/68. Sqn Ldr 1/7/84. Retd GD(G) 1/7/87.
LUNDY F.K. Born 28/12/31. Commd 6/12/51. Flt Lt 5/6/57. Retd GD 11/4/70.
LUNGLEY S.D. Born 29/1/60. Commd 28/6/79. Wg Cdr 1/7/97. Retd GD 1/7/00.
LUNN A.R. Born 6/7/63. Commd 28/7/88. Flt Lt 28/1/95. Retd OPS SPT(INT) 27/5/04.
LUNN L.G. AFC. Born 27/1/23. Commd 14/9/43. Sqn Ldr 1/1/66. Retd GD 27/1/79.
LUNN R. Born 24/2/47. Commd 28/10/66. Wg Cdr 1/1/91. Retd GD 14/9/96.
LUNNON-WOOD A.K. Born 31/10/53. Commd 18/4/72. Sqn Ldr 1/7/87. Retd FLY(P) 31/1/05.
LUNT C.C. BA. Born 26/11/60. Commd 11/9/83. Sqn Ldr 1/7/94. Retd GD 11/11/99.
LUNT J.D. BA. Born 13/3/41. Commd 9/9/63. Gp Capt 1/1/87. Retd GD 13/4/96.
LUPA H.T. BSc MB ChB DAvMed MRAeS. Born 2/2/59. Commd 6/10/81. Wg Cdr 2/8/97. Retd MED 7/10/99.
LUPTON K.V. Born 17/10/26. Commd 20/11/58. Flt Lt 20/11/63. Retd GD 29/3/69.
LUSCOMBE M.W.J. Born 11/11/28. Commd 3/6/65. Flt Lt 3/6/68. Retd GD 11/11/78.
LUSHER H.G. Born 31/1/49. Commd 16/8/68. Sqn Ldr 1/1/89. Retd GD 1/1/92.
LUSSEY D. Born 19/12/45. Commd 22/7/66. Flt Lt 15/12/72. Retd SY 19/12/83.
LUTER B.C. MA. Born 23/5/36. Commd 12/9/58. Sqn Ldr 12/3/69. Retd ADMIN 23/5/93.
LUTKIN J.R. Born 30/8/46. Commd 20/9/68. Flt Lt 13/9/72. Retd GD 3/4/76.
LUTMAN A.J.A. Born 12/5/31. Commd 1/10/58. Sqn Ldr 1/7/69. Retd ADMIN 25/8/82.
LUTO A.T. CEng MIEE MCMI. Born 16/6/32. Commd 20/12/57. Sqn Ldr 1/7/67. Retd ENG 16/6/87.
LUTON M. Born 29/10/58. Commd 20/5/82. Wg Cdr 1/7/00. Retd GD 23/5/03.
LUTON S. BSc. Born 29/10/60. Commd 30/8/87. Sqn Ldr 1/7/02. Retd ADMIN (TRG) 1/7/05.
LUTTON D.R. Born 4/10/64. Commd 26/10/90. Flt Lt 22/6/94. Retd OPS SPT 4/10/02.
LUXTON J.D. BEM. Born 14/9/43. Commd 8/9/77. Sqn Ldr 1/1/86. Retd ENG 14/9/97.
LUXTON P.A. BEng. Born 17/6/62. Commd 18/3/84. Sqn Ldr 1/7/94. Retd GD 17/6/00.
LYALL R.W. Born 9/1/43. Commd 6/7/62. Sqn Ldr 1/1/72. Retd GD 9/1/81.
LYDALL R. Born 3/2/38. Commd 6/7/62. Sqn Ldr 1/1/72. Retd GD 12/5/92.
LYDDON-JONES G.D. Born 8/3/35. Commd 19/9/59. Flt Lt 4/5/65. Retd GD(G) 17/8/79.
LYDIATE B.W. Born 28/3/33. Commd 29/12/51. Sqn Ldr 1/7/68. Retd GD 1/11/87.
LYDIATE D. MSc FCIPD CertEd. Born 2/6/51. Commd 5/1/86. Sqn Ldr 1/7/94. Retd ADMIN 5/1/02.
LYNAS C.T. OBE FIIP MCMI. Born 24/6/20. Commd 24/11/43. Wg Cdr 1/1/68. Retd ENG 30/6/73.
LYNCH D. Born 27/1/31. Commd 26/7/51. Flt Lt 14/3/61. Retd RGT 27/1/69.
LYNCH H.A.M. BA. Born 26/8/74. Commd 10/8/97. Flt Lt 10/2/00. Retd ADMIN (SEC) 8/9/03.
LYNCH J. Born 1/4/13. Commd 2/9/45. Flt Lt 4/1/51. Retd SUP 3/4/55.
LYNCH P.R.G. MBE. Born 6/8/10. Commd 30/10/42. Sqn Ldr 1/7/51. Retd SUP 15/8/59. rtg Wg Cdr.
LYNCH W. CEng MIMechE MRAeS. Born 29/8/43. Commd 26/5/67. Sqn Ldr 1/7/78. Retd ENG 29/8/83.
LYNDON R.J. Born 16/4/37. Commd 11/11/65. Flt Lt 6/10/71. Retd GD(G) 1/4/86.
LYNE M.D. CB AFC** MRAeS. Born 23/3/19. Commd 29/7/39. AVM 1/7/66. Retd GD 10/4/71.
LYNHAM C.R. BA. Born 5/4/74. Commd 2/8/95. Fg Offr 15/7/95. Retd GD 13/5/00.
LYNN G.S. MBE MCMI. Born 18/7/44. Commd 2/8/73. Wg Cdr 1/1/88. Retd ENG 31/3/94.
LYNN J.R. Born 14/7/29. Commd 29/7/54. Flt Lt 5/2/60. Retd GD 27/4/70.
LYNN T. Born 24/6/43. Commd 12/1/62. Flt Lt 26/7/67. Retd GD 27/10/75.
LYON A.F. BA. Born 8/2/36. Commd 10/12/57. Flt Lt 18/6/63. Retd GD 8/2/94.
LYON R.T.F. CEng MIMechE MIProdE MRAeS CDipAF. Born 23/8/28. Commd 11/2/53. Sqn Ldr 1/1/67.
    Retd ENG 23/8/78. Re-instated 9/9/81 to 9/9/84.
LYONS C.W. AFM. Born 19/12/24. Commd 4/6/59. Sqn Ldr 1/7/73. Retd GD 19/12/79.
LYONS D. Born 4/6/59. Commd 15/6/83. Sqn Ldr 1/7/95. Retd ENG 4/6/99.
LYONS J.H.J. BSc MCIPD. Born 22/8/56. Commd 13/4/80. Sqn Ldr 1/7/94. Retd ADMIN 2/12/96.
LYONS J.P. Born 14/3/33. Commd 26/3/64. Flt Lt 26/3/70. Retd ADMIN 30/11/86.
LYONS T.R.H. Born 4/2/33. Commd 27/2/52. Flt Lt 26/6/56. Retd GD 4/2/71. Re-instated 17/9/80 to 1/5/84.
LYSTER D.G. DSO DFC AFC*. Born 16/4/11. Commd 1/4/40. Gp Capt 1/1/56. Retd GD 7/1/61.
LYSTER J.M. MCIPD. Born 22/10/46. Commd 6/1/96. Wg Cdr 1/7/98. Retd ADMIN 22/10/01.
LYTHABY R. Born 26/4/45. Commd 24/6/71. Wg Cdr 1/1/92. Retd ENG 26/4/00.
LYTHGOE M.R. Born 21/8/47. Commd 11/8/67. Flt Lt 11/2/73. Retd GD 9/5/76.
LYTTLE R.E. MCMI. Born 2/6/46. Commd 21/9/72. Wg Cdr 1/1/00. Retd ADMIN 1/1/03.
LYTTLE R.I.S. Born 1/6/50. Commd 24/6/71. Flt Lt 1/12/75. Retd GD 22/10/94.

M

M'KENZIE-HALL J.E. MVO. Born 7/6/23. Commd 27/2/43. Flt Lt 26/5/55. Retd GD 6/3/64. rtg Sqn Ldr.
MAAN M.H. MSc BSc MCMI. Born 15/9/45. Commd 1/3/68. Wg Cdr 1/1/85. Retd ENG 14/3/96.
MABBETT D.W. BSc. Born 26/8/58. Commd 5/9/76. Sqn Ldr 1/1/89. Retd GD 26/9/96.
MABBOTT J.E. Born 1/3/43. Commd 1/10/69. Sqn Ldr 1/1/82. Retd GD 1/3/86.
MABBOTT R.G.S. Born 21/1/35. Commd 10/9/70. Wg Cdr 1/7/90. Retd ADMIN 24/7/91.
MABEN A. LDS. Born 21/8/12. Commd 7/1/35. Sqn Ldr 1/7/46. Retd DEL 14/5/50.
MABLY J.R. MA. Born 11/7/22. Commd 4/4/61. Sqn Ldr 6/3/63. Retd EDN 22/9/70.
MACALLISTER J.D. LRCS LRCP. Born 1/6/21. Commd 23/11/53. Wg Cdr 21/1/66. Retd MED 19/9/77.
MACANGUS A. BSc. Born 6/4/61. Commd 5/9/82. Flt Lt 15/10/83. Retd GD 5/3/91.
MACARTE M.A. Born 4/4/54. Commd 6/12/87. Flt Lt 6/11/85. Retd ADMIN 9/5/96.
MACARTNEY S.M.J. BSc. Born 2/9/48. Commd 15/9/69. Wg Cdr 1/1/92. Retd GD 2/9/03.
MACAULAY J.W. Born 4/8/66. Commd 16/6/88. Flt Lt 16/12/93. Retd GD 14/9/96.
MACAULAY L.K. BA. Born 27/10/58. Commd 28/9/80. Sqn Ldr 1/1/94. Retd ADMIN 31/7/00.
MACAULEY G.W. Born 5/4/55. Commd 5/4/79. Flt Lt 5/10/84. Retd GD 27/11/94.
MACAUSLAND G.H. Born 17/2/56. Commd 11/9/86. Flt Lt 11/9/88. Retd ENG 11/9/94.
MACBEAN A. Born 3/7/51. Commd 10/2/72. Sqn Ldr 1/1/87. Retd SUP 1/1/90.
MACBEAN A.A. Born 12/8/23. Commd 16/3/45. Flt Lt 4/6/53. Retd GD 1/5/66.
MACBEAN J.A.M. MBE FINucE. Born 24/7/20. Commd 23/9/43. Wg Cdr 1/7/65. Retd ENG 24/7/75.
MACBRAYNE D. Born 8/11/48. Commd 24/4/70. Sqn Ldr 1/1/84. Retd GD(G) 8/11/92.
MACBRAYNE K.J. Born 13/8/42. Commd 7/6/68. Flt Lt 7/6/70. Retd GD 13/7/74.
MACCALLUM G.W. BA. Born 23/5/48. Commd 9/8/79. Sqn Ldr 1/7/86. Retd ENG 1/10/90.
MACCONNACHIE A. Born 8/3/31. Commd 31/12/52. Sqn Ldr 1/7/71. Retd GD(G) 8/3/86.
MACCORKINDALE P.B. OBE. Born 11/6/24. Commd 17/6/45. Gp Capt 1/1/73. Retd GD 3/5/75.
MACDERMID M. Born 11/11/27. Commd 14/11/50. Wg Cdr 1/7/71. Retd GD 1/9/79.
MACDONALD A.J. BA. Born 7/11/41. Commd 30/8/66. Flt Lt 30/5/68. Retd GD 22/4/83.
MACDONALD A.R. MSc BA MCIPS MCMI. Born 12/6/44. Commd 15/7/66. Sqn Ldr 1/1/78. Retd SUP 1/11/84.
MACDONALD A.R. Born 12/3/63. Commd 22/6/86. Flt Lt 22/6/92. Retd ADMIN 22/6/02.
MACDONALD C.M. Born 14/9/12. Commd 13/11/41. Flt Lt 20/11/45. Retd ENG 27/12/51.
MACDONALD D.C. BSc. Born 23/10/64. Commd 11/9/83. APO 11/9/83. Retd GD 1/2/88.
MACDONALD E.P. Born 1/7/18. Commd 13/7/40. Sqn Offr 1/7/53. Retd SEC 15/1/55.
MACDONALD G.A. Born 14/11/20. Commd 24/1/63. Flt Lt 24/1/68. Retd ENG 14/11/73.
MACDONALD G.B. Born 5/12/47. Commd 23/8/87. Flt Lt 23/4/91. Retd ENG 31/7/01.
MACDONALD G.D. CEng FRAeS FCMI. Born 20/5/26. Commd 27/9/50. Gp Capt 1/1/74. Retd ENG 20/7/81.
MACDONALD G.W.B. MSc FICD. Born 16/11/51. Commd 28/7/88. Sqn Ldr 1/1/98. Retd MED SPT 16/11/01.
MACDONALD I.A. Born 25/3/60. Commd 11/1/79. Sqn Ldr 1/7/91. Retd GD 25/3/98.
MACDONALD I.N.M. AFC. Born 1/9/18. Commd 17/12/38. Wg Cdr 1/7/51. Retd GD 29/3/60.
MACDONALD I.T. MA. Born 22/12/47. Commd 17/1/73. Flt Lt 17/10/73. Retd ADMIN 22/7/76.
MACDONALD J. Born 23/2/47. Commd 25/2/66. Flt Lt 8/3/72. Retd GD 21/4/73.
MACDONALD J.A. BSc. Born 28/8/32. Commd 2/2/56. Sqn Ldr 2/8/66. Retd ADMIN 28/3/86.
MACDONALD J.A. Born 12/3/65. Commd 8/12/83. Fg Offr 8/6/86. Retd GD(G) 7/7/88.
MACDONALD J.B. BTech. Born 7/6/62. Commd 31/8/80. Sqn Ldr 1/7/01. Retd FLY(P) 31/8/03.
MACDONALD J.H. MSc FInstPet. Born 29/10/44. Commd 23/1/64. Wg Cdr 1/1/88. Retd SUP 29/10/99.
MACDONALD J.N. MBE. Born 25/8/21. Commd 18/4/44. Sqn Ldr 1/7/60. Retd GD 4/4/75.
MACDONALD M.J.A. Born 16/6/57. Commd 2/6/77. Sqn Ldr 1/7/89. Retd GD 14/9/96.
MACDONALD N.A. Born 27/4/42. Commd 15/8/85. Flt Lt 15/8/89. Retd SUP 2/4/93.
MACDONALD R.McD. MBE. Born 8/5/25. Commd 9/6/48. Gp Capt 1/7/73. Retd SEC 27/3/76.
MACDONALD R.P. Born 14/2/41. Commd 6/5/65. Flt Lt 6/12/68. Retd SUP 14/2/79.
MACDONALD W. Born 4/7/25. Commd 23/12/61. Sqn Ldr 1/1/73. Retd GD 5/7/77.
MACDONALD-BENNETT T.I. Born 28/2/45. Commd 31/1/64. Flt Lt 31/7/69. Retd GD 3/11/72.
MACDOUGALL D.J. AFC. Born 26/7/25. Commd 30/7/52. Sqn Ldr 1/9/65. Retd GD 26/7/76.
MACDOUGALL N. MBE. Born 31/8/44. Commd 18/10/79. Sqn Ldr 1/1/90. Retd SY 14/9/96.
MACDOUGALL N.R.H. Born 16/7/47. Commd 17/2/67. Sqn Ldr 1/7/86. Retd GD 12/3/93.
MACE B.H. Born 22/3/32. Commd 2/7/52. Flt Lt 5/11/58. Retd GD 22/3/70.
MACE J.L. MIDPM MCMI. Born 13/4/37. Commd 8/7/65. Wg Cdr 1/7/84. Retd SUP 13/4/94.
MACE J.R. BA DPhysEd. Born 19/10/35. Commd 14/5/63. Wg Cdr 1/1/86. Retd ADMIN 19/10/90.
MACE K.B. Born 8/6/43. Commd 28/7/64. Sqn Ldr 1/1/73. Retd GD 8/6/81. Re-instated on Retired List 3/9/85.
MACEVOY R.I. Born 17/11/43. Commd 2/8/68. Wg Cdr 1/7/94. Retd OPS SPT 1/1/98.
MACEY E.H. OBE. Born 4/4/36. Commd 23/2/55. AVM 1/7/85. Retd GD 9/4/91.
MACFADYEN I.D. CB OBE FRAeS. Born 19/2/42. Commd 30/7/63. AM 26/8/94. Retd GD 19/2/99.
MACFARLANE G.A. MBE MCMI. Born 17/3/23. Commd 3/8/50. Wg Cdr 1/7/66. Retd SUP 1/11/67.
MACFARLANE G.J. Born 25/2/59. Commd 15/6/83. Flt Lt 15/12/88. Retd GD 14/2/99.

MACFARLANE N.G. DSO. Born 5/12/15. Commd 7/3/38. Wg Cdr 1/1/51. Retd GD 18/4/58.
MACFARLANE N.I. Born 22/7/56. Commd 11/5/78. Flt Lt 27/8/82. Retd GD 23/12/96.
MACGOWAN W.E. Born 13/2/34. Commd 23/9/66. Flt Lt 23/9/72. Retd GD 20/8/84.
MACGREGOR A. BA MCIT MCMI. Born 30/7/32. Commd 27/7/54. Sqn Ldr 1/1/67. Retd GD 30/7/87.
MACGREGOR A.N. Born 18/7/44. Commd 31/1/64. Gp Capt 1/1/92. Retd GD 18/11/99.
MACGREGOR I. Born 30/11/31. Commd 11/3/65. Sqn Ldr 1/1/77. Retd ADMIN 10/7/82.
MACGREGOR J.P. Born 8/12/28. Commd 8/11/51. Flt Lt 23/2/57. Retd GD 8/12/83.
MACGREGOR S.W. BA. Born 31/1/36. Commd 6/8/63. Sqn Ldr 25/9/69. Retd EDN 6/8/79.
MACHEJ S.J. DFC. Born 23/9/19. Commd 1/9/45. Sqn Ldr 1/7/55. Retd GD 19/12/58.
MACHEN P.C. MA MSc CEng MIEE. Born 24/11/36. Commd 30/9/56. Sqn Ldr 1/7/68. Retd ENG 24/11/74.
MACHIN P.J. Born 2/11/26. Commd 4/7/51. Flt Lt 18/6/58. Retd GD(G) 2/11/64.
MACHRAY J. Born 22/2/33. Commd 1/3/57. Wg Cdr 1/1/77. Retd ENG 22/2/88.
MACINNES D.M. MCIPS MCMI. Born 13/8/39. Commd 29/7/65. Sqn Ldr 1/1/76. Retd SUP 1/1/79.
    Re-instated 27/8/80. Sqn Ldr 27/8/77. Retd SUP 1/6/90.
MACINTOSH A.G. Born 16/3/47. Commd 19/7/84. Flt Lt 19/7/88. Retd GD(G) 14/3/96.
MACINTYRE J.S. MA. Born 14/11/32. Commd 11/4/57. Sqn Ldr 21/6/63. Retd ADMIN 14/11/87.
MACINTYRE T.A. Born 5/7/37. Commd 27/2/56. Gp Capt 1/1/79. Retd GD(G) 6/9/89.
MACIVER D. Born 16/6/24. Commd 3/11/44. Wg Cdr 1/7/62. Retd GD 29/1/72.
MACIVER J. Born 11/4/48. Commd 12/7/79. Wg Cdr 1/7/97. Retd GD 11/4/03.
MACK D.R. MBA BSc CEng MIEE. Born 24/9/57. Commd 5/9/82. Sqn Ldr 1/1/91. Retd ENG 26/2/95.
MACKAY A.A. Born 14/7/38. Commd 13/12/60. Flt Lt 26/2/64. Retd GD 14/7/76.
MACKAY A.J. MBE DFC. Born 5/2/22. Commd 1/1/45. Wg Cdr 1/1/65. Retd SUP 25/11/72.
MACKAY A.S.G. BSc. Born 15/4/53. Commd 15/11/72. Sqn Ldr 1/7/88. Retd ENG 1/7/91.
MACKAY D.J. BSc IEng AMRAeS. Born 7/12/63. Commd 19/12/91. Sqn Ldr 1/7/01. Retd ENG 18/7/02.
MACKAY D.M. BA. Born 10/10/60. Commd 25/11/84. Flt Lt 25/5/88. Retd OPS SPT 25/11/00.
MACKAY D.W.D. AFC BSc. Born 22/3/57. Commd 21/10/79. Sqn Ldr 1/1/91. Retd GD 21/10/95.
MACKAY E.D. Born 23/12/23. Commd 28/7/44. Sqn Ldr 1/10/55. Retd GD 8/9/73.
MACKAY E.O. MBE MCMI. Born 26/10/18. Commd 15/11/43. Wg Cdr 1/7/67. Retd GD(G) 12/3/71.
MACKAY F.D. Born 17/1/59. Commd 27/3/80. Flt Lt 5/7/86. Retd ADMIN 17/1/97.
MACKAY F.G. BSc. Born 25/5/19. Commd 21/7/43. Sqn Ldr 1/1/55. Retd GD 25/5/74.
MACKAY G.A. MBE. Born 28/12/39. Commd 2/8/73. Sqn Ldr 1/1/83. Retd ENG 28/12/89.
MACKAY G.D. Born 10/3/18. Commd 19/7/51. Flt Lt 1/8/58. Retd SUP 1/11/63.
MACKAY H.G. CB OBE AFC BSc FRAeS. Born 3/10/47. Commd 3/1/69. AVM 1/1/01. Retd GD 3/10/02.
MACKAY L.W. Born 17/10/64. Commd 19/12/85. Flt Lt 19/6/91. Retd GD 14/3/97.
MACKAY N.F. Born 1/1/33. Commd 17/1/52. Flt Lt 24/7/57. Retd GD 1/1/71.
MACKAY N.G. Born 7/1/57. Commd 15/10/81. Sqn Ldr 1/7/93. Retd SUP 14/3/97.
MACKAY S.M. AFC. Born 17/11/22. Commd 20/5/42. Wg Cdr 1/7/58. Retd GD 31/3/62.
MACKAY W.D. MCSP GradDipPhysio. Born 19/4/47. Commd 2/6/77. Flt Lt 2/6/83. Retd MED(T) 2/6/85.
    Re-entered 2/3/87. Sqn Ldr 2/3/91. Retd MED(T) 6/6/97.
MACKENZIE D. DFC. Born 9/3/12. Commd 12/10/36. Sqn Ldr 1/7/52. Retd GD 12/10/56.
MACKENZIE D.S. The Rev. Born 18/1/45. Commd 21/4/74. Retd Wg Cdr 31/7/02.
MACKENZIE G.C. Born 20/10/56. Commd 28/6/79. Sqn Ldr 1/1/92. Retd SUP 26/2/01.
MACKENZIE H.D. Born 15/10/45. Commd 10/6/66. Sqn Ldr 1/7/78. Retd GD 26/6/96.
MACKENZIE I.J. CEng MIERE MCMI. Born 26/7/40. Commd 22/10/63. Sqn Ldr 1/1/75. Retd ENG 31/3/84.
MACKENZIE J. Born 7/11/49. Commd 27/3/86. Flt Lt 27/3/90. Retd ENG 2/6/93.
MACKENZIE J.L. Born 27/6/53. Commd 25/10/73. Flt Lt 9/3/80. Retd GD(G) 24/10/81. Re-instated 9/11/83.
MACKENZIE K. Born 1/1/31. Commd 28/7/67. Flt Lt 28/7/68. Retd EDN 28/7/75.
MACKENZIE K. MA MSc CEng MRAeS. Born 9/7/55. Commd 2/9/73. Gp Capt 1/7/02. Retd GD 1/8/04.
MACKENZIE K.C. Born 12/7/38. Commd 4/12/67. Flt Lt 13/10/71. Retd SEC 7/9/74.
MACKENZIE K.I. Born 22/12/42. Commd 15/6/62. Flt Lt 11/11/67. Retd GD 22/1/80.
MACKENZIE K.P. Born 21/12/17. Commd 17/12/38. Wg Cdr 1/7/50. Retd GD 29/5/59.
MACKENZIE K.T.W. Born 27/2/18. Commd 23/3/50. Sqn Ldr 1/1/60. Retd GD 27/2/58.
MACKENZIE K.W. DFC AFC AE FCMI. Born 8/6/16. Commd 24/4/40. Wg Cdr 1/1/54. Retd GD 1/7/67.
MACKENZIE M.R. BSc. Born 15/12/45. Commd 13/9/71. Sqn Ldr 1/1/87. Retd ADMIN 19/11/01.
MACKENZIE P.S. Born 22/5/39. Commd 22/1/63. Flt Lt 12/6/69. Retd SUP 22/5/89.
MACKENZIE R.P. Born 27/1/55. Commd 5/1/78. Flt Lt 5/7/84. Retd GD(G) 20/6/93.
MACKENZIE T.A. Born 13/6/28. Commd 8/12/48. Flt Lt 1/12/54. Retd GD 13/6/66.
MACKENZIE-CROOKS R.B. Born 4/1/43. Commd 30/7/43. Sqn Ldr 1/1/73. Retd GD 2/6/80.
MACKEY A.E. BEM. Born 28/5/16. Commd 9/4/45. Sqn Ldr 1/7/56. Retd SUP 10/8/67.
MACKEY D.J. Born 15/3/59. Commd 20/9/79. Flt Lt 20/3/86. Retd SUP 16/3/94.
MACKEY J. BDS LDSRCS FISM FCMI. Born 24/10/36. Commd 17/5/56. AVM 1/1/88. Retd DEL 14/4/97.
MACKICHAN A.S. MSc BSc CEng FIMechE FRAeS. Born 6/9/43. Commd 15/7/65. Gp Capt 1/7/88.
    Retd ENG 6/9/98.
MACKIE A.C.L. CBE DFC*. Born 3/8/22. Commd 11/5/41. A Cdre 1/7/66. Retd GD 30/9/68.
MACKIE D.F. Born 20/9/22. Commd 11/8/45. Flt Lt 29/11/51. Retd GD 1/9/57.
MACKIE E.D. Born 3/11/52. Commd 6/7/86. Wg Cdr 1/7/03. Retd GD 27/5/04.

MACKIE I.G. Born 2/12/35. Commd 23/3/55. Flt Lt 1/3/61. Retd GD 23/3/87.
MACKIE W.S. MSc BSc BEng CEng MIIE MIEE. Born 6/2/62. Commd 3/8/88. Flt Lt 15/7/91. Retd ENG 6/2/01.
MACKINLAY G. CEng MIEE. Born 10/12/42. Commd 15/7/65. Wg Cdr 1/7/80. Retd ENG 10/12/97.
MACKINNON A.J. Born 8/3/30. Commd 1/8/51. Wg Cdr 1/7/74. Retd GD 26/8/84.
MACKINNON M.S. Born 12/3/32. Commd 16/9/55. Fg Offr 16/9/57. Retd GD 22/12/59.
MACKINNON N.J. Born 10/2/43. Commd 26/11/81. Flt Lt 26/11/85. Retd OPS SPT 10/2/98.
MACKINNON R.J.N. Born 7/12/54. Commd 28/2/80. Wg Cdr 1/7/97. Retd ADMIN 11/5/00.
MACKINNON W. Born 21/12/23. Commd 31/3/45. Flt Lt 4/6/53. Retd GD 1/11/67.
MACKINTOSH A.M. BSc. Born 6/6/30. Commd 18/11/53. Gp Capt 1/1/76. Retd ENG 31/12/82.
MACKINTOSH E.K. MA CEng MIEE. Born 5/7/36. Commd 30/9/55. Sqn Ldr 1/7/67. Retd ENG 5/7/74.
MACKINTOSH J. Born 6/1/23. Commd 10/2/45. Sqn Ldr 1/1/57. Retd GD 6/1/72.
MACKINTOSH M.F. Born 1/9/21. Commd 9/6/43. Flt Lt 20/4/55. Retd GD(G) 19/12/57.
MACKLEY B. Born 29/10/32. Commd 23/8/51. Flt Lt 1/6/62. Retd GD(G) 30/1/72.
MACKREATH J. BSc. Born 28/4/51. Commd 9/9/69. Gp Capt 1/7/97. Retd ENG 2/4/99.
MACKRETH A.J.B. Born 21/7/12. Commd 31/7/43. Flt Lt 31/7/45. Retd GD 18/11/45.
MACLACHLAN A.C. MRCGP DPH DIH. Born 17/4/31. Commd 26/9/54. Wg Cdr 16/8/67. Retd MED 3/2/78.
MACLACHLAN A.J.C. CEng MRAeS. Born 19/10/41. Commd 2/3/61. Wg Cdr 1/7/88. Retd ENG 19/10/96.
MACLACHLAN M.R.F. Born 30/11/39. Commd 6/3/63. Flt Lt 9/5/67. Retd PRT 1/10/75.
MACLACHLAN N.K. Born 1/1/38. Commd 6/7/62. Flt Lt 12/11/69. Retd GD 13/3/78.
MACLACHLAN R. AFC. Born 4/6/23. Commd 28/9/51. Sqn Ldr 1/1/68. Retd GD 4/6/83.
MACLAINE M.J. AFC. Born 26/8/46. Commd 5/11/70. Sqn Ldr 1/1/84. Retd GD 20/7/92.
MACLAREN I.N. Born 13/2/18. Commd 26/6/39. Flt Lt 29/11/51. Retd GD(G) 31/3/62.
MACLAREN M. Born 20/6/45. Commd 19/8/66. Flt Lt 14/5/72. Retd GD 20/6/86.
MACLAREN R.B. MB ChB DIH. Born 23/10/29. Commd 3/3/57. Wg Cdr 3/3/70. Retd MED 3/3/73.
MACLAUGHLIN D.S. BSc. Born 14/12/40. Commd 25/9/62. Flt Lt 25/7/66. Retd ENG 11/10/72.
MACLEAN E.J. MBE. Born 11/5/49. Commd 19/9/71. Wg Cdr 1/7/90. Retd ENG 19/2/01.
MACLEAN H. BSc. Born 14/11/43. Commd 28/9/64. Sqn Ldr 1/1/76. Retd GD 14/11/81.
MACLEAN J. MBE MCMI. Born 16/6/26. Commd 23/6/60. Wg Cdr 1/1/76. Retd SY 27/5/77.
MACLEARY I.S. Born 20/8/36. Commd 9/5/66. Flt Lt 9/5/71. Retd ADMIN 9/5/82.
MACLEMAN R. BSc. Born 30/3/54. Commd 30/10/72. Wg Cdr 1/7/96. Retd GD 28/2/03.
MACLENNAN A.O. Born 20/9/44. Commd 22/5/70. Sqn Ldr 1/7/85. Retd SY(RGT) 1/7/88.
MACLENNAN A.R. IEng MIIE. Born 11/2/66. Commd 21/12/89. Sqn Ldr 1/7/01. Retd ENGINEER 1/7/04.
MACLENNAN D. Born 24/7/35. Commd 3/7/56. Gp Capt 1/1/81. Retd GD 7/4/90.
MACLENNAN D.A.F. The Rev. OBE BD. Born 6/5/34. Commd 5/8/64. Retd Wg Cdr 6/11/89.
MACLENNAN K.M. Born 13/3/42. Commd 30/5/69. Sqn Ldr 1/7/90. Retd GD 13/12/02.
MACLENNAN S.W. Born 17/3/65. Commd 11/10/84. Flt Lt 11/4/91. Retd OPS SPT(FLTOPS) 17/11/04.
MACLEOD A.M. MB ChB DPM. Born 9/5/27. Commd 18/9/55. Wg Cdr 23/8/62. Retd MED 8/4/68.
MACLEOD A.M. The Rev. MA. Born 12/7/20. Commd 18/11/47. Retd Wg Cdr 12/7/75.
MACLEOD C.J. BSc. Born 1/2/36. Commd 14/6/63. Sqn Ldr 19/2/68. Retd ADMIN 16/4/82.
MACLEOD D.F. CEng MIEE. Born 2/11/38. Commd 24/9/59. Gp Capt 1/7/91. Retd ENG 1/7/94.
MACLEOD D.H. Born 25/7/61. Commd 20/10/83. Sqn Ldr 1/1/93. Retd GD 25/7/99.
MACLEOD D.H. MB ChB DTM&H. Born 5/10/32. Commd 3/11/56. Wg Cdr 3/11/69. Retd MED 2/4/80.
MACLEOD E. Born 28/1/47. Commd 16/12/66. Plt Offr 13/4/67. Retd GD 18/1/68. Re-entered 12/8/81. Sqn Ldr 10/7/98.
   Retd OPS SPT(ATC) 3/4/04.
MACLEOD G.G. Born 17/5/46. Commd 23/4/87. Flt Lt 23/4/91. Retd ENG 2/4/93.
MACLEOD I.S. Born 27/4/61. Commd 28/2/80. Flt Lt 28/8/86. Retd GD(G) 1/6/93.
MACLEOD I.S. BA BA MIDPM MBCS. Born 23/6/42. Commd 18/8/61. Flt Lt 18/2/67. Retd GD 1/10/88.
MACLEOD M.D. Born 22/4/37. Commd 10/3/77. Sqn Ldr 1/1/86. Retd ENG 5/10/92.
MACLEOD M.M. Born 15/1/51. Commd 3/12/70. Sqn Ldr 1/7/83. Retd GD 15/1/89.
MACLEOD N. BSc. Born 10/5/54. Commd 30/10/72. Wg Cdr 1/7/90. Retd ADMIN 5/12/93.
MACLEOD N.M. OBE. Born 31/3/46. Commd 4/5/72. Gp Capt 1/1/94. Retd ADMIN 14/3/96.
MACLEOD R.M. IEng MILT AMRAeS. Born 17/6/57. Commd 30/8/84. Sqn Ldr 1/7/96. Retd SUP 8/4/00.
MACLEOD W.J.R. Born 3/2/51. Commd 10/9/70. Flt Lt 10/3/76. Retd GD 3/2/89.
MACMILLAN C.A. Born 11/3/43. Commd 16/11/61. Sqn Ldr 1/1/80. Retd GD(G) 31/3/94.
MACMILLAN D.R. Born 23/9/39. Commd 2/8/81. Flt Lt 12/11/70. Retd GD 31/10/89.
MACMILLAN I.C. MA. Born 15/6/41. Commd 17/8/64. Wg Cdr 1/7/84. Retd GD 15/6/96.
MACMILLAN-BELL H.I. Born 22/10/33. Commd 8/4/53. Fg Offr 3/3/55. Retd GD 1/10/57.
MACNAB A.J. MA BCom FCMA MInstAM MCMI AMS. Born 18/8/54. Commd 14/1/73. Sqn Ldr 1/7/87.
   Retd ADMIN 4/5/00.
MACNAUGHT R.L.F. BSc IEng MIIE. Born 15/7/57. Commd 28/7/95. Flt Lt 28/7/99. Retd ENGINEER 1/3/04.
MACNEILL C.C. The Rev. OBE BA. Born 27/9/30. Commd 7/6/62. Retd Wg Cdr 6/6/84.
MACNICOL N.R. Born 24/1/32. Commd 15/12/53. Flt Lt 15/6/56. Retd GD 1/1/76.
MACNISH N.K. Born 6/8/42. Commd 24/2/61. Flt Lt 9/2/68. Retd GD 31/10/81.
MACPHERSON A.M. Born 3/1/61. Commd 23/10/86. Sqn Ldr 1/1/97. Retd OPS SPT 1/1/00.
MACPHERSON C.S. Born 24/5/43. Commd 3/8/62. Flt Lt 3/2/68. Retd GD 5/12/75.
MACPHERSON D.A. BA. Born 12/1/47. Commd 16/1/72. Flt Lt 16/10/75. Retd SEC 3/10/78.

MACPHERSON I.A. Born 18/10/36. Commd 5/7/73. Sqn Ldr 1/7/88. Retd ENG 18/10/94.
MACPHERSON I.S. DFC. Born 1/11/28. Commd 14/12/49. Sqn Ldr 1/1/61. Retd GD 10/1/70.
MACPHERSON J.D.V. Born 18/3/26. Commd 17/1/52. Wg Cdr 1/1/69. Retd GD 7/8/79.
MACPHERSON J.H. MCMI. Born 14/3/44. Commd 18/7/63. Sqn Ldr 1/1/75. Retd SUP 30/8/95.
MACQUILLAN P.A. Born 10/5/43. Commd 29/3/62. Plt Offr 20/3/63. Retd ENG 19/12/64.
MACRAE A. Born 9/5/60. Commd 17/7/87. Flt Lt 21/11/89. Retd ENG 9/5/98.
MACRAE A.S. Born 6/7/40. Commd 31/8/62. Flt Lt 29/2/68. Retd GD 6/7/78.
MACRAE I.R. Born 16/2/36. Commd 11/11/71. Sqn Ldr 1/1/87. Retd ADMIN 1/1/89.
MACRAE J.P.R. Born 12/12/32. Commd 11/8/53. Flt Lt 5/10/60. Retd GD 12/12/70.
MACRAE J.R.A. BSc. Born 7/7/57. Commd 12/8/79. Sqn Ldr 1/1/91. Retd GD 7/4/98.
MACRAE K. MBE. Born 8/10/19. Commd 28/7/49. Wg Cdr 1/1/66. Retd SUP 8/10/74.
MACRAE M.K. Born 17/10/20. Commd 22/6/50. Gp Capt 1/7/72. Retd SEC 17/10/85.
MACRO E.L. OBE MCMI. Born 5/3/20. Commd 3/4/39. Wg Cdr 1/7/59. Retd SUP 31/5/69.
MACTAGGART J.G. Born 12/1/42. Commd 15/9/61. Flt Lt 15/3/67. Retd GD 12/1/80.
MACTAGGART W.K. CBE BSc CEng FIMechE FRAeS FCMI. Born 15/1/29. Commd 1/4/52. AVM 1/1/78.
   Retd ENG 7/5/80.
MADDEN F.A.P. Born 31/7/26. Commd 21/11/50. Sqn Ldr 1/1/66. Retd GD 28/11/75.
MADDEN J.M. MSc CEng MIEE. Born 17/12/52. Commd 25/9/71. Wg Cdr 1/1/89. Retd ENG 1/1/92.
MADDEN P. Born 11/3/34. Commd 6/4/72. Flt Lt 6/4/75. Retd GD 10/4/79.
MADDERN T. BA. Born 13/4/38. Commd 23/9/59. Wg Cdr 1/1/80. Retd GD 6/4/83.
MADDEX N.W.S. Born 26/9/37. Commd 4/11/82. Sqn Ldr 1/7/90. Retd ENG 4/11/92.
MADDIESON D.A. Born 3/7/29. Commd 12/3/64. Flt Lt 12/3/69. Retd GD 4/7/78.
MADDIESON G.S. Born 9/12/54. Commd 8/5/86. Sqn Ldr 1/1/94. Retd ENG 9/12/98.
MADDOCK T.W. Born 20/6/22. Commd 16/10/43. Flt Lt 16/4/47. Retd GD 20/6/65.
MADDOCKS B.J. Born 12/7/42. Commd 18/10/62. Wg Cdr 1/1/91. Retd GD 2/4/93.
MADDOCKS D. Born 23/11/52. Commd 10/12/91. Flt Lt 19/12/95. Retd OPS SPT(ATC) 24/9/03.
MADDOX A.D. Born 3/3/51. Commd 16/3/73. Flt Lt 16/3/76. Retd GD 23/2/83.
MADDOX C.J. BSc. Born 20/8/38. Commd 14/10/71. Sqn Ldr 14/4/78. Retd EDN 14/10/79.
MADDOX D.A. Born 17/3/24. Commd 21/1/45. Gp Capt 1/1/68. Retd GD 17/3/79.
MADELIN I. Born 12/4/31. Commd 18/6/52. Gp Capt 1/7/79. Retd GD 12/7/86.
MADEN W.B. Born 13/2/38. Commd 15/12/59. Flt Lt 15/6/62. Retd GD 21/5/65.
MADER E.C. Born 25/3/19. Commd 23/5/63. Flt Lt 23/5/66. Retd GD(G) 15/6/73.
MADER P.R. BSc. Born 24/2/54. Commd 17/9/72. Sqn Ldr 1/1/89. Retd ADMIN 24/2/92.
MADERSON C.W. Born 12/10/19. Commd 24/4/43. Sqn Ldr 1/7/67. Retd SEC 12/10/64.
MADGE A.W. MSc BSc MRAeS. Born 18/9/61. Commd 2/9/79. Wg Cdr 1/1/97. Retd ENG 1/1/00.
MADGE E.W. Born 21/2/38. Commd 13/12/79. Sqn Ldr 1/1/90. Retd ENG 21/2/96.
MADOC-JONES H. BA. Born 29/11/29. Commd 1/11/50. Wg Cdr 1/1/71. Retd SEC 29/11/79.
MAEER K.W. Born 15/9/46. Commd 28/4/65. Flt Lt 17/3/71. Retd GD 25/9/92.
MAFFETT S.A.H. Born 18/2/41. Commd 19/12/61. Sqn Ldr 1/7/70. Retd GD 18/2/79.
MAGEE D.J. Born 19/8/44. Commd 14/6/63. Wg Cdr 1/1/91. Retd GD 2/4/93.
MAGEE F. Born 17/9/15. Commd 25/8/60. Flt Lt 25/8/63. Retd ENG 26/2/67.
MAGEE G.D. Born 30/12/51. Commd 10/4/71. Sqn Ldr 1/1/86. Retd GD 30/12/89.
MAGEE K.F. Born 11/7/58. Commd 11/1/79. Flt Lt 11/7/84. Retd GD 11/7/96.
MAGEE M.F. MCMI. Born 12/6/34. Commd 17/9/53. Sqn Ldr 1/7/66. Retd ADMIN 12/6/92.
MAGEE M.J. BSc. Born 27/5/59. Commd 5/1/79. Sqn Ldr 1/7/93. Retd GD 27/5/97.
MAGGS C.A. Born 12/3/65. Commd 18/11/90. Flt Lt 18/11/90. Retd GD 14/9/96.
MAGGS E.A. Born 21/3/23. Commd 6/1/45. Flt Lt 19/11/53. Retd GD 28/7/68.
MAGGS K.J. Born 1/5/22. Commd 27/1/55. Flt Lt 27/1/61. Retd GD 1/5/77.
MAGGS W.J. CB OBE MA. Born 2/2/14. Commd 2/1/39. AVM 1/1/67. Retd SUP 10/10/69.
MAGILL P. Born 25/3/47. Commd 21/2/74. Flt Lt 21/2/76. Retd GD 25/3/85.
MAGILL P.G. Born 22/1/45. Commd 31/1/64. Flt Lt 30/10/69. Retd GD 18/6/75.
MAGILL T.N. BA. Born 8/12/59. Commd 11/1/79. Flt Lt 11/6/87. Retd SUP 14/9/96.
MAGOR D.H. Born 27/10/30. Commd 25/5/50. Gp Capt 1/1/78. Retd GD 2/8/83.
MAGUIRE F.M. Born 24/2/39. Commd 25/3/64. Flt Lt 1/7/68. Retd GD 7/3/77.
MAGUIRE J.H. MBE. Born 4/3/19. Commd 16/12/43. Sqn Ldr 1/1/56. Retd ENG 22/3/68.
MAGUIRE R.C. BA. Born 28/3/66. Commd 18/2/90. Flt Lt 18/8/93. Retd SY 31/8/96.
MAGURN J.P. Born 5/5/30. Commd 18/2/54. Flt Lt 1/1/61. Retd PRT 29/4/69.
MAHAFFEY B.S. BA. Born 25/4/46. Commd 19/9/71. Wg Cdr 1/7/86. Retd GD 25/4/04.
MAHENDRAN R. Born 31/8/33. Commd 3/2/65. Sqn Ldr 1/7/71. Retd GD 3/2/81.
MAHER B.J.L. Born 15/8/39. Commd 1/8/63. Flt Lt 1/8/64. Retd GD 14/2/76.
MAHER T.M. BEng. Born 23/5/61. Commd 2/8/85. Sqn Ldr 1/1/96. Retd ENG 23/5/99.
MAHGHAN C.G. CB CBE AFC. Born 3/2/23. Commd 16/3/47. AVM 1/1/75. Retd GD 3/3/78.
MAHON A.G. Born 11/2/42. Commd 17/12/63. Flt Lt 25/7/66. Retd GD 11/2/80.
MAHON A.W.L. MBE CEng MRAeS. Born 4/12/14. Commd 7/10/43. Wg Cdr 1/1/64. Retd ENG 4/6/67.
MAHONEY M. MB ChB FRCS(Glas). Born 18/7/34. Commd 8/8/62. A Cdre 2/5/94. Retd MED 1/1/97.
MAHONEY M.F. MA BSc. Born 25/1/57. Commd 12/8/79. Sqn Ldr 1/7/88. Retd GD 12/8/95.

MAHONEY P.J. BA. Born 7/9/60. Commd 18/3/84. Sqn Ldr 1/1/96. Retd ADMIN 17/6/02.
MAIDMAN N. Born 23/9/35. Commd 7/5/64. Flt Lt 1/7/68. Retd ENG 23/1/74.
MAIDMENT L.J. DFM. Born 27/3/19. Commd 21/9/42. Flt Lt 21/3/46. Retd GD 9/5/53.
MAILLARD P.B. Born 24/5/33. Commd 27/2/52. Sqn Ldr 1/7/86. Retd GD 14/10/87.
MAIN B.J. MMar. Born 26/7/37. Commd 14/9/65. Wg Cdr 1/7/80. Retd MAR 1/4/86.
MAIN D.MacP. Born 27/2/44. Commd 2/8/68. Sqn Ldr 1/1/76. Retd ENG 27/2/82.
MAIN J.B. CB OBE BSc CEng FIEE FIIE(elec) FRAeS. Born 28/1/41. Commd 30/9/60. AVM 1/1/94.
    Retd ENG 12/4/96.
MAINPRICE M.C. Born 1/6/17. Commd 23/1/39. Sqn Ldr 1/8/47. Retd SUP 3/2/60.
MAIR J.W. MVO MSc CEng MRAeS. Born 11/6/36. Commd 19/2/63. Wg Cdr 1/7/76. Retd ENG 23/7/86.
MAIR L. Born 21/1/34. Commd 29/4/53. A Cdre 1/1/83. Retd GD 1/5/87.
MAIR T.J. MA MEd. Born 11/11/16. Commd 6/1/49. Gp Capt 1/7/68. Retd EDN 11/11/71.
MAISEY J.H. LLB FCIS. Born 25/7/23. Commd 28/8/42. Wg Cdr 1/7/73. Retd ADMIN 31/12/76.
MAISH W.B. MRAeS. Born 21/1/34. Commd 29/4/53. A Cdre 1/1/83. Retd GD 1/5/87.
MAISNER A. CB CBE AFC. Born 26/7/21. Commd 1/9/48. A Cdre 1/1/72. Retd GD 14/1/77. rtg AVM.
MAITLAND J.E. Born 1/4/33. Commd 15/12/53. Gp Capt 1/7/80. Retd GD 1/5/93.
MAITLAND J.R. Born 11/10/14. Commd 3/9/46. Sqn Ldr 1/4/56. Retd GD 6/6/58.
MAITLAND P.J. AFC. Born 31/5/39. Commd 15/12/59. Sqn Ldr 1/1/68. Retd GD 23/9/77.
MAITLAND-CONLON G.D. Born 24/12/36. Commd 14/5/80. Flt Lt 14/5/74. Retd SY 16/7/87.
MAITLAND-TITTERTON L. MCMI. Born 28/5/31. Commd 12/9/63. Flt Lt 12/9/69. Retd ENG 28/5/89.
MAJOR D.R. Born 11/8/40. Commd 22/8/61. Sqn Ldr 1/7/86. Retd GD 13/12/93.
MAJOR G.H. Born 26/9/09. Commd 11/5/43. Flt Lt 13/9/50. Retd SUP 28/2/59.
MAJOR P.C.A. Born 24/9/24. Commd 4/5/50. Wg Cdr 1/7/72. Retd GD 24/9/79.
MAJOR P.C.J. Born 11/4/53. Commd 19/3/81. Sqn Ldr 1/7/89. Retd ENG 26/12/95.
MAJOR W.T. MA. Born 13/4/23. Commd 14/5/45. Flt Lt 2/1/61. Retd EDN 9/1/63.
MAKEPEACE R.M.T. Born 28/12/41. Commd 3/1/64. Flt Lt 9/2/68. Retd GD 28/12/79.
MAKIN B.G. Born 12/1/46. Commd 9/12/75. Sqn Ldr 1/1/86. Retd ADMIN (SEC) 12/1/04.
MAKINSON-SANDERS J. BA. Born 21/2/75. Commd 4/4/99. Flt Lt 4/10/01. Retd ADMIN (SEC) 31/12/03.
MAKINSON-SANDERS J.M.F. Born 18/2/47. Commd 1/3/68. Flt Lt 1/3/71. Retd GD 26/5/72.
MALCOLM R.A. BSc. Born 6/11/47. Commd 1/9/70. Flt Lt 1/12/70. Retd GD 1/9/82.
MALIN D.P. DFC. Born 1/5/37. Commd 1/4/58. Flt Lt 1/10/60. Retd GD 19/4/69.
MALIN I.G.L. Born 30/8/54. Commd 5/7/73. Flt Lt 5/1/79. Retd GD 10/4/88.
MALING J.P. Born 10/10/31. Commd 30/7/80. Sqn Ldr 30/5/68. Retd SUP 10/4/92.
MALINGS R.C. BA. Born 29/1/26. Commd 26/9/57. Flt Lt 26/9/63. Retd ADMIN 29/1/86.
MALINS H.R. Born 12/4/11. Commd 7/10/43. Flt Lt 7/4/47. Retd ENG 12/5/58.
MALINS L.A. DSO DFC. Born 20/6/20. Commd 10/6/41. Gp Capt 1/7/61. Retd GD 1/3/66.
MALINS W.E.V. DFC. Born 26/9/15. Commd 4/6/38. Wg Cdr 1/7/51. Retd GD 8/5/52.
MALLABAND P.D. BSc. Born 1/12/50. Commd 15/9/69. Flt Lt 15/12/73. Retd GD 24/5/75.
MALLEN I. Born 26/4/43. Commd 28/4/65. Flt Lt 17/3/71. Retd GD 1/9/82.
MALLET M.H. Born 4/5/20. Commd 15/4/57. Flt Lt 15/4/57. Retd SEC 4/5/75.
MALLETT D.R. Born 21/7/24. Commd 25/2/44. Sqn Ldr 1/1/59. Retd GD 31/8/63.
MALLETT E. MA. Born 23/10/25. Commd 29/9/48. Sqn Ldr 1/1/65. Retd SUP 31/7/68.
MALLETT F.A. Born 17/8/33. Commd 6/4/54. Wg Cdr 1/1/70. Retd GD 10/1/76.
MALLINDER A. Born 23/7/34. Commd 18/8/61. Flt Lt 26/7/67. Retd GD 23/7/72.
MALLINSON J.M. Born 25/11/33. Commd 27/10/67. Flt Lt 27/10/69. Retd GD(G) 27/10/75.
MALLINSON L. BEM. Born 16/6/16. Commd 25/8/55. Sqn Ldr 1/1/67. Retd ENG 16/6/73.
MALLINSON P. Born 24/10/35. Commd 2/2/68. Flt Lt 8/3/72. Retd GD 9/8/73.
MALLISON J.E. Born 1/8/23. Commd 3/8/61. Flt Lt 3/8/66. Retd GD(G) 1/8/74.
MALLORIE T.W. BSc. Born 7/12/54. Commd 16/9/73. Sqn Ldr 1/7/85. Retd GD 7/12/93.
MALONE D. Born 23/6/39. Commd 17/7/64. Flt Lt 8/1/69. Retd GD 23/6/77.
MALONE E.A. Born 20/11/49. Commd 22/6/75. Wg Cdr 1/7/91. Retd ADMIN 14/3/96.
MALONE M. MA. Born 17/7/53. Commd 25/9/71. Sqn Ldr 1/7/84. Retd GD 1/3/92.
MALONEY G.M. FCMI. Born 2/2/24. Commd 19/5/44. Gp Capt 1/1/73. Retd GD 27/3/76.
MALONEY G.T.O. Born 4/5/22. Commd 22/6/45. Sqn Ldr 1/7/60. Retd ADMIN 30/3/77.
MALONEY T. CEng MIEE MRAeS. Born 23/11/35. Commd 3/4/58. Wg Cdr 1/7/78. Retd ENG 23/11/93.
MALPASS C.P. MB BS MRCS LRCP FRCS(Glas). Born 31/7/37. Commd 11/1/65. Sqn Ldr 15/6/72.
    Retd MED 31/7/76.
MALPASS D.J. BSc FCMI. Born 17/9/34. Commd 6/12/56. Gp Capt 1/1/83. Retd ADMIN 27/4/86.
MALSTER A.A. Born 6/12/15. Commd 17/8/40. Flt Lt 1/9/45. Retd SEC 5/6/55. rtg Sqn Ldr.
MALTBY M.J. BA. Born 23/6/39. Commd 1/1/61. Sqn Ldr 1/1/74. Retd GD 2/10/77.
MALYON J.N. BSc MCMI MCIPD. Born 28/12/31. Commd 25/8/55. Sqn Ldr 25/2/65. Retd EDN 25/8/71.
MAMMEN J.H. Born 22/10/28. Commd 22/1/52. Flt Lt 22/7/56. Retd GD 22/10/66.
MANCLARK R.J. LLB. Born 17/5/52. Commd 11/8/74. Flt Lt 11/11/75. Retd GD 11/8/90.
MANDER J.G. MB BS. Born 5/10/27. Commd 29/6/53. Wg Cdr 2/6/64. Retd MED 29/6/69.
MANDER M. BA. Born 16/1/62. Commd 31/8/80. Plt Offr 15/10/81. Retd GD 15/8/84.
MANDER R.M.J. Born 15/11/46. Commd 1/11/79. Flt Lt 21/12/81. Retd ENG 16/6/97.

MANDER S.G. Born 28/8/49. Commd 1/4/71. Sqn Ldr 1/7/86. Retd GD 7/4/01.
MANDERSON D.J.H. BSc. Born 17/12/50. Commd 13/9/70. Sqn Ldr 1/1/85. Retd ENG 17/12/88.
MANDLEY C.J. BA RGN. Born 14/5/62. Commd 4/7/97. Sqn Ldr 1/1/99. Retd ADMIN (SEC) 2/4/05.
MANGAN M.T. BSc. Born 26/7/64. Commd 26/4/87. Flt Lt 26/10/89. Retd FLY(N) 26/4/03.
MANGER M.J. MSc BEng CEng MIEE. Born 13/9/62. Commd 3/3/85. Sqn Ldr 1/1/98. Retd ENGINEER 3/3/05.
MANLEY R.B. Born 5/10/42. Commd 12/7/62. Flt Lt 12/10/68. Retd SEC 1/10/75.
MANN A.H. Born 5/8/48. Commd 1/8/69. Flt Lt 1/2/75. Retd SY 5/8/86.
MANN A.S. DFC. Born 14/6/19. Commd 5/9/37. Gp Capt 1/1/67. Retd GD 14/6/74.
MANN C.F. MSc BSc CPhys CEng. Born 26/2/51. Commd 14/6/81. Sqn Ldr 1/1/88. Retd ADMIN 30/11/01.
MANN J.R. MBE BSc. Born 27/9/52. Commd 30/10/72. Sqn Ldr 1/1/89. Retd GD 1/1/92.
MANN M.C. Born 19/3/53. Commd 25/9/71. Wg Cdr 1/7/88. Retd GD 1/7/90.
MANN S.P. Born 29/7/57. Commd 1/11/79. Flt Lt 1/5/85. Retd GD(G) 29/7/95.
MANN T. BA. Born 1/2/33. Commd 9/6/55. Sqn Ldr 4/3/66. Retd EDN 6/9/71.
MANN W. Born 1/7/25. Commd 15/3/05. Fg Offr 15/3/53. Retd SEC 12/10/55.
MANNERS J.G. Born 19/3/32. Commd 8/10/70. Sqn Ldr 1/7/82. Retd ENG 30/4/90.
MANNERS W.J.E. Born 4/8/24. Commd 25/8/44. Flt Lt 29/11/51. Retd GD 1/3/68.
MANNERS-SPENCER J.M. BSc. Born 1/11/39. Commd 1/10/62. Flt Lt 1/7/64. Retd GD 6/10/72.
MANNING B. Born 20/9/41. Commd 14/8/64. Flt Lt 15/4/70. Retd GD 1/7/87.
MANNING E.T.J. OBE CEng MRAeS MCMI. Born 1/3/30. Commd 11/6/53. Gp Capt 1/7/80. Retd ENG 10/9/82.
MANNING G.A.K. MB BCh MRCGP DRCOG MRAeS. Born 4/4/55. Commd 14/2/78. Wg Cdr 1/8/93.
    Retd MED 14/2/94.
MANNING J.F. AFC ALCM. Born 6/3/21. Commd 28/7/43. Wg Cdr 1/1/60. Retd GD 6/3/68.
MANNING J.G. Born 24/5/09. Commd 13/3/47. Fg Offr 13/3/47. Retd SUP 21/6/48.
MANNING P. Born 13/11/42. Commd 31/10/69. Sqn Ldr 1/7/79. Retd ADMIN 2/6/96.
MANNING R.I. DFC. Born 16/5/18. Commd 14/7/43. Sqn Ldr 1/7/56. Retd ENG 17/8/63.
MANNING R.J. Born 5/3/37. Commd 29/7/58. Wg Cdr 1/7/79. Retd GD 1/4/91.
MANNING S.C. Born 11/9/54. Commd 15/3/73. Flt Lt 15/9/78. Retd GD 8/12/88.
MANNING W.E. Born 10/1/31. Commd 17/5/62. Flt Lt 1/4/66. Retd SUP 5/6/90.
MANNINGS E.J. Born 9/5/47. Commd 5/3/65. Sqn Ldr 1/1/84. Retd GD 9/5/91.
MANNINGS G.N. Born 13/4/25. Commd 11/6/53. Sqn Ldr 1/1/73. Retd GD 13/4/83.
MANNINGS R.P. Born 21/11/33. Commd 16/12/53. Flt Lt 16/6/58. Retd GD 21/11/71.
MANNION C.J.M. Born 8/4/49. Commd 20/9/68. Flt Lt 20/3/74. Retd GD 8/6/87.
MANNION D.T. Born 13/9/63. Commd 4/12/86. Flt Lt 17/11/90. Retd GD 13/9/01.
MANNS K.R. OBE. Born 8/10/14. Commd 22/11/43. Wg Cdr 1/7/60. Retd ADMIN 13/4/70.
MANOCHA S.D.H. Born 4/10/39. Commd 19/1/66. Wg Cdr 1/1/85. Retd ENG 2/4/90.
MANS K.D.R. Born 10/2/46. Commd 26/5/67. Flt Lt 18/2/70. Retd GD 5/1/77.
MANSBRIDGE P.A. Born 26/2/37. Commd 8/6/62. Flt Lt 26/7/67. Retd GD 1/5/74.
MANSER A.G. Born 27/3/20. Commd 8/4/44. Flt Lt 7/6/51. Retd GD 31/7/61.
MANSER R.C.H. Born 23/7/43. Commd 17/12/65. Sqn Ldr 1/1/89. Retd GD 22/9/94.
MANSER R.J. Born 8/12/44. Commd 13/2/86. Flt Lt 13/8/90. Retd ENG 31/5/92.
MANSFIELD B.R. Born 13/3/49. Commd 16/8/68. Flt Lt 16/2/74. Retd GD 1/7/87.
MANSFIELD E.A. MA MSc CEng MRAeS. Born 14/4/32. Commd 26/9/53. Gp Capt 1/7/77. Retd ENG 14/4/89.
MANSFIELD G.W. Born 21/9/49. Commd 29/8/72. Flt Lt 29/11/72. Retd GD 26/10/77.
MANSFIELD K.P. Born 11/7/59. Commd 23/10/78. Flt Lt 15/12/87. Retd ENG 31/3/94.
MANSFIELD R.A. MSc BSc (Eur Ing) CEng MBCS. Born 27/1/56. Commd 15/9/74. Sqn Ldr 1/7/91.
    Retd ENG 27/1/01.
MANSFIELD R.J. Born 1/4/14. Commd 9/5/40. Sqn Ldr 1/8/47. Retd GD 9/5/57.
MANSON J.McG.C. Born 20/3/41. Commd 26/11/60. Flt Lt 26/5/71. Retd GD 20/3/79.
MANSON M.LeM. Born 18/12/15. Commd 13/12/41. Sqn Ldr 1/1/52. Retd ENG 15/9/52.
MANSON R.J.M. MMar MNI. Born 31/3/25. Commd 24/4/57. Sqn Ldr 24/4/65. Retd MAR 1/6/79.
MANTLE W.E. The Rev. MA. Born 16/5/17. Commd 1/9/43. Retd Gp Capt 26/8/73.
MANTON G.A.L. Born 18/6/10. Commd 26/6/31. Gp Capt 1/1/49. Retd GD 26/6/60.
MANTON S.R. Born 17/1/55. Commd 8/9/77. Flt Lt 8/3/83. Retd GD 14/2/93.
MANVILLE K.D. Born 25/4/44. Commd 3/7/80. Sqn Ldr 1/1/89. Retd SUP 14/3/00.
MAPLE D.C. The Rev. Born 30/7/34. Commd 22/8/71. Retd Sqn Ldr 13/11/75.
MAPP C. Born 12/1/10. Commd 4/9/41. Flt Lt 21/3/45. Retd ENG 10/4/46. rtg Sqn Ldr.
MAPP N.J. MCMI. Born 29/1/33. Commd 9/4/53. Sqn Ldr 1/1/70. Retd GD 10/9/91.
MARCH B.J. BSc LLB. Born 14/11/36. Commd 14/8/62. Sqn Ldr 1/3/70. Retd EDN 14/8/78.
MARCH K.C.W. Born 28/2/62. Commd 19/3/81. Sqn Ldr 1/7/99. Retd FLY(P) 3/11/04.
MARCH V.R. Born 12/5/50. Commd 15/9/69. Flt Lt 15/10/75. Retd ENG 12/5/91.
MARCHANT D.J.S. MBE BSc. Born 29/7/37. Commd 28/9/60. Sqn Ldr 1/7/85. Retd GD 29/7/95.
MARCHANT R.J. Born 14/9/34. Commd 9/4/53. Flt Lt 26/8/58. Retd GD 14/9/72.
MARCHBANK C.D. BSc. Born 23/5/61. Commd 13/2/83. Flt Lt 13/11/84. Retd GD 14/3/96.
MARCHINGTON F. MIEE DipEE. Born 9/11/37. Commd 24/2/67. Wg Cdr 1/7/89. Retd ENG 1/3/93.
MAREK G.J. Born 28/4/50. Commd 28/9/89. Flt Lt 28/9/93. Retd SUP 14/3/96.
MARENGO-ROWE A.J. MB BS MRCS LRCP. Born 20/8/36. Commd 4/2/64. Flt Lt 1/1/63. Retd MED 30/9/67.

MARGAILLAN R.M. Born 5/4/35. Commd 10/2/56. Flt Lt 7/3/62. Retd GD 5/4/73.
MARGETTS A. Born 25/4/31. Commd 17/12/52. Flt Lt 21/10/59. Retd GD 12/5/69.
MARGETTS P.R. BSc. Born 14/1/61. Commd 2/9/79. Flt Lt 15/4/84. Retd GD 21/3/00.
MARGIOTTA G.J. Born 28/12/51. Commd 13/9/70. Flt Lt 12/2/80. Retd GD 29/7/94.
MARGIOTTA G.L. BA. Born 29/8/39. Commd 9/9/63. Wg Cdr 1/1/92. Retd GD 6/7/94.
MARKER T.J. AFC. Born 19/7/41. Commd 12/7/68. Flt Lt 4/1/71. Retd GD 19/7/96.
MARKEY A.H.C. CEng MRAeS FINucE MCMI. Born 16/8/21. Commd 21/10/43. Wg Cdr 1/7/63. Retd ENG 1/11/77.
MARKEY M.C. MA. Born 9/10/39. Commd 9/11/60. Wg Cdr 1/7/77. Retd ADMIN 26/4/80.
MARKEY M.J.W. Born 2/6/40. Commd 10/2/59. Wg Cdr 1/1/86. Retd SY 3/4/93.
MARKEY P.D. OBE MSc BA FCIPS FILT FCMI. Born 28/3/43. Commd 17/12/64. AVM 1/7/95. Retd SUP 28/8/97.
MARKS B.J. OBE FCA. Born 30/4/31. Commd 13/7/59. Wg Cdr 1/7/74. Retd ADMIN 24/7/86.
MARKS K.G. AACCA. Born 30/6/24. Commd 12/9/43. Sqn Ldr 1/4/58. Retd SEC 30/6/62.
MARKS M.H. MBE CEng MRAeS MInstD MCMI. Born 17/4/63. Commd 28/2/88. Sqn Ldr 1/7/95.
    Retd ENG 17/4/01.
MARKS N.J. Born 5/11/58. Commd 11/9/77. Flt Lt 4/3/84. Retd GD 2/11/86. Re-entered 12/10/87. Flt Lt 22/1/85.
    Retd GD 5/11/96.
MARKS P.C. Born 11/3/59. Commd 15/6/83. Sqn Ldr 1/7/94. Retd ADMIN 9/8/99.
MARKS P.J. Born 16/7/44. Commd 22/2/63. Flt Lt 22/8/68. Retd GD 16/7/01.
MARKS T.J. Born 25/9/45. Commd 5/11/65. Flt Lt 25/3/71. Retd GD 2/6/76.
MARKWELL E. Born 17/8/23. Commd 11/2/44. Sqn Ldr 1/1/68. Retd GD 29/3/78.
MARLAND R.C. BL. Born 17/8/40. Commd 22/4/63. Flt Lt 20/1/68. Retd GD 22/4/79.
MARLOW D.C. Born 23/9/46. Commd 1/3/68. Flt Lt 1/3/71. Retd GD 23/9/83.
MARLOW D.E.G. Born 31/1/26. Commd 25/10/46. Flt Lt 29/6/50. Retd GD 31/7/63.
MARLOW-SPALDING M.J. Born 13/5/47. Commd 6/4/72. Gp Capt 1/1/94. Retd ENG 14/3/97.
MARMAN C.S. MMar. Born 25/7/46. Commd 24/3/74. Flt Lt 24/3/74. Retd GD 14/3/96.
MARMAN P.G. AFC. Born 12/3/21. Commd 31/7/44. Sqn Ldr 1/10/55. Retd GD 29/9/62.
MARMENT H.V. MCMI. Born 10/9/36. Commd 9/7/55. Sqn Ldr 1/1/85. Retd ADMIN 1/9/89.
MARMION J.C. OBE FCMI. Born 25/3/24. Commd 30/6/44. Gp Capt 1/1/70. Retd GD 25/3/79.
MARMONT A.E. Born 27/8/29. Commd 10/3/64. Flt Lt 10/3/64. Retd GD 10/3/72.
MARNANE W.R. BA. Born 5/11/44. Commd 19/8/65. Sqn Ldr 1/1/84. Retd GD(G) 31/8/94.
MARQUIS L.W. Born 23/3/31. Commd 21/2/60. Flt Lt 21/2/74. Retd GD(G) 11/9/76.
MARQUIS R.J. Born 10/3/59. Commd 9/5/91. Flt Lt 9/5/93. Retd ADMIN 31/10/95.
MARR D.G. MBE CEng MRAeS MCMI. Born 7/2/38. Commd 2/2/60. Wg Cdr 1/7/78. Retd ENG 3/4/91.
MARR D.S.B. AFC* BSc MRAeS. Born 12/11/40. Commd 9/9/63. Wg Cdr 1/7/78. Retd GD 1/7/81.
MARR J. Born 20/8/19. Commd 21/10/54. Sqn Ldr 1/7/68. Retd ENG 20/8/69.
MARR P.M. Born 31/3/15. Commd 24/1/45. Flt Offr 2/7/52. Retd SEC 16/9/61.
MARREN L. Born 21/10/19. Commd 12/12/46. Sqn Ldr 1/7/67. Retd SUP 21/10/74.
MARRIOTT G. Born 9/10/32. Commd 10/9/52. Flt Lt 25/12/75. Retd GD 9/10/92.
MARRIOTT G.T. BTech. Born 12/1/43. Commd 6/4/67. Sqn Ldr 1/7/79. Retd ENG 6/11/83.
MARRIOTT J.F.H. Born 25/5/34. Commd 26/7/55. Wg Cdr 1/1/78. Retd GD 3/4/88.
MARRIOTT M.B.R. Born 3/11/44. Commd 29/11/63. Sqn Ldr 1/1/93. Retd GD 31/10/00.
MARRIOTT N. DFC. Born 4/1/22. Commd 26/2/44. Sqn Ldr 1/10/54. Retd GD 24/3/61.
MARRIOTT W.H.E. Born 4/8/11. Commd 6/6/41. Sqn Ldr 1/7/49. Retd SEC 24/1/59. rtg Wg Cdr.
MARRIOTT W.J. OBE. Born 26/7/24. Commd 25/8/44. Wg Cdr 1/7/60. Retd GD 28/2/76.
MARRISON C.G. Born 10/12/58. Commd 2/3/78. Wg Cdr 1/7/95. Retd GD 10/12/02.
MARRISON S. Born 17/9/11. Commd 28/11/40. Flt Lt 9/8/45. Retd ENG 20/11/47. rtg Sqn Ldr.
MARRS A.W. Born 6/3/42. Commd 9/9/63. Flt Lt 9/3/68. Retd GD 6/3/80.
MARSDEN B.P. BSc. Born 24/10/29. Commd 21/2/52. Sqn Ldr 1/1/63. Retd ENG 24/10/67.
MARSDEN C.R. Born 16/4/39. Commd 22/2/63. Sqn Ldr 1/1/79. Retd GD 28/7/90.
MARSDEN H. Born 16/11/28. Commd 29/4/71. Sqn Ldr 1/7/83. Retd ADMIN 15/3/85.
MARSDEN H.N. Born 27/7/27. Commd 16/12/43. Sqn Ldr 1/7/58. Retd ENG 20/2/74.
MARSDEN J. MBE. Born 20/11/18. Commd 6/9/56. Flt Lt 6/9/59. Retd CAT 20/11/73.
MARSDEN J.R. Born 10/11/41. Commd 19/6/70. Sqn Ldr 1/7/77. Retd ENG 22/7/93.
MARSDEN J.W. BSc MRINA. Born 26/1/50. Commd 14/10/71. Sqn Ldr 1/7/92. Retd OPS SPT 30/10/00.
MARSDEN M.R. Born 5/3/16. Commd 5/6/58. Flt Offr 5/6/63. Retd PRT 5/9/67.
MARSDEN T.E. BSc. Born 26/11/46. Commd 19/11/72. Flt Lt 19/8/74. Retd GD 31/3/95.
MARSDEN W. Born 18/1/36. Commd 30/4/59. Flt Lt 15/2/65. Retd GD 29/9/89.
MARSH D.A. Born 18/7/43. Commd 1/11/63. Sqn Ldr 1/7/89. Retd GD 18/7/00.
MARSH D.H. Born 6/8/31. Commd 20/12/51. Flt Lt 4/4/57. Retd GD 6/8/91.
MARSH D.T. Born 6/4/33. Commd 25/8/55. Flt Lt 21/10/59. Retd EDN 26/1/66.
MARSH E.P. Born 12/8/30. Commd 17/1/52. Flt Lt 24/7/57. Retd GD 12/8/68.
MARSH J.C. Born 19/1/46. Commd 26/5/67. Flt Lt 18/2/70. Retd GD 24/2/77.
MARSH L. DFM. Born 29/10/21. Commd 30/11/44. Sqn Ldr 1/1/69. Retd SY 29/10/76.
MARSH M.J. OBE. Born 30/4/31. Commd 20/1/51. Wg Cdr 1/7/74. Retd GD 30/4/86.
MARSH N. Born 18/7/47. Commd 28/4/67. Sqn Ldr 1/7/83. Retd ENG 18/7/97.
MARSH P.A. Born 9/4/32. Commd 10/9/52. Flt Lt 7/2/58. Retd GD 9/4/70.

MARSH P.E. Born 6/1/21. Commd 6/2/56. Flt Lt 6/2/56. Retd CAT 17/1/67.
MARSH P.E. Born 18/10/33. Commd 17/1/52. Flt Lt 22/5/57. Retd GD(G) 17/5/80.
MARSH P.M. OBE. Born 24/6/25. Commd 9/6/45. Wg Cdr 1/1/65. Retd GD 24/6/78.
MARSH S. Born 15/4/24. Commd 12/2/53. Flt Lt 12/8/56. Retd GD 15/4/82.
MARSH T.P. Born 24/11/50. Commd 25/2/72. Sqn Ldr 1/1/87. Retd GD 1/1/90.
MARSHALL A.C. MIMechE MRAeS. Born 29/4/22. Commd 23/9/43. Sqn Ldr 1/4/56. Retd ENG 30/6/64.
MARSHALL A.F. Born 18/11/36. Commd 27/10/54. Flt Lt 1/3/61. Retd GD 2/3/87.
MARSHALL A.J. Born 5/11/34. Commd 28/2/57. Flt Lt 21/6/63. Retd GD(G) 1/5/64.
MARSHALL A.K. AFC. Born 27/8/19. Commd 10/3/44. Sqn Ldr 1/1/56. Retd GD 21/8/59.
MARSHALL A.R. Born 16/11/23. Commd 7/9/61. Sqn Ldr 1/7/73. Retd ENG 16/10/75.
MARSHALL A.S. Born 21/1/55. Commd 28/8/75. Flt Lt 28/2/81. Retd GD 14/3/96.
MARSHALL B.E. Born 25/2/33. Commd 3/6/65. Flt Lt 1/9/70. Retd MED(SEC) 13/3/76.
MARSHALL D. Born 24/3/33. Commd 3/4/59. Flt Lt 3/4/63. Retd ADMIN 19/2/77.
MARSHALL D. BA. Born 12/3/37. Commd 27/8/58. Sqn Ldr 27/2/69. Retd EDN 3/10/78.
MARSHALL D.A. MIEH MCMI. Born 7/2/35. Commd 9/10/75. Sqn Ldr 21/4/84. Retd MED(T) 1/4/89.
MARSHALL D.A. BEM. Born 14/4/38. Commd 20/11/75. Flt Lt 20/11/80. Retd SUP 14/8/88.
MARSHALL D.B. Born 21/12/45. Commd 6/11/64. Flt Lt 6/10/71. Retd GD 1/1/75.
MARSHALL D.F. Born 13/9/38. Commd 10/2/59. Sqn Ldr 1/7/71. Retd GD 13/11/77.
MARSHALL D.J. Born 13/2/48. Commd 3/5/68. Sqn Ldr 1/7/01. Retd FLY(N) 1/7/03.
MARSHALL E.E.H. Born 24/3/19. Commd 11/2/52. Flt Lt 11/2/52. Retd RGT 12/7/58.
MARSHALL E.W.T. Born 3/9/31. Commd 12/6/51. Flt Lt 12/3/56. Retd GD 3/9/89.
MARSHALL F.G. Born 27/11/35. Commd 1/12/54. Sqn Ldr 1/1/68. Retd GD 16/4/76.
MARSHALL F.W.C. BA DPhysEd MCMI. Born 11/2/39. Commd 10/9/63. Wg Cdr 1/7/78. Retd ADMIN 9/11/90.
MARSHALL G. Born 30/10/42. Commd 29/3/68. Sqn Ldr 1/1/85. Retd GD 1/11/93.
MARSHALL H. AFC. Born 24/6/24. Commd 17/5/56. Flt Lt 17/5/62. Retd GD 31/3/74. rtg Sqn Ldr.
MARSHALL H. OBE DFC. Born 19/5/31. Commd 20/6/51. Gp Capt 1/1/80. Retd GD 19/5/86.
MARSHALL I. Born 26/8/36. Commd 23/12/60. Wg Cdr 1/1/90. Retd GD 1/1/93.
MARSHALL J. MBE MCMI. Born 2/9/20. Commd 17/6/54. Sqn Ldr 1/7/65. Retd ENG 1/6/73.
MARSHALL J. CBE MVO BEng CEng MRAeS. Born 12/4/35. Commd 27/9/57. A Cdre 1/7/83. Retd ENG 1/5/88.
MARSHALL J.A. Born 31/10/41. Commd 6/7/62. Flt Lt 1/7/69. Retd GD 31/10/79.
MARSHALL J.C. Born 23/11/27. Commd 13/2/64. Sqn Ldr 1/7/74. Retd ENG 23/11/87.
MARSHALL J.C.W. Born 20/8/42. Commd 29/11/63. Wg Cdr 1/1/97. Retd GD 20/8/97.
MARSHALL J.D. Born 13/7/49. Commd 9/12/71. Sqn Ldr 1/7/73. Retd GD 13/7/99.
MARSHALL J.McE. Born 8/4/20. Commd 25/2/43. Flt Lt 5/9/48. Retd SEC 25/4/64.
MARSHALL J.W. OBE. Born 24/11/39. Commd 11/8/67. Wg Cdr 1/1/84. Retd GD 31/3/95.
MARSHALL K. Born 8/10/45. Commd 3/3/67. Sqn Ldr 1/7/78. Retd GD 8/10/83.
MARSHALL L. Born 24/10/21. Commd 17/10/57. Flt Lt 1/4/63. Retd ENG 25/7/63.
MARSHALL L.J. MBE. Born 23/1/46. Commd 18/8/67. Wg Cdr 1/7/84. Retd GD 23/1/90.
MARSHALL N.G.S. Born 7/3/23. Commd 31/5/49. Wg Cdr 1/1/66. Retd GD 7/3/78.
MARSHALL N.P.H. Born 2/3/54. Commd 28/7/88. Flt Lt 28/7/90. Retd ENG 1/4/93.
MARSHALL P.J. Born 28/4/61. Commd 12/9/86. Sqn Ldr 1/7/98. Retd ADMIN (SEC) 28/11/03.
MARSHALL P.M. FCIPD. Born 3/8/37. Commd 6/9/56. Gp Capt 1/1/88. Retd ADMIN 30/9/91.
MARSHALL P.S. BEng BSc CEng MIEE. Born 10/5/61. Commd 7/8/87. Flt Lt 13/7/92. Retd ENG 2/1/03.
MARSHALL R. OBE. Born 16/9/21. Commd 9/11/43. Wg Cdr 1/7/66. Retd GD(G) 17/8/76.
MARSHALL R. Born 14/5/56. Commd 28/8/75. Flt Lt 28/2/81. Retd GD 14/5/94.
MARSHALL R.A. Born 22/10/48. Commd 12/7/68. Flt Lt 12/7/74. Retd GD(G) 21/10/86.
MARSHALL R.A. Born 23/6/43. Commd 3/10/69. Sqn Ldr 1/1/93. Retd GD 22/10/97.
MARSHALL R.B.D. Born 29/11/30. Commd 12/12/51. Flt Lt 28/4/58. Retd GD 19/7/68.
MARSHALL R.H. Born 1/9/31. Commd 7/9/61. Sqn Ldr 1/7/74. Retd ENG 6/11/82.
MARSHALL R.J. Born 28/5/54. Commd 14/1/88. Flt Lt 14/1/90. Retd ENG 14/1/02.
MARSHALL R.W. Born 19/1/15. Commd 9/5/41. Wg Cdr 1/7/58. Retd SEC 15/6/66.
MARSHALL S. BA. Born 19/10/60. Commd 26/9/82. Sqn Ldr 1/1/96. Retd FLY(P) 19/10/04.
MARSHALL S.A. MB BCh BAO DavMed. Born 29/8/36. Commd 27/11/63. Wg Cdr 7/6/75. Retd MED 26/9/94.
MARSHALL S.J. Born 24/1/25. Commd 18/6/44. Flt Lt 18/12/47. Retd GD 24/1/64.
MARSHALL S.O.O. Born 23/9/22. Commd 4/8/50. Sqn Ldr 1/1/61. Retd SUP 24/4/68.
MARSHALL T.A. MSc BSc CEng MIMechE. Born 15/2/62. Commd 29/9/83. Sqn Ldr 1/7/99. Retd ENG 1/7/02.
MARSHALL T.B. Born 13/6/55. Commd 22/11/73. Flt Lt 6/4/80. Retd GD(G) 30/9/82.
MARSHALL W.G. FAAI MCMI. Born 1/1/35. Commd 29/7/65. Sqn Ldr 1/1/78. Retd SEC 1/10/81.
MARSHALL-HARDY R.F. Born 20/5/19. Commd 26/10/43. Sqn Ldr 1/4/55. Retd GD 20/5/62.
MARSHALL-HASDELL D.J. Born 6/1/54. Commd 16/11/72. Sqn Ldr 1/7/84. Retd GD 25/1/86.
MARSHFIELD M.J. BA. Born 5/4/56. Commd 8/2/81. Flt Lt 8/5/83. Retd ADMIN 11/12/88.
MARSKELL P.R. BSc. Born 11/2/55. Commd 2/9/75. Flt Lt 15/10/77. Retd GD 15/7/88.
MARSON M.J.C. Born 18/4/39. Commd 31/7/58. Flt Lt 14/11/66. Retd GD 13/4/77.
MARSTON P. MBE BA MRAeS. Born 18/3/42. Commd 11/11/71. Sqn Ldr 1/1/89. Retd GD 18/3/97.
MARSTON R. AFC . Born 20/11/47. Commd 21/9/72. Gp Capt 1/7/01. Retd GD 20/5/05.
MARSTON S.W. Born 9/10/48. Commd 3/5/68. Flt Lt 3/11/73. Retd GD 1/2/88.

MART K. BEng. Born 16/4/61. Commd 28/8/83. Sqn Ldr 1/1/95. Retd ENG 16/4/99.
MARTER A.D. Born 9/6/46. Commd 2/4/65. Sqn Ldr 1/7/84. Retd ENG 26/2/99.
MARTIN A.G. Born 5/5/40. Commd 11/10/84. Flt Lt 1/3/87. Retd SUP 5/5/95.
MARTIN A.G. BSc. Born 1/8/61. Commd 5/2/84. Flt Lt 5/8/86. Retd GD 5/2/96.
MARTIN A.H. CEng MIMechE. Born 17/7/24. Commd 10/9/51. Flt Lt 10/3/54. Retd ENG 9/2/66.
MARTIN A.I.J. Born 8/2/33. Commd 17/1/69. Flt Lt 17/1/74. Retd ENG 8/2/88.
MARTIN A.M. Born 5/4/41. Commd 23/2/68. Wg Cdr 1/1/87. Retd GD 5/4/93.
MARTIN A.P. BSc. Born 15/1/58. Commd 11/12/83. Sqn Ldr 1/7/96. Retd SUP 11/12/99.
MARTIN A.R. Born 27/5/28. Commd 1/8/51. Wg Cdr 1/7/69. Retd ADMIN 1/12/76.
MARTIN B.S. Born 17/8/20. Commd 24/4/42. Wg Cdr 1/7/60. Retd GD 29/10/74.
MARTIN C.E.H. CEng MRAeS MCMI. Born 16/8/31. Commd 18/7/63. Sqn Ldr 1/7/73. Retd ENG 16/8/81.
MARTIN C.G.A. Born 28/1/25. Commd 4/4/59. Flt Lt 25/7/66. Retd GD 18/5/75.
MARTIN C.J. MSc BSc(Eng) CEng MIEE. Born 27/10/50. Commd 19/11/72. Flt Lt 19/2/76. Retd ENG 1/10/89.
MARTIN D. Born 19/8/20. Commd 6/3/53. Flt Lt 6/3/58. Retd GD 19/8/70.
MARTIN D.A. Born 17/1/46. Commd 2/8/68. Sqn Ldr 1/7/78. Retd GD 1/3/99.
MARTIN D.C. Born 14/10/42. Commd 9/3/62. Sqn Ldr 1/1/75. Retd GD 14/10/83.
MARTIN D.D. OBE BSc. Born 4/7/20. Commd 6/3/39. Sqn Ldr 1/1/49. Retd GD 1/7/73. rtg Wg Cdr.
MARTIN D.D. Born 5/10/47. Commd 6/4/72. Flt Lt 6/10/77. Retd GD 13/12/87.
MARTIN D.F. MCMI. Born 11/2/21. Commd 23/10/43. Sqn Ldr 1/7/65. Retd GD(G) 11/2/76.
MARTIN D.J. BSc. Born 2/3/64. Commd 11/9/83. Flt Lt 15/1/88. Retd FLY(P) 7/4/03.
MARTIN D.J.G. BA MRAeS MCMI. Born 27/2/30. Commd 9/8/55. Sqn Ldr 1/7/67. Retd GD 3/1/85.
MARTIN D.J.Y. MCMI. Born 9/9/49. Commd 2/6/77. Sqn Ldr 1/1/84. Retd SY 9/9/87.
MARTIN F.B. DFM. Born 2/5/21. Commd 19/6/44. Flt Lt 21/7/61. Retd GD 30/3/68.
MARTIN F.R. BA. Born 21/8/34. Commd 9/8/57. Flt Lt 26/2/64. Retd EDN 25/12/65.
MARTIN G.E. Born 7/11/19. Commd 17/6/54. Flt Lt 1/1/63. Retd ENG 5/7/69.
MARTIN G.G. MBE. Born 28/4/54. Commd 18/1/73. Gp Capt 1/7/95. Retd ADMIN 6/12/98.
MARTIN G.N. BSc. Born 13/10/34. Commd 28/8/58. Sqn Ldr 1/7/69. Retd ADMIN 21/8/85.
MARTIN H.B. MCMI. Born 20/5/47. Commd 24/6/71. Sqn Ldr 1/1/85. Retd SUP 11/2/97.
MARTIN H.F. Born 21/6/16. Commd 1/9/45. Flt Lt 1/9/45. Retd GD(G) 21/6/66.
MARTIN H.L. Born 15/9/29. Commd 2/7/52. Flt Lt 27/11/57. Retd GD 5/2/68.
MARTIN I.R. AFC*. Born 4/2/32. Commd 4/7/51. Gp Capt 1/7/72. Retd GD 31/5/75.
MARTIN J. PhD MSc. Born 14/4/46. Commd 16/1/72. Flt Lt 16/1/73. Retd ADMIN 16/1/76. Re-entered 2/9/81.
  Wg Cdr 1/1/01. Retd ENG 1/1/03.
MARTIN J.A. MBE MIIM MCMI. Born 21/8/32. Commd 18/1/84. Sqn Ldr 20/5/81. Retd ENG 21/2/92.
MARTIN J.C.P. Born 26/9/60. Commd 6/11/80. Sqn Ldr 1/7/94. Retd OPS SPT 26/9/98.
MARTIN J.D. BA. Born 19/9/46. Commd 2/4/65. Wg Cdr 1/1/90. Retd GD 14/1/01.
MARTIN J.F. Born 26/8/23. Commd 2/8/43. Flt Lt 2/9/46. Retd GD 26/8/66.
MARTIN J.F.S. AFC BSc. Born 13/12/38. Commd 28/9/60. Gp Capt 1/7/89. Retd GD 1/7/91.
MARTIN J.H. DFC. Born 24/7/24. Commd 28/2/57. Flt Lt 28/2/63. Retd GD 24/7/74.
MARTIN J.H. MCMI. Born 25/3/29. Commd 12/12/51. Wg Cdr 1/7/81. Retd SUP 1/7/84.
MARTIN J.L. Born 27/6/32. Commd 7/5/52. Flt Lt 2/10/57. Retd GD 27/12/70.
MARTIN J.S. CBE BDS. Born 14/4/31. Commd 16/9/56. A Cdre 1/7/86. Retd DEL 31/12/90.
MARTIN K. OBE BA. Born 21/10/24. Commd 4/12/50. Gp Capt 1/1/72. Retd ENG 21/4/82.
MARTIN K.L. Born 23/4/60. Commd 4/9/81. Sqn Ldr 1/7/96. Retd OPS SPT 3/6/02.
MARTIN L.G.P. CBE FCMI. Born 28/7/20. Commd 8/3/43. A Cdre 1/7/72. Retd GD 27/11/76.
MARTIN L.S. Born 6/1/21. Commd 27/4/44. Wg Cdr 1/7/69. Retd ENG 6/1/76.
MARTIN M.F. Born 12/3/39. Commd 2/5/59. Flt Lt 2/11/64. Retd GD 12/3/77.
MARTIN M.L. MCMI. Born 13/12/50. Commd 11/6/81. Sqn Ldr 1/1/90. Retd ENGINEER 6/4/05.
MARTIN P. BA. Born 29/1/49. Commd 3/1/68. Sqn Ldr 1/7/95. Retd FLY(P) 14/3/05.
MARTIN P. Born 20/4/52. Commd 16/2/89. Flt Lt 16/2/93. Retd ENG 3/4/93.
MARTIN P.G. Born 20/7/33. Commd 4/6/44. Fg Offr 4/6/64. Retd ENG 10/10/69. rtg Flt Lt.
MARTIN P.G. Born 4/2/34. Commd 15/10/52. Sqn Ldr 1/1/69. Retd SUP 4/2/73.
MARTIN P.J. BSc. Born 31/8/43. Commd 29/11/81. Sqn Ldr 1/1/90. Retd ENG 14/9/96.
MARTIN P.S. DFC. Born 13/10/35. Commd 17/12/57. Sqn Ldr 1/7/66. Retd GD 25/1/69.
MARTIN R.F. DFC* AFC. Born 26/7/18. Commd 29/7/39. Wg Cdr 1/1/51. Retd GD 1/7/53.
MARTIN R.F.H. Born 17/2/23. Commd 7/3/42. Sqn Ldr 1/1/53. Retd GD 17/2/66.
MARTIN R.J. Born 30/1/33. Commd 9/4/52. Gp Capt 1/7/82. Retd GD(G) 30/1/88.
MARTIN R.J.W. Born 8/7/20. Commd 17/8/50. Flt Lt 17/2/55. Retd RGT 2/5/68. rtg Sqn Ldr.
MARTIN R.M. Born 14/9/21. Commd 27/4/40. Gp Capt 1/7/69. Retd SEC 14/9/75.
MARTIN R.R. Born 11/3/32. Commd 17/12/52. Flt Lt 17/6/55. Retd GD 26/4/61.
MARTIN S.E. MILT. Born 5/5/45. Commd 9/3/66. Sqn Ldr 1/1/84. Retd SUP 5/5/00.
MARTIN S.H. OBE. Born 9/11/19. Commd 1/5/42. Wg Cdr 1/7/58. Retd GD 2/6/68.
MARTIN S.J. BSc. Born 24/11/55. Commd 15/9/74. Flt Lt 15/10/78. Retd GD 15/7/89.
MARTIN S.L. Born 22/7/56. Commd 5/4/79. Flt Lt 5/10/84. Retd GD 30/4/96.
MARTIN S.V. BSc CEng MRAeS DLUT. Born 13/4/50. Commd 8/11/68. Wg Cdr 1/7/87. Retd ENG 1/7/90.
MARTIN T.C.D. Born 5/11/38. Commd 7/5/64. Flt Lt 10/2/67. Retd ENG 5/11/76.

MARTIN T.J. Born 22/2/36. Commd 17/3/67. Flt Lt 17/3/69. Retd GD 17/3/75.
MARTIN T.T. Born 14/1/47. Commd 23/9/65. Sqn Ldr 1/7/80. Retd SY 14/1/85.
MARTIN W.B. Born 21/6/59. Commd 18/11/78. Flt Lt 18/11/83. Retd GD 1/7/89.
MARTIN W.D. BA. Born 4/7/44. Commd 16/1/67. Sqn Ldr 1/1/76. Retd GD 1/5/84.
MARTIN W.D.E. Born 9/1/22. Commd 21/6/56. Flt Lt 21/6/62. Retd GD 1/3/68.
MARTIN W.L. Born 19/9/14. Commd 15/7/43. Flt Lt 5/4/49. Retd SEC 1/3/68.
MARTIN-JONES I.L. MSc. Born 14/3/29. Commd 18/10/51. Wg Cdr 1/1/69. Retd ENG 14/3/84.
MARTIN-POPE A. Born 7/9/28. Commd 6/3/67. Sqn Ldr 1/7/77. Retd ENG 7/9/89.
MARTIN-SMITH P.R. Born 10/8/46. Commd 18/8/67. Wg Cdr 1/1/90. Retd GD 14/3/97.
MARTINDALE A.R. CB BA FCMI. Born 20/1/30. Commd 3/5/51. AVM 1/1/83. Retd SUP 20/1/85.
MARTINDALE I. Born 4/2/48. Commd 8/9/83. Sqn Ldr 1/1/93. Retd ENGINEER 4/2/03.
MARTINDALE I.C. Born 3/12/45. Commd 6/5/66. Fg Offr 6/5/68. Retd GD 6/6/70.
MARTINDALE J.H. Born 17/9/44. Commd 1/4/71. Flt Lt 1/4/73. Retd SUP 28/6/75.
MARTINS M.D. Born 11/2/33. Commd 4/5/72. Flt Lt 4/5/76. Retd GD(G) 11/5/88.
MARTYN C.A. Born 9/5/55. Commd 17/9/72. Sqn Ldr 1/7/87. Retd GD 1/8/95.
MARTYN K.P. Born 30/3/28. Commd 8/11/68. Flt Lt 8/11/71. Retd GD 1/4/76.
MARTYN R.D. Born 15/4/32. Commd 28/2/54. Wg Cdr 1/7/75. Retd ADMIN 6/7/77.
MARTYN W.J. Born 18/4/23. Commd 10/12/47. Flt Lt 12/8/56. Retd GD 31/3/62.
MARVELL C.B. BEng CEng MIEE. Born 12/2/67. Commd 2/8/85. Sqn Ldr 1/1/99. Retd ENGINEER 12/2/05.
MARWOOD I.F. BSc(Eng). Born 11/11/53. Commd 2/9/73. Sqn Ldr 1/1/85. Retd ENG 11/11/91.
MARWOOD K.M. AFM. Born 4/1/30. Commd 10/11/53. Wg Cdr 1/1/77. Retd GD 4/1/85.
MASEFIELD B.J. Born 19/5/43. Commd 28/6/76. Sqn Ldr 1/7/91. Retd GD 31/12/93.
MASEFIELD R.M. Born 12/7/43. Commd 17/5/62. Sqn Ldr 1/1/80. Retd GD 12/7/87.
MASHEDER M.A. Born 4/3/47. Commd 17/2/67. Flt Lt 17/8/72. Retd GD 4/3/85.
MASKELL C.J. BSc CEng MIMechE. Born 2/10/44. Commd 15/7/66. Gp Capt 1/1/90. Retd ENG 14/9/96.
MASKELL H.H.A. Born 27/1/14. Commd 25/5/50. Flt Lt 25/11/53. Retd CAT 27/1/61.
MASKELL N.W. CEng FIEE FCMI MRAeS. Born 10/4/20. Commd 16/8/41. Gp Capt 1/7/65. Retd ENG 10/4/75.
MASLEN K.C. Born 2/3/21. Commd 16/8/44. Flt Lt 13/11/57. Retd GD 30/1/69.
MASLIN D. Born 2/1/42. Commd 18/12/62. Flt Lt 18/6/65. Retd GD 1/7/70.
MASON A.L. Born 31/8/18. Commd 3/3/42. Flt Lt 20/11/50. Retd SEC 21/11/61.
MASON A.R. MRIN. Born 23/9/29. Commd 12/9/51. Gp Capt 1/1/74. Retd GD 23/9/84.
MASON B. Born 13/3/31. Commd 24/10/51. Flt Lt 13/4/60. Retd GD(G) 13/3/86.
MASON B.H.D. Born 19/3/35. Commd 17/6/54. Sqn Ldr 1/1/72. Retd GD 31/1/84.
MASON B.I. OBE FCMI. Born 17/5/37. Commd 1/4/58. Wg Cdr 1/1/80. Retd ADMIN 25/4/90.
MASON B.J. MA MCMI. Born 22/1/35. Commd 12/9/58. Sqn Ldr 12/3/65. Retd EDN 12/9/74.
MASON B.T. MBE. Born 8/3/46. Commd 20/9/79. Flt Lt 20/9/81. Retd ENG 19/9/87. Re-entrant 16/10/89. Sqn Ldr 1/1/92.
    Retd ENG 14/3/96.
MASON D. BSc. Born 17/2/62. Commd 14/10/84. Sqn Ldr 1/1/98. Retd GD 1/1/01.
MASON D. BA. Born 25/1/35. Commd 29/7/65. Sqn Ldr 3/10/73. Retd EDN 1/11/75.
MASON D.R. MBE LLB. Born 15/3/59. Commd 20/12/80. Wg Cdr 1/1/96. Retd GD 1/1/99.
MASON D.R. Born 10/4/46. Commd 9/3/72. Sqn Ldr 1/7/83. Retd GD 10/1/87.
MASON F.K. Born 4/9/28. Commd 11/4/51. Fg Offr 11/4/53. Retd GD(G) 20/7/56.
MASON G. Born 20/7/63. Commd 15/10/81. Sqn Ldr 1/1/98. Retd GD 20/7/01.
MASON G.A. DFC FCMI. Born 20/12/21. Commd 20/8/42. A Cdre 1/1/72. Retd GD 26/3/77.
MASON G.E. Born 3/3/33. Commd 21/11/51. Flt Lt 6/3/57. Retd GD 3/3/71.
MASON G.J.A. Born 24/11/05. Commd 26/5/42. Fg Offr 1/1/43. Retd ENG 9/3/46. rtg Flt Lt.
MASON G.L. Born 14/11/45. Commd 22/9/64. Sqn Ldr 1/1/76. Retd SUP 1/10/79.
MASON I.M. Born 9/4/44. Commd 17/12/65. Flt Lt 17/3/71. Retd GD 22/10/94.
MASON J. Born 3/2/48. Commd 23/9/66. Sqn Ldr 1/7/84. Retd SUP 1/7/96.
MASON J.K.F. CBE MD BChir MRCPath DCP DMJ DTM&H. Born 19/12/19. Commd 12/8/43. Gp Capt 1/7/63.
    Retd MED 14/8/73.
MASON J.S. CBE CEng MRAeS. Born 25/10/17. Commd 20/9/40. A Cdre 1/1/69. Retd ENG 5/12/72.
MASON J.W. Born 25/2/16. Commd 5/11/42. Flt Lt 5/5/46. Retd ENG 9/1/54.
MASON K. Born 19/2/48. Commd 14/2/69. Flt Lt 14/8/74. Retd GD 1/7/00.
MASON M.D. Born 5/7/39. Commd 22/8/59. Fg Offr 22/8/62. Retd GD(G) 20/11/66. Re-instated 26/8/70.
    Sqn Ldr 17/7/89. Retd GD(G) 3/5/94.
MASON M.D.L. BSc CEng MIEE MIMechE MRAeS MCMI. Born 1/6/38. Commd 30/7/59. Sqn Ldr 1/1/71.
    Retd ENG 1/6/76.
MASON M.I. Born 13/3/67. Commd 12/3/87. Flt Lt 12/9/93. Retd OPS SPT(REGT) 13/3/05.
MASON M.S. OBE. Born 24/5/45. Commd 23/11/78. Gp Capt 1/7/95. Retd ENG 28/9/96.
MASON N.C. MA MSc MB BChir DAvMed AFOM. Born 17/3/46. Commd 29/4/68. Wg Cdr 10/9/84.
    Retd MED 29/4/90.
MASON N.J. Born 1/4/30. Commd 1/8/51. Fg Offr 1/8/53. Retd SEC 1/5/57.
MASON P.F. MB ChB FRCS(Edin) DAvMed. Born 5/11/59. Commd 21/7/81. Wg Cdr 1/8/97. Retd MED 1/10/99.
MASON P.J. Born 18/4/38. Commd 11/6/60. Sqn Ldr 1/7/83. Retd GD 18/4/93.
MASON P.J. BA. Born 8/6/61. Commd 2/9/79. Sqn Ldr 1/7/93. Retd ADMIN 14/9/96.

MASON P.J.D. Born 20/9/50. Commd 20/12/73. Sqn Ldr 1/7/88. Retd GD 14/11/91.
MASON R.A. CB CBE MA. Born 22/10/32. Commd 29/6/56. AVM 1/1/86. Retd ADMIN 22/4/89.
MASON R.J. Born 9/3/51. Commd 5/11/70. Flt Lt 5/5/75. Retd GD 2/2/82.
MASON R.L. BSc. Born 4/9/30. Commd 18/2/54. Sqn Ldr 1/1/65. Retd ENG 4/9/80.
MASON R.S. MBE ACIS. Born 12/3/20. Commd 18/3/43. Wg Cdr 1/7/62. Retd SEC 13/1/68.
MASON S. Born 30/6/24. Commd 29/10/64. Flt Lt 29/10/67. Retd GD 30/6/84.
MASON S.B. Born 22/5/58. Commd 29/7/83. Flt Lt 19/8/86. Retd GD 22/5/96.
MASON T. Born 27/8/37. Commd 28/2/56. Sqn Ldr 1/7/70. Retd GD 27/8/84.
MASON T.C.W. Born 20/5/36. Commd 10/2/72. Flt Lt 10/2/78. Retd ENG 16/4/91.
MASON W.M. DSO DFC. Born 2/6/14. Commd 10/1/42. Wg Cdr 1/7/54. Retd GD 5/7/61.
MASSEY A.J. Born 7/1/67. Commd 31/7/86. Fg Offr 31/7/88. Retd GD 1/7/91.
MASSEY C. MCIPD MCMI. Born 30/7/33. Commd 11/12/52. Sqn Ldr 1/1/68. Retd ADMIN 24/9/76.
MASSEY C.J. Born 4/12/45. Commd 22/5/70. Flt Lt 22/11/75. Retd GD 20/1/92.
MASSEY G.W. Born 31/8/22. Commd 11/2/44. Sqn Ldr 1/10/54. Retd GD 31/8/71.
MASSEY R.G. MCMI. Born 10/12/42. Commd 22/7/71. Sqn Ldr 1/7/80. Retd ADMIN 10/12/97.
MASSEY W.J. MBE. Born 21/4/32. Commd 9/4/52. Wg Cdr 1/1/81. Retd GD 2/1/86.
MASSIE G.A. Born 11/5/30. Commd 14/11/51. Wg Cdr 1/1/72. Retd GD 14/5/83.
MASSIE G.W.S. Born 21/4/42. Commd 12/1/61. Flt Lt 1/7/68. Retd SEC 28/6/73.
MASTERMAN C.S. CEng MRAeS MIMechE. Born 29/6/42. Commd 24/9/64. Sqn Ldr 1/1/75. Retd ENG 29/6/80.
MASTERMAN D.L. MA. Born 7/7/41. Commd 6/9/65. Sqn Ldr 1/1/78. Retd GD 6/9/81.
MASTERMAN P.G. Born 7/3/35. Commd 19/8/53. Wg Cdr 1/1/78. Retd GD 1/1/86.
MASTERS B.M. Born 20/11/28. Commd 4/8/54. Flt Lt 21/10/59. Retd GD 20/11/83.
MASTERS C.W. Born 3/5/56. Commd 2/8/90. Sqn Ldr 1/7/98. Retd SUP 1/7/01.
MASTERS M.C.H. BA. Born 24/11/59. Commd 26/9/82. Flt Lt 26/12/83. Retd GD 26/9/98.
MASTERS M.I. BSc. Born 27/3/47. Commd 17/12/72. Flt Lt 17/6/73. Retd GD 11/9/74.
MASTERS S.M. Born 16/8/61. Commd 14/8/80. Sqn Ldr 1/7/93. Retd GD 1/10/98.
MASTERTON R.G. BSc MB ChB MRCPath MCMI DipGUM. Born 19/4/53. Commd 14/5/74. Sqn Ldr 1/8/83.
    Retd MED 19/4/91.
MASTIN P.J. Born 5/9/28. Commd 23/9/66. Flt Lt 8/1/69. Retd SEC 23/9/74.
MATCHAM G.M. Born 30/3/25. Commd 1/10/50. Wg Cdr 1/7/66. Retd GD 30/3/80.
MATES W.A.J. MDA MCIPS. Born 1/11/48. Commd 30/6/70. Sqn Ldr 1/1/83. Retd SUP 18/12/90.
MATHER D.A. BA. Born 7/12/67. Commd 15/9/85. Flt Lt 15/1/91. Retd GD 15/7/00.
MATHERS B.H. Born 18/2/35. Commd 18/5/56. Sqn Ldr 1/7/72. Retd SUP 18/2/93.
MATHERS D.K. Born 22/4/22. Commd 12/4/45. Flt Lt 4/6/53. Retd GD 26/4/77.
MATHESON N.G. Born 10/3/50. Commd 26/2/71. Wg Cdr 1/1/90. Retd GD 10/3/94.
MATHEWS A.T. BSc CEng MRAeS. Born 22/3/13. Commd 26/9/39. Wg Cdr 1/7/55. Retd EDN 22/3/68.
MATHEWS J. CEng MRAeS MIEE MCMI. Born 5/12/22. Commd 17/2/44. A Cdre 1/1/75. Retd ENG 1/11/77.
MATHEWS M.F.J. AFC. Born 8/8/22. Commd 25/9/42. Wg Cdr 1/1/63. Retd GD 8/8/77.
MATHIAS D.A. BSc. Born 9/8/46. Commd 3/11/74. Flt Lt 3/8/78. Retd ADMIN 6/11/82.
MATHIE A.R.C. Born 10/5/44. Commd 24/6/65. Wg Cdr 1/7/89. Retd GD 3/4/92.
MATHIESON D. Born 12/12/59. Commd 14/8/80. Flt Lt 14/2/86. Retd GD 12/12/97.
MATHIESON K.R. BSc. Born 9/4/41. Commd 1/10/62. Sqn Ldr 1/1/76. Retd GD 9/4/79.
MATHIESON P. BSc. Born 3/7/63. Commd 7/6/87. Sqn Ldr 1/1/99. Retd ADMIN (SEC) 1/11/03.
MATON J.C. Born 1/7/44. Commd 1/4/71. Sqn Ldr 1/1/80. Retd ADMIN 1/1/83.
MATSON H.J.D. AFC. Born 10/10/15. Commd 27/6/38. Sqn Ldr 1/9/45. Retd GD 27/12/58. rtg Wg Cdr.
MATSON K.E. BA DipEd. Born 22/9/40. Commd 2/1/67. Wg Cdr 1/1/85. Retd ADMIN 5/4/91.
MATSON R.E. Born 3/1/40. Commd 12/7/63. Flt Lt 12/1/69. Retd GD 1/10/90.
MATTEY G.L. CBE DFC AFC. Born 10/3/18. Commd 15/6/40. Gp Capt 1/7/63. Retd GD 2/6/66.
MATTHEW A.L. DFC. Born 28/3/22. Commd 31/8/43. Sqn Ldr 1/7/57. Retd GD 28/3/65.
MATTHEWMAN D.G. Born 5/6/61. Commd 26/9/90. Flt Lt 26/9/92. Retd ADMIN 20/2/97.
MATTHEWS A.G. Born 17/2/29. Commd 24/9/52. Flt Lt 21/2/58. Retd GD 11/9/76.
MATTHEWS A.P. OBE. Born 7/9/48. Commd 1/8/69. Gp Capt 1/7/89. Retd SUP 1/4/91.
MATTHEWS A.R. Born 28/9/45. Commd 6/5/66. Wg Cdr 1/1/91. Retd GD 31/3/94.
MATTHEWS C.D. Born 13/9/25. Commd 24/1/52. Flt Lt 1/10/58. Retd SUP 5/10/68.
MATTHEWS D.C. BSc. Born 19/7/54. Commd 6/3/77. Sqn Ldr 1/7/84. Retd GD 11/3/89. Re-entrant 7/1/91.
    Sqn Ldr 29/4/86. Retd GD 14/3/96.
MATTHEWS D.J. Born 25/1/38. Commd 27/2/67. Flt Lt 29/6/74. Retd ENG 29/6/80.
MATTHEWS D.J.P. DFC. Born 15/3/22. Commd 9/8/43. Sqn Ldr 1/7/66. Retd GD(G) 29/9/70.
MATTHEWS D.O. BPharm FDS BDS LDSRCS. Born 21/8/34. Commd 7/2/58. A Cdre 1/7/90. Retd DEL 14/8/93.
MATTHEWS E. OBE. Born 9/8/27. Commd 13/2/52. Wg Cdr 1/7/69. Retd GD 3/4/77.
MATTHEWS G.L. Born 24/3/61. Commd 5/4/79. Flt Lt 5/10/84. Retd GD 1/4/87.
MATTHEWS G.R. Born 18/9/44. Commd 4/12/64. Flt Lt 4/5/72. Retd GD 7/10/76.
MATTHEWS I.D. Born 10/7/49. Commd 11/8/77. Sqn Ldr 1/1/87. Retd ENG 1/1/90.
MATTHEWS J. Born 28/10/38. Commd 29/11/63. Flt Lt 9/2/68. Retd GD 28/10/76.
MATTHEWS J.B. Born 21/7/20. Commd 5/11/52. Sqn Ldr 1/7/73. Retd GD 21/7/84.
MATTHEWS J.G. CBE AFC. Born 5/1/24. Commd 20/9/47. A Cdre 1/7/74. Retd GD 2/8/77.

MATTHEWS L.T. Born 20/10/46. Commd 11/9/64. Flt Lt 10/3/70. Retd GD 22/10/76.
MATTHEWS L.U. MCMI. Born 20/3/26. Commd 17/7/46. Gp Capt 1/1/75. Retd GD 16/5/78.
MATTHEWS M.J. BA MBCS MCMI. Born 25/9/32. Commd 14/12/54. Wg Cdr 1/1/76. Retd ADMIN 14/8/87.
MATTHEWS N. Born 8/1/36. Commd 11/3/65. Sqn Ldr 1/1/84. Retd GD(G) 8/1/91.
MATTHEWS N. Born 21/4/61. Commd 18/3/87. Sqn Ldr 1/1/95. Retd ENG 21/4/99.
MATTHEWS P.B. Born 11/6/16. Commd 30/3/44. Flt Lt 30/9/48. Retd GD(G) 11/6/69.
MATTHEWS R.L. Born 31/10/26. Commd 12/2/53. Flt Lt 12/8/56. Retd GD(G) 2/11/82.
MATTHEWS R.T. Born 14/12/21. Commd 19/5/49. Sqn Ldr 1/1/64. Retd SUP 14/12/76.
MATTHEWS S.I. Born 3/8/46. Commd 29/11/68. Sqn Ldr 1/1/95. Retd GD 31/5/98.
MATTHEWS T.J. BSc. Born 19/10/48. Commd 23/11/78. Sqn Ldr 1/7/87. Retd ENGINEER 19/10/03.
MATTHEWSON D.A.J. Born 27/5/43. Commd 2/4/65. Flt Lt 2/10/70. Retd GD 6/10/72.
MATTICK A.A. MSc BSc. Born 16/4/48. Commd 12/12/71. Sqn Ldr 12/6/79. Retd ADMIN 6/1/95.
MATTICK A.D. Born 10/9/23. Commd 26/9/57. Sqn Ldr 1/7/75. Retd ENG 29/4/78.
MATTIMOE I.C. BSc. Born 24/6/52. Commd 13/9/70. Sqn Ldr 1/7/84. Retd GD 24/6/90.
MATTOCK A.V. Born 9/12/23. Commd 23/9/44. Flt Lt 18/10/49. Retd GD 5/1/67.
MATTOCK J.E. Born 10/5/14. Commd 30/9/42. Sqn Offr 1/7/53. Retd SUP 10/5/63.
MAUD J.M. Born 22/12/25. Commd 27/4/45. Wg Cdr 1/1/65. Retd GD 7/8/76.
MAUDE A.F. Born 6/7/23. Commd 30/12/42. Flt Lt 30/12/44. Retd GD(G) 1/2/74.
MAUDE J.V. CEng MIMechE MRAeS. Born 20/8/37. Commd 28/7/60. Sqn Ldr 1/7/69. Retd ENG 19/8/89.
MAUGHAN C.G. CB CBE AFC. Born 3/3/23. Commd 14/3/49. AVM 1/1/75. Retd GD 3/3/78.
MAUGHAN M. MSc BSc. Born 16/7/48. Commd 13/2/72. Sqn Ldr 13/4/79. Retd ADMIN 13/2/91.
MAULTBY J.M. BA. Born 17/12/36. Commd 2/10/58. Sqn Ldr 1/1/71. Retd GD 17/12/94.
MAUND H.G. Born 8/5/39. Commd 29/2/60. Flt Lt 25/7/66. Retd GD(G) 8/5/77.
MAUNDER M.J. Born 2/3/43. Commd 3/11/69. Wg Cdr 1/7/86. Retd ENG 30/6/98.
MAUNDER R.A. Born 26/7/37. Commd 5/11/70. Flt Lt 5/11/72. Retd SUP 5/11/79.
MAUNDERS D.A. Born 12/9/23. Commd 28/9/55. Flt Lt 25/8/61. Retd GD 31/12/68.
MAUNSELL-THOMAS J.R. Born 11/8/37. Commd 29/7/58. Flt Lt 29/1/61. Retd GD 9/11/68.
MAURICE D.J. FCA. Born 26/11/39. Commd 10/12/63. Wg Cdr 1/7/78. Retd SEC 1/7/81.
MAURICE-JONES D.W. MA. Born 10/8/37. Commd 24/8/59. Gp Capt 1/7/84. Retd GD 10/8/94.
MAVIN A.V. Born 30/12/40. Commd 6/9/68. Flt Lt 6/9/70. Retd GD 10/1/91.
MAVOR R.I.D. Born 23/10/66. Commd 27/3/86. Sqn Ldr 1/1/98. Retd GD 1/2/99.
MAW J.M.T. Born 21/6/36. Commd 22/1/55. Flt Lt 18/10/62. Retd GD 4/8/81.
MAWBY A. Born 17/10/34. Commd 9/7/57. Flt Lt 17/1/68. Retd GD(G) 10/6/83.
MAWBY A.J. OBE BSc. Born 8/12/44. Commd 30/8/66. Wg Cdr 1/1/87. Retd GD 8/12/00.
MAWDSLEY D.E. Born 25/9/43. Commd 21/10/66. Wg Cdr 1/1/81. Retd ENG 21/5/93.
MAWDSLEY J. Born 1/11/13. Commd 22/4/43. Flt Lt 22/10/46. Retd ENG 1/5/54.
MAWER J. Born 22/3/29. Commd 26/10/50. Sqn Ldr 1/1/64. Retd SUP 22/9/88.
MAWHINNEY J. Born 7/8/43. Commd 17/12/64. Sqn Ldr 1/7/75. Retd GD 7/8/81.
MAWSON E.F.P. Born 1/7/57. Commd 24/7/81. Sqn Ldr 1/7/91. Retd ENG 1/7/95.
MAWSON S.J. BDS MCMI. Born 28/1/48. Commd 5/1/69. Wg Cdr 24/1/84. Retd DEL 11/5/93.
MAX R.D. DSO DFC. Born 24/11/18. Commd 23/8/38. Gp Capt 1/1/60. Retd GD 24/11/68.
MAXEY I.H. MSc BA. Born 28/10/43. Commd 26/11/81. Sqn Ldr 1/1/90. Retd ENG 6/4/96.
MAXWELL A.M.L. LLB. Born 15/6/38. Commd 12/12/59. Wg Cdr 1/7/87. Retd GD 28/10/90.
MAXWELL I.A. BSc. Born 30/6/50. Commd 13/9/70. Sqn Ldr 1/1/87. Retd GD 1/1/90.
MAXWELL J. Born 22/5/21. Commd 15/5/42. Wg Cdr 1/7/69. Retd GD(G) 30/3/78.
MAXWELL T.J. DFC. Born 10/6/24. Commd 29/7/44. Flt Lt 4/2/56. Retd GD(G) 28/7/76.
MAXWELL W.A. MB BS FRCS(Edin) MRCS(Eng) LRCP. Born 26/7/52. Commd 5/12/72. Wg Cdr 9/2/90.
 Retd MED 1/10/91.
MAY A. Born 13/2/18. Commd 13/5/42. Sqn Ldr 1/1/54. Retd ENG 24/2/67.
MAY D.McM. Born 6/2/20. Commd 7/11/46. Fg Offr 7/11/47. Retd SEC 7/4/50.
MAY D.R. Born 6/4/31. Commd 30/7/52. Flt Lt 27/12/57. Retd GD 6/4/69.
MAY D.T. Born 18/4/38. Commd 24/7/61. Flt Lt 1/4/66. Retd GD 15/3/72.
MAY J.A.G. CB CBE. Born 12/11/41. Commd 9/3/62. AVM 1/1/93. Retd GD 12/4/97.
MAY J.E. BSc(Eng). Born 17/6/63. Commd 29/9/85. Flt Lt 29/3/88. Retd GD 23/4/02.
MAY J.W. DFC. Born 8/7/22. Commd 17/4/43. Flt Lt 17/10/46. Retd GD 18/1/50.
MAY J.W. Born 6/11/34. Commd 24/11/60. Flt Lt 24/11/60. Retd GD 1/4/69.
MAY M.M. Born 7/1/55. Commd 11/5/80. Flt Lt 8/3/81. Retd RGT 30/9/81.
MAY N. Born 4/11/46. Commd 17/2/67. Sqn Ldr 1/1/87. Retd GD 27/7/00.
MAY N.P. Born 17/8/34. Commd 30/9/65. Flt Lt 30/9/65. Retd GD 4/9/76.
MAY P. Born 25/11/25. Commd 28/11/46. Flt Lt 17/5/56. Retd RGT 29/5/59.
MAYALL P.V. CBE FCMI. Born 18/4/31. Commd 31/8/51. A Cdre 1/1/83. Retd GD 18/4/86.
MAYBURY P.L. MA MB BCh FFCM MFOM. Born 10/8/28. Commd 24/10/54. Gp Capt 1/1/76. Retd MED 11/12/82.
 rtg A Cdre.
MAYCOCK R.E. Born 14/4/26. Commd 18/5/61. Flt Lt 18/5/67. Retd ENG 14/4/86.
MAYDWELL W.S.G. DSO DFC. Born 18/7/13. Commd 19/5/37. Wg Cdr 1/10/46. Retd GD 12/3/58. rtg Gp Capt.
MAYER W.L.M. AFC. Born 1/7/41. Commd 31/1/64. Wg Cdr 1/1/82. Retd GD 30/6/92.

MAYERS B.J.W. Born 25/3/46. Commd 27/3/75. Flt Lt 27/3/77. Retd GD 25/3/84.
MAYERS C. Born 27/3/21. Commd 8/1/44. Flt Lt 7/4/58. Retd GD 31/7/68.
MAYES H.E.B. Born 17/6/36. Commd 9/4/57. Sqn Ldr 1/7/69. Retd GD 7/11/75.
MAYES J.E.C. Born 24/2/34. Commd 9/11/54. Sqn Ldr 1/7/65. Retd GD 30/10/71.
MAYES M.W. Born 18/6/21. Commd 24/2/44. Flt Lt 4/6/53. Retd GD(G) 15/6/65.
MAYES P.W. Born 9/9/36. Commd 2/5/59. Wg Cdr 1/1/78. Retd GD 9/11/91.
MAYES R. BSc. Born 11/6/46. Commd 8/9/69. Flt Lt 8/6/71. Retd GD 23/12/86.
MAYES R.W. OBE PhD BSc CChem FRSC. Born 15/8/43. Commd 14/8/77. Wg Cdr 1/1/95. Retd MED(T) 15/8/99.
MAYHEW J.B. Born 26/7/31. Commd 11/9/56. Flt Lt 11/3/62. Retd GD 26/7/69.
MAYHEW S.M. Born 31/8/70. Commd 22/6/89. Flt Lt 22/12/95. Retd OPS SPT(ATC) 31/7/03.
MAYNARD G. Born 17/4/23. Commd 27/3/45. Flt Lt 24/1/66. Retd GD 18/4/73.
MAYNARD G.J.D. CBE. Born 30/6/42. Commd 17/12/63. A Cdre 1/7/90. Retd SUP 30/6/97.
MAYNARD J.C. BA. Born 16/3/60. Commd 3/10/78. Flt Lt 15/10/82. Retd GD 3/10/98.
MAYNARD J.J. Born 18/4/34. Commd 26/11/52. Wg Cdr 1/1/75. Retd GD 18/10/89.
MAYNARD L.C. OBE MCMI. Born 7/7/22. Commd 13/12/43. Wg Cdr 1/7/61. Retd GD 9/1/69.
MAYNARD L.H. CBE. Born 2/4/07. Commd 18/4/40. Gp Offr 1/7/52. Retd SEC 23/6/62.
MAYNARD M.J. BSc. Born 23/2/37. Commd 1/2/60. Sqn Ldr 1/8/67. Retd EDN 1/2/76.
MAYNARD M.R. Born 28/2/59. Commd 24/9/92. Flt Lt 24/9/98. Retd MED(T) 31/10/00.
MAYNARD P. BSc. Born 2/6/57. Commd 17/8/80. Flt Lt 17/5/82. Retd GD 17/8/96.
MAYNE J.L. Born 30/7/52. Commd 11/9/86. Flt Lt 11/9/88. Retd GD 16/2/97.
MAYNE K.M. Born 12/10/57. Commd 20/9/79. Sqn Ldr 1/1/90. Retd ADMIN 1/11/95.
MAYNE L.S.H. Born 17/10/46. Commd 6/10/69. Wg Cdr 1/7/92. Retd ADMIN 14/3/97.
MAYNER B.G. Born 31/8/34. Commd 30/7/52. Sqn Ldr 1/7/83. Retd GD 31/8/89.
MAYNERD D. BSc. Born 28/5/47. Commd 19/2/73. Flt Lt 19/5/73. Retd GD 20/7/77.
MAYO A.M. MSc CEng MIERE MITD CertEd. Born 12/8/42. Commd 11/8/77. Sqn Ldr 1/1/84. Retd ADMIN 2/10/88.
MAYO J.M.A. Born 18/3/47. Commd 18/4/74. Wg Cdr 1/1/88. Retd SUP 15/11/96.
MAYS E.J. Born 14/7/42. Commd 15/10/81. Sqn Ldr 1/7/91. Retd ENG 14/7/98.
MAYS J.S. Born 12/7/37. Commd 20/8/55. Wg Cdr 1/7/80. Retd SUP 15/6/90.
MAZURK J.E. Born 22/2/45. Commd 15/7/66. Flt Lt 15/1/69. Retd GD 4/3/75.
MCADAM D.W. DFC. Born 18/5/17. Commd 20/6/43. Sqn Ldr 1/10/54. Retd GD 12/7/60.
MCADAM P.A. Born 29/5/31. Commd 9/4/53. Flt Lt 18/8/58. Retd GD 29/5/69.
MCALEESE J. Born 21/1/51. Commd 11/11/71. Fg Offr 11/11/73. Retd GD 30/8/75.
MCALISTER D. Born 1/3/45. Commd 17/2/67. Flt Lt 4/11/70. Retd GD 2/3/76.
MCALL D. MDA. Born 8/5/59. Commd 11/6/81. Wg Cdr 1/1/97. Retd ADMIN 2/7/01.
MCALLEN K.A. AFC. Born 6/1/23. Commd 3/12/59. Flt Lt 3/12/62. Retd GD 2/7/68.
MCALLISTER C.P. Born 11/9/18. Commd 27/3/47. Flt Lt 27/9/51. Retd SUP 13/9/67.
MCALLISTER D. Born 8/4/50. Commd 19/9/71. Sqn Ldr 1/1/81. Retd ADMIN 8/4/88.
MCALLISTER V.S. MA. Born 19/7/17. Commd 16/2/49. Sqn Ldr 20/3/59. Retd EDN 10/5/72.
MCANDREW S. CEng MIMechE MRAeS. Born 23/11/44. Commd 15/7/66. Sqn Ldr 1/7/79. Retd ENG 14/3/96.
MCARDLE L. DFC. Born 14/8/21. Commd 5/3/41. Wg Cdr 1/7/59. Retd GD 30/7/65.
MCARDLE M.P. Born 2/5/44. Commd 29/11/63. Flt Lt 29/5/69. Retd GD 15/8/70.
MCAREAVEY H.I.B. Born 26/3/42. Commd 22/2/63. Flt Lt 8/1/69. Retd GD 28/3/79.
MCARTHUR D.A. Born 26/5/34. Commd 5/4/55. Sqn Ldr 1/7/64. Retd GD 26/5/72.
MCARTHUR J.A. AFC. Born 14/2/30. Commd 11/4/51. Sqn Ldr 1/1/59. Retd GD 14/2/68.
MCARTHUR W.P. Born 2/2/44. Commd 7/2/71. Sqn Ldr 1/7/83. Retd ENG 7/2/89.
MCATHEY G. BA. Born 19/4/37. Commd 6/2/67. Sqn Ldr 8/10/75. Retd ADMIN 4/4/89.
MCAULEY D. Born 12/7/65. Commd 8/6/84. Sqn Ldr 1/7/99. Retd FLY(P) 31/10/03.
MCAULEY G.M. Born 23/6/44. Commd 25/6/65. Flt Lt 23/12/69. Retd GD 1/11/77.
MCAULIFFE K.M.F. Born 31/12/53. Commd 9/10/75. Sqn Ldr 1/1/88. Retd GD 31/12/91.
MCAUSLAN D.N. BSc. Born 29/5/36. Commd 1/10/57. Sqn Ldr 1/1/71. Retd GD 1/6/84.
MCAVOY G.B. The Rev. MBE MA BA. Born 9/6/41. Commd 7/10/68. Retd Wg Cdr 31/12/95.
MCBEATH M. Born 4/12/42. Commd 19/1/64. Flt Lt 19/7/68. Retd GD 28/6/93.
MCBOYLE J.H. BSc. Born 13/12/54. Commd 20/5/79. Flt Lt 20/8/79. Retd GD 17/12/88.
MCBRIDE I.A.D. BSc. Born 21/8/39. Commd 11/6/62. Flt Lt 30/9/63. Retd GD 3/7/91.
MCBRIEN T. Born 27/4/53. Commd 8/12/83. Flt Lt 8/12/85. Retd ENG 8/12/97.
MCBURNEY A.E. Born 28/2/49. Commd 19/12/77. Sqn Ldr 1/7/84. Retd ADMIN (SEC) 28/8/04.
MCBURNEY K.M. Born 3/3/46. Commd 18/8/67. Sqn Ldr 1/1/80. Retd GD 3/3/97.
MCCABE B.A. Born 18/10/23. Commd 1/4/45. Flt Lt 27/5/54. Retd GD 22/7/65.
MCCABE E.T. OBE CEng MRAeS. Born 7/5/14. Commd 17/8/40. Gp Capt 1/1/60. Retd ENG 7/5/69.
MCCABE J. Born 10/6/50. Commd 15/8/89. Flt Lt 15/8/69. Retd ADMIN 30/7/93.
MCCABE J. OBE. Born 1/6/34. Commd 4/6/52. Wg Cdr 1/1/85. Retd GD 31/1/87.
MCCABE M.J. Born 31/8/36. Commd 23/7/58. Sqn Ldr 1/1/68. Retd ENG 29/7/77. Re-instated 29/10/79.
　　Sqn Ldr 3/4/70. Retd ENG 31/8/91.
MCCAFFERTY J.B. MB BS DMRD FRCR. Born 23/4/34. Commd 20/9/59. Wg Cdr 24/7/72. Retd MED 1/5/79.
MCCAFFREY W.F. Born 8/1/32. Commd 3/11/60. Flt Lt 3/11/65. Retd PI 2/11/85.

MCCAIG D.P.F. MBE AFC. Born 4/10/22. Commd 4/7/43. Flt Lt 4/7/45. Retd GD 3/3/47. Re-employed 8/5/80.
   Sqn Ldr 1/4/56. Retd GD 4/10/65.
MCCAIG P.E. MA. Born 18/8/32. Commd 14/10/59. Sqn Ldr 1/1/70. Retd ADMIN 4/5/84.
MCCAIRNS C.J. Born 7/3/48. Commd 1/3/68. Sqn Ldr 1/1/78. Retd GD 7/3/86.
MCCALL D.R. BSc CEng MinstP MIEE. Born 14/8/24. Commd 16/6/48. Wg Cdr 1/4/69. Retd EDN 7/11/75.
MCCALL S.D. Born 27/5/65. Commd 30/8/84. Flt Lt 20/2/90. Retd GD 14/3/96.
MCCALLUM D.P. Born 8/11/65. Commd 17/8/92. Flt Lt 23/10/92. Retd FLY(N) 8/11/03.
MCCALLUM H.H. Born 12/8/23. Commd 2/9/43. Flt Lt 2/3/47. Retd ENG 22/8/57.
MCCALLUM J.M. AFC. Born 7/11/19. Commd 11/1/45. Flt Lt 19/8/68. Retd GD 27/11/74.
MCCALLUM K.R. Born 18/3/46. Commd 20/9/68. Sqn Ldr 1/1/88. Retd GD 10/6/90.
MCCALLUM M.W. Born 4/6/32. Commd 9/11/54. Flt Lt 5/10/60. Retd GD 9/10/70.
MCCALLUM N.K. DFC AFC. Born 24/9/20. Commd 1/9/45. Sqn Ldr 1/1/50. Retd GD 25/4/58.
MCCAMBRIDGE D. Born 22/4/58. Commd 11/9/77. Flt Lt 19/8/68. Retd GD 21/3/92.
MCCAMBRIDGE P.A. Born 10/12/58. Commd 2/2/78. Flt Lt 2/8/83. Retd GD 12/12/88.
MCCANDLESS B.C. CB CBE MSc BSc CEng FIEE FRAeS. Born 14/5/44. Commd 15/7/65. AVM 1/1/96.
   Retd ENG 14/5/99.
MCCANDLESS D.C. Born 29/3/45. Commd 27/3/86. Flt Lt 27/3/90. Retd ENG 29/3/00.
MCCANN C.J. Born 19/7/50. Commd 22/8/76. Sqn Ldr 18/4/82. Retd LGL 17/9/85.
MCCANN D.F.P. Born 15/5/38. Commd 29/4/71. Sqn Ldr 1/7/89. Retd ENG 15/5/93.
MCCANN D.G. BA. Born 1/12/30. Commd 6/10/53. Sqn Ldr 1/1/63. Retd GD 1/10/69.
MCCANN D.T. OBE. Born 1/12/32. Commd 9/4/52. Wg Cdr 1/1/75. Retd GD 31/7/89.
MCCANN M.C. MISM MILT. Born 2/2/49. Commd 27/3/86. Sqn Ldr 1/7/96. Retd SUP 7/1/99.
MCCANN R.E. Born 24/8/50. Commd 24/8/72. Flt Lt 24/2/79. Retd GD(G) 24/8/88.
MCCARNEY E.S. Born 19/8/64. Commd 8/9/83. Sqn Ldr 1/7/99. Retd OPS SPT 19/8/02.
MCCARRY K.J. BSc. Born 30/3/64. Commd 29/9/83. Flt Lt 15/1/88. Retd GD 15/10/98.
MCCARTHEY J.V. Born 27/10/40. Commd 31/7/62. Flt Lt 31/1/65. Retd GD 15/1/72.
MCCARTHY B. Born 15/4/29. Commd 1/9/70. Flt Lt 26/5/57. Retd GD 15/4/67.
MCCARTHY B. DPhysEd MHCIMA MCMI. Born 11/5/26. Commd 18/5/55. Sqn Ldr 1/7/76. Retd CAT 1/7/79.
MCCARTHY D. Born 23/3/44. Commd 23/3/67. Flt Lt 23/9/72. Retd GD 6/4/76.
MCCARTHY J. Born 21/10/21. Commd 14/4/45. Flt Lt 7/6/51. Retd SEC 31/10/64. Re-employed 1/8/69 to 2/3/76.
MCCARTHY J. BSc. Born 28/5/31. Commd 28/1/54. Gp Capt 1/1/80. Retd ADMIN 2/9/85.
MCCARTHY J.P. MCMI. Born 28/6/20. Commd 22/9/55. Sqn Ldr 1/7/66. Retd ENG 23/7/73.
MCCARTHY J.V. Born 27/10/40. Commd 31/7/62. Flt Lt 31/1/65. Retd GD 15/1/72.
MCCARTHY M.B. Born 27/8/46. Commd 21/4/77. Sqn Ldr 1/1/90. Retd ENG 27/8/01.
MCCARTHY M.D. Born 28/3/47. Commd 23/3/67. Sqn Ldr 1/7/82. Retd SUP 28/3/91.
MCCARTHY R.F. Born 15/4/34. Commd 27/2/70. Sqn Ldr 1/1/81. Retd GD(G) 30/4/85.
MCCARTHY R.J. BSc. Born 3/8/55. Commd 1/9/74. Sqn Ldr 1/7/90. Retd GD 3/8/99.
MCCARTHY S.F. BSc. Born 23/12/65. Commd 13/6/95. Flt Lt 11/4/90. Retd FLY(P) 23/12/03.
MCCARTHY W.J. MBE. Born 29/9/46. Commd 2/3/78. Wg Cdr 1/7/95. Retd GD 1/12/01.
MCCARTNEY A. Born 25/12/14. Commd 15/10/42. Flt Lt 4/6/53. Retd GD(G) 31/12/65.
MCCARTNEY J. Born 1/10/46. Commd 1/8/69. Flt Lt 1/11/73. Retd ENG 18/8/77.
MCCARTNEY J.A. Born 29/1/68. Commd 16/6/88. Flt Lt 16/12/94. Retd ADMIN 14/3/97.
MCCARTNEY R.J. Born 4/9/44. Commd 27/9/73. Wg Cdr 1/1/86. Retd ADMIN 1/11/88.
MCCARTY R.S. Born 16/1/25. Commd 25/4/51. Flt Lt 14/11/56. Retd GD 16/10/66.
MCCASKIE T.B. OBE MCMI. Born 24/11/23. Commd 1/12/44. Wg Cdr 1/7/65. Retd ADMIN 28/5/76.
MCCAUGHEY J.R. BSc. Born 12/9/51. Commd 15/9/69. Sqn Ldr 1/7/83. Retd GD 1/1/89.
MCCAUSLAND A.G. Born 8/8/33. Commd 27/9/51. Flt Lt 17/6/57. Retd GD 8/8/76.
MCCAUSLAND W.J. AFM. Born 4/6/24. Commd 27/5/54. Flt Lt 26/5/59. Retd GD 30/9/67.
MCCAY D.D. Born 24/9/49. Commd 9/11/89. Sqn Ldr 1/1/00. Retd MED SPT 3/4/02.
MCCHESNEY W.E. Born 2/2/10. Commd 17/6/41. Sqn Ldr 1/1/52. Retd SEC 29/11/58.
MCCLARTY J.J.W. CEng MIEE. Born 16/1/46. Commd 27/6/71. Gp Capt 1/1/94. Retd ENG 14/9/96.
MCCLAY M.P. Born 1/9/20. Commd 10/11/41. Flt Offr 1/9/45. Retd SEC 13/10/51.
MCCLEAN F.W. Born 15/1/20. Commd 5/5/60. Flt Lt 5/5/65. Retd ENG 7/10/67.
MCCLEERY C.W.V. MA CEng MIEE. Born 1/2/35. Commd 25/9/54. Sqn Ldr 1/1/68. Retd ENG 2/2/85.
MCCLELLAND D.M. Born 15/9/51. Commd 29/6/72. Flt Lt 29/6/78. Retd OPS SPT(ATC) 5/5/04.
MCCLELLAND I.W. Born 29/3/59. Commd 25/8/80. Flt Lt 22/2/86. Retd GD 17/5/96.
MCCLEMENT D.J. Born 6/6/43. Commd 20/8/65. Flt Lt 20/2/71. Retd GD 28/10/81.
MCCLEN D. AFC. Born 25/11/32. Commd 27/9/51. Gp Capt 1/1/72. Retd GD 1/9/75.
MCCLORY F. OBE. Born 27/5/29. Commd 6/12/51. Gp Capt 1/1/79. Retd GD 2/10/82.
MCCLOSKEY P.W.J. Born 13/3/47. Commd 11/4/85. Sqn Ldr 1/7/95. Retd ENGINEER 13/3/05.
MCCLOUD R.C. Born 15/12/43. Commd 14/6/63. Sqn Ldr 3/1/79. Retd GD(P) 15/12/87. Re-entered 31/5/89.
   Sqn Ldr 18/6/80. Retd FLY(P) 31/5/04.
MCCLUGGAGE W. Born 24/12/25. Commd 20/5/53. Flt Lt 15/9/58. Retd GD 3/5/69.
MCCLUGGAGE W.A. MSc BSc. Born 12/6/55. Commd 1/9/74. Wg Cdr 1/7/94. Retd ENG 12/6/99.
MCCLUNEY J.G. Born 3/11/37. Commd 1/4/58. Sqn Ldr 1/7/68. Retd GD 1/6/01.
MCCLURE-HALL G. MA BA MCMI. Born 26/1/48. Commd 1/6/72. Gp Capt 1/1/92. Retd MED(SEC) 14/3/96.

MCCLUSKEY C.J. MB ChB FRCOG. Born 6/3/40. Commd 22/4/63. Gp Capt 1/10/89. Retd MED 14/9/96.
MCCLUSKEY P.D. Born 31/7/34. Commd 4/3/71. Flt Lt 4/3/73. Retd PRT 4/3/79.
MCCLUSKEY R. AFC DPhysEd. Born 23/5/39. Commd 31/10/61. Wg Cdr 1/1/83. Retd ADMIN 3/10/93.
MCCLYMONT D. BSc. Born 5/7/59. Commd 26/7/81. Sqn Ldr 1/1/92. Retd GD 26/7/97.
MCCLYMONT G.J. Born 15/7/58. Commd 17/5/79. Sqn Ldr 1/7/91. Retd GD 15/7/96.
MCCLYMONT W. Born 23/8/18. Commd 26/10/43. Sqn Ldr 1/7/55. Retd GD 29/3/58.
MCCOMAS J.F. Born 27/5/34. Commd 1/4/53. Flt Lt 2/11/59. Retd GD 27/5/72.
MCCOMBE A.B. Born 18/3/60. Commd 20/9/79. Wg Cdr 1/1/01. Retd OPS SPT 1/1/03.
MCCOMBIE I.M. BSc. Born 18/6/65. Commd 28/10/86. Flt Lt 26/4/89. Retd GD 26/10/98.
MCCOMBIE J.W. CBE. Born 25/5/10. Commd 2/9/41. Gp Capt 1/1/60. Retd ENG 25/5/65.
MCCOMISKY J. Born 26/7/47. Commd 17/5/79. Flt Lt 17/5/81. Retd ADMIN 17/5/87.
MCCONCHIE R.P. Born 9/6/33. Commd 30/1/52. Flt Lt 16/6/57. Retd GD 9/6/71.
MCCONE H. Born 1/9/34. Commd 2/7/64. Flt Lt 2/7/66. Retd SEC 30/9/72.
MCCONKIE R.K. Born 14/7/39. Commd 21/4/67. Flt Lt 21/4/69. Retd GD(G) 14/7/77.
MCCONNELL D.L. MSc MB ChB DAvMed. Born 23/12/49. Commd 8/5/80. Gp Capt 1/7/99. Retd MEDICAL 18/7/03.
MCCONNELL H.D. Born 19/3/30. Commd 1/6/63. Wg Cdr 1/7/76. Retd PRT 3/1/79.
MCCONNELL J.W. MCMI. Born 6/12/22. Commd 17/4/47. Sqn Ldr 1/7/68. Retd SUP 6/12/77.
MCCONNELL P.E. Born 2/9/38. Commd 11/9/58. Flt Lt 15/2/65. Retd ADMIN 2/9/76.
MCCONNELL R. BA. Born 12/11/48. Commd 3/1/69. A Cdre 1/1/99. Retd ADMIN 5/4/02.
MCCONNON D. BA. Born 27/5/33. Commd 7/9/56. Sqn Ldr 7/3/66. Retd EDN 8/9/73.
MCCORD A.W. IEng. Born 18/7/39. Commd 3/11/77. Sqn Ldr 1/7/87. Retd ENG 18/7/97.
MCCORD B. Born 24/2/44. Commd 16/6/69. Sqn Ldr 1/7/80. Retd SY 16/6/85.
MCCORD T.N. Born 10/10/42. Commd 24/4/64. Flt Lt 12/11/69. Retd GD 14/1/73.
MCCORKLE J.F. AFM. Born 10/12/21. Commd 10/8/55. Flt Lt 10/8/60. Retd GD 2/3/65.
MCCORMACK J.J. Born 8/6/33. Commd 9/3/66. Flt Lt 9/3/72. Retd GD(G) 8/6/88.
MCCORMACK-WHITE C. Born 4/6/52. Commd 30/3/89. Sqn Ldr 1/7/99. Retd ADMIN 19/10/02.
MCCORMICK D.G. BSc MInstP. Born 30/9/45. Commd 16/1/72. Flt Lt 16/10/72. Retd GD 30/9/00.
MCCORMICK D.W. BSc. Born 14/2/54. Commd 25/9/71. Wg Cdr 1/7/91. Retd ENG 20/11/02.
MCCORMICK J.C.H. MSc BSc. Born 31/10/61. Commd 22/7/84. Flt Lt 22/1/88. Retd ENG 30/9/96.
MCCORMICK M.J. Born 14/6/36. Commd 27/3/75. Sqn Ldr 1/1/89. Retd GD 14/6/94.
MCCORMICK R.A. BSc. Born 24/1/62. Commd 29/9/85. Sqn Ldr 1/1/02. Retd FLY(N) 8/4/04.
MCCORMICK R.P. Born 11/10/33. Commd 17/5/62. Sqn Ldr 1/7/77. Retd GD(G) 12/10/83.
MCCOUBREY I.A. MB ChB FFOM FCMI MRCGP DAvMed MRAeS. Born 8/7/46. Commd 24/7/73. A Cdre 1/7/96. Retd MED 18/4/97.
MCCOURT J. MBE. Born 9/8/41. Commd 13/12/79. Sqn Ldr 1/7/88. Retd ENG 10/5/95.
MCCOWAN N.C. Born 30/12/63. Commd 19/12/85. Flt Lt 19/6/91. Retd GD 30/12/01.
MCCOY R. Born 22/8/42. Commd 11/10/84. Flt Lt 11/10/88. Retd ENG 31/3/94.
MCCRACKEN A.W. MB ChB MCPath DCP DTM&H. Born 24/11/31. Commd 3/3/57. Sqn Ldr 1/4/62. Retd MED 30/3/68.
MCCRAE D.I. MA. Born 29/11/41. Commd 7/12/65. Wg Cdr 1/1/91. Retd GD 29/11/96.
MCCRAN J.B. Born 28/4/49. Commd 22/9/88. Flt Lt 22/9/92. Retd ADMIN 14/3/96.
MCCRANN R.J.D. Born 29/5/35. Commd 6/2/64. Flt Lt 21/10/59. Retd GD 29/5/93.
MCCREA W.E. DFC BSc. Born 3/4/21. Commd 27/3/43. Wg Cdr 1/7/64. Retd EDN 13/5/72.
MCCREADY L.L.J. Born 19/1/53. Commd 12/4/73. Sqn Ldr 1/1/86. Retd GD 7/10/86.
MCCREANNEY T. MBE. Born 23/12/60. Commd 16/12/86. Sqn Ldr 1/7/90. Retd ENG 15/7/99.
MCCREERY A.J. Born 10/4/37. Commd 5/6/56. A Cdre 1/1/86. Retd GD 11/3/88.
MCCREITH S. AFC* MRAeS. Born 11/6/19. Commd 3/7/42. Wg Cdr 1/1/58. Retd GD 11/6/66.
MCCRIMMON N.A. Born 5/10/41. Commd 25/7/59. Sqn Ldr 1/7/72. Retd GD 5/10/79. Re-entered 29/10/80. Sqn Ldr 25/7/73. Retd GD 5/10/96.
MCCRINDLE M.K. BSc DPhysEd FCMI. Born 28/4/32. Commd 18/11/54. Wg Cdr 1/1/74. Retd SUP 7/4/85.
MCCRORIE J.D. Born 22/1/38. Commd 16/11/61. Sqn Ldr 1/7/72. Retd PRT 1/10/75.
MCCRORIE R.F. Born 30/4/42. Commd 21/10/65. Sqn Ldr 1/7/77. Retd ADMIN 30/6/96.
MCCRUDDEN K.M. Born 10/3/16. Commd 16/4/35. Flt Lt 1/3/45. Retd GD(G) 10/3/66. rtg Sqn Ldr.
MCCULLAGH E.A. MCMI. Born 22/5/31. Commd 12/3/52. Sqn Ldr 1/7/65. Retd GD(G) 22/5/86.
MCCULLOCH I.J. Born 4/9/46. Commd 23/3/66. Sqn Ldr 1/1/84. Retd ADMIN 1/11/89.
MCCULLOCH J.D.C. Born 28/8/20. Commd 18/11/54. Sqn Ldr 1/7/69. Retd SEC 28/8/75.
MCCULLOCH J.W. BEng. Born 28/11/39. Commd 30/9/59. Wg Cdr 1/7/77. Retd ENG 28/11/94.
MCCULLOCH R.A. BA. Born 9/5/50. Commd 24/3/74. Sqn Ldr 1/1/86. Retd ADMIN 24/3/90.
MCCULLOCH T. Born 14/6/40. Commd 20/12/73. Flt Lt 12/12/75. Retd SEC 20/12/81.
MCCULLOCH T.A. Born 30/8/22. Commd 2/12/44. Sqn Ldr 1/10/55. Retd GD 30/8/71.
MCCULLOUCH S.D. Born 13/4/47. Commd 18/11/66. Wg Cdr 1/1/85. Retd GD(G) 13/4/91.
MCCUMISKEY G.P. DPhysEd. Born 8/3/26. Commd 16/5/51. Flt Lt 16/5/55. Retd PE 14/5/67.
MCCUNN W.J. BSc CEng MIERE DipSoton. Born 12/3/72. Commd 12/9/61. Sqn Ldr 12/3/72. Retd ADMIN 20/1/89.
MCCURDY R. DFC*. Born 19/9/18. Commd 4/10/42. Sqn Ldr 1/1/64. Retd GD(G) 30/3/76.
MCCUTCHEON G. BSc. Born 2/9/64. Commd 8/5/88. Flt Lt 8/11/90. Retd SY 8/8/94.
MCCUTCHEON G. MCIPD MCMI. Born 22/9/34. Commd 30/8/66. Sqn Ldr 1/7/77. Retd ADMIN 22/2/92.

MCDADE B. BA. Born 17/8/49. Commd 8/9/77. Sqn Ldr 1/1/85. Retd ENG 1/1/88.
MCDEAN W. Born 13/9/19. Commd 29/8/45. Sqn Ldr 1/1/54. Retd RGT 30/4/61.
MCDERMID B.D. MSc MBA BEng CEng MRAeS. Born 27/1/59. Commd 16/9/84. Sqn Ldr 1/1/95.
    Retd ENGINEER 18/6/04.
MCDERMOTT A.R. BSc CEng MRAeS. Born 2/1/41. Commd 9/11/64. Sqn Ldr 1/7/76. Retd ENG 9/11/80.
MCDERMOTT J.G.S. Born 24/1/45. Commd 23/10/86. Flt Lt 23/10/90. Retd SUP 14/3/96.
MCDERMOTT K.T. BA. Born 20/11/34. Commd 22/5/59. Wg Cdr 1/1/77. Retd ADMIN 14/2/85.
MCDERMOTT P.A.C. DFC DFM. Born 4/3/20. Commd 7/4/42. Wg Cdr 1/1/57. Retd GD 30/4/66.
MCDICKEN A.A. Born 15/3/45. Commd 1/4/66. Sqn Ldr 1/7/76. Retd GD 10/1/81.
MCDILL J.M. MCMI. Born 7/2/30. Commd 26/11/64. Sqn Ldr 1/7/77. Retd ADMIN 7/2/88.
MCDINNES J.K. BSc. Born 27/8/62. Commd 11/12/83. Flt Lt 11/6/86. Retd GD 14/9/96.
MCDONALD A.P. Born 6/10/29. Commd 6/1/49. Flt Lt 10/4/56. Retd GD 6/10/67.
MCDONALD A.W. Born 30/9/33. Commd 9/4/52. Wg Cdr 1/7/79. Retd GD 6/10/84.
MCDONALD B.A.D.McK. AFC*. Born 9/5/30. Commd 4/6/59. Sqn Ldr 1/7/71. Retd GD 9/5/90.
MCDONALD D. MBE MA BD. Born 6/3/29. Commd 6/8/63. Sqn Ldr 14/2/66. Retd ADMIN 6/8/82.
MCDONALD F.J. Born 28/5/44. Commd 31/1/64. Flt Lt 31/7/69. Retd GD 26/7/75.
MCDONALD G.M. Born 13/4/51. Commd 14/1/88. Flt Lt 14/1/92. Retd ADMIN 14/3/96.
MCDONALD I. Born 6/2/38. Commd 22/10/63. Sqn Ldr 9/10/74. Retd EDN 1/10/79.
MCDONALD I. Born 23/9/32. Commd 14/8/56. Sqn Ldr 1/1/84. Retd GD 23/9/92.
MCDONALD I.A. Born 21/12/20. Commd 7/11/51. Flt Lt 16/8/61. Retd GD(G) 7/8/65.
MCDONALD I.J. MA. Born 19/9/47. Commd 11/9/77. Sqn Ldr 1/7/88. Retd ADMIN 1/10/01.
MCDONALD J. FCMI. Born 13/12/33. Commd 17/9/53. Gp Capt 1/7/80. Retd SUP 18/4/84.
MCDONALD J.E. Born 1/3/30. Commd 5/5/51. Sqn Ldr 1/1/62. Retd GD 28/11/75. rtg Wg Cdr.
MCDONALD K. Born 21/6/33. Commd 5/4/55. Flt Lt 13/11/57. Retd GD 21/6/71. rtg Sqn Ldr.
MCDONALD K.J. OBE DFC. Born 1/3/14. Commd 13/7/36. Gp Capt 1/1/56. Retd GD 12/11/57.
MCDONALD M. Born 4/7/65. Commd 16/6/88. Flt Lt 16/12/93. Retd FLY(P) 14/2/04.
MCDONALD M. Born 10/8/56. Commd 12/10/78. Sqn Ldr 1/7/88. Retd GD 10/8/94.
MCDONALD M.M. Born 16/11/42. Commd 29/10/60. Flt Lt 15/4/70. Retd GD(G) 16/11/80.
MCDONALD R. Born 23/8/24. Commd 17/3/45. Wg Cdr 1/1/68. Retd PE 1/12/72.
MCDONALD S.G. MHCIMA. Born 5/8/32. Commd 1/10/60. Sqn Ldr 1/7/69. Retd CAT 14/10/83.
MCDONALD T.P. OBE. Born 16/4/49. Commd 24/6/71. Gp Capt 1/7/02. Retd GD 30/6/05.
MCDONALD W. DFC FCIS. Born 30/5/21. Commd 7/10/43. Sqn Ldr 1/7/56. Retd SEC 28/1/76.
MCDONALD-GIBSON J.H. Born 25/5/49. Commd 20/5/82. Flt Lt 20/11/88. Retd OPS SPT 18/1/98.
MCDONALD-WEBB I.D. Born 8/9/60. Commd 22/5/80. Sqn Ldr 1/7/94. Retd GD 8/9/98.
MCDONNELL A.J. Born 22/9/23. Commd 11/12/44. Sqn Ldr 1/1/71. Retd GD 25/6/73.
MCDONNELL D.K.L. OBE. Born 27/1/46. Commd 31/1/64. Gp Capt 1/1/94. Retd GD 28/2/01.
MCDONNELL F.E. OBE. Born 9/2/16. Commd 3/4/39. Wg Cdr 1/7/54. Retd SUP 31/5/61.
MCDONNELL J.F. Born 29/3/23. Commd 30/11/44. Flt Lt 10/11/55. Retd GD 8/1/66.
MCDONNELL J.F. Born 26/4/28. Commd 22/7/50. Wg Cdr 1/1/72. Retd RGT 27/4/78.
MCDONNELL J.J. Born 21/5/23. Commd 24/2/67. Flt Lt 24/2/72. Retd ENG 1/3/78.
MCDONNELL N.J. Born 13/2/56. Commd 22/5/80. Sqn Ldr 1/6/90. Retd GD 1/8/99.
MCDOUGALL A.D. Born 17/10/50. Commd 17/7/70. Flt Lt 17/1/77. Retd ADMIN 17/10/88.
MCDOUGALL C.N. DFC. Born 17/3/35. Commd 30/4/62. Sqn Ldr 1/1/82. Retd GD 6/2/89.
MCDOUGALL D.J. Born 24/5/48. Commd 9/12/71. Flt Lt 9/6/77. Retd GD 14/3/97.
MCDOUGALL J.S. Born 26/3/50. Commd 24/4/70. Sqn Ldr 1/1/83. Retd SY(PRT) 26/3/88.
MCDOUGALL M.R.L. Born 10/10/45. Commd 10/6/66. Flt Lt 4/5/72. Retd GD 25/4/76.
MCDOWELL C.B. Born 15/1/47. Commd 16/12/66. Sqn Ldr 1/7/80. Retd ENG 16/12/00.
MCDOWELL S.R. Born 28/12/27. Commd 17/7/58. Flt Lt 17/7/64. Retd SEC 21/11/66.
MCEACHERN W.H. DFC DFM. Born 16/5/24. Commd 4/6/59. Sqn Ldr 1/1/70. Retd GD 31/5/73.
MCELHAW T.J. BA MCMI. Born 14/10/26. Commd 3/5/46. Wg Cdr 1/1/65. Retd GD 14/10/81.
MCELLIGOTT D.P. AM MBE BA. Born 26/5/25. Commd 17/7/46. Flt Lt 17/7/52. Retd RGT 31/12/66.
MCELROY G.E. MDA BSc CEng MRAeS. Born 15/8/57. Commd 5/4/83. Gp Capt 1/7/01. Retd GD 17/10/04.
MCELWAIN J.D.de S. OBE BSc CEng MRAeS. Born 7/9/17. Commd 20/9/40. Wg Cdr 1/7/56. Retd ENG 21/9/74.
MCENERY J.N. Born 12/12/44. Commd 18/11/66. Sqn Ldr 1/1/84. Retd SUP 1/10/91.
MCERLEAN L. BSc. Born 18/10/58. Commd 30/10/83. Sqn Ldr 1/7/95. Retd SUP 30/10/99.
MCEVOY J. Born 24/6/31. Commd 15/11/51. Sqn Ldr 1/1/82. Retd GD 24/6/89.
MCEVOY J.J. Born 1/1/63. Commd 14/4/85. Sqn Ldr 1/7/99. Retd OPS SPT 1/7/02.
MCEVOY J.R.N. MBE. Born 1/4/40. Commd 1/8/61. Sqn Ldr 1/7/76. Retd GD 11/4/95.
MCEWAN A.R. Born 22/12/38. Commd 22/5/75. Sqn Ldr 1/1/86. Retd ADMIN 1/10/87.
MCEWAN P.D. Born 8/12/42. Commd 28/2/64. Flt Lt 15/4/70. Retd GD 11/5/97.
MCEWEN N.D. AFC FCMI. Born 7/11/33. Commd 3/9/52. A Cdre 1/1/84. Retd GD 2/8/87.
MCEWEN R.A. Born 29/11/34. Commd 3/6/65. Wg Cdr 1/7/81. Retd SUP 29/11/89.
MCEWEN W. Born 25/8/23. Commd 6/1/55. Flt Lt 6/1/58. Retd GD 25/8/73.
MCFADYEN A.G. BA. Born 18/11/55. Commd 29/11/81. Sqn Ldr 1/1/91. Retd OPS SPT 27/11/01.
MCFADYEN M.A. BSc. Born 25/10/48. Commd 15/9/69. Flt Lt 15/10/70. Retd ENG 25/10/86.
MCFADZEAN J.B. BSc. Born 27/7/58. Commd 22/3/81. Flt Lt 22/6/81. Retd GD 5/6/90.

MCFARLAND J. Born 19/9/24. Commd 21/6/56. Sqn Ldr 1/7/71. Retd GD 19/9/82.
MCFARLANE C.W.R. Born 26/5/48. Commd 22/9/69. Flt Lt 26/5/75. Retd ENG 2/8/76.
MCFARLANE I.M. The Rev. BA. Born 16/9/46. Commd 5/4/81. Retd Sqn Ldr 4/10/91.
MCFARLANE N. Born 23/11/33. Commd 16/7/52. Flt Lt 16/8/61. Retd GD 12/2/74.
MCFARLANE R. DSO DFC*. Born 12/7/14. Commd 3/11/41. Gp Capt 1/7/56. Retd GD 30/6/62.
MCFARLANE S.C. Born 13/4/35. Commd 1/11/79. Flt Lt 1/11/82. Retd ADMIN 10/8/87.
MCFETRIDGE W. Born 9/1/17. Commd 16/11/43. Flt Lt 16/5/47. Retd GD 9/1/60.
MCGAHAN P.J. MISM MCMI. Born 3/12/55. Commd 22/5/75. Wg Cdr 1/1/94. Retd ADMIN 4/12/98.
MCGARRY T.P. OBE DFC. Born 6/3/19. Commd 21/9/42. Gp Capt 1/7/68. Retd GD 9/3/74.
MCGARVEY J. MBE BSc. Born 21/3/37. Commd 25/7/57. Sqn Ldr 1/1/69. Retd ENG 31/12/76. rtg Wg Cdr.
MCGEE P.C.T. Born 6/3/22. Commd 9/8/44. Flt Lt 18/2/52. Retd SUP 17/9/66.
MCGEORGE W. Born 30/1/45. Commd 21/12/67. Flt Lt 9/3/74. Retd SEC 28/6/75.
MCGEOUGH P.J.R. Born 28/3/46. Commd 13/2/86. Sqn Ldr 1/1/96. Retd ENG 14/9/96.
MCGETTIGAN F.H.P. Born 23/8/42. Commd 19/7/84. Sqn Ldr 1/1/92. Retd SUP 23/8/97.
MCGETTRICK J.J. Born 10/11/48. Commd 8/12/83. Flt Lt 8/12/87. Retd ADMIN 1/9/90.
MCGHEE C.B. DFC. Born 26/9/21. Commd 7/3/42. Flt Lt 7/9/45. Retd ENG 18/6/55. rtg Sqn Ldr.
MCGHIE D.C.P. Born 21/10/55. Commd 19/12/91. Flt Lt 19/12/95. Retd ENGINEER 25/5/04.
MCGIBBON C.W. BSc. Born 10/1/46. Commd 27/10/70. Flt Lt 27/7/71. Retd GD 5/9/91.
MCGILCHRIST D.G. Born 23/5/39. Commd 21/7/61. Flt Lt 21/1/67. Retd GD 23/5/77.
MCGILL B.J. Born 8/2/34. Commd 26/7/55. Wg Cdr 1/1/74. Retd SUP 2/9/80.
MCGILL D.P.K. OBE CEng MRAeS. Born 31/8/42. Commd 15/7/64. A Cdre 1/7/92. Retd ENG 5/4/95.
MCGINTY M.T. BSc. Born 27/2/51. Commd 25/9/71. Wg Cdr 1/1/87. Retd PRT 8/12/91.
MCGLARY S. Born 9/11/53. Commd 14/1/88. Sqn Ldr 1/7/97. Retd ENG 14/1/02.
MCGLASHAN K.B. AFC. Born 28/8/20. Commd 18/3/39. Sqn Ldr 1/1/49. Retd GD 29/8/58.
MCGLENNON D.M. Born 6/1/65. Commd 8/5/88. Flt Lt 8/5/94. Retd ADMIN 1/11/96.
MCGONIGLE F. MBE. Born 16/7/20. Commd 9/1/45. Wg Cdr 1/7/67. Retd SUP 16/7/75.
MCGONIGLE N. Born 1/1/58. Commd 5/9/76. Wg Cdr 1/1/96. Retd OPS SPT 21/4/01.
MCGOUGH W.H. MCMI. Born 1/4/25. Commd 21/10/65. Flt Lt 21/10/71. Retd GD(G) 1/4/80. rtg Sqn Ldr.
MCGOWAN A. MA. Born 18/11/59. Commd 18/10/81. Sqn Ldr 1/1/91. Retd SY 14/3/96.
MCGOWAN G. Born 24/3/17. Commd 27/8/52. Flt Lt 27/8/57. Retd GD(G) 3/5/67.
MCGOWAN R.B. Born 17/9/18. Commd 7/5/44. Sqn Ldr 1/7/56. Retd GD 27/11/58.
MCGOWAN R.C. Born 26/5/49. Commd 21/7/68. Flt Lt 12/1/74. Retd GD 16/9/78.
MCGRAN A.J.V. IEng. Born 23/9/34. Commd 19/8/71. Sqn Ldr 1/7/87. Retd ENG 23/9/94.
MCGRANAGHAN J.A. MA. Born 3/12/40. Commd 9/9/63. Flt Lt 9/6/65. Retd GD 27/2/74.
MCGRATH A. BA. Born 3/10/39. Commd 23/3/66. Sqn Ldr 1/1/85. Retd GD(G) 2/4/91.
MCGRATH A.P. Born 12/9/43. Commd 24/6/65. Fg Offr 24/12/65. Retd SUP 19/9/70.
MCGRATH H.P. Born 10/9/12. Commd 8/7/43. Sqn Ldr 1/7/54. Retd ENG 10/9/62.
MCGRATH J.G. BSc. Born 1/11/60. Commd 14/10/84. Flt Lt 14/4/86. Retd GD 1/11/01.
MCGRATH K.E. Born 1/7/13. Commd 29/3/42. Fg Offr 7/3/47. Retd GD(G) 1/11/53.
MCGRATH P.A. AFC. Born 14/6/21. Commd 17/3/43. Flt Lt 17/9/46. Retd GD 14/6/54.
MCGRATH W.J. Born 17/5/48. Commd 27/2/70. Wg Cdr 1/1/91. Retd SUP 5/12/96.
MCGREEVY T. OBE CEng FCMI MRAeS. Born 10/5/18. Commd 15/12/41. Gp Capt 1/7/67. Retd ENG 10/5/73.
MCGREGOR A. BA. Born 25/7/59. Commd 11/4/82. Sqn Ldr 1/7/96. Retd OPS SPT 1/7/99.
MCGREGOR A.D. Born 3/5/34. Commd 17/12/52. Flt Lt 12/5/58. Retd GD(G) 1/2/73.
MCGREGOR A.E.I. Born 17/2/45. Commd 8/1/65. Sqn Ldr 1/7/77. Retd GD 14/3/97.
MCGREGOR A.J. DSO AE*. Born 23/11/20. Commd 18/6/40. Wg Cdr 1/1/71. Retd GD(G) 23/11/76.
MCGREGOR D.R.H. MRAeS. Born 29/8/42. Commd 30/7/63. Gp Capt 1/7/84. Retd GD 28/7/93.
MCGREGOR G.L. Born 26/12/59. Commd 11/10/84. Sqn Ldr 1/7/97. Retd OPS SPT 1/7/00.
MCGREGOR I. Born 10/9/66. Commd 4/7/85. Sqn Ldr 1/7/01. Retd FLY(P) 10/9/04.
MCGREGOR I.F. BSc. Born 17/6/55. Commd 15/9/74. Flt Lt 30/5/78. Retd GD 15/1/91.
MCGREGOR I.J. Born 18/10/15. Commd 6/1/44. Flt Lt 26/5/55. Retd GD(G) 9/7/66.
MCGREGOR I.M. MA. Born 17/2/56. Commd 30/10/83. Sqn Ldr 1/1/92. Retd ADMIN 30/10/99.
MCGREGOR M.D. MA. Born 5/10/12. Commd 3/11/43. Wg Offr 1/1/64. Retd EDN 5/10/67.
MCGREGOR R.R. Born 5/10/43. Commd 28/4/65. Flt Lt 4/11/70. Retd GD 1/4/78.
MCGREGOR S.M. Born 7/4/21. Commd 16/3/47. Wg Cdr 1/1/61. Retd GD 7/7/64.
MCGREGOR-EDWARDS N. BA. Born 3/4/51. Commd 3/1/71. Sqn Ldr 1/7/87. Retd ADMIN 1/7/90.
MCGRORY J.I. MBE. Born 31/7/27. Commd 14/12/44. Sqn Ldr 1/1/66. Retd GD 31/7/76.
MCGRORY J.M. Born 2/5/39. Commd 3/11/77. Sqn Ldr 1/1/88. Retd GD 3/10/93.
MCGRORY W.J. Born 22/1/34. Commd 24/9/52. Flt Lt 1/4/58. Retd GD(G) 6/4/83.
MCGUIGAN M.P. BA. Born 4/11/57. Commd 6/11/87. Wg Cdr 1/7/03. Retd GD 15/10/04.
MCGUIGAN R.J.A. Born 25/10/31. Commd 22/11/56. Wg Cdr 1/1/75. Retd ENG 27/10/81.
MCGUINNESS G.P. BSc. Born 20/2/63. Commd 22/7/84. Flt Lt 22/1/87. Retd GD 14/4/92.
MCGUIRE A.B. MBE. Born 16/5/28. Commd 5/4/50. A Cdre 1/1/80. Retd SY 1/8/81.
MCGUIRE A.C. Born 22/5/21. Commd 23/2/44. Flt Lt 23/8/47. Retd GD 22/2/66.
MCGUIRE E.J. MB BS FFCM FCMI MFOM MRAeS. Born 7/12/24. Commd 29/6/50. A Cdre 18/1/75.
    Retd MED 2/4/81.

MCGUIRE K. Born 21/11/47. Commd 31/7/70. Sqn Ldr 1/1/96. Retd GD 23/9/01.
MCGUIRE R.P. Born 21/9/52. Commd 12/7/79. Flt Lt 7/4/82. Retd GD 21/9/90.
MCGUIRK T. Born 18/11/24. Commd 5/11/59. Flt Lt 1/1/75. Retd GD(G) 31/8/77.
MCHENDRY J. Born 4/9/43. Commd 11/4/85. Flt Lt 11/4/89. Retd ADMIN 14/3/96.
MCHUGH A.L. Born 14/1/44. Commd 6/4/62. Sqn Ldr 1/1/73. Retd GD 15/1/82.
MCILROY C.D.R. Born 28/2/55. Commd 17/7/75. Sqn Ldr 1/1/89. Retd GD 28/2/93.
MCILROY W.A. BSc CEng MRAeS AFIMA. Born 17/9/21. Commd 25/8/42. Sqn Ldr 1/1/58. Retd ENG 18/5/76.
MCILWAINE G.L. BSc. Born 18/8/42. Commd 28/9/64. Fg Offr 15/4/65. Retd GD 23/9/67.
MCILWRAITH A. LLB MCMI. Born 23/4/28. Commd 4/2/64. Sqn Ldr 1/7/71. Retd ADMIN 23/4/83.
MCINNES A. Born 24/2/46. Commd 11/2/65. Sqn Ldr 1/1/78. Retd SY 24/2/84.
MCINROY T. Born 13/10/10. Commd 11/2/43. Flt Lt 29/6/50. Retd GD(G) 13/10/65.
MCINTEE B.M. BSc. Born 23/9/44. Commd 28/9/64. Wg Cdr 1/1/87. Retd ENG 1/10/93.
MCINTOSH A.A. DFC MA. Born 13/8/19. Commd 15/3/43. Gp Capt 1/7/67. Retd EDN 13/8/74.
MCINTOSH E.A. Born 30/10/30. Commd 10/3/59. Sqn Ldr 1/7/70. Retd ADMIN 30/10/87.
MCINTOSH G.J. AFC. Born 19/2/36. Commd 26/8/63. Sqn Ldr 1/1/73. Retd GD 10/9/89.
MCINTOSH H.N.M. The Rev. MA. Born 24/8/22. Commd 22/3/61. Retd Wg Cdr 22/3/66.
MCINTOSH I.C.R. Born 7/6/32. Commd 6/4/54. Sqn Ldr 1/1/69. Retd GD 26/8/77.
MCINTYRE A.G. AFC. Born 4/1/17. Commd 9/4/40. Sqn Ldr 1/7/56. Retd GD 30/1/59.
MCINTYRE A.J. Born 16/4/36. Commd 19/8/65. Flt Lt 19/8/67. Retd GD 17/4/86.
MCINTYRE D. Born 19/11/33. Commd 27/7/54. Flt Lt 27/1/57. Retd GD 1/5/68.
MCINTYRE D.M. Born 10/1/50. Commd 27/2/70. Flt Lt 27/8/75. Retd GD 10/1/88.
MCINTYRE D.R. Born 24/7/40. Commd 3/11/77. Sqn Ldr 1/1/90. Retd ENG 24/7/95.
MCINTYRE I.G. MSc BDS FDSRCSEd MGDSRCS(Eng) DDPHRCS FCMI. Born 9/7/43. Commd 17/9/61. AVM 1/7/97.
    Retd DEL 20/4/01.
MCINTYRE M.E. BSc. Born 26/9/51. Commd 7/11/76. Sqn Ldr 1/1/87. Retd ENG 7/11/92.
MCINTYRE R.S. FCIS MBCS. Born 18/6/40. Commd 1/4/65. Wg Cdr 1/1/85. Retd ADMIN 18/6/95.
MCINTYRE T.F. Born 2/7/30. Commd 12/7/62. Flt Lt 12/7/68. Retd ENG 2/1/73.
MCINTYRE W.J.J.H. Born 28/6/43. Commd 1/10/65. Flt Lt 17/3/71. Retd ADMIN 28/6/98.
MCKAVANAGH D.J. The Rev. MA BD AKC. Born 2/3/51. Commd 26/1/87. Retd Sqn Ldr 31/12/99.
MCKAY A. Born 10/2/46. Commd 26/5/67. Gp Capt 1/1/87. Retd GD 10/2/90.
MCKAY D. Born 9/3/33. Commd 4/10/51. Sqn Ldr 1/1/73. Retd GD(G) 11/10/74.
MCKAY D.S. Born 17/11/50. Commd 23/8/89. Flt Lt 30/3/93. Retd OPS SPT 6/6/00.
MCKAY G.W. Born 2/10/45. Commd 28/4/65. Flt Lt 28/10/70. Retd GD 14/9/96.
MCKAY I.F. BSc. Born 27/6/51. Commd 13/11/72. Sqn Ldr 1/7/85. Retd GD 27/6/89.
MCKAY I.J. MBE BEM. Born 1/4/39. Commd 17/7/87. Sqn Ldr 1/7/94. Retd FLY(ENG) 2/4/05.
MCKAY J.T. LHA MCMI. Born 27/5/29. Commd 8/7/65. Flt Lt 28/4/69. Retd MED(SEC) 9/11/74. rtg Sqn Ldr.
MCKAY R. Born 8/9/20. Commd 9/9/54. Flt Lt 9/9/57. Retd SUP 8/9/75.
MCKAY R. CEng MIMechE MRAeS. Born 14/8/34. Commd 9/11/65. Sqn Ldr 1/1/83. Retd ENG 14/8/92.
MCKAY R.A. Born 26/10/20. Commd 28/8/47. Sqn Ldr 1/4/55. Retd GD(G) 31/10/70. rtg Wg Cdr.
MCKEATING G.E.D. BSc. Born 15/5/50. Commd 15/9/69. Sqn Ldr 1/7/85. Retd GD 1/7/88.
MCKECHNIE E.M. CBE MRCS LRCP. Born 20/8/17. Commd 22/6/44. A Cdre 1/7/72. Retd MED 29/10/76.
MCKEE C. BA. Born 24/11/72. Commd 28/10/01. Flt Lt 11/2/99. Retd ADMIN (CAT) 25/10/03.
MCKEE I.K. AFC*. Born 5/4/34. Commd 21/10/53. Gp Capt 1/1/87. Retd GD 5/4/89.
MCKEE W.L. MCMI. Born 28/3/40. Commd 25/7/60. Wg Cdr 1/1/85. Retd GD 28/3/95.
MCKEEVER L. Born 4/2/27. Commd 21/10/66. Flt Lt 21/10/72. Retd SUP 4/2/83.
MCKEITH T.N. Born 24/6/65. Commd 28/3/91. Flt Lt 28/3/93. Retd FLY(P) 24/6/03.
MCKELLAR P. Born 14/6/42. Commd 22/5/64. Flt Lt 22/11/69. Retd GD 14/6/80.
MCKELVIE A.S. MBE MIIM MCMI. Born 18/11/35. Commd 4/5/72. Sqn Ldr 1/1/84. Retd SUP 3/1/91.
MCKELVIE K.J. Born 29/1/50. Commd 18/4/74. Flt Lt 18/12/77. Retd GD 29/1/90.
MCKENDRICK D.I. Born 26/6/45. Commd 19/6/64. Sqn Ldr 1/7/80. Retd GD 6/7/99.
MCKENNA D.H.T. BSc. Born 15/9/60. Commd 8/10/81. Flt Lt 15/10/84. Retd GD 14/9/96.
MCKENNA J. MCMI. Born 26/9/31. Commd 27/1/55. Sqn Ldr 1/7/70. Retd SEC 1/7/75.
MCKENNA J.F. Born 7/10/38. Commd 18/8/61. Fg Offr 18/8/63. Retd GD 26/2/65.
MCKENNA M.J. MBE. Born 26/4/46. Commd 23/2/68. Sqn Ldr 1/7/87. Retd GD 26/8/01.
MCKENNA S.M. Born 3/4/63. Commd 10/5/90. Flt Lt 15/2/93. Retd ENG 3/4/01.
MCKENNA T. BSc. Born 4/12/34. Commd 10/9/63. Sqn Ldr 1/1/71. Retd ENG 4/12/92.
MCKENNEY R.R. DFC. Born 3/7/21. Commd 30/7/49. Flt Lt 30/1/52. Retd GD(G) 31/7/70.
MCKENZIE I. BA CEng MIEE MRAeS. Born 1/4/39. Commd 18/7/61. Sqn Ldr 1/7/73. Retd ENG 1/10/94.
MCKENZIE I. BSc MB ChB DAvMed. Born 9/5/55. Commd 14/2/83. Wg Cdr 3/5/95. Retd MED 14/9/96.
MCKENZIE J. Born 12/7/47. Commd 1/8/69. Sqn Ldr 1/7/84. Retd ENG 12/7/91.
MCKENZIE J. CEng MIMechE MRAeS. Born 24/3/37. Commd 10/9/63. Sqn Ldr 15/2/70. Retd EDN 10/9/79.
MCKENZIE L.B. MB ChB. Born 9/3/31. Commd 14/10/56. Wg Cdr 14/10/69. Retd MED 14/10/72.
MCKENZIE L.E. DFC. Born 23/6/20. Commd 3/3/43. Sqn Ldr 1/7/65. Retd GD(G) 23/6/75.
MCKEON A.J.M. CBE AFC. Born 3/2/44. Commd 21/12/62. A Cdre 1/1/92. Retd GD 22/12/95.
MCKEOWN D.M. MBE MIIM MCMI. Born 10/8/34. Commd 23/3/65. Wg Cdr 1/7/82. Retd ENG 1/5/85.
MCKEOWN G.M. Born 30/10/54. Commd 21/2/74. Sqn Ldr 1/7/89. Retd OPS SPT 30/10/98.

MCKEOWN I. MBE. Born 12/7/25. Commd 28/2/57. Sqn Ldr 1/1/70. Retd ADMIN 12/7/83.
MCKEOWN J.D.P. Born 22/9/51. Commd 4/5/72. Flt Lt 12/4/77. Retd OPS SPT 1/1/98.
MCKEOWN J.K. The Rev. BA. Born 13/4/10. Commd 15/7/41. Retd Wg Cdr 15/3/63.
MCKEVITT M. MBE . Born 22/4/48. Commd 11/4/85. Sqn Ldr 1/7/00. Retd ENGINEER 22/4/05.
MCKIE-SMITH S. Born 12/6/45. Commd 28/11/69. Flt Lt 28/5/75. Retd GD 14/7/87. Re-instated 1/3/91. Flt Lt 13/1/79. Retd GD 1/8/94.
MCKIERNAN C.J. BA MBIFM. Born 13/9/61. Commd 19/6/88. Sqn Ldr 1/1/96. Retd ADMIN (SEC) 19/6/04.
MCKILLEN J.D.B. Born 7/10/45. Commd 26/4/84. Sqn Ldr 1/7/94. Retd ADMIN 5/4/99.
MCKINLAY K.P. MB BS MRCP MRCS LRCP. Born 17/6/57. Commd 28/5/86. Wg Cdr 4/8/94. Retd MED 15/10/97.
MCKINLAY P. MA BEd. Born 24/3/50. Commd 20/5/79. Sqn Ldr 1/1/86. Retd ADMIN 1/2/96.
MCKINLAY R.C. AFC. Born 30/4/42. Commd 30/7/63. Wg Cdr 1/7/78. Retd GD 1/7/81.
MCKINLEY J.P.J. Born 3/8/11. Commd 17/3/41. Sqn Ldr 1/4/56. Retd ENG 11/3/67.
MCKINLEY M.S.J. Born 2/10/41. Commd 31/7/62. Sqn Ldr 1/1/73. Retd GD 2/10/79.
MCKINNON P.D. Born 22/7/42. Commd 6/5/65. Flt Lt 2/10/71. Retd GD 2/2/81.
MCKINSTRY P.E.G. Born 30/12/33. Commd 6/4/54. Flt Lt 6/4/59. Retd SUP 6/7/67.
MCKNIGHT R.J.N. BA. Born 22/3/36. Commd 14/10/63. Flt Lt 14/10/63. Retd GD 22/3/74.
MCLACHLAN A.C. Born 19/7/45. Commd 2/3/78. Flt Lt 2/3/80. Retd GD 26/11/84.
MCLACHLAN A.L. Born 3/12/30. Commd 26/5/55. Flt Lt 26/11/60. Retd GD(G) 3/12/68. Re-instated 20/9/71. Flt Lt 13/9/63. Retd GD(G) 3/12/88.
MCLACHLAN G.G. MBE. Born 3/10/34. Commd 10/12/52. Wg Cdr 1/1/81. Retd GD 3/10/89.
MCLACHLAN P. MSc BEng CEng MIEE. Born 13/5/61. Commd 10/6/84. Wg Cdr 1/1/98. Retd ENG 1/1/00.
MCLACHLAN T.A.G. Born 27/12/25. Commd 14/4/49. Sqn Ldr 1/1/60. Retd GD 30/12/68.
MCLARDY W. Born 12/6/33. Commd 9/4/52. Flt Lt 5/9/57. Retd GD 12/6/71.
MCLAREN B.G. MSc MBA MCMI. Born 3/11/47. Commd 27/2/75. Gp Capt 1/1/96. Retd GD 24/8/01.
MCLAREN B.K. Born 21/5/34. Commd 16/4/57. Wg Cdr 1/1/84. Retd GD 21/5/92.
MCLAREN C.A.B. MB ChB FFARCS. Born 11/2/28. Commd 30/3/53. A Cdre 1/6/87. Retd MED 11/2/93.
MCLAREN J. Born 11/12/45. Commd 16/8/68. Flt Lt 16/2/74. Retd GD 24/9/76.
MCLAREN J.C.E. Born 2/8/28. Commd 27/10/67. Sqn Ldr 1/7/80. Retd ENG 2/8/84.
MCLAREN M.R. Born 23/12/60. Commd 16/6/88. Sqn Ldr 1/7/96. Retd OPS SPT 1/7/99.
MCLAREN S.A. Born 16/3/61. Commd 8/4/82. Sqn Ldr 1/1/94. Retd GD 16/3/99.
MCLAUCHLAN R.H. Born 11/4/21. Commd 1/7/45. Flt Lt 19/11/53. Retd GD 1/10/68.
MCLAUGHLAN K.B. The Rev. BD PhL. Born 3/5/30. Commd 3/7/67. Retd Wg Cdr 30/11/87.
MCLAUGHLIN A.N. MA BSc. Born 20/3/62. Commd 14/9/80. Wg Cdr 1/7/98. Retd GD 19/11/01.
MCLAUGHLIN G. Born 22/2/53. Commd 1/11/79. Flt Lt 29/9/82. Retd GD(G) 22/2/91.
MCLAUGHLIN M. Born 13/3/48. Commd 7/3/71. Gp Capt 1/7/90. Retd PRT 8/3/92.
MCLAUGHLIN P.C. Born 7/10/41. Commd 21/12/62. Flt Lt 1/7/68. Retd GD 7/10/79.
MCLAUGHLIN R. Born 15/1/40. Commd 24/8/72. Wg Cdr 1/1/91. Retd GD(G) 15/1/95.
MCLAUGHLIN R.P. MCMI. Born 23/9/30. Commd 22/10/54. Flt Lt 22/4/60. Retd GD 29/6/70.
MCLAUGHLIN S. AFC BSc. Born 1/12/59. Commd 9/11/78. Flt Lt 15/4/81. Retd GD 1/12/97.
MCLAUGHLIN S.J. Born 16/10/63. Commd 4/12/86. Flt Lt 4/6/92. Retd GD 12/5/02.
MCLAUGHLIN W. MSc BEng. Born 24/4/63. Commd 2/8/89. Flt Lt 15/7/92. Retd ENGINEER 29/7/03.
MCLEA C.D. Born 1/12/44. Commd 29/4/71. Flt Lt 1/4/74. Retd GD 14/9/96.
MCLEAN A.H. BSc. Born 3/9/50. Commd 9/9/69. Sqn Ldr 1/1/85. Retd GD 3/9/88.
MCLEAN A.I. Born 13/12/31. Commd 19/8/71. Flt Lt 19/8/73. Retd SUP 3/12/86.
MCLEAN A.K. Born 8/2/30. Commd 19/8/53. Flt Lt 25/2/59. Retd GD 26/8/73.
MCLEAN D. PhD CEng MIEE. Born 22/1/36. Commd 27/6/58. Sqn Ldr 27/6/70. Retd EDN 27/6/74.
MCLEAN G. Born 6/7/41. Commd 17/7/70. Sqn Ldr 1/1/78. Retd ENG 1/1/81.
MCLEAN G.M. Born 2/12/21. Commd 24/8/43. Wg Cdr 1/1/62. Retd ENG 2/12/76.
MCLEAN I. Born 10/4/40. Commd 3/1/64. Flt Lt 22/5/71. Retd GD 13/4/77.
MCLEAN I.J. Born 5/3/62. Commd 5/2/81. Sqn Ldr 1/7/94. Retd GD 5/3/00.
MCLEAN K. Born 21/8/51. Commd 22/6/89. Flt Lt 22/6/93. Retd MED(SEC) 14/3/96.
MCLEAN Q. Born 4/1/43. Commd 24/4/70. Flt Lt 4/5/72. Retd GD(G) 4/1/81. Re-entrant 22/4/87. Flt Lt 20/8/78. Retd GD(G) 14/3/96.
MCLEAN W.T. Born 3/12/41. Commd 31/1/64. Flt Lt 4/5/72. Retd GD 31/8/75.
MCLEISH I. Born 10/8/46. Commd 21/1/66. Flt Lt 21/7/72. Retd GD 31/8/84.
MCLELLAN A.M.K. Born 28/10/53. Commd 31/7/86. Flt Lt 31/7/88. Retd ENG 31/7/00.
MCLELLAN J.P. Born 21/4/21. Commd 9/8/56. Flt Lt 9/8/56. Retd SUP 21/4/71.
MCLELLAN M.J. BSc. Born 26/10/52. Commd 30/10/72. Flt Lt 15/4/80. Retd ENG 1/4/95.
MCLELLAN R. AFC BSc MRAeS. Born 20/1/51. Commd 24/3/74. Wg Cdr 1/1/90. Retd GD 1/6/93.
MCLEOD G. AFC. Born 27/9/46. Commd 2/8/68. Wg Cdr 1/7/84. Retd GD 27/9/90.
MCLEOD H.G. DFC. Born 27/10/15. Commd 3/7/42. Flt Lt 3/1/47. Retd GD(G) 8/11/65.
MCLEOD J. FCMI. Born 29/3/33. Commd 6/4/54. Gp Capt 1/7/77. Retd GD 29/3/93.
MCLEOD J.H. Born 6/7/45. Commd 19/8/71. Flt Lt 19/8/73. Retd GD(G) 6/7/83.
MCLEOD P. CEng MRAeS. Born 29/3/33. Commd 6/4/54. Wg Cdr 1/1/76. Retd ENG 25/1/84.
MCLEOD R. The Rev. MA BD. Born 7/11/17. Commd 12/12/46. Retd Wg Cdr 7/2/73.
MCLINTOCK I. MSc BSc CDipAF. Born 2/6/60. Commd 13/8/87. Sqn Ldr 1/1/94. Retd ADMIN (SEC) 12/7/03.

MCLOUGHLIN A.J. Born 1/1/47. Commd 17/12/64. Flt Lt 17/6/70. Retd GD 4/1/77.
MCLOUGHLIN J.A. MBE MA. Born 28/8/50. Commd 23/9/68. A Cdre 1/1/99. Retd ADMIN 6/11/02.
MCLOUGHLIN J.E. MBE BEM. Born 26/1/31. Commd 17/3/67. Sqn Ldr 1/7/76. Retd SY 2/4/84.
MCLOUGHLIN K.H. MB BCh BAO FFARCS(Ire). Born 5/3/55. Commd 13/10/85. Wg Cdr 1/8/93. Retd MED 14/5/02.
MCLUCKIE R. Born 8/5/39. Commd 8/6/62. Flt Lt 1/4/66. Retd GD 8/5/75.
MCLURCAN D.C. Born 8/10/34. Commd 27/1/67. Flt Lt 27/1/73. Retd ADMIN 6/11/76.
MCLUSKIE I.R. OBE MSc. Born 30/8/48. Commd 2/6/67. Gp Capt 1/1/97. Retd GD 7/4/00.
MCMAHON D. BSc. Born 1/3/62. Commd 31/7/83. Flt Lt 31/1/87. Retd ENG 31/3/94.
MCMAHON M. BSc. Born 21/12/58. Commd 29/8/77. Sqn Ldr 1/7/93. Retd ENG 26/5/97.
MCMANUS S.J. Born 20/3/44. Commd 21/7/65. Flt Lt 21/1/71. Retd GD 5/4/77. Re-entered 20/4/83. Sqn Ldr 1/7/89.
    Retd OPS SPT(FC) 20/3/04.
MCMASTER H. AFC AFM. Born 29/8/24. Commd 25/8/49. Sqn Ldr 1/7/63. Retd GD 14/5/73.
MCMASTER L. Born 21/3/29. Commd 29/10/52. Flt Lt 15/8/62. Retd GD 21/3/87.
MCMASTER T.H.L. Born 25/6/48. Commd 20/9/79. Sqn Ldr 1/1/89. Retd ENG 3/9/99.
MCMELLIN G.F. OBE BSc. Born 6/11/40. Commd 1/10/62. Gp Capt 1/1/90. Retd GD 6/11/95.
MCMICHAEL A.F. Born 18/6/35. Commd 13/7/61. Wg Cdr 1/1/78. Retd GD(G) 18/6/90.
MCMILLAN A. Born 29/10/32. Commd 12/7/51. Flt Lt 13/11/57. Retd GD 29/10/70.
MCMILLAN E.L. CBE AFC. Born 4/3/16. Commd 30/4/41. Gp Capt 1/7/58. Retd GD 4/6/66.
MCMILLAN M. MSc BEng CEng MIEE. Born 28/2/60. Commd 2/8/85. Sqn Ldr 1/1/96. Retd ENG 31/7/99.
MCMILLEN W.R. Born 13/1/48. Commd 15/8/85. Sqn Ldr 1/7/94. Retd ENGINEER 13/1/05.
MCMINN J.M. BSc CEng MRAeS. Born 16/10/30. Commd 15/10/52. Gp Capt 1/1/79. Retd GD 30/7/83.
MCMORLAND J. Born 15/12/31. Commd 24/12/64. Flt Lt 24/12/65. Retd EDN 25/10/68.
MCMULLEN E.L. MBE. Born 14/6/20. Commd 13/6/44. Sqn Ldr 1/7/52. Retd RGT 14/6/65.
MCMULLEN H.D. Born 29/4/44. Commd 1/4/66. Flt Lt 1/10/72. Retd GD(G) 29/4/82.
MCMURRAY G.B.N. Born 8/5/35. Commd 1/10/57. Flt Lt 26/2/64. Retd GD 3/10/76.
MCMURRAY W.A. Born 24/7/52. Commd 20/12/90. Flt Lt 20/12/94. Retd ENG 3/4/95.
MCNABNEY V. GM. Born 27/9/25. Commd 16/9/50. Gp Capt 1/1/72. Retd GD 27/9/80.
MCNAE C. Born 29/11/48. Commd 23/3/67. Flt Lt 23/9/72. Retd GD 14/3/96.
MCNAIR R.D. MCMI. Born 29/12/24. Commd 19/12/49. Wg Cdr 1/1/70. Retd SUP 19/9/74.
MCNALLY L.C. CEng MIEE MRAeS. Born 16/9/38. Commd 24/11/60. Sqn Ldr 1/7/77. Retd ENG 31/8/94.
MCNALLY N.F. BSc. Born 1/7/18. Commd 16/2/44. Flt Offr 7/4/48. Retd EDN 1/3/52.
MCNAMARA P.T. BA. Born 9/12/53. Commd 17/9/72. Flt Lt 15/10/76. Retd GD 25/8/77.
MCNAMARA P.V.P. Born 17/2/44. Commd 10/5/90. Flt Lt 10/5/94. Retd ENG 17/2/01.
MCNAUGHTAN J.M. Born 14/2/47. Commd 21/1/66. Flt Lt 21/7/71. Retd GD 14/2/85.
MCNAUGHTON S. Born 16/5/48. Commd 25/9/80. Sqn Ldr 1/1/88. Retd ADMIN 29/1/90.
MCNEE I.R. MBE. Born 25/6/42. Commd 15/3/87. Flt Lt 15/9/90. Retd ENG 25/6/97.
MCNEIL I. MA. Born 8/9/56. Commd 15/3/87. Flt Lt 15/9/90. Retd ADMIN 29/7/92.
MCNEIL I.W.P. Born 30/9/45. Commd 3/3/67. A Cdre 1/7/96. Retd OPS SPT 7/8/99.
MCNEIL J.J. Born 3/7/46. Commd 10/1/69. Sqn Ldr 1/1/87. Retd GD 3/7/01.
MCNEILE A.D.C. Born 24/4/44. Commd 3/8/62. Sqn Ldr 1/1/76. Retd GD 24/2/79.
MCNEILL K. Born 15/7/39. Commd 22/7/66. Flt Lt 8/11/69. Retd ENG 15/7/77.
MCNEISH J. The Rev. Born 13/9/34. Commd 31/1/66. Retd Sqn Ldr 26/8/72.
MCNICHOL D. MCMI. Born 25/3/24. Commd 28/5/47. Wg Cdr 1/7/68. Retd SUP 6/7/74.
MCNICHOLL A.L. Born 23/9/42. Commd 1/4/66. Flt Lt 1/10/71. Retd GD 3/8/76.
MCNISH A.F. BA. Born 2/5/57. Commd 9/11/80. Wg Cdr 1/1/96. Retd ADMIN 1/1/99.
MCPARTLIN M.J. Born 9/11/42. Commd 20/5/82. Flt Lt 1/3/87. Retd SUP 1/11/87.
MCPHAIL G.J. Born 25/3/21. Commd 1/12/44. Flt Lt 19/9/57. Retd GD(G) 29/12/73.
MCPHEE A. MCMI. Born 11/6/46. Commd 4/5/72. Sqn Ldr 1/7/85. Retd ADMIN 30/9/98.
MCPHEE J. AFC. Born 3/8/19. Commd 16/10/42. Flt Lt 4/12/52. Retd GD 1/6/68.
MCPHEE K.J. BA CEng FIEE. Born 18/8/39. Commd 24/9/59. Gp Capt 1/7/88. Retd ENG 18/8/94.
MCPHERSON G. AFM. Born 15/10/10. Commd 16/4/41. Sqn Ldr 1/7/53. Retd GD(G) 15/10/60.
MCPHIE R.A. Born 6/7/22. Commd 4/3/46. Sqn Ldr 1/7/56. Retd GD 6/7/65.
MCQUADE L.P. BA. Born 5/9/54. Commd 30/8/78. Sqn Ldr 1/1/91. Retd GD 30/8/94.
MCQUIGG C.J.W. BA. Born 17/4/46. Commd 11/4/85. Sqn Ldr 1/1/96. Retd GD 17/4/01.
MCQUILLAN A.R. BA. Born 12/1/33. Commd 11/10/51. Sqn Ldr 1/1/63. Retd GD 22/4/77.
MCQUILLAN C.J. OBE CEng MRAeS. Born 15/5/41. Commd 17/5/62. Gp Capt 1/1/88. Retd ENG 15/5/96.
MCQUILLAN D. Born 5/10/44. Commd 24/6/65. Wg Cdr 1/7/87. Retd GD 14/9/96.
MCQUINN D.E. Born 30/9/37. Commd 1/11/57. Fg Offr 1/11/57. Retd GD 19/7/63.
MCRAE J. Born 14/5/41. Commd 4/10/63. Sqn Ldr 1/1/75. Retd GD 8/10/94.
MCROBB J.McK. Born 14/6/28. Commd 27/8/64. Sqn Ldr 1/1/80. Retd SUP 14/6/83.
MCROBB K.D. AFC. Born 26/3/33. Commd 28/3/53. Sqn Ldr 1/7/80. Retd GD 8/11/87.
MCROBBIE G.L. Born 16/6/44. Commd 22/2/63. A Cdre 1/7/97. Retd GD 1/12/98.
MCROBERTS D.D. MA. Born 28/3/57. Commd 18/11/79. Flt Lt 18/2/82. Retd ADMIN 1/6/90.
MCSHERRY A.L. BSc. Born 11/7/55. Commd 16/9/73. Wg Cdr 1/1/00. Retd GD 31/7/03.
MCSORLEY D.F.H. Born 17/5/44. Commd 17/2/67. Flt Lt 17/8/72. Retd GD 31/10/82.
MCSORLEY T. Born 23/1/42. Commd 10/2/72. Flt Lt 10/2/74. Retd GD 23/1/97.

MCTAGGART P.P. BEd. Born 4/2/60. Commd 26/4/87. Flt Lt 26/10/90. Retd ADMIN 1/12/96.
MCTAVISH D.I. MBE. Born 23/1/35. Commd 23/6/67. Sqn Ldr 1/1/75. Retd ENG 23/1/90.
MCTEER A.H. Born 10/10/44. Commd 17/3/67. Sqn Ldr 1/7/85. Retd GD(G) 14/8/94.
MCTEER D. MCMI. Born 21/4/47. Commd 2/8/68. Gp Capt 1/7/94. Retd ADMIN 14/9/96.
MCTEER T. Born 21/8/19. Commd 31/10/63. Flt Lt 31/10/66. Retd PE 21/8/74.
MCTIGHE M.G. Born 12/8/49. Commd 15/8/85. Flt Lt 15/8/89. Retd ENG 2/5/94.
MCTURK J.McE. Born 1/12/22. Commd 1/5/52. Flt Lt 14/11/56. Retd GD 14/10/70.
MCVIE J. Born 16/10/33. Commd 10/4/56. Sqn Ldr 1/1/64. Retd GD 16/10/71.
MCVITIE A.McK. Born 8/2/28. Commd 10/1/51. Sqn Ldr 1/1/61. Retd GD 29/2/68.
MCWICKER J.S. AFM. Born 25/2/24. Commd 4/5/50. Flt Lt 4/11/53. Retd GD 1/10/68.
MCWILLIAM A.C. DPhysEd. Born 17/11/23. Commd 3/2/51. Flt Lt 22/5/57. Retd PE 31/1/67.
MCWILLIAMS J.B. Born 8/10/21. Commd 16/10/42. Sqn Ldr 1/7/53. Retd GD 8/10/64.
MEACHAM H.W. Born 30/10/21. Commd 24/9/59. Flt Lt 24/9/64. Retd ENG 30/10/73.
MEACHAM R.L. Born 17/3/44. Commd 17/1/85. Sqn Ldr 1/7/93. Retd ADMIN 17/3/99.
MEAD C. Born 22/7/41. Commd 10/11/61. Flt Lt 22/1/67. Retd GD 22/7/79.
MEAD D.J. BSc. Born 30/3/49. Commd 24/9/67. Flt Lt 15/10/72. Retd GD 30/3/87.
MEAD S.B. Born 21/3/32. Commd 4/7/51. Fg Offr 3/5/53. Retd GD 1/8/70.
MEADE S.C. OBE. Born 4/4/61. Commd 13/3/80. Wg Cdr 1/7/99. Retd GD 1/6/02.
MEADER J.C. Born 6/2/34. Commd 11/4/54. Wg Cdr 1/7/78. Retd GD(G) 6/2/89.
MEADLEY B.A.F. Born 27/4/30. Commd 12/12/51. Flt Lt 12/6/54. Retd GD 27/4/68.
MEADOWS C.J. Born 17/3/47. Commd 18/12/80. Flt Lt 18/12/82. Retd GD 7/12/96.
MEADOWS F.W.G. Born 15/10/23. Commd 13/2/58. Sqn Ldr 1/7/72. Retd GD 15/10/83.
MEADOWS J. OBE MCMI. Born 20/7/29. Commd 11/4/51. Gp Capt 1/7/76. Retd SUP 21/7/79.
MEADOWS L. MBE. Born 9/8/22. Commd 24/1/52. Sqn Ldr 1/7/73. Retd GD 9/12/76.
MEADOWS M. AFC. Born 4/2/33. Commd 8/11/51. Flt Lt 23/2/57. Retd GD 4/2/71.
MEADOWS N.R. Born 6/1/53. Commd 1/7/82. Flt Lt 15/6/86. Retd ADMIN 29/11/93.
MEADS R.H.F. Born 20/9/61. Commd 14/8/80. Flt Lt 14/2/87. Retd SUP 1/10/91.
MEADWELL D.M. Born 14/12/41. Commd 8/12/61. Wg Cdr 1/1/93. Retd GD 14/12/96.
MEAGHER J.K. CEng MRAeS. Born 1/11/56. Commd 28/2/80. Gp Capt 1/1/00. Retd ENG 10/1/01.
MEAKIN C.J. Born 5/11/43. Commd 13/10/61. Wg Cdr 1/1/89. Retd GD 21/7/92.
MEALING D.L. DFM. Born 8/7/19. Commd 5/7/43. Flt Lt 5/1/47. Retd GD 9/5/53.
MEARS J.A. AFM. Born 16/6/19. Commd 28/1/60. Flt Lt 28/1/65. Retd GD(G) 16/6/77.
MEARS W.A. BA. Born 11/3/34. Commd 17/12/52. Gp Capt 1/7/80. Retd GD 9/4/86.
MEATON R.A.H. BA. Born 9/3/51. Commd 24/1/72. Flt Lt 15/10/76. Retd SEC 3/2/79.
MEATS E.N. CBE BSc. Born 11/12/29. Commd 19/8/53. A Cdre 1/1/80. Retd ADMIN 11/12/84.
MEATYARD M.J. Born 19/3/51. Commd 4/2/71. Flt Lt 4/8/77. Retd GD(G) 19/3/89.
MECKIFF J.L. Born 20/9/33. Commd 31/7/45. Sqn Ldr 1/7/57. Retd GD 20/9/66.
MEDCALF D. Born 30/5/58. Commd 10/5/90. Flt Lt 10/5/92. Retd ADMIN 10/5/98.
MEDCRAFT A.J. Born 3/3/48. Commd 2/2/78. Flt Lt 15/10/80. Retd SY 28/12/86.
MEDD-SYGROVE B.F. Born 30/9/57. Commd 6/7/80. Flt Lt 6/7/86. Retd ADMIN 31/3/94.
MEDDINGS E.J. Born 5/6/23. Commd 4/5/50. Flt Lt 19/11/53. Retd GD 1/6/68.
MEDFORD A.W. BSc. Born 23/3/50. Commd 15/9/69. Wg Cdr 1/7/89. Retd GD 23/3/05.
MEDHURST I.B. Born 8/11/42. Commd 12/9/63. Sqn Ldr 1/7/92. Retd ADMIN 31/7/96.
MEDHURST P.W. Born 26/7/50. Commd 25/2/72. Flt Lt 25/2/75. Retd GD 26/7/88.
MEDLAND C.G. Born 9/5/44. Commd 28/2/66. Flt Lt 28/2/70. Retd GD 9/7/82. rtg Sqn Ldr.
MEDLAND L.G. MSc CEng MRAeS MCMI. Born 3/11/35. Commd 1/2/63. Sqn Ldr 1/1/70. Retd ENG 3/11/93.
MEDLAND W.J. Born 17/5/49. Commd 4/3/71. Sqn Ldr 1/1/88. Retd FLY(N) 17/5/04.
MEDWAY P.W. Born 21/2/49. Commd 2/6/77. Fg Offr 2/6/77. Retd SY 1/7/78.
MEDWORTH J.C.O. Born 3/10/18. Commd 25/4/43. Flt Lt 25/6/52. Retd GD(G) 1/8/64.
MEE E.D. MBE. Born 9/4/24. Commd 25/3/54. Flt Lt 17/5/56. Retd GD 9/4/84.
MEE R.I. Born 19/7/16. Commd 25/8/55. Sqn Ldr 1/1/68. Retd ENG 19/7/71.
MEE V.A. BSc. Born 2/6/50. Commd 14/12/72. Sqn Ldr 1/1/91. Retd GD 19/1/97.
MEEHAN J. Born 6/7/46. Commd 23/9/67. Wg Cdr 1/1/87. Retd GD 14/3/96.
MEEHAN K.T. Born 20/4/33. Commd 24/1/52. Sqn Ldr 1/1/66. Retd GD 20/4/71.
MEEHAN M. Born 12/12/19. Commd 2/10/43. Wg Cdr 1/1/66. Retd RGT 1/4/61.
MEEK J.B.S. MCMI. Born 24/5/38. Commd 28/7/59. Wg Cdr 1/7/79. Retd ADMIN 24/5/93.
MEEK S.A. BSc. Born 8/3/65. Commd 19/7/87. Flt Lt 19/1/89. Retd GD 23/5/89.
MEEKS J.E. MRAeS. Born 8/9/32. Commd 19/4/51. Flt Lt 25/1/57. Retd ENG 8/9/70.
MEELBOOM D.J.A. Born 6/8/45. Commd 1/6/72. Flt Lt 1/12/77. Retd GD 2/4/93.
MEGARRY J.B. Born 7/12/54. Commd 12/2/76. Sqn Ldr 1/1/88. Retd GD 7/12/92.
MEGGS H.G. Born 6/6/32. Commd 28/9/61. Flt Lt 28/9/66. Retd GD 1/10/76.
MEICHAN W.F. CEng MRAeS. Born 16/1/29. Commd 30/7/53. Sqn Ldr 1/1/66. Retd GD 30/4/77.
MEIKLEJOHN A.A. Born 13/9/38. Commd 9/3/66. Flt Lt 4/5/72. Retd ENG 24/7/77.
MEIKLEJOHN I.R. BA. Born 10/4/47. Commd 10/1/71. Flt Lt 10/10/74. Retd GD(G) 10/10/93.
MEIKLEJOHN J.S. Born 2/1/21. Commd 19/3/43. Sqn Ldr 1/1/56. Retd GD 30/3/68.
MEJOR J.G. DFC. Born 12/7/21. Commd 20/3/42. Sqn Ldr 1/1/53. Retd GD 12/7/64.

MELBOURNE A.P. Born 14/6/25. Commd 25/5/45. Sqn Ldr 1/1/62. Retd GD 26/8/77.
MELDON M. Born 14/8/47. Commd 28/4/67. Flt Lt 28/10/72. Retd GD 4/11/84.
MELDRUM R.S. Born 26/4/37. Commd 8/1/59. Flt Lt 15/2/65. Retd GD 1/9/65.
MELDRUM R.S. MCIPS MCMI. Born 4/11/38. Commd 15/7/58. Sqn Ldr 1/7/70. Retd SUP 8/8/78.
MELHUISH P. Born 14/11/49. Commd 11/11/71. Wg Cdr 1/1/97. Retd GD 5/1/04.
MELLERS J. DFC. Born 15/3/25. Commd 16/3/45. Gp Capt 1/1/71. Retd GD 13/7/73.
MELLET P.C. MBE. Born 24/2/24. Commd 28/1/44. Sqn Ldr 1/7/57. Retd GD 24/2/73.
MELLING P. BSc CEng MRAeS ACGI. Born 6/12/47. Commd 22/3/81. Sqn Ldr 1/1/88. Retd ENG 16/6/00.
MELLISH P.J. MBE. Born 2/4/33. Commd 29/12/51. Wg Cdr 1/7/82. Retd GD 30/9/91.
MELLOR D.B. MA DMS CertEd. Born 7/9/51. Commd 17/12/79. Wg Cdr 1/7/99. Retd GD 2/2/05.
MELLOR E.V. MBE MRAeS. Born 4/1/29. Commd 26/7/50. Gp Capt 1/1/76. Retd GD 4/1/84.
MELLOR H.L. AFC. Born 31/10/18. Commd 19/1/43. Sqn Ldr 1/7/59. Retd GD 31/7/62.
MELLOR P.R. DFC*. Born 11/5/21. Commd 14/3/42. Flt Lt 19/4/45. Retd GD(G) 11/5/67.
MELLOR S.I. Born 19/7/48. Commd 18/1/73. Flt Lt 18/7/75. Retd GD 19/7/86.
MELLOR S.S. Born 22/2/25. Commd 4/10/56. Sqn Ldr 1/7/73. Retd GD(G) 22/2/83.
MELLOR T.K. MB BCh BDS FDSRCPS FRCS(Ed). Born 17/11/54. Commd 8/1/84. Wg Cdr 13/2/92. Retd DEL 8/1/00.
MELLORS W.C. Born 28/2/49. Commd 20/9/79. Flt Lt 20/9/81. Retd ADMIN 30/9/94.
MELROSE D.G.A. MBE. Born 28/5/22. Commd 25/4/43. Wg Cdr 1/7/68. Retd SEC 8/4/75.
MELROSE J.F.C. DFC. Born 11/2/20. Commd 20/8/41. Wg Cdr 1/1/61. Retd GD 10/4/72. rtg Gp Capt.
MELSOM C.J. BSc. Born 26/12/38. Commd 19/2/63. Flt Lt 19/11/66. Retd ENG 19/2/79.
MELTON N.H. Born 18/6/44. Commd 30/4/67. Flt Lt 30/4/71. Retd GD 30/4/89.
MELVILLE K.I. Born 7/12/61. Commd 11/4/85. Flt Lt 11/10/91. Retd SUP 31/3/94.
MELVILLE R.K.C. Born 28/10/38. Commd 25/7/60. Flt Lt 6/3/63. Retd GD 28/12/69.
MELVILLE-JACKSON A. Born 17/8/47. Commd 1/3/68. Sqn Ldr 1/7/83. Retd FLY(P) 17/8/04.
MELVILLE-JACKSON G.H. DFC BA. Born 23/11/19. Commd 22/6/40. Wg Cdr 1/1/58. Retd GD 29/9/68.
MELVIN A.L. BSc. Born 15/5/33. Commd 8/8/56. Sqn Ldr 25/4/66. Retd ADMIN 15/5/93.
MELVIN N. Born 19/8/19. Commd 27/2/47. Flt Lt 27/8/51. Retd GD(G) 29/10/66.
MELVIN W.J. Born 1/1/44. Commd 1/3/71. Sqn Ldr 1/1/83. Retd ADMIN 3/7/87.
MENEAR G.H. Born 7/6/26. Commd 2/10/58. Flt Lt 2/10/63. Retd GD(G) 7/6/76.
MENEZES G.L. Born 25/8/41. Commd 3/3/68. Flt Lt 4/11/70. Retd GD 25/8/79.
MENZIES A.R. Born 31/10/34. Commd 13/7/59. Flt Lt 6/3/63. Retd PE 19/6/73.
MENZIES P.D. Commd 2/3/45. Born 5/4/24. Sqn Ldr 1/7/55. Retd GD 31/3/75.
MENZIES R.C. Born 2/9/16. Commd 15/6/42. Flt Lt 3/10/49. Retd GD 11/11/58.
MERCER A. Born 28/7/17. Commd 26/1/42. Sqn Ldr 1/1/54. Retd ENG 29/10/66.
MERCER B.P.W. AFC*. Born 19/1/29. Commd 29/1/48. Sqn Ldr 1/1/60. Retd GD 19/1/67.
MERCER J.D. Born 8/5/23. Commd 17/1/49. Flt Lt 13/4/60. Retd GD 26/3/62.
MERCER M.J. Born 18/8/33. Commd 30/7/52. Flt Lt 5/11/58. Retd GD 18/8/88.
MERCER M.J. Born 11/3/57. Commd 17/5/79. Wg Cdr 1/1/98. Retd GD 3/4/04.
MERCER P.R. MSc BSc CEng MIEE. Born 5/1/54. Commd 3/9/72. Sqn Ldr 1/7/85. Retd ENG 1/4/93.
MERCER R.N. Born 9/2/47. Commd 8/12/83. Sqn Ldr 1/1/92. Retd ADMIN 1/7/93.
MERCER T.J. Born 20/2/43. Commd 14/6/63. Flt Lt 14/12/68. Retd GD 28/12/73.
MERCER W.H. Born 29/5/19. Commd 27/5/54. Flt Lt 22/7/57. Retd GD 6/3/64.
MERCH-CHAMMON E. MBE CEng MIERE. Born 22/3/18. Commd 14/4/41. Wg Cdr 1/7/63. Retd ENG 6/7/67.
MERCHANT C.F.P. CEng MIERE MCMI. Born 5/11/42. Commd 15/7/64. Wg Cdr 1/7/83. Retd ENG 5/11/86.
MEREDITH R.G. Born 5/6/38. Commd 28/7/59. Sqn Ldr 1/1/70. Retd SUP 1/10/87.
MEREDITH W.D. Born 2/8/17. Commd 15/1/44. Fg Offr 30/11/47. Retd GD 14/12/54. rtg Flt Lt.
MERIDEW K.J. Born 17/7/64. Commd 3/3/84. Fg Offr 15/9/86. Retd GD(G) 30/4/88.
MERIFIELD P.J. Born 15/10/48. Commd 16/8/68. Flt Lt 16/2/74. Retd GD 1/10/94.
MERRELL D. BSc DipSoton. Born 2/10/37. Commd 1/1/63. Sqn Ldr 1/3/69. Retd EDN 1/1/79.
MERRETT K.D. Born 26/7/33. Commd 1/7/52. Flt Lt 22/5/57. Retd GD 26/7/88.
MERRICK C.S. Born 24/11/68. Commd 5/5/88. Flt Lt 24/3/95. Retd ADMIN 14/3/97.
MERRICK R.E. MCIPD ACIB. Born 18/6/52. Commd 17/1/82. Flt Lt 17/10/85. Retd ADMIN (SEC) 17/1/05.
MERRICK R.H. BA. Born 29/12/50. Commd 15/9/69. Flt Lt 15/4/76. Retd SEC 1/9/79.
MERRIFIELD A.J. MB BS FFARCS MRCS LRCP MIBiol DA. Born 4/8/26. Commd 1/5/51. A Cdre 1/1/82.
   Retd MED 1/6/87.
MERRIFIELD W.G.J. Born 3/9/20. Commd 2/9/45. Sqn Ldr 1/7/60. Retd SEC 1/7/68.
MERRILL E. Born 15/12/16. Commd 21/5/41. Flt Lt 1/9/45. Retd SUP 18/12/53. rtg Sqn Ldr.
MERRILL M. Born 6/8/59. Commd 22/2/79. Flt Lt 22/8/84. Retd GD 6/8/97.
MERRIMAN D.A.P. MA BA. Born 6/12/37. Commd 31/7/61. Sqn Ldr 1/7/71. Retd GD 1/2/88.
MERRIMAN E.W. CBE DFM FCMI. Born 12/8/20. Commd 15/12/42. A Cdre 1/7/71. Retd GD 1/5/74.
MERRIMAN H.A. CBE AFC* FRAeS. Born 17/5/29. Commd 1/8/51. AVM 1/1/81. Retd GD 20/10/84.
MERRIMAN J.L. Born 27/6/46. Commd 21/10/66. Sqn Ldr 1/1/82. Retd OPS SPT 2/6/99.
MERRIMAN P.A. BSc. Born 14/5/43. Commd 15/7/65. Sqn Ldr 1/1/74. Retd ENG 14/5/81.
MERRITT B.W. Born 22/6/42. Commd 8/10/70. Flt Lt 8/10/72. Retd GD 22/6/80.
MERRITT J.C. MB BS MRCGP DRCOG DAvMed. Born 22/10/48. Commd 27/7/70. Wg Cdr 11/7/87.
   Retd MED 6/11/88.

MERRY J.E.N. Born 18/4/36. Commd 22/1/55. Sqn Ldr 1/1/67. Retd GD 9/8/77.
MERRY J.F. Born 27/10/34. Commd 5/4/55. Sqn Ldr 1/1/68. Retd GD 27/10/89.
MERRY R.T.G. MB BS FRCP MRCPsych DRCOG. Born 25/10/37. Commd 26/9/71. Sqn Ldr 7/5/70.
     Retd MED 26/8/76. Re-entered 20/8/80. A Cdre 1/2/99. Retd MED 25/10/02.
MERRYWEATHER D.V. Born 7/10/47. Commd 17/3/67. Sqn Ldr 1/7/90. Retd OPS SPT 6/10/02.
MERVYN-JONES C.F. DFO DFC. Born 12/5/18. Commd 15/6/40. Wg Cdr 1/7/52. Retd GD 14/5/60.
MESSAGE S.A. Born 7/4/13. Commd 30/1/47. Plt Offr 30/1/47. Retd SUP 1/11/48.
MESTON P. Born 23/12/16. Commd 31/7/37. Wg Cdr 1/1/49. Retd GD 30/6/58.
METCALF M.J. Born 7/1/54. Commd 9/12/91. Sqn Ldr 1/7/84. Retd GD 7/1/92. rtg Wg Cdr.
METCALF V.K. DFC. Born 30/11/25. Commd 1/3/57. Wg Cdr 1/1/67. Retd GD 1/5/76.
METCALFE F.D. Born 1/1/23. Commd 23/4/47. Wg Cdr 1/1/75. Retd SEC 1/1/78.
METCALFE G. Born 9/4/29. Commd 23/1/64. Flt Lt 23/1/69. Retd GD(G) 10/4/79.
METCALFE P.J. MCMI. Born 6/6/34. Commd 29/10/64. Sqn Ldr 1/7/79. Retd ENG 6/6/94.
METCALFE R. Born 16/2/47. Commd 25/2/66. Wg Cdr 1/7/90. Retd GD 31/3/95.
METHERELL M.J. BA. Born 5/6/37. Commd 2/10/58. Wg Cdr 1/1/81. Retd GD 5/6/92.
MEWES A. Born 11/2/53. Commd 2/2/75. Sqn Ldr 1/1/89. Retd ENG 1/1/92.
MEYER B.G. DFC. Born 17/8/17. Commd 9/8/37. Sqn Ldr 1/7/70. Retd SEC 1/7/73.
MEYER K. Born 21/1/15. Commd 17/3/55. Flt Lt 17/3/58. Retd ENG 22/1/70.
MEYER M.S. Born 17/2/45. Commd 9/12/76. Wg Cdr 1/7/93. Retd ADMIN 17/5/00.
MEYER R.H. BSc. Born 26/4/59. Commd 9/11/80. Sqn Ldr 1/1/90. Retd SY 14/3/97.
MEYER R.J. Born 27/9/45. Commd 19/6/70. Flt Lt 17/10/76. Retd GD(G) 1/4/89.
MEYER T.P. Born 27/6/23. Commd 27/8/45. Flt Lt 27/2/48. Retd GD 27/6/66.
MEYERS T.K. Born 11/12/30. Commd 22/12/53. Flt Lt 21/10/59. Retd GD 11/12/68.
MEYNELL C.S. BSc. Born 15/2/53. Commd 17/9/72. Flt Lt 15/4/79. Retd ENG 9/8/83.
MEYRICK R.R.F. Born 27/6/36. Commd 26/1/56. Sqn Ldr 1/7/71. Retd SUP 1/10/77.
MIALL M.J.D. Born 25/9/42. Commd 12/1/62. Sqn Ldr 1/7/88. Retd GD 19/4/00.
MICALLEF D. MCIT MCMI. Born 11/1/45. Commd 26/8/66. Wg Cdr 1/1/92. Retd SUP 11/1/00.
MICALLEF-EYNAUD M.A. Born 11/10/48. Commd 27/2/70. Sqn Ldr 1/1/80. Retd GD 11/10/86.
MICHAEL J.J. Born 7/8/19. Commd 13/3/47. Sqn Ldr 1/1/67. Retd SEC 28/2/73.
MICHAELS T.J. Born 9/11/42. Commd 12/7/63. Flt Lt 12/1/69. Retd GD 1/1/75.
MICHIE I.G. Born 3/8/31. Commd 17/1/52. Flt Lt 24/7/57. Retd GD 3/8/69.
MICKLEBURGH G.H. MITD. Born 11/11/28. Commd 31/12/62. Wg Cdr 1/7/77. Retd GD(G) 11/5/85.
MICKLEBURGH-SAUNDERS R.J. Born 1/6/13. Commd 29/4/43. Flt Lt 29/10/46. Retd ENG 5/12/53.
MIDDA M. BDS FDSRCS. Born 24/2/37. Commd 6/1/63. Sqn Ldr 13/11/65. Retd DEL 31/8/71.
MIDDLEBROOK G. MBE. Born 13/9/26. Commd 25/10/46. Wg Cdr 1/7/67. Retd GD 11/9/76.
MIDDLEBROOK P.T. Born 7/2/37. Commd 26/5/61. Flt Lt 10/2/67. Retd GD 9/9/79.
MIDDLEMAS R. Born 7/2/54. Commd 10/3/77. Flt Lt 10/9/82. Retd GD 15/12/92.
MIDDLEMIST M.J. Born 18/2/31. Commd 11/11/50. Wg Cdr 1/1/72. Retd GD 10/12/85.
MIDDLETON A. Born 15/7/33. Commd 20/3/52. Flt Lt 17/12/58. Retd SUP 26/6/64.
MIDDLETON B.D. BA. Born 19/4/55. Commd 16/9/73. Flt Lt 15/10/79. Retd ADMIN 22/2/83.
MIDDLETON C.L. Born 25/4/39. Commd 9/2/62. Flt Lt 9/8/67. Retd GD 1/6/79.
MIDDLETON G.W. Born 18/9/62. Commd 25/2/82. Flt Lt 25/8/87. Retd GD 18/9/00.
MIDDLETON H.K.W. BA FCMI MCIPD. Born 7/2/44. Commd 15/7/66. Gp Capt 1/1/89. Retd ADMIN 30/6/93.
MIDDLETON I.S. MBA BA. Born 12/4/57. Commd 3/9/78. Gp Capt 1/7/00. Retd GD 8/1/04.
MIDDLETON J. Born 19/10/29. Commd 28/6/50. Flt Lt 14/5/56. Retd GD 19/10/67.
MIDDLETON J. MBE MCMI. Born 3/5/27. Commd 24/9/64. Sqn Ldr 1/1/76. Retd ENG 31/3/78.
MIDDLETON J. Born 21/9/48. Commd 31/7/70. Gp Capt 1/1/98. Retd GD 30/7/01.
MIDDLETON J.B. BSc. Born 25/2/55. Commd 1/7/74. Flt Lt 15/10/78. Retd GD 25/1/94.
MIDDLETON J.G. Born 16/3/34. Commd 21/5/52. Flt Lt 16/10/57. Retd GD 16/3/93.
MIDDLETON K.S. LLB. Born 25/10/45. Commd 18/8/67. Sqn Ldr 1/7/82. Retd ADMIN 1/7/85.
MIDDLETON L.M. Born 23/10/12. Commd 23/7/32. Plt Offr 23/7/32. Retd GD 5/4/33.
MIDDLETON N. Born 9/3/29. Commd 25/6/66. Flt Lt 25/6/71. Retd SUP 9/7/83.
MIDDLETON P.G. Born 24/1/45. Commd 24/6/76. Sqn Ldr 1/7/94. Retd OPS SPT 1/7/99.
MIDDLETON P.G. Born 15/9/26. Commd 15/5/46. Wg Cdr 1/1/67. Retd GD 20/12/75.
MIDDLETON R. AFC. Born 11/8/06. Commd 2/5/40. Sqn Ldr 23/11/43. Retd GD 11/7/46. rtg Wg Cdr.
MIDDLETON R.J. BSc. Born 21/9/49. Commd 2/1/77. Sqn Ldr 1/1/89. Retd GD(G) 2/1/93.
MIDDLETON W.I.C. MBE. Born 1/3/37. Commd 18/6/62. Sqn Ldr 1/1/76. Retd SUP 26/10/82.
MIDDLETON Y.M. Born 1/7/35. Commd 14/10/59. Fg Offr 14/10/59. Retd CAT 23/7/64.
MIDDLETON-JONES D.L. Born 23/9/29. Commd 3/9/52. Flt Lt 10/3/58. Retd GD 22/10/72. Re-instated 3/9/80.
     Flt Lt 23/5/68. Retd GD 23/9/89.
MIDDLEWEEK C.A.T. Born 4/8/32. Commd 15/6/61. Sqn Ldr 1/7/77. Retd GD(G) 4/8/87.
MIDDLEWICK J.N. BEd DPhysEd. Born 15/10/47. Commd 11/4/74. Sqn Ldr 1/7/89. Retd ADMIN 1/7/92.
MIDWINTER R.H. BSc MRAeS. Born 25/4/54. Commd 3/9/72. Sqn Ldr 1/7/87. Retd GD 25/6/92.
MIERS R.J.P. Born 5/10/31. Commd 28/9/51. Gp Capt 1/1/78. Retd GD 7/10/81.
MIGHALL R.T.W. OBE MSc BA. Born 4/7/40. Commd 19/12/61. Wg Cdr 1/7/80. Retd SUP 2/4/93.
MILBORROW G.C. MS MCMI. Born 2/8/40. Commd 6/10/60. Sqn Ldr 1/1/72. Retd SUP 2/8/78.

MILBURN E.J. BA. Born 18/2/64. Commd 26/4/87. Flt Lt 26/10/90. Retd ADMIN 1/8/99.
MILBURN R.L. BSc. Born 18/11/49. Commd 23/9/68. Flt Lt 15/4/73. Retd FLY(P) 18/11/04.
MILEMAN D. Born 25/7/38. Commd 14/2/66. Flt Lt 14/2/66. Retd GD 25/7/76.
MILES A.F. Born 5/9/51. Commd 15/2/77. Flt Lt 15/2/83. Retd ADMIN 14/2/93.
MILES A.P. BSc. Born 20/8/37. Commd 17/10/71. Sqn Ldr 1/1/78. Retd ENG 30/9/93.
MILES C.G. Born 25/4/15. Commd 9/8/37. Sqn Ldr 1/9/45. Retd ENG 5/5/64. rtg Wg Cdr.
MILES C.G. BA. Born 6/5/56. Commd 25/2/79. Flt Lt 25/5/80. Retd GD 25/2/95.
MILES C.R. MBE. Born 27/4/32. Commd 18/7/63. Sqn Ldr 1/7/77. Retd ENG 27/4/92.
MILES D.B.G. MBE. Born 28/3/18. Commd 14/1/40. Sqn Ldr 1/8/47. Retd ENG 1/10/50.
MILES D.M. Born 16/8/45. Commd 28/11/67. Plt Offr 28/11/68. Retd GD 20/7/69.
MILES G.C.M. MA MSc. Born 1/4/36. Commd 25/9/54. Sqn Ldr 1/7/66. Retd ENG 1/4/74.
MILES H.G.K. Born 24/3/22. Commd 24/11/60. Sqn Ldr 1/7/71. Retd SEC 1/10/74.
MILES J.E. Born 5/7/09. Commd 12/11/42. Flt Lt 25/11/45. rtg Flt Lt.
MILES J.T. BA. Born 20/7/33. Commd 9/8/54. Sqn Ldr 1/1/77. Retd GD 6/1/86.
MILES K.F.G.E. Born 14/8/40. Commd 19/12/61. Wg Cdr 1/1/87. Retd GD 31/3/97.
MILES K.H. AFC MCMI. Born 13/9/23. Commd 27/5/44. Wg Cdr 1/1/62. Retd GD 31/8/73.
MILES K.V. Born 19/11/18. Commd 15/4/43. Flt Lt 15/10/46. Retd ENG 8/9/53.
MILES L.A. Born 27/3/19. Commd 7/5/53. Sqn Ldr 1/7/65. Retd ENG 4/12/71.
MILES M.J. Born 21/5/26. Commd 4/7/51. Flt Lt 17/10/56. Retd GD 25/5/76.
MILES M.W. Born 24/2/39. Commd 8/11/62. Sqn Ldr 1/1/74. Retd ADMIN 15/9/82.
MILES P.G. MBE BSc. Born 9/1/46. Commd 2/4/65. Sqn Ldr 1/1/80. Retd FLY(P) 9/1/04.
MILES P.R. Born 28/11/59. Commd 30/3/89. Flt Lt 30/3/91. Retd ENG 14/3/97.
MILES R. Born 3/3/29. Commd 27/8/52. Flt Lt 29/4/59. Retd GD 3/3/89.
MILES R.M. Born 8/2/42. Commd 9/7/66. Sqn Ldr 1/7/76. Retd ENG 8/2/80.
MILES T. AFC. Born 1/2/41. Commd 4/12/64. Flt Lt 4/6/70. Retd GD 17/8/80.
MILL P.D. Born 16/11/58. Commd 22/5/80. Flt Lt 22/11/86. Retd SY 16/11/96.
MILLAR D.G. BSc. Born 3/4/50. Commd 6/1/71. Wg Cdr 1/7/87. Retd GD 1/7/90.
MILLAR G.H. CEng MIERE. Born 23/5/23. Commd 11/2/44. Wg Cdr 1/7/73. Retd ENG 23/5/79.
MILLAR G.M. Born 7/7/19. Commd 25/11/43. Sqn Ldr 1/1/56. Retd ENG 7/7/70.
MILLAR I.P. MSc BSc CEng MRAeS. Born 8/8/58. Commd 12/2/79. Sqn Ldr 1/1/91. Retd ENG 1/4/97.
MILLAR J.H. BA. Born 26/1/58. Commd 5/9/76. Flt Lt 15/10/82. Retd ADMIN 1/9/85.
MILLAR L.R. BSc. Born 30/6/41. Commd 9/9/63. Flt Lt 9/12/64. Retd GD 9/9/79.
MILLAR M.J. Born 1/1/50. Commd 9/12/71. Flt Lt 9/6/77. Retd GD 26/2/83.
MILLAR M.K. Born 2/2/42. Commd 25/2/66. Flt Lt 25/3/71. Retd GD 4/10/81.
MILLAR P. CB FRAeS MInstD. Born 20/6/42. Commd 30/7/63. AVM 1/1/95. Retd GD 31/5/98.
MILLAR W.I. Born 15/11/48. Commd 24/2/67. Sqn Ldr 1/1/79. Retd SUP 17/1/81.
MILLARD I.J. Born 13/7/44. Commd 20/10/67. Sqn Ldr 1/7/82. Retd ENG 13/6/93.
MILLARD L.E. BSc. Born 18/5/63. Commd 22/7/84. Plt Offr 22/7/84. Retd GD 28/1/85.
MILLARD P. Born 1/4/37. Commd 20/8/55. Flt Lt 1/3/61. Retd GD 1/4/75.
MILLARD P. DPhysEd. Born 10/3/46. Commd 7/8/67. Sqn Ldr 1/1/81. Retd ADMIN 1/9/85.
MILLARD V.F.E. Born 20/10/34. Commd 27/2/70. Sqn Ldr 1/1/83. Retd GD(G) 31/7/89.
MILLER A. Born 26/3/14. Commd 10/1/38. Wg Cdr 1/7/50. Retd SUP 20/4/59.
MILLER A.D. MRAeS. Born 17/4/16. Commd 1/4/40. Wg Cdr 1/1/56. Retd ENG 31/8/63. rtg Gp Capt.
MILLER A.S. Born 25/12/48. Commd 31/7/70. Flt Lt 31/7/73. Retd GD 5/7/01.
MILLER A.T. Born 15/1/44. Commd 8/1/65. Flt Lt 8/7/70. Retd GD 1/6/94.
MILLER A.V. Born 16/8/37. Commd 23/9/66. Flt Lt 23/9/68. Retd GD 16/8/95.
MILLER C. Born 23/4/59. Commd 20/7/78. Wg Cdr 1/7/95. Retd GD 9/4/01.
MILLER C.E.C. Born 29/4/34. Commd 17/5/60. Flt Lt 17/5/60. Retd GD 13/3/64.
MILLER C.J. Born 17/5/42. Commd 30/7/64. Flt Lt 1/7/91. Retd OPS SPT 17/5/97.
MILLER D. Born 31/3/61. Commd 7/10/91. Flt Lt 27/7/88. Retd GD(G) 14/3/96.
MILLER D. Born 25/3/38. Commd 11/11/66. Flt Lt 26/7/69. Retd GD(G) 1/11/85.
MILLER D.G. Born 3/9/37. Commd 14/8/64. Flt Lt 8/1/69. Retd GD 6/6/80.
MILLER D.S. BA. Born 20/9/49. Commd 8/11/68. Sqn Ldr 1/7/84. Retd GD 20/3/87.
MILLER E.C. Born 5/1/31. Commd 6/12/51. Flt Lt 27/3/57. Retd GD(G) 7/7/81.
MILLER G.C. BTech. Born 29/12/57. Commd 28/9/80. Flt Lt 28/12/80. Retd GD 28/9/96.
MILLER G.R. Born 10/8/47. Commd 28/2/69. Flt Lt 8/3/72. Retd GD 10/8/02.
MILLER H. Born 6/2/21. Commd 28/7/43. Wg Cdr 1/7/64. Retd GD 14/2/76.
MILLER H. MSc. Born 15/4/75. Commd 27/9/02. Flt Lt 4/10/00. Retd ADMIN (TRG) 17/8/03.
MILLER I.E. MCMI. Born 3/7/21. Commd 12/5/41. Wg Cdr 1/1/61. Retd SEC 3/11/73.
MILLER J. CBE DFC AFC FCA. Born 3/12/21. Commd 3/7/42. A Cdre 1/7/66. Retd GD 5/4/69.
MILLER J.G. The Rev. BEd. Born 29/3/40. Commd 22/5/83. Retd Sqn Ldr 31/10/88.
MILLER J.I. Born 12/2/32. Commd 17/5/51. Sqn Ldr 1/1/64. Retd GD 12/2/70.
MILLER J.J. CB BL. Born 27/4/28. Commd 6/9/47. AVM 1/1/79. Retd ADMIN 27/4/83.
MILLER J.W. CEng MRAeS. Born 22/4/21. Commd 25/1/45. Sqn Ldr 1/10/56. Retd ENG 30/3/78.
MILLER M.H. CBE AFC. Born 14/1/28. Commd 29/9/49. A Cdre 1/7/76. Retd GD 22/8/81.
MILLER P.A. BSc(Eng) CEng MRAeS ACGI. Born 15/1/46. Commd 1/1/67. Sqn Ldr 1/7/79. Retd ENG 15/1/90.

MILLER P.C. CEng MIMechE. Born 7/10/36. Commd 16/11/59. Wg Cdr 1/7/77. Retd ENG 3/4/90.
MILLER P.C.R. BSc. Born 5/4/65. Commd 9/12/95. Flt Lt 26/10/89. Retd FLY(P) 6/12/03.
MILLER P.E. Born 2/1/45. Commd 19/12/63. Sqn Ldr 1/7/81. Retd GD(G) 2/1/89.
MILLER P.J. BSc(Eng) CEng MRAeS. Born 10/9/39. Commd 20/9/60. A Cdre 1/7/90. Retd ENG 11/12/93.
MILLER P.L. Born 21/12/35. Commd 14/1/54. Sqn Ldr 1/1/72. Retd GD 21/12/89.
MILLER R. Born 23/3/42. Commd 15/3/84. Sqn Ldr 1/7/94. Retd ADMIN 1/7/97.
MILLER R. Born 6/9/38. Commd 8/6/62. Flt Lt 1/7/68. Retd GD 13/2/78. Re-instated 11/1/84. Flt Lt 29/5/74.
    Retd GD 6/9/63.
MILLER R. MBA BA MCMI. Born 18/10/33. Commd 6/5/55. Sqn Ldr 1/1/73. Retd GD 1/10/78. Re-instated 11/11/81.
    Sqn Ldr 11/2/76. Retd GD 18/10/91.
MILLER R.A. Born 11/8/21. Commd 15/1/43. Sqn Ldr 1/7/73. Retd GD 11/8/76.
MILLER R.A. OBE FCMI FRAeS. Born 12/7/36. Commd 2/4/57. A Cdre 1/1/83. Retd GD 1/3/84.
MILLER R.C. Born 5/1/43. Commd 26/5/67. Sqn Ldr 1/7/82. Retd ENG 1/7/85.
MILLER R.E. BA PGCE FRGS. Born 20/12/47. Commd 2/8/68. Flt Lt 2/2/74. Retd GD 1/5/76. Re-instated 1/10/80.
    Flt Lt 5/7/78. Retd GD(G) 22/5/95.
MILLER R.L. OBE BSc CEng MIMechE. Born 7/12/63. Commd 13/1/92. Wg Cdr 1/7/00. Retd GD 1/7/03.
MILLER S. BEng. Born 16/4/65. Commd 2/8/89. Flt Lt 23/8/92. Retd ENGINEER 16/4/03.
MILLER S. BSc. Born 25/6/41. Commd 6/1/64. Sqn Ldr 1/7/74. Retd GD 3/3/78.
MILLER S.J. CEng MIMechE MRAeS. Born 12/9/40. Commd 17/7/62. Sqn Ldr 1/1/74. Retd ENG 12/9/95.
MILLER T.F.K. BSc. Born 14/5/45. Commd 22/9/65. Flt Lt 15/10/68. Retd GD 14/5/83.
MILLER T.W.L. AFC. Born 11/12/52. Commd 1/6/72. Sqn Ldr 1/1/84. Retd GD 11/12/90.
MILLER W.H. DFC. Born 27/9/21. Commd 27/10/43. Flt Lt 27/4/47. Retd GD 18/9/56.
MILLER W.J. Born 31/7/37. Commd 7/7/67. Flt Lt 12/11/69. Retd GD 31/7/75.
MILLICAN J.A. The Rev. MA. Born 25/2/23. Commd 6/3/50. Retd Sqn Ldr 1/10/61.
MILLIGAN D. BSc. Born 11/1/56. Commd 23/4/87. Sqn Ldr 1/1/94. Retd ENG 1/3/99.
MILLIGAN F. Born 11/3/39. Commd 31/7/62. Sqn Ldr 1/7/72. Retd GD 11/3/94.
MILLIGAN G.M. BA. Born 9/12/47. Commd 6/12/70. Sqn Ldr 6/6/78. Retd ADMIN 6/12/86.
MILLIGAN J. Born 8/9/37. Commd 22/8/59. Sqn Ldr 1/1/74. Retd GD 13/8/88.
MILLIGAN J.L. MA MB BCh MRCS LRCP MRCP DPhysMed. Born 28/3/27. Commd 3/1/52. Wg Cdr 4/7/63.
    Retd MED 17/12/68. Re-entered 11/12/87. Wg Cdr 17/12/94. Retd DEL 10/2/98. Re-instated 16/6/86.
    Flt Lt 19/11/79. Retd GD(G) 19/8/91.
MILLIGAN M.J. CBE FRAeS. Born 18/8/38. Commd 2/4/57. A Cdre 1/1/88. Retd GD 18/8/93.
MILLIKIN P.M. MBE. Born 7/3/46. Commd 8/1/65. Sqn Ldr 1/7/92. Retd GD 1/6/01.
MILLINGTON N.D. MSc BChD BDS MGDSRCS(Eng). Born 22/6/58. Commd 1/2/81. Flt Lt 10/12/81.
    Retd DEL 10/12/86. Re-entered 11/12/87. Wg Cdr 17/12/94. Retd DEL 10/2/98.
MILLINGTON R.J. MCMI. Born 18/8/38. Commd 24/1/74. Flt Lt 24/1/78. Retd GD(G) 20/8/84. Re-instated 16/6/86.
    Flt Lt 19/11/79. Retd GD(G) 19/8/91.
MILLINGTON T.J. Born 14/1/65. Commd 24/6/90. Fg Offr 24/6/92. Retd ADMIN 27/6/96.
MILLINS T. Born 8/12/62. Commd 30/7/92. Flt Lt 30/7/94. Retd ENG 14/9/96.
MILLMAN A.R. Born 4/9/31. Commd 19/4/51. Flt Lt 17/10/56. Retd GD 4/9/69.
MILLMAN B. MBE. Born 19/5/10. Commd 14/1/43. Flt Lt 4/12/52. Retd SUP 6/6/59.
MILLNER R. Born 13/7/62. Commd 28/4/84. Flt Lt 29/4/89. Retd ENG 21/5/94.
MILLO J.R. Born 12/2/51. Commd 24/1/74. Flt Lt 24/7/79. Retd GD 14/9/96.
MILLOY P.D.G. MEng BSc. Born 6/9/47. Commd 16/1/72. Wg Cdr 1/7/90. Retd ENG 4/6/99.
MILLS A. Born 23/11/21. Commd 24/9/44. Flt Lt 24/9/50. Retd PE 1/2/68.
MILLS A. Born 25/10/16. Commd 3/4/39. Wg Cdr 1/7/59. Retd SUP 29/10/66.
MILLS A.A.K. Born 1/9/40. Commd 10/11/61. Flt Lt 10/5/67. Retd GD 1/9/78.
MILLS A.J. AFC. Born 27/10/17. Commd 20/12/43. Flt Lt 20/6/47. Retd GD 29/3/58.
MILLS A.M. Born 21/3/43. Commd 17/5/79. Sqn Ldr 1/1/02. Retd FLY(AEO) 21/3/05.
MILLS A.R. MBE. Born 16/9/40. Commd 13/12/79. Sqn Ldr 1/1/88. Retd ENG 31/5/97.
MILLS B.A. Born 19/12/39. Commd 19/7/84. Flt Lt 19/7/88. Retd ENGINEER 14/9/92.
MILLS B.C. Born 5/1/31. Commd 12/12/51. Sqn Ldr 1/1/66. Retd GD 14/1/69.
MILLS B.J. Born 13/12/51. Commd 6/4/72. Sqn Ldr 1/7/82. Retd GD 13/12/89.
MILLS C. Born 15/7/55. Commd 20/12/90. Flt Lt 20/12/94. Retd OPS SPT 31/12/00.
MILLS C.J. BA. Born 5/2/65. Commd 4/10/83. Flt Lt 15/1/89. Retd GD 17/10/98.
MILLS D.C. Born 7/4/31. Commd 4/6/52. Sqn Ldr 1/7/86. Retd GD 1/7/89.
MILLS D.H. Born 23/5/30. Commd 12/12/51. Sqn Ldr 1/7/65. Retd GD 16/4/73.
MILLS D.L. BA PGCE. Born 15/12/71. Commd 21/8/00. Flt Lt 1/12/00. Retd ADMIN (SEC) 19/6/03.
MILLS D.R.S. Born 9/6/30. Commd 28/2/52. Flt Lt 5/9/57. Retd GD 9/6/68.
MILLS D.T. Born 5/7/32. Commd 21/11/51. Sqn Ldr 1/1/67. Retd GD 1/10/74.
MILLS H.W. DFM. Born 24/2/20. Commd 6/4/43. Flt Lt 6/4/45. Retd GD(G) 24/2/75. rtg Sqn Ldr.
MILLS J.A. Born 5/9/56. Commd 4/9/81. Flt Lt 9/6/85. Retd GD(G) 23/9/94.
MILLS J.E. Born 30/4/43. Commd 3/5/68. Flt Lt 3/11/74. Retd SUP 27/11/83.
MILLS J.M. BSc DipSoton. Born 7/7/34. Commd 27/9/57. Wg Cdr 27/3/75. Retd EDN 6/12/75.
MILLS K. Born 13/8/31. Commd 2/7/52. Flt Lt 27/11/57. Retd GD 2/7/88.
MILLS K.A. Born 18/11/30. Commd 13/2/64. Flt Lt 13/2/69. Retd GD 1/8/74.

MILLS K.W. AFC BSc. Born 30/8/41. Commd 17/8/64. Gp Capt 1/1/90. Retd GD 30/8/93.
MILLS L.C. Born 13/2/35. Commd 24/5/53. Flt Lt 7/10/58. Retd GD 13/2/73. rtg Sqn Ldr.
MILLS M.H. BSc CEng MIEE MinstP. Born 9/3/38. Commd 25/9/59. Sqn Ldr 1/1/68. Retd ENG 9/3/76.
MILLS O. Born 7/3/29. Commd 25/8/60. Sqn Ldr 1/7/80. Retd ADMIN 7/3/84.
MILLS P.S. CEng MRAeS. Born 1/9/22. Commd 9/7/44. Sqn Ldr 1/10/55. Retd ENG 1/2/75.
MILLS R. MBE MA MSc BA JP. Born 8/8/26. Commd 13/2/47. Sqn Ldr 7/7/61. Retd EDN 25/2/67.
MILLS R. Born 10/11/15. Commd 21/6/56. Sqn Ldr 1/1/66. Retd SEC 1/1/68.
MILLS R.B. Born 27/4/41. Commd 5/4/79. Sqn Ldr 1/1/91. Retd ENG 27/4/96.
MILLS R.F. Born 31/3/34. Commd 28/1/54. Wg Cdr 1/7/76. Retd SUP 31/3/89.
MILLS R.H.F. Born 20/9/18. Commd 1/2/49. Flt Lt 22/12/49. Retd SEC 20/9/73.
MILLS R.L. OBE. Born 24/4/21. Commd 2/6/49. Wg Cdr 1/7/64. Retd ENG 20/4/76.
MILLS R.M. Born 15/9/72. Commd 19/12/91. Flt Lt 19/6/97. Retd FLY(P) 30/4/03.
MILLS R.S. Born 1/4/33. Commd 6/12/51. Sqn Ldr 1/7/75. Retd ADMIN 1/4/78.
MILLS T.J. Born 28/9/36. Commd 8/4/60. Fg Offr 8/4/61. Retd GD 1/7/66.
MILLS V.R. MHCIMA. Born 5/8/30. Commd 24/2/67. Flt Lt 24/2/72. Retd ADMIN 1/2/77.
MILLS W.H. DFC. Born 28/7/20. Commd 22/7/42. Wg Cdr 1/7/58. Retd GD 28/7/67.
MILLSON A.E. DSO DFC. Born 18/4/21. Commd 3/4/41. Sqn Ldr 1/7/61. Retd GD 30/8/67. rtg Wg Cdr.
MILLWARD G.W. CEng MIEE. Born 20/9/42. Commd 14/9/65. Sqn Ldr 1/1/75. Retd ENG 14/9/81.
MILLWARD P. Born 16/2/60. Commd 8/9/83. Sqn Ldr 1/7/96. Retd OPS SPT 1/7/99.
MILNE A.R. DPhysEd. Born 26/11/48. Commd 13/9/70. Flt Lt 3/6/75. Retd GD 7/12/82.
MILNE D. MA MCMI. Born 9/3/30. Commd 10/5/53. Wg Cdr 1/7/74. Retd ADMIN 6/4/82.
MILNE D. Born 16/10/13. Commd 20/2/43. Fg Offr 20/8/43. Retd ENG 27/1/47. rtg Flt Lt.
MILNE D.F. BSc. Born 4/12/56. Commd 30/8/78. Sqn Ldr 1/7/94. Retd GD 4/12/00.
MILNE D.J. MCMI. Born 30/10/32. Commd 28/2/57. Flt Lt 1/3/63. Retd PI 22/4/81.
MILNE G.C. Born 7/1/45. Commd 18/11/66. Wg Cdr 1/1/86. Retd GD(G) 7/11/94.
MILNE I.A. MA MA. Born 18/9/51. Commd 19/11/74. Air Cdre 1/7/02. Retd GD 1/7/05.
MILNE W.C. FCMI. Born 11/2/29. Commd 22/8/51. A Cdre 1/1/80. Retd GD 11/2/84.
MILNE-SMITH D.H. Born 6/2/47. Commd 21/1/66. Gp Capt 1/1/94. Retd GD 11/10/02.
MILNER D.C. Born 4/10/23. Commd 21/4/45. Flt Lt 7/6/51. Retd GD 4/10/78.
MILNER D.H. Born 30/1/41. Commd 28/2/85. Flt Lt 28/2/89. Retd ENG 30/1/96.
MILNER G.S. BSc. Born 20/4/64. Commd 26/10/86. Flt Lt 26/4/89. Retd GD 14/3/96.
MILNER P. Born 29/4/34. Commd 5/7/68. Sqn Ldr 1/1/75. Retd ENG 29/4/94.
MILNES J.P. BEd. Born 22/11/46. Commd 30/7/72. Wg Cdr 1/7/91. Retd ADMIN 26/9/01.
MILNES P.R. Born 18/3/58. Commd 4/9/81. Flt Lt 11/3/84. Retd GD 23/9/99.
MILNES S.D. MB BS MRCGP MRCS(Eng) LRCP DAvMed DIMC AFOM MRAeS. Born 16/2/48. Commd 9/5/71. Wg Cdr 20/6/88. Retd MED 14/3/97.
MILROY W.H. PhD BTh MCIPD MBIFM. Born 8/2/56. Commd 14/6/89. Wg Cdr 1/7/98. Retd GD 1/11/03.
MILSOM R.A. Born 20/4/15. Commd 2/4/40. Sqn Ldr 1/7/53. Retd SUP 29/4/64.
MILSOM R.J. OBE. Born 9/12/43. Commd 17/12/64. Sqn Ldr 1/1/85. Retd GD 8/12/98.
MILTON F.H.P. Born 18/9/21. Commd 9/11/47. Sqn Ldr 1/1/52. Retd RGT 29/5/58.
MILTON G.J. BSc. Born 23/7/55. Commd 19/3/78. Flt Lt 19/12/79. Retd GD 19/3/90.
MILTON I. Born 21/12/52. Commd 10/2/72. Flt Lt 10/8/77. Retd GD 1/5/90.
MILTON R.B.G. Born 24/1/47. Commd 1/3/68. Sqn Ldr 1/1/82. Retd GD 2/9/86.
MILWARD P.H. Born 17/8/43. Commd 6/5/66. Flt Lt 4/5/72. Retd GD 13/12/81.
MILWARD R.A. OBE DFC*. Born 7/10/16. Commd 16/4/35. Wg Cdr 1/7/47. Retd GD 2/5/59.
MIMMACK S.B. Born 18/6/44. Commd 1/4/65. Sqn Ldr 1/1/82. Retd GD(G) 18/6/88.
MINARDS R.P. LLB. Born 21/7/44. Commd 20/8/67. Flt Lt 20/11/68. Retd GD 20/8/89.
MINGAYE B. Born 15/9/31. Commd 17/5/51. Flt Lt 6/9/56. Retd GD 15/9/69.
MINIHANE T.R. Born 10/4/26. Commd 29/6/50. Sqn Ldr 1/1/60. Retd ENG 15/5/64.
MINNIGIN G.A.F. DCM MM. Born 21/8/20. Commd 15/11/48. Wg Cdr 1/7/62. Retd RGT 21/8/75.
MINNIS H. Born 31/1/26. Commd 22/2/46. Sqn Ldr 1/7/56. Retd GD 31/1/64.
MINNS D.G. Born 16/5/32. Commd 16/9/71. Flt Lt 16/9/73. Retd ENG 31/3/79.
MINNS P. BA. Born 23/8/19. Commd 4/1/50. Flt Lt 1/9/45. Retd ENG 11/1/62. rtg Sqn Ldr.
MINSHULL J.S. Born 24/12/54. Commd 26/9/91. Flt Lt 26/9/95. Retd ENG 20/4/98.
MINTER J.M. Born 6/12/34. Commd 9/6/54. Sqn Ldr 1/1/69. Retd SUP 1/4/88.
MINTER P.C. CEng MIEE MCMI. Born 9/1/47. Commd 1/8/69. Sqn Ldr 1/7/87. Retd ENG 9/1/91.
MINTEY D.T.H. Born 30/11/10. Commd 17/12/41. Fg Offr 22/3/43. Retd ENG 28/12/45. rtg Flt Lt.
MINTON K.H. BSc(Econ) FCMI. Born 13/1/45. Commd 3/3/67. A Cdre 1/7/91. Retd ADMIN 2/12/94.
MINTON L.A. Born 28/7/40. Commd 15/2/73. Flt Lt 15/2/75. Retd SUP 15/2/81. Re-instated 11/5/83. Sqn Ldr 1/1/87. Retd SUP 31/7/90.
MIRANDA D.A. Born 18/2/58. Commd 6/10/94. Flt Lt 6/10/98. Retd MED SUP 31/1/03.
MISKELLY I.D. Born 16/9/58. Commd 16/12/79. Flt Lt 16/6/86. Retd SUP 16/9/96.
MISKELLY I.R. Born 13/10/46. Commd 18/8/67. Wg Cdr 1/1/89. Retd GD 9/5/03.
MITCHAM D.T. Born 11/6/46. Commd 21/1/68. Flt Lt 21/7/75. Retd SUP 11/6/87.
MITCHELL A.A. Born 12/9/21. Commd 9/7/59. Flt Lt 9/7/64. Retd ENG 12/9/76.
MITCHELL A.L. BDS. Born 20/9/40. Commd 24/6/62. Wg Cdr 29/7/77. Retd DEL 20/9/78.

MITCHELL A.N. MBE. Born 2/9/48. Commd 27/2/70. Wg Cdr 1/7/90. Retd GD 16/2/02.
MITCHELL A.P. Born 2/6/48. Commd 28/7/67. Sqn Ldr 1/1/89. Retd ADMIN 1/8/95.
MITCHELL A.S. Born 18/10/32. Commd 1/3/56. Flt Lt 11/5/62. Retd GD 20/7/71.
MITCHELL A.T. MB BS MRCP(UK). Born 15/2/57. Commd 5/10/79. Wg Cdr 10/8/94. Retd MED 5/10/95.
MITCHELL B. Born 17/5/48. Commd 7/6/73. Flt Lt 7/12/78. Retd GD 22/10/94.
MITCHELL B.K. Born 1/12/43. Commd 17/3/67. Flt Lt 17/6/73. Retd ADMIN 29/11/82.
MITCHELL B.T. MIDPM MCIPS MCMI. Born 17/9/33. Commd 31/7/56. Wg Cdr 1/7/75. Retd SUP 17/9/92.
MITCHELL B.W. Born 16/4/42. Commd 24/4/64. Flt Lt 5/5/90. Retd GD 6/8/93.
MITCHELL C. BA. Born 11/5/43. Commd 28/7/64. Sqn Ldr 1/7/72. Retd GD 11/5/87.
MITCHELL C.A. Born 28/5/45. Commd 8/9/77. Flt Lt 8/9/79. Retd ENG 8/9/85.
MITCHELL C.C. CEng MIMechE MRAeS. Born 22/8/39. Commd 28/7/60. Wg Cdr 1/7/78. Retd ENG 22/8/94.
MITCHELL C.N.C. Born 25/9/25. Commd 20/7/50. Sqn Ldr 1/1/60. Retd GD 25/9/80.
MITCHELL D. Born 6/2/33. Commd 16/7/52. Flt Lt 12/12/57. Retd GD 6/2/71.
MITCHELL D.A. Born 21/11/43. Commd 25/3/64. Sqn Ldr 1/7/76. Retd GD 23/7/82.
MITCHELL D.C. MBE. Born 3/11/24. Commd 25/5/45. Wg Cdr 1/1/65. Retd GD 29/9/72.
MITCHELL D.J. Born 3/6/26. Commd 22/2/46. Sqn Ldr 1/1/60. Retd GD 1/6/68.
MITCHELL D.J.G. BSc. Born 27/6/65. Commd 1/4/85. Flt Lt 15/1/89. Retd FLY(P) 27/6/03.
MITCHELL E.T. Born 28/1/30. Commd 17/3/67. Flt Lt 17/3/72. Retd ENG 2/10/74.
MITCHELL F.A. Born 9/11/56. Commd 1/12/77. Flt Lt 9/4/84. Retd GD(G) 1/12/85. Re-entered 18/10/91. Flt Lt 6/6/89. Retd DPS SPT 3/3/01.
MITCHELL F.W. Born 12/2/38. Commd 28/7/59. A Cdre 1/1/89. Retd GD 20/9/92.
MITCHELL F.G. Born 8/10/66. Commd 8/5/86. Flt Lt 8/11/91. Retd FLY(N) 8/10/04.
MITCHELL G. Born 23/10/12. Commd 14/2/41. Flt Lt 27/8/44. Retd ASD 30/1/46. rtg Sqn Ldr.
MITCHELL G. MB ChB MRCP MRCP(Edin). Born 10/4/32. Commd 19/5/56. Sqn Ldr 1/4/62. Retd MED 26/11/66.
MITCHELL G.D. OBE BA. Born 23/1/35. Commd 28/7/60. Wg Cdr 1/1/78. Retd GD 23/1/90.
MITCHELL G.D. Born 8/9/27. Commd 28/8/50. Flt Lt 28/2/55. Retd GD 8/9/82.
MITCHELL G.F. Born 28/4/42. Commd 14/8/70. Sqn Ldr 1/7/89. Retd ADMIN 1/9/93.
MITCHELL G.G. Born 10/5/37. Commd 12/12/59. Flt Lt 12/6/65. Retd GD 25/8/75.
MITCHELL G.H.C. Born 29/8/29. Commd 6/11/47. Flt Lt 26/5/55. Retd GD 31/12/74. Re-instated 8/10/79 to 29/8/87. rtg Sqn Ldr.
MITCHELL G.H.E. CBE BA. Born 14/6/37. Commd 4/7/57. A Cdre 1/1/88. Retd ADMIN 14/6/92.
MITCHELL G.M. Born 17/7/62. Commd 19/12/91. Flt Lt 19/12/93. Retd ADMIN 15/11/96.
MITCHELL H.F.S. DFC. Born 2/11/16. Commd 21/3/43. Flt Lt 19/7/53. Retd GD(G) 9/3/62.
MITCHELL H.G. Born 1/5/30. Commd 12/11/55. Flt Lt 12/5/61. Retd GD 18/4/84. rtg Sqn Ldr.
MITCHELL I.A. Born 25/12/41. Commd 5/6/67. Sqn Ldr 1/1/79. Retd ENG 25/12/82.
MITCHELL J. Born 26/3/30. Commd 27/2/52. Wg Cdr 1/1/74. Retd GD 4/4/82.
MITCHELL J.B. CBE AFC. Born 24/11/30. Commd 11/6/53. A Cdre 1/1/82. Retd GD 2/7/84.
MITCHELL J.E.F. DFC. Born 27/11/18. Commd 28/7/42. Sqn Ldr 1/7/57. Retd GD 19/4/58.
MITCHELL J.H. Born 15/9/21. Commd 27/1/55. Sqn Ldr 1/7/69. Retd ENG 30/9/71.
MITCHELL J.I. Born 5/3/56. Commd 29/1/87. Flt Lt 29/1/89. Retd GD 1/2/02.
MITCHELL J.L. LVO DFC AFC AE. Born 12/11/18. Commd 21/4/40. A Cdre 1/7/68. Retd GD 1/9/74.
MITCHELL J.N. MSc MB BS MFOM DAvMed. Born 21/12/35. Commd 28/4/63. Gp Capt 1/1/85. Retd MED 31/7/85.
MITCHELL J.N.S. MB ChB FRCP DCH. Born 16/12/26. Commd 29/9/50. Gp Capt 29/9/70. Retd MED 12/1/80.
MITCHELL J.R. Born 15/8/55. Commd 15/3/84. Flt Lt 15/3/86. Retd ADMIN 15/8/93.
MITCHELL J.T. Born 29/8/31. Commd 27/5/53. Flt Lt 11/11/58. Retd GD 29/8/69.
MITCHELL J.W. Born 17/5/31. Commd 11/4/63. Sqn Ldr 1/7/74. Retd SUP 30/11/84.
MITCHELL M. BDS. Born 21/1/63. Commd 19/1/86. Wg Cdr 19/7/98. Retd DEL 19/1/02.
MITCHELL M. Born 3/8/47. Commd 2/8/68. Gp Capt 1/1/94. Retd GD 3/8/04.
MITCHELL N. Born 20/1/46. Commd 15/10/81. Sqn Ldr 1/7/91. Retd ENG 15/9/00.
MITCHELL P. MBE. Born 8/9/42. Commd 4/7/69. Wg Cdr 1/7/92. Retd ENG 8/9/97.
MITCHELL P.M. Born 17/11/22. Commd 30/6/44. Sqn Ldr 1/1/55. Retd GD 9/12/61.
MITCHELL P.W. Born 4/11/64. Commd 28/7/93. Flt Lt 29/7/95. Retd ADMIN 4/11/02.
MITCHELL R. Born 22/5/40. Commd 18/12/62. Sqn Ldr 1/7/75. Retd SUP 1/7/78.
MITCHELL R.A. Born 29/11/45. Commd 2/6/67. Sqn Ldr 1/7/94. Retd ADMIN 30/11/01.
MITCHELL R.A.K. BSc. Born 30/9/44. Commd 26/5/67. Sqn Ldr 1/7/74. Retd ENG 1/6/76.
MITCHELL R.C. MBE. Born 14/10/18. Commd 9/7/53. Sqn Ldr 1/7/63. Retd ENG 18/4/70.
MITCHELL R.F. Born 13/2/33. Commd 22/5/61. Sqn Ldr 1/7/79. Retd ADMIN 13/2/88.
MITCHELL R.H. Born 25/6/33. Commd 24/2/67. Flt Lt 1/1/73. Retd ENG 1/10/74.
MITCHELL R.J. MBE CEng MIEE. Born 23/2/19. Commd 18/7/41. Sqn Ldr 1/1/53. Retd ENG 23/1/56.
MITCHELL R.P.G. Born 5/12/33. Commd 13/8/52. Flt Lt 20/7/58. Retd GD 5/4/72.
MITCHELL R.S. Born 8/12/29. Commd 28/6/51. Sqn Ldr 1/7/64. Retd GD 26/2/85.
MITCHELL S.A. DFC. Born 14/7/61. Commd 5/1/83. Sqn Ldr 1/1/98. Retd GD 1/2/02.
MITCHELL T.A. Born 15/9/49. Commd 3/10/74. Flt Lt 3/4/80. Retd GD 20/5/90.
MITCHELL T.S. Born 10/4/37. Commd 19/7/57. Flt Lt 3/12/63. Retd SUP 11/2/66.
MITCHELL V.D. Born 25/4/35. Commd 26/5/67. Sqn Ldr 1/7/77. Retd GD(G) 25/4/85.
MITCHELL V.M. Born 1/6/57. Commd 3/7/80. Flt Lt 3/1/87. Retd SUP 4/3/89.

MITCHELL W. Born 25/2/17. Commd 26/11/43. Flt Lt 26/5/47. Retd GD 1/9/50.
MITCHELMORE A. Born 12/10/16. Commd 25/9/43. Sqn Ldr 1/1/55. Retd GD(G) 31/8/61.
MITCHEM M.M. DFM. Born 15/9/20. Commd 9/10/44. Flt Lt 9/4/49. Retd SUP 15/9/75.
MITCHENER A.W. MCIPS. Born 27/3/32. Commd 2/10/67. Sqn Ldr 1/7/73. Retd SUP 6/8/83.
MITCHISON B. MSc BSc. Born 18/12/62. Commd 5/9/82. Sqn Ldr 1/1/97. Retd ENG 18/12/00.
MLEJNECKY F. Born 10/12/18. Commd 20/10/43. Flt Lt 7/6/51. Retd GD 28/10/68.
MOBBERLEY D. AFC. Born 24/2/26. Commd 19/6/52. Sqn Ldr 1/8/65. Retd GD 3/9/68.
MOCHAN J.P. Born 13/1/48. Commd 13/1/67. Sqn Ldr 1/7/90. Retd GD 31/7/02.
MOCKFORD M.D. OBE. Born 21/9/34. Commd 19/8/65. Wg Cdr 1/7/86. Retd PI 21/9/89.
MOFFAT A. Born 17/4/36. Commd 3/8/62. Sqn Ldr 1/7/87. Retd GD 17/4/96.
MOFFAT D.F. OBE. Born 21/10/28. Commd 16/1/52. Gp Capt 1/1/74. Retd GD 29/3/78.
MOFFAT D.F. Born 1/11/35. Commd 3/1/56. Flt Lt 3/7/61. Retd GD 2/11/79.
MOFFAT H.J. AFC. Born 26/6/33. Commd 27/2/52. Sqn Ldr 1/7/70. Retd GD 21/6/73.
MOFFAT J.R. CEng MIProdE. Born 6/4/46. Commd 17/12/72. Wg Cdr 1/7/88. Retd ENG 6/4/91.
MOFFAT P.M. Born 19/2/41. Commd 3/7/80. Flt Lt 3/7/85. Retd ENG 30/3/94.
MOFFAT W. Born 23/7/54. Commd 8/5/86. Flt Lt 8/5/88. Retd OPS SPT 8/5/00.
MOFFATT A. Born 24/4/50. Commd 14/2/69. Flt Lt 14/8/74. Retd GD 28/9/74.
MOFFATT G.W. Born 15/3/37. Commd 21/7/61. Sqn Ldr 1/7/72. Retd GD 4/5/88.
MOFFETT I.F. Born 11/4/47. Commd 29/7/65. Sqn Ldr 1/7/83. Retd GD(G) 11/4/91.
MOFFETT M.T. MSc BSc. Born 5/6/47. Commd 16/10/72. Wg Cdr 1/7/86. Retd ENG 1/7/89.
MOFFITT A.J. Born 27/11/64. Commd 8/12/83. Fg Offr 2/6/86. Retd SUP 19/1/90.
MOFFITT F.J. Born 30/11/40. Commd 22/2/63. Flt Lt 1/8/72. Retd GD 30/11/90.
MOGER B. Born 3/2/35. Commd 15/9/60. Sqn Ldr 1/1/72. Retd SEC 1/1/75.
MOGFORD F.L. Born 8/11/46. Commd 28/4/67. Wg Cdr 1/7/90. Retd GD 8/11/01.
MOHAMMED H.A. Born 27/9/47. Commd 4/6/87. Flt Lt 4/6/91. Retd OPS SPT 31/1/99.
MOINET A.N. Born 5/12/46. Commd 10/5/90. Flt Lt 10/5/94. Retd ENGINEER 5/12/04.
MOIR A.D. OBE MVO BSc MRIN. Born 3/11/46. Commd 23/3/69. Wg Cdr 1/1/88. Retd GD 10/5/94.
MOIR I. BSc CEng MIEE MRAeS. Born 31/8/42. Commd 15/7/63. Sqn Ldr 1/1/75. Retd ENG 31/8/80.
MOIR J.McG. MA. Born 28/3/44. Commd 28/9/64. Flt Lt 15/4/67. Retd GD 14/4/72.
MOLE B.F. Born 9/9/43. Commd 1/3/68. Sqn Ldr 1/7/81. Retd ADMIN 1/10/86.
MOLES J.G. MCMI. Born 2/11/26. Commd 25/8/60. Sqn Ldr 1/7/71. Retd ENG 1/9/78.
MOLES J.W. BEM. Born 21/4/25. Commd 14/11/57. Flt Lt 14/11/63. Retd ENG 17/1/70.
MOLESWORTH D.W. CEng MIEE MRAeS. Born 13/3/30. Commd 28/7/53. Sqn Ldr 1/7/67. Retd ENG 13/9/92.
MOLESWORTH J.E.N. Born 28/4/26. Commd 19/3/47. Flt Lt 17/5/56. Retd RGT 31/8/58.
MOLLAND A. Born 1/11/36. Commd 25/3/55. Flt Lt 7/8/64. Retd GD 1/11/74.
MOLLAND H. Born 13/12/32. Commd 17/5/51. Flt Lt 22/5/57. Retd GD 13/12/69.
MOLLE D.C. Born 24/1/49. Commd 16/2/89. Sqn Ldr 1/1/00. Retd ENGINEER 24/1/04.
MOLLISON A. Born 21/1/21. Commd 7/4/55. Sqn Ldr 1/7/66. Retd ENG 21/10/72.
MOLLISON K.B. Born 25/7/33. Commd 26/4/62. Flt Lt 26/4/62. Retd GD 25/7/88.
MOLLOY B. ACIS MCMI. Born 18/5/31. Commd 31/10/71. Sqn Ldr 31/10/71. Retd SUP 18/5/91.
MOLLOY G.J. BA. Born 10/11/58. Commd 17/8/80. Sqn Ldr 1/7/89. Retd GD 1/10/99.
MOLLOY M.A. Born 21/4/41. Commd 14/6/63. Gp Capt 1/7/90. Retd GD 22/1/97.
MOLONEY P.A. Born 20/4/59. Commd 12/10/78. Flt Lt 12/4/84. Retd GD 20/4/97.
MOLONEY P.S. Born 17/5/38. Commd 22/9/58. Flt Lt 14/4/65. Retd SUP 17/5/76.
MOLONEY T.F. AFM. Born 10/8/26. Commd 18/11/66. Flt Lt 18/11/71. Retd RGT 2/10/79.
MOLYNEAUX M. Born 6/1/47. Commd 18/11/66. Flt Lt 18/3/73. Retd GD(G) 25/4/80.
MOLYNEUX E.T.U. BA. Born 27/8/70. Commd 11/9/88. Flt Lt 15/1/94. Retd FLY(P) 22/7/03.
MOLYNEUX R. Born 22/1/25. Commd 16/3/45. Flt Lt 4/1/51. Retd GD 1/5/68.
MONAGHAN G.A. Born 3/2/46. Commd 11/8/67. Wg Cdr 1/7/87. Retd GD 4/5/01.
MONAGHAN G.M.J. BTech. Born 30/11/56. Commd 30/8/78. Sqn Ldr 1/1/89. Retd GD 30/11/94.
MONAGHAN S.H. Born 7/7/48. Commd 28/2/69. Flt Lt 28/2/72. Retd GD 17/9/82.
MONAHAN J.D. Offr 23/6/49. Commd 25/10/73. Plt Offr 12/8/67. Retd PRT 17/10/75.
MONCASTER C.J. BSc. Born 8/4/54. Commd 17/9/72. Wg Cdr 1/1/94. Retd GD 8/4/98.
MONFORT G.R. Born 3/9/44. Commd 25/4/69. Flt Lt 25/10/75. Retd OPS SPT 3/2/00.
MONICO J.D. Born 24/1/21. Commd 15/4/43. Flt Lt 9/1/47. Retd ENG 9/1/47. rtg Flt Lt.
MONK B. Born 17/3/44. Commd 5/11/70. Sqn Ldr 1/1/79. Retd GD 1/4/90.
MONK D. Born 3/6/43. Commd 14/4/69. Sqn Ldr 1/1/79. Retd ENG 1/6/89.
MONK K.L. MCIPD. Born 20/6/34. Commd 5/11/70. Sqn Ldr 1/1/78. Retd ENG 22/12/89.
MONK M.A.N. Born 1/10/47. Commd 2/2/68. Flt Lt 23/5/74. Retd GD(G) 1/10/85.
MONK M.J. Born 4/9/43. Commd 8/1/65. Flt Lt 8/7/70. Retd GD 1/10/76.
MONK W.G. Born 11/7/23. Commd 7/7/55. Flt Lt 25/2/60. Retd GD 31/5/72.
MONKHOUSE K.E.J. MA CEng FIEE. Born 2/6/38. Commd 30/9/58. A Cdre 1/1/87. Retd ENG 2/6/93.
MONKS M.R. FCMI. Born 2/11/38. Commd 28/8/59. Gp Capt 1/7/85. Retd GD 30/11/89.
MONSON K.G. MCMI. Born 26/3/36. Commd 12/11/54. Wg Cdr 1/7/73. Retd GD 11/7/78.
MONTAGU C.B. MSc BSc CEng MIMechE. Born 18/5/50. Commd 26/2/71. Gp Capt 1/7/99. Retd GD 18/5/05.
MONTAGU-SMITH A.M. DL. Born 17/7/15. Commd 15/3/35. Wg Cdr 1/7/47. Retd GD 1/1/61. rtg Gp Capt.

MONTAGUE E. Born 29/5/26. Commd 8/4/57. Sqn Ldr 1/1/65. Retd SEC 8/5/68.
MONTAGUE G.T. CertEd. Born 22/7/44. Commd 20/12/73. Sqn Ldr 1/1/89. Retd SUP 22/7/99.
MONTAGUE P. Born 24/4/16. Commd 18/1/48. Flt Lt 4/6/53. Retd SUP 1/5/65.
MONTAGUE R.M.B. BSc. Born 1/6/39. Commd 22/5/62. A Cdre 1/7/90. Retd ADMIN 1/6/94.
MONTALTO R. Born 20/8/28. Commd 14/5/53. Flt Lt 14/4/59. Retd SUP 20/8/66.
MONTEITH D.J. BA. Born 7/11/51. Commd 13/9/70. Flt Lt 13/6/76. Retd RGT 6/7/80.
MONTEITH-HODGE D. MCMI. Born 11/9/27. Commd 10/9/52. Sqn Ldr 1/7/65. Retd PE 14/4/73.
MONTGOMERIE I.E.D. Born 31/5/40. Commd 13/12/60. Flt Lt 13/6/63. Retd GD 30/8/71.
MONTGOMERY A. BA. Born 16/12/32. Commd 6/8/63. Sqn Ldr 9/2/68. Retd ADMIN 6/8/79.
MONTGOMERY A.C. OBE MA. Born 1/8/46. Commd 6/10/69. Gp Capt 1/1/95. Retd GD 3/1/97.
MONTGOMERY B.G. BA. Born 31/10/31. Commd 20/11/56. Flt Lt 20/8/58. Retd GD 24/7/72.
MONTGOMERY C.M. Born 28/4/45. Commd 24/4/64. Flt Lt 24/10/69. Retd GD 22/10/82.
MONTGOMERY D.A. MB BS MRCS LRCP DCP MRCPath. Born 24/3/33. Commd 11/8/57. Wg Cdr 11/8/70.
    Retd MED 11/8/73.
MONTGOMERY D.M. BA. Born 18/2/47. Commd 22/6/70. Flt Lt 22/3/72. Retd GD 1/4/75.
MONTGOMERY G.P.F. MBE. Born 9/6/39. Commd 8/9/77. Sqn Ldr 1/1/85. Retd ENG 8/6/92.
MONTGOMERY R.A. Born 15/1/17. Commd 6/1/42. Flt Lt 1/9/45. Retd ENG 15/1/66.
MONTGOMERY R.S. BSc. Born 25/10/49. Commd 16/12/79. Flt Lt 16/12/80. Retd ADMIN 16/12/95.
MONTGOMERY-SAUNDERS F.W.L. Born 26/8/28. Commd 10/11/49. Flt Lt 21/9/55. Retd GD 26/8/66.
MOODY D.B. Born 22/1/52. Commd 15/10/81. Sqn Ldr 1/1/90. Retd SUPPLY 26/1/04.
MOODY D.W. Born 26/3/28. Commd 13/1/72. Flt Lt 13/1/75. Retd ENG 5/4/79.
MOODY H. Born 30/1/22. Commd 17/3/67. Flt Lt 17/3/70. Retd ENG 23/9/72.
MOODY J.K. BSc. Born 24/9/46. Commd 1/7/82. Sqn Ldr 1/1/90. Retd GD 24/9/02.
MOON A.J.F. Born 26/10/41. Commd 6/4/62. Flt Lt 1/7/68. Retd GD 23/8/75.
MOON H.H. Born 21/6/19. Commd 27/4/41. Sqn Ldr 1/8/47. Retd GD 29/7/58.
MOON P.A.H. Born 9/6/20. Commd 2/2/52. Gp Capt 1/1/70. Retd SEC 9/6/75.
MOON S. Born 17/12/52. Commd 10/5/90. Flt Lt 10/5/94. Retd OPS SPT(ATC) 31/1/05.
MOONEY A.G.P. Born 18/1/40. Commd 16/9/71. Flt Lt 16/9/73. Retd SEC 16/9/79.
MOONEY D.L. MVO. Born 21/3/41. Commd 15/9/61. Sqn Ldr 1/7/88. Retd GD 22/3/91.
MOONEY F.C. Born 21/2/50. Commd 2/8/90. Fg Offr 2/8/90. Retd ENG 1/6/93.
MOONEY G. Born 6/11/38. Commd 27/5/71. Flt Lt 27/5/73. Retd GD 30/9/76.
MOONEY J. Born 23/12/45. Commd 28/6/79. Flt Lt 28/6/81. Retd GD 1/3/94.
MOONEY P.M. Born 13/10/49. Commd 11/4/85. Flt Lt 11/4/89. Retd SY 31/3/94.
MOONEY R.T. BSc. Born 26/9/38. Commd 8/6/62. Sqn Ldr 1/7/72. Retd GD 26/9/93.
MOORCROFT B. DSO DFC MA. Born 26/4/21. Commd 5/6/43. Wg Cdr 1/7/61. Retd GD 26/10/68.
MOORCROFT G.E. Born 19/2/37. Commd 22/7/71. Flt Lt 16/4/74. Retd ENG 22/7/79.
MOORCROFT P. Born 10/10/58. Commd 29/3/90. Flt Lt 29/3/92. Retd ADMIN 29/3/00.
MOORE A. Born 28/12/47. Commd 28/7/88. Flt Lt 28/7/92. Retd SY 31/10/95.
MOORE A.G. Born 9/2/38. Commd 26/10/62. Flt Lt 26/4/68. Retd GD 31/10/89.
MOORE B.A. MA MSc MIEE. Born 23/8/57. Commd 5/8/76. Sqn Ldr 1/1/87. Retd ENG 18/12/90.
MOORE B.D. OBE BSc CEng MRAeS MCMI. Born 28/3/25. Commd 18/10/50. Gp Capt 1/7/73. Retd ENG 28/10/78.
MOORE C. Born 6/11/29. Commd 18/11/66. Flt Lt 18/11/69. Retd GD 1/5/76.
MOORE C.M. Born 2/4/42. Commd 17/3/67. Gp Capt 1/7/89. Retd ADMIN 3/4/96.
MOORE C.S. CB OBE. Born 27/2/10. Commd 20/12/30. A Cdre 1/7/54. Retd GD 23/7/62. rtg AVM.
MOORE C.T. CBE. Born 1/1/43. Commd 17/12/64. Gp Capt 1/1/86. Retd GD 2/4/93.
MOORE D. Born 28/6/23. Commd 1/10/43. Flt Lt 19/11/53. Retd GD 18/11/64.
MOORE D. Born 8/11/35. Commd 23/11/78. Flt Lt 23/11/81. Retd SY 24/10/87.
MOORE D.G.McL. Born 7/5/20. Commd 22/9/49. Sqn Ldr 1/1/61. Retd ENG 12/10/73.
MOORE D.H. MBE. Born 29/5/35. Commd 12/12/59. Sqn Ldr 1/1/86. Retd GD 3/1/95.
MOORE D.R. BSc. Born 18/6/62. Commd 28/4/84. Flt Lt 29/10/87. Retd ENG 14/9/96.
MOORE E.T. Born 13/6/25. Commd 15/12/44. Gp Capt 1/7/76. Retd SUP 13/6/80.
MOORE F.A. Born 4/8/24. Commd 8/7/54. Flt Lt 7/7/59. Retd GD 4/8/79.
MOORE F.T. MIPM MCMI. Born 2/10/34. Commd 12/7/63. Wg Cdr 1/7/80. Retd ADMIN 20/4/85.
MOORE G.A. Born 7/8/41. Commd 4/2/71. Sqn Ldr 1/1/87. Retd GD 7/8/96.
MOORE G.C. Born 18/5/30. Commd 24/1/52. Flt Lt 15/5/57. Retd GD 10/1/76.
MOORE G.C. Born 19/7/32. Commd 5/11/52. Flt Lt 24/3/58. Retd GD 22/3/74.
MOORE G.J.P. BSc DipEurHum DipAppSS. Born 18/10/51. Commd 28/6/79. Wg Cdr 1/7/94. Retd ADMIN 13/11/02.
MOORE G.J.T. Born 27/4/41. Commd 3/7/80. Sqn Ldr 1/1/90. Retd SUP 26/2/94.
MOORE G.R. MA CEng MRAeS MIERE DipEl. Born 18/9/27. Commd 25/11/48. Sqn Ldr 1/1/61. Retd ENG 18/9/65.
MOORE G.S. MSc. Born 5/6/41. Commd 12/6/62. Wg Cdr 1/1/91. Retd SUP 6/10/91.
MOORE J. Born 6/10/28. Commd 12/9/50. Flt Lt 12/3/55. Retd GD 6/10/85.
MOORE J.C. BSc CEng MIEE ACGI. Born 16/9/40. Commd 30/9/59. Sqn Ldr 1/1/70. Retd ENG 16/9/78.
MOORE J.C. Born 1/7/16. Commd 17/6/40. Flt Offr 1/9/45. Retd SEC 27/8/50. rtg Sqn Offr.
MOORE J.M. Born 24/3/48. Commd 24/11/67. Flt Lt 19/9/74. Retd GD(G) 2/2/87.
MOORE K.B. Born 13/1/46. Commd 4/12/64. Gp Capt 1/7/88. Retd GD 18/4/91.
MOORE K.M. CEng MIERE. Born 3/10/31. Commd 23/3/66. Flt Lt 1/7/68. Retd ENG 23/3/74.

MOORE L. Born 21/4/18. Commd 4/12/43. Sqn Ldr 1/10/54. Retd GD 21/9/58.
MOORE M. Born 18/4/37. Commd 27/2/56. Wg Cdr 1/7/76. Retd GD(G) 1/10/86.
MOORE M.A. Born 18/10/32. Commd 14/12/54. Plt Offr 14/12/54. Retd GD 6/9/56.
MOORE M.A. Born 29/12/44. Commd 4/5/72. Sqn Ldr 1/1/81. Retd ADMIN 29/12/88.
MOORE M.C.C. Born 10/3/49. Commd 3/10/69. Wg Cdr 1/7/97. Retd GD 10/3/04.
MOORE M.J. Born 10/5/33. Commd 10/9/54. Flt Lt 16/8/61. Retd GD 4/10/78.
MOORE M.L. BSc. Born 21/7/61. Commd 11/12/83. Flt Lt 11/6/86. Retd GD 19/4/02.
MOORE N. MSc BSc. Born 23/4/67. Commd 1/9/85. Flt Lt 15/1/91. Retd FLY(N) 23/4/05.
MOORE N.C. MD BCh MRCPsych DPM. Born 1/8/38. Commd 24/9/62. Wg Cdr 3/8/78. Retd MED 5/11/83.
MOORE N.D. Born 4/2/53. Commd 10/2/72. Sqn Ldr 1/1/85. Retd SUP 4/2/91.
MOORE P.J. Born 29/9/46. Commd 19/8/66. Gp Capt 1/7/91. Retd GD 7/1/95.
MOORE P.M. MILT. Born 19/7/44. Commd 25/2/82. Sqn Ldr 1/7/90. Retd SUP 27/11/95.
MOORE R. Born 29/12/40. Commd 18/12/62. Sqn Ldr 1/1/84. Retd GD 7/12/93.
MOORE R.C. Born 13/12/42. Commd 30/7/63. Wg Cdr 1/1/87. Retd GD 13/12/97.
MOORE R.D. Born 16/10/22. Commd 5/3/43. Flt Lt 5/5/49. Retd GD 20/10/49.
MOORE R.F. BEM. Born 25/2/37. Commd 9/10/75. Sqn Ldr 1/1/86. Retd ENG 1/5/91.
MOORE R.J. Born 1/10/47. Commd 23/3/67. Flt Lt 23/9/72. Retd GD 14/5/90.
MOORE R.M. Born 13/5/44. Commd 13/1/67. Flt Lt 13/7/72. Retd GD 26/9/82.
MOORE R.P. Born 5/12/35. Commd 28/11/69. Flt Lt 11/5/72. Retd GD 17/12/73.
MOORE T. MA BSc MINucE MCMI. Born 27/4/17. Commd 23/9/43. Sqn Ldr 1/1/59. Retd ENG 27/4/66.
MOORE T.S. Born 16/8/41. Commd 9/8/79. Sqn Ldr 1/1/87. Retd ADMIN 21/6/96.
MOORE W.J. Born 26/12/63. Commd 19/7/84. Flt Lt 19/1/90. Retd GD 14/3/97.
MOOREHOUSE M.G. BSc(Eng) MIIM ACGI. Born 8/1/38. Commd 14/4/69. Sqn Ldr 1/7/79. Retd ENG 14/4/85.
MOORES D.S. BSc. Born 14/10/50. Commd 1/11/71. Flt Lt 1/2/73. Retd GD 20/12/88.
MOORES F.S. DFC. Born 1/12/15. Commd 21/6/43. Flt Lt 21/12/46. Retd ENG 15/9/53.
MOORES G.J.E. OBE. Born 11/7/31. Commd 14/10/51. Wg Cdr 1/7/70. Retd GD 29/5/76.
MOORES P.W. BSc. Born 16/5/48. Commd 1/9/71. Sqn Ldr 1/7/80. Retd ENG 31/10/87.
MOORHEAD M.D. BSc. Born 13/6/46. Commd 28/9/64. Flt Lt 22/6/72. Retd ENG 30/3/78.
MOORHOUSE G.H. Born 27/9/24. Commd 20/4/50. Flt Lt 20/10/53. Retd GD 27/9/62.
MOORS E.H. Born 26/12/30. Commd 25/5/50. Sqn Ldr 1/1/64. Retd GD 27/5/69.
MORALEE G.C. Born 3/10/23. Commd 6/1/45. Flt Lt 6/7/48. Retd GD 3/4/69.
MORALEE P.J. Born 26/5/46. Commd 27/2/70. Sqn Ldr 1/1/84. Retd SY 1/10/88. Re-entered 27/2/70. Sqn Ldr 28/5/86.
  Retd OPS SPT 26/5/01.
MORAN J. Born 10/4/42. Commd 19/6/86. Sqn Ldr 1/7/92. Retd ADMIN 1/7/98.
MORAN L.E. DFC. Born 23/7/20. Commd 8/8/43. Sqn Ldr 1/1/61. Retd GD 27/11/64.
MORAN M.F. MB BCh MChOtol BAO DLO MRAeS. Born 18/4/27. Commd 24/10/54. AVM 17/10/88.
  Retd MED 3/12/91.
MORAN S.F. Born 22/12/23. Commd 3/5/46. Flt Lt 29/6/50. Retd GD 25/12/66.
MORBLY-HARDINGE W.P. Born 18/6/32. Commd 6/9/68. Flt Lt 6/9/73. Retd ENG 13/7/82.
MOREAU R.D. Born 19/2/26. Commd 25/5/50. Sqn Ldr 1/7/68. Retd Pl 13/9/80.
MORECOMBE L.G. Born 9/1/33. Commd 24/1/52. Flt Lt 15/8/57. Retd GD 9/1/88.
MORELAND A.C. Born 6/10/10. Commd 25/4/41. Sqn Ldr 1/7/49. Retd SUP 25/10/59.
MORELAND D.H. FCMI. Born 2/11/30. Commd 3/11/51. Flt Lt 3/5/56. Retd ADMIN 2/11/68. Re-employed 26/2/71.
  Sqn Ldr 1/1/79. Retd 16/4/84.
MOREN L.A. Born 22/6/28. Commd 6/10/60. Sqn Ldr 1/1/78. Retd GD 1/8/78.
MORFFEW C.G. Born 27/9/47. Commd 30/5/69. Wg Cdr 1/7/90. Retd GD 11/3/02.
MORFILL E.R. Born 19/2/12. Commd 2/8/41. Sqn Ldr 1/7/53. Retd ENG 19/8/61.
MORFILL P.F. DFM. Born 11/12/14. Commd 15/1/42. Sqn Ldr 1/7/53. Retd GD 4/2/58.
MORFORD D.J. Born 28/3/29. Commd 17/5/62. Sqn Ldr 1/7/73. Retd ENG 28/3/89.
MORGAN A.I. BSc. Born 8/4/37. Commd 2/10/58. Sqn Ldr 1/7/68. Retd GD 11/12/77.
MORGAN A.J.M. OBE CEng MIERE MCMI. Born 13/1/22. Commd 29/5/43. Wg Cdr 1/1/62. Retd ENG 30/11/72.
MORGAN A.M. MB BChir DO FRCS. Born 6/10/30. Commd 5/5/57. Gp Capt 5/5/80. Retd MED 1/3/83.
MORGAN B. MBE. Born 15/6/10. Commd 21/8/41. Wg Cdr 1/7/52. Retd SEC 15/6/62.
MORGAN B. Born 24/11/41. Commd 11/5/62. Flt Lt 11/11/67. Retd GD 1/10/76.
MORGAN B.C. Born 12/12/53. Commd 27/3/86. Flt Lt 27/3/88. Retd SUP 14/3/96.
MORGAN B.E. MBE DPhysEd. Born 4/3/35. Commd 21/9/59. Sqn Ldr 1/7/71. Retd SUP 7/2/88.
MORGAN B.V. Born 8/4/26. Commd 23/12/54. Flt Offr 7/3/62. Retd SUP 15/7/65.
MORGAN C.J. AFC* FCMI. Born 10/3/25. Commd 7/7/49. Wg Cdr 1/7/64. Retd GD 10/3/80.
MORGAN C.R. Born 26/1/47. Commd 24/3/83. Sqn Ldr 1/1/92. Retd ENG 17/9/01.
MORGAN C.R. Born 7/2/51. Commd 24/6/71. Air Cdre 1/1/02. Retd GD 1/7/04.
MORGAN C.W. Born 15/3/35. Commd 3/10/70. Flt Lt 8/10/75. Retd GD 15/2/78.
MORGAN D. Born 15/4/47. Commd 29/7/83. Sqn Ldr 1/7/49. Retd ADMIN 15/4/98.
MORGAN D.J. Born 5/3/36. Commd 7/5/64. Flt Lt 7/5/66. Retd ENG 5/3/74. Re-instated 1/4/81. Flt Lt 3/6/73.
  Retd ENG 23/2/91.
MORGAN D.R. Born 21/5/44. Commd 4/7/85. Sqn Ldr 1/7/91. Retd GD 21/5/00.
MORGAN D.R. BA. Born 6/11/17. Commd 25/8/47. Wg Cdr 1/7/63. Retd EDN 16/4/68.

MORGAN G. BSc. Born 5/3/52. Commd 2/9/73. Flt Lt 2/12/74. Retd GD 5/3/90.
MORGAN G.I. BSc CEng MIProdE. Born 26/11/54. Commd 17/1/82. Sqn Ldr 1/1/91. Retd ENG 17/1/98.
MORGAN G.O. DPhysEd. Born 15/10/41. Commd 30/8/66. Wg Cdr 1/7/90. Retd ADMIN 15/10/96.
MORGAN G.R. Born 21/11/49. Commd 3/8/86. Flt Lt 3/8/84. Retd ADMIN 3/8/02.
MORGAN G.R.T. MA CEng MRAeS. Born 24/2/40. Commd 30/9/59. Wg Cdr 1/1/79. Retd ENG 31/10/92.
MORGAN G.W. Born 12/4/24. Commd 16/11/61. Sqn Ldr 1/1/75. Retd ENG 12/4/78.
MORGAN H.E. Born 2/1/47. Commd 14/8/80. Flt Lt 14/8/82. Retd ENG 14/8/88.
MORGAN H.S. Born 11/6/28. Commd 26/9/57. Flt Lt 26/3/61. Retd GD 29/3/69.
MORGAN I.L. Born 17/3/42. Commd 24/3/61. Wg Cdr 1/1/90. Retd GD 17/3/97.
MORGAN J. Born 11/6/45. Commd 17/12/65. Wg Cdr 1/7/85. Retd GD 8/6/90.
MORGAN J.A. Born 26/1/39. Commd 28/7/60. Gp Capt 1/7/87. Retd ENG 26/1/94.
MORGAN J.A. CBE. Born 1/9/31. Commd 15/12/53. A Cdre 1/1/84. Retd GD 1/1/87.
MORGAN J.C. Born 9/9/30. Commd 26/7/51. Flt Lt 14/11/56. Retd GD 12/3/71.
MORGAN J.D. Born 20/7/52. Commd 17/1/85. Flt Lt 17/7/87. Retd ENG 17/1/93.
MORGAN J.D. Born 26/2/20. Commd 20/5/43. Flt Lt 10/7/47. Retd ENG 30/6/55.
MORGAN J.G. Born 25/8/29. Commd 24/6/53. Sqn Ldr 1/1/68. Retd GD 25/8/84.
MORGAN J.L. Born 6/8/45. Commd 24/6/76. Wg Cdr 1/1/97. Retd GD 6/8/00.
MORGAN J.M. BSc. Born 23/8/35. Commd 18/12/56. Flt Lt 8/7/59. Retd GD 23/8/73.
MORGAN J.R. Born 5/4/38. Commd 28/7/59. Sqn Ldr 1/1/69. Retd GD 30/6/81.
MORGAN J.R. MHCIMA. Born 13/10/50. Commd 19/9/71. Wg Cdr 1/1/89. Retd ADMIN 21/2/02.
MORGAN J.T. Born 16/2/29. Commd 23/10/56. Flt Lt 23/4/62. Retd GD 16/2/67.
MORGAN J.T. Born 18/6/45. Commd 8/1/65. Flt Lt 8/7/70. Retd GD 11/8/76.
MORGAN J.V. BSc. Born 15/9/48. Commd 19/9/71. Wg Cdr 1/7/93. Retd SUP 29/11/99.
MORGAN K.C. Born 25/6/33. Commd 9/8/51. Flt Lt 11/11/63. Retd GD 11/11/71.
MORGAN K.J.W. Born 14/10/35. Commd 6/1/54. Flt Lt 6/7/59. Retd GD(G) 14/10/90.
MORGAN L.R. Born 19/6/34. Commd 5/4/55. Sqn Ldr 1/7/68. Retd GD 5/9/76.
MORGAN M.C.W. BA MB BChir DA LRCP MRCS. Born 1/6/36. Commd 3/9/62. Flt Lt 3/9/62. Retd MED 9/4/67.
MORGAN M.L. Born 11/2/45. Commd 26/5/67. Sqn Ldr 1/1/93. Retd ADMIN 1/1/96.
MORGAN M.W. ACII. Born 20/4/44. Commd 3/5/68. Sqn Ldr 1/1/86. Retd GD(G) 31/3/94.
MORGAN N. Born 21/2/46. Commd 25/2/66. Sqn Ldr 1/1/92. Retd GD 18/5/96.
MORGAN P. Born 19/6/31. Commd 16/7/52. Flt Lt 12/12/57. Retd GD 31/7/76.
MORGAN P. Born 11/6/41. Commd 14/6/63. Flt Lt 14/12/68. Retd GD 11/6/79.
MORGAN P.K. BA. Born 19/10/43. Commd 6/1/69. Flt Lt 6/1/70. Retd EDN 17/8/74.
MORGAN R.A. Born 15/4/26. Commd 9/8/48. Sqn Ldr 1/1/70. Retd SY 1/10/76.
MORGAN R.G. MCMI. Born 9/5/35. Commd 31/7/56. Wg Cdr 1/1/73. Retd ADMIN 2/4/80.
MORGAN R.J.L. CEng MRAeS MCMI. Born 14/8/41. Commd 17/7/62. Sqn Ldr 1/7/76. Retd ENG 1/4/89.
MORGAN R.R. Born 5/8/35. Commd 22/7/66. Sqn Ldr 1/1/81. Retd GD 5/8/90.
MORGAN S.H. Born 30/4/44. Commd 28/11/69. Sqn Ldr 1/1/95. Retd GD 30/4/99.
MORGAN S.K. CEng MIEE. Born 2/4/37. Commd 7/11/58. Gp Capt 1/1/84. Retd ENG 7/5/88.
MORGAN S.P. BSc. Born 21/10/53. Commd 3/9/72. Sqn Ldr 1/1/81. Retd GD 21/10/91.
MORGAN T. Born 27/1/25. Commd 25/8/55. Flt Lt 25/8/61. Retd GD 28/9/68.
MORGAN T.E. Born 9/9/52. Commd 4/3/71. Flt Lt 10/7/77. Retd GD(G) 26/9/78. Re-instated 9/4/80. Flt Lt 21/1/79. Retd GD(G) 31/1/86.
MORGAN T.J. CEng. Born 7/4/37. Commd 30/7/59. Gp Capt 1/1/80. Retd ENG 7/4/87.
MORGAN T.R. Born 28/5/34. Commd 26/7/55. A Cdre 1/1/82. Retd ADMIN 9/11/85.
MORGAN V.J. Born 5/7/27. Commd 9/3/50. Wg Cdr 1/7/68. Retd GD 5/7/82.
MORGAN W.B.C. Born 30/11/25. Commd 6/3/42. Flt Lt 6/9/55. Retd GD 2/5/80.
MORGAN W.W. Born 19/12/50. Commd 25/2/72. Flt Lt 25/2/75. Retd GD 25/2/88.
MORGAN-JONES J.I. MBE. Born 4/6/34. Commd 19/11/53. Wg Cdr 1/1/79. Retd SY(RGT) 20/4/89.
MORGANS A.W. Born 17/7/34. Commd 3/6/65. Sqn Ldr 1/1/84. Retd GD 1/5/87.
MORGANS B.T. MB BCh FRCSEng. Born 31/5/43. Commd 30/6/71. Air Cdre 21/8/96. Retd MEDICAL 1/5/03.
MORGANS J.M.C. Born 2/2/33. Commd 4/10/57. Flt Lt 4/4/57. Retd GD 2/2/88.
MORGANTI D.J. Born 7/10/34. Commd 12/3/64. Sqn Ldr 1/7/80. Retd GD 7/10/94.
MORIARTY P.D.R. Born 17/4/40. Commd 1/3/68. Sqn Ldr 1/7/81. Retd ADMIN 1/10/86.
MORISON I.C. Born 15/5/58. Commd 20/7/78. Sqn Ldr 1/1/90. Retd GD 13/9/96.
MORISON R.B. DFC AFC. Born 7/12/20. Commd 23/12/39. Gp Capt 1/7/59. Retd GD 31/7/65.
MORISON R.T. CBE. Born 20/8/16. Commd 19/7/40. AVM 1/1/70. Retd ENG 19/4/72.
MORLEY B.G. Born 3/2/31. Commd 16/7/52. Flt Lt 12/12/57. Retd GD(G) 3/2/86.
MORLEY D. Born 14/3/47. Commd 14/7/66. Flt Lt 8/3/72. Retd GD 28/8/76.
MORLEY E. MBE. Born 27/3/45. Commd 8/9/77. Sqn Ldr 1/1/89. Retd ENG 27/3/02.
MORLEY G.E. MB ChB DIH. Born 1/10/27. Commd 3/1/52. Wg Cdr 5/10/64. Retd MED 21/1/71.
MORLEY J. The Rev. AKC. Born 5/11/43. Commd 8/11/77. Retd Wg Cdr 8/5/93.
MORLEY J.F. Born 6/1/42. Commd 22/2/79. Flt Lt 22/2/82. Retd GD 20/7/92.
MORLEY J.R. MBE. Born 13/12/36. Commd 6/4/72. Sqn Ldr 1/1/87. Retd ENG 13/12/94.
MORLEY J.R.D. MBE . Born 28/3/47. Commd 13/1/67. Gp Capt 1/1/93. Retd GD 28/1/03.
MORLEY P. Born 24/8/33. Commd 15/6/53. Flt Lt 17/9/58. Retd GD 24/8/88.

MORLEY P.R. Born 24/10/46. Commd 3/3/67. Wg Cdr 1/1/89. Retd GD 14/9/96.
MORLEY R.E. DFC. Born 24/5/24. Commd 10/10/44. Sqn Ldr 1/1/56. Retd GD 24/5/62.
MORLEY R.H. MBE. Born 11/4/23. Commd 30/5/45. Sqn Ldr 1/1/56. Retd GD 11/4/66.
MORLEY R.J. Born 4/8/47. Commd 4/3/71. Flt Lt 12/8/77. Retd ADMIN 9/11/86.
MORLEY-MOWER G.F. DFC AFC. Born 5/5/18. Commd 29/11/37. Wg Cdr 1/1/53. Retd GD 15/8/68.
MORONEY W.J. RMN. Born 20/2/37. Commd 17/3/67. Gp Capt 1/7/89. Retd MED(SEC) 9/12/91.
MORRELL P.B. Born 4/4/46. Commd 1/3/68. Wg Cdr 1/7/88. Retd SUP 27/11/00.
MORRELL P.R. Born 5/12/32. Commd 24/10/51. Sqn Ldr 1/1/68. Retd GD 1/7/71.
MORRELL S.T. Born 16/11/48. Commd 31/7/70. Flt Lt 31/7/73. Retd GD 7/9/74.
MORRIS Sir Alec KBE CB BSc CEng FIEE FRAeS DipEl. Born 11/3/26. Commd 8/2/49. AM 1/7/81. Retd ENG 1/7/83.
MORRIS A.G. BSc CEng MIEE. Born 7/4/55. Commd 16/9/73. Sqn Ldr 1/1/91. Retd ENG 17/5/98.
MORRIS A.J.S. BSc. Born 26/3/67. Commd 24/10/85. Flt Lt 15/1/93. Retd ENG 15/7/01.
MORRIS A.M.D. MSc. Born 12/9/46. Commd 21/5/65. Gp Capt 1/1/94. Retd GD 12/9/01.
MORRIS A.R. BA. Born 1/11/54. Commd 2/9/73. Sqn Ldr 1/7/86. Retd GD 1/11/92.
MORRIS A.S. Born 14/10/37. Commd 22/2/63. Flt Lt 25/7/66. Retd GD 14/10/75.
MORRIS A.S.J. MCMI. Born 6/6/18. Commd 30/1/47. Sqn Ldr 1/7/66. Retd SEC 30/9/71.
MORRIS B. MCIPD MCMI. Born 18/1/36. Commd 19/8/71. Sqn Ldr 1/7/89. Retd ADMIN 24/11/91.
MORRIS B. Born 25/2/43. Commd 29/3/62. Flt Lt 29/9/68. Retd ENG 29/3/69.
MORRIS B.A. Born 19/12/47. Commd 24/3/83. Flt Lt 24/3/87. Retd ENG 31/3/94.
MORRIS B.G. OBE. Born 30/3/13. Commd 16/3/34. Wg Cdr 1/10/46. Retd GD 19/6/54.
MORRIS B.S. OBE AFC. Born 21/8/45. Commd 28/2/64. Gp Capt 1/7/90. Retd GD 30/9/00.
MORRIS C. Born 26/4/33. Commd 26/6/56. Wg Cdr 1/1/82. Retd ENG 11/9/86.
MORRIS C.H. Born 26/8/55. Commd 21/4/77. Sqn Ldr 1/7/88. Retd ADMIN 26/8/93.
MORRIS C.J. OBE FRIN. Born 9/7/48. Commd 1/8/69. Gp Capt 1/7/91. Retd GD 9/4/04.
MORRIS D. BA MRAeS. Born 20/9/31. Commd 9/4/53. Sqn Ldr 1/1/68. Retd GD 9/7/89.
MORRIS D.B. BSc. Born 14/8/36. Commd 16/1/72. Sqn Ldr 16/1/72. Retd ENG 14/8/94.
MORRIS D.G. Born 28/3/42. Commd 26/11/60. Wg Cdr 1/1/88. Retd GD 1/7/95.
MORRIS D.G.A. Born 20/6/22. Commd 19/7/56. Flt Lt 12/4/60. Retd GD(G) 20/6/77.
MORRIS D.H. DFM. Born 2/10/20. Commd 31/10/43. Flt Lt 7/6/51. Retd PI 31/7/74.
MORRIS D.L. FFA MCMI. Born 30/3/53. Commd 2/8/73. Sqn Ldr 1/1/90. Retd ADMIN 1/1/93.
MORRIS D.M. BSc(Eng) CEng MIEE MRAeS. Born 4/1/43. Commd 30/9/61. Wg Cdr 1/1/90. Retd ENG 30/1/97.
MORRIS D.S. Born 6/10/66. Commd 6/1/95. Sqn Ldr 1/7/00. Retd ADMIN (CAT) 6/4/05.
MORRIS E. FAAI MCMI. Born 18/6/38. Commd 1/11/56. Wg Cdr 1/1/79. Retd ADMIN 5/4/88.
MORRIS E.J. CB CBE DSO DFC FCMI. Born 6/4/15. Commd 5/9/37. A Cdre 1/1/63. Retd GD 16/7/68.
MORRIS E.W.J. MCMI. Born 21/9/28. Commd 6/4/50. Wg Cdr 1/1/69. Retd GD 21/9/83.
MORRIS F.N. Born 21/12/13. Commd 17/6/40. Sqn Ldr 1/7/56. Retd SEC 8/1/63.
MORRIS G. Born 7/9/41. Commd 14/8/80. Sqn Ldr 1/7/90. Retd ENG 1/8/93.
MORRIS G.E. Born 22/4/17. Commd 7/4/40. Wg Cdr 1/7/53. Retd GD(G) 29/5/70.
MORRIS G.M. Born 8/8/41. Commd 12/7/62. Wg Cdr 1/1/86. Retd ADMIN 2/7/94.
MORRIS G.W. Born 12/12/42. Commd 24/3/61. Sqn Ldr 1/7/94. Retd GD 14/9/96.
MORRIS H.D. Born 7/12/31. Commd 30/7/64. Flt Lt 30/7/70. Retd ADMIN 18/1/84.
MORRIS H.R. Born 22/11/34. Commd 31/3/64. Sqn Ldr 1/7/84. Retd GD(G) 21/11/89.
MORRIS I.J. MBE CertFE. Born 30/3/48. Commd 28/9/89. Sqn Ldr 1/1/99. Retd ADMIN (SEC) 1/8/04.
MORRIS J. CBE BSc. Born 8/7/36. Commd 1/10/57. AVM 1/1/90. Retd GD 1/1/92.
MORRIS J. Born 7/3/22. Commd 27/11/52. Flt Offr 27/11/58. Retd SEC 1/5/68.
MORRIS J.B. Born 24/2/49. Commd 24/4/80. Flt Lt 24/4/82. Retd ADMIN 24/4/88.
MORRIS J.E. Born 12/9/32. Commd 29/10/69. Sqn Ldr 1/1/76. Retd ENG 13/12/84.
MORRIS J.R. Born 15/11/39. Commd 22/7/71. Sqn Ldr 1/7/79. Retd GD(G) 1/5/86.
MORRIS K. Born 6/12/36. Commd 3/5/68. Flt Lt 6/10/71. Retd GD 20/7/88.
MORRIS K.E. BA. Born 4/4/70. Commd 10/10/93. Fg Offr 10/10/92. Retd GD 13/10/95.
MORRIS K.J.H. BA. Born 26/6/57. Commd 19/9/76. Sqn Ldr 1/1/87. Retd SY 31/3/90.
MORRIS K.L. Born 8/7/25. Commd 19/10/45. Sqn Ldr 1/1/61. Retd GD 19/7/83.
MORRIS K.R. The Rev. Born 20/7/35. Commd 15/9/65. Retd Wg Cdr 26/2/83.
MORRIS L.C. Born 6/10/10. Commd 4/4/43. Fg Offr 4/10/43. Retd ENG 29/1/46.
MORRIS L.J. MHCIMA. Born 30/10/16. Commd 2/8/45. Wg Cdr 1/1/60. Retd CAT 30/10/71.
MORRIS L.P. Born 6/9/51. Commd 9/3/76. Flt Lt 9/12/79. Retd ADMIN 1/6/86.
MORRIS M.R. Born 8/5/54. Commd 11/9/86. Flt Lt 11/9/88. Retd SY 11/9/94.
MORRIS N.C. Born 17/10/29. Commd 21/10/66. Flt Lt 21/10/71. Retd ENG 31/1/81.
MORRIS P.A. Born 14/6/56. Commd 26/4/84. Wg Cdr 1/7/98. Retd GD 20/12/02.
MORRIS P.A. Born 28/6/66. Commd 23/10/86. Sqn Ldr 1/7/00. Retd FLY(P) 28/6/04.
MORRIS P.G. Born 29/6/25. Commd 7/9/61. Flt Lt 7/9/64. Retd GD 2/7/68.
MORRIS P.K. Born 22/1/67. Commd 10/2/93. Flt Lt 27/10/93. Retd OPS SPT(FC) 22/1/05.
MORRIS P.L. Born 26/2/47. Commd 9/3/66. Sqn Ldr 1/7/90. Retd GD(G) 14/9/96.
MORRIS P.M. BA. Born 15/7/58. Commd 1/8/90. Sqn Ldr 1/7/01. Retd ADMIN (TRG) 1/7/04.
MORRIS R. OBE MA CEng FIEE DipEl. Born 6/7/24. Commd 11/11/43. Gp Capt 1/1/70. Retd ENG 30/3/77.
MORRIS R. Born 30/12/43. Commd 19/6/64. Flt Lt 17/3/71. Retd GD 30/12/81.

MORRIS R.H. Born 10/3/49. Commd 29/8/72. Flt Lt 29/8/76. Retd PE 31/12/79.
MORRIS R.H.J. Born 28/11/37. Commd 20/11/56. Flt Lt 20/5/62. Retd GD 28/11/75.
MORRIS R.I. Born 26/10/39. Commd 19/12/61. Sqn Ldr 1/7/70. Retd GD 15/12/79.
MORRIS R.J. Born 6/12/47. Commd 28/10/66. Sqn Ldr 1/1/80. Retd GD 6/12/84.
MORRIS R.V. CBE AFC. Born 24/9/49. Commd 14/2/69. AVM 1/1/01. Retd GD 30/4/02.
MORRIS S.C. Born 22/2/64. Commd 13/2/86. Flt Lt 2/3/90. Retd GD 22/2/02.
MORRIS S.J. BA. Born 10/12/51. Commd 25/9/71. Gp Capt 1/7/95. Retd ADMIN 3/12/97.
MORRIS S.P. Born 13/5/50. Commd 8/10/70. Flt Lt 8/4/76. Retd GD 20/5/81.
MORRIS T.F. Born 19/2/20. Commd 29/9/41. Flt Lt 27/12/50. Retd SEC 4/9/61.
MORRIS T.G. Born 12/6/35. Commd 30/5/59. Sqn Ldr 1/7/72. Retd GD 12/6/90.
MORRIS T.W. Born 9/7/28. Commd 30/9/49. Flt Lt 28/8/55. Retd GD 9/7/66.
MORRIS-TURNER J.M. Born 2/8/51. Commd 27/7/72. Flt Lt 13/1/79. Retd GD(G) 2/8/89.
MORRISH D.C. BA. Born 28/12/32. Commd 12/9/56. Sqn Ldr 12/3/64. Retd EDN 31/12/72.
MORRISH P.J. Born 16/4/27. Commd 18/7/61. Fg Offr 18/7/63. Retd SEC 1/11/63.
MORRISON D. Born 7/5/45. Commd 3/8/87. Sqn Ldr 1/7/93. Retd OPS SPT(ATC) 4/8/03.
MORRISON D.J. MEd BSc PGCE CBiol MIBiol MCIPD. Born 16/10/51. Commd 20/1/80. Sqn Ldr 1/1/88.
    Retd ADMIN 20/1/96.
MORRISON D.M. Born 3/12/43. Commd 21/5/65. Flt Lt 26/9/71. Retd GD 13/4/76.
MORRISON D.M. Born 28/7/22. Commd 14/6/42. Flt Lt 16/3/53. Retd GD(G) 28/7/77. rtg Sqn Ldr.
MORRISON D.P. Born 4/7/21. Commd 27/7/43. Sqn Ldr 1/4/55. Retd GD 4/7/64.
MORRISON F.G. The Rev. Born 12/2/37. Commd 6/6/66. Retd Wg Cdr 6/6/82.
MORRISON G.J. Born 6/3/49. Commd 8/1/76. Sqn Ldr 1/7/84. Retd ENG 3/12/01.
MORRISON G.M. MBE. Born 9/12/33. Commd 21/10/53. Sqn Ldr 1/1/65. Retd GD 9/12/71.
MORRISON I.N. BSc. Born 17/12/65. Commd 3/1/88. Flt Lt 3/7/90. Retd GD 14/3/97.
MORRISON J. MB BSc ChB MRCGP. Born 6/10/41. Commd 29/6/64. Sqn Ldr 15/8/72. Retd MED 19/7/80.
MORRISON P.J. MCMI. Born 31/7/41. Commd 16/4/63. Flt Lt 31/7/68. Retd RGT 31/7/79. rtg Sqn Ldr.
MORRISON W.J.O. AFC MRAeS. Born 15/10/23. Commd 8/11/44. Gp Capt 1/1/67. Retd GD 14/2/73.
MORRISS R.A. Born 19/5/37. Commd 11/12/58. Sqn Ldr 1/7/73. Retd ADMIN 1/7/76.
MORRISSEY B.M. Born 10/5/15. Commd 25/7/44. Flt Lt 10/11/55. Retd GD(G) 4/8/60.
MORRISSEY M.J. Born 20/9/34. Commd 12/11/57. Flt Lt 21/5/63. Retd GD 20/9/72.
MORROW M.McA. Born 6/3/42. Commd 25/11/63. Fg Offr 3/10/65. Retd GD 27/11/68.
MORROW W.K.D. OBE . Born 6/10/49. Commd 17/7/70. Gp Capt 1/1/98. Retd GD 6/4/05.
MORS P.L. Born 16/5/47. Commd 28/9/64. Sqn Ldr 1/1/77. Retd ENG 16/5/83.
MORSE R.B.J.S. Born 11/12/17. Commd 4/4/45. Flt Lt 7/6/51. Retd RGT 30/9/58.
MORTEN P.G. Born 8/12/30. Commd 17/10/57. Flt Lt 17/4/62. Retd GD 30/8/69.
MORTER D. Born 8/7/30. Commd 21/3/51. Flt Lt 21/9/55. Retd GD 8/7/68.
MORTIMER A.P. Born 25/5/44. Commd 26/9/85. Flt Lt 26/9/87. Retd FLY(ENG) 25/5/04.
MORTIMER B.W. Born 26/4/38. Commd 12/7/63. Sqn Ldr 1/7/74. Retd GD(G) 1/7/77.
MORTIMER C.P. The Rev. Born 18/4/38. Commd 27/3/77. Retd Wg Cdr 30/6/93.
MORTIMER E.L. Born 19/2/26. Commd 3/12/56. Flt Lt 3/12/56. Retd PRT 30/6/66.
MORTIMER I. BSc. Born 12/5/49. Commd 19/2/73. Sqn Ldr 1/1/83. Retd GD 19/2/89.
MORTIMER J.C.S. Born 4/12/44. Commd 8/5/86. Sqn Ldr 1/7/94. Retd ENG 14/3/96.
MORTIMER M. Born 11/5/32. Commd 8/7/65. Flt Lt 9/7/71. Retd SY 1/10/76.
MORTIMORE G.T. Born 8/1/24. Commd 23/7/43. Flt Lt 23/1/47. Retd GD 8/1/70.
MORTLOCK D.F. Born 21/4/36. Commd 12/9/63. Gp Capt 1/7/84. Retd SUP 28/7/86.
MORTLOCK G.E. Born 29/12/25. Commd 11/10/51. Flt Lt 25/1/57. Retd GD 1/10/75.
MORTON A.M. BSc. Born 7/12/37. Commd 11/11/59. Sqn Ldr 1/7/70. Retd ADMIN 29/5/76.
MORTON C.C.R. Born 12/4/25. Commd 4/6/64. Sqn Ldr 1/1/77. Retd ENG 12/4/85.
MORTON F.de C.G. Born 22/4/18. Commd 27/4/41. Flt Lt 9/6/47. Retd SEC 1/7/55. rtg Sqn Ldr.
MORTON G. MCIPS. Born 2/12/47. Commd 22/9/67. Gp Capt 1/7/95. Retd SUP 2/12/02.
MORTON G.S. Born 17/2/46. Commd 8/1/65. Flt Lt 8/7/70. Retd GD(G) 1/3/74.
MORTON J.E. MSc BTech CEng MRAeS CertEd. Born 2/2/49. Commd 2/1/77. Sqn Ldr 1/7/85.
    Retd ADMIN 14/3/96.
MORTON S.J. Born 7/2/45. Commd 31/1/64. Sqn Ldr 1/1/85. Retd GD 14/9/96.
MORTON W.H. Born 9/2/07. Commd 30/1/47. Fg Offr 30/1/49. Retd SEC 18/1/52.
MOSELEY A.G. Born 11/4/25. Commd 14/6/49. Flt Lt 14/12/53. Retd GD 21/9/64.
MOSELEY D.A.R. Born 20/9/24. Commd 19/10/59. Flt Lt 19/10/59. Retd ADMIN 20/9/82.
MOSES H.H. MBE. Born 5/5/39. Commd 3/9/60. Gp Capt 1/1/90. Retd GD 5/1/95.
MOSEY E. MBE. Born 3/10/13. Commd 18/11/54. Flt Lt 18/11/57. Retd ENG 3/10/68.
MOSLEY C.P. Born 15/7/61. Commd 11/6/81. Flt Lt 11/12/86. Retd GD 15/1/93.
MOSS A. DFM. Born 26/8/20. Commd 26/9/57. Sqn Ldr 1/7/71. Retd ENG 26/8/75.
MOSS A.S. Born 4/4/65. Commd 2/8/90. Sqn Ldr 1/1/00. Retd ENG 5/4/02.
MOSS B.G. Born 3/1/37. Commd 10/1/37. Sqn Ldr 1/1/86. Retd ENG 23/2/92.
MOSS D.E. BA. Born 4/5/62. Commd 14/3/88. Flt Lt 16/3/86. Retd FLY(N) 30/4/04.
MOSS D.M. Born 24/6/47. Commd 1/3/68. Gp Capt 1/1/96. Retd GD 24/6/02.
MOSS D.R.K. Born 4/8/66. Commd 28/7/88. Flt Lt 28/1/94. Retd FLY(P) 12/10/03.

MOSS G. OBE AFC. Born 22/6/23. Commd 29/4/44. Gp Capt 1/1/71. Retd GD 3/11/73.
MOSS I.E. CEng MRAeS. Born 5/2/27. Commd 20/2/72. Sqn Ldr 20/2/72. Retd ENG 22/4/90.
MOSS J.B. Born 5/7/45. Commd 22/7/68. Plt Offr 22/7/68. Retd CAT 29/12/68.
MOSS M. Born 6/6/35. Commd 24/8/72. Sqn Ldr 1/7/82. Retd ADMIN 26/7/85.
MOSS M.S. BEM BA. Born 20/4/49. Commd 23/4/87. Sqn Ldr 1/7/96. Retd ENG 1/9/02.
MOSS P. MCSP. Born 30/1/30. Commd 2/3/61. Wg Cdr 1/7/76. Retd MED 28/10/77.
MOSS P.S. Born 23/7/44. Commd 9/8/63. Plt Offr 9/8/64. Retd GD 19/8/65.
MOSSFORD A.R. LGSM ARCM. Born 28/7/38. Commd 8/8/74. Sqn Ldr 18/8/84. Retd DM 14/4/95.
MOSSMAN G.K. CBE. Born 10/10/27. Commd 27/7/49. Gp Capt 1/7/73. Retd GD 1/2/78.
MOSSMAN P.J. Born 28/6/42. Commd 16/12/63. Plt Offr 21/3/64. Retd GD(G) 1/10/65.
MOTT A.J. OBE CEng FIEE MRAeS. Born 27/2/08. Commd 15/2/40. Wg Cdr 1/7/47. Retd ENG 27/2/63.
MOTT B.W. Born 4/3/35. Commd 2/2/68. Sqn Ldr 8/10/75. Retd ADMIN 2/4/84.
MOTT W.H.M. Born 19/9/44. Commd 17/12/65. Flt Lt 8/1/69. Retd GD 19/9/88.
MOULD A.J. MBE. Born 22/3/11. Commd 26/10/36. Sqn Ldr 1/1/60. Retd GD(G) 1/1/63. rtg Wg Cdr.
MOULD H.J. CEng MRAeS. Born 29/9/26. Commd 29/4/54. Sqn Ldr 1/7/65. Retd ENG 1/10/76.
MOULD J.E.M. CBE. Born 12/11/14. Commd 23/1/39. A Cdre 1/7/66. Retd SUP 29/1/70.
MOULD S.G. Born 3/6/49. Commd 31/7/70. Flt Lt 31/7/73. Retd GD 7/2/88.
MOULD T.W. BEM. Born 11/12/20. Commd 27/8/59. Flt Lt 27/8/64. Retd ENG 11/12/76.
MOULDEN K.A. Born 27/12/32. Commd 26/12/51. Flt Lt 26/6/46. Retd GD 27/12/70.
MOULE A.L. BSc. Born 6/12/47. Commd 14/5/73. Sqn Ldr 1/1/85. Retd GD 14/6/98.
MOULE D.E. DFC. Born 28/12/56. Commd 6/11/80. Sqn Ldr 1/7/89. Retd GD 7/7/97.
MOULE D.G. Born 27/10/32. Commd 26/3/52. Wg Cdr 1/7/83. Retd GD 1/1/87.
MOULES P.L. BA. Born 27/3/50. Commd 15/9/69. Wg Cdr 1/7/86. Retd GD 27/3/91.
MOULES P.S. AFC. Born 23/4/23. Commd 23/7/43. Sqn Ldr 1/7/66. Retd GD 23/4/83.
MOULL A.P. BA. Born 27/4/35. Commd 25/2/64. Flt Lt 13/2/69. Retd SUP 8/1/83.
MOULTON J.E. Born 22/3/43. Commd 14/6/63. Wg Cdr 1/1/85. Retd SUP 22/3/98.
MOULTON L.H. CB DFC CEng FIEE FCMI. Born 3/12/15. Commd 26/4/41. AVM 1/1/69. Retd ENG 15/3/71.
MOUNFIELD P.A. MB BS MRCOG. Born 4/12/31. Commd 8/9/57. Wg Cdr 8/9/70. Retd MED 8/9/73.
MOUNSEY J.A.B. MBE MRCS LRCP FCMI. Born 14/9/20. Commd 23/5/46. Gp Capt 1/1/67. Retd MED 31/3/78.
MOUNSEY J.S. Born 29/10/28. Commd 18/2/60. Flt Lt 18/2/65. Retd ENG 18/2/68.
MOUNT C.J. CBE DSO DFC BA. Born 14/12/13. Commd 26/12/36. A Cdre 1/1/58. Retd GD 26/12/66.
MOUNTAIN D. Born 20/10/41. Commd 11/5/78. Flt Lt 11/5/80. Retd ENG 11/5/86.
MOUNTAIN J.B. MBE. Born 6/10/30. Commd 6/12/51. Wg Cdr 1/1/71. Retd GD 30/5/78.
MOUNTAIN P. Born 18/11/38. Commd 20/11/75. Flt Lt 20/11/78. Retd GD 3/9/89.
MOUNTER D.J. BSc. Born 6/2/43. Commd 8/4/68. Flt Lt 6/10/71. Retd ENG 16/6/89.
MOUNTFORD J.C.M. AFC. Born 20/2/21. Commd 10/7/39. Sqn Ldr 1/1/49. Retd GD 25/3/58.
MOWAT I. Born 19/1/52. Commd 20/9/79. Wg Cdr 1/7/99. Retd GD 23/9/04.
MOWAT J. Born 14/3/47. Commd 5/11/65. Flt Lt 4/5/72. Retd GD 2/6/76.
MOWBRAY F.J. CEng MIEE. Born 19/12/09. Commd 24/7/41. Wg Cdr 1/7/54. Retd ENG 19/12/64.
MOWBRAY R.G. BSc. Born 8/1/58. Commd 28/9/80. Flt Lt 28/12/81. Retd GD 28/9/96.
MOXAM L.R. MBE. Born 24/9/31. Commd 27/6/51. Sqn Ldr 1/1/63. Retd GD 31/12/64.
MOXEY B.W. BSc. Born 12/11/51. Commd 13/9/70. Sqn Ldr 1/1/81. Retd ADMIN 12/11/89.
MOXLEY C.E. The Rev. MA. Born 28/10/09. Commd 1/9/44. Retd Wg Cdr 21/10/50. Recalled 1/12/52 to 16/10/65. Gp Capt.
MOXON R.H. Born 9/2/44. Commd 11/11/65. Flt Lt 9/2/71. Retd ADMIN 9/2/82.
MOY D.B. BA. Born 31/10/33. Commd 1/1/63. Sqn Ldr 1/3/68. Retd ADMIN 1/1/79.
MOYCE D.J. Born 28/1/32. Commd 30/4/62. Wg Cdr 1/7/77. Retd GD(G) 28/1/87.
MOYES D.D. Born 1/4/34. Commd 8/5/53. Flt Lt 10/9/58. Retd GD 30/9/77. Reistated 3/6/81. Flt Lt 14/5/62. Retd GD 1/4/89.
MOYES W. MBE. Born 6/1/25. Commd 30/9/48. Sqn Ldr 1/4/56. Retd ENG 6/1/80.
MUDDLE A.R. Born 27/6/35. Commd 4/5/72. Sqn Ldr 1/7/84. Retd ENG 8/8/86.
MUDE K.H. DFM. Born 2/2/22. Commd 16/7/04. Sqn Ldr 1/7/60. Retd GD 30/6/73.
MUDFORD J.J. Born 9/5/29. Commd 16/12/52. Sqn Ldr 1/7/63. Retd GD 16/12/68.
MUDGE R.F. Born 10/11/33. Commd 18/3/53. Wg Cdr 1/7/70. Retd GD 26/1/82.
MUDGE R.P. Born 13/3/21. Commd 22/10/53. Sqn Ldr 1/1/72. Retd ENG 30/8/75.
MUGFORD C.F. Born 6/3/35. Commd 22/7/53. Flt Lt 28/7/59. Retd GD 31/3/74.
MUGFORD D.M.T. BSc. Born 20/11/41. Commd 10/4/67. Sqn Ldr 1/1/74. Retd ENG 10/4/83.
MUGRIDGE C.A. Born 26/5/43. Commd 14/6/63. Flt Lt 14/12/68. Retd GD 2/3/76.
MUGRIDGE J.R. Born 21/5/42. Commd 17/12/64. Flt Lt 17/12/69. Retd SUP 21/7/83.
MUIR D.W.F. Born 15/4/26. Commd 22/2/46. Flt Lt 22/8/49. Retd GD 15/4/64.
MUIR J. Born 5/1/34. Commd 21/10/66. Flt Lt 21/10/71. Retd ENG 5/1/89.
MUIR J.N. Born 30/4/47. Commd 20/9/79. Sqn Ldr 1/1/89. Retd ADMIN (SEC) 30/4/03.
MUIR J.S.C. Born 23/10/37. Commd 10/2/56. Wg Cdr 1/1/81. Retd GD 23/10/92.
MUIR R.W. Born 19/8/40. Commd 25/1/63. Flt Lt 8/1/69. Retd GD 2/10/78.
MUIRHEAD G.K. DFM. Born 22/3/20. Commd 10/6/41. Sqn Ldr 1/7/57. Retd GD 22/3/69.
MULCAHY P.L. Born 28/4/58. Commd 22/2/79. Sqn Ldr 1/7/89. Retd GD 17/12/96.

MULDOWNEY A.J. Born 8/2/60. Commd 23/4/87. Flt Lt 23/4/89. Retd ENG 8/2/98.
MULGREW K. Born 25/12/56. Commd 20/12/90. Flt Lt 20/12/92. Retd GD 5/1/01.
MULHALL T.A. Born 29/9/51. Commd 15/8/85. Sqn Ldr 1/7/95. Retd ENG 22/1/98.
MULHEARN K.J. The Rev. Born 12/8/26. Commd 18/10/61. Retd Gp Capt 18/10/77.
MULHOLLAND H. Born 3/5/10. Commd 6/9/46. Flt Lt 6/9/46. Retd PRT 6/11/59. rtg Sqn Ldr.
MULHOLLAND-FENTON L.G. ACMA. Born 13/5/63. Commd 5/8/96. Sqn Ldr 1/1/00. Retd SUPPLY 22/8/03.
MULINDER W.D. AFC. Born 23/1/34. Commd 23/9/63. Wg Cdr 1/1/79. Retd GD 24/9/88.
MULKERN A.M.M. BSc. Born 20/8/47. Commd 23/9/68. Sqn Ldr 1/1/83. Retd ADMIN 1/1/86.
MULKERN P.F. Born 30/9/44. Commd 25/2/66. Sqn Ldr 1/1/93. Retd GD 12/4/95.
MULLAN J.A. BEM. Born 8/3/42. Commd 23/5/85. Sqn Ldr 1/7/94. Retd ADMIN 8/3/97.
MULLAN J.P. Born 2/8/47. Commd 5/11/65. Flt Lt 4/5/72. Retd GD 14/3/97.
MULLANEY J.M. FCMI LHSM. Born 17/6/34. Commd 22/5/70. Wg Cdr 1/1/85. Retd MED(SEC) 3/1/87.
MULLARKEY D. MBE. Born 29/8/28. Commd 5/4/50. Wg Cdr 1/7/64. Retd GD 9/4/81.
MULLEN A. Born 15/4/65. Commd 19/7/84. Flt Lt 19/1/90. Retd FLY(P) 15/4/03.
MULLEN A.B. Born 13/12/43. Commd 9/3/62. Sqn Ldr 1/7/74. Retd SUP 9/9/76.
MULLEN B.J. BSc. Born 16/11/47. Commd 1/11/71. Flt Lt 1/8/73. Retd GD 1/4/92.
MULLEN E.H. Born 7/3/76. Commd 6/2/97. Flt Lt 6/8/03. Retd OPS SPT(FLTOPS) 12/2/04.
MULLEN J. Born 28/1/20. Commd 14/3/57. Sqn Ldr 1/7/67. Retd ENG 31/7/70.
MULLEN J.V. Born 26/3/47. Commd 29/4/71. Flt Lt 3/12/84. Retd GD(G) 4/4/95.
MULLEN N.H. Born 27/4/26. Commd 12/3/64. Flt Lt 12/3/67. Retd GD 17/1/76.
MULLEN P.J.P. MB ChB. Born 24/5/57. Commd 18/10/77. Wg Cdr 1/9/94. Retd MED 14/3/96.
MULLEN T.A.F. Born 22/4/47. Commd 1/8/68. Flt Lt 6/10/71. Retd GD 22/4/91.
MULLEN W.F. BA CEng FIEE FRAeS. Born 24/12/36. Commd 24/7/57. Gp Capt 1/1/81. Retd ENG 6/4/90.
MULLER J.E. BSc. Born 31/3/38. Commd 25/1/71. Flt Lt 25/1/71. Retd EDN 2/9/72.
MULLER M.E. Born 27/7/48. Commd 31/8/78. Flt Lt 31/8/82. Retd ADMIN 1/5/94.
MULLETT C. MBE. Born 24/5/22. Commd 25/6/65. Flt Lt 25/6/71. Retd ADMIN 28/1/78.
MULLEY J.L. BSc. Born 18/6/45. Commd 2/3/70. Flt Lt 2/6/73. Retd ENG 2/3/86.
MULLIGAN G.H. MBE MBA MCMI. Born 25/10/44. Commd 5/11/70. Sqn Ldr 1/7/83. Retd FLY(N) 25/10/04.
MULLIGAN S.K. Born 17/1/36. Commd 27/6/59. Flt Lt 27/12/64. Retd GD 1/5/79.
MULLINEAUX R.H. FCMI. Born 12/12/25. Commd 29/6/50. Gp Capt 1/1/76. Retd GD 3/4/79.
MULLINGER J.R. Born 25/4/44. Commd 1/4/71. Sqn Ldr 1/1/92. Retd ADMIN 25/4/00.
MULLINGS N.W. BSc. Born 20/3/59. Commd 3/8/86. Wg Cdr 1/7/01. Retd GD 1/7/04.
MULLINGS W.M. Born 17/5/22. Commd 10/3/49. Flt Lt 19/11/53. Retd PE 3/5/64.
MULLINS R.D. AFC. Born 1/3/25. Commd 1/9/44. Wg Cdr 1/1/66. Retd PE 1/9/73.
MULLOOLY J.B. Born 30/5/33. Commd 28/1/53. Flt Lt 17/6/58. Retd GD(G) 9/8/87.
MULVENNEY W. BA. Born 1/12/40. Commd 6/8/63. Wg Cdr 1/7/85. Retd ADMIN 1/2/91.
MUMBY L.R. OBE. Born 3/8/14. Commd 2/1/39. Gp Capt 1/1/62. Retd SUP 3/8/69.
MUMFORD A. CVO OBE. Born 8/3/36. Commd 9/4/57. Gp Capt 1/7/80. Retd GD 1/6/88.
MUMFORD J.S. BDS. Born 5/11/39. Commd 24/7/62. Wg Cdr 12/12/76. Retd DEL 24/7/78.
MUMFORD P. Born 21/6/37. Commd 15/9/65. Flt Lt 4/1/71. Retd GD(G) 22/12/87.
MUMME I.G.T. Born 18/1/46. Commd 18/11/66. Flt Lt 18/3/73. Retd SUP 18/11/01.
MUMMERY B.W. BSc. Born 20/6/39. Commd 27/6/59. Flt Lt 27/12/64. Retd GD 5/11/78.
MUNCASTER A. Born 31/3/51. Commd 21/9/72. Flt Lt 21/3/79. Retd GD(G) 1/4/80.
MUNCASTER G.A. Born 14/6/30. Commd 17/12/52. Sqn Ldr 1/7/62. Retd GD 21/5/76.
MUNDAY A.J. BDS LDSRCS. Born 24/10/32. Commd 14/9/58. Wg Cdr 17/3/71. Retd DEL 1/3/91.
MUNDAY B. Born 10/7/42. Commd 3/11/77. Flt Lt 3/11/79. Retd GD 31/3/94.
MUNDAY D.A.P. MCMI. Born 5/11/36. Commd 30/7/57. Sqn Ldr 1/1/68. Retd SUP 5/11/74.
MUNDAY J.R. Born 9/4/48. Commd 2/1/70. Flt Lt 2/7/75. Retd GD 9/4/86.
MUNDAY K.N. Born 27/12/39. Commd 14/8/80. Flt Lt 14/8/83. Retd GD 27/12/94.
MUNDAY S.P. Born 18/9/56. Commd 22/2/88. Sqn Ldr 1/1/97. Retd SUP 22/9/02.
MUNDAY V.D. BSc. Born 2/9/39. Commd 19/2/63. Sqn Ldr 1/7/73. Retd SUP 2/9/94.
MUNDEN M.A. Born 5/11/32. Commd 13/9/51. Flt Lt 4/1/57. Retd GD 18/12/83.
MUNDY A.H. Born 31/5/20. Commd 31/5/43. Flt Lt 30/11/46. Retd GD 30/11/60.
MUNDY C.P. Born 5/7/23. Commd 20/8/43. Sqn Ldr 1/1/57. Retd GD 31/7/58.
MUNDY D. Born 5/9/43. Commd 8/1/76. Sqn Ldr 1/7/83. Retd ADMIN 8/1/90. Re-entered 2/9/94. Sqn Ldr 23/2/88. Retd ADMIN 5/9/99.
MUNDY D.A.P. AMCMI. Born 5/11/36. Commd 30/7/57. Sqn Ldr 1/1/68. Retd SUP 5/11/74.
MUNDY J.D. DFC. Born 14/5/19. Commd 23/1/39. Sqn Ldr 1/8/47. Retd GD 14/5/58.
MUNDY R.F. Born 7/5/35. Commd 9/4/57. Wg Cdr 1/7/73. Retd GD 28/7/89.
MUNGAVIN G.C. The Rev. Born 26/2/27. Commd 6/3/62. Retd Wg Cdr 6/3/75.
MUNN B.P. Born 4/2/47. Commd 7/7/67. Fg Offr 7/7/69. Retd GD 3/10/70.
MUNN B.R.H. Born 26/11/22. Commd 2/10/43. Flt Lt 2/4/47. Retd GD 26/11/65.
MUNN K.A.A. Born 3/4/25. Commd 31/3/45. Sqn Ldr 1/7/72. Retd GD 3/4/76.
MUNNELLY H.M. Born 20/6/62. Commd 30/8/84. Sqn Ldr 1/7/95. Retd GD 20/6/00.
MUNNS P.N. BEng. Born 29/11/67. Commd 17/2/91. Flt Lt 17/8/92. Retd FLY(P) 17/2/03.
MUNNS R.C. MA CEng MIEE. Born 12/10/53. Commd 2/11/75. Sqn Ldr 1/1/86. Retd ENG 2/11/94.

MUNNS S.A.E. OBE DFM. Born 30/5/19. Commd 5/2/42. Wg Cdr 1/7/58. Retd GD 30/5/74.
MUNRO A.J. Born 4/5/30. Commd 13/8/52. Flt Lt 9/1/58. Retd GD 4/7/71.
MUNRO A.L.D. BSc. Born 11/10/41. Commd 22/9/63. Sqn Ldr 1/1/81. Retd ENG 2/4/92.
MUNRO A.W. The Rev. MA BD. Born 7/8/49. Commd 11/6/78. Retd Wg Cdr 11/6/94.
MUNRO C.A. BSc(Eng). Born 15/1/62. Commd 14/9/80. Flt Lt 15/4/85. Retd GD 15/1/00.
MUNRO D.G. AFM. Born 4/3/24. Commd 17/3/55. Flt Lt 17/3/61. Retd GD 28/6/68.
MUNRO J. Born 7/3/34. Commd 1/1/64. Sqn Ldr 1/7/74. Retd GD 1/9/87.
MUNRO M.R. BSc CEng MRAeS. Born 18/2/48. Commd 18/9/66. Wg Cdr 1/1/88. Retd ENG 1/8/98.
MUNRO P. Born 15/11/18. Commd 4/3/54. Flt Lt 4/3/57. Retd SEC 16/11/67.
MUNSLOW C.H.J. Born 18/4/40. Commd 25/2/65. Flt Lt 25/2/69. Retd SUP 18/4/78. Re-instated 11/6/79.
    Flt Lt 20/4/70. Retd SUP 19/4/90.
MUNSLOW W. BEng. Born 24/3/61. Commd 13/7/90. Flt Lt 15/7/93. Retd ENG 24/3/99.
MUNSON D.H.G. BSc CEng MRAeS. Born 15/11/25. Commd 18/7/49. Sqn Ldr 1/1/57. Retd ENG 15/11/80.
MUNT M.H. Born 4/1/31. Commd 5/7/53. Flt Lt 29/4/59. Retd GD 4/1/69.
MUNYARD R.S. AFC. Born 10/3/43. Commd 19/8/66. Flt Lt 1/3/69. Retd GD 10/3/81.
MURCHIE I.T.A. MSc MIMechE FRAeS. Born 11/12/22. Commd 15/4/43. Wg Cdr 1/1/60. Retd ENG 22/6/68.
MURCHIE J.W. Born 4/4/17. Commd 31/1/44. Flt Lt 31/7/48. Retd SUP 16/6/66. rtg Sqn Ldr.
MURCUTT B.J. MCMI. Born 3/4/34. Commd 8/7/65. Sqn Ldr 1/7/80. Retd SY 9/4/85.
MURDEN M.A. CEng MIMechE MIProdE MRAeS. Born 1/12/35. Commd 24/7/57. Sqn Ldr 1/7/66.
    Retd ENG 29/12/73.
MURDOCH C.J.B. AFM. Born 16/5/25. Commd 18/10/62. Flt Lt 18/10/65. Retd GD 31/3/74.
MURDOCH M.A. Born 22/8/54. Commd 17/5/79. Sqn Ldr 1/7/90. Retd GD 1/1/94.
MURDOCK A.E. Born 9/12/14. Commd 30/5/46. Flt Lt 30/11/50. Retd SEC 9/12/63.
MURDOCK B. Born 7/9/47. Commd 20/12/73. Flt Lt 3/4/76. Retd GD 22/4/94.
MURFITT K.P. Born 20/8/32. Commd 2/1/54. Flt Lt 5/10/60. Retd GD 20/8/87.
MURKIN D.A. BEM. Born 8/2/32. Commd 29/7/65. Flt Lt 29/7/71. Retd SY 7/8/82.
MURKIN S.D. AFC. Born 9/12/52. Commd 21/4/77. Sqn Ldr 1/7/89. Retd GD 8/12/96. Re-entered 4/11/97.
    Wg Cdr 1/1/00. Retd GD 12/4/02.
MURKOWSKI A.S. Born 19/4/20. Commd 17/5/56. Flt Lt 17/5/59. Retd GD 19/4/75.
MURLAND H.F. MCMI. Born 12/4/23. Commd 12/7/44. Sqn Ldr 1/7/65. Retd SEC 4/4/70.
MURLEY H.T. DFC AFC* MRAeS. Born 9/9/23. Commd 10/5/44. Wg Cdr 1/1/62. Retd GD 31/3/75.
MURPHY A. Born 11/8/56. Commd 16/9/76. Sqn Ldr 1/1/89. Retd GD 1/5/95.
MURPHY B.M.P. BSc MRAeS. Born 16/9/41. Commd 4/10/65. Sqn Ldr 1/7/91. Retd GD 16/9/96.
MURPHY D.H. BA FRCS(Glas) MRCS LRCP. Born 31/7/30. Commd 7/7/57. Gp Capt 1/2/82. Retd MED 8/7/86.
MURPHY D.T. Born 8/2/31. Commd 12/1/61. Flt Lt 12/1/66. Retd GD 8/2/88.
MURPHY J.C. Born 12/1/48. Commd 23/9/66. Wg Cdr 1/7/91. Retd SY 31/3/94.
MURPHY J.E.T. OBE. Born 18/3/17. Commd 23/1/39. Sqn Ldr 1/7/48. Retd SUP 27/5/53. rtg Wg Cdr.
MURPHY J.J. Born 2/8/57. Commd 12/10/78. Flt Lt 12/4/84. Retd GD 25/6/90.
MURPHY J.N. Born 25/12/28. Commd 13/12/50. Flt Lt 13/6/53. Retd GD 25/12/66.
MURPHY K.P. Born 12/2/24. Commd 3/6/57. Flt Lt 1/3/61. Retd SUP 2/12/75.
MURPHY M.J. IEng. Born 24/12/40. Commd 9/2/66. Sqn Ldr 1/7/76. Retd ENG 24/12/95.
MURPHY M.L. Born 7/5/60. Commd 8/4/82. Flt Lt 8/10/87. Retd GD 11/8/89.
MURPHY P.B. CEng MIEE. Born 5/1/42. Commd 23/6/67. Wg Cdr 1/7/84. Retd ENG 29/12/95.
MURPHY S.D.A. BDS. Born 10/11/38. Commd 9/6/63. Wg Cdr 9/6/76. Retd DEL 29/6/88.
MURPHY S.P. MA CEng MIEE MCMI. Born 9/12/51. Commd 13/9/70. Wg Cdr 1/7/90. Retd ENG 14/9/96.
MURPHY T.G. Born 4/11/32. Commd 23/8/51. Flt Lt 31/1/59. Retd GD 1/10/76.
MURPHY T.J. Born 4/3/13. Commd 15/5/58. Flt Lt 15/5/63. Retd ENG 15/5/68.
MURRAY A. Born 11/10/58. Commd 14/2/99. Flt Lt 14/2/99. Retd OPS SPT(FLTOPS) 19/7/04.
MURRAY A.D. AFC. Born 18/11/46. Commd 2/6/67. Flt Lt 2/12/72. Retd GD 7/4/79.
MURRAY A.R. MA CEng MRAeS. Born 1/12/30. Commd 26/9/53. Gp Capt 1/7/81. Retd ENG 3/4/85.
MURRAY A.S. BSc. Born 12/6/47. Commd 20/4/71. Sqn Ldr 1/1/84. Retd GD 30/12/88.
MURRAY C. OBE. Born 28/5/15. Commd 23/1/39. Gp Capt 1/7/66. Retd SUP 28/5/70.
MURRAY C. BSc. Born 24/2/41. Commd 25/1/63. Flt Lt 3/10/67. Retd ENG 24/8/82.
MURRAY C.G. Born 19/5/45. Commd 4/6/64. Flt Lt 20/10/70. Retd GD(G) 19/5/83.
MURRAY D. MB BS MRCP. Born 29/5/43. Commd 16/9/63. Gp Capt 19/8/91. Retd MED 14/3/96.
MURRAY D.C. MA. Born 6/8/41. Commd 11/3/62. Fg Offr 15/4/63. Retd GD 14/9/65.
MURRAY F.G. Born 27/2/25. Commd 6/3/57. Flt Lt 21/8/63. Retd SUP 26/6/72.
MURRAY G.S. Born 22/11/22. Commd 25/5/44. Sqn Ldr 1/7/70. Retd GD 1/5/73.
MURRAY I.R. Born 28/1/47. Commd 11/4/85. Sqn Ldr 1/1/94. Retd MED(T) 16/8/98.
MURRAY J.R. Born 9/9/35. Commd 9/7/57. Sqn Ldr 1/7/70. Retd GD 6/1/84.
MURRAY K.F.C. Born 11/3/55. Commd 3/7/80. Sqn Ldr 1/1/90. Retd SUP 11/3/95.
MURRAY L.C. Born 15/10/19. Commd 17/12/43. Flt Lt 29/11/51. Retd GD(G) 2/10/63.
MURRAY M.J. Born 5/2/53. Commd 27/1/77. Sqn Ldr 1/1/88. Retd ADMIN 9/8/98.
MURRAY M.R. Born 1/9/34. Commd 15/6/53. Sqn Ldr 1/7/90. Retd GD 29/7/93.
MURRAY P.A.L. Born 16/5/21. Commd 22/8/41. Flt Lt 1/9/45. Retd SEC 29/1/56.
MURRAY P.G.E. FCMI MRAeS. Born 22/5/37. Commd 22/7/66. Wg Cdr 1/1/79. Retd MED(T) 1/12/86.

MURRAY P.S. BSc. Born 25/7/52. Commd 6/4/72. Sqn Ldr 1/1/85. Retd GD 17/1/86.
MURRAY R.A. MBE MCMI. Born 19/5/40. Commd 9/3/62. Wg Cdr 1/7/84. Retd SY 16/5/91.
MURRAY T.C. DSO DFC*. Born 31/5/18. Commd 17/12/38. Wg Cdr 1/7/50. Retd GD 13/5/59.
MURRAY T.J. Born 4/12/43. Commd 16/9/67. Gp Capt 1/7/93. Retd GD 4/12/98.
MURRAY-ROCHARD A.L. OBE. Born 2/5/25. Commd 7/3/46. Wg Cdr 1/1/64. Retd ENG 30/11/78.
MURRELL G.M. Born 14/4/37. Commd 8/10/70. Sqn Ldr 1/7/80. Retd GD 25/5/84.
MURRIE J. The Rev. BD. Born 13/1/26. Commd 1/9/54. Retd Wg Cdr 1/9/70.
MURROW J.S. Born 22/5/29. Commd 11/3/65. Sqn Ldr 1/7/76. Retd GD 22/5/87.
MURTAGH M.L. BA. Born 12/2/53. Commd 18/10/81. Flt Lt 18/1/85. Retd ADMIN 18/10/97.
MURTON B. BSc. Born 7/4/40. Commd 2/1/67. Sqn Ldr 2/2/73. Retd ADMIN 1/11/77.
MURTY J.K. BSc. Born 12/5/50. Commd 3/10/68. Sqn Ldr 1/7/85. Retd GD 13/7/00.
MURZYN J.F. Born 10/7/19. Commd 14/11/57. Flt Lt 14/11/60. Retd GD(G) 11/9/65.
MUSE R.W. Born 24/4/45. Commd 13/1/67. Flt Lt 13/7/72. Retd OPS SPT 15/12/98.
MUSGRAVE A.B. BSc. Born 5/2/29. Commd 16/6/53. Sqn Ldr 1/1/61. Retd GD 16/6/69.
MUSGRAVE C.M. Born 27/10/42. Commd 15/7/63. Wg Cdr 1/1/79. Retd ENG 1/1/82.
MUSGRAVE J.R. MC. Born 15/11/15. Commd 11/10/41. Flt Lt 11/10/43. Retd LGL 1/11/49.
MUSGRAVE J.R. DSO TD. Born 22/6/18. Commd 12/11/41. Gp Capt 1/1/67. Retd GD 31/3/70.
MUSGRAVE W. Born 27/12/22. Commd 17/2/47. Flt Lt 9/6/52. Retd GD 26/7/61.
MUSGROVE A.C. AFC*. Born 10/1/20. Commd 29/3/48. Sqn Ldr 1/9/65. Retd GD 1/2/73.
MUSGROVE S.A. Born 11/11/33. Commd 12/3/52. Flt Lt 10/7/57. Retd GD 11/11/71.
MUSHENS A. Born 25/7/34. Commd 8/10/52. Flt Lt 6/3/58. Retd GD 25/7/89.
MUSKER C.N. CEng MIMechE. Born 3/8/30. Commd 24/3/69. Wg Cdr 1/1/75. Retd ENG 2/4/82.
MUSSARD R.W. MSc BSc CEng MIMechE. Born 25/1/50. Commd 26/2/71. Sqn Ldr 1/7/85. Retd ENG 1/10/92.
MUSSELWHITE M.N. MBE IEng MIIE. Born 9/8/49. Commd 5/7/73. Sqn Ldr 1/1/90. Retd ENGINEER 9/8/04.
MUSTARD J.E.M. BSc. Born 5/5/47. Commd 1/9/70. Sqn Ldr 1/1/86. Retd GD 1/1/89.
MUTCH P. MSc BEd. Born 27/6/58. Commd 23/9/79. Sqn Ldr 1/1/89. Retd ADMIN 14/3/97.
MUTCH T. Born 22/7/24. Commd 14/2/63. Flt Lt 14/2/66. Retd GD 1/11/73.
MUTSAARS J.A.B. Born 2/11/31. Commd 26/3/59. Wg Cdr 1/1/79. Retd GD 2/11/88.
MUTTON R.F. Born 18/4/10. Commd 17/4/47. Flt Lt 19/6/52. Retd SUP 10/1/56.
MUTTY D.J. Born 3/10/63. Commd 11/9/86. Flt Lt 11/3/92. Retd FLY(P) 12/5/04.
MYALL D.M. Born 18/1/45. Commd 2/8/68. Flt Lt 1/7/79. Retd ENG 18/1/00.
MYATT W.G. AFC. Born 17/4/24. Commd 26/2/45. Flt Lt 26/8/48. Retd GD 17/4/62.
MYERS A.B. Born 12/1/70. Commd 30/3/89. Flt Lt 30/9/93. Retd GD 21/12/96.
MYERS F.J. Born 28/7/24. Commd 7/5/53. Sqn Ldr 1/9/65. Retd GD 31/3/74.
MYERS G. Born 28/5/25. Commd 22/5/45. Sqn Ldr 1/7/56. Retd GD 2/7/74.
MYERS J.R. LLB. Born 2/5/36. Commd 10/10/58. Wg Cdr 1/1/81. Retd ADMIN 1/12/91.
MYERS J.R. Born 29/5/45. Commd 10/1/69. Flt Lt 10/7/74. Retd GD 19/8/84.
MYERS L.E. Born 6/12/48. Commd 22/12/67. Flt Lt 22/6/73. Retd GD 6/12/86.
MYERS N. Born 14/3/14. Commd 17/4/47. Sqn Ldr 1/1/70. Retd SUP 1/1/73.
MYLES W.S. Born 6/4/37. Commd 21/10/66. Flt Lt 27/1/69. Retd SEC 6/4/75.

N

NADIN J.L. Born 3/11/48. Commd 8/6/84. Sqn Ldr 1/7/92. Retd SUP 14/3/96.
NADIN W.V. AFC*. Born 24/5/23. Commd 18/2/60. Flt Lt 1/4/63. Retd GD 24/5/83.
NAGLE P.M. Born 4/6/38. Commd 3/9/60. Flt Lt 3/3/66. Retd GD 4/6/76.
NAIDO B.S. Born 11/5/40. Commd 10/11/61. Sqn Ldr 1/1/74. Retd GD 11/5/78.
NAILARD A.C.L. BSc. Born 22/5/61. Commd 16/9/79. Flt Lt 15/10/83. Retd GD 22/2/96.
NAILE L.S. Born 18/2/29. Commd 19/4/51. Flt Lt 17/10/56. Retd GD 18/2/67.
NAILER R.G. OBE CEng FIMechE. Born 6/5/45. Commd 15/7/66. Gp Capt 1/7/89. Retd ENG 1/9/91.
NAIRN R.McF. Born 22/12/29. Commd 6/6/57. Flt Lt 7/3/62. Retd GD 22/12/67.
NAISH D.J. Born 14/9/31. Commd 11/3/65. Fg Offr 2/11/66. Retd MED(T) 20/9/69.
NANCARROW J.H. Born 14/5/14. Commd 12/9/38. Gp Capt 1/7/58. Retd SUP 12/6/70.
NANCE E.J. OBE. Born 30/3/36. Commd 17/12/57. Wg Cdr 1/7/73. Retd GD 7/7/78.
NANNERY C.J. Born 6/5/47. Commd 8/1/76. Sqn Ldr 1/7/83. Retd SUP 19/3/88.
NAPIER J.J. Born 11/4/43. Commd 2/6/67. Flt Lt 2/6/71. Retd GD 4/6/83.
NAPIER M.J.W. BSc(Eng). Born 20/9/59. Commd 4/9/78. Sqn Ldr 1/1/92. Retd GD 20/9/97.
NAPIER R.W. MBE. Born 4/5/32. Commd 22/7/66. Sqn Ldr 1/1/75. Retd ENG 17/7/82.
NAPLES W.B.B. MCMI. Born 25/12/20. Commd 9/10/42. Sqn Ldr 1/10/55. Retd GD 25/12/69.
NARDONE S.G. Born 22/6/65. Commd 15/2/90. Flt Lt 3/3/92. Retd GD 14/3/96.
NARSEY A.K. BEng. Born 23/1/61. Commd 23/8/88. Flt Lt 15/7/91. Retd ENG 23/1/99.
NASH A. Born 31/7/46. Commd 2/12/66. Flt Lt 2/6/72. Retd GD 1/10/89.
NASH A.J. MA. Born 31/12/59. Commd 9/8/79. Wg Cdr 1/1/99. Retd GD 5/4/02.
NASH A.STJ. Born 22/4/65. Commd 26/4/84. Flt Lt 26/10/89. Retd GD 3/4/97.
NASH C.C. BA. Born 11/4/46. Commd 12/4/73. Wg Cdr 1/7/90. Retd OPS SPT 11/4/01.
NASH F.C. Born 26/12/41. Commd 17/7/70. Flt Lt 17/7/72. Retd GD(G) 26/12/79.
NASH H.W. MBE MA. Born 25/6/59. Commd 8/9/83. Wg Cdr 1/7/98. Retd GD 31/12/02.
NASH J.A. Born 28/6/57. Commd 23/11/78. Sqn Ldr 1/7/91. Retd GD 5/4/99.
NASH J.M. Born 19/5/36. Commd 27/7/61. Sqn Ldr 1/1/72. Retd GD 4/11/86.
NASH L. BSc. Born 9/12/40. Commd 6/9/63. Flt Lt 18/12/67. Retd GD 18/6/79.
NASH L.A. CEng MRAeS. Born 8/12/32. Commd 22/7/55. Wg Cdr 1/7/76. Retd ENG 30/4/83.
NASH M.A. MBA BSc. Born 12/7/57. Commd 14/9/75. Sqn Ldr 1/1/88. Retd SY 12/7/95.
NASH M.C. Born 26/1/33. Commd 12/7/51. Flt Lt 11/1/57. Retd GD 26/1/88.
NASH M.R. AFC. Born 14/4/31. Commd 4/6/52. Sqn Ldr 1/1/65. Retd GD 3/2/76.
NASH P. Born 14/4/56. Commd 27/3/75. Flt Lt 27/9/81. Retd GD(G) 14/4/94.
NASH P.J. MB ChB FFARCS DA. Born 21/4/44. Commd 29/6/64. Sqn Ldr 30/7/73. Retd MED 3/1/76.
NASH T.H.S. Born 23/7/38. Commd 28/11/60. Flt Lt 28/5/66. Retd GD 28/11/76.
NASH T.J. OBE AFC FCMI MRAeS. Born 21/5/37. Commd 28/1/58. Gp Capt 1/7/80. Retd GD 31/10/83.
NAST M.J. Born 3/12/22. Commd 13/7/61. Flt Lt 13/7/64. Retd GD 14/10/72.
NATION B.H.G. Born 15/5/18. Commd 24/9/44. Flt Lt 24/3/48. Retd GD 15/5/61.
NATTRASS D.H. BSc MCIT MILT. Born 7/6/57. Commd 3/5/81. Flt Lt 3/11/84. Retd SUP 14/9/96.
NATTRASS T. CBE AFC*. Born 21/4/41. Commd 11/6/60. A Cdre 1/1/89. Retd GD 2/11/91.
NAUGHTON E.B. The Rev. Born 26/1/34. Commd 18/7/66. Retd Wg Cdr 18/7/85.
NAYAR V.K. Born 30/12/41. Commd 8/7/65. Sqn Ldr 1/1/75. Retd SUP 1/10/85.
NAYLOR C. OBE. Born 27/5/32. Commd 18/2/54. Wg Cdr 1/1/75. Retd SUP 27/5/87.
NAYLOR M.L. AFC. Born 9/2/47. Commd 21/1/66. Sqn Ldr 1/1/83. Retd GD 1/1/86.
NAYLOR P.W. CEng MIMechE MRAeS. Born 17/5/39. Commd 18/7/61. Sqn Ldr 1/1/72. Retd ENG 20/7/91.
NAYLOR R. Born 7/11/20. Commd 9/6/55. Sqn Ldr 1/1/65. Retd GD(G) 1/6/70.
NAZ P.G. OBE. Born 2/6/35. Commd 8/7/53. A Cdre 1/1/87. Retd GD 4/9/90.
NEAL A.E. AFC FCMI. Born 17/7/48. Commd 21/4/67. A Cdre 1/7/96. Retd GD 18/5/01.
NEAL B.R. FCMI. Born 14/4/46. Commd 2/8/68. Wg Cdr 1/1/89. Retd GD 14/4/03.
NEAL D. Born 14/5/24. Commd 18/2/60. Flt Lt 18/2/65. Retd GD 14/5/79.
NEAL J.S. Born 13/5/38. Commd 1/4/76. Sqn Ldr 1/1/91. Retd GD 1/1/94.
NEAL K.L.H. BA. Born 3/2/51. Commd 24/9/72. Flt Lt 24/6/76. Retd GD(G) 31/3/82.
NEAL L.A. MD MB BCh MRCGP DRCOG. Born 4/1/58. Commd 1/8/82. Sqn Ldr 1/8/87. Retd MED 1/8/90.
   Re-entered 18/10/91. Wg Cdr 18/10/96. Retd MED 1/11/00.
NEAL N.J. MSc MSc. Born 17/8/50. Commd 14/4/85. Sqn Ldr 1/1/92. Retd ADMIN (TRG) 2/12/04.
NEAL N.McD. MBE. Born 9/5/22. Commd 1/5/47. Wg Cdr 1/7/73. Retd SUP 6/7/75.
NEAL P.M. Born 1/7/18. Commd 2/9/42. Sqn Offr 1/1/51. Retd SEC 21/10/58.
NEALE A. MBE. Born 9/1/42. Commd 23/11/78. Sqn Ldr 1/7/88. Retd ENG 2/4/93.
NEALE A. OBE. Born 1/9/32. Commd 28/7/53. Gp Capt 1/1/80. Retd GD 2/9/86.
NEALE J.C. Born 8/2/35. Commd 17/1/69. Flt Lt 6/10/71. Retd GD 1/3/74.
NEALEY J.R. Born 15/6/36. Commd 1/12/77. Sqn Ldr 1/1/88. Retd ENG 15/6/94.
NEATE K.S. Born 23/7/26. Commd 4/6/64. Sqn Ldr 1/1/77. Retd GD 23/7/84.

NEATE R.G. Born 5/7/18. Commd 12/2/44. Wg Cdr 1/7/61. Retd SEC 30/10/64.
NEDVED V. MBE DFC. Born 27/3/17. Commd 2/8/40. Sqn Ldr 1/7/55. Retd GD 1/10/58. rtg Wg Cdr.
NEEDHAM A. Born 15/5/24. Commd 14/11/49. Flt Lt 24/10/57. Retd SEC 31/8/68.
NEEDHAM A.J. Born 21/10/44. Commd 13/2/64. Gp Capt 1/1/91. Retd GD(G) 21/10/94.
NEEDHAM D.A. BA. Born 27/9/41. Commd 30/7/63. Gp Capt 1/1/90. Retd GD 1/2/94.
NEEDHAM D.E.B. Born 30/3/32. Commd 27/11/55. Flt Lt 6/3/63. Retd SUP 12/1/71.
NEEDHAM D.G. Born 30/4/53. Commd 21/8/72. Sqn Ldr 1/1/84. Retd GD 30/4/91.
NEEDHAM E.G. Born 20/12/48. Commd 10/2/72. Flt Lt 10/8/77. Retd FLY(N) 20/12/03.
NEEDHAM J.R.M. MCMI. Born 28/12/40. Commd 29/7/65. Sqn Ldr 1/7/79. Retd SUP 28/12/95.
NEEDHAM R.S. MCMI. Born 7/4/17. Commd 4/7/42. Sqn Ldr 1/1/64. Retd GD(G) 7/4/75.
NEEDHAM R.W.L. Born 18/6/23. Commd 3/6/44. Flt Lt 26/1/59. Retd SEC 18/6/72.
NEGUS T.W. OBE BDS FDSRCSEd LDSRCS. Born 10/1/43. Commd 29/12/63. A Cdre 1/1/94. Retd DEL 2/4/02.
NEIGHBOUR A.J. Born 14/10/47. Commd 29/8/72. Flt Lt 29/8/76. Retd ADMIN 29/8/77. Re-instated 25/9/83.
    Sqn Ldr 1/7/88. Retd ADMIN 31/3/94.
NEIL D.J. Born 29/2/28. Commd 26/5/60. Flt Lt 26/5/65. Retd GD 1/1/76.
NEIL M.J. MBE. Born 18/6/33. Commd 17/1/52. Sqn Ldr 1/7/65. Retd GD 1/1/94.
NEIL P.I.A. Born 29/9/50. Commd 25/2/72. Sqn Ldr 1/7/83. Retd GD 29/9/88.
NEILL A. BSc. Born 27/1/61. Commd 5/9/82. Sqn Ldr 1/1/94. Retd GD 27/1/99.
NEILL C.E. Born 21/12/33. Commd 20/12/51. Sqn Ldr 1/1/69. Retd GD 31/1/71.
NEILSON D.E. Born 15/6/38. Commd 3/11/77. Sqn Ldr 1/1/89. Retd ENG 11/12/91.
NEL L.H.A. Born 11/6/36. Commd 1/4/58. Flt Lt 16/8/61. Retd GD 13/6/69.
NELLIST G. MCMI. Born 20/11/21. Commd 5/8/43. Flt Lt 4/12/52. Retd GD 1/5/74.
NELSON A.F. Born 23/4/40. Commd 22/5/75. Flt Lt 22/5/78. Retd GD 23/4/95.
NELSON A.G. Born 12/1/30. Commd 26/5/60. Flt Lt 26/5/66. Retd ENG 25/1/85.
NELSON B.J.R. Born 22/6/47. Commd 16/12/66. Wg Cdr 1/7/88. Retd ENG 22/6/02.
NELSON C.R. MA. Born 14/4/51. Commd 6/7/80. Sqn Ldr 1/1/88. Retd ADMIN 14/3/96.
NELSON E.L. Born 23/7/21. Commd 5/8/44. Sqn Ldr 1/1/69. Retd SUP 23/7/76.
NELSON I.H. Born 24/2/39. Commd 29/4/58. Sqn Ldr 1/1/75. Retd GD 1/1/78.
NELSON P.A. Born 30/5/40. Commd 13/12/60. Flt Lt 13/6/63. Retd GD 30/5/78.
NELSON P.E. AFC. Born 27/2/24. Commd 27/2/51. Sqn Ldr 1/7/69. Retd GD 27/2/84.
NELSON R.B. Born 28/4/37. Commd 17/12/57. Sqn Ldr 1/1/69. Retd GD 18/12/81. Re-entered 19/4/85.
    Sqn Ldr 3/5/72. Retd GD 28/4/97.
NELSON T.G. MA. Born 10/7/32. Commd 1/10/54. Sqn Ldr 1/4/66. Retd EDN 25/9/73.
NELSON T.J. MCMI. Born 20/12/35. Commd 30/7/57. Sqn Ldr 1/7/66. Retd GD 4/4/80.
NELSON-EDWARDS G.H. DFC. Born 8/3/18. Commd 26/9/39. Wg Cdr 1/7/53. Retd GD 30/9/60.
NEO C.K. BSc CEng MRAeS. Born 28/4/47. Commd 1/8/69. Sqn Ldr 1/7/80. Retd ENG 28/4/85.
NEQUEST D. OBE. Born 30/5/46. Commd 5/3/65. Wg Cdr 1/1/90. Retd GD 20/10/96.
NESBITT B.D. Born 23/6/46. Commd 10/6/66. Sqn Ldr 1/1/81. Retd GD(G) 1/7/87.
NESBITT J.R. Born 31/3/29. Commd 30/7/53. Flt Lt 30/1/58. Retd GD 3/8/76.
NESBITT R.C. Born 27/12/28. Commd 8/11/62. Sqn Ldr 1/1/76. Retd ENG 2/12/80.
NESBITT R.C. Born 6/2/53. Commd 25/2/88. Sqn Ldr 1/1/97. Retd ENGINEER 22/4/05.
NESBITT-JONES J.A. BA. Born 29/8/69. Commd 4/9/00. Flt Lt 5/4/00. Retd ADMIN (TRG) 15/3/04.
NESS A.M. Born 29/4/59. Commd 20/7/78. Fg Offr 20/1/81. Retd GD(G) 22/11/82.
NESS G.G. Born 28/1/27. Commd 7/5/52. Flt Lt 2/10/57. Retd GD 1/8/75. rtg Sqn Ldr.
NETHAWAY M.F.J. MInstD. Born 28/8/46. Commd 10/5/73. Wg Cdr 1/7/94. Retd ENG 28/8/01.
NETHERTON-SINCLAIR D.A. BA DPhysEd MCIPD. Born 21/7/46. Commd 29/8/72. Sqn Ldr 28/2/77.
    Retd ADMIN 29/8/88.
NETTLESHIP G.W. MRIN MCMI. Born 18/12/28. Commd 4/6/52. Flt Lt 30/10/57. Retd GD 18/12/83.
NETTLEY R.E.W. BA. Born 9/11/27. Commd 25/5/50. Wg Cdr 1/7/67. Retd GD 14/3/78.
NEUBROCH H. OBE FCMI. Born 7/5/23. Commd 14/5/43. Gp Capt 1/1/66. Retd GD 7/5/78.
NEVE A.C.P. MBE MCMI. Born 12/11/23. Commd 1/1/45. Sqn Ldr 1/7/61. Retd SEC 12/11/83.
NEVE R. CEng MRAeS. Born 21/11/39. Commd 28/7/60. Sqn Ldr 1/7/69. Retd ENG 21/11/77. Re-instated 3/6/81.
    Sqn Ldr 11/1/73. Retd ENG 21/11/94.
NEVE W.J. Born 2/5/20. Commd 19/8/42. Sqn Ldr 1/1/63. Retd ENG 4/7/70.
NEVES R.E.H. Born 5/11/32. Commd 28/7/53. Gp Capt 1/7/83. Retd ADMIN 5/11/87.
NEVILL J.E. OBE FCMI MRAeS. Born 27/10/35. Commd 31/7/56. A Cdre 1/7/82. Retd GD 3/4/89.
NEVILLE A.J. DFC. Born 22/11/20. Commd 27/5/42. Sqn Ldr 1/1/67. Retd GD 22/11/75.
NEVILLE J. Born 14/10/33. Commd 3/3/54. Flt Lt 3/9/59. Retd GD 14/10/71.
NEVILLE R.E. MCMI. Born 15/9/32. Commd 21/5/52. Gp Capt 1/1/78. Retd GD(G) 31/10/81.
NEVILLE T.M. Born 4/7/52. Commd 7/1/71. Sqn Ldr 1/1/85. Retd GD 4/9/90.
NEVISON W. Born 30/10/42. Commd 28/7/64. Wg Cdr 1/1/90. Retd GD 2/4/93.
NEW P.A. Born 16/11/48. Commd 2/6/67. Sqn Ldr 1/7/85. Retd GD 1/7/88.
NEW R. Born 22/10/25. Commd 12/12/47. Wg Cdr 1/7/65. Retd GD 12/12/67.
NEWALL D. Born 4/3/43. Commd 28/7/64. Flt Lt 10/2/67. Retd GD 18/10/75.
NEWALL E.R. Born 17/11/44. Commd 8/1/65. Flt Lt 22/8/70. Retd GD(G) 17/11/82. Re-entered 5/5/87. Flt Lt 7/2/75.
    Retd OPS SPT 29/4/99.

NEWBERRY G. OBE. Born 24/12/18. Commd 13/2/42. Wg Cdr 1/7/56. Retd GD 26/6/73. rtg Gp Capt.
NEWBERRY T.W. Born 13/6/14. Commd 26/6/41. Sqn Ldr 1/8/47. Retd GD 3/7/57.
NEWBERRY D.E. BSc. Born 26/5/55. Commd 2/9/73. Flt Lt 15/10/77. Retd GD 26/5/93.
NEWBERY J.H. DFC. Born 14/1/24. Commd 6/2/51. Sqn Ldr 1/1/75. Retd GD 14/1/82.
NEWBERY M.J. Born 26/10/56. Commd 14/7/77. Flt Lt 14/1/83. Retd GD 26/10/94.
NEWBOLD S.P. BSc. Born 1/10/57. Commd 28/9/80. Flt Lt 28/12/81. Retd GD 28/9/92.
NEWBOULD A.M. BA. Born 3/4/34. Commd 3/8/55. Sqn Ldr 3/2/64. Retd EDN 30/6/78.
NEWBURY R.D. BSc. Born 5/1/44. Commd 17/5/63. Sqn Ldr 1/7/77. Retd ENG 5/1/85.
NEWBY A.J. Born 27/8/13. Commd 27/9/45. Fg Offr 27/3/46. Retd ENG 3/9/46.
NEWBY G.W.E. MCIPD MCMI. Born 30/8/22. Commd 15/4/44. Wg Cdr 1/1/66. Retd ADMIN 30/3/77.
NEWBY J.C. MCMI. Born 26/4/30. Commd 26/7/51. Wg Cdr 1/1/67. Retd GD 18/11/72.
NEWCOMBE A.M. MBE. Born 27/12/48. Commd 4/7/69. Sqn Ldr 1/7/86. Retd ADMIN 7/1/02.
NEWELL D. OBE FCMI. Born 15/6/24. Commd 11/2/44. Gp Capt 1/7/71. Retd GD(G) 4/4/76.
NEWELL D.L. Born 15/11/22. Commd 13/4/45. Flt Lt 13/10/48. Retd SUP 16/11/73.
NEWELL R.G. Born 16/4/32. Commd 15/8/51. Sqn Ldr 1/1/75. Retd GD 16/4/87.
NEWEY V.H. BSc. Born 10/5/60. Commd 23/5/82. Flt Lt 23/11/85. Retd ADMIN 24/9/88.
NEWINGTON-IRVING N.J.N. Born 24/3/38. Commd 28/7/60. Flt Lt 1/4/66. Retd SEC 3/8/67.
NEWITT A.E. DFC. Born 1/8/17. Commd 25/10/37. Sqn Ldr 1/1/51. Retd GD 29/11/57. rtg Wg Cdr.
NEWLAND D.J. MCIPS. Born 5/2/52. Commd 11/5/89. Sqn Ldr 1/7/01. Retd SUPPLY 16/8/04.
NEWLAND J.C. Born 10/10/44. Commd 15/7/66. Wg Cdr 1/1/85. Retd ADMIN 10/10/88.
NEWLANDS R.M. Born 4/11/36. Commd 10/9/70. Flt Lt 10/9/72. Retd SUP 10/9/78.
NEWMAN B.E. Born 27/12/39. Commd 11/5/62. Fg Offr 11/5/64. Retd GD 25/10/64.
NEWMAN B.H. Born 1/2/37. Commd 9/10/75. Sqn Ldr 1/1/84. Retd SUP 1/2/87.
NEWMAN C.J. Born 24/3/15. Commd 5/5/55. Sqn Ldr 31/12/63. Retd MED(T) 24/3/68.
NEWMAN C.J.V. LDS. Born 8/4/40. Commd 20/9/59. Wg Cdr 1/7/76. Retd DEL 8/4/78.
NEWMAN C.R. MB BS MRCP. Born 17/3/35. Commd 6/11/60. Wg Cdr 17/8/72. Retd MED 1/1/73.
NEWMAN C.R. Born 4/6/39. Commd 22/7/71. Flt Lt 22/7/72. Retd EDN 2/10/79.
NEWMAN D.A. Born 21/11/33. Commd 23/9/66. Flt Lt 23/9/71. Retd ENG 21/11/88.
NEWMAN E. Born 12/11/29. Commd 5/11/52. Sqn Ldr 1/7/63. Retd GD 12/11/89.
NEWMAN G.S. Born 3/8/36. Commd 30/7/64. Wg Cdr 1/1/84. Retd GD(G) 1/8/88.
NEWMAN H.W.A. CEng MRAeS. Born 2/3/20. Commd 19/8/42. Sqn Ldr 1/7/53. Retd ENG 2/3/75.
NEWMAN K. MBE. Born 4/8/31. Commd 4/2/53. Sqn Ldr 1/1/70. Retd GD 9/9/86.
NEWMAN K.J. MBE DFC. Born 4/7/22. Commd 25/2/44. Wg Cdr 1/1/69. Retd SEC 10/11/73.
NEWMAN M.C. Born 27/4/27. Commd 4/7/51. Sqn Ldr 1/1/60. Retd GD 27/4/65.
NEWMAN M.J. Born 11/7/31. Commd 21/5/53. Sqn Ldr 1/1/68. Retd SUP 11/7/88.
NEWMAN N.J. Born 17/1/47. Commd 4/9/81. Sqn Ldr 1/1/91. Retd GD 17/1/97.
NEWMAN P.M. OBE. Born 13/6/35. Commd 24/2/67. Wg Cdr 1/7/81. Retd ADMIN 2/4/87.
NEWMAN R.A. Born 15/6/28. Commd 3/5/68. Sqn Ldr 1/7/82. Retd ENG 15/6/86.
NEWMAN R.A. Born 20/10/42. Commd 21/5/65. Sqn Ldr 1/7/90. Retd GD 20/10/97.
NEWMAN R.D. Born 23/11/43. Commd 9/12/71. Flt Lt 9/12/73. Retd GD(G) 14/3/96.
NEWMAN R.H. Born 3/10/34. Commd 6/5/65. Sqn Ldr 1/7/82. Retd GD 1/5/89.
NEWMAN T.C.M. MA. Born 27/6/55. Commd 30/10/77. Sqn Ldr 1/1/89. Retd GD 30/10/93.
NEWMAN T.J. Born 1/3/30. Commd 9/8/51. Wg Cdr 1/1/77. Retd GD 1/3/85.
NEWMAN T.M. Born 15/7/42. Commd 4/10/63. Flt Lt 15/1/68. Retd GD 15/7/80.
NEWMAN T.P. BSc. Born 2/3/48. Commd 3/1/69. Sqn Ldr 1/1/82. Retd GD 2/3/86.
NEWMAN W.A. BA BA ACIS. Born 21/10/37. Commd 17/8/59. Wg Cdr 1/1/80. Retd GD 18/8/88.
NEWNHAM P.R. Born 28/4/61. Commd 30/4/81. Flt Lt 30/10/85. Retd GD 1/6/92.
NEWNS A.F.P. CEng MIEE MCMI. Born 7/3/45. Commd 16/6/74. Wg Cdr 1/7/90. Retd ENG 16/6/93.
NEWRICK C.W. MA MB BChir FRCPath DCP. Born 23/6/37. Commd 2/9/64. Gp Capt 29/6/86. Retd MED 14/9/96.
NEWSOME C.P. BEd MCIPD. Born 20/3/56. Commd 21/10/79. Sqn Ldr 1/1/88. Retd ADMIN 14/3/96.
NEWSOME P.R. Born 10/1/33. Commd 4/6/52. Sqn Ldr 1/1/65. Retd GD 1/5/76.
NEWSTEAD T.J. Born 12/6/48. Commd 8/9/83. Wg Cdr 1/1/05. Retd GD 1/1/05.
NEWTON A.C. Born 30/8/60. Commd 13/12/79. Flt Lt 13/6/84. Retd GD 1/4/96.
NEWTON A.J. BEM. Born 24/12/45. Commd 16/6/88. Flt Lt 16/6/92. Retd ENG 3/4/93.
NEWTON B.H. CB CVO OBE FCMI. Born 1/4/32. Commd 28/7/53. AVM 1/1/85. Retd GD 9/6/89.
NEWTON B.V. Born 25/11/18. Commd 17/9/41. Flt Lt 1/1/47. Retd GD 1/1/47. Retd GD 16/6/53.
NEWTON D.R. Born 6/11/36. Commd 8/10/63. Flt Lt 8/10/63. Retd GD 8/10/79.
NEWTON D.W. Born 21/9/30. Commd 23/4/52. Flt Lt 5/11/58. Retd GD 15/9/72.
NEWTON E.J.C. BA. Born 5/11/56. Commd 14/10/84. Flt Lt 14/4/87. Retd ADMIN 1/10/89. Re-entered 5/3/90.
    Flt Lt 16/9/87. Retd ADMIN 18/3/01.
NEWTON F.A.B. MBE MRAeS MCMI. Born 26/12/17. Commd 2/1/45. Sqn Ldr 1/1/56. Retd GD 5/4/72.
NEWTON G.A. MBE. Born 23/9/30. Commd 19/12/63. Flt Lt 19/12/69. Retd SEC 4/10/75.
NEWTON G.S. Born 4/5/31. Commd 6/12/51. Wg Cdr 1/1/83. Retd GD 30/8/91.
NEWTON J.K. MSc BSc CEng MIMechE MRAeS. Born 22/4/45. Commd 15/7/66. Gp Capt 1/1/90.
    Retd ENG 22/4/00.
NEWTON J.M. Born 1/6/56. Commd 17/7/75. Flt Lt 17/1/81. Retd GD 1/6/94.

NEWTON J.R. Born 15/7/50. Commd 1/6/72. Flt Lt 1/12/77. Retd GD 15/7/88.
NEWTON M.D. Born 12/11/54. Commd 15/2/90. Sqn Ldr 1/7/01. Retd ENGINEER 18/4/05.
NEWTON N.D. Born 5/6/64. Commd 23/10/86. Flt Lt 23/4/92. Retd GD 23/12/02.
NEWTON P.A. BSc. Born 27/8/50. Commd 4/5/70. Flt Lt 15/4/73. Retd GD 27/8/88.
NEWTON P.C. Born 27/12/40. Commd 8/6/62. Flt Lt 15/4/70. Retd GD 4/1/72.
NEWTON P.E. Born 13/5/33. Commd 24/7/57. Sqn Ldr 1/7/67. Retd ENG 13/5/71.
NEWTON R.J. BSc(Eng). Born 24/7/45. Commd 26/9/66. Flt Lt 24/1/68. Retd GD 25/10/97.
NEWTON R.T. BEng. Born 15/3/64. Commd 18/8/85. Sqn Ldr 1/7/96. Retd GD 12/4/02.
NEWTON S.A.E. Born 17/9/29. Commd 16/11/51. Wg Cdr 1/7/69. Retd GD 17/10/79.
NEWTON T.J.B. Born 6/1/40. Commd 26/10/62. Flt Lt 26/4/68. Retd GD 10/7/78.
NEWTON W. Born 16/4/13. Commd 1/8/43. Flt Lt 7/6/51. Retd SEC 8/5/65.
NEWTON W.J. Born 3/10/33. Commd 23/7/52. Flt Lt 10/1/63. Retd GD 21/3/75.
NEYHAUL N.J. BA. Born 20/10/60. Commd 4/1/83. Flt Lt 4/7/86. Retd GD(G) 20/12/95.
NIAS T.J. IEng MIIE. Born 10/9/41. Commd 17/7/62. Wg Cdr 1/1/86. Retd ENG 10/9/96.
NIBLETT D.R. MCIPD. Born 13/5/43. Commd 22/9/67. Sqn Ldr 1/1/85. Retd SY 3/4/93.
NIBLOCK L.N. Born 12/6/39. Commd 8/6/84. Flt Lt 1/3/87. Retd GD 23/10/90.
NICE B.A. Born 5/12/31. Commd 5/5/54. Flt Lt 5/11/59. Retd GD 15/2/71.
NICHOL A.J. Born 12/11/63. Commd 4/12/86. Flt Lt 21/8/89. Retd GD 14/3/96.
NICHOL C.R. Born 13/5/60. Commd 11/1/79. Flt Lt 11/7/84. Retd GD 13/5/98.
NICHOL G.R. BSc. Born 11/6/51. Commd 2/9/73. Flt Lt 2/6/74. Retd GD 14/12/90.
NICHOL R.S. Born 30/10/21. Commd 20/12/44. Wg Cdr 1/7/61. Retd GD 12/7/70.
NICHOL W.E. Born 10/12/27. Commd 14/11/51. Flt Lt 14/5/56. Retd GD 7/6/68.
NICHOLAS A.F. MBE. Born 10/4/29. Commd 3/5/56. Wg Cdr 1/7/77. Retd GD 10/4/84.
NICHOLAS E.F. Born 4/4/16. Commd 2/10/44. Flt Lt 2/4/48. Retd GD(G) 20/5/71. rtg Sqn Ldr.
NICHOLAS H.J.H. Born 3/7/20. Commd 2/2/56. Flt Lt 2/2/59. Retd RGT 19/8/67.
NICHOLAS J.A. Born 26/12/23. Commd 25/8/44. Sqn Ldr 1/4/58. Retd SEC 31/3/62.
NICHOLAS J.J.R. MCMI. Born 11/6/60. Commd 4/6/87. Sqn Ldr 1/1/00. Retd OPS SPT(ATC) 2/6/03.
NICHOLAS K.E. Born 5/4/38. Commd 26/5/67. Sqn Ldr 1/1/89. Retd GD 22/9/92.
NICHOLL S.M. CB CBE AFC BA FRAeS. Born 15/11/46. Commd 22/9/65. AVM 1/7/98. Retd GD 15/11/01.
NICHOLLS A.C. MCMI. Born 3/1/34. Commd 24/1/63. Wg Cdr 1/7/80. Retd ADMIN 31/10/88.
NICHOLLS C.A. Born 19/10/50. Commd 22/5/70. Sqn Ldr 1/1/86. Retd GD 1/1/89.
NICHOLLS C.E. Born 21/9/50. Commd 10/1/69. Flt Lt 10/7/74. Retd GD 1/11/75.
NICHOLLS C.H. Born 3/11/52. Commd 1/4/71. Flt Lt 1/10/76. Retd GD 1/10/81.
NICHOLLS D.H. MA MRAeS. Born 7/10/41. Commd 9/11/64. Gp Capt 1/7/91. Retd GD 7/10/96.
NICHOLLS Sir John KCB CBE DFC AFC. Born 5/7/26. Commd 14/6/46. AM 1/1/78. Retd GD 31/7/80.
NICHOLLS J.A. Born 31/7/10. Commd 17/1/41. Flt Lt 1/7/43. Retd ENG 8/1/46. rtg Sqn Ldr.
NICHOLLS P. MBA. Born 16/12/51. Commd 30/8/84. Sqn Ldr 1/1/92. Retd ENGINEER 16/8/04.
NICHOLLS P.M. Born 4/12/44. Commd 29/12/64. Flt Lt 11/12/71. Retd SUP 7/6/93.
NICHOLLS S. AFM. Born 26/3/26. Commd 15/5/58. Flt Lt 15/5/63. Retd GD 26/3/76.
NICHOLS A. Born 18/4/49. Commd 4/6/87. Fg Offr 13/9/86. Retd MED 4/6/90.
NICHOLS B. Born 18/6/61. Commd 26/11/81. Sqn Ldr 1/7/97. Retd OPS SPT 1/7/00.
NICHOLS B.A. Born 27/12/49. Commd 10/3/77. Flt Lt 10/3/79. Retd GD 18/5/86.
NICHOLS B.G. Born 16/3/39. Commd 18/2/58. Flt Lt 21/8/63. Retd GD 20/11/69. Re-instated 19/3/79. Flt Lt 19/3/79. Retd GD 2/4/90.
NICHOLS C.E. BSc. Born 30/11/43. Commd 28/9/64. Flt Lt 15/4/67. Retd PI 30/11/81.
NICHOLS D.A.G. Born 5/9/42. Commd 31/10/74. Flt Lt 31/10/76. Retd PI 6/9/85.
NICHOLS E. Born 20/2/47. Commd 29/8/72. Flt Lt 24/2/75. Retd GD 14/9/96.
NICHOLS G.C. DFC. Born 19/6/24. Commd 20/11/43. Flt Lt 20/5/47. Retd GD 26/4/50.
NICHOLS J.A. Born 27/5/39. Commd 18/8/61. Flt Lt 18/2/67. Retd GD 27/5/94.
NICHOLS M.J. MilSec. Born 3/7/51. Commd 10/9/70. Flt Lt 1/8/76. Retd SY(PRT) 3/7/89.
NICHOLS M.R. Born 7/2/46. Commd 31/10/69. Sqn Ldr 1/1/78. Retd GD 14/9/96.
NICHOLS P.D.H. CEng MIMechE. Born 13/9/36. Commd 23/7/58. Sqn Ldr 1/7/67. Retd ENG 13/9/74.
NICHOLS T.W. Born 20/9/35. Commd 18/8/61. Flt Lt 18/2/67. Retd GD 2/5/77.
NICHOLS W.H. BSc. Born 5/12/63. Commd 18/9/89. Flt Lt 6/9/89. Retd FLY(N) 19/7/03.
NICHOLSON A.A. CBE LVO MA FRAeS. Born 27/6/46. Commd 22/9/65. AVM 1/1/99. Retd GD 27/6/00.
NICHOLSON A.A.N. CBE AE FCMI. Born 8/3/19. Commd 3/10/39. A Cdre 1/1/66. Retd GD 11/12/70.
NICHOLSON A.C.M. BA. Born 20/6/44. Commd 28/9/64. Flt Lt 15/4/69. Retd GD 19/7/84.
NICHOLSON A.N. OBE PhD MD DSc MB ChB FRCPath FRCP FRCP(Edin) FFOM FRAeS. Born 26/7/34. Commd 4/9/60. A Cdre 18/7/90. Retd MED 1/6/99.
NICHOLSON C.E. Born 21/8/23. Commd 6/7/49. Flt Lt 6/7/53. Retd SEC 25/4/64.
NICHOLSON E.H.J. MBE BSc CEng. Born 28/11/65. Commd 15/9/86. Sqn Ldr 1/7/01. Retd ENGINEER 1/7/04.
NICHOLSON G.D. BA. Born 15/12/62. Commd 2/9/84. Flt Lt 2/3/88. Retd SUP 14/6/96.
NICHOLSON H.B. Born 11/10/32. Commd 8/10/52. Sqn Ldr 1/7/78. Retd GD(G) 1/2/83.
NICHOLSON I.G. Born 28/2/42. Commd 24/4/64. Fg Offr 24/4/66. Retd GD 24/8/68.
NICHOLSON J.M. Born 8/5/22. Commd 20/11/42. Flt Lt 24/12/48. Retd GD 19/6/54.
NICHOLSON M.H. Born 1/7/18. Commd 13/12/44. Flt Offr 29/11/51. Retd SEC 2/6/61.

NICHOLSON M.J. Born 27/9/49. Commd 28/2/82. Wg Cdr 1/7/99. Retd ADMIN 23/1/01.
NICHOLSON R.P. Born 14/12/27. Commd 14/11/51. Sqn Ldr 1/7/67. Retd GD 15/8/78.
NICHOLSON S.J. Born 15/3/59. Commd 21/6/90. Flt Lt 21/6/92. Retd SUP 14/3/96.
NICHOLSON W.F. FCMI. Born 9/12/31. Commd 16/7/52. Wg Cdr 1/1/77. Retd GD(G) 21/1/80.
NICKERSON G.J. MIIE(elec). Born 12/3/47. Commd 1/7/82. Flt Lt 1/3/87. Retd ENG 1/1/92.
NICKLEN F.J. Born 25/3/37. Commd 12/12/59. Flt Lt 1/4/66. Retd GD(G) 25/3/75.
NICKLES N.F. Born 2/3/53. Commd 6/4/72. Flt Lt 6/10/77. Retd GD 2/3/91.
NICKLIN J.G. Born 15/11/30. Commd 10/12/52. Flt Lt 17/8/58. Retd GD 15/11/68.
NICKOLLS M.H. Born 8/7/18. Commd 27/10/43. Sqn Ldr 1/7/66. Retd SEC 9/8/68.
NICKS J. BA. Born 30/7/32. Commd 10/9/70. Flt Lt 10/9/74. Retd ENG 3/8/82.
NICKS M. MA BL. Born 30/3/45. Commd 13/8/72. Wg Cdr 13/8/82. Retd LGL 16/9/91.
NICKSON R.E. FCMI. Born 27/4/40. Commd 1/8/61. Wg Cdr 1/1/83. Retd GD 27/4/95.
NICKSON V.J. AFC MCMI. Born 11/3/32. Commd 11/10/51. Sqn Ldr 1/1/66. Retd GD 24/11/73.
NICOL B.E. MBE BA. Born 1/2/32. Commd 1/2/56. Gp Capt 1/1/84. Retd ADMIN 30/8/86.
NICOL D.J. MSc MCIT DPhysEd. Born 22/12/44. Commd 13/9/70. Wg Cdr 1/1/88. Retd SUP 13/9/92.
NICOL J. Born 19/3/36. Commd 29/7/55. Flt Lt 29/1/61. Retd PI 20/3/84.
NICOL J.B. MBE BEM. Born 20/11/21. Commd 18/7/63. Flt Lt 18/7/68. Retd PRT 3/4/80.
NICOL L.A. Born 2/8/62. Commd 30/4/81. Flt Lt 30/10/86. Retd GD 17/12/99.
NICOLL C.A. Born 7/6/20. Commd 27/10/40. Sqn Ldr 1/7/70. Retd GD 7/6/75.
NICOLL D.A.P. BSc MB ChB. Born 30/4/52. Commd 6/4/78. Wg Cdr 4/8/93. Retd MED 14/3/96.
NICOLL G.F. Born 11/9/29. Commd 14/8/70. Sqn Ldr 1/7/85. Retd GD 11/9/89.
NICOLL I.T. BSc CEng MRAeS MCMI. Born 31/3/38. Commd 30/9/57. Gp Capt 1/7/88. Retd ENG 31/3/93.
NICOLLE B.P. Born 27/12/40. Commd 31/7/62. Wg Cdr 1/1/84. Retd GD 2/4/93.
NICOLLE B.R. Born 27/3/43. Commd 13/10/61. Sqn Ldr 1/1/91. Retd GD 31/3/93.
NICOLSON D.A.V. DFM. Born 12/1/24. Commd 30/7/44. Sqn Ldr 1/7/56. Retd RGT 12/1/69.
NICOLSON J.A. Born 15/11/47. Commd 28/11/74. Sqn Ldr 1/1/94. Retd OPS SPT(ATC) 15/7/03.
NIEASS E.L. MBE. Born 2/7/24. Commd 17/6/45. Wg Cdr 1/1/71. Retd GD 2/7/79.
NIEL E.C. Born 29/5/33. Commd 8/1/56. Flt Lt 7/8/64. Retd SEC 6/9/73. rtg Sqn Ldr
NIELAND I.R.J. BA. Born 5/5/36. Commd 28/1/58. Wg Cdr 1/1/82. Retd GD 7/5/87.
NIELD R. CBE. Born 24/4/37. Commd 19/12/59. Gp Capt 1/1/86. Retd GD 23/1/92.
NIELSEN D.N. Born 9/1/20. Commd 2/6/43. Flt Lt 2/12/46. Retd ENG 8/5/54.
NIEZRECKI W.T. AFC DFM. Born 9/3/20. Commd 17/12/53. Sqn Ldr 1/1/72. Retd GD 9/3/75.
NIGHTINGALE A.L. BSc(Eng). Born 3/4/62. Commd 31/8/80. Flt Lt 15/10/84. Retd GD 3/4/00.
NIGHTINGALE H.H. Born 5/3/40. Commd 28/4/61. Sqn Ldr 1/1/76. Retd GD 1/7/78.
NIGHTINGALE J.H. Born 25/2/33. Commd 11/4/58. Sqn Ldr 1/1/74. Retd ENG 1/6/77.
NIGHTINGALE V.E. Born 14/10/40. Commd 8/12/61. Sqn Ldr 1/1/77. Retd GD 1/1/80.
NIMICK P.G. BEng. Born 17/5/64. Commd 3/8/88. Flt Lt 7/9/91. Retd ENGINEER 17/5/04.
NISBET D.J. Born 19/9/39. Commd 6/5/83. Flt Lt 6/5/87. Retd GD(G) 19/9/95.
NISBET G.McL. BSc(Eng). Born 20/4/52. Commd 11/5/75. Wg Cdr 1/1/91. Retd ENG 27/11/98.
NIVEN D.M. CB CBE BSc. Born 18/9/46. Commd 18/8/68. AVM 1/7/98. Retd GD 31/1/03.
NIVEN D.S.R. Born 23/11/26. Commd 16/11/61. Sqn Ldr 1/7/72. Retd ENG 19/8/78.
NIVEN J. DFC. Born 12/4/20. Commd 29/4/42. Sqn Ldr 1/10/55. Retd GD 3/9/58.
NIX S.W. Born 20/9/30. Commd 29/10/64. Sqn Ldr 1/1/86. Retd ENG 1/1/89.
NIXON A. Born 19/12/63. Commd 16/6/88. Flt Lt 11/7/91. Retd FLY(N) 30/4/04.
NIXON A.F. Born 19/9/38. Commd 1/8/61. Flt Lt 26/2/64. Retd GD 19/9/76.
NIXON D.P.M. MA. Born 12/5/40. Commd 1/10/62. Flt Lt 1/1/64. Retd GD 1/6/70.
NIXON E.J. Born 20/6/28. Commd 21/12/67. Flt Lt 21/12/72. Retd ENG 20/6/86.
NIXON F. Born 25/7/27. Commd 15/12/49. Sqn Ldr 1/7/62. Retd GD 12/1/76.
NIXON F.B. Born 12/4/32. Commd 17/9/52. Flt Lt 22/5/57. Retd GD 23/5/70.
NIXON J.D. Born 13/11/31. Commd 5/2/57. Flt Lt 7/8/62. Retd GD 14/5/71.
NIXON K.C.D. AFC. Born 31/10/23. Commd 17/1/45. Gp Capt 1/1/69. Retd GD 18/10/75.
NIXON M.A. Born 3/2/40. Commd 12/7/62. Sqn Ldr 1/4/75. Retd GD 20/5/86.
NIXON P.M.B. Born 6/6/45. Commd 28/5/66. Gp Capt 1/1/92. Retd GD(G) 14/9/96.
NIXON P.T. Born 3/9/66. Commd 25/9/88. Flt Lt 25/9/93. Retd OPS SPT(ATC) 25/9/04.
NOAKE E.L. BEM. Born 8/1/23. Commd 9/3/66. Flt Lt 9/3/71. Retd GD 17/7/71.
NOAKES J.E.P. Born 31/7/40. Commd 17/7/70. Flt Lt 17/7/72. Retd ENG 1/4/78.
NOBLE B.A. Born 8/2/57. Commd 13/12/79. Flt Lt 1/8/83. Retd SUP 8/2/95.
NOBLE B.J. AFC. Born 11/11/29. Commd 16/11/51. Sqn Ldr 1/7/62. Retd GD 12/12/83.
NOBLE D. Born 14/11/48. Commd 21/3/69. Flt Lt 1/4/75. Retd ENG 1/11/77. Re-instated 25/11/81. Sqn Ldr 1/7/87. Retd ENG 1/7/90.
NOBLE E. Born 16/6/28. Commd 30/3/61. Sqn Ldr 1/7/74. Retd GD(G) 26/10/77.
NOBLE K.G. BSc. Born 15/6/59. Commd 17/8/80. Sqn Ldr 1/7/90. Retd GD 15/6/97.
NOBLE M.A. Born 2/7/34. Commd 5/4/55. Sqn Ldr 1/7/65. Retd GD 2/7/72.
NOBLE P.R. BSc. Born 24/8/54. Commd 7/1/74. Flt Lt 15/10/78. Retd GD 1/1/87.
NOBLE R. The Rev. BA BD. Born 28/9/43. Commd 26/9/71. Retd Wg Cdr 28/9/98.
NOBLE R.F. DFC. Born 27/8/18. Commd 13/10/41. Sqn Ldr 1/7/49. Retd GD 16/2/58.

NOCKELS R.L. Born 25/3/30. Commd 3/6/65. Flt Lt 3/6/70. Retd ENG 1/12/83.
NOCKLES A.G. BSc. Born 21/2/52. Commd 30/3/75. Flt Lt 30/6/76. Retd GD 30/9/91.
NOCKOLDS M.D.S. Born 10/12/45. Commd 2/6/77. Sqn Ldr 1/7/91. Retd GD 30/11/93.
NOKES D.J. Born 2/2/20. Commd 3/11/41. Flt Lt 19/2/46. Retd ENG 10/10/53.
NOLAN B.N. Born 20/12/41. Commd 23/9/66. Sqn Ldr 1/1/77. Retd GD 26/4/79.
NOLAN F.P. BSc. Born 22/7/53. Commd 23/5/82. Sqn Ldr 1/7/91. Retd ENG 25/10/94.
NOLAN G.L. Born 22/11/53. Commd 3/9/72. Sqn Ldr 1/1/88. Retd SUP 22/11/91.
NOLAN J. Born 9/10/11. Commd 13/5/43. Sqn Ldr 1/7/60. Retd ENG 9/1/67.
NOLAN M.P. Born 1/9/34. Commd 25/2/53. Flt Lt 17/8/58. Retd GD 1/9/92.
NOLAN T.J. Born 6/3/48. Commd 20/9/68. Flt Lt 20/3/74. Retd GD 6/3/86.
NOON A.J. CEng BSc MIMechE MRAeS. Born 4/2/30. Commd 26/9/53. Sqn Ldr 1/7/63. Retd ENG 4/2/68.
NOONE J.M. Born 20/4/66. Commd 14/8/91. Sqn Ldr 1/7/02. Retd OPS SPT(ATC) 1/7/05.
NOOTT D.A.C. Born 25/9/39. Commd 9/1/64. Flt Lt 18/9/68. Retd GD 25/9/77.
NORBURY E.G. Born 2/11/44. Commd 3/3/67. Sqn Ldr 1/1/82. Retd GD 2/11/99.
NORCROSS H.S.L.T. DFC. Born 7/1/17. Commd 14/1/43. Sqn Ldr 1/7/56. Retd GD(G) 7/1/73.
NORCROSS T.R. Born 17/7/32. Commd 28/11/51. Sqn Ldr 1/1/82. Retd GD 30/9/82.
NORFOLK A.H.J. AFC. Born 15/12/44. Commd 31/1/64. Flt Lt 4/5/72. Retd GD 1/4/92.
NORGAN K.A. BSc. Born 25/11/42. Commd 12/1/62. Flt Lt 12/7/67. Retd GD 6/5/72. Re-entered 6/9/76.
    Sqn Ldr 1/7/87. Retd ENG 25/11/97.
NORMAN A.A. Born 8/1/33. Commd 26/3/52. Sqn Ldr 1/7/70. Retd GD 6/12/84.
NORMAN A.P. DFC. Born 19/5/24. Commd 10/12/43. Wg Cdr 1/1/68. Retd GD 30/10/72.
NORMAN E.H.A. BEM. Born 9/10/40. Commd 10/3/77. Sqn Ldr 1/7/90. Retd GD 13/12/96.
NORMAN F.L.G. FHCIMA MCMI. Born 30/7/25. Commd 9/4/52. Sqn Ldr 1/1/74. Retd CAT 4/10/75.
NORMAN G.P. Born 10/3/22. Commd 28/5/46. Flt Lt 6/9/55. Retd GD(G) 31/8/68.
NORMAN I.A.W. Born 20/5/63. Commd 23/9/82. Sqn Ldr 1/1/96. Retd GD 20/5/01.
NORMAN K.P. Born 5/1/30. Commd 9/4/52. Flt Lt 21/10/59. Retd GD 28/3/70.
NORMAN M.J. Born 14/5/31. Commd 6/12/51. Flt Lt 22/5/57. Retd GD 14/7/91.
NORMAN M.J.S. MBE. Born 4/8/30. Commd 26/9/51. Wg Cdr 1/7/72. Retd GD 4/8/85.
NORMAN N.G.E. Born 22/7/35. Commd 23/9/66. Flt Lt 23/9/72. Retd SUP 1/11/74.
NORMAN P.B. Born 10/7/31. Commd 17/5/62. Flt Lt 17/5/68. Retd ENG 2/4/82.
NORMAN R.F. Born 9/11/33. Commd 16/7/52. Sqn Ldr 1/7/79. Retd GD 9/11/88.
NORMAN S.C. CEng MIMechE. Born 14/1/35. Commd 19/2/59. Sqn Ldr 1/7/66. Retd ENG 19/2/75.
NORMILE J.P. Born 14/10/51. Commd 15/12/88. Flt Lt 15/12/92. Retd ENG 3/4/93.
NORREYS W.L. Born 15/4/23. Commd 26/3/45. Flt Lt 10/11/55. Retd GD 15/4/66.
NORRIE S.D. Born 20/11/54. Commd 28/8/75. Flt Lt 28/2/81. Retd GD 20/11/92.
NORRIS B.J. The Rev. BA. Born 28/6/46. Commd 17/5/81. Retd Sqn Ldr 31/12/86.
NORRIS D.F.G. Born 23/6/23. Commd 19/7/51. Sqn Ldr 1/7/62. Retd GD 23/6/78.
NORRIS E.R. Born 29/9/36. Commd 14/1/65. Sqn Ldr 1/1/73. Retd GD 30/4/87.
NORRIS G.B.H. CBE FFA FCMI. Born 10/6/26. Commd 9/8/47. Gp Capt 1/7/74. Retd SEC 10/6/81.
NORRIS G.L. Born 20/9/40. Commd 6/7/62. Flt Lt 6/1/68. Retd GD 20/9/78.
NORRIS M.A. MBE. Born 17/1/44. Commd 25/6/65. Flt Lt 17/3/71. Retd GD 26/1/73. Re-entered 22/3/74.
    Wg Cdr 1/1/91. Retd GD 17/1/99.
NORRIS M.W. MInstPet MRAeS. Born 3/8/47. Commd 12/10/78. Wg Cdr 1/7/94. Retd GD 31/7/03.
NORRIS P. MB ChB. Born 28/9/28. Commd 30/3/53. Wg Cdr 16/1/65. Retd MED 30/3/69.
NORRIS P.G. Born 28/11/45. Commd 15/7/66. Sqn Ldr 1/7/76. Retd ENG 28/11/83. Re-entered 13/9/85.
    Sqn Ldr 8/4/78. Retd ENG 28/11/01.
NORRIS R.A.D. Born 22/2/47. Commd 1/3/68. Sqn Ldr 1/7/79. Retd ENG 22/2/91.
NORRISS D.K. Born 17/6/46. Commd 8/1/65. A Cdre 1/1/96. Retd GD 15/6/00.
NORRISS Sir Peter KBE CB AFC MA FRAeS. Born 22/4/44. Commd 5/1/66. AM 30/10/98. Retd GD 22/3/01.
NORRISS R.C. BSc. Born 7/11/50. Commd 15/9/69. Flt Lt 15/4/74. Retd GD 7/11/88.
NORSWORTHY R.J. CEng MIEE DUS MCMI. Born 8/1/34. Commd 7/9/56. Wg Cdr 1/7/71. Retd ENG 31/3/78.
NORTH B.P. MBE MCMI. Born 17/1/40. Commd 7/5/64. Sqn Ldr 1/1/72. Retd ENG 1/4/78. Re-instated 7/11/79.
    Wg Cdr 1/7/85. Retd ENG 23/6/90.
NORTH D.E. Born 2/12/44. Commd 15/7/66. Gp Capt 1/1/91. Retd GD 1/9/97.
NORTH G.P. OBE. Born 25/1/44. Commd 11/7/62. Wg Cdr 1/7/85. Retd GD 31/3/94.
NORTH J.L. Born 7/4/58. Commd 11/1/79. Flt Lt 11/7/85. Retd GD(G) 7/4/96.
NORTH M.A. Born 28/8/62. Commd 11/12/83. Flt Lt 11/12/88. Retd ADMIN 14/3/96.
NORTH N.M. MBE. Born 27/12/22. Commd 2/9/44. Flt Lt 17/5/56. Retd GD 18/10/67. Re-employed SUP 21/12/69 to
    28/6/75 and 19/12/79 to 27/11/82.
NORTH P.G. MA BA. Born 1/3/47. Commd 8/2/81. Sqn Ldr 1/1/88. Retd ADMIN 14/9/96.
NORTH R.J. Born 30/10/47. Commd 27/2/70. Flt Lt 27/8/72. Retd GD 30/10/91.
NORTH R.P. Born 1/9/33. Commd 30/4/52. Flt Lt 24/11/57. Retd GD 1/9/70.
NORTH R.W.H. Born 10/3/50. Commd 31/10/69. Sqn Ldr 1/1/88. Retd GD 1/1/91.
NORTH V.M. BA. Born 18/12/47. Commd 8/4/79. Sqn Ldr 1/1/86. Retd ADMIN 8/6/87.
NORTH-LEWIS C.D. DSO DFC*. Born 13/3/18. Commd 4/12/40. A Cdre 1/1/64. Retd GD 1/2/71.
NORTHCOTE R. OBE BA. Born 21/10/45. Commd 15/7/66. Gp Capt 1/7/89. Retd GD 9/4/91.

NORTHCOTT D.S. Born 8/11/29. Commd 22/7/70. Fg Offr 22/7/70. Retd ENG 1/11/74.
NORTHEY H. MVO. Born 27/11/46. Commd 2/8/68. Wg Cdr 1/1/92. Retd GD 2/5/98.
NORTHMORE W.J.J. CBE CEng MIERE MRAeS. Born 10/7/29. Commd 8/2/51. A Cdre 1/1/82. Retd ENG 10/7/84.
NORTHWOOD R.J. Born 9/3/38. Commd 25/6/66. Sqn Ldr 1/1/81. Retd GD 9/3/93.
NORTON B.K. Born 22/3/58. Commd 17/1/85. Flt Lt 17/1/89. Retd ENG 30/9/02.
NORTON D.M. Born 1/7/19. Commd 6/10/41. Flt Offr 1/9/45. Retd SEC 21/10/59.
NORTON G.E. Born 23/12/30. Commd 1/4/53. Flt Lt 21/10/59. Retd GD 2/10/71.
NORTON H.G.P. Born 3/7/45. Commd 25/2/66. Sqn Ldr 1/1/83. Retd GD 1/1/86.
NORTON J. ACIS. Born 12/7/31. Commd 9/8/60. Wg Cdr 1/7/79. Retd SEC 21/11/81.
NORTON J.R. Born 5/6/55. Commd 5/1/78. Sqn Ldr 1/1/94. Retd GD 3/11/01.
NORTON W.H.W. MBE. Born 17/4/33. Commd 17/1/52. Sqn Ldr 1/7/66. Retd GD 17/4/93.
NORTON W.L. BSc. Born 10/1/40. Commd 1/10/62. Sqn Ldr 1/7/71. Retd GD 1/10/78.
NORTON-SMITH P. CBE DFC AFC. Born 18/5/15. Commd 2/11/40. Gp Capt 1/1/59. Retd GD 8/6/65.
NOTMAN E.J. Born 26/12/67. Commd 10/5/90. Fg Offr 10/5/92. Retd GD 31/3/94.
NOTMAN R.F. Born 25/6/30. Commd 19/8/65. Sqn Ldr 1/1/77. Retd SUP 10/9/82.
NOTT R.E. Born 2/11/53. Commd 22/2/79. Sqn Ldr 1/1/93. Retd OPS SPT(ATC) 15/9/04.
NOTTAGE G.W. LLB. Born 6/3/45. Commd 3/3/67. Wg Cdr 1/7/87. Retd GD 31/12/92.
NOTTAGE S.M. Born 1/7/18. Commd 4/12/40. Sqn Offr 1/1/51. Retd SEC 12/3/52.
NOTTINGHAM J. Born 1/1/40. Commd 31/7/62. Sqn Ldr 1/1/76. Retd GD 1/1/79.
NOUJAIM S.C.J. Born 23/12/60. Commd 29/7/83. Flt Lt 29/1/89. Retd GD 14/2/99.
NOWAKOWSKI J. Born 26/3/21. Commd 15/10/46. Sqn Ldr 1/7/57. Retd GD 27/3/64.
NOWELL J. Born 25/7/41. Commd 27/3/70. Flt Lt 8/3/72. Retd GD 25/7/79.
NOWELL J.W. Born 12/5/32. Commd 28/7/53. Sqn Ldr 1/7/64. Retd GD 3/7/70.
NOYCE B.F. Born 7/3/22. Commd 2/3/52. Flt Offr 20/9/56. Retd SEC 20/2/60.
NOYCE D.J. BA. Born 11/11/39. Commd 15/1/63. Gp Capt 1/7/85. Retd SY(PRT) 2/1/90.
NOYCE N.A. MBE. Born 8/2/22. Commd 29/8/42. Sqn Ldr 1/7/72. Retd GD(G) 15/3/77.
NOYES K.W.T. MBE. Born 17/11/35. Commd 7/1/71. Sqn Ldr 1/7/80. Retd SY 17/11/93.
NOYES L.B. AFC. Born 20/11/09. Commd 1/4/40. Sqn Ldr 1/7/51. Retd GD(G) 14/1/60. rtg Wg Cdr.
NUDDS C. Born 3/7/48. Commd 15/2/73. Flt Lt 17/11/75. Retd GD(G) 30/7/86. Re-instated 5/10/87. Flt Lt 18/2/77. Retd GD(G) 6/1/92.
NUGENT N.A.D. Born 6/11/26. Commd 16/6/53. Wg Cdr 1/7/70. Retd GD 30/10/76.
NUGENT S.G. Born 17/3/63. Commd 26/9/90. Flt Lt 26/9/92. Retd OPS SPT 17/3/01.
NUNN A.B.C. Born 24/5/14. Commd 31/12/41. Sqn Ldr 1/8/47. Retd GD 25/12/54.
NUNN B.E. OBE BA. Born 6/8/41. Commd 1/10/62. Gp Capt 1/1/87. Retd GD 7/4/93.
NUNN I.D. Born 6/1/25. Commd 7/9/61. Sqn Ldr 1/1/77. Retd ENG 6/1/80.
NUNN J.L. DFC BSc MRAeS. Born 11/4/19. Commd 3/10/39. Wg Cdr 1/1/54. Retd GD 11/4/66.
NUNN J.M. Born 14/1/36. Commd 22/10/54. Wg Cdr 1/7/79. Retd GD 22/9/89.
NURSAW D. Born 27/5/29. Commd 26/7/50. Flt Lt 26/1/53. Retd GD 27/5/67.
NURSE W.F. Born 7/11/20. Commd 15/4/44. Flt Lt 15/4/50. Retd GD 7/11/58. rtg Sqn Ldr.
NUSSEY A.S. Born 25/8/48. Commd 27/2/70. Sqn Ldr 1/7/83. Retd GD 13/4/96.
NUTKINS J.H. BSc. Born 5/11/41. Commd 22/9/65. Sqn Ldr 1/1/75. Retd GD 21/12/82.
NUTT P.J. CEng MRAeS. Born 4/3/44. Commd 15/7/65. Gp Capt 1/7/86. Retd ENG 1/7/89.
NUTT R.D. Born 5/8/35. Commd 11/2/55. Flt Lt 7/3/62. Retd GD 5/8/73.
NUTTALL J.A. Born 10/9/54. Commd 20/9/79. Sqn Ldr 1/1/92. Retd GD 1/10/97.
NUTTALL R. OBE CEng MRAeS FCMI. Born 7/5/19. Commd 8/7/43. Wg Cdr 1/1/64. Retd ENG 16/1/75. rtg Gp Capt.
NUTTALL W.C. BA. Born 11/11/37. Commd 13/10/64. Sqn Ldr 13/4/70. Retd ADMIN 13/10/80.
NUTTER R. Born 3/8/45. Commd 31/1/64. Flt Lt 15/4/70. Retd GD 3/8/83.

O

O'BRIAN P.G.StG. OBE DFC*. Born 16/9/17. Commd 18/12/37. Gp Capt 1/7/56. Retd GD 18/7/59.
O'BRIEN C.M.P. BA. Born 5/10/48. Commd 1/11/71. Sqn Ldr 1/7/90. Retd GD 16/10/00.
O'BRIEN D.C.T. Born 30/3/45. Commd 27/10/67. Flt Lt 30/3/72. Retd GD 4/5/76.
O'BRIEN E.T. Born 26/1/51. Commd 6/4/72. Sqn Ldr 1/1/89. Retd GD(G) 1/1/92.
O'BRIEN G.P. Born 16/3/31. Commd 28/11/51. Sqn Ldr 1/1/66. Retd GD 9/8/75.
O'BRIEN J.J. Born 19/7/18. Commd 17/6/54. Flt Lt 17/6/57. Retd GD(G) 25/5/71.
O'BRIEN J.J. Born 1/12/37. Commd 15/6/61. Flt Lt 19/11/66. Retd GD 21/11/76.
O'BRIEN J.P. BA. Born 23/5/34. Commd 26/5/67. Sqn Ldr 1/1/74. Retd ENG 7/4/87.
O'BRIEN J.W.A. Born 21/6/47. Commd 14/8/70. Flt Lt 14/2/77. Retd GD(G) 31/3/86.
O'BRIEN K.S. MBE. Born 7/7/25. Commd 12/9/56. Sqn Ldr 1/9/65. Retd GD 8/9/82.
O'BRIEN P.F.J. IEng Ing EurEta MIIE. Born 17/4/64. Commd 29/3/92. Flt Lt 26/11/92. Retd ENGINEER 11/7/03.
O'BRIEN R.P. CB OBE BA FRAeS. Born 1/11/41. Commd 31/7/62. AVM 1/7/92. Retd GD 5/12/98.
O'BRIEN T.M. Born 8/7/50. Commd 10/5/90. Flt Lt 10/5/94. Retd OPS SPT 10/9/00.
O'CALLAGHAN B.A. Born 1/1/24. Commd 7/7/54. Flt Lt 7/7/59. Retd GD 9/12/68.
O'CARROLL J.J. Born 22/8/28. Commd 12/4/73. Flt Lt 12/4/78. Retd ENG 19/9/86.
O'CARROLL J.V. Born 14/2/54. Commd 8/8/74. Flt Lt 23/2/81. Retd OPS SPT 14/2/99.
O'CONNELL C.D. Born 5/2/49. Commd 31/7/70. Wg Cdr 1/1/99. Retd GD 30/9/04.
O'CONNELL P.M. MCMI. Born 18/5/53. Commd 11/9/86. Sqn Ldr 1/7/94. Retd ENG 17/11/01.
O'CONNOR A.C. Born 28/8/66. Commd 15/12/88. Sqn Ldr 1/7/00. Retd FLY(P) 28/8/04.
O'CONNOR I.M. BSc MB MCh BAO DPH DOMS. Born 5/7/18. Commd 2/4/51. Gp Capt 2/4/65. Retd MED 5/7/83.
O'CONNOR M.J. OBE. Born 8/12/46. Commd 1/3/68. Wg Cdr 1/1/88. Retd GD 2/12/96.
O'CONNOR P.D.T. CEng MRAeS. Born 7/3/37. Commd 30/7/59. Sqn Ldr 1/7/68. Retd ENG 7/3/75.
O'CONNOR S. DFC AFC AFM. Born 26/5/22. Commd 21/10/54. Sqn Ldr 1/9/65. Retd GD 26/5/77.
O'DELL P.M.H. Born 20/1/64. Commd 11/10/84. Sqn Ldr 1/7/97. Retd GD 20/1/02.
O'DOHERTY P.J. Born 28/2/42. Commd 13/2/69. Flt Lt 24/6/73. Retd GD(G) 28/2/80.
O'DONNELL J. MA. Born 22/6/47. Commd 17/7/77. Sqn Ldr 1/1/89. Retd ADMIN 17/7/93.
O'DONNELL J.J. BDS LDSRCS. Born 18/4/60. Commd 1/9/85. Wg Cdr 3/3/97. Retd DEL 1/9/01.
O'DONNELL M. Born 29/9/27. Commd 1/7/50. Flt Lt 1/1/55. Retd GD 31/8/79.
O'DONNELL N. Born 23/12/49. Commd 28/9/89. Sqn Ldr 1/7/99. Retd ADMIN (SEC) 12/4/04.
O'DONNELL P. Born 6/4/25. Commd 27/9/51. Flt Lt 13/6/58. Retd SUP 6/4/74.
O'DONNELL R.E. BSc AIB. Born 20/12/44. Commd 9/4/72. Sqn Ldr 1/1/85. Retd ADMIN 20/12/99.
O'DONOGHUE E. Born 15/11/23. Commd 30/4/43. Flt Lt 20/3/51. Retd GD(G) 19/2/76.
O'DONOVAN G.P. Born 7/3/31. Commd 15/10/52. Sqn Ldr 1/1/68. Retd GD 1/1/71.
O'DONOVAN G.W. DSO DFC. Born 24/3/21. Commd 27/2/43. Sqn Ldr 1/7/52. Retd GD 30/6/61.
O'DONOVAN M. Born 16/7/46. Commd 1/11/79. Flt Lt 13/8/73. Retd GD 9/11/85.
O'DWYER D. Born 4/4/42. Commd 23/6/67. Wg Cdr 1/7/86. Retd SUP 5/5/97.
O'DWYER-RUSSELL J.D. OBE. Born 31/8/30. Commd 31/8/50. Wg Cdr 1/1/73. Retd SY 31/8/85.
O'DWYER-RUSSELL T.D. Born 20/10/55. Commd 27/3/75. Flt Lt 22/10/80. Retd GD 8/2/91.
O'FLINN P. Born 6/6/36. Commd 30/7/64. Flt Lt 24/6/77. Retd GD(G) 25/9/82.
O'FLYNN F.J. Born 16/2/43. Commd 25/1/63. Sqn Ldr 1/7/75. Retd GD 4/6/95.
O'FLYNN F.M.G. Born 10/1/24. Commd 23/9/66. Flt Lt 23/9/72. Retd SEC 15/1/74.
O'FLYNN P. Born 15/12/56. Commd 30/9/81. Flt Lt 13/7/84. Retd ENG 29/12/94.
O'GRADY M.J. Born 29/8/38. Commd 24/4/70. Wg Cdr 1/1/89. Retd GD(G) 29/8/93.
O'HAGAN M. CEng MIERE. Born 7/8/24. Commd 1/11/45. Sqn Ldr 1/7/59. Retd ENG 19/9/64.
O'HAGAN M.P.A. Born 1/2/44. Commd 21/10/65. Wg Cdr 1/1/88. Retd GD(G) 2/12/96.
O'HAGAN V.W.J. BA CertEd. Born 16/7/41. Commd 1/8/66. Sqn Ldr 1/3/72. Retd ADMIN 1/8/88.
　　Re-entered 11/12/89. Sqn Ldr 1/7/73. Retd ADMIN 16/7/96.
O'HANLON M.J. Born 1/10/47. Commd 12/3/87. Flt Lt 12/3/91. Retd OPS SPT 8/10/99.
O'HARA J. AFC. Born 20/10/19. Commd 16/12/44. Flt Lt 16/6/48. Retd GD(G) 20/10/75.
O'HARA L. MBA BA. Born 6/6/36. Commd 18/7/60. Wg Cdr 1/1/75. Retd SUP 16/11/82.
O'HARA R.MCM. Born 14/4/39. Commd 12/10/75. Flt Lt 12/10/81. Retd GD(G) 14/4/94.
O'HARE B. BCom MITD MCMI. Born 20/5/34. Commd 30/12/58. Wg Cdr 1/7/78. Retd ADMIN 1/10/84.
O'LEARY D. DFC. Born 8/10/20. Commd 27/9/42. Sqn Ldr 1/1/56. Retd GD(G) 8/4/71.
O'LEARY D.A. Born 6/6/33. Commd 8/10/70. Flt Lt 8/10/73. Retd GD(G) 6/6/93.
O'LEARY D.A. Born 18/4/25. Commd 8/11/51. Flt Lt 6/3/57. Retd GD(G) 7/1/78.
O'LEARY J.D. Born 10/1/21. Commd 12/5/43. Flt Lt 12/5/45. Retd GD(G) 1/2/73.
O'LEARY M.J. Born 28/11/31. Commd 3/8/61. Flt Lt 3/8/67. Retd GD 28/11/91.
O'LEARY T.O. Born 4/10/29. Commd 20/12/57. Flt Lt 20/12/63. Retd GD 28/3/69.
O'LOUGHLIN B.D. Born 10/6/66. Commd 23/5/85. Flt Lt 23/11/90. Retd GD 14/3/96.
O'MAHONY J.P.S. Born 18/10/30. Commd 30/8/50. Sqn Ldr 1/1/68. Retd GD 15/4/76.
O'MAHONY O.R. Born 10/7/39. Commd 20/8/65. Flt Lt 6/7/68. Retd GD 10/7/77.

O'MALLEY F. Born 3/12/29. Commd 28/5/66. Flt Lt 28/5/72. Retd ADMIN 1/3/83.
O'MALLEY F.P. Born 17/7/16. Commd 29/7/43. Sqn Ldr 1/7/54. Retd ENG 17/7/72.
O'MARA R.J. BSc. Born 8/1/66. Commd 8/6/87. Flt Lt 15/1/91. Retd GD 1/5/96.
O'NEILL A.M.J. CEng FIMechE FRAeS. Born 27/3/43. Commd 6/4/62. Gp Capt 1/7/88. Retd ENG 6/8/94.
O'NEILL B. Born 10/12/46. Commd 1/6/72. Flt Lt 30/9/78. Retd GD(G) 14/8/88.
O'NEILL C.O. Born 11/7/52. Commd 29/6/72. Flt Lt 9/12/78. Retd GD(G) 11/7/90.
O'NEILL D.W.J. MRCS LRCP. Born 11/6/23. Commd 17/10/46. Flt Lt 10/8/47. Retd MED 30/4/54. rtg Sqn Ldr.
O'NEILL E. Born 9/2/16. Commd 9/11/50. Sqn Ldr 1/1/66. Retd SEC 1/7/70.
O'NEILL H.F. DFC*. Born 19/9/20. Commd 29/8/38. Gp Capt 1/1/62. Retd GD 3/12/66.
O'NEILL J. Born 31/5/47. Commd 5/11/70. Flt Lt 1/4/74. Retd GD 31/5/85.
O'NEILL J. Born 11/4/14. Commd 12/9/38. Wg Cdr 1/1/51. Retd SUP 15/9/58.
O'NEILL J.A. DFC. Born 7/10/15. Commd 15/3/35. Wg Cdr 1/7/47. Retd GD 29/11/57. rtg Gp Capt.
O'NEILL J.P.H. MBE AFC. Born 6/1/31. Commd 24/1/52. Wg Cdr 1/1/74. Retd GD 1/4/85.
O'NEILL K.B. BSc CEng MIMechE MRAeS. Born 5/8/40. Commd 17/10/71. Sqn Ldr 1/7/89. Retd ENG 5/8/95.
O'NEILL M.T.C. MCMI. Born 5/10/43. Commd 4/7/69. Sqn Ldr 1/2/93. Retd SUP 1/2/93.
O'NEILL P.J. Born 17/3/27. Commd 25/8/60. Fg Offr 25/8/60. Retd SEC 25/7/65.
O'NEILL S.J. MBE. Born 1/12/28. Commd 19/12/63. Sqn Ldr 1/7/76. Retd ENG 2/7/82.
O'NEILL T.J. Born 12/6/53. Commd 5/2/81. Flt Lt 4/3/85. Retd ENG 30/3/92.
O'NEILL W.I. MCMI. Born 15/7/23. Commd 21/4/44. Wg Cdr 1/7/73. Retd SY 20/11/76.
O'REGAN C.A. Born 12/12/20. Commd 19/7/57. Sqn Ldr 1/7/72. Retd ENG 12/12/75.
O'REILLY B.J. MB ChB. Born 2/11/54. Commd 20/1/76. Wg Cdr 1/8/92. Retd MED 14/3/96.
O'REILLY C. OBE. Born 1/4/28. Commd 21/12/48. Wg Cdr 1/1/71. Retd SUP 1/4/83.
O'REILLY F. Born 23/7/49. Commd 27/7/89. Flt Lt 27/7/93. Retd SUP 9/9/96.
O'REILLY J.J. Born 2/7/32. Commd 15/9/60. Flt Lt 15/3/65. Retd GD 2/7/70.
O'REILLY M.J. BA. Born 4/9/54. Commd 20/1/80. Sqn Ldr 1/1/95. Retd GD 1/2/99.
O'REILLY P.J. CB BSc CEng FIEE FRAeS. Born 26/4/46. Commd 19/5/69. AVM 1/7/96. Retd ENG 24/4/99.
O'RIORDAN J.A. Born 14/9/25. Commd 30/4/59. Flt Lt 30/10/63. Retd GD 31/3/70.
O'ROURKE M.J. Born 26/10/38. Commd 28/5/57. Flt Lt 19/6/64. Retd GD 20/1/68.
O'SHEA N. Born 20/12/28. Commd 24/9/52. Sqn Ldr 1/7/70. Retd GD 3/1/76.
O'SHEA P.R. BEng. Born 6/6/58. Commd 2/8/85. Flt Lt 15/7/88. Retd ENG 6/6/96.
O'SHEA S.M. The Rev. Born 26/6/23. Commd 15/4/58. Retd Wg Cdr 15/10/74.
O'SULLIVAN J.B.P. MA. Born 30/5/33. Commd 22/11/56. Gp Capt 1/7/84. Retd ADMIN 5/9/87.
O'SULLIVAN K.M. Born 24/2/52. Commd 14/8/70. Fg Offr 14/8/72. Retd GD 12/9/75.
O'SULLIVAN V.F. MCMI. Born 11/11/42. Commd 26/10/62. Sqn Ldr 1/1/74. Retd GD 18/5/86.
O'TOOLE E.F. MBE CEng MIEE MRAeS MCMI. Born 3/9/35. Commd 7/9/61. Sqn Ldr 11/4/84. Retd ENG 3/9/94.
O'TOOLE L. Born 23/10/32. Commd 3/9/80. Sqn Ldr 2/11/71. Retd SUP 23/4/92.
OAKDEN D.I. Born 12/6/34. Commd 15/11/55. Gp Capt 1/7/80. Retd GD 8/3/88.
OAKES E.R. Born 12/4/23. Commd 14/11/57. Flt Lt 1/4/63. Retd GD 1/9/67.
OAKES M.S. BSc. Born 11/7/54. Commd 7/3/72. Flt Lt 15/4/77. Retd GD 2/2/93.
OAKES P.A. BSc. Born 24/5/66. Commd 30/8/87. Flt Lt 28/2/90. Retd GD 14/3/97.
OAKES S.L. Born 1/12/41. Commd 1/6/72. Sqn Ldr 1/7/79. Retd SY 1/6/86.
OAKEY T.W. AFC BSc. Born 20/10/24. Commd 4/9/50. Wg Cdr 1/1/62. Retd GD 20/10/79.
OAKLEY D. BSc. Born 16/4/50. Commd 15/9/69. Flt Lt 15/12/73. Retd GD 16/4/88.
OAKLEY J. OBE. Born 11/4/20. Commd 9/11/43. Gp Capt 1/7/71. Retd GD(G) 11/12/75.
OAKLEY P.A. MBE. Born 5/7/23. Commd 6/6/52. Sqn Ldr 1/1/63. Retd GD 8/7/67.
OAKLEY S. MSc BA MCIPS MILDM. Born 4/4/49. Commd 23/9/68. Sqn Ldr 1/1/87. Retd SUP 31/3/94.
OAKLEY W.W. Born 17/2/14. Commd 24/7/46. Fg Offr 24/7/47. Retd SEC 17/4/55.
OART J.H. Born 22/7/43. Commd 20/10/83. Flt Lt 20/10/87. Retd ENG 2/7/93.
OATES A.S.H. Born 3/3/11. Commd 19/7/45. Fg Offr 19/1/46. Retd ASD 28/9/46.
OATES L.H. MBE. Born 19/6/12. Commd 30/11/41. Sqn Ldr 1/7/54. Retd ENG 19/6/67. rtg Wg Cdr.
OATES N.A. BA. Born 11/2/57. Commd 15/9/74. Flt Lt 15/10/80. Retd ENG 9/8/83.
OATES V. Born 18/5/23. Commd 3/8/61. Sqn Ldr 1/7/71. Retd GD 19/9/77.
OATEY A.H. DUS CEng MIEE. Born 29/11/35. Commd 24/7/57. Sqn Ldr 1/7/66. Retd ENG 2/5/79.
OATEY W.R. Born 26/2/34. Commd 6/9/55. Sqn Ldr 1/7/69. Retd GD 30/6/76.
OBERTELLI A.J.A. Born 20/1/49. Commd 24/7/71. Flt Lt 24/12/75. Retd GD 8/3/87.
OCKLEFORD C.E. LDS RCS(Edin). Born 23/12/19. Commd 9/1/42. Gp Capt 1/1/65. Retd DEL 1/12/83.
ODBERT R.M. BSc MB ChB MRCGP DCH DRCOG DAvMed MRAeS. Born 6/4/50. Commd 4/9/73. Sqn Ldr 1/8/82.
    Retd MED 6/3/90.
ODDEY M.J.L. BSc CEng MIMechE MCMI. Born 1/12/58. Commd 1/9/77. Wg Cdr 1/1/94. Retd ENG 1/1/97.
ODDY S.J. BSc. Born 31/3/51. Commd 15/9/69. Sqn Ldr 1/1/85. Retd GD 31/3/89.
ODELL P.M.H. Born 20/1/64. Commd 11/10/84. Sqn Ldr 1/7/97. Retd GD 20/1/02.
ODLING P.J. Born 3/3/35. Commd 24/6/53. Sqn Ldr 1/1/68. Retd GD 12/7/75.
OFFORD R.E. Born 11/10/32. Commd 31/5/51. Flt Lt 28/11/56. Retd GD 17/10/69.
OFFORD R.J. AFC FCMI. Born 17/9/31. Commd 8/8/52. A Cdre 1/7/80. Retd GD 17/9/86.
OFFORD R.J. BCom. Born 10/6/60. Commd 15/8/82. Sqn Ldr 1/1/94. Retd GD 15/8/98.
OGDEN G. Born 17/8/44. Commd 6/5/65. Wg Cdr 1/1/85. Retd ADMIN 19/8/93.

OGDEN S. Born 20/12/64. Commd 28/7/88. Sqn Ldr 1/7/98. Retd SUPPLY 20/12/03.
OGIER T.H. Born 17/7/49. Commd 8/9/77. Flt Lt 24/5/80. Retd ENG 17/7/87.
OGILVIE I.M. MB ChB MFCM DPH. Born 5/8/26. Commd 3/5/49. A Cdre 1/5/78. Retd MED 1/8/80.
OGILVIE J.G. Born 2/10/46. Commd 18/8/67. Sqn Ldr 1/1/76. Retd GD 1/1/80.
OGILVIE T. BSc. Born 16/1/32. Commd 25/9/62. Wg Cdr 1/7/77. Retd ENG 14/9/86.
OGLE J.R.N. MCMI. Born 1/5/41. Commd 18/12/62. Sqn Ldr 1/1/76. Retd SUP 2/6/82.
OKE G.J. Born 2/5/36. Commd 10/3/60. Sqn Ldr 1/7/74. Retd SUP 2/5/91.
OLD D.G. Born 19/6/30. Commd 15/6/61. Flt Lt 15/6/67. Retd RGT 14/10/80.
OLD D.M. BSc. Born 12/10/51. Commd 13/9/70. Sqn Ldr 1/7/86. Retd GD 12/10/89.
OLDAKER R.W. BSc. Born 11/11/55. Commd 15/9/74. Wg Cdr 1/7/93. Retd SUP 11/11/02.
OLDFIELD A.J. Born 11/6/41. Commd 15/9/61. Flt Lt 11/12/66. Retd GD 11/6/79.
OLDFIELD D. BA. Born 27/10/56. Commd 8/4/79. Sqn Ldr 1/1/87. Retd ADMIN 14/3/96.
OLDFIELD J.E. Born 17/6/45. Commd 2/6/67. Sqn Ldr 1/7/91. Retd GD 3/2/97.
OLDHAM J.B. Born 19/12/44. Commd 14/8/64. Flt Lt 14/2/70. Retd GD 31/12/75.
OLDING R.C. CBE DSC. Born 29/11/32. Commd 6/10/57. Gp Capt 1/1/79. Retd GD 31/12/84.
OLDLAND E.F. BSc. Born 11/6/19. Commd 23/7/48. Sqn Ldr 23/12/53. Retd EDN 21/2/63.
OLDROYD A.W. DFC AFC. Born 20/9/16. Commd 29/6/36. Wg Cdr 1/7/47. Retd GD 20/9/63.
OLIVE R.B. AFC. Born 20/3/30. Commd 2/2/56. Sqn Ldr 1/7/83. Retd GD 20/3/88.
OLIVER A.R. BA MIQA AMRAeS. Born 11/12/38. Commd 13/12/60. Wg Cdr 1/1/86. Retd ENG 5/6/90.
OLIVER B.R. DFC. Born 23/4/33. Commd 20/11/56. Sqn Ldr 1/1/67. Retd GD 7/4/77.
OLIVER C.E. Born 5/12/24. Commd 13/2/47. Sqn Ldr 1/7/59. Retd SUP 5/12/61.
OLIVER D.R. MB ChB. Born 25/11/27. Commd 11/4/56. Flt Lt 11/4/57. Retd MED 30/3/61.
OLIVER D.R. DFC MCMI. Born 20/2/22. Commd 11/8/43. Sqn Ldr 1/1/56. Retd GD 20/12/71.
OLIVER D.S. Born 26/9/39. Commd 1/4/68. Flt Lt 7/8/69. Retd ENG 23/10/80.
OLIVER E.J. Born 20/5/49. Commd 31/8/75. Sqn Ldr 1/1/90. Retd ADMIN 1/9/93.
OLIVER G.W. MCMI. Born 15/2/23. Commd 5/8/44. Wg Cdr 1/1/68. Retd GD(G) 15/3/73.
OLIVER H.W. Born 17/1/41. Commd 29/10/63. Sqn Ldr 1/7/78. Retd GD 1/7/81.
OLIVER J. Born 2/1/24. Commd 3/2/45. Flt Lt 3/8/48. Retd GD 4/4/62.
OLIVER J.R. MSc MBCS. Born 11/12/38. Commd 13/12/60. Wg Cdr 1/7/80. Retd GD 25/9/89.
OLIVER K.H. LDSRCS. Born 16/2/34. Commd 25/10/59. Wg Cdr 1/8/72. Retd DEL 31/8/80.
OLIVER K.L. Born 5/3/54. Commd 19/12/61. Fg Offr 19/12/91. Retd ENG 3/4/93.
OLIVER K.M. Born 12/12/28. Commd 13/7/49. Gp Capt 1/7/72. Retd RGT 12/12/78.
OLIVER K.P. BSc. Born 12/4/51. Commd 13/9/70. Sqn Ldr 1/7/86. Retd GD 11/7/89.
OLIVER M.A. Born 9/1/62. Commd 4/9/81. Flt Lt 4/3/87. Retd GD 28/2/00.
OLIVER M.E. Born 20/2/51. Commd 29/4/71. Sqn Ldr 1/1/86. Retd ADMIN 20/2/89.
OLIVER M.S. MSc BSc. Born 4/8/47. Commd 18/9/66. Gp Capt 1/1/91. Retd SUP 7/10/97.
OLIVER N.W.J. MB BS DObstRCOG MRCP. Born 6/8/33. Commd 16/6/57. Wg Cdr 9/5/70. Retd MED 1/1/70.
OLIVER P.A. MIDPM MCMI. Born 27/12/39. Commd 22/5/70. Sqn Ldr 1/7/82. Retd SUP 5/1/86.
OLIVER P.L. Born 30/6/30. Commd 13/9/50. Sqn Ldr 1/1/62. Retd GD 30/6/68.
OLIVER P.M. Born 5/9/47. Commd 9/3/72. Fg Offr 9/3/74. Retd GD 18/9/76.
OLIVER S.G. Born 5/11/57. Commd 29/4/03. Flt Lt 21/5/94. Retd OPS SPT(INT) 6/2/04.
OLIVER S.W.StJ. BSc. Born 26/12/51. Commd 30/5/76. Wg Cdr 1/7/90. Retd ENG 31/5/02.
OLLIFF N.J. BSc. Born 20/9/47. Commd 19/5/74. Flt Lt 19/2/77. Retd ENG 1/4/81.
OLLIVER T. MBE. Born 3/7/21. Commd 15/6/61. Sqn Ldr 1/7/73. Retd ENG 3/7/76.
OLLIVER T. MSc BDS. Born 16/4/47. Commd 8/12/74. Gp Capt 6/8/97. Retd DEL 15/10/99.
OLSON W.H. Born 10/2/25. Commd 1/4/45. Sqn Ldr 1/1/62. Retd GD 27/4/68.
OLVER M.K. Born 31/1/47. Commd 30/5/69. Flt Lt 4/8/64. Retd GD(G) 14/3/96.
ONGLEY C.G. Born 3/6/33. Commd 30/1/52. Flt Lt 29/5/57. Retd GD 13/12/71.
ONLEY M.J. BSc. Born 12/5/59. Commd 17/1/82. Sqn Ldr 1/1/92. Retd GD 17/1/98.
ONSLOW G.H. Born 4/10/28. Commd 29/7/49. Flt Lt 20/11/58. Retd RGT 5/3/68.
OPENSHAW D. BSc. Born 12/5/34. Commd 24/8/56. Sqn Ldr 24/2/66. Retd EDN 24/8/72.
OPENSHAW I.K. BSc. Born 11/7/31. Commd 16/1/72. Sqn Ldr 16/1/72. Retd ENG 11/7/93.
OPIE B.W. FCIPD FCMI. Born 5/11/31. Commd 17/12/52. A Cdre 1/7/80. Retd ADMIN 3/4/85.
ORAM G. BEng CEng MIEE. Born 11/8/65. Commd 3/9/89. Flt Lt 20/4/93. Retd ENGINEER 10/12/03.
ORAM K.M. Born 13/7/43. Commd 27/3/86. Flt Lt 27/3/90. Retd ENG 31/3/94.
ORANGE N.G. MBE. Born 15/6/35. Commd 23/9/66. Sqn Ldr 1/7/80. Retd ADMIN 16/4/89.
ORCHARD D.F. Born 29/6/24. Commd 1/10/43. Sqn Ldr 1/7/56. Retd GD 29/6/62.
ORCHARD H.F. Born 7/1/23. Commd 3/6/43. Sqn Ldr 1/1/56. Retd SUP 26/12/61.
ORCHARD N.A. MSc BDS MGDSRCS(Eng). Born 26/10/47. Commd 14/9/69. Wg Cdr 26/11/84. Retd DEL 14/3/97.
ORD G.E. CBE FCMI. Born 19/8/31. Commd 21/5/52. Gp Capt 1/1/77. Retd GD 30/12/84.
ORD I.G.L. Born 14/2/44. Commd 28/4/65. Sqn Ldr 1/1/78. Retd GD 14/2/82.
ORDISH G.A. Born 15/4/47. Commd 29/7/65. Wg Cdr 1/1/92. Retd OPS SPT 19/1/02.
ORGAN M.J. BEd. Born 22/5/56. Commd 3/3/85. Sqn Ldr 1/7/95. Retd ADMIN (SEC) 26/9/04.
ORME B.M. Born 25/10/45. Commd 29/10/64. Fg Offr 29/4/67. Retd ENG 2/1/71.
ORME C.J. Born 18/6/46. Commd 17/12/64. Sqn Ldr 1/7/78. Retd ENG 14/3/96.
ORME D.I. Born 8/7/61. Commd 11/10/93. Flt Lt 11/10/95. Retd ENG 20/11/02.

ORME J.P. CEng MIMechE. Born 15/3/38. Commd 19/9/71. Flt Lt 19/9/72. Retd ENG 29/9/89.
ORME K.P. AFC BSc MRAeS. Born 17/3/43. Commd 17/4/64. Sqn Ldr 1/1/75. Retd GD 17/3/81.
ORMEROD A.J. Born 22/2/48. Commd 7/1/71. Fg Offr 7/1/73. Retd GD 15/5/75.
ORMEROD J.A. Born 29/3/21. Commd 9/7/41. Sqn Ldr 1/1/59. Retd GD 29/3/64.
ORMEROD J.M. Born 23/1/23. Commd 4/6/64. Flt Lt 4/6/69. Retd ENG 1/11/69.
ORMISTON J.A. Born 12/6/71. Commd 28/3/91. Flt Lt 28/9/96. Retd FLY(P) 13/2/04.
ORMISTON T.McN. DFC. Born 30/11/17. Commd 17/4/39. Sqn Ldr 1/10/54. Retd GD 26/11/57.
ORMROD W. CBE MSc CEng MRAeS. Born 21/1/26. Commd 22/2/46. A Cdre 1/1/75. Retd ENG 3/5/77.
ORMSHAW B.H. Born 29/11/34. Commd 20/2/59. Flt Lt 26/7/67. Retd ENG 20/2/75.
ORR B.J. Born 23/7/46. Commd 1/4/65. Sqn Ldr 1/1/90. Retd GD(G) 31/5/93.
ORR J.S. MBE. Born 1/1/43. Commd 1/4/76. Sqn Ldr 1/1/92. Retd GD 1/2/98.
ORR K.B. Born 16/11/18. Commd 14/1/41. Sqn Ldr 1/1/57. Retd GD 12/6/59.
ORR M.K. Born 5/12/27. Commd 30/9/50. Flt Lt 10/2/57. Retd GD 7/12/66.
ORR N.W. Born 16/11/19. Commd 14/1/41. Sqn Ldr 1/7/54. Retd GD 9/9/58.
ORR W.R. Born 21/8/13. Commd 13/9/42. Flt Lt 13/3/46. Retd ENG 1/1/54.
ORREY M.I. Born 14/10/30. Commd 3/5/51. Sqn Ldr 1/7/70. Retd GD(G) 15/2/85.
ORRICK R. Born 4/9/22. Commd 1/4/45. Flt Lt 10/11/55. Retd GD(G) 7/9/72.
ORRINGE D.A. Born 26/4/44. Commd 24/4/64. Flt Lt 24/10/69. Retd GD 29/11/75.
ORSLER T.B. Born 17/12/32. Commd 29/10/52. Flt Lt 14/8/59. Retd SUP 1/8/78.
ORTON A.A. Born 10/8/46. Commd 19/8/66. Flt Lt 4/5/72. Retd GD 10/8/84.
ORTON P.D. Born 4/9/32. Commd 28/7/53. Flt Lt 28/1/56. Retd GD 30/12/59.
ORWELL S.J. Born 10/7/49. Commd 31/7/70. Wg Cdr 1/7/96. Retd GD 10/7/04.
ORWIN C.W. CEng MRAeS MCMI. Born 13/2/23. Commd 23/2/50. Wg Cdr 1/1/72. Retd ENG 31/3/77.
ORYTL R. BSc. Born 16/1/60. Commd 11/9/83. Flt Lt 7/11/88. Retd GD 14/3/97.
OSBORN D.R. Born 23/10/33. Commd 26/3/52. Flt Lt 7/8/57. Retd GD 23/10/71.
OSBORN M.P. Born 19/12/40. Commd 30/5/59. Sqn Ldr 1/7/80. Retd GD(G) 19/12/95.
OSBORN P. Born 1/1/48. Commd 28/2/69. Flt Lt 28/2/72. Retd GD 2/11/87.
OSBORN P.D. Born 19/11/29. Commd 17/5/51. Sqn Ldr 1/7/67. Retd GD 31/5/74.
OSBORN T.G.R. CBE. Born 17/4/36. Commd 14/7/54. A Cdre 1/7/88. Retd GD 17/4/91.
OSBORNE C.E.W. Born 8/5/31. Commd 19/1/70. Sqn Ldr 1/1/77. Retd GD 8/5/89.
OSBORNE D.G. BA. Born 7/9/48. Commd 22/6/70. Flt Lt 22/3/72. Retd GD 30/8/74.
OSBORNE I.W.S. DPhysEd. Born 16/12/45. Commd 13/9/70. Flt Lt 13/9/74. Retd ADMIN 1/10/82.
OSBORNE M.N. Born 14/9/33. Commd 13/12/55. Flt Lt 18/8/59. Retd GD 28/4/70.
OSBORNE N.G. BSc. Born 5/12/51. Commd 13/9/70. Sqn Ldr 1/7/85. Retd GD 5/12/89.
OSBORNE P.B. DFC. Born 17/7/23. Commd 29/11/48. Sqn Ldr 1/7/74. Retd GD 30/6/78.
OSBORNE P.E. Born 28/6/46. Commd 3/3/67. Flt Lt 3/9/69. Retd GD 28/6/84.
OSBORNE P.R.P. Born 22/5/28. Commd 1/12/49. Flt Lt 2/11/55. Retd GD 22/5/66.
OSBORNE R.A. CertEd. Born 9/4/46. Commd 22/4/79. Sqn Ldr 1/7/91. Retd ADMIN 3/8/00.
OSBORNE R.W. Born 6/7/40. Commd 26/5/61. Flt Lt 26/11/66. Retd GD 1/11/77.
OSBORNE R.W. Born 21/4/46. Commd 2/4/65. Flt Lt 2/10/70. Retd GD 21/4/84.
OSBORNE S.C. Born 31/1/43. Commd 1/3/62. Flt Lt 8/1/69. Retd GD(G) 30/1/96.
OSBORNE S.R. Born 8/7/65. Commd 19/7/84. Flt Lt 19/1/90. Retd GD 14/3/96.
OSBORNE T.E. Born 9/2/55. Commd 26/5/87. Wg Cdr 1/1/99. Retd GD 30/8/04.
OSBORNE T.F. Born 24/5/46. Commd 11/6/81. Flt Lt 11/6/84. Retd GD 1/8/86.
OSMAN A.J. Born 8/6/66. Commd 23/5/85. Sqn Ldr 1/1/97. Retd OPS SPT(REGT) 18/4/05.
OSMAN M.R. Born 2/6/66. Commd 11/9/86. Wg Cdr 1/1/02. Retd GD 26/1/05.
OSMENT D.E.T. Born 14/10/16. Commd 7/3/38. Sqn Ldr 1/8/47. Retd SEC 14/10/65.
OSMENT D.G. MBE. Born 2/2/33. Commd 12/3/64. Sqn Ldr 1/7/74. Retd GD 13/11/81.
OSTERBERG R.D. FCIS MBCS. Born 22/4/30. Commd 19/6/52. Gp Capt 1/1/77. Retd SEC 23/9/78.
OSTRIDGE C.P. Born 24/12/29. Commd 17/1/52. Flt Lt 8/5/57. Retd GD 24/12/67.
OSWALD T.J. Born 11/2/43. Commd 20/8/65. Sqn Ldr 1/7/88. Retd GD 11/2/98.
OSWELL Q.M.B. Born 30/10/35. Commd 10/4/56. Wg Cdr 1/1/81. Retd GD 30/10/90.
OSZCZYK M.S. BSc CertEd. Born 8/4/55. Commd 6/9/81. Flt Lt 6/9/82. Retd ADMIN 6/9/97.
OTLEY L.J. Born 7/10/24. Commd 24/3/44. Flt Lt 24/9/47. Retd GD 21/12/63. rtg Sqn Ldr.
OTLEY-DOE C.E. MSc. Born 26/1/61. Commd 21/12/89. Wg Cdr 1/1/03. Retd GD 5/4/04.
OTLEY-DOE D.L. Born 21/6/66. Commd 16/5/94. Flt Lt 28/1/95. Retd OPS SPT(ATC) 21/6/04.
OTRIDGE B. Born 1/3/50. Commd 30/5/69. Sqn Ldr 1/7/87. Retd ENG 1/7/90.
OTRIDGE D. Born 5/4/43. Commd 10/6/66. Flt Lt 14/2/69. Retd GD 5/4/98.
OTTAWAY K.P. BA MCIPD. Born 9/12/54. Commd 24/1/74. Sqn Ldr 1/1/89. Retd SY 9/12/92.
OTTER G.R. MBE. Born 5/8/16. Commd 6/9/56. Sqn Ldr 1/1/66. Retd ENG 23/12/72.
OUGHTON G.J. BSc CEng MRAeS. Born 8/11/45. Commd 15/7/66. Gp Capt 1/7/92. Retd ENG 22/10/94.
OUGHTON M.D. Born 22/2/57. Commd 8/5/86. Flt Lt 8/11/92. Retd OPS SPT(FLTOPS) 11/11/03.
OULTON P.D. Born 6/9/37. Commd 28/7/59. A Cdre 1/1/89. Retd GD 6/9/92.
OUSTON R.J. Born 2/1/37. Commd 16/4/57. Wg Cdr 1/7/88. Retd GD 13/1/91.
OUTEN D.R. Born 28/11/52. Commd 11/7/74. Sqn Ldr 1/7/91. Retd ADMIN 17/3/97.
OVEL W.E. BSc. Born 13/10/50. Commd 15/9/69. Sqn Ldr 1/7/85. Retd GD 14/3/96.

OVENDEN D.A. RVM IEng FIIE MCMI. Born 7/9/43. Commd 14/8/80. Sqn Ldr 1/7/89. Retd ENG 25/10/97.
OVENDEN L.R.J. AFC. Born 28/8/17. Commd 15/1/41. Sqn Ldr 1/8/47. Retd GD 26/8/58.
OVENS A.J. OBE BSc. Born 12/2/52. Commd 10/1/72. Gp Capt 1/7/96. Retd GD 25/4/04.
OVENS J.L.P. Born 18/7/80. Commd 6/12/51. Sqn Offr 1/7/66. Retd SEC 1/7/69.
OVER F. MA MSc BA AFIMA. Born 20/11/32. Commd 2/3/57. Sqn Ldr 1/11/68. Retd EDN 23/10/75.
OVERALL R.H.T. Born 23/5/31. Commd 17/12/52. Sqn Ldr 1/1/67. Retd ADMIN 23/5/86.
OVEREND A.P.J. BA. Born 1/7/43. Commd 31/10/66. Fg Offr 11/11/66. Retd EDN 12/7/68.
OVERSBY G. Born 15/12/12. Commd 6/11/41. Flt Lt 4/11/46. Retd ENG 28/4/58.
OVERTON C.R. Born 16/6/14. Commd 4/11/43. Sqn Ldr 1/10/55. Retd ENG 16/6/63.
OVERTON D.G. MSc BA CPhys MInstP. Born 5/4/48. Commd 7/12/86. Sqn Ldr 1/7/01. Retd ADMIN (TRG) 1/7/03.
OVERY L.R. Born 13/8/34. Commd 13/2/60. Flt Lt 13/8/65. Retd GD 22/9/75.
OWEN A. Born 5/5/56. Commd 11/8/77. Flt Lt 24/3/81. Retd GD 1/7/86.
OWEN A.J. DFC* AFC DFM. Born 8/7/22. Commd 11/3/43. Wg Cdr 1/1/60. Retd GD 8/7/69.
OWEN C.R.W. Born 20/10/25. Commd 7/7/52. Flt Lt 7/7/52. Retd ENG 20/10/63.
OWEN D. BA. Born 7/9/40. Commd 31/3/64. Sqn Ldr 31/3/73. Retd ADMIN 31/3/80.
OWEN D.C. Born 2/12/31. Commd 6/9/79. Sqn Ldr 9/7/75. Retd ADMIN 2/12/86.
OWEN D.J. Born 22/9/62. Commd 14/1/92. Sqn Ldr 1/1/01. Retd OPS SPT(INT) 1/1/04.
OWEN D.P. Born 15/2/50. Commd 26/9/85. Flt Lt 26/9/89. Retd ENG 6/3/93.
OWEN E.I. Born 14/9/20. Commd 23/4/45. Flt Lt 11/8/55. Retd GD 2/7/68.
OWEN G.M. MBE. Born 26/4/17. Commd 1/9/41. Wg Offr 1/7/61. Retd CAT 10/7/63.
OWEN G.W. Born 20/4/17. Commd 17/7/46. Fg Offr 17/7/47. Retd RGT 25/5/49.
OWEN H. Born 4/6/21. Commd 20/9/44. Flt Lt 1/4/51. Retd SEC 15/7/55.
OWEN J.H. Born 3/2/44. Commd 26/3/64. Sqn Ldr 1/1/79. Retd ADMIN 3/2/88.
OWEN J.K. CEng MIMechE MRAeS. Born 17/4/38. Commd 30/7/59. Sqn Ldr 1/1/71. Retd ENG 17/4/76.
OWEN J.R. Born 19/1/45. Commd 27/3/80. Flt Lt 27/3/80. Retd ENG 1/10/94.
OWEN J.R. AFC. Born 15/9/37. Commd 28/7/59. Sqn Ldr 1/7/68. Retd GD 15/9/75.
OWEN J.S. Born 6/10/18. Commd 29/3/39. Wg Cdr 1/7/54. Retd GD 10/6/64. rtg Gp Capt.
OWEN M.C. Born 30/3/48. Commd 17/2/67. Flt Lt 18/7/73. Retd GD(G) 30/9/78.
OWEN M.J. MSc BSc CEng MIEE MRIN MRAeS MCMI ACGI. Born 17/3/43. Commd 6/10/74. Sqn Ldr 1/7/84. Retd ENG 15/4/94.
OWEN N.C. MCIPD MCMI. Born 15/9/45. Commd 7/7/69. Sqn Ldr 1/1/86. Retd RGT 7/7/91.
OWEN N.T. Born 8/7/20. Commd 29/3/44. Flt Lt 17/3/49. Retd GD(G) 26/12/53.
OWEN P.C. Born 9/11/57. Commd 8/12/83. Sqn Ldr 1/1/93. Retd ADMIN 2/12/97.
OWEN P.L.T. OBE MA DipSoton CEng FIEE. Born 16/12/33. Commd 26/9/53. A Cdre 1/7/78. Retd ENG 3/4/81.
OWEN P.S. Born 7/9/47. Commd 23/3/67. Gp Capt 1/7/92. Retd GD 1/4/00.
OWEN R.C. CEng MIEE DipElEng. Born 7/7/49. Commd 17/10/71. Wg Cdr 1/1/90. Retd ENG 7/12/96.
OWEN R.L. Born 18/4/50. Commd 27/3/75. Flt Lt 9/8/79. Retd PI 14/5/89.
OWEN W.K. BA. Born 29/11/65. Commd 16/9/84. Flt Lt 15/1/90. Retd GD 15/7/99.
OWEN W.T. BA. Born 13/7/27. Commd 10/2/49. Wg Cdr 1/1/70. Retd SEC 1/11/74.
OWENS D.T. FCMI. Born 30/9/23. Commd 2/2/45. Gp Capt 1/7/73. Retd SUP 30/6/77.
OWENS D.W.L. Born 13/10/31. Commd 11/9/52. Gp Capt 1/7/84. Retd GD(G) 1/7/87.
OWENS J.A. Born 18/7/64. Commd 4/6/92. Flt Lt 25/2/94. Retd OPS SPT(ATC) 27/4/03.
OWENS W.D. Born 10/6/54. Commd 27/8/87. Flt Lt 27/8/89. Retd SUP 14/3/96.
OWENS W.J. Born 25/6/21. Commd 23/12/61. Flt Lt 23/12/66. Retd ENG 31/12/74.
OWER P.C. MSc BDS MGDSRCS(Ed) MGDSRCS(Eng). Born 24/12/55. Commd 22/6/80. Wg Cdr 28/2/92. Retd DEL 22/6/96.
OWERS A.J. BA. Born 14/3/62. Commd 25/1/82. Sqn Ldr 1/7/96. Retd GD 1/12/00.
OWGAN D.F. Born 23/12/40. Commd 5/11/70. Flt Lt 5/11/72. Retd GD(G) 22/12/78.
OXBORROW G.E. Born 28/12/55. Commd 17/8/80. Sqn Ldr 1/9/90. Retd ADMIN 14/3/96.
OXBORROW M.D. Born 30/5/52. Commd 11/1/79. Flt Lt 21/2/83. Retd GD 20/12/97.
OXBORROW R.J. AHSM. Born 5/12/45. Commd 3/7/80. Sqn Ldr 1/1/87. Retd MED(SEC) 1/8/92.
OXBY D.A. DSO DFC DFM*. Born 10/6/20. Commd 31/10/42. Wg Cdr 1/7/57. Retd GD 11/3/69.
OXENHAM D.O. Born 29/9/25. Commd 14/12/50. Sqn Ldr 1/1/67. Retd GD 25/9/75.
OXER H.F. MA MB BChir MRCS FFARCS LRCP DA. Born 16/4/32. Commd 14/10/58. Wg Cdr 13/10/71. Retd MED 10/9/75.
OXLEE D.D. OBE. Born 3/7/34. Commd 29/7/65. Wg Cdr 1/1/81. Retd PI 10/1/86.
OXLEE G.J. OBE BA MRAeS MCMI. Born 30/3/36. Commd 21/10/65. Gp Capt 1/1/85. Retd PI 9/8/87.
OXLEY C.D.A. AFC MCMI. Born 10/9/23. Commd 6/1/45. Wg Cdr 1/1/74. Retd GD(G) 31/3/77.
OXLEY J.D. BSc CEng MIEE. Born 23/7/24. Commd 17/9/57. Sqn Ldr 1/1/63. Retd ENG 1/6/78.
OXLEY J.F. Born 20/11/41. Commd 27/1/61. Flt Lt 9/2/68. Retd GD(G) 14/9/92.
OXLEY M. Born 13/7/29. Commd 3/11/60. Flt Lt 3/11/65. Retd GD 1/6/68.
OXLEY R.G. Born 31/1/45. Commd 3/3/67. Flt Lt 12/11/69. Retd GD 7/5/76.
OXTOBY P.A. Born 2/8/24. Commd 1/11/43. Sqn Ldr 1/7/59. Retd CAT 30/5/70.
OYSTON J.K. MB BS FRCS. Born 13/1/25. Commd 29/9/50. Wg Cdr 1/4/62. Retd MED 1/11/69.
OZANNE D.T.F. Born 26/5/34. Commd 26/7/55. Flt Lt 29/4/59. Retd GD 26/5/72.
OZANNE J.F. Born 28/11/30. Commd 18/10/62. Sqn Ldr 1/1/78. Retd ENG 28/11/83.
O'HARA L. MBE. Born 6/6/36. Commd 18/7/60. Wg Cdr 1/1/75. Retd SUP 16/11/82.

P

PACK J.M. CBE. Born 5/3/31. Commd 14/4/53. A Cdre 1/1/78. Retd GD 1/8/86.
PACKER D.G.L. BSc DipSoton CEng MIEE MCMI. Born 3/10/30. Commd 24/9/52. Wg Cdr 3/10/70. Retd EDN 3/1/76.
PACKER F.W.J. Born 19/3/30. Commd 21/11/51. Flt Lt 6/3/57. Retd GD 19/3/68.
PACKMAN D. FInstPet FCMI FCIPS FRGS. Born 26/8/38. Commd 15/12/59. Gp Capt 1/7/85. Retd SUP 23/5/87.
PACKWOOD E.W.H. ACIS MCMI. Born 8/9/27. Commd 17/3/49. Gp Capt 1/7/77. Retd SEC 8/9/79.
PADBURY D.W. Born 22/7/30. Commd 13/2/52. Sqn Ldr 1/7/76. Retd GD 22/7/88.
PADDON A.E. BEd. Born 24/1/51. Commd 3/9/78. Sqn Ldr 1/1/89. Retd ADMIN 1/10/94.
PADGET P.I. LDS. Born 4/4/19. Commd 3/10/41. Wg Cdr 1/1/57. Retd DEL 31/10/72.
PADLEY P.G. Born 3/9/33. Commd 8/9/54. Wg Cdr 1/7/70. Retd GD 15/6/73.
PAGE A.M. BA. Born 21/10/56. Commd 5/5/77. Flt Lt 15/10/79. Retd GD 14/8/88.
PAGE B.S. Born 6/11/48. Commd 1/8/69. Gp Capt 1/7/98. Retd GD 6/11/03.
PAGE C.I. Born 10/12/54. Commd 18/4/74. Flt Lt 14/9/80. Retd GD(G) 28/5/82. Re-instated 25/4/84. Flt Lt 12/8/82. Retd GD(G) 14/3/96.
PAGE G.J. Born 7/11/30. Commd 21/8/54. Sqn Ldr 1/7/66. Retd GD 14/3/74.
PAGE G.M.B. BSc. Born 2/10/46. Commd 6/10/69. Wg Cdr 1/1/89. Retd GD 14/9/96.
PAGE J.S. Born 2/7/47. Commd 2/1/70. Sqn Ldr 1/1/88. Retd SY 14/3/96.
PAGE M.D. BSc. Born 22/9/61. Commd 29/4/84. Flt Lt 29/10/87. Retd SUP 14/9/96.
PAGE M.R. Born 22/12/64. Commd 10/5/90. Sqn Ldr 1/7/98. Retd ADMIN 22/12/02.
PAGE R.J. MCMI. Born 8/8/24. Commd 13/6/46. Sqn Ldr 1/1/60. Retd RGT 15/7/78.
PAGE R.S. Born 11/5/58. Commd 4/9/81. Flt Lt 4/3/88. Retd SUP 31/3/94.
PAGE S.L. BSc MCMI. Born 30/12/21. Commd 27/3/43. Wg Cdr 1/7/65. Retd ADMIN 30/12/76.
PAGE T.J. DFM. Born 24/1/22. Commd 19/7/44. Sqn Ldr 1/4/58. Retd SEC 10/5/68.
PAGE T.S. CEng MIEE. Born 10/11/43. Commd 15/7/65. Sqn Ldr 1/7/76. Retd ADMIN 10/11/87.
PAGE W.F. OBE AFC FCMI. Born 21/1/33. Commd 23/4/52. Gp Capt 1/1/77. Retd GD 2/1/91.
PAGET J.W.F. Born 29/5/29. Commd 5/7/53. Flt Lt 25/11/58. Retd GD 4/4/70.
PAICE R.H. Born 22/5/38. Commd 10/11/61. Flt Lt 1/4/66. Retd GD 1/4/76.
PAIN E.J. Born 20/6/34. Commd 7/1/71. Fg Offr 7/1/71. Retd ENG 14/1/76. rtg Flt Lt.
PAIN H. Born 27/8/21. Commd 18/11/43. Flt Lt 17/4/46. Retd GD(G) 31/8/73. rtg Sqn Ldr.
PAIN K.V. Born 8/1/38. Commd 16/5/74. Sqn Ldr 1/1/86. Retd ADMIN 14/10/89.
PAINES D.A.M. Born 14/7/31. Commd 10/12/52. Flt Lt 29/4/59. Retd GD 6/5/72.
PAINES J.D.B. MSc BA BA. Born 20/7/63. Commd 12/3/99. Sqn Ldr 1/7/00. Retd FLY(P) 28/2/04.
PAINTER A.S. Born 7/1/37. Commd 6/9/63. Sqn Ldr 1/1/76. Retd GD 18/6/79.
PAINTER K.P. Born 20/4/38. Commd 23/1/64. Flt Lt 8/8/66. Retd ADMIN 20/4/76.
PAINTING C.H. Born 11/1/29. Commd 3/11/05. Flt Lt 3/5/56. Retd GD 11/1/87.
PAISEY M.A.C. BA. Born 6/8/64. Commd 9/9/82. Flt Lt 15/10/86. Retd GD 15/7/97.
PAISH C.M. BA. Born 1/4/37. Commd 2/10/58. Sqn Ldr 1/7/68. Retd GD 10/10/88.
PAISH S.C. BA. Born 29/12/61. Commd 29/9/85. Flt Lt 29/3/87. Retd GD 29/9/01.
PAISLEY C.J. MIDPM. Born 27/5/46. Commd 23/9/66. Sqn Ldr 1/1/80. Retd SUP 27/5/90.
PAISLEY E.J. CEng MRAeS MIMechE. Born 13/1/33. Commd 8/2/57. Sqn Ldr 1/7/65. Retd ENG 8/2/73.
PAKES F. Born 7/8/19. Commd 29/4/43. Wg Cdr 1/7/69. Retd ENG 7/8/74.
PAKULA K. BSc. Born 7/2/20. Commd 5/4/49. Flt Lt 4/12/52. Retd GD(G) 22/11/65.
PALETHORPE H.W.O. Born 29/3/09. Commd 1/4/40. Flt Lt 1/4/42. Retd GD 21/12/45.
PALEY M.A. Born 25/8/41. Commd 12/3/60. Wg Cdr 1/1/86. Retd GD 25/6/94.
PALFREY M.J. Born 29/7/45. Commd 16/9/76. Flt Lt 16/9/78. Retd ENG 16/9/84.
PALIN G.R. PhD BSc CEng MRAeS. Born 23/4/30. Commd 28/10/55. Wg Cdr 28/3/70. Retd EDN 30/9/75.
PALIN Sir Roger KCB OBE MA FRAeS FCIPD. Born 8/7/38. Commd 21/1/63. ACM 22/4/91. Retd GD 1/7/93.
PALLISTER C.A.J. Born 19/10/39. Commd 14/11/59. Sqn Ldr 1/7/74. Retd GD 19/10/77.
PALLISTER I. BSc. Born 17/12/51. Commd 13/9/70. Wg Cdr 1/1/97. Retd GD 22/11/04.
PALLISTER M.A. BA MB BChir MRCGP MFCM MRCS LRCP DTM&H DPH DIH. Born 5/10/30. Commd 3/3/57. A Cdre 1/1/85. Retd MED 5/4/89.
PALMER A. MCMI. Born 27/3/21. Commd 29/6/44. Sqn Ldr 1/7/70. Retd SEC 27/3/76.
PALMER A.G. Born 11/9/10. Commd 10/8/44. Flt Lt 29/6/50. Retd SUP 6/1/58.
PALMER A.V.E. Born 11/10/23. Commd 3/4/45. Wg Cdr 1/1/65. Retd GD 2/4/74.
PALMER A.V.H. OBE. Born 23/5/22. Commd 28/7/49. Wg Cdr 1/1/66. Retd ENG 23/5/77.
PALMER A.V.M. MBE. Born 20/3/40. Commd 3/6/65. Sqn Ldr 1/1/75. Retd ADMIN 20/3/78.
PALMER B. Born 14/11/32. Commd 12/2/53. Wg Cdr 1/1/76. Retd GD(G) 4/12/82.
PALMER B.G. BA BEd. Born 20/8/47. Commd 4/9/72. Wg Cdr 1/7/90. Retd GD(G) 31/3/94.
PALMER B.J. BA. Born 18/5/20. Commd 19/10/49. Sqn Ldr 19/11/59. Retd EDN 1/11/64.
PALMER C.R. MBE AFC. Born 31/7/22. Commd 30/12/45. Sqn Ldr 1/7/66. Retd GD 1/4/73.
PALMER D.J. BSc. Born 18/12/50. Commd 28/8/73. Sqn Ldr 1/7/84. Retd ENG 14/9/90.
PALMER G.A.W. Born 6/12/32. Commd 26/3/64. Sqn Ldr 1/7/78. Retd ADMIN 12/5/89.

PALMER G.P. Born 22/11/38. Commd 17/3/67. Flt Lt 17/3/73. Retd ENG 1/9/76.
PALMER J. MBE. Born 11/9/18. Commd 15/4/43. Flt Lt 15/10/46. Retd ENG 19/6/54.
PALMER J.F. Born 17/11/19. Commd 22/8/46. Sqn Ldr 1/7/62. Retd ENG 16/11/74.
PALMER J.K. OBE. Born 10/6/30. Commd 27/9/51. Gp Capt 1/1/80. Retd GD 5/3/83.
PALMER L.J. Born 27/9/20. Commd 19/3/43. Sqn Ldr 1/7/54. Retd GD 1/4/61.
PALMER L.O. Born 3/6/13. Commd 12/8/43. Sqn Ldr 1/7/60. Retd ENG 3/6/69.
PALMER L.V. DPhysEd. Born 31/12/43. Commd 14/9/65. Wg Cdr 1/1/86. Retd ADMIN 14/3/96.
PALMER M.J.S. Born 23/11/42. Commd 23/6/67. A Cdre 1/7/91. Retd ENG 1/5/94.
PALMER M.W. BSc. Born 13/7/58. Commd 28/9/80. Wg Cdr 1/1/97. Retd SUP 28/9/02.
PALMER P.E. Born 15/3/49. Commd 11/11/71. Flt Lt 11/5/77. Retd FLY(P) 30/4/03.
PALMER R.C. Born 25/5/33. Commd 1/6/72. Flt Lt 1/6/75. Retd GD 25/5/88.
PALMER R.S. Born 2/2/33. Commd 21/11/51. Sqn Ldr 1/1/66. Retd SEC 2/2/71.
PALMER S.J. MCMI. Born 17/2/19. Commd 23/8/45. Sqn Ldr 1/7/62. Retd SEC 17/2/74.
PALMER S.J. OBE DFC MCMI. Born 21/9/22. Commd 3/9/43. Wg Cdr 1/7/66. Retd ADMIN 21/11/77.
PALMER T.J. Born 9/5/20. Commd 12/9/47. Sqn Ldr 1/7/68. Retd SEC 9/5/75.
PALMER W.J. Born 21/12/43. Commd 8/12/83. Sqn Ldr 31/12/96. Retd ENG 31/7/98.
PALOMEQUE A.G. BA MHCIMA DipAT. Born 4/10/62. Commd 7/12/86. Sqn Ldr 1/1/98. Retd ADMIN 7/12/02.
PAMPLIN B.P. Born 27/4/35. Commd 7/3/54. Wg Cdr 1/7/72. Retd GD(G) 3/4/82.
PANKHURST D.M. Born 30/5/28. Commd 19/3/62. Flt Lt 19/3/62. Retd GD 23/9/72.
PANTER W.J. Born 27/6/26. Commd 1/10/64. Flt Lt 1/10/64. Retd GD(G) 1/9/82.
PANTING P.D. BA. Born 3/5/24. Commd 24/10/45. Sqn Ldr 11/6/59. Retd EDN 31/8/68.
PANTON A. BSc. Born 21/7/63. Commd 2/9/84. Sqn Ldr 1/7/99. Retd ENGINEER 21/7/04.
PANTON A.D. CB OBE DFC. Born 2/11/16. Commd 18/12/37. A Cdre 1/7/67. Retd GD 18/12/72.
PANTON I.E. Born 25/4/53. Commd 18/1/73. Flt Lt 28/6/79. Retd ADMIN 25/4/91.
PANTON I.H. FCMI MInstAM. Born 23/12/28. Commd 23/4/53. Gp Capt 1/7/79. Retd GD 23/12/83.
PAPPIN V.G.H. BEd. Born 19/5/58. Commd 9/11/80. Flt Lt 9/11/84. Retd ADMIN 9/11/89.
PAPWORTH P.M. Born 5/5/33. Commd 5/4/55. Wg Cdr 1/7/75. Retd GD 1/10/83.
PAPWORTH P.R. Born 20/5/38. Commd 14/3/57. Flt Lt 14/6/63. Retd SEC 5/11/69.
PAPWORTH R.D.J. MB ChB DA. Born 5/1/41. Commd 18/7/71. Wg Cdr 5/5/79. Retd MED 20/8/87.
PARDO P.J. Born 4/7/49. Commd 8/10/70. Flt Lt 4/1/75. Retd GD 5/7/75.
PARFIT K.J. FCMI MCIPD. Born 20/3/24. Commd 3/9/43. Gp Capt 1/7/71. Retd GD 31/3/78.
PARFIT S.M. BSc. Born 31/3/64. Commd 30/3/86. Flt Lt 30/9/89. Retd ADMIN 14/9/96.
PARFITT I.G. Born 23/7/43. Commd 21/7/65. Flt Lt 11/8/70. Retd GD 15/5/84.
PARFITT R. Born 7/10/28. Commd 9/4/52. Flt Lt 9/10/54. Retd GD 25/5/56.
PARFITT R.A. ACMA. Born 17/10/23. Commd 22/3/45. Sqn Ldr 1/1/58. Retd GD 17/1/67.
PARFITT S.J.R. BSc. Born 22/12/52. Commd 30/9/73. Sqn Ldr 1/1/87. Retd GD 22/12/90.
PARHAM W.J. MBE. Born 16/2/18. Commd 30/8/45. Gp Capt 1/1/70. Retd SUP 16/2/73.
PARIS R.N. Born 4/12/24. Commd 26/2/51. Flt Lt 10/11/55. Retd GD 4/12/79.
PARISH G.E. Born 14/12/11. Commd 7/8/41. Fg Offr 7/8/41. Retd GD 22/2/46.
PARK A.J. CBE. Born 7/10/34. Commd 27/5/53. A Cdre 1/7/88. Retd GD 1/7/94.
PARK A.J. Born 10/6/48. Commd 1/8/69. Sqn Ldr 1/7/82. Retd GD 10/11/86.
PARK A.R. Born 6/9/64. Commd 15/3/84. Sqn Ldr 1/7/96. Retd OPS SPT 6/9/02.
PARK C.S. BSc. Born 28/8/74. Commd 8/2/98. Flt Lt 8/8/01. Retd ADMIN (SEC) 31/3/03.
PARK K.W. Born 23/3/55. Commd 6/10/77. Sqn Ldr 1/1/94. Retd GD 19/6/99.
PARK L. DFC. Born 7/5/22. Commd 30/10/43. Sqn Ldr 1/1/68. Retd GD(G) 31/3/77.
PARKER A.D. BSc. Born 25/4/52. Commd 11/1/76. Flt Lt 11/4/77. Retd GD 11/1/92.
PARKER A.F.B. Born 3/10/22. Commd 6/9/56. Flt Lt 6/9/62. Retd GD 28/12/63.
PARKER A.L. Born 27/6/47. Commd 20/10/67. Sqn Ldr 1/1/88. Retd FLY(N) 27/6/05.
PARKER A.P. Born 10/10/44. Commd 31/1/64. Flt Lt 31/7/69. Retd GD 12/8/70.
PARKER A.S. BA. Born 16/6/28. Commd 6/3/52. Sqn Ldr 6/9/61. Retd EDN 21/11/67.
PARKER C.J. BSc. Born 16/12/54. Commd 7/1/74. Flt Lt 15/4/78. Retd GD 15/7/88.
PARKER D.A. CEng MRAeS. Born 13/2/33. Commd 22/5/59. Wg Cdr 1/7/77. Retd ENG 17/12/83.
PARKER D.E. Born 9/3/31. Commd 21/10/66. Sqn Ldr 19/10/76. Retd MED(T) 1/6/80.
PARKER D.J. Born 21/7/36. Commd 13/2/60. Flt Lt 13/8/65. Retd GD 1/5/89.
PARKER D.M. MBE MB ChB. Born 6/5/29. Commd 21/11/54. Wg Cdr 4/5/67. Retd MED 21/11/70.
PARKER E.R. Born 15/5/37. Commd 24/1/74. Flt Lt 24/1/78. Retd GD(G) 29/11/82.
PARKER F.E. FIIE. Born 15/6/48. Commd 5/7/73. Wg Cdr 1/7/89. Retd ENG 14/3/97.
PARKER G.A. CEng MRAeS. Born 4/2/29. Commd 5/11/52. Flt Lt 5/11/57. Retd ENG 5/11/68.
PARKER G.B. Born 19/9/57. Commd 26/11/81. Flt Lt 26/5/87. Retd GD 19/1/89.
PARKER G.E. Born 13/6/10. Commd 24/10/41. Flt Lt 18/11/57. Retd SEC 28/6/62.
PARKER G.H. Born 6/6/48. Commd 13/2/86. Sqn Ldr 1/7/01. Retd ENGINEER 31/8/04.
PARKER G.R. MSc BSc. Born 6/12/40. Commd 31/12/63. Wg Cdr 1/1/84. Retd ADMIN 6/12/95.
PARKER H.B. Born 26/6/29. Commd 23/8/56. Fg Offr 23/11/58. Retd SEC 2/6/61.
PARKER H.M. FAAI MCMI. Born 3/12/31. Commd 31/5/51. Wg Cdr 1/1/81. Retd ADMIN 2/11/85.
PARKER J.A. MBE. Born 22/5/21. Commd 27/1/44. Gp Capt 1/7/68. Retd ENG 27/3/76.
PARKER J.C.L. Born 29/4/46. Commd 1/3/68. Flt Lt 8/3/72. Retd GD 10/1/75.

PARKER J.E. Born 15/2/53. Commd 15/12/88. Flt Lt 15/12/92. Retd ENG 17/4/93.
PARKER J.E. Born 21/3/49. Commd 11/8/69. Wg Cdr 1/1/90. Retd GD 21/3/04.
PARKER J.G. Born 5/2/64. Commd 19/6/86. Flt Lt 19/12/91. Retd FLY(P) 19/6/03.
PARKER J.I. AFC. Born 14/9/22. Commd 18/12/43. Wg Cdr 1/7/59. Retd GD 14/9/69.
PARKER J.J. Born 12/5/31. Commd 9/4/52. Sqn Ldr 1/7/67. Retd GD 9/12/75.
PARKER J.J. Born 25/3/36. Commd 29/11/63. Flt Lt 26/7/67. Retd GD 25/3/74.
PARKER J.R. Born 12/4/39. Commd 4/11/63. Flt Lt 29/7/67. Retd PI 12/4/77.
PARKER J.W. Born 9/12/48. Commd 21/2/74. Sqn Ldr 1/7/83. Retd ADMIN 9/12/86.
PARKER J.W.G. Born 12/11/20. Commd 11/7/43. Sqn Ldr 1/7/68. Retd ENG 12/11/75.
PARKER L.H.T. CEng MRAeS. Born 6/3/33. Commd 8/2/57. Wg Cdr 1/7/75. Retd ENG 4/2/86.
PARKER M.A. BSc. Born 11/7/63. Commd 30/8/81. Flt Lt 15/4/86. Retd GD 3/11/00.
PARKER M.J. BSc. Born 6/3/51. Commd 13/9/70. Sqn Ldr 1/7/84. Retd ENG 6/3/89.
PARKER N.A. Born 26/2/31. Commd 9/3/50. Flt Lt 18/2/58. Retd GD 26/2/69.
PARKER O.B. Born 11/11/16. Commd 7/1/43. Wg Cdr 1/7/61. Retd ENG 11/11/71.
PARKER R. Born 26/1/43. Commd 24/3/61. Wg Cdr 1/7/87. Retd GD 26/1/98.
PARKER R. Born 14/7/15. Commd 26/11/53. Sqn Ldr 1/1/64. Retd SUP 14/7/70.
PARKER R.C. Born 16/5/31. Commd 25/5/05. Gp Capt 1/1/79. Retd GD 16/5/86.
PARKER R.G. BA. Born 23/12/47. Commd 19/9/71. Wg Cdr 1/1/95. Retd ADMIN 23/12/02.
PARKER R.G. Born 8/12/49. Commd 20/10/85. Flt Lt 20/10/85. Retd ADMIN 20/10/91.
PARKER S.C.B. DFC MCIPS MCMI. Born 9/12/22. Commd 20/8/44. Wg Cdr 1/7/71. Retd SUP 9/12/77.
PARKER S.R. Born 28/8/67. Commd 24/7/97. Flt Lt 24/7/99. Retd OPS SPT(ATC) 30/8/04.
PARKER T.E. Born 25/6/63. Commd 4/11/82. Flt Lt 31/3/89. Retd SUP 14/3/96.
PARKER T.J. Born 22/3/63. Commd 8/4/82. Sqn Ldr 1/1/01. Retd GD 11/10/02.
PARKER W.D. Born 19/8/22. Commd 4/9/58. Flt Lt 4/9/61. Retd PI 19/9/74.
PARKER W.I. MCMI. Born 24/5/40. Commd 18/5/61. Flt Lt 28/12/66. Retd GD 8/10/70. Re-employed 11/7/69.
    Retd ADMIN Sqn Ldr 6/4/83.
PARKER W.M. Born 19/6/34. Commd 26/10/61. Wg Cdr 1/7/79. Retd GD 19/6/89.
PARKER-ASHLEY A.N.S. MA BSc MRAeS. Born 18/11/38. Commd 9/9/63. Wg Cdr 1/1/78. Retd GD 12/9/83.
PARKER-EATON R.G. MBE MCMI. Born 21/11/31. Commd 20/10/50. Wg Cdr 1/7/67. Retd SUP 13/7/74.
PARKER-HOARE M.J. Born 12/2/35. Commd 9/2/66. Flt Lt 9/2/72. Retd ADMIN 30/9/78.
PARKES A. BSc. Born 20/1/33. Commd 22/1/54. Gp Capt 1/1/80. Retd GD 20/1/91.
PARKES W.B. Born 27/4/19. Commd 18/2/23. Flt Lt 18/8/46. Retd GD 21/6/50.
PARKHOUSE R.C.L. Born 4/2/21. Commd 7/3/40. Sqn Ldr 1/1/54. Retd SEC 31/8/73.
PARKHURST C.R. Born 24/5/49. Commd 4/7/69. Wg Cdr 1/7/89. Retd GD 24/5/04.
PARKIN A.G. Born 25/5/47. Commd 29/7/65. Sqn Ldr 1/1/84. Retd GD(G) 1/3/93.
PARKIN C.S. Born 28/8/38. Commd 15/12/59. Sqn Ldr 1/7/70. Retd SUP 28/8/76.
PARKIN E.G. Born 21/4/17. Commd 26/5/40. Flt Lt 1/12/53. Retd GD(G) 21/4/72.
PARKIN H.V. Born 3/9/17. Commd 5/10/43. Flt Lt 27/5/54. Retd GD 1/4/62.
PARKIN J. Born 27/5/42. Commd 31/1/80. Sqn Ldr 1/7/90. Retd ENG 14/3/96.
PARKIN L.W.R. MBE MCMI. Born 22/5/32. Commd 12/9/63. Wg Cdr 1/1/84. Retd ENG 22/5/92.
PARKIN M. Born 31/7/49. Commd 22/5/75. Sqn Ldr 1/7/86. Retd GD 15/4/95.
PARKIN N.D. MB BS MRCS LRCP MRCPath DCP. Born 12/8/31. Commd 2/7/52. Wg Cdr 11/6/72. Retd MED 23/5/76.
PARKIN R.D. MBE MMAR. Born 11/2/32. Commd 13/11/62. Wg Cdr 1/1/77. Retd MAR 13/11/80.
PARKINSON C.L. MA. Born 26/3/29. Commd 10/9/51. A Cdre 1/1/77. Retd ENG 14/8/79.
PARKINSON D. Born 18/5/38. Commd 2/4/64. Flt Lt 1/7/69. Retd GD 18/5/76.
PARKINSON D. DFM MCMI. Born 27/8/24. Commd 3/11/44. Sqn Ldr 1/1/71. Retd SEC 23/7/79.
PARKINSON D.J. Born 5/9/35. Commd 12/3/60. Flt Lt 12/9/65. Retd GD 5/9/90.
PARKINSON G.E. MA BSc. Born 6/4/65. Commd 1/6/92. Sqn Ldr 1/1/01. Retd ADMIN (TRG) 6/4/03.
PARKINSON J. Born 10/5/45. Commd 22/11/84. Flt Lt 22/11/88. Retd SUP 12/7/93.
PARKINSON J.B. Born 29/11/34. Commd 16/11/56. Gp Capt 1/7/81. Retd GD 1/1/87.
PARKINSON R.C.C. FHCIMA FCMI. Born 24/10/43. Commd 9/3/66. Wg Cdr 1/7/85. Retd ADMIN 2/6/93.
PARKINSON R.K. Born 12/11/23. Commd 3/11/44. Sqn Ldr 1/4/55. Retd GD 12/11/91.
PARKINSON T.W. Born 5/10/45. Commd 15/7/66. Wg Cdr 1/1/81. Retd ENG 12/12/84.
PARKINSON W.N. MA BSc CEng MIMechE MCIPD. Born 26/4/58. Commd 19/6/88. Sqn Ldr 1/1/95.
    Retd ADMIN (TRG) 19/6/04.
PARKS H.E. DPhysEd. Born 23/12/24. Commd 13/8/52. Flt Lt 13/8/56. Retd PE 1/4/72. rtg Sqn Ldr.
PARKS P.J. MBE. Born 1/1/20. Commd 22/9/49. Sqn Ldr 1/7/61. Retd ENG 1/1/75.
PARKYN J.E. Born 16/12/47. Commd 24/6/76. Flt Lt 24/6/79. Retd ADMIN 6/12/85.
PARLOR S.M. BSc. Born 7/6/66. Commd 11/2/93. Flt Lt 4/10/95. Retd ADMIN (P ED) 4/4/05.
PARLOUR A.W. DFC. Born 3/9/22. Commd 24/8/43. Flt Lt 27/7/47. Retd GD 1/10/60.
PARMEE R.J. MCMI. Born 12/5/48. Commd 18/1/73. Sqn Ldr 1/7/87. Retd ADMIN 1/9/99.
PARMINTER L.M.T. Born 12/2/64. Commd 8/12/83. Flt Lt 2/6/90. Retd GD 19/5/00.
PARNABY J.D. BA LLB. Born 1/7/41. Commd 26/5/70. Wg Cdr 1/1/89. Retd ADMIN 1/7/96.
PARNELL F.G. Born 26/12/40. Commd 8/4/82. Flt Lt 1/3/87. Retd ENG 26/12/95.
PARNELL J.T.W. Born 25/9/10. Commd 25/4/40. Fg Offr 4/1/41. Retd ASD 3/12/45. rtg Sqn Ldr.
PARNELL M.A. BSc MRAeS MRIN. Born 6/7/55. Commd 16/9/73. Flt Lt 15/4/78. Retd GD 25/7/93.

PARNELL-HOPKINSON C. The Rev. Born 1/8/46. Commd 19/2/84. Retd Wg Cdr 1/8/01.
PARR A.W. AFC. Born 17/10/33. Commd 23/7/52. Wg Cdr 1/7/73. Retd GD 29/5/88.
PARR D. Born 9/10/49. Commd 8/8/69. Sqn Ldr 1/1/87. Retd SUP 9/10/90.
PARR G. Born 26/8/39. Commd 24/2/64. Flt Lt 4/11/70. Retd GD 7/10/79.
PARR G.E.R. Born 23/11/19. Commd 26/8/42. Sqn Ldr 1/7/53. Retd GD 20/11/59.
PARR J.J.E. Born 12/2/49. Commd 27/2/70. Wg Cdr 1/7/90. Retd GD 14/9/96.
PARR J.L. AIB. Born 17/10/42. Commd 4/9/87. Wg Cdr 1/1/91. Retd ADMIN 1/7/93.
PARR J.M. Born 29/11/32. Commd 20/10/55. Sqn Ldr 1/7/80. Retd ADMIN 17/1/89.
PARR R.I. Born 29/12/44. Commd 18/11/66. Fg Offr 29/12/67. Retd GD 14/2/70.
PARRATT D. Born 3/4/29. Commd 14/12/49. Gp Capt 1/7/73. Retd GD 4/3/80.
PARRINI A.L. Born 11/9/46. Commd 25/6/66. Sqn Ldr 1/7/83. Retd SUP 11/9/90.
PARROTT D.N.H. Born 26/1/18. Commd 2/6/44. Flt Lt 18/9/48. Retd GD(G) 26/1/73.
PARRY C.H. Born 18/3/25. Commd 17/11/44. Gp Capt 1/1/77. Retd GD 18/3/80.
PARRY D.G. MBE BA. Born 18/5/62. Commd 31/8/80. Wg Cdr 1/1/97. Retd ADMIN 1/10/99.
PARRY D.J. DFC. Born 8/10/21. Commd 10/9/43. Flt Lt 10/9/49. Retd GD(G) 8/10/71.
PARRY D.J. MRAeS. Born 28/12/34. Commd 10/2/56. Sqn Ldr 1/1/68. Retd GD 28/12/72.
PARRY D.M. Born 12/7/33. Commd 1/8/69. Sqn Ldr 1/7/79. Retd SEC 12/7/83.
PARRY G.F. CEng MIEE. Born 1/4/38. Commd 23/1/64. Gp Capt 1/1/85. Retd ENG 10/4/88.
PARRY G.R. Born 11/12/54. Commd 16/2/89. Flt Lt 16/2/91. Retd ENG 16/2/97.
PARRY I.E. MCMI. Born 22/12/21. Commd 15/10/43. Sqn Ldr 1/7/60. Retd SUP 1/10/70.
PARRY I.J. Born 22/5/38. Commd 6/10/77. Flt Lt 6/10/83. Retd MED(SEC) 22/5/88.
PARRY I.S. BSc MS CEng MIEE. Born 10/5/38. Commd 30/9/57. Wg Cdr 1/7/74. Retd ENG 19/12/81.
PARRY I.T. Born 8/9/41. Commd 20/7/66. Flt Lt 1/7/69. Retd GD 8/9/96.
PARRY J.K. BSc. Born 21/12/40. Commd 2/10/61. Sqn Ldr 1/7/70. Retd GD 21/12/78.
PARRY M.L.P. Born 4/12/40. Commd 22/3/63. Flt Lt 4/6/66. Retd GD 29/4/78.
PARRY N.M.S. Born 25/11/43. Commd 12/7/63. Flt Lt 8/9/70. Retd GD 3/1/76.
PARRY P.W.P. MBE. Born 19/3/48. Commd 29/3/68. Sqn Ldr 1/1/81. Retd RGT 19/6/92.
PARRY R. Born 30/11/62. Commd 2/2/84. Flt Lt 2/8/89. Retd GD 14/3/96.
PARRY R.D. Born 17/12/48. Commd 31/7/70. Flt Lt 31/7/73. Retd GD 17/12/86.
PARRY R.M. BEng. Born 4/3/65. Commd 31/7/90. Sqn Ldr 1/1/02. Retd ENGINEER 1/1/05.
PARRY-EVANS Sir David GCB CBE. Born 19/7/35. Commd 4/12/56. ACM 1/7/89. Retd GD 29/2/92.
PARRY-EVANS R. Born 31/10/23. Commd 16/7/56. Flt Lt 16/7/56. Retd CAT 11/3/67.
PARSLEY R.R.C. OBE. Born 22/3/43. Commd 17/12/65. Wg Cdr 1/7/84. Retd GD 22/3/98.
PARSLOW A. IEng FRAeS. Born 5/9/37. Commd 1/9/85. Sqn Ldr 1/1/88. Retd ENG 25/10/91.
PARSONS B.K. Born 11/9/45. Commd 6/9/63. Wg Cdr 1/1/82. Retd GD 1/1/85.
PARSONS B.W. CBE DFC AFC FCMI. Born 12/4/20. Commd 5/12/42. A Cdre 1/7/70. Retd GD 26/8/75.
PARSONS C.A. MB BS FRCS FRCR LRCP DMRD. Born 1/10/40. Commd 10/9/62. Sqn Ldr 18/2/71.
    Retd MED 1/10/76.
PARSONS C.H.J. TD. Born 29/3/20. Commd 31/10/47. Sqn Ldr 1/7/52. Retd RGT 15/11/58.
PARSONS C.J. MCMI. Born 6/2/45. Commd 6/5/65. Wg Cdr 1/1/88. Retd ADMIN 24/1/98.
PARSONS C.K. BSc. Born 7/6/43. Commd 19/11/64. Flt Lt 6/6/67. Retd GD 29/3/74.
PARSONS D. Born 1/10/52. Commd 15/8/85. Flt Lt 15/8/87. Retd SUP 14/3/96.
PARSONS D.L. Born 2/5/34. Commd 14/12/54. Sqn Ldr 1/7/65. Retd GD 31/12/71.
PARSONS D.W. MVO FCMI. Born 27/11/35. Commd 12/1/55. Wg Cdr 1/7/72. Retd GD 3/4/80.
PARSONS E. Born 14/9/39. Commd 14/5/60. Flt Lt 14/11/65. Retd GD 5/2/78.
PARSONS E.A. Born 21/1/37. Commd 3/5/68. Sqn Ldr 1/1/78. Retd ADMIN 1/4/84.
PARSONS F.H. BA. Born 1/9/23. Commd 24/9/63. Sqn Ldr 24/3/67. Retd EDN 24/9/79.
PARSONS G.A. BA. Born 23/10/62. Commd 16/2/86. Flt Lt 16/8/89. Retd OPS SPT 4/4/02.
PARSONS G.C. MSc BSc ARCS. Born 20/8/42. Commd 28/9/80. Sqn Ldr 1/1/88. Retd ADMIN 20/8/97.
PARSONS J.B. MB BS MRCS LRCP FFARCS. Born 21/1/26. Commd 4/1/51. Wg Cdr 26/6/63. Retd MED 25/12/68.
PARSONS J.D. Born 13/2/28. Commd 1/6/49. Flt Lt 8/1/59. Retd GD 13/2/66.
PARSONS M. MBE DPhysEd. Born 18/6/44. Commd 17/8/68. Sqn Ldr 1/7/81. Retd ADMIN 1/5/94.
PARSONS P.I. Born 28/2/49. Commd 31/7/70. Flt Lt 31/7/76. Retd SY 28/2/93.
PARSONS P.M. Born 26/11/20. Commd 3/10/45. Flt Offr 3/10/51. Retd SEC 5/6/65.
PARSONS R.M. Born 10/7/46. Commd 6/5/83. Sqn Ldr 1/1/91. Retd ENG 1/9/98.
PARSONS S.R. OBE CEng MRAeS. Born 28/7/39. Commd 7/5/64. Gp Capt 1/7/82. Retd ENG 26/11/84.
PARTINGTON G.R. BEM. Born 13/11/42. Commd 2/2/65. Sqn Ldr 1/1/78. Retd ENG 2/2/83.
PARTINGTON J.A. MBE BSc. Born 8/6/38. Commd 13/11/62. Wg Cdr 1/1/82. Retd ENG 8/6/93.
PARTINGTON T.G. BSc(Eng). Born 17/5/55. Commd 2/9/73. Flt Lt 15/10/77. Retd GD 15/7/88.
PARTRIDGE B.C. MBE. Born 1/11/22. Commd 29/3/56. Sqn Ldr 1/1/70. Retd ENG 31/10/73.
PARTRIDGE B.L. Born 9/10/22. Commd 1/1/43. Wg Cdr 1/1/59. Retd GD 9/7/61.
PARTRIDGE D.J. Born 24/12/71. Commd 17/9/90. Fg Offr 15/7/92. Retd GD 1/5/95.
PARTRIDGE J.E. DSO DFC*. Born 23/3/14. Commd 1/5/42. Sqn Ldr 1/7/58. Retd SEC 6/4/69. rtg Wg Cdr.
PARTRIDGE J.M. Born 10/9/26. Commd 25/8/60. Sqn Ldr 1/1/72. Retd ENG 10/9/81.
PARTRIDGE R.H. Born 27/11/44. Commd 25/3/64. Flt Lt 12/11/69. Retd GD 30/9/78.
PARTRIDGE R.W. Born 22/2/54. Commd 1/12/77. Flt Lt 1/6/84. Retd SUP 15/8/93.

PARTRIDGE R.W. BSc. Born 21/7/56. Commd 3/1/82. Flt Lt 23/6/82. Retd ENG 11/2/93.
PARTRIDGE S.J. Born 7/4/57. Commd 28/10/76. Flt Lt 28/4/83. Retd SY 7/4/95.
PASCALL A.R.J. Born 23/9/39. Commd 23/6/64. Wg Cdr 1/1/80. Retd ADMIN 22/7/87.
PASCO D. Born 21/9/37. Commd 17/10/59. Sqn Ldr 1/7/71. Retd GD 30/10/76.
PASCOE D.T.C. CEng MIEE. Born 8/4/17. Commd 18/7/46. Sqn Ldr 28/8/59. Retd ENG 8/4/72.
PASCOE P.W. AFC. Born 18/1/34. Commd 5/11/52. Flt Lt 24/3/58. Retd GD 30/9/77.
PASCOE S.V. Born 2/10/18. Commd 5/11/42. Flt Lt 17/5/56. Retd GD(G) 29/3/61.
PASH N.E. Born 25/1/20. Commd 27/9/46. Flt Lt 19/11/53. Retd GD 7/10/61.
PASKETT G. Born 16/6/46. Commd 4/12/64. Flt Lt 4/6/70. Retd GD 3/12/75.
PASS D.M. BA. Born 7/8/35. Commd 8/8/58. Sqn Ldr 8/2/68. Retd ADMIN 7/8/93.
PASS L. MBE. Born 26/4/22. Commd 6/10/60. Sqn Ldr 1/1/70. Retd ENG 30/7/73.
PASSBY D.C. BA DipEd. Born 9/5/33. Commd 26/1/56. Sqn Ldr 22/6/65. Retd ADMIN 9/5/88.
PASSFIELD R.F. Born 17/8/32. Commd 13/9/51. Sqn Ldr 1/7/80. Retd GD 17/8/92.
PATCH T.J. MSc BA CDipAF. Born 16/7/59. Commd 11/9/77. Wg Cdr 1/7/95. Retd SUP 1/6/02.
PATCHETT C.H. Born 19/12/50. Commd 28/11/74. Flt Lt 28/5/80. Retd GD 12/8/90.
PATCHING C. BSc. Born 20/6/63. Commd 13/9/81. Sqn Ldr 1/7/95. Retd ADMIN 20/6/02.
PATCHING E.J. Born 22/7/61. Commd 8/9/83. Flt Lt 8/3/89. Retd GD 22/10/99.
PATEL M.R. OBE BSc CEng MRAeS. Born 10/2/44. Commd 6/10/71. Wg Cdr 1/1/88. Retd ENG 5/10/02.
PATERSON A.W. Born 17/7/26. Commd 25/10/46. Flt Lt 25/4/50. Retd GD 21/1/59.
PATERSON C.R. Born 19/9/38. Commd 25/7/60. Sqn Ldr 1/7/70. Retd GD 19/9/93.
PATERSON D.F.M. BA. Born 27/2/54. Commd 14/11/76. Flt Lt 14/8/77. Retd GD 14/11/88.
PATERSON D.S. Born 11/7/20. Commd 20/12/57. Flt Lt 20/12/63. Retd CAT 17/7/70.
PATERSON G.A. BSc CEng FCMI FRAeS FIEE. Born 29/5/48. Commd 27/2/70. Gp Capt 1/7/94. Retd GD 29/5/03.
PATERSON G.H. DPhysEd. Born 18/9/29. Commd 21/12/52. Flt Lt 21/12/57. Retd PE 4/1/68. rtg Sqn Ldr.
PATERSON J. LLB. Born 7/5/40. Commd 10/2/59. Flt Lt 12/8/64. Retd GD 7/5/78.
PATERSON J.G. MB ChB FRCR DMRD. Born 14/7/37. Commd 3/3/63. Wg Cdr 7/9/75. Retd MED 3/3/79.
PATERSON L.C. MSc BSc CPhys MInstP CEng. Born 10/9/50. Commd 25/5/80. Wg Cdr 1/1/94. Retd ADMIN 25/5/96.
PATERSON M. LLB. Born 5/1/57. Commd 17/8/80. Flt Lt 17/11/80. Retd GD 14/3/96.
PATERSON M. DFC. Born 15/4/15. Commd 5/2/41. Wg Cdr 1/1/55. Retd GD 9/12/66.
PATERSON N.S. Born 14/1/22. Commd 17/7/46. Flt Lt 19/11/53. Retd RGT 25/1/67.
PATON B.J. Born 7/8/50. Commd 15/9/69. Sqn Ldr 1/1/87. Retd GD 1/1/90.
PATON D.McL. MRAeS MCMI. Born 17/8/44. Commd 17/5/63. Wg Cdr 1/7/88. Retd GD 1/10/91.
PATON G. Born 25/1/58. Commd 26/11/81. Sqn Ldr 1/1/94. Retd GD 1/1/97.
PATON J.A. Born 20/6/22. Commd 9/7/44. Sqn Ldr 1/1/58. Retd GD 28/2/61.
PATON M.A. Born 10/10/62. Commd 11/5/86. Flt Lt 11/5/92. Retd ADMIN 2/9/99.
PATON N. BEd MHCIMA. Born 30/3/48. Commd 20/1/80. Fg Offr 20/4/79. Retd ADMIN 14/4/81.
PATRICK D.A. Born 2/10/23. Commd 23/2/49. Flt Lt 14/10/52. Retd GD 30/6/67.
PATRICK D.R. Born 9/7/29. Commd 12/9/50. Sqn Ldr 1/1/61. Retd GD 5/7/76.
PATRICK G.A. Born 7/11/30. Commd 20/12/51. Flt Lt 8/12/66. Retd GD 18/4/72.
PATRICK H.N. Born 22/10/43. Commd 14/8/64. Sqn Ldr 1/1/83. Retd GD 30/9/89.
PATRICK I.W. Born 26/9/42. Commd 2/2/68. Sqn Ldr 1/1/90. Retd GD(G) 19/12/92.
PATRICK J.W. Born 9/10/24. Commd 8/9/44. Flt Lt 8/3/48. Retd GD 9/10/62.
PATRICK K.B. Born 3/8/45. Commd 3/9/65. Sqn Ldr 1/7/81. Retd GD 1/7/84.
PATRICK R.A. Born 21/3/44. Commd 6/5/65. Flt Lt 8/3/72. Retd GD(G) 21/3/82.
PATRICK R.C. DFC* AFC. Born 8/10/17. Commd 14/12/38. Wg Cdr 1/7/55. Retd GD 10/10/64.
PATRICK R.I. Born 9/12/47. Commd 11/8/67. Flt Lt 11/5/73. Retd GD 16/6/85.
PATRICK S.N. BSc. Born 17/4/61. Commd 26/5/85. Sqn Ldr 1/7/00. Retd OPS SPT(ATC) 1/7/03.
PATTEN T.J. MA. Born 23/3/41. Commd 30/12/63. Sqn Ldr 1/1/76. Retd SEC 30/3/81.
PATTEN V.E.G. MCMI. Born 23/1/39. Commd 20/1/63. Wg Cdr 1/7/83. Retd ENG 1/8/89.
PATTENDEN G.E.P. LLB FCIS. Born 31/12/47. Commd 22/7/71. Wg Cdr 1/7/99. Retd ADMIN 30/9/01.
PATTERSON A.H.R. Born 8/10/29. Commd 21/6/56. Flt Lt 21/12/59. Retd GD 30/9/77.
PATTERSON D.H. Born 21/7/51. Commd 4/2/71. Sqn Ldr 1/7/88. Retd GD 1/7/91.
PATTERSON E.J.A. OBE. Born 14/5/23. Commd 28/8/42. Wg Cdr 1/1/61. Retd GD 31/3/78.
PATTERSON G. Born 30/10/23. Commd 2/10/50. Flt Lt 26/9/56. Retd GD 31/3/62.
PATTERSON H. MBE. Born 18/3/20. Commd 14/1/48. Flt Lt 14/7/51. Retd SUP 3/4/57.
PATTERSON J. Born 20/12/15. Commd 8/10/42. Flt Lt 8/4/46. Retd ENG 23/12/64.
PATTERSON J.A. Born 28/11/20. Commd 24/3/44. Flt Lt 7/6/51. Retd SEC 28/11/69.
PATTERSON J.R. CEng MIEE. Born 30/6/43. Commd 18/7/63. Wg Cdr 1/1/88. Retd ENG 18/7/97.
PATTERSON L.J. BSc. Born 30/8/60. Commd 15/5/79. Flt Lt 15/4/82. Retd GD 8/10/96.
PATTERSON M. MBE. Born 30/4/39. Commd 26/10/62. Sqn Ldr 1/7/77. Retd GD 14/5/90.
PATTERSON M.G. MSc BSc(EurIng) CEng MRAeS. Born 13/10/53. Commd 17/9/72. Sqn Ldr 1/1/85.
    Retd ENG 3/12/96.
PATTERSON P.J. MRIN MCMI. Born 18/10/36. Commd 28/2/56. Wg Cdr 1/1/80. Retd GD 10/12/86.
PATTERSON R. Born 16/8/36. Commd 5/3/57. Flt Lt 6/3/63. Retd GD 10/9/74.
PATTERSON R. Born 3/9/44. Commd 7/7/67. Flt Lt 7/1/73. Retd GD 31/3/95.
PATTERSON S. Born 7/3/23. Commd 28/5/66. Flt Lt 28/5/71. Retd ENG 7/3/78.

PATTIE A.S. CBE FHCIMA. Born 10/3/17. Commd 17/10/41. Gp Capt 1/7/66. Retd CAT 10/3/72.
PATTINSON A.G.S. Born 5/5/31. Commd 27/6/51. Flt Lt 27/12/55. Retd GD 9/1/60.
PATTINSON I.D. OBE MA CEng MIEE MRAeS DipEL. Born 21/2/28. Commd 19/2/51. Wg Cdr 1/1/75. Retd ENG 4/1/83.
PATTINSON R.W.B. Born 17/1/42. Commd 14/9/64. Flt Lt 4/5/72. Retd GD 14/9/80.
PATTISON F. Born 2/5/50. Commd 28/7/88. Flt Lt 28/7/92. Retd ENG 1/9/00.
PATTISON G.E. Born 16/12/48. Commd 7/1/73. Flt Lt 4/3/76. Retd MAR 1/4/86.
PATTISON J. Born 9/3/29. Commd 28/3/63. Sqn Ldr 10/10/73. Retd MED(SEC) 28/5/75.
PATTRICK R.V. BEM. Born 19/5/25. Commd 30/7/59. Wg Cdr 1/1/77. Retd ENG 28/4/79.
PAUL D.M. Born 22/5/40. Commd 19/12/61. Wg Cdr 1/7/91. Retd GD 2/6/95.
PAUL G.J.C. CB DFC. Born 31/10/07. Commd 20/6/27. A Cdre 1/1/54. Retd GD 6/10/58.
PAUL I.S.M. DipEl. Born 19/11/13. Commd 26/2/53. Flt Lt 26/2/58. Retd ENG 15/12/69.
PAUL R.E. AFC. Born 11/3/22. Commd 10/4/43. Sqn Ldr 1/7/54. Retd GD 11/3/71.
PAULETTE P.D.A. Born 8/9/30. Commd 28/2/57. Flt Lt 28/8/61. Retd GD 8/9/68.
PAVELEY D.J. BA CertEd. Born 12/5/64. Commd 11/10/87. Flt Lt 11/4/90. Retd ADMIN (P ED) 11/10/03.
PAVELEY R.G. BEd. Born 8/1/35. Commd 9/2/55. Flt Lt 10/8/60. Retd GD 8/1/73. Re-instated 15/4/81. Flt Lt 15/11/68. Retd GD 6/5/90.
PAVEY C.W.J. Born 8/10/16. Commd 30/7/46. Flt Lt 20/7/54. Retd GD(G) 8/10/73.
PAVEY F.T. Born 1/7/20. Commd 16/11/61. Flt Lt 16/11/64. Retd GD 1/7/75.
PAVEY M.T. The Rev. ALCD. Born 29/2/32. Commd 1/1/64. Retd Wg Cdr 1/1/80.
PAVEY R.E. Born 26/1/44. Commd 19/4/63. Wg Cdr 1/1/84. Retd GD(G) 31/3/94.
PAVIS E.J. DPhysEd. Born 8/4/36. Commd 14/8/62. Sqn Ldr 1/1/80. Retd ADMIN 1/2/86.
PAWLEY D.E. BA MCIPD. Born 15/4/39. Commd 10/9/63. Sqn Ldr 10/9/75. Retd ADMIN 20/10/84.
PAWSON A.W. MCMI. Born 25/5/19. Commd 21/4/44. Wg Cdr 1/7/62. Retd ENG 20/5/75.
PAWSON J.B. Born 29/6/40. Commd 5/5/69. Wg Cdr 1/7/83. Retd GD(G) 14/7/85.
PAWSON P.T. Born 18/10/46. Commd 31/7/86. Flt Lt 31/7/90. Retd ENGINEER 18/10/03.
PAWSON T.W. Born 4/5/32. Commd 7/9/61. Wg Cdr 1/1/79. Retd GD 31/12/83.
PAXTON J.L. Born 1/6/31. Commd 3/8/51. Wg Cdr 1/7/80. Retd SUP 2/6/84.
PAXTON T.R. Born 26/5/50. Commd 14/2/69. Sqn Ldr 1/7/88. Retd GD 1/7/91.
PAYLING J.D. Born 13/7/30. Commd 28/7/49. Gp Capt 1/7/72. Retd GD 7/4/79.
PAYN A.J. OBE. Born 11/9/18. Commd 17/12/38. Wg Cdr 1/1/51. Retd GD 11/9/67.
PAYN A.L. Born 1/11/61. Commd 5/2/81. Wg Cdr 1/1/98. Retd ADMIN 1/1/01.
PAYNE A.V. Born 13/5/44. Commd 1/4/66. Flt Lt 1/10/71. Retd GD 29/8/98.
PAYNE B.E.N. Born 12/3/32. Commd 22/1/54. Sqn Ldr 1/7/71. Retd SUP 1/8/85.
PAYNE D. Born 7/6/36. Commd 12/3/60. Flt Lt 12/9/65. Retd GD 7/6/74.
PAYNE F.L. Born 23/9/10. Commd 7/11/40. Flt Lt 1/4/46. Retd ENG 28/4/47. rtg Sqn Ldr.
PAYNE F.P.G. Born 24/9/14. Commd 22/5/44. Flt Lt 22/11/47. Retd GD 21/9/53.
PAYNE G. Born 19/1/25. Commd 6/6/57. Flt Lt 1/4/63. Retd GD 1/10/68.
PAYNE G.W. Born 14/2/29. Commd 26/7/50. Sqn Ldr 1/1/62. Retd GD 14/2/84.
PAYNE H.W. Born 25/5/10. Commd 27/1/44. Flt Lt 30/4/55. Retd GD(G) 31/3/62.
PAYNE J.M. The Rev. MA. Born 13/2/17. Commd 7/12/44. Retd Gp Capt 7/3/72.
PAYNE K.W. Born 12/8/29. Commd 17/5/51. Sqn Ldr 1/1/64. Retd GD 12/8/84.
PAYNE M.A. Born 7/3/56. Commd 27/3/86. Fg Offr 23/11/84. Retd SUP 11/6/88.
PAYNE M.J. Born 8/2/58. Commd 23/10/86. Sqn Ldr 1/1/00. Retd OPS SPT(REGT) 1/1/04.
PAYNE M.T. Born 9/5/35. Commd 19/8/58. Flt Lt 24/9/65. Retd GD 22/5/74.
PAYNE N.G. DFC. Born 31/1/22. Commd 3/9/42. Sqn Ldr 1/1/59. Retd SEC 1/1/66.
PAYNE R. AFC. Born 24/1/44. Commd 22/3/63. Flt Lt 22/9/68. Retd GD 24/1/82.
PAYNE R.A. BA. Born 3/5/60. Commd 15/8/82. Flt Lt 15/11/83. Retd GD 15/8/98.
PAYNE R.E.G. Born 20/11/25. Commd 25/10/50. Sqn Ldr 1/7/63. Retd GD 19/3/76.
PAYNE R.H. Born 20/5/20. Commd 25/2/42. Sqn Ldr 1/7/66. Retd GD 2/7/68.
PAYNE R.J. Born 10/5/31. Commd 17/10/71. Flt Lt 17/5/74. Retd ENG 10/5/89.
PAYNE R.L. MCMI. Born 20/6/34. Commd 23/9/65. Sqn Ldr 1/7/79. Retd ADMIN 10/8/87.
PAYNE R.N. MA BA. Born 1/12/38. Commd 30/9/57. Wg Cdr 1/7/79. Retd ENG 28/9/94.
PAYNE R.W. AFC. Born 23/9/22. Commd 15/10/44. Wg Cdr 1/1/60. Retd GD 23/9/77.
PAYNE S.M. Born 28/4/59. Commd 2/11/88. Flt Lt 2/11/90. Retd OPS SPT(ATC) 28/4/03.
PAYNE S.R. Born 1/5/61. Commd 15/10/81. Flt Lt 15/4/88. Retd ADMIN 14/3/97.
PAYTON D. Born 19/3/44. Commd 31/1/64. Sqn Ldr 1/1/77. Retd GD 19/3/82.
PEACE B.W. Born 12/6/28. Commd 12/8/52. Flt Lt 12/5/58. Retd GD 12/6/66.
PEACE N.A. Born 20/8/29. Commd 3/10/69. Sqn Ldr 1/1/79. Retd ENG 20/8/87.
PEACEY A.W.D. Born 6/3/29. Commd 5/12/51. Sqn Ldr 1/1/68. Retd GD 25/6/76.
PEACH R.M. MRIN. Born 6/1/43. Commd 28/10/66. Wg Cdr 1/1/85. Retd GD 2/4/93.
PEACHEY M.J. BSc CEng MIMechE. Born 4/1/43. Commd 15/7/65. Sqn Ldr 1/1/74. Retd ENG 21/8/76.
PEACOCK D.A. DFC. Born 28/12/17. Commd 21/12/36. Sqn Ldr 1/7/50. Retd GD 7/2/58. rtg Wg Cdr.
PEACOCK J.A. Born 18/11/34. Commd 21/10/66. Flt Lt 12/11/69. Retd GD(G) 18/11/94.
PEACOCK J.C. Born 28/11/64. Commd 21/12/89. Sqn Ldr 1/7/99. Retd ENG 28/11/02.
PEACOCK J.H. Born 23/1/32. Commd 27/6/63. Flt Lt 27/6/63. Retd GD 15/8/68.

PEACOCK P. Born 30/7/52. Commd 15/3/73. Wg Cdr 1/1/88. Retd ADMIN 1/1/91.
PEACOCK P.G. CBE BSc. Born 27/3/29. Commd 26/10/50. A Cdre 1/7/80. Retd GD 27/3/84.
PEACOCK T.C.W. Born 4/10/21. Commd 22/10/59. Sqn Ldr 1/7/70. Retd GD 4/10/76.
PEACOCK T.H. Born 20/6/44. Commd 20/1/64. Flt Lt 11/12/69. Retd GD 3/9/76.
PEACOCK T.J. LLB. Born 15/11/55. Commd 17/8/80. Flt Lt 5/6/84. Retd SY 17/8/96.
PEACOCK W.T. Born 7/4/35. Commd 27/3/70. Flt Lt 4/5/72. Retd SUP 1/5/85.
PEACOCK-EDWARDS R.S. CBE AFC FRAeS FCMI. Born 27/1/45. Commd 21/5/65. A Cdre 1/7/94. Retd GD 27/1/00.
PEAKE A.D. Born 16/11/33. Commd 4/2/53. Flt Lt 1/7/58. Retd SUP 29/5/76.
PEAKE F. Born 17/5/15. Commd 18/3/43. Sqn Ldr 1/1/63. Retd ENG 7/5/70.
PEAKER A.B. CEng MRAeS. Born 25/6/22. Commd 17/1/44. Wg Cdr 1/1/69. Retd ENG 25/6/77.
PEAKER M.G. Born 20/5/39. Commd 24/11/59. Gp Capt 1/1/84. Retd GD 20/5/94.
PEAKMAN R. BSc. Born 4/7/41. Commd 13/10/64. Sqn Ldr 13/4/74. Retd ADMIN 22/10/94.
PEAPLE T.D. Born 22/4/38. Commd 19/1/66. Flt Lt 1/4/69. Retd ENG 1/8/91.
PEARCE A.A. MRAeS. Born 11/5/22. Commd 6/7/44. Sqn Ldr 1/4/55. Retd GD 31/8/68.
PEARCE A.C. MSc BSc PGCE DIC. Born 22/2/61. Commd 28/9/83. Sqn Ldr 1/1/93. Retd ADMIN 28/9/99.
PEARCE A.F. Born 19/9/43. Commd 11/11/65. Sqn Ldr 1/7/79. Retd GD(G) 19/9/87.
PEARCE A.G. Born 8/6/40. Commd 31/7/62. Sqn Ldr 1/1/72. Retd GD 8/6/95.
PEARCE B.P.J. Born 29/5/46. Commd 26/5/67. Sqn Ldr 1/1/78. Retd ENG 29/5/84.
PEARCE C.F. CEng MIEE. Born 4/8/13. Commd 15/7/33. Wg Cdr 1/7/47. Retd ENG 1/11/52. rtg Gp Capt.
PEARCE D. Born 1/7/19. Commd 10/2/43. Flt Offr 26/5/53. Retd GD(G) 28/2/58.
PEARCE F.W. DFC. Born 8/5/21. Commd 18/7/44. Sqn Ldr 1/1/67. Retd GD 8/11/75.
PEARCE G.A. Born 27/3/36. Commd 12/11/54. Flt Lt 1/3/61. Retd GD 27/3/74.
PEARCE G.C. Born 7/3/36. Commd 22/1/54. Flt Lt 7/8/64. Retd GD 28/10/86.
PEARCE G.M. BA. Born 27/4/35. Commd 5/5/54. Sqn Ldr 1/1/71. Retd GD 1/8/77.
PEARCE J. Born 10/2/47. Commd 9/12/76. Wg Cdr 1/1/93. Retd ADMIN 13/11/00.
PEARCE J.F.L. MBE. Born 24/9/26. Commd 11/3/65. Sqn Ldr 1/7/75. Retd ENG 24/9/84.
PEARCE J.H. Born 6/6/24. Commd 26/11/43. Sqn Ldr 1/4/55. Retd GD 1/5/68.
PEARCE M.J. BSc. Born 27/2/51. Commd 15/9/69. Sqn Ldr 1/1/84. Retd GD 27/2/89.
PEARCE M.S. BSc CEng MIEE. Born 28/2/46. Commd 26/5/67. Wg Cdr 1/7/87. Retd GD 31/7/03.
PEARCE N.G. MSc BSc. Born 22/9/59. Commd 18/8/85. Sqn Ldr 1/1/95. Retd SUP 18/8/01.
PEARCE P. MBA BSc CEng MRAeS CDipAF. Born 10/1/63. Commd 22/10/84. Sqn Ldr 1/7/97.
    Retd ENGINEER 1/9/03.
PEARCE R.A. Born 18/2/37. Commd 18/8/61. Flt Lt 1/4/66. Retd GD 29/9/73.
PEARCE R.D. Born 11/3/21. Commd 4/10/43. Sqn Ldr 1/7/70. Retd GD 11/3/76.
PEARCE R.S. Born 1/6/60. Commd 4/9/81. Sqn Ldr 1/7/93. Retd GD 1/6/98.
PEARCE W.E.R. Born 22/7/57. Commd 15/6/83. Flt Lt 5/8/85. Retd GD 22/7/95.
PEARMAN L. MBE MM. Born 29/3/21. Commd 11/6/44. Wg Cdr 1/1/61. Retd SUP 1/6/68.
PEARS H. DFC. Born 30/5/23. Commd 10/11/42. Sqn Ldr 1/1/53. Retd GD 30/5/66.
PEARSE J.G. Born 22/5/14. Commd 1/5/42. Wg Cdr 1/7/60. Retd SEC 18/1/69.
PEARSE W.J. CEng MRAeS. Born 5/3/37. Commd 11/10/60. Wg Cdr 1/7/79. Retd ENG 16/4/89.
PEARSE W.T.D. Born 14/11/32. Commd 10/5/73. Sqn Ldr 1/1/87. Retd ENG 25/4/92.
PEARSON A.D.G. Born 1/3/37. Commd 27/7/72. Sqn Ldr 27/1/76. Retd ADMIN 3/1/88.
PEARSON C.R. Born 7/3/60. Commd 11/5/78. Flt Lt 11/11/83. Retd GD 1/10/90.
PEARSON D.A.W. MHCIMA. Born 6/4/49. Commd 9/12/74. Gp Capt 1/7/99. Retd GD 6/4/04.
PEARSON E. Born 16/11/34. Commd 29/10/52. Sqn Ldr 1/7/65. Retd GD 22/2/79.
PEARSON F.J.C. Born 16/1/31. Commd 16/8/52. Flt Lt 13/11/57. Retd GD 5/5/78.
PEARSON F.MacC. Born 17/3/39. Commd 12/11/57. Wg Cdr 1/1/81. Retd GD 17/3/94.
PEARSON F.R. Born 25/4/31. Commd 28/6/51. Flt Lt 10/10/56. Retd GD 25/4/69.
PEARSON G. Born 12/3/14. Commd 25/11/43. Flt Lt 25/5/47. Retd SEC 24/7/62.
PEARSON G. Born 31/3/31. Commd 19/7/51. Sqn Ldr 1/1/65. Retd GD 28/11/75.
PEARSON G.S. MBE ACIS MCMI. Born 6/11/46. Commd 27/5/71. Wg Cdr 1/7/88. Retd ADMIN 19/6/93.
PEARSON I.D. Born 11/12/44. Commd 9/3/72. Flt Lt 3/5/77. Retd ADMIN 1/9/78.
PEARSON J.D. BSc. Born 30/1/54. Commd 9/10/75. Flt Lt 15/4/78. Retd GD 15/7/89.
PEARSON J.McL. Born 14/3/20. Commd 25/5/49. Flt Lt 4/12/52. Retd GD(G) 18/3/75.
PEARSON J.P. Born 21/7/42. Commd 6/4/72. Flt Lt 6/4/74. Retd GD 1/11/93.
PEARSON J.W. Born 25/1/48. Commd 1/8/69. Sqn Ldr 1/1/86. Retd GD(G) 1/10/92.
PEARSON M.F.V. Born 30/7/17. Commd 28/12/44. Sqn Ldr 1/1/55. Retd RGT 6/5/58.
PEARSON M.L. MEng. Born 18/12/70. Commd 14/12/89. Fg Offr 15/1/92. Retd ENG 5/8/97.
PEARSON N.A.J. Born 20/3/65. Commd 15/3/84. Flt Lt 15/9/89. Retd GD 14/3/96.
PEARSON N.F. BSc CEng MRAeS. Born 21/12/61. Commd 2/2/84. Sqn Ldr 1/1/97. Retd ENG 3/1/02.
PEARSON N.J. MA FRAeS FCMI. Born 17/2/46. Commd 4/7/69. Gp Capt 1/1/96. Retd OPS SPT 1/7/01.
PEARSON R.A.J. Born 10/3/38. Commd 28/2/57. Wg Cdr 1/7/77. Retd GD 10/3/93.
PEARSON R.F. MBE. Born 2/12/23. Commd 5/12/43. Wg Cdr 1/1/75. Retd ENG 2/12/78.
PEARSON R.J.H. AFC. Born 18/5/24. Commd 28/9/44. Flt Lt 16/1/50. Retd GD(G) 8/6/54.
PEARSON R.M. Born 9/9/30. Commd 1/8/51. Flt Lt 1/8/56. Retd SUP 9/9/68.
PEARSON R.S. Born 4/2/59. Commd 11/6/81. Sqn Ldr 1/6/90. Retd GD 1/2/97.

PEARSON S.D. Born 5/11/61. Commd 6/11/80. Sqn Ldr 1/1/93. Retd GD 5/11/99.
PEARSON S.J. MCIPS MILogDip. Born 25/6/58. Commd 25/2/88. Sqn Ldr 1/1/96. Retd SUP 1/2/02.
PEARSON S.W. Born 3/3/45. Commd 27/9/73. Flt Lt 27/9/75. Retd SY 11/7/82.
PEARSON T. Born 22/9/52. Commd 17/12/64. Flt Lt 9/2/68. Retd GD 22/9/80.
PEARSON T.A. Born 23/3/39. Commd 15/12/59. Wg Cdr 1/7/78. Retd GD 29/9/89.
PEART H. Born 21/11/42. Commd 25/2/88. Flt Lt 25/2/92. Retd ENG 2/5/93.
PEART J.W. Born 10/1/63. Commd 10/5/90. Flt Lt 10/5/92. Retd ADMIN 10/1/01.
PEART R. AFC. Born 7/9/46. Commd 14/7/66. Sqn Ldr 1/7/78. Retd GD 8/11/84.
PEART-JACKSON W.J.P. Born 10/5/28. Commd 2/5/61. Sqn Ldr 27/8/69. Retd ADMIN 2/9/77.
PEARTON F.W. FCMI. Born 25/10/22. Commd 26/5/60. Flt Lt 26/5/63. Retd ENG 2/6/73.
PEASE A.K.F. BSc. Born 16/2/62. Commd 15/7/82. Sqn Ldr 1/7/96. Retd GD 16/2/00.
PEASE C.T. Born 5/5/55. Commd 28/7/93. Sqn Ldr 1/7/02. Retd ENGINEER 1/12/04.
PEASE E.I. MBE CEng MIEE AMCMI. Born 1/4/34. Commd 20/12/57. Wg Cdr 1/7/72. Retd ENG 19/4/84.
PEASLEY G.K. AFC. Born 4/6/33. Commd 19/7/51. Gp Capt 1/1/79. Retd GD 2/9/84.
PEASLEY W.R. DFC. Born 1/5/20. Commd 17/6/42. Flt Lt 22/5/49. Retd GD 19/11/54.
PEAT K.S. Born 27/8/23. Commd 20/1/45. Flt Lt 20/7/48. Retd GD 27/8/61.
PEATY B. BSc. Born 20/7/38. Commd 26/10/62. Flt Lt 26/4/68. Retd GD 10/7/78.
PEBERDY R.J. OBE CEng MIEE. Born 19/8/31. Commd 22/7/55. Gp Capt 1/1/81. Retd ENG 4/10/83.
PECK G. AFC BSc. Born 27/9/49. Commd 3/10/68. Sqn Ldr 1/7/80. Retd GD 12/2/83.
PECK G.C. AFC. Born 1/12/22. Commd 12/1/61. Sqn Ldr 1/7/73. Retd GD 1/12/77.
PECK R.E.F. Born 4/4/23. Commd 22/9/49. Sqn Ldr 1/1/69. Retd ENG 26/3/76.
PECK R.J. Born 13/11/47. Commd 27/2/70. Flt Lt 27/8/75. Retd GD 13/11/85.
PECKETT D.S. MEng BSc CEng MIEE. Born 24/5/48. Commd 28/2/69. Wg Cdr 1/7/87. Retd ENG 31/3/94.
PEDLEY M. Born 30/9/46. Commd 5/2/65. Flt Lt 5/8/70. Retd GD 30/9/01.
PEDLEY M.G.F. OBE DSO DFC. Born 17/11/15. Commd 6/8/35. Wg Cdr 1/7/47. Retd GD 31/12/57. rtg Gp Capt.
PEDLEY N.M. Born 11/10/46. Commd 9/8/68. Flt Lt 4/5/72. Retd GD 21/9/86.
PEDLEY T.F. BSc CEng MRAeS. Born 25/5/56. Commd 14/1/79. Sqn Ldr 1/7/87. Retd ENG 9/12/96.
PEDRICK D.W. BA MBCS. Born 2/4/46. Commd 23/9/66. Wg Cdr 1/1/87. Retd ENG 2/4/90.
PEEBLES A.D. Born 5/11/40. Commd 11/6/60. Flt Lt 11/12/65. Retd GD 5/11/78.
PEEBLES J.S. Born 9/11/20. Commd 10/8/48. Flt Lt 10/8/56. Retd MAR 20/6/57.
PEEKE-VOUT J.M. Born 9/6/46. Commd 19/1/66. Flt Lt 19/7/72. Retd ENG 28/3/75.
PEEL D.B. Born 26/2/62. Commd 28/9/89. Sqn Ldr 1/7/01. Retd ADMIN 15/8/02.
PEEL G.W. Born 20/12/13. Commd 1/1/34. Wg Cdr 5/10/45. Retd ENG 25/1/46. rtg Gp Capt.
PEEL J. BA FCMI FInstPET MCIPS. Born 8/1/31. Commd 12/12/51. Gp Capt 1/7/74. Retd SUP 1/7/81.
PEEL J.R.A. DSO DFC. Born 17/10/11. Commd 23/7/32. Wg Cdr 1/10/46. Retd GD 20/1/48. rtg Gp Capt.
PEELE R.A. Born 5/5/46. Commd 2/8/68. Flt Lt 2/2/71. Retd GD 8/11/75.
PEER R.C. MBE. Born 13/5/44. Commd 10/3/69. Sqn Ldr 1/7/83. Retd ENG 13/5/99.
PEET E.D. Born 8/5/43. Commd 9/2/62. Flt Lt 9/8/67. Retd GD 8/5/80.
PEET W.W. DFC. Born 24/7/20. Commd 11/7/49. Flt Lt 1/8/55. Retd GD(G) 9/3/65.
PEFFERS F.G.C. Born 23/11/29. Commd 13/9/51. Sqn Ldr 1/1/68. Retd GD 2/3/76.
PEGG B.P.R. Born 10/9/30. Commd 24/1/52. Flt Lt 13/11/57. Retd GD 1/12/82.
PEGG R.F. Born 17/7/42. Commd 24/8/72. Flt Lt 24/8/74. Retd GD(G) 24/8/80.
PEGNALL B.E.A. Born 15/4/44. Commd 3/3/67. A Cdre 1/7/92. Retd GD 14/12/95.
PEGRUM R.G. Born 22/1/45. Commd 3/1/64. Sqn Ldr 1/7/79. Retd GD 22/1/03.
PEILE C.T.B. MRAeS. Born 21/5/32. Commd 28/7/53. Wg Cdr 1/1/77. Retd GD 22/5/90.
PEIRSE Sir Richard KCVO CB. Born 16/3/31. Commd 9/4/52. AVM 1/7/82. Retd GD 16/6/88.
PEIRSE R.E. Born 21/7/44. Commd 21/5/65. Fg Offr 21/5/67. Retd GD 17/11/68.
PELCOT A.F. Born 31/1/53. Commd 28/7/88. Flt Lt 28/7/92. Retd SY 5/8/96.
PELLANT W.R.G. The Rev. AKC. Born 2/2/14. Commd 21/4/48. Retd Gp Capt 24/10/71.
PELLING A.H. Born 21/5/33. Commd 27/6/66. Flt Lt 22/7/68. Retd ENG 22/7/74.
PELLS D.E.W. Born 29/10/41. Commd 19/4/63. Flt Lt 19/10/68. Retd GD 30/4/94.
PELLY M.L. Born 1/7/18. Commd 15/3/50. Fg Offr 15/3/52. Retd SEC 1/6/54.
PEMBERTON A.J.R. Born 15/4/25. Commd 29/9/50. Sqn Ldr 1/1/72. Retd GD(G) 15/4/83.
PEMBERTON A.M. Born 24/4/57. Commd 28/10/76. Flt Lt 28/4/82. Retd GD 24/4/95.
PEMBERTON B.M. MCMI. Born 12/5/28. Commd 28/10/63. Sqn Ldr 1/7/69. Retd SUP 18/5/79.
PEMBERTON C.M.G. Born 1/2/51. Commd 8/8/69. Flt Lt 8/2/75. Retd GD 4/10/77.
PEMBERTON D.L. Born 13/2/37. Commd 27/9/73. Sqn Ldr 1/7/84. Retd GD(G) 7/10/91.
PEMBERTON J. Born 6/3/21. Commd 28/12/44. Flt Lt 11/5/60. Retd GD 24/1/62.
PEMBERTON-PIGOTT T.N.J. MCIT MILT. Born 14/11/46. Commd 13/8/72. Wg Cdr 1/1/90. Retd SUP 2/4/01.
PEMBREY T.E.C. Born 7/6/50. Commd 25/2/72. Flt Lt 25/2/75. Retd GD 6/7/87.
PENDER H.K. Born 12/8/59. Commd 15/8/85. Flt Lt 15/2/87. Retd GD 14/9/96.
PENDLEBURY B.A. Born 16/12/32. Commd 4/3/71. Flt Lt 4/3/73. Retd SUP 16/12/87.
PENDLEBURY P. Born 4/7/32. Commd 26/3/64. Sqn Ldr 1/1/85. Retd ADMIN 20/1/87.
PENDLETON G. Born 19/6/39. Commd 24/2/61. Flt Lt 24/8/66. Retd GD 19/6/77.
PENDRED G.L. Born 8/3/24. Commd 13/11/43. Gp Capt 1/1/69. Retd GD 16/4/73.
PENDREGAUST R. Born 8/5/82. Commd 24/7/81. Flt Lt 24/1/87. Retd GD 8/3/92.

PENDRY J.B. Born 1/3/37. Commd 19/8/65. Flt Lt 18/5/71. Retd GD 18/5/84.
PENFOLD A.B. Born 25/2/47. Commd 14/9/65. Flt Lt 1/3/71. Retd GD 8/1/83.
PENGELLY G.R. Born 19/4/35. Commd 7/7/55. A Cdre 1/7/85. Retd SUP 29/1/90.
PENGILLEY D.R. BTech MRAeS. Born 17/10/46. Commd 28/2/72. Sqn Ldr 1/1/85. Retd GD 28/2/88.
PENKETH W.J. BSc. Born 26/1/48. Commd 1/9/71. Wg Cdr 1/7/97. Retd ENG 17/12/99.
PENLEY-MARTIN J.R. Born 27/3/33. Commd 30/4/52. Flt Lt 6/11/57. Retd GD 27/3/76.
PENLEY-MARTIN J.R.M. Born 7/4/59. Commd 25/2/88. Flt Lt 25/2/90. Retd ENG 7/4/97.
PENMAN G.H. Born 19/11/27. Commd 17/5/62. Sqn Ldr 1/1/77. Retd GD(G) 19/5/83.
PENMAN J.McA. MB ChB MRCPsych DPM. Born 8/3/33. Commd 4/9/58. Wg Cdr 24/9/71. Retd MED 6/10/76.
PENMAN J.O.R. BSc CEng MIEE MRAeS. Born 17/4/37. Commd 7/12/61. Wg Cdr 1/7/86. Retd ENG 6/4/89.
PENN K. Born 8/4/33. Commd 19/7/51. Flt Lt 9/11/56. Retd GD(G) 8/4/88.
PENNA C. DFM. Born 10/6/22. Commd 29/1/44. Sqn Ldr 1/1/70. Retd SEC 10/6/72.
PENNELL C.W. MBE MCMI. Born 11/10/41. Commd 31/10/69. Gp Capt 1/1/90. Retd PRT 12/10/91.
PENNELL M.E. BSc. Born 26/2/43. Commd 30/9/62. Sqn Ldr 1/1/74. Retd ENG 26/2/81.
PENNEY B.J. Born 28/2/54. Commd 10/5/90. Flt Lt 10/5/94. Retd ENG 14/3/96.
PENNIALL R.G. MBE. Born 3/9/32. Commd 14/5/53. Wg Cdr 1/1/76. Retd ADMIN 1/8/87.
PENNINGTON A.J. MCMI. Born 3/2/50. Commd 26/2/71. Gp Capt 1/7/99. Retd GD 15/4/05.
PENNINGTON G.C. Born 4/7/57. Commd 26/9/90. Flt Lt 26/9/92. Retd ENG 16/11/98.
PENNINGTON G.H. OBE BSc CEng MIEE MRAeS. Born 29/12/21. Commd 12/9/49. Wg Cdr 29/12/62. Retd EDN 7/1/68.
PENNINGTON G.J. Born 12/10/55. Commd 8/6/84. Flt Lt 8/6/86. Retd ADMIN 15/12/92.
PENNY A.T. Born 1/9/48. Commd 31/7/70. Sqn Ldr 1/1/86. Retd FLY(N) 1/9/03.
PENNY C.R. BSc. Born 8/8/38. Commd 21/12/62. Flt Lt 1/1/66. Retd GD 30/11/74.
PENNY F.C.B. AFM. Born 3/7/22. Commd 25/5/54. Flt Lt 27/5/57. Retd GD 1/10/68.
PENNY H.A. OBE FCMI. Born 1/2/22. Commd 18/12/42. Gp Capt 1/1/68. Retd SEC 5/1/70.
PENNY J.A. Born 19/7/22. Commd 5/2/48. Flt Lt 5/8/51. Retd SEC 19/7/71.
PENNY J.C. Born 22/12/21. Commd 30/10/42. Sqn Ldr 1/7/73. Retd ADMIN 31/3/77.
PENNY K.C. Born 23/3/31. Commd 14/1/53. Flt Lt 3/6/58. Retd GD 8/4/69.
PENNY L.S. BA. Born 8/6/40. Commd 19/12/61. Wg Cdr 1/7/78. Retd GD 1/7/81.
PENNY S.D. BA BSc CEng MBCS MIEE MRAeS. Born 3/1/58. Commd 19/9/76. Wg Cdr 1/7/94. Retd ENG 1/7/97.
PENNYFATHER P.R. MCMI. Born 1/5/24. Commd 15/12/44. Sqn Ldr 1/10/57. Retd SEC 1/5/79.
PENRICE C. BSc. Born 9/4/59. Commd 17/3/79. Sqn Ldr 1/7/92. Retd GD 23/6/98.
PENROSE A. DFC* CGM. Born 6/5/20. Commd 21/4/45. Flt Lt 5/6/58. Retd GD(G) 1/4/65.
PENROSE J.D. DLC CEng FRAeS FRSA. Born 1/5/30. Commd 19/6/50. Flt Lt 13/11/57. Retd GD 30/9/61.
PENRY K.R. MCMI. Born 28/12/21. Commd 20/11/42. Wg Cdr 1/1/59. Retd GD 28/12/68.
PENTON-VOAK B.E. Born 1/7/40. Commd 22/2/63. Sqn Ldr 1/7/87. Retd ADMIN 11/8/95.
PENTON-VOAK M.J. Born 15/1/43. Commd 8/6/62. Wg Cdr 1/1/91. Retd GD 15/1/98.
PENTYCROSS F.A. Born 4/3/17. Commd 27/6/36. Sqn Ldr 1/8/47. Retd GD 27/3/60.
PEPPER A.C. Born 9/9/41. Commd 20/9/79. Sqn Ldr 1/7/89. Retd SUP 19/6/93.
PEPPER D.J.S. CEng MRAeS MCMI. Born 12/11/39. Commd 2/2/65. Sqn Ldr 1/7/76. Retd ENG 2/2/87.
PEPPER S.P. Born 23/9/51. Commd 4/3/71. Flt Lt 4/9/76. Retd GD 23/9/89.
PERCIVAL S.H. BEd. Born 22/4/48. Commd 29/8/72. Sqn Ldr 1/7/89. Retd ADMIN 14/3/96.
PERCY T.E. BSc. Born 5/7/44. Commd 18/8/68. Flt Lt 18/5/70. Retd GD 31/1/76.
PERDUE G.S. Born 4/9/24. Commd 2/5/49. Flt Lt 27/3/55. Retd GD 4/9/62.
PERERA M.D.M. Born 28/9/32. Commd 29/12/65. Flt Lt 29/12/65. Retd SUP 29/12/81.
PERFECT A.A. MCMI. Born 15/6/43. Commd 5/7/68. Wg Cdr 1/1/94. Retd OPS SPT 4/4/00.
PERIGO J.D. Born 23/9/34. Commd 13/2/64. Sqn Ldr 1/1/85. Retd ADMIN 26/7/87.
PERKIN K.A. Born 6/5/18. Commd 19/8/40. Sqn Ldr 1/7/53. Retd GD 29/10/58.
PERKIN-BALL R.W.K. Born 24/8/44. Commd 25/10/73. Flt Lt 25/10/75. Retd GD(G) 24/8/82.
PERKINS C.T. Born 26/5/47. Commd 21/4/77. Sqn Ldr 1/1/98. Retd GD 26/5/01.
PERKINS D.A. Born 8/10/25. Commd 21/12/45. Sqn Ldr 1/1/57. Retd GD 28/1/77.
PERKINS I.M. MBE MRCS MFCM LRCP FCMI. Born 15/12/20. Commd 30/7/48. AVM 31/3/78. Retd MED 15/12/80.
PERKINS L.J. Born 12/12/31. Commd 14/8/53. Flt Lt 23/1/58. Retd GD 12/12/69.
PERKINS M. Born 29/9/36. Commd 29/7/58. Sqn Ldr 1/7/70. Retd SUP 14/1/83.
PERKINS N.J. Born 18/1/60. Commd 22/2/79. Flt Lt 22/8/85. Retd GD(G) 22/8/87. Re-entered 19/4/91. Flt Lt 17/10/86. Retd OPS SPT 1/10/97.
PERKINS R.C. MBE. Born 20/3/35. Commd 16/11/61. Wg Cdr 1/7/80. Retd SEC 30/7/83.
PERKINS R.H. Born 29/8/24. Commd 29/3/45. Flt Lt 3/2/53. Retd GD 3/1/66.
PERKINS R.L. BA. Born 12/1/47. Commd 13/9/71. Plt Offr 13/9/71. Retd GD 3/1/66.
PERKINS S.J. OBE AFC FCMI. Born 13/4/23. Commd 3/7/42. Gp Capt 1/1/69. Retd GD 1/11/75.
PERKINS S.J.B. Born 6/8/56. Commd 15/6/83. Flt Lt 15/12/89. Retd GD(G) 1/1/96.
PERKS G.D. DFC. Born 19/9/18. Commd 23/4/53. Flt Lt 14/9/47. Retd GD 27/7/58.
PERKS M.J. Born 8/8/48. Commd 17/1/69. Flt Lt 21/5/75. Retd SUP 8/8/86.
PERKS R.I. CEng MIERE. Born 26/12/21. Commd 31/5/43. Wg Cdr 1/7/67. Retd ENG 29/6/74.
PERKS R.J. FCIS. Born 6/9/49. Commd 10/9/70. Sqn Ldr 1/7/94. Retd ADMIN 29/10/02.
PERKS T.A.N. Born 25/11/48. Commd 7/6/73. Flt Lt 13/8/78. Retd GD(G) 19/4/87.

PERMAN A.E. ACIS. Born 9/7/31. Commd 3/6/65. Flt Lt 3/6/70. Retd SEC 9/7/75.
PEROU R.L. Born 8/7/37. Commd 12/8/59. Fg Offr 12/8/59. Retd ENG 18/1/64.
PEROWNE B.I.S. AFC. Born 25/12/22. Commd 30/4/43. Sqn Ldr 1/1/60. Retd GD 25/6/73.
PERRETT M.J. OBE. Born 7/11/44. Commd 29/11/63. Gp Capt 1/7/94. Retd GD 31/5/01.
PERRETT M.W. MInstPS. Born 10/1/36. Commd 14/10/75. Flt Lt 14/10/75. Retd SUP 2/2/86.
PERRETT S.D. Born 18/1/64. Commd 23/5/85. Sqn Ldr 1/1/00. Retd FLY(P) 18/4/03.
PERRIDGE M.J. BSc CEng MIEE. Born 8/8/42. Commd 15/7/63. Gp Capt 1/7/90. Retd ENG 31/3/94.
PERRIN D.R. OBE DFC. Born 19/1/21. Commd 17/6/43. Wg Cdr 1/1/73. Retd SEC 19/1/76.
PERRIN F. Born 31/8/16. Commd 14/11/46. Sqn Ldr 1/7/62. Retd SUP 15/3/69.
PERRIN G.M. MBE. Born 1/10/33. Commd 18/6/52. Sqn Ldr 1/7/68. Retd GD 27/2/76.
PERRIN J.E. Born 23/4/20. Commd 23/3/50. Sqn Ldr 1/1/72. Retd ENG 22/4/73.
PERRIN N.A. BA CEng FRAeS. Born 30/9/30. Commd 29/11/51. AVM 1/7/84. Retd ENG 1/7/86.
PERRIN N.A. Born 10/10/66. Commd 16/10/90. Flt Lt 15/6/94. Retd FLY(P) 3/4/03.
PERRINS W.J. Born 13/8/55. Commd 17/7/75. Flt Lt 17/1/81. Retd GD 13/1/94.
PERRIS A.J.B. Born 27/12/44. Commd 19/8/66. Flt Lt 4/11/70. Retd GD 1/1/76.
PERROTT D.J.S. Born 25/11/42. Commd 29/6/72. Sqn Ldr 1/1/81. Retd ENG 14/7/86.
PERROTT P.J. AFC. Born 22/5/33. Commd 13/2/52. Flt Lt 12/6/57. Retd GD 22/5/71.
PERRY A.D. Born 2/11/29. Commd 17/5/62. Sqn Ldr 1/7/77. Retd GD 2/11/87.
PERRY B.V. Born 7/6/46. Commd 18/8/67. Flt Lt 18/8/70. Retd GD 4/10/77. Re-instated 22/7/81. Sqn Ldr 1/7/86. Retd GD 1/7/89.
PERRY C. BSc. Born 17/10/59. Commd 5/2/84. Flt Lt 5/8/86. Retd GD 5/2/00.
PERRY C.C. Born 18/11/55. Commd 8/12/83. Sqn Ldr 1/7/93. Retd SY 1/7/96.
PERRY D.J. MBE. Born 31/8/26. Commd 2/8/50. Sqn Ldr 1/1/75. Retd GD 30/3/78.
PERRY E.A. Born 23/3/44. Commd 5/2/65. Flt Lt 23/9/69. Retd GD 1/5/76.
PERRY F.G. Born 30/6/13. Commd 21/10/54. Flt Lt 21/10/57. Retd ENG 2/7/68.
PERRY F.G. Born 30/1/34. Commd 4/6/52. Flt Lt 30/10/57. Retd GD 6/4/59.
PERRY G.L. MS BSc CEng MRAeS MCMI ACGI. Born 31/12/44. Commd 22/9/63. Wg Cdr 1/1/81. Retd ENG 1/1/84.
PERRY K.H. DSO AFC. Born 25/3/22. Commd 22/10/43. Sqn Ldr 1/7/55. Retd GD 25/3/65.
PERRY P.J. MSc BSc(Eng) CEng MRAeS. Born 22/9/39. Commd 30/9/59. Wg Cdr 1/1/79. Retd ENG 19/1/90.
PERRY P.N. AFC*. Born 7/1/38. Commd 28/2/56. Flt Lt 21/8/63. Retd GD 24/11/78.
PERRY R.C. MBE. Born 14/7/34. Commd 22/7/66. Sqn Ldr 1/7/85. Retd ENG 1/10/91.
PERRY R.G. Born 10/3/29. Commd 26/7/50. Sqn Ldr 1/7/59. Retd GD 1/9/74.
PERRY R.N. Born 2/5/46. Commd 1/4/65. Sqn Ldr 1/7/76. Retd GD(G) 2/5/90.
PERRY R.S.N. MA. Born 8/9/49. Commd 22/4/71. Gp Capt 1/1/91. Retd SUP 1/5/92.
PERRY S.G. Born 20/2/34. Commd 25/2/53. Wg Cdr 1/1/74. Retd GD 30/8/80.
PERRY T.D. Born 26/12/33. Commd 13/2/52. Sqn Ldr 1/1/68. Retd GD 26/12/88.
PERRYMAN J.G. Born 31/5/60. Commd 21/9/89. Sqn Ldr 1/1/98. Retd SUP 8/1/03.
PERRYMAN N.F. Born 3/7/15. Commd 30/6/43. Sqn Ldr 1/7/63. Retd GD(G) 28/8/65.
PERT G. Born 2/9/56. Commd 11/5/89. Flt Lt 11/5/91. Retd ENG 11/5/97.
PERTWEE H.R.P. DFC MCMI. Born 15/2/23. Commd 7/2/42. Sqn Ldr 1/1/51. Retd SUP 15/2/72.
PETCH C.S.F. MSc BSc. Born 26/10/58. Commd 29/8/77. Sqn Ldr 1/1/90. Retd ENG 1/5/00.
PETERS A.D.A. Born 14/9/23. Commd 25/11/53. Flt Lt 25/11/58. Retd GD 11/4/68.
PETERS A.J. Born 7/3/54. Commd 24/8/80. Sqn Ldr 1/7/94. Retd GD 14/3/96.
PETERS C.E. DFC. Born 15/2/21. Commd 28/7/43. Flt Lt 26/5/55. Retd GD 28/9/68.
PETERS D.B. Born 4/10/58. Commd 11/1/79. Sqn Ldr 11/7/84. Retd GD 4/10/96.
PETERS E.A. Born 29/7/30. Commd 12/12/51. Sqn Ldr 1/1/62. Retd GD 29/7/68.
PETERS G.F. Born 14/10/29. Commd 26/3/53. Sqn Ldr 1/1/69. Retd GD 22/5/76.
PETERS J.G. BSc. Born 30/12/61. Commd 14/9/80. Sqn Ldr 1/7/97. Retd GD 1/7/00.
PETERS L.J. Born 1/2/13. Commd 2/12/41. Flt Lt 4/9/45. Retd ENG 20/9/47. rtg Sqn Ldr.
PETERS N.P. MA. Born 20/5/61. Commd 1/11/79. Gp Capt 1/1/03. Retd GD 1/3/05.
PETERS P. OBE DFC. Born 29/12/16. Commd 26/3/38. Wg Cdr 1/7/52. Retd GD 17/1/72.
PETERS P.H.J. AFC. Born 1/11/31. Commd 4/4/51. Sqn Ldr 1/7/61. Retd GD 12/6/85.
PETERS P.W. DFC AFC. Born 24/1/16. Commd 6/3/39. Sqn Ldr 1/8/47. Retd GD 3/3/53.
PETERS R.G. CB. Born 22/8/40. Commd 1/8/61. AVM 1/1/91. Retd GD 1/7/93.
PETERS R.S. Born 17/3/26. Commd 20/12/46. Sqn Ldr 1/1/58. Retd GD 17/3/64.
PETERSON C.M. Born 2/4/20. Commd 28/2/46. Flt Lt 15/12/49. Retd ENG 27/5/68.
PETERSON G.K. CEng MRAeS. Born 3/6/47. Commd 22/11/73. Sqn Ldr 1/7/85. Retd ENGINEER 3/6/05.
PETERSON M.G. BA. Born 13/11/77. Commd 2/4/00. Flt Lt 2/10/02. Retd FLY(P) 21/10/03.
PETERSON R.V. Born 29/9/20. Commd 26/9/57. Sqn Ldr 1/7/68. Retd ENG 18/9/73.
PETGRAVE-JOHNSON A.G. BA. Born 14/4/35. Commd 12/2/54. Flt Lt 13/4/60. Retd GD 31/3/61.
PETHARD J.W.G. Born 2/8/42. Commd 24/3/61. Flt Lt 24/9/66. Retd GD 1/10/88.
PETHERAM C.J. MCMI. Born 3/4/28. Commd 27/9/49. Sqn Ldr 1/7/59. Retd GD 4/4/78.
PETHICK M. Born 26/12/33. Commd 24/9/52. Sqn Ldr 1/1/75. Retd GD(G) 17/11/77.
PETRE B. Born 26/10/46. Commd 4/7/85. Flt Lt 4/7/89. Retd ENG 6/12/97.
PETRE G.W. DFC AFC. Born 17/12/16. Commd 30/7/38. Gp Capt 1/1/57. Retd GD 17/12/66.
PETRIE I.J.N. BSc. Born 24/3/59. Commd 9/11/80. Flt Lt 9/8/81. Retd ENG 11/3/90.

PETRIE K.R. Born 29/2/36. Commd 2/9/55. Wg Cdr 1/1/80. Retd GD 1/3/91.
PETRIE M.A. Born 20/10/59. Commd 5/2/81. Flt Lt 1/6/85. Retd GD 6/3/90.
PETTERSON G.C. Born 7/1/27. Commd 3/6/54. Flt Lt 3/12/56. Retd GD 9/1/65.
PETTET M.J. CEng MRAeS. Born 30/5/34. Commd 26/9/53. Sqn Ldr 1/7/67. Retd ENG 1/6/84.
PETTIFER J.K. MA CEng MIEE. Born 18/5/35. Commd 26/9/53. Wg Cdr 1/1/72. Retd ENG 10/6/85.
PETTIFER M.I. OBE BSc. Born 4/11/48. Commd 24/1/71. Gp Capt 1/7/97. Retd ADMIN 1/6/01.
PETTIFER W.E. Born 12/9/22. Commd 11/3/43. Wg Cdr 1/1/61. Retd GD 25/5/68.
PETTINGER D.C. MCMI. Born 4/9/33. Commd 1/10/62. Sqn Ldr 1/1/70. Retd GD 15/10/83.
PETTIT A.C. Born 15/7/15. Commd 20/8/43. Flt Lt 11/11/54. Retd PE 28/8/63.
PETTIT B.D. Born 30/3/33. Commd 21/8/61. Flt Lt 21/8/61. Retd GD 30/3/91.
PETTMAN L.O. Born 26/5/30. Commd 26/11/64. Flt Lt 26/11/65. Retd EDN 26/11/72.
PETTS J.E. Born 4/5/33. Commd 17/12/52. Sqn Ldr 1/1/80. Retd GD 5/5/91.
PETTY D.A. MA MA CertEd. Born 28/10/45. Commd 30/7/72. Sqn Ldr 30/1/79. Retd ADMIN 14/3/96.
PETTY S.H. Born 20/8/55. Commd 11/8/77. Flt Lt 11/2/83. Retd GD 31/3/87.
PEXTON B.L. Born 18/6/34. Commd 24/2/55. Wg Cdr 1/1/74. Retd SY 31/12/85.
PEXTON D.L. MCMI. Born 28/11/35. Commd 22/1/55. Sqn Ldr 1/1/71. Retd ADMIN 27/4/87.
PEYCKE E.C. Born 11/11/48. Commd 10/1/69. Flt Lt 10/7/74. Retd GD 1/1/77.
PFANDER K.N. Born 18/6/48. Commd 10/9/70. Fg Offr 10/9/72. Retd GD 25/1/75.
PHAIR E.N. The Rev. Born 5/10/15. Commd 24/3/43. Retd Sqn Ldr 24/10/53.
PHARAOH M.H. Born 8/6/38. Commd 30/7/59. Wg Cdr 1/7/89. Retd ENG 8/11/93.
PHEASANT V.A. MBE. Born 2/7/40. Commd 24/9/64. Sqn Ldr 1/1/74. Retd GD 6/1/85.
PHILBEY B. Born 25/7/29. Commd 8/11/50. Flt Lt 14/5/56. Retd GD 25/7/67.
PHILIP A.C. MBE. Born 19/12/11. Commd 22/7/41. Sqn Ldr 1/7/53. Retd SEC 24/2/61.
PHILIP A.F. MSc BSc(Eng). Born 9/3/46. Commd 27/10/70. Sqn Ldr 1/1/90. Retd FLY(P) 9/3/04.
PHILIP P.H. Born 22/2/27. Commd 11/6/53. Sqn Ldr 1/7/67. Retd GD 22/2/82.
PHILIP R.J. Born 21/9/42. Commd 28/2/85. Sqn Ldr 1/7/93. Retd ADMIN 21/9/97.
PHILLIP E.M. Born 22/7/20. Commd 29/7/42. Flt Offr 29/1/47. Retd SEC 14/5/53.
PHILLIPS A. Born 8/3/23. Commd 16/9/44. Sqn Ldr 1/7/55. Retd GD 8/3/66.
PHILLIPS A.B. Born 5/4/60. Commd 14/10/88. Sqn Ldr 1/7/95. Retd SUPPLY 5/4/04.
PHILLIPS A.D.S. OBE FCMI. Born 14/8/20. Commd 4/4/46. Gp Capt 1/7/70. Retd ENG 3/7/73.
PHILLIPS A.J. Born 23/12/40. Commd 18/8/61. Flt Lt 23/12/67. Retd GD(G) 23/2/81. Re-instated 30/4/90.
   Flt Lt 30/4/88. Retd GD(G) 23/12/95.
PHILLIPS A.L. BA. Born 22/9/43. Commd 26/5/67. Flt Lt 24/10/70. Retd ENG 22/9/81.
PHILLIPS B.A. MBE MRAeS. Born 30/3/28. Commd 27/7/49. Sqn Ldr 1/1/62. Retd ENG 30/3/66.
PHILLIPS C.H.P. Born 31/1/20. Commd 19/6/43. Flt Lt 19/12/46. Retd GD 31/1/63.
PHILLIPS C.M. BA. Born 18/7/44. Commd 9/10/64. Flt Lt 9/4/70. Retd GD 18/7/94.
PHILLIPS D.B. BA BSc. Born 18/2/34. Commd 22/8/58. Sqn Ldr 17/5/67. Retd ADMIN 17/7/76. Re-instated 22/10/79.
   Sqn Ldr 22/8/70. Retd ADMIN 18/2/89.
PHILLIPS D.H. OBE. Born 6/9/44. Commd 17/12/65. Gp Capt 1/7/89. Retd GD 27/11/93.
PHILLIPS D.J. CEng MRAeS MCMI. Born 15/2/35. Commd 27/2/58. Wg Cdr 1/7/75. Retd ENG 3/4/79.
PHILLIPS D.M. Born 23/8/35. Commd 14/4/54. Flt Lt 7/7/61. Retd SUP 15/2/67.
PHILLIPS D.R. FIFA ACIS. Born 9/11/44. Commd 30/7/64. Wg Cdr 1/1/87. Retd ADMIN 4/4/90.
PHILLIPS F.H. Born 10/4/17. Commd 3/8/43. Flt Lt 29/1/52. Retd GD(G) 10/5/56.
PHILLIPS G.M. MBE. Born 5/7/24. Commd 26/9/51. Sqn Ldr 1/1/69. Retd GD 5/7/79.
PHILLIPS G.T. BSc. Born 9/10/45. Commd 25/7/71. Sqn Ldr 1/7/84. Retd ADMIN 1/2/98.
PHILLIPS G.W. BSc. Born 1/2/52. Commd 2/9/84. Sqn Ldr 1/1/93. Retd GD 1/10/97.
PHILLIPS H. Born 4/1/35. Commd 17/1/52. Flt Lt 16/11/63. Retd GD 30/9/75.
PHILLIPS J.F. Born 11/3/42. Commd 29/10/64. Sqn Ldr 1/1/82. Retd GD(G) 1/10/89.
PHILLIPS J.H. MCMI. Born 16/1/25. Commd 3/5/46. Wg Cdr 1/7/64. Retd ADMIN 16/12/69. Re-employed 20/1/72 to
   16/1/82. Sqn Ldr 6/5/58.
PHILLIPS J.J. Born 1/5/43. Commd 15/10/81. Flt Lt 15/10/86. Retd ENG 1/2/98.
PHILLIPS J.S.S. Born 20/12/35. Commd 5/11/62. Sqn Ldr 1/7/73. Retd GD 7/4/81.
PHILLIPS K. Born 19/9/53. Commd 1/12/77. Sqn Ldr 1/7/86. Retd ADMIN 19/9/91.
PHILLIPS K.H. Born 11/4/21. Commd 6/12/56. Flt Lt 6/12/59. Retd ENG 26/9/64.
PHILLIPS M.J. MB ChB DCP DTM&H MRCPath. Born 24/2/31. Commd 8/2/56. Wg Cdr 8/2/69. Retd MED 30/6/72.
PHILLIPS M.J. BSc(Eng). Born 5/7/44. Commd 28/9/64. Flt Lt 5/7/67. Retd GD 5/7/82.
PHILLIPS M.T. Born 4/5/44. Commd 17/12/65. Gp Capt 1/1/94. Retd GD 14/3/96.
PHILLIPS N.R. BSc. Born 25/12/46. Commd 15/9/71. Sqn Ldr 1/7/84. Retd ENG 15/9/87.
PHILLIPS O.R. MCMI. Born 9/3/28. Commd 11/6/52. Sqn Ldr 1/1/63. Retd GD 24/9/76.
PHILLIPS P.C. BSc. Born 16/12/29. Commd 24/1/52. Wg Cdr 1/7/72. Retd ENG 21/1/81.
PHILLIPS P.K. Born 8/5/45. Commd 2/3/78. Sqn Ldr 1/1/88. Retd SUP 2/3/92.
PHILLIPS P.L. BSc CEng MRAeS. Born 7/10/40. Commd 15/8/82. Sqn Ldr 1/7/89. Retd ENG 4/1/02.
PHILLIPS R.A. BSc. Born 11/10/45. Commd 29/11/74. Sqn Ldr 1/7/91. Retd GD 11/10/04.
PHILLIPS R.C. MB ChB MRCGP DRCOG. Born 6/12/55. Commd 9/6/85. Wg Cdr 8/1/95. Retd MED 9/6/01.
PHILLIPS R.H. Born 18/2/10. Commd 9/12/43. Flt Lt 9/6/47. Retd ENG 1/9/50.
PHILLIPS R.J. Born 16/3/19. Commd 10/10/46. Wg Cdr 1/1/69. Retd SUP 30/9/72.

PHILLIPS S.A. Born 12/3/60. Commd 11/1/79. Sqn Ldr 1/1/91. Retd GD 12/3/98.
PHILLIPS S.B. Born 1/5/14. Commd 11/2/44. Fg Offr 5/11/48. Retd GD(G) 18/6/50. rtg Flt Lt.
PHILLIPS T. Born 4/12/14. Commd 6/6/40. Wg Cdr 1/1/56. Retd SEC 21/6/61.
PHILLIPS T. Born 4/10/33. Commd 28/11/69. Sqn Ldr 1/1/80. Retd ENG 5/11/85.
PHILLIPSON J.McD. BA. Born 28/1/62. Commd 14/9/80. Flt Lt 15/10/84. Retd GD 15/7/95.
PHILLIPSON P.R. Born 26/9/55. Commd 19/3/81. Flt Lt 16/5/85. Retd OPS SPT 26/9/99.
PHILLPOTTS M.J. AMBCS. Born 19/11/46. Commd 5/1/70. Sqn Ldr 1/1/81. Retd ENG 1/10/92.
PHILO P.D.G. MILDM MCIT MILT MCMI. Born 15/1/38. Commd 5/5/60. Wg Cdr 1/7/74. Retd ENG 15/1/76.
  Re-instated 25/11/80. Sqn Ldr 1/1/88. Retd ENG 15/1/93.
PHILP G. Born 11/10/46. Commd 21/4/77. Sqn Ldr 1/1/88. Retd GD 30/10/96.
PHILP W.A. Born 28/4/32. Commd 11/6/52. Sqn Ldr 1/1/65. Retd ADMIN 6/9/77.
PHILPOTT A.J. Born 13/3/53. Commd 22/11/84. Flt Lt 22/11/86. Retd ENG 22/11/92.
PHILPOTT I.M. Born 18/8/35. Commd 21/10/54. Flt Lt 21/10/60. Retd RGT 18/8/73.
PHILPOTT R.J. Born 16/7/19. Commd 18/11/41. Sqn Ldr 1/1/68. Retd GD(G) 16/7/75.
PHILPOTT W.F. Born 29/3/20. Commd 15/9/60. Flt Lt 15/9/65. Retd ENG 29/3/75.
PHIPPEN J. Born 6/9/36. Commd 20/6/63. Sqn Ldr 1/7/71. Retd SEC 2/10/79.
PHIPPS A.L. BSc. Born 28/4/64. Commd 14/9/86. Flt Lt 14/3/89. Retd FLY(P) 2/6/04.
PHIPPS A.R.P. Born 8/11/39. Commd 25/7/60. Wg Cdr 1/1/77. Retd GD 9/11/84.
PHIPPS K.H. BA. Born 17/1/62. Commd 3/1/88. Flt Lt 3/7/91. Retd ADMIN (SEC) 1/1/94. Re-entered 8/11/00.
  Flt Lt 1/8/96. Retd ADMIN 31/3/04.
PHIPPS L.W. CB AFC. Born 17/4/30. Commd 26/10/50. AVM 1/1/80. Retd GD 20/4/84.
PHYSICK M.D. BSc. Born 24/6/63. Commd 18/8/85. Flt Lt 18/2/87. Retd GD 18/8/01.
PHYSICK M.J. Born 12/3/61. Commd 16/9/79. Sqn Ldr 1/1/96. Retd GD 22/12/99.
PICHEL-JUAN M. Born 2/3/48. Commd 26/8/76. Flt Lt 1/12/75. Retd GD 19/11/93.
PICK K. Born 23/8/49. Commd 26/9/90. Flt Lt 26/9/94. Retd ENGINEER 31/10/03.
PICK R.E. CEng MIM ARSM. Born 23/2/33. Commd 30/12/63. Sqn Ldr 1/1/70. Retd ENG 23/5/91.
PICK S.J. Born 1/7/55. Commd 17/1/85. Sqn Ldr 1/1/92. Retd SUP 1/1/95.
PICKARD A.C. BA. Born 18/3/61. Commd 31/7/83. Flt Lt 31/1/86. Retd GD 30/4/00.
PICKARD C.F. Born 23/3/28. Commd 14/12/49. Gp Capt 1/7/75. Retd GD 4/4/80.
PICKARD H.H. MBE BSc. Born 18/12/21. Commd 11/11/43. A Cdre 1/7/73. Retd ADMIN 18/12/76.
PICKAVANCE M.J. Born 3/1/61. Commd 3/10/79. Flt Lt 11/3/89. Retd GD 3/1/99.
PICKAVANCE P. CEng MRAeS. Born 6/9/34. Commd 5/6/67. Sqn Ldr 1/1/78. Retd ENG 5/6/83.
PICKAVANCE R. MSc BSc CEng MIEE. Born 4/3/50. Commd 15/9/69. Wg Cdr 1/1/02. Retd GD 4/3/05.
PICKEN B.W. MCMI. Born 24/7/30. Commd 4/7/51. Sqn Ldr 1/1/75. Retd GD(G) 6/4/83.
PICKERELL I.W. Born 26/3/51. Commd 21/10/81. Sqn Ldr 1/1/86. Retd GD 24/8/91.
PICKERILL R.A. OBE MA BSc CEng MIMechE MBCS. Born 10/2/57. Commd 14/9/75. Gp Capt 1/7/00.
  Retd GD 3/5/04.
PICKERING J.H.T. Born 11/8/14. Commd 31/8/36. Wg Cdr 1/1/49. Retd GD(G) 31/5/68.
PICKERING J.M. Born 25/2/48. Commd 3/11/77. Sqn Ldr 1/1/91. Retd ENG 14/3/97.
PICKERING R.J. BSc. Born 15/5/48. Commd 1/9/70. Sqn Ldr 1/1/82. Retd FLY(P) 15/5/03.
PICKERSGILL J.N.M. Born 5/8/31. Commd 28/7/53. Flt Lt 22/5/57. Retd GD 5/8/69.
PICKETT R.E. Born 15/12/54. Commd 22/5/75. Flt Lt 22/11/80. Retd GD 16/12/95.
PICKING A.W. MVO. Born 31/7/31. Commd 28/9/51. Sqn Ldr 1/1/65. Retd GD 31/1/71.
PICKLES T. Born 2/4/48. Commd 26/5/67. Sqn Ldr 1/1/81. Retd SUPPLY 2/5/03.
PICKMERE O.D. Born 25/4/26. Commd 6/12/51. Flt Lt 27/3/57. Retd GD 4/8/66.
PICKNETT A.J. DFC. Born 28/1/21. Commd 14/2/40. Wg Cdr 1/1/56. Retd GD 28/1/68.
PICKTHALL C.R. Born 30/12/49. Commd 24/8/72. Sqn Ldr 1/1/87. Retd GD(G) 14/3/96.
PICKTHALL M.A. Born 4/11/45. Commd 20/8/65. Flt Lt 20/2/71. Retd GD 19/11/88.
PICTON R.S. MSc BSc. Born 20/4/46. Commd 17/10/71. Sqn Ldr 17/4/77. Retd ADMIN 17/10/87.
PIDDLESDEN M.O. Born 29/9/32. Commd 23/8/51. Flt Lt 23/2/57. Retd GD 29/1/72.
PIELOW A.N. MCMI. Born 17/7/44. Commd 5/9/69. Flt Lt 7/3/76. Retd ADMIN 1/7/94.
PIERCE B.A.J. Born 27/7/28. Commd 5/7/68. Sqn Ldr 1/7/78. Retd ENG 4/4/85.
PIERCE C.G.H. BA. Born 29/7/31. Commd 9/4/52. Gp Capt 1/7/80. Retd ADMIN 6/4/83.
PIERCE D.H. Born 22/5/37. Commd 8/5/56. Flt Lt 7/5/62. Retd GD 7/5/78.
PIERCE D.J.B. MBE. Born 2/6/38. Commd 17/1/60. Gp Capt 1/1/91. Retd GD 1/1/93.
PIERCE D.P. MIEH. Born 30/12/60. Commd 4/6/87. Flt Lt 4/6/93. Retd MED(T) 31/10/95.
PIERCE F.S.J. Born 26/9/27. Commd 13/3/48. Flt Lt 11/11/54. Retd GD 26/9/65.
PIERCE J.W. MRAeS. Born 21/6/44. Commd 24/6/65. Wg Cdr 1/1/91. Retd GD 15/3/04.
PIERCE S.L. MBE. Born 1/3/32. Commd 30/7/52. Sqn Ldr 1/7/78. Retd GD 1/3/90.
PIERCE T.R.B. CBE. Born 14/9/19. Commd 4/4/38. A Cdre 1/1/66. Retd GD 3/10/70.
PIERCEY V.G. Born 14/7/21. Commd 6/6/46. Wg Cdr 1/7/67. Retd ENG 14/7/76.
PIERSE J.W. Born 12/11/34. Commd 2/7/64. Flt Lt 2/7/70. Retd GD 16/1/74.
PIERSON M.J.W. MBE MRAeS MBCS MMS MCMI. Born 6/10/31. Commd 24/5/53. Gp Capt 1/1/80.
  Retd GD 14/7/86.
PIESING C.C. Born 8/2/14. Commd 13/3/47. Flt Lt 29/11/51. Retd CAT 11/3/52.
PIFF B.S.J. MBE. Born 22/9/20. Commd 13/8/41. Sqn Ldr 1/7/55. Retd GD 22/9/63.

PIFF R.E.G. CEng MRAeS. Born 20/3/16. Commd 11/2/42. Wg Cdr 1/1/59. Retd ENG 11/4/71.
PIGDON J.E. Born 27/9/29. Commd 13/2/52. Sqn Ldr 1/7/68. Retd GD 27/2/76.
PIKE D. BSc ACGI. Born 28/11/43. Commd 22/9/63. Flt Lt 15/4/68. Retd GD 28/11/81.
PIKE D.H.O. MCMI. Born 26/5/22. Commd 3/4/59. Flt Lt 3/4/64. Retd ENG 26/5/77. rtg Sqn Ldr.
PIKE D.J. Born 22/5/38. Commd 30/12/59. Flt Lt 30/6/65. Retd GD 1/9/71.
PIKE E. Born 10/4/22. Commd 9/6/55. Flt Lt 9/6/60. Retd GD 1/10/68.
PIKE F.W. MBE. Born 7/9/42. Commd 19/10/65. Wg Cdr 1/1/82. Retd ENG 19/10/87.
PIKE H.E. Born 23/8/20. Commd 24/10/46. Sqn Ldr 1/1/68. Retd SUP 23/8/75.
PIKE J. MSc. Born 30/5/59. Commd 5/2/81. Wg Cdr 1/1/99. Retd GD 30/5/03.
PIKE J.E. PhD MSc BSc. Born 27/6/45. Commd 14/6/71. Flt Lt 3/10/73. Retd ENG 1/12/78.
PIKE J.R. CEng MIMechE MRAeS. Born 28/6/35. Commd 10/8/65. Sqn Ldr 1/1/77. Retd ENG 30/4/90.
PIKE P.C.G. MCMI. Born 3/8/50. Commd 3/10/74. Sqn Ldr 1/7/86. Retd GD 20/5/90.
PIKE R.G. Born 12/7/43. Commd 28/7/64. Flt Lt 28/1/67. Retd GD 12/7/81.
PIKE W.F.J. Born 6/11/30. Commd 30/4/50. Sqn Ldr 1/1/76. Retd GD 14/10/84.
PIKE W.J. MSc MB BS MRCSEng MRCGP MFOM LRCP DRCOG DAvMed. Born 31/12/44. Commd 27/6/75.
    AVM 1/7/02. Retd MEDICAL 31/12/04.
PIKE W.M. Born 12/10/48. Commd 3/12/74. Fg Offr 31/12/76. Retd SEC 29/7/78.
PILBEAM K.A. Born 22/10/35. Commd 18/10/62. Wg Cdr 1/1/88. Retd GD 22/10/93.
PILCHER C.E.C. BSc. Born 10/9/47. Commd 2/8/68. Flt Lt 2/5/73. Retd ENG 21/3/75.
PILCHER R.D. Born 9/6/25. Commd 28/7/45. Sqn Ldr 1/1/60. Retd GD 8/1/76.
PILCHER-CLAYTON J.K. Born 15/10/11. Commd 23/9/41. Sqn Ldr 1/7/55. Retd ENG 15/10/60.
PILE B.L. BA. Born 7/8/52. Commd 17/9/72. Wg Cdr 1/7/90. Retd OPS SPT 1/11/98.
PILE R.L.C. LLM FIMLS DMLM. Born 11/10/40. Commd 2/6/77. Sqn Ldr 27/3/87. Retd MED(T) 12/11/90.
PILGRAM G.R. CEng MRAeS MMS. Born 6/12/35. Commd 5/7/68. Sqn Ldr 1/1/77. Retd ENG 16/2/91.
PILGREM R.A. Born 26/2/30. Commd 22/7/71. Flt Lt 22/7/76. Retd ENG 7/9/82.
PILGRIM-MORRIS G.J. BSc(Econ) FInstAM. Born 19/5/45. Commd 18/8/67. Wg Cdr 1/7/89. Retd ADMIN 19/5/01.
PILGRIM-MORRIS J.S. Born 30/12/36. Commd 16/10/58. Wg Cdr 1/7/81. Retd GD 6/9/86.
PILKINGTON A.J. Born 3/1/42. Commd 6/5/66. Sqn Ldr 1/7/80. Retd GD 3/1/97.
PILKINGTON J.L. BSc(Eng). Born 26/11/51. Commd 16/9/73. Wg Cdr 1/7/93. Retd ENG 20/9/99.
PILKINGTON M.G. Born 29/12/51. Commd 20/7/78. Sqn Ldr 1/1/92. Retd GD 14/3/97.
PILKINGTON M.J. CB CBE. Born 9/10/37. Commd 17/11/58. AVM 1/7/86. Retd GD 18/12/92.
PILKINGTON P.P. Born 20/11/29. Commd 26/8/66. Flt Lt 26/8/69. Retd GD 6/1/76.
PILLAI S.N. BSc. Born 19/11/60. Commd 14/9/80. Flt Lt 15/1/86. Retd GD 27/9/99.
PILLEY R. Born 12/8/46. Commd 26/5/67. Flt Lt 18/2/70. Retd GD 2/6/78.
PIM R.S. BSc. Born 6/6/58. Commd 29/9/85. Flt Lt 29/3/86. Retd ADMIN 29/9/01.
PIMM D.M.J. Born 2/5/46. Commd 16/9/76. Sqn Ldr 1/1/88. Retd ENG 24/8/92.
PINCHES L.J.E. Born 12/10/40. Commd 14/5/60. Flt Lt 14/11/65. Retd GD 12/10/78.
PINCHIN R.P. Born 26/4/57. Commd 24/6/76. Flt Lt 24/12/81. Retd GD 3/10/93.
PINDER S.P.H. MB BS DAvMed DFFP. Born 15/2/53. Commd 13/4/86. Wg Cdr 13/4/92. Retd MED 14/3/96.
PINE D. Born 2/9/24. Commd 6/10/44. Sqn Ldr 1/7/55. Retd GD 2/7/76.
PINE R.D.H. Born 25/6/49. Commd 25/2/72. Flt Lt 25/2/75. Retd GD 28/4/89.
PINFOLD H.M. Born 5/2/13. Commd 14/9/34. Gp Capt 1/7/53. Retd GD 1/10/68.
PINGREE B.J.W. MSc BSc MB ChB. Born 13/8/38. Commd 13/8/60. Sqn Ldr 5/2/74. Retd MED 4/2/75.
PINK A.W. OBE. Born 8/8/17. Commd 19/6/47. Wg Cdr 1/1/56. Retd PRT 8/8/67.
PINK J.R. Born 27/4/39. Commd 14/5/57. Gp Capt 1/7/84. Retd SUP 27/4/94.
PINK N.R. Born 3/8/29. Commd 5/7/68. Flt Lt 5/7/73. Retd ENG 3/8/79.
PINK T.J. OBE MCIPD. Born 22/8/46. Commd 16/1/72. Gp Capt 1/1/94. Retd ADMIN 22/8/96.
PINKEY K. Born 27/8/39. Commd 14/10/71. Sqn Ldr 1/7/90. Retd ENG 27/8/94.
PINKS C.N.R. Born 6/2/23. Commd 26/3/59. Flt Lt 1/4/63. Retd GD 6/2/78.
PINN D.L. MBE. Born 28/11/25. Commd 14/4/49. Sqn Ldr 1/1/59. Retd GD 30/9/75.
PINNELL C.P. Born 11/5/44. Commd 9/11/70. Wg Cdr 1/4/81. Retd LGL 9/11/86.
PINNER K.S.R. MCMI. Born 15/7/33. Commd 2/6/67. Sqn Ldr 1/1/73. Retd ADMIN 28/2/86.
PINNEY P.G. CVO. Born 27/8/39. Commd 13/12/60. Gp Capt 1/7/86. Retd GD 22/5/94.
PINNINGTON A. Born 31/12/44. Commd 27/2/75. Flt Lt 27/2/77. Retd GD 8/6/96.
PINNINGTON J.F. Born 3/2/24. Commd 8/1/45. Wg Cdr 1/1/61. Retd GD 31/3/73. rtg Gp Capt.
PINNOCK R.E. Born 21/1/23. Commd 13/7/61. Sqn Ldr 1/1/74. Retd ENG 21/1/78.
PINTCHES J.R. Born 15/9/31. Commd 20/12/51. Flt Lt 14/5/58. Retd GD 15/9/86.
PIPE G.K. Born 17/8/45. Commd 25/3/64. Flt Lt 25/9/69. Retd GD 2/4/92.
PIPE P.J. Born 16/2/33. Commd 2/4/56. Flt Lt 1/1/77. Retd GD 16/2/91.
PIPER A.H. DFC. Born 4/4/16. Commd 5/6/41. Sqn Ldr 1/8/47. Retd GD 24/1/58.
PIPER A.L. Born 10/4/51. Commd 6/10/77. Flt Lt 15/10/79. Retd ENG 10/4/89.
PIPER C. Born 24/2/40. Commd 21/1/66. Flt Lt 8/3/72. Retd GD(G) 1/1/75.
PIPER C.J. Born 1/5/48. Commd 30/5/69. Fg Offr 1/5/71. Retd ENG 10/4/75.
PIPER J.F.G. Born 15/8/22. Commd 17/3/55. Plt Offr 17/3/55. Retd GD 28/5/60.
PIPER K.R. Born 29/7/37. Commd 5/12/63. Flt Lt 15/4/70. Retd GD(G) 10/9/79.
PIPER L.R. Born 8/1/38. Commd 1/10/60. Sqn Ldr 1/7/75. Retd GD 8/1/96.

PIPER R. MBE. Born 23/6/41. Commd 6/9/68. Sqn Ldr 1/7/80. Retd GD 29/6/91.
PIPER R.J. Born 4/3/33. Commd 6/12/51. Flt Lt 27/3/57. Retd GD 24/9/75.
PIPER S.A.J. MBE. Born 5/10/25. Commd 18/10/62. Sqn Ldr 1/1/74. Retd GD 5/10/83.
PIPPET E.F. OBE. Born 23/10/15. Commd 15/3/35. Wg Cdr 1/7/47. Retd GD 23/10/70. rtg Gp Capt.
PITCAIRN-HILL F.C. Born 17/11/30. Commd 26/11/52. Flt Lt 5/10/60. Retd GD(G) 17/11/85.
PITCAIRN-HILL T.H. Born 26/12/15. Commd 19/3/42. Sqn Ldr 1/7/53. Retd ENG 28/10/68.
PITCHER A. CEng MIMechE MCMI. Born 13/3/30. Commd 15/11/51. Wg Cdr 1/7/74. Retd ENG 5/12/81.
PITCHER G. Born 3/7/41. Commd 12/1/62. Flt Lt 3/1/67. Retd GD 28/2/73.
PITCHER P.C. Born 31/7/48. Commd 19/8/66. Flt Lt 4/5/72. Retd GD 9/10/95.
PITCHFORK G.R. MBE BA FRAeS. Born 4/2/39. Commd 1/8/61. A Cdre 1/1/90. Retd GD 3/10/94.
PITICK G. Born 26/9/44. Commd 17/2/67. Flt Lt 17/8/72. Retd GD 1/10/84.
PITKIN J.M. BSc CEng MRAeS. Born 1/11/62. Commd 31/8/80. Sqn Ldr 1/1/92. Retd ENG 1/11/99.
PITMAN D.C.J. Born 30/1/32. Commd 16/12/66. Flt Lt 16/12/71. Retd GD 30/1/82.
PITMAN R.J.G. MSc. Born 30/10/34. Commd 23/10/62. Sqn Ldr 30/9/72. Retd EDN 1/10/79.
PITT J.G. Born 3/2/65. Commd 11/9/86. Flt Lt 11/3/93. Retd ADMIN 14/9/96.
PITT M.R. Born 13/3/50. Commd 14/8/70. Sqn Ldr 1/7/86. Retd GD 1/7/89.
PITT-BROWN W. CBE DFC* AFC FCMI. Born 3/7/18. Commd 30/7/38. A Cdre 1/7/61. Retd GD 3/4/69.
PITTAWAY R.A. Born 25/10/47. Commd 2/6/67. Sqn Ldr 1/7/85. Retd GD 14/9/96.
PITTAWAY S.F. Born 19/12/60. Commd 20/10/83. Flt Lt 1/10/87. Retd GD 20/6/99.
PITTER A.M. Born 28/12/69. Commd 29/7/91. Flt Lt 29/1/98. Retd ADMIN (SEC) 11/3/03.
PITTS A. Born 8/12/47. Commd 2/12/66. Flt Lt 2/6/72. Retd GD 10/1/99.
PITTS J. Born 24/12/44. Commd 5/3/65. Wg Cdr 1/1/90. Retd GD 24/12/04.
PITTS R.F. Born 24/8/58. Commd 11/9/86. Flt Lt 11/9/88. Retd GD(G) 24/8/96.
PITTS R.J.M. Born 2/8/59. Commd 6/11/80. Flt Lt 6/5/86. Retd GD 1/1/01.
PITTSON K.T. Born 2/5/49. Commd 8/6/84. Sqn Ldr 1/1/95. Retd ADMIN 15/11/99.
PIXTON G.W. DFC AFC . Born 14/6/51. Commd 4/5/72. Gp Capt 1/1/99. Retd GD 15/8/03.
PLACE R.T. Born 15/4/27. Commd 8/10/52. Flt Lt 6/3/58. Retd GD 27/5/68.
PLAISTOW C.M. Born 3/7/30. Commd 14/11/51. Flt Lt 14/5/56. Retd GD 2/8/73.
PLANK N.F. Born 3/2/39. Commd 8/8/74. Flt Lt 8/8/76. Retd ENG 7/4/83.
PLANT M.E. Born 20/6/42. Commd 14/8/70. Flt Lt 14/8/72. Retd GD 20/6/97.
PLANT R. Born 7/12/65. Commd 28/2/85. Flt Lt 28/8/91. Retd SUP 14/3/97.
PLANTEROSE P.J. MVO. Born 16/2/39. Commd 30/9/58. Gp Capt 1/1/90. Retd GD 20/4/92.
PLATER L.W. BA. Born 27/12/47. Commd 9/12/71. Sqn Ldr 1/7/85. Retd GD 1/7/88.
PLATER R.F. Born 30/8/27. Commd 1/11/50. Flt Lt 1/5/55. Retd GD 30/3/68.
PLATT B.D. Born 12/3/24. Commd 27/10/55. Flt Lt 27/10/61. Retd PI 12/3/79.
PLATT E.A. BA. Born 30/10/33. Commd 25/8/55. Sqn Ldr 30/4/63. Retd EDN 30/10/71.
PLATT J.C. MCMI. Born 5/6/22. Commd 2/10/43. Wg Cdr 1/1/69. Retd GD(G) 5/6/77.
PLATT J.C. BA. Born 2/4/47. Commd 22/9/68. Gp Capt 1/1/96. Retd GD 2/4/02.
PLATT K.J.G. CEng MIEE. Born 5/10/49. Commd 26/2/71. Sqn Ldr 1/7/83. Retd GD 24/10/87.
PLATTS F.J. OBE FIMS. Born 15/5/32. Commd 30/7/64. Wg Cdr 1/1/80. Retd GD(G) 1/1/85.
PLATTS J.T. MSc BEng. Born 24/10/62. Commd 16/2/86. Flt Lt 16/8/88. Retd ADMIN 14/3/97.
PLAYLE L.C.W. Born 16/2/52. Commd 29/4/71. Flt Lt 29/10/76. Retd GD 16/2/90.
PLEASANCE H.P. OBE DFC*. Born 12/4/14. Commd 11/5/36. Gp Capt 1/7/55. Retd GD 1/12/60.
PLEASANT A.M. Born 26/3/39. Commd 19/2/76. Flt Lt 19/2/81. Retd GD(G) 5/5/93.
PLEDGER Sir Malcolm. Born 24/7/48. Commd 18/9/66 ACM 2/9/02. Retd GD 18/4/05.
PLEDGER P.V. OBE. Born 24/3/27. Commd 8/4/49. Gp Capt 1/1/68. Retd GD 2/1/70.
PLENDERLEITH B.C. Born 27/9/50. Commd 8/12/83. Flt Lt 8/12/85. Retd ADMIN 14/3/97.
PLESSIS R.J.N. Born 1/7/37. Commd 30/10/61. Flt Lt 30/10/61. Retd GD 17/2/68.
PLESTED I.J. Born 16/7/47. Commd 21/5/65. Flt Lt 21/11/70. Retd GD 15/12/84.
PLEWS J.G. BA. Born 5/8/46. Commd 11/5/78. Flt Lt 11/5/80. Retd GD 21/11/98.
PLIMMER H.L. DFC*. Born 3/3/12. Commd 4/4/42. Sqn Ldr 1/7/53. Retd PE 1/9/60.
PLIMMER M. Born 6/8/39. Commd 19/1/66. Sqn Ldr 1/7/76. Retd ENG 1/7/79.
PLINSTON F.A. DFC. Born 29/4/19. Commd 17/12/38. Sqn Ldr 1/6/45. Retd GD 16/5/58.
PLOSZEK H.R. AFC. Born 6/5/36. Commd 17/12/57. Sqn Ldr 1/7/69. Retd GD 18/6/90.
PLOWMAN C.G. CEng MIMechE MRAeS. Born 17/5/37. Commd 25/9/59. Gp Capt 1/1/85. Retd ENG 17/5/92.
PLOWMAN K.F. Born 18/1/23. Commd 13/6/46. Flt Lt 13/6/52. Retd RGT 18/1/61.
PLOWMAN P.E. Born 26/10/39. Commd 4/4/59. Sqn Ldr 1/7/73. Retd SUP 8/11/82.
PLOWMAN R.L. LDSRCS. Born 28/8/57. Commd 30/9/79. Wg Cdr 1/12/94. Retd DEL 30/9/95.
PLOWMAN R.T.F. BA. Born 10/7/28. Commd 12/10/52. Sqn Ldr 1/7/62. Retd GD 12/10/68.
PLOWMAN W.S. BA MCIPD. Born 11/2/48. Commd 31/8/78. Sqn Ldr 1/7/85. Retd ADMIN 14/3/97.
PLOWRIGHT H.D.W. MB BS MRCS MRCOG LRCP DObstRCOG. Born 26/3/34. Commd 12/6/60. Sqn Ldr 16/3/64. Retd MED 2/8/69.
PLOWS D.M. BSc. Born 28/3/46. Commd 14/4/67. Flt Lt 1/6/71. Retd GD 3/2/76.
PLUCK M.F.E.W. Born 30/11/44. Commd 2/4/65. Flt Lt 2/10/70. Retd GD 30/11/82.
PLUCK N.S. MCMI. Born 10/8/30. Commd 21/2/52. Sqn Ldr 1/7/66. Retd SEC 1/7/69.
PLUMB A.A. Born 4/11/36. Commd 25/10/73. Sqn Ldr 1/7/83. Retd PI 4/10/83.

PLUMB F.A. Born 3/1/33. Commd 13/9/51. Sqn Ldr 1/1/67. Retd GD 31/1/71.
PLUMB J.V. Born 10/10/52. Commd 27/7/72. Wg Cdr 1/1/98. Retd GD 1/11/04.
PLUMB K.J. BSc. Born 1/12/52. Commd 20/1/80. Sqn Ldr 1/1/88. Retd ADMIN 14/3/97.
PLUMB R.G. FCCS. Born 7/4/17. Commd 21/2/57. Flt Lt 23/9/59. Retd SEC 4/4/70.
PLUMBLEY E.P. Born 4/10/21. Commd 5/9/57. Flt Lt 26/11/61. Retd ENG 30/12/72.
PLUME J.M. Born 16/5/58. Commd 22/11/84. Flt Lt 14/5/89. Retd ADMIN 9/7/00.
PLUME M.A.P. Born 4/7/16. Commd 1/3/62. Flt Lt 1/3/65. Retd CAT 31/12/71.
PLUME P.S. BTech CEng MIMechE. Born 29/1/50. Commd 2/9/73. Sqn Ldr 1/1/83. Retd ENG 2/9/89.
PLUMLEY J.H. BSc. Born 9/5/48. Commd 3/1/69. Wg Cdr 1/1/94. Retd GD 5/5/00.
PLUMMER A.J.W. Born 8/8/42. Commd 25/10/87. Flt Lt 25/10/89. Retd ADMIN 19/8/91.
PLUMMER B. MBE. Born 1/1/36. Commd 18/8/54. Sqn Ldr 1/7/81. Retd GD 1/1/96.
PLUMMER J.H.C. MBE FCMI MBCS. Born 30/5/23. Commd 23/10/43. A Cdre 1/1/74. Retd ADMIN 1/9/76.
PLUMMER K.G. BSc. Born 2/1/56. Commd 15/10/78. Sqn Ldr 1/1/91. Retd GD 14/9/96.
PLUMMER R.A. MCIPS. Born 9/7/42. Commd 29/3/68. Gp Capt 1/7/90. Retd SUP 9/7/97.
PLUNKETT P.A. BSc. Born 7/2/42. Commd 14/9/64. Flt Lt 14/6/66. Retd GD 14/9/80.
PLUNKETT P.N.O. BSc. Born 28/8/45. Commd 5/1/66. Gp Capt 1/1/90. Retd GD 30/9/98.
POATE C.D. Born 30/7/50. Commd 26/2/71. Fg Offr 26/2/72. Retd GD 15/6/73.
POCKNELL D. Born 1/10/19. Commd 5/4/43. Sqn Ldr 1/7/56. Retd ENG 1/10/68.
POCOCK D.A. CBE. Born 5/7/20. Commd 25/7/41. AVM 1/1/73. Retd RGT 5/7/75.
POCOCK R.C. Born 23/9/18. Commd 5/3/43. Flt Lt 5/9/46. Retd GD 15/10/57. rtg Sqn Ldr.
POCOCK R.W. MCMI. Born 11/5/30. Commd 30/7/53. Wg Cdr 1/7/75. Retd SUP 21/4/84.
PODEVIN C. Born 4/1/12. Commd 12/8/43. Fg Offr 12/2/44. Retd ENG 9/2/46.
PODGER C.J. Born 3/5/34. Commd 12/7/55. Sqn Ldr 1/1/68. Retd GD 1/5/82.
PODMORE W.F. MCMI. Born 18/8/20. Commd 30/8/62. Flt Lt 30/8/67. Retd ENG 18/8/75.
POGMORE J.R. MB BS MRCS MRCOG LRCP DObstRCOG. Born 12/6/42. Commd 22/4/63. Wg Cdr 2/1/80.
    Retd MED 12/6/80.
POIL R.W. The Rev. AKC. Born 9/11/30. Commd 17/1/52. Retd Wg Cdr 10/12/76.
POINTER A.R.B. MBE. Born 15/10/17. Commd 18/4/43. Flt Lt 18/10/46. Retd GD(G) 2/8/69.
POLAK E. Born 22/2/20. Commd 12/4/44. Flt Lt 27/5/54. Retd GD(G) 22/2/60.
POLAND E.R. Born 20/4/25. Commd 29/4/44. Flt Lt 4/12/52. Retd SUP 1/2/58.
POLDEN D.B. DFM. Born 29/1/23. Commd 10/9/43. Sqn Ldr 1/7/67. Retd GD(G) 2/10/76.
POLE F.G. BSc. Born 25/5/47. Commd 6/10/69. Sqn Ldr 1/1/83. Retd GD 1/1/86.
POLE F.G. CEng MIMechE MRAeS MCMI. Born 26/7/36. Commd 12/9/58. Flt Lt 21/6/64. Retd ENG 21/8/77.
POLHILL J. Born 29/9/12. Commd 31/12/41. Sqn Ldr 1/10/55. Retd ENG 29/9/67.
POLLARD C.S. BSc. Born 28/12/62. Commd 22/5/89. Sqn Ldr 1/7/00. Retd OPS SPT(FC) 1/7/03.
POLLARD D.M. BSc. Born 22/12/72. Commd 9/4/95. Flt Lt 9/10/97. Retd FLY(P) 3/4/03.
POLLARD D.W. BSc. Born 20/11/46. Commd 26/5/67. Flt Lt 18/11/71. Retd ENG 16/10/75.
POLLARD E.H. Born 3/2/18. Commd 14/9/44. Sqn Ldr 1/1/56. Retd ENG 12/3/73.
POLLARD J.T. Born 14/2/31. Commd 15/10/52. Flt Lt 5/11/58. Retd GD 14/2/69.
POLLARD K.G. Born 5/4/20. Commd 11/9/43. Flt Lt 19/6/52. Retd RGT 5/4/65.
POLLARD K.G. Born 17/10/37. Commd 13/10/61. Sqn Ldr 1/7/72. Retd GD 7/4/79.
POLLARD N.A. Born 18/12/28. Commd 22/7/50. Wg Cdr 1/7/77. Retd SY 13/11/82.
POLLEY I.W.M. CEng MIMechE. Born 13/9/37. Commd 10/12/63. Sqn Ldr 1/1/71. Retd ENG 10/12/79.
POLLINGTON D. AFC. Born 26/12/46. Commd 1/3/68. Gp Capt 1/1/00. Retd GD 3/1/02.
POLLINGTON J.E. MCMI. Born 27/1/23. Commd 5/10/50. Wg Cdr 1/7/65. Retd GD 31/3/73.
POLLITT A.M. MBE. Born 18/5/15. Commd 19/4/41. Sqn Ldr 1/7/60. Retd GD(G) 28/5/70.
POLLOCK A.J. Born 7/10/58. Commd 13/9/88. Gp Capt 1/1/00. Retd 28/4/03.
POLLOCK A.R. Born 13/3/36. Commd 10/4/56. Flt Lt 10/10/58. Retd GD 24/10/68.
POLLOCK D.P. Born 10/9/38. Commd 4/9/60. Wg Cdr 1/7/77. Retd GD(G) 10/9/93.
POLLOCK H.A. MBE MCMI. Born 9/11/21. Commd 9/5/46. Sqn Ldr 1/1/63. Retd ENG 1/12/77.
POLLOCK H.A.J. Born 9/4/24. Commd 7/11/44. Flt Lt 14/12/54. Retd GD(G) 16/5/65.
POLLOCK J. Born 17/6/25. Commd 9/7/59. Flt Lt 9/7/65. Retd ACB 30/4/66.
POLLOCK J. Born 24/2/34. Commd 3/12/70. Flt Lt 3/12/73. Retd GD 24/5/92.
POLLOCK N.J.C. OBE. Born 5/1/18. Commd 29/6/41. Sqn Ldr 1/1/54. Retd SEC 7/1/65.
POLLOCK N.R. MBE. Born 29/12/23. Commd 21/10/54. Sqn Ldr 1/7/70. Retd GD 30/4/84.
POLLOCK S.J.C. Born 10/9/46. Commd 9/3/72. Flt Lt 9/3/77. Retd ENG 15/11/87.
POLWARTH J.B. BA. Born 23/12/59. Commd 7/11/82. Flt Lt 7/2/83. Retd GD 1/4/93.
POMEROY A.I. Born 11/7/65. Commd 14/11/91. Flt Lt 2/2/93. Retd FLY(P) 11/7/03.
POMEROY C.A. Born 3/12/42. Commd 14/7/66. Sqn Ldr 1/7/77. Retd GD 3/12/80.
POMFRET C.J. BSc(Tech) CEng MIMechE MCMI. Born 13/12/54. Commd 16/9/73. Sqn Ldr 1/7/86. Retd ENG 27/3/96.
POMFRET S. Born 1/7/31. Commd 2/5/51. Wg Cdr 1/7/68. Retd GD 1/7/87.
POND G.R. Born 20/4/29. Commd 11/10/50. Flt Lt 1/5/55. Retd GD 14/11/75.
POND M.R. Born 25/2/39. Commd 31/10/69. Flt Lt 31/10/71. Retd ENG 1/4/78.
PONSFORD R.A. LRAM ARCM. Born 22/10/19. Commd 28/3/59. Sqn Ldr 13/12/67. Retd DM 22/10/74.
PONTING A.J. LLB. Born 21/1/35. Commd 25/11/60. Flt Lt 18/2/70. Retd SUP 10/2/78.
PONTON W.H. Born 24/8/20. Commd 19/1/46. Sqn Ldr 1/1/68. Retd GD(G) 24/8/75.

POOK J.J. MBE DFC. Born 20/4/45. Commd 15/7/66. Sqn Ldr 1/1/79. Retd GD 15/6/97.
POOL G.L. Born 19/9/23. Commd 28/5/47. Flt Lt 19/11/53. Retd GD 27/6/65.
POOL I. Born 3/9/59. Commd 9/5/91. Flt Lt 9/5/93. Retd GD(G) 14/3/96.
POOLE A.N. Born 28/1/45. Commd 31/10/74. Sqn Ldr 1/7/91. Retd GD(G) 1/4/94.
POOLE D. Born 2/5/50. Commd 6/11/72. Flt Lt 11/11/76. Retd GD(G) 26/8/86.
POOLE D. Born 1/8/16. Commd 21/10/54. Flt Lt 21/10/57. Retd SEC 1/8/73.
POOLE D.R. BSc. Born 17/5/60. Commd 6/9/81. Sqn Ldr 1/7/91. Retd GD 17/5/98.
POOLE F.A.G. MA BSc. Born 22/2/21. Commd 1/1/50. Sqn Ldr 1/11/55. Retd EDN 15/9/61.
POOLE F.W. Born 14/3/20. Commd 17/5/56. Flt Lt 17/5/62. Retd SEC 25/6/65.
POOLE G.M. Born 9/2/34. Commd 24/2/67. Flt Lt 24/2/72. Retd GD 19/4/79.
POOLE J. Born 16/6/21. Commd 1/11/56. Sqn Ldr 1/1/69. Retd ENG 16/6/76.
POOLE N.P. Born 18/5/47. Commd 11/8/67. Sqn Ldr 1/7/84. Retd GD 2/1/99.
POOLE P.B. Born 1/7/21. Commd 29/10/53. Fg Offr 29/10/55. Retd SEC 15/3/57.
POOLE R. Born 15/11/13. Commd 19/9/44. Flt Lt 19/6/52. Retd RGT 1/5/58.
POOLE R.S.G. Born 24/5/27. Commd 20/12/46. Flt Lt 4/1/51. Retd GD 31/10/75.
POOLER M.J. Born 23/2/49. Commd 27/2/70. Flt Lt 27/8/75. Retd GD 23/2/91.
POOLEY A.F.V. Born 21/5/46. Commd 31/10/69. Sqn Ldr 1/1/86. Retd GD 16/6/91.
POOLEY J.D.A. Born 8/11/32. Commd 23/4/52. Flt Lt 19/9/57. Retd GD 8/11/70.
POOLEY T.T. Born 9/10/45. Commd 7/11/85. Sqn Ldr 1/7/96. Retd ENG 23/3/01.
POOTS R. Born 26/11/51. Commd 21/2/74. Sqn Ldr 1/7/88. Retd GD 1/7/91.
POPE B.J. Born 10/10/58. Commd 22/5/80. Flt Lt 22/10/86. Retd SUP 1/7/89.
POPE B.T. Born 4/12/40. Commd 27/7/72. Sqn Ldr 25/11/77. Retd ADMIN 27/7/81.
POPE C.A. MA PGCE FRGS MCIPD DipEdTech. Born 18/3/55. Commd 8/4/79. Sqn Ldr 1/7/89. Retd ADMIN 8/4/01.
POPE F.R. MBE. Born 29/3/15. Commd 22/4/43. Sqn Ldr 1/7/56. Retd ENG 31/3/65.
POPE G.B. Born 8/3/17. Commd 5/6/43. Sqn Ldr 1/1/65. Retd SUP 8/3/74.
POPE I.G. MHCIMA. Born 9/3/53. Commd 30/3/75. Sqn Ldr 1/1/88. Retd ADMIN 30/3/91.
POPE J.R. BSc. Born 14/5/52. Commd 13/9/70. Sqn Ldr 1/7/87. Retd GD 1/7/90.
POPE K. Born 28/8/53. Commd 16/5/74. Flt Lt 17/8/80. Retd GD(G) 28/8/92.
POPE L.C. Born 29/3/28. Commd 14/5/53. Flt Lt 14/11/56. Retd GD 29/3/66.
POPE L.D. DFC. Born 1/1/22. Commd 24/6/43. Sqn Ldr 1/1/68. Retd GD 1/8/73.
POPE L.R. Born 18/12/30. Commd 28/6/51. Flt Lt 14/5/58. Retd SEC 28/12/68.
POPE R. Born 24/2/39. Commd 1/4/66. Flt Lt 1/10/70. Retd GD 7/6/77.
POPE W.H. OBE. Born 27/7/21. Commd 31/7/42. A Cdre 1/7/73. Retd GD(G) 27/7/76.
POPE W.J. OBE CEng MRAeS MCMI. Born 4/12/19. Commd 19/8/42. Wg Cdr 1/1/60. Retd ENG 4/12/74.
POPEJOY G.E. Born 13/4/13. Commd 8/4/43. Sqn Ldr 1/1/57. Retd ENG 13/4/68.
POPHAM M.H. Born 29/11/33. Commd 8/4/82. Sqn Ldr 1/1/90. Retd ENG 1/9/93.
POPPITT B.P. MCMI. Born 6/7/35. Commd 25/9/62. Sqn Ldr 1/1/71. Retd ENG 25/9/75.
POPPLE J.R. Born 23/11/56. Commd 25/11/82. Sqn Ldr 1/7/92. Retd SUP 19/12/97.
POPPLE R.T. MBE MCIPD MCMI. Born 26/1/31. Commd 19/6/52. Wg Cdr 1/7/76. Retd SEC 1/9/78.
PORTEOUS T.C. AFC. Born 23/7/38. Commd 15/12/59. Sqn Ldr 1/1/69. Retd GD 27/8/75.
PORTER A.H. OBE CEng MRAeS FCMI. Born 14/9/12. Commd 20/2/41. Gp Capt 1/7/62. Retd ENG 14/9/66.
PORTER A.V. Born 26/8/41. Commd 29/11/63. Flt Lt 1/7/69. Retd GD 28/2/70.
PORTER E.J. BSc. Born 21/1/58. Commd 31/8/75. Flt Lt 15/10/81. Retd ADMIN 15/7/91.
PORTER E.O. Born 3/7/17. Commd 30/7/38. Sqn Ldr 1/3/42. Retd GD 28/1/48.
PORTER G. BA. Born 15/10/24. Commd 23/8/50. Sqn Ldr 15/10/58. Retd EDN 11/9/65.
PORTER H.R. CEng MRAeS. Born 26/6/14. Commd 12/11/42. Sqn Ldr 1/7/53. Retd ENG 26/6/69.
PORTER J.A. OBE BA. Born 20/11/42. Commd 9/2/62. Gp Capt 1/1/90. Retd GD 2/4/93.
PORTER J.A. OBE BSc DipSoton CEng FIEE FRAeS. Born 29/9/34. Commd 26/9/53. AVM 1/7/84. Retd ENG 6/2/89.
PORTER J.W. Born 20/4/40. Commd 24/4/64. Sqn Ldr 1/7/75. Retd GD 1/7/78.
PORTER L.J. Born 3/10/20. Commd 18/10/47. Flt Lt 4/1/51. Retd GD(G) 27/9/75.
PORTER M.D. Born 27/5/35. Commd 10/4/56. Flt Lt 5/11/58. Retd GD 10/4/92.
PORTER M.J. Born 14/10/37. Commd 15/12/59. Sqn Ldr 1/1/73. Retd ADMIN 30/11/90.
PORTER W. Born 4/6/23. Commd 24/4/45. Flt Lt 4/1/51. Retd GD 29/10/61.
PORTER W.W. The Rev. BD. Born 2/3/27. Commd 20/10/65. Retd Wg Cdr 20/10/81.
POSKITT L.A. Born 23/11/18. Commd 24/12/44. Fg Offr 24/12/45. Retd GD(G) 26/9/52. rtg Flt Lt.
POSTANCE R. CEng MIERE. Born 29/7/44. Commd 24/1/63. Flt Lt 24/7/69. Retd ENG 29/7/82.
POSTLETHWAITE J.P. Born 29/11/35. Commd 2/4/57. Sqn Ldr 1/1/70. Retd GD 1/10/77.
POTESTA T.C. OBE. Born 9/6/38. Commd 5/11/59. Gp Capt 1/1/86. Retd ADMIN 9/11/89.
POTHAN G.M. Born 4/4/40. Commd 4/11/51. Flt Lt 1/11/61. Retd CAT 16/11/70.
POTOCKI W.J. DFC. Born 9/6/19. Commd 1/11/45. Sqn Ldr 1/7/53. Retd GD 31/5/56.
POTTAGE J. OBE. Born 23/11/38. Commd 16/1/60. Wg Cdr 1/7/84. Retd GD(G) 23/11/93.
POTTER A. Born 8/11/31. Commd 13/8/52. Sqn Ldr 1/1/81. Retd GD 8/11/89.
POTTER A.W. Born 9/10/33. Commd 8/7/53. Sqn Ldr 1/1/79. Retd GD 9/10/88.
POTTER B. Born 15/5/39. Commd 15/12/59. Flt Lt 15/8/62. Retd GD 31/7/69.
POTTER C.E. Born 25/3/40. Commd 13/12/79. Sqn Ldr 1/1/89. Retd ENG 25/3/95.
POTTER C.J. BSc. Born 23/3/53. Commd 28/9/80. Sqn Ldr 1/1/87. Retd ENG 28/3/97.

POTTER D.D. Born 9/5/30. Commd 19/7/51. Flt Lt 22/6/59. Retd GD 30/9/77.
POTTER D.J. BA. Born 23/10/66. Commd 20/2/88. Flt Lt 15/1/91. Retd FLY(P) 23/1/05.
POTTER D.M. BA. Born 16/5/34. Commd 8/10/70. Flt Lt 8/10/71. Retd EDN 3/1/76.
POTTER D.N.R. MPhil BEd. Born 23/5/51. Commd 28/12/80. Sqn Ldr 1/1/89. Retd ADMIN (SEC) 17/5/04.
POTTER G.J. Born 9/3/38. Commd 18/8/61. Flt Lt 25/7/66. Retd GD 9/3/93.
POTTER I.P.G. BSc CEng MIEE. Born 17/2/49. Commd 27/2/70. Sqn Ldr 1/1/86. Retd ENG 1/5/94.
POTTER J. MA MSc MBCS MRAeS. Born 23/12/43. Commd 6/9/65. Sqn Ldr 28/6/74. Retd ADMIN 30/1/82.
POTTER J.E. Born 23/12/11. Commd 9/4/41. Wg Cdr 1/7/56. Retd ENG 23/6/65.
POTTER J.G. MDA BSc. Born 7/1/54. Commd 18/11/73. Wg Cdr 1/1/92. Retd SUP 16/7/95.
POTTER J.R. BSc. Born 16/2/42. Commd 26/9/71. Sqn Ldr 1/7/88. Retd GD 31/3/93.
POTTER M.W. BSc. Born 9/8/47. Commd 2/8/68. Sqn Ldr 1/7/79. Retd ENG 29/4/86.
POTTER R.A. Born 13/5/45. Commd 11/3/68. Flt Lt 11/6/71. Retd SEC 31/5/75.
POTTER S.B. BSc. Born 1/5/57. Commd 2/3/80. Sqn Ldr 1/7/89. Retd GD 1/10/96.
POTTLE W.M. BSc. Born 25/12/37. Commd 4/9/59. Sqn Ldr 4/3/70. Retd EDN 25/12/75.
POTTS A.N. Born 30/9/62. Commd 11/4/85. Flt Lt 11/10/90. Retd GD 14/3/96.
POTTS A.T. Born 10/6/44. Commd 12/7/79. Sqn Ldr 1/1/90. Retd SUP 10/6/99.
POTTS C.J. Born 1/7/22. Commd 9/12/42. Flt Offr 28/5/49. Retd SEC 14/6/55.
POTTS D.A. BA. Born 20/12/64. Commd 20/4/93. Sqn Ldr 1/7/98. Retd ADMIN (SEC) 7/5/05.
POTTS D.S. Born 16/4/64. Commd 24/9/92. Flt Lt 14/6/95. Retd SUP 16/4/02.
POTTS J.A. Born 21/11/43. Commd 31/8/62. Flt Lt 15/4/71. Retd ADMIN 18/3/94.
POTTS N.H. Born 15/4/15. Commd 17/7/43. Sqn Ldr 1/1/55. Retd SEC 4/9/61.
POUGHER-HEMSLEY P.R. BA FCIPD MCMI MRAeS. Born 30/4/48. Commd 28/2/69. Wg Cdr 1/1/90. Retd GD 14/3/97.
POULSON A. Born 28/11/19. Commd 1/3/51. Sqn Ldr 1/7/61. Retd SEC 28/1/69.
POULSON H.F. Born 18/2/20. Commd 21/6/43. Sqn Ldr 1/7/59. Retd ENG 18/2/75.
POULTER J.M. BSc. Born 1/8/45. Commd 16/1/72. Wg Cdr 1/1/88. Retd ADMIN 1/8/00.
POULTER K. Born 31/7/46. Commd 25/6/65. Flt Lt 25/3/71. Retd GD 14/3/96.
POULTER L.G. Born 25/4/47. Commd 28/2/69. Flt Lt 8/3/72. Retd GD 25/4/85.
POULTER R.A. MS BSc. Born 9/2/46. Commd 26/5/67. Sqn Ldr 1/7/76. Retd ENG 9/2/84.
POULTER R.G. Born 29/2/24. Commd 13/9/51. Flt Lt 22/5/57. Retd GD 30/8/66.
POULTON B.J. AFC. Born 3/5/44. Commd 6/4/62. A Cdre 1/1/96. Retd GD 2/5/97.
POULTON S. BSc. Born 22/11/46. Commd 22/10/72. Sqn Ldr 1/1/89. Retd ENG 22/11/01.
POUNDS B. BEM. Born 4/5/29. Commd 30/1/70. Flt Lt 30/1/74. Retd ENG 5/5/79.
POUNTAIN S.G. CEng MRAeS MCMI. Born 6/1/30. Commd 4/2/53. Wg Cdr 1/7/73. Retd ENG 15/5/80.
POUNTNEY F.K. Born 9/2/43. Commd 8/10/70. Wg Cdr 1/7/87. Retd GD(G) 11/4/91.
POVAH A.J. Born 11/10/20. Commd 23/8/56. Flt Lt 10/8/60. Retd GD 1/5/68.
POVEY K.C. Born 7/4/31. Commd 27/6/51. Flt Lt 14/11/56. Retd GD 8/6/71.
POVEY R.W. MB BS FRCS LRCP. Born 11/4/21. Commd 19/8/56. A Cdre 1/1/79. Retd MED 24/10/83.
POWELL A.E. Born 19/6/46. Commd 28/7/67. Sqn Ldr 1/7/78. Retd ADMIN 19/6/90.
POWELL D.J. OBE BA MInstPet MCMI. Born 15/7/43. Commd 28/7/64. Wg Cdr 1/7/84. Retd SUP 15/7/93.
POWELL E. Born 3/2/30. Commd 21/9/50. Sqn Ldr 1/1/67. Retd GD 3/2/85.
POWELL G.R. Born 15/6/26. Commd 28/7/67. Flt Lt 28/7/72. Retd ENG 7/10/75.
POWELL H.F. Born 5/12/10. Commd 27/5/43. Wg Cdr 1/1/63. Retd ENG 12/1/66.
POWELL J.B. Born 27/6/46. Commd 24/4/80. Sqn Ldr 1/7/90. Retd ADMIN (SEC) 2/3/03.
POWELL J.F. OBE MA. Born 12/6/15. Commd 18/4/39. AVM 1/7/68. Retd EDN 4/5/72.
POWELL J.R. Born 2/10/24. Commd 4/5/50. Sqn Ldr 1/1/61. Retd GD 1/10/73.
POWELL L.G. Born 2/5/54. Commd 17/9/72. Sqn Ldr 1/7/91. Retd ENG 2/5/98.
POWELL L.R. Born 25/7/47. Commd 10/12/65. Wg Cdr 1/7/94. Retd GD 2/11/01.
POWELL M. Born 10/7/40. Commd 28/7/67. Flt Lt 1/7/89. Retd GD 15/5/94.
POWELL M. BEng. Born 5/1/58. Commd 26/2/87. Flt Lt 28/3/81. Retd FLY(P) 31/1/05.
POWELL M.B. MCMI. Born 12/5/38. Commd 26/5/67. Sqn Ldr 1/7/83. Retd ENG 12/5/96.
POWELL M.B. BTech. Born 27/12/62. Commd 5/1/86. Flt Lt 5/7/87. Retd OPS SPT 5/1/02.
POWELL R.F.B. Born 30/10/20. Commd 23/4/42. Wg Cdr 1/7/56. Retd GD 30/10/67.
POWELL R.G. MCMI. Born 19/1/46. Commd 31/1/64. Wg Cdr 1/1/90. Retd GD 22/4/94.
POWER F. Born 5/2/62. Commd 19/3/81. Flt Lt 19/9/87. Retd OPS SPT 5/2/00.
POWER J. Born 12/4/37. Commd 23/9/66. Flt Lt 23/9/68. Retd GD 12/4/75.
POWER M. Born 25/12/51. Commd 28/7/88. Flt Lt 28/7/92. Retd GD(G) 9/8/96.
POWER M.D. MA. Born 7/2/52. Commd 24/6/73. Flt Lt 15/10/74. Retd GD 23/12/82.
POWIS B.R. Born 24/6/26. Commd 23/9/65. Flt Lt 23/9/68. Retd GD 31/7/82.
POWLES E.C. AFC. Born 19/4/21. Commd 21/4/45. Flt Lt 30/6/49. Retd GD 22/6/53.
POWLES R.T. Born 6/4/57. Commd 8/9/77. Flt Lt 8/3/84. Retd SY 6/4/85.
POWLEY R.H. MSc. Born 30/12/44. Commd 6/5/65. Gp Capt 1/1/92. Retd SUP 3/12/96.
POWLING R.H.C. Born 2/11/20. Commd 12/9/40. Wg Cdr 1/1/61. Retd GD 1/6/73.
POWNALL D.J. Born 7/4/32. Commd 17/5/51. Sqn Ldr 1/7/64. Retd SY 7/4/87.
POWNER W.H. DPhysEd. Born 7/7/29. Commd 18/4/56. Sqn Ldr 1/7/70. Retd PE 7/7/79.
POYNDER S.C.R. Born 27/8/50. Commd 4/2/71. Flt Lt 4/8/76. Retd GD 1/6/78.

POYNTER L.W. OBE CEng FIMechE MRAeS MCMI. Born 4/1/41. Commd 11/4/63. Gp Capt 1/7/89. Retd ENG 29/6/96.
POYNTZ S.J. Born 6/2/49. Commd 1/7/82. Wg Cdr 1/1/94. Retd GD 16/10/03.
POYSER G.F. Born 10/5/32. Commd 27/7/54. Wg Cdr 1/7/76. Retd GD 10/5/87.
POZYCZKA T.A. MB BS MROG. Born 11/9/48. Commd 27/1/69. Wg Cdr 22/12/85. Retd MED 11/9/86.
PRAGNELL D.J. Born 9/1/37. Commd 10/3/77. Flt Lt 10/3/81. Retd ENG 3/4/87.
PRAGNELL G.R. Born 8/5/31. Commd 2/7/52. Flt Lt 21/10/59. Retd GD 8/5/69.
PRANDLE A.L. Born 28/3/13. Commd 23/4/43. Fg Offr 19/6/48. Retd GD(G) 19/7/51. rtg Sqn Ldr.
PRATCHETT I.A.V. LLB IEng. Born 7/9/39. Commd 22/3/81. Flt Lt 22/3/83. Retd ENG 22/3/97.
PRATLEY C.W. OBE CEng FIEE. Born 7/11/45. Commd 26/5/67. Gp Capt 1/7/97. Retd ENG 7/11/00.
PRATT B.C. Born 22/10/37. Commd 29/9/55. Wg Cdr 1/1/85. Retd GD(G) 30/8/88.
PRATT B.G. Born 24/2/34. Commd 15/6/53. Flt Lt 17/9/58. Retd GD 24/2/72.
PRATT C.W. Born 23/6/43. Commd 23/6/67. Wg Cdr 1/1/88. Retd ADMIN 1/10/91.
PRATT G.L. Born 25/8/33. Commd 25/9/52. Flt Lt 27/2/59. Retd RGT 10/11/70. rtg Sqn Ldr.
PRATT J.W. MHCIMA. Born 15/7/21. Commd 7/9/61. Flt Lt 7/9/67. Retd CAT 16/6/73.
PRATT P.L. Born 22/3/58. Commd 12/10/78. Flt Lt 12/4/84. Retd GD 1/3/89.
PRATT R.W. BSc. Born 30/11/43. Commd 30/8/66. Flt Lt 30/11/67. Retd GD 29/7/72.
PRATT S.J. MCIPD MCMI. Born 9/1/36. Commd 4/4/54. Sqn Ldr 1/7/68. Retd GD 25/11/75.
PRATT W.C. Born 16/8/23. Commd 17/12/53. Flt Lt 17/12/59. Retd GD(G) 1/9/72.
PRATT W.E. Born 22/6/20. Commd 11/7/46. Flt Lt 11/1/51. Retd SEC 30/9/67.
PRATTIS P.A. Born 8/5/44. Commd 24/4/64. Flt Lt 4/11/70. Retd GD 8/5/82.
PREDDY L. AFC. Born 24/9/20. Commd 16/4/43. Wg Cdr 1/7/58. Retd GD 24/9/63.
PREECE C.D. OBE AFC. Born 30/4/26. Commd 22/1/48. Gp Capt 1/7/78. Retd GD 30/4/84.
PREECE C.P. Born 12/11/52. Commd 9/3/72. Flt Lt 9/3/77. Retd GD 12/3/82.
PREECE J.M. Born 7/10/36. Commd 19/4/55. Sqn Ldr 1/1/72. Retd GD 1/1/75.
PRENTICE J.M. BSc. Born 20/1/54. Commd 19/6/77. Flt Lt 19/3/78. Retd GD 19/12/93.
PRENTICE J.T. MCMI. Born 25/4/20. Commd 5/4/43. Wg Cdr 1/7/60. Retd SUP 26/1/71.
PRENTON C.G. The Rev. Born 8/4/33. Commd 1/1/63. Retd Wg Cdr 21/8/83.
PRESCOTT F.B. Born 7/8/49. Commd 11/7/74. Sqn Ldr 1/1/87. Retd GD 24/3/90. Re-entered 19/8/91. Sqn Ldr 28/5/88. Retd GD 26/2/00.
PRESCOTT M.E. BA DMS FCIS. Born 5/1/53. Commd 28/12/80. Flt Lt 28/12/82. Retd ADMIN 9/1/91.
PRESLAND P.N. Born 3/4/43. Commd 28/7/64. Gp Capt 1/7/88. Retd GD 1/6/93.
PRESNAIL A.P. Born 16/5/26. Commd 15/6/50. Sqn Ldr 1/7/59. Retd GD 3/7/79.
PRESS C.H. CEng MRAeS. Born 3/6/15. Commd 14/12/35. Gp Capt 1/7/57. Retd ENG 3/6/70.
PRESS L.G. OBE AFC**. Born 1/3/19. Commd 21/10/41. Wg Cdr 1/1/58. Retd GD 1/7/69.
PRESSLEY P.L.W. AFC. Born 23/2/32. Commd 26/9/51. Sqn Ldr 1/7/71. Retd GD 31/10/88.
PREST R. Born 24/12/49. Commd 20/6/68. Flt Lt 20/3/74. Retd GD 4/1/80.
PRESTON C.J. Born 2/5/35. Commd 21/10/53. Flt Lt 21/4/59. Retd GD 8/5/73.
PRESTON J.M. Born 5/8/30. Commd 11/4/51. Flt Lt 11/1/54. Retd GD 14/5/60.
PRESTON J.S. FCMI. Born 11/12/33. Commd 20/12/51. Gp Capt 1/7/79. Retd GD 20/1/84.
PRESTON M. MA. Born 9/2/63. Commd 29/9/85. Sqn Ldr 1/7/96. Retd GD 29/12/01.
PRESTON M.H. Born 7/7/45. Commd 6/11/64. Flt Lt 6/5/70. Retd GD 12/1/77.
PRESTON P. BEd MCIPD MRAeS. Born 12/8/52. Commd 30/10/83. Sqn Ldr 1/1/90. Retd ADMIN 14/3/96.
PRESTON P.P. Born 16/4/59. Commd 24/7/81. Flt Lt 24/1/87. Retd GD 14/3/96.
PRESTON T.S. BSc. Born 14/4/13. Commd 4/4/39. Flt Lt 1/6/47. Retd EDN 25/9/48.
PREW R.A. MRAeS. Born 7/12/12. Commd 15/5/40. Sqn Ldr 1/1/52. Retd ENG 28/8/58.
PREWETT C.L. Born 25/5/40. Commd 6/12/70. Flt Lt 6/12/72. Retd ENG 30/10/81.
PRICE A.C. Born 14/5/42. Commd 5/11/70. Flt Lt 5/11/72. Retd GD(G) 14/5/80.
PRICE A.C. BSc. Born 1/8/57. Commd 31/8/75. Flt Lt 15/10/81. Retd GD(G) 20/2/88.
PRICE A.J. BSc BSc. Born 22/7/61. Commd 5/2/80. Flt Lt 15/1/86. Retd GD(G) 31/5/92.
PRICE A.R. Born 23/2/40. Commd 22/5/70. Sqn Ldr 1/7/78. Retd ENG 7/4/91.
PRICE A.S. Born 16/1/46. Commd 1/3/68. Sqn Ldr 1/1/83. Retd GD 30/4/89.
PRICE A.W. Born 3/8/36. Commd 20/11/56. Flt Lt 20/5/62. Retd GD 3/8/74.
PRICE B.H. BSc. Born 3/2/32. Commd 8/5/56. Gp Capt 1/7/76. Retd ENG 3/2/89.
PRICE B.W. OBE MSc BSc FCMI MRAeS. Born 9/1/42. Commd 12/11/63. Wg Cdr 1/1/78. Retd SUP 9/1/97.
PRICE C.F. Born 25/7/16. Commd 3/7/41. Wg Cdr 1/1/55. Retd RGT 25/7/66.
PRICE C.P. MA. Born 28/12/44. Commd 13/8/72. Sqn Ldr 13/8/77. Retd LGL 8/1/82.
PRICE D. The Rev. BA. Born 30/1/23. Commd 4/1/56. Retd Sqn Ldr 6/9/68.
PRICE D.J. MSc BSc. Born 11/11/51. Commd 20/5/79. Flt Lt 20/5/80. Retd ADMIN 4/1/91.
PRICE D.R. Born 15/2/47. Commd 10/12/65. Flt Lt 10/6/71. Retd GD 4/8/72.
PRICE D.S. MBE. Born 10/6/25. Commd 6/11/52. Flt Lt 17/5/56. Retd GD 24/3/61.
PRICE F.H. Born 8/11/11. Commd 10/12/42. Sqn Ldr 1/7/54. Retd SUP 29/11/60.
PRICE F.W. The Rev. BA. Born 22/4/22. Commd 11/11/52. Retd Wg Cdr 11/11/68.
PRICE G.C. Born 19/6/30. Commd 25/11/53. Sqn Ldr 1/1/78. Retd GD 19/6/88.
PRICE H.T. Born 9/8/27. Commd 27/7/49. Wg Cdr 1/1/69. Retd GD 15/11/77.
PRICE J. BSc AFIMA. Born 6/12/33. Commd 22/11/57. Wg Cdr 1/1/83. Retd ADMIN 2/4/87.

PRICE J.A. Born 24/3/53. Commd 11/9/86. Flt Lt 11/12/88. Retd GD 11/9/94.
PRICE J.A.B. Born 26/4/63. Commd 8/4/82. Flt Lt 8/10/87. Retd GD 13/3/92.
PRICE J.D.H. Born 3/6/30. Commd 1/12/50. Flt Lt 25/3/57. Retd GD 19/6/68.
PRICE J.L. AFC MRAeS FCMI. Born 18/8/29. Commd 13/12/50. Gp Capt 1/1/73. Retd GD 3/1/80.
PRICE J.S.B. CBE. Born 11/2/38. Commd 15/12/59. Gp Capt 1/7/81. Retd GD 12/5/87.
PRICE J.W. CBE FCMI MRAeS. Born 26/1/30. Commd 26/7/50. AVM 1/1/83. Retd GD 1/8/84.
PRICE K.O.N. Born 22/8/42. Commd 17/12/63. Flt Lt 4/11/70. Retd GD 22/8/80.
PRICE N.F. Born 12/4/44. Commd 27/8/64. Flt Lt 27/2/71. Retd ENG 12/4/83.
PRICE N.R.C. Born 29/5/31. Commd 9/4/52. Wg Cdr 1/7/67. Retd GD 18/1/78.
PRICE N.S. Born 16/3/14. Commd 28/3/47. Flt Lt 28/9/51. Retd SUP 30/9/58.
PRICE P.J. BSc. Born 7/8/58. Commd 5/2/84. Sqn Ldr 1/7/95. Retd ADMIN 28/8/96.
PRICE P.W.McL. Born 28/8/49. Commd 23/2/68. Sqn Ldr 1/7/83. Retd GD 28/8/87. Re-entered 2/9/88. Wg Cdr 1/7/93. Retd GD 14/9/96.
PRICE R.A. MBE. Born 8/3/30. Commd 1/10/54. Flt Lt 1/4/60. Retd GD 8/3/92.
PRICE R.C. Born 5/2/24. Commd 25/8/60. Sqn Ldr 1/7/71. Retd ENG 5/2/79.
PRICE R.G. Born 21/4/64. Commd 4/12/86. Flt Lt 11/5/90. Retd GD 21/4/02.
PRICE R.G. DFC* FCMI MIPM. Born 9/1/22. Commd 31/8/42. Gp Capt 1/1/66. Retd GD 9/4/73.
PRICE R.G. CB FCMI. Born 18/7/28. Commd 27/7/49. AVM 1/1/82. Retd GD 1/1/84.
PRICE R.L. MBA MCMI. Born 21/10/57. Commd 14/4/85. Flt Lt 14/4/90. Retd ADMIN 14/3/97.
PRICE R.W. Born 31/8/21. Commd 5/9/44. Sqn Ldr 1/1/67. Retd GD 31/8/73.
PRICE S.T.G. AFM. Born 12/10/25. Commd 15/12/49. Sqn Ldr 1/1/60. Retd GD 31/3/75.
PRICE T. Born 1/3/47. Commd 2/6/67. Flt Lt 2/12/72. Retd GD 1/3/85.
PRICE T.R. BSc. Born 18/1/62. Commd 14/10/84. Flt Lt 14/4/87. Retd GD 14/10/96.
PRICE W.L. MB BCh. Born 21/4/16. Commd 18/7/41. Sqn Ldr 9/8/48. Retd MED 28/1/50.
PRICE W.S. MBE MCMI. Born 30/3/29. Commd 19/1/50. Sqn Ldr 1/7/63. Retd SEC 3/4/79.
PRICE-BROWN A.M.R. MB BS. Born 12/7/64. Commd 26/1/98. Fg Off 15/7/01. Retd MEDICAL 4/8/03.
PRICE-REES T.E. Born 12/12/43. Commd 20/10/67. Flt Lt 15/7/71. Retd GD 1/11/75.
PRICE-WALKER C.D. Born 30/8/42. Commd 28/2/80. Flt Lt 28/2/80. Retd ENG 5/2/97.
PRICHARD D.L. DSO. Born 15/11/16. Commd 16/8/39. Wg Cdr 1/7/54. Retd GD 29/11/63.
PRICHARD G.W. Born 30/5/41. Commd 26/10/62. Flt Lt 15/4/70. Retd GD 30/5/79.
PRICKETT F.M. MRAeS. Born 13/7/16. Commd 20/4/50. Sqn Ldr 1/7/61. Retd ENG 13/7/71.
PRICKETT Sir Thomas KCB DSO DFC. Born 31/7/13. Commd 9/1/38. ACM 15/6/69. Retd GD 1/10/70.
PRIDDLE A.L. BSc. Born 29/12/58. Commd 6/9/81. Flt Lt 6/12/81. Retd GD 6/9/97.
PRIDE I.McC. MBE. Born 13/1/45. Commd 14/8/64. Flt Lt 4/5/72. Retd OPS SPT 13/1/00.
PRIDEAUX J.A. Born 6/4/39. Commd 4/4/59. Gp Capt 1/1/86. Retd GD 21/4/90.
PRIDMORE D.W.R. Born 23/12/22. Commd 8/3/54. Sqn Ldr 1/1/73. Retd ADMIN 23/12/77.
PRIER R.G. DFC. Born 25/10/12. Commd 16/12/33. Wg Cdr 1/10/46. Retd GD 21/1/58.
PRIEST B. BA. Born 17/10/40. Commd 31/7/62. Sqn Ldr 1/1/73. Retd GD 8/4/79.
PRIEST J.R. Born 8/1/30. Commd 10/10/63. Flt Lt 10/10/68. Retd GD 18/9/69.
PRIEST J.S.D. Born 11/9/48. Commd 16/8/68. Flt Lt 16/2/74. Retd GD 3/11/02.
PRIEST J.S.D. Born 24/12/49. Commd 20/9/68. Flt Lt 16/2/74. Retd GD 4/1/80.
PRIESTLEY D.E. MSc CEng FIEE FCIPD. Born 28/5/34. Commd 7/9/56. Gp Capt 1/7/83. Retd ADMIN 28/5/89.
PRIESTLEY H. Born 6/5/23. Commd 7/10/44. Flt Lt 26/5/55. Retd GD(G) 31/5/70.
PRIESTLEY I. Born 10/6/39. Commd 20/9/79. Sqn Ldr 1/9/79. Retd SY 10/6/94.
PRIESTLEY J.C. Born 3/6/32. Commd 21/1/71. Sqn Ldr 1/7/82. Retd SY 3/6/87.
PRIMER R. Born 1/4/16. Commd 6/9/43. Flt Lt 1/1/50. Retd GD(G) 1/4/66.
PRIMETT M.N. MA. Born 24/3/58. Commd 11/6/81. Gp Capt 1/1/02. Retd GD 3/4/04.
PRIMROSE J. AFC DPhysEd. Born 24/3/25. Commd 17/12/51. Sqn Ldr 1/7/58. Retd GD 2/7/68. Re-instated 22/10/80 to 24/3/85.
PRINCE H.J.D. AFC. Born 28/2/34. Commd 3/3/54. Sqn Ldr 1/1/70. Retd GD 15/3/86.
PRINCE J.T. Born 6/9/40. Commd 2/5/59. Flt Lt 20/6/69. Retd GD 6/9/95.
PRINCE M.J. Born 11/5/60. Commd 15/12/88. Flt Lt 15/12/90. Retd ENG 11/5/98.
PRINCE R.M. Born 13/1/37. Commd 15/3/73. Sqn Ldr 1/1/87. Retd GD 13/1/92.
PRINCE R.S. Born 1/5/56. Commd 16/6/88. Flt Lt 16/6/90. Retd ENG 16/6/96.
PRING A.J. Born 6/11/12. Commd 9/4/53. Flt Lt 1/1/58. Retd GD 6/11/61.
PRING R.M. Born 4/12/45. Commd 1/7/82. Flt Lt 1/7/85. Retd GD 4/12/00.
PRINGLE Sir Charles KBE MA FEng Hon FRAeS. Born 6/6/19. Commd 4/4/41. AM 1/7/73. Retd ENG 6/6/76.
PRINGLE M.A. Born 12/12/33. Commd 11/6/52. Sqn Ldr 1/1/72. Retd GD 3/11/81.
PRINGLE R. Born 24/8/47. Commd 9/12/71. Flt Lt 9/6/77. Retd GD 19/9/79.
PRINGUER D.C. Born 16/7/40. Commd 9/7/60. Flt Lt 9/1/66. Retd GD 16/7/95.
PRINT C.P. MSc. Born 16/1/60. Commd 25/11/84. Flt Lt 25/5/87. Retd OPS SPT 25/11/00.
PRIOR A.R.J. MBE BSc MB BS. Born 3/11/52. Commd 19/11/74. Wg Cdr 1/8/92. Retd MED 2/4/98.
PRIOR B.M.G. Born 5/11/32. Commd 24/9/52. Flt Lt 14/11/58. Retd GD(G) 5/11/92.
PRIOR F.R.J. Born 3/4/37. Commd 19/6/70. Sqn Ldr 1/1/77. Retd ENG 13/12/90.
PRIOR H. Born 18/2/36. Commd 4/3/71. Sqn Ldr 1/1/86. Retd GD 6/2/91.
PRIOR I.R. BA AMBCS. Born 11/3/44. Commd 25/3/64. Wg Cdr 1/1/89. Retd GD 26/11/94.

PRIOR K.S. MB BS FRCGP MFOM MRCS(Eng) LRCP DAvMed. Born 23/8/40. Commd 13/8/62. A Cdre 1/7/92. Retd MED 14/3/96.
PRIOR M.R. Born 23/8/60. Commd 27/3/80. Sqn Ldr 1/7/92. Retd GD 23/8/98.
PRIOR P.E. OBE AFC. Born 3/11/21. Commd 16/3/43. Wg Cdr 1/7/64. Retd GD 30/5/77.
PRIOR P.N. MBE BA. Born 15/11/33. Commd 3/9/59. Wg Cdr 1/7/78. Retd SUP 25/4/81.
PRIOR R.G. Born 2/3/30. Commd 21/2/52. Flt Lt 21/2/58. Retd GD(G) 20/7/68.
PRIOR V. Born 9/4/32. Commd 12/11/57. Flt Lt 21/5/63. Retd GD 28/12/77.
PRISSICK H. Born 19/11/52. Commd 25/9/71. Sqn Ldr 1/7/88. Retd GD 20/4/93.
PRISSICK M. CBE. Born 11/6/49. Commd 25/2/72. A Cdre 1/7/99. Retd GD 11/7/01.
PRITCHARD A. Born 12/5/29. Commd 23/9/66. Flt Lt 23/9/69. Retd GD 12/5/76.
PRITCHARD A.R. MSc BEng CEng MIMechE. Born 10/8/52. Commd 16/5/72. Sqn Ldr 1/7/85. Retd ENG 1/5/91.
PRITCHARD A.W. FCIPD FCMI. Born 8/7/40. Commd 27/6/59. Sqn Ldr 1/7/88. Retd ADMIN 8/1/97.
PRITCHARD D. Born 25/4/44. Commd 6/9/63. Flt Lt 6/3/69. Retd GD 25/4/82.
PRITCHARD D.B. Born 19/10/19. Commd 23/10/42. Sqn Ldr 1/1/57. Retd GD 14/3/61.
PRITCHARD D.M. Born 23/9/60. Commd 18/12/80. Sqn Ldr 1/7/93. Retd GD 23/9/98.
PRITCHARD G.S.B. MA CEng MRAeS. Born 23/4/41. Commd 30/9/60. Wg Cdr 1/7/84. Retd ENG 23/4/96.
PRITCHARD J.E. Born 24/2/42. Commd 28/4/61. Flt Lt 13/1/72. Retd GD 24/2/80.
PRITCHARD M. MCMI. Born 25/4/44. Commd 31/10/63. Sqn Ldr 1/7/74. Retd ADMIN 3/10/97.
PRITCHARD-SMITH S. Born 6/11/23. Commd 3/6/53. Flt Lt 14/5/58. Retd CAT 6/11/72.
PRITCHETT A.J. BSc. Born 6/6/61. Commd 4/1/83. Flt Lt 4/10/84. Retd GD 14/3/96.
PRITT M.G. Born 9/3/43. Commd 1/12/69. Sqn Ldr 1/7/83. Retd ADMIN 9/3/99.
PROBERT C.G. Born 19/1/40. Commd 4/11/81. Flt Lt 13/4/67. Retd GD(G) 12/12/86. Re-instated 4/11/81 to 12/12/86.
PROBERT H.A. MBE MA. Born 23/12/26. Commd 4/11/48. A Cdre 1/7/76. Retd ADMIN 1/10/78.
PROBERT R.J. MCMI. Born 18/7/30. Commd 24/7/52. Sqn Ldr 1/7/65. Retd SUP 3/4/81.
PROBERT R.L. Born 25/7/40. Commd 9/4/60. Flt Lt 9/10/65. Retd GD 25/7/78.
PROBERT T.V. Born 15/10/30. Commd 13/9/51. Flt Lt 4/1/57. Retd GD 15/10/68.
PROBERT V.C.M. Born 24/2/35. Commd 1/8/69. Flt Lt 6/10/71. Retd ADMIN 1/8/77.
PROBYN P.J. FCMI. Born 23/1/24. Commd 6/9/47. Gp Capt 1/1/71. Retd SUP 31/3/78.
PROCOPIDES M.D. BSc. Born 1/6/50. Commd 7/11/76. Sqn Ldr 1/7/86. Retd GD 1/1/01.
PROCTER J.H. MBE BA. Born 5/7/37. Commd 4/9/59. Sqn Ldr 4/3/68. Retd EDN 4/9/75.
PROCTER K.J.M. BSc (Eur Ing) CEng FIEE FRAeS FCMI. Born 7/3/44. Commd 30/9/62. A Cdre 1/1/97. Retd ENG 7/4/00.
PROCTOR C.T. BA CEng MIEE. Born 19/12/37. Commd 28/7/60. Flt Lt 19/10/65. Retd ENG 4/7/90.
PROCTOR D.A. Born 5/3/32. Commd 17/5/51. Flt Lt 19/12/56. Retd GD 7/5/70.
PROCTOR G.P. Born 3/2/29. Commd 23/6/60. Wg Cdr 1/7/81. Retd ENG 3/2/87.
PROCTOR J.W. Born 27/3/20. Commd 5/11/43. Flt Lt 10/1/50. Retd GD 25/12/63.
PROCTOR R.G. MBE. Born 22/12/24. Commd 17/6/45. Wg Cdr 1/7/65. Retd SUP 22/12/79.
PROCTOR R.S. BSc CEng MIEE. Born 5/6/46. Commd 26/5/70. Sqn Ldr 1/7/79. Retd ENG 26/5/86.
PROFIT G.R. OBE AFC MRAeS. Born 31/10/40. Commd 23/6/61. A Cdre 1/7/87. Retd GD 2/11/90.
PROOPS R.A. FIMLT. Born 23/1/30. Commd 1/2/62. Sqn Ldr 25/6/73. Retd MED(T) 30/10/75.
PROSSER C.J. BEng. Born 11/5/68. Commd 17/2/91. Fg Offr 17/2/89. Retd GD 21/10/92.
PROSSER W.H. Born 31/5/34. Commd 11/11/60. Flt Lt 11/11/60. Retd GD 30/7/65.
PROSSER-HIGDON D.R. Born 28/3/27. Commd 25/8/54. Wg Cdr 1/1/69. Retd PRT 8/6/76. rtg Gp Capt.
PROTHERO F.J. Born 5/5/22. Commd 15/6/50. Flt Lt 15/12/53. Retd GD 28/7/73.
PROTHERO R.M. MRAeS MCMI. Born 30/5/39. Commd 21/10/60. Wg Cdr 1/1/84. Retd GD 30/5/94.
PROUD P. BA. Born 16/1/32. Commd 19/8/54. Sqn Ldr 17/2/63. Retd EDN 30/8/70.
PROUDLOCK J.R.C. Born 20/10/16. Commd 4/12/42. Gp Capt 1/1/65. Retd PRT 29/6/68.
PROUDLOVE F.W. Born 15/3/15. Commd 14/1/42. Flt Lt 1/9/45. Retd ENG 1/8/53.
PROUT C.D. BSc. Born 26/12/59. Commd 26/9/82. Flt Lt 26/12/85. Retd ENG 26/9/87.
PROUT K.E. IEng FIIE. Born 27/1/51. Commd 5/2/81. Sqn Ldr 1/7/90. Retd ENG 10/10/99.
PROUT R.A. BSc. Born 6/7/47. Commd 28/10/73. Flt Lt 28/1/75. Retd GD 19/3/81.
PROVAN G.G. Born 30/9/40. Commd 31/10/74. Flt Lt 31/10/76. Retd SY 31/10/82.
PROWTING N.H. Born 6/7/22. Commd 21/11/47. Flt Lt 4/12/52. Retd GD 3/1/64.
PRUNIER A.P. BSc. Born 29/10/48. Commd 5/2/84. Sqn Ldr 1/1/89. Retd ADMIN 5/2/00.
PRYCE G.O. AIIP. Born 26/4/20. Commd 6/10/60. Flt Lt 6/10/65. Retd ENG 8/4/72.
PRYCE K.E. BA. Born 26/10/41. Commd 11/10/70. Sqn Ldr 1/7/83. Retd SUP 1/7/96.
PRYCE R.N. CEng MIEE. Born 19/11/21. Commd 22/11/56. Sqn Ldr 1/7/66. Retd ENG 19/11/76.
PRYOR-JONES A.J.W. Born 30/5/42. Commd 11/1/79. Flt Lt 1/1/82. Retd GD 9/11/96.
PUCKERING J.N. Born 3/8/36. Commd 16/12/58. Sqn Ldr 1/7/67. Retd GD 3/8/74.
PUDDY R.J. Born 5/11/52. Commd 20/1/80. Sqn Ldr 1/1/88. Retd ADMIN 14/3/96.
PUDNEY K.W. Born 21/5/45. Commd 8/1/76. Sqn Ldr 1/1/87. Retd MED(SEC) 1/9/92. rtg Wg Cdr.
PUDWELL J.S. Born 4/1/31. Commd 11/11/50. Flt Lt 11/5/55. Retd GD(G) 4/1/93.
PUGH G.A.W. BDS. Born 13/10/44. Commd 1/6/72. Sqn Ldr 10/1/75. Retd DEL 1/9/76.
PUGH H. Born 7/10/23. Commd 26/11/43. Flt Lt 26/11/49. Retd SEC 5/3/62.
PUGH H.A. BSc. Born 4/4/56. Commd 12/8/79. Flt Lt 12/11/80. Retd GD 12/8/95.
PUGH J.D. Born 20/3/34. Commd 14/12/54. Wg Cdr 1/7/72. Retd GD 16/9/87.

PUGH J.R. Born 27/4/47. Commd 18/8/67. Flt Lt 4/11/70. Retd GD 28/8/75.
PUGH K.W.T. AFC CEng MRAeS FCMI. Born 22/8/20. Commd 18/10/41. Gp Capt 1/7/61. Retd GD 22/8/72.
PUGH M.A.P. OBE AFC. Born 27/4/33. Commd 28/2/52. Wg Cdr 1/7/77. Retd GD 27/4/93.
PUGH P.M.D. MCMI. Born 20/9/48. Commd 16/12/66. Flt Lt 16/6/73. Retd SUP 1/9/77. Re-entered 3/3/81.
    Sqn Ldr 1/7/84. Retd SUP 5/3/97.
PUGH R.M. AFC. Born 25/6/21. Commd 23/10/39. Sqn Ldr 1/1/51. Retd GD 28/9/68.
PULFORD J.F. Born 30/3/61. Commd 8/10/87. Flt Lt 8/10/89. Retd ADMIN 31/5/99.
PULFREY A.J. Born 11/11/48. Commd 17/7/70. Wg Cdr 1/1/89. Retd GD 25/4/01.
PULFREY J.M. Born 20/2/60. Commd 17/5/79. Flt Lt 17/11/85. Retd GD 17/5/86. Re-entered 16/5/90. Flt Lt 15/11/89.
    Retd OPS SPT 19/2/01.
PULL S.J. Born 2/11/46. Commd 6/5/66. Flt Lt 6/11/71. Retd GD 2/11/84.
PULLAN J.R. OBE FCA. Born 17/1/14. Commd 29/7/39. Wg Cdr 1/7/55. Retd SEC 6/3/61.
PULLAN M.G.A. Born 7/4/49. Commd 29/6/72. Flt Lt 29/12/77. Retd GD 13/3/88.
PULLEN F.F. MBE. Born 29/11/46. Commd 23/9/68. Sqn Ldr 1/7/85. Retd SUP 14/3/96.
PULLEN J.A. MCMI. Born 20/1/38. Commd 24/6/71. Sqn Ldr 1/7/82. Retd ENG 20/1/88.
PULLEN L.R. Born 24/3/20. Commd 6/6/57. Flt Lt 6/6/60. Retd ENG 6/6/70.
PULLEN S.K. Born 14/5/62. Commd 15/10/81. Flt Lt 15/4/87. Retd GD 14/5/00.
PULLEY N.S. Born 3/5/32. Commd 9/4/52. Flt Lt 15/2/65. Retd GD(G) 31/12/85.
PULLEYBLANK B.A. Born 15/3/47. Commd 10/5/73. Flt Lt 10/5/75. Retd GD 14/3/96.
PULLIN R.W. Born 31/7/33. Commd 10/9/70. Flt Lt 10/9/74. Retd GD 14/1/76.
PUNCHER C.L.G. MBE. Born 28/5/11. Commd 30/10/42. Sqn Ldr 1/7/51. Retd SUP 28/5/60.
PURCELL J. Born 5/1/38. Commd 29/7/58. Sqn Ldr 1/7/69. Retd SUP 5/1/76.
PURCELL J.D. AFC. Born 8/7/26. Commd 31/7/50. Flt Lt 16/5/56. Retd GD 28/10/65.
PURCHASE G.W. BSc. Born 21/5/52. Commd 13/9/70. Flt Lt 15/4/75. Retd GD 21/5/90.
PURCHASE W. MBE. Born 19/11/36. Commd 7/11/58. Sqn Ldr 1/1/73. Retd GD 19/11/94.
PURDIE M.J. Born 5/11/44. Commd 17/12/65. Wg Cdr 1/1/83. Retd GD 31/3/94.
PURDUE E.G. Born 16/4/22. Commd 22/8/63. Sqn Ldr 1/1/72. Retd ENG 25/8/73.
PURDY R.B. Born 22/4/43. Commd 17/7/64. Flt Lt 17/1/70. Retd GD 22/4/81.
PURKIS E.F.J. CEng MRAeS MCMI. Born 26/2/40. Commd 15/7/63. Flt Lt 26/7/67. Retd ENG 26/2/78.
PURNELL I.J. Born 7/9/48. Commd 5/8/76. Wg Cdr 1/1/90. Retd ENG 10/8/96.
PURNELL T.L.G. Born 29/4/62. Commd 30/4/81. Flt Lt 30/10/86. Retd GD 29/4/00.
PURSE J.M. BSc. Born 9/5/61. Commd 26/9/82. Flt Lt 26/12/83. Retd GD 31/8/95.
PURSER B.L. MCMI. Born 13/5/23. Commd 4/12/42. Sqn Ldr 1/1/67. Retd PI 31/12/77.
PURSER H.E. ACIS. Born 28/1/36. Commd 22/10/59. Wg Cdr 1/1/83. Retd ADMIN 12/8/86.
PURSER M.M. BSc CEng MRAeS. Born 10/7/44. Commd 22/9/63. Sqn Ldr 1/1/77. Retd ENG 10/7/82.
PURT M.B.D. Born 5/4/50. Commd 31/7/70. Flt Lt 31/7/73. Retd GD 27/7/79.
PURVES G.F. Born 21/10/22. Commd 27/3/43. Flt Lt 15/3/47. Retd SEC 30/3/62.
PURVES N.L. BSc. Born 11/5/66. Commd 1/4/87. Sqn Ldr 1/1/01. Retd FLY(P) 11/5/04.
PUSEY C.H. MBE. Born 8/12/12. Commd 18/7/46. Sqn Ldr 1/7/57. Retd SUP 28/4/67.
PUSEY F.R. OBE MCMI. Born 5/3/20. Commd 21/4/45. Wg Cdr 1/7/62. Retd GD(G) 5/3/75.
PUSEY W.A.S. Born 31/8/40. Commd 8/9/83. Flt Lt 8/9/87. Retd GD(G) 31/8/95.
PYE A.C. DPhysEd. Born 6/2/27. Commd 18/4/56. Flt Lt 18/4/60. Retd PE 20/1/71.
PYE A.J. Born 4/5/47. Commd 9/2/66. A Cdre 1/1/97. Retd SUP 2/12/99.
PYE C.R. MSc BSc CEng MRAeS. Born 1/6/46. Commd 2/7/72. Gp Capt 1/1/95. Retd ENG 14/9/96.
PYLE G.S. Born 24/6/44. Commd 3/3/67. Sqn Ldr 1/1/78. Retd GD 24/6/82.
PYLE M.W. Born 7/3/43. Commd 15/7/66. Flt Lt 15/7/68. Retd GD 6/4/76.
PYM J.M.E. AFC. Born 2/12/41. Commd 18/12/62. Sqn Ldr 1/1/78. Retd GD 1/1/81. Re-instated on Retired List
    13/11/88.
PYNE A.R. BA. Born 5/10/46. Commd 28/2/72. Flt Lt 28/5/73. Retd GD 28/2/88.
PYNE G.L. MCMI. Born 10/5/31. Commd 30/5/61. Sqn Ldr 1/7/75. Retd SUP 1/9/83.
PYNN D. BSc. Born 3/2/48. Commd 4/6/72. Sqn Ldr 1/1/84. Retd GD 4/6/88.
PYPER G.D. BSc. Born 5/11/49. Commd 17/1/72. Sqn Ldr 1/7/83. Retd GD 17/1/88.
PYPER H.H. Born 7/5/54. Commd 20/12/73. Wg Cdr 1/7/90. Retd OPS SPT 13/2/99.
PYPER J. Born 21/6/45. Commd 15/7/66. Sqn Ldr 1/7/75. Retd GD 1/7/89.
PYPER S.E. BSc. Born 12/12/51. Commd 14/11/76. Flt Lt 14/2/80. Retd GD(G) 19/7/87.
PYRAH R.E. Born 23/3/31. Commd 14/4/53. Flt Lt 17/5/56. Retd GD 23/3/69.
PYSDEN G.T. Born 2/8/30. Commd 18/5/61. Sqn Ldr 1/7/71. Retd ENG 15/8/84.

Q

QUAID C.F. FInstPet MCMI. Born 29/12/42. Commd 12/3/64. Sqn Ldr 1/7/76. Retd SUP 26/5/82.
QUAID P.D. Born 27/2/40. Commd 14/8/70. Flt Lt 14/8/72. Retd GD 14/8/78.
QUAIFE C.M. OBE. Born 15/3/35. Commd 9/4/57. Wg Cdr 1/1/78. Retd GD 1/2/86.
QUAINTMERE P.J. Born 29/9/41. Commd 12/4/66. Sqn Ldr 1/1/77. Retd GD(G) 29/3/94.
QUANT J.A. MB BS BDS FDSRCS(Eng) MRCS(Eng) LRCP. Born 19/1/33. Commd 16/6/57. A Cdre 1/1/85.
   Retd DEL 6/4/90.
QUANT P. MHCIMA. Born 17/2/33. Commd 22/5/59. Sqn Ldr 1/1/69. Retd CAT 22/5/75.
QUANTICK D.J. Born 1/8/46. Commd 22/11/73. Flt Lt 22/11/75. Retd GD(G) 1/8/91.
QUARMBY D.A. BEng CEng MIEE. Born 9/6/60. Commd 16/9/84. Flt Lt 30/12/87. Retd ENG 9/6/98.
QUARTERMAINE R.W. MSc CEng MRAeS. Born 10/4/35. Commd 25/7/56. Wg Cdr 1/7/76. Retd MED 8/4/87.
QUARTERMAN R.J. Born 4/2/35. Commd 31/1/54. Retd GD 3/4/81.
QUARTLY A.F. BSc. Born 3/1/44. Commd 22/9/64. Flt Lt 6/6/67. Retd GD 29/3/74.
QUATERMASS-LEWIS G.M. Born 21/11/35. Commd 12/1/55. Flt Lt 31/5/61. Retd RGT 21/1/74.
QUAYLE C.E.G. Born 8/12/32. Commd 28/7/53. Sqn Ldr 1/7/69. Retd SUP 1/10/79.
QUELCH N. ACCS. Born 7/1/15. Commd 12/2/43. Sqn Ldr 1/1/55. Retd SEC 23/3/63.
QUERZANI J.F.G.R. Born 16/5/36. Commd 1/8/69. Sqn Ldr 1/7/81. Retd GD 13/9/89.
QUESTED E. MBE. Born 25/8/11. Commd 22/1/42. Fg Offr 22/3/43. Retd MED 26/7/46.
QUICK D.A.G. BSc. Born 23/5/52. Commd 13/9/70. Sqn Ldr 1/1/85. Retd ADMIN 23/5/90.
QUICK D.M. Born 14/11/44. Commd 19/11/87. Flt Lt 19/11/89. Retd ADMIN 5/4/99.
QUICK F.C. Born 23/3/20. Commd 21/10/54. Sqn Ldr 1/1/71. Retd SEC 23/3/75.
QUICK G.H. Born 21/3/23. Commd 19/1/44. Sqn Ldr 1/1/58. Retd GD 21/3/66.
QUICK G.J. BSc. Born 13/11/49. Commd 15/9/69. Flt Lt 15/6/75. Retd GD(G) 1/7/82. Re-entered 19/10/87. Flt Lt 3/10/80.
   Retd GD(G) 24/7/96.
QUICK M.C. Born 22/1/47. Commd 4/12/86. Flt Lt 4/12/88. Retd GD(G) 14/3/96.
QUICK M.E.H. MCMI. Born 9/3/40. Commd 27/3/75. Flt Lt 27/3/80. Retd ENG 31/3/83.
QUICK P.E. Born 18/7/54. Commd 16/9/76. Flt Lt 1/3/81. Retd GD 31/1/02.
QUILL T.C. Born 6/10/18. Commd 29/7/42. Wg Cdr 1/7/62. Retd GD(G) 6/10/68.
QUIN K.C. Born 15/6/39. Commd 13/12/60. Flt Lt 13/6/63. Retd GD 15/3/77. rtg Sqn Ldr.
QUIN P.L. OBE LLB FCMI MCIPD. Born 15/1/33. Commd 7/12/56. Gp Capt 1/7/82. Retd ADMIN 10/3/84.
QUINCEY N.J. Born 12/8/49. Commd 13/2/86. Sqn Ldr 1/7/94. Retd MED(SEC) 10/12/98.
QUINE J.D. Born 16/4/25. Commd 4/7/57. Flt Lt 1/4/63. Retd GD 15/4/76.
QUINLAN M.A. BSc. Born 16/5/62. Commd 14/10/84. Flt Lt 14/4/87. Retd GD 14/10/00.
QUINLAN P.J. Born 5/6/43. Commd 8/1/76. Flt Lt 8/1/78. Retd GD 2/4/93.
QUINN A.E. Born 8/8/19. Commd 21/9/44. Flt Lt 30/6/49. Retd PRT 1/12/62.
QUINN G.W. BA. Born 27/4/41. Commd 23/11/78. Flt Lt 23/11/88. Retd ENG 24/7/91.
QUINN P.N. Born 15/4/43. Commd 21/1/66. Fg Offr 21/1/68. Retd GD 1/3/69.
QUINN P.R. BA. Born 27/4/34. Commd 29/10/64. Sqn Ldr 1/7/75. Retd MED 1/9/87.
QUINN S.E. Born 16/5/14. Commd 17/6/42. Flt Lt 14/2/47. Retd SUP 20/10/55.
QUINNELL J.P. Born 19/7/47. Commd 16/8/68. Flt Lt 16/2/74. Retd GD 9/9/75.
QUINTIN-BAXENDALE B.W. Born 5/1/40. Commd 10/3/77. Sqn Ldr 1/1/91. Retd GD 5/1/95.
QUINTON A.A.G. MRCS LRCP DAvMed AFOM. Born 14/3/42. Commd 16/9/63. Wg Cdr 31/7/80. Retd MED 1/9/88.
QUINTON C.D. MCMI. Born 19/5/29. Commd 8/2/54. Wg Cdr 1/1/75. Retd SEC 4/4/81.
QUINTON J.B. BSc MInstP MCMI. Born 9/6/34. Commd 1/3/56. Gp Capt 1/1/75. Retd ENG 29/9/79.
QUINTRELL G.H.A. Born 17/7/36. Commd 28/5/66. Flt Lt 28/5/68. Retd PRT 1/12/73.

R

RABBITTS H.W. Born 4/8/20. Commd 25/8/55. Sqn Ldr 1/7/67. Retd ENG 4/8/70.
RABY K.W. Born 24/5/30. Commd 2/7/52. Flt Lt 27/11/57. Retd GD 1/7/64.
RABY P. FCCS. Born 3/6/14. Commd 17/4/39. Wg Cdr 1/1/57. Retd SEC 31/10/63.
RACE F.G. Born 12/8/28. Commd 5/11/70. Flt Lt 5/11/72. Retd ENG 12/8/83.
RACKHAM M.A. Born 22/4/52. Commd 22/5/75. Flt Lt 22/11/80. Retd GD 3/2/91.
RACKHAM R.D. Born 6/5/45. Commd 20/7/78. Sqn Ldr 1/1/87. Retd ENG 14/3/96.
RACKSTRAW A. Born 30/5/37. Commd 1/4/58. Wg Cdr 1/7/76. Retd SUP 18/10/87.
RADBOURNE B.M. BSc MB ChB DA FFARCS. Born 1/7/23. Commd 9/12/48. Wg Cdr 9/12/60. Retd MED 1/5/63.
RADCLIFFE N. Born 18/10/33. Commd 21/10/66. Flt Lt 21/10/72. Retd SUP 31/10/74.
RADD J. Born 20/6/16. Commd 1/2/48. Flt Lt 1/2/48. Retd PE 5/8/64.
RADFORD H.R. Born 25/4/28. Commd 26/7/50. Sqn Ldr 1/7/58. Retd GD 28/12/63.
RADFORD L.P.G. Born 22/7/60. Commd 22/2/79. Flt Lt 22/8/83. Retd GD 5/11/89.
RADFORD P.J. Born 6/11/38. Commd 22/11/73. Flt Lt 22/11/78. Retd ADMIN 5/11/84.
RADFORTH A.M. Born 31/12/54. Commd 15/3/73. Sqn Ldr 1/1/88. Retd OPS SPT 31/12/98.
RADFORTH M.A. Born 3/7/42. Commd 30/7/63. Sqn Ldr 1/1/89. Retd GD 3/7/98.
RADICE J.V. OBE MCMI. Born 18/12/30. Commd 27/6/51. Wg Cdr 1/1/70. Retd GD 27/4/85.
RADLEY B. CEng MRAeS. Born 6/1/23. Commd 7/9/45. Flt Lt 30/6/49. Retd GD 1/8/52.
RADLEY R.S. DFC AFC FCMI. Born 18/3/19. Commd 10/8/40. Sqn Ldr 1/7/60. Retd GD 18/3/74.
RADNOR A.E. Born 10/1/33. Commd 23/8/51. Wg Cdr 1/7/72. Retd GD 10/1/91.
RADTKE J.W.J. Born 10/2/19. Commd 29/7/48. Flt Lt 18/5/56. Retd GD(G) 10/7/68.
RAE C.N. Born 16/2/57. Commd 24/6/84. Flt Lt 25/10/82. Retd GD 30/4/88.
RAE I.E. Born 30/3/46. Commd 23/2/68. Flt Lt 20/9/73. Retd GD 1/11/74.
RAE J. MVO. Born 14/7/36. Commd 14/10/71. Sqn Ldr 1/1/84. Retd ENG 4/7/94.
RAE K.M.C.K. Born 14/6/38. Commd 24/2/61. Sqn Ldr 1/1/87. Retd GD 14/6/96.
RAE T.M.c.M. AFM. Born 29/7/25. Commd 18/5/61. Flt Lt 18/5/64. Retd GD 29/7/83.
RAE W.C. CB. Born 22/6/40. Commd 23/12/58. AVM 1/1/92. Retd GD 22/6/95.
RAEBURN P.D. Born 2/12/34. Commd 13/12/55. Sqn Ldr 1/7/65. Retd GD 1/10/80.
RAEBURN R.M. Born 27/5/31. Commd 7/3/51. Sqn Ldr 1/7/63. Retd GD 3/5/77.
RAESIDE J.F. Born 5/7/38. Commd 13/12/60. Sqn Ldr 1/7/71. Retd ADMIN 9/1/78.
RAESIDE J.M. Born 6/1/24. Commd 29/7/65. Flt Lt 29/7/70. Retd GD(G) 6/1/79.
RAFFEL J.W. BSc CEng MIMechE MIEE MINucE. Born 19/1/34. Commd 17/6/62. Sqn Ldr 1/1/68.
   Retd ENG 17/7/78. Re-instated 3/12/79 to 14/1/85.
RAFFERTY M.D. Born 8/6/25. Commd 21/5/47. Sqn Ldr 1/7/57. Retd GD 4/6/73.
RAFTERY R.G. Born 18/1/31. Commd 17/5/51. Flt Lt 6/9/56. Retd GD 27/4/70.
RAGG W.L. Born 2/5/42. Commd 15/3/79. Sqn Ldr 1/1/89. Retd GD 2/11/97.
RAGLAN J.B. Born 19/12/36. Commd 9/7/60. Sqn Ldr 1/1/76. Retd GD 19/12/91.
RAIKES P.F.J. Born 3/5/38. Commd 18/7/63. Wg Cdr 1/1/81. Retd GD(G) 3/5/93.
RAIMONDO J.V. MSc BSc. Born 29/11/47. Commd 1/8/69. Sqn Ldr 1/1/80. Retd ENG 1/10/87.
RAINBIRD T. Born 26/9/31. Commd 5/3/57. Flt Lt 5/9/62. Retd GD 7/4/72.
RAINBOW A.D. Born 26/12/32. Commd 5/9/69. Flt Lt 5/9/73. Retd ENG 31/3/87.
RAINBOW C.A. ACIS. Born 5/3/31. Commd 28/7/59. Gp Capt 1/7/81. Retd ADMIN 11/11/86.
RAINBOW E. BSc DipSoton CEng MIEE MCMI. Born 28/8/33. Commd 22/12/55. Wg Cdr 1/1/74. Retd ENG 30/9/83.
RAINE P.D. MSc BSc CEng MIEE. Born 21/11/62. Commd 29/1/82. Sqn Ldr 1/7/94. Retd ENG 21/11/00.
RAINE P.J.W. DFC. Born 2/11/21. Commd 21/12/42. Flt Lt 21/6/46. Retd SEC 1/7/60.
RAINE-BISHOP N.N. BSc CEng MIMeche. Born 19/11/64. Commd 5/9/82. Fg Offr 15/4/84. Retd ENG 12/7/86.
RAINFORD D.J. MBE MB BS FRCP FFOM FRAeS MRCS. Born 27/7/46. Commd 25/7/66. A Cdre 21/7/96.
   Retd MED 4/10/02.
RAISON R.M. Born 29/9/51. Commd 23/10/86. Sqn Ldr 1/7/93. Retd ADMIN 14/3/96.
RAIT D.M. Born 2/12/47. Commd 2/2/78. Wg Cdr 1/1/97. Retd ENG 1/12/00.
RAJAPAKSHA H. Born 7/3/34. Commd 19/6/67. Flt Lt 19/6/67. Retd GD 15/12/73.
RAKE A.C. Born 7/9/57. Commd 14/7/77. Flt Lt 14/1/83. Retd GD 18/6/96.
RAKE D.S.V. OBE AFC*. Born 26/5/22. Commd 19/6/42. Gp Capt 1/7/64. Retd GD 26/3/76.
RALEY A.J. MBE. Born 6/6/35. Commd 4/9/61. Wg Cdr 1/1/80. Retd GD 6/6/91.
RALLS A.W. BA. Born 7/9/54. Commd 29/11/81. Flt Lt 28/2/83. Retd SUP 14/3/97.
RALPH A. BSc. Born 21/5/59. Commd 29/11/81. Flt Lt 28/2/83. Retd GD 29/11/97.
RALPH J.A. Born 10/11/30. Commd 23/12/53. Flt Lt 23/12/59. Retd GD(G) 10/11/92.
RAMAGE L.M. Born 6/11/57. Commd 31/1/80. Sqn Ldr 1/7/93. Retd GD 14/9/96.
RAMIREZ R. AFC. Born 26/4/24. Commd 7/7/49. Wg Cdr 1/1/67. Retd GD 28/12/72.
RAMSAY A.C. Born 16/5/30. Commd 24/1/52. Sqn Ldr 1/7/63. Retd GD 17/5/84.
RAMSAY A.W.D. Born 9/12/25. Commd 6/9/51. Flt Lt 14/11/56. Retd PRT 9/12/72.
RAMSAY I.A. Born 30/7/41. Commd 4/2/71. Sqn Ldr 1/1/86. Retd GD(G) 16/9/94.

RAMSAY I.G. Born 16/6/46. Commd 11/2/65. Sqn Ldr 1/1/77. Retd GD(G) 22/10/94.
RAMSAY J.G. Born 23/1/32. Commd 13/8/52. Flt Lt 9/1/58. Retd GD 1/12/85.
RAMSBOTTOM A. MIDPM. Born 8/5/48. Commd 13/1/67. Sqn Ldr 1/7/80. Retd ADMIN 8/5/86.
RAMSBOTTOM B.D. BDS. Born 2/4/47. Commd 29/9/68. Wg Cdr 10/6/83. Retd DEL 2/4/85.
RAMSBOTTOM D.H. Born 24/6/19. Commd 28/7/49. Sqn Ldr 1/1/64. Retd SEC 31/10/67.
RAMSBOTTOM R.W. Born 23/9/32. Commd 31/1/51. Flt Lt 31/10/56. Retd GD 23/9/70.
RAMSBOTTOM T.A. Born 13/6/40. Commd 28/4/64. Flt Lt 4/11/70. Retd ENG 28/4/83.
RAMSDALE R. Born 21/5/33. Commd 12/3/52. Flt Lt 2/4/62. Retd GD 2/4/78.
RAMSDEN A. AFM. Born 26/1/23. Commd 14/3/57. Flt Lt 14/3/63. Retd GD 29/6/68.
RAMSDEN D.R. BSc. Born 18/2/56. Commd 30/10/77. Flt Lt 30/1/79. Retd GD 30/10/89.
RAMSEY I.A.F. Born 28/10/49. Commd 15/1/79. Flt Lt 10/10/86. Retd SY 31/1/94.
RAMSEY N.G.C. DFC. Born 16/12/19. Commd 2/2/42. Flt Lt 20/7/48. Retd GD 4/3/61.
RAMSEY S. Born 27/9/59. Commd 15/6/83. Sqn Ldr 1/1/92. Retd ENG 8/2/98.
RAMSHAW F.M. Born 25/6/43. Commd 19/4/63. Sqn Ldr 1/7/93. Retd GD 23/4/97.
RAMSHAW G.D. BSc CEng DipSoton MIEE. Born 5/2/34. Commd 24/8/56. Wg Cdr 24/2/74. Retd ADMIN 29/9/84.
RAMUS A.A. Born 21/11/29. Commd 11/4/51. Wg Cdr 1/1/68. Retd GD 15/7/85.
RANASINGHE D.J.C. MCMI. Born 25/9/30. Commd 28/2/66. Sqn Ldr 1/1/72. Retd SUP 3/7/84.
RANCE B.H. MSc MB ChB MFOM. Born 20/9/29. Commd 16/6/57. Wg Cdr 16/6/70. Retd MED 16/7/83.
RANCE F.S. Born 2/6/43. Commd 6/4/62. Gp Capt 1/7/90. Retd GD 2/6/98.
RAND M.D. Born 22/5/43. Commd 3/1/64. Flt Lt 4/5/72. Retd GD 25/6/76.
RANDALL A.M. Born 11/5/61. Commd 2/9/79. Sqn Ldr 1/7/93. Retd GD 11/5/99.
RANDALL B.A. Born 17/8/36. Commd 5/7/68. Flt Lt 5/7/70. Retd ENG 5/7/76.
RANDALL D.J. Born 13/4/50. Commd 3/7/83. Flt Lt 12/6/75. Retd GD 19/4/88.
RANDALL H.C. DFC. Born 2/9/18. Commd 29/7/39. Wg Cdr 1/1/52. Retd GD 2/9/65.
RANDALL N.O. BA. Born 11/5/50. Commd 22/8/76. Sqn Ldr 1/1/84. Retd ADMIN 22/8/92.
RANDALL R.W. Born 10/1/33. Commd 9/10/58. Sqn Ldr 1/1/69. Retd SY(PRT) 15/11/73.
RANDEL J. Born 16/11/45. Commd 15/6/83. Flt Lt 15/6/87. Retd ENG 17/6/94.
RANDELL E.J. Born 10/4/30. Commd 18/5/56. Sqn Ldr 1/7/78. Retd GD 10/4/88.
RANDERSON R.N. MA BSc. Born 28/7/55. Commd 22/8/76. Wg Cdr 1/7/96. Retd GD 26/9/03.
RANDLE R.R. PhD BSc CEng MIEE. Born 5/7/29. Commd 9/12/54. Wg Cdr 1/7/69. Retd ENG 1/7/72.
RANDLE W.S.O. CBE AFC DFM FRAeS FCMI. Born 17/5/21. Commd 30/3/43. Gp Capt 1/1/64. Retd GD 1/4/72.
RANDLES S. Born 25/4/56. Commd 1/12/77. Wg Cdr 1/1/96. Retd GD 25/4/00.
RANDOLPH P.McD. Born 16/5/29. Commd 5/4/50. Wg Cdr 1/7/69. Retd SUP 1/10/77.
RANDS A.J. Born 6/3/64. Commd 6/5/83. Flt Lt 6/11/88. Retd GD 14/3/96.
RANDS E.G. FCMI. Born 19/2/14. Commd 13/10/37. Gp Capt 1/7/59. Retd SEC 28/7/69.
RANDS J.E. OBE. Born 23/11/59. Commd 5/4/79. Sqn Ldr 1/1/91. Retd GD 23/11/97.
RANKIN A.F. Born 5/3/32. Commd 19/11/52. Flt Lt 5/11/58. Retd GD 1/11/75.
RANKIN C.L. Born 23/7/39. Commd 25/6/57. Flt Lt 31/1/68. Retd GD 1/10/77.
RANKIN M.E. Born 7/11/33. Commd 27/7/54. Sqn Ldr 1/1/65. Retd GD 11/11/71.
RANKIN R. Born 3/4/33. Commd 17/3/54. Flt Lt 17/9/59. Retd GD 3/4/71.
RANKINE S.K. BSc. Born 22/11/52. Commd 25/9/71. Sqn Ldr 1/1/85. Retd ENG 1/10/91.
RANSCOMBE G.L. Born 27/9/29. Commd 9/4/52. Flt Lt 26/5/55. Retd GD 30/9/66.
RANSCOMBE J.W. Born 1/7/27. Commd 3/8/61. Flt Lt 3/8/67. Retd SUP 1/6/74.
RANSLEY B.M. Born 29/8/32. Commd 17/1/69. Wg Cdr 1/7/88. Retd PRT 1/7/91.
RANSOM D.C. Born 8/4/33. Commd 26/3/52. Flt Lt 7/8/57. Retd GD(G) 8/4/93.
RANSOM G. MSc BA. Born 25/7/43. Commd 17/1/82. Sqn Ldr 1/1/91. Retd ENG 25/7/98.
RANSOM W.H. Born 11/8/21. Commd 8/2/44. Sqn Ldr 1/7/61. Retd GD(G) 11/8/76.
RANSOME R.L. Born 26/9/61. Commd 11/6/81. Flt Lt 11/12/86. Retd GD 26/9/99.
RANSON G. Born 12/2/43. Commd 26/4/84. Flt Lt 26/4/88. Retd ENG 2/4/93.
RAPER S.P. Born 9/9/63. Commd 11/10/91. Flt Lt 28/10/94. Retd OPS SPT(ATC) 3/10/03.
RAPHAEL B. AFC. Born 3/9/43. Commd 21/12/62. Sqn Ldr 1/7/76. Retd GD 31/3/94.
RAPHAEL W.G. Born 18/7/19. Commd 1/9/45. Flt Lt 1/9/45. Retd GD 31/3/62.
RAPKINS L.B. Born 14/10/41. Commd 14/8/70. Flt Lt 13/10/72. Retd GD(G) 16/12/74.
RAPLEY C. Born 14/7/57. Commd 16/2/86. Flt Lt 16/8/89. Retd ENG 14/3/97.
RAPSON A.H. Born 21/8/45. Commd 16/8/68. Flt Lt 16/2/74. Retd GD 6/5/85.
RAPSON P.E. DFC. Born 21/11/15. Commd 10/4/42. Flt Lt 5/7/50. Retd SEC 1/9/62.
RATCLIFFE D. Born 13/11/61. Commd 24/4/80. Flt Lt 24/10/85. Retd GD 12/5/99.
RATCLIFFE P.A. BSc. Born 28/9/66. Commd 2/11/88. Sqn Ldr 1/1/01. Retd OPS SPT(FC) 28/9/04.
RATCLIFFE R.H. Born 27/1/25. Commd 4/10/56. Plt Offr 4/10/56. Retd GD 30/9/59.
RATCLIFFE W.D. Born 31/1/26. Commd 11/7/47. Sqn Ldr 1/1/59. Retd RGT 30/10/65.
RATH N.T. Born 4/4/52. Commd 16/1/00. Flt Lt 16/1/00. Retd FLY(AEO) 1/2/05.
RATHBONE C.W.H. Born 16/5/53. Commd 16/6/72. Sqn Ldr 1/7/89. Retd GD 1/7/92.
RATHMELL C.W. DFC. Born 19/10/20. Commd 6/2/44. Sqn Ldr 1/7/70. Retd SUP 3/12/70.
RATNARAJA E.C.L.M. Born 25/4/40. Commd 5/4/61. Flt Lt 15/6/67. Retd SEC 6/3/73.
RATTUE J.M. MSc BSc. Born 28/12/56. Commd 2/3/80. Sqn Ldr 1/7/90. Retd ADMIN 14/3/96.
RAVEN G.W. Born 18/1/63. Commd 30/8/84. Fg Offr 12/11/85. Retd SUP 1/10/88.

RAVEN J. Born 17/3/13. Commd 1/2/40. Fg Offr 13/3/47. Retd SUP 5/12/56. rtg Sqn Ldr.
RAVENHILL S.M. Born 27/12/15. Commd 13/1/48. Sqn Ldr 1/7/52. Retd SUP 27/12/72.
RAVENSCROFT K. Born 17/12/32. Commd 17/10/57. Flt Lt 17/4/62. Retd GD 17/12/92.
RAW R. Born 22/4/26. Commd 21/5/52. Flt Lt 1/9/59. Retd MAR 3/4/68.
RAWLES G.K. BSc. Born 22/10/56. Commd 25/5/80. Flt Lt 25/8/81. Retd GD 11/11/96.
RAWLINGS P.A. Born 23/12/46. Commd 2/4/65. Flt Lt 20/10/70. Retd GD 1/1/77.
RAWLINS S.J. DFC FCMI. Born 25/7/21. Commd 5/8/39. Gp Capt 1/1/66. Retd GD 27/3/76.
RAWLINSON A.C. OBE DFC* AFC. Born 31/7/18. Commd 1/9/45. Wg Cdr 1/7/52. Retd GD 13/11/61. rtg Gp Capt.
RAWLINSON H. DFC. Born 14/4/20. Commd 3/7/41. Flt Lt 16/5/48. Retd GD 25/8/65.
RAWLL C.C.G. MB ChB DTM&H. Born 18/8/30. Commd 29/8/54. Wg Cdr 29/8/67. Retd MED 5/9/70.
RAWTHORNE C. Born 18/7/53. Commd 5/7/73. Sqn Ldr 1/1/86. Retd GD 18/7/91.
RAY A.P. MSc BSc CEng MIEE MRAeS MCMI MCIPD. Born 25/8/38. Commd 31/12/63. Sqn Ldr 23/4/70.
    Retd ADMIN 1/3/84.
RAY D.A. Born 23/1/47. Commd 1/3/68. Gp Capt 1/1/93. Retd GD 30/8/02.
RAY D.W. Born 19/12/33. Commd 21/5/52. Flt Lt 16/10/57. Retd GD 19/12/71. rtg Sqn Ldr.
RAY E.G. Born 31/10/35. Commd 21/4/67. Sqn Ldr 1/7/81. Retd ENG 31/8/88.
RAY F.G.A. Born 10/9/37. Commd 6/9/63. Flt Lt 8/1/69. Retd GD 10/9/75.
RAY J.A. Born 6/3/33. Commd 11/3/65. Sqn Ldr 14/5/76. Retd MED(SEC) 18/3/85.
RAY J.M.A. Born 2/5/26. Commd 21/9/56. Sqn Ldr 1/1/73. Retd RGT 9/7/80.
RAY P.R. Born 22/6/45. Commd 11/8/67. Wg Cdr 1/1/91. Retd GD 5/7/99.
RAY R.L.G. AFC. Born 6/7/25. Commd 1/3/49. Sqn Ldr 1/7/72. Retd GD 6/7/80.
RAYBOULD K. Born 9/5/36. Commd 27/5/71. Sqn Ldr 1/7/85. Retd ADMIN 2/1/91.
RAYDEN R.S. Born 12/8/16. Commd 18/7/43. Sqn Ldr 1/1/66. Retd ENG 12/8/70.
RAYFIELD G. BA CIMS FMS FInstAM MCMI. Born 25/3/43. Commd 24/6/65. Wg Cdr 1/1/93. Retd GD 20/12/97.
RAYMENT A.G. Born 8/5/44. Commd 24/4/64. Sqn Ldr 1/7/80. Retd GD 2/4/93.
RAYMOND P.E. BSc. Born 25/9/24. Commd 24/1/45. Gp Capt 1/1/72. Retd ADMIN 26/3/77.
RAYMOND-BARKER G.G.C. Born 30/4/26. Commd 25/10/46. Flt Lt 19/6/52. Retd GD 22/3/68.
RAYMONT G.J. Born 10/6/48. Commd 10/9/70. Flt Lt 10/3/77. Retd SY 10/6/86.
RAYNER A. Born 12/4/61. Commd 8/12/83. Flt Lt 20/2/92. Retd RGT 20/2/92.
RAYNER C.M. Born 9/9/52. Commd 20/12/73. Sqn Ldr 1/7/84. Retd GD 9/9/90.
RAYNER G.W. BA. Born 12/5/29. Commd 26/10/50. Wg Cdr 1/7/68. Retd EDN 12/5/79.
RAYNER H.J. DFC AFC. Born 15/7/14. Commd 22/5/41. Wg Cdr 1/7/54. Retd GD 29/9/61.
RAYNER H.R. MSc MBCS. Born 5/9/50. Commd 19/9/71. Sqn Ldr 1/7/84. Retd SUP 30/9/89.
RAYNER K.E.J. Born 5/1/38. Commd 29/10/60. Sqn Ldr 1/7/72. Retd GD 5/1/76. Re-instated 6/3/77. Retd 31/7/83.
RAYNER M.O. OBE CEng MRAeS MCMI. Born 26/2/19. Commd 28/3/46. Wg Cdr 1/7/62. Retd ENG 18/5/74.
RAYNER P.R. AFC. Born 15/1/34. Commd 17/2/53. Flt Lt 10/3/58. Retd GD 2/10/78.
RAYNHAM H.D. AFC. Born 2/11/39. Commd 21/3/84. Flt Lt 3/2/81. Retd GD 2/11/94.
RAYNOR R.N. BA BTech CEng MRAeS MCMI. Born 22/11/53. Commd 30/9/73. Sqn Ldr 1/1/84.
    Retd ENG 22/11/91.
RAYSON C.J.A. MBE MB BS MRCGP MHSM MRCS LRCP DObstRCOG DAvMed AFOM. Born 11/7/48.
    Commd 29/9/69. Gp Capt 1/1/96. Retd MED 12/7/98.
RAYSON M.J. LVO. Born 19/7/30. Commd 24/10/51. A Cdre 1/7/82. Retd GD 19/7/85.
REA A.P. MMAR. Born 16/6/37. Commd 28/4/64. Sqn Ldr 1/7/78. Retd SUP 16/6/92.
REA P.B. Born 6/8/23. Commd 1/4/49. Flt Lt 25/2/53. Retd GD 31/3/62.
REA T.J. BA. Born 12/2/50. Commd 16/12/79. Flt Lt 16/12/80. Retd ADMIN 16/12/95.
READ A.C.L. Born 17/7/44. Commd 14/1/65. Flt Lt 15/4/71. Retd SEC 10/8/74.
READ A.R. Born 5/6/38. Commd 15/5/63. Gp Capt 1/7/86. Retd SUP 11/2/89.
READ C.A. Born 25/7/27. Commd 7/5/52. Flt Lt 7/2/58. Retd GD 25/7/65.
READ D. Born 12/4/20. Commd 15/2/45. Sqn Ldr 1/1/61. Retd SUP 11/6/65.
READ D. Born 11/10/24. Commd 12/4/51. Flt Lt 1/1/53. Retd PRT 18/2/59.
READ D.C. Born 8/4/37. Commd 2/12/55. Gp Capt 1/1/84. Retd GD 3/6/87.
READ D.G. Born 12/3/37. Commd 8/8/60. Flt Lt 8/2/66. Retd GD 8/8/76.
READ D.J. Born 31/10/42. Commd 6/6/66. Sqn Ldr 1/1/83. Retd ADMIN 5/6/86.
READ D.J. MA MCIPD MCMI. Born 25/2/33. Commd 24/8/56. Gp Capt 1/1/80. Retd ADMIN 16/11/87.
READ G.J. Born 6/1/24. Commd 10/7/45. Sqn Ldr 1/7/60. Retd GD 7/1/75.
READ H.G. Born 28/8/20. Commd 14/10/42. Sqn Ldr 1/1/70. Retd SEC 28/8/75.
READ J.A. CertEd. Born 4/5/50. Commd 29/8/72. Sqn Ldr 1/7/89. Retd ADMIN 7/4/01.
READ J.R.J. The Rev. BA. Born 15/3/39. Commd 30/4/72. Retd Wg Cdr 30/4/88.
READ J.S. Born 13/10/20. Commd 17/5/43. Sqn Ldr 1/7/59. Retd GD 13/10/75.
READ K.R.L. Born 26/10/39. Commd 19/12/61. Flt Lt 7/8/64. Retd 26/10/77. Re-entered 2/4/80. Sqn Ldr 1/1/91.
    Retd GD 26/10/99.
READ M.G. Born 27/3/30. Commd 17/5/51. Flt Lt 6/9/56. Retd GD 25/7/70.
READ M.S. Born 21/7/31. Commd 23/5/51. Flt Lt 15/3/56. Retd GD 21/7/69.
READ N.R. Born 28/5/36. Commd 29/4/58. Sqn Ldr 1/1/77. Retd GD 3/10/87.
READ S.G. MBA CMILT. Born 23/8/67. Commd 7/4/92. Sqn Ldr 1/7/97. Retd SUPPLY 24/8/04.
READ S.J. Born 3/6/61. Commd 5/2/88. Sqn Ldr 1/7/97. Retd FLY(N) 3/6/05.

READE C.S. Born 28/4/15. Commd 17/8/39. Sqn Ldr 1/8/47. Retd SUP 17/5/64.
READE M. Born 28/11/30. Commd 23/11/53. Sqn Ldr 1/7/67. Retd GD 30/4/76.
READER B.A. Born 17/11/32. Commd 6/4/54. Flt Lt 14/11/56. Retd GD 17/11/70.
READER D.C. PhD BSc MB BS MRCS LRCP. Born 7/6/35. Commd 3/3/63. Gp Capt 3/3/86. Retd MED 2/1/99.
READER D.M. MA CEng FCMI MRAeS. Born 11/4/34. Commd 26/9/53. A Cdre 1/7/81. Retd ENG 27/6/86.
READHEAD N.J. Born 25/2/56. Commd 14/7/77. Fg Offr 14/7/79. Retd GD 6/1/82.
READING J.H. MB BS MRCS LRCP DTM&H. Born 26/4/26. Commd 1/9/52. Wg Cdr 31/1/64. Retd MED 1/9/68.
READING R.W. MCIPS MCMI. Born 24/2/50. Commd 2/5/69. Sqn Ldr 1/7/84. Retd SUP 24/2/88.
READMAN A.B. Born 3/5/40. Commd 5/11/70. Sqn Ldr 5/5/77. Retd ADMIN 5/11/80.
READMAN E. MBCS. Born 2/2/32. Commd 25/6/66. Flt Lt 25/6/71. Retd ENG 1/2/84.
READY M.S. BA. Born 17/7/65. Commd 9/9/97. Flt Lt 7/6/89. Retd FLY(P) 17/7/03.
READYHOOF K.C. Born 10/5/30. Commd 28/6/51. Flt Lt 10/10/56. Retd GD 10/5/68.
REASON D.J. MCMI. Born 11/7/42. Commd 31/1/64. Wg Cdr 1/7/88. Retd ADMIN 25/10/92.
REAY G.E. DFM. Born 29/8/22. Commd 10/1/45. Flt Lt 10/7/48. Retd GD 29/8/65.
REAY W. MSc BDS FDSRCS(Ed) MOrthRCSE LDS DOrthRCS. Born 6/9/45. Commd 16/4/74. Gp Capt 22/12/92. Retd DEL 16/4/96.
REDDIN G. Born 25/9/31. Commd 16/7/52. Flt Lt 17/7/61. Retd GD 13/8/70.
REDDING J.S. Born 20/9/30. Commd 28/6/51. Sqn Ldr 1/7/76. Retd GD 20/9/88.
REDDING R.F. MBE. Born 5/6/25. Commd 22/9/44. Wg Cdr 1/7/70. Retd GD 3/4/76.
REDDISH J. Born 15/2/24. Commd 10/4/51. Sqn Ldr 1/7/73. Retd GD 15/2/79.
REDDY P.E. Born 12/11/42. Commd 17/12/63. Flt Lt 26/7/67. Retd GD 12/11/80.
REDDYHOFF F.D. BSc. Born 15/1/31. Commd 31/8/64. Sqn Ldr 1/3/68. Retd EDN 9/5/81.
REDFERN A. BA. Born 29/7/31. Commd 4/9/59. Wg Cdr 1/1/74. Retd MAR 1/1/77.
REDFERN J.C. DPhysEd. Born 24/7/46. Commd 18/1/73. Flt Lt 18/7/79. Retd SY(PRT) 3/7/88.
REDFORD J. Born 6/9/41. Commd 8/6/62. Flt Lt 8/12/67. Retd GD 6/9/79.
REDGRAVE M.StJ. Born 6/2/52. Commd 23/4/87. Flt Lt 23/4/89. Retd GD 31/3/97.
REDLEY T.A. Born 26/6/25. Commd 14/11/49. Sqn Ldr 1/1/63. Retd SUP 26/6/82.
REDMAN A.R. Born 20/9/33. Commd 21/5/52. Sqn Ldr 1/7/84. Retd GD 29/5/87.
REDMOND C.F.S. Born 18/8/42. Commd 17/12/64. Flt Lt 26/7/67. Retd GD 13/7/74.
REDMOND D.J. Born 8/5/23. Commd 19/7/56. Sqn Ldr 1/7/66. Retd ENG 8/5/78.
REDMOND T. Born 27/6/48. Commd 4/7/85. Flt Lt 4/7/89. Retd GD(G) 29/7/94.
REDMONDS C. Born 9/6/33. Commd 7/7/55. Flt Lt 9/2/57. Retd GD 9/6/71.
REDMORE M.A. Born 22/6/42. Commd 11/5/62. Sqn Ldr 1/7/74. Retd GD 22/6/97.
REECE J.R. Born 11/6/34. Commd 8/10/70. Flt Lt 8/10/73. Retd GD 4/7/84.
REECE R.A. DFC DFM. Born 2/11/14. Commd 9/8/40. Sqn Ldr 1/8/47. Retd GD 21/2/58.
REED A.C. OBE MA. Born 6/5/35. Commd 1/10/57. Wg Cdr 1/7/81. Retd GD 15/4/87.
REED A.D. BSc. Born 16/5/60. Commd 19/6/83. Sqn Ldr 1/7/93. Retd GD 19/6/99.
REED A.G. IEng FIIE MCMI. Born 14/6/45. Commd 1/4/76. Wg Cdr 1/7/99. Retd ENG 14/6/00.
REED A.J.H. Born 21/12/41. Commd 3/8/62. Flt Lt 8/1/69. Retd GD 21/12/79.
REED D.J. BA PGCE. Born 30/8/60. Commd 11/5/86. Sqn Ldr 1/1/95. Retd ADMIN 11/8/02.
REED D.W.M. Born 12/3/34. Commd 9/7/55. Flt Lt 15/8/62. Retd GD 1/10/80.
REED G.E. Born 24/10/10. Commd 11/2/43. Fg Offr 11/8/43. Retd ASD 8/1/46. rtg Flt Lt.
REED I.P. Born 27/9/20. Commd 1/6/42. Flt Lt 29/6/50. Retd RGT 27/10/65.
REED K.B. Born 21/5/39. Commd 1/7/82. Flt Lt 1/3/87. Retd ADMIN 28/1/90.
REED M.B. MCMI. Born 5/6/31. Commd 7/6/60. Sqn Ldr 1/1/70. Retd SUP 15/8/84.
REED P.F. OBE CEng MRAeS. Born 26/4/23. Commd 20/2/43. Wg Cdr 1/1/69. Retd ENG 6/4/74.
REED P.J. BSc. Born 10/2/63. Commd 10/11/85. Flt Lt 10/5/89. Retd ADMIN 1/11/96.
REED S. MIDPM MCIPS. Born 15/3/40. Commd 19/12/61. Wg Cdr 1/7/86. Retd SUP 15/3/95.
REED S.C. MSc BSc. Born 29/12/63. Commd 5/9/82. Sqn Ldr 1/1/95. Retd ENG 29/12/01.
REED T.A. BSc. Born 1/5/44. Commd 15/7/66. Sqn Ldr 1/7/75. Retd ENG 11/11/75.
REED T.W. Born 7/3/19. Commd 27/10/55. Fg Offr 27/10/58. Retd ENG 9/10/61.
REED-PURVIS H. CB OBE BSc. Born 1/7/28. Commd 19/7/51. AVM 1/1/80. Retd SY 4/9/83.
REEDER F.E. CEng MIEE MCMI. Born 15/9/20. Commd 2/12/43. Sqn Ldr 1/7/66. Retd ENG 1/5/73.
REEDER M.P. Born 2/6/61. Commd 30/8/84. Flt Lt 1/3/91. Retd ADMIN 30/11/96.
REEDER R.W. Born 7/10/22. Commd 14/1/44. Flt Lt 19/6/52. Retd GD 31/3/74.
REEH D. BSc. Born 17/1/51. Commd 15/9/69. Sqn Ldr 1/7/82. Retd GD 1/7/85.
REEKIE G.L. Born 20/8/44. Commd 14/7/66. Sqn Ldr 1/1/87. Retd GD 20/8/99.
REEN P.J. Born 23/6/23. Commd 4/10/45. Sqn Ldr 1/7/56. Retd ENG 29/9/61.
REES B.G. Born 17/4/49. Commd 2/11/88. Sqn Ldr 1/7/97. Retd ENG 31/10/99.
REES C.D. Born 17/4/53. Commd 2/9/73. Sqn Ldr 1/1/90. Retd ADMIN 1/1/93.
REES C.D. Born 23/3/32. Commd 1/10/60. Sqn Ldr 1/7/78. Retd RGT 8/6/84.
REES D. Born 28/7/58. Commd 29/11/81. Flt Lt 29/11/85. Retd PRT 2/4/92.
REES D.L. DPhysEd. Born 23/4/54. Commd 3/7/80. Flt Lt 17/1/83. Retd GD 1/7/93.
REES D.W. BSc. Born 28/11/48. Commd 1/9/70. Wg Cdr 1/7/88. Retd GD 19/5/92.
REES E.I. Born 16/9/56. Commd 19/3/81. Sqn Ldr 30/5/95. Retd SY 10/11/96.
REES G. CEng MIEE MRAeS. Born 1/8/29. Commd 27/2/52. Gp Capt 1/7/78. Retd ENG 13/4/84.

REES G.D. BSc. Born 19/11/49. Commd 15/9/69. Flt Lt 15/12/73. Retd FLY(P) 19/11/04.
REES G.G.M. Born 12/8/36. Commd 19/8/71. Sqn Ldr 1/1/83. Retd ENG 1/10/87.
REES G.T. Born 3/9/18. Commd 17/10/57. Sqn Ldr 1/7/66. Retd ENG 31/10/70.
REES H. OBE BSc CEng MIEE. Born 11/9/49. Commd 28/9/70. Gp Capt 2/3/90. Retd ENG 11/9/93.
REES H.K. Born 2/2/21. Commd 13/1/42. Wg Cdr 1/7/58. Retd GD 2/2/68.
REES J. FCMI MRAeS. Born 30/6/25. Commd 3/3/45. Gp Capt 1/1/74. Retd SUP 1/1/76.
REES J. AFC. Born 13/2/22. Commd 7/6/44. Flt Lt 7/12/47. Retd GD 21/10/56.
REES K.M. Born 14/2/46. Commd 18/8/67. Flt Lt 18/2/73. Retd SUP 2/4/75.
REES M.S. Born 17/2/49. Commd 27/2/70. Sqn Ldr 1/1/88. Retd FLY(P) 17/2/04.
REES O.R. Born 7/12/47. Commd 24/11/67. Sqn Ldr 1/1/95. Retd GD 14/9/96.
REES P.A. BSc CEng MRAeS. Born 23/8/63. Commd 3/8/86. Sqn Ldr 1/7/99. Retd ENGINEER 3/8/03.
REES R.A. MA DCAe CEng MIEE. Born 26/1/36. Commd 30/9/55. Flt Lt 21/8/63. Retd ENG 26/1/74.
REES R.J. BSc MCMI. Born 15/6/32. Commd 25/8/55. Wg Cdr 1/1/84. Retd ADMIN 15/6/87.
REES S.A.L. CEng MIMechE MRAeS MCMI. Born 23/1/29. Commd 5/12/51. Gp Capt 1/7/73. Retd ENG 11/8/79.
REES S.C. Born 22/4/61. Commd 5/5/88. Flt Lt 3/1/94. Retd ADMIN 14/3/97.
REES S.T. Born 24/10/59. Commd 19/2/88. Flt Lt 28/10/86. Retd GD 25/11/95.
REES V. DFC. Born 7/8/17. Commd 21/1/38. Wg Cdr 1/1/52. Retd GD 7/8/72.
REES V. Born 2/12/40. Commd 21/3/62. Sqn Ldr 1/1/74. Retd SUP 1/7/79.
REES V.J. MBE MA BSc DipEl. Born 18/6/23. Commd 20/3/47. Sqn Ldr 24/8/59. Retd EDN 24/8/65.
REESE N.P. BSc. Born 27/10/59. Commd 3/8/86. Flt Lt 3/10/89. Retd ENG 3/8/02.
REEVE J.D. Born 19/6/34. Commd 16/7/57. Flt Lt 1/4/63. Retd GD 5/2/77.
REEVE K.A. Born 22/5/27. Commd 4/4/51. Flt Lt 4/10/55. Retd GD 22/5/65.
REEVE N.P. Born 14/9/44. Commd 7/6/73. Sqn Ldr 1/7/91. Retd OPS SPT 11/7/01.
REEVE R.J. Born 18/12/47. Commd 1/3/68. Sqn Ldr 1/7/80. Retd GD 26/5/98.
REEVE S. Born 18/3/22. Commd 23/12/61. Flt Lt 23/12/66. Retd SUP 29/4/72.
REEVE T.J. Born 21/4/62. Commd 30/6/91. Flt Lt 24/10/89. Retd GD 14/3/96.
REEVE W.G. Born 29/1/20. Commd 28/7/43. Sqn Ldr 1/7/69. Retd SEC 13/5/72.
REEVES A.J.W. CEng MRAeS. Born 6/9/38. Commd 28/7/60. Wg Cdr 1/7/76. Retd ENG 16/5/91.
REEVES B.M. Born 15/11/55. Commd 13/12/79. Flt Lt 13/8/85. Retd SY 13/8/95.
REEVES E.E. MBE. Born 1/12/28. Commd 25/8/49. Wg Cdr 1/1/70. Retd GD 10/1/79.
REEVES F.J. Born 8/3/27. Commd 15/12/49. Sqn Ldr 1/7/72. Retd GD 8/3/83.
REEVES J.W. Born 29/4/46. Commd 1/7/82. Sqn Ldr 1/7/94. Retd FLY(AEO) 29/4/04.
REEVES M.J. Born 8/1/53. Commd 22/11/73. Flt Lt 22/5/79. Retd GD 8/1/91.
REFFOLD C.N. Born 9/5/52. Commd 16/9/71. Flt Lt 16/3/77. Retd GD 25/10/86.
REGAN J.Q. MA LLB. Born 17/9/43. Commd 23/9/68. Sqn Ldr 23/3/76. Retd ADMIN 16/9/94.
REGAN T.P. MSc CEng MIEE MRAeS. Born 30/10/39. Commd 18/7/61. Gp Capt 1/7/81. Retd ENG 3/7/83.
REGESTER M.J.C. Born 16/6/25. Commd 19/10/45. Flt Lt 19/10/51. Retd SUP 16/6/63.
REID A.G. Born 18/7/24. Commd 13/5/44. Sqn Ldr 1/1/55. Retd GD 18/7/62.
REID B.A. MB ChB MRCOG MRCGP MFFP DCH. Born 3/4/57. Commd 24/2/81. Wg Cdr 1/8/94. Retd MED 14/3/96.
REID B.K. Born 2/10/39. Commd 25/3/64. Flt Lt 15/4/70. Retd GD 2/10/71.
REID C.A.W. Born 24/3/42. Commd 21/12/62. Wg Cdr 1/1/83. Retd GD 22/4/94.
REID D.C. MRAeS. Born 20/4/43. Commd 22/2/63. Wg Cdr 1/1/90. Retd GD 20/4/98.
REID D.C. Born 3/5/52. Commd 4/2/71. Sqn Ldr 1/7/88. Retd GD 1/7/91.
REID D.E.MacD. BSc. Born 8/2/59. Commd 9/11/80. Sqn Ldr 1/7/92. Retd GD 29/7/97.
REID D.F.S. Born 25/1/49. Commd 29/3/68. Flt Lt 29/9/79. Retd ADMIN 13/12/96.
REID D.W. Born 10/2/43. Commd 19/8/71. Sqn Ldr 1/7/80. Retd ENG 5/9/88.
REID G.G. Born 2/9/48. Commd 28/2/69. Sqn Ldr 1/7/81. Retd GD 1/1/83.
REID G.M. DFC. Born 5/11/22. Commd 20/7/44. Flt Lt 20/1/48. Retd GD 28/9/49.
REID H. Born 24/7/43. Commd 31/1/64. Gp Capt 1/7/95. Retd GD 24/9/99.
REID I.A. MA. Born 2/5/37. Commd 1/5/61. Sqn Ldr 1/1/68. Retd GD 2/5/95.
REID J. Born 17/7/40. Commd 20/7/78. Flt Lt 20/7/81. Retd GD 16/1/93.
REID J.A. Born 28/2/54. Commd 10/5/90. Flt Lt 10/5/92. Retd OPS SPT 10/11/99.
REID J.A.R.M. CEng FRAeS FINucE FCMI. Born 21/7/17. Commd 9/7/38. Gp Capt 1/1/59. Retd ENG 17/8/72.
REID K. Born 19/7/46. Commd 5/2/65. Sqn Ldr 1/1/83. Retd GD 19/7/90.
REID M. Born 29/6/43. Commd 3/3/67. Flt Lt 8/3/72. Retd SUP 24/4/82.
REID M. Born 31/3/39. Commd 31/8/78. Flt Lt 31/8/82. Retd ADMIN 31/1/85.
REID M.C. Born 18/5/42. Commd 30/1/70. Sqn Ldr 1/1/77. Retd ENG 18/10/80.
REID M.D.C. Born 11/5/30. Commd 15/9/60. Sqn Ldr 1/7/80. Retd ADMIN 11/5/85.
REID P.D. BSc. Born 12/12/60. Commd 10/10/83. Flt Lt 30/4/85. Retd GD 30/10/95.
REID R. Born 25/2/14. Commd 10/7/47. Sqn Ldr 1/7/62. Retd CAT 28/9/68.
REID R.G. Born 30/9/18. Commd 17/8/39. Flt Lt 1/7/48. Retd SUP 30/1/55.
REID R.L. CBE CEng MIMechE. Born 17/2/35. Commd 31/12/62. A Cdre 1/7/83. Retd ENG 16/5/88.
REID W.McK. PhD BSc. Born 8/6/53. Commd 28/9/80. Wg Cdr 1/7/99. Retd ENG 28/9/02.
REILLEY M.I.S. Born 5/9/45. Commd 15/9/67. Flt Lt 15/3/73. Retd GD 14/9/96.
REILLY D.P. Born 17/7/33. Commd 20/5/53. Gp Capt 1/7/84. Retd GD 25/6/85.
REILLY I. OBE BA. Born 7/4/44. Commd 17/12/65. Wg Cdr 1/7/85. Retd GD 14/3/96.

REINECK C.H. OBE. Born 23/5/37. Commd 26/8/57. A Cdre 1/7/85. Retd GD 1/9/90.
REITH C.G. Born 23/2/30. Commd 7/5/52. Flt Lt 2/10/57. Retd GD 6/10/67.
REITH R.G. MA. Born 1/10/58. Commd 20/7/87. Wg Cdr 1/7/00. Retd GD 13/6/04.
REIZ J.M. Born 4/8/56. Commd 16/9/76. Flt Lt 20/1/83. Retd ADMIN 5/8/86.
REJDER B. FCMI. Born 11/12/24. Commd 3/11/44. Wg Cdr 1/1/62. Retd GD 11/12/79.
RELF B.R.F. DipEurHum AIPM. Born 23/12/42. Commd 18/8/61. Sqn Ldr 1/1/81. Retd OPS SPT 23/12/97.
RELF J.A. Born 23/5/43. Commd 15/7/64. Sqn Ldr 1/7/78. Retd ENG 3/4/82.
RELFE R.I. BSc. Born 27/2/51. Commd 13/9/70. Sqn Ldr 1/7/85. Retd ADMIN 27/2/89.
RELPH W. OBE. Born 15/8/13. Commd 22/9/49. Wg Cdr 27/2/65. Retd MED(T) 15/8/68.
REMFRY K.R.M. MBE. Born 19/3/21. Commd 4/5/45. Flt Lt 19/5/52. Retd GD 7/5/70.
REMINGTON N.R. Born 1/10/44. Commd 29/1/72. Flt Lt 29/12/77. Retd GD 14/2/88.
REMLINGER M.J. Born 3/1/48. Commd 28/2/69. Gp Capt 1/1/94. Retd GD 15/5/01.
REMNANT D.McL. Born 16/5/30. Commd 8/6/49. Gp Capt 1/7/71. Retd SUP 12/12/73.
RENAUD-WRIGHT M.StJ. Born 24/3/17. Commd 5/11/42. Flt Lt 5/5/46. Retd ENG 1/1/60.
RENFREW S.C. Born 30/6/46. Commd 13/1/67. Sqn Ldr 1/7/91. Retd SUP 29/3/96.
RENKIN P.H. Born 28/9/19. Commd 8/6/49. Gp Capt 1/7/71. Retd SUP 12/12/73.
RENNIE C.A. DFM. Born 29/12/19. Commd 19/1/43. Wg Cdr 1/1/59. Retd GD 29/12/74.
RENNIE J. MA BSc FCIPD FCMI. Born 12/10/40. Commd 6/1/69. Gp Capt 1/1/89. Retd ADMIN 15/7/95.
RENOWDEN G.R. The Venerable. CB BA LTh. Born 13/8/29. Commd 15/1/58. Retd AVM 8/10/88.
RENSHAW A. Born 29/11/47. Commd 3/12/70. Wg Cdr 1/7/92. Retd ENG 1/11/01.
RENSHAW E.C. Born 13/9/40. Commd 4/7/69. Flt Lt 4/7/71. Retd ENG 18/3/72.
RENSHAW G.R. Born 10/9/31. Commd 31/5/51. Flt Lt 20/9/56. Retd GD 8/8/65.
RENSHAW J. BSc. Born 20/6/59. Commd 28/9/80. Plt Offr 28/12/78. Retd ENG 31/3/82.
RENSHAW J.D.E. Born 7/1/30. Commd 14/4/53. Flt Lt 14/4/58. Retd SEC 7/7/68.
RENSHAW J.L. Born 27/7/53. Commd 14/1/88. Flt Lt 14/1/90. Retd ENG 14/1/96.
RENSHAW S.J. Born 22/4/51. Commd 26/11/81. Flt Lt 26/5/88. Retd OPS SPT 27/7/97.
RENTON H.F. CB LLD MA. Born 13/3/31. Commd 9/6/55. A Cdre 1/7/80. Retd ADMIN 13/3/86.
RENTON R.A. Born 25/12/38. Commd 31/8/60. Sqn Ldr 1/1/73. Retd GD 2/10/77.
RENWICK A.W. Born 20/6/49. Commd 22/9/69. Fg Offr 22/3/72. Retd ENG 30/1/76.
RENWICK C.H. DPhysEd. Born 3/9/35. Commd 13/11/62. Wg Cdr 1/1/86. Retd ADMIN 19/1/89.
RENYARD B. CEng MIMechE MRAeS MCMI. Born 8/4/38. Commd 28/7/60. Wg Cdr 1/7/76. Retd ENG 3/5/90.
REST P.A. Born 14/12/37. Commd 28/9/60. Flt Lt 28/3/71. Retd GD 28/9/76.
RETALLACK M. MBE. Born 25/4/27. Commd 14/11/57. Flt Lt 14/5/62. Retd GD 25/4/87.
REVELL J.D. BSc. Born 11/7/44. Commd 15/7/66. Sqn Ldr 1/1/80. Retd ENG 11/7/88.
REVELL M. FRSA FCIPD MCMI. Born 25/6/47. Commd 17/1/82. Flt Lt 17/7/84. Retd ADMIN (SEC) 25/6/05.
REVILL R. BA. Born 10/1/42. Commd 10/5/71. Sqn Ldr 1/7/06. Retd ADMIN 1/1/94.
REVITT E.D. DFC. Born 18/10/19. Commd 20/9/42. Sqn Ldr 1/1/64. Retd GD(G) 31/1/67.
REVNELL B.J. Born 4/3/33. Commd 6/12/51. Sqn Ldr 1/7/68. Retd GD 1/7/71.
REX A.J. BSc. Born 12/5/54. Commd 30/5/76. Flt Lt 20/8/77. Retd GD 14/3/89.
REXFORD-WELCH S.C. MA MSc MRCS LRCP. Born 27/10/15. Commd 1/6/49. Gp Capt 13/7/68. Retd MED 27/10/80.
REY M. Born 24/11/33. Commd 26/5/67. Sqn Ldr 1/1/75. Retd ENG 1/4/79.
REYNER K. FCMI FITD. Born 26/11/35. Commd 26/7/56. Gp Capt 1/7/82. Retd SY 18/6/86.
REYNISH T.K.D. Born 11/10/39. Commd 8/2/91. Sqn Ldr 8/2/91. Retd GD 11/10/94.
REYNOLDS A.J. Born 15/4/46. Commd 10/6/66. Flt Lt 8/3/72. Retd GD 1/10/76.
REYNOLDS A.L. Born 2/3/49. Commd 6/4/72. Sqn Ldr 1/1/85. Retd GD 6/7/88.
REYNOLDS B.R. Born 5/8/35. Commd 9/12/53. Sqn Ldr 1/1/70. Retd GD 5/8/90.
REYNOLDS C. DFC. Born 6/10/21. Commd 2/8/44. Flt Lt 16/5/49. Retd GD(G) 31/3/62.
REYNOLDS D.A. Born 16/4/15. Commd 4/11/43. Sqn Ldr 1/7/62. Retd ENG 15/8/64.
REYNOLDS E. Born 9/3/31. Commd 15/12/53. Flt Lt 15/6/56. Retd GD 1/7/58.
REYNOLDS G.F. Born 21/4/34. Commd 21/10/66. Wg Cdr 1/1/84. Retd SUP 21/4/89.
REYNOLDS G.L. BSc. Born 12/11/43. Commd 13/4/64. Flt Lt 15/4/67. Retd GD 12/4/75.
REYNOLDS J. DPhysEd. Born 2/4/33. Commd 28/2/57. Gp Capt 1/1/85. Retd ADMIN 2/4/88.
REYNOLDS J.C. MB BS MRCS MRCP. Born 8/4/51. Commd 20/2/73. Sqn Ldr 13/7/81. Retd MED 23/8/89.
REYNOLDS J.R. Born 28/2/33. Commd 22/7/71. Flt Lt 22/7/73. Retd ENG 22/7/79.
REYNOLDS J.T. Born 21/12/29. Commd 26/3/52. Flt Lt 26/9/56. Retd GD 21/12/67.
REYNOLDS M. BSc(Eng). Born 31/7/47. Commd 13/1/74. Sqn Ldr 1/7/87. Retd FLY(N) 31/7/04.
REYNOLDS N.S.B. BEM. Born 5/10/22. Commd 11/2/65. Flt Lt 11/2/70. Retd ENG 5/10/77.
REYNOLDS P. DFC*. Born 30/10/21. Commd 11/5/41. Wg Cdr 1/7/57. Retd GD 23/10/68.
REYNOLDS P. Born 22/1/44. Commd 22/2/63. Sqn Ldr 1/1/81. Retd GD 1/7/84.
REYNOLDS P.A. CertEd. Born 4/7/46. Commd 17/10/71. Wg Cdr 1/1/92. Retd ADMIN 13/9/96.
REYNOLDS P.F. Born 21/12/34. Commd 14/1/65. Flt Lt 14/1/71. Retd SUP 1/11/75.
REYNOLDS P.G.H. Born 18/10/16. Commd 1/11/44. Flt Lt 16/5/60. Retd GD(G) 25/11/66.
REYNOLDS P.J. Born 1/2/44. Commd 16/8/68. Flt Lt 16/2/74. Retd GD 6/5/87.
REYNOLDS S. BA. Born 1/1/49. Commd 22/2/71. Flt Lt 22/5/74. Retd ADMIN 22/2/87.
REYNOLDS S.K. Born 10/11/42. Commd 5/9/69. Sqn Ldr 1/7/76. Retd GD 6/6/84.

REYNOLDS T.F. CEng MIMechE. Born 17/6/36. Commd 17/11/58. Gp Capt 1/7/83. Retd ENG 18/6/86.
RHIND H.A. Born 12/3/44. Commd 15/7/65. Flt Lt 15/7/70. Retd ENG 27/11/76.
RHIND J.R. Born 10/5/28. Commd 31/1/51. Sqn Ldr 1/1/63. Retd GD 12/1/67.
RHODES A.D. Born 28/6/56. Commd 4/6/87. Flt Lt 4/6/89. Retd GD(G) 4/6/95.
RHODES A.F.P. Born 4/4/45. Commd 1/4/66. Flt Lt 1/10/71. Retd GD 3/1/76.
RHODES D.B.D. MBE CEng MRAeS MCMI. Born 13/12/20. Commd 26/9/57. Sqn Ldr 1/7/68. Retd ENG 5/6/75.
RHODES G.K. Born 27/6/34. Commd 18/11/66. Sqn Ldr 1/1/79. Retd ENG 1/10/85.
RHODES K.D. BA MCMI. Born 29/6/44. Commd 24/6/65. Wg Cdr 1/7/84. Retd GD 30/3/94.
RHODES M.D. Born 6/4/36. Commd 23/6/67. Wg Cdr 1/7/84. Retd ENG 6/4/94.
RHODES R.G. MBE AFC. Born 11/7/29. Commd 9/3/66. Sqn Ldr 1/7/76. Retd GD 11/7/89.
RHODES R.H.N. AFC MRAeS. Born 1/12/43. Commd 26/10/62. Wg Cdr 1/1/82. Retd GD 6/1/86.
RHODES R.L. Born 27/3/47. Commd 24/7/81. Flt Lt 24/7/83. Retd GD 24/7/89.
RHODES W. Born 30/11/43. Commd 22/3/63. Flt Lt 8/1/69. Retd GD 27/8/81.
RHYDDERCH R.D. MB BCh FFARCS DA. Born 26/5/44. Commd 15/9/69. Sqn Ldr 5/9/73. Retd MED 1/12/78.
RICCOMINI G.C. Born 23/3/23. Commd 20/11/43. Sqn Ldr 1/1/66. Retd GD(G) 31/3/76.
RICE B. BEM. Born 2/5/39. Commd 1/7/82. Sqn Ldr 1/7/91. Retd SY 1/7/94.
RICE D.J.C. Born 7/5/42. Commd 22/3/63. Flt Lt 22/9/68. Retd GD 7/5/80.
RICE K.N. Born 6/6/25. Commd 17/8/45. Sqn Ldr 1/1/57. Retd GD 6/6/68.
RICE L.G. Born 14/10/23. Commd 27/8/59. Flt Lt 27/8/64. Retd ENG 30/4/76.
RICE P.D. Born 20/1/46. Commd 23/9/66. Flt Lt 23/3/72. Retd GD 13/3/76.
RICE R.G. Born 22/12/20. Commd 23/7/56. Flt Lt 23/7/56. Retd SEC 30/12/72.
RICE V.J. BA IEng. Born 7/6/42. Commd 3/7/80. Sqn Ldr 1/7/88. Retd ENG 7/6/97.
RICE W. OBE. Born 1/8/46. Commd 22/7/66. Wg Cdr 1/7/91. Retd ADMIN 1/8/01.
RICH N.L. BSc. Born 21/12/53. Commd 17/9/72. Sqn Ldr 1/1/89. Retd ENG 1/5/02.
RICH P.C.A. MCMI. Born 23/11/14. Commd 18/9/40. Wg Cdr 1/7/61. Retd SUP 24/1/70.
RICHARD D.M. CBE MRAeS. Born 19/10/33. Commd 27/7/54. A Cdre 1/7/84. Retd GD 19/10/88.
RICHARDS A.J. OBE. Born 21/5/38. Commd 10/7/57. Wg Cdr 1/7/72. Retd GD 21/6/77.
RICHARDS B. Born 2/5/50. Commd 26/9/90. Flt Lt 26/9/94. Retd ENG 3/3/01.
RICHARDS D. BA. Born 13/11/31. Commd 15/11/55. Sqn Ldr 1/7/64. Retd GD 15/11/71.
RICHARDS D. Born 7/7/39. Commd 23/12/58. Sqn Ldr 1/1/73. Retd ENG 7/7/77.
RICHARDS D.A. DFC. Born 2/4/23. Commd 28/5/44. Flt Lt 28/11/47. Retd GD 1/5/68.
RICHARDS E. Born 15/1/25. Commd 15/12/49. Sqn Ldr 1/7/71. Retd PI 30/6/78.
RICHARDS G. AFC. Born 11/12/20. Commd 5/7/43. Sqn Ldr 1/7/66. Retd GD 11/12/75.
RICHARDS G.A.T. MA. Born 18/6/18. Commd 15/3/41. Wg Cdr 1/1/67. Retd EDN 9/9/69.
RICHARDS G.E.A. Born 8/2/36. Commd 22/10/59. Flt Lt 22/1/66. Retd SUP 8/2/74.
RICHARDS G.T.G. Born 30/9/23. Commd 4/11/44. Sqn Ldr 1/10/55. Retd GD 1/4/61.
RICHARDS J. Born 12/7/39. Commd 16/7/84. Sqn Ldr 1/1/92. Retd GD 12/7/94.
RICHARDS J. BSc. Born 16/3/35. Commd 5/7/60. Sqn Ldr 9/6/70. Retd EDN 14/8/75.
RICHARDS J. BA DPhysEd. Born 12/5/34. Commd 7/9/56. Sqn Ldr 7/3/64. Retd EDN 9/9/75.
RICHARDS J.M. Born 20/4/42. Commd 24/2/61. Flt Lt 24/8/66. Retd GD 14/2/76.
RICHARDS J.T.G. MA MCMI. Born 1/10/35. Commd 11/4/58. Sqn Ldr 14/4/66. Retd EDN 26/6/74.
RICHARDS K.D. Born 10/2/45. Commd 22/5/64. Flt Lt 22/11/69. Retd GD 10/2/00.
RICHARDS M. Born 25/1/45. Commd 10/9/70. Flt Lt 3/12/76. Retd PRT 29/9/78.
RICHARDS M.E. Born 21/1/48. Commd 5/1/78. Sqn Ldr 1/1/92. Retd FLY(AEO) 21/1/05.
RICHARDS M.J. MRIN MCMI. Born 20/12/33. Commd 9/4/52. Wg Cdr 1/1/79. Retd GD 30/4/85.
RICHARDS P.B.M. Born 27/4/42. Commd 28/7/64. Gp Capt 1/7/87. Retd SUP 27/4/97.
RICHARDS R.B. Born 5/9/42. Commd 19/4/63. Wg Cdr 1/1/86. Retd GD 2/1/93.
RICHARDS R.E. Born 23/1/52. Commd 7/1/71. Flt Lt 7/7/77. Retd GD(G) 23/1/90.
RICHARDS R.G.H. Born 3/5/44. Commd 28/2/80. Flt Lt 28/2/84. Retd ENG 3/5/88.
RICHARDS R.J. The Rev. BA. Born 25/1/16. Commd 19/1/43. Retd Wg Cdr 25/1/71.
RICHARDS R.R.V. BA. Born 17/4/28. Commd 19/10/49. Sqn Ldr 1/7/62. Retd SEC 17/4/66.
RICHARDS R.S. Born 26/8/28. Commd 9/4/52. Flt Lt 9/1/58. Retd GD 27/8/66.
RICHARDS S.M. BSc. Born 11/3/53. Commd 25/9/71. Sqn Ldr 1/7/88. Retd ENG 1/7/91.
RICHARDS S.R. Born 16/4/54. Commd 20/10/83. Wg Cdr 1/7/01. Retd ENG 15/9/02.
RICHARDS S.W. MBE. Born 17/6/43. Commd 17/7/70. Wg Cdr 1/1/84. Retd ADMIN 17/6/87.
RICHARDSON A. Born 12/12/42. Commd 14/2/65. Flt Lt 6/12/69. Retd GD 12/12/80.
RICHARDSON A. Born 26/1/39. Commd 9/12/76. Sqn Ldr 9/12/82. Retd MED(T) 9/12/84.
RICHARDSON A.D. Born 21/9/47. Commd 5/11/65. Sqn Ldr 1/1/94. Retd GD 4/7/02.
RICHARDSON A.G. Born 3/1/33. Commd 6/4/59. Flt Lt 6/4/59. Retd GD 3/1/93.
RICHARDSON A.G. Born 28/8/51. Commd 13/9/70. Flt Lt 22/1/79. Retd GD 28/8/89.
RICHARDSON A.J. Born 4/5/28. Commd 8/11/51. Sqn Ldr 1/1/69. Retd GD(G) 2/8/80.
RICHARDSON A.K. Born 20/4/48. Commd 2/2/70. Wg Cdr 1/7/90. Retd GD 20/4/03.
RICHARDSON A.M. BSc. Born 21/2/63. Commd 2/9/84. Flt Lt 2/3/88. Retd ADMIN 14/9/96.
RICHARDSON A.P. Born 26/11/19. Commd 29/1/44. Flt Lt 24/9/47. Retd GD 17/7/58.
RICHARDSON B. Born 27/7/45. Commd 5/2/65. Fg Offr 5/2/67. Retd GD 28/2/70.
RICHARDSON B.T. MBE. Born 24/2/51. Commd 23/4/87. Sqn Ldr 1/1/97. Retd ADMIN 21/4/98.

RICHARDSON C.G. Born 10/7/34. Commd 5/4/55. Sqn Ldr 1/1/71. Retd GD 1/1/74.
RICHARDSON C.H. MILT DipMgmt. Born 25/1/58. Commd 19/9/76. Flt Lt 19/3/83. Retd SUP 25/1/99.
RICHARDSON D. Born 28/7/35. Commd 31/5/56. Flt Lt 20/10/61. Retd SUP 1/3/78.
RICHARDSON D.A. Born 11/10/49. Commd 22/7/71. Fg Offr 22/7/73. Retd GD 2/9/76.
RICHARDSON D.J. BSc. Born 16/9/51. Commd 29/4/84. Sqn Ldr 1/7/88. Retd ADMIN 14/3/97.
RICHARDSON D.L. Born 21/6/53. Commd 17/9/72. Flt Lt 7/4/80. Retd GD 21/6/91.
RICHARDSON D.L. Born 15/7/26. Commd 21/6/50. Flt Lt 21/12/54. Retd GD 2/3/76.
RICHARDSON F.R.J. DFM AIIP. Born 26/8/23. Commd 10/10/44. Wg Cdr 1/7/70. Retd ENG 26/8/81.
RICHARDSON F.S. Born 31/1/66. Commd 23/8/90. Flt Lt 15/9/90. Retd OPS SPT(REGT) 31/1/04.
RICHARDSON F.W. Born 27/8/27. Commd 25/4/51. Flt Lt 25/1/57. Retd GD 17/4/67.
RICHARDSON G. Born 16/9/49. Commd 30/5/69. Sqn Ldr 1/7/81. Retd GD 16/9/87.
RICHARDSON G.F. BSc. Born 2/5/52. Commd 13/1/74. Sqn Ldr 1/1/89. Retd FLY(N) 2/5/03.
RICHARDSON G.L. BSc. Born 16/5/53. Commd 13/2/77. Flt Lt 13/8/79. Retd SUP 13/2/93.
RICHARDSON J. MBE AFC FCMI. Born 26/2/24. Commd 27/3/45. Gp Capt 1/1/68. Retd GD 26/9/75.
RICHARDSON J. Born 17/4/34. Commd 19/1/66. Sqn Ldr 19/1/78. Retd MED(T) 20/5/86.
RICHARDSON J.B. DFC. Born 7/4/15. Commd 26/1/44. Flt Lt 26/7/47. Retd GD 21/8/58.
RICHARDSON J.E. Born 18/9/23. Commd 25/5/45. Flt Lt 4/12/52. Retd GD 26/6/67.
RICHARDSON J.F. Born 18/2/30. Commd 20/12/51. Flt Lt 22/5/57. Retd GD 18/2/73.
RICHARDSON J.J.D. BA CEng MRAeS MCMI. Born 27/6/29. Commd 12/7/62. Sqn Ldr 1/1/73. Retd ENG 27/6/89.
RICHARDSON J.W. Born 3/9/33. Commd 21/1/54. Sqn Ldr 1/7/68. Retd GD 30/9/73.
RICHARDSON K.P. BA. Born 11/12/44. Commd 11/8/77. Flt Lt 1/1/85. Retd ADMIN 31/3/94.
RICHARDSON K.R. OBE DFC MCMI. Born 30/1/22. Commd 26/10/44. Wg Cdr 1/7/61. Retd GD 30/1/77.
RICHARDSON M.G. OBE . Born 10/6/49. Commd 3/10/69. Wg Cdr 1/1/92. Retd GD 10/6/04.
RICHARDSON N.J. Born 2/4/22. Commd 7/5/47. Flt Lt 4/6/53. Retd GD 2/7/65.
RICHARDSON P.D. BA MISM MCMI. Born 4/11/61. Commd 29/4/84. Flt Lt 29/10/87. Retd OPS SPT 29/4/00.
RICHARDSON P.D. Born 13/7/15. Commd 23/12/42. Flt Lt 19/2/47. Retd GD 1/4/58.
RICHARDSON R. Born 3/4/47. Commd 13/1/67. Flt Lt 13/7/72. Retd GD 3/4/85.
RICHARDSON R.A. Born 23/7/21. Commd 21/2/48. Flt Lt 4/6/53. Retd GD 2/4/68.
RICHARDSON S.A. Born 14/9/61. Commd 30/4/81. Sqn Ldr 1/1/96. Retd GD 14/9/99.
RICHARDSON W.A. BSc CEng MIMechE. Born 2/3/42. Commd 15/7/63. Gp Capt 1/1/86. Retd ENG 25/2/89.
RICHES H.F. Born 24/3/22. Commd 19/10/49. Sqn Ldr 19/10/57. Retd MAR 8/7/61.
RICHES P.M. Born 20/7/48. Commd 28/2/69. Sqn Ldr 1/1/96. Retd FLY(N) 20/7/03.
RICHEY F.A. MSc BA. Born 21/11/49. Commd 17/10/71. Wg Cdr 1/7/91. Retd GD 21/5/05.
RICHFORD H.C. DFC. Born 30/8/23. Commd 21/8/44. Sqn Ldr 1/1/58. Retd GD 10/10/66.
RICHMOND D.E. Born 24/8/37. Commd 5/3/57. Sqn Ldr 1/1/74. Retd ENG 24/8/87.
RICHMOND G. Born 4/5/43. Commd 5/7/68. Sqn Ldr 1/7/76. Retd ENG 2/11/83.
RICHMOND K.A. Born 6/6/30. Commd 23/9/53. Sqn Ldr 23/3/64. Retd ADMIN 6/6/85.
RICHMOND P. Born 20/2/39. Commd 7/7/64. Flt Lt 19/8/64. Retd GD 20/2/77.
RICHMOND S.P. Born 18/1/48. Commd 28/2/69. Sqn Ldr 1/1/81. Retd SUP 17/7/86.
RICHMOND W. Born 21/9/24. Commd 24/11/60. Flt Lt 24/11/63. Retd ADMIN 1/9/76.
RICKABY A.J. Born 13/4/41. Commd 2/3/61. Sqn Ldr 1/1/75. Retd SEC 13/4/79.
RICKARD D.K. Born 15/7/70. Commd 28/4/61. Sqn Ldr 1/1/72. Retd GD 15/7/78.
RICKARD F.P. Born 21/4/38. Commd 4/2/71. Flt Lt 4/2/73. Retd GD 1/1/90.
RICKARD F.W. Born 26/11/21. Commd 30/1/45. Flt Lt 11/6/53. Retd GD 10/5/67.
RICKARD M.W. Born 3/1/75. Commd 6/10/94. Flt Lt 6/4/01. Retd ADMIN (SEC) 1/9/03.
RICKARD P.E. Born 12/1/48. Commd 19/8/66. Sqn Ldr 1/7/83. Retd GD 1/7/86.
RICKARDS F.B. Born 16/8/29. Commd 5/12/51. Flt Lt 5/6/56. Retd GD 31/1/76. rtg Sqn Ldr.
RICKARDS T.J. Born 24/4/48. Commd 15/2/90. Flt Lt 15/2/94. Retd ENGINEER 24/4/03.
RICKETT R.C.A. Born 16/3/27. Commd 8/4/53. Flt Lt 26/3/67. Retd GD 9/7/73.
RICKETTS H.P. Born 29/6/13. Commd 10/12/42. Flt Lt 10/6/46. Retd ENG 19/3/47. rtg Sqn Ldr.
RICKETTS M.P. Born 26/6/33. Commd 6/4/72. Flt Lt 6/4/78. Retd ADMIN 6/4/84.
RICKINSON J. Born 31/7/41. Commd 7/11/85. Flt Lt 7/11/87. Retd ENG 31/7/96.
RICKWOOD R.P. MBE. Born 18/4/36. Commd 2/8/68. Sqn Ldr 1/1/77. Retd ENG 5/1/79.
RICKWOOD S.R. Born 17/12/45. Commd 15/6/83. Sqn Ldr 1/1/92. Retd ENGINEER 17/12/03.
RIDDELL G. BSc. Born 1/6/60. Commd 4/1/79. Sqn Ldr 1/1/94. Retd GD 31/3/99.
RIDDELL M.A.D. DFC DFM. Born 25/7/21. Commd 31/7/42. Flt Lt 31/1/46. Retd GD 26/7/54. rtg Sqn Ldr.
RIDDELL M.E.M. Born 13/7/13. Commd 27/10/41. Wg Offr 1/7/62. Retd SEC 13/6/68.
RIDDELL T. Born 23/5/51. Commd 2/1/75. Sqn Ldr 1/1/86. Retd GD 23/9/90.
RIDDETT G.O. BSc. Born 27/12/46. Commd 18/4/69. Flt Lt 15/4/71. Retd GD 1/4/89.
RIDE M.M. Born 31/12/26. Commd 28/2/51. Flt Lt 16/2/57. Retd GD 17/10/66.
RIDEAL E.C. OBE. Born 23/6/20. Commd 7/1/42. Sqn Ldr 1/1/56. Retd SEC 23/6/69.
RIDER W.J. BEd. Born 18/10/14. Commd 21/1/43. Sqn Ldr 1/7/63. Retd ENG 6/8/66.
RIDGE A.A.G. AFC. Born 12/12/24. Commd 17/10/57. Flt Lt 2/12/63. Retd GD 31/3/71.
RIDGEWAY F. MBE. Born 16/1/20. Commd 18/8/43. Wg Cdr 1/1/66. Retd SEC 1/2/74.
RIDGEWELL R.J. Born 8/1/18. Commd 8/7/54. Flt Lt 8/7/60. Retd GD(G) 11/4/74.
RIDGLEY M.G. Born 4/7/33. Commd 13/2/52. Flt Lt 12/6/57. Retd GD 4/7/71.

RIDGWAY C.A. Born 19/8/23. Commd 22/9/50. Flt Lt 22/9/54. Retd GD(G) 31/1/69.
RIDLER A.W. MA. Born 2/7/58. Commd 1/4/90. Flt Lt 1/10/91. Retd ADMIN 14/3/97.
RIDLEY C.R.A. BSc. Born 22/9/59. Commd 19/6/83. Flt Lt 19/12/85. Retd GD 21/3/00.
RIDLEY J.W. CEng MRAeS MCMI. Born 30/5/23. Commd 2/10/58. Sqn Ldr 1/7/73. Retd ENG 26/3/77.
RIDLEY K.C. Born 2/7/56. Commd 19/7/84. Flt Lt 19/7/86. Retd GD 3/12/96.
RIDLEY N.M. MBE. Born 28/9/31. Commd 12/8/54. Sqn Ldr 1/7/72. Retd SUP 29/9/81.
RIDLEY R.A. BSc. Born 16/11/42. Commd 15/7/64. Sqn Ldr 1/1/76. Retd ENG 16/11/80.
RIDLEY R.G. Born 23/2/27. Commd 9/3/50. Sqn Ldr 1/1/65. Retd GD 23/2/85.
RIDOUT H.J. Born 9/11/30. Commd 12/12/51. Sqn Ldr 1/7/60. Retd GD 9/11/68.
RIDOUT T.A.F. Born 5/2/23. Commd 20/6/45. Flt Lt 29/6/50. Retd GD 23/6/57.
RIDPATH F.T. Born 5/9/30. Commd 26/3/52. Flt Lt 14/9/60. Retd GD(G) 5/9/80.
RIGBY D.G.L. Born 31/5/26. Commd 16/7/52. Flt Lt 12/12/57. Retd GD 31/5/64.
RIGBY D.H. Born 17/5/34. Commd 29/10/52. Flt Lt 24/3/58. Retd GD 17/5/72.
RIGBY D.S. Born 27/4/45. Commd 21/1/66. Sqn Ldr 1/7/90. Retd GD 14/3/97.
RIGBY F.M. Born 17/11/29. Commd 20/12/51. Flt Lt 22/5/57. Retd GD 17/11/67.
RIGBY J.C.H. BA. Born 26/1/55. Commd 2/3/80. Flt Lt 2/6/83. Retd SY 1/10/93.
RIGBY P. Born 18/2/52. Commd 28/2/85. Flt Lt 28/2/87. Retd ENG 1/7/94.
RIGBY W.T.L. Born 16/10/23. Commd 29/6/50. Sqn Ldr 1/7/71. Retd GD 16/10/78.
RIGDEN K.F. BA. Born 2/8/54. Commd 30/10/77. Flt Lt 30/7/79. Retd GD 30/10/89.
RIGG E.C. MBE AFC MRAeS. Born 21/4/26. Commd 25/10/46. Wg Cdr 1/7/65. Retd GD 18/5/76.
RIGG H.W.J. AFC MRAeS. Born 28/7/34. Commd 10/4/56. Wg Cdr 1/7/76. Retd GD 12/7/85.
RIGG M.D. Born 9/6/43. Commd 14/7/66. Flt Lt 14/1/72. Retd GD 7/4/76.
RILEY B.A. Born 14/8/33. Commd 18/6/52. Wg Cdr 1/1/78. Retd GD 1/5/87.
RILEY D. Born 29/5/32. Commd 16/4/54. Flt Lt 13/4/60. Retd GD 15/6/72.
RILEY D. BSc. Born 4/12/35. Commd 20/10/69. Sqn Ldr 3/10/73. Retd ADMIN 4/12/85.
RILEY D.C. Born 8/8/58. Commd 21/4/77. Sqn Ldr 1/7/90. Retd GD 8/8/96.
RILEY D.G. Born 15/4/33. Commd 17/1/52. Wg Cdr 1/7/79. Retd GD 27/6/92.
RILEY D.J. BSc. Born 1/3/63. Commd 25/11/84. Flt Lt 25/5/87. Retd GD 1/3/01.
RILEY G.G. Born 24/11/60. Commd 13/12/79. Sqn Ldr 1/7/92. Retd GD 24/11/98.
RILEY H.R. CEng FCMI MIERE MRAeS. Born 18/2/29. Commd 22/3/51. Gp Capt 1/7/73. Retd ENG 6/11/82.
RILEY J.A. MBE. Born 13/6/28. Commd 14/2/63. Sqn Ldr 1/7/74. Retd ENG 5/11/77. Re-instated 25/3/81 to 1/12/84.
RILEY J.T. Born 12/2/22. Commd 2/11/44. Flt Lt 17/9/51. Retd GD 12/2/65.
RILEY L.J. BA. Born 28/5/23. Commd 6/11/52. Sqn Ldr 1/7/67. Retd GD 30/9/73.
RILEY P.J. BA. Born 3/2/64. Commd 7/6/87. Sqn Ldr 1/1/01. Retd OPS SPT(ATC) 1/1/04.
RILEY P.M. Born 26/9/40. Commd 28/2/61. Sqn Ldr 1/7/70. Retd GD 31/12/77.
RILEY R.J. Born 24/4/27. Commd 2/6/47. Sqn Ldr 1/1/60. Retd SUP 24/4/65.
RILEY S.C. Born 15/6/51. Commd 28/11/69. Flt Lt 28/5/75. Retd GD 30/6/88.
RILEY T. Born 20/8/30. Commd 13/1/56. Flt Lt 14/5/61. Retd GD 20/8/68. Re-employed GD(G) 13/9/74 to 11/2/75.
RILEY T.J. Born 1/10/57. Commd 10/3/77. Flt Lt 10/9/82. Retd GD 1/10/95.
RILEY W.A. Born 27/5/48. Commd 7/6/68. Sqn Ldr 1/1/80. Retd ENG 27/5/86.
RILEY W.L. Born 29/3/22. Commd 22/10/43. Flt Lt 30/10/53. Retd SUP 31/3/62.
RIMER F.J. Born 30/1/08. Commd 17/1/40. Sqn Ldr 1/7/51. Retd ENG 30/1/57.
RIMINGTON R. Born 27/8/31. Commd 14/11/51. Sqn Ldr 1/7/63. Retd GD 27/8/69.
RIMINI F.M. BEM. Born 10/3/34. Commd 27/3/70. Sqn Ldr 16/8/80. Retd MED(T) 4/1/88.
RIMMER B.A. Born 12/6/29. Commd 23/2/54. Flt Lt 23/8/59. Retd GD 8/11/77.
RIMMER F. Born 24/7/23. Commd 4/9/46. Sqn Ldr 1/1/61. Retd GD 24/2/67.
RIMMER J.A.J. BSc. Born 20/7/57. Commd 14/9/75. Wg Cdr 1/1/95. Retd GD 31/12/03.
RIMMER T. Born 3/11/21. Commd 27/1/44. Flt Lt 27/7/47. Retd ENG 26/4/56. rtg Sqn Ldr.
RIMMER T.W. CB OBE MA FRAeS. Born 16/12/48. Commd 13/9/71. AVM 1/1/99. Retd GD 7/2/04.
RING M.M.D. BEM. Born 25/4/24. Commd 12/3/64. Flt Lt 12/3/69. Retd SUP 25/4/79.
RINGER A.W. CBE MVO AFC* MCMI. Born 22/8/21. Commd 17/1/45. Gp Capt 1/1/71. Retd GD 17/9/76.
RINGLAND D.C.M. BSc. Born 15/1/53. Commd 28/1/73. Sqn Ldr 1/7/87. Retd GD 28/1/97.
RINGROSE G.E. BSc. Born 19/10/30. Commd 5/11/52. Sqn Ldr 1/1/63. Retd ENG 5/11/68.
RIORDAN D.P. DFC. Born 17/9/32. Commd 19/7/51. Flt Lt 29/4/59. Retd GD 17/9/87.
RIORDAN M.H. BA. Born 21/11/33. Commd 26/9/56. Flt Lt 26/3/63. Retd EDN 3/1/68.
RIORDAN R.D. Born 18/12/43. Commd 21/9/72. Sqn Ldr 1/1/90. Retd GD(G) 18/12/91.
RIPLEY G. Born 16/4/48. Commd 11/5/78. Flt Lt 11/5/80. Retd OPS SPT(FC) 16/4/03.
RIPLEY M.B.H. CEng. Born 25/2/38. Commd 8/6/63. Sqn Ldr 1/7/76. Retd ENG 20/1/89.
RIPPENGAL A.V. DFC DFM. Born 13/9/22. Commd 3/9/43. Flt Lt 7/6/51. Retd GD 13/9/77.
RIPPIN G.W. Born 17/8/34. Commd 30/7/52. Sqn Ldr 1/1/80. Retd GD 17/8/89.
RIPPON D. Born 22/12/49. Commd 31/7/86. Wg Cdr 1/7/97. Retd MEDICAL SUPPORT 22/12/04.
RISBY A.E. Born 6/1/25. Commd 5/7/62. Sqn Ldr 1/7/76. Retd GD 31/1/74.
RISDALE N.L. DFC BSc. Born 9/4/59. Commd 28/12/80. Sqn Ldr 1/7/90. Retd GD 9/4/97.
RISELEY E.A. Born 26/1/23. Commd 16/6/44. Sqn Ldr 1/1/55. Retd GD 26/1/78.
RISELEY-PRICHARD J.M. BSc. Born 2/2/63. Commd 11/7/91. Sqn Ldr 1/7/95. Retd ADMIN (PROVSY) 1/2/03.
RISELEY-PRICHARD R.A. MA BM BCh FFCM FCMI. Born 19/2/25. Commd 1/3/51. AVM 1/1/81. Retd MED 19/2/85.

RITCH D.N.S. BSc. Born 11/6/63. Commd 1/4/85. Flt Lt 15/1/88. Retd GD 11/6/01.
RITCHIE F.G. Born 19/5/20. Commd 16/2/45. Flt Lt 16/8/48. Retd GD(G) 29/6/62.
RITCHIE J.M.B. Born 27/1/47. Commd 6/5/66. Sqn Ldr 1/1/84. Retd GD 27/1/02.
RITCHIE P. LLB. Born 16/10/35. Commd 28/11/58. Wg Cdr 16/10/73. Retd LGL 28/11/74.
RITCHIE P.W. Born 27/3/47. Commd 11/8/67. Flt Lt 11/2/73. Retd GD 1/7/90.
RITCHIE W.B.C. MBE. Born 8/1/33. Commd 21/5/52. Sqn Ldr 1/7/83. Retd GD 8/1/91.
RIVERS J.L.S. Born 16/12/22. Commd 11/4/57. Sqn Ldr 1/7/70. Retd ENG 22/7/82.
RIVETT F.L. Born 13/10/37. Commd 24/4/56. Flt Lt 21/8/63. Retd GD 31/10/64.
RIX D.A. Born 9/4/44. Commd 12/7/63. Flt Lt 30/4/69. Retd GD 9/4/82. rtg Sqn Ldr.
RIXOM J.A. BSc. Born 24/6/32. Commd 1/3/61. A Cdre 1/1/81. Retd ENG 24/8/87.
RIXON J.J. Born 22/7/52. Commd 8/5/86. Flt Lt 8/5/88. Retd SUP 14/3/96.
RIXSON S.R. Born 19/5/52. Commd 9/10/75. Sqn Ldr 1/7/89. Retd GD 14/9/96.
ROACH A. Born 15/5/23. Commd 9/1/46. Flt Lt 15/12/53. Retd GD 15/6/66.
ROACH C.J. Born 28/4/44. Commd 21/4/67. Flt Lt 6/9/73. Retd GD(G) 1/7/92.
ROACHE R.B. DFC*. Born 16/7/21. Commd 19/2/41. Gp Capt 1/7/65. Retd GD 14/2/70.
ROBB A.M. Born 12/2/66. Commd 19/11/87. Flt Lt 19/5/94. Retd OPS SPT(ATC) 12/2/04.
ROBB B.S. Born 11/12/56. Commd 2/2/84. Flt Lt 14/3/86. Retd GD 1/6/98.
ROBB G.P. MBE. Born 7/12/24. Commd 13/12/68. Flt Lt 13/12/73. Retd ENG 7/12/84.
ROBB J.W. Born 7/1/38. Commd 25/7/59. Flt Lt 25/1/65. Retd GD 25/7/85.
ROBB R.C. OBE MB ChB MFCM DPhysMed DPH DIH. Born 30/5/22. Commd 17/10/46. A Cdre 1/1/73.
    Retd MED 1/7/76.
ROBBIE P.J. OBE. Born 11/4/46. Commd 3/3/67. Gp Capt 1/7/94. Retd GD 14/8/96.
ROBBINS C.J. Born 18/8/49. Commd 27/8/87. Flt Lt 27/8/91. Retd ENGINEER 8/4/04.
ROBBINS F.M. CEng MIEE. Born 12/7/36. Commd 23/7/58. Sqn Ldr 1/1/68. Retd ENG 29/12/79.
ROBBINS J.A. Born 16/8/34. Commd 14/2/56. Flt Lt 14/8/61. Retd GD 16/8/72.
ROBBINS J.S. ACT(Bath) FHCIMA. Born 5/9/34. Commd 2/10/62. Sqn Ldr 1/7/74. Retd ADMIN 29/9/84.
ROBERSON N.J. Born 27/9/40. Commd 25/6/66. Flt Lt 8/1/69. Retd GD 27/9/95.
ROBERSON S.C. Born 16/2/36. Commd 17/6/54. Sqn Ldr 1/7/85. Retd GD 16/2/94.
ROBERTS A. Born 14/11/45. Commd 26/5/67. Flt Lt 18/2/70. Retd GD 14/11/83.
ROBERTS A.J. BSc MB BS MRCGP DAvMed. Born 23/4/60. Commd 15/12/82. Wg Cdr 1/2/99. Retd MED 15/12/00.
ROBERTS A.J. Born 29/10/29. Commd 20/12/51. Flt Lt 8/4/57. Retd GD 29/10/67.
ROBERTS A.J. Born 25/8/57. Commd 15/3/79. Flt Lt 27/12/82. Retd GD 25/8/95.
ROBERTS A.J.A. DFC. Born 23/12/15. Commd 24/4/41. Sqn Ldr 1/8/47. Retd GD 23/12/57.
ROBERTS A.L. CB CBE AFC FRAeS. Born 19/5/38. Commd 16/12/58. AVM 1/1/87. Retd GD 5/4/94.
ROBERTS A.L.N. Born 20/5/28. Commd 14/8/70. Flt Lt 14/8/73. Retd GD 20/5/83.
ROBERTS A.M. AFC. Born 16/4/47. Commd 18/8/67. Sqn Ldr 1/7/80. Retd GD 16/4/85.
ROBERTS A.W. DPhysEd. Born 9/5/28. Commd 5/5/54. Wg Cdr 1/1/80. Retd ADMIN 14/6/83.
ROBERTS B.E. Born 16/8/81. Commd 5/8/76. Flt Lt 5/8/78. Retd ENG 5/8/84.
ROBERTS B.E.W. Born 18/1/17. Commd 29/7/53. Sqn Ldr 1/1/69. Retd GD(G) 1/9/70.
ROBERTS B.H. BEM. Born 6/4/21. Commd 27/4/61. Flt Lt 27/4/66. Retd SEC 1/4/70.
ROBERTS C. Born 9/2/49. Commd 31/7/70. Flt Lt 31/7/73. Retd GD 9/2/87.
ROBERTS C.F. Born 13/4/45. Commd 22/5/64. Flt Lt 22/11/69. Retd GD 1/11/79.
ROBERTS C.P. Born 22/5/38. Commd 18/12/56. Sqn Ldr 1/7/89. Retd GD 22/5/96.
ROBERTS C.S. MA MSc BSc. Born 13/5/61. Commd 18/7/86. Wg Cdr 1/7/99. Retd GD 28/2/05.
ROBERTS D. Born 30/11/47. Commd 24/2/67. Wg Cdr 1/1/85. Retd OPS SPT 30/12/02.
ROBERTS D. MBCS MCIPD CertEd. Born 13/11/43. Commd 30/10/83. Sqn Ldr 1/7/90. Retd ADMIN 1/11/95.
ROBERTS D. DFC AFC. Born 6/5/23. Commd 20/2/43. Gp Capt 1/7/64. Retd GD 6/5/78.
ROBERTS D. Born 22/8/29. Commd 8/10/52. Flt Lt 26/8/57. Retd GD 22/8/67.
ROBERTS D.A. Born 20/11/35. Commd 27/1/77. Flt Lt 27/1/82. Retd ADMIN 20/9/86.
ROBERTS D.G. Born 1/9/65. Commd 22/9/88. Flt Lt 22/3/94. Retd FLY(P) 1/7/05.
ROBERTS D.G. Born 30/3/45. Commd 31/1/64. Sqn Ldr 1/1/92. Retd FLY(P) 30/3/03.
ROBERTS D.P. MA MRAeS. Born 11/11/24. Commd 11/2/44. Sqn Ldr 1/10/56. Retd ENG 10/4/65.
ROBERTS D.W. BSc. Born 13/8/49. Commd 20/1/80. Sqn Ldr 1/7/91. Retd ADMIN 14/3/97.
ROBERTS E. Born 20/10/47. Commd 8/12/83. Flt Lt 8/12/87. Retd ADMIN 10/3/91.
ROBERTS E.H. Born 7/8/29. Commd 3/9/52. Sqn Ldr 1/7/69. Retd GD 7/8/84.
ROBERTS E.W. Born 12/11/16. Commd 29/5/46. Flt Lt 29/11/50. Retd SEC 28/5/64.
ROBERTS F. Born 14/7/22. Commd 26/5/60. Flt Lt 26/5/63. Retd GD(G) 14/7/77.
ROBERTS F.E. Born 1/7/16. Commd 3/2/40. Sqn Offr 1/7/54. Retd SUP 26/8/55.
ROBERTS G. MA. Born 12/3/32. Commd 11/8/53. Sqn Ldr 1/7/62. Retd GD 7/4/72.
ROBERTS G.D. Born 10/4/35. Commd 14/7/66. Sqn Ldr 1/7/80. Retd GD 1/2/92.
ROBERTS G.P. Born 8/6/25. Commd 31/8/45. Wg Cdr 1/7/71. Retd GD 9/12/75.
ROBERTS H. MSc BSc CPhys MInstP. Born 12/3/65. Commd 3/6/93. Sqn Ldr 1/1/98. Retd ENGINEER 12/3/03.
ROBERTS H.D. BSc(Eng). Born 20/9/59. Commd 4/9/78. Flt Lt 15/10/82. Retd GD 13/4/93.
ROBERTS H.G. Born 9/9/12. Commd 28/5/45. Fg Offr 10/3/54. Retd GD(G) 11/6/60.
ROBERTS I.F. Born 16/8/49. Commd 8/8/69. Flt Lt 8/2/75. Retd GD 4/10/88.
ROBERTS J. DFM. Born 10/9/22. Commd 14/11/43. Flt Lt 14/5/47. Retd GD 10/9/60.

ROBERTS J.C. The Rev. BA. Born 8/10/50. Commd 26/6/77. Retd Wg Cdr 26/6/93.
ROBERTS J.G. DFC DFM. Born 25/2/21. Commd 10/7/42. Wg Cdr 1/1/58. Retd GD 26/7/60.
ROBERTS J.L. MBE. Born 10/8/33. Commd 6/6/57. Wg Cdr 1/7/77. Retd PRT 10/8/91.
ROBERTS J.L. Born 11/10/37. Commd 2/3/61. Flt Lt 5/10/65. Retd SY 1/10/77.
ROBERTS J.M. CEng MIMechE MRAeS MCMI. Born 20/10/29. Commd 28/10/56. Gp Capt 1/1/79.
   Retd ENG 20/10/84.
ROBERTS J.N. Born 24/12/35. Commd 9/2/66. Sqn Ldr 1/1/73. Retd PRT 1/10/74.
ROBERTS L.A. Born 10/1/16. Commd 21/9/50. Sqn Ldr 1/7/59. Retd ENG 10/1/74.
ROBERTS M.C. Born 5/6/43. Commd 17/12/65. Sqn Ldr 1/1/76. Retd SUP 14/6/84.
ROBERTS M.G. The Rev. BA. Born 22/9/13. Commd 1/11/46. Retd Wg Cdr 22/9/68.
ROBERTS M.H.W. Born 18/9/40. Commd 3/2/64. Sqn Ldr 1/7/80. Retd SUP 2/4/93.
ROBERTS N.J. FISM MInstAM MCMI. Born 17/2/55. Commd 15/8/85. Sqn Ldr 1/1/96. Retd ADMIN 15/8/99.
ROBERTS O.J. Born 7/1/54. Commd 15/8/85. Sqn Ldr 1/7/00. Retd GD 28/5/05.
ROBERTS P. Born 6/9/57. Commd 24/6/76. Gp Capt 1/1/99. Retd OPS SPT 12/4/01.
ROBERTS P.A. BSc. Born 20/3/56. Commd 1/7/79. Sqn Ldr 1/7/95. Retd OPS SPT 1/7/01.
ROBERTS P.A. Born 3/2/31. Commd 4/7/51. Wg Cdr 1/7/73. Retd GD 20/6/85.
ROBERTS P.A.B. MSc BSc CEng MRAeS MIQA. Born 25/7/51. Commd 25/2/72. Sqn Ldr 1/1/84. Retd ENG 1/10/90.
ROBERTS P.B. Born 2/6/34. Commd 4/2/53. Flt Lt 24/6/58. Retd GD 2/6/92.
ROBERTS P.E. Born 4/6/39. Commd 22/7/71. Flt Lt 22/7/73. Retd ENG 4/6/81.
ROBERTS P.H.P. Born 20/8/22. Commd 28/11/43. Sqn Ldr 1/10/54. Retd GD 21/11/60.
ROBERTS P.J. Born 1/5/60. Commd 17/5/79. Sqn Ldr 1/1/96. Retd GD 6/6/00.
ROBERTS P.J. MB BS MRCS LRCP DA. Born 10/10/46. Commd 8/8/71. Wg Cdr 21/1/87. Retd MED 18/12/92.
ROBERTS P.K. Born 22/1/56. Commd 15/3/84. Flt Lt 15/3/86. Retd ENG 1/6/94.
ROBERTS P.M. Born 12/3/58. Commd 27/1/77. Flt Lt 27/7/82. Retd GD 1/6/89.
ROBERTS R.D. OBE CEng MRAeS FCMI. Born 29/3/20. Commd 19/8/42. Gp Capt 1/7/70. Retd ENG 29/3/75.
ROBERTS R.E. Born 11/3/41. Commd 13/2/79. Sqn Ldr 1/1/88. Retd ENG 16/9/93.
ROBERTS R.J. MBE. Born 11/5/32. Commd 14/4/53. Sqn Ldr 1/7/64. Retd GD 24/1/86.
ROBERTS R.L.A. DFM. Born 25/5/25. Commd 19/9/44. Gp Capt 1/7/74. Retd ADMIN 25/5/80.
ROBERTS R.W. MInstAM. Born 4/6/50. Commd 29/11/81. Wg Cdr 1/7/99. Retd GD 4/6/05.
ROBERTS S.B. Born 18/6/37. Commd 26/3/64. Flt Lt 25/7/70. Retd GD(G) 1/6/81.
ROBERTS S.G. BA. Born 3/8/57. Commd 23/9/79. Flt Lt 23/12/81. Retd PI 13/12/82.
ROBERTS T.A. DFC. Born 21/6/21. Commd 1/5/42. Flt Lt 1/11/45. Retd GD 15/5/55.
ROBERTS T.K. Born 30/9/37. Commd 11/11/71. Flt Lt 11/11/73. Retd GD(G) 12/11/76.
ROBERTS V.J. MInstAM(Dip) MCMI. Born 24/5/43. Commd 8/10/70. Flt Lt 8/10/72. Retd SEC 24/5/81. rtg Sqn Ldr.
ROBERTS W.A.B. OBE. Born 4/7/44. Commd 29/11/63. Wg Cdr 1/1/87. Retd GD 4/7/00.
ROBERTS W.J. OBE CEng FIERE DipEl. Born 19/5/23. Commd 14/10/43. Wg Cdr 1/7/61. Retd ENG 19/5/73.
ROBERTS W.J.H. Born 12/10/21. Commd 13/7/44. Gp Capt 1/1/68. Retd GD 30/1/77.
ROBERTS W.R. Born 6/4/20. Commd 23/9/43. Sqn Ldr 1/1/63. Retd ENG 7/4/75.
ROBERTSHAW K. LLB. Born 18/3/43. Commd 6/9/65. Wg Cdr 1/1/85. Retd GD 31/3/93.
ROBERTSHAW R.J. BSc. Born 24/10/56. Commd 31/8/75. Flt Lt 15/10/79. Retd GD 15/3/91.
ROBERTSHAW S. Born 1/10/57. Commd 11/4/85. Flt Lt 11/4/87. Retd GD(G) 1/10/95.
ROBERTSON A. MITD MIPM MCMI. Born 13/1/35. Commd 22/5/59. Wg Cdr 1/7/79. Retd ADMIN 21/10/87.
ROBERTSON A.J.L. Born 19/4/45. Commd 24/4/70. Sqn Ldr 1/1/82. Retd GD(G) 1/12/85.
ROBERTSON A.R. BSc. Born 26/3/84. Commd 11/9/77. Flt Lt 11/6/78. Retd GD 11/9/93.
ROBERTSON B.H. Born 1/7/14. Commd 16/6/41. Flt Lt 1/9/45. Retd SEC 20/8/51.
ROBERTSON C.D. Born 26/6/60. Commd 15/2/90. Flt Lt 25/7/92. Retd ENG 31/3/99.
ROBERTSON D.C. BSc. Born 7/2/63. Commd 2/9/84. Sqn Ldr 1/1/98. Retd GD 7/2/01.
ROBERTSON D.G.W. Born 14/9/24. Commd 3/5/51. Flt Lt 14/11/56. Retd GD 14/9/62.
ROBERTSON D.H. Born 20/5/30. Commd 9/11/55. Flt Lt 1/10/67. Retd GD 2/7/69.
ROBERTSON D.S.T. MBE. Born 5/5/24. Commd 4/10/51. Sqn Ldr 1/7/62. Retd ADMIN 1/9/77.
ROBERTSON E. Born 24/9/43. Commd 20/7/78. Flt Lt 20/7/80. Retd GD(G) 20/7/86.
ROBERTSON E.S. CEng MRAeS MCMI. Born 18/6/19. Commd 9/8/42. Wg Cdr 1/7/70. Retd ENG 18/6/74.
ROBERTSON G. MPhil BA CEng MIEE. Born 9/5/48. Commd 28/2/69. Wg Cdr 1/7/90. Retd ENG 4/12/98.
ROBERTSON G. Born 23/7/43. Commd 28/2/85. Sqn Ldr 1/7/94. Retd ENG 24/10/97.
ROBERTSON G. Born 3/2/35. Commd 17/12/52. Sqn Ldr 1/1/66. Retd GD 10/3/89.
ROBERTSON G.A. CBE BA FRAeS FRSA. Born 22/2/45. Commd 15/7/66. AM 18/3/96. Retd GD 9/12/98.
ROBERTSON G.B. AFC BSc. Born 18/11/41. Commd 22/9/63. Wg Cdr 1/7/77. Retd GD 1/7/80.
ROBERTSON G.M. Born 24/3/47. Commd 25/8/67. Fg Offr 25/2/70. Retd ENG 14/9/72.
ROBERTSON H.D. Born 18/3/15. Commd 27/3/44. Flt Lt 6/10/48. Retd ENG 21/4/64.
ROBERTSON I.K. Born 7/1/31. Commd 21/1/54. Flt Lt 8/6/59. Retd GD 7/1/69.
ROBERTSON I.M. Born 26/9/45. Commd 15/7/66. Wg Cdr 1/1/86. Retd GD 26/9/00.
ROBERTSON I.McK. BSc MBCS. Born 23/4/43. Commd 10/7/67. Sqn Ldr 1/7/79. Retd ENG 10/7/83.
ROBERTSON J.MacG. Born 14/4/26. Commd 8/4/49. Gp Capt 1/1/71. Retd GD 26/5/72.
ROBERTSON J.N. Born 19/12/27. Commd 16/2/53. Flt Lt 5/11/58. Retd GD 16/2/69.
ROBERTSON K.F. Born 25/12/38. Commd 16/11/59. Sqn Ldr 1/7/71. Retd GD 28/1/72.
ROBERTSON L.A. MBE. Born 15/6/23. Commd 15/5/42. Flt Lt 1/8/51. Retd GD 31/7/57.

ROBERTSON M.J. BSc CEng MRAeS. Born 21/7/48. Commd 13/9/71. Flt Lt 15/4/76. Retd ENG 13/9/87.
ROBERTSON N.A. Born 18/7/46. Commd 23/9/66. Flt Lt 4/5/72. Retd GD 1/4/89.
ROBERTSON N.D. BA. Born 11/5/56. Commd 6/10/75. Flt Lt 15/10/78. Retd GD 15/7/90.
ROBERTSON P.W. MD ChB. Born 6/11/23. Commd 12/8/48. Wg Cdr 1/5/60. Retd MED 30/12/67.
ROBERTSON R.F. MCMI. Born 17/10/35. Commd 30/7/57. Gp Capt 1/7/79. Retd SUP 5/5/90.
ROBERTSON R.J. Born 23/11/23. Commd 8/11/62. Sqn Ldr 1/7/72. Retd ENG 15/5/75.
ROBERTSON R.McC. MA. Born 9/12/22. Commd 17/4/45. Sqn Ldr 17/8/61. Retd EDN 19/5/71.
ROBERTSON R.S. MBE. Born 1/2/34. Commd 5/11/70. Sqn Ldr 1/1/80. Retd ADMIN 17/6/84.
ROBERTSON V.C. Born 31/8/39. Commd 2/10/61. Sqn Ldr 1/1/74. Retd GD 1/10/88.
ROBERTSON W.D. CBE. Born 24/6/22. Commd 10/7/43. A Cdre 1/1/69. Retd GD 29/1/77.
ROBINS I.H.R. MBE MRAeS MCMI. Born 10/4/39. Commd 18/2/58. Wg Cdr 1/1/86. Retd GD 31/5/90.
ROBINS V.A. DFC. Born 19/6/22. Commd 15/4/43. Sqn Ldr 1/7/65. Retd GD 20/6/73.
ROBINSON A. Born 5/6/16. Commd 21/6/45. Flt Lt 21/12/49. Retd CAT 5/6/71.
ROBINSON A.J. Born 6/4/37. Commd 29/7/55. Sqn Ldr 1/1/83. Retd GD 27/7/91.
ROBINSON A.R. Born 13/3/41. Commd 21/5/65. Flt Lt 21/11/71. Retd GD(G) 29/11/94.
ROBINSON A.T. Born 3/5/20. Commd 29/1/46. Flt Lt 29/7/50. Retd RGT 11/2/58.
ROBINSON B. Born 29/12/33. Commd 26/10/61. Fg Offr 26/10/61. Retd GD 25/7/65.
ROBINSON B.L. FCMI. Born 2/7/36. Commd 7/12/54. AVM 1/7/89. Retd GD 2/7/91.
ROBINSON C.A. Born 8/6/61. Commd 14/1/82. Flt Lt 14/7/87. Retd GD 14/3/96.
ROBINSON C.A. Born 31/8/48. Commd 8/11/68. Sqn Ldr 1/7/83. Retd RGT 1/10/90.
ROBINSON C.B.G. AFC. Born 29/9/11. Commd 7/9/36. Wg Cdr 1/10/46. Retd GD 20/4/48.
ROBINSON C.I. Born 6/7/43. Commd 14/9/64. Flt Lt 14/3/70. Retd GD 31/3/93.
ROBINSON C.P. Born 26/11/37. Commd 22/1/57. Flt Lt 7/8/64. Retd GD 29/4/78.
ROBINSON C.R.N. Born 30/7/54. Commd 5/7/73. Flt Lt 5/1/79. Retd GD 21/7/79.
ROBINSON D.A. MBE. Born 12/6/64. Commd 15/12/88. Flt Lt 14/12/91. Retd ENG 12/6/02.
ROBINSON D.A. Born 17/4/50. Commd 10/2/72. Plt Offr 10/2/72. Retd GD(G) 26/6/73.
ROBINSON D.B. Born 26/7/27. Commd 8/4/49. Wg Cdr 1/1/63. Retd GD 26/7/82. rtg Gp Capt.
ROBINSON D.C. FCMI MInstPS. Born 12/11/28. Commd 5/4/50. A Cdre 1/7/78. Retd SUP 12/11/83.
ROBINSON D.E. Born 8/10/42. Commd 2/5/69. Flt Lt 30/8/75. Retd SUP 7/1/85.
ROBINSON D.F. BSc. Born 17/1/49. Commd 28/2/82. Sqn Ldr 1/1/88. Retd ENG 27/7/01.
ROBINSON D.G. MBE FTCL LRAM ARCO(CHM) ARCM. Born 4/9/31. Commd 18/3/60. Flt Lt 18/3/66.
   Retd DM 9/2/72.
ROBINSON D.G. Born 14/9/41. Commd 25/1/63. Sqn Ldr 1/7/75. Retd GD 14/9/79.
ROBINSON D.J. MA IEng MIIE. Born 28/9/47. Commd 27/7/72. Wg Cdr 1/7/91. Retd GD 28/9/03.
ROBINSON D.McL. Born 16/9/35. Commd 20/8/55. Sqn Ldr 1/1/68. Retd GD 16/9/73.
ROBINSON E. OBE. Born 20/1/22. Commd 6/11/42. Sqn Ldr 1/4/55. Retd GD 20/1/65.
ROBINSON E.T. BEM. Born 29/4/22. Commd 6/10/60. Sqn Ldr 1/1/70. Retd ENG 7/7/72.
ROBINSON F.G.M. MBE CEng FRAeS MIMechE. Born 5/6/28. Commd 5/12/51. A Cdre 1/7/81. Retd ENG 1/7/83.
ROBINSON G.G. Born 8/4/21. Commd 21/10/43. Sqn Ldr 1/7/69. Retd GD(G) 30/3/78.
ROBINSON G.H. Born 12/6/22. Commd 29/6/43. Flt Lt 14/1/51. Retd GD 28/6/66.
ROBINSON H.R. Born 18/3/32. Commd 6/12/51. Sqn Ldr 1/7/72. Retd GD(G) 9/12/83.
ROBINSON I.D. BSc CEng MIMechE. Born 29/6/57. Commd 2/1/75. Flt Lt 15/4/81. Retd ENG 29/6/95.
ROBINSON I.G. BA. Born 14/4/56. Commd 19/6/83. Flt Lt 19/12/85. Retd GD 19/6/99.
ROBINSON I.L.J. CEng MRAeS MCMI. Born 17/6/20. Commd 25/8/55. Sqn Ldr 1/7/67. Retd ENG 17/6/75.
ROBINSON J. RMN. Born 12/4/57. Commd 21/7/85. Flt Lt 21/1/92. Retd MED SPT 21/7/02.
ROBINSON J. DPhysEd. Born 28/3/31. Commd 13/4/56. Flt Lt 13/4/60. Retd PE 13/4/62.
ROBINSON J.A. AFC MRAeS. Born 8/3/32. Commd 17/12/52. Wg Cdr 1/1/72. Retd GD 3/1/78.
ROBINSON J.B. AFC*. Born 29/3/34. Commd 10/9/52. Sqn Ldr 1/1/71. Retd GD 30/12/74.
ROBINSON J.H. Born 29/9/21. Commd 15/9/60. Flt Lt 15/9/65. Retd ENG 6/4/68.
ROBINSON J.H. Born 16/2/33. Commd 8/10/70. Sqn Ldr 1/1/84. Retd ENG 21/4/92.
ROBINSON J.L. MA BA BA CertEd. Born 9/3/37. Commd 13/9/70. Wg Cdr 1/7/85. Retd ADMIN 25/10/89.
ROBINSON J.L. BA. Born 16/10/72. Commd 10/8/97. Flt Lt 10/2/01. Retd OPS SPT(INT) 10/9/03.
ROBINSON J.L. BA. Born 16/10/72. Commd 10/8/97. Flt Lt 10/2/01. Retd OPS SPT(INT) 15/9/03.
ROBINSON J.M. Born 24/2/31. Commd 24/6/55. Flt Lt 6/3/63. Retd GD(G) 24/8/92.
ROBINSON J.R. AFC. Born 2/8/19. Commd 20/10/41. Sqn Ldr 1/1/52. Retd GD 2/8/62.
ROBINSON J.S. Born 6/6/42. Commd 17/12/63. Sqn Ldr 1/1/75. Retd GD 6/6/82.
ROBINSON K. BSc. Born 20/3/41. Commd 1/3/62. Wg Cdr 1/7/86. Retd SY(PRT) 1/7/88.
ROBINSON K.H.A. Born 6/12/34. Commd 24/4/70. Flt Lt 24/4/75. Retd ENG 26/4/75.
ROBINSON K.W. MB BCh MRCGP DRCOG DAvMed. Born 9/3/47. Commd 25/11/68. Sqn Ldr 16/8/77.
   Retd MED 27/5/85.
ROBINSON L.A. Born 26/9/34. Commd 8/9/58. Sqn Ldr 1/1/90. Retd GD 26/9/92.
ROBINSON L.T. Born 24/11/23. Commd 2/6/44. Flt Lt 29/6/50. Retd GD 24/11/66.
ROBINSON L.W. Born 30/9/24. Commd 8/11/62. Flt Lt 8/11/67. Retd GD(G) 1/10/74.
ROBINSON M. BSc CEng MRAeS. Born 22/3/57. Commd 17/7/87. Sqn Ldr 1/7/96. Retd ENG 10/4/00.
ROBINSON M.H. BSc. Born 28/5/35. Commd 5/2/57. Flt Lt 5/11/58. Retd GD 15/4/64.

ROBINSON M.I. BSc. Born 9/12/60. Commd 11/9/83. Flt Lt 11/3/86. Retd GD 16/12/95.
ROBINSON M.J. BTech CEng MIMechE. Born 14/2/59. Commd 13/2/83. Sqn Ldr 1/1/93. Retd ENG 13/2/99.
ROBINSON M.L.R. MA. Born 27/6/59. Commd 4/9/78. Flt Lt 15/10/82. Retd GD 27/6/97.
ROBINSON M.M.J. CB FCMI. Born 11/2/27. Commd 7/4/48. AVM 1/7/80. Retd GD 1/7/82.
ROBINSON M.W. Born 31/12/48. Commd 24/6/71. Flt Lt 24/12/76. Retd GD 31/12/86.
ROBINSON N. Born 26/4/22. Commd 18/8/44. Flt Lt 10/7/48. Retd GD 31/3/62.
ROBINSON N.C. MA. Born 13/11/72. Commd 11/8/96. Flt Lt 11/2/99. Retd OPS SPT(ATC) 1/1/04.
ROBINSON N.S. BA. Born 12/1/48. Commd 22/2/79. Flt Lt 22/2/81. Retd FLY(AEO) 29/4/05.
ROBINSON P. BSc. Born 15/1/64. Commd 15/3/87. Sqn Ldr 1/7/99. Retd FLY(P) 15/3/03.
ROBINSON P.A. OBE FRAeS. Born 8/8/49. Commd 27/2/70. AVM 1/7/02. Retd GD 8/8/04.
ROBINSON P.B. Born 6/7/26. Commd 16/5/49. Sqn Ldr 1/1/61. Retd RGT 6/10/67.
ROBINSON P.G. BSc. Born 24/10/44. Commd 15/7/66. Sqn Ldr 1/1/78. Retd ENG 24/12/88.
ROBINSON P.H.J. Born 26/4/34. Commd 28/3/60. Sqn Ldr 1/1/73. Retd GD 26/4/89.
ROBINSON P.N. Born 15/4/45. Commd 11/11/65. Wg Cdr 1/7/88. Retd ENG 14/4/98.
ROBINSON P.T. BA BSc. Born 9/6/38. Commd 8/8/58. Sqn Ldr 9/12/67. Retd ADMIN 9/6/76.
ROBINSON R. MBE. Born 21/6/21. Commd 20/9/49. Sqn Ldr 1/7/69. Retd SEC 21/6/81.
ROBINSON R.F.A. Born 28/3/50. Commd 16/1/00. Flt Lt 16/1/00. Retd OPS SPT(FLTOPS) 28/3/05.
ROBINSON R.G. Born 2/6/24. Commd 30/7/64. Flt Lt 30/7/67. Retd GD 10/6/82.
ROBINSON R.M. Born 3/9/44. Commd 11/9/64. Flt Lt 8/3/72. Retd GD 29/9/88.
ROBINSON R.P. Born 5/12/44. Commd 20/8/65. Sqn Ldr 1/7/86. Retd GD 2/4/93.
ROBINSON S. FCA MCMI. Born 26/1/16. Commd 29/7/39. Wg Cdr 1/1/56. Retd SEC 29/7/63.
ROBINSON S. Born 26/6/43. Commd 17/5/63. Sqn Ldr 1/7/87. Retd FLY(P) 26/6/03.
ROBINSON T. BSc. Born 31/7/63. Commd 22/6/86. Flt Lt 22/12/88. Retd GD 22/6/98.
ROBINSON T. Born 23/5/45. Commd 23/9/68. Flt Lt 23/3/73. Retd ENG 31/3/76.
ROBINSON T.A. MBE. Born 15/12/24. Commd 11/1/51. Wg Cdr 1/7/70. Retd GD 15/12/82.
ROBINSON T.D. Born 22/9/64. Commd 13/5/84. Flt Lt 15/9/89. Retd GD 10/12/96.
ROBINSON W. MBE. Born 10/1/17. Commd 23/9/43. Sqn Ldr 1/1/62. Retd ENG 11/10/69.
ROBINSON W.E. MBE MCMI. Born 1/1/21. Commd 18/5/61. Sqn Ldr 1/7/69. Retd ENG 11/4/79.
ROBINSON W.W. CEng MIEE. Born 22/1/45. Commd 15/7/65. Gp Capt 1/1/91. Retd ENG 14/9/96.
ROBINSON-BROWN S.J. Born 18/12/57. Commd 5/4/79. Flt Lt 13/9/85. Retd SY 1/10/87.
ROBSON A.J.R. DFC. Born 27/7/22. Commd 13/3/44. Flt Lt 13/9/47. Retd SEC 31/12/65.
ROBSON A.N. Born 8/4/35. Commd 7/5/59. Sqn Ldr 1/1/74. Retd ADMIN 1/7/80.
ROBSON B. MSc BSc CEng MRAeS. Born 20/8/38. Commd 30/9/58. Wg Cdr 1/1/80. Retd ENG 3/10/92.
ROBSON J. Born 4/8/46. Commd 12/3/87. Sqn Ldr 1/1/98. Retd GD 1/7/99.
ROBSON J.D. MA. Born 25/10/31. Commd 17/10/54. Sqn Ldr 1/1/68. Retd SEC 1/1/71.
ROBSON K. MCMI. Born 30/6/33. Commd 10/10/63. Wg Cdr 1/7/80. Retd ENG 3/7/84.
ROBSON K. Born 9/3/59. Commd 8/9/77. Flt Lt 8/3/83. Retd GD 9/3/97.
ROBSON R. Born 2/7/45. Commd 17/7/64. Flt Lt 17/1/70. Retd GD 4/10/92.
ROBSON R.A.M. MCMI AIL. Born 23/9/52. Commd 3/12/70. Sqn Ldr 1/1/84. Retd ADMIN 31/1/90.
ROBSON R.H. MA. Born 2/8/29. Commd 12/12/51. Flt Lt 12/6/54. Retd GD 30/8/67.
ROBSON R.M. OBE FCMI. Born 22/4/35. Commd 28/7/55. AVM 1/7/87. Retd GD 7/11/87.
ROBSON S.M. Born 21/4/46. Commd 8/8/69. Sqn Ldr 1/1/85. Retd ENG 1/1/88.
ROBSON T.D. BA MCMI DipEd. Born 23/9/42. Commd 13/6/66. Sqn Ldr 1/1/87. Retd ADMIN 7/4/97.
ROBSON W. BA. Born 2/5/36. Commd 27/8/58. Flt Lt 12/1/65. Retd GD 23/6/77.
ROCH J.W. DFC. Born 30/10/13. Commd 5/11/42. Sqn Ldr 1/10/57. Retd SEC 12/11/68.
ROCHARD E.B. Born 3/7/23. Commd 4/3/43. Flt Lt 7/6/51. Retd RGT 29/2/60.
ROCHE J.P. Born 10/8/28. Commd 29/3/68. Fg Offr 29/3/68. Retd SEC 2/6/73.
ROCHE P.J. Born 21/8/29. Commd 23/12/61. Flt Lt 23/12/67. Retd GD 21/8/84.
ROCHE T.J. BA. Born 30/3/60. Commd 4/8/78. Sqn Ldr 1/7/91. Retd GD 30/3/98.
ROCHESTER E. MCMI. Born 10/8/35. Commd 26/5/61. Gp Capt 1/7/82. Retd GD(G) 19/9/89.
ROCHESTER G.W. Born 15/3/28. Commd 18/9/47. Flt Lt 10/11/55. Retd RGT 15/3/66.
ROCHFORT B.J.J. FCIPD FCMI. Born 7/7/38. Commd 4/10/56. Wg Cdr 1/1/77. Retd SY 7/7/86.
ROCHFORT J. Born 22/4/45. Commd 4/12/64. Flt Lt 4/6/70. Retd GD 1/4/87.
ROCK K.G. FCIPD MCMI. Born 7/10/34. Commd 14/5/60. Flt Lt 14/11/65. Retd GD 2/4/75.
ROCKALL R.M. Born 4/6/33. Commd 15/9/60. Flt Lt 15/3/65. Retd GD 4/6/71.
ROCKEL L.A. Born 11/4/45. Commd 21/7/65. Flt Lt 8/3/72. Retd GD 8/10/83.
ROCKINGHAM P. Born 4/8/20. Commd 22/9/55. Flt Lt 22/9/61. Retd GD(G) 4/8/70.
ROCKLIFFE E.A. Born 7/12/20. Commd 29/9/41. Sqn Ldr 1/1/50. Retd GD 1/1/58.
ROCKLIFFE-FIDLER G.N. Born 13/11/65. Commd 26/9/91. Flt Lt 15/3/95. Retd SUPPLY 13/11/03.
RODDA S.G. Born 27/2/46. Commd 11/11/71. Wg Cdr 1/1/94. Retd GD 27/2/01.
RODEN R.F. Born 31/12/27. Commd 30/9/53. Flt Lt 7/7/59. Retd GD 14/10/73.
RODEN T.G.V. MRCS LRCP DPH. Born 8/1/20. Commd 14/11/40. Wg Cdr 23/2/62. Retd MED 23/1/63.
RODFORD J.D. BSc. Born 23/6/45. Commd 5/1/66. Wg Cdr 1/1/90. Retd GD 23/6/03.
RODGER A.L. Born 25/6/63. Commd 23/10/86. Flt Lt 23/4/94. Retd OPS SPT 23/6/02.
RODGER M.W. BA. Born 29/5/35. Commd 27/4/70. Sqn Ldr 31/12/72. Retd ADMIN 27/4/87.
RODGER R.H. Born 11/7/10. Commd 14/1/43. Flt Lt 27/10/58. Retd SUP 16/2/62.

RODGERS D.L. BA. Born 18/11/47. Commd 21/1/66. Wg Cdr 1/1/87. Retd GD 18/11/91.
RODGERS I.A. Born 8/4/43. Commd 9/12/65. Sqn Ldr 1/7/79. Retd ADMIN 1/7/82.
RODGERS J.B. MSc BSc CEng FIMA FCA MRAeS. Born 5/10/30. Commd 28/5/57. Wg Cdr 28/7/73. Retd ADMIN 28/4/76.
RODGERS J.D. Born 23/1/63. Commd 16/12/82. Sqn Ldr 1/1/98. Retd OPS SPT 23/1/01.
RODGERS M. Born 26/10/46. Commd 10/12/69. Wg Cdr 1/7/93. Retd GD 13/12/04.
RODGERS M.M. BCom. Born 16/9/26. Commd 17/5/50. Flt Offr 17/11/55. Retd SEC 29/7/60.
RODGERS P.J. MBE. Born 25/11/43. Commd 9/8/63. Gp Capt 1/1/97. Retd OPS SPT 25/11/98.
RODWAY J. Born 4/11/46. Commd 11/9/64. Plt Offr 11/9/65. Retd GD 2/9/66.
ROE M. Born 27/6/44. Commd 20/9/68. Flt Lt 20/3/74. Retd GD 31/12/84.
ROE S.J.B. Born 21/6/18. Commd 19/10/43. Sqn Ldr 1/7/63. Retd PE 21/6/73.
ROEBUCK A.F. Born 30/6/45. Commd 5/3/65. Flt Lt 5/9/70. Retd GD 29/3/74.
ROEBUCK R.F. FCIS. Born 6/9/42. Commd 9/12/65. Sqn Ldr 1/7/80. Retd ADMIN 18/6/93.
ROFFEY H.H. Born 28/2/24. Commd 18/4/44. Sqn Ldr 1/7/60. Retd GD 28/2/79.
ROGAN T.J. Born 21/9/41. Commd 12/1/62. Flt Lt 1/7/68. Retd GD 31/8/80.
ROGERS A.C. Born 26/1/41. Commd 5/3/65. Flt Lt 5/9/70. Retd GD 24/3/73.
ROGERS A.P. Born 20/11/54. Commd 3/10/74. Fg Offr 3/4/77. Retd ADMIN 17/2/78.
ROGERS B.A. Born 25/1/34. Commd 26/7/55. Flt Lt 26/7/60. Retd SEC 25/1/72.
ROGERS B.N. Born 16/11/37. Commd 29/7/58. Sqn Ldr 1/7/69. Retd GD 1/2/90.
ROGERS C. Born 16/2/54. Commd 2/8/90. Flt Lt 2/8/94. Retd ENG 14/9/96.
ROGERS C.G. DFC. Born 16/2/23. Commd 22/1/43. Flt Lt 22/7/46. Retd GD 22/8/64.
ROGERS D.R. Born 27/8/58. Commd 5/4/79. Flt Lt 5/10/84. Retd GD 5/4/87.
ROGERS E.W. Born 27/7/47. Commd 8/10/87. Flt Lt 8/10/91. Retd ENG 6/6/00.
ROGERS G.A. Born 23/12/51. Commd 12/4/73. Flt Lt 12/10/78. Retd GD 16/1/82.
ROGERS G.B. Born 17/4/40. Commd 19/8/58. Wg Cdr 1/7/77. Retd GD(G) 6/3/85.
ROGERS G.F. BA MCIPD. Born 7/5/52. Commd 28/12/71. Sqn Ldr 1/1/86. Retd ADMIN 1/10/89.
ROGERS J. Born 27/8/22. Commd 27/1/43. Flt Offr 27/1/48. Retd GD(G) 15/3/52.
ROGERS Sir John KCB CBE CCMI FRAeS. Born 11/1/28. Commd 5/4/50. ACM 1/1/84. Retd GD 31/3/86.
ROGERS J.E.G. Born 17/12/29. Commd 2/7/52. Flt Lt 4/5/60. Retd SUP 25/7/73.
ROGERS J.H. AFC MCMI. Born 6/2/24. Commd 1/10/43. Wg Cdr 1/7/61. Retd GD 29/10/76.
ROGERS J.K. OBE FCMI. Born 20/1/24. Commd 20/8/43. Gp Capt 1/1/71. Retd GD(G) 31/3/78.
ROGERS J.N. Born 30/4/52. Commd 4/3/71. Flt Lt 4/9/76. Retd GD 1/10/79.
ROGERS J.P. Born 8/4/46. Commd 9/10/75. Gp Capt 21/3/94. Retd ADMIN 20/1/96.
ROGERS J.S. BEng. Born 5/7/73. Commd 6/4/97. Fg Offr 6/4/96. Retd GD 19/7/00.
ROGERS K.B. DFC AFC. Born 11/10/22. Commd 11/9/43. Wg Cdr 1/1/59. Retd GD 16/7/66.
ROGERS L. BSc. Born 16/9/46. Commd 11/5/71. Flt Lt 11/2/72. Retd GD 11/5/87.
ROGERS L.R. Born 21/10/19. Commd 26/9/50. Sqn Ldr 1/7/64. Retd SUP 9/9/68.
ROGERS M.A. OBE. Born 3/10/47. Commd 30/5/71. Gp Capt 1/7/95. Retd ENG 11/12/99.
ROGERS M.H. MB ChB MFCM DRCOG AFOM FCMI. Born 26/7/30. Commd 29/8/54. A Cdre 1/7/81. Retd MED 5/4/85.
ROGERS M.J. Born 12/4/26. Commd 16/11/51. Flt Lt 16/5/56. Retd GD 12/4/64.
ROGERS N.C. Born 14/11/58. Commd 18/10/81. Sqn Ldr 1/7/93. Retd GD 18/10/97.
ROGERS P.A. DipPE. Born 24/12/46. Commd 22/8/71. Flt Lt 22/8/75. Retd ADMIN 22/8/87.
ROGERS P.C.H. Born 22/10/61. Commd 6/11/80. Flt Lt 6/5/86. Retd GD 3/1/99.
ROGERS P.F. OBE BA. Born 28/5/32. Commd 28/2/52. Gp Capt 1/7/78. Retd GD 2/10/86.
ROGERS P.J. BA. Born 13/11/49. Commd 13/9/70. Sqn Ldr 1/1/85. Retd GD 1/1/88.
ROGERS P.L. Born 11/8/42. Commd 30/8/62. Flt Lt 8/1/69. Retd ADMIN 11/8/80.
ROGERS P.M. Born 5/7/37. Commd 30/5/69. Flt Lt 30/5/71. Retd GD 26/7/74.
ROGERS R.J. Born 8/11/46. Commd 11/9/64. Flt Lt 11/3/70. Retd GD 10/11/96.
ROGERS R.J. Born 19/9/34. Commd 10/9/52. Wg Cdr 1/7/79. Retd GD 31/8/86.
ROGERS R.M. MCMI. Born 31/3/20. Commd 24/3/39. Sqn Ldr 1/1/61. Retd SUP 31/3/75.
ROGERS R.S. Born 21/11/50. Commd 3/1/70. Flt Lt 30/7/75. Retd GD 21/11/88.
ROGERS T.V. Born 19/9/43. Commd 22/3/63. Wg Cdr 1/1/86. Retd GD 19/9/98.
ROGERS W.G. MBE. Born 26/12/14. Commd 3/12/42. Flt Lt 16/8/61. Retd ENG 26/12/71.
ROGERSON A.C. MA. Born 1/5/37. Commd 3/9/59. Sqn Ldr 1/3/68. Retd ADMIN 18/1/77.
ROGERSON C.S. BA. Born 8/12/61. Commd 2/9/84. Sqn Ldr 1/1/93. Retd ADMIN 2/9/00.
ROGERSON J.T.G. MB ChB FFARCS DA. Born 28/1/40. Commd 3/2/65. Gp Capt 22/4/86. Retd MED 11/10/95.
ROGERSON M. MBE MA MBA. Born 18/2/64. Commd 20/10/83. Wg Cdr 1/7/99. Retd GD 1/2/03.
ROGERSON P.H. Born 20/2/10. Commd 24/2/44. Flt Lt 24/8/87. Retd ENG 1/1/59.
ROKOSZ S.T. AFC. Born 9/11/18. Commd 28/11/47. Flt Lt 18/5/56. Retd GD 29/1/58.
ROLFE C.I. Born 18/11/13. Commd 1/4/40. Sqn Ldr 1/8/47. Retd GD 1/4/56.
ROLFE G.D. Born 26/4/42. Commd 18/8/61. Sqn Ldr 1/7/76. Retd GD 26/7/80.
ROLFE G.H. CVO CBE. Born 10/12/40. Commd 31/7/62. Gp Capt 1/1/83. Retd GD 10/12/95.
ROLFE P.J.A. Born 9/12/47. Commd 30/5/69. Flt Lt 30/11/74. Retd GD 30/6/85.
ROLFE P.P. Born 19/5/42. Commd 31/1/64. Sqn Ldr 1/7/74. Retd GD 19/5/80.
ROLLIN N. Born 4/10/22. Commd 28/2/44. Wg Cdr 1/7/71. Retd SUP 30/3/77.

ROLLINS J.W. MB BS MRCPhys MRCS LRCP DPM. Born 27/9/35. Commd 12/6/60. Gp Capt 12/12/82.
Retd MED 27/9/85.
ROLLINS M.S. Born 3/2/33. Commd 9/4/52. Flt Lt 20/7/58. Retd PI 8/12/84.
ROLLO T.R.D. Born 15/12/46. Commd 2/2/68. Flt Lt 12/4/74. Retd SEC 31/8/74.
ROLLO W.S. Born 17/5/43. Commd 24/1/63. Sqn Ldr 1/1/76. Retd SUP 17/5/84.
ROLPH D.A. MBE. Born 20/9/34. Commd 5/11/52. Gp Capt 1/7/86. Retd GD 8/5/89.
ROLPH T.C. BSc. Born 14/10/53. Commd 8/1/76. Flt Lt 15/4/79. Retd GD 8/1/92.
ROMAN P.M. Born 14/7/44. Commd 14/7/66. Flt Lt 15/4/70. Retd GD 14/4/82.
ROMNEY F.C. Born 31/7/29. Commd 14/10/51. Sqn Ldr 1/1/63. Retd GD 2/8/79.
RONAYNE D.C. Born 13/6/42. Commd 12/7/63. Flt Lt 12/1/69. Retd GD 6/1/80.
RONDEL G.J. Born 23/1/29. Commd 2/1/52. Flt Lt 2/10/57. Retd GD 23/1/67.
RONDOT M.J. Born 7/2/48. Commd 22/12/67. Sqn Ldr 1/7/86. Retd GD(G) 4/7/92.
ROOKE W.D. Born 7/4/23. Commd 16/5/57. Flt Lt 16/5/64. Retd GD 30/5/64.
ROOM P.A. MBE BSc. Born 12/5/52. Commd 25/9/71. Flt Lt 23/9/79. Retd ENG 19/11/82.
ROOME D.C. OBE FRAeS. Born 30/11/46. Commd 21/7/65. Gp Capt 1/1/97. Retd GD 6/4/01.
ROOMS P.L.P. Born 19/8/40. Commd 18/7/61. Sqn Ldr 1/7/70. Retd ENG 19/8/78. rtg Wg Cdr.
ROOMS W.S. OBE BSc (Eur Ing) CEng MIEE MRAeS. Born 17/7/54. Commd 17/9/72. Gp Capt 1/1/96.
Retd ENG 29/4/99.
ROONEY A.J. BSc. Born 1/9/65. Commd 11/5/89. Sqn Ldr 1/1/00. Retd FLY(P) 9/1/05.
ROONEY E.S. Born 27/6/22. Commd 11/5/43. Flt Lt 11/5/45. Retd GD 17/7/46. Re-employed 3/10/49. Sqn Ldr 1/7/60.
Retd GD 6/8/65.
ROONEY J. BSc. Born 16/10/53. Commd 7/11/76. Flt Lt 7/8/77. Retd GD 30/4/00.
ROONEY M.A. DFC. Born 6/4/21. Commd 11/1/44. Flt Lt 27/5/60. Retd GD 6/4/76.
ROONEY P. BA DPhysEd. Born 15/2/46. Commd 19/8/68. Wg Cdr 1/1/96. Retd ADMIN 8/4/01.
ROOTES J.G. BSc. Born 25/3/46. Commd 26/5/67. Sqn Ldr 1/1/77. Retd ENG 25/3/84.
ROOTHAM J. Born 18/3/22. Commd 5/6/60. Flt Lt 5/5/65. Retd ENG 2/6/73.
ROOUM J.E. CBE AFC. Born 14/10/42. Commd 23/12/60. A Cdre 1/7/91. Retd GD 11/11/97.
ROPE B.A. Born 9/9/44. Commd 26/4/84. Sqn Ldr 1/7/92. Retd ENG 9/9/99.
ROPER C.F.K. AFM. Born 17/10/22. Commd 17/6/54. Flt Lt 17/6/60. Retd GD 1/1/65.
ROPER N. OBE ACIS. Born 3/5/34. Commd 17/6/63. Gp Capt 1/7/80. Retd ADMIN 1/8/84.
RORK G.D. CEng MRAeS. Born 15/6/34. Commd 23/7/58. Wg Cdr 1/7/76. Retd ENG 8/9/88.
ROSBOTHAM K. BEng. Born 1/7/65. Commd 31/7/91. Flt Lt 15/7/94. Retd ENGINEER 1/7/03.
ROSBOTTOM P.M. CEng MRAeS. Born 16/7/39. Commd 25/6/66. Sqn Ldr 1/7/75. Retd ENG 24/7/89.
ROSCILLI G.A. CEng MIProdE MRAeS. Born 1/9/40. Commd 14/9/65. Sqn Ldr 1/7/76. Retd ENG 2/7/93.
ROSCOE B.J. BSc. Born 26/8/55. Commd 17/7/77. Flt Lt 17/10/78. Retd GD 17/7/89.
ROSCOE C.W. Born 21/5/51. Commd 22/6/89. Flt Lt 22/6/91. Retd ADMIN 22/6/97.
ROSE A.E. Born 30/1/44. Commd 8/8/69. Fg Offr 8/8/71. Retd GD 1/6/73.
ROSE B. MBE MMar. Born 11/6/21. Commd 4/1/50. Sqn Ldr 4/1/58. Retd MAR 4/1/66.
ROSE I.A. Born 10/6/62. Commd 24/7/81. Sqn Ldr 1/7/92. Retd GD 10/6/00.
ROSE J. OBE MIISec. Born 15/9/45. Commd 21/10/66. Gp Capt 1/7/91. Retd ADMIN 20/7/97.
ROSE L. CEng FRAeS FCMI. Born 15/9/14. Commd 15/12/34. Gp Capt 1/7/64. Retd ENG 15/9/69.
ROSE L.G. BSc. Born 7/9/45. Commd 18/7/66. Flt Lt 1/7/69. Retd GD 21/12/74.
ROSE M.A. Born 6/1/42. Commd 28/4/61. Flt Lt 1/7/68. Retd GD 6/1/80.
ROSE N.E. AFC* MCMI. Born 30/5/24. Commd 27/5/54. Sqn Ldr 1/1/68. Retd GD 30/5/84.
ROSE O.M. MBE. Born 25/8/32. Commd 11/2/65. Sqn Ldr 1/7/77. Retd ENG 11/4/92.
ROSE P.S. MSc BEng. Born 6/11/64. Commd 15/8/84. Sqn Ldr 1/7/97. Retd ENG 6/11/02.
ROSE P.W. Born 21/7/30. Commd 9/4/52. Flt Lt 9/4/57. Retd SEC 21/7/68.
ROSE R. Born 12/10/23. Commd 13/7/61. Flt Lt 13/7/66. Retd ENG 1/12/73.
ROSE R.I.L. Born 22/11/31. Commd 14/4/53. Flt Lt 14/10/55. Retd GD 23/8/69.
ROSE S.A. BA. Born 25/11/56. Commd 20/5/79. Flt Lt 20/8/82. Retd ADMIN 26/4/83.
ROSE V. Born 17/11/20. Commd 26/9/57. Sqn Ldr 1/7/68. Retd ENG 17/11/70.
ROSEDALE J.R. Born 10/3/54. Commd 24/4/87. Flt Lt 23/4/89. Retd ENG 3/4/93.
ROSEFIELD L. Born 8/8/33. Commd 18/6/52. Flt Lt 14/5/58. Retd SUP 8/8/73.
ROSENORN-LANNG M.J. Born 5/2/31. Commd 23/2/51. Sqn Ldr 1/1/70. Retd GD 5/2/86.
ROSER P.W. CB MBE FRAeS. Born 11/7/48. Commd 28/2/69. AVM 1/1/00. Retd GD 26/9/03.
ROSIE K.S. Born 26/4/62. Commd 28/2/81. Flt Lt 5/8/87. Retd OPS SPT 31/12/01.
ROSIE P.I. Born 25/8/56. Commd 24/4/80. Sqn Ldr 1/7/90. Retd FLY(P) 10/4/05.
ROSS A. Born 31/7/13. Commd 4/2/43. Fg Offr 1/4/45. Retd SEC 18/2/58. rtg Flt Lt.
ROSS A. Born 24/9/37. Commd 2/3/61. Sqn Ldr 1/7/73. Retd ADMIN 5/6/89.
ROSS A.J. BSc. Born 6/1/61. Commd 2/9/79. Sqn Ldr 1/7/94. Retd GD 6/1/99.
ROSS A.J. Born 24/2/40. Commd 13/12/60. Sqn Ldr 1/7/69. Retd GD 24/2/78.
ROSS A.N. BSc. Born 19/3/66. Commd 29/9/84. Flt Lt 15/1/90. Retd GD 15/7/99.
ROSS A.Q.M. BA. Born 4/2/42. Commd 31/7/62. Flt Lt 15/2/65. Retd GD 30/11/74.
ROSS C.J. Born 13/6/30. Commd 17/3/67. Flt Lt 17/3/72. Retd GD(G) 25/9/75.
ROSS C.W. Born 23/2/29. Commd 1/3/62. Sqn Ldr 1/1/74. Retd SEC 23/2/79.
ROSS D. FInstAM MCIPD. Born 30/9/42. Commd 5/1/78. Sqn Ldr 1/7/89. Retd ADMIN 12/7/97.

ROSS D.H. Born 24/2/23. Commd 13/2/47. Flt Lt 19/11/53. Retd GD 22/3/62.
ROSS D.McD. Born 22/1/44. Commd 17/2/67. Sqn Ldr 1/7/94. Retd FLY(P) 22/1/04.
ROSS G. BSc. Born 17/7/31. Commd 30/6/54. Gp Capt 1/7/80. Retd GD 17/10/86.
ROSS G.B. MA. Born 6/6/49. Commd 10/4/68. Flt Lt 15/4/72. Retd GD 3/2/81.
ROSS G.I.M. Born 26/5/26. Commd 17/11/47. Flt Lt 4/12/52. Retd RGT 26/5/64.
ROSS I.B. Born 8/4/31. Commd 31/5/51. Sqn Ldr 1/1/81. Retd ADMIN 8/4/86.
ROSS I.J. Born 28/3/37. Commd 14/5/63. Fg Offr 14/5/63. Retd EDN 31/8/66.
ROSS J. AFC. Born 13/11/23. Commd 5/5/47. Sqn Ldr 1/7/58. Retd GD 13/11/66.
ROSS J. Born 15/12/31. Commd 5/7/68. Sqn Ldr 1/1/80. Retd ADMIN 19/11/86.
ROSS J.B. MB ChB DTM&H. Born 3/7/12. Commd 3/1/38. A Cdre 1/7/64. Retd MED 16/6/70.
ROSS J.H. MBE. Born 21/11/31. Commd 24/9/64. Sqn Ldr 1/1/77. Retd ENG 21/5/92.
ROSS J.W. Born 6/5/56. Commd 28/8/75. Sqn Ldr 1/1/94. Retd FLY(N) 30/6/04.
ROSS M.G. MILT. Born 4/6/55. Commd 8/11/90. Flt Lt 8/11/94. Retd SUP 14/9/96.
ROSS N. MB ChB DRCOG DAvMed. Born 16/2/60. Commd 18/12/80. Wg Cdr 1/8/97. Retd MED 16/2/01.
ROSS N.F. BSc. Born 27/3/59. Commd 27/9/79. Flt Lt 15/10/81. Retd GD 22/1/93.
ROSS P.S. Born 20/3/46. Commd 1/10/65. Flt Lt 1/4/71. Retd GD 1/11/76.
ROSS R. Born 20/11/46. Commd 21/7/65. Sqn Ldr 1/1/84. Retd FLY(N) 7/4/03.
ROSS R.A. BSc. Born 24/2/65. Commd 3/8/86. Sqn Ldr 1/1/98. Retd FLY(P) 5/1/04.
ROSS T.A. Born 11/7/13. Commd 6/4/46. Flt Lt 11/11/54. Retd SEC 1/4/66.
ROSS T.G. Born 15/5/12. Commd 30/5/46. Fg Offr 30/5/46. Retd ASD 10/11/47.
ROSS W.G. AFC. Born 3/2/11. Commd 1/5/42. Flt Lt 1/5/44. Retd GD 24/1/47.
ROSS-SMITH J.M. CEng MIMechE MIProdE MRAeS MCMI. Born 12/2/35. Commd 14/9/65. Wg Cdr 1/7/80.
    Retd ENG 1/6/87.
ROSS-THOMSON A.J. Born 19/8/59. Commd 18/12/80. Sqn Ldr 1/7/99. Retd FLY(P) 31/3/05.
ROSSER M.J. MB BS DAvMed. Born 5/11/48. Commd 26/10/70. Wg Cdr 15/7/88. Retd MED 9/2/89.
ROSSER W.J. DFC. Born 18/2/17. Commd 7/8/41. Flt Lt 27/5/54. Retd SEC 20/2/72.
ROSSIE M.D. Born 17/6/38. Commd 14/11/59. Flt Lt 14/5/65. Retd GD 17/6/93.
ROSTRON J.D. Born 14/7/41. Commd 18/11/81. Flt Lt 3/4/93. Retd GD 2/4/93.
ROTHERAM R.C. OBE DFC. Born 27/8/17. Commd 30/7/38. Wg Cdr 1/7/50. Retd GD 27/8/72.
ROTHERY D.R. Born 30/1/34. Commd 26/11/52. Sqn Ldr 1/1/72. Retd GD 30/1/92.
ROTHWELL I.P. Born 4/12/33. Commd 23/7/52. Flt Lt 13/4/60. Retd GD 4/12/71.
ROTHWELL M.J. Born 19/1/49. Commd 27/5/71. Flt Lt 27/11/76. Retd GD 8/2/87.
ROUGEAU R.G. Born 22/2/34. Commd 29/1/58. Fg Offr 29/1/58. Retd GD 26/9/64.
ROUGH M.J.A. Born 17/1/47. Commd 12/2/66. Sqn Ldr 1/1/83. Retd GD 1/1/86.
ROUGH N.M. Born 28/8/44. Commd 6/10/69. Sqn Ldr 1/1/92. Retd GD 22/4/94.
ROUGHTON J.G.A. Born 8/7/45. Commd 8/7/65. Sqn Ldr 1/7/80. Retd ADMIN 18/10/93.
ROULSTON S.P. Born 5/2/58. Commd 28/7/94. Flt Lt 28/7/96. Retd OPS SPT(PROVSY) 9/2/05.
ROUND P. Born 19/10/61. Commd 8/12/83. Fg Offr 17/5/86. Retd ADMIN 31/3/89.
ROUND P.M. LLB. Born 20/8/52. Commd 13/2/77. Sqn Ldr 1/1/91. Retd SY 14/9/96.
ROUNDS T.W.B. Born 6/6/48. Commd 26/2/71. Sqn Ldr 1/7/84. Retd FLY(N) 6/6/04.
ROURKE P.J. Born 14/3/35. Commd 19/8/53. Flt Lt 25/12/58. Retd GD 14/3/73.
ROURKE T.K. MCMI. Born 21/12/23. Commd 26/11/43. Sqn Ldr 1/1/59. Retd SUP 21/6/76.
ROURKE T.W. Born 4/2/48. Commd 15/9/67. Flt Lt 15/3/73. Retd GD 22/7/76.
ROUSE E.G.C. Born 28/12/44. Commd 3/3/67. Sqn Ldr 1/1/78. Retd FLY(P) 28/12/04.
ROUSE G.G. Born 17/12/22. Commd 4/9/58. Flt Lt 4/9/63. Retd ENG 31/5/73.
ROUSELL R.H. Born 27/2/26. Commd 20/10/49. Flt Lt 20/4/53. Retd GD 14/9/68.
ROUSSEAU N.A.B. Born 8/10/42. Commd 11/5/78. Sqn Ldr 1/7/94. Retd GD 1/7/98.
ROUSSEL G.T. Born 10/6/20. Commd 16/1/50. Flt Lt 16/1/50. Retd SUP 10/6/69.
ROUTH J.E. MRCS LRCP DPH. Born 23/7/25. Commd 24/11/50. Wg Cdr 3/5/63. Retd MED 28/4/76.
ROUTIER J.S. Born 15/1/29. Commd 12/9/63. Flt Lt 12/9/68. Retd ENG 15/6/82.
ROUTLEDGE B.L. Born 21/5/50. Commd 4/3/71. Fg Offr 4/9/73. Retd PI 30/6/77.
ROUTLEDGE G.C. Born 21/7/46. Commd 15/10/81. Flt Lt 1/3/87. Retd ENG 19/9/87.
ROUTLEDGE J. MCMI. Born 22/6/35. Commd 28/5/66. Wg Cdr 1/7/85. Retd ADMIN 25/10/89.
ROWBOTHAM B. DFC. Born 3/7/22. Commd 25/6/53. Sqn Ldr 1/1/67. Retd GD 31/3/74.
ROWDEN A.H. Born 22/7/15. Commd 17/4/47. Flt Lt 17/10/51. Retd SEC 22/7/64.
ROWDEN B.P. BEM MCMI. Born 1/8/26. Commd 8/4/53. Sqn Ldr 1/1/65. Retd GD 2/12/75.
ROWE B.E. MBE. Born 11/8/30. Commd 12/9/63. Sqn Ldr 1/7/76. Retd ENG 6/7/87.
ROWE C. MCMI. Born 4/4/35. Commd 27/9/57. Wg Cdr 1/7/84. Retd GD(G) 4/4/90.
ROWE C.J. Born 11/1/43. Commd 31/3/65. Gp Capt 1/7/90. Retd SUP 11/1/96.
ROWE D.F. Born 1/10/38. Commd 25/8/67. Sqn Ldr 1/1/82. Retd ENG 10/4/91.
ROWE D.H.G. Born 7/6/43. Commd 17/12/65. Flt Lt 8/1/69. Retd GD 9/8/75.
ROWE D.H.W. Born 23/11/40. Commd 20/11/75. Sqn Ldr 1/7/91. Retd SUP 30/4/95.
ROWE D.J. LVO. Born 18/9/32. Commd 27/8/52. Sqn Ldr 1/1/74. Retd GD 12/3/92.
ROWE E.M.C. Born 1/1/30. Commd 4/7/51. Flt Lt 21/3/58. Retd GD(G) 30/8/80.
ROWE J.E. Born 21/5/23. Commd 12/6/58. Flt Lt 12/6/63. Retd SEC 3/4/74.
ROWE K.A. BSc. Born 15/12/52. Commd 14/1/74. Flt Lt 15/10/77. Retd ENG 3/12/85.

ROWE K.O. Born 14/9/31. Commd 2/7/52. Flt Lt 14/5/58. Retd GD(G) 14/9/86.
ROWE L.E. BSc(Eng). Born 26/10/31. Commd 30/1/58. Wg Cdr 1/1/76. Retd ENG 1/5/82.
ROWE L.W.H. Born 23/11/30. Commd 13/8/52. Wg Cdr 1/7/71. Retd GD 23/11/85.
ROWE M.P. MB BCh DAvMed. Born 22/8/44. Commd 9/5/71. Sqn Ldr 9/8/76. Retd MED 6/2/90.
ROWE R. Born 26/5/20. Commd 16/4/45. Flt Lt 18/5/56. Retd CAT 26/5/73.
ROWE R.G. MA CEng MRAeS. Born 10/3/27. Commd 24/8/50. Wg Cdr 1/7/71. Retd ENG 5/2/75.
ROWE T. IEng MCIPS. Born 13/12/42. Commd 9/3/72. Wg Cdr 1/7/88. Retd SUP 22/5/93.
ROWE T.H. Born 28/11/20. Commd 14/11/49. Flt Lt 14/11/49. Retd SUP 28/11/69.
ROWELL J.D. Born 1/8/28. Commd 30/5/51. Sqn Ldr 1/7/61. Retd GD 1/4/73.
ROWELL K. Born 30/8/25. Commd 7/7/55. Sqn Ldr 1/7/70. Retd ADMIN 27/10/76.
ROWELL P.A. AFC. Born 27/9/19. Commd 6/1/42. Flt Lt 1/9/45. Retd GD 1/4/50.
ROWELL P.W. Born 14/11/45. Commd 3/5/68. Flt Lt 3/11/73. Retd GD 2/9/75.
ROWLAND A.D. BA MCIPS. Born 24/1/44. Commd 5/2/65. Flt Lt 6/10/71. Retd GD(G) 30/9/89.
ROWLAND C.J. BSc(Eng) CEng MRAeS. Born 9/8/42. Commd 30/9/61. Wg Cdr 1/1/79. Retd ENG 4/4/93.
ROWLAND G.C. Born 1/9/19. Commd 25/5/50. Wg Cdr 1/7/70. Retd SEC 1/1/75.
ROWLAND J.D.G. AFC. Born 26/4/39. Commd 25/7/60. Flt Lt 25/1/68. Retd GD 26/4/94.
ROWLAND J.N. DSO DFC*. Born 28/12/19. Commd 7/3/40. Flt Lt 7/9/43. Retd GD 2/1/47.
ROWLAND L.M. LLB. Born 23/4/75. Commd 2/4/00. Flt Lt 2/4/03. Retd OPS SPT(PROVSY) 21/7/03.
ROWLANDS B.A. MBE. Born 24/1/44. Commd 5/2/65. Flt Lt 6/10/71. Retd GD(G) 30/9/89.
ROWLANDS G.F.R. Born 25/3/50. Commd 27/3/70. Flt Lt 27/9/75. Retd GD 25/3/88.
ROWLANDS Sir John KBE BSc CEng FRAeS MInstP. Born 23/9/15. Commd 4/4/39. AM 1/7/71. Retd ENG 1/7/73.
ROWLANDS J.A. MSc CEng MIMechE MRAeS. Born 15/2/40. Commd 18/7/61. Wg Cdr 1/1/78. Retd ENG 2/9/94.
ROWLANDS J.B. Born 20/3/20. Commd 22/12/44. Flt Lt 22/6/48. Retd GD 20/3/74.
ROWLANDS P. BSc MB BCh MRCP DCH. Born 25/9/30. Commd 21/8/55. Wg Cdr 4/8/68. Retd MED 21/8/71.
ROWLANDS P.G. Born 16/1/50. Commd 14/9/75. Wg Cdr 1/7/90. Retd ADMIN 7/1/97.
ROWLANDS R. Born 23/8/50. Commd 24/7/81. Flt Lt 24/7/83. Retd ENG 27/2/90.
ROWLANDS R.E. Born 13/9/33. Commd 11/10/51. Flt Lt 1/3/61. Retd GD 1/2/71.
ROWLEY E. Born 30/9/43. Commd 21/10/65. Sqn Ldr 1/7/79. Retd ENG 30/9/98.
ROWLEY M.J.B. Born 13/12/39. Commd 18/7/61. Wg Cdr 1/1/80. Retd ENG 1/1/90.
ROWLEY P.S. Born 11/1/30. Commd 4/7/69. Flt Lt 4/7/72. Retd GD(G) 2/4/75.
ROWLEY T.G.S. Born 11/10/65. Commd 4/7/85. Flt Lt 4/1/91. Retd FLY(P) 11/4/04.
ROWLEY W.E. Born 13/9/29. Commd 21/10/66. Sqn Ldr 1/1/79. Retd ENG 14/11/81.
ROWLEY-BROOKE P.S.J. BA. Born 9/6/46. Commd 1/3/68. Sqn Ldr 1/1/82. Retd ENG 9/6/01.
ROWNEY N.A. Born 11/12/12. Commd 12/8/41. Flt Lt 1/9/45. Retd ENG 23/5/54.
ROWNEY P.J. Born 5/9/49. Commd 4/7/69. Wg Cdr 1/7/96. Retd GD 27/5/03.
ROWNTREE C.G. BSc CEng MIMechE. Born 26/3/46. Commd 28/9/64. Wg Cdr 1/1/87. Retd ENG 6/5/90.
ROWNTREE M.P. Born 22/4/45. Commd 8/7/65. Sqn Ldr 1/7/83. Retd ENG 1/10/89.
ROWORTH D.W. Born 5/7/35. Commd 26/10/59. Flt Lt 26/4/61. Retd GD 30/9/77.
ROWSON D.J. Born 23/2/47. Commd 27/7/72. Flt Lt 27/1/78. Retd GD 5/11/89.
ROXBERRY A.E. Born 1/7/30. Commd 7/12/50. Fg Offr 7/12/52. Retd SEC 2/5/55.
ROXBERRY D.K. Born 21/12/26. Commd 14/6/46. Sqn Ldr 1/1/57. Retd GD 3/10/75.
ROXBURGH D.A. MB ChB DMRD. Born 24/2/39. Commd 23/9/63. Wg Cdr 1/12/78. Retd MED 2/2/81.
ROXBURGH D.K. BSc. Born 25/8/64. Commd 1/2/87. Flt Lt 1/8/88. Retd FLY(P) 14/3/04.
ROXBURGH E.M. Born 13/12/27. Commd 16/10/52. Flt Lt 16/10/58. Retd SEC 17/1/69.
ROXBURGH I.D. AFC AFM. Born 5/9/17. Commd 26/3/41. Sqn Ldr 1/1/51. Retd GD 1/11/57.
ROY J.G. Born 26/10/33. Commd 25/10/73. Flt Lt 25/10/75. Retd GD 26/4/84.
ROY L.T. Born 17/11/29. Commd 18/5/61. Sqn Ldr 1/7/72. Retd SUP 2/9/81.
ROYAL E.G. Born 18/6/20. Commd 12/8/54. Sqn Ldr 1/7/69. Retd GD(G) 18/6/75.
ROYCE M.J. Born 21/8/63. Commd 25/2/82. Flt Lt 25/8/87. Retd GD 21/8/01.
ROYLE A.P. BEng. Born 9/10/59. Commd 4/1/83. Flt Lt 4/7/83. Retd GD 4/1/99.
ROYLE G.A. MSc BSc. Born 21/3/61. Commd 16/9/79. Sqn Ldr 1/1/92. Retd ENG 21/3/99.
ROYLE P. MB BS FFARCS. Born 31/1/53. Commd 2/9/75. Wg Cdr 4/8/90. Retd MED 21/3/93.
RUBENSTEIN M. MSc CEng MRAeS. Born 16/12/53. Commd 10/6/84. Flt Lt 10/12/82. Retd ENG 10/6/00.
RUDD A.W. Born 24/6/29. Commd 2/7/52. Flt Lt 8/1/58. Retd GD 22/1/68.
RUDD D.I. Born 24/6/48. Commd 20/5/82. Sqn Ldr 1/1/92. Retd ADMIN 31/3/94.
RUDD M.C. AFC. Born 12/5/49. Commd 1/4/69. A Cdre 1/7/95. Retd GD 3/12/97.
RUDD M.J. Born 20/8/51. Commd 16/3/73. Sqn Ldr 1/7/94. Retd ADMIN 1/10/01.
RUDD P.C. Born 18/9/18. Commd 10/12/42. Flt Lt 10/6/47. Retd RGT 26/8/58. rtg Sqn Ldr.
RUDDICK D.R. MA. Born 23/4/39. Commd 1/10/62. Sqn Ldr 1/7/77. Retd GD 1/10/80.
RUDIN J. BSc(Eng). Born 20/10/37. Commd 26/11/60. Sqn Ldr 1/1/83. Retd GD 1/1/96.
RUDOLPH F.R.C. Born 6/11/40. Commd 30/5/69. Wg Cdr 1/7/84. Retd ADMIN 11/7/94.
RUFF C.E. MBE. Born 20/9/19. Commd 20/10/55. Sqn Ldr 1/7/65. Retd GD 20/9/74.
RUFF P.J. MBE. Born 11/7/33. Commd 8/7/65. Sqn Ldr 1/1/79. Retd SY 15/3/87.
RUFFLE D.M. Born 5/7/30. Commd 2/7/52. Flt Lt 17/12/59. Retd SEC 5/7/68.
RUGG D.E. Born 3/10/24. Commd 6/3/52. Sqn Ldr 1/1/69. Retd GD 3/10/84.
RULE A.E. Born 8/3/43. Commd 13/1/67. Flt Lt 13/7/72. Retd GD 1/8/90.

RULE D.W. MBE. Born 23/1/29. Commd 26/5/67. Wg Cdr 1/1/81. Retd ADMIN 26/2/83.
RULE T.W. Born 4/6/43. Commd 27/10/67. Flt Lt 27/4/74. Retd SUP 11/7/83.
RUMBOL R.W. Born 3/10/32. Commd 31/5/51. Flt Lt 28/11/56. Retd GD 3/10/70.
RUMBOLD B.J. The Rev. CertEd. Born 30/6/43. Commd 20/6/77. Retd Wg Cdr 1/9/94.
RUMENS K.R. Born 22/7/66. Commd 4/7/85. Sqn Ldr 1/1/02. Retd FLY(P) 1/1/05.
RUNACRES K.B. Born 30/8/40. Commd 27/7/72. Sqn Ldr 1/7/82. Retd ENG 30/8/95.
RUNCHMAN F.E. Born 11/1/22. Commd 29/11/43. Sqn Ldr 1/4/55. Retd GD 22/2/65.
RUNDLE A.F. Born 2/11/46. Commd 1/4/69. Fg Offr 1/4/71. Retd GD 16/12/71.
RUSE D.E.McG. Born 14/9/24. Commd 19/1/56. Sqn Offr 1/7/67. Retd SEC 18/10/75.
RUSE N.F. Born 23/2/13. Commd 10/11/41. Wg Cdr 1/1/60. Retd ENG 23/2/65.
RUSH F.C.I. Born 7/11/53. Commd 20/7/78. Flt Lt 20/1/84. Retd GD 1/10/95.
RUSH J.M. BA. Born 20/5/41. Commd 11/11/71. Sqn Ldr 1/1/89. Retd GD(G) 20/5/96.
RUSH W.J. MBE BA. Born 10/5/43. Commd 24/6/76. Wg Cdr 1/7/90. Retd ENG 3/4/97.
RUSHER D.H.S. DSO. Born 18/3/15. Commd 15/12/34. Wg Cdr 1/7/47. Retd GD 1/1/48.
RUSHFORTH R.N. Born 2/12/28. Commd 9/3/66. Sqn Ldr 1/1/77. Retd ENG 3/12/82.
RUSHMERE M.J. Born 5/6/48. Commd 27/3/70. Flt Lt 5/6/75. Retd SUP 5/6/88.
RUSHTON P. Born 3/12/51. Commd 24/8/72. Flt Lt 1/9/78. Retd GD 9/2/82.
RUSHTON W.L. Born 8/6/33. Commd 19/8/71. Sqn Ldr 1/7/82. Retd ENG 8/6/93.
RUSHWORTH D.W. Born 25/2/30. Commd 18/5/61. Flt Lt 18/5/67. Retd SEC 31/7/68.
RUSHWORTH G.F. Born 12/2/36. Commd 24/3/61. Flt Lt 10/2/67. Retd GD 12/2/74.
RUSKELL C.M. BSc. Born 18/1/51. Commd 15/9/69. Sqn Ldr 1/7/85. Retd ENGINEER 3/9/04.
RUSKELL K. MBE DFC. Born 14/6/22. Commd 9/10/42. Sqn Ldr 1/7/54. Retd ADMIN 1/9/76.
RUSKELL R.M.F. Born 18/7/48. Commd 2/6/67. Flt Lt 2/12/72. Retd GD 28/2/76.
RUSLING N.C. BA. Born 13/12/47. Commd 18/9/66. Gp Capt 1/7/93. Retd GD 13/12/02.
RUSSELL A. BA. Born 1/10/50. Commd 27/3/86. Flt Lt 27/3/90. Retd GD 14/3/96.
RUSSELL A. Born 1/10/12. Commd 1/4/45. Flt Lt 14/11/56. Retd SEC 1/10/67.
RUSSELL A.J. Born 23/12/30. Commd 1/3/62. Flt Lt 1/3/68. Retd ENG 1/9/73.
RUSSELL A.K.M. Born 21/9/38. Commd 27/1/67. Wg Cdr 1/7/87. Retd ADMIN 31/12/91.
RUSSELL B. Born 14/10/50. Commd 2/11/88. Flt Lt 2/11/92. Retd ADMIN 13/1/96.
RUSSELL G.L. BSc. Born 22/9/48. Commd 1/2/87. Flt Lt 1/2/87. Retd ADMIN 14/12/96.
RUSSELL H. MBE. Born 20/7/09. Commd 6/9/47. Sqn Ldr 1/7/60. Retd SUP 20/7/64.
RUSSELL I.J.L. BSc. Born 8/3/65. Commd 16/9/84. Flt Lt 15/1/90. Retd FLY(P) 31/3/05.
RUSSELL J.D. Born 25/7/20. Commd 9/2/43. Flt Lt 13/6/51. Retd GD(G) 17/12/69.
RUSSELL J.H. Born 17/7/37. Commd 25/1/63. Sqn Ldr 1/1/75. Retd SUP 2/10/78.
RUSSELL J.R. Born 22/8/46. Commd 21/4/67. Flt Lt 29/7/73. Retd OPS SPT 22/8/01.
RUSSELL J.T.A. Born 20/6/32. Commd 16/7/52. Sqn Ldr 1/1/77. Retd GD(G) 1/6/86.
RUSSELL L.D.A. Born 31/5/40. Commd 30/5/59. Flt Lt 30/11/64. Retd GD 1/7/77.
RUSSELL L.J. Born 29/1/30. Commd 13/12/50. Sqn Ldr 1/1/59. Retd GD 30/10/70. rtg Wg Cdr.
RUSSELL M.E.J. Born 15/6/40. Commd 21/7/61. Flt Lt 21/1/67. Retd GD 1/10/81.
RUSSELL M.I. Born 31/3/34. Commd 27/8/52. Flt Lt 14/5/58. Retd GD 2/3/63.
RUSSELL M.J. OBE. Born 28/3/47. Commd 23/9/66. Wg Cdr 1/7/87. Retd GD 14/12/96.
RUSSELL M.W.J. Born 14/5/44. Commd 15/7/65. Sqn Ldr 1/7/83. Retd ENG 1/10/85.
RUSSELL R.B. Born 11/12/45. Commd 22/7/81. Flt Lt 22/1/77. Retd GD 8/3/87.
RUSSELL R.J. AFC. Born 30/4/32. Commd 28/1/53. Sqn Ldr 1/7/86. Retd GD 23/2/91.
RUSSELL R.M. BA. Born 1/12/44. Commd 26/11/81. Sqn Ldr 1/1/90. Retd ADMIN 31/7/98.
RUSSELL S.I. BEng. Born 13/2/66. Commd 3/8/93. Flt Lt 15/7/96. Retd ENGINEER 13/2/04.
RUSSELL T.A.E. Born 29/3/21. Commd 6/8/43. Flt Lt 1/1/49. Retd PRT 1/10/65.
RUSSELL W. Born 4/10/42. Commd 28/2/80. Sqn Ldr 1/1/91. Retd GD(G) 12/7/96.
RUSSELL W.B. MB ChB DRCOG DAvMed DPH MFOM. Born 18/5/33. Commd 24/5/59. Gp Capt 1/1/83.
    Retd MED 21/9/85.
RUSSELL-BISHOP R.G. Born 16/9/13. Commd 29/6/50. Sqn Ldr 29/6/62. Retd MED(T) 4/12/67.
RUSSELL-SMITH C.P. BSc CEng MRAeS. Born 16/11/41. Commd 24/9/63. Sqn Ldr 1/1/72. Retd ENG 16/11/96.
RUSSELL-SMITH S.J. Born 27/9/24. Commd 30/6/44. Flt Lt 16/8/61. Retd GD(G) 28/11/73.
RUSSUM K. AFC. Born 12/10/22. Commd 9/9/44. Wg Cdr 1/1/68. Retd GD 25/3/77.
RUST J.D. Born 5/1/39. Commd 25/7/60. Wg Cdr 1/1/78. Retd GD 1/2/82.
RUST T.J. Born 15/6/67. Commd 31/7/86. Sqn Ldr 1/7/97. Retd FLY(P) 15/6/05.
RUST V.R. Born 25/3/29. Commd 7/7/55. Flt Lt 7/1/59. Retd GD 25/3/84.
RUSTIN C.C. AFC* BSc CEng MRAeS. Born 14/5/32. Commd 14/11/57. Wg Cdr 1/1/74. Retd GD 14/5/87.
RUSTON A.M. CBE DFC. Born 2/3/20. Commd 8/10/39. A Cdre 1/1/65. Retd GD 2/4/70.
RUSTON C. Born 29/3/47. Commd 10/12/65. Flt Lt 8/3/72. Retd GD 14/3/96.
RUSTON N.D. Born 14/4/50. Commd 30/7/92. Fg Offr 30/7/92. Retd ENG 31/3/94.
RUSTON P.E. MCIPS MCMI. Born 21/10/34. Commd 30/8/60. Wg Cdr 1/7/76. Retd SUP 18/4/86.
RUTHEN P.L. MBE BSc CEng MRAeS. Born 13/7/34. Commd 1/10/57. Sqn Ldr 29/3/71. Retd ADMIN 13/7/92.
RUTHERDALE R.J. Born 9/1/53. Commd 27/7/89. Flt Lt 27/7/93. Retd OPS SPT 1/10/01.
RUTHERFORD B.E. Born 22/3/25. Commd 17/1/51. Flt Lt 17/10/56. Retd GD 29/8/65.
RUTHERFORD D.A. BA. Born 7/5/53. Commd 25/6/66. Sqn Ldr 1/7/80. Retd MAR 1/4/86.

RUTHERFORD I. Born 5/4/39. Commd 7/1/58. Flt Lt 9/7/62. Retd GD 5/4/95.
RUTHVEN J.C. Born 31/8/37. Commd 16/12/66. Flt Lt 16/12/68. Retd GD(G) 31/8/93.
RUTLEDGE B. Born 22/11/38. Commd 12/3/60. Wg Cdr 1/1/87. Retd GD 22/11/93.
RUTLEDGE G.A. BA. Born 24/11/47. Commd 28/2/69. Flt Lt 28/2/72. Retd GD 14/7/92.
RUTLEY F.G. BSc. Born 26/6/63. Commd 30/8/87. Flt Lt 30/8/88. Retd ADMIN 14/3/97.
RUTSON G.M. Born 14/8/45. Commd 5/11/65. Flt Lt 5/5/71. Retd GD 15/2/76.
RUTTER A.S. BSc(Eng) CEng MRAeS. Born 18/7/49. Commd 26/2/71. Sqn Ldr 1/1/85. Retd ENGINEER 20/7/03.
RUTTER I.T. MBE. Born 8/8/24. Commd 6/9/56. Sqn Ldr 1/7/68. Retd GD 8/8/84.
RUTTER K.J. Born 21/7/62. Commd 22/9/88. Flt Lt 22/3/94. Retd FLY(P) 4/4/05.
RYALL F.D. Born 14/9/56. Commd 5/8/76. Wg Cdr 1/1/96. Retd GD 14/9/01.
RYALL K.J. DFC MCMI. Born 8/11/23. Commd 4/11/43. Wg Cdr 1/1/69. Retd GD 31/3/78.
RYALL M. CEng CPhys MInstP. Born 17/7/44. Commd 10/3/69. Gp Capt 1/1/99. Retd ENG 17/9/99.
RYALL P.J. Born 15/4/33. Commd 17/5/56. Flt Lt 11/10/62. Retd GD 1/9/85.
RYAN B.F. Born 6/1/22. Commd 4/9/43. Sqn Ldr 1/4/56. Retd GD 30/1/71.
RYAN J.A. Born 21/5/26. Commd 14/6/46. Wg Cdr 1/1/64. Retd GD 1/11/75.
RYAN K.J. OBE. Born 8/10/25. Commd 15/12/49. Wg Cdr 1/7/67. Retd GD 8/10/83.
RYAN M.A.F. Born 28/7/36. Commd 17/12/57. Wg Cdr 1/1/77. Retd GD 19/4/84.
RYAN M.C. Born 19/7/37. Commd 2/2/68. Flt Lt 2/2/70. Retd SEC 2/2/76.
RYAN P.A. Born 14/7/42. Commd 13/7/61. Gp Capt 1/1/86. Retd SY 12/2/94.
RYAN P.W. Born 18/6/39. Commd 30/5/59. Flt Lt 30/11/64. Retd GD 18/6/77.
RYAN T.P.F. MHCIMA. Born 8/7/46. Commd 4/9/67. Flt Lt 4/9/72. Retd ADMIN 1/9/76.
RYAN W.A. Born 18/2/20. Commd 17/5/56. Flt Lt 17/5/62. Retd GD(G) 30/4/66.
RYAN W.F. Born 20/9/23. Commd 2/10/58. Flt Lt 2/10/64. Retd PRT 5/1/74. rtg Sqn Ldr.
RYANS P.T. CEng MIMechE MRAeS. Born 31/5/32. Commd 3/8/55. Gp Capt 1/7/79. Retd ENG 7/4/84.
RYANS R.B. Born 3/7/44. Commd 21/12/62. Flt Lt 21/6/68. Retd GD 3/7/82.
RYCROFT D.H. CEng MIEE. Born 11/12/42. Commd 6/1/69. Flt Lt 4/5/72. Retd ENG 11/12/97.
RYDER A.N. Born 25/5/50. Commd 17/7/70. Flt Lt 17/1/76. Retd GD 12/7/78.
RYDER A.S. BA. Born 9/4/66. Commd 27/8/92. Flt Lt 15/1/91. Retd FLY(P) 9/4/04.
RYDER D.J. Born 13/3/20. Commd 8/4/44. Sqn Ldr 1/7/66. Retd SUP 13/3/75.
RYDER E.J. MSc. Born 26/8/14. Commd 26/12/37. Wg Cdr 1/7/48. Retd ENG 1/9/66.
RYDER R.E.T. BSc. Born 5/2/51. Commd 15/9/69. Sqn Ldr 1/7/84. Retd ENG 6/12/89.
RYDER S.F. Born 22/5/31. Commd 23/4/52. Flt Lt 14/11/56. Retd GD 22/5/69.
RYE W.J. AFC. Born 11/10/08. Commd 26/8/40. Sqn Ldr 1/1/51. Retd GD(G) 11/10/58. rtg Wg Cdr.
RYGALSKI S.A. Born 3/3/63. Commd 13/8/82. Sqn Ldr 1/7/96. Retd SUP 3/3/01.
RYLE A.E. OBE AFC FCMI. Born 5/6/35. Commd 27/2/58. Gp Capt 1/1/84. Retd GD 5/6/95.
RYLES D.S. Born 12/7/32. Commd 13/8/52. Flt Lt 9/1/58. Retd GD 12/7/70. Re-instated 23/12/81 to 1/7/85.
RYLES M.T. MB ChB MSc MRCGP DRCOG DAvMed DOcc Med. Born 25/3/60. Commd 14/11/91. Wg Cdr 1/8/97. Retd MEDICAL 25/6/05.
RYMARZ R.J.G. MA MSc BSc CertEd. Born 15/12/49. Commd 18/4/71. Wg Cdr 1/7/88. Retd ADMIN 14/9/96.

S

SAADY D.J. BA. Born 27/6/38. Commd 30/9/58. Sqn Ldr 1/1/70. Retd ENG 27/6/76.
SAAR R.C. MBE MCMI. Born 30/5/39. Commd 7/1/58. Sqn Ldr 1/1/71. Retd GD 30/5/77.
SABAN J.T. Born 15/8/30. Commd 17/3/55. Wg Cdr 1/1/76. Retd SUP 15/8/85.
SABBEN J.M.H. BMet CEng MRAeS. Born 9/12/40. Commd 12/3/63. Wg Cdr 1/7/79. Retd ENG 12/3/85.
SABIN J.R. BSc CEng MIEE. Born 1/11/44. Commd 13/9/71. Sqn Ldr 1/1/82. Retd GD 13/9/87.
SABINE M.S. Born 8/2/40. Commd 1/8/61. Sqn Ldr 1/7/75. Retd GD 1/7/78.
SABOURIN P.C. BA. Born 23/4/60. Commd 7/11/82. Flt Lt 7/8/86. Retd ENG 7/11/87.
SACH J.L. BEng. Born 5/7/76. Commd 10/10/00. Flt Lt 5/4/01. Retd ENGINEER 27/4/03.
SACHEDINA K.A. BSc. Born 4/2/61. Commd 26/9/82. Sqn Ldr 1/1/97. Retd GD 1/1/00.
SACKETT P.D.M. Born 22/4/41. Commd 6/4/62. Fg Offr 6/4/64. Retd GD 14/5/65.
SADDLETON D.S. BA. Born 13/2/38. Commd 16/1/72. Sqn Ldr 16/7/75. Retd ADMIN 19/12/87.
SADDLETON P.E.J. Born 29/12/33. Commd 4/4/54. Wg Cdr 1/1/75. Retd GD(G) 25/11/85.
SADLER A.E. Born 18/4/27. Commd 31/1/51. Sqn Ldr 1/1/64. Retd GD 18/4/85.
SADLER A.G. Born 25/4/33. Commd 29/9/51. Flt Lt 15/1/57. Retd GD 25/4/71.
SADLER B. BSc. Born 11/4/58. Commd 28/9/80. Flt Lt 28/6/81. Retd GD 31/1/93.
SADLER E.C. Born 29/2/32. Commd 23/4/52. Flt Lt 19/9/57. Retd GD 29/2/92.
SADLER G.B. MSc BSc CEng MRAeS MBCS MCMI. Born 19/11/51. Commd 13/9/70. Sqn Ldr 1/7/85.
　　Retd ENG 1/12/92.
SADLER I.F. Born 3/6/49. Commd 15/8/77. Sqn Ldr 1/1/88. Retd SY 15/8/93.
SADLER J. Born 6/12/09. Commd 14/10/43. Flt Lt 14/4/48. Retd SEC 21/9/53.
SADLER J.M. Born 15/7/44. Commd 5/2/81. Sqn Ldr 1/7/92. Retd ENG 17/6/96.
SADLER J.R. Born 22/4/43. Commd 22/2/63. Flt Lt 22/8/68. Retd GD 9/11/81.
SADLER-HALL M.M. MA. Born 28/12/35. Commd 14/9/65. Flt Lt 14/9/66. Retd EDN 1/10/71.
SAER J.M.H. Born 1/4/51. Commd 23/9/79. Flt Lt 23/9/83. Retd ADMIN 23/9/95.
SAGE D.J. BA. Born 11/12/45. Commd 17/1/72. Flt Lt 17/10/75. Retd ENG 17/1/88.
SAGE G.D. Born 11/11/32. Commd 17/7/70. Flt Lt 17/7/73. Retd PI 1/9/84.
SAIFURRAHMAN Z.A. BSc CEng MRAeS. Born 20/2/47. Commd 1/8/69. Flt Lt 13/7/73. Retd ENG 20/2/85.
SAINSBURY D.J. MSc BEd. Born 5/5/53. Commd 25/5/80. Wg Cdr 1/1/99. Retd ADMIN 25/5/02.
SAINSBURY N.M. IEng AMRAeS. Born 7/6/60. Commd 15/12/88. Sqn Ldr 1/7/97. Retd ENGINEER 7/6/04.
SAKER J. Born 8/10/34. Commd 10/9/52. Flt Lt 23/3/58. Retd GD 8/10/92.
SAKER R.N.J. MBE CDipAF. Born 24/12/31. Commd 29/3/51. Wg Cdr 1/1/80. Retd GD 16/5/83.
SALE M.J. MCMI. Born 7/12/43. Commd 31/10/69. Wg Cdr 1/1/88. Retd SUP 1/5/93.
SALISBURY J. BSc MInstP MCIPD. Born 10/6/37. Commd 13/11/62. Sqn Ldr 24/3/70. Retd ADMIN 13/11/82.
　　Re-instated 31/8/83. Sqn Ldr 23/4/70. Retd ADMIN 22/5/91.
SALISBURY K.J. Born 20/11/16. Commd 15/5/47. Sqn Ldr 1/4/58. Retd SEC 30/11/71.
SALISBURY K.W.N. Born 4/11/48. Commd 31/7/70. Fg Offr 31/7/71. Retd SEC 31/12/75. rtg Flt Lt.
SALKELD D. BSc. Born 3/11/28. Commd 20/10/49. Wg Cdr 1/7/67. Retd ENG 11/12/75.
SALKELD P. Born 13/4/51. Commd 7/1/71. Fg Offr 7/1/73. Retd GD 23/11/73.
SALMON J.F. BA. Born 14/11/43. Commd 30/9/63. Flt Lt 15/10/69. Retd ENG 4/9/71.
SALMON R.D. Born 7/6/62. Commd 30/4/81. Flt Lt 30/10/86. Retd GD 23/6/89.
SALMON R.S. MCMI. Born 25/3/24. Commd 21/6/44. Gp Capt 1/7/72. Retd GD 7/4/79.
SALMON S.E. CEng MIEE MRAeS. Born 25/1/40. Commd 18/7/61. Sqn Ldr 1/1/71. Retd ENG 11/2/77.
SALMOND J.J.W. Born 20/12/26. Commd 14/6/46. Flt Lt 15/12/49. Retd GD 2/5/50.
SALMOND J.S.R. Born 20/6/31. Commd 14/4/53. Flt Lt 14/10/55. Retd GD 20/6/86.
SALT G.S. Born 23/4/45. Commd 9/8/79. Flt Lt 9/8/81. Retd GD(G) 9/8/87.
SALT R.M. MBE AFC. Born 25/7/32. Commd 14/4/53. Sqn Ldr 1/7/66. Retd GD 25/7/70.
SALTER A. Born 15/6/34. Commd 5/4/55. Gp Capt 1/7/83. Retd GD 15/6/89.
SALTER A.G. DFC. Born 13/7/16. Commd 10/5/37. Sqn Ldr 1/8/47. Retd GD 27/1/58.
SALTER D.G. CEng MIEE. Born 26/5/24. Commd 24/10/43. Sqn Ldr 1/1/56. Retd ENG 26/11/77.
SALTER G.A. Born 17/9/23. Commd 10/4/51. Flt Lt 10/10/54. Retd GD 9/4/73.
SALTER L.A. Born 22/2/43. Commd 3/10/69. Fg Offr 3/4/72. Retd GD(G) 3/10/73.
SALTER M.G. MBE MBA BA CEng FRAeS. Born 12/4/48. Commd 24/4/70. Wg Cdr 1/7/91. Retd GD 1/8/03.
SALTER R.M. Born 19/12/45. Commd 30/4/81. Flt Lt 30/4/85. Retd ENG 22/9/97.
SALTER T.A. MBE BSc(Eng) CEng MRAeS MCMI DNCL. Born 13/5/42. Commd 1/9/64. Wg Cdr 1/1/87.
　　Retd ENG 13/5/97.
SALUSBURY D.J. BA. Born 6/9/43. Commd 6/6/66. Gp Capt 1/7/94. Retd SY 1/9/96.
SALWEY C.H. Born 5/8/34. Commd 26/7/55. Flt Lt 1/1/66. Retd GD 5/8/92.
SAMARASINGHE S.N. Born 4/5/26. Commd 28/2/66. Flt Lt 28/2/66. Retd SEC 17/11/81.
SAMBROOK G. Born 6/8/47. Commd 1/3/68. Flt Lt 1/3/71. Retd GD 6/8/85.
SAMES C.R. Born 2/10/46. Commd 28/2/85. Flt Lt 28/2/89. Retd ADMIN 1/4/92.
SAMES D.W. BSc. Born 25/5/35. Commd 28/9/60. Sqn Ldr 1/1/68. Retd GD 21/9/84.

SAMPLE W.C.H.M. Born 27/9/50. Commd 27/3/70. Flt Lt 27/9/75. Retd GD 14/9/76.
SAMPSON C.F.J. BSc AMBCS. Born 6/4/46. Commd 13/9/70. Wg Cdr 1/7/90. Retd ADMIN 14/3/96.
SAMPSON D.P. DFC. Born 5/2/22. Commd 16/7/42. Sqn Ldr 1/7/51. Retd GD 5/2/65. rtg Wg Cdr.
SAMPSON I.W. Born 24/9/40. Commd 6/7/62. Sqn Ldr 1/1/81. Retd GD 24/9/95.
SAMPSON J.A. Born 5/2/31. Commd 10/12/52. Flt Lt 1/11/61. Retd GD 3/11/67.
SAMPSON J.R. AFC. Born 1/5/46. Commd 13/5/88. Flt Lt 23/12/71. Retd GD 14/5/94.
SAMPSON R.B. Born 24/1/15. Commd 13/4/44. Flt Lt 13/10/47. Retd ENG 24/1/64.
SAMPSON T.R. Born 7/5/46. Commd 24/4/64. Sqn Ldr 1/1/81. Retd GD(G) 7/5/91.
SAMUEL D.L. DPhysEd. Born 10/5/38. Commd 3/1/63. Sqn Ldr 1/1/74. Retd PE 3/7/79.
SAMUEL E.G. BSc CEng MIMechE. Born 25/11/48. Commd 27/2/70. Gp Capt 1/7/92. Retd GD 25/11/03.
SAMUELS D.M.A. Born 30/7/32. Commd 14/4/53. Flt Lt 14/10/55. Retd GD 30/7/70.
SAMUELS T.C. Born 31/5/19. Commd 17/1/50. Flt Lt 29/11/51. Retd GD 15/7/62.
SAND R.P.D. Born 26/8/35. Commd 2/10/53. Flt Lt 5/10/60. Retd GD(G) 26/8/73. Re-instated 3/12/80. Flt Lt 12/1/68.
    Retd GD(G) 8/9/90.
SANDBACH L. Born 23/9/26. Commd 27/9/51. Flt Lt 11/1/57. Retd GD 3/11/69.
SANDEMAN C.A. Born 19/4/47. Commd 20/10/83. Sqn Ldr 1/7/92. Retd ENG 2/1/99.
SANDERS A.A.J. DFC AFC. Born 30/9/20. Commd 7/3/40. Wg Cdr 1/1/54. Retd GD 30/9/67.
SANDERS A.E. Born 25/8/29. Commd 15/9/50. Flt Lt 5/6/56. Retd GD 25/8/67.
SANDERS J.F. BSc. Born 28/5/11. Commd 25/4/39. Gp Capt 1/1/64. Retd EDN 28/2/69.
SANDERS J.T. MBE. Born 13/1/52. Commd 4/5/72. Sqn Ldr 1/1/92. Retd FLY(N) 20/4/04.
SANDERS M.F. Born 8/9/45. Commd 16/9/76. Sqn Ldr 1/7/84. Retd ENG 2/12/96.
SANDERS N.B. Born 1/6/41. Commd 22/8/63. Flt Lt 15/4/70. Retd SUP 1/6/79.
SANDERS P.J.G. Born 4/2/44. Commd 24/6/65. Flt Lt 24/12/67. Retd GD 4/9/82.
SANDERS P.T. MSc BA. Born 27/2/50. Commd 8/9/77. Sqn Ldr 1/1/84. Retd ADMIN 27/8/88.
SANDERS R.F. Born 30/11/45. Commd 4/6/72. Sqn Ldr 1/7/84. Retd ENG 4/6/88.
SANDERS R.S. DFC AFC*. Born 14/12/22. Commd 20/11/42. Wg Cdr 1/1/58. Retd GD 14/12/77.
SANDERSON C.E. BA. Born 16/12/60. Commd 16/9/79. Flt Lt 15/4/86. Retd SUP 1/10/89.
SANDERSON F.A.S. Born 8/3/33. Commd 23/9/65. Flt Lt 23/9/71. Retd SUP 8/8/80.
SANDERSON G. Born 24/6/30. Commd 14/2/63. Flt Lt 14/2/69. Retd ADMIN 24/6/68.
SANDERSON M.D. Born 21/8/40. Commd 19/10/62. Flt Lt 19/5/67. Retd ENG 19/10/81.
SANDERSON P.R. Born 19/9/27. Commd 8/4/49. Sqn Ldr 1/7/60. Retd GD 28/6/68.
SANDERSON P.R. Born 18/7/29. Commd 24/9/64. Flt Lt 24/9/69. Retd ENG 1/9/73.
SANDERSON R. BA MBA. Born 8/4/42. Commd 6/8/63. Sqn Ldr 6/8/75. Retd ADMIN 2/10/82.
SANDERSON S.P. Born 15/4/56. Commd 14/8/80. Sqn Ldr 1/7/87. Retd ENG 15/4/94.
SANDERSON-MILLER M.S. Born 25/3/42. Commd 30/1/75. Sqn Ldr 1/1/84. Retd ENG 21/4/88.
SANDFORD B.V. Born 24/8/43. Commd 24/6/65. Flt Lt 24/12/67. Retd GD 2/4/96.
SANDFORD J. BSc MRAeS DCAe. Born 20/5/24. Commd 10/9/47. Wg Cdr 20/5/65. Retd EDN 1/8/70.
SANDFORD R.F. Born 22/10/45. Commd 26/5/67. Flt Lt 18/2/70. Retd GD 7/10/76.
SANDMANN G. Born 14/1/28. Commd 2/12/54. Flt Lt 2/12/59. Retd GD 13/10/69.
SANDOE R.J. Born 30/11/39. Commd 30/3/65. Sqn Ldr 1/7/76. Retd ENG 30/11/95.
SANDOM C.W. MSc BEng CEng MIEE. Born 24/7/61. Commd 7/8/87. Flt Lt 15/7/90. Retd ENG 9/9/00.
SANDON R.A. Born 8/9/62. Commd 15/8/89. Flt Lt 11/5/91. Retd OPS SPT 12/9/98.
SANDS L. Born 16/7/22. Commd 14/4/60. Flt Lt 14/4/60. Retd GD 16/7/77. rtg Sqn Ldr.
SANDS P.L. Born 20/9/30. Commd 26/8/66. Flt Lt 26/8/71. Retd ENG 8/8/74.
SANDS R.P. Born 30/8/45. Commd 1/4/65. Sqn Ldr 1/1/86. Retd GD(G) 30/8/89.
SANDYS J.F. Born 6/7/34. Commd 5/7/66. Sqn Ldr 1/7/82. Retd GD 7/8/89.
SANFORD-CASEY B.M. BA. Born 7/5/45. Commd 17/3/65. Wg Cdr 1/1/90. Retd GD 13/8/94.
SANKEY C.V. Born 28/2/33. Commd 27/9/51. Sqn Ldr 1/1/70. Retd GD 7/5/76.
SANSOM F.B. Born 5/7/39. Commd 29/7/65. Sqn Ldr 1/7/74. Retd ENG 5/7/77.
SANSOM M.D. Born 4/8/31. Commd 5/7/51. Sqn Ldr 1/1/67. Retd ADMIN 4/11/85.
SANSOME G.E. CEng MIMechE MRAeS. Born 25/2/28. Commd 4/4/61. Sqn Ldr 1/7/67. Retd ENG 25/8/91.
SANSOME N.F.E. Born 22/9/37. Commd 15/2/73. Flt Lt 15/2/77. Retd GD(G) 22/9/87.
SAPSFORD J.W. CEng MIMechE MCMI. Born 28/6/29. Commd 3/10/61. Sqn Ldr 1/1/70. Retd ENG 3/10/77.
SARBUTT D.W. BEM. Born 1/4/16. Commd 26/9/57. Sqn Ldr 1/1/66. Retd ENG 16/1/71.
SARGEANT A.R. Born 1/3/34. Commd 29/4/53. Sqn Ldr 1/1/67. Retd GD 28/1/77.
SARGEANT B. Born 7/6/41. Commd 23/9/66. Flt Lt 1/7/69. Retd GD(G) 7/6/79.
SARGEANT R.A. Born 24/4/46. Commd 14/7/66. Wg Cdr 1/1/91. Retd GD 20/7/96.
SARGEANT R.M. CEng MIEE. Born 23/2/29. Commd 5/9/57. Sqn Ldr 1/7/65. Retd ENG 23/2/89.
SARGENT D. Born 18/2/44. Commd 7/6/68. Sqn Ldr 1/1/86. Retd GD 11/3/99.
SARGENT D.M. Born 21/11/36. Commd 24/1/63. Sqn Ldr 1/7/74. Retd ADMIN 18/10/87.
SARGENT J. Born 19/5/48. Commd 1/8/69. Flt Lt 8/3/72. Retd GD 19/5/86.
SARGENT K.G. Born 5/8/21. Commd 6/12/56. Flt Lt 23/11/61. Retd GD 5/8/76.
SARGENT M.W. Born 2/10/48. Commd 21/3/69. Flt Lt 19/7/75. Retd SEC 1/4/78.
SARGENT R.H. Born 16/12/47. Commd 2/8/68. Sqn Ldr 1/1/81. Retd GD 16/12/91.
SARJEANT C.J. Born 22/12/54. Commd 4/6/87. Flt Lt 4/6/89. Retd GD 22/12/98.
SATCHWELL G.F. MRAeS. Born 8/1/21. Commd 1/11/41. Wg Cdr 1/7/60. Retd ENG 14/10/61.

SATHERLEY A. Born 24/9/14. Commd 21/9/50. Flt Lt 21/3/54. Retd ENG 15/10/66.
SATOW A.R. Born 1/3/27. Commd 2/3/49. Sqn Ldr 1/1/58. Retd GD 1/3/65.
SATTERLY R.D. Born 1/11/31. Commd 29/3/62. Flt Lt 29/3/66. Retd PRT 1/11/69.
SATTERTHWAITE W.E. OBE CEng MIEE. Born 1/8/16. Commd 16/3/44. Wg Cdr 1/1/62. Retd ENG 12/9/71.
SAUNBY C.C. Born 21/10/44. Commd 15/7/66. Flt Lt 15/1/69. Retd GD 29/8/74.
SAUNDBY R.P. MMedSci MB ChB MFCM MFOM MRAeS. Born 31/5/32. Commd 26/3/54. A Cdre 1/7/86.
   Retd MED 31/5/91.
SAUNDERS A.E. Born 25/2/52. Commd 20/1/80. Flt Lt 20/1/84. Retd ADMIN 20/1/96.
SAUNDERS A.E.J. BA. Born 11/4/62. Commd 30/3/86. Flt Lt 30/9/88. Retd OPS SPT 30/3/02.
SAUNDERS A.F. Born 9/2/32. Commd 5/3/57. Flt Lt 6/3/63. Retd GD 6/5/76.
SAUNDERS C. Born 22/6/14. Commd 18/11/40. Sqn Ldr 1/8/47. Retd SEC 22/6/63.
SAUNDERS D.A. CBE MSc BSc CEng FIEE. Born 14/11/33. Commd 10/1/57. AVM 1/7/87. Retd ENG 5/4/90.
SAUNDERS D.J. CBE MSc BSc CEng FIMechE FRAeS. Born 12/6/43. Commd 15/7/64. AVM 1/7/91.
   Retd ENG 1/9/97.
SAUNDERS D.M.C. Born 21/7/55. Commd 30/1/75. Flt Lt 30/7/81. Retd ADMIN 17/9/85.
SAUNDERS E.J. IEng MIIE. Born 1/7/56. Commd 22/11/84. Sqn Ldr 1/7/95. Retd ENG 15/10/00.
SAUNDERS E.M. Born 11/12/65. Commd 8/11/90. Flt Lt 8/5/96. Retd GD 10/2/00.
SAUNDERS F.A. Born 17/2/15. Commd 20/5/43. Flt Lt 20/11/46. Retd GD 1/9/57.
SAUNDERS J. Born 10/9/36. Commd 31/8/62. Flt Lt 29/2/68. Retd GD 15/5/78.
SAUNDERS J.D. BSc. Born 19/5/41. Commd 9/11/64. Flt Lt 9/2/66. Retd GD 19/5/96.
SAUNDERS J.R. Born 14/9/22. Commd 1/11/41. Gp Capt 1/1/66. Retd GD 15/3/70.
SAUNDERS M.B. MSc BDS MGDSRCS(Eng). Born 26/2/63. Commd 19/1/86. Wg Cdr 11/7/98. Retd DEL 19/1/02.
SAUNDERS M.G. Born 10/5/45. Commd 5/2/65. Wg Cdr 1/1/90. Retd GD 10/5/00.
SAUNDERS N.J. Born 20/7/54. Commd 17/9/72. Fg Offr 2/9/75. Retd GD 20/10/77.
SAUNDERS P. DFC. Born 28/9/17. Commd 18/5/41. Sqn Ldr 1/1/53. Retd GD 26/1/58.
SAUNDERS P.C.H. Born 20/5/49. Commd 19/12/85. Sqn Ldr 1/7/02. Retd ADMIN (P ED) 1/7/04.
SAUNDERS R.F. Born 17/5/33. Commd 8/5/53. Gp Capt 1/7/81. Retd GD 17/5/88.
SAUNDERS R.H.G. CEng MIMechE MIEE. Born 30/1/25. Commd 13/11/62. Sqn Ldr 13/5/66. Retd EDN 13/11/78.
SAUNDERS R.L. MA. Born 24/8/07. Commd 4/7/39. Sqn Ldr 1/9/47. Retd EDN 1/9/67.
SAUNDERS R.M. Born 5/5/39. Commd 26/8/66. Sqn Ldr 1/7/78. Retd SEC 7/8/81.
SAUNDERS R.V. Born 20/3/09. Commd 30/7/43. Fg Offr 30/1/44. Retd ENG 3/11/45.
SAUNDERS T.B.J. MBE. Born 17/9/30. Commd 21/6/56. Sqn Ldr 1/7/69. Retd GD 13/6/84.
SAUNDERS-DAVIES D.A.P. FCMI. Born 9/12/24. Commd 23/9/44. Gp Capt 1/1/71. Retd GD 29/3/76.
SAUZIER J.R.D. OBE CEng MIERE. Born 23/8/43. Commd 15/7/65. Wg Cdr 1/1/83. Retd ENG 23/8/87.
SAVAGE G.P.J. BA. Born 6/5/42. Commd 16/9/76. Flt Lt 16/9/78. Retd ENG 16/9/84.
SAVAGE J.D.C. MSc BSc. Born 26/1/62. Commd 5/9/82. Sqn Ldr 1/1/98. Retd ENG 1/1/01.
SAVAGE M.H. Born 2/6/22. Commd 27/1/45. Sqn Ldr 1/10/55. Retd GD 16/9/60.
SAVAGE S. Born 21/9/43. Commd 1/4/65. Flt Lt 1/10/70. Retd GD 28/8/82. Re-entered 1/7/85. Sqn Ldr 1/7/98.
   Retd FLY(N) 1/12/03.
SAVAGE T.I.B. Born 14/3/69. Commd 17/1/85. Fg Offr 29/3/87. Retd SY 1/10/90. rtg Flt Lt.
SAVIGAR N.J.L. Born 28/7/52. Commd 15/3/73. Wg Cdr 1/7/87. Retd GD 28/7/90.
SAVILL M.S. Born 4/2/37. Commd 9/7/62. Flt Lt 28/7/65. Retd GD 28/1/73.
SAVILLE H.W. Born 18/3/16. Commd 11/8/54. Flt Lt 11/8/59. Retd GD(G) 10/4/66.
SAVILLE I. BSc. Born 12/7/55. Commd 15/9/74. Flt Lt 15/4/79. Retd GD 14/9/96.
SAVVA E. Born 6/6/22. Commd 2/7/47. Sqn Ldr 1/7/58. Retd SEC 26/1/63.
SAW A.J.A. BSc CEng MRAeS MIEE. Born 26/11/41. Commd 15/7/63. Sqn Ldr 1/1/72. Retd ENG 26/11/80.
SAWARD D. OBE. Born 6/6/13. Commd 28/7/34. Wg Cdr 8/10/43. Retd ENG 8/8/45. rtg Gp Capt.
SAWDEN D. Born 26/8/32. Commd 19/7/51. Sqn Ldr 1/1/63. Retd GD 9/4/84.
SAWLE THOMAS M.I. Born 12/8/43. Commd 12/7/63. Flt Lt 20/6/70. Retd GD 12/8/84.
SAWYER A. OBE. Born 6/11/48. Commd 5/11/70. Gp Capt 1/7/96. Retd GD 2/7/02.
SAWYER A.V. DFC. Born 28/12/12. Commd 16/12/33. Wg Cdr 28/10/43. Retd GD 13/8/46. rtg Gp Capt.
SAWYER D.J. MRAeS. Born 4/3/41. Commd 31/1/65. Flt Lt 31/1/65. Retd GD 30/10/82.
SAWYER G.P. MBE BEng. Born 31/10/65. Commd 11/6/93. Sqn Ldr 1/1/01. Retd FLY(P) 22/2/04.
SAWYER J.H. Born 20/7/21. Commd 22/11/43. Flt Lt 22/5/47. Retd GD 20/7/76.
SAWYER J.N. CBE. Born 29/10/34. Commd 5/4/55. Gp Capt 1/1/84. Retd GD 29/10/89.
SAWYER L.R. Born 24/8/34. Commd 10/9/52. Flt Lt 14/5/58. Retd GD 24/8/72.
SAWYER M.N. AFC. Born 16/12/37. Commd 18/1/56. Sqn Ldr 1/1/83. Retd GD 20/12/88.
SAWYER P.G. AFC. Born 15/4/27. Commd 20/10/49. Sqn Ldr 1/7/59. Retd GD 15/4/82.
SAWYER P.J. Born 28/1/35. Commd 13/12/55. Sqn Ldr 1/1/68. Retd GD 1/10/76.
SAWYER R. MBE. Born 4/6/26. Commd 27/8/59. Wg Cdr 1/7/75. Retd SUP 31/10/78.
SAWYER R.G. MA BSc MCMI. Born 15/3/36. Commd 22/11/57. Sqn Ldr 5/12/66. Retd EDN 1/10/78.
SAXBY G. BSc AIIP. Born 4/11/25. Commd 16/12/66. Sqn Ldr 13/2/72. Retd EDN 1/5/74.
SAXBY R.L. BSc. Born 26/3/35. Commd 20/12/57. Sqn Ldr 20/6/68. Retd EDN 12/9/73.
SAXTON D.W. MB ChB MRCOG. Born 4/6/52. Commd 16/7/74. Sqn Ldr 15/8/83. Retd MED 1/12/90.
SAXTON K.L.W. MBE MCMI. Born 25/2/28. Commd 28/7/60. Sqn Ldr 1/7/73. Retd ENG 16/4/76.
SAXTON P.J. BA. Born 6/8/47. Commd 1/1/67. Flt Lt 15/10/70. Retd GD 1/2/77.

SAY D.I. Born 3/11/47. Commd 7/7/67. Plt Offr 7/7/68. Retd GD 2/5/69.
SAYE J.G. Born 3/10/37. Commd 16/12/58. Gp Capt 1/1/82. Retd GD 21/1/90.
SAYER M.H.W. BSc CEng MIEE. Born 5/2/39. Commd 30/9/58. Sqn Ldr 7/4/72. Retd ENG 5/2/94.
SAYER M.J. FRIN. Born 17/8/43. Commd 9/3/62. Sqn Ldr 1/1/74. Retd GD 13/3/00.
SAYER R. Born 10/1/43. Commd 5/2/81. Sqn Ldr 1/7/89. Retd ADMIN 1/10/93.
SAYERS J.L. DFC*. Born 21/2/21. Commd 17/11/49. Sqn Ldr 1/1/69. Retd GD(G) 31/8/71.
SAYERS R.C. Born 23/7/38. Commd 6/8/60. Flt Lt 6/2/66. Retd GD 23/7/76.
SAYFRITZ H.V. Born 3/12/22. Commd 14/7/44. Wg Cdr 1/1/63. Retd GD 18/3/77.
SCALES E.J. Born 24/3/33. Commd 25/10/51. Sqn Ldr 1/1/71. Retd GD 31/5/84.
SCAMBLER J.A. FCMI. Born 8/7/32. Commd 26/3/52. Gp Capt 1/7/76. Retd GD 3/4/85.
SCAMMELL N.R. Born 14/1/47. Commd 1/8/69. Flt Lt 8/3/72. Retd GD 19/5/86.
SCAMMELLS J.R. Born 13/10/18. Commd 30/5/46. Flt Lt 4/1/51. Retd GD(G) 13/10/71. rtg Sqn Ldr.
SCANLON F.P. MSc BSc. Born 13/12/58. Commd 11/9/77. Sqn Ldr 1/1/90. Retd GD 13/5/00.
SCANLON J.T. CEng FCMI MRAeS. Born 22/3/22. Commd 21/10/42. Gp Capt 1/7/67. Retd ENG 22/3/77.
SCANNELL K.H.E. BSc. Born 2/6/55. Commd 5/2/84. Sqn Ldr 1/7/94. Retd ENG 23/2/02.
SCARD G.T. BA. Born 13/5/45. Commd 3/1/64. Wg Cdr 1/1/91. Retd GD 13/5/00.
SCARFF B.H. Born 9/11/20. Commd 24/2/43. Sqn Ldr 1/1/71. Retd GD 15/5/74.
SCARFFE M.G. Born 2/1/54. Commd 7/6/73. Sqn Ldr 1/1/90. Retd FLY(N) 14/12/04.
SCARGILL P.N. Born 23/1/50. Commd 27/2/70. Fg Offr 27/8/72. Retd SEC 4/1/75.
SCARLETT A.P. Born 22/11/46. Commd 28/7/67. Sqn Ldr 1/7/85. Retd SUP 18/9/90.
SCARLETT R. Born 8/9/29. Commd 18/9/50. Flt Lt 5/6/56. Retd GD 8/9/67.
SCARLETT R.W.J. Born 16/9/21. Commd 10/12/43. Sqn Ldr 1/1/67. Retd GD 7/4/73.
SCARRATT R.G. Born 13/4/21. Commd 31/7/58. Sqn Ldr 1/7/69. Retd SEC 1/10/71.
SCASE E.H. MBE. Born 22/7/38. Commd 27/9/73. Sqn Ldr 1/7/82. Retd ADMIN 23/7/88.
SCATES E.A. Born 19/1/23. Commd 5/5/60. Flt Lt 5/5/63. Retd GD(G) 19/1/78.
SCEATS J.M. Born 12/5/33. Commd 26/3/53. Flt Lt 26/9/57. Retd GD 12/5/71.
SCHAUER B.J.A. Born 6/5/32. Commd 23/10/56. Flt Lt 22/4/62. Retd GD 6/5/70.
SCHENK K.S.R. Born 23/9/68. Commd 10/5/90. Fg Offr 10/11/92. Retd ADMIN 14/3/97.
SCHIMMEL A.A. Born 8/4/51. Commd 22/7/71. Flt Lt 22/1/77. Retd GD 8/4/89.
SCHLUSSLER K.A. BE. Born 17/9/39. Commd 21/1/66. Flt Lt 24/11/69. Retd GD 20/7/75.
SCHOFIELD A.V. Born 11/5/35. Commd 11/3/68. Wg Cdr 1/1/87. Retd PRT 11/5/90.
SCHOFIELD B.S. Born 13/9/41. Commd 29/9/78. Sqn Ldr 1/1/90. Retd ADMIN 13/3/97.
SCHOFIELD J.F. Born 7/4/32. Commd 6/12/51. Flt Lt 27/3/57. Retd GD 7/4/45.
SCHOFIELD J.M. Born 14/1/54. Commd 9/8/79. Flt Lt 26/10/81. Retd SUP 14/1/92.
SCHOFIELD M.L. Born 6/3/45. Commd 19/6/64. Wg Cdr 1/1/85. Retd GD 6/3/89.
SCHOFIELD S.B. MSc BSc CEng MRAeS. Born 26/5/48. Commd 19/2/73. Air Cdre 1/7/00. Retd GD 26/5/03.
SCHOFIELD T.J. BSc(Eng). Born 9/5/60. Commd 18/3/84. Flt Lt 18/9/87. Retd RGT 11/5/90.
SCHOLEFIELD J.N. MCMI. Born 28/12/47. Commd 16/9/76. Wg Cdr 1/7/91. Retd ADMIN 1/5/98.
SCHOLES M. MBE DFM. Born 17/10/24. Commd 29/8/44. Wg Cdr 1/7/72. Retd ADMIN 25/3/78.
SCHOLLAR A.J. MCIPD. Born 17/1/35. Commd 2/2/56. Wg Cdr 1/7/75. Retd ADMIN 2/4/87.
SCHONER N.J. MSc BSc. Born 13/9/61. Commd 6/10/83. Flt Lt 22/7/88. Retd ENG 13/4/00.
SCHOOLING N.J. Born 14/3/35. Commd 16/1/72. Sqn Ldr 16/1/72. Retd SUP 16/1/88.
SCHRANZ P.J. FRCSEd(Orth) MRCS(Eng) LRCP. Born 23/2/58. Commd 15/2/79. Wg Cdr 1/8/95.
  Retd MED 30/11/96.
SCHROETER N.S. MMar MNI. Born 1/4/48. Commd 30/3/75. Flt Lt 30/3/75. Retd GD 14/12/96.
SCHUCK K. Born 6/3/21. Commd 1/12/44. Flt Lt 15/10/52. Retd GD 19/6/65.
SCHULKINS N.B. MBE BSc CEng MIMechE MRIN. Born 11/9/53. Commd 17/9/72. Sqn Ldr 1/1/88.
  Retd ENG 11/9/91.
SCHULMAN C.J. DFM. Born 9/8/17. Commd 12/1/43. Flt Lt 31/8/56. Retd GD(G) 19/2/69.
SCHULTZ K. BSc. Born 11/2/51. Commd 15/9/69. Sqn Ldr 1/1/87. Retd GD 3/1/89.
SCHWAIGER I.L. Born 24/5/30. Commd 1/8/51. Sqn Ldr 1/7/60. Retd GD 24/6/68.
SCHYNS M.G.B. Born 18/2/22. Commd 1/12/49. Flt Lt 20/3/61. Retd SEC 18/2/79.
SCOBBIE D.M. Born 8/7/38. Commd 15/9/60. Flt Lt 26/7/67. Retd GD 8/7/76.
SCOFFHAM P.D. AFC . Born 19/8/48. Commd 27/2/70. Gp Capt 1/1/98. Retd GD 19/8/03.
SCOFIELD K.H. BSc. Born 5/1/56. Commd 1/9/80. Flt Lt 12/12/82. Retd GD(G) 1/10/87.
SCOGGINS I.M. MA CEng MRAeS. Born 20/7/36. Commd 30/9/55. Sqn Ldr 1/7/67. Retd ENG 28/7/74.
SCORER L. DFC. Born 18/4/19. Commd 30/3/42. Flt Lt 19/6/52. Retd GD 25/5/62.
SCOREY A.T. Born 28/11/26. Commd 9/1/47. Flt Lt 17/3/57. Retd GD 15/1/67.
SCOTCHMER L.E.H. OBE. Born 29/10/23. Commd 14/5/43. Gp Capt 1/1/69. Retd GD 30/3/78.
SCOTHERN D. Born 4/1/42. Commd 10/3/77. Sqn Ldr 1/1/88. Retd ENG 4/1/97.
SCOTHERN M. CertEd. Born 20/9/45. Commd 12/10/78. Sqn Ldr 1/1/87. Retd ENG 3/4/97.
SCOTLAND A. MBE. Born 16/11/36. Commd 2/2/68. Sqn Ldr 1/7/76. Retd GD 1/5/87.
SCOTT A. MBE. Born 11/5/23. Commd 14/3/49. Sqn Ldr 1/1/73. Retd GD 11/5/83.
SCOTT A.D. BSc CEng MRAeS. Born 20/9/39. Commd 30/9/59. Flt Lt 15/4/66. Retd ENG 20/9/94.
SCOTT A.G. MBE. Born 26/11/21. Commd 26/11/43. Sqn Ldr 1/1/65. Retd GD(G) 1/1/71.
SCOTT A.G. CEng MIEE. Born 20/4/48. Commd 17/9/72. Sqn Ldr 1/7/80. Retd ENG 31/5/86.

SCOTT A.H. DFM. Born 27/7/21. Commd 13/3/43. Sqn Ldr 1/7/69. Retd GD(G) 27/7/76.
SCOTT A.M. Born 20/12/21. Commd 5/9/42. Flt Lt 3/10/48. Retd SEC 12/9/67.
SCOTT A.M.O. BA. Born 3/11/47. Commd 24/9/67. Wg Cdr 1/1/95. Retd GD 6/5/05.
SCOTT B.C. AFC. Born 27/12/51. Commd 24/6/71. Sqn Ldr 1/7/85. Retd GD 27/12/89.
SCOTT C. Born 18/3/39. Commd 11/8/77. Flt Lt 11/8/78. Retd ADMIN 28/11/88.
SCOTT C.F.S. Born 1/6/08. Commd 28/1/43. Flt Lt 2/9/45. Retd ENG 1/6/57.
SCOTT C.L.M. Born 31/5/27. Commd 27/7/49. Flt Lt 27/1/52. Retd GD 31/5/65.
SCOTT D.H. Born 7/7/36. Commd 17/12/57. Sqn Ldr 1/7/72. Retd GD 1/7/75.
SCOTT D.I. MBE FRIN FCMI. Born 24/7/32. Commd 19/4/51. Gp Capt 1/1/84. Retd GD 27/10/86.
SCOTT D.J. MA BA MB BChir MRCP DCH. Born 25/10/50. Commd 9/1/72. Wg Cdr 9/9/88. Retd MED 9/1/89.
SCOTT D.M. BA. Born 31/5/60. Commd 12/10/79. Sqn Ldr 1/1/92. Retd ADMIN 14/3/96.
SCOTT D.M. Born 20/10/21. Commd 27/1/43. Flt Offr 24/2/56. Retd SEC 5/8/62.
SCOTT D.N. BSc. Born 27/3/58. Commd 27/9/78. Flt Lt 15/4/81. Retd GD 30/9/00.
SCOTT D.R. DFC AFC. Born 12/7/21. Commd 7/9/43. Flt Lt 7/3/47. Retd GD 12/7/67.
SCOTT D.S. Born 21/4/20. Commd 4/11/43. Flt Lt 4/5/47. Retd ENG 1/12/64.
SCOTT D.W. MBE CEng MRAeS. Born 19/4/25. Commd 4/2/48. Wg Cdr 1/1/69. Retd ENG 12/4/79.
SCOTT E.J. Born 5/3/34. Commd 18/2/53. Sqn Ldr 1/7/81. Retd GD 15/4/87.
SCOTT F. MBE FCMI. Born 2/12/32. Commd 17/1/52. Gp Capt 1/7/76. Retd GD 4/4/80.
SCOTT G. Born 7/12/04. Commd 10/12/42. Flg Offr 10/12/42. Retd ENG 1/9/47. rtg Flt Lt.
SCOTT G. BSc. Born 10/3/37. Commd 22/1/59. Sqn Ldr 4/10/72. Retd EDN 10/3/75.
SCOTT H.C. MBE. Born 8/7/15. Commd 3/6/42. Sqn Ldr 1/1/56. Retd GD(G) 27/3/61.
SCOTT I.F. BA. Born 4/3/47. Commd 1/9/70. Flt Lt 1/6/71. Retd GD 1/9/82.
SCOTT I.G. ACMA. Born 16/3/33. Commd 20/6/63. Sqn Ldr 1/7/74. Retd ADMIN 1/11/77.
SCOTT I.L. Born 6/6/24. Commd 1/10/43. Sqn Ldr 1/1/56. Retd GD 6/6/62.
SCOTT I.P. Born 29/12/50. Commd 21/9/72. Flt Lt 21/3/78. Retd GD 29/12/88.
SCOTT I.W. Born 29/9/47. Commd 1/7/82. Flt Lt 1/7/84. Retd GD 1/7/91.
SCOTT J. MCIPS MCMI. Born 25/3/42. Commd 27/1/67. Wg Cdr 1/1/89. Retd SUP 25/3/97.
SCOTT J. Born 5/11/17. Commd 14/12/43. Flt Lt 10/11/55. Retd GD(G) 31/12/65.
SCOTT J.B. Born 14/8/65. Commd 28/7/95. Flt Lt 28/7/97. Retd ADMIN (TRG) 14/8/03.
SCOTT J.F.H. Born 11/3/22. Commd 22/4/45. Wg Cdr 1/1/72. Retd SUP 11/3/77.
SCOTT J.H.L. Born 26/1/44. Commd 28/9/62. Fg Offr 28/9/64. Retd GD 14/11/67.
SCOTT J.R. Born 28/7/28. Commd 8/5/50. Flt Lt 1/6/59. Retd GD 1/6/67.
SCOTT J.S. Born 5/1/13. Commd 18/12/43. Flt Lt 18/12/45. Retd GD 4/7/46.
SCOTT J.S.W. DPhysEd. Born 2/2/46. Commd 19/8/68. Sqn Ldr 1/1/88. Retd ADMIN 2/4/97.
SCOTT K.F. Born 12/3/22. Commd 21/6/56. Flt Lt 21/6/59. Retd GD 1/3/74. rtg Sqn Ldr.
SCOTT L. Born 14/9/21. Commd 20/4/50. Flt Lt 20/10/53. Retd GD 14/9/76.
SCOTT L.K. Born 7/11/47. Commd 29/3/68. Fg Offr 29/3/70. Retd GD 13/1/72.
SCOTT P. BEM. Born 17/4/17. Commd 11/4/57. Flt Lt 1/4/63. Retd ENG 17/4/72.
SCOTT P. Born 21/6/46. Commd 2/1/70. Flt Lt 2/7/76. Retd ADMIN 11/8/85.
SCOTT P.H.L. AFC. Born 27/2/24. Commd 21/1/45. A Cdre 1/1/73. Retd GD 29/3/77.
SCOTT P.J. MSc BSc. Born 24/1/58. Commd 5/9/76. Sqn Ldr 1/1/90. Retd ENG 7/4/01.
SCOTT P.J. CB MSc BSc CEng FIMechE FRAeS. Born 4/4/49. Commd 1/8/69. AVM 1/7/99. Retd GD 4/4/04.
SCOTT P.R. Born 24/4/58. Commd 11/6/81. Flt Lt 11/12/87. Retd GD(G) 9/2/97.
SCOTT R. Born 1/2/56. Commd 19/7/84. Flt Lt 13/5/87. Retd ADMIN 1/2/94.
SCOTT R.A. Born 30/12/35. Commd 12/12/59. Flt Lt 13/1/67. Retd GD 29/1/76.
SCOTT R.E. LLB. Born 17/1/58. Commd 31/8/75. Flt Lt 15/10/79. Retd GD 1/4/88.
SCOTT R.G. AFC. Born 13/2/32. Commd 14/1/60. Sqn Ldr 1/7/77. Retd GD 30/9/82.
SCOTT R.J. MA. Born 18/8/33. Commd 24/2/55. Sqn Ldr 18/2/63. Retd EDN 1/9/71.
SCOTT R.J.S. BA. Born 18/7/39. Commd 18/7/61. Sqn Ldr 1/7/80. Retd ENG 18/3/92.
SCOTT R.T.D. Born 25/5/22. Commd 20/7/50. Flt Lt 1/7/67. Retd GD 25/5/77.
SCOTT R.W. CEng MIMechE MRAeS. Born 17/12/37. Commd 23/7/58. Wg Cdr 1/7/77. Retd ENG 3/7/79.
SCOTT S. Born 23/2/56. Commd 9/5/91. Flt Lt 9/5/95. Retd ENG 1/10/99.
SCOTT T.F. CEng MIMechE. Born 3/9/37. Commd 2/5/66. Sqn Ldr 14/5/72. Retd ADMIN 2/5/76.
SCOTT T.I. BEM. Born 31/10/38. Commd 18/4/74. Sqn Ldr 1/1/84. Retd ENG 18/8/90.
SCOTT T.McM. BA MCMI. Born 12/3/34. Commd 5/9/69. Wg Cdr 1/7/85. Retd ADMIN 1/2/90.
SCOTT W.A. MBE. Born 21/10/18. Commd 9/8/45. Sqn Ldr 1/7/66. Retd SEC 9/6/73.
SCOTT W.J. BSc. Born 13/4/53. Commd 7/10/73. Sqn Ldr 1/7/87. Retd ADMIN 25/11/00.
SCOTT W.L. Born 26/3/55. Commd 25/9/83. Flt Lt 23/5/79. Retd GD 1/12/89.
SCOTT W.L.M. Born 16/3/24. Commd 12/11/43. Gp Capt 1/7/68. Retd GD 16/3/79.
SCOTT W.P. CEng MIEE. Born 23/3/40. Commd 15/7/63. Wg Cdr 1/1/78. Retd ENG 6/1/81.
SCOTT-NELSON R.J. Dip PE. Born 23/5/44. Commd 16/8/70. Flt Lt 16/8/74. Retd ADMIN 16/8/86.
SCOTT-SKINNER S.M. Born 7/2/51. Commd 16/3/73. Flt Lt 16/3/76. Retd GD 7/2/89.
SCOTTING P.A. Born 8/8/61. Commd 20/6/91. Flt Lt 20/6/93. Retd ADMIN 4/12/96.
SCOTTON A.H. Born 22/2/34. Commd 27/2/52. Flt Lt 26/6/57. Retd GD(G) 26/4/80.
SCOULLER D.C. AFC MRAeS. Born 9/4/35. Commd 30/7/57. Gp Capt 1/7/83. Retd GD 9/4/89.
SCOWEN B.J. DFC. Born 29/4/21. Commd 11/11/44. Wg Cdr 1/1/69. Retd GD 4/7/72.

SCRAGG W.A. Born 8/1/42. Commd 14/5/60. Sqn Ldr 1/7/91. Retd GD 8/1/97.
SCRANCHER P.J. Born 24/12/48. Commd 26/9/90. Flt Lt 26/9/92. Retd SUP 1/1/00.
SCREECH P.V. BA. Born 1/11/54. Commd 11/12/83. Sqn Ldr 1/1/92. Retd ADMIN 11/12/00.
SCRIMGEOUR D. McL CBE. Born 14/5/27. Commd 3/9/47. A Cdre 1/7/76. Retd GD 14/5/82.
SCRIMGEOUR J. MBE BEM. Born 12/2/20. Commd 23/2/50. Sqn Ldr 1/7/58. Retd SEC 31/8/68.
SCRIMSHAW K.A. Born 29/5/61. Commd 19/12/91. Fg Offr 19/6/94. Retd ADMIN 23/1/97.
SCRIVEN A.W. Born 4/11/29. Commd 19/6/70. Flt Lt 19/6/72. Retd SUP 4/11/87.
SCRIVENER F.M.H. Born 26/3/24. Commd 28/5/57. Sqn Ldr 1/7/69. Retd SUP 30/6/78.
SCRIVENER R.J. Born 8/3/44. Commd 29/11/63. Flt Lt 29/5/69. Retd GD 8/3/88.
SCRIVENS E.R. MCMI. Born 26/8/18. Commd 30/12/43. Sqn Ldr 1/1/62. Retd ENG 9/9/73.
SCROGGS T.W.M. Born 1/11/32. Commd 14/12/54. Flt Lt 14/12/59. Retd ADMIN 1/11/87.
SCULLION J.L. MCMI. Born 30/10/31. Commd 16/11/61. Wg Cdr 1/1/80. Retd ENG 29/4/83.
SCULLION P.J. MCMI. Born 7/4/45. Commd 21/1/73. Sqn Ldr 1/1/81. Retd ENG 14/3/97.
SCULLY J.M. MBE. Born 1/10/46. Commd 9/8/79. Sqn Ldr 1/1/89. Retd ENG 1/10/01.
SCUTT J.B. Born 20/4/20. Commd 9/7/59. Sqn Ldr 1/7/70. Retd ENG 30/4/73.
SEABOURNE E.W. DFC. Born 26/8/19. Commd 12/8/41. Sqn Ldr 1/8/47. Retd SEC 2/12/60.
SEABROOK G.L. CB FCA. Born 25/8/09. Commd 7/6/33. AVM 1/1/64. Retd SEC 29/6/66.
SEABROOK S.E. Born 5/2/22. Commd 5/5/60. Sqn Ldr 1/7/70. Retd ENG 9/9/72.
SEABY E.W. ACIS. Born 25/4/38. Commd 6/9/68. Flt Lt 6/9/70. Retd ADMIN 6/9/76.
SEAGER K.D. Born 13/12/63. Commd 24/3/83. Flt Lt 24/9/88. Retd GD 14/3/96.
SEAL C.T. BPharm. Born 29/2/64. Commd 11/10/87. Sqn Ldr 1/7/00. Retd FLY(P) 7/1/05.
SEALE D.R. MCMI. Born 14/4/32. Commd 24/1/52. Wg Cdr 1/1/75. Retd GD 5/11/85.
SEALEY A.D. Born 4/2/69. Commd 2/11/88. Flt Lt 2/5/94. Retd GD 30/3/00.
SEALEY H.G. MVO. Born 9/2/26. Commd 10/2/52. Sqn Ldr 1/7/67. Retd GD 8/5/76.
SEALY J.L. Born 4/6/39. Commd 18/8/61. Fg Offr 18/8/63. Retd GD 25/9/65.
SEAMAN G. Born 27/4/41. Commd 24/4/77. Flt Lt 21/4/80. Retd GD 22/4/94.
SEAR D.A. Born 13/7/21. Commd 18/11/54. Sqn Ldr 1/7/66. Retd ENG 13/1/77.
SEARLE J.F. BSc CEng MIMechE. Born 13/8/43. Commd 29/8/72. Sqn Ldr 1/7/90. Retd ENG 31/3/94.
SEARLE N.F. MRAeS. Born 19/2/20. Commd 23/9/43. Wg Cdr 1/1/61. Retd ENG 4/5/68.
SEARLE P.E. Born 6/4/43. Commd 4/3/71. Sqn Ldr 1/7/79. Retd SUP 6/4/98.
SEARLE R.E. Born 1/6/46. Commd 22/7/71. Sqn Ldr 1/7/80. Retd ENG 1/6/90.
SEARLE R.J. CEng MRAeS. Born 18/3/36. Commd 25/2/64. Sqn Ldr 1/7/81. Retd ENG 21/3/90.
SEARLE R.W. Born 3/5/46. Commd 5/3/65. Flt Lt 5/9/70. Retd GD 1/1/80.
SEARS R.H. Born 27/11/44. Commd 2/2/84. Sqn Ldr 1/1/93. Retd ADMIN 27/11/99.
SEARS R.W. Born 25/2/48. Commd 28/2/69. Sqn Ldr 1/7/85. Retd GD 25/2/89.
SEATON C.M. Born 19/11/44. Commd 26/4/84. Flt Lt 1/3/87. Retd GD 22/6/99.
SEATON D.H. DFC AFC*. Born 19/5/21. Commd 20/8/41. Gp Capt 1/7/60. Retd GD 20/5/64.
SEATON D.J. MBE. Born 8/8/45. Commd 7/6/68. Sqn Ldr 1/7/81. Retd ENG 8/6/97.
SEATON D.J. BSc. Born 18/4/53. Commd 30/8/78. Sqn Ldr 1/1/89. Retd ENG 30/8/94.
SEAWARD G.L. Born 29/9/48. Commd 27/7/72. Wg Cdr 1/1/02. Retd GD 30/6/04.
SEAWARD P.V.A. DMS MRIN MCMI. Born 17/9/46. Commd 16/12/66. Flt Lt 25/2/73. Retd ADMIN 17/9/84.
    Re-entered 21/7/86. Flt Lt 28/12/74. Retd ADMIN 17/9/01.
SEAWARD P.V.A. MRIN MCMI. Born 17/9/46. Commd 16/12/66. Flt Lt 25/2/73. Retd ADMIN 17/9/84.
SEBLEY T.P.H. Born 7/11/50. Commd 4/3/71. Sqn Ldr 1/7/86. Retd SY 14/9/96.
SEBRIGHT A.L. Born 20/5/32. Commd 28/6/51. Sqn Ldr 1/1/64. Retd GD 12/11/76.
SECKER J.C. Born 12/12/50. Commd 3/11/77. Wg Cdr 1/7/92. Retd GD 8/4/05.
SECKER R.L. Born 22/8/12. Commd 18/10/43. Flt Lt 18/4/47. Retd ENG 23/9/55.
SEDDON H. Born 6/3/50. Commd 4/5/72. Sqn Ldr 1/1/93. Retd GD 14/9/96.
SEDGLEY B.A. Born 17/4/25. Commd 24/1/52. Flt Lt 18/8/57. Retd GD 17/4/63.
SEDGWICK P.A. BSc. Born 18/2/39. Commd 1/10/62. Sqn Ldr 1/7/71. Retd GD 1/10/78.
SEDMAN D.M. Born 10/4/45. Commd 10/12/65. Wg Cdr 1/7/91. Retd GD 10/4/00.
SEEGER J.E.R. Born 21/6/42. Commd 24/3/61. Flt Lt 24/9/66. Retd GD 30/1/73.
SEEKINGS M.R.J. Born 23/9/33. Commd 9/4/57. Flt Lt 9/4/62. Retd SEC 15/2/68.
SEELEY A.H. Born 20/9/31. Commd 30/7/52. Flt Lt 27/12/57. Retd GD 20/9/69.
SEFTON J. Born 23/1/49. Commd 31/7/70. Flt Lt 31/7/73. Retd GD 22/10/94.
SEGGER W.M. Born 5/12/13. Commd 22/9/41. Fg Offr 29/9/45. Retd SUP 18/1/63. rtg Sqn Offr.
SEIDELIN R. MA DM BCh MRCP DPM. Born 24/1/24. Commd 29/9/50. Wg Cdr 13/12/60. Retd MED 13/12/68.
SELBY F. Born 4/3/29. Commd 17/5/51. Flt Lt 6/9/56. Retd GD 4/3/67.
SELBY M.J. Born 24/1/47. Commd 28/11/69. Wg Cdr 1/1/90. Retd GD 14/3/96.
SELBY R.C. MCIPS MCMI. Born 13/4/32. Commd 17/5/62. Sqn Ldr 1/7/73. Retd SUP 3/10/78.
SELBY-DAVIES R. BA. Born 9/9/42. Commd 13/6/71. Flt Lt 13/3/75. Retd OPS SPT 9/9/97.
SELBY-GREEN A.G. Born 19/1/59. Commd 17/9/84. Flt Lt 19/7/86. Retd GD 6/9/89.
SELDON F.P. Born 18/1/58. Commd 15/2/90. Flt Lt 15/2/92. Retd OPS SPT 28/7/98.
SELDON J.L. MA MSc MTech. Born 4/12/35. Commd 25/9/54. Sqn Ldr 1/1/69. Retd ENG 4/12/73.
SELDON P.R. Born 15/7/32. Commd 6/12/51. Flt Lt 27/3/57. Retd GD 15/7/87.
SELDON R.J.B. Born 11/9/30. Commd 21/4/54. Flt Lt 16/8/61. Retd RGT 22/5/70.

SELF A.W. MSc. Born 14/3/42. Commd 9/3/72. Sqn Ldr 15/10/80. Retd ADMIN 2/10/84.
SELF F.J.A. MA. Born 26/6/56. Commd 15/10/78. Flt Lt 15/10/84. Retd ADMIN 15/10/86.
SELLAR J.C. BDS. Born 15/4/47. Commd 18/12/67. Sqn Ldr 23/12/74. Retd DEL 1/10/76.
SELLARS N.A. Born 4/1/20. Commd 29/11/37. Wg Cdr 1/7/55. Retd GD 1/10/68.
SELLARS R.J. MHCIMA. Born 10/4/33. Commd 17/1/52. Sqn Ldr 1/7/73. Retd ADMIN 1/7/76.
SELLER M.A.E. Born 8/2/40. Commd 13/10/61. Wg Cdr 1/1/81. Retd GD 26/10/90.
SELLERS B. BSc CEng MIMechE MRAeS MCMI. Born 30/12/38. Commd 30/9/57. Sqn Ldr 1/7/71.
    Retd ENG 30/9/80.
SELVARAJAH G. Born 21/1/41. Commd 29/12/69. Flt Lt 29/12/69. Retd GD(G) 21/1/96.
SELVARATNAM S. CEng MIEE MRAeS MCMI AMIMechE. Born 25/9/44. Commd 13/4/80. Sqn Ldr 1/1/89.
    Retd ENG 14/3/97.
SELVES M.J. Born 27/7/46. Commd 8/1/65. Flt Lt 8/7/70. Retd GD 27/7/85.
SELWAY A.D.M. Born 8/8/48. Commd 27/3/70. Fg Offr 13/8/72. Retd SY 10/7/76.
SEMARK A.M. Born 22/11/42. Commd 6/7/62. Flt Lt 1/7/68. Retd GD 22/11/80.
SEMPLE A.W. Born 14/10/44. Commd 3/3/67. Wg Cdr 1/1/91. Retd GD 10/10/00.
SEMPLE I. Born 22/11/35. Commd 14/7/54. Gp Capt 1/7/85. Retd GD 31/7/89.
SEMPLE N. Born 3/9/46. Commd 26/5/67. Flt Lt 18/8/72. Retd ENG 3/10/78.
SENIOR G.G. BA. Born 29/10/49. Commd 12/8/79. Flt Lt 12/8/81. Retd ADMIN 12/8/89.
SENIOR J.A. Born 9/6/20. Commd 29/8/45. Flt Lt 30/11/60. Retd RGT 9/6/65.
SENIOR J.E. BSc. Born 17/1/46. Commd 28/9/64. Flt Lt 15/10/69. Retd GD 17/1/84.
SENIOR R. Born 10/2/29. Commd 12/9/51. Sqn Ldr 1/7/77. Retd GD 10/2/84.
SENIOR S.E. MBE. Born 10/4/60. Commd 13/8/82. Sqn Ldr 1/7/93. Retd ADMIN 12/4/98.
SENTANCE G.A. MBE FCIS FCCS MCMI. Born 29/6/15. Commd 21/11/41. Wg Cdr 1/1/59. Retd SEC 3/4/68.
SEPHTON A.J. BSc. Born 13/1/50. Commd 15/9/69. Flt Lt 15/4/74. Retd GD 1/7/89.
SEPPINGS C.E. Born 21/6/21. Commd 18/9/47. Flt Lt 1/1/55. Retd PRT 31/8/63.
SERCOMBE C.B. Born 14/10/24. Commd 14/4/49. Flt Lt 14/10/52. Retd GD 31/1/62.
SERCOMBE S.P.R. Born 15/6/20. Commd 4/11/44. Flt Lt 5/11/58. Retd SEC 2/7/75.
SERGEANT R.E. Born 8/11/41. Commd 4/11/82. Sqn Ldr 1/1/92. Retd ENG 8/11/96.
SERRELL-COOKE J. MCMI. Born 9/7/34. Commd 14/12/54. Sqn Ldr 1/1/79. Retd ADMIN 14/9/84.
SEVERN J.G. Born 15/9/17. Commd 17/5/56. Flt Lt 17/5/62. Retd SUP 30/5/70.
SEVERN P.J. Born 4/12/42. Commd 10/11/61. Flt Lt 26/7/67. Retd GD 1/7/77.
SEVERNE Sir John KCVO OBE AFC DL. Born 15/8/25. Commd 19/10/45. AVM 1/7/78. Retd GD 15/8/80.
SEVERS A.D. Born 12/4/65. Commd 15/3/84. Flt Lt 15/9/89. Retd GD 14/3/96.
SEVIOUR C.D. BSc. Born 29/7/48. Commd 13/12/68. Sqn Ldr 1/7/83. Retd ENGINEER 29/7/03.
SEWARD D.J. AFC CCMI. Born 25/1/31. Commd 25/10/50. Gp Capt 1/7/79. Retd GD 25/1/81.
SEWARD R.F. Born 12/2/53. Commd 21/6/90. Flt Lt 21/6/94. Retd ENG 14/9/96.
SEWART A. Born 21/1/19. Commd 26/4/45. Flt Lt 26/10/49. Retd GD(G) 1/12/63. rtg Sqn Ldr.
SEWELL E.F.W. Born 10/1/21. Commd 6/2/44. Flt Lt 7/6/51. Retd GD 19/7/55.
SEWELL J. BA FRGS. Born 14/6/40. Commd 14/5/62. Wg Cdr 1/7/87. Retd GD 6/12/92.
SEWELL J.E. MBE MCMI. Born 4/2/28. Commd 9/8/51. Wg Cdr 1/1/67. Retd GD 8/4/78. rtg Gp Capt.
SEWELL M.K. DFC AFC. Born 22/3/14. Commd 4/6/38. Wg Cdr 1/7/47. Retd GD 4/4/61.
SEXSTONE C.L. Born 2/7/48. Commd 13/2/72. Gp Capt 1/7/94. Retd ADMIN 14/9/96.
SEXTON K.R.F. MBE CEng MIProdE MRAeS. Born 17/10/37. Commd 9/2/66. Sqn Ldr 1/1/77. Retd ENG 24/12/91.
SEYD M.V. Born 25/10/40. Commd 18/12/62. Flt Lt 26/7/67. Retd GD 25/10/78.
SEYMOUR A.C.P. Born 1/11/39. Commd 28/3/63. A Cdre 1/7/90. Retd SY 1/1/94.
SEYMOUR C.C.B. Born 12/9/38. Commd 21/8/62. Wg Cdr 1/1/80. Retd GD 14/9/92.
SEYMOUR C.R. Born 1/7/45. Commd 3/3/67. Wg Cdr 1/7/86. Retd SUP 1/7/89.
SEYMOUR D.W. Born 29/4/37. Commd 29/8/60. Sqn Ldr 1/3/71. Retd ADMIN 29/4/92.
SEYMOUR J.M. Born 17/8/39. Commd 9/4/72. Flt Lt 9/10/76. Retd ADMIN 9/4/88.
SEYMOUR P.J. OBE FCMI. Born 26/5/43. Commd 24/6/65. Gp Capt 1/1/90. Retd ADMIN 22/4/94.
SEYMOUR-COOKE T.C. DFC AFC DFM. Born 23/7/21. Commd 2/8/41. Flt Lt 22/10/47. Retd GD 19/7/52. rtg Sqn Ldr.
SHACKELL J.M. Born 6/5/53. Commd 14/12/72. Wg Cdr 1/1/94. Retd OPS SPT 1/2/01.
SHACKLETON J. Born 15/6/20. Commd 24/5/51. Flt Lt 24/11/55. Retd GD(G) 20/6/62.
SHACKLEY G.J. MSc BSc CEng MIEE. Born 9/4/45. Commd 6/9/81. Sqn Ldr 1/1/90. Retd ENG 6/9/97.
SHADBOLT B.M. Born 26/10/37. Commd 3/7/56. Flt Lt 3/1/62. Retd GD 1/8/64.
SHAFE A.C. AFC. Born 15/3/22. Commd 16/3/44. Sqn Ldr 1/7/68. Retd GD 13/5/77.
SHAKESPEAR J.G.W. Born 13/7/20. Commd 20/6/56. Flt Lt 20/6/56. Retd SEC 1/12/63. Re-employed 29/4/71 to
    13/7/75.
SHAKESPEARE R. Born 8/3/30. Commd 23/10/62. Sqn Ldr 23/10/67. Retd EDN 23/10/78.
SHALLCROSS P.S. Born 24/8/28. Commd 13/2/64. Flt Lt 13/2/69. Retd ENG 21/4/76.
SHAMBROOK P. BEng. Born 14/12/56. Commd 2/8/85. Flt Lt 15/7/88. Retd ENG 14/12/94.
SHANAHAN D.W. DFC. Born 4/6/20. Commd 25/6/42. Flt Lt 28/1/46. Retd GD 8/7/63.
SHANKLAND D. Born 7/8/46. Commd 12/2/68. Sqn Ldr 1/7/96. Retd GD 2/4/01.
SHANKS C.J.A. Born 22/1/52. Commd 4/2/71. Flt Lt 4/8/76. Retd GD 22/4/89.
SHANKS C.R. DFC. Born 10/4/20. Commd 16/6/44. Flt Lt 13/3/51. Retd GD 28/9/68.
SHANNON D.M. OBE. Born 18/2/45. Commd 28/4/65. Gp Capt 1/1/95. Retd GD 28/2/00.

SHANNON H. DFC. Born 9/11/18. Commd 27/7/40. Sqn Ldr 1/1/53. Retd GD 12/12/57.
SHANNON M.S. MEd BSc. Born 28/6/38. Commd 31/12/63. Sqn Ldr 1/3/71. Retd ADMIN 14/8/82.
SHANNON T.S. BSc. Born 30/9/60. Commd 2/9/79. Sqn Ldr 1/1/92. Retd ENG 30/9/98.
SHAPLAND J.A. BA. Born 25/11/65. Commd 14/6/86. Flt Lt 15/1/90. Retd GD 14/3/96.
SHARKEY J.B. BA. Born 23/8/42. Commd 19/9/71. Wg Cdr 1/1/89. Retd SUP 19/9/93.
SHARLAND R.E. Born 19/11/65. Commd 17/7/87. Flt Lt 17/1/94. Retd OPS SPT(FC) 2/4/04.
SHARMA A. MB ChB DTM&H. Born 14/10/51. Commd 31/3/88. Wg Cdr 28/9/90. Retd MED 29/10/96.
SHARMA R.K. Born 7/12/39. Commd 29/11/63. Flt Lt 29/5/69. Retd GD 13/8/79.
SHARMAN A.J. AFC. Born 5/2/24. Commd 1/10/43. Sqn Ldr 1/7/54. Retd GD 13/10/59.
SHARMAN M.R. Born 13/11/51. Commd 29/4/71. Flt Lt 29/10/76. Retd GD 14/4/89.
SHARMAN P.B. Born 12/11/44. Commd 26/5/67. Sqn Ldr 1/1/84. Retd FLY(P) 31/3/05.
SHARMAN P.R. BSc. Born 19/10/64. Commd 22/1/87. Sqn Ldr 1/7/00. Retd FLY(P) 30/6/04.
SHARP A.L. MCMI. Born 27/5/22. Commd 10/8/43. Wg Cdr 1/1/62. Retd SEC 28/9/68.
SHARP A.T. BA. Born 10/3/18. Commd 5/10/53. Flt Lt 13/11/57. Retd PI 10/3/73.
SHARP C. MSc MB BS MRCGP MRCP MRCS DCH DAvMed AFOM MRAeS. Born 5/3/52. Commd 29/10/78.
    Wg Cdr 5/4/89. Retd MED 23/7/95.
SHARP D.J. AFC BSc. Born 23/10/45. Commd 2/4/65. Sqn Ldr 1/1/83. Retd GD 23/10/00.
SHARP E. Born 23/12/32. Commd 27/9/51. Flt Lt 11/1/57. Retd GD 30/6/73.
SHARP F. Born 24/5/25. Commd 29/4/57. Flt Lt 29/4/57. Retd GD 19/5/69.
SHARP G.R. PhD MB ChB. Born 11/4/35. Commd 30/9/62. Wg Cdr 30/9/72. Retd MED 16/3/82.
SHARP J.A.H. Born 25/8/52. Commd 19/3/78. Wg Cdr 1/1/96. Retd ENG 1/5/98.
SHARP J.S. BEng. Born 9/6/57. Commd 16/9/84. Flt Lt 11/10/86. Retd ENG 9/6/95.
SHARP J.T. Born 11/5/29. Commd 21/11/51. Sqn Ldr 1/1/77. Retd GD 11/5/84.
SHARP K.G. DSC. Born 25/1/13. Commd 23/12/35. Sqn Ldr 1/1/61. Retd SEC 30/4/63.
SHARP P.A. Born 6/10/54. Commd 1/9/92. Flt Lt 27/1/95. Retd MED(T) 14/9/96.
SHARP P.E. CEng MIEE. Born 6/9/40. Commd 7/3/65. Sqn Ldr 1/7/78. Retd ENG 1/7/81.
SHARP R.J. Born 15/12/47. Commd 31/7/70. Gp Capt 1/1/95. Retd GD 1/11/96.
SHARP W.T.H. Born 2/2/10. Commd 22/2/42. Sqn Ldr 1/1/51. Retd CAT 22/2/59. rtg Wg Cdr.
SHARPE C.D. Born 3/11/31. Commd 30/7/52. Sqn Ldr 1/7/61. Retd GD 24/6/66.
SHARPE C.E. BA. Born 15/1/58. Commd 28/12/80. Flt Lt 28/12/86. Retd ADMIN 28/12/88. Re-entered 4/7/89.
    Flt Lt 28/6/84. Retd ADMIN 13/10/96.
SHARPE D.E. Born 24/6/23. Commd 27/2/44. Flt Lt 27/8/47. Retd ENG 24/7/61.
SHARPE D.E. Born 8/5/41. Commd 19/6/70. Flt Lt 19/6/72. Retd ENG 1/10/84.
SHARPE D.I. Born 20/4/58. Commd 29/11/81. Sqn Ldr 1/1/90. Retd ENG 29/11/97.
SHARPE D.R. BSc. Born 9/6/57. Commd 13/5/76. Flt Lt 15/10/81. Retd ENG 20/7/90.
SHARPE G.C. BA. Born 18/10/44. Commd 23/3/67. Flt Lt 23/9/72. Retd GD 18/10/82.
SHARPE G.M. MA CEng MIEE MRAeS MCMI. Born 21/4/38. Commd 30/9/58. Sqn Ldr 1/1/95. Retd ENG 21/4/96.
SHARPE H.C. BEM. Born 15/9/19. Commd 29/1/43. Flt Lt 7/6/51. Retd GD(G) 1/4/65.
SHARPE J.H. MBE MRAeS MCMI. Born 11/10/42. Commd 27/3/80. Sqn Ldr 1/7/88. Retd ADMIN 11/10/02.
SHARPE K.A. Born 9/10/20. Commd 29/4/43. Sqn Ldr 1/7/54. Retd ENG 4/1/64.
SHARPE M.C. Born 10/1/42. Commd 27/1/61. Sqn Ldr 1/7/74. Retd GD 10/1/97.
SHARPE M.F. Born 2/10/36. Commd 13/2/60. Sqn Ldr 1/7/71. Retd ADMIN 1/10/87.
SHARPE S.D. Born 26/4/32. Commd 2/5/69. Sqn Ldr 1/7/77. Retd GD(G) 1/5/82.
SHARPE W.G.D. Born 7/4/29. Commd 21/5/52. Flt Lt 16/10/57. Retd GD 30/10/67.
SHARPLES D. BA MCIPD MCMI. Born 1/7/41. Commd 22/2/71. Wg Cdr 1/7/88. Retd SY 1/7/96.
SHARPLES E.J. Born 21/9/23. Commd 15/2/45. Sqn Ldr 1/7/70. Retd GD 21/9/78.
SHARRATT J.G. Born 4/2/17. Commd 18/6/42. Sqn Ldr 1/7/52. Retd SEC 4/2/72.
SHATFORD W.F. Born 28/2/48. Commd 15/2/90. Flt Lt 15/2/94. Retd ENGINEER 28/2/03.
SHAW A. Born 28/12/41. Commd 4/7/64. Sqn Ldr 1/7/87. Retd GD 28/12/96.
SHAW A.G. BSc(Eng) CEng MIEE. Born 6/8/40. Commd 30/9/59. Gp Capt 1/7/91. Retd ENG 6/8/95.
SHAW A.G. Born 24/8/33. Commd 4/7/64. Sqn Ldr 4/7/71. Retd EDN 4/7/73.
SHAW A.T. Born 21/9/23. Commd 19/5/49. Sqn Ldr 1/7/62. Retd GD 30/6/78.
SHAW B. MSc BSc CEng MIMechE MRAeS MCMI. Born 1/4/51. Commd 15/9/69. Sqn Ldr 1/1/85.
    Retd ENG 1/5/90.
SHAW B.W.B. MA DCAe CEng MIMechE MRAeS. Born 22/2/27. Commd 5/11/52. Sqn Ldr 1/1/62.
    Retd ENG 5/11/68.
SHAW C.F. Born 4/8/43. Commd 29/8/72. Wg Cdr 1/1/96. Retd ADMIN 14/9/96.
SHAW C.J. BSc(Eng). Born 7/11/34. Commd 26/9/53. Sqn Ldr 1/7/70. Retd ENG 27/1/86.
SHAW C.P. BSc. Born 25/5/44. Commd 17/7/64. Flt Lt 17/3/71. Retd GD 25/5/82.
SHAW D. BA. Born 19/10/36. Commd 20/9/60. Sqn Ldr 20/3/69. Retd ADMIN 20/9/76.
SHAW D.A. BSc CEng MRAeS. Born 7/6/53. Commd 3/10/76. Sqn Ldr 1/7/91. Retd ENG 3/10/98.
SHAW D.C. Born 11/3/23. Commd 13/3/46. Flt Lt 4/6/54. Retd GD 25/9/66.
SHAW D.S. OBE. Born 14/4/42. Commd 21/10/66. Sqn Ldr 1/1/84. Retd GD 1/12/86.
SHAW E.J. AFC. Born 28/4/26. Commd 25/10/46. Wg Cdr 1/1/78. Retd GD 1/5/80.
SHAW G.A. BSc. Born 12/7/61. Commd 16/10/80. Sqn Ldr 1/7/91. Retd ADMIN 14/3/96.
SHAW H.F. Born 28/2/22. Commd 27/1/44. Wg Cdr 1/1/65. Retd GD(G) 10/8/73.

SHAW H.J. Born 2/1/33. Commd 9/8/51. Sqn Ldr 1/7/67. Retd GD 24/4/76.
SHAW J. Born 6/7/28. Commd 13/2/52. Flt Lt 13/11/56. Retd GD 6/7/66.
SHAW J.C. Born 27/7/16. Commd 8/10/42. Sqn Ldr 1/7/59. Retd ENG 13/8/66.
SHAW J.L. MBE. Born 4/6/33. Commd 3/8/61. Sqn Ldr 1/7/79. Retd GD 4/6/88.
SHAW K.D. MBE MSc FCIS. Born 22/11/47. Commd 11/11/71. Wg Cdr 1/7/88. Retd ADMIN 2/4/96.
SHAW K.G. Born 3/7/23. Commd 24/9/44. Flt Lt 7/6/51. Retd GD 4/9/62.
SHAW K.W. Born 11/8/55. Commd 24/7/81. Flt Lt 24/7/83. Retd GD 1/12/95.
SHAW M. CEng MRAeS. Born 8/3/36. Commd 24/7/57. Flt Lt 6/3/63. Retd ENG 1/10/77.
SHAW M. BA. Born 18/9/33. Commd 9/8/57. Sqn Ldr 9/2/67. Retd ADMIN 26/11/85.
SHAW M.J.F. CBE. Born 11/4/37. Commd 28/7/59. Gp Capt 1/7/79. Retd GD 6/4/92.
SHAW M.P.G.L. Born 16/12/41. Commd 18/12/62. Sqn Ldr 1/7/77. Retd GD 1/11/80.
SHAW P.A.T. Born 8/12/35. Commd 17/3/67. Flt Lt 17/3/69. Retd GD 30/8/75.
SHAW P.J. BSc. Born 20/5/50. Commd 22/8/71. Sqn Ldr 1/7/86. Retd ADMIN 1/7/89.
SHAW P.R. Born 13/5/60. Commd 26/11/81. Flt Lt 26/5/87. Retd GD 1/4/90.
SHAW P.W. Born 5/7/24. Commd 1/10/43. Sqn Ldr 1/1/58. Retd GD 1/6/68.
SHAW R.H. DFC. Born 6/7/12. Commd 23/7/32. Gp Capt 1/1/52. Retd GD 18/3/54.
SHAW S. Born 16/11/35. Commd 1/10/62. Flt Lt 1/4/68. Retd GD 25/2/72.
SHAW T.J.H. BSc CEng MIMechE. Born 15/12/45. Commd 1/10/70. Sqn Ldr 1/7/83. Retd ENG 15/12/00.
SHAW W. Born 1/8/14. Commd 24/10/46. Fg Offr 24/10/47. Retd ENG 27/1/48.
SHAW CLOSE C.C. BA. Born 22/1/22. Commd 23/10/51. Sqn Ldr 23/8/58. Retd EDN 28/4/64.
SHAWE M.P. Born 6/3/25. Commd 4/2/48. Sqn Ldr 1/7/65. Retd RGT 6/3/80.
SHEARD M.J.B. BSc. Born 21/8/65. Commd 26/1/98. Flt Lt 11/4/89. Retd FLY(P) 11/10/03.
SHEARD M.S. MSc BSc CEng MIEE. Born 16/11/62. Commd 13/9/81. Wg Cdr 1/1/97. Retd ENG 16/11/00.
SHEARDOWN R.D. OBE. Born 8/10/11. Commd 3/6/41. Sqn Ldr 1/7/53. Retd SEC 9/8/58.
SHEARER R. DPhysEd. Born 13/7/30. Commd 2/1/52. Flt Lt 13/7/56. Retd PE 13/7/68.
SHEARER R.A. MA BSc CEng MRAeS MCMI MIEE. Born 20/8/58. Commd 5/9/76. Gp Capt 1/7/02. Retd GD 15/9/04.
SHEARER T. Born 11/5/51. Commd 4/5/72. Sqn Ldr 1/7/86. Retd SY(RGT) 1/7/89.
SHEARMAN A. Born 1/9/59. Commd 20/3/90. Flt Lt 29/3/92. Retd SUP 13/9/96.
SHEARN M.R. BSc. Born 22/9/47. Commd 13/9/70. Sqn Ldr 15/1/79. Retd ADMIN 13/9/86.
SHEARS A.J. MBE . Born 21/5/49. Commd 29/7/83. Wg Cdr 1/7/01. Retd GD 21/5/04.
SHEARS P.E. BSc. Born 9/4/66. Commd 15/9/86. Flt Lt 15/1/93. Retd ADMIN 14/9/96.
SHEARS P.M. BEng MRAeS. Born 14/4/64. Commd 3/9/89. Sqn Ldr 1/1/00. Retd ENG 1/1/03.
SHEARWOOD M. AIIP. Born 17/8/39. Commd 4/7/66. Flt Lt 4/7/72. Retd ENG 4/7/82.
SHEASBY R.K. Born 13/1/38. Commd 22/1/57. Flt Lt 15/8/62. Retd GD 1/2/79.
SHEATH J.M. Born 16/3/38. Commd 4/6/64. Sqn Ldr 1/1/81. Retd GD 1/1/86.
SHEATH N.T. Born 11/1/63. Commd 8/4/82. Flt Lt 8/10/87. Retd GD 22/6/02.
SHEDDEN J. The Rev. CBE BD. Born 23/6/43. Commd 3/3/86. Retd Gp Capt 23/6/98.
SHEEHAN A.J. MB BS FRCS DLO. Born 19/1/34. Commd 7/3/63. Wg Cdr 1/2/74. Retd MED 6/1/81.
SHEEHAN M.J. Born 1/2/40. Commd 22/5/70. Wg Cdr 1/1/90. Retd MED(SEC) 1/11/93.
SHEEHAN W.J.L. DFC MRAeS MCMI. Born 7/6/21. Commd 25/7/44. Wg Cdr 1/7/61. Retd GD 29/9/72.
SHEELEY G.J. Born 26/7/53. Commd 14/7/77. Flt Lt 14/1/82. Retd GD 14/9/85.
SHEELEY I.M. Born 21/3/57. Commd 14/7/77. Wg Cdr 1/7/96. Retd OPS SPT 21/3/01.
SHEEN D.J. Born 18/10/41. Commd 28/4/61. Flt Lt 26/7/67. Retd GD 18/10/79.
SHEFFIELD C.J. Born 12/6/45. Commd 11/10/84. Flt Lt 11/10/88. Retd ENG 12/6/00.
SHEFFIELD I.V. Born 15/9/46. Commd 7/1/71. Fg Offr 7/1/73. Retd GD 22/7/75.
SHEFFIELD R.J. Born 6/4/47. Commd 11/4/85. Flt Lt 11/4/89. Retd GD(G) 14/3/96.
SHEILD H.J. DFC*. Born 30/9/16. Commd 1/9/45. Sqn Ldr 1/7/49. Retd GD 30/9/58.
SHELBOURN R.J. Born 7/12/46. Commd 12/7/68. Flt Lt 12/1/72. Retd GD 4/4/78.
SHELDON J.G. BSc(Econ). Born 28/11/36. Commd 2/10/58. Gp Capt 1/7/87. Retd GD 29/7/94.
SHELDON K.J. Born 8/8/45. Commd 1/12/77. Sqn Ldr 1/1/90. Retd ADMIN 8/8/00.
SHELDON K.J. MB ChB MRCGP DOcc Med. Born 22/5/61. Commd 14/2/90. Wg Cdr 9/9/98. Retd MEDICAL 19/3/04.
SHELDON M. Born 14/12/61. Commd 23/4/87. Sqn Ldr 1/1/99. Retd FLY(P) 1/7/03.
SHELDRAKE R.J. BSc. Born 30/1/49. Commd 1/11/71. Flt Lt 1/8/75. Retd ENG 1/11/87.
SHELL K.E. BSc CEng MRAeS. Born 20/10/45. Commd 26/5/67. Sqn Ldr 1/7/79. Retd ENG 20/10/89.
SHELLEY D. Born 20/10/21. Commd 30/11/50. Wg Cdr 1/1/68. Retd GD(G) 6/11/76.
SHELLEY E.A. Born 6/5/33. Commd 26/8/66. Flt Lt 26/8/71. Retd GD 8/11/75.
SHELLEY G.H.D. Born 4/8/27. Commd 31/5/30. Sqn Ldr 1/1/64. Retd GD 1/9/73.
SHELLEY J.A.F. BA MCMI. Born 19/1/30. Commd 15/12/49. Wg Cdr 1/7/68. Retd GD 19/1/85.
SHELLEY K.D. Born 23/3/54. Commd 21/12/89. Flt Lt 21/12/93. Retd ENG 6/2/96.
SHELLEY L.P. Born 18/6/25. Commd 10/5/46. Flt Lt 10/5/52. Retd RGT 29/5/59.
SHELLEY P.A.J. MBE DPhys Ed. Born 23/5/23. Commd 15/7/43. Gp Capt 1/7/75. Retd EDN 29/3/78.
SHELLEY P.C. Born 8/12/32. Commd 24/6/71. Flt Lt 24/6/76. Retd ADMIN 6/4/87.
SHELLEY T.G. Born 23/2/26. Commd 30/7/52. Flt Lt 27/12/56. Retd GD 1/5/67.
SHELTON E.R.A. MCMI. Born 30/10/26. Commd 23/8/46. Sqn Ldr 1/1/60. Retd SEC 26/7/75.
SHELTON J.R. BA MBCS. Born 3/2/55. Commd 7/11/76. Sqn Ldr 1/1/89. Retd SUP 3/2/93.

SHELTON-SMITH K.C. BEng. Born 24/3/60. Commd 1/7/82. Flt Lt 13/8/86. Retd ENG 24/9/98.
SHENTON J.H. Born 8/2/26. Commd 24/4/50. Flt Lt 11/11/54. Retd GD 24/4/66.
SHENTON R.T. Born 10/11/27. Commd 12/3/64. Sqn Ldr 31/8/74. Retd MED 1/6/78.
SHEPARD G.R.A. MSc BSc CEng MIEE. Born 24/3/45. Commd 14/9/66. Sqn Ldr 15/1/77. Retd ADMIN 24/3/83.
SHEPARD M.J.W. Born 19/12/44. Commd 18/11/66. Sqn Ldr 1/7/79. Retd ENG 19/12/82. Re-entered 3/1/86.
    Sqn Ldr 15/7/82. Retd ENG 19/12/99.
SHEPARD R.W.R. BEM. Born 14/10/11. Commd 25/3/54. Sqn Ldr 1/7/63. Retd ENG 14/10/66.
SHEPHARD I. CEng MIEE. Born 25/9/41. Commd 15/7/63. Sqn Ldr 1/7/74. Retd ENG 25/9/79.
SHEPHARD R.G. MA. Born 11/3/47. Commd 27/10/70. Flt Lt 27/1/74. Retd ADMIN 14/3/96.
SHEPHERD A. Born 5/10/22. Commd 15/9/47. Flt Lt 25/11/53. Retd GD 5/10/67.
SHEPHERD A.E. Born 19/2/26. Commd 22/2/46. Sqn Ldr 1/7/56. Retd GD 1/3/75.
SHEPHERD D.J. Born 4/3/67. Commd 7/11/91. Flt Lt 4/9/94. Retd FLY(P) 4/3/05.
SHEPHERD D.N. DFC. Born 31/10/20. Commd 23/7/41. Wg Cdr 1/1/59. Retd GD 30/11/64.
SHEPHERD J.M.P. Born 12/8/36. Commd 23/9/66. Flt Lt 23/9/72. Retd GD(G) 11/1/90.
SHEPHERD P. Born 8/5/53. Commd 1/6/72. Wg Cdr 1/7/90. Retd GD 16/8/03.
SHEPHERD R.G. Born 5/8/18. Commd 4/3/43. Flt Lt 4/9/46. Retd ENG 5/8/73.
SHEPHERD R.W. MCIPS AIDPM. Born 21/3/37. Commd 11/4/63. Wg Cdr 1/7/89. Retd SUP 22/7/91.
SHEPHERD S.G. BSc. Born 23/4/45. Commd 28/9/64. Flt Lt 15/10/68. Retd GD 31/8/74.
SHEPHERD-SMITH M.A. Born 2/10/41. Commd 11/6/60. Sqn Ldr 1/1/79. Retd GD 2/12/96.
SHEPPARD A.J. AFC. Born 8/4/39. Commd 25/7/60. Wg Cdr 1/1/90. Retd GD 8/4/94.
SHEPPARD B. Born 21/2/32. Commd 13/8/52. Flt Lt 1/10/67. Retd GD 31/3/74.
SHEPPARD C.W. Born 18/8/08. Commd 11/3/41. Sqn Ldr 1/8/47. Retd ENG 4/5/56.
SHEPPARD J.D. Born 24/5/39. Commd 19/10/72. Flt Lt 19/10/74. Retd GD(G) 19/10/80.
SHEPPARD P.B. Born 30/8/31. Commd 25/6/66. Flt Lt 25/6/71. Retd GD 30/9/84.
SHEPPARD P.R. BEM. Born 17/8/49. Commd 5/5/88. Sqn Ldr 1/7/99. Retd ENG 27/5/02.
SHEPPARD R.F. Born 10/12/22. Commd 12/11/51. Wg Cdr 1/7/73. Retd ADMIN 10/12/77.
SHEPPARD T.H. MBE. Born 16/10/33. Commd 27/5/54. Sqn Ldr 1/7/64. Retd GD 27/2/76.
SHEPPARD W.P. Born 8/9/31. Commd 16/1/52. Flt Lt 16/7/56. Retd GD 10/12/70.
SHEPPERSON R.A. Born 29/6/39. Commd 27/1/67. Sqn Ldr 1/1/74. Retd SUP 29/6/77.
SHEPPHARD A. Born 11/2/29. Commd 10/7/52. Flt Lt 22/6/59. Retd GD 1/7/75. rtg Sqn Ldr.
SHERBURN J. DFC. Born 18/8/24. Commd 19/6/47. Flt Lt 15/4/57. Retd GD 18/8/62.
SHERET G.L. MA. Born 29/5/28. Commd 6/9/50. Wg Cdr 1/1/68. Retd GD 6/11/70.
SHERISTON J.H. Born 9/6/21. Commd 14/9/43. Sqn Ldr 1/7/58. Retd GD 9/8/76.
SHERIT K.L. MA MSc CEng FCIPD MInstMC. Born 1/10/53. Commd 17/8/80. Gp Capt 1/7/96. Retd ADMIN 17/8/02.
SHERLOCK B.A. Born 4/4/34. Commd 1/11/56. Sqn Ldr 1/1/85. Retd GD 1/3/88.
SHERLOCK W.P. Born 29/11/33. Commd 13/8/52. Sqn Ldr 1/1/75. Retd GD 29/11/88.
SHERMAN-BALL G.A. FCMI. Born 7/6/34. Commd 12/8/54. Gp Capt 1/1/85. Retd ADMIN 1/10/87.
SHERRARD J.L. BEM MCMI. Born 18/4/21. Commd 28/2/46. Wg Cdr 1/7/66. Retd ENG 14/9/74.
SHERRIFF H.M. MB ChB FRCS. Born 13/4/41. Commd 1/4/63. Wg Cdr 10/8/80. Retd MED 8/5/82.
SHERRIFF P.A. Born 11/1/63. Commd 8/6/84. Flt Lt 1/6/89. Retd GD 14/9/96.
SHERRINGTON A.S. Born 27/9/42. Commd 29/3/62. Flt Lt 29/6/68. Retd SEC 30/4/71.
SHERRINGTON C.F. BSc. Born 16/9/52. Commd 17/1/74. Flt Lt 15/10/75. Retd GD 27/4/77.
SHERRINGTON T.B. CB OBE FCMI MHCIMA. Born 30/4/42. Commd 12/9/63. AVM 1/1/92. Retd ADMIN 30/9/97.
SHERWIN B. Born 18/10/22. Commd 1/6/45. Sqn Ldr 1/4/56. Retd GD 27/5/66.
SHERWIN V.G. Born 29/5/23. Commd 6/6/57. Flt Lt 1/4/63. Retd GD 3/3/69.
SHERWOOD C.A. Born 4/10/21. Commd 24/6/44. Sqn Ldr 1/10/57. Retd SEC 4/10/73.
SHEVELS A.A. Born 22/4/46. Commd 8/9/77. Sqn Ldr 1/7/87. Retd ENG 22/4/01.
SHEVLIN B.J.M. Born 19/3/48. Commd 26/5/67. Flt Lt 4/11/73. Retd SUP 19/3/89.
SHEWRY M. Born 17/7/48. Commd 1/8/69. Sqn Ldr 1/7/85. Retd SY(RGT) 1/7/89.
SHIEBER N.W. Born 25/4/38. Commd 5/8/76. Sqn Ldr 1/7/89. Retd ADMIN 25/4/90.
SHIELDS D. Born 16/12/50. Commd 17/5/79. Flt Lt 17/5/81. Retd ADMIN 16/12/88.
SHIELDS F.L. Born 22/12/28. Commd 6/10/60. Sqn Ldr 1/7/75. Retd GD 22/6/84.
SHIELDS G. Born 10/6/43. Commd 24/6/65. Sqn Ldr 1/1/78. Retd GD 10/6/81.
SHIELDS M.H. FCMI. Born 4/3/45. Commd 24/11/67. Gp Capt 1/7/93. Retd OPS SPT 4/3/00.
SHIELDS M.T.C. Born 21/12/19. Commd 1/6/42. Flt Lt 1/12/46. Retd SEC 21/12/74.
SHIELDS P.L. Born 18/12/65. Commd 25/6/91. Sqn Ldr 1/1/01. Retd SUPPLY 1/1/04.
SHIELDS R. Born 22/5/58. Commd 26/2/79. Wg Cdr 1/1/96. Retd ADMIN 22/5/02.
SHIELDS R.M. MVO . Born 4/4/48. Commd 23/9/66. Sqn Ldr 1/7/83. Retd FLY(N) 4/4/04.
SHIELDS W. Born 11/7/24. Commd 28/8/51. Sqn Ldr 1/7/68. Retd GD 11/7/82.
SHIELLS I.M. Born 26/4/56. Commd 22/5/80. Flt Lt 18/7/83. Retd GD 14/9/96.
SHIELS J.P. Born 19/3/38. Commd 23/9/65. Flt Lt 23/9/67. Retd GD 2/5/75.
SHILLITO J.A. Born 21/10/18. Commd 13/9/45. Sqn Ldr 1/1/55. Retd SEC 30/8/69.
SHILLITO P. MSc BSc CEng MIEE. Born 6/1/61. Commd 18/3/84. Sqn Ldr 1/1/92. Retd ENG 18/6/01.
SHILTON P.R. Born 7/8/53. Commd 18/1/73. Plt Offr 18/1/74. Retd GD 14/9/47.
SHIMELL C.R. MSc BSc CEng MIMechE ACGI. Born 2/5/54. Commd 3/9/72. Sqn Ldr 1/1/86. Retd ENG 2/5/92.
SHIMMONS R.W. Born 24/12/44. Commd 15/7/66. Wg Cdr 1/7/85. Retd GD 30/6/89.

SHINE M.E. Born 10/1/35. Commd 10/12/52. Sqn Ldr 1/1/65. Retd GD 31/5/76.
SHINGLES A.G. DFC. Born 18/10/22. Commd 18/10/44. Flt Lt 18/4/48. Retd GD 25/11/67.
SHIPLEY G.V. Born 10/7/36. Commd 7/12/54. Flt Lt 15/6/60. Retd GD 10/7/74.
SHIPMAN K.E.W. Born 18/6/35. Commd 24/2/55. Sqn Ldr 1/7/70. Retd GD 1/7/73.
SHIPMAN N.M. Born 14/6/31. Commd 12/7/62. Flt Lt 12/7/68. Retd ADMIN 13/7/68. Re-instated 30/4/80 to 13/7/85.
SHIPPEN J.M. BSc. Born 24/2/61. Commd 29/7/83. Sqn Ldr 1/7/99. Retd ENG 26/11/00.
SHIPTON A.J. Born 20/11/33. Commd 4/9/58. Wg Cdr 1/7/77. Retd SEC 1/12/78.
SHIPWAY G.T. Born 2/11/33. Commd 30/1/52. Flt Lt 29/5/57. Retd GD 2/11/71.
SHIRLEY M.J. AMCMI. Born 11/3/33. Commd 3/5/54. Sqn Ldr 1/7/68. Retd ADMIN 1/12/78.
SHIRREFF A.C. Born 12/2/19. Commd 12/9/41. Sqn Ldr 1/1/51. Retd GD 1/5/58.
SHOEBRIDGE R.B. Born 14/9/42. Commd 31/1/64. Flt Lt 6/10/71. Retd GD 14/9/80.
SHOOLBRAID W.G.H. Born 20/4/28. Commd 4/9/58. Sqn Ldr 1/1/69. Retd ENG 4/11/78.
SHOPLAND A.W. BSc. Born 2/11/63. Commd 19/7/87. Flt Lt 19/1/90. Retd GD 14/9/96.
SHORE G.B. BSc. Born 3/2/30. Commd 15/10/52. Wg Cdr 3/9/70. Retd EDN 21/11/81.
SHORE W.A. BA. Born 13/3/51. Commd 6/10/74. Flt Lt 6/7/78. Retd SY 19/1/85.
SHOREMAN A. Born 3/1/15. Commd 28/5/42. Flt Lt 28/4/47. Retd GD(G) 3/1/65.
SHORRICK N. BSc MCIPD MCMI. Born 25/2/33. Commd 20/9/57. Wg Cdr 1/1/84. Retd ADMIN 23/9/87.
SHORROCK G.C. MBE. Born 12/9/41. Commd 30/7/63. Sqn Ldr 1/7/75. Retd GD 12/9/79.
SHORROCK K.J. Born 17/3/33. Commd 27/8/52. Sqn Ldr 1/1/64. Retd GD 19/4/77.
SHORROCKS C.E. Born 7/8/35. Commd 17/3/67. Flt Lt 17/3/69. Retd RGT 31/10/79.
SHORT A.F. OBE MCIPD. Born 25/2/44. Commd 20/6/63. Gp Capt 1/7/88. Retd ADMIN 25/2/94.
SHORT B.E. Born 27/3/30. Commd 25/6/53. Flt Lt 25/12/57. Retd GD 27/3/66. rtg Sqn Ldr.
SHORT C.D. BSc. Born 24/9/49. Commd 23/9/68. Flt Lt 15/10/74. Retd ENG 22/9/81.
SHORT C.J.G. Born 23/2/22. Commd 25/3/44. Sqn Ldr 1/1/55. Retd GD 29/7/66.
SHORT D.A.W. Born 15/7/26. Commd 30/7/59. Flt Lt 30/7/64. Retd ENG 31/7/75.
SHORT D.J. Born 11/10/36. Commd 13/11/61. Fg Offr 3/11/63. Retd GD 27/1/68.
SHORT F.D. Born 23/5/43. Commd 11/9/64. Flt Lt 4/5/72. Retd GD 1/5/76.
SHORT F.R. MA. Born 18/11/17. Commd 3/1/51. Wg Cdr 1/1/66. Retd EDN 2/12/72.
SHORT H. Born 25/12/44. Commd 14/2/69. Sqn Ldr 1/1/80. Retd GD 25/6/90.
SHORT J.A.V. MCMI. Born 12/1/24. Commd 24/8/44. Gp Capt 1/1/76. Retd GD(G) 31/3/78.
SHORT J.C. Born 16/5/57. Commd 4/9/81. Flt Lt 16/7/84. Retd GD(G) 23/6/95.
SHORT J.H. ACMA. Born 14/7/37. Commd 21/10/65. Sqn Ldr 1/7/73. Retd ADMIN 14/7/77.
SHORT M. MBE AFC. Born 5/9/25. Commd 1/4/52. Gp Capt 1/7/74. Retd GD 5/12/80.
SHORT M.A. Born 31/5/62. Commd 24/4/80. Sqn Ldr 1/1/93. Retd ADMIN 22/11/00.
SHORT R.M. Born 24/2/36. Commd 14/10/71. Flt Lt 14/10/73. Retd SUP 14/10/79.
SHORTER B. Born 2/12/47. Commd 21/4/67. Sqn Ldr 1/1/81. Retd SUP 2/12/91.
SHORTHOUSE A.Q. Born 17/4/30. Commd 26/2/53. Flt Lt 26/8/57. Retd GD 17/4/68.
SHREEVE C.J. Born 18/5/48. Commd 7/6/68. Flt Lt 7/12/74. Retd ENG 31/8/77.
SHREEVE P.A. BSc. Born 6/8/51. Commd 15/9/69. Flt Lt 15/10/75. Retd ENG 31/8/78.
SHRIMPTON P.H,W.D. Born 30/7/37. Commd 29/7/58. Sqn Ldr 1/7/68. Retd SUP 30/11/77.
SHUSTER R.C. AFC. Born 2/9/44. Commd 15/7/66. Flt Lt 15/1/69. Retd GD 26/9/97.
SHUTLER M.J. BA. Born 13/8/47. Commd 13/12/68. Flt Lt 13/8/74. Retd ENG 1/1/87.
SHUTT S. BSc. Born 21/3/57. Commd 19/9/76. Sqn Ldr 1/1/93. Retd GD 1/1/96.
SHUTTLEWORTH F.N. MB ChB DOMS. Born 18/8/13. Commd 24/10/39. Gp Capt 1/7/61. Retd MED 1/4/64.
SIBBALD M.C. Born 19/10/45. Commd 9/3/65. Flt Lt 4/5/72. Retd GD 12/6/73.
SIBBONS F.T. Born 5/12/10. Commd 24/11/41. Flt Lt 3/12/46. Retd SUP 5/12/59. rtg Sqn Ldr.
SIBLEY J.C. Born 7/8/47. Commd 25/4/69. Flt Lt 25/10/74. Retd GD 1/11/75.
SIBLEY M.E. Born 8/2/37. Commd 3/7/80. Flt Lt 3/7/82. Retd GD 28/3/88.
SIBREE B.O. Born 21/8/22. Commd 23/7/43. Flt Lt 23/7/45. Retd GD 1/7/75.
SIDDLE P. Born 18/12/23. Commd 6/10/60. Flt Lt 6/10/65. Retd ENG 31/3/78. rtg Sqn Ldr.
SIDDLE V.J. Born 19/5/42. Commd 17/5/63. Plt Offr 16/9/64. Retd SUP 30/12/66.
SIDDONS G.A. Born 30/6/55. Commd 10/3/77. Flt Lt 30/7/83. Retd GD(G) 30/6/93.
SIDDOWAY A.P. Born 26/6/57. Commd 13/8/82. Flt Lt 19/1/85. Retd GD(G) 1/4/96.
SIDEBOTHAM B. Born 6/2/41. Commd 10/10/63. Wg Cdr 1/1/78. Retd GD 22/5/93.
SIDEBOTTOM T.G. OBE FCIS FCIPD. Born 11/11/43. Commd 9/4/65. Gp Capt 1/7/89. Retd ADMIN 27/10/94.
SIDEY R.M. CEng MIMechE. Born 12/6/25. Commd 25/9/62. Sqn Ldr 1/7/71. Retd ENG 12/6/83.
SIDLOW H. Born 27/9/29. Commd 27/8/52. Flt Lt 23/1/58. Retd GD 2/4/84.
SIDWELL T.V. Born 6/12/33. Commd 6/2/52. Flt Lt 2/1/61. Retd GD(G) 2/1/77. Re-instated 20/5/81. Flt Lt 20/5/65. Retd GD(G) 6/12/88.
SIEDLE L.D.C. Born 7/12/46. Commd 11/3/65. Flt Lt 7/1/72. Retd RGT 25/8/72.
SIERWALD R.C. Born 2/3/42. Commd 30/7/63. Sqn Ldr 1/1/76. Retd GD 2/6/97.
SIEVWRIGHT J.M. Born 8/10/26. Commd 25/5/53. Flt Lt 24/3/60. Retd GD(G) 14/10/65. Re-instated 6/12/71. Sqn Ldr 1/1/76. Retd GD(G) 8/10/86.
SIGLEY G.C. Born 29/12/45. Commd 2/6/77. Sqn Ldr 1/1/88. Retd GD 14/9/96.
SILANDER S. Born 25/5/45. Commd 8/6/84. Flt Lt 1/3/87. Retd GD 1/5/94.
SILCOX J.F. Born 28/9/46. Commd 2/4/65. Flt Lt 4/11/70. Retd GD 20/10/76.

SILK A.E.T. Born 12/9/32. Commd 4/3/71. Sqn Ldr 1/7/80. Retd GD 29/2/84.
SILK D.J. MA PhD CEng FIEE. Born 15/12/43. Commd 30/9/62. Wg Cdr 1/1/78. Retd ENG 15/12/84. rtg Gp Capt.
SILLARS R.B. FCMI. Born 16/4/23. Commd 1/5/43. Gp Capt 1/1/69. Retd GD 22/9/73.
SILLENCE M. Born 2/4/42. Commd 24/1/63. Sqn Ldr 1/1/74. Retd ADMIN 2/4/80.
SILLINCE B. Born 15/5/27. Commd 15/5/58. Sqn Ldr 1/7/71. Retd ENG 2/5/78.
SILLITOE C.S. Born 19/4/33. Commd 26/3/52. Flt Lt 13/4/60. Retd GD 19/4/71.
SILLS B.T. MCMI. Born 21/3/36. Commd 9/4/57. A Cdre 1/1/86. Retd GD 6/7/91.
SILVANI M.J. Born 4/7/31. Commd 1/5/52. Flt Lt 11/5/58. Retd GD 14/7/69.
SILVER C.S. CEng MIEE MRAeS. Born 15/10/31. Commd 7/6/51. Wg Cdr 1/1/74. Retd ENG 15/10/81.
SILVERTAND J.M. Born 16/7/44. Commd 1/4/66. Fg Offr 1/4/68. Retd GD 1/7/71.
SILVESTER A.E. MA FCMI. Born 21/8/29. Commd 22/10/52. Gp Capt 1/1/75. Retd EDN 14/1/81.
SIM S.R. Born 5/10/21. Commd 21/5/44. Sqn Ldr 1/4/55. Retd GD 18/5/74.
SIMICH M.F.R. Born 6/10/45. Commd 21/4/67. Flt Lt 21/10/72. Retd GD 29/6/74.
SIMKIN D.P.M. Born 17/12/23. Commd 7/7/49. Sqn Ldr 1/7/60. Retd GD 1/7/63.
SIMKINS K.I. BSc. Born 28/8/47. Commd 1/9/70. Flt Lt 1/6/71. Retd GD 1/3/76.
SIMMONDS E.L. Born 1/6/22. Commd 13/1/52. Flt Lt 13/7/55. Retd GD 22/4/64.
SIMMONDS J.E. Born 8/12/20. Commd 23/4/41. Sqn Ldr 1/7/54. Retd GD 16/12/68.
SIMMONDS J.J. MCMI. Born 13/2/31. Commd 18/8/54. Wg Cdr 1/7/75. Retd SUP 30/6/84.
SIMMONDS P.A.A. Born 9/4/37. Commd 23/6/61. Flt Lt 23/6/67. Retd GD 5/12/92.
SIMMONS D.C.H. CBE AFC MA FCMI. Born 11/12/21. Commd 14/3/42. A Cdre 1/7/70. Retd GD 11/12/76.
SIMMONS D.J. LDSRCS MCMI. Born 2/10/32. Commd 25/9/60. Wg Cdr 9/10/72. Retd DEL 2/10/91.
SIMMONS E.N. Born 22/11/20. Commd 29/9/44. Flt Lt 22/3/48. Retd GD 22/11/75.
SIMMONS I.A. Born 11/7/29. Commd 1/8/51. Sqn Ldr 1/1/60. Retd GD 27/7/67.
SIMMONS J.N. Born 24/12/30. Commd 31/8/50. Sqn Ldr 1/1/79. Retd GD 24/12/88.
SIMMONS L.H. Born 27/9/21. Commd 10/5/46. Sqn Ldr 1/7/71. Retd RGT 8/4/72.
SIMMONS Sir Michael KCB AFC. Born 8/5/37. Commd 29/7/58. AM 3/4/89. Retd GD 5/12/92.
SIMMONS P.J. Born 24/3/34. Commd 5/11/70. Sqn Ldr 1/1/80. Retd ENG 11/9/84.
SIMMS D.A.G. BSc. Born 19/12/52. Commd 11/7/76. Flt Lt 10/9/78. Retd ADMIN 3/10/78.
SIMMS J.B. Born 29/7/35. Commd 5/11/70. Sqn Ldr 28/10/81. Retd MED(SEC) 31/8/86.
SIMMS J.G. Born 8/2/25. Commd 28/1/54. Sqn Ldr 1/1/68. Retd GD 31/10/77.
SIMMS P.J. Born 20/8/40. Commd 29/9/87. Flt Lt 13/5/76. Retd ADMIN 29/9/95.
SIMON B.J. Born 7/8/45. Commd 26/5/67. Wg Cdr 1/7/87. Retd SUP 14/9/96.
SIMONIS H.R. Born 7/5/38. Commd 6/8/60. Flt Lt 6/2/66. Retd GD 1/10/81.
SIMONS C.A.E. FCMI. Born 15/7/27. Commd 2/3/49. Gp Capt 1/7/70. Retd GD 13/11/82.
SIMONS R.W.B. OBE MILDM MCMI. Born 12/2/32. Commd 6/6/57. Gp Capt 1/7/84. Retd SUP 1/7/89.
SIMPKIN M.L. OBE MCIPD. Born 9/6/47. Commd 22/1/67. Gp Capt 1/7/91. Retd ADMIN 27/4/94.
SIMPSON A. Born 28/4/46. Commd 4/1/68. Flt Lt 1/12/76. Retd OPS SPT 1/6/98.
SIMPSON A.B. Born 12/6/33. Commd 28/6/51. Flt Lt 10/10/56. Retd GD 31/5/93.
SIMPSON A.C. Born 25/8/44. Commd 19/8/66. Flt Lt 17/3/71. Retd GD 13/11/82. Re-entered 5/1/90. Flt Lt 5/1/87.
    Retd GD 25/8/01.
SIMPSON A.D. Born 9/5/54. Commd 17/7/75. Sqn Ldr 1/7/88. Retd ADMIN 9/5/92.
SIMPSON A.J. BA. Born 10/3/67. Commd 1/9/85. Flt Lt 15/1/91. Retd GD 14/9/96.
SIMPSON A.W. Born 3/10/43. Commd 1/11/63. Flt Lt 1/7/69. Retd GD 21/6/76.
SIMPSON B. Born 24/11/44. Commd 11/6/81. Flt Lt 11/6/85. Retd ENG 14/4/89.
SIMPSON B.S. Born 3/3/50. Commd 26/2/71. Flt Lt 26/8/76. Retd SUP 1/9/78.
SIMPSON C.A. AFC. Born 29/3/31. Commd 21/11/50. Wg Cdr 1/1/74. Retd GD 3/4/85.
SIMPSON C.E. DFC. Born 22/6/20. Commd 21/10/41. Sqn Ldr 1/7/60. Retd GD 30/3/68.
SIMPSON C.E. MSc MB ChB MFOM MFCM. Born 24/9/29. Commd 6/3/55. AVM 1/7/86. Retd MED 3/4/89.
SIMPSON D.A. BA DPhysEd. Born 4/3/33. Commd 24/5/65. Sqn Ldr 24/5/65. Retd ADMIN 4/3/88.
SIMPSON D.A. BSc. Born 31/5/55. Commd 30/9/73. Gp Capt 1/7/03. Retd GD 1/7/05.
SIMPSON D.C. BA MIL DipTrans. Born 5/11/45. Commd 24/9/67. Sqn Ldr 1/7/88. Retd ADMIN 22/10/94.
SIMPSON D.C. MB ChB FRCS LRCP. Born 15/6/56. Commd 24/11/85. Wg Cdr 10/4/94. Retd MED 14/3/96.
SIMPSON D.J. Born 25/3/32. Commd 18/5/61. Flt Lt 18/5/66. Retd GD(G) 1/1/83.
SIMPSON E.V.C. Born 25/9/18. Commd 23/3/50. Wg Cdr 1/7/70. Retd ENG 25/9/73.
SIMPSON G.A.D. MCMI. Born 22/3/28. Commd 3/1/51. Wg Cdr 1/1/71. Retd GD 1/10/76.
SIMPSON G.D. CBE AFC FRAeS. Born 10/4/48. Commd 28/2/69. Air Cdre 1/7/97. Retd GD 10/4/03.
SIMPSON G.P. Born 6/7/36. Commd 11/2/55. Sqn Ldr 1/1/82. Retd GD 6/7/91.
SIMPSON H.R. MA PhD CEng FBCS MIEE. Born 17/6/35. Commd 25/9/54. Gp Capt 1/7/74. Retd ENG 1/10/80.
SIMPSON J. BA MSc. Born 15/5/35. Commd 18/7/63. Sqn Ldr 18/4/71. Retd ADMIN 4/11/85.
SIMPSON J.A. DFC AFC. Born 15/10/18. Commd 25/5/43. Sqn Ldr 1/1/54. Retd GD 20/12/57.
SIMPSON J.C. MBE MSc DipUS FINucE MInstP MCMI. Born 4/4/27. Commd 18/7/49. Sqn Ldr 1/7/63.
    Retd SY 27/11/76.
SIMPSON J.H. MBE. Born 19/7/55. Commd 18/4/74. Sqn Ldr 1/1/89. Retd GD(G) 19/7/93.
SIMPSON J.H. DFC. Born 23/5/20. Commd 3/3/42. Flt Lt 3/9/45. Retd GD 15/7/48. rtg Wg Cdr.
SIMPSON J.H. Born 22/9/48. Commd 11/10/84. Flt Lt 1/10/88. Retd ENG 19/12/96.
SIMPSON J.M. Born 15/4/28. Commd 30/3/61. Flt Lt 30/3/66. Retd GD 15/4/73.

SIMPSON K.C.H. Born 9/5/40. Commd 19/12/61. Sqn Ldr 1/7/73. Retd GD 1/6/79.
SIMPSON K.W. Born 23/9/23. Commd 11/11/44. Gp Capt 1/7/70. Retd GD 1/10/76.
SIMPSON M.J. Born 29/5/51. Commd 30/1/70. Flt Lt 13/6/76. Retd GD(G) 2/6/81.
SIMPSON M.R. Born 4/6/40. Commd 17/7/64. Flt Lt 15/4/70. Retd GD 2/4/93.
SIMPSON P.J.H. Born 8/6/39. Commd 14/12/72. Flt Lt 14/12/74. Retd SEC 14/12/80.
SIMPSON R. MSc BSc CEng MIEE. Born 13/7/63. Commd 5/9/82. Sqn Ldr 1/1/93. Retd ENG 14/9/01.
SIMPSON R.A.L. Born 8/5/18. Commd 10/8/44. Sqn Ldr 1/1/59. Retd SEC 6/3/65.
SIMPSON R.C. CBE. Born 30/6/24. Commd 3/8/49. Gp Capt 1/7/70. Retd GD 30/6/80. rtg A Cdre.
SIMPSON R.C.R. MSc FBCS FCMI. Born 22/6/49. Commd 28/11/74. Gp Capt 1/7/01. Retd GD 22/6/04.
SIMPSON R.G. BTech. Born 25/9/56. Commd 17/8/80. Flt Lt 17/11/80. Retd GD 17/8/96.
SIMPSON T.D. Born 21/2/65. Commd 19/7/84. Sqn Ldr 1/7/97. Retd FLY(P) 21/2/03.
SIMPSON W.G. OBE MCIPS MCIT MILT MCMI. Born 12/5/48. Commd 1/8/69. Wg Cdr 1/1/85. Retd SUP 11/12/88.
SIMPSON W.J. DFC MCMI. Born 31/5/23. Commd 7/12/48. Wg Cdr 1/1/61. Retd GD 11/4/74.
SIMS A.G. BA. Born 18/7/41. Commd 24/7/81. Sqn Ldr 1/1/89. Retd ADMIN 18/7/96.
SIMS A.G. Born 18/6/50. Commd 26/2/71. Flt Lt 26/2/74. Retd GD 19/6/80.
SIMS G. BA. Born 28/4/54. Commd 11/9/77. Sqn Ldr 1/1/89. Retd GD 11/9/93.
SIMS G.N. DFC MCMI. Born 25/12/22. Commd 20/8/44. Wg Cdr 1/7/65. Retd GD 25/4/74.
SIMS J.F. MCMI. Born 27/8/33. Commd 19/4/60. Sqn Ldr 1/1/70. Retd SUP 27/8/88.
SIMS J.L.M. Born 10/5/39. Commd 11/5/62. Sqn Ldr 1/7/72. Retd GD 1/10/81. Re-instated 9/3/83. Sqn Ldr 6/12/73. Retd GD 31/8/89.
SIMS J.R. MBE MA. Born 18/5/24. Commd 6/4/45. Flt Lt 22/6/52. Retd GD 18/5/67. rtg Sqn Ldr.
SIMS M. MISM MHSM CertMHS. Born 29/12/49. Commd 30/3/89. Flt Lt 30/3/93. Retd MED(SEC) 14/3/96.
SIMS M.R.C. Born 9/6/42. Commd 18/12/62. Flt Lt 18/4/68. Retd GD 9/6/82.
SIMS P.G.D. BSc(Eng) CEng MIMechE MRAeS MCMI. Born 9/11/38. Commd 24/9/63. Sqn Ldr 1/1/72. Retd ENG 24/9/82. Re-instated 21/7/86. Sqn Ldr 27/10/75. Retd ENG 4/9/90
SIMS T.R. MSc. Born 17/10/37. Commd 12/3/64. Sqn Ldr 1/1/72. Retd ENG 26/9/81.
SINCLAIR A.J. Born 25/4/36. Commd 26/11/60. Flt Lt 1/4/66. Retd GD 25/4/74.
SINCLAIR A.R. BA. Born 20/7/51. Commd 15/9/69. Sqn Ldr 1/7/84. Retd GD 20/7/89.
SINCLAIR G.A. BSc. Born 21/11/54. Commd 1/8/76. Sqn Ldr 1/7/96. Retd GD 21/11/98.
SINCLAIR G.L. DFC. Born 15/8/16. Commd 1/3/37. Wg Cdr 1/1/51. Retd GD 23/12/57.
SINCLAIR I.R. Born 20/3/39. Commd 15/12/59. Flt Lt 15/8/62. Retd GD 20/3/77.
SINCLAIR J.G. Born 6/5/19. Commd 22/9/49. Flt Lt 11/11/54. Retd SUP 6/5/68.
SINCLAIR J.J. MCMI AIIP. Born 23/8/27. Commd 26/8/66. Sqn Ldr 1/7/81. Retd ENG 23/8/85.
SINCLAIR P. Born 27/3/23. Commd 7/9/61. Flt Lt 7/9/67. Retd SEC 1/5/74.
SINCLAIR P.L. MCMI. Born 17/9/43. Commd 27/2/70. Sqn Ldr 1/1/88. Retd OPS SPT 13/4/01.
SINCLAIR R.E. Born 8/12/45. Commd 2/4/65. Sqn Ldr 1/1/89. Retd GD 1/6/98.
SINCLAIR-DAY I.E. Born 3/1/32. Commd 17/10/57. Flt Lt 17/2/63. Retd GD(G) 13/3/71.
SINDALL T.H. Born 8/7/41. Commd 31/7/62. Sqn Ldr 1/7/73. Retd GD 6/1/79.
SINEL M.L. Born 31/1/33. Commd 6/4/54. Sqn Ldr 1/1/63. Retd GD 31/1/71.
SINFIELD A.T. Born 1/8/39. Commd 30/4/81. Sqn Ldr 1/7/94. Retd ADMIN 31/3/99.
SINGH A. BSc. Born 16/7/57. Commd 14/9/75. Flt Lt 15/4/80. Retd GD 15/7/90.
SINGH V. Born 1/9/31. Commd 8/10/52. Flt Lt 1/3/61. Retd GD 1/9/69.
SINGLETON A.P. MBE MCMI. Born 8/4/43. Commd 19/12/63. Wg Cdr 1/1/83. Retd ADMIN 15/5/93.
SINGLETON D.F.K. BA MSc CEng MIEE. Born 15/12/47. Commd 24/9/67. Sqn Ldr 1/1/80. Retd ENG 15/12/85.
SINGLETON J.R.M. Born 27/3/44. Commd 22/7/66. Flt Lt 27/3/71. Retd SEC 1/11/72. Re-entered 18/6/80. Wg Cdr 1/7/96. Retd ADMIN 6/7/98.
SINGLETON P.H. Born 25/10/35. Commd 26/10/61. Sqn Ldr 1/1/77. Retd GD 31/5/88.
SINGLETON P.M. MCIPD. Born 15/12/49. Commd 1/8/69. Wg Cdr 1/1/90. Retd OPS SPT 9/7/99.
SINGLETON S.D. CEng MRAeS. Born 6/12/20. Commd 7/1/43. Wg Cdr 1/7/65. Retd ENG 6/12/75.
SINGLETON S.L. Born 15/10/49. Commd 7/6/68. Fg Offr 21/9/70. Retd GD 7/6/74. Re-entered 30/8/79. Wg Cdr 1/7/96. Retd ADMIN 22/12/99.
SINGLETON-HOBBS G.A. Born 23/9/53. Commd 28/10/76. Flt Lt 28/4/83. Retd ADMIN 4/8/98.
SINKER A. BSc. Born 26/7/41. Commd 9/9/63. Flt Lt 9/6/65. Retd GD 9/9/79.
SINKER D.R.G. BSc. Born 2/3/60. Commd 18/3/84. Flt Lt 18/9/86. Retd GD 18/12/00.
SINKINSON I. BA. Born 4/6/46. Commd 26/6/86. Sqn Ldr 1/1/91. Retd ENG 11/12/96.
SIRCUS R.J. Born 15/2/48. Commd 19/6/70. Flt Lt 17/10/76. Retd ADMIN 1/8/80.
SISMORE E.B. DSO DFC** AFC AE* FCMI. Born 23/6/21. Commd 29/8/42. A Cdre 1/7/71. Retd GD 23/6/76.
SITUNAYAKE S.M.V. Born 25/3/31. Commd 28/9/64. Sqn Ldr 1/7/70. Retd GD 1/11/87.
SIVITER C.E. Born 16/5/48. Commd 30/5/69. Flt Lt 16/11/73. Retd GD 27/12/75.
SIVITER D. Born 19/3/31. Commd 26/3/53. Flt Lt 5/8/58. Retd GD 19/3/69.
SIVYER S.W. BSc. Born 10/10/54. Commd 3/8/86. Flt Lt 3/8/85. Retd ADMIN 10/3/87.
SIZELAND G.E. MBE. Born 27/7/29. Commd 24/11/67. Sqn Ldr 1/7/80. Retd ADMIN 27/2/84.
SIZER W.M. DFC*. Born 23/2/20. Commd 7/5/38. Sqn Ldr 1/1/50. Retd GD 23/2/63. rtg Wg Cdr.
SKEA A.F. MA. Born 10/4/41. Commd 22/2/63. Sqn Ldr 1/1/75. Retd GD 10/4/79.
SKEA P.E. Born 21/12/42. Commd 16/9/81. Sqn Ldr 1/1/84. Retd ENG 30/9/94.
SKEHILL J.M. Born 1/7/15. Commd 17/11/41. Flt Offr 1/9/45. Retd SEC 29/5/53.

SKELLAND D.J. Born 17/12/33. Commd 27/1/67. Sqn Ldr 1/1/77. Retd SUP 17/12/90.
SKELLERN C.I.B. BEd FITD. Born 28/3/41. Commd 5/10/66. Wg Cdr 1/7/87. Retd ADMIN 13/7/94.
SKELLEY M.H. Born 1/7/18. Commd 9/12/42. Flt Offr 9/12/47. Retd SEC 7/2/55.
SKELLEY R.P. Born 20/3/38. Commd 16/12/58. A Cdre 1/7/90. Retd GD 1/7/93.
SKELLON R.C. Born 13/3/16. Commd 19/1/39. Wg Cdr 1/1/57. Retd SEC 28/4/62.
SKELTON A.M. Born 20/4/48. Commd 29/3/68. Flt Lt 20/10/73. Retd FLY(P) 20/4/03.
SKELTON C.D. Born 3/4/11. Commd 8/11/44. Sqn Ldr 1/1/62. Retd GD(G) 20/4/66.
SKELTON S.S. Born 20/4/29. Commd 3/8/49. Flt Lt 3/7/55. Retd GD 20/7/67.
SKENE A.J. Born 21/8/44. Commd 7/7/67. Flt Lt 7/1/73. Retd GD 21/8/02.
SKERRETT C.G.H. Born 6/11/25. Commd 3/11/60. Sqn Ldr 1/10/66. Retd EDN 1/1/72.
SKILLICORN B.W. AFC. Born 16/2/43. Commd 7/12/64. Flt Lt 12/11/69. Retd GD 15/2/98.
SKILTON J.A. DFC. Born 24/6/20. Commd 3/3/44. Flt Lt 3/9/47. Retd GD 22/7/58.
SKINGSLEY Sir Anthony GBE KCB MA. Born 19/10/33. Commd 8/7/55. ACM 1/5/89. Retd GD 31/12/92.
SKINNER A.H. MCMI. Born 30/8/38. Commd 19/9/58. Sqn Ldr 1/1/73. Retd GD 2/10/77.
SKINNER D. Born 30/10/29. Commd 20/1/51. Flt Lt 20/7/55. Retd GD 29/2/84.
SKINNER D.A. Born 8/4/43. Commd 11/8/67. Flt Lt 4/5/72. Retd GD 9/8/76.
SKINNER D.R. Born 11/6/50. Commd 25/2/72. Wg Cdr 1/7/94. Retd GD 11/6/05.
SKINNER E.J. Born 21/1/29. Commd 11/3/53. Flt Lt 7/3/62. Retd GD 22/1/67.
SKINNER G. CBE MSc BSc CEng FILT FIMechE FCMI MRAeS. Born 16/9/45. Commd 28/9/64. AVM 1/7/99.
   Retd ENG 16/9/00.
SKINNER H.H. FCMI. Born 4/8/32. Commd 26/1/55. Wg Cdr 1/7/76. Retd GD 4/8/87.
SKINNER H.M. Born 5/5/34. Commd 2/9/55. Flt Lt 2/3/61. Retd GD 5/5/72.
SKINNER J.D. PhD BTech AdvDipEd(Open). Born 2/1/44. Commd 13/9/70. Wg Cdr 1/7/89. Retd ADMIN 11/4/99.
SKINNER J.D. Born 12/12/32. Commd 31/3/60. Wg Cdr 1/7/79. Retd ADMIN 12/12/87.
SKINNER K.E. Born 18/5/44. Commd 5/11/65. Wg Cdr 1/1/88. Retd GD 9/12/96.
SKINNER M.W. Born 30/9/49. Commd 2/9/87. Sqn Ldr 1/1/91. Retd ENGINEER 30/9/04.
SKINNER P.D. Born 27/2/41. Commd 27/1/61. Flt Lt 27/7/66. Retd GD 28/9/74.
SKINNER R.J. Born 31/5/24. Commd 4/5/50. Sqn Ldr 1/7/70. Retd GD(G) 31/5/79.
SKINNER T.A. MB BS. Born 7/1/58. Commd 19/2/84. Wg Cdr 19/2/96. Retd MED 31/3/00.
SKIPP J.S. Born 31/5/55. Commd 9/8/79. Flt Lt 6/10/81. Retd GD 14/3/97.
SKIPSEY M.R. BSc. Born 3/5/39. Commd 19/4/63. Sqn Ldr 1/1/71. Retd ENG 30/1/79.
SKITCH R.E. DFC. Born 8/7/22. Commd 30/1/42. Sqn Ldr 1/4/55. Retd GD 5/9/55.
SKLIROS M.P. The Rev. MA. Born 15/4/33. Commd 15/8/65. Retd Sqn Ldr 15/9/77.
SKOYLES R.W. BA. Born 27/1/60. Commd 20/10/80. Sqn Ldr 1/7/94. Retd ADMIN 12/4/97.
SKRINE J.R. Born 22/12/23. Commd 21/6/45. Flt Lt 21/12/48. Retd GD 22/12/66.
SKUODAS L.J. BEd BSc. Born 8/9/58. Commd 14/10/84. Flt Lt 14/4/84. Retd ADMIN 14/10/00.
SLACK A.J. BSc. Born 26/10/59. Commd 29/11/81. Flt Lt 29/5/85. Retd ADMIN 19/1/91.
SLACK M.R.G. BSc. Born 7/5/57. Commd 24/9/75. Sqn Ldr 1/1/90. Retd ENG 2/3/96.
SLACK R.A. CEng MRAeS. Born 18/4/43. Commd 26/5/67. Sqn Ldr 1/7/76. Retd ENG 18/4/81.
SLADDEN D.L. Born 20/7/21. Commd 1/9/45. Wg Cdr 1/1/54. Retd RGT 24/9/60.
SLADDEN R.E.A. Born 9/10/29. Commd 18/9/68. Flt Lt 20/8/58. Retd GD 9/10/84.
SLADE D.G. Born 10/8/29. Commd 30/7/52. Gp Capt 1/7/70. Retd GD 10/12/82.
SLADE D.R. BSc. Born 16/1/34. Commd 23/9/63. Flt Lt 18/11/63. Retd ENG 23/9/79.
SLADE R.G.S. Born 1/10/39. Commd 1/8/61. Sqn Ldr 1/1/76. Retd GD 1/1/79.
SLADER E.D. BSc. Born 13/5/58. Commd 9/11/80. Flt Lt 9/5/82. Retd GD 9/11/96.
SLANEY G.H.W. Born 16/2/32. Commd 13/8/52. Flt Lt 16/8/61. Retd GD 16/2/70.
SLATER A. BA. Born 7/4/58. Commd 18/10/81. Sqn Ldr 1/1/96. Retd OPS SPT 1/1/99.
SLATER C.E. MBE DFC AFC. Born 9/4/22. Commd 25/8/55. Sqn Ldr 1/7/67. Retd GD 5/3/77.
SLATER E.W. Born 28/2/13. Commd 21/10/54. Flt Lt 21/4/59. Retd ENG 28/2/68.
SLATER F.W. Born 6/3/23. Commd 20/6/63. Flt Lt 20/6/66. Retd ENG 18/10/73.
SLATER G. MSc BSc CEng MIEE MRAeS. Born 26/12/50. Commd 23/9/68. Sqn Ldr 1/7/81. Retd ENG 26/12/88.
SLATER J.C. Born 12/5/53. Commd 5/7/68. Fg Offr 5/1/71. Retd SUP 15/12/72.
SLATER J.K. Born 11/9/48. Commd 3/5/68. Flt Lt 3/11/73. Retd GD 4/4/78.
SLATER K.G. Born 17/9/26. Commd 29/8/51. Sqn Ldr 14/2/66. Retd EDN 10/2/67.
SLATER R.J. Born 13/2/45. Commd 4/2/71. Gp Capt 1/7/91. Retd ADMIN 13/2/00.
SLATER S. DSO OBE DFC*. Born 29/9/21. Commd 10/4/43. Gp Capt 1/1/65. Retd GD 1/7/70.
SLATER S.A. Born 7/12/50. Commd 16/11/72. Sqn Ldr 1/1/85. Retd GD 7/12/88.
SLATER T.G. Born 13/10/59. Commd 21/12/89. Flt Lt 21/12/91. Retd OPS SPT 21/12/97.
SLATTER A.T. Born 28/4/38. Commd 20/6/63. Flt Lt 1/4/66. Retd GD 28/4/76.
SLATTER C. BSc(Eng). Born 29/9/49. Commd 2/7/72. Sqn Ldr 1/1/87. Retd GD 18/9/00.
SLATTER D.A. MBE. Born 28/2/34. Commd 11/10/79. Sqn Ldr 1/1/86. Retd ADMIN 28/2/92.
SLATTERY D.P. Born 2/5/25. Commd 23/3/50. Flt Lt 27/5/54. Retd GD 2/5/63.
SLAUGHTER F.W. Born 21/11/22. Commd 17/9/43. Sqn Ldr 1/7/54. Retd GD 21/11/77.
SLAWSON P.R. Born 19/12/45. Commd 28/2/69. Sqn Ldr 1/7/80. Retd ENG 19/12/83.
SLAYTER R.P. Born 20/5/37. Commd 16/12/58. Wg Cdr 1/1/88. Retd SUP 20/5/92.
SLEDMERE F.W. AFC FCMI. Born 3/4/22. Commd 18/12/43. Gp Capt 1/1/69. Retd GD 3/4/75.

SLEEMAN E. Born 28/12/18. Commd 26/7/43. Sqn Ldr 1/7/56. Retd GD 11/7/58.
SLESSOR J.A.G. CVO DL. Born 14/8/25. Commd 19/10/45. Gp Capt 1/1/70. Retd GD 31/1/78.
SLINGER A.P. OBE. Born 19/6/35. Commd 13/7/61. Wg Cdr 1/1/81. Retd GD 19/6/93.
SLINGSBY G.G. Born 24/7/28. Commd 29/11/50. Sqn Ldr 1/1/76. Retd GD 24/7/86.
SLINN G.K. BSc. Born 4/1/40. Commd 7/9/66. Sqn Ldr 1/7/74. Retd ENG 4/1/95.
SLOAN C.H. AFC. Born 24/7/26. Commd 25/10/46. Sqn Ldr 1/7/56. Retd GD 24/10/65.
SLOAN D. DFC MCMI. Born 23/2/21. Commd 1/5/42. Sqn Ldr 1/7/63. Retd SEC 1/11/74.
SLOAN M.A. BSc. Born 23/5/74. Commd 6/4/97. Flt Lt 6/10/00. Retd ADMIN (SEC) 19/6/03.
SLOAN N.P. Born 6/2/66. Commd 20/5/90. Sqn Ldr 1/1/00. Retd ADMIN (SEC) 20/5/04.
SLOAN R.A. BTech. Born 15/5/55. Commd 8/1/78. Flt Lt 8/10/78. Retd GD 8/1/94.
SLOAN R.W. BSc. Born 6/4/20. Commd 14/5/43. Wg Cdr 29/12/66. Retd EDN 6/4/75.
SLOAN S.N. MVO DFC CGM. Born 25/10/22. Commd 24/5/43. Flt Lt 24/11/46. Retd GD 17/8/51.
SLOANE I.R.F. BSc. Born 19/9/52. Commd 2/10/72. Flt Lt 15/4/78. Retd GD 20/11/81.
SLOCOMBE P.H. Born 5/10/46. Commd 27/1/77. Flt Lt 27/1/79. Retd MED(SEC) 21/12/85.
SLOCUM G.D. Born 21/11/46. Commd 10/6/66. Sqn Ldr 1/7/80. Retd GD 21/11/84.
SLOGROVE R.P. BA. Born 1/11/45. Commd 15/7/66. Flt Lt 15/10/70. Retd SUP 10/3/76. rtg Sqn Ldr.
SLOSS D.J. Born 16/12/44. Commd 14/8/80. Flt Lt 14/8/82. Retd GD(G) 1/10/88.
SLOSS I. CEng FRAeS. Born 3/8/46. Commd 2/10/66. A Cdre 1/1/97. Retd ENG 2/4/00.
SLOSS R.P. MA. Born 5/11/27. Commd 25/8/54. Wg Cdr 1/4/69. Retd EDN 1/4/73.
SLOUGH D. Born 14/11/40. Commd 24/6/76. Sqn Ldr 1/1/86. Retd ADMIN 1/10/87.
SLY K.B. Born 24/2/24. Commd 23/10/51. Flt Lt 11/11/54. Retd GD 30/3/63.
SMAIL T.W. DFC. Born 16/8/23. Commd 18/12/42. Flt Lt 22/2/50. Retd GD 29/12/67.
SMAILES A.A. AFC. Born 10/5/23. Commd 20/12/43. Wg Cdr 1/1/60. Retd GD 8/1/65.
SMAILES M.S. Born 4/9/58. Commd 11/5/78. Sqn Ldr 1/7/94. Retd OPS SPT 1/1/02.
SMAILES R.A.C. Born 28/12/37. Commd 20/12/56. Flt Lt 20/12/62. Retd RGT 31/12/71.
SMALE A.M. Born 20/6/62. Commd 30/4/81. Flt Lt 30/10/86. Retd GD 1/10/89.
SMALE D.J. MBE MCMI. Born 13/5/36. Commd 17/7/70. Wg Cdr 1/7/90. Retd ADMIN 26/5/92.
SMALE K.C. Born 26/8/25. Commd 11/10/51. Flt Lt 25/1/57. Retd GD 28/9/68.
SMALE L.W. Born 27/4/14. Commd 26/9/57. Flt Lt 26/9/60. Retd SEC 24/5/67.
SMALE M.J. IEng MIIE. Born 21/5/55. Commd 8/5/86. Flt Lt 8/5/88. Retd ENG 20/8/01.
SMALES K.P. DSO DFC FCMI. Born 7/1/17. Commd 18/5/37. Gp Capt 1/7/58. Retd GD 21/3/68.
SMALL A. Born 13/11/35. Commd 26/9/57. Sqn Ldr 1/1/68. Retd ENG 13/11/80.
SMALL A.R. Born 30/5/30. Commd 25/10/51. Flt Lt 13/11/57. Retd GD 30/5/85.
SMALL I.Mack. BA. Born 15/5/56. Commd 19/9/76. Flt Lt 15/4/80. Retd GD 15/7/90.
SMALL I.T. Born 10/6/33. Commd 26/3/52. Sqn Ldr 1/1/71. Retd GD 1/11/84.
SMALL J.A. BA. Born 24/1/49. Commd 13/2/72. Sqn Ldr 1/1/90. Retd ADMIN 13/7/96.
SMALL K.A. Born 9/12/32. Commd 4/10/51. Flt Lt 5/11/58. Retd GD 9/12/70.
SMALL M.F. Born 1/8/45. Commd 6/11/80. Sqn Ldr 1/7/94. Retd ENG 14/6/96.
SMALL M.K. MSc BSc. Born 17/2/64. Commd 14/4/85. Wg Cdr 1/7/01. Retd GD 17/2/05.
SMALL R. BA. Born 18/1/47. Commd 9/12/71. Flt Lt 9/6/77. Retd GD 14/3/96.
SMALL S.J. Born 12/5/63. Commd 8/4/82. Fg Offr 8/10/84. Retd GD(G) 11/7/86.
SMALL V.W. MCMI. Born 18/9/33. Commd 26/11/52. Gp Capt 1/1/85. Retd GD 18/9/88.
SMALL W. DFC. Born 18/3/23. Commd 9/11/43. Flt Lt 6/7/56. Retd GD(G) 30/3/74.
SMALLEY J.E. Born 11/10/20. Commd 19/11/42. Gp Capt 1/1/73. Retd SUP 10/11/75.
SMALLEY R.G. Born 10/2/32. Commd 23/8/51. Wg Cdr 1/1/72. Retd GD 30/9/85.
SMALLMAN A.P. DSO AFC. Born 27/6/19. Commd 7/11/40. Wg Cdr 1/1/56. Retd GD 18/3/57.
SMART A.M. Born 8/3/40. Commd 6/9/63. Sqn Ldr 1/7/74. Retd GD 8/3/80.
SMART D.M. Born 30/9/45. Commd 20/5/82. Sqn Ldr 1/7/90. Retd ADMIN 27/2/97.
SMART G.A. MBE AFC. Born 24/4/37. Commd 15/4/55. A Cdre 1/1/87. Retd GD 8/4/89.
SMART G.J. MSc BDS MGDSRCS(Ed) LDSRCS. Born 12/5/54. Commd 22/2/81. Wg Cdr 3/8/89. Retd DEL 22/2/97.
SMART H.S. BA. Born 5/4/45. Commd 14/7/69. Flt Lt 14/10/70. Retd GD 22/10/94.
SMART M.C.N. AFC. Born 9/11/26. Commd 3/9/47. Gp Capt 1/1/75. Retd GD 6/12/81.
SMART M.D. BA FCIPD. Born 18/3/42. Commd 15/12/60. AVM 1/9/96. Retd ADMIN 25/4/98.
SMART R.J.R. Born 24/8/57. Commd 5/4/79. Flt Lt 16/9/82. Retd GD 24/10/95.
SMART R.T. MCMI. Born 28/4/16. Commd 1/5/47. Sqn Ldr 1/7/58. Retd SUP 28/4/74.
SMEATON G.T. OBE. Born 30/10/27. Commd 9/12/48. A Cdre 1/1/79. Retd GD 7/7/79.
SMEDLEY A.W.A. Born 8/6/31. Commd 14/3/57. Sqn Ldr 1/7/67. Retd GD 24/9/76.
SMEDLEY W.M. OBE CEng MRAeS. Born 14/4/20. Commd 19/8/42. Gp Capt 1/7/66. Retd ENG 14/4/75.
SMEETH E.F. Born 10/10/23. Commd 11/10/53. Flt Lt 29/6/50. Retd GD 10/10/83.
SMEETON J. Born 20/7/21. Commd 19/7/51. Flt Lt 19/1/55. Retd ENG 28/4/62.
SMEETON R. OBE. Born 4/7/30. Commd 9/6/55. Wg Cdr 1/7/78. Retd ENG 3/4/84.
SMERDON G.R.B. BSc. Born 4/8/61. Commd 19/6/83. Flt Lt 19/12/85. Retd GD 4/3/00.
SMERDON R.E.W. Born 25/11/22. Commd 37/7/43. Sqn Ldr 1/1/56. Retd GD 25/11/71.
SMERDON T.R. Born 22/2/31. Commd 17/3/67. Sqn Ldr 1/1/78. Retd ENG 12/8/85.
SMETHURST H.C. BA. Born 17/4/60. Commd 4/9/78. Flt Lt 15/10/82. Retd GD 15/7/93.
SMIRTHWAITE S.M. BSc. Born 19/2/58. Commd 17/8/80. Flt Lt 17/11/81. Retd GD 17/8/96.

SMIRTHWAITE S.P. BSc. Born 30/6/55. Commd 16/9/73. Flt Lt 15/4/78. Retd GD 15/7/88.
SMITH A. BSc. Born 22/1/58. Commd 23/9/79. Flt Lt 23/12/80. Retd GD 12/1/93.
SMITH A. The Rt Rev Mgr. Born 29/3/41. Commd 18/9/77. Retd Gp Capt 21/4/97.
SMITH A. MBE. Born 21/12/39. Commd 29/6/72. Sqn Ldr 1/1/80. Retd ADMIN 21/12/94.
SMITH A.C. Born 1/9/22. Commd 28/8/45. Flt Lt 28/8/49. Retd GD 5/3/52.
SMITH A.C. Born 25/5/25. Commd 21/2/52. Flt Lt 21/8/55. Retd GD 25/5/63.
SMITH A.E. CEng MIMechE. Born 1/7/37. Commd 24/9/64. Flt Lt 24/9/66. Retd ENG 1/7/75.
SMITH A.G. Born 16/4/62. Commd 18/12/80. Flt Lt 18/6/86. Retd GD 14/9/96.
SMITH A.G. Born 3/12/42. Commd 9/9/63. Flt Lt 17/3/71. Retd GD 3/12/80.
SMITH A.G. AFC. Born 25/12/10. Commd 19/8/40. Sqn Ldr 1/7/50. Retd GD(G) 3/3/59.
SMITH A.I.A. Born 1/4/40. Commd 4/4/59. Sqn Ldr 1/1/70. Retd GD 1/4/78.
SMITH A.J. Born 11/1/31. Commd 17/12/52. Flt Lt 12/5/58. Retd GD(G) 11/1/86.
SMITH A.J. Born 23/2/14. Commd 14/1/43. Retd GD 28/3/46. rtg Sqn Ldr.
SMITH A.J. OBE BSc CEng FRAeS MIMechE. Born 13/6/53. Commd 2/3/76. AVM 1/7/02. Retd GD 1/1/05.
SMITH A.J.E. Born 16/7/46. Commd 21/10/66. Fg Offr 21/4/69. Retd RGT 16/9/72.
SMITH A.J.F. MBE. Born 5/10/26. Commd 29/5/52. Sqn Ldr 1/7/68. Retd GD 5/10/87.
SMITH A.M. Born 6/6/40. Commd 21/4/77. Sqn Ldr 1/7/92. Retd ENG 6/6/95.
SMITH A.M. Born 5/10/67. Commd 9/5/91. Fg Offr 17/10/93. Retd ADMIN 14/3/97.
SMITH A.M. Born 31/1/25. Commd 12/10/55. Flt Offr 12/10/59. Retd CAT 17/3/62.
SMITH A.M. BSc. Born 6/6/65. Commd 14/9/86. Flt Lt 14/3/89. Retd FLY(P) 13/4/04.
SMITH A.M.W. Born 24/6/28. Commd 8/8/62. Flt Lt 1/4/66. Retd RGT 11/7/71.
SMITH A.P. Born 1/11/63. Commd 9/10/95. Sqn Ldr 1/7/00. Retd FLY(P) 1/9/03.
SMITH A.P.D. Born 28/7/46. Commd 14/7/66. Flt Lt 14/1/72. Retd GD 14/3/96.
SMITH A.R. Born 27/12/42. Commd 18/1/73. Sqn Ldr 1/7/81. Retd ADMIN 15/6/96.
SMITH A.R. Born 17/10/49. Commd 22/5/75. Sqn Ldr 1/1/88. Retd OPS SPT(ATC) 17/10/04.
SMITH A.R.S. DFC FCMI. Born 18/5/23. Commd 2/1/44. Flt Lt 2/7/47. Retd GD 13/4/59.
SMITH A.W. Born 21/8/62. Commd 30/3/00. Flt Lt 30/3/04. Retd FLY(P) 28/11/04.
SMITH A.W.S. Born 16/5/47. Commd 21/7/65. Fg Offr 21/7/67. Retd GD 17/2/69.
SMITH B. BA. Born 12/6/37. Commd 30/12/55. Sqn Ldr 1/7/73. Retd GD 30/4/88.
SMITH B. The Rev. Born 15/7/44. Commd 18/9/77. Retd Gp Capt 15/7/95.
SMITH B.E. Born 26/5/37. Commd 9/12/65. Sqn Ldr 15/9/73. Retd EDN 26/5/75.
SMITH B.H. Born 3/6/44. Commd 4/5/72. Flt Lt 2/5/79. Retd GD(G) 3/6/82. Re-entrant 1/6/87. Sqn Ldr 1/7/92.
  Retd GD(G) 14/3/96.
SMITH B.I. Born 17/8/59. Commd 5/1/78. Sqn Ldr 1/7/90. Retd GD 17/8/97.
SMITH B.M. BSc. Born 27/7/21. Commd 1/9/53. Wg Cdr 17/10/61. Retd EDN 11/6/66.
SMITH B.N. Born 5/8/28. Commd 31/1/51. Fg Offr 31/1/52. Retd GD 11/12/54.
SMITH B.S. Born 7/2/61. Commd 4/12/86. Flt Lt 12/5/89. Retd GD 7/2/99.
SMITH B.S. Born 31/3/33. Commd 15/6/53. Flt Lt 14/10/58. Retd GD 9/7/71.
SMITH C.A. Born 25/2/44. Commd 19/5/69. Sqn Ldr 1/7/77. Retd ENG 19/5/85.
SMITH C.C. Born 12/11/21. Commd 12/6/58. Sqn Ldr 1/7/69. Retd ENG 17/3/78.
SMITH C.D. MBE DFC. Born 31/12/20. Commd 18/8/44. Flt Lt 4/12/52. Retd GD(G) 5/4/63.
SMITH C.D. MA. Born 14/4/49. Commd 15/9/69. Wg Cdr 1/7/88. Retd ADMIN 14/3/96.
SMITH C.E. Born 3/1/40. Commd 29/7/68. Flt Lt 24/6/73. Retd ENG 24/1/81.
SMITH C.F. AFC. Born 21/2/13. Commd 30/5/42. Flt Lt 30/5/44. Retd GD 6/12/46.
SMITH C.J. BTech. Born 14/12/51. Commd 3/11/74. Sqn Ldr 1/7/87. Retd GD 3/11/90.
SMITH C.J. BSc. Born 17/10/63. Commd 26/5/85. Flt Lt 26/11/87. Retd GD 17/10/01.
SMITH C.J. Born 17/8/60. Commd 6/11/80. Flt Lt 8/2/87. Retd GD 14/9/87.
SMITH C.J.D. BSc. Born 12/5/58. Commd 17/8/80. Sqn Ldr 1/1/90. Retd ENG 17/8/96.
SMITH C.J.L. Born 6/4/49. Commd 1/12/77. Wg Cdr 1/7/99. Retd GD 9/5/03.
SMITH C.R. Born 1/12/30. Commd 24/9/64. Sqn Ldr 1/7/75. Retd ENG 1/12/88.
SMITH C.W. Born 17/5/35. Commd 3/12/70. Sqn Ldr 1/7/85. Retd ADMIN 17/5/90.
SMITH D. BSc. Born 30/4/38. Commd 15/2/60. Flt Lt 15/8/65. Retd GD 30/4/76.
SMITH D. Born 10/4/46. Commd 5/7/68. Flt Lt 21/11/74. Retd SY 10/4/84.
SMITH D. Born 14/2/39. Commd 3/11/77. Flt Lt 3/11/82. Retd ENG 15/2/89.
SMITH D. MBA MSc BSc MCIPD MCMI. Born 15/11/57. Commd 22/7/84. Sqn Ldr 1/7/90. Retd ADMIN 28/2/97.
SMITH D. Born 10/11/42. Commd 25/6/66. Wg Cdr 1/7/86. Retd ENG 1/10/89.
SMITH D.A. BSc. Born 27/2/52. Commd 3/9/72. Sqn Ldr 1/7/84. Retd ENG 27/2/90.
SMITH D.A. Born 25/9/21. Commd 27/4/61. Flt Lt 27/4/66. Retd ENG 25/9/73.
SMITH D.C. Born 21/2/45. Commd 19/7/84. Sqn Ldr 1/7/94. Retd ADMIN 17/5/96.
SMITH D.C. OBE. Born 17/9/42. Commd 8/6/62. Gp Capt 1/7/90. Retd GD 8/6/93.
SMITH D.E.S. MBCS MCMI. Born 26/4/30. Commd 14/1/06. Wg Cdr 1/7/76. Retd ADMIN 26/4/85.
SMITH D.F. Born 13/9/33. Commd 31/1/61. Sqn Ldr 1/1/72. Retd SUP 3/1/77.
SMITH D.F. Born 3/2/30. Commd 17/12/52. Sqn Ldr 1/1/62. Retd GD 19/3/76.
SMITH D.G. Born 29/4/47. Commd 7/6/68. Flt Lt 7/12/73. Retd GD 30/4/76.
SMITH D.H. Born 31/3/38. Commd 6/7/59. Sqn Ldr 1/7/71. Retd GD 2/4/88.
SMITH D.J. Born 4/7/33. Commd 10/10/63. Flt Lt 1/4/66. Retd SEC 10/10/71.

SMITH D.J. MB BS MRCS LRCP. Born 25/6/35. Commd 12/6/60. Wg Cdr 14/5/73. Retd MED 12/6/76.
SMITH D.J. Born 14/6/33. Commd 27/8/52. Sqn Ldr 1/1/69. Retd GD 23/4/88.
SMITH D.J. Born 1/9/24. Commd 21/10/54. Sqn Ldr 1/7/73. Retd GD 1/3/77.
SMITH D.M. OBE. Born 21/8/36. Commd 27/8/64. Gp Capt 1/1/85. Retd ADMIN 27/10/89.
SMITH D.M. Born 1/7/24. Commd 5/7/51. Fg Offr 5/7/53. Retd SEC 6/11/54.
SMITH D.P.J. CBE DFC. Born 17/5/22. Commd 22/6/43. Gp Capt 1/1/67. Retd GD(G) 26/3/77.
SMITH D.R. Born 10/9/40. Commd 1/4/71. Flt Lt 1/4/73. Retd GD(G) 1/10/87.
SMITH D.S. Born 30/8/30. Commd 2/5/51. Sqn Ldr 1/7/63. Retd GD 19/12/75.
SMITH D.W. Born 29/6/24. Commd 9/6/45. Wg Cdr 1/1/63. Retd GD 29/4/78.
SMITH D.W. BSc. Born 2/6/44. Commd 16/1/67. Flt Lt 16/4/68. Retd GD 29/5/76.
SMITH D.W.H. AFC. Born 23/2/24. Commd 12/11/43. Gp Capt 1/7/69. Retd GD 27/11/70.
SMITH E.D. BSc. Born 4/4/18. Commd 7/6/40. Gp Capt 1/7/61. Retd ENG 15/9/69.
SMITH E.D. DFC. Born 18/9/56. Commd 5/8/76. Sqn Ldr 1/1/93. Retd GD 1/1/96.
SMITH E.E. MA. Born 25/8/74. Commd 24/8/99. Flt Lt 13/2/99. Retd OPS SPT(FLTOPS) 1/9/03.
SMITH E.G. Born 11/1/15. Commd 30/8/41. Sqn Ldr 1/7/51. Retd GD(G) 15/1/62.
SMITH E.J. Born 10/8/20. Commd 19/12/59. Flt Lt 19/12/65. Retd ENG 15/3/69.
SMITH E.J. Born 20/2/42. Commd 23/3/67. Sqn Ldr 1/1/89. Retd GD 2/2/97.
SMITH E.J.E. OBE. Born 2/10/34. Commd 31/7/56. Wg Cdr 1/7/71. Retd GD 1/7/74.
SMITH E.S. Born 12/5/18. Commd 12/6/40. Sqn Ldr 1/7/52. Retd GD 31/12/57.
SMITH F. Born 27/4/21. Commd 24/2/44. Flt Lt 24/8/47. Retd GD 27/4/64.
SMITH F.A. MCIPS MCMI. Born 22/12/29. Commd 4/10/51. Wg Cdr 1/7/75. Retd SUP 4/4/80.
SMITH F.J. BA MCMI DPhysEd. Born 3/9/32. Commd 26/1/56. Wg Cdr 1/1/79. Retd ADMIN 2/4/85.
SMITH F.L. Born 28/5/21. Commd 7/12/44. Flt Lt 9/12/55. Retd GD(G) 13/4/76.
SMITH F.R. Born 6/2/20. Commd 20/4/50. Flt Lt 20/10/54. Retd SEC 20/4/70.
SMITH F.W.M. Born 5/12/32. Commd 27/9/71. Flt Lt 11/1/57. Retd GD 30/4/93.
SMITH G. Born 4/9/22. Commd 31/7/58. Sqn Ldr 1/7/70. Retd ENG 4/9/73.
SMITH G. Born 6/6/31. Commd 8/7/65. Flt Lt 8/7/71. Retd PRT 14/4/72.
SMITH G. Born 5/9/38. Commd 30/1/75. Flt Lt 30/1/80. Retd GD(G) 31/12/84.
SMITH G.A. Born 6/12/35. Commd 19/1/66. Flt Lt 19/1/68. Retd ENG 19/1/74.
SMITH G.A. Born 30/4/39. Commd 4/11/82. Flt Lt 1/3/87. Retd ENG 30/4/94.
SMITH G.A.R. BEng. Born 30/1/64. Commd 2/8/85. Flt Lt 1/11/90. Retd ENG 2/12/95.
SMITH G.D. Born 31/7/41. Commd 8/12/83. Sqn Ldr 1/7/94. Retd ENG 1/7/97.
SMITH G.F. Born 17/5/44. Commd 14/6/63. Sqn Ldr 1/1/80. Retd GD 29/7/93.
SMITH G.G. Born 19/4/21. Commd 26/5/46. Flt Lt 25/11/48. Retd GD 1/10/55.
SMITH G.H. Born 5/8/25. Commd 27/1/55. Flt Lt 27/1/61. Retd SEC 6/8/70.
SMITH G.H. Born 12/5/23. Commd 13/10/48. Flt Lt 27/8/67. Retd GD 12/5/78. Re-instated 28/8/79 to 12/5/83.
SMITH G.J.E. BSc. Born 9/10/49. Commd 1/11/71. Flt Lt 1/2/73. Retd GD 1/11/91.
SMITH G.M. Born 14/5/46. Commd 25/2/82. Sqn Ldr 1/7/91. Retd SUP 6/4/98.
SMITH G.McD. MBE BSc. Born 17/6/48. Commd 20/1/71. Flt Lt 20/10/73. Retd ENG 31/3/94.
SMITH G.N. CEng MRAeS MIEE. Born 25/3/37. Commd 30/7/59. Sqn Ldr 1/7/68. Retd ENG 25/3/75.
SMITH G.N. MCSP DipTP. Born 5/8/50. Commd 30/4/81. Fg Offr 30/4/83. Retd MED(T) 1/9/86.
SMITH G.P. Born 27/3/55. Commd 8/8/76. Flt Lt 5/2/83. Retd SY 27/3/93.
SMITH G.P. Born 7/3/46. Commd 1/3/68. Wg Cdr 1/1/87. Retd GD 10/6/01.
SMITH G.T. Born 25/2/38. Commd 14/3/57. Flt Lt 19/6/63. Retd SEC 30/8/69.
SMITH G.T. Born 6/9/37. Commd 23/6/67. Sqn Ldr 1/1/87. Retd GD 17/1/90.
SMITH G.W. Born 9/10/52. Commd 28/2/85. Flt Lt 28/2/87. Retd ENG 1/10/93.
SMITH G.W. MBE. Born 19/12/19. Commd 25/10/43. Sqn Ldr 1/7/66. Retd GD 3/12/68.
SMITH G.W. Born 22/6/42. Commd 17/7/75. Flt Lt 17/7/77. Retd ENG 17/7/83.
SMITH G.W.T. MA MB BChir MRCS LRCP FRCS(Edin) DO. Born 18/3/37. Commd 20/9/59. Wg Cdr 19/6/68.
   Retd MED 20/9/75.
SMITH H. DFC AFC. Born 17/4/23. Commd 9/2/44. Wg Cdr 1/7/62. Retd GD 18/4/68.
SMITH H.A. Born 18/3/64. Commd 28/3/88. Sqn Ldr 1/7/99. Retd MEDICAL SUPPORT 2/2/05.
SMITH H.B. Born 8/1/49. Commd 11/11/71. Sqn Ldr 1/7/86. Retd SUP 1/7/89.
SMITH H.C. Born 30/10/37. Commd 24/6/71. Flt Lt 24/6/73. Retd ENG 1/10/85.
SMITH H.D. MCMI FInstPet. Born 7/7/24. Commd 8/9/44. Sqn Ldr 1/7/65. Retd SUP 10/10/78.
SMITH H.G. BA CertEd. Born 4/12/54. Commd 14/3/85. Sqn Ldr 1/7/94. Retd OPS SPT(ATC) 1/5/05.
SMITH H.J. MBE DFC. Born 8/10/18. Commd 20/10/42. Flt Lt 30/7/47. Retd CAT 15/2/61.
SMITH H.J. BSc. Born 14/5/32. Commd 13/8/52. Flt Lt 18/5/58. Retd GD 1/5/86.
SMITH H.R. BA CEng MRAeS. Born 30/9/42. Commd 30/9/61. Wg Cdr 1/7/89. Retd ENG 2/8/93.
SMITH H.R. Born 8/7/22. Commd 11/8/44. Flt Lt 11/2/48. Retd GD 5/8/60.
SMITH I.D. Born 3/4/49. Commd 20/9/68. Flt Lt 20/3/74. Retd GD 28/9/86.
SMITH I.E. Born 22/12/23. Commd 16/5/45. Wg Cdr 1/1/68. Retd SUP 1/11/72.
SMITH I.G. Born 4/9/54. Commd 6/10/77. Flt Lt 6/4/83. Retd GD 28/3/93.
SMITH I.P. BSc CEng MRAeS. Born 16/3/46. Commd 26/5/67. Sqn Ldr 1/7/80. Retd ENG 16/9/84.
SMITH I.T.G. BEng. Born 29/4/62. Commd 3/9/90. Flt Lt 4/4/95. Retd ENGINEER 18/4/03.

SMITH J. Born 24/9/41. Commd 11/8/67. Sqn Ldr 1/7/76. Retd ADMIN 3/4/82. Re-entered 5/11/90. Sqn Ldr 2/2/85.
Retd ADMIN 5/6/98.
SMITH J. BA. Born 17/8/62. Commd 10/11/85. Flt Lt 10/5/89. Retd ADMIN 10/11/91.
SMITH J. Born 24/9/41. Commd 9/7/66. Sqn Ldr 1/7/76. Retd ADMIN 2/4/82.
SMITH J. BSc BM BCh MRCPath DCP. Born 2/8/39. Commd 20/1/64. Wg Cdr 2/9/79. Retd MED 20/1/82.
SMITH J.A. Born 4/4/30. Commd 29/3/50. Flt Lt 29/9/54. Retd GD 4/4/68.
SMITH J.A. Born 4/6/38. Commd 26/5/60. Flt Lt 10/2/67. Retd GD 4/6/76.
SMITH J.A. Born 10/5/25. Commd 11/1/51. Sqn Ldr 1/1/68. Retd GD 10/5/80.
SMITH J.C.I. Born 13/10/58. Commd 22/3/81. Sqn Ldr 1/7/94. Retd ADMIN 14/3/97.
SMITH J.D. MEd BSc. Born 26/6/36. Commd 20/2/59. Sqn Ldr 17/5/68. Retd ADMIN 18/9/82.
SMITH J.E. CB CBE AFC. Born 8/6/24. Commd 6/3/50. AVM 1/1/78. Retd GD 3/4/81.
SMITH J.E. Born 11/11/43. Commd 2/2/84. Flt Lt 2/2/88. Retd ADMIN 14/3/97.
SMITH J.F. Born 19/2/22. Commd 6/10/60. Sqn Ldr 1/7/73. Retd ENG 1/10/75.
SMITH J.F. CEng MIMechE MRAeS. Born 11/10/38. Commd 30/7/59. Wg Cdr 1/1/78. Retd ENG 13/10/81.
SMITH J.J. MSc MRAeS. Born 5/7/56. Commd 20/5/82. Sqn Ldr 1/7/92. Retd ENGINEER 4/3/03.
SMITH J.M. Born 6/11/71. Commd 5/10/95. Plt Offr 5/10/96. Retd GD 26/7/97.
SMITH J.M. Born 12/9/27. Commd 4/9/58. Sqn Ldr 1/1/70. Retd ENG 13/1/73.
SMITH J.M. BSc. Born 11/8/60. Commd 25/10/87. Flt Lt 11/8/88. Retd GD(G) 21/3/91.
SMITH J.P. Born 22/3/37. Commd 10/2/72. Flt Lt 10/2/74. Retd GD 22/3/95.
SMITH J.R. Born 8/12/46. Commd 19/6/70. Flt Lt 30/1/74. Retd GD 4/11/75.
SMITH J.R. Born 31/12/37. Commd 2/1/67. Flt Lt 23/12/71. Retd ADMIN 13/2/82.
SMITH J.W.C. Born 17/2/15. Commd 22/4/43. Flt Lt 22/10/46. Retd ENG 17/2/64.
SMITH J.W.G. CBE DFC. Born 11/5/22. Commd 10/11/42. Gp Capt 1/1/72. Retd GD(G) 11/5/77.
SMITH J.W.G. Born 26/3/36. Commd 22/8/58. Flt Lt 26/7/64. Retd GD 22/8/74.
SMITH J.W.R. Born 23/10/14. Commd 30/1/47. Fg Offr 30/1/49. Retd SUP 1/9/52.
SMITH K. Born 20/1/24. Commd 11/5/45. Sqn Ldr 1/1/57. Retd GD 20/1/67.
SMITH K. BSc. Born 1/4/48. Commd 18/9/96. Wg Cdr 1/7/90. Retd GD 7/10/98.
SMITH K.A. BSc. Born 12/6/60. Commd 13/2/83. Wg Cdr 1/1/01. Retd GD 1/4/05.
SMITH K.B. Born 9/10/28. Commd 1/8/51. Plt Offr 1/8/51. Retd GD 14/6/52.
SMITH K.B. Born 29/7/50. Commd 30/5/69. Flt Lt 30/11/74. Retd GD 29/1/83.
SMITH K.C. BEM. Born 22/10/21. Commd 12/6/58. Flt Lt 12/6/64. Retd ENG 4/8/73.
SMITH K.E. Born 31/7/40. Commd 5/4/71. Flt Lt 5/4/71. Retd SUP 5/10/79.
SMITH K.G. Born 30/11/56. Commd 27/1/77. Sqn Ldr 1/1/89. Retd GD 11/11/95.
SMITH K.P. BA. Born 16/5/47. Commd 11/8/69. Flt Lt 11/8/75. Retd GD 17/1/76. Re-entered 8/2/79. Wg Cdr 1/7/94.
Retd OPS SPT 8/2/01.
SMITH K.R. Born 29/5/58. Commd 6/11/80. Flt Lt 21/4/86. Retd ADMIN 30/4/94.
SMITH K.W.E. Born 6/5/53. Commd 22/7/71. Sqn Ldr 1/7/87. Retd RGT 16/2/91.
SMITH L. Born 28/5/28. Commd 25/6/66. Flt Lt 25/6/71. Retd SEC 31/5/74.
SMITH L.F. Born 13/4/23. Commd 26/3/59. Flt Lt 26/3/64. Retd GD 7/4/73.
SMITH L.O. Born 17/2/26. Commd 31/5/50. Sqn Ldr 1/1/73. Retd GD(G) 17/2/86.
SMITH M.F. Born 9/2/29. Commd 9/4/52. Flt Lt 5/11/58. Retd GD 2/12/75.
SMITH M.H. Born 8/2/38. Commd 28/7/59. Gp Capt 1/7/82. Retd GD 1/2/89.
SMITH M.J. MCIPD MCMI. Born 4/6/46. Commd 8/9/69. Wg Cdr 1/1/87. Retd ADMIN 5/11/90.
SMITH M.J. Born 8/4/47. Commd 24/11/67. Flt Lt 24/5/73. Retd GD 22/4/94.
SMITH M.J. BSc. Born 27/7/38. Commd 22/8/61. Sqn Ldr 22/2/69. Retd ADMIN 27/7/93.
SMITH M.J.M. Born 26/11/44. Commd 7/7/67. Flt Lt 7/7/74. Retd SUP 8/5/83.
SMITH M.L. BA. Born 22/4/46. Commd 28/10/66. Wg Cdr 1/7/90. Retd GD 3/12/96.
SMITH M.R. CBE. Born 28/5/39. Commd 15/12/59. Gp Capt 1/1/89. Retd GD 1/8/93.
SMITH M.R. MCMI. Born 28/2/53. Commd 19/10/75. Sqn Ldr 1/7/84. Retd PRT 19/10/91.
SMITH M.T. Born 16/6/47. Commd 9/5/91. Flt Lt 9/5/95. Retd ADMIN 22/7/98.
SMITH M.V. Born 19/6/46. Commd 26/5/67. Flt Lt 18/2/70. Retd GD 30/11/77.
SMITH N.B. Born 21/6/43. Commd 15/7/66. Flt Lt 15/1/69. Retd GD 20/6/81.
SMITH N.C.R. BSc. Born 16/5/52. Commd 20/2/75. Flt Lt 15/10/80. Retd ENG 20/2/91.
SMITH N.F.G. BA FCMI MInstPkg MCIPS. Born 13/2/33. Commd 20/11/52. Wg Cdr 1/1/72. Retd SUP 26/5/78.
SMITH N.H.J. DFC. Born 15/4/18. Commd 1/5/39. Flt Lt 1/9/45. Retd GD 29/3/58. rtg Wg Cdr.
SMITH N.J. MSc BSc. Born 15/9/56. Commd 8/1/84. Sqn Ldr 1/1/93. Retd ENG 8/1/00.
SMITH N.S. Born 21/11/31. Commd 27/3/52. Flt Lt 27/12/57. Retd GD 21/11/69.
SMITH P. MBA BTech. Born 19/9/53. Commd 3/9/72. Sqn Ldr 1/7/88. Retd GD 14/9/96.
SMITH P. MBE FCMI MCIPD. Born 29/2/24. Commd 29/4/44. Gp Capt 1/7/69. Retd GD 1/3/79.
SMITH P. Born 15/4/43. Commd 24/6/65. Sqn Ldr 1/1/75. Retd GD 15/4/81.
SMITH P.A. Born 20/9/47. Commd 2/8/90. Sqn Ldr 1/1/99. Retd ADMIN 20/9/02.
SMITH P.A. Born 13/11/46. Commd 22/8/71. Flt Lt 22/11/74. Retd ENG 22/8/87.
SMITH P.A. BSc FRIN. Born 18/2/47. Commd 1/3/68. Gp Capt 1/1/94. Retd GD 13/1/01.
SMITH P.B. Born 16/11/30. Commd 19/3/52. Flt Lt 19/9/56. Retd GD 16/11/68.
SMITH P.B. Born 6/11/60. Commd 6/11/80. Flt Lt 6/5/87. Retd GD(G) 1/10/91.
SMITH P.C. Born 26/9/48. Commd 7/1/71. Flt Lt 7/7/76. Retd GD 14/3/96.

SMITH P.D. BA. Born 14/12/63. Commd 30/3/86. Flt Lt 30/9/88. Retd FLY(P) 14/2/04.
SMITH P.D.B. LLB. Born 31/1/31. Commd 11/5/51. Flt Lt 11/5/57. Retd SEC 31/7/59.
SMITH P.F. MBE. Born 8/1/18. Commd 15/1/42. Wg Cdr 1/1/61. Retd SEC 8/1/68.
SMITH P.G. Born 25/12/46. Commd 25/4/69. Flt Lt 25/10/74. Retd GD 20/8/76.
SMITH P.G. CEng MRAeS. Born 16/3/20. Commd 10/2/49. Wg Cdr 1/7/65. Retd ENG 1/11/72.
SMITH P.J. Born 12/7/32. Commd 11/10/51. Gp Capt 1/7/77. Retd SY 12/7/87.
SMITH P.J. CEng MIEE. Born 29/6/42. Commd 28/2/66. Sqn Ldr 1/7/76. Retd ENG 28/2/82.
SMITH P.J. Born 27/2/44. Commd 19/6/70. Flt Lt 19/6/72. Retd GD 8/4/76.
SMITH P.J. Born 9/10/48. Commd 11/5/89. Flt Lt 11/5/93. Retd ENGINEER 9/10/03.
SMITH P.S. MSc CertEd. Born 18/1/46. Commd 2/7/72. Sqn Ldr 1/1/87. Retd FLY(N) 1/4/04.
SMITH R. Born 26/3/33. Commd 28/6/51. Flt Lt 10/10/56. Retd GD 15/8/74.
SMITH R.A. BSc. Born 3/12/54. Commd 31/1/80. Flt Lt 29/5/86. Retd GD(G) 1/10/96.
SMITH R.A. MA FCMI FCIPD. Born 9/1/37. Commd 22/8/58. Gp Capt 1/1/86. Retd ADMIN 30/9/90.
SMITH R.A. Born 19/11/39. Commd 2/5/59. Flt Lt 2/11/64. Retd GD 14/1/71. Re-employed 30/4/72. Retd SUP 1/7/78.
SMITH R.B. DPhysEd. Born 7/3/44. Commd 19/8/68. Sqn Ldr 1/1/81. Retd GD 7/1/97.
SMITH R.B. Born 27/12/41. Commd 11/7/61. Flt Lt 11/1/67. Retd GD 7/9/73.
SMITH R.B. Born 24/10/41. Commd 26/5/61. Sqn Ldr 1/7/78. Retd GD 1/8/90.
SMITH R.C. Born 3/9/43. Commd 5/2/65. Sqn Ldr 1/1/87. Retd GD 3/9/00.
SMITH R.D.D. MCMI. Born 9/8/30. Commd 17/7/51. Sqn Ldr 1/1/63. Retd GD 17/8/73.
SMITH R.F.L.H. Born 2/11/48. Commd 15/4/73. Sqn Ldr 1/1/85. Retd ADMIN 15/4/89.
SMITH R.G. Born 18/10/23. Commd 12/9/58. Flt Lt 1/4/63. Retd GD 1/8/68.
SMITH R.G. Born 26/1/19. Commd 27/3/42. Sqn Ldr 1/7/54. Retd GD 3/7/59.
SMITH R.G. MA MCMI. Born 12/5/54. Commd 3/9/72. Wg Cdr 1/7/89. Retd RGT 1/7/92.
SMITH R.H. Born 22/5/21. Commd 17/4/42. Flt Lt 27/5/54. Retd GD(G) 5/10/67.
SMITH R.H. OBE CEng MIEE MCMI. Born 24/2/21. Commd 22/8/46. Gp Capt 1/1/74. Retd ENG 30/3/78.
SMITH R.H. OBE. Born 14/9/17. Commd 14/9/37. Wg Cdr 1/1/49. Retd GD 29/9/59.
SMITH R.H. FCMI. Born 11/7/42. Commd 26/5/61. Gp Capt 1/1/88. Retd ADMIN 11/7/97.
SMITH R.J. Born 12/5/42. Commd 22/5/80. Flt Lt 22/5/83. Retd GD 2/4/93.
SMITH R.J. Born 10/8/32. Commd 19/4/51. Sqn Ldr 1/7/63. Retd GD 10/8/70.
SMITH R.J.D. Born 3/6/42. Commd 8/6/62. Flt Lt 8/12/67. Retd GD 28/8/76.
SMITH R.K. Born 13/6/45. Commd 28/11/69. Flt Lt 17/8/73. Retd GD 14/6/77.
SMITH R.L. BSc MInstP. Born 8/5/34. Commd 20/5/59. Gp Capt 1/1/77. Retd ENG 2/5/87.
SMITH R.M. BSc. Born 13/3/44. Commd 30/5/71. Sqn Ldr 1/7/78. Retd GD 13/3/99.
SMITH R.M. Born 11/10/36. Commd 4/9/59. Wg Cdr 1/7/79. Retd ADMIN 6/4/83.
SMITH R.M. Born 14/7/29. Commd 17/1/51. Flt Lt 14/11/56. Retd GD 14/7/67.
SMITH R.N. OBE. Born 24/12/15. Commd 14/9/34. Wg Cdr 1/7/47. Retd GD 30/6/57.
SMITH R.S. Born 31/7/44. Commd 15/7/65. Sqn Ldr 1/1/77. Retd ENG 31/7/82. Re-instated 24/4/87. Sqn Ldr 28/9/81.
  Retd ENG 11/10/90.
SMITH R.T.D. AFM. Born 13/2/21. Commd 4/9/58. Flt Lt 4/9/63. Retd PE 22/8/74. rtg Sqn Ldr.
SMITH R.W. Born 22/11/25. Commd 21/9/50. Flt Lt 21/3/54. Retd GD 23/11/73.
SMITH R.W. DBE CEng MIMechE MRAeS. Born 1/6/37. Commd 30/4/59. Wg Cdr 1/7/75. Retd ENG 25/9/91.
SMITH R.W. Born 17/5/45. Commd 27/10/67. Flt Lt 24/2/74. Retd GD(G) 17/5/83.
SMITH S. Born 30/10/53. Commd 20/12/73. Flt Lt 20/6/79. Retd GD 30/10/91.
SMITH S.A. Born 9/11/45. Commd 11/11/65. Flt Lt 11/5/71. Retd GD(G) 9/11/83.
SMITH S.C. Born 7/9/52. Commd 30/8/73. Sqn Ldr 1/1/88. Retd GD 1/10/97.
SMITH S.C. Born 9/11/61. Commd 20/10/83. Flt Lt 20/4/90. Retd ADMIN 14/3/97.
SMITH S.C. MBE MIIM MCMI. Born 26/7/25. Commd 18/6/56. Sqn Ldr 1/1/72. Retd MAR 26/7/79.
SMITH S.C. BSc. Born 5/5/56. Commd 14/1/79. Flt Lt 14/10/80. Retd GD 14/1/87.
SMITH S.E. Born 23/10/60. Commd 24/7/81. Sqn Ldr 1/7/96. Retd GD 1/7/99.
SMITH S.E. MBE MBA BEd MCIPD MCMI. Born 13/6/56. Commd 23/5/82. Wg Cdr 1/1/95. Retd ADMIN 20/9/99.
SMITH S.G. Born 1/3/14. Commd 28/2/57. Flt Lt 28/2/60. Retd ACB 1/1/66.
SMITH S.J. Born 19/3/44. Commd 29/4/71. Sqn Ldr 1/7/80. Retd ENG 31/7/93.
SMITH S.K. Born 3/8/59. Commd 5/1/78. Sqn Ldr 1/7/90. Retd OPS SPT 5/12/98.
SMITH S.L. Born 29/3/60. Commd 11/1/79. Sqn Ldr 1/7/95. Retd GD 1/7/98.
SMITH S.R.F. Born 8/3/61. Commd 28/7/94. Flt Lt 28/7/96. Retd OPS SPT 11/5/00.
SMITH S.R.R. Born 25/6/14. Commd 10/10/34. Wg Cdr 1/7/47. Retd GD 25/6/58.
SMITH S.W. MBE. Born 19/1/27. Commd 12/3/52. Flt Lt 1/3/61. Retd GD 19/1/87.
SMITH S.W.G. BSc. Born 13/6/23. Commd 23/12/43. Sqn Ldr 1/7/56. Retd EDN 11/1/73.
SMITH T.D. Born 2/7/36. Commd 26/8/66. Fg Offr 26/8/66. Retd GD(G) 18/7/69.
SMITH T.G. Born 11/12/19. Commd 16/8/41. Flt Lt 31/1/47. Retd GD 2/9/50.
SMITH T.G. Born 1/10/36. Commd 1/11/79. Flt Lt 1/11/82. Retd GD(G) 1/10/88.
SMITH T.J. BSc CEng FIMechE MRAeS. Born 20/12/42. Commd 4/1/71. Wg Cdr 1/7/91. Retd ENG 1/10/93.
SMITH T.M. Born 5/6/41. Commd 15/2/73. Sqn Ldr 1/1/81. Retd SUP 15/2/90.
SMITH T.R.C. Born 27/8/43. Commd 12/7/63. Sqn Ldr 1/1/82. Retd GD 14/3/96.
SMITH V. MSc MBA BEd FRAeS FCIPD FCMI MBCS. Born 27/2/58. Commd 26/10/86. Gp Capt 1/1/01.
  Retd GD 1/7/04.

SMITH V.G. LLB(Lond) LLB BL. Born 25/7/33. Commd 4/4/60. Sqn Ldr 1/1/65. Retd EDN 4/4/73.
SMITH W. Born 29/5/56. Commd 31/8/78. Wg Cdr 1/1/94. Retd ADMIN 29/5/00.
SMITH W. Born 22/9/56. Commd 30/8/84. Flt Lt 18/2/87. Retd SUP 22/4/94.
SMITH W. Born 21/1/16. Commd 6/9/45. Flt Lt 29/6/50. Retd SUP 31/8/63.
SMITH W.H. Born 5/10/18. Commd 29/8/45. Fg Offr 29/8/46. Retd RGT 5/5/50. rtg Flt Lt.
SMITH W.H. MB BS FRCR MRCS LRCP DMR(D). Born 21/4/47. Commd 22/1/68. Wg Cdr 2/7/84. Retd MED 21/4/85.
SMITH W.H.H. Born 28/8/08. Commd 2/12/40. Flt Lt 6/12/44. Retd ENG 6/1/46. rtg Sqn Ldr.
SMITH W.J. DFC. Born 9/2/13. Commd 13/7/36. Wg Cdr 1/10/46. Retd GD 14/2/58.
SMITH W.M. MB ChB MRCGP. Born 28/2/44. Commd 25/7/66. Sqn Ldr 7/8/75. Retd MED 25/7/82.
SMITH-CARINGTON J.H. AFC. Born 26/10/21. Commd 14/3/42. Wg Cdr 1/7/60. Retd GD 26/10/71.
SMITHER M.J.B. Born 24/8/39. Commd 18/7/61. Sqn Ldr 1/7/70. Retd ENG 3/1/78.
SMITHSON F.M. Born 4/12/23. BSc. Born 8/6/50. Commd 8/4/44. Flt Lt 10/11/55. Retd GD 4/12/66.
SMITHSON J.D. BSc. Born 8/6/50. Commd 23/9/68. Sqn Ldr 1/1/91. Retd FLY(P) 8/6/05.
SMITHSON P.C. MSc BEd. Born 25/5/54. Commd 17/1/82. Wg Cdr 1/1/98. Retd ADMIN 5/12/98.
SMITHSON W.J. Born 2/11/33. Commd 20/12/51. Flt Lt 4/4/57. Retd GD(G) 17/1/73.
SMITZ A.J. DFC. Born 12/10/11. Commd 26/3/40. Sqn Ldr 1/1/60. Retd GD(G) 1/8/60.
SMORTHIT N.M. BSc. Born 23/8/62. Commd 2/4/84. Flt Lt 15/1/87. Retd GD 23/8/00.
SMOUT P.F. AFC DPhysEd. Born 1/6/47. Commd 19/8/68. Wg Cdr 1/7/97. Retd ADMIN 3/7/99.
SMULOVIC P.S.V. BSc. Born 22/11/46. Commd 15/6/83. Sqn Ldr 1/7/95. Retd ENG 24/1/98.
SMURTHWAITE R. CEng MIEE. Born 2/1/18. Commd 8/10/42. Sqn Ldr 1/7/53. Retd ENG 1/9/70.
SMUTS J.A. Born 24/9/36. Commd 18/2/58. Flt Lt 18/2/65. Retd GD(G) 24/9/74.
SMYTH A.J.M. OBE DFC BSc. Born 17/2/15. Commd 21/2/37. Gp Capt 1/7/55. Retd GD 6/10/61.
SMYTH A.J.N. BEcon. Born 18/10/53. Commd 27/3/77. Sqn Ldr 1/7/88. Retd GD 30/4/95. Re-entered 10/4/00.
 Sqn Ldr 10/7/89. Retd FLY(P) 1/8/04.
SMYTH A.T. Born 28/3/54. Commd 7/7/80. Wg Cdr 1/1/95. Retd ADMIN 9/7/98.
SMYTH D.F. Born 23/10/39. Commd 26/9/83. Flt Lt 6/5/87. Retd SY 23/10/94.
SMYTH D.M. Born 2/3/66. Commd 26/9/90. Flt Lt 26/9/92. Retd FLY(N) 31/3/04.
SMYTH G.H. Born 5/6/24. Commd 20/4/50. Sqn Ldr 1/1/75. Retd GD 5/6/79.
SMYTH G.T. Born 4/5/12. Commd 5/11/42. Flt Lt 5/5/46. Retd ENG 15/9/59. rtg Sqn Ldr.
SMYTH J.A. BChD. Born 21/10/57. Commd 1/10/78. Wg Cdr 14/3/93. Retd DEL 21/10/96.
SMYTH P.J. Born 15/8/49. Commd 10/1/69. Sqn Ldr 1/1/01. Retd FLY(N) 15/8/04.
SMYTH P.M. BSc. Born 27/2/49. Commd 24/9/72. Flt Lt 24/6/73. Retd GD 24/9/88. Re-entered 3/1/89. Flt Lt 3/10/73.
 Retd FLY(P) 30/1/04.
SMYTH P.N. Born 21/9/27. Commd 19/7/56. Sqn Ldr 1/1/72. Retd ENG 14/5/80.
SMYTH R.H. AFC. Born 27/1/22. Commd 5/8/42. Sqn Ldr 1/7/54. Retd GD 31/10/61.
SMYTH R.J.V. DFC. Born 14/2/20. Commd 24/6/41. Wg Cdr 1/1/59. Retd GD 14/2/67.
SMYTH S.G. MBE . Born 17/8/48. Commd 7/1/71. Wg Cdr 1/1/01. Retd GD 4/10/03.
SMYTH T.A. Born 7/5/35. Commd 3/12/54. Flt Lt 3/6/60. Retd GD 7/5/73.
SMYTH W.L. MBE MCMI. Born 12/9/25. Commd 26/12/51. Wg Cdr 1/7/68. Retd GD 12/9/80.
SMYTHE G. Born 25/9/24. Commd 11/11/50. Flt Lt 11/5/55. Retd GD 3/4/74.
SMYTHE P.J. Born 17/3/30. Commd 15/4/55. Flt Lt 1/3/61. Retd GD 17/3/91.
SMYTHE R.F.W. Born 27/2/34. Commd 27/1/67. Fg Offr 27/1/67. Retd RGT 29/9/72.
SMYTHE W.V. Born 21/10/20. Commd 10/3/44. Flt Lt 9/7/56. Retd GD(G) 23/5/69.
SNADDEN W.R. Born 19/2/42. Commd 28/2/64. Flt Lt 28/8/69. Retd GD 19/2/80.
SNAPE B.R.R. OBE. Born 9/11/08. Commd 12/12/41. Sqn Ldr 1/7/52. Retd SEC 15/4/58.
SNAPE D.E. Born 9/6/23. Commd 10/2/45. Flt Lt 10/8/48. Retd GD(G) 31/3/62.
SNAPE K.R. Born 23/4/37. Commd 19/2/57. Flt Lt 19/8/62. Retd GD(G) 23/4/75.
SNAPE R.A. Born 19/6/51. Commd 10/2/72. Flt Lt 22/6/78. Retd ADMIN 19/12/89.
SNARE R.T.F. Born 23/9/32. Commd 26/9/51. Sqn Ldr 1/1/65. Retd GD 23/9/70.
SNASHALL S.M. BEng. Born 30/1/67. Commd 15/9/85. Sqn Ldr 1/1/00. Retd FLY(P) 30/1/05.
SNEDDON H.M. Born 17/5/24. Commd 26/5/60. Sqn Ldr 1/7/71. Retd ENG 1/9/73.
SNEDDON J. Born 25/7/30. Commd 21/11/51. Flt Lt 13/11/57. Retd GD 25/10/68.
SNEDDON M.I. BSc CEng MIEE. Born 7/7/59. Commd 26/9/82. Flt Lt 1/11/85. Retd ENG 26/9/98.
SNEDDON P.A. BSc. Born 25/1/51. Commd 8/4/73. Sqn Ldr 1/1/84. Retd GD 8/4/89.
SNEDDON S.R. BSc. Born 22/6/63. Commd 7/12/86. Flt Lt 7/6/90. Retd OPS SPT 7/12/02.
SNEDDON T.J. Born 30/3/42. Commd 8/12/61. Wg Cdr 1/1/84. Retd GD 22/12/89.
SNELDERS F.M. Born 20/7/45. Commd 27/3/70. Sqn Ldr 1/1/84. Retd GD 20/7/01.
SNELGROVE P.S. Born 28/12/47. Commd 11/10/84. Flt Lt 11/10/88. Retd SUP 1/10/93.
SNELL A.M. BA CertEd. Born 7/8/53. Commd 2/11/88. Flt Lt 2/11/90. Retd ADMIN 2/11/96.
SNELL J.D. Born 3/7/46. Commd 18/8/67. Sqn Ldr 1/1/82. Retd GD 3/7/91.
SNELL P.R. BA. Born 12/9/54. Commd 6/11/77. Sqn Ldr 1/7/90. Retd GD 1/6/95.
SNELL R.W.K. Born 12/3/36. Commd 22/10/54. Flt Lt 7/3/62. Retd GD 12/3/74.
SNELL S. Born 9/7/19. Commd 10/2/45. Flt Lt 23/3/47. Retd ENG 7/11/53.
SNELL V.A. Born 8/2/69. Commd 29/3/90. Plt Offr 13/7/90. Retd ADMIN 15/11/91.
SNELLER J.A.J. MA CEng MRAeS. Born 6/3/57. Commd 1/7/82. Wg Cdr 1/1/96. Retd ENG 6/3/01.
SNELLER K.G. AFC. Born 3/10/20. Commd 21/6/56. Sqn Ldr 1/7/72. Retd GD 25/10/75.

SNELLER R.G.J. DFC. Born 25/11/21. Commd 21/6/50. Flt Lt 21/12/54. Retd GD 30/3/68.
SNELLING G.E. MCMI. Born 12/11/25. Commd 9/2/66. Sqn Ldr 1/7/77. Retd ENG 12/11/83.
SNELLING M.H.B. AFC MA. Born 12/12/41. Commd 30/9/60. Flt Lt 22/2/66. Retd GD 29/12/73.
SNELLING R.F.S. CEng MIMechE. Born 22/8/35. Commd 11/6/63. Flt Lt 10/2/67. Retd ENG 22/8/93.
SNOOK P. MBE. Born 14/1/43. Commd 11/8/67. Flt Lt 12/11/69. Retd GD 14/1/00.
SNOW D.B. Born 15/10/53. Commd 18/1/73. Sqn Ldr 1/1/88. Retd GD 15/10/91.
SNOW I.P. Born 30/11/47. Commd 27/1/77. Sqn Ldr 1/7/84. Retd SUP 1/10/89.
SNOW J.W. Born 8/10/21. Commd 20/4/50. Fg Offr 20/4/51. Retd ENG 12/10/54.
SNOWDEN J.S. BA. Born 12/4/49. Commd 15/3/73. Sqn Ldr 1/1/84. Retd GD(G) 14/3/96.
SNOWDEN R.W. Born 29/4/48. Commd 11/9/86. Flt Lt 11/9/90. Retd ENG 21/10/99.
SNOWDON E. Born 8/2/18. Commd 6/11/58. Flt Lt 6/11/64. Retd ENG 1/6/66.
SOAMES-WARING D. Born 25/4/31. Commd 3/5/68. Flt Lt 3/5/71. Retd GD 3/7/73.
SOAR D.E. Born 3/11/28. Commd 11/1/76. Retd ENG 6/8/80.
SOBEY B.L. BA CEng MCMI MIEE. Born 9/12/48. Commd 2/7/72. Air Cdre 1/7/00. Retd GD 9/12/03.
SODEAU M.D. Born 17/9/64. Commd 2/8/90. Flt Lt 16/5/94. Retd FLY(P) 20/4/03.
SODEN E. BSc. Born 27/7/42. Commd 30/9/61. Flt Lt 9/2/68. Retd ENG 29/12/73.
SOFFE C.R. BSc. Born 1/6/65. Commd 28/8/83. Flt Lt 15/1/89. Retd GD 15/7/98.
SOLE M.A. Born 23/9/50. Commd 20/9/69. Fg Offr 20/3/72. Retd GD(G) 22/11/74.
SOLIS P. Born 15/5/39. Commd 7/5/68. Flt Lt 17/3/71. Retd AD 15/5/94.
SOLLEY D.C. BSc. Born 26/5/62. Commd 11/9/83. Flt Lt 11/3/87. Retd ADMIN 5/12/87.
SOLLITT A.G. Born 11/4/46. Commd 26/5/67. Sqn Ldr 1/1/76. Retd GD 27/7/99.
SOLLITT S. AFC. Born 27/10/21. Commd 29/6/50. Flt Lt 29/12/53. Retd GD 2/1/68.
SOLOMON S.P.E. Born 25/12/50. Commd 1/1/71. Sqn Ldr 1/7/85. Retd GD 25/12/88.
SOMERFIELD P.J. Born 25/4/45. Commd 5/2/65. Flt Lt 6/10/71. Retd GD 22/10/94.
SOMERS-JOCE D.R. Born 30/3/32. Commd 28/6/51. Flt Lt 9/3/57. Retd GD 29/5/76.
SOMERVELL M.J.S. CEng MRAeS MCMI. Born 15/6/30. Commd 4/8/53. Wg Cdr 1/7/74. Retd ENG 17/6/80.
SOMERVILLE A.D. Born 6/7/62. Commd 8/9/83. Sqn Ldr 1/7/98. Retd GD 1/7/01.
SOMERVILLE P.C. Born 4/11/41. Commd 1/11/79. Sqn Ldr 1/1/92. Retd SY 27/6/94.
SOMMER V.M. Born 1/7/20. Commd 25/8/41. Sqn Offr 1/7/50. Retd SEC 16/9/57.
SOUCH G. Born 6/7/29. Commd 11/4/51. Fg Offr 11/4/52. Retd GD 12/3/53.
SOULSBY R. Born 11/6/26. Commd 23/1/59. Flt Lt 18/3/64. Retd EDN 25/5/66.
SOULSBY R.N. Born 10/2/45. Commd 28/2/64. Flt Lt 28/8/69. Retd GD 10/2/83.
SOUNESS F.S. DFC. Born 31/8/30. Commd 17/5/51. Flt Lt 6/9/56. Retd GD 31/12/69. Re-instated 18/6/80 to 31/8/87.
SOUTAR Sir Charles KBE MB BS LMSSA MFCM DPH DIH. Born 12/6/20. Commd 2/5/46. AM 31/3/78.
  Retd MED 12/6/81.
SOUTER J.O. Born 6/11/27. Commd 25/8/60. Sqn Ldr 1/7/72. Retd ADMIN 6/11/82.
SOUTER K.P. Born 12/6/19. Commd 6/7/42. Flt Lt 9/1/50. Retd GD 25/4/58.
SOUTH A.A. MBE CertEd DPhysEd. Born 28/1/48. Commd 8/12/76. Sqn Ldr 1/1/89. Retd ADMIN 28/1/03.
SOUTH G.J. DSO DFC FCMI. Born 21/10/22. Commd 28/2/43. Gp Capt 1/1/66. Retd GD 2/3/73.
SOUTH P.G. BA. Born 26/6/25. Commd 10/3/45. Gp Capt 1/1/68. Retd GD 14/8/71.
SOUTHALL J.D. Born 20/12/19. Commd 20/5/44. Flt Lt 20/5/47. Retd ENG 15/10/56.
SOUTHAM T.H. Born 15/8/49. Commd 7/6/73. Sqn Ldr 1/1/86. Retd GD 1/7/94.
SOUTHCOMBE W.R. Born 11/12/42. Commd 22/3/63. Wg Cdr 1/1/88. Retd GD 31/3/99.
SOUTHERN D.F. Born 3/7/31. Commd 3/7/31. Sqn Ldr 1/7/86. Retd GD 3/7/92.
SOUTHERN J.M. Born 27/6/58. Commd 1/7/82. Flt Lt 27/5/85. Retd GD 20/4/92.
SOUTHERN P. BSc. Born 27/9/61. Commd 20/1/85. Flt Lt 20/7/87. Retd GD 20/1/01.
SOUTHERN S. Born 28/4/60. Commd 17/5/79. Sqn Ldr 1/7/97. Retd ADMIN 30/6/99.
SOUTHERN T. Born 17/9/18. Commd 22/9/41. Sqn Offr 1/9/45. Retd SEC 17/5/56.
SOUTHGATE H.C. CB CBE. Born 30/10/21. Commd 23/9/43. AVM 1/1/74. Retd SUP 30/10/76.
SOUTHGATE M.R. Born 1/6/33. Commd 22/7/54. Sqn Ldr 1/1/71. Retd GD 25/6/86.
SOUTHON V.A. Born 3/4/29. Commd 13/12/50. Flt Lt 13/6/53. Retd GD 3/4/67.
SOUTHWELL B.G. Born 16/3/32. Commd 19/7/51. Flt Lt 14/11/56. Retd GD 14/1/70.
SOUTHWELL D.W. Born 31/7/23. Commd 7/11/46. Flt Lt 7/5/51. Retd SEC 6/2/58.
SOUTHWELL F.R. Born 26/11/24. Commd 20/4/50. Wg Cdr 1/7/71. Retd SEC 11/8/81.
SOUTHWICK E.E. BEM. Born 20/4/30. Commd 17/4/73. Sqn Ldr 1/1/83. Retd ENG 12/2/87.
SOUTHWOOD D.R. AFC BSc. Born 15/6/55. Commd 2/9/73. Sqn Ldr 1/7/89. Retd GD 15/6/99.
SOUTHWOULD B.W. BA. Born 26/6/45. Commd 29/11/63. Flt Lt 29/5/69. Retd GD 26/6/00.
SOWDEN P. Born 31/10/31. Commd 27/8/64. Wg Cdr 1/7/81. Retd ADMIN 1/2/80.
SOWDEN P.J. CEng MRAeS. Born 14/10/38. Commd 30/7/59. Sqn Ldr 1/7/78. Retd ENG 17/2/89.
SOWDEN R.E. BSc. Born 7/11/54. Commd 15/10/78. Sqn Ldr 1/7/92. Retd ENG 1/12/96.
SOWELLS E.J. MBE. Born 17/9/43. Commd 27/7/72. Wg Cdr 1/7/89. Retd ENG 15/1/94.
SOWELLS W.T. Born 16/5/39. Commd 7/2/61. Flt Lt 1/1/92. Retd ENG 16/5/94.
SOWERBY R.F. MB ChB MRCGP DavMed MFOM. Born 17/6/31. Commd 5/4/59. Gp Capt 1/1/82. Retd MED 7/9/84.
SOWERBY W.B. MVO. Born 1/3/33. Commd 4/7/51. Sqn Ldr 1/7/78. Retd GD 28/11/86.
SOWLER D.J. AFC. Born 22/4/44. Commd 24/6/65. Sqn Ldr 1/7/76. Retd GD 30/9/81.
SOWOOD P.J. MA PhD MBA BM BCh DAvMed. Born 23/2/53. Commd 20/1/76. Wg Cdr 1/8/92. Retd MED 20/1/96.

SOWREY Sir Frederick KCB CBE AFC. Born 14/9/22. Commd 20/8/41. AM 1/1/78. Retd GD 5/4/80.
SOWREY J.A. DFC AFC MRAeS. Born 5/1/20. Commd 7/3/40. Gp Capt 1/7/61. Retd GD 18/6/68. rtg A Cdre.
SPALDING R.M. Born 27/8/48. Commd 1/8/69. Gp Capt 1/1/94. Retd ADMIN 14/3/96.
SPALDING M.B. Born 15/8/23. Commd 21/4/44. Wg Cdr 1/7/62. Retd GD 1/10/68.
SPANDLER R.B. Born 13/8/37. Commd 21/8/68. Sqn Ldr 1/1/79. Retd ADMIN 13/8/95.
SPANDLEY T.A. Born 25/12/60. Commd 31/1/80. Sqn Ldr 1/1/90. Retd GD 25/12/98.
SPANNER C.A. Born 2/8/42. Commd 12/1/62. Sqn Ldr 1/1/77. Retd GD 18/12/95.
SPARKES P. Born 20/2/65. Commd 16/6/88. Flt Lt 16/12/93. Retd GD 14/3/97.
SPARKES P.D. BSc CEng MIEE. Born 12/2/40. Commd 10/12/63. Sqn Ldr 1/7/74. Retd ENG 1/10/88.
SPARKES R.G. MBE DFC. Born 12/5/22. Commd 12/11/43. Wg Cdr 1/1/69. Retd GD(G) 31/3/77.
SPARKES R.M. Born 5/4/33. Commd 19/7/51. Wg Cdr 1/7/70. Retd GD 18/7/87.
SPARKES R.W. MBE DFC MCMI. Born 11/3/21. Commd 3/9/43. Wg Cdr 1/7/68. Retd SUP 11/3/76.
SPARKS J.C. BA CertEd. Born 11/12/52. Commd 30/3/86. Sqn Ldr 1/1/94. Retd ADMIN 30/3/02.
SPARKS J.P. AE BSc CEng MRAeS. Born 30/9/23. Commd 24/2/45. Sqn Ldr 1/7/62. Retd ENG 30/3/78.
SPARKS M. LRCP LRFPS. Born 9/8/16. Commd 25/7/41. Gp Capt 1/1/66. Retd MED 9/8/74.
SPARKS M.J. MCMI. Born 13/5/35. Commd 25/6/66. Sqn Ldr 1/7/75. Retd GD 16/3/87.
SPARKS M.N. AFC. Born 30/12/20. Commd 20/9/47. Flt Lt 29/6/50. Retd GD 13/11/67.
SPARKS W. MBE. Born 10/10/19. Commd 20/6/43. Flt Lt 19/6/52. Retd GD(G) 10/10/74.
SPARROW E.M. DFC AFC MCMI. Born 18/2/22. Commd 8/5/42. Wg Cdr 1/1/60. Retd GD 18/2/69.
SPARROW K.A. Born 15/12/62. Commd 29/5/97. Flt Lt 29/5/99. Retd OPS SPT(FLTOPS) 29/5/05.
SPARROW M.J. Born 4/3/32. Commd 10/9/52. Sqn Ldr 1/1/69. Retd GD 1/5/76.
SPARROW M.V.D. Born 25/5/45. Commd 18/8/67. Sqn Ldr 1/1/88. Retd FLY(P) 25/5/03.
SPATCHER J.L. AFC. Born 12/1/33. Commd 6/4/54. Sqn Ldr 1/7/63. Retd GD 12/1/71.
SPEAIGHT P.D. Born 20/5/49. Commd 13/8/82. Flt Lt 13/8/84. Retd ENG 13/8/90.
SPEAKE P.J. Born 1/7/29. Commd 1/6/61. Flt Offr 1/6/63. Retd SEC 18/7/63.
SPEAKMAN N.A. Born 21/6/61. Commd 8/12/83. Flt Lt 8/6/89. Retd GD 1/10/00.
SPEAR C.W.P. Born 27/4/43. Commd 15/7/64. Wg Cdr 1/7/89. Retd ENG 27/4/98.
SPEAR J.R. BSc. Born 30/3/58. Commd 5/9/76. Flt Lt 15/10/80. Retd GD 14/9/96.
SPEAREY W.W. Born 16/5/20. Commd 11/9/42. Sqn Ldr 1/1/71. Retd Pl 16/5/75.
SPEARPOINT A. MCMI. Born 25/1/48. Commd 2/1/75. Wg Cdr 1/1/93. Retd GD 30/9/03.
SPEARS P.A. AFC. Born 14/4/50. Commd 19/6/70. Sqn Ldr 1/7/87. Retd GD 1/7/90.
SPEED B.N.J. OBE FCMI MIL. Born 16/9/40. Commd 6/8/60. A Cdre 1/7/87. Retd GD 16/9/95.
SPEED M.D. Born 6/12/44. Commd 28/9/62. Gp Capt 1/7/90. Retd GD 31/3/94.
SPEEDIE A. Born 24/4/21. Commd 14/2/46. Sqn Ldr 1/7/60. Retd ENG 24/4/71.
SPEER K.G. Born 21/6/28. Commd 14/1/53. Flt Lt 3/6/58. Retd GD 25/8/68.
SPEIGHT M.J. BSc. Born 16/7/64. Commd 10/11/85. Flt Lt 10/5/88. Retd GD 26/5/99.
SPEIGHT W. MBE. Born 11/1/46. Commd 1/7/82. Sqn Ldr 1/7/91. Retd GD 7/9/98.
SPEIRS J.P. Born 7/4/32. Commd 25/6/57. Flt Lt 6/3/63. Retd GD 25/3/73.
SPENCE A. BTech. Born 16/9/57. Commd 8/2/81. Flt Lt 8/5/81. Retd GD 7/12/93.
SPENCE A.J. MBE FCMI. Born 9/5/21. Commd 13/3/47. Gp Capt 1/7/71. Retd SUP 9/5/76.
SPENCE B.G. BA IEng. Born 27/9/44. Commd 12/7/79. Sqn Ldr 1/1/92. Retd ENG 19/5/97.
SPENCE E.L. Born 1/7/37. Commd 24/4/60. Flt Offr 7/8/64. Retd CAT 31/12/65.
SPENCE J.F. Born 8/2/43. Commd 22/5/70. Sqn Ldr 1/1/82. Retd GD(G) 9/2/89.
SPENCE J.U. Born 21/12/28. Commd 18/5/55. Sqn Ldr 1/1/67. Retd SEC 18/5/71.
SPENCE N.M. Born 25/6/43. Commd 1/6/72. Sqn Ldr 1/1/84. Retd GD(G) 1/10/86.
SPENCER A.W. Born 20/12/29. Commd 7/5/52. Sqn Ldr 1/1/79. Retd GD(G) 20/12/89.
SPENCER C. Born 29/11/32. Commd 11/5/59. Wg Cdr 1/1/73. Retd SUP 14/2/76.
SPENCER C.L.B. Born 9/8/20. Commd 14/3/46. Wg Cdr 1/7/68. Retd ENG 4/4/75.
SPENCER C.R. AFC DFM. Born 10/9/16. Commd 10/7/43. Flt Lt 9/6/50. Retd GD(G) 14/5/63.
SPENCER C.R.C. Born 16/10/25. Commd 6/12/46. Sqn Ldr 1/7/56. Retd GD 1/2/68.
SPENCER D.E. Born 29/12/22. Commd 29/3/45. Gp Capt 1/1/75. Retd SUP 29/12/77.
SPENCER D.G. Born 15/2/28. Commd 18/9/48. Flt Lt 8/5/57. Retd GD 11/5/67.
SPENCER F.A. OBE FCMI MCIPS. Born 22/11/27. Commd 31/7/58. Gp Capt 1/7/78. Retd SUP 22/11/82.
SPENCER F.L. Born 19/5/19. Commd 3/7/44. Sqn Ldr 1/4/56. Retd GD 18/11/58.
SPENCER G.B. MCMI. Born 7/12/33. Commd 20/12/51. Sqn Ldr 1/7/64. Retd GD 1/6/86.
SPENCER J.D. BA. Born 29/3/29. Commd 27/6/64. Sqn Ldr 1/7/77. Retd ADMIN 29/3/84.
SPENCER J.H. CBE AFC MCIPD. Born 2/10/39. Commd 3/6/58. A Cdre 1/7/90. Retd GD 2/10/95.
SPENCER J.R. ACIS. Born 11/5/50. Commd 7/6/73. Sqn Ldr 1/1/84. Retd ADMIN 2/4/94.
SPENCER J.R.C. Born 17/5/24. Commd 13/1/44. Sqn Ldr 1/7/57. Retd ENG 17/5/73.
SPENCER J.W.C. MSc BSc CEng MIMechE. Born 11/5/50. Commd 26/2/71. Wg Cdr 1/7/95. Retd GD 11/5/05.
SPENCER K. BA MInstAM(Dip). Born 6/8/46. Commd 13/2/72. Sqn Ldr 1/1/84. Retd ADMIN 2/12/96.
SPENCER M. Born 28/1/50. Commd 4/3/81. Flt Lt 30/4/83. Retd ENG 11/7/85.
SPENCER P.D. Born 15/12/54. Commd 30/6/78. Wg Cdr 1/7/93. Retd GD 31/10/98.
SPENCER R.E. Born 14/5/30. Commd 7/5/52. Flt Lt 2/10/57. Retd GD 2/9/71.
SPENCER T.D. MBE. Born 29/12/16. Commd 26/2/42. Sqn Ldr 1/1/53. Retd ENG 29/12/65.
SPERANDEO F. Born 17/7/30. Commd 21/10/65. Sqn Ldr 1/7/76. Retd ADMIN 6/4/83.

SPERRING P.J. Born 15/6/49. Commd 2/1/75. Wg Cdr 1/7/90. Retd ENG 30/4/94.
SPIBY D.W. DFM. Born 7/7/21. Commd 1/10/43. Flt Lt 7/6/51. Retd GD(G) 1/5/69.
SPICE P.C. Born 18/11/22. Commd 23/12/44. Wg Cdr 1/7/69. Retd ENG 18/11/77.
SPICER M.J. BSc. Born 11/10/36. Commd 22/8/61. Flt Lt 10/6/63. Retd EDN 1/9/68.
SPIERS P. Born 15/6/31. Commd 29/3/68. Flt Lt 29/3/71. Retd GD 15/6/86.
SPIERS P.H. Born 14/12/13. Commd 15/6/44. Flt Lt 3/10/51. Retd ENG 16/4/56.
SPIERS R.J. MB BS MRCS LRCP DAvMed. Born 18/5/51. Commd 21/11/71. Wg Cdr 9/7/89. Retd MED 23/3/90.
SPIERS R.J. OBE FRAeS. Born 8/11/28. Commd 14/12/49. A Cdre 1/1/79. Retd GD 8/11/83.
SPIEWAKOWSKI M.J. Born 8/7/48. Commd 10/2/72. Sqn Ldr 1/7/82. Retd ENG 8/7/86.
SPIGHT B.F. Born 12/11/34. Commd 5/5/60. Flt Lt 5/11/64. Retd GD 12/11/72.
SPIGHT P.J.U. Born 12/12/44. Commd 11/5/78. Sqn Ldr 1/7/91. Retd ADMIN 12/12/98.
SPILLANE J.P. OBE CEng MIMechE MRAeS DCAe. Born 18/11/18. Commd 10/11/42. Wg Cdr 1/7/60.
    Retd ENG 5/7/66.
SPILLER N.B. Born 15/8/46. Commd 18/8/67. Gp Capt 1/1/97. Retd GD 21/9/04.
SPILSBURY D.A. Born 6/5/45. Commd 11/9/64. Wg Cdr 1/1/91. Retd GD 12/7/99.
SPILSBURY D.R. MRAeS. Born 28/1/15. Commd 28/10/43. Wg Cdr 1/7/65. Retd ENG 11/8/70.
SPINK C.R. CB CBE FCMI FRAeS. Born 17/5/46. Commd 2/8/68. Air Mshl 19/6/00. Retd GD 14/6/03.
SPINK D.J. Born 1/1/33. Commd 27/9/51. Sqn Ldr 1/7/67. Retd GD 1/1/71.
SPINK P.L. Born 3/11/47. Commd 30/1/68. Flt Lt 25/5/74. Retd GD 3/11/00.
SPINKS A.J. BSc. Born 4/4/33. Commd 14/11/57. Wg Cdr 1/7/72. Retd ENG 30/11/88.
SPINKS L.G. Born 10/2/30. Commd 23/9/66. Flt Lt 23/9/71. Retd GD 10/2/85.
SPIRES B. Born 8/1/48. Commd 2/11/88. Sqn Ldr 1/7/94. Retd FLY(ALM) 23/9/03.
SPIRIT H.E. BSc. Born 25/2/45. Commd 21/1/68. Sqn Ldr 1/1/94. Retd FLY(P) 31/8/04.
SPITTAL M.J. MB ChB. Born 15/2/60. Commd 19/11/81. Wg Cdr 1/8/97. Retd MED 1/10/98.
SPITTLES T.W. Born 14/5/34. Commd 24/5/53. Sqn Ldr 1/1/87. Retd GD 14/5/89.
SPOFFORTH J.S. Born 29/3/40. Commd 21/10/66. Flt Lt 21/1/73. Retd ADMIN 4/7/82.
SPOFFORTH P.A.M. Born 6/8/47. Commd 2/8/68. Sqn Ldr 1/7/82. Retd GD 6/8/85.
SPONG D.B. BSc. Born 4/1/55. Commd 30/9/73. Flt Lt 15/10/76. Retd GD 7/4/88.
SPOONER C. Born 9/12/25. Commd 27/6/51. Flt Lt 27/12/55. Retd GD 9/12/79.
SPOONER R.H. Born 19/3/46. Commd 8/11/68. Wg Cdr 1/1/90. Retd ADMIN 14/3/96.
SPOONER R.J.S. AFC. Born 6/3/22. Commd 17/9/43. Wg Cdr 1/1/60. Retd GD 2/5/68.
SPOOR S.J. AFC. Born 20/11/43. Commd 6/5/66. Sqn Ldr 1/7/81. Retd GD 24/7/89.
SPOTTISWOOD J.D. CB CVO AFC MA. Born 27/5/34. Commd 11/6/52. AVM 1/1/84. Retd GD 27/5/89.
SPRACKLING B.J. DFC. Born 9/7/22. Commd 3/8/43. Sqn Ldr 1/7/57. Retd GD 9/7/65.
SPRACKLING J.M. Born 11/12/38. Commd 7/1/58. Wg Cdr 1/1/83. Retd GD 4/11/89.
SPRAGG B.J. DFC. Born 2/12/23. Commd 14/4/44. Wg Cdr 1/7/69. Retd GD 1/5/74.
SPRAGG R.E. Born 15/2/32. Commd 29/10/64. Sqn Ldr 1/10/71. Retd EDN 29/10/72.
SPRAGUE D.J. Born 6/11/59. Commd 20/9/79. Sqn Ldr 1/1/94. Retd GD 1/3/99.
SPREADBURY J.A. Born 12/5/29. Commd 28/11/49. Flt Lt 27/12/55. Retd GD 12/5/67.
SPRECKLEY G.C. Born 10/3/44. Commd 12/7/63. Sqn Ldr 1/1/92. Retd GD 10/3/99.
SPRENT J.C. Born 10/9/31. Commd 27/6/51. Gp Capt 1/1/78. Retd GD 30/4/86.
SPRINGATE L.T. AFM. Born 18/5/43. Commd 29/4/77. Flt Lt 29/4/73. Retd GD 18/5/81.
SPRINGETT R. FRAeS MILT. Born 9/4/44. Commd 26/3/64. Gp Capt 1/7/93. Retd SUP 9/4/99.
SPRINGETT R.J. OBE BSc BA. Born 13/5/38. Commd 1/1/61. Gp Capt 1/7/92. Retd GD 13/2/94.
SPRINKS P.L.E. MCMI. Born 24/9/41. Commd 2/8/68. Sqn Ldr 1/7/77. Retd ENG 1/7/80. Re-entered 8/12/82.
    Wg Cdr 1/1/91. Retd ENG 1/2/97.
SPROSEN B.J. Born 21/1/39. Commd 22/2/63. Wg Cdr 1/7/84. Retd GD 21/10/88.
SPRULES R.K. Born 4/5/34. Commd 24/2/67. Flt Lt 4/5/72. Retd ENG 24/2/75.
SPURLING T.A. Born 3/8/34. Commd 30/12/55. Flt Lt 30/6/61. Retd GD 3/8/72.
SPURR C.B. Born 16/8/24. Commd 8/7/54. Flt Lt 8/1/58. Retd GD 15/5/64.
SPURRELL G.L. MPhil BA MCIPS. Born 7/3/40. Commd 13/2/64. Gp Capt 1/7/91. Retd SUP 7/3/95.
SPURWAY B. Born 7/1/39. Commd 5/11/70. Sqn Ldr 1/1/84. Retd GD 18/7/89.
SQUIRE G.L.G. FCMI. Born 1/1/34. Commd 22/7/66. Sqn Ldr 1/7/84. Retd SUP 1/1/93.
SQUIRE P.C. MSc BSc(Eng) CEng MRAeS. Born 16/8/37. Commd 22/8/58. Wg Cdr 1/7/78. Retd ADMIN 22/8/91.
SQUIRE Sir Peter GCB DFC AFC DSc FRAeS. Born 7/10/45. Commd 15/7/66. ACM 29/3/99. Retd GD 5/12/03.
SQUIRE R. Born 10/11/50. Commd 8/10/70. Flt Lt 16/1/77. Retd ADMIN 12/2/77.
SQUIRE R.F.G. Born 10/4/26. Commd 12/12/51. Flt Lt 12/6/56. Retd GD 10/10/69.
SQUIRES B.W. Born 14/10/42. Commd 2/1/75. Flt Lt 2/1/77. Retd ADMIN 15/11/87.
SQUIRES D.H. BSc. Born 1/12/52. Commd 6/7/80. Flt Lt 6/10/82. Retd SUP 2/4/93.
SQUIRES D.J. Born 20/11/66. Commd 31/7/86. Flt Lt 31/1/92. Retd FLY(N) 20/11/04.
SQUIRES E.J.J. Born 9/7/22. Commd 10/2/45. Sqn Ldr 1/7/53. Retd PRT 31/3/62.
SQUIRES P.J. MSc BEng CEng MIEE. Born 20/12/52. Commd 13/4/80. Sqn Ldr 1/1/91. Retd ENG 1/10/99.
SQUIRES S.B. Born 27/5/59. Commd 28/7/88. Flt Lt 28/7/90. Retd ADMIN 27/5/98.
SQUIRRELL C.R.R. Born 12/3/23. Commd 26/5/60. Sqn Ldr 1/7/72. Retd ENG 30/10/76.
ST AUBYN B.J. Born 20/1/32. Commd 6/4/54. Gp Capt 1/1/79. Retd GD 8/11/85.
ST CLAIR B.E. Born 17/10/33. Commd 23/7/52. Wg Cdr 1/1/75. Retd GD 1/2/84.

ST GEORGE CAREY G.M. BA. Born 11/2/60. Commd 5/2/84. Flt Lt 5/5/86. Retd SUP 14/3/96.
ST JOHN BROWN T. Born 9/3/34. Commd 8/10/52. Sqn Ldr 1/1/70. Retd SEC 22/10/74.
STABLEFORD B.T. Born 29/1/43. Commd 17/12/64. Flt Lt 8/1/69. Retd GD 31/5/70.
STABLER A.M. Born 20/1/32. Commd 23/4/52. Sqn Ldr 1/7/70. Retd GD 1/10/73.
STABLES A.J. CBE FRAeS. Born 1/3/45. Commd 3/3/67. AVM 1/1/95. Retd GD 29/1/01.
STABLES D.H. MA. Born 26/10/33. Commd 3/9/62. Wg Cdr 1/7/75. Retd ADMIN 4/4/88.
STACEY A.C.E. MB BS MRCGP MRCS LRCP DCH DRCOG DAvMed. Born 4/11/46. Commd 2/8/68. Sqn Ldr 8/6/80.
    Retd MED 6/4/86.
STACEY A.D. Born 7/3/32. Commd 9/7/54. Sqn Ldr 1/1/70. Retd GD 7/3/87.
STACEY C.C.D. BSc. Born 20/3/50. Commd 23/9/68. Wg Cdr 1/1/92. Retd OPS SPT 24/7/98.
STACEY C.F. Born 20/5/47. Commd 11/8/67. Flt Lt 11/2/73. Retd GD 25/9/75.
STACEY F.P.S. Born 6/3/16. Commd 16/4/44. Sqn Ldr 1/7/63. Retd PRT 29/5/60.
STACEY P.M. Born 22/7/17. Commd 13/3/45. Flt Lt 14/8/55. Retd GD 14/5/61.
STACEY T.B. Born 9/3/36. Commd 14/2/63. Flt Lt 16/5/68. Retd GD(G) 9/3/94.
STAFF F.R.C. MBE. Born 23/3/24. Commd 24/6/44. Sqn Ldr 1/1/57. Retd GD 23/7/67.
STAFF W.J. Born 20/9/34. Commd 16/4/80. Flt Lt 15/5/77. Retd ENG 6/4/93.
STAFF-BRETT J. Born 20/12/14. Commd 4/3/43. Wg Cdr 1/1/59. Retd ENG 25/5/68.
STAFFERTON P. MCIPD AIIP. Born 2/12/42. Commd 2/6/67. Sqn Ldr 1/7/82. Retd ENG 2/12/97.
STAFFORD J.W. Born 11/6/50. Commd 4/3/71. Sqn Ldr 1/1/84. Retd ENG 11/6/88.
STAGG C.M. Born 25/11/51. Commd 10/4/73. Sqn Ldr 1/1/87. Retd GD 5/5/90.
STAGG G.A.H. Born 8/6/44. Commd 6/12/70. Sqn Ldr 1/1/81. Retd GD(G) 12/4/90.
STAGG J.G. MCMI. Born 24/1/36. Commd 16/2/61. Wg Cdr 1/7/80. Retd ADMIN 15/10/88.
STAINCLIFFE C.D. Born 31/5/49. Commd 26/7/01. Sqn Ldr 1/1/89. Retd ADMIN 15/7/01.
STAINES H.C. ACA. Born 17/10/14. Commd 10/6/38. Sqn Ldr 1/6/45. Retd SEC 20/7/48. rtg Wg Cdr.
STAINTON R. BSc. Born 4/9/35. Commd 30/8/60. Sqn Ldr 3/5/70. Retd ADMIN 4/9/93.
STAITE T.J. Born 14/8/16. Commd 17/4/47. Flt Lt 29/11/51. Retd SUP 29/2/64. rtg Sqn Ldr.
STALEY J.R. Born 17/5/26. Commd 16/7/52. Flt Lt 12/12/57. Retd GD 4/3/68.
STALEY R.L. Born 4/8/35. Commd 23/1/64. Flt Lt 1/4/71. Retd GD 4/8/73.
STALEY R.V. Born 23/4/28. Commd 26/9/51. Flt Lt 26/3/54. Retd GD 1/5/59.
STALKER A.D.J. Born 5/12/65. Commd 11/9/86. Sqn Ldr 1/7/01. Retd ADMIN (SEC) 1/7/04.
STALKER R.H. Born 21/1/33. Commd 25/10/51. Flt Lt 25/4/57. Retd GD 26/1/71.
STALLAN D.C. Born 3/5/42. Commd 3/8/62. Flt Lt 3/2/68. Retd GD 9/6/79.
STALLWOOD G. Born 27/8/52. Commd 16/6/92. Flt Lt 16/6/94. Retd GD 18/7/00.
STAMER P.T. Born 19/11/51. Commd 25/9/71. Flt Lt 14/4/80. Retd PI 11/7/89.
STAMFORD M.C. Born 4/5/23. Commd 19/5/44. Sqn Ldr 1/7/62. Retd PE 14/9/68.
STAMFORD M.C.R. MBA BA MCMI. Born 30/1/56. Commd 19/9/74. Flt Lt 27/7/82. Retd ADMIN 15/10/96.
STAMMERS C.V. OBE. Born 6/2/08. Commd 7/11/40. Wg Cdr 1/1/49. Retd ENG 6/2/62.
STAMMERS H.J. Born 25/1/19. Commd 9/8/43. Flt Lt 9/2/47. Retd GD 12/2/53.
STAMMERS J.B. BA. Born 28/3/62. Commd 9/3/86. Flt Lt 5/8/86. Retd GD 28/10/91.
STAMP P.A. Born 11/5/44. Commd 29/11/63. Wg Cdr 1/7/85. Retd SUP 17/9/94.
STAMP P.G. Born 22/8/46. Commd 2/12/66. Sqn Ldr 1/1/79. Retd ENG 22/8/84.
STAMP R.A. Born 16/3/13. Commd 28/3/46. Flt Lt 28/9/50. Retd SUP 6/5/54.
STAMP R.J. Born 19/2/59. Commd 20/12/90. Flt Lt 20/12/92. Retd GD 1/8/01.
STAMP R.J.M. MA. Born 8/12/44. Commd 25/7/71. Flt Lt 25/10/73. Retd ADMIN 25/7/87.
STAMPER C. Born 23/12/20. Commd 17/7/42. Flt Lt 11/5/46. Retd ENG 23/3/54.
STANBRIDGE T.F.S. Born 27/6/27. Commd 19/8/71. Flt Lt 19/8/74. Retd SY 27/6/87.
STANDEN B.E. Born 1/8/32. Commd 13/6/61. Flt Lt 13/6/61. Retd GD 13/6/77.
STANDEN K.J. Born 13/4/34. Commd 24/5/53. Flt Lt 10/9/58. Retd GD 3/4/76.
STANDHAM C.F. Born 24/10/42. Commd 16/12/66. Flt Lt 16/6/73. Retd ENG 30/8/82.
STANDING M.G.T. MCMI. Born 8/3/44. Commd 27/8/64. Sqn Ldr 1/1/76. Retd ADMIN 8/3/82.
STANDLEY S. BA. Born 12/12/40. Commd 22/9/63. Sqn Ldr 1/1/73. Retd GD 23/9/79.
STANFORD F.G. Born 28/4/26. Commd 22/3/51. Sqn Ldr 1/7/74. Retd GD 28/4/81.
STANFORD K.J. DFM. Born 5/1/20. Commd 1/9/45. Sqn Ldr 1/1/51. Retd GD 5/1/63.
STANFORD R.K. BEd MCIPD. Born 11/7/52. Commd 5/2/84. Flt Lt 5/8/83. Retd ADMIN 1/2/97.
STANGER G.A.B. Born 20/2/33. Commd 8/10/70. Flt Lt 8/10/73. Retd GD 17/4/84.
STANGROOM D.A. AFC. Born 19/10/41. Commd 9/2/62. Wg Cdr 1/1/86. Retd GD 19/10/96.
STANIER B. Born 6/7/44. Commd 8/5/86. Flt Lt 8/5/90. Retd SY 2/4/93.
STANIFORD W.A. Born 30/4/55. Commd 8/8/74. Sqn Ldr 1/7/86. Retd GD(G) 2/5/87.
STANIFORTH J.I. Born 12/2/38. Commd 4/10/63. Wg Cdr 1/1/86. Retd GD 12/2/94.
STANLEY D.J. Born 28/2/49. Commd 2/6/77. Gp Capt 1/7/95. Retd ADMIN 1/11/99.
STANLEY D.R. BA. Born 18/4/46. Commd 18/8/67. Sqn Ldr 1/1/81. Retd GD 18/4/84.
STANLEY D.T. OBE. Born 6/5/14. Commd 31/12/41. Sqn Ldr 1/7/55. Retd ENG 6/5/69.
STANLEY K. Born 19/4/45. Commd 3/1/64. Flt Lt 4/5/72. Retd GD 1/9/76.
STANLEY R.A. MB BS FRCS LRCP. Born 8/1/46. Commd 27/7/70. Wg Cdr 12/1/85. Retd MED 8/1/96.
STANLEY R.L. MBE. Born 5/5/28. Commd 16/5/49. Sqn Ldr 1/7/63. Retd RGT 7/5/74.
STANMORE R. Born 11/9/34. Commd 25/6/66. Flt Lt 25/6/72. Retd GD(G) 1/10/80.

STANNARD B.M. Born 3/11/55. Commd 28/10/76. Sqn Ldr 1/1/89. Retd ADMIN 11/4/95.
STANNARD D.G. Born 21/9/35. Commd 29/3/56. Flt Lt 24/10/61. Retd GD 30/6/92.
STANNARD H.G. Born 25/2/24. Commd 6/9/56. Flt Lt 6/9/62. Retd GD(G) 31/10/64.
STANNARD P.W. OBE BSc. Born 20/6/44. Commd 22/9/63. Wg Cdr 1/1/89. Retd GD 22/4/94.
STANNING P. Born 1/1/32. Commd 10/12/52. Flt Lt 5/5/58. Retd GD 2/6/77. rtg Sqn Ldr.
STANNIS J.S. Born 16/12/14. Commd 3/3/48. Flt Lt 17/4/53. Retd SUP 25/10/58.
STANSFIELD C.E. Born 7/4/14. Commd 24/10/40. Flt Lt 1/9/45. Retd GD(G) 7/4/64. rtg Sqn Ldr.
STANSFIELD R. Born 28/5/24. Commd 28/1/44. Sqn Ldr 1/1/57. Retd GD 28/5/62.
STANTON N.D. BSc. Born 9/6/74. Commd 23/11/94. Flt Lt 15/1/98. Retd FLY(P) 22/1/05.
STANTON R.H. MVO MRAeS MRIN. Born 6/1/45. Commd 21/1/66. Sqn Ldr 1/1/92. Retd GD 14/3/96.
STANTON S. Born 17/6/51. Commd 25/2/72. Sqn Ldr 1/1/85. Retd GD 17/6/88.
STANTON V.H. Born 9/5/26. Commd 4/7/57. Sqn Ldr 1/7/68. Retd GD 29/10/75.
STANWAY M.I. Born 12/1/30. Commd 20/4/50. Wg Cdr 1/1/73. Retd GD 12/1/85.
STANYON D. Born 16/9/33. Commd 28/9/54. Wg Cdr 1/7/74. Retd ADMIN 19/7/88.
STANYON P. BSc CertFE. Born 13/4/48. Commd 19/6/86. Flt Lt 19/6/88. Retd ADMIN (TRG) 15/8/03.
STAPLEFORD H.P. CEng FIMechE MRAeS. Born 14/1/20. Commd 19/8/42. Gp Capt 1/7/64. Retd ENG 7/4/68.
STAPLES J. CEng MIEE. Born 10/11/35. Commd 13/7/61. Sqn Ldr 1/7/70. Retd ENG 10/11/73.
STAPLES J.E. DFM. Born 12/1/21. Commd 30/11/43. Flt Lt 30/5/47. Retd GD 28/9/68.
STAPLES T.N. OBE DFM. Born 12/1/20. Commd 27/6/41. Wg Cdr 1/7/58. Retd GD(G) 6/9/65.
STAPLETON D.C. CB CBE DFC AFC. Born 15/1/18. Commd 18/5/36. AVM 1/7/63. Retd GD 16/7/68.
STAPLETON E.J. Born 10/9/28. Commd 8/11/62. Flt Lt 8/11/68. Retd SEC 5/10/74.
STAPLETON E.J. MBE MInstPet MCIPS MCMI. Born 5/1/45. Commd 3/3/67. Wg Cdr 1/7/84. Retd SUP 5/1/89.
STAPLETON L.A. Born 20/8/26. Commd 6/4/50. Sqn Ldr 1/9/65. Retd GD 31/10/73.
STAPLETON W. CBE. Born 27/6/20. Commd 20/8/38. Wg Cdr 1/7/54. Retd GD 12/9/64.
STAPLEY V.A. OBE DFC. Born 22/2/22. Commd 19/4/44. Wg Cdr 1/1/67. Retd GD(G) 22/2/77.
STAPPARD J.A. AFC. Born 28/4/29. Commd 26/9/54. Sqn Ldr 1/1/68. Retd GD 28/6/92.
STARK F.H.B. Born 6/7/33. Commd 27/5/53. Sqn Ldr 1/7/67. Retd GD 12/11/76.
STARK L.W.F. DFC* AFC. Born 16/11/20. Commd 12/6/43. Flt Lt 12/12/46. Retd GD 16/11/63. rtg Sqn Ldr.
STARK R.A. MCMI. Born 20/9/34. Commd 9/5/54. Sqn Ldr 1/7/69. Retd ADMIN 3/4/82.
STARK R.F. MB ChB. Born 16/12/23. Commd 30/10/43. Wg Cdr 8/11/63. Retd MED 2/1/70.
STARKEY D.A.J. MCMI. Born 24/12/29. Commd 22/10/53. Gp Capt 1/1/77. Retd SUP 24/12/84.
STARKEY F.E. Born 23/9/31. Commd 26/3/52. Flt Lt 7/8/57. Retd GD(G) 28/4/78.
STARKEY I.D. BA. Born 11/1/48. Commd 27/3/70. Sqn Ldr 1/1/84. Retd ADMIN 1/1/87.
STARLING J. Born 22/12/61. Commd 26/3/92. Flt Lt 26/3/94. Retd SUP 12/4/96.
STARLING M.C. Born 23/6/42. Commd 29/11/63. Sqn Ldr 1/7/88. Retd GD 23/6/00.
STARLING N.A. BA. Born 1/4/63. Commd 5/9/82. Flt Lt 15/10/88. Retd ENG 6/10/91.
STARLING R.F. DFC. Born 10/5/22. Commd 27/2/42. Wg Cdr 1/7/58. Retd GD 10/5/64.
STARR W.K. DPhysEd. Born 16/5/43. Commd 6/12/70. Fg Offr 6/12/70. Retd EDN 17/8/74.
START D.A. Born 1/11/36. Commd 25/6/66. Flt Lt 25/6/68. Retd GD 1/11/74.
STATHAM C.R. LLB. Born 7/8/50. Commd 25/2/79. Wg Cdr 1/1/93. Retd ADMIN 14/3/97.
STATHAM G.A. MBE. Born 25/4/26. Commd 26/3/52. Flt Lt 31/7/57. Retd GD 25/4/86.
STATHAM R.H.G. Born 22/3/36. Commd 4/12/56. Flt Lt 12/6/62. Retd GD 22/3/74.
STAVELEY A.T. Born 12/9/14. Commd 1/3/37. Wg Cdr 1/7/52. Retd GD 12/9/61.
STAVERS L.W. Born 17/8/18. Commd 22/2/42. Flt Lt 22/6/47. Retd SEC 17/8/67.
STAVERT C.M. AFC. Born 10/8/21. Commd 26/6/39. Sqn Ldr 1/7/53. Retd GD 15/8/64.
STEAD B.A. BSc CEng MRAeS MCMI ACGI. Born 20/4/33. Commd 8/11/53. Wg Cdr 1/7/69. Retd GD 1/2/73.
STEAD J.R. MSc BSc. Born 3/7/62. Commd 14/9/80. Wg Cdr 1/1/01. Retd ENG 1/1/03.
STEAN P.M. Born 26/2/41. Commd 23/12/58. A Cdre 1/1/90. Retd GD 2/4/96.
STEAR Sir Michael KCB CBE DL MA FRAeS. Born 11/10/38. Commd 1/10/62. ACM 27/8/92. Retd GD 11/10/96.
STEDMAN D.W.S. Born 20/11/27. Commd 5/12/51. Flt Lt 5/6/56. Retd GD 19/8/73.
STEED F.S. CEng MIEE. Born 7/12/19. Commd 8/5/41. Flt Lt 1/9/45. Retd ENG 27/10/56. rtg Sqn Ldr.
STEED M.W. Born 13/3/42. Commd 6/7/62. Flt Lt 6/1/68. Retd GD(G) 30/12/72.
STEED R.E. Born 3/11/25. Commd 1/5/52. Sqn Ldr 1/1/62. Retd GD 13/12/75.
STEEDMAN A. AFC. Born 10/9/23. Commd 20/2/45. Wg Cdr 1/7/62. Retd GD 29/9/72.
STEEL A.J. Born 29/4/44. Commd 15/7/66. Flt Lt 15/1/69. Retd GD 29/4/82.
STEEL B.B. BSc. Born 24/10/55. Commd 24/1/74. Sqn Ldr 1/7/92. Retd FLY(N) 2/8/04.
STEEL D.J. MBE BSc. Born 2/3/61. Commd 15/8/82. Sqn Ldr 1/1/93. Retd GD 2/3/99.
STEEL M.K. Born 24/10/43. Commd 4/10/63. Flt Lt 1/7/69. Retd GD 9/1/94.
STEEL N.G. Born 27/12/36. Commd 17/12/57. Flt Lt 17/6/60. Retd GD 18/11/68.
STEEL W. Born 20/1/29. Commd 1/2/62. Flt Lt 1/2/67. Retd CAT 6/10/72.
STEEL W.H. BEng. Born 13/9/65. Commd 25/9/88. Flt Lt 25/3/91. Retd GD 14/3/96.
STEELE A.G. CBE AFC*. Born 2/10/23. Commd 16/4/43. A Cdre 1/7/72. Retd GD 1/7/78.
STEELE A.J. Born 27/12/48. Commd 15/9/67. Flt Lt 15/3/73. Retd GD 1/10/88.
STEELE G. Born 11/9/21. Commd 11/6/43. Flt Lt 11/12/46. Retd GD 4/6/65.
STEELE J. Born 22/10/42. Commd 11/4/85. Flt Lt 11/4/89. Retd ENG 22/10/97.
STEELE R.J. Born 26/2/16. Commd 11/8/44. Sqn Ldr 1/7/58. Retd PE 26/2/71.

STEELE W.P. BSc. Born 7/7/34. Commd 4/2/64. Sqn Ldr 1/7/68. Retd ADMIN 6/11/86.
STEELE-MORGAN M.D. Born 17/10/29. Commd 4/10/56. Flt Lt 5/10/60. Retd GD(G) 30/6/70.
STEEN B.A. MBE. Born 1/8/47. Commd 18/1/73. Sqn Ldr 1/1/84. Retd GD 17/5/88.
STEENSON J.E. Born 3/12/47. Commd 2/8/68. Sqn Ldr 1/7/80. Retd GD 3/1/85.
STEER D.G. Born 3/5/47. Commd 5/4/79. Flt Lt 5/4/81. Retd GD 1/10/89.
STEER E.R.A. Born 8/12/23. Commd 12/8/54. Flt Lt 12/2/58. Retd GD 22/5/68.
STEER G.W. MBE. Born 11/3/22. Commd 23/6/60. Sqn Ldr 1/1/69. Retd ENG 11/3/77.
STEER J.H. OBE. Born 8/6/07. Commd 3/8/40. Sqn Ldr 1/8/47. Retd ENG 8/6/56.
STEER J.W.M. MSc. Born 10/11/27. Commd 18/4/50. Sqn Ldr 1/1/63. Retd ENG 27/5/78.
STEER M.J. FCIPD FCMI. Born 21/5/47. Commd 10/7/90. Gp Capt 1/1/90. Retd ADMIN 2/12/97.
STEER M.J.W. Born 28/9/59. Commd 8/9/83. Flt Lt 8/3/89. Retd GD 14/3/96.
STEER W.H. Born 1/4/49. Commd 26/9/83. Flt Lt 26/9/89. Retd ENG 3/4/92.
STEFF-LANGSTON J.A. MBE FCMI. Born 5/11/26. Commd 25/10/46. Gp Capt 1/1/69. Retd GD 10/6/78.
STEGGALL G. Born 20/3/31. Commd 25/5/50. Flt Lt 6/10/56. Retd GD 1/9/84.
STEGGLES R.H. Born 18/3/21. Commd 21/1/67. Flt Lt 27/1/72. Retd ENG 1/1/74.
STEIB D.E. Born 1/7/20. Commd 27/10/41. Flt Offr 1/9/45. Retd SEC 24/6/53.
STEIN E.D. Born 6/5/38. Commd 23/9/59. Gp Capt 1/1/93. Retd GD 6/7/93.
STEIN N.J.A. BA. Born 13/7/60. Commd 6/9/81. Flt Lt 6/12/82. Retd GD 14/3/96.
STEINER P.H. MILT. Born 30/3/48. Commd 25/6/66. Wg Cdr 1/7/95. Retd GD 17/4/03.
STEINFURTH O.R. Born 20/9/19. Commd 4/8/41. Flt Offr 1/9/45. Retd SEC 1/10/64.
STELLITANO W. Born 20/6/45. Commd 5/5/88. Flt Lt 5/5/92. Retd ENG 20/6/02.
STELLMACHER C.A. BSc. Born 13/8/45. Commd 6/9/81. Sqn Ldr 1/1/88. Retd ADMIN 26/10/96.
STENNER A.B. BSc. Born 14/4/33. Commd 20/10/55. Sqn Ldr 20/4/63. Retd EDN 7/7/71.
STENNETT R.A. Born 25/7/47. Commd 13/12/79. Flt Lt 13/12/81. Retd GD 30/8/88.
STENNING S.A. Born 1/9/58. Commd 31/8/78. Sqn Ldr 1/1/91. Retd SY 14/3/96.
STENSON R. BA. Born 20/1/46. Commd 20/8/65. Flt Lt 20/2/71. Retd OPS SPT 18/5/98.
STEPHEN C.D. Born 15/3/43. Commd 28/4/67. Sqn Ldr 1/1/77. Retd GD 15/3/81.
STEPHEN H.F. Born 3/5/17. Commd 6/10/59. Flt Lt 6/10/65. Retd ENG 19/8/67.
STEPHENS A. Born 22/1/32. Commd 23/12/61. Flt Lt 23/12/67. Retd GD 22/1/87.
STEPHENS A.B. BA MCMI. Born 24/6/38. Commd 31/7/62. Gp Capt 1/1/90. Retd GD 18/6/92.
STEPHENS A.P. Born 29/10/44. Commd 31/1/64. Wg Cdr 1/7/91. Retd GD 29/10/04.
STEPHENS A.R. Born 3/4/35. Commd 19/7/57. Flt Lt 1/7/61. Retd PRT 1/10/66.
STEPHENS A.T. LLB. Born 19/11/35. Commd 23/10/59. Wg Cdr 1/1/80. Retd ADMIN 19/11/90.
STEPHENS C.M. BSc. Born 11/10/57. Commd 19/9/76. Sqn Ldr 1/7/87. Retd GD 12/12/89.
STEPHENS F.C. Born 26/7/34. Commd 13/6/62. Flt Lt 1/10/67. Retd GD 13/6/84.
STEPHENS F.P. MB BS MRCS LRCP DPM. Born 22/12/27. Commd 27/10/52. Wg Cdr 6/1/64. Retd MED 27/10/68.
STEPHENS G.R. MSc BSc CEng MRAeS ACGI. Born 24/4/45. Commd 28/9/64. Sqn Ldr 1/7/80. Retd ENG 1/7/83.
STEPHENS H.O. Born 7/3/20. Commd 19/6/41. Sqn Ldr 1/1/58. Retd ENG 20/6/73.
STEPHENS I.G.C. CEng MIEE. Born 5/4/21. Commd 12/4/51. Sqn Ldr 1/7/60. Retd ENG 19/12/64.
STEPHENS J.A.T. Born 16/12/58. Commd 9/8/79. Sqn Ldr 1/1/93. Retd GD 16/4/97.
STEPHENS J.B. Born 14/1/26. Commd 27/6/51. Flt Lt 27/12/54. Retd GD 14/1/69.
STEPHENS M.A. Born 12/12/43. Commd 7/1/71. Wg Cdr 1/7/90. Retd SY 1/2/92.
STEPHENS M.C. BSc. Born 18/1/63. Commd 3/2/84. Sqn Ldr 1/1/97. Retd GD 18/1/01.
STEPHENS M.J. Born 6/10/59. Commd 24/3/83. Flt Lt 19/1/89. Retd OPS SPT 18/5/98.
STEPHENS M.M. DSO DFC**. Born 20/10/19. Commd 23/12/39. Gp Capt 1/7/58. Retd GD 10/11/60.
STEPHENS M.R. Born 24/5/55. Commd 16/5/74. Flt Lt 16/11/79. Retd GD 24/5/93.
STEPHENS R.D. Born 14/5/14. Commd 21/1/39. Gp Capt 1/7/65. Retd SUP 14/5/69.
STEPHENS R.J. BSc CEng FIEE. Born 18/10/44. Commd 3/10/66. Wg Cdr 1/1/89. Retd ENG 18/10/00.
STEPHENS T.G. BA. Born 26/4/32. Commd 5/5/55. Sqn Ldr 17/2/65. Retd EDN 6/7/70.
STEPHENS T.W. BSc. Born 12/6/42. Commd 10/7/67. Sqn Ldr 1/3/74. Retd EDN 15/11/83.
STEPHENS W.C. DFM. Born 27/7/16. Commd 20/3/43. Flt Lt 14/1/52. Retd GD(G) 5/7/67.
STEPHENS W.L. Born 19/3/10. Commd 29/10/42. Fg Offr 29/6/43. Retd ASD 27/11/46. rtg Flt Lt.
STEPHENSON A.D.G. DFC AFC. Born 17/4/18. Commd 6/10/38. Flt Lt 1/9/45. Retd GD 3/12/57. rtg Sqn Ldr.
STEPHENSON A.H. Born 13/8/36. Commd 5/2/57. Sqn Ldr 1/7/72. Retd GD 13/2/93.
STEPHENSON D.J.A. MHCIMA. Born 25/6/46. Commd 14/4/69. Sqn Ldr 1/7/79. Retd ADMIN 14/3/96.
STEPHENSON E.V. Born 20/10/14. Commd 2/5/44. Flt Lt 14/11/56. Retd SUP 20/10/63.
STEPHENSON G.D. Born 1/7/21. Commd 21/3/45. Flt Offr 1/1/50. Retd PRT 24/9/55.
STEPHENSON G.G. Born 5/6/36. Commd 20/12/57. Flt Lt 2/1/60. Retd GD 27/5/66.
STEPHENSON H. Born 23/3/59. Commd 8/4/82. Fg Offr 11/2/83. Retd PI 1/12/86.
STEPHENSON J.W.N. Born 10/12/36. Commd 28/11/69. Flt Lt 8/3/72. Retd GD(G) 11/1/91.
STEPHENSON L.J. Born 8/11/37. Commd 28/7/67. Flt Lt 12/4/73. Retd GD(G) 31/5/85.
STEPHENSON M.J. Born 18/8/46. Commd 4/3/71. Sqn Ldr 1/1/80. Retd SUP 18/8/83.
STEPHENSON M.P. Born 24/4/59. Commd 24/7/81. Flt Lt 24/1/88. Retd SUP 1/10/91.
STEPHENSON M.P.H. Born 21/9/25. Commd 17/12/45. Flt Lt 29/11/51. Retd GD 1/2/57.
STEPHENSON P.J.T. DFC. Born 25/8/18. Commd 18/6/40. Sqn Ldr 1/9/45. Retd GD 31/7/55. rtg Wg Cdr.
STEPHENSON R.V. Born 4/1/28. Commd 8/4/49. Sqn Ldr 1/1/62. Retd GD 4/1/66.

STEPHENSON T.B. CB DipEl. Born 18/8/26. Commd 13/9/45. AVM 1/1/80. Retd ENG 9/10/82.
STEPHENSON W. Born 26/4/24. Commd 19/9/44. Wg Cdr 1/7/66. Retd GD 30/3/78.
STEPHENSON-OLIVER J.N. Born 28/7/38. Commd 8/1/57. Wg Cdr 1/7/79. Retd GD 11/5/85.
STEPNEY M.S. Born 1/6/47. Commd 8/9/83. Sqn Ldr 1/7/92. Retd SUP 14/3/96.
STEPNIEWSKI T.Z. BEM. Born 2/4/23. Commd 5/12/63. Flt Lt 5/12/66. Retd GD(G) 1/7/74.
STEPTOE B.E. BA MCMI. Born 14/12/32. Commd 29/12/53. Sqn Ldr 1/1/68. Retd SEC 28/2/71.
STERLING N. Born 24/8/31. Commd 10/9/52. Flt Lt 7/2/58. Retd GD 19/10/70.
STERLING S.C. Born 22/2/34. Commd 22/1/57. Sqn Ldr 1/1/70. Retd GD 24/3/76.
STERN P.A.P. Born 9/12/41. Commd 12/7/63. Flt Lt 12/1/69. Retd GD 9/12/79.
STERNE G. Born 17/4/34. Commd 26/11/52. Flt Lt 2/6/58. Retd GD 17/4/92.
STEVEN D.A. Born 4/6/57. Commd 21/4/77. Flt Lt 21/10/82. Retd GD 4/6/95.
STEVEN W. Born 5/12/21. Commd 22/9/49. Wg Cdr 1/7/69. Retd SUP 5/12/76.
STEVENS A.C. Born 30/8/53. Commd 1/6/72. Flt Lt 1/12/77. Retd GD 1/9/82.
STEVENS A.H. Born 26/2/33. Commd 19/12/63. Flt Lt 19/12/68. Retd ENG 4/11/72.
STEVENS A.R. Born 20/3/31. Commd 31/8/50. Flt Lt 31/8/56. Retd SEC 20/3/69.
STEVENS B.A. Born 6/3/28. Commd 17/1/49. Flt Lt 6/5/55. Retd GD 1/4/73.
STEVENS B.R. The Rev MA LLM. Born 7/8/49. Commd 13/9/87. Retd Sqn Ldr 13/9/93.
STEVENS C.D. Born 19/5/47. Commd 2/8/68. Sqn Ldr 1/1/86. Retd GD 14/3/96.
STEVENS C.F. Born 18/9/33. Commd 27/8/52. Flt Lt 14/5/58. Retd GD 18/9/70.
STEVENS C.N. Born 12/7/49. Commd 7/11/91. Flt Lt 7/11/95. Retd ENGINEER 12/7/04.
STEVENS D.B.L. MCMI. Born 4/2/42. Commd 23/12/61. Sqn Ldr 1/1/73. Retd SUP 1/5/84.
STEVENS D.G. BSc MB BS MRCGP MRCPsych. Born 22/4/51. Commd 18/11/75. Wg Cdr 4/2/93. Retd MED 14/3/96.
STEVENS D.J. CEng MRAeS. Born 16/8/39. Commd 6/2/67. Sqn Ldr 1/1/76. Retd ENG 16/8/94.
STEVENS E.R. Born 27/1/31. Commd 11/2/64. Sqn Ldr 1/7/76. Retd ENG 4/4/80.
STEVENS G. Born 21/8/17. Commd 16/1/43. Flt Lt 16/7/46. Retd GD(G) 4/5/68.
STEVENS I.H. MA. Born 28/4/63. Commd 30/8/81. Flt Lt 15/4/88. Retd ADMIN 7/7/91.
STEVENS I.P. Born 15/11/30. Commd 1/8/51. Wg Cdr 1/7/76. Retd SUP 12/6/82.
STEVENS J.D. Born 7/4/30. Commd 23/2/55. Sqn Ldr 1/1/67. Retd GD 30/4/76.
STEVENS J.E. MBE BSc CEng MRAeS MCMI. Born 30/5/48. Commd 19/7/71. Wg Cdr 1/7/96. Retd ENG 10/4/99.
STEVENS J.F.V. Born 12/1/15. Commd 14/2/46. Flt Lt 4/1/51. Retd SUP 12/12/53.
STEVENS J.M.S. Born 29/2/24. Commd 13/1/54. Fg Offr 13/1/54. Retd CAT 22/1/57.
STEVENS M. Born 25/8/45. Commd 4/5/72. Flt Lt 4/11/78. Retd GD(G) 15/11/93.
STEVENS M.C. BSc. Born 2/2/63. Commd 20/2/75. Gp Capt 1/7/97. Retd GD 13/1/05.
STEVENS M.M.J. DFC. Born 1/11/15. Commd 15/3/35. Sqn Ldr 1/12/40. Retd GD 10/12/45. rtg Wg Cdr.
STEVENS M.R. Born 14/1/49. Commd 13/1/72. Flt Lt 13/7/77. Retd GD 20/9/87.
STEVENS M.R.J. BSc(Eng) CEng MIEE MRAeS. Born 16/7/40. Commd 30/9/60. Sqn Ldr 1/1/72. Retd ENG 16/7/95.
STEVENS P.D.B. BA FCMI. Born 17/9/20. Commd 29/10/38. Gp Capt 1/7/64. Retd GD 17/10/72.
STEVENS P.E. MB BS MRCP(UK). Born 13/7/56. Commd 18/10/77. Sqn Ldr 1/8/86. Retd MED 13/7/94.
STEVENS P.J. OBE MD MRCPath ChB DCP DTM&H. Born 11/8/26. Commd 29/9/50. Wg Cdr 1/4/62. Retd MED 30/6/70.
STEVENS P.J. Born 26/1/53. Commd 22/5/75. Flt Lt 22/11/80. Retd GD 3/2/91.
STEVENS R. Born 14/12/30. Commd 7/9/61. Sqn Ldr 1/7/72. Retd SUP 31/8/74.
STEVENS R.W. The Rev. AKC. Born 15/12/36. Commd 2/9/63. Retd Wg Cdr 2/9/79.
STEVENS W.C.H. Born 1/11/11. Commd 5/6/42. Sqn Ldr 1/7/60. Retd ENG 29/8/63.
STEVENS W.F.J. MBE DFC AFC. Born 1/11/18. Commd 10/7/43. Sqn Ldr 1/7/62. Retd GD 1/11/73.
STEVENS-HOARE P. Born 7/11/22. Commd 21/10/54. Flt Lt 21/4/58. Retd GD(G) 23/10/70.
STEVENSON A. Born 24/8/15. Commd 12/6/47. Flt Lt 12/12/50. Retd ENG 24/11/62.
STEVENSON A.G. Born 20/9/36. Commd 17/5/63. Flt Lt 12/11/67. Retd GD 20/9/94.
STEVENSON A.L. Born 11/5/20. Commd 21/6/56. Sqn Ldr 1/1/69. Retd GD 11/5/77.
STEVENSON B.L. DPhysEd. Born 27/7/48. Commd 24/4/77. Sqn Ldr 1/7/90. Retd ADMIN 31/3/94.
STEVENSON C. BSc. Born 6/11/54. Commd 8/1/78. Flt Lt 8/4/80. Retd ENG 27/5/85.
STEVENSON D.A. Born 21/11/22. Commd 30/10/43. Flt Lt 30/4/47. Retd GD 2/6/54.
STEVENSON D.A. BSc. Born 7/4/33. Commd 18/10/55. Sqn Ldr 1/7/65. Retd GD 18/10/71.
STEVENSON D.L. DFC. Born 13/10/20. Commd 2/8/41. Sqn Ldr 1/1/57. Retd GD 13/10/69.
STEVENSON G.P. Born 6/5/20. Commd 6/3/52. Sqn Ldr 1/1/62. Retd ENG 20/3/76.
STEVENSON J. Born 4/7/32. Commd 28/6/51. Sqn Ldr 1/1/78. Retd GD 4/7/90.
STEVENSON J. Born 5/1/47. Commd 29/3/68. Sqn Ldr 1/1/88. Retd GD 5/1/02.
STEVENSON J.C. Born 5/12/12. Commd 19/4/37. Wg Cdr 1/7/52. Retd GD 18/2/60.
STEVENSON J.M. CBE FCIT FILT FCIPS FCMI. Born 27/7/26. Commd 13/3/47. A Cdre 1/7/75. Retd SUP 27/7/81.
STEVENSON N. MHCIMA. Born 15/6/24. Commd 2/7/47. Sqn Ldr 1/7/69. Retd CAT 15/6/79.
STEVENSON P.R. CEng MIEE. Born 3/7/43. Commd 6/11/67. Sqn Ldr 1/7/76. Retd ENG 6/11/89.
STEVENSON R.M. BSc CEng MIEE MCMI. Born 20/12/47. Commd 1/11/70. Sqn Ldr 1/1/81. Retd ENG 1/11/86.
STEVENSON R.W.H. Born 4/6/18. Commd 21/1/38. Sqn Ldr 1/6/45. Retd GD 26/10/48.
STEVENSON S.T. Born 2/2/14. Commd 13/8/41. Flt Lt 1/9/45. Retd ENG 13/2/48.
STEWARD I.B.M. BSc. Born 1/11/49. Commd 13/10/71. Sqn Ldr 1/7/80. Retd ENG 1/11/87.
STEWARD M.J. Born 15/10/37. Commd 16/1/60. Flt Lt 16/7/65. Retd GD 13/8/78.

STEWART A.G. Born 17/7/49. Commd 5/5/88. Sqn Ldr 1/1/96. Retd ADMIN 3/8/02.
STEWART A.G. Born 7/5/72. Commd 24/9/92. Flt Lt 24/3/99. Retd SUPPLY 15/4/03.
STEWART A.J. MRAeS MCMI. Born 9/10/54. Commd 28/10/73. Wg Cdr 1/1/97. Retd GD 11/9/03.
STEWART A.R. MBE. Born 17/6/17. Commd 23/2/50. Sqn Ldr 1/7/59. Retd SEC 1/12/70.
STEWART A.W.J. Born 19/5/51. Commd 25/2/72. Wg Cdr 1/1/93. Retd GD 6/4/98.
STEWART C.E. BSc MCIPS. Born 13/9/61. Commd 5/2/84. Sqn Ldr 1/1/92. Retd SUP 5/2/00.
STEWART C.G. Born 2/4/26. Commd 30/4/53. Flt Lt 30/4/53. Retd GD 30/4/69.
STEWART D. Born 29/1/42. Commd 1/4/65. Wg Cdr 1/1/88. Retd GD 29/1/97.
STEWART D. CEng FRAeS. Born 3/1/29. Commd 4/2/64. Gp Capt 1/7/76. Retd ENG 3/1/86.
STEWART D.McG. Born 16/9/19. Commd 18/10/45. Flt Lt 19/11/53. Retd GD(G) 30/9/64.
STEWART D.McL. Born 6/10/41. Commd 2/7/64. Sqn Ldr 1/7/78. Retd SUP 1/7/84.
STEWART D.R. MA. Born 7/2/40. Commd 26/2/63. Sqn Ldr 1/1/74. Retd SEC 26/5/81.
STEWART G. BA. Born 24/9/42. Commd 27/1/61. Wg Cdr 1/1/85. Retd GD(G) 14/3/96.
STEWART G. Born 14/6/48. Commd 27/7/72. Flt Lt 13/1/79. Retd GD(G) 17/1/88.
STEWART G.H. BSc. Born 14/5/22. Commd 19/7/44. Sqn Ldr 1/1/59. Retd GD 31/7/68.
STEWART H. Born 26/10/43. Commd 10/3/77. Wg Cdr 1/7/98. Retd GD 23/8/00.
STEWART I.G. Born 1/3/47. Commd 4/11/82. Sqn Ldr 1/7/94. Retd ENG 13/7/97.
STEWART I.G.M. Born 29/4/33. Commd 19/12/63. Sqn Ldr 1/7/84. Retd GD 29/4/93.
STEWART I.M. CB AFC LLB FRAeS. Born 27/7/45. Commd 3/11/69. AVM 1/1/97. Retd GD 25/1/04.
STEWART I.McL. LMSSA DPM. Born 15/1/27. Commd 7/1/54. Sqn Ldr 7/1/61. Retd MED 29/10/62.
STEWART J. MRIN. Born 9/3/35. Commd 6/1/64. Sqn Ldr 1/7/83. Retd GD 12/4/90.
STEWART J.A. BA. Born 26/9/45. Commd 31/1/64. Wg Cdr 1/1/85. Retd GD 26/9/89.
STEWART J.A. BEng. Born 13/1/61. Commd 18/86. Flt Lt 15/7/89. Retd ENG 13/1/99.
STEWART J.A. BA. Born 8/3/57. Commd 6/10/94. Flt Lt 6/10/96. Retd GD 22/5/01.
STEWART J.F. Born 22/10/25. Commd 20/7/45. Gp Capt 1/7/77. Retd GD 22/1/81.
STEWART J.G. Born 17/5/62. Commd 15/8/85. Flt Lt 31/1/90. Retd SUP 17/5/00.
STEWART J.M. Born 3/5/53. Commd 9/12/76. Sqn Ldr 1/7/90. Retd ADMIN 3/5/97.
STEWART J.W. Born 8/10/46. Commd 26/5/67. Gp Capt 1/1/97. Retd ENG 8/10/01.
STEWART K.A. Born 15/6/31. Commd 18/11/66. Flt Lt 18/11/71. Retd ENG 29/6/74.
STEWART K.J. Born 25/3/22. Commd 5/9/42. Flt Lt 21/3/51. Retd GD 7/8/63.
STEWART L. BDS. Born 9/7/40. Commd 18/9/60. Sqn Ldr 5/6/70. Retd DEL 9/7/78.
STEWART M. Born 13/3/62. Commd 8/4/82. Sqn Ldr 1/7/94. Retd OPS SPT 13/3/00.
STEWART N.R. Born 26/1/46. Commd 5/2/65. Sqn Ldr 1/1/97. Retd GD 26/1/01.
STEWART P.C. Born 13/6/32. Commd 13/6/66. Flt Lt 26/7/76. Retd GD 1/11/84.
STEWART P.M.G. Born 8/12/36. Commd 29/10/57. Flt Lt 29/4/63. Retd GD 24/7/69. Re-instated 22/6/70. Flt Lt 22/6/70.
    Retd GD 8/12/94.
STEWART R. MCIPS MCMI. Born 8/12/22. Commd 31/10/63. Sqn Ldr 1/1/74. Retd SUP 8/12/77.
STEWART R.J. MBE . Born 11/8/46. Commd 1/3/68. Sqn Ldr 1/1/94. Retd FLY(N) 11/8/03.
STEWART S. Born 3/7/11. Commd 8/5/44. Fg Offr 20/8/46. Retd ENG 17/11/47. Re-employed 1/3/49. Flt Lt 18/5/56.
    Retd 29/7/63.
STEWART S.G. Born 12/2/57. Commd 31/8/75. Sqn Ldr 1/7/90. Retd GD 1/10/95.
STEWART S.H. Born 22/7/44. Commd 21/4/77. Flt Lt 21/4/79. Retd GD 31/12/94.
STEWART T.W. Born 21/10/32. Commd 9/10/75. Fg Offr 9/10/75. Retd SEC 17/10/78.
STEWART-RATTRAY I.J. Born 7/2/38. Commd 28/5/66. Sqn Ldr 1/1/76. Retd GD 1/1/79.
STEWART-SMITH J.T. Born 8/10/39. Commd 19/8/65. Flt Lt 2/12/67. Retd SEC 11/7/70.
STICK D.H. CEng MRAeS. Born 28/8/38. Commd 16/4/63. Sqn Ldr 1/1/76. Retd ENG 16/4/82.
STICKINGS T.J. Born 27/3/35. Commd 7/6/68. Flt Lt 7/6/70. Retd ENG 21/6/76.
STICKLAND R.E. BA. Born 1/7/37. Commd 13/2/64. Wg Cdr 1/1/79. Retd ENG 22/10/88.
STICKLEY E.G. IEng FIIE. Born 14/3/43. Commd 24/8/72. Sqn Ldr 1/7/80. Retd ENG 14/3/87.
STIFF P.A. Born 28/7/21. Commd 18/9/42. Flt Lt 18/3/46. Retd SEC 1/11/53.
STILES B.N. Born 13/11/22. Commd 12/2/44. Flt Lt 4/1/51. Retd GD 5/8/62.
STILL J.B. Born 16/3/54. Commd 7/6/73. Flt Lt 7/12/79. Retd GD(G) 16/3/92.
STILLMAN D.J. DPhysEd. Born 19/4/47. Commd 10/1/71. Sqn Ldr 1/1/89. Retd ADMIN 1/5/94.
STILLWELL F. Born 8/8/23. Commd 5/3/46. Sqn Ldr 1/7/58. Retd GD 31/12/74.
STILWELL N.J. Born 27/10/45. Commd 16/8/68. Flt Lt 16/2/74. Retd GD 27/10/02.
STILWELL N.S.E. Born 3/1/62. Commd 11/6/81. Flt Lt 11/12/86. Retd GD 14/3/96.
STIMPSON C.W. Born 3/12/49. Commd 26/2/71. Flt Lt 26/2/74. Retd GD 22/5/81.
STIMSON R. Born 14/3/19. Commd 21/2/46. Wg Cdr 1/1/65. Retd SUP 28/6/69.
STINCHCOMBE A.B. FCMI. Born 26/7/27. Commd 8/4/49. Gp Capt 1/7/72. Retd GD 1/1/77.
STINGEMORE G.P. Born 24/1/60. Commd 5/8/86. Flt Lt 13/1/89. Retd GD 24/3/99.
STINTON D. MBE MRAeS. Born 9/12/27. Commd 8/6/53. Sqn Ldr 1/1/63. Retd GD 8/6/69.
STINTON J.G. Born 1/12/30. Commd 24/1/52. Flt Lt 15/5/57. Retd GD 1/12/68.
STIRLING J.C. DPhysEd MCMI. Born 23/9/42. Commd 27/4/65. Sqn Ldr 1/1/79. Retd GD 1/5/93.
STIRRUP J. MBE MCMI. Born 4/10/26. Commd 25/5/50. Wg Cdr 1/7/67. Retd GD 4/4/81.
STIRRUP M.A. Born 16/9/44. Commd 11/10/70. Flt Lt 11/10/76. Retd ADMIN 6/5/77.
STIRTON I.N. Born 8/10/64. Commd 30/8/84. Flt Lt 28/2/90. Retd GD 22/1/03.

STIRZAKER P.J. Born 6/11/43. Commd 5/9/69. Flt Lt 3/4/72. Retd RGT 6/11/81.
STOALING A.P. Born 26/11/53. Commd 16/5/74. Flt Lt 16/11/79. Retd GD 26/11/91.
STOAT B.E. MBE. Born 8/2/32. Commd 13/8/52. Flt Lt 20/2/58. Retd GD 6/10/72.
STOBART B.A.W. Born 9/11/25. Commd 14/3/47. Sqn Ldr 1/7/58. Retd GD 9/11/63.
STOBART G. Born 14/10/63. Commd 8/12/83. Sqn Ldr 1/1/00. Retd GD 14/10/01.
STOBART R.H. MILT. Born 20/5/64. Commd 13/2/86. Sqn Ldr 1/7/97. Retd SUP 20/5/02.
STOCK B. MCMI. Born 19/7/33. Commd 25/3/54. Wg Cdr 1/7/84. Retd ADMIN 13/6/87.
STOCK C.J. Born 23/10/41. Commd 24/1/63. Sqn Ldr 1/1/79. Retd GD(G) 1/1/82.
STOCK I.M. BSc. Born 25/1/51. Commd 11/12/83. Sqn Ldr 1/1/99. Retd ADMIN 1/1/02.
STOCKER E.E. DSO DFC CEng MIMechE. Born 31/8/22. Commd 19/1/43. Flt Lt 19/7/46. Retd GD 10/9/56.
STOCKER A. Born 24/5/32. Commd 26/8/54. Gp Capt 1/1/82. Retd GD 17/9/84.
STOCKER S.C. BSc. Born 24/11/65. Commd 16/9/84. Sqn Ldr 1/7/01. Retd FLY(P) 1/10/04.
STOCKER T.A.J. MBE MSc DipEl FCMI. Born 30/10/22. Commd 11/11/43. Gp Capt 1/7/69. Retd ENG 16/12/72.
STOCKHAM J.J. Born 2/9/54. Commd 5/7/73. Fg Offr 5/7/75. Retd GD 7/8/78.
STOCKILL J.A. BA. Born 15/8/48. Commd 31/7/70. Flt Lt 31/1/76. Retd SEC 29/3/78.
STOCKING R. Born 24/1/23. Commd 22/10/59. Sqn Ldr 1/7/74. Retd ENG 10/7/76.
STOCKINGS J.D. BSc. Born 26/2/65. Commd 19/7/87. Flt Lt 19/1/90. Retd GD 19/7/99.
STOCKLEY T.P. Born 14/6/41. Commd 17/12/63. Sqn Ldr 1/1/76. Retd GD 14/6/79.
STOCKMAN B.T. MBE. Born 23/4/33. Commd 8/7/65. Flt Lt 8/7/71. Retd GD(G) 23/4/88.
STOCKS M. Born 23/5/52. Commd 4/7/57. Flt Lt 4/1/62. Retd GD(G) 25/10/86.
STOCKTING J. BSc DipEL CEng MIEE MRAeS. Born 15/11/28. Commd 27/10/54. Wg Cdr 1/7/73. Retd ENG 11/4/81.
STOCKTON B.J. BA. Born 1/6/27. Commd 29/8/56. Wg Cdr 1/1/72. Retd EDN 2/5/79.
STOCKTON I.D. BSc. Born 6/8/57. Commd 28/9/86. Flt Lt 5/2/86. Retd GD 28/9/02.
STOCKTON N.A. BEng. Born 17/8/61. Commd 2/8/89. Flt Lt 15/7/92. Retd ENG 17/8/02.
STOCKWELL G.D. Born 3/10/28. Commd 2/9/50. Flt Lt 7/11/57. Retd GD 3/10/66.
STOCKWELL J.M. Born 25/6/39. Commd 8/12/61. Flt Lt 1/4/66. Retd GD 25/6/77.
STODDART P.J. BSc. Born 5/12/59. Commd 4/1/83. Flt Lt 4/10/85. Retd ENG 1/3/91.
STODDART-STONES G. Born 9/9/21. Commd 29/10/43. Flt Lt 4/1/51. Retd GD 9/9/64.
STODDART-STONES R.C.E. Born 6/1/15. Commd 30/8/51. Flt Offr 30/8/57. Retd SUP 23/4/66.
STOKER D.J. MB BS MRCS MRCP. Born 22/3/28. Commd 3/7/52. Wg Cdr 15/6/64. Retd MED 3/7/68.
STOKER W.I.C. Born 6/11/35. Commd 17/12/57. Wg Cdr 1/1/75. Retd GD 18/1/86.
STOKER W.L. Born 12/12/34. Commd 1/3/68. Flt Lt 12/2/73. Retd MED(SEC) 12/12/73.
STOKES B.J. IEng FIIE. Born 1/6/47. Commd 31/8/78. Wg Cdr 1/1/96. Retd ENG 4/12/99.
STOKES B.P.L. Born 17/3/39. Commd 6/4/62. Sqn Ldr 1/7/85. Retd GD 17/3/94.
STOKES D.G. Born 15/10/13. Commd 28/7/34. Gp Capt 1/1/51. Retd GD 12/6/59.
STOKES F. Born 27/7/27. Commd 3/7/50. Sqn Ldr 1/1/63. Retd GD 1/1/66.
STOKES F.J. Born 22/8/46. Commd 28/10/66. Flt Lt 8/3/72. Retd GD 14/3/96.
STOKES J.A. BSc CEng MIEE. Born 27/10/62. Commd 1/10/84. Sqn Ldr 1/1/94. Retd ENG 27/10/00.
STOKES J.E. MBE. Born 21/1/36. Commd 21/10/65. Sqn Ldr 1/1/74. Retd ENG 1/10/94.
STOKES M.J. Born 3/1/46. Commd 26/5/67. Wg Cdr 1/7/91. Retd GD 2/4/97.
STOKES M.J. The Rev Born 2/12/34. Commd 24/6/68. Retd Wg Cdr 2/12/89.
STOKES P.D. MA CEng MRAeS. Born 2/7/40. Commd 30/9/60. Wg Cdr 1/1/78. Retd ENG 1/5/89.
STOKES P.M. MBE . Born 23/6/61. Commd 29/7/83. Wg Cdr 1/7/01. Retd GD 23/6/05.
STOKES R.C.W. Born 10/11/30. Commd 28/6/50. Sqn Ldr 1/1/77. Retd GD 4/11/85.
STOKES R.J.S. MBE MSc BSc. Born 22/1/53. Commd 3/9/72. Wg Cdr 1/7/87. Retd ENG 22/1/91.
STOKLE N. BA CEng MIEE. Born 3/11/12. Commd 31/1/46. Flt Lt 31/7/48. Retd ENG 3/11/61.
STOLTON A.T. Born 29/1/63. Commd 14/1/82. Flt Lt 14/7/88. Retd ADMIN 14/3/97.
STONE D.R. MCIPS MCMI. Born 25/1/33. Commd 21/5/53. Sqn Ldr 1/1/88. Retd SUP 25/1/91.
STONE D.S. Born 4/4/48. Commd 21/4/67. Flt Lt 21/10/73. Retd SUP 14/6/75.
STONE E.N. MBE MMar. Born 6/12/20. Commd 4/1/50. Wg Cdr 1/7/64. Retd MAR 4/10/72.
STONE G.E.J. Born 6/7/52. Commd 29/6/72. Sqn Ldr 1/7/88. Retd ADMIN 1/7/91.
STONE G.L. MILT. Born 24/11/77. Commd 24/7/97. Fg Off 24/1/00. Retd SUPPLY 3/4/03.
STONE J. Born 28/4/45. Commd 29/11/68. Sqn Ldr 1/7/80. Retd GD 28/9/86.
STONE J.L. Born 21/6/26. Commd 4/7/64. Sqn Ldr 4/1/69. Retd EDN 4/7/74.
STONE J.L.H.B. Born 16/4/34. Commd 17/7/70. Sqn Ldr 1/7/83. Retd ENG 16/4/92.
STONE N.L.M. MINucE MCMI. Born 13/5/20. Commd 6/6/57. Sqn Ldr 1/7/74. Retd ENG 3/7/76.
STONE P.T. BSc. Born 12/2/64. Commd 5/9/82. Fg Offr 4/10/83. Retd ENG 10/4/87.
STONE R. OBE MCMI. Born 27/7/21. Commd 19/8/42. Gp Capt 1/1/70. Retd ENG 27/7/76.
STONE R.C. Born 30/12/58. Commd 14/1/82. Flt Lt 14/7/88. Retd SUP 4/5/97.
STONE R.D. OBE. Born 4/4/46. Commd 28/4/67. Wg Cdr 1/1/89. Retd GD 4/4/01.
STONE R.D. AFC. Born 30/4/33. Commd 11/10/51. A Cdre 1/7/81. Retd GD 22/8/83.
STONEHOUSE G.G. Born 11/8/30. Commd 20/12/62. Flt Lt 20/12/68. Retd SEC 1/11/72.
STONEMAN W.J. DFM MCMI. Born 8/9/23. Commd 26/10/44. Sqn Ldr 1/1/71. Retd SEC 8/9/79.
STONER J.F.B. Born 30/4/19. Commd 18/11/43. Wg Cdr 1/7/61. Retd GD 30/4/74.
STONER M.B. AFC. Born 29/8/47. Commd 28/2/69. Wg Cdr 1/7/91. Retd GD 14/9/96.
STONER M.P. Born 1/2/56. Commd 20/5/82. Flt Lt 11/12/84. Retd GD(G) 1/2/94.

STONER R.A. BSc. Born 11/4/63. Commd 2/9/84. Flt Lt 2/3/87. Retd GD 11/4/01.
STONES A.J. Born 5/2/42. Commd 11/5/62. Fg Offr 11/5/64. Retd GD 30/5/69.
STONES C.E. Born 10/4/24. Commd 30/1/47. Flt Lt 4/12/52. Retd GD 10/4/62.
STONES J. Born 19/8/25. Commd 12/1/61. Flt Lt 12/1/64. Retd GD 17/6/67.
STONES S. MBE. Born 2/7/25. Commd 31/10/63. Sqn Ldr 1/1/74. Retd SUP 2/7/83.
STONHAM J.F.G. DFC. Born 5/11/22. Commd 20/11/43. Sqn Ldr 1/7/58. Retd GD 5/11/71.
STONOR Sir Thomas KCB BSc. Born 5/3/36. Commd 23/9/59. AM 30/9/88. Retd GD 19/10/91.
STOPFORTH P.J. Born 24/1/66. Commd 4/6/87. Sqn Ldr 1/1/01. Retd FLY(N) 20/10/04.
STORAR A.A. MBE. Born 26/4/14. Commd 9/11/42. Wg Cdr 1/1/62. Retd SUP 26/4/70.
STORER J.S. Born 15/10/62. Commd 23/5/85. Sqn Ldr 1/7/97. Retd GD 21/1/01.
STORER R.A.E. BSc. Born 9/11/33. Commd 25/9/56. Wg Cdr 1/1/75. Retd GD 9/11/88.
STOREY E.S. Born 2/4/21. Commd 11/9/43. Sqn Ldr 1/7/57. Retd GD 2/4/64.
STOREY G.J. OBE AFC FCMI. Born 6/7/23. Commd 21/8/43. Gp Capt 1/7/67. Retd GD 6/1/69.
STOREY P.J. OBE FCIS MCMI. Born 12/9/41. Commd 31/3/64. Wg Cdr 1/7/82. Retd ADMIN 12/9/92.
STOREY R.R. BSc. Born 7/8/48. Commd 28/9/67. Sqn Ldr 1/1/79. Retd SUPPLY 7/8/03.
STORRS R. Born 4/3/67. Commd 12/3/87. Fg Offr 12/3/89. Retd GD 5/10/90.
STORY J.F. Born 31/12/19. Commd 19/8/42. Flt Lt 19/2/46. Retd ENG 31/12/68.
STOTT B.J. Born 20/10/37. Commd 14/8/56. Flt Lt 26/2/64. Retd GD 20/10/75.
STOTT D.F. Born 30/5/33. Commd 17/7/56. Flt Lt 6/2/63. Retd SEC 10/4/72.
STOTT J.E. Born 30/5/50. Commd 19/12/85. Flt Lt 19/12/89. Retd GD(G) 14/3/96.
STOUT A.R. Born 9/1/38. Commd 4/10/63. Flt Lt 1/4/71. Retd GD 9/1/76.
STOUT T.A. BSc. Born 15/11/63. Commd 10/11/85. Sqn Ldr 1/1/99. Retd GD 1/1/02.
STOVES W. Born 25/5/17. Commd 16/6/43. Flt Lt 31/1/47. Retd GD 1/3/50.
STOW D.R. Born 8/7/35. Commd 24/11/60. Flt Lt 25/7/66. Retd SEC 8/7/73.
STOWELL P.T. Born 6/12/30. Commd 27/6/51. Flt Lt 27/3/56. Retd GD 6/12/73.
STRACHAN A. Born 7/3/59. Commd 17/5/79. Flt Lt 17/11/84. Retd GD 7/3/97.
STRACHAN C.H. Born 14/8/35. Commd 25/7/56. Sqn Ldr 1/1/68. Retd ENG 14/8/73.
STRACHAN I.W. MBE AFC FRAeS. Born 3/5/38. Commd 28/7/59. Wg Cdr 1/7/77. Retd GD 3/5/93.
STRACHAN J.S. BSc. Born 2/2/60. Commd 17/10/80. Flt Lt 15/10/84. Retd ADMIN 22/7/85.
STRACHAN M. Born 31/5/54. Commd 24/6/76. Flt Lt 11/11/82. Retd ADMIN 31/5/92.
STRACHAN R.W.S. Born 28/3/33. Commd 12/4/73. Flt Lt 12/4/77. Retd GD(G) 2/4/93.
STRACHAN V.F. Born 16/6/45. Commd 6/5/66. Flt Lt 8/3/72. Retd GD 16/6/83.
STRAFFORD H. Born 28/12/36. Commd 14/2/63. Sqn Ldr 1/1/70. Retd GD 1/10/77.
STRAFFORD R.A. Born 13/7/34. Commd 2/10/58. Sqn Ldr 1/7/70. Retd GD 1/10/77.
STRANG A.J.M. BA BSc. Born 14/1/47. Commd 13/2/72. Sqn Ldr 1/1/82. Retd GD 14/4/02.
STRANG F.A. MBE BEd. Born 3/5/58. Commd 10/6/84. Flt Lt 10/12/86. Retd ADMIN 30/6/94.
STRANGE J.E. Born 14/5/23. Commd 16/6/44. Flt Lt 27/5/54. Retd GD 17/4/68.
STRANGEWAY E.J. AFC. Born 2/5/26. Commd 3/5/46. Wg Cdr 1/1/68. Retd GD 27/9/75.
STRATTON D.R. MCMI. Born 1/3/25. Commd 5/1/45. Sqn Ldr 1/4/56. Retd GD 30/11/75.
STRATTON G.F. MRCS LRCP DAvMed. Born 31/3/46. Commd 26/9/66. Flt Lt 29/12/71. Retd MED 29/12/76.
     Re-entered 5/11/80. Wg Cdr 4/4/85. Retd MED 14/3/97.
STRATTON J.G. AFM. Born 15/11/23. Commd 6/1/55. Flt Lt 6/1/61. Retd GD 1/8/68.
STRATTON N. Born 12/5/42. Commd 26/3/64. Flt Lt 12/5/69. Retd SUP 16/7/71.
STRAUGHAN B.J.J. Born 20/1/33. Commd 16/7/52. Sqn Ldr 1/1/71. Retd GD 20/1/88.
STRAUGHAN G.A. MSc. Born 20/2/49. Commd 24/3/74. Sqn Ldr 1/7/83. Retd ENG 1/7/91.
STRAUGHTON R. DPhysEd. Born 14/10/38. Commd 2/2/65. Flt Lt 2/2/69. Retd ADMIN 24/5/76.
STRAW D.P.E. Born 6/9/42. Commd 11/5/62. Wg Cdr 1/7/88. Retd GD 6/9/97.
STRAW K. BSc CEng MIEE. Born 24/4/58. Commd 30/8/81. Sqn Ldr 1/1/92. Retd ENGINEER 18/7/03.
STRAWSON C.R. Born 17/12/33. Commd 3/9/52. Sqn Ldr 1/1/79. Retd GD 17/12/88.
STREET G.N. OBE. Born 11/3/17. Commd 3/4/39. Wg Cdr 1/1/57. Retd SUP 3/4/67.
STREET H.G. Born 22/9/20. Commd 21/6/56. Sqn Ldr 1/1/68. Retd ENG 22/9/82.
STREET R. Born 7/4/23. Commd 16/10/43. Sqn Ldr 1/1/57. Retd GD 7/4/66.
STREETER J.F. Born 14/4/53. Commd 27/2/75. Flt Lt 27/8/80. Retd GD 14/10/91.
STRETCH A.G. DFM. Born 27/8/20. Commd 3/6/44. Flt Lt 3/12/47. Retd GD 17/11/54.
STRETEN M.W. BSc. Born 12/2/43. Commd 22/9/63. Wg Cdr 1/1/82. Retd GD 12/2/98.
STRETTON R.S.J. Born 13/8/29. Commd 19/12/52. Flt Lt 13/2/61. Retd GD 13/2/69.
STREVENS C.J. BDS. Born 5/3/44. Commd 28/12/66. Wg Cdr 23/12/82. Retd DEL 28/12/82.
STRICKLAND A.W. Born 19/6/24. Commd 10/3/44. Sqn Ldr 1/7/56. Retd GD 4/7/68.
STRICKLAND D. Born 21/5/51. Commd 25/8/71. Wg Cdr 1/7/91. Retd ADMIN 31/5/98.
STRICKLAND K.N. Born 29/1/54. Commd 22/8/76. Gp Capt 1/7/04. Retd GD 1/12/04.
STRICKLAND V.J. Born 9/8/41. Commd 24/2/61. Flt Lt 24/8/66. Retd GD 9/8/80.
STRIKE I.D. Born 20/1/35. Commd 8/5/53. Sqn Ldr 1/1/85. Retd GD 31/1/90.
STRINGER B. Born 5/1/30. Commd 6/12/56. Sqn Ldr 1/1/74. Retd GD(G) 31/1/78.
STRINGFELLOW C.H. MBE. Born 16/1/24. Commd 9/7/59. Sqn Ldr 1/1/72. Retd ENG 11/10/77.
STRODE T.M. Born 4/12/64. Commd 28/9/89. Sqn Ldr 1/7/00. Retd FLY(P) 31/8/03.
STRONG C.J. Born 3/8/32. Commd 9/4/52. Wg Cdr 1/7/80. Retd GD 3/8/87.

STRONG D.M. CB AFC. Born 30/9/13. Commd 6/1/36. A Cdre 1/1/60. Retd GD 6/4/66.
STRONG J.F. MBE. Born 8/3/33. Commd 6/12/51. Wg Cdr 1/1/74. Retd GD 1/10/77.
STRONG W.J. Born 4/11/20. Commd 13/6/46. Flt Lt 13/12/50. Retd RGT 8/6/74.
STRONGE F.W.T. Born 17/5/38. Commd 29/11/63. Flt Lt 8/1/69. Retd ADMIN 17/5/76.
STRONGMAN E. BSc. Born 23/11/49. Commd 23/9/68. Sqn Ldr 1/7/83. Retd GD 24/11/86.
STROUD A.E. Born 24/10/29. Commd 25/8/49. Wg Cdr 1/1/73. Retd GD 15/7/83.
STROUD H.M. Born 30/4/37. Commd 28/7/59. Wg Cdr 1/1/82. Retd ADMIN 5/10/90.
STROUD J.K. Born 22/2/34. Commd 23/6/67. Flt Lt 8/3/72. Retd ENG 23/6/75.
STROUD K. Born 21/3/46. Commd 7/6/68. Flt Lt 7/12/74. Retd GD(G) 1/10/91.
. STROUD M.H.McM. Born 16/12/45. Commd 5/4/79. Flt Lt 5/4/81. Retd GD(AEO) 7/12/87.
STRUDWICK A.S.R. CB DFC. Born 16/4/21. Commd 9/6/42. A Cdre 1/7/67. Retd GD 29/3/76.
STRUTHERS I. BSc. Born 3/8/50. Commd 18/4/71. Flt Lt 15/4/74. Retd GD 20/11/81.
STUART A.F. Born 29/8/50. Commd 27/3/70. Wg Cdr 1/7/90. Retd GD 15/1/00.
STUART D.J. Born 16/10/33. Commd 10/3/54. Flt Lt 16/10/60. Retd GD 16/10/71.
STUART D.W. MB BS FRCS (Edin) FRCS DLO. Born 23/12/21. Commd 27/2/47. Wg Cdr 27/2/59.
  Retd MED 28/11/60.
STUART E.M. BSc. Born 9/10/53. Commd 13/2/77. Wg Cdr 1/1/92. Retd ADMIN 27/9/96.
STUART H.J. The Venerable CB MA. Born 16/11/26. Commd 18/5/55. Retd AVM 11/7/83.
STUART J.C. Born 7/12/19. Commd 20/1/44. Flt Lt 20/7/47. Retd GD 8/6/64.
STUART J.C. DFC. Born 5/3/21. Commd 25/6/44. Sqn Ldr 1/1/54. Retd GD 3/4/64.
STUART J.E. MBE. Born 31/7/30. Commd 26/3/53. Sqn Ldr 1/1/76. Retd ADMIN 5/9/81.
STUART J.R. Born 11/9/30. Commd 19/7/57. Sqn Ldr 1/7/71. Retd GD(G) 1/10/74.
STUART M.D. Born 2/10/31. Commd 2/7/52. Flt Lt 5/11/58. Retd GD 2/10/69.
STUART T.B. CEng MIMechE MIProdE. Born 4/3/32. Commd 19/5/69. Sqn Ldr 1/7/79. Retd ENG 4/3/93.
STUART-PAUL Sir Roland KBE. Born 7/11/34. Commd 10/4/56. AM 7/11/89. Retd GD 1/4/92.
STUBBINGS D.H. Born 25/12/21. Commd 17/10/57. Sqn Ldr 1/7/69. Retd ENG 15/4/72.
STUBBINGTON J.E.G. CEng MIEE MRAeS. Born 17/5/40. Commd 18/7/61. Wg Cdr 1/7/83. Retd ENG 1/3/85.
STUBBS B.H. Born 5/1/30. Commd 30/1/52. Flt Lt 29/5/57. Retd GD 5/1/68.
STUBBS K. Born 9/5/40. Commd 26/10/62. Wg Cdr 1/7/84. Retd SUP 9/5/95.
STUBBS R.H. Born 2/1/25. Commd 3/11/44. Sqn Ldr 1/7/72. Retd GD 2/10/75.
STUBINGS R.A. Born 26/7/26. Commd 15/6/50. Sqn Ldr 1/7/60. Retd GD 30/4/76.
STUDWELL H.E. BEM. Born 30/9/28. Commd 30/7/59. Wg Cdr 1/7/78. Retd ENG 30/9/83.
STUMP E.R. CEng MIEE MRAeS. Born 7/6/28. Commd 4/10/56. Flt Lt 4/4/60. Retd ENG 7/6/66. rtg Sqn Ldr.
STUNELL P. Born 10/4/47. Commd 20/10/83. Flt Lt 20/10/87. Retd ENG 14/9/96.
STUPPLES D.W. BA MSc CEng MIEE. Born 15/12/43. Commd 6/4/72. Sqn Ldr 1/1/79. Retd ENG 1/10/84.
STURGEON A.R. MRAeS. Born 24/11/22. Commd 14/3/44. Flt Lt 14/9/47. Retd ENG 24/11/60.
STURGEON B. Born 15/3/43. Commd 16/9/76. Sqn Ldr 1/1/86. Retd ADMIN 31/3/99.
STURGEON D.W. Born 4/12/19. Commd 4/12/42. Flt Lt 4/6/46. Retd GD 12/2/58.
STURGESS A.P. Born 25/11/54. Commd 20/10/83. Flt Lt 20/10/85. Retd OPS SPT 25/11/98.
STURGESS I.T. Born 25/5/49. Commd 27/2/70. Flt Lt 27/2/73. Retd GD 25/5/87.
STURGESS T.N. Born 25/12/46. Commd 27/5/78. Sqn Ldr 1/7/91. Retd SUP 14/3/96.
STURMAN A.V.H. Born 25/7/23. Commd 1/6/45. Flt Lt 4/6/53. Retd GD 22/12/69.
STURMAN G.G. Born 23/6/44. Commd 23/3/67. Flt Lt 23/9/72. Retd GD 31/10/82.
STURMAN R.J. Born 4/11/46. Commd 23/6/67. Gp Capt 1/1/94. Retd OPS SPT 6/4/02.
STURNHAM B.J. LRAM ARCM. Born 29/3/35. Commd 21/12/67. Flt Lt 17/3/73. Retd DM 30/4/77.
STURROCK D. MB ChB MSc. Born 3/5/26. Commd 1/3/51. Gp Capt 1/3/73. Retd MED 28/3/75.
STURT C.J. OBE MCMI. Born 6/1/39. Commd 28/7/59. Gp Capt 1/1/84. Retd GD 12/11/90.
STURT P.G. Born 25/1/42. Commd 31/7/62. Gp Capt 1/1/91. Retd GD 26/8/96.
STUTTARD J. Born 8/3/49. Commd 20/9/68. Flt Lt 20/3/74. Retd GD 3/3/81.
STUTTERS G.A. MILT. Born 27/2/48. Commd 26/9/91. Flt Lt 26/9/95. Retd SUPPLY 27/2/03.
STYLES A.F. Born 10/10/36. Commd 2/8/68. Flt Lt 17/3/71. Retd GD 2/8/76.
STYLES A.J.P. BSc. Born 14/4/45. Commd 15/7/66. Sqn Ldr 1/7/77. Retd ENG 14/4/83.
STYLES F.R. Born 7/2/39. Commd 15/12/59. Wg Cdr 1/1/84. Retd GD 7/2/94.
STYLES J.C. Born 14/11/46. Commd 22/7/71. Sqn Ldr 1/1/80. Retd SY 14/11/90. Re-entered 1/10/91. Sqn Ldr 18/11/80.
  Retd ADMIN 14/9/99.
STYLES K.L. Born 24/3/33. Commd 27/8/52. Sqn Ldr 1/1/66. Retd GD 29/3/71.
STYLES L.F. Born 18/4/15. Commd 3/4/39. Sqn Ldr 1/8/47. Retd SUP 18/4/64. rtg Wg Cdr.
STYLES P.L. BA. Born 5/9/34. Commd 14/8/70. Fg Offr 14/8/70. Retd ENG 30/3/78. rtg Flt Lt.
SUCKLING C.A. MBE BSc CEng MIEE. Born 1/3/48. Commd 26/2/71. Gp Capt 1/7/98. Retd GD 1/3/03.
SUDBOROUGH N.J. CB OBE FCIPD. Born 23/3/48. Commd 13/1/67. AVM 1/7/00. Retd GD 6/1/03.
SUDLOW R.A.A. Born 1/4/50. Commd 31/7/70. Flt Lt 31/1/74. Retd GD 1/4/88.
SUFFOLK R.N. Born 17/7/52. Commd 9/3/72. Flt Lt 9/9/77. Retd GD 1/7/90.
SUFFOLK T.F. Born 15/10/44. Commd 21/7/65. Wg Cdr 1/1/90. Retd GD(G) 2/4/94.
SUGDEN R.B. Born 5/11/51. Commd 22/7/71. Fg Offr 22/7/73. Retd GD 14/9/76.
SUGG M.R. Born 17/2/33. Commd 23/3/66. Flt Lt 23/3/71. Retd SUP 30/9/79.
SUGGATE J.R. BSc. Born 18/1/27. Commd 25/4/62. Wg Cdr 1/7/72. Retd ENG 18/1/82.

SULAIMAN BIN S. Born 25/3/34. Commd 1/4/58. Flt Lt 1/3/61. Retd GD 30/9/65.
SULLIVAN D.G. Born 15/4/33. Commd 14/3/57. Gp Capt 1/7/80. Retd ADMIN 15/4/89.
SULLIVAN J.B. Born 30/3/33. Commd 10/12/52. Flt Lt 29/4/59. Retd GD 29/8/64.
SULLIVAN J.I.H. Born 26/1/15. Commd 6/10/41. Flt Offr 1/9/45. Retd SEC 14/11/57.
SULLIVAN L. Born 16/5/48. Commd 10/6/66. Sqn Ldr 1/1/81. Retd FLY(N) 16/5/05.
SULLIVAN M. Born 21/12/36. Commd 26/5/67. Wg Cdr 1/7/90. Retd SUP 4/1/91.
SULLIVAN M. Born 5/7/54. Commd 21/3/74. Sqn Ldr 1/1/87. Retd SUP 5/7/92.
SULLY A.K. Born 19/7/53. Commd 27/7/72. Sqn Ldr 1/1/89. Retd FLY(N) 2/4/05.
SULLY D.S. BEng. Born 6/1/60. Commd 4/7/82. Flt Lt 4/4/84. Retd GD 4/7/98.
SUMMERS J.J. Born 25/3/63. Commd 15/3/84. Flt Lt 21/7/90. Retd SUP 1/11/96.
SUMMERS J.R. Born 20/10/35. Commd 23/9/65. Sqn Ldr 1/7/73. Retd SEC 1/11/78.
SUMMERS N.J. MSc BSc. Born 9/3/63. Commd 30/8/81. Sqn Ldr 1/1/95. Retd ENG 26/10/98.
SUMMERS P.G. MEng BA. Born 5/6/45. Commd 1/3/68. Sqn Ldr 1/1/82. Retd ENG 1/10/86.
SUMMERS R.G.B. OBE. Born 18/10/21. Commd 1/5/42. Wg Cdr 1/1/58. Retd GD 18/10/68.
SUMMERS T.J. Born 13/7/47. Commd 1/8/69. Flt Lt 1/2/72. Retd GD 13/7/85.
SUMNER A.J. MA. Born 17/5/52. Commd 13/9/70. Flt Lt 15/4/75. Retd GD 15/7/85. Re-instated 22/1/86.
  Flt Lt 22/10/75. Retd GD 17/5/90.
SUMNER A.W. Born 7/12/47. Commd 17/2/67. Wg Cdr 1/7/91. Retd GD 1/7/97.
SUMNER D.G. Born 22/2/54. Commd 15/10/81. Flt Lt 15/10/83. Retd OPS SPT 22/2/98.
SUMNER D.P.T. Born 17/8/43. Commd 25/3/64. Flt Lt 15/4/70. Retd GD 17/8/81.
SUMNER E.C. MInstAM MCMI DMS AInstAM. Born 18/1/50. Commd 15/8/85. Sqn Ldr 1/1/94. Retd ADMIN (SEC)
  18/1/05.
SUMNER S.A. Born 2/6/33. Commd 17/1/52. Flt Lt 24/7/57. Retd GD 3/6/76. Re-instated 1/4/81. Retd GD 17/10/86.
SUNDARAM V.K. BSc. Born 9/4/44. Commd 2/8/71. Flt Lt 2/2/75. Retd ADMIN 2/12/85.
SUNDERLAND R. Born 10/12/52. Commd 1/6/72. Sqn Ldr 1/7/85. Retd GD 10/12/90.
SUNLEY A.W. Born 13/5/43. Commd 14/8/70. Flt Lt 24/3/74. Retd GD 13/5/76.
SUNNUCKS P.J. Born 9/7/32. Commd 19/4/51. Wg Cdr 1/7/79. Retd GD 9/7/84.
SUREN I.E. Born 5/4/29. Commd 2/8/50. Sqn Ldr 1/7/60. Retd GD 17/2/68.
SURMAN P.J. Born 9/11/35. Commd 8/7/54. Sqn Ldr 1/1/67. Retd SEC 9/11/73.
SURR R.A. BA. Born 22/3/55. Commd 14/8/86. Sqn Ldr 1/7/94. Retd ADMIN 14/9/02.
SURTEES G.C. MA BSc. Born 16/6/61. Commd 30/10/83. Flt Lt 30/4/87. Retd ADMIN 14/3/96.
SURTEES W. DFC. Born 16/7/14. Commd 26/3/38. Wg Cdr 1/1/53. Retd GD 1/12/57.
SUSANS B. Born 20/4/49. Commd 3/7/80. Sqn Ldr 1/1/89. Retd ENG 28/12/96.
SUSSUM G.E. Born 20/6/39. Commd 18/2/58. Sqn Ldr 1/7/73. Retd GD 2/9/89.
SUTCLIFFE D.M. Born 10/8/48. Commd 23/3/67. Sqn Ldr 1/1/96. Retd FLY(P) 10/2/05.
SUTCLIFFE D.W. MBE. Born 4/3/43. Commd 31/10/63. Wg Cdr 1/7/84. Retd SY 5/1/95.
SUTCLIFFE G.D. Born 19/6/22. Commd 23/1/43. Sqn Ldr 1/10/54. Retd GD 19/6/71.
SUTCLIFFE R. MCMI. Born 24/11/27. Commd 14/1/65. Flt Lt 14/1/71. Retd PRT 1/11/72.
SUTHERLAND D.J.L. BSc. Born 4/5/55. Commd 30/10/83. Flt Lt 30/4/87. Retd ADMIN 30/10/99.
SUTHERLAND G. BSc. Born 22/3/33. Commd 24/4/57. Sqn Ldr 24/7/66. Retd EDN 24/4/73.
SUTHERLAND G.B. Born 18/4/09. Commd 2/11/42. Flt Lt 2/5/46. Retd SEC 6/1/58.
SUTHERLAND G.MacL. MCMI. Born 28/1/30. Commd 29/11/51. Wg Cdr 1/1/79. Retd SY 1/12/83.
SUTHERLAND J.G. Born 14/8/49. Commd 26/2/71. Fg Offr 26/2/72. Retd SUP 20/8/76.
SUTHERLAND J.G. Born 21/12/55. Commd 28/10/76. Flt Lt 28/4/82. Retd GD 29/12/84.
SUTHERLAND J.W. MA. Born 11/5/46. Commd 16/8/70. Wg Cdr 1/1/88. Retd ADMIN 14/3/97.
SUTHERLAND M.A. MBE. Born 23/7/33. Commd 26/2/53. Gp Capt 1/7/79. Retd GD 23/7/88.
SUTHERLAND M.J. BSc. Born 27/8/62. Commd 31/8/80. Flt Lt 15/10/84. Retd GD 14/9/96.
SUTHERLAND M.J. BSc. Born 16/2/51. Commd 13/9/70. Plt Offr 15/7/74. Retd SUP 25/2/75.
SUTHERLAND R. MSc BSc. Born 16/6/71. Flt Lt 15/1/76. Retd ADMIN 10/1/90.
SUTHERLAND T.G.G. Born 12/7/34. Commd 19/2/76. Flt Lt 19/2/79. Retd PI 17/4/89.
SUTHERLAND W.J.S. Born 15/12/18. Commd 7/8/43. Sqn Ldr 1/1/54. Retd GD 7/2/58.
SUTTIE A.J. MInstAM. Born 18/4/49. Commd 23/11/78. Sqn Ldr 1/1/87. Retd ADMIN 31/1/97.
SUTTLE C.E.P. OBE BSc CEng FIEE FRCO. Born 9/7/13. Commd 17/10/39. Gp Capt 9/7/59. Retd EDN 9/7/73.
  rtg A Cdre.
SUTTON G.E. Born 18/2/31. Commd 19/7/57. Flt Lt 19/1/62. Retd GD 31/7/68.
SUTTON H.T. OBE DFC. Born 21/1/14. Commd 19/10/34. Wg Cdr 1/7/57. Retd SEC 17/2/66. rtg Gp Capt.
SUTTON I. MBE CEng MRAeS MCMI. Born 6/5/24. Commd 17/10/57. Sqn Ldr 1/7/71. Retd ENG 9/5/78.
SUTTON Sir John KCB. Born 9/7/32. Commd 22/3/51. AM 1/1/86. Retd GD 5/7/89.
SUTTON J.C.K. MBE CEng MRAeS. Born 23/6/15. Commd 15/5/41. Sqn Ldr 1/1/52. Retd ENG 23/6/70.
  rtg Wg Cdr.
SUTTON J.D.D. Born 4/3/35. Commd 22/5/70. Flt Lt 22/5/73. Retd GD 2/6/76.
SUTTON M.C. Born 7/12/63. Commd 15/6/83. Sqn Ldr 1/1/96. Retd GD 7/12/01.
SUTTON M.P.J. Born 1/11/45. Commd 21/1/66. Flt Lt 3/6/71. Retd GD 2/11/82.
SUTTON P. Born 25/11/36. Commd 7/5/64. Sqn Ldr 1/7/73. Retd ENG 25/11/94.
SUTTON P.D. MB BS FRCR DMR(D). Born 29/6/21. Commd 16/1/47. A Cdre 1/1/80. Retd MED 30/6/83.
SUTTON R.J. Born 18/10/47. Commd 14/2/91. Flt Lt 14/2/93. Retd GD 19/10/98.

SUTTON W.A. Born 5/10/22. Commd 23/6/44. Flt Lt 23/12/47. Retd GD 28/11/58.
SVENSSON I.A.G. Born 29/5/31. Commd 30/7/52. Sqn Ldr 1/1/64. Retd GD 29/5/69.
SVETLIK L. Born 23/3/17. Commd 28/2/42. Flt Lt 18/5/56. Retd GD(G) 28/7/66.
SWABY S.J. Born 29/12/43. Commd 16/12/82. Flt Lt 16/12/85. Retd GD(G) 14/3/96.
SWAFFER D.C. Born 10/5/46. Commd 15/3/79. Flt Lt 15/3/81. Retd GD 30/1/96.
SWAFFIELD J. Born 3/6/24. Commd 30/12/44. Sqn Ldr 1/1/61. Retd CAT 1/10/66.
SWAFFIELD N. Born 5/8/41. Commd 13/12/68. Sqn Ldr 1/1/85. Retd SUP 1/1/88.
SWAIN B.L. Born 5/11/45. Commd 11/5/78. Wg Cdr 1/7/91. Retd ADMIN 5/11/00.
SWAIN C.M. Born 19/3/38. Commd 29/6/72. Flt Offr 29/12/72. Retd GD(G) 2/10/74.
SWAIN G.G. BA. Born 19/8/47. Commd 25/2/68. Flt Lt 8/3/72. Retd GD(G) 19/8/91.
SWAIN J. Born 26/2/41. Commd 19/12/61. Flt Lt 19/6/64. Retd GD 1/9/73.
SWAIN J.A. Born 27/2/35. Commd 11/6/60. Flt Lt 11/12/65. Retd GD 27/2/73.
SWAIN J.G.G. BDS. Born 20/1/46. Commd 28/12/66. Wg Cdr 18/12/81. Retd DEL 8/6/98.
SWAIN CD P.D. Born 8/5/26. Commd 1/10/56. Flt Lt 23/2/56. Retd ADMIN 1/10/80.
SWAITHES C.W.C. Born 12/12/34. Commd 25/1/66. Wg Cdr 1/1/80. Retd SUP 1/6/92.
SWALES F.L. Born 28/2/28. Commd 25/4/51. Flt Lt 25/1/57. Retd GD 28/2/66.
SWALWELL L.C. Born 27/1/28. Commd 14/12/49. Gp Capt 1/1/73. Retd GD 1/11/75.
SWAN A.J. MBE QGM MIExpE. Born 5/11/42. Commd 23/11/78. Sqn Ldr 1/1/89. Retd ENG 1/6/92.
SWAN D.A. FCIS. Born 23/10/34. Commd 20/6/61. Sqn Ldr 1/1/72. Retd SEC 10/7/79.
SWANCOTT N.A.J. Born 22/4/63. Commd 26/11/81. Flt Lt 26/5/87. Retd GD 1/10/90.
SWANN R.N. Born 20/7/41. Commd 8/12/61. Sqn Ldr 1/1/76. Retd GD 20/7/79.
SWANSON B.G. Born 29/2/32. Commd 19/7/51. Wg Cdr 1/7/83. Retd GD 1/3/87.
SWANSON S.J. Born 7/6/30. Commd 24/2/67. Flt Lt 24/2/70. Retd GD 7/6/88.
SWANWICK G.W. Born 10/11/15. Commd 7/10/41. Wg Cdr 1/1/60. Retd SEC 30/4/70.
SWAPP G.D. OBE MA. Born 25/5/31. Commd 21/10/54. Wg Cdr 1/1/70. Retd ADMIN 31/12/83.
SWARBRICK D.L. Born 17/5/30. Commd 18/5/61. Sqn Ldr 1/7/83. Retd ENG 17/5/80.
SWART D.W. OBE MCMI. Born 9/8/25. Commd 20/12/51. Wg Cdr 1/1/65. Retd GD 1/10/74.
SWART L. CBE AFC. Born 28/11/32. Commd 12/7/51. A Cdre 1/7/80. Retd GD 28/11/87.
SWASH M.G. Born 27/5/44. Commd 15/6/83. Sqn Ldr 1/7/91. Retd ENG 27/9/96.
SWASH W.P. Born 3/9/38. Commd 9/8/63. Flt Lt 26/7/67. Retd GD(G) 3/9/76.
SWATKINS I.R. BA. Born 4/12/57. Commd 22/2/81. Sqn Ldr 1/7/91. Retd ADMIN (SEC) 22/2/03.
SWATTON B.P. Born 11/4/41. Commd 18/12/62. Wg Cdr 1/1/81. Retd SUP 2/4/93.
SWATTON P.J. Born 4/5/35. Commd 13/5/53. Sqn Ldr 1/1/86. Retd GD 3/2/89.
SWEENEY A.E. AFC. Born 11/1/22. Commd 19/5/44. Wg Cdr 1/1/70. Retd GD 6/2/77.
SWEENEY C.M. Born 15/11/48. Commd 4/3/71. Gp Capt 1/7/95. Retd GD 31/1/01.
SWEENEY L.J. Born 27/5/27. Commd 7/7/49. Sqn Ldr 1/1/68. Retd GD 27/5/85.
SWEENEY M. Born 11/4/53. Commd 9/12/71. Flt Lt 9/6/77. Retd GD 20/4/83.
SWEET I.D. MSc BSc. Born 2/4/49. Commd 4/10/71. Sqn Ldr 1/7/83. Retd ENG 1/10/90.
SWEET J. BA. Born 25/9/29. Commd 21/5/52. Sqn Ldr 1/1/65. Retd GD 1/1/68.
SWEETING J. MA. Born 27/7/37. Commd 29/12/65. Flt Lt 29/9/68. Retd ADMIN 27/7/92.
SWEETING J.M. Born 5/8/38. Commd 2/5/68. Fg Offr 2/5/68. Retd SEC 29/11/69.
SWEETING R.F. DFC. Born 16/3/20. Commd 17/5/41. Sqn Ldr 1/7/49. Retd GD 21/5/58.
SWEETLOVE G.G. MBE. Born 20/4/26. Commd 12/1/61. Sqn Ldr 1/1/75. Retd GD 21/4/76.
SWEETMAN J.E. Born 3/3/48. Commd 2/12/66. Flt Lt 2/6/72. Retd GD 3/3/86.
SWEPSON D. Born 1/2/33. Commd 28/1/53. Flt Lt 17/8/58. Retd GD 1/2/71.
SWETMAN K.M. TD. Born 9/5/44. Commd 13/4/86. Flt Lt 13/12/87. Retd ADMIN 13/4/98.
SWETTENHAM W.A. Born 27/2/33. Commd 8/11/51. Flt Lt 23/2/57. Retd GD(G) 27/2/71.
SWIFT A.N. BA. Born 12/9/56. Commd 14/9/75. Flt Lt 15/10/79. Retd GD 15/7/90.
SWIFT D.J. Born 5/4/32. Commd 17/7/61. Flt Lt 17/7/61. Retd GD 17/7/65.
SWIFT D.S. Born 2/11/44. Commd 6/12/65. Flt Lt 26/2/72. Retd GD(G) 2/11/82.
SWIFT G.R. Born 14/8/45. Commd 5/2/65. Flt Lt 5/8/70. Retd GD 4/4/78.
SWINBURN W.H. AIIP. Born 23/2/20. Commd 2/6/44. Flt Lt 2/6/46. Retd GD 23/2/75.
SWINDEN J. MSc BSc CEng MIEE. Born 8/6/41. Commd 30/9/62. Wg Cdr 1/1/85. Retd ENG 2/4/93.
SWINDLE E.S. Born 13/2/57. Commd 22/11/84. Flt Lt 18/6/87. Retd ENG 13/2/95.
SWINDLEHURST P.W. CEng FCIPD MIMechE MRAeS. Born 11/6/36. Commd 17/5/60. Wg Cdr 1/1/73. Retd ENG 17/10/87.
SWINDLEHURST W. Born 29/6/47. Commd 17/1/85. Sqn Ldr 1/7/97. Retd FLY(AEO) 29/6/03.
SWINEY M.J.E. OBE. Born 19/8/26. Commd 14/6/46. A Cdre 1/1/74. Retd GD 3/4/80.
SWINGLEHURST F.H. Born 22/4/20. Commd 27/10/41. Flt Lt 19/2/46. Retd ENG 5/1/54.
SWINHOE M.H. Born 31/12/45. Commd 3/3/67. Sqn Ldr 1/7/82. Retd GD 31/12/89.
SWINNERTON D. Born 17/9/53. Commd 9/11/89. Fg Offr 9/11/89. Retd SUP 1/6/93. rtg Flt Lt.
SWINSCOE B.D. BSc. Born 21/6/48. Commd 28/2/69. Flt Lt 28/11/73. Retd ENG 1/10/86.
SWIRES R.I. MB ChB DAvMed. Born 30/11/33. Commd 15/2/59. Wg Cdr 17/6/71. Retd MED 15/2/75.
SYDENHAM J.R. Born 28/4/20. Commd 16/10/46. Flt Lt 16/4/51. Retd SEC 24/7/54.
SYDNEY J. MCMI. Born 29/2/20. Commd 8/10/42. Sqn Ldr 1/1/63. Retd ENG 16/2/74.
SYDNEY P.H. Born 19/1/21. Commd 14/10/42. Flt Offr 24/2/50. Retd SEC 16/2/55.

SYKES F. MBE. Born 26/8/17. Commd 27/10/55. Sqn Ldr 1/1/65. Retd ENG 18/10/67.
SYKES L.J. CEng MIMechE MRAeS. Born 6/1/35. Commd 25/10/57. Wg Cdr 1/7/77. Retd ENG 30/4/86.
SYKES M.J. Born 9/5/44. Commd 25/3/64. Flt Lt 25/9/69. Retd GD 9/5/82.
SYKES N. Born 26/6/33. Commd 8/2/57. Wg Cdr 1/1/71. Retd ENG 1/1/74.
SYKES R.L. Born 15/3/23. Commd 7/8/45. Flt Lt 4/6/53. Retd GD(G) 15/3/78.
SYLVESTER P.A.M. OBE BEM MCMI. Born 10/11/20. Commd 25/5/50. Wg Cdr 1/7/69. Retd SUP 10/4/75.
SYME J. Born 13/6/19. Commd 6/9/45. Sqn Ldr 1/1/56. Retd ENG 21/9/74.
SYME T.S. DFC DPhysEd. Born 28/5/28. Commd 6/4/50. Sqn Ldr 1/7/62. Retd GD 27/4/68.
SYMES D.B. Born 2/12/45. Commd 28/4/67. Gp Capt 1/7/91. Retd GD 2/4/98.
SYMES G.D. BA. Born 7/10/49. Commd 15/9/69. Sqn Ldr 1/1/83. Retd ADMIN 10/4/01.
SYMES K.A. BEM. Born 13/4/32. Commd 17/3/67. Sqn Ldr 1/1/78. Retd ADMIN 13/4/82.
SYMES L.F. Born 27/3/24. Commd 6/8/43. Sqn Ldr 24/10/62. Retd EDN 28/6/78.
SYMES P.J. Born 30/5/38. Commd 15/12/59. Sqn Ldr 1/7/75. Retd SEC 1/7/78.
SYMMANS T. Born 29/4/48. Commd 25/4/69. Plt Offr 29/4/69. Retd GD 19/8/70. Re-entered 1/11/81. Flt Lt 1/11/89.
    Retd OPS SPT 1/11/97.
SYMONDS D.C. AFC. Born 10/4/50. Commd 7/6/68. Wg Cdr 1/1/85. Retd GD 10/4/89.
SYMONDS J.B. MCIPD. Born 18/6/42. Commd 21/10/65. A Cdre 1/1/94. Retd ADMIN 18/6/97.
SYMONDS K.W.P. AFM. Born 20/8/24. Commd 26/10/61. Sqn Ldr 1/7/74. Retd ENG 20/8/82.
SYMONDS P.C. OBE FCMI MRAeS. Born 5/3/40. Commd 7/5/64. Gp Capt 1/1/90. Retd ENG 5/3/96.
SYMONDSON B.F. Born 7/4/37. Commd 27/11/55. Sqn Ldr 1/1/69. Retd ADMIN 7/12/77.
SYMONS A.J.P. MCMI. Born 26/9/40. Commd 11/10/70. Sqn Ldr 1/1/82. Retd ADMIN 11/10/90.
SYMONS B.R. Born 18/4/47. Commd 17/2/67. Sqn Ldr 1/7/92. Retd GD 18/4/00.
SYMONS D. Born 1/1/36. Commd 30/7/57. Wg Cdr 1/7/85. Retd GD 2/7/87.
SYMONS F. Born 10/4/38. Commd 27/10/67. Flt Lt 7/10/72. Retd SUP 19/3/81.
SYMONS J.C. Born 11/3/35. Commd 27/5/64. Sqn Ldr 1/1/72. Retd ENG 8/4/85.
SYNDERCOMBE M.R.L. Born 16/5/58. Commd 2/6/77. Sqn Ldr 1/1/94. Retd GD 1/1/97.
SYNNOTT B.P. Born 20/10/45. Commd 15/7/66. Wg Cdr 1/8/82. Retd GD 1/1/85.
SYVRET-THOMPSON D.G. Born 27/7/30. Commd 9/7/54. Flt Lt 28/7/65. Retd GD 2/11/82.
SZOTA B. Born 16/10/18. Commd 7/2/57. Sqn Ldr 1/7/70. Retd GD 16/10/73.
SZYMANSKI A.R. Born 12/6/67. Commd 9/11/89. Flt Lt 9/5/95. Retd GD 16/1/02.

T

TABARD P.G. Born 13/2/21. Commd 15/6/44. Flt Lt 11/11/54. Retd GD 18/1/63.
TABBERER N.J.H. Born 21/8/37. Commd 18/1/56. Flt Lt 16/8/61. Retd GD 21/8/75. rtg Sqn Ldr.
TABER T.E. Born 27/6/20. Commd 1/8/43. Flt Lt 21/11/50. Retd SEC 27/6/69.
TABERHAM M.C. BEng. Born 29/6/58. Commd 19/9/76. Flt Lt 15/10/80. Retd GD 29/2/92.
TABERNACLE J.M. Born 20/4/30. Commd 1/8/51. Flt Lt 11/11/54. Retd GD 20/7/68.
TABOR K.J. Born 29/7/25. Commd 25/5/45. Sqn Ldr 1/4/56. Retd GD 29/7/63.
TACEY A. Born 13/8/23. Commd 27/5/54. Flt Lt 27/5/60. Retd GD 1/8/68.
TACQ A.R.L. Born 10/1/18. Commd 24/3/44. Flt Lt 7/6/51. Retd GD(G) 19/2/68.
TAGG J.K.S. Born 3/11/38. Commd 8/5/60. Flt Lt 26/7/67. Retd GD 3/11/76.
TAGGART A.W.McM. AFC BA MRAeS. Born 26/9/45. Commd 1/4/66. Sqn Ldr 1/7/80. Retd GD 6/1/93.
TAGGART M.P. BSc. Born 2/10/54. Commd 16/9/73. Flt Lt 15/4/78. Retd GD 14/9/96.
TAILBY A.J. BSc. Born 19/3/58. Commd 7/1/76. Sqn Ldr 1/1/90. Retd GD 19/3/96.
TAINSH G.H. Born 30/1/47. Commd 1/3/68. Flt Lt 6/10/71. Retd GD 16/12/75.
TAIT A.P.W. Born 12/2/40. Commd 1/10/60. Flt Lt 26/7/67. Retd GD 7/9/78.
TAIT J. LLB. Born 21/4/34. Commd 6/7/60. Sqn Ldr 13/12/71. Retd EDN 30/9/78.
TAIT J.B. DSO*** DFC*. Born 9/12/16. Commd 1/8/36. Gp Capt 1/1/53. Retd GD 9/12/66.
TAIT J.D. BSc. Born 1/5/63. Commd 24/8/92. Sqn Ldr 1/1/01. Retd OPS SPT(FC) 1/1/05.
TAIT P.C. Born 3/12/42. Commd 9/3/62. Flt Lt 9/9/67. Retd GD 3/12/80.
TAIT S.A. Born 5/8/81. Commd 20/10/83. Flt Lt 20/4/89. Retd GD 17/7/00.
TAIT W.A.K. Born 21/1/34. Commd 15/6/53. Flt Lt 12/9/58. Retd GD 4/9/72.
TAIT W.A.M. Born 27/7/41. Commd 23/6/61. Sqn Ldr 1/1/73. Retd GD 27/7/79.
TAIT W.B. Born 2/5/37. Commd 17/7/64. Flt Lt 9/2/68. Retd GD 27/1/79.
TAIT W.C. Born 27/1/44. Commd 20/5/68. Flt Lt 4/5/72. Retd ADMIN 20/5/87.
TAITE R.G. Born 30/6/42. Commd 9/2/62. Flt Lt 9/8/67. Retd GD 30/6/79.
TALBOT E.C.S. BSc. Born 22/8/46. Commd 7/1/68. Flt Lt 15/4/70. Retd GD 2/3/76.
TALBOT G.A. Born 3/9/34. Commd 10/4/56. Sqn Ldr 1/7/68. Retd GD 28/11/75.
TALBOT-WILLIAMS A.T. MA. Born 29/5/24. Commd 26/6/44. Gp Capt 1/1/66. Retd GD 30/4/71.
TALL E.H. Born 2/5/25. Commd 1/4/65. Flt Lt 1/4/68. Retd GD 1/11/77.
TALLACK L.E. Born 20/11/61. Commd 8/6/84. Flt Lt 2/3/89. Retd GD 14/9/96.
TALLETT A.S. MCIPD. Born 14/4/31. Commd 17/5/51. Wg Cdr 1/7/71. Retd GD 30/6/85.
TALLISS J.G. Born 18/7/30. Commd 6/12/51. Flt Lt 5/6/57. Retd GD 18/7/68. Re-instated 17/12/80. Flt Lt 4/11/70.
    Retd GD 19/10/90.
TALTON H. Born 4/3/33. Commd 22/8/61. Wg Cdr 1/7/76. Retd GD(G) 4/3/88.
TAMBLIN P.A. Born 25/9/45. Commd 11/10/84. Flt Lt 11/10/88. Retd ENG 10/4/93.
TAMBLIN P.J. CB BA CCMI. Born 11/1/26. Commd 11/7/51. A Cdre 1/1/77. Retd ADMIN 22/4/80.
TAMBLING D.W. Born 20/7/21. Commd 27/2/47. Sqn Ldr 1/1/64. Retd SUP 20/7/71.
TAME F.W. Born 24/8/18. Commd 16/1/47. Wg Cdr 1/1/64. Retd SUP 19/10/68.
TAME P.A. Born 23/8/45. Commd 10/12/65. Fg Offr 10/12/68. Retd GD(G) 1/10/71.
TAME P.H. Born 10/1/43. Commd 22/2/63. Sqn Ldr 1/1/77. Retd GD 8/6/97.
TAMS F.A.B. OBE. Born 19/2/14. Commd 1/4/40. Wg Cdr 1/1/54. Retd GD 20/2/59.
TAMSETT C.H. Born 30/11/17. Commd 20/11/43. Wg Cdr 1/1/61. Retd SUP 13/9/69.
TANDY R. MSc BSc CEng MIEE. Born 12/1/64. Commd 11/11/82. Sqn Ldr 1/1/98. Retd ENG 12/1/02.
TANK J.S.R. BSc. Born 25/3/63. Commd 22/7/84. Sqn Ldr 1/7/98. Retd GD 1/7/01.
TANNER A.J. IEng MInstLM MIIE. Born 25/8/50. Commd 2/8/90. Flt Lt 2/8/94. Retd ENGINEER 31/1/04.
TANNER A.T. Born 5/12/23. Commd 9/8/48. Flt Lt 20/11/53. Retd GD 5/10/68.
TANNER B.D. Born 6/4/35. Commd 28/7/60. Wg Cdr 1/1/80. Retd GD 19/6/84.
TANNER C.E. DPhysEd. Born 20/11/40. Commd 1/9/64. Flt Lt 1/9/68. Retd PE 28/2/73.
TANNER D.W. Born 29/8/46. Commd 1/4/71. Flt Lt 1/10/76. Retd GD 14/12/96.
TANNER J.R. Born 29/11/22. Commd 27/3/45. Gp Capt 1/7/74. Retd GD 31/3/77.
TANNER M.R. Born 30/6/42. Commd 17/9/63. Sqn Ldr 1/1/75. Retd GD 30/6/80.
TAPE S.F. Born 2/7/58. Commd 4/7/85. Flt Lt 4/7/87. Retd OPS SPT 2/7/02.
TAPLIN F.M.N. OBE. Born 11/7/24. Commd 16/3/47. Wg Cdr 1/7/65. Retd GD 11/7/79.
TAPLIN R.K. MBE BSc(Econ) FILT MCIPS MIMIS MBCS MIL MRAeS MCMI. Born 3/12/48. Commd 27/1/70.
    Wg Cdr 1/1/97. Retd SUP 25/2/00.
TAPPER K.F.W. MBE. Born 25/5/21. Commd 17/4/43. Wg Cdr 1/1/58. Retd GD 15/10/66.
TAPSON I.R. BEng. Born 3/6/65. Commd 1/9/85. Flt Lt 15/1/91. Retd ENGINEER 3/9/03.
TAPSTER I.R. MCIPD. Born 9/6/30. Commd 1/8/51. Sqn Ldr 1/7/72. Retd SEC 1/8/74.
TARGETT S.R. Born 18/3/62. Commd 4/9/81. Sqn Ldr 1/7/95. Retd SUP 18/3/00.
TARLING R.G.R. Born 7/8/16. Commd 24/11/41. Flt Lt 1/9/45. Retd GD(G) 29/11/58.
TARLTON S.W. MB BS MRCS LRCP MRCPath DCP DTM&H. Born 5/1/32. Commd 11/8/57. Wg Cdr 26/7/70.
    Retd MED 11/8/73.

TARRAN O.A. Born 18/12/27. Commd 16/7/52. Flt Lt 12/12/57. Retd GD 21/1/76. rtg Sqn Ldr.
TARRANT D.L. Born 27/11/40. Commd 11/8/77. Flt Lt 11/8/82. Retd GD(G) 1/11/88.
TARRANT K.W.J. DFC*. Born 30/12/17. Commd 17/8/40. Gp Capt 1/1/68. Retd GD 29/12/70.
TARRY A.W. Born 24/2/22. Commd 25/2/44. Wg Cdr 1/1/60. Retd GD 28/9/68.
TARWID A.S. MBE. Born 15/10/21. Commd 23/4/53. Sqn Ldr 1/1/67. Retd GD 15/10/76.
TASKER D. Born 14/9/15. Commd 24/5/43. Sqn Ldr 1/1/61. Retd GD(G) 28/11/64.
TASKER D.R. BA. Born 10/9/50. Commd 11/10/84. Sqn Ldr 1/1/91. Retd ENG 11/10/98.
TASKER J.C. Born 24/11/33. Commd 18/2/60. Sqn Ldr 1/7/74. Retd SUP 24/11/92.
TASKER T.M. Born 13/9/47. Commd 19/6/70. Sqn Ldr 1/1/86. Retd GD(G) 13/9/91.
TASSELL D.M. BSc. Born 10/11/61. Commd 26/4/84. Sqn Ldr 1/7/96. Retd ENG 10/11/99.
TATE A. Born 19/9/33. Commd 28/3/60. Sqn Ldr 1/1/66. Retd GD 19/9/71.
TATE F.H. AFM. Born 25/9/23. Commd 17/5/62. Flt Lt 17/5/65. Retd GD 25/9/78.
TATE J.S. Born 21/8/40. Commd 10/11/61. Flt Lt 10/5/67. Retd GD 3/9/76.
TATE P. Born 10/3/32. Commd 14/11/51. Flt Lt 14/5/56. Retd GD 31/12/92.
TATTERSALL J. BSc. Born 7/1/31. Commd 9/12/54. Sqn Ldr 9/6/65. Retd EDN 10/1/81.
TATTON R.I. Born 26/10/47. Commd 28/6/81. Sqn Ldr 1/1/87. Retd GD(G) 1/10/89.
TAUNTON R.E. Born 25/1/49. Commd 21/2/69. Flt Lt 26/6/75. Retd SY 25/1/87.
TAVANYAR E.A. Born 1/7/21. Commd 24/8/50. Flt Offr 24/8/56. Retd SEC 1/3/57.
TAVANYAR T.G. BA. Born 24/7/66. Commd 8/5/88. Flt Lt 8/11/91. Retd SUP 14/9/96.
TAVNER C.C. MIPR. Born 9/1/39. Commd 9/9/59. Wg Cdr 1/1/86. Retd GD 9/1/94.
TAYLER G.G. CEng MIERE. Born 12/5/16. Commd 27/9/40. Sqn Ldr 1/1/52. Retd ENG 30/5/64.
TAYLER J.S. Born 27/10/36. Commd 4/5/72. Flt Lt 4/5/75. Retd GD(G) 29/7/89.
TAYLOR A. Born 11/12/39. Commd 9/10/64. Plt Offr 9/10/65. Retd GD 21/8/66.
TAYLOR A. Born 8/1/43. Commd 24/1/74. Flt Lt 24/1/76. Retd SY 24/1/83.
TAYLOR A. Born 31/8/33. Commd 9/4/52. Sqn Ldr 1/7/68. Retd GD 31/8/71.
TAYLOR A. MSc. Born 16/5/31. Commd 2/7/52. Sqn Ldr 5/7/67. Retd EDN 26/10/75.
TAYLOR A.A. Born 22/3/21. Commd 14/5/45. Sqn Ldr 1/7/58. Retd GD 22/3/71.
TAYLOR A.C. Born 1/4/50. Commd 23/5/85. Sqn Ldr 1/1/01. Retd SUPPLY 1/4/05.
TAYLOR A.G.S. BA MCollP MCIPD AdDipEd. Born 24/5/53. Commd 17/8/80. Flt Lt 17/8/81. Retd ADMIN 17/8/96.
TAYLOR A.H. BSc. Born 16/5/63. Commd 25/11/84. Flt Lt 25/5/87. Retd GD 16/11/01.
TAYLOR A.J. Born 22/9/48. Commd 8/10/87. Flt Lt 8/10/89. Retd ADMIN 14/3/96.
TAYLOR A.J. BA. Born 24/12/40. Commd 18/5/65. Sqn Ldr 1/7/85. Retd ADMIN 28/6/86.
TAYLOR A.J. BEng. Born 6/6/62. Commd 16/9/84. Flt Lt 3/5/89. Retd ENG 6/8/00.
TAYLOR A.M. BSc. Born 29/3/47. Commd 17/1/72. Sqn Ldr 1/7/86. Retd GD 1/7/89.
TAYLOR A.R. BSc. Born 26/1/49. Commd 27/2/70. Sqn Ldr 1/1/80. Retd ENG 26/1/89.
TAYLOR A.S.H. MInstAM. Born 3/1/46. Commd 8/9/69. Sqn Ldr 1/1/81. Retd SY 8/11/85.
TAYLOR A.T.H. BSc MCMI. Born 3/10/39. Commd 2/10/61. Sqn Ldr 1/1/73. Retd GD 14/5/82.
TAYLOR A.W. Born 20/6/38. Commd 11/6/81. Flt Lt 11/12/83. Retd GD(G) 20/6/93.
TAYLOR B. BA. Born 9/5/38. Commd 6/4/62. Flt Lt 7/7/63. Retd GD 10/5/88.
TAYLOR B. Born 22/4/44. Commd 5/2/65. Sqn Ldr 1/1/77. Retd GD 22/4/88.
TAYLOR B.C. Born 5/4/31. Commd 25/8/67. Flt Lt 25/8/73. Retd ADMIN 30/4/76.
TAYLOR B.P. Born 3/1/53. Commd 6/4/72. Sqn Ldr 1/7/89. Retd GD 1/7/92.
TAYLOR B.T. Born 27/9/39. Commd 29/4/58. Flt Lt 5/11/63. Retd GD 3/4/79. Re-instated 21/9/84. Flt Lt 25/4/69. Retd GD 15/12/90.
TAYLOR C. Born 18/2/22. Commd 8/7/54. Sqn Ldr 1/7/68. Retd GD 18/2/77.
TAYLOR C. Born 23/1/17. Commd 9/4/43. Flt Lt 1/10/51. Retd GD(G) 29/11/61. rtg Sqn Ldr.
TAYLOR C.C. Born 3/3/33. Commd 15/12/53. Wg Cdr 1/1/85. Retd ADMIN 3/3/88.
TAYLOR C.E.B. Born 27/7/36. Commd 5/5/58. Sqn Ldr 1/1/82. Retd GD 27/7/91.
TAYLOR C.H. Born 22/8/29. Commd 18/1/50. Sqn Ldr 1/7/62. Retd GD 22/8/67.
TAYLOR C.J. MBE. Born 18/5/44. Commd 10/6/66. Sqn Ldr 1/1/80. Retd GD 6/8/98.
TAYLOR C.M. Born 7/11/66. Commd 15/12/88. Flt Lt 26/12/93. Retd ENGINEER 12/6/03.
TAYLOR C.R. OBE. Born 25/12/10. Commd 24/3/33. Wg Cdr 4/7/44. Retd GD 6/4/46. rtg Gp Capt.
TAYLOR C.R.V. Born 8/9/32. Commd 26/12/51. Flt Lt 14/11/56. Retd GD 8/11/75.
TAYLOR D. Born 14/7/31. Commd 19/6/53. Sqn Ldr 1/7/71. Retd ENG 14/7/81.
TAYLOR D. Born 9/6/54. Commd 27/7/72. Flt Lt 27/1/79. Retd GD(G) 9/6/92.
TAYLOR D.A. Born 21/1/26. Commd 29/6/50. Sqn Ldr 1/1/66. Retd GD 21/1/76.
TAYLOR D.A. Born 31/12/58. Commd 12/10/78. Sqn Ldr 1/1/89. Retd GD 30/6/99.
TAYLOR D.A. Born 14/5/51. Commd 9/12/76. Flt Lt 21/6/80. Retd FLY(N) 30/9/03.
TAYLOR D.A.J. BEM CEng MRAeS. Born 8/7/22. Commd 28/7/60. Sqn Ldr 1/1/72. Retd ENG 30/6/78.
TAYLOR D.B. Born 6/3/34. Commd 7/5/52. Flt Lt 2/10/57. Retd GD 1/5/84.
TAYLOR D.E. Born 7/4/30. Commd 28/11/51. Flt Lt 28/5/56. Retd GD 14/5/84.
TAYLOR D.H. BSc. Born 10/11/34. Commd 26/3/56. Sqn Ldr 1/1/69. Retd GD 10/11/72.
TAYLOR D.H.E. Born 16/9/25. Commd 21/5/46. Sqn Ldr 1/1/61. Retd GD 5/3/76.
TAYLOR D.I.W. FIFA. Born 12/12/50. Commd 28/12/80. Flt Lt 4/7/84. Retd ADMIN 17/9/89.
TAYLOR D.J. Born 5/4/44. Commd 8/1/69. Sqn Ldr 1/7/85. Retd GD 29/11/93.

TAYLOR D.J. Born 13/1/31. Commd 18/5/70. Sqn Ldr 1/1/74. Retd ADMIN 22/5/82.
TAYLOR D.J. Born 3/9/50. Commd 25/2/72. Wg Cdr 1/7/90. Retd SUP 14/5/94.
TAYLOR D.J.J. Born 4/1/27. Commd 13/9/50. Flt Lt 13/3/55. Retd GD 4/1/85.
TAYLOR D.J.W. Born 5/2/40. Commd 13/12/60. Flt Lt 13/6/63. Retd GD 21/8/64.
TAYLOR D.L. Born 24/8/45. Commd 2/4/65. Flt Lt 8/4/72. Retd SUP 24/8/83.
TAYLOR D.M.c. Born 18/12/40. Commd 29/6/72. Flt Lt 29/6/74. Retd ENG 3/11/77.
TAYLOR D.P. BSc. Born 26/3/66. Commd 16/9/84. Flt Lt 15/1/90. Retd GD 15/7/99.
TAYLOR D.W. Born 10/7/30. Commd 26/8/66. Flt Lt 26/8/07. Retd SUP 29/4/78.
TAYLOR D.W. BSc. Born 26/8/49. Commd 27/2/70. Flt Lt 27/11/74. Retd ENG 26/8/87.
TAYLOR E.A. BA. Born 31/8/29. Commd 26/9/50. Wg Cdr 1/1/68. Retd GD 3/4/80.
TAYLOR E.C. DFC. Born 24/10/23. Commd 13/12/44. Sqn Ldr 1/1/73. Retd GD 18/7/78.
TAYLOR E.W. BA DPhysEd. Born 27/6/22. Commd 24/4/47. Sqn Ldr 1/1/60. Retd PE 2/5/63.
TAYLOR F.H. Born 10/11/42. Commd 10/12/75. Sqn Ldr 1/7/87. Retd ENG 10/12/91.
TAYLOR G. Born 7/11/29. Commd 1/3/57. Flt Lt 1/3/61. Retd GD 26/6/84.
TAYLOR G. Born 29/5/34. Commd 16/7/52. Sqn Ldr 1/1/67. Retd GD 27/11/76.
TAYLOR G.C. BSc. Born 21/9/44. Commd 8/9/69. Sqn Ldr 8/3/77. Retd ADMIN 8/9/85.
TAYLOR G.L. Born 28/6/24. Commd 12/10/52. Flt Lt 1/7/56. Retd PRT 22/4/70.
TAYLOR G.P. CEng MRAeS MIEE. Born 2/3/40. Commd 17/7/62. Sqn Ldr 1/7/72. Retd ENG 2/3/78.
TAYLOR G.S. BSc. Born 16/10/27. Commd 22/12/49. Flt Lt 10/11/52. Retd GD 16/10/65.
TAYLOR G.T. Born 14/3/24. Commd 4/6/47. Flt Lt 25/3/56. Retd GD 31/3/62.
TAYLOR G.T. Born 6/3/43. Commd 15/7/66. Sqn Ldr 1/1/97. Retd GD 30/10/97.
TAYLOR G.W. Born 20/1/33. Commd 4/10/51. Flt Lt 1/11/61. Retd GD 20/12/72.
TAYLOR H. Born 25/12/21. Commd 4/10/45. Flt Lt 4/4/49. Retd GD 10/12/66.
TAYLOR H. Born 3/9/11. Commd 28/5/41. Flt Lt 1/9/45. Retd ASD 25/11/49.
TAYLOR H. Born 1/7/29. Commd 2/5/51. Flt Lt 2/11/55. Retd GD 1/7/67.
TAYLOR H.N. Born 13/2/38. Commd 9/3/62. Flt Lt 1/7/69. Retd GD 20/10/77.
TAYLOR H.W. DFC. Born 27/8/20. Commd 24/10/41. Sqn Ldr 1/1/58. Retd GD 27/8/75.
TAYLOR J. Born 7/5/33. Commd 26/3/52. Flt Lt 1/8/57. Retd GD 8/5/71.
TAYLOR J. Born 5/12/41. Commd 28/2/85. Sqn Ldr 1/7/93. Retd ENG 5/12/96.
TAYLOR J.C.E. Born 10/5/59. Commd 15/3/84. Fg Offr 15/9/86. Retd GD(G) 14/5/89.
TAYLOR J.D. CEng MIMechE. Born 12/3/34. Commd 12/4/65. Sqn Ldr 1/7/71. Retd ENG 2/3/93.
TAYLOR J.E. Born 6/7/63. Commd 17/7/87. Flt Lt 12/10/89. Retd FLY(P) 6/1/04.
TAYLOR J.J. Born 18/8/22. Commd 29/8/44. Flt Lt 4/10/48. Retd GD 22/9/67.
TAYLOR J.J.T. Born 20/4/51. Commd 16/3/73. Flt Lt 16/3/76. Retd GD 31/12/84.
TAYLOR J.K.I. Born 2/4/35. Commd 14/11/71. Sqn Ldr 4/9/83. Retd ADMIN 14/11/87.
TAYLOR J.M. Born 5/7/19. Commd 29/7/39. Flt Lt 3/9/41. Retd GD 24/2/46.
TAYLOR J.M. Born 10/10/29. Commd 19/4/51. Flt Lt 30/1/61. Retd GD 31/7/64.
TAYLOR J.N.H. Born 7/7/54. Commd 2/9/73. Sqn Ldr 1/1/91. Retd ADMIN 1/1/94.
TAYLOR J.W.J. Born 21/3/33. Commd 4/6/52. Sqn Ldr 1/1/64. Retd GD 21/6/92.
TAYLOR K.B. Born 13/10/49. Commd 3/12/70. Sqn Ldr 1/1/83. Retd GD 14/3/97.
TAYLOR K.R. IEng MIIE. Born 29/10/53. Commd 31/7/86. Sqn Ldr 1/7/96. Retd ENGINEER 6/1/05.
TAYLOR L.C. Born 25/6/26. Commd 15/10/53. Flt Lt 15/4/57. Retd GD 30/9/77.
TAYLOR L.E.K. BA. Born 23/2/70. Commd 1/12/96. Fg Offr 1/6/96. Retd SUP 28/3/00.
TAYLOR L.I.A. Born 21/1/28. Commd 27/7/49. Sqn Ldr 1/7/61. Retd GD 30/5/64.
TAYLOR L.W. BSc. Born 6/7/55. Commd 6/3/77. Flt Lt 6/12/78. Retd GD 6/3/89.
TAYLOR M. Born 15/8/58. Commd 15/2/90. Flt Lt 15/2/92. Retd ENG 31/3/94.
TAYLOR M. Born 13/5/30. Commd 5/9/57. Flt Lt 5/3/62. Retd GD 28/3/69.
TAYLOR M.A. BEM. Born 30/7/36. Commd 12/4/73. Sqn Ldr 1/7/84. Retd ENG 30/7/95.
TAYLOR M.B. Born 13/2/60. Commd 23/4/78. Flt Lt 23/10/83. Retd GD 18/4/87.
TAYLOR M.B. BDS. Born 21/6/45. Commd 20/1/74. Wg Cdr 13/2/83. Retd DEL 20/1/90.
TAYLOR M.C. Born 26/6/39. Commd 6/4/62. Sqn Ldr 1/1/75. Retd GD 1/1/78.
TAYLOR M.D. Born 20/4/47. Commd 9/2/66. Flt Lt 18/6/72. Retd GD(G) 1/10/75.
TAYLOR M.F.H. Born 17/7/45. Commd 8/6/84. Sqn Ldr 1/7/97. Retd ADMIN 2/7/99.
TAYLOR M.F.W. BSc. Born 1/6/53. Commd 26/4/72. Flt Lt 15/10/78. Retd GD 1/6/91.
TAYLOR M.H. MSc BSc CEng MIEE. Born 30/9/30. Commd 2/1/62. Wg Cdr 1/1/79. Retd ADMIN 28/8/83.
TAYLOR M.J. BSc. Born 9/4/54. Commd 3/9/72. Sqn Ldr 1/1/91. Retd GD 9/4/98.
TAYLOR M.J. Born 23/8/39. Commd 11/11/71. Sqn Ldr 1/1/85. Retd GD 7/2/90.
TAYLOR M.J. Born 25/10/31. Commd 4/6/52. Sqn Ldr 1/1/67. Retd GD 1/1/70.
TAYLOR M.J.C. Born 2/6/33. Commd 12/1/54. Wg Cdr 1/7/79. Retd GD 2/6/88.
TAYLOR M.S. BSc CEng MRAeS. Born 7/3/49. Commd 27/2/70. Wg Cdr 1/1/87. Retd ENG 14/3/96.
TAYLOR N.E. MA BSc FRAeS. Born 6/12/47. Commd 9/8/71. A Cdre 1/1/98. Retd GD 13/5/02.
TAYLOR N.H. Born 7/1/34. Commd 10/12/52. Flt Lt 5/5/58. Retd GD(G) 4/9/89.
TAYLOR N.I. Born 20/9/33. Commd 19/10/80. Sqn Ldr 1/7/84. Retd ADMIN 25/1/87.
TAYLOR N.R. Born 3/9/60. Commd 19/7/84. Flt Lt 19/1/89. Retd GD 19/3/00.
TAYLOR N.S. Born 1/11/21. Commd 21/11/44. Flt Lt 21/5/48. Retd GD 29/3/68.
TAYLOR O.G. MA CEng FCMI MIEE. Born 11/5/28. Commd 25/11/48. Wg Cdr 1/7/63. Retd ENG 11/5/65.

TAYLOR P. OBE CEng MRAeS. Born 26/8/33. Commd 24/9/64. Wg Cdr 1/7/76. Retd ENG 26/8/83.
TAYLOR P. Born 15/11/46. Commd 15/9/67. Flt Lt 15/3/73. Retd GD 1/5/93.
TAYLOR P. Born 1/12/47. Commd 21/4/67. Flt Lt 29/7/73. Retd GD(G) 1/12/85.
TAYLOR P. Born 8/1/64. Commd 24/3/83. Sqn Ldr 1/7/94. Retd GD 25/9/01.
TAYLOR P.C. OBE BA. Born 6/7/45. Commd 23/9/66. Wg Cdr 1/7/87. Retd SUP 6/1/00.
TAYLOR P.F. BA. Born 9/2/62. Commd 14/10/84. Flt Lt 14/4/87. Retd GD 14/10/00.
TAYLOR P.F. Born 14/6/46. Commd 7/7/67. Flt Lt 7/1/73. Retd GD 14/6/01.
TAYLOR P.G. Born 6/6/22. Commd 11/1/43. Flt Lt 15/7/47. Retd SEC 11/6/55.
TAYLOR P.G. MA FCMI. Born 6/10/35. Commd 12/9/58. Gp Capt 1/7/84. Retd ADMIN 4/4/88.
TAYLOR P.L. Born 25/6/57. Commd 14/7/77. Flt Lt 14/1/83. Retd GD 2/7/87.
TAYLOR P.P.W. CBE AFC. Born 2/1/37. Commd 29/7/58. A Cdre 1/1/84. Retd GD 1/1/87.
TAYLOR P.R. Born 13/10/21. Commd 4/3/43. Sqn Ldr 1/1/54. Retd ENG 10/5/58.
TAYLOR P.T. AFC. Born 28/11/29. Commd 21/4/54. Sqn Ldr 1/1/69. Retd GD 1/7/73.
TAYLOR P.W. MCMI. Born 27/10/39. Commd 24/4/70. Flt Lt 24/4/77. Retd MED(SEC) 8/1/33. Re-instated 28/9/83.
    Sqn Ldr 1/7/85. Retd MED(SEC) 28/9/88.
TAYLOR R. Born 7/2/40. Commd 29/4/58. Sqn Ldr 1/1/76. Retd GD 1/5/94.
TAYLOR R. Born 19/4/52. Commd 4/3/71. Sqn Ldr 1/1/89. Retd GD 1/1/92.
TAYLOR R.B. Born 5/6/30. Commd 27/8/52. Flt Lt 23/1/58. Retd GD 22/5/76.
TAYLOR R.C. Born 4/3/33. Commd 9/4/52. Sqn Ldr 1/7/65. Retd GD 1/6/73.
TAYLOR R.C. Born 1/1/67. Commd 31/7/86. APO 31/7/86. Retd GD 22/3/87.
TAYLOR R.D.G. BSc. Born 25/2/41. Commd 19/6/64. Flt Lt 19/9/65. Retd GD 15/2/96.
TAYLOR R.E.T. Born 25/1/28. Commd 1/7/53. Flt Lt 26/11/58. Retd GD 6/1/69.
TAYLOR R.F. Born 1/10/14. Commd 18/11/43. Sqn Ldr 1/7/58. Retd ENG 1/10/69.
TAYLOR R.G. Born 24/5/44. Commd 20/8/65. Sqn Ldr 1/7/76. Retd GD 24/5/88.
TAYLOR R.H. MRAeS. Born 2/4/21. Commd 19/8/42. Sqn Ldr 1/7/54. Retd ENG 20/12/69.
TAYLOR R.H. The Rev BA. Born 10/7/27. Commd 1/6/61. Retd Wg Cdr 10/4/83.
TAYLOR R.H.W. Born 12/12/25. Commd 16/12/66. Flt Lt 16/12/69. Retd GD 14/1/76.
TAYLOR R.I. BSc. Born 5/6/51. Commd 8/9/74. Sqn Ldr 1/7/88. Retd ENG 31/1/95.
TAYLOR R.J.M. Born 17/11/44. Commd 26/10/62. Sqn Ldr 1/1/78. Retd OPS SPT 4/2/99.
TAYLOR R.K. MCMI. Born 7/10/30. Commd 17/1/52. Sqn Ldr 1/7/67. Retd GD 28/11/75.
TAYLOR R.M. BSc. Born 30/12/49. Commd 3/1/71. Flt Lt 15/10/72. Retd GD 30/12/87.
TAYLOR R.P. BSc(Eng) CEng MIMechE MCMI. Born 17/3/36. Commd 12/3/60. Wg Cdr 1/7/79. Retd ENG 4/2/89.
TAYLOR R.R. OBE MBE DL. Born 14/6/32. Commd 28/6/51. Sqn Ldr 1/7/66. Retd GD 30/6/73.
TAYLOR R.S. Born 14/6/47. Commd 6/5/66. Flt Lt 4/5/72. Retd GD 14/6/85.
TAYLOR R.W. BSc. Born 26/3/58. Commd 28/9/80. Sqn Ldr 1/1/93. Retd GD 28/9/96.
TAYLOR S. Born 5/7/22. Commd 20/10/55. Flt Lt 22/2/59. Retd ENG 2/6/73.
TAYLOR S. Born 20/1/18. Commd 21/10/54. Sqn Ldr 5/3/65. Retd MED(T) 8/7/68.
TAYLOR S.C. CBE. Born 22/4/20. Commd 21/9/44. Gp Capt 1/7/69. Retd ENG 22/4/75.
TAYLOR S.C. BSc BDS MGDSRCS(Eng). Born 23/12/52. Commd 25/9/71. Sqn Ldr 22/5/87. Retd DEL 23/3/92.
TAYLOR S.D. MCIPD. Born 17/9/30. Commd 4/1/54. Wg Cdr 1/1/83. Retd GD 17/9/85.
TAYLOR S.E. Born 6/2/17. Commd 1/1/51. Flt Lt 17/5/56. Retd CAT 17/11/58.
TAYLOR S.J. Born 15/9/51. Commd 3/5/79. Flt Lt 17/2/86. Retd GD 18/7/01.
TAYLOR S.J. Born 30/10/64. Commd 16/6/88. Fg Offr 12/10/88. Retd ADMIN 30/11/91.
TAYLOR S.L. Born 25/2/21. Commd 21/11/42. Flt Lt 21/11/47. Retd SEC 29/7/60.
TAYLOR S.McC. BSc. Born 3/8/37. Commd 23/9/59. Wg Cdr 1/1/85. Retd GD 6/12/91.
TAYLOR T. Born 2/1/19. Commd 5/8/42. Sqn Ldr 1/1/53. Retd ENG 2/1/74.
TAYLOR T.C. Born 27/12/32. Commd 4/10/51. Sqn Ldr 1/1/66. Retd GD 27/12/70.
TAYLOR T.D. Born 18/4/44. Commd 22/5/64. Flt Lt 12/11/69. Retd GD 18/4/82.
TAYLOR T.H. Born 6/7/42. Commd 19/6/64. Flt Lt 1/7/69. Retd GD 1/8/94.
TAYLOR T.R.B. The Rev. MA. Born 23/1/23. Commd 18/8/49. Retd Wg Cdr 18/8/65.
TAYLOR V.W.C. DFC. Born 26/7/19. Commd 1/5/42. Flt Lt 1/11/46. Retd SEC 12/12/53. rtg Sqn Ldr.
TAYLOR W. Born 16/5/20. Commd 3/2/43. Flt Lt 25/9/46. Retd GD 22/3/63.
TAYLOR W.C. OBE CEng MRAeS. Born 3/6/20. Commd 19/8/42. A Cdre 1/1/72. Retd ENG 3/6/75.
TAYLOR W.F. Born 20/10/35. Commd 7/3/61. Flt Lt 1/4/66. Retd GD 29/4/75.
TAYLOR W.G. Born 30/5/39. Commd 24/4/77. Flt Lt 21/4/80. Retd GD(G) 30/5/94.
TAYLOR W.H. DUS CEng MIEE. Born 8/8/31. Commd 2/9/53. Sqn Ldr 1/7/65. Retd ENG 2/9/69.
TAYLOR W.J. OBE MRAeS. Born 31/1/51. Commd 22/11/73. Gp Capt 1/7/93. Retd ENG 6/4/01.
TAYLOR W.S. MSc CEng. Born 24/1/53. Commd 13/2/77. Sqn Ldr 1/7/86. Retd ENG 13/2/96.
TAYLOR W.W. Born 24/1/31. Commd 29/4/71. Flt Lt 29/4/76. Retd GD 1/7/86.
TEAGER J.E.W. OBE AFC. Born 12/8/21. Commd 28/9/43. Gp Capt 1/7/70. Retd GD 16/7/75.
TEAGER J.F.N. Born 21/3/58. Commd 21/4/77. Wg Cdr 1/7/94. Retd GD 1/1/98.
TEALE C. BSc. Born 26/6/60. Commd 4/9/78. Flt Lt 15/10/82. Retd GD 7/6/89.
TEAR R.C. MBE BSc(Eng) CEng MIMechE MRAeS. Born 11/6/30. Commd 6/5/53. Gp Capt 1/7/79.
    Retd ENG 2/4/85.
TEASDALE R.J. BDS. Born 21/6/38. Commd 13/7/66. Wg Cdr 11/1/78. Retd DEL 24/6/96.
TEATHER J.B. Born 27/10/44. Commd 31/1/64. Flt Lt 12/11/69. Retd GD 27/10/83.

TEBB B.A. Born 27/5/45. Commd 29/11/63. Sqn Ldr 1/7/79. Retd GD 27/5/83.
TEBBOTH J.G. Born 25/4/31. Commd 29/7/65. Flt Lt 11/4/70. Retd MED(T) 4/9/75.
TEBBS C.R. Born 25/6/45. Commd 4/5/72. Sqn Ldr 1/7/81. Retd ADMIN 1/12/88.
TEBBS J.W. BA. Born 26/1/35. Commd 2/1/62. Wg Cdr 1/7/84. Retd ADMIN 3/8/87.
TEBBS N.A. Born 22/6/38. Commd 7/12/61. Flt Lt 1/4/66. Retd GD 22/6/76.
TEBBUTT K. AFC. Born 7/8/23. Commd 12/11/43. Sqn Ldr 1/1/55. Retd GD 16/9/61.
TEDDER C.J. Born 4/3/24. Commd 16/9/44. Sqn Ldr 1/7/55. Retd GD 4/3/73.
TEHAN B.M. Born 6/2/33. Commd 18/6/52. Sqn Ldr 1/1/66. Retd GD 27/10/73.
TELFER-SMITH S.R. MBA BSc DIC. Born 10/8/60. Commd 29/9/85. Sqn Ldr 1/1/92. Retd ADMIN 14/3/96.
TELFORD A.M. Born 12/8/58. Commd 8/9/77. Flt Lt 8/3/84. Retd SY 12/8/96.
TELFORD C.M. Born 29/12/24. Commd 29/12/49. Flt Lt 29/6/53. Retd GD 29/12/62.
TELFORD F.G. Born 14/12/40. Commd 15/9/67. Flt Lt 6/10/71. Retd GD(G) 14/12/78.
TELFORD G.M. BSc. Born 21/4/54. Commd 17/9/72. Wg Cdr 1/1/94. Retd GD 28/9/01.
TELFORD M. Born 9/2/30. Commd 4/7/64. Sqn Ldr 5/10/68. Retd EDN 31/8/72.
TELFORD M.A. AFC. Born 20/1/36. Commd 9/6/54. Flt Lt 28/7/65. Retd GD 3/10/78.
TELLIS R.C.L. Born 27/6/40. Commd 23/3/67. Flt Lt 23/9/72. Retd GD 27/6/95.
TEMPERO K. Born 4/9/23. Commd 28/1/45. Sqn Ldr 1/7/61. Retd GD(G) 31/3/77.
TEMPLE A.I. MSc BA. Born 24/7/48. Commd 12/3/72. Wg Cdr 1/7/91. Retd SUP 14/3/97.
TEMPLE M.L.L. Born 7/1/44. Commd 21/1/66. Sqn Ldr 1/7/93. Retd FLY(P) 7/1/04.
TEMPLE T.C. Born 22/12/33. Commd 15/6/53. Sqn Ldr 1/1/78. Retd PI 2/12/84.
TEMPLE-SMITH M.N. Born 10/8/57. Commd 24/7/81. Flt Lt 24/1/87. Retd GD 23/3/97.
TEMPLETON J.B. Born 19/11/36. Commd 21/10/64. Flt Lt 21/10/64. Retd GD 23/5/67.
TEMPLETON R.J. Born 14/5/16. Commd 8/1/47. Sqn Ldr 1/1/60. Retd CAT 14/5/66.
TEMPLETON W.V. BSc CEng MRAeS MIEE. Born 24/1/40. Commd 30/9/59. Sqn Ldr 1/1/76. Retd ENG 2/4/91.
TENCH N.R. MBE. Born 16/8/45. Commd 4/10/63. Wg Cdr 1/1/89. Retd GD 27/8/04.
TENISON-COLLINS J.A. BSc. Born 24/7/58. Commd 11/9/77. Flt Lt 15/4/82. Retd GD 24/7/96.
TENNANT E.A. DFC. Born 25/2/22. Commd 3/12/42. Flt Lt 3/6/46. Retd GD 16/6/53. rtg Sqn Ldr.
TERNOUTH M.L. Born 25/10/49. Commd 4/7/69. Flt Lt 4/1/75. Retd GD 25/10/87. Re-entered 1/3/89. Sqn Ldr 1/7/96.
   Retd GD 4/3/01.
TERRETT A.L. Born 24/10/39. Commd 19/12/61. Gp Capt 1/7/92. Retd GD 24/10/94.
TERRETT J.D. Born 10/11/51. Commd 26/11/81. Sqn Ldr 1/7/94. Retd ENGINEER 31/12/04.
TERRETT P.E. OBE LLB. Born 8/2/34. Commd 30/1/58. Gp Capt 1/1/81. Retd ADMIN 18/7/88.
TERRY Sir Colin KBE CB BSc(Eng) CEng FRAeS FRSA FILT FCGI. Born 8/8/43. Commd 30/9/62. AM 11/7/97.
   Retd ENG 7/8/99.
TERRY C.J. Born 21/10/50. Commd 4/3/71. Flt Lt 4/9/76. Retd GD 1/3/94.
TERRY Sir Peter GCB AFC. Born 18/10/26. Commd 17/7/46. ACM 1/3/81. Retd GD 18/10/84.
TERRY R.B. BSc CEng MRAeS. Born 16/8/29. Commd 15/11/51. Sqn Ldr 1/7/62. Retd ENG 16/8/67.
TETLEY J.F.H. Born 5/2/32. Commd 14/4/53. AVM 1/7/84. Retd GD 3/4/87.
TETLEY W. Born 17/11/12. Commd 6/6/44. Fg Offr 20/9/51. Retd CAT 3/12/64.
TETLOW H.H. Born 22/3/23. Commd 27/8/59. Flt Lt 27/8/65. Retd ENG 10/12/74.
TETLOW P.E. Born 9/8/24. Commd 30/3/61. Flt Lt 30/3/64. Retd GD(G) 5/7/68.
TETTMAR R.E. MB BS MRCPath MRCS LRCP DPath. Born 28/6/47. Commd 10/11/69. Sqn Ldr 26/7/78.
   Retd MED 10/11/85.
TEW B. Born 13/12/33. Commd 20/1/56. Sqn Ldr 1/1/78. Retd GD(G) 1/12/85.
TEW D.H. Born 22/4/24. Commd 19/7/56. Sqn Ldr 1/7/69. Retd GD 22/4/82.
TEW M.R.N. BSc. Born 27/9/47. Commd 11/5/71. Sqn Ldr 1/7/82. Retd GD 21/6/99.
TEW P.A. Born 13/2/47. Commd 28/2/69. Flt Lt 8/3/72. Retd GD 13/2/85.
THACKER J. BSc. Born 8/9/53. Commd 17/7/72. Sqn Ldr 1/7/86. Retd ADMIN 17/7/93.
THACKER J.H. Born 6/3/20. Commd 24/10/45. Sqn Ldr 1/7/56. Retd RGT 28/1/61.
THACKER R. Born 16/11/32. Commd 13/9/51. Flt Lt 30/1/57. Retd GD 30/1/74.
THAIN G.T. DFC. Born 12/7/18. Commd 3/11/40. Wg Cdr 1/1/55. Retd GD 26/8/65.
THAIN J.W. MRAeS. Born 29/6/19. Commd 27/4/44. Flt Lt 11/5/48. Retd GD 12/1/63.
THAIN M.C. Born 8/1/44. Commd 30/5/69. Flt Lt 15/11/71. Retd GD 8/1/83. Re-instated 3/7/85. Flt Lt 9/5/74.
   Retd GD 22/10/94.
THATCHER M.F. AFM. Born 23/5/37. Commd 3/10/69. Flt Lt 4/5/72. Retd GD 14/1/75.
THAYER F.E. MBE MCMI. Born 4/4/21. Commd 5/2/43. Sqn Ldr 1/1/66. Retd GD(G) 4/4/74.
THEAKSON A.E. Born 16/5/34. Commd 6/6/64. Flt Lt 6/6/66. Retd GD 6/6/72.
THEED A.J.M. Born 20/7/40. Commd 25/8/60. Flt Lt 27/7/67. Retd RGT 20/7/78.
THEOBALD D.A. Born 19/11/49. Commd 1/4/71. Flt Lt 1/10/76. Retd GD 30/1/81.
THEOBALD R.M. Born 4/10/33. Commd 29/10/64. Sqn Ldr 1/7/79. Retd ENG 4/10/89.
THILTHORPE R. Born 18/11/43. Commd 8/12/61. Sqn Ldr 1/1/77. Retd GD 15/10/87.
THIRD D. MSc BSc CEng MIEE. Born 23/6/41. Commd 1/8/66. Sqn Ldr 6/10/71. Retd ADMIN 1/8/82.
THIRKETTLE A. BSc FCMI. Born 22/11/31. Commd 24/9/52. Gp Capt 1/1/73. Retd ENG 25/9/76.
THIRLE J. AFC. Born 8/1/32. Commd 12/9/56. Sqn Ldr 1/1/67. Retd PE 12/9/72.
THIRLWALL C. OBE AFC BA. Born 11/7/44. Commd 14/8/64. Gp Capt 1/7/94. Retd GD 11/7/99.
THIRLWELL J.D. OBE DFC. Born 31/10/19. Commd 7/3/40. Gp Capt 1/1/61. Retd GD 20/7/68.

THIRNBECK J.R. Born 16/9/29. Commd 11/4/51. Sqn Ldr 1/7/64. Retd SEC 16/9/67.
THISTLETHWAITE K. Born 24/9/55. Commd 15/3/84. Wg Cdr 1/7/96. Retd SUP 24/9/99.
THOLEN P.J. Born 5/3/61. Commd 24/4/80. Flt Lt 24/10/85. Retd GD 9/1/92.
THOM I. BA MCIPD CertFE. Born 22/5/54. Commd 14/2/99. Flt Lt 14/2/99. Retd ADMIN (TRG) 25/12/04.
THOM M.I. MA CEng MRAeS MIEE. Born 24/5/35. Commd 25/9/54. Gp Capt 1/1/76. Retd ENG 1/6/78.
THOMAS A. Born 9/3/44. Commd 25/9/80. Sqn Ldr 1/7/94. Retd SUP 7/1/98.
THOMAS A.C. BA DPhysEd. Born 10/6/36. Commd 10/9/63. Sqn Ldr 17/10/71. Retd EDN 10/9/79.
THOMAS A.F. Born 7/4/10. Commd 30/8/41. Flt Lt 26/5/55. Retd CAT 24/5/62.
THOMAS A.J. Born 26/5/43. Commd 11/4/85. Sqn Ldr 1/1/01. Retd FLY(AEO) 26/5/03.
THOMAS A.L. Born 16/12/30. Commd 1/4/53. Flt Lt 5/11/56. Retd GD 16/12/68.
THOMAS A.R. Born 26/2/45. Commd 14/6/63. Sqn Ldr 1/1/85. Retd GD 22/12/95.
THOMAS A.T. Born 16/4/35. Commd 14/8/70. Flt Lt 14/8/72. Retd SY 1/10/76.
THOMAS A.V. Born 25/12/31. Commd 25/9/56. Flt Lt 25/3/62. Retd GD 25/12/89.
THOMAS A.W.G. Born 27/5/22. Commd 5/8/44. Flt Lt 22/7/48. Retd GD 31/3/74.
THOMAS B. Born 7/1/26. Commd 23/2/50. Flt Lt 27/5/54. Retd GD(G) 7/1/69.
THOMAS B. Born 15/6/63. Commd 8/11/90. Flt Lt 8/11/92. Retd ADMIN 14/3/97.
THOMAS B.A. Born 4/12/31. Commd 2/5/59. Flt Lt 2/11/64. Retd GD 28/11/69.
THOMAS C. Born 17/6/23. Commd 18/10/51. Sqn Ldr 1/7/74. Retd GD 17/6/83.
THOMAS C.B. Born 24/12/47. Commd 13/9/70. Flt Lt 13/3/76. Retd GD 15/7/76.
THOMAS C.C. BSc. Born 12/1/59. Commd 5/9/76. Sqn Ldr 1/7/93. Retd GD 12/1/03.
THOMAS C.P. BSc. Born 9/9/33. Commd 10/2/59. Flt Lt 15/8/62. Retd GD 7/11/74.
THOMAS C.S. BA MCMI. Born 16/11/42. Commd 14/9/64. Gp Capt 1/7/92. Retd GD 10/2/96.
THOMAS D. Born 10/5/22. Commd 19/6/43. Flt Lt 14/11/48. Retd GD 1/5/61.
THOMAS D.A. CEng MRAeS MCMI. Born 10/6/18. Commd 2/6/49. Sqn Ldr 1/1/59. Retd ENG 11/6/68.
THOMAS D.A. Born 21/2/43. Commd 17/7/64. Flt Lt 4/5/72. Retd GD 21/2/81.
THOMAS D.C. Born 26/12/37. Commd 7/1/58. Sqn Ldr 1/7/72. Retd GD 26/12/95.
THOMAS D.D. Born 15/3/46. Commd 29/3/68. Flt Lt 29/9/73. Retd GD 15/3/87.
THOMAS D.G. BSc. Born 6/7/49. Commd 5/7/83. Sqn Ldr 1/1/98. Retd GD 6/7/02.
THOMAS D.H. MSc. Born 8/1/44. Commd 30/8/66. Sqn Ldr 1/7/78. Retd GD 30/8/88.
THOMAS D.J. Born 29/6/37. Commd 27/8/64. Flt Lt 27/8/66. Retd GD 25/6/75.
THOMAS D.L.J. Born 4/7/45. Commd 29/11/63. Flt Lt 29/5/69. Retd GD 1/11/79.
THOMAS D.M. MSc BEng CEng MRAeS. Born 19/9/66. Commd 3/8/88. Sqn Ldr 1/1/99. Retd ENGINEER 19/9/04.
THOMAS E.B. Born 27/3/31. Commd 26/12/51. Sqn Ldr 1/1/67. Retd GD 19/12/75.
THOMAS E.B. Born 2/10/23. Commd 1/5/44. Flt Lt 1/5/46. Retd GD(G) 9/8/72.
THOMAS E.J.M. DPhysEd. Born 13/2/34. Commd 25/9/62. Sqn Ldr 1/7/74. Retd ADMIN 13/2/89.
THOMAS E.L. Born 28/2/36. Commd 25/6/66. Sqn Ldr 1/1/74. Retd GD 31/7/87.
THOMAS F.A. DFC AFC FCMI. Born 30/10/21. Commd 10/11/42. Wg Cdr 1/1/63. Retd GD 1/10/73. rtg Gp Capt.
THOMAS F.B. Born 8/2/36. Commd 3/8/61. Flt Lt 1/4/66. Retd ADMIN 30/4/76.
THOMAS F.D. Born 17/8/22. Commd 8/1/53. Flt Lt 21/7/56. Retd GD 1/7/73.
THOMAS F.W. Born 4/8/13. Commd 21/10/35. Flt Lt 1/6/45. Retd SEC 1/5/48. rtg Sqn Ldr.
THOMAS G. Born 28/4/54. Commd 15/2/73. Sqn Ldr 1/1/88. Retd GD 14/12/93.
THOMAS G. BSc. Born 5/4/40. Commd 14/9/64. Flt Lt 14/6/66. Retd GD 14/9/80.
THOMAS G.E. MBE FRIN. Born 28/6/47. Commd 11/8/67. Sqn Ldr 1/1/98. Retd GD 28/6/02.
THOMAS G.J.R. Born 10/2/50. Commd 29/8/72. Flt Lt 29/8/76. Retd ADMIN 29/8/88.
THOMAS H. Born 2/1/35. Commd 1/4/53. Flt Lt 21/10/59. Retd GD 2/1/90.
THOMAS H. Born 4/5/48. Commd 4/3/81. Wg Cdr 1/7/00. Retd GD 4/5/03.
THOMAS H.A. Born 21/5/42. Commd 12/7/63. Flt Lt 12/1/69. Retd GD 2/4/93.
THOMAS I. Born 16/9/36. Commd 8/4/65. Fg Offr 8/4/65. Retd RGT 7/1/70.
THOMAS I. Born 17/12/41. Commd 9/2/62. Sqn Ldr 1/1/77. Retd GD 1/1/80.
THOMAS I.J. Born 15/3/33. Commd 3/1/61. Wg Cdr 1/1/78. Retd ADMIN 29/9/85.
THOMAS I.M. The Rev. MA. Born 3/1/50. Commd 2/1/77. Retd Wg Cdr 3/1/01.
THOMAS J. MBE. Born 10/3/31. Commd 9/4/52. Sqn Ldr 1/7/74. Retd GD 10/3/93.
THOMAS J. Born 13/4/17. Commd 17/10/57. Flt Lt 1/4/63. Retd ENG 15/7/67.
THOMAS J.A. Born 15/6/38. Commd 30/7/59. Flt Lt 30/1/63. Retd GD 24/4/89.
THOMAS J.A. Born 28/3/46. Commd 25/8/67. Wg Cdr 1/1/88. Retd GD 28/4/03.
THOMAS J.B.P. Born 28/3/11. Commd 3/3/33. Wg Cdr 1/7/47. Retd GD 21/10/49. rtg Gp Capt.
THOMAS J.E. MA. Born 10/2/23. Commd 8/4/53. Sqn Ldr 8/10/60. Retd EDN 21/7/67.
THOMAS J.F. BA. Born 29/12/43. Commd 21/4/67. Wg Cdr 1/1/86. Retd ADMIN 3/1/89.
THOMAS J.M. MEng BSc. Born 15/9/45. Commd 1/9/71. Flt Lt 1/8/73. Retd ENG 26/10/79.
THOMAS J.V. BSc. Born 4/6/47. Commd 2/7/72. Flt Lt 2/10/73. Retd GD 2/7/88.
THOMAS K.D. BSc. Born 26/7/49. Commd 23/9/68. Sqn Ldr 1/7/95. Retd GD 31/8/99.
THOMAS K.I. MBE. Born 10/6/14. Commd 14/1/42. Sqn Ldr 1/7/53. Retd ENG 10/6/63.
THOMAS M. Born 24/10/42. Commd 3/8/62. Flt Lt 1/7/69. Retd GD 31/1/76.
THOMAS M. Born 4/9/18. Commd 24/3/44. Flt Lt 4/1/51. Retd SEC 23/10/65.
THOMAS M. Born 4/9/18. Commd 3/6/42. Flt Offr 3/12/46. Retd SEC 21/3/61.
THOMAS M.E. Born 18/1/43. Commd 13/1/67. Flt Lt 13/7/72. Retd GD 28/6/75. Re-instated 5/6/78. Retd 3/9/85.

THOMAS M.G. Born 13/5/34. Commd 5/4/55. Sqn Ldr 1/1/72. Retd GD 14/5/88.
THOMAS M.K. MSc BDS MGDSRCS(Eng). Born 17/4/54. Commd 10/9/78. Wg Cdr 12/1/91. Retd DEL 10/12/95.
THOMAS M.O. MEd MSc Dip Soton. Born 1/11/34. Commd 7/9/56. Sqn Ldr 1/5/65. Retd ADMIN 4/5/83.
THOMAS N.A. Born 19/9/52. Commd 9/3/72. Sqn Ldr 1/7/91. Retd OPS SPT(ATC) 13/4/04.
THOMAS N.C. CEng MIEE MRAeSae. Born 29/4/41. Commd 17/7/62. Sqn Ldr 1/7/71. Retd ENG 29/4/79.
THOMAS N.N. MA CEng Dip El MIEE. Born 28/9/31. Commd 26/9/53. Flt Lt 1/1/75. Retd ENG 28/9/86.
THOMAS O.G. AFC. Born 17/3/20. Commd 1/12/44. Flt Lt 1/6/48. Retd GD(G) 26/8/67.
THOMAS P. AFC. Born 21/2/26. Commd 17/12/45. Sqn Ldr 1/1/63. Retd GD 1/1/66.
THOMAS P.D. BSc. Born 5/1/63. Commd 18/8/85. Flt Lt 18/2/89. Retd ENG 18/8/01.
THOMAS P.E.H. AFC. Born 13/12/19. Commd 3/11/40. Wg Cdr 1/7/58. Retd GD 6/2/65.
THOMAS P.H. Born 25/2/29. Commd 14/1/53. Fg Offr 28/4/55. Retd GD 5/6/59.
THOMAS P.J. MBE. Born 4/3/36. Commd 3/12/59. Sqn Ldr 1/7/70. Retd GD 29/11/86.
THOMAS P.M. BA. Born 30/7/44. Commd 28/3/67. Flt Lt 28/3/69. Retd GD 31/3/93.
THOMAS P.M.H. Born 21/8/32. Commd 10/12/52. Flt Lt 18/10/60. Retd GD 9/4/75.
THOMAS P.W. BSc. Born 5/8/57. Commd 12/8/79. Flt Lt 12/11/79. Retd GD 28/1/88.
THOMAS R.D. Born 22/2/35. Commd 22/7/66. Flt Lt 22/7/71. Retd ENG 1/12/73.
THOMAS R.G. MBE CEng MRAeS MCMI. Born 26/8/19. Commd 5/10/50. Wg Cdr 1/1/68. Retd ENG 1/5/75.
THOMAS R.H. DFC. Born 5/7/20. Commd 17/1/45. Flt Lt 14/10/60. Retd GD(G) 1/5/75. rtg Sqn Ldr.
THOMAS R.J.M. Born 27/5/47. Commd 21/1/66. Sqn Ldr 1/7/93. Retd GD 27/5/98.
THOMAS R.L. MRAeS. Born 31/3/37. Commd 1/4/58. Sqn Ldr 1/1/69. Retd GD 31/3/75.
THOMAS R.M. OBE AFC FRAeS. Born 3/5/49. Commd 27/2/70. Gp Capt 1/7/95. Retd GD 1/8/99.
THOMAS R.M. Born 19/6/40. Commd 17/7/64. Flt Lt 17/1/70. Retd GD 1/4/80.
THOMAS R.S. BTech. Born 6/5/49. Commd 2/8/71. Sqn Ldr 1/7/85. Retd GD 1/7/88.
THOMAS R.W. Born 10/7/23. Commd 15/6/61. Flt Lt 15/6/64. Retd GD 10/7/83.
THOMAS S.E. MBE. Born 20/6/53. Commd 19/7/84. Sqn Ldr 1/1/91. Retd GD 1/8/00.
THOMAS S.J. AFC*. Born 11/4/20. Commd 2/1/42. Flt Lt 23/8/47. Retd GD 31/3/62. rtg Sqn Ldr.
THOMAS S.R. Born 25/2/60. Commd 28/6/79. Sqn Ldr 1/1/93. Retd FLY(P) 25/2/04.
THOMAS T. Born 17/12/17. Commd 3/2/44. Sqn Ldr 1/7/55. Retd ENG 1/4/66.
THOMAS T.J.S. The Rev. BA. Born 17/12/21. Commd 8/10/51. Retd Gp Capt 22/12/76.
THOMAS T.P. Born 5/12/14. Commd 29/9/41. Flt Lt 18/7/48. Retd GD(G) 5/12/64.
THOMAS V. MB BCh MRCGP DRCOG DAvMed AFOM. Born 18/5/45. Commd 22/1/68. Wg Cdr 16/1/87. Retd MED 18/5/95.
THOMAS W. BEM. Born 21/3/30. Commd 27/8/64. Sqn Ldr 1/7/80. Retd ENG 21/3/90.
THOMAS W.E. OBE AFC. Born 15/6/21. Commd 26/1/41. Wg Cdr 1/7/60. Retd GD 1/5/67.
THOMAS W.E. Born 16/5/21. Commd 3/7/42. Flt Lt 3/1/46. Retd PI 16/5/76.
THOMAS W.E.W. MCMI. Born 6/2/25. Commd 31/7/58. Sqn Ldr 1/1/71. Retd SEC 1/8/79.
THOMAS W.J. Born 16/3/11. Commd 16/3/44. Flt Lt 16/9/47. Retd ENG 19/12/48. Re-employed 5/1/53 to 5/1/58.
THOMAS W.K. Born 17/2/17. Commd 12/9/42. Sqn Ldr 1/7/70. Retd SEC 30/6/73.
THOMPSON A. Born 27/4/23. Commd 4/10/51. Sqn Ldr 1/1/62. Retd GD 1/1/65.
THOMPSON A. BSc. Born 7/2/49. Commd 13/9/71. Wg Cdr 1/1/93. Retd GD 7/2/99.
THOMPSON A. BSc CEng MIEE. Born 24/9/47. Commd 2/9/73. Sqn Ldr 1/7/81. Retd ENG 2/9/89.
THOMPSON A.B. CEng MRAeS. Born 5/12/25. Commd 6/3/52. Gp Capt 1/7/72. Retd ENG 9/12/75.
THOMPSON A.C. BA. Born 13/2/61. Commd 11/9/83. Flt Lt 11/3/86. Retd ADMIN 4/7/87.
THOMPSON A.I. MCMI. Born 12/6/23. Commd 6/10/44. Wg Cdr 1/7/72. Retd GD 12/6/78.
THOMPSON A.J. Born 25/7/29. Commd 20/3/52. Flt Lt 27/9/57. Retd GD 25/7/72. rtg Sqn Ldr.
THOMPSON A.J. Born 3/8/49. Commd 1/7/82. Wg Cdr 1/7/01. Retd GD 5/5/04.
THOMPSON A.L.C. Born 22/5/26. Commd 21/5/46. Gp Capt 1/1/77. Retd PRT 1/3/80.
THOMPSON A.R. MBE MPhil BA FCMI MCIPD. Born 6/1/46. Commd 15/4/66. Gp Capt 1/1/89. Retd ADMIN 10/5/94.
THOMPSON B. Born 18/8/29. Commd 21/5/52. Flt Lt 16/10/57. Retd GD 16/10/67.
THOMPSON B.A.W. Born 4/12/44. Commd 27/5/71. Flt Lt 18/9/77. Retd SUP 9/11/86.
THOMPSON B.D. Born 25/5/32. Commd 11/4/54. Sqn Ldr 1/7/77. Retd GD(G) 1/9/82.
THOMPSON C.F.P. Born 28/9/25. Commd 13/6/46. Sqn Ldr 1/1/59. Retd GD 28/6/68.
THOMPSON C.J. Born 20/2/45. Commd 5/2/65. Flt Lt 5/8/70. Retd GD 21/2/76.
THOMPSON C.M. BSc. Born 11/4/65. Commd 26/10/86. Sqn Ldr 1/7/96. Retd ENGINEER 11/4/05.
THOMPSON C.V. MS BSc CEng. Born 27/5/44. Commd 15/7/65. A Cdre 1/7/91. Retd ENG 27/9/96.
THOMPSON C.W. Born 30/3/44. Commd 19/8/66. Sqn Ldr 1/7/94. Retd FLY(P) 30/3/04.
THOMPSON D. BEM. Born 16/7/29. Commd 24/2/67. Flt Lt 24/2/72. Retd PRT 1/4/73.
THOMPSON D.R. Born 29/4/49. Commd 26/2/71. Wg Cdr 1/7/92. Retd GD 29/4/04.
THOMPSON G. BA. Born 20/8/29. Commd 25/8/54. Sqn Ldr 1/1/65. Retd SUP 6/11/65.
THOMPSON G.A. Born 22/8/47. Commd 21/1/66. Sqn Ldr 1/1/79. Retd GD 22/8/85.
THOMPSON G.C. Born 6/11/41. Commd 22/2/63. Flt Lt 22/8/68. Retd GD 6/11/96.
THOMPSON G.J. BA. Born 6/11/53. Commd 7/3/74. Sqn Ldr 1/7/98. Retd SUP 31/8/01.
THOMPSON H. MCMI. Born 30/11/48. Commd 31/10/74. Sqn Ldr 1/1/85. Retd PRT 1/10/89.
THOMPSON J. Born 22/4/30. Commd 5/7/53. Flt Lt 7/4/55. Retd GD 28/2/69.
THOMPSON J.A. Born 5/4/49. Commd 11/6/81. Flt Lt 11/6/83. Retd SUP 11/6/89.

THOMPSON J.E. MBE. Born 11/5/16. Commd 17/4/40. Flt Lt 29/4/48. Retd SEC 7/12/49. rtg Sqn Ldr.
THOMPSON J.E. Born 3/8/34. Commd 26/5/67. Sqn Ldr 1/7/81. Retd ENG 1/8/90.
THOMPSON J.W.C. Born 18/3/39. Commd 2/5/69. Fg Offr 2/11/71. Retd ENG 1/7/75.
THOMPSON K.S. Born 28/10/62. Commd 14/1/82. Sqn Ldr 1/1/96. Retd OPS SPT 28/10/00.
THOMPSON L.D. Born 9/1/61. Commd 23/9/82. Flt Lt 23/3/89. Retd SY 1/2/93.
THOMPSON M.H. Born 2/2/47. Commd 20/12/90. Flt Lt 20/12/94. Retd ENG 2/2/02.
THOMPSON M.J. MILT CertEd. Born 21/6/49. Commd 7/9/82. Sqn Ldr 1/1/90. Retd SUPPLY 31/7/03.
THOMPSON N.J. MA BA. Born 26/1/48. Commd 30/3/80. Flt Lt 30/3/81. Retd ADMIN 30/3/96.
THOMPSON P.A. Born 6/1/43. Commd 9/10/64. Flt Lt 6/7/68. Retd GD 21/9/74.
THOMPSON P.A.S. OBE DFC. Born 18/11/22. Commd 8/11/41. Wg Cdr 1/1/60. Retd GD 18/11/69.
THOMPSON P.D. Born 3/3/43. Commd 17/12/65. Flt Lt 17/6/68. Retd GD 3/9/70.
THOMPSON P.F. DFC. Born 3/3/21. Commd 6/3/44. Flt Lt 6/9/47. Retd GD 3/3/64.
THOMPSON P.J. Born 24/10/31. Commd 26/12/51. Sqn Ldr 1/1/70. Retd GD 1/2/85.
THOMPSON P.R. Born 24/6/63. Commd 9/12/84. Flt Lt 14/3/96. Retd GD(G) 14/3/96.
THOMPSON P.R. Born 25/12/41. Commd 23/12/60. Flt Lt 23/6/66. Retd GD 25/12/79.
THOMPSON R.G. Born 29/8/29. Commd 10/1/50. Flt Lt 11/11/54. Retd GD 29/8/67.
THOMPSON R.J. DFC. Born 18/1/25. Commd 17/11/44. Flt Lt 17/5/48. Retd GD 17/1/63.
THOMPSON R.J. Born 25/8/39. Commd 2/1/70. Flt Lt 2/1/72. Retd PI 2/1/78.
THOMPSON R.J. Born 19/4/35. Commd 7/5/64. Wg Cdr 1/7/81. Retd ENG 31/12/85.
THOMPSON R.M. MSERT. Born 26/11/56. Commd 4/7/85. Sqn Ldr 1/7/95. Retd ADMIN 26/11/00.
THOMPSON R.P. Born 31/8/55. Commd 16/9/73. Sqn Ldr 1/1/91. Retd ADMIN 29/1/94.
THOMPSON R.V. MSc MILT. Born 15/11/49. Commd 25/2/72. Wg Cdr 1/7/92. Retd GD 15/11/04.
THOMPSON R.W. Born 24/7/43. Commd 5/1/78. Sqn Ldr 1/7/87. Retd FLY(AEO) 24/7/03.
THOMPSON S.E. Born 11/4/14. Commd 10/9/51. Flt Lt 10/9/51. Retd SEC 11/4/69.
THOMPSON S.W. BSc. Born 8/3/63. Commd 19/7/87. Flt Lt 19/1/90. Retd GD 24/9/96.
THOMPSON T.A. Born 23/3/47. Commd 8/9/83. Wg Cdr 1/7/01. Retd GD 1/7/03.
THOMPSON T.L. BSc. Born 8/11/18. Commd 30/12/42. Sqn Ldr 9/3/55. Retd EDN 1/2/68.
THOMPSON T.L. MCMI. Born 24/7/23. Commd 25/1/51. Sqn Ldr 1/1/67. Retd GD 20/4/73.
THOMPSON T.P. Born 3/4/29. Commd 4/6/52. Sqn Ldr 1/7/63. Retd GD 8/1/68.
THOMPSON V. Born 21/3/47. Commd 10/11/74. Wg Cdr 1/1/96. Retd GD(G) 14/9/96.
THOMPSON V.R. AFC. Born 12/10/31. Commd 2/7/52. Sqn Ldr 1/7/69. Retd GD 1/7/72.
THOMPSON W.L. Born 20/3/27. Commd 7/5/53. Flt Lt 7/11/57. Retd GD 20/3/87.
THOMPSTONE R.R. Born 19/7/21. Commd 29/5/52. Flt Lt 14/6/61. Retd SUP 30/4/66.
THOMSON A.D. BSc. Born 10/10/53. Commd 30/9/73. Flt Lt 15/10/78. Retd ENG 24/3/86.
THOMSON A.R. Born 12/5/33. Commd 1/12/53. Flt Lt 19/12/58. Retd GD 12/5/71.
THOMSON A.S. Born 24/3/22. Commd 3/10/49. Flt Lt 26/8/56. Retd GD 19/7/66.
THOMSON B.R. Born 20/9/47. Commd 8/11/68. Flt Lt 1/10/75. Retd OPS SPT 20/9/02.
THOMSON C.G.A. Born 5/3/64. Commd 9/11/89. Flt Lt 7/2/93. Retd ADMIN 5/3/02.
THOMSON C.R. BSc CEng MIEE. Born 31/7/61. Commd 18/3/84. Sqn Ldr 1/7/95. Retd ENG 18/3/00.
THOMSON D.A. Born 22/1/45. Commd 23/3/67. Wg Cdr 1/7/89. Retd GD 14/3/96.
THOMSON G.C. BSc. Born 15/7/60. Commd 26/9/82. Flt Lt 26/12/83. Retd GD 26/9/98.
THOMSON G.E. Born 9/2/31. Commd 29/12/51. Flt Lt 29/6/56. Retd GD 9/2/69.
THOMSON H.G. AFC*. Born 7/2/31. Commd 13/5/53. Flt Lt 5/11/58. Retd GD 31/8/72.
THOMSON I. Born 25/7/36. Commd 5/6/56. Gp Capt 1/7/82. Retd GD 23/6/90.
THOMSON I.D.L. Born 12/2/42. Commd 29/11/63. Sqn Ldr 1/1/81. Retd GD 12/2/97.
THOMSON I.R. MBE. Born 12/9/44. Commd 10/5/90. Flt Lt 10/5/94. Retd ENG 21/1/99.
THOMSON J. Born 9/5/38. Commd 16/5/74. Sqn Ldr 1/1/84. Retd ENG 28/5/90.
THOMSON J.A.S. Born 17/9/29. Commd 1/8/51. Wg Cdr 1/1/73. Retd GD 17/9/84.
THOMSON J.D. MSc BSc CEng MIEE DIC. Born 21/5/47. Commd 14/11/76. Sqn Ldr 1/7/84. Retd ADMIN 17/9/94.
THOMSON J.I.S. Born 16/6/33. Commd 25/7/59. Flt Lt 13/5/66. Retd GD(G) 10/3/68.
THOMSON J.K.B. BSc. Born 10/10/53. Commd 26/10/75. Flt Lt 26/7/77. Retd GD 26/10/87.
THOMSON J.P.A. MA MSc. Born 3/7/38. Commd 30/9/58. Sqn Ldr 1/1/72. Retd ENG 30/11/90.
THOMSON K.G. Born 25/3/17. Commd 23/9/43. Wg Cdr 1/1/61. Retd ENG 7/4/70.
THOMSON L.A.J. Born 2/2/61. Commd 29/7/91. Flt Lt 29/7/93. Retd SUP 14/2/97.
THOMSON P.A. AFC. Born 26/6/24. Commd 4/5/45. Wg Cdr 1/7/67. Retd GD 29/6/74.
THOMSON R. Born 2/5/23. Commd 10/12/45. Sqn Ldr 1/7/57. Retd GD(G) 1/10/63.
THOMSON T.R. Born 18/11/21. Commd 17/4/43. Sqn Ldr 1/1/70. Retd GD(G) 18/11/76.
THOMSON W.M.S. MB ChB DCH. Born 3/12/25. Commd 3/3/49. Wg Cdr 1/4/62. Retd MED 18/3/68.
THORBURN A.R. Born 26/11/10. Commd 10/12/42. Fg Offr 11/3/44. Retd ENG 21/3/49. rtg Flt Lt.
THORBURN G.G. OBE BA. Born 2/9/30. Commd 19/8/54. Gp Capt 1/1/82. Retd ADMIN 4/11/84.
THORBURN N.R. BDS. Born 22/7/57. Commd 12/3/78. Wg Cdr 10/12/92. Retd DEL 22/7/95.
THORINGTON S. Born 17/3/57. Commd 11/9/80. Wg Cdr 1/1/93. Retd ADMIN 17/3/95.
THORLEY L.R. Born 21/11/45. Commd 15/10/81. Sqn Ldr 1/7/97. Retd ENG 18/10/00.
THORLEY M.A. MRAeS. Born 5/12/44. Commd 7/1/71. Wg Cdr 1/7/89. Retd ENG 27/4/96.
THORMAN D.L. Born 6/7/21. Commd 22/1/43. Flt Lt 6/6/49. Retd GD 6/7/64.
THORN G.W. MBE. Born 5/9/16. Commd 15/11/45. Sqn Ldr 1/7/67. Retd CAT 12/9/69.

THORN P.F.C.A. Born 15/7/27. Commd 5/2/62. Flt Lt 5/2/62. Retd GD 15/7/87.
THORN T.G. AFC FRAes. Born 21/9/42. Commd 28/7/64. A Cdre 1/7/90. Retd GD 28/12/95.
THORNALLEY A.H. Born 20/7/23. Commd 22/1/45. Wg Cdr 1/7/70. Retd SUP 29/3/78.
THORNBERRY S.C.C. Born 19/2/50. Commd 2/1/70. Flt Lt 2/7/75. Retd GD 19/2/88.
THORNE A.C. Born 3/1/35. Commd 15/2/72. Flt Lt 15/2/78. Retd MAR 10/4/86.
THORNE B.A.R. Born 12/2/39. Commd 27/2/75. Sqn Ldr 1/7/86. Retd SUP 12/2/94.
THORNE J.B. OBE FCMI. Born 25/3/37. Commd 22/10/59. A Cdre 1/1/88. Retd ADMIN 1/1/90.
THORNE N.C. AFC*. Born 6/6/24. Commd 26/11/43. Wg Cdr 1/7/59. Retd GD 6/6/71.
THORNE P.D. OBE AFC** FRAeS. Born 3/6/23. Commd 3/7/42. A Cdre 1/7/74. Retd GD 3/6/78.
THORNE R.E.J. Born 27/9/46. Commd 20/10/83. Flt Lt 20/10/87. Retd ENG 1/1/97.
THORNE-THORNE L. Born 28/4/43. Commd 8/10/70. Fg Offr 9/1/73. Retd SEC 30/8/75.
THORNEYCROFT G.N. Born 1/1/34. Commd 6/2/56. Flt Lt 26/2/64. Retd GD 1/7/66.
THORNHAM A.B. Born 9/7/59. Commd 18/12/80. Sqn Ldr 1/1/94. Retd ADMIN 9/7/97.
THORNHILL C. DFC. Born 13/4/14. Commd 16/4/44. Flt Lt 16/10/47. Retd GD 20/7/53.
THORNICROFT E.F. AFC DFM. Born 28/9/13. Commd 24/9/41. Sqn Ldr 1/8/47. Retd ENG 28/9/68. rtg Wg Cdr.
THORNLEY H.V. Born 15/3/18. Commd 9/8/45. Flt Lt 9/2/49. Retd GD(G) 15/4/68.
THORNLEY J.F. BEM IEng FIEIE. Born 5/4/45. Commd 24/3/83. Sqn Ldr 1/7/93. Retd ENG 2/4/99.
THORNTHWAITE A.P. Born 16/2/51. Commd 3/12/70. Sqn Ldr 1/7/88. Retd GD 1/7/91.
THORNTON A.E. Born 10/10/57. Commd 11/6/81. Flt Lt 6/7/86. Retd SY 10/10/95.
THORNTON D.L.F. OBE. Born 12/4/28. Commd 11/4/51. A Cdre 1/1/80. Retd GD 12/4/83.
THORNTON E. Born 14/9/20. Commd 17/5/62. Sqn Ldr 1/7/72. Retd SUP 14/9/73.
THORNTON G.F. DFC. Born 17/6/22. Commd 25/9/42. Flt Lt 25/3/46. Retd GD(G) 21/12/49.
THORNTON J.B. OBE. Born 30/11/33. Commd 26/11/52. Wg Cdr 1/1/77. Retd GD 24/1/89.
THORNTON J.G. Born 26/12/41. Commd 18/8/61. Flt Lt 18/2/67. Retd GD 26/12/79.
THORNTON M.E. Born 17/2/48. Commd 16/9/71. Wg Cdr 1/7/90. Retd SY 1/3/94.
THORNTON P.D. BEng. Born 3/7/60. Commd 2/8/85. Flt Lt 21/10/89. Retd ENG 31/3/94.
THORNTON P.J. Born 7/12/44. Commd 19/8/71. Flt Lt 19/2/78. Retd ADMIN 3/7/83.
THORNTON R.W. MBE. Born 27/2/14. Commd 1/2/45. Flt Lt 27/10/61. Retd ENG 7/1/67.
THORNTON T. Born 17/8/34. Commd 16/1/61. Wg Cdr 1/7/80. Retd GD 17/8/89.
THORNTON Z. Born 1/7/16. Commd 29/9/41. Flt Offr 1/9/45. Retd SEC 30/11/51.
THORNTON-HENSHAW G.StJ.M. MCIPD. Born 25/11/54. Commd 8/1/76. Sqn Ldr 1/7/87. Retd ADMIN 25/5/93.
THOROGOOD A.N.J. Born 29/12/56. Commd 27/2/83. Sqn Ldr 1/7/96. Retd GD 27/2/99.
THOROGOOD L.A. DFC. Born 13/5/19. Commd 14/8/41. Flt Lt 14/2/45. Retd GD(G) 1/6/64. rtg Sqn Ldr.
THORP J.M. BSc. Born 22/5/75. Commd 13/10/95. Flt Lt 15/1/00. Retd OPS SPT(REGT) 1/2/04.
THORP R.J. Born 12/3/23. Commd 16/9/44. Gp Capt 1/1/70. Retd SUP 12/3/78.
THORPE A.A.P. MCMI. Born 26/10/42. Commd 23/5/63. Wg Cdr 1/7/86. Retd ENG 10/4/97.
THORPE A.J. Born 13/9/46. Commd 28/4/65. Wg Cdr 1/7/87. Retd GD 13/9/01.
THORPE G.S.E. Born 30/8/41. Commd 5/4/79. Sqn Ldr 1/7/89. Retd ENG 30/8/96.
THORPE H.R. Born 19/8/11. Commd 4/10/45. Flt Lt 15/12/49. Retd ENG 19/8/66. rtg Sqn Ldr.
THORPE J.W. AFC. Born 19/3/45. Commd 22/3/63. Gp Capt 1/1/96. Retd GD 10/4/99.
THORPE M.P. BSc. Born 18/6/62. Commd 14/10/84. Flt Lt 14/4/88. Retd ENG 14/10/00.
THORPE P.N. Born 6/12/32. Commd 19/2/64. Sqn Ldr 1/1/83. Retd GD 6/12/92.
THORPE R.B. Born 2/3/35. Commd 9/5/54. Fg Offr 9/5/56. Retd GD 19/12/61.
THOW D.P. BSc CEng MRAeS MIMechE MCMI. Born 10/12/50. Commd 15/9/69. Wg Cdr 1/1/90.
 Retd ENG 6/12/01.
THRALE T. Born 3/12/61. Commd 15/8/85. Sqn Ldr 1/7/96. Retd FLY(N) 4/12/04.
THRASHER A.H.W. Born 9/4/30. Commd 11/1/51. Flt Lt 15/2/54. Retd GD 9/4/68.
THREADGOULD A. AFC. Born 8/8/46. Commd 10/10/65. Gp Capt 1/7/91. Retd GD 1/12/95.
THREAPLETON M.R. Born 25/9/55. Commd 25/8/82. Flt Lt 29/6/84. Retd GD 2/10/87.
THREAPLETON N.E. BSc. Born 4/11/51. Commd 13/2/77. Gp Capt 1/7/97. Retd GD 19/7/02.
THRELFALL T.J. BA. Born 12/12/34. Commd 10/2/54. Flt Lt 9/6/61. Retd GD 29/5/71.
THRIPP G. OBE. Born 27/12/12. Commd 16/12/33. Wg Cdr 15/3/45. Retd GD 25/3/47.
THROP K. CEng MIEE. Born 6/8/36. Commd 23/3/66. Sqn Ldr 1/1/74. Retd ENG 28/10/91.
THROSBY M. Born 29/11/65. Commd 4/7/85. Sqn Ldr 1/1/00. Retd OPS SPT(ATC) 29/11/03.
THROWER B.S. Born 2/6/46. Commd 28/8/75. Wg Cdr 1/7/91. Retd ENG 31/10/97.
THROWER G. Born 15/1/31. Commd 26/6/51. Flt Lt 10/10/56. Retd GD 19/1/69.
THRUSH J.P. Born 3/10/20. Commd 17/2/44. Sqn Ldr 1/1/56. Retd SEC 16/6/61.
THRUSSELL B. Born 19/3/31. Commd 17/12/52. Flt Lt 17/6/55. Retd GD 19/3/69.
THURLEY A.P. AFC. Born 25/8/54. Commd 22/5/75. Sqn Ldr 1/7/88. Retd GD 25/2/94.
THURLOW P.R. Born 24/2/45. Commd 24/11/67. Flt Lt 21/8/71. Retd GD 19/5/76.
THURSTON G.L. MA. Born 13/11/45. Commd 8/2/69. Wg Cdr 1/1/90. Retd GD 12/2/96.
THURSTON N. LVO. Born 25/9/47. Commd 12/7/68. Wg Cdr 1/1/92. Retd GD 14/9/96.
THURSTON N.C. Born 13/12/31. Commd 31/5/31. Wg Cdr 1/7/84. Retd GD(G) 13/12/91.
THURTLE I.C. Born 22/8/63. Commd 20/6/91. Flt Lt 20/6/93. Retd GD 22/8/01.
THWAITE A.R. Born 12/12/33. Commd 21/4/67. Sqn Ldr 1/7/78. Retd ENG 31/12/83.
THWAITE W. Born 11/10/29. Commd 1/3/62. Flt Lt 1/3/68. Retd SEC 1/9/73.

THWAITES G.J. MBE MCMI. Born 27/4/21. Commd 25/9/46. Sqn Ldr 1/7/63. Retd SEC 28/7/70.
TIBBLE M.R. Born 12/7/44. Commd 28/9/62. Flt Lt 28/3/68. Retd GD 28/2/76.
TICKELL C.R.B. Born 9/12/35. Commd 9/4/57. Sqn Ldr 1/1/70. Retd GD 8/9/77.
TICKNER D. Born 28/8/32. Commd 10/10/51. Flt Lt 1/2/60. Retd GD(G) 5/4/83.
TIDBALL C.J. Born 6/6/45. Commd 3/3/67. Sqn Ldr 1/1/81. Retd GD 6/6/00.
TIDMAN W.A. Born 8/12/20. Commd 13/3/47. Wg Cdr 1/7/71. Retd SUP 26/1/76.
TIDY D.P. MA. Born 17/4/23. Commd 13/11/62. Sqn Ldr 15/2/65. Retd EDN 30/7/66.
TIERNAN F. Born 30/6/46. Commd 8/1/65. Wg Cdr 1/1/91. Retd GD 18/7/00.
TIERNEY H.F. Born 28/9/38. Commd 28/10/76. Sqn Ldr 1/1/87. Retd SUP 28/9/93.
TIERNEY J.E. Born 3/6/31. Commd 27/7/54. Flt Lt 27/7/59. Retd SUP 3/6/69.
TIERNEY R. BSc. Born 17/9/41. Commd 6/9/65. Sqn Ldr 1/1/73. Retd GD 21/9/91.
TILFORD D.C. MBE MRIN. Born 3/11/37. Commd 2/10/58. Sqn Ldr 1/1/86. Retd GD 3/11/92.
TILFORD R.S. Born 26/4/43. Commd 9/2/62. Flt Lt 9/8/67. Retd GD 27/8/76.
TILL M.A.C. Born 6/4/19. Commd 22/6/46. Flt Lt 29/11/51. Retd SEC 12/5/59.
TILLEARD J.R. Born 5/9/20. Commd 22/9/49. Sqn Ldr 1/1/59. Retd ENG 17/1/62.
TILLER B.R. Born 8/6/31. Commd 24/1/63. Wg Cdr 1/1/85. Retd ENG 8/6/89.
TILLEY D. BSc. Born 7/8/73. Commd 2/11/92. APO 2/11/92. Retd GD 30/10/94.
TILLING E.J. Born 17/12/60. Commd 10/2/94. Flt Lt 26/11/98. Retd MED(T) 31/12/02.
TILLMAN A.K. CEng MIEE. Born 21/5/38. Commd 30/7/59. Wg Cdr 1/7/84. Retd GD 16/7/91.
TILLOTSON N.J. Born 27/12/43. Commd 28/9/62. Flt Lt 28/3/68. Retd GD 27/12/81.
TILLOTSON R.G.W. Born 3/9/42. Commd 23/5/63. Flt Lt 1/4/70. Retd GD 3/9/80.
TILSLEY E.C.F. Born 23/8/26. Commd 11/4/57. Flt Lt 11/10/61. Retd GD 10/1/73.
TILSLEY L. Born 1/7/22. Commd 13/6/45. Fg Offr 13/6/47. Retd SEC 4/3/54.
TILSON D.R. Born 12/1/41. Commd 7/6/68. Wg Cdr 1/1/92. Retd ENG 12/1/96.
TILSTONE P.J. MCMI. Born 1/10/48. Commd 17/7/70. Sqn Ldr 1/7/85. Retd GD 1/10/92.
TILY C.N.J. MSc MBCS DIC AFIMA. Born 1/10/38. Commd 20/9/60. Sqn Ldr 20/3/71. Retd ADMIN 1/10/85.
TILY M.F. Born 3/4/40. Commd 17/7/70. Flt Lt 17/7/76. Retd MED(SEC) 3/1/79.
TIMBERS C.J. Born 30/6/68. Commd 17/9/89. Flt Lt 15/1/94. Retd ADMIN 12/6/98.
TIMBERS H.A. Born 17/7/46. Commd 2/12/66. Flt Lt 4/5/72. Retd GD 17/7/01.
TIMBERS M.D. Born 24/11/33. Commd 17/10/59. Sqn Ldr 1/1/73. Retd GD 24/11/88.
TIMILTY J. Born 16/7/24. Commd 23/9/44. Flt Lt 19/8/49. Retd GD 12/12/62.
TIMLETT R.J. Born 18/10/25. Commd 26/9/51. Flt Lt 26/3/56. Retd GD 18/10/63.
TIMMINS D.L. Born 3/9/14. Commd 18/4/48. Flt Lt 18/4/48. Retd SEC 3/9/63.
TIMMS G. Born 5/2/49. Commd 27/2/70. Sqn Ldr 1/1/82. Retd GD 1/3/86.
TIMMS G.W. MBE. Born 13/7/32. Commd 27/8/52. Wg Cdr 1/7/82. Retd GD 13/7/94.
TIMMS N.J. BEd. Born 22/7/46. Commd 22/9/74. Sqn Ldr 1/7/85. Retd ADMIN 31/3/94.
TIMMS W. MCMI. Born 6/5/18. Commd 17/6/54. Sqn Ldr 1/7/67. Retd ENG 6/5/73.
TINDAL N.H.J. Born 7/3/11. Commd 10/10/31. Wg Cdr 1/10/46. Retd GD 20/3/48. rtg Gp Capt.
TINDALE A.B. Born 20/4/44. Commd 30/7/64. Flt Lt 30/1/70. Retd SUP 5/11/94.
TINDALE M. Born 23/4/39. Commd 14/6/63. Flt Lt 14/12/68. Retd GD 26/2/79.
TINDALL P.L. Born 15/11/30. Commd 14/11/51. Sqn Ldr 1/7/68. Retd GD 1/7/71.
TINGAY C.D. MBE AFC. Born 20/9/55. Commd 31/8/78. Sqn Ldr 1/1/90. Retd GD 20/9/93.
TINGLE M.W. MBE. Born 13/2/46. Commd 6/11/64. Sqn Ldr 1/1/78. Retd GD 31/5/85.
TINGLE N.B. BA. Born 17/8/50. Commd 26/2/71. Sqn Ldr 1/7/83. Retd ADMIN 17/8/94.
TINKLER C. MBE. Born 21/2/25. Commd 28/1/60. Flt Lt 28/1/65. Retd GD 21/2/74.
TINLEY M.F.J. CBE AE FCMI. Born 28/7/31. Commd 30/8/50. Gp Capt 1/7/76. Retd GD 10/5/83.
TINSLEY I.C. BDS LDSRCS. Born 9/2/45. Commd 8/9/63. Wg Cdr 25/7/81. Retd DEL 9/2/83.
TINSLEY M.U. Born 15/8/13. Commd 10/4/41. Flt Lt 1/9/45. Retd ENG 1/9/53. rtg Sqn Ldr.
TINSON M.S. Born 17/4/44. Commd 6/6/66. Flt Lt 17/10/69. Retd GD 18/4/81.
TIPPELL E.A. Born 23/8/23. Commd 15/12/44. Sqn Ldr 1/4/56. Retd GD 23/11/66.
TIPPEN M.W. Born 3/5/36. Commd 21/8/55. Wg Cdr 1/7/78. Retd GD(G) 1/8/90.
TIPPER G.J. MHCIMA. Born 25/11/46. Commd 25/11/68. Sqn Ldr 1/7/84. Retd ADMIN 14/3/86.
TIPPER M.S. Born 10/5/40. Commd 7/7/67. Flt Lt 4/5/72. Retd GD 10/5/78.
TIPPETT C.M. Born 23/10/51. Commd 28/9/80. Sqn Ldr 1/7/95. Retd ADMIN 1/7/98.
TIPTON J.E. DFC* LLB. Born 15/9/17. Commd 13/7/42. Wg Cdr 1/1/58. Retd GD 30/9/65.
TISBURY J.A. MBE MCMI. Born 7/1/45. Commd 27/1/77. Sqn Ldr 1/7/85. Retd ADMIN 6/4/98.
TISDALE D.N.P. Born 27/5/52. Commd 18/10/81. Sqn Ldr 1/7/90. Retd SUP 14/3/97.
TISSINGTON B.R. Born 18/8/50. Commd 29/3/90. Flt Lt 29/3/94. Retd SUP 20/6/02.
TITCHEN B.J. FCMI MRIN. Born 4/8/45. Commd 28/4/65. Gp Capt 1/1/94. Retd GD 4/8/00.
TITE I.D.C. AFC. Born 13/5/36. Commd 29/7/58. Sqn Ldr 1/7/70. Retd GD 29/3/75.
TITTERTON M.V. Born 30/8/44. Commd 22/5/64. Flt Lt 22/11/69. Retd GD 31/10/75.
TIVENAN W.H. Born 30/10/28. Commd 18/5/61. Sqn Ldr 1/7/80. Retd ENG 30/10/86.
TIWANA K.S. Born 14/7/49. Commd 31/7/86. Flt Lt 31/7/88. Retd ENG 31/7/94.
TIWARI A. MSc. Born 26/12/46. Commd 11/7/76. Flt Lt 11/1/78. Retd ENG 11/7/93.
TIWARI I.B. MB BS FRCS(Ed). Born 13/11/35. Commd 24/3/69. Gp Capt 4/4/85. Retd MED 2/12/97.
TIZZARD A.P. AFM. Born 5/3/26. Commd 14/1/65. Flt Lt 14/1/68. Retd GD 3/11/73.

TIZZARD D.W. Born 11/11/51. Commd 5/8/76. Flt Lt 19/4/80. Retd GD 28/3/90.
TOAL K.G. Born 25/5/43. Commd 4/12/64. Flt Lt 4/5/72. Retd GD 25/5/81.
TOAL S. BSc. Born 16/11/44. Commd 5/5/68. Flt Lt 5/2/70. Retd GD 29/5/76.
TODD A.G. Born 5/2/07. Commd 17/2/44. Fg Offr 17/2/44. Retd ENG 29/12/45.
TODD B. MBE. Born 17/4/44. Commd 15/7/65. Wg Cdr 1/8/83. Retd ENG 12/2/97.
TODD B. Born 9/11/31. Commd 12/9/63. Flt Lt 12/9/68. Retd GD 18/1/86.
TODD D. MBE BSc. Born 13/5/50. Commd 21/1/73. Gp Capt 1/7/00. Retd GD 2/2/04.
TODD D.E. Born 24/8/30. Commd 3/7/53. Sqn Ldr 1/7/66. Retd GD 4/7/69.
TODD G.P. Born 30/4/43. Commd 22/8/63. Wg Cdr 1/7/86. Retd SUP 30/9/90.
TODD G.R. Born 10/12/60. Commd 24/7/81. Flt Lt 24/1/87. Retd GD 14/3/96.
TODD J.O. MB ChB MRCPsych MRCGP DAvMed AFOM. Born 24/9/56. Commd 18/10/77. Wg Cdr 1/8/93.
    Retd MED 14/3/96.
TODD M.D. Born 5/2/43. Commd 28/4/61. Wg Cdr 1/7/82. Retd GD 3/10/90.
TODD P.R. Born 22/5/38. Commd 26/8/66. Flt Lt 13/11/71. Retd GD(G) 11/5/82.
TODD R.H. MCMI. Born 25/9/21. Commd 10/5/46. Wg Cdr 1/7/66. Retd SUP 25/9/76.
TODD R.M. MB ChB FRCS. Born 18/11/31. Commd 4/2/57. Wg Cdr 4/2/70. Retd MED 4/2/73.
TODD W.D. Born 6/2/29. Commd 16/11/61. Wg Cdr 1/7/83. Retd GD(G) 6/2/89.
TODMAN D.A.W. DFC. Born 6/6/30. Commd 13/5/53. Sqn Ldr 1/7/66. Retd GD 1/10/69.
TOFI P.M. Born 13/9/57. Commd 1/7/82. Sqn Ldr 1/7/95. Retd ADMIN 1/12/01.
TOFTS S.W. MA BA PGCE. Born 19/11/55. Commd 20/1/80. Wg Cdr 1/7/95. Retd ADMIN 31/1/99.
TOGNERI R. MSc BA BSc. Born 10/11/50. Commd 15/9/69. Sqn Ldr 1/7/86. Retd GD 10/11/94.
TOLAN E.P. DFM MCMI. Born 10/5/23. Commd 20/3/44. Sqn Ldr 1/7/66. Retd SUP 30/8/75.
TOLCHER A.R. Born 24/2/36. Commd 2/5/55. Gp Capt 1/7/85. Retd GD 24/4/92.
TOLFREE D.J. MIOSH. Born 9/7/31. Commd 21/10/66. Flt Lt 21/10/71. Retd ENG 4/6/90.
TOLHURST A.C. Born 10/6/38. Commd 25/7/60. Gp Capt 1/1/84. Retd GD 14/11/88.
TOLLADAY B.E. BA. Born 11/6/43. Commd 17/12/64. Sqn Ldr 1/1/85. Retd ENG 2/5/93.
TOLMAN P.A. AFC. Born 22/8/52. Commd 3/12/70. Sqn Ldr 1/1/86. Retd GD 22/8/89.
TOM M.D. Born 14/6/43. Commd 21/12/62. Flt Lt 15/4/70. Retd GD 15/4/76.
TOMALIN A.M. Born 2/5/43. Commd 17/12/65. Sqn Ldr 1/1/79. Retd GD 2/5/98.
TOMALIN S.W.StJ. ACIS MCMI. Born 23/12/29. Commd 23/10/59. Sqn Ldr 1/7/71. Retd SUP 23/10/75.
TOMBLESON D.A.L. BA MRAeS. Born 4/4/46. Commd 1/3/68. Wg Cdr 1/1/85. Retd ENG 4/4/90.
TOMBLESON W.T. Born 18/3/12. Commd 17/3/49. Flt Lt 17/9/52. Retd SEC 21/4/59.
TOMBLIN H.C.W. Born 6/9/18. Commd 7/10/43. Sqn Ldr 1/7/58. Retd ENG 15/9/74.
TOMES J.N. CBE BA. Born 7/2/13. Commd 24/8/33. A Cdre 1/7/57. Retd GD 23/3/63.
TOMKINS M.G. MBE MCIPD. Born 5/10/31. Commd 30/7/52. A Cdre 1/7/84. Retd ADMIN 5/10/86.
TOMKINS S.J. BEng. Born 18/3/46. Commd 20/8/67. Sqn Ldr 1/1/82. Retd GD 18/3/90.
TOMLIN R.A. MBE. Born 18/12/25. Commd 1/11/50. Wg Cdr 1/7/68. Retd GD 31/8/73.
TOMLIN R.C. Born 13/5/50. Commd 4/5/70. Sqn Ldr 1/1/88. Retd GD 7/9/92.
TOMLINS D. Born 18/10/32. Commd 8/10/70. Flt Lt 8/10/73. Retd GD 27/3/77.
TOMLINSON A.J.W. Born 1/7/27. Commd 18/11/53. Flt Offr 18/11/57. Retd CAT 29/8/64.
TOMLINSON B.J. BSc. Born 19/1/35. Commd 3/4/59. Sqn Ldr 21/2/67. Retd EDN 3/4/75.
TOMLINSON C.A. AFC* MRAeS. Born 26/5/24. Commd 11/11/43. Sqn Ldr 1/7/56. Retd GD 1/6/68.
TOMLINSON G.J. BSc. Born 22/3/50. Commd 9/8/71. Sqn Ldr 1/7/84. Retd GD 9/1/86.
TOMLINSON K.S. Born 29/12/51. Commd 27/5/71. Fg Offr 16/10/73. Retd GD(G) 27/5/76. Re-entered 13/9/91.
    Flt Lt 19/9/97. Retd OPS SPT(ATC) 15/4/04.
TOMLINSON M.A. Born 6/12/42. Commd 5/9/69. Flt Lt 5/9/71. Retd GD 6/12/80.
TOMLINSON M.C. Born 23/2/33. Commd 24/10/51. Flt Lt 1/6/64. Retd GD 1/6/72.
TOMLINSON M.I. Born 26/9/59. Commd 7/11/85. Flt Lt 7/11/87. Retd GD 26/9/99.
TOMLINSON N.F. Born 21/4/31. Commd 8/7/54. Flt Lt 6/8/59. Retd SUP 14/8/73.
TOMLINSON P.F. BEd. Born 20/9/49. Commd 4/11/73. Flt Lt 4/8/76. Retd ADMIN 4/11/89.
TOMLINSON R. Born 9/4/29. Commd 29/10/64. Sqn Ldr 23/5/71. Retd EDN 29/10/72.
TOMLINSON S. Born 8/9/54. Commd 3/7/80. Flt Lt 30/6/83. Retd SUP 8/9/92.
TOMLINSON W. BEM. Born 20/11/19. Commd 22/9/55. Sqn Ldr 1/1/67. Retd PRT 20/11/74.
TOMPKINS G.J. MBE. Born 20/6/32. Commd 28/6/51. Flt Lt 10/10/56. Retd GD 28/6/70.
TOMPKINS K.W. Born 23/9/48. Commd 10/2/72. Fg Offr 10/2/72. Retd SEC 11/12/72.
TOMPKINS R.C. MBE. Born 2/7/34. Commd 26/7/55. Wg Cdr 1/7/82. Retd GD 2/7/89.
TOMPKINSON D.J. Born 30/3/32. Commd 5/5/54. Flt Lt 1/10/67. Retd GD 30/3/88.
TOMPSON G.L. Born 14/3/49. Commd 7/1/71. Sqn Ldr 1/7/84. Retd GD 17/12/87.
TONES M.D. Born 1/1/44. Commd 31/10/69. Wg Cdr 1/7/86. Retd GD 16/6/92.
TONG R.C. OBE. Born 23/6/40. Commd 18/2/60. Gp Capt 1/7/91. Retd ADMIN 23/6/95.
TONKIN S.M. MA. Born 1/11/59. Commd 18/4/79. Flt Lt 15/10/84. Retd ADMIN 1/8/89.
TONKINSON B.J. Born 4/5/36. Commd 4/1/56. Flt Lt 6/3/63. Retd GD 2/8/69.
TONKS J.E.W. Born 27/4/18. Commd 6/11/54. Flt Lt 6/11/63. Retd ENG 27/4/73.
TOOGOOD G. Born 27/6/09. Commd 1/1/42. Sqn Ldr 1/1/49. Retd ENG 27/6/58.
TOOGOOD H. Born 5/2/20. Commd 24/10/41. Flt Lt 19/2/47. Retd SEC 1/3/62.
TOOGOOD W.G. BEM. Born 27/3/20. Commd 5/4/43. Sqn Ldr 1/1/55. Retd ENG 2/5/70.

TOOGOOD W.R. Born 5/3/48. Commd 16/12/66. Sqn Ldr 1/1/91. Retd OPS SPT 1/5/98.
TOOMER H.S. Born 20/3/23. Commd 9/7/59. Sqn Ldr 1/1/71. Retd ENG 20/2/78.
TOOMEY J.P. MA. Born 15/9/34. Commd 12/7/57. Sqn Ldr 15/3/64. Retd EDN 12/7/73.
TOON D.A. CBE. Born 11/4/25. Commd 29/7/48. Gp Capt 1/1/72. Retd GD 11/12/80.
TOOTAL P.S.E. OBE. Born 7/6/41. Commd 18/12/62. Gp Capt 1/1/85. Retd GD 7/4/93.
TOOTELL W. Born 20/8/31. Commd 13/9/51. Sqn Ldr 1/7/69. Retd SUP 23/7/86.
TOOTS R.I. Born 15/2/56. Commd 7/11/85. Flt Lt 7/5/92. Retd ADMIN 8/7/97.
TOPAZ T.K. Born 27/2/34. Commd 3/6/65. Flt Lt 3/6/70. Retd GD 7/12/74.
TOPHAM A.G. Born 8/2/33. Commd 6/6/57. Sqn Ldr 1/1/69. Retd GD 21/7/86.
TOPHAM C.R. BSc. Born 21/1/57. Commd 31/8/75. Sqn Ldr 1/7/90. Retd GD 21/1/95.
TOPHAM K.D. Born 21/4/63. Commd 26/8/90. Flt Lt 4/10/90. Retd OPS SPT 21/4/01.
TOPHAM M. MA. Born 26/7/28. Commd 17/11/49. Sqn Ldr 1/12/65. Retd EDN 14/7/67.
TOPHAM M.W. MBE. Born 27/4/38. Commd 23/11/78. Flt Lt 23/11/83. Retd ENG 27/4/96.
TOPHAM R. Born 8/3/30. Commd 9/8/51. Sqn Ldr 1/7/72. Retd GD(G) 8/3/85.
TOPLISS G.W. DFC. Born 20/7/14. Commd 10/1/38. Wg Cdr 1/1/51. Retd GD 10/10/61.
TOPP K.F. MSc CEng MRAeS. Born 8/8/35. Commd 26/9/71. Sqn Ldr 26/9/71. Retd ENG 26/9/87.
TOPP R.L. AFC**. Born 15/5/23. Commd 22/9/44. A Cdre 1/7/70. Retd GD 31/3/78.
TOPPER L. Born 27/7/21. Commd 14/11/43. Flt Lt 4/12/52. Retd GD 18/5/65.
TOPPING I.B. Born 15/3/34. Commd 18/6/52. Sqn Ldr 1/1/67. Retd GD 15/3/72.
TORDOFF L.W. MBE. Born 27/1/11. Commd 22/8/41. Flt Lt 1/9/45. Retd SUP 1/9/50. rtg Sqn Ldr.
TORODE A.S. OBE MB ChB FRCP DPhysMed. Born 15/6/41. Commd 20/1/64. Gp Capt 6/10/90. Retd MED 14/3/96.
TORPY G.L. MBE. Born 14/9/32. Commd 20/12/51. Flt Lt 22/5/57. Retd GD 1/9/73.
TORRENS R.G. OBE BSc CEng MRAeS MCMI. Born 27/5/58. Commd 5/9/76. Wg Cdr 1/1/93. Retd ENG 3/4/99.
TOSE A. BA. Born 18/6/77. Commd 25/10/01. Flt Lt 9/2/02. Retd SUPPLY 30/9/03.
TOSH D.A. BMet. Born 6/11/61. Commd 11/9/83. Flt Lt 11/3/87. Retd ADMIN 29/10/96.
TOSHNEY J.J. BSc. Born 15/4/50. Commd 30/10/72. Flt Lt 15/4/76. Retd ENG 30/10/88.
TOSSELL J.H. FCIPS FCMI MCIT MILT. Born 15/8/35. Commd 24/1/63. A Cdre 1/7/86. Retd SUP 31/5/89.
TOTTMAN S.H. Born 25/4/31. Commd 14/4/53. Wg Cdr 1/7/74. Retd SUP 28/6/82.
TOULL G.R. MSc BSc CEng FIEE MCMI. Born 13/12/31. Commd 18/2/54. Gp Capt 1/7/75. Retd ENG 26/4/83.
TOURLE M.J. MCIPS MCMI. Born 26/8/41. Commd 30/7/59. Wg Cdr 1/1/84. Retd SUP 25/4/93.
TOUT E.S.T. MBE. Born 6/1/27. Commd 24/9/64. Sqn Ldr 1/1/76. Retd ENG 3/4/79.
TOUZEL M. Born 26/1/57. Commd 5/8/76. Flt Lt 5/2/82. Retd GD 16/4/95.
TOVEY B.A. Born 25/8/30. Commd 17/2/58. Sqn Ldr 1/1/80. Retd GD(G) 25/8/85.
TOWEY J.V. OBE BA MCMI. Born 15/9/33. Commd 12/7/57. Wg Cdr 1/1/74. Retd ADMIN 22/12/85.
TOWLE C.M. Born 13/9/46. Commd 11/7/74. Fg Offr 15/10/74. Retd SEC 17/3/79.
TOWLER B.A. Born 22/5/43. Commd 4/10/63. Flt Lt 29/1/69. Retd GD 2/11/76.
TOWLER B.M. Born 29/3/59. Commd 2/2/78. Sqn Ldr 1/7/92. Retd SUP 17/2/96.
TOWLER J.B. FCMI. Born 23/8/23. Commd 15/10/43. Wg Cdr 1/7/66. Retd GD 15/2/77.
TOWLER J.L.W. Born 22/11/24. Commd 4/9/46. A Cdre 1/1/77. Retd GD 29/4/78.
TOWN C.G. Born 14/1/30. Commd 27/2/75. Flt Lt 27/2/78. Retd SUP 27/2/88.
TOWNEND G. BSc PGCE. Born 27/4/67. Commd 3/9/89. Flt Lt 15/1/92. Retd ADMIN 5/8/99.
TOWNEND I.A. Born 30/1/61. Commd 26/11/81. Sqn Ldr 1/7/96. Retd ADMIN 1/7/99.
TOWNEND-DYSON E.B. Born 19/10/08. Commd 30/8/41. Sqn Ldr 1/7/49. Retd SEC 30/11/57.
TOWNLEY C. MA BA MCMI MCIPD. Born 7/9/34. Commd 12/9/61. Sqn Ldr 12/9/73. Retd ADMIN 14/10/84.
TOWNLEY C.P. Born 8/10/17. Commd 28/8/41. Flt Lt 1/9/45. Retd ENG 8/10/73.
TOWNLEY R. BSc. Born 13/9/31. Commd 5/2/68. Flt Lt 5/2/68. Retd EDN 6/2/73.
TOWNS D. BEM MInstPet. Born 20/11/50. Commd 2/11/88. Flt Lt 2/11/92. Retd SUP 1/8/96.
TOWNSEND B.K. DFC. Born 28/9/15. Commd 5/1/40. Flt Lt 20/7/46. Retd GD 25/10/70. rtg Sqn Ldr.
TOWNSEND D. Born 10/9/23. Commd 1/12/44. Flt Lt 1/6/48. Retd GD 10/9/66.
TOWNSEND D.F. Born 8/4/24. Commd 23/8/45. Flt Lt 1/1/56. Retd SEC 31/5/69.
TOWNSEND G.R. Born 11/3/19. Commd 12/11/43. Flt Lt 12/5/48. Retd SEC 30/11/55. rtg Sqn Ldr.
TOWNSEND J.A. Born 2/7/36. Commd 17/5/56. Flt Lt 17/5/62. Retd SEC 14/10/75.
TOWNSEND J.E. Born 13/3/20. Commd 11/4/42. Flt Lt 1/1/55. Retd GD 30/6/58.
TOWNSEND J.F. Born 20/1/13. Commd 2/4/63. Flt Lt 2/4/56. Retd ENG 31/8/67.
TOWNSEND J.G. Born 12/2/44. Commd 24/6/71. Flt Lt 24/6/73. Retd GD(G) 1/5/85.
TOWNSEND J.W. Born 25/9/30. Commd 22/7/71. Flt Lt 22/7/72. Retd EDN 30/9/78.
TOWNSEND M.E. MA. Born 29/7/23. Commd 11/2/44. Sqn Ldr 1/1/59. Retd GD 2/3/68.
TOWNSEND R.M. Born 26/9/51. Commd 13/1/72. Plt Offr 13/1/73. Retd GD 3/10/73.
TOWNSHEND D.P. Born 3/3/60. Commd 13/8/84. Flt Lt 13/6/86. Retd OPS SPT(FC) 3/3/04.
TOWNSON J. MBE. Born 23/8/24. Commd 22/11/44. Sqn Ldr 1/4/56. Retd GD 23/8/73.
TOY R.D. IEng MIIE. Born 23/4/39. Commd 9/3/72. Wg Cdr 1/1/92. Retd ENG 1/1/95.
TOYNE S. MBE. Born 8/1/32. Commd 29/11/55. Sqn Ldr 1/1/67. Retd GD 31/8/87.
TOZER C.S. Born 9/2/22. Commd 29/10/43. Flt Lt 29/4/47. Retd GD 18/5/48.
TRACE M.R. OBE MA FRAeS. Born 11/9/47. Commd 23/9/68. Gp Capt 1/1/94. Retd GD 5/7/01.
TRACY A.J. BA. Born 28/2/59. Commd 29/8/77. Flt Lt 15/4/82. Retd GD 15/7/92.
TRACY J.P. Born 31/12/48. Commd 21/3/69. Fg Offr 21/3/71. Retd GD 26/9/73.

TRACY R.F. Born 16/7/23. Commd 8/5/45. Sqn Ldr 1/7/68. Retd GD 16/7/78.
TRAGHEIM J.A. Born 24/10/30. Commd 23/9/65. Flt Lt 23/9/70. Retd ENG 1/2/75.
TRAINER E.J. Born 23/10/23. Commd 1/2/50. Flt Lt 3/5/56. Retd GD 28/10/66.
TRANT H.B. MBE. Born 14/12/23. Commd 3/9/53. Wg Cdr 1/7/77. Retd ADMIN 19/1/80.
TRANTER N.A. Born 27/6/22. Commd 12/6/58. Flt Lt 12/6/63. Retd GD(G) 1/10/75.
TRANTER S.G.R. BSc. Born 4/4/58. Commd 12/8/79. Sqn Ldr 1/7/90. Retd GD 4/4/96.
TRANTHAM I.D. Born 11/4/44. Commd 8/4/82. Sqn Ldr 1/7/91. Retd ENG 1/9/94.
TRATHEN A.M. Born 23/10/34. Commd 7/5/64. Sqn Ldr 1/1/73. Retd ENG 1/1/76.
TRAVERS D.C. Born 16/2/39. Commd 29/10/62. Fg Offr 28/6/63. Retd GD 17/8/86.
TRAVERS D.L.M. LDS. Born 8/8/17. Commd 18/1/45. Gp Capt 1/1/67. Retd DEL 20/11/69.
TRAVERS P.R. MB BS MRCS LRCP DPhysMed. Born 16/2/19. Commd 17/6/43. Wg Cdr 18/8/57. Retd MED 9/1/66.
TRAVERS SMITH I. DSO . Born 14/11/46. Commd 1/4/66. Gp Capt 1/7/94. Retd GD 14/2/05.
TRAVERSE A.J. DSM. Born 10/7/23. Commd 25/9/52. Sqn Ldr 1/1/71. Retd GD(G) 26/1/77.
TRAVIS E.B. BA. Born 22/3/26. Commd 6/11/62. Sqn Ldr 14/2/66. Retd EDN 6/11/73.
TRAVIS R.C. MBE BSc CEng FIEE FRAeS. Born 26/8/30. Commd 21/12/52. Gp Capt 1/7/79. Retd ADMIN 4/4/85.
TRAYLOR A.G. Born 2/10/44. Commd 29/11/63. Sqn Ldr 1/7/82. Retd GD 2/10/99.
TREADWELL E.A. BSc. Born 28/11/46. Commd 20/4/71. Flt Lt 20/1/72. Retd GD 30/8/75.
TREANOR B.G. Born 29/4/49. Commd 19/7/84. Sqn Ldr 1/1/94. Retd SUPPLY 1/11/03.
TREDRAY N.P.K. Born 9/8/47. Commd 23/2/68. Sqn Ldr 1/1/99. Retd GD 10/8/01.
TREDRE A.F. MB BS MRCP MRCS. Born 15/10/34. Commd 3/2/64. Gp Capt 3/2/84. Retd MED 14/2/89.
TREEN M.A. Born 29/9/40. Commd 28/4/67. Flt Lt 15/4/70. Retd GD 3/11/76.
TREGASKIS N.R. Born 27/10/42. Commd 3/8/62. Sqn Ldr 1/7/77. Retd GD 27/10/80.
TREGEAR R.M. CEng MIEE MRAeS. Born 12/6/31. Commd 30/12/63. Sqn Ldr 1/1/69. Retd ENG 12/6/91.
TREMAINE J. MSc BEng CEng MIEE. Born 2/1/67. Commd 1/9/85. Sqn Ldr 1/7/98. Retd ENGINEER 15/5/05.
TREMBLING G.E.J. DFM. Born 18/2/24. Commd 7/7/54. Flt Lt 7/7/59. Retd GD 2/1/69.
TRENCH B.W. Born 17/1/44. Commd 22/7/66. Wg Cdr 1/1/88. Retd SUP 6/8/98.
TREVAINS C.J. OBE. Born 27/5/26. Commd 15/12/49. Wg Cdr 1/7/67. Retd GD 3/4/80.
TREVAINS G.E. CEng MIEE. Born 12/1/22. Commd 22/9/49. Wg Cdr 1/7/67. Retd ENG 1/2/79.
TREVASKUS R. Born 3/7/46. Commd 11/1/79. Flt Lt 11/1/81. Retd GD 19/1/93.
TREVELYAN R.F. Born 16/9/19. Commd 4/11/43. Flt Lt 4/5/47. Retd ENG 22/11/47.
TREVELYAN R.S. Born 14/11/20. Commd 24/12/48. Flt Lt 24/12/48. Retd RGT 1/10/57.
TREVERTON V.J. BSc. Born 24/10/56. Commd 31/8/75. Sqn Ldr 1/7/89. Retd GD 24/10/94.
TREVETT A.D. Born 3/5/54. Commd 7/6/73. Wg Cdr 1/1/95. Retd GD 1/7/03.
TREVIS A.C.E. Born 6/7/44. Commd 13/1/67. Flt Lt 13/7/72. Retd GD 22/8/82.
TREW D.H. Born 16/5/30. Commd 1/1/61. Sqn Ldr 23/9/71. Retd ADMIN 14/9/82.
TREWEEK A. Born 26/3/31. Commd 23/1/58. Flt Lt 28/10/58. Retd GD 1/5/84.
TREWENACK R.W.L. AFC. Born 26/3/24. Commd 4/4/50. Flt Lt 19/11/53. Retd GD 11/2/68. rtg Sqn Ldr.
TREWIN I.A. (Eur Ing) CEng MIEE. Born 5/11/44. Commd 9/11/65. Wg Cdr 1/1/88. Retd ENG 17/5/99.
TREWINNARD L.P. Born 9/8/49. Commd 31/7/70. Flt Lt 31/7/73. Retd GD 31/3/95.
TRIBE D.H. Born 27/11/30. Commd 2/7/64. Wg Cdr 1/1/83. Retd ADMIN 3/4/85.
TRIBE D.M. MInstAM MCMI DipMgmt. Born 2/6/65. Commd 8/10/87. Flt Lt 19/7/92. Retd ADMIN (SEC) 2/6/03.
TRICCAS A.P.P. Born 29/6/36. Commd 10/3/77. Sqn Ldr 1/7/90. Retd ENG 1/7/93.
TRICK P.A.R. CEng MRAeS MCMI. Born 11/9/19. Commd 26/9/57. Sqn Ldr 1/1/71. Retd ENG 11/9/74.
TRICKER G.E. Born 16/4/24. Commd 15/2/45. Sqn Ldr 1/1/57. Retd GD 10/2/68.
TRICKETT C.L. DFC. Born 19/7/13. Commd 31/3/41. Sqn Ldr 1/8/47. Retd GD 19/7/56.
TRIGG C.J. MBE MSc BSc CEng MRAeS MCMI. Born 26/10/54. Commd 2/9/73. Wg Cdr 1/1/92.
   Retd ENG 26/10/98.
TRIGG N.E. CEng MRAeS MIMechE. Born 9/9/36. Commd 28/7/60. Wg Cdr 1/7/64. Retd ENG 16/12/77.
TRIGG R. Born 22/2/33. Commd 27/6/59. Flt Lt 27/12/69. Retd GD 6/2/75.
TRIGG R.S. DFC. Born 14/3/22. Commd 23/4/40. Flt Lt 19/11/53. Retd GD 31/8/62.
TRILLO W. Born 13/4/36. Commd 9/12/71. Sqn Ldr 1/1/86. Retd ENG 8/7/90.
TRIMBLE E.N. Born 28/7/44. Commd 31/8/78. Wg Cdr 1/7/90. Retd ADMIN 31/5/94.
TRIMMER R.M. PhD MSc BDS. Born 9/6/41. Commd 30/12/62. Wg Cdr 26/11/77. Retd DEL 16/8/85.
TRINDER R.R.S. Born 16/4/51. Commd 15/9/69. Sqn Ldr 1/7/83. Retd GD 16/4/89.
TRIPLOW P.H.J. Born 9/4/32. Commd 19/7/56. Flt Lt 19/1/61. Retd GD 9/4/70.
TRIPP G.T. OBE BA. Born 17/3/33. Commd 12/3/52. Gp Capt 1/7/80. Retd GD 17/4/86.
TRIPP M.J. Born 6/2/43. Commd 16/12/68. Flt Lt 22/10/73. Retd GD(G) 18/3/83. Re-entrant 26/9/84. Flt Lt 2/5/75.
   Retd GD(G) 14/3/96.
TRIPP R.J. BSc MCMI. Born 15/3/49. Commd 19/2/73. Gp Capt 1/1/96. Retd GD 22/7/03.
TRIPP R.N. Born 17/4/44. Commd 22/5/64. Flt Lt 22/11/69. Retd GD 30/9/76.
TRIPTREE D.W. AFC. Born 24/9/16. Commd 15/4/39. Wg Cdr 1/7/54. Retd GD 6/11/63.
TRITTON J.W. AFC. Born 13/11/31. Commd 15/8/51. Gp Capt 1/1/81. Retd GD 4/8/87.
TROAKE M.S. CEng MRAeS. Born 21/8/31. Commd 10/10/51. Sqn Ldr 1/7/66. Retd ENG 4/10/75.
   Re-instated 19/8/81. Sqn Ldr 16/5/72. Retd ENG 27/9/88.
TROBE K.M.W. Born 22/5/22. Commd 9/7/43. Flt Lt 19/11/53. Retd GD 22/5/77.
TROKE C.B. Born 22/7/45. Commd 11/8/67. Wg Cdr 1/7/91. Retd GD 22/7/00.

TROMP J.E. Born 14/8/23. Commd 5/5/60. Flt Lt 5/5/65. Retd RGT 10/8/68.
TROTMAN A.J. Born 14/6/48. Commd 19/8/66. Flt Lt 19/2/72. Retd GD 14/6/86.
TROTMAN A.J.E. Born 27/8/50. Commd 13/4/80. Sqn Ldr 1/1/88. Retd ADMIN 14/3/97.
TROTMAN D.A. AFC FCMI. Born 28/11/21. Commd 19/6/42. A Cdre 1/1/68. Retd GD 28/11/76.
TROTMAN J. OBE. Born 6/7/15. Commd 1/5/39. Wg Cdr 1/1/58. Retd SUP 1/8/72.
TROTT D.T. BSc. Born 5/3/63. Commd 14/10/84. Flt Lt 14/4/87. Retd GD 5/7/01.
TROTTER D. Born 11/5/44. Commd 18/7/63. Flt Lt 20/3/70. Retd GD 11/5/82.
TROTTER E.W. Born 14/9/35. Commd 9/3/72. Sqn Ldr 1/7/83. Retd ENG 2/4/88.
TROTTER K. Born 7/8/17. Commd 6/6/57. Flt Lt 6/6/60. Retd PE 5/12/70. rtg Sqn Ldr.
TROTTER K.R.A. BSc(Eng) CEng MIEE. Born 31/12/42. Commd 30/12/62. Gp Capt 1/1/90. Retd ENG 18/4/95.
TROTTER R. DFC. Born 22/6/22. Commd 19/7/44. Flt Lt 19/1/48. Retd PI 17/10/72.
TROTTER R.W.D. Born 18/7/47. Commd 21/5/65. Wg Cdr 1/7/88. Retd GD 31/10/92.
TROUGHTON-SMITH S.H. Born 19/11/20. Commd 31/10/38. Wg Cdr 1/1/62. Retd SUP 1/9/67.
TROUT A.J. Born 20/10/43. Commd 4/12/64. Sqn Ldr 1/1/94. Retd GD 20/10/02.
TROWBRIDGE K.R. BSc. Born 23/8/50. Commd 3/10/72. Flt Lt 3/1/74. Retd GD 3/10/88.
TROWERN F.A. OBE AFC MCMI. Born 28/8/32. Commd 26/7/51. Wg Cdr 1/7/76. Retd GD 1/9/83.
TROWERN R.M. Born 12/9/36. Commd 15/12/59. Wg Cdr 1/1/87. Retd GD 30/11/89.
TROWN E. Born 16/11/33. Commd 31/12/52. Flt Lt 12/2/60. Retd GD 11/12/71.
TRUBSHAW E.B. MVO. Born 29/1/24. Commd 5/12/43. Flt Lt 5/6/47. Retd GD 22/4/50.
TRUDGILL M.J.A. MB BCh MRCGP DipIMC DAvMed MRAeS. Born 6/1/66. Commd 12/8/93. Wg Cdr 1/8/03.
    Retd MEDICAL 6/1/04.
TRUELOVE O.J. MBE CEng FRAeS MIMechE. Born 24/10/37. Commd 30/7/59. A Cdre 1/7/86. Retd ENG 10/11/89.
TRUELOVE P.A. Born 4/1/33. Commd 4/3/63. Sqn Ldr 18/4/70. Retd ADMIN 4/1/88.
TRUEMAN D.A. Born 7/9/42. Commd 20/11/75. Sqn Ldr 1/1/84. Retd GD 7/9/97.
TRUEMAN D.W. Born 26/2/43. Commd 4/6/64. Sqn Ldr 1/1/78. Retd GD 26/2/81.
TRUEMAN G.F.R. BSc CEng MIProdE. Born 16/1/38. Commd 1/9/70. Sqn Ldr 1/1/77. Retd ENG 1/9/86.
    Re-instated 16/11/87. Sqn Ldr 18/3/78. Retd ENG 10/7/90.
TRUEPENNY L.K. Born 30/1/35. Commd 4/2/71. Flt Lt 4/2/76. Retd SUP 30/1/93.
TRULUCK V.G. Born 18/11/35. Commd 5/7/68. Flt Lt 5/7/70. Retd ENG 5/7/76.
TRUMPER M.G. CEng MIMechE MRAeS. Born 9/6/38. Commd 12/12/59. Wg Cdr 1/1/79. Retd ENG 9/6/93.
TRUMPESS B.E. BA DipEd. Born 21/6/32. Commd 7/9/56. Sqn Ldr 7/3/66. Retd EDN 7/9/72.
TRUNDLE L. Born 27/9/17. Commd 19/7/57. Sqn Ldr 1/1/66. Retd ENG 20/5/72.
TRUSCOTT E.M. Born 2/3/42. Commd 9/2/62. Flt Lt 9/8/67. Retd GD 15/2/69.
TRUSCOTT J.A.W. Born 2/5/45. Commd 20/12/90. Flt Lt 20/12/94. Retd ADMIN 7/4/96.
TRUSCOTT J.C. Born 31/1/20. Commd 30/6/42. Flt Lt 30/12/45. Retd GD 27/1/47.
TRUSCOTT T.T. BSc. Born 9/1/34. Commd 30/1/58. Sqn Ldr 9/8/68. Retd EDN 5/5/75.
TRUSLER D.G.M. Born 2/7/45. Commd 28/4/65. Flt Lt 28/10/70. Retd GD 8/12/76.
TRUSSLER J.D. BA. Born 6/12/40. Commd 24/6/71. Wg Cdr 1/7/89. Retd ENG 9/12/95.
TUCK D.T. CEng MIEE. Born 14/7/46. Commd 26/10/75. Sqn Ldr 1/1/89. Retd ENG 1/10/96.
TUCK J. Born 15/4/18. Commd 5/6/43. Sqn Ldr 1/1/58. Retd SUP 29/7/72.
TUCKER D.E. FINucE. Born 17/11/23. Commd 16/5/57. Sqn Ldr 1/1/70. Retd ENG 1/8/74.
TUCKER D.K. MSc CEng MRAeS MIEE. Born 13/10/38. Commd 18/7/61. Sqn Ldr 1/1/71. Retd ENG 14/10/75.
TUCKER D.R. BA. Born 13/6/48. Commd 11/7/74. Flt Lt 27/9/76. Retd ENG 13/6/86.
TUCKER E.G.F. Born 16/7/25. Commd 23/6/44. Sqn Ldr 1/1/73. Retd GD(G) 18/3/77.
TUCKER J. Born 30/4/33. Commd 16/9/53. Sqn Ldr 1/1/67. Retd GD 30/4/71.
TUCKER J.A. Born 9/11/33. Commd 21/5/52. Sqn Ldr 1/7/70. Retd GD 1/7/73.
TUCKER J.A. Born 6/10/29. Commd 15/12/53. Flt Lt 14/11/56. Retd GD 6/10/67.
TUCKER J.M. DPhysEd. Born 6/5/40. Commd 18/5/65. Flt Lt 4/5/72. Retd PE 18/5/81.
TUCKER J.McD. Born 9/12/15. Commd 1/7/42. Sqn Offr 1/1/54. Retd SEC 27/11/60.
TUCKER J.R. FCMI. Born 30/1/30. Commd 13/2/52. Wg Cdr 1/7/69. Retd GD 30/1/85.
TUCKER M.J. Born 30/10/43. Commd 23/11/78. Flt Lt 23/11/83. Retd ENG 30/10/88.
TUCKER R.C. Born 21/4/38. Commd 6/4/72. Sqn Ldr 1/7/87. Retd ENG 21/4/93.
TUCKER S.S.P. BSc. Born 18/3/59. Commd 28/12/80. Flt Lt 28/9/82. Retd ENG 25/10/89.
TUCKER V.P. BA. Born 2/4/60. Commd 19/7/87. Flt Lt 19/7/87. Retd ADMIN 14/3/97.
TUCKER W.H. AFC. Born 6/6/22. Commd 10/7/45. Sqn Ldr 1/7/72. Retd GD 31/7/73.
TUCKEY J.T. Born 18/7/32. Commd 6/4/54. Sqn Ldr 1/7/72. Retd ADMIN 18/7/87.
TUCKFIELD L.S. Born 17/4/63. Commd 19/7/84. Flt Lt 19/7/89. Retd GD 17/4/01.
TUDNO-JONES M. Born 3/5/63. Commd 15/3/84. Flt Lt 15/9/90. Retd ADMIN 14/3/97.
TUDOR E.W.D. Born 2/12/32. Commd 6/12/51. Flt Lt 27/3/57. Retd GD(G) 2/12/70. Re-instated 11/1/74. Flt Lt 6/5/60.
    Retd GD(G) 11/1/90.
TUDOR N.J. MSc BEng CEng MIEE. Born 9/9/64. Commd 26/10/83. Sqn Ldr 1/1/00. Retd ENGINEER 9/9/03.
TUFF J.M. Born 6/9/64. Commd 19/12/85. Flt Lt 23/4/92. Retd ADMIN 2/4/93.
TUFFIN P.E. Born 27/3/44. Commd 21/2/74. Sqn Ldr 1/1/82. Retd ENG 1/1/85. Re-instated 8/12/86. Sqn Ldr 8/12/83.
    Retd ENG 5/6/93.
TUFFIN R. Born 24/9/27. Commd 2/3/49. Flt Lt 4/12/53. Retd GD 1/4/65.
TUFFS N.R. MBE. Born 4/9/53. Commd 13/1/92. Sqn Ldr 1/7/85. Retd GD 15/12/91.

TUKE L.L. Born 13/11/27. Commd 8/4/49. Sqn Ldr 1/1/58. Retd GD 7/4/68.
TUKE P. Born 10/10/33. Commd 23/7/52. Flt Lt 11/5/58. Retd GD 30/11/70.
TULETT G.A. Born 25/5/35. Commd 17/12/64. Sqn Ldr 24/9/72. Retd EDN 2/4/79.
TULIP J.A. Born 21/8/34. Commd 5/11/52. Flt Lt 26/7/67. Retd GD 1/4/73.
TULK J.A. Born 16/8/30. Commd 9/4/52. Flt Lt 9/10/54. Retd GD 6/10/68.
TULL G.A. Born 16/7/25. Commd 2/8/51. Sqn Ldr 1/1/74. Retd GD 16/7/83.
TULL G.A.J. Born 27/2/47. Commd 6/5/66. Wg Cdr 1/7/98. Retd GD 27/2/05.
TULLO M.B. Born 2/2/39. Commd 28/4/60. Sqn Ldr 1/1/72. Retd ADMIN 1/12/82.
TULLOCK E.P. Born 16/12/66. Commd 2/11/88. Sqn Ldr 1/1/02. Retd ADMIN (SEC) 1/1/05.
TULLY K.F. Born 8/6/47. Commd 22/12/67. Sqn Ldr 1/1/88. Retd OPS SPT 8/6/02.
TUNALEY M.A. Born 28/7/62. Commd 26/11/81. Flt Lt 26/5/88. Retd OPS SPT(FC) 28/7/03.
TUNBRIDGE P.A. (Eur Ing) CEng MIMechE. Born 1/12/21. Commd 30/1/47. Flt Lt 30/11/51. Retd ENG 17/7/55.
TUNLEY N.E. Born 17/2/43. Commd 15/9/67. Flt Lt 15/3/73. Retd GD 22/10/94.
TUNNAH J.E. BEM MCMI. Born 9/2/41. Commd 24/1/74. Flt Lt 24/1/76. Retd RGT 10/7/84.
TUNNICLIFF R. Born 4/2/29. Commd 25/8/67. Flt Lt 25/8/72. Retd SEC 6/7/79.
TUNNICLIFFE A.R. Born 11/8/33. Commd 30/7/57. Flt Lt 15/2/63. Retd GD 3/5/73.
TUNSTALL P.D. Born 1/12/18. Commd 24/11/37. Sqn Ldr 1/8/47. Retd GD 3/12/57.
TUPPEN H.J. BDS LDSRCS. Born 9/10/33. Commd 7/6/59. Gp Capt 1/7/82. Retd DEL 9/4/94.
TURBIN R.W. Born 17/6/37. Commd 10/4/56. Flt Lt 6/3/63. Retd GD 17/6/75.
TURBITT D. BSc. Born 11/10/49. Commd 15/9/69. Flt Lt 15/10/73. Retd GD 19/4/02.
TURFERY P. MBE MCMI. Born 6/2/43. Commd 19/10/72. Gp Capt 1/7/88. Retd ADMIN 1/3/90.
TURFF M.F. Born 8/9/48. Commd 19/9/71. Flt Lt 19/9/76. Retd ENG 19/9/87.
TURFREY G.P. Born 25/11/48. Commd 29/3/68. Flt Lt 29/9/73. Retd GD 1/5/94.
TURGOOSE R. BSc. Born 19/10/39. Commd 2/10/61. Sqn Ldr 1/1/73. Retd GD 19/10/94.
TURK E.P. MB BChir MRCPath. Born 15/4/48. Commd 26/10/70. Wg Cdr 23/6/87. Retd MED 14/3/96.
TURLEY G.J. DFM. Born 25/11/23. Commd 8/7/54. Sqn Ldr 1/1/69. Retd GD 1/6/73.
TURNBULL A. BSc. Born 7/8/59. Commd 6/9/81. Flt Lt 6/12/83. Retd ENG 1/10/87.
TURNBULL E. Born 10/7/23. Commd 26/5/60. Flt Lt 26/5/65. Retd ENG 9/7/77.
TURNBULL G.J. BSc MB ChB MRCP MRCPsych. Born 22/12/48. Commd 29/11/70. Wg Cdr 1/8/87. Retd MED 20/8/93.
TURNBULL I.F. Born 11/9/53. Commd 9/3/72. Flt Lt 5/8/78. Retd GD(G) 11/9/91.
TURNBULL J.D. Born 25/12/21. Commd 24/6/43. Flt Lt 31/12/56. Retd SUP 3/7/66.
TURNBULL J.G. Born 23/3/47. Commd 1/3/68. Flt Lt 1/3/71. Retd GD 19/4/83.
TURNBULL K. BSc. Born 6/6/61. Commd 2/9/79. Flt Lt 15/4/84. Retd GD 6/6/99.
TURNBULL L.J. Born 1/1/26. Commd 21/10/54. Flt Lt 21/10/60. Retd GD 1/1/76.
TURNBULL R.T. Born 30/7/43. Commd 9/3/62. Sqn Ldr 1/1/94. Retd GD 30/7/98.
TURNBULL T.R.C. Born 22/2/36. Commd 21/7/55. Sqn Ldr 1/7/71. Retd SEC 1/7/74.
TURNBULL W.N.O. Born 5/7/57. Commd 19/8/91. Flt Lt 15/12/80. Retd ENG 3/11/92.
TURNER A. MBE MCMI. Born 14/11/40. Commd 28/5/66. Wg Cdr 1/7/88. Retd GD 4/7/95.
TURNER A.D. FCMI. Born 30/5/37. Commd 18/12/56. Gp Capt 1/1/84. Retd GD 1/12/88.
TURNER A.D.H. BSc. Born 2/9/46. Commd 18/8/68. Flt Lt 18/2/73. Retd GD 2/9/84.
TURNER A.J. Born 30/12/40. Commd 6/7/62. Flt Lt 6/1/68. Retd GD 30/12/78.
TURNER B.L.StC. FCMI. Born 15/9/32. Commd 14/12/54. Wg Cdr 1/7/80. Retd ADMIN 31/10/88.
TURNER C.A. Born 5/2/34. Commd 5/7/53. Sqn Ldr 1/7/66. Retd GD 5/2/89.
TURNER C.F.L. BEM. Born 23/10/16. Commd 1/4/43. Sqn Ldr 1/7/55. Retd ENG 21/12/68.
TURNER C.J. BSc. Born 5/6/48. Commd 4/1/68. Sqn Ldr 1/7/81. Retd GD 1/8/92.
TURNER C.McA. BSc. Born 5/11/50. Commd 3/1/74. Flt Lt 15/10/75. Retd GD 3/1/90.
TURNER C.R. AFC. Born 2/9/17. Commd 30/7/42. Sqn Ldr 1/1/54. Retd GD 7/1/58.
TURNER D.G.L. Born 20/9/44. Commd 21/3/69. Flt Lt 8/3/72. Retd GD 7/9/89.
TURNER D.J. MSc BEng CEng MIMechE. Born 15/1/63. Commd 16/9/84. Sqn Ldr 1/1/95. Retd ENG 15/1/01.
TURNER D.J. Born 8/2/36. Commd 6/1/64. Flt Lt 1/4/66. Retd GD 8/2/74.
TURNER D.J. BSc(Eng) CEng MIMechE. Born 8/8/34. Commd 1/2/60. Sqn Ldr 1/7/70. Retd ENG 1/8/88.
TURNER D.M. BA. Born 31/12/53. Commd 19/11/78. Flt Lt 19/3/79. Retd GD 14/3/97.
TURNER D.W.T. BA. Born 10/4/33. Commd 19/11/52. Flt Lt 15/4/58. Retd GD 10/4/92.
TURNER G. Born 27/7/14. Commd 10/10/46. Fg Offr 10/10/48. Retd SUP 20/12/49. rtg Flt Lt.
TURNER G. BEM MCMI. Born 26/6/29. Commd 16/11/61. Sqn Ldr 1/1/73. Retd ADMIN 23/9/82.
TURNER G.C. MRAeS. Born 22/1/10. Commd 2/9/41. Wg Cdr 1/1/57. Retd ENG 22/3/62.
TURNER G.C. MB ChB FRCP DCH. Born 13/5/32. Commd 17/8/58. A Cdre 8/4/89. Retd MED 6/4/92.
TURNER G.E. Born 21/8/28. Commd 1/7/53. Flt Lt 11/12/58. Retd GD 1/7/76.
TURNER G.F. DFC. Born 10/4/21. Commd 15/5/42. Sqn Ldr 1/1/54. Retd GD 10/4/64.
TURNER G.J. Born 19/3/59. Commd 15/3/84. Flt Lt 15/9/90. Retd OPS SPT 31/10/01.
TURNER G.M. AFC. Born 29/9/33. Commd 27/7/54. Sqn Ldr 1/7/65. Retd GD 27/7/68.
TURNER G.R. Born 14/6/47. Commd 11/7/74. Sqn Ldr 1/1/81. Retd ENG 14/6/85.
TURNER G.W. OBE DFM. Born 3/12/19. Commd 20/7/42. Wg Cdr 1/7/60. Retd GD 3/12/74.
TURNER H.T. DFC. Born 23/4/21. Commd 27/10/43. Flt Lt 27/4/47. Retd GD 14/6/76.
TURNER H.W. Born 24/5/22. Commd 4/5/50. Flt Lt 4/11/53. Retd GD 24/5/65.

TURNER I.R. MMar. Born 21/3/20. Commd 19/10/49. Sqn Ldr 19/10/57. Retd MAR 19/10/65.
TURNER J. MSc BSc CEng MRAeS. Born 18/9/45. Commd 22/10/72. Gp Capt 1/1/92. Retd ENG 15/6/99.
TURNER J. BA. Born 11/10/52. Commd 26/4/72. Sqn Ldr 1/1/87. Retd GD 11/10/90.
TURNER J. Born 1/7/19. Commd 17/11/43. Flt Offr 17/11/49. Retd SUP 20/5/54.
TURNER J.A. Born 5/7/41. Commd 9/3/62. Flt Lt 5/1/67. Retd GD 5/7/79.
TURNER J.A. Born 15/3/30. Commd 23/2/50. Wg Cdr 1/1/70. Retd ADMIN 15/3/85.
TURNER J.A. BEd. Born 12/3/62. Commd 11/9/83. Flt Lt 11/3/87. Retd ADMIN 12/3/00.
TURNER J.H. Born 1/10/22. Commd 20/3/43. Gp Capt 1/7/68. Retd ADMIN 1/10/77.
TURNER J.H. MVO. Born 11/4/34. Commd 26/7/55. Wg Cdr 1/1/76. Retd GD 11/5/84.
TURNER J.McC. Born 15/3/47. Commd 8/6/84. Fg Offr 8/6/83. Retd ADMIN 1/12/87.
TURNER L.H. BEng. Born 16/2/54. Commd 19/7/87. Flt Lt 19/1/90. Retd ADMIN 14/3/97.
TURNER M. MCMI. Born 3/11/28. Commd 16/10/52. Sqn Ldr 1/7/68. Retd ADMIN 7/11/83.
TURNER M.C. MCMI. Born 16/6/38. Commd 25/7/60. Sqn Ldr 1/7/72. Retd GD 9/4/90.
TURNER M.J. Born 28/1/62. Commd 21/6/90. Sqn Ldr 1/7/99. Retd SUP 1/7/02.
TURNER M.J. Born 4/6/43. Commd 28/8/75. Sqn Ldr 1/1/86. Retd ENG 30/11/87.
TURNER N.M. BA. Born 16/6/55. Commd 9/1/80. Retd SY 10/4/96.
TURNER P. CB. Born 29/12/24. Commd 30/4/45. AVM 1/7/76. Retd SEC 29/12/79.
TURNER P. Born 11/2/48. Commd 11/10/70. Fg Offr 24/11/71. Retd GD 31/1/72.
TURNER P.E. Born 8/4/32. Commd 26/12/51. Sqn Ldr 1/1/79. Retd GD 8/4/92.
TURNER P.J. BSc. Born 15/9/45. Commd 17/1/72. Flt Lt 17/10/73. Retd GD 12/5/88.
TURNER P.R. BA. Born 25/12/54. Commd 14/8/77. Flt Lt 14/11/78. Retd GD 14/8/89.
TURNER P.R. The Venerable. CB MTh BA AKC. Born 8/3/42. Commd 22/6/70. Retd AVM 13/12/98.
TURNER P.W. Born 24/5/60. Commd 15/1/83. Flt Lt 4/12/86. Retd GD(G) 13/12/86.
TURNER P.W. Born 16/9/48. Commd 29/3/68. Wg Cdr 1/1/86. Retd SUP 1/1/89.
TURNER R. Born 19/6/45. Commd 2/12/66. Sqn Ldr 1/7/80. Retd GD 30/4/94.
TURNER R.A.N. CEng MIMechE. Born 17/10/29. Commd 14/8/61. Sqn Ldr 26/2/64. Retd EDN 21/9/68.
TURNER R.A.P. Born 28/8/14. Commd 18/4/41. Sqn Ldr 1/8/47. Retd SEC 1/4/55.
TURNER R.E. Born 12/5/36. Commd 10/8/55. Wg Cdr 1/7/76. Retd GD 10/2/82.
TURNER R.E. Born 31/8/42. Commd 1/10/60. Wg Cdr 1/7/83. Retd GD 31/8/86.
TURNER R.M. MBE. Born 12/8/38. Commd 30/9/58. Sqn Ldr 1/7/69. Retd GD 12/8/76.
TURNER S.C. Born 8/8/60. Commd 25/2/82. Sqn Ldr 1/1/96. Retd GD 1/1/99.
TURNER S.C. CEng MIEE MCMI. Born 13/7/20. Commd 18/7/46. Sqn Ldr 1/1/57. Retd ENG 13/7/70.
TURNER S.C.G. BSc(Econ) MCMI. Born 17/6/56. Commd 5/9/76. Wg Cdr 1/7/99. Retd GD 2/12/02.
TURNER S.W. BA. Born 23/3/57. Commd 2/10/75. Wg Cdr 1/7/94. Retd GD 5/4/96.
TURNER W.A. MSc MRAeS. Born 1/5/38. Commd 5/7/60. Flt Lt 5/1/63. Retd ADMIN 5/7/76.
TURNER W.L. Born 23/3/19. Commd 6/11/41. Flt Lt 19/11/51. Retd ENG 5/9/57.
TURNER W.R. Born 25/1/20. Commd 17/7/46. Fg Offr 17/7/48. Retd RGT 10/1/56.
TURNHAM J.A. Born 14/5/33. Commd 20/12/57. Wg Cdr 1/7/77. Retd ADMIN 14/5/88.
TURNILL T.W. Born 22/7/34. Commd 10/4/56. Sqn Ldr 1/7/69. Retd GD 22/7/92.
TURPIN R.H. OBE. Born 17/8/36. Commd 27/10/67. Wg Cdr 1/7/91. Retd GD 1/7/94.
TURPY J.R. Born 4/4/45. Commd 26/3/64. Sqn Ldr 1/7/79. Retd ADMIN 4/4/89.
TURVILL P.A. BSc CEng MIMechE. Born 15/10/52. Commd 1/9/74. Wg Cdr 1/1/92. Retd ENG 1/6/02.
TUSON R.L.B. Born 9/4/36. Commd 2/5/59. Sqn Ldr 1/7/71. Retd GD 9/4/91.
TUTHILL A.R. Born 17/8/28. Commd 13/7/61. Flt Lt 13/7/66. Retd ENG 1/2/69.
TUTHILL D.E. MBE. Born 29/9/33. Commd 30/1/52. Sqn Ldr 1/7/79. Retd GD 29/9/91.
TUTIN F. Born 3/5/37. Commd 1/12/77. Sqn Ldr 1/7/88. Retd ENG 2/7/90.
TUTT J.R. Born 14/5/51. Commd 24/4/70. Flt Lt 24/10/76. Retd RGT 1/7/78.
TUTTON P.E. Born 30/8/32. Commd 18/10/62. Flt Lt 18/10/67. Retd GD(G) 30/8/87.
TUXFORD R. AFC. Born 30/3/49. Commd 27/2/70. Sqn Ldr 1/1/82. Retd GD 30/3/87.
TUXWORTH N.C. Born 12/4/10. Commd 30/7/41. Sqn Ldr 1/7/52. Retd SEC 1/2/58.
TWEEDIE D. Born 19/11/19. Commd 30/7/53. Sqn Ldr 1/7/63. Retd ENG 1/8/74.
TWEEDIE J.M. Born 5/2/31. Commd 7/8/52. Flt Lt 5/11/73. Retd GD 23/4/76.
TWEEDIE K.A. MBE CEng MIEE. Born 24/3/16. Commd 11/4/46. Sqn Ldr 1/10/56. Retd ENG 24/3/71.
TWEEDLEY J.McM. MBE. Born 17/9/36. Commd 27/3/75. Sqn Ldr 1/1/86. Retd ENG 1/5/89.
TWELFTREE J.C. Born 22/5/35. Commd 15/5/57. Flt Lt 6/3/63. Retd GD 17/7/65.
TWELVETREE T. Born 21/6/62. Commd 11/6/81. Flt Lt 11/12/86. Retd GD 21/6/00.
TWIBILL M.T. MMAR MNI. Born 5/8/26. Commd 9/10/56. Sqn Ldr 9/10/64. Retd MAR 5/8/81.
TWIGG A. Born 22/5/27. Commd 3/9/47. Wg Cdr 1/1/66. Retd GD 3/10/78.
TWIGGER A.R. Born 18/8/23. Commd 13/6/51. Sqn Ldr 1/7/63. Retd GD 18/8/83.
TWINE N.E. Born 11/1/48. Commd 13/12/79. Sqn Ldr 1/7/89. Retd ENG 11/1/03.
TWISS B.C. MA CEng MIMechE DCAe. Born 18/4/26. Commd 31/8/48. Sqn Ldr 1/1/58. Retd ENG 4/5/65.
TWIST J.N. BA. Born 15/4/56. Commd 16/6/82. Flt Lt 20/8/82. Retd SUP 31/8/84.
TWYMAN C.D. BSc. Born 6/6/46. Commd 13/4/66. Sqn Ldr 1/7/80. Retd SUP 6/6/84.
TYACK E.W. CBE FRAeS. Born 23/4/44. Commd 22/5/64. A Cdre 1/1/92. Retd GD 3/12/99.
TYACK G.E. MTech BSc CEng MIEE MBCS MCMI. Born 23/12/40. Commd 10/9/63. Wg Cdr 1/7/79.
  Retd ENG 29/9/97.

TYDEMAN R.J. Born 10/3/48. Commd 28/2/69. Sqn Ldr 1/7/81. Retd GD 21/1/89.
TYE A.C. MCMI. Born 28/5/26. Commd 2/11/49. Wg Cdr 1/1/72. Retd GD 28/5/81.
TYE J. Born 9/6/38. Commd 26/10/62. Flt Lt 26/4/68. Retd GD 9/1/81.
TYLDESLEY A.M. MRAeS. Born 22/12/33. Commd 17/8/55. Sqn Ldr 1/7/66. Retd GD 22/12/88.
TYLER G.A. BA. Born 18/4/42. Commd 14/9/64. Flt Lt 14/6/66. Retd GD 14/9/80.
TYLER J.C. Born 18/1/30. Commd 8/7/65. Flt Lt 8/7/70. Retd SY 26/8/77.
TYLER J.D. MBE. Born 23/5/49. Commd 27/3/70. Sqn Ldr 1/7/85. Retd GD 14/3/97.
TYLER M.W.R.H. Born 31/8/24. Commd 14/1/46. Sqn Ldr 1/1/60. Retd GD 8/10/67.
TYLER P.G. OBE FCMI. Born 21/12/19. Commd 31/10/39. A Cdre 1/1/71. Retd SUP 27/1/73.
TYLER R.C. Born 21/1/33. Commd 10/12/52. Flt Lt 5/5/58. Retd GD 21/1/71.
TYLER W. DFC. Born 18/5/20. Commd 21/8/42. Flt Lt 21/2/46. Retd GD 18/5/63.
TYNDALL W.F.C. Born 18/4/42. Commd 24/6/65. Flt Lt 9/2/68. Retd GD 30/9/80.
TYRRELL A.J. MSc BEng. Born 10/3/62. Commd 1/8/86. Sqn Ldr 1/1/98. Retd ENGINEER 5/4/04.
TYRRELL G.M. Born 26/9/44. Commd 16/6/69. Flt Lt 16/3/71. Retd GD 16/6/91.
TYRRELL J.J. Born 7/4/35. Commd 26/7/55. Flt Lt 14/5/58. Retd GD 1/1/69.
TYRRELL M.J.M. MMar. Born 17/10/40. Commd 6/1/69. Wg Cdr 1/7/84. Retd MAR 1/4/86.
TYSON J. Born 24/4/24. Commd 3/11/44. Sqn Ldr 1/7/58. Retd GD 24/4/73.
TYSON P.N. BSc. Born 9/4/62. Commd 13/5/81. Flt Lt 15/10/84. Retd GD 15/7/95.
TYSON-WOODCOCK P.J.E. Born 24/7/40. Commd 9/12/65. Sqn Ldr 1/7/78. Retd ADMIN 31/8/90.
TYZAZK J.E.V. CBE. Born 11/1/04. Commd 10/1/29. Wg Cdr 31/7/42. Retd SUP 9/2/46. rtg Gp Capt.

U

UDY R.J. Born 21/6/41. Commd 1/2/62. Flt Lt 1/7/69. Retd GD(G) 21/6/79.
UNDERDOWN M. Born 26/7/42. Commd 1/4/66. Flt Lt 28/8/68. Retd GD 26/7/80.
UNDERDOWN P.J. Born 12/1/31. Commd 14/4/53. Flt Lt 14/10/55. Retd GD 12/1/69.
UNDERHILL C.D. BSc. Born 25/10/52. Commd 28/1/73. Flt Lt 15/4/76. Retd GD 25/10/90.
UNDERHILL P.W. BTech CEng MIMechE. Born 19/5/48. Commd 5/12/73. Sqn Ldr 1/1/84. Retd ENG 5/12/89.
UNDERWOOD J.K. Born 9/1/20. Commd 18/12/43. Flt Lt 18/6/47. Retd GD 29/1/58.
UNDERWOOD M.H. Born 18/4/33. Commd 12/4/73. Sqn Ldr 1/7/82. Retd ENG 2/1/86.
UNDERWOOD P.G. BSc. Born 2/9/58. Commd 17/8/80. Flt Lt 17/5/82. Retd GD 2/9/96.
UNDERWOOD R. Born 19/6/63. Commd 15/6/83. Flt Lt 15/12/88. Retd GD 19/6/01.
UNDERWOOD R.J. Born 1/7/28. Commd 24/9/64. Fg Offr 24/9/65. Retd CAT 31/1/68.
UNDERWOOD S.C. Born 21/5/59. Commd 28/2/80. Flt Lt 28/8/85. Retd GD 21/10/99.
UNDERWOOD S.T. OBE. Born 4/4/17. Commd 5/12/41. Wg Cdr 1/7/55. Retd GD 4/4/72.
UNDERWOOD T.H. Born 31/3/43. Commd 23/12/61. Wg Cdr 1/1/84. Retd ADMIN 1/1/94.
UNDERWOOD T.M. Born 10/2/26. Commd 23/1/60. Flt Lt 23/1/65. Retd GD(G) 30/6/78.
UNDERWOOD W.B. MBE MCMI. Born 9/10/32. Commd 15/5/58. Sqn Ldr 1/1/69. Retd SUP 16/1/84.
UNSTED B.G.W. Born 2/7/32. Commd 1/4/53. Flt Lt 17/3/59. Retd GD 2/7/70.
UNSWORTH G.W. BA. Born 15/1/31. Commd 26/3/53. Flt Lt 26/6/54. Retd GD 15/1/69.
UNWIN C.R. MBE DPhysEd. Born 3/6/39. Commd 18/5/65. Flt Lt 8/3/72. Retd GD 18/5/81. Re-instated 24/3/86.
    Flt Lt 11/1/77. Retd GD 9/10/93.
UNWIN G.C. DSO DFM*. Born 18/1/13. Commd 31/7/41. Wg Cdr 1/1/54. Retd GD 18/1/61.
UNWIN J.N.B. Born 18/6/24. Commd 8/9/44. Sqn Ldr 1/7/55. Retd GD 18/6/67.
UPFOLD P.E. Born 6/8/32. Commd 28/11/74. Sqn Ldr 21/11/82. Retd MED 6/8/87.
UPHAM J.A. MSc BSc CEng FCIPD MIEE MBCS DIC CDipAF. Born 17/3/46. Commd 19/9/71. Gp Capt 1/1/99.
    Retd ADMIN 31/7/01.
UPRICHARD J.L. CBE. Born 31/12/43. Commd 8/3/65. A Cdre 1/7/94. Retd GD 31/12/98.
UPRICHARD R.J.H. MA MCMI. Born 31/12/22. Commd 9/7/43. Gp Capt 1/7/68. Retd GD 31/12/73.
UPSHALL F.W. Born 4/5/07. Commd 15/10/41. Sqn Ldr 1/7/55. Retd GD 18/6/67.
UPSON P.A. BSc. Born 28/4/60. Commd 4/9/78. Flt Lt 15/4/85. Retd SY(RGT) 16/12/88.
UPTON C.E. MSc MCIT MILT. Born 11/2/43. Commd 17/12/65. Wg Cdr 1/1/82. Retd SUP 14/4/91.
UPTON G.T.G. Born 18/10/25. Commd 19/10/45. Flt Lt 4/4/51. Retd GD 18/10/63.
UPTON R.T. MBE. Born 8/6/26. Commd 1/1/73. Flt Lt 1/1/73. Retd GD 25/10/78.
UREN E.F. CEng MIMechE. Born 1/6/40. Commd 18/7/61. Wg Cdr 1/7/79. Retd ENG 1/6/90.
UREN J.C. Born 27/3/60. Commd 22/2/79. Sqn Ldr 1/1/98. Retd GD 1/1/01.
URQUHART J.M. MB ChB DPH. Born 1/10/18. Commd 2/7/42. Gp Capt 1/7/63. Retd MED 3/10/68.
URQUHART M.M.A. Born 26/6/49. Commd 6/2/79. Gp Capt 1/1/99. Retd GD 26/6/04.
URRY F.A. Born 6/1/22. Commd 5/7/68. Flt Lt 1/1/73. Retd ENG 5/7/78.
URRY M.W. Born 13/8/41. Commd 2/1/75. Sqn Ldr 1/1/84. Retd ENG 2/1/86.
USHERWOOD W.P. MCIPS. Born 19/10/27. Commd 1/10/57. Sqn Ldr 1/7/67. Retd SUP 3/1/80.
USSHER C.W.J. MRCS LRCP. Born 13/7/22. Commd 2/12/47. Flt Lt 2/12/48. Retd MED 1/4/53. rtg Sqn Ldr.
UTTLEY J.R.S. MSc CEng MIMechE. Born 2/4/46. Commd 21/1/73. Sqn Ldr 1/7/85. Retd ENG 21/1/89.
UTTON K.H.G. Born 30/4/22. Commd 16/3/45. Flt Lt 16/9/48. Retd GD 9/5/65.

V

VACHA I.D. Born 14/11/48. Commd 31/7/70. Gp Capt 1/7/00. Retd GD 14/11/03.
VALE D.L. BSc. Born 21/1/50. Commd 28/2/72. Flt Lt 28/11/75. Retd GD(G) 28/2/88.
VALE G.G. Born 4/7/47. Commd 23/11/78. Sqn Ldr 1/1/92. Retd ENG 13/4/96.
VALE J.B. Born 2/8/34. Commd 27/5/53. Flt Lt 17/9/58. Retd GD(G) 2/8/89.
VALE P.N. BSc. Born 16/6/50. Commd 25/2/72. Flt Lt 25/11/76. Retd ENG 1/9/00.
VALENTINE D.G.A. Born 6/7/18. Commd 3/8/44. Gp Capt 1/7/69. Retd SUP 6/7/73.
VALENTINE D.J.B. Born 26/8/36. Commd 13/7/61. Gp Capt 1/7/86. Retd ADMIN 2/5/91.
VALENTINE L.F. Born 18/3/20. Commd 6/3/44. Flt Lt 6/3/50. Retd SEC 18/3/75.
VALENTINE M.C. Born 23/9/45. Commd 9/12/65. Wg Cdr 1/1/87. Retd OPS SPT 23/9/00.
VALENTINE M.R. Born 26/12/23. Commd 16/10/44. Flt Lt 2/4/49. Retd SEC 31/3/62.
VALENTINE R.G. Born 11/11/34. Commd 27/3/56. Flt Lt 19/6/62. Retd GD 11/11/72. rtg Sqn Ldr.
VALLANCE A.G.B. CB OBE MPhil FRAeS. Born 7/4/48. Commd 28/2/69. AVM 1/7/00. Retd GD 2/2/05.
VALLANCE C.G. BSc. Born 6/8/48. Commd 15/6/70. Sqn Ldr 1/1/82. Retd ENG 6/8/86.
VAN DER VEEN M. MA CEng FIEE. Born 22/1/46. Commd 28/9/64. AVM 1/1/96. Retd ENG 3/1/98.
VAN GEENE R.G. Born 24/8/49. Commd 29/11/68. Flt Lt 29/5/75. Retd GD 24/8/87.
VAN HINSBERGH P.J. Born 31/1/22. Commd 11/4/57. Sqn Ldr 1/1/72. Retd GD 31/1/82.
VAN PUYENBROEK J.E. Born 27/6/18. Commd 14/12/42. Sqn Ldr 1/1/59. Retd ENG 27/3/63.
VAN REE G. BDS. Born 27/5/51. Commd 3/9/72. Wg Cdr 6/12/87. Retd DEL 8/6/96.
VAN WARMELO W. MBE BSc. Born 16/3/36. Commd 5/3/57. Wg Cdr 1/1/85. Retd GD 27/2/87.
VAN WYK P.D. Born 2/7/37. Commd 27/2/60. Flt Lt 27/11/60. Retd GD 1/10/64.
VANGUCCI P.C. AFC FCMI. Born 29/8/31. Commd 11/1/51. Gp Capt 1/7/77. Retd GD 5/11/84.
VANSTONE D.J. FCMI. Born 13/4/19. Commd 1/6/44. Gp Capt 1/7/67. Retd ENG 13/4/74.
VANT W.J. Born 28/6/48. Commd 14/8/70. Wg Cdr 1/7/88. Retd GD(G) 1/10/92.
VARCOE D.H. Born 1/7/23. Commd 12/10/55. Flt Offr 12/4/61. Retd SEC 12/5/67.
VARDY S.J. MB ChB FRCSEd. Born 7/8/53. Commd 5/11/79. Wg Cdr 1/8/96. Retd MED 2/4/00.
VAREY A.J. Born 24/1/47. Commd 1/3/68. Wg Cdr 1/7/85. Retd ENG 8/5/91.
VAREY H.R.S. Born 9/8/50. Commd 19/6/70. Flt Lt 17/10/76. Retd SEC 7/4/79.
VARLEY G.A. Born 23/2/61. Commd 26/11/81. Sqn Ldr 1/7/95. Retd OPS SPT(ATC) 23/2/05.
VARLEY G.W. BSc FRCS(Ed) MB ChB. Born 30/5/58. Commd 25/9/80. Sqn Ldr 1/8/89. Retd MED 25/9/96.
VARLEY P.W.R. Born 19/1/24. Commd 27/4/45. Flt Lt 29/6/50. Retd GD 28/4/55.
VARLEY R.W. ACIS. Born 20/4/32. Commd 2/8/51. Sqn Ldr 1/1/71. Retd ADMIN 1/10/77.
VARTY L. Born 3/12/25. Commd 26/3/52. Flt Lt 31/7/57. Retd GD 3/12/63.
VARY C.E. Born 28/2/43. Commd 19/11/62. Wg Cdr 1/7/90. Retd GD 3/3/97.
VASEY C.A. FCMI. Born 20/9/28. Commd 11/4/51. Gp Capt 1/7/76. Retd GD 21/1/82.
VASS A. Born 9/4/45. Commd 19/10/72. Sqn Ldr 1/7/83. Retd OPS SPT 9/4/02.
VASS D.C. MBE FRAes FCMI MCIPD. Born 7/3/50. Commd 4/7/69. A Cdre 1/1/00. Retd GD 12/1/02.
VASSE D.G. Born 17/6/25. Commd 28/7/45. Sqn Ldr 1/1/57. Retd GD 29/6/68.
VATCHER A.R. SRN RNT. Born 11/3/35. Commd 11/11/65. Flt Lt 11/11/71. Retd MED(T) 31/8/74.
VAUGHAN A.H. OBE BA. Born 3/12/49. Commd 15/9/69. A Cdre 1/1/97. Retd ADMIN 1/2/99.
VAUGHAN B.R. Born 5/3/37. Commd 12/1/61. Sqn Ldr 1/1/73. Retd SEC 7/4/81.
VAUGHAN J.C. Born 9/1/25. Commd 2/1/51. Sqn Ldr 1/1/66. Retd GD(G) 9/1/83.
VAUGHAN K.H. Born 29/6/22. Commd 7/6/44. Flt Lt 7/12/47. Retd GD 29/6/77.
VAUGHAN M.C.M. CBE. Born 12/6/16. Commd 24/6/43. Gp Capt 1/7/65. Retd SEC 8/1/73. rtg A Cdre.
VAUGHAN S.A. Born 12/10/56. Commd 22/11/84. Sqn Ldr 1/7/94. Retd ENG 1/7/97.
VAUGHAN-LANE T. MB ChB FRCS. Born 9/4/47. Commd 27/1/69. Sqn Ldr 10/7/77. Retd MED 9/6/85.
VAUGHAN-SMITH N.V. BSc CEng MIEE MRAeS. Born 20/5/48. Commd 28/2/69. Gp Capt 1/1/02. Retd GD 30/4/05.
VAUGHNLEY A.G. Born 5/2/62. Commd 28/9/89. Flt Lt 28/9/91. Retd GD 5/2/00.
VAUTIER B. Born 20/7/52. Commd 27/2/75. Flt Lt 27/8/81. Retd ADMIN 4/11/90.
VAUTIER E.A. Born 21/2/22. Commd 19/10/44. Sqn Ldr 1/1/59. Retd CAT 14/12/67.
VAUX J.M.S. Born 27/4/22. Commd 28/5/43. Sqn Ldr 1/7/58. Retd GD 27/4/65.
VAUX S.D. Born 1/4/50. Commd 8/10/87. Flt Lt 8/10/91. Retd SUP 1/2/97.
VEAL P.J. Born 25/6/38. Commd 28/7/59. Sqn Ldr 1/7/82. Retd GD 25/6/95.
VEALL J.J. Born 21/9/26. Commd 2/3/49. Flt Lt 9/6/52. Retd GD 21/9/69.
VEARNCOMBE M.G. Born 8/8/55. Commd 22/2/79. Wg Cdr 1/1/97. Retd ADMIN 1/2/98.
VELLA J.F. MCMI. Born 6/5/33. Commd 6/4/54. Wg Cdr 1/1/80. Retd SUP 27/11/84.
VELLA R.A. BSc MIEE. Born 14/10/61. Commd 9/11/89. Sqn Ldr 1/7/99. Retd ENG 1/7/02.
VELTMAN D.R. BA. Born 15/7/44. Commd 20/10/83. Flt Lt 20/10/85. Retd ADMIN 20/10/91.
VENABLES W.A. MBE. Born 31/10/19. Commd 2/6/49. Flt Lt 2/12/52. Retd SEC 31/7/66.
VENDRELL J. MMar. Born 19/1/17. Commd 12/7/56. Sqn Ldr 12/7/64. Retd MAR 19/1/72.
VENIER A.L. MVO. Born 14/5/30. Commd 20/12/51. Wg Cdr 1/1/84. Retd GD 14/5/85.
VENMAN A.J. Born 12/2/38. Commd 2/1/75. Sqn Ldr 2/1/87. Retd MED(T) 12/2/93.

VENN K.F. CEng MRaeS MCMI DCAe. Born 30/1/21. Commd 19/8/42. Wg Cdr 1/7/59. Retd ENG 31/5/69.
VENN M.G.P. OBE MB BS MFOM DAvMed MRaeS MCMI. Born 29/4/31. Commd 6/1/57. A Cdre 1/7/84. Retd MED 1/2/85.
VENNER R. MBA IEng AMRaeS. Born 17/7/54. Commd 11/10/84. Wg Cdr 1/1/02. Retd GD 8/4/05.
VENTHAM V. BSc. Born 30/1/34. Commd 23/8/55. Flt Lt 23/5/57. Retd GD 30/1/72.
VENTURA M.R.C. Born 12/10/37. Commd 2/8/68. Flt Lt 2/8/70. Retd SUP 2/8/76.
VENUS L.C. Born 22/7/58. Commd 19/10/81. Sqn Ldr 1/1/94. Retd ADMIN 19/10/97.
VERDON-ROE R. Born 23/7/25. Commd 29/1/46. Flt Lt 6/2/54. Retd GD 1/7/57.
VERGNANO P.N. Born 7/11/52. Commd 30/3/75. Sqn Ldr 1/7/86. Retd ADMIN 14/3/97.
VERNAL J. Born 6/9/45. Commd 21/4/67. Sqn Ldr 1/7/83. Retd GD 8/11/95.
VERNER A.D. Born 7/3/43. Commd 29/11/68. Sqn Ldr 1/1/99. Retd FLY(N) 7/3/03.
VERNON A.R. MB BS. Born 27/4/55. Commd 18/11/75. Sqn Ldr 1/8/84. Retd MED 1/2/86.
VERNON F.L.A. MRCS LRCP FRCOG. Born 17/10/18. Commd 4/1/54. Gp Capt 1/12/66. Retd MED 1/2/70.
VERNON J. Born 8/4/37. Commd 4/1/56. Sqn Ldr 1/1/70. Retd GD 6/2/91.
VERNON P.A. Born 9/10/48. Commd 29/4/71. Sqn Ldr 1/1/86. Retd GD 1/1/89.
VERNON R.K. BEM. Born 15/9/47. Commd 8/9/83. Flt Lt 8/9/87. Retd ENG 2/12/98.
VERRALL W.H. Born 22/12/19. Commd 22/9/55. Sqn Ldr 1/7/67. Retd ENG 27/12/74.
VERRALLS W.A. DFC. Born 18/3/14. Commd 8/5/43. Flt Lt 21/2/56. Retd GD(G) 18/3/69.
VERRIER P.C. DPhysEd. Born 5/10/37. Commd 8/12/64. Flt Lt 9/2/68. Retd PE 27/5/81.
VERRIL M. Born 8/2/42. Commd 22/5/64. Sqn Ldr 1/1/93. Retd GD 28/11/95.
VERTH J.W. MSc BA CEng MRaeS MIEE DIC. Born 6/5/55. Commd 11/10/84. Sqn Ldr 1/1/92. Retd ENG 16/12/02.
VICK J.W. DFC. Born 30/1/17. Commd 10/8/44. Wg Cdr 1/1/66. Retd GD(G) 17/2/72.
VICKERS A.G.W. Born 2/1/25. Commd 2/3/61. Flt Lt 2/3/66. Retd GD 1/6/73. Re-instated 19/10/78 to 2/1/83.
VICKERS D.R. MBE BA CEng MIMechE MCMI. Born 28/1/42. Commd 13/10/64. Wg Cdr 1/7/77. Retd ENG 13/10/83.
VICKERS F.J. Born 21/4/23. Commd 4/6/44. Sqn Ldr 1/7/56. Retd GD 31/3/62.
VICKERS M.A. AFC. Born 22/5/23. Commd 1/10/47. Sqn Ldr 1/7/67. Retd GD 22/5/78.
VICKERY L.D. Born 14/2/16. Commd 10/6/39. Wg Cdr 1/1/63. Retd SEC 14/4/66.
VICKERY L.J. Born 17/9/21. Commd 6/9/56. Sqn Ldr 1/1/69. Retd ENG 15/9/73.
VICKERY R.A. Born 2/4/28. Commd 30/7/52. Flt Lt 27/12/57. Retd GD 2/4/66.
VIELLE E.E. OBE MRaeS. Born 29/4/13. Commd 28/7/34. Gp Capt 1/1/51. Retd GD 14/11/57.
VIEROD D. Born 23/10/29. Commd 3/5/68. Flt Lt 3/5/73. Retd ENG 23/10/87.
VIGAR J.A. Born 5/4/31. Commd 20/10/53. Flt Lt 22/10/57. Retd GD 1/1/70.
VIGORS T.A. DFC. Born 22/3/21. Commd 23/12/39. Sqn Ldr 24/1/44. Retd GD 8/11/46. rtg Wg Cdr.
VILLIERS P. BEng. Born 11/7/66. Commd 3/9/90. Flt Lt 25/2/94. Retd ENGINEER 11/7/04.
VIMPANY R.N. MBE. Born 18/4/23. Commd 28/12/43. Sqn Ldr 1/1/64. Retd GD 1/1/67.
VINALES J. Born 8/8/45. Commd 28/4/65. Sqn Ldr 1/1/83. Retd GD 1/7/94.
VINCE D.G. Born 3/5/24. Commd 13/3/46. Flt Lt 13/3/52. Retd RGT 3/5/62.
VINCENT F. OBE MWSOM MCMI. Born 13/7/24. Commd 31/12/44. Gp Capt 1/1/75. Retd SEC 13/7/79.
VINCENT H.A. Born 14/3/59. Commd 8/11/89. Flt Lt 9/11/91. Retd ADMIN 23/4/94.
VINCENT H.McC. Born 12/5/24. Commd 9/3/50. Flt Lt 27/5/54. Retd GD 12/5/67.
VINCENT J.C. BSc. Born 30/9/54. Commd 3/9/72. Wg Cdr 1/1/95. Retd GD 30/9/98.
VINCENT M.D. Born 3/4/47. Commd 23/3/67. Flt Lt 23/9/72. Retd GD 8/12/76.
VINCENT R.E. BSc CEng MRaeS MCMI. Born 27/7/49. Commd 24/9/72. Sqn Ldr 1/1/84. Retd ENG 24/9/88.
VINCENT R.J. MCMI. Born 27/10/29. Commd 28/6/51. Sqn Ldr 1/1/67. Retd GD 1/7/73.
VINCENTI J.H. MD. Born 26/12/26. Commd 5/7/54. Sqn Ldr 1/2/61. Retd MED 22/2/65.
VINCENTI N. MD FRCS FRCS(Glas) DLO. Born 4/12/26. Commd 5/2/56. Gp Capt 20/2/73. Retd MED 5/2/84.
VINE A.W. MBE AFC AFM. Born 12/3/22. Commd 4/7/57. Sqn Ldr 1/1/67. Retd GD 12/3/77.
VINE A.W. Born 21/2/42. Commd 27/1/67. Flt Lt 27/1/69. Retd GD 9/4/83.
VINE D.C. Born 27/7/49. Commd 7/11/85. Sqn Ldr 1/1/92. Retd GD 14/3/97.
VINE E. AFC*. Born 16/2/22. Commd 24/1/52. Flt Lt 15/5/57. Retd GD 1/11/74.
VINEY E.C. Born 16/6/43. Commd 21/5/65. Flt Lt 21/11/69. Retd GD 16/6/81.
VINEY R.C. Born 13/3/40. Commd 17/7/62. Sqn Ldr 1/7/77. Retd ENG 13/3/95.
VINNICOMBE K. Born 7/2/36. Commd 3/1/61. Flt Lt 15/9/65. Retd ADMIN 7/2/94.
VIRASINGHE I.A.K. Born 26/1/34. Commd 15/9/65. Flt Lt 15/9/65. Retd SEC 6/2/75.
VIRGO I. MSc BTech CEng MRaes. Born 22/10/52. Commd 25/9/71. Sqn Ldr 1/7/87. Retd ENG 31/7/96.
VISAGIE P.W. LLB. Born 1/12/48. Commd 30/6/74. Wg Cdr 1/12/84. Retd LGL 30/6/90.
VITTLES S.R. Born 18/3/42. Commd 19/6/64. Flt Lt 19/12/69. Retd GD 18/3/80.
VIVASH E.P. BA MCMI. Born 26/8/35. Commd 2/10/57. Sqn Ldr 2/4/66. Retd ADMIN 26/8/85.
VIVIAN H.D. Born 4/4/22. Commd 22/7/42. Flt Offr 22/1/47. Retd SEC 20/8/57.
VIVIAN J.A. MA. Born 7/12/26. Commd 11/2/63. Flt Lt 28/7/65. Retd ADMIN 13/2/79.
VIZARD A.E. Born 23/4/54. Commd 21/4/77. Flt Lt 21/10/82. Retd GD 2/1/93.
VOADEN J.H. CEng MIEE MCMI. Born 28/9/35. Commd 17/5/60. Sqn Ldr 1/7/67. Retd ENG 17/5/76.
VOCKINS V.V. Born 28/9/17. Commd 17/10/41. Sqn Ldr 1/7/62. Retd ENG 28/9/72.
VOIGT P.G.O. Born 25/12/63. Commd 23/10/86. Flt Lt 23/4/92. Retd GD 23/6/02.
VOLLBORTH P.W. Born 21/3/33. Commd 5/12/51. Sqn Ldr 1/7/68. Retd ADMIN 4/10/84.

VOLLER E.B. Born 17/3/36. Commd 30/7/57. Flt Lt 26/2/64. Retd GD 17/3/74.
VOLTZENLOGEL P.N. MCIT MILT. Born 3/3/58. Commd 21/4/77. Wg Cdr 1/7/97. Retd SUP 3/3/02.
VOLWERK J.M. Born 17/8/45. Commd 15/8/85. Sqn Ldr 1/7/92. Retd ADMIN 14/3/96.
VON BAUMANN A.G. Born 10/6/23. Commd 27/10/55. Flt Lt 27/10/61. Retd GD 31/12/77.
VON PATZELT M.G. Born 23/12/19. Commd 6/5/43. Sqn Ldr 1/1/60. Retd SEC 23/12/68.
VOSE W.L. Born 19/11/54. Commd 20/5/82. Wg Cdr 1/1/97. Retd GD 19/4/03.
VOSPER J.R. Born 31/3/13. Commd 19/11/42. Flt Lt 19/5/46. Retd ENG 31/3/62.
VOUSDEN R.J.C. MRAeS. Born 4/3/44. Commd 9/8/63. Sqn Ldr 1/7/81. Retd GD 1/1/96.
VOUTE N.M. Born 15/4/49. Commd 28/11/69. Flt Lt 15/10/74. Retd GD 15/4/87.
VOYLE A.J. BSc. Born 9/11/41. Commd 15/7/63. Sqn Ldr 1/7/75. Retd ENG 9/11/79.
VOYSEY A. BSc. Born 27/6/57. Commd 14/9/75. Sqn Ldr 1/7/89. Retd ENG 27/6/95.
VOYSEY F.W. Born 13/12/27. Commd 15/12/49. Flt Lt 15/6/53. Retd GD 26/7/68.
VRACAS B.H. BA. Born 14/7/56. Commd 15/9/74. Flt Lt 15/10/78. Retd GD 1/12/85.

W

WADDELL A.D. MBE MCIT MILT. Born 25/5/47. Commd 21/10/66. Wg Cdr 1/7/85. Retd SUP 14/3/97.
WADDELL C.P. Born 26/9/15. Commd 8/7/41. Wg Cdr 1/1/54. Retd GD(G) 20/7/65.
WADDINGHAM J. Born 28/6/27. Commd 30/7/53. Flt Lt 30/1/58. Retd GD 28/6/70.
WADDINGTON B. Born 29/11/48. Commd 4/7/69. Flt Lt 4/1/75. Retd GD 9/6/86.
WADDINGTON J.F. AFC. Born 13/11/42. Commd 7/7/67. Sqn Ldr 1/7/87. Retd GD 22/4/94.
WADDINGTON W.D.B. DFC. Born 8/8/19. Commd 25/8/40. Flt Lt 1/9/45. Retd GD 8/8/62. rtg Sqn Ldr.
WADE B.R.M. DFC. Born 15/9/21. Commd 9/10/39. Wg Cdr 1/1/59. Retd GD 15/9/68.
WADE G.M. MBE. Born 17/12/22. Commd 9/11/43. Flt Lt 4/1/51. Retd SEC 10/4/62.
WADE G.N. Born 15/8/38. Commd 31/7/62. Flt Lt 15/2/65. Retd GD(G) 16/8/75.
WADE J.M. BA. Born 6/12/38. Commd 25/10/73. Flt Lt 25/10/75. Retd GD(G) 25/10/81. Re-instated 13/10/86.
  Flt Lt 3/10/80. Retd GD(G) 24/1/90.
WADE J.P.A. DFC. Born 11/7/23. Commd 27/11/43. Flt Lt 4/1/51. Retd SUP 21/8/57.
WADE N.L. DFC. Born 11/7/23. Commd 27/11/45. Flt Lt 27/11/49. Retd SUP 16/1/65.
WADE R.D. Born 7/7/50. Commd 15/8/85. Flt Lt 15/8/89. Retd GD 31/3/94.
WADEY G.D. Born 28/5/33. Commd 2/3/59. Flt Lt 1/3/61. Retd GD 28/5/93.
WADLEY R.E.A. Born 19/9/36. Commd 27/4/65. Sqn Ldr 1/1/91. Retd ADMIN 1/1/94.
WADSWORTH D.A. Born 24/2/44. Commd 24/6/65. Sqn Ldr 1/7/74. Retd GD 31/3/94.
WAGGETT A.V. Born 29/9/33. Commd 27/2/70. Sqn Ldr 1/7/81. Retd ENG 29/9/88.
WAGHORN C.P. MSc BA MCIT MILT. Born 6/10/54. Commd 17/6/79. Sqn Ldr 1/1/90. Retd SUP 17/6/95.
WAGHORN E.W. Born 27/7/25. Commd 26/3/64. Flt Lt 26/4/69. Retd PE 1/2/74.
WAGNER F.P.G. Born 26/1/35. Commd 20/1/56. Flt Lt 20/7/61. Retd GD(G) 27/1/72. Re-employed Flt Lt 5/4/74 to
  1/4/78.
WAGNER P.R. MB BS MRCS LRCP. Born 10/8/23. Commd 1/9/49. Wg Cdr 1/4/62. Retd MED 1/9/65.
WAGSTAFF L.E. Born 8/5/37. Commd 18/5/55. Flt Lt 1/8/61. Retd GD 8/5/65.
WAGSTAFF M.F. Born 10/10/41. Commd 23/9/65. Sqn Ldr 1/7/77. Retd SEC 10/2/79.
WAGSTAFF R. BSc. Born 5/2/40. Commd 30/6/62. Flt Lt 30/6/67. Retd ENG 31/3/80.
WAGSTAFFE B. IEng AMRAeS. Born 28/5/35. Commd 5/7/68. Sqn Ldr 1/7/77. Retd ENG 28/5/90.
WAIN M.R. BA. Born 7/7/42. Commd 22/7/68. Wg Cdr 1/7/87. Retd ENG 22/7/90.
WAIN R.M. Born 9/8/33. Commd 28/9/54. Flt Lt 28/3/59. Retd GD 5/4/75.
WAINMAN H. BA. Born 17/1/42. Commd 10/11/61. Flt Lt 12/10/71. Retd GD 16/1/94.
WAINWRIGHT E.H. Born 19/3/24. Commd 3/11/44. Sqn Ldr 1/1/71. Retd GD(G) 28/10/77.
WAINWRIGHT G.C. BSc MRAeS. Born 19/9/16. Commd 21/6/40. Wg Cdr 1/7/56. Retd ENG 24/12/64.
WAINWRIGHT M.T. AFC. Born 15/3/19. Commd 27/9/37. Sqn Ldr 1/7/53. Retd GD 31/3/58.
WAINWRIGHT N.D. Born 2/10/58. Commd 31/8/78. Sqn Ldr 1/1/93. Retd GD 10/6/00.
WAINWRIGHT R.N. Born 18/4/52. Commd 25/9/71. Flt Lt 9/3/80. Retd GD 18/4/90.
WAINWRIGHT W.A. BSc. Born 5/7/43. Commd 14/9/64. Sqn Ldr 1/1/76. Retd GD 5/7/81.
WAITE B. Born 22/10/47. Commd 9/2/81. Sqn Ldr 1/7/94. Retd ADMIN 1/7/97.
WAITE E. MRAeS. Born 5/6/23. Commd 4/5/50. Wg Cdr 1/7/71. Retd ENG 30/3/77.
WAITE G. MCMI. Born 12/12/18. Commd 5/10/44. Wg Cdr 1/7/62. Retd SUP 27/2/71.
WAITE G.W. Born 4/9/45. Commd 20/8/65. Flt Lt 6/10/71. Retd GD 4/9/00.
WAITE W.E. MBE. Born 14/4/31. Commd 26/3/52. Sqn Ldr 1/7/64. Retd GD 1/12/73. rtg Wg Cdr.
WAITT C.B. BA. Born 4/8/58. Commd 29/11/81. Wg Cdr 1/7/96. Retd SUP 1/7/99.
WAKEFIELD A.J. CEng MIMechE MIOSH. Born 12/12/36. Commd 30/5/71. Sqn Ldr 1/7/90. Retd ENG 12/12/94.
WAKEFIELD C.P. Born 28/11/33. Commd 13/8/52. Flt Lt 9/1/58. Retd GD 28/11/71.
WAKEFIELD D.C. Born 21/6/36. Commd 23/3/66. Flt Lt 23/3/68. Retd PE 11/9/73.
WAKEFIELD D.K. BSc. Born 20/4/49. Commd 2/1/70. Flt Lt 15/10/72. Retd GD 20/4/87.
WAKEFORD D.B.W. CEng MIMechE. Born 10/2/35. Commd 7/11/58. Wg Cdr 1/7/80. Retd ENG 6/12/85.
WAKEFORD Sir Richard KCB MVO OBE AFC. Born 20/4/22. Commd 7/3/42. AM 1/7/75. Retd GD 31/3/78.
WAKELIN R.H.W. Born 4/4/43. Commd 24/6/65. Sqn Ldr 1/7/77. Retd SUP 4/4/81.
WAKELY P.A. MB BS MRCS LRCP. Born 12/8/44. Commd 13/9/65. Sqn Ldr 26/6/74. Retd MED 24/1/76.
WAKELY B. BSc. Born 9/4/47. Commd 28/2/69. Gp Capt 1/1/99. Retd ENG 18/9/00.
WAKEMAN R. DFC. Born 14/10/18. Commd 8/9/44. Flt Lt 19/6/55. Retd GD(G) 10/6/69.
WAKERLEY D.G. BSc BChD LDS. Born 9/5/35. Commd 22/11/57. Wg Cdr 22/7/66. Retd DEL 4/3/77.
WAKLING B.G.E. Born 14/4/44. Commd 21/12/62. Sqn Ldr 1/7/75. Retd GD 21/12/82.
WALDECK A.C. Born 3/10/40. Commd 28/6/68. Flt Lt 2/8/70. Retd GD(G) 5/10/77.
WALDEN C.T. Born 21/2/27. Commd 19/7/51. Wg Cdr 1/7/68. Retd GD 30/10/70.
WALDEN G.F. DFC. Born 14/4/21. Commd 29/7/45. Sqn Ldr 1/7/70. Retd GD(G) 14/4/76.
WALDER C.L. MSc. Born 29/10/53. Commd 19/6/86. Sqn Ldr 1/1/96. Retd ENGINEER 1/5/04.
WALDING J.K. BA. Born 16/9/37. Commd 29/10/60. Flt Lt 29/4/66. Retd GD 12/7/76.
WALDRON A.P. CBE AFC. Born 8/9/47. Commd 21/1/66. A Cdre 1/1/98. Retd GD 8/9/02.
WALDWYN C.R. MSc BSc CEng MIIE MRAeS. Born 11/12/60. Commd 4/2/81. Sqn Ldr 1/7/94. Retd ENG 11/12/98.

WALENTOWICZ J. Born 4/8/20. Commd 7/1/48. Flt Lt 10/11/55. Retd GD 1/10/69.
WALES D.H. AFC. Born 11/6/22. Commd 23/7/41. Flt Lt 17/12/51. Retd GD 4/3/63.
WALES K.C.G. BSc CEng MIMechE MRAeS. Born 18/11/33. Commd 25/1/71. Flt Lt 25/8/70. Retd ENG 25/1/87.
WALFORD G.B. OBE. Born 13/4/16. Commd 10/5/37. Gp Capt 1/1/58. Retd GD 31/3/67.
WALKER A. BSc. Born 9/10/49. Commd 1/11/71. Sqn Ldr 1/1/86. Retd GD 1/1/89.
WALKER A. Born 29/6/56. Commd 16/2/89. Flt Lt 17/9/94. Retd MED(T) 14/9/96.
WALKER A.A. Born 6/3/39. Commd 16/12/68. Sqn Ldr 1/12/68. Retd GD 6/4/89.
WALKER A.C. Born 3/9/16. Commd 25/5/55. Sqn Ldr 1/1/68. Retd ENG 3/9/73.
WALKER A.D. Born 24/7/39. Commd 30/5/59. Sqn Ldr 1/7/74. Retd SUP 1/10/86.
WALKER A.E. Born 28/6/20. Commd 3/8/61. Flt Lt 3/8/67. Retd RGT 1/6/74.
WALKER A.F. BSc. Born 11/9/56. Commd 13/5/76. Sqn Ldr 1/7/88. Retd GD 15/6/96.
WALKER A.R. BSc. Born 10/11/59. Commd 5/1/86. Flt Lt 15/3/90. Retd ENG 10/11/97.
WALKER B.C. Born 9/7/35. Commd 17/3/55. Sqn Ldr 1/7/72. Retd ADMIN 19/5/89.
WALKER C.B. Born 25/12/50. Commd 13/5/81. Sqn Ldr 1/7/89. Retd GD(G) 14/3/96.
WALKER C.G. Born 8/7/52. Commd 10/2/72. Sqn Ldr 1/1/89. Retd OPS SPT 8/5/02.
WALKER C.P. Born 28/4/62. Commd 15/8/89. Flt Lt 12/2/92. Retd OPS SPT 28/4/00.
WALKER C.S. Born 21/2/14. Commd 6/1/44. Flt Lt 6/7/47. Retd GD 1/3/52.
WALKER D.B. Born 30/7/32. Commd 29/12/51. Flt Lt 25/4/57. Retd GD 30/7/70.
WALKER D.C. Born 26/12/17. Commd 2/1/39. Sqn Ldr 1/7/48. Retd SUP 26/12/66. rtg Wg Cdr.
WALKER D.J. Born 24/12/60. Commd 23/7/98. Flt Lt 23/7/02. Retd OPS SPT(REGT) 2/3/04.
WALKER E.S. Born 7/12/41. Commd 19/12/85. Flt Lt 19/12/87. Retd GD 7/12/01.
WALKER G.B. Born 15/12/30. Commd 12/10/54. Flt Lt 12/4/60. Retd GD 12/10/70.
WALKER G.F. BSc. Born 5/11/42. Commd 15/7/63. Sqn Ldr 1/7/72. Retd ENG 15/11/75.
WALKER G.R. Born 10/10/40. Commd 12/1/62. Sqn Ldr 1/7/74. Retd GD 10/10/95.
WALKER G.R. AFC. Born 4/3/22. Commd 22/2/46. Flt Lt 4/1/51. Retd GD 4/3/77.
WALKER H.G.A. Born 28/6/55. Commd 2/2/78. Flt Lt 2/8/83. Retd GD 14/3/96.
WALKER H.H. BEM. Born 15/7/38. Commd 18/4/74. Sqn Ldr 1/1/85. Retd ENG 15/7/93.
WALKER H.J. Born 5/9/45. Commd 14/10/71. Flt Lt 14/10/73. Retd GD 5/9/83.
WALKER I.D. Born 21/3/56. Commd 17/5/79. Sqn Ldr 1/1/92. Retd ADMIN 17/5/95.
WALKER Sir John KCB CBE AFC FRAeS. Born 26/5/36. Commd 31/7/56. AM 18/10/91. Retd GD 5/1/95.
WALKER J.F. Born 11/3/23. Commd 11/2/44. Sqn Ldr 1/4/56. Retd GD 11/3/72.
WALKER J.G. Born 6/4/39. Commd 9/3/62. Fg Offr 25/7/62. Retd RGT 27/5/68.
WALKER J.J. Born 12/4/29. Commd 28/2/49. Flt Lt 2/2/55. Retd GD 12/4/67.
WALKER J.M. Born 3/11/44. Commd 13/2/64. Gp Capt 1/1/88. Retd SUP 14/9/96.
WALKER J.N. Born 12/1/46. Commd 5/6/67. Sqn Ldr 1/7/77. Retd ENG 12/1/84.
WALKER J.S. Born 27/7/42. Commd 8/6/62. Flt Lt 8/12/67. Retd GD 3/2/76.
WALKER K. Born 11/3/34. Commd 23/8/55. Sqn Ldr 1/1/88. Retd GD 1/1/91.
WALKER K.J. BSc CEng MIMechE. Born 18/2/47. Commd 30/3/75. Sqn Ldr 1/7/83. Retd ENG 1/4/02.
WALKER M.D. Born 9/3/45. Commd 25/3/64. Flt Lt 25/9/69. Retd GD 24/2/94.
WALKER M.J. Born 24/2/53. Commd 15/10/81. Flt Lt 15/10/84. Retd GD(G) 15/4/91.
WALKER M.J.C. BA. Born 15/12/28. Commd 28/9/55. Flt Lt 28/9/55. Retd GD 6/10/69.
WALKER M.J.H. BA MCIT MILT MCMI. Born 20/7/34. Commd 13/12/55. Wg Cdr 1/1/76. Retd SUP 1/3/89.
WALKER M.V. MA. Born 17/5/33. Commd 14/10/59. Sqn Ldr 1/7/73. Retd ADMIN 17/5/88.
WALKER N.E.D. Born 15/12/35. Commd 16/4/54. Flt Lt 16/10/59. Retd GD 15/12/73.
WALKER N.E.N. Born 11/8/32. Commd 1/10/54. Flt Lt 1/10/67. Retd GD(G) 11/8/70.
WALKER P.F.H. Born 5/3/39. Commd 25/7/60. Sqn Ldr 1/7/72. Retd GD 5/3/77.
WALKER P.G. Born 21/7/29. Commd 30/7/52. Flt Lt 30/4/55. Retd GD 22/7/67.
WALKER R. Born 26/5/29. Commd 8/2/49. Flt Lt 12/1/55. Retd GD 4/12/57.
WALKER R. Born 14/7/39. Commd 20/9/81. Flt Lt 20/10/78. Retd ADMIN 20/9/89.
WALKER R.B. Born 13/11/44. Commd 24/2/67. Flt Lt 31/8/72. Retd ADMIN 13/11/82.
WALKER R.B. MBE. Born 22/9/20. Commd 6/9/45. Flt Lt 6/9/51. Retd SEC 1/5/64.
WALKER R.D. Born 11/7/34. Commd 2/7/52. Sqn Ldr 1/1/64. Retd GD 11/7/72.
WALKER R.J.E. CEng MIMechE MRAeS. Born 19/12/23. Commd 6/1/44. Sqn Ldr 1/1/56. Retd ENG 16/1/74.
WALKER R.K. Born 14/5/43. Commd 13/6/71. Flt Lt 13/6/71. Retd EDN 14/1/76.
WALKER R.L. Born 30/3/20. Commd 22/5/47. Wg Cdr 1/7/69. Retd SUP 1/8/74.
WALKER R.M. Born 7/11/43. Commd 3/8/62. Sqn Ldr 1/1/89. Retd GD 6/9/96.
WALKER R.P.H. BSc. Born 14/11/49. Commd 28/2/72. Flt Lt 28/5/73. Retd GD 28/2/88.
WALKER R.T. Born 15/9/31. Commd 23/2/55. Flt Lt 18/6/61. Retd GD 6/10/70.
WALKER S. SRN RCNT RNT. Born 1/3/37. Commd 10/5/73. Fg Offr 30/8/74. Retd MED(T) 11/9/76.
WALKER S. BA. Born 7/4/52. Commd 13/9/70. Flt Lt 15/10/75. Retd GD 10/5/82.
WALKER S. AFC. Born 15/7/24. Commd 13/5/44. Gp Capt 1/1/72. Retd GD 15/7/79.
WALKER S.A. Born 22/11/63. Commd 2/11/88. Flt Lt 4/9/91. Retd OPS SPT 22/11/01.
WALKER S.G. Born 11/7/58. Commd 13/8/82. Flt Lt 13/2/89. Retd OPS SPT 12/4/98.
WALKER S.L. Born 27/11/50. Commd 24/2/74. Sqn Ldr 1/1/87. Retd SUP 14/3/96.
WALKER S.T. MBE BSc. Born 13/4/61. Commd 2/9/79. Flt Lt 15/10/83. Retd GD 13/4/99.
WALKER S.T.E. Born 25/4/49. Commd 27/2/70. Flt Lt 27/2/73. Retd GD 17/9/75.

WALKER T.W. MBE. Born 9/4/63. Commd 2/9/84. Sqn Ldr 1/7/94. Retd GD 9/4/01.
WALKER-NORTHWOOD P.A. Born 4/9/67. Commd 4/6/87. Flt Lt 4/12/92. Retd GD 14/3/97.
WALKERLEY R.A. BTech. Born 7/1/50. Commd 15/9/69. Sqn Ldr 1/1/86. Retd ENG 1/1/89.
WALKINGTON I.R. BA. Born 5/12/27. Commd 9/12/48. Wg Cdr 1/7/70. Retd SEC 4/3/75.
WALL A.J. CEng MRAeS. Born 7/4/58. Commd 20/5/82. Sqn Ldr 1/1/91. Retd ENG 7/12/97.
WALL A.L. Born 1/11/40. Commd 18/12/62. Sqn Ldr 1/1/75. Retd GD 12/1/80.
WALL B.L.E. Born 13/12/28. Commd 13/12/50. Sqn Ldr 1/1/63. Retd SEC 6/3/76.
WALL D.A. BSc. Born 8/10/66. Commd 12/5/91. Flt Lt 12/11/93. Retd FLY(N) 16/11/03.
WALL F.J.J. Born 11/10/26. Commd 21/11/51. Flt Lt 21/5/56. Retd GD 30/11/70.
WALL G.P. MBA BSc(Eng) CEng MRAes. Born 3/2/61. Commd 23/11/81. Wg Cdr 1/7/98. Retd ENG 1/12/00.
WALL J. Born 16/9/23. Commd 14/11/49. Sqn Ldr 1/4/61. Retd EDN 31/10/70.
WALL L.F.E. Born 20/1/14. Commd 21/9/40. Flt Offr 29/11/48. Retd SEC 1/12/67.
WALL M.W. Born 16/1/49. Commd 1/3/70. Wg Cdr 1/3/71. Retd MED 1/3/87.
WALL S.A. Born 31/3/64. Commd 15/3/84. Flt Lt 15/9/89. Retd GD 2/4/01.
WALLACE A.B. Born 11/5/47. Commd 3/10/69. Sqn Ldr 1/1/86. Retd GD 21/2/93.
WALLACE A.F. CBE DFC. Born 22/8/21. Commd 23/12/40. Gp Capt 1/7/64. Retd GD 15/6/69.
WALLACE A.F. AFC. Born 23/11/20. Commd 11/9/42. Sqn Ldr 1/7/67. Retd GD 23/11/75.
WALLACE B. Born 7/12/34. Commd 21/4/67. Flt Lt 21/4/69. Retd ENG 21/4/75.
WALLACE D.B. MBE. Born 14/3/48. Commd 10/6/66. Wg Cdr 1/1/95. Retd GD 31/5/01.
WALLACE D.O.W. Born 30/9/46. Commd 4/5/72. Wg Cdr 1/1/87. Retd ADMIN 14/3/96.
WALLACE D.S. The Rev. Born 5/9/25. Commd 20/1/51. Retd Wg Cdr 5/9/80.
WALLACE H.C. OBE. Born 24/7/16. Commd 11/7/41. Wg Cdr 30/4/68. Retd MED(SEC) 24/1/73.
WALLACE I.R. BSc. Born 7/11/34. Commd 20/9/57. Sqn Ldr 3/9/67. Retd EDN 20/9/73.
WALLACE J.A. Born 15/7/22. Commd 20/10/55. Flt Lt 1/3/59. Retd ENG 1/5/76.
WALLACE J.E.V. BSc(Eng). Born 27/9/43. Commd 14/4/69. Sqn Ldr 1/7/77. Retd ENG 14/4/91.
WALLACE J.R. BSc. Born 7/1/33. Commd 13/6/71. Sqn Ldr 13/6/71. Retd ENG 13/10/89.
WALLACE M.F. BSc. Born 6/12/54. Commd 6/3/77. Flt Lt 6/12/78. Retd GD 21/9/93.
WALLACE N.A. Born 29/7/51. Commd 13/1/72. Flt Lt 13/7/77. Retd GD 28/10/88.
WALLACE R. Born 12/1/26. Commd 26/3/52. Sqn Ldr 1/7/63. Retd GD 1/9/76.
WALLACE R.L. CBE AFC. Born 28/2/09. Commd 14/12/29. Gp Capt 1/7/47. Retd GD 28/4/53.
WALLANE E.L. Born 27/7/22. Commd 8/8/43. Sqn Ldr 1/1/54. Retd GD 27/7/65.
WALLBANK D.J. Born 5/5/53. Commd 14/12/72. Flt Lt 14/6/79. Retd GD(G) 5/5/91.
WALLBANK H. Born 21/4/25. Commd 7/5/52. Sqn Ldr 1/7/73. Retd GD 21/4/83.
WALLBANK N. Born 13/5/25. Commd 3/3/45. Flt Lt 3/3/51. Retd RGT 3/5/59.
WALLBUTTON B.C. CEng FIEE. Born 11/12/34. Commd 22/8/58. Sqn Ldr 30/7/67. Retd ADMIN 12/4/91.
WALLEN G.S. Born 20/9/38. Commd 6/5/65. Sqn Ldr 1/1/76. Retd ADMIN 20/9/93.
WALLER A.D. LDS. Born 20/10/41. Commd 18/9/60. Sqn Ldr 17/9/69. Retd DEL 31/12/74.
WALLER C.J.N. IEng FIIE AMRAeS. Born 14/4/45. Commd 23/11/78. Sqn Ldr 1/1/91. Retd ENG 14/4/02.
WALLER D.E. Born 5/7/29. Commd 4/6/52. Flt Lt 21/1/59. Retd SUP 14/1/68.
WALLER D.M. FCMI. Born 6/7/37. Commd 29/7/58. A Cdre 1/1/85. Retd SUP 1/8/90.
WALLER D.R. Born 10/5/45. Commd 5/11/70. Sqn Ldr 1/1/85. Retd SUP 19/8/87.
WALLER E.A. BA CEng MIEE MBCS. Born 31/8/46. Commd 13/9/70. Flt Lt 13/12/73. Retd ENG 13/9/86.
WALLER I.M. Born 27/12/34. Commd 18/3/53. Flt Lt 29/4/59. Retd GD 27/12/72.
WALLER K.S. MA. Born 13/1/75. Commd 4/4/99. Flt Lt 4/10/01. Retd ADMIN (SEC) 20/5/03.
WALLER P.F. BA. Born 8/7/50. Commd 26/10/86. Fg Offr 26/4/86. Retd ADMIN 21/8/88.
WALLER P.J.C. Born 3/10/49. Commd 27/5/71. Fg Offr 27/5/73. Retd GD 4/1/74.
WALLIKER D.J. CBE. Born 26/1/19. Commd 17/4/39. A Cdre 1/1/70. Retd SUP 26/1/74.
WALLIKER J.A. Born 24/8/47. Commd 28/2/69. Sqn Ldr 1/7/78. Retd GD 11/12/85.
WALLIKER P.A. BA. Born 12/2/44. Commd 17/12/65. Flt Lt 17/9/67. Retd GD 12/2/82.
WALLINGTON R.M.A. Born 22/3/44. Commd 17/7/64. Flt Lt 4/11/70. Retd GD 15/4/77.
WALLINGTON W.P. Born 19/12/34. Commd 28/1/53. Flt Lt 5/11/58. Retd GD 1/1/90.
WALLIS B. Born 21/8/30. Commd 9/4/52. Flt Lt 21/8/57. Retd GD 21/8/71.
WALLIS E.F. MBE. Born 13/3/30. Commd 13/2/52. Sqn Ldr 1/1/76. Retd GD 13/3/88.
WALLIS G.E. Born 17/11/37. Commd 14/8/65. Flt Lt 14/8/67. Retd GD 18/2/75.
WALLIS J.G. Born 14/10/28. Commd 22/7/50. Fg Offr 22/7/52. Retd RGT 7/12/58.
WALLIS K.H. MRAeS. Born 26/4/16. Commd 1/2/40. Wg Cdr 1/7/58. Retd ENG 30/5/64.
WALLIS P. Born 14/11/41. Commd 21/7/61. Sqn Ldr 1/1/87. Retd GD 14/11/96.
WALLIS P.E. Born 31/5/47. Commd 17/10/71. Flt Lt 17/4/76. Retd ENG 17/10/87.
WALLIS R. Born 10/7/42. Commd 17/12/63. Sqn Ldr 1/1/76. Retd ADMIN 15/9/95.
WALLIS R.J. Born 25/10/46. Commd 20/10/67. Wg Cdr 1/1/88. Retd SUP 14/3/97.
WALLIS T.T. Born 16/10/35. Commd 19/9/55. Gp Capt 1/1/87. Retd RGT 6/4/90.
WALLIS J.A. Born 14/8/43. Commd 27/1/77. Sqn Ldr 1/7/91. Retd GD 15/8/94.
WALMSLEY C.R. MBE. Born 18/11/21. Commd 15/9/60. Sqn Ldr 1/1/69. Retd ENG 20/11/71.
WALMSLEY F. MCMI. Born 21/12/29. Commd 28/12/51. Sqn Ldr 1/7/74. Retd ADMIN 1/9/82.
WALMSLEY H.E. DFC*. Born 14/12/22. Commd 4/1/43. Gp Capt 1/7/63. Retd GD 14/10/71.
WALMSLEY I.H.F. Born 1/4/29. Commd 26/7/50. Sqn Ldr 1/7/65. Retd GD 1/4/71.

WALMSLEY J. Born 19/12/46. Commd 3/1/64. Wg Cdr 1/1/90. Retd GD 1/11/94.
WALMSLEY J.D. Born 14/2/44. Commd 10/6/66. Sqn Ldr 1/7/79. Retd GD 1/12/89.
WALMSLEY M.J.P. MVO. Born 22/6/31. Commd 17/12/52. Sqn Ldr 1/1/63. Retd GD 22/6/69.
WALMSLEY P. BSc. Born 17/6/56. Commd 14/8/77. Sqn Ldr 1/1/88. Retd GD 28/3/91.
WALNE K. BSc. Born 5/11/46. Commd 28/2/72. Wg Cdr 1/1/95. Retd GD 19/4/04.
WALPOLE J.J. Born 26/10/42. Commd 28/3/63. Sqn Ldr 1/7/78. Retd GD(G) 1/7/81.
WALPOLE N.J.R. OBE. Born 20/2/34. Commd 14/12/54. Gp Capt 1/1/80. Retd GD 31/7/88.
WALSH A.W. Born 28/1/48. Commd 15/3/84. Sqn Ldr 1/7/94. Retd ADMIN 28/1/03.
WALSH D.B. Born 16/11/45. Commd 17/7/70. Flt Lt 17/1/76. Retd GD 22/10/94.
WALSH G.A. Born 8/6/47. Commd 24/7/81. Sqn Ldr 1/1/89. Retd ADMIN 14/3/97.
WALSH J.F. Born 27/9/61. Commd 20/9/88. Flt Lt 5/11/86. Retd ADMIN 6/4/93.
WALSH J.N. Born 18/4/24. Commd 13/7/61. Flt Lt 13/7/64. Retd GD 23/4/69.
WALSH J.P. BA. Born 29/5/47. Commd 22/8/71. Flt Lt 22/11/72. Retd GD 30/9/75.
WALSH J.W. Born 16/5/29. Commd 16/1/52. Flt Lt 4/2/59. Retd GD(G) 16/5/67.
WALSH K.M. Born 2/9/44. Commd 24/4/70. Sqn Ldr 1/1/82. Retd GD(G) 3/12/85. Re-instated on Retired List 22/1/88.
WALSH L.M.P. BSc. Born 21/4/49. Commd 22/9/71. Gp Capt 1/7/99. Retd ENG 17/2/02.
WALSH M. MBE. Born 1/7/12. Commd 17/6/40. Sqn Offr 1/2/49. Retd SUP 1/5/56.
WALSH N.R. BSc. Born 13/5/61. Commd 27/3/83. Flt Lt 27/6/84. Retd GD 30/10/99.
WALSH P. Born 11/11/42. Commd 12/4/73. Flt Lt 12/4/75. Retd GD 10/11/97.
WALSHE N.R. Born 30/3/52. Commd 5/7/73. Flt Lt 30/3/79. Retd GD(G) 2/5/80.
WALSTER R.A. BSc. Born 2/2/48. Commd 24/9/67. Sqn Ldr 1/1/86. Retd ENG 2/2/92.
WALTER D. Born 26/5/31. Commd 9/7/53. Flt Lt 13/4/60. Retd SUP 26/5/69. rtg Sqn Ldr.
WALTER D.J. Born 11/9/25. Commd 25/8/55. Flt Lt 25/8/61. Retd GD 1/10/68.
WALTER E.J. Born 23/12/34. Commd 30/7/57. Flt Lt 30/7/62. Retd SEC 16/1/65.
WALTER J.N. MBE CEng MIMechE. Born 2/1/35. Commd 5/10/56. Gp Capt 1/7/79. Retd ENG 5/10/87.
WALTER N.E. Born 30/10/36. Commd 22/7/71. Sqn Ldr 3/10/79. Retd ADMIN 22/7/85.
WALTER N.W. Born 5/7/25. Commd 26/5/45. Sqn Ldr 1/7/70. Retd SUP 29/1/77.
WALTERS B.S. AFC. Born 7/8/49. Commd 17/7/70. Flt Lt 17/1/76. Retd GD 7/8/86.
WALTERS J.K. Born 15/3/40. Commd 24/3/61. Gp Capt 1/1/87. Retd GD 15/3/95.
WALTERS M. Born 3/7/26. Commd 20/7/50. Flt Lt 20/1/54. Retd GD 1/8/68.
WALTERS P. MTech CEng MIEE MRAeS. Born 20/3/42. Commd 15/7/64. Sqn Ldr 1/7/74. Retd ENG 20/3/97.
WALTERS R.H. CEng MRAeS MIEE. Born 2/1/32. Commd 24/2/55. Wg Cdr 1/7/78. Retd ENG 1/6/90.
WALTERS R.J. BSc. Born 17/10/46. Commd 11/5/71. Sqn Ldr 1/7/84. Retd GD 17/10/01.
WALTERS-MORGAN W.M. Born 7/4/35. Commd 17/5/56. Sqn Ldr 1/1/68. Retd PRT 7/4/73.
WALTHAM D.L. Born 29/8/33. Commd 21/5/52. Flt Lt 26/11/57. Retd GD 29/8/71.
WALTHAM J.D. Born 12/2/36. Commd 10/9/70. Sqn Ldr 1/1/82. Retd GD 18/3/86.
WALTON A. Born 9/9/30. Commd 30/3/52. Flt Lt 29/10/57. Retd GD 9/9/68.
WALTON A.D. Born 1/4/49. Commd 26/10/67. Flt Lt 20/4/73. Retd GD 1/4/87.
WALTON B.K. Born 6/10/40. Commd 2/5/59. Sqn Ldr 1/7/71. Retd GD 6/10/78.
WALTON D. Born 14/4/44. Commd 11/4/85. Flt Lt 11/4/89. Retd ENG 14/12/90.
WALTON D.E. DFC. Born 16/5/22. Commd 27/3/44. Flt Lt 27/9/47. Retd GD 16/5/65.
WALTON E.J. MCMI ACIS. Born 19/12/35. Commd 15/2/56. Sqn Ldr 1/7/68. Retd SEC 19/12/73.
WALTON H.A. Born 14/11/15. Commd 8/7/43. Sqn Ldr 1/7/60. Retd ENG 31/8/68.
WALTON J. CEng MIMechE MRAeS. Born 6/7/31. Commd 28/3/66. Sqn Ldr 1/7/74. Retd ENG 6/7/89.
WALTON J. MBE. Born 20/6/39. Commd 19/8/65. Sqn Ldr 1/7/77. Retd PRT 14/2/91.
WALTON J. IEng AFSLAET. Born 16/5/53. Commd 26/11/81. Sqn Ldr 1/1/90. Retd ENGINEER 31/8/04.
WALTON J.H. AFC. Born 14/3/23. Commd 5/8/43. Gp Capt 1/7/67. Retd GD 5/4/72.
WALTON J.T. MBE. Born 4/7/31. Commd 6/9/68. Sqn Ldr 1/7/78. Retd ENG 30/10/82.
WALTON K.G. Born 21/8/64. Commd 19/6/86. Flt Lt 19/12/92. Retd OPS SPT 21/8/02.
WALTON P. MSc BSc. Born 17/3/47. Commd 26/1/79. Sqn Ldr 1/7/86. Retd ADMIN (TRG) 17/3/05.
WALTON P.R. Born 29/12/36. Commd 15/2/56. Flt Lt 15/8/61. Retd GD 29/12/74.
WALTON P.R.C. Born 8/3/52. Commd 22/5/70. Sqn Ldr 1/1/85. Retd ADMIN 7/6/89.
WALTON R.D. Born 10/3/22. Commd 19/6/42. Wg Cdr 1/1/61. Retd GD 28/7/68. rtg Gp Capt.
WALTON S.B. BEM. Born 21/9/31. Commd 8/7/65. Flt Lt 14/8/73. Retd SEC 20/9/75.
WALTON W.C. DFC. Born 23/12/20. Commd 26/3/42. Flt Lt 26/9/45. Retd GD 16/6/53.
WALWYN-JAMES D.H. MA BSc DPhil DCAe CEng MRAeS FRIC. Born 18/5/28. Commd 11/6/56. Wg Cdr 1/4/69. Retd EDN 14/5/69.
WANKLYN D.C. AIIP. Born 28/6/25. Commd 21/3/51. Flt Lt 21/9/55. Retd ENG 5/5/79.
WANSTALL B.N. OBE AIPD. Born 5/11/29. Commd 27/6/51. Wg Cdr 1/1/75. Retd GD 8/5/82.
WANT N.D. OBE. Born 9/6/35. Commd 1/10/54. Wg Cdr 1/1/80. Retd GD 1/9/91.
WAPLE C.A. BSc. Born 2/9/76. Commd 1/9/97. Fg Offr 15/7/97. Retd GD 2/5/00.
WAPLINGTON R.J.W. Born 10/10/36. Commd 23/7/58. Flt Lt 15/2/65. Retd ENG 12/8/67.
WAPPAT F. BEM. Born 22/6/30. Commd 7/1/71. Sqn Ldr 1/1/79. Retd ADMIN 16/5/84.
WARBOYS K.J. Born 22/6/43. Commd 3/1/64. Flt Lt 3/7/69. Retd GD 1/9/76.
WARBURTON G.R. Born 28/12/46. Commd 1/10/65. Wg Cdr 1/1/95. Retd GD 15/5/02.

WARBURTON K.C. Born 12/8/22. Commd 31/5/48. Fg Offr 19/5/50. Retd GD 9/10/54.
WARBURTON P.L. Born 30/7/61. Commd 8/12/83. Flt Lt 11/3/91. Retd GD 30/7/99.
WARBURTON R.G. Born 10/5/42. Commd 31/7/86. Flt Lt 31/7/90. Retd ENG 10/5/97.
WARBURTON S.A. Born 28/1/41. Commd 24/3/61. Sqn Ldr 1/7/72. Retd GD 7/2/95.
WARBY D.A.J. MBE MSc BEd MCMI. Born 8/12/52. Commd 23/5/83. Sqn Ldr 1/7/95. Retd ADMIN 31/1/03.
WARD A. Born 29/4/35. Commd 2/3/61. Sqn Ldr 1/7/72. Retd GD 11/5/84.
WARD A.F. OBE. Born 6/6/12. Commd 2/12/40. Gp Capt 1/7/58. Retd ENG 6/6/67.
WARD A.M. Born 12/5/48. Commd 16/8/68. Sqn Ldr 1/1/01. Retd FLY(P) 12/5/03.
WARD A.S. BSc. Born 16/9/55. Commd 31/7/79. Flt Lt 30/1/79. Retd GD 4/2/90.
WARD A.W. MBE BSc. Born 1/1/49. Commd 6/12/70. Wg Cdr 1/7/95. Retd ADMIN 23/5/00.
WARD B.A. BSc DIC ARCS MRAeS. Born 29/9/26. Commd 10/2/49. Gp Capt 1/1/75. Retd ENG 31/3/77.
WARD B.C. Born 15/5/37. Commd 7/5/64. Sqn Ldr 1/1/74. Retd MED 16/5/87.
WARD C.D. Born 12/4/57. Commd 21/6/90. Flt Lt 21/6/92. Retd ENG 21/6/98.
WARD C.E. Born 20/1/58. Commd 8/9/77. Flt Lt 17/12/83. Retd ADMIN 2/11/89.
WARD C.J. Born 19/9/33. Commd 31/10/74. Flt Lt 31/10/79. Retd GD(G) 19/9/94.
WARD D. BA BSc. Born 21/9/42. Commd 6/9/65. Sqn Ldr 1/1/86. Retd GD 21/9/00.
WARD D. MA MCMI. Born 20/1/34. Commd 22/2/60. Gp Capt 1/7/84. Retd GD 20/1/89.
WARD D.A. MCMI. Born 17/2/36. Commd 17/3/67. Sqn Ldr 1/7/79. Retd ADMIN 1/6/87.
WARD D.A. Born 9/10/26. Commd 15/5/47. Sqn Ldr 1/1/62. Retd GD 13/7/67.
WARD D.J. Born 23/2/26. Commd 11/8/48. Wg Cdr 1/1/73. Retd GD 23/8/83.
WARD D.J. BA. Born 19/4/54. Commd 25/2/79. Flt Lt 25/5/81. Retd ADMIN 31/7/88.
WARD D.S. Born 25/9/33. Commd 14/11/59. Flt Lt 14/5/65. Retd GD 1/9/74.
WARD E. BA MB BCh MFCM DPH. Born 30/7/26. Commd 1/9/52. Gp Capt 1/1/74. Retd MED 1/2/77.
WARD E. Born 20/10/39. Commd 8/5/64. Flt Lt 8/5/68. Retd SUP 8/9/70.
WARD E.W. MBE. Born 22/1/41. Commd 29/3/68. Gp Capt 1/1/91. Retd GD 12/7/93.
WARD G.E. MBE. Born 2/3/55. Commd 23/11/78. Sqn Ldr 1/7/90. Retd GD(G) 1/7/93.
WARD G.R. MSc. Born 27/4/43. Commd 8/9/69. Flt Lt 8/3/70. Retd ENG 8/11/75.
WARD J. BSc CEng MRAeS ACGI MICE. Born 7/8/33. Commd 16/1/57. Wg Cdr 1/7/76. Retd ENG 24/12/77.
WARD J. Born 28/7/22. Commd 1/8/50. Flt Lt 23/10/56. Retd GD 7/12/66.
WARD J. Born 19/4/28. Commd 12/8/54. Sqn Ldr 1/1/77. Retd GD 19/4/88.
WARD J.A. AFC FCMI. Born 29/4/43. Commd 8/6/62. Wg Cdr 1/1/84. Retd GD 2/4/93.
WARD J.A. Born 18/10/39. Commd 21/12/67. Flt Lt 11/2/71. Retd SUP 18/10/77.
WARD J.C.W. BMet. Born 16/6/59. Commd 25/8/80. Flt Lt 15/4/83. Retd GD 16/6/97.
WARD J.D.R. BSc. Born 28/7/64. Commd 15/9/85. Sqn Ldr 1/1/00. Retd FLY(P) 1/10/04.
WARD J.H. Born 8/5/15. Commd 9/7/38. Flt Lt 1/4/47. Retd LGL 15/3/49. rtg Sqn Ldr.
WARD J.K. Born 27/1/67. Commd 2/12/91. Sqn Ldr 1/1/02. Retd FLY(P) 27/1/05.
WARD J.L. Born 23/5/48. Commd 22/5/75. Sqn Ldr 1/7/87. Retd ADMIN 17/5/95.
WARD J.M. Born 14/3/42. Commd 11/11/71. Flt Lt 11/11/73. Retd GD(G) 1/4/87.
WARD J.R. Born 27/11/41. Commd 11/9/64. Sqn Ldr 1/1/94. Retd GD 27/11/96.
WARD J.R. Born 31/10/30. Commd 13/5/53. Gp Capt 1/1/81. Retd GD 26/8/83.
WARD K.A. Born 3/3/35. Commd 8/7/53. Flt Lt 8/1/59. Retd GD 3/3/73. rtg Sqn Ldr.
WARD K.M.M. LLB. Born 21/6/56. Commd 14/10/81. Flt Lt 21/1/84. Retd SY 2/10/85.
WARD L.H. Born 17/12/19. Commd 17/4/47. Flt Lt 29/11/51. Retd SUP 17/8/53.
WARD L.M. Born 5/5/56. Commd 15/8/85. Flt Lt 15/8/85. Retd SUP 5/5/94.
WARD L.W. BA. Born 22/3/32. Commd 9/9/59. Sqn Ldr 9/9/69. Retd ADMIN 22/3/92.
WARD M. CEng MIEE. Born 15/10/37. Commd 9/12/65. Sqn Ldr 1/1/74. Retd ENG 2/4/88.
WARD M.C. Born 20/10/44. Commd 9/8/63. Flt Lt 1/7/69. Retd GD 14/6/75.
WARD M.D. Born 6/1/47. Commd 2/12/68. Sqn Ldr 1/1/81. Retd ENG 6/1/85.
WARD M.G. Born 5/7/40. Commd 23/6/67. Sqn Ldr 1/7/74. Retd SEC 5/7/78.
WARD M.J. Born 15/1/47. Commd 11/10/84. Flt Lt 11/10/88. Retd OPS SPT 24/8/98.
WARD M.J. Born 24/4/46. Commd 26/5/67. Sqn Ldr 1/7/81. Retd ENG 24/4/90.
WARD M.T. Born 17/4/50. Commd 6/4/72. Flt Lt 6/10/78. Retd GD(G) 1/6/88.
WARD M.W. OBE MB BS FRCS(Edin). Born 2/10/40. Commd 11/3/68. Gp Capt 6/7/89. Retd MED 23/10/96.
WARD N.A. BSc. Born 19/11/55. Commd 13/4/80. Flt Lt 13/1/83. Retd GD(G) 13/4/96.
WARD N.A. BSc. Born 22/2/53. Commd 28/12/71. Flt Lt 15/4/76. Retd GD 2/2/91.
WARD O.A. Born 22/9/18. Commd 17/1/49. Gp Capt 1/1/67. Retd RGT 22/9/73.
WARD P. Born 6/5/33. Commd 26/11/56. Flt Lt 2/6/58. Retd GD 11/6/72.
WARD P.A. Born 5/9/33. Commd 3/10/69. Flt Lt 3/10/72. Retd GD(G) 4/10/74.
WARD R. MCMI. Born 11/2/34. Commd 8/7/52. Flt Lt 20/11/57. Retd GD 11/8/72.
WARD R.A.P. The Rev. Born 17/1/53. Commd 19/7/82. Retd Wg Cdr 19/7/98.
WARD R.J. BSc. Born 25/7/59. Commd 17/8/80. Sqn Ldr 1/1/95. Retd GD 11/6/97.
WARD R.J. Born 6/7/41. Commd 30/7/63. Wg Cdr 1/1/87. Retd GD 2/11/90.
WARD S. Born 23/1/30. Commd 29/12/51. Wg Cdr 1/1/80. Retd GD 17/11/84.
WARD S.J. BSc. Born 5/10/65. Commd 29/1/86. Flt Lt 15/1/90. Retd GD 15/7/99.
WARD T. Born 31/8/25. Commd 19/12/63. Flt Lt 19/12/66. Retd GD 28/3/69.
WARD T.C. BSc. Born 23/12/38. Commd 25/3/64. Sqn Ldr 1/7/78. Retd GD 1/7/81.

WARD T.D. FCMI. Born 20/7/30. Commd 11/6/53. Gp Capt 1/1/73. Retd ENG 1/11/78.
WARD V.H. Born 10/6/51. Commd 18/10/79. Sqn Ldr 1/1/91. Retd SUPPLY 1/7/03.
WARD W. Born 15/7/45. Commd 28/11/69. Flt Lt 4/5/72. Retd GD 15/7/83.
WARD-DUTTON I. Born 8/8/41. Commd 24/11/67. Wg Cdr 1/1/85. Retd ENG 8/8/91.
WARD-SUMNER M.D. MBE. Born 27/10/06. Commd 21/7/41. Sqn Offr 1/7/50. Retd SEC 18/3/56.
WARDELL H.H. Born 12/9/16. Commd 15/1/42. Sqn Ldr 1/7/61. Retd ENG 30/6/65.
WARDEN G.M. Born 14/2/25. Commd 12/3/64. Flt Lt 12/3/67. Retd GD 16/1/76.
WARDEN R.H. BSc. Born 10/5/50. Commd 12/12/71. Flt Lt 12/3/76. Retd SEC 2/10/79.
WARDHAUGH R.C. Born 2/1/49. Commd 27/2/70. Sqn Ldr 1/1/83. Retd GD 2/1/87.
WARDILL D.H. CEng MIEE MIMechE. Born 3/3/36. Commd 8/8/58. Gp Capt 1/7/79. Retd ENG 3/3/91.
WARDILL J.C. MCMI. Born 23/12/20. Commd 26/11/41. Sqn Ldr 1/1/60. Retd SUP 23/12/75.
WARDILL J.D. BA MB BChir DMRD. Born 15/11/31. Commd 13/4/58. Sqn Ldr 13/4/63. Retd MED 1/10/68.
WARDILL T.C. Born 30/1/48. Commd 11/10/72. Gp Capt 1/7/00. Retd ADMIN 30/1/03.
WARDLAW K. Born 19/6/47. Commd 26/9/90. Flt Lt 26/9/94. Retd ADMIN 31/3/99.
WARDLE J.C.R. MMedSci MB BS MRCS LRCP DRCOG. Born 2/5/31. Commd 17/9/72. Wg Cdr 7/4/74.
  Retd MED 2/11/89.
WARDLE P.R. BSc. Born 25/10/41. Commd 19/8/63. Flt Lt 19/12/68. Retd ENG 19/10/81.
WARDMAN C.T. Born 11/9/13. Commd 1/1/37. Sqn Ldr 1/12/43. Retd SUP 5/3/46. rtg Wg Cdr.
WARDROP A.L. Born 20/12/30. Commd 12/9/63. Sqn Ldr 1/1/74. Retd ENG 1/10/85.
WARDROP T. BSc. Born 8/7/61. Commd 1/2/87. Flt Lt 1/8/89. Retd FLY(N) 1/2/03.
WARE A. Born 27/4/44. Commd 15/7/66. Wg Cdr 1/1/90. Retd GD 27/4/00.
WARE A.S. Born 3/4/20. Commd 27/2/44. Flt Lt 27/8/47. Retd GD 1/10/62.
WARE C.C. Born 4/11/40. Commd 24/8/70. Flt Lt 12/7/65. Retd GD 4/11/95.
WARE D.J. BSc. Born 13/3/65. Commd 14/9/86. Flt Lt 14/3/89. Retd FLY(N) 19/1/04.
WARE D.R. MBE DFC AFC. Born 13/9/22. Commd 5/11/43. Sqn Ldr 1/10/54. Retd GD 15/2/64.
WARE E.M. DFC. Born 24/10/16. Commd 24/10/36. Sqn Ldr 1/6/41. Retd GD 30/8/50. rtg Wg Cdr.
WARE G.W.H. DFM. Born 28/2/19. Commd 22/7/43. Wg Cdr 1/7/70. Retd ENG 1/11/73.
WARE I.H. Born 4/3/49. Commd 7/2/79. Sqn Ldr 1/7/91. Retd OPS SPT(REGT) 4/3/04.
WARE M.H. Born 1/10/22. Commd 3/7/43. Sqn Ldr 1/7/67. Retd GD 1/10/77.
WARE M.W. BA MCMI. Born 10/11/32. Commd 3/10/66. Sqn Ldr 1/9/73. Retd ADMIN 12/4/83.
WARE S.J. The Rev. BA. Born 5/4/55. Commd 23/11/95. Retd Wg Cdr 8/4/05.
WAREHAM F. Born 14/2/50. Commd 12/3/87. Flt Lt 1/2/93. Retd SUP 2/4/00.
WAREHAM M.J. Born 12/11/64. Commd 26/9/90. Flt Lt 12/8/94. Retd FLY(N) 24/3/03.
WAREHAM P.J. BEd. Born 23/11/53. Commd 19/3/78. Flt Lt 19/6/78. Retd GD 14/3/96.
WAREHAM R.J.E. Born 11/5/22. Commd 4/5/50. Sqn Ldr 1/1/72. Retd GD 11/5/82.
WARGENT M.G. Born 10/2/46. Commd 5/3/65. Sqn Ldr 1/7/82. Retd GD 10/9/90.
WARHAFTIG W. MBE CEng FIMechE FRAeS FCMI. Born 29/4/26. Commd 18/4/51. Gp Capt 1/1/75.
  Retd ENG 29/4/81.
WARING D.A. AFC . Born 29/6/45. Commd 5/2/65. Sqn Ldr 1/1/81. Retd FLY(P) 31/10/03.
WARING S.L. Born 5/10/45. Commd 25/6/65. Flt Lt 25/12/70. Retd GD 5/10/83.
WARMINGTON M.A. BSc. Born 10/7/61. Commd 7/10/82. Wg Cdr 1/1/02. Retd GD 1/1/04.
WARMINGTON W.I. DFC. Born 17/5/22. Commd 4/3/43. Flt Lt 17/5/56. Retd GD 3/11/63.
WARNE P.C. Born 9/10/31. Commd 29/10/52. Flt Lt 3/3/59. Retd GD 9/10/69.
WARNE P.F. Born 8/3/41. Commd 25/8/67. Flt Lt 18/11/73. Retd SEC 3/5/75.
WARNEFORD D. MBE. Born 6/12/42. Commd 23/11/78. Sqn Ldr 1/1/88. Retd ENG 14/3/96.
WARNER A. Born 31/1/40. Commd 30/5/69. Sqn Ldr 1/1/78. Retd ENG 1/4/90.
WARNER A.E. Born 13/6/33. Commd 8/11/51. Flt Lt 23/2/57. Retd GD 24/2/73.
WARNER B.J. Born 22/6/49. Commd 31/7/86. Flt Lt 31/7/90. Retd ADMIN 14/3/96.
WARNER D.B. Born 14/5/32. Commd 5/7/53. Flt Lt 5/11/58. Retd GD 14/5/70.
WARNER D.L. BSc. Born 14/2/56. Commd 15/9/74. Sqn Ldr 1/7/86. Retd GD 1/10/88.
WARNER D.M. Born 21/5/18. Commd 28/11/48. Flt Lt 27/5/54. Retd GD(G) 1/8/63.
WARNER I. Born 7/5/21. Commd 18/12/43. Flt Offr 8/12/49. Retd SEC 11/8/51.
WARNER K.B. Born 19/11/28. Commd 2/5/51. Sqn Ldr 1/7/68. Retd SUP 19/11/83.
WARNER M.P. Born 22/7/43. Commd 24/8/72. Flt Lt 24/8/72. Retd SY 1/2/93.
WARNER N.G. Born 7/1/43. Commd 17/12/64. Sqn Ldr 1/7/77. Retd GD 9/1/75.
WARNER R.T. Born 20/5/46. Commd 11/5/78. Flt Lt 11/5/80. Retd GD 11/5/86.
WARNER T.F. Born 14/6/44. Commd 17/5/63. Flt Lt 17/11/68. Retd GD 1/1/76.
WARNES A.E. MA BSc CEng MIEE. Born 11/4/53. Commd 24/6/72. Air Cdre 1/7/02. Retd GD 20/1/05.
WARNES N.J. MBE LRAM ARCM. Born 6/7/28. Commd 28/3/60. Sqn Ldr 30/7/71. Retd DM 15/9/73.
WARNOCK J.D. Born 17/8/54. Commd 11/6/81. Sqn Ldr 1/7/91. Retd SUP 1/7/94.
WARNOCK J.S. MCMI. Born 22/4/45. Commd 18/11/66. Sqn Ldr 1/7/80. Retd ADMIN 1/7/83.
WARNOCK J.T.D. BSc. Born 2/2/54. Commd 8/1/78. Flt Lt 8/10/78. Retd GD 2/2/92.
WARNOCK T.S. Born 27/12/44. Commd 23/9/66. Flt Lt 23/3/72. Retd GD(G) 27/12/82.
WARR C.B. Born 12/10/24. Commd 4/1/45. Flt Lt 27/5/54. Retd GD 31/3/67.
WARR S.A. BEng. Born 10/10/65. Commd 3/8/88. Sqn Ldr 1/7/02. Retd ENGINEER 28/2/04.
WARREN A.Y. MSc MB BS MRCPath. Born 30/6/59. Commd 24/9/84. Sqn Ldr 1/8/93. Retd MED 4/5/01.

WARREN C. MBE DFC. Born 15/11/18. Commd 1/10/39. Sqn Ldr 1/6/45. Retd GD 14/12/57. rtg Wg Cdr.
WARREN C.A. Born 11/11/71. Commd 3/6/93. Flt Lt 3/12/98. Retd FLY(P) 4/3/04.
WARREN D. MBE. Born 30/12/35. Commd 21/10/66. Wg Cdr 1/1/85. Retd ADMIN 1/7/88.
WARREN D.C. Born 24/3/44. Commd 25/4/69. Flt Lt 1/1/73. Retd GD 22/10/94.
WARREN D.G. DFC. Born 11/7/16. Commd 7/10/35. Flt Lt 11/12/46. Retd GD(G) 11/7/66. rtg Wg Cdr.
WARREN D.H. Born 9/9/29. Commd 30/7/52. Gp Capt 1/7/75. Retd GD 9/9/84.
WARREN D.J. Born 4/12/44. Commd 3/10/66. Sqn Ldr 1/1/75. Retd ADMIN 6/4/85.
WARREN J. Born 24/1/43. Commd 28/4/65. Sqn Ldr 1/1/80. Retd GD 4/5/94.
WARREN J.C.A. Born 5/8/27. Commd 15/9/60. Sqn Ldr 1/1/74. Retd ENG 1/12/76.
WARREN J.D. Born 6/6/55. Commd 8/9/83. Sqn Ldr 1/7/02. Retd FLY(P) 4/4/03.
WARREN J.J. Born 18/7/37. Commd 17/3/67. Flt Lt 18/7/92. Retd GD 18/7/92.
WARREN M.D. BSc. Born 7/5/64. Commd 29/9/85. Sqn Ldr 1/1/99. Retd GD 7/5/02.
WARREN P.A. Born 26/3/58. Commd 21/4/77. Flt Lt 21/10/82. Retd GD 30/8/88.
WARREN P.F.F. BA. Born 23/9/33. Commd 5/10/56. Sqn Ldr 5/4/65. Retd EDN 5/10/72.
WARREN P.H. BSc. Born 22/3/61. Commd 20/1/85. Flt Lt 20/7/88. Retd GD(G) 19/1/90.
WARREN P.J. BEng. Born 7/8/49. Commd 24/3/74. Sqn Ldr 1/7/96. Retd GD 21/11/00.
WARREN P.J. Born 11/9/46. Commd 20/10/67. Sqn Ldr 1/7/79. Retd GD 11/9/84.
WARREN R.J. Born 3/10/32. Commd 13/8/52. Flt Lt 9/1/58. Retd GD 3/10/70.
WARREN R.S. Born 16/3/25. Commd 23/8/56. Flt Lt 23/2/61. Retd GD 2/1/68.
WARREN T.A. Born 2/1/23. Commd 25/9/43. Sqn Ldr 1/4/56. Retd GD 2/1/78.
WARREN T.B. Born 28/7/33. Commd 28/1/53. Flt Lt 29/4/59. Retd GD 27/1/72.
WARREN-SMITH C.D. BSc MB BS FRCS. Born 23/2/51. Commd 20/2/73. Wg Cdr 11/1/90. Retd MED 1/1/92.
WARREN-WILSON J.P. BA. Born 6/10/54. Commd 24/7/77. Sqn Ldr 1/7/87. Retd GD 24/7/93.
WARRICK N.M. FIAP MCMI. Born 18/4/56. Commd 27/2/75. Wg Cdr 1/1/97. Retd OPS SPT 19/4/01.
WARRINGTON L. BA BSc. Born 21/2/55. Commd 3/9/72. Sqn Ldr 1/1/90. Retd ENG 21/2/93.
WARRINGTON L.M. Born 22/1/49. Commd 31/7/70. Flt Lt 31/7/73. Retd GD 22/6/87.
WARRINGTON V.L. OBE MA. Born 2/7/34. Commd 11/9/57. A Cdre 1/7/84. Retd GD 1/8/88.
WARSAP B.L. OBE. Born 2/12/38. Commd 18/12/56. Wg Cdr 1/7/80. Retd GD 2/12/93.
WARTON K.F. Born 13/3/40. Commd 9/7/59. Flt Lt 19/2/65. Retd GD 13/3/78.
WARWICK C.B.L. MBE. Born 10/12/16. Commd 10/6/44. Sqn Ldr 1/7/66. Retd GD(G) 10/12/73.
WARWICK J.L. Born 11/6/28. Commd 1/3/62. Flt Lt 1/3/68. Retd PE 16/6/78.
WARWICK K. MA MSc. Born 13/11/72. Commd 6/8/99. Flt Lt 1/12/99. Retd ADMIN (SEC) 22/4/03.
WARWICK M. Born 16/1/45. Commd 8/9/83. Sqn Ldr 1/7/91. Retd ENG 1/3/93.
WARWICK P.H. Born 13/6/21. Commd 27/5/54. Flt Lt 26/5/59. Retd GD 13/6/68.
WARWICK R.A. OBE MCMI. Born 16/10/28. Commd 7/11/51. Wg Cdr 1/1/76. Retd GD 16/10/83.
WARWICK-SPAUL C.B.R. MCMI. Born 11/11/18. Commd 17/4/39. Sqn Ldr 1/1/68. Retd SUP 11/11/73.
WARWOOD M. Born 26/7/37. Commd 24/9/64. Sqn Ldr 1/1/73. Retd GD(G) 30/4/83.
WASHBOURN R.O. Born 20/2/33. Commd 22/8/61. Sqn Ldr 1/7/71. Retd ENG 20/2/88.
WASHBOURNE A.E. Born 5/9/47. Commd 3/1/82. Flt Lt 24/12/76. Retd GD 3/1/99.
WASHINGTON F.J. Born 14/7/33. Commd 26/7/51. Flt Lt 24/4/57. Retd GD 17/10/84.
WASHINGTON I.P. Born 12/3/33. Commd 16/12/66. Flt Lt 16/12/71. Retd GD 12/3/89.
WASHINGTON-SMITH J.P. Born 22/9/51. Commd 31/8/78. Wg Cdr 1/7/93. Retd ENG 1/10/99.
WASHINGTON-SMITH M.H. BEd. Born 20/7/55. Commd 8/1/78. Wg Cdr 1/1/94. Retd ADMIN 14/3/97.
WASLEY R.J. Born 4/3/24. Commd 23/1/45. Wg Cdr 1/7/69. Retd SEC 30/6/78.
WASS E.A. AE* MCMI. Born 8/10/20. Commd 9/11/44. Sqn Ldr 1/1/59. Retd SUP 8/10/75.
WASSELL R.A. Born 28/10/48. Commd 11/10/70. Sqn Ldr 1/7/86. Retd ENG 14/3/97.
WATERER E.C. MCMI. Born 22/3/24. Commd 2/11/45. Sqn Ldr 1/4/56. Retd GD 22/3/73.
WATERFALL E.J. Born 27/10/47. Commd 1/8/69. Flt Lt 1/8/72. Retd GD 7/10/78.
WATERFALL R.T.F. MBE. Born 2/8/27. Commd 20/9/48. Wg Cdr 1/1/74. Retd SY 4/8/81.
WATERFIELD C.D. MCMI. Born 17/10/33. Commd 26/3/52. Wg Cdr 1/1/74. Retd GD 1/1/85.
WATERHOUSE C. BSc. Born 5/5/65. Commd 1/4/85. Flt Lt 15/1/89. Retd GD 15/7/98.
WATERHOUSE I.J. Born 21/11/44. Commd 4/8/82. Sqn Ldr 1/7/90. Retd ENG 1/1/95.
WATERMAN D.G.G. FIL. Born 14/11/35. Commd 1/4/58. Sqn Ldr 1/7/74. Retd ADMIN 29/4/91.
WATERMEYER A.E. Born 24/9/66. Commd 19/6/88. Flt Lt 19/6/94. Retd ADMIN 14/9/96.
WATERS A.P.J. Born 19/8/29. Commd 8/9/49. Flt Lt 8/3/53. Retd GD 19/8/67.
WATERS B.L. Born 30/9/36. Commd 14/12/55. Sqn Ldr 1/1/69. Retd GD 30/9/74.
WATERS G.J. Born 8/4/34. Commd 16/9/53. Flt Lt 13/4/60. Retd GD 8/4/72.
WATERS I.F. Born 14/8/43. Commd 23/11/78. Sqn Ldr 1/1/89. Retd ENG 31/3/93.
WATERS I.R. MRCS LRCP. Born 12/3/16. Commd 24/2/44. Flt Lt 24/2/44. Retd MED 14/9/48. rtg Sqn Ldr.
WATERS J. MHCIMA. Born 5/5/37. Commd 6/9/56. Wg Cdr 1/1/76. Retd ADMIN 6/5/77.
WATERS J.C. Born 31/10/33. Commd 14/12/54. Sqn Ldr 1/1/66. Retd GD 31/10/71.
WATERS J.D. CEng MRAeS. Born 13/8/42. Commd 7/5/65. Gp Capt 1/1/91. Retd ENG 14/9/96.
WATERS L. Born 25/8/35. Commd 19/6/70. Flt Lt 19/6/72. Retd SUP 19/6/78.
WATERS R.C.J. Born 5/7/20. Commd 29/8/38. Flt Lt 1/1/52. Retd SEC 26/8/67.
WATERS R.D. Born 24/6/57. Commd 31/7/81. Flt Lt 11/12/86. Retd GD 9/2/97.
WATERS R.S. MBE. Born 23/9/44. Commd 7/1/75. Wg Cdr 1/7/92. Retd GD(G) 31/3/94.

WATERSON M.R.G. Born 19/11/40. Commd 26/10/62. Flt Lt 26/4/68. Retd GD 19/11/78.
WATERWORTH A. Born 11/6/43. Commd 27/5/71. Flt Lt 27/5/73. Retd GD 6/12/74. Re-employed 14/11/76.
Flt Lt 25/4/75. Retd ADMIN 4/11/84.
WATKIN E.W. Born 9/8/33. Commd 13/2/52. Flt Lt 12/6/57. Retd GD(G) 9/8/93.
WATKIN G. Born 17/4/49. Commd 2/2/70. Wg Cdr 1/7/94. Retd OPS SPT 31/1/98.
WATKIN J.S. BEng CEng MRAeS. Born 30/11/70. Commd 17/9/89. Flt Lt 15/1/96. Retd ENG 17/9/01.
WATKIN-JONES H. DFC. Born 8/3/23. Commd 1/1/49. Sqn Ldr 1/1/59. Retd GD 8/3/66.
WATKINS A.R. BA MCMI. Born 3/4/37. Commd 19/2/56. Wg Cdr 1/1/77. Retd GD 1/9/87.
WATKINS D.G. BA MIMIS MCT MRIN CertEd. Born 30/4/30. Commd 2/7/52. Flt Lt 27/11/57. Retd GD 9/12/75.
WATKINS M. Born 16/9/41. Commd 24/11/67. Sqn Ldr 1/7/87. Retd GD 8/12/95.
WATKINS M.J. Born 17/5/45. Commd 10/5/71. Wg Cdr 1/1/92. Retd ADMIN 19/6/93.
WATKINS M.W. Born 21/6/46. Commd 4/12/64. Flt Lt 4/11/70. Retd GD 28/2/85.
WATKINS T. Born 10/1/18. Commd 24/4/42. Flt Lt 18/9/49. Retd GD(G) 10/1/68.
WATKINS T.C.S. BEng. Born 21/1/74. Commd 29/7/98. Flt Lt 13/5/99. Retd ENGINEER 17/3/03.
WATKINS W.M. OBE. Born 3/11/37. Commd 11/9/61. Gp Capt 1/7/92. Retd GD 3/11/92.
WATLING P.R. BSc. Born 3/9/54. Commd 2/9/73. Sqn Ldr 1/1/88. Retd GD 3/9/92.
WATRET W. Born 14/8/22. Commd 15/9/60. Sqn Ldr 1/1/73. Retd ENG 14/8/77.
WATSON A. BSc. Born 1/2/36. Commd 20/2/59. Flt Lt 20/11/62. Retd ENG 20/2/75.
WATSON A.H. Born 28/10/22. Commd 23/11/44. Sqn Ldr 1/1/71. Retd GD(G) 31/3/77.
WATSON A.L. BA MBCS. Born 9/5/34. Commd 13/12/55. Wg Cdr 1/7/72. Retd SUP 9/5/89.
WATSON A.M. BSc. Born 20/10/43. Commd 30/8/66. Wg Cdr 1/7/90. Retd GD 20/10/98.
WATSON A.V. Born 16/4/42. Commd 19/3/65. Flt Lt 19/9/68. Retd GD 16/4/80.
WATSON B.R. Born 26/9/44. Commd 5/1/70. Wg Cdr 1/7/91. Retd ADMIN 25/8/96.
WATSON B.W. Born 13/3/30. Commd 16/12/51. Flt Lt 27/3/57. Retd GD(G) 13/3/88.
WATSON C.C. Born 9/8/42. Commd 9/12/76. Sqn Ldr 1/1/82. Retd ADMIN 10/7/85.
WATSON C.J. MBE CEng MIEE MRAeS. Born 11/7/38. Commd 30/7/59. Gp Capt 1/7/89. Retd ENG 11/7/93.
WATSON C.W.D. Born 7/3/45. Commd 26/5/67. Flt Lt 18/2/70. Retd GD 1/5/84.
WATSON D. CEng MIEE MRAeS. Born 8/5/40. Commd 19/12/63. Gp Capt 1/7/91. Retd ENG 8/5/95.
WATSON D. Born 5/2/44. Commd 5/7/73. Sqn Ldr 1/7/90. Retd ENG 6/1/96.
WATSON D.A. Born 10/3/30. Commd 12/3/52. Sqn Ldr 1/1/69. Retd GD 10/9/91.
WATSON D.F.D. BA. Born 23/12/46. Commd 1/10/65. Flt Lt 1/4/71. Retd GD 31/12/86.
WATSON D.Q. DFC MCMI. Born 1/6/15. Commd 1/5/42. Wg Cdr 1/7/59. Retd SEC 15/6/70.
WATSON D.R.McK. MBE MCMI. Born 28/4/33. Commd 13/8/52. Gp Capt 1/1/79. Retd GD 28/4/88.
WATSON E.E. Born 11/2/22. Commd 24/4/44. Sqn Ldr 1/10/57. Retd ADMIN 11/2/82.
WATSON F. Born 14/11/29. Commd 11/3/65. Flt Lt 11/3/68. Retd GD 31/7/76.
WATSON F.C. Born 25/1/19. Commd 15/4/43. Sqn Ldr 1/4/56. Retd ENG 2/12/67.
WATSON G. BSc CEng MRAes. Born 30/10/26. Commd 17/3/49. A Cdre 1/7/74. Retd ENG 8/4/78.
WATSON G. Born 26/4/34. Commd 10/12/57. Sqn Ldr 1/1/69. Retd GD 13/7/87.
WATSON G.C. AIPM. Born 24/6/47. Commd 2/8/73. Flt Lt 22/11/79. Retd ADMIN 16/4/89.
WATSON G.M. BSc. Born 23/2/55. Commd 30/10/77. Flt Lt 30/7/79. Retd GD 30/11/89.
WATSON G.M. BSc CEng MIMechE. Born 24/11/49. Commd 16/5/72. Gp Capt 1/1/99. Retd GD 9/6/03.
WATSON G.V. MRAeS. Born 12/11/18. Commd 15/4/43. Sqn Ldr 1/1/62. Retd ENG 23/1/71.
WATSON H.E.E. Born 15/7/30. Commd 24/9/52. Flt Lt 21/2/58. Retd GD 30/9/77.
WATSON J. Born 10/3/49. Commd 21/3/69. Sqn Ldr 1/1/89. Retd SUP 10/3/93.
WATSON J. Born 5/8/47. Commd 10/12/65. Flt Lt 10/6/71. Retd GD 13/9/75.
WATSON J. AFC. Born 26/8/39. Commd 14/11/59. Sqn Ldr 1/7/72. Retd GD 12/10/79.
WATSON J.A. Born 4/4/25. Commd 24/5/51. Sqn Ldr 1/1/68. Retd GD 1/7/73.
WATSON J.A. Born 10/5/34. Commd 4/7/69. Flt Lt 4/7/75. Retd GD(G) 15/11/84.
WATSON K. Born 24/6/56. Commd 9/12/76. Fg Offr 1/5/78. Retd ADMIN 30/6/82.
WATSON K.I. Born 8/4/32. Commd 2/8/51. Wg Cdr 1/1/73. Retd GD 18/11/86.
WATSON K.J. BSc. Born 29/8/60. Commd 28/2/82. Wg Cdr 1/7/00. Retd GD 1/7/02.
WATSON K.R. FIMLS. Born 7/2/39. Commd 8/1/76. Sqn Ldr 25/8/86. Retd MED(T) 1/7/90.
WATSON K.T. DFC. Born 13/8/15. Commd 21/2/42. Sqn Ldr 1/8/47. Retd GD 30/11/51.
WATSON L. Born 16/11/21. Commd 27/4/61. Flt Lt 27/4/66. Retd ENG 16/11/71.
WATSON M. Born 26/6/33. Commd 7/8/59. Flt Lt 7/8/63. Retd PE 7/8/75.
WATSON M.J. BSc(Eng). Born 9/8/45. Commd 20/1/80. Flt Lt 20/7/76. Retd ADMIN 20/1/96.
WATSON M.W.B. MRCS LRCP DObstRCOG. Born 19/4/27. Commd 3/7/52. Wg Cdr 13/5/64. Retd MED 3/7/68.
WATSON N.M. Born 28/2/47. Commd 7/7/67. Sqn Ldr 1/7/93. Retd GD 28/10/02.
WATSON P.A. Born 5/11/38. Commd 25/8/60. Flt Lt 25/2/67. Retd GD 5/11/76.
WATSON P.H. MA. Born 7/6/34. Commd 1/9/70. Flt Lt 1/9/70. Retd GD(G) 14/2/79.
WATSON P.K. BA MRAeS. Born 29/9/27. Commd 24/5/49. Sqn Ldr 1/1/62. Retd ENG 29/9/65.
WATSON P.L. FCMI DPhysEd. Born 11/2/46. Commd 16/8/70. Gp Capt 1/1/98. Retd ADMIN 11/2/01.
WATSON P.M. BSc. Born 25/7/62. Commd 4/9/80. Flt Lt 14/10/84. Retd GD 15/7/95.
WATSON P.R. Born 14/2/41. Commd 22/5/75. Wg Cdr 1/7/90. Retd ADMIN 14/2/96.
WATSON R.L. Born 7/2/33. Commd 27/9/51. Wg Cdr 1/7/70. Retd GD 1/2/78.
WATSON S. Born 26/8/34. Commd 27/5/53. Flt Lt 17/9/58. Retd GD 26/8/71.

WATSON S.W. IEng MIIE. Born 19/11/46. Commd 15/3/84. Sqn Ldr 1/7/97. Retd ENG 31/1/98.
WATSON T.H. BA. Born 7/6/35. Commd 23/10/56. Gp Capt 1/7/80. Retd GD 8/4/87.
WATSON T.J. Born 11/12/51. Commd 16/3/73. Sqn Ldr 1/1/84. Retd SUP 11/12/89.
WATSON T.M. Born 15/12/36. Commd 6/5/65. Sqn Ldr 1/1/75. Retd ADMIN 19/11/77.
WATSON W. Born 7/7/21. Commd 5/3/46. Flt Lt 5/3/52. Retd SEC 6/3/76.
WATT A.W. Born 6/9/51. Commd 9/11/89. Sqn Ldr 1/1/02. Retd ADMIN (SEC) 1/6/04.
WATT B.A. Born 31/5/50. Commd 28/2/71. Wg Cdr 1/7/87. Retd SUP 1/7/90.
WATT B.M.W. BSc. Born 28/7/42. Commd 10/9/63. Flt Lt 10/9/69. Retd SEC 14/9/73.
WATT D.R. Born 3/11/22. Commd 3/7/42. Wg Cdr 1/7/70. Retd ENG 1/12/77.
WATT F. BSc. Born 1/1/44. Commd 20/10/66. Flt Lt 5/4/71. Retd GD 30/10/75.
WATT H.J. MA. Born 20/1/59. Commd 9/11/80. Flt Lt 9/2/81. Retd GD 20/1/97.
WATT J. Born 6/10/23. Commd 9/5/44. Flt Lt 10/11/55. Retd GD 29/3/69.
WATT J. MBE. Born 10/6/27. Commd 3/11/60. Sqn Ldr 1/1/74. Retd ENG 2/10/79.
WATT J.A. Born 15/12/33. Commd 8/10/52. Flt Lt 6/3/58. Retd GD 6/11/64.
WATT J.D. Born 23/3/51. Commd 18/4/74. Sqn Ldr 1/7/87. Retd ENG 14/3/96.
WATT J.G. Born 8/10/45. Commd 19/8/66. Flt Lt 4/5/72. Retd GD 8/10/83.
WATT J.J. Born 19/2/33. Commd 27/2/52. Flt Lt 26/6/57. Retd GD 19/2/71.
WATT M.A. RMN. Born 23/4/57. Commd 17/7/87. Flt Lt 8/9/92. Retd MED(SEC) 14/3/96.
WATT T.B. Born 30/9/20. Commd 27/5/44. Flt Lt 27/5/46. Retd PI 30/9/75.
WATTAM D.M. BSc. Born 3/4/64. Commd 8/1/96. Flt Lt 14/3/88. Retd FLY(P) 21/4/03.
WATTERS P.T. MB BCh BAO FFARCS DA. Born 19/8/30. Commd 13/4/58. Wg Cdr 13/10/68. Retd MED 15/4/75.
WATTERS T.W. Born 24/4/33. Commd 20/3/52. Wg Cdr 1/7/77. Retd SUP 24/4/86.
WATTERSON M.E. Born 28/10/42. Commd 26/5/67. Fg Offr 26/5/67. Retd ENG 9/8/69.
WATTON P.J.L. MBE CEng MRAeS. Born 14/6/35. Commd 2/11/56. Sqn Ldr 1/1/68. Retd ENG 23/4/86.
WATTON R.J. MILT. Born 11/10/53. Commd 21/1/80. Sqn Ldr 1/7/91. Retd SUPPLY 31/3/03.
WATTS A.F. Born 9/9/35. Commd 22/7/71. Flt Lt 22/7/73. Retd GD(G) 22/7/79.
WATTS A.R.M. OBE BA. Born 7/9/16. Commd 3/2/47. Wg Cdr 1/1/59. Retd EDN 8/9/66.
WATTS D.A. Born 3/4/59. Commd 19/6/86. Flt Lt 19/6/88. Retd ENG 1/2/94.
WATTS D.A. Born 26/10/31. Commd 4/11/53. Flt Lt 9/5/57. Retd GD 16/2/73.
WATTS E.J. MBE. Born 8/4/09. Commd 24/10/40. Wg Cdr 1/1/53. Retd ENG 27/5/64.
WATTS F.H.A. DFC. Born 26/2/20. Commd 13/12/43. Flt Lt 18/12/47. Retd GD 14/7/64.
WATTS H.D. Born 22/1/56. Commd 22/5/75. Sqn Ldr 1/7/86. Retd ADMIN 7/6/91.
WATTS J.A. BA. Born 19/5/55. Commd 16/9/73. Flt Lt 15/10/77. Retd GD 15/7/88.
WATTS J.M. Born 11/10/23. Commd 28/5/52. Flt Lt 10/2/55. Retd ADMIN 20/2/82.
WATTS J.R. Born 28/7/32. Commd 15/12/53. Wg Cdr 1/7/73. Retd ADMIN 28/5/84.
WATTS J.W. Born 29/9/33. Commd 2/2/68. Flt Lt 8/3/72. Retd GD 30/3/78.
WATTS M.E.T. Born 13/12/13. Commd 21/5/47. Flt Lt 21/11/51. Retd SUP 31/12/62.
WATTS M.H.F. Born 23/12/47. Commd 24/4/70. Flt Lt 23/1/74. Retd GD 22/10/94.
WATTS M.J. Born 7/12/32. Commd 23/12/52. Sqn Ldr 1/1/69. Retd GD 1/1/72.
WATTS M.W. BSc MCMI. Born 26/5/35. Commd 27/8/58. Sqn Ldr 1/7/66. Retd ENG 13/12/88.
WATTS R.F. BA. Born 13/9/14. Commd 4/6/38. Gp Capt 1/7/57. Retd GD 4/10/64.
WATTS R.J. Born 7/8/47. Commd 2/8/68. Flt Lt 2/8/71. Retd GD 24/9/86.
WATTS T.R. Born 17/4/52. Commd 22/7/71. Sqn Ldr 1/7/83. Retd GD 17/4/89.
WATTS-PHILLIPS J.E. OBE BSc MRAeS. Born 11/8/34. Commd 1/10/57. Wg Cdr 1/1/79. Retd GD 17/2/82.
WAUCHOPE F.A. Born 22/2/59. Commd 3/7/80. Fg Offr 3/1/83. Retd SY 23/4/83.
WAUGH P. Born 25/11/66. Commd 25/2/88. Flt Lt 25/8/93. Retd FLY(P) 1/2/05.
WAUGH W.J. Born 9/3/17. Commd 1/5/39. Flt Lt 1/9/45. Retd SUP 9/3/66. rtg Sqn Ldr.
WAY D.H. LHA MCMI. Born 27/5/35. Commd 19/1/66. Wg Cdr 1/1/83. Retd MED(SEC) 28/12/85.
WAY P.D. Born 31/3/59. Commd 23/3/81. Sqn Ldr 1/7/91. Retd ADMIN 31/3/97.
WEARDEN S.F. BEng. Born 27/5/56. Commd 8/4/79. Sqn Ldr 1/1/92. Retd ENG 8/4/95.
WEARING S.H. Born 25/1/56. Commd 9/10/75. Flt Lt 9/4/81. Retd GD 21/7/88.
WEATHERALL K. Born 28/3/27. Commd 25/6/66. Flt Lt 25/6/69. Retd ENG 18/8/78.
WEATHERHEAD E.P. Born 27/12/39. Commd 24/6/76. Sqn Ldr 1/1/89. Retd ADMIN 1/1/90.
WEATHERILL P.G. BEM. Born 9/9/48. Commd 2/11/88. Flt Lt 2/11/92. Retd ADMIN 14/3/97.
WEATHERILT P.F. Born 7/7/36. Commd 24/7/57. Sqn Ldr 1/1/66. Retd ENG 7/7/74.
WEATHERLY B.D. Born 8/10/32. Commd 31/5/51. Wg Cdr 1/1/77. Retd GD 8/10/82.
WEATHERSTON S.A. Born 15/3/54. Commd 11/7/74. Sqn Ldr 1/1/85. Retd GD 15/3/92.
WEAVER A. Born 17/7/40. Commd 18/12/62. Sqn Ldr 1/7/79. Retd ADMIN 1/6/87.
WEAVER A.V. Born 7/4/42. Commd 9/3/62. Flt Lt 9/9/67. Retd GD 7/4/80.
WEAVER B.J. OBE. Born 12/5/35. Commd 7/5/64. Wg Cdr 1/1/78. Retd ENG 12/5/89.
WEAVER G.T. MBE. Born 24/3/39. Commd 27/3/70. Flt Lt 27/3/72. Retd ENG 1/10/92.
WEAVER I.W. Born 31/1/60. Commd 8/9/83. Flt Lt 8/3/85. Retd GD 4/12/97.
WEAVER P.A. BSc CEng MCMI MRAeS MMS. Born 12/10/52. Commd 13/9/70. Sqn Ldr 1/1/82. Retd ENG 12/10/90.
WEAVER-SMITH M. MSc CDip AF AIPD. Born 27/11/31. Commd 9/3/56. Sqn Ldr 17/2/63. Retd ADMIN 27/11/86.
WEAVILL A.D. BEd. Born 19/4/54. Commd 30/10/77. Sqn Ldr 1/1/87. Retd SY 30/10/93.
WEBB A. Born 23/1/16. Commd 18/4/45. Fg Offr 28/7/48. Retd SEC 8/5/52.

WEBB A.C. Born 4/6/40. Commd 13/10/61. Flt Lt 1/4/66. Retd GD 1/5/76.
WEBB A.E.P. AFC. Born 14/3/43. Commd 9/2/62. Wg Cdr 1/7/86. Retd GD 2/4/93.
WEBB B. Born 16/8/31. Commd 28/2/57. Sqn Ldr 1/7/67. Retd GD 1/7/70.
WEBB B.P. Born 26/3/46. Commd 11/10/84. Flt Lt 11/10/88. Retd OPS SPT 26/3/01.
WEBB C. MBA BSc CEng MIMechE MRAeS. Born 17/3/61. Commd 22/3/84. Wg Cdr 1/7/01. Retd ENG 1/8/02.
WEBB D. Born 22/12/46. Commd 1/3/68. Sqn Ldr 1/1/83. Retd GD 22/4/94.
WEBB D. Born 16/4/47. Commd 21/1/66. Flt Lt 4/5/72. Retd GD 1/10/86.
WEBB D.B. DFC. Born 30/5/20. Commd 17/11/42. Sqn Ldr 1/7/53. Retd GD 30/5/63.
WEBB D.F. Born 14/6/31. Commd 5/9/55. Flt Lt 7/3/62. Retd GD 5/9/69.
WEBB D.F. Born 26/8/16. Commd 18/11/54. Flt Lt 18/11/57. Retd CAT 30/4/69.
WEBB D.G. DFM. Born 14/12/23. Commd 30/5/44. Wg Cdr 1/1/66. Retd SEC 20/6/78.
WEBB D.J. Born 22/9/46. Commd 28/2/69. Flt Lt 23/5/73. Retd ENG 8/4/74.
WEBB D.J. Born 18/8/41. Commd 21/10/65. Flt Lt 8/4/72. Retd SUP 12/1/81.
WEBB E.A.H. DMS FISM MInstAM MCIPD MCMI. Born 18/4/43. Commd 23/7/80. Sqn Ldr 1/7/88. Retd ADMIN 18/4/98.
WEBB E.J. Born 23/8/22. Commd 3/7/44. Sqn Ldr 1/1/55. Retd GD 23/8/65.
WEBB G.S.R. Born 13/12/25. Commd 2/7/52. Sqn Ldr 1/7/71. Retd GD 31/10/75.
WEBB H. Born 30/12/20. Commd 18/5/61. Flt Lt 18/5/64. Retd PRT 30/12/67.
WEBB J. Born 23/11/51. Commd 20/9/71. Sqn Ldr 1/1/88. Retd GD 14/4/91.
WEBB J.A.L. DFC. Born 25/3/20. Commd 15/5/44. Flt Lt 19/2/48. Retd SEC 23/5/75.
WEBB J.F. MCMI. Born 10/2/29. Commd 3/8/50. Wg Cdr 1/7/76. Retd SEC 3/7/79.
WEBB J.G. CEng MRAeS MCMI. Born 17/11/18. Commd 26/5/44. Wg Cdr 1/1/65. Retd ENG 17/11/73.
WEBB J.J. Born 10/4/37. Commd 21/6/60. Flt Lt 21/8/63. Retd GD 2/2/68.
WEBB M.F.D. Born 24/3/46. Commd 22/5/64. Sqn Ldr 1/1/84. Retd GD 24/3/90.
WEBB M.J. Born 15/9/33. Commd 2/7/52. Sqn Ldr 1/7/69. Retd GD 27/5/77.
WEBB M.J. Born 21/10/49. Commd 2/5/71. Wg Cdr 1/1/91. Retd ADMIN 14/3/97.
WEBB P.C. CBE DFC. Born 10/3/18. Commd 1/9/45. Gp Capt 1/7/63. Retd GD 18/3/73. rtg A Cdre.
WEBB P.M.G. Born 13/11/40. Commd 21/7/65. Flt Lt 19/3/68. Retd SY(PRT) 13/11/78.
WEBB P.R. Born 31/12/44. Commd 7/5/64. Sqn Ldr 1/1/78. Retd GD(G) 31/12/88.
WEBB P.R.A. MCMI. Born 11/11/34. Commd 24/9/52. Wg Cdr 1/7/80. Retd GD 1/9/86.
WEBB R.B. Born 27/3/57. Commd 15/3/79. Sqn Ldr 1/1/89. Retd GD 27/3/95.
WEBB R.J. Born 13/4/33. Commd 11/10/51. Flt Lt 25/1/57. Retd GD 13/4/71.
WEBB R.K. Born 28/6/39. Commd 3/6/58. Flt Lt 5/12/63. Retd GD 1/10/85.
WEBB R.T. BM MRCGP DRCOG DAvMed. Born 15/11/54. Commd 1/8/79. Wg Cdr 1/8/92. Retd MED 1/8/95.
WEBB T.M. AFC MRAeS. Born 22/4/42. Commd 24/2/61. Gp Capt 1/7/87. Retd GD 30/6/73.
WEBB W.E. MCMI. Born 17/11/29. Commd 24/1/63. Sqn Ldr 1/7/74. Retd ENG 17/11/89.
WEBBER M.J. AFC BSc. Born 16/4/39. Commd 21/9/60. Wg Cdr 1/1/74. Retd GD 2/10/77.
WEBLEY D.L. BTech. Born 18/10/42. Commd 30/8/66. Sqn Ldr 1/7/77. Retd GD 18/10/02.
WEBLEY E.J. Born 20/9/38. Commd 6/11/67. Sqn Ldr 1/7/80. Retd SUP 20/9/93.
WEBLEY S.K. Born 3/12/55. Commd 12/10/78. Flt Lt 12/4/84. Retd GD 12/6/94.
WEBSTER A. Born 28/7/30. Commd 25/9/52. Flt Lt 26/3/56. Retd GD 28/7/68.
WEBSTER A.J. Born 17/9/20. Commd 16/9/44. Wg Cdr 1/7/60. Retd GD(G) 17/9/75.
WEBSTER A.J.E. Born 22/9/66. Commd 31/7/92. Sqn Ldr 1/7/99. Retd OPS SPT(ATC) 22/9/04.
WEBSTER A.K. Born 6/11/42. Commd 28/7/64. Flt Lt 10/2/67. Retd GD 6/11/80.
WEBSTER A.M. Born 2/10/22. Commd 29/3/62. Flt Lt 29/3/65. Retd GD 30/6/73.
WEBSTER C.J. Born 6/6/44. Commd 18/9/63. Sqn Ldr 1/1/74. Retd GD(G) 6/6/82.
WEBSTER C.M.F. Born 6/11/29. Commd 20/10/49. Flt Lt 20/4/53. Retd GD 6/11/89.
WEBSTER C.S. Born 3/5/65. Commd 22/9/88. Flt Lt 22/3/95. Retd SUP 14/3/97.
WEBSTER D.J. Born 8/4/24. Commd 19/10/49. Flt Lt 19/10/55. Retd SEC 16/6/63.
WEBSTER D.S. MBE. Born 29/2/56. Commd 27/1/77. Flt Lt 2/7/83. Retd OPS SPT 31/1/00.
WEBSTER E.E. Born 15/3/51. Commd 1/4/76. Wg Cdr 1/7/00. Retd OPS SPT 18/5/02.
WEBSTER J.J. AFC. Born 14/10/20. Commd 16/9/42. Sqn Ldr 1/7/66. Retd GD 10/5/68.
WEBSTER M. Born 15/4/35. Commd 29/10/57. Flt Lt 29/4/63. Retd GD 15/4/73. rtg Sqn Ldr.
WEBSTER M. MBE. Born 12/7/27. Commd 23/2/51. Sqn Ldr 1/7/75. Retd GD 12/7/82.
WEBSTER P.E. MBE . Born 24/10/65. Commd 23/5/85. Sqn Ldr 1/1/99. Retd FLY(N) 7/5/04.
WEBSTER R. MSc CEng MIEE. Born 24/12/32. Commd 22/5/62. Sqn Ldr 22/1/69. Retd ADMIN 21/10/85.
WEBSTER R.A. Born 6/10/42. Commd 2/1/75. Flt Lt 2/1/77. Retd GD(G) 2/1/83.
WEBSTER R.E. Born 25/6/29. Commd 14/12/49. Sqn Ldr 1/1/61. Retd GD 25/6/67.
WEBSTER R.E. MB BS MRCPath. Born 27/1/59. Commd 9/4/85. Sqn Ldr 27/11/88. Retd MED 14/3/96.
WEBSTER R.J. MBE. Born 30/9/56. Commd 14/1/88. Sqn Ldr 1/1/97. Retd OPS SPT 1/6/01.
WEBSTER R.K. MSc BDS. Born 3/10/44. Commd 8/9/63. Sqn Ldr 22/12/71. Retd DEL 21/9/79.
WEBSTER R.M. CEng MIEE MRAeS. Born 19/6/42. Commd 15/7/63. Wg Cdr 1/1/90. Retd ENG 27/9/94.
WEBSTER S.M.R. Born 24/11/30. Commd 19/11/52. Flt Lt 15/4/58. Retd GD 1/5/70.
WEDDERBURN A.C. MBE DPhysEd. Born 30/10/30. Commd 23/4/52. Sqn Ldr 1/1/70. Retd GD 30/10/90.
WEDDLE I. Born 21/3/38. Commd 15/12/59. Wg Cdr 1/1/86. Retd GD 4/5/92.
WEDGE R.E. CBE BSc FRAeS MInstD. Born 22/6/44. Commd 5/1/66. Gp Capt 1/7/91. Retd GD 1/2/00.

WEDGWOOD P.W. Born 6/1/21. Commd 23/5/63. Flt Lt 23/5/66. Retd SEC 1/8/68.
WEEDEN B.A. Born 25/3/34. Commd 14/12/54. Sqn Ldr 1/7/64. Retd GD 29/8/73.
WEEDEN J. CB LLB. Born 21/6/49. Commd 30/6/74. AVM 1/7/97. Retd LGL 1/10/02.
WEEDING D.E. CEng MIMechE MRAeS. Born 30/8/30. Commd 24/9/52. Sqn Ldr 1/1/63. Retd ENG 22/10/68.
WEEDON H.F. Born 31/7/27. Commd 3/6/65. Flt Lt 3/6/68. Retd GD 31/7/82.
WEEDON R.C. Born 26/8/29. Commd 8/11/51. Flt Lt 23/2/57. Retd GD 30/4/76.
WEEKES C.D. Born 14/2/28. Commd 11/4/51. Flt Lt 16/12/58. Retd GD(G) 14/2/66.
WEEKS D.T. Born 4/12/30. Commd 1/8/68. Flt Lt 1/8/74. Retd ENG 9/1/81.
WEEKS E.T. Born 23/3/32. Commd 28/6/51. Wg Cdr 1/1/78. Retd GD(G) 23/3/87.
WEEKS R.L. CEng MRAeS. Born 31/10/39. Commd 22/5/62. Sqn Ldr 1/7/73. Retd ENG 22/5/78.
WEEKS R.M.H. Born 4/4/64. Commd 27/3/86. Flt Lt 27/9/91. Retd GD 4/4/02.
WEEKS S.G. Born 28/12/61. Commd 15/6/83. Flt Lt 18/12/89. Retd GD(G) 14/3/96.
WEERASINGHE N.E. Born 3/1/31. Commd 22/5/62. Fg Offr 12/12/51. Retd GD 21/5/55.
WEETMAN A. Born 24/1/23. Commd 6/12/56. Flt Lt 6/12/62. Retd GD 28/3/70.
WEIGALL S.H.D. Born 7/3/28. Commd 5/4/50. Wg Cdr 1/1/67. Retd ADMIN 2/8/80.
WEIGHT C.D. Born 27/9/56. Commd 31/1/80. Flt Lt 2/8/84. Retd GD(G) 27/9/94.
WEIGHT P.E. Born 8/9/46. Commd 1/3/68. Sqn Ldr 1/1/82. Retd ENG 8/9/01.
WEIGHTMAN W.A. Born 1/10/25. Commd 12/7/56. Flt Lt 10/2/58. Retd RGT 13/5/70.
WEIL T.O. DFC. Born 25/3/17. Commd 25/9/42. Flt Lt 26/3/46. Retd GD(G) 25/3/64.
WEINDLING M.R. Born 14/1/48. Commd 21/3/69. Sqn Ldr 1/7/84. Retd ENG 14/1/92.
WEIR A.A. Born 2/10/30. Commd 25/10/53. Wg Cdr 1/1/78. Retd GD(G) 9/4/85.
WEIR A.A.McP. Born 24/4/40. Commd 9/3/62. Flt Lt 9/9/67. Retd GD 24/4/78.
WEIR C.F. Born 22/1/24. Commd 12/3/52. Flt Lt 10/7/56. Retd GD 18/9/67.
WEIR D.M. Born 1/4/33. Commd 10/9/52. Flt Lt 7/2/58. Retd GD 1/4/71.
WEIR I. Born 21/11/36. Commd 1/10/60. Sqn Ldr 1/7/88. Retd GD 1/8/89.
WEIR N.A. Born 4/4/59. Commd 24/11/85. Flt Lt 6/4/88. Retd GD 14/3/96.
WEIR R.S. AFC DPhysEd. Born 1/5/53. Commd 17/7/77. Flt Lt 17/1/83. Retd GD 17/7/93.
WEISS A.P.W. Born 24/9/37. Commd 16/11/59. Flt Lt 9/12/64. Retd GD 25/8/66.
WEISS R.M.J. Born 9/9/63. Commd 17/1/85. Flt Lt 17/7/90. Retd GD 18/12/92.
WELBERRY J. BEM. Born 26/12/46. Commd 16/6/88. Sqn Ldr 1/1/00. Retd ENG 1/1/03.
WELBURN M. Born 28/4/53. Commd 24/3/83. Wg Cdr 1/1/96. Retd ENG 3/6/02.
WELBY P.J. MCMI. Born 29/4/32. Commd 14/12/54. Wg Cdr 1/1/80. Retd SUP 9/2/85.
WELCH A.L. BSc CEng MRAeS. Born 5/5/43. Commd 9/10/67. Sqn Ldr 1/7/77. Retd ENG 9/11/86.
WELCH E.C.A. Born 23/8/32. Commd 26/7/51. Flt Lt 14/11/56. Retd GD 23/8/70.
WELCH F.I. AFC. Born 23/2/34. Commd 23/4/52. Sqn Ldr 1/1/64. Retd GD 26/2/94.
WELCH J. DFC. Born 13/9/19. Commd 3/7/41. Sqn Ldr 1/1/51. Retd GD 26/12/58. rtg Wg Cdr.
WELCH J. Born 17/1/32. Commd 7/5/52. Flt Lt 14/5/58. Retd GD 17/1/70.
WELCH W.H. Born 15/1/44. Commd 30/8/84. Flt Lt 30/8/88. Retd SY 1/10/91.
WELCOMME R.G. CEng MRAeS. Born 18/2/22. Commd 17/2/44. Wg Cdr 1/7/65. Retd ENG 18/2/77.
WELDING T.E. MBE. Born 31/10/16. Commd 1/7/43. Sqn Ldr 1/7/56. Retd ENG 31/10/73.
WELFORD F.L. DFC. Born 23/5/21. Commd 13/9/46. Sqn Ldr 1/1/57. Retd GD 23/5/64.
WELFORD L. Born 26/7/34. Commd 16/6/51. Sqn Ldr 1/1/70. Retd GD 30/9/78.
WELHAM J.B. CEng MIMechE MCMI. Born 9/4/48. Commd 28/2/69. Sqn Ldr 1/7/79. Retd ENG 9/4/86.
WELLEN W.M.J. MBE. Born 29/9/26. Commd 17/10/57. Flt Lt 1/4/63. Retd GD 30/9/75.
WELLER A.G. AFC. Born 19/4/25. Commd 21/1/45. Sqn Ldr 1/7/58. Retd GD 19/4/63.
WELLER B.I. MSc BDS MGDSRCS(Ed) LDSRCS(Eng). Born 22/11/56. Commd 23/11/80. Wg Cdr 12/2/93. Retd DEL 23/11/96.
WELLER J.B. Born 19/12/43. Commd 6/4/62. Flt Lt 6/10/67. Retd GD 31/3/94.
WELLER M.G. MBE BEM. Born 31/3/31. Commd 24/1/63. Flt Lt 24/1/69. Retd ENG 19/10/69.
WELLER P.F. Born 19/10/09. Commd 10/7/41. Wg Cdr 1/11/55. Retd ENG 8/12/59.
WELLER P.L. MA BA. Born 5/11/41. Commd 27/3/80. Sqn Ldr 1/1/87. Retd ADMIN 1/1/90.
WELLER V.A. BA BSc PGCE. Born 12/1/55. Commd 14/8/77. Sqn Ldr 1/1/88. Retd ADMIN 14/3/97.
WELLERD J.A. Born 14/11/33. Commd 3/9/52. Sqn Ldr 1/1/71. Retd GD 4/5/79.
WELLICOME B.W. Born 28/12/26. Commd 25/10/46. Sqn Ldr 1/7/61. Retd GD 13/4/68.
WELLINGHAM J.B. MA CEng FRAeS FCMI. Born 21/6/25. Commd 14/2/46. A Cdre 1/1/72. Retd ENG 31/3/78.
WELLINGS I.B. Born 18/6/44. Commd 22/5/64. Wg Cdr 1/7/90. Retd GD 19/4/96.
WELLINGS N.D. Born 5/3/66. Commd 19/11/87. Flt Lt 19/5/94. Retd SUP 26/3/01.
WELLINGTON R.T. Born 21/2/35. Commd 24/11/65. Flt Lt 24/11/65. Retd GD 18/5/76.
WELLS A.S. Born 9/9/55. Commd 11/7/79. Flt Lt 11/7/84. Retd GD 5/11/88.
WELLS D. Born 28/7/36. Commd 17/1/69. Sqn Ldr 29/1/80. Retd MED(SEC) 28/2/85.
WELLS E.P. DSO DFC*. Born 26/7/16. Commd 1/9/45. Gp Capt 1/1/59. Retd GD 15/6/60.
WELLS F. Born 27/4/34. Commd 1/2/62. Flt Lt 1/4/66. Retd GD 27/4/72.
WELLS G. Born 15/2/34. Commd 11/6/60. Sqn Ldr 1/7/85. Retd GD 14/8/86.
WELLS G.C.D. MA CEng MRAeS. Born 26/2/38. Commd 30/9/56. Sqn Ldr 1/1/68. Retd ENG 26/2/76.
WELLS J. MCIPS. Born 26/4/42. Commd 2/1/70. Wg Cdr 1/7/87. Retd SUP 1/9/97.
WELLS J.C.A. SRN RMN RNT. Born 12/2/38. Commd 9/10/67. Flt Lt 9/10/73. Retd MED(T) 29/9/75.

WELLS J.T. MCMI. Born 1/12/33. Commd 16/4/54. Sqn Ldr 1/7/79. Retd ADMIN 1/12/88.
WELLS J.W. BSc. Born 11/12/62. Commd 2/9/84. Flt Lt 2/9/89. Retd ENG 11/12/00.
WELLS K.J. DFC. Born 26/11/24. Commd 27/5/44. Wg Cdr 1/1/65. Retd GD 8/2/77.
WELLS M.P. Born 20/10/30. Commd 21/3/51. Sqn Ldr 1/7/61. Retd GD 20/10/68.
WELLS O.J. Born 10/3/22. Commd 22/10/41. Wg Cdr 1/1/56. Retd GD 28/4/56.
WELLS P.J. Born 31/5/25. Commd 16/2/45. Gp Capt 1/7/72. Retd GD 1/10/77.
WELLS R. Born 18/11/32. Commd 6/2/52. Flt Lt 14/8/57. Retd GD 1/7/76. rtg Sqn Ldr.
WELLS R.J. Born 14/9/35. Commd 3/3/54. Sqn Ldr 1/1/67. Retd GD 17/6/77.
WELLS R.W. BA. Born 8/12/61. Commd 19/8/90. Flt Lt 19/2/94. Retd ADMIN 14/3/96.
WELLS W.J.E. BA. Born 25/3/49. Commd 22/7/84. Flt Lt 24/4/86. Retd ADMIN 25/4/93.
WELLS W.J.G. Born 17/6/33. Commd 27/8/62. Sqn Ldr 1/7/84. Retd GD 6/12/85.
WELLSPRING P.J.C. BSc. Born 19/9/39. Commd 28/11/66. Flt Lt 28/8/70. Retd GD(G) 28/11/82.
WELLUM G.H.A. DFC. Born 4/8/21. Commd 23/10/39. Flt Lt 1/9/45. Retd GD 30/6/61. rtg Sqn Ldr.
WELPLY P.M.C. Born 3/5/34. Commd 25/3/54. Wg Cdr 1/1/81. Retd ADMIN 30/10/84.
WELSH J. Born 13/10/36. Commd 5/2/57. Flt Lt 15/8/62. Retd GD 13/10/74.
WELSH M. BSc. Born 8/12/65. Commd 1/4/86. Flt Lt 15/1/89. Retd GD 15/7/99.
WELSH S.A. Born 19/2/42. Commd 11/8/67. Flt Lt 11/2/74. Retd GD(G) 1/5/83.
WELSTEAD E.H. Born 30/8/41. Commd 11/5/62. Fg Offr 11/5/64. Retd GD 28/1/72.
WELTON A.J. Born 18/2/42. Commd 23/9/66. Sqn Ldr 11/7/86. Retd SUP 18/2/97.
WELTON R.L. SRN RCNT RNT. Born 18/6/21. Commd 17/7/70. Flt Lt 17/7/76. Retd MED(T) 31/7/76.
WELVAERT A.L.S. AFM. Born 27/7/17. Commd 27/3/52. Flt Lt 27/9/55. Retd GD(G) 27/2/65.
WENHAM P.L. BSc. Born 16/5/59. Commd 11/9/77. Flt Lt 15/4/82. Retd GD 16/5/97.
WENHAM W.T. Born 30/8/26. Commd 28/6/60. Flt Lt 28/7/65. Retd ENG 1/9/77.
WENSLEY C.C. Born 5/12/46. Commd 9/12/71. Sqn Ldr 1/1/99. Retd GD 2/7/02.
WENSLEY E. Born 16/6/36. Commd 28/5/66. Wg Cdr 1/7/83. Retd SY(PRT) 9/1/89.
WENSLEY G. Born 2/8/42. Commd 4/10/63. Wg Cdr 1/1/84. Retd GD 2/8/97.
WERB D.G. Born 19/4/42. Commd 27/7/64. Wg Cdr 1/1/85. Retd GD 18/4/94.
WERE J.M. Born 4/2/29. Commd 5/9/69. Flt Lt 5/9/73. Retd SUP 5/9/74.
WESKETT B.W. MCMI. Born 8/7/31. Commd 14/4/53. Sqn Ldr 1/1/65. Retd GD(G) 8/7/69. Re-employed 19/2/71 to 6/11/71.
WESLEY C.J. Born 15/11/48. Commd 22/12/67. Sqn Ldr 1/1/96. Retd GD 1/7/00.
WESLEY D.M. OBE FInstPet. Born 29/9/46. Commd 24/2/67. Gp Capt 1/7/93. Retd SUP 29/9/01.
WESSON P.G. BA. Born 8/5/57. Commd 22/3/81. Flt Lt 22/6/81. Retd GD 22/3/97.
WEST A.E. Born 31/7/28. Commd 18/9/47. Flt Lt 9/6/54. Retd RGT 31/7/66.
WEST A.G. Born 25/7/15. Commd 10/1/42. Wg Cdr 1/1/62. Retd SUP 1/8/70.
WEST A.M. BSc. Born 19/4/49. Commd 15/9/69. Sqn Ldr 1/7/82. Retd ADMIN 12/7/87.
WEST B.L. MCMI. Born 13/2/35. Commd 17/3/55. Flt Lt 17/3/61. Retd SEC 13/2/73.
WEST C.D.P. Born 26/10/44. Commd 11/9/64. Flt Lt 15/4/70. Retd GD 28/8/75.
WEST D.R. DFC. Born 1/1/21. Commd 27/3/39. Flt Lt 1/9/45. Retd GD 1/12/61. rtg Sqn Ldr.
WEST D.R. OBE CEng MRAeS MIEE. Born 20/5/35. Commd 30/7/59. Gp Capt 1/1/85. Retd ENG 1/1/87.
WEST D.R. MA CEng MRAeS. Born 3/5/38. Commd 6/8/80. Sqn Ldr 23/9/75. Retd ENG 1/6/92.
WEST F.P. Born 9/2/30. Commd 30/7/52. Sqn Ldr 1/7/75. Retd SUP 3/1/89.
WEST F.P. Born 1/7/23. Commd 7/2/45. Flt Offr 29/11/51. Retd SUP 1/10/55.
WEST F.T. FCMI. Born 4/12/32. Commd 13/9/51. Wg Cdr 1/1/74. Retd GD 2/4/86.
WEST G.T. Born 12/12/38. Commd 28/11/60. Sqn Ldr 1/1/73. Retd GD 12/12/76.
WEST H.J. DSO DFC. Born 17/4/23. Commd 27/2/44. Sqn Ldr 1/1/58. Retd GD 17/4/72.
WEST H.R.A. Born 19/7/21. Commd 21/4/44. Sqn Ldr 1/1/67. Retd GD(G) 1/7/69.
WEST I.J. Born 31/7/58. Commd 17/7/87. Sqn Ldr 1/1/95. Retd ADMIN 1/5/00.
WEST I.W. MHCIMA. Born 22/9/53. Commd 8/1/78. Sqn Ldr 1/1/89. Retd ADMIN 8/1/94.
WEST J.G. Born 21/2/43. Commd 27/9/73. Flt Lt 27/9/74. Retd ENG 27/9/81.
WEST J.S. BEd. Born 25/12/53. Commd 18/3/84. Sqn Ldr 1/7/94. Retd ADMIN 14/3/97.
WEST K.D. Born 22/11/53. Commd 8/10/87. Flt Lt 8/10/89. Retd SUP 8/10/95.
WEST M.E. Born 9/1/41. Commd 25/8/67. Sqn Ldr 1/1/78. Retd SUP 2/4/93.
WEST M.J. Born 3/10/33. Commd 31/7/58. Wg Cdr 1/1/75. Retd ADMIN 11/2/86.
WEST P. Born 13/7/51. Commd 4/9/90. Sqn Ldr 4/9/88. Retd ENG 20/9/96.
WEST P. Born 22/5/36. Commd 7/5/64. Sqn Ldr 1/7/71. Retd ENG 22/5/94.
WEST P.J. MBE. Born 21/7/33. Commd 28/1/60. Wg Cdr 1/7/80. Retd GD 2/9/85.
WEST P.R. BSc. Born 16/5/51. Commd 13/11/72. Flt Lt 15/4/74. Retd GD 16/5/89.
WEST P.T. OBE CEng MIEE MRAeS. Born 28/1/40. Commd 20/8/60. Wg Cdr 1/7/84. Retd ENG 28/1/95.
WEST R.J. Born 16/9/47. Commd 28/2/69. Sqn Ldr 1/7/80. Retd ADMIN 16/9/85.
WEST S.J. Born 13/3/30. Commd 11/4/51. Sqn Ldr 1/1/59. Retd GD 10/6/77.
WEST T.A. Born 15/9/31. Commd 8/5/53. Flt Lt 26/8/58. Retd GD 15/9/69.
WEST-JONES G.S. Born 21/5/24. Commd 3/6/44. Flt Lt 3/12/47. Retd GD 21/5/62.
WESTBROOK L.H. Born 21/4/23. Commd 16/1/45. Flt Lt 19/11/53. Retd GD 28/6/68.
WESTBY N. MBE DFC AFC. Born 29/8/23. Commd 1/6/44. Flt Lt 1/12/47. Retd GD 29/8/66.
WESTCOTT D.A. Born 21/9/22. Commd 29/4/44. Flt Lt 23/5/48. Retd GD 21/9/77.

WESTELL H.L. Born 23/10/32. Commd 12/7/51. Flt Lt 13/11/61. Retd GD 4/11/75.
WESTERN G.R. Born 1/5/52. Commd 25/2/88. Sqn Ldr 1/7/01. Retd ADMIN 29/12/01.
WESTHEAD W.A. Born 13/2/29. Commd 4/6/52. Sqn Ldr 1/7/69. Retd GD 13/2/84.
WESTLAKE G.H. DSO DFC FCMI. Born 21/4/18. Commd 24/8/40. Gp Capt 1/7/61. Retd GD 25/7/69.
WESTLEY M.D. Born 15/3/37. Commd 10/2/59. Flt Lt 1/4/66. Retd SEC 15/3/75.
WESTLEY P.W. BA. Born 20/11/52. Commd 17/1/82. Flt Lt 17/1/83. Retd ADMIN 14/3/96.
WESTOBY B.J. Born 24/12/32. Commd 27/9/51. Gp Capt 1/7/78. Retd GD 24/12/91.
WESTON C.T. BEng. Born 29/1/69. Commd 6/9/87. Flt Lt 15/1/94. Retd ENG 6/4/00.
WESTON D. Born 20/1/31. Commd 6/1/51. Flt Lt 25/7/56. Retd GD 20/1/74.
WESTON D.J. BSc. Born 29/5/50. Commd 15/9/69. Sqn Ldr 1/7/85. Retd GD 1/7/88.
WESTON F.G. MBE. Born 13/10/07. Commd 17/1/42. Flt Lt 1/9/45. Retd ENG 9/5/53.
WESTON G.A.C. Born 10/10/55. Commd 27/3/80. Flt Lt 5/6/82. Retd GD 3/12/97.
WESTON G.E. Born 14/1/15. Commd 21/2/46. Flt Lt 21/8/50. Retd SUP 16/2/64.
WESTON I. Born 25/3/46. Commd 5/3/65. Flt Lt 5/9/70. Retd GD 3/12/85.
WESTON I.J. The Rev. MBE. Born 28/4/45. Commd 18/9/77. Retd Wg Cdr 28/4/00.
WESTON J.R. BSc. Born 18/2/58. Commd 18/10/81. Flt Lt 18/7/82. Retd GD 18/10/97.
WESTON K.J. Born 7/6/45. Commd 9/12/76. Sqn Ldr 1/7/89. Retd ENG 31/3/94.
WESTON M.R. Born 5/2/35. Commd 9/7/57. Flt Lt 17/1/63. Retd PI 10/9/76.
WESTON P.J. Born 11/9/62. Commd 26/4/84. Flt Lt 21/10/87. Retd GD 11/4/01.
WESTON R.I. Born 5/11/21. Commd 14/5/54. Flt Lt 14/5/59. Retd ENG 30/9/61.
WESTWELL D.K. Born 29/1/37. Commd 5/12/63. Sqn Ldr 1/7/73. Retd ADMIN 2/2/87.
WESTWOOD C. Born 10/4/32. Commd 29/4/53. Flt Lt 30/9/58. Retd GD 1/9/77.
WESTWOOD D.B. AFC. Born 27/5/30. Commd 5/9/69. Flt Lt 5/9/72. Retd GD 30/5/84.
WESTWOOD H.C. OBE. Born 28/10/04. Commd 30/5/40. Wg Cdr 1/7/47. Retd GD(G) 28/10/56.
WESTWOOD H.J. Born 11/10/21. Commd 4/6/56. Flt Lt 4/6/56. Retd GD(G) 11/10/76.
WESTWOOD M.P. OBE. Born 29/8/44. Commd 19/4/63. Wg Cdr 1/1/91. Retd GD 29/8/01.
WETHERELL I. Born 17/4/33. Commd 28/11/74. Flt Lt 28/11/77. Retd GD(G) 3/6/85.
WETTON D.N. Born 12/11/38. Commd 25/7/60. Flt Lt 25/1/63. Retd GD 12/11/76.
WETTON G.R. Born 21/8/32. Commd 29/7/65. Flt Lt 29/7/70. Retd GD 21/8/87.
WHALEY L.E.S. DFC. Born 15/1/14. Commd 21/6/42. Sqn Ldr 1/7/52. Retd SEC 16/7/60.
WHALEY R.K.J. BA. Born 17/2/44. Commd 24/6/65. Flt Lt 24/12/67. Retd GD 24/4/76. Re-instated 22/4/81.
    Flt Lt 22/12/72. Retd GD 6/8/93.
WHALLEY F. Born 31/1/32. Commd 22/8/51. Flt Lt 22/2/56. Retd GD 31/1/70.
WHARRAD M.F. Born 2/10/44. Commd 4/7/69. Flt Lt 6/10/71. Retd GD 31/12/76.
WHARRIER I. BSc. Born 8/8/62. Commd 5/9/82. Flt Lt 5/11/87. Retd ENG 8/8/00.
WHARTON A.N.R. MCIPS. Born 5/8/48. Commd 27/2/70. Sqn Ldr 1/1/83. Retd SUP 5/8/92.
WHARTON B.K. MRCS LRCP DPM. Born 9/12/27. Commd 27/4/53. Wg Cdr 3/4/65. Retd MED 27/4/70.
WHARTON N.J. Born 8/1/46. Commd 19/6/64. Flt Lt 19/12/69. Retd GD 8/1/84.
WHATLEY A.E. Born 20/2/24. Commd 7/7/54. Flt Lt 7/7/59. Retd GD 1/10/68.
WHATLING D. Born 5/1/47. Commd 1/10/65. Sqn Ldr 1/1/81. Retd GD 11/8/84.
WHATLING L. Born 30/5/51. Commd 4/2/71. Flt Lt 4/8/76. Retd GD 13/10/81. Re-instated 24/11/82. Flt Lt 16/9/77.
    Retd GD 11/6/90.
WHATMORE A.G. Born 12/6/49. Commd 10/1/69. Sqn Ldr 1/7/99. Retd FLY(N) 31/10/04.
WHEALE R.D.J. MBE BA AKC MCMI. Born 7/12/37. Commd 8/12/64. Sqn Ldr 2/6/69. Retd ADMIN 7/12/93.
WHEATLEY P.E. Born 28/5/56. Commd 10/3/77. Flt Lt 10/9/82. Retd GD 28/5/94.
WHEATLEY R.A. Born 2/6/21. Commd 26/2/54. Flt Lt 26/2/59. Retd ENG 27/8/63.
WHEATLEY R.B. Born 10/8/60. Commd 23/4/87. Sqn Ldr 9/5/97. Retd GD 10/8/98.
WHEATLEY T.M.K. Born 29/4/44. Commd 26/10/62. Sqn Ldr 1/7/77. Retd GD 29/4/99.
WHEATON B.C. Born 13/4/34. Commd 26/8/66. Flt Lt 26/8/68. Retd ENG 26/8/74.
WHEELDON D.A.A. Born 8/6/55. Commd 8/8/74. Sqn Ldr 1/7/87. Retd SUP 27/2/96.
WHEELDON G.R. AFC. Born 28/12/16. Commd 5/5/43. Sqn Ldr 1/1/54. Retd SEC 28/12/65.
WHEELER A.E.C. DFC*. Born 29/1/18. Commd 6/9/41. Sqn Ldr 1/7/49. Retd GD 28/12/57.
WHEELER A.J. BSc. Born 4/4/60. Commd 18/10/81. Flt Lt 10/10/87. Retd OPS SPT 7/4/00.
WHEELER B.V. Born 7/1/48. Commd 2/8/68. Sqn Ldr 1/7/82. Retd GD 7/1/86.
WHEELER D.A. LLB. Born 22/2/47. Commd 8/1/65. Sqn Ldr 1/1/77. Retd GD 1/1/87.
WHEELER D.J. BSc. Born 28/3/66. Commd 2/9/84. Flt Lt 15/1/90. Retd GD 15/1/00.
WHEELER G.C. BSc. Born 4/8/39. Commd 4/12/64. Flt Lt 4/9/66. Retd GD 11/7/72.
WHEELER J.A. Born 28/9/33. Commd 2/7/52. Sqn Ldr 1/1/70. Retd GD 28/11/75. Re-instated 1/4/80. Sqn Ldr 5/5/74.
    Retd GD 28/9/88.
WHEELER J.P. Born 15/6/24. Commd 12/11/43. Flt Lt 27/12/56. Retd ENG 30/7/68.
WHEELER J.R. MCMI. Born 5/10/38. Commd 7/1/58. Wg Cdr 1/1/90. Retd GD 5/10/93.
WHEELER L.E. BEd. Born 22/1/50. Commd 7/12/75. Flt Lt 7/9/78. Retd ADMIN 12/7/85.
WHEELER L.W.F. Born 4/7/30. Commd 21/5/52. AVM 1/7/83. Retd GD 2/7/84.
WHEELER M.A. Born 13/10/64. Commd 17/7/87. Flt Lt 17/2/92. Retd FLY(P) 21/3/04.
WHEELER Sir Neil GCB CBE DSO DFC* AFC FRAeS. Born 8/7/17. Commd 31/7/37. ACM 11/3/72. Retd GD 3/1/76.
WHEELER O.J. Born 6/7/48. Commd 7/6/68. Flt Lt 7/12/73. Retd FLY(N) 6/7/03.

WHEELER P.A. Born 28/9/45. Commd 31/3/70. Flt Lt 30/6/73. Retd ENG 31/3/86.
WHEELER R.L. Born 21/4/36. Commd 26/8/66. Flt Lt 26/8/68. Retd GD 26/8/74.
WHEELER R.R. Born 30/7/21. Commd 10/10/44. Flt Lt 11/8/48. Retd GD 30/8/64.
WHEELER S.C. Born 27/1/67. Commd 16/6/88. Flt Lt 5/11/94. Retd OPS SPT(ATC) 27/1/05.
WHEELER T.W. Born 27/4/43. Commd 24/4/83. Flt Lt 24/3/87. Retd ENG 28/4/93.
WHEELER W.J. Born 4/5/27. Commd 21/10/66. Flt Lt 21/10/71. Retd ENG 29/1/72.
WHEELER W.M. Born 19/10/27. Commd 9/8/51. Sqn Ldr 1/7/69. Retd GD 15/11/75.
WHEELEY J.M. Born 11/6/42. Commd 1/2/62. Flt Lt 1/8/68. Retd ADMIN 11/6/80.
WHEELIKER P.G. MBA FIFA MCMI. Born 10/6/52. Commd 25/5/80. Flt Lt 25/8/83. Retd SUP 2/4/93.
WHELAN A.R. BA. Born 13/10/34. Commd 8/8/58. Flt Lt 30/6/64. Retd GD 8/8/74.
WHELAN J.B.D. Born 21/7/44. Commd 8/1/76. Flt Lt 8/1/78. Retd ADMIN 8/1/84.
WHELAN J.F. Born 31/5/35. Commd 30/7/57. Flt Lt 15/2/63. Retd GD 31/5/93.
WHELAN P.N. Born 12/2/56. Commd 22/5/80. Flt Lt 22/11/85. Retd GD 21/1/96.
WHELLER J.V. Born 14/2/47. Commd 25/2/66. Flt Lt 25/8/72. Retd GD(G) 14/2/88.
WHERRETT M.J. Born 3/2/49. Commd 18/4/69. Flt Lt 13/9/74. Retd GD 14/3/96.
WHERRY G.H. OBE DFC. Born 13/12/18. Commd 3/5/37. Wg Cdr 1/7/51. Retd GD 13/5/68.
WHERRY I.L. Born 22/7/44. Commd 13/2/64. Flt Lt 20/6/70. Retd GD(G) 22/7/82.
WHIGHT M.G. Born 21/4/46. Commd 26/4/84. Sqn Ldr 1/7/93. Retd ENG 14/3/96.
WHIGHT R.A. Born 30/1/48. Commd 17/2/67. Wg Cdr 1/1/90. Retd GD 14/9/96.
WHILEY K.C.H. MBE. Born 31/10/22. Commd 10/7/45. Sqn Ldr 1/1/62. Retd ENG 1/6/73.
WHIPPY S.W. Born 21/8/31. Commd 5/9/57. Sqn Ldr 1/7/77. Retd ADMIN 11/5/84.
WHITAKER A.J.W. Born 23/4/33. Commd 27/7/54. Sqn Ldr 1/7/64. Retd GD 23/4/71.
WHITAKER C.L. Born 22/2/46. Commd 26/5/67. Wg Cdr 1/7/86. Retd GD 23/2/90.
WHITAKER D. CEng MIMechE. Born 16/2/39. Commd 1/8/66. Wg Cdr 1/7/88. Retd ENG 16/7/94.
WHITAKER E.J. Born 5/1/49. Commd 2/12/66. Sqn Ldr 1/7/89. Retd GD 14/3/97.
WHITAKER J.G. BSc CEng MRAeS. Born 14/4/26. Commd 6/11/47. Gp Capt 1/1/74. Retd ENG 14/8/79.
WHITAKER P.K. Born 2/5/17. Commd 11/4/46. Flt Lt 29/6/50. Retd ENG 2/5/66.
WHITBREAD J.E. Born 24/9/45. Commd 19/6/86. Flt Lt 19/6/90. Retd ENG 1/6/93.
WHITBREAD P.C.A. Born 20/1/48. Commd 14/10/71. Sqn Ldr 1/1/90. Retd GD 1/12/00.
WHITBREAD P.H. MIMechE. Born 11/1/30. Commd 4/7/60. Sqn Ldr 1/7/67. Retd ENG 5/7/89.
WHITBURN C.H. Born 8/2/20. Commd 21/4/45. Flt Lt 30/6/49. Retd GD 8/2/63.
WHITBY D.E. MBE. Born 1/6/21. Commd 23/9/65. Sqn Ldr 1/1/76. Retd ENG 1/6/81.
WHITBY M.S. Born 11/12/46. Commd 20/8/65. Flt Lt 4/5/72. Retd PI 31/12/83.
WHITBY P.G. Born 13/9/16. Commd 10/5/37. Flt Lt 1/12/42. Retd SEC 27/9/65. rtg Sqn Ldr.
WHITCHURCH A.R. MMar. Born 19/12/35. Commd 31/3/64. Sqn Ldr 2/10/74. Retd MAR 1/4/86.
WHITCHURCH P.A. Born 28/4/65. Commd 19/7/84. Fg Offr 19/1/87. Retd GD(G) 1/5/90.
WHITE A. MBE FCMI MCIPD. Born 2/7/23. Commd 12/6/47. Gp Capt 1/7/71. Retd SEC 4/5/74.
WHITE A.D.M. Born 26/3/45. Commd 2/3/78. Flt Lt 2/3/80. Retd SUP 2/3/86.
WHITE A.E. Born 27/1/38. Commd 7/11/62. Flt Lt 4/5/72. Retd GD 1/5/74.
WHITE A.J. Born 6/11/28. Commd 27/1/67. Flt Lt 27/1/72. Retd ENG 6/11/86.
WHITE A.J. Born 13/3/42. Commd 6/4/62. Flt Lt 6/10/67. Retd GD 13/3/80.
WHITE A.J. BA. Born 2/1/49. Commd 22/9/74. Sqn Ldr 1/1/84. Retd ADMIN 22/9/90.
WHITE A.J. Born 12/3/61. Commd 26/11/81. Flt Lt 26/5/87. Retd GD 31/8/89.
WHITE A.M. MSc BSc MInstP. Born 11/11/34. Commd 4/9/67. Sqn Ldr 4/3/71. Retd ADMIN 4/9/83.
WHITE C.B. Born 31/1/20. Commd 9/8/45. Wg Cdr 1/7/64. Retd ENG 15/4/71.
WHITE C.F. DPhysEd. Born 9/2/40. Commd 31/12/63. Flt Lt 31/12/67. Retd ADMIN 29/6/82.
WHITE C.P. Born 13/10/49. Commd 27/2/70. Flt Lt 27/8/75. Retd GD 13/10/87.
WHITE C.R. Born 2/3/24. Commd 6/10/45. Flt Lt 30/6/49. Retd GD 2/9/68.
WHITE C.S. BA. Born 11/9/56. Commd 26/11/78. Flt Lt 26/8/80. Retd GD 26/11/86.
WHITE D. DFC. Born 6/6/22. Commd 8/11/41. Flt Lt 1/9/45. Retd GD 11/4/54. rtg Sqn Ldr.
WHITE D.A. MB ChB FRCS FFARCS DRCOG. Born 7/12/48. Commd 14/3/82. Wg Cdr 14/3/88. Retd MED 14/3/98.
WHITE D.A.C. Born 28/8/42. Commd 31/10/69. Flt Lt 4/5/72. Retd OPS SPT 28/2/98.
WHITE D.B. Born 3/2/34. Commd 24/9/52. Wg Cdr 1/1/77. Retd GD 10/8/87.
WHITE D.H. Born 21/2/48. Commd 25/4/69. Gp Capt 1/1/98. Retd GD 21/2/05.
WHITE D.J. Born 19/1/55. Commd 20/9/79. Sqn Ldr 1/7/93. Retd GD(G) 22/5/95.
WHITE D.J. MB BS FRCOG. Born 1/6/22. Commd 5/8/52. Gp Capt 8/4/71. Retd MED 2/4/85.
WHITE D.S. Born 5/6/27. Commd 27/7/49. Sqn Ldr 1/1/59. Retd GD 1/3/68.
WHITE D.W. Born 10/6/23. Commd 25/8/44. Flt Lt 6/1/52. Retd GD 3/7/62.
WHITE E.J. DFM. Born 25/10/22. Commd 23/2/45. Sqn Ldr 1/7/53. Retd SUP 26/10/73.
WHITE F.H. MCMI. Born 20/9/25. Commd 19/8/65. Sqn Ldr 1/1/76. Retd ENG 20/9/78.
WHITE F.W.L. MBE BSc. Born 3/12/35. Commd 27/11/58. Sqn Ldr 1/7/67. Retd ENG 3/5/75.
WHITE G.A. CB AFC LLB FRAeS. Born 11/3/32. Commd 17/3/54. AVM 1/1/83. Retd GD 3/4/87.
WHITE G.A. Born 30/1/60. Commd 5/5/88. Flt Lt 5/5/94. Retd MED(T) 14/9/96.
WHITE G.E. MBE. Born 6/5/35. Commd 19/1/66. Flt Lt 8/1/69. Retd ENG 19/1/74.
WHITE H.J. Born 27/5/22. Commd 28/7/60. Flt Lt 28/7/63. Retd SEC 30/9/67.
WHITE I. AInstAM. Born 5/1/62. Commd 30/10/83. Flt Lt 30/4/89. Retd ADMIN 14/3/96.

WHITE J. Born 25/1/32. Commd 15/6/64. Sqn Ldr 1/7/74. Retd GD(G) 21/4/86.
WHITE J.B. MA. Born 4/4/37. Commd 20/9/55. Wg Cdr 1/1/75. Retd ENG 10/12/79.
WHITE J.C. Born 9/11/21. Commd 21/6/56. Sqn Ldr 1/7/70. Retd ENG 1/3/78.
WHITE J.F. BA. Born 19/6/44. Commd 16/2/69. Flt Lt 16/5/70. Retd GD 28/2/76.
WHITE J.F. Born 17/8/42. Commd 6/9/63. Flt Lt 6/3/69. Retd GD 17/8/76.
WHITE J.J. Born 19/1/25. Commd 10/3/60. Flt Lt 10/3/65. Retd GD 28/9/68.
WHITE J.J. Born 25/3/65. Commd 7/11/85. Flt Lt 7/5/92. Retd OPS SPT(FC) 3/4/03.
WHITE J.K. MInstAM. Born 6/1/38. Commd 2/2/68. Sqn Ldr 1/7/76. Retd ADMIN 6/1/93.
WHITE J.P. BSc. Born 12/3/59. Commd 23/5/82. Wg Cdr 1/1/01. Retd GD 23/5/04.
WHITE J.R. Born 5/8/20. Commd 6/7/55. Flt Lt 1/12/59. Retd GD(G) 1/11/73.
WHITE J.S. Born 22/10/22. Commd 23/3/66. Flt Lt 23/3/71. Retd ENG 22/10/77.
WHITE J.V. Born 2/8/16. Commd 21/6/45. Fg Offr 30/1/47. Retd SUP 26/7/47. rtg Flt Lt.
WHITE J.W. CBE FRAeS FCMI. Born 21/2/48. Commd 17/2/67. Gp Capt 1/1/97. Retd GD 21/7/03.
WHITE J.W. MBE CEng MRAeS. Born 29/1/14. Commd 25/4/40. Gp Capt 1/1/58. Retd ENG 12/11/66.
WHITE K.J. BSc. Born 10/4/64. Commd 26/10/86. Flt Lt 26/4/90. Retd SUP 14/3/97.
WHITE L.D. Born 18/4/58. Commd 23/5/85. Flt Lt 23/5/87. Retd GD 18/4/96.
WHITE L.E. Born 3/8/38. Commd 9/2/62. Sqn Ldr 1/7/89. Retd GD 3/8/93.
WHITE M. Born 16/8/24. Commd 4/9/48. Flt Lt 29/12/53. Retd GD 16/8/68.
WHITE M.G.F. OBE. Born 18/11/52. Commd 9/3/72. A Cdre 1/1/97. Retd GD 15/8/01.
WHITE M.J. Born 2/2/43. Commd 28/4/61. Gp Capt 1/1/91. Retd GD 2/1/96.
WHITE M.J.F. Born 12/6/35. Commd 9/4/57. Sqn Ldr 1/7/70. Retd GD 1/7/73.
WHITE M.V. Born 20/10/49. Commd 21/3/69. Flt Lt 21/9/75. Retd GD(G) 20/10/87.
WHITE M.W. Born 6/7/43. Commd 17/7/70. Sqn Ldr 1/7/78. Retd SY 6/7/87.
WHITE N.K. BSc MB ChB. Born 18/9/56. Commd 25/9/80. Sqn Ldr 1/8/89. Retd MED 29/5/97.
WHITE P.J. IEng FIIE. Born 16/7/53. Commd 8/12/83. Wg Cdr 1/1/01. Retd GD 26/7/03.
WHITE R.C. Born 12/6/52. Commd 1/6/72. Flt Lt 1/12/77. Retd GD 12/6/90.
WHITE R.D.R. BSc. Born 7/6/58. Commd 26/7/81. Flt Lt 20/10/81. Retd GD 20/10/00.
WHITE R.G.J. OBE. Born 5/10/13. Commd 10/1/38. Wg Cdr 1/1/49. Retd SUP 1/8/50.
WHITE R.J. BSc CEng MRAeS. Born 4/9/42. Commd 15/7/64. Sqn Ldr 1/7/76. Retd ENG 31/5/98.
WHITE R.J. MCMI. Born 11/1/31. Commd 9/3/50. Wg Cdr 1/7/80. Retd ADMIN 11/1/86.
WHITE R.W. MBE. Born 17/10/46. Commd 18/11/66. Wg Cdr 1/1/91. Retd OPS SPT 1/12/00.
WHITE R.W. BSc. Born 5/10/42. Commd 15/7/64. Flt Lt 15/10/68. Retd ENG 5/10/69.
WHITE S.E. Born 18/10/59. Commd 5/4/79. Flt Lt 5/10/85. Retd GD(G) 1/6/86.
WHITE S.G.R. MRAeS. Born 25/1/20. Commd 15/7/43. Sqn Ldr 1/1/55. Retd ENG 12/10/63.
WHITE S.J. Born 18/2/36. Commd 26/11/60. Flt Lt 1/4/66. Retd GD 3/10/79.
WHITE S.M.F. Born 6/2/16. Commd 23/12/43. Sqn Ldr 1/1/57. Retd SEC 19/7/64.
WHITE T.A. BSc. Born 2/5/62. Commd 12/3/87. Flt Lt 2/9/91. Retd ENG 2/5/00.
WHITE T.P. CB CEng FIEE DL. Born 1/5/32. Commd 1/7/54. AVM 1/7/83. Retd ENG 1/5/87.
WHITE V.G.B. Born 21/10/09. Commd 31/7/41. Flt Lt 1/7/44. Retd GD 20/12/45. rtg Sqn Ldr.
WHITE W.B. DPhysEd MCMI. Born 27/5/31. Commd 12/9/56. Wg Cdr 1/1/74. Retd ADMIN 24/12/85.
WHITE W.R.J. Born 8/5/21. Commd 30/3/43. Sqn Ldr 1/1/71. Retd GD 8/5/76.
WHITEAR G.S. Born 20/3/47. Commd 2/8/68. Flt Lt 6/10/71. Retd GD 1/9/77.
WHITEHEAD D.J.B. AFC. Born 4/10/23. Commd 18/6/46. Wg Cdr 1/7/63. Retd GD 4/10/78.
WHITEHEAD G.E. BSc. Born 5/9/44. Commd 19/9/71. Sqn Ldr 1/7/88. Retd ENG 5/9/99.
WHITEHEAD H.A.L. Born 27/7/36. Commd 23/11/78. Sqn Ldr 1/7/89. Retd ENG 29/5/92.
WHITEHEAD L.J. Born 14/8/56. Commd 28/11/74. Sqn Ldr 1/1/88. Retd SY 14/11/95.
WHITEHEAD M.D. BTech. Born 4/7/59. Commd 26/9/82. Sqn Ldr 1/7/94. Retd GD 1/5/01.
WHITEHEAD P.F. Born 28/2/52. Commd 10/5/73. Flt Lt 10/11/78. Retd GD 28/2/90.
WHITEHOUSE L.J. Born 6/7/54. Commd 19/12/85. Flt Lt 19/12/87. Retd ADMIN 19/12/93.
WHITEHOUSE M.B. BSc. Born 4/12/48. Commd 18/9/66. Wg Cdr 1/1/95. Retd GD 4/12/03.
WHITEHOUSE T.F. Born 21/8/42. Commd 30/7/64. Flt Lt 30/1/71. Retd ENG 10/6/76.
WHITEHURST G.R. BSc. Born 26/1/53. Commd 25/7/76. Flt Lt 25/10/77. Retd GD 25/4/97.
WHITEIGHT L.J.S. Born 1/11/22. Commd 23/8/56. Sqn Ldr 1/7/71. Retd GD 23/3/76.
WHITELAW P.T. Born 6/5/30. Commd 2/7/52. Flt Lt 14/5/58. Retd GD 6/5/68.
WHITELEGG J.W. MBE BSc CEng MIMechE MIEE MRAeS. Born 6/6/16. Commd 27/9/45. Sqn Ldr 1/1/58.
    Retd ENG 1/1/64.
WHITELEGG P.J. Born 3/3/58. Commd 2/8/90. Flt Lt 2/8/92. Retd ENG 2/8/98.
WHITELEY A.M. Born 24/8/55. Commd 28/6/79. Sqn Ldr 1/1/90. Retd ENG 24/8/99.
WHITELEY D.L. Born 15/6/40. Commd 16/1/60. Sqn Ldr 1/7/71. Retd GD 15/6/78.
WHITELEY G.E. DSO. Born 22/5/16. Commd 22/10/42. Flt Lt 22/2/46. Retd SEC 23/5/65.
WHITELEY H. Born 23/9/14. Commd 9/8/41. Sqn Ldr 1/7/52. Retd ENG 23/9/63.
WHITELEY M.C. CEng MRAeS MCMI. Born 15/5/35. Commd 27/5/56. Sqn Ldr 1/7/66. Retd ENG 15/5/73.
WHITELOCK C.F. Born 20/3/14. Commd 30/3/42. Sqn Ldr 1/1/53. Retd ENG 20/12/61.
WHITEMAN D.M. Born 27/4/44. Commd 22/5/64. Flt Lt 15/4/70. Retd GD 10/3/76.
WHITEMAN M.N. Born 28/4/37. Commd 14/5/57. Sqn Ldr 1/1/72. Retd GD 28/4/75.
WHITESIDE B. Born 24/10/17. Commd 13/3/46. Flt Lt 13/9/50. Retd RGT 26/2/58.

WHITESIDE T.C.D. MBE PhD MB ChB MRCP FRAeS FCMI. Born 2/7/21. Commd 11/7/46. Gp Capt 25/2/68. Retd MED 15/5/79.
WHITEWRIGHT I.S. BA. Born 2/10/27. Commd 10/12/63. Sqn Ldr 10/6/67. Retd EDN 10/12/79.
WHITFIELD G.F. Born 19/1/27. Commd 19/12/63. Flt Lt 19/12/66. Retd GD 19/1/82.
WHITFIELD J.J. Born 6/8/45. Commd 5/2/65. Gp Capt 1/7/90. Retd GD 2/7/94.
WHITFIELD N.M. Born 7/2/37. Commd 18/3/81. Flt Lt 13/10/79. Retd ENG 24/10/87.
WHITFIELD P.C. MA BA MCIPD. Born 31/7/37. Commd 1/1/63. Sqn Ldr 27/10/70. Retd ADMIN 1/10/77.
WHITFORD T.J. Born 12/10/32. Commd 23/8/51. Flt Lt 23/2/57. Retd GD 12/10/70.
WHITING A. Born 5/4/35. Commd 11/5/78. Flt Lt 11/5/81. Retd ENG 17/4/87.
WHITING T.A. DFC. Born 31/8/17. Commd 17/1/40. Wg Cdr 1/7/54. Retd GD 6/11/67.
WHITINGTON R.B. Born 20/12/27. Commd 19/12/63. Sqn Ldr 1/7/75. Retd ENG 1/7/80.
WHITLING N.R.W. Born 31/3/37. Commd 16/12/58. Sqn Ldr 1/7/69. Retd GD 14/12/75.
WHITLOCK A.J. OBE. Born 25/9/24. Commd 12/5/47. Gp Capt 1/7/70. Retd GD 25/9/82.
WHITMAN D.C. Born 11/1/33. Commd 5/4/55. Wg Cdr 1/1/74. Retd GD 11/1/88.
WHITMELL M.A. BSc. Born 31/10/59. Commd 18/10/81. Flt Lt 18/7/85. Retd SUP 4/3/86.
WHITNEY B.H. BSc. Born 11/3/39. Commd 2/8/60. Flt Lt 2/2/65. Retd ENG 6/3/66.
WHITNEY J.M. Born 26/4/38. Commd 17/7/70. Flt Lt 17/7/72. Retd SUP 17/7/79.
WHITNEY J.R.A. AFC MRAeS. Born 28/12/44. Commd 25/3/64. Wg Cdr 1/7/86. Retd GD 28/12/04.
WHITSON A.C. MCMI. Born 7/5/32. Commd 15/12/53. Sqn Ldr 1/7/68. Retd GD 1/1/71.
WHITSTON J.R. Born 8/8/46. Commd 5/2/65. Wg Cdr 1/1/88. Retd GD 1/2/01.
WHITTAKER A.W. CEng MIMechE MRAeS MIEE. Born 25/8/34. Commd 10/10/60. Wg Cdr 1/1/76. Retd ENG 30/9/83.
WHITTAKER C.R. Born 13/3/58. Commd 5/2/81. Sqn Ldr 1/7/94. Retd GD 5/4/99.
WHITTAKER D. CB MBE. Born 25/6/33. Commd 20/3/52. AVM 1/7/86. Retd GD 4/4/89.
WHITTAKER G. Born 4/8/24. Commd 7/4/44. Flt Lt 7/10/47. Retd GD 26/8/58.
WHITTAKER G.L. Born 25/6/41. Commd 11/11/71. Flt Lt 11/11/73. Retd GD(G) 11/11/79.
WHITTAKER K. Born 29/4/55. Commd 9/8/79. Flt Lt 9/2/85. Retd GD 6/5/95.
WHITTAKER N.S. Born 2/7/31. Commd 29/4/53. Flt Lt 26/11/58. Retd GD 2/7/69.
WHITTAKER P. Born 20/5/52. Commd 5/4/79. Sqn Ldr 1/1/94. Retd GD(G) 14/3/96.
WHITTAKER P.J. Born 16/2/25. Commd 26/8/45. Sqn Ldr 1/7/59. Retd GD 16/2/63.
WHITTAKER R.A. Born 1/2/46. Commd 7/1/71. Flt Lt 7/7/77. Retd GD(G) 14/9/86.
WHITTAKER R.N. MBE. Born 27/3/33. Commd 10/4/52. A Cdre 1/7/84. Retd SUP 27/3/88.
WHITTAKER T.B. MBE. Born 25/11/17. Commd 3/5/56. Sqn Ldr 1/1/66. Retd PRT 1/9/70.
WHITTAKER W.A. Born 21/8/42. Commd 7/6/68. Wg Cdr 1/7/90. Retd ENG 12/4/93.
WHITTAM J.R. Born 25/2/34. Commd 27/7/54. Sqn Ldr 1/1/64. Retd GD 25/2/72.
WHITTAM R. Born 2/10/21. Commd 5/12/42. Wg Cdr 1/1/61. Retd GD 2/10/76. rtg Gp Capt.
WHITTEN E.W. Born 31/1/32. Commd 31/10/61. Flt Lt 31/10/61. Retd ENG 12/10/67.
WHITTICASE R.J. BA. Born 23/5/44. Commd 10/12/65. Flt Lt 10/6/71. Retd GD 23/5/82.
WHITTINGHAM H.W. MA MB ChB MRCS LRCP DTM&H. Born 11/10/14. Commd 28/9/39. Gp Capt 1/1/60. Retd MED 11/10/72.
WHITTINGHAM I.C. Born 26/10/58. Commd 2/2/84. Sqn Ldr 1/7/92. Retd ADMIN 1/7/97.
WHITTINGHAM J. Born 14/4/55. Commd 16/5/74. Wg Cdr 1/7/94. Retd GD 14/6/99.
WHITTINGHAM L.F. OBE. Born 10/10/23. Commd 17/4/44. Wg Cdr 1/7/74. Retd GD 10/10/78.
WHITTINGHAM R.J. FRAeS FCMI. Born 16/2/44. Commd 15/7/65. Gp Capt 1/7/91. Retd ENG 10/6/01.
WHITTINGHAM T.H. MITD. Born 8/2/34. Commd 3/4/56. Gp Capt 1/1/86. Retd GD 31/3/86.
WHITTINGTON L.M. AFC. Born 13/11/21. Commd 6/4/43. Flt Lt 6/10/46. Retd GD 22/8/53. rtg Sqn Ldr.
WHITTLE G.G. DFM. Born 15/9/23. Commd 27/9/43. Sqn Ldr 1/1/56. Retd GD 28/12/61.
WHITTLE R. CEng MRAeS. Born 14/9/38. Commd 2/1/62. Flt Lt 1/5/66. Retd ENG 2/1/78.
WHITTLE T.J. Born 10/11/46. Commd 6/5/68. Flt Lt 2/3/73. Retd GD 14/8/90.
WHITTOME K.J. Born 6/8/34. Commd 19/11/52. Flt Lt 15/4/58. Retd GD 6/8/72.
WHITTON B. MBE. Born 27/5/48. Commd 11/10/84. Sqn Ldr 1/7/94. Retd ADMIN 14/3/97.
WHITTON D.J. MBE BA. Born 28/2/23. Commd 29/5/45. Flt Lt 3/9/53. Retd SEC 1/10/64.
WHITTON J.G. BSc. Born 2/1/51. Commd 30/9/73. Sqn Ldr 1/7/86. Retd GD 27/12/89.
WHITWAM A.S.J. Born 19/10/30. Commd 15/12/53. Flt Lt 15/6/56. Retd GD 9/8/75. rtg Sqn Ldr.
WHITWELL J.K. Born 5/2/29. Commd 15/2/51. Sqn Ldr 1/1/63. Retd ENG 26/6/65.
WHITWORTH R.E.S. Born 12/1/36. Commd 27/8/64. Wg Cdr 1/7/79. Retd SUP 31/12/82.
WHOLEY R.E. Born 16/2/45. Commd 22/5/64. Wg Cdr 1/1/88. Retd GD 3/2/01.
WHYBRO M.J. Born 19/11/41. Commd 12/1/62. Sqn Ldr 1/1/79. Retd GD 1/10/94.
WHYBROW P.G. BA. Born 1/7/14. Commd 10/3/41. Sqn Offr 1/1/50. Retd SEC 7/4/55.
WHYMAN A.J. Born 18/3/16. Commd 18/6/44. Sqn Ldr 1/7/62. Retd GD(G) 19/3/66.
WHYNACHT K.A. DFC AFC. Born 30/11/23. Commd 8/8/47. Sqn Ldr 1/1/75. Retd GD(G) 30/11/78.
WHYTE A. FIISec MIOSH MCMI. Born 29/7/42. Commd 4/12/64. Wg Cdr 1/7/91. Retd SY 1/9/93.
WHYTE A.B. MSc CEng MIEE MRAeS. Born 12/11/25. Commd 19/10/49. Wg Cdr 17/2/71. Retd EDN 13/7/73.
WHYTE A.J. BSc. Born 12/4/60. Commd 5/2/84. Flt Lt 5/8/86. Retd GD 17/12/96.
WHYTE R.A. Born 13/6/30. Commd 16/11/51. Sqn Ldr 1/7/62. Retd GD 14/12/71.
WHYTE S.G. Born 26/5/63. Commd 11/6/81. Flt Lt 11/12/87. Retd ADMIN 9/8/91.

WHYTE W.L. Born 19/1/46. Commd 2/12/66. Wg Cdr 1/1/86. Retd GD 26/11/97.
WICK K.L. Born 14/3/31. Commd 17/1/69. Flt Lt 17/1/73. Retd ENG 30/11/74. Re-instated 22/10/80. Sqn Ldr 1/1/87.
    Retd ENG 31/7/89.
WICKENS S.G. Born 12/1/64. Commd 29/7/83. Flt Lt 12/10/90. Retd SUP 14/3/96.
WICKES A.J. Born 8/2/44. Commd 17/5/63. Flt Lt 8/1/69. Retd GD 1/10/77.
WICKES N.A. DFC AFC. Born 30/7/24. Commd 16/2/49. Sqn Ldr 1/7/57. Retd GD 30/7/67.
WICKHAM A.A. BA BA FCMI. Born 21/10/35. Commd 12/1/55. Wg Cdr 1/1/74. Retd GD 21/10/90.
WICKMAN P.R. Born 6/10/52. Commd 16/5/74. Flt Lt 16/11/79. Retd GD 6/10/90.
WICKS C.H. Born 18/11/17. Commd 28/1/43. Sqn Ldr 1/7/62. Retd ENG 18/11/73.
WICKSON A. Born 1/5/10. Commd 27/5/47. Flt Lt 27/11/51. Retd SUP 1/5/67.
WICKSON K.M. MCMI. Born 23/12/24. Commd 14/7/44. Sqn Ldr 1/1/58. Retd GD 23/12/67.
WIDD P.L. Born 15/11/39. Commd 28/3/63. Flt Lt 1/7/69. Retd SEC 14/2/76.
WIDDESS J.D.McM. MBE. Born 16/9/44. Commd 25/3/64. Sqn Ldr 1/7/79. Retd GD 16/9/00.
WIDDICOMBE R.A.L. Born 29/5/27. Commd 11/11/65. Flt Lt 11/11/70. Retd ENG 29/5/82.
WIDDISON G.C. Born 12/6/21. Commd 15/12/52. Flt Lt 15/12/52. Retd ENG 3/11/61.
WIDDOWS S.C. CB DFC. Born 4/10/09. Commd 25/7/31. A Cdre 1/1/55. Retd GD 29/12/58.
WIDDOWSON M.K. Born 10/5/46. Commd 25/3/64. A Cdre 1/7/92. Retd GD 14/9/96.
WIENER J.S. Born 1/8/63. Commd 29/3/90. Flt Lt 29/3/92. Retd ADMIN 3/9/02.
WIER T. AFC. Born 2/1/20. Commd 12/10/48. Flt Lt 12/10/48. Retd GD(G) 2/1/75.
WIFFIN R.K. OBE BA FTCL LRAM ARCM. Born 9/8/54. Commd 14/1/82. Wg Cdr 1/7/98. Retd MUSIC 4/4/03.
WIGGANS I.R. Born 7/8/64. Commd 9/11/89. Sqn Ldr 1/1/02. Retd OPS SPT(ATC) 1/1/05.
WIGGINS B.D. MBE BSc CEng MIMechE MRAeS MCMI. Born 7/7/29. Commd 5/12/60. Wg Cdr 1/7/75.
    Retd ENG 13/11/79.
WIGGINS R.M. Born 14/4/46. Commd 31/3/70. Sqn Ldr 1/7/86. Retd ENG 1/10/89.
WIGGINS T.E. Born 18/3/37. Commd 22/8/62. Sqn Ldr 1/1/71. Retd GD 18/3/95.
WIGGLE J.G. Born 29/5/55. Commd 30/9/73. Sqn Ldr 1/1/95. Retd GD 20/5/96.
WIGHT-BOYCOTT A.B. OBE. Born 7/4/46. Commd 3/3/67. Gp Capt 1/1/95. Retd GD 14/9/96.
WIGHTMAN C.L. Born 4/4/38. Commd 6/1/61. Flt Lt 6/7/65. Retd GD 16/4/66.
WIGHTMAN R.A. Born 3/10/36. Commd 4/12/58. Flt Lt 14/2/66. Retd GD 4/12/74.
WIGHTMAN W.K. AFC. Born 13/1/24. Commd 28/1/44. Flt Lt 28/7/47. Retd GD 1/6/77.
WIGHTON J.P. Born 28/8/30. Commd 27/2/52. Flt Lt 26/6/57. Retd GD 6/6/71.
WIGMORE B.T. Born 14/1/41. Commd 27/7/64. Wg Cdr 1/7/89. Retd GD(G) 4/7/89.
WIGMORE W.I.C. Born 18/12/38. Commd 14/4/59. Sqn Ldr 1/7/86. Retd GD 27/2/91.
WIKELEY J.D. MCIPS MCMI. Born 2/2/25. Commd 30/4/72. Sqn Ldr 30/4/72. Retd SUP 2/2/85.
WILBERFORCE B.D. MB ChB MRCS LRVP. Born 11/8/16. Commd 18/11/43. Wg Cdr 1/4/62. Retd MED 1/7/69.
WILBRAHAM W.H. Born 12/4/37. Commd 18/7/61. Flt Lt 1/4/66. Retd GD 19/1/91.
WILBY D.J.G. AFC. Born 20/5/47. Commd 21/7/65. A Cdre 1/7/96. Retd GD 24/7/00.
WILBY P.J. CEng MRAeS. Born 17/12/37. Commd 29/10/64. Sqn Ldr 5/8/72. Retd EDN 17/12/75.
WILBY S.K. Born 5/7/50. Commd 28/2/85. Sqn Ldr 1/7/00. Retd ENG 31/7/02.
WILCOCK C.J.M. Born 6/7/44. Commd 9/8/63. Sqn Ldr 1/7/77. Retd GD 12/3/89.
WILCOCK J. Born 6/6/33. Commd 27/1/67. Sqn Ldr 1/1/78. Retd ENG 7/6/83.
WILCOCK M.D. Born 24/9/63. Commd 23/4/87. Flt Lt 21/8/93. Retd ADMIN 31/10/96.
WILCOCK N.J. BSc(Eng). Born 4/12/50. Commd 15/9/69. Sqn Ldr 1/7/98. Retd FLY(P) 8/8/03.
WILCOCK P.J. MBE. Born 5/2/49. Commd 24/8/72. Sqn Ldr 1/7/83. Retd GD 3/1/89.
WILCOX A.T. Born 30/5/16. Commd 28/4/45. Flt Lt 4/1/51. Retd SUP 30/8/64.
WILCOX B. Born 6/7/33. Commd 29/11/65. Flt Lt 29/11/65. Retd GD 6/7/88.
WILCOX J.R. Born 9/1/22. Commd 12/9/58. Sqn Ldr 15/4/70. Retd ADMIN 9/1/82.
WILCOX L.J.C. AFC AFM. Born 14/1/24. Commd 21/2/69. Flt Lt 21/2/72. Retd GD(G) 21/2/79.
WILCOX N.H. Born 21/7/40. Commd 11/11/67. Flt Lt 11/11/67. Retd GD 1/11/68.
WILCOX P.H. MBE. Born 28/9/43. Commd 23/3/63. Sqn Ldr 1/1/81. Retd GD 1/10/00.
WILCOX R.J.V. Born 26/10/44. Commd 21/8/68. Gp Capt 1/1/91. Retd ADMIN 31/3/94.
WILCOX W.J. Born 11/8/32. Commd 9/12/76. Flt Lt 9/12/79. Retd ADMIN 30/7/88.
WILD F.J. CEng MIMechE. Born 26/1/33. Commd 21/10/55. Gp Capt 1/1/76. Retd ENG 21/6/86.
WILD G.L. BSc. Born 11/5/65. Commd 25/6/89. Flt Lt 25/12/92. Retd ADMIN 14/9/96.
WILD J. Born 15/7/27. Commd 1/10/52. Gp Capt 1/7/79. Retd GD 2/4/80.
WILD J.E. Born 5/11/64. Commd 3/8/93. Flt Lt 13/12/96. Retd ENG 5/11/02.
WILD J.G. Born 8/9/40. Commd 14/7/66. Sqn Ldr 1/7/87. Retd GD 2/4/93.
WILD J.M. BA. Born 21/9/56. Commd 18/11/79. Flt Lt 18/5/83. Retd SY 18/11/95.
WILD M.S. Born 31/8/35. Commd 21/10/53. Gp Capt 1/1/89. Retd GD 4/7/89.
WILD N.N. LLB. Born 6/4/48. Commd 27/4/70. Flt Lt 27/1/74. Retd SEC 1/4/78.
WILD P.R. AFC. Born 29/7/34. Commd 18/8/54. Flt Lt 5/10/60. Retd GD 29/7/72. Re-instated 5/11/80 to 31/7/84.
WILDE A. Born 21/4/29. Commd 7/5/51. Flt Lt 7/5/51. Retd SUP 21/4/84.
WILDE C.D. Born 8/9/33. Commd 9/2/66. Sqn Ldr 1/7/81. Retd ENG 8/9/91.
WILDE P.H. Born 26/7/22. Commd 30/9/43. Flt Lt 30/3/47. Retd ENG 2/8/55.
WILDE P.J. Born 31/10/32. Commd 17/5/51. Flt Lt 6/9/56. Retd GD 1/5/74.
WILDEMAN M. BA. Born 6/9/61. Commd 25/11/84. Flt Lt 25/5/86. Retd GD 25/11/96.

WILDER S.R. Born 1/2/63. Commd 22/11/84. APO 22/11/84. Retd GD 6/9/85.
WILDERS R.H.J. Born 24/8/25. Commd 2/7/52. Flt Lt 3/6/59. Retd SEC 8/3/69.
WILDERSPIN K.L. BSc CEng MIEE MRAeS DLUT. Born 29/9/54. Commd 16/9/73. Gp Capt 20/12/96. Retd ENG 4/12/98.
WILDIG R.B. Born 5/3/22. Commd 4/4/49. Flt Lt 30/1/57. Retd GD 6/8/65.
WILDING A. MSc CEng MIMechE MRAeS. Born 28/9/27. Commd 30/5/58. Wg Cdr 17/2/73. Retd ADMIN 30/9/76.
WILDING A.C. BSc. Born 20/3/59. Commd 7/11/82. Wg Cdr 1/7/96. Retd ENG 11/7/99.
WILDING R.G. AFM. Born 3/5/20. Commd 27/1/55. Flt Lt 27/1/61. Retd GD 29/6/68.
WILDING S.W. CBE. Born 3/8/19. Commd 30/8/43. A Cdre 1/7/71. Retd SUP 3/8/74.
WILDMAN J.C. Born 1/2/45. Commd 1/3/68. Wg Cdr 1/1/87. Retd ENG 11/12/96.
WILDMAN P.G. BA FRAeS. Born 10/2/47. Commd 22/9/65. Gp Capt 1/1/93. Retd GD 18/2/03.
WILDMAN W.A. MBE. Born 2/7/44. Commd 1/4/76. Sqn Ldr 1/1/83. Retd ADMIN 1/8/84. Re-instated 1/10/85. Sqn Ldr 2/3/84. Retd ADMIN 1/4/88.
WILDRIDGE D.B. BSc. Born 4/4/51. Commd 15/9/69. Flt Lt 15/4/74. Retd GD 4/4/89.
WILDS P.J. Born 2/5/33. Commd 11/2/65. Sqn Ldr 1/1/80. Retd GD 1/8/84.
WILDSMITH D.A. Born 31/10/42. Commd 9/8/63. Flt Lt 9/8/68. Retd GD 1/7/76.
WILES C.W. Born 26/2/22. Commd 27/2/47. Flt Lt 11/11/54. Retd GD 26/2/65.
WILES R.A. BSc MCIPD MCMI PGCE. Born 30/10/32. Commd 23/11/56. Wg Cdr 1/7/78. Retd ADMIN 30/10/87.
WILKES I.F. BSc. Born 20/2/56. Commd 1/9/74. Flt Lt 15/10/78. Retd GD 15/7/89.
WILKES J.D. Born 2/7/44. Commd 1/4/76. Sqn Ldr 1/1/83. Retd ADMIN 1/8/84. Re-instated 1/10/85. Sqn Ldr 2/3/84. Retd ADMIN 1/4/88.
WILKES V.T.M. DFC. Born 29/1/21. Commd 31/12/44. Flt Lt 7/6/51. Retd SUP 15/8/54.
WILKEY R.C. Born 22/12/49. Commd 10/7/4. Sqn Ldr 1/1/88. Retd OPS SPT 18/9/98.
WILKIE I.H. Born 23/6/37. Commd 17/7/58. Wg Cdr 1/7/81. Retd ADMIN 17/7/87.
WILKIN L. Born 24/1/48. Commd 24/2/67. Sqn Ldr 1/1/82. Retd GD(G) 11/10/85.
WILKIN R. Born 3/11/45. Commd 1/11/85. Sqn Ldr 1/1/90. Retd FLY(P) 3/11/03.
WILKINS C.J. BSc. Born 10/11/51. Commd 13/9/70. Flt Lt 15/4/77. Retd GD(G) 23/9/80.
WILKINS F.J. MA CEng MRAeS MIMechE. Born 20/3/24. Commd 21/6/50. Sqn Ldr 21/6/60. Retd EDN 21/6/66.
WILKINS M.E. IEng MIIE. Born 26/5/65. Commd 19/12/91. Flt Lt 19/12/93. Retd ENGINEER 26/5/03.
WILKINS M.J. BSc CEng MRAeS. Born 31/12/43. Commd 14/9/69. Wg Cdr 1/7/87. Retd ENG 30/11/01.
WILKINS N.E. DFC MCMI. Born 10/1/25. Commd 25/3/44. Wg Cdr 1/1/63. Retd GD 3/1/76.
WILKINS P.A. FCMI MIPM. Born 30/6/45. Commd 31/10/63. Gp Capt 1/7/91. Retd ADMIN 14/6/94.
WILKINS R.A.W. Born 26/5/52. Commd 19/10/72. Wg Cdr 1/1/96. Retd OPS SPT 11/8/02.
WILKINS R.J. Born 3/10/30. Commd 10/3/60. Flt Lt 10/9/63. Retd GD 3/10/68.
WILKINSON A.C. Born 19/2/34. Commd 22/5/59. Sqn Ldr 22/9/69. Retd EDN 8/10/74.
WILKINSON A.C. BSc. Born 12/3/66. Commd 19/7/87. Sqn Ldr 1/7/01. Retd OPS SPT(REGT) 1/7/04.
WILKINSON A.L. Born 18/8/35. Commd 30/6/54. Sqn Ldr 1/7/67. Retd SUP 18/8/73.
WILKINSON A.T.B. MBE BA FCMI MRAeS MCIPS MIMIS. Born 19/4/43. Commd 30/1/70. Wg Cdr 1/1/96. Retd SUP 19/4/98.
WILKINSON C.J. BSc. Born 6/7/65. Commd 11/9/83. Flt Lt 15/1/89. Retd GD 15/7/98.
WILKINSON C.S. FCA. Born 16/6/43. Commd 17/12/64. Flt Lt 15/4/70. Retd GD 14/4/71.
WILKINSON D.J. BSc. Born 23/3/49. Commd 27/1/70. Sqn Ldr 1/7/82. Retd GD 25/2/89.
WILKINSON F.B. BEM. Born 30/3/22. Commd 15/9/60. Flt Lt 15/9/65. Retd ENG 4/7/73.
WILKINSON G. Born 27/12/34. Commd 2/3/61. Sqn Ldr 1/1/73. Retd ENG 27/12/92.
WILKINSON G.C. AFC. Born 7/11/26. Commd 29/12/48. Flt Lt 21/12/54. Retd GD 1/7/59.
WILKINSON I.D. FCMI. Born 8/4/32. Commd 27/7/54. A Cdre 1/7/81. Retd SUP 4/8/84.
WILKINSON J. AFC. Born 21/9/31. Commd 30/7/52. A Cdre 1/7/83. Retd GD 1/8/86.
WILKINSON J.H.B. Born 26/8/35. Commd 27/1/61. Flt Lt 1/7/68. Retd GD 25/8/73.
WILKINSON J.N. Born 22/10/45. Commd 17/7/64. Flt Lt 4/5/72. Retd GD 12/12/98.
WILKINSON J.N. BA. Born 17/2/62. Commd 14/9/80. Flt Lt 15/10/86. Retd SUP 1/10/89.
WILKINSON K. MA BSc CertEd. Born 1/6/48. Commd 3/1/88. Flt Lt 3/7/84. Retd ADMIN (TRG) 3/1/04.
WILKINSON K.G. BSc. Born 29/9/46. Commd 13/9/70. Wg Cdr 1/7/90. Retd GD(G) 1/1/97.
WILKINSON K.J. Born 31/1/29. Commd 12/12/51. Flt Lt 12/12/56. Retd SUP 31/1/67. rtg Sqn Ldr.
WILKINSON M. BA PGCE MIL. Born 15/8/53. Commd 29/9/85. Sqn Ldr 1/7/94. Retd ADMIN 29/9/01.
WILKINSON P.A. MRCS LRCP. Born 3/3/11. Commd 3/5/37. Gp Capt 1/10/57. Retd MED 3/12/69.
WILKINSON P.J. CVO MA FRAeS. Born 8/6/38. Commd 10/1/57. Plt Offr 8/3/57. Retd GD(G) 21/10/58. Re-entered 11/9/61. A Cdre 1/7/91. Retd GD 30/10/96.
WILKINSON R.E. LRAM ARCM. Born 28/1/42. Commd 9/12/76. Wg Cdr 1/7/95. Retd DM 1/6/98.
WILKINSON R.J. FCMI. Born 4/04/34. Commd 24/9/52. Gp Capt 1/1/78. Retd SUP 6/5/88.
WILKINSON R.S. Born 17/2/39. Commd 28/1/58. Flt Lt 30/7/63. Retd GD 17/2/77.
WILKINSON S. Born 24/2/21. Commd 6/3/45. Sqn Ldr 1/1/72. Retd GD 1/9/73.
WILKINSON S.N. MSc BSc CEng MRAeS. Born 28/8/65. Commd 19/6/88. Sqn Ldr 1/7/00. Retd ENGINEER 19/6/04.
WILKINSON T.H. Born 23/8/40. Commd 9/12/76. Flt Lt 9/12/81. Retd SUP 3/2/85.
WILKINSON W. OBE CEng FCMI MIEE. Born 9/5/18. Commd 29/4/43. Gp Capt 1/1/67. Retd ENG 9/5/73.
WILKINSON W.A. MCMI. Born 16/11/23. Commd 1/4/44. Wg Cdr 1/7/75. Retd ADMIN 29/3/78.
WILKINSON W.H. MRCS LRCP. Born 5/5/25. Commd 29/6/53. Wg Cdr 29/6/64. Retd MED 29/6/69.
WILKS B.P. BEM MLitt. Born 21/12/42. Commd 20/5/82. Flt Lt 20/5/86. Retd ADMIN 21/12/97.

WILKS C.E. Born 26/4/29. Commd 4/10/51. Flt Lt 14/7/57. Retd GD 22/6/74.
WILKS J.E.G. Born 19/8/19. Commd 31/1/46. Flt Lt 7/6/51. Retd ENG 22/5/63.
WILL B.V. BSc. Born 2/1/47. Commd 24/4/77. Sqn Ldr 1/7/85. Retd ADMIN 24/4/93.
WILL J.A. MBE. Born 18/2/26. Commd 20/12/51. Flt Lt 4/4/57. Retd GD 18/2/69.
WILLANS R.J. MCMI. Born 31/8/33. Commd 19/12/63. Sqn Ldr 1/1/78. Retd ENG 6/4/85.
WILLBOND T.C. Born 15/11/46. Commd 11/11/65. Sqn Ldr 1/1/90. Retd GD(G) 14/9/96.
WILLCOX L.T.H. Born 1/12/44. Commd 6/11/64. Flt Lt 6/5/70. Retd GD 21/7/76.
WILLDER K.B.S. CBE BSc CEng FIEE. Born 12/1/18. Commd 31/3/40. A Cdre 1/7/64. Retd ENG 12/1/73.
WILLERTON A. Born 9/3/60. Commd 28/7/88. Sqn Ldr 1/1/97. Retd ADMIN 31/10/01.
WILLETS D.F. Born 13/11/36. Commd 28/10/76. Flt Lt 28/10/77. Retd ADMIN 23/8/83.
WILLETTS W.J. Born 19/2/17. Commd 5/10/44. Flt Lt 5/4/48. Retd ENG 29/9/62. rtg Sqn Ldr.
WILLEY J.R. Born 3/1/47. Commd 1/4/66. Sqn Ldr 1/7/82. Retd GD 1/7/85.
WILLEY R.StJ.F. Born 22/11/33. Commd 24/6/53. Flt Lt 21/10/59. Retd GD 22/11/71.
WILLIAMS A. BSc DCAe MRAeS. Born 5/2/29. Commd 30/9/54. Wg Cdr 30/9/69. Retd EDN 2/3/76.
WILLIAMS A.E. Born 4/6/13. Commd 28/2/57. Flt Lt 28/2/60. Retd ACB 1/11/65.
WILLIAMS A.F. Born 15/9/36. Commd 24/8/55. Flt Lt 22/10/60. Retd GD 18/5/67.
WILLIAMS A.F.E. ACIS. Born 6/8/51. Commd 13/2/77. Wg Cdr 1/7/94. Retd ADMIN 14/9/96.
WILLIAMS A.G. Born 6/2/44. Commd 24/6/65. Sqn Ldr 1/1/74. Retd ADMIN 6/2/82.
WILLIAMS A.H. Born 10/3/49. Commd 9/7/79. Flt Lt 16/3/75. Retd GD 22/10/94.
WILLIAMS A.H. BSc MCMI. Born 8/6/46. Commd 4/6/72. Sqn Ldr 1/7/83. Retd GD 8/6/01.
WILLIAMS A.P. BA. Born 9/6/60. Commd 7/5/92. Flt Lt 7/5/94. Retd ADMIN 14/3/97.
WILLIAMS B. Born 27/1/45. Commd 14/1/88. Flt Lt 14/1/92. Retd ADMIN 30/4/98.
WILLIAMS B. Born 17/8/47. Commd 21/10/66. Flt Lt 25/2/73. Retd GD(G) 2/4/75.
WILLIAMS B.G. MSc BA FCMI. Born 14/4/33. Commd 25/8/55. Gp Capt 1/1/76. Retd SUP 3/4/82.
WILLIAMS C. OBE. Born 24/10/30. Commd 30/7/53. Wg Cdr 1/7/74. Retd GD 27/8/84.
WILLIAMS C.D. BSc. Born 27/6/62. Commd 2/9/84. Sqn Ldr 1/7/97. Retd GD 2/9/00.
WILLIAMS C.D. Born 2/7/64. Commd 15/10/84. Flt Lt 15/4/90. Retd FLY(P) 27/9/04.
WILLIAMS C.J. BChD MCMI. Born 25/7/55. Commd 30/10/77. Sqn Ldr 16/3/84. Retd DEL 31/5/89.
WILLIAMS C.J.A. Born 26/8/37. Commd 7/2/57. Sqn Ldr 1/1/86. Retd GD 26/8/87.
WILLIAMS C.L. Born 29/12/29. Commd 30/7/52. Flt Lt 2/3/58. Retd GD 18/9/68.
WILLIAMS D. Born 27/5/33. Commd 21/11/51. Sqn Ldr 1/7/75. Retd GD 27/5/93.
WILLIAMS D. MA DCAe. Born 12/5/33. Commd 26/9/53. Sqn Ldr 1/7/66. Retd ENG 12/5/71.
WILLIAMS D. OBE BSc CEng MRAeS. Born 22/6/39. Commd 22/8/61. Gp Capt 1/1/86. Retd ENG 22/6/94.
WILLIAMS D. Born 10/12/32. Commd 25/10/57. Sqn Ldr 25/10/68. Retd EDN 25/10/73.
WILLIAMS D.A. AFC. Born 19/12/44. Commd 28/4/65. Gp Capt 1/1/91. Retd GD 28/7/00.
WILLIAMS D.C. OBE. Born 6/11/46. Commd 18/7/68. Wg Cdr 1/1/90. Retd GD 9/9/00.
WILLIAMS D.G. BA. Born 12/7/40. Commd 18/3/63. Sqn Ldr 12/9/71. Retd EDN 12/3/79.
WILLIAMS D.G. Born 28/6/27. Commd 22/8/63. Wg Cdr 1/7/77. Retd MED(SEC) 21/7/79.
WILLIAMS D.H. Born 4/4/28. Commd 27/7/49. Sqn Ldr 1/7/59. Retd GD 1/9/72.
WILLIAMS D.H. MCMI. Born 16/8/20. Commd 21/9/50. Sqn Ldr 1/7/63. Retd SUP 16/8/73.
WILLIAMS D.I. Born 3/2/64. Commd 17/11/91. Sqn Ldr 1/7/95. Retd FLY(P) 3/11/03.
WILLIAMS D.J. BA. Born 19/12/37. Commd 7/8/59. Flt Lt 26/2/64. Retd EDN 8/5/65.
WILLIAMS D.J. BSc CEng MRAeS. Born 7/5/32. Commd 29/4/54. Wg Cdr 1/7/71. Retd ENG 22/4/85.
WILLIAMS D.L. BSc CEng MIEE. Born 15/9/41. Commd 5/10/70. Wg Cdr 1/1/87. Retd ENG 15/9/96.
WILLIAMS D.M. MA MSc. Born 23/6/55. Commd 30/8/78. Wg Cdr 1/1/91. Retd SUP 30/8/94.
WILLIAMS D.M. Born 22/1/22. Commd 25/1/51. Gp Capt 1/1/72. Retd SEC 22/1/77.
WILLIAMS D.R. OBE FCMI. Born 12/5/49. Commd 26/2/71. Air Cdre 1/7/99. Retd GD 14/7/03.
WILLIAMS D.S. Born 24/8/30. Commd 8/4/63. Sqn Ldr 1/7/74. Retd ADMIN 24/8/87.
WILLIAMS D.W. Born 31/7/27. Commd 21/11/51. Sqn Ldr 1/1/67. Retd GD 29/10/75.
WILLIAMS E. MCMI. Born 14/12/22. Commd 14/11/48. Flt Lt 29/6/50. Retd ADMIN 31/12/82.
WILLIAMS E.C.A. Born 9/11/42. Commd 9/2/66. Flt Lt 30/4/72. Retd ADMIN 31/3/94.
WILLIAMS E.H.C. Born 7/6/30. Commd 10/4/52. Sqn Ldr 1/7/62. Retd GD 7/6/68.
WILLIAMS E.M. Born 10/6/25. Commd 8/9/44. Flt Lt 4/12/52. Retd GD 31/12/68.
WILLIAMS E.M. Born 12/12/17. Commd 12/1/49. Flt Lt 12/1/55. Retd SEC 23/8/69.
WILLIAMS E.S. CBE. Born 27/9/24. Commd 7/7/49. A Cdre 1/7/79. Retd GD 23/11/81.
WILLIAMS F.J.B. MB ChB FRCR DMRD. Born 1/2/42. Commd 16/9/63. Sqn Ldr 4/8/72. Retd MED 1/2/80.
WILLIAMS G.A. OBE. Born 24/2/58. Commd 20/7/78. Wg Cdr 1/7/96. Retd ADMIN 24/8/02.
WILLIAMS G.C. AFC* FRAeS. Born 4/6/31. Commd 17/12/57. AVM 1/7/87. Retd GD 4/4/91.
WILLIAMS G.E. CEng MRAeS. Born 29/9/29. Commd 5/12/51. Sqn Ldr 1/7/65. Retd ENG 2/6/81.
WILLIAMS G.H. LVO. Born 6/3/39. Commd 14/5/60. Sqn Ldr 1/1/72. Retd GD 16/6/95.
WILLIAMS G.J. BSc. Born 26/12/63. Commd 25/3/83. Flt Lt 15/1/88. Retd GD 27/8/02.
WILLIAMS G.J. Born 13/11/52. Commd 9/3/72. Sqn Ldr 1/7/81. Retd GD 13/11/90.
WILLIAMS G.J.C. Born 24/9/30. Commd 2/5/57. Flt Lt 7/7/61. Retd SEC 22/1/73.
WILLIAMS G.L. Born 25/6/19. Commd 10/1/46. Sqn Ldr 1/7/65. Retd ENG 9/4/74.
WILLIAMS H.C.J. Born 11/7/43. Commd 12/7/63. Flt Lt 12/1/69. Retd GD 11/7/87.
WILLIAMS H.M. Born 11/9/54. Commd 22/5/75. Sqn Ldr 1/1/91. Retd GD 11/9/98.

WILLIAMS I.A. BEd. Born 16/1/58. Commd 5/2/84. Sqn Ldr 1/1/98. Retd ADMIN 1/1/01.
WILLIAMS I.D. BA. Born 14/4/37. Commd 11/6/63. Sqn Ldr 11/12/73. Retd EDN 11/10/81.
WILLIAMS I.G. MCMI. Born 28/4/21. Commd 22/9/55. Sqn Ldr 1/7/63. Retd ENG 28/4/76.
WILLIAMS I.R. Born 24/7/57. Commd 22/2/79. Sqn Ldr 1/7/89. Retd GD 24/7/01.
WILLIAMS I.S. BSc. Born 22/6/58. Commd 27/3/83. Flt Lt 27/6/85. Retd SUP 22/3/96.
WILLIAMS J. Born 6/12/46. Commd 1/11/81. Flt Lt 1/11/86. Retd ENG 1/11/97.
WILLIAMS J.A. OBE. Born 3/3/29. Commd 13/12/50. Wg Cdr 1/7/75. Retd GD 3/3/84.
WILLIAMS J.A. Born 31/5/48. Commd 5/11/70. Flt Lt 6/5/77. Retd ADMIN 20/7/86.
WILLIAMS J.A. Born 15/9/26. Commd 7/3/51. Sqn Ldr 1/7/67. Retd GD 15/9/86.
WILLIAMS J.A. Born 19/2/23. Commd 4/5/50. Flt Lt 1/11/53. Retd GD 19/4/63.
WILLIAMS J.D. MCMI. Born 26/11/25. Commd 25/5/50. Wg Cdr 1/1/68. Retd GD 5/1/77.
WILLIAMS J.E. BA. Born 8/5/27. Commd 4/8/64. Sqn Ldr 10/2/67. Retd ADMIN 22/8/86.
WILLIAMS J.G. MBE. Born 16/4/46. Commd 2/4/65. Wg Cdr 1/7/96. Retd GD 1/1/01.
WILLIAMS J.G. BSc. Born 26/10/30. Commd 6/11/52. Sqn Ldr 26/10/63. Retd ADMIN 21/10/76.
WILLIAMS J.K. BA. Born 2/5/56. Commd 6/11/77. Sqn Ldr 1/1/89. Retd GD 2/5/00.
WILLIAMS J.K. Born 17/4/22. Commd 15/6/50. Sqn Ldr 1/1/67. Retd GD 30/6/76.
WILLIAMS J.M. BSc. Born 1/5/54. Commd 30/10/72. Flt Lt 15/10/75. Retd ENG 25/6/86.
WILLIAMS J.N. OBE CEng MIEE. Born 4/1/23. Commd 21/5/43. Gp Capt 1/7/74. Retd ENG 4/1/78.
WILLIAMS J.W. BSc. Born 30/1/38. Commd 26/11/60. Flt Lt 26/5/66. Retd GD 30/1/94.
WILLIAMS K. MCMI. Born 24/2/44. Commd 14/8/80. Sqn Ldr 1/1/92. Retd MED(SEC) 25/9/98.
WILLIAMS K.G. BA MRCS LRCP. Born 23/6/26. Commd 27/10/56. Flt Lt 27/10/51. Retd MED 1/5/57. rtg Sqn Ldr.
WILLIAMS K.J. Born 19/9/43. Commd 30/1/70. Sqn Ldr 1/7/79. Retd ENG 1/11/93.
WILLIAMS K.L.D. Born 5/5/43. Commd 23/11/78. Sqn Ldr 1/7/89. Retd ADMIN 5/5/98.
WILLIAMS L.P. MSc BSc. Born 21/6/63. Commd 7/8/95. Flt Lt 27/2/93. Retd FLY(N) 20/7/04.
WILLIAMS M. Born 30/7/37. Commd 26/11/56. Flt Lt 3/1/62. Retd GD 30/7/75.
WILLIAMS M.A. Born 22/9/53. Commd 8/8/74. Wg Cdr 1/1/94. Retd GD 1/7/99.
WILLIAMS M.A. Born 16/12/59. Commd 22/2/79. Flt Lt 22/8/84. Retd GD 16/12/97.
WILLIAMS M.D. Born 23/3/50. Commd 17/5/79. Sqn Ldr 1/7/90. Retd ENG 14/3/96.
WILLIAMS M.F. Born 19/4/42. Commd 6/5/81. Flt Lt 12/8/68. Retd GD 2/4/93.
WILLIAMS M.G. CEng MIEE. Born 7/3/33. Commd 8/2/57. Sqn Ldr 1/1/68. Retd ENG 13/2/74.
WILLIAMS M.G.E. AFC. Born 6/11/24. Commd 12/6/45. Flt Lt 12/12/48. Retd GD 8/4/64.
WILLIAMS M.J. Born 15/11/45. Commd 26/4/84. Sqn Ldr 1/7/92. Retd ADMIN 19/7/94.
WILLIAMS M.J. CEng MIEE MRAeS MCMI. Born 4/11/42. Commd 11/3/65. Sqn Ldr 1/7/77. Retd ENG 4/11/80.
WILLIAMS M.M. Born 24/5/59. Commd 22/7/99. Flt Lt 22/7/01. Retd FLY(P) 10/9/04.
WILLIAMS M.R. MA FCMI. Born 9/8/29. Commd 31/8/54. A Cdre 1/1/78. Retd GD 9/8/84.
WILLIAMS M.T. Born 7/9/35. Commd 14/2/58. Fg Offr 4/3/60. Retd GD 11/3/64.
WILLIAMS M.W. Born 2/1/36. Commd 20/8/58. Flt Lt 7/8/64. Retd GD 15/9/67.
WILLIAMS N.E. BEM LCIPD. Born 12/7/49. Commd 14/2/99. Flt Lt 14/2/99. Retd ADMIN (SEC) 12/7/04.
WILLIAMS N.H. Born 25/12/43. Commd 17/5/63. Wg Cdr 1/7/87. Retd OPS SPT 25/12/98.
WILLIAMS N.M. BA. Born 9/10/26. Commd 17/11/49. Sqn Ldr 1/4/61. Retd EDN 30/4/66.
WILLIAMS N.P. BSc. Born 4/3/65. Commd 8/5/88. Flt Lt 8/11/90. Retd FLY(P) 8/5/04.
WILLIAMS N.R. AFC. Born 10/3/33. Commd 15/11/51. Sqn Ldr 1/7/65. Retd GD 10/3/71.
WILLIAMS O.M. CEng MRAeS. Born 25/6/48. Commd 28/2/69. Sqn Ldr 1/1/80. Retd ENG 25/6/86.
WILLIAMS P. Born 26/5/37. Commd 28/4/61. Fg Offr 28/4/63. Retd GD 30/7/65.
WILLIAMS P.D. BTech. Born 18/1/51. Commd 11/8/74. Sqn Ldr 1/7/88. Retd GD 14/7/92.
WILLIAMS P.F. DPhysEd. Born 19/7/31. Commd 6/1/58. Wg Cdr 1/1/75. Retd ADMIN 6/7/85.
WILLIAMS P.G. BSc. Born 23/2/54. Commd 3/8/75. Flt Lt 3/5/77. Retd GD 23/2/92.
WILLIAMS P.L. MSc BSc CEng MIEE. Born 24/2/65. Commd 28/8/83. Sqn Ldr 1/7/98. Retd ENGINEER 24/2/03.
WILLIAMS P.R.B. Born 8/9/47. Commd 23/6/67. Wg Cdr 8/9/02. Retd ADMIN 8/9/02.
WILLIAMS P.V. Born 15/1/24. Commd 7/5/53. Flt Lt 13/11/57. Retd GD 6/9/69.
WILLIAMS R. BSc(Eng). Born 30/6/40. Commd 30/9/59. Sqn Ldr 1/1/71. Retd ENG 30/6/95.
WILLIAMS R.A. BSc. Born 24/2/68. Commd 7/1/90. Flt Lt 7/7/92. Retd GD 7/10/93.
WILLIAMS R.C. BSc. Born 29/9/53. Commd 28/9/80. Sqn Ldr 1/1/91. Retd SUP 14/11/96.
WILLIAMS R.C. MB ChB DAvMed. Born 31/7/51. Commd 18/7/72. Wg Cdr 24/9/88. Retd MED 31/7/89.
WILLIAMS R.C. MB MRCS LRCP DAvMed. Born 27/3/33. Commd 15/2/59. Wg Cdr 15/2/72. Retd MED 5/7/76.
WILLIAMS R.E. Born 31/1/41. Commd 1/8/61. Gp Capt 1/1/90. Retd GD 29/2/96.
WILLIAMS R.G. BA. Born 15/11/52. Commd 25/9/71. Wg Cdr 1/7/91. Retd SUP 14/3/97.
WILLIAMS R.G.C. Born 3/8/39. Commd 6/7/62. Sqn Ldr 1/7/84. Retd GD 3/8/94.
WILLIAMS R.G.L. Born 19/6/43. Commd 17/12/65. Sqn Ldr 1/1/73. Retd GD 19/6/81.
WILLIAMS R.H. Born 19/4/33. Commd 29/12/51. Flt Lt 2/1/62. Retd GD 1/7/76.
WILLIAMS R.J. Born 23/2/13. Commd 27/5/42. Sqn Ldr 1/7/57. Retd GD(G) 17/4/59.
WILLIAMS R.J.R. Born 30/12/24. Commd 31/3/45. Sqn Ldr 1/1/65. Retd GD 10/6/77.
WILLIAMS R.McC. DFC. Born 10/4/21. Commd 20/10/42. Flt Lt 14/3/51. Retd GD 10/4/76.
WILLIAMS R.N. Born 27/12/48. Commd 11/11/71. Wg Cdr 1/1/97. Retd GD 27/12/03.
WILLIAMS R.N. Born 27/12/48. Commd 11/11/71. Wg Cdr 1/1/97. Retd GD 27/12/03.
WILLIAMS R.S. Born 5/12/36. Commd 28/2/56. Sqn Ldr 1/1/73. Retd GD 3/4/87.

WILLIAMS R.T. Born 11/2/36. Commd 12/1/67. Sqn Ldr 1/1/73. Retd GD 11/2/91.
WILLIAMS R.T. BSc. Born 17/4/29. Commd 24/10/51. Flt Lt 24/7/55. Retd ENG 2/9/80.
WILLIAMS S. Born 17/4/22. Commd 30/12/42. Sqn Ldr 1/1/72. Retd SUP 17/4/73.
WILLIAMS S.B. Born 31/10/41. Commd 9/12/65. Sqn Ldr 1/1/75. Retd ENG 2/11/82.
WILLIAMS S.B. BSc. Born 9/4/61. Commd 31/7/83. Flt Lt 31/1/87. Retd OPS SPT(ATC) 19/5/03.
WILLIAMS S.C. BSc. Born 24/5/64. Commd 18/8/85. Sqn Ldr 1/1/99. Retd GD 24/5/02.
WILLIAMS S.C. Born 30/11/21. Commd 18/10/62. Flt Lt 18/10/65. Retd GD 30/11/76.
WILLIAMS S.D.P. Born 4/12/60. Commd 31/1/80. Flt Lt 31/7/85. Retd GD 13/9/88.
WILLIAMS S.R. BA BEd. Born 27/5/51. Commd 8/12/83. Sqn Ldr 1/1/91. Retd ADMIN 1/1/94.
WILLIAMS S.T. BA. Born 18/7/66. Commd 8/1/89. Sqn Ldr 1/7/99. Retd FLY(P) 8/1/05.
WILLIAMS T. MBE. Born 26/7/18. Commd 29/7/48. Sqn Ldr 1/1/58. Retd SEC 26/7/65.
WILLIAMS T.C. MA. Born 30/4/25. Commd 4/1/56. Sqn Ldr 17/8/61. Retd EDN 22/12/67.
WILLIAMS T.C. Born 30/9/25. Commd 14/1/65. Flt Lt 14/1/68. Retd GD 30/9/75.
WILLIAMS T.G. BSc. Born 4/6/60. Commd 4/9/78. Flt Lt 15/4/84. Retd GD 4/6/98.
WILLIAMS T.I. BEM. Born 30/12/19. Commd 15/6/61. Sqn Ldr 1/7/71. Retd SEC 30/12/74.
WILLIAMS T.J.C. Born 21/12/28. Commd 27/8/52. Sqn Ldr 1/1/70. Retd GD 31/10/75.
WILLIAMS T.R.D. BSc. Born 11/8/44. Commd 30/7/72. Sqn Ldr 30/1/75. Retd ADMIN 30/10/88.
WILLIAMS V.J. MBE BSc. Born 15/1/48. Commd 5/1/70. Sqn Ldr 1/1/89. Retd OPS SPT 22/4/02.
WILLIAMS W.B. LDS. Born 19/6/24. Commd 19/6/47. Wg Cdr 1/4/62. Retd DEL 8/3/73.
WILLIAMS W.M. Born 1/7/30. Commd 22/2/57. Flt Offr 27/2/61. Retd CAT 27/3/65.
WILLIAMSON B.T. Born 18/12/50. Commd 21/2/74. Sqn Ldr 1/7/88. Retd OPS SPT 29/4/01.
WILLIAMSON C.K. Born 29/7/30. Commd 4/10/50. Flt Lt 4/4/55. Retd GD 25/7/68.
WILLIAMSON C.M. MA MSc CEng MRAeS CDipAF. Born 16/4/55. Commd 24/9/76. Wg Cdr 1/7/94.
    Retd ENG 6/4/01.
WILLIAMSON C.R. Born 2/4/46. Commd 20/8/65. Wg Cdr 1/1/90. Retd GD 9/8/97.
WILLIAMSON D.L. Born 17/8/59. Commd 26/11/81. Flt Lt 26/5/88. Retd SY 28/7/93.
WILLIAMSON E.C. BA FCMI. Born 21/4/40. Commd 31/7/62. Gp Capt 1/7/88. Retd SY 1/8/93.
WILLIAMSON I.G. Born 31/3/35. Commd 8/11/68. Flt Lt 8/11/70. Retd SUP 1/5/74.
WILLIAMSON J. Born 9/10/44. Commd 28/6/64. Flt Lt 28/8/69. Retd FLY(N) 9/10/04.
WILLIAMSON J.A. Born 1/7/14. Commd 8/7/42. Flt Offr 8/1/47. Retd SEC 18/6/51.
WILLIAMSON J.H.S. Born 8/2/34. Commd 29/10/52. Flt Lt 24/3/58. Retd GD 8/2/72.
WILLIAMSON J.I.T. Born 25/11/23. Commd 3/8/50. Flt Lt 3/2/54. Retd GD 21/4/56.
WILLIAMSON J.S. Born 29/10/28. Commd 18/10/62. Flt Lt 18/10/68. Retd ENG 1/6/79.
WILLIAMSON M.B. BSc CEng MIEE MCMI. Born 20/9/64. Commd 24/1/85. Wg Cdr 1/7/01. Retd ENG 1/10/02.
WILLIAMSON M.C. Born 12/12/47. Commd 28/2/69. Sqn Ldr 1/1/93. Retd GD 14/3/96.
WILLIAMSON M.E. Born 12/10/44. Commd 9/7/72. Wg Cdr 1/1/90. Retd ADMIN 14/9/96.
WILLIAMSON M.E. OBE. Born 13/4/37. Commd 28/7/59. Gp Capt 1/1/86. Retd GD 2/7/88.
WILLIAMSON N.P. Born 7/4/60. Commd 11/5/86. Sqn Ldr 1/1/99. Retd ENG 11/5/02.
WILLIAMSON P.P. BSc. Born 3/1/43. Commd 6/9/65. Sqn Ldr 1/7/92. Retd GD 31/12/95.
WILLIAMSON R. DFM. Born 8/3/22. Commd 30/11/43. Flt Lt 30/11/49. Retd SEC 25/6/55.
WILLIAMSON R.D. Born 2/12/31. Commd 19/8/53. Sqn Ldr 1/1/64. Retd GD 2/12/69.
WILLIAMSON W.H. Born 5/11/28. Commd 9/1/52. Wg Cdr 1/7/67. Retd ENG 1/7/70.
WILLIAMSON W.M. BA DipPE. Born 18/10/48. Commd 22/8/71. Flt Lt 22/8/75. Retd ADMIN 22/8/87.
WILLIAMSON-NOBLE S.M.D. MA MS CEng FRAeS. Born 18/5/43. Commd 30/9/62. A Cdre 1/1/93.
    Retd ENG 1/8/97.
WILLIES D.A. Born 6/2/41. Commd 14/5/60. Flt Lt 1/4/70. Retd GD(G) 29/10/91.
WILLIMENT A.R. Born 13/5/36. Commd 8/11/68. Wg Cdr 1/7/88. Retd MED(T) 1/1/93.
WILLING M.J. Born 24/8/43. Commd 13/10/61. Flt Lt 9/2/68. Retd GD 8/4/77. rtg Sqn Ldr.
WILLINGALE D.J. Born 20/3/46. Commd 28/4/67. Flt Lt 16/4/77. Retd GD(G) 25/1/94.
WILLINGHAM Y. Born 12/2/63. Commd 14/9/83. Flt Lt 20/1/92. Retd OPS SPT(ATC) 5/4/04.
WILLINGS A.L. BA. Born 3/7/34. Commd 5/4/55. Flt Lt 14/5/58. Retd GD 7/4/79.
WILLIS A.L. BA. Born 30/4/48. Commd 7/1/87. Retd Wg Cdr 30/4/03.
WILLIS A.P. Born 12/2/49. Commd 21/12/67. Sqn Ldr 1/1/89. Retd SUP 14/3/96.
WILLIS A.R. Born 5/12/58. Commd 3/2/85. Flt Lt 14/3/83. Retd GD 5/12/96.
WILLIS B.H.P. Born 17/7/33. Commd 8/9/55. Flt Lt 13/4/60. Retd GD 17/7/71.
WILLIS C.J. Born 15/6/56. Commd 23/10/86. Flt Lt 10/1/89. Retd ADMIN 14/3/96.
WILLIS C.V.D. DSO OBE DFC. Born 9/11/16. Commd 30/7/38. Gp Capt 1/7/56. Retd GD 3/3/65. rtg A Cdre.
WILLIS D. MCSP GradDipPhysio. Born 23/4/39. Commd 21/2/74. Sqn Ldr 3/2/85. Retd MED(T) 20/9/91.
WILLIS D.G. BA. Born 22/8/26. Commd 6/9/56. Flt Lt 6/3/60. Retd GD(G) 8/4/66.
WILLIS D.J. AFC. Born 14/6/39. Commd 25/7/60. Sqn Ldr 1/7/71. Retd GD 14/6/77.
WILLIS D.J.R. MBE CEng MIMechE. Born 13/8/25. Commd 4/9/58. Flt Lt 4/9/63. Retd ENG 5/9/73.
WILLIS G. Born 30/4/30. Commd 13/12/52. Sqn Ldr 1/1/66. Retd GD 1/1/69.
WILLIS G.E. BSc FRAeS. Born 25/10/49. Commd 11/3/73. AVM 1/1/02. Retd GD 25/10/04.
WILLIS G.F. Born 7/3/49. Commd 31/8/78. Sqn Ldr 1/1/91. Retd GD(G) 1/1/93.
WILLIS G.W. FInstPet MCMI. Born 21/2/25. Commd 14/5/49. Wg Cdr 1/7/74. Retd SUP 21/2/80.
WILLIS Sir John GBE KCB. Born 27/10/37. Commd 29/7/58. ACM 4/4/95. Retd GD 10/1/98.

WILLIS J.M. BSc. Born 10/4/42. Commd 1/9/65. Flt Lt 1/6/67. Retd GD 22/10/94.
WILLIS M.E. MSc IEng MIIE LCGI. Born 30/9/52. Commd 29/1/87. Wg Cdr 1/1/01. Retd GD 14/11/03.
WILLIS P.A. Born 22/11/59. Commd 1/11/79. Wg Cdr 1/7/99. Retd GD 17/6/05.
WILLIS R.D. Born 16/5/29. Commd 7/9/61. Sqn Ldr 1/1/74. Retd ENG 19/5/79.
WILLIS-FLEMING R.C. Born 11/12/36. Commd 18/2/58. Wg Cdr 1/7/84. Retd GD(G) 11/12/91.
WILLIS-RICHARDS J.W. MBE. Born 15/10/19. Commd 10/6/41. Sqn Ldr 1/1/58. Retd GD 15/10/62.
WILLISON D.J. BSc. Born 4/7/43. Commd 17/8/64. Gp Capt 1/1/89. Retd GD 7/4/93.
WILLMAN W.T. BA MCMI. Born 16/11/42. Commd 28/7/64. Sqn Ldr 1/1/73. Retd GD 18/12/82. rtg Wg Cdr.
WILLMER C.J. Born 9/4/47. Commd 2/12/66. Sqn Ldr 1/1/85. Retd GD 1/1/88.
WILLMOTT B. Born 26/10/46. Commd 1/3/68. Flt Lt 4/5/72. Retd GD 26/10/84.
WILLMOTT G. Born 12/8/29. Commd 5/1/60. Sqn Ldr 1/7/72. Retd SUP 15/4/91.
WILLMOTT J. Born 19/2/52. Commd 16/3/73. Flt Lt 16/3/76. Retd GD 19/2/80.
WILLMOTT J.R.M. Born 30/6/41. Commd 28/9/61. Sqn Ldr 1/1/73. Retd GD 30/6/79.
WILLMOTT N.P. Born 29/9/51. Commd 14/10/71. Wg Cdr 1/1/89. Retd OPS SPT 1/10/99.
WILLMOTT R.A. Born 26/6/44. Commd 2/2/84. Flt Lt 2/2/88. Retd ADMIN 2/12/97.
WILLMOTT T.W. DFC. Born 28/7/17. Commd 4/3/42. Sqn Ldr 1/4/56. Retd GD 5/8/60.
WILLOUGHBY D.F. Born 21/2/40. Commd 3/8/62. Flt Lt 15/4/70. Retd GD 21/2/95.
WILLOUGHBY M.L. BSc. Born 30/9/48. Commd 1/12/71. Sqn Ldr 1/7/88. Retd ENG 1/12/93.
WILLOUGHBY-CRISP G.A. Born 5/9/44. Commd 29/4/71. Flt Lt 29/4/73. Retd GD 12/9/91.
WILLS A.M. CVO OBE. Born 21/9/43. Commd 28/7/64. Gp Capt 1/7/83. Retd GD 31/3/94.
WILLS A.P. DFC. Born 14/4/22. Commd 23/7/41. Sqn Ldr 1/7/50. Retd GD 27/4/52.
WILLS K.E. CEng MIMechE MRAeS. Born 8/1/26. Commd 4/5/50. Sqn Ldr 1/7/62. Retd ENG 10/1/76.
WILLS R.E. Born 3/11/46. Commd 2/6/67. Flt Lt 2/12/72. Retd GD 3/11/84.
WILLS R.P. BSc. Born 7/12/57. Commd 16/12/79. Flt Lt 16/3/81. Retd GD 9/10/89.
WILLSMER M.J. Born 18/4/45. Commd 12/7/68. Flt Lt 12/1/74. Retd GD 14/3/96.
WILLSON G.R. MBE. Born 11/11/26. Commd 24/10/46. Sqn Ldr 1/7/60. Retd GD 31/12/84.
WILLSON P.A. Born 21/6/58. Commd 1/4/99. Flt Lt 1/4/01. Retd GD 29/10/02.
WILLSON R.A. Born 12/6/46. Commd 5/3/65. Flt Lt 24/12/70. Retd GD 17/3/77.
WILLSON S. Born 27/1/65. Commd 28/2/85. Flt Lt 28/8/90. Retd GD 27/1/03.
WILLSON-PEPPER A.C. Born 7/6/31. Commd 14/7/53. Flt Lt 17/1/58. Retd GD 7/6/68.
WILLY K.R. CBE BA FBCS MMS MCIPS. Born 25/1/25. Commd 30/1/47. A Cdre 1/1/74. Retd SUP 25/1/80.
WILMERS D.H. Born 12/9/46. Commd 1/7/82. Sqn Ldr 1/1/91. Retd ADMIN 1/11/02.
WILMOT A.G. CEng MIEE MCMI. Born 10/7/22. Commd 15/2/51. Wg Cdr 1/1/68. Retd ENG 10/7/77.
WILMOT C.J. Born 27/6/34. Commd 13/12/55. Flt Lt 13/6/58. Retd GD 1/10/71.
WILMOT J.C. MRAeS MCMI. Born 14/3/42. Commd 12/1/61. Sqn Ldr 1/1/76. Retd GD(G) 30/9/88.
WILMOTT C.J. Born 26/7/36. Commd 14/1/65. Flt Lt 26/7/67. Retd SEC 26/7/74.
WILMSHURST A.K. Born 28/7/30. Commd 13/2/52. Sqn Ldr 1/7/69. Retd GD 1/9/77.
WILMSHURST-SMITH S.M. Born 11/1/56. Commd 27/2/75. Sqn Ldr 1/1/88. Retd ADMIN 28/6/93.
WILSHIRE P.J. Born 29/11/40. Commd 20/11/75. Flt Lt 20/11/77. Retd GD(G) 20/11/83.
WILSON Sir Andrew KCB AFC FRAeS. Born 27/2/41. Commd 31/7/62. ACM 16/4/93. Retd GD 26/8/95.
WILSON A. Born 16/1/50. Commd 24/3/83. Wg Cdr 1/7/97. Retd GD 16/1/05.
WILSON A.D. Born 21/12/42. Commd 25/6/65. Flt Lt 25/12/70. Retd GD 8/3/81.
WILSON A.E. Born 19/1/34. Commd 16/9/71. Sqn Ldr 1/1/80. Retd SUP 19/1/84.
WILSON A.H.P. CEng MRAeS MIEE. Born 21/10/36. Commd 23/7/58. Sqn Ldr 1/1/69. Retd ENG 21/10/74.
WILSON A.J. Born 29/6/38. Commd 27/1/64. Flt Lt 27/1/64. Retd GD 11/2/65.
WILSON A.J. Born 1/7/51. Commd 30/1/70. Flt Lt 30/7/72. Retd GD 1/7/89.
WILSON A.J.H. MCMI. Born 11/2/23. Commd 27/3/47. Wg Cdr 1/7/74. Retd SUP 11/2/78.
WILSON A.L. MSc BSc CEng MBCS. Born 26/7/58. Commd 25/1/77. Wg Cdr 1/1/96. Retd ENG 1/1/99.
WILSON A.P. LLB. Born 19/8/52. Commd 25/2/79. Wg Cdr 1/1/92. Retd SY 14/3/96.
WILSON A.R. DSO. Born 22/9/19. Commd 2/3/41. Wg Cdr 1/1/58. Retd GD 22/9/74.
WILSON A.R. MB ChB MFCM DAvMed. Born 22/2/32. Commd 3/11/57. Wg Cdr 3/11/70. Retd MED 1/1/75.
WILSON A.R. Born 1/5/39. Commd 11/4/57. Sqn Ldr 1/7/70. Retd SEC 1/7/73.
WILSON A.R.E. Born 4/5/34. Commd 13/7/61. Flt Lt 1/4/66. Retd SEC 4/5/72.
WILSON B. Born 22/4/39. Commd 5/2/57. Wg Cdr 1/1/80. Retd GD 16/12/89.
WILSON B. Born 21/1/33. Commd 11/10/51. Flt Lt 25/1/57. Retd GD 21/1/71.
WILSON B.A. Born 14/11/40. Commd 28/4/65. Flt Lt 1/7/69. Retd GD 3/5/78.
WILSON B.C.F. Born 26/4/33. Commd 5/11/70. Wg Cdr 1/7/85. Retd GD(G) 26/4/93.
WILSON B.G.R. Born 31/12/59. Commd 1/11/79. Flt Lt 1/5/85. Retd GD 31/12/97.
WILSON C.B. Born 23/2/43. Commd 23/2/64. Fg Offr 23/2/65. Retd GD 26/5/67.
WILSON C.B. BSc. Born 17/10/62. Commd 16/2/86. Flt Lt 16/8/88. Retd FLY(N) 16/8/03.
WILSON D. MDA MCIPS. Born 22/1/48. Commd 7/3/71. Wg Cdr 1/7/91. Retd SUP 14/3/97.
WILSON D.C. McH. Born 22/1/42. Commd 1/6/72. Flt Lt 1/12/77. Retd GD 29/10/82.
WILSON D.F. BA. Born 24/5/50. Commd 13/2/72. Wg Cdr 1/1/88. Retd ADMIN 25/10/96.
WILSON D.G. MBE BSc CEng MIMechE. Born 27/3/49. Commd 26/2/71. Wg Cdr 1/7/91. Retd GD 24/5/04.
WILSON D.J. Born 5/3/45. Commd 31/1/64. Flt Lt 4/11/70. Retd GD 1/9/76.
WILSON D.J. BSc. Born 4/9/62. Commd 18/10/83. Sqn Ldr 1/7/95. Retd ENG 1/3/02.

WILSON D.S. Born 22/5/45. Commd 29/11/63. Sqn Ldr 1/1/81. Retd GD 1/2/85.
WILSON E. Born 27/9/23. Commd 5/5/44. Flt Lt 5/11/47. Retd GD 28/12/64.
WILSON E.R. BSc. Born 18/1/53. Commd 14/9/75. Flt Lt 14/6/78. Retd GD(G) 14/9/91.
WILSON F.M. Born 4/7/42. Commd 8/12/61. Flt Lt 8/6/67. Retd GD 28/7/72.
WILSON G. BSc. Born 6/12/63. Commd 29/9/85. Sqn Ldr 1/7/96. Retd ADMIN 24/3/02.
WILSON G.A. BEM. Born 28/12/46. Commd 24/4/84. Sqn Ldr 1/7/94. Retd ENG 18/6/01.
WILSON G.B. BSc CEng MIEE. Born 26/3/32. Commd 23/9/55. Wg Cdr 1/7/73. Retd ENG 1/1/81.
WILSON G.D. Born 8/11/64. Commd 13/12/93. Flt Lt 2/5/95. Retd OPS SPT(ATC) 28/3/04.
WILSON G.E. BA. Born 12/5/27. Commd 25/9/62. Sqn Ldr 15/2/65. Retd ADMIN 25/9/78. Re-instated 6/8/80 to
    12/5/84.
WILSON G.J. MC. Born 14/8/26. Commd 17/7/47. Wg Cdr 1/1/71. Retd RGT 14/8/84.
WILSON G.K. BSc. Born 16/3/60. Commd 7/11/82. Sqn Ldr 1/7/95. Retd GD 7/11/98.
WILSON G.S. PhD MSc BDS DGDPRCS. Born 9/11/42. Commd 25/3/54. Gp Capt 1/7/74. Retd DEL 4/11/93.
WILSON G.W. MCMI. Born 20/9/24. Commd 22/8/63. Sqn Ldr 1/7/73. Retd ENG 20/9/79.
WILSON H.A. Born 12/11/38. Commd 9/2/62. Wg Cdr 1/1/83. Retd GD 3/1/90.
WILSON H.F. FHCIMA. Born 23/11/17. Commd 7/6/43. Sqn Ldr 1/7/65. Retd CAT 14/11/72.
WILSON I.A.B. MBE MBCS. Born 14/5/49. Commd 31/7/70. Sqn Ldr 1/1/87. Retd GD(G) 17/6/94.
WILSON I.K.A.G. Born 1/4/42. Commd 21/5/65. Flt Lt 4/5/72. Retd GD 8/2/81.
WILSON I.N. Born 25/4/24. Commd 10/3/44. Flt Lt 28/12/47. Retd GD 13/5/67.
WILSON J. Born 15/6/37. Commd 24/2/67. Sqn Ldr 1/1/74. Retd ADMIN 12/11/87.
WILSON J.B. MSc BSc. Born 28/2/31. Commd 24/9/52. Sqn Ldr 7/7/66. Retd EDN 12/10/74.
WILSON J.C. Born 6/3/33. Commd 26/3/59. Sqn Ldr 1/7/71. Retd GD 6/3/91.
WILSON J.D. Born 18/3/26. Commd 18/3/53. Flt Lt 24/7/58. Retd GD 23/9/68.
WILSON J.D. Born 24/12/33. Commd 27/10/67. Flt Lt 12/11/69. Retd GD 24/12/88.
WILSON J.E.S. MVO. Born 7/10/22. Commd 14/3/49. Wg Cdr 1/1/62. Retd SY 26/3/77.
WILSON J.F. Born 5/2/26. Commd 14/3/47. Flt Lt 7/6/51. Retd GD 5/2/64.
WILSON J.G. Born 28/10/40. Commd 3/11/77. Sqn Ldr 1/1/85. Retd ENG 28/10/95.
WILSON J.G. Born 21/9/19. Commd 10/11/42. Sqn Ldr 1/4/55. Retd GD 17/7/59.
WILSON J.G. Born 16/1/17. Commd 28/3/46. Sqn Ldr 1/1/57. Retd SUP 31/5/63. rtg Wg Cdr.
WILSON J.H. The Venerable. CB MA. Born 14/2/24. Commd 10/10/50. Retd AVM 15/9/80.
WILSON J.H.M. BSc. Born 4/1/66. Commd 30/8/87. Flt Lt 28/2/90. Retd GD 14/3/97.
WILSON J.H.W. Born 3/3/33. Commd 18/6/52. Sqn Ldr 1/7/80. Retd GD 3/3/91.
WILSON J.R. Born 21/8/48. Commd 11/8/77. Sqn Ldr 1/1/89. Retd ADMIN 1/5/02.
WILSON J.S. Born 21/6/47. Commd 2/8/68. Wg Cdr 1/7/90. Retd GD 20/5/98.
WILSON J.U. MB BS. Born 18/3/55. Commd 19/7/77. Sqn Ldr 1/2/86. Retd MED 9/7/93.
WILSON J.W. BSc(Eng). Born 5/8/32. Commd 24/8/59. Flt Lt 24/5/61. Retd GD(G) 5/8/90.
WILSON K. Born 20/3/21. Commd 16/3/45. Flt Lt 14/11/55. Retd SUP 25/7/64.
WILSON K.H. AFM. Born 23/4/24. Commd 14/1/54. Flt Lt 14/1/60. Retd GD 30/6/65.
WILSON K.J. Born 28/2/30. Commd 26/11/52. Sqn Ldr 1/1/66. Retd GD 1/7/73.
WILSON L.B. Born 16/3/19. Commd 28/2/46. Flt Lt 29/6/50. Retd ENG 24/7/54.
WILSON L.R. Born 9/12/63. Commd 30/8/84. Flt Lt 1/3/91. Retd ADMIN 20/7/91.
WILSON M.A. BSc. Born 23/12/65. Commd 15/9/86. Flt Lt 15/1/91. Retd GD 15/7/00.
WILSON M.A.S. MA. Born 5/2/49. Commd 14/7/69. Flt Lt 14/4/73. Retd SEC 27/6/75.
WILSON M.C.G. Born 23/4/43. Commd 28/7/64. A Cdre 1/1/92. Retd SUP 14/9/96.
WILSON M.E. Born 24/8/47. Commd 6/1/69. Wg Cdr 1/7/94. Retd ENG 6/4/01.
WILSON M.G. Born 7/7/50. Commd 26/2/71. Sqn Ldr 1/7/85. Retd GD 7/7/88.
WILSON M.J. BA. Born 29/10/32. Commd 3/8/55. Sqn Ldr 17/2/63. Retd EDN 3/8/71.
WILSON M.P. Born 15/9/40. Commd 26/10/61. Flt Lt 15/11/67. Retd SUP 15/11/77.
WILSON M.R. BSc. Born 24/3/57. Commd 14/9/75. Flt Lt 15/4/80. Retd GD 30/9/92.
WILSON N. Born 16/9/34. Commd 25/9/54. Flt Lt 4/6/62. Retd GD 16/9/72.
WILSON P. Born 8/9/31. Commd 14/11/51. Flt Lt 14/5/56. Retd GD 8/9/69.
WILSON P. Born 8/2/65. Commd 8/11/90. Flt Lt 17/11/95. Retd ENG 8/2/03.
WILSON P.A. Born 28/5/55. Commd 20/9/79. Flt Lt 25/10/81. Retd GD 28/5/93.
WILSON P.D. MCMI. Born 3/6/47. Commd 6/4/72. Wg Cdr 1/7/91. Retd ADMIN 14/9/96.
WILSON P.G.C. AFC MRAeS. Born 23/4/29. Commd 26/9/51. Gp Capt 1/7/73. Retd GD 23/12/81.
WILSON P.M. OBE CEng MRAeS MCMI. Born 17/4/31. Commd 25/3/54. Gp Capt 1/7/74. Retd ENG 28/5/77.
WILSON P.R. BSc AMRAeS. Born 24/4/59. Commd 4/7/82. Flt Lt 4/4/84. Retd GD 31/8/98.
WILSON R. Born 5/7/36. Commd 31/7/55. Sqn Ldr 1/1/68. Retd GD 5/7/74.
WILSON R.A. Born 5/6/65. Commd 13/2/86. Flt Lt 13/8/91. Retd FLY(P) 10/9/03.
WILSON R.C. Born 15/6/48. Commd 22/12/67. Wg Cdr 1/7/89. Retd GD 28/3/93.
WILSON R.G. Born 1/1/50. Commd 10/2/72. Fg Offr 10/2/74. Retd GD 13/1/76.
WILSON R.J. MTech CEng MIMechE MRAeS. Born 12/4/38. Commd 30/7/59. Sqn Ldr 1/1/70. Retd ENG 4/11/78.
    Re-instated 4/1/80. Sqn Ldr 13/6/71. Retd ENG 1/7/90.
WILSON R.L. CEng MIEE. Born 3/4/43. Commd 26/5/67. Wg Cdr 1/1/92. Retd ENG 2/8/93.
WILSON R.L. Born 9/10/47. Commd 28/4/67. Fg Offr 28/4/69. Retd GD 2/12/71.
WILSON R.M. BA MRAeS MCMI. Born 22/4/44. Commd 29/11/63. Sqn Ldr 1/7/81. Retd GD 22/4/99.

WILSON R.N. Born 8/5/32. Commd 5/12/60. Sqn Ldr 1/7/68. Retd GD 1/4/73.
WILSON R.R. Born 7/1/22. Commd 7/2/47. Fg Offr 16/2/49. Retd GD 12/9/52.
WILSON R.V. Born 8/5/45. Commd 27/11/65. Flt Lt 4/5/72. Retd GD 12/4/76.
WILSON R.V.W. BSc. Born 16/5/46. Commd 17/9/67. Sqn Ldr 1/7/81. Retd ENG 16/5/90.
WILSON S. BSc. Born 14/10/58. Commd 29/8/77. Sqn Ldr 1/1/91. Retd GD 14/10/96.
WILSON S.G.W. Born 29/6/45. Commd 25/6/65. Flt Lt 17/3/71. Retd GD 25/4/76.
WILSON S.J. BSc. Born 18/1/62. Commd 10/11/85. Flt Lt 10/5/89. Retd SUP 15/12/90.
WILSON S.J. BA. Born 8/9/70. Commd 10/4/94. Flt Lt 10/10/96. Retd ADMIN (SEC) 23/4/03.
WILSON S.P. Born 11/2/47. Commd 16/11/72. Flt Lt 16/5/77. Retd GD 1/5/91.
WILSON S.R. MCMI. Born 19/1/33. Commd 12/9/63. Sqn Ldr 1/1/74. Retd ADMIN 31/3/85.
WILSON T.A. Born 5/8/43. Commd 12/1/62. Flt Lt 12/7/67. Retd GD 15/4/76.
WILSON T.H.W. CEng MRAeS MIEE. Born 20/7/38. Commd 9/3/66. Sqn Ldr 1/1/73. Retd ENG 29/9/81.
WILSON T.I. The Rev. Born 25/10/30. Commd 16/1/57. Retd Wg Cdr 8/11/85.
WILSON T.M. BEM. Born 23/9/32. Commd 4/7/69. Sqn Ldr 1/7/80. Retd ADMIN 24/9/82.
WILSON W. Born 17/6/23. Commd 10/3/41. Sqn Ldr 1/7/71. Retd GD 17/6/81.
WILSON W. BSc. Born 1/2/54. Commd 8/4/79. Flt Lt 8/1/83. Retd ADMIN 1/5/85.
WILSON W.J. Born 7/10/40. Commd 4/9/81. Sqn Ldr 1/1/90. Retd SY 7/10/95.
WILSON W.J.Mc. AFM. Born 19/6/24. Commd 17/5/56. Sqn Ldr 1/7/71. Retd GD 1/10/77.
WILSON-CLARK F.K. Born 15/2/43. Commd 8/6/62. Flt Lt 9/2/68. Retd GD 15/2/81.
WILTON M.S.J. Born 23/3/17. Commd 4/4/38. Flt Lt 1/9/45. Retd SEC 19/10/52. rtg Sqn Ldr.
WILTON-JONES A.M. Born 8/4/49. Commd 18/1/73. Plt Offr 19/4/73. Retd PI 28/2/75.
WILTSHIER J.R. DPhysEd. Born 15/12/23. Commd 8/8/51. Flt Lt 8/8/55. Retd ADMIN 31/8/65.
WILTSHIRE J. OBE CEng MIMechE MRAeS MCMI. Born 22/12/31. Commd 16/5/57. Wg Cdr 1/7/78.
　　Retd ENG 31/8/86.
WILTSHIRE J.R. DPhysEd. Born 15/12/23. Commd 8/8/51. Flt Lt 8/8/55. Retd PE 31/8/65.
WILTSHIRE P.A. Born 5/7/61. Commd 10/8/81. Flt Lt 15/4/87. Retd GD 14/3/96.
WINCH C.A.H. Born 28/6/21. Commd 9/1/43. Flt Lt 9/7/46. Retd GD 31/12/55.
WINCH G.E. CBE FCMI. Born 27/7/35. Commd 3/5/56. A Cdre 1/7/87. Retd SY 27/7/90.
WINCH H.J. Born 20/4/18. Commd 15/2/39. Sqn Ldr 1/7/43. Retd ENG 1/5/46. rtg Wg Cdr.
WINCHURCH J.C.G. Born 29/5/37. Commd 23/1/64. Sqn Ldr 1/1/78. Retd ADMIN 10/4/82.
WINDEATT M.C. Born 23/11/40. Commd 17/5/79. Flt Lt 17/5/82. Retd GD 19/1/94.
WINDER P.D. Born 31/5/50. Commd 16/9/71. Flt Lt 16/3/77. Retd GD 31/5/88.
WINDER P.L. Born 1/8/43. Commd 17/5/63. Flt Lt 17/11/68. Retd GD 4/9/70.
WINDLE M.N. ADC MA CEng MIMechE. Born 15/6/43. Commd 30/9/61. Gp Capt 1/1/83. Retd ENG 10/10/86.
WINDLE R.E. AFC. Born 30/3/22. Commd 21/2/44. Flt Lt 21/8/47. Retd GD 30/6/61.
WINDSOR B.J. Born 12/9/33. Commd 28/9/54. Flt Lt 28/9/56. Retd GD 30/9/64.
WINDSOR G.E.J. BEd. Born 23/3/58. Commd 19/6/83. Sqn Ldr 1/1/89. Retd ADMIN 23/6/89.
WINDSOR P.J. BSc CEng MRAeS. Born 20/7/59. Commd 26/9/82. Sqn Ldr 1/7/94. Retd ENG 26/9/98.
WINEPRESS F.J. Born 17/1/22. Commd 21/12/44. Sqn Ldr 1/7/69. Retd SUP 25/6/73.
WINFIELD D. BSc CertEd. Born 23/9/52. Commd 9/11/80. Sqn Ldr 1/1/90. Retd ADMIN 14/3/96.
WINFIELD R.G. Born 21/1/25. Commd 3/12/59. Sqn Ldr 1/1/76. Retd GD 21/1/83.
WING L. MBE BA MCMI. Born 28/10/32. Commd 12/7/51. A Cdre 1/1/85. Retd GD 28/10/87.
WING W.M.G. MBE DFM. Born 12/2/19. Commd 31/8/42. Sqn Ldr 1/1/54. Retd SEC 22/7/67.
WINGATE J.B. Born 25/8/24. Commd 11/2/44. Flt Lt 11/8/47. Retd GD 25/8/62.
WINGATE N.R.J. AFC. Born 26/5/34. Commd 28/11/60. Sqn Ldr 1/1/81. Retd GD 5/4/85.
WINGFIELD J.D.T. Born 12/9/39. Commd 25/7/60. Sqn Ldr 1/1/73. Retd GD 30/4/74.
WINGHAM A. MB BS DRCOG. Born 13/12/58. Commd 13/2/80. Wg Cdr 3/8/97. Retd MED 1/9/01.
WINGROVE G.E. MSc BSc. Born 26/10/58. Commd 11/9/77. Wg Cdr 1/1/00. Retd GD 12/4/03.
WINKLES A.R.C. Born 17/2/45. Commd 28/2/64. Wg Cdr 1/1/83. Retd GD 1/7/01.
WINKLEY C.H. Born 9/7/55. Commd 6/11/80. Flt Lt 6/5/87. Retd SY 31/3/94.
WINKS S.W. Born 26/11/16. Commd 9/7/59. Flt Lt 9/7/62. Retd ENG 28/11/70.
WINKWORTH R.J. LDSRCS. Born 4/5/37. Commd 9/6/63. Gp Capt 1/1/84. Retd DEL 9/6/94.
WINLOW R.S. Born 3/1/22. Commd 9/8/47. Sqn Ldr 1/7/59. Retd SUP 14/12/63.
WINN S. Born 31/12/18. Commd 18/9/47. Flt Lt 19/6/52. Retd SEC 30/9/67.
WINN S.B. Born 3/9/24. Commd 11/9/44. Sqn Ldr 1/1/55. Retd GD 14/1/57.
WINN-MORGAN T.M. BSc. Born 28/5/56. Commd 15/9/74. Sqn Ldr 1/7/94. Retd ENG 1/8/96.
WINNING R.M.J. Born 14/3/43. Commd 17/3/67. Wg Cdr 1/7/87. Retd OPS SPT 14/3/98.
WINSHIP J.H.A. Born 15/9/31. Commd 28/12/51. Wg Cdr 1/1/66. Retd GD 1/5/69.
WINSKILL Sir Archie KCVO CBE DFC* AE. Born 24/1/17. Commd 15/8/40. A Cdre 1/7/63. Retd GD 18/12/68.
WINSLAND C.G. OBE. Born 21/6/40. Commd 26/5/67. A Cdre 1/7/94. Retd ADMIN 13/5/99.
WINSTANLEY K. Born 8/3/39. Commd 26/5/61. Sqn Ldr 1/7/74. Retd GD 1/7/77.
WINSTON D.G. Born 8/9/34. Commd 31/1/72. Flt Lt 13/1/77. Retd GD(G) 7/3/86.
WINSTONE T.J. Born 6/9/44. Commd 31/1/64. Flt Lt 4/11/70. Retd GD 31/1/76.
WINTER C.B. Born 12/1/54. Commd 30/1/75. Sqn Ldr 1/1/88. Retd SY 14/3/96.
WINTER C.R. DFC. Born 2/6/23. Commd 5/12/43. Sqn Ldr 1/1/55. Retd GD 11/10/56.
WINTER D. Born 18/5/39. Commd 12/2/59. Flt Lt 12/5/65. Retd SEC 8/10/74.

WINTER E. Born 11/6/42. Commd 25/6/66. Flt Lt 25/6/68. Retd GD 31/1/75.
WINTER K.R. Born 9/5/40. Commd 1/8/61. Wg Cdr 1/1/85. Retd GD 9/5/95.
WINTER Y.E. BSc. Born 1/7/20. Commd 12/10/55. Flt Offr 12/4/61. Retd SEC 12/8/67.
WINTERBOTTOM D. Born 30/4/31. Commd 26/7/51. Sqn Ldr 1/1/84. Retd GD 30/4/93.
WINTERBOTTOM D.F. Born 6/1/23. Commd 26/9/57. Flt Lt 26/9/63. Retd SEC 1/8/70.
WINTERBOURNE J.S. MBE AFC. Born 16/1/25. Commd 7/5/53. Sqn Ldr 1/7/72. Retd GD 24/1/85.
WINTERBOURNE S.J. Born 12/12/57. Commd 3/11/77. Sqn Ldr 1/7/90. Retd ADMIN 12/6/97.
WINTERFORD D.A. Born 4/7/23. Commd 3/3/44. Sqn Ldr 1/7/57. Retd GD 12/2/67.
WINTERHALDER V.N. BSc. Born 23/11/41. Commd 15/7/64. Flt Lt 22/5/68. Retd ENG 23/11/79.
WINTERMEYER M.J. BSc. Born 5/3/63. Commd 18/8/85. Flt Lt 18/2/88. Retd GD 18/8/01.
WINTERS A.L. Born 3/5/35. Commd 28/5/66. Flt Lt 28/5/72. Retd PRT 1/4/76.
WINTERS I.J.E. Born 30/4/66. Commd 14/1/88. Flt Lt 12/3/92. Retd ADMIN 14/9/96.
WINTERSGILL D. Born 13/12/42. Commd 20/7/65. Flt Lt 6/10/71. Retd ENG 20/7/81.
WINTERTON I.T. CEng MIEE. Born 9/6/38. Commd 18/10/62. Flt Lt 14/11/67. Retd ENG 9/6/76.
WINTERTON R.M. MSc BSc CPhys MInstP MCMI. Born 24/6/54. Commd 8/4/79. Wg Cdr 1/7/94.
   Retd ADMIN 14/3/97.
WIRDNAM A.R.J. Born 15/9/38. Commd 26/10/62. Flt Lt 26/4/67. Retd GD 10/7/78.
WIRDNAM K.A.C. Born 13/9/28. Commd 1/8/51. A Cdre 1/7/76. Retd GD 13/9/83.
WISBY W.G. Born 13/8/14. Commd 26/11/53. Flt Lt 26/11/56. Retd GD 13/8/69.
WISE A.M. Born 9/12/58. Commd 19/7/84. Flt Lt 19/1/91. Retd ADMIN 3/1/93.
WISE A.N. LVO MBE BA. Born 1/8/43. Commd 17/12/65. Gp Capt 1/7/90. Retd GD 1/8/98.
WISEMAN E.A. Born 14/4/18. Commd 10/10/46. Sqn Ldr 1/1/59. Retd SUP 13/7/68.
WISEMAN H. Born 1/7/24. Commd 12/1/49. Flt Offr 12/1/55. Retd SUP 30/9/55.
WISEMAN N. BSc MIExpE DipEd AIL. Born 22/7/46. Commd 2/5/71. Wg Cdr 1/7/89. Retd ENG 14/9/96.
WISEMAN R.A. BSc. Born 26/6/54. Commd 13/2/77. Flt Lt 13/5/78. Retd GD 14/3/97.
WISHART R. BSc. Born 10/7/55. Commd 3/9/72. Flt Lt 15/4/80. Retd ENG 15/7/88.
WISHART S.R. Born 22/8/45. Commd 16/9/71. Flt Lt 16/3/77. Retd GD 29/7/77.
WISMARK M.R.S. MBE. Born 22/10/34. Commd 25/7/56. Wg Cdr 1/7/74. Retd ENG 2/9/75.
WISTOW D.J. MBE. Born 2/2/24. Commd 23/3/51. Sqn Ldr 1/1/70. Retd GD 1/4/73.
WITCHALL S.C. Born 5/4/24. Commd 28/7/60. Flt Lt 28/7/63. Retd GD 5/4/84.
WITCHELL W.J.H. Born 14/3/17. Commd 8/7/48. Sqn Ldr 1/1/52. Retd RGT 31/3/58.
WITHERINGTON A.A. Born 29/9/20. Commd 31/8/44. Gp Capt 1/1/67. Retd PRT 29/9/75.
WITHEROW J.H. MCIPD MCMI. Born 10/6/27. Commd 1/6/49. Sqn Ldr 1/1/67. Retd SY 10/6/82.
WITHEROW M.S. FCMI. Born 17/8/36. Commd 21/6/56. A Cdre 1/7/86. Retd RGT 23/11/90.
WITHERS A.F. Born 14/1/44. Commd 26/5/67. Flt Lt 15/4/70. Retd GD 4/1/86.
WITHERS B.R. MBE AFC. Born 22/9/46. Commd 25/2/66. Sqn Ldr 1/1/88. Retd GD 12/9/01.
WITHERS P.A.G. Born 5/5/23. Commd 29/5/43. Sqn Ldr 1/1/53. Retd GD 10/6/61.
WITHERS R.B. Born 3/12/30. Commd 13/7/61. Flt Lt 13/7/67. Retd SEC 20/9/69.
WITHERS R.M. BEng. Born 5/3/65. Commd 31/7/91. Sqn Ldr 1/1/02. Retd ENGINEER 1/1/05.
WITHERS W.F.M. DFC. Born 12/1/46. Commd 18/8/68. Sqn Ldr 1/1/87. Retd GD 26/9/91.
WITHEY V.R. Born 11/10/21. Commd 15/8/44. Wg Cdr 1/7/67. Retd SUP 27/3/76.
WITHINGTON A.M. Born 17/9/36. Commd 15/4/55. Sqn Ldr 1/1/71. Retd GD 17/9/74.
WITHINGTON B. BSc. Born 12/1/51. Commd 22/9/74. Sqn Ldr 1/7/83. Retd ADMIN 9/12/90.
WITTIN-HAYDEN L.J. DFC AFC. Born 23/11/19. Commd 15/11/44. Sqn Ldr 1/1/68. Retd GD 30/9/70.
WITTON H. Born 15/12/29. Commd 10/9/69. Sqn Ldr 1/7/80. Retd ENG 30/10/81.
WITTS D.R. Born 27/9/40. Commd 23/9/87. Flt Lt 1/1/70. Retd GD(G) 28/11/88.
WITTS S.M. MB ChB DRCOG. Born 23/11/59. Commd 31/1/88. Flt Lt 31/1/88. Retd MED 6/7/88.
WOBER H.A. MB BS MFOM DRCOG DAvMed MRAeS. Born 6/6/39. Commd 10/9/62. A Cdre 1/1/92.
   Retd MED 1/6/97.
WOLFF J.M. MBE. Born 16/1/38. Commd 7/6/68. Flt Lt 7/6/70. Retd GD 7/6/76.
WOLLASTON K.F. Born 19/2/35. Commd 11/6/63. Sqn Ldr 1/7/72. Retd CAT 11/6/79.
WOLLERT C.A.L. Born 29/7/28. Commd 28/6/51. Flt Lt 10/6/63. Retd GD 1/3/68.
WOLLEY J.H. MBE. Born 3/4/31. Commd 25/9/51. Sqn Ldr 1/1/70. Retd GD 3/4/93.
WOLSEY A.K. Born 18/7/49. Commd 27/5/71. Sqn Ldr 1/7/85. Retd ADMIN 30/9/97.
WOLSTENHOLE A. Born 10/8/32. Commd 5/7/53. Flt Lt 7/3/62. Retd GD(G) 10/8/87.
WOLSTENHOLME H. Born 14/1/32. Commd 22/8/51. Sqn Ldr 1/1/62. Retd GD 14/4/71. rtg Wg Cdr.
WOLSTENHOLME R.A. Born 11/3/32. Commd 10/9/52. Flt Lt 7/2/58. Retd GD 11/3/70.
WOMACK J. BSc. Born 11/5/49. Commd 17/1/72. Flt Lt 17/10/75. Retd SUP 17/1/88.
WOMPHREY P. Born 29/10/39. Commd 17/9/57. Sqn Ldr 1/1/71. Retd GD 29/10/90.
WOOBERRY D.E. Born 22/1/36. Commd 24/7/57. Flt Lt 15/4/62. Retd ENG 8/6/70.
WOOD A. Born 29/6/61. Commd 14/2/88. Sqn Ldr 1/1/97. Retd ENGINEER 14/2/04.
WOOD A.C.M. Born 31/7/52. Commd 26/10/62. Flt Lt 4/5/72. Retd GD 31/7/76.
WOOD A.H. BSc. Born 8/11/31. Commd 24/2/55. Sqn Ldr 17/2/63. Retd EDN 11/11/70.
WOOD A.MCF. Born 3/8/46. Commd 27/3/75. Sqn Ldr 1/7/89. Retd GD(G) 14/9/96.
WOOD A.S. BSc. Born 29/3/59. Commd 1/2/87. Flt Lt 1/8/86. Retd ADMIN 14/3/97.
WOOD A.W. Born 1/10/63. Commd 19/12/91. Flt Lt 19/12/93. Retd ENG 15/3/99.

WOOD A.W. Born 10/3/45. Commd 26/11/64. Flt Lt 15/4/71. Retd SUP 5/7/75.
WOOD B. Born 22/10/49. Commd 23/9/68. Plt Offr 8/11/71. Retd GD 6/4/73.
WOOD B.L. OBE. Born 11/12/36. Commd 30/12/54. Gp Capt 1/1/90. Retd GD 1/2/91.
WOOD C.C. Born 26/9/48. Commd 29/6/72. Plt Offr 29/6/73. Retd GD 8/2/74.
WOOD C.L. Born 2/2/42. Commd 11/6/81. Flt Lt 11/6/86. Retd ENG 31/3/94.
WOOD C.R.S. Born 24/11/41. Commd 15/7/64. Wg Cdr 1/7/88. Retd ENG 11/10/99.
WOOD D. OBE MCMI. Born 5/10/19. Commd 30/5/44. Wg Cdr 1/7/65. Retd GD 5/10/74.
WOOD D. BA FTCL LGSM ARCM. Born 3/11/37. Commd 28/6/79. Sqn Ldr 5/7/88. Retd DM 1/5/91.
WOOD D. Born 30/12/23. Commd 30/11/44. Sqn Ldr 1/1/56. Retd GD 30/12/61.
WOOD D.A. Born 15/1/53. Commd 15/3/73. Fg Offr 15/9/75. Retd SY 18/8/76.
WOOD D.A. BA. Born 20/3/42. Commd 1/10/67. Sqn Ldr 5/7/75. Retd ADMIN 5/1/83.
WOOD D.A. Born 30/1/28. Commd 23/4/53. Sqn Ldr 1/1/63. Retd GD 9/7/73.
WOOD D.A. Born 6/3/34. Commd 5/2/57. Sqn Ldr 1/7/80. Retd ADMIN 10/7/86.
WOOD D.D. Born 22/2/48. Commd 5/4/79. Flt Lt 5/4/81. Retd GD 30/11/91.
WOOD D.G. Born 20/3/32. Commd 4/10/56. Flt Lt 4/4/61. Retd GD 1/5/75. Re-entered 23/4/80. Flt Lt 27/3/66. Retd GD(G) 1/5/85.
WOOD D.H. MCMI. Born 26/2/30. Commd 12/12/51. Wg Cdr 1/7/76. Retd GD 12/11/84.
WOOD D.J. CEng MRAeS. Born 5/2/19. Commd 28/10/43. Sqn Ldr 1/10/55. Retd ENG 8/2/69.
WOOD D.L. BSc CEng MIEE MRAeS. Born 13/6/21. Commd 18/3/43. Sqn Ldr 1/1/54. Retd ENG 10/8/61.
WOOD D.M. Born 10/8/57. Commd 5/8/76. Wg Cdr 1/1/97. Retd GD 10/8/01.
WOOD E. Born 2/1/35. Commd 29/7/55. Flt Lt 16/8/61. Retd GD 2/1/73.
WOOD E.G. Born 13/10/37. Commd 2/4/57. Sqn Ldr 1/7/69. Retd GD 30/9/80.
WOOD E.J.C. Born 21/1/36. Commd 1/1/76. Retd ENG 4/7/77.
WOOD E.T. Born 11/6/24. Commd 15/12/44. Sqn Ldr 1/7/59. Retd GD 12/6/68.
WOOD F.R. AFC. Born 31/3/25. Commd 15/12/49. Flt Lt 19/11/53. Retd GD 31/3/63.
WOOD G. CBE. Born 3/9/39. Commd 1/10/64. A Cdre 1/7/91. Retd GD(G) 3/9/94.
WOOD G.P. Born 29/6/60. Commd 29/1/87. Flt Lt 23/4/89. Retd SUP 29/6/98.
WOOD H.R. Born 1/4/20. Commd 2/10/58. Flt Lt 2/10/63. Retd ENG 4/7/70.
WOOD H.W. Born 24/5/23. Commd 26/6/44. Flt Lt 7/6/51. Retd PE 29/1/53.
WOOD I. Born 4/3/46. Commd 18/8/70. Flt Lt 18/2/76. Retd GD 17/8/86.
WOOD I.J. Born 11/6/48. Commd 27/5/68. Fg Offr 10/8/70. Retd SEC 2/2/74.
WOOD J. DFM. Born 4/8/13. Commd 31/7/41. Wg Cdr 1/7/47. Retd GD 2/5/58.
WOOD J.B.H. Born 7/11/39. Commd 19/12/61. Flt Lt 10/2/67. Retd GD 7/11/77.
WOOD J.E. Born 11/3/23. Commd 23/12/43. Flt Lt 27/5/54. Retd PE 11/3/71.
WOOD J.F. BA. Born 12/8/41. Commd 7/7/67. Flt Lt 12/1/70. Retd GD 12/8/79. Re-entered 13/8/80. Flt Lt 13/1/71. Retd GD 12/8/96.
WOOD J.M. CEng MIEE. Born 11/5/43. Commd 21/1/66. Flt Lt 21/7/72. Retd ENG 5/10/87.
WOOD J.P. CBE. Born 7/3/32. Commd 1/3/51. A Cdre 1/1/79. Retd ADMIN 1/4/83.
WOOD J.R. Born 20/10/64. Commd 30/8/84. Flt Lt 20/2/90. Retd GD 20/10/02.
WOOD J.W. MBE. Born 14/1/17. Commd 22/7/44. Wg Cdr 1/1/69. Retd GD(G) 14/1/74.
WOOD K.G. BSc. Born 29/6/43. Commd 27/10/68. Sqn Ldr 1/7/88. Retd GD 22/6/93.
WOOD M. BSc. Born 5/8/53. Commd 6/3/77. Flt Lt 6/12/78. Retd GD 6/3/89.
WOOD M.A. Born 4/11/40. Commd 17/12/63. Gp Capt 1/1/90. Retd GD 4/11/90.
WOOD M.A. Born 8/3/53. Commd 29/4/71. Sqn Ldr 1/7/99. Retd FLY(N) 3/10/03.
WOOD M.E. Born 4/10/48. Commd 2/6/67. Sqn Ldr 1/7/83. Retd GD 6/11/86.
WOOD M.H. MBE. Born 11/9/44. Commd 10/12/65. Wg Cdr 1/1/94. Retd GD 10/10/97.
WOOD M.J. Born 14/2/56. Commd 23/11/78. Flt Lt 2/1/83. Retd SY 14/2/94.
WOOD M.J. MInstPet. Born 12/9/48. Commd 2/11/88. Sqn Ldr 1/1/01. Retd SUPPLY 12/9/03.
WOOD M.L. Born 30/12/46. Commd 10/12/65. Flt Lt 4/5/72. Retd GD 28/9/73.
WOOD M.P. BSc. Born 19/3/57. Commd 12/10/78. Flt Lt 15/10/79. Retd GD 10/6/95.
WOOD M.S. BA. Born 26/10/61. Commd 30/10/83. Flt Lt 30/4/87. Retd OPS SPT 30/10/99.
WOOD N.R. CBE BSc MRAeS. Born 21/7/49. Commd 23/9/68. Air Cdre 1/7/00. Retd GD 31/8/03.
WOOD P. MBE. Born 10/8/57. Commd 24/3/83. Wg Cdr 1/7/94. Retd SY 14/3/96.
WOOD P.C. Born 23/11/39. Commd 31/8/62. Flt Lt 29/2/68. Retd GD 15/5/78.
WOOD P.D. Born 27/7/23. Commd 11/8/44. Wg Cdr 1/1/72. Retd GD(G) 1/12/77.
WOOD P.E. Born 17/7/29. Commd 27/10/55. Flt Lt 21/10/59. Retd ENG 1/12/61.
WOOD P.J. Born 17/10/48. Commd 16/8/68. Flt Lt 16/2/74. Retd GD 17/10/86.
WOOD P.L. CEng MRAeS. Born 3/8/38. Commd 28/4/64. Wg Cdr 1/7/90. Retd ENG 18/2/94.
WOOD P.M. Born 8/5/58. Commd 21/4/77. Wg Cdr 1/7/96. Retd OPS SPT 8/5/02.
WOOD P.R. Born 8/4/44. Commd 28/4/65. Sqn Ldr 1/1/78. Retd GD 8/4/82.
WOOD R. BSc(Eng) CEng MRAeS. Born 26/9/41. Commd 30/9/61. Wg Cdr 1/7/79. Retd ENG 3/4/93.
WOOD R. MBE. Born 15/5/14. Commd 14/11/46. Sqn Ldr 1/1/62. Retd SUP 15/5/69.
WOOD R. MCMI. Born 15/5/21. Commd 28/8/46. Wg Cdr 1/1/72. Retd GD(G) 13/4/74.
WOOD R.A. MBE MCIT MILT. Born 25/11/43. Commd 13/2/64. Wg Cdr 1/1/83. Retd SUP 25/11/87.
WOOD R.B. Born 23/2/45. Commd 4/11/82. Sqn Ldr 1/7/91. Retd ENG 20/8/98.
WOOD R.C. OBE AFC. Born 11/11/29. Commd 18/6/76. Gp Capt 1/1/80. Retd GD 7/11/84.

WOOD R.H. OBE. Born 24/1/36. Commd 1/2/56. AVM 1/1/88. Retd GD 3/4/90.
WOOD R.J. BSc CEng MIEE. Born 19/6/45. Commd 15/7/66. Sqn Ldr 1/1/77. Retd ENG 19/6/83.
WOOD R.P. BA. Born 8/4/51. Commd 19/2/73. Flt Lt 19/5/74. Retd GD 8/4/89.
WOOD R.R. Born 14/11/27. Commd 4/2/71. Flt Lt 4/2/74. Retd SUP 14/11/82.
WOOD R.S. McP. Born 12/5/47. Commd 25/2/66. Flt Lt 6/10/71. Retd GD 12/5/85.
WOOD S. MHCIMA. Born 29/6/52. Commd 18/11/75. Air Cdre 1/7/01. Retd GD 7/8/03.
WOOD S.J. BSc. Born 1/2/53. Commd 25/9/71. Sqn Ldr 1/1/87. Retd GD 1/2/91.
WOOD T.A.K. Born 6/11/32. Commd 28/6/51. Flt Lt 10/1/57. Retd GD 6/11/92.
WOOD T.C. Born 2/6/21. Commd 6/9/56. Flt Lt 6/9/59. Retd ADMIN 2/6/76.
WOOD T.J. Born 16/10/48. Commd 31/7/70. Gp Capt 1/1/98. Retd GD 27/2/02.
WOOD W. Born 22/7/40. Commd 31/7/62. Sqn Ldr 1/7/71. Retd GD 22/7/78.
WOOD W.C. AFC AFM. Born 25/12/21. Commd 20/4/50. Flt Lt 20/10/53. Retd GD 1/5/61.
WOOD W.J.H. Born 8/9/44. Commd 17/10/71. Sqn Ldr 1/7/84. Retd ENG 17/10/87.
WOOD W.R. Born 11/7/20. Commd 6/11/58. Flt Lt 6/11/63. Retd RGT 11/7/75.
WOODACRE R.W. Born 23/5/39. Commd 9/7/59. Flt Lt 10/2/67. Retd GD 14/9/68.
WOODARD J.F. CBE FCMI. Born 5/6/31. Commd 30/9/53. Gp Capt 1/7/77. Retd GD 5/6/84.
WOODBERRY M.A.S. Born 10/4/38. Commd 10/9/70. Sqn Ldr 1/7/88. Retd ADMIN 10/4/93.
WOODBRIDGE D.A.S. MBE MRAeS. Born 14/1/20. Commd 15/4/43. Sqn Ldr 1/7/58. Retd ENG 1/10/63.
WOODCOCK A.D. DFC* MRAeS. Born 26/2/23. Commd 10/12/43. Wg Cdr 1/7/60. Retd GD 4/9/69.
WOODCOCK A.W.D. MBE. Born 8/6/24. Commd 20/2/45. Wg Cdr 1/1/72. Retd ADMIN 29/3/78.
WOODCOCK B.N. BTech. Born 3/2/48. Commd 10/4/68. Sqn Ldr 1/7/78. Retd ENG 4/5/01.
WOODCOCK J.A. BDS. Born 14/7/58. Commd 22/2/81. Sqn Ldr 16/1/86. Retd DEL 22/2/86.
WOODCOCK J.D. Born 12/2/18. Commd 24/3/43. Flt Lt 24/9/47. Retd GD(G) 25/4/69.
WOODCRAFT R.G. AFC. Born 29/8/13. Commd 2/5/40. Sqn Ldr 1/7/53. Retd GD(G) 29/8/63.
WOODCRAFT R.W. Born 4/11/20. Commd 19/8/42. Sqn Ldr 1/7/59. Retd ENG 4/11/75.
WOODFIELD R.W. Born 31/5/48. Commd 15/8/85. Flt Lt 15/8/89. Retd ENG 1/2/95.
WOODFORD A.A.G. CB BA. Born 6/1/39. Commd 28/7/59. AVM 1/1/88. Retd GD 2/6/92.
WOODGATE A.M. BEng. Born 1/2/63. Commd 3/9/90. Flt Lt 15/7/93. Retd ENGINEER 1/2/04.
WOODGATE L. Born 3/7/28. Commd 4/6/64. Flt Lt 4/6/69. Retd ENG 1/8/78. Re-instated 4/3/81 to 4/3/84.
WOODHAM P.R. Born 25/3/26. Commd 14/1/53. Sqn Ldr 1/7/71. Retd GD 3/8/74.
WOODHAMS M.W. Born 16/11/31. Commd 17/5/51. Flt Lt 6/9/56. Retd GD 10/10/64.
WOODHEAD R.W.A. Born 8/4/39. Commd 13/12/60. Sqn Ldr 1/7/77. Retd GD 8/4/94.
WOODHOUSE C.H.D. Born 4/7/45. Commd 25/1/71. Flt Lt 16/1/74. Retd GD(G) 19/7/89.
WOODHOUSE G. Born 23/12/40. Commd 22/5/80. Flt Lt 22/5/83. Retd GD 9/7/91.
WOODHOUSE J.E. Born 4/1/46. Commd 2/11/88. Flt Lt 2/11/92. Retd ENG 1/5/93.
WOODHOUSE J.M. BA. Born 22/12/65. Commd 10/11/91. Flt Lt 10/5/94. Retd ADMIN 14/3/96.
WOODHOUSE R. Born 13/11/20. Commd 14/1/44. Flt Lt 14/7/47. Retd GD(G) 7/2/56.
WOODHOUSE R. Born 25/5/32. Commd 7/5/52. Flt Lt 2/10/57. Retd GD 25/5/70.
WOODHOUSE S.H. Born 4/2/31. Commd 1/3/51. Sqn Ldr 1/1/63. Retd SEC 4/2/69.
WOODHOUSE W.K. Born 4/12/51. Commd 26/3/72. Sqn Ldr 1/1/85. Retd SY(RGT) 4/12/89.
WOODIER J.L. Born 6/3/33. Commd 18/11/66. Flt Lt 18/11/72. Retd SEC 16/12/72.
WOODING G.P.C. BA. Born 1/1/51. Commd 15/9/69. Wg Cdr 1/1/88. Retd ADMIN 7/12/91.
WOODING R.J. DPhysEd. Born 21/6/49. Commd 16/8/70. Sqn Ldr 1/1/88. Retd ADMIN 1/10/91.
WOODIWISS M.J. Born 9/9/42. Commd 4/2/71. Flt Lt 6/4/75. Retd ADMIN 5/12/82.
WOODLAND C.R. Born 25/3/44. Commd 5/9/88. Sqn Ldr 1/1/92. Retd ENGINEER 25/3/03.
WOODLEY G.J. OBE. Born 18/5/46. Commd 1/3/68. A Cdre 1/1/96. Retd ENG 31/12/96.
WOODLEY G.V. Born 18/8/36. Commd 25/6/66. Flt Lt 4/11/70. Retd SUP 18/8/74.
WOODLEY M.E. Born 2/9/46. Commd 2/8/68. Sqn Ldr 1/7/81. Retd GD 2/9/90.
WOODLEY R.J.R. Born 7/7/23. Commd 6/9/56. Sqn Ldr 1/7/69. Retd GD 3/9/73.
WOODMAN A.W.K. Born 4/4/27. Commd 20/6/51. Flt Lt 20/12/55. Retd GD 4/4/65.
WOODMAN C.M. BA. Born 17/4/56. Commd 14/1/79. Wg Cdr 1/7/93. Retd ADMIN 23/8/95.
WOODMAN D.D. MA BA CEng MIEE MRAeS. Born 18/5/54. Commd 3/9/72. Wg Cdr 1/7/91. Retd ENG 1/7/94.
WOODMAN P.M. Born 2/1/44. Commd 2/3/78. Sqn Ldr 1/7/89. Retd GD 23/12/96.
WOODROFFE R.J. MBE. Born 12/6/50. Commd 19/8/71. Wg Cdr 1/7/89. Retd ADMIN 2/11/01.
WOODRUFF A.F. Born 27/11/56. Commd 6/5/83. Flt Lt 18/10/85. Retd SY 27/11/94.
WOODRUFF D.B. Born 30/6/33. Commd 2/6/52. Flt Lt 29/4/60. Retd GD 18/9/70.
WOODS A.E.G. AFC. Born 19/1/23. Commd 24/3/44. Wg Cdr 1/7/65. Retd GD 1/7/75.
WOODS A.J. BA. Born 30/9/38. Commd 9/3/72. Wg Cdr 1/7/89. Retd ADMIN 30/9/93.
WOODS C. Born 1/7/43. Commd 11/5/62. Flt Lt 11/11/67. Retd GD 31/12/74.
WOODS C.J. MSc BSc(Eng) CEng MIMechE MRAeS. Born 22/8/47. Commd 22/9/65. Wg Cdr 1/7/89. Retd ENG 22/8/02.
WOODS D. CBE CEng MRAeS MCMI. Born 10/4/24. Commd 7/4/46. Gp Capt 1/7/72. Retd ENG 28/8/76.
WOODS D.J. MBCS MCMI. Born 14/9/32. Commd 15/12/53. Gp Capt 1/7/84. Retd SUP 14/9/87.
WOODS G. Born 5/5/36. Commd 7/12/61. Wg Cdr 1/1/79. Retd GD(G) 16/12/81. Re-instated on Retired List 24/11/89.
WOODS G.C. Born 4/5/46. Commd 21/7/65. Flt Lt 21/1/71. Retd GD 18/12/73.

WOODS G.P. Born 15/4/35. Commd 19/8/53. Sqn Ldr 1/7/80. Retd GD 15/4/93.
WOODS J. CChem MRSC. Born 28/8/37. Commd 25/7/71. Sqn Ldr 1/1/80. Retd ENG 28/8/95.
WOODS J. Born 18/9/41. Commd 22/2/63. Flt Lt 22/8/68. Retd GD 18/9/79.
WOODS J.C. Born 16/8/22. Commd 25/2/44. Wg Cdr 1/7/66. Retd GD 6/3/76.
WOODS J.R. BSc. Born 26/9/50. Commd 28/2/72. Sqn Ldr 1/1/84. Retd GD 26/9/88.
WOODS J.W. Born 16/12/28. Commd 5/7/68. Flt Lt 5/7/73. Retd ENG 16/12/89.
WOODS K.B. BSc DipEl. Born 10/11/21. Commd 31/10/41. Sqn Ldr 10/11/55. Retd EDN 31/8/63.
WOODS L.A. Born 2/3/50. Commd 11/11/71. Sqn Ldr 1/1/84. Retd ADMIN 2/3/88.
WOODS P.A.A. MSc. Born 3/11/45. Commd 18/8/67. Wg Cdr 1/7/87. Retd SUP 14/3/97.
WOODS P.R. Born 20/7/38. Commd 24/7/71. Sqn Ldr 1/7/80. Retd ENG 20/7/93.
WOODS R.D. Born 2/12/53. Commd 11/8/77. Flt Lt 11/2/83. Retd GD 14/3/97.
WOODS R.J.A. Born 15/5/20. Commd 13/5/44. Sqn Ldr 1/9/65. Retd GD 15/5/68.
WOODS T.A. Born 14/7/58. Commd 15/8/85. Sqn Ldr 1/7/95. Retd ENG 20/5/99.
WOODS T.J.A. Born 1/3/63. Commd 8/4/82. Sqn Ldr 1/7/98. Retd GD 1/7/01.
WOODS T.L. Born 17/7/48. Commd 11/6/81. Wg Cdr 1/7/92. Retd MED SPT 1/10/02.
WOODS W.E. Born 5/11/31. Commd 17/12/52. Flt Lt 17/6/55. Retd GD 5/11/69.
WOODWARD B.S.A. MCMI. Born 12/12/31. Commd 2/7/52. Sqn Ldr 1/1/70. Retd GD 30/4/83.
WOODWARD D.A. Born 12/6/52. Commd 25/9/71. Plt Offr 25/9/73. Retd GD 25/9/74.
WOODWARD D.A. BA. Born 7/4/56. Commd 2/3/80. Flt Lt 2/9/83. Retd SUP 2/3/96.
WOODWARD F.H. ACIS. Born 27/2/21. Commd 22/9/44. Flt Lt 22/9/50. Retd SEC 28/2/55.
WOODWARD R.A. Born 7/10/14. Commd 17/5/56. Flt Lt 17/5/59. Retd ENG 16/9/66.
WOODWARD R.C. Born 7/1/43. Commd 23/12/60. Wg Cdr 1/1/85. Retd GD 2/4/93.
WOOFF K.C. Born 19/6/59. Commd 29/7/83. Flt Lt 29/1/89. Retd GD 13/9/99.
WOOLCOCK P.R. Born 26/1/25. Commd 28/7/44. Flt Lt 11/11/54. Retd GD 16/1/76.
WOOLDRIDGE D. Born 28/2/44. Commd 4/7/69. Sqn Ldr 1/1/82. Retd GD 2/7/93.
WOOLDRIDGE M. Born 3/11/41. Commd 18/12/65. Flt Lt 8/3/72. Retd GD 22/10/94.
WOOLDRIDGE M.G.L. MA. Born 15/7/50. Commd 19/2/73. Wg Cdr 1/7/91. Retd SUP 14/3/97.
WOOLER K. Born 19/4/54. Commd 6/10/77. Flt Lt 6/4/83. Retd GD 1/5/90.
WOOLF D. Born 24/1/39. Commd 21/2/69. Flt Lt 25/12/74. Retd MED(SEC) 22/2/77.
WOOLFORD K.C. BA. Born 15/3/44. Commd 29/7/65. Sqn Ldr 1/7/79. Retd GD 1/7/82.
WOOLFORD P.R. MBA (Eur Ing) CEng FRSA MRAeS MInstD MCMI. Born 25/4/44. Commd 27/3/70. Wg Cdr 1/7/88.
    Retd ENG 25/4/99.
WOOLFORD R.F. Born 12/8/33. Commd 19/8/71. Sqn Ldr 19/2/78. Retd ADMIN 13/8/86.
WOOLFREY A.G.J. Born 12/11/31. Commd 19/6/52. Sqn Ldr 1/7/82. Retd GD 12/5/92.
WOOLGAR D.C. Born 18/9/40. Commd 26/8/66. Flt Lt 7/12/68. Retd ENG 18/9/78.
WOOLLACOTT R.N. MBE. Born 4/9/43. Commd 28/7/64. Wg Cdr 1/1/89. Retd GD 26/6/01.
WOOLLAM R.J. Born 2/7/47. Commd 29/6/72. Flt Lt 29/12/77. Retd GD 13/3/88.
WOOLLER J. Born 10/8/22. Commd 1/6/44. Sqn Ldr 1/1/73. Retd ENG 10/8/77.
WOOLLETT R. Born 1/5/30. Commd 5/9/57. Flt Lt 5/3/62. Retd GD 19/1/63.
WOOLLEY F.E. Born 14/3/13. Commd 12/12/46. Flt Lt 12/6/51. Retd SUP 14/3/62. rtg Sqn Ldr.
WOOLLEY G.A. OBE AFC. Born 16/5/45. Commd 21/7/65. Gp Capt 1/1/94. Retd GD 14/3/96.
WOOLLEY H.H. MBE. Born 18/7/31. Commd 16/12/51. Sqn Ldr 1/1/71. Retd GD(G) 18/7/86.
WOOLLEY J.C. BSc. Born 15/7/54. Commd 15/9/54. Flt Lt 15/4/61. Retd ENG 28/12/67.
WOOLLEY J.M. Born 9/7/47. Commd 16/8/68. Sqn Ldr 1/7/81. Retd GD 9/7/85.
WOOLLEY R. Born 26/5/56. Commd 7/11/91. Flt Lt 7/11/95. Retd MED(SEC) 15/10/97.
WOOLLEY W. Born 19/9/32. Commd 30/7/52. Flt Lt 27/12/57. Retd GD 19/9/91.
WOOLLISCROFT D.G. MB BS MRCGP DRCOG DAvMed AFOM. Born 1/2/57. Commd 21/8/80. Wg Cdr 1/8/94.
    Retd MED 21/8/96.
WOOLMAN M.A. Born 6/10/66. Commd 25/2/88. Flt Lt 25/8/93. Retd GD 14/3/97.
WOOLSTON P.C.G. BEM. Born 11/8/20. Commd 27/10/55. Sqn Ldr 1/1/69. Retd GD(G) 30/4/74.
WOOLVEN C.G. CEng MRAeS. Born 17/1/20. Commd 27/4/44. Sqn Ldr 1/7/65. Retd ENG 17/9/70.
WOOLVEN R.E. Born 1/9/37. Commd 19/9/59. Sqn Ldr 1/1/71. Retd GD 21/10/78.
WOOSEY D.C. Born 25/10/55. Commd 11/4/85. Wg Cdr 1/1/00. Retd GD 8/9/02.
WOOSTER J.L. Born 20/5/31. Commd 10/10/51. Flt Lt 10/4/56. Retd GD 20/5/69.
WOOTTON D.G. CChemMRSC FIBMS. Born 17/11/39. Commd 27/3/70. Flt Lt 27/3/76. Retd MED(T) 31/12/77.
WORBY I.A.N. Born 6/9/28. Commd 5/4/50. Gp Capt 1/7/77. Retd GD 29/5/82.
WORDSWORTH J.C.R. MHCIMA. Born 15/6/27. Commd 15/8/62. Flt Lt 14/2/66. Retd CAT 20/11/74.
WORLEY D.C. Born 21/1/67. Commd 27/8/87. Flt Lt 27/2/93. Retd GD 14/9/96.
WORMALD I.A. Born 31/3/38. Commd 10/11/61. Sqn Ldr 1/1/74. Retd GD 1/1/77. Re-instated 11/10/76 to 11/10/87.
WORRALL G.G. Born 7/7/33. Commd 13/8/52. Flt Lt 9/1/58. Retd GD 7/7/72.
WORRALL J.A. OBE MCMI. Born 21/6/27. Commd 7/12/49. Wg Cdr 1/1/65. Retd GD 22/6/82.
WORSELL G.A.W. BA. Born 1/5/30. Commd 19/8/53. Sqn Ldr 17/2/63. Retd EDN 19/8/69.
WORSLEY G.A. Born 6/12/34. Commd 8/9/69. Sqn Ldr 1/7/79. Retd SY 8/9/85.
WORSLEY S.E. LLB. Born 23/2/75. Commd 1/2/01. Flt Lt 1/2/01. Retd LEGAL 31/8/03.
WORSLEY W.E. Born 6/11/35. Commd 27/4/61. Flt Lt 1/7/68. Retd SUP 12/1/75. rtg Sqn Ldr.
WORT M.J. MB BS BMedSci FFARCS. Born 26/2/53. Commd 17/9/74. Wg Cdr 20/7/91. Retd MED 21/10/91.

WORT P.L. Born 8/10/32. Commd 27/8/52. Flt Lt 23/1/58. Retd GD 20/8/76.
WORTH A.J.S. Born 29/7/48. Commd 10/2/72. Flt Lt 15/7/75. Retd GD(G) 29/7/86.
WORTH A.M. BDS LDSRCS. Born 12/9/43. Commd 23/8/61. Flt Lt 23/12/64. Retd DEL 28/9/68.
WORTHINGTON D.R. CEng MIEE MRaeS MCMI. Born 10/8/33. Commd 22/7/55. Sqn Ldr 1/7/66. Retd ENG 14/12/71.
WORTHINGTON I.J. BA CEng MIEE. Born 22/4/40. Commd 30/9/59. Wg Cdr 1/7/82. Retd ENG 1/3/94.
WORTHINGTON I.R. Born 23/11/51. Commd 9/12/71. Flt Lt 25/11/78. Retd SY(RGT) 23/11/89.
WORTHINGTON P.L.B. PhD MSc BSc BSc. Born 20/3/44. Commd 20/1/80. Flt Lt 20/1/81. Retd ADMIN 1/1/85.
WORTHINGTON P.M. MBE. Born 8/10/28. Commd 27/7/49. Sqn Ldr 1/1/61. Retd GD 8/10/66.
WORTHINGTON P.S. Born 20/6/37. Commd 3/10/69. Sqn Ldr 1/1/76. Retd GD(G) 1/1/79.
WORTHINGTON R.B. MBE. Born 6/4/15. Commd 16/12/43. Sqn Ldr 1/1/70. Retd SEC 1/1/73.
WORTHY E.A. Born 23/10/21. Commd 24/4/43. Flt Lt 5/10/60. Retd GD(G) 31/1/76.
WORTLEY M.G. Born 24/7/41. Commd 22/2/63. Flt Lt 22/8/68. Retd GD 24/7/96.
WOSKETT S.W.K. AFM MCMI. Born 24/10/28. Commd 19/12/59. Sqn Ldr 1/1/77. Retd ADMIN 24/10/83.
WOTHERSPOON A.S. Born 16/3/30. Commd 27/9/51. Flt Lt 11/1/57. Retd GD 16/3/68.
WRAIGHT M.J. Born 27/4/33. Commd 17/1/52. Sqn Ldr 1/1/71. Retd GD 27/4/88.
WRANGHAM J. Born 4/12/32. Commd 26/3/52. Flt Lt 31/7/57. Retd GD 22/3/71.
WRATTEN Sir William GBE CB AFC CCMI FRaeS. Born 15/8/39. Commd 13/12/60. ACM 1/9/94. Retd GD 5/11/97.
WRAY A.F. Born 12/2/35. Commd 14/1/53. Wg Cdr 1/1/76. Retd GD 16/6/81.
WRAY H.L. BSc. Born 23/5/67. Commd 6/11/88. Sqn Ldr 1/1/96. Retd ENG 10/9/01.
WRAY P. BSc CEng MIEE. Born 24/5/46. Commd 26/5/67. Wg Cdr 1/1/82. Retd ENG 10/12/86.
WRAY P.M. BEng. Born 19/6/64. Commd 5/8/92. Sqn Ldr 1/1/02. Retd ENGINEER 1/1/05.
WREN C.A. MSc BSc(Eng). Born 17/4/62. Commd 14/9/80. Sqn Ldr 1/7/91. Retd ENGINEER 1/7/03.
WREN C.G. Born 4/5/48. Commd 23/2/68. Flt Lt 23/8/73. Retd GD 4/5/82.
WREN D. Born 2/6/21. Commd 30/7/59. Flt Lt 27/2/63. Retd ENG 4/9/71.
WREN R.J. Born 6/7/59. Commd 11/8/77. Sqn Ldr 1/7/93. Retd GD 8/5/98.
WRENN M.J. Born 25/6/66. Commd 28/2/85. Flt Lt 28/8/91. Retd OPS SPT(ATC) 25/6/04.
WRIDE G.B. Born 16/5/53. Commd 21/12/89. Flt Lt 21/12/93. Retd ENG 1/11/94.
WRIGHT A. Born 5/4/24. Commd 8/9/43. Sqn Ldr 1/7/55. Retd GD 5/4/73.
WRIGHT A.A.H. Born 1/8/22. Commd 25/5/50. Sqn Ldr 1/1/70. Retd GD 1/8/73.
WRIGHT A.B. Born 29/5/46. Commd 29/10/64. Fg Offr 7/5/67. Retd RGT 1/9/71.
WRIGHT A.C. Born 30/3/24. Commd 18/9/48. Flt Lt 3/7/54. Retd GD 30/3/67.
WRIGHT A.J. BA MCMI. Born 1/1/42. Commd 24/2/61. Sqn Ldr 1/1/79. Retd GD 1/7/98.
WRIGHT A.J. DFC MRIN MCMI. Born 27/7/22. Commd 6/11/42. Wg Cdr 1/1/66. Retd GD(G) 3/1/76.
WRIGHT A.J.W. Born 8/10/40. Commd 26/5/61. Flt Lt 26/11/66. Retd GD 8/10/78.
WRIGHT A.L. CEng MRAeS. Born 20/9/27. Commd 27/6/57. Wg Cdr 1/1/77. Retd EDN 19/5/79.
WRIGHT A.O. MBE CEng MRAeS. Born 8/10/37. Commd 30/7/59. Wg Cdr 1/7/88. Retd ENG 8/10/90.
WRIGHT A.R. DFC* AFC. Born 12/2/20. Commd 23/10/39. Wg Cdr 1/7/52. Retd GD 12/2/67. rtg Gp Capt.
WRIGHT A.R. Born 10/5/48. Commd 29/9/69. Flt Lt 10/5/75. Retd OPS SPT(ATC) 10/5/03.
WRIGHT A.W.A. Born 4/8/31. Commd 27/6/51. Flt Lt 27/12/55. Retd GD 4/8/89.
WRIGHT B.A. CBE AFC. Born 22/11/40. Commd 11/9/64. Gp Capt 1/1/84. Retd GD 22/11/95.
WRIGHT B.W. BA. Born 19/3/57. Commd 22/3/81. Flt Lt 22/6/81. Retd GD 12/2/91.
WRIGHT C.H. Born 8/4/37. Commd 3/11/60. Sqn Ldr 1/1/72. Retd GD 12/7/90.
WRIGHT C.J. BA MCMI. Born 15/10/57. Commd 22/3/81. Flt Lt 22/9/84. Retd ADMIN 22/3/97.
WRIGHT D. MMar. Born 24/6/35. Commd 9/3/62. Flt Lt 9/9/67. Retd GD 24/6/93.
WRIGHT D. AFC. Born 28/9/28. Commd 27/7/49. Wg Cdr 1/1/65. Retd GD 28/9/83.
WRIGHT D. MCMI. Born 23/11/33. Commd 13/8/52. Flt Lt 20/2/58. Retd GD 23/11/71.
WRIGHT D. Born 30/6/26. Commd 13/8/52. Flt Lt 9/1/58. Retd GD 29/6/68.
WRIGHT D.B. Born 4/12/30. Commd 19/8/53. Flt Lt 20/2/59. Retd GD 15/1/64.
WRIGHT D.D. Born 11/5/38. Commd 26/5/67. Flt Lt 30/10/69. Retd ADMIN 11/5/76.
WRIGHT D.H. LDSRCS. Born 5/5/36. Commd 22/5/60. Wg Cdr 17/4/73. Retd DEL 15/6/93.
WRIGHT D.K. DPhysEd. Born 20/6/35. Commd 7/2/57. Gp Capt 1/1/91. Retd ADMIN 20/4/91.
WRIGHT D.W. Born 16/2/38. Commd 24/11/60. Sqn Ldr 1/7/71. Retd SUP 1/8/78.
WRIGHT D.W. Born 22/9/57. Commd 20/1/85. Fg Offr 20/1/87. Retd ADMIN 30/4/90.
WRIGHT E.H. Born 15/4/32. Commd 27/8/52. Sqn Ldr 1/1/67. Retd GD 3/9/85.
WRIGHT E.W. CBE DFC DFM. Born 21/9/19. Commd 18/12/40. A Cdre 1/7/66. Retd GD 21/7/73.
WRIGHT F. Born 3/11/19. Commd 13/2/47. Flt Lt 13/8/51. Retd SUP 6/11/68.
WRIGHT F.C. MBE MIPD. Born 22/1/23. Commd 9/7/43. Sqn Ldr 1/1/70. Retd ADMIN 22/1/78.
WRIGHT F.G. BEM. Born 7/2/35. Commd 24/2/67. Flt Lt 24/2/73. Retd PRT 2/4/75.
WRIGHT G.C. Born 29/2/40. Commd 22/4/73. Flt Lt 22/10/73. Retd GD 11/3/78.
WRIGHT G.J. Born 13/12/14. Commd 15/12/34. Wg Cdr 1/7/47. Retd 1/11/49. rtg Gp Capt.
WRIGHT G.J. Born 13/2/40. Commd 28/10/68. Sqn Ldr 1/7/78. Retd CAT 28/10/84.
WRIGHT G.W.F. Born 5/1/46. Commd 18/8/67. Flt Lt 18/8/70. Retd GD 24/4/75.
WRIGHT H.T. Born 3/9/17. Commd 6/6/44. Flt Lt 6/12/47. Retd ENG 31/12/64.
WRIGHT I.H. Born 4/10/41. Commd 20/10/68. Sqn Ldr 1/7/79. Retd GD 10/7/83.
WRIGHT I.M. BSc. Born 15/4/61. Commd 2/9/79. Flt Lt 15/10/83. Retd GD 15/4/99.
WRIGHT J. MBE. Born 28/11/41. Commd 16/9/71. Wg Cdr 1/1/88. Retd MED(SEC) 30/6/90.

WRIGHT J. Born 15/11/33. Commd 14/12/54. Sqn Ldr 1/7/68. Retd GD 15/11/71.
WRIGHT J. BSc. Born 16/2/66. Commd 11/10/84. Flt Lt 15/1/90. Retd FLY(N) 16/2/04.
WRIGHT J.S. Born 9/3/20. Commd 10/3/45. Sqn Ldr 1/1/68. Retd SEC 9/9/75.
WRIGHT J.W.F. Born 11/5/26. Commd 21/12/45. Flt Lt 30/6/49. Retd GD 26/10/52.
WRIGHT K.B. Born 8/12/23. Commd 11/2/44. Flt Lt 11/8/47. Retd GD 8/12/61.
WRIGHT K.M. Born 1/10/65. Commd 21/6/90. Sqn Ldr 1/7/01. Retd ENGINEER 1/7/04.
WRIGHT L.H. MBE MCMI. Born 5/5/31. Commd 17/5/62. Sqn Ldr 1/7/75. Retd ADMIN 19/1/84.
WRIGHT L.J. Born 11/3/28. Commd 17/5/51. Sqn Ldr 1/7/62. Retd GD 25/10/75.
WRIGHT M.A.B.K. Born 3/7/53. Commd 16/9/71. Flt Lt 16/3/77. Retd GD 3/1/92.
WRIGHT M.C. Born 31/5/39. Commd 13/12/60. Flt Lt 13/6/63. Retd GD 31/12/69.
WRIGHT M.C.StJ. Born 31/12/41. Commd 24/2/67. Sqn Ldr 1/7/81. Retd ENG 31/12/96.
WRIGHT M.D. MBE. Born 25/6/27. Commd 30/8/48. Wg Cdr 1/1/73. Retd PRT 1/6/78.
WRIGHT M.H. Born 29/1/49. Commd 31/3/70. Flt Lt 31/3/75. Retd GD 14/3/96.
WRIGHT N. Born 26/2/29. Commd 23/2/50. Flt Lt 18/5/59. Retd GD 26/2/67.
WRIGHT N. BSc. Born 8/4/35. Commd 25/2/64. Sqn Ldr 25/3/70. Retd ADMIN 25/2/83.
WRIGHT N.J. Born 4/10/41. Commd 28/7/60. Wg Cdr 1/7/83. Retd ADMIN 4/10/91.
WRIGHT O.D. BA. Born 15/4/49. Commd 8/11/68. Wg Cdr 1/1/94. Retd GD 14/3/97.
WRIGHT P. Born 29/11/38. Commd 25/11/78. Flt Lt 23/11/84. Retd SY 1/10/86.
WRIGHT P.C. Born 9/10/45. Commd 2/8/68. Fg Offr 9/11/70. Retd GD(G) 6/4/74.
WRIGHT P.D. BA. Born 4/7/26. Commd 4/10/50. Wg Cdr 1/7/63. Retd GD 1/11/80. rtg Gp Capt.
WRIGHT P.H.F. Born 12/7/32. Commd 10/4/56. Flt Lt 10/10/61. Retd GD 10/10/75.
WRIGHT P.J. Born 18/5/32. Commd 28/11/51. Sqn Ldr 1/7/65. Retd GD 14/8/72.
WRIGHT P.J. Born 18/3/48. Commd 19/8/66. Sqn Ldr 1/1/81. Retd GD 18/3/86.
WRIGHT P.M. Born 5/2/63. Commd 20/5/82. Flt Lt 20/11/87. Retd GD 29/11/91.
WRIGHT R. Born 28/7/35. Commd 27/1/67. Sqn Ldr 1/7/82. Retd ENG 3/11/85.
WRIGHT R.C. Born 23/1/43. Commd 28/7/64. Sqn Ldr 1/1/78. Retd GD 2/4/93.
WRIGHT R.H. Born 23/11/21. Commd 13/7/61. Flt Lt 13/7/66. Retd ENG 5/4/75.
WRIGHT R.J. Born 20/7/44. Commd 5/11/70. Flt Lt 1/4/74. Retd GD 20/7/82.
WRIGHT R.M. Born 14/7/39. Commd 11/5/62. Flt Lt 11/11/67. Retd GD 14/7/97.
WRIGHT R.StL. Born 7/5/28. Commd 28/2/57. Sqn Ldr 1/7/68. Retd GD 15/7/72.
WRIGHT R.W. MB ChB. Born 11/1/23. Commd 22/9/44. Wg Cdr 5/9/64. Retd MED 12/2/68.
WRIGHT R.W.J. Born 2/5/36. Commd 10/8/55. Sqn Ldr 1/7/81. Retd GD 2/7/89.
WRIGHT S.G. DFC. Born 6/7/22. Commd 16/8/46. Flt Lt 29/6/50. Retd GD 7/7/55.
WRIGHT S.G. Born 20/5/37. Commd 24/4/61. Flt Lt 25/5/61. Retd GD 24/4/77.
WRIGHT S.J. Born 12/3/35. Commd 23/11/78. Flt Lt 23/11/83. Retd PI 4/1/86.
WRIGHT S.R.A. Born 25/6/51. Commd 8/4/82. Sqn Ldr 1/7/92. Retd ADMIN 30/9/99.
WRIGHT T.B. BA. Born 10/2/43. Commd 22/7/71. Wg Cdr 1/1/86. Retd ENG 10/2/98.
WRIGHT W.J.R. Born 19/3/35. Commd 23/5/63. Flt Lt 26/10/69. Retd GD(G) 20/2/79.
WRIGHT W.W. BA BA DipEd. Born 5/10/42. Commd 8/1/68. Wg Cdr 1/1/87. Retd ADMIN 29/8/94.
WRIGHT-NOOTH P.H. Born 24/10/26. Commd 3/8/66. Flt Lt 15/3/68. Retd ADMIN 3/8/82.
WRIGHTON P.J. MRIN. Born 27/10/44. Commd 14/7/66. Wg Cdr 1/7/88. Retd GD 2/4/93.
WRIGLEY D.A. Born 17/12/47. Commd 2/8/68. Sqn Ldr 1/1/92. Retd ENG 12/6/01.
WRIGLEY S.A. Born 19/3/44. Commd 15/7/66. Gp Capt 1/1/96. Retd GD 19/3/99.
WRINCH N.P.H. Born 11/10/53. Commd 5/8/76. Fg Offr 5/8/78. Retd GD 9/12/81.
WYATT A.R. MSc. Born 2/2/45. Commd 16/9/76. Sqn Ldr 1/7/84. Retd ADMIN 16/9/89.
WYATT A.S.t.C. Born 24/8/27. Commd 1/6/50. Sqn Ldr 1/1/61. Retd GD 24/9/76.
WYATT A.V. Born 15/2/43. Commd 21/1/66. Sqn Ldr 1/1/92. Retd GD 15/2/98.
WYATT D.A. Born 3/2/61. Commd 31/1/80. Sqn Ldr 1/1/92. Retd GD 4/2/98.
WYATT D.P.P. BSc. Born 19/2/66. Commd 11/10/84. Flt Lt 15/1/90. Retd GD 15/7/99.
WYATT D.R. MBE. Born 3/10/40. Commd 15/3/79. Sqn Ldr 1/7/89. Retd ENG 3/10/95.
WYATT G.M. DFC. Born 24/9/15. Commd 30/9/35. Wg Cdr 1/7/47. Retd GD 24/9/55. rtg Gp Capt.
WYATT J.W. BSc CEng MRAeS. Born 27/2/37. Commd 30/9/56. Wg Cdr 1/7/76. Retd ENG 30/8/80.
WYATT S.G. BSc. Born 16/3/61. Commd 1/9/83. Flt Lt 11/3/86. Retd GD 14/3/97.
WYATT S.J. Born 21/8/53. Commd 11/8/77. Flt Lt 11/2/83. Retd GD 1/10/98.
WYDRA S.P. BSc. Born 6/2/53. Commd 13/11/72. Flt Lt 15/10/74. Retd GD 15/7/85.
WYER E.J. Born 11/12/47. Commd 31/7/70. Sqn Ldr 1/1/84. Retd GD 12/12/91.
WYER R.F.E. Born 22/11/43. Commd 22/3/63. Flt Lt 22/9/68. Retd GD 2/12/75.
WYLAM B.B. Born 28/9/35. Commd 27/1/55. Flt Lt 1/3/61. Retd SEC 28/9/73.
WYLD H. Born 28/1/33. Commd 9/4/52. Flt Lt 5/9/57. Retd GD 28/1/76.
WYLD J.R. Born 16/3/31. Commd 8/11/51. Sqn Ldr 1/7/69. Retd GD 30/9/77.
WYLDE R.C. Born 25/9/29. Commd 10/12/52. Flt Lt 5/5/58. Retd GD 23/6/68.
WYLIE M.D. Born 13/12/46. Commd 2/8/68. Sqn Ldr 1/1/92. Retd GD 31/1/01.
WYLIE M.D. DFC. Born 28/2/22. Commd 15/1/41. Wg Cdr 1/1/58. Retd GD 30/8/69. rtg Gp Capt.
WYLLIE D.G.V. Born 13/1/30. Commd 1/12/53. Flt Lt 1/3/61. Retd GD 1/12/69.
WYLLIE H.A. LDSRCS. Born 17/6/33. Commd 20/11/60. Sqn Ldr 20/7/65. Retd DEL 26/8/70.
WYMAN A.R.A. Born 21/1/33. Commd 5/9/69. Flt Lt 5/9/71. Retd ENG 5/9/77.

WYN-JONES E.W. BSc. Born 9/3/56. Commd 6/9/81. Wg Cdr 1/1/96. Retd ADMIN 7/4/00.
WYNELL-MAYOW J. Born 21/4/21. Commd 1/11/56. Sqn Ldr 1/1/69. Retd ENG 21/4/76.
WYNESS J.A. MA. Born 11/5/56. Commd 19/7/87. Flt Lt 19/1/87. Retd ADMIN 2/10/91.
WYNESS R.F. DFM. Born 2/10/12. Commd 3/10/40. Sqn Ldr 1/8/47. Retd GD 2/10/55.
WYNN D.I. MBE CertEd. Born 25/12/47. Commd 4/5/72. Sqn Ldr 1/1/88. Retd ADMIN 1/5/00.
WYNN J.K. Born 8/11/60. Commd 19/7/84. Flt Lt 13/12/86. Retd FLY(N) 11/12/03.
WYNN L.L.W. Born 13/12/12. Commd 10/10/46. Fg Offr 10/10/47. Retd SUP 12/5/58.
WYNN M.J. DPhysEd. Born 3/10/40. Commd 31/1/66. Wg Cdr 1/7/81. Retd ADMIN 31/1/88.
WYNN-PARRY C.B. MBE MA DM BCh FRCP DPhysMed. Born 11/10/24. Commd 7/10/48. Gp Capt 1/5/68.
    Retd MED 3/4/76.
WYNNE D.J. Born 5/6/38. Commd 2/7/62. Flt Lt 16/8/63. Retd GD 8/9/67.
WYNNE D.T. Born 26/2/36. Commd 10/2/72. Flt Lt 10/2/75. Retd ADMIN 1/9/87.
WYNNE G. Born 2/5/24. Commd 10/3/44. Flt Lt 10/3/49. Retd GD 2/5/67.
WYNNE J.E. Born 31/1/43. Commd 26/5/60. Sqn Ldr 1/1/71. Retd ENG 31/1/81.
WYNNE J.G. DFC. Born 8/5/21. Commd 19/12/41. Wg Cdr 1/7/60. Retd GD 28/7/73.
WYNNE-JONES D. The Rev. Commd 31/5/56. Retd Sqn Ldr 13/1/05.
WYPER D.J. MB ChB DRCOG DAvMed MRAeS. Born 13/2/51. Commd 14/5/74. Wg Cdr 18/2/90.
    Retd MED 19/9/96.
WYRILL R.P.S. Born 20/5/16. Commd 7/10/35. Wg Cdr 1/7/47. Retd GD 29/12/59.
WYSE D. Born 2/6/52. Commd 7/11/91. Fg Offr 7/11/91. Retd SUP 7/1/96.
WYVER C.C. Born 4/7/47. Commd 25/4/69. Flt Lt 4/1/73. Retd GD 12/5/88.

Y

YAPP A.R.E. CEng MIEE MRAeS. Born 16/10/36. Commd 30/5/59. Sqn Ldr 1/1/72. Retd GD 6/2/75.
YARDLEY J.H.G. Born 9/6/11. Commd 17/2/45. Flt Lt 17/2/51. Retd SUP 12/5/58.
YARRAM M.F. BSc. Born 24/6/47. Commd 26/5/70. Sqn Ldr 1/7/81. Retd SUP 1/6/00.
YARROW S.W.S. MCMI. Born 18/2/41. Commd 18/12/62. Wg Cdr 1/7/85. Retd GD 18/2/96.
YARROW T.B.J. MBE BSc. Born 27/5/49. Commd 15/9/69. Wg Cdr 1/1/94. Retd GD 14/3/97.
YARWOOD S.N. BA. Born 3/2/71. Commd 21/6/95. Flt Lt 12/8/98. Retd SUPPLY 23/3/03.
YARWOOD T. MInstAM MCMI. Born 1/8/39. Commd 16/5/74. Sqn Ldr 1/7/85. Retd ADMIN 1/8/94.
YATES B. Born 22/7/39. Commd 24/6/71. Flt Lt 24/6/73. Retd ENG 24/6/79.
YATES C.E.J. BSc. Born 1/2/57. Commd 17/8/79. Sqn Ldr 1/7/90. Retd GD 13/10/95.
YATES D.N. Born 3/2/23. Commd 30/10/43. Flt Lt 4/12/52. Retd GD 2/8/63. Re-instated 20/1/64. Retd 10/12/75.
    rtg Sqn Ldr.
YATES D.P. OBE. Born 9/7/46. Commd 18/11/66. Gp Capt 1/1/99. Retd ENG 2/1/01.
YATES G.W. Born 21/2/21. Commd 31/3/60. Flt Lt 31/3/63. Retd ENG 1/5/73.
YATES H.F. Born 9/8/15. Commd 2/8/45. Flt Lt 4/1/51. Retd SEC 24/10/53.
YATES J.A. Born 22/6/51. Commd 22/10/72. Sqn Ldr 1/7/85. Retd ADMIN 1/10/91.
YATES J.B. CEng MRAeS. Born 29/9/17. Commd 19/8/42. Wg Cdr 1/7/58. Retd ENG 30/3/68.
YATES J.R. Born 25/4/24. Commd 3/11/45. Sqn Ldr 1/7/55. Retd GD 14/8/65.
YATES J.W.L. Born 4/9/27. Commd 7/8/59. Sqn Ldr 30/12/66. Retd EDN 7/8/75.
YATES M.J. BSc. Born 19/3/57. Commd 28/12/80. Sqn Ldr 1/1/89. Retd ADMIN 14/3/97.
YATES P.N. Born 18/6/34. Commd 22/8/59. Flt Lt 22/2/65. Retd GD 31/8/72.
YATES P.W. Born 22/2/55. Commd 9/12/76. Flt Lt 30/4/83. Retd GD(G) 22/2/93.
YATES R. Born 20/2/45. Commd 22/2/63. Sqn Ldr 1/1/88. Retd GD 21/7/98.
YATES R.G. Born 19/8/49. Commd 1/6/72. Flt Lt 6/6/75. Retd GD 19/8/87.
YATES V.W. Born 19/7/44. Commd 15/7/66. Flt Lt 15/1/69. Retd GD 3/7/70.
YATES W.H. Born 1/11/31. Commd 25/2/53. Flt Lt 7/3/62. Retd GD(G) 2/11/82.
YATES-EARL J.E. Born 31/10/19. Commd 11/2/43. Sqn Ldr 1/7/59. Retd GD(G) 31/10/74.
YAXLEY R.E. MCMI. Born 22/10/24. Commd 14/1/57. Flt Lt 24/4/60. Retd SUP 22/10/79.
YEARDLEY J.N. Born 11/4/48. Commd 4/6/87. Flt Lt 4/6/91. Retd ENG 1/7/93.
YEARWOOD G.D.e.L. Born 2/10/34. Commd 12/3/60. Sqn Ldr 1/7/82. Retd GD(AEO) 2/10/89.
YEARWOOD H.G. Born 26/4/21. Commd 10/12/42. Sqn Ldr 1/7/52. Retd RGT 1/10/58.
YEATES A.G. Born 5/11/45. Commd 6/11/67. Gp Capt 1/1/89. Retd ENG 2/4/94.
YEATS P.N. Born 21/3/59. Commd 2/4/84. Flt Lt 19/10/83. Retd GD 21/3/97.
YEE Y.S. BSc CEng MIMechE MRAeS. Born 30/11/44. Commd 9/11/80. Flt Lt 9/11/78. Retd ENG 9/11/96.
YELDHAM A. MBE. Born 12/6/53. Commd 27/7/72. Wg Cdr 1/7/89. Retd ADMIN 1/11/92.
YELDHAM N.S. Born 12/3/47. Commd 22/12/67. Wg Cdr 1/1/89. Retd GD 12/6/02.
YELDHAM R.E.D. Born 23/4/34. Commd 9/4/52. Flt Lt 5/9/57. Retd GD 23/4/71.
YEO C.J. AFC. Born 24/5/46. Commd 10/12/65. Sqn Ldr 1/7/78. Retd GD 17/11/78.
YEO P.G.R. Born 24/10/37. Commd 18/8/61. Wg Cdr 1/1/81. Retd GD 30/9/83.
YEOMANS J.A. MCMI. Born 25/3/23. Commd 28/3/46. Wg Cdr 1/1/66. Retd GD 25/9/76.
YEOMANS K.T. Born 29/7/29. Commd 27/2/52. Flt Lt 27/11/57. Retd GD 29/7/67.
YERBY R.K. Born 17/6/45. Commd 26/4/84. Sqn Ldr 1/7/94. Retd ENG 14/6/96.
YETMAN F.B. BA. Born 12/2/28. Commd 4/10/50. A Cdre 1/7/78. Retd GD 1/5/79.
YORK A.E.C. BA. Born 22/10/22. Commd 8/1/52. Gp Capt 1/7/70. Retd EDN 27/10/73.
YORK D.A. Born 5/12/36. Commd 12/6/57. Fg Offr 17/9/59. Retd GD 6/12/65.
YORK G.A. Born 1/7/41. Commd 7/6/64. Flt Lt 1/1/67. Retd GD 1/7/79. Re-entrant 6/7/86. Flt Lt 4/1/74.
    Retd GD 1/7/96.
YORK H. Born 4/5/19. Commd 2/3/43. Flt Lt 2/3/49. Retd SEC 4/5/68.
YORK M.W. MSc CEng MIEE. Born 28/10/46. Commd 3/2/71. Flt Lt 3/11/72. Retd ENG 6/9/80.
YORK V.W. DFC. Born 4/3/21. Commd 11/6/44. Wg Cdr 1/7/70. Retd SUP 4/3/76.
YORKE D.J. FBIFM. Born 5/6/47. Commd 19/7/84. Sqn Ldr 1/1/96. Retd ADMIN 3/8/01.
YOUD W.E. Born 8/9/26. Commd 18/6/52. Flt Lt 17/12/57. Retd GD 8/9/64.
YOUDAN D. MCMI. Born 20/7/35. Commd 8/7/54. Wg Cdr 1/1/78. Retd SUP 3/4/84.
YOUINGS A.W. Born 11/4/10. Commd 3/6/41. Fg Offr 5/8/42. Retd ENG 27/11/45. rtg Sqn Ldr.
YOULDON K.C. CEng MIMechE. Born 26/12/33. Commd 24/9/59. Wg Cdr 1/7/79. Retd ENG 26/12/88.
YOUNG A.C.M.N. Born 30/12/42. Commd 6/7/62. Flt Lt 15/4/70. Retd GD 20/12/93.
YOUNG A.G. Born 15/9/38. Commd 20/12/60. Flt Lt 1/4/66. Retd GD 15/9/76.
YOUNG A.J. Born 21/2/60. Commd 22/2/79. Flt Lt 22/8/84. Retd GD 1/4/90.
YOUNG A.M. BA. Born 22/5/59. Commd 4/9/78. Flt Lt 14/10/82. Retd GD 22/8/97.
YOUNG A.V.M. Born 8/3/50. Commd 25/2/72. Fg Offr 25/2/73. Retd SEC 20/9/75.
YOUNG B. Born 27/1/47. Commd 1/3/68. Sqn Ldr 1/7/82. Retd GD 1/7/91.
YOUNG B.C. Born 24/2/47. Commd 17/1/69. Flt Lt 27/11/75. Retd GD(G) 24/2/85.

YOUNG C. MHCIMA. Born 29/9/64. Commd 14/9/86. Sqn Ldr 1/7/98. Retd ADMIN 29/9/02.
YOUNG D.C. Born 4/3/36. Commd 8/1/59. Sqn Ldr 1/1/72. Retd GD 1/6/77.
YOUNG D.H. Born 7/8/22. Commd 22/10/41. Sqn Ldr 1/4/55. Retd GD 7/8/65.
YOUNG D.J. MSc BSc CEng MIMechE. Born 29/7/57. Commd 3/5/81. Sqn Ldr 1/1/91. Retd ENG 27/7/01.
YOUNG D.J. Born 27/4/47. Commd 2/12/66. Flt Lt 2/6/72. Retd GD 27/4/85.
YOUNG D.R. Born 23/12/26. Commd 3/5/46. Wg Cdr 1/1/69. Retd GD 8/11/75.
YOUNG G.A. Born 12/6/45. Commd 1/10/65. Sqn Ldr 1/1/79. Retd GD 12/6/83.
YOUNG G.D. MSc BSc CEng MIEE. Born 29/8/41. Commd 22/10/63. Sqn Ldr 28/3/73. Retd EDN 22/10/79.
YOUNG G.E. Born 11/5/25. Commd 4/10/77. Flt Lt 1/1/56. Retd GD 23/9/77.
YOUNG G.K. MBE BSc CEng MCIPD MRAeS. Born 10/12/32. Commd 1/7/61. Wg Cdr 1/7/80. Retd ADMIN 1/8/82.
YOUNG G.L. Born 30/1/47. Commd 1/2/89. Sqn Ldr 1/7/99. Retd GD 18/9/00.
YOUNG G.P. Born 23/2/25. Commd 22/1/45. Flt Lt 21/7/48. Retd GD 23/2/63.
YOUNG G.W.V. Born 10/4/17. Commd 20/10/55. Flt Lt 20/10/58. Retd GD 9/2/65.
YOUNG H.M. Born 19/8/49. Commd 30/5/69. Flt Lt 30/11/74. Retd GD 19/9/92.
YOUNG I. BSc. Born 31/10/46. Commd 19/11/72. Sqn Ldr 1/7/81. Retd GD 1/9/89.
YOUNG I.F. MB ChB DMRD. Born 6/5/31. Commd 6/5/56. Sqn Ldr 1/4/62. Retd MED 6/4/68.
YOUNG J. OBE. Born 16/9/42. Commd 22/8/71. Wg Cdr 1/7/86. Retd ADMIN 2/10/91.
YOUNG J.A. Born 13/9/32. Commd 31/5/51. Flt Lt 5/10/60. Retd GD 3/10/71. rtg Sqn Ldr.
YOUNG J.G.P. Born 3/8/34. Commd 5/11/52. Flt Lt 1/3/61. Retd GD 1/2/78.
YOUNG J.M. MBE. Born 12/7/36. Commd 19/6/70. Sqn Ldr 1/7/77. Retd ADMIN 10/8/87.
YOUNG J.R. Born 15/10/30. Commd 4/6/53. Flt Lt 19/11/58. Retd GD 29/3/69.
YOUNG J.R. Born 21/10/22. Commd 3/12/43. Sqn Ldr 1/1/72. Retd GD 31/3/74.
YOUNG J.W.C.N. Born 21/9/15. Commd 3/4/39. Wg Cdr 1/7/56. Retd SUP 31/5/61.
YOUNG L.C. DFC. Born 1/6/20. Commd 3/2/44. Flt Lt 27/6/51. Retd GD 27/9/55.
YOUNG M. BSc(Eng). Born 28/12/45. Commd 28/9/64. Sqn Ldr 1/1/81. Retd GD 14/10/85. Re-entered 3/8/90.
Sqn Ldr 21/10/85. Retd GD 30/5/01.
YOUNG M. MBE. Born 25/10/45. Commd 24/4/70. Wg Cdr 1/7/89. Retd GD 2/7/93.
YOUNG M.J.R. MA BA CertEd MCIPD. Born 28/1/47. Commd 24/1/74. Flt Lt 8/6/80. Retd GD(G) 1/10/89.
Re-entered 13/3/91. Flt Lt 18/11/81. Retd OPS SPT 1/6/98.
YOUNG M.M. MBE. Born 3/2/27. Commd 8/7/54. Flt Lt 8/1/58. Retd GD 4/8/73.
YOUNG N.F. Born 7/12/60. Commd 11/4/85. Flt Lt 19/7/88. Retd GD 22/8/01.
YOUNG P. Born 8/10/47. Commd 28/11/74. Flt Lt 28/5/07. Retd GD 8/10/85.
YOUNG P. MBE. Born 1/7/14. Commd 22/7/42. Flt Offr 22/1/47. Retd SEC 23/6/52.
YOUNG P.A. Born 27/7/44. Commd 8/10/87. Flt Lt 8/10/91. Retd ENG 2/7/93.
YOUNG P.J. Born 28/5/25. Commd 26/5/54. Sqn Ldr 1/1/66. Retd GD 10/12/76.
YOUNG P.J.J. Born 14/4/51. Commd 1/4/71. Sqn Ldr 1/7/86. Retd GD 1/7/89.
YOUNG P.W.F. Born 23/4/41. Commd 3/1/68. Flt Lt 14/10/73. Retd SUP 2/7/80.
YOUNG R.B. BSc. Born 17/12/48. Commd 13/6/71. Flt Lt 15/10/72. Retd GD 13/6/87.
YOUNG R.J. BEM. Born 9/2/48. Commd 22/5/80. Flt Lt 22/5/82. Retd SUP 20/5/88.
YOUNG R.S.E. BSc. Born 8/7/60. Commd 10/2/82. Flt Lt 15/10/84. Retd GD 14/9/95.
YOUNG R.W. Born 5/6/42. Commd 20/9/68. Flt Lt 12/5/72. Retd GD 1/4/76.
YOUNG R.W.R. MBE CEng MRAeS MCMI. Born 28/2/35. Commd 25/7/56. Wg Cdr 1/7/75. Retd ENG 3/4/85.
YOUNG S. Born 3/10/59. Commd 6/5/83. Wg Cdr 1/7/98. Retd GD 1/10/00.
YOUNG S. MA CEng MIEE CertEd. Born 14/11/54. Commd 16/12/79. Sqn Ldr 1/1/90. Retd ENG 16/12/01.
YOUNG S.J. Born 12/3/62. Commd 11/6/81. Wg Cdr 1/7/99. Retd GD 31/10/01.
YOUNG T.B. BSc CEng MIEE. Born 20/10/59. Commd 6/9/81. Sqn Ldr 1/7/90. Retd ENG 20/10/97.
YOUNG T.G. OBE BEng MRAeS. Born 17/6/11. Commd 29/9/33. Wg Cdr 1/7/47. Retd ENG 20/6/63. rtg Gp Capt.
YOUNG W.A. MCMI. Born 8/10/19. Commd 9/7/38. Sqn Ldr 1/7/53. Retd GD 15/4/71.
YOUNG W.B.C. Born 25/6/22. Commd 4/11/44. Sqn Ldr 1/7/57. Retd GD 31/8/63.
YOUNG W.H.S. Born 18/10/13. Commd 19/6/42. Sqn Ldr 1/7/52. Retd SUP 18/1/69.
YOUNGMAN M.A. Born 27/8/61. Commd 24/7/81. Sqn Ldr 1/7/98. Retd GD 20/1/02.
YULE A.J. Born 1/9/57. Commd 6/11/80. Sqn Ldr 1/7/90. Retd GD 7/7/96.
YULE M.R. Born 30/6/42. Commd 17/12/63. Wg Cdr 1/7/85. Retd SUP 7/7/96.

Z

ZAJAC W.J. Born 17/12/18. Commd 3/1/49. Flt Lt 3/1/49. Retd GD(G) 20/1/74.
ZALA E.D. AFC. Born 16/5/23. Commd 28/5/43. Sqn Ldr 1/7/68. Retd GD 31/3/74.
ZANKER M.W. Born 16/2/62. Commd 26/11/81. Flt Lt 26/5/87. Retd GD 16/2/00.
ZARRAGA H.P. Born 9/2/40. Commd 14/8/64. Flt Lt 14/2/70. Retd GD 1/7/80.
ZAVALA-SUAREZ C.M.R. MCMI. Born 19/4/26. Commd 11/12/64. Flt Lt 12/2/63. Retd SUP 19/4/83.
ZBROZEK F. MSc BSc. Born 22/10/47. Commd 2/9/73. Sqn Ldr 2/3/79. Retd ADMIN 2/9/89.
ZELENY A.P. MBE. Born 11/10/14. Commd 23/6/41. Flt Lt 10/11/50. Retd GD(G) 15/11/71. rtg Sqn Ldr.
ZINKUS V.J. BA MILT. Born 5/9/57. Commd 31/1/80. Flt Lt 31/7/86. Retd SUP 24/9/95.
ZMITROWICZ K. Born 8/9/24. Commd 4/6/64. Flt Lt 4/6/67. Retd GD 29/6/74.
ZMITROWICZ Z. Born 12/6/22. Commd 2/3/61. Flt Lt 2/3/64. Retd GD 12/6/73.
ZOTOV D.V. MBE. Born 2/11/39. Commd 19/12/61. Sqn Ldr 1/1/72. Retd GD 3/12/76.
ZOTOV N.V. CEng MIEE. Born 20/12/45. Commd 30/11/64. Sqn Ldr 1/7/79. Retd ENG 23/4/93.

LIST OF RETIRED OFFICERS OF THE PRINCESS MARY'S ROYAL AIR FORCE NURSING SERVICE

A'COURT M.E. SRN. Born 28/3/19. Sqn Offr 31/5/57. Retd 31/5/61.
ALDERSON G.P. SRN SCM. Born 30/11/36. Sqn Offr 6/7/70. Retd 1/10/71.
AMBROSE L.A. SRN. Born 5/5/32. Sqn Offr 22/5/69. Retd 31/7/71.
ANDERSON K. SRN. Born 1/7/37. Flt Offr 14/9/64. Retd 19/8/67.
ARIS M.S. SRN. Born 1/12/18. Sqn Offr 2/11/55. Retd 26/11/60.
ARNOLD P.A. SRN. Born 17/3/42. Flt Offr 8/5/68. Retd 4/7/75.
ASHTON D.F.Mac. SRN. Born 21/6/30. Sqn Offr 7/1/68. Retd 5/11/73.
AYLWARD S.J. SRN SCM. Born 9/4/31. Sqn Offr 5/11/66. Retd 9/6/73.
BAKER C.A. RGN RM. Born 15/9/59. Commd 9/10/91. Sqn Ldr 4/10/95. Retd 8/12/03.
BAKER S.M. ARRC SRN. Born 2/12/31. Sqn Offr 2/5/65. Retd 22/7/75.
BALDOCK G.A. Born 30/6/41. Sqn Ldr 15/11/76. Retd 28/7/82.
BALDWIN P.A. SRN SCM. Born 1/7/31. Flt Offr 14/8/63. Retd 15/4/67.
BALDWIN R. SRN SCM. Born 8/3/35. Sqn Offr 9/8/69. Retd 13/12/71.
BARNES M. RGN. Born 18/1/59. Commd 15/7/92. Sqn Ldr 8/4/96. Retd 6/12/03.
BECKWITH C.A. ARRC RM. Born 8/1/52. Sqn Ldr 4/3/88. Retd 14/3/96.
BEDFORD S.T. BSc RGN. Born 5/5/71. Commd 8/7/00. Flt Lt 22/7/00. Retd 28/12/03.
BELL H.S. MSc RGN RNT. Born 17/2/65. Commd 3/2/00. Flt Lt 3/2/98. Retd 31/8/03.
BENNETT J.M. SCM. Born 27/4/57. Flt Lt 7/4/83. Retd 8/7/87.
BENNETT K.M. SRN. Born 4/3/22. Flt Offr 28/6/50. Retd 6/7/58.
BENNETT M.M. Born 5/10/45. Sqn Ldr 13/5/83. Retd 10/9/88.
BIRD M.T. ARRC SRN. Born 1/6/25. Sqn Ldr 3/11/62. Retd 1/6/80.
BLACKWOOD M.F. SRN. Born 8/8/05. Sqn Offr 14/6/52. Retd 14/9/60.
BLAKE O.C. RRC SRN RNT. Born 10/7/20. Wg Offr 1/7/65. Retd 12/9/67.
BOASE J.N.M. ARRC. Born 27/9/44. Sqn Ldr 9/12/77. Retd 27/9/88.
BONSEY B.M.N. ARRC SRN. Born 22/2/24. Sqn Offr 3/11/62. Retd 4/11/76.
BOWLER R.A. SRN SCM. Born 18/5/36. Flt Offr 3/2/66. Retd 31/5/71.
BRADLEY M.M. SRN RFN SCM. Born 2/9/13. Sqn Offr 26/3/54. Retd 26/9/68.
BREWSTER-LIDDLE J.J.G. Born 11/9/56. Fg Offr 2/1/90. Retd 1/1/96.
BROWN H.C. SRN. Born 7/3/11. Sister 1/4/41. Retd 19/7/50.
BROWN J.B. ARRC SRN SCM. Born 8/11/29. Sqn Offr 5/4/66. Retd 18/11/73.
BROWN M. RM. Born 27/2/43. Sqn Ldr 18/8/79. Retd 17/9/88.
BRUCE J.H. ARRC SCM. Born 5/3/50. Sqn Ldr 1/6/85. Retd 15/2/86.
BRUMPTON N.J. Born 2/8/58. Sqn Ldr 7/4/92. Retd 1/10/95.
BUDGE M.A. SRN SCM. Born 19/11/13. Sqn Offr 15/6/55. Retd 15/12/68.
BULL C.P.I. ARRC RM. Born 22/12/35. Wg Cdr 1/1/85. Retd 22/12/90.
BUNCE F.C. SRN SCM. Born 25/4/17. Sqn Offr 25/5/58. Retd 3/8/64.
BYRNE S.P.A. SRN. Born 19/7/10. Sister 16/10/40. Retd 17/6/49. rtg Senior Sister
CALLCOTT S.T. RRC RGN RM. Born 25/2/61. Commd 21/4/93. Wg Cdr 1/7/01. Retd 1/7/04.
CAPEWELL C.E. SRN. Born 19/9/34. Sqn Offr 19/5/69. Retd 20/12/69.
CARMICHAEL I.R. ARRC SRN SCM. Born 18/11/27. Sqn Offr 10/2/69. Retd 10/2/75.
CARTWRIGHT J. SRN. Born 1/7/24. Flt Offr 17/11/60. Retd 5/5/67.
CASTLE M.A. SRN SCM. Born 8/7/38. Flt Offr 3/12/64. Retd 26/6/70.
CHANDLER M.F.R. SRN. Born 22/10/19. Flt Offr 13/6/49. Retd 4/4/52.
CHEW L. RRC . Born 9/5/49. Commd 14/5/84. Wg Cdr 1/1/97. Retd 25/8/04.
CHURCH E.J. SRN RM. Born 7/5/59. Sqn Ldr 6/3/93. Retd 14/3/96.
CLARKSON S.E. Born 29/1/53. Sqn Ldr 18/5/86. Retd 20/4/91.
COGGINS V.M. SRN. Born 10/2/19. Sqn Offr 4/7/62. Retd 20/2/74.
COGHLAN A.J. ARRC SRN. Born 15/5/20. Wg Offr 1/7/70. Retd 15/5/75.
COLAM P.F. ARRC SRN SCM. Born 14/11/27. Sqn Offr 3/5/64. Retd 3/5/70.
COOKSON H.M. ARRC SRN. Born 23/4/21. Sqn Offr 1/4/62. Retd 13/9/74.
COOPER J. RM. Born 4/7/47. Sqn Ldr 31/5/83. Retd 3/5/91.
CORAM M.P.E. SRN SCM. Born 24/12/29. Sqn Offr 7/10/67. Retd 29/10/73.
COUSINS S.J. SRN. Born 28/1/57. Sqn Ldr 24/10/91. Retd 14/3/96.
COWDEN C.E. SRN. Born 17/2/30. Flt Offr 29/7/68. Retd 31/10/72.
COX A.C.W. RRC. Born 18/8/48. Sqn Ldr 11/4/88. Retd 22/5/88.

CROSSLAND B.A. SRN. Born 28/2/53. Sqn Ldr 9/4/87. Retd 14/3/96.
CROSTHWAITE R.G.C. SRN. Born 28/5/15. Flt Offr 12/10/50. Retd 21/1/52.
CUFF J.M. SRN. Born 18/9/28. Flt Offr 2/2/57. Retd 25/3/60.
DANIELS J.M. SRN. Born 22/1/19. Sqn Offr 5/6/61. Retd 5/6/65.
DAVERN C.C. SCM. Born 26/12/30. Sqn Offr 12/11/67. Retd 24/11/78.
DAVIES G.M. ARRC SRN RSCN. Born 28/4/14. Sqn Offr 9/1/53. Retd 28/4/69.
DAVIES M.D. SRN. Born 11/6/34. Flt Offr 5/1/67. Retd 3/6/75.
DENNETT E.D. ARRC. Born 31/7/31. Wg Cdr 1/7/80. Retd 29/4/85.
DOUGLAS J. SRN. Born 14/8/30. Sqn Offr 8/7/67. Retd 10/7/73.
DUCAT-AMOS B.M. CB RRC. Born 2/2/21. A Cdt 1/7/72. Retd 29/11/78.
DUNCAN M.B. SRN RFN. Born 25/2/19. Sqn Offr 5/6/62. Retd 29/6/68.
DUNN M.K. ARRC SRN SCM. Born 22/10/22. Sqn Offr 3/7/64. Retd 23/10/72.
DURAND I.M.L. SRN. Born 15/12/13. Sister 15/3/40. Retd 4/4/45.
DUTCH B.J. SRN. Born 1/7/25. Sqn Offr 1/4/62. Retd 8/10/67.
DUTHIE I.M. SRN SCM. Born 1/7/28. Flt Offr 1/4/62. Retd 31/7/65.
EASTBURN E.A. Born 15/10/58. Sqn Ldr 30/5/93. Retd 13/11/99.
EASTON K.H. SRN SCM. Born 29/6/33. Sqn Offr 20/10/68. Retd 20/10/74.
EASY P.J. Born 2/12/47. Sqn Ldr 12/2/82. Retd 13/8/88.
EDMUNDS-JONES J. RRC RSCN. Born 24/5/38. Sqn Offr 19/3/78. Retd 31/12/88.
EILLEY E.M. SRN RMN. Born 23/5/36. Sqn Offr 1/5/71. Retd 26/10/74.
ELLIS P.M. SRN. Born 1/7/28. Flt Offr 3/5/58. Retd 7/4/62.
EMERSON J.M. ARRC SRN. Born 3/5/21. Wg Offr 1/7/68. Retd 10/10/70.
FERN M.C. SRN SCM. Born 20/3/38. Sqn Offr 3/4/73. Retd 29/6/80.
FINUCANE E.M. SRN RFN. Born 6/1/14. Sqn Offr 11/6/56. Retd 6/1/67.
FIRTH M.J. SRN. Born 4/9/24. Flt Offr 20/9/52. Retd 1/3/60.
FIRTH S.M. RRC SCM. Born 24/1/31. Gp Capt 1/1/82. Retd 1/9/87.
FLEMING R.A. SRN. Born 21/7/56. Flt Lt 12/7/82. Retd 17/5/85.
FORWARD B.J. ARRC BA RNT CertEd. Born 27/1/48. Commd 6/10/77. Gp Capt 1/7/98. Retd 31/7/03.
FRANCIS D. SRN. Born 26/4/22. Sqn Offr 22/7/57. Retd 15/7/70.
FRASER C.A. SRN. Born 1/7/34. Flt Offr 4/7/62. Retd 30/7/67.
FROUDE H. RM. Born 23/1/51. Sqn Ldr 1/6/85. Retd 10/11/93.
FRUDE M.J. MBE SCM. Born 26/9/27. Sqn Ldr 5/8/68. Retd 26/9/82.
FUDGE L.M. RM. Born 12/11/47. Sqn Ldr 4/9/81. Retd 14/3/97.
FURLONG D.M. SRN. Born 11/7/52. Sqn Ldr 1/1/86. Retd 25/1/92.
GIBBONS O.E.V. MBE SRN. Born 28/2/15. Sister 1/4/41. Retd 9/9/50.
GILES Dame Pauline DBE RRC SRN SCM. Born 17/9/12. A Cdt 1/9/66. Retd 12/10/70.
GOLDING A.B. ARRC. Born 2/10/32. Wg Cdr 1/1/85. Retd 1/1/88.
GOODFELLOW N.S. RM. Born 3/7/43. Sqn Ldr 22/6/81. Retd 5/7/98.
GOSTLING M.P. RRC. Born 7/5/24. Wg Offr 1/7/76. Retd 7/5/79.
GOULDING C.R. SRN. Born 3/12/23. Sqn Offr 5/11/60. Retd 2/12/76.
GOWSELL D.A.S.W. SRN. Born 1/7/26. Flt Offr 5/3/56. Retd 19/10/58.
GRAHAM M.R. SRN. Born 1/4/17. Flt Offr 9/12/49. Retd 28/9/52.
GRIFFITH J.D. SRN. Born 1/7/27. Sqn Offr 1/4/62. Retd 25/8/66.
GRIMMER K.L. RGN. Born 19/2/71. Commd 18/8/00. Flt Lt 9/3/00. Retd 30/8/03.
GULLIVER V.J. SRN SCM. Born 17/2/41. Flt Offr 4/12/69. Retd 5/7/75.
GUMLEY C.J.G. RRC SCM RNT. Born 24/9/27. Wg Offr 1/1/69. Retd 1/9/79.
GURNEY M.C. SRN. Born 3/5/14. Sister 14/9/40. Retd 11/9/45.
GWYTHER M.E. SRN. Born 3/10/31. Sqn Offr 10/11/66. Retd 1/9/71.
HALL A.R. Born 21/3/41. Sqn Ldr 1/5/75. Retd 6/7/95.
HANCOCK E.M. RRC RM. Born 5/4/37. Gp Capt 1/7/89. Retd 5/4/94.
HAND V.M. RRC. Born 2/4/44. Flt Lt 2/10/69. Retd 2/10/71. Re-entered 10/7/72. A Cdre 1/7/95. Retd 1/7/97.
HANSON G.H. Born 9/11/47. Sqn Ldr 1/7/85. Retd 11/1/87.
HARDY K. SRN. Born 21/8/12. Sister 4/7/40. Retd 31/7/49. rtg Senior Sister.
HARRIS E.M. ARRC DN RCNT RNT. Born 26/6/29. Sqn Offr 8/8/70. Retd 26/6/84.
HARRIS I.J. CB RRC SCM. Born 26/9/26. A Cdre 1/1/82. Retd 26/11/84.
HARRIS M.A. SRN RSCN. Born 18/1/33. Flt Offr 4/9/63. Retd 12/11/70.
HARRISON C.B. DN. Born 13/12/35. Sqn Ldr 17/3/73. Retd 1/10/85.
HARRISON M.J. SRN SCM. Born 27/6/33. Sqn Offr 4/4/71. Retd 20/4/74.
HAWKE G.L. ARRC SRN. Born 14/5/25. Sqn Ldr 3/5/64. Retd 14/5/80.
HAZELGROVE A. SRN SCM. Born 10/8/35. Flt Offr 8/4/65. Retd 3/1/69.
HENDERSON C.A. ARRC RM. Born 30/11/57. Commd 23/7/90. Sqn Ldr 26/12/91. Retd 21/11/04.
HERD M.E. SRN SCM. Born 31/5/40. Sqn Ldr 24/7/74. Retd 7/9/80.
HIGGS M. ARRC SRN. Born 1/10/29. Sqn Offr 30/10/65. Retd 1/7/77.
HILL D.M.W. MSc BSc RMN FInstLM. Born 16/2/55. Commd 4/6/87. Wg Cdr 1/7/03. Retd 7/3/05.
HINSON P.J. SRN. Born 4/1/58. Sqn Ldr 21/5/92. Retd 14/3/96.
HIRST R.B. SRN SCM. Born 25/6/39. Flt Offr 8/2/67. Retd 31/1/73.

HOGLAND J.R. ARRC SRN. Born 1/7/20. Sqn Offr 21/7/57. Retd 12/6/65.
HOLLIDAY G. ARRC. Born 23/2/50. Sqn Ldr 25/9/88. Retd 14/3/96.
HOLLINGDALE P.M. SRN SRCN. Born 23/10/25. Sqn Offr 22/6/63. Retd 30/4/69.
HOLT E.B. SCM. Born 8/7/47. Flt Offr 23/10/73. Retd 29/8/81.
HOPE D.P. SRN. Born 1/7/24. Sqn Offr 1/4/62. Retd 25/11/66.
HOPKINS K.J. ARRC SCM. Born 19/10/37. Sqn Ldr 13/8/74. Retd 7/2/82.
HORN A.M. SRN. Born 27/1/13. Sister 1/5/40. Retd 1/4/45.
HOYLE H. ARRC RM. Born 19/10/60. Sqn Ldr 16/6/94. Retd 3/2/01.
HURST L. ARRC MA BSc CertFE. Born 10/7/60. Sqn Ldr 3/2/95. Retd 9/6/01.
HUTCHINS D. ARRC SRN SCM. Born 20/7/30. Sqn Offr 23/9/67. Retd 23/9/75.
IBBOTT B.A. SRN SCM. Born 1/8/38. Flt Offr 3/12/64. Retd 3/12/70.
JAMIESON L.N. ARRC SRN. Born 23/7/10. Sister 1/10/39. Retd 1/12/48. rtg Senior Sister.
JOHNS B.M.A. ARRC SRN. Born 1/8/21. Sqn Offr 7/7/58. Retd 1/8/74.
JOHNSON F.M. SRN RFN. Born 30/3/21. Sqn Offr 27/5/58. Retd 1/6/66.
JOHNSTON M.E. ARRC RM. Born 7/8/33. Sqn Ldr 15/11/69. Retd 7/8/88.
JONES J.A. RM. Born 1/12/61. Sqn Ldr 27/1/96. Retd 28/9/02.
JOY S.N. ARRC SCM RSCN. Born 24/2/38. Sqn Ldr 2/8/78. Retd 5/6/83.
JOY W.E. ARRC RSCN. Born 6/4/52. Sqn Ldr 22/1/88. Retd 25/6/94.
KEEBLE C.L. RM. Born 23/2/60. Sqn Ldr 14/5/93. Retd 14/3/96.
KELL H.E. AARC SCM. Born 6/6/45. Sqn Ldr 1/7/80. Retd 25/1/87.
KEMP H.M. SRN SCM. Born 21/3/30. Sqn Offr 16/7/66. Retd 12/8/73.
KENEFICK L.M. SRN. Born 16/10/17. Sqn Offr 20/6/58. Retd 31/3/59.
KENT D.M. SRN. Born 5/2/21. Flt Offr 21/3/53. Retd 13/8/60.
KIDMAN E.F. RM. Born 17/5/47. Sqn Ldr 22/3/83. Retd 15/12/92.
KING A.G. SRN RNT. Born 21/4/37. Flt Offr 4/12/63. Retd 31/8/71.
KING E.E.E. SRN. Born 3/7/13. Sqn Offr 24/6/57. Retd 20/7/66.
KING I.E. ARRC SCM. Born 31/1/31. Sqn Ldr 21/7/67. Retd 31/1/86.
KINGSTON M.A. SRN. Born 16/4/16. Sqn Offr 1/4/62. Retd 16/4/71.
KIRK M.L. SRN. Born 5/3/26. Flt Offr 1/12/55. Retd 20/11/60.
KIRKHAM O.A. SRN. Born 1/7/26. Sqn Offr 1/4/62. Retd 16/11/66.
KRUSIN A.M. ARRC SRN RSCN SCM. Born 16/1/13. Gp Offr 1/7/66. Retd 22/4/69.
LA-ROCHE A. SCM. Born 25/6/52. Flt Offr 15/9/79. Retd 1/8/85.
LANE D.E. MBE ARRC. Born 22/10/23. Sqn Offr 15/7/66. Retd 22/10/78.
LAURENCE R. Born 26/3/54. Sqn Ldr 23/5/91. Retd 31/8/00.
LAY E. ARRC SRN. Born 8/1/17. Sqn Offr 5/7/54. Retd 8/1/67.
LEIPER J. SRN. Born 7/11/11. Sister 4/1/40. Retd 20/7/49. rtg Senior Sister.
LEVICK C. ARRC. Born 5/10/42. Sqn Offr 23/2/78. Retd 7/2/85.
LEWIS-BOWEN A.J. RM. Born 10/2/53. Sqn Ldr 11/8/88. Retd 28/1/95.
MACBAIN C.M.C. SRN. Born 6/8/15. Flt Offr 1/2/49. Retd 14/2/52.
MACKAY D.E. SRN. Born 25/3/13. Sister 6/3/40. Retd 5/3/45.
MACMILLAN M. SRN. Born 1/7/21. Flt Offr 11/6/60. Retd 13/10/64.
MANNING R.C. RM. Born 11/10/41. Wg Cdr 1/1/88. Retd 11/10/96.
MAPP Y.E. RM. Born 14/3/41. Sqn Ldr 5/6/82. Retd 26/11/88.
MARSH M.A. SRN SCM. Born 1/7/19. Sqn Offr 1/10/60. Retd 1/10/64.
MARTIN E.E. SRN. Born 3/10/30. Flt Offr 1/11/60. Retd 29/3/65.
MASON C.M. SRN. Born 21/5/33. Sqn Offr 27/9/69. Retd 13/2/71.
MASSAM R. ARRC SRN. Born 28/7/19. Wg Offr 1/7/70. Retd 28/7/74.
MATCHETT J.K. SRN. Born 11/9/27. Sqn Offr 16/2/63. Retd 16/2/69.
MCCABE I.M. SRN. Born 14/2/39. Sqn Ldr 1/7/81. Retd 1/6/83.
MCCANN D.C. RGN. Born 30/5/66. Commd 1/4/99. Flt Lt 12/9/98. Retd 2/9/04.
MCCARDLE J. SRN RFN SCM. Born 7/12/12. Sqn Offr 8/1/55. Retd 8/1/68.
MCCREADY N. SRN. Born 1/7/23. Flt Offr 14/9/57. Retd 1/8/60.
MCCULLOCH J. Born 24/12/57. Sqn Ldr 18/2/93. Retd 1/8/98.
MCLEAN M.McK. SRN. Born 27/9/23. Flt Offr 16/5/59. Retd 31/8/61.
MCLUCKIE M.D. SRN. Born 9/4/37. Flt Offr 6/4/66. Retd 31/12/72.
MCNAIR M.K. SRN RFN. Born 18/4/16. Wg Offr 1/1/67. Retd 18/4/71.
MCPHAIL A. ARRC SRN. Born 1/7/17. Sqn Offr 30/8/60. Retd 24/7/65.
MCPHERSON M.S. SRN RSCN. Born 20/10/12. Sqn Offr 9/6/54. Retd 20/10/65.
MCTEAR V.L. Born 1/7/37. Sqn Offr 17/12/72. Retd 4/2/79.
METCALFE J. ARRC SRN SCM. Born 19/7/27. Sqn Offr 1/2/66. Retd 1/2/72.
METCALFE J. CB RRC SRN SCM. Born 8/1/23. A Cdre 1/1/79. Retd 29/11/81.
MILLAR M.M. SCM. Born 30/11/34. Wg Cdr 1/7/80. Retd 1/7/83.
MITCHELL L.M. SRN. Born 26/2/12. Sister 1/8/40. Retd 12/4/45.
MOENS A.R. SRN. Born 4/2/25. Sqn Offr 1/4/62. Retd 15/4/63.
MOFFATT A. RRC SRN. Born 24/4/25. Sqn Ldr 19/8/68. Retd 24/4/80.
MORGAN G. Born 29/10/52. Flt Lt 25/3/86. Retd 12/12/88.

MORGAN K.A. SCM. Born 8/12/43. Sqn Offr 4/1/79. Retd 2/2/86.
MOSELEY P.M. SCM RSCN. Born 21/1/41. Sqn Offr 15/12/80. Retd 24/11/81.
MYLES A.P. Born 29/12/44. Flt Lt 8/4/77. Retd 29/12/82.
NEEHAM D.R. Born 9/7/48. Sqn Ldr 4/7/84. Retd 6/2/89.
NEWBROOK W.A. SRN. Born 20/3/18. Sqn Offr 20/11/59. Retd 20/11/66.
NEWTON C.A. SRN. Born 1/7/34. Flt Offr 6/10/61. Retd 14/11/63.
NEWTON C.M. SRN. Born 31/12/60. Sqn Ldr 18/5/95. Retd 14/3/96.
O'CONNOR M.M. RRC SRN SCM. Born 26/4/25. Gp Capt 1/7/76. Retd 26/4/80.
O'DONOVAN M. SRN. Born 18/2/18. Flt Offr 1/2/49. Retd 23/10/54.
O'KEEFFE J.J. Born 16/4/42. Sqn Ldr 6/4/85. Retd 31/3/93.
O'LEARY T.P. Born 30/7/40. Flt Lt 4/4/81. Retd 4/4/87.
OAKMAN J. ARRC. Born 6/1/54. Sqn Ldr 12/12/87. Retd 14/3/96.
ORR A.M. RRC RSCN. Born 22/7/35. Wg Cdr 1/7/88. Retd 1/1/92.
OSBORNE D.B. SRN RSCN. Born 30/3/57. Sqn Ldr 24/1/94. Retd 14/3/96.
OVENS E.R.K. SRN SCM. Born 27/3/21. Sqn Offr 21/11/65. Retd 21/11/71.
OXBOROUGH C.V. ARRC. Born 15/9/34. Sqn Offr 24/6/74. Retd 24/6/84.
PAGE M.M. SRN. Born 1/7/28. Flt Offr 1/10/57. Retd 18/2/62.
PARKER B.J. SRN RFN. Born 1/7/30. Flt Offr 1/10/60. Retd 5/9/66.
PARTINGTON R.A.L. RRC RM. Born 14/6/33. Wg Cdr 1/1/80. Retd 14/6/88.
PEDDER M.E. Born 11/4/40. Wg Cdr 1/7/85. Retd 11/4/95.
PENNY F.A. SRN. Born 19/6/41. Sqn Offr 17/12/74. Retd 18/11/75.
PENROSE R.A. RRC SRN. Born 18/6/25. Wg Cdr 1/1/73. Retd 18/6/80.
PERKINS J.B. BA DN RNT CertEd. Born 31/10/48. Sqn Ldr 13/4/92. Retd 14/3/97.
PERKINS S.J. Born 24/3/33. Sqn Ldr 30/10/72. Retd 7/4/83.
PETTIFER S.M. SRN. Born 27/2/48. Flt Offr 15/8/73. Retd 1/1/80.
PIRIE M.L. ARRC SCM. Born 16/5/42. Sqn Offr 11/4/78. Retd 9/6/85.
POULTER J.R. SRN. Born 15/3/47. Flt Lt 13/3/82. Retd 22/2/86.
PRICE C.V. RRC SRN. Born 2/12/16. Sqn Offr 4/10/60. Retd 2/12/71.
PROUD E.B. ARRC RM. Born 22/5/52. Sqn Ldr 23/7/88. Retd 28/6/97.
REED A.A. RRC. Born 25/1/30. A Cdre 1/1/85. Retd 25/8/85.
REID R.A. OBE ARRC RM DipHE. Born 26/4/46. Commd 14/5/82. Gp Capt 1/1/02. Retd 10/2/04.
REILLY P.J. Born 18/11/57. Sqn Ldr 23/7/92. Retd 14/9/96.
RICHARDSON L.Y. RGN DipHE. Born 8/2/66. Commd 1/10/98. Flt Lt 14/3/98. Retd 21/4/04.
RICHARDSON V. RM. Born 8/7/44. Commd 6/10/74. Sqn Offr 28/4/83. Retd 18/5/95.
ROBINSON P. SCM. Born 29/3/44. Sqn Offr 2/6/79. Retd 23/2/87.
RODDY A. SRN. Born 1/7/25. Flt Offr 23/7/57. Retd 5/12/64.
ROE B.A. SRN. Born 1/7/30. Flt Offr 29/5/58. Retd 30/11/61.
ROQUES L.M. ARRC SRN. Born 1/1/12. Wg Offr 1/1/61. Retd 10/4/61.
ROSCOE F.G. RGN. Born 18/12/61. Commd 7/8/91. Sqn Ldr 5/7/96. Retd 31/7/04.
ROSE M.F. SRN SCM. Born 2/2/32. Sqn Offr 21/3/67. Retd 2/7/72.
RUSSELL D.D. SRN. Born 28/7/18. Flt Offr 23/7/49. Retd 20/9/54.
RYAN E.F.T.H. SRN. Born 28/2/14. Sqn Offr 6/1/54. Retd 10/10/57.
SABINI D.L. SRN. Born 14/11/53. Sqn Ldr 26/2/89. Retd 7/10/89.
SANDISON E.A. RRC. Born 23/11/40. Gp Capt 1/1/88. Retd 30/11/91.
SANSOME A.J. SRN. Born 10/9/54. Sqn Ldr 6/1/88. Retd 3/10/92.
SCOFIELD A.J. ARRC. Born 1/7/48. Wg Cdr 1/1/92. Retd 1/7/98.
SCOTT L.R. Born 9/1/55. Flt Lt 23/9/81. Retd 21/2/83.
SCOTT M.M. SRN. Born 1/7/31. Flt Offr 1/4/62. Retd 1/8/64.
SEXTON R. ARRC RM. Born 9/9/52. Sqn Ldr 7/7/86. Retd 3/2/89.
SHANNON F. Born 16/3/53. Sqn Ldr 20/12/90. Retd 2/11/96.
SHAW M.J. MSc BSc CertEd(RNT). Born 23/2/48. Sqn Ldr 3/12/92. Retd 7/5/99.
SHAW M.M. RRC RM. Born 7/4/33. Gp Capt 1/1/85. Retd 31/8/88.
SHELDON M.A. ARRC. Born 19/10/25. Sqn Offr 20/9/67. Retd 19/10/80.
SHIMELL J.M. Born 11/6/50. Flt Offr 15/8/79. Retd 31/8/85.
SILCOCK V.M.J. RRC SRN. Born 17/10/20. Wg Offr 1/1/68. Retd 31/1/70.
SILVERTHORNE E. RM. Born 13/6/35. Sqn Offr 2/12/73. Retd 2/12/79.
SIMACEK J.J. Born 11/7/46. Flt Lt 3/4/82. Retd 1/5/87.
SIMKIN M.J. SRN SCM. Born 29/1/39. Flt Offr 4/1/67. Retd 17/11/73.
SIMPSON G.M.C. RRC. Born 12/8/42. Wg Cdr 1/7/85. Retd 13/3/89.
SIMPSON J. ARRC. Born 30/9/40. Sqn Offr 29/10/76. Retd 15/9/85.
SINKER J.E. SRN RM. Born 12/6/50. Sqn Ldr 22/5/85. Retd 7/5/89.
SLADE C.E. SRN SCM. Born 22/5/35. Sqn Offr 9/2/69. Retd 12/7/69.
SMALL I.A. SRN. Born 20/3/23. Flt Offr 1/5/55. Retd 9/1/60.
SMEDLEY J.D. RRC. Born 17/3/28. Wg Cdr 1/7/78. Retd 17/3/83.
SMITH J.A. RM. Born 14/11/52. Commd 27/7/82. Sqn Ldr 22/7/87. Retd 3/5/04.
SMITH T.A. RRC. Born 21/11/43. Sqn Ldr 11/1/87. Retd 14/3/97.

SOPER B. SRN. Born 15/2/22. Sqn Offr 26/2/59. Retd 23/9/59.
SOUTHERN-ROBERTS D. SRN. Born 22/1/42. Sqn Ldr 6/4/84. Retd 6/10/85.
STACEY R.C. RM. Born 20/12/56. Sqn Ldr 19/3/93. Retd 14/3/97.
STAINER S.M. SRN. Born 29/9/40. Flt Offr 1/9/66. Retd 31/8/70.
STALKER M.MacD. ARRC SRN. Born 1/7/29. Flt Offr 20/12/56. Retd 7/8/63.
STEEL I.B. SRN SCM. Born 11/6/22. Sqn Offr 15/9/61. Retd 4/4/72.
STEER P. Born 27/3/56. Flt Lt 16/1/93. Retd 14/3/96.
STEWART J.M. SCM RSCN. Born 16/1/34. Sqn Offr 31/5/72. Retd 4/10/81.
STONES P. ARRC RM. Born 24/11/35. Sqn Offr 13/4/76. Retd 24/11/90.
SURRIDGE P.D. MBE ARRC RM. Born 24/4/43. Sqn Ldr 12/1/77. Retd 9/10/94.
SWINDLEHURST P.A. SRN. Born 5/12/40. Sqn Ldr 15/12/74. Retd 1/8/80.
SYKES J.E.A. SRN. Born 10/6/35. Flt Offr 3/10/62. Retd 22/9/63.
TAIT I.J. SRN RFN. Born 1/7/25. Flt Offr 11/11/61. Retd 1/6/65.
TAYLOR A.M. SRN RSCN. Born 7/12/29. Sqn Offr 6/2/67. Retd 20/2/72.
TAYLOR J.L. Born 18/5/48. Flt Lt 7/8/79. Retd 22/6/84.
THOMAS K. SRN SCM. Born 26/5/13. Sqn Offr 10/2/51. Retd 10/2/65.
TIBBIT D.G.W. Born 1/10/50. Flt Lt 22/5/81. Retd 1/10/88.
TOOP J.M. SRN. Born 13/4/28. Sqn Offr 1/5/71. Retd 1/5/77.
TRICK D.M. RRC SRN. Born 14/1/13. Wg Offr 26/6/63. Retd 14/1/68.
TUCKER D.R. Born 11/6/53. Sqn Ldr 20/2/90. Retd 14/9/96.
TYLER M.H. RSCN. Born 13/4/35. Sqn Offr 8/5/79. Retd 11/8/85.
UPFOLD M.M.A. ARRC RM. Born 13/2/36. Sqn Ldr 8/2/75. Retd 8/2/88.
UTLEY S. RRC. Born 1/1/46. Wg Cdr 1/7/89. Retd 14/12/96.
WALKER E.K. Born 20/1/56. Flt Lt 20/8/83. Retd 13/11/86.
WALSH D.M. SRN. Born 1/7/31. Flt Offr 7/11/60. Retd 6/2/64.
WALSH M.B. ARRC SRN. Born 15/8/20. Wg Offr 1/1/70. Retd 15/8/75.
WALSH M.D. SRN SCM. Born 12/4/28. Sqn Offr 23/2/69. Retd 23/2/75.
WATSON A. SRN. Born 25/3/40. Flt Offr 6/2/67. Retd 7/11/70.
WATSON E.M. SRN. Born 18/1/27. Sqn Offr 29/4/67. Retd 29/4/77.
WATSON J.A. SRN. Born 10/6/42. Sqn Offr 22/1/76. Retd 28/5/76.
WATT M.V. SRN. Born 2/3/31. Sqn Offr 1/6/66. Retd 2/6/81.
WEEKS L. Born 8/1/48. Sqn Ldr 5/4/87. Retd 1/10/87.
WELBY M.M.C. SRN. Born 1/7/34. Flt Offr 1/4/62. Retd 21/10/66.
WELFORD A.M. RRC RM. Born 25/6/45. Wg Cdr 1/7/92. Retd 25/6/00.
WESTMAN D.M. BA RNT SCM. Born 3/9/46. Sqn Ldr 27/3/80. Retd 15/9/85.
WHITE M.E. ARRC . Born 28/9/48. Commd 21/2/84. Wg Cdr 1/7/98. Retd 11/6/05.
WHITE N.A. SRN. Born 1/7/21. Flt Offr 18/6/59. Retd 11/11/61.
WILLCOX F.H. ARRC SRN. Born 24/4/12. Flt Offr 1/2/49. Retd 1/4/52.
WILLIAMS R.H. RRC. Born 13/10/44. A Cdre 1/7/99. Retd 2/7/01.
WILLLIAMS E.E.R. SRN. Born 7/4/20. Flt Offr 7/3/54. Retd 17/3/85.
WILSON M. SRN SCM. Born 1/5/39. Flt Offr 28/4/66. Retd 26/6/73.
WINTER C. SRN. Born 16/12/46. Sqn Ldr 22/7/82. Retd 14/3/96.
WOOD M. MBE SRN. Born 14/6/28. Sqn Offr 14/2/63. Retd 3/12/67.
WOOD M.J. SRN SCM. Born 1/7/36. Flt Offr 4/4/63. Retd 20/3/67.
WOODBRIDGE V.T. Born 12/10/59. Sqn Ldr 24/9/94. Retd 14/9/96.
WRIGHT D.H. SRN. Born 28/2/20. Sqn Offr 9/8/56. Retd 31/1/59.
WRIGHT S.W. SRN. Born 4/12/39. Flt Offr 20/5/70. Retd 31/3/76.
WRIGHT V.D. ARRC SCM. Born 19/4/36. Sqn Ldr 9/12/73. Retd 5/6/83.
WYATT J.B. Born 3/6/43. Sqn Ldr 8/11/86. Retd 21/3/88.
WYATT K.N. SRN. Born 4/3/24. Sqn Offr 1/4/62. Retd 10/4/67.
YOUNG M.J. ARRC SRN RSCN. Born 30/8/28. Sqn Offr 31/12/67. Retd 12/6/73.

OBITUARY

Retired Officers whose deaths have been reported since July 2005

ROYAL AIR FORCE

Name	Date of Death
AIKEN Sir John KCB ACM	31.5.05
ALLEN B.J. Flt Lt	5.3.05
ALMOND G. Sqn Ldr	11.4.05
AMOR R.L. AFC Sqn Ldr	16.1.05
ANDERSON E.W. Flt Lt	28.7.04
ANDERSON H.S. Flt Lt	27.5.05
ANSCOMBE P.C. AFC DFM Flt Lt	10.3.05
APPLEGARTH E.W. Flt Lt	3.11.04
ARCHER R.N. OBE Wg Cdr	8.4.05
AUSTIN M.F. MA FCII MCMI DMS Flt Lt	26.7.04
BABBINGTON F.T. Flt Lt	9.1.05
BACON G.M.c.A. A Cdre	8.2.05
BAILEY S.W. Flt Lt	10.5.05
BAKER J.D. Sqn Ldr	19.8.04
BALDWIN E. DSO OBE DFC DFM Wg Cdr	18.10.04
BALDWIN R.M. Sqn Ldr	31.12.04
BALMER C.H. Sqn Ldr	3.9.04
BARRINGTON F.N. Sqn Ldr	11.4.04
BARTLETT W.E. MBE Flt Lt	6.10.04
BASTARD L.G.A. AFC Gp Capt	15.1.05
BATHO C.J. Flt Lt	25.5.05
BATTEY E.F. BA Sqn Ldr	15.8.04
BATTY W.G. MB ChB DObstRCOG DAvMed Wg Cdr	30.5.04
BAUCHOP J.S. Fg Offr	6.11.04
BEAUGEARD G.G. Gp Capt	27.4.05
BEDDOW W.D. AFC Flt Lt	23.2.05
BENT R.W. Flt Lt	18.3.05
BICKNELL J. Wg Cdr	9.12.04
BINKS A.F. DFC Wg Cdr	8.4.05
BIRD T.E. Fg Offr	14.4.05
BLACKWELL S.A. Flt Lt	11.12.04
BLISS J.E. ACIS Sqn Ldr	27.6.04
BOOKER R. BA Wg Cdr	18.5.05
BOOTH K.S. OBE AFC Wg Cdr	2.9.04
BOSLEY G. Flt Lt	23.4.05
BOTT J.M. Flt Lt	24.11.04
BOYD J.M.c.I. Sqn Ldr	12.5.05
BRAY H.S. AFC Flt Lt	29.12.04
BREAKES A. MBE MCMI Wg Cdr	12.12.04
BRIDGES R.B. Gp Capt	26.3.05
BRISTOW G.A. Sqn Ldr	11.2.05
BRISTOW P.D. BSc Sqn Ldr	31.8.04
BROGAN J.A. Flt Lt	11.2.05
BROOKS W.T. OBE DSO AFC A Cdre .	31.12.04
BROUGH J.E. MCMI Wg Cdr	19.3.05
BROWNRIGG H.C. Flt Lt	12.9.04
BRUNSKILL F. Flt Lt	10.12.04
BRUNTON F.A.McK. Wg Cdr	1.1.05
BRUSTER A.G. Flt Lt	20.1.05

Name	Date of Death
BUDD C.B. BSc CEng DIC MIMechE MRAeS ACGI Gp Capt	24.1.05
BUNTING M.C. MBE Gp Capt	14.11.04
BURGESS J.N. MMar MNI FCMI Gp Capt	30.12.04
BURNS P. Sqn Ldr	22.3.05
BURROWS C.E. Flt Lt	18.3.05
BURTON F. Sqn Ldr	28.4.05
BUTLER C.G.M. Flt Lt	20.7.04
BUTLER D.O. DFC Wg Cdr	1.3.05
BUTLER I.B. DFC AFC Gp Capt	26.1.05
CANDLISH E.G.J. MRIN MCMI Sqn Ldr	5.9.04
CANTON N.E. MBE DFC Sqn Ldr	31.8.04
CAREY F.R. CBE DFC** AFC DFM Gp Capt	6.12.04
CARMAN R. MBE CEng MIEE MCMI Sqn Ldr	2.12.04
CARPENTER J.M.V. DFC* Flt Lt	11.2.05
CARROLL B.P. Flt Lt	2.12.04
CARTER P. Gp Capt	11.4.05
CARTER R.F. MCMI Wg Cdr	30.4.04
CARTWRIGHT J. OBE Wg Cdr	22.4.05
CARWARDINE A.J. Flt Lt	9.4.05
CATTLEY J.E. Flt Lt	23.7.04
CHAPLE P.J.S. Flt Lt	10.5.05
CHATFIELD R.M. DFC Sqn Ldr	8.6.04
CHEESEMAN H.J.R. MCMI Sqn Ldr ..	27.6.04
CHIGNALL G.N.V. MBE FCMI Gp Capt	11.7.04
CHIVERS F.A.E. DipEE Sqn Ldr	5.11.04
CHIVERS J. Flt Lt	23.1.05
CHRISTIE M.R. Sqn Ldr	21.11.04
CLAPHAM J.R. CEng MRAeS Sqn Ldr	10.10.04
CLARK F.J. Sqn Ldr	30.1.05
CLARK T.B. Flt Lt	22.3.05
CLARKE J.L. Flt Lt	25.6.04
CLIFFORD P. MBE Flt Lt	10.3.05
COCKLE C.E. Wg Cdr	14.8.04
COFFEY P.V. MBE Sqn Ldr	15.5.05
COGAN L.E. Sqn Ldr	1.1.05
COLBOURNE R. GM Flt Lt	26.2.05
COLEMAN K.H. Flt Lt	10.8.04
COLLENETTE R.M.C. Flt Lt	25.6.04
COLLINS E.A.H. Flt Lt	2.10.04
COLLINS P.M. Flt Lt	9.3.05
COLLINS W.R. Sqn Ldr	7.5.05
COOPER C.C.F. DFC Wg Cdr	28.12.04
CORCK R.G. Flt Lt	12.12.04
COTTERILL F. BSc Sqn Ldr	4.11.04
COUCHThe Rev J.H. Gp Capt	2.1.05
COUPAR W.G. Sqn Ldr	26.10.04
COWAN R.C. BEM CEng MRAeS Sqn Ldr	9.12.04

Name	Date of Death
CRESSY F.J. Flt Lt	8.1.05
CROUCH A.W. Flt Lt	13.9.04
CROWLESMITH J.D. MB BS MRCS MFCM LRCP DCH FCMI Gp Capt	20.7.04
CURTIS N.F. OBE Gp Capt	24.7.04
CURTIS S.A. MBE Sqn Ldr	30.3.05
D'AVOINE J.A.S. Flt Lt	26.2.05
DALTON B. Sqn Ldr	23.9.04
DALTON R.W. DFM Sqn Ldr	29.6.04
DARNELL E.A. Wg Cdr	4.3.05
DAVIES A.E. Wg Cdr	26.11.04
DAVIES D. Flt Lt	19.3.05
DAVIES J.D.E. Wg Cdr	17.6.04
DAVIS L.A. Flt Lt	29.6.04
DAWSON L. Flt Lt	8.9.04
DAWSON S.C. Wg Cdr	4.3.05
DAYKIN V. Flt Lt	4.10.04
DE SALIS J.P.F. Flt Lt	13.1.05
DENNEHY J. Sqn Ldr	20.10.04
DICKSON E.D. Flt Lt	9.9.04
DITCHFIELD G.F. BEM Flt Lt	14.4.05
DIXON H.M. Flt Lt	29.4.05
DOBBIE J.B. Flt Lt	11.4.05
DODSON H.J. AFC Gp Capt	29.12.04
DOHERTY M.V. BA MRCS LRCP DAvMed Wg Cdr	19.5.04
DONNELLY G.L. DFM Flt Lt	1.1.05
DONOGHUE E.C. AFC Flt Lt	6.12.04
DOUBEK J. Flt Lt	18.3.05
DOUGLAS G.S.A. Flt Lt	12.5.05
DOUGLASS A.G. OBE AFC Sqn Ldr	11.11.04
DUNN A.G. BSc Sqn Ldr	26.11.04
DUNN Sir Patrick KBE CB DFC AM	17.6.04
DUNN T.U. MRAeS Wg Cdr	12.5.05
EGGLETON M.H.A. Flt Lt	26.4.05
ELLERBECK H.W. Flt Lt	1.11.04
ELLIS E. BA Sqn Ldr	14.4.05
ELMER J.C. Flt Lt	29.12.04
EMERY E.W.C. Flt Lt	21.8.04
ENSTONE A.W.J. MBE Flt Lt	26.12.04
EVANS A. Flt Lt	1.9.04
EVANS D.R. Flt Lt	29.3.05
EVANS I.H. Flt Lt	2.1.05
FAIRBAIRN D.I. OBE Wg Cdr	17.5.05
FERN B.E. Sqn Ldr	1.1.05
FITZPATRICK H.G. Flt Lt	21.3.05
FLEMING W.B. Wg Cdr	25.4.05
FORBES R.C. Flt Lt	30.3.05
FOWLER J.W. Flt Lt	19.1.05
FOWLER R.O. Flt Lt	18.4.05
FRANKLYN R.V.B. Wg Cdr	7.2.05
FRASER I. Gp Cdr	21.1.05
FRY A.B. DFC Flt Lt	3.11.04
FRY J.R. Flt Lt	14.11.04
GARLAND D.J. AE BSc MIEE Gp Capt	12.1.05
GARTON-HORSLEY C.I.M. Flt Offr	2.1.05
GIBBONS J.S. Sqn Ldr	24.5.05
GIBSON P.H. MBE MA FCMI Wg Cdr	5.4.05
GILBERT R.M.R. Sqn Ldr	6.2.05
GILL P. Sqn Ldr	20.7.04
GILLIATT P. OBE Wg Cdr	3.7.04
GLAZIER W.T. Sqn Ldr	9.2.05
GODFREY S.H. Flt Lt	11.3.05

Name	Date of Death
GOODWIN D. Flt Lt	13.1.05
GOSSE P.M. MC Wg Cdr	8.12.04
GRANT D.S. MRCS LRCP Gp Capt	26.10.04
GRAVES P.L. MSc BSc Gp Capt	30.5.05
GREEN J.E. MCMI Sqn Ldr	12.11.04
GREEN P. MBE Wg Cdr	7.2.05
GREEN R.C. Sqn Ldr	16.1.05
GREGORY H. Flt Lt	23.1.05
GRISTWOOD P.E. Flt Lt	22.8.04
GUILE H.W. MCMI Wg Cdr	14.5.05
HAMILL J.I. Wg Cdr	4.1.05
HANAFIN B.D. DFC Sqn Ldr	12.4.05
HANNAH F.J. Flt Lt	15.2.05
HARDING W.H. Flt Lt	28.2.05
HARRINGTON R.G. AFM Flt Lt	13.1.04
HARRIS The Rt Rev Mgr J.B. Gp Capt	16.12.04
HARRIS L.R. BEM AIIP Sqn Ldr	23.5.05
HARRISON W.A.S. OBE MCMI Wg Cdr	4.5.05
HARWOOD R.A. Flt Lt	9.2.05
HASSAN W.E. MB BS MFCM DPH Gp Capt	13.2.05
HATHAWAY R.T. Flt Lt	1.10.04
HAY J.B. Flt Lt	28.8.04
HEALEY N.V.O. MCIPS MInstAM MCMI Sqn Ldr	18.12.04
HEDLEY C.H. DFC Flt Lt	27.12.04
HEMMING I.G.S. CB CBE FCMI A Cdre	28.3.05
HEMMINGS J.A. Flt Lt	2.5.05
HENCE R.H.J. CEng MIEE MCMI Wg Cdr	13.11.04
HENDERSON R. OBE Wg Cdr	6.1.05
HENDY C. Flt Lt	30.3.05
HERN H.R. Flt Lt	18.1.05
HESLOP G. Flt Lt	18.1.05
HEWITT H.B. Flt Lt	8.3.05
HIGGINS J.E.N. Sqn Ldr	18.5.05
HILTON L.J. Wg Cdr	4.12.04
HOLKHAM-JENNER E.G. MCMI Sqn Ldr	14.4.05
HOLMAN D.C.L. Sqn Ldr	31.12.04
HOLMES R.D. MCMI Sqn Ldr	26.2.05
HOPKINS G.H. Sqn Ldr	4.3.05
HORNE G.E. Wg Cdr	20.2.05
HORSFALL J.E. Sqn Ldr	30.1.05
HOWARD H.R. Flt Lt	16.11.04
HULL G.N. Flt Lt	21.4.05
HUNT P.A. Flt Lt	16.2.05
HUNT P.C. Flt Lt	26.3.05
HUNT S.J. Sqn Ldr	26.3.05
INNES R.A. Sqn Ldr	6.4.05
IVELAW-CHAMPAN J. Flt Lt	20.11.04
JARRETT H.W. Sqn Ldr	31.8.04
JARVIS D. Sqn Ldr	31.1.05
JOHNSON G.W. DFC* MRAeS Wg Cdr	28.7.04
JOHNSTONE T. Sqn Ldr	4.1.05
JONES P.H. MBE Sqn Ldr	12.1.05
JONES R.A. Gp Capt	3.1.05
JONES R.F. Flt Lt	17.1.05
KALKHOVEN D.G. Flt Lt	28.2.05
KAY N. Sqn Ldr	6.5.04
KEAREY J.A. Flt Lt	3.2.05
KELSEY W. MRAeS Flt Lt	25.12.04
KILDUFF J.E. CBE FCMI MRIN Gp Capt	5.5.05

Name	Date of Death
KING J.K. MCMI Wg Cdr	13.11.04
KING S.E. A Cdre	14.9.04
KINGON A.M. MBE MB BS MRCP	
MRCS Wg Cdr	12.12.04
KNELL C.L.F. Flt Lt	1.1.05
KOGUT S.A. Flt Lt	2.2.05
LAWS P.E. Sqn Ldr	27.10.04
LEDWARD H.T.R. Flt Lt	29.11.04
LEIGHTON D.G. MCMI Sqn Ldr	17.12.04
LEWIS H.E. MRCS LRCP Wg Cdr	25.1.05
LEWIS S.R. Flt Lt	20.5.05
LIGHT D.C. MRCS LRCP DMRD	
Gp Capt	18.4.05
LIVETT D.J. MBE Flt Lt	30.4.04
LOADER C.G. AFC Flt Lt	19.11.04
LUCIE-SMITH H.J. Wg Cdr	9.4.05
LUSH N.A. Flt Lt	3.11.04
MACKIE G. Wg Cdr	4.1.05
MALLINSON J.D. AFC Wg Cdr	20.12.04
MANLEY A. Flt Lt	25.10.04
MANSON R.E.B. Sqn Ldr	8.10.04
MARSHALL P.F. CB OBE A Cdre	4.2.05
MARSHALL V.E. Sqn Ldr	26.1.05
MARTIN H.V. Sqn Ldr	2.12.04
MARTYN A.G. Sqn Ldr	22.3.05
MCCOLL A.H.McN. Sqn Ldr	6.10.04
MCDONOUGH J.I. Wg Cdr	2.12.04
MCGOWAN R.R. AFC Sqn Ldr	13.7.04
MCGRATH T. Flt Lt	10.5.05
MCNEILL J.E. BEM Sqn Ldr	15.7.04
METCALFE N.E. Sqn Ldr	23.4.05
MEWIS W.D. MBE Sqn Ldr	11.10.04
MIDWOOD J. Wg Cdr	27.12.04
MOODY R. Flt Lt	13.5.05
MORGAN G.L.O. DPhysEd Flt Lt	13.3.05
MORGAN J.M. DFC Wg Cdr	7.12.04
MORGAN L. CEng MRAeS MCMI	
Gp Capt	19.12.04
MORRELL P. Sqn Ldr	5.1.05
MORRIS P.J. BEM Flt Lt	20.4.05
MUNRO R.V.A. AFC* Sqn Ldr	25.10.04
NELSON C.T.M. MBE MCMI Wg Cdr ..	17.5.05
NICKLES F.R. Sqn Ldr	4.1.05
NORTH G.N. AFC Sqn Ldr	7.1.05
O'BRIEN J.D. Wg Cdr	1.8.04
O'SULLIVAN J.H. Flt Lt	31.3.05
O'SULLIVAN J.T. OBE Gp Capt	19.10.04
OLIVER D. GM Flt Lt	28.10.04
OLIVER J.F. OBE Wg Cdr	28.11.04
ORBELL P.A. MA MCMI Sqn Ldr	4.11.04
PALLOT C.G. Sqn Ldr	29.1.05
PARKER S. FInstPet Sqn Ldr	23.2.05
PARRATT R. MBE Sqn Ldr	7.7.04
PELLY A.E. Sqn Ldr	23.1.05
PENMAN D.J. OBE DSO DFC Wg Cdr .	27.11.04
PENNEY N.W. DFC Flt Lt	14.8.04
PENNY L. Sqn Ldr	13.4.05
PETTS N.R. Flt Lt	16.11.04
PHILLIPS P. Flt Lt	11.11.04
PONTET-PICCOLOMINI D.R.A. Flt Lt ..	13.8.04
POOLE J.V. Flt Lt	19.12.04
POPAY H.I. DFM* Sqn Ldr	16.11.04
POTTER M.G. DFC Flt Lt	29.9.04

Name	Date of Death
POWER A.G. Flt Lt	8.12.04
POWER G.H.D.A. MRCS LRCP Sqn Ldr	4.12.04
RAVENHALL J.M. Flt Lt	23.7.04
RAWCLIFFE E.C. Flt Lt	24.9.04
REEVES D.V. Sqn Ldr	10.11.04
RIGG S.M. MB ChB Wg Cdr	14.9.04
ROOM C.A. Sqn Ldr	5.12.04
RUMP F. CBE Gp Capt	2.1.05
SANDERSON C. Flt Lt	1.3.05
SANDERSON C.P. Sqn Ldr	28.8.04
SANDERSON-MILLER A.F.J. Flt Lt ...	12.10.04
SANDS J. Sqn Ldr	31.1.05
SAYERS G.F.H. DFC AFC Flt Lt	2.10.04
SCANDRETT C.F. MCMI Flt Lt	17.2.05
SEMMENS W.C. Flt Lt	26.3.05
SEYMOUR R.G. Wg Cdr	24.6.04
SHARMAN B.B. Flt Lt	15.10.04
SHARMAN E.V. Flt Lt	18.10.04
SHAW G.W. MBE Flt Lt	1.11.04
SHEARER J. OBE Wg Cdr	21.6.04
SHEPHERD J.R. OBE DFC Wg Cdr ...	2.2.05
SIM V.A. MBE Sqn Ldr	20.6.04
SIMPSON R.A. Sqn Ldr	11.12.04
SKILLINGS D.H.A. Flt Lt	1.2.05
SMART R.E. Sqn Ldr	17.10.04
SMITH A.C.L. Flt Lt	11.12.04
SMITH R.A. Flt Lt	24.11.04
SMITH W.G. Sqn Ldr	3.7.04
SPENCER J. MBE Wg Cdr	21.11.04
SPIKINS B.C. Sqn Ldr	7.11.04
SPRAGG E.G. Sqn Ldr	12.1.05
SPURGEON J.H. DFC* AFC Flt Lt	4.1.05
STEPHENS R. MBE Sqn Ldr	20.7.04
STEVENS W. MCMI Sqn Ldr	30.11.04
STEWART M. FCMI Wg Cdr	30.11.04
STICKLAND G.C. MRAeS Sqn Ldr ...	6.12.04
STIRLAND G. Sqn Ldr	13.12.04
STOWE J.R. Wg Cdr	16.8.04
STRANGE D.J. Fg Offr	26.12.04
STREET R.J. Gp Capt	12.6.04
SYMES L. Sqn Ldr	2.12.04
TALBOT G.S. BA Sqn Ldr	30.1.05
TAYLER R.H. Flt Lt	30.8.04
TAYLOR D.H. Flt Lt	26.1.05
TEMPLE G.F. Flt Lt	24.9.04
TEMPLEMAN-ROOKE B.A. DSO DFC*	
AFC Sqn Ldr	28.7.04
TEMPLING B.C. Flt Lt	22.11.04
THACKRAY H.W. Sqn Ldr	2.3.05
THOMAS D.M. Flt Lt	21.7.04
THOMAS H.S. Sqn Ldr	1.10.04
THORNBOROUGH R.J. Flt Lt	11.2.05
THORNE J.N. Sqn Ldr	21.12.04
THURBON M.T. CEng MRAeS MIERE	
MIEE Wg Cdr	14.6.04
TOMPKINS R.N. LDSRCS Wg Cdr ...	23.6.04
TRAHAIR F.T. MBE FCCS Sqn Ldr ...	14.9.04
TUFT W.J. MBE MCIPD FCMI Gp Capt	1.5.04
TUHILL P.J. DFC Flt Lt	26.4.04
TWIDLE H.W. MBE Flt Lt	29.1.05
VERE R.P. Flt Lt	3.1.05
VYE H.J. Flt Lt	13.10.04
WADAMS G.V. AFC Flt Lt	16.5.04

Name	Date of Death
WALKER J.L. AFC Sqn Ldr	11.9.04
WALLACE J.S.M.c.C. MBE Flt Lt	3.12.04
WALLINGTON W.J. Flt Lt	25.9.04
WARD C.R. MBE BSc Wg Cdr	18.2.05
WARD D.A. BSc MRAeS Sqn Ldr	10.9.04
WARE C.C.G. Flt Lt	19.9.04
WARNER C.E. Flt Lt	23.8.04
WATKINS M.R. BSc Flt Lt	22.8.04
WATTON A.J. DFC Flt Lt	24.8.04
WELCH A.H.E. DFC TD CEng MIEE MRAeS MCMI Sqn Ldr	2.2.05
WEST L.J.T. AFC Sqn Ldr	16.3.05
WHICHELO A.E. Flt Lt	28.1.05
WHITE K.G. MCMI Sqn Ldr	10.12.04
WHITSUN-JONES D.D. Flt Lt	10.1.05
WHITTINGTON R.S. Sqn Ldr	20.10.04
WILKIE P. MBE Sqn Ldr	3.1.05
WILKINSON E.A.F. Sqn Ldr	28.10.04
WILLCOCKS H.J. DCAe Sqn Ldr	10.6.04
WILLIAMS H.W.T. Flt Lt	18.7.04
WILLIAMS J. Flt Lt	14.9.04
WILLIAMS J.A. Flt Lt	1.8.04
WILLIAMS J.H.H. Flt Lt	7.3.05
WILLIAMS M.J. BSc ARTC Sqn Ldr	24.2.04
WILLIAMS R.A. Wg Cdr	11.6.04
WILLSON J.R. Sqn Ldr	7.3.05
WILSON A.L. AFC Sqn Ldr	12.9.04
WILSON L.D. DSO DFC AFC Wg Cdr	6.6.04
WILSON P.F. Flt Lt	2.1.05
WINCH A.G.W. DFC Flt Lt	18.2.05
WINKS H. Flt Lt	2.12.04
WISEMAN W.E. MBE DFC Flt Lt	30.1.05
WOLSEY W.E. FCA Gp Capt	3.3.05
WOOD L. MBE DFM Wg Cdr	25.10.04
WOOD T.C. DFC Sqn Ldr	14.1.04
WOODS J.J. DFC Sqn Ldr	17.7.04
WOOLFREY A.R.G. Sqn Ldr	16.10.04
WOOLLEY F.C. MBE Wg Cdr	19.2.05
WRAGG K.H. Flt Lt	17.9.04
WRAY C.D. Flt Lt	8.3.05
WRIGHT H.H. DFM Flt Lt	28.2.05
YOUNG F. Flt Lt	5.1.03
YOUNGER W.G.W. Flt Lt	8.1.05

Princess Mary's Royal Air Force Nursing Service

BURTON M.M. SRN Sqn Offr	4.4.05
CHEEL Z.M. ARRC Wg Cdr	10.2.05
GREEN E.M. SRN Sqn Offr	22.4.05

Printed in the United Kingdom for The Stationery Office
181876 10/05 C13 10170